I0796550

OBJECTS TELL STORIES

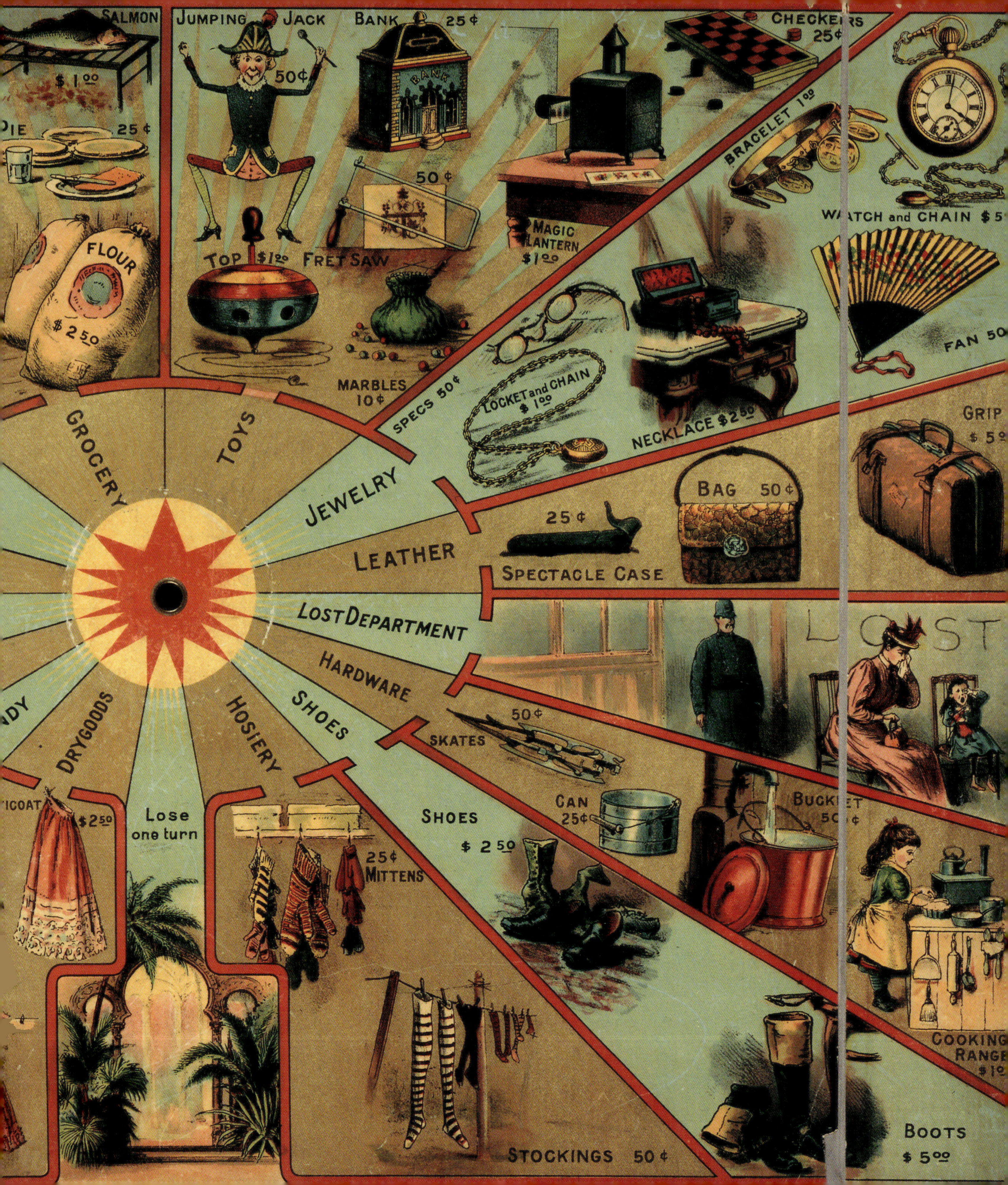
SALMON
$1.00
PIE 25¢
FLOUR
$2.50
JUMPING JACK
50¢
BANK 25¢
BANK
50¢
TOP $1.00
FRET SAW
MARBLES
10¢
CHECKERS
25¢
MAGIC
LANTERN
$1.00
BRACELET 1.00
WATCH and CHAIN $5
FAN 50
SPECS 50¢
LOCKET and CHAIN
$1.00
NECKLACE $2.50
GRIP
$5
BAG 50¢
25¢
SPECTACLE CASE
GROCERY
TOYS
JEWELRY
LEATHER
LOST DEPARTMENT
HARDWARE
SHOES
HOSIERY
DRYGOODS
NDY
LOST
50¢
SKATES
CAN
25¢
BUCKET
50¢
ICOAT
$2.50
Lose
one turn
25¢
MITTENS
SHOES
$2.50
COOKING
RANGE
$10
STOCKINGS 50¢
BOOTS
$5.00

OBJECTS TELL STORIES

Treasures from THE NEW YORK HISTORICAL

Valerie Paley

With editorial contributions by
Jeanne Gutierrez, Tessa Bangs, and
the staff of The New York Historical

The New York Historical
In association with D Giles Limited

First published in 2025 by GILES
An imprint of D Giles Limited
66 High Street
Lewes, BN7 1XG, UK
gilesltd.com

This publication has been generously supported by the Martin J. Gross Family Foundation

Library of Congress Control Number: 2025915834

ISBN Hardcover: 978-1-917273-04-6

For The New York Historical:
Project Curator: Valerie Paley, PhD, Senior Vice President and Sue Ann Weinberg Director, Patricia D. Klingenstein Library
Project Editors: Jeanne Gutierrez and Tessa Bangs
Photographs by Glenn Castellano and Eleanor Gillers

For D Giles Limited:
Copy-edited and proofread by Sarah Kane
Designed by Helen Swansbourne
Produced by GILES, an imprint of D Giles Limited
Printed and bound in Europe

Cover: Béatrice Coron (b. 1956), *Hi Five! Stories from the Five Boroughs: Manhattan*, 2019, hand-cut Tyvek, The New York Historical, Purchase, Coaching Club Acquisition Fund, 2019.96

Frontispiece: McLoughlin Brothers (1854–1921), The Game of Playing Department Store, 1898 (detail of cat. 154)

This page: Martin Wong (1946–1999), *Canal Street*, 1992 (detail of cat. 95)

Opposite page: Betye Saar (b. 1926), *Extreme Times Call for Extreme Heroines*, 2017 (detail of cat. 13)

MIX
Paper | Supporting responsible forestry
FSC® C118234
FSC
www.fsc.org

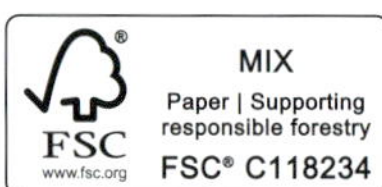

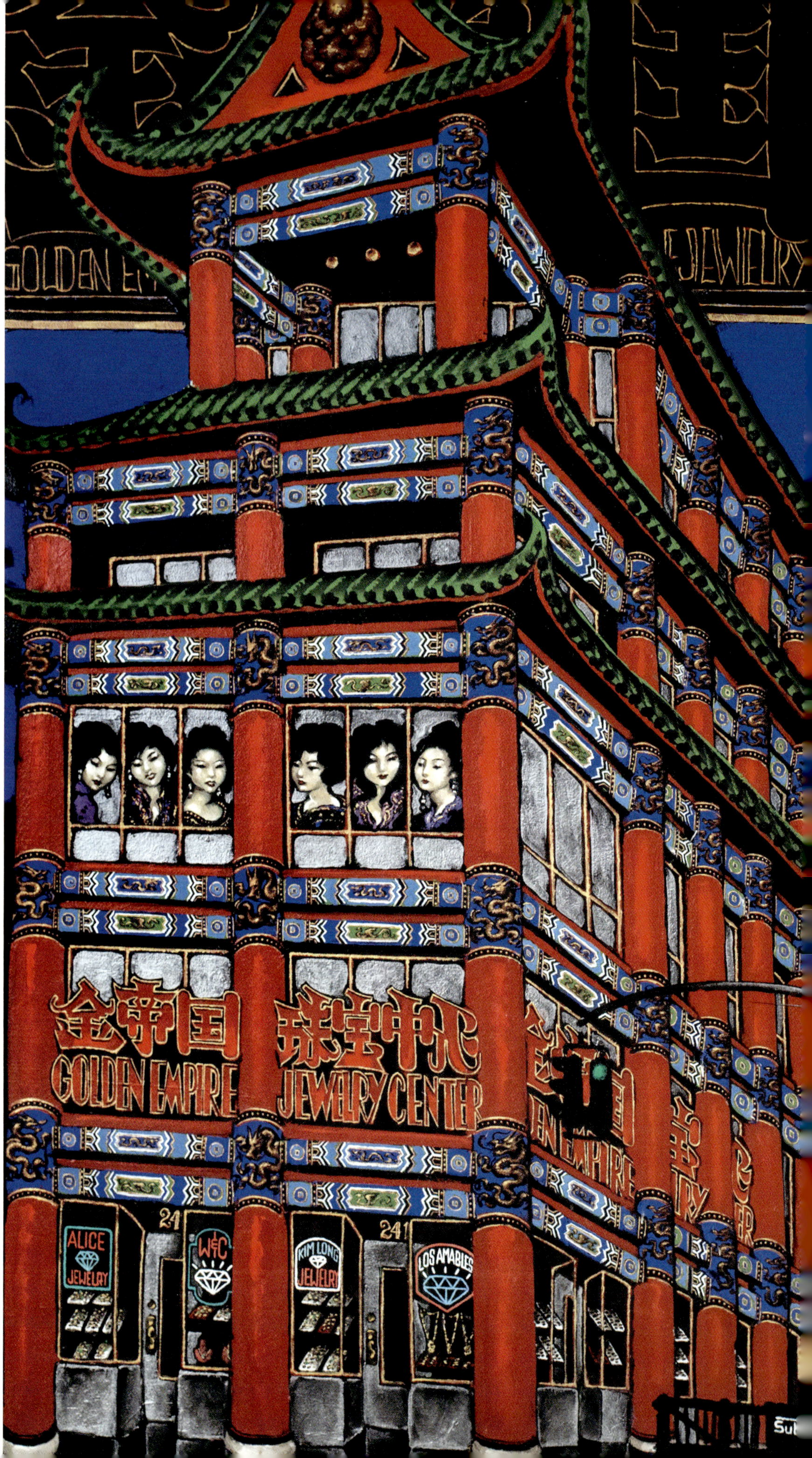

Contents

PREFACE

MARTIN J. GROSS
Martin J. Gross Family Foundation

Institutions embody their founders' vision and their influence on the broader culture in which they exist. The New York Historical is no exception. It has collected objects of significant historical importance since 1804 and serves as a resource for those engaged in the serious study of history. This volume's portrayal of the people, places, and things in its museum and library offers a magnificent window into its treasures.

However, the history of an institution is not exhausted by what it contains, but by how it endured. In this regard, The New York Historical has a fascinating story to tell—one that includes changes in organizational structure, periods of adversity, and ultimately, its flourishing. In short, it is a story about vision, dedicated leadership, and managerial execution.

About two decades after its founding in 1804, the fledgling historical society faced financial struggles. To survive, it needed public funding, which it did not pursue again until the late 1980s. Even without a permanent home until 1857, The New York Historical grew faster than other leading cultural institutions. However, its dedication to relying solely on private financial contributions for its annual operations put it on a challenging path. After a century of quiet existence, in 1935 it received a $4.5 million bequest from Mary Gardiner Thompson. Soon after, the membership organization changed its internal structure and established a self-perpetuating board of trustees.

Thompson's bequest offered a financial cushion and a 40-year respite from implementing proper managerial accountability until the funds were depleted in the early 1970s. The challenges were most severe in the early 1990s, when the organization's restructuring could have resulted in its liquidation. Luckily, this outcome was avoided, thanks to steady improvements in physical spaces, programming, and a business model under more responsible leadership.

A dramatic change in The New York Historical's profile occurred at the turn of the 20th century when Richard Gilder and Roger Hertog introduced their own vision to the museum and library. They recognized the immense potential of New York's first cultural institution to promote a deeper appreciation for history in the city they loved. Key aspects of their plan included forming a core group to serve on the board that shared their vision and were willing to dedicate time, effort, and resources. They also developed a marketing strategy that featured innovative programming to meet their objectives.

Perhaps most critical was the decision to hire Louise Mirrer as President and CEO in 2004. She is the longest-serving president in the institution's history. During her tenure, she has provided steady and enlightened leadership. In 2011, she oversaw a $100 million capital campaign to modernize the Central Park West headquarters. Among her many accomplishments are initiating special projects on Citizenship and the Presidency and overseeing the expansion of the institution's visitation to over 500,000 annually, along with numerous other groundbreaking exhibitions and initiatives like the DiMenna Children's History Museum and the Center for Women's History, the first of its kind in the nation within a major museum. The opening of the Tang Wing for American Democracy in 2026 continues this extraordinary trajectory.

Gilder and Hertog's vision for leadership at the board level has been sustained by the tenures of Chair Pam B. Schafler from 2013 to 2022 and Agnes Hsu-Tang, who began as Board Chair in 2022. Together with staff, they have transformed a struggling historical society into a vibrant institution benefiting New York and the nation.

Charles-Balthazar-Julien Fevret de Saint-Mémin (1770–1852)
Unidentified Osage Warrior Wearing Bird Headdress, 1807
(detail of cat. 32)

INTRODUCTION

LOUISE MIRRER
President and CEO, The New York Historical

It is a rare cultural institution that can boast of a vision that, for nearly two-and-one-quarter centuries, has stood the test of time. But from its establishment in 1804 to the present day, The New York Historical has adhered to its founders' principal design to "collect and preserve" in consideration of the wisdom that "[w]ithout the aid of original records and authentic documents history would be nothing more than a well-combined series of ingenious conjectures and amusing fables."

This book is in part a tribute to the eleven men whose inspired idea was to document their own time and place. Prescient in a city that had barely recovered from the ravages of British occupation, at a time when colleges and universities stocked their libraries and fashioned their curricula to fit a classical, not contemporary, mold, they frenetically collected the effects of their own historical moment and their personal roles in it, so that future generations might understand what happened and why. Their extraordinary consciousness of the importance of original materials would set in motion a trajectory that promoted The New York Historical as an institution that could, in the words of James Madison, "afford the best aids in procuring and presenting the materials, otherwise but too perishable, from which a faithful history of our country must be formed."

To be sure, The New York Historical's founders had a powerful vision for the institution. Over the years, our librarians and curators so diligently accomplished the tasks they set in motion that we have seen a near-constant and often precipitous need to increase our physical space. This year marks the conclusion of our latest effort to accommodate the veritable cornucopia of art, artifacts, and documents that constitute our collections' current state: our beautiful new Tang Wing for American Democracy, designed by Robert A.M. Stern. The new Tang Wing will enable us to better use our collections to tell the myriad stories of Americans and the nation they call home. The Tang Wing will also celebrate our American democracy, to which our institution, founded by those who fought for its freedoms and privileges, is fervently committed to sustain. Though our founders might be surprised by some of the directions our collecting has taken in the modern age, they would, I think, be reassured by our dedication to preservation and education, and by our fierce devotion to history and our nation's finest ideals, which remain the same.

This book is also a tribute to the generosity of my longtime friend and former New York Historical Trustee, Martin Gross. Marty is passionate about books, and it is a pleasure and an honor to thank him for his inspired idea that we should have a new volume to feature our rich collections, and our thinking about what they say. My colleague, Valerie Paley, Sue Ann Weinberg Director of our Patricia D. Klingenstein Library, took this project on, despite an already overfilled plate. I want to thank her for her willingness always to apply her many talents to The New York Historical, and also for her colleagueship since my arrival more than two decades ago as President and CEO. I also want to acknowledge The New York Historical Board of Trustees, led by Chair Dr. Agnes Hsu-Tang, whose inimitable sensitivity around the importance of projects of intellectual and creative merit is exemplified by this book.

Fig. 1
Robert A.M. Stern Architects (founded 1969)
Site Rendering, The New York Historical Tang Wing for American Democracy, View Along West 76th Street Looking Northeast, 2023
Courtesy of Zubatkin Owner Representation

ACKNOWLEDGMENTS

The dedicated scholarship of our curators, archivists, educators, postdocs, pre-doctoral fellows, and interns laid the groundwork for this book, which would not have been possible without their erudition and deep knowledge of The New York Historical museum and library collections. We acknowledge and thank Nina Nazionale, Allison Robinson, and Nicole Mahoney, whose editorial selections inform this book, along with the current and former staff of The New York Historical, whose written work is reflected in these pages.

Jean Ashton
Maurita Baldock
Keren Ben-Horin
Salonee Bhaman
Cynthia Copeland
Rachel Corbman
Anna Danziger Halperin
Marybeth De Filippis
Joseph Ditta
La-Kisha Emmanuel
Olive Eng
Jonah Estess
Jessica Fletcher
Anne Garner
Julie Golia
Sarah Gordon
Leslie Hayes
Margaret Heilbrun
Margi K. Hofer
Kathleen Hulser
Wendy N.E. Ikemoto
Angela long
Dominique Jean-Louis
Chandler Jenrette
Nick Juravich
Marybeth Kavanagh
Rebecca Klassen
Andrew Kryzak
Marilyn Kushner
Sarah Levy
Sarah Litvin
Regan Loggans
Nicole Mahoney
Meredith Mann
Sandra Markham
Andrea Marpillero-Colomina
Hope McCaffrey
Kerrie Mitchell
Gina Modero
Laura Mogulescu
Nina Nazionale
Caitlin O'Keefe
Akane Okoshi
Roberta J.M. Olson
Kim Orcutt
Edward O'Reilly
Emily Pazar
Cristian Petru Panaite
Tamar Rabinowitz
Henry Raine
Mujtaba Raja
Jan Ramirez
Marci Reaven
Jill Reichenbach
Clare Richfield
Samantha Rijkers
Allison Robinson
Luis Rodriguez
Michael Ryan
Allyson Schettino
Debra Schmidt Bach
Joanna Scutts
Justine Shakespeare
Russell Shorto
Marlena Slowik
Jacqueline Smith
Maggie B. Solarz
Dakota Stevens
Jenn Tham
Mike Thornton
Crystal Toscano
Mariam Touba
Lilly Tuttle
Alisa Wade
Rachel Walman
Marjorie Waters
Amy Weinstein
Lily Wong
Timothy Wroten
Jenny Zeng

We also acknowledge and thank the scholars, advisors, and consultants whose work with our collections has informed our own scholarship and contributed to the making of this book.

Claire Bellerjeau
Ira Berlin
Anna Mae Duane
Lauren Hewes
Harold Holzer
Cynthia Lee
Richard Rabinowitz
Sam Roberts
Thomas Thurston
Nan Wolverton

Opposite:
Red Grooms (b. 1937)
On Your Mark, Get Set, Go!, 2002
Color lithograph
Patricia D. Klingenstein Library, The New York Historical, Purchase, Henry Luce Fund, 2004

B.A.T. Red Grooms 2002

PEOPLE

PEOPLE

VALERIE PALEY

In November 1804, eleven prominent men across the social, cultural, and political spectrum of New York City, all witnesses to the American Revolution, met to discuss forming an organization to collect and publish manuscript papers chronicling the new nation's founding. Gathered at the behest of John Pintard, a merchant with preservationist proclivities, they recognized the need to take action to archive their historical moment and preserve future access by rescuing the records of the past that had been relegated to "the dust and obscurity of private repositories."

Their responsibility was clear. "The cause of truth is interesting to all men," they stated, "and those who possess the means, however small, of preventing error or elucidating obscure facts will confer a benefit on mankind by communicating them to the world." A little over a decade earlier, Pintard had expressed his concerns about the scattering of American records—and their casual destruction and neglect—in a conversation with the leaders who would eventually establish the nation's first historical society in Massachusetts. Now it was New York's turn to heed the call "to discover, procure, and preserve whatever may relate to the natural, civil, literary, and ecclesiastical history of the United States in general, and of [New York State] in particular."

Thus, the New-York Historical Society was born, founded by individuals who shared mutual beliefs and interests, working together for the common good—embodying the very definition of "society" itself. The institution, now The New York Historical, has remained true to its founding principles, navigating historical turns as it enters its third century, outlasting the hyphen in the city's name and even the original spirit of the term "society."

For over two hundred years, these collections have fundamentally represented the efforts of many people. Beyond the origin story of the foresight and perseverance of the institution's founders and funders, this section of *Objects Tell Stories* presents a selection of other individuals' narratives—the artists, writers, and makers whose work is held here; the historical figures whose words, deeds, ideas, and images are embedded in the things they left behind and the art that depicts them; and the collectors and curators whose legacy and purpose it is to bring these stories to life.

Previous spread:
Unidentified photographer
Caesar, an Enslaved Man, 1851
Daguerreotype
Patricia D. Klingenstein Library, The New York Historical

This is by no means an exhaustive survey. Still, it encourages contemplation beyond an arbitrary classification of the types of objects and the range of people who reflected and continue to reflect the dynamics of society at large at a particular moment.

For example, loosely grouped in the "Artists & Creators" section, rare silver objects showcase the exceptional work of individual artisans and implicitly reveal the political affiliations of both artist and owner. A two-foot-wide 18th-century salver featuring the city's seal was crafted by Swiss-born silversmith and loyalist Lewis Fueter and presented to Captain Thomas Sowers by British Royal Governor William Tryon (cat. 2). In contrast, a piece of domestic silver from the same period—a "cann," or mug—was made by notable colonial silversmith Myer Myers, a member of the Jewish community, and owned by Presbyterian minister Alexander McWhorter, a passionate patriot of the American cause who served as a chaplain in Washington's army (cat. 3).

Unusual biographical connections abound. Gilbert Stuart, the renowned portraitist known for his iconic images of George Washington, is represented here by a different type of work on paper: a letter containing a plea to the esteemed painter Benjamin West, who subsequently took on the struggling young artist as his apprentice and assistant (cat. 4). The story of 19th-century operatic superstar Jenny Lind, famously promoted by entrepreneur P.T. Barnum, is depicted not in her image but with a mother-of-pearl fan she once held (cat. 6), while the intrepid Bill Cunningham, the beloved 20th-century fashion and society photographer, is embodied in his bike, which he used to traverse the city to travel from assignment to assignment (cat. 11).

The New York Historical, home to the first Center for Women's History of its kind in the United States, has long embraced women's stories as essential to understanding the full scope of the American narrative. Here, the works of women artists tell complex tales of adversity, activism, and identity that go beyond the character and quality of the works themselves. Designer Clara Driscoll and her staff at the Women's Glass Cutting Department at Tiffany Studios toiled in anonymity during the late 19th and early 20th centuries to create iconic Tiffany lamps that elegantly illuminated upper-middle-class homes while also empowering the women artisans with salaries that provided them with the financial means to live independent lives in the city (cat. 8). Similarly, the spiritedly entrepreneurial Jessie Tarbox Beals, one of America's first photojournalists, sold souvenir postcards that captured her distinctly bohemian Greenwich Village neighborhood in the 1910s (cat. 9). Graffiti artist Lady Pink made her mark beginning in the 1980s through a bold and assertive persona, and used that spirit to artistically encourage people to vote during a live spray-painting session on an enormous canvas outside City Hall for a National Voter Registration Day event in 2014 (cat. 12). Contemporary assemblage artist Betye Saar emerged at the intersection of the feminist and Black art movements of the 1970s and became known for creating highly charged political pieces that challenge race and gender stereotypes (cat. 13). Kay WalkingStick, an artist of mixed Anglo and Indigenous heritage, has engaged with themes including feminism, spirituality, landscape, her Cherokee heritage, and Native American history, which are embedded in her work, including the monumental *Niagara* (cat. 14).

Under the heading "Writers" is a remarkable variety of creators and formats. Jupiter Hammon, the first published African American author in the United States, is represented by a poem discovered in The New York Historical's library some two centuries after he put pen to paper (cat. 15). Born on

Long Island in 1711, Hammon could read and write—an unusual thing for an enslaved person. In this rare example of his work, he expresses themes of salvation and redemption, reflecting his religious upbringing. In contrast, there are two documents from archives of more considerable size and scope: the original 1923 prospectus for the weekly newsmagazine *TIME* (cat. 25), and a page from Robert A. Caro's 1971 planning calendar (cat. 26). Both express journalistic discipline and efficiency: *TIME*'s mandate to condense information on all important subjects into roughly 100 short articles per issue (none exceeding 400 words), and Caro's record of the number of words he produced on a given month for his monumental, Pulitzer Prize–winning 1974 biography of Robert Moses, *The Power Broker.* The New York Historical holds the complete records of Time Inc., providing a detailed perspective of 20th-century history in an estimated seven million documents and artifacts. And through more than a hundred boxes of notes, manuscript drafts, scrapbooks, correspondence, and other files, the Robert A. Caro Archive documents the work and process of a writer whose name is synonymous with dedicated research.

The Patricia D. Klingenstein Library holds the fourth-largest collection of American newspapers published before 1820, along with nearly complete runs of 19th-century commercial dailies and some obscure periodicals expressing political, religious, and ethnic viewpoints. Featured here are five notable publications that convey not only news but also the implicit stories of their publishers. Samuel Eli Cornish and John Brown Russwurm's *Freedom's Journal* was the first Black-owned and -operated newspaper published in the United States, debuting in 1827, the same year that New York abolished slavery (cat. 17). The following year, Elias Boudinott, a young missionary-educated Cherokee, launched the *Cherokee Phoenix, & Indians' Advocate*, the first newspaper written and published by a Native American nation (cat. 18). Victoria Woodhull, perhaps best known as an outspoken leader of the American women's suffrage movement, was also the publisher of *Woodhull & Claflin's Weekly* with her sister, Tennessee Claflin, in the 1870s. Backed by Cornelius Vanderbilt, it was one of the first newspapers published by women in the United States (cat. 22). The makeshift *Prison Times*, a handwritten, four-page publication, was produced in a Civil War prison camp. One of four known copies of the first and only issue of this newspaper, it describes the daily activities of a community of Confederate prisoners (cat. 21). Finally, in 1883, Chinese-born Wong Chin Foo began publishing *Mei hua shin bao*, the first Chinese-language newspaper on the East Coast of the United States (cat. 23). Everywhere, he sought to debunk anti-Chinese stereotypes and defend Chinese Americans' claims to equal rights.

The "Politicians" section showcases a lively and diverse collection of representatives from the 18th through the 21st centuries. It ranges from a selection of unique documents commemorating the highly contentious process of writing, signing, and ratifying the United States Constitution in the 1780s (cat. 29 and cat. 30), to one of New York congresswoman Bella Abzug's distinctive hats from the 1970s (cat. 37). Familiar and famous 19th-century figures like Abraham Lincoln and Boss Tweed are also present, along with Gayę̈twahgeh (Cornplanter), the 18th-century Onöndowa'ga:' (Seneca) chief and Native American diplomat (cat. 31), as well as an unidentified Osage delegate who visited Washington after the Louisiana Purchase in the early 19th century (cat. 32). New York congresswoman Carolyn Maloney's 2021 Met Gala gown transcends its utility as a "red carpet" garment to illustrate the longevity of women's suffrage and activist iconography (cat. 38).

Yet perhaps no image of a politician stirs as much curiosity and controversy as the striking portrait of an early 18th-century woman once believed to be Edward Hyde, Viscount Cornbury, the British governor of New York and New Jersey (cat. 27). Universally detested, he was said to be an unapologetic cross-dresser, a legend that stood for over two centuries until only recently. The endurance of this now-debunked story raises a tantalizing question about early American identity. During a time when affiliations were shifting from local to national, it may still have been unclear what defined being American, but it certainly was not the aristocracy rejected by colonial revolutionaries, as represented by British Lord Cornbury.

As with all the individuals memorialized in this section, among the "Activists & Revolutionaries" are exceptional examples: John Peter Zenger, the printer whose 1735 trial for seditious libel became a major landmark in the development of a free press; the abolitionists Frederick Douglass and Sojourner Truth; women activists Elizabeth Cady Stanton, Muriel Fox, and Edie Windsor, and more.

But equally potent are the documents that imply impactful collective action: the 547 New Yorkers who in 1776 signed a petition pledging their loyalty to the Crown; the group of white citizens who founded the New-York Manumission Society in 1785 to publicly lobby for the abolition of slavery; the Greenwich Village mothers who joined a grassroots movement started by community activist Shirley Hayes to save Washington Square Park from Robert Moses's wrecking ball in 1959; and the "Occupy Wall Street" activists who encamped in New York's Zuccotti Park in 2011.

There is a certain intimacy to examining the people depicted here through objects that not only represent their lives, but also possess the power to convey broader stories that place the past in context. Sometimes, they leave us with more questions than answers. We can gaze into the eyes of Caesar, whose 1851 daguerreotype entered The New York Historical's collections in 1926, yet we cannot know the circumstances surrounding the image's creation. Although it has been with us for almost 100 years, what little we do know about Caesar is complicated by unreliable narrators and gaps in the historical record. Was he truly born enslaved in 1737? Was he truly the last person north of the Mason-Dixon line to die a slave, as he is often mythologized? All we can do is meet Caesar's direct, piercing gaze, contemplate his self-possessed presentation, and ask what his image reveals about Black manhood in the decades after New York's gradual abolition of chattel slavery.

Ultimately, items like these that end up in museum and library collections often arise from unique circumstances, all thanks to the efforts of individuals. Both donors and curators continually enhance collections with new depictions and explorations of thematic interests, which can significantly influence our historical understanding.

Tracy 168 (Michael Tracy, 1958–2023)
Borne to be Wild Style, 2001
Graphite and ink on watercolor paper
The New York Historical, Gift courtesy of
Regina Serniak Stewart, 2012.20.31 (detail)

ARTISTS & CREATORS

1

CHARLES WILLSON PEALE (1741–1827)

The Peale Family, 1773–1809

Oil on canvas
The New York Historical, Gift of Thomas Jefferson Bryan, 1867.298

Conceived in the early 1770s, Charles Willson Peale's monumental family portrait helped cement his position as a master portraitist. It caught John Adams's eye during a studio visit in Philadelphia in 1776, and he later wrote admiringly to Abigail Adams about the "pleasant cheerfulness" depicted in the faces of the artist's loved ones, and the "strong family attachments and natural affections" between them. Peale positioned himself at the left of the composition, holding his palette and supervising a drawing made by his brothers, St. George and James. At center, Rachel Brewer Peale, the artist's first wife, holds their daughter, Margaret. Peale's mother, Margaret, his sister, Elizabeth, and his daughter, Eleanor, are seated at right. Standing behind the table are Peale's sister, Margaret Jane, and the family nurse, Peggy Durgan. (Not included in the family portrait are the mixed-race family enslaved by the Peales: Lucy, Scarborough, and their son Moses Williams.)

Peale had studied art in London before returning to America, just before the Revolutionary War. He fought—and flourished—on the battlefield, receiving commissions to paint George Washington and other officers. This "Gallery of Great Men" became the nucleus of Peale's Philadelphia Museum, which the artist opened in 1784. The museum also displayed thousands of natural history specimens, Native American works, and historical relics, alongside hundreds of paintings. Though initially very popular, Peale's Museum fell on hard times in the mid-1800s, and the collections were eventually dispersed. In 1854, art patron Thomas Jefferson Bryan purchased a number of paintings—including this one—and later donated them to The New York Historical.

2

LEWIS FUETER (1746–1784)

Salver presented to Captain Thomas Sowers (1740–1774), 1772–73

New York City
Silver
The New York Historical, Gift of J. Lawrence Aspinwall, 1928.24

Measuring nearly two feet across, this silver salver, engraved with the Seal of the City of New York, was presented to Captain Thomas Sowers by Royal Governor William Tryon (1729–1788) and the General Assembly of New York. Sowers was a British army engineer who had fought the French and allied Native American nations during the Seven Years' War. Familiar with the dangers posed by Britain's imperial rivals, Sowers was instrumental in repairing the Battery at the tip of Manhattan, shoring up a critical defense for the British colonies, for which he received this salver as a token of thanks.

Like Sowers, the Swiss-born silversmith Lewis Fueter was loyal to the British crown—a stance that ensured a steady stream of commissions from the royal government. However, as the Revolutionary War progressed, his political views grew increasingly unpopular, and he fled New York when the British evacuated the city in 1783.

3

MYER MYERS (1723–1795)

Cann owned by Reverend Alexander McWhorter (1734–1807), ca. 1750–65

New York City
Silver
The New York Historical, Gift of George C. McWhorter, 1895.12

This is one of 28 known canns manufactured by colonial silversmith Myer Myers. It was the first piece of domestic silver acquired by The New York Historical, serving as the foundation of a now-extensive collection. Myers created important pieces for elite colonial families, including Presbyterian minister Reverend Alexander McWhorter. An ardent patriot, McWhorter joined George Washington's army and eventually became chaplain of Henry Knox's artillery brigade.

Myers was a member of Manhattan's Jewish community, present since 1654 when 23 Jewish refugees fleeing Brazil arrived in Dutch New Amsterdam. Though they faced discrimination, these early Jewish arrivals successfully petitioned the government for the right to worship, own property, and trade freely. By the end of his long life, Myer Myers would see his right to full political equality enshrined in Article VI of the Constitution, and his religious liberty confirmed by the First Amendment.

4

GILBERT STUART (1755–1828)

Letter to Benjamin West (1738–1820), 1776

No. 30 Grace Church St. [London]
Manuscript
Patricia D. Klingenstein Library, The New York Historical

Today, Gilbert Stuart is acclaimed as one of America's most accomplished portrait painters. But in 1776, he was 21 years old, recently arrived in England, and, literally, a starving artist: "For some time I have been reduc'd to one miserable meal a day & frequently not even that," he complained. The recipient of Stuart's plea was Benjamin West, an American-born artist who studied in Italy before settling in London, where he became one of the first American painters to garner acclaim beyond his place of birth. By 1776, West was a charter member of the Royal Academy, eventually receiving over 60 commissions from King George III. Stuart's letter produced the desired result: for five years, he served as West's apprentice and assistant before opening his own studio.

In 1793, Stuart decided to return to the United States, and pursued a sitting with George Washington. He produced several portraits of the first president, as well as other prominent Americans, including John Jay, Dolley Madison, Thomas Jefferson, John Quincy Adams, and Louisa Adams. West remained in London, where he trained many other American artists—among them Charles Willson Peale, Ralph Earle, John Trumbull, and Thomas Sully.

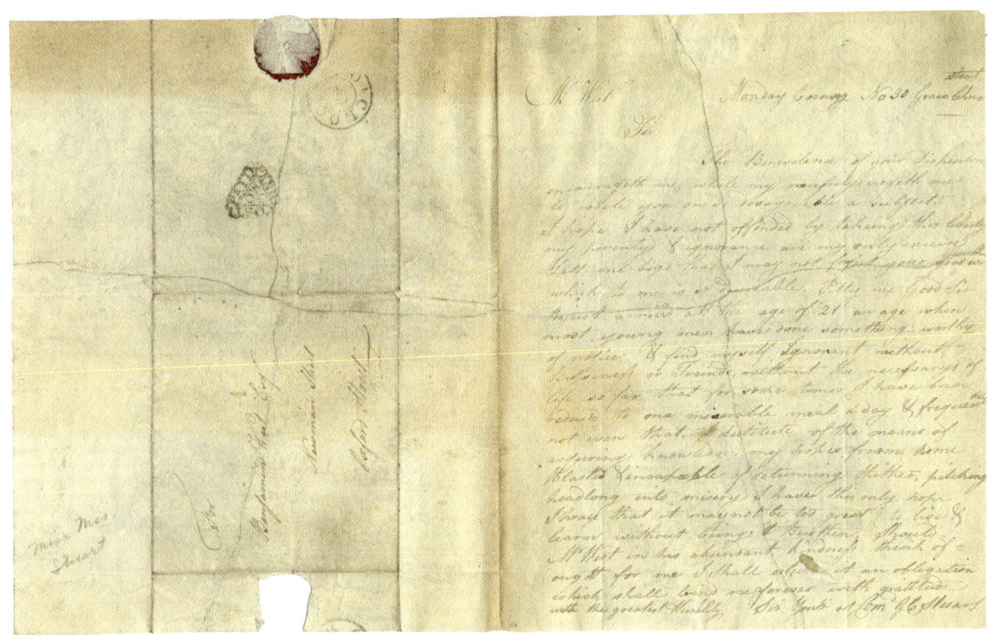

Mr West — Monday Evening No 30 Grace Church street

Sir

The Benevolence of your Disposition encourageth me, while my necessity urgeth me to write you on so disagreeable a subject. I hope I have not offended by taking this liberty my poverty & ignorance are my only excuse Lett me beg that I may not forfeit your good will which to me is so desirable. Pitty me Good Sir I've just arrived at the age of 21 an age when most young men have done something worthy of notice & find myself Ignorant without business or Friends, without the necessarys of life so far that for some time I have been reduc'd to one miserable meal a day & frequently not even that, destitute of the means of acquiring knowledge, my hopes from home blasted & incapable of returning thither, pitching headlong into misery I have this only hope I pray that it may not be too great to live & learn without being a Burthen. Should Mr West in his abundant kindness think of aught for me I shall esteem it an obligation which shall bind me forever with gratitude with the greatest Humility Sir Your obt Servt G C Stuart

recto

verso

5

THOMAS W. COMMERAW (ca. 1771–1823)

Jug, ca. 1797–1819

New York City
Salt-glazed stoneware, cobalt oxide
The New York Historical, Purchased from Elie Nadelman, 1937.820. The conservation of this object was supported through the NYSCA/GHHN Conservation Treatment Grant Program administered by Greater Hudson Heritage Network. This program is made possible by the New York State Council on the Arts with support from the Office of the Governor and the New York State Legislature. Additional support provided by the Robert David Lion Gardiner Foundation.

Thomas W. Commeraw was born enslaved to German immigrant potter William Crolius, and likely learned his craft from a member of Crolius's family. Crolius died when Thomas was eight, manumitting Commeraw and his family in his will. Between 1797 and 1819, Commeraw operated his own successful workshop, located at Corlears Hook on the East River. He produced thousands of utilitarian vessels that were used to store everything from beer and cider to milk, molasses, and meat, boldly branding them with his name, location, and distinctive swag-and-tassel embellishments.

Commeraw, the only Black master potter in New York at the time, rose to prominence as an entrepreneur, property owner, and advocate for his community, fighting political and economic discrimination. However, the War of 1812 caused a financial downturn that eventually put Commeraw out of business. In 1820, he traveled to Sierra Leone on a ship sponsored by the American Colonization Society, which promoted the "return" of free African Americans to Africa. Hoping to found a Black republic, the group was instead devastated by malaria. After two years of hardship, Commeraw and his surviving family returned to the United States.

6

UNIDENTIFIED MAKER

Fan owned by Jenny Lind (1820–1887), ca. 1850

Mother-of-pearl, silk, lace, metal, embroidery thread, paint, rhinestones
The New York Historical, Gift of Leonidas Westervelt, 1945.181

Soprano Johanna Maria "Jenny" Lind earned widespread acclaim in the 1840s as "the Swedish Nightingale." At age 28, Lind planned to retire from her successful European career—but then she received a tantalizing offer from American entrepreneur P.T. Barnum. The proprietor of Barnum's American Museum in Manhattan proposed an 18-month American tour; the contract would give Lind control over her program and accompanists, plus $1,000 per performance. Lind accepted, and Barnum threw himself into promoting her, appealing to a vast middle-class audience by focusing not only on Lind's artistry, but her "womanly" values, such as modesty, morality, and generosity. The relentless publicity proved successful: thousands of people crowded New York Harbor to watch Lind's arrival, and an auction to attend her debut drove ticket prices up to $200 per person. A craze for all things Lind—from opera glasses to paper dolls—swept the country. She performed 150 concerts throughout the United States, accompanied by the Norwegian violinist Ole Bull. According to The New York Historical's records, Lind presented this fan to Bull during her celebrated, and lucrative, tour.

Fig. 2a–c
Unidentified German artist
Jenny Lind paper doll and costumes, ca. 1850
Lithograph on paper
Patricia D. Klingenstein Library, The New York Historical

7

JOHN ROGERS (1829–1904)

The Slave Auction, 1859

New York City
Painted plaster
The New York Historical, Gift of Samuel V. Hoffman, 1928.28

The artist and entrepreneur John Rogers was famous for his narrative figural sculpture groups, mass-produced in plaster and sold to a broad audience of upper- and middle-class Americans. He considered this small sculpture of an enslaved family about to be torn apart "the most powerful group" he had ever made. He offered it for sale at a pivotal moment—just two weeks after John Brown's execution for attempting to capture the federal arsenal at Harper's Ferry in a bid to liberate enslaved Virginians. But Rogers misjudged his audience: he was familiar with the abolitionist fervor of his New England home and had not counted on New York's strong commercial ties to the South. He wrote in dismay that "*The Slave Auction* tells such a strong story that none of the stores will receive it . . . for fear of offending their Southern customers." Rogers only made a few sales among anti-slavery activists, but the work circulated widely as an image in popular culture and an idea in public memory, primarily in the form of album photographs, stereo views, and cartes-de-visite. *The Slave Auction* launched Rogers's career and gave him a reputation for moral courage. Indeed, the group was often lauded as "*Uncle Tom's Cabin* in plaster."

8

CLARA DRISCOLL (1861–1944), designer
TIFFANY STUDIOS (1902–1932), maker

Dragonfly table lamp, designed ca. 1900–06

New York City
Leaded glass, bronze
The New York Historical, Gift of Dr. Egon Neustadt, N84.113

The history behind Tiffany Studios' iconic lamps offers a fascinating look at the often-hidden contributions of women in the arts. Louis Comfort Tiffany (1848–1933) is considered the artistic genius behind Tiffany Studios; however, he was not the exclusive designer of its lamps, windows, and other luxury objects. In fact, Clara Driscoll, head of the Women's Glass Cutting Department from 1892 to 1909, was behind many of the firm's famous leaded-glass shade designs. Driscoll and her staff, who called themselves the "Tiffany Girls," labored in anonymity but were well compensated. The women's weekly salary of $35 was on par with that of Tiffany's unionized male designers, a reflection of his regard for their abilities. This *Dragonfly* shade, a popular model designed by Driscoll, was priced at $175 in Tiffany's 1906 price list. Considering that the average hourly wage in 1906 was only around 17 cents, these lamps were unattainable for all but the most affluent consumers.

By the 1930s, however, tastes had changed. The Great Depression sapped the market for luxury goods, and the famous Tiffany glassworks in Corona, Queens, closed its doors. In 1935, Dr. Egon Neustadt, a Vienna-born orthodontist and real estate developer, began collecting Tiffany lamps, buying his first piece at a secondhand shop for only $12.50. Neustadt eventually amassed the world's largest private collection of Tiffany lamps, over 350 in all, plus hundreds of crates of uncut glass. The Neustadt Collection was first displayed at The New York Historical in 1983; 132 lamps were donated in the following year. These pieces are now showcased in the interactive Gallery of Tiffany Lamps, which opened in 2017.

9

JESSIE TARBOX BEALS (1870–1942)

Beals at Work, 1904

Gelatin silver print
Patricia D. Klingenstein Library, The New York Historical

Jessie Tarbox Beals, one of the first American women photojournalists, published her freelance work in newspapers and magazines such as *Town and Country*, *Harper's Bazaar*, the *Christian Science Monitor*, *McClure's*, and the *New York Times*. Despite this, Beals died deeply impoverished, and for many years afterwards her daughter struggled to find publishers or exhibitors for her work.

Beals started shooting as a teenager in 1888, and became the staff photographer for two small Buffalo, New York, papers in 1902. Two years later, she lugged her unwieldy kit—a 50-pound box camera, glass negatives, and tripods—to photograph the 1904 World's Fair in St. Louis, doggedly pursuing a portrait of President Theodore Roosevelt and capturing the novelty of airships in flight. Moving to New York City, Beals plunged into Progressive-era Greenwich Village where she photographed artists, authors, restaurateurs, reformers, suffragists, shopkeepers, and *bons vivants*. The entrepreneurial photographer sold these images as souvenir postcards, capitalizing on the public's fascination with her famously bohemian neighborhood. A consummate self-promoter, Beals also took many photographs of herself, posing with her camera equipment, which helped cement her status as a professional photojournalist. As she wrote in 1904, all a woman needed to succeed in the field was "health and strength, a fair photographic outfit, and the ability to hustle, which is the most necessary qualification." Alongside her images of women doctors, advertisers, scientists, journalists, and a judge, these self-portraits helped create a visual language of female professionalism.

BOOTHS
AND
OPERATOR
BOOTHS
AND
OPERATOR

10

ENIT ZERNER KAUFMAN (1897–1961)

Marian Anderson (1897–1993), ca. 1940–45

Watercolor, gouache, white tempera, and charcoal on heavy watercolor paper
The New York Historical, Gift of Mrs. Enit Kaufman, 1947.216

In 1939, Marian Anderson, a celebrated African American contralto, was forbidden to perform at the 3,700-seat Constitution Hall in Washington, DC. The nation's capital was still racially segregated—and the venue only booked white performers. A group of Anderson's outraged supporters, including First Lady Eleanor Roosevelt and activist Mary McLeod Bethune, arranged for her concert to take place at the Lincoln Memorial instead. Approximately 75,000 people gathered on the National Mall to hear Anderson sing "My Country, 'Tis of Thee," and millions more tuned in on the radio.

That very same year, portraitist Enit Zerner Kaufman, born near Vienna, moved to New York with her husband from Paris, after the advent of World War II disrupted her life and career. Kaufman published this depiction of Anderson in her 1946 book *American Portraits*, the only Black woman included.

Anderson devoted much of her life to improving prospects for Black people in the performing arts. In 1955, she became the first African American to sing at New York's Metropolitan Opera, and she returned to the Lincoln Memorial for the March on Washington in 1963, singing "He's Got the Whole World in His Hands."

11

BIRIA (founded 1976), manufacturer
CIEL BICYCLES (founded ca. 1987), retailer

Bicycle with light and lock belonging to Bill Cunningham, ca. 2002

Aluminum, other metals, rubber, plastic
The New York Historical, Gift of Louise Doktor, 2017.13.1

William John "Bill" Cunningham (1929–2016) was a longstanding *New York Times* photographer and journalist known for his candid shots of up-to-the-minute fashion trends. Photos for his "On the Street" column were often captured at a favorite vantage point on the corner of Fifth Avenue and 57th Street, while his other column, "Evening Hours," required his attendance at up to 20 galas per week. As *Vogue* editor-in-chief Anna Wintour once remarked, "We all get dressed for Bill."

Cunningham started his career as a milliner, creating fanciful hats under the name William J. As fashion became less formal and more individualistic, he found his calling as a photographer and began contributing regularly to *The New York Times* in the 1970s, joining the staff in 1994, citing a need for health insurance. Cunningham dressed invariably in a blue worker's jacket, khaki pants, and sneakers, and lived until 2010 in a studio above Carnegie Hall, sleeping on a single-size cot. This bicycle is one of 30 that he owned over his many years of activity, replacing them as they got wrecked or stolen. Cunningham also owned a series of Nikon cameras, and used this one through the end of his career. Cunningham's archive, including tens of thousands of photographs, negatives, slides, contact sheets, and memorabilia, found a permanent home at The New York Historical in 2025.

Fig. 3
Nikon (founded 1917)
Camera with lens belonging to Bill Cunningham, ca. 2012
Metal, rubber, glass, plastic
The New York Historical, Gift of Louise Doktor, 2017.13.3

12

LADY PINK (Sandra Fabrera, b. 1964)

VOTE, 2014

Acrylic spray paint on canvas
The New York Historical, Purchase, Coaching Club Acquisition Fund, 2021.6

Born in Ecuador and raised in Queens, Lady Pink began her career as a graffiti artist in 1979, tagging subway cars. She had her work first exhibited in galleries and museums while still attending the High School of Art and Design in Manhattan, and was featured in the influential 1983 hip-hop film *Wild Style*. As a young woman in a male-dominated scene, she made her mark with a fearless and assertive persona. Today, she is known as "The First Lady of Graffiti" for her early, influential role.

The League of Women Voters of the City of New York commissioned Lady Pink to execute this canvas in a live painting session during a National Voter Registration Day event outside City Hall. Because the non-partisan advocacy group, founded in 1919, was also celebrating its 95th anniversary, Lady Pink incorporated imagery from the long history of the suffrage movement into the mural.

League of Women Voters of N.Y.C.
VOTE

13

BETYE SAAR (b. 1926)

Extreme Times Call for Extreme Heroines, 2017

Mixed media and wood figure on vintage washboard, clock
The New York Historical, Purchased through the generosity of Louise Mirrer; Ernest Tollerson and Katrinka Leefmans; Pam and Scott Schafler; Marilynn Gelfman Karp; Margi and Andrew Hofer; Linda S. Ferber; Frances Ann Schulman; Nicole, Nathan, and Brian Wagner; an anonymous donor; and members of the Frederick Douglass Council. Additional support provided through the Women Artists Fund in memory of Mildred Mirrer, 2019.76

Betye Saar is a contemporary assemblage artist who collects found and vintage objects and combines them into three-dimensional collages. She emerged at the intersection of the feminist and Black art movements of the 1970s, and became known for creating highly charged political pieces that challenge race and gender stereotypes. Saar's breakout piece and best-known assemblage, *The Liberation of Aunt Jemima* (1972), features a grossly caricatured Jim Crow–era figurine of the famous pancake-making "mammy." By arming it with a rifle and gun, Saar transformed an object designed to denigrate into a heroine liberating herself from that very denigration. This piece, *Extreme Times Call for Extreme Heroines*, belongs to a series of washboard assemblages that Saar has been creating since 1997. These works honor washerwomen who worked 16 hours per day in steamy conditions—laundry being one of the few types of jobs readily available to Black women in the decades between abolition and the Civil Rights Movement.

recto

verso

14

KAY WALKINGSTICK (b. 1935)

Niagara, 2022

Oil on panel in two parts
The New York Historical, Purchased through the generosity of Agnes Hsu-Tang and Oscar Tang; Nancy Newcomb; an anonymous donor; Barry Barnett; Helen Appel; Belinda and Charles Bralver; Dorothy Tapper Goldman; Margi and Andrew Hofer; Louise Mirrer; Jennifer and John Monsky; Suzanne Peck and Brian Friedman; Pam and Scott Schafler; Barbara and Elliott Wagner; and Linda Ferber, 2023.2ab

Kay WalkingStick's prolific career has spanned more than four decades. An artist of mixed Anglo and Indigenous heritage and an enrolled citizen of Cherokee Nation, she engages with a diversity of themes, including feminism, spirituality, landscape, her Cherokee heritage, and Native American history at large. *Niagara* is one of few paintings in which WalkingStick features New York, where she was born and raised, studied (at Pratt Institute's School of Art), and came of age as an artist.

Niagara is a resplendent landscape, a political statement, and a reclamation. The geometric band running across the lower right is inspired by a piece of Kanien'kehá:ka (Mohawk) pottery by artist Steve Smith; the pattern also appears in Onöndowa'ga:' (Seneca) and Onõñda'gega' (Onondaga) art. WalkingStick overlays it upon the falls in honor of the Haudenosaunee at large—the confederacy of Indigenous nations that inhabits the Niagara region. "I'm hoping that people see my present work as a statement about the beauty and the importance of our planet," said WalkingStick. "All of the land here in this continent is Indian land. . . . It's all Indian territory. And that's an important thing for people to recognize."

Thomas Sully (1783–1872)
Woman and Child Reading, Folio 20 in the John Ludlow Morton Album, 1831
Graphite and gray wash on card, bound into an album
The New York Historical, Bequest of Emily Ellison Post, 1944.384

WRITERS

15

JUPITER HAMMON (1711–ca. 1806)

An Evening Thought. Salvation by Christ, with Penetential [sic] Cries: Composed by Jupiter Hammon, a Negro belonging to Mr Lloyd, of Queen's-Village, on Long-Island, the 25th of December, 1760

Possibly New York: Hugh Gaine, 1760
Broadside
Patricia D. Klingenstein Library, The New York Historical

Jupiter Hammon, born on October 17, 1711, in the Manor of Queens Village on Long Island, was enslaved at birth by Henry Lloyd (1685–1763) and remained enslaved by four generations of Lloyd's descendants. The family had strong ties to Anglican and Congregational churches, which encouraged Bible-reading among enslaved men and women. Hammon learned to read, and, though it was unusual for enslaved persons to learn how to write, he also became an accomplished author, publishing four poems and three essays in his lifetime. In one composition, "An Address to the Negroes in New York State," written when he was nearly 70 and printed as a 22-page pamphlet, Hammon reflected on the hypocrisy of slaveholders who fought in the Revolutionary War: "I must say that I have hoped that God would open their eyes, when they were so much engaged for liberty, to think of the state of the poor blacks, and to pity us."

"An Evening Thought," written when Hammon was about 50, focuses on the theme of salvation that characterizes much of his work. Discovered at The New York Historical in 1905, the poem is the first known work published by an African American.

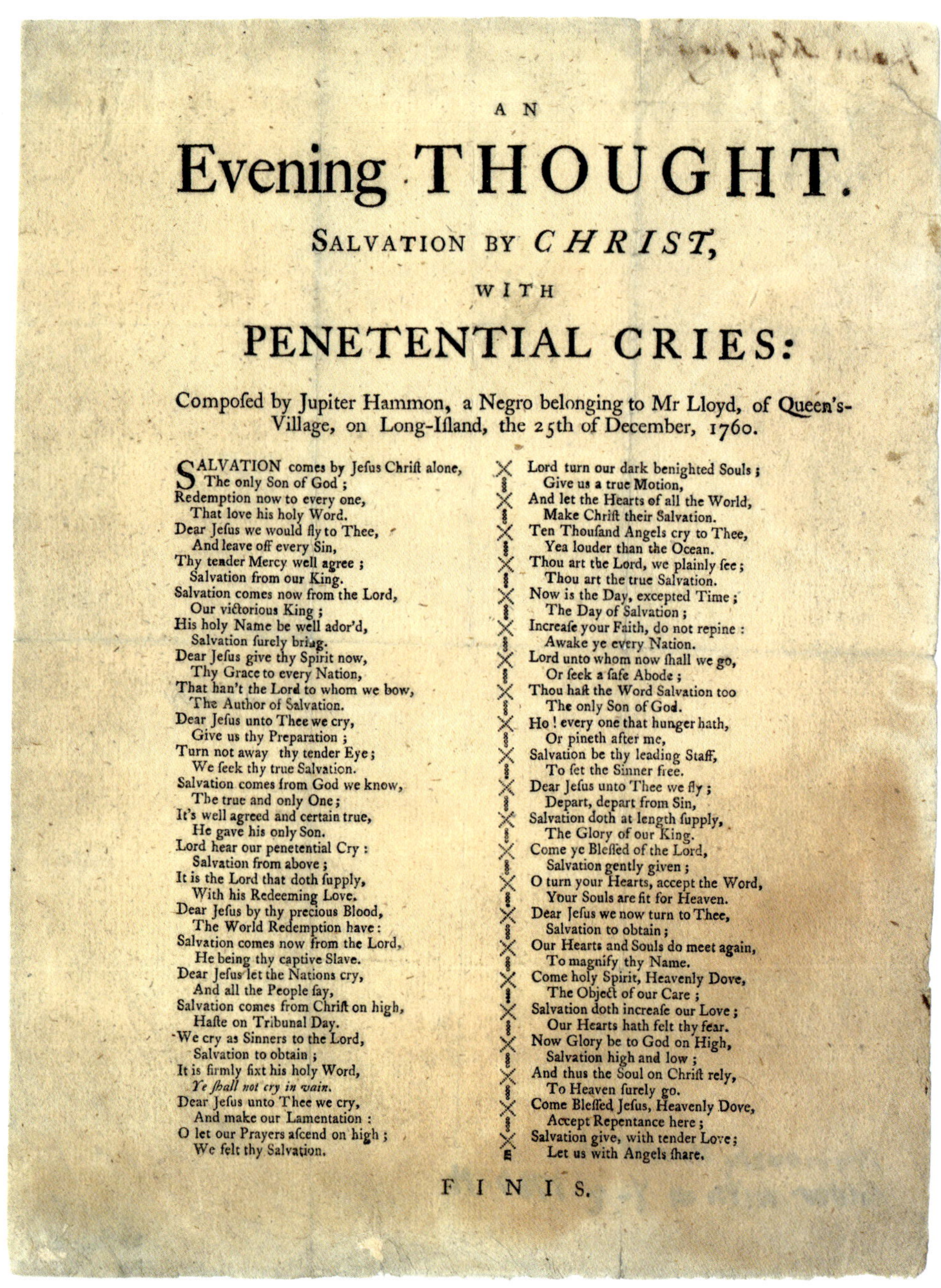

A N

Evening THOUGHT.

SALVATION BY *CHRIST*,

WITH

PENETENTIAL CRIES:

Compoſed by Jupiter Hammon, a Negro belonging to Mr Lloyd, of Queen's-Village, on Long-Iſland, the 25th of December, 1760.

SALVATION comes by Jeſus Chriſt alone,
The only Son of God;
Redemption now to every one,
That love his holy Word.
Dear Jeſus we would fly to Thee,
And leave off every Sin,
Thy tender Mercy well agree;
Salvation from our King.
Salvation comes now from the Lord,
Our victorious King;
His holy Name be well ador'd,
Salvation ſurely bring.
Dear Jeſus give thy Spirit now,
Thy Grace to every Nation,
That han't the Lord to whom we bow,
The Author of Salvation.
Dear Jeſus unto Thee we cry,
Give us thy Preparation;
Turn not away thy tender Eye;
We ſeek thy true Salvation.
Salvation comes from God we know,
The true and only One;
It's well agreed and certain true,
He gave his only Son.
Lord hear our penetential Cry:
Salvation from above;
It is the Lord that doth ſupply,
With his Redeeming Love.
Dear Jeſus by thy precious Blood,
The World Redemption have:
Salvation comes now from the Lord,
He being thy captive Slave.
Dear Jeſus let the Nations cry,
And all the People ſay,
Salvation comes from Chriſt on high,
Haſte on Tribunal Day.
We cry as Sinners to the Lord,
Salvation to obtain;
It is firmly fixt his holy Word,
Ye ſhall not cry in vain.
Dear Jeſus unto Thee we cry,
And make our Lamentation:
O let our Prayers aſcend on high;
We felt thy Salvation.
Lord turn our dark benighted Souls;
Give us a true Motion,
And let the Hearts of all the World,
Make Chriſt their Salvation.
Ten Thouſand Angels cry to Thee,
Yea louder than the Ocean.
Thou art the Lord, we plainly ſee;
Thou art the true Salvation.
Now is the Day, excepted Time;
The Day of Salvation;
Increaſe your Faith, do not repine:
Awake ye every Nation.
Lord unto whom now ſhall we go,
Or ſeek a ſafe Abode;
Thou haſt the Word Salvation too
The only Son of God.
Ho! every one that hunger hath,
Or pineth after me,
Salvation be thy leading Staff,
To ſet the Sinner free.
Dear Jeſus unto Thee we fly;
Depart, depart from Sin,
Salvation doth at length ſupply,
The Glory of our King.
Come ye Bleſſed of the Lord,
Salvation gently given;
O turn your Hearts, accept the Word,
Your Souls are fit for Heaven.
Dear Jeſus we now turn to Thee,
Salvation to obtain;
Our Hearts and Souls do meet again,
To magnify thy Name.
Come holy Spirit, Heavenly Dove,
The Object of our Care;
Salvation doth increaſe our Love;
Our Hearts hath felt thy fear.
Now Glory be to God on High,
Salvation high and low;
And thus the Soul on Chriſt rely,
To Heaven ſurely go.
Come Bleſſed Jeſus, Heavenly Dove,
Accept Repentance here;
Salvation give, with tender Love;
Let us with Angels ſhare.

F I N I S.

16

REMBRANDT PEALE (1778–1860)

Thomas Jefferson (1743–1826), 1805

Oil on linen
The New York Historical, Gift of Thomas Jefferson Bryan, 1867.306

Thomas Jefferson's place in United States history is unquestionably central and yet deeply complicated. He wrote eloquently on the nation's foundational principles while enslaving hundreds of people, some of whom were his own children, born to Sally Hemings, an enslaved woman.

A member of the affluent planter class, Jefferson received a "gentleman's education," studying Greek, Latin, and law before entering politics. In 1775, as tension grew between the British crown and the American colonies, Jefferson was elected to the Second Continental Congress, where he served on the five-member committee that produced the Declaration of Independence. Drawing on his legal studies and existing documents, including his own draft of a constitution for the state of Virginia, Jefferson wrote a "rough draught" of the Declaration in just a few days, including its famous Preamble:

> We hold these truths to be self-evident, that all men are created equal, that they are endowed by their Creator with certain unalienable Rights, that among these are Life, Liberty and the pursuit of Happiness.

Jefferson was serving as the nation's third president in 1805, when Rembrandt Peale traveled to Washington to paint this portrait. It hung in Peale's Philadelphia Museum until 1854, when art collector Thomas Jefferson Bryan purchased it; it was later given by him to The New York Historical.

17

SAMUEL E. CORNISH (1795–1858) and
JOHN B. RUSSWURM (1799–1851), publishers

Freedom's Journal: "Righteousness Exalteth a Nation", Vol. I, No. 3

New York, March 30, 1827
Patricia D. Klingenstein Library, The New York Historical

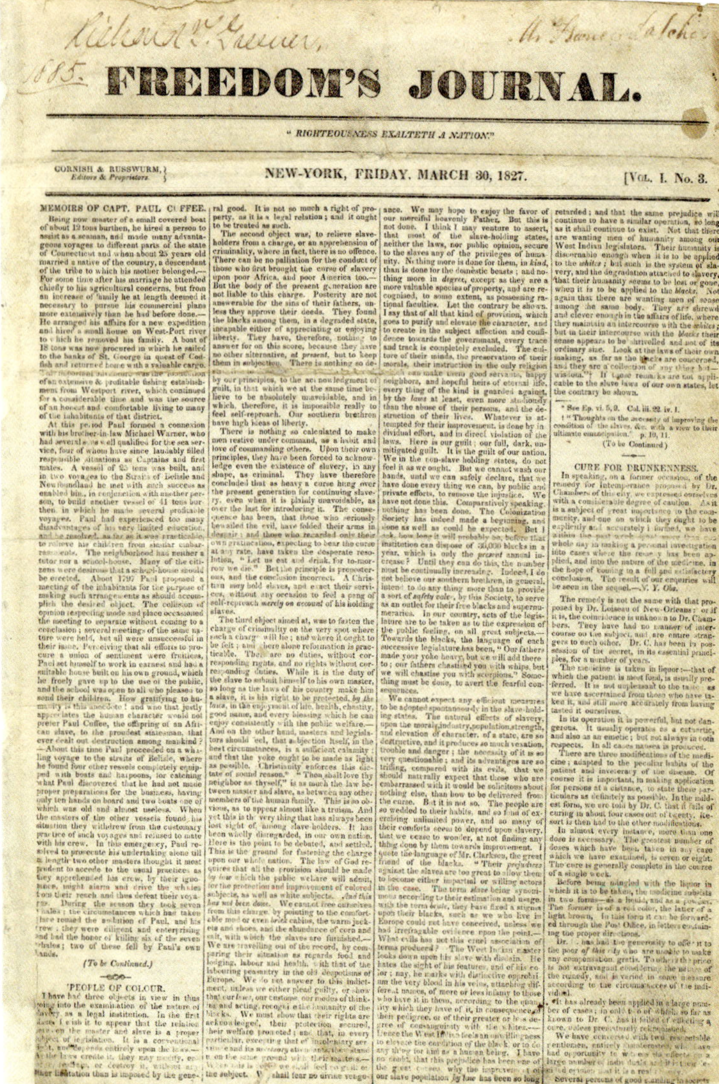

FREEDOM'S JOURNAL.

"RIGHTEOUSNESS EXALTETH A NATION."

CORNISH & RUSSWURM, Editors & Proprietors. NEW-YORK, FRIDAY, MARCH 30, 1827. [VOL. I. No. 3.

MEMOIRS OF CAPT. PAUL CUFFEE.

PEOPLE OF COLOUR.

CURE FOR DRUNKENNESS.

Freedom's Journal was the first Black-owned and -operated newspaper published in the United States. Appearing in the same year that New York abolished slavery, *Freedom's Journal* was intended to inform, educate, and uplift the free Black community. The paper advocated for African Americans' political rights, including the vote, and worked to counter harmful stereotypes disseminated by the white press.

The paper's senior publisher, Samuel Eli Cornish, was a free Black man and an ordained minister who founded the first Black Presbyterian Church in New York City. John Brown Russwurm, his publishing partner, was born in Jamaica to an enslaved Black woman and a white plantation owner, and became one of the first Black college graduates in the United States. Their paper circulated as far afield as Haiti, Canada, and Europe. However, after Cornish resigned in September 1827, Russwurm began using *Freedom's Journal* to promote the colonization movement. This controversial stance lost the paper many readers; it folded in 1829 and Russwurm emigrated to Liberia, where he lived until his death.

Fig. 4
Francis Kearney (1785–1837), engraver
Reverend Samuel Cornish (1795–1858)
Steel engraving
Philadelphia: J. How, 1825
Patricia D. Klingenstein Library, The New York Historical, Gift of Daniel Parish Jr., 1901

Though he resigned from *Freedom's Journal*, Samuel Cornish continued his involvement in the Black press. After John Russwurm departed for Liberia, Cornish attempted to revive their pioneering newspaper under the name *Rights of All*; however, it only lasted for one year. Cornish also edited the *Weekly Advocate* (later the *Colored American*), a monthly magazine dedicated to the emerging Black middle class. Meanwhile, Cornish was also active in the growing abolitionist movement, becoming a founding member of the American Anti-Slavery Society in 1833. Via publications and public lectures, this radical organization called for immediate, uncompensated emancipation, as well as boycotts of products made by enslaved labor.

18

ELIAS BOUDINOTT (ᎦᎴᎩᎾ ᎤᏩᏘ, Cherokee, 1802–1839), publisher

Cherokee Phoenix, & Indians' Advocate, Vol. III, No. 40

New Echota, Georgia: The Cherokee Nation, March 12, 1831
Patricia D. Klingenstein Library, The New York Historical

The first Native North American language to be written in syllabic form was Tsalagi, or Cherokee, spoken by a large and powerful nation with ancestral homelands in the southeastern United States. The Cherokee syllabary was devised by the Cherokee intellectual and inventor Sikwâ'y (Sequoyah) in the first decades of the 1800s; the set of characters transformed spoken Cherokee into a language that could be both written and read. Soon, more Cherokee were literate in Tsalagi than their white neighbors were in English. In 1827, Cherokee Nation published a written Constitution, and the *Cherokee Phoenix, & Indians' Advocate*, the first newspaper written and published by a Native American nation, appeared in 1828. Edited by a young missionary-educated Cherokee named Elias Boudinott (Galangina), the paper played an important role in Cherokee Nation's resistance to white encroachment as a new means of communication, a rallying symbol, and an avenue to reach potential white allies.

By the 1830s, much of the Cherokee territory had been violently appropriated, and Cherokee culture, traditions, and sovereignty were under attack. The state of Georgia annexed Cherokee lands and abolished the tribal government, courts, and laws. When the US Supreme Court declared such actions unconstitutional, President Andrew Jackson refused to enforce the ruling. Believing that removal was now inevitable, in 1835 Boudinott joined a small group in signing the Treaty of New Echota, which ceded all Cherokee territory east of the Mississippi in exchange for lands in present-day Oklahoma. Soon after, the Cherokee people were forcibly relocated; the Trail of Tears claimed an estimated 4,000 Cherokee lives. Boudinott and two other signatories of the Treaty of New Echota were killed the following year.

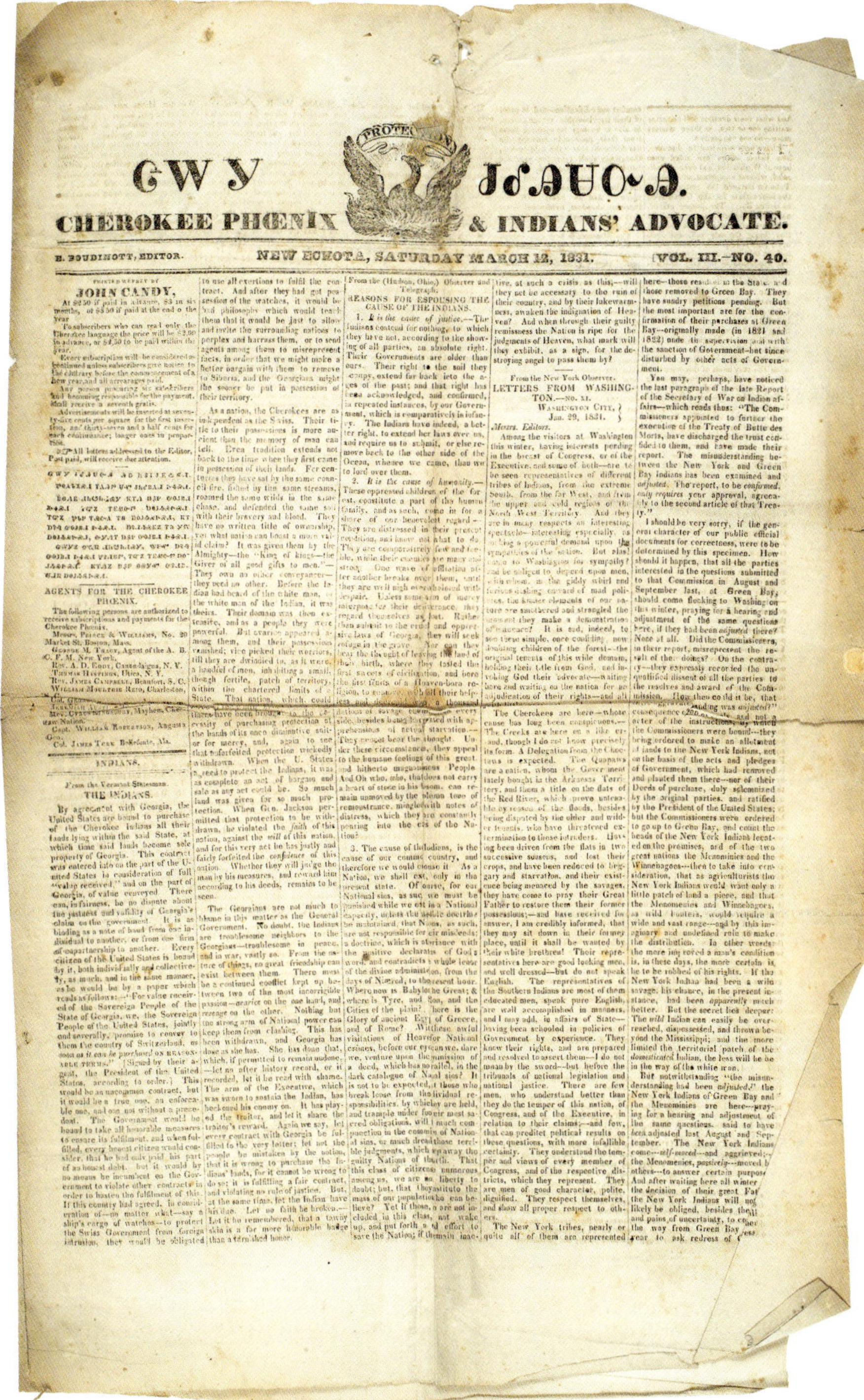

ᏣᎳᎩ ᏧᎴᎯᏌᏅᎯ.
CHEROKEE PHŒNIX & INDIANS' ADVOCATE.

E. BOUDINOTT, EDITOR. NEW ECHOTA, SATURDAY MARCH 12, 1831. VOL. III.—NO. 40.

19

WALT WHITMAN (1819–1892)

Letter to Samuel Baldwin Haskell (1810–1876) and Rosalinda Derby Haskell (1812–1894), July 27, 1863

Washington, DC
Patricia D. Klingenstein Library, The New York Historical

In summer 1863, only a few weeks after the battles of Gettysburg and Vicksburg turned the tide of the Civil War, an army hospital volunteer composed a letter to a couple in Breesport, New York: "Your son Erastus Haskell, of Company K, 41st New York, is now lying sick with typhoid fever," he informed them. The volunteer was Walt Whitman, at that time already well known as an essayist, journalist, and poet. His groundbreaking collection *Leaves of Grass*, first published in 1855, had already gone through several printings, despite controversy surrounding its sexually explicit language and homoerotic imagery.

Whitman was passionately pro-Union. Although he was too old to join the army, his brothers George and Andrew both served, and Whitman initially traveled from Brooklyn to Washington to search for George among the casualties of the battle of Fredericksburg. Shocked by the suffering of the wounded, Whitman plunged into writing—not only to the families of individual soldiers, but also to the Northern press, raising public awareness about poor conditions inside military hospitals.

Less than two weeks later, Whitman wrote again to the Haskells: "Dear friends, I thought it would be soothing to you to have a few lines about the last days of your son." Erastus had not suffered alone, Whitman assured them. "There was hardly a day but I was with him a portion of the time," fanning him to relieve the oppressive heat and keeping him company. Whitman considered Haskell and his fellow Union soldiers "the real precious and royal ones of this land, giving themselves up, aye, even their young & precious lives, in their country's cause." Such sentiments inspired Ralph Waldo Emerson to deem Whitman's poems "more deeply American, democratic, & in the interest of political liberty, than those of any other poet."

Fig. 5
Mathew B. Brady Studio (1844–1873)
Walt Whitman (1819–1892), 1870
Albumen silver print
Patricia D. Klingenstein Library,
The New York Historical

Washington
July 27 1863
Mr & Mrs Haskell
Your son Erastus Haskell of Co K 141st New York, is now lying sick with typhoid fever here in hospital. I have been with him quite a good deal from day to day, was with him yesterday & indeed almost every day, & feel much interested in the young man. He has been very sick, & seems to be so now, as I should judge, but the doctor says he will recover. I had a talk with the doctor yesterday & he says so still. But Erastus seems to me very sick, & I thought I would write to you. He had some one write to you about two weeks ago, but has received no answer. Erastus does not talk much, so I do not understand much about his affairs. I am merely a friend.

July 16, 1947

the address of Erastus is
Ward E, Armory Square Hospital
Washington
DC

Should you wish to write to me direct
Walt Whitman
care Major Hapgood, paymaster
U S A cor 15th & F st
Washington
DC

Upon second thought I enclose you an envelope &c to send your letter to Erastus — put a stamp on it & write soon. I suppose you know he has been sick a great deal since he has been in the service.

20

CLARA HARRIS (1834–1883)

Letter to Mary, April 25, 1865

Washington, DC
Patricia D. Klingenstein Library, The New York Historical

Washington April 25th
My dear Mary:
I received your kind note last week, & should have answered it before, but that I have really felt, as though could not settle myself quietly, even to the performance of such a slight duty as that. Henry has been suffering a great deal with his arm, but it is now

doing very well, — the knife went from the elbow nearly to the shoulder, inside, — cutting an artery, nerves & veins — He bled so profusely as to make him very weak. My whole clothing, as I sat in the box was saturated literally with blood, & my hands & face — You may imagine what a scene — poor Mrs Lincoln all through that dreadful night

Clara Harris, daughter of Ira Harris, a US senator from New York, accompanied Abraham and Mary Todd Lincoln to Ford's Theater on the night of April 14, 1865. There, she witnessed the assassination of the nation's 16th president. Her fiancé, Henry Reed Rathbone, was stabbed while grappling with Lincoln's murderer, John Wilkes Booth. Harris joined those who accompanied the mortally injured Lincoln as he was moved to a house across the street from the theater, and remained at Mary Lincoln's side until her husband died the next morning. Her letter describes the harrowing events, the grief of the widowed first lady, and the severity of Rathbone's wound.

After the terrible night of Lincoln's death, Harris and Rathbone tried to move on. However, Rathbone was plagued with guilt for surviving the assassination and believed that he should have done more to prevent the tragedy. His mental health declined, and he began to suffer from hallucinations. On Christmas Eve in 1883, while living in Germany, he shot Clara and stabbed himself several times with a knife. Clara died from the attack, and Henry was committed to an asylum for the criminally insane.

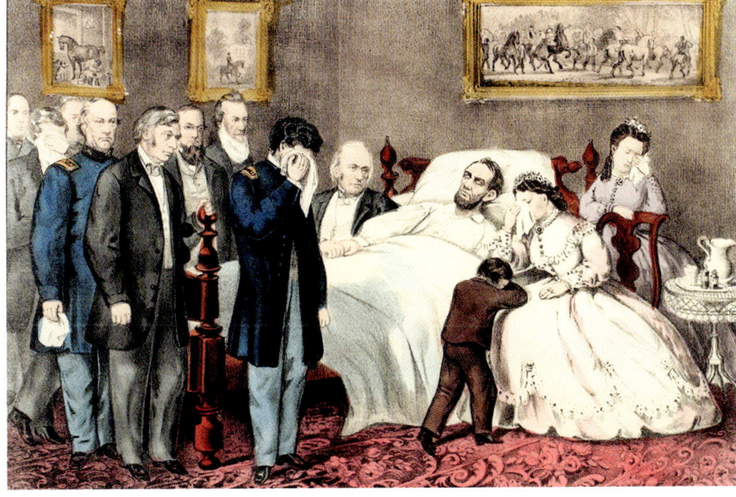

Fig. 6
Unidentified artist
Death of President Lincoln at Washington, D.C. April 15, 1865. The Nation's Martyr.
Colored lithograph
New York: Currier & Ives, 1865
Patricia D. Klingenstein Library,
The New York Historical

21

JOHN W. HIBBS, WILLIAM H. BENNETT, GEORGE S. THOMAS, and ABORN HARRIS, editors and publishers

Prison Times, Vol. 1, No. 1

Fort Delaware prison camp, Division 27, 1865
Patricia D. Klingenstein Library, The New York Historical

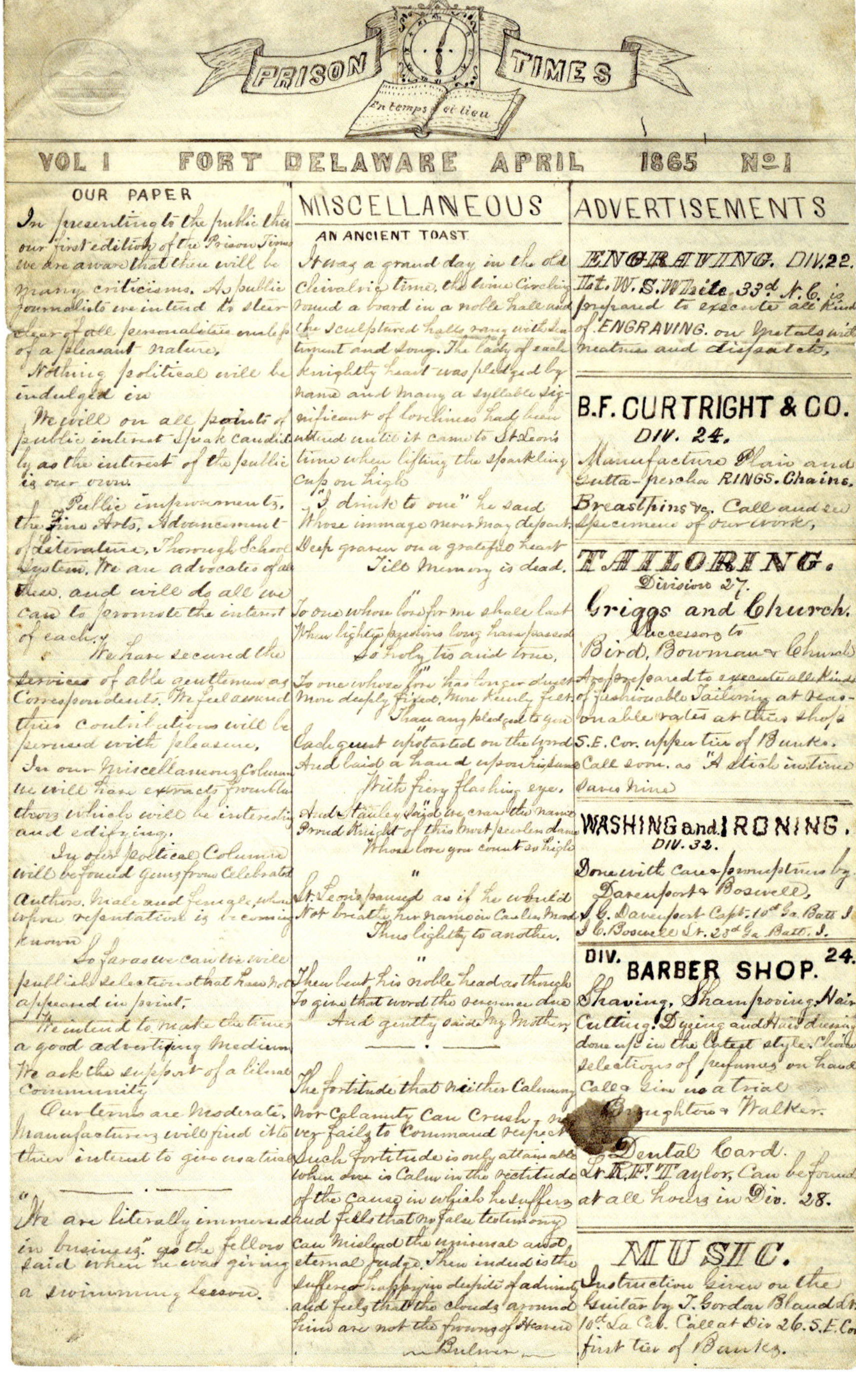

PRISON TIMES

En temps et lieu

VOL I FORT DELAWARE APRIL 1865 No 1

OUR PAPER

In presenting to the public this our first edition of the Prison Times we are aware that there will be many criticisms. As public journalists we intend to steer clear of all personalities unless of a pleasant nature.

Nothing political will be indulged in.

We will on all points of public interest speak candidly as the interest of the public is our own.

Public improvements, the Fine Arts, Advancement of Literature, Thorough School System. We are advocates of all these, and will do all we can to promote the interest of each.

We have secured the services of able gentlemen as Correspondents. We feel assured their contributions will be perused with pleasure.

In our Miscellaneous Column we will have extracts from authors which will be interesting and edifying.

In our Poetical Column will be found gems from Celebrated Authors, Male and female, whose reputation is becoming known.

So far as we can we will publish selections that have not appeared in print.

We intend to make the Times a good advertising Medium. We ask the support of a liberal Community.

Our terms are Moderate. Manufacturers will find it to their interest to give us a trial.

— · —

"We are literally immersed in business" as the fellow said when he was giving a swimming lesson.

MISCELLANEOUS

AN ANCIENT TOAST

It was a grand day in the old Chivalric time, the wine circling round a board in a noble hall and the sculptured halls rang with sentiment and song. The lady of each knightly heart was pledged by name and many a syllable significant of loveliness had been uttered until it came to St. Leon's time when lifting the sparkling cup on high

"I drink to one" he said
Whose image never may depart.
Deep graven on a grateful heart
Till memory is dead.

"To one whose love for me shall last
When lighter passions long have passed
So holy 'tis and true,

To one whose love has longer dwelt
More deeply fixed, more keenly felt
Than any pledged to you."

Each guest upstarted on the word
And laid a hand upon his sword
With fiery flashing eye.
And Stanley said "we crave the name
Proud Knight of this most peerless dame
Whose love you count so high."

St. Leon paused as if he would
Not breathe her name in careless mood
Thus lightly to another.
Then bent his noble head as though
To give that word the reverence due
And gently said "My Mother."

— · —

The fortitude that neither Calumny nor Calamity can crush, never fails to command respect. Such fortitude is only attainable when one is Calm in the rectitude of the cause in which he suffers and feels that no false testimony can mislead the universal and eternal judge. Then indeed is the sufferer happy in despite of adversity and feels that the clouds around him are not the frowns of Heaven

— Bulwer —

ADVERTISEMENTS

ENGRAVING. DIV. 22.
Lt. W. S. White 33d N. C. is prepared to execute all kinds of ENGRAVING on Metals with neatness and dispatch.

B.F. CURTRIGHT & CO.
DIV. 24.
Manufacture Plain and Gutta-percha RINGS. Chains. Breastpins &c. Call and see specimens of our work.

TAILORING.
Division 27.
Griggs and Church.
Successors to
Bird, Bowman & Church
Are prepared to execute all kinds of fashionable Tailoring at reasonable rates at their shop S.E. Cor. upper tier of Bunks. Call soon, as "A stitch in time saves nine"

WASHING and IRONING.
DIV. 32.
Done with care & promptness by
Davenport & Boswell.
J. G. Davenport Capt. 10th Ga. Batt. I.
J. C. Boswell Lt. 23d Ga. Batt. I.

DIV. 24.
BARBER SHOP.
Shaving, Shampooing, Hair Cutting. Dyeing and Hair dressing done up in the latest style. Choice selections of perfumes on hand. Call & give us a trial
[illegible]ughton & Walker.

Dental Card.
Lt. R. F. Taylor, Can be found at all hours in Div. 28.

MUSIC.
Instruction Given on the Guitar by J. Gordon Bland Lt. 10th La. Cav. Call at Div 26. S.E. Cor. first tier of Bunks.

This is one of four known copies of the first and only issue of *Prison Times*, a four-page newspaper handwritten at a prison camp on Pea Patch Island in the Delaware River. Many of the detainees at Fort Delaware had been captured at Gettysburg; the paper's editors and proprietors were all Confederate officers.

The newspaper reflects the prisoners' attempts to re-create their civilian lives. Alongside original articles, announcements, and a camp directory, it includes poems, notices for a chess club, a debating society, and a Christian Association, plus advertisements for shoe repairs, haircuts, and laundry service. The prison camp was overcrowded and unsanitary; epidemics of cholera, typhoid, and smallpox periodically swept through the population—and yet the prisoners' greatest fear was isolation and abandonment. Although the lead editorial promised "to keep our readers posted upon all the events of our little world . . . and afford them every facility of knowing who is here and what is being done," it also wrote plaintively of the lack of contact with "the 'Great World' outside."

22

VICTORIA CLAFLIN WOODHULL (1838–1927) and TENNESSEE CLAFLIN (1844–1923), publishers

Woodhull & Claflin's Weekly: Progress! Free Thought! Untrammeled Lives! Breaking the Way for Future Generations, Vol. 2, No. 23, whole No. 49

New York, April 22, 1871
Patricia D. Klingenstein Library, The New York Historical

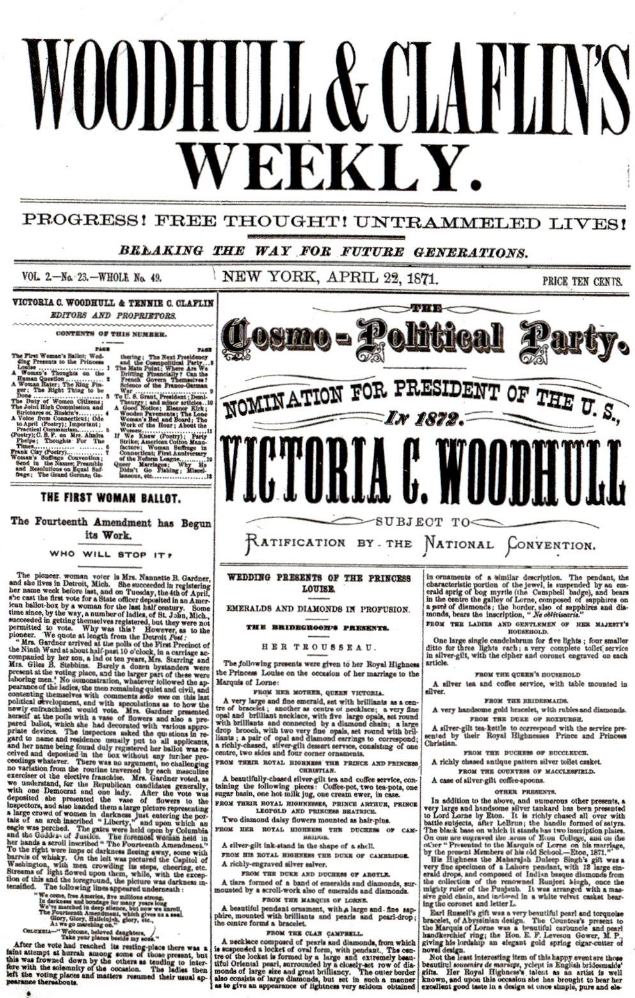

WOODHULL & CLAFLIN'S WEEKLY.

PROGRESS! FREE THOUGHT! UNTRAMMELED LIVES!

BREAKING THE WAY FOR FUTURE GENERATIONS.

VOL. 2.—No. 23.—WHOLE No. 49. NEW YORK, APRIL 22, 1871. PRICE TEN CENTS.

VICTORIA C. WOODHULL & TENNIE C. CLAFLIN
EDITORS AND PROPRIETORS.

CONTENTS OF THIS NUMBER.

	PAGE
The First Woman's Ballot; Wedding Presents to the Princess Louise	1
A Woman's Thoughts on the Human Question	2
A Woman Hater; The Ring Finger; The Right Thing to be Done	3
The Duty of Women Citizens; The Joint High Commission and Strictures on Ruskin's	4
A Voice from Connecticut; Ode to April (Poetry); Important; Practical Communism	5
(Poetry); C. B. P. on Mrs. Almira Phelps; Thoughts For The Times	6
Frank Clay (Poetry)	7
Woman's Suffrage Convention; Send in the Names; Preamble and Resolutions on Equal Suffrage; The Grand German Gathering; The Next Presidency and the Cosmopolitical Party	8
The Main Point; Where Are We Drifting Financially? Can the French Govern Themselves? Science of the Franco-German War	9
To U. S. Grant, President; Demi-Theurgy; and minor articles	10
A Good Notice; Eleanor Kirk; Wooden Pavements; The Lone Woman's Bed and Board; The Work of the Hour; About the Women	11
If We Knew (Poetry); Party Strike; American Cotton Manufacture; Woman Suffrage in Connecticut; First Anniversary of the Reform League	12
Queer Marriages; Why He Didn't Go Fishing; Miscellaneous, etc.	13

THE

Cosmo-Political Party.

NOMINATION FOR PRESIDENT OF THE U. S.,

IN 1872.

VICTORIA C. WOODHULL

SUBJECT TO

RATIFICATION BY THE NATIONAL CONVENTION.

THE FIRST WOMAN BALLOT.

The Fourteenth Amendment has Begun its Work.

WHO WILL STOP IT?

The pioneer woman voter is Mrs. Nannette B. Gardner, and she lives in Detroit, Mich. She succeeded in registering her name week before last, and on Tuesday, the 4th of April, she cast the first vote for a State officer deposited in an American ballot-box by a woman for the last half century. Some time since, by the way, a number of ladies, of St. John, Mich., succeeded in getting themselves registered, but they were not permitted to vote. Why was this? However, as to the pioneer. We quote at length from the Detroit *Post*:

"Mrs. Gardner arrived at the polls of the First Precinct of the Ninth Ward at about half-past 10 o'clock, in a carriage accompanied by her son, a lad of ten years, Mrs. Starring and Mrs. Giles B. Stebbins. Barely a dozen bystanders were present at the voting place, and the larger part of these were laboring men.' No demonstration, whatever followed the appearance of the ladies, the men remaining quiet and civil, and contenting themselves with comments *sotto voce* on this last political development, and with speculations as to how the newly enfranchised would vote. Mrs. Gardner presented herself at the polls with a vase of flowers and also a prepared ballot, which she had decorated with various appropriate devices. The inspectors asked the questions in regard to name and residence usually put to all applicants, and her name being found duly registered her ballot was received and deposited in the box without any further proceedings whatever. There was no argument, no challenging no variation from the routine traversed by each masculine exerciser of the elective franchise. Mrs. Gardner voted, as we understand, for the Republican candidates generally, with one Democrat and one lady. After the vote was deposited she presented the vase of flowers to the inspectors, and also handed them a large picture representing a large crowd of women in darkness just entering the portals of an arch inscribed "Liberty," and upon which an eagle was perched. The gates were held open by Columbia and the Goddess of Justice. The foremost woman held in her hands a scroll inscribed "The Fourteenth Amendment." To the right were imps of darkness fleeing away, some with barrels of whisky. On the left was pictured the Capitol of Washington, with men crowding its steps, cheering, etc. Streams of light flowed upon them, while, with the exception of this and the foreground, the picture was darkness intensified. The following lines appeared underneath:

"We come, free America, five millions strong,
In darkness and bondage for many years long
We've marched in deep silence, but now we enroll,
The Fourteenth Amendment, which gives us a seal.
Glory, Glory, Hallelujah, glory, etc.,
As we go marching on."

COLUMBIA—"Welcome, beloved daughters,
Take your places beside my sons."

After the vote had reached its resting-place there was a faint attempt at hurrah among some of those present, but this was frowned down by the others as tending to interfere with the solemnity of the occasion. The ladies then left the voting places and matters resumed their usual appearance thereabouts.

WEDDING PRESENTS OF THE PRINCESS LOUISE.

EMERALDS AND DIAMONDS IN PROFUSION.

THE BRIDEGROOM'S PRESENTS.

HER TROUSSEAU.

The following presents were given to her Royal Highness the Princess Louise on the occasion of her marriage to the Marquis of Lorne:

FROM HER MOTHER, QUEEN VICTORIA.

A very large and fine emerald, set with brilliants as a centre of bracelet; another as centre of necklace; a very fine opal and brilliant necklace, with five large opals, set round with brilliants and connected by a diamond chain; a large drop brooch, with two very fine opals, set round with brilliants; a pair of opal and diamond earrings to correspond; a richly-chased, silver-gilt dessert service, consisting of one centre, two sides and four corner ornaments.

FROM THEIR ROYAL HIGHNESS THE PRINCE AND PRINCESS CHRISTIAN.

A beautifully-chased silver-gilt tea and coffee service, containing the following pieces: Coffee-pot, two tea-pots, one sugar basin, one hot milk jug, one cream ewer, in case.

FROM THEIR ROYAL HIGHNESSES, PRINCE ARTHUR, PRINCE LEOPOLD AND PRINCESS BEATRICE.

Two diamond daisy flowers mounted as hair-pins.

FROM HER ROYAL HIGHNESS THE DUCHESS OF CAMBRIDGE.

A silver-gilt ink-stand in the shape of a shell.

FROM HIS ROYAL HIGHNESS THE DUKE OF CAMBRIDGE.

A richly-engraved silver salver.

FROM THE DUKE AND DUCHESS OF ARGYLE.

A tiara formed of a band of emeralds and diamonds, surmounted by a scroll-work also of emeralds and diamonds.

FROM THE MARQUIS OF LORNE.

A beautiful pendant ornament, with a large and fine sapphire, mounted with brilliants and pearls and pearl-drop; the centre forms a bracelet.

FROM THE CLAN CAMPBELL.

A necklace composed of pearls and diamonds, from which is suspended a locket of oval form, with pendant. The centre of the locket is formed by a large and extremely beautiful Oriental pearl, surrounded by a closely-set row of diamonds of large size and great brilliancy. The outer border also consists of large diamonds, but set in such a manner as to give an appearance of lightness very seldom obtained in ornaments of a similar description. The pendant, the characteristic portion of the jewel, is suspended by an emerald sprig of bog myrtle (the Campbell badge), and bears in the centre the galley of Lorne, composed of sapphires on a pavé of diamonds; the border, also of sapphires and diamonds, bears the inscription, "*Ne obliviscaris.*"

FROM THE LADIES AND GENTLEMEN OF HER MAJESTY'S HOUSEHOLD.

One large single candelabrum for five lights; four smaller ditto for three lights each; a very complete toilet service in silver-gilt, with the cipher and coronet engraved on each article.

FROM THE QUEEN'S HOUSEHOLD

A silver tea and coffee service, with table mounted in silver.

FROM THE BRIDESMAIDS.

A very handsome gold bracelet, with rubies and diamonds.

FROM THE DUKE OF ROXBURGH.

A silver-gilt tea-kettle to correspond with the service presented by their Royal Highnesses Prince and Princess Christian.

FROM THE DUCHESS OF BUCCLEUCH.

A richly chased antique pattern silver toilet casket.

FROM THE COUNTESS OF MACCLESFIELD.

A case of silver-gilt coffee-spoons.

OTHER PRESENTS.

In addition to the above, and numerous other presents, a very large and handsome silver tankard has been presented to Lord Lorne by Eton. It is richly chased all over with battle subjects, after LeBrun; the handle formed of satyrs. The black base on which it stands has two inscription plates. On one are engraved the arms of Eton College, and on the other "Presented to the Marquis of Lorne on his marriage, by the present Members of his old School.—Eton, 1871."

His Highness the Maharajah Duleep Singh's gift was a very fine specimen of a Lahore pendant, with 13 large emerald drops, and composed of Indian basque diamonds from the collection of the renowned Runjeet Singh, once the mighty ruler of the Punjaub. It was arranged with a massive gold chain, and inclosed in a white velvet casket bearing the coronet and letter L.

Earl Russell's gift was a very beautiful pearl and torquoise bracelet, of Abyssinian design. The Countess's present to the Marquis of Lorne was a beautiful carbuncle and pearl handkerchief ring; the Hon. E. F. Leveson Gower, M. P., giving his lordship an elegant gold spring cigar-cutter of novel design.

Not the least interesting item of this happy event are those beautiful *souvenirs de mariage*, yclept in English bridesmaids' gifts. Her Royal Highness's talent as an artist is well known, and upon this occasion she has brought to bear her excellent good taste in a design at once simple, pure and ele-

Victoria Claflin Woodhull, later Victoria Woodhull Martin, was an American leader of the women's suffrage movement. With financial backing from the multimillionaire Cornelius Vanderbilt, she and her sister, Tennessee Claflin, were also the first women to open a Wall Street brokerage firm. The sisters used their profits to fund *Woodhull & Claflin's Weekly*, which appeared on May 14, 1870—one of the first newspapers published by women in the United States. The sisters advocated for a variety of controversial topics: vegetarianism, spiritualism, socialism, and women's political rights. As the headline pictured blared, Woodhull ran for president of the United States in 1872, almost 50 years before ratification of the 19th Amendment.

Perhaps the newspaper's most contentious subject was "free love," the right of women and men to marry, divorce, and bear children without government interference or formal legal ties. When critiqued by Henry Ward Beecher, first minister of Brooklyn's Plymouth Church, Woodhull used her paper to blast him for hypocrisy and expose Beecher's sexual affair with congregant Elizabeth Richards Tilton, the wife of Beecher's close friend and colleague Theodore Tilton. In the wake of the scandal, both Woodhull and Claflin were arrested under the 1873 Comstock Act for distributing obscene material through the mail. The scandal dragged on for years, eventually bankrupting Woodhull. *Woodhull & Claflin's Weekly* ceased publication in 1876.

Fig. 7
Mathew B. Brady Studio
(1844–1873)
Victoria Claflin Woodhull (1838–1927), ca. 1870
Carte-de-visite
Patricia D. Klingenstein Library,
The New York Historical

23

WONG CHIN FOO (1847–1898), editor

Mei hua shin bao (Chinese American), Vol. 1, No. 1

New York: Enterprise P. Co., February 3, 1883
Patricia D. Klingenstein Library, The New York Historical

循環新報

光緒八年歲次壬午十二月貳拾柒日第壹號

美華新報

美華館舖在紐約咀啉街第壹佰捌拾玖號又壹佰玖拾壹號開張

耶蘇降世壹千八百八十三年

The CHINESE AMERICAN.

WONG CHING FOO, Editor.

Entered at the New York P. O. as Second Class Matter.

Enterprise P. Co., (E. B. COLE, F. P. COLE) Managers.
189 & 191 CHATHAM ST.

Vol. I. Single Copies 5 Cents. NEW YORK, SATURDAY, FEBRUARY 3, 1883. Yearly Rates $2.50 No. 1.

事屬傳聞省垣自仰忠街等處大道田祿以後各處大街時聞火儆於是謠言四起或謂火星下墜或謂火龍降臨茲將所聞錄之以供衆覽聞初一晚十三甫黃姓書館學徒在館中飲酒為樂忽然瞥見火球一顆從空中下墜倏忽不見學徒等驚譁不已莫不走避此一事也又聞初二日早有紅雀一羣約六七十頭形如白鴿而毛羽全紅集于十弍三甫庵之工人多見之約越点鐘之久然後飛去此又其一事也又聞南海縣屬近小塘鄉有村名荔枝園者於晚間十分点鐘見有火龍一条長約十餘丈從空際垂於村內其光熊熊人多驚異越刻乃滅所聞如是未知確否姑錄以資談柄

由上海新報云

啓聞昨於本年九月初七日有文稱說扗京有段奇事世所罕聞者謂云緬甸國王曾有大白象一隻身高丈餘形威兇猛向屬人性剋下以為珍奇之物貢献天朝 皇駕受之內有文武官僚欲將試而使之被象鞭死其員於是 聖上發怒命擊死象掘地而掩之以伸衆官之冤云

女色迷魂

脂紅粉白每易迷魂柳綠花艷多能揖魄尋花問柳之輩蜂狂蝶浪之徒視歡場為樂窩竟入迷津之局者良可慨哉觀於番人此段孽賬可為貪色者儆也現本埠禮拜四日番人新聞云謂[illegible]有一番人名叫嚼嚕珠者家有餘資已為冠者乃慕少艾自詡風流目前現在他本街閒遊柳巷尋花但見朱門半推忽有女子娉婷美貌年光十七正應及笄乃覯男子私約苟合之歡故常常而見之夜去明來將臨半載未幾而今有孕矣又將近分娩於是女子見姦夫之富豪將欲索勒姦夫以孕難之求此財以充用資奈姦夫之不听何于是稟官究治姦夫入獄後又引弄二番亦已冠者亦以此孕謂二番之種以言難之於今審訊前之姦夫此二番聞之亦怒特為他証人贏此女子捕其入獄云

When Wong Chin Foo was left destitute as a teenager in northern China, he was taken in by American missionaries. He converted to their Baptist faith, learned to speak English, and spent a year studying in the United States. He returned to China briefly, but departed again in 1873 during an uprising against the Qing Dynasty. Once back in the US, Wong supported himself by traveling the country to educate the public about Chinese culture. In 1874, he became a US citizen in Michigan (one of the few states where Chinese naturalization was possible), and in 1880 he registered to vote, later adopting Western clothing and hairstyles.

In 1883, Wong began publishing *Mei hua shin bao*, the first Chinese-language newspaper on the East Coast. He also contributed articles to English-language publications such as *Harper's Weekly*, the *North American Review*, the *New York Herald*, and the *New York Sun*. Everywhere, he sought to debunk anti-Chinese stereotypes and defend Chinese Americans' claims to equal rights. Pugnacious and publicity-savvy, Wong went toe-to-toe with Denis Kearney, a prominent advocate for the 1882 Chinese Exclusion Act. In 1887, the two men appeared together in New York to discuss the "China Question." Journalists from around the country watched as both went on the offensive, producing an event that was more of a shouting match than a debate. All the newspaper articles agreed that Wong had won, but US policy toward Chinese immigration remained unchanged until 1943.

24

LANGSTON HUGHES (1901–1967)

“Seven Moments of Love: An Un-sonnet Sequence in Blues”, 1939

Typescript
Patricia D. Klingenstein Library, The New York Historical

In 1939, the Harlem Suitcase Theater put on a bare-bones, experimental production of *Don’t You Want to Be Free?*—an epic depiction of Black history written and directed by Langston Hughes, a founding member of the theater. Already known internationally as a writer and cultural figure, Hughes inscribed this typescript copy of “Seven Moments of Love” to one of the evening’s featured actors: his friend Robert Earl Jones, a former prizefighter who would go on to a career in film (a calling that his son, actor James Earl Jones, also pursued).

The Harlem Suitcase Theater, never a great financial success, closed after the 1939–40 season, but Hughes’s writing career continued apace. He wrote a Hollywood script, finished his autobiography, *The Big Sea*, and continued to write poetry—including his 1942 volume, *Shakespeare in Harlem*, which opened with “Seven Moments of Love.” With these poems, Hughes returned to the themes and imagery of his groundbreaking early work, fusing them with the traditional sonnet form to express Black American voices and experiences.

Fig. 8
Bernard Gotfryd (1924–2016)
Langston Hughes (1901–1967), ca. 1962
Gelatin silver print
Patricia D. Klingenstein Library, The New York Historical

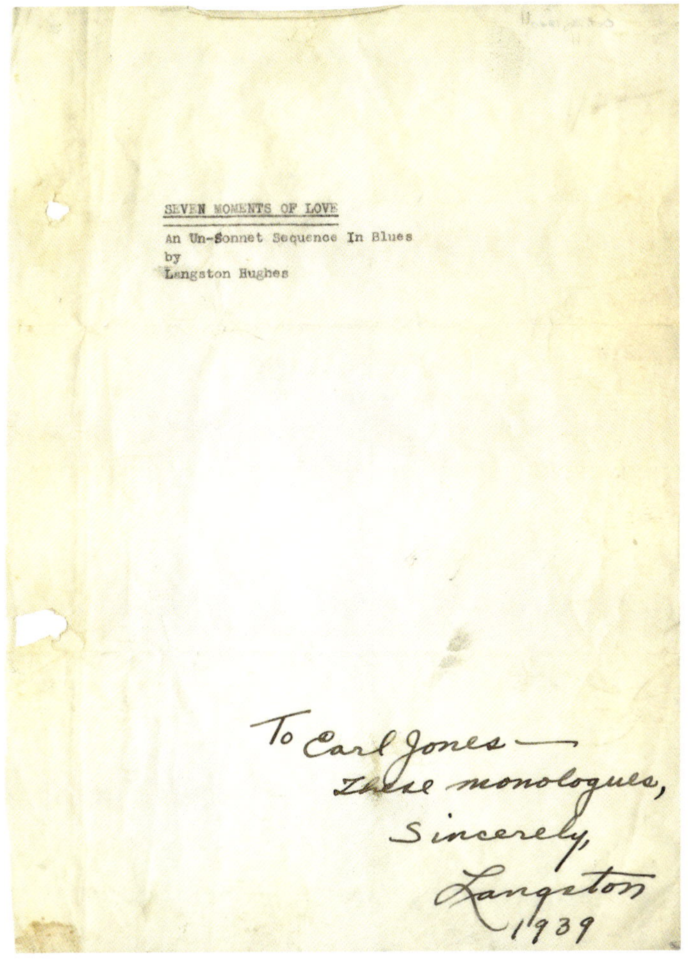

SEVEN MOMENTS OF LOVE
An Un-Sonnet Sequence In Blues
by
Langston Hughes

To Carl Jones —
These monologues,
Sincerely,
Langston
1939

II.

SUPPER TIME

I look in the kettle, the kettle is dry.
Look in the bread box, nothing but a fly.
Turn on the light and look real good!
I would make a fire but there ain't no wood.
Look at that water dripping in the sink.
Listen at my heart beats trying to think.
Listen at my footprints walking on the floor.
That place where your trunk was, ain't no trunk no more.
Place where your clothes hung's empty and bare.
Stay away if you want to, and see if I care!
If I had a fire I'd make me some tea
And set down and drink it, myself and me.
Lawd! I got to find me a woman for the WPA—
Cause if I don't they'll cut down my pay.

25

Prospectus for *TIME* magazine, 1923

Typescript
Patricia D. Klingenstein Library, The New York Historical, Gift of Time Inc.

(For private circulation)

T I M E
The Weekly News-Magazine
(A Prospectus)

THE ARGUMENT

Although daily journalism has been more highly developed in the United States than in any other country of the world --

Although foreigners marvel at the excellence of our periodicals, World's Work, Century, Literary Digest, Outlook, and the rest --

People in America are, for the most part, poorly informed.

This is not the fault of the daily newspapers; they print all the news.

It is not the fault of the weekly "reviews"; they adequately develop and comment on the news.

To say with the facile cynic that it is the fault of the people themselves is to beg the question.

People are uninformed BECAUSE NO PUBLICATION HAS ADAPTED ITSELF TO THE TIME WHICH BUSY MEN ARE ABLE TO SPEND ON SIMPLY KEEPING INFORMED.

T I M E is a weekly news-magazine, aimed to serve the modern necessity of keeping people informed, created on a new principle of COMPLETE ORGANIZATION.

T I M E is interested - not in how much it includes between its cover - but in HOW MUCH IT GETS OFF ITS PAGES INTO THE MINDS OF ITS READERS.

A media empire was born on March 3, 1923, when the first issue of *TIME* hit newsstands. The magazine was the brainchild of co-founders Henry R. Luce (1898–1967) and Briton Hadden (1898–1929), Hotchkiss and Yale classmates who served together during World War I. Their mission was "to inform many people who would not otherwise be informed; and to inform all people in a manner in which they have never been informed before," by addressing America's most valued commodity, constantly exhausted by the demands of a modern world: time.

TIME emerged during the era of scientific management. Henry Ford began his automobile assembly line in 1913, and its step-by-step, routinized process is a clear parallel to *TIME*'s journalistic efficiency. It sought to gather "all available information on all subjects of importance and general interest" from "virtually every magazine and newspaper of note in the world," then distill it to approximately 100 short articles, none over 400 words in length. Like Ford's cars, this streamlined process yielded an economical price: *TIME* launched with a cost of 15 cents per issue.

26

ROBERT A. CARO (b. 1935)

Planning calendar, 1971

Patricia D. Klingenstein Library, The New York Historical,
The Robert A. Caro Archive

Robert Caro's career has been marked by the publication of monumental biographies, each requiring an astonishing level of commitment and productivity. For *The Power Broker*, his Pulitzer Prize–winning biography of New York's "master builder," Robert Moses, Caro spent seven years conducting hundreds of interviews; poring over decades of newspapers, magazines, and promotional materials; digging through dozens of public and private archives; outlining; writing; and revising. (Ina Caro, Robert's wife and a crucial collaborator in the project, even sold their house to help fund the work.) In 1974, when *The Power Broker* was published to great acclaim, its 1,296 pages pushed the limits of what a binding could physically hold—even though the manuscript had been cut down by about one-third, with Caro and his editor, Robert Gottlieb, excising 350,000 words.

Caro set a goal of writing 1,000 words per day during his work on *The Power Broker*, tracking his progress in the pages of a small planning calendar. This document provides an intriguing record of how Caro's writing practice progressed. Alongside the other materials in the Robert A. Caro Archive, it is evidence of Caro's journalistic rigor, dedication to research, and nuanced understanding of power which have inspired generations of readers and garnered nearly every major literary honor.

Unidentified artist
Congressional Pugilists, 1798
Etching
Patricia D. Klingenstein Library,
The New York Historical

POLITICIANS

27

UNIDENTIFIED ARTIST

Portrait of an Unidentified Person, ca. 1710

Oil on canvas
The New York Historical, Purchase, 1952.80

Typical of provincial British portraiture of the early 18th century, this painting of a person in feminine attire had long been identified as a likeness of Edward Hyde (1661–1723), who carried the title Viscount Cornbury and was appointed governor of the Province of New York and New Jersey by his cousin, Queen Anne, in 1702. Serving as governor until 1708, Lord Cornbury was reported to have been "universally detested," and a fondness for cross-dressing accompanied his reputation as "half-witted." Popular legend alluded to the governor discrediting his office by publicly appearing in women's attire, strolling Broadway—even opening the Assembly—in his wife's clothes. Hyde is also said to have held his state levees at New York, and received his visitors, dressed in a woman's court costume, because he represented the person of a female sovereign: his cousin, Queen Anne. Recent scholarship has corrected some of the slanderous characterizations of Cornbury's gubernatorial abilities by his 19th-century detractors, and the portrait has been reclaimed as that of a woman. However, the identities of both the sitter and the painter remain a mystery.

28

UNIDENTIFIED MAKER

Wooden leg of Gouverneur Morris (1752–1816), ca. 1780

Philadelphia, Pennsylvania
Oak, leather, metal
The New York Historical, Gift of Mrs. Frederick Menzies, 1954.148

Although Gouverneur Morris hailed from a prominent New York family with Loyalist sympathies, he became a devoted patriot during the Revolutionary War. As a member of New York's Provincial Congress and Committee of Safety, he worked tirelessly to fund the war effort. A delegate to the Continental Congress, Morris coordinated with George Washington in organizing and advocating for the Continental Army after an eye-opening visit to the winter camp at Valley Forge. Morris's experiences led him to believe in a powerful central government, which he fought for as a representative of Pennsylvania at the 1787 Constitutional Convention. There, he helped shape a strong executive branch, crafted the Preamble to the Constitution, and gave more speeches than any other delegate. Often his oratory condemned the institution of slavery and decried the hypocrisy of the Three-Fifths Compromise, which gave disproportionate representation to slaveholding states. Morris went on to serve as minister to France during the French Revolution, a US senator representing New York, and chair of the Erie Canal Commission. A close friend and ally of Alexander Hamilton, he gave the eulogy at Hamilton's funeral.

Persistent rumors alleged that the tall, handsome, and notoriously amorous Morris lost his left leg after jumping out a window to escape a jealous husband; in reality, his injury was the result of a carriage accident when he was 28.

29a

William Livingston's (1723–1790) copy of the second draft of the United States Constitution with his annotations, 1787

Patricia D. Klingenstein Library, The New York Historical

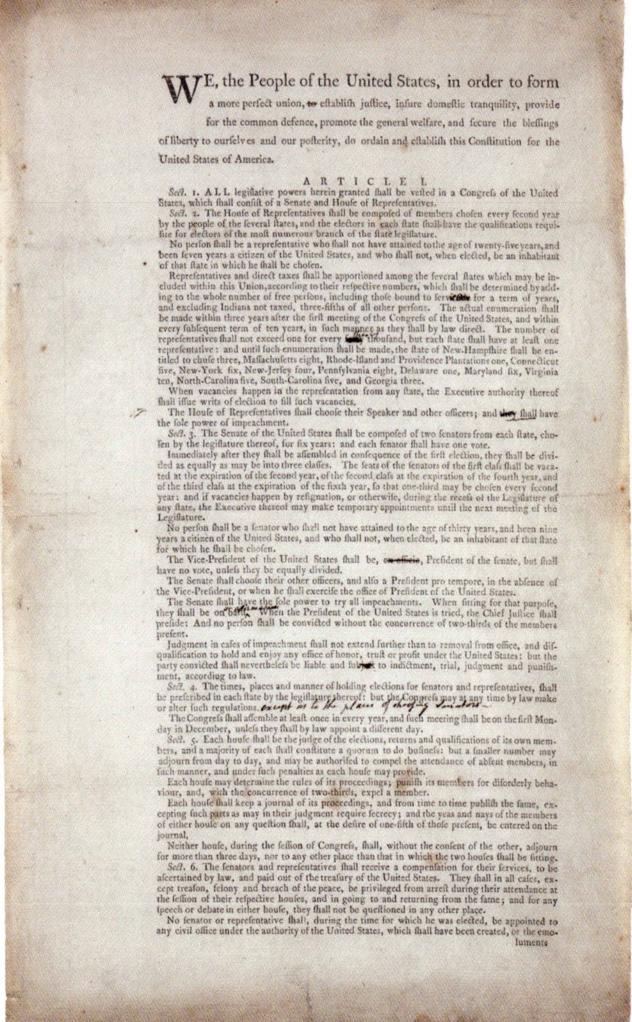

WE, the People of the United States, in order to form a more perfect union, to eſtabliſh juſtice, inſure domeſtic tranquility, provide for the common defence, promote the general welfare, and ſecure the bleſſings of liberty to ourſelves and our poſterity, do ordain and eſtabliſh this Conſtitution for the United States of America.

A R T I C L E I.

Sect. 1. ALL legiſlative powers herein granted ſhall be veſted in a Congreſs of the United States, which ſhall conſiſt of a Senate and Houſe of Repreſentatives.

Sect. 2. The Houſe of Repreſentatives ſhall be compoſed of members choſen every ſecond year by the people of the ſeveral ſtates, and the electors in each ſtate ſhall have the qualifications requiſite for electors of the moſt numerous branch of the ſtate legiſlature.

No perſon ſhall be a repreſentative who ſhall not have attained to the age of twenty-five years, and been ſeven years a citizen of the United States, and who ſhall not, when elected, be an inhabitant of that ſtate in which he ſhall be choſen.

Repreſentatives and direct taxes ſhall be apportioned among the ſeveral ſtates which may be included within this Union, according to their reſpective numbers, which ſhall be determined by adding to the whole number of free perſons, including thoſe bound to ſervitude for a term of years, and excluding Indians not taxed, three-fifths of all other perſons. The actual enumeration ſhall be made within three years after the firſt meeting of the Congreſs of the United States, and within every ſubſequent term of ten years, in ſuch manner as they ſhall by law direct. The number of repreſentatives ſhall not exceed one for every forty thouſand, but each ſtate ſhall have at leaſt one repreſentative: and until ſuch enumeration ſhall be made, the ſtate of New-Hampſhire ſhall be entitled to chuſe three, Maſſachuſetts eight, Rhode-Iſland and Providence Plantations one, Connecticut five, New-York ſix, New-Jerſey four, Pennſylvania eight, Delaware one, Maryland ſix, Virginia ten, North-Carolina five, South-Carolina five, and Georgia three.

When vacancies happen in the repreſentation from any ſtate, the Executive authority thereof ſhall iſſue writs of election to fill ſuch vacancies.

The Houſe of Repreſentatives ſhall chooſe their Speaker and other officers; and they ſhall have the ſole power of impeachment.

Sect. 3. The Senate of the United States ſhall be compoſed of two ſenators from each ſtate, choſen by the legiſlature thereof, for ſix years: and each ſenator ſhall have one vote.

Immediately after they ſhall be aſſembled in conſequence of the firſt election, they ſhall be divided as equally as may be into three claſſes. The ſeats of the ſenators of the firſt claſs ſhall be vacated at the expiration of the ſecond year, of the ſecond claſs at the expiration of the fourth year, and of the third claſs at the expiration of the ſixth year, ſo that one-third may be choſen every ſecond year: and if vacancies happen by reſignation, or otherwiſe, during the receſs of the Legiſlature of any ſtate, the Executive thereof may make temporary appointments until the next meeting of the Legiſlature.

No perſon ſhall be a ſenator who ſhall not have attained to the age of thirty years, and been nine years a citizen of the United States, and who ſhall not, when elected, be an inhabitant of that ſtate for which he ſhall be choſen.

The Vice-Preſident of the United States ſhall be, ex officio, Preſident of the ſenate, but ſhall have no vote, unleſs they be equally divided.

The Senate ſhall chooſe their other officers, and alſo a Preſident pro tempore, in the abſence of the Vice-Preſident, or when he ſhall exerciſe the office of Preſident of the United States.

The Senate ſhall have the ſole power to try all impeachments. When ſitting for that purpoſe, they ſhall be on oath. When the Preſident of the United States is tried, the Chief Juſtice ſhall preſide: And no perſon ſhall be convicted without the concurrence of two-thirds of the members preſent.

Judgment in caſes of impeachment ſhall not extend further than to removal from office, and diſqualification to hold and enjoy any office of honor, truſt or profit under the United States: but the party convicted ſhall nevertheleſs be liable and ſubject to indictment, trial, judgment and puniſhment, according to law.

Sect. 4. The times, places and manner of holding elections for ſenators and repreſentatives, ſhall be preſcribed in each ſtate by the legiſlature thereof: but the Congreſs may at any time by law make or alter ſuch regulations, except as to the places of chuſing Senators.

The Congreſs ſhall aſſemble at leaſt once in every year, and ſuch meeting ſhall be on the firſt Monday in December, unleſs they ſhall by law appoint a different day.

Sect. 5. Each houſe ſhall be the judge of the elections, returns and qualifications of its own members, and a majority of each ſhall conſtitute a quorum to do buſineſs: but a ſmaller number may adjourn from day to day, and may be authoriſed to compel the attendance of abſent members, in ſuch manner, and under ſuch penalties as each houſe may provide.

Each houſe may determine the rules of its proceedings; puniſh its members for diſorderly behaviour, and, with the concurrence of two-thirds, expel a member.

Each houſe ſhall keep a journal of its proceedings, and from time to time publiſh the ſame, excepting ſuch parts as may in their judgment require ſecrecy; and the yeas and nays of the members of either houſe on any queſtion ſhall, at the deſire of one-fifth of thoſe preſent, be entered on the journal.

Neither houſe, during the ſeſſion of Congreſs, ſhall, without the conſent of the other, adjourn for more than three days, nor to any other place than that in which the two houſes ſhall be ſitting.

Sect. 6. The ſenators and repreſentatives ſhall receive a compenſation for their ſervices, to be aſcertained by law, and paid out of the treaſury of the United States. They ſhall in all caſes, except treaſon, felony and breach of the peace, be privileged from arreſt during their attendance at the ſeſſion of their reſpective houſes, and in going to and returning from the ſame; and for any ſpeech or debate in either houſe, they ſhall not be queſtioned in any other place.

No ſenator or repreſentative ſhall, during the time for which he was elected, be appointed to any civil office under the authority of the United States, which ſhall have been created, or the emoluments

29b

JOHN LANSING JR. (1754–1829?)

Notebooks from the Constitutional Convention, 1787

Patricia D. Klingenstein Library, The New York Historical

This selection of documents commemorates the highly contentious process of writing, signing, and ratifying the United States Constitution. William Livingston, who served as governor of New Jersey from 1776 to 1790 and was also a member of the New Jersey Delegation to the 1787 Constitutional Convention in Philadelphia, left a copy of the second draft of the Constitution thickly annotated with the changes and compromises that appear in the final version, which Livingston signed. In contrast, New York delegate John Lansing opposed the Constitution. His notebooks, among the rare surviving first hand accounts of the proceedings, record his distress as the Convention went beyond its mandate in establishing a new government, rather than simply amending the Articles of Confederation, as charged.

30a

JOHN JAY (1745–1829)

Draft of *Federalist Number 64, In Relation to Foreign Nations*, ca. 1788

Manuscript
Patricia D. Klingenstein Library, The New York Historical

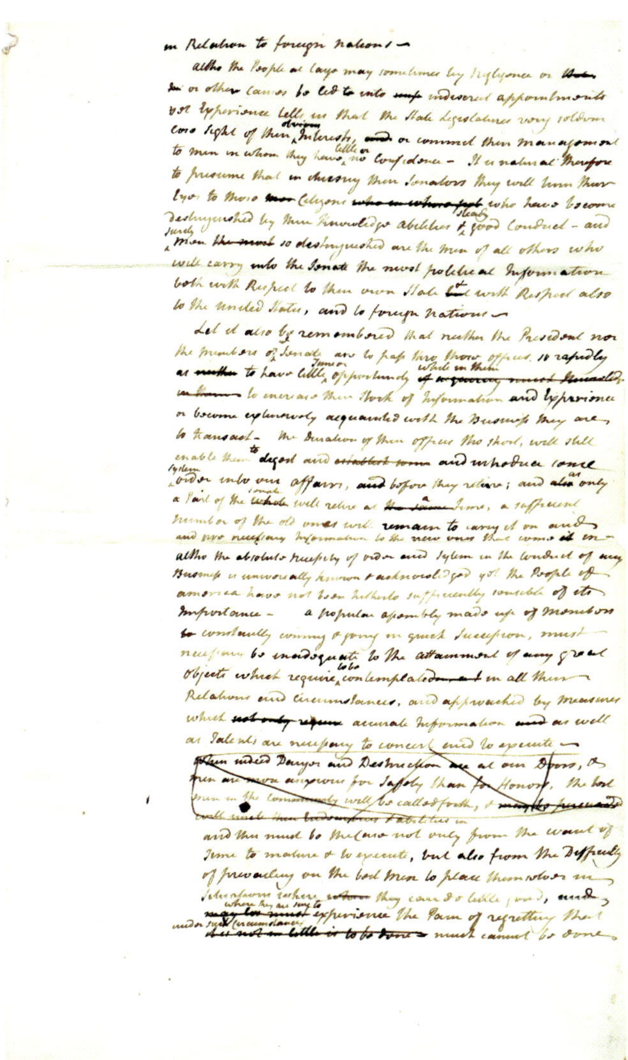

30b

ALEXANDER HAMILTON (1757–1804), JOHN JAY (1745–1829), AND JAMES MADISON (1751–1836)

John Pintard's (1759–1844) copy of *The Federalist*

New York: J. and A. M'Lean, 1787
Patricia D. Klingenstein Library, The New York Historical

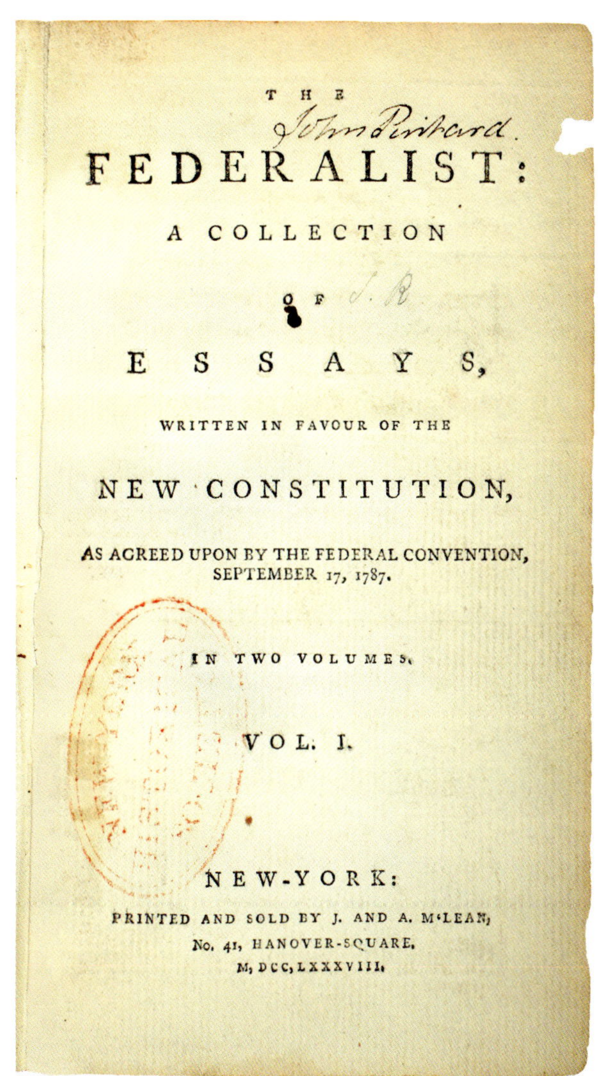

THE
John Pintard.
FEDERALIST:
A COLLECTION
OF
ESSAYS,
WRITTEN IN FAVOUR OF THE
NEW CONSTITUTION,
AS AGREED UPON BY THE FEDERAL CONVENTION,
SEPTEMBER 17, 1787.
IN TWO VOLUMES.
VOL. I.
NEW-YORK:
PRINTED AND SOLD BY J. AND A. M'LEAN,
No. 41, HANOVER-SQUARE,
M,DCC,LXXXVIII.

To promote the case for ratification to the public, Alexander Hamilton, James Madison, and John Jay wrote 85 essays, each anonymously signed "Publius," which are now collectively known as *The Federalist Papers.* These essays were first published in newspapers and then issued in two volumes. This draft of *Federalist Number 64*, written in John Jay's hand, argues that the Constitution must provide for senatorial approval of treaties. The essay bore the number 63 when it was first published on March 5, 1788, but was renumbered 64 in the first collected edition, published March 22, 1788. John Pintard donated his copy of the first complete edition of *The Federalist* published in book form to The New York Historical.

31

F. BARTOLI (1783–1796)

Gayḗtwahgeh (Cornplanter, 1732/1742–1836), 1796

Oil on canvas
The New York Historical, Gift of Thomas Jefferson Bryan, 1867.314

This portrait of Gayḗtwahgeh (Cornplanter) likely commemorates his May 1786 meeting with the US Congress in New York. It was a high-stakes occasion: among the Haudenosaunee nations, the Kanien'kehá:ka (Mohawk), Gayogo̱hó:nǫʔ (Cayuga), and Onöndowa'ga:' (Seneca) had allied with the British during the American Revolution, and, as a result, were not included in the 1783 Treaty of Paris which ended the war. Instead, in the following year the federal government dictated the separate Treaty of Fort Stanwix, which established the first reservation territory in the United States and compelled the Kanien'kehá:ka, Gayogo̱hó:nǫʔ, and Onöndowa'ga:' to cede their interest in lands beyond the reservation boundaries.

Gayḗtwahgeh is pictured wearing pieces of regalia presented to him by the "Council of the Thirteen Fires," which signaled the establishment of peaceful relations between the Onöndowa'ga:' chief and the young republic. In addition to bestowing these gifts, Congress gave Gayḗtwahgeh assurances that both the British and Americans wanted peace with the Native Americans and would respect the boundaries of land assigned to them by treaty. However, the US government rarely enforced these treaty rights, especially after completion of the Erie Canal in 1825, which made nearby Onöndowa'ga:' lands highly attractive to non-Native speculators. The Onöndowa'ga:' people waged a decades-long lobbying and legal campaign to preserve their lands from federal, state, and private encroachment, and prevent their forced removal to Kansas.

31

32

CHARLES-BALTHAZAR-JULIEN FEVRET DE SAINT-MÉMIN (1770–1852)

Unidentified Osage Warrior Wearing Bird Headdress, 1807

Charcoal with stumping, Conté crayon, black pastel, and black and white chalk on pink prepared paper, nailed over canvas to a wooden strainer
The New York Historical, Purchase, Elizabeth DeMilt Fund, 1860.91

This stunning life-size drawing belongs to a group of eight portraits of Indigenous Americans (six men and two women) by Charles-Balthazar-Julien Fevret de Saint-Mémin in The New York Historical's collection. The subjects were members of official delegations from the Ni-u-kon-ska (Osage) and Numakiki (Mandan). They visited Washington, DC, three times between 1804 and 1807 with the dual purpose of meeting President Thomas Jefferson and establishing trade after the Louisiana Purchase suddenly made their lands part of the United States. While in Washington, itinerant artist Saint-Mémin drew their portraits.

The delegates had no way of knowing that the changes that would transform the United States during the 19th century would bring enormous losses to their people. Smallpox epidemics decimated the Numakiki, while a series of treaties gradually stripped away Ni-u-kon-ska Nation lands. In the 1870s, the Ni-u-kon-ska were forcibly removed to "Indian Territory" in today's Oklahoma, where many of their descendants live today.

33a

ABRAHAM LINCOLN (1809–1865)

By the President of the United States of America. A Proclamation.

Broadside
Philadelphia: Frederick Leypoldt, 1864
Patricia D. Klingenstein Library, The New York Historical

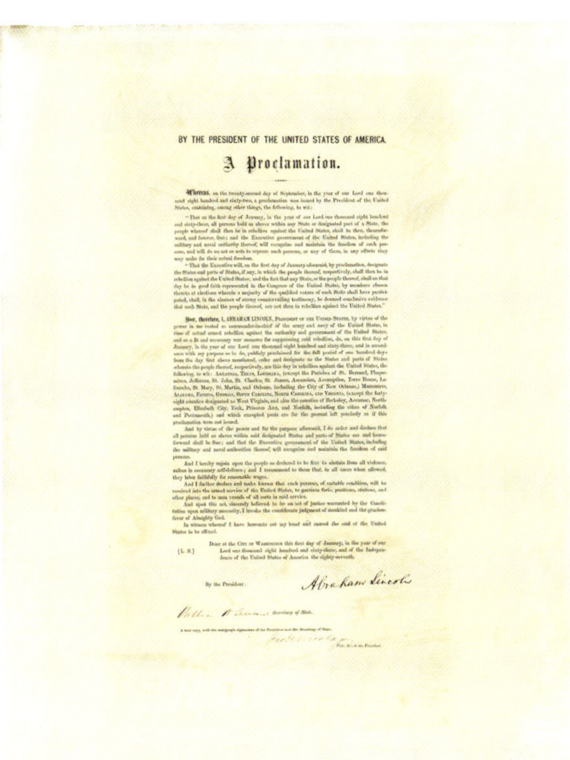

BY THE PRESIDENT OF THE UNITED STATES OF AMERICA.

A Proclamation.

Abraham Lincoln's Emancipation Proclamation, which went into effect on January 1, 1863, was a major step toward the abolition of slavery in the United States and a pivotal moment in the Civil War. "If my name ever goes into history, it will be for this act, and my whole soul is in it," he remarked at the moment of signing.

This copy is known as the Leland-Boker edition of the Emancipation Proclamation, after the two men who arranged for its printing by Frederick Leypoldt. Only 48 were made, and each was autographed by Lincoln, secretary of state William Seward, and John Nicolay, private secretary to the president. They were offered for sale, priced at $10 each, at the Philadelphia Great Central Sanitary Fair of June 7–29, 1864. Over a hundred thousand visitors attended the Fair—yet not all of the Leland-Boker replicas of the Emancipation Proclamation sold, perhaps a reflection on Lincoln's unpopularity after three years of war. Indeed, Lincoln himself doubted that he would win re-election that fall.

33b

ABRAHAM LINCOLN (1809–1865)

The Inaugural Address of President Abraham Lincoln, Delivered at the National Capitol, March 4th, 1865

Broadside
Patricia D. Klingenstein Library, The New York Historical

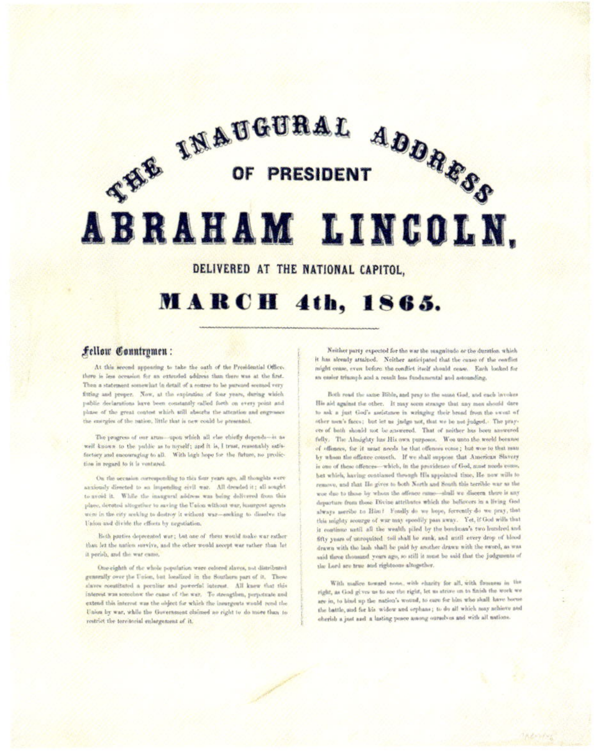

THE INAUGURAL ADDRESS OF PRESIDENT

ABRAHAM LINCOLN,

DELIVERED AT THE NATIONAL CAPITOL,

MARCH 4th, 1865.

Fellow Countrymen:

Of course Lincoln emerged victorious in 1864, and delivered his Second Inaugural Address at the National Capitol on March 4, 1865. This blue-inked broadside is the first printing of one of the best-known political speeches in US history. Exhausted yet determined, Lincoln re-interpreted America's founding and lit the way for "peace among ourselves" after the long and bloody Civil War:

> With malice toward none, with charity for all, with firmness in the right, as God gives us to see the right, let us strive on to finish the work we are in, to bind up the nation's wound, to care for him who shall have borne the battle, and for his widow and orphans; to do all which may achieve and cherish a just and a lasting peace among ourselves and with all nations.

After Lincoln's death on April 15, all subsequent printings of this address were done in black ink.

34

CORNWALL KIRKPATRICK (1814–1890) and WILLIAM WALLACE KIRKPATRICK (1828–1896), artists
ANNA POTTERY (active 1859–1896), manufacturer

Snake jug, 1871

Anna, Illinois
Salt-glazed stoneware
The New York Historical, Gift of Mrs. Thomas Nast, 1906.6ab

This jug was created as a gift for Thomas Nast, the renowned political caricaturist. The swirling mass of snakes and heads represents the ring of notoriously corrupt New York City politicians headquartered at Tammany Hall and headed by William Magear "Boss" Tweed (1823–1878). Nast was well known for skewering Tweed and his cronies in the pages of *Harper's Weekly*. Thanks in large part to Nast's public campaign, Tweed was arrested in 1871, and in 1873 he went on trial in the Tweed Courthouse, which had come to symbolize his corrupt practices. Graft, theft, and kickbacks had inflated the building's cost to $12 million, making it the most expensive public building in the US; $5 million of the money had gone straight into Tweed's own pocket. In contrast, the United States had purchased the territory of Alaska for $7.2 million less than ten years before.

Tweed was convicted on numerous charges and served a reduced, one-year jail sentence before being arrested and imprisoned again in a civil suit brought by the City of New York to recover $6 million in embezzled funds. Tweed escaped from Ludlow Street Jail during a home visit in 1875, and fled to Spain, after which a $10,000 reward was issued. Spanish officials, familiar with Nast's work, recognized Tweed and apprehended him. He returned to prison in New York in 1876, and died there two years later.

Fig. 9
J. & E. Stevens Company (1843–ca. 1940), manufacturer
John Hall (active late 19th century), designer
Tammany mechanical bank, ca. 1873
Cromwell, Connecticut
Iron, paint
The New York Historical, Purchased from Elie Nadelman, 1937.1237

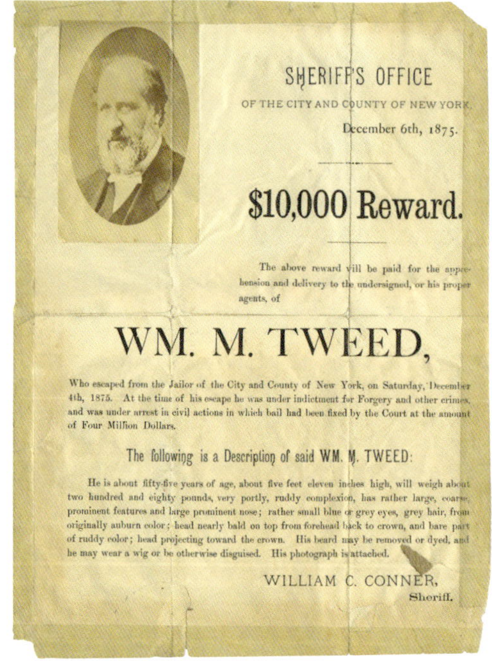

SHERIFF'S OFFICE
OF THE CITY AND COUNTY OF NEW YORK,
December 6th, 1875.

$10,000 Reward.

The above reward will be paid for the apprehension and delivery to the undersigned, or his proper agents, of

WM. M. TWEED,

Who escaped from the Jailor of the City and County of New York, on Saturday, December 4th, 1875. At the time of his escape he was under indictment for Forgery and other crimes, and was under arrest in civil actions in which bail had been fixed by the Court at the amount of Four Million Dollars.

The following is a Description of said WM. M. TWEED:

He is about fifty-five years of age, about five feet eleven inches high, will weigh about two hundred and eighty pounds, very portly, ruddy complexion, has rather large, coarse, prominent features and large prominent nose; rather small blue or grey eyes, grey hair, from originally auburn color; head nearly bald on top from forehead back to crown, and bare part of ruddy color; head projecting toward the crown. His beard may be removed or dyed, and he may wear a wig or be otherwise disguised. His photograph is attached.

WILLIAM C. CONNER,
Sheriff.

Fig. 10
William C. Conner (active late 19th century)
Sheriff's Office of the City and County of New York, December 6th, 1875. $10,000 Reward.
New York City
Patricia D. Klingenstein Library, The New York Historical

34

35

UNIDENTIFIED MAKER

Suffrage pennant, ca. 1913

Wool
The New York Historical, Purchased through the generosity of Elizabeth B. Dater and William Mitchell Jennings Jr., 2015.39

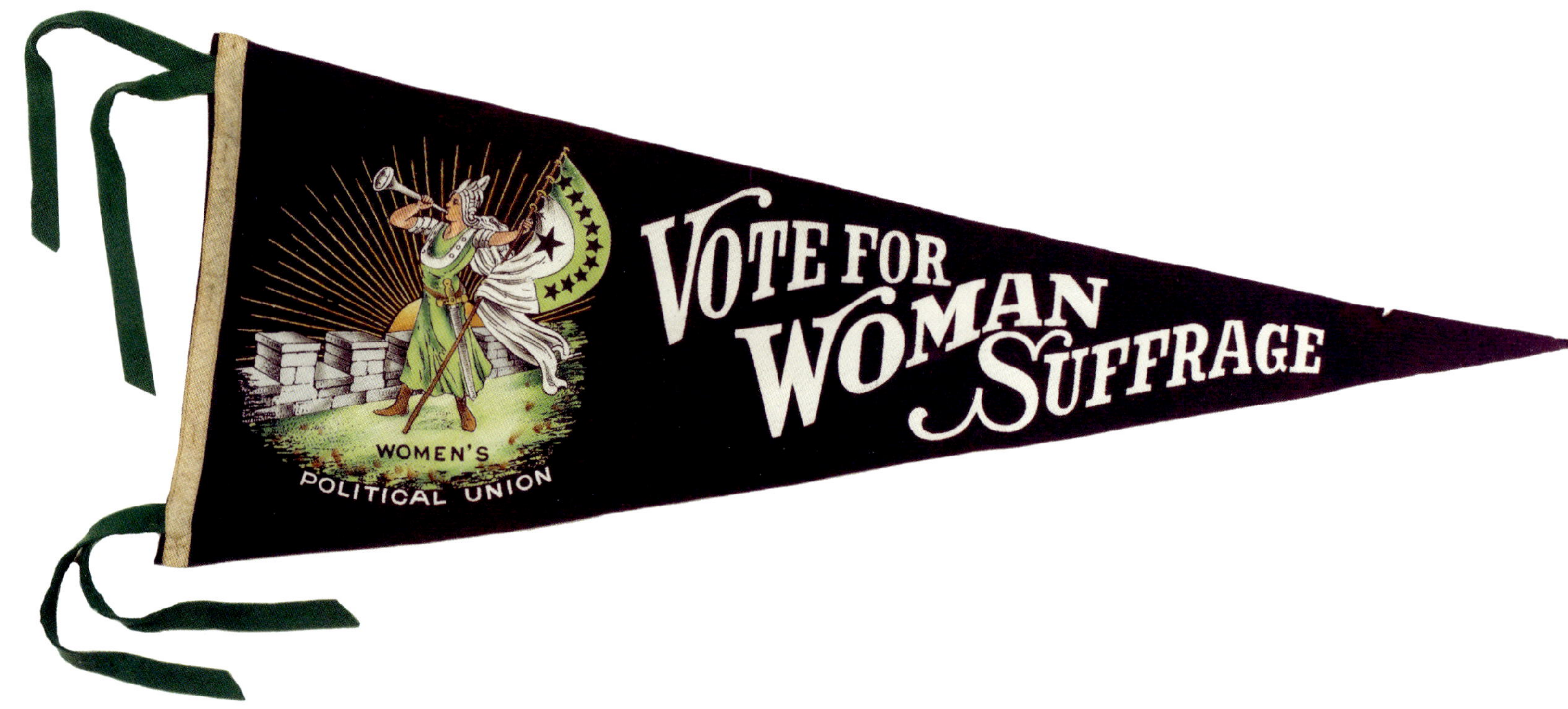

An armored maiden stands on ramparts at dawn, sounding a clarion call to arms in the long battle for women's suffrage. To the movement's followers, the imagery on this suffrage pennant, created ca. 1913 for the New York City–based Women's Political Union (WPU), also signaled the organization's connections to British suffrage groups. WPU founder Harriot Eaton Stanton Blatch (1856–1940), the daughter of suffragist Elizabeth Cady Stanton, lived in England for 20 years. During this time, she was deeply influenced by the British Women's Social and Political Union (WSPU) and its founder, Emmeline Pankhurst. WSPU members were notorious for their civil disobedience and dramatic actions: they slashed paintings at the National Gallery in London, smashed windows at government offices, and went on hunger strike when imprisoned. Blatch returned to New York in 1902, bringing the WSPU's purple, green, and white color scheme with her. The "Bugler Girl" was adopted from a 1908 design by Caroline Watts for the National Union of Women's Suffrage Societies, another British organization.

Originally called the Equality League for Self-Supporting Women, the WPU brought thousands of wage-earning women into the suffrage movement. It also pioneered some new, attention-grabbing strategies. Suffrage shops in New York City sold branded merchandise, while thousands of garment workers, laundresses, and "factory girls" joined suffrage parades, marching with banners and pennants like this one. New York State denied women the vote in 1915, but a successful referendum in 1917 gave suffragists a major victory, paving the way for the passage of the 19th Amendment to the US Constitution in 1920.

36

TIFFANY & CO. (founded 1837)

Cigar box belonging to Alfred E. Smith (1873–1944), 1929

New York City
Silver
The New York Historical, Purchase, 2004.49

This humidor, consisting of nearly 12 pounds of silver and taking at least four artisans over 104 hours to complete, was presented in 1930 to Alfred E. Smith. The four-time New York State governor, 1928 Democratic Party presidential candidate, and renowned cigar aficionado began working at age 14, slinging fish at the Fulton Market to support his family. Smith's political ascent was facilitated by the notorious Tammany machine, but, following his election to the New York State Assembly, he became famous for his legislative savvy and dedication to progressive reform. After 146 workers died in the 1911 Triangle Shirtwaist factory fire, Smith's crusade against unsafe workplaces helped him win the Assembly speakership, and, soon afterwards, his first term as governor.

Smith's enormous popularity in New York did not carry over into the rest of the country: his bid for the presidency failed in large part because he was considered pro-Catholic and pro-immigrant, and because he supported the repeal of Prohibition. Newspaper publisher Paul Block editorialized, "If the people of the United States knew you as we know you, they would know the Al Smith whose career is an inspiration to every true American, whose accomplishments are a tribute to American idealism, and whose success is a proof of American opportunity." These laudatory words were engraved on the underside of the cigar box's lid.

37

UNIDENTIFIED MAKER

Hat worn by Bella Savitzky Abzug (1920–1998), 1970s

Italy
Straw, mesh fabric
The New York Historical, Gift of Judge Emily Jane Goodman, 2018.3

A lifelong New Yorker, Bella Savitzky Abzug was born in the Bronx to Jewish immigrants, attended Hunter College, and received a scholarship to Columbia Law School at a time when women lawyers faced intense discrimination. To avoid being overlooked and ignored in chambers or in court, she donned attention-grabbing hats: as she later explained, "It was the only way they would take you seriously." Even as fashions changed and hats fell out of favor, Abzug remained famous for her signature wide-brimmed *chapeaux*.

Abzug's focus on labor law and civil rights cases led her to activism in 1961, when she helped to found Women Strike for Peace, a national organization against nuclear testing and the Vietnam War. In 1970, at age 50, she ran for Congress and was elected to the first of three terms. As a representative, Abzug was a leading advocate for the passage of the Equal Rights Amendment and sponsored the 1974 Equality Act, protecting gay Americans from discrimination. Her relentlessness earned her the nickname "Battling Bella." Although Abzug's later campaigns for US Senate and New York City mayor were unsuccessful, she is credited with paving the way for future generations of women in politics.

38

GASSAN ANTONIOS (b. 1969), designer

Gown worn by Representative Carolyn B. Maloney to the Met Gala, 2021

Polyester/silk satin, polyester/silk Chantilly lace, nylon underlayer, acetate lining, glass beads, PVC sequins with reflective coating
The New York Historical, Gift of Gassan Antonios (Antonios Couture), 2023.31

Every aspect of this floor-length gown references American women's long campaign to pass the Equal Rights Amendment. The ERA, first proposed by Alice Paul and other members of the National Woman's Party in 1923, has been introduced in every session of Congress since. Passage of the ERA would enshrine equality before the law, regardless of sex, in the US Constitution.

Support for the ERA gained momentum in the late 1960s with the growth of the women's liberation movement. It passed Congress in 1972 when women legislators (including New York representatives Bella Abzug and Shirley Chisholm) advocated for its passage. However, the amendment bogged down in state-level campaigns for ratification, falling three states short by its initial 1982 deadline. In 2020, as part of the centennial of the 19th Amendment, Congress once again pushed to put the ERA back on the legislative table. Carolyn B. Maloney (b. 1946), then serving as a Democratic representative for New York, was central to this effort—and she used the platform of the Metropolitan Museum of Art's Costume Institute Gala to spread the message. The white, green, purple, and gold of her gown incorporates the history of women's activism by using colors associated with the early 20th-century suffragist movements in England and the United States. The letters "ERA" on the front of the skirt, though made of Chantilly lace and applied with sequins and beaded embroidery, recall the handmade demonstration banners carried by suffragists, and the long trains of the dress echo their sashes. Maloney added a circular handbag to the ensemble with the words "ERA YES," a reference to pin-back buttons worn by activists in the 1970s.

Bettina von Zwehl (b. 1971)
Meditations in an Emergency, #14, 2018
Gelatin silver print, hand-printed
Patricia D. Klingenstein Library,
The New York Historical

ACTIVISTS & REVOLUTIONARIES

39

JOHN PETER ZENGER (1697–1746), printer

The New-York Weekly Journal: Containing the Freshest Advices, Foreign, and Domestick, No. XLVII

New York, September 23, 1734
Patricia D. Klingenstein Library, The New York Historical

When the independent *New-York Weekly Journal* appeared in 1733, it became the second newspaper published in the Province of New York—but it was the first to take on New York's powerful provincial governor, William Cosby. The paper was started by attorneys William Smith and James Alexander, opponents of Cosby and allies of New York's Chief Justice Lewis Morris, who had also clashed with Cosby and been removed from office.

Cosby chose to retaliate against the *Journal*'s relatively powerless printer, John Peter Zenger, a German immigrant. In November 1734, Zenger was arrested on charges of seditious libel. Smith and Alexander, disbarred by Cosby, were unavailable to defend him, and Cosby's allies on the Supreme Court set an impossibly high bail. Zenger was forced to languish in jail for almost a year. (While he was imprisoned, his wife Anna kept the *New-York Weekly Journal* going, making her the first woman in New York to publish a newspaper.) Attorney Andrew Hamilton of Philadelphia won Zenger's eventual acquittal in August 1735, in what is considered a major landmark in the development of a free press, later enshrined in the Bill of Rights. Gouverneur Morris, the grandson of Chief Justice Lewis Morris, deemed the verdict in *Crown v. Zenger* "the germ of American freedom, the morning star of that liberty which subsequently revolutionized America."

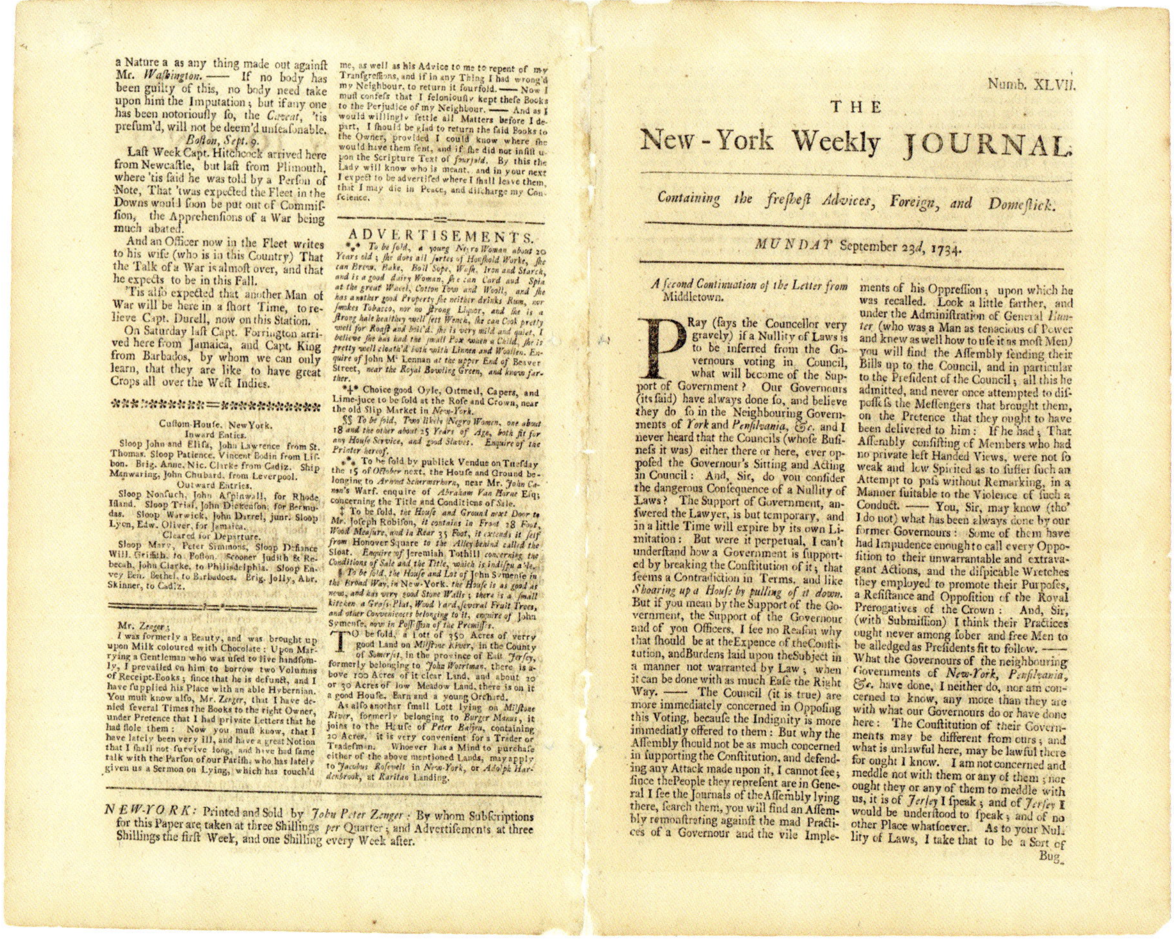

a Nature a as any thing made out againſt Mr. *Waſhington.* —— If no body has been guilty of this, no body need take upon him the Imputation; but if any one has been notoriouſly ſo, the *Caveat*, 'tis preſum'd, will not be deem'd unſeaſonable.

Boſton, Sept. 9.

Laſt Week Capt. Hitchcock arrived here from Newcaſtle, but laſt from Plimouth, where 'tis ſaid he was told by a Perſon of Note, That 'twas expected the Fleet in the Downs would ſoon be put out of Commiſſion, the Apprehenſions of a War being much abated.

And an Officer now in the Fleet writes to his wife (who is in this Country) That the Talk of a War is almoſt over, and that he expects to be in this Fall.

'Tis alſo expected that another Man of War will be here in a ſhort Time, to relieve Capt. Durell, now on this Station.

On Saturday laſt Capt. Forrington arrived here from Jamaica, and Capt. King from Barbados, by whom we can only learn, that they are like to have great Crops all over the Weſt Indies.

Cuſtom-Houſe, New York.
Inward Entries.

Sloop John and Eliſa, John Lawrence from St. Thomas. Sloop Patience, Vincent Bodin from Liſbon. Brig. Anne, Nic. Clarke from Cadiz. Ship Manwaring, John Chubard, from Leverpool.

Outward Entries.

Sloop Nonſuch, John Aſpinwall, for Rhode Iſland. Sloop Trial, John Dickenſon, for Bermudas. Sloop Warwick, John Darrel, junr. Sloop Lyon, Edw. Oliver, for Jamaica.

Cleared for Departure.

Sloop Mary, Peter Simmons, Sloop Defiance Will. Griffith, to Boſton. Scooner Judith & Rebecah, John Clarke, to Philadelphia. Sloop Envey Ben. Bethel, to Barbadoes. Brig. Jolly, Abr. Skinner, to Cadiz.

Mr. *Zenger*;

I was formerly a Beauty, and was brought up upon Milk coloured with Chocolate: Upon Marrying a Gentleman who was uſed to live handſomly, I prevailed on him to borrow two Volumns of Receipt-Books; ſince that he is defunct, and I have ſupplied his Place with an able Hybernian. You muſt know alſo, Mr. *Zenger*, that I have denied ſeveral Times the Books to the right Owner, under Pretence that I had private Letters that he had ſtole them: Now you muſt know, that I have lately been very ill, and have a great Notion that I ſhall not ſurvive long, and have had ſame talk with the Parſon of our Pariſh, who has lately given us a Sermon on Lying, which has touch'd me, as well as his Advice to me to repent of my Tranſgreſſions, and if in any Thing I had wrong'd my Neighbour, to return it fourfold. —— Now I muſt confeſs that I feloniouſly kept theſe Books to the Perjudice of my Neighbour. —— And as I would willingly ſettle all Matters before I depart, I ſhould be glad to return the ſaid Books to the Owner, provided I could know where ſhe would have them ſent, and if ſhe did not inſiſt upon the Scripture Text of *fourfold.* By this the Lady will know who is meant, and in your next I expect to be advertiſed where I ſhall leave them, that I may die in Peace, and diſcharge my Conſcience.

ADVERTISEMENTS.

*** *To be ſold, a young Negro Woman about* 20 *Years old; ſhe does all ſortes of Houſhold Worke, ſhe can Brew, Bake, Boil Sope, Waſh, Iron and Starch, and is a good dairy Woman, ſhe can Card and Spin at the great Wheel, Cotton Tow and Wooll, and ſhe has another good Property ſhe neither drinks Rum, nor ſmokes Tobacco, nor no ſtrong Liquor, and ſhe is a ſtrong hale healthey well ſett Wench, ſhe can Cook pretty well for Roaſt and boil'd, ſhe is very mild and quiet, I believe ſhe has had the ſmall Pox when a Child, ſhe is pretty well cloath'd both with Linnen and Woollen. Enquire of* John Mc Lennan *at the upper End of* Beaver Street, *near the Royal Bowling Green, and know farther.*

† Choice good Oyle, Oatmeal, Capers, and Lime-juce to be ſold at the Roſe and Crown, near the old Slip Market in *New-York.*

§§ *To be ſold, Two likely Negro Women, one about* 18 *and the other about* 25 *Years of Age, both fit for any Houſe Service, and good Slaves. Enquire of the Printer hereof.*

*** To be ſold by publick Vendue on Tueſday the 15 of *October* next, the Houſe and Ground belonging to *Arnout Schermerhorn*, near Mr. *John Cannon's* Warf. enquire of *Abraham Van Horne* Eſq; concerning the Title and Conditions of Sale.

‡ To be ſold, *the Houſe and Ground next Door to* Mr. Joſeph Robiſon, *it contains in Front* 28 *Foot, Wood Meaſure, and in Rear* 35 *Foot, it extends it ſelf from* Honover Square *to the Alley behind called the* Sloat. *Enquire of* Jeremiah Tothill *concerning the Conditions of Sale and the Title, which is indiſputable.*

§ *To be ſold, the Houſe and Lot of* John Symenſe *in the Broad Way, in* New-York. *the Houſe is as good as new, and has very good Stone Walls; there is a ſmall kitchen a Graſs-Plat, Wood Yard, ſeveral Fruit Trees, and other Conveniences belonging to it, enquire of* John Symenſe, *now in Poſſeſſion of the Premiſſes.*

TO be ſold, a Lott of 350 Acres of verry good Land on *Milſtone River*, in the County of *Somerſet*, in the province of Eaſt *Jerſey*, formerly belonging to *John Woortman*, there is above 100 Acres of it clear Land, and about 20 or 30 Acres of low Meadow Land, there is on it a good Houſe, Barn and a young Orchard.

As alſo another ſmall Lott lying on *Milſtone River*, formerly belonging to *Burger Maaus*, it joins to the Houſe of *Peter Balyeu*, containing 20 Acres, it is very convenient for a Trader or Tradeſman. Whoever has a Mind to purchaſe either of the above mentioned Lands, may apply to *Jacobus Roſevelt* in *New-York*, or *Adolph Hardenbrook*, at *Raritan* Landing.

NEW-YORK: Printed and Sold by *John Peter Zenger*: By whom Subſcriptions for this Paper are taken at three Shillings *per* Quarter; and Advertiſements at three Shillings the firſt Week, and one Shilling every Week after.

Numb. XLVII.

THE
New-York Weekly JOURNAL.

Containing the freſheſt Advices, Foreign, and Domeſtick.

MUNDAY September 23*d*, 1734.

A ſecond Continuation of the Letter from Middletown.

PRay (ſays the Councellor very gravely) if a Nullity of Laws is to be inferred from the Governours voting in Council, what will become of the Support of Government? Our Governours (its ſaid) have always done ſo, and believe they do ſo in the Neighbouring Governments of *York* and *Penſilvania*, *&c.* and I never heard that the Councils (whoſe Buſineſs it was) either there or here, ever oppoſed the Governour's Sitting and Acting in Council: And, Sir, do you conſider the dangerous Conſequence of a Nullity of Laws? The Support of Government, anſwered the Lawyer, is but temporary, and in a little Time will expire by its own Limitation: But were it perpetual, I can't underſtand how a Government is ſupported by breaking the Conſtitution of it; that ſeems a Contradiction in Terms, and like *Shoaring up a Houſe by pulling of it down.* But if you mean by the Support of the Government, the Support of the Governour and of you Officers, I ſee no Reaſon why that ſhould be at the Expence of the Conſtitution, and Burdens laid upon the Subject in a manner not warranted by Law; when it can be done with as much Eaſe the Right Way. —— The Council (it is true) are more immediately concerned in Oppoſing this Voting, becauſe the Indignity is more immediatly offered to them: But why the Aſſembly ſhould not be as much concerned in ſupporting the Conſtitution, and defending any Attack made upon it, I cannot ſee; ſince the People they repreſent are in General I ſee the Journals of the Aſſembly lying there, ſearch them, you will find an Aſſembly remonſtrating againſt the mad Practices of a Governour and the vile Implements of his Oppreſſion; upon which he was recalled. Look a little farther, and under the Adminiſtration of General *Hunter* (who was a Man as tenacious of Power and knew as well how to uſe it as moſt Men) you will find the Aſſembly ſending their Bills up to the Council, and in particular to the Preſident of the Council; all this he admitted, and never once attempted to diſpoſſeſs the Meſſengers that brought them, on the Pretence that they ought to have been delivered to him: If he had; That Aſſembly conſiſting of Members who had no private left Handed Views, were not ſo weak and low Spirited as to ſuffer ſuch an Attempt to paſs without Remarking, in a Manner ſuitable to the Violence of ſuch a Conduct. —— You, Sir, may know (tho' I do not) what has been always done by our former Governours: Some of them have had Impudence enough to call every Oppoſition to their unwarrantable and extravagant Actions, and the diſpicable Wretches they employed to promote their Purpoſes, a Reſiſtance and Oppoſition of the Royal Prerogatives of the Crown: And, Sir, (with Submiſſion) I think their Practices ought never among ſober and free Men to be alledged as Preſidents fit to follow. —— What the Governours of the neighbouring Governments of *New-York*, *Penſilvania*, *&c.* have done, I neither do, nor am concerned to know, any more than they are with what our Governours do or have done here: The Conſtitution of their Governments may be different from ours; and what is unlawful here, may be lawful there for ought I know. I am not concerned and meddle not with them or any of them; nor ought they or any of them to meddle with us, it is of *Jerſey* I ſpeak; and of *Jerſey* I would be underſtood to ſpeak; and of no other Place whatſoever. As to your Nullity of Laws, I take that to be a Sort of

Bug-

40a

In Congress, July 4, 1776. A Declaration by the Representatives of the United States of America, in General Congress Assembled

Broadside
New York: Hugh Gaine, 1776
Patricia D. Klingenstein Library, The New York Historical

40b

In Congress, July 4, 1776. A Declaration by the Representatives of the United States of America, in General Congress Assembled

Broadside
Likely New York by unknown printer, 1776
Patricia D. Klingenstein Library, The New York Historical

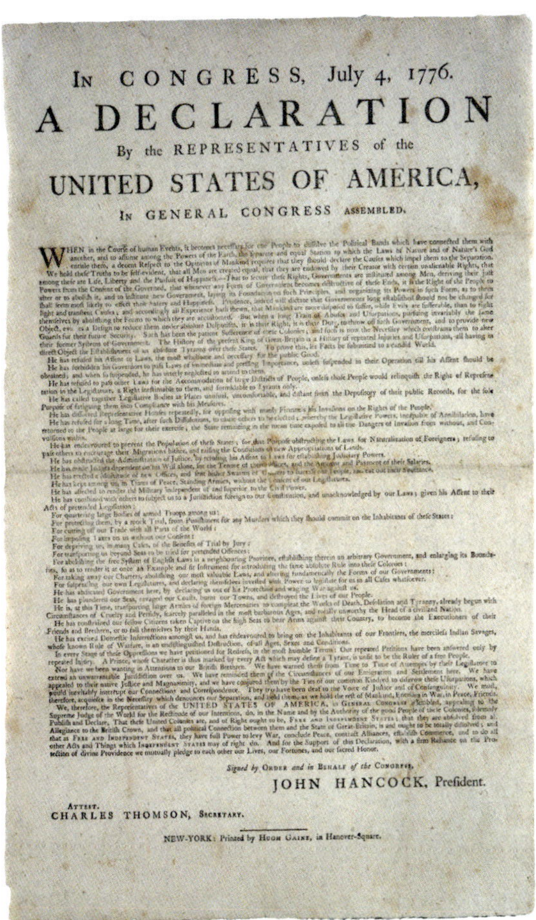

IN CONGRESS, July 4, 1776.
A DECLARATION
By the REPRESENTATIVES of the
UNITED STATES OF AMERICA,
IN GENERAL CONGRESS ASSEMBLED.

Signed by ORDER *and in* BEHALF *of the* CONGRESS,
JOHN HANCOCK, President.

ATTEST.
CHARLES THOMSON, SECRETARY.

NEW-YORK: Printed by HUGH GAINE, in Hanover-Square.

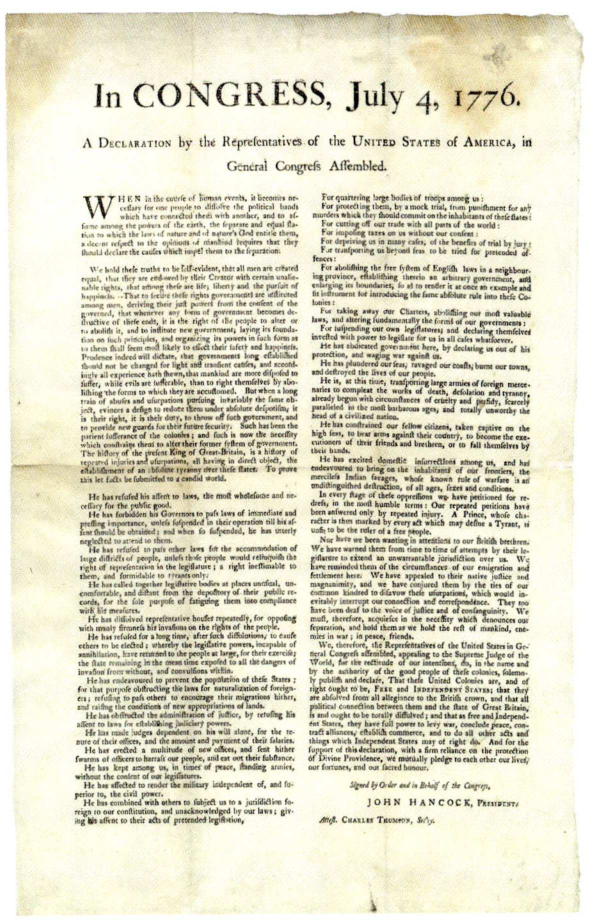

In CONGRESS, July 4, 1776.

A DECLARATION by the Repreſentatives of the UNITED STATES of AMERICA, in General Congreſs Aſſembled.

Signed by Order and in Behalf of the Congreſs,
JOHN HANCOCK, PRESIDENT.
Atteſt. CHARLES THOMSON, *Sec'y.*

On July 4, 1776, the Continental Congress in Philadelphia issued a document asserting the necessity of a permanent separation from Britain, and advocating for independence. Five days later, on July 9, General George Washington ordered it to be read aloud to his troops and to New Yorkers at various outdoor spots. It was received with cheers and prompted a crowd to rush to Bowling Green to dismantle the statue of King George. But despite this show of patriotism, New York—and New Yorkers—were deeply divided during the Revolutionary War.

Washington would have read a printing of the Declaration of Independence made by John Dunlap of Philadelphia, 200 copies of which had been distributed to colonial governors and commanders of the Continental Army. The New York Historical holds two New York printings, one by Hugh Gaine, editor of the *New-York Mercury*. Gaine, who had immigrated to New York from Ireland in 1744 and established his own press and bookshop in 1757, printed the Declaration on paper watermarked with the royal seal. Gaine fled the city during the first months of the British occupation but soon returned, using his press for the Loyalist cause, for which he is often remembered as a turncoat. The New York Historical is the only library that holds a copy of the other broadside, done by an unknown printer on an unknown date.

41

Petition of 547 Loyalists from New York City, 1776

Manuscript
Patricia D. Klingenstein Library, The New York Historical

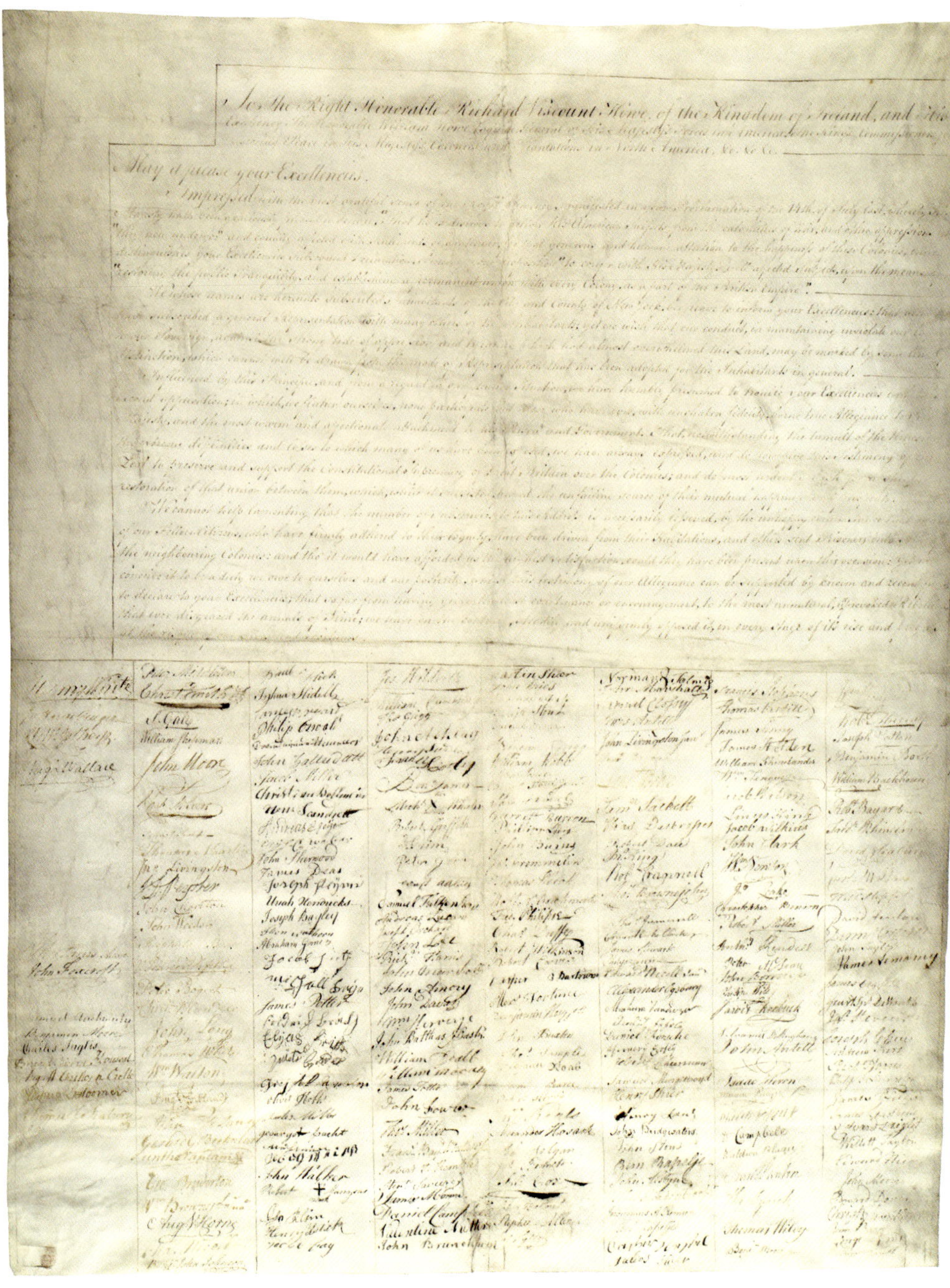

This unique petition of November 28, 1776, bears the signatures of 547 Loyalists from New York City. Known as the "Loyalist declaration of dependence," it was the second petition sent to London and addressed to Royal Commissioners Richard and William Howe from Loyalists seeking special protection under British occupation. Their first petition, for the suspension of martial law, went unanswered; in this second, insisting that they had risked their lives and fortunes opposing "the most unnatural, unprovoked rebellion, that ever disgraced the annals of time," the Loyalists sought only "some level of distinction" from the "inhabitants in general." Little improved for the Loyalists, however, and they suffered additionally from the demoralizing effects of inflation, wartime profiteering, street violence, and the city's general dirt and stench.

42

NEW-YORK MANUMISSION SOCIETY (1785–1849)

Minutes of the New-York Manumission Society, Volume 6, January 25, 1785–November 21, 1797

Patricia D. Klingenstein Library, The New York Historical

1785.
2mo. 4th

William Backhouse
William Carman
Thomas Burling Cabinet Maker
Thomas Bowne
Leonard M. Cutting
John Keese

Chairman — A Chairman being proposed, the Hon. John Jay Esquire was unanimously appointed —

Rules. — Mr Troup, from the Committee, appointed at the former meeting to draw up Rules for the Government of the Society; reported that they had prepared them and desired Leave to read the same - which being read, and others added, the whole, after Debate thereon were agreed to - Which said Rules, with the Reasons for instituting the said Society prefixed thereto, are as follows.

Principles. — The benevolent Creator and Father of Men having given to them all, an equal Right to Life, Liberty and Property; no Sovereign Power, on Earth, can justly deprive them of either; but in Conformity to impartial Government and Laws to which they have expressly or tacitly consented -

Objects of the Society. — It is our Duty therefore, both as free Citizens and Christians, not only to regard, with Compassion, the Injustice done to those, among us, who are held as Slaves, but to

1785
2mo. 4th

to endeavour, by lawful ways and means, to enable them to Share, equally with us, in that civil and religious Liberty with which an indulgent Providence has blessed these States; and to which these, our Brethren, are by Nature, as much entitled as ourselves.

Kidnapping — The Violent Attempts lately made to seize, and export for Sale, several free Negroes who were peaceably following their respective Occupations, in this City, must excite the Indignation of every Friend to Humanity, and ought to receive exemplary Punishment.

Helpless situation of the Negroes. — The Hope of Impunity is, too often, an invincible temptation to Transgression; and as the helpless Condition of the Persons alluded to doubtless exposed them to the Outrage they experienced; so it is probable that the like Circumstances may again expose them and others to similar Violences. - Destitute of Friends and of knowledge; struggling with Poverty and accustomed to Submission they are under great disadvantages in Asserting their Rights. -

Motives. — These Considerations induce us to form ourselves into a Society to be Stiled. A Society for promoting the Manumission of Slaves and protecting such of them as have been or may be Liberated.

Name. — And that the Objects of the Society may be pursued with Uniformity and Propriety we have agreed that it shall be regulated by the

In 1785, a group of New York's leading white citizens founded the New-York Society for Promoting the Manumission of Slaves, and Protecting Such of Them as Have Been, or May Be Liberated, commonly referred to as the New-York Manumission Society. Its members included Quakers, professionals, merchants, and political figures—many of whom, ironically, were also slave owners. The society's mission was to publicly lobby for the abolition of slavery and manumission of enslaved people in New York State, and to advocate on behalf of those already freed. More specifically, the society provided legal assistance to illegally enslaved Black men and women, prosecuted slave owners who were guilty of mistreating the enslaved, and supported efforts to enforce laws banning the sale of enslaved people. Additionally, it sought to strengthen legislation against the transportation of enslaved people to and from New York State. The society founded the African Free School in 1787, ultimately turning it over to the New York public school system in 1834. It helped to bring about the Gradual Emancipation Law of 1799 and its counterpart in 1817, which officially ended slavery in New York ten years later.

43

SAMUEL WOOD (1760–1844), publisher
ALEXANDER ANDERSON (1775–1870), engraver

Injured Humanity: Being a Representation of What the Unhappy Children of Africa Endure from Those Who Call Themselves Christians

Broadside
New York: Samuel Wood, ca. 1805–08
Patricia D. Klingenstein Library, The New York Historical

New York publisher Samuel Wood produced this illustrated broadside in the hope of effecting a boycott of the West Indian trade in enslaved people. The text and illustrations also appeared in *The Mirror of Misery; or, Tyranny Exposed*, first issued by Wood in 1807. Wood, like many of the earliest American anti-slavery advocates, belonged to the Quaker faith and employed a variety of its arguments against slavery: it was immoral, un-Christian, made a mockery of the foundational rights that Americans had fought to gain, and was innately inhumane and cruel. The engravings by Alexander Anderson graphically depicted whippings, torture devices, and the forced separation of families.

On January 1, 1808, an act banning the international slave trade and the importation of enslaved people—signed into law the previous year by President Thomas Jefferson—went into effect. Though little remembered today, the 1808 ban is notable as the first time that the US government acknowledged the evils of slavery. Many anti-slavery advocates hoped that it would be the first step on the road to gradual emancipation, but this proved not to be the case. Instead, the institution of slavery expanded into the recently purchased Louisiana Territory, prompting a series of political crises that eventually culminated in the Civil War.

INJURED HUMANITY;

BEING

A Representation of what the unhappy Children of Africa endure from those who call themselves

CHRISTIANS.

The husband and wife, after being sold to different purchasers, violently separated; probably never to see each other more.

When slaves are purchased by the planters, they are generally marked on the breast with a red hot iron.

A representation of a slave at work cruelly accoutred, with a Head-frame and Mouth-piece to prevent his eating—with Boots and Spurs round his legs, and half a hundred weight chained to his body to prevent his absconding.

The manner of fixing the slaves on a ladder to be flogged, which is also occasionally laid flat on the ground for severer punishment.

THE respectable and increasing numbers of those, who, from motives of humanity, have concurred in rejecting the produce of West-India slavery, cannot but afford a subject of the sincerest joy to every friend of mankind. Even those who, from motives of interest, still favour or engage in the trade, have been obliged to be silent upon the injustice of first procuring the Negroes, and have not had the hardiness to excuse or palliate the horrors of the *middle passage*: but still they assert, that the treatment the slaves meet with in the West-Indies amply counterbalances their previous sufferings; nay, they have not scrupled to extol a state of servitude as a happy asylum from African despotism, and calmly maintain, that the condition of the labouring poor in England is much harder than that of the Negroes in the West-India islands. Upon this ground, the opposers of slavery are willing to meet its advocates, and the design of the following extracts is to enable the public to form an impartial and decisive judgment on the subject.

WHEN a ship arrives at the port in the West-Indies, the slaves are exposed to sale, (except those who are very ill, they being left in the yard to perish by disease or hunger.) The healthy are disposed of by public auction, the sickly by scramble. The sale by scramble is thus described; the ship being darkened by sails, the purchasers are admitted, who, rushing forward with the ferocity of brutes, seize as many slaves as they have occasion for. In none of the sales, is any care taken to prevent the separation of relatives or friends; but husbands and wives, parents and children, are parted with as little concern as sheep and lambs by the butcher. Abstract of the evidence, as laid before a committee of the British parliament, page 46 and 47.

With respect to the *general* treatment of the slaves, Mr. Woolrich says, that he never knew the *best* master in the West-Indies use his slaves so well, as the *worst* master his servants in England. Abstract of the evidence, see page 53.

To come to a more *particular* description of their treatment, it will be proper to divide them into different classes: the first consisting of those bought for the use of the *plantations*: the second of the *in* and *out-door* slaves.

The field slaves are called out by daylight to their work: if they are not out in time, they are flogged. When put to their work, they perform it in rows, and, without exception, under the whip of drivers, a certain number of whom are allotted to each gang. Such is the *mode* of their labour: as to the time of it, they begin at daylight, and continue with two intermissions (one for half an hour in the morning, the other for two hours at noon) till sunset. Besides this, they are expected to range about and pick grass for the cattle, either during their two hours *rest* at noon, or after the fatigues of the day.

Sir G. Young adds, that women were, in general, considered to miscarry, from the cruel treatment they met with; and Captain Hall says, that he has seen a woman seated to give suck to her child, roused from that situation by a severe blow from the cart-whip. Abstract of the evidence, see page 53, 54, 55.

The above account of their labour is confined to that season of the year which is termed *out of crop*. In the crop season, the labour is of much longer duration. Mr. Dalrymple says, they are obliged to work as long as they can, that is, as long as they can keep awake or stand. Sometimes, through excess of fatigue, they fall asleep, when it has happened to those who feed the mills, that their arms have been caught therein and torn off. Mr. Cook, on the same subject, states, that they work, in general, eighteen hours out of the twenty-four: he knew a girl lose her hand by the mill while feeding it, being overcome with sleep, she dropped against the rollers. Abstract of the evidence, page 55, 56.

To this account of their labour, it should be added, that it appears, that on some estates, the slaves have Sunday and Saturday afternoon to themselves; on others, Sunday only, and on others, only Sunday in part. It appears again, that *in crop*, on no estate have they more than Sunday for the cultivation of their own lands. Abstract of the evidence, page 56.

The point next to be considered is the *food* of the slaves, which appears to be subject to no rule; on some estates, they are allowed land; on others, provisions; and some are allowed provisions and land jointly. The best allowance is at Barbadoes, of which the following is the account. The slaves, in general, says Gen. Tottenham, appeared to be ill fed: each slave had one pint of grain for 24 hours, and sometimes, half a rotten herring. When the herrings were *unfit for the whites*, they were bought up *for the slaves*. Nine pints of corn, and one pound of salt-fish a week, are, in general, the utmost allowance. As a proof that some have not food enough, Mr. Cook says, that he has known both Africans and Creoles eat the putrid carcasses of animals *through want*. Abstract of the evidence, page 57 and 58.

As to the accusation of their being *thieves*, all the evidences maintain, that it was on account of their being *half starved*. Abstract of the evidence, p. 58.

Concerning the *property* of the field-slaves, all the evidences agree in asserting, that they never heard of a field-slave amassing such a sum as enabled him to purchase his freedom. Abstract of the evidence, page 60.

Having now described the state of the plantation, it will be proper to say a few words on that of the *in* and *out-door* slaves.

The *in-door* slaves are allowed to be better clothed and fed, and less worked, than the plantation; on account, however, of being constantly exposed to the cruelty and caprice of their masters and mistresses, their lives are rendered so wretched, that they not unfrequently wish to be sent to the field: the *out-door* slaves are porters, coopers, &c. who are obliged to bring to their masters a certain sum every day.

The ordinary punishments of the slaves are inflicted by the whip and cow-skin. This, says Mr. Woolrich, is generally made of plaited cow-skin, with a thick strong lash, it is so formidable an instrument, that some of the overseers can by means of it take skin off a horse's back, he has seen them lay the marks of it into a deal board: the incisions (according to Dr. Harrison and the Dean of Middleham) are sometimes so deep that you may lay your finger into the wounds, and are such as no time can erase. As a farther proof of the *severity* of the punishments, the following facts are adduced. Mr. Fitzmaurice has known pregnant women so severely whipped, as to have miscarried in consequence of it. Davidson knew a negro girl die of a mortification of her wounds two days after whipping. Dr. Jackson recollects a negro dying under the lash, or soon after. Abstract of the evidence, see page 66 and 67.

We now proceed to the *extraordinary* punishments, in the infliction of which, malice, fury, and all the worst passions of the human mind, rage with unbridled license. Benevolence recoils at the dreadful perspective, and can scarce collect composure to disclose the bloody catalogue.

Captain Rap has known slaves severely punished, then put into the stocks, a cattle chain of sixty or seventy pounds weight put on them, and a large collar round their necks, and a weight of fifty-six pounds fastened to the chain, when they were driven afield: the collars are formed with two, three, or four projections, which hinder them from lying down to sleep.

A *negro* man, in Jamaica, (says Dr. Harrison) was put on the picket so long, as to cause a mortification of his foot and hand, on suspicion of robbing his master, a public officer, of a sum of money, which it afterwards appeared *the master had taken himself.* Yet the master was privy to the punishment, and the slave had no compensation. Abstract of the evidence, page 69.

Mr. Fitzmaurice mentions the practice of dropping hot lead upon the slaves, which he saw performed by a planter of the name of Rushie in Jamaica, this same man, in three years, destroyed by severity *forty negroes out of sixty.* The rest of the conduct of this planter was suppressed by the house of commons, as containing circumstances *too horrible to be given to the world.*

An overseer on the estate where Mr. J. Turry was, in Granada, threw a slave *into the boiling cane juice,* who died in four days.

Captain Cook relates, that he saw a woman named Rachel Lauder, beat a slave most unmercifully, and would have murdered her, had she not been prevented; the girl's crime was, the not bringing money enough from on board of a ship, *whither she had been sent by her mistress, for the purpose of prostitution.*

Lieutenant Davidson relates, that the wife of the clergyman at Port-Royal, used to drop hot sealing-wax on her negroes after flogging; he was sent for as surgeon to one of them whose breast was terribly burnt.

If it should be asked, for what offences the punishments cited have taken place, the following answer may be given:

Under the head of *ordinary* punishments, the slaves appear to have suffered for not coming to the field in time, not picking a sufficient quantity of grass, for staying too long of an errand, and theft, to which they were often driven by hunger.

Under the head of *extraordinary* punishments, the following have been alleged as reasons: for running away, for breaking a plate, or to extort confession in the moments of passion, and one on a diabolical pretence, which the master held out to the world to conceal *his own villainy, and which he knew to be false.* Women punish their slaves for being found pregnant, for not bringing home the *full wages of prostitution,* and others, without *even the allegation of a fault.*

All the facts that have been now adduced are of unquestionable authority, having been extracted from the evidence laid before the house of commons by eye-witnesses of the facts. Let now every honest man lay his hand on his breast, and seriously reflect, whether he is justifiable in countenancing such barbarities; or whether he ought not to reject, with horror, the smallest participation in such infernal transactions. To the weaker sex, whose amiable characteristic it is, to be "tremblingly alive" to every tale of wo, the friends of the abolition return their warmest acknowledgments, for the zeal with which many of them have espoused the cause of humanity, and for the noble example they have shewn, in rejecting the produce of slavery and misery.

The manner of yoking the slaves by the Mandingoes, or African slave merchants, who usually march annually in eight or ten parties, from the river Gambia to Bambarra; each party having from one hundred to one hundred and fifty slaves.

The Log-Yokes are made of the roots of trees, so heavy as to make it extremely difficult for the persons who wear them to walk, much more to escape or run away.

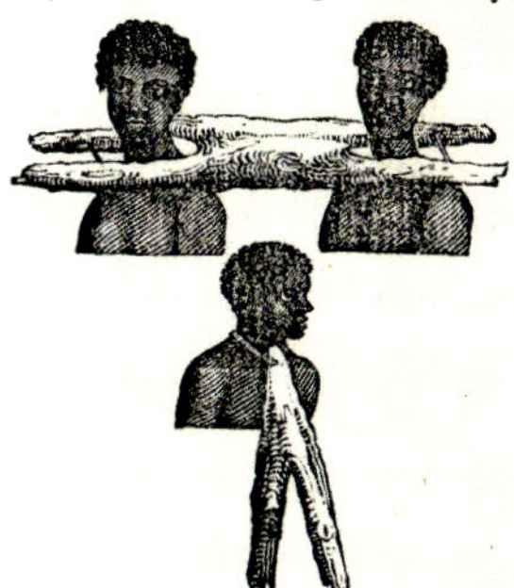

A front and profile view of an African's head, with the mouth-piece and necklace, the hooks round which are placed to prevent an escape when pursued in the woods, and to hinder them from laying down the head to procure rest.—At A is a flat iron which goes into the mouth, and so effectually keeps down the tongue, that nothing can be swallowed, not even the saliva, a passage for which is made through holes in the mouth-plate.

An enlarged view of the mouth-piece, which, when long worn, becomes so heated, as frequently to bring off the skin along with it.

A view of the leg-bolts or shackles, as put upon the legs of the slaves on ship-board, in the middle passage.

An enlarged view of the boots and spurs, as used at some plantations in Antigua.

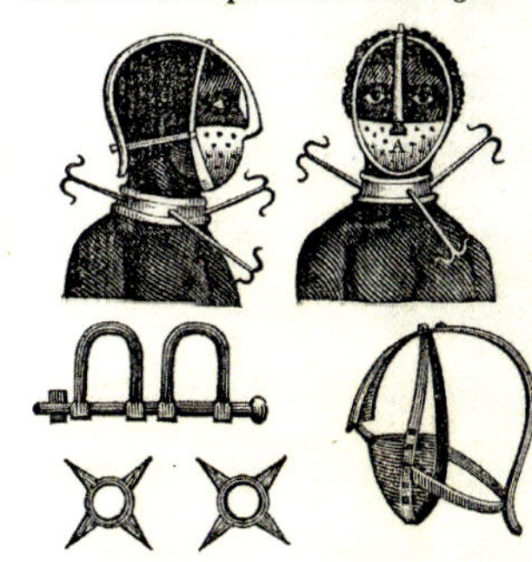

Another method in which the poor victims are placed to be flogged.

PRINTED AND SOLD BY SAMUEL WOOD, NO. 362, PEARL-STREET.

44

FREDERICK DOUGLASS (1818–1895)

Men of Color, to Arms!

Broadside
Rochester, New York: March 2, 1863
Patricia D. Klingenstein Library, The New York Historical

While the Second Confiscation Act and the Militia Act had allowed "persons of African descent" in "rebellious states" to serve in the Union Army beginning in 1862, it was President Abraham Lincoln's Emancipation Proclamation that threw open the door for Northern Black men eager to enlist. In this broadside, originally published as an editorial in *Douglass' Monthly*, the abolitionist, author, and orator Frederick Douglass—recognizing that military service would cement Black men's claims to citizenship—exhorted them to fight for the Union. "Who would be free themselves must strike the blow," he wrote. "I urge you to fly to arms, and smite with death the power that would bury the Government and your liberty in the same hopeless grave." Chiding his home state of New York for its laggard response, Douglass advised Black men to "get at the throat of treason and Slavery" by enlisting in the 54th Massachusetts Infantry, the first Black regiment raised in the North. Black soldiers would serve under white officers in segregated regiments, but Douglass promised that his readers would receive "the same wages, the same rations, the same equipment, the same protection, and the same bounty secured to white soldiers." However, it took a year for Lincoln to make good on the promise of equal pay.

In April 1863, Douglass's own sons Charles and Lewis enlisted with the 54th Massachusetts Infantry, and in July of that year Lewis was severely wounded when the 54th Massachusetts led an attack against Fort Wagner, South Carolina. Their bravery under fire won nationwide accolades and inspired yet more Black men to enlist. By the end of the Civil War, over 180,000 Black soldiers and 18,000 Black sailors would serve in the United States Colored Troops.

Fig. 10
Unidentified photographer
Frederick Douglass (1818–1895), late 19th century
Carte-de-visite
Patricia D. Klingenstein Library, The New York Historical

MEN OF COLOR, TO ARMS!

A Call by Frederick Douglass.

When first the Rebel cannon shattered the walls of Sumter, and drove away its starving garrison, I predicted that the war then and there inaugurated would not be fought out entirely by white men. Every month's experience during these two dreary years has confirmed that opinion. A war undertaken and brazenly carried on for the perpetual enslavement of colored men, calls logically and loudly upon colored men to help to suppress it. Only a moderate share of sagacity was needed to see that the arm of the slave was the best defence against the arm of the slaveholder. Hence with every reverse to the National arms, with every exulting shout of victory raised by the slaveholding Rebels, I have implored the imperilled nation to unchain against her foes her powerful black hand. Slowly and reluctantly that appeal is beginning to be heeded. Stop not now to complain that it was not heeded sooner. It may, or it may not have been best—that it should not. This is not the time to discuss that question. Leave it to the future. When the war is over, the country is saved, peace is established, and the black man's rights are secured, as they will be, history with an impartial hand, will dispose of that and sundry other questions. Action! action! not criticism, is the plain duty of this hour. Words are now useful only as they stimulate to blows. The office of speech now is only to point out when, where and how to strike to the best advantage. There is no time for delay. The tide is at flood that leads on to fortune. From east to west, from north to south the sky is written all over with "now or never." Liberty won by white men would lack half its lustre. Who would be free themselves must strike the blow. Better even to die free than to live slaves. This is the sentiment of every brave colored man among us. There are weak and cowardly men in all nations. We have them among us. They will tell you that this is the "whiteman's war;" that you will be "better off after than before the war;" that the getting of you into the army is to "sacrifice you on the first opportunity." Believe them not—cowards themselves, they do not wish to have their cowardice shamed by your brave example. Leave them to their timidity, or to whatever other motive may hold them back.

I have not thought lightly of the words I am now addressing to you. The counsel I give comes of close observation of the great struggle now in progress—and of the deep conviction that this is your hour and mine.

In good earnest, then, and after the best deliberation, I, now, for the first time during the war, feel at liberty to call and counsel you to arms. By every consideration which binds you to your enslaved fellow countrymen, and the peace and welfare of your country; by every aspiration which you cherish for the freedom and equality of yourselves and your children; by all the ties of blood and identity which make us one with the brave black men now fighting our battles in Louisiana, in South Carolina, I urge you to fly to arms, and smite with death the power that would bury the Government and your liberty in the same hopeless grave. I wish I could tell you that the State of New York calls you to this high honor. For the moment her constituted authorities are silent on the subject. They will speak by and by, and doubtless on the right side; but we are not compelled to wait for her. We can get at the throat of treason and Slavery through the State of Massachusetts.

She was first in the war of Independence; first to break the chains of her slaves; first to make the black man equal before the law; first to admit colored children to her common schools, and she was the first to answer with her blood the alarm cry of the nation—when its capital was menaced by rebels. You know her patriotic Governor, and you know Charles Sumner—I need add no more.

Massachusetts now welcomes you to arms as her soldiers. She has but a small colored population from which to recruit. She has full leave of the General Government to send one regiment to the war, and she has undertaken to do it. Go quickly and help fill up this first colored regiment from the North. I am authorized to assure you that you will receive the same wages, the same rations, the same equipments, the same protection, the same treatment and the same bounty secured to white soldiers. You will be led by able and skillful officers—men who will take especial pride in your efficiency and success. They will be quick to accord to you all the honor you shall merit by your valor—and see that your rights and feelings are respected by other soldiers. I have assured myself on these points—and can speak with authority. More than twenty years unswerving devotion to our common cause, may give me some humble claim to be trusted at this momentous crisis.

I will not argue. To do so implies hesitation and doubt, and you do not hesitate. You do not doubt. The day dawns—the morning star is bright upon the horizon! The iron gate of our prison stands half open. One gallant rush from the North will fling it wide open, while four millions of our brothers and sisters shall march out into Liberty! The chance is now given you to end in a day the bondage of centuries, and to rise in one bound from social degradation to the plane of common equality with all other varieties of men. Remember Denmark Vesey of Charleston. Remember Nathaniel Turner of South Hampton; remember Shields, Green, and Copeland, who followed noble John Brown, and fell as glorious martyrs for the cause of the slaves. Remember that in a contest with oppression, the Almighty has no attribute which can take sides with oppressors. The case is before you. This is our golden opportunity—let us accept it—and forever wipe out the dark reproaches unsparingly hurled against us by our enemies. Win for ourselves the gratitude of our country—and the best blessings of our prosperity through all time. The nucleus of this first regiment is now in camp at Readville, a short distance from Boston. I will undertake to forward to Boston all persons adjudged fit to be mustered into this regiment, who shall apply to me at any time within the next two weeks.

FREDERICK DOUGLASS.

Rochester, March 2, 1863.

45

UNIDENTIFIED PHOTOGRAPHER

Sojourner Truth (d. 1883), 1864

Albumen print carte-de-visite
Patricia D. Klingenstein Library,
The New York Historical

Born into slavery in Dutch-speaking New York, Isabella Baufree should have gained her legal freedom when New York's Gradual Emancipation Law took effect in 1827. When her enslaver failed to honor the law, she self-emancipated, finding work in New York City as a domestic laborer and then waging a historic legal battle to free her youngest child from enslavement. A profound religious experience called Baufree to pursue life as an itinerant preacher; she renamed herself Sojourner Truth in 1843. Truth championed the political rights of African American women and men, encouraging women's rights advocates to include Black women in their work. In 1851, at a women's rights convention in Ohio, Truth delivered a ringing speech now known as "Ain't I a Woman," borrowing examples from her life to describe Black women's combined strength and femininity. The *New York Independent* republished the speech in 1863, though it was rewritten in stereotyped dialect.

To support her speaking tour across the country, Sojourner Truth sold copies of her autobiography and portraits of herself. The words at the bottom of her carte-de-visite are a bold and important statement in an era when the photographer would otherwise have owned the image rights. Truth also used props to invoke the visual culture of white middle-class womanhood, subverting the idea of racial hierarchy. She wore a shawl and bonnet and posed with a book—an important symbol of literacy, even though she could neither read nor write.

46

SUSAN B. ANTHONY (1820–1906), proprietor
ELIZABETH CADY STANTON (1815–1902), editor

The Revolution: Principle, Not Policy: Justice, Not Favors, Vol. I, No. 1

New York, January 8, 1868
Patricia D. Klingenstein Library, The New York Historical

Suffragists Susan B. Anthony and Elizabeth Cady Stanton, along with co-editor Parker Pillsbury, published the inaugural issue of the *Revolution* in New York on Wednesday, January 8, 1868. It was the organ of the National Party of New America and a vehicle in Stanton and Anthony's long fight for women's suffrage. The first issue listed the paper's ambitious goals, among which was "Educated Suffrage, Irrespective of Sex or Color."

The 15th Amendment, first proposed in 1868, promised voting rights to all men, regardless of race or previous enslavement. In the *Revolution*, Stanton argued that the proposed amendment was unfair because it guaranteed that all men (including those recently freed from slavery and newly arrived immigrants) would receive voting rights, but women—even native-born educated white women—would not. While both Stanton and Anthony had been abolitionists, they spoke openly and publicly about their opposition to the 15th Amendment, often using racist, nativist, and classist language. At the time, this was a problematic but not uncommon stance among white suffragists.

The debate over the 15th Amendment led to a split between the two women and their colleague Frederick Douglass, a staunch supporter of women's suffrage. He was so outraged by the women's responses to the 15th Amendment that he spoke out against Stanton at the May 1869 convention of the American Equal Rights Association (AERA). Stanton and Anthony left the AERA shortly after the convention and formed the National Woman Suffrage Association (NWSA). While the NWSA did not prohibit Black women from joining at the national level, local organizations could, and did, reject their participation.

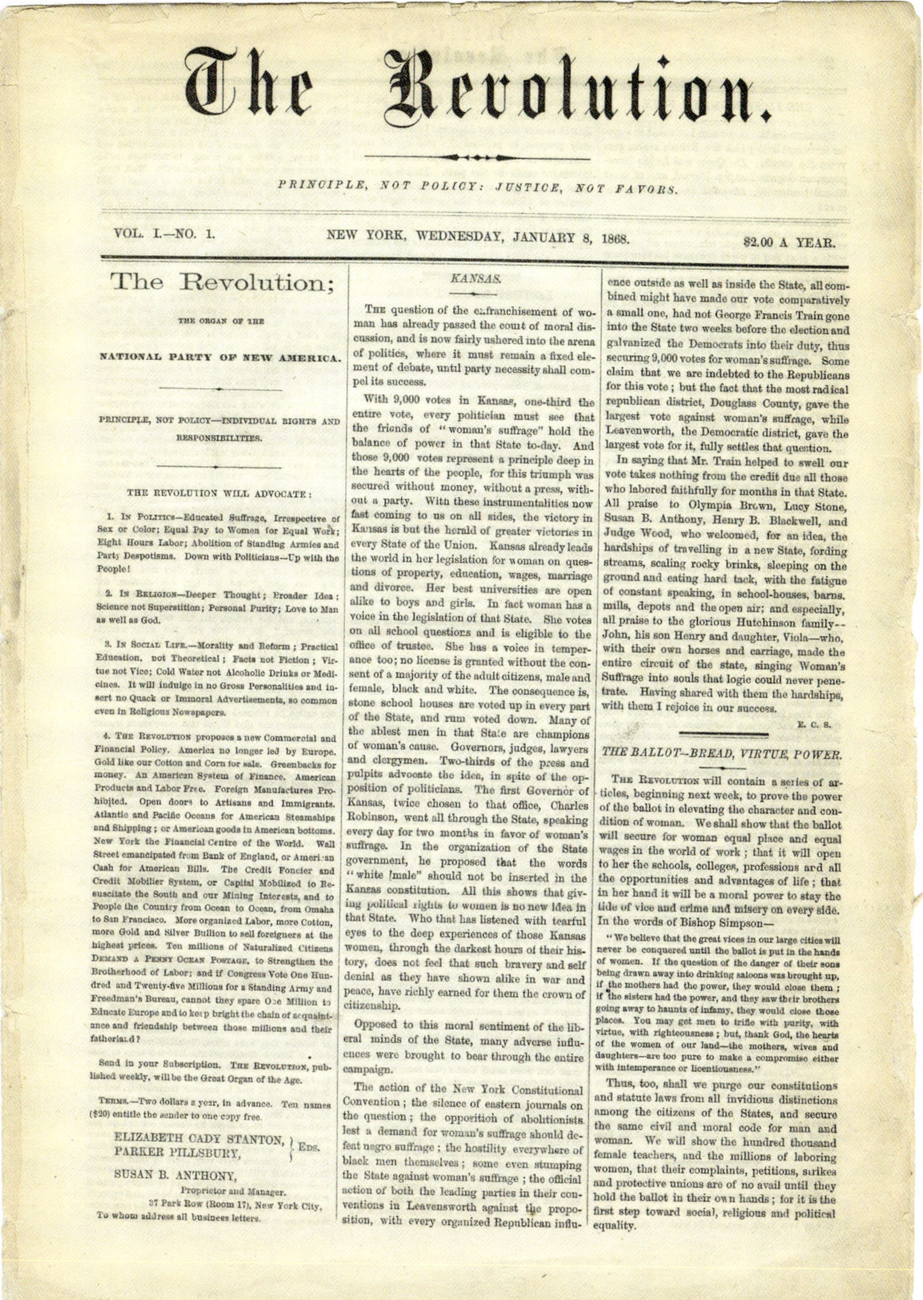

The Revolution.

PRINCIPLE, NOT POLICY: JUSTICE, NOT FAVORS.

VOL. I.—NO. 1. NEW YORK, WEDNESDAY, JANUARY 8, 1868. $2.00 A YEAR.

The Revolution;

THE ORGAN OF THE

NATIONAL PARTY OF NEW AMERICA.

PRINCIPLE, NOT POLICY—INDIVIDUAL RIGHTS AND RESPONSIBILITIES.

THE REVOLUTION WILL ADVOCATE:

1. IN POLITICS—Educated Suffrage, Irrespective of Sex or Color; Equal Pay to Women for Equal Work; Eight Hours Labor; Abolition of Standing Armies and Party Despotisms. Down with Politicians—Up with the People!

2. IN RELIGION—Deeper Thought; Broader Idea; Science not Superstition; Personal Purity; Love to Man as well as God.

3. IN SOCIAL LIFE.—Morality and Reform; Practical Education, not Theoretical; Facts not Fiction; Virtue not Vice; Cold Water not Alcoholic Drinks or Medicines. It will indulge in no Gross Personalities and insert no Quack or Immoral Advertisements, so common even in Religious Newspapers.

4. THE REVOLUTION proposes a new Commercial and Financial Policy. America no longer led by Europe. Gold like our Cotton and Corn for sale. Greenbacks for money. An American System of Finance. American Products and Labor Free. Foreign Manufactures Prohibited. Open doors to Artisans and Immigrants. Atlantic and Pacific Oceans for American Steamships and Shipping; or American goods in American bottoms. New York the Financial Centre of the World. Wall Street emancipated from Bank of England, or American Cash for American Bills. The Credit Foncier and Credit Mobilier System, or Capital Mobilized to Resuscitate the South and our Mining Interests, and to People the Country from Ocean to Ocean, from Omaha to San Francisco. More organized Labor, more Cotton, more Gold and Silver Bullion to sell foreigners at the highest prices. Ten millions of Naturalized Citizens DEMAND A PENNY OCEAN POSTAGE, to Strengthen the Brotherhood of Labor; and if Congress Vote One Hundred and Twenty-five Millions for a Standing Army and Freedman's Bureau, cannot they spare One Million to Educate Europe and to keep bright the chain of acquaintance and friendship between those millions and their fatherland?

Send in your Subscription. THE REVOLUTION, published weekly, will be the Great Organ of the Age.

TERMS.—Two dollars a year, in advance. Ten names ($20) entitle the sender to one copy free.

ELIZABETH CADY STANTON, } EDS.
PARKER PILLSBURY, }

SUSAN B. ANTHONY,
Proprietor and Manager.
37 Park Row (Room 17), New York City,
To whom address all business letters.

KANSAS.

THE question of the enfranchisement of woman has already passed the court of moral discussion, and is now fairly ushered into the arena of politics, where it must remain a fixed element of debate, until party necessity shall compel its success.

With 9,000 votes in Kansas, one-third the entire vote, every politician must see that the friends of "woman's suffrage" hold the balance of power in that State to-day. And those 9,000 votes represent a principle deep in the hearts of the people, for this triumph was secured without money, without a press, without a party. With these instrumentalities now fast coming to us on all sides, the victory in Kansas is but the herald of greater victories in every State of the Union. Kansas already leads the world in her legislation for woman on questions of property, education, wages, marriage and divorce. Her best universities are open alike to boys and girls. In fact woman has a voice in the legislation of that State. She votes on all school questions and is eligible to the office of trustee. She has a voice in temperance too; no license is granted without the consent of a majority of the adult citizens, male and female, black and white. The consequence is, stone school houses are voted up in every part of the State, and rum voted down. Many of the ablest men in that State are champions of woman's cause. Governors, judges, lawyers and clergymen. Two-thirds of the press and pulpits advocate the idea, in spite of the opposition of politicians. The first Governor of Kansas, twice chosen to that office, Charles Robinson, went all through the State, speaking every day for two months in favor of woman's suffrage. In the organization of the State government, he proposed that the words "white male" should not be inserted in the Kansas constitution. All this shows that giving political rights to women is no new idea in that State. Who that has listened with tearful eyes to the deep experiences of those Kansas women, through the darkest hours of their history, does not feel that such bravery and self denial as they have shown alike in war and peace, have richly earned for them the crown of citizenship.

Opposed to this moral sentiment of the liberal minds of the State, many adverse influences were brought to bear through the entire campaign.

The action of the New York Constitutional Convention; the silence of eastern journals on the question; the opposition of abolitionists lest a demand for woman's suffrage should defeat negro suffrage; the hostility everywhere of black men themselves; some even stumping the State against woman's suffrage; the official action of both the leading parties in their conventions in Leavensworth against the proposition, with every organized Republican influence outside as well as inside the State, all combined might have made our vote comparatively a small one, had not George Francis Train gone into the State two weeks before the election and galvanized the Democrats into their duty, thus securing 9,000 votes for woman's suffrage. Some claim that we are indebted to the Republicans for this vote; but the fact that the most radical republican district, Douglass County, gave the largest vote against woman's suffrage, while Leavenworth, the Democratic district, gave the largest vote for it, fully settles that question.

In saying that Mr. Train helped to swell our vote takes nothing from the credit due all those who labored faithfully for months in that State. All praise to Olympia Brown, Lucy Stone, Susan B. Anthony, Henry B. Blackwell, and Judge Wood, who welcomed, for an idea, the hardships of travelling in a new State, fording streams, scaling rocky brinks, sleeping on the ground and eating hard tack, with the fatigue of constant speaking, in school-houses, barns, mills, depots and the open air; and especially, all praise to the glorious Hutchinson family—John, his son Henry and daughter, Viola—who, with their own horses and carriage, made the entire circuit of the state, singing Woman's Suffrage into souls that logic could never penetrate. Having shared with them the hardships, with them I rejoice in our success.

E. C. S.

THE BALLOT—BREAD, VIRTUE, POWER.

THE REVOLUTION will contain a series of articles, beginning next week, to prove the power of the ballot in elevating the character and condition of woman. We shall show that the ballot will secure for woman equal place and equal wages in the world of work; that it will open to her the schools, colleges, professions and all the opportunities and advantages of life; that in her hand it will be a moral power to stay the tide of vice and crime and misery on every side. In the words of Bishop Simpson—

"We believe that the great vices in our large cities will never be conquered until the ballot is put in the hands of women. If the question of the danger of their sons being drawn away into drinking saloons was brought up, if the mothers had the power, they would close them; if the sisters had the power, and they saw their brothers going away to haunts of infamy, they would close those places. You may get men to trifle with purity, with virtue, with righteousness; but, thank God, the hearts of the women of our land—the mothers, wives and daughters—are too pure to make a compromise either with intemperance or licentiousness."

Thus, too, shall we purge our constitutions and statute laws from all invidious distinctions among the citizens of the States, and secure the same civil and moral code for man and woman. We will show the hundred thousand female teachers, and the millions of laboring women, that their complaints, petitions, strikes and protective unions are of no avail until they hold the ballot in their own hands; for it is the first step toward social, religious and political equality.

47

SHIRLEY HAYES (1912–2002)

"Save the Square!" poster, 1959

Patricia D. Klingenstein Library, The New York Historical, Shirley Hayes Papers

Shirley Hayes was a community activist for most of her life. A long-time resident of Greenwich Village, she is best known for her yearslong fight to save Washington Square Park after New York City's powerful parks commissioner, Robert Moses, proposed expanding the road running through the park into a four-lane highway. When local mothers heard how this would increase traffic and diminish recreation space, they gathered in the park playground to begin formulating their opposition. Hayes, who regularly brought her four sons to play in the park, co-founded and chaired the Washington Square Park Committee to stop Moses, who was dumbfounded by this organized opposition. At one Board of Estimate meeting, he rebuked, "There is nobody against this—NOBODY, NOBODY, NOBODY, but a bunch of, a bunch of MOTHERS!" In fact, the Washington Square Park Committee had many prominent allies, including former first lady Eleanor Roosevelt, then-congressman John Lindsay, and Jane Jacobs, the renowned author of *The Death and Life of Great American Cities* (1961). After years of campaigning, the city listened to Hayes and her allies, permanently closing the existing road in 1959—an early success for grassroots organizing against top-down planning.

47

SAVE THE SQUARE!
WIENER
SEND POSTCARDS TO
BORO PRES. HULAN E. JACK
MAYOR ROBERT F. WAGNER
c/o WASHINGTON SQUARE PARK COMMITTEE
24 EAST 11 STREET, N.Y.C.
No Parkway Thru Washington Square Park
CLOSE THE PARK TO ALL TRAFFIC
Courtesy of the Pickwick Offset Press - A Village Firm

48

FRED McDARRAH (1926–2007)

Marsha P. Johnson (1945–1992), Fourth Christopher Street Liberation Day March, New York, New York, June 24, 1973

Archival pigment print
Patricia D. Klingenstein Library, The New York Historical, Gift of the Goldman Sonnenfeldt Family

Fred McDarrah, the first staff photographer at the *Village Voice*, took this portrait of radical activist, sex worker, and self-described "street queen" Marsha P. Johnson at the 1973 Christopher Street Liberation Day March (a forerunner of NYC Pride). Johnson was marching with Sylvia Rivera (1951–2002) and other members of Street Transvestite Action Revolutionaries (STAR), the organization they had co-founded in 1970. Johnson carried a poster protesting the incarceration of LGBTQ+ people at a time when gay sex was illegal, cruising was criminalized, and an 1845 law against "criminal impersonation" was used to surveil, harass, and arrest New Yorkers whose appearance did not conform with gender and class norms: cross-dressers, drag queens, butches, "female impersonators," and people who might now identify as trans, genderfluid, or nonbinary.

Johnson was on the front lines of the fight against such discriminatory treatment—not only by protesting, marching, and speaking out, but by providing direct services to the people who were most impacted. From November 1970 to July 1971, Johnson, Rivera, and others organized STAR House, a short-lived but impactful shelter for gender non-conforming, queer, and homeless sex workers and youth, located in a derelict building on East Second Street. As LGBTQ+ activist Agosto Machado, who first met Johnson in the early 1960s, later recalled, "Marsha galvanized and encouraged us. . . . She was always a role model in courage."

49

UNIDENTIFIED MAKER

“Suffragette-style” or “Mexican Wedding” dress worn by Muriel Fox (b. 1928), 1970s

Cotton, synthetic fabric, lace
The New York Historical, Gift of Muriel Fox, Veteran Feminists of America, 2018.5

This dress was worn by feminist activist Muriel Fox while leading two major marches organized by the National Organization for Women (NOW) in support of the Equal Rights Amendment (ERA). The first march took place on July 9, 1978, in Washington, DC, and was the single largest demonstration in support of the ERA in US history. Marchers included NOW founder Betty Friedan, Gloria Steinem, Dick Gregory, and Fox, who carried a NOW banner styled after suffrage banners from the early 20th century, with stripes of yellow, white, and purple. Fox grabbed the hand of seven-year-old Brooke Shafran and led the march with her, an image of which was memorialized on a NOW medallion.

Fox wore the dress again in Chicago at a Mother’s Day march in 1980, shortly after her own mother’s death. The image of her leading that march, bearing an ERA banner, is one of the most iconic images of the struggle to pass an equal rights amendment. At both marches, and at other ERA demonstrations, the flowing white dresses worn by Fox and others harkened back to the early 20th-century suffrage movement. However, conservative grassroots organizers, believing that the ERA’s passage would undermine the traditional family and eliminate gender-specific privileges such as child support and male-only draft conscription, mobilized to block it. Ultimately, the ERA passed 35 state legislatures, falling just short of the 38 needed to become law.

50

UNIDENTIFIED MAKER

We Are the 99% People that R[ule?] the World, 2011

Purple and multicolored paint and black marker on white poster board
Patricia D. Klingenstein Library, The New York Historical, Gift of Grace Davie, 2019

On September 17, 2011, approximately 1,000 activists marched through lower Manhattan, eventually settling in a small plaza called Zuccotti Park. There, they created an encampment complete with tents, a library of donated books, drumming circles, and a free "people's kitchen." Chanting "We are the 99%," Occupy Wall Street was a reaction to the global financial crisis of 2008–09 and the profound economic malaise that followed. It soon spread to other US cities, and even internationally.

The Occupy encampment itself was short-lived, and its many critics point out that it failed to effect substantial reforms in the banking industry, the financial sector, or the regulation of corporations' political spending. Yet others argue that Occupy Wall Street was transformative in other ways: it raised awareness of economic inequality, protested the concentration of wealth at the top of the economic ladder, facilitated the rise of left-leaning politicians (such as the Bronx-born US representative Alexandria Ocasio-Cortez) and, arguably, helped provide a model for other protest movements in the age of social media.

51

Scarf worn by Edie Windsor at the Supreme Court, ca. 2013

Silk, cotton
The New York Historical, Estate of Edith S. Windsor and Thea C. Spyer by The Judith M. Kasen-Windsor Trust, 2024.38.3

In 2013, activist Edith "Edie" Windsor (1929–2017) secured a landmark victory in the fight for marriage equality when her Supreme Court case forced the federal government to recognize same-sex marriages. Windsor and Thea Spyer (1931–2009) were engaged for 40 years. They met in 1963 in Greenwich Village, and in 1967 Spyer proposed to Windsor, though same-sex relationships were illegal at that time. Over the years, the couple participated in the gay liberation movement and the long fight to overturn discriminatory laws.

In 1993, New York City broadened domestic partnership laws to include same-sex couples, so Windsor and Spyer went to City Hall. However, in 1996 the US Congress passed the Defense of Marriage Act (DOMA), defining "marriage" as "between one man and one woman." It also allowed states to refuse to recognize same-sex marriages granted in other states.

In 2007, doctors told Spyer, who had been diagnosed with multiple sclerosis, that she had less than a year to live. Windsor and Spyer traveled to Canada to legally marry. New York recognized their union, but, when Spyer died, Windsor received a huge inheritance tax bill on their joint property—one she wouldn't have gotten had the federal government recognized their marriage. Windsor filed a lawsuit challenging the section of DOMA that defined marriage, saying that it violated the principles of equal protection found in the due process clause of the US Constitution's Fifth Amendment. Windsor wore this scarf over a pinstriped suit on June 27, 2013, when the Supreme Court determined that the section was unconstitutional, clearing the way for nationwide recognition of same-sex marriages.

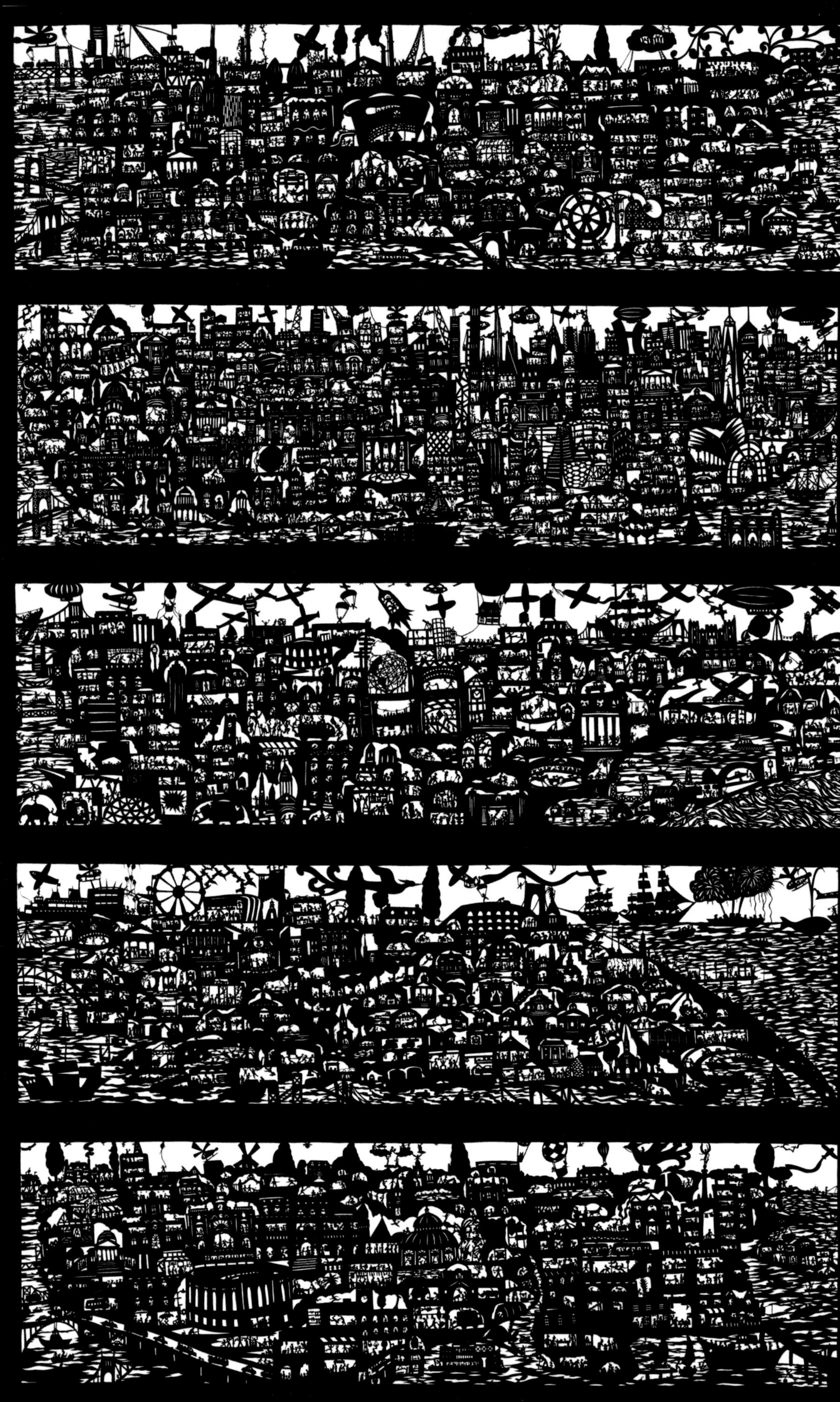

PLACES

PLACES

VALERIE PALEY

Some objects have the power to capture place, time, and space, transporting us into the past: a map, an architectural drawing, a building fragment, a photograph, a sculptural ornament. Researchers and museum visitors alike can reflect on this notion by homing in, zooming out, and closing in again on such documentary evidence of the past at The New York Historical. In this section of *Objects Tell Stories*, the narrative of a semi-mythic American natural landscape evolves and progresses into the built environment that came to be known as New York City—and beyond.

Of the many prized holdings of The New York Historical, the 1803 authorization for the Louisiana Purchase stands out for both its simplicity and its power to narrate a complex story (cat. 76). The one-page document bears Napoleon's signature, among others, authorizing negotiations to take place with future American president James Monroe and Robert R. Livingston, in whose papers the certificate was discovered. The stained right corner is said to have been marked by the Madeira wine used to toast the proceedings, which granted the United States vital control over shipping on the Mississippi River, along with 828,000 square miles of land—roughly doubling the country's size and having far-reaching geopolitical and societal implications for the fledgling nation.

Closer to home, some three decades later, Thomas Cole secured a commission from New York merchant Luman Reed to execute a cycle of five paintings that the young artist had longed to create. The resulting series, *The Course of Empire* (ca. 1834), captures the early 19th-century tensions and inherent anxieties as the "savage" landscape transforms into a civilization that rises, collapses, and reverts to its natural state (cat. 78). Locally, that unblemished land is described in more technical terms in the earliest-known survey of Long Island: a 1670 manuscript map by Robert Ryder (cat. 74). It depicts the contours of what would become modern New York City and the shorelines of Connecticut and New Jersey.

Previous spread:
Béatrice Coron (b. 1956), ***Hi Five! Stories from the Five Boroughs***, 2019
Hand-cut Tyvek

Brooklyn
The New York Historical, Purchased through the generosity of Pam and Scott Schafler in honor of Rhoda Bressler's milestone birthday, 2020.24

Manhattan
The New York Historical, Purchase, Coaching Club Acquisition Fund, 2019.96

Queens
The New York Historical, Purchase, F.S. Ellis Fund, 2022.3.2

Staten Island
The New York Historical, Purchase, F.S. Ellis Fund, 2022.3.3

The Bronx
The New York Historical, Purchase, F.S. Ellis Fund, 2022.3.1

Contemporary New Yorkers are left now to commune with an alternative kind of rugged countryside, as captured in the city's public parks. In many ways, however, Central Park, the great 19th-century exemplar of urban green space, is as much a built environment as the city that developed around it. Frederick Law Olmsted and Calvert Vaux's Greensward Plan won the 1857 competition to design the park, but it is intriguing to imagine that the same 843-acre oasis could have been laid out quite differently had John Rink's entry (cat. 79) been chosen.

Interestingly, if the 1811 Commissioners' Plan had been followed faithfully, New Yorkers would have wound up with an even smaller percentage of open space. The plan created order out of the randomness of nature and the idiosyncrasies of the forms of former Native and Dutch settlements. The resulting grid over the island of Manhattan marked and regulated the city's street patterns without regard for the land's variations and became a conduit for the city's northward expansion and economic growth. As the grid extended its reach, some New Yorkers increasingly called for parks, while a new generation of city dwellers, most of whom were immigrants seeking opportunity, were relegated to substandard tenement housing in retrofitted older single-family homes and small buildings downtown. In 1899, Lawrence Veiller and the Charity Organization Society documented the city's most impoverished neighborhoods in data-filled maps that would lead to some of the most consequential housing reform legislation of the 20th century (cat. 92).

On an individual level, however, the streets themselves are part of the city's very soul, and their evolution and development are thoroughly documented in The New York Historical's collections. For instance, the two decades between the 1731 Lyne Plan of the city and its 1755 update show steady growth, with new byways and buildings, both private and public, shaping the outlines of place and space that still faintly correspond to the silhouette of the modern city (cat. 86). By focusing on these locales more intimately and with vivid immediacy, we appreciate the people and buildings of Dey Street that Baroness Hyde de Neuville sketched during her family's travels in the 1810s (cat. 87); the areas of Five Points and Madison Square captured photographically in the 1840s and '50s (cats. 88 and 89); or long-gone places and events around the five boroughs depicted in chromolithograph postcards used for souvenir correspondence in the decades surrounding the turn of the 20th century (cat. 71). More recent photographic portrayals reveal familiar neighborhoods along with characters and contexts that nostalgically evoke the recent past, such as Arlene Gottfried's images of Coney Island (cat. 81) and Eugene Gordon's of Jackson Heights, Queens, from the late 20th century (cat. 93).

Few places on Earth can claim as many streets as Manhattan that symbolize conceptual understandings of place: Wall Street for finance, Madison Avenue for advertising, Fifth Avenue for department stores, Park Avenue for private wealth, Seventh Avenue for fashion and the garment industry, and Broadway for theater and entertainment. The mythic stature of these thoroughfares may have outlived the reality of what continues to transpire there, but the persistence of this shorthand reflects New York's historical and cultural preeminence.

For example, William Holbrook Beard's iconic painting, *The Bulls and Bears in the Market* (1879), energetically depicts the New York Stock Exchange as it appeared in the 1870s (cat. 91). Created after the Panic of 1873, which triggered the worst depression in 19th-century America, the painting anthropomorphizes aggressive ("bullish") and conservative ("bearish") investors, visually defining the terminology that reputedly was popularized on Wall Street during that era.

Identifying the location as part of a historic district, an unassuming street sign for Christopher Street, just a few blocks north and a century later, evokes a similar power to capture the character of a neighborhood and its history (cat. 94). Greenwich Village was long associated with its reputation as an American "bohemia" and hub for the city's artistic, literary, and cultural life before the area was designated as a historic district in 1969, during the emergence of the historic preservation movement. The Village was also a center for 20th-century countercultural crusades, including, but not limited to, the struggle for LGBTQ+ rights. The Stonewall Uprising marked the flashpoint for the movement, also in 1969, ignited by a raid on a bar on Christopher Street, near the site of the long-gone Harry Howard Hose Company No. 55 firehouse, which a century earlier had been adorned with the monumental wooden sculpture of its namesake fire chief (cat. 68).

Indeed, historians and others have noted that little structural evidence of the city's distant past remains on its streets, due to its success as a metropolis in moving "ever upward" (echoing New York State's motto). Corporate progress has involved tearing down, building larger, dismantling, and then constructing even bigger enhancements to the built environment. This tacit acceptance of impermanence led to indifference toward the aesthetics and historical significance of earlier times, until the destruction of Pennsylvania Station in 1963. The demolition of the Beaux-Arts masterpiece provoked international outrage and sparked the architectural preservation movement in the city and beyond. The New York Historical is the primary repository for the work of the McKim, Mead, and White architectural firm, and its drawings and business records detail the creation of the storied New York City train station and countless other projects from the Gilded Age.

Such markers of a "lost" New York abound at The New York Historical. Since the arrival of Delmonico's in the 1830s, restaurants in the city have served as a "see and be seen" cultural space. Alongside collections of ephemera like matchbooks, business cards, and ashtrays that document long-gone dining establishments, two representative objects best convey this story here. The Four Seasons restaurant in Mies van der Rohe's 1958 Seagram Building was the ostensible birthplace of the business "power lunch." Its scene-setting, monumental Pablo Picasso backdrop had once been a stage curtain for the 1919 ballet *Le Tricorne*, commissioned by Serge Diaghilev for the Ballets Russes (cat. 62). The Four Seasons' interiors were landmarked in 1989, but the unprotected Picasso was subsequently entrusted to The New York Historical. The Upper East Side bar and restaurant Elaine's was no less of a scene. It functioned for 46 years as a "saloon salon" for actors, authors, and celebrities until its closure in 2011. The sign that hung outside its door is all that remains of that iconic pub, also included in the museum's collections (cat. 63).

Francis Guy's *Tontine Coffee House* (cat. 55) illustrates a different kind of drinking establishment. In the 18th century, coffeehouses served as more than mere venues for refreshment; they functioned as vibrant social, mercantile, and political hubs where people gathered to conduct business and discuss current events. Located at the bustling intersection of Wall and Water Streets, the Tontine Coffee House even housed the New York Stock Exchange shortly after its formation. The original building survived the Great Fire of 1835 but was demolished 20 years later to make way for a larger structure. Where ships once docked, perceptible in the distance of the painting, is now landfill.

Indeed, we are fortunate to have disembodied relics as totems of a specific time and place. It is often forgotten that New York City was the first capital of the United States, but The New York Historical possesses several items from George

Washington's April 30, 1789, inauguration, which allow us to evoke that day in our imaginations. Notably, part of the railing from Federal Hall, where Washington took the oath of office and delivered his inaugural address, remains (cat. 54). Not far from this spot, at the city's Bowling Green in July 1776, Continental soldiers joined patriotic New Yorkers in tearing down a lead equestrian monument of their king, George III. This statue was transported to Litchfield, Connecticut, where local women and children melted it down into 42,088 bullets for the Revolutionary War. The statue's tail, however, survives in The New York Historical's collections (cat. 67).

The ensuing century witnessed rapid expansion and significant social and commercial change. Elements of the built environment that emerged during this period may still be visible today, thanks in large part to landmarks protection, but the creation stories of both famous and everyday architectural projects are documented here. The circa 1837 trade sign for John Butler Snook's architectural office, depicting the façade of a Greek temple, barely hints at the crucial role Snook played throughout his 60-year career in shaping the streetscape of downtown Manhattan (cat. 58). He designed several notable buildings, churches, and residences—now demolished—but most of his work consisted of tenements, warehouses, and commercial structures—including some of the historically significant cast-iron architecture in the area now known as SoHo.

In some instances, only fragments remain as evidence of a place. One surviving architectural remnant is a piece of the façade of James Bogardus's Edgar Laing Stores (cat. 59), which, by most accounts, was the first cast-iron building in New York City. Located at the intersection of Washington and Murray Streets, it was dismantled before the Landmarks Commission designated the Cast Iron Historic District. Nearby in SoHo, in 1986, the artist Keith Haring opened the Pop Shop at 292 Lafayette Street to make his work accessible to a wide audience. Haring covered the interior of the space—ceiling, walls, even the floor—with a continuous mural in his signature graffiti-inflected style; however, the ceiling is the only original portion that still exists (cat. 65).

Finally, no event in recent memory, except perhaps for the COVID-19 pandemic, has taken as significant a toll on the psyche of New York City as the destruction of the World Trade Center during the terrorist attacks on September 11, 2001. Reminiscent of its founding motivation to preserve evidence of America's founding period, The New York Historical activated its staff to collect the remnants of the disaster's aftermath. The institutional initiative which came to be known as "History Responds" continues to gather objects that capture an unfolding history as it happens, when it happens. Images of the Twin Towers abound in The New York Historical's collections, along with architectural drawings of its stairwells. But a mangled desk clock recovered from the Fresh Kills landfill in Staten Island perhaps best encapsulates this moment, and the devastation of place (cat. 66). It stopped at 9:04 a.m., almost exactly the time that the South Tower of the World Trade Center was struck by United Airlines Flight 175. Fifty-six minutes later, the South Tower collapsed.

H.N. Tiemann & Co. (1880–1916)
Interior of Grant's Tomb, Riverside Drive at 122nd Street, New York City, ca. 1897
Glass plate negative
Patricia D. Klingenstein Library,
The New York Historical

BUILDINGS & ARCHITECTURE

52

ATTRIBUTED TO EVERT DUYCKINCK I (1621–ca. 1703)

Stained-glass window, ca. 1656

New York City
Glass
The New York Historical, Gift of Mrs. Howard C. Robbins, 1951.414b

These are two of a small group of stained-glass windows attributed to Evert Duyckinck that are thought to have been made for the First Reformed Dutch Church, built in Albany, New York, in 1656 and torn down in 1715. One window, ornamented with a coat of arms depicting three ostriches on a vert field, was later removed from a house on Eighth Street in New York City and found by Mrs. Howard Robbins in a wrecker's yard. She used the window in her Dutch Revival house at Sneden's Landing on the Hudson River before donating it to The New York Historical.

In 17th-century Europe, stained-glass makers were respected craftsmen who underwent years of training and might belong to the same guild as glass engravers and glass painters, gilders, goldsmiths, and illuminators. While the guilds provided useful business networks and a system of mutual aid, it was expensive and sometimes difficult to advance through the ranks from journeyman to master of one's own shop. Perhaps that is part of the reason why Duyckinck, one of the first artists in the colonial period to produce fine glasswork in North America, emigrated with his family, arriving in 1638.

ATTRIBUTED TO EVERT DUYCKINCK I (1621–ca. 1703)

Stained-glass window, ca. 1656

New York City
Glass
The New York Historical, Gift of Mrs. Howard C. Robbins, 1951.414a

53

ATTRIBUTED TO STEPHEN DWIGHT (ca. 1736–1788)

Chimneypiece, ca. 1767

New York City
White pine
The New York Historical, Gift of James W. Beekman, 1874.8

The Beekman family of New York traced its roots to a Dutch ancestor who arrived in 1647. The Beekmans served in both the Dutch and British colonial administrations, held significant amounts of property, and quickly rose to affluence. By 1763–64, James Beekman (1732–1807), a dry-goods merchant, could afford to build one of New York's finest rococo residences: a country house that he named Mount Pleasant, located at today's 51st Street and overlooking the East River. The mansion was so large and well situated that it was used as a headquarters by General William Howe during the British occupation of New York City. The patriot spy Nathan Hale is said to have been imprisoned in the greenhouse and hanged in a nearby orchard.

When the mansion was torn down in 1874, the carved and painted chimneypiece that graced the mansion's drawing room was presented to The New York Historical by James William Beekman. The coat of arms is said to have ornamented the front parlor, and the tiles may have been installed in the nursery.

Fig. 12
Unidentified maker
Delftware fireplace tiles from the Beekman mansion, 1725–75
England or Holland
Tin-glazed earthenware
The New York Historical, Permanent loan from the Beekman Family Association, Z.770j, Z.770g, Z.770p

Fig. 13
Attributed to Stephen Dwight (ca. 1736–1788)
Beekman family coat of arms, 1760–70
Probably New York
Wood, paint, gilding
The New York Historical, Permanent loan from the Beekman Family Association, 1962.63

54

UNIDENTIFIED MAKER

Railing from Federal Hall, 1788–89

New York City
Iron, paint
The New York Historical, Gift of the Chamber of Commerce of the State of New York, 1884.3

George Washington was inaugurated as the first president of the United States on April 30, 1789, while standing on the balcony of Federal Hall, located on Wall Street in New York City. Built in 1703 and originally known as City Hall, the building was renamed after the ratification of the Constitution in 1788. It housed the federal government until the national capital moved from New York to Philadelphia in 1790. The original building was torn down in 1812. (In 1842, a new building on the site became the first US Customs House, and later a US Sub-Treasury; it is now a National Memorial.) During the demolition of Federal Hall, the center section of the balcony railing was salvaged and incorporated into a portico on the Administrative Building at Bellevue Hospital. It was removed in 1883, and presented to The New York Historical the following year.

Fig. 14
Unidentified maker
Armchair, 1785–89
New York City
Mahogany with pine and poplar
The New York Historical, Gift of Edmund B. Southwick, 1916.7

This mahogany armchair came from the Senate chamber in Federal Hall, where it was used by George Washington while delivering his inaugural address to members of Congress after being sworn in as president. Washington expressed his humility at having been entrusted with such a weighty responsibility, pledging that the executive branch would uphold the highest standards of private morality and strive to earn the affection of his fellow citizens and the respect of the world. The chair was subsequently used for the presidential inaugurations of Ulysses S. Grant in 1873 and James A. Garfield in 1881.

Fig. 15
Giuseppe Guidicini (1812–1868)
President Washington Taking the Oath, Federal Hall, 1789, 1839
Oil on fine linen
The New York Historical, Purchase, X.269

In 1839, The New York Historical commissioned Italian painter Giuseppe Guidicini to create a "transparency" commemorating the semicentennial of Washington's inauguration. Guidicini painted the scene upon a thin sheet of linen, treated with oil. A candle burning behind the work illuminated it to "brilliant effect." Transparencies were a common feature of 19th-century political events, but, because of their delicate and flammable materials, they rarely survived.

55

FRANCIS GUY (1760–1820)

Tontine Coffee House, New York City, ca. 1797

Oil on linen
The New York Historical, Purchase, The Louis Durr Fund, Sponsored by Laurie and Sy Sternberg, 1907.32

In 1797, Francis Guy, one of the first artists in America to specialize in landscapes, depicted the financial crossroads of 18th-century New York: the Tontine Coffee House, located at the intersection of Wall and Water Streets. The second floor of the establishment functioned as the home of the New York Stock Exchange.

The coffeehouse was named after a type of joint investment called a tontine. The tontine association founded by New York's merchants in 1790 allowed them to raise significant amounts of capital at a time when the city had only one bank. Records held by The New York Historical's Patricia D. Klingenstein Library show that 203 shares in the tontine were sold at $200 each to fund construction of the building in 1792–94. The Tontine Coffee House quickly became a crucial meeting place where merchants and traders socialized, exchanged information, and bargained over cargo from ships arriving at the East River wharves, visible in the background of this painting. These cargoes included enslaved men and women, who were bought and sold at the Meal Market across the street.

56

JOHN MCCOMB JR. (1763–1853)

New York City Hall, Front Elevation, 1802

Ink, wash, graphite
Patricia D. Klingenstein Library, The New York Historical

John McComb was New York City's principal architect from 1800 until his retirement in the 1820s, and is remembered as one of the most important architects in the United States during the Federal period. The eldest child of John McComb Sr. (1734–1811), who was also an architect in colonial and post-Revolutionary New York City, McComb Jr. became his father's assistant in 1783. By 1790 he was commissioned to build a residence for the new United States president. The building was not finished when the federal government moved to Pennsylvania, but New York's governors used the house until 1797. McComb designed opulent houses for New York's elite, including Senator Rufus King, Reverend Benjamin Moore, and Alexander Hamilton; he also built lighthouses at Montauk Point, Eaton's Neck, and Cape Henry, Virginia, which still exist today.

In 1800, the New York City Common Council held a design competition for a new City Hall. McComb, in consultation with the French architect Joseph François Mangin, made 105 drawings, all of which are preserved in The New York Historical's Patricia D. Klingenstein Library. The City Council awarded Mangin and McComb the top prize of $350 in 1802, and McComb was subsequently named chief architect and superintendent of construction. As soon as the building was completed in 1811, it was recognized as one of the finest public buildings in America, and has remained one of the nation's architectural treasures.

57

UNIDENTIFIED MAKER

Steeple ball from the Garden Street Church destroyed in the Great Fire, ca. 1693

United States
Wood, metal, paint
The New York Historical, Gift of Edgar F. Ronig, D. D., 1936.418

The Garden Street Dutch Reformed Church, located on what is now Exchange Place, was constructed in 1693. It was built to replace the Fort Amsterdam church, which became an Anglican church for English soldiers after the British takeover of New Netherland in 1664. The congregation was granted a full charter as the Dutch Church in America by King William III of England in May 1696. A second church was built on the same site in 1807; it housed the bell belonging to the original church, which had been cast in 1674.

This second church building was destroyed in the Great Fire of 1835, which blazed across 23 city blocks on December 16 and 17, burning nearly a quarter of New York's business district and many of the few remaining Dutch buildings. Freezing temperatures hindered firefighters' efforts to combat the flames, which destroyed 650 buildings and $20 million of property, per the handwriting on the steeple ball, which was given to the donor by Dr. George Alexander, minister of the First Presbyterian Church.

Fig. 16
Nicolino Calyo (1799–1884)
View of the Ruins after the Great Fire in New-York, December 16th and 17th 1835, as Seen from Exchange Place, 1836
Gouache on heavy paper
The New York Historical, Thomas Jefferson Bryan Fund, 1980.54

The Italian artist Nicolino Calyo made several paintings of the 1835 fire; this scene reveals the extent of the destruction along Exchange Place, looking east. The façade of the old Garden Street Dutch Reformed Church is visible on the left, its entrance protected from looters by guards.

58

UNIDENTIFIED MAKER

Architect's sign, ca. 1837

New York City
Wood
The New York Historical, Gift of Mr. Thomas E. Snook Jr., 1953.197

This trade sign, depicting the façade of a Greek temple, hung in front of the office of architect John Butler Snook (1815–1901), whose career as a practicing architect in New York City spanned nearly 60 years. Snook served as an apprentice in his father's carpentry business, and was largely self-taught as an architect, establishing his firm in 1837. In 1842, he joined the firm of Joseph Trench, and in less than five years became the firm's junior partner. Snook played an instrumental role in developing the streetscape of downtown Manhattan. Among his notable buildings were the A.T. Stewart "Marble Palace" (1845–46), the Grand Central Depot (1869–71), and the Metropolitan Hotel (1849–52). He also designed churches, residences, and hospitals. While Snook did not specialize in one type of structure, the majority of his work was in tenements, warehouses, and commercial buildings—including some of the historically significant cast-iron architecture in the area now known as SoHo.

59

JAMES BOGARDUS (1800–1874)

Architectural ornament from the Laing Stores, 1849

Iron, wood
The New York Historical, Gift of Dr. Winston R. Weisman, 1990.5b

This cast-iron fragment represents one of the most important examples of a notable New York City building type. The Edgar Laing Stores, at the intersection of Washington and Murray Streets, was constructed in 1849. According to historians, it was the first cast-iron building in New York City, and a significant example of the work of noted cast-iron designer James Bogardus. This architectural fragment illustrates the elaborate ornamentation typically found on cast-iron façades, with a foliate scroll design and two beasts' heads flanking a fanciful *mascaron*, or face, crowned with grapes.

By the early 1970s, city officials were debating SoHo's fate. The neighborhood then housed light industry, such as garment and printing firms, as well as a growing number of artists' studios. The preservationist Margot Gayle (1908–2008) became a vocal proponent for landmarking the area, emphasizing its technologically innovative and visually ornate 19th-century cast-iron architecture. To build grassroots support, Gayle founded the Friends of Cast Iron Architecture in 1970. For $3, members received a button and a small magnet that could be used to test building façades for cast iron. Gayle and other activists (including this object's donor, architectural historian Winston R. Weisman) prevailed in 1973 when the Landmarks Commission designated 26 blocks in SoHo the Cast Iron Historic District. However, the Laing building had already been dismantled to make way for a proposed new City University campus. The disassembled façade went into storage, but in two separate incidents (1974 and 1977) most of the pieces were stolen and sold for scrap in the Bronx. The *New York Times* dubbed the loss "perhaps the most darkly comical episode" in Landmarks Commission history.

Fig. 17
Unidentified maker
Tab button, ca. 1970s
Metal
The New York Historical, Z.3599.3

60

THOMAS R. JOHNSON (d. 1915)

Woolworth Building presentation drawing, depicting an earlier proposed design, Cass Gilbert, architect, 1910

Graphite and colored pencil on board
Patricia D. Klingenstein Library, The New York Historical

Architect Cass Gilbert (1859–1934) designed Manhattan's United States Custom House (1901–07) and the 24-story building at 90 West Street (1905–07). However, his most famous design was the Woolworth Building (1911–13), an elegant Gothic-style edifice with a terra-cotta exterior installed over a steel frame. Though often described as a "Cathedral of Commerce," Gilbert later disputed this characterization, stating that his design was inspired by civic and commercial models: medieval guildhalls, city halls, and even the British Houses of Parliament. Still, he wrote, "the Woolworth Tower stands on its merits, for I know of no prototype." It was the tallest building in the world from 1913 to 1930 and housed the headquarters of F.W. Woolworth and Company, a hugely successful five-and-dime retailer. Located in a major shopping district, near City Hall Park and opposite the Post Office, the tower served as an advertisement all its own, garnering publicity and attention from the start: President Woodrow Wilson attended the opening ceremony.

Gilbert went on to design other buildings in New York, including the New York Life Insurance Company Building (1925–28) and the US Courthouse (1936), which was completed after his death. Gilbert also completed designs for the George Washington Memorial Bridge (1927–31), but they proved to be too expensive and were never used.

61

JULES CROW (active early 20th century)

Pennsylvania Station Interior, 1906

Watercolor, ink, and graphite on paper
Patricia D. Klingenstein Library, The New York Historical

Architectural historian Vincent Scully wrote that to arrive in New York City through the original Pennsylvania Station was to enter it like a god. The architectural firm McKim, Mead, and White designed the station for the Pennsylvania Railroad. In 1879, Charles McKim (1847–1909), William Rutherford Mead (1846–1928), and Stanford White (1853–1906) established their partnership in New York City and soon became the premier architectural firm in the United States, renowned for their neoclassical Beaux-Arts buildings. This presentation drawing, painted by Jules Crow in 1906, depicts Penn Station's 148-foot-high coffered ceiling, modeled after ancient Roman baths, that soared above travelers in the waiting room. The station opened in 1910 and stood for only 54 years. Its demolition, beginning in 1963, sparked the creation of the New York City Landmarks Preservation Commission two years later.

The McKim, Mead, and White Architectural Collection is one of the largest and most significant held by the Patricia D. Klingenstein Library at The New York Historical, consisting of more than 61,000 architectural drawings and 1,500 photographs, as well as 54 ledgers, 30 photo albums, scrapbooks, over 300 original line drawings, and 700 boxes of correspondence.

Fig. 18
De W.C. Ward (1873–1937), photographer
Adolph A. Weinman (1870–1952), sculptor
***Night*, clock figure from Pennsylvania Station**, ca. 1910
Photographic print
Patricia D. Klingenstein Library, The New York Historical

NEW YORK
TRENTON

62

PABLO PICASSO (1881–1973)

Curtain for the ballet *Le Tricorne*, 1919

Tempera on canvas
The New York Historical, Gift of New York Landmarks Conservancy, Courtesy of Vivendi Universal, Sponsored by Leonard A. Lauder, 2015.22

Pablo Picasso created this monumental stage curtain for the ballet *Le Tricorne*, fulfilling a commission from impresario Serge Diaghilev, founder of the avant-garde Ballets Russes. Although the Ballets Russes never performed *Le Tricorne* in New York, and Picasso himself never traveled to the United States, the curtain became a notable city landmark.

In 1928, the chronically cash-strapped Diaghilev sold the curtain to a private collector. Phyllis Lambert, architectural historian and daughter of Samuel Bronfman, CEO of the Seagram Company, acquired the curtain in 1957, and it was installed in The Four Seasons restaurant in the Seagram Building, designed by Ludwig Mies van der Rohe and Philip Johnson. The elegant establishment attracted crowds of wealthy and influential New Yorkers, leading *Vanity Fair* to call it "absolute ground zero for power lunching." The Four Seasons interiors were given landmark status by the City in 1989, but, as a freestanding work of art, the Picasso was left unprotected. In 2005, Lambert gifted the curtain to the New York Landmarks Conservancy, which subsequently entrusted it to The New York Historical. In 2014, the curtain was installed in its new home in The New York Historical's Dexter Hall.

Fig. 19
Emil Antonucci (1929–2006), designer
The Four Seasons matchbook, after 1959
Cardboard, wood, striker, adhesive
The New York Historical, Gift of Lila A. Morris, 2008.47.181

Brooklyn-born graphic designer Emil Antonucci created The Four Seasons logo in 1959, and it was used until the restaurant left the Seagram Building in 2016.

Fig. 20
Ludwig Mies van der Rohe (1886–1969), designer
Knoll International (founded 1938), maker
***Brno* armchair**, designed 1958
East Greenville, Pennsylvania
Stainless steel, wool upholstery
The New York Historical, Gift of The Four Seasons Restaurant, 2016.47.1

Ludwig Mies van der Rohe's *Brno* armchair, upholstered in a midnight-blue shade unique to The Four Seasons, served as the primary seating in both dining areas, the Pool Room and the Grill Room.

PICASSO
PINXIT 1919

63

UNIDENTIFIED MAKER

Sign from Elaine's restaurant, 1963

Metal (possibly galvanized steel), Plexiglas
The New York Historical, Gift of the Estate of Elaine Kaufman, 2012.5

This sign hung in front of the iconic Upper East Side restaurant Elaine's until its closing in 2011. As Diane Becker, co-executor of the estate of restaurant owner Elaine Kaufman (1929–2010), explained to the *New York Times*, "The Elaine's sign hung over Second Avenue for nearly 50 years as a beacon welcoming anyone and everyone who wanted to have fun, if only for a night. . . . I want New Yorkers to remember the siren song of Elaine's and all that Elaine and Elaine's gave the city." In 1963, Kaufman scraped together $5,000 to buy an Austro-Hungarian bar on Second Avenue and transformed it into one of the most famous night spots in America. The "saloon salon" attracted the likes of Woody Allen (table 8), Jacqueline Kennedy (table 10), and William Styron (table 4). Kaufman died in December 2010 at the age of 81. Becker, then the restaurant manager, inherited Elaine's and attempted to keep it running. However, by April 2011, Becker had determined that it was no longer a viable business, and it closed forever the next month.

64

PARADISE GARAGE (1976–1987)

Membership card for Simon R. Newey, 1979

New York City
Plastic, paper
The New York Historical, Gift of Bob Newey - photos NYC, 2020.5.2

Paradise Garage, dubbed the "Gay-rage," was located in a former parking garage at 84 King Street in SoHo. The building was purchased in 1976, and opened to the public in 1977. Like many of the LGBTQ+ nightlife venues that arose in New York City after the 1969 Stonewall uprising, Paradise Garage operated as a private club, which allowed it to avoid the State Liquor Authority's licensing requirements and earn revenue through paid memberships. It also helped assure personal safety, cultivate a sense of exclusivity, and foster feelings of belonging. This membership card, from 1979, belonged to Simon Robert "Bob" Newey, who worked in the fashion industry and began going to clubs in 1969.

The Garage's resident superstar, DJ Larry Levan (1954–1992), designed an award-winning sound system which was said to be the best in New York. Levan was frequently compared to a preacher in a church, able to speak directly to the crowd via his music. He is now widely considered a progenitor of house music. The club served no alcohol or food, which exempted it from city rules governing bar hours and allowed its patrons, who were primarily Black and Latino, to dance all night. Paradise Garage closed after ten years, only two months before owner Michael Brody died of AIDS-related complications in 1987. The building was demolished in 2018.

65

KEITH HARING (1958–1990)

Pop Shop ceiling, 1986

Acrylic and latex on drywall with aluminum armature
The New York Historical, Gift of the Keith Haring Foundation, Inc., 2011.17a-j

Keith Haring was synonymous with New York's downtown art scene in the 1980s. With encouragement from Andy Warhol, and defying criticism that his work would become overly commercial, Haring opened the Pop Shop at 292 Lafayette Street in SoHo in 1986 with the goal of making his art accessible to a wide range of people, as part of "an extended performance." The Pop Shop blurred contemporary lines between culture and commerce, high and low art, public and private spaces. Haring covered the interior of the shop—ceiling, walls, even the floor—with a single continuous mural in his signature graffiti-inflected style, boldly executed in black and white. After the artist's death from AIDS-related causes in 1990, the Keith Haring Foundation continued to run the Pop Shop until 2005, when rent increases forced it to close. During its 19 years in operation, the shop's floor and walls required extensive repainting, making the ceiling the only original portion of the mural in existence.

66

UNIDENTIFIED MAKER

Desk clock, ca. 2000

The New York Historical, Gift of Federal Bureau of Investigation, Birmingham, Alabama, 2002.58.1

The Twin Towers of the World Trade Center were a prominent part of the New York City skyline. When completed in 1973, they became the tallest buildings in New York, symbolizing the central role of the United States in the global economy.

This desk clock was destroyed in the terrorist attacks of September 11, 2001, that killed nearly 3,000 people. It stopped at 9:04 a.m., almost exactly the time that the South Tower of the World Trade Center was struck by United Airlines Flight 175. Fifty-six minutes later, the South Tower collapsed.

In the wake of the attacks, almost two million tons of material from the Ground Zero site was brought to the Fresh Kills landfill in Staten Island, where hundreds of FBI and NYPD personnel sorted through it—often by hand—searching for human remains, personal effects, and forensic evidence. An FBI special agent was inspired to donate this clock, which was found during the Fresh Kills recovery operation, after seeing a television documentary that discussed The New York Historical's "History Responds" collecting initiative, launched immediately following the attacks to preserve and interpret the unimaginable events of that day.

Ground Zero is now a memorial plaza, and the Twin Towers' footprints are occupied by two waterfall pools, surrounded by bronze walls etched with the names of those lost on 9/11 and in February 1993, when an earlier terrorist attack on the World Trade Center killed six. Designed by architect Michael Arad and landscape architect Peter Walker, the memorial, which opened on the tenth anniversary of the 9/11 attacks, is entitled *Reflecting Absence*. Arad's 9/11 Memorial papers, records, and sketches are part of the Patricia D. Klingenstein Library's collections.

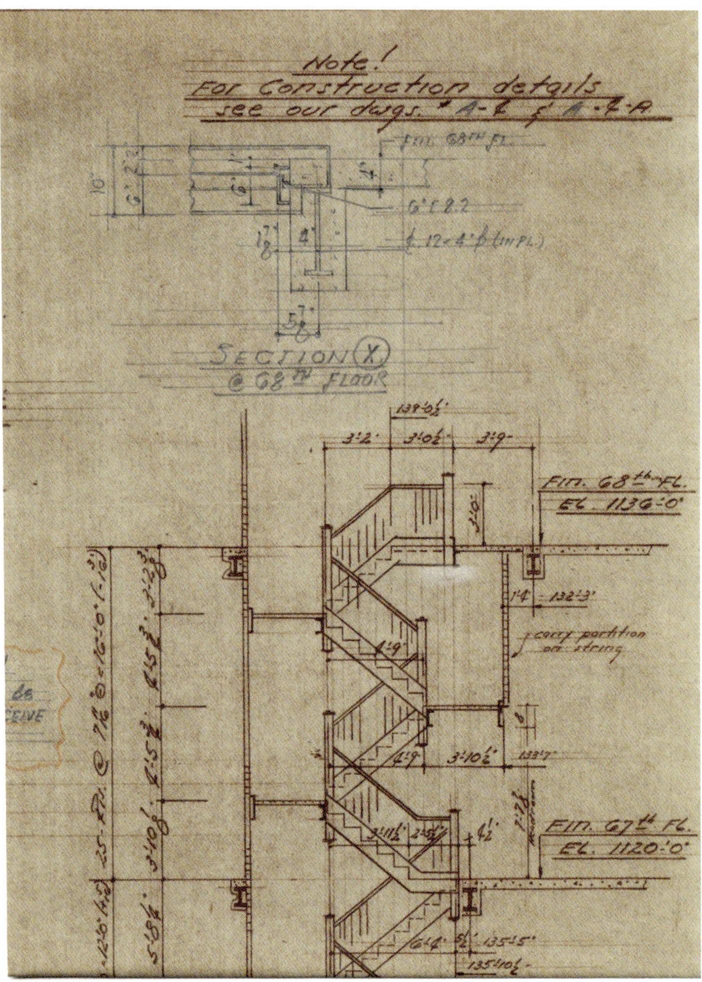

Fig. 21
Adler & Neilson Architectural Iron Works (incorporated 1920)
Drawing A2G title block, *Stair No. 2 - 66th to 68th FLS. @ Revised Location*, 1969–73
Patricia D. Klingenstein Library, The New York Historical

The New York Historical houses the Adler & Neilson Architectural Iron Works Collection, the records of a firm that worked on many New York City landmarks, including the LaGuardia and John F. Kennedy airports, the Brooklyn Army Terminal, The Museum of Modern Art, Rockefeller Center, the Federal Reserve Bank of New York, the 1939 and 1963 World's Fairs, and the World Trade Center. Designed by Japanese American architect Minoru Yamasaki (1912–1986), the Twin Towers' exterior walls consisted of load-bearing steel columns, built to withstand wind, earthquakes, and impact—including horizontal strikes by commercial aircraft—while interior columns at the buildings' core areas housed the elevators and stairwells.

Staff archivists recently discovered four boxes of architectural drawings, dating from between 1969 and 1973, that detail the interior stairwells of the Twin Towers. During the terrorist attacks of September 11, 2001, these stairs quickly became the only means of egress from the buildings.

66

Henry Augustus Lukeman (1871–1935)
Maquette for Straus Memorial, Straus Park, New York City, 1915
Plaster and graphite
The New York Historical, Gift of Joseph and Paula Bidwell McNay, 2021.10.1

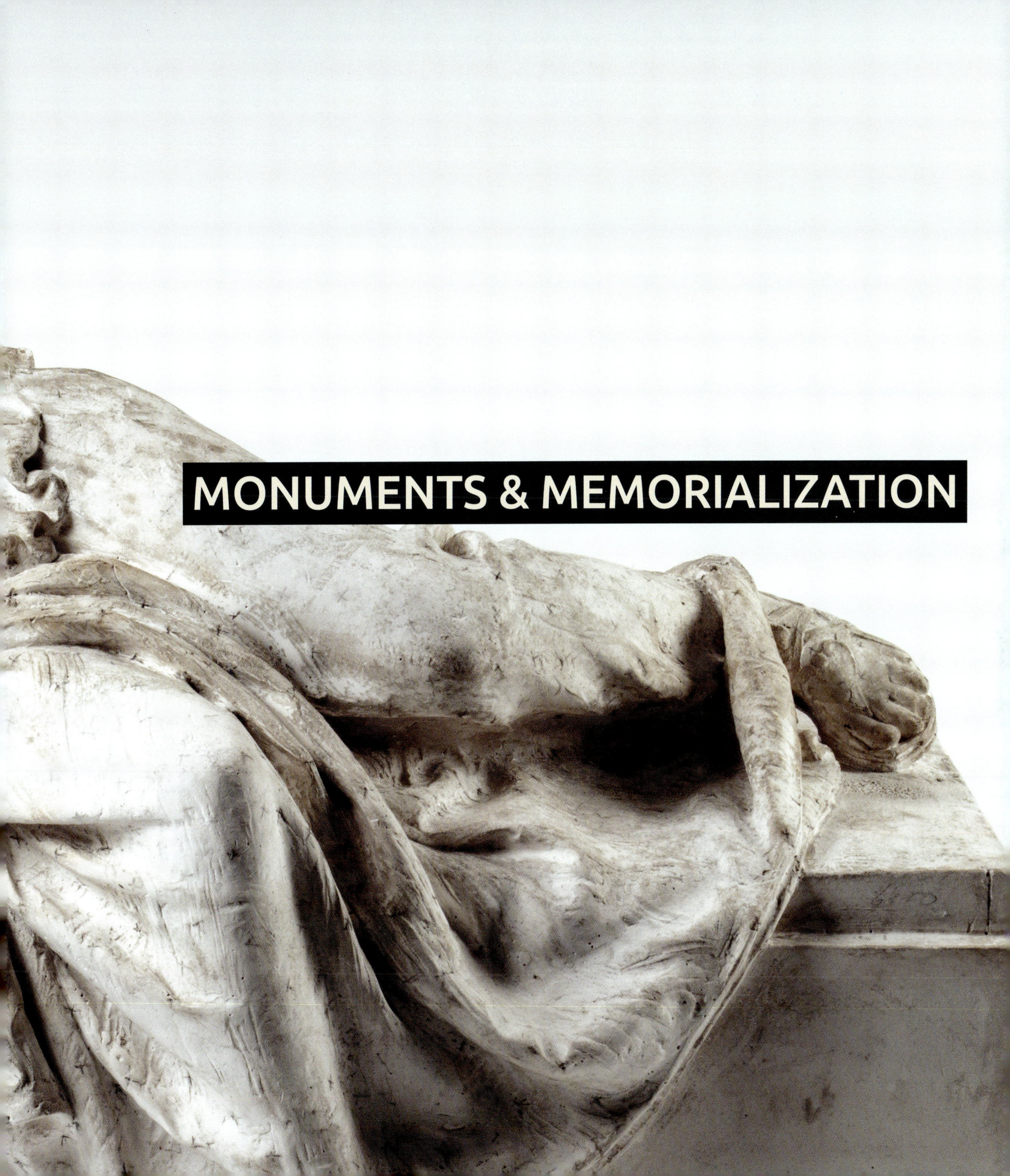

MONUMENTS & MEMORIALIZATION

67

JOSEPH WILTON (1722–1803)

Tail fragment of the equestrian statue of King George III, 1770–76

New York City and England
Lead
The New York Historical, Purchase, 1878.6

After a public reading of the Declaration of Independence on July 9, 1776, Continental soldiers joined patriotic New Yorkers in tearing down an equestrian statue of King George III on the Bowling Green at the southern tip of Manhattan. Soon afterwards, the residents of Litchfield, Connecticut, received an unusual delivery: four thousand pounds of gilded lead, the remnants of the statue. Litchfield was a crucial munitions depot, and the town's records show that patriotic women and children melted the lead down into 42,088 bullets. "His Statue here has been pulled down to make Musket Ball of, so that his Troops will probably have melted Majesty fired at them," quipped New Yorker Ebenezer Hazard in a July 12, 1776, letter. In contrast, it is believed that some Connecticut Loyalists hid bits of the statue in and around their homes, for fragments such as the one pictured here were later found buried in the area.

Fig. 22
Johannes Adam Simon Oertel (1823–1909)
Pulling Down the Statue of King George III, New York City, 1852–53
Oil on canvas
The New York Historical, Gift of Samuel V. Hoffman, 1925.6

68

UNIDENTIFIED MAKER

Fire Chief Harry Howard (1822–1896), ca. 1855

New York City
Painted wood
The New York Historical, Purchased from Elie Nadelman, 1937.328. Conservation made possible with the generous support of John S. Tamagni in honor of his grandfather Arthur Searle, NYFD, 1886–1909, 1937.328

This monumental statue depicts fire chief Harry Howard (1822–1896) trumpeting orders to members of his company while gesturing them towards a blaze. One of the most celebrated firefighters in New York City history, Howard was revered for his bravery and credited with saving many lives. He rose from humble beginnings, starting as a teenage "runner" for Peterson Engine Company No. 15, headquartered on Chrystie Street between Canal and Bayard. In 1850, members of the Atlantic Hose Company No. 14 elected him foreman. Located on Elizabeth Street near the Old Bowery Theater, this company was manned by "Bowery Boys," working-class nativists who, according to Howard's obituary, took "prominent part" in a deadly street riot in July 1857, battling Irish residents of the Five Points neighborhood.

In 1857, Howard attained the position of chief engineer, the highest rank in the all-volunteer force. He resigned in 1860, following a stroke, and spent the rest of his life advocating on behalf of firefighters.

Originally placed atop the Harry Howard Hose Company No. 55 at 115 Christopher Street in New York City, this sculpture subsequently ornamented three other fire headquarters before taking its place in the entry gallery of Elie Nadelman's Museum of Folk Art and Peasant Arts, located in the Riverdale section of the Bronx. Nadelman (1882–1946), an avant-garde sculptor, and his wife Viola Speiss Flannery (1878–1962) began collecting folk art in the early 1900s. The New York Historical purchased the Nadelmans' folk art collection of 15,000 objects in 1937.

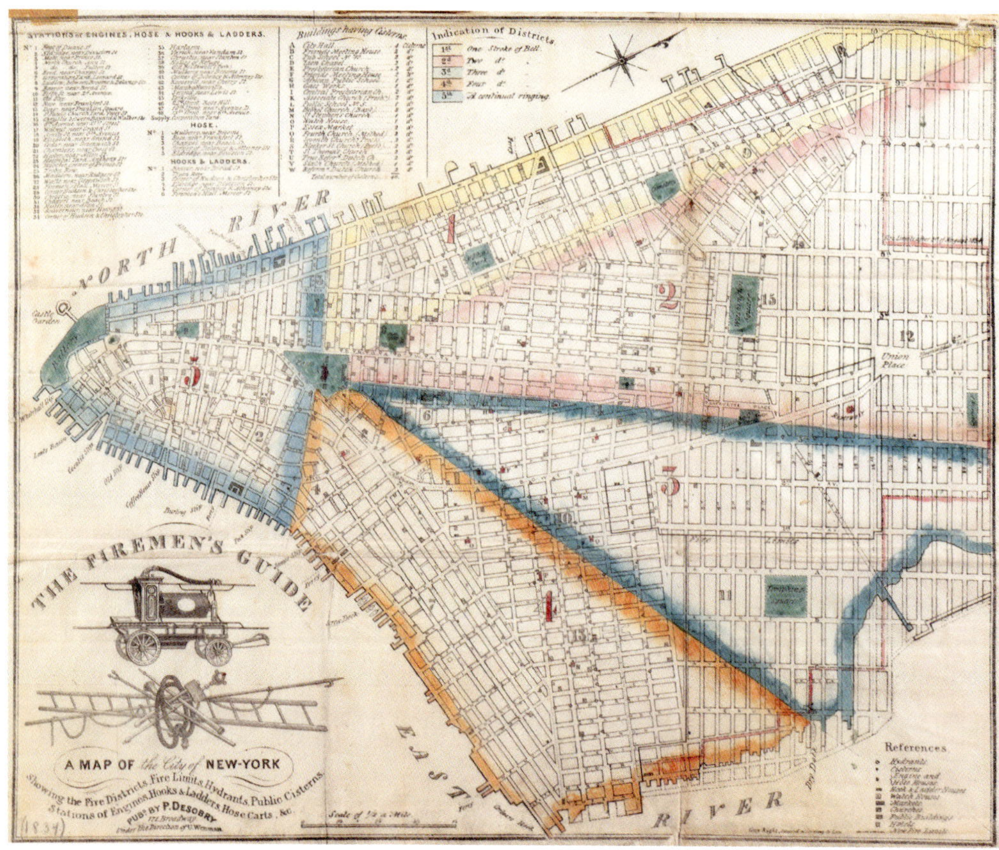

Fig. 23
The Firemen's Guide
Hand-colored map
New York: P. Desobry under the direction of U. Wenman, 1834
Patricia D. Klingenstein Library, The New York Historical

69

FRÉDÉRIC-AUGUSTE BARTHOLDI (1834–1904), designer
AVOIRON & CIE (1876–1886), maker

Model of *Liberty Enlightening the World*, ca. 1879–83

Paris, France
Copper-plated zinc
The New York Historical, Gift of Mr. George A. Zabriskie, 1942.346

The idea of the Statue of Liberty emerged at the end of the American Civil War, when the French abolitionist and historian Édouard de Laboulaye (1811–1883) first proposed the monumental gift. One of his associates was the neoclassical sculptor Frédéric-Auguste Bartholdi, whose design incorporated broken shackles and chains under Lady Liberty's feet. These were powerful symbols that had long been associated with the abolitionist cause.

Liberty Enlightening the World was intended for presentation to the United States on July 4, 1876, in honor of the nation's centennial, but only the 30-foot raised arm and torch were constructed in time to be displayed at the International Centennial Exhibition in Philadelphia. Though the exhibition generated great enthusiasm for the project, the US still had to build a suitable pedestal for the statue, and fundraising remained sluggish. In 1883, the popular poet and activist Emma Lazarus, the daughter of Jewish immigrants, donated her poem "The New Colossus" to a charitable auction to raise money for the statue's pedestal, helping to shift the statue's symbolism towards hospitality and opportunity for immigrants. Newspaperman—and immigrant—Joseph Pulitzer also helped with this campaign, prompting 120,000 people to collectively donate over $100,000 to the cause. In his call for donations, Pulitzer wrote, "Let us not wait for the millionaires to give us this money. It is not a gift from the millionaires of France to the millionaires of America, but a gift of the whole people of France to the whole people of America." In part through these efforts, the Statue of Liberty became synonymous with the immigrant experience and character of New York and the United States.

When the completed statue was finally unveiled in New York Harbor on October 28, 1886, over one million people watched a parade of more than 20,000 marchers commemorating the event. At the time of the dedication, the Statue of Liberty was the tallest structure in New York, reaching 305 feet. It remains a potent symbol of both New York and the nation.

70

MARIA EWING SHERMAN FITCH (1851–1913)

Grand Army Quilt, ca. 1888

Edgewood, Pennsylvania
Silk, wool, cotton
The New York Historical, Given in honor of Carl Schenker Jr., Conservation sponsored by Anne Richardson Johnson, Frank Richardson, Thomas F. Richardson, Beth Gutcheon Clements, Susan Sherman Richardson, and John S. Richardson, 2014.12

This crazy quilt by Maria ("Minnie") Ewing Sherman Fitch commemorates the military legacy of her father, Major General William Tecumseh Sherman (1820–1891). Known by Sherman descendants as the Grand Army Quilt in reference to the Civil War veterans' fraternal organization, Fitch's hand-sewn homage is strewn with embroidered military insignia denoting Union Army branches and ranks, and corps badges (worn by soldiers on their uniforms) with accompanying corps numbers. Fitch incorporated two reunion ribbons, presumably her father's, among the patchwork. Sherman commanded the Department of the Cumberland from 1861 to 1862, the Army of the Tennessee from October 1863 to March 1864, and the Military Division of the Mississippi—comprising the Tennessee, Cumberland, and Ohio departments—from 1864 to 1866. He succeeded Ulysses S. Grant as commanding general of the army in 1869 and retired in 1883.

Crazy quilts were typically created as showpieces, and the Grand Army Quilt's highly unusual shape suggests a non-functional purpose, most likely to display on a parlor surface. The quilt shares its name with the plazas marking the main entrance to Brooklyn's Prospect Park as well as the southeastern entrance to Manhattan's Central Park, two of the many physical monuments and memorials to the Union Army across New York City. At Central Park's Grand Army Plaza, a statue of General Sherman by Augustus Saint-Gaudens (1848–1907) adorns the space.

Fig. 24
Robert L. Bracklow (1849–1919), photographer
The Sherman Monument at Grand Army Plaza in Manhattan, New York City, 1903
Print from glass plate negative
Patricia D. Klingenstein Library,
The New York Historical

71

THADDEUS WILKERSON (1871–1943)

Night Scene, Naval Parade, Hudson-Fulton Celebration, 1909

Photo postcard
Patricia D. Klingenstein Library, The New York Historical, Bob Stonehill Collection of New York City Postcards

Three hundred years after Henry Hudson arrived in New York Harbor, and one hundred years after the successful launch of Robert Fulton's steamboat service to Albany, New York City hosted the Hudson-Fulton Celebration, a two-week-long, million-dollar extravaganza of parades, concerts, flyovers, fireworks, and commemorative merchandise. Led by a committee including J.P. Morgan and Andrew Carnegie, the event lauded New York as both a global city and the heart of American progress; as a port, it was vital to international and national commerce, central to the nation's emerging identity as a world power. The celebration attracted millions of spectators, New Yorkers and tourists alike.

This rare postcard by photographer Thaddeus Wilkerson shows the "naval rendezvous" of September 25, which featured "mercantile and pleasure craft, encircling the great international fleet" of warships. The spectacle went on into the night, as huge audiences lined Riverside Park to glimpse the illuminated flotilla. On October 1, the ships began heading north towards Albany, accompanied by replicas of Hudson's ship *Halve Maen* (Half Moon), built in Amsterdam and gifted to the US by the Netherlands, and Fulton's steamship *Clermont*, constructed locally by the Staten Island Shipbuilding Company. The New York Historical houses a comprehensive collection of 32,000 such postcards of New York City, assembled by collector Bob Stonehill.

72

AUGUSTA SAVAGE (1892–1962)

Lift Every Voice and Sing (The Harp), ca. 1939

White metal cast with a black patina
The New York Historical, Purchase, Coaching Club Acquisition Fund, 2019.90

Artist, activist, and educator Augusta Savage was an important figure in the Harlem Renaissance who devoted much of her life to advancing Black artists and their careers. Savage moved from Florida to New York in 1921, attended the Cooper Union School of Art, and won a scholarship to further study in Paris. Upon her return to New York City in 1932, she opened the Savage Studio of Arts and Crafts in Harlem, becoming an influential teacher. She co-founded the Harlem Artists Guild in 1935 and became the first director of the WPA-funded Harlem Community Art Center in 1937. *Lift Every Voice and Sing* is Savage's signature work, the only commission from a Black woman artist at the 1939 New York World's Fair, which spread across what is now Flushing Meadows–Corona Park in Queens and was visited by nearly 45 million people.

Lift Every Voice and Sing takes the form of a harp, and casts the singers as instruments of God. "Lift Every Voice and Sing" was originally a poem written by Savage's friend James Weldon Johnson in 1900. It was set to music by his brother John Rosamond Johnson in 1905, and declared the "Negro National Anthem" by the NAACP in 1919. Savage's original 16-foot sculpture was an extraordinary accomplishment that defied systemic period sexism and the institutionalized racism of Jim Crow. *Lift Every Voice and Sing*, one of the fair's most popular works of art, received high praise in the press—yet the sculpture was demolished after the event, for Savage lacked the funds to cast the original work in bronze or pay for a facility to store it. *Lift Every Voice and Sing* survives only through small-scale replicas like this one.

73

ALISON SAAR (b. 1956)

Maquette for *Swing Low: Harriet Tubman Memorial*, 2007

Bronze
The New York Historical, Purchase, 2009.34

This 2007 maquette is a study for Alison Saar's *Swing Low: Harriet Tubman Memorial*—a monument to the celebrated African American abolitionist who escaped slavery in 1849 and repeatedly risked her life to complete an estimated 13 trips back to her native Maryland to help others toward freedom. During the Civil War, Tubman continued her work alongside the Union Army, gathering information and liberating enslaved people through a network of spies, pilots, and soldiers. She planned the June 1863 Combahee River Raid, commanding a group of Black soldiers who freed almost 800 enslaved people while suffering no casualties.

Alison Saar, the daughter of noted artist Betye Saar, is a sculptor, mixed-media, and installation artist whose work explores Black female identity and the African diaspora. Saar's composition likens Tubman to the Underground Railroad. Her petticoat forms the front grate of a train; on her skirt ride the faces, belongings, and shoeprints of those she helped escape from bondage. When the full-size statue, which stands over ten feet tall, was installed in 2008, *Swing Low* became the first public monument to an African American woman in New York City. It is located in Harlem, at the intersection of Frederick Douglass Boulevard, West 122nd Street, and St. Nicholas Avenue, now called Harriet Tubman Triangle.

Fig. 25
Alison Saar (b. 1956)
Design for objects and Underground Railroad passengers in skirt (archival material related to *Swing Low*), 2004
Pencil on paper
The New York Historical, Purchased through the generosity of Charles and Belinda Bralver, 2020.39.3

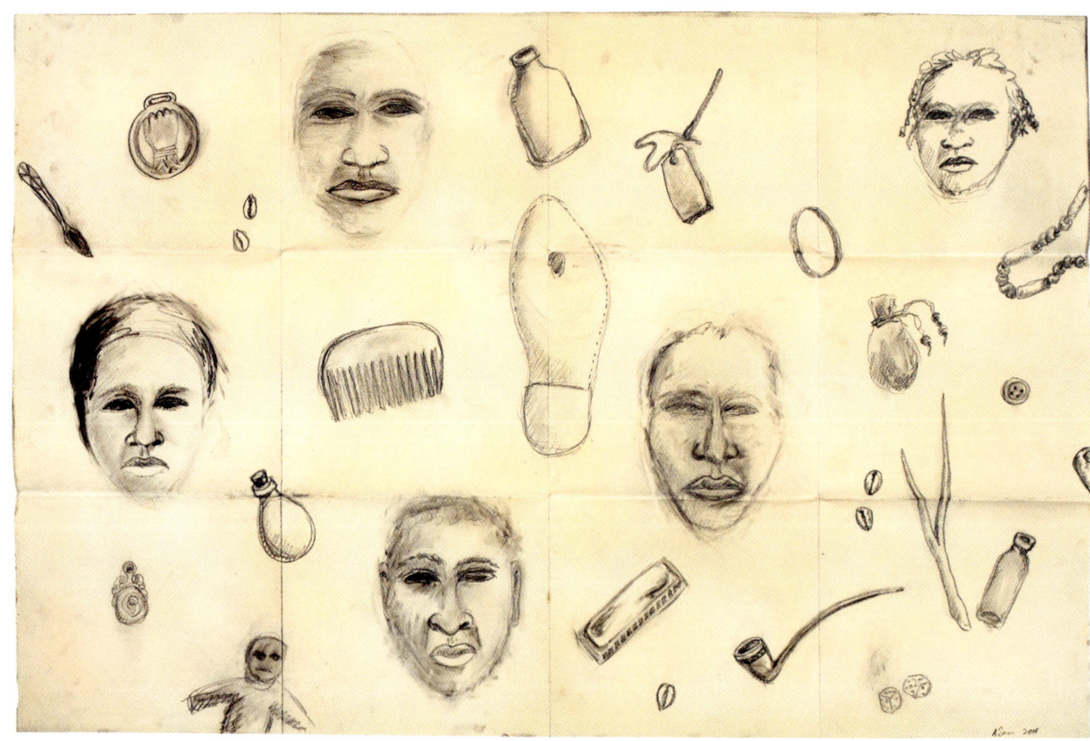

Asher B. Durand (1796–1886)
Study of Four Trees with Rocks, Hague, Lake George, New York, ca. 1862
Graphite on gray paper
The New York Historical,
Gift of Miss Nora Durand Woodman, 1918.169

NATURE & ENVIRONMENT

ROBERT RYDER (d. 1681?), surveyor

Map of Long Island and Adjacent Areas of Connecticut, New York, and New Jersey, 1670

Manuscript map
Patricia D. Klingenstein Library, The New York Historical

This is the manuscript of the earliest known survey of Long Island as far east as Riverhead. A shoreline map, it shows most of Long Island, all of modern New York City, and the shorelines of Connecticut and New Jersey. The map marks the rocky coast in red, gives place names, and outlines the various colonies in different colors. The date "ANNO DOMINI 1670" is embedded in cartouche decoration. Robert Ryder's map depicts Long Island as a sparsely populated stretch of land settled by farmers and fishermen, but it was in fact home to many Native American communities, including the Shinnecock, Secatogue, and Unkechaug, who still reside there today.

75

MANHATTAN WATER COMPANY (1799–1955)

Section of water pipe, 1800–40

New York City
Wood, iron
The New York Historical, Gift of Mr. J.W. Rutherford, 1907, X.47

This piece of wooden pipe was installed by the Manhattan Water Company, founded by Aaron Burr in 1799. While it was originally envisioned by public officials as a provider of pure water to Lower Manhattan from north of New York City, the company's goals were never realized—its only source of water was a modest well near the Collect Pond, a spring-fed freshwater pool in today's Chinatown. By 1800, it was thoroughly polluted by refuse from nearby slaughterhouses, tanneries, breweries, and other manufacturers: the water quality was poor, outbreaks of disease frequent, and many people were forced to purchase water from peddlers instead. However, a clause in the company's charter allowed Burr to form a bank, creating a rival to Alexander Hamilton's Bank of the United States. The Bank of the Manhattan Company became the second commercial bank in New York City (and is claimed by JPMorganChase as its earliest predecessor institution), but the two banks' rivalry was a factor in the ultimately fatal duel between Hamilton and Burr.

76

NAPOLEON BONAPARTE (1769–1821), CHARLES MAURICE DE TALLEYRAND-PÉRIGORD (1754–1838), AND HUGUES-BERNARD MARET (1763–1839)

Authorization for the sale of the Louisiana Territory, April 24, 1803

Manuscript with seal
Patricia D. Klingenstein Library, The New York Historical

This document authorizes the sale of the Louisiana Territory and bears the signatures of Napoleon, Emperor of the French; Foreign Minister Charles Maurice de Talleyrand-Périgord; and Secretary of State Hugues-Bernard Maret. It granted François, marquis de Barbé-Marbois, the authority to negotiate with Robert Livingston, United States minister to France, and future president James Monroe. The Louisiana Purchase Treaty was signed six days later, on April 30, 1803. The treaty would sell the Louisiana Territory from the French to the Americans for $15 million, giving the US vital control over shipping on the Mississippi River, plus 828,000 square miles of land—an amount that would roughly double the size of the United States—at about four cents per acre.

The stain on the right of the authorization is thought to be Madeira wine, used to toast the prospective sale. Festivities aside, however, the Louisiana Purchase would have profound consequences, especially for the people who were not party to the negotiations: Native American nations who would be forcibly displaced by white settlers, and enslaved African Americans. The spread of slavery into the Western states carved from the Louisiana Purchase would precipitate a nationwide political crisis and, eventually, the Civil War.

76

Au Nom du Peuple Français

Bonaparte, Premier Consul

Ayant pour but de resserrer les liens d'amitié qui unissent la France et les États-unis d'Amérique et de régler des objets de discussion relatifs à l'exécution de la Convention conclue le huit Vendémiaire an neuf entre les deux États; prenant entière confiance dans la fidélité du Citoyen Barbé-Marbois, Ministre du Trésor public et dans son dévouement pour le service de la République; lui donne plein et absolu pouvoir, Commission et mandement spécial, pour, au nom du Peuple français, et avec Monsieur James Monroë, Ministre Plénipotentiaire extraordinaire des États-unis d'Amérique, pareillement munis de pouvoirs en bonne et due forme, convenir, arrêter, conclure et signer tels Traités, Articles, Conventions, déclarations et autres actes qu'il avisera bon être; promettant, au nom du Peuple français, de tenir ferme et stable, accomplir et exécuter ponctuellement tout ce que le dit Plénipotentiaire aura promis et signé en vertu du présent Pouvoir, comme aussi d'en faire expédier les Lettres de ratification en bonne forme et de les faire délivrer pour être échangées dans le tems dont il sera convenu. En foi de quoi sont données les présentes, signées, contresignées et munies du sceau de la République.

Monsieur Robert- Robert-Livingston Ministre Plénipotentiaire
ch. mau. talleyrand

À St. Cloud le quatre floréal an onze de la République française vingt quatre avril mil huit cent trois.

Bonaparte

Le Ministre des Relations Extérieures,
ch. mau. talleyrand

Par le Premier Consul
Le Secrétaire d'État
Hugues B. Maret

77

JOHN JAMES AUDUBON (1785–1851)

Carolina Parakeet (Conuropsis carolinensis), Study for Plate 26 of "The Birds of America", ca. 1825

Watercolor, graphite, pastel, gouache, and black ink with scraping and selective glazing on paper, laid on card
The New York Historical, Purchased for the Society by public subscription from Mrs. John J. Audubon, 1863.17.26

The New York Historical holds John James Audubon's original watercolor models for *The Birds of America* (1827–38), a landmark publication comprising 435 lifelike and life-sized images glorifying the beauty of North American birds in the wild; as well as the corresponding plates from the double elephant–folio series, engraved by Robert Havell Jr.; and the reduced octavo-edition. While Audubon's work spurred early conservation efforts and remains central to both environmental activism and the history of American art, it was produced within a complex system of racial oppression. Audubon was a slaveholder and defender of slaveholders' rights, and he also enabled projects of scientific racism.

This watercolor, made in Louisiana, features a sprightly group of Carolina parakeets (*Conuropsis carolinensis*), the only parrot endemic to North America. The birds once flocked in vast numbers—and were shot in equally vast quantities by farmers seeking to protect their crops. Further decimated by habitat loss, the pet trade, and hatmakers' demands for their colorful feathers, the Carolina parakeet was declared extinct in 1939.

78

THOMAS COLE (1801–1848)

The Course of Empire: The Savage State, ca. 1834

Oil on canvas
The New York Historical, Gift of the New-York Gallery of the Fine Arts, 1858.1

In the late 1820s, the young Thomas Cole quickly built a successful career as a painter of Hudson River landscapes. But he harbored ambitions of turning the landscape form to a larger purpose. As early as 1827, he conceived a cycle of paintings that would illustrate the rise and fall of a civilization, and a few years later he began sketching and developing his ideas. In 1833, he secured a commission from New York merchant Luman Reed to create five paintings for the art gallery in his home. In the resulting series, *The Course of Empire*, a civilization appears, matures, and collapses. Cole's cyclical view of history was inspired by Lord Byron's Romantic poem, *Childe Harold's Pilgrimage*: "First freedom, then glory; when that fails, wealth, vice, corruption." The artist's distinctly pessimistic vision differed from that of many of his peers; in the early years of the United States' history, its future was considered limitless.

Although it depicts a wilderness, several elements in the first painting, *The Savage State*, commence the symbolic systems that trace the arc of civilization. The sun rises over the water, signaling a new day. Cole identified the season as springtime, and depicted the rudiments of society: men banding together for the hunt, as well as the beginnings of the arts in the making of canoes, huts, and music.

Fig. 26a
Thomas Cole (1801–1848)
The Course of Empire: The Arcadian or Pastoral State, ca. 1834
Oil on canvas
The New York Historical, Gift of the New-York Gallery of the Fine Arts, 1858.2

The second painting in Cole's series imagines society in a state of ideal balance between man and nature.

Fig. 26b
Thomas Cole (1801–1848)
The Course of Empire: The Consummation of Empire, 1835–36
Oil on canvas
The New York Historical, Gift of the New-York Gallery of the Fine Arts, 1858.3

In the third painting of Cole's series, nature has been subjugated to the needs of humanity. Cole's elaborate and overbuilt city is a visually stunning creation, but the artist meant the scene as a warning.

Fig. 26c
Thomas Cole (1801–1848)
The Course of Empire: Destruction, 1836
Oil on canvas
The New York Historical, Gift of the New-York Gallery of the Fine Arts, 1858.4

The fourth and most dramatic image in the *Course of Empire* cycle depicts the utter ruin of Cole's civilization. Cole's vision recalls the terror and destruction wrought in New York by the Great Fire of 1835.

Fig. 26d
Thomas Cole (1801–1848)
The Course of Empire: Desolation, 1836
Oil on canvas
The New York Historical, Gift of the New-York Gallery of the Fine Arts, 1858.5

The last of Cole's five canvases captures the exquisite stillness of a world without humankind. The sun is setting and nature is again reclaiming the landscape.

79

JOHN RINK (active mid-19th century)

Plan of the Central Park, New York: Entry No. 4 in the Competition, March 20, 1858

Ink and colored washes on paper
Patricia D. Klingenstein Library, The New York Historical

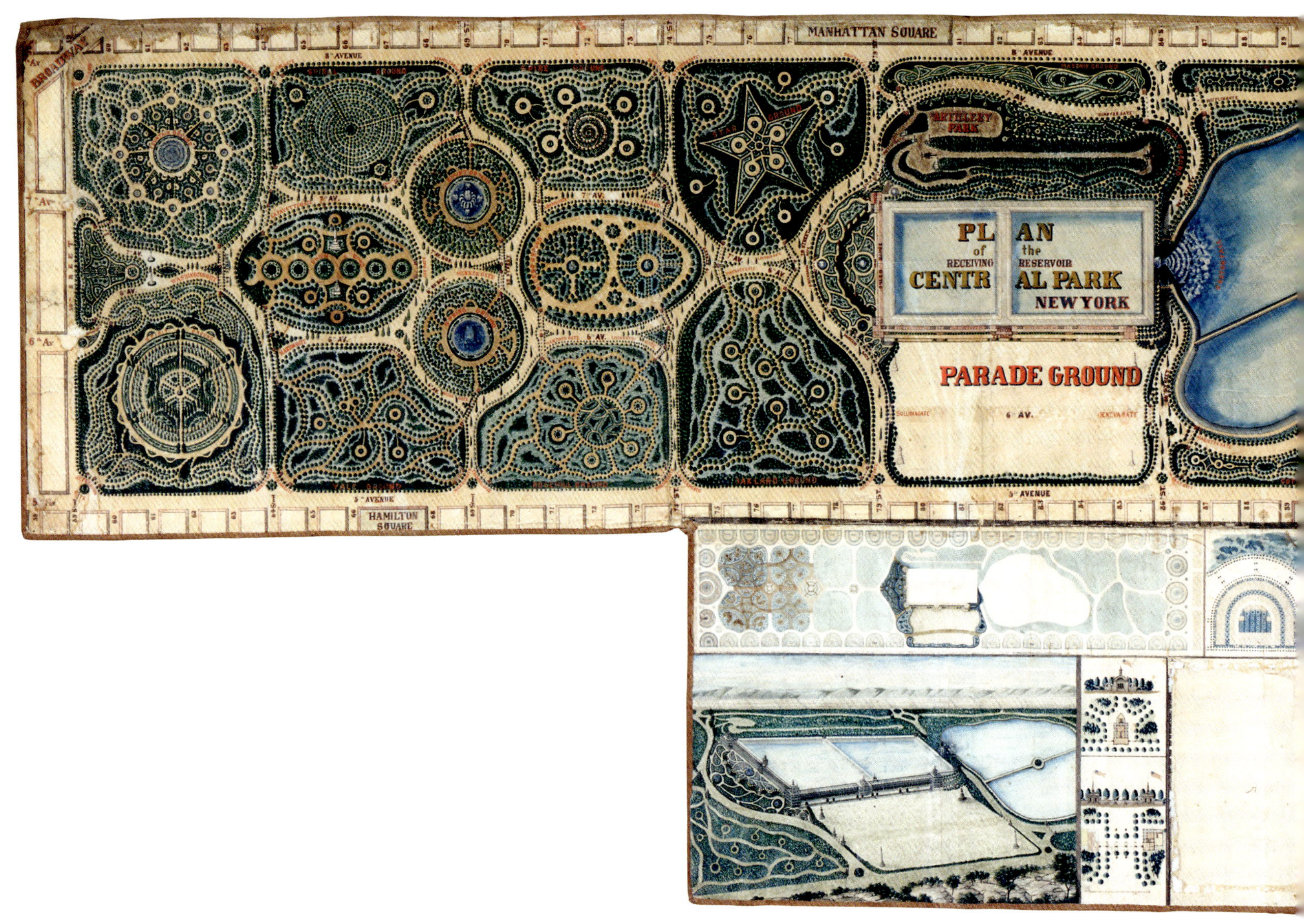

79

Between 1825 and 1857, the land in what is now Central Park was home to a community largely made up of African Americans. Known as Seneca Village, it lay roughly between 82nd and 89th Streets, and Seventh and Eighth Avenues. However, in 1853 the New York City government approved a plan to take the land using eminent domain. While the government offered to pay owners what it claimed was the fair value of their land, many Black landowners believed the government did not appraise it highly enough. They also had more to lose than their property: at this time, Black New Yorkers could only vote if they owned at least $250 worth of property, which meant that losing their homes often meant losing their enfranchisement.

In 1857, the Board of Commissioners of Central Park announced a design competition for the park that had been approved and purchased in 1853, with a reward of $2,000 for the winner. As part of the competition, John Rink, likely an engineer in the employ of the park commissioners, submitted this entry, number four of the 33 total submissions, only five of which survive today.

Rink's design, which is over eight feet long, favored symmetry and formality. It was characterized by formal gardens designated by their shapes, like the Star Ground and Spiral Ground. Roads and entrance gates were named after United States presidents and patriots. It shows reservoirs, a parade ground, roads, plantings, and a monumental museum building (precursor of the Metropolitan Museum of Art) proposed for the south and east flanks of the Yorkville Reservoir. Ultimately, however, it was the open, flowing Greensward Plan submitted by Frederick Law Olmsted and Calvert Vaux that won the competition.

Fig. 27
John Bachmann (1814–1896)
Birds Eye View of the Central Park, New-York, 1865
Lithograph
Patricia D. Klingenstein Library, The New York Historical

The Swiss-born John Bachmann was among the first printmakers to depict bird's-eye views in the United States. Although they appear to be captured from above, bird's-eye views were actually mathematically compiled on a grid using hundreds of sketches done on the ground. Bachmann's skillful use of the bird's-eye view helped popularize it as a way of portraying modern urban geography, and launched a new genre of American printmaking. His view of Central Park shows the pastures and woods that were key to Olmsted and Vaux's Greensward Plan, providing a reprieve from the crowded city in the background.

80

ERNEST LAWSON (1873–1939)

High Bridge Aqueduct, after 1928

Oil on canvas
The New York Historical, Promised gift of Elie and Sarah Hirschfeld, Scenes of New York City, IL2021.51.20

The oldest bridge in New York City, High Bridge opened in 1848 as part of a large and complex water distribution system known as the Croton Aqueduct. A massive engineering feat, the aqueduct conveyed fresh water from the Croton River in Westchester County southward to the rapidly growing city of New York, helping diminish the spread of communicable disease. High Bridge, which carried the water across the Harlem River from the Bronx into Upper Manhattan, was originally built as a series of 16 stone arches resembling an ancient Roman aqueduct. In 1928, five of the narrow masonry arches were replaced by a single wide steel arch to facilitate navigation along the river. However, rather than lauding the aqueduct as a technological triumph over nature, Ernest Lawson filtered his view of the bridge through a scrim of young saplings, setting the structure within a larger pastoral landscape that only hints at modern transformation.

For eight years beginning in 1898, Lawson lived near the High Bridge in Washington Heights, then a sparsely populated area at the edges of the city. Lawson's landscapes did not highlight the recognized public landmarks of early-20th-century industrial New York, but explored the overlooked excavation sites, squatter homes, docks, and steel bridges on its fringes.

81

ARLENE GOTTFRIED (1950–2017)

Under the Boardwalk, Coney Island, 1976

Gelatin silver print
Patricia D. Klingenstein Library, The New York Historical, Gift of Sally Klingenstein Martell

New York is ringed by beaches—Brighton, Manhattan, Orchard, Rockaway, Jacob Riis, Midland, Coney Island. As the city grew increasingly populous in the late 19th century, residents began flocking to the seaside in search of ocean views, cool breezes, and recreation; hotels, amusement parks, boardwalks, and bathing facilities sprang up to cater to the demand.

However, the question of who should have access to the beaches, and what kinds of activities would be welcome there, has long been contentious. When Coney Island opened its famous amusement parks, middle-class reformers questioned the morality of rides like the "Blowhole Theater," which featured jets of air that lifted women's skirts. In the mid-20th century, police patrolled Jacob Riis Park in Queens, harassing gay and lesbian New Yorkers who gathered there to sunbathe and cruise. Parks commissioner Robert Moses, who derided Coney Island and the Rockaways as only fit for "honky-tonk catchpenny amusement resorts," relocated many of the city's neediest people to these peripheral areas as part of his "urban renewal" projects: families on public assistance, the disabled, and the elderly. By the 1970s, the beaches, like the city overall, had developed a reputation as overcrowded, run-down, and rather seedy. Yet at the same time, the beaches (and beachgoers) inspired some of New York's greatest photographers, including the Brooklyn-born Arlene Gottfried, whose work is pictured here. Gottfried credited her ability to connect with strangers to her childhood in Coney Island and "exposure to all kinds of people."

82

UNIDENTIFIED PHOTOGRAPHER

Elizabeth Barlow Rogers, Henry Stern, and Jane Present, ca. 1983

Photographic print
Patricia D. Klingenstein Library, The New York Historical

After one hundred years of use, Central Park, built according to Frederick Law Olmsted and Calvert Vaux's famous Greensward Plan between 1858 and 1876, was in disrepair. In the depths of New York's fiscal crisis in the 1970s, the park lawns were worn down to bare dirt, broken playground equipment went unrepaired, trash went uncollected, and even Bethesda Fountain was dry and graffitied. In 1979, parks commissioner Gordon Davis named Upper West Side resident Elizabeth Barlow Rogers (b. 1936) the first Central Park administrator. With a graduate degree in city planning and an abiding scholarly interest in Olmsted's landscape architecture, Rogers was already working to raise private funds for the restoration of Central Park. In 1980, the city partnered with these advocates to form the nonprofit Central Park Conservancy (CPC), one of the first public–private partnerships established by then-mayor Ed Koch. Since then, public–private partnerships like the CPC have been replicated throughout New York City.

With Rogers at the helm, the CPC raised hundreds of millions of dollars to restore and revitalize every part of Central Park. In 1983, the CPC began sponsoring "You Gotta Have Park" weekends, featuring everything from children's puppet performances to croquet tournaments. Hundreds of volunteers (including parks commissioner Henry Stern, pictured here with Rogers and CPC trustee Jane Present) fanned out across Central Park, asking attendees to donate small sums towards the park's upkeep and encouraging them to feel invested in preserving and maintaining its beauty. Rogers's papers and other archival collections charting the Conservancy's establishment reside in the Patricia D. Klingenstein Library.

83

ANNA EGGLETON (b. 1990)

Flaco at The New York Historical, 2024

Digital watercolor and pencil on paper
The New York Historical, Commissioned by and Gift of Agnes Hsu-Tang, PhD and Oscar Tang for the 220th anniversary of The New York Historical

When Flaco the Eurasian eagle-owl flew out of the Central Park Zoo through a hole cut in his enclosure, some said that vandals had irresponsibly released him into a dangerous urban habitat. They argued that, having been hatched in captivity and raised in an aviary, the 13-year-old owl was not prepared to fly, hunt, or survive. Against all odds, however, Flaco defied capture and thrived, making a home for himself in Manhattan.

Unfortunately, on February 23, 2024, Flaco died after either colliding with or falling from a building on West 89th Street. Postmortem testing revealed that he had been severely weakened by pigeon herpesvirus and rat poison. These would likely have been fatal, even without the traumatic injury, and may have predisposed him to collide with the building. (According to the NYC Bird Alliance, an estimated quarter of a million birds die each year in the city from hitting windows.) In his honor, the New York State Bird Safe Buildings Act, first introduced in 2023, was renamed the FLACO Act (Feathered Lives Also Count). It would require bird-friendly construction on state-owned and -leased buildings. In 2024, the City Council piloted a rat contraceptive program, in part to prevent raptors like Flaco from ingesting poison-riddled rodents.

McSpedon & Baker, lithographers
Five Points, 1827
Engraved for *Valentine's Manual*, 1855
Patricia D. Klingenstein Library,
The New York Historical

STREETS & NEIGHBORHOODS

84

PETER STUYVESANT (1592–1672)

Property deed issued to Manuel de Spangie by Peter Stuyvesant, January 18, 1651

Manuscript with seal
Patricia D. Klingenstein Library, The New York Historical

In 1644, the New Netherland director Willem Kieft and the Council of New Amsterdam granted conditional freedom to 11 of the men enslaved by the Dutch West India Company. Their wives were also granted "half-freedom" on the same terms, meaning that they could be re-enslaved if they did not pay yearly dues of grain, beans, peas, and hogs: 20 guilders' worth of foodstuffs. Their children remained enslaved. The newly emancipated people were granted parcels of land north of the Dutch settlement, near the Fresh Pond, along paths that would later become Broadway and the Bowery.

In 1649, Manuel de Spangie (or de Spanje), an enslaved man, purchased his freedom from his owner, Philip Jansz Ringo, for three hundred guilders, payable in three yearly installments. Two years later, this property deed, issued by Peter Stuyvesant, the last Dutch governor of the colony, made Manuel de Spangie another of Manhattan's early Black landowners. Manuel de Spangie's four-acre property was possibly located near today's Prince Street.

85

DANIEL DENTON (ca. 1626–1703)

A Brief Description of New-York: Formerly Called New-Netherlands

London: Printed for John Hancock, at the first shop in Popes-Head Alley in Cornhil at the three Bibles, and William Bradley at the three Bibles in the Minories, 1670
Patricia D. Klingenstein Library, The New York Historical

Daniel Denton wrote this pamphlet in 1670, the first work promoting the settlement of New York by the English after the capture of New Netherland from the Dutch. Born in England, Denton traveled extensively in North America during his long lifetime, eventually living and holding public office in Massachusetts, New Jersey, and New York, though he spent most of his career in Jamaica, Queens. His 25-page pamphlet, published in London, painted an appealing picture of opportunity in Britain's new colony: "here is hundreds, nay thousands of Acres, that would invite inhabitants," he wrote, promising that even "those which fortune hath frowned upon in *England*" could help themselves to "such a quantity of Land, that he may weary himself with walking over his fields of Corn, and all sorts of Grain." Despite his optimism, Denton must certainly have been aware of the bloody conflicts between Dutch settlers and Native Americans. However, he dismissed the possibility of future strife, asserting, "where the English come to settle, a Divine Hand makes way for them: by removing or cutting off the Indians, either by Wars one with the other, or by some raging mortal Disease."

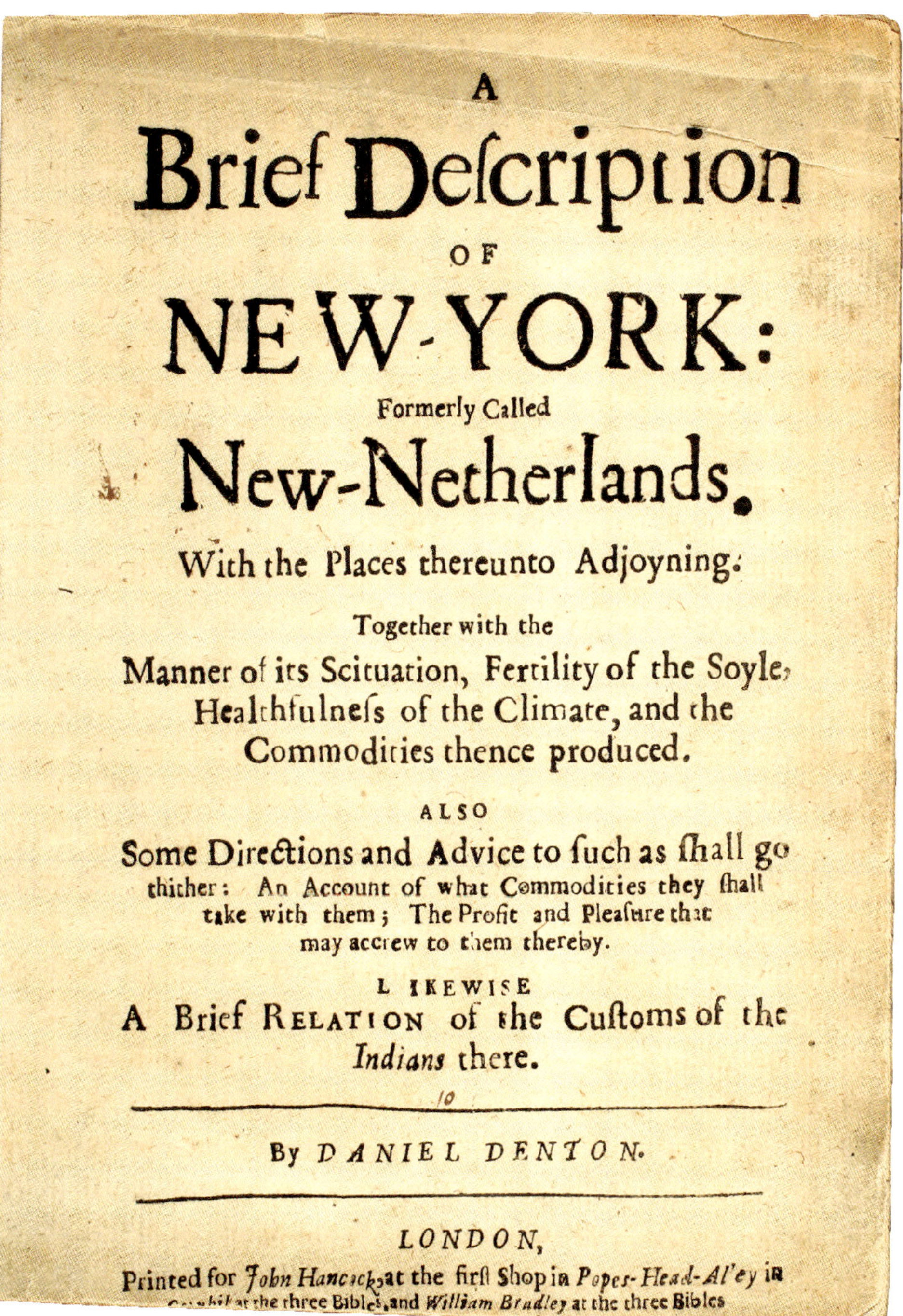
A

Brief Deſcription

OF

NEW-YORK:

Formerly Called

New-Netherlands.

With the Places thereunto Adjoyning.

Together with the

Manner of its Scituation, Fertility of the Soyle, Healthfulneſs of the Climate, and the Commodities thence produced.

ALSO

Some Directions and Advice to ſuch as ſhall go thither: An Account of what Commodities they ſhall take with them; The Profit and Pleaſure that may accrew to them thereby.

LIKEWISE

A Brief RELATION of the Cuſtoms of the *Indians* there.

By *DANIEL DENTON*.

LONDON,

Printed for *John Hancock*, at the firſt Shop in *Popes-Head-Alley* in Cornhil at the three Bibles, and *William Bradley* at the three Bibles

86a

JAMES LYNE (active 1728–1744), surveyor

A Plan of the City of New York from an Actual Survey, Made by James Lyne

New York: William Bradford, 1731
Patricia D. Klingenstein Library, The New York Historical

86b

FRANCIS W. MAERSCHALCK (d. 1776), surveyor

A Plan of the City of New York from an Actual Survey

New York: Printed, engraved for and sold by G. Duyckinck, 1755
Patricia D. Klingenstein Library, The New York Historical

The 1731 Lyne Bradford map is the first plan of New York printed in the city itself. It depicts lower Manhattan, and has an index at the upper left listing many different houses of worship (among them a Jewish synagogue, Baptist and Quaker meeting-houses, and Dutch, French, and English churches) as well as the Governor's House, the Custom House, and several different marketplaces—including the Meal Market, where enslaved people were bought and sold.

In 1755, a new map was engraved from a survey by Francis W. Maerschalck. It reused the 1731 copperplate used by James Lyne and William Bradford, updated to reflect the city's rapid growth: street names were changed, new streets added, and shading used to indicate new buildings. It was engraved for, printed, and sold by Gerardus Duyckinck, who added a second plate to depict the expansion of the city. A line running vertically between the words "Fresh" and "Water" marks where impressions from the two plates meet.

Many of the churches, markets, and public buildings depicted in the 1731 Lyne Bradford map are still present, but the Maerschalck plan notably includes the location of the "Negroes Buriel Ground." Both enslaved and free people of African descent lived and worked in 18th-century New York; at the time this map was made they constituted between 15 and 20 percent of the population. Approximately 20,000 of them were interred in the African Burial Ground, but, when the land was sold in the 1790s, a later leveling project buried the graves under 25 feet of fill. They lay nearly forgotten until 1991, when construction of an office tower at 290 Broadway uncovered skeletal remains. Two years later, the African Burial Ground was named a New York City Landmark, and in 2006 it became a National Historic Monument.

Both of these maps were presented to The New York Historical by founder John Pintard in 1807.

a

b

87

ANNE-MARGUÉRITE-JOSÉPHINE-HENRIETTE ROUILLÉ DE MARIGNY (1771–1849)

Dey Street on the Hudson River, New York City, 1810

Watercolor, graphite, black chalk, black and brown ink, and gouache on paper
The New York Historical, Thomas Jefferson Bryan Fund, 1982.5

Anne-Marguérite-Joséphine-Henriette Rouillé de Marigny, Baroness Hyde de Neuville, was born to a wealthy and aristocratic family in France. A self-taught artist who specialized in drawings and watercolors, she survived the French Revolution and Robespierre's Reign of Terror, but her husband's royalist politics forced the couple to live as fugitives under Napoleon. She was able to win her husband a sentence of exile, rather than death, and the couple landed in New York City in 1807. From there, they traveled up the Hudson River and explored upstate New York. Henriette kept a visual diary of the people and places she encountered, leaving behind a substantial body of work.

From 1810 to 1814 Baroness Hyde de Neuville and her husband lived at 61 Dey Street. At the time, New York still resembled a small fishing village, but, as she observed New York Harbor's growing vigor and the diversity of its street life, she created this record of its maritime and commercial activity. The couple purchased an estate in Brunswick, New Jersey, in 1811; their Dey Street address was convenient to the steamboat ferry, introduced by Robert Fulton in 1812, which ran from Cortlandt Street, one block to the south, across the Hudson River to Paulus Hook.

Dey Street is currently one east–west block between Church and Broadway and no longer extends to the Hudson River. Its western reaches were demolished to make way for the World Trade Center in the late 1960s.

88

UNIDENTIFIED MAKER

195–99 Chatham Square and 9–17 East Broadway, New York City, ca. 1842–65

Ambrotype
Patricia D. Klingenstein Library, The New York Historical

This mid-19th-century New York City street scene, complete with advertisements, pedestrians, commercial buildings, and vehicles, was captured in an ambrotype. Though somewhat resembling daguerreotypes, ambrotypes were faster and cheaper to produce and became very popular, especially in America. This one depicts Chatham Square, where eight streets converge—including East Broadway, the Bowery, and Mott Street—making it a longstanding hub of commercial and transit activity. First known as a horse-market, Chatham Square would later become an anchor of Manhattan's Chinatown. However, 19th-century Chatham Square was a notorious district of brothels, cheap hotels, saloons, theaters, and music halls, forming one edge of the historic Five Points neighborhood. Five Points was one of the first integrated neighborhoods in the United States, largely populated by Black and Irish New Yorkers, but it was also widely known as the worst slum in America.

Five Points' poor living conditions were the result of mass industrialization, urbanization, and lack of oversight. As people flooded into the city, the working class and poor, predominantly immigrants and people of color, occupied the less desirable city center where greedy landlords built cheap structures to house them. In these areas, extended families might live together in a single room, and the air was polluted by the exhaust from nearby factories. It was not until the 20th century that New York began to regulate the development of its built environment. The Tenement House Act passed in 1901, the first local zoning law in the United States was adopted in 1916, and the City Planning Commission was established in 1936.

89a

VICTOR PREVOST (1820–1881)

Looking toward Madison Square from Rear Window of 28 East 28th Street, Showing Adrian Iselin's House and Stable Then Building, Copy Two, before 1906

Gelatin silver contact print
Patricia D. Klingenstein Library, The New York Historical, Gift of Eugene Hoffman

Victor Prevost captured this image looking toward Madison Square from the rear window of his home at 28 East 28th Street. Among other buildings, the photograph shows the property of wealthy financier Adrian Iselin, son of Swiss immigrants who made a fortune after the Civil War through investments in railroads, mining, and real estate. His socially prominent family lived at 23 East 26th Street, between Madison and Fifth Avenue, facing Madison Square Park. Formally opened in 1847 and extensively refurbished in 1870, Madison Square Park was ringed by elegant mansions and would become a center of upscale culture in Gilded Age New York. The famous restaurant Delmonico's, where the city elite hosted sumptuous dinner parties and balls, opened a new location on Fifth Avenue at 26th Street in 1876. The original Madison Square Garden, built in 1879, was replaced in 1891 by a Beaux-Arts masterpiece designed by architect Stanford White, featuring a massive main hall, a 1,200-seat theater, a 1,500-seat concert hall, and a rooftop cabaret.

Prevost was born in France in 1820 and moved to New York City in 1850. In 1853, he opened a photography studio at 627 Broadway, between Houston and Bleecker Streets, becoming one of the few photographers in the United States producing calotypes, a photographic process that relied on paper negatives. His surviving calotypes are rare examples of early paper photographs of New York City. The New York Historical collection includes 44 original 19th-century negatives, as well as later prints made from these negatives.

89b

VICTOR PREVOST (1820–1881)

Looking toward Madison Square from Rear Window of 28 East 28th Street, Showing Adrian Iselin's House and Stable Then Building, 1854

Original calotype negative
Patricia D. Klingenstein Library, The New York Historical

Atlas of the Borough of Manhattan – City of New York, Desk and Library Edition, Plate 91

Philadelphia: G.W. Bromley & Co., 1916
Patricia D. Klingenstein Library, The New York Historical

In 1807, the New York State legislature empowered Commissioners John Rutherford, Simeon De Witt, and Gouverneur Morris to lay out a plan for the city's growth. Although most of the city's population still lived south of Canal Street, with the aid of surveyor John Randel Jr. they envisioned a grid system that would extend from Houston Street to 155th Street in Harlem. Widespread use of eminent domain allowed the city to overcome the objections of private landowners, and the grid spread northward over the course of 60 years, facilitating growth, shaping the fabric of the city, and creating a booming market for real estate.

The city's rapid growth created a concurrent need for insurance, especially after the terrible fire of 1835 bankrupted nearly every insurance company in New York. By the mid-1800s, fire insurance maps such as the one pictured here had been widely adopted. They provided necessary and detailed information to underwriters about streets, lots, nearby transit, infrastructure, and buildings, including purpose (residences, department stores, schools, hotels), size (the notation 4B indicated a four-story building with a basement, for example), and materials. The pink color that dominates this particular map, showing 12 blocks of the Upper West Side bounded by West 71st Street, Central Park West, West 77th Street, and Amsterdam Avenue, indicates that the buildings were made of brick. The New York Historical's current building, begun in 1903 and completed in 1908, can be seen at the top right corner. Atlases such as these are indispensable to scholars researching the city's growth and development.

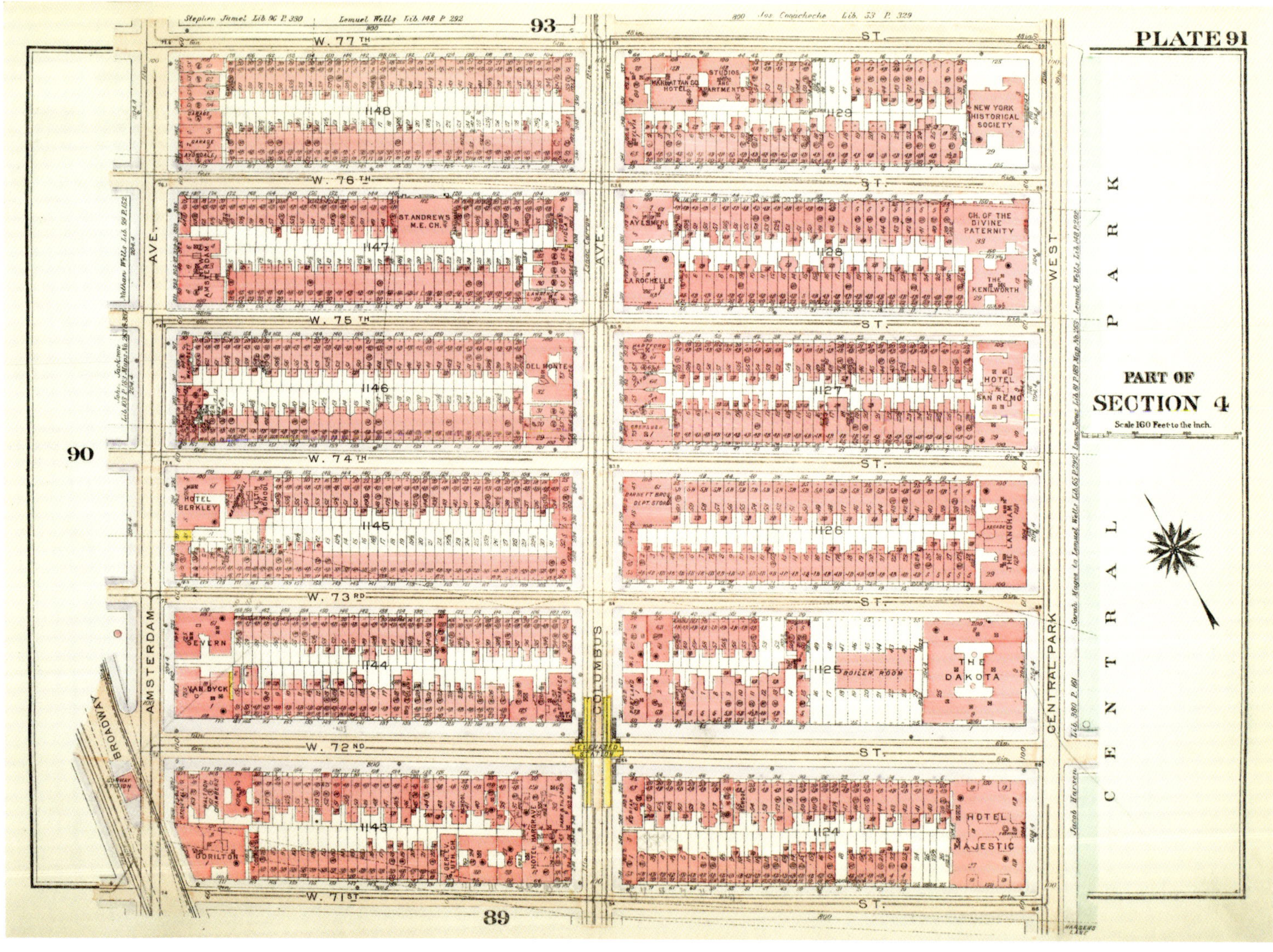

91

WILLIAM HOLBROOK BEARD (1824–1900)

The Bulls and Bears in the Market, 1879

Oil on linen
The New York Historical, Purchase, Thomas Jefferson Bryan Fund, 1971.104

In 1653, seeking to fortify New Amsterdam against the British, Governor Peter Stuyvesant ordered the construction of an earth and log wall along the settlement's northern boundary. The wall, which was mostly built by enslaved and free Black workers, now gives its name to Wall Street in New York's financial district—the setting of *The Bulls and Bears in the Market*.

William Holbrook Beard worked in New York City from 1859 until his death and is considered one of America's finest animal painters. In this, as in many of his paintings, he used animals to mimic and satirize human behavior. The bears symbolize "bearish" (conservative) investors, while bulls represent "bullish" (aggressive) investors. These terms came into usage on Wall Street in the late 19th century. Beard may have been inspired in part by the stock market crash of 1873, which produced 19th-century America's worst economic depression. This 1879 oil painting is set in Broad Street, looking north. The New York Stock Exchange occupied the building at the left from 1865 until its demolition in 1901. The current New York Stock Exchange was constructed partially on the same site in 1903. The neoclassical building at the top right of the painting is the US Sub-Treasury, formerly the Customs House, built on the site of the old Federal Hall, and now the Federal Hall National Memorial.

LAWRENCE VEILLER (1872–1959) and the
CHARITY ORGANIZATION SOCIETY (founded 1882)

"Prevalence of Disease" map series no. 4, 1899

Manuscript map
Patricia D. Klingenstein Library, The New York Historical

Conceived by housing reformer Lawrence Veiller and produced in conjunction with the Charity Organization Society, the Tenement House Exhibition opened on Fifth Avenue near 38th Street in February 1900, in order to educate the public about substandard housing in New York City. On display were photographs, charts, models, and over one hundred hand-colored maps that documented Manhattan's most impoverished neighborhoods. More than 10,000 people attended the exhibition during its two-week run; it then traveled to other cities, including the Paris Exposition of 1900. The heightened awareness generated by the exhibition led to some of the most consequential housing reform legislation of the 20th century, beginning with the Tenement Law of 1901. The law led to the majority of new tenement buildings being constructed on larger lots, and the inclusion of windows and toilets. This was intended to improve ventilation and sanitation, curtailing the spread of infectious diseases.

To make the maps, Veiller and his assistants began by tracing the outlines of streets and blocks from existing maps. They depicted neighborhoods throughout Manhattan, from the Battery to Harlem, in two series: "Strongholds of Poverty" and "Prevalence of Disease." This particular map illustrates the presence of several infectious diseases, including tuberculosis, typhoid fever, scarlet fever, and diphtheria, in the tenement house district bounded by the Bowery, Essex, Division, and Rivington Streets.

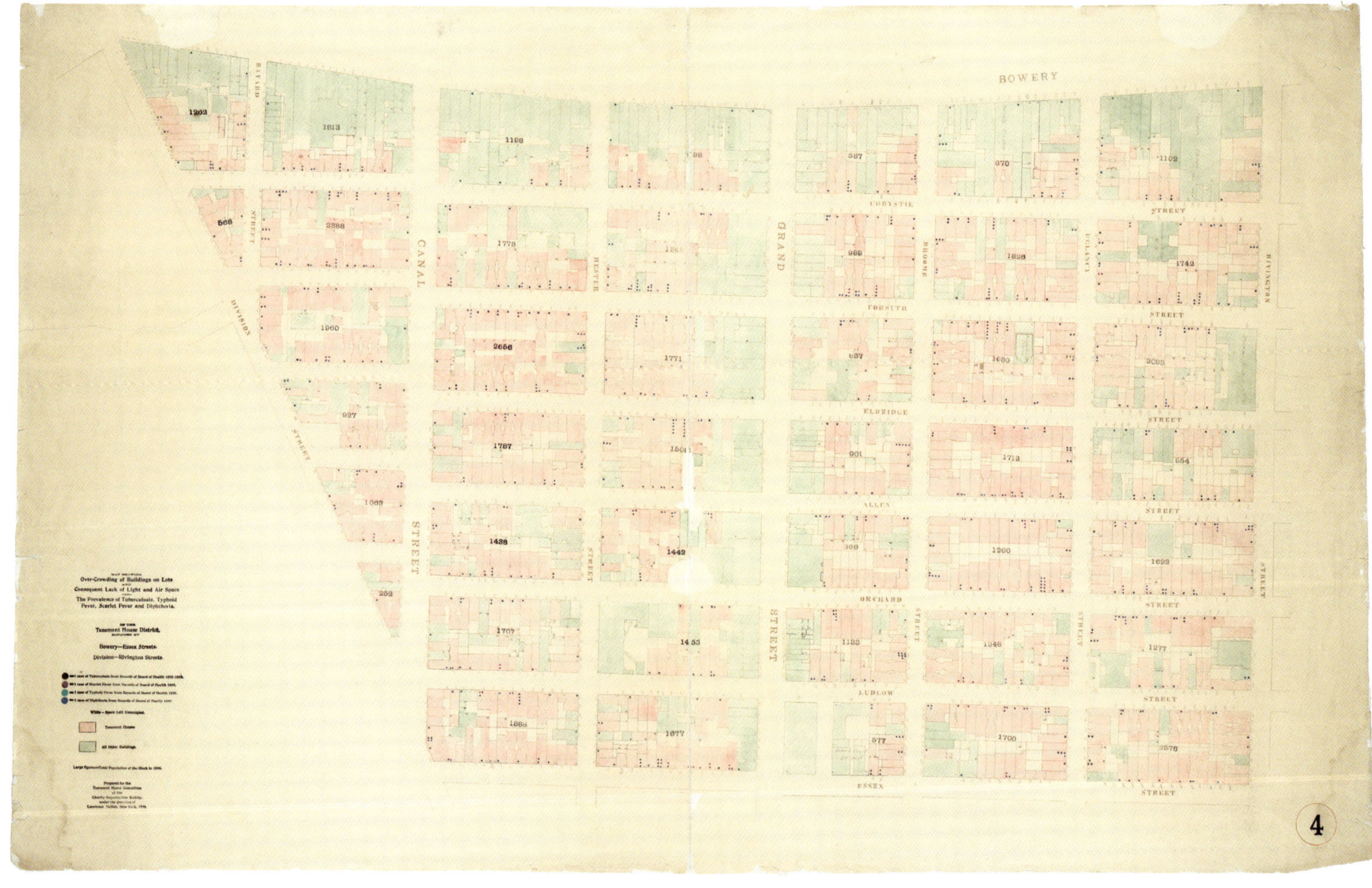

93

EUGENE GORDON (1923–2008)

New York – Jackson Heights, Queens, 1984

Gelatin silver print
Patricia D. Klingenstein Library, The New York Historical

Eugene Gordon started his career as a photographer taking stock images for textbooks and other publications. He traveled extensively in his personal life and documented his wanderings as he did, continuing this project throughout New York City—most extensively at home in Queens, where he printed his photographs in his own darkroom. Some of Gordon's favorite subjects were street scenes, parades, protests, and festivals. The images show New Yorkers going about their lives amid the shifting ethnic makeup of a vibrant city. This photograph captures a street corner in Jackson Heights, which saw an influx of South Asian immigrants starting in the 1970s, shortly after President Lyndon B. Johnson signed the Immigration and Nationality Act of 1965, while seated in front of the Statue of Liberty. Also known as Hart-Cellar Act, this law abolished the national quota system and transformed US demographics. Jackson Heights is now famous as one of the most diverse places in the world, with over 160 languages spoken.

The Eugene Gordon Photograph Collection, containing over 700 gelatin silver prints, is an invaluable record of the street life, religious groups, buildings, businesses, and public events of New York City from the 1970s to the 1990s.

94

Street sign, ca. 1990

New York City
Metal
The New York Historical, Gift of Steven H. Jaffe, 2003.54

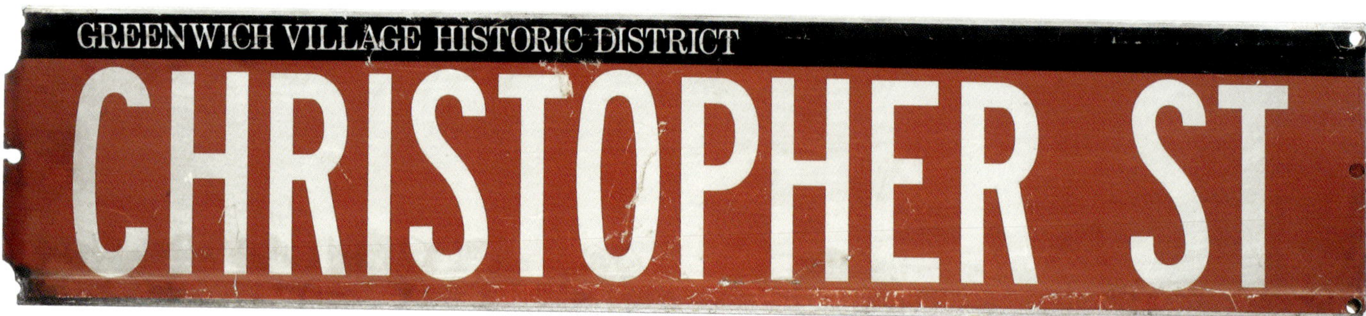

When the Greenwich Village Historic District was officially dedicated in 1969, the designation report mentioned the area's architectural distinctions, but focused on its significance as an artistic, literary, and cultural hub. From the early 1800s onward, Greenwich Village was not only home to individual luminaries, but also institutions and businesses that allowed like-minded people to mingle. By the early 20th century, inexpensive housing and a bohemian reputation made the Village a destination for writers and artists of all kinds; gay men and lesbians flocked there as well. By the 1960s, the Village was packed with venues devoted to jazz, folk music, and Beat poetry; civil rights and anti-Vietnam War protests joined other movements—such as suffrage and workers' rights—that had long found expression there.

In June 1969, the Stonewall Uprising—a flashpoint in the struggle for LGBTQ+ rights—erupted from a routine police raid of an unlicensed, Mafia-run gay bar on Christopher Street. The Stonewall Inn was dingy and served weak, overpriced drinks, but it was one of the few venues where gay and lesbian patrons could dance together at a time when such behavior was automatically considered "disorderly conduct." As police forced patrons out of the bar in the wee hours of Saturday, June 28, community members began to fight back, leading to a series of protests over several days. Since then, New York's annual Pride march has commemorated the anniversary of the 1969 uprising.

This street sign was retrieved by the donor when it fell from its post at the corner of Christopher Street and Seventh Avenue, near Sheridan Square.

Fig. 28
National Park Service (founded 1916), maker
Stonewall fan, 2016
Paper, wood
The New York Historical, History Responds Collecting Initiative, 2018.54

In 1999, Stonewall became the first LGBT site in the country to be listed on the National Register of Historic Places, and the following year it was named a National Historic Landmark. In June 2016, the Stonewall Inn was designated a national monument, the first dedicated to LGBTQ+ history.

95

MARTIN WONG (1946–1999)

Canal Street, 1992

New York City
Acrylic on canvas
The New York Historical, Purchase, Watson Fund, 2000.6ab
Copyright Martin Wong Foundation

Canal Street, now one of the busiest streets in Manhattan's Chinatown, was named after the canal built in 1810 to drain the fetid Collect Pond. Chinatown itself began as a tiny enclave between Pell and Doyer Streets and the lower part of Mott Street, populated by itinerant Chinese sailors and merchants. The completion of the transcontinental railroad in 1869, followed by violence against the Chinese in the West, led to New York City's Chinatown population expanding to more than 2,000 by the 1870s. Today it reaches north to Kenmare and Delancey Streets, east to Allen Street, south to East and Worth Streets, and west to Broadway. In the late 20th century, other Chinatowns emerged in Flushing, Queens, and Sunset Park, Brooklyn.

Artist Martin Wong was born in Portland, Oregon, and raised in San Francisco. He moved to New York's Lower East Side in 1978, becoming a prominent figure in the downtown arts scene. Wong died of AIDS-related causes in 1999. He painted this vivid impression, one of a series inspired by the streetscapes of Chinatowns in New York and San Francisco, as part of his efforts to locate himself as a Chinese American, gay activist, and West Coast émigré within an ethnic community. In this reality-bending composition, two almost identical red brick commercial buildings stand side by side at the intersection of Canal and Center Streets, separated by an impossibly narrow cross street.

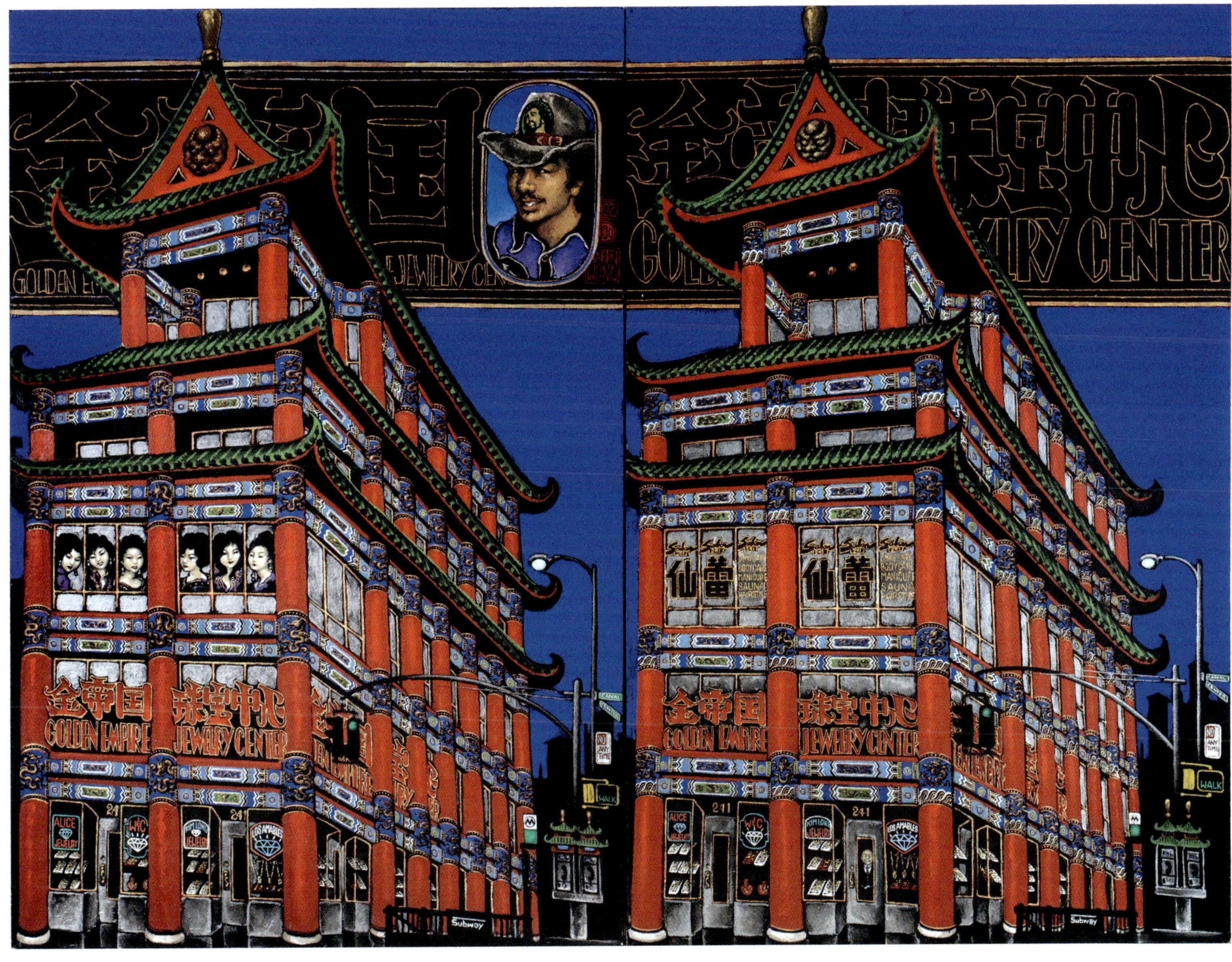

THINGS

THINGS

VALERIE PALEY

History can be a litany of facts and dates, a chain of recorded events that collectively form the content of textbooks. Yet, history can also unfold as a dramatic, visceral story, a narrative that delves into the past to uncover meaning for the present. The material evidence that remains from specific times and places—in objects, documents, and images—attests to the certainty that history, indeed, happened once upon a time.

These things can be affecting, even if, collected together, they sometimes can resemble the clutter of an attic. However, as three-dimensional, primary source documents touched by real people, they are also authentic tokens. In museum collections, objects can thus serve as potent witnesses to the past, representing, among other things, the individuals who owned and utilized them and the events they saw.

When the New-York Historical Society was founded in 1804, there were no real museums in the city. Following the founders' initial call for donations of "whatever may relate" to the nation's history, the library flourished dramatically, partly because it was one of the few secure repositories for rare books and manuscripts. There were even fewer sites for the public display of valuable paintings and artworks. Therefore, until the Metropolitan Museum opened in 1872, it remained the most significant art museum in the city. Because there was no institutional rival for contributions in these early decades of The New York Historical's existence, the collections are rich in unique examples of documents, books, art, and material culture from the 19th century and earlier. In this section of *Objects Tell Stories*, we highlight some of these most famous things, along with treasures, both great and small, of more recent vintage.

Of towering historical substance, "Christian Charitie: A Modell Hereof" (more commonly called "A Model of Christian Charity," cat. 137) is a foundational document of the United States, frequently cited in discussions of American exceptionalism. The New York Historical's copy of John Winthrop's 1630 lay sermon is the earliest-known manuscript version and serves as the basis for all published editions, the first of which did not appear until 1838. For over two centuries, political figures have invoked this text to express idealistic

---

Previous spread:
Unidentified artist
Excelsior, last quarter of 18th century
Oil on linen
The New York Historical, X.731

themes of unity and optimism, encapsulated in the image of "a city upon a hill."

Indeed, many of the earliest documents in the collection are religious in nature. The extinct language of the Timucua, a Native American people, is known through only nine surviving primary sources (cat. 136). Five are held by The New York Historical, including two catechisms and two devotional texts in Spanish and Timucua from the early 1600s. In 1766, the first Jewish prayer book published in North America was also the first to be translated into English, after Isaac Pinto, a Sephardic merchant and scholar, recognized that many fellow members of Congregation Shearith Israel in New York could not understand the Hebrew service (cat. 138).

The phrase "George Washington Slept Here" may be a tired cliché, but during the Revolutionary War, when the general was not offered more comfortable shelter, three folding stools connected by a piece of canvas served as his camp bed (cat. 128). Barely long enough to accommodate Washington's six-foot-two-inch frame, this makeshift cot stands as evidence of the even greater hardships faced by the battle-weary, poorly supplied troops, the circumstances of whom Washington repeatedly reported to Congress around 1777.

Any copy of the 1770s-era map of North America by John Mitchell is impressive in size, scale, and content. It provides an accurate cartographic description of Britain's territorial holdings in North America at the time. The copy at The New York Historical is marked up with red lines, indicating the demarcations of potential boundaries negotiated in 1782–83 for the Treaty of Paris, which formally ended the Revolution and recognized American independence (cat. 127). Only three copies of the red-lined Mitchell map are known to exist. The New York Historical's was used by John Jay, who negotiated on behalf of the United States alongside John Adams and Benjamin Franklin. Such remarkable, history-defining treasures abound in the collections, most often donated by the institution's early leaders and their descendants.

The story of the bitter rivalry between Alexander Hamilton and Aaron Burr had already achieved mythic status in history books long before it was popularized on the Broadway stage. On the morning of July 11, 1804, the men arrived in Weehawken, New Jersey, for their legendary duel, adhering to the rules laid out by Hamilton's second, Nathaniel Pendleton. The procedural arrangements in Pendleton's handwriting for the duel, along with the exchange of letters between Hamilton and Burr leading up to it, are housed in the Patricia D. Klingenstein Library (cat. 129).

Before dawn on that fateful summer day, Hamilton boarded a boat bound for Weehawken accompanied by two friends and four oarsmen. As the sun rose and the vessel pulled into the current, he looked back at lower Manhattan and remarked, "It's going to be a great city someday." Some two decades later, that destiny would be sealed with the opening of the Erie Canal, which fundamentally transformed and defined New York. The city became the nation's chief port, facilitating trade and commerce from the interior and connecting it to the Atlantic Ocean. The project was the brainchild of DeWitt Clinton (1769–1828), a founding member of The New York Historical, who inaugurated the canal's completion in 1825 by "marrying" the waters of Lake Erie to the Atlantic Ocean. The decoratively painted keg he used for this ceremony is a small but historically outsized gem in the collection (cat. 108).

After the canal opened, the East River became a crucial waterway that facilitated the rapid industrial, cultural, and population boom on New York's eastern shore—today's Brooklyn and Queens. Less than a century later, the New York City subway system encouraged residential development in northern Manhattan and enhanced the interconnectivity of the city's boroughs. The creation of this rapid transit system marked nothing short of the emergence of the modern city, ranking among the great urban achievements of the 20th century.

On October 27, 1904, Mayor George B. McClellan Jr. launched the subway's maiden voyage by pressing a sterling silver subway controller, now one of The New York Historical's treasures (cat. 110). Additionally, apart from tokens and other subway ephemera, the Patricia D. Klingenstein Library holds over 71,000 photographic prints documenting the construction of the subway and its surface extensions in Manhattan, the Bronx, Brooklyn, and Queens (fig. 31). This collection provides an extensive survey of commercial and residential structures along subway routes, as well as glimpses of everyday street life.

It is fascinating to reflect on the mundane activities captured in such images from a century or more ago, and perhaps gain a deeper understanding of how easily one's own moments can be overlooked as worthy of preservation. Appeals to the public to keep and donate papers and other things flourished during the first 150 years of The New York Historical's existence. "Every day records are burned or thrown away which might be saved if historical societies could afford to employ field agents to seek them out and ask for them," Alexander J. Wall, the institution's then-director, wrote in 1944.

Lieutenant Colonel Ely S. Parker was one such field agent. On April 9, 1865, General Ulysses S. Grant wrote a letter to General Robert E. Lee at Appomattox Court House, Virginia, detailing the terms of surrender for Lee's army, effectively bringing an end to the Civil War. As Grant's military secretary, Parker supplied the writing materials: a pen and a manifold order book with yellow sheets of copy paper—a primitive form of carbon paper. According to Parker, Grant's handwritten lines produced "3 or 4 impressions" of the original document. Lee studied it, looked relieved, and accepted its terms. Graciously shaking hands with the gathered staff, he paused at Parker, a prominent member of the Tonawanda Seneca Nation. "I see that there is at least one real American here," Lee remarked. "General, today we are all Americans," Parker responded. Grant handed him one of the sheets as a keepsake, a monumental document that is now part of The New York Historical collections (cat. 132).

Although formal period images of Ely Parker exist, the one we display in this volume is a strikingly unfinished-looking one by Mathew B. Brady, the best-known photographer of his generation. The Patricia D. Klingenstein Library holds thousands of Brady portraits of notable figures from the 19th century. Perhaps the most fascinating are part of a collection of over 5,000 fragile and unmounted prints that served as the "file photographs" of Brady's renowned New York City studio, with the sitter's surname inscribed in pencil on the emulsion. Kept in near-total darkness and unidentified for 150 years, the images remain as fresh, clear, and immediate as the day they were created. Parker chose to accessorize the Western attire of his formal portrait with a symbol of his heritage: a mammoth silver peace medal that George Washington presented to his ancestor Sa-go-ye-wa-tha, or Red Jacket, chief of the Seneca Wolf Clan, in 1792 (fig. 34).

The American Civil War (1861–65) was the largest and deadliest conflict fought on American soil. By 1863, the initial enthusiasm for the war had vanished, and the Union struggled to recruit enough soldiers. In response, President Lincoln instituted the nation's first conscription act and draft. In New York, the draft ignited one of the worst urban riots in American history. For four days, a mob terrorized the city's African American population, beating and murdering innocent civilians and destroying property—including the Colored Orphan Asylum.

One of The New York Historical's prized possessions is the only known draft wheel to survive the July 1863 New York City

Draft Riots (cat. 131). This object and its contents—small cards bearing the handwritten names and addresses of potential conscripts—have survived as witnesses to a tumultuous time. However, as powerful on a more intimate scale is one of the few items that survived the sacking of the Colored Orphan Asylum: a scorched Bible clutched by a young girl as a mob closed in on her and a group of other children (fig. 33). The asylum was founded in 1836 by Quaker women from the New-York Manumission Society, itself established in 1785 by several leading white citizens. Its mission was to publicly advocate for the abolition of slavery and the manumission of enslaved people in New York State, as well as to support those already freed. Among the society's other major achievements was the founding in 1787 of the African Free School, dedicated to educating Black children in preparation for life as free citizens. The records of the Orphan Asylum, the Manumission Society, and the Free School are all part of the holdings of the Patricia D. Klingenstein Library.

The complete records of these important 19th-century organizations were foundational to The New York Historical's early collecting and have served as exceptional resources for scholars of the period. More recent donations of similar scope and scale continue to abound, such as the records of the Women's Sports Foundation, established in 1974 by Billie Jean King to advance the lives of women and girls through sport and activity. Of great related importance is the athlete's own archive, which includes documents, scrapbooks, publications, photographs, memorabilia, and artifacts that she generated and collected throughout her life and career as an athlete, advocate for equality, and public figure.

Sometimes, the smallest things tell a story in the mightiest way. The 1765 Stamp Act was a British law that directly taxed the American colonies for printed materials, leading to the famous cry of "taxation without representation," serving as both a dress rehearsal and the opening episode of the American Revolution. The tax stamp measures only about an inch in size (cat. 147). Fragments of objects from the 18th and 19th centuries, excavated from the backyard of the Ear Inn, New York City's oldest continuously operating bar, were once discarded as garbage. In a broader sense, however, these artifacts also reflect the lives of the inhabitants of the residential and commercial building over the centuries, as well as the commitment of The New York Historical staff to advancing the field of urban archaeology (cat. 148). A strip of yellowed New York Stock Exchange ticker tape from October 29, 1929, Black Tuesday, succinctly captures the peak of the stock market crash, the collapse of the US economy, and the beginning of the Great Depression. It reads: "Total sales today 16,388,700. Good night" (cat. 155).

These things, both big and small, unique or merely representative of a time and place, constitute a democracy of objects that collectively tell the story of a civilization left behind by citizens of both the distant and more recent past. As descendants, academics, or history enthusiasts, we, in fact, are caretakers of these collections, which inform us of the achievements, great and small, of our literal and figurative ancestors.

For over 220 years and counting, The New York Historical has amassed millions of things. The more famous among them—the John James Audubon watercolors, the documents from the founding era, the Hudson River School paintings, for example—are prominently displayed and well known. The lesser-known items rest quietly beneath the same roof, awaiting further exploration by a scholar or curator motivated by a hunch, an obsession, a research project, or perhaps simply the inspiration that those unique moments of discovery can bring.

Arthur W. Grumbine (1901–1998)
Chinese New Year, New York City, 1948
Gelatin silver print
Patricia D. Klingenstein Library,
The New York Historical

CEREMONIES & TRADITIONS

96

BENJAMIN WYNKOOP (ca. 1675–1751)

Brandywine bowl (*brandewijnkom*), ca. 1700

New York City
Silver
The New York Historical, Bequest of Catharine Augusta De Peyster, 1911.38

The brandywine bowl, a decorative vessel favored by elite families of Dutch descent, embodies the perpetuation of Dutch tradition in New York. They are most commonly associated with the Dutch ritual of the *kindermaal*, a celebratory feast held in honor of a mother and her newborn child. This silver bowl is engraved with three sets of initials, which trace the bowl's ownership through six generations of the De Peyster family, all the way down to Catharine Augusta De Peyster (1835–1911), the donor. The earliest set of initials indicates that the bowl was made to celebrate the birth of one of the children of New York City merchant Cornelis De Peyster and his wife, Maria Bancker, who married in 1694.

97

UNIDENTIFIED MAKER

Wedding dress worn by Cornelia De Peyster Teller (1690–1756), ca. 1712, with several alterations into the 20th century

Possibly England or United States
Silk brocade, needlepoint lace, silk chiffon
The New York Historical, Gift of Mrs. Arthur T. Sutcliffe, 1949.115a

This wedding dress was worn by Cornelia De Peyster, daughter of Isaac and Maria (Van Ball) De Peyster, on October 12, 1712, when she married Oliver Stephen Teller (1685–1729), son of Andres and Sophia (Van Cortlandt) Teller. The marriage united two influential New Amsterdam families. Before the 1840 wedding of Queen Victoria of England, it was not common for brides to dress in head-to-toe white. Instead, a bride wore whatever color she preferred, like this fashionable yellow silk brocade, and paired it with white accessories such as shoes, fans, and even quilted petticoats.

Weddings in colonial America took place between late December and early February when most wealthy families were wintering near each other in the city. Unlike today, the wedding was held during the day at the bride's parents' home. As a result, wedding dresses tended to be informal day garments, suitable for the bride's everyday wardrobe after her wedding day. The imported fabric of this dress, featuring an English-style floral pattern, was possibly designed by the famed British textile designer Anna Maria Garthwaite.

Over the course of two centuries, the dress underwent several alterations, most recently for Alice Crary Sutcliffe's wedding on April 30, 1908. Originally the dress was a *robe à l'anglaise*, a fashionable style that was worn over a matching petticoat like a robe and pinned to the side of a matching stomacher. This triangular front panel did not survive and was likely repurposed into the front fitted bodice. The needlepoint net and lace flounces were most likely added in the early 20th century.

HENRY BARCLAY (1715–1764)

“Register of baptisms, marriages, communicants & funerals begun by Henry Barclay at Fort Hunter, January 26th, 1734/5”, 1735–46

Manuscript
Patricia D. Klingenstein Library, The New York Historical

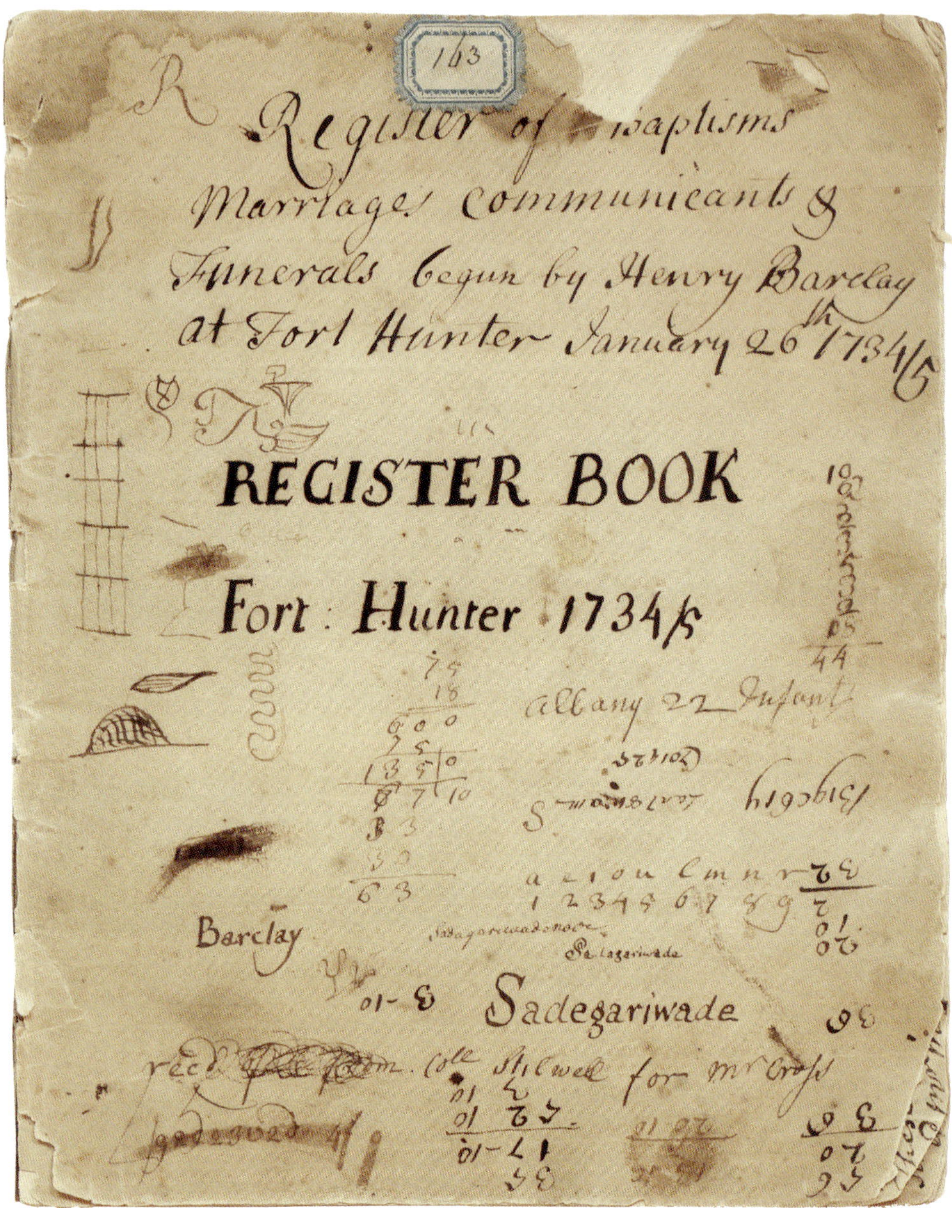
Register of baptisms
Marriages communicants &
Funerals begun by Henry Barclay
at Fort Hunter January 26th 1734/5

REGISTER BOOK

Fort: Hunter 1734/5

Albany 22 Infants

Barclay

Sadegariwade

In 1711, Queen Anne ordered the construction of Fort Hunter in New York, near Schenectady, at the behest of ambassadors from the Kanien’kehá:ka (Mohawk) Nation—Britain’s allies in their ongoing colonial contest with France over North American territories. The fort included an Anglican chapel, intended as a buffer against encroachment by French Catholics, and became a hub for various missionaries, like Henry Barclay.

Barclay’s father Thomas had been one of Fort Hunter’s earliest missionaries, and Henry followed in his footsteps after graduating from Yale. Henry was appointed catechist, or religious instructor, to the Kanien’kehá:ka at Fort Hunter in 1736. He was subsequently ordained in England, and sent back by the Society for the Propagation of the Gospel as a missionary in Albany and Fort Hunter in 1738. Barclay tended a diverse congregation of English, Irish, and Dutch, enslaved Black people, and the Kanien’kehá:ka to whom he was proselytizing. His handwritten “Register of baptisms, marriages, communicants & funerals,” totaling 69 pages, provides a material record of this work.

Barclay left Fort Hunter in 1746, two years after Britain and France officially opened hostilities in King George’s War. The fighting primarily took place in present-day Canada, Maine, and Massachusetts, but northern New York also saw skirmishes and raids between the Europeans and Indigenous nations. Despite their alliance, the Kanien’kehá:ka distrusted Barclay and the British, with good reason: conflicts over land had already begun. As rector, Barclay had been granted the right to use 300 acres of land, but upon his departure tried to sell it as his own property. The Kanien’kehá:ka objected, and Barclay eventually turned the land over to the Society for the Propagation of the Gospel.

99

PIERRE CHARLES L'ENFANT (1754–1825), designer
JOHN COOK (active 1797–1825), maker

Ribbon badge, ca. 1802

New York City
Silk, gold, enamel
The New York Historical, Gift of Miss Frances Jay, Mrs. Alexander Duer Harvey, Mrs. Lloyd Kirkham Garrison, and Mrs. Lawrence W. Fox in memory of Mrs. Pierre Jay (Louisa Shaw Barlow), 1972.12ab

This badge belonged to Matthew Clarkson (1758–1825), an original member of the Society of the Cincinnati. It appears in a portrait of Clarkson by Gilbert Stuart at the Metropolitan Museum of Art. The Cincinnati, founded in 1783 by Major-General Henry Knox and other officers, was dedicated to preserving the ideologies of the American Revolution. The name was inspired by the fifth-century Roman hero Lucius Quinctius Cincinnatus, who sacrificed his private interests to serve the Republic and famously renounced his sweeping militaristic powers. George Washington, who resigned from the army in 1784 and refused to seek a third term as president in 1796, was widely hailed as the American Cincinnatus.

The original medal, which was distributed to Revolutionary War officers, was designed by Major Pierre Charles L'Enfant. The die was cut in Paris in 1784. This ribbon badge was made in New York City around 1802 and is one of only five known surviving examples. It takes the form of an eagle with outstretched wings, crowned by a laurel wreath, and contains an enameled image of Cincinnatus receiving a sword.

100

CLEMENT CLARKE MOORE (1779–1863)

"A visit from St. Nicholas, Clement C. Moore, 1862 March 13th, originally written many years ago"

Holograph manuscript
Patricia D. Klingenstein Library, The New York Historical

'Twas the night before Christmas, when all through
the house
Not a creature was stirring, not even a mouse;
The stockings were hung by the chimney with care,
In hopes that St. Nicholas soon would be there;
The children were nestled all snug in their beds,
While visions of sugar-plums danced in their heads;
And Mamma in her 'kerchief, and I in my cap,
Had just settled our brains for a long winter's nap;
When out on the lawn there arose such a clatter,
I sprang from the bed to see what what was the matter.
Away to the window I flew like a flash,
Tore open the shutters and threw up the sash.
The moon, on the breast of the new-fallen snow,
Gave the lustre of mid-day to objects below,
When, what to my wondering eyes should appear,
But a miniature sleigh, and eight tiny rein-deer,
With a little old driver, so lively and quick,
I knew in a moment it must be St. Nick.
More rapid than eagles his coursers they came,
And he whistled, and shouted, and called them by name;
"Now, Dasher! now, Dancer! now, Prancer and Vixen!
On, Comet! on, Cupid! on, Donder and Blitzen!
To the top of the porch! to the top of the wall!
Now dash away! dash away! dash away all!"

Theologian and Hebrew scholar Clement C. Moore is thought to have composed the famous Christmas poem "A Visit from St. Nicholas" on December 22, 1822, at his Manhattan home on West 24th Street. Many years later, it was written out by the author at the suggestion of The New York Historical librarian George H. Moore, who wished to add a holograph copy of the poem to the collection. The three pages were accompanied by a cover letter from art patron Thomas W.C. Moore, presenting the enclosed manuscript and relaying the circumstances of the poem's original composition and publication 40 years earlier. (Despite their identical surnames, the three men were not related.) "A Visit from St. Nicholas" was originally published anonymously in the Troy, New York, *Sentinel* in 1823, and Moore publicly acknowledged the poem as his in 1838. Although Moore's claim has occasionally been disputed, he is widely accepted as the author.

"A Visit from St. Nicholas" provided inspiration for today's Santa Claus: a red-cheeked and red-suited "jolly old elf," who drives a flying sleigh pulled by eight famous reindeer. But Moore's "St. Nicholas" was very different from the historical St. Nicholas of Myra (or Bari), who died on December 6, 343 CE, in modern-day Turkey. He is said to have performed many good deeds in his lifetime, and was celebrated as the patron saint of sailors, merchants, archers, brewers, pawnbrokers, students, and children. St. Nicholas is honored in the Netherlands with a holiday called Sinterklaas, which Dutch settlers brought with them to New Amsterdam. Over time, the feast of Sinterklaas blended with British and German folk traditions, giving shape to today's Christmas celebrations.

101

JOSÉ MARIA MORA (ca. 1849–1926)

Mrs. Cornelius Vanderbilt II (Alice Claypoole Gwynne) as "Electric Light" at the Vanderbilt Ball, 1883

Cabinet card
Patricia D. Klingenstein Library, The New York Historical

The period from the end of the Civil War to the close of the 19th century is often referred to as the Gilded Age: a period of rapid industrialization and technological advancement that significantly increased the number of American millionaires, but was also marked by profound economic inequality.

Many of these *nouveaux riches* families sought admission to "The Four Hundred," a select list defined by Mrs. Caroline Schermerhorn Astor, a descendant of two of New York's oldest and most prominent Dutch families, and the unquestioned leader of New York society. Determined to reach the top, Alva and William Vanderbilt (grandson of the multimillionaire railroad and shipping titan Cornelius Vanderbilt) built a massive Fifth Avenue mansion designed by architect Richard Morris Hunt, filled it with imported European furniture and fine art, and threw a massive costume ball for 1,200 guests. Alva invited journalists to preview the excesses of the party; they reported that the Vanderbilts spent $65,000 on champagne and $11,000 on flowers. The total cost? An estimated $250,000, or approximately $6 million in today's money. Mrs. Astor and her daughter were among the attendees.

Cuban-born society photographer José Maria Mora captured the outfits. Far from the flimsy Halloween costumes of today, the fancy dresses on display at the Vanderbilt Ball were haute couture masterpieces. Alva's sister-in-law, Mrs. Alice Vanderbilt, for example, wore a yellow satin "Electric Light" gown, a Parisian creation from the atelier of Charles Frederick Worth. It was even equipped with batteries so that it would really light up.

102

MEAVE THOMPSON GEDNEY (1863–1905)

Mrs. Bradley Martin (Cornelia Sherman, 1845–1920), 1897

Watercolor on ivory, silver gilt
The New York Historical, Gift of the Estate of Peter Marié, 1905.156

The great fortunes amassed in the late 19th century fed a resurgence in American portraiture as a record of riches and mark of status. This included a new interest in portrait miniatures: exquisitely detailed watercolors done on ivory, small enough to fit in the palm of the hand. The New York society figure Peter Marié commissioned over three hundred of these tiny jewel-like portraits, believing that the women of his elite circle epitomized female beauty.

This portrait miniature captures the sumptuous costume worn by Cornelia Sherman Martin, who hosted a controversial costume ball at the Waldorf Hotel on February 10, 1897. She dressed as Mary, Queen of Scots, in an extravagant ensemble which included jewels that had once belonged to Empress Josephine of France. Her husband Bradley Martin dressed as Louis XV.

The event drew widespread criticism from those who thought it an ostentatious display of wealth and excess at a time when the nation was still struggling with the aftermath of the Panic of 1893: a series of bank runs and failures, followed by years of high unemployment and economic contractions. Labor unrest swept the country, with strikes among coal miners, iron and steel workers, and railroad employees. The 1894 Pullman Strike brought rail travel to a standstill across much of the nation and sent labor leader Eugene V. Debs to prison on conspiracy charges, where, he wrote, "the first glimmerings of Socialism" began to spark in his political consciousness. It is small wonder that Reverend Dr. William S. Rainsford, rector of St. George's Protestant Episcopal Church in New York, caused a press frenzy for criticizing the Martin ball from his pulpit and warning that such events gave ammunition to "socialistic agitators."

102

103

CHILDE HASSAM (1859–1935)

The Fourth of July, 1916 (The Greatest Display of the American Flag Ever Seen in New York, Climax of the Preparedness Parade in May), 1916

Oil on canvas
The New York Historical, Gift of Richard Gilder, 2016.31

This monumental painting by American Impressionist Childe Hassam depicts Fifth Avenue in New York bedecked with dozens of American flags in celebration of Independence Day, 1916. The artist was a committed supporter of the Preparedness Movement, which advocated for a strengthened national defense after the outbreak of war in Europe in July 1914—despite official declarations of neutrality and a strong strain of anti-interventionism among the American people.

Nevertheless, proponents of the preparedness cause staged parades in cities across the country for the next two years. Witnessing one such parade in May 1916, Hassam commented: "I looked up the Avenue and saw those wonderful flags waving, and I painted a series of flag pictures after that." This is the second of Hassam's flag pictures. The full title of this painting, *The Fourth of July, 1916 (The Greatest Display of the American Flag Ever Seen in New York, Climax of the Preparedness Parade in May)*, conflates the annual Fourth of July celebration with the nationalistic fervor created by the Preparedness Movement. Threats to American ships from German submarines, plus the decoding of the Zimmerman Telegram, shifted US attitudes, and the United States entered the war in 1917. In the following year, Fifth Avenue was designated the "Avenue of the Allies."

104

UNIDENTIFIED MAKER
SURMA BOOKS AND MUSIC CO. (1918–2016), retailer

Pysanka (Ukrainian Easter egg), 1990–2016

Goose egg shell, dyes
The New York Historical, Gift of the Surmach Family, 2017.5.8

For nearly a century, Surma Books & Music Co., named for a Ukrainian woodwind instrument, was a cultural hub for New York City's Little Ukraine, an immigrant-centered community in the East Village. Based around Seventh Street, and historically bounded by Second Avenue, Houston Street, Third Avenue, and 14th Street, the area has reflected the ebb and flow of Ukrainian immigration over the course of a century, from the late 19th century through the 20th.

Myron Surmach Sr., the founder of Surma, exemplified this history. He arrived at Ellis Island from Ukraine in 1910 and settled in New York City after working various odd jobs in New Jersey and Pennsylvania. He opened his shop in 1918 to sell clothing and Ukrainian books, but as increasing numbers of Ukrainians fled war, political instability, and famine, Surma soon evolved into a general store, selling everything from phonographs to washing machines, as well as services such as letter reading. Originally located on Avenue A, in 1943, the store moved to its longtime location at 11 East Seventh Street, in time to welcome a second wave of Ukrainian immigrants after the Second World War.

During the folk revival of the 1950s and '60s, around the time that Surmach's son, Myron Jr. (1932–2003) assumed the business, the store's offerings shifted toward products such as ceramics, religious icons, embroidered shirts, and hand-carved wooden objects. The perpetuation of artistic practices, such as decorating *pysanky*, along with foodways and faith traditions, keeps diasporic communities such as Little Ukraine connected to the traditions of their home nations, through generations. In so doing, they help form the culture of New York City and its environs.

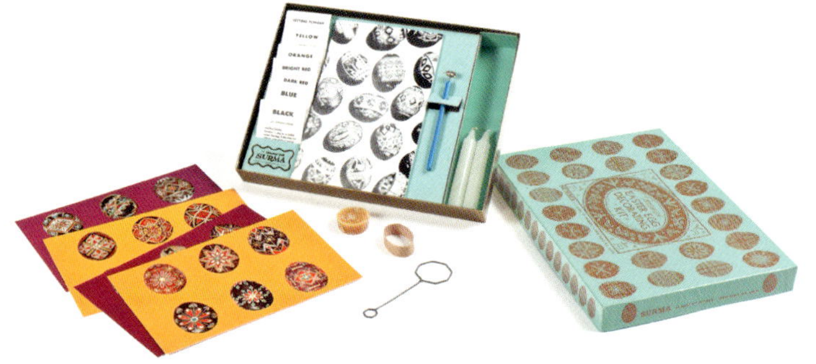

Fig. 29
Yaroslava Surmach Mills (1926–2009), artist
Surma Books and Music Co. (1918–2016), retailer
Ukrainian Easter egg decorating kit, ca. 1957–80
New York City
Cardboard, paper, dyes, plastic, waxes, metal
The New York Historical, Gift of the Surmach Family, 2017.5.1

105

NOOKART.COM

Adam & Steve wedding cake topper, 2007

China
Plastic, paint, metal
The New York Historical, Gift of Ulysses Grant Dietz in honor of Gary N. Berger, 2020.26

This wedding cake topper was gifted to The New York Historical by Ulysses Grant Dietz, Chief Curator Emeritus of the Newark Museum, in response to a call for the donation of a same-sex marriage wedding cake topper. Dietz (the great-great-grandson of US president Ulysses Grant), and his husband, Gary Berger, have been together for 45 years. As Dietz explained, prior to the legalization of same-sex marriage, "an older generation of gay men who never expected to get married . . . used symbols our own way without regard to the larger world." Over the years, the couple marked their commitment to each other in several different ways, including a 2007 civil union ceremony, suggested by Dietz's mother, for which this cake topper was given to Dietz by his older brother as "somewhat of a joke." Dietz and Berger officially married on October 21, 2013, the first day that same-sex marriages became legal in the state of New Jersey.

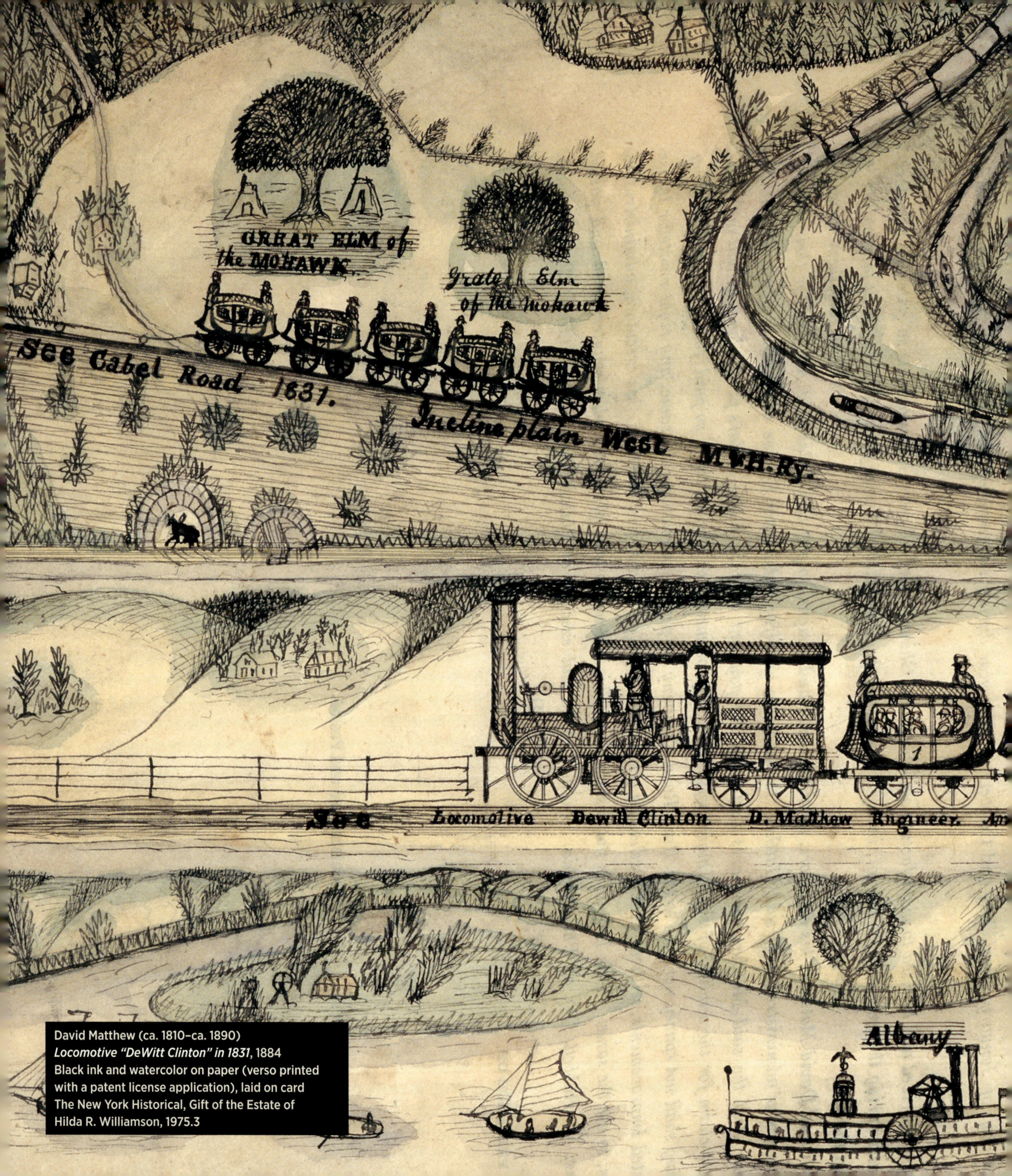

David Matthew (ca. 1810–ca. 1890)
Locomotive "DeWitt Clinton" in 1831, 1884
Black ink and watercolor on paper (verso printed with a patent license application), laid on card
The New York Historical, Gift of the Estate of Hilda R. Williamson, 1975.3

TRANSPORTATION & TRAVEL

106

BEEKMAN FAMILY, former owner

Beekman family coach, ca. 1770

England
Wood (ash and spruce by analysis), iron, leather
The New York Historical, Gift of Gerard Beekman, 1911.25

When New York merchant James Beekman acquired this coach in 1771, it became the crown jewel of a horse-drawn fleet that already included a chaise, chariot, and phaeton. Much as luxury cars are used to signal status and wealth today, various types of horse-drawn vehicles did the same for 18th-century New Yorkers: from the economical gig (an open, two-wheeled, self-driven vehicle pulled by one horse) to splendid coaches like this one. It features a luxurious enclosed body, accommodation for up to six passengers, and would have been driven by a liveried coachman, accompanied by a footman, and drawn by a minimum of two horses—the prestige vehicle of the 18th century. Beekman's account book records that he purchased the coach for £138, and made additional expenditures for painting the family coat of arms on the doors and varnishing the surface. Gerard Beekman, the great-grandson of James Beekman, donated the family coach to The New York Historical in 1911.

107

UNIDENTIFIED MAKER

Bell from the *Clermont*, 1800–07

United States
Iron, wood, paint
The New York Historical, Gift of Alfred Van Santvoord Olcott, 1949.177

This bell is said to have been used on Robert Fulton's steamboat *Clermont*, the first commercially successful steamboat in the United States. Built at Corlears Hook and equipped with a steam engine specially ordered from British manufacturers Boulton and Watt, in 1807, the *Clermont* made its initial run to Albany, New York—a distance of 150 miles—in just over 30 hours, less than half the time it took to make the journey aboard a sail-powered river sloop.

With financial backing from the powerful Chancellor Robert R. Livingston Jr., Fulton began service between New York City and Albany in September 1807. Livingston and Fulton held a monopoly over steamboat transportation in the waters around New York until 1820, when, in the landmark case *Gibbons v. Ogden*, the US Supreme Court ruled that Congress held the power to regulate interstate commerce under the Commerce Clause of the Constitution.

The *Clermont* retired in 1814, but a replica was built for the 1909 Hudson-Fulton Celebration. According to Eben E. Olcott, father of the donor and chairman of the Clermont Committee of the Hudson-Fulton Exhibition, this bell was used on the original *Clermont* in its first year of operation.

108

UNIDENTIFIED MAKER

Keg from the Erie Canal celebration, ca. 1825

United States
Oak, metal, paint
The New York Historical, X.48

DeWitt Clinton (1769–1828), a founding member of The New York Historical, used this keg to "marry" the waters of Lake Erie and the Atlantic Ocean at Sandy Hook on October 26, 1825, at a celebration of the completion of the Erie Canal, his brainchild.

This canal, the final link between the Great Lakes and the eastern coastline, was an unprecedented feat of ingenuity, engineering, and construction. Nine thousand workers labored for eight years with picks and shovels, digging a 363-mile-long trench, four feet deep and 40 feet wide. The uneven terrain demanded a series of locks and aqueducts. But the Erie Canal also required radical public policy decisions and deep-pocketed investors. Fortunately, its greatest champion, DeWitt Clinton, who had served as a US senator and mayor of New York City, was elected governor of New York in 1816. His issue of municipal bonds, guaranteed by the state, helped finance the project—and the canal was so successful that the bonds were all repaid by 1836.

The opening of the Erie Canal fundamentally transformed and defined New York. The city became the nation's chief port, bringing trade and commerce from the nation's interior and connecting it to the Atlantic Ocean. The East River became an infrastructural waterway, enabling the rapid development of New York's eastern shore—today's Brooklyn and Queens.

109

EDWARD YORKE MCCAULEY (1827–1894)

Diary, 1853–54

Manuscript
Patricia D. Klingenstein Library, The New York Historical

69

Prince's Barge

were told that the survey was necessary, and could not be carried on without touching ashore,
but as far as the boats' crews being in danger, it would be safer for any parties
belligerently inclined, to leave them alone, for they would hardly take a
hard knock without giving one in return: Of course they gave the matter
up, after a little conversation a good feeling was created, and one of the Officials
went so far as to shew, with great show of Secrecy, a Japanese Chart of Yeddo
Bay. I went below and procured a sheet of tracing paper; having pencils &c

Edward Yorke McCauley served as a midshipman aboard the USS *Powhatan*, Commodore Matthew Perry's flagship during his expedition to Japan in the 1850s. At this time, ocean travel was beginning its dramatic shift from sail power to steam power. Although ocean voyages still took long, arduous weeks, if not months, ships were beginning to escape the vagaries of wind and ocean currents—although Navy steamships like the *Powhatan* would also carry sails for the next 30 years.

The Perry Expedition, made up of several vessels including the *Powhatan*, intended to end Japan's two-century-old policy of self-isolation with a commercial treaty. McCauley's illustrated diary is a rare first-hand account containing observations written and illustrated from February 1853 to June 1854. The diary suggests that McCauley was genuinely interested in the people he encountered, and that he possessed at least some desire to make a serious record of them. However, in several journal entries, what McCauley may have intended as humorous vignettes instead serve as prime examples of the chauvinism and nationalism that troubled many encounters along the journey.

Perry's expedition marked the beginning of a period of intense political and economic change within Japan, while beyond its borders a craze for Japanese products influenced Western fashions, architecture, and the arts. McCauley himself went on to a long career in the United States Navy: he was aboard the USS *Niagara* when it laid the first transatlantic telegraph cable in 1857–58, served throughout the Civil War, and later rose through the ranks to become rear admiral and commander of the Pacific Squadron.

110

TIFFANY & CO. (founded 1837)

Controller handle, 1904

New York City
Silver, steel, ebony
The New York Historical, Gift of George B. McClellan, 1922.103

New York City mayor George B. McClellan Jr. used this sterling silver subway controller to start the city's first subway train on its maiden voyage on October 27, 1904. He was so intoxicated by the speed of the train that he raced through the scheduled station stop at 42nd Street and continued uptown. Mayor McClellan's inaugural ride officially opened the New York City subway system—but it looked quite different from today.

The city had awarded a subway construction contract to the Interborough Rapid Transit Company (IRT) in 1900. The company built a 9.1-mile line featuring 28 stations, from City Hall to 145th Street, the first of three initial lines that ultimately formed what we now recognize as the MTA-run subway system. It soon expanded into the Bronx, Brooklyn, and Queens. Meanwhile, another privately owned company, Brooklyn Rapid Transit Company (BRT, later known as the BMT) built additional lines. Though there were a few free transfers at certain points, riders often had to pay another fare, usually five cents, to transfer to a different line.

Fig. 30
Unidentified maker
New York City subway token, 1953
Brass
The New York Historical, Gift of Jordan and Kathy Wouk, 2020.12.1

The NYC subway token was once a de facto symbol of daily city life. Subway tokens went into use on July 25, 1953, when the fare was raised to 15 cents and could no longer be paid with a single coin. Rather than having riders use three nickels, the MTA introduced a dime-sized token worth 15 cents. Known as the "Small Y-token," the cut-out "Y" in the center was intended to discourage counterfeiting. Plastic MetroCards, introduced in 1994, completely replaced subway tokens in 2003, at which point the discontinued tokens became sentimental mementoes for New Yorkers and tourists alike.

In 1913, the IRT signed a contract with rival BMT, and split management of the subway system. All subway lines were consolidated into one agency by 1940, with the IRT and the BMT joining the Independent City-Owned Subway System (IND), which was managed by the New York City Board of Transportation. In 1953, the Board of Transportation was replaced with today's New York City Transit Authority, which in 1968 became part of the Metropolitan Transit Authority (MTA). The New York City subway system is now the largest in the United States, encompassing over 800 miles of track and 472 stations. The system operates continuously, 24 hours a day, and regularly carries over one billion people annually.

Fig. 31
Unidentified photographer
East 16th Street and Fourth Avenue, Manhattan, 1901
Patricia D. Klingenstein Library, The New York Historical
Photograph © New York Transit Museum

Early subway tunnels were constructed via the "cut-and-cover" method pictured here: the street was torn up, the tunnel constructed relatively near the surface, and then paved over again. Later tunnel projects went deeper, boring through bedrock to minimize disruption at street level and avoid existing utilities. The New York Historical's Subway Construction Photograph Collection documents the building of the system in over 71,000 photographs.

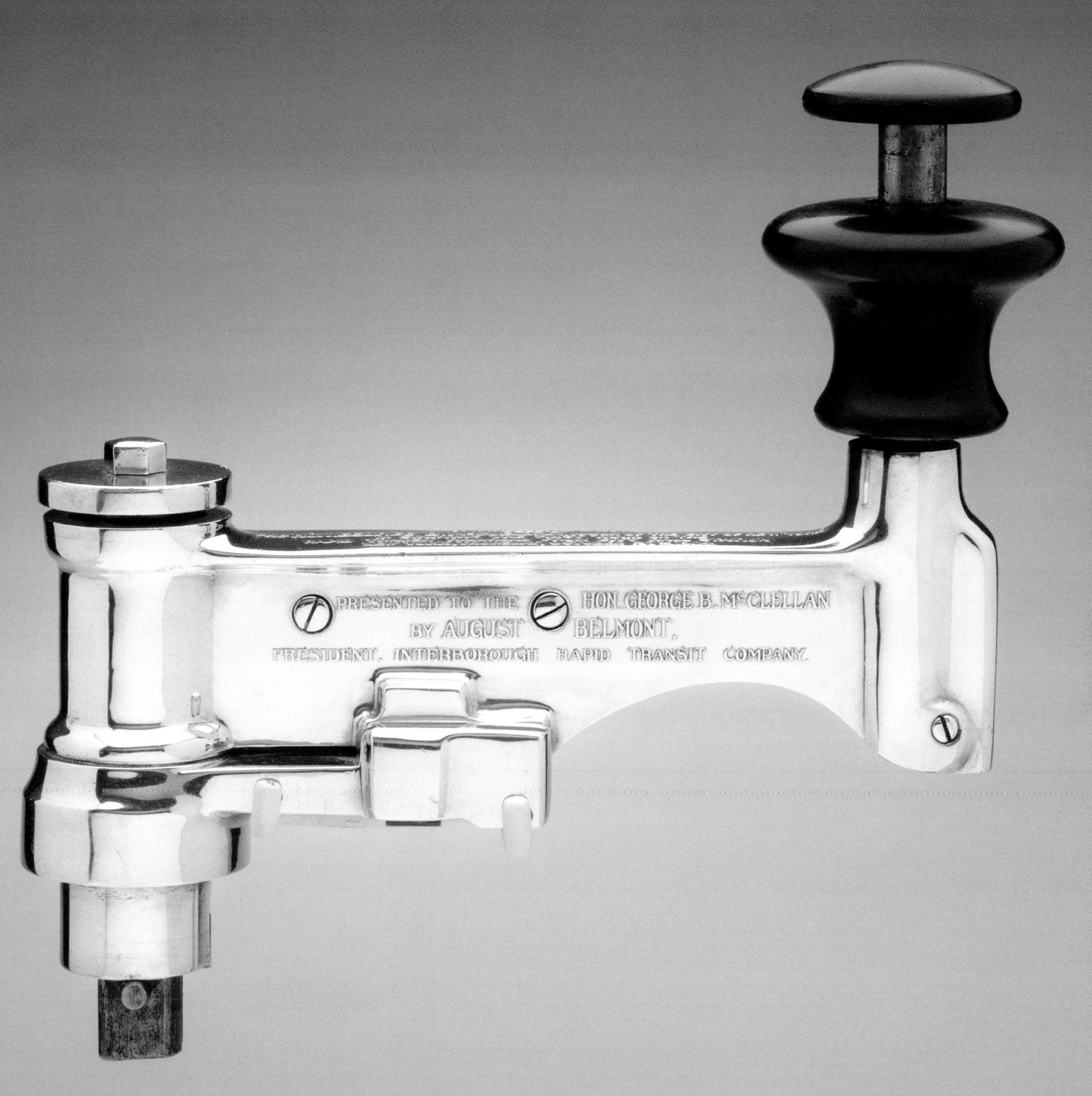
PRESENTED TO THE HON. GEORGE B. McCLELLAN
BY AUGUST BELMONT,
PRESIDENT, INTERBOROUGH RAPID TRANSIT COMPANY.

111a

LIONEL (founded 1900)

Steeplecab locomotive, 1915–16

Metal, paint, glass
The New York Historical, Jerni Collection, acquired with generous support from Bloomberg Philanthropies, Richard Gilder, and an anonymous donor, 2014.31.2887.1

111b

H.E. BOUCHER MFG. CO. (1901–43)

Dining car, 1925–30

United States
Various metals, plastic
The New York Historical, Jerni Collection, acquired with generous support from Bloomberg Philanthropies, Richard Gilder, and an anonymous donor, 2014.31.1285.2

111c

UNIDENTIFIED MAKER

Refrigerator car, ca. 1930–40s

Plastic, metal, wood
The New York Historical, Jerni Collection, acquired with generous support from Bloomberg Philanthropies, Richard Gilder, and an anonymous donor, 2014.31.2632

The Jerni Collection, acquired by The New York Historical in 2014, chronicles a century of toy train design and experimentation, with unique, handcrafted, and hand-painted pieces dating from approximately 1850 to 1940. Objects from the Jerni Collection illustrate in miniature how changes in railroad technology affected Americans' lives on scales large and small.

Toy trains appeared in the 1830s, not long after their real-life counterparts began to revolutionize the transport of goods and people across the United States. The first Railroad Land Grant Act was signed into law in 1850, and track construction proliferated. By 1869, the completion of the Transcontinental Railroad allowed passengers to cross the United States in a matter of days, rather than months. With the rise of train travel, railroad magnate George Pullman introduced luxurious sleeping cars in 1865, and in 1868 he rolled out the first dining car, named after a famous New York City restaurant: Delmonico's. Around the same time, refrigerator cars transformed the way in which food was transported around the country. By the 1870s, New York City shops could be stocked with oranges and grapes from California, or meat and dairy from the Midwest.

Trains were not only for interstate hauls, however—as infrastructure improved in the late 19th century, more and more people began commuting to New York from the suburbs of Long Island, Westchester, Connecticut, and New Jersey. A fatal crash in the smoky tunnels beneath Park Avenue prompted the New York Central Railroad to electrify the trains running to Grand Central; the state legislature went one step further and banned steam trains from Manhattan entirely. This prohibition went into effect in 1908, and by 1912, electric locomotives, such as the one pictured here, powered the daily commute in most major cities in the United States.

112

FINNIGAN'S LTD. (1830–1988), maker

Gentleman's dressing case with travel cover and accessories, ca. 1919

Cover: canvas, crocodile skin, paper; dressing case: crocodile skin, leather, brass, other metals; accessories: silver, gilding, brass, stainless steel, cork, horsehair, ivory, velvet, other metals
The New York Historical, Gift of Oscar L. Tang and Dr. Agnes Hsu-Tang, in honor of the late Shirley Young, 2022.12

This luxurious traveling case belonged to Dr. Wellington Koo, a statesman, diplomat, and judge who was instrumental in expanding China's relationship with European countries and the United States. Vi-Kyuin (V.K.) Wellington Koo (1888–1985) was born near Shanghai and traveled extensively throughout his life. Between 1905 and 1912, Koo attended Columbia University, earning a BA and MA in political science, followed by a PhD in international law and diplomacy. Over his 70-year career, he served as China's minister to the United States and Cuba, and was one of five members of the Chinese delegation to the 1919 Paris Peace Conference that produced the Treaty of Versailles, bringing an end to World War I. He served as an acting president and acting premier of China; and was the Chinese ambassador to Great Britain, France, and the United States. Dr. Koo was also a founding delegate of the United Nations, the first to sign the UN Charter in 1945, and a representative to the UN General Assembly. He became a judge on the International Court of Justice at The Hague in 1956, and served as vice president of that body until he retired in 1967.

It is possible that Koo purchased or received this dressing case as a gift around 1921, when he was stationed in Great Britain. Traveling dressing cases evolved from the heavy trunks and *portmanteaux* of the 18th century. With the advent of railroad, steamship, and motor car travel, dressing cases were redesigned to be hand-carried. Essentially portable dressing rooms, they were stocked with bottles, jars, boxes, mirrors, clothing and hair brushes, manicuring tools, portable inkwells, clocks, barometers, corkscrews, button hooks, scissors, mechanical pencils, and boot jacks.

113

UNIDENTIFIED MAKER

Jim Crow bus sign, ca. 1930–50

Wood, brass, paint
The New York Historical, Purchase, 2015.25

This painted sign was used on a bus or trolley in the American South, probably in Texas, during the 1930s or 1940s. It is a powerful artifact of the Jim Crow era, during which state and local laws mandated racial segregation in public facilities, including public transportation. The sign's metal dowel allowed it to be easily moved from the back of one bus seat to another as needed, enabling white passengers to control the location of Black passengers and number of available seats.

An estimated six million African Americans left the Jim Crow South during the period of the Great Migration (1910–70), and New York City was one of their primary destinations. Although racial segregation in the North was generally not formally codified in state or local law, practices such as racially restrictive real estate covenants, "redlining," and discriminatory hiring ensured that many northern cities, including New York, became bastions of de facto segregation.

114

ENOC PEREZ (b. 1967)

Study for *TWA Terminal, Kennedy Airport*, 2006

Watercolor and black ink on paper
The New York Historical. Promised gift of Elie and Sarah Hirschfeld, Scenes of New York City, IL2021.51.125

Puerto Rican–born Enoc Perez is best known for his paintings and drawings of modernist architectural landmarks, such as this large preparatory watercolor of Eero Saarinen's celebrated TWA Terminal which opened in 1962 at Idlewild, now John F. Kennedy International Airport. Designed for Trans World Airlines by the architectural firm of Eero Saarinen and Associates, the pioneering thin-shell roof is supported by four Y-shaped piers, creating a prominent, wing-shaped profile that evokes a bird about to take flight. The original interior consisted of an open, three-level, sculptured space filled with walls of windows, opening onto vistas of departing and arriving jets. Two futuristic, tube-shaped, red-carpeted departure and arrival corridors extended outward from the terminal to the gates.

Although portions of the original complex have been demolished, Saarinen's masterpiece has been renovated and repurposed as the TWA Hotel. Both the interior and the exterior of the TWA Terminal—which evoke the 1960s Space Race and the go-go age—were declared New York City Landmarks in 1994, and listed on the National Register of Historic Places in 2005.

Charles Gilbert Hine (1859–1931)
Digging Ditches, ca. 1883–1908
Platinum print
Patricia D. Klingenstein Library,
The New York Historical

WORK & LABOR

115

UNIDENTIFIED MAKER

Baby walker, 1700–50

Probably the Netherlands
Cherry
The New York Historical, Purchased from Elie Nadelman, 1937, INV.14959

This baby walker resembles a form popular in the Netherlands called a *loopwagen*. As early as the 15th century, they helped toddlers learn to walk and encouraged erect posture, which carried moral overtones of upright character. Dutch book illustrations and paintings of the 17th and 18th centuries show similar baby walkers and attest to their popularity. Like their 20th-century counterparts, they gave toddlers circumscribed mobility (preventing dangerous stumbles into hot fireplaces or stoves) while allowing their caregivers to carry on with other household tasks. With regular usage, wooden baby walkers like this 18th-century European example suffered considerable wear and tear, and few American examples are known. This rare surviving object was once part of the Elie Nadelman Folk Art collection.

MARY ALEXANDER (1693–1760)

Fabric samples, 1726–60

Cotton, paper, with manuscript annotations
Patricia D. Klingenstein Library, The New York Historical

These fabric swatches belonged to merchant and trader Mary Alexander. The granddaughter of a famed female merchant, Alexander made her own fortune importing dry goods, china, and groceries from London for retail in New York. Her elite family connections enabled her to establish lines of credit and trade networks that reached across the Atlantic, as far as India and China, where desirable fabrics such as silk and cotton chintz were made.

Mary Alexander was born in New York City in 1693. In 1711, she married Samuel Prevoost, an importer. The couple had three children and together ran their mercantile business. Mary contributed much of her inheritance to the business and generally acted as a business partner with her husband. After Prevoost's death around 1720, Mary married James Alexander, an attorney and politician. She had seven more children in her second marriage, though only five lived to adulthood, and continued to run the Prevoost business. She sold goods in her store in front of their mansion on Broad Street and became one of the leading merchants in New York City. Mary was a prominent member of colonial society and is reputed to have served as an informal advisor to many New York politicians.

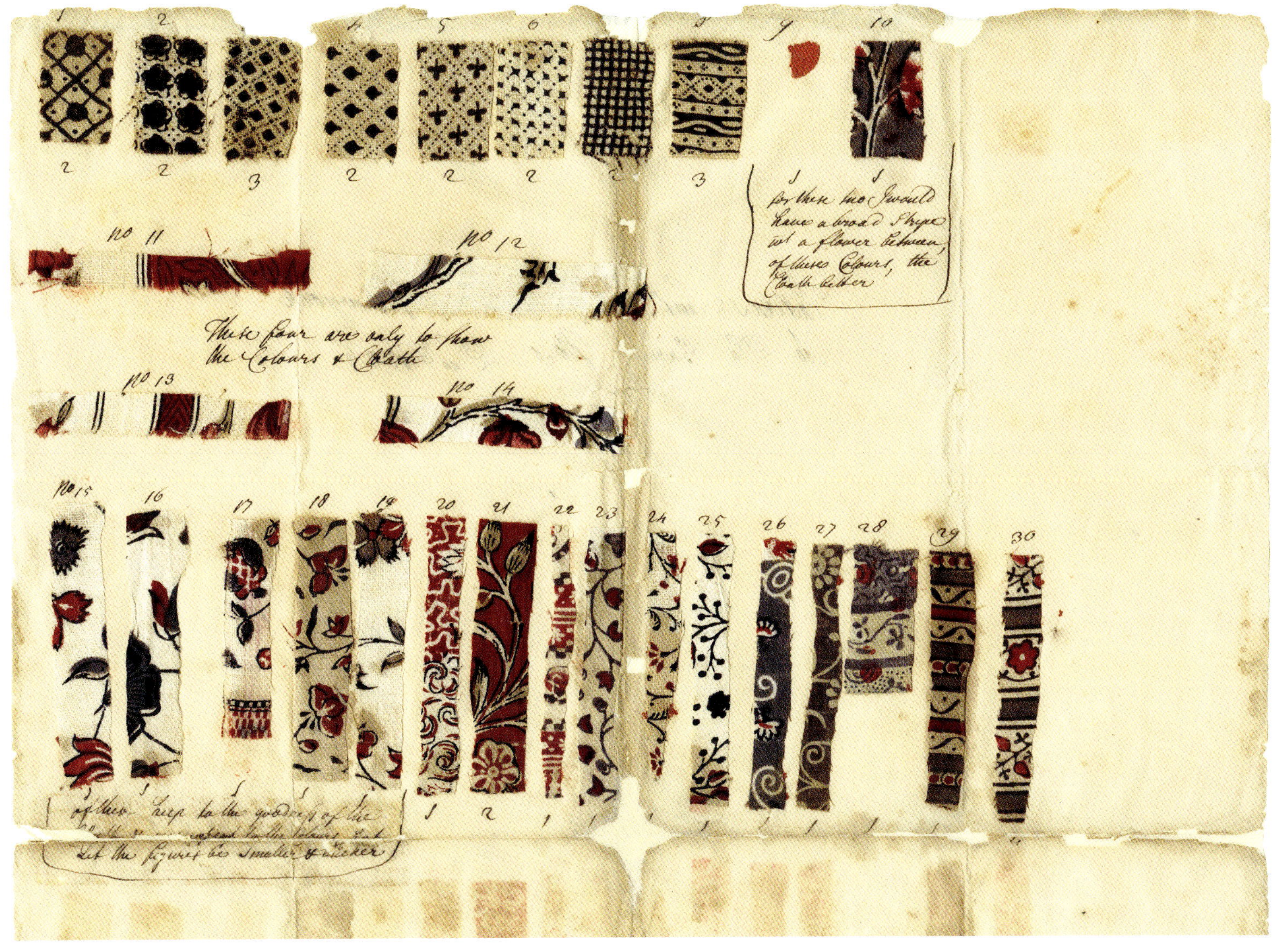

117

Birth certificate of Amanda, born to a "Negro Woman Slave named Phillis" belonging to Ann Helme of New York City, 1807

Manuscript
Patricia D. Klingenstein Library, The New York Historical

For more than two centuries, New York was the capital of American slavery. Prior to 1827, New York City had the largest enslaved population of any city outside of the South, and its economy was built on the labor and trade of enslaved persons.

The Patricia D. Klingenstein Library contains nearly 250 birth certificates such as the one pictured here, written for children like Amanda who were born to enslaved women in New York City between 1800 and 1818. The records show that many slave owners were white women. Though their economic and legal rights were constrained by the principle of coverture, white women were active participants in the slave trade. Indeed, the first Married Women's Property Act in the US was passed in Mississippi in 1839, largely to protect women's rights to "her property in such slaves, and their natural increase"—in other words, their children.

Since the late 17th century, the legal status of children—free or enslaved—had been based on the status of their mothers. However, political considerations forced a change. In 1799, New York passed a Gradual Emancipation Law that freed enslaved children born after July 4, 1799, but indentured them until they were young adults. In 1817, a new law passed that would free persons born into slavery before 1799, but not until 1827.

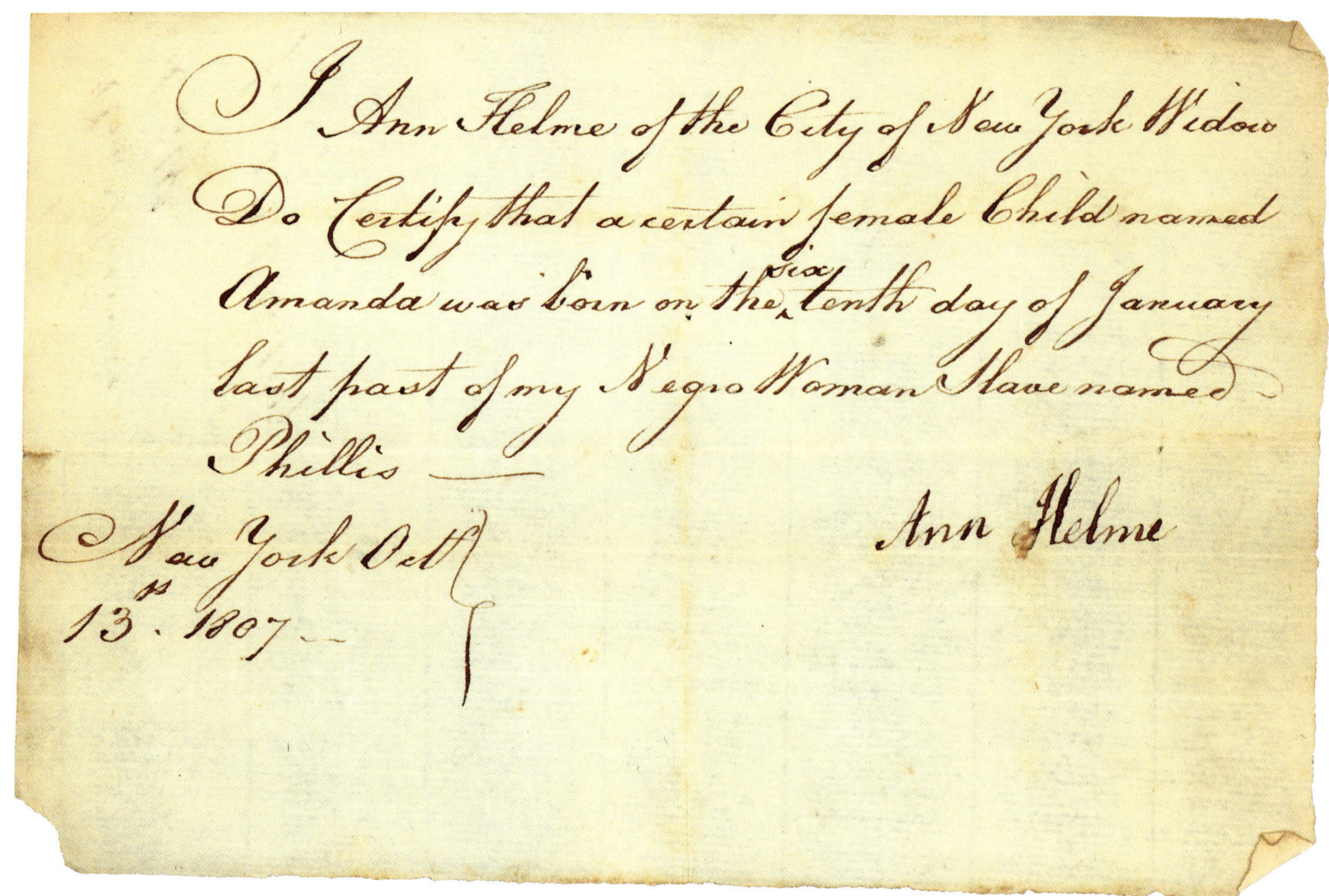

I Ann Helme of the City of New York Widow Do Certify that a certain female Child named Amanda was born on the sixtenth day of January last past of my Negro Woman Slave named Phillis —

Ann Helme

New York Octr 13. 1807 —

118a

ANTHONY MEUCCI (active 1818–37)

Pierre Toussaint (ca. 1781–1853), ca. 1825

Watercolor on ivory
The New York Historical, Gift of Miss Georgina Schuyler, 1920.4

Born into enslavement in Saint-Domingue, today's Haiti, Pierre Toussaint was brought to New York about 1797 by Jean Bérard, a wealthy French landowner fleeing the uprising of enslaved people that had begun six years earlier. Bérard returned to Haiti but died there unexpectedly, leaving Marie Bérard, his young widow, destitute in New York. Until her death in 1807, Toussaint supported her, as well as his own family, as one of the most successful and fashionable hairdressers in New York City—a status reflected in his dark coat, high-collared shirt, and white cravat. A devout Catholic and philanthropist, Toussaint donated to the construction of Old Saint Patrick's Cathedral, orphanages, and other institutions.

118b

ANTHONY MEUCCI (active 1818–37)

Mrs. Pierre Toussaint (Juliette Noel, ca. 1786–1851), ca. 1825

Watercolor on ivory
The New York Historical, Gift of Miss Georgina Schuyler, 1920.5

In 1811, four years after gaining his own freedom upon his enslaver's death, Toussaint purchased the freedom of Juliette Noel, the daughter of a nurse in a French family, and they were married. She is depicted wearing a stylish lace-trimmed gown, but she also wears coral jewelry and a headwrap fashioned from a Madras-plaid handkerchief—adornments rooted in her Afro-Caribbean heritage. Like her husband, Juliette Toussaint practiced philanthropy, providing funds to purchase a Lower Manhattan meeting house for the New York African Society for Mutual Relief. This mutual aid society, founded in 1808, supported Black schools and provided assistance to the sick, widowed, and orphaned.

119

LADIES' CHRISTIAN UNION (founded 1858)

Young Women's Home, Ladies' Christian Union, 27 and 28 North Washington Square, New York City, ca. 1898

Patricia D. Klingenstein Library, The New York Historical

The Ladies' Christian Union (LCU) was founded in 1858 by philanthropist Caroline Roberts. Its original aim was to hold prayer meetings for the young unmarried women flooding into New York City in search of employment and opportunity. However, it soon became apparent that the more pressing need was for safe and affordable housing for working women, which the organization provided for the next 140 years. Sage House, originally called the Young Women's Home, was the LCU's oldest. It was originally located on Amity Street (now West Third Street), moved to East 14th Street, and in 1868 moved again, to the Washington Square North location pictured here. Soon after, in 1870, the Young Ladies' Branch, an auxiliary of the LCU, reorganized independently as the Young Women's Christian Association (YWCA).

Sage House was joined by other residences, whose early occupants included teachers, seamstresses, governesses, telegraph operators, and milliners, while the 20th century saw drama students, secretaries, librarians, and eventually, business and engineering students. The last LCU homes closed to the public in 2000–01, but the organization survives today as a grant-making foundation dedicated to helping female students afford housing in New York City while preparing for careers that serve the community.

120

MADAM C.J. WALKER MANUFACTURING CO.

Madam C.J. Walker's Vegetable Shampoo, ca. 1910–20

Tin, paper
The New York Historical, Gift of Lisa Kugelman in memory of Thomas P. Kugelman, 2015.36ab

Entrepreneur Madam C.J. Walker (1867–1919), born Sarah Breedlove to formerly enslaved parents in Louisiana, was a pioneer in the Black hair-care and cosmetics industry, a leading philanthropist in the African American community, and the first female self-made millionaire in the US. She founded the Madam C.J. Walker Manufacturing Company in Denver in 1906, later moving to Indianapolis, and began selling Madam Walker's Wonderful Hair Grower, a scalp conditioning and healing formula which she claimed had been revealed to her in a dream. Her Vegetable Shampoo was also introduced that year, followed by Tetter Salve (a dandruff treatment) and Glossine (a protective ointment for hair straightened with a hot comb). Walker marketed her products throughout the country through door-to-door sales, demonstrations in churches and lodges, and the education of Walker "hair culturists" at her training schools—a business strategy that empowered Black women to find work and support themselves outside of domestic labor. Walker settled in Harlem in 1916, continuing to oversee her Indianapolis-based beauty empire from the New York office, and became heavily involved in the social and political life of Harlem.

Walker also used her immense fortune to fight Jim Crow and help African Americans achieve full citizenship. She supported local organizations such as orphanages, settlement houses, and elder-care centers that focused on the day-to-day needs of Black Americans, and contributed to the preservation of Frederick Douglass's home. Just before her death in 1919, she made a large donation to the NAACP, which was then fighting to pass a national anti-lynching bill. The NAACP later credited her gift with helping the organization survive the Great Depression.

121

UNIDENTIFIED MAKER

Buttoned shoe, ca. 1915

Leather, beads, buttons
The New York Historical,
Gift of Stuart Weitzman,
IL2016.62.25

The first decades of the 20th century witnessed a revolution in the way women dressed, moved, and behaved in public. As the floor-length gowns of the late 1800s gave way to the shorter skirts and slim silhouettes of the Jazz Age, women's feet and legs became a new focal point. Beaded and buttoned shoes grew enormously popular, and the demand for new footwear expanded rapidly.

By 1900, nearly every American shoe was made in a mechanized factory, and one-third of shoe-factory laborers were women who had a robust history of activism. Indeed, the first national union of working women had been organized in 1868 by women in the footwear industry: the Daughters of St. Crispin, named after the patron saint of shoemakers. With the support of the all-male Knights of St. Crispin, the women went on strike in the shoemaking city of Lynn, Massachusetts, in 1871, successfully fighting against wage cuts for skilled workers. "We are freeborn American women," one shoemaker wrote, "and when they attempt to tell us what to do we will rise in our might, and three thousand voices will tell them what we will do."

A small stamp on the sole of this fashionable beaded shoe bears the mark of the International Boot & Shoe Workers Union, established in 1895 and considered radical for its time. By 1904, its constitution called for "uniform wages for the same class of work, regardless of sex."

122

INTERNATIONAL LADIES' GARMENT WORKERS' UNION (founded 1900)

Pin-back button, 1970–95

Metal, paper, Mylar
The New York Historical, Gift of Irwin Silver, 2003.97.16

Founded by working-class immigrants in 1900, the International Ladies Garment Workers Union (ILGWU) organized to protect and promote the rights of workers in the growing women's garment industry. From its inception, 85% of ILGWU members were women, predominantly immigrants. Through pioneering education and healthcare programs for workers and their families, the organization advanced a notion that workers' rights and women's rights are inextricably linked. The Chinese characters on this pin-back button reflect the change in the ethnicity of garment workers from predominantly Jewish and Italian, to Latinx and Chinese.

One of the earliest programs created by the ILGWU was the first-ever Union Health Center, established in New York in 1914 to provide medical care to union members and their families. Following the passage of the restrictive Immigration Act of 1925, which prevented undocumented migrants from traveling back and forth between Europe and the United States, the union provided citizenship classes for its Italian and Jewish undocumented immigrant workers. Later, the union played a key role in President Ronald Reagan's Immigration Reform and Control Act (IRCA), which opened up a new path for citizenship for undocumented immigrants who had been in the country since 1982. The ILGWU lobbied for the act and provided substantial counseling on immigration issues for workers.

123

TED TINLING (1910–1990)

Philadelphia Freedoms tennis dress worn by Billie Jean King (b. 1943), ca. 1974

Synthetic textile
The New York Historical, Billie Jean King Collection, 2019.14.3

In the 1970s, Billie Jean King's relentless activism for gender equality changed the face of American sports. She protested women's unequal pay by forming the Virginia Slims all-female tennis tournament and playing as one of its "Original 9." In 1974, King co-founded the World Team Tennis (WTT), the first tournament to include mixed-gender teams. She served as player and coach for the first Philadelphia Freedoms team during the inaugural season of the tournament, becoming the first woman to coach a professional team with male players.

The Freedoms' opening game drew thousands of people who came to see King's famously powerful serve. The tournament provided opportunities for female players to compete for equal prize money alongside their male counterparts. In keeping with King's vision to make tennis more diverse, WTT's matches also broke with tradition by encouraging the audience to cheer loudly for their teams. It was a rare opportunity for female and male players to train and compete on equal footing, helping give rise to tennis superstars such as Venus Williams, member of the team for three seasons between 2006 and 2009.

British designer Ted Tinling created this dress, featuring the Liberty Bell, for King and her team to wear during the inaugural match of the Philadelphia Freedoms. Tinling, who fondly called King "Madame Superstar," made some of her most iconic outfits as she ascended to unprecedented fame, including the dress she wore to face Bobby Riggs in the 1973 "Battle of the Sexes."

Attributed to Albert Berghaus (active ca. 1859–1880)
24 Weeks on the Potomac, cartoon for *Frank Leslie's Illustrated Newspaper* (February 1, 1862); verso: study for the same subject, 1862
Black ink over graphite on ivory paper
The New York Historical, Purchase, James B. Wilbur Fund, 1945.580.82

WAR & CONFLICT

on the Potomac.

124

DUTCH STATES GENERAL

Writ of mandamus issued to Peter Stuyvesant, April 28, 1648

Manuscript with seal
Patricia D. Klingenstein Library, The New York Historical

De Staten Generael der Vereenichde Nederlanden

Ter ordonnantie vande Hooghgemelte Heeren Staten Generael

This legal document of April 28, 1648, concerns the case of Cornelis Melyn and Jochem Pietersz Cuyter. Melyn had held the patroonship of Staten Island since 1640; Cuyter (or Kuyter) held 400 acres of land along the Hudson River. Both were prosperous and influential, and among the Dutch settlers who suffered losses in the war waged by Willem Kieft, the director of New Netherland from 1638 to 1647. Kieft persecuted and massacred Native Americans "unjustly and contrary to all international law." Their subsequent retaliation led to "Kieft's War," with devastating losses on both sides. When Kieft sought to hire mercenaries to defend the colony, Melyn and Cuyter were part of the group that argued against the tax hikes that would be needed to enact Kieft's plan.

According to Kieft's successor, Peter Stuyvesant, Melyn and Cuyter went one step too far when they sent a "Remonstrance" to the Netherlands complaining about Kieft. Stuyvesant accused both men of insubordination and slander, and banished them from the colony. However, the Dutch States General found in Melyn and Cuyter's favor and strongly condemned both their treatment and the Native Americans' treatment at the hands of Kieft. The States General issued this writ of mandamus to compel Stuyvesant's cooperation and reverse the sentence against Melyn and Cuyter, allowing them to return to New Amsterdam.

125

COTTON MATHER (1663–1728)

The Wonders of the Invisible World: Being an Account of the Tryals of Several Witches, Lately Executed in New-England: and of Several Remarkable Curiosities therein Occurring

London: Printed first, at Bostun [*sic*] in New-England; and reprinted at London, for John Dunton, at the Raven in the Poultry, 1693
Patricia D. Klingenstein Library, The New York Historical

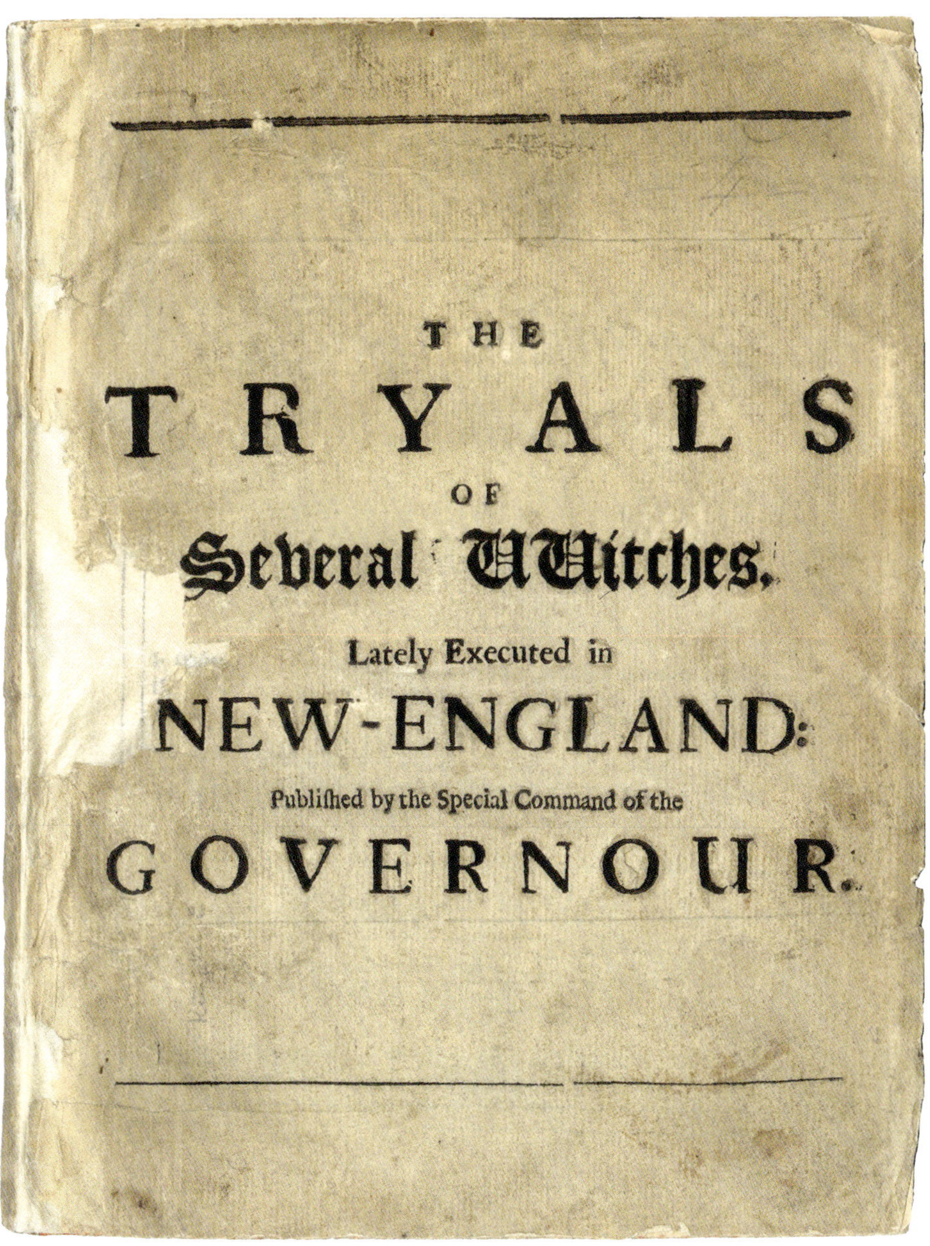
THE
TRYALS
OF
Several Witches,
Lately Executed in
NEW-ENGLAND:
Publiſhed by the Special Command of the
GOVERNOUR.

The Wonders of the Invisible World is Cotton Mather's account of the Salem witch trials. The accusations in Salem, Massachusetts, began early in 1692 and spiraled until October of that year, eventually ensnaring 170 people who were accused of conspiring with Satan to unleash *maleficia* (harmful magic) against their neighbors. By the time the trials concluded in 1693, 19 of the accused would be executed, while six others died in prison.

Cotton Mather, the son of prominent Puritan Increase Mather, was a Congregational minister in Boston, like his father. Although he was not directly involved in the Salem trials, Mather used this text to describe and justify the verdicts and executions. The book, which was printed first in Boston in 1692 and then in London the following year, fanned the belief in witchcraft, already widespread in colonial Massachusetts at the end of the 17th century. But Mather also evinced skepticism about the Salem court's most controversial practice: the admission of spectral evidence, derived from visions, dreams, and other supernatural sources.

PAUL REVERE (1735–1818)

The Bloody Massacre Perpetrated in King-Street Boston on March 5th 1770, by a Party of the 29th Regt., 1770

Hand-colored engraving
Patricia D. Klingenstein Library, The New York Historical

Paul Revere issued this famous print less than a month after the Boston Massacre, and it became an important piece of visual propaganda for colonial Americans. The New York Historical's copy is one of the rare versions that show Crispus Attucks as a Black man. He was an American stevedore of African and Native American descent, widely regarded as the first person killed in the Boston Massacre and thus the first American to die in the American Revolution.

A Revolutionary activist, Revere was a member of the Sons of Liberty, a secret group opposed to British colonial policy, including taxation, that kept track of British troop movements and warships in the harbor. He was also a master craftsman specializing in metalwork, including copperplate engravings and fashionable and functional objects made from silver, gold, brass, bronze, and copper. Over two hundred copies of Revere's engraving were printed and sent throughout America and Europe, spreading news of the massacre and stoking revolutionary fervor in the colonies.

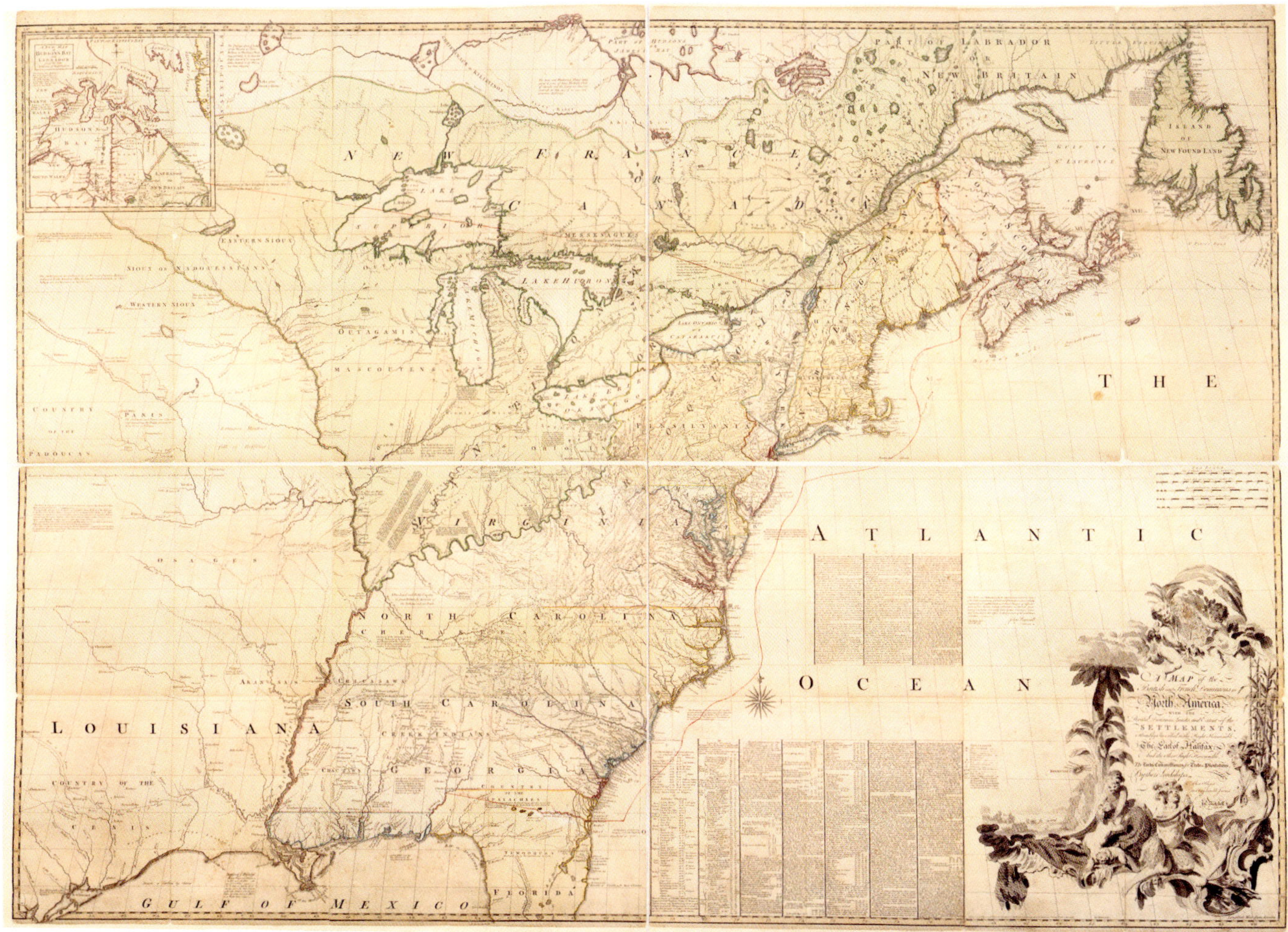

127

JOHN MITCHELL (1711–1768)

A Map of the British and French Dominions in North America, with the Roads, Distances, Limits, and Extent of the Settlements, Humbly Inscribed to the Right Honourable the Earl of Halifax, and the Other Right Honourable the Lords Commissioners for Trade & Plantations, 1773

First impression of third edition, with hand-drawn red lines
Patricia D. Klingenstein Library, The New York Historical

First published in London in 1755, John Mitchell's map was the most impressive and accurate cartographic description of Britain's territorial holdings in North America. The historical significance of the map increased exponentially when it was used to demarcate potential boundaries during the negotiation of the Treaty of Paris, 1782–83, which formally ended the Revolution and recognized US independence. Representatives from Britain, the United States of America, and Spain each brought a copy of the Mitchell map to the negotiations. Red lines were hand-drawn on the maps to identify potential boundaries. Only three copies of the red-lined Mitchell map are known to exist. This map was used by John Jay, who negotiated on behalf of the United States along with John Adams and Benjamin Franklin. It was donated to The New York Historical by his son, Peter Augustus Jay, during his tenure as president of the institution, 1840–42.

128

UNIDENTIFIED MAKER

Camp bed, ca. 1775–77

Probably United States
Wood, canvas, iron
The New York Historical, Gift of Ernest Livingston McCrackan, 1871.8

George Washington's Revolutionary War camp bed was made of three folding stools. Stretching six-and-a-half feet long, it barely fit the six-foot-two-inch General Washington. He may have slept on this rudimentary bed during the harsh winter of 1777–78, which the Continental Army spent encamped at Valley Forge. At that low point in the war, the troops were battle-weary and poorly supplied. Washington's letters mention shortages of every kind: horses and wagons; clothes and shoes; flour and soap. Without extensive reforms, Washington wrote, the army would have no choice but to "starve—dissolve—or disperse" by the time fighting resumed. The Continental Congress heeded Washington's dire warnings. In June 1778, the army marched out again with settled supply issues, a reorganized army, and new military skills. Even more welcome was news of a formal alliance with France, which would help turn the tide of the war.

According to the donor's great-aunt, Mrs. Francis A. Livingston (Catharine Roosevelt Kissam), this camp bed was given by Washington to his recording secretary, Richard Varick (1753–1831), at the close of the Revolutionary War.

NATHANIEL PENDLETON (1756–1821)

Second statement of the regulations for the duel between Aaron Burr and Alexander Hamilton, July 11, 1804

Manuscript
Patricia D. Klingenstein Library, The New York Historical

Bitter rivals Alexander Hamilton and Aaron Burr arrived in Weehawken, New Jersey, for their legendary duel, just before seven in the morning on July 11, 1804, in separate boats. Following the rules laid out in this letter by Hamilton's second, Nathaniel Pendleton, they left the oarsmen and attending physician David Hosack on the banks of the Hudson River so that they would not bear witness to illegalities about to take place: dueling was forbidden by law in both New York and New Jersey.

Hamilton and Burr climbed to a bluff above the river, where their seconds carved out ten paces. Hamilton, as the challenged party, chose his weapon: a flintlock pistol which may have been used by his son Philip at his own fatal duel at the same site. Pendleton and William Van Ness, Burr's second, offered conflicting stories of which man shot first, but Hamilton's bullet lodged in a tree trunk many feet away from Burr, while Burr's bullet lodged in Hamilton's abdomen—a painful and ultimately fatal wound.

The duel came after decades of personal, professional, and political disagreements between the men, even though they mingled in similar social circles. They belonged to different political parties, but their mutual hostility also resulted from financial competition: Burr founded the Manhattan Company in 1799 as a rival to Hamilton's Bank of New York. Their duel resulted from a series of insults and challenges laundered through rumor and the political press.

News of Hamilton's fall was posted at Tontine Coffee House, and New Yorkers reeled with sadness and disbelief. The event prompted the decline of dueling in New York and across the country.

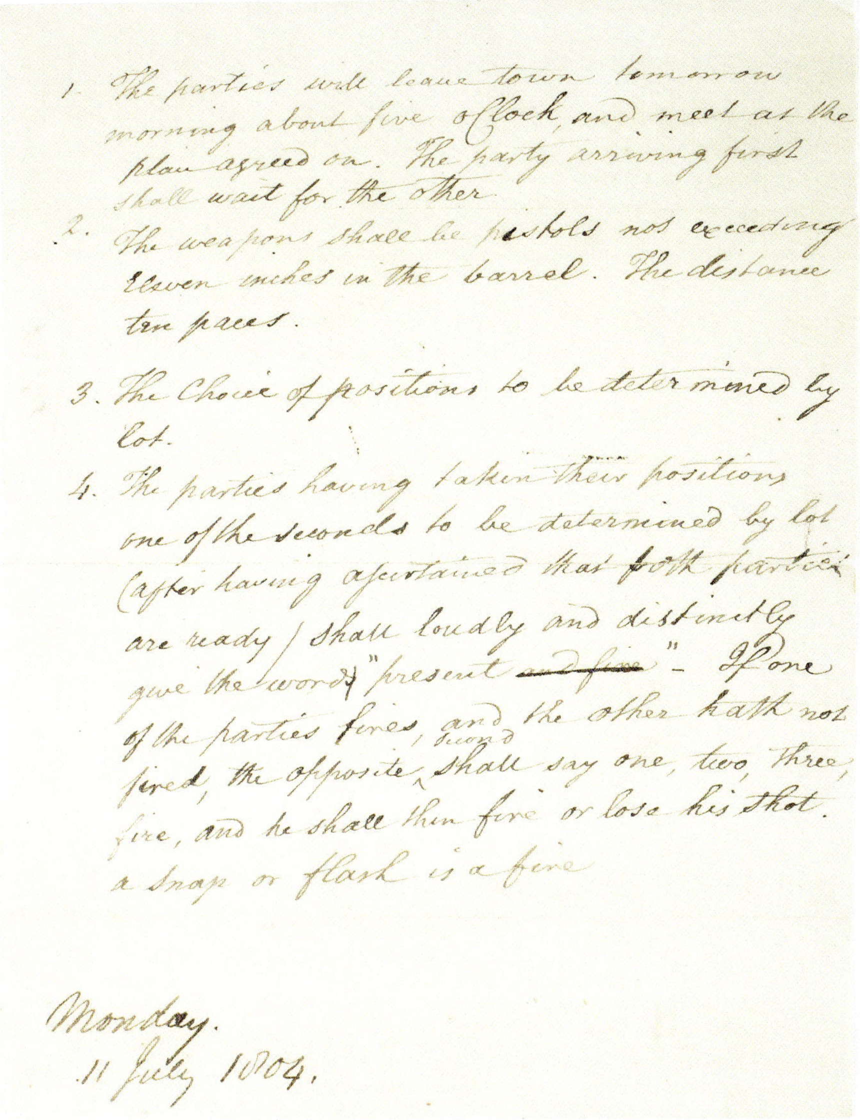

1. The parties will leave town tomorrow morning about five o'clock, and meet at the place agreed on. The party arriving first shall wait for the other

2. The weapons shall be pistols not exceeding Eleven inches in the barrel. The distance ten paces.

3. The Choice of positions to be determined by Lot.

4. The parties having taken their positions one of the seconds to be determined by lot (after having ascertained that both parties are ready) shall loudly and distinctly give the word "present ~~and fire~~" - If one of the parties fires, and the other hath not fired, the opposite second shall say one, two, three, fire, and he shall then fire or lose his shot. a Snap or flash is a fire

Monday.
11 July 1804.

Fig. 32
Unidentified maker
Mourning ring, 1805
United States
Gold, hair, leather, satin, velvet
The New York Historical, Gift of Mr. B. Pendleton Rogers, 1961.5ab

This ring contains the hair of Alexander Hamilton. While on his deathbed, Hamilton's wife Elizabeth clipped locks of her husband's hair, as did many families of prominent figures who distributed locks of hair to friends and close associates. The following year, she arranged to have this memorial ring made for Nathaniel Pendleton, Hamilton's second during his famous 1804 duel with Aaron Burr. In a letter, Elizabeth Hamilton requested that Pendleton wear the ring with its "precious Lock of his hair . . . in Remembrance of your beloved friend."

130

SARAH R. BLUNT (active Civil War)

Letter to Mary Blunt, March 4, 1862

Point Lookout, Maryland
Manuscript
Patricia D. Klingenstein Library, The New York Historical

During the Civil War, Sarah R. Blunt left her home in Brooklyn to serve as a nurse in the military hospitals at Point Lookout, Maryland, and Harper's Ferry, Virginia. She wrote over one hundred pages of correspondence to her family, describing her living conditions and the wounded soldiers she cared for. In this letter, dated March 4, 1862, she wrote to her mother about a man, "not in uniform," who came to the hospital in search of a formerly enslaved woman named Charlotte Bet, who was working there as a cleaner. When the man "kept poking his head in the door," another hospital worker named Mrs. Gibbons

Point Lookout Md.
Wednesday - March 4th 62

Dear Mother,

Last night I received Eliza's letter and the Times - thank father for the last - I am always glad to get any thing now a day - This evening I was going to write cousin Augusta but could not find my ink and so will write her to morrow - The wine will be most acceptable and I think it is very kind of her to send it hope she will put books in too for the poor fellows seem to care for reading more than any thing else - Miss Platt & I are superintending the cleaning of our ward - this week we have found contrabands to do it - You know though what how much work they do -

This morning while I was showing Charlotte Bet how to clean a window I noticed a man, not in uniform, looking in the door - As he did not belong there I told Charlotte Bet to shut the door, but just then Mrs. Gibbons came along with Dr Stevens, and while we were all talking this same man kept poking his head into the door. finally Mrs G. turned round and asked him what he was here. he said he wanted to see the girl in there! pointing to where Charlotte Bet was - As she belonged to his brother in law and he wanted to take her back with him. Mrs. G. asked C. if she wanted to go 'I guess no missus' So Mrs G asked his name &c. - and finding it was not Jones who says is the only Union man in the county she told him he was a rebel and inquired what his business was. The man pointed to Bet and claimed that she was his brother-in-law's property. "Mrs. G," wrote Blunt, then called the man "a rebel," and informed him that "he had no right, even if he was not one, to take the slave."

Bet was one of four "contrabands" working in the Point Lookout hospital. The military term referred to enslaved men and women who escaped behind Union lines. Union officers realized that their self-emancipation weakened the Confederacy, and, in August 1861, Congress passed the First Confiscation Act, freeing slaves whose labor had been used to support the Confederate Army. Just nine days after this letter was written, Congress passed an Article of War prohibiting officers in the Union Army or Navy from returning any contraband slaves to their owners, effectively overturning the Fugitive Slave Act and setting the stage for Lincoln's Emancipation Proclamation. By the end of the Civil War, an estimated half a million formerly enslaved people were contributing to the Union cause as nurses, cooks, orderlies, builders, and spies.

that he had no right, even if he
was not one to take the slave, as the
order from Government was that no
slave should be sent or taken out
of the military lines unless they
wished to go. The man then went off
quick enough — (So many are in my
room talking that I hardly know
what I'm writing & so I leave it therefore
to you to make an interesting tale out
of it.) Tell Effie I was delighted
with her letter and to morrow I shall
write her one. Kiss the three little
children for me. I would give lots
to see them and all
Frank, our man, has just come
in to say there were no letters for any
of us. Sorry. It is pleasant to be rewarded
after a toilsome day by a letter
but if you wont — why I am too
far away to make you feel a fuss
Kiss Pinkie and dont spend too

much time killing fleas.
How is Millie Hyde — I hope better.
My love to all Aunt Mary's family
And our own too. Cousin Eliza did
With much love
Your affectionate daughter
Sarah R. Blunt
P.S. I wish you could look out
of my window this evening. The
moon reflects the water Chesapeake
is shining right down on the Bay
& so it seems almost as if we
were on ship board looking out
of our cabin window so near
are we to the water.
Please write if you dont I
wont come home at all.
I shall always number my letters
so that you can know when any
are lost
Nat.
Send me Jane Eyre. It is in my writing desk
if it belongs to Aunt Mary for I think she would let me
have it for men who have nothing [illegible] to do

131

UNIDENTIFIED MAKER

Draft wheel, ca. 1863

New York City
Wood, metal
The New York Historical, Gift of Frederic C. Wagner, 1865.6

By 1863, the initial enthusiasm for the Civil War had vanished, and the Union struggled to recruit enough soldiers. In response, President Lincoln instituted the nation's first conscription act and draft, which went into effect in New York City on July 11. All men between the ages of 20 and 35, and all unmarried men between the ages of 35 and 45 whose names were selected were required to serve in the military, unless they paid a $300 exemption fee. This drum-shaped wheel was used in the draft lottery held on July 13 in the Seventh Congressional District (the East Side below 14th Street and above Rivington Street). The draft touched off the worst urban riots in American history. For four days a mob terrorized the city's African American population, beating and murdering innocent civilians, and destroying property—including the Colored Orphan Asylum.

Founded in 1836 by Quaker women from the New-York Manumission Society and located in a large, well-appointed building on Fifth Avenue between 43rd and 44th Streets, the Colored Orphan Asylum at that time housed 233 orphaned and homeless children, some of whom were the children of Black Union soldiers. Only moments before the mob broke in, the children were hastily evacuated by their teachers. The crowd plundered the Asylum, looting everything from furniture to baby clothes, then set fire to the building despite the pleas of administrators. According to a handwritten account among the institution's records, one of the only things saved was a Bible, which a little girl carried away with her.

Union soldiers had to be called in from Gettysburg to put an end to the chaos, and the official citywide death toll was 119, although many historians estimate it was even higher. This is the only known draft wheel to survive the New York City Draft Riots.

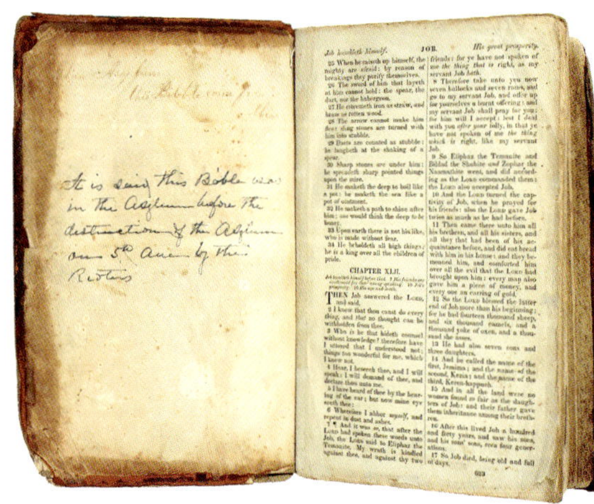

Fig. 33
Association for the Benefit of Colored Orphans (founded 1836)
Bible used at the Colored Orphan Asylum, ca. 1863
Patricia D. Klingenstein Library, The New York Historical

ULYSSES S. GRANT (1822–1885)

Letter to Robert E. Lee (1807–1870), April 9, 1865

New York City
Manifold impression in the hand of Ulysses S. Grant, with revisions by Ely S. Parker, October 21, 1880
Patricia D. Klingenstein Library, The New York Historical

On April 9, 1865, General Ulysses S. Grant wrote a letter for General Robert E. Lee at Appomattox Court House, detailing the terms of surrender of Lee's army. Lee studied the document—a mere five sentences—and appeared relieved. The terms stated that Lee's army must surrender its military property, including military-issued arms and artillery, and must sign paroles "not to take up arms against the Government of the United States." Lee's agreement effectively ended the war in Virginia, though fighting continued across the South for several weeks.

This is one of the original impressions from the manifold on which Grant wrote the terms of surrender, with interlinear revisions by Lieutenant Colonel Ely S. Parker (1828–1895), a prominent member of the Tonawanda Seneca Nation who acted as Grant's military secretary. Parker provided the writing materials: a manifold order book with yellow sheets of copy paper and a pen. Grant's handwritten lines created, according to Parker, "3 or 4 impressions" of the original.

Fig. 34
Mathew B. Brady Studio (1844–1873)
Ha-sa-no-an-da (Ely Samuel Parker, 1828–1895), ca. 1851
Salted paper and albumen print
Patricia D. Klingenstein Library,
The New York Historical

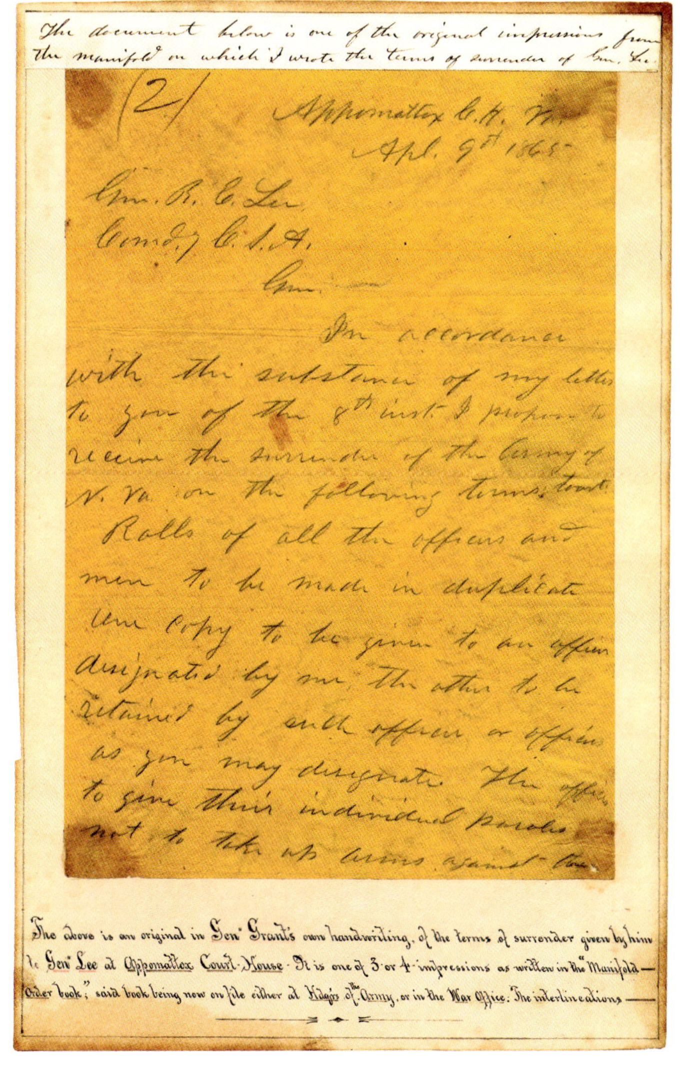

The document below is one of the original impressions from the manifold on which I wrote the terms of surrender of Gen. Lee

(2)

Appomattox C.H. Va.
Apl. 9th 1865

Gen. R. E. Lee
Comdg C.S.A.
Gen.

In accordance with the substance of my letter to you of the 8th inst. I propose to receive the surrender of the Army of N. Va. on the following terms, towit:

Rolls of all the officers and men to be made in duplicate one copy to be given to an officer designated by me, the other to be retained by such officer or officers as you may designate. The officers to give their individual paroles not to take up arms against the

The above is an original in Genl Grant's own handwriting, of the terms of surrender given by him to Genl Lee at Appomattox Court-House. It is one of 3 or 4 impressions as written in the "Manifold—Order book"; said book being now on file either at Hdqrs of the Army, or in the War Office. The interlineations—

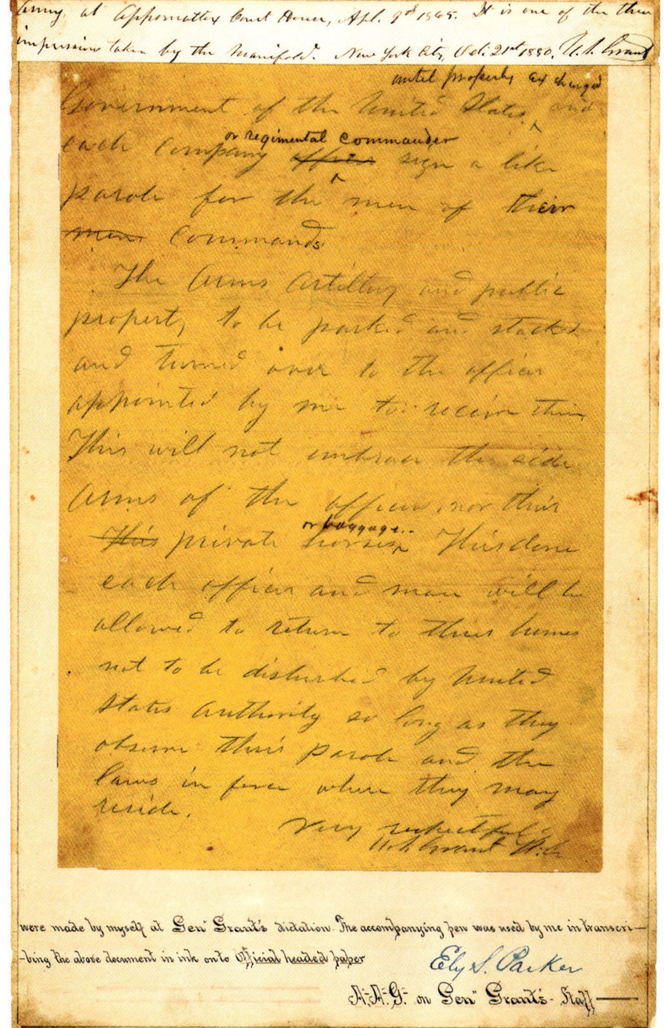

Army at Appomattox Court House, Apl. 9th 1865. It is one of the three impressions taken by the Manifold. New York City, Oct. 21st 1880. U. S. Grant

Government of the United States, until properly exchanged and each Company ~~Officer~~ or regimental commander sign a like parole for the men of their ~~men~~ Commands.

The Arms, Artillery and public property to be parked and stacked and turned over to the officer appointed by me to receive them. This will not embrace the side arms of the officers, nor their ~~this~~ private horses or baggage. This done each officer and man will be allowed to return to their homes not to be disturbed by United States authority so long as they observe their parole and the laws in force where they may reside.

Very respectfully
U. S. Grant Lt. Gn.

were made by myself at Genl Grant's dictation. The accompanying pen was used by me in transcribing the above document in ink onto Official headed paper

Ely S. Parker
A.A.G. on Genl Grant's Staff

133

UNIDENTIFIED MAKER

Slave shackles, ca. 1866

Georgia, United States
Steel
The New York Historical, Gift of Mrs. Carroll Beckwith, 1921.20

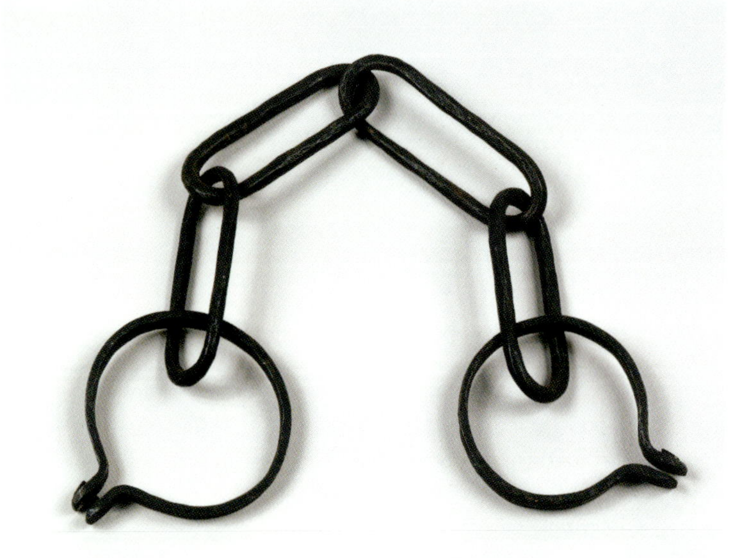

According to a letter accompanying their donation to The New York Historical in 1921, these shackles were cut off enslaved teenager Mary Horn of Americus, Georgia, by Colonel William W. Badger of the 176th Regiment New York Volunteers, more than a year after Lincoln issued the Emancipation Proclamation: based on when the regiment was in Georgia, in either 1865 or 1866. Mary is said to have been enslaved by a Judge Horn, who riveted the irons around her ankles with his own hands to prevent her from walking to the next plantation to see her beloved, George. George begged Badger to free Mary from her shackles and supposedly held her over an anvil while Badger cut them off. Badger stated that he married the couple after cutting off the shackles.

134

UNIDENTIFIED MAKER

Brassard, ca. 1915

Linen, wool, metal
The New York Historical, Gift of Adelaide Milton de Groot, 1942.207

World War I greatly expanded women's official capacities within the US military, from the "Hello Girls" of the Army Signal Corps to the "Lady Hellcats" of the Marine Reserve. And, as in previous wars, thousands of women also served as nurses. Whether affiliated with the army, the navy, the Red Cross, or another volunteer organization, nurses found themselves responding to the horrific casualties of trench warfare. Adelaide Milton de Groot, a wealthy New Yorker, wore this brassard as a Red Cross volunteer in France during World War I. Despite concerted efforts to professionalize nursing in the mid-19th century, World War I catalyzed large numbers of volunteer nurses without formal training. Indeed, some male leaders welcomed society women as nursing volunteers, reasoning that they would happily return to their homes once the war ended rather than seek paid employment. Nevertheless, women's wartime work helped to justify the 1920 passage of the 19th Amendment that secured women's right to vote in the United States.

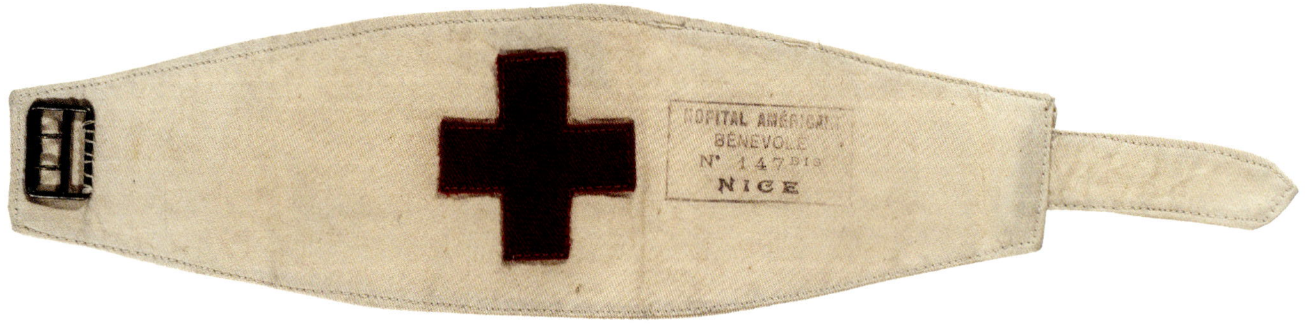

135

CLAIRE MCCARDELL (1905–1958), designer
SAKS FIFTH AVENUE (founded 1867), retailer

Civil Defense uniform worn by Ann L. Adikes (1896–1956), 1942

New York City
Wool, silk, metal
The New York Historical, Gift of the Mayor's Committee, 1946.89a, b

During World War II, American women across the nation contributed to the war effort both abroad and at home, serving in every branch of the armed services. More than 100,000 women became Navy WAVES (Women Accepted for Volunteer Emergency Service), and the Women's Army Corp (WAC) saw 150,000 enrollees. The Marine Corps and the Coast Guard both formed Women's Reserves, and, while the WASPS (Women Airforce Service Pilots) were technically a civilian organization, they were essential to Air Force operations as test pilots, trainers, and transporters.

Women were also involved on the home front. In 1941, the Office of Civilian Defense (OCD), an organization headed by New York City mayor Fiorello LaGuardia, called for volunteers to prepare the city for a possible German attack by air. Twelve thousand women enlisted during the first two months of training alone, serving as auxiliary firefighters, firewatchers, and fire wardens. The New York Historical's collection includes this OCD uniform, worn by Ann L. Adikes from 1942 to 1945. The blue wool skirt and single-breasted coat, fastened with gold buttons cast with the Great Seal of the United States, was sold at Saks Fifth Avenue and designed by New York–based designer Claire McCardell. McCardell's focus on reasonably priced, ready-to-wear "separates" in dynamic and easy-to-move-in materials such as denim and wool jersey allowed her to pivot quickly to making uniforms, even amid wartime rationing.

Work Projects Administration (New York City)
Education and Recreation District Office
Women Learning the Principles of Design, Adult Education Program, New York City, 1938
Photographic print
Patricia D. Klingenstein Library,
The New York Historical

TEACHING & LEARNING

FRANCISCO PAREJA (d. 1628), printer

Catechismo y breve exposición de la doctrina christiana

Mexico City: Con licencia de los superiores, en Mexico: En casa de la viuda de Pedro Balli, 1612
Patricia D. Klingenstein Library, The New York Historical

The extinct language of the Timucua, a Native American people who lived in what is now central and northern Florida and southern Georgia, is known through only nine surviving primary sources, most of them from the early 17th century. Five of these works are held by The New York Historical, including two catechisms in Spanish and Timucua written by the Franciscan missionary Francisco Pareja, printed in Mexico City in 1612, and two devotional texts by Gregorio de Movilla, also a missionary to the Timucua people, printed in Mexico City in 1635.

Timucua, the primary language of the region at the time of European settlement in the late 1500s, was lost by the early 1700s. It is believed by some scholars to be a language "isolate," that is, a language that is not related to any other language—and most of the Timucua-language books are "unique," in that they survive in only one copy. These rare works were donated to The New York Historical by the heirs of Thomas Buckingham Smith (1810–1871), a lawyer, diplomat, antiquarian, and author who served as secretary to the governor of the Territory of Florida and as a member of the Florida Territorial Legislative Council. He sought opportunities to work at the United States embassies in Mexico and Spain, which gave him the opportunity to collect manuscripts and rare books relating to his interests in Spanish North America and Native American languages and culture.

CATECHISMO.
Y BREVE EXPO-
SICION DE LA DOC-
trina Chriſtiana.
Muy vtil y neceſſaria, aſi para los Eſpañoles, como para los Naturales, en Lengua Caſtellana, y Timuquana, en modo de preguntas, y reſpueſtas. Cõpueſto por el P. F. Franciſco Pareja de la Orden de N. Seraphico P.S. Frãciſco, Padre dela Cuſtodia de S. Elena de la Florida.

137

ATTRIBUTED TO JOHN WINTHROP (1588–1649)

“A modell of Christian charity, written on boarde the Arrabella, on the Attlantick Ocean”, 1630

Manuscript
Patricia D. Klingenstein Library, The New York Historical

This is the earliest surviving text of “Christian Charitie: A Modell Hereof” (more commonly called “A Model of Christian Charity”), a lay sermon commonly attributed to the Puritan John Winthrop. The once-unheralded manuscript came to The New York Historical from Francis Bayard Winthrop, a descendant, in 1809. No other contemporary manuscript of Winthrop’s famous sermon is known, and this copy is the basis of all the published editions, the first of which did not appear until 1838.

Winthrop led a large group of emigrants from England across the Atlantic in 1630, and served as the first governor of the Massachusetts Bay Colony. The sermon is one of America’s founding documents and is often used as a reference point for “American exceptionalism,” principally due to its biblical reference from Matthew 5:14 “that wee shall be as a citty upon a hill.” While the body of the sermon itself is consistent with a 17th-century document, nowhere does it name an author, nor the circumstances of its writing.

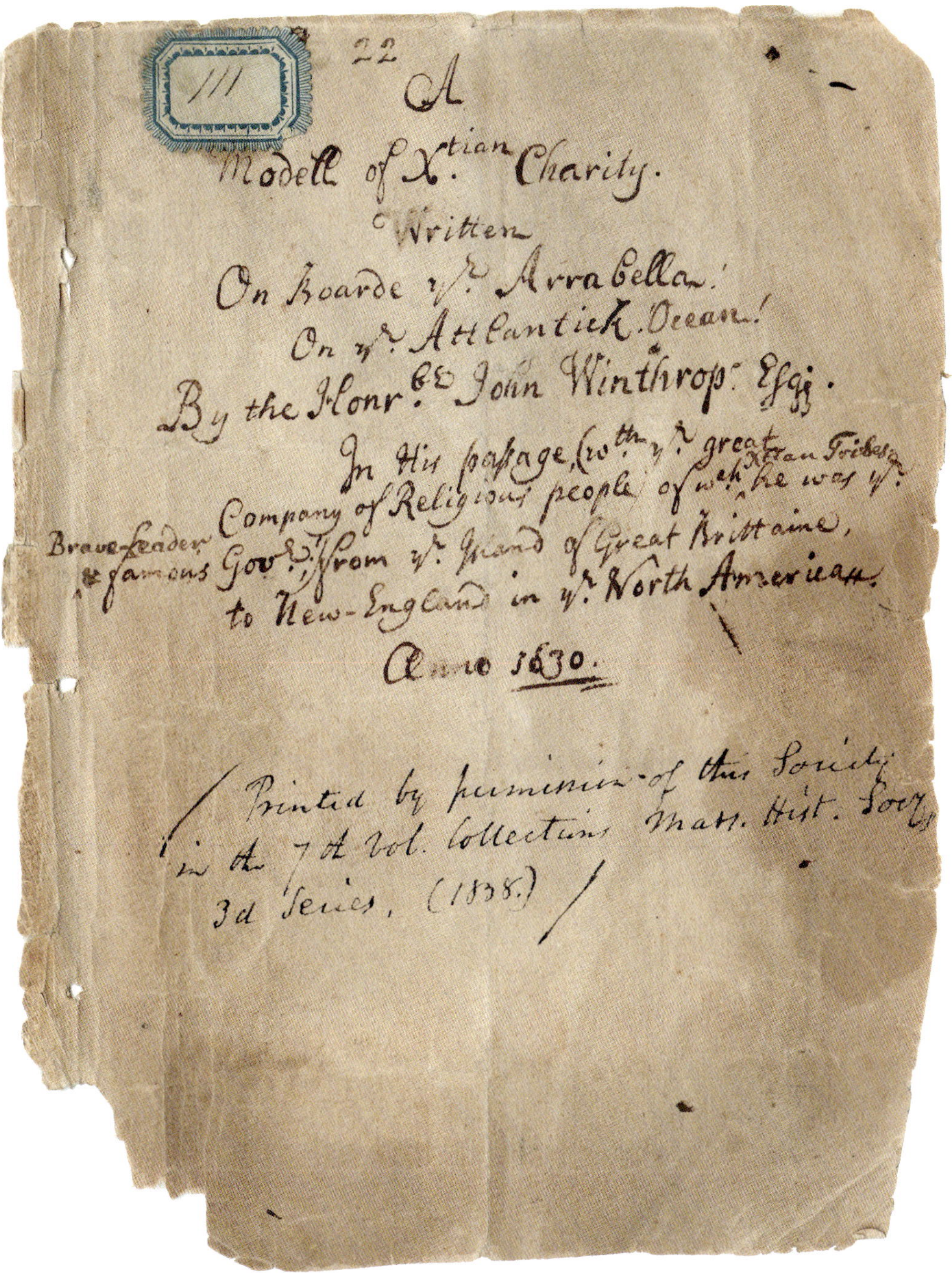

111

22

A
Modell of Xtian Charity.
Written
On Boarde ye Arrabella.
On ye Attlantick Ocean.
By the Honrble John Winthrop Esqr.
In His passage, (with ye great Company of Religious people, of wch Xtian Tribes he was ye Brave Leader & famous Govr;) from ye Island of Great Brittaine, to New-England in ye North America.
Anno 1630.

(Printed by permission of this Society in the 7th Vol. Collections Mass. Hist. Socy 3d Series, (1838.)

138

ISAAC PINTO (1720–1791), translator

Prayers for Shabbath, Rosh-Hashanah, and Kippur; or, The Sabbath, the Beginning of the Year, and the Day of Atonements

New York: John Holt, 1766
Patricia D. Klingenstein Library, The New York Historical

The first Jewish prayer book to be published in North America was also the first to be translated into English, after Isaac Pinto, a Sephardic merchant and scholar, realized that many fellow members of Congregation Shearith Israel in New York could not understand the Hebrew service. In 1766, he completed a translation of all the prayers recited on the weekly Sabbath and the yearly holidays. As Pinto wrote in the preface, services would still be conducted in Hebrew, "the sacred tongue with which God chose to reveal himself to our ancestors," but now those members who did not understand Hebrew could follow along in English.

Congregation Shearith Israel, the oldest Jewish congregation in North America and the only Jewish congregation in New York until 1825, was founded by Brazilian émigrés, many descended from Jews who, facing persecution and expulsion, had fled the Iberian peninsula at the end of the 15th century. Pinto's book, despite being written in English, therefore followed Spanish-Portuguese customs—though it also included a prayer for King George III and the royal family of England.

PRAYERS
FOR
SHABBATH, ROSH-HASHANAH, AND KIPPUR,
OR
The SABBATH, the BEGINNING of the YEAR,
AND
The DAY of ATONEMENTS;
WITH
The AMIDAH and MUSAPH of the MOADIM,
OR
SOLEMN SEASONS.
According to the Order of the Spanish and Portuguese Jews.

TRANSLATED BY *ISAAC PINTO.*

And for him printed by JOHN HOLT, in New-York,
A. M. 5526.

139

SARAH JANEWAY VAN ZANDT (1771–1841)

Sampler, 1783

New York City
Linen, silk
The New York Historical, Purchased through the generosity of Donna and Marvin Schwartz, 2014.5

Samplers have a long history, developing over time from personal reference tools into an important component of women's formal education. By the 17th century, the vocabulary of sampler motifs had become international, due in part to the popularity of pattern books that circulated throughout Europe and made their way to America. This sampler, made by eleven-year-old Sarah Ann Janeway of New York City, belongs to an identifiable type made from the 1740s to the 1830s. They were mostly worked by wealthy New York City girls of Dutch descent and composed of both biblical and secular motifs.

Sarah was the eldest daughter of Auftje "Effie" Ten Eyck and George Janeway, a member of the Committee of Sixty in 1775 and the subsequent Committee of One Hundred. His service as a captain in New York's Revolutionary War militia led to the front door of their home being painted with a red "R," for "Rebel," shortly after the British occupation of New York City in September 1776. When Sarah completed this sampler in May 1783, the British had already surrendered, but the Treaty of Paris was still under negotiation and the British had not yet evacuated. On Evacuation Day that November, George Janeway signed a letter congratulating George Washington from the "Citizens of New York, who have returned from exile."

140

JAMES MCCUNE SMITH (1813–1865)

"An address delivered by James M. Smith, aged 11 years, in the New York African Free School, to General La Fayette, on the day he visited the institution", September 10, 1824

Manuscript
Patricia D. Klingenstein Library, The New York Historical

In order to further the objectives of its organization, the New-York Manumission Society founded the New York African Free School in 1787. The school was devoted to the education of Black boys and girls as preparation for life as free citizens. Beginning with a single schoolhouse on Cliff Street, the African Free School ultimately boasted seven school buildings around the city. The New-York Manumission Society's role ebbed with the end of slavery in New York, and oversight of the African Free Schools turned over to the New York Public School Society in 1834. All the schools subsequently became part of the public school system in 1847.

The fourth volume of the records of the New York African Free School contains penmanship and drawing studies by the students from 1816 to 1826, including this speech given by James McCune Smith in 1824 to mark the visit of the Marquis de Lafayette. Smith, who was born during New York's gradual emancipation, was an exceptionally bright student, and his being selected to address the visiting Revolutionary War hero was a great honor. Smith was freed in 1827 by New York's Emancipation Act, and went on to become the first African American to earn a medical degree. It was granted by the University of Glasgow after US medical schools refused to admit him. He returned to New York in 1837, opened the first Black-owned pharmacy in the United States, and became a prominent physician and abolitionist.

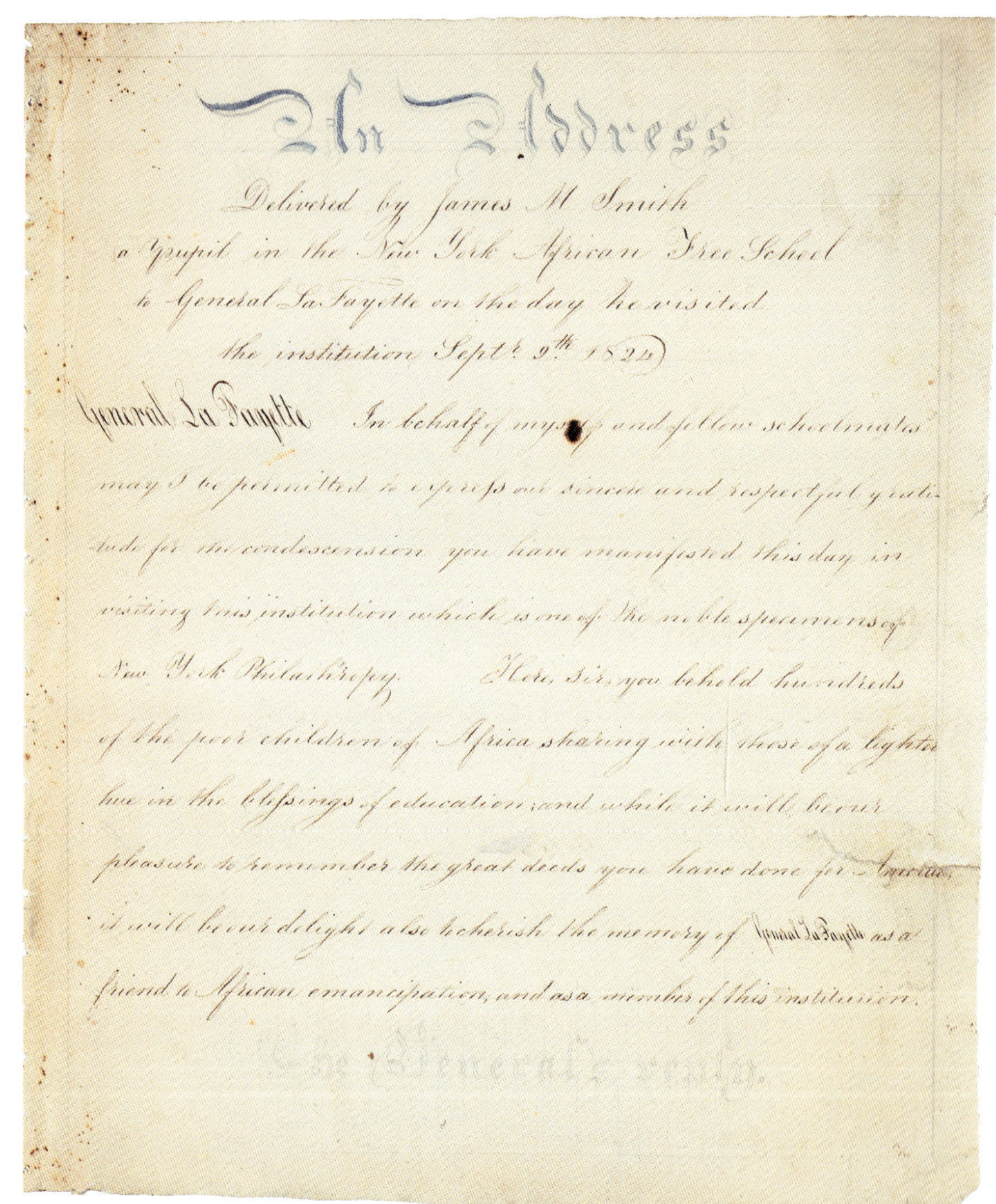

An Address

Delivered by James M Smith
a pupil in the New York African Free School
to General La Fayette on the day he visited
the institution Septr 9th 1824

General La Fayette In behalf of myself and fellow schoolmates may I be permitted to express our sincere and respectful gratitude for the condescension you have manifested this day in visiting this institution which is one of the noble specimens of New York Philanthropy. Here, Sir, you behold hundreds of the poor children of Africa sharing with those of a lighter hue in the blessings of education; and while it will be our pleasure to remember the great deeds you have done for America, it will be our delight also to cherish the memory of General La Fayette as a friend to African emancipation, and as a member of this institution.

141

HORACE GREELEY (1811–1872)

Letter to Henry David Thoreau (1817–1862), November 4, 1856

Washington, DC
Manuscript
Patricia D. Klingenstein Library,
The New York Historical

Henry David Thoreau is best remembered as a writer, but in 1838 he spent a brief time teaching in his hometown of Concord, Massachusetts. Unlike most other educators of his time, Thoreau eschewed corporal punishment, lectures, and rote memorization in favor of practical, hands-on experience and time spent in nature. The future resident of Walden Pond spent part of 1843 at Castleton, Staten Island, tutoring Ralph Waldo Emerson's nephew Willie, but he struggled to embrace New York City and returned to Concord after six months.

In 1856, Horace Greeley, editor and publisher of the *New-York Tribune*, wrote to Thoreau, asking if he would tutor two of his young children, then aged seven and five. By this time, Greeley was an extremely influential figure: the *Tribune*, which he founded in 1841 as a Whig newspaper, was nationally known for its political reporting, intellectual appeal, and reformist positions. A vocal opponent of slavery and an advocate for workers' rights, Greeley also published the work of Transcendentalist authors like Margaret Fuller and Ralph Waldo Emerson and served as Thoreau's literary agent.

Greeley's letter assured Thoreau that the Greeley house was miles from the crowded city, and that Thoreau's unconventional method of teaching would be welcome: "Mrs. Greeley thinks highly of you," Greeley wrote, "and sympathizes with your views more fully than I do." Nevertheless, Thoreau did not accept Greeley's offer of employment.

142

UNIDENTIFIED MAKER

Topsy-turvy doll, 1890–1905

Textile, paint
The New York Historical, Gift of Katharine Prentis Murphy, 1961.30

The hallmark of the topsy-turvy doll is that the two torsos are unified by a skirt that can be flipped, one over the other, creating the dolls' central design feature: the ability to obscure one side in order to play with the other. Although many surviving examples like this one were handmade, mass-manufactured examples proliferated during the early to mid-20th century. These were sometimes marketed as "Topsy and Eva" dolls, a reference to two characters from Harriet Beecher Stowe's famous anti-slavery novel *Uncle Tom's Cabin*: Topsy, an enslaved Black girl, and Eva, the daughter of her enslaver.

Objects in The New York Historical's collections reflect the time in which they were produced. Although collection items that depict or reflect hate, racism, discrimination, or stereotypes may be offensive and disturbing, they provide historical insights into the realities of daily life in New York and the nation.

143

UNIDENTIFIED MAKER

New York City public school door knob, 1905–25

Brass
The New York Historical, Gift of Marilynn Karp, in honor of Ivan C. Karp, 2020.22

Cast bronze door knobs like this example were common fixtures in New York City's public schools during the early 1900s. Little is known about their design or manufacture, but they may have been associated with an effort to expand and standardize the city-wide school system. Public schools in New York City had their origins in the African Free Schools and other charitable educational institutions, such as those run by the Free School Society, later called the Public School Society, which the Manumission Society turned the African Free Schools over to in 1834. In 1853, the society officially merged with the Board of Education. Central consolidation and expansion continued over the years. During the 1970s and '80s, as older schools were remodeled or closed, these knobs became collectible mementoes of city life. This brass knob, with its oval handle, dates to 1905–25, and was purchased by the donor in 1965.

144

LEWIS WICKES HINE (1874–1940)

Young Women Sewing, Italian School, James Memorial Building, 152–166 Hester Street, ca. 1928

Patricia D. Klingenstein Library, The New York Historical, Children's Aid Society Collection

The Children's Aid Society (CAS) was founded in February 1853 by a group of nine men including Protestant minister Charles Loring Brace, who became its secretary. At a time when unprecedented numbers of people were arriving in New York, the founders feared a strain on the city's resources; they also expressed concern that impoverished children were turning to crime or barely surviving as street sweepers, peddlers, or rag-pickers. Brace was particularly concerned about "poor, neglected, and ignorant" girls, who, he wrote, would "naturally and inevitably" become prostitutes. The CAS founders believed that education, gainful work, and a wholesome family atmosphere would transform New York's street children into self-reliant members of society.

The Children's Aid Society Collection fills over 1,000 archival boxes. It includes financial, legal, and real estate records; diaries and memoirs; documentation of the many different programs run by CAS, and thousands of photographs. These photographs depict children celebrating holidays at various lodging houses for homeless youths, playing at recreational clubs and camps, receiving medical and dental services, and studying at the CAS-operated industrial schools in disadvantaged neighborhoods across the city, from the Henrietta School on West 63rd Street in the Black neighborhood of San Juan Hill, to the Italian School on Hester Street in the Lower East Side.

Boys learned vocational skills such as woodworking, metalworking, shoe repair, typesetting, and hand-lettering, while girls learned sewing, hatmaking, laundering, and other domestic tasks. Such jobs conformed to middle-class expectations and values, but domestic work and the garment trades did not necessarily pay enough to keep girls housed, as the society's own records proved. Over half of the homeless young women who sought temporary lodging at the Elizabeth Home for Girls listed their occupations as "domestic," and many others were milliners or dressmakers.

145

UNIDENTIFIED MAKER

World War II student identification tag, ca. 1942

Bakelite
The New York Historical, Gift of Marilyn Sambol Moskowitz, 2011.12

During World War II, the safety of New York's students became the responsibility of New York schools. Principals and teachers received training in civilian defense and first aid; the Board of Education distributed emergency equipment to teachers; air raid drills became part of the classroom routine; and the School Defense Council arranged for public, private, and parochial school students to wear identification tags around their necks. By July 1942, 1,600,000 children had received tags, each bearing their name, date of birth, school district, and a serial number. This example was given to Marilyn Sambol Moskowitz (b. 1937), a student at Brooklyn's P.S. 225. Similar to the metal "dog tags" issued to soldiers, these student tags were meant to be worn in case of emergency or evacuation.

Students contributed to the war effort as well: for example, the government-sponsored High School Victory Corps trained teenagers for roles in the armed forces, merchant marine, and nursing corps. Even young children could collect cans or cooking grease for defense factories to convert into equipment and ammunition, grow vegetables in backyard victory gardens, or save up to buy defense bonds.

Frederick Kelly (1905–1999)
Willoughby's, New York, 1961
Gelatin silver print
Patricia D. Klingenstein Library,
The New York Historical

COMMERCE & INDUSTRY

146

LYDIA A. WALLACE-CHAVEZ (Unkechaug, Kainai Blackfoot, b. 1979) for Wampum Magic

Two Row wampum belt, 2022

Mastic, New York
Quahog, whelk (shells), hide
The New York Historical, Purchase, F.S. Ellis Fund, 2022.32.1

Wampum has long played an important role in Haudenosaunee culture. Created with purple and white beads made from quahog clam and whelk shells, wampum belts are physical representations of the laws accompanying agreements and discussions between nations. The Two Row wampum belt is a visual representation of the first agreement made in ca. 1613 in upstate New York between the Haudenosaunee and Dutch traders. An expression of mutual respect and cooperation, the Two Row's parallel lines of purple beads represent the two cultures traveling side by side in a spirit of peace, friendship, and non-interference. Algonquian peoples living along the Atlantic coast, like the Unkechaug, made wampum beads through a painstaking process of hand-drilling and traded them with their Haudenosaunee neighbors. The craft tradition remains alive today: Lydia Wallace-Chavez created this belt using the same tools and techniques as her Unkechaug ancestors.

147

British tax stamp, two shillings, sixpence, reign of George III, 1760–1820

Parchment fragment with tin strip (recto and verso)
Patricia D. Klingenstein Library, The New York Historical

In 1765, the British Parliament imposed the Stamp Act upon the North American colonies. The tax applied to pamphlets, almanacs, diplomas, newspapers, playing cards, and dice—but also documents such as deeds, wills, and clearance for ships. Without these, even the most routine commercial and legal transactions could not occur. Implementation and compliance with the Stamp Act was difficult and complicated: paper came in various sizes and prices, and different denominations of stamps were required for business transactions of varying value. The paper itself was manufactured in England and required payment in hard currency, which was in short supply.

Colonial newspapers, which were expected to absorb the stamp surcharge for both their folio paper and for each advertisement, whipped up the colonists' fury against the Stamp Act, resulting in a boycott so successful that few examples of tax stamps exist. The colonists' reaction to the Stamp Act and to the tax stamps themselves was at once a dress rehearsal for, and the opening episode of, the American Revolution.

recto

verso

148a–e

Artifacts from the Ear Inn, 1750–2000

Shell, glass, ceramic, metal, plastic
The New York Historical, Gift of Martin Sheridan and Richard Hayman and the Ear Inn, 2011.18c.6 [oyster shell], 2011.18s.3 [chamber pot fragment], 2011.18.11 [thimble], 2011.18s.6 [bottle neck], 2011.18.13 [guitar pick]

These objects were excavated from the backyard of the historic James Brown house at 326 Spring Street in Greenwich Village, now the home of the Ear Inn restaurant and pub. The building was constructed around 1817 and has since been continuously occupied as a mixed-use building, both residential and commercial. At various points, it may have been a tobacco shop, apothecary, speakeasy, boarding house, or brothel—though it now houses New York City's oldest continuously operating bar. Excavations in 2010 in the building's basement, including an area that was likely the site of a privy before the building was extended to cover the entire yard, yielded thousands of artifacts, from animal bones and oyster shells to bottle caps and cigar ends that shed light on the diets, habits, and daily life of previous owners and tenants. The bulk of the artifacts date to the mid- to late 19th century.

149

ABEL BUELL (1742–1825), diemaker
JAMES JARVIS (active 1786–ca. 1790), minter

Fugio cent, 1787

Copper
New Haven, Connecticut
The New York Historical, Gift of Albert C. Todaro, 2005.4.1

The first copper coins ever minted by the United States are named after the Latin inscription *fugio* on the obverse, which coupled with the sundial motif and the words "Mind your business" loosely translates to "Time flies, so attend to your business." The reverse bears a design of 13 chain links and the inscription "We Are One," referring to the newly united country. The motifs are associated with Benjamin Franklin, and appeared on the Continental paper currency issued during the Revolutionary War. These Fugio cents were minted in 1787, the year the Constitution was ratified, but they were never widely circulated because the unscrupulous minter, James Jarvis, made the coins underweight.

Under British rule, the colonists faced a constant shortage of specie: Britain limited the importation of gold and silver coins, and banned colonial production. British pence, Spanish *reales*, and Dutch *stuivers* circulated in North America, but British mercantile policies encouraged the flow of money into British coffers. Colonists therefore relied heavily on commodities as a medium of exchange, from beaver pelts to tobacco to wampum. After winning independence, the new US government confronted a monetary crisis: the Articles of Confederation permitted each state and the federal government to issue its own coinage, which led to an overwhelming flood of counterfeits. Under the Constitution, Congress retained the right to coin money, passing the Coinage Act and establishing the US Mint in 1792.

obverse

reverse

150

UNIDENTIFIED MAKER

Pewterers' banner, 1788

New York City
Painted silk
The New York Historical, Gift of James S. Haring, 1903.12; important support for conservation of the banner was provided by The Sherman Fairchild Foundation, the Greater Hudson Heritage Network, Jeff R. Bridgman American Antiques, Morris W. Offit, the Pewter Collectors Club of America, Dr. and Mrs. Donald M. Herr, Bette Wolf, the Dutch Pewter Society, Edward McManus, Diane Markunas, and Sylvia J. Sillers

This banner was carried by the Society of Pewterers of the City of New York in the Federal Procession of July 23, 1788, which celebrated the ratification of the Constitution of the United States. New York was a center of early pewter production, but British laws had made it difficult and costly to import tin and other necessary raw materials. Independence freed the American pewterers from these restrictions, which had been intended to discourage colonial manufacturers from competing with their British counterparts.

The ratification of the Constitution empowered President George Washington's first Treasury Secretary, Alexander Hamilton, to promote the development of American industry. Hamilton levied taxes on imported goods, encouraged the immigration of skilled artisans from Europe, and pressed for the federal government to invest in manufacturing. The inscription on the banner, which reads, in part, "All Art Shall Flourish in Columbia's Land," seems to anticipate Hamilton's economic program.

This object is one of the only banners known to have survived from the celebratory parades held in such cities as Baltimore, Charleston, Philadelphia, and Boston. It descended in the family of pewterer William J. Elsworth (1746–1814/1816), who presumably carried it during the New York procession.

151

JOHN WESLEY JARVIS (1780–1840)

Harmon Hendricks (1771–1838), ca. 1815–25

Oil on wood panel
The New York Historical, Gift of Ruth Hendricks Schulson, 2012.28.9

Harmon Hendricks was a prominent member of the Sephardic Jewish community in New York and a pioneer in the American copper industry. He began working in his father Uriah's business as an apprentice, becoming a partner in 1792 at age 20. Uriah had originally been a dry-goods merchant, but eventually specialized in importing iron and copper goods. Harmon grew especially interested in the metals trade and took over the family business after Uriah's death from yellow fever in 1798.

In the 1760s, the British Navy had discovered that cladding ships' hulls in sheets of copper protected them from wood-boring mollusks, leading to a surge in demand from shipwrights. However, with the outbreak of the Napoleonic Wars, British copper became difficult to procure. Realizing that a ready supply of copper was now a matter of national security, Hendricks shifted his focus from importing the metal to producing it himself, a decision that became all the more urgent with the British blockade of the American coast during the War of 1812. Hendricks worked with Paul Revere, Robert Fulton, and other American metalsmiths and manufacturers to find solutions for the shortage of quality copper. In 1814, he purchased the Soho Copper Works in Belleville, New Jersey, supplying not only the US Navy (which required 12,000 feet of copper sheathing for each of its six frigates) but the rest of the booming maritime industry, as well—including merchant vessels and commercial steamboats like Fulton's.

Later generations of Hendrickses would provide copper for new industries and products, from railroads to light bulbs to telegraph cables. The Patricia D. Klingenstein Library at The New York Historical holds over 250 years of Hendricks family records that illustrate the growth of this crucial American industry.

152

To Emigrants and Others. 100,000 Acres of Land for Sale

New York: Henry Ludwig, printer, 1837
Broadside
Patricia D. Klingenstein Library, The New York Historical

This advertisement, published in 1837 in English and in German, was written on behalf of a group of wealthy land buyers—businessmen, financiers, and bankers—and targeted towards "emigrants and others" seeking new lands in which to settle. It announced that the investors had just bought 400,000 acres of land from the Holland Land Company, and advertised the sale of 100,000 of those acres in the western New York counties of Genesee, Cattaraugus, and Allegany. The fact that this land had been expropriated from the Haudenosaunee over the course of many decades went unmentioned.

Instead, the broadside trumpeted the health and productivity of the land, and the presence of villages, schools, churches, and marketplaces. Yet the real selling point was the in-progress construction of the Genesee Valley Canal, which would eventually connect with the Erie Canal. The new landowners blithely assured readers that "public improvements," including railroads, would soon be built, and that Congress would act to improve access and navigation on the nearby Allegheny River—but the question of whether or not the federal government should subsidize such transportation projects was in fact one of the major political debates of the early 19th century.

It is likely that the new landowners hoped to flip the acreage for a substantial profit. However, 1837 marked the bursting of a real estate bubble and the start of a financial crisis that kicked off a multi-year economic downturn. The Panic of 1837 brought widespread hardship, poverty, homelessness, downward social mobility, and hunger; death and desertion broke up families. These economic woes were popularly understood to have been brought about by speculations in land, such as the one advertised here.

To Emigrants and Others.

100,000 Acres of Land

FOR SALE.

The Subscribers having recently purchased 400,000 Acres of Land of the Holland Land Co., situated in the counties of *Genesee*, *Cataraugus*, and *Alleghany*, in the south-westerly part of this State, now offer for sale, in lots to suit purchasers, 100,000 acres of the tract. This portion of the State is peculiarly healthy. The surface of the country is generally hilly, interspersed with valleys of deep and rich alluvion, and well watered with springs and streams. The soil is especially adapted to grazing, and yields bountifully of most kinds of grain usually cultivated in the western part of this State. The timber is various, consisting of Beech, Maple, Hickory, White and Black Oak, Chestnut, Cucumber, &c., and in many parts extensive groves of valuable White Pine.

The Genesee Valley Canal connecting with the Erie Canal at Rochester, and terminating at the Alleghany River, is now under construction by the State, which goes through a large portion of this tract. The New-York and Erie Rail-Road, which will be constructed at no very remote period, passes through these lands. The Alleghany River, already the channel of an important trade in Lumber, will this year be surveyed under a law of Congress, with reference to the improvement of the navigation to the Ohio and Mississippi.—These various public improvements present advantages for this section of the State which will facilitate the agricultural and mechanical improvements, and give free access to the best market for their surplus produce.

The counties in which these lands are situated are already inhabited by a large population, and contain numerous and flourishing villages, so that in most cases, settlers can have the advantages at once of schools and churches, and of easy access to convenient places for market and the transaction of business. The subscribers feel confident, that, taking into view healthfulness of climate, fertility of soil, easiness of access, and convenience to market, a combination of attractions are offered to settlers, which few portions of this country present.

For particulars inquire of NICHOLAS DEVEREUX, at Utica, or ASHER TYLER, Agent of the Proprietors at Ellicottville, Cataraugus Co.

NICHOLAS DEVEREUX, Utica,
GOOLD HOYT, 27, Park Place, New-York.
RUFUS L. LORD, Exchange Place, "
NEVINS, TOWNSEND & Co. 42, Wall-st. "
THOMAS SUFFERN, 71, Washington Square, "
WILLIAM KENT, 43, Liberty-street, "
CHARLES HOYT, 42, Pine-street, "
JAMES Mc BRIDE, 5, College Place, "
and others,
} *Proprietors.*

D. O. MACOMBER, Agent, No. 4, South-st. N. Y.

Distances from New-York to Ellicottville.

To Albany by Steamboat, 145 miles.—Fare, $1, and on Towboats, 50 cents.

To Rochester on the Erie Canal, 270 miles.—Fare, 2¼ cents per mile and found.

To York Landing on the Genesee River, 42 miles.—Fare, 25 cents.

To Ellicottville by wagons prepared for the purpose, 63 miles.—Fare, allowing 200 lbs baggage to each person, $2 12½ cents.

Whole expense for six persons from New-York to Ellicottville, (520 miles,) $57 72, or $9 62 cts., each. This includes board on the Canal. Children under 12 years of age, half-price.

At Rochester and at York Landing every arrangement is made for the forwarding of settlers without delay, and in the most economical and comfortable manner. Apply at *No. 4, South-st.* (Up-Stairs,) where every information will be given.

New-York, May, 1837.

Henry Ludwig, Printer, corner of Vesey and Greenwich-sts. N. Y.

153

UNIDENTIFIED HAUDENOSAUNEE ARTIST

Haudenosaunee beaded pincushion, 1890–1910

Possibly New York or Canada
Cotton, glass beads, linen, paper, metal paillettes, plant material
The New York Historical, Gift of Arnold and Dora Stern, 2017.53.1

In the early 1800s, Haudenosaunee (Iroquois) beadworkers began ornamenting pincushions, purses, picture frames, card holders, and keepsakes with multiple rows of glass beads sewed over velvet or wool to create a mounded effect. Haudenosaunee designs often feature flowers, leaves, and other woodland motifs, but this pincushion adds an eagle and two American flags, indicating that it was created for the souvenir market that sprang up around Niagara Falls in the latter half of the 19th century.

Niagara had long been an important site for fur traders, bringing Indigenous nations together and also attracting French *voyageurs*. Glass beads were among the commodities exchanged for animal pelts and hides, in addition to metal tools, European fabrics, and firearms. However, after the Revolutionary War, the 1784 Treaty of Fort Stanwix forced the Haudenosaunee to cede their interest in lands beyond their newly established reservation boundaries, which allowed a wave of non-Native settlers and speculators to steal, coerce, and forcefully appropriate much of the land around Niagara Falls. The completion of the Erie Canal in 1825 facilitated travel to the area; railroads followed in later decades, and Niagara was soon crowded with non-Native tourists eager to take in the stunning vistas.

Bounded by reservations that represented a tiny fraction of their original territory and largely unable to subsist via hunting, fishing, and trapping, Haudenosaunee beadworkers developed an important new source of income and a sophisticated business model to meet skyrocketing demand. Their exquisite work, blending Western materials, popular motifs, and Indigenous artistry, disproved widespread stereotypes that dismissed Indigenous people as "unskilled" and "uncivilized." This pincushion represents the survival and adaptive skill of Indigenous artistry within an international marketplace. Today, such pieces are highly sought after by collectors and institutions.

154

MCLOUGHLIN BROTHERS (1854–1921)

The Game of Playing Department Store, 1898

New York City
Cardboard, wood, paper
The New York Historical, The Liman Collection, 2000.715

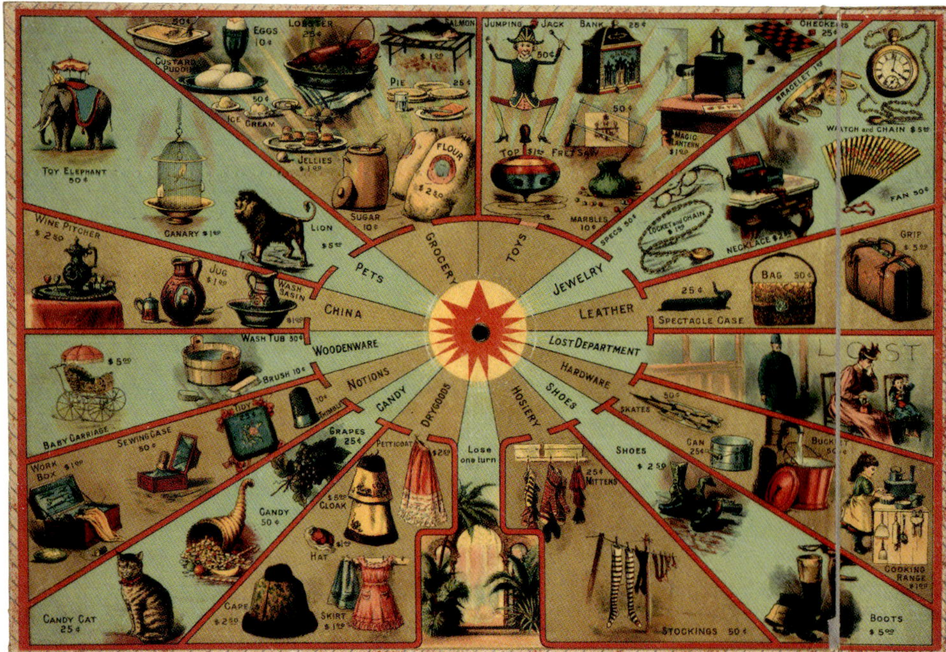

Years before Lizzie Magie created The Landlord's Game (later known as Monopoly, perhaps one of the most popular board games ever invented), a plethora of board games aimed to educate Americans about proper consumption habits. The Game of Playing Department Store was inspired by the growth of shopping emporiums selling a wide variety of goods under one roof. While the consumption of fashionable goods was seen by some as frivolous and immoral, department stores promoted themselves as respectable, middle-class spaces, providing an array of free services and social events for the city's growing middle class—especially women. Indeed, New York's renowned shopping district, along Broadway, Fifth, and Sixth Avenues between 15th and 24th Streets, was widely known as "The Ladies' Mile." The McLoughlin Brothers' game combined excitement for the dizzying array of newly available goods with the morality of restraint: it encouraged players to accumulate the greatest quantity of purchases while spending their money as economically as possible.

In the late 19th century, as work moved out of middle-class homes to factories and offices, the parlor became a space for families to spend their leisure time together. The growing demand for genteel entertainment, coupled with technological advancements in color lithography, fueled a robust market for board games, and New York City soon became a prominent center of board game manufacturing.

155

UNIDENTIFIED MAKER

Total sales today 16,388,700. Good night, October 29, 1929

New York City
Ticker tape
Patricia D. Klingenstein Library, The New York Historical

This is the closing ticker tape from the New York Stock Exchange on October 29, 1929: the infamous date of the stock market crash that signaled the beginning of the Great Depression. The tape listed the total sales from that day—16,388,700—followed by "Good night." Known as "Black Tuesday," October 29 kicked off the collapse of the US economy. By the fall of 1932, the Dow Jones Industrial Average, an important stock market index, lost 89 percent of its value. As Americans lost faith in their banking system, they began withdrawing their meager remaining funds en masse. "Bank runs," as they were dubbed, caused thousands of banks to shutter their doors; their coffers were emptied. As banks failed, so did businesses, leaving millions out of work. By March 1933, 30 percent of the US civilian labor force was unemployed, the highest percentage in American history.

TOTAL SALES TODAY 16.388.700. GOOD NIGHT OCT 29 1929

156

GREGG BARNES (b. 1965), designer
T.O. DEY (founded 1926), maker

Kinky Boots, ca. 2013

New York City
Patent, metallic, possibly alligator, and other leathers; rubber, textile, metal
The New York Historical, Gift of *Kinky Boots*, 2017.6ab

"The sex is in the heel / Fierce as you can make it / The sex is the appeal," sings Lola, the drag queen at the heart of the musical *Kinky Boots.* The hit Broadway show, created by New Yorkers Harvey Fierstein (who wrote the book) and pop singer Cyndi Lauper (music and lyrics), was inspired by the true story of a struggling shoe factory that survived by producing high-heeled fetish footwear built for men. Costume designer Gregg Barnes and custom shoemaker T.O. Dey created over 150 pairs of boots for the musical's 20 lead actors and chorus members, strong enough to endure a grueling eight-performance-a-week schedule. In 2018, *Playbill* reported that some of the boots made for the original Broadway company were still in use, more than five years later. This pair was worn by actor and dancer Kevin Smith Kirkwood.

In 2013, *Kinky Boots* was nominated for 13 Tony Awards, winning six, including Best Musical. Lauper won for Best Original Score, lead actor Billy Porter won Best Actor, and Barnes was nominated for Best Costume Design. The popularity of musicals like *Kinky Boots* has contributed significantly to the economic engine that is Broadway: the Department of Labor recently estimated that Broadway contributed well over $12 billion to the New York City economy, and generated over 12,000 direct jobs—many of them unionized—and over 74,000 indirect jobs in tourism and hospitality.

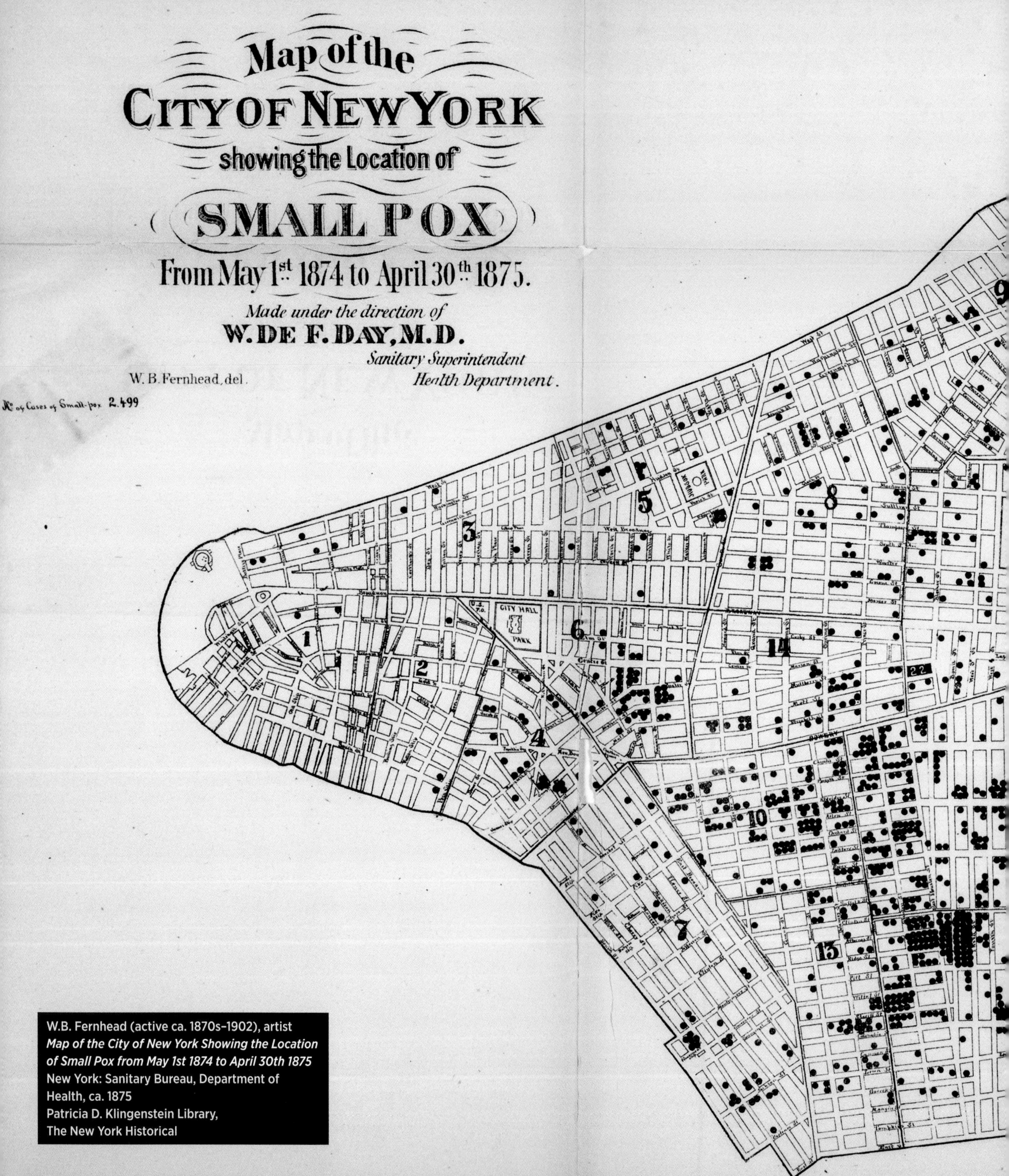

W.B. Fernhead (active ca. 1870s–1902), artist
Map of the City of New York Showing the Location of Small Pox from May 1st 1874 to April 30th 1875
New York: Sanitary Bureau, Department of Health, ca. 1875
Patricia D. Klingenstein Library, The New York Historical

HEALTH & MEDICINE

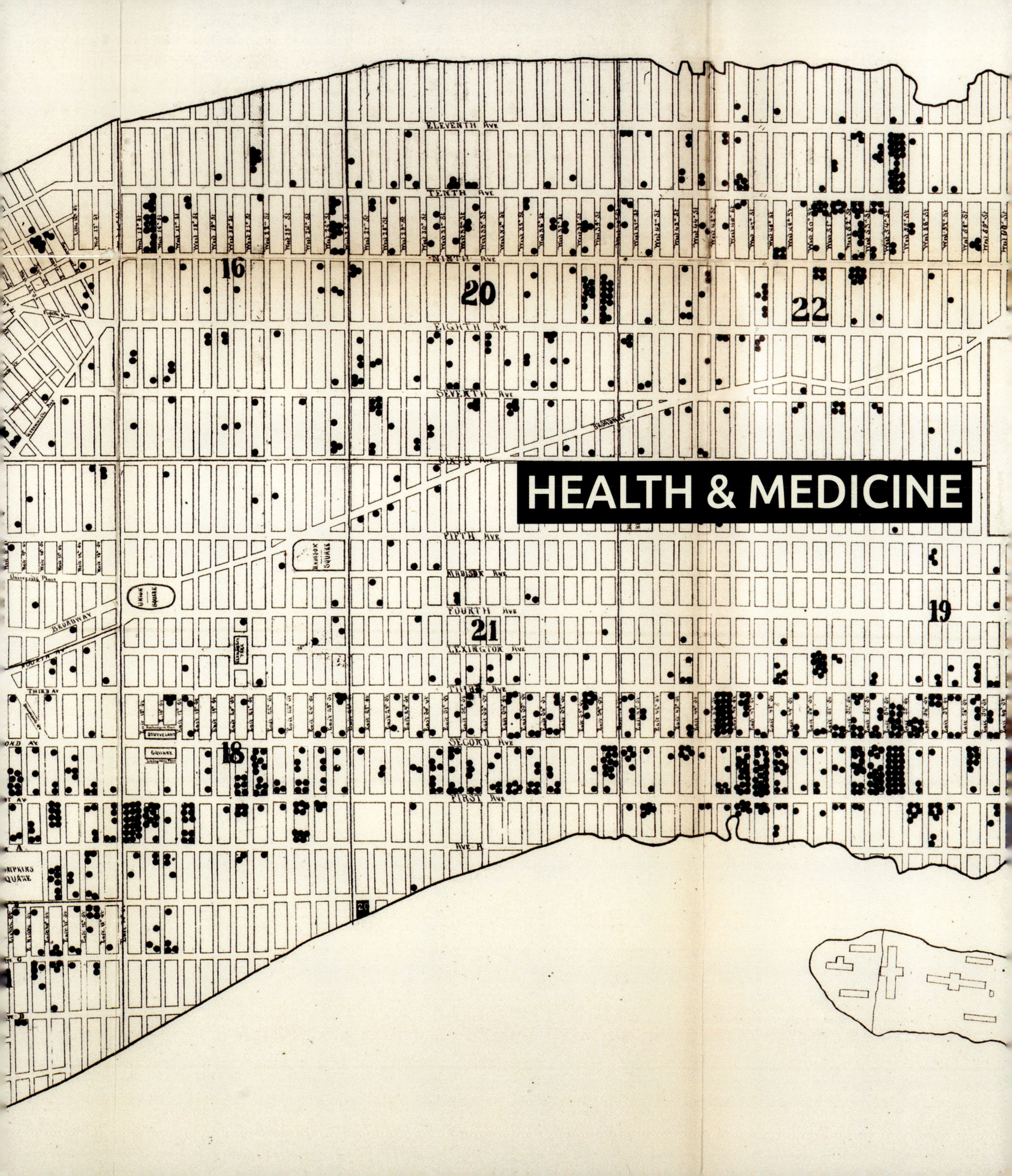

157

ALEXANDER ANDERSON (1775–1870)

"A Medical Grammar", ca. 1775

Manuscript
Patricia D. Klingenstein Library, The New York Historical

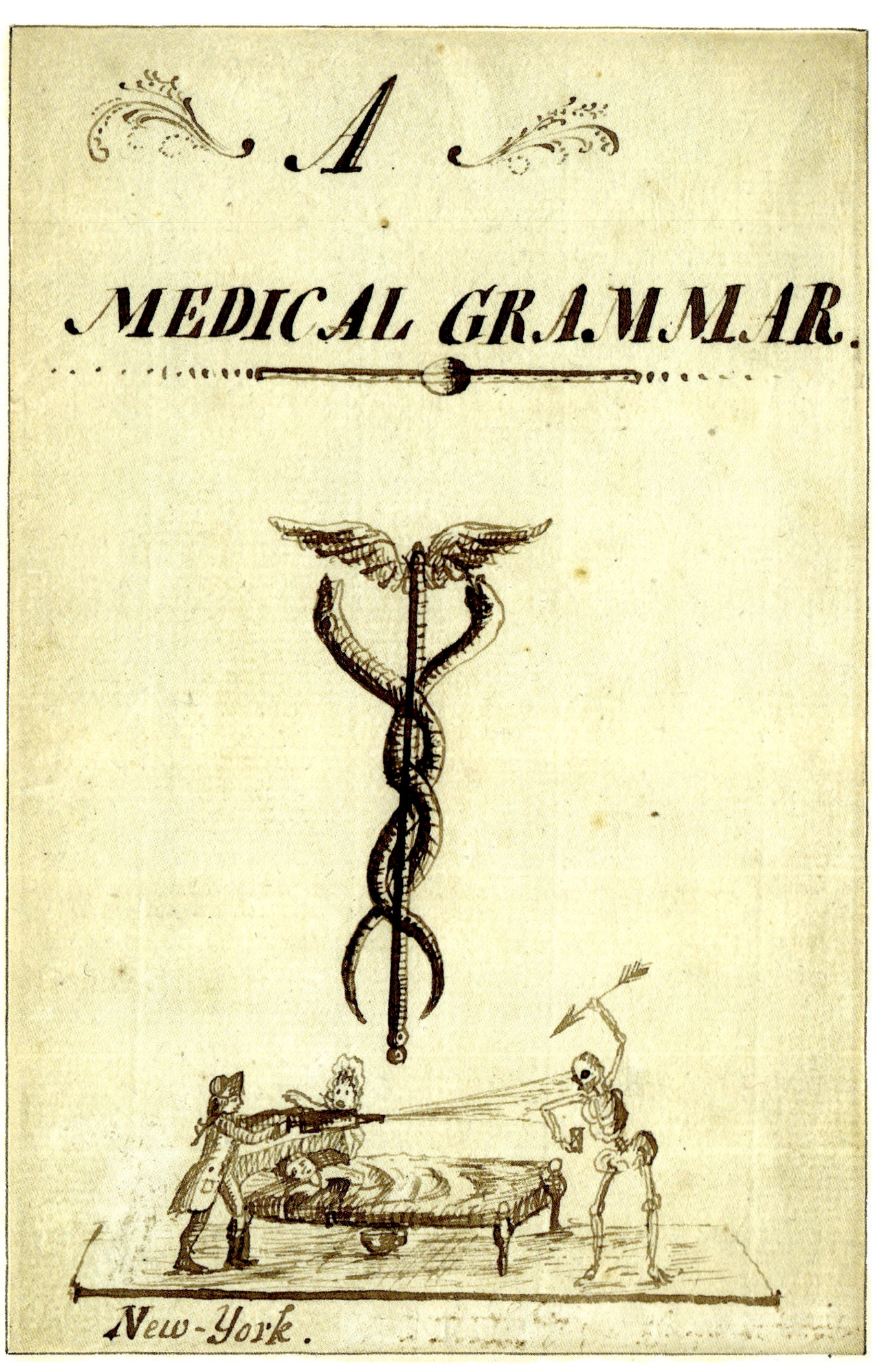

Alexander Anderson was a New York City physician and illustrator. He is known for being not only the first physician at Bellevue Hospital, established in 1795 to treat patients during a yellow fever epidemic, but also one of the first American wood engravers. This manuscript features three pen-and-ink drawings done by Dr. Anderson when he was 20 years old, relating to his medical practice and his interest in engraving: dramatic and humorous sketches of armed soldiers fighting back visages of illness and death with rifles and pistols. "A Medical Grammar" is a basic and short treatise of medical science and surgery, as understood in the 1790s. One might imagine Anderson intended it to be a helpful resource for his studies.

158

UNIDENTIFIED MAKER

Medicine box, 1820–70

London, England
Metal
The New York Historical, Z.1508

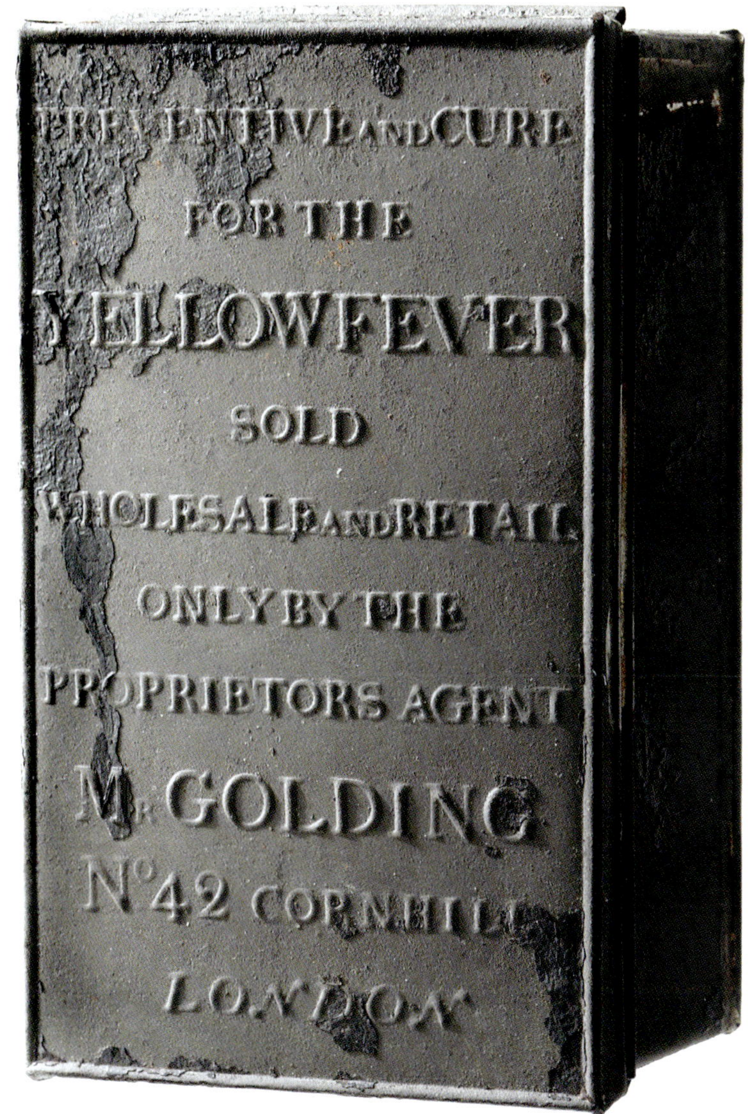

This box originally contained medicine that claimed to prevent and cure yellow fever, one of the deadliest infectious diseases of the 18th and 19th centuries, which kills by causing internal and external hemorrhage. Unfortunately for patients, the "treatments" for yellow fever involved bloodletting and "medicines" such as calomel (mercury chloride), which were useless at best and poisonous at worst. Doctors did not learn how to prevent yellow fever until 1937, and there is no cure even today.

Perhaps as early as 1668, before it even had a name, a "fatal epidemic" of what most historians believe was yellow fever swept through New York City. The first undisputed outbreak of yellow fever raged in Charleston and Philadelphia in 1699, prompting Pennsylvania to pass the first quarantine law in the colonies in the following year. Thereafter, throughout the 18th century, there were frequent epidemics of yellow fever in America, including no less than ten in New York City alone.

The New York City Board of Health was founded in response to an outbreak in 1805, and was empowered to evacuate areas where infection was widespread, and to quarantine patients. Because doctors did not realize that yellow fever was transmitted by mosquitoes, impoverished New Yorkers and recent immigrants, crowded together in unsanitary conditions, were often blamed for spreading the disease.

Fig. 35
John Henri Isaac Browere (1798–1834)
David Hosack, MD (1769–1835), ca. 1825–30
Painted plaster
The New York Historical, Gift of Dr. John W. Francis, 1832.2

A native New Yorker, David Hosack was a noted physician and one of the city's most prominent citizens. As a young doctor, he distinguished himself during the yellow fever epidemic of 1797–98, and he was the attending physician at the duel between Aaron Burr and Alexander Hamilton. He was a biographer and historian as well as a founder and the fourth president of The New York Historical.

159

CALEB S. WOODHULL (1792–1866), mayor of New York
JAMES KELLY, chairman of the Sanatory [*sic*] Committee

Notice. Preventives of Cholera! Published by Order of the Sanatory Committee, under the Sanction of the Medical Counsel [sic]

New York: unknown printer, 1849
Broadside
Patricia D. Klingenstein Library, The New York Historical

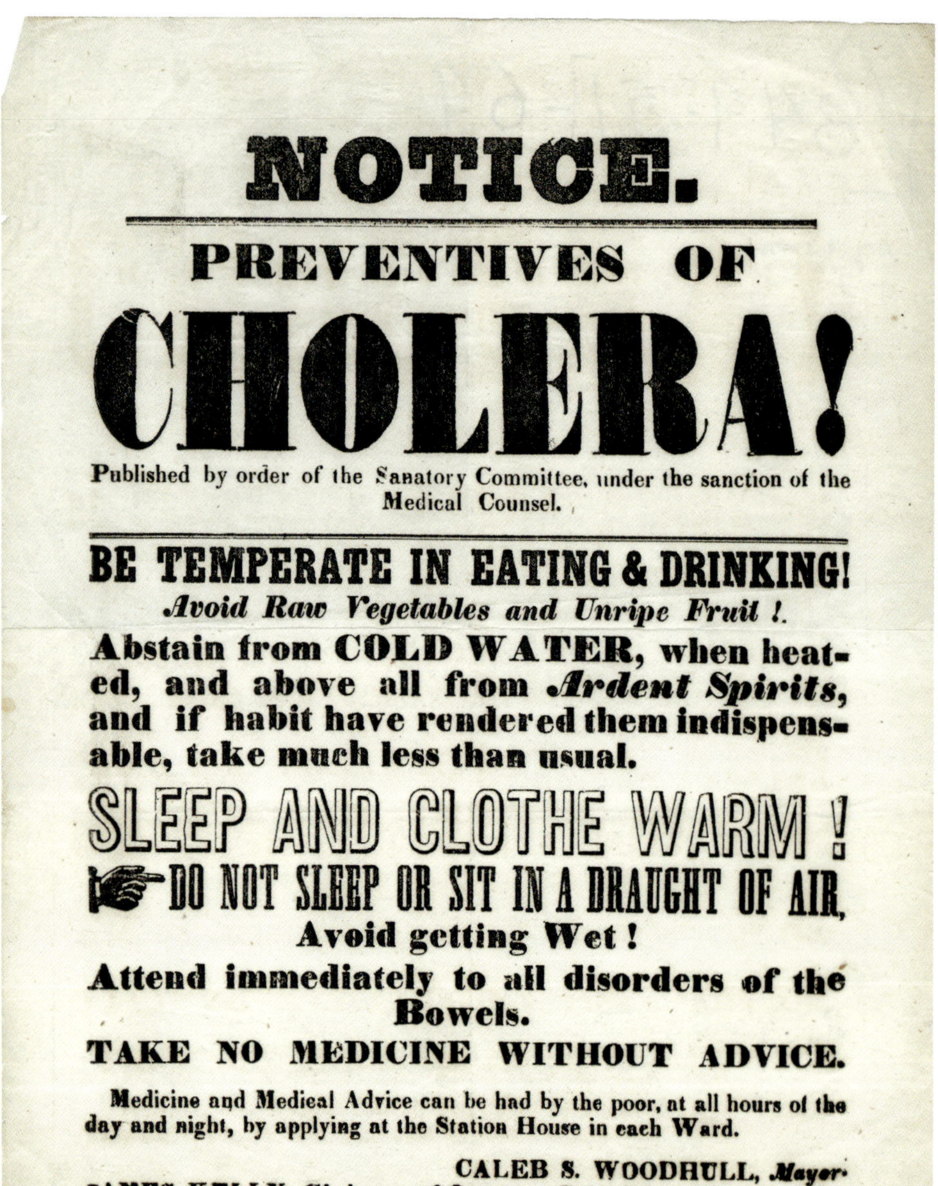
NOTICE.

PREVENTIVES OF

CHOLERA!

Published by order of the Sanatory Committee, under the sanction of the Medical Counsel.

BE TEMPERATE IN EATING & DRINKING!

Avoid Raw Vegetables and Unripe Fruit !.

Abstain from COLD WATER, when heated, and above all from *Ardent Spirits*, and if habit have rendered them indispensable, take much less than usual.

SLEEP AND CLOTHE WARM !

DO NOT SLEEP OR SIT IN A DRAUGHT OF AIR,

Avoid getting Wet !

Attend immediately to all disorders of the Bowels.

TAKE NO MEDICINE WITHOUT ADVICE.

Medicine and Medical Advice can be had by the poor, at all hours of the day and night, by applying at the Station House in each Ward.

CALEB S. WOODHULL, *Mayor.*
JAMES KELLY, *Chairman of Sanatory Committee.*

Likely relating to New York's cholera epidemic of 1849, this broadside advising prevention of cholera was signed by Caleb S. Woodhull, mayor of New York from 1849 to 1851, and James Kelly, the chairman of the Sanitary Committee. Directives from physicians and boards of health circulated widely, but such public service announcements were often speculative, misleading, or simply wrong.

Until the mid-19th century, health professionals did not know that cholera was caused by the consumption of contaminated food and water. Ships could spread outbreaks of cholera worldwide, and, as a major port, New York saw devastating cholera epidemics in 1832, 1849, and 1854. In response, the city began implementing sanitary measures to contain the disease. These included disinfecting homes and privies, clearing streets and vacant lots of manure, and, most importantly, constructing miles upon miles of sewers.

S/S Chalmette

CERTIFICATE OF PROTECTION FROM SMALLPOX

Havana, CUBA, JUL 18 1902, 1901

This is to certify that ......
a native of ......, going to ......,
age ......, color ......, sex ......, has produced satisfactory
evidence to me that ...... is protected from smallpox by ......
successful vaccination ......, revaccination ......, or vaccination on this
date, or a previous attack of the disease, and that ...... is in good health at
the present time.

Baggage to be at ...... by ...... m. day ...... sailing.

PERSONAL DESCRIPTION.

Height,
Weight,
Bald, or partly bald.
Hair, straight, curly,
Moustache,
Chin beard,
Side whiskers,
Eyes,
Form,

John Donaldson.
Signature for identification.

Surgeon, U. S. M. H. S.

160

US MARINE HOSPITAL SERVICE (founded 1798)

Certificate of protection from smallpox, 1901–02

Printed with manuscript annotations
Patricia D. Klingenstein Library, The New York Historical, Bella C. Landauer Collection

For at least 3,000 years, smallpox—a highly contagious, disfiguring, and often lethal disease—swept through urban and rural communities alike in terrifying epidemics. Among populations with exposure and immunity to the variola virus, smallpox regularly killed one-third of those infected, but when European colonists brought smallpox to the Western Hemisphere, "virgin soil" outbreaks among Native American nations sometimes reached mortality rates of 90 percent. There was no cure for smallpox, and for centuries the only way to contain an outbreak was to quarantine anyone exposed. However, variola carried within itself the seeds of its own destruction: people who survived smallpox seldom suffered from it again, nor could they transmit it to others. In the early 18th century, Europeans learned how to induce a mild case of smallpox by transferring a small amount of pus from an infected person to a small incision in the skin of a healthy person. This practice, called inoculation or variolation, was already known in China, India, parts of Africa, and present-day Turkey; it was soon transmitted to Britain's American colonies. Cotton Mather, Benjamin Franklin, Thomas Jefferson, and George Washington were all proponents of the procedure.

In 1796, British physician Edward Jenner demonstrated that exposure to the much less virulent cowpox virus conferred immunity against smallpox. This new procedure, known as vaccination, was widely adopted by public health officials: vaccines were mandated for schoolchildren and military personnel, and travelers were required to carry proof of vaccination, such as the certificate pictured here. After World War II, the newly formed World Health Organization (WHO) embarked upon a global campaign to eradicate smallpox. In 1980, WHO declared victory, marking a major milestone in global health.

161

SHEPARD & DUDLEY (ca. 1870–94), manufacturers

Medical kit owned by Dr. Grace Louise Merritt Vicario (1865–1945), ca. 1888–94

New York
Metal, leather, cotton
The New York Historical, Gift of the Jagger Merritt Vicario Family, 2019.10a-r

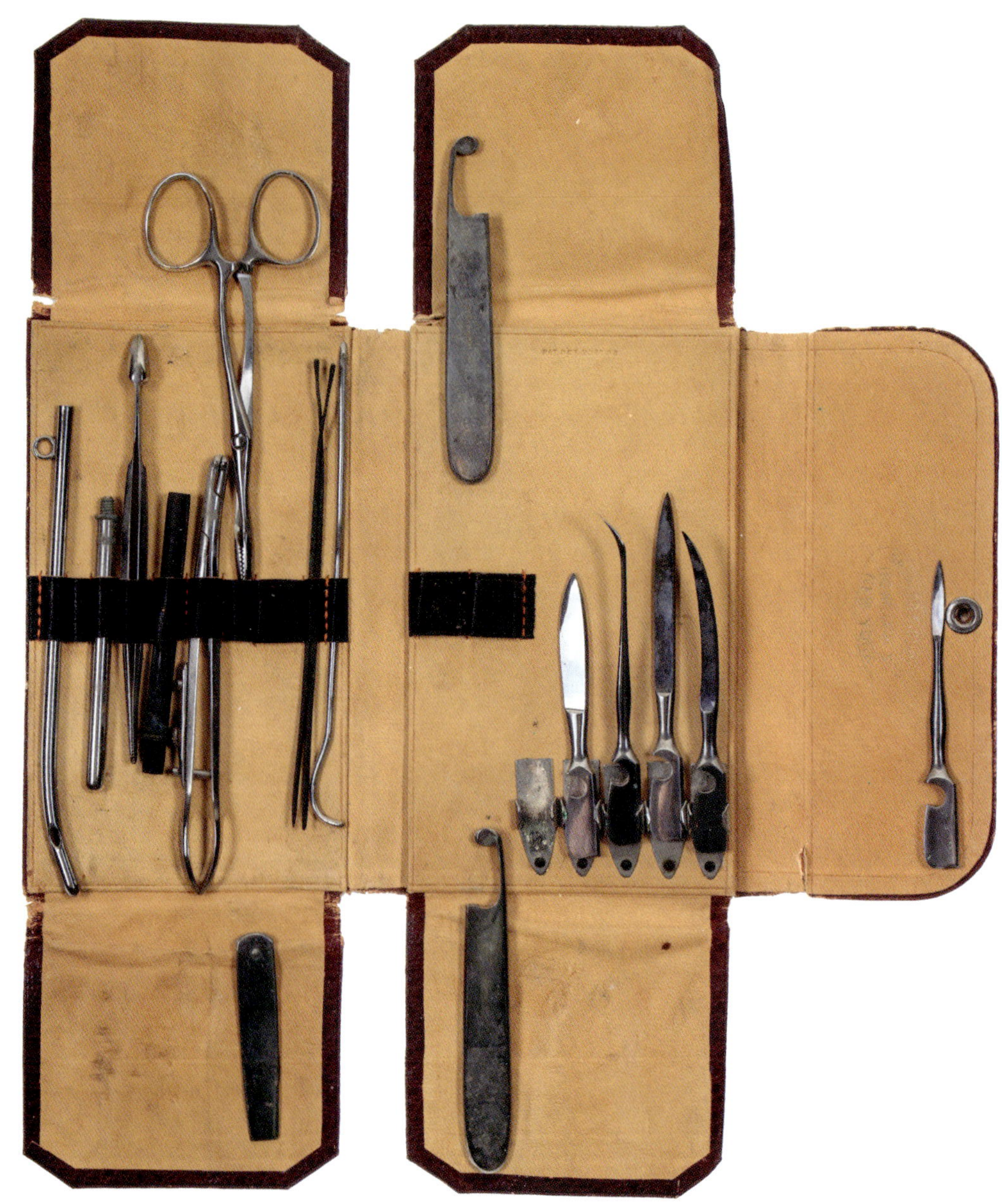

This kit belonged to Dr. Grace Louise Merritt Vicario, an 1892 graduate of the Woman's Medical College of the New York Infirmary for Women and Children. It was founded by Elizabeth Blackwell, who in 1849 became the first woman to receive an MD from a US medical school. She opened her hospital for impoverished New Yorkers in 1857, and in 1868 the affiliated Woman's Medical College accepted its first 15 students. One of the central goals of the college was to give poor women the opportunity to consult "a physician of their own sex," a unique mission that prioritized the training of women nurses and doctors to address hygiene and health among the families packed into New York City's crowded tenements. As more medical schools around the country began to embrace coeducation, the Woman's Medical College closed in 1899, and the New York Infirmary for Women and Children became part of what is now New York-Presbyterian Hospital.

Until the late 19th century, surgical tool handles were made of materials like wood, composite, horn, or ivory, and were set in velvet-lined, mahogany cases. With advances in surgical knowledge on bacterial infection—namely, the transfer of bacteria through contact—the medical field began to focus on aseptic techniques. Twentieth-century tool manufacturers transitioned to materials that supported the creation of a sterile environment and could withstand steaming or antiseptic solutions.

162

UNIDENTIFIED MAKER

Calf brace worn by Franklin D. Roosevelt (1882–1945), ca. 1940

United States
Leather, steel
The New York Historical, Purchase, 2002.76

This lower-leg brace was one of many used by Franklin Delano Roosevelt. Born into an affluent and politically well-connected family in Hyde Park, New York, he contracted polio in 1921, when he was 39 years old. Polio is a highly infectious disease that affects the nervous system and can result in permanent paralysis or death. Epidemics were frequent, and, by the mid-20th century, the virus killed or paralyzed half a million individuals per year. Despite paralysis of both legs, FDR was determined to walk again and sought out numerous cures, from mineral baths to braces. Heavy steel braces allowed him to walk short distances, and lower-leg braces helped to prevent atrophy of his leg muscles. This calf brace came from the estate of Roosevelt's White House secretary, Grace Tully.

First elected to the presidency in 1932, Roosevelt is the only president to serve more than two terms. He is remembered for leading the US through the Great Depression and World War II, for his wife Eleanor's humanitarian efforts, and for promulgating the New Deal—which expanded the federal government's power and responsibilities towards its citizens with programs such as Social Security and laws like the Fair Labor Standard Act. Roosevelt, the only physically disabled US president, was also the founder of the National Foundation for Infantile Paralysis (now known as the March of Dimes).

It was not until the 1950s, when Jonas Salk introduced the first successful polio vaccine, that the number of polio cases worldwide went from tens of thousands per year to hundreds. Polio was even eradicated in New York State in 1979—but in 2022, amid increased skepticism and misinformation about the efficacy of vaccines, it reappeared.

163

SILENCE = DEATH COLLECTIVE (founded 1986), designers

ACT UP stickers, ca. 1987–2000

Paper
The New York Historical, Bella C. Landauer Collection, 2002.1.1547

The spread of HIV/AIDS was first clinically observed in 1981, after an unprecedented number of gay men in New York and California sought treatment for a rare lung infection and rare form of skin cancer. The media originally dubbed the syndrome GRID (gay-related immune deficiency), blamed the epidemic on sexual "deviancy," and circulated misinformation about how the disease spread. Many people—even medical professionals—refused to touch a person with HIV/AIDS, share kisses, food, or even the same bathroom. As a result, people with HIV/AIDS often found themselves isolated and stigmatized. By 1989, more than 27,000 people had died of complications from AIDS, and, until the mid-1990s, there was no effective treatment.

The epidemic catalyzed a mass movement of AIDS advocacy and the formation of many activist groups. One such organization was AIDS Coalition to Unleash Power, or ACT UP. Founded in New York in 1987 after a fiery call to action by playwright Larry Kramer, the group used dramatic demonstrations and "zaps" to pressure pharmaceutical companies, the FDA, and public officials to accelerate their response to the AIDS crisis. They deployed a pink triangle graphic, a historical reference to the symbol that identified gay prisoners in Nazi concentration camps, and the unforgettable slogan, SILENCE=DEATH.

164

TIM OKAMURA (b. 1968)

Nurse Tracey, 2021

Oil on linen
The New York Historical, Purchased through the generosity of Susan and Robert Klein, 2020.33

Nurse Tracey belongs to a larger portrait series of essential workers laboring on the front lines of the coronavirus pandemic. The series was inspired by contemporary Canadian-born artist Tim Okamura's own bout with COVID-19 during the height of the outbreak in New York in the spring of 2020, and it features doctors and nurses from Manhattan and Brooklyn hospitals. This portrait, which recalls the inspirational "We Can Do It!" poster from World War II, replaces the iconic factory worker with Tracey-Ann Knight, DNP, RN—a woman originally from Jamaica, who now works as nurse manager at NYU Langone Health in Brooklyn. Its focus on a woman of color brings to the fore the racial dimensions of the pandemic—both the large number of people of color who risked their lives to fight the disease and its disproportionate toll on communities of color.

Janssen Pharmaceuticals of Johnson & Johnson developed the first single-shot vaccine to receive FDA emergency use authorization for preventing COVID-19. One of the first doses in the nation, drawn from this vial, was given on March 3, 2021, to a volunteer patient at Northwell Health's South Shore University Hospital in Bay Shore, Long Island.

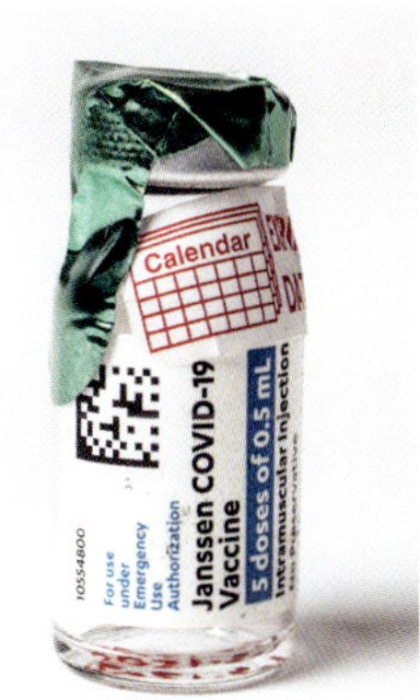

Fig. 36
Janssen Pharmaceuticals of Johnson & Johnson (founded 1953)
First administered Johnson & Johnson COVID-19 vaccine vial, 2021
Glass, plastic, foil, paper
The New York Historical, Gift of Northwell Health, 2021.2.1

STEINBERG
65

INDEX

Page numbers in *italics* refer to the illustrations

Opposite:
Saul Steinberg (1914–1999)
Landscapes with Palaces, 1965
Acrylic paint, watercolor, colored pencils, crayon, black ink, and rubber stamps on paper
Promised gift of Elie and Sarah Hirschfeld, Scenes of New York City, IL2021.51.89

HISTORIA

LOS ACONTECIMIENTOS QUE CAMBIARON EL MUNDO

AÑO A AÑO

HISTORIA

LOS ACONTECIMIENTOS QUE CAMBIARON EL MUNDO

AÑO A AÑO

SEGUNDA EDICIÓN

Edición de arte
Sharon Spencer

Edición
Annie Moss

Coordinación de arte
Michael Duffy

Coordinación editorial
Angeles Gavira y Rohan Sinha

Diseño de cubiertas
Suhita Dharamjit

Coordinación de cubiertas
Priyanka Sharma

Desarrollo de cubiertas
Sophia MTT

Edición de cubiertas
Saloni Talwar

Coordinación de maquetación
Vishal Bhatia

Preproducción y producción
Gillian Reid

Diseño de maqueta
Anita Yadav

Coordinación de producción
Andy Hilliard

Dirección de arte
Karen Self

Subdirección de publicaciones
Liz Wheeler

Dirección de publicaciones
Jonathan Metcalf

Una producción de Dynamo Limited para DK
Cathedral Court, Southernhay E, Exeter, EX1 1AF

Publicado originalmente en Gran Bretaña en 2011 por Dorling Kindersley Limited
DK, One Embassy Gardens, 8 Viaduct Gardens, London, SW11 7B

Parte de Penguin Random House

Título original: *History Year by Year*
Segunda edición 2024

ISBN: 978-0-5938-4808-1

Impreso en Emiratos Árabes Unidos

www.dkespañol.com

PRIMERA EDICIÓN

Edición de arte
Sudakshina Basu, Balwant Singh y Ina Stradins

Coordinación editorial
Soma B. Chowdhury, Peter Frances, Angeles Gavira y Janet Mohun

Edición de arte de proyecto
Paul Drislane, Alison Gardner, Anna Hall y Francis Wong

Edición de proyecto
Lara Maiklem, Ruth O'Rourke-Jones, Peter Preston y David Summers

Diseño
Mini Dhawan, Riccie Janus, Fiona Macdonald, Anjana Nair, Pallavi Narain y Duncan Turner

Edición
Rahul Ganguly, Corinne Masciocchi, Lizzie Munsey, Martyn Page, Laura Palosuo, Gill Pitts, Steve Setford, Nikki Simms, Alison Sturgeon, Miezan van Zyl, Laura Wheadon y Victoria Wiggins

Asistentes de diseño
Showmik Chakraborty, Arushi Nayar, Neha Sharma y Pooja Verma

Asistentes de edición
Sudeshna Dasgupta, Sam Priddy y Himanshi Sharma

Coordinación de producción
Mandy Inness

Producción editorial
Ben Marcus

Apoyo técnico creativo
Adam Brackenbury

Índice temático
Hilary Bird

Iconografía
Ria Jones y Liz Moore

Coordinación de edición de arte
Michelle Baxter y Arunesh Talapatra

Diseño de cubierta
Mark Cavanagh

Dirección de maquetación
Balwant Singh

Cartografía
Encompass Graphics Limited

Dirección de producción
Pankaj Sharma

Dirección editorial
Sarah Larter y Rohan Sinha

Diseño de maqueta
Rajesh Singh Adhikari, Shankar Prasad, Arjinder Singh y Tanveer Abbas Zaidi

Dirección de arte
Phil Ormerod

Dirección de publicaciones
Jonathan Metcalf

Coordinación de diseño de maqueta
Dheeraj Arora y Jagtar Singh

SMITHSONIAN INSTITUTION

Coordinación de proyecto
Ellen Nanney

DE LA EDICIÓN EN ESPAÑOL

Servicios editoriales
deleatur, s.l.

Coordinación de proyecto
Marina Alcione

Traducción
Montserrat Asensio, Antón Corriente, Gemma Deza y José Luis López Angón

Dirección editorial
Elsa Vicente

Este libro se ha impreso con papel certificado por el Forest Stewardship Council™ como parte del compromiso de DK por un futuro sostenible.
Para más información, visita www.dk.com/our-green-pledge.

COLABORADORES

ORÍGENES HUMANOS
Fiona Coward
Investigadora de la Royal Holloway University de Londres; colaboró en la obra *Prehistoria*, de DK.
Texto adicional de Jane McIntosh

PRIMERAS CIVILIZACIONES
Jen Green
Autora de más de 250 libros sobre diversos temas, desde historia y geografía hasta naturaleza y medio ambiente.
Texto adicional de Jane McIntosh

LA ÉPOCA CLÁSICA
Philip Parker
Historiador y escritor; entre sus obras destacan *The Empire Stops Here* e *Historia del mundo*, de DK.

COMERCIO E INVENCIONES
Joel Levy
Escritor especializado en historia e historia de la ciencia; autor de *Lost Cities* y *Lost Histories*, entre otras obras.

REFORMA Y EXPLORACIÓN
Thomas Cussans
Escritor y colaborador del diario *The Times*; ha escrito para DK *Timelines of World History* e *Historia*.
Texto adicional de Frank Ritter

LA ERA DE LAS REVOLUCIONES
Carrie Gibson
Escritora y colaboradora de los diarios *The Guardian* y *The Observer*, es doctorada en historia de los siglos XVIII y XIX por la Universidad de Cambridge (RU).

TECNOLOGÍA Y SUPERPOTENCIAS
R.G. Grant
Escritor de historia con más de veinte libros publicados, entre los que figuran *Batalla*, *Soldado* e *Historia*, de DK.

Sally Regan
Colaboradora de varias obras de DK, como *Historia*, *La Segunda Guerra Mundial* y *Ciencia*; documentalista premiada entre cuyos films destacan *Shell Shock* y *Bomber Command* para Channel 4.

GLOSARIO
Richard Beatty

ASESORES

Jane McIntosh
8 MA–700 a. C.
Profesora de la Facultad de Estudios Asiáticos y de Oriente Medio de la Universidad de Cambridge (RU).

Neville Morley
700 a. C.–599 d. C.
Profesor de Historia Antigua en la Facultad de Humanidades de la Universidad de Bristol (RU).

Roger Collins
600–1449
Profesor honorario de la Facultad de Historia, Cultura Clásica y Arqueología de la Universidad de Edimburgo (RU).

David Parrott
1450–1749
Profesor de Historia y lector del New College de la Universidad de Oxford (RU).

Michael Broers
1750–1913
Profesor y tutor del Lady Margaret Hall College de la Universidad de Oxford (RU).

Richard Overy
1914–ACTUALIDAD
Profesor de Historia de la Universidad de Exeter (RU).

SMITHSONIAN

Los colaboradores de este organismo son historiadores y profesionales especializados de los siguientes museos:

Museo Nacional del Aire y el Espacio
Este museo de la Smithsonian Institution es uno de los más populares del mundo. Su propósito es instruir y estimular a sus visitantes mediante la conservación y exhibición de artefactos aeronáuticos y espaciales.

Museo Nacional de Historia Estadounidense
Este museo de la Smithsonian Institution dedica sus colecciones y becas a fomentar el conocimiento de la nación y de sus numerosos pueblos.

Museo Nacional de Historia Natural
Este museo es el más visitado del mundo de su clase y el que más público atrae del complejo museístico de la Smithsonian Institution.

CONTENIDO

Introducción

Como le sucede a mucha gente, mi entusiasmo inicial por la historia se concentraba en fechas y sucesos: 1815 y Waterloo; 1588 y la derrota de la Armada Invencible; la caída de Constantinopla en 1453... Algunas tenían connotaciones personales: el 1 de julio de 1916, mi abuelo, sirviendo como artillero, perdió a muchos de sus mejores amigos en el primer día de la batalla del Somme.

Desde su comienzo, la historia fue moldeada como una grandiosa crónica de acontecimientos y acciones, obra a menudo de protagonistas heroicos, y destinada a cautivar la imaginación al estilo de una novela épica. Pero a lo largo del siglo XX creció entre los historiadores el escepticismo hacia la «historia del hecho». Lo habitual era que esos hechos fueran batallas, tratados y conflictos políticos; una narración que excluía las vidas de la mayoría de los hombres, mujeres y niños. Como reacción, los historiadores se centraron en las continuidades culturales, sociales y económicas, buscando sus pistas en los objetos cotidianos, los registros comerciales, y en los relatos de niños y ancianos. El resultado fue, ciertamente, una narración más rica y diversa sobre la experiencia humana, pero que a menudo eliminaba la percepción del cambio a lo largo del tiempo.

Este libro muestra que la historia construida sobre una cronología no tiene por qué ser un simple recuento de guerras y conquistas, de tratados y traiciones. Todo ello está presente aquí, pero también están las fechas de las innovaciones intelectuales y tecnológicas, la creación de obras de arte clave, los cambios cruciales en la estructura de la agricultura, la exploración y el comercio. Se trata de una estimulante y detallada narración de la creatividad humana, así como de su aterradora capacidad destructora; de descubrimientos y conocimientos tanto como de desastres naturales e insensatez humana. Profusamente ilustrados y sucintamente explicados, los acontecimientos clave de la historia, desde el inicio mismo de la agricultura hasta los últimos descubrimientos en astrofísica, son presentados en la que probablemente sea la más exhaustiva cronología recopilada hasta la fecha.

La contribución de este libro a la comprensión de la historia global ha sido tan excitante para mí como ayudar a elaborarlo y escoger entre todos los aspectos de la historia de la humanidad para componer esta cronología. A lo largo de *Historia año a año*, los diversos acontecimientos, descubrimientos y logros sucedidos en Europa y América del Norte se ofrecen enfrentados a sucesos igualmente trascendentales en Oriente Próximo, Asia, África, América del Sur o el Pacífico. Es una historia que estimula la percepción de un mundo más amplio al ubicar lado a lado los sucesos de todo el mundo, y al recordarnos que descubrimientos y progreso, logros de organización social y desafíos al poder establecido no son monopolio del mundo occidental, sino que son tan probables en India o Egipto como en Francia y España.

El diseño de este libro ofrece una oportunidad única de poder apreciar una historia global de la humanidad en todas sus facetas. Espero que el lector disfrute tanto leyéndolo y usándolo de fuente de referencia como yo he disfrutado planificándolo y escribiéndolo.

DAVID PARROTT
Universidad de Oxford

La última ciudad de los incas
Encaramada a 2430 m sobre el nivel del mar, en los Andes peruanos, la ciudadela inca de Machu Picchu fue construida probablemente en el siglo XV, y abandonada en el XVI.

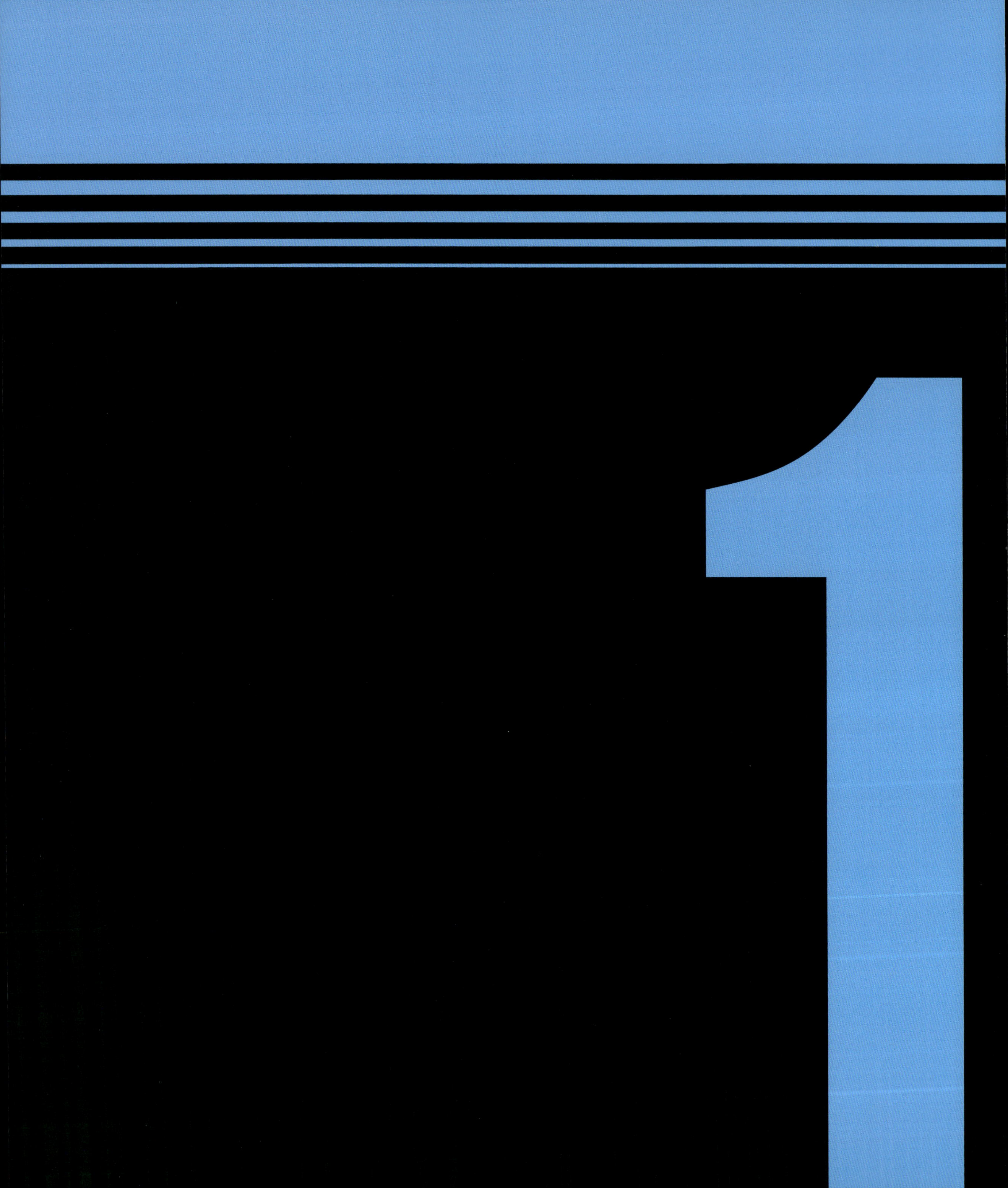

ORÍGENES HUMANOS

8 MA–3000 a.C.

8–4,5 MA

4,5–2 MA

2–1,8 MA

1,8–1,6 MA

La garganta de Olduvai (Tanzania) es un área de gran importancia arqueológica, llamado a veces «cuna de la humanidad». Con esta región se asocian al menos dos especies de homininos tempranos.

LAS DIFERENCIAS ENTRE EL ADN Y LAS PROTEÍNAS EN SANGRE de humanos y otros simios sugieren que nuestro linaje se separó del de otros chimpancés hace unos 6 MA. Solo hay unos pocos especímenes fósiles de esta época: ***Sahelanthropus tchadensis*** (7,1–6,8 MA), ***Orrorin tugenensis*** (6,1–5,8 MA) y dos especies de ***Ardipithecus***, *kadabba* (5,8–5,2 MA) y *ramidus* (4,8–4,2 MA). Todas estas especies estaban adaptadas para trepar a los árboles. Aunque las más tardías pudieran ser **bípedas**, no es seguro que fueran antepasados de los humanos. Dado que las especies están en **evolución constante** y los individuos varían, es difícil decidir a qué especie atribuir fósiles aislados y fragmentarios y establecer el parentesco entre ellas. Sin embargo, estos fósiles nos ofrecen un atisbo de los miembros más antiguos de la familia humana que vivieron en los bosques y sabanas de África.

7 MA ÉPOCA DE LA APARICIÓN DEL **PRIMER** ANCESTRO **HUMANO**

VARIAS ESPECIES DE AUSTRALOPITECINOS habitaron en África hace 4,2–2 MA. Aunque caminaran erguidos la mayor parte del tiempo, eran bastante **pequeños y simiescos**, y aún pasaban algún tiempo en los árboles. Su cerebro era similar en tamaño al del chimpancé actual, y algunos parecen haber usado **útiles líticos**; los más antiguos, de hace **3,3 MA**, proceden de Kenia, pero se han hallado huesos con marcas de corte por herramientas líticas asociados con ***Australopithecus afarensis*** de hace 3,4 MA. Los descendientes de los australopitecinos adoptaron dos modos de vida distintos: los del género ***Paranthropus*** tenían potentes mandíbulas y dientes grandes para comer alimentos vegetales duros; ***Homo rudolfensis*** y ***H. habilis*** parecen haber ingerido **más proteínas** y haber usado herramientas para extraer el tuétano de huesos largos que obtenían de presas ya muertas por animales carnívoros.

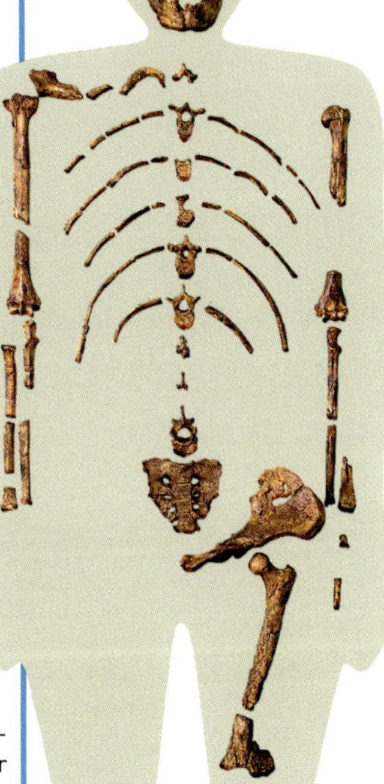

Lucy
Este inusual esqueleto completo de Australopithecus afarensis, *hallado en Etiopía en 1974, debe su nombre a la canción de los Beatles* Lucy in the sky with diamonds.

EL MODO DE VIDA DE LOS PARANTROPINOS no tuvo éxito finalmente, y se **extinguieron** tras unos **1,2 MA**. Pasados 2 MA, antiguas especies humanas prosperaron y se multiplicaron. *H. habilis* y *H. rudolfensis* no diferían mucho de los australopitecinos.

Fue con ***H. ergaster*** (2 MA) cuando nuestros antepasados empezaron a **parecerse más a nosotros**: alto y esbelto, pudo ser el primer homínino (término que incluye a humanos actuales y sus ancestros) sin mucho vello corporal. Sus **cerebros eran mayores** que los de sus antepasados, perdieron las últimas especializaciones arborícolas y se adaptaron por completo a caminar y correr.

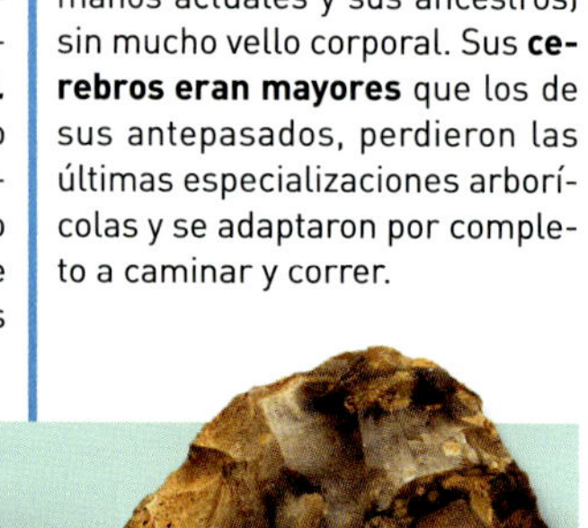

HERRAMIENTAS

Diversos animales usan objetos naturales como herramientas, pero solo consta la manufactura de útiles líticos entre los homininos. Los más antiguos, llamados olduvayenses por el lugar donde se descubrieron, son simples lascas cortantes obtenidas al golpear guijarros con un percutor. Útiles posteriores, como los bifaces achelenses, requieren mayor habilidad. La manufactura de herramientas pudo ser un factor en la evolución del cerebro humano.

NO MUCHO DESPUÉS DE APARECER, *H. ergaster* (en Asia, *H. erectus*) se expandió **fuera de África**, llegando al sureste asiático hace 1,8–1,6 MA y a China hace 1,7 MA. La presencia de una especie emparentada de rasgos arcaicos, ***H. georgicus***, en Dmanisi (Georgia) hace **1,8 MA** podría indicar una difusión de homininos anterior. Útiles líticos de hace hasta 2,1 MA hallados en Shangshazui y Lantian (Gongwangling), en China, respaldan esta teoría, y también los rasgos reminiscentes de *H. habilis* del muy posterior ***H. floresiensis*** de Liang Bua, en la isla indonesia de Flores, que apunta a que sus antepasados se marcharon de África antes que *H. ergaster/erectus*.

Habitar más al norte exigía una **forma de vida distinta** a la de la

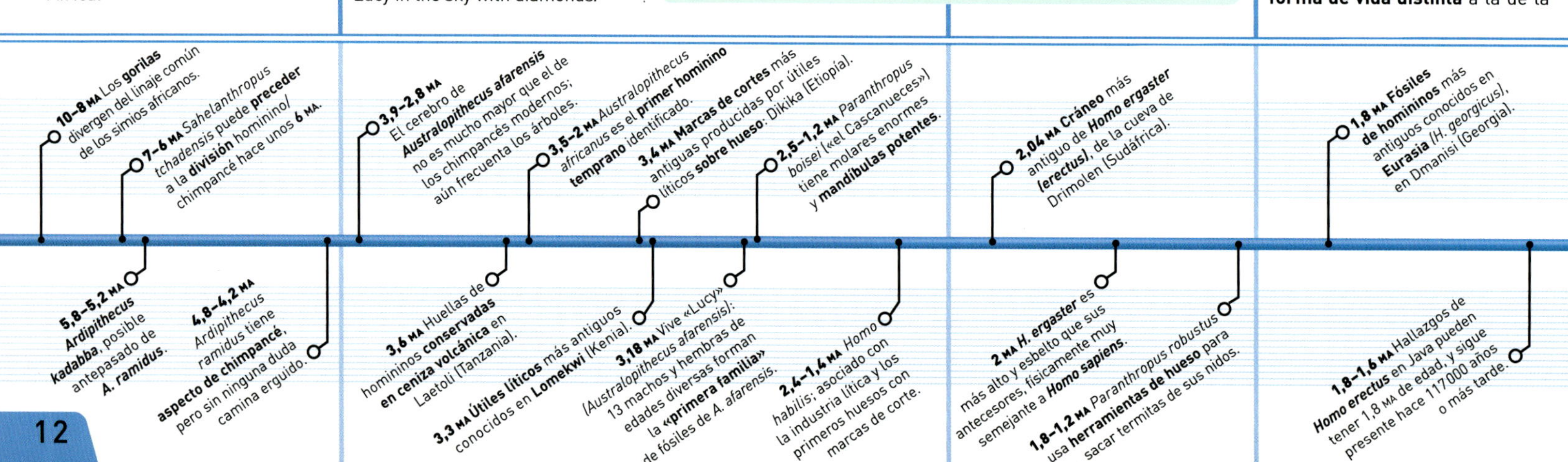

1,6–0,4 MA

400 000–160 000 AÑOS

« TODOS LOS SERES HUMANOS **DESCIENDEN DE ANTEPASADOS COMUNES** QUE VIVIERON EN ÁFRICA HACE MENOS DE 200 000 AÑOS. **»**

Stephen Jay Gould, paleontólogo estadounidense, en *Acabo de llegar. El final de un principio en historia natural* (2002).

Homininos fuera de África
Nuestros antepasados más antiguos evolucionaron en África. Aquí se muestran las posibles rutas de dispersión, con la edad de los fósiles más antiguos conocidos en cada región.

sabana africana. El clima era más árido, y los entornos, más estacionales, con una variación marcada de los recursos alimenticios a lo largo del año. La relativa escasez de plantas comestibles habría obligado a los homininos a competir por **proteínas animales**, más difíciles de obtener. Para **sobrevivir** en estas regiones tuvieron que recorrer distancias mayores y **colaborar**, compartiendo recursos e información.

MIENTRAS HOMO ERECTUS PROSPERABA en el este y sureste de Asia hasta hace 150 000 años, llegaron a Europa descendientes de *H. ergaster*. Los fósiles de ***H. antecessor*** hallados en España son de hace 1,2 MA; las herramientas de Italia, de hace 1,6 MA; y las huellas y herramientas de Inglaterra, de hace 0,95–0,7 MA. Las marcas en los huesos de *H. antecessor* de Atapuerca (España) sugieren que pudo darse el canibalismo, y los pocos enclaves conocidos de estos colonos indican que tal vez no pudieran prosperar en un medio extraño. Hace 600 000 años, ***H. heidelbergensis*** se había difundido mucho más por Europa. Parecen haber sido buenos cazadores y carroñeros.

Los hallazgos de **bifaces achelenses** de *H. ergaster* y *H. erectus* han abundado en África y Eurasia, y no tanto en Asia oriental. Esto demuestra la capacidad para aprender **habilidades complejas** y transmitirlos a lo largo de generaciones. Para hacer estos útiles tuvieron que concebir las piedras como hojas (o lascas) y, para ello, debieron de elegir y transportar piedra de calidad. Los bifaces sirvieron para muchas actividades, pero también como signo de identidad **individual o grupal**, al reflejar la fuerza y destreza de sus creadores.

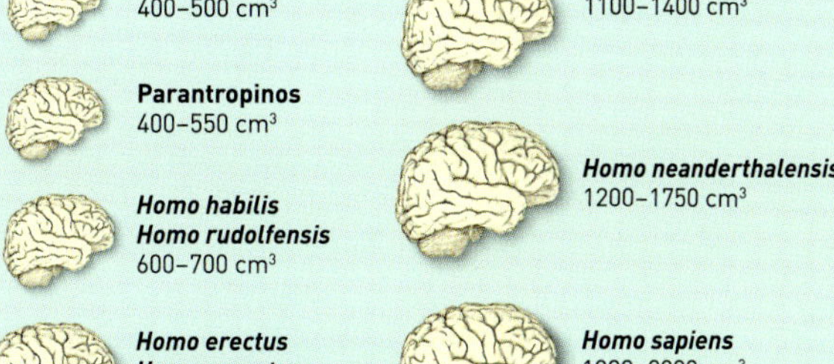

CAPACIDAD CRANEAL EN HOMININOS

Los humanos tienen un cerebro desproporcionadamente grande para un primate de su tamaño, y los arqueólogos difieren en cuanto al cómo y al porqué de su expansión. El cambio a dietas más grasas y calóricas, como el tuétano y la carne, pudo «impulsar» el crecimiento encefálico, además de exigir utensilios más complejos y una caza y recolección más eficaces. Las habilidades sociales fueron también parte del proceso, pues el periodo de crianza más largo que los niños necesitaban para desarrollar cerebros mayores exigió reforzar la cooperación grupal y los vínculos de pareja.

Enterrar a los muertos
Los neandertales solían ser respetuosos con sus muertos. Algunos fueron enterrados en tumbas, como en la cueva de Kebara (Israel), que data de 60 000 a. C.

HACE UNOS 400 000 AÑOS, *H. heidelbergensis* había evolucionado a ***H. neanderthalensis***, que vivió en Europa y el oeste de Asia, y a los denisovanos, que se expandieron por Siberia y Asia oriental, pero dejaron poco rastro.

Los neandertales eran **más bajos y fornidos** que los humanos modernos, y de cerebro tan grande o incluso más, pero de forma ligeramente distinta. Eran **muy hábiles** fabricando útiles líticos y lanzas pesadas, con las que cazaban con éxito presas grandes y peligrosas, como caballos y bisontes.

Los neandertales daban un trato especial a sus muertos, enterramiento incluido, y tenían cierto comportamiento simbólico expresado en adornos personales simples y piezas de arte abstracto. Hacían ropa y diversos útiles líticos, y también construían refugios. Es difícil determinar si hablaban, pero estudios recientes indican una capacidad auditiva que podría ser un indicio de que usaran lenguaje hablado.

En África, desde hace alrededor de 300 000 años, los fósiles de homininos van revelando gradualmente los rasgos esqueléticos de *Homo sapiens*: arcos supraorbitales menores, cráneo más alto y redondeado y mentón. La nueva datación de los fósiles de Jebel Irhoud (Marruecos) indican que el norte de África fue también una zona importante para estos primeros *H. sapiens*. En Olorgesailie, en el valle del Rift de África, se hallaron pruebas de grandes cambios climáticos y ambientales iniciados hace 400 000 años y que probablemente favorecieron evoluciones importantes en el comportamiento de los homininos hacia una mayor cooperación social e innovación tecnológica hace alrededor de 320 000 años.

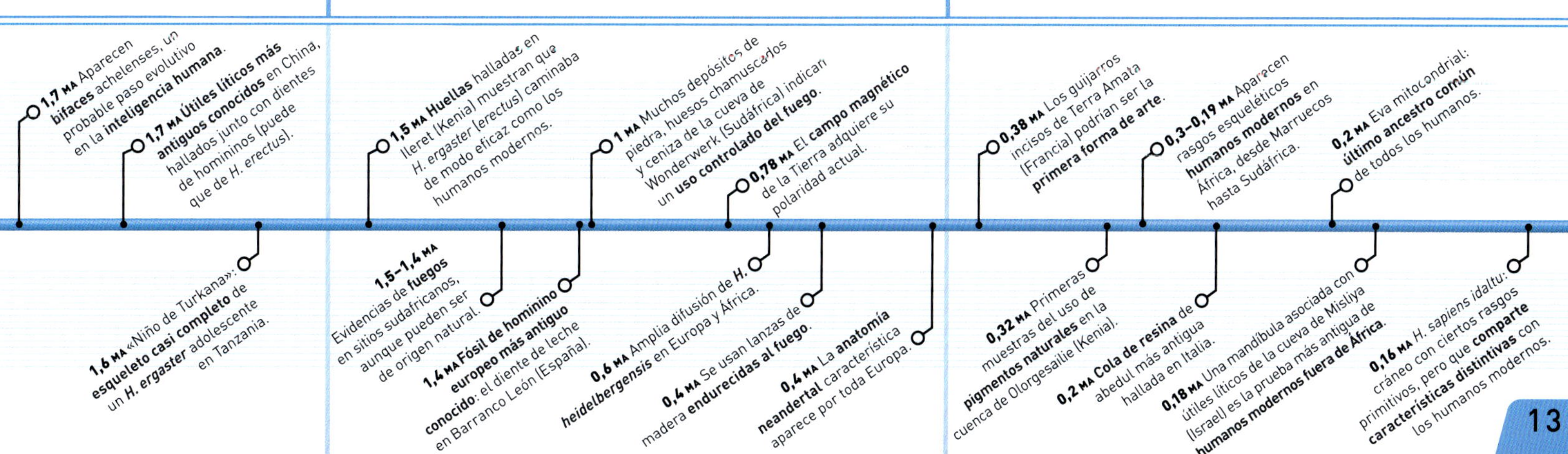

COLONIZACIÓN DEL PLANETA

DIFUSIÓN DE LOS HUMANOS MODERNOS ALREDEDOR DEL MUNDO

Pruebas esqueléticas y de ADN indican que nuestra especie, *Homo sapiens*, evolucionó en África y luego se difundió por el mundo. Los primeros rastros posibles de humanos modernos fuera de África son fósiles y útiles líticos de hace 180 000 años hallados en Israel.

En la colonización del mundo por *H. sapiens* hubo muchas paradas, inicios, algunas retiradas y distintas oleadas de grupos en ciertas áreas. En Asia oriental se hallaron fósiles y útiles líticos datados en 120 000–63 000 años, pero los estudios del ADN apuntan a la extinción de estos primeros colonos: todos los humanos actuales descienden de humanos modernos que vivieron en África o la abandonaron por Asia occidental hace 60 000–50 000 años. Algunos pudieron seguir la ruta meridional y costera por Arabia y el sur de Asia hasta China y el sureste asiático. Australia se comenzó a habitar después de hace 50 000 años, y su interior árido, antes de hace 30 000. Otros avanzaron por el interior en muchas direcciones, llegando algunos a Siberia hace unos 40 000 años. A Europa llegaron grupos desde Anatolia, o bien hasta más al norte desde Asia central, en varias oleadas, pero solo los llegados desde hace unos 35 000 años contribuyeron al acervo genético europeo actual. Los *H. sapiens* llegados al norte desde China hace unos 36 000 años se mezclaron con grupos en el noreste de Siberia, pasaron a Beringia, la tierra hoy sumergida bajo el estrecho de Bering entre Siberia y Alaska, expuesta por el bajo nivel del mar durante la última glaciación. Algunos pudieron ir al sur por la costa hace unos 17 000 años al comenzar a retroceder el hielo, y otros pudieron avanzar por el interior, al abrirse un corredor hace 14 000 años. Las características puntas de lanza Clovis (talladas por ambos lados) eran comunes por toda América del Norte hace 12 000 años, y por tanto había allí humanos modernos entonces, pero se conocen también enclaves más antiguos, incluidos algunos en América del Sur.

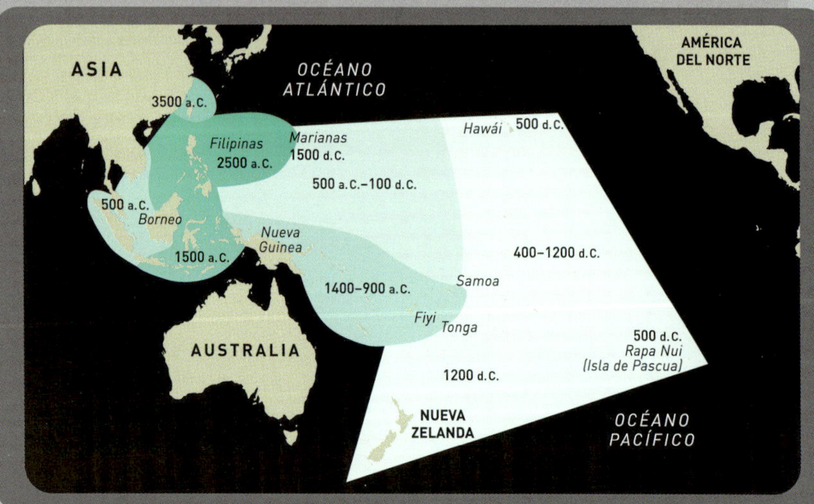

ÚLTIMAS LLEGADAS

Las islas de Oceanía se hallan entre las últimas partes del mundo colonizadas, a través de Filipinas, por agricultores austronesios procedentes de Taiwán. Las islas más remotas del norte y este de Micronesia y Polinesia permanecieron inhabitadas hasta después de 700 d.C., y Nueva Zelanda no fue poblada sino hasta 1200 d.C.

Rastreo lingüístico
A menudo puede rastrearse la difusión de las lenguas para reflejar los movimientos de población. En este mapa se muestra la difusión de hablantes austronesios en Oceanía. Algunas zonas occidentales ya habían sido pobladas con anterioridad.

Marcha global
Las pruebas esqueléticas y genéticas indican que los humanos modernos surgieron en África y desde allí se extendieron por el mundo, como refleja el mapa. En su expansión por el mundo, los humanos se encontraron y cruzaron con otros homininos arcaicos en épocas y lugares diversos, de los que los enclaves más antiguos en cada continente aparecen entre paréntesis.

Estas pinturas rupestres de Lascaux (Francia) son de hace unos 17 000 años. Muchas pinturas rupestres son de época similar, pero algunas fueron obra de antiguos *Homo sapiens* hace unos 39 000 años en Asia.

HUMANOS MODERNOS EMIGRARON AL NORTE, a Asia occidental, antes de hace 100 000 años. Son probables dispersiones múltiples por Eurasia desde hace 120 000 años, por distintas rutas. Los primeros humanos modernos en Asia oriental pudieron encontrarse con grupos de *H. erectus*, presentes en China y el sureste asiático hasta hace unos 100 000 años, y quizá más tarde.

Excavaciones en Indonesia en 2003 revelaron que **homininos extremadamente pequeños** y altamente especializados, quizá descendientes de *H. erectus*, vivieron en la isla de **Flores** hace entre 100 000 y 50 000 años. Fragmentos de mandíbulas y dientes posiblemente emparentados en otro yacimiento isleño apuntan a que esta especie, ***H. floresiensis***, viviera allí desde hace 700 000 años.

300 000

EL NÚMERO DE AÑOS DE **PREDOMINIO** DE LOS **NEANDERTALES** EN EUROPA Y ASIA OCCIDENTAL

El análisis de huesos de la **cueva de Denisova**, en Rusia, reveló ADN distinto del de neandertales y humanos modernos, de un hominino («**denisovano**») que vivió allí hace 250 000–60 000 años.

Núcleo preparado y lasca
Los neandertales y otros homininos preparaban un núcleo de piedra antes de extraer una lasca afilada. En Europa esta técnica es conocida como musteriense.

Pruebas arqueológicas y genéticas apoyan la llegada de humanos modernos a Asia oriental antes de hace 74 000 años, cuando la erupción masiva del **volcán Toba** en Indonesia desencadenó un **«invierno volcánico»** global. Los análisis de ADN indican que muchos grupos humanos se extinguieron en esta época.

La arqueología indica una aceleración de la tasa de **desarrollo cultural** humano en África hace 100 000 años, con un avance marcado hace *c.* 60 000–50 000 años. Las **innovaciones** consistieron en prácticas complejas de caza, una tecnología de útiles flexible a base de lascas largas de sílex extraídas de núcleos preparados y, hace 40 000 años, pequeños segmentos de lasca para **herramientas compuestas**, junto con herramientas en una amplia gama de otros materiales para tareas específicas en lugar de para usos múltiples.

Comportamientos humanos modernos, como el arte figurativo (no abstracto) y las redes extensas de contactos social, reflejan el desarrollo de un lenguaje capaz de **expresar el pensamiento abstracto**, que permitió comunicar y transmitir conocimientos y habilidades, y tuvo un papel clave en la innovación. Tales desarrollos condujeron a un gran aumento de la población, que probablemente dio lugar a las migraciones que siguieron al clima más benigno posterior a las glaciaciones de hace 65 000 años. Las pruebas genéticas indican que los emigrados, originarios de África, se cruzaron con neandertales en Asia occidental, y por ello toda la población humana actual salvo los africanos conserva entre un 1 % y un 4 % de material genético neandertal.

Después de hace unos 60 000 años, los humanos modernos se difundieron rápidamente por el mundo, alcanzando **Australia** hace 50 000 años; **Europa** en varias oleadas entre hace 54 000 y 35 000 años; **Siberia** hace 40 000 años; y **América** antes de hace 12 000 años. Se cruzaron con denisovanos en el sureste asiático. Cuando *H. sapiens* comenzó a migrar, en el mundo vivían otras especies humanas. Hace 15 000 años, todas salvo *H. sapiens* estaban **extintas**.

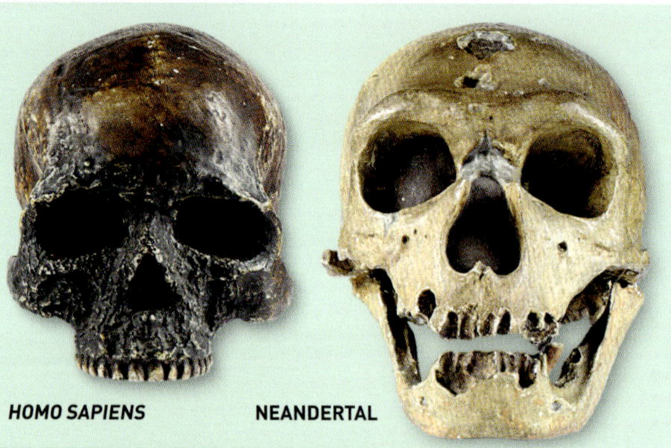

HOMO SAPIENS **NEANDERTAL**

HUMANOS MODERNOS Y NEANDERTALES

El cráneo de los neandertales (dcha.) era ligeramente mayor que el humano moderno (izda.), pero la frente era más baja e inclinada, y un doble arco óseo sobre los ojos formaba crestas superciliares robustas. La parte inferior de la cara, proyectada, carecía de mentón. En conjunto, los esqueletos neandertales revelan que eran mucho más musculados que los humanos modernos, y físicamente muy activos, pero no especializados para el clima frío como antes se creía.

« LOS NEANDERTALES **NO ERAN HOMBRES-MONO** [...] ERAN **TAN HUMANOS COMO NOSOTROS,** PERO REPRESENTABAN UN **TIPO DISTINTO DE HUMANIDAD**. »

Chris Stringer y Clive Gamble, de *En busca de los neandertales* (1993)

EN EUROPA, LOS HUMANOS MODERNOS coincidieron con los neandertales, que sobrevivieron hasta hace 40 000 años en algunos lugares. Por qué y cómo **desaparecieron los neandertales** es una de las cuestiones más debatidas de la arqueología. Hay pocas pruebas de interacción violenta entre las especies, y la comparación del ADN indica **algún grado de cruzamiento** entre ellas, todo ello, o en su mayor parte, anterior a la migración de los humanos modernos desde Asia occidental. En esqueletos neandertales se han detectado deficiencias periódicas en la dieta, lo cual apunta a una existencia difícil. Los humanos modernos pudieron **superarles en la competencia** por el **alimento y las materias primas** en condiciones de cambio climático rápido. Los hábitats de la época fueron muy inestables, e incluso un aumento leve en la competencia pudo tener consecuencias importantes.

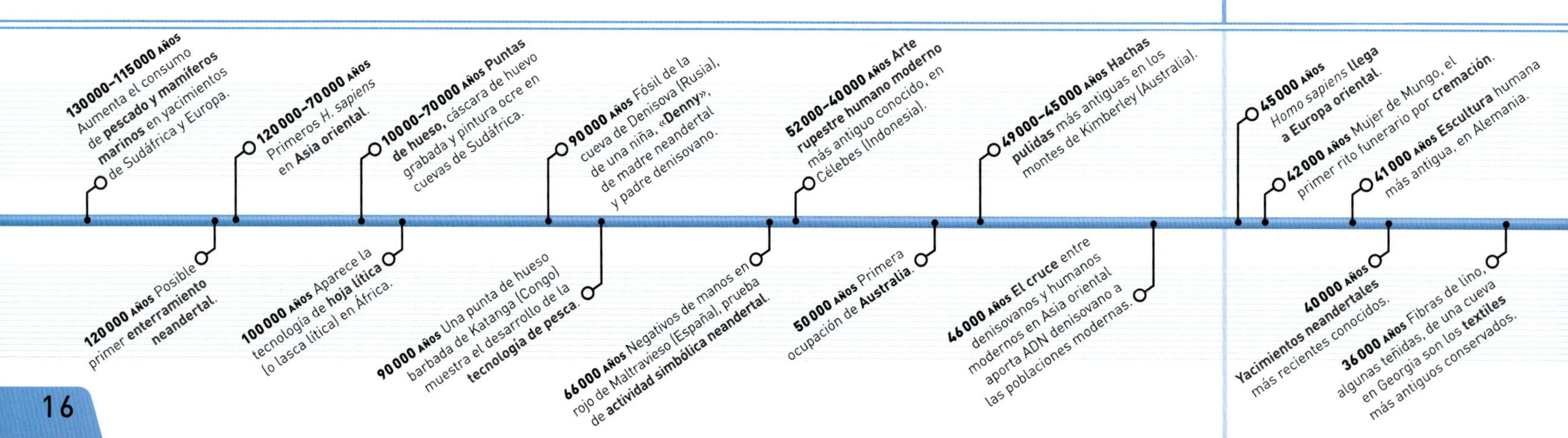

Aunque coexistieran con los humanos modernos durante 5000–10 000 años en Europa, los **grupos sociales neandertales eran reducidos**, y su densidad de población era escasa; y es probable que el gran número de humanos modernos asentados en Eurasia, con su **estilo de vida eficiente y sus grupos sociales extensos**, les superase en la competencia. Además, el **intercambio de recursos e información** facilitado por el uso del lenguaje y los símbolos entre los humanos modernos, junto con lo planificado y flexible de sus tecnologías, hicieron que *H. sapiens* fuera más capaz de soportar cambios climáticos que los neandertales.

Actualmente se considera que la explicación más probable de la **extinción neandertal** fuera una combinación de condiciones ambientales adversas y una reproducción más lenta.

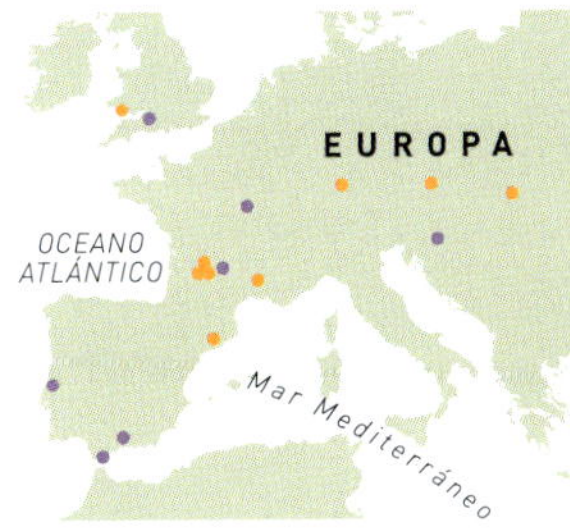

Alcance neandertal y moderno
Humanos modernos y neandertales coexistieron durante varios miles de años. El mapa muestra los lugares donde interactuaron en Europa.

EXTENSIÓN MÁXIMA DE LA ÚLTIMA GLACIACIÓN

El clima europeo fue cada vez más frío a partir de 23 000 a. C. Durante el último máximo glacial (hace 21 000–18 000 años), casquetes glaciares cubrían el norte de Europa; en cambio, en el sur, los extensos herbazales poco arbolados eran buenos terrenos de caza para los grupos humanos capaces de sobrevivir al frío.

LA CULTURA GRAVETIENSE de Europa y Rusia (hace 28 000–21 000 años) es conocida por sus yacimientos elaborados, a menudo con estructuras y enterramientos complejos, bisutería, tallas de marfil y cuerno e impresiones de material tejido. En estos lugares se hallaron también algunos de los objetos cerámicos más antiguos conocidos, entre ellos las famosas estatuillas llamadas **«venus»**, que pudieron ser amuletos de fertilidad o religiosos, o bien objetos intercambiados entre grupos sociales regionales durante el **máximo glacial**.

Estatuilla de venus
Estas figurillas talladas son de mujeres en todas las fases de la vida. Esta es la de Willendorf (Austria).

vientre exagerado

EN EL PICO DEL MÁXIMO glacial, con las capas de hielo en su máxima extensión, los humanos que habitaban más al norte y en las montañas se retiraron a áreas que ofrecían más refugio, como ocurrió en Europa en los actuales norte de España y suroeste de Francia, donde a este periodo se le llama Solutrense. Es probable **una desaparición global de muchos grupos**, pero algunos resistieron en lugares más abrigados. Para sobrevivir en tales condiciones debían dedicar mucho tiempo y esfuerzo a la caza. Entre sus armas hay puntas líticas en forma de hojas. Aunque sean pocas las pruebas, aparte de agujas de hueso finamente trabajadas, debieron emplear **prendas ajustadas** para conservar el calor. Tal vez más importante, estos cazadores debían vivir atentos a predecir e interceptar los movimientos de manadas de grandes mamíferos para tener **éxito en la caza**, una cuestión de vida o muerte.

EN EUROPA, SOFISTICADAS PUNTAS, agujas y arpones de hueso y cuerno caracterizan la industria de la cultura magdaleniense, que practicaba la caza de diversas especies, sobre todo del reno.

El Magdaleniense (18 000–12 000 años) es famoso por sus bellos objetos de arte, grabados y **pinturas rupestres**. Hay muchas teorías en cuanto a su significado y finalidad. La mayoría de los negativos de manos son de mujeres, un indicio de que pudieran ser ellas quienes crearan la mayor parte de este arte rupestre. La mayoría de las pinturas no representan animales de la zona, y por tanto no tenían como fin el éxito en la caza. Podrían ser un registro de información real o simbólica acerca del mundo en que vivían sus creadores de modos que aún no comprendemos. La inaccesibilidad de algunas pinturas y sus figuras medio humanas y medio animales podría apuntar a rituales chamánicos, y las huellas de pies de niños en estos lugares, a ritos iniciáticos. De otro modo, las pinturas y los objetos podían quizá afirmar la identidad grupal y territorial, ya que el número de yacimientos arqueológicos de la época apunta a un aumento de la población, así como a una posible intensificación de la competencia por los recursos.

Un aumento de las temperaturas causó la **retirada de los casquetes glaciares** que cubrían el norte de Europa y partes del norte de Asia, áreas rápidamente recolonizadas. Algunos grupos habían llegado ya a América del Norte por Alaska en esta época. Más al este, en China y en el área de la cultura jomon de Japón, aparecen algunas de las primeras ollas de arcilla hace entre 20 000 y 18 000 años.

Pinturas rupestres de Altamira
Esta pintura paleolítica de un bisonte se descubrió en el sitio rupestre de Altamira (España).

36 000–28 000 AÑOS En Europa, algunas tecnologías apuntan al **intercambio cultural**.

35 000 AÑOS La tecnología auriñacense está asentada en toda Europa.

32 000 AÑOS Serie de magníficos **retratos de animales** en la cueva de Chauvet (Francia).

32 000 AÑOS *Homo sapiens* más antiguos en **Japón**.

28 000–21 000 AÑOS Culmina la **cultura gravetiense**, con esculturas cerámicas.

27 000 AÑOS Yacimientos complejos de cazadores-recolectores en la **llanura rusa**.

26 000 AÑOS Inicio de la **tecnología cerámica** con horno en Dolni Vestonice (República Checa).

21 000–18 000 AÑOS Último **máximo glacial**.

21 000 AÑOS Aparece la **industria solutrense**.

18 000 AÑOS Aparece la **industria magdaleniense**.

17 000 AÑOS Pinturas de la cueva de **Lascaux** (Francia).

17 000 AÑOS El *átlatl* (lanzadardos) más antiguo conocido, hallado en **Combe Saunière** (Francia).

16 000–15 000 AÑOS Comienza la recolonización de zonas de **Europa** septentrional **abandonadas** por las malas condiciones climáticas.

15 000 AÑOS Monte Verde (Chile): yacimiento sudamericano de polémica datación temprana.

14 000 AÑOS Incremento **de la pesca** con arpones de cuerno.

La arquitectura megalítica (megalito significa «gran piedra») fue usada para crear monumentos y tumbas en la Europa neolítica. Entre sus creaciones en torno al 3000 a. C. se hallan los crómlech (círculos de piedra), como este de Castlerigg, en el norte de Inglaterra.

Densidad de población
En el este de Asia, la población creció rápidamente entre 13 000 y 6400 a. C.

EL ABRUPTO AUMENTO DE TEMPERATURA entre hace 12 700 y 10 800 años **fundió los casquetes glaciares** septentrionales, produciendo un aumento del nivel del mar y de la pluviosidad, y la formación de lagos; esto favoreció la **extensión de bosques y herbazales** y proporcionó nuevas oportunidades a las comunidades cazadoras-recolectoras. Las zonas inundadas por el aumento del nivel del mar, así como lagos y ríos, eran **ricas fuentes de alimento**. Las praderas mantenían a grandes manadas, y los márgenes de los bosques proveían de alimento vegetal y caza. Casi todos **los cazadores-recolectores se desplazaban estacionalmente** para explotar recursos en distintas zonas, pero los lugares privilegiados, como los estuarios, podían mantener a una comunidad todo el año. Una de esas regiones era la costa de Perú y Chile, donde la fría corriente de Humboldt proporcionaba abundancia de pesca. Allí habitaban **comunidades estables** en 7000 a. C., entre ellas la de **chinchorro**, creadora de las primeras momias conocidas (*véase* recuadro).

Otra zona favorable fue Oriente Próximo; su vegetación incluía **cereales silvestres que se podían almacenar** para abastecer a toda una comunidad a lo largo del año, complementados con otras fuentes alimenticias como la caza. Un periodo de frío y de sequía (10 800–9600 a. C.) provocó una brusco descenso en la disponibilidad de cereal silvestre, lo que empujó a algunas comunidades a recurrir a su cultivo.

La agricultura comenzó en muchas partes del mundo en diferentes momentos y aprovechando los recursos locales. La domesticación de plantas y animales se difundió por intercambio entre grupos vecinos y colonización de nuevas tierras por comunidades de granjeros. La agricultura no fue un descubrimiento: los cazadores-recolectores poseían un profundo conocimiento de las plantas y animales de los que dependían, y solían tomar medidas para **aumentar la productividad**. La labranza fue, pues, una elección hecha para mejorar la productividad local, a menudo a costa de más trabajo y riesgo. Las razones para cultivar la tierra pudieron incluir la extensión del tiempo de residencia en un asentamiento, el aporte de un extra de comida para celebraciones o poblaciones crecientes, o bien aumentar la cantidad de alimentos preferidos o decrecientes.

Los cereales fueron básicos para la agricultura temprana. La cebada y el trigo se domesticaron en Oriente Próximo y llegaron hasta el norte de África, Europa y el centro y sur de Asia. El mijo común y el menor, en el valle del río Amarillo; y el arroz en el valle del Yangtsé, ambos en China; desde allí se extendieron al este y sureste asiáticos. En África, se domesticaron otras variedades de mijo y el arroz africano pasado 3000 a. C. En América, el cereal principal fue el maíz; sin embargo, aunque ya se cultivaba en 6700 a. C., hasta 2000 a. C. no sería lo bastante productivo para sustentar a comunidades permanentes. En muchas partes del mundo se cultivaron **legumbres y verduras** junto a los cereales.

El cultivo de **tubérculos**, como la mandioca y el ñame, y de **árboles** comenzó ya en fechas tempranas en zonas húmedas tropicales de las tierras altas de Nueva Guinea y en bosques húmedos de América Central y el norte de América del Sur.

Ovejas, cabras, cerdos y vacas se domesticaron en Eurasia y África, en principio solo por su carne. Sin embargo, en América solo había animales adecuados para la domesticación en los Andes: llamas, conejos de Indias y alpacas. Las **aves**, en especial gallinas, patos y pavos,

«Dios pez» de Lepenski Vir
La pesca sustentó un asentamiento de cazadores-recolectores a orillas del Danubio serbio. Sus habitantes tallaron estos hombres-peces, probablemente dioses.

Cráneo de ciervo de Star Carr
Tocado de cabeza procedente de un enclave de cazadores-recolectores en Inglaterra; pudo utilizarse en rituales de caza.

11 500–9000 a. C. Rápida **colonización de América** por parte de pueblos que utilizan microlitos y, más tarde, herramientas de la cultura de Clovis.

10 800–9600 a. C. Periodo frío del Dryas reciente, probablemente causado por la fusión de los casquetes glaciares; ascenso muy rápido de temperatura pasado el año 9600 a. C.

10 500 a. C. Primeros **cereales domesticados:** centeno en Siria; trigo y cebada ya en 8000 a. C.

9500–8000 a. C. Cazadores-recolectores erigen ejemplos de arquitectura monumental en **Göbekli Tepe** y **Karahan Tepe** (Turquía).

9000 a. C. Primeros **animales domesticados** en Asia occidental.

9000–8200 a. C. Los restos en **Chipre** indican la colonización de la isla y el **transporte en barca** de ovejas, cabras, vacas y cerdos.

9000–3000 a. C. El aumento de pluviosidad produce el **«Sáhara verde»:** lagos, ríos y herbazales en torno al norte de África.

8500–7300 a. C. Construcción de un **muro de piedra** en torno a **Jericó** (Israel), probablemente como protección contra inundaciones, y no con fines militares.

8000 a. C. Primeros asentamientos agrícolas en el valle del río Amarillo (**China**); cultivan **mijo**.

8000 a. C. Domesticación de la calabaza en Mesoamérica, **calabaza y frijol** en Ecuador.

7000 a. C. Domesticación del cebú en Mehrgarh (al oeste de Pakistán) por cultivadores de trigo, cebada y legumbres.

7000 a. C. Cultivos amazónicos, como los **cacahuetes**, crecen en la costa de Perú, por lo que hubo un cultivo anterior en la Amazonia.

7000 a. C. Domesticación de bovinos por comunidades de cazadores-pescadores del Sáhara verde.

7000 a. C. Cultivos de **banana, taro y ñame** en las tierras altas de Nueva Guinea.

6700 a. C. Domesticación del **maíz** en México a partir del teosinte silvestre.

también fueron criadas en el Viejo y el Nuevo Mundo. Hacia 6500 a.C., vacas, ovejas y cabras eran criadas **por su leche**, además de por su carne; y el ganado vacuno se empleaba como tiro de **arado**, lo que permitió cultivos más extensos. La cría **lanar** empezó en Oriente Próximo, y se extendió con rapidez a Europa y Asia central. El uso de **animales de carga** como llamas y asnos permitió el transporte a larga distancia.

La agricultura era más productiva que el forrajeo, y podía sustentar **comunidades mayores**. El sedentarismo también contribuyó a favorecer el **crecimiento demográfico**. Muchas aldeas agrícolas tempranas de Oriente Próximo alcanzaron un tamaño considerable; la más importante fue **Chatal Huyuk**, en Turquía, ocupada *c.* 7400–6200 a.C. y que alcanzó los ocho mil habitantes. A sus casas apiñadas, decoradas con pinturas y figuras de cabezas de animales, se accedía con escalerillas desde el techo.

« EL **NEOLÍTICO** FUE… UN PUNTO EN UN CONTINUO DE **MAYOR CONTROL ECONÓMICO** DE LOS RECURSOS… DESDE EL **CARROÑEO** HASTA… LA **AGRICULTURA**. »

Clive Gamble, en *Origins and revolutions: human identity in earliest prehistory* (2007)

Pasado 7000 a.C., los **granjeros** se extendieron desde Turquía al sureste y centro de Europa, mientras que los cazadores-recolectores del Mediterráneo adoptaban gradualmente la agricultura con cultivos y animales de Oriente Próximo. Hacia 3500 a.C. casi toda Europa había abrazado la agricultura.

A partir de 5000 a.C. se construyeron en Europa occidental y septentrional cámaras mortuorias de piedra de formas diversas, a menudo recubiertas con túmulos de tierra: los **megalitos**. Casi todas eran tumbas colectivas.

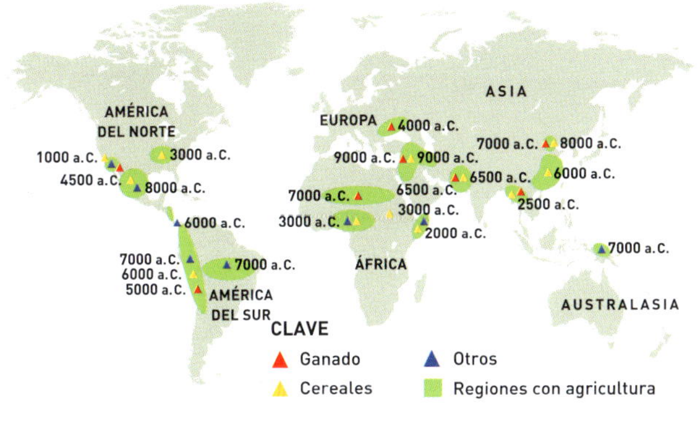

La expansión de la agricultura
El cultivo de plantas y la domesticación de animales empezaron en distintas zonas del mundo y en diferentes momentos, de forma independiente.

El cobre y el oro nativos (puros en estado natural) comenzaron a moldearse en Oriente Próximo por forja en frío antes de 8000 a.C. Sobre 7000 a.C. ya se **fundían menas** con el fin de obtener el mineral, y para 6000 a.C. se vaciaban el cobre y el plomo. En principio, los metales se convertían en pequeños objetos que podían denotar prestigio y estatus. Pero luego el cobre empezó a usarse para crear **herramientas**, y *c.* 4200 a.C. se seleccionaban deliberadamente menas de cobre con arsénico para conseguir un metal más duro. La adición de estaño propiciaba una aleación más resistente, el **bronce**, que ya se utilizaba en Oriente Próximo en 3200 a.C.

El desarrollo de **técnicas de control del agua** permitió a los granjeros de Oriente Próximo colonizar las llanuras del sur de **Mesopotamia**, donde la agricultura dependía por completo de la irrigación pero era sumamente productiva. Hacia mediados del IV milenio a.C. la región estaba densamente poblada, y las aldeas empezaban a convertirse en **ciudades**, con artesanos especializados. Creció la demanda de materias primas, incluidas las menas metálicas, a menudo procedentes de fuentes distantes. Se desarrolló una **red comercial** que se extendía desde Egipto, a través de Oriente Próximo, hasta los límites montañosos del sur de Asia. A lo largo de la ruta, algunas ciudades controlaban fuentes de materias primas o puntos estratégicos. En la vanguardia de este desarrollo estuvo **Sumer**, en el sur de Mesopotamia; pero también en **Elam** (suroeste de Irán) y **Egipto** crecía la complejidad social, religiosa, económica y política. En estas tres regiones se desarrollaron, antes de 3000 a.C., **sistemas de escritura** usados para controlar las transacciones económicas y los títulos de propiedad. La primera escritura pictográfica conocida (*c.* 3300 a.C.) procede de **Uruk**, en Sumer, un inmenso y complejo asentamiento merecidamente conocido como la **primera ciudad de la historia**.

MOMIAS CHINCHORRO

Las primeras momias no proceden de Egipto, sino de la costa norte de Chile, una región árida donde existen momias naturales de 7000 a.C. Los chinchorro iniciaron la momificación artificial pasado 5000 a.C. Eliminaban la carne, recomponían y reforzaban el esqueleto, rellenaban la piel con materia vegetal, y la recubrían con arcilla que pintaban con manganeso negro u ocre rojo. Solamente eran momificados algunos individuos, en especial niños.

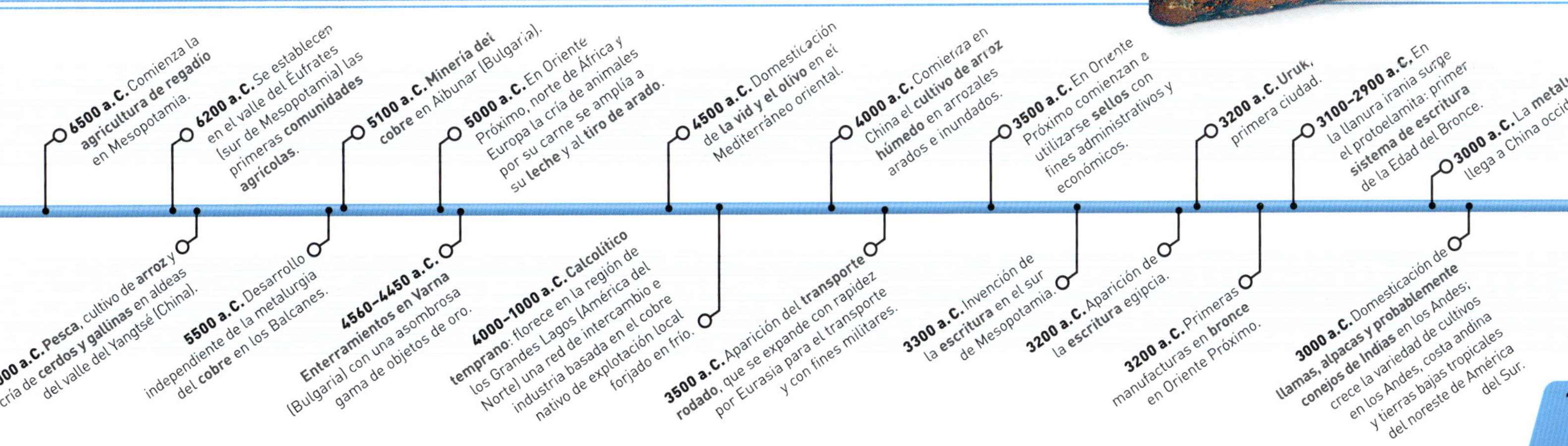

Cabeza de hacha de cobre
El oro y el cobre fueron los primeros metales trabajados. Su uso se generalizó en Europa c. 2500 a.C.

Fragmento de cerámica
4000 a. C. • RUMANÍA
Las distintas culturas pueden ser identificadas por sus formas únicas de decorar objetos: este fragmento es típico de la cultura de Cucuteni-Tripolje.

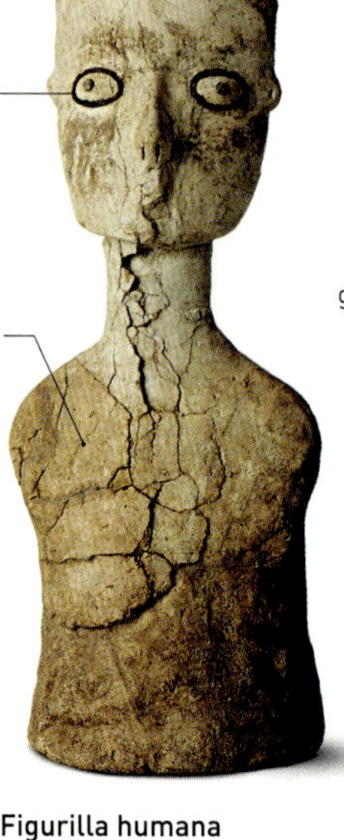

Figurilla humana
6750–6500 a. C. • JORDANIA
Esta gran estatuilla de 'Ain Ghazal es una de las varias procedentes de Oriente Próximo que pudieron representar antepasados o dioses.

Placa de esquisto
4000 a. C. • PORTUGAL
No está claro el simbolismo de las placas grabadas neolíticas como esta, aunque se cree que eran elaboradas para enterrarlas junto a los muertos.

Hueso grabado
13 000–8000 a. C. • FRANCIA
A menudo los artistas paleolíticos grababan, además de pintar, sus representaciones de animales; como esta escena de caza de un bisonte, procedente de Laugerie-Basse.

PUEBLOS PREHISTÓRICOS

LOS HUMANOS TEMPRANOS SE DIFERENCIAN POR LAS MATERIAS PRIMAS QUE USARON PARA CREAR HERRAMIENTAS, ARMAS Y ADORNOS

Tradicionalmente, la prehistoria se divide en las edades de Piedra, Bronce y Hierro; pero las primeras tecnologías emplearon otro tipo de materiales, como madera, cuero y fibras vegetales, de los que poco ha perdurado.

Además de su utilidad para la supervivencia y subsistencia, los objetos creados por los pueblos prehistóricos fueron importantes en sus vidas sociales. Los distintos grupos desarrollaron formas propias de elaborar y decorar objetos, y sus diseños característicos pudieron convertirse en señas de identidad o símbolos de estatus. El comercio e intercambio de objetos fue otro medio vital para establecer relaciones y jerarquías entre individuos y grupos.

Útil olduvayense
2,6–1,7 MA • ÁFRICA
Las primeras herramientas líticas fueron simples lascas de bordes afilados obtenidas al golpear un guijarro con un percutor.

Núcleo y lascas
100 000 a. C. en adelante • MUY EXTENDIDO
Los primeros humanos modernos crearon hojas uniformes que podían enmangarse en madera o cuerno, o utilizarse a mano como útiles para diversos fines.

cabeza dentada
hecha de cuerno

Arpón de cuerno
8000 a. C. • REINO UNIDO
La cabeza de este arpón está unida a un largo mango para lancear peces: un recurso alimenticio clave cuando subía el nivel del mar, como al final de la última glaciación.

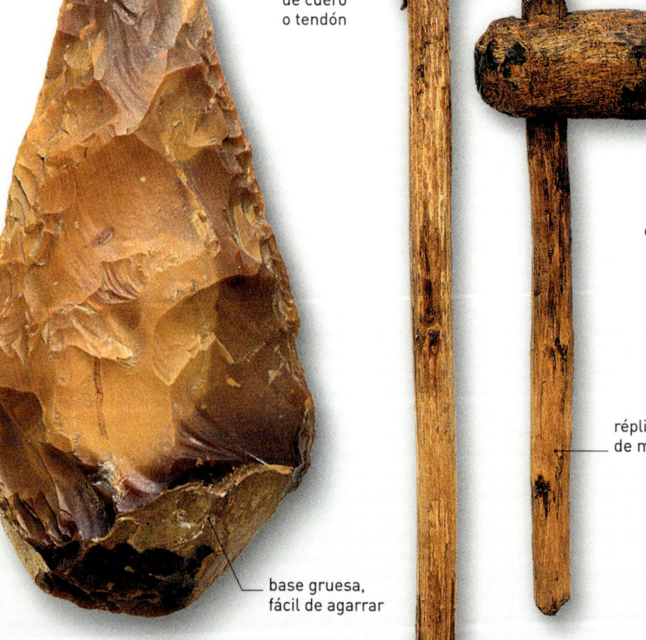

Bifaz de sílex
400 000 a. C. • REINO UNIDO
Los bifaces, como este de Swanscombe, eran hábilmente producidos y tenían múltiples utilidades; entre ellas, trabajar la madera y despiezar animales.

Útiles con cabezas de azuela
11 660–4000 a. C. • EUROPA
Estas azuelas mesolíticas se usaban para extraer raíces o cortar madera en los bosques que cubrieron Europa tras la última glaciación.

Caja funeraria de arcilla
4000 a. C. • ASIA OCCIDENTAL
Una práctica funeraria calcolítica (Edad del Cobre) implicaba permitir la descomposición del muerto al aire para luego recoger sus huesos y meterlos en cajas de arcilla.

Propulsor labrado
10 500 a. C. • FRANCIA
Los propulsores o estólicas, como este de Montastruc, permitían a los cazadores arrojar los venablos a mayor distancia y con más fuerza. A menudo estaban tallados con formas animales; aquí, un mamut lanudo hecho de cuerno.

Venus de Lespugue
24 000–22 000 a. C. • FRANCIA
Esta figurilla de marfil de Lespugue, en los Pirineos, es una de muchas estatuillas que representan a Venus y que realzan la figura de mujeres embarazadas o que han sido madres de muchos hijos.

Cabeza momificada
7000–3000 a. C. • PERÚ
En los climas muy secos los cuerpos pueden momificarse. Algunas de las momias más antiguas proceden de los desiertos peruanos.

Joyería en oro
4560–4450 a. C. • BULGARIA
En la necrópolis de Varna se han hallado más de tres mil piezas de algunas de las joyas de oro más antiguas conocidas, casi todas enterradas con hombres de la élite.

Aperos agrícolas
9500 a. C.-1834 d. C. • MUY EXTENDIDO
Los cereales, primero silvestres y luego domesticados, eran segados con hoces como estas, hasta que fueron reemplazadas debido a la invención de la cosechadora.

Sello neolítico
7500–5700 a. C. • ANATOLIA
Sellos como este, del asentamiento de Chatal Huyuk, se usaron en el Neolítico para estampar diseños decorativos sobre piel o ropa.

Útiles de confección
6500 a. C. • ORIGEN DESCONOCIDO
Aunque los tejidos existían ya *c.* 26 000 a. C., los telares grandes aparecieron durante el Neolítico medio. Las pesas mantenían tensos los hilos verticales, y los horizontales se tejían con husos de hueso.

2

PRIMERAS CIVILIZACIONES 3000–700 a.C.

Este periodo contempló el surgimiento de civilizaciones complejas. En los valles fértiles de Egipto, India, Oriente Próximo y China prosperaron comunidades y se desarrolló el comercio. Europa, América Central y América del Sur también florecieron en esta época.

3000–2700 a. C.

Stonehenge, en el sur de Inglaterra, era un lugar ceremonial hacia 2900 a. C. Un anillo exterior de arenisca azulada en un antiguo recinto de tierra se dispuso más tarde dentro del círculo de piedra sarsen de la imagen.

60 MILLARES
POBLACIÓN DE LA CIUDAD DE **URUK**
c. 2800 a. C.

DURANTE LA SEGUNDA MITAD DEL IV MILENIO A. C. surgieron las primeras civilizaciones, primero en Asia occidental y el norte de África, y más tarde en el sur de Asia. También se desarrollaron en China, a principios del II milenio a. C. En 3000 a. C. existían ya las **primeras ciudades** en el sur de **Mesopotamia** (actual Iraq). En esta región de las llanuras del bajo Éufrates se habían asentado en *c.* 6200 a. C. agricultores que empleaban sistemas de regadío simples. Durante el IV milenio hubo grandes avances en la tecnología agrícola y la productividad resultante. **Sistemas de regadío** cada vez más **sofisticados** abastecieron los campos cultivados con el arado, útil de reciente invención y tirado por bueyes y asnos domesticados también hacía poco, los cuales tiraban también de carros rodados inventados alrededor de 3500 a. C. Los excedentes liberaron a algunos de la vida agrícola, permitiendo la especialización en profesiones como el sacerdocio, la artesanía, el comercio y la administración. Se formó la primera sociedad jerárquica del mundo, dirigida al principio por sacerdotes. La oveja lanuda, criada por primera vez en esta época, abasteció a una **industria textil creciente** para uso doméstico y exportación. Surgieron muchos pueblos, y, en 3400 a. C., Uruk era ya una ciudad. Otras, entre ellas Ur y Nippur, ya en 3000 a. C. dominaban cada una sus áreas circundantes, y, durante los siglos siguientes, **Sumeria** (la zona meridional de la región) fue un mosaico de ciudades-estado en competencia gobernadas por reyes. La **metalurgia** había comenzado en el oeste de Asia ya en el IX milenio a. C.; y, en 3000 a. C., los sumerios comenzaron a manufacturar bronce, aleación de cobre con estaño importado del lejano Afganistán.

En **Egipto**, alrededor de 3100 a. C., a orillas del río Nilo nació una de las **civilizaciones antiguas más complejas**. El Nilo formaba una estrecha franja de llanuras aluviales, terrenos cultivables que cada inundación anual cubría de limo negro. El año agrícola egipcio empezaba en otoño, cuando decrecía el río, y los agricultores plantaban trigo, cebada, alubias y lentejas en el suelo fértil.

Hacia el final del IV milenio a. C., de las comunidades agrícolas habían surgido dos reinos: **el Alto Egipto**, al sur, y el **Bajo Egipto**, al norte. El rey **Narmer** unió ambos hacia 3100 a. C. Se supone que a Narmer le sucedió **Menes**, pero los historiadores dudan si Menes fue otro nombre del propio Narmer. A Menes se le atribuye la fundación de la capital de Egipto, Menfis, y de la primera dinastía egipcia.

Como en Mesopotamia, una agricultura eficiente trajo la prosperidad y la especialización que permitieron el desarrollo de **las artes, la artesanía, la ingeniería y la primera medicina**. El periodo protodinástico de Egipto (*c.* 3100–2686 a. C.) incluía ya muchos de los aspectos célebres de la cultura egipcia: la escritura **jeroglífica**, una **religión** sofisticada y la creencia en el más allá, así como la conservación de los muertos mediante la **momificación**. Se desarrolló una sociedad jerárquica compleja, con el faraón, al que se atribuía carácter semidivino, en la cima. Los faraones gobernaban con ayuda de un ministro principal (visir), gobernadores regionales (nomarcas) y un personal muy numeroso de funcionarios menores, como sacerdotes, recaudadores de impuestos y escribas.

En China estaban surgiendo sociedades estratificadas, como Longshan, en el valle del Huang He (río Amarillo), y Liangzhu, más al sur, en el valle del bajo Yangtsé. El cultivo del **arroz y del mijo** ya se había generalizado; el mijo era el alimento básico en el norte, y el arroz, en el sur. También empezaban a cultivarse árboles frutales y otros cultivos, como la soja. Fibras como las del **bambú y la seda** se emplearon para producir cestas y textiles, y floreció también la **talla del jade**, que alcanzó gran sofisticación en Liangzhu, donde comenzó también la **técnica del lacado** hacia 2800 a. C. En ambas regiones, la jerarquía social emergente se refleja en algunas grandes tumbas con cientos de artículos de lujo, como objetos de bronce o cobre, producidos en varias regiones del norte antes de 2500 a. C.

A partir de *c.* 3000 a. C., la expansión de pueblos de la **región de las estepas**, por el Danubio hasta Europa central y desde Ucrania hasta el norte y este de Europa, dejó enterramientos individuales bajo túmulos, con adornos y armas de cobre, vehículos rodados y, al norte, un tipo de cerámica cordada singular. Hay también pruebas genéticas de este nuevo aporte, al que se atribuye la introducción de las lenguas indoeuropeas en Europa. En Europa occidental, unas tradiciones más antiguas de construcción de tumbas y un interés creciente por la observación astronómica dieron lugar a la nueva **tradición megalítica**, consistente en erigir dólmenes, crómlech, monolitos y tumbas con atributos astronómicos. Entre ellos se cuentan Newgrange (Irlanda), Stonehenge (Inglaterra) y Carnac (Francia).

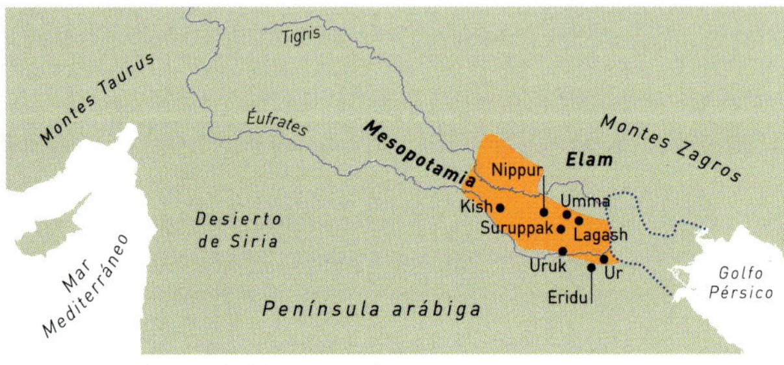

Ciudades antiguas de Mesopotamia
Sumeria, al sur de Mesopotamia, fue el lugar de la primera civilización urbana del mundo desde c. 3000 a. C. Su éxito agrícola favoreció el desarrollo de una sociedad compleja.

CLAVE
- Ciudades-estado en el periodo dinástico arcaico
- Antigua línea de la costa

Paleta de Narmer
Esta placa tallada de pizarra arenosa verde describe el triunfo del legendario rey Narmer del Alto Egipto sobre sus enemigos.

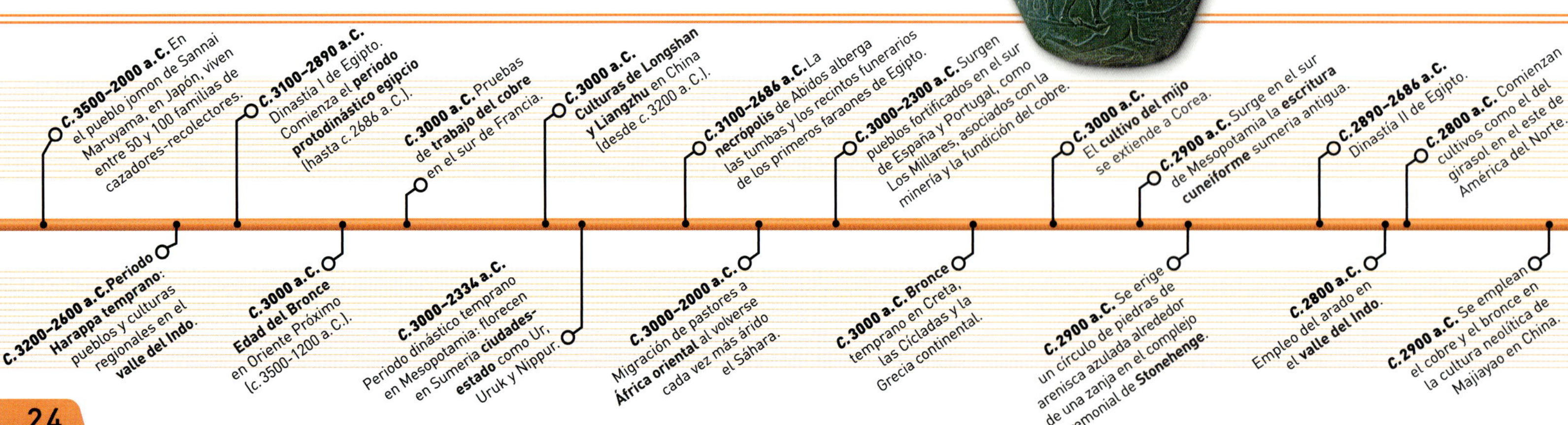

2700–2500 a. C.

Las tres pirámides de Guiza se construyeron para los faraones Keops (Jufu), Kefrén (Jafra) y Micerino (Menkaura) entre 2589 y 2503 a. C. Las protegía la Gran Esfinge, cuyas facciones podrían ser las de Kefrén.

2,3 MILLONES NÚMERO DE **BLOQUES** USADOS EN **LA GRAN PIRÁMIDE** DE GUIZA

Estandarte de Ur
Esta caja tiene dos paneles laterales: uno representa la guerra; el otro (en la imagen), tiempos de paz.

EL SUR DE MESOPOTAMIA era un mosaico de más de 40 ciudades-estado, siendo las más importantes Ur, Uruk, Nippur y Kish. **El comercio floreció** gracias a una red de ríos y canales, y se mantuvieron relaciones comerciales con Anatolia (actual Turquía), Irán y Afganistán, intercambiando grano, madera, minerales, herramientas, cerámica y textiles. La población **sumeria** era singular por ser **predominantemente urbana**. En Ur, Uruk y otros centros se vivía en casas apiñadas de ladrillos de adobe. El templo en el centro de la ciudad era el foco religioso y hogar del dios local, y en el recinto que lo rodeaba vivían los sacerdotes, al frente de propiedades e industrias. Entre 2600 y 2450 a. C., en el gran **cementerio de Ur** se enterraron 16 personas importantes –quizá de la realeza–, con rituales de sacrificios humanos y acompañados de tesoros, como el **estandarte de Ur**, adornado con elaborados diseños hechos con materiales preciosos.

La **primera escritura pictográfica** surgió en Sumeria (*c.* 3300 a. C.) por la necesidad de mantener registros económicos y administrativos. A partir de los pictogramas (imágenes que representan palabras o ideas), hacia *c.* 2900 a. C. se desarrolló la escritura llamada **cuneiforme**, en la que los escribas marcaban impresiones en forma de cuña en tablillas de arcilla blanda con cañas afiladas. La gran densidad de población del sur de Mesopotamia llevó a la competencia por los recursos naturales, a **conflictos** por la tierra y el agua y a forjar y romper alianzas entre ciudades.

Tablilla cuneiforme
El inventario de signos empleados en la escritura cuneiforme se fue reduciendo mucho con el tiempo.

Los primeros signos de **civilización en América** se dieron en las costas de Perú y en los Andes en *c.* 3500–3000 a. C. **Granjeros andinos** cultivaron patatas y quinoa, y criaron alpacas y llamas. En el interior de valles costeros se cultivó algodón, además de maíz, alubias, guayaba, aguacate y batata, mientras comunidades costeras pesqueras explotaban los ricos recursos marinos. Surgieron **ciudades**, como Caral (*c.* 2800), como centros ceremoniales con plataformas piramidales de piedras y barro, asociadas a patios circulares excavados. En Áspero, en la costa, había al menos once de estas plataformas.

En la **llanura del Indo** se asentaron en el IV milenio a. C. agricultores que desarrollaron cierta **tecnología para controlar inundaciones**. Hacia 2600 a. C., grandes cambios acompañaron el surgimiento de la **civilización del valle del Indo**. **Mohenjo-Daro**, en el propio Indo, y **Harappa**, al noreste, fueron ciudades preeminentes, con 100 000 y 60 000 habitantes, respectivamente.

En **Egipto**, el ascenso al trono del faraón Sanajt en 2686 a. C. marcó el inicio de la dinastía III y del **Imperio Antiguo**, una época de fuerte gobierno centralizado en la que se **construyeron pirámides**. Estos monumentos magníficos eran **tumbas reales**; en el periodo protodinástico se había enterrado a los faraones bajo plataformas de adobe llamadas mastabas. Hacia 2650 a. C. se terminó para el rey Zoser **la pirámide escalonada de Saqqara**, considerada la primera. Diseñada por el arquitecto Imhotep, tenía el aspecto de seis mastabas de piedra, una sobre otra.

Poco después aparecieron las pirámides de perfil liso, de las que las mayores son las tres **pirámides de Guiza**. Estas hazañas de la ingeniería no las construyeron esclavos, como antes se creía, sino equipos a tiempo completo de artesanos y canteros, con la ayuda de campesinos que prestaban servicio al Estado durante la inundación del Nilo. Se cortaban bloques enormes de piedra (los inferiores de 6–10 toneladas, los superiores de 1–2 toneladas) en las canteras locales, se transportaban sobre trineos, y se izaban por rampas, cada vez más altas a medida que avanzaba la construcción.

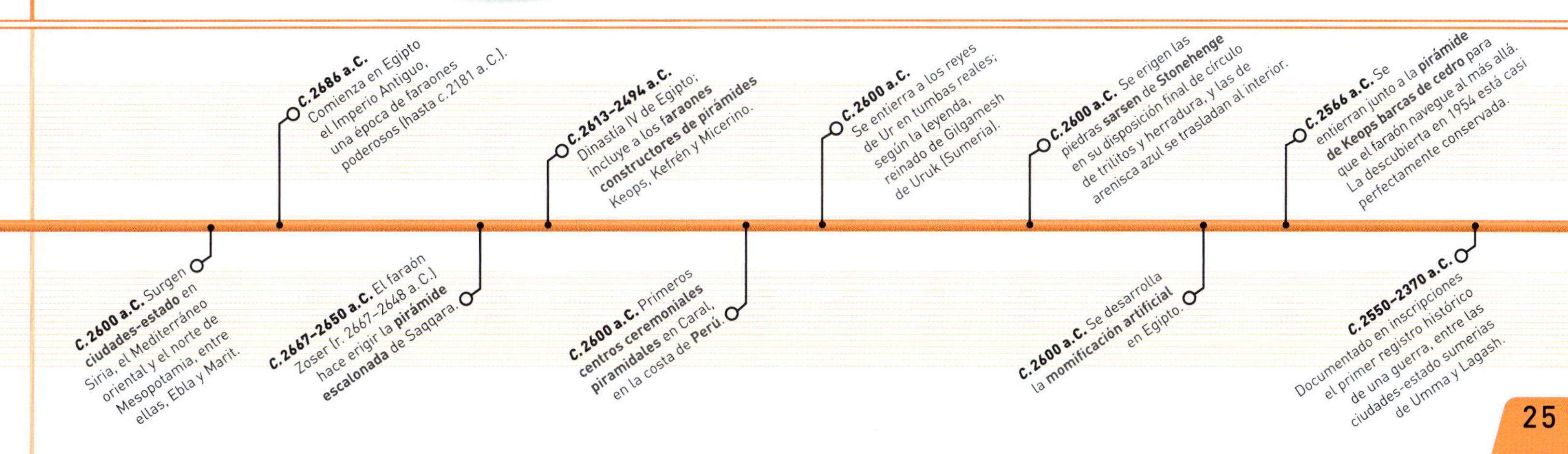

2500–2350 a.C.

Ruinas de la ciudadela de Mohenjo-Daro, compuesta por varios edificios. Fue construida sobre una plataforma para protegerla de las inundaciones del Indo.

EN LA SEGUNDA MITAD DEL III MILENIO A.C. siguieron desarrollándose civilizaciones en Oriente Medio, en Egipto y en el sur de Asia, y surgieron sociedades complejas en China, Europa y América del Sur.

En el sur de Asia, la **civilización del Indo** (*véase* 2700–2500 a.C.) llegó a su madurez *c.* 2600 a.C., extendiéndose 1700 km de este a oeste y 1300 km de norte a sur. La prosperidad de la región estaba basada en la agricultura, la minería, la artesanía y el comercio. Entre los más de cien sitios excavados en ella se encuentran las ciudades de Mohenjo-Daro, Harappa y Dholavira.

Mohenjo-Daro y **Harappa** eran ciudades **bien planificadas**, diseñadas en cuadrícula. Estaban protegidas por muros de adobe y dominadas por una **ciudadela** que controlaba una «ciudad baja» de edificios públicos y **casas adosadas** de una o dos plantas. Las zonas residenciales parecían estar divididas por industrias, como alfarería, bisutería y metalurgia.

Además, las ciudades del Indo contaron con el **sistema de tuberías más avanzado** de todo el mundo antiguo, con pozos cerrados y desagües cubiertos bajo las calles que recibían las aguas residuales de las letrinas.

Estos centros urbanos estaban conectados por extensas **redes comerciales**. Los mercaderes aportaban productos manufacturados de los valles a las regiones circundantes a cambio de menas metálicas, piedras preciosas y madera. Las rutas comerciales de larga distancia llegaron a Mesopotamia y Afganistán.

En torno a 2500 a.C. apareció en sellos y cerámicas la **escritura del Indo**, compuesta por cientos de signos. Los intentos por descifrarla han fracasado; de ahí que muchos aspectos de esta cultura sigan siendo un misterio.

En Oriente Medio, **Mesopotamia** (*véase* 2700–2500 a.C.) seguía siendo un mosaico de pequeñas pero **poderosas ciudades-estado**, cada una de las cuales controlaba sus tierras circundantes, donde se cultivaban cebada, legumbres y dátiles. Más al oeste florecían ciudades-estado en Siria y el Mediterráneo oriental. Entre las ciudades mesopotámicas existió una **red comercial** que sugiere cierta colaboración, pero también eran frecuentes los **conflictos armados**.

Shortugai
Himalaya
Indo
Meseta iraní
Ropar
Banawali
Harappa
Rhakighari
Kalibangan
Nausharo
Valle del Indo
Mohenjo-Daro
Montes Zagros
Chanhu-Daro
Dholavira
Indo
Golfo Pérsico
Sutkagen Dor
Lothal
Kuntasi
Mar Arábigo

Civilización del Indo
Las excavaciones indican que la civilización del Indo cubrió una extensión mayor que Mesopotamia y Egipto juntas.

CLAVE
- Zona de civilización urbana
- Centros urbanos
- Antigua costa

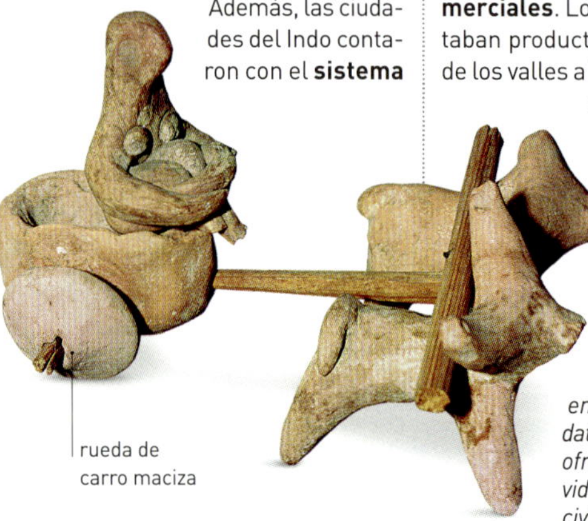

Vidas agrícolas
Este modelo en arcilla de un carro de bueyes hallado en Mohenjo-Daro y datado c. *2500–1900 a.C. ofrece una visión de la vida campesina en la civilización del Indo.*

2350–2200 a.C.

El gran túmulo de creta de Silbury Hill, en Wiltshire (Inglaterra), es el mayor de Europa. Su finalidad, sin embargo, se desconoce.

EN MESOPOTAMIA APARECIÓ UNA NUEVA POTENCIA: el **rey Sargón** (*c.* 2334–2279 a.C.) nacido en la ciudad norteña de **Acad**, derrotó a Lugalzagesi de Umma y se convirtió en rey de Sumer. A lo largo de sucesivas campañas hacia el Mediterráneo oriental, en Siria y Anatolia, Sargón consiguió levantar el **primer imperio de la historia**, que se extendería desde el Mediterráneo oriental hasta el golfo Pérsico: el Imperio acadio.

Sargón y sus sucesores dejaron constancia de sus conquistas y logros en numerosas inscripciones. Su nombre significa «**rey legítimo**», lo que llevó a algunos estudiosos a creer que tomó el poder por la fuerza. Sargón hablaba acadio, una lengua semítica que reemplazó al sumerio como idioma oficial del imperio.

El gobierno acadio era impuesto por medio de gobernadores regionales que recaudaban tributos. La **debilidad del imperio** radicaba en la ausencia de **fronteras** defendibles, y se vio sometido a **ataques** regulares de las **tribus montañesas** vecinas. Naram-Sin, nieto de Sargón, extendió el imperio, pero este solo duraría cuatro generaciones antes de caer abatido por los ataques. El reinado de Sargón estableció la práctica del control burocrático estatal y reguló muchos aspectos de la vida económica.

En **Egipto**, este periodo coincide con el **debilitamiento** del poder real en el **Imperio Antiguo** (*véase* 2700–2500 a.C.) a favor de los gobernadores locales (**nomarcas**) que administraban las distintas zonas del valle y el delta del Nilo. Al sur de la primera catarata del Nilo crecía el **poder** del **reino de Kush**, surgido en torno a la ciudad de Kerma, en la tercera catarata. Hacia el final de la **dinastía VI** (c. 2181 a.C.),

> « BAJO SU MANO **LOS PUEBLOS** SE CONTENTARON CON SUS PRADOS, Y **LA TIERRA SE REGOCIJÓ**. »
>
> **Inscripción de Lugalzagesi**, rey de Sumer, describiendo su reinado

EDAD DEL BRONCE EUROPEA

La cultura de Únětice de Bohemia y Polonia desarrolló el trabajo del bronce hacia 2300 a.C. con minas en los Cárpatos y en Europa central. También se desarrolló independientemente en la Europa atlántica hacia 2100 a.C. Era un metal duro, adecuado para armas, armaduras y herramientas, como esta hacha. La industria del bronce estimuló el comercio, lo cual aumentó las interconexiones en Europa.

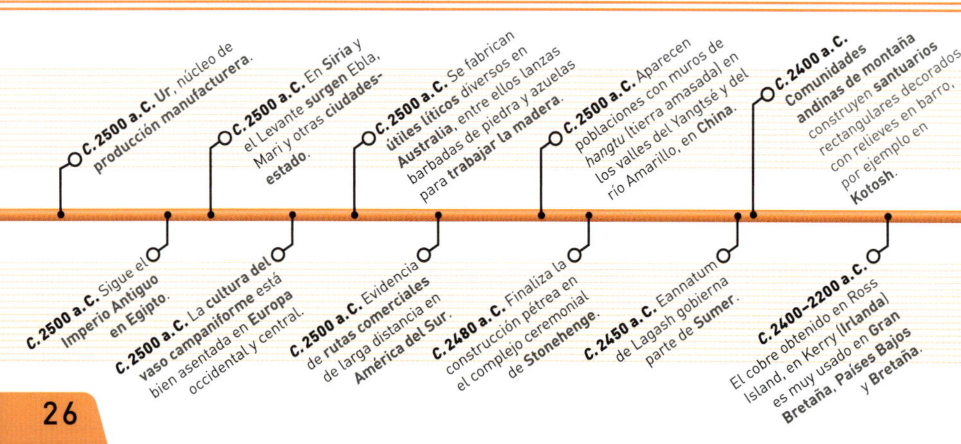

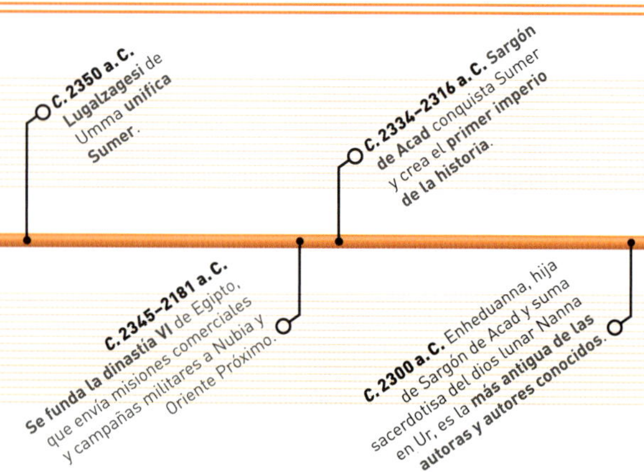

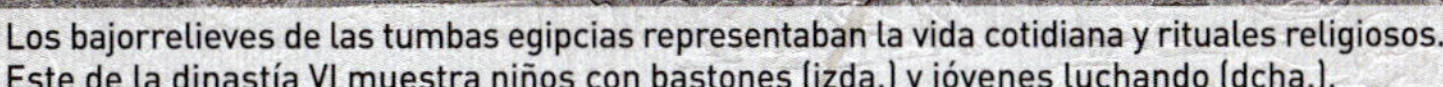

Los bajorrelieves de las tumbas egipcias representaban la vida cotidiana y rituales religiosos. Este de la dinastía VI muestra niños con bastones (izda.) y jóvenes luchando (dcha.).

la autoridad de los reyes egipcios ya había sido socavada.

En **Europa occidental** floreció la cultura del **vaso campaniforme**, así llamada por la forma de la **cerámica** característica hallada en las tumbas. Surgió *c.* 2900 a.C., probablemente en Iberia, y se difundió primero a Francia por mar. En 2500 a.C. llegó a Europa occidental y central. Hacia 2300 a.C., la **tecnología del bronce** del Mediterráneo y Centroeuropa empezó a **propagarse** al norte siguiendo los cursos del **Rin** y del **Danubio**; sociedades cada vez más militarizadas usaban el bronce para crear armas, lo que desencadenó la aparición de **jefaturas** en toda Europa.

A medida que iban creciendo las poblaciones, también comenzó a intensificarse la **competencia** por la **tierra** y los **recursos**. Los campos se cercaron, la agricultura se expandió y se construyeron muros fronterizos. En muchas zonas se erigieron estructuras imponentes, como los **túmulos funerarios**.

En **América del Sur** las sociedades se desarrollaron en dos regiones separadas: los **valles** del altiplano y las **llanuras altas** en los **Andes**, y la **costa del Pacífico** y los valles interiores. Las culturas andinas estaban basadas en **la agricultura y en el pastoreo**. **Asentamientos costeros** como Áspero, en Perú, dependían de la **pesca**, e intercambiaban pescado seco por cultivos, algodón para textiles, hilo y redes de pesca y calabazas como boyas con comunidades del interior.

Rey guerrero acadio
Esta máscara de bronce de un rey acadio pudo representar a Sargón I o a su nieto, Naram-Sin, que extendió el imperio de Sargón.

REYES DÉBILES POSTERIORES permitieron a muchas **ciudades-estado sumerias**, como **Uruk**, **Ur** y **Lagash**, separarse del Imperio acadio en 2193 a.C. Los **guti** de los montes Zagros atacaron a menudo al menguante imperio, y lo conquistaron en 2154 a.C. Una coalición de ciudades-estado sumerias acabó por expulsarlos. Bajo **Ur-Nammu de Ur** (r. 2112–2095 a.C.), los ejércitos sumerios conquistaron **Elam** y las regiones orientales y crearon un vasto imperio nuevo. Ur-Nammu fundó la **tercera dinastía de Ur**, que supuso la **reactivación del poder sumerio**, además de un gran **renacimiento** cultural. Los eruditos sumerios diseñaron un método de cómputo basado en unidades de 60 que todavía hoy en día se refleja en la división de la hora en 60 minutos, el minuto en 60 segundos y el círculo en 360 grados.

Ur-Nammu también encargó la construcción del **primer zigurat** en Ur: una imponente estructura escalonada y rematada por un templo. Los zigurats acabarían siendo una característica de la arquitectura antigua en el sur de Mesopotamia.

El **Imperio Antiguo** egipcio se hundió en torno a 2181 a.C., después de una serie de desastres naturales que provocaron hambrunas, las cuales socavaron la autoridad real, de la cual se pensaba que debía garantizar las inundaciones anuales que fertilizaban el valle del Nilo. El poder de Menfis, la capital del Imperio Antiguo, quedó completamente desautorizado cuando nomarcas y nobles se hicieron con el control de las provincias. Esto inició una época de **agitación** conocida como **Primer Periodo Intermedio**, la primera de las tres etapas de incertidumbre en la historia egipcia. Durante aproximadamente 140 años, algunos reinos como Henen-nesut (Egipto central) se disputaron el poder con Uaset (Tebas, en el sur de Egipto). Ya en 2040 a.C., el rey tebano **Mentuhotep II** derrotó a sus rivales y **reunificó Egipto**, lo que dio comienzo al **Imperio Medio**.

Alrededor de 2000 a.C., la productividad agrícola aumentó marcadamente en el valle del río Amarillo en China con la evolución del arroz de alto rendimiento y la introducción del trigo, la cebada y el ganado ovino y bovino del oeste de Asia. Según la tradición histórica china, Yu el Grande **fundó** la **primera dinastía**, la de los **Xia**. Sin embargo, **no se ha encontrado ninguna prueba arqueológica** que confirme la existencia de un **estado centralizado** en China durante esta época.

Por último, hacia el final del III milenio a.C. estaba naciendo la **primera civilización europea** en la isla de **Creta**. Conocida como **civilización minoica**, prosperó a través del **comercio** y de la **agricultura**. Las granjas cretenses producían importantes cantidades de trigo, aceitunas, vino y lana, que podían ser transportados fácilmente por mar. Los minoicos también exportaban trabajos en bronce, cerámica y tintes. En 2000 a.C. Creta albergaba varios pequeños reinos.

Cerámica de Longshan
Este elegante trípode muestra las patas cónicas y los patrones enroscados típicos de la cultura de Longshan.

100 MILLARDOS
POBLACIÓN PROBABLE DE LA CIUDAD DE **UR** *c.* 2100 a.C.

c. 2300 a.C. Comienza la **Edad del Bronce** en **Europa central**.

c. 2300 a.C. Comienza la Edad del Bronce en el sur de Europa, Italia y los Balcanes.

c. 2278–2184 a.C. Reinado de **Pepi II**, de la dinastía VI de **Egipto**.

c. 2200 a.C. El **oro** y el **estaño** de **Cornualles** se explotan y comercializan ampliamente.

c. 2200 a.C. Pueblos probablemente procedentes de **Siberia** se asientan en el **Ártico**.

c. 2181 a.C. Comienza el **Primer Periodo Intermedio** en Egipto (hasta 2040 a.C.)

2119 a.C. Una coalición de **ciudades-estado sumerias** dirigida por **Utu-hegal** de Uruk expulsa a los **guti** y recupera el control de **Acad**.

c. 2112–2004 a.C. La **Tercera Dinastía de Ur** combina una gran **creatividad cultural** y un amplio **comercio marítimo** con una **burocracia excesiva**.

c. 2100–1800 a.C. La cultura de Sintashta, en **Kazajistán**, desarrolla la **equitación** y los **carros** ligeros y rápidos de **ruedas con radios**.

c. 2070 a.C. Según la tradición china, **Yu el Grande funda la dinastía Xia** en el este de **China**; se dice que duró hasta 1766 a.C.

c. 2040 a.C. Mentuhotep III de Tebas derrota a sus rivales y **reunifica Egipto**.

c. 2040 a.C. Mentuhotep II establece una nueva **capital** en Itj-tawy, cerca de Menfis; comienza el **Imperio Medio**.

2004 a.C. La ciudad de **Ur cae** en manos de los elamitas; fin de la **dinastía de Ur**.

los jeroglíficos son signos gráficos

la escritura hierática se lee de derecha a izquierda

el papiro se obtiene prensando tiras de la planta en varias capas

la ilustración muestra un sacerdote realizando una ofrenda al dios Osiris

Jeroglífico y escritura hierática egipcios
Este antiguo papiro manuscrito egipcio muestra dos formas de escritura: la hierática (izda.) y la jeroglífica (dcha., sobre las dos figuras). La escritura hierática es una versión simplificada que facilita la lectura y escritura de la compleja escritura jeroglífica, en la cual los signos tienen una acusada forma pictórica.

Prehistoria
Pictogramas
Las imágenes pintadas en cuevas hace 25 000 años son precursoras de la escritura, al registrar información que luego podía ser entendida por otros.

Imágenes rupestres de los pueblo ancestrales.

3300 a.C.
Cuneiforme
La primera escritura propiamente dicha fue creada por los sumerios de Mesopotamia. Escrita con cañas afiladas, producía signos en forma de cuña sobre tablillas de arcilla húmeda que se endurecían al secarlas.

Tablilla mesopotámica

***C.* 3300 a.C.**
Jeroglíficos egipcios
Empleada primero para registros administrativos, esta escritura representa palabras y sílabas con signos pictóricos estilizados, junto con determinativos (mudos) que ayudan a interpretar otros signos.

***C.* 1900 a.C.**
Escritura china
La primera escritura china nos ha llegado sobre huesos de oráculo usados en adivinación. Esta escritura todavía se utiliza hoy; consta de 50 000 caracteres que representan palabras.

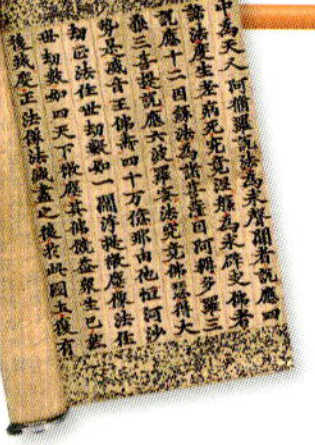

Rollo de papel chino

Siglo VIII a.C.
Alfabeto griego
Los primeros alfabetos, que solo utilizaban consonantes, aparecieron en el Levante *c.* 1150 a.C. Uno de ellos, el fenicio, pasó a los griegos, que le añadieron las vocales, a través del comercio.

Tablilla encerada griega

***C.* 600 a.C.**
Escritura mesoamericana
Esta escritura se usó con fines fines religiosos y en calendarios. Las inscripciones zapotecas tienen nombres y fechas, un antecedente de la escritura maya clásica en la que los reyes registraron sus biografías.

100 d.C.
Alfabeto latino
Los romanos adaptaron el griego a la escritura latina. El Imperio romano lo difundió por toda Europa, y fue usado tanto para la correspondencia oficial como para la personal.

Rollo de pergamino chino

HISTORIA DE LA ESCRITURA

DE LAS PINTURAS RUPESTRES A LA ERA DIGITAL, LA ESCRITURA HA SIDO SIEMPRE PARTE IMPORTANTE DE NUESTRA CIVILIZACIÓN

El surgimiento de la escritura supuso un avance asombroso, pues permitió la comunicación a distancia y el registro de información para la posteridad. La escritura evolucionó por separado en distintas culturas: en Mesopotamia, Egipto y el valle del Indo antes de 2500 a. C.; luego en Creta, China y Mesoamérica.

Algunos estudiosos consideran que las pinturas rupestres prehistóricas constituyen una forma de escritura. La primera escritura propiamente dicha fue creada por los sumerios en Mesopotamia (hoy Iraq) *c.* 3300 a. C. Pronto, otras culturas desarrollaron sistemas escritos, normalmente para mantener registros económicos o temporales. A medida que evolucionaba, la escritura sirvió para reforzar el poder real. Muchos textos tempranos, incluidos los monumentales sobre piedra, glorifican las proezas de los reyes y atribuyen sus éxitos a la aprobación divina.

Los sistemas de escritura pueden dividirse en tres tipos, según la función de los signos usados: logográfico, silábico y alfabético; aunque algunos hacen uso de dos tipos de signos. En la escritura logográfica cada signo representa una palabra, un ejemplo es la escritura china, aunque también usa signos silábicos. Su inconveniente es que precisa muchos símbolos (el chino tiene 50 000 caracteres). En la silábica, los signos representan sílabas; necesita una cantidad menor, pero aún importante, de signos: 700 en la cuneiforme babilónica. En la alfabética, cada signo representa un sonido; en ella se precisan muchos menos signos: normalmente, unos 26. Los primeros alfabetos surgieron entre 1450 y 1150 a. C. en el Mediterráneo oriental. Durante años, la difusión de la escritura estuvo limitada a las élites, pero la invención de la imprenta lo cambió todo. A finales del siglo XX, la escritura se hizo electrónica con la introducción de los procesadores de texto. En la década de 1990, Internet supuso una nueva revolución en la difusión de la información.

Textos antiguos en un mundo digital
Hoy podemos acceder digitalmente a textos antiguos. Aquí una estudiante examina una copia digital del Codex Sinaiticus, *manuscrito en griego hace más de 1600 años.*

Mosaico romano

Señal actual

SIGNOS PICTOGRÁFICOS

Los pictogramas, o signos pictóricos, son una antigua forma de comunicación. Algunos estudiosos no los consideran escritura «auténtica» porque no comunican el sonido de palabras en idioma alguno. Las imágenes superiores, por ejemplo –de una casa romana en Pompeya, datada en 79 d. C., y de una señal actual–, trasmiten un aviso idéntico. Este símbolo puede ser leído en cualquier idioma, por ejemplo como *canis*, *chien*, *Hund* o *perro*. Aunque las palabras comunican la misma idea, reproducen los sonidos de lenguas distintas: latín, francés, alemán y español. Los pictogramas tienen un uso limitado, pero muy extendido, y aparecen por ejemplo en señales de tráfico, mapas y etiquetas de ropa.

Siglo IV
Códices
El códice, o manuscrito en forma de libro, fue reemplazando gradualmente al pergamino. Desarrollado por los romanos, su empleo se extendió gracias a la religión cristiana.

Siglo VII
Escritura árabe
El alfabeto árabe fue usado para escribir el Corán, libro sagrado del islam. Su uso se propagó gracias a la fe islámica hasta llegar a ser una de las escrituras más difundidas del mundo.

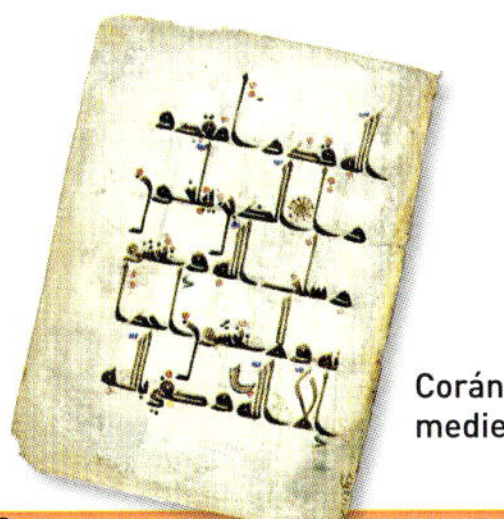

Corán medieval

Siglos VII–IX
Manuscritos iluminados
La escritura se difundió al inicio de la Edad Media gracias a la copia de textos cristianos. Los manuscritos iluminados, muy decorados, tenían letras capitulares ornamentadas e ilustraciones marginales.

Libro de Durrow

***C.* 1450**
Invención de la imprenta
El trabajo que supone copiar a mano limitaba la difusión de la escritura. La invención de los tipos móviles en China por Pi Sheng hacia 1040 d. C. derivó en la creación de la imprenta por Gutenberg, que hizo mucho más accesible la escritura en Europa.

1867–1868
La máquina de escribir
El inventor estadounidense Christopher L. Sholes ayudó a construir la primera máquina de escribir. La patente fue vendida a Remington, que puso las primeras máquinas a la venta en 1874.

Remington Model I

1884
La pluma estilográfica
El inventor estadounidense L. E. Waterman produjo la primera pluma estilográfica útil, que reemplazó con rapidez a la de ave. En 1943, Lászlo Biró patentó el bolígrafo.

Pluma estilográfica Waterman

1971
Escritura en la era digital
En 1971 Ray Tomlinson envió el primer mensaje electrónico de un ordenador a otro. En la década de 1980, la difusión de los ordenadores personales popularizó este sistema.

1990–actualidad
Mensajes de texto
En la década de 1990 se envían los primeros mensajes de texto por teléfono móvil, sistema que se hará muy popular en la década siguiente. En 2009 se habían enviado más de 1,5 billones de mensajes.

Smartphone

Los jeroglíficos egipcios incluían el uso de signos pictóricos que representan palabras y sílabas. Esta muestra es de una caja mortuoria del Imperio Medio.

LA CIVILIZACIÓN MINOICA, a la que dio nombre el legendario rey Minos, **floreció** en la **isla egea** de **Creta** a principios del II milenio a. C., y alcanzó su cénit entre 2000 y 1600 a. C. Se cree que la **prosperidad** de Creta fue el resultado de una agricultura productiva y de la **exportación de alfarería, textiles, alimentos y bienes de lujo** a Egipto, Chipre y áreas del Mediterráneo oriental y del Egeo. Los minoicos fundaron colonias en muchas partes del mar Egeo, entre ellas las islas de Citera, Tera, Melos y Rodas, así como en Mileto (Asia Menor).

Las tierras de cultivo en Creta estaban bajo el control de ciudades con **palacios centrales**, talleres, edificios administrativos y religiosos y almacenes estatales. A juzgar por los restos conservados, fueron particularmente impresionantes los palacios de Cnosos, Festos, Malia y Zacros. Hacia 1700 a. C., un terremoto destruyó los palacios. El de **Cnosos** se **reconstruyó** a una escala aún más magnífica que antes, lo cual sugiere que dominaba toda la isla. El palacio era de cinco plantas, con estancias que daban a patios interiores. Se cree que este laberíntico complejo dio origen al laberinto de la **leyenda del Minotauro**, monstruo con cabeza de toro. Sin duda, los toros eran parte de las ceremonias minoicas. Las **deidades** veneradas en los altares minoicos parecen haber sido **femeninas**, siendo la más popular una **diosa de la naturaleza**; pero los detalles de la cultura minoica continúan siendo un misterio, pues sus tipos de escritura, llamadas jeroglífico cretense y lineal A, no se han podido descifrar aún.

En Egipto, el faraón Mentuhotep II reunificó el país hacia el final del III milenio, pero la segunda época de gobierno poderoso y centralizado no llegaría hasta **Amenemes I**, desde *c.* 1985 a. C., durante el Imperio Medio. En 1965 a. C., su sucesor, **Senusret I**, conquistó **Nubia**, al sur, llevando así los límites de Egipto hasta la segunda catarata del Nilo. Nubia aportó a Egipto oro, cobre y esclavos, y el ejército egipcio empleó mercenarios nubios. Un siglo más tarde, **Senusret III** conquistó el **Mediterráneo oriental**.

El **Imperio Medio egipcio** tuvo un carácter **más democrático** que el Imperio Antiguo. Los faraones se presentaban más como conductores del Estado que como monarcas absolutos. El proceso de momificación, antes exclusivo de los faraones, se **permitía también al pueblo llano**. Para conservar el cuerpo como hogar permanente del espíritu, se extraían los órganos vitales, se desecaba el cuerpo con natrón, se rellenaba con lino y se envolvía con vendajes.

40
DÍAS ERAN NECESARIOS PARA PODER **MOMIFICAR** UN **CUERPO**

Toro embistiendo
Los rituales minoicos incluían el salto del toro. Este fresco de Cnosos se remonta a c. 1500 a. C.

Bronce Xia
Placa de bronce del periodo Xia, hallada en Erlitou. La adorna un mosaico de turquesas, y se cree que representa las escamas de un dragón.

SEGÚN LA TRADICIÓN, LA PRIMERA DINASTÍA CHINA fue la de los **Xia**, que se supone llegó al poder en 2070 a. C. tras una gran inundación en el valle del **río Amarillo**. No hay pruebas de ello, aunque hallazgos recientes apuntan a que hubo una gran inundación alrededor de 1920 a. C. Hoy se cree que Erlitou (provincia de Henan) fue la capital Xia. Los arqueólo-

20 000
TABLILLAS DE ARCILLA SE HAN ENCONTRADO HASTA AHORA EN **MARI**

C. 2000–1750 a. C. Tras la caída del imperio de Ur III, **Estados rivales de Mesopotamia** compiten por el poder. Se imponen Isin y, luego, Larsa en el sur.

C. 2000 a. C. Cultivo de maíz, alubias y calabazas en el suroeste de América del Norte; se crean largas rutas comerciales.

C. 2000 a. C. Desde el área de la estepa se difunden la práctica de **montar a caballo** y los **carros** tirados por caballos, lo cual revoluciona la guerra y el transporte.

C. 2000 a. C. El cultivo del **mijo perla** se asienta en la **región del Sahel**, en África.

C. 1985–1795 a. C. La necrópolis de **Tebas** contiene las tumbas de **faraones** del **Imperio Medio** y del **Imperio Nuevo**.

C. 1985–1965 a. C. El faraón Amenemes I lleva la estabilidad a Egipto durante el **Imperio Medio**.

C. 1985–1795 a. C. Los **faraones de la XII Dinastía** egipcia hacen de la ciudad sagrada de Tebas la capital del **Alto Egipto**.

1965 a. C. Sensusret I de Egipto conquista Nubia y extiende su reino hasta la segunda catarata del Nilo.

C. 1900 a. C. Surge como ciudad **Erlitou** en la región del río Amarillo.

C. 1900 a. C. Establecimiento de pueblos y pequeños reinos en **Anatolia**.

C. 1900 a. C. Comienza la escritura entre los **minoicos**, tanto en **jeroglífico cretense** como **lineal A**.

C. 1900–1700 a. C. Declive de la **civilización del Indo**; gradualmente se abandonan sus ciudades.

C. 1894 a. C. Fundación de la primera dinastía de **Babilonia**.

C. 1877 a. C. Se construye la ciudad amurallada de Kahun para albergar a los trabajadores del culto mortuorio del faraón Senusret II (1877–1870 a. C.), enterrado en la pirámide de Lahun.

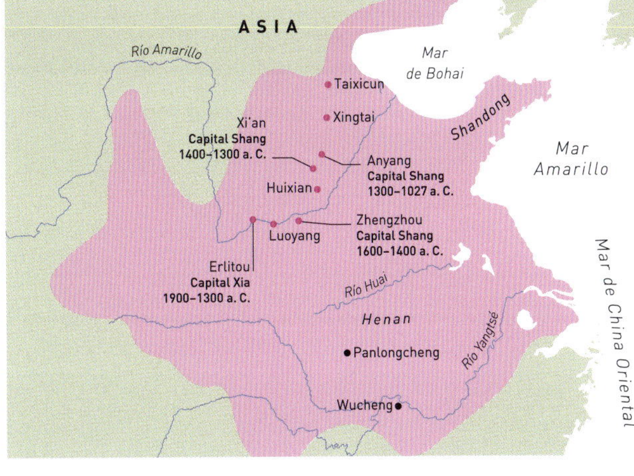

CLAVE
Área de influencia Shang
• Ciudad Shang

China Xia y Shang
El curso medio del río Amarillo fue el corazón de la civilización Xia y Shang entre c. 2100 a.C. y 1100 a.C. Desde allí se difundió su influencia cultural, como el trabajo en bronce.

gos descubrieron allí vasijas de bronce y un **complejo palaciego** construido sobre una plataforma de tierra compactada alrededor de 1900 a.C. A la dinastía Xia le sucedió la **Shang** alrededor de 1600 a.C. Muchos rasgos de la sociedad china posterior, como una **burocracia** sólida y la **veneración de los antepasados**, se remontan a los Shang.

En el sur de Asia, la **civilización del Indo**, que prosperó durante el III milenio (*véase* 2500–2350 a.C.), entró **en declive** hacia *c.* 1800 a.C. Los estudiosos lo atribuyen en parte a cambios en el régimen fluvial de los ríos que alimentaban los regadíos. Parece que **las ciudades fueron asoladas por enfermedades** como el cólera y la malaria. El comercio con Mesopotamia también decayó, y la importancia creciente de algunos cultivos, como el mijo y el arroz, cambió las prácticas agrícolas. Todos estos factores parecen haber llevado a un **declive de la cultura urbana**, caracterizada por la escritura y una burocracia centralizada, en favor de una **cultura rural**.

En América del Sur, alrededor de 1800 a.C. se practicaba el cultivo a gran escala a lo largo de la costa del Pacífico. **Enormes complejos ceremoniales** dominaban asentamientos importantes, como **El Paraíso** y **Sechín Alto**, en Perú. Largas rutas comerciales comunicaban las poblaciones costeras con comunidades en los valles andinos al este y más allá. En Perú comenzó a fabricarse **cerámica** para cocinar alimentos como tubérculos y alubias a partir de 2000 a.C.

En Oriente Próximo, a la caída de la tercera dinastía de Ur siguió la lucha por el poder entre las ciudades-estado. **Assur**, en la ribera del Tigris, controló una lucrativa red comercial en el siglo XIX a.C., en la que se intercambiaban textiles de Mesopotamia y estaño afgano por plata de Anatolia. Los reyes amorreos gobernaron muchos Estados, entre ellos: Larsa, que dominó el sur de Mesopotamia; Babilonia, cuya primera dinastía fue fundada en 1894 a.C.; y Mari, en el Éufrates medio. En 1813–1781 a.C., otro rey amorreo, **Samsi-Adad**, fundó un **reino** en la alta Mesopotamia. Las tablillas de arcilla de Mari registran detalles administrativos y políticos de la vida bajo Samsi-Adad, y se conservan también muchos textos literarios de la época, como unas copias de la versión Ur III del poema *Epopeya de Gilgamesh*, una de las obras literarias más antiguas que se conservan.

Héroe sumerio
Tablillas y petroglifos del periodo paleobabilónico registraron la Epopeya de Gilgamesh, *poema narrativo transmitido por la tradición oral.*

« SI UN HOMBRE LIBRE **VACIÓ** EL **OJO** DE OTRO **HOMBRE LIBRE**, SE LE **VACIARÁ** UN OJO. »

Código de Hammurabi, rey de Babilonia

LA CIUDAD-ESTADO DE BABILONIA SURGIÓ y creció en importancia entre 2000 y 1800 a.C. Gobernada por **Hammurabi** desde 1790 a.C., se convirtió en un Estado vasallo de **Samsi-Adad**, pero, tras la muerte de este, su débil sucesor **Ishme-Dagan** fue vasallo de Hammurabi, quien dirigió una coalición contra los Estados más poderosos de la época. En 1764 a.C., Hammurabi y sus aliados hicieron retroceder a los elamitas al este, y en 1762 a.C. conquistaron Eshnunna, más al norte. Su mayor logro, en 1763 a.C., fue derrotar a Larsa, que controlaba el sur de Mesopotamia. En 1757–1755 a.C., Hammurabi se volvió contra su aliado principal, la ciudad de Mari, la cual saqueó, completando así el control de un imperio que abarcaba todo el sur y centro de Mesopotamia.

Hammurabi introdujo el código legal babilonio en sus dominios. Sus 282 leyes regulaban la propiedad, la familia, el comercio y el trabajo. El **código de Hammurabi** es famoso por sus leyes punitivas, que prescribían castigos de dureza igual a la del delito cometido: el «ojo por ojo». Hoy, sin embargo, dicho código se entiende más como una declaración de principios morales que como un sistema judicial impuesto. Como tal, obligaba tanto a los ricos y poderosos como al pueblo llano, y exhortaba al fuerte para que se abstuviera de oprimir al más débil.

Grabado en piedra
El código de Hammurabi fue inscrito en pilares de piedra llamados estelas. En esta se muestra al dios de la justicia, Shamash (dcha.), dictando leyes al rey.

C. 1830 a.C. Un incendio **destruye** el **área comercial** de los mercaderes asirios en Kanesh (Anatolia), aunque, irónicamente, **se salvan** sus archivos, de más de **25 000 tablillas de arcilla**.

1813–1781 a.C. Reinado de Samsi-Adad; conquista el norte de Mesopotamia y funda un **reino en la Alta Mesopotamia** con capital en Shubat-Enlil.

C. 1800 a.C. Se abandona el gran **centro ceremonial de Caral**, en Perú.

C. 1800 a.C. Aparecen **tumbas de élite** en Europa central, bajo túmulos y con bienes de lujo.

C. 1800–1600 a.C. El **disco celeste de Nebra**, con la **luna**, el **sol** y las **constelaciones**, es usado en **observaciones astronómicas** en el centro de Alemania en la Edad del Bronce.

C. 1800–1400 a.C. La **escritura protosinaítica** aparece y se desarrolla como primer alfabeto consonántico (abyad), en Sinaí y, luego, en Canaán.

C. 1800 a.C. La introducción de la **rueda de alfarero** en la Creta minoica inicia la **producción en masa** de cerámica de alta calidad.

C. 1800 a.C. Producción regular de objetos de hierro en Kaman-Kalehöyük (Anatolia).

C. 1800 a.C. Construcción del centro ceremonial de **La Florida** en **Perú**; se encuentra aquí la **cerámica más antigua de Perú**.

C. 1800 a.C. Comienza el asentamiento en San Lorenzo, más tarde un gran centro ceremonial olmeca en Mesoamérica.

1792–1750 a.C. Reinado de **Hammurabi** de Babilonia; establece el **Imperio babilonio** en Mesopotamia y promulga un código legal aplicable en todo el imperio.

C. 1725 a.C. Fin del Imperio Medio egipcio en medio de disturbios; comienza el **Segundo Periodo Intermedio** (1650–1550 a.C.)

C. 1700 a.C. Las **ofrendas votivas** depositadas en una fuente sagrada en El Manatí, en la región mesoamericana del Golfo, representan los **inicios de la cultura olmeca**.

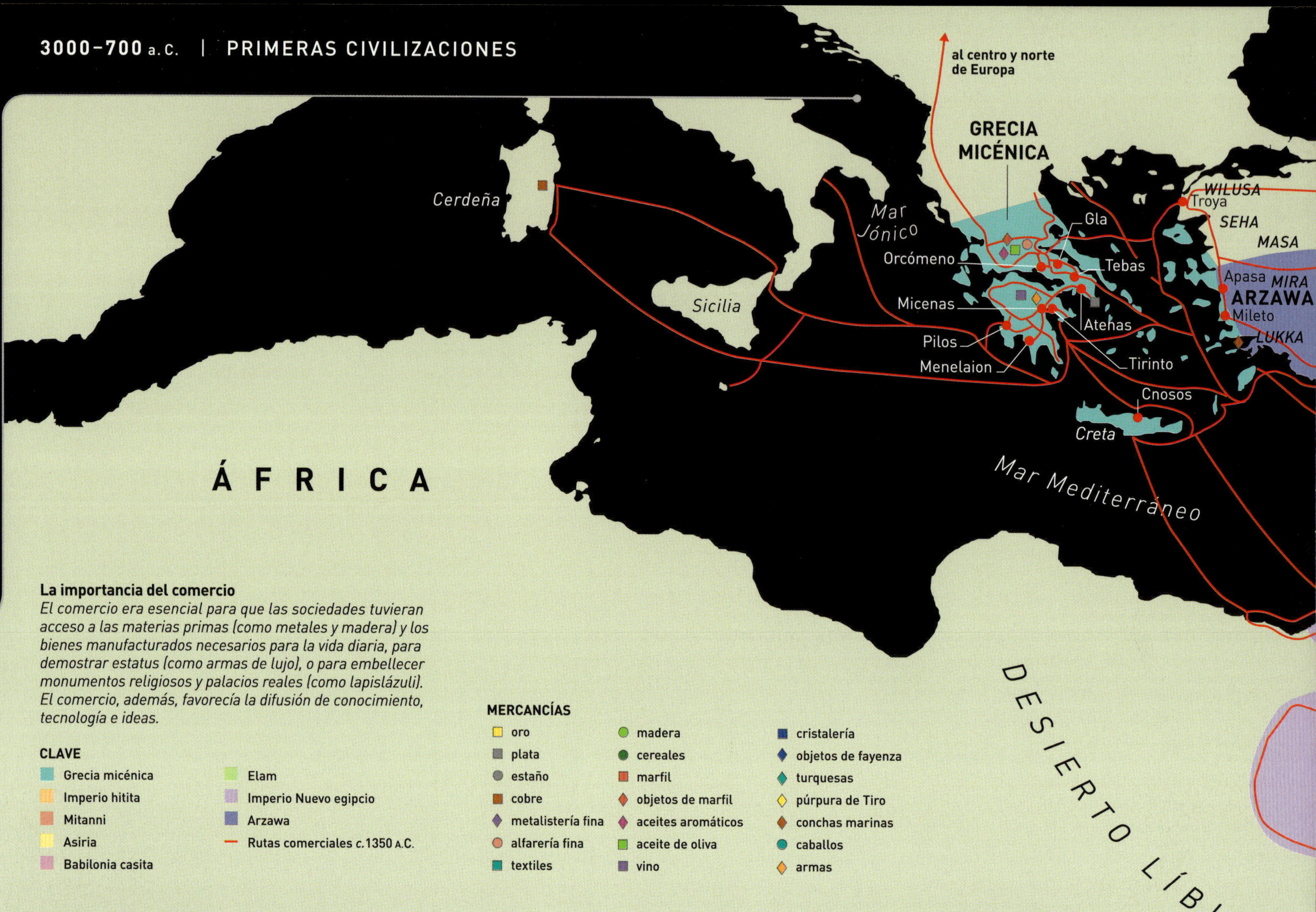

al centro y norte de Europa

GRECIA MICÉNICA

Cerdeña

Mar Jónico

Sicilia

Orcómeno

Gla

Tebas

Micenas

Atenas

Pilos

Menelaion

Tirinto

Cnosos

Creta

WILUSA

Troya

SEHA

MASA

Apasa

MIRA

ARZAWA

Mileto

LUKKA

ÁFRICA

Mar Mediterráneo

DESIERTO LÍBICO

al África subsahariana

La importancia del comercio
El comercio era esencial para que las sociedades tuvieran acceso a las materias primas (como metales y madera) y los bienes manufacturados necesarios para la vida diaria, para demostrar estatus (como armas de lujo), o para embellecer monumentos religiosos y palacios reales (como lapislázuli). El comercio, además, favorecía la difusión de conocimiento, tecnología e ideas.

CLAVE
- Grecia micénica
- Imperio hitita
- Mitanni
- Asiria
- Babilonia casita
- Elam
- Imperio Nuevo egipcio
- Arzawa
- Rutas comerciales c. 1350 a. C.

MERCANCÍAS
- oro
- plata
- estaño
- cobre
- metalistería fina
- alfarería fina
- textiles
- madera
- cereales
- marfil
- objetos de marfil
- aceites aromáticos
- aceite de oliva
- vino
- cristalería
- objetos de fayenza
- turquesas
- púrpura de Tiro
- conchas marinas
- caballos
- armas

IMPERIOS ANTIGUOS

EL NACIMIENTO DE LAS SOCIEDADES AVANZADAS

En el III milenio a. C. surgieron estados en Egipto, Mesopotamia y el Indo. En el II milenio, la sociedad urbana ya se había consolidado en Oriente Medio y poderosos estados competían por el control de la tierra; por contraste, en el sur de Asia desaparecían pueblos. En América y China nacían sociedades complejas.

La excepcional productividad agrícola de los valles de los ríos Nilo, Éufrates, Indo (p. 26) y Amarillo (p. 31) desempeñó un papel clave en el surgimiento precoz de civilizaciones en esas regiones. Lo mismo que el comercio internacional, que además fue importante para el desarrollo de las primeras civilizaciones del Nuevo Mundo. El comercio también permitió prosperar a muchas sociedades vecinas: a lo largo del tiempo desarrollaron culturas complejas cada vez más focalizadas en los centros urbanos y entraron en competencia por recursos y mercados. La diplomacia fue esencial para el funcionamiento fluido de las redes comerciales internacionales y para el éxito en las pugnas de poder entre estados. Cartas reales encontradas en Ajetatón (Amarna), la capital egipcia, ofrecen un cuadro fascinante de las relaciones entre los reyes de los dos grandes estados rivales del Mediterráneo oriental en el siglo XIV a. C.

« DURANTE **LARGO TIEMPO** HEMOS MANTENIDO BUENAS RELACIONES ENTRE NUESTROS **REYES**. »

Rey babilonio Burnaburiash II al faraón egipcio Ajnatón; de las cartas de Amarna (siglo XIV a. C.)

EL PANORAMA MUNDIAL

Durante el II milenio a. C. se extendieron el urbanismo y las sociedades complejas. Aunque compartían muchos rasgos, como el comercio, una alta productividad agrícola, poblaciones densas y necesidades de administración, las sociedades urbanas adoptaron formas distintas. Los grandes complejos ceremoniales con suburbios residenciales de América fueron focos de una región más amplia, conectada por una religión y un comercio compartidos.

Centros avanzados
Este mapa muestra las civilizaciones tanto establecidas como emergentes al final del II milenio a. C. Las sociedades de granjeros y cazadores-recolectores ocupaban otras regiones.

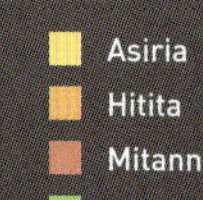

CLAVE
- Chavín
- Olmeca
- Shang
- Micenas
- Egipto
- Babilonia
- Asiria
- Hitita
- Mitanni
- Elam

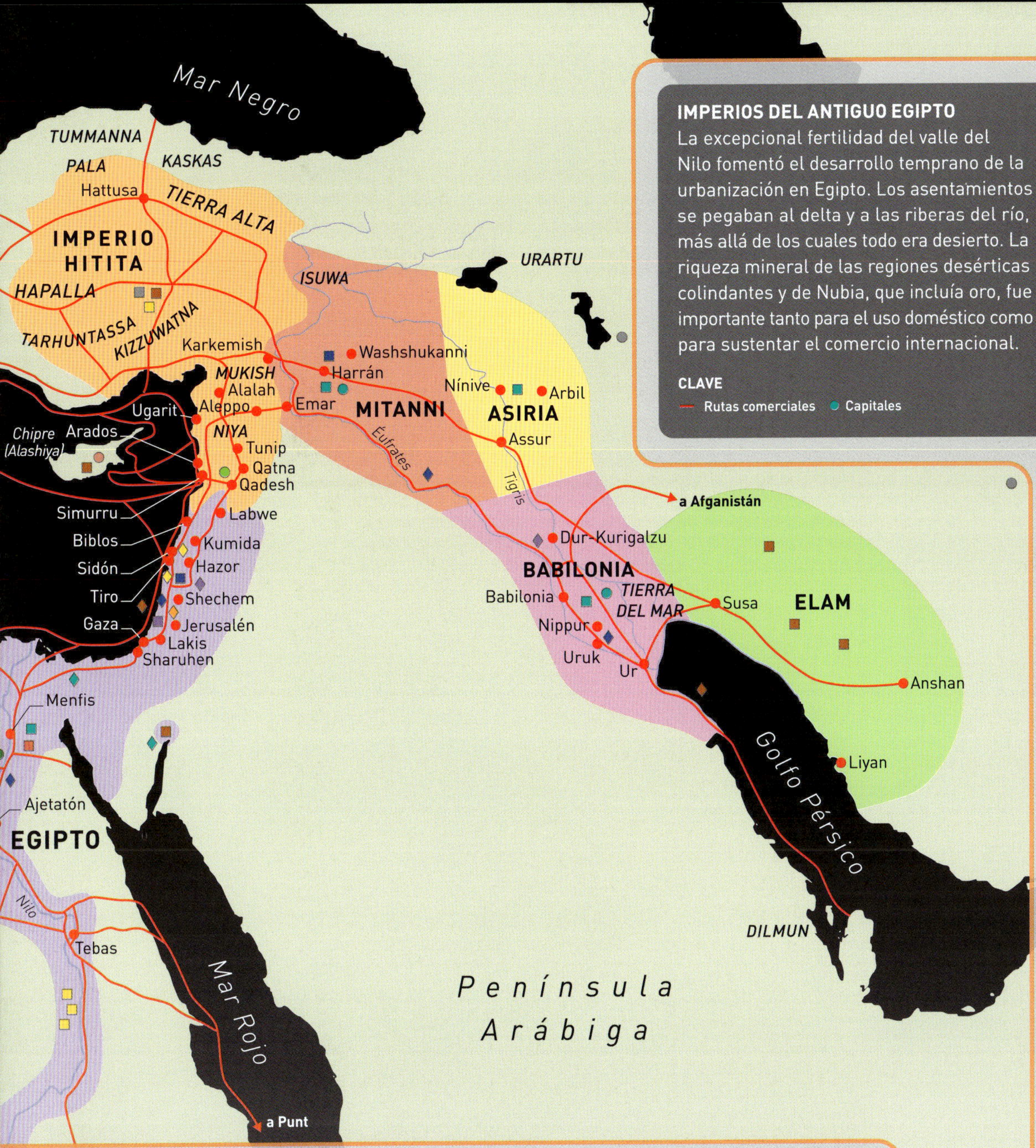

Mar Negro
TUMMANNA
PALA
KASKAS
Hattusa
TIERRA ALTA
IMPERIO HITITA
HAPALLA
ISUWA
URARTU
TARHUNTASSA
KIZZUWATNA
Karkemish
Washshukanni
Harrán
MUKISH
Alalah
Nínive
Arbil
Ugarit
Aleppo
Emar
MITANNI
ASIRIA
Chipre (Alashiya)
Arados
NIYA
Tunip
Assur
Qatna
Qadesh
Éufrates
Tigris
Simurru
Labwe
a Afganistán
Biblos
Kumida
Dur-Kurigalzu
Sidón
Hazor
BABILONIA
Tiro
Shechem
Babilonia
TIERRA DEL MAR
Susa
ELAM
Gaza
Jerusalén
Nippur
Lakis
Sharuhen
Uruk
Ur
Anshan
Menfis
Golfo Pérsico
Liyan
Ajetatón
EGIPTO
Nilo
DILMUN
Tebas
Península Arábiga
Mar Rojo
a Punt

IMPERIOS DEL ANTIGUO EGIPTO

La excepcional fertilidad del valle del Nilo fomentó el desarrollo temprano de la urbanización en Egipto. Los asentamientos se pegaban al delta y a las riberas del río, más allá de los cuales todo era desierto. La riqueza mineral de las regiones desérticas colindantes y de Nubia, que incluía oro, fue importante tanto para el uso doméstico como para sustentar el comercio internacional.

CLAVE

— Rutas comerciales ● Capitales

Chipre
Mar Mediterráneo
Delta del Nilo
BAJO
Guiza
Menfis
Saqqara
EGIPTO
Sinaí
Desierto Oriental
Nilo
DESIERTO OCCIDENTAL
Abidos
ALTO EGIPTO
Elefantina
Mar Rojo
MEDJA
NUBIA
SATJU
YAM
SÁHARA
DESIERTO DE NUBIA

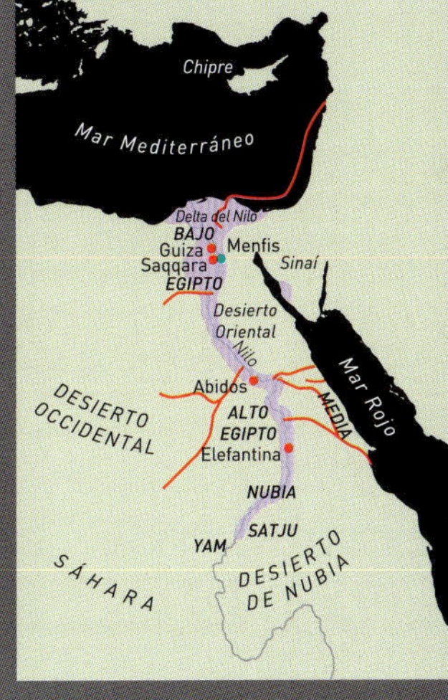

Imperio Antiguo *c.* 2686–2181 a. C.
Los gobernantes ejercen un control centralizado y disponen de recursos impresionantes, como demuestran las pirámides de Guiza.

Chipre
Mar Mediterráneo
Avaris (Tell el-Daba)
capital c. 1650–1550 a.C.
BAJO
Menfis
EGIPTO
Sinaí
Iti-tawy
capital c. 1985–1650 a.C.
Desierto Oriental
Nilo
Waset (Tebas)
Karnak
Mar Rojo
DESIERTO OCCIDENTAL
capital c. 2055–1985 a.C. y c. 1650–1550 a.C.
ALTO EGIPTO
NUBIA
WAWAT
SÁHARA
DESIERTO DE NUBIA
KUSH

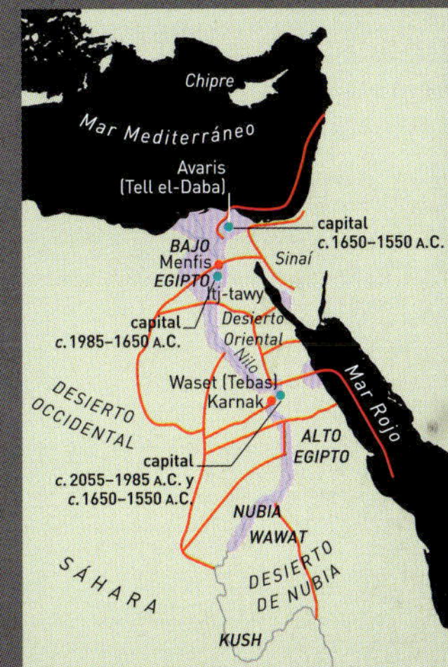

Impero Medio *c.* 2040–1640 a. C.
Las tumbas decoradas constatan una vida próspera bajo la estable dinastía XII, pero el estado se desintegra con los faraones posteriores.

Chipre
Mar Mediterráneo
Per-Ramsés (Qantir)
capital c. 1279–1069 a.C.
BAJO EGIPTO
Menfis
Sinaí
capital c. 1333–1279 a.C.
Desierto Oriental
Ajetatón (Amarna)
capital c. 1349–1333 a.C.
Nilo
Waset (Tebas)
Mar Rojo
DESIERTO OCCIDENTAL
ALTO EGIPTO
capital c. 1550–1349 a.C.
NUBIA
SÁHARA
DESIERTO DE NUBIA
KUSH

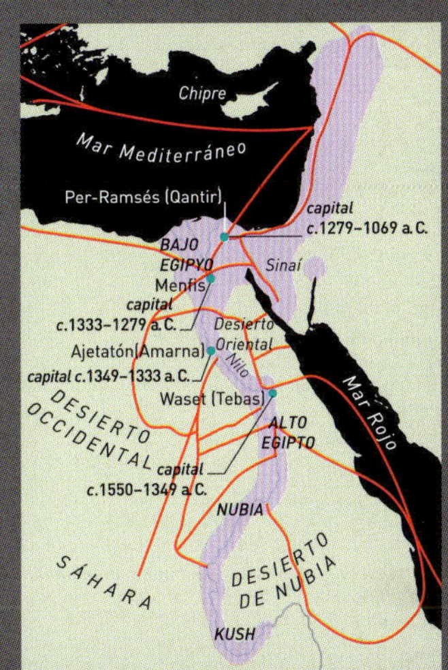

Imperio Nuevo *c.* 1550–1069 a. C.
Egipto alcanza la cima de su poder, conquista Nubia y el Mediterráneo oriental y erige abundantes templos.

Siberia
Hattusa
Micenas
Anyang
Xi'an
Babilonia
Assur
Susa
Menfis
Zhengzhou
OCÉANO ATLÁNTICO
OCÉANO PACÍFICO
SÁHARA
San Lorenzo
Chavín de Huántar
OCÉANO ATLÁNTICO
OCÉANO ÍNDICO
OCÉANO PACÍFICO

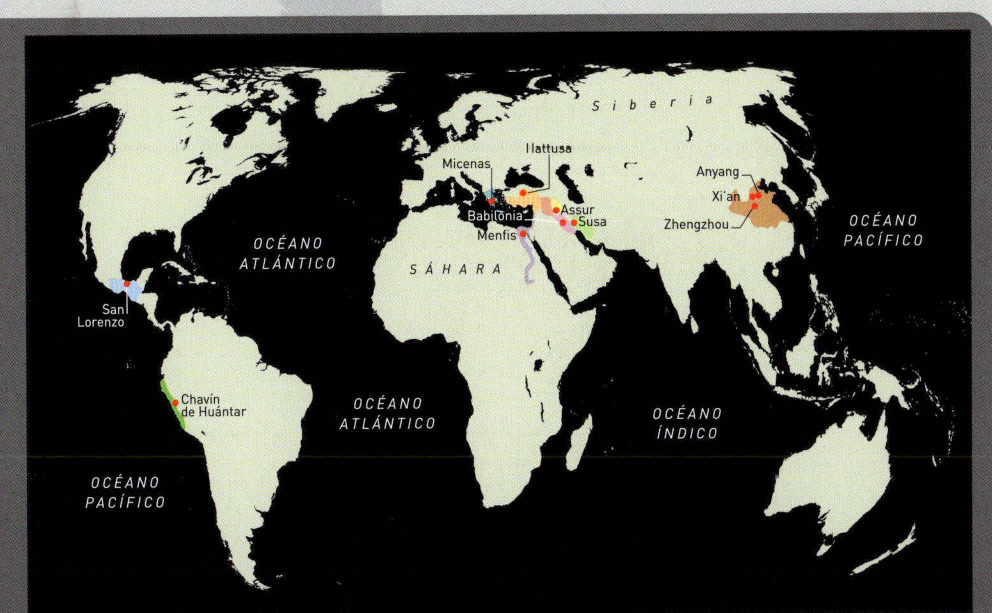

1650–1550 a.C.

Hattusa, la capital hitita, fue fundada por Hattusil I en 1650 a.C. y destruida en 1180 a.C.

TRAS LA MUERTE DE HAMMURABI en 1750 a.C., el Imperio babilonio (*véase* 1850–1790 a.C.) decayó, a la vez que ascendían otras potencias, como los **hurritas** de Mitani, en Siria, y los **hititas**, en Anatolia. Ya en 1650 a.C., los hititas habían logrado crear un extenso reino en la Anatolia central, con capital en Hattusa. Este pueblo había desarrollado técnicas avanzadas de **trabajo del bronce y del hierro**, y eran también renombrados como **guerreros feroces**. El rey hitita **Mursil I** (r. 1620–1590 a.C.) expandió su imperio hasta el Mediterráneo oriental, y en 1595 a.C. **atacó Babilonia**, pero fue asesinado poco después, y el imperio quedó reducido durante un siglo.

En Egipto, el **Imperio Medio** (*véase* 2000–1850 a.C.) **decaía** en 1670 a.C., en parte a causa de inundaciones irregulares del Nilo. Con el aumento de poder de los nomarcas, estalló la **guerra civil**, y los pueblos vecinos no tardaron en aprovechar la agitación. Los **nubios** recuperaron tierras ocupadas por Egipto, y, en 1650 a.C., los **hicsos** del Mediterráneo oriental conquistaron el Bajo Egipto. El Alto Egipto siguió bajo el control de los faraones.

SIDERURGIA

En 2000 a.C. ya se producía hierro en Anatolia, metal usado en objetos de lujo, como el adorno de esta caja de Acemhöyük. Los hititas, que monopolizaban su manufactura, lo exportaban como material caro y de prestigio. Desde alrededor de 1200 a.C. se produjo acero dulce, convirtiendo el hierro en un metal duro y práctico para herramientas. Su uso se difundió: llegó a Grecia en torno a 1200 a.C., y a Europa Central, antes de 800 a.C.

Hombre y animal
El Imperio hitita fue famoso por su artesanía en bronce, y sus armas y artefactos se vendían a buen precio. Esta estatuilla de un hombre y un caballo fue probablemente un encargo.

1550–1400 a.C.

Construido a lo largo de 300 años, el complejo ceremonial de Karnak (Egipto) incluye el mayor templo del mundo, dedicado a Amón-Ra, dios protector de los faraones.

EN *C.* 1550 a.C., EL REY TEBANO AMOSIS I (r. 1550–1525 a.C.) logró **expulsar** a los **hicsos** del Bajo Egipto e inició el tercer periodo de gobierno estable en Egipto, el **Imperio Nuevo** (*c.* 1550–1070 a.C.). En esta época, los **reyes egipcios** adoptaron el **título de faraón** («gran casa»). Sucesivos faraones guerreros emprendieron campañas militares para expandir de nuevo Egipto. **Tutmés I** (r. 1504–1492 a.C.) hizo retirarse al sur a los **nubios** y recuperó el Sinaí y parte de Siria y Palestina. Bajo **Tutmés III** (r. 1479–1425 a.C.), Egipto controló una franja a lo largo de la costa mediterránea y el norte del Éufrates (p. 33).

2000
ES EL NÚMERO DE NOMBRES DE DIOSES Y DIOSAS EN EL ANTIGUO EGIPTO

Los Estados conquistados pagaban tributos anuales enormes, y parte de ellos se destinaron a construir uno de los mayores **recintos religiosos** del mundo, en **Karnak**, y el magnífico templo funerario de la **reina Hatsepsut** (r. 1473–1458 a.C.).

La **religión egipcia** era muy compleja. Cada aldea, pueblo y distrito tenían una deidad protectora propia. En la pintura y escultura, muchos dioses aparecen con cabeza de animal, como representación de sus atributos. Por ejemplo, el dios halcón Horus protegía al faraón, y el dios Tot, con cabeza de ibis, a los escribas.

Hacia 1600 a.C. surgía en la Grecia continental una nueva civilización, llamada **micénica**, por el palacio fortificado de Micenas, supuesto hogar del mítico rey Agamenón, de la *Ilíada* de Homero. Probablemente, los micénicos se llamaron a sí mismos *ahhiyawa*. Enterramientos bien surtidos, como

Máscara de oro
El arqueólogo alemán Heinrich Schliemann halló esta máscara funeraria en una tumba de Micenas, y afirmó que pertenecía al rey Agamenón.

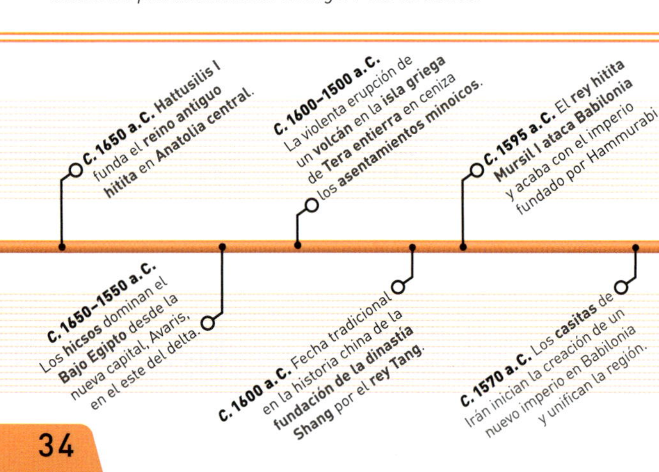

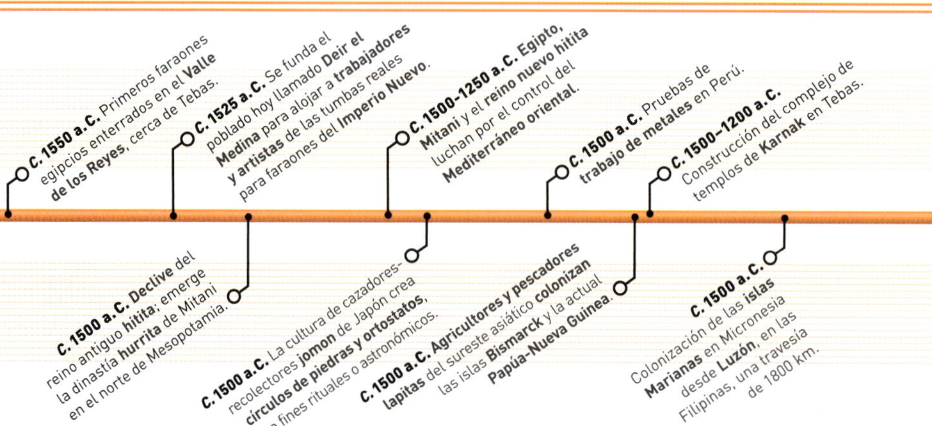

las tumbas de fosas de Micenas reflejan una aristocracia guerrera. Sus **tierras** eran un **mosaico de pequeños reinos**, cada uno dominado más tarde por un palacio-ciudadela como los de Micenas, Tirinto y Pilos. Extendieron su influencia a través del comercio. Tras el hundimiento del Imperio minoico hacia 1450 a. C., los micénicos se apoderaron de varios lugares antes controlados por los minoicos, entre ellos, Cnosos. Después de 1400 a. C. controlaron también sus rutas comerciales y **fundaron asentamientos** en Rodas, Kos y la península de Anatolia.

Los micénicos heredaron las artes y la artesanía minoicos, y adaptaron la **escritura lineal A** para escribir en su propia lengua, una forma arcaica de griego. Fueron **grandes comerciantes**, y se aventuraron hasta Sicilia e Italia. En un barco que se cree de origen cananeo, naufragado frente a las costas de Ulubu-run (Turquía), se encontraron estaño de Irán o Afganistán, lingotes de vidrio de Canaán, cobre y alfarería de Chipre, marfil y joyas de Egipto y espadas micénicas.

En **Oriente Próximo**, los **casitas** se apoderaron de Babilonia, y en 1475 a. C. tenían un imperio estable que duró hasta 1155 a. C. Mantuvieron por lo general buenas relaciones con sus vecinos **Elam**, al este, y **Mitani**, que en 1500 a. C. gobernaba todo el norte de Mesopotamia. Egipto controlaba gran parte del este del Mediterráneo, lo cual causó enfrentamientos frecuentes con Mitani. Hacia 1400 a. C., en Anatolia surgió el **reino nuevo hitita**, de poder creciente. Con el declive de Mitani a partir de 1380 a. C., los hititas y el **Estado en ascenso de Asiria** se fueron repartiendo su territorio, lo cual acabó por hacer entrar en conflicto a los hititas con Egipto en el Mediterráneo oriental.

En China, la **cultura Shang** (*véase* 1850–1790 a. C.) floreció a partir de *c.* 1600 a. C., y sus reyes dominaron una gran parte de China central; sin embargo tuvieron que defender el reino de la amenaza de las tribus nómadas del norte. **Murallas defensivas** rodeaban las **capitales Shang** (la capital fue trasladada varias veces), y se enterraba a sus reyes y nobles en tumbas con ajuares funerarios fabulosos y sacrificios rituales humanos. Se cree que la sociedad Shang estaba bien organizada y altamente jerarquizada. La escritura surgió alrededor de 1400 a. C. La mayoría de los ejemplos de **escritura temprana** son **huesos oraculares**, un testimonio de que los reyes Shang consultaban a los antepasados para las decisiones importantes. Las preguntas sobre el futuro se inscribían en un hueso de buey o un caparazón de tortuga, que luego se golpeaban con una herramienta caliente de metal. Se creía que el modo en que se rompía el hueso daba la respuesta.

Civilizaciones del Egeo
Hacia 1450 a. C., la influencia de los micénicos se extendía por todo el mar Egeo, y controlaban también muchos lugares antes minoicos.

CLAVE
- Asentamiento micénico
- Palacio micénico

Tutankamón fue enterrado con un tesoro fabuloso. Este detalle del trono del faraón lo muestra siendo ungido por su esposa Anjesenamón.

EN *C.* 1352 a. C., AMENOFIS IV se convirtió en **faraón de Egipto**. Reformador religioso, rompió con la religión tradicional y con su panteón de dioses, e **inició** el **culto a un dios único**, el disco solar **Atón**. Cambió su nombre por el de Ajnatón («espíritu viviente de Atón») y fundó una **nueva capital** entre Tebas y Menfis, a la que llamó Ajetatón («horizonte de Atón»).

Se cree que sus reformas religiosas fueron muy impopulares, sobre todo entre la influyente élite sacerdotal. Después de su muerte en *c.* 1336 a. C., ascendió al trono su hijo de nueve años **Tutankamón**, quien restableció los dioses antiguos y abandonó la nueva capital. Se cree que Tutankamón murió bajo extrañas circunstancias a los 18 años de edad, y fue enterrado precipitadamente en una tumba menor. Durante años se atribuyó su muerte a un golpe en la cabeza, pero las pruebas más recientes apuntan a una septicemia después de haberse roto la pierna, complicada por su mala salud: padeció malaria, además de males congénitos debidos a su origen incestuoso.

Desde la década de 1570 a. C. se enterró a los faraones en **tumbas** excavadas en la roca del **Valle de los Reyes**, en la ribera oeste del Nilo, con la esperanza de protegerlas de los ladrones, pero casi todas fueron **despojadas** de sus riquezas. En 1922, sin embargo, el arqueólogo británico Howard Carter descubrió prácticamente **intacta** la **tumba de Tutankamón**. En la cámara mortuoria había cuatro capillas doradas, y contenían el **sarcófago y la momia** del faraón con una máscara de oro macizo. En las otras estancias se hallaron joyas, estatuas doradas, muebles e instrumentos musicales.

Culto al sol
Ajnatón instituyó el culto al disco solar Atón. En este bajorrelieve, hallado en Ajetatón (actual Amarna), se le ve adorando al sol junto a su esposa Nefertiti.

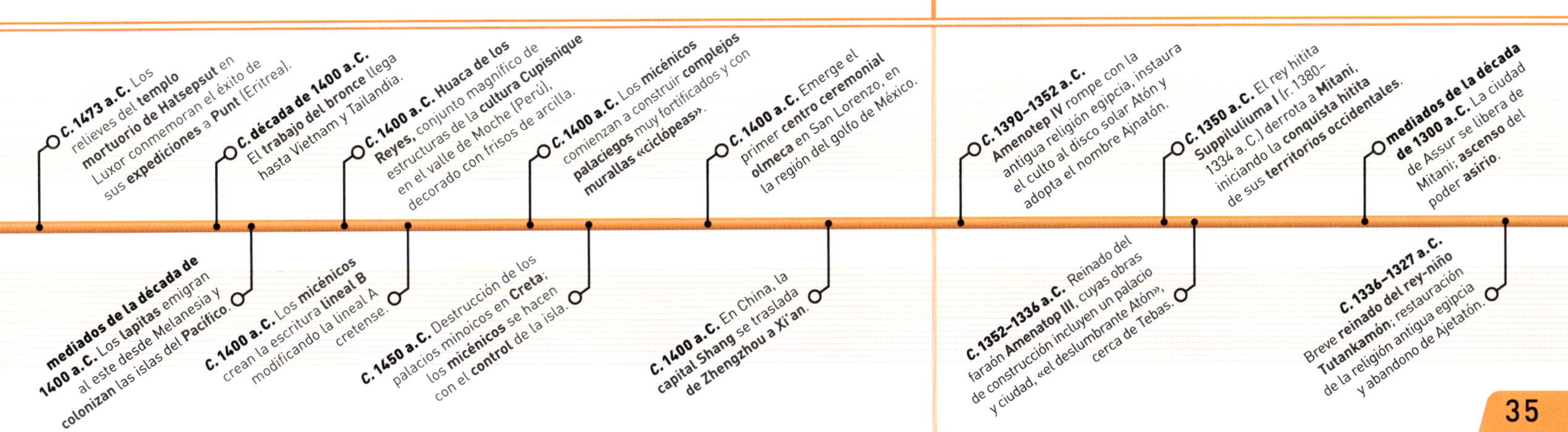

1300–1200 a.C.

En la fachada del templo de Ramsés II en Abu Simbel hay cuatro estatuas sedentes colosales del faraón, pero la segunda (desde la izda.) fue destruida.

HACIA FINALES DEL II MILENIO a.C. el Mediterráneo oriental y Oriente Próximo eran un **mosaico de imperios** que comprendía Egipto, Babilonia, Elam, Asiria y el reino hitita en Anatolia. Las fronteras fluctuaban en la pugna de cada reino por imponerse a sus vecinos por conquista o diplomacia. Hubiera guerra o paz, permanecieron intactas las **rutas comerciales vitales** por las que llegaba a la región el cobre para fabricar **bronce**.

Una zona habitual de conflicto fue el norte del **Mediterráneo oriental** (hoy Siria y Líbano), arrebatado a Egipto por los hititas, que habían ocupado el oeste de Mitani (*véase* 1550–1400 a.C.). En el siglo XII a.C., el faraón Seti I y su hijo **Ramsés II** lanzaron campañas para recuperarlo. El reinado de Ramsés (r. 1279–1213 a.C.) fue una época de **estabilidad y prosperidad** en Egipto. Mediante una combinación de guerra, diplomacia y matrimonios estratégicos, Ramsés trató de extender la influencia egipcia en Oriente Próximo. En la década de 1270 a.C. mantuvo una serie de guerras contra el rey hitita Muwatallis II, de las que la más famosa fue la **batalla de Qadesh** (*c.* 1274 a.C.). Ramsés proclamó su victoria, pero hoy se cree que el resultado de la batalla fue indeciso, y que los hititas conservaron la región.

« TÚ, **GRAN GUERRERO** SIN IGUAL, **VICTORIOSO** A OJOS DE TODO EL MUNDO. »

Inscripción conmemorativa de la victoria de Ramsés II en Qadesh

Propaganda antigua
En este detalle del templo de Ramsés II en Abu Simbel, el faraón dispara su arco mientras se enfrenta solo al ejército hitita en la batalla de Qadesh.

En 1259 a.C., tras nuevas campañas en Siria, Ramsés cambió de táctica, negoció un **tratado de paz pionero** con el nuevo rey hitita, **Hattusil III**, y tomó en matrimonio a dos princesas hititas (tuvo ocho esposas en total). Después del tratado, Ramsés mantuvo una correspondencia amistosa con el rey hitita, registrada en acadio en escritura cuneiforme sobre tablillas de arcilla.

Ramsés emprendió también un programa ambicioso de **construcción de monumentos**. En la frontera del sur de Egipto con Nubia construyó el magnífico templo de **Abu Simbel**, y en el Bajo Egipto fundó la nueva capital de **Pi-Ramsés**, aunque Tebas, en el Alto Egipto, siguió siendo un centro importante. Al oeste de Tebas construyó un vasto templo funerario que fue también palacio, corte y centro del saber.

El final del II milenio a.C. vio resurgir a Assur en el hoy llamado **Imperio asirio medio** (1350–1000 a.C.). Después de la muerte de Samsi-Adad y el colapso del reino de la Alta Mesopotamia, Assur recuperó la independencia, pero fue luego sometida por Mitani. El renacimiento de Assur comenzó bajo **Assur-Uballit I** (r. 1363–1328 a.C.), quien la liberó del poder de Mitani y fundó un reino en el norte de Mesopotamia. Sus sucesores, Salmanasar I y Tukulti-Ninurta I, siguieron ganando territorios y expandieron el reino hacia el oeste, conquistando el este de Mitani y, brevemente, de 1225 a 1216 a.C., Babilonia, al sureste.

En Grecia alcanzaron su apogeo los palacios y reinos **micénicos**, con amplias redes comerciales.

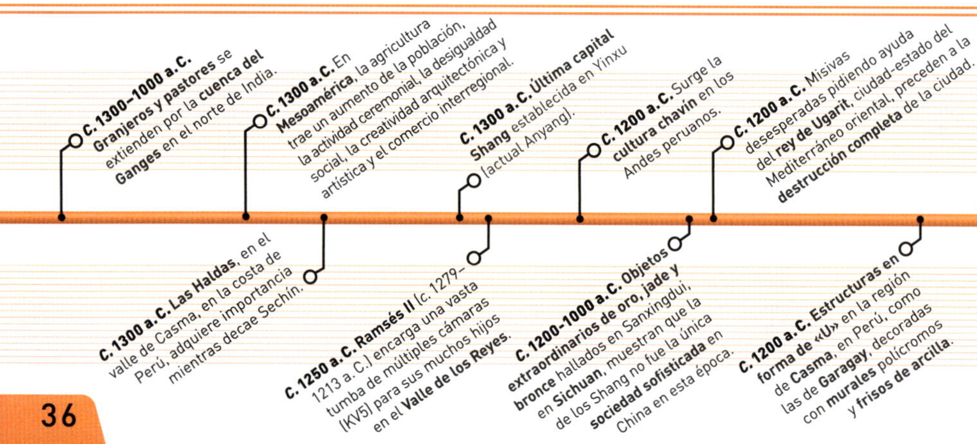

1200–1100 a.C.

Los bloques empleados para construir estos muros de Micenas, hoy en ruinas, eran tan enormes que civilizaciones posteriores las creyeron obra de gigantes.

ENTRE *c.* 1250 Y 1050 a.C., muchas de las **potencias** dominantes en Oriente Próximo durante siglos entraron en **declive**, y algunas desaparecieron por completo. En el Mediterráneo oriental comenzó una **época convulsa**: Chipre, Egipto, Anatolia, Canaán y Siria fueron atacados, y muchas ciudades costeras fueron saqueadas. Los ataques suelen atribuirse a las oleadas migratorias de los llamados pueblos del mar. Los escritos de la época dan pocas pistas sobre su identidad, pero es probable que procedieran de diversas partes del Mediterráneo central y oriental. En 1178 a.C., el faraón Ramsés III los expulsó del Bajo Egipto.

Cada vez hay más pruebas de que dichas migraciones fueron el resultado, y no la causa, de la nefasta situación a partir de *c.* 1250 a.C. Hubo una serie de terremotos en *c.* 1225–1175 a.C. El cambio climático trajo sequía, malas cosechas y hambre, obligando a algunas comunidades marítimas a emigrar o dedicarse a la piratería. Los Estados desestabilizados fueron presa más fácil, y la capital hitita, Hattusa, fue saqueada en *c.* 1180 a.C., probablemente por sus enemigos tradicionales del norte, los kaskas. Los hititas perdieron sus posesiones en el Mediterráneo oriental, y el imperio quedó fragmentado.

Hacia 1200 a.C., los reinos micénicos sufrieron un periodo tumultuoso, resultado tanto de la desintegración interna como de las amenazas exteriores. Se reforzaron las defensas de muchos palacios, y, por los escritos de Pilos, consta el temor de la población a los ataques por mar. En 1100 a.C., la mayoría de los palacios micénicos habían sido saqueados y abandonados.

En la Edad del Bronce Final predominó en parte de Europa la **cultura de los campos de urnas**, cuyo nombre alude a la práctica de incinerar a los muertos y enterrar sus restos en urnas funerarias, a veces acompañadas por ricos ajuares. Surgió en la **región del Danubio** en 1300 a.C., y en los siglos siguientes se extendió a Italia y al centro y este de Europa.

Entre 1200 y 700 a.C. la **tecnología del hierro** se propagó desde Grecia a Europa central. El hierro reemplazó rápidamente al bronce en armas y herramientas, poniendo fin a la **Edad del Bronce**.

En Mesoamérica, la primera gran civilización de la región, la **olmeca**,

« LLEGARON **AUDACES** EN SUS NAVES DE GUERRA DESDE EL **CENTRO DEL MAR**, Y NADIE ERA CAPAZ DE RESISTIRLES. »

Inscripción de **Ramsés II** (r. 1279–1213 a.C.), referente a los pueblos del mar

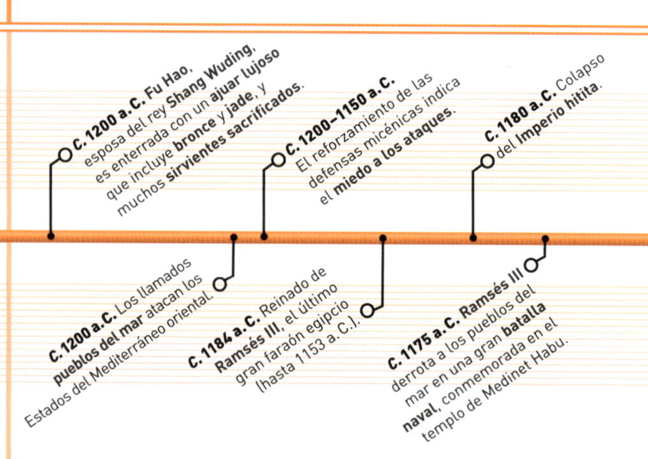

1100–1000 a.C.

« CUANDO TODOS LOS DESEOS DEL CORAZÓN SE DESVANECEN, EL MORTAL SE HACE INMORTAL. »

Krishna Yajur Veda

prosperaba en las tierras bajas costeras del golfo de México. Los **olmecas** construyeron centros ceremoniales como San Lorenzo, templos y casas sobre montículos de tierra, y tallaron enormes cabezas de piedra cubiertas con cascos, probablemente efigies de sus soberanos. También establecieron rutas comerciales de larga distancia. En el Perú contemporáneo se fundó el centro ceremonial de montaña de Chavín de Huántar (*véase* 900–800 a.C.), mientras decaían centros costeros como Cerro Sechín.

Guerrero de piedra
Las tallas monumentales de los templos de Cerro Sechín, en la costa peruana, muestran guerreros, víctimas torturadas y sacrificios humanos.

EL FINAL DEL II MILENIO TRAJO CONSIGO GRANDES CAMBIOS en las relaciones de poder en Oriente Próximo. En 1070 a.C. finalizó el Imperio Nuevo egipcio, y el país entró en la época de agitación del **Tercer Periodo Intermedio**, que duró hasta 747 a.C. (*véase* 800–700 a.C.). Los historiadores creen que el poder de los faraones se vio erosionado por una élite sacerdotal que obtuvo el control en muchas zonas. En 1000 a.C., todos los territorios ganados por los faraones del Imperio Nuevo se habían perdido.

En **Mesopotamia** se desataron **guerras frecuentes** entre babilonios, asirios y elamitas, y la región sufrió incursiones devastadoras de los nómadas arameos desde el oeste.

Mientras tanto, otras potencias emergían en la zona, como un pueblo de lengua semítica, los **cananeos**, que habitaba en el Mediterráneo oriental desde hacía siglos, en ciudades-estado que controlaban su territorio circundante. Eran marinos experimentados, con un papel central en el comercio internacional. A partir de 1100 a.C., puertos cananeos como Arados, Biblos, Tiro y Sidón ampliaron su actividad, estableciendo puestos comerciales y colonias por todo el Mediterráneo oriental. Comerciaban con cedro del Líbano, objetos de vidrio y marfil, minerales metálicos y, lo más importante, el costoso tinte púrpura obtenido del caracol marino *Murex brandaris*. De este artículo procede su nombre en griego, *phoinikós* (de *phoinix*, «púrpura»), del que deriva **fenicios**.

En **China**, una nueva dinastía reemplazó a los Shang en 1046 a.C., cuando el rey Wu de los Zhou derrotó al último gobernante Shang, Di-Xin. La **dinastía Zhou** reinaría en China durante **700 años**. Esta larga era suele dividirse en dos periodos: Zhou Oriental y Zhou Occidental. Durante la primera, la capital fue Zongzhou. Esta fue una **época de prosperidad** y fuerte poder centralizado. El territorio Zhou se dividió en feudos, concedidos a los nobles de confianza a cambio de apoyo militar. Continuaron muchos aspectos de la tradición china ya presentes en el periodo Shang, como el culto a los antepasados y los huesos oraculares.

Mientras tanto, en **Japón**, la **cultura jomon** siguió siendo de cazadores-recolectores, aunque prósperos y sedentarios. Su nombre deriva de las marcas de cuerda seca –*jomon*– que adornan su cerámica.

Después de la decadencia de los pueblos y ciudades de la civilización del Indo (*véase* 1850-1790 a.C.), florecieron comunidades menores de agricultores y pastores en el **norte de India**. En 1200 a.C. estaban emigrando a la **cuenca del Ganges**, y estableciendo asentamientos mixtos donde se cultivaba arroz y se criaban animales, como vacas y caballos. Los textos sagrados indios más antiguos, los **Vedas**, transmitidos oralmente durante muchos siglos, reflejan este periodo. Se compusieron en **sánscrito** (idioma **indoeuropeo** emparentado con las lenguas iranias y casi todas las europeas), el antepasado de muchos idiomas hoy hablados en el sur de Asia, como el hindi y el urdu. Aunque los Vedas sean en gran parte escritos y constituyan himnos religiosos, la información geográfica que contienen no solo describe la expansión gradual de agricultores y pastores trashumantes desde el Punyab hasta la cuenca del Ganges, sino que también informa sobre conflictos con otros grupos, y sobre la vida local de la época. La **división de la sociedad** en ***varnas***, o **castas**, por ejemplo, se describe en los Vedas, apareciendo por primera vez en el Libro X del *Rigveda*, aunque nada en el texto indique que el sistema fuera hereditario en la época.

Sello de una cultura
En este ejemplar de cerámica jomon tardía, el cuenco y el pie muestran las marcas características de cuerdas que dan nombre al periodo.

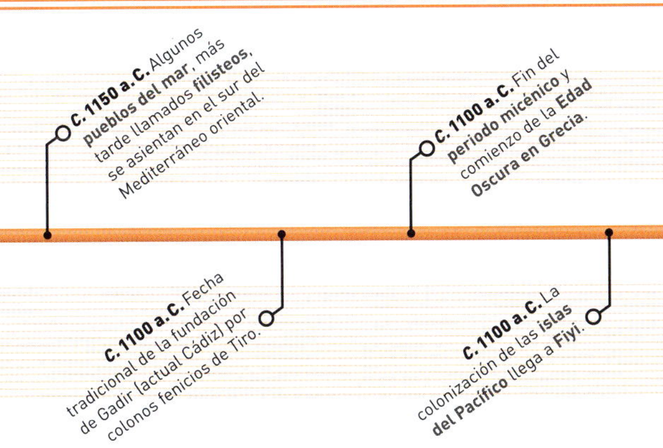

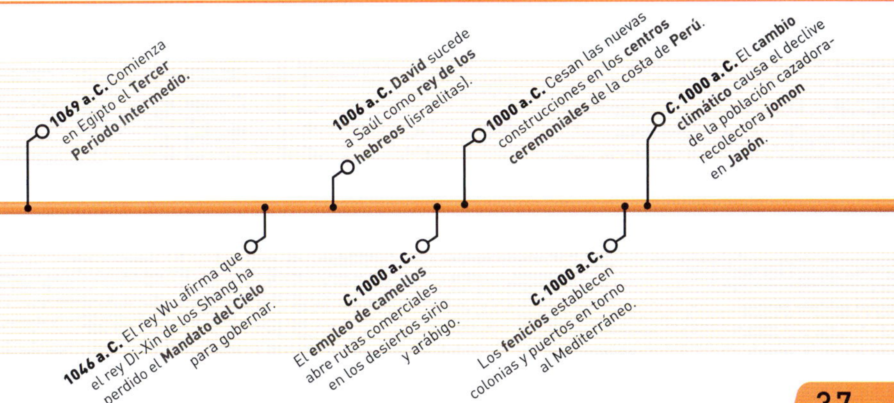

Estatuilla de gato
C. 600 a.C.
Estatuilla de cobre sobre base de madera. Los gatos estaban vinculados a la diosa Bastet, protectora del faraón. Una perforación en la nariz sostenía originalmente un anillo.

Estatua con estela
C. 1360 a.C.
Representación de un alto sacerdote de Amón sosteniendo una estela o losa tallada. La estela se utilizaba como losa sepulcral o marcador conmemorativo. La inscripción es un himno al dios Sol y una lista de dignatarios locales.

Caja decorada de Perpauty
C. 1370 a.C.
Caja de madera de sicómoro; perteneció a un hombre llamado Perpauty y pudo contener lino. Pintada por los cuatro costados, el mostrado aquí presenta a Perpauty y su esposa recibiendo presentes de su hijo y sus tres hijas.

Frasco con forma de pato
C. 1700 a.C.
Tarro labrado en forma de pato, que parece atado y desplumado. Probablemente contenía alguna pasta cosmética, tal vez pintura de ojos, que sería extraída y untada con un tapón-aplicador, ahora perdido.

ANTIGUO EGIPTO

UNA NOTABLE CIVILIZACIÓN VISTA A PARTIR DE SUS TESOROS Y OBJETOS COTIDIANOS

Artefactos creados hace más de dos mil años atestiguan las habilidades de los artesanos egipcios. También reflejan la riqueza egipcia y su red comercial, a través de la cual se importaban ébano, lapislázuli y marfil.

Muchos de los objetos mostrados aquí fueron usados en la vida diaria por egipcios acomodados. Reflejan la creencia en un más allá y la práctica de enterrar las posesiones que, se creía, emplearía el espíritu del muerto en la otra vida. Los gobernantes eran enterrados junto a grandes tesoros, pero casi todas sus tumbas fueron despojadas de sus riquezas, bien en la antigüedad, bien más recientemente.

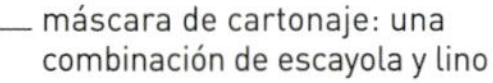

Shabtis
1292–1190 a.C.
Estatuillas de sirvientes, llamadas shabtis, colocadas habitualmente en las tumbas. Los egipcios creían que cobrarían vida para servir al espíritu del muerto en su próxima vida.

Máscara funeraria
C. 1500 a.C.
Esta máscara pudo cubrir la cabeza de una momia. Los egipcios momificaban los cuerpos porque el espíritu del difunto no podría sobrevivir a menos que tuviera un cuerpo al cual volver.

Shabti momiforme
C. 1300 a.C.
Gran figura de shabti labrada en madera. Las herramientas que porta son símbolos tradicionales de realeza; el escarabeo representa al dios Jepri.

Chacal o perro momificado
C. 600 a.C.
Los chacales y, a partir del siglo VIII a.C., los perros se momificaban en honor a Anubis, el dios con cabeza de chacal que presidía funerales y embalsamamientos.

incrustación de lapislázuli

Collares
C. 1550–1069 a. C.
Los artesanos egipcios tenían acceso a metales preciosos y a piedras semipreciosas. Los collares se usaban en la vida diaria y también eran enterrados con el difunto.

Pendientes de botón y arete
C. 1550–1069 a. C.
Una vez creada la forma básica de estos pendientes, se envolvía con hebras de vidrio de colores muy contrastados; los botones requerían grandes perforaciones en el lóbulo de la oreja.

Peine de madera
C. 300 a. C.
Peine a doble cara con filas de púas largas y cortas alternas. Muchos egipcios llevaban el pelo corto y utilizaban peluca. Los peines se usaban para peinar el pelo natural y la peluca.

Cucharilla cosmética
C. 1360 a. C.
Cucharilla para pasta cosmética tallada en esquisto con la forma de un íbice con la cabeza girada sobre el lomo, de forma que los cuernos rectos tocaran el cuenco.

Amuleto
912–343 a. C.
El udjat simbolizaba el ojo del dios Horus. Este talismán se colocaba sobre la momia con el fin de proteger el espíritu del muerto en el más allá. También simbolizaba la regeneración.

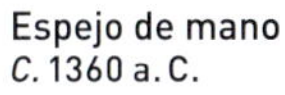

Espejo de mano
C. 1360 a. C.
Montura de madera para espejo; sujetaba un disco de bronce pulido. El mango está tallado con forma de columna papiriforme y rematado con el dios Bes, una deidad popular.

Amuleto con figura masculina
C. 2200 a. C.
Amuleto dorado con un dios varón arrodillado sosteniendo en sus manos dos hojas de palma. Seguramente Heh, el dios de la eternidad. Las hojas muestran muescas que representan años.

Amuletos de rana
C. 1360 a. C.
La rana era símbolo de vida y de fertilidad. Las mujeres llevaban estos fetiches para atraer la suerte. Están hechos en fayenza azul (loza fina) con detalles de oro.

el disco representa el sol

incrustaciones en celdillas de oro

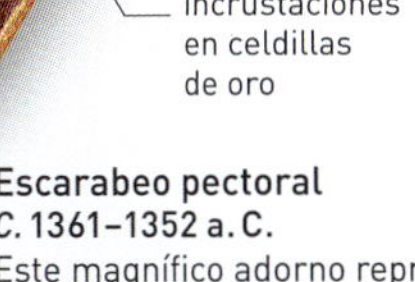

Escarabeo pectoral
C. 1361–1352 a. C.
Este magnífico adorno representa al dios escarabajo Jepri rodeando el disco solar rojo. Proviene de la tumba de Tutankamón.

Escarabajo alado
644–322 a. C.
Los escarabeos eran amuletos de la fortuna. El escarabajo, símbolo de renacimiento, era un modelo de joyería en el antiguo Egipto.

1000–900 a.C.

Durante el reinado del rey Salomón, mediado el siglo x a.C., Meggido (en el actual Israel) fue una importante fortaleza y centro administrativo israelita.

EN EL SIGLO X A.C. PROSIGUIÓ EL DECLIVE de las principales potencias de Oriente Medio. Egipto y Asiria se habían debilitado, permitiendo el ascenso del efímero pero históricamente importante **reino de Israel**. Los israelitas eran pastores nómadas de lengua semítica que, según la Biblia, llegaron a la tierra de Canaán en el siglo XIII a.C. Allí chocaron con los nativos filisteos y cananeos. Alrededor del año 1000 a.C., el **rey David** (r. 1006–965 a.C.) **unió a las tribus de Israel** y estableció su capital en **Jerusalén**. El hijo de David, **Salomón** (r. *c.* 965–931 a.C.), amplió sus territorios y construyó un magnífico templo-palacio en la capital, aunque a su muerte el reino se dividió en dos. Finalmente, Israel y luego Judá serían parte del Imperio asirio.

Grabado en oro
Esta placa dorada con el símbolo protector del ojo udjat procede del reinado de Psusenas I, faraón de la dinastía XXI, momento en que Egipto se hallaba dividido.

SALMANASAR III (858–824 a.C.)

En el siglo IX a.C., el rey asirio Salmanasar III logró consolidar y proteger su imperio gracias a campañas en contra de las tribus mesopotámicas, Israel y Judá, Siria, Urartu y Anatolia. Este obelisco de caliza negra conmemora sus hazañas y las de su *turtanu* (general en jefe), Dayyan-Assur. En él se detalla, en escritura cuneiforme, los distintos tributos impuestos a los pueblos conquistados.

En esa misma época, **Asiria** empezaba a resurgir como una gran **potencia** en **Mesopotamia**. El rey Assur-Dan II (r. 934–912 a.C.) promovió la agricultura, logrando de esa manera aumentar la prosperidad; su sucesor, Adad-Nirari II, amplió el territorio asirio, recuperando tierras que habían pertenecido al Imperio Medio durante el siglo XIII a.C.

900–800 a.C.

El jaguar aparece en muchas religiones mesoamericanas y sudamericanas. Aquí, aparece en un bajorrelieve procedente de Chavín de Huántar.

EN EL SIGLO IX A.C. LA CULTURA OLMECA SEGUÍA DESARROLLÁNDOSE en Mesoamérica. San Lorenzo fue destruida hacia 900 a.C., y **La Venta**, al noreste, se convirtió en el **principal centro olmeca**. Este enorme asentamiento estaba dominado por una pirámide de 34 m de altura, antecesora de los templos mayas. Los olmecas probablemente diseñaron una escritura de **glifos**, la primera de esta región. Su influencia se difundió por Mesoamérica, hasta alcanzar a otras culturas que en ese momento empezaban a florecer: los **zapotecas** y los **mayas**.

En el valle del Ohio (este de América del Norte) empezaba el desarrollo de la **cultura adena**, caracterizada por los terraplenes rituales y túmulos, donde se han hallado objetos de artesanía fina.

En el distante sur, la **cultura chavín** había surgido en los Andes peruanos *c.* 1200 a.C., y se extendió a la costa. **Hábiles ingenieros y arquitectos**, construyeron canales y nivelaron pendientes tanto para el cultivo como para la construcción. Su asentamiento principal, **Chavín de Huántar**, situado a gran altura en los Andes, parece haber sido centro de peregrinación de un culto a seres sobrenaturales, en parte humanos y en parte animales. Su dios principal, el «dios de los báculos», solía ser representado con colmillos.

En **Europa**, el **hierro reemplazaba** gradualmente al **bronce** como metal preferido para la fabricación de armas y herramientas. La zona más próxima a **Hallstatt** (Austria) se convirtió en el centro de una cultura temprana del hierro surgida a partir de la cultura de los campos de urnas (*véase* 1200–1100 a.C.). Los caudillos de Hallstatt dominaban los trabajos locales de extracción de sal y hierro. Vivían en colinas fortificadas y eran enterrados con ricos ajuares funerarios.

Durante el siglo IX a.C., los **fenicios** adquirieron gran poder e influencia. Sus conocimientos como navegantes y su habilidad para realizar largas travesías marítimas les dieron acceso a todo el Mediterráneo. Fundaron colonias en busca de materias primas en la actual Cádiz, Sicilia, Cerdeña y lugares de la costa del norte de África, como Cartago (actual Túnez). Esta red comercial dio a conocer el **alfabeto** fenicio por todo el ámbito del **Mediterráneo**.

En Oriente Medio el **Imperio neoasirio** iniciaba su expansión y, uno tras otro, Israel, Judá y los estados de las vecinas Siria y Fenicia cayeron bajo control asirio.

Ofrendas funerarias
Broche de la Edad del Hierro hallado en un enterramiento en Hallstatt (Austria). El tipo de joyas asociadas sugiere que la tumba era de una mujer.

La región mediterránea
Este mapa de la región mediterránea en el siglo VIII a.C. muestra las colonias establecidas por las civilizaciones dominantes en la época, incluidos fenicios y griegos.

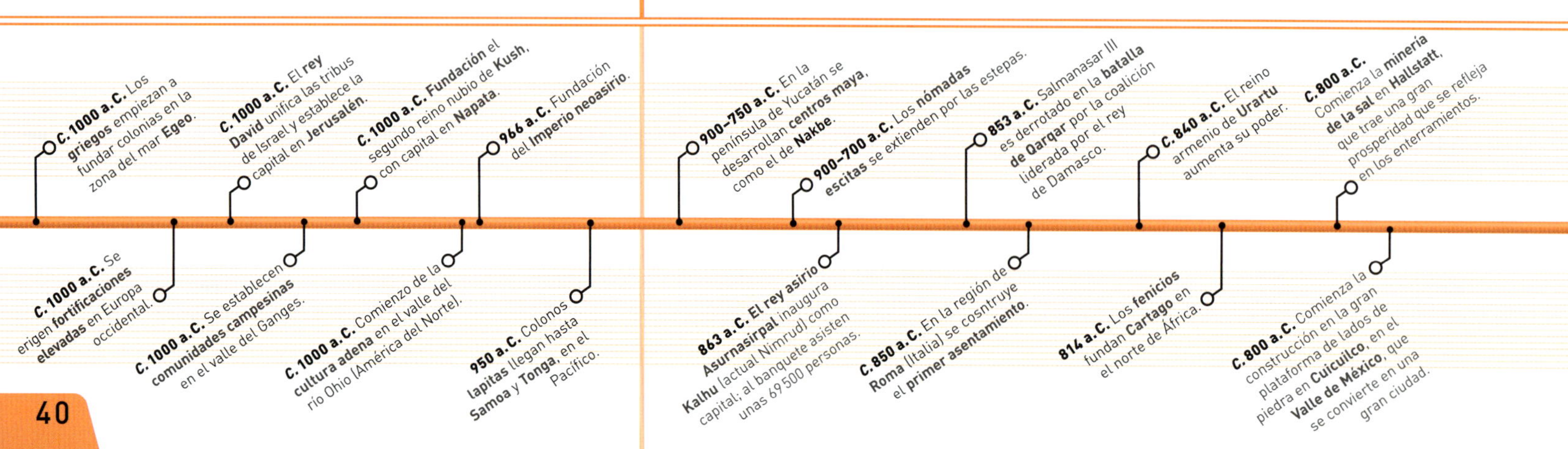

En 705 a.C. la capital asiria se trasladó a Nínive. Este relieve en piedra muestra un banquete del rey asirio y de su reina en los jardines del palacio real.

ASIRIA CONTINUÓ CON SU POLÍTICA AGRESIVA a lo largo del siglo VIII a.C., conquistando pequeños estados en Oriente Medio y reduciéndolos a provincias. Su éxito se basaba en un **ejército disciplinado** y técnicamente muy avanzado, así como en una **eficiente burocracia**. Los pueblos conquistados debían pagar gravosos tributos, y las revueltas eran aplastadas. Las naciones especialmente problemáticas sufría deportaciones: una gran cantidad de sus pobladores eran reasentados en otras regiones del imperio.

Tras un periodo caracterizado por gobiernos débiles durante la primera mitad del siglo, Tiglatpileser III (r. 744–727 a.C.) recuperó las pérdidas asirias. Su sucesor, **Sargón II** (r. 722–704 a.C.) realizó campañas en Irán y Anatolia, conquistó Babilonia y, en 714 a.C., derrotó al estado armenio de Urartu. También venció a los israelitas, y llevó a las «diez tribus perdidas» de Israel al norte de Mesopotamia.

Urna ritual
Los herreros zhou fueron grandes artesanos del metal. Este recipiente de bronce, que data del siglo VIII a.C. pertenece al periodo de la dinastía Zhou Oriental.

En **China**, la capital zhou se desplazó a Luoyang, en el este, en 770 a.C.; esto marcó el comienzo de la **dinastía Zhou Oriental**, que duró hasta 256 a.C. El control real se había debilitado a medida que los señores con grandes feudos se hacían más poderosos. Ahora, el control central se desintegró y los **señores de la guerra rivales** luchaban entre sí. A pesar del caos, esta fue una época de avance técnico y cultural: las herramientas de hierro incrementaron la eficiencia agrícola y la producción de alimentos, las poblaciones y las ciudades crecieron, y empezaron a **desarrollarse la filosofía**, **las artes y la literatura**.

En Egipto todavía continuaba la agitación del Tercer Periodo Intermedio. Desde 850 a.C. el reino se había enredado en una destructiva guerra civil, y ahora estaba dividido en pequeños estados. Ya en el siglo VIII a.C., **Piye** (r. 747–716 a.C.), rey de Kush (Nubia), consiguió **conquistar** el Alto y el Bajo **Egipto**, unificándolos bajo el **dominio de los kushitas**.

En el Mediterráneo, la influencia fenicia continuó expandiéndose mientras la ciudad de **Cartago**, ubicada en el norte de África, se hacía **más poderosa**. Grecia empezaba a salir de la Edad Oscura posterior a la caída de Micenas. En la Grecia continental empezaron a surgir ciudades-estado, o **polis**, en torno a ciudadelas elevadas. Para aumentar sus territorios, estas polis fundaron colonias en las costas del Egeo; pese a que la rivalidad entre ellas era a menudo intensa, comenzó a surgir una **identidad y una cultura griegas**: todo los griegos eran identificados como «helenos». En 776 a.C. se celebraron en **Olimpia** los primeros juegos panhelénicos en honor a Zeus. Mediado el siglo VIII a.C., los griegos habían adoptado el alfabeto fenicio para su propia lengua, y es muy probable que los poemas épicos de Homero, la *Ilíada* y la *Odisea* –hasta entonces transmitidos oralmente–, fueran escritos poco después.

Estatua kushita
Estatua de alabastro del periodo kushita de Egipto. Amenirdis I, hermana de Piye y de Shabako (r. c. 716–702 a.C.), sostiene un mayal, símbolo tradicional de realeza egipcia.

En el siglo VIII a.C. el **centro de Italia** era un mosaico de pequeños estados regidos por los **etruscos** –primera civilización autóctona italiana– y por tribus itálicas como latinos, umbríos y sabinos. Se piensa que **Roma** fue fundada por el jefe latino **Rómulo** en 753 a.C. En sus primeros días, la ciudad, construida sobre siete colinas, fue regida por diversos pueblos, entre ellos etruscos, latinos y sabinos.

Hallazgo de los gemelos
Esta obra de Charles de La Fosse describe la leyenda de Rómulo y Remo, abandonados al nacer y amamantados por una loba antes de ser rescatados por unos pastores.

« TAMAÑA **EMPRESA** ERA **FUNDAR** LA **RAZA ROMANA**. »

Virgilio, *Eneida*. Libro I, canto 33

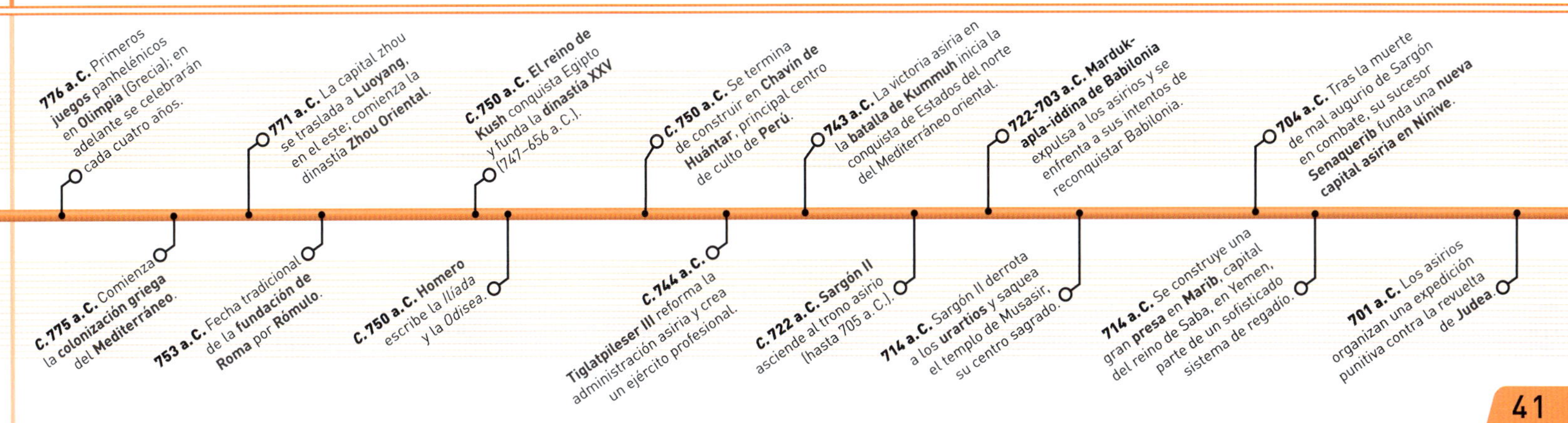

LA ÉPOCA CLÁSICA
700 a.C.–599 d.C.

La aparición de civilizaciones culturalmente dinámicas en Grecia, Persia, China e India, y más adelante Roma, marcó el inició de la época clásica. La influencia de sus avances en la ciencia, el arte y la política aún se siente hoy.

700–676 a. C.

« POR DOQUIER **BUSCABA** ALGUNA EXCUSA PARA **PROVOCAR LA GUERRA. »**

Tito Livio, *Historia de Roma.* Libro I, XXI; sobre Tulio Hostilio, tercer rey de Roma

EN CHINA, LA CIUDAD DE LUOYANG CAYÓ EN MANOS DE LOS SHEN en 771 a. C., y la capital zhou occidental se trasladó a Chengzhou, en el este. Desde allí, la dinastía Zhou oriental continuaría reinando nominalmente sobre **una China fragmentada** hasta en 148 estados. A partir de 700 a. C. los zhou serían gobernados por una serie de emperadores títeres, mientras que el poder real descansaba sobre el **ba** («el mayor») entre los estados vecinos. El estado de Qi obtuvo la supremacía bajo el mandato de **Huan Gong** (r. 685–643 a. C.), pero se debilitó tras su muerte debido a la **pugna de poder** entre sus cinco hijos, lo que permitió a **Jin Wen Gong** (r. 636–628 a. C.) convertirse en ba. A finales de siglo, el poder en China alternaba entre los **estados de Qi, Jin, Qin y Chu.**

Faraón nubio
Taharka reinó 19 años en Egipto antes de que una invasión asiria lo obligara a regresar a Nubia en 671 a. C.

7 ERA EL NÚMERO DE LOS **REYES** DE **ROMA**

Por otro lado, en Italia, la **ciudad-estado de Roma** comenzaba a adquirir un núcleo urbano y se inició la construcción del **primer foro**. Al segundo rey romano, **Numa Pompilio** (r. 715–674 a. C.), históricamente se le atribuye el establecimiento en Roma de un calendario y del primer sacerdocio.

En Asia occidental **continuaba la expansión de los asirios**, que los enfrentó a Egipto, cuyo apoyo intermitente a los rebeldes contra el gobierno asirio en Siria supuso un foco de tensión permanente. En 671 a. C., el rey asirio Asaradón logró **capturar la capital real egipcia**, Menfis. Sin embargo, el control asirio sobre Egipto era débil, y el faraón nubio **Taharka** expulsó a los invasores.

Alrededor de 700 a. C., el pueblo **etrusco** inició su expansión hacia el sur desde las actuales Toscana y Umbría. Pese a que su idioma apenas ha podido ser descifrado, sus lujosas tumbas indican una **rica cultura material**. Durante su expansión fundaron ciudades como Capua, pero **chocaron** con las colonias griegas y con Roma. Mucho más poderosos en un principio, los etruscos se encontraban **políticamente desunidos**, y una larga **serie de guerras** con los romanos se volvieron contra ellos.

c. 700 a. C. Los nómadas **escitas** empiezan a establecer **poblados permanentes** en las estepas occidentales.

c. 700 a. C. Primeras **inscripciones etruscas**.

700 a. C. Senaquerib de Asiria **asedia Jerusalén**, pero debe regresar a Asiria para sofocar una revuelta.

c. 700 a. C. Comienza el **periodo arcaico** en **Grecia**.

700 a. C. La **cultura adena** empieza a florecer en el curso superior del Ohio.

690 a. C. El rey nubio **Taharka**, faraón de Egipto; instaura la dinastía XXV.

689 a. C. El rey asirio **Senaquerib destruye Babilonia**.

681 a. C. Senaquerib de Asiria es **asesinado**; Asaradón asciende al trono.

675–651 a. C.

Pirámides de la necrópolis de Nuri (Sudán), que fue lugar de enterramiento de los reyes napateos y meroítas desde *c.* 650 a. C.

ENTRE 664 Y 663 A. C., ASSURBANIPAL (r. 668–627 a. C.) coordinó una campaña para derrotar a los egipcios que se habían rebelado contra el poder asirio y para extender su control hasta Tebas (hoy Luxor) en el sur. Esta no fue la última revuelta contra los asirios: solo diez años después, el rey vasallo de Sais, **Samético I** (r. 664–610 a. C.) también se sublevó contra sus señores asirios, expulsándolos y fundando la dinastía XXVI, bajo la cual **Egipto pudo recuperar** de nuevo **su independencia**. Después del declive final del poder asirio, que tuvo lugar en 609 a. C., el **faraón Necao II** (610–595 a. C.) pudo fijar una posición estable en Palestina.

En aquella época, en Grecia se iniciaba el **auge** de algunas de sus **ciudades-estado**, en especial de **Atenas, Esparta y Corinto**; en esta última surgió un nuevo tipo de gobernante, el «tirano», a partir del derrocamiento de los reyes baquíadas en 658 a. C. El nuevo rey,

« TAHARKA EL IMPÍO LLEGÓ A **OCUPAR EGIPTO. »**

Assurbanipal, relato de la conquista de Egipto (664 a. C.)

Cipselo (r. *c.* 657–627 a. C.), se basó en la fuerza de la personalidad, más que en la aprobación divina, y estableció una dinastía bajo la cual **Corinto disfrutó de siete décadas de hegemonía** y creó colonias por todo el Mediterráneo occidental. Otros tiranos tomaron el poder en otras ciudades griegas, sustituyendo el gobierno de los aristócratas.

En los límites del mundo griego, en Asia Menor occidental, el **reino de Lidia** aumentaba su poder bajo el gobierno de su primer gran rey, **Giges** (685–647 a. C.), quien se alió con Assurbanipal de Asiria a fin de rechazar la amenaza sobre sus dos reinos de los invasores cimerios en 668–665 a. C.; sin embargo, posteriormente ayudaría a Samético I de Egipto en su revuelta contra los asirios. Giges también adoptó una postura muy agresiva hacia sus vecinos, los griegos jonios de Mileto y Esmirna.

Según la tradición japonesa, **Jimmu Tenno**, descendiente de la diosa del sol **Amateratsu** y primer emperador, ascendió al trono en 660 a. C. El relato de su viaje desde Honshu, en el sur, hacia su reino cerca de Nara, en el este, es legendario, pero pudo hacerse eco de sucesos reales del periodo **ya-**

ASSURBANIPAL (r. 668–627 a. C.)

Inicialmente, compartió reinado sobre Asiria con su hermano, Shamash-shum-ukin. Después de frustrar la revuelta de este en 648 a. C., llevó a cabo una gran expansión de los dominios asirios. Además de anexionarse Egipto, atacó Elam, cuya capital, Susa, saqueó en 647 a. C. Los años finales de su reinado no igualaron los éxitos militares del principio; tras su muerte, la pugna entre sus dos hijos debilitó el Imperio asirio.

30 000 ES EL NÚMERO DE **TABLILLAS DE ARCILLA** QUE SE DESCUBRIERON EN LA **BIBLIOTECA DE NÍNIVE**, EN EL REINO ASIRIO DE **ASSURBANIPAL**

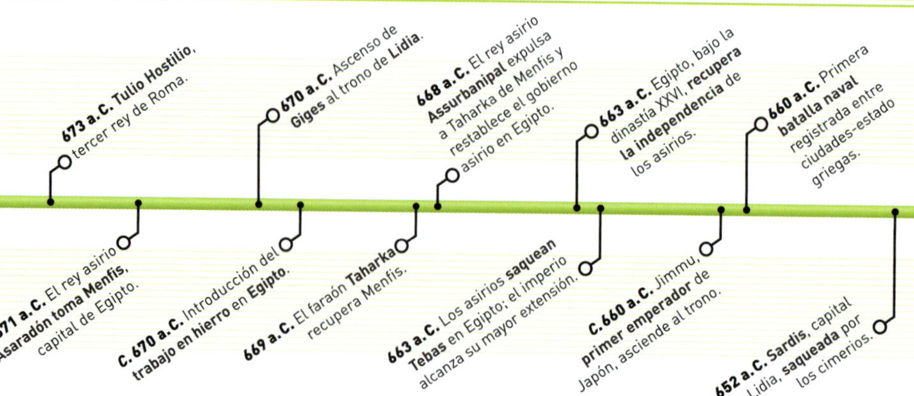

650–601 a.C.

Friso con leones en la avenida de las Procesiones de Babilonia, que fue construida *c.* 600 a.C. y atravesaba el centro de la ciudad hasta la Puerta de Ishtar.

El Imperio asirio
Desde su centro en torno a Assur y Nínive, el Imperio asirio creció hasta abarcar Babilonia, Media, Urartu, Elam, Siria y Egipto.

yoi, después de 100 a.C., cuando los jefes tribales empezaron a **consolidar sus territorios**.

El tercer rey de Roma, llamado **Tulio Hostilio** (r. 673–642 a.C.), resultó ser mucho más beligerante que su predecesor, Numa Pompilio, e inició una serie de batallas contra su vecina Alba Longa que condujo a la destrucción de esa ciudad y a la deportación de su población a Roma en la que sería la **primera gran expansión romana**. El cuarto rey, **Anco Marcio** (r. 642–617 a.C.) extendió el territorio romano hacia la costa y fundó el puerto romano de Ostia, situado en la desembocadura del río Tíber. Su sucesor, **Tarquinio Prisco** (r. 616–578 a.C.), se convirtió en uno de los mayores reyes de la ciudad. De ascendencia etrusca –un claro signo de la gran influencia etrusca sobre la primitiva Roma–, consiguió una serie de victorias sobre sabinos, latinos y etruscos, todo ellos competidores de Roma por el dominio sobre la Italia central. También se dice que fue él quien instauró los juegos públicos romanos.

EN 691 A.C. LOS ASIRIOS HABÍAN CONQUISTADO finalmente Babilonia, destruyendo parcialmente la ciudad. Su reconstrucción empezó bajo Asaradón (r. 680–669 a.C.) y en 652 a.C. ya había recuperado su importancia y se convertía en núcleo de **una revuelta** conducida por Shamash-shum-ukin contra su hermano menor, Assurbanipal. Costó **cuatro años de guerra** reprimir tanto a los babilonios como a sus aliados elamitas, y la lucha terminó consumiendo la capacidad asiria para mantener su imperio. En 630 a.C. los asirios ya habían perdido Egipto y Palestina, y en 626 a.C. los **babilonios lograban recuperar su independencia**. En 616 a.C. Babilonia ya era lo bastante fuerte para, ayudada por los medos (cuya base estaba situada en el noroeste de Irán), invadir Asiria. En 612 a.C. babilonios, medos y escitas saquearon Nínive, la capital asiria. El **Imperio asirio se desmoronó**. Un remanente de su ejército se reagrupó, estableciendo un pequeño reino en torno a Harrán, pero en 609 a.C. también este había caído.

Los **escitas** formaban parte de una cultura de **jinetes nómadas** que controlaba un enorme territorio en las estepas del norte del Cáucaso desde *c.* 800 a.C. En 652 a.C. sometieron a los medos, y el rey escita Bartatua se hizo lo bastante influyente como para recibir a una princesa asiria como esposa. La **alianza con Asiria** perduró durante todo el reinado de su hijo Madyes, pero en torno a 615 a.C. los escitas cambiaron de bando y desempeñaron un **rol fundamental en la destrucción de Asiria**. Los sometidos medos no tardaron en volverse contra ellos, y hacia 590 a.C. los escitas se retiraron hacia el norte.

En el mundo griego crecía el **establecimiento de colonias** por el Mediterráneo. Entre las primeras estuvieron las italianas, como **Siracusa**, que fue fundada *c.* 733 a.C. También fundaron **Cirene** (en Libia) *c.* 630 a.C., y **Massalia** (Marsella) *c.* 600 a.C. Llegaron incluso a alcanzar España, por el oeste, y las costas del mar Negro.

Mientras tanto, en la propia Grecia, la **ciudad-estado de Esparta** estaba estableciendo su predominio en el Peloponeso; en 669 a.C., después de sufrir una derrota frente a Argos, los espartanos decidieron promover una profunda reforma militar y obtuvieron la victoria contra los mesenios (660–650 a.C.). En 600 a.C. **Esparta ya había conquistado** el sur del Peloponeso, establecido un sistema social estratificado y convertido a los mesenios en ilotas (una especie de esclavos).

La futura rival de Esparta, **Atenas**, unificó gradualmente bajo su control la región del Ática durante el siglo VIII a.C. La monarquía hereditaria fue sustituida por un sistema de nueve arcontes elegidos anualmente. Poco después de una dura revuelta popular contra Cilón, que tuvo lugar en 632 a.C., Atenas recibió su primer código legal, elaborado por Dracón en 621 a.C. La llamada **ley draconiana** sería famosa por la severidad de los castigos que prescribía.

En el sur de Egipto, el **estado de Napata** se convirtió en una potencia de primera magnitud: conquistó Egipto bajo el mandato de Pianjy (r. 747–716 a.C.), y lo controló hasta después de la muerte de Taharka (r. 690–664 a.C.).

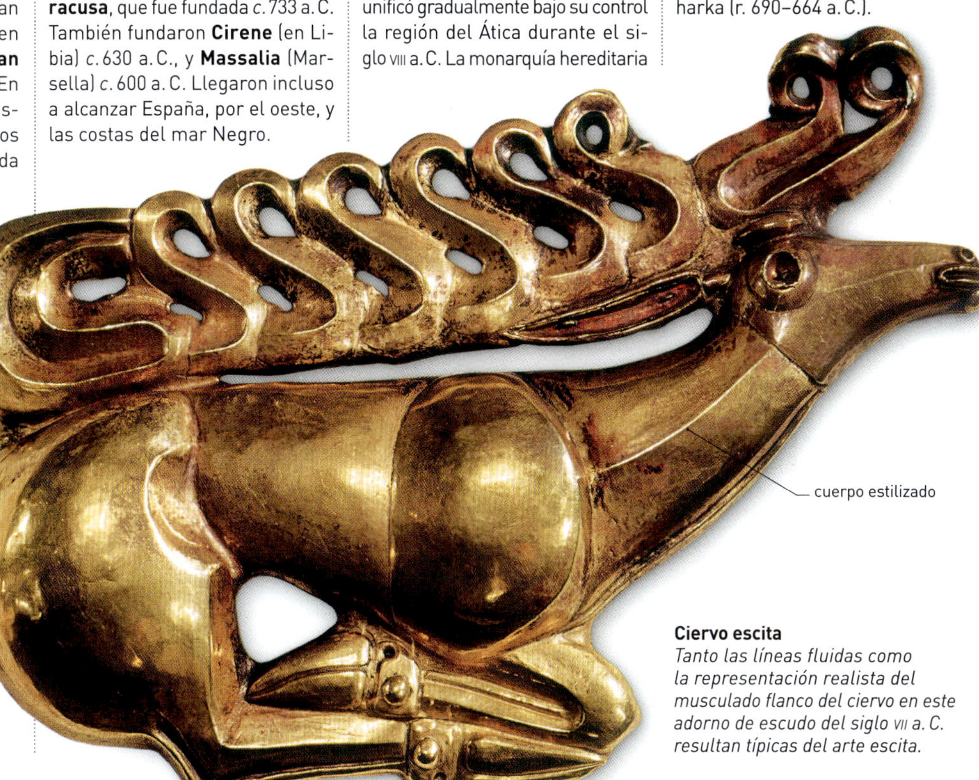

Ciervo escita
Tanta las líneas fluidas como la representación realista del musculado flanco del ciervo en este adorno de escudo del siglo VII a.C. resultan típicas del arte escita.

652 a.C. La **rebelión babilonia** amenaza el control asirio, pero es sofocada (hasta 649 a.C.).

C. 650 a.C. Comienza la **época de los tiranos** en las ciudades-estado griegas.

C. 650 a.C. La tecnología del hierro llega a la **China zhou**.

650 a.C. Primeras monedas acuñadas en **Lidia**.

647 a.C. Assurbanipal **saquea Susa**.

648 a.C. Babilonia se rinde a Assurbanipal.

630 a.C. Esparta en **guerra** con **Mesenia**.

631 a.C. Muerte de **Assurbanipal**.

630 a.C. Fundación de la colonia griega de **Cirene** (en la actual Libia).

626 a.C. Nabopolasar asciende al trono babilonio e instaura el Imperio neobabilónico (o caldeo).

625 a.C. Periandro, hijo de Cípselo, toma el poder como tirano de Corinto.

621 a.C. Código de Dracón: primeras leyes escritas de Atenas.

620 a.C. Fundación de la colonia griega de **Tartessos** en España.

616 a.C. El etrusco Tarquinio, **rey de Roma**.

615 a.C. Los **medos**, potencia emergente, **derrotan** a los **escitas**.

612 a.C. El **Imperio asirio se hunde** bajo los ataques de medos y babilonios.

609 a.C. Harrán, estado residual asirio, es capturado por babilonios y medos: el estado asirio desaparece definitivamente.

608 a.C. El faraón **Necao II** invade **Judá**.

605 a.C. Nabucodonosor II accede al trono de Babilonia.

604 a.C. Fecha tradicional de nacimiento de **Laozi**, fundador del **taoísmo**.

600–551 a.C.

Vista medieval de Jerusalén, capturada por los babilonios en 597 a.C. Diez años después fue tomada de nuevo y destruida en su mayor parte. Tras ambos asedios, muchos de sus habitantes fueron deportados a Babilonia.

TRAS HABER AYUDADO A DESTRUIR EL IMPERIO ASIRIO, Nabopolasar (r. 626–605 a.C.), el primer rey del **Imperio neobabilónico**, embelleció la ciudad de Babilonia. Su hijo, Nabucodonosor II (r. 605–562 a.C.) derrotó a los egipcios en 605 a.C., restauró el principal zigurat de Babilonia y ordenó la construcción de los famosos jardines colgantes. El último rey neobabilonio, **Nabónido** (r. 556–539 a.C.), trasladó la corte al oasis árabe de Tema; durante su reinado **creció el descontento** entre los babilonios.

Los medos del noroeste de Persia (Irán) consolidaron su reino bajo **Ciáxares** (r. 624–585 a.C.), y contribuyeron a la destrucción del Imperio asirio en 612 a.C. El último rey medo, Astiages (r. 584–550 a.C.) hizo campaña en Azerbaiyán y controló territorios tan al oeste como Lidia (Turquía). Sin embargo, en la década de 550 a.C., Media se encontró bajo la fuerte presión de los babilonios por el sur y de la nueva potencia persa.

El reino de Judá había actuado durante largo tiempo como tapón a la expansión hacia occidente de asirios y babilonios. En **597 a.C.**, Nabucodonosor II **tomó Jerusalén** y depuso al rey Jeconías, instalando en el trono a Sedecías; este se terminó rebelando contra el poder babilonio y sufrió un **nuevo asedio** en **587 a.C.** Gran parte de la ciudad fue arrasada, el templo judío destruido por completo, y muchos de sus habitantes deportados al **exilio** en Babilonia.

En **Atenas** (*c.* 594 a.C.) finalizó un periodo de conflictos sociales gracias a las reformas de **Solón**, en especial un **código legal** que protegía los derechos de propiedad de los pobres, abolía la esclavitud por deudas y moderaba los aspectos más extremos de las **leyes draconianas** (*véase* 650–601 a.C.). En torno a 560 a.C., Pisístrato se hizo con el poder y gobernó como **tirano**. Desterrado por dos veces, regresó en 547 a.C. y consolidó un régimen estable.

La **ciudad griega** de Mileto asistió el inicio del **pensamiento filosófico occidental** *c.* 600 a.C. Tales (n. *c.* 624 a.C.), que trató de comprender la naturaleza básica del universo, concluyó que su principio fundamental era el agua.

Legislador y reformador
Esta imagen muestra al estadista y legislador griego Solón como maestro. Sus reformas empezaron a socavar el poder de la aristocracia en Atenas.

550–501 a.C.

Asia central se convirtió en baluarte de las creencias budistas. Estas pinturas rupestres en Dunhuang (China) ilustran diversas parábolas budistas.

CIRO, REY DEL PEQUEÑO REINO DE PERSIS (o Fars), situado en el oeste de Persia (Irán), **se rebeló** contra los señores medos en **559 a.C.** En 550 a.C. ya había logrado conquistar la capital meda, Ecbatana, y derrocó a su rey, Astiages. Temeroso del **creciente poder de Persia**, el **rey Creso** de Lidia combatió a Ciro, pero este avanzó hacia el oeste y, en 547 a.C., derrotó a los lidios en el río Halys (Kizil Irmak) y se anexionó Asia Menor.

Ciro tomó Babilonia en 539 a.C., con lo que obtuvo gran parte de Mesopotamia y convirtió el **Imperio persa** en el mayor de Oriente Medio. **Ciro murió** en 530 a.C. mientras luchaba en el actual Turkmenistán, y fue sucedido por su hijo **Cambises**.

En 526 a.C. Cambises envió sus **ejércitos hacia Egipto**. El faraón Amosis II acababa de morir y su sucesor, Samético III, aún no había consolidado su puesto. Cambises derrotó al ejército egipcio en Pelusio (525 a.C.) y **tomó Menfis, la capital real**. Se proclamó a sí mismo faraón y, a continuación, sometió el sur de Egipto. El dominio persa sobre Egipto duraría hasta 401 a.C.

Cambises falleció en 522 a.C. y, después de la breve rebelión de su hermano menor Bardiya (Esmerdis), o de alguien que se hacía pasar por él, el trono fue ocupado por un noble persa, **Darío**. Estallaron entonces revueltas generalizadas, incluso en Media, pero Darío las sofocó. Entre 519 y 515 a.C., Darío **expandió el Imperio persa** anexionándose territorios en Asia central y en la frontera con **India**, donde el poder político estaba reunido en torno a los **mahajanapadas**, un grupo formado por 16 poderosos reinos, de los cuales Magadha era

Darío I el Grande
Este friso muestra al rey Darío entronizado y portando los símbolos del poder. Darío fue sucedido por su hijo Jerjes.

« LIBRÉ **19 BATALLAS** EN **UN** SOLO **AÑO**... Y EN TODAS **VENCÍ**. »

Inscripción de Behistún, erigida por **Darío I**

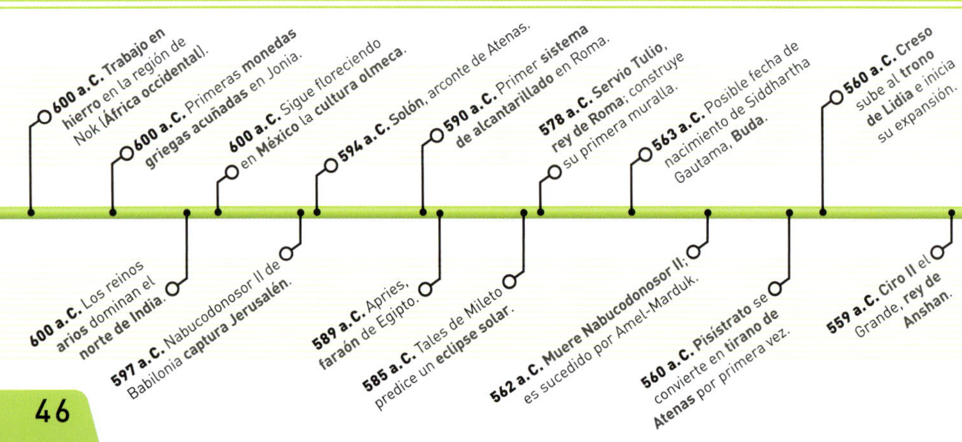

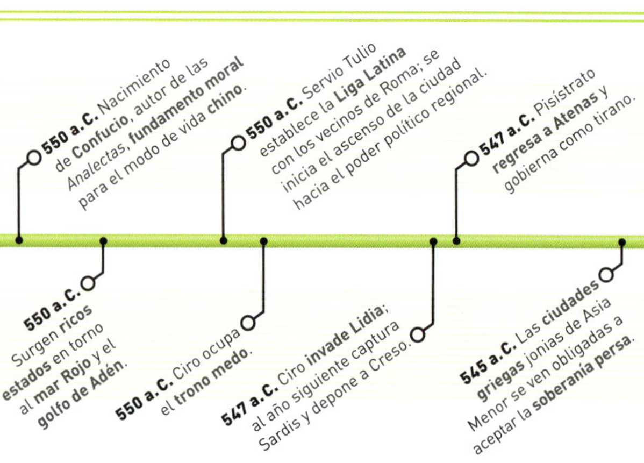

« NI LA **MUERTE SERÁ TEMIDA** POR AQUEL QUE HA VIVIDO SABIAMENTE. **»**

Siddhartha Gautama, el Buda (563–483 a. C.)

482

DURACIÓN EN **AÑOS** DE LA **REPÚBLICA ROMANA**

el más importante. Posteriormente, el rey Darío también consiguió subyugar a la mayor parte de las ciudades-estado griegas en Jonia antes de **llegar hasta Europa** en 513 a. C. para conquistar Tracia.

Mientras tanto, en Italia, Servio Tulio (r. 578–535 a. C.), **sexto rey de Roma** y de quien se dice que fue esclavo, había sucedido a Tarquinio Prisco. Durante su reinado implantó numerosas e **importantes reformas**: fijó las fronteras formales de la ciudad y dividió a los romanos en cuatro tribus –un sistema que se extendería a medida que crecía el territorio–, y también en **clases en función del patrimonio**. La población quedó de esta manera dividida por el equipamiento que podían permitirse y por su papel en el ejército romano. Los más ricos debían combatir en la caballería, las clases altas en la infantería pesada y los pobres como tropas ligeras auxiliares. Los votos de las clases superiores tenían mucho más peso en la asamblea popular. El **último rey de Roma**, Tarquinio el Soberbio (r. 534–509 a. C.), era etrusco. Preocupados por la **creciente tiranía** de su reinado, un grupo de aristócratas romanos dirigidos por Lucio Junio Bruto (su sobrino) y Lucio Tarquinio Colatino (su primo) persuadió al ejército y cerró las puertas de la ciudad al rey, que fue depuesto. Los nuevos líderes **establecieron una república** en la que la autoridad suprema era ostentada por dos magistrados llamados **cónsules**, cuyo poder era limitado mediante la **elección anual** de nuevos cónsules por la asamblea.

CIRO EL GRANDE
(r. 559–530 a. C.)

Poco se sabe acerca de los primeros años de Ciro. Gobernaba el reino de Fars cuando dirigió una revuelta contra Astiages, su señor medo. Al derrotarlo, se coronó rey de los medos. Después siguió expandiendo la influencia persa con la conquista de Lidia. A fin de presentarse como el regente ideal en las ciudades que conquistaba, Ciro adaptaba las ideas locales sobre la realeza. Murió en 530 a. C.

En algún momento en torno al año 530 a. C., **Siddhartha Gautama**, un príncipe indio de Kapilvastu (hoy en Nepal), tuvo una revelación religiosa y decidió rechazar su educación noble para embarcarse en una búsqueda de la «iluminación». Seis años después la recibió, y empezó a predicar una vía de ascetismo moderado para conseguir la liberación del sufrimiento de la vida material. Es conocido como el Buda («el despierto», en sánscrito) y sus seguidores, que empezaron a ser llamados **budistas**, difundieron su doctrina y su pensamiento por toda el Asia meridional y, hacia finales del siglo III d. C., por China y, posteriormente, por Corea, Japón y el Sureste Asiático.

Confucio (o K'ung Fu-tzu) nació hacia 551 a. C., en un momento de enorme inestabilidad política durante el **periodo de las Primaveras y Otoños** (770–481 a. C.) Totalmente consagrado al estudio desde los quince años, la **filosofía política** que desarrolló refleja aquel tiempo turbulento. Enseñaba que el hombre superior (o *junzi*) debía respetar a los demás y **no infligir daño innecesario**. Su filosofía, que fue desarrollada por sus discípulos, enseñaba el respeto a los ancianos y se convirtió en la piedra angular del posterior sistema imperial.

La élite persa
Estos arqueros del palacio de Darío en Susa eran la élite del ejército persa, que incluía representantes de provincias tan lejanas como Etiopía y Afganistán.

540 a. C. Nace Mahavira, fundador de la **religión jainista**.

540 a. C. Comienza el **reinado de Bimbisara** en Magadha.

539 a. C. Rebelión en **Babilonia**. Ciro entra en la ciudad y la anexiona.

538 a. C. Ciro **ocupa Jerusalén** y permite el regreso de los judíos exiliados en Babilonia.

535 a. C. Batalla naval entre griegos y cartagineses frente a Alalia (Aleria, Córcega).

534 a. C. Sube al trono Tarquinio el Soberbio, **último rey de Roma**.

533 a. C. Los ejércitos de Ciro el Grande invaden el **norte de India**.

530 a. C. Ciro muere durante su campaña contra los masagetas.

525 a. C. Cambises invade Egipto, **derrota a los egipcios** en Pelusio, captura Menfis y depone al faraón Samético III, dando fin a la dinastía saíta.

521 a. C. Ascenso de **Darío I** al trono persa tras la **guerra civil**.

538–515 a. C. Reconstrucción del templo de Jerusalén, quemado en **587 a. C.**

520 a. C. Tarquinio el Soberbio inicia la construcción del **Capitolio** en Roma.

520 a. C. Darío I **sofoca una revuelta** en Babilonia y completa el canal que conecta el Nilo con el mar Rojo.

515 a. C. Darío construye su **residencia real** en Susa, antigua capital elamita.

514 a. C. Revuelta fallida de Harmodio y Aristogitón contra los pisistrátidas, descendientes de Pisístrato, en Atenas.

510 a. C. Los alcmeónidas **expulsan a Pisístrato** de Atenas con la ayuda del rey de Esparta.

509 a. C. Los romanos expulsan a Tarquinio el Soberbio e instauran la **república**.

507 a. C. Clístenes establece el **gobierno democrático** en Atenas.

504 a. C. Tarquinio el Soberbio intenta **tomar Roma**, pero fracasa.

Antefija con Medusa
FECHA DESCONOCIDA
Esta antefija de terracota –adorno colocado en las cornisas o aleros de tejados– muestra el rostro de Medusa, la criatura mítica cuya mirada convertía a los hombres en piedra.

Casco corintio
600–500 a. C.
El casco corintio, forjado con una única lámina de bronce, fue el tipo más común en Grecia en el periodo 750–300 a. C.

Punta de lanza
600–400 a. C.
Los hoplitas griegos (infantería armada) portaban una lanza larga *(dori)*, de la que aquí se ve la hoja.

GRECIA ANTIGUA

DE LO FUNCIONAL A LO DECORATIVO, LOS GRIEGOS CREARON UN ARTE DE GRAN BELLEZA

Aunque los griegos produjeron un grandioso arte monumental, objetos menores como joyería, instrumentos musicales, armas y jarrones muestran su amor por las formas intrincadas y la ornamentación a lo largo de todos los periodos de su historia.

El arte griego pasó por varias fases que se reflejan en todos los aspectos de su producción artística, pero especialmente en los jarrones. En el estilo geométrico (*c.* 850–700 a. C.) la decoración se componía básicamente de formas geométricas; fue seguido por el orientalizante (*c.* 700–600 a. C.), con temas animales y florales y, finalmente, a partir de 600 a. C., por las representaciones más naturalistas del estilo clásico.

Espejo de bronce
490–460 a. C.
Este espejo ricamente decorado muestra la imagen de Afrodita flanqueada por dos erotes.

Pendientes de oro
420–400 a. C.
Delicados pendientes de filigrana de oro con figuras de barcos y sirenas (criaturas míticas cuyas hermosas voces atraían a la muerte a los marinos incautos).

Címbalos de bronce
500–400 a. C.
Tenían forma de campana o copa, y se representaban a menudo en los jarrones en manos de sátiros o de mujeres en festejos dionisíacos.

Tapa de espejo y fíbula
420–400 a. C.
La fíbula (broche) y la cadena de plata pudieron servir para ajustar una capa. El reverso del espejo muestra a Afrodita con el dios Pan, mitad macho cabrío.

Aulos
400 a. C.
En origen, este instrumento de viento era doble (uno de sus caramillos se ha perdido) y se tocaba a través de una caña.

Broche de oro
650–600 a. C.
Broche con forma de halcón datado en un periodo de fuerte influencia de Asia occidental y Egipto en Grecia.

Figurilla ecuestre beocia
550 a. C.
El diseño de este jinete y su caballo muestra un aire arcaico en comparación con la producción de terracotas beocias de los dos siglos posteriores (dcha.).

Figurilla beocia
400–200 a. C.
Esta terracota de una mujer sosteniendo un jarrón procede de Beocia, donde la tradición de tales esculturas se inició ya en el siglo VIII a. C.

Ostracón
***C.* 475–470 a. C.**
En Atenas, los políticos podían ser castigados al ostracismo (exilio) por votación pública. El voto con el nombre del político a desterrar se inscribía en un fragmento de cerámica.

Disco
600–500 a. C.
Este fino disco de bronce perteneció a un atleta llamado Exoidas. Después de conseguir una victoria con él en un certamen deportivo, se lo dedicó a los semidioses Cástor y Pólux.

Ánfora ateniense
540–530 a. C.
Un ánfora era un tipo de vasija usado para almacenar vino. Esta está decorada con la técnica de figuras negras, precedente del estilo de figuras rojas.

Ascos ático
425–400 a. C.
El ascos era un tipo de vasija para verter líquidos como aceite, con la forma típica de una bota de vino. El dibujo, del estilo de figuras rojas, se hizo popular *c.* 530 a. C.

Esquifos ático
525–500 a. C.
Este vaso muestra a unos recién casados de pie sobre un carro, rodeados de sirvientes. Está pintado en el estilo de figuras negras.

Píxide de Apulia
500–400 a. C.
El píxide se utilizaba a menudo para guardar pequeñas joyas y cosméticos. Este ejemplar del sur de Italia está decorado con formas geométricas.

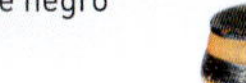

Lequito ático
480–470 a. C.
A menudo las vasijas mostraban escenas mitológicas. En este, decorado con figuras negras, la diosa Atenea derriba a un gigante.

Epíquisis
375–340 a. C.
Esta vasija de larga embocadura se usaba para servir vino. El ejemplar mostrado, del sur de Italia, tiene la base decorada con galones blancos.

« SON **BUENAS NUEVAS**... SI LOS PERSAS **OCULTAN EL SOL**, PODREMOS COMBATIR **A LA SOMBRA**. »

Heródoto, historiador griego, en su *Historias*, citando palabras atribuidas al espartano Dieneces al tener noticias de que los arqueros persas disparaban tantas flechas que estas ocultarían el sol

Esta pintura del siglo XIX muestra al rey espartano Leónidas I (centro, de frente) en la batalla de las Termópilas (480 a.C.). El nombre de este desfiladero se convirtió en sinónimo de resistencia heroica contra fuerzas superiores.

Los plebeyos abandonan Roma
La salida de la plebe (en el grabado, a la izda.) amenazaba con fragmentar Roma, por lo que los patricios (dcha.) cedieron parte de su poder político.

LAS CIUDADES-ESTADO JONIAS de Anatolia occidental habían estado sometidas al Imperio persa desde que Ciro conquistó Lidia, su potencia dominante anterior, en 547 a.C. (*véase* 550–501 a.C.). En 499 a.C., **Aristágoras**, señor de Mileto, se desplazó a la Grecia continental con el fin de atraer aliados para un **levantamiento** contra los persas. Esparta rechazó su petición, y solo Atenas y Eretria enviaron tropas. Un ataque fallido sobre Sardes llevó a los atenienses a retirarse. A partir de 497 a.C., los jonios perdieron terreno frente a la **ofensiva terrestre de los persas**. La muerte de Aristágoras aquel año minó la unidad de los jonios, y tras la derrota en la **batalla naval de Lade** (494 a.C.), la revuelta fracasó, y al año siguiente los persas se apoderaron de Mileto.

600
PERSIA

353
JONIA

La batalla de Lade
La armada jonia griega combatió con denuedo en Lade, pero la deserción de los samios, pactada con los persas, llevó a la derrota total.

En Italia, la **joven república romana** fue sacudida por la **disensión social** cuando, en 494 a.C., los plebeyos (grupos sociales inferiores) abandonaron Roma en masa como protesta por el trato que les dispensaban los patricios (grupos sociales superiores), y amenazaron con crear un estado alternativo. Solo accedieron a regresar tras el reconocimiento oficial de sus propios representantes, los tribunos.

EL REINO DE MAGADHA adquirió mucha importancia en el norte de India bajo el reinado de **Bimbisara** (r. 543–491 a.C.), protector de Gautama **Buda** (*c.* 563–*c.* 486 a.C.), fundador del budismo (*véase* 550–501 a.C.). Áyata Shatru (r. 491–461 a.C.), hijo de Bimbisara, fortaleció la capital real en Rajagriha y construyó un **centro en Pataligrama**, a orillas del Ganges, que más adelante se convertiría en **Pataliputra, capital real maurya**. Con la conquista de Kosala y Kashi, y la anexión de la confederación vrijji, Áyata Shatru convirtió Magadha en la **potencia dominante** en la llanura del Ganges.

En China, el sistema político de Primaveras y Otoños dio paso al **periodo de los Reinos Combatientes** (481–221 a.C.), durante el cual siete estados se enfrentaron en un ciclo constante de maniobras diplomáticas para debilitar al contrario, interrumpido periódicamente por estallidos bélicos.

En 490 a.C., **Darío I** (548–486 a.C.) de Persia decidió vengarse de los griegos continentales por su apoyo a la revuelta jonia. Envió una **inmensa expedición naval** al mando de Artafernes y Datis que, partiendo de Cilicia, tomó tierra en Naxos antes de apoderarse de Eretria, que había ayudado a los jonios en el año 499 a.C. Aunque los **atenienses** pidieron ayuda a Esparta, solo la recibieron de Platea, que envió un refuerzo de mil hombres. Asesorados por su general Milcíades II el Joven (550–489 a.C.), los atenienses optaron por salir al encuentro de los **persas**, en lugar de esperar su asedio. En 490 a.C., en **Maratón**, los hoplitas (infantería pesada) grie-

Ritón persa con león alado
El Imperio persa disfrutó de vastas riquezas, como muestran objetos de la vida diaria como este vaso dorado. Se dedicaron enormes recursos a la conquista de Grecia.

7
NÚMERO DE LOS **REINOS COMBATIENTES**

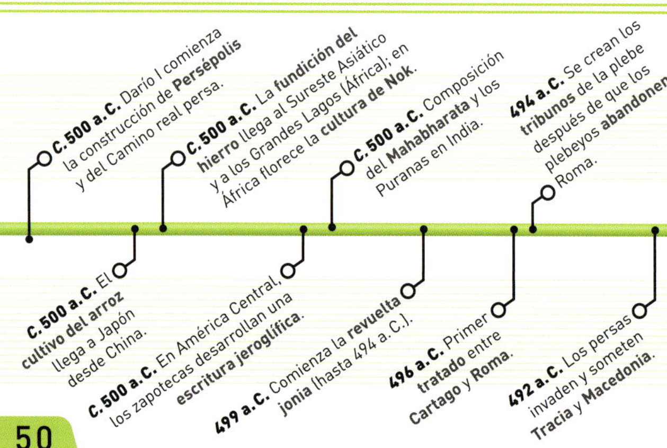

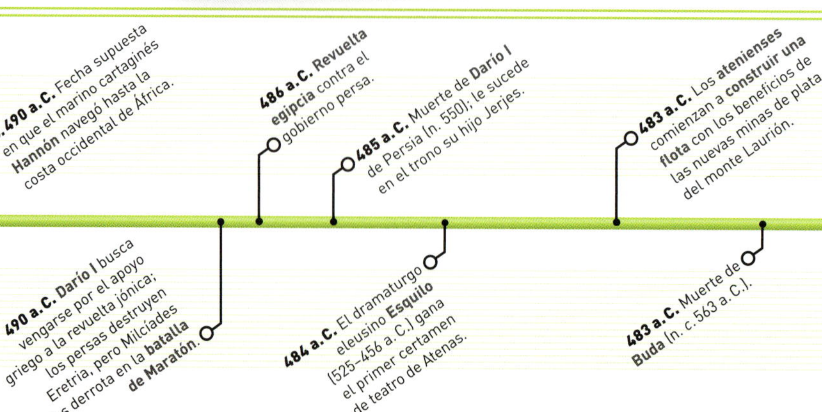

gos cargaron frontalmente contra una fuerza persa muy superior, obteniendo una **victoria impensable** con la que terminó la primera guerra médica.

La castigada fuerza expedicionaria persa se retiró de Grecia después de Maratón, pero en 481 a.C., **Jerjes I** (519–465 a.C.) envió un nuevo ejército que cruzó el Helesponto (cerca de la actual Estambul) y avanzó hacia Atenas desde el norte. Muchas ciudades septentrionales prefirieron someterse, pero Atenas y Esparta formaron una liga de ciudades sureñas. En 480 a.C., la **heroica defensa** del paso de las **Termópilas** por el rey espartano Leónidas I (donde murió junto con trescientos espartanos) dio tiempo a la evacuación de Atenas. Los persas arrasaron la ciudad, pero poco después la flota ateniense, al mando de **Temístocles** (*véase* recuadro) infligía una importante derrota a la fuerza naval de Jerjes en **Salamina**. Esta victoria griega fue seguida, en junio de 479 a.C., por la terrestre de Platea, en Beocia, y la naval de Mícala, frente a la costa jonia, finalizando así la segunda guerra médica. Luego los griegos pasaron a la ofensiva, y en 478–477 a.C. encadenaron una serie de victorias en Jonia y Citio (Chipre) que **invirtieron gran parte de los avances persas**.

Las guerras médicas
Aunque las fuerzas persas eran muchísimo más numerosas, las griegas ganaron combates terrestres y navales cruciales.

Después de las derrotas iniciales de los persas en 480–479 a.C., Atenas trató de formalizar una **confederación contra los persas**. En torno a 477 a.C. se estableció una tesorería en la isla de Delos, donde se depositaban fondos y se celebraban encuentros regulares. Sin embargo, esta **Liga de Delos** no tardó en ser sino un imperio ateniense, y Esparta y sus aliados se negaron a participar.

TEMÍSTOCLES (*c.* 524–460 a.C.)

Inteligente político y estratega, convenció a los atenienses para usar las riquezas de una mina de plata encontrada en Laurión en 483 a.C. para duplicar el tamaño de su armada. No obstante, pasada la victoria naval de Salamina, los celos crecientes de sus rivales políticos le acabaron condenando al ostracismo (exilio por voto público) *c.* 470 a.C.

> « EL **GRAN COMBATE** HA LLEGADO. »
>
> **Heródoto**, historiador griego, en su *Historias*, citando al general espartano Pausanias antes de la batalla de Platea (479 a.C.)

LOS ATENIENSES DISFRUTARON DE ÉXITOS tempranos bajo el liderazgo de Cimón (510–450 a.C.) al arrebatar a los persas Eyón, a orillas del río Estrimón (Anatolia), en 476 a.C., y en el ataque a Caristos, en Eubea (que se había rendido a los persas), en 470 a.C. En torno a esas fechas, un intento de la isla de Naxos por abandonar la Liga de Delos fue sofocado con dureza por una fuerza expedicionaria ateniense. En 466 a.C., las tropas atenienses obtuvieron una **gran victoria sobre los persas** en el río Eurimedonte, en el sur de Anatolia, estableciendo la supremacía ateniense en el Egeo.

Pericles (*c.* 495–429 a.C.), el estadista ateniense y principal responsable de hacer de Atenas el centro político y cultural de Grecia, intentó procesar sin éxito a Cimón en 463 a.C., bajo la acusación de desatender la oportunidad de conquistar Macedonia. A partir de esa maniobra, el **planteamiento expansionista** ateniense de Pericles resultó ya evidente. Cuando el líder principal de los demócratas, Efialtes, fue asesinado en 461 a.C., Pericles, su protegido, ocupó rápidamente su lugar.

Los persas intentaron periódicamente sobornar a los espartanos para que lanzaran ataques contra Atenas, pero en principio con poco éxito. En 464 a.C., una **revuelta de los ilotas mesenios** (siervos) en el Peloponeso occidental disuadió incluso más a los espartanos de cualquier intento de contener el poder creciente de la liga. Los mesenios apenas recibieron ayuda exterior y en 462 a.C., su último bastión en el monte Itome había sido reducido. Poco tiempo después estallaría abiertamente el conflicto entre Esparta y Atenas, y sus aliados respectivos. La **primera guerra del Peloponeso** no tuvo un resultado concluyente; finalizó en 451 a.C. con un tratado por cinco años, extendido en 446 a.C. en la **paz de los Treinta Años**.

Tesoro ateniense en Delos
Todos los miembros de la Liga de Delos debían depositar fondos en la tesorería de Delos, pero la contribución más importante era la de Atenas.

Mientras tanto, la parte occidental del mundo griego estaba ganando importancia, marcada por el ascenso de la ciudad-estado siciliana de **Siracusa**. Bajo una serie de hábiles gobernantes (tiranos) iniciada con **Gelón** (r. 485–478 a.C.) y su hermano **Hierón I** (r. 478–467 a.C.), las fuerzas siracusanas sometieron a Acragas y expandieron su territorio en torno a Catania. Aunque el hermano menor de Hierón, **Trasíbulo**, fue expulsado en 466 a.C., los siracusanos retuvieron su posición dominante en Sicilia más allá de la década de 450 a.C.

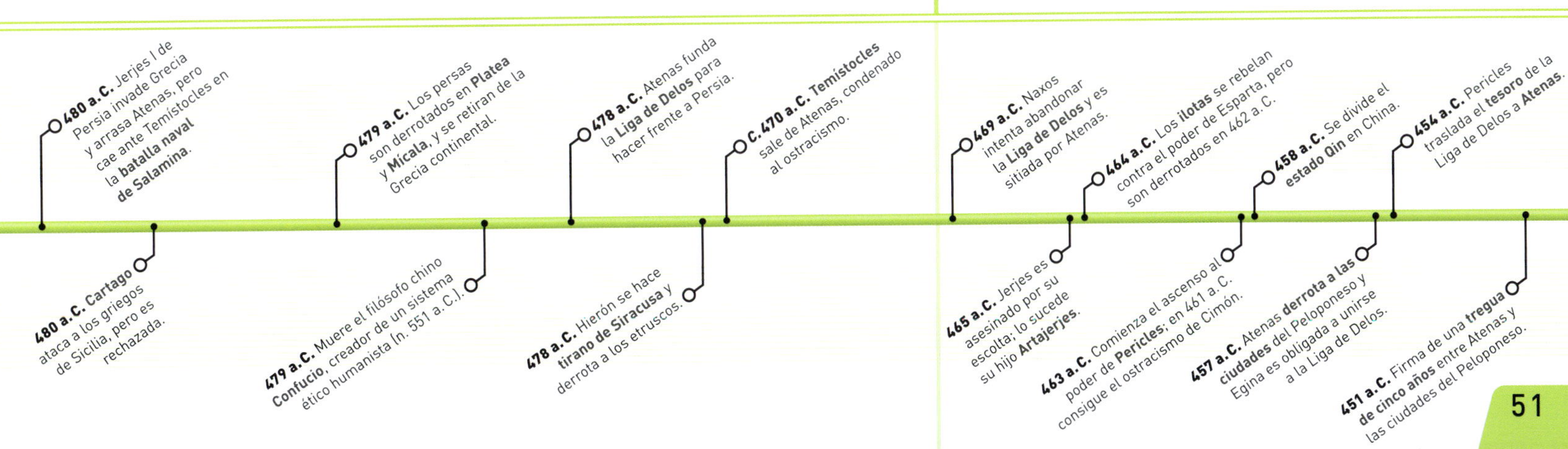

450–431 a.C.

430–404 a.C.

A finales del siglo v, la ciudad mexicana de Monte Albán comenzó la construcción de sus edificios públicos, antecesores de sus magníficas pirámides posteriores, mostradas aquí.

EN LA REPÚBLICA ROMANA, las dos clases sociales –patricios y plebeyos (*véase* 500–491 a.C.)– todavía seguían divididas. Ambos bandos llegaron a un acuerdo en 451 a.C., nombrando un grupo de diez hombres (**decenviros**) que gobernarían Roma al margen de la constitución normal. En 449 a.C., el decenvirato promulgó las **leyes de las Doce Tablas**, que conformaron la base de toda la legislación romana.

Alrededor de 450 a.C. emergió en Europa central una **nueva cultura céltica**, llamada **La Tène**, que sustituyó a la anterior dominante de Hallstatt. Regida por una aristocracia guerrera que enterraba a sus muertos con espadas, lanzas y carros funerarios, tuvo centros importantes en Bohemia y en torno a los ríos Marne y Mosela (actual Francia).

12

NÚMERO DE **TABLAS** DE LA LEY **ROMANA**

En Oaxaca (costa pacífica de México), poco antes de 450 a.C. surgió un nuevo centro en **Monte Albán**. Esta protociudad, en una colina que dominaba el valle de Oaxaca, atrajo a las gentes de las aldeas agrícolas circundantes. Albergaba **grandes edificaciones públicas** –entre ellas pirámides truncadas, grandes plazas y canchas de juego de pelota– así como elaboradas tumbas. En 150 años, Monte Albán alcanzó una población aproximada de 17000 personas, que la convirtió en la **mayor ciudad de Mesoamérica**.

Figura zapoteca de Monte Albán
Esta elaborada cerámica de una deidad es típica de la producción de Monte Albán, que llegó a ser el enclave principal en México en el siglo v a.C.

ATENAS Y ESPARTA YA SE HABÍAN ENFRENTADO CON ANTERIORIDAD (*véase* 475–451 a.C.). El Imperio ateniense poseía **primacía naval**, ya que incluía la mayor parte de las islas y ciudades costeras del norte y este del mar Egeo. Por su parte, Esparta dirigía una alianza de ciudades independientes del Peloponeso y Grecia central, además de Corinto, y tenía el **ejército más poderoso**.

Pese a la Paz de los Treinta Años de 446 a.C., las tensiones continuaron. En 433 a.C., Atentas apoyó a Córcira en una disputa con Corinto; los corintios persuadieron a Esparta de que esto **violaba la paz**, y Esparta emitió un ultimátum que Atenas rechazó. Atenas, dirigida en un principio por Pericles, tuvo éxito inicialmente en la **guerra del Peloponeso** (431–404 a.C.), y en 427 a.C. capturó a una numerosa fuerza espartana en Pilos, al suroeste de Esparta. Pericles murió en la **peste devastadora** que asoló y debilitó gravemente Atenas en 430 a.C. Ninguno de los bandos lograba una victoria decisiva, y en 421 a.C. acordaron la **paz de Nicias**, que debía durar 50 años. La tregua quedó pronto en entredicho. Corinto se negó a reconocerla, y llegaron al poder partidarios de la guerra tanto en Esparta como en Atenas, liderados en esta última por el joven y ambicioso **Alcibíades** (450–404 a.C.). Ambos bandos trataron de obtener ventaja sin abandonar por completo el tratado. En 418 a.C., los aliados de Esparta lograron una **victoria clave en Mantinea** contra la alianza de Atenas y Argos. Atenas devolvió el golpe en 416 a.C.

« EL **IMPERIO** QUE POSEÉIS ES YA **COMO UNA TIRANÍA**, QUE PARECE INJUSTO DETENTAR, PERO QUE ES **PELIGROSO** PERDER. »

Tucídides, historiador griego, en su *Historia de la guerra del Peloponeso*, II. 63, relatando un discurso de Pericles a los atenienses

SÓCRATES (469–399 a.C.)

Fue uno de los mayores filósofos griegos. Pese a que sirvió al Consejo de Atenas, su desafío a la moral establecida en una época de inestabilidad política le granjeó poderosos enemigos. Rechazó preparar una defensa convencional contra la acusación de impiedad y corrupción de la juventud ateniense, y fue sentenciado a morir ingiriendo cicuta.

c. 450 a.C. Surge la cultura de **La Tène** en Europa central.

c. 450 a.C. Enterramientos de nómadas de las estepas en Pazyryk (Siberia) y Noin-Ula (Mongolia).

c. 450 a.C. Comienza la construcción de la ciudad zapoteca de **Monte Albán** en México.

449 a.C. Paz de Calias entre griegos y persas.

449 a.C. Adopción oficial de las **leyes de las Doce Tablas** en Roma.

449 a.C. Pericles inicia la construcción de los **Muros Largos** entre Atenas y su puerto, el Pireo.

447 a.C. Comienza la construcción de un nuevo **Partenón** (acaba en 432 a.C.).

433 a.C. Atenas intercede por **Corfú** en su disputa con **Corinto**, provocando las represalias espartanas.

431 a.C. Esparta da un **ultimátum a Atenas**, pero Pericles convence a los atenienses para que lo rechacen.

430 a.C. Esparta invade el Ática; en Atenas, asolada por la **peste**, mueren miles de personas.

c. 428 a.C. Nace el filósofo griego **Platón** (m. c. 347 a.C.).

427 a.C. La ciudad de **Platea**, aliada ateniense, se somete a Esparta.

423 a.C. Muerte de Artajerjes I; **Darío II**, rey de Persia.

423 a.C. Tregua de un año en la guerra entre Atenas y Esparta (extendida en 422 a.C.).

421 a.C. La **paz de Nicias** entre Atenas y Esparta detiene temporalmente la guerra del Peloponeso.

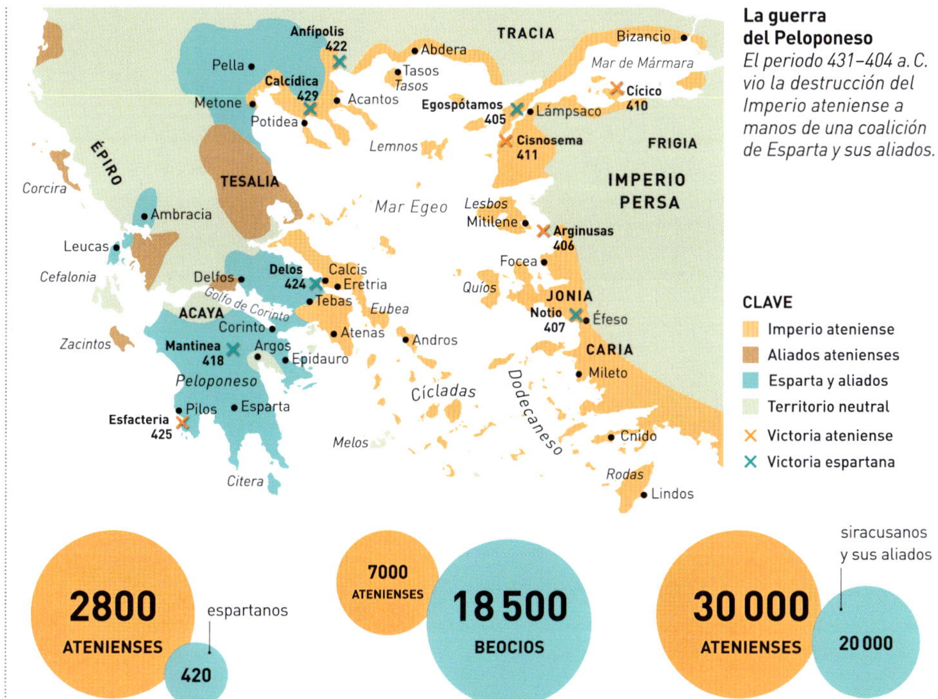

La guerra del Peloponeso
El periodo 431–404 a. C. vio la destrucción del Imperio ateniense a manos de una coalición de Esparta y sus aliados.

CLAVE
- Imperio ateniense
- Aliados atenienses
- Esparta y aliados
- Territorio neutral
- Victoria ateniense
- Victoria espartana

BATALLA DE ESFACTERIA 425 a. C. | **BATALLA DE DELOS 424 a. C.** | **SITIO DE SIRACUSA 415–413 a. C.**

con la toma de Melos –la única isla importante del Egeo que no controlaba–, pero se excedió fatalmente en 415 a. C. en la expedición contra Siracusa en Sicilia, que supuso la **total destrucción** de sus fuerzas en 413 a. C. Mientras tanto, los espartanos fortificaron Decelia en el Ática, desde donde podían asolar a voluntad el territorio ateniense.

En 412 a. C., una alianza con Persia fortaleció aún más la posición de Esparta, y el régimen democrático de Atenas fue brevemente derribado en 411 a. C. La democracia fue restaurada al año siguiente pero, a pesar de las victorias atenienses en Cícico (410 a. C.) y Arginusas (406 a. C.), la **destrucción total de la flota ateniense en Egospótamos**, frente a las costas de Jonia (405 a. C.), dejó a Atenas indefensa. Los espartanos sitiaron la ciudad y, a pesar de su férrea resistencia, **los atenienses fueron obligados a rendirse**. Atenas fue entonces despojada del resto de su flota y, en 404 a. C., se instaló para gobernarla el proespartano consejo de los Treinta Tiranos.

En el reino de Magadha (noreste de **India**), tras la muerte de Áyata Shatru (*c.* 459 a. C.) y una serie de gobernantes incompetentes, se desvanecía (*c.* 413 a. C.) la dinastía Haryanka fundada por Bimbisara. **Shishunaga fundó una nueva dinastía**, que sería responsable de administrar la transferencia de la capital real de Magadha a **Pataliputra**. La dinastía Shishunaga solamente duraría sesenta años.

403–381 a.C.

TRAS SU VICTORIA EN LA GUERRA DEL PELOPONESO, Esparta se vio involucrada en un conflicto con Persia sobre la autonomía de las ciudades griegas jonias. Durante la década de 390 a. C., luchas esporádicas y negociaciones fallidas desviaron la atención de Esparta sobre el debilitamiento de su posición en la Grecia continental. La **paz de Antálcidas**, un tratado definitivo con Persia en 386 a. C., privó de autonomía a los jonios, pero permitió a Esparta anular toda amenaza a su supremacía: en 385 a. C. atacó Mantinea, en el Peloponeso central, y en 383 a. C. ocupó Tebas. El poder espartano parecía inexpugnable.

En Persia, la **muerte de Darío II** (r. 423–404 a. C.) fue seguida por una breve guerra civil cuando Ciro el Joven trató de derrocar a **Artajerjes II** (r. 404–358 a. C.), su hermano mayor. Ciro fue derrotado y muerto en la **batalla de Cunaxa** (401 a.C), después de la cual unos diez mil de sus mercenarios griegos quedaron aislados en el norte de Mesopotamia. Al mando de **Jenofonte**, los griegos marcharon hacia las costas del mar Negro y alcanzaron la seguridad de Trapezonte (Trebisonda o Trabzon, en la actual Turquía), una hazaña que su comandante inmortalizó en la obra *Anábasis*.

En Italia, **los romanos extendieron su territorio** y en 396 a. C. se anexionaron Veyes, cuya sumisión representó el **final de la amenaza etrusca**. Sin embargo, *c.* 390 a. C. un ejército galo que había estado atacando la ciudad etrusca de Clusium giró hacia el sur, derrotó a los romanos en la batalla de Alia y saqueó **Roma**. El desastre obsesionaría a los romanos durante siglos.

Pintura funeraria etrusca
El idioma etrusco apenas se ha podido descifrar, por lo que gran parte de lo que sabemos sobre su cultura procede de los frescos de sus tumbas.

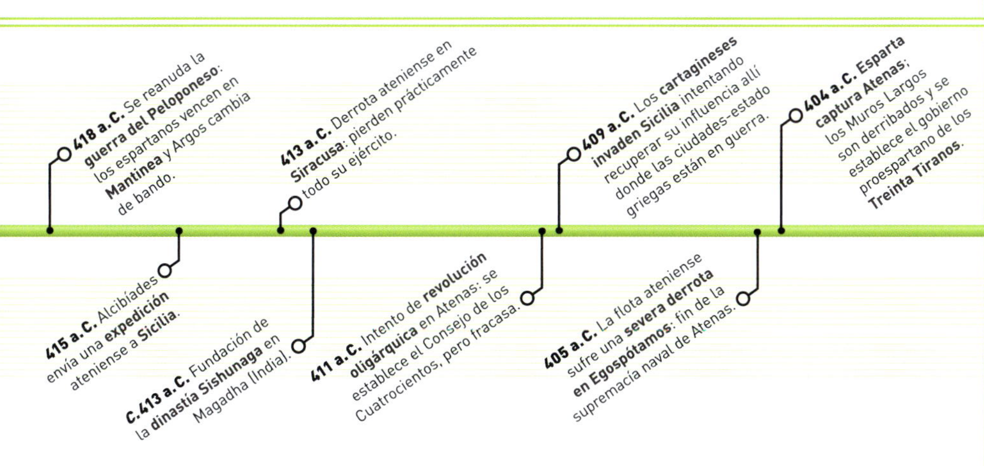

403 a. C. Se disuelve el consejo de los Treinta Tiranos; **restauración de la democracia**.

399 a. C. Ejecución de **Sócrates**, filósofo griego.

401 a. C. Jenofonte dirige desde Babilonia al mar Negro a diez mil mercenarios griegos que apoyaban la revuelta persa.

398–397 a. C. Dionisio I de Siracusa derrota a los cartagineses.

399 a. C. Egipto se separa de Persia; comienza la dinastía XXIX.

396 a. C. Los romanos capturan la ciudad etrusca de **Veyes**.

384 a. C. Platón termina el ***Banquete*** y funda la Academia.

386 a. C. Esparta y Persia firman la **paz de Antálcidas**.

383 a. C. Se reanuda la guerra entre **Cartago** y **Dionisio de Siracusa**.

Hebilla de Sutton Hoo

remache liso conectado con pasador deslizante por detrás

chapa circular en la base de la lengüeta de la hebilla

entrelazado animal con resalte de círculos

La hebilla de Sutton Hoo
Hecha de oro macizo y decorada con un patrón de animales entrelazados, esta hebilla de cinturón fue encontrada en un barco funerario del siglo VII en Anglia Oriental (Reino Unido).

perfil de cabeza de ave

patrón entrelazado central

serpientes entrelazadas que se muerden la cola

Prehistoria
Uso de mena de cobre
En Irán occidental y Anatolia, el cobre es martillado o batido para darle forma en objetos pequeños, como cuentas.

Mena de cobre

***C.* 1500–1200 a.C.**
Refinamiento del vaciado en bronce
Se desarrollan nuevas técnicas para vaciar y adornar vasijas de bronce; por ejemplo, batiendo el interior.

Caldero shang

***C.* 900 a.C.–100 d.C.**
Uso del hierro
La fundición del hierro, que permite crear útiles y armas más robustos, pasa de Anatolia occidental a Grecia *c.* 900 a.C. y a África occidental *c.* 400 a.C.

Armas de hierro

***C.* 100–700**
Metalistería anglosajona
El trabajo en metal anglosajón alcanzó una gran sofisticación; con frecuencia se utilizaron formas animales como decoración.

2600–2400 a.C.
Uso de lámina de cobre batido
Los métodos previos de fundición del cobre se refinan, lo que permite batirlo aún en caliente para lograr formas más complejas.

Toro sumerio en cobre

***C.* 1500–30 a.C.**
Refinado del oro
Los antiguos egipcios aprendieron a separar el oro puro de la plata *c.* 1500 a.C. y empezaron a usarlo más ampliamente con fines decorativos.

Máscara funeraria de Tutankamón

***C.* 640–500 a.C.**
El metal como moneda
Las monedas de metal (hechas con una aleación de oro y plata) se usaron primero en Lidia (en la actual Turquía) *c.* 640 a.C. Los griegos adoptaron la idea y la extendieron por el Mediterráneo.

Moneda griega

HISTORIA DE LA METALURGIA

YA SEA EN OBJETOS COTIDIANOS O EN MÁQUINAS COMPLEJAS, LOS METALES SON VITALES PARA NUESTRA CIVILIZACIÓN

Desde su primer uso conocido en el VIII milenio a. C., los metales han desempeñado un papel clave en la producción de una vasta gama de objetos; incluso hoy, con la disponibilidad de sofisticados polímeros y compuestos, siguen permeando cada aspecto de la civilización contemporánea.

Alrededor del año 7000 a. C., los minerales naturales, y en especial el cobre, empezaron a usarse para crear elementos pequeños, como alfileres, en el oeste de Irán y el este de Anatolia. Se hacían martillando o batiendo el metal para darle forma. El cobre caliente es más maleable, lo cual probablemente se descubrió de forma accidental al dejar caer metal al fuego. Pero lo que condujo al empleo de metales a gran escala fue la introducción de la fundición en crisol.

EL DESARROLLO DE ALEACIONES

En torno a 3000 a. C. se produjo la primera aleación: el bronce. Obtenido al fundir estaño y cobre en un crisol, es más resistente y se trabaja mejor que sus componentes individuales por separado, y siguió siendo el metal principal en herramientas y armas hasta la introducción de la fundición del hierro *c.* 1250 a. C. La técnica para fundir hierro puro no fue inventada hasta el siglo XIX, de modo que los primeros objetos de este metal se lograban fundiendo mineral de hierro para obtener una «flor de hierro» impura, separando luego las piezas y soldándolas después en un horno. Este método de producción continuó en boga hasta la introducción del horno de cuba en Europa durante el siglo XV. La revolución industrial del siglo XVIII aportó nuevas técnicas y el empleo de coque en los hornos; pero sería el convertidor (1856), invento del británico Henry Bessemer, lo que permitiría la producción a gran escala de acero, una aleación hierro-carbono de gran resistencia y calidad. Más tarde, avanzada la revolución industrial, progresos adicionales permitirían producir otros metales, como aluminio, magnesio y titanio, cuya ligereza y resistencia desempeñaron un papel central en el desarrollo de la aviación y la industria espacial.

1083 °C

PUNTO DE FUSIÓN DEL **COBRE**. CUANDO SE **ALEA** CON **ESTAÑO**, **DESCIENDE** A 950 °C

CÓMO SE PRODUCEN LAS ALEACIONES

Una aleación es una mezcla de metales o de un metal con un no metal (como hierro y carbono en el acero). Existen aleaciones naturales, pero las sintéticas no fueron creadas hasta *c.* 3000 a. C., al fundir cobre con estaño para producir bronce. La técnica se difundió, llegando a Mesopotamia poco después de 3000 a. C. y a Egipto *c.* 2000 a. C., o posiblemente antes.

700–800
Fabricación de espadas
En Europa, los espaderos desarrollan armas más sólidas uniendo capas sucesivas de hierro con carbono añadido, o batiendo finas láminas de hierro y luego fundiéndolas

Espada vikinga

800–1300/1450
Objetos cristianos en metales preciosos
Los objetos sagrados cristianos medievales, como crucifijos y relicarios, se elaboraban en oro y otros metales preciosos, a menudo con incrustación de gemas.

Altar de Verdún

***C.* siglo XV**
Armas de metal colado
El desarrollo del hierro colado halla un uso inmediato en la artillería por su robustez y la posibilidad de usarlo para crear formas como tubos.

Cañón medieval

1810
Hojalata
El inventor británico Peter Durand patenta la hojalata para conservar alimentos. Su patente era para una lata de hierro revestida de estaño para evitar su oxidación.

1856
Convertidor Bessemer
El británico Henry Bessemer inventa un convertidor que permite la producción a gran escala de acero de alta calidad.

Convertidor Bessemer

Lockheed blackbird

1910
Papel de aluminio
Se produce la primera hoja de aluminio, facilitada por la invención en 1886 de un método para producir el metal en serie al aplicar una corriente eléctrica al metal fundido.

Década de 1950
Aeronave de titanio
Dada su relación resistencia-peso, el titanio empieza a usarse ampliamente en aeronáutica militar. En la actualidad se usa igualmente en la civil.

380–371 a.C.

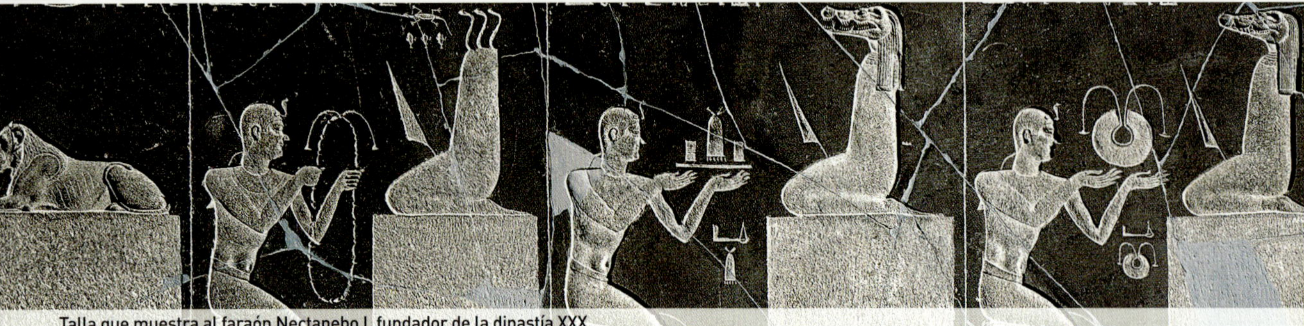

Talla que muestra al faraón Nectanebo I, fundador de la dinastía XXX, realizando ofrendas a varios dioses; entre ellos, el dios cocodrilo Sobek.

DESPUÉS DE LA REBELIÓN DE AMIRTEO, fundador de la dinastía XXVIII en 404 a.C., Egipto se había desembarazado del control de Persia. Sin embargo, los persas no habían renunciado a Egipto. **Nectanebo I** estableció la dinastía XXX en 380 a.C. y en 373 a.C. repelió la fuerza enviada por los persas y sus aliados griegos. La atención persa sobre Egipto fue desviada en la década siguiente por la **rebelión de los sátrapas**, la cual fue agravada en parte por las campañas llevadas a cabo entre 361–360 a.C. por Teos, hijo de Nectanebo I, en la Palestina dominada por Persia. Teos fue derrocado por **Nectanebo II** (r. 359–343 a.C.), quien siguió inmiscuyéndose en las guerras civiles persas. En una imprudente intervención (346 a.C.) envió tropas para ayudar a una sublevación en Sidón (Líbano). En respuesta, **Artajerjes III** de Persia marchó sobre el delta del Nilo en 343 a.C. y Egipto fue derrotado al cabo de dos años; de nuevo bajo el control persa, nunca volvería a tener una dinastía de faraones nativos.

150 PAREJAS FORMABAN EL **BATALLÓN SAGRADO**, UNIDAD DE ÉLITE **TEBANA**

11 000 ESPARTANOS, MERCENARIOS Y ALIADOS

9000 TEBANOS Y ALIADOS

Batalla de Leuctra
Los ejércitos de hoplitas griegos solían situar a los mejores hombres en el flanco derecho. En Leuctra, los tebanos concentraron sus fuerzas en el izquierdo para enfrentarse a las tropas espartanas y desbaratarlas.

En Grecia, la **ocupación espartana de Tebas**, iniciada en 383 a.C., tuvo una vida muy corta. En 379 a.C. fue asesinado el **polemarca** (gobernador) espartano, y los tebanos expulsaron a la guarnición espartana con ayuda de dos generales atenienses llegados para ayudar bajo su propia iniciativa. Como represalia, el rey espartano **Cleómbroto I** (r. 380–371) envió una expedición que no consiguió retomar Tebas, pero alarmó tanto a los atenienses que ejecutaron a uno de los generales y desterraron al otro, abandonando temporalmente su alianza con Tebas. Los **espartanos invadieron la región de Beocia** en 378–377 a.C., pero lograron pocos progresos. Ese acto hizo que los atenienses revivieran su alianza con Tebas e intentaran establecer una **segunda confederación ateniense** con el fin de oponerse a Esparta. En 375 a.C., Tebas, Atenas y Esparta firmaron una paz común que sería rota casi de inmediato. A partir de ese momento los tebanos tomaron la iniciativa, apoyados en una nueva fuerza de élite de ciudadanos soldados, el **Batallón Sagrado**, formado por 150 parejas de hombres. Este grupo complementaba a los mercenarios que formaban los cuerpos de combate principales en las guerras entre ciudades-estado griegas. Los intentos tebanos por conquistar la Fócida y retener el control de Beocia irritaron a Esparta e hicieron fracasar el intento ateniense de mediar en una paz en 372 a.C. En 371 a.C., y bajo la brillante táctica de su general **Epaminondas**, el ejército tebano libró una batalla en **Leuctra** (Grecia central) que consiguió aplastar a las falanges espartanas. **Tebas**, a merced de Esparta solo ocho años atrás, era ahora la **potencia dominante en Grecia**.

Templo de Tot
Situado en Hermópolis, en el Alto Egipto, el templo de Tot fue construido durante el Imperio Nuevo, pero se reformó en el siglo IV *a.C.*

En Sicilia, **Siracusa** siguió floreciendo bajo la mano firme de **Dionisio I** (405–367 a.C.), que libró la tercera de una serie de guerras contra Cartago en 383–375 a.C. En principio, la guerra no fue favorable para Dionisio, que perdió su flota en una tormenta. Los esfuerzos cartagineses por armar una expedición a Sicilia se vieron dificultados por la peste en 379 a.C. y por una revuelta de las ciudades sometidas de Libia, por lo que no enviaron tropas hasta 377 a.C. Dionisio, que había estado luchando contra los aliados de Cartago en el sur de Italia, regresó a Sicilia y **aplastó a las tropas de Magón**: se dice que murieron diez mil hombres en la contienda. Dionisio permitió la retirada del resto, que se reagrupó y regresó un año después al mando de Himilcón, hijo de Magón, para infligir una hiriente derrota a los siracusanos. Exhaustos, ambos bandos **firmaron una paz** en 375 a.C. que dejaba a Dionisio el este de Sicilia y zonas del sur de Italia.

370–356 a.C.

Ruinas de Tebas, ciudad-estado dominante en Grecia durante la década de 360 a.C.

LOS ATENIENSES MEDIARON en una **paz general** en Grecia en 371 a.C. No obstante, Tebas no participó en ella y dirigió una coalición que **invadió Esparta** en 370–369 a.C. Mesenia quedó finalmente fuera del control espartano; pero el logro de nuevas victorias tebanas se vio dificultado por la deposición de **Epaminondas**, juzgado por aceptar un supuesto soborno a cambio de no atacar la ciudad de Esparta. Repuesto Epaminondas, en 367 a.C. los tebanos consiguieron el apoyo persa para su alianza antiespartana, y una **invasión posterior del Peloponeso** en 366 a.C. atrajo nuevos miembros a la coalición. Sin embargo, el éxito tebano descansaba en exceso en la personalidad de un solo hombre, y cuando Epaminondas falleció en combate en

Teatro antiguo
El Odeón era un templo construido en Mesene, ciudad fundada por Epaminondas de Tebas en 367 a.C.

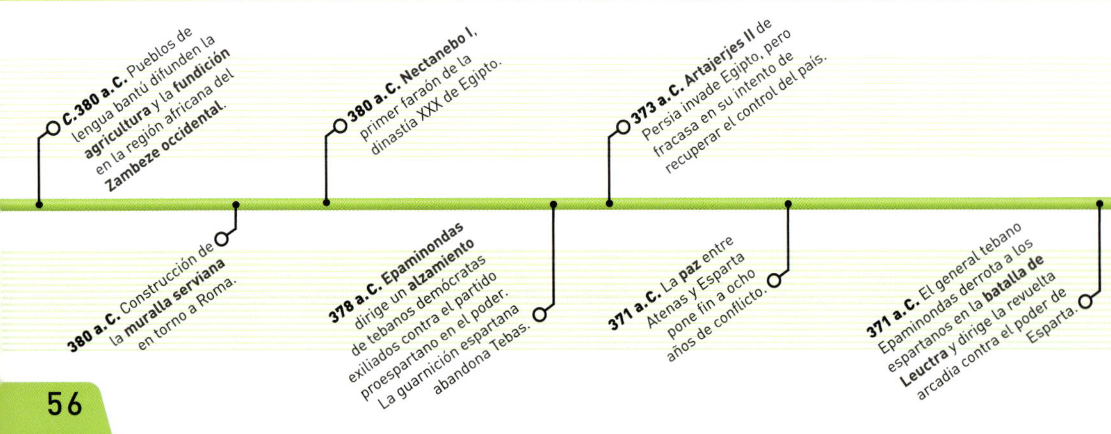

371 a.C. El general tebano Epaminondas derrota a los espartanos en la **batalla de Leuctra** y dirige la revuelta arcadia contra el poder de Esparta.

369 a.C. Epaminondas invade **Mesenia**.

360 a.C. Comienza en el Imperio persa la **rebelión de los sátrapas** (gobernadores).

362 a.C. La **batalla de Mantinea** marca el eclipse del poder espartano.

« UN EJÉRCITO DE CIERVOS **DIRIGIDO POR UN LEÓN** ES MUCHO MÁS TEMIBLE QUE UN EJÉRCITO DE LEONES **DIRIGIDO POR UN CIERVO. »**

Frase atribuida a Filipo II, rey de Macedonia (siglo IV a.C.)

362 a.C., el poder de Tebas declinó rápidamente.

En India, la **dinastía Nanda** comenzó su **expansión** en la década de 370 a.C., y siguió hasta permitirle arrebatar el poder a los Shishunaga (345 a.C.). El fundador de la dinastía, **Mahapadma Nanda**, conquistó gran parte del norte de India y reunió un inmenso ejército. Aplicó un eficaz sistema administrativo con recaudadores nombrados directamente y emprendió obras de regadío. Pero el derrocamiento en 321 a.C. de Dhana Nanda fue seguido por la **absorción del Imperio Nanda por el Imperio Maurya**.

El **estado de Chu**, en el Yangtsé medio, era el más meridional de los **reinos combatientes** chinos. A lo largo del siglo V a.C. se anexionó otros estados, convirtiéndose así en la potencia dominante *c.* 380 a.C. En 366 a.C., una rotunda victoria del estado de **Qin** contra los ejércitos de **Han y Wei**, seguida por otra derrota de Wei en la **batalla de Shimen** (364 a.C), condujeron al debilitamiento de Chu y al traslado hacia el este de Daliang, la capital real de Wei. Un revitalizado Wei consiguió el poder suficiente como para obligar a los gobernantes de otros cuatro reinos combatientes a concurrir a su corte en 356 a.C. Pero la supremacía de Wei fue efímera, y las derrotas sufridas frente a los ejércitos de Qi en Guiling y Maling (353 y 341 a.C.) lo redujeron al vasallaje.

88
EDAD DE **MAHAPADMA NANDA** AL MORIR

EN 359 A.C. MORÍA PERDICAS III de Macedonia; su sucesor fue **Filipo II** (r. 359–336 a.C.), quien empezó a cambiar la posición de un reino que otros griegos consideraban menor. En 357 a.C. hizo su mayor conquista: Anfípolis, en Tracia. Se vio envuelto en la **tercera guerra sagrada** (356–346 a.C.), desencadenada por las supuestas violaciones de Esparta y Fócida del oráculo de Delfos, y la utilizó para consolidar su lugar en el juego de poder de la Grecia central y el Peloponeso. En la década de 340 a.C. fortaleció su posición en Tesalia y se involucró en disputas insignificantes entre ciudades-estado cuyas facciones rivales se volvían hacia él o hacia Atenas en busca de apoyo. En el año 340 a.C. estalló una **guerra abierta** entre Filipo y la alianza Atenas-Tebas. Dos años más tarde, **derrotaba a los atenienses** en Queronea y aniquilaba al Batallón Sagrado tebano (*véase* 380–371 a.C.). El poder macedonio era indiscutible en Grecia.

En Italia central, la **constante expansión** de Roma provocó la alarma entre sus vecinos y condujo a un conflicto de seis años con Tibur (Tívoli) durante la década de 360 a.C. En 341 a.C. se declaró una **guerra general entre Roma y los latinos** que habitaban la región actual del Lazio, en torno a Roma: los romanos acababan de salir de otra guerra contra los samnitas, un pueblo de los Apeninos centrales, y los latinos aprovecharon el estado de agotamiento en el que estos se encontraban para lanzar un ataque. Durante el primer año de guerra, en una batalla junto al Vesubio, se dice que el cónsul Publio Decio Mus dedicó su cuerpo a los dioses del inframundo y llevó a cabo una carga suicida contra las filas latinas que invirtió el designio del combate a favor de los romanos. Los **romanos habían derrotado a la Liga Latina** en 338 a.C. Las condiciones de paz, con muchos latinos que obtuvieron la ciudadanía romana, fueron benignas. La liga fue disuelta y muchas de las antiguas ciudades latinas fueron absorbidas por el estado romano, lo que acercó más aún a Roma el control total de la Italia central.

En 350 a.C., la **cultura de Chavín** del sur de Perú estaba en su apogeo. Se expandió a zonas costeras y montañosas vecinas, y difundió su iconografía característica de seres en parte humanos y en parte felinos, representados en piedra, material textil y cerámica.

FILIPO II DE MACEDONIA (382–336 a.C.)

El rey Filipo II reformó el ejército macedonio y obligó a las ciudades griegas a unirse a la Liga de Corinto, bajo su control. Tras su regreso a Macedonia, tomó una nueva esposa, Cleopatra, pero fue apuñalado hasta la muerte durante los banquetes posiblemente por orden de su hijo Alejandro Magno, que temía perder su posición si Cleopatra le daba otro heredero a Filipo.

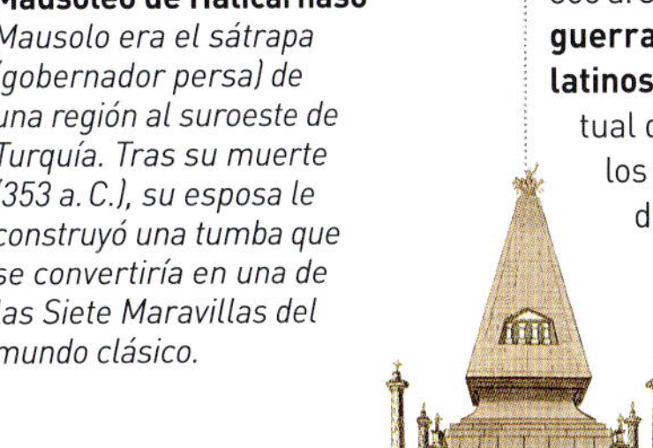

Mausoleo de Halicarnaso
Mausolo era el sátrapa (gobernador persa) de una región al suroeste de Turquía. Tras su muerte (353 a.C.), su esposa le construyó una tumba que se convertiría en una de las Siete Maravillas del mundo clásico.

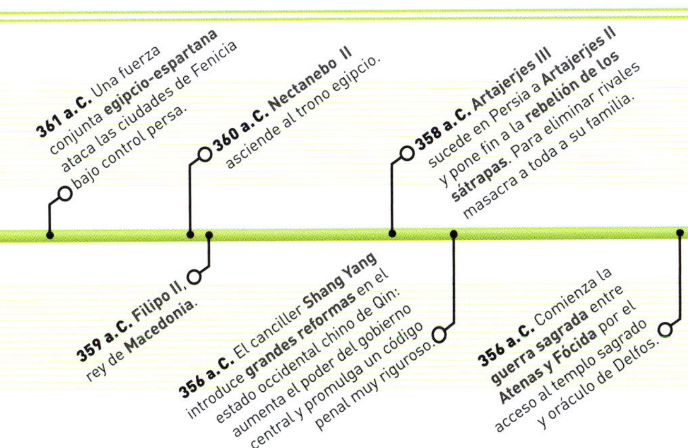

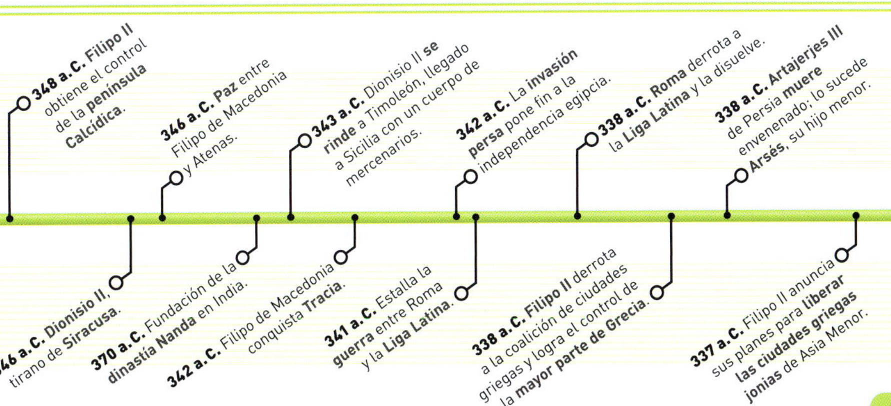

361 a.C. Una fuerza conjunta **egipcio-espartana** ataca las ciudades de Fenicia bajo control persa.

360 a.C. Nectanebo II asciende al trono egipcio.

359 a.C. Filipo II, rey de **Macedonia**.

358 a.C. Artajerjes III sucede en Persia a **Artajerjes II** y pone fin a la **rebelión de los sátrapas**. Para eliminar rivales masacra a toda a su familia.

356 a.C. El canciller **Shang Yang** introduce **grandes reformas** en el estado occidental chino de Qin: aumenta el poder del gobierno central y promulga un código penal muy riguroso.

356 a.C. Comienza la **guerra sagrada** entre **Atenas y Fócida** por el acceso al templo sagrado y oráculo de Delfos.

348 a.C. Filipo II obtiene el control de la **península Calcídica**.

346 a.C. Dionisio II, tirano de **Siracusa**.

346 a.C. Paz entre Filipo de Macedonia y Atenas.

370 a.C. Fundación de la **dinastía Nanda** en India.

343 a.C. Dionisio II **se rinde** a Timoleón, llegado a Sicilia con un cuerpo de mercenarios.

342 a.C. Filipo de Macedonia conquista **Tracia**.

342 a.C. La **invasión persa** pone fin a la independencia egipcia.

341 a.C. Estalla la **guerra** entre Roma y la **Liga Latina**.

338 a.C. Roma derrota a la **Liga Latina** y la disuelve.

338 a.C. Filipo II derrota a la coalición de ciudades griegas y logra el control de la **mayor parte de Grecia**.

338 a.C. Artajerjes III de Persia **muere** envenenado; lo sucede **Arsés**, su hijo menor.

337 a.C. Filipo II anuncia sus planes para **liberar las ciudades griegas** jonias de Asia Menor.

A pesar de verse superado en número, Alejandro Magno, mostrado aquí sobre su caballo Bucéfalo, hizo en Issos un uso brillante de la caballería para lograr una asombrosa victoria sobre Darío III.

Ruinas de Persépolis
La capital ceremonial persa de Persépolis fue arrasada hasta los cimientos por las tropas de Alejandro en 330 a. C.

TRAS EL ASESINATO DE FILIPO DE MACEDONIA en 336 a. C. (*véase* 355–337 a. C.), su hijo Alejandro (conocido comúnmente como Alejandro Magno) fue rey de Macedonia. Al año siguiente, Alejandro invadió Tracia, pero el rumor de su asesinato causó una gran revuelta centrada en la ciudad griega de Tebas, apoyada por **Darío III de Persia** (r. 336–330 a. C.). Alejandro reaccionó pronto derrotando a los tebanos y arrasando la ciudad. Los demás Estados subordinados a Macedonia no tardaron en someterse. En 334 a. C. se lanzó sobre Anatolia, donde ya había establecido un ejército macedonio, reuniendo una fuerza de unos 43 000 hombres en infantería y 6000 en caballería. Aunque estas cifras eran ridículas frente a las de los sátrapas locales, la caballería de Alejandro rompió las líneas del **sátrapa Arsames** en el río Gránico (noroeste de Turquía), y avanzó hacia el corazón del Imperio persa. En 333 a. C., en Issos (norte de Siria), derrotó a un ejército comandado por el propio Darío III. En 331 a. C. volvía a derrotarlo en **Gaugamela** (en el actual Iraq). Al año siguiente, Darío era apuñalado por **Besso**, uno de sus generales. Alejandro parecía haber logrado el control del vasto Imperio persa.

Aristóteles
El filósofo griego Aristóteles fue empleado por Filipo II como tutor de Alejandro.

TRAS LA MUERTE DE DARÍO, Besso se autoproclamó rey de Persia (como **Artajerjes V**), pero algunos sátrapas se sometieron a Alejandro, y no a él. En 330–329 a. C., Alejandro persiguió a Besso hasta las regiones más orientales del Imperio persa, penetrando en Bactriana, más allá del Hindu Kush. Finalmente, en Sogdiana, al norte del río Oxus, los nobles locales liderados por el jefe sogdiano **Espitamenes** traicionaron a Besso y lo entregaron a Alejandro. Sin embargo, una vez que este siguió su marcha hacia el norte, Espitamenes se rebeló; a Alejandro le costó un año de dura campaña liberar el **sitio de Maracanda** (Samarcanda) y pacificar Sogdiana, aunque la fortaleza de la «roca sogdiana» consiguió resistir hasta 327 a. C. Más tarde, Alejandro cruzó el valle de Kabul y, al año siguiente, consiguió derrotar al gobernante local, **Poros**, en el río Hidaspes. Sus planes de penetrar más en India fueron frustrados por sus soldados que, desmoralizados y diezmados por la enfermedad, se amotinaron y exigieron volver a casa. Una parte del ejército lo hizo por mar, al mando de Nearco, pero un destacamento marchó con Alejandro a través del duro desierto de Gedrosia, sufriendo enormes pérdidas. Llegaron a Persia central a principios de 324 a. C., pero Alejandro, que aún planeaba llevar a cabo nuevas expediciones en el interior de Arabia, moría preso de fiebres en Babilonia en junio de 323 a. C.; tenía 33 años.

En el centro de Italia, los samnitas de los Apeninos centromeridionales, que ya habían sido derrotados por los romanos en 342–340 a. C., luchaban en la **segunda guerra samnita** (326–304 a. C.). El avance de los romanos en la Campania después de la abolición de la **Liga Latina** en 338 a. C. alarmó a los samnitas, y el emplazamiento de una colonia en sus tierras en 328 a. C., sumado a las tensiones por el control de Neapolis (Nápoles), condujo a la **guerra abierta** en 326 a. C. En 321 a. C., los samnitas derrotaron a los romanos en las **Horcas Caudinas**. Los romanos fueron humillados al verse obligados a inclinarse y «pasar bajo el yugo» (un arco hecho con sus lanzas capturadas). Pasaron cuatro años de paz antes de que reanudaran la guerra y, a pesar de la obstinada resistencia de los samnitas, finalmente los romanos vencieron en 304 a. C.

Conquistas de Alejandro Magno
Alejandro penetró hasta el último rincón del Imperio persa. Para cimentar su poder fundó una serie de nuevas ciudades, casi todas a partir de su propio nombre; en especial Alejandría, en Egipto.

CONQUISTAS DE ALEJANDRO
Imperio macedonio 336-323 a.C.
Trayecto de las fuerzas de Alejandro

30
EDAD AL MORIR DE **BUCÉFALO, CABALLO FAVORITO** DE ALEJANDRO MAGNO

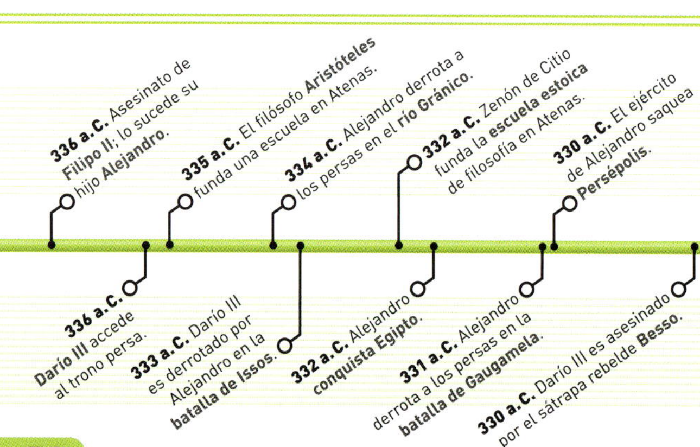

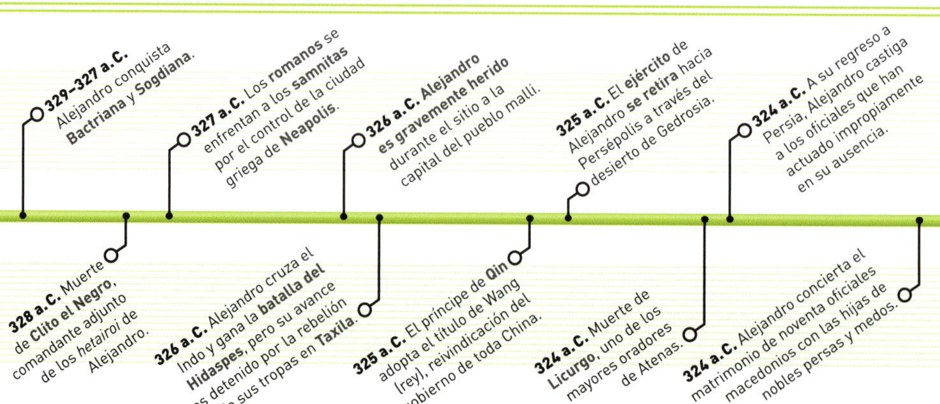

322–301 a.C.

« EL MÁS **FUERTE**. »

Alejandro Magno, en su lecho de muerte, en respuesta a la pregunta sobre quién le sucedería

Yelmo de estilo samnita
Algunos gladiadores romanos usaban casco, espada y escudo inspirados en el estilo de armadura samnita.

ALEJANDRO MAGNO no había establecido una sucesión ordenada a su muerte en 323 a.C., y sus generales más experimentados también habían muerto, menos Antípatro, que había permanecido como regente en Macedonia. Roxana, la esposa de Alejandro, estaba embarazada, y Arrideo, su hermanastro, era deficiente mental; una **camarilla de generales** presentes ante su lecho de muerte –**Tolomeo, Casandro, Seleuco y Lisímaco**– urdieron una solución por la que Alejandro IV (323–311 a.C.), el hijo recién nacido de Roxana, compartiría nominalmente el trono con Arrideo, que se convirtió en **Filipo III**. En realidad, esta camarilla militar se repartió el imperio entre ellos mismos y otros cuatro generales: **Perdicas** surgió como poder en el centro; **Antípatro y Crátero** se repartieron Europa; **Antígono Monoftalmos** («el tuerto») asumió las riendas de Frigia; **Tolomeo** se hizo con el poder en Egipto, mientras que **Seleuco y Casandro** fueron a puestos de gobierno.

Estos generales, que fueron conocidos como los **diádocos** (sucesores), lucharon en una larga serie de guerras por el control del antiguo imperio de Alejandro Magno. Al principio, contra Perdicas, que fue asesinado en 320 a.C. A continuación ascendió al poder Antípatro, aunque por un corto periodo de tiempo, pues falleció de muerte natural en 319 a.C. Esto permitió a Antígono intentar el asalto al poder frente a los cuatro jugadores restantes: Casandro en Macedonia, Tolomeo en Egipto, Lisímaco en Tracia y Seleuco en Babilonia. La guerra entre grupos se desarrolló sin resultados hasta 311 a.C.; al reanudarse en 307 a.C., parecía que Antígono había logrado una cierta primacía sobre el resto; sin embargo, en 301 a.C., **Lisímaco aplastó al ejército antigónida** en Ipsos, y se anexionó gran parte de sus territorios, consolidando así una **división tripartita** del imperio entre él mismo y los otros dos diádocos, Tolomeo y Seleuco.

80 000
ANTÍGONO

75 000
LISÍMACO

Batalla de Ipsos
Aunque en ligera desventaja, Lisímaco desplegó sus arqueros contra el flanco enemigo, causando la desbandada de la infantería de Antígono.

En India, en torno a 320 a.C., **Chandragupta Maurya** (r. *c.* 320–297 a.C.) destronó al último de los nandas (*véase* 370–356 a.C.) y se convirtió en señor de Magadha y la llanura del Ganges. Gobernante enérgico, absorbió gradualmente las regiones periféricas del Imperio Nanda, extendiendo su control hasta las regiones de Gujarat y el Punjab. En 305 a.C., quince años después de su victoria sobre el último regente nanda, inició una campaña contra **Seleuco**, uno de los sucesores de Alejandro, que finalizó en 303 a.C. con un tratado por el cual los griegos cedían a Chandragupta el control del este de Afganistán y el Baluchistán. Una vez establecido el **Imperio Maurya** en 307 a.C., Chandragupta decidió abdicar en su hijo **Bindusara** (r. 297–272 a.C.), se convirtió al jainismo y, finalmente, se dejó morir de inanición.

En China, el filósofo **Mencio** (o Meng Zi, *c.* 372–289 a.C.) llegó a la corte de Wei *c.* 320, y se ganó con rapidez reputación como el «segundo sabio» de la **tradición confuciana**. Casi todo lo que se sabe de Mencio procede del ***Shiji***, historia escrita en forma de diálogos con varios reyes de la época. Mencio enfatizaba el valor del *de* (virtud) en un rey y, de forma más práctica, recomendaba impuestos bajos, castigos menos severos y asegurar que el pueblo tuviese suficiente comida. Creía que, si un rey actuaba con benevolencia, todos desearían ser gobernados por él, y por tanto no tendría necesidad de conquistas. La opinión bondadosa de Mencio sobre la naturaleza humana tenía un gran atractivo, y sus opiniones políticas fueron muy influyentes en época de la **dinastía Song** (960–1279 d.C.). Adelantado al pensamiento moderno, defendió el concepto de que no existe guerra justa.

ALEJANDRO MAGNO (356–323 a.C.)

A los veinte años, Alejandro heredó de su padre gran parte de Grecia; a su muerte, solo trece años después, su imperio abarcaba una vasta región desde el río Indo en el este hasta Iliria en el oeste. Fue un general brillante, pero propenso a la violencia impulsiva. Su adopción del ritual de la corte persa le distanció de muchos nativos macedonios, y su negativa a nombrar sucesor resultó fatal.

323 a.C. Alejandro muere en Babilonia; su imperio empieza a desintegrarse entre facciones en guerra.

323 a.C. Estalla en Tesalia la **guerra lamiaca (o griega)** entre los macedonios y Atenas y sus aliados.

322 a.C. Muerte de **Demóstenes**, uno de los grandes oradores atenienses.

321 a.C. Los samnitas derrotan al ejército romano en las **Horcas Caudinas**.

321 a.C. Atenas es derrotada por **Antípatro**; los términos de la paz suponen el fin de la **democracia ateniense**.

320 a.C. Tolomeo se anexiona Judea y Siria.

315 a.C. Asesinato de **Olimpia**, madre de Alejandro.

312 a.C. Apio Claudio construye el primer acueducto de Roma.

311 a.C. Los sucesores de Alejandro acuerdan la **división del imperio**.

311 a.C. Muerte de **Alejandro IV**, hijo de Alejandro Magno.

308 a.C. Último enterramiento real de un rey **kushita**, Natasen, en Napata.

307 a.C. Atenas cae bajo el control **macedonio**.

306 a.C. Tolomeo I es **derrotado** frente a Salamina (Chipre) por los griegos al mando de Demetrio.

305 a.C. Seleuco se impone en Persia y Anatolia, fundando la **dinastía seléucida**.

304 a.C. Fin de la **segunda guerra samnita**: aunque Roma vence, no consigue nuevos territorios.

303 a.C. Chandragupta Maurya firma un **tratado de paz** con Seleuco.

301 a.C. Lisímaco y Seleuco derrotan a **Antígono**, que resulta muerto, en la **batalla de Ipsos**.

300–281 a.C.

El faro de Alejandría fue construido bajo Tolomeo II *c.* 280 a.C. Guiaba a los barcos hacia el puerto de Alejandría durante la noche.

EN ITALIA ESTALLÓ una **tercera guerra** entre **romanos y samnitas** (298 a.C.), provocada aparentemente por el acoso de los samnitas a sus vecinos, los lucanos. Pese a dos victorias romanas en 297 a.C., los samnitas, en esta ocasión aliados con los galos, aún pudieron reunir un inmenso ejército en 295 a.C. en **Sentinum**. El igualmente enorme

275

AÑOS QUE REINÓ EN EGIPTO LA **DINASTÍA TOLEMAICA**

ejército romano –unos 45 000 hombres, el mayor que nunca habían reunido– se vio amenazado con la derrota hasta que el cónsul romano **Publio Decio Mus** se ofreció a sí mismo y al ejército enemigo como víctimas sacrificiales a los dioses del inframundo y lideró una **carga suicida** que rompió las filas samnitas. En 293 y 292 a.C. prosiguieron las victorias romanas, y dos años más tarde los samnitas se rendían definitivamente y sus dominios eran anexionados por Roma, cuyo territorio se extendía ahora por toda la península Itálica hasta el mar Adriático.

Demetrio Poliorcetes (*c.* 337–283 a.C.), hijo de Antígono (*véase* 322–301 a.C.), estaba recomponiendo su poder desde las bases en las islas del Egeo y Chipre. Fue capaz de explotar la necesidad de **Seleuco**, en Babilonia, de encontrar aliados contra el ahora todopoderoso **Lisímaco**. Demetrio **invadió Macedonia** en 294 a.C.; su rey Casandro había muerto tres años antes dejando a sus dos jóvenes hijos enfrentados en una **guerra civil**. Después atacó los territorios asiáticos de Lisímaco, pero en 292 a.C. tuvo que regresar a Grecia por una revuelta en Etolia. Aunque ya la había sofocado en 289 a.C., la flota egipcia tolemaica había capturado casi todas sus bases insulares. Se retiró a Asia y murió en 283 a.C., cautivo de Seleuco.

Tolomeo había heredado la posición más débil entre los sucesores de Alejandro. En 306 a.C., una derrota naval frente a Demetrio Poliorcetes confinó temporalmente sus ambiciones a Egipto. Sin embargo, usó con astucia los mecanismos de poder existentes allí para establecerse como faraón a la antigua usanza, y creó una administración que combinaba lo mejor de las tradiciones griega y egipcia. En fecha tan temprana como 295 a.C., su fuerza naval había recuperado y conquistado gran parte del Egeo. En Egipto su posición era tan segura que, al morir en 283 a.C., legó el reino a su hijo Tolomeo II Filadelfo (r. 283–245 a.C.), el segundo rey de una dinastía tolemaica que reinaría en Egipto hasta el año 30 d.C.

280–266 a.C.

> « OTRA VICTORIA ASÍ Y **ESTAMOS PERDIDOS.** »
>
> **Pirro,** rey del estado griego de Epiro (279 a.C).

EN 281 A.C., LA PETICIÓN de protección contra los romanos de los enviados de Tarento, en el sur de Italia, dio a **Pirro**, rey del estado griego de Epiro, la excusa perfecta para satisfacer sus ambiciones e intervenir en la región. Llegó con un ejército de más de 25 000 hombres que incluía elefantes de guerra. En 280 a.C. derrotó a los romanos en el **río Siris** (actual río Sinno), pero el senado romano rechazó la oferta de paz. Al año siguiente volvió a vencer en **Ausculum**, pero sus bajas fueron tan graves que aquello parecía más una derrota. Tras invadir Sicilia, Pirro se retiró a **Epiro** en 275 a.C., con una inmensa pérdida de tropas y sin haber logrado ganancias territoriales.

La derrota y **muerte de Lisímaco** en 281 a.C. en la guerra contra

Pirro de Epiro
Pese a sus muchas campañas, cuando Pirro murió regía un reino poco mayor que el que había heredado.

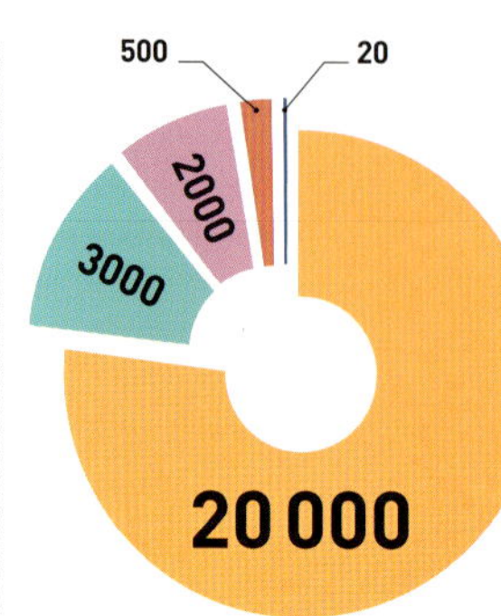

CLAVE
- Infantería
- Caballería
- Arqueros
- Honderos
- Elefantes de guerra

Ejército de Pirro
El ejército llevado por Pirro a Italia incluía una pequeña cantidad de elefantes, cuya presencia provocó el pánico entre la caballería romana.

Seleuco y el posterior asesinato del diádoco no tardaron en provocar la inestabilidad entre el **Imperio seléucida** (en aquel momento regido por su hijo **Antíoco I**) y el rey egipcio **Tolomeo II Filadelfo**. Finalmente, en 274 a.C. estallaba la **primera guerra siria** entre ambos. Los egipcios resultaron victoriosos en el conflicto y se anexionaron parte de la costa siria y del sur de Anatolia. Esta posición fue invertida en parte por las pérdidas egipcias en la **segunda guerra siria** (260–253 a.C.), y luego recuperada en la **tercera** (246–241 a.C.), en la que lucharon el seléucida **Antíoco II** y **Tolomeo III**. Estas tres debilitadoras contiendas dejaron especialmente vulnerables a los seléucidas frente al creciente poder de **Partia**.

265–241 a.C.

Roma derrotó a la armada cartaginesa en la batalla de Mylae (260 a.C.).

EN INDIA, el ascenso al trono de Asoka (*c.* 294–232 a.C.) en 268 a.C. había marcado un punto clave para el **Imperio Maurya**. A la muerte de Bindusara (*véase* 322–301 a.C.), su hijo Asoka debió librar una **guerra civil** de cuatro años contra sus hermanos antes de acceder al trono. Unos ocho años después lanzó una campaña contra **Kalinga** (actual Orissa), tan sangrienta que se dice que murieron unas cien mil personas. Esta matanza golpeó la conciencia de Asoka de tal forma que rechazó para siempre la guerra y fomentó el concepto budista del ***dharma***, en su sentido de virtud o piedad. Bajo su patrocinio se reunió el **tercer concilio budista** (*c.* 250 a.C.) y buscó la expansión al exterior de sus ideas, intercambiando misiones diplomáticas con reyes extranjeros como **Antíoco II de Siria** y **Tolomeo II de Egipto**. A su muerte, en 232 a.C., el Imperio Maurya había alcanzado su mayor extensión y parecía seguro.

En china, **Zhao Zheng** sucedió a su padre en el trono Qin en 246 a.C. A partir de 228 a.C., hábilmente aconsejado por su **canciller Li Si**, desencadenó una guerra de conquista contra el resto de los **reinos combatientes** (*véase* 370–356 a.C.). Zhao y Yan no tardaron en caer; los ejércitos de Qin capturaron Wei y, en 223 a.C., se apoderaron de Chu. Únicamente resistía Qi, pero fue también anexionado en 221 a.C. por Zhao Zheng, que así se convirtió en señor de toda China. Ese mismo año se proclamó *shi huangdi* («primer emperador») de la nueva **dinastía Qin**, con el nombre de Shi Huangdi.

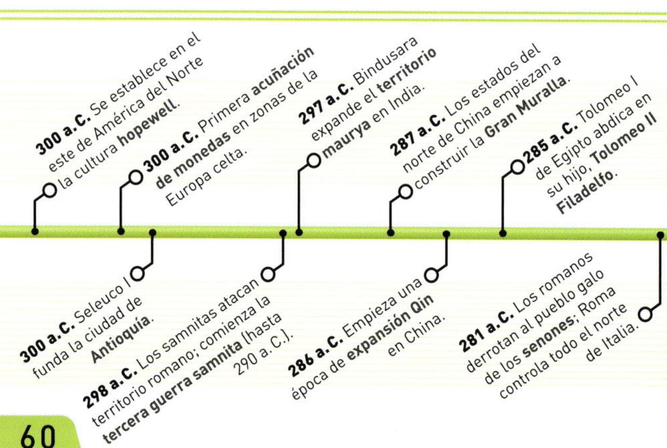

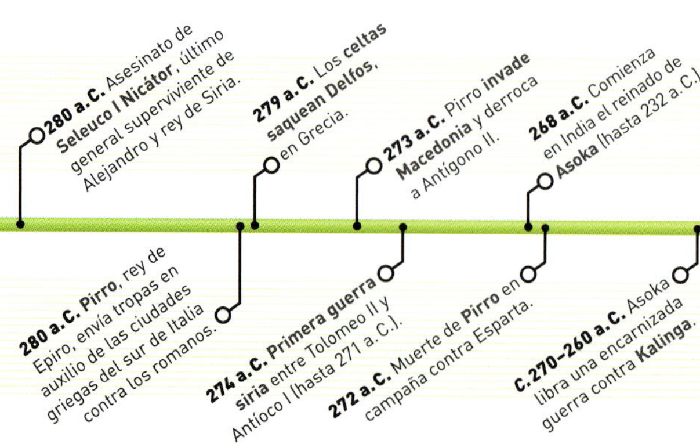

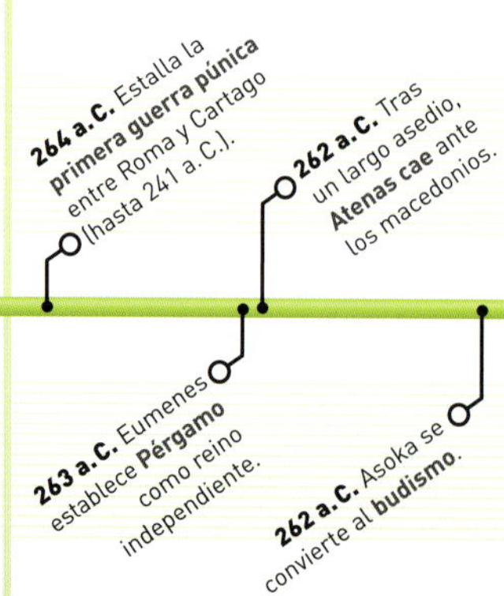

23 AÑOS DURACIÓN DE LA **PRIMERA GUERRA PÚNICA**

LA RELIGIÓN ROMANA

La religión inicial romana combinaba la adoración a grandes dioses como Neptuno (mostrado aquí) con la de deidades locales. Había varios tipos de sacerdotes: los *augures* leían los designios divinos en señales como el vuelo de las aves; los *haruspices* hacían predicciones a partir de entrañas de animales sacrificados; y los *pontifices* controlaban el complejo calendario de festivales religiosos. En sus hogares, los romanos tenían altares para los dioses domésticos y los espíritus de sus ancestros.

En Persia, la dinastía seléucida griega, que había heredado la región tras la muerte de Alejandro Magno en 323 a. C., se enfrentó desde 280 a. C. a una serie de incursiones nómadas. **Antíoco I** (r. *c.* 292–261 a. C.) expulsó a los nómadas, pero las guerras con Egipto (280–272 y 260–253 a. C.) pusieron a prueba los recursos del reino. Al la muerte de **Antíoco II** (r. 280–246 a. C.) estalló la guerra civil entre Berenice, viuda del rey, y su primera esposa Laodice. Esto condujo a la **secesión de Bactriana bajo Diodoto y de Partia bajo Andrágoras**. Aprovechando esta inestabilidad, los nómadas parnos, liderados por **Arsaces**, entraron en Partia mediada la década de 240 a. C.

En la rivalidad sobre Sicilia, donde los cartagineses habían poseído colonias desde el siglo VIII a. C., se encuentra el origen de la **primera guerra púnica** (264–241 a. C.), un conflicto entre Roma y la potencia norteafricana de Cartago. En 264 a. C., Roma envió un ejército de apoyo a los **mamertinos** –un grupo de mercenarios del sur de Italia que ocupaba la ciudad siciliana de Messina (Mesina)– en su conflicto con Siracusa, que al mismo tiempo era apoyada por Cartago. La resistencia cartaginesa fue tan enconada que los romanos apenas realizaron progresos. Sin embargo, la suerte romana cambió con la construcción de su primera flota. En 260 a. C. obtuvieron una victoria de gran importancia en **Mylae**, pero en 256 a. C. una invasión romana del norte de África fracasó en la captura de Cartago debido a la ineptitud del cónsul Régulo. En tierra, los romanos tomaron uno a uno los bastiones cartagineses; en 249 a. C. solamente resistía **Drepanum**, en el oeste de la isla, donde una gran **victoria naval cartaginesa** retrasó la causa romana. Sin embargo, en 242 a. C. una nueva flota romana aparecía frente a las costas de Drepanum y acababa tomándola, y al año siguiente aplastaba a la armada cartaginesa en las **islas Egates**. Tal derrota obligó a **Amílcar Barca**, el general cartaginés, a solicitar la paz. Los términos de la misma implicaban el abandono de Sicilia por parte de Cartago; las esferas de influencia de ambos bandos, empero, se mantuvieron incómodamente solapadas, plantando de esta manera la semilla de dos futuros conflictos.

Gran estupa de Sanchi
Esta estupa budista en la India central fue iniciada por Asoka, el emperador Maurya, en el siglo III a. C.

« SI **NO** QUIEREN **COMER**, ¡HACED QUE **BEBAN**! »

Publio Claudio Pulcher, cónsul y general romano, al ordenar ahogar a los pollos sagrados cuando se negaron a comer antes de la batalla de Drepanum (249 a. C.)

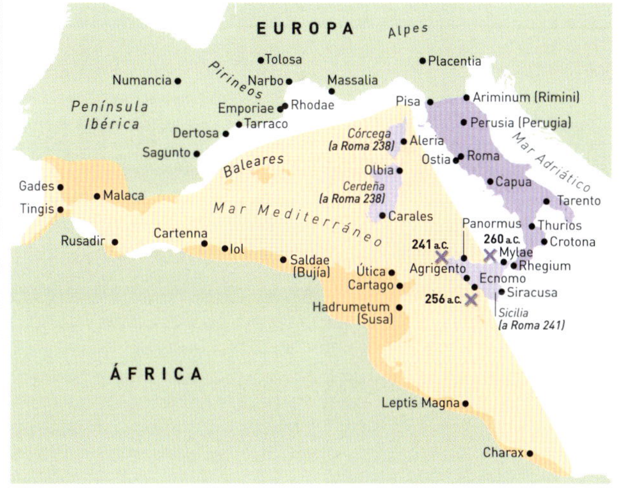

CLAVE
- Imperio cartaginés en 264 a. C.
- Territorio romano en 264 a. C.
- Ganancias romanas (238 a. C.)
- × Victoria romana

La primera guerra púnica
Las dos décadas de combates se concentraron en torno a Sicilia, pero también hubo invasiones romanas en el norte de África y en Cerdeña.

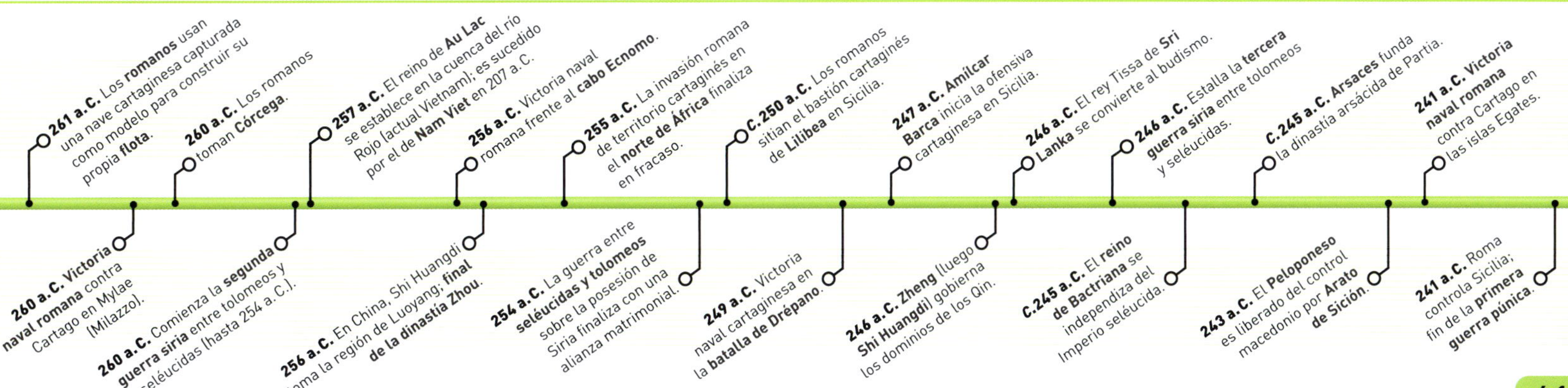

36 NÚMERO DE COMANDANCIAS (REGIONES) FIJADAS POR EL EMPERADOR SHI HUANGDI

EN 221 A.C., SHI HUANGDI, el primer emperador de China, dividió su imperio en 36 comandancias por consejo de su ministro **Li Si**. Los desposeídos aristócratas y nobles de los anteriores enemigos de Qin fueron trasladados a la capital, Xianyang, para mantenerlos controlados. Para fomentar el sentimiento de unidad, Li Si unificó la escritura y los sistemas de pesos y medidas para toda China. Se hicieron nuevas conquistas en el norte (219 a.C.) y el sur (214 a.C.), y se enviaron miles de colonos a los nuevos territorios. Shi Huangdi trató con dureza a la oposición: impuso la **quema de libros** en 213 a.C., en la que ardieron los escritos de los filósofos opuestos al estado Qin, y en 212 a.C. ordenó el asesinato brutal de intelectuales opositores.

Tras la **primera guerra púnica** (*véase* 264–241 a.C.), con Sicilia y Cerdeña perdidas, Cartago dirigió su atención a **Iberia**. En 237 a.C. fue enviado **Amílcar**, que no tardó en conquistar casi todo el sur; aunque murió en combate contra los **oretanos**, una tribu celta, para entonces ya había logrado tanto un **nuevo imperio** para Cartago como una poderosa zona de influencia para su familia, los **bárcidas**.

Supresión de la oposición
Esta acuarela sobre seda muestra a Shi Huangdi, primer emperador de China, supervisando la quema de libros y la ejecución de eruditos.

A pesar de su victoria en la primera guerra púnica, la posición romana en el norte de Italia continuaba siendo débil. En 226 a.C., las tribus celtas de **insubros y boyos** trataron de expulsarlos, pero un año después, en la **batalla de Telamón**, quedaron atrapados entre dos ejércitos romanos y fueron derrotados. Aunque los boyos aceptaron la derrota en 224 a.C. y los insubros pidieron la paz dos años después, los romanos la rechazaron y siguieron atacando en busca de una victoria total. El rey de los boyos murió en combate cuerpo a cuerpo con un cónsul romano, y su capital, **Mediolanum** (Milán), fue tomada. En 218 a.C. los romanos establecieron colonias en territorio celta, entre ellas Placentia (Piacenza).

Seleuco II (r. 246–225 a.C.) no pudo sofocar una revuelta liderada por **Arsaces** (*véase* 265–241 a.C.) en Parthava (Partia) –antigua satrapía en el noreste del Imperio seléucida–, y en la región del actual Irán surgió un **reino parto** independiente. Los partos se anexionaron gradualmente nuevos territorios hacia occidente, en especial bajo **Mitrídates I** (r. 171–138 a.C.). A principios del siglo I a.C. solo quedaba bajo control seléucida una pequeña porción de Siria.

Esta representación de Aníbal cruzando los Alpes se atribuye al pintor italiano Jacopo Ripanda. Sorprendentemente, los 37 elefantes sobrevivieron al paso de las montañas.

Segunda guerra púnica
Los tres teatros de operaciones principales fueron la península Ibérica, Italia y el norte de África. En 203 a.C. los cartagineses quedaron limitados a África.

SEGUNDA GUERRA PÚNICA 218–202 a.C.

- Imperio cartaginés 218 a.C.
- Territorio cartaginés 200 a.C.
- Territorio romano 218 a.C.
- Territorio romano 200 a.C.
- Territorio massaliota 218 a.C.
- × Victoria cartaginesa
- × Victoria romana
- → Aníbal (219–202 a.C.)
- → Asdrúbal (208–207 a.C.)
- → Escipión el Africano (210–206 y 204–202 a.C.)

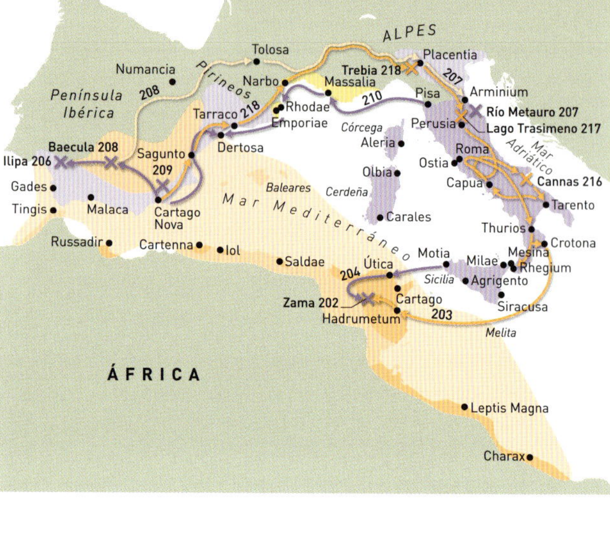

ALARMADOS POR LA EXPANSIÓN CARTAGINESA EN IBERIA, los romanos enviaron en 226 a.C. una embajada a **Asdrúbal** –hijo de Amílcar y nuevo comandante bárcida allí– y se aseguraron un acuerdo según el cual los cartagineses no cruzarían al norte del río Ebro. Roma, a cambio, aceptaba el río como frontera sur; pero al mismo tiempo forjaba alianzas con ciudades del sur, como Sagunto. Asdrúbal fue asesinado en el 221 a.C.; dos años más tarde, **Aníbal**, su hermano y sucesor, atacaba Sagunto y desencadenaba la **segunda guerra púnica** (219–201 a.C.).

Frente a la perspectiva de que Roma enviara un ejército a Iberia y otro desde Sicilia al norte de África, Aníbal decidió golpear primero: con 50 000 infantes, 9000 jinetes y 37 elefantes, marchó hacia el norte de Iberia, cruzó los Pirineos, atravesó el sur de la Galia y –ante el asombro romano– **cruzó los Alpes**. Aunque ahora solo contaba con la mitad de las fuerzas con las que salió, su presencia estimuló la rebelión de los celtas del norte de Italia, y en el invierno de 218 a.C. aplastó a un ejército romano en **Trebia**. Al año siguiente derrotó a otra importante fuerza en el **lago Trasimeno**, dando muerte a unos quince mil romanos, entre ellos uno de sus cónsules. Enfrentados a numerosas **deserciones** entre las ciudades aliadas, Roma debió recurrir a tácticas dilatorias para poder contener a Aníbal; sin embargo, la medida resultó efímera, y en 216 a.C. los romanos sufrían una

Batalla de Cannas
Unos 35 000 romanos sobrevivieron a esta batalla, pero la mitad fueron capturados por los cartagineses, y muchos fueron vendidos como esclavos.

SOLDADOS (EN MILES): 0, 20, 40, 60, 80, 100
50 000 bajas
6000 bajas
Romano · Cartaginés
EJÉRCITOS

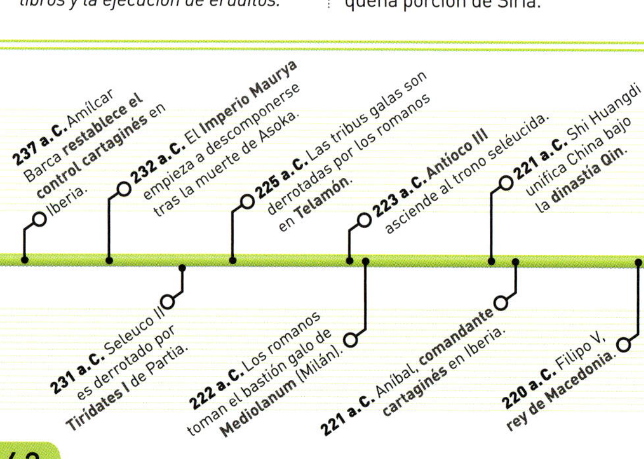

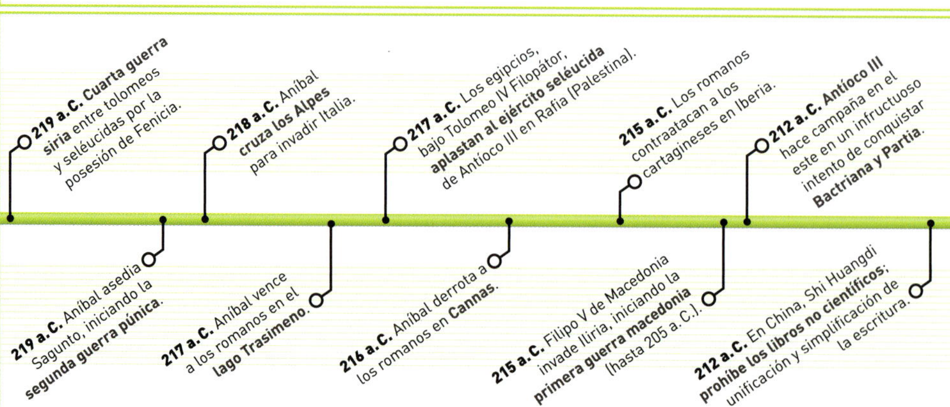

210–201 a.C.

Después de su muerte, el primer emperador Qin fue enterrado en un inmenso mausoleo en el cual se colocó un ejército de ocho mil figuras de soldados de terracota, de unos 2 m cada una.

ANÍBAL (247–182 a.C.)

Pese a sus brillantes tácticas, Aníbal carecía de habilidad estratégica para convertir su cadena de victorias sobre los romanos a partir de 218 a.C. en una victoria final. Después de la rendición de Cartago en 201 a.C., sirvió como sufete (magistrado máximo) de la ciudad hasta que en 195 a.C. los romanos le obligaron a exiliarse. Después ofreció sus servicios a distintos enemigos de Roma antes de envenenarse en Bitinia.

de las peores derrotas de su historia en **Cannas**, en la que Aníbal mató a cincuenta mil hombres. Al no marchar hacia Roma de inmediato, el avance cartaginés perdió intensidad. Pese a que Aníbal ocupó gran parte del sur de Italia, incluida la ciudad clave de Capua (211 a.C.), en 212 Roma ya había formado 25 nuevas legiones, y estaba lista para devolver los golpes a Cartago.

CUANDO SHI HUANGDI FALLECIÓ en 210 a.C., el resentimiento contra su gobierno autocrático estalló en una serie de revueltas campesinas. Varios reinos se separaron del central, mientras que las fuerzas contrarias a los Qin hallaban en **Xiang Yu** a un dotado líder militar. En 208 a.C. fue ejecutado Li Si, y un nuevo ejército al mando de **Liu Bang**, de origen campesino, se alzó para desafiar a los Qin. Hacia 206 a.C. el **Imperio Qin** se había fragmentado, y Xiang Yu y Liu Bang estaban en guerra. Xiang Yu se suicidó en 202 a.C., tras ser derrotado en **Gaixia**. Ya sin oposición alguna, Liu Bang se declaró emperador con el nombre de **Gaodi**, primer gobernante de la **dinastía Han** (*véase* 200–171 a.C.).

Con Aníbal haciendo pocos progresos en el **sur de Italia**, los romanos se embarcaron en una política de eliminación de aliados de Cartago. **Filipo V de Macedonia** fue su primer objetivo, cuyos ataques sobre Iliria en 215 a.C. habían provocado la primera guerra macedonia (215–205 a.C.) con Roma. Los romanos se aliaron en 211 a.C. con los etolios, que combatían a los macedonios por tierra mientras Roma realizaba ataques navales. La invasión de **Etolia** por Filipo en 207 a.C. obligó a los etolios a firmar la paz al año siguiente, y aunque los romanos enviaron tropas de refresco en 205 a.C., la guerra finalizó con un reconocimiento del **statu quo** entre ambos bandos.

En Iberia, los romanos habían retomado **Sagunto** en 212 a.C., pero una derrota desastrosa al año siguiente, en la que murieron los dos cónsules, parecía a punto de arruinar la posición romana en la zona. El senado envió a Iberia al joven general **Publio Cornelio Escipión** (c. 236–183 a.C.), quien tomó la capital cartaginesa de **Cartago Nova** (Cartagena) y en 206 a.C., en **Ilipa**, venció a un gran ejército cartaginés.

En 207 a.C., **Asdrúbal**, hermano de Aníbal, era derrotado y muerto en el **río Metauro**, al norte de Italia, privando a Aníbal de refuerzos cruciales. Para 204 a.C., muchos de sus aliados del sur habían desertado, y cuando Escipión desembarcó con sus tropas en **Útica** (norte de África), los cartagineses convocaron a Aníbal para repeler la amenaza sobre la propia **Cartago**. Los romanos ofrecieron unos términos de paz relativamente indulgentes, pero Cartago los rechazó y Escipión fue tomando sus ciudades una tras otra. Ayudado por el príncipe númida Masinisa, **Escipión derrotó al último ejército de Aníbal** en Zama, en 202 a.C. Las condiciones de paz que tuvieron que aceptar los cartagineses fueron entonces mucho más duras: perdieron todos sus territorios excepto una estrecha franja de tierra en torno a la propia Cartago; su flota quedó reducida a solo diez naves; no podían iniciar guerra alguna fuera de África, y en el interior debían contar con el permiso de Roma para hacerlo. Un tributo anual de diez mil talentos completaba la humillación al que había sido el mayor enemigo de Roma.

La continencia de Escipión
Escipión fue famoso por su clemencia. En esta pintura de Federico de Madrazo devuelve a una mujer cartaginesa a su prometido.

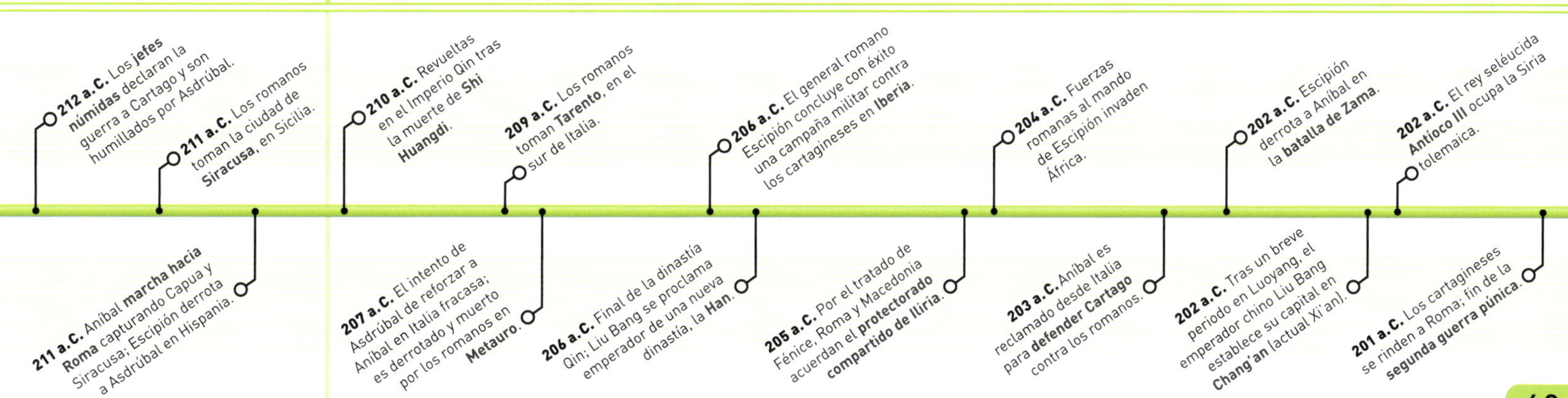

Moneda ateniense
El tetradracma ateniense de plata tenía la imagen de una lechuza por una cara y la cabeza de Atenea por la otra. También tenía grabadas las letras griegas ATHE para identificar su ciudad de origen.

Prehistoria
Ganado como capital
En la prehistoria se utilizaba el ganado vacuno como moneda, y a veces ovejas o pollos servían como valor fraccionario.

Buey

1200 a. C.
Conchas-moneda
El uso de conchas de caurí como moneda, iniciado en las Maldivas, se difundió por el Pacífico y llegó a África en el siglo XIX.

Conchas de caurí

1000–500 a. C.
Herramienta-moneda
En China se hacían miniaturas en metal de útiles cotidianos (perforados para ensartarlos) que se usaban como moneda.

Cuchillo monetario

***C.* 640–630 a. C.**
Primeras monedas
El estado de Lidia acuñó las primeras monedas auténticas en electro (aleación de oro y plata) y las grabó con la imagen de un león o un ciervo.

Monedas lidias

465–454 a. C.
Monedas griegas
Casi cada ciudad-estado griega acuñaba su propia moneda, a menudo con el nombre de la ciudad grabado. La plata reemplazó al electro como metal principal.

27 a. C.–14 d. C.
Áureo de Augusto
Julio César reformó el sistema monetario romano y emitió una nueva versión de la moneda de oro, el áureo, con un valor de 25 denarios de plata.

Áureo

HISTORIA DEL DINERO

LA ADOPCIÓN DEL DINERO PERMITIÓ A SOCIEDADES ANTIGUAS PROSPERAR Y CONVERTIRSE EN CIVILIZACIONES COMPLEJAS

A medida que las sociedades se hacían más complejas, surgió la necesidad de un sistema de cambio para la adquisición de bienes. El dinero cumplió ese papel, y evolucionó del ganado a metales preciosos y, finalmente, a monedas y billetes. Hoy, con las tarjetas de crédito y las transacciones electrónicas, es un medio de cambio aún más abstracto.

Las primeras formas de dinero –usadas en el pago de sanciones y en intercambios rituales, como las dotes– incluían elementos físicos como el ganado. En el milenio IV a. C., el crecimiento del comercio en Egipto y Mesopotamia impulsó nuevas formas de pago. Durante miles de años se usaron los metales preciosos, a veces en forma de barras o lingotes. El código legal del rey babilonio Hammurabi menciona préstamos pagados en plata. En 640 a. C., en el reino de Lidia (Asia Menor), se inventó la moneda, que luego se extendió al mundo griego. En época romana ya se había adoptado un sistema de tres metales, con monedas de oro, plata y bronce (las de menor valor). Las monedas solían llevar la efigie del soberano o de un dios en una cara, e imágenes simbólicas en la otra, con fines propagandísticos, además de fiscales.

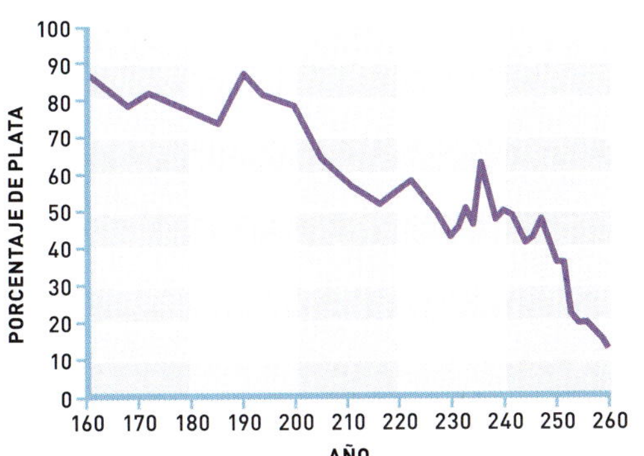

Degradación de la moneda romana
Debido a la inflación, el gasto excesivo y el poco control en la acuñación, la pureza del denario romano cayó de un 90 % de plata bajo Marco Aurelio (r. 161–180) a un 4 % durante el reinado de Galieno (r. 260–268).

PAPEL DE CAMBIO

El papel moneda empezó a usarse en China en *c.* 1189, durante la dinastía Jin. Los billetes permitían expresar valores elevados, y por ello eran más convenientes que las monedas. Bancos respaldados por gobiernos empezaron a emitir billetes, intercambiables en teoría por su cantidad equivalente en lingotes de oro (un sistema conocido como patrón oro). Pero la crisis económica posterior a la Primera Guerra Mundial obligó a los países a abandonarlo. El valor «real» de billetes y monedas se hizo nominal, basado más bien en la confianza de que podían ser intercambiados por bienes. La proliferación de las tarjetas de crédito a partir de la década de 1950 llevó esta etapa más allá, cuando el comprador no tuvo que transferir nada, solo el compromiso de pago en una fecha posterior.

COMERCIO Y PAPEL MONEDA

El crecimiento del papel moneda en Europa tras la Edad Media fue alimentado por las necesidades comerciales. Los mercaderes podían depositar fondos en un banco y recibían un pagaré que les permitía retirar esa cantidad en cualquier ciudad donde el banco tuviera sucursal. Las grandes familias banqueras, como los Médicis, eran tan ricas que podían financiar con sus préstamos las campañas militares de los reyes europeos.

806–821
Papel moneda
El emperador Xiazong emitió en China los primeros billetes durante una época de escasez de cobre. La dinastía Jin emitió los primeros billetes reales *c.* 1189.

Billete de la dinastía Song

1158
El cambio
Enrique II de Inglaterra creó una acuñación de alta calidad basada en el penique de plata; tenía el diseño de una cruz y duraría un siglo.

Penique de plata

1519
Táleros
La moneda acuñada con plata de la mina Joachimsthal (Bohemia) se hizo corriente en los imperios español y austriaco de los Habsburgo.

Tálero de Joachimsthal

Siglo XVII
Cheque moderno
En el siglo XVII se generalizó en Europa el uso de cheques, a menudo respaldados por joyeros.

1694
Primer billete bancario
El Banco de Inglaterra se fundó para financiar la creciente deuda nacional, y emitió los primeros billetes bancarios, respaldados con sus propias reservas de oro.

Primer billete de un dólar

1862
Primer billete de dólar
El Tesoro de EE. UU. emitió los primeros billetes de circulación nacional. Eran conocidos como «lechugas» por su color verde brillante.

1949
Tarjetas de crédito y débito
Las tarjetas de crédito aparecieron en EE. UU. (1949); las de débito, que operan como dinero electrónico, lo hicieron en la década de 1980.

Tarjetas de crédito

2009
Criptomoneda
Aparece el bitcoin, la primera criptomoneda descentralizada (no emitida por un banco central, y existente solo en forma electrónica). Algunos lo ven como el futuro del dinero; otros, como mera especulación.

200–171 a.C.

El séquito real de Gaodi, primer emperador Han, representado en las montañas de China. Gaodi fue uno de los pocos gobernantes chinos de extracción campesina.

EL PRIMER EMPERADOR HAN DE CHINA, GAODI, murió en 195 a.C., cuando su sucesor, Huidi, tenía tan solo quince años. Huidi cayó bajo el dominio de su madre, la emperatriz Lu Hou, que se hizo con el poder a la prematura muerte de Huidi, en 188 a.C. Bajo el reinado de Lu Hou, **China fue invadida** por los xiongnu del norte y por el reino de Nanyue desde el sur. La **estabilidad no sería recuperada** hasta el reinado de Wendi (r. 180–157 a.C.), hijo de Gaodi. El número de comandancias (regiones) bajo el control central Han había ascendido de 13 a 40 en 143 a.C.

13

NÚMERO DE **REGIONES** QUE COMPONÍAN LA **CHINA HAN**

En Japón, el periodo **yayoi medio** (200 a.C.–100 d.C.) supuso un aumento de población –posiblemente llegó a las 600 000 personas– y el principio de la **consolidación política en el Japón central**, en especial en torno a la cuenca del bajo Nara (cerca de Osaka).

En **India**, la **dinastía Sunga** tomó el poder en Magadha en 185 a.C., cuando su fundador, Pusyamitra Sunga (r. 185–149 a.C.), ex general maurya, asesinó al último rey de esta dinastía (*véase* 265–241 a.C.). Se dice que persiguió a los budistas, lo que marcó el principio del declive de esta religión en su India natal. También luchó en una **larga serie de guerras** con los vecinos de Magadha, entre ellos los **satavahana**, los **kalinga** y los reinos **indogriegos** de Bactriana.

Bactriana (en el actual Afganistán) se liberó del control de los seléucidas alrededor de 250 a.C., y la gobernó una serie de reyes griegos, comenzando por Diodoto. En India surgió otra **dinastía indogriega** que ganó poder bajo **Menandro I** (c. 165–130 a.C.), importante benefactor del budismo. Con los reyes indogriegos emergió en torno a Gandhara una nueva **escuela artística** que fusionó la iconografía budista con el naturalismo griego. Gradualmente, estos griegos orientales fueron cayendo bajo la presión de los nómadas escitas y tocarios, y en 125 a.C. Bactriana se derrumbó. El último reino indogriego del Punjab sobrevivió hasta 10 d.C.

La victoria romana sobre Filipo V de Macedonia (*véase* 210–201 a.C.) en la **segunda guerra macedonia** (200–196 a.C.) no condujo a adquisiciones permanentes en Grecia, y Roma retiró sus tropas en 194 a.C. Después de la muerte de Filipo en 179 a.C., su hijo Perseo presidió el deterioro de las relaciones con Roma, y en 171 a.C. dio comienzo la **tercera guerra macedonia**. Las campañas iniciales romanas apenas lograron más que la defección de sus aliados griegos; sin embargo, el enfoque más disciplinado del cónsul **Emilio Paulo Macedónico** (*véase* 170–147 a.C.) cosechó mejores resultados.

patrones y formas geométricos

Jarrón yayoi
El periodo yayoi de la historia japonesa (c. 300 a.C.–250 d.C.) recibe el nombre del lugar donde se encontró por primera vez su cerámica, cerca de Tokio.

170–147 a.C.

Pintura mural que muestra la revuelta de Judas Macabeo en Jerusalén.

LA TERCERA GUERRA MACEDONIA finalizó en 168 a.C., cuando Paulo derrotó a Perseo en la **batalla de Pidna**. Una purga de elementos antirromanos barrió las ciudades griegas, y Macedonia fue dividida en cuatro repúblicas para impedir que recuperara su poder.

En 149 a.C. los intentos espartanos por implicar a Roma en una disputa con la **Liga Aquea** (un grupo de ciudades-estado griegas) coincidieron con una revuelta antirromana en Macedonia; derrotados los macedonios en 148 a.C., los romanos dirigieron su atención a los aqueos. El cónsul Lucio Mumio aplastó con rapidez a los aqueos y tomó Corinto, que arrasó hasta los cimientos. Las diversas ligas de ciudades griegas fueron disueltas y **Grecia perdió su independencia**, convirtiéndose en la provincia romana de **Acaya**.

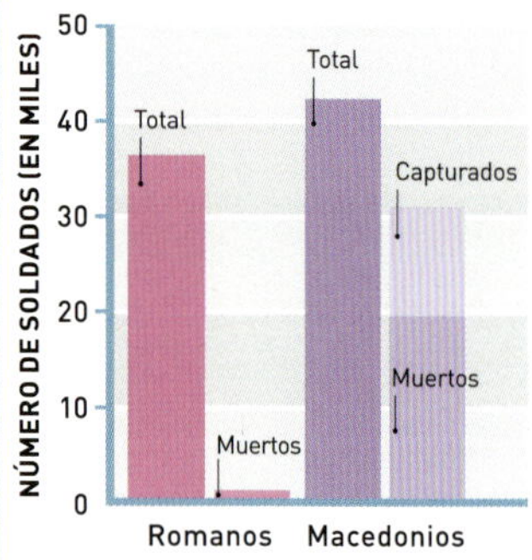

Batalla de Pidna
El ejército de Filipo V, dirigido por su hijo Perseo, fue destruido en Pidna. Los romanos mataron a unos 20 000 macedonios y capturaron a 11 000.

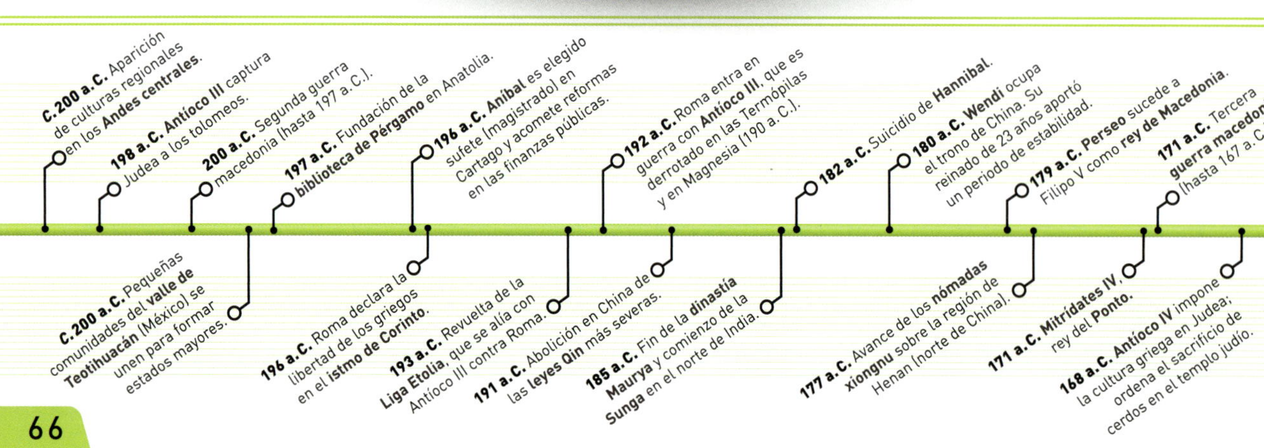

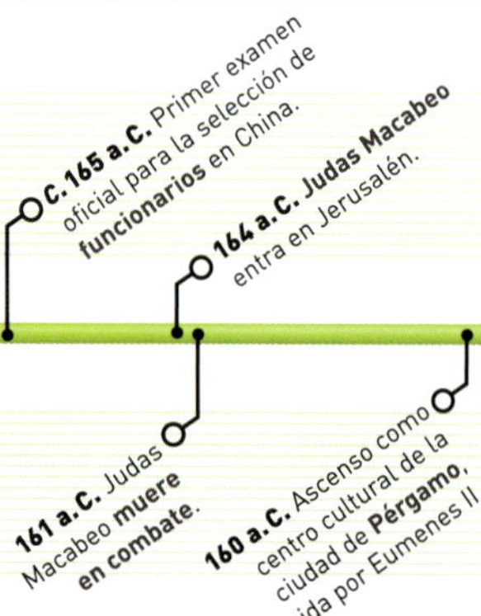

Ruinas de Cartago, incendiada y maldita ritualmente tras su captura en 146 a.C. Cerca de ella se fundó una nueva ciudad romana en torno a 48 a.C.

Tras acabar la segunda guerra púnica en 202 a.C., los romanos habían permitido que su aliado, el rey Masinisa de Numidia, traspasara los límites del territorio cartaginés. Las condiciones de paz que pusieron fin a la guerra prohibían a

« CARTAGO DEBE SER **DESTRUIDA. »**

Catón el Viejo, senador romano

Cartago emprender una guerra sin la aprobación romana. Impedidos para actuar, los cartagineses se vieron reducidos a enviar **embajadas a Roma** para protestar por los actos de Masinisa. Pero Roma apoyó a su aliado, e incluso el resultado de una de las embajadas, en 162 a.C., fue

Estela cartaginesa
Estela votiva del tofet (santuario-necrópolis) de Cartago que muestra a Tanit, la Astarté de los fenicios.

imponer a Cartago el pago de una sanción de 500 talentos anuales. En 151 a.C., el gobierno cartaginés envió una fuerza militar para liberar una población asediada por Masinisa, y Roma reaccionó **declarando la guerra**. Esta fue la **tercera guerra púnica** (149–146 a.C.), una guerra que había sido alentada en Roma por el senador **Catón el Viejo**, quien en diversas intervenciones en el senado había reclamado la destrucción de Cartago. Los dos primeros años de guerra pasaron entre ineficaces ataques romanos a pueblos en torno a Cartago. En 147 a.C., el nombramiento de un nuevo comandante, **Escipión Emiliano**, iba a transformar el curso de la guerra en menos de un año.

En 168 a.C., el rey seléucida **Antíoco IV** prohibió las prácticas religiosas judías en Judea, lo que condujo a la **revuelta de Judas Macabeo** y sus hermanos. En 164 a.C. entraron en Jerusalén, reconsagraron el templo y restablecieron el judaísmo. El **Imperio seléucida** continuó decayendo (*véase* 280–266 a.C.) con el derrocamiento del rey Demetrio I en 150 a.C. por Alejandro Balas, que fue rápidamente seguido por la **pérdida de las satrapías** (provincias) clave de Media y Susiana.

LA REPÚBLICA ROMANA

Tras el derrocamiento del último rey en 507 a.C., Roma se convirtió en una república dirigida por dos cónsules elegidos anualmente, que pasaron a ser apoyados por otros magistrados (pretores y cuestores) y por los tribunos de la plebe, cuyo papel era proteger los derechos de las clases inferiores. Luego las elecciones para el consulado fueron criticadas porque el cargo conllevaba un gran potencial para el enriquecimiento personal y familiar. Con el ascenso de Julio César a dictador en 27 a.C. el cargo perdió todo poder real, y se convirtió en un premio para los favoritos imperiales.

« ME ESTREMECE PENSAR QUE ALGÚN DÍA ALGUIEN PUEDA DAR LA MISMA ORDEN PARA ROMA. »

Escipión Emiliano, general y cónsul romano, al dar la orden de incendiar Cartago, según los apotegmas de Plutarco

EN CHINA, LAS INCURSIONES DE LAS TRIBUS NÓMADAS XIONGNU amenazaban seriamente la frontera norte de la dinastía Han desde 177 a.C. En 139 a.C., el enviado imperial Zhang Qian partió hacia Asia central en busca de **posibles aliados** contra los xiongnu. Su épico viaje ayudó a explorar vías para la expansión china hasta alcanzar Dunhuang, así como permitió fundar **nuevas comandancias en Asia central** ya en 104 a.C. Zhang Qian fue capturado por los xiongnu y pasó varios años prisionero antes de escapar. Bajo el emperador Wudi (141–87 a.C.) los chinos lanzaron **una serie de ofensivas** contra ellos, en particular en los años 121 y 119 a.C., tras las cuales la paz reinó en las fronteras durante casi veinte años.

En Asia occidental, el mermado y casi indefenso **dominio seléucida** (*véase* 170–147 a.C.) fue desgarrado por las guerras civiles y cayó presa de la injerencia de los partos, los asmoneos y, cada vez más, los romanos. En 142 a.C., los macabeos expulsaron a la guarnición seléucida de Jerusalén y establecieron un **reino asmoneo** semiautónomo en el que gobernó una dinastía judía hasta que los romanos tomaron Jerusalén en 63 a.C.

En la **península Ibérica**, hacia 174 a.C. los romanos habían conquistado gran parte del sur de España y parte de Portugal, donde los lusitanos resistieron vigorosamente; a la revuelta de uno de sus líderes, Viriato (147 a.C.) se unieron en 144 a.C. varias tribus celtíberas. Esta rebelión se extinguió después del asesinato de Viriato en 140 a.C. En 133 a.C., y tras un encarnizado asedio, cayó finalmente Numancia, centro principal de la revuelta. Sus pobladores fueron vendidos como esclavos y Roma obtuvo el control de toda Iberia excepto el extremo norte de España.

La **tercera guerra púnica** finalizó cuando Escipión Emiliano bloqueó el puerto de Cartago antes de lanzar un exitoso **ataque sobre la ciudad** en la primavera del año 146 a.C. Los últimos defensores cartagineses perdieron la vida entre las llamas del templo de la ciudad. La caída de Cartago acabó con 118 años de luchas contra Roma; la ciudad fue totalmente arrasada y su población fue deportada para impedir cualquier resurgimiento cartaginés.

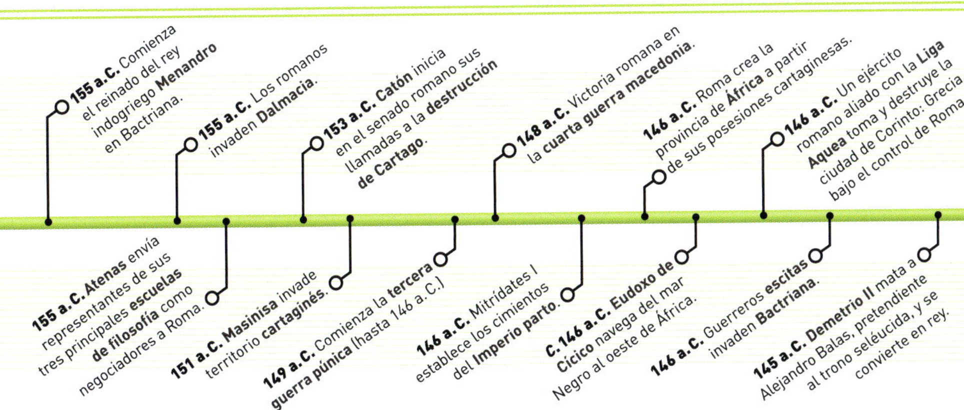

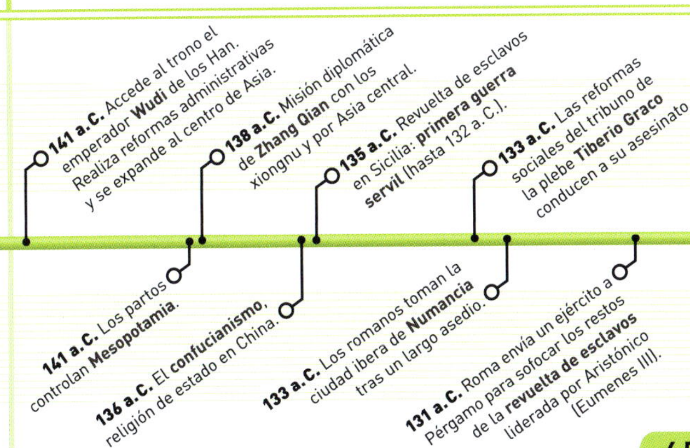

130–111 a.C.

« POR MÁS QUE INTENTES DEMORARLA, ESTÁS DESTINADO A ENCONTRAR LA MISMA MUERTE QUE YO. »

Tiberio Graco, político romano, hablando a su hermano Cayo en un sueño, según un discurso de Cicerón

LAS TRIBUS SAKA (ESCITAS) invadieron el Punjab (norte de India) hacia 125 a.C. Gradualmente, fueron **ocupando más territorio** hasta dar fin al breve periodo de unidad indogriega (*véase* 200–171 a.C.) sobre 110 a.C., durante el reinado de Antialcidas. Dirigidos por el rey Maues, los saka ocuparon el reino de Gandhara y su capital, Taxila (*c.* 80 a.C.). El reino saka se hundió después de la muerte de **Maues** (*c.* 60 a.C.), pero fue revivido bajo su hijo **Azes I** (r. 58–*c.* 30 a.C.), que conquistó gran parte del norte de India. Los saka conservaron esta región hasta el ascenso del Imperio kusana durante el siglo I d.C.

Bajorrelieve de Amravati
Esta escultura muestra la vida de Buda. Procede de Amravati, en Andhra Pradesh (sureste de India), una de las capitales de los Satavahana.

En el centro y sur de India los **satavahana** comenzaron su ascenso al poder tras la desintegración del Imperio Maurya en el siglo II a.C. (*véase* 200–171 a.C.). Desde su capital en el **Decán**, el sexto rey satavahana, **Satakarni II**, extendió considerablemente sus dominios *c.* 50 a.C., aunque tanto él como los reyes siguientes tuvieron que contener las amenazas saka y kusana del noroeste.

En **Roma** estalló la agitación social por la gestión de la tierra pública realizada por el gobierno. **Tiberio Sempronio Graco**, que en 133 a.C. era tribuno de la plebe, pretendía asegurar la entrega de estas parcelas a las familias más pobres. Cuando el senado obstruyó sus planes, trató de prolongar su tribunado para conseguir su objetivo. Una **turba organizada por senadores** opuestos a estos planes lo golpeó hasta la muerte en el Foro. **Cayo**, hermano de Tiberio, fue nombrado **tribuno en 123 a.C.**, e intentó concluir la obra de su hermano. También redujo el papel del senado en la administración de justicia e impulsó una ley para permitir la venta subvencionada de grano a los pobres. En 122 a.C., el senado declaró a **Cayo enemigo del estado** por sus planes para extender la ciudadanía en Italia: él se suicidó, y miles de sus seguidores políticos fueron ejecutados.

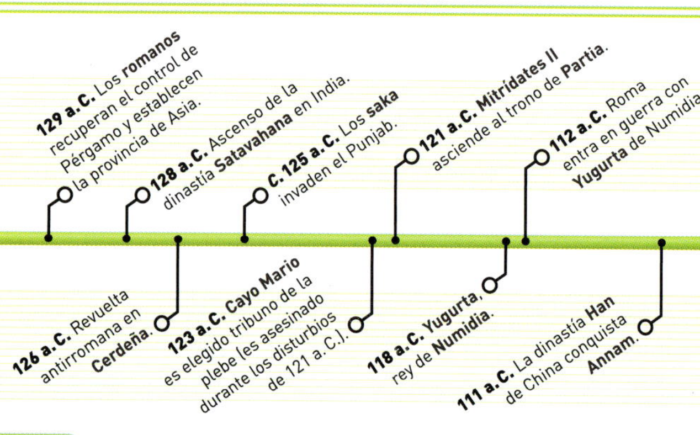

110–191 a.C.

Pintura sobre seda del siglo XVII sobre los emperadores chinos; representa al emperador Wudi de los Han acogiendo a un erudito.

EN PALESTINA, EL REINO ASMONEO (*véase* 146–131 a.C.) había seguido su expansión hasta la **caída de Jerusalén** a manos del seléucida Antíoco VII en 131 a.C. Sin embargo, durante el reinado de Juan Hircán (r. 134–104 a.C.) recuperó gran parte del territorio perdido. **Alejandro Janneo** (r. 103–76 a.C.) amplió el reino hasta ocupar la casi totalidad del actual Israel y Cisjordania. Después de las derrotas de 84 a.C. ante el rey nabateo Aretas III y de los conflictos internos surgidos tras la muerte de Alejandro, los asmoneos fueron cada vez más vulnerables a la injerencia romana.

En el **norte de África**, los romanos afrontaron un serio desafío a la muerte en 118 a.C. de Micipsa, hijo de su antiguo aliado Masinisa de Numidia (*véase* 170–147 a.C.); ordenaron que el reino fuera dividido entre sus hijos y su sobrino **Yugurta**. Este rechazó el trato, asesinando a un primo y atacando al otro, Aderbal, que huyó a Roma. Tras una breve división de Numidia entre ambos, Yugurta renovó sus ataques contra su primo, lo que involucró a los romanos. A partir de 109 a.C. se sucedieron varios años de campañas desastrosas hasta que Roma envió a **Quinto Cecilio Metelo**, que capturó los bastiones de Yugurta uno tras otro. Finalmente, atrapado en el extremo occidental de su territorio, Yugurta fue entregado a los romanos por su suegro, **Boco I de Mauritania**.

En la Galia, dos tribus germánicas, **cimbrios y teutones**, venían derrotando a los romanos desde 107 a.C., de manera notable en Arausio (105 a.C.), donde **Roma perdió** ochenta mil hombres. A su regreso del norte África, Cayo Mario tomo el mando de la defensa contra los germanos, y en 102 a.C. derrotó a los teutones en Aquae Sextiae para, a continuación, aplastar a los cimbrios en la **batalla de Vercellae** (101 a.C.). Al año siguiente obtuvo su sexto consulado: una recompensa sin precedentes.

En China, el **emperador Wudi de los Han** (r. 141–87 a.C.) fortaleció el sistema administrativo del imperio al instaurar **ideas del con-**

« BIEN HACES EN CONSIDERAR TUYA LA AUTORIDAD, YA QUE LA HAS COMPRADO. »

El padre de Julio César censura al futuro dictador Sila por haber comprado corruptamente el cargo de pretor en 94 a.C., según **Plutarco** en *Vidas paralelas*

REFORMAS MILITARES ROMANAS

En el siglo II a.C., el ejército romano estaba teniendo dificultades para el reclutamiento entre las clases acaudaladas tradicionales. Cayo Mario solucionó el problema abriendo el ejército a todo ciudadano, al margen sus propiedades. El águila se convirtió en el estandarte universal de las legiones romanas por primera vez, y las propias legiones fueron reformadas como fuerza de infantería pesada. La infantería ligera y la caballería se organizaron como unidades «auxiliares», reclutadas entre no ciudadanos.

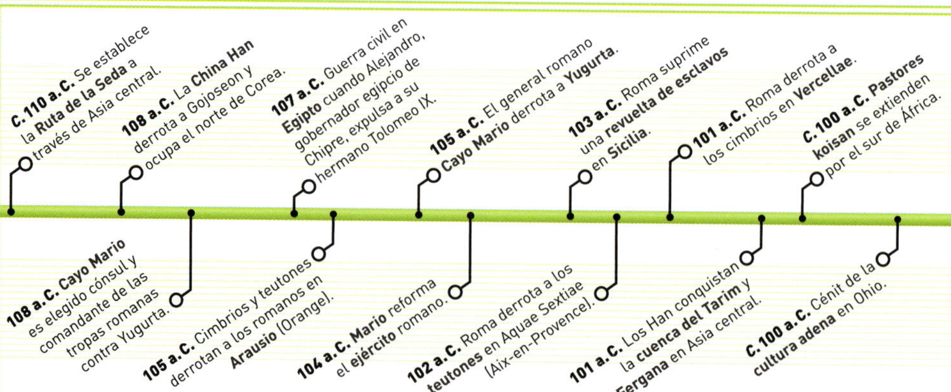

90–71 a.C.

El castro Maiden Castle (RU) sufrió varias fases de reconstrucción tras su inicio *c.* 600 a. C., y alcanzó su forma final unos 500 años después.

Capturado en piedra
En el pasado se pensó que las estelas de los Danzantes, en Monte Albán, representaban a bailarines; hoy se cree que son cuerpos mutilados de enemigos capturados en combate.

fucianismo. En 136 a. C. se habían establecido posiciones oficiales para académicos, consolidando el dominio total de la casa regente sobre la vida intelectual de China. En 106 a. C., **Wudi nombró a trece inspectores regionales** para controlar la conducta de los funcionarios, elevó los impuestos y prohibió la acuñación privada de moneda. Sus ejércitos avanzaron profundamente en Asia central; en 108 a. C., el Imperio Han había alcanzado su **máxima extensión**.

En **México**, la población de **Monte Albán** alcanzaba los diecisiete mil habitantes hacia el año 100 a. C. Su dominio empezaba a superar las inmediaciones del **valle de Oaxaca**, y en la ciudad se construían grandes plataformas de piedra y monumentos públicos.

TRAS SU VICTORIA EN VERCELLAE (*véase* 110–91 a. C.), Mario se convirtió en el político dominante en Roma; pero el brutal comportamiento de su aliado Lucio Saturnino, tribuno de la plebe, provocó al senado. La **violencia política** desencadenada hizo que Mario marchara con su ejército sobre Roma en 100 a. C.; Saturnino fue asesinado durante los disturbios subsiguientes. A medida que menguaba el poder de Mario, crecía el descontento entre los italianos sin ciudadanía romana. En 91 a. C., estalló en la **guerra social**. **Lucio Sila** (*c.* 138–78 a. C.), protegido de Mario, asumió un papel clave en la supresión de la revuelta, que se produjo principalmente **a lo largo de 88 a. C.**, aunque Roma hizo ciertas concesiones a los rebeldes. En 88 a. C. Sila fue elegido cónsul, y ese mismo año, mientras esperaba para zarpar hacia Grecia para combatir la amenaza del rey del Ponto, **Mitrídates VI**, supo que el senado había votado por Mario para dirigir la campaña. Enfurecido, Sila entró en Roma con sus tropas y se hizo con el poder. En 87 a. C. emprendió su lucha contra Mitrídates, y en 84 a. C. ya lo había expulsado de Grecia. Volvió a Roma, derrotó al resto de sus oponentes (incluido un envejecido Mario), y en 82 a. C. fue **nombrado dictador**. Sila se vengó de los seguidores de Mario, designó a la mayoría de los senadores y restó poder a los tribunos. Las fuerzas contrarias a Sila apoyaron a **Quinto Sertorio**, que había huido a Hispania. Tras la muerte de Sila en 78 a. C., el senado envió a **Pompeyo** a ocuparse de Sertorio, pero sus esfuerzos militares fueron infructuosos, y solo el asesinato de Sertorio le permitiría volver victorioso a Roma en 71 a. C.

En 73 a. C. estalló cerca de Nápoles una **revuelta de esclavos** liderada por el gladiador **Espartaco**, que creció hasta convertirse en la más grave que Roma había enfrentado nunca. Los rebeldes fueron acorralados finalmente en el sur de Italia y derrotados por el general **Marco Licinio Craso** en 71 a. C.

En el siglo I a. C., los pueblos celtas del sur de Britania habían empezado a extender sus **castros** en *oppida* («pueblos») defendidos por grandes fortificaciones. Los *oppida* más grandes eran formidables obstáculos para los atacantes, y algunos fueron capitales reales.

La rebelión de Espartaco
Craso crucificó esclavos a lo largo de la vía Apia, que conducía a Roma, como aviso a cualquiera que planeara una insurrección similar.

Escudo celta britano (siglo I a. C.)
Fue descubierto en el río Támesis, donde probablemente fue arrojado como ofrenda a un dios del río.

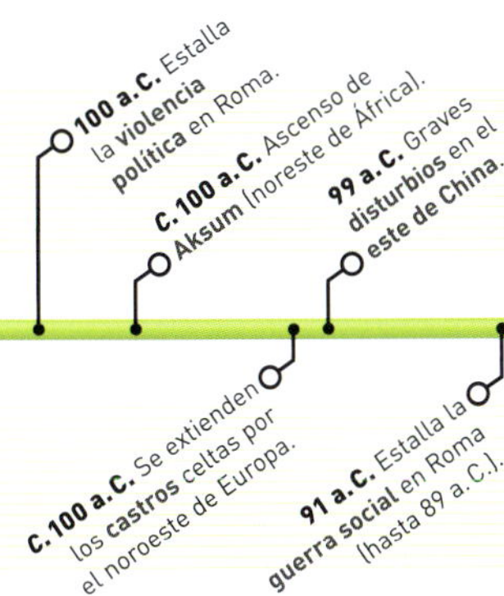

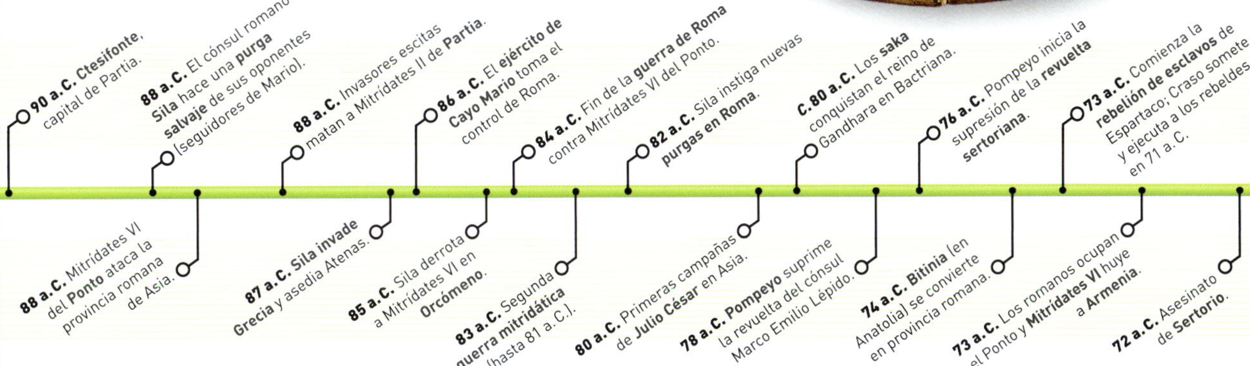

70–61 a. C.

Mound City, en Ohio (EE. UU.), contiene un grupo de más de veinte montículos funerarios de la cultura hopewell.

DESPUÉS DE SU REGRESO A ITALIA, POMPEYO (*véase* 90–71 a. C.) fue elegido **cónsul** para ese año, a pesar de no tener aún la edad legal. Cuando volvió a estallar la guerra con **Mitrídates del Ponto**, los romanos, al mando del general **Lúculo**, lo obligaron a retirarse a Armenia, gobernada por su yerno Tigranes II. Sin embargo, las tropas de Lúculo **se amotinaron en 68 a. C.**, y **Pompeyo** fue enviado a reemplazarlo. Tigranes se entregó y Mitrídates se retiró al norte del mar Negro. Conseguido su objetivo, Pompeyo entró en Siria, donde depuso al último rey seléucida y **capturó Jerusalén**.

En China, la **dinastía Han** abandonó las políticas reformadoras de **Zhaodi** (r. 87–74 a. C.) y **Xuandi** (r. 74–49 a. C.). La **familia Huo**, que había dominado el gobierno durante décadas, fue eliminada del poder y sus principales miembros, ejecutados. Se recortó el gasto oficial y las agresivas expediciones al Asia central fueron sustituidas por el

3

NÚMERO DE **TRIUNFOS** MILITARES CONCEDIDOS A **POMPEYO**

establecimiento de **pequeñas colonias permanentes**.

En **México**, la ciudad de **Cuicuilco**, en el sur del valle de México, fue destruida por un volcán en algún momento del siglo I a. C. Su desaparición allanó el camino para que **Teotihuacán** afirmase su control sobre todo el valle y se convirtiera en la potencia dominante en México durante más de 500 años.

A finales del siglo I a. C., los **pueblos adena** de Ohio, en el este de América del Norte, empezaban a convertirse en la **cultura hopewell**. Estos pueblos vivían de la caza y la recolección, pero también construyeron elaborados túmulos (montículos funerarios) para sus jefes.

Pájaro hopewell
Las pipas de arcilla, a menudo con formas de aves, eran uno de los productos característicos de la cultura hopewell.

60–51 a. C.

Reconstrucción de las murallas de Alesia, donde César obligó a rendirse a Vercingetórix.

CAYO JULIO CÉSAR FUE NOMBRADO CÓNSUL de Roma por primera vez en 59 a. C. Cumplida su propretura en Hispania, era muy popular entre los équites (acaudalados no senadores), pero la oposición hacia él en el senado (y el obstruccionismo de su cocónsul Bíbulo) lo empujaron a unirse a **Pompeyo** y **Craso**; los tres dominarían Roma, como **Primer Triunvirato**, hasta 53 a. C.

En 58 a. C. fue nombrado gobernador de la Galia Narbonense, la zona sur de la Galia, ocupada por Roma. Aprovechó la migración de los **helvecios** a través de la Galia para cruzar los Alpes y derrotar a su rey **Ariovisto**. César regresó a Roma, pero dejó a su lugarteniente Labieno en la Galia, y al año siguiente avanzó para derrotar a las tribus **belgas** del noroeste. En el año 55 a. C. ya había sometido gran parte del país y adquirido una vasta nueva provincia para Roma sin haber recibido aprobación alguna del senado.

En 56 a. C. estalló una **revuelta antirromana** entre los **vénetos** del norte de la Galia, aparentemente apoyados por las tribus celtas de Britania. César respondió desplazando dos legiones a Britania en

César en el Louvre
Esta estatua con la corona de laurel de general victorioso es parte del culto a la personalidad de César.

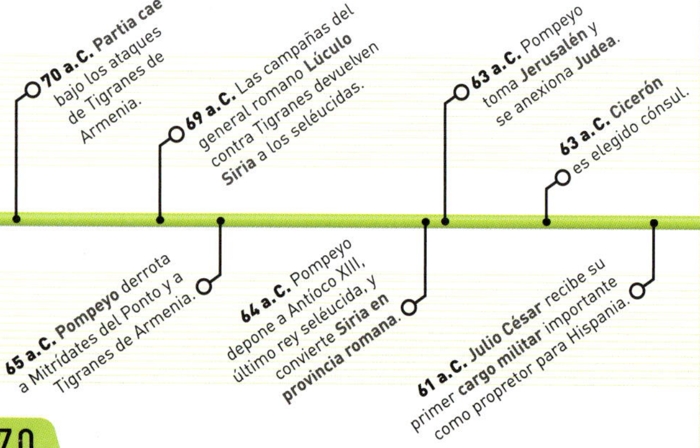

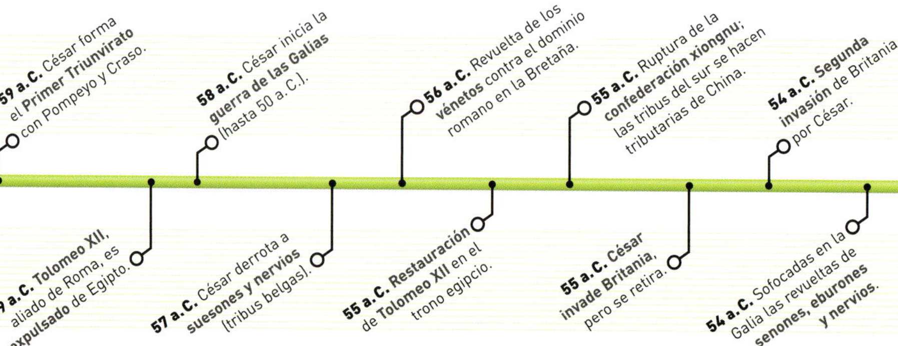

« [CÉSAR] SOÑÓ QUE SE REMONTABA SOBRE LAS NUBES, Y PONÍA SU MANO EN LA DE JÚPITER. »

Suetonio, en *Vida de los doce césares*, relata el sueño de Julio César la noche previa a su asesinato en el senado (44 a. C.)

55 a. C. Una tormenta impidió la llegada de refuerzos, obligándole a retirarse, pero al año siguiente volvió con cinco legiones (unos treinta mil hombres). Al inicio, los britanos no ofrecieron resistencia, pero más tarde, dirigidos por **Cassivelanus**, jefe de los catavelaunos, se opusieron vigorosamente al avance romano en todo el recorrido hasta el Támesis. Cuando cayó el baluarte de Cassivelanus en Wheathampstead, este pidió la paz, y César regresó a Roma con rehenes y la promesa del pago de tributo.

A finales de 54 a. C., poco después de la segunda expedición de César a Britania, estalló en la Galia otra revuelta que, esta vez liderada por los **senones**, iba a aniquilar gran parte de las fuerzas romanas. Tras aplastar la revuelta, la atención de César fue desviada por la situación en Roma, donde la **violencia política** había provocado el asesinato de su antiguo aliado Clodio, y donde Pompeyo había sido elegido cónsul único, rompiendo así el triunvirato. Los **carnutos**, alentados por la confusión en Roma, se rebelaron en la Galia, y a ellos se unieron los arvernos, dirigidos por **Vercingetórix**, que venció a Labieno en varias escaramuzas, e incluso al propio César en Gergovia; pero en septiembre de 52 a. C. quedó cercado en **Alesia**. Los romanos construyeron una muralla en torno a su posición y lograron rechazar a las tropas de refuerzo galas. Perdida toda esperanza, **Vercingetórix se rindió** y fue llevado a Roma, donde sería estrangulado en 46 a. C. tras ser mostrado durante el desfile triunfal de César.

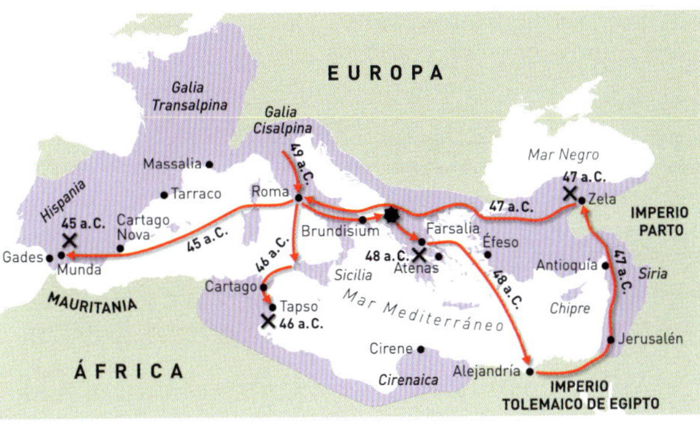

CLAVE

- Movimientos de César
- Asedio
- Victorias de César

Guerras civiles romanas
César obtuvo Italia con facilidad, pero debió luchar duramente para superar a Pompeyo en su bastión griego, y después a los hijos de este y sus restantes seguidores en África e Hispania.

CÉSAR ACABÓ CON LA REVUELTA GALA a finales de 50 a. C., pero para entonces el **triunvirato** estaba concluido: los partidarios de Pompeyo se habían vuelto contra César, y Craso murió en combate en 53 a. C. El senado ordenó a César disolver su ejército, o sería declarado enemigo del estado. Su respuesta fue **cruzar el río Rubicón** y entrar en Italia con sus tropas en 49 a. C. Esta ilegalidad constituía una **declaración de guerra** contra el senado.

Mientras **César marchaba hacia Roma**, las ciudades se sometían a su paso, lo cual obligó a Pompeyo a huir de Roma a Grecia. César se dirigió a Hispania, donde, en agosto de 49 a. C., consiguió que las legiones leales a Pompeyo se rindieran. En diciembre partió hacia Grecia en busca de Pompeyo. En julio, César sufrió una derrota en la batalla de **Dirraquio**, pero contraatacó y venció en **Farsalia**. Pompeyo se refugió en Egipto, donde fue asesinado por orden de **Tolomeo XIII**, quien esperaba congraciarse así con César, aunque en vano. César se alió con la hermana de Tolomeo, **Cleopatra**, depuesta por él, la cual logró así recuperar el trono.

« ALEA IACTA EST. »

«La suerte está echada»
César a sus tropas al cruzar el Rubicón (49 a. C.). De las *Vidas paralelas* de Plutarco

César regresó a Roma, donde obtuvo fondos confiscando las propiedades de los partidarios de Pompeyo. A finales de 47 a. C. se embarcó hacia África y allí derrotó a un nuevo ejército pompeyano en **Tapso** (actual Túnez). Los hijos de Pompeyo, Cneo y Sexto, huyeron a Hispania para continuar la resistencia desde allí, y César se anexionó el reino de Juba de Mauritania, que los había apoyado. Luego partió hacia Hispania, y en marzo de 45 a. C. derrotó a Cneo en **Munda**, dando fin de hecho a la guerra civil.

En aquel momento César era todopoderoso. Fue **nombrado dictador en 49 a. C.**, y en 47 a. C. le fue concedido el cargo de por vida. La preocupación por su poder –en particular el temor de que planeara proclamarse rey– llevó a unos sesenta conspiradores a agruparse en torno a los senadores **Marco Bruto y Casio Longino**. La conspiración culminó con el asesinato de César en el **idus de marzo** (15 de marzo), justo antes de que tuviera lugar la sesión del senado. Si los conspiradores habían esperado hacerse con el poder, pronto se desengañaron: **Marco Antonio**, uno de los principales partidarios de César, llegó al foro, mientras **Octavio**, sobrino nieto e hijo adoptivo del asesinado, recibía el apoyo general para ocupar el cargo de su padre.

En India, **Kalinga** (actual Orissa), que había sido reino cliente del Imperio Maurya (*véase* 200–171 a. C.), ganó importancia bajo el gobierno de **Kharavela** mediado el siglo I a. C. Kharavela expandió el reino hacia el norte y el este, conquistando la capital sunga de Pataliputra en Magadha. Defendió la religión india del jainismo y estableció **contactos comerciales** a gran distancia, hasta el Sureste Asiático.

El asesinato de César
Los conspiradores abaten a César con sus dagas. César, mientras cae, ve a Bruto, su antiguo protegido, y exclama: «¿Tú también, hijo mío?».

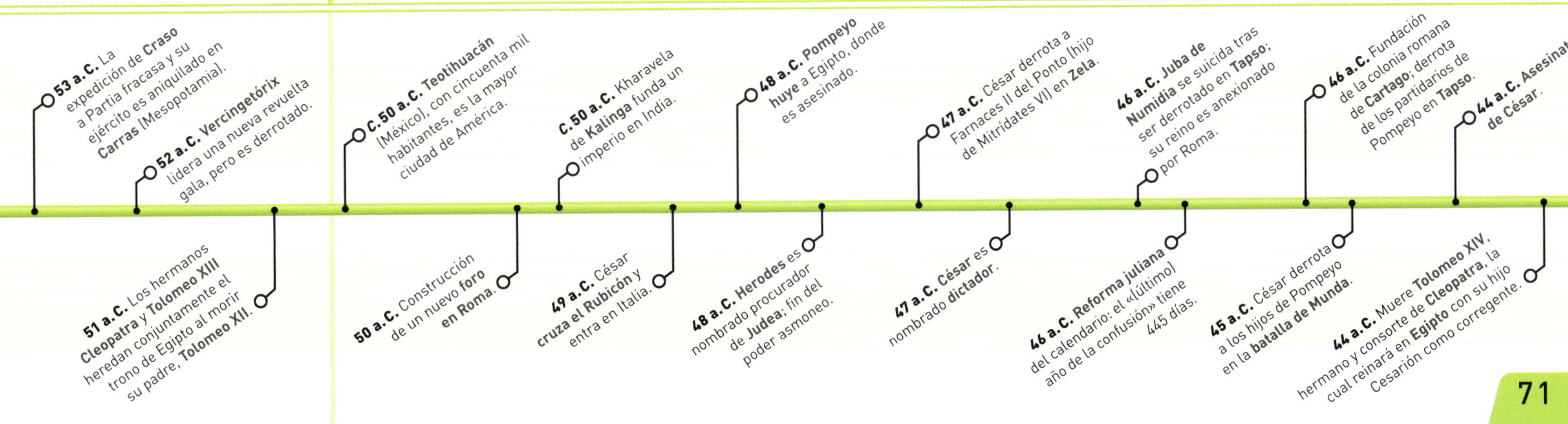

43–28 a.C.

Esta pintura del siglo XVIII muestra a Marco Antonio huyendo de la batalla de Actium en 31 a.C. Como consecuencia, muchos de sus seguidores se pasaron al bando de Octavio.

EN ROMA, EL PERIODO POSTERIOR AL ASESINATO de **Julio César** supuso una tensión creciente entre **Marco Antonio** y **Octavio**, a quien muchos veían como sucesor legítimo de César. Aliado en un principio con el Senado, Octavio combatió en **Mutina** (Módena) a las fuerzas de Marco Antonio, que asediaban allí a Décimo Bruto, uno de los asesinos de César. Marco Antonio se vio obligado a retirarse a la Galia. Cuando el senado votó el traspaso de las tropas de Octavio a Décimo Bruto, aquel se dio cuenta de que estaba siendo marginado, y formó una alianza con Marco Antonio y **Marco Lépido**, el gobernador de la Galia Transalpina, que daría lugar al **Segundo Triunvirato**.

El triunvirato lanzó una campaña militar contra **Casio y Marco Bruto**, otros dos de los asesinos de César, que habían acaparado gran parte del territorio oriental. En 42 a.C., Marco Antonio y Octavio los derrotaron en **Filipos**, al norte de Grecia, lo que provocó el suicidio de Casio. Tres semanas después destruyeron los restos del ejército de Marco Bruto. Marco Antonio se quedó en el este hasta 40 a.C., año en que regresó a Italia para intentar debilitar el **poder creciente de Octavio**. Sus dos ejércitos se negaron a enfrentarse, lo que provocó una **división de facto del Imperio**, con Marco Antonio gobernando Oriente y Octavio, Occidente; Lépido tuvo que conformarse con África. El **triunvirato fue renovado** por otros cinco años en 38 a.C., pero estaba claro que el conflicto entre Octavio y Marco Antonio no se iba a posponer mucho tiempo.

10 AÑOS GOBERNÓ EN ROMA EL **SEGUNDO TRIUNVIRATO**

Sin embargo, Marco Antonio estaba ocupado con una **guerra contra los partos** que, aliados con los restos del ejército de Casio, atacaron **Siria** en 39 a.C. En 36 a.C., Marco Antonio invadió la misma **Partia** –aparentemente para recuperar las águilas legionarias capturadas por los partos en la **batalla de Carras** (53 a.C.)– y avanzó hacia su capital, Fraata; pero no tenía recursos suficientes para llevar a cabo un asedio.

Cleopatra VII Thea Filopátor
Como se ve en este retrato, Cleopatra –reina del Egipto tolemaico durante 21 años– adoptaba la apariencia de la diosa egipcia Isis.

Número de naves: Octavio 400; Marco Antonio y Cleopatra 230 (aprox.)
(Eje: 0, 100, 200, 350, 400, 500 – NÚMERO DE NAVES; Octavio; Marco Antonio y Cleopatra)

Batalla de Actium
La flota de Octavio superaba en número a la de Marco Antonio y Cleopatra; sus naves eran más pequeñas y manejables, y sus tripulaciones estaban mejor entrenadas.

En 33 a.C. **expiró el triunvirato**, y Octavio consiguió que el senado declarase a Marco Antonio **enemigo del estado**. A este último le había hecho impopular su relación con **Cleopatra**, que había sobrevivido a sus dos hermanos y reinaba en Egipto. Octavio se atrajo rápidamente a la opinión pública, y reunió una flota que destruyó la fuerza naval de Marco Antonio en Actium , frente a la costa occidental de Grecia, en septiembre de 31 a. C. El ejército de Marco Antonio **se unió a Octavio** y él **huyó a Egipto** con Cleopatra, donde Octavio los alcanzó en el verano de 30 a.C. El militar romano y la reina egipcia **se suicidaron**, y Egipto fue anexionado al Imperio romano. Ahora **Octavio era el amo indiscutido** de todo el mundo romano.

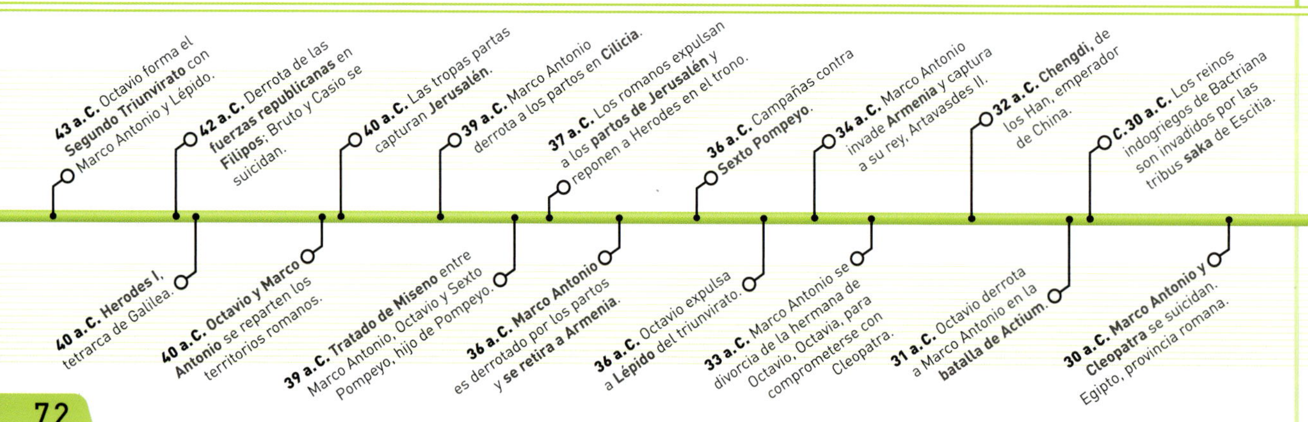

27–20 a.C.

Augusto construyó un nuevo Foro en Roma, con un grandioso templo de Marte.

DERROTADOS SUS ENEMIGOS, Octavio no tomó el título de dictador, como había hecho César, sino que gobernó informalmente como *princeps*: **primer ciudadano**. Tras adquirir el control de las legiones de Marco Antonio, ahora poseía un ejército de 500 000 hombres; desmanteló más de la mitad, quedándose con 28 legiones (unos 150 000 soldados), y estableció al resto en colonias italianas y exteriores. **Restauró el senado**, renunciando en apariencia a todos sus poderes. La respuesta del senado fue otorgarle el control personal de Egipto, Galia, Cilicia (actual Turquía), Hispania y Siria; se le concedió el título de **augusto** (que incorporó al nombre) y, fortaleciendo más aún su posición, fue cónsul de 27 a 23 a.C. En ese tiempo, el senado votó la concesión de **poderes adicionales** para Augusto, entre ellos el de *imperium maius* (23 a.C.), que le concedía la autoridad suprema en las provincias que aún no gobernaba, y los poderes permanentes de un **tribuno de la plebe**. Aunque en teoría el senado era la autoridad suprema, en la práctica nadie podía igualar el poder de Augusto, **primer emperador romano**.

El **norte de África** había opuesto una fuerte resistencia tanto a Julio César como a Augusto, que estableció allí a muchos veteranos del ejército. En 25 a.C., concedió Mauritania (noroeste de África) a **Juba II de Numidia**, cuya esposa era hija de Marco Antonio y Cleopatra, y que demostró ser un fiable **aliado de Roma**. Aun así, Augusto envió una guarnición al norte de África, donde permaneció 300 años.

27 a.C. Octavio recibe el título de **augusto**, y se convierte en el **primer emperador romano**.

26–19 a.C. Revuelta contra Roma de los **cántabros** en el norte de Hispania.

27 a.C. Marcus Agripa completa la conquista romana del norte de Hispania.

25–24 a.C. Elio Galo fracasa en la conquista de Arabia Félix (Yemen).

20–10 a.C.

La Maison Carrée, en Nimes (sur de Francia), es uno de los templos romanos mejor conservados. Fue construida *c.* 16 a.C. por Marco Vipsanio Agripa.

En el Asia occidental, **Augusto** permitió que **Herodes I** mantuviera el trono de Galilea, aun cuando este había apoyado a Marco Antonio. Incluso le concedió **territorios adicionales** que incluían parte de Siria y Gaza. Herodes, que había sido nombrado por Marco Antonio en 42 a.C., y que en 37 a.C. ya había conquistado los restos del **reino asmoneo** (*véase* 146–131 a.C.), fue un **aliado de confianza** de Roma hasta su muerte, en 4 a.C.

El emperador Augusto
Augusto, revestido aquí con la toga de sacerdote, adquirió el título de pontifex maximus *(sacerdote mayor) a la muerte de Lépido, en 12 a.C.*

« [ÉL] PUDO **ALABARSE** DE DEJARLA DE **MÁRMOL** HABIÉNDOLA RECIBIDO DE **LADRILLO**. **»**

Suetonio, en *Vida de los doce césares*, sobre el embellecimiento de Roma por Augusto

LOS ÉXITOS DE AUGUSTO descansaron en gran parte en la capacidad de **Marco Vipsanio Agripa**, que ascendió desde una familia menor hasta llegar a cónsul en 37, 28 y 27 a.C. Tras casarse con Julia, hija de Augusto, Agripa recibió varias promociones, entre ellas la de tribuno de la plebe en 18 a.C. El heredero de Augusto murió en 25 a.C., por lo que este **adoptó a los hijos de Agripa**, dándoles los nuevos nombres de **Cayo y Lucio César**. Agripa parecía destinado a suceder a Augusto, pero falleció inesperadamente en 12 a.C., dejando abierta la **cuestión sucesoria**.

Con su amenaza de **invadir Partia** en 20 a.C., Augusto había urdido el retorno de los estandartes romanos capturados por los partos en **Carras** (53 a.C.). En 16 a.C., el gobernador romano de Macedonia empezó a avanzar hacia el río Danubio, y a partir de 12 a.C., **Tiberio**, hijastro de Augusto e hijo de Livia, su segunda esposa, se desplazó al norte desde Iliria para crear la provincia romana de **Panonia** (hoy Austria y Hungría). En el periodo comprendido entre 12 y 9 a.C., **Druso**, hermano de Tiberio, impulsó el control romano al otro lado del Rin, hacia el Elba, donde murió. Sobre estas fechas, Roma se anexionó las provincias de **Retia** (en la actual Suiza) y **Nórica** (entre los Alpes y el Danubio), **desplazando las fronteras del imperio** al menos hasta la línea de los ríos Rin y Danubio.

Los partidarios de Tiberio, ahora el **general más influyente**, intentaron que este desplazara a Lucio y Cayo como herederos de Augusto; el propio emperador hizo poco por resolver el problema de la sucesión.

9–1 a.C.

« MANDÉ AL **EXILIO A LOS ASESINOS DE MI PADRE**... Y **LOS VENCÍ** EN DOS BATALLAS. **»**

Res gestae divi Augusti, testamento de **Augusto**, grabado en un templo de Ancyra (Ankara, Turquía)

EN 9 A.C. DRUSO YA HABÍA DERROTADO a las principales tribus germanas y había alcanzado el río Elba. Tras su muerte, Augusto nombró a **Tiberio** para reemplazarlo. Tiberio obtuvo en 8 a.C. una serie de victorias, pero luego **renunció** misteriosamente **a sus cargos** y se exilió en Rodas. Esto dejó a Cayo y Lucio César (menores de edad) como **herederos aparentes** del imperio.

En China, durante el **reinado de Yuandi** (48–33 a.C.) siguieron los recortes económicos iniciados bajo **Xuandi** (*véase* 70–61 a.C.). Algunos reinos semiindependientes que los primeros Han habían suprimido empezaron a resurgir. Yuandi y sus sucesores, **Chengdi** (r. 33–7 a.C.) y **Aidi** (r. 7–1 a.C.), crearon numerosos **marquesados**, muchos de los cuales eran cedidos a los hijos de los nuevos reyes, lo que debilitó el control central del estado. Chengdi no tuvo **heredero varón**, por lo que lo sucedió su medio sobrino Aidi en 7 a.C. Esto causó la **disensión** entre los nobles cuyos candidatos al trono habían sido ignorados.

El **reino nabateo** del norte de Arabia aumentó su riqueza gracias al control del comercio de especias desde el sur, y alcanzó su mayor poder bajo **Málico I** (*c.* 59–*c.* 30 a.C.), mediado el siglo I a.C. Luego afrontó la amenaza de **Herodes I** sobre su frontera norte. Una disputa sucesoria entre **Aretas IV** y su primer ministro **Sileo** llevó a Roma a interesarse en la región en 9–8 a.C. Una expedición liderada por Cayo César se anexionó la región de los nabateos durante un breve periodo en 3–1 a.C., pero los romanos se retiraron, permitiendo a este pueblo un siglo más de independencia.

El Tesoro de Petra
El Khazné está entre los mejores monumentos de Petra. Excavado en la pared de un farallón, pudo ser una tumba real, tal vez de Aretas IV (c. 9 a.C.–40 d.C.).

LA LITERATURA ROMANA EN TIEMPOS DE AUGUSTO

El final de la República y el reinado de Augusto fueron una edad de oro en las letras latinas. El orador Cicerón y el historiador Salustio marcaron la cumbre de la última literatura republicana. Tras el ascenso de Augusto al poder, los poetas Virgilio (dcha.; 70–19 a.C.), autor de las *Églogas* y del poema épico *Eneida*, y Horacio (65–8 a.C.), autor de las *Odas* y del *Canto secular*, florecieron bajo el patrocinio de Mecenas, amigo íntimo del emperador.

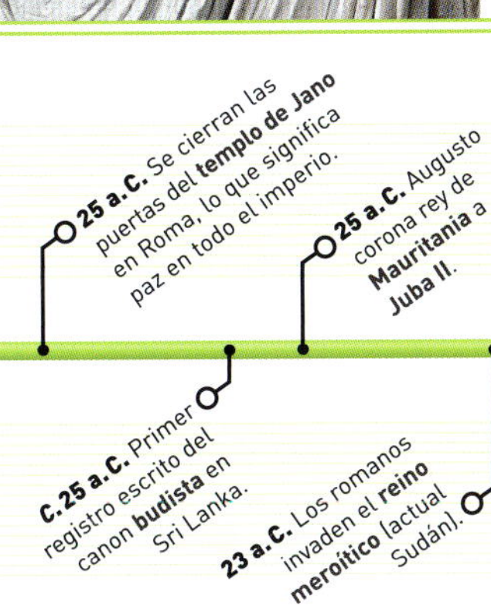

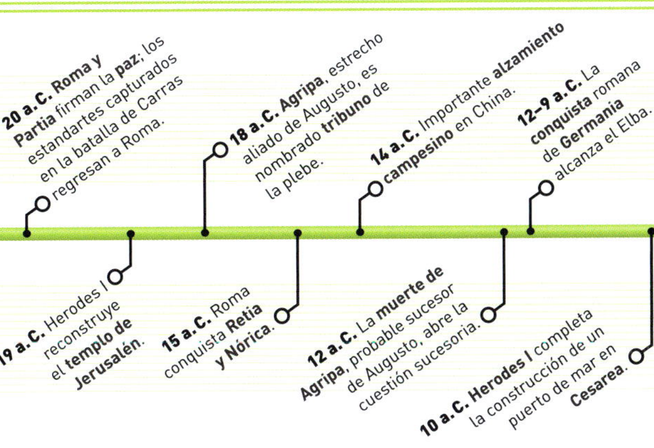

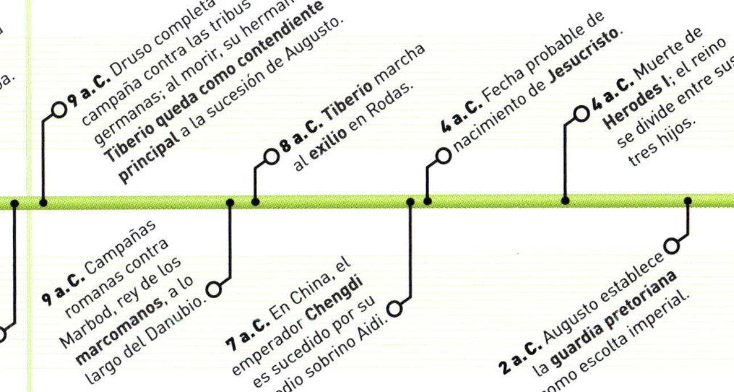

EL AUGE DEL IMPERIO ROMANO

DE CIUDAD A REPÚBLICA Y DE REPÚBLICA A IMPERIO DOMINANTE EN EUROPA

Poco después de su fundación en 753 a. C., la ciudad de Roma empezó a luchar con los pueblos vecinos para lograr más territorio. Gradualmente, los romanos se vieron implicados en campañas en la península Itálica y más allá. En el siglo I d. C., el Imperio romano ya era el más grande nunca visto en Europa.

El crecimiento inicial de los territorios romanos fue lento, con guerras contra sus vecinos que con frecuencia amenazaron la existencia de la propia Roma. Los romanos controlaban la Italia central en 290 a. C., y empezaban a expandirse por la península. La rivalidad con Cartago condujo a las tres guerras púnicas (264–146 a. C.), pero las victorias condujeron a la adquisición de territorios en Sicilia, Cerdeña, Hispania y el mismo norte de África.

Las campañas lanzadas en los Balcanes a inicios del siglo II a. C. llevaron a la anexión de gran parte de Grecia en 146 a. C. El ritmo de expansión se aceleró durante los años finales de la república, a medida que los generales competían por el poder político y usaban sus éxitos militares para reforzar sus posiciones en Roma. Fue en este periodo (58–50 a. C.) cuando Pompeyo se anexionó Siria y Julio César conquistó gran parte de la Galia.

El colapso de la República romana y la llegada de Augusto, el primer emperador, en 27 a. C., no acabaron con la expansión del imperio. La búsqueda de seguridad en las fronteras existentes se materializó en una ampliación aún mayor de las mismas. Las últimas adquisiciones a gran escala se realizaron en tiempos de Claudio, que dirigió la invasión de Britania en 43 d. C., y de Trajano, que conquistó nuevas provincias en Dacia (la actual Rumanía) y Mesopotamia entre 106 y 117 d. C.

«NO PONGO A SUS DOMINIOS LÍMITE EN EL ESPACIO NI EL TIEMPO.»

Virgilio, poeta romano (70–19 a. C.); el dios Júpiter profetiza la futura grandeza de Roma en la *Eneida*.

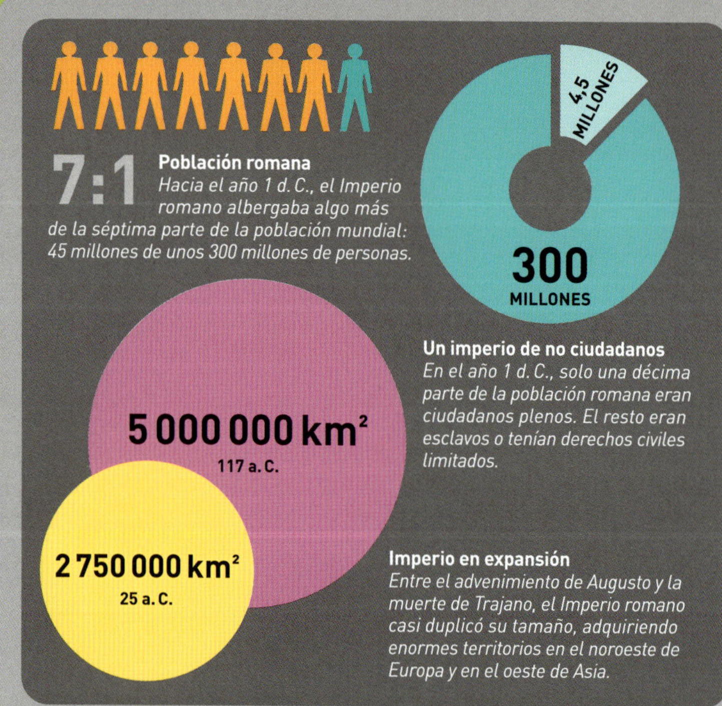

7:1 **Población romana**
Hacia el año 1 d. C., el Imperio romano albergaba algo más de la séptima parte de la población mundial: 45 millones de unos 300 millones de personas.

Un imperio de no ciudadanos
En el año 1 d. C., solo una décima parte de la población romana eran ciudadanos plenos. El resto eran esclavos o tenían derechos civiles limitados.

Imperio en expansión
Entre el advenimiento de Augusto y la muerte de Trajano, el Imperio romano casi duplicó su tamaño, adquiriendo enormes territorios en el noroeste de Europa y en el oeste de Asia.

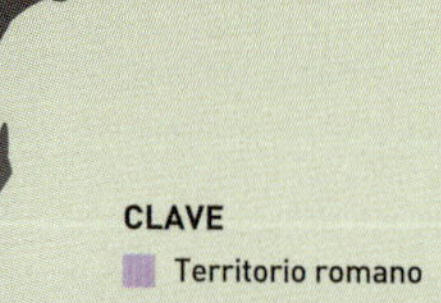

100 D. C.
En torno a 100 d. C., el Mediterráneo se había convertido en un «lago» romano, y la ocupación de territorios en el noroeste y centro de Europa había empujado la frontera norte del imperio hasta el Rin y el Danubio.

UN IMPERIO CRECIENTE

La conquista de Italia les llevó a los romanos casi 500 años, pero en solo la mitad de ese tiempo aumentaron sus territorios hasta incluir Hispania, Galia, parte de Germania, casi todos los Balcanes, y grandes zonas del norte África y el oeste de Asia. En el siglo siguiente ocuparon Mauritania, Britania y Dacia, y pequeñas regiones del oeste asiático; pero a partir de 250 d. C., el imperio comenzó a contraerse.

240 a. C. Los romanos controlaron gran parte de la península Itálica. La victoria en la primera guerra púnica (264–241 a. C.) supuso nuevas tierras en Sicilia, pero Roma aún hallaba resistencia en el norte de Italia.

10 000 KILÓMETROS

LONGITUD APROXIMADA DE LAS **FRONTERAS ROMANAS** EN SU **MÁXIMA EXTENSIÓN**

Caledonia
Hibernia
Mar del Norte
Mar Báltico
Eboracum
Lindum
Camulodonum
BRITANIA
Londinium
Colonia Agripina
Germania
Burgundios
GERMANIA INFERIOR
Augusta Treverorum
Durocortorum
Mogontiacum
Sármatas
LIONENSE
BÉLGICA
GERMANIA SUPERIOR
Marcomanos
Cuados
Virdobona
Carnuntum
Brigetio
MOSIA INFERIOR
REINO DEL BÓSFORO
Lugdunum
RECIA
NÓRICA
Virunum
PANONIA SUPERIOR
Aquineum
Apulum
AQUITANIA
Aquilea
PANONIA INFERIOR
Roxolanos
Mediolanum
DACIA
Durostorum
Mar Negro
ALPES GRAYOS Y PENINOS
ALPES COTIOS
Sirmium
Viminacium
NARBONENSE
ALPES MARÍTIMOS
Ravena
DALMACIA
MODESIA SUPERIOR
Trapezonte
NENSE
Massilia
Bizancio
Filipópolis
PONTO-BITINIA
Córcega
Roma
TRACIA
Samosata
Ancyra
Baleares
Aleria
ITALIA
Tesalónica
MACEDONIA
CAPADOCIA
Cerdeña
ÉPIRO
ASIA
Zeugma
Valentia
Carales
Messana
GALACIA
Cartago Nova
Delfos
Éfeso
CILICIA
Corinto
Mileto
LICIA
Antioquía
Útica
Mar Mediterráneo
Sicilia
ACAYA
MAURITANIA CESARIANA
Siracusa
Esparta
Atenas
Chipre
SIRIA
Cartago
Damasco
Thugga
Creta
Tiro
JUDEA
Jerusalén
Bostra
Sabratha
ÁFRICA
Ptolemaida
Leptis Magna
Alejandría
Petra
Cirene
ARABIA
Sáhara
CIRENE Y CRETA
Menfis
EGIPTO
Mar Rojo

200 a.C. La victoria sobre Cartago en la segunda guerra púnica aportó nuevas posesiones en la península Ibérica y Cerdeña. Hacia 200 a.C. se había ganado una posición en el noroeste de Grecia.

120 a.C. La mayor parte de la península Ibérica había caído bajo posesión romana, así como el territorio cartaginés en el norte de África, Grecia y partes de Anatolia occidental.

60 a.C. En 96 a.C. se habían logrado nuevos territorios en el norte de África, y en 63 a.C. se anexionaron Siria y parte de Palestina. También se ensancharon las fronteras en Anatolia.

14 d.C. Las fronteras romanas se habían expandido hasta incluir la Galia más allá de los Alpes, las nuevas provincias de Retia y Nórica (Suiza, sur de Alemania y Austria), Panonia (Hungría) y Egipto.

« QUINTILIO VARO, DEVUÉLVEME **MIS LEGIONES.** »

Emperador Augusto, al saber de la derrota romana en el bosque de Teutoburgo (9 d. C.)

WANG MANG TENÍA A SU CARGO EL EJÉRCITO Y EL GOBIERNO chinos bajo el **emperador Pingdi** (r. 1 a. C.–6 d. C.), y consolidó su influencia casando a su hija con el joven emperador. A la muerte de Pingdi, gran parte de la nobleza rechazó la elección de sucesor de Wang y se **sublevó**. Wang los aplastó con facilidad y en 9 d. C. tomó el título de **primer emperador Xin**. Reformó el sistema monetario, prohibió la venta privada de esclavos, reorganizó las comandancias (regiones administrativas chinas) y reinstauró varios monopolios del estado. En 4–11, graves inundaciones del río Amarillo provocaron **hambrunas y revueltas** en las zonas rurales. En 23, los campesinos rebeldes llamados los **Cejas Rojas**, unieron sus fuerzas con los leales a los Han y aplastaron a los ejércitos de Wang Mang. Tras la caída de la capital, Chang'an, **Gengshi** se convirtió en emperador de la **dinastía Han restaurada**, quien trasladó la capital a Luoyang.

28
DISTINTOS **TIPOS** DE **MONEDAS** ACUÑADAS POR **WANG MANG**

Tiberio (*véase* 20–10 a. C.) regresó a Germania en 4 d. C. para someter a las tribus locales. Los **marcomanos resistían**, pero un ataque planeado contra ellos en 6 d. C. debió ser pospuesto debido a una revuelta en Panonia que costó tres años sofocar. Un nuevo comandante romano, **Quintilio Varo**, fue enviado a Germania, pero su **gobierno corrupto** encolerizó a las tribus. En el año 9, Varo fue emboscado en el bosque de Teutoburgo y sus tres legiones resultaron aniquiladas. Augusto ordenó la **retirada hasta el Rin**, donde la frontera romana permaneció 400 años.

Refuerzo del poder
En vez de ampliar las conquistas romanas, Tiberio se concentró en fortalecer el imperio existente.

Cuando el emperador Augusto (*véase* 27–20 a. C.) murió en el año 14, su sucesor obvio era **Tiberio** (Lucio y Cayo César habían muerto), que ya poseía la mayor parte de los poderes de Augusto y tenía la **lealtad de la guardia pretoriana**, el cuerpo de élite con base en Roma creado por Augusto. Aunque hubo movimientos en el senado para **restaurar la república**, Tiberio los acalló con rapidez. Su reinado (hasta 37) fue tranquilo en casa. **Germánico**, su sobrino, realizó intensas campañas en Germania hasta 16, pero sus esfuerzos no condujeron a la recuperación de territorios más allá del Rin, y murió envenenado en 19. Cuando en 23 murió Druso, el hijo de Tiberio, el emperador, **cansado de la vida pública**, se retiró a la isla de Capri. **Sejano**, al mando de la guardia pretoriana, asumió el poder de facto en asuntos diarios, pero su gobierno era tiránico y en 31 Tiberio reafirmó súbitamente su puesto e hizo ejecutar a Sejano.

Puente de Tiberio en Rímini (Italia)
Este puente terminado en el reinado de Tiberio llevaba a la vía Emilia (que iba de Ariminum a Placentia) cruzando el río Marecchia.

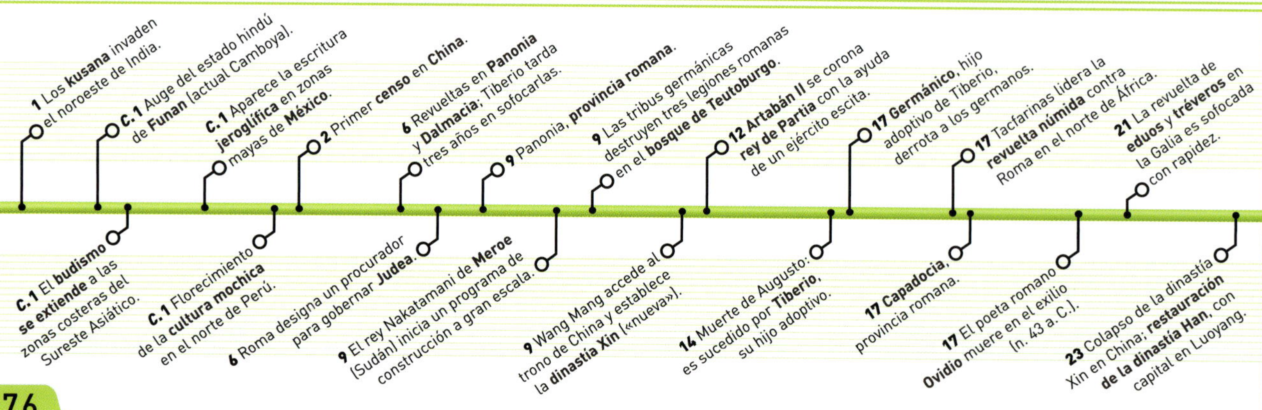

EL REINADO DE GENGSHI COMO EMPERADOR CHINO fue efímero. Marginó a los Cejas Rojas y enfureció a muchos nobles y burócratas al trasladar de nuevo la capital de Luoyang a **Chang'an**. En 25 d. C., cuando Chang'an fue saqueada por los Cejas Rojas, Gengshi ya había perdido el control de gran parte de China. Fue depuesto y reemplazado por **Guang Wudi** (25–57), considerado el primer emperador **Han oriental**. El nuevo gobernante tuvo que afrontar una **guerra civil**; en 27 ya había derrotado a los Cejas Rojas, pero hasta el año 36 no lograría imponerse al último de los **señores de la guerra** contrarios a él. En 37 suprimió todos los reinos que se habían levantado contra sus predecesores, excepto tres, y res-

CLAVE
- China Qin en 206 a. C.
- Territorio añadido por la dinastía Han entre 206 a. C. y 9 d. C.
- Gran Muralla bajo los Han

El Imperio de los Han
Al inicio de la dinastía de los Han Orientales en 25 d. C., el dominio chino se internaba en Asia central; gran parte de este territorio había sido obtenido por los Han Occidentales.

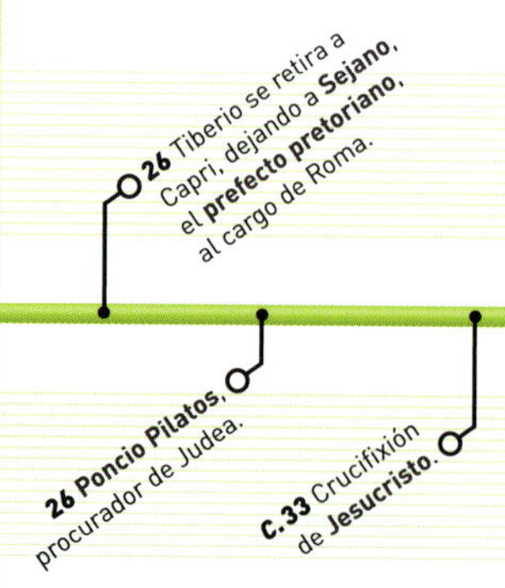

Este friso del periodo Han oriental chino muestra una comitiva que incluye carros tirados por caballos.

JESUCRISTO (*C.* 4 a. C.–33 d. C.)

Jesús, un carpintero de Nazaret, comenzó a predicar hacia los treinta años. Enseñó dentro de la tradición judía, llamando a la reforma del templo y al amor al prójimo por encima de la estricta observancia de la ley religiosa. Reunió a su alrededor a un grupo de doce discípulos, pero fue blanco de los judíos conservadores, temerosos de su creciente influencia. Las autoridades romanas de Judea ordenaron su crucifixión en el año 33. Sus discípulos continuaron difundiendo sus enseñanzas.

tableció Luoyang como capital. Se enfrentó a nuevas tensiones con los **xiongnu** en la frontera norte, pero no logró aprovechar la división de estos en dos **bandos rivales** hasta el año 49.

A la muerte de Tiberio, en 37 d. C., el **Imperio romano** volvía a enfrentarse a una **sucesión incierta**. Tiberio había nombrado dos herederos, pero Gemelo no tardó en ser desplazado por la popularidad entre el senado y el ejército de Cayo, apodado **Calígula** («pequeña cáliga»). La conducta de este como emperador se hizo cada vez más errática: asesinó a Gemelo y a muchos de los seguidores de Tiberio. También condenó a muerte al marido de su hermana, su primer heredero. Después de visitar a las legiones del Rin en 39, mandó desplazarlas hasta la costa continental frente a Britania para lanzar una invasión; una vez allí, simplemente los puso a recoger conchas en la playa.

Los **reinos judíos** independientes de Palestina se hundieron a medida que aumentaba el poder romano, lo que fue fermento de un poderoso cambio religioso. **Juan el Bautista** predicó en la década de 20 d. C., y fue seguido en torno al año 30 por un nuevo predicador: **Jesucristo**. Tras la muerte de este en 33, sus discípulos empezaron a extender su mensaje. Hacia el año 50 se habían establecido comunidades de cristianos –así eran conocidos los seguidores de Jesús– en todo el occidente de Asia, con grupos especialmente nutridos en Antioquía y la primera aparición de **cristianos en Roma**.

EN INDIA, GRUPOS DE NÓMADAS TOCARIOS (o yuezhi) ocuparon tierras en Bactriana liderados por Kujula Kadfises (30–80 d. C.), que fundó el **Imperio kusana** y conquistó parte de Gandhara. A pesar de que se conocen muy pocos detalles del reinado de Kujula Kadfises, **acuñó monedas** imitando los modelos griego y romano, lo cual demuestra que Bactriana y el noroeste de India continuaba siendo en gran parte un **cruce de caminos cultural**.

En el noroeste de Europa, un grupo de oficiales descontentos de la guardia pretoriana **asesinaron a Calígula** en enero de 41, hartos de su conducta cruel e irracional (*véase* 24–40). En 43, el nuevo emperador **Claudio** (r. 41–54) envió una fuerza de cuatro legiones, dirigidas por **Aulo Placio**, gobernador de Panonia, a **conquistar Britania**. Los romanos desembarcaron sin oposición en Rutupias (Richborough), avanzaron sobre Londinium y tomaron Camalodunum (Colchester), capital del líder principal de la resistencia britana, **Caractaco**. Claudio en persona hizo una breve aparición en Camalodunum antes de regresar a Roma a disfrutar de la gloria de haber **adquirido una nueva provincia**. En 47, los romanos detuvieron brevemente su conquista de Britania al alcanzar una línea formada aproximadamente por el río Humber en el este y el Severn en el oeste. Empezaron a establecer **fortalezas legionarias** en su nueva provincia, entre ellas las de Exeter y Lincoln. El sustituto de Placio, **Publio Escápula**, invadió Gales, donde Caractaco continuaba resistiendo, y en el año 50 derrotó a un ejército formado por siluros y ordovicos. Caratacco se retiró a la supuesta seguridad ofrecida por los brigantes, en el norte de Inglaterra. Pero la reina brigante, **Cartimandua**, lo entregó a los romanos. La Britania romana quedaría relativamente tranquila durante una década.

Catacumba cristiana (Roma)
Los primeros cristianos romanos no tenían cementerios. Empezaron a enterrar a sus muertos en complejos subterráneos llamados catacumbas.

La década de 40 contempló una pugna en la **comunidad cristiana** primitiva entre quienes deseaban permanecer dentro de la tradición judía y los que, dirigidos por **Pablo**, promovían la inclusión de gentiles (no judíos) en la Iglesia cristiana. En 46, Pablo inició una serie de **viajes misioneros** que lo llevaron a través de Anatolia y Grecia hasta Roma, donde fue **martirizado** unos veinte años después. Predicador carismático, Pablo escribió además una serie de influyentes **epístolas** (cartas) a diversos grupos incipientes de cristianos. Al atraer a un grupo más amplio que el de los judíos dentro del imperio, Pablo se aseguró de que el **cristianismo** se extendiera lo suficiente para sobrevivir a la **persecución** que comenzarían a sufrir bajo el emperador Nerón en 65. A finales del siglo IV, el cristianismo ya era la **religión mayoritaria** del Imperio romano.

EL EMPERADOR CLAUDIO (10 a. C.–54 a. C.)

Tío de Calígula, Claudio era impensable como candidato a emperador. Pero resultó ser un gobernante inteligente y enérgico: sofocó dos revueltas en 42 d. C., tras lo cual ordenó la ejecución de más de 300 senadores. Fue desafortunado en la elección de esposa: ordenó ejecutar a la tercera, Mesalina, por sus infidelidades, y se dice que la siguiente, su sobrina Agripina, lo envenenó.

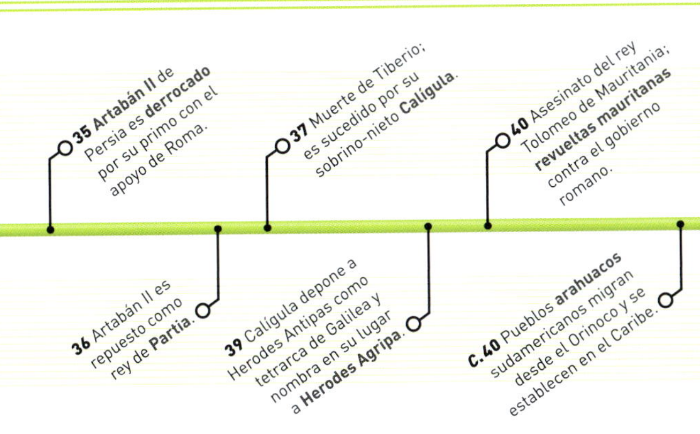

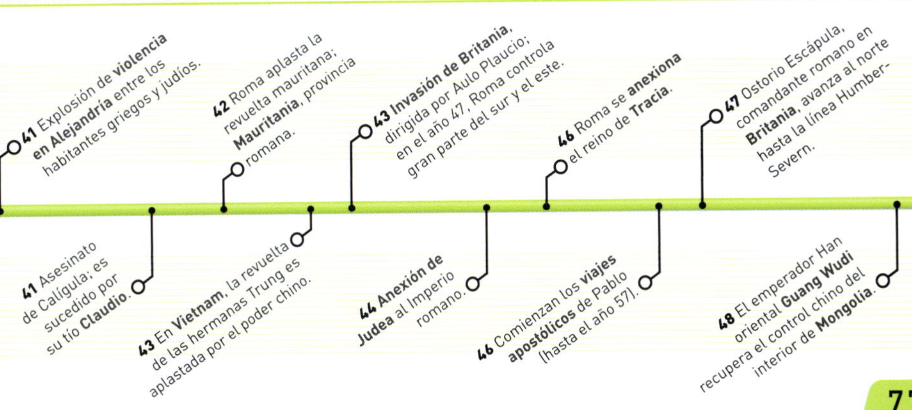

70 MIL
FUERON LAS **VÍCTIMAS** DEL **EJÉRCITO DE BOADICEA** DURANTE LA **REVUELTA DE LOS ICENOS**

Ruinas de Masada, el último bastión de la revuelta judía contra Roma iniciada en el año 66.

A LA MUERTE DE CLAUDIO EN 54, el trono imperial romano recayó en **Nerón** (37–68), su yerno e hijo adoptivo. El reinado del joven emperador comenzó bien, con su promesa al senado de que evitaría tomar medidas arbitrarias. Pero el primer signo de su tiranía surgió en 59, cuando hizo asesinar a su madre **Agripina** (15–59). En 62, **Tigelino** (*c.* 10–69) tomó el mando como prefecto de pretorio (comandante de la guardia pretoriana). Tigelino fomentó el lado menos deseable de la personalidad de Nerón, cuyo gobierno se hizo cada vez más despótico. Tras un **incendio** que destruyó gran parte de Roma en 64, se dice que Nerón se cobró una terrible venganza sobre la pequeña población cristiana de la ciudad, por entonces un chivo expiatorio conveniente. Luego, durante la reconstrucción de Roma, se ganó la antipatía de varios senadores al incautarse de sus tierras para construirse un nuevo palacio. También impuso nuevos impuestos sobre Palestina, lo que dio pie a una **revuelta judía** en el año 66.

En **Britania**, los romanos se enfrentaron a una revuelta grave de los icenos en el año 60. Al morir el rey de los **icenos**, dejó sus dominios tanto a sus dos hijas como a Nerón, esperando seguir cooperando con Roma. La revuelta estalló al ignorar Roma su voluntad y anexionarse el reino. La reina viuda **Boadicea** marchó sobre Camulodunum (Colchester) al frente de un ejército. **Suetonio Paulino**, gobernador de Britania, estaba de campaña en Gales y, para cuando regresó, Camulodunum había sido arrasada por los icenos. A continuación, los rebeldes incendiaron Londinium (Londres) y Verulamium (Saint Albans) antes de ser finalmente retenidos y derrotados por Paulino. Se dice que los icenos perdieron ochenta mil guerreros y que la propia Boadicea fue capturada, pero que murió, posiblemente envenenada, poco después.

Boadicea
Esta estatua de Boadicea se alza en el exterior del parlamento británico en Londres, una ciudad arrasada por la reina icena.

EN EL ESTE, Roma se enfrentó a nuevos problemas con Partia sobre la región fronteriza de **Armenia**, en cuyo trono el rey parto había instalado a su propio candidato, **Tirídates**, en 53. En 58, una fuerza romana invadió Armenia, tomó su capital Artaxata y Tigranocerta, y coronó a **Tigranes VI**, un rey pro romano; sin embargo, su desacertada invasión de un aliado parto en 61 condujo a su deposición, y Tirídates I fue repuesto. En 62, un nuevo ejército romano sufrió una rotunda derrota a manos de los partos, y solo una incursión del ejército romano en la propia Armenia al año siguiente logró acabar con la guerra. Se permitió que Tirídates mantuviera el trono, siempre que viajara a Roma para obtener la aprobación de Nerón, lo cual hizo en 66.

La posición de **Nerón** como emperador empezaba a ser cada vez más precaria cuando **Calpurnio Pisón** lideró una conspiración contra él en 64, la cual provocó que Nerón ordenara muchas ejecuciones, incluidas las de varios senadores. A principios de 68 estalló una revuelta liderada por **Cayo Julio Vindex**, gobernador de la Galia Lugdunense; y un poco más adelante, la legión con base en Hispania proclamó emperador a su gobernador, **Sulpicio Galba**. La revuelta de Vindex fue sofocada por **Verginio Rufo**, gobernador de Germania, pero **Nerón**, aterrado por la idea de que Rufo sería el siguiente en reclamar su trono, **se suicidó**.

Tras la muerte de Nerón siguió una rápida sucesión de emperadores, que hizo del año 69 el **«año de los cuatro emperadores»**. En primer lugar, la guardia pretoriana reconoció a **Galba** (3 a. C.–69 d. C.), pero este se hizo impopular cuando rechazó otorgar el donativo, una prima tradicional que el nuevo emperador pagaba a la guardia cuando accedía al trono. En enero de 69 se sublevaba **Aulo Vitelio**, gobernador de la Germania Superior; y **Salvio Otón** (32–69), uno de los primeros seguidores de Galba, encolerizado porque este nombró a otro senador como heredero, hizo que lo asesinaran y ocupó el trono. En abril, los ejércitos de Otón y Vitelio chocaban en Bedriacum, cerca de Cremona (norte de Italia), con la victoria del segundo. Otón se suicidó, pero Vitelio no tardó en

Invasión romana
Cuando los romanos derribaron finalmente los muros de Masada, todos sus defensores, excepto siete, se suicidaron para no caer en manos romanas.

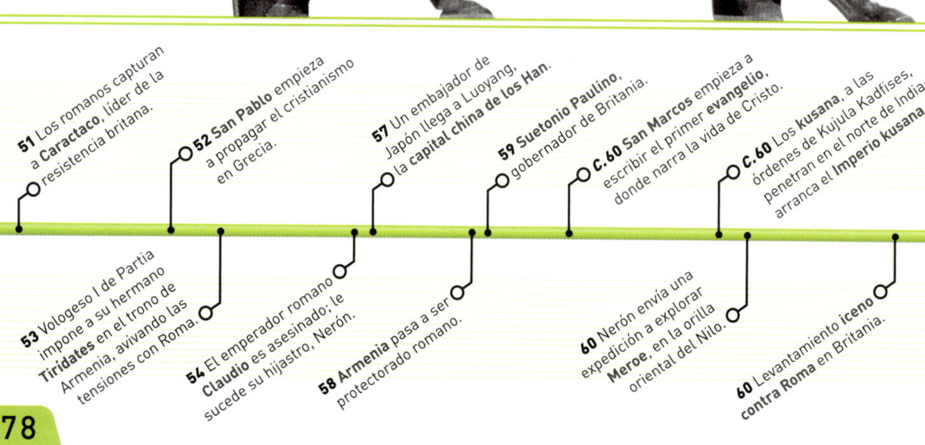

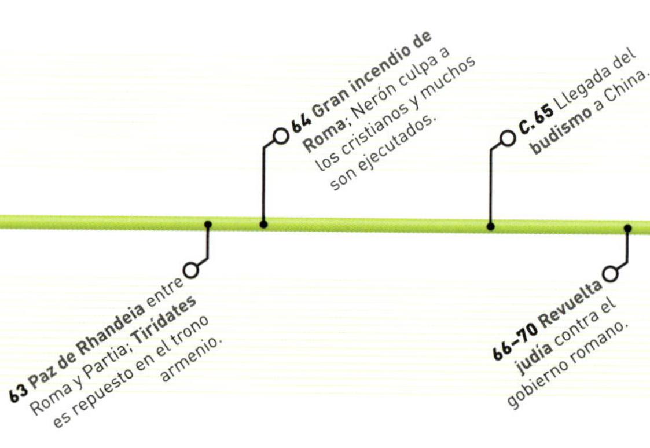

73–90

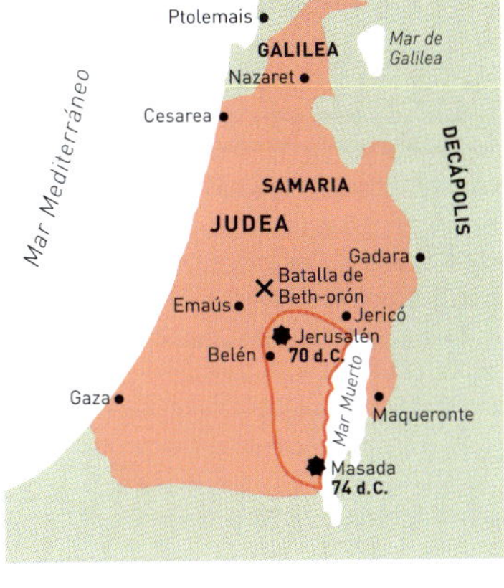

Rebeliones judías entre 66 y 74
Aunque en 66 los rebeldes lograron controlar gran parte de Palestina, en 69 ya habían perdido el control de toda la región excepto los alrededores de Jerusalén.

afrontar una nueva conspiración cuando **Tito Flavio Vespasiano** (9–79), general encargado de sofocar la revuelta judía, se estableció a sí mismo como emperador. Todo el Oriente y los Balcanes se le unieron de inmediato. En octubre se libró la segunda **batalla de Bedriacum**, en la que fueron aplastadas las tropas de Vitelio. En diciembre de 69, los ejércitos de Vespasiano tomaban Roma; Vitelio fue ejecutado poco después. Roma volvía a tener un **dirigente indiscutido**.

Vespasiano maniobró con rapidez para restablecer la lealtad del ejército, disolviendo la guardia pretoriana de Vitelio y reclutando otra. También debió afrontar una grave revuelta en el Rin, donde **Julio Civilis**, un noble bátavo, unió sus fuerzas a las de legionarios disidentes y estuvo a punto de establecer un **Imperio galo** independiente.

Judea llevaba bajo gobierno directo romano desde la muerte del rey Herodes Agripa I en 44. El dominio extranjero y la insensibilidad romana hacia las leyes judías eran fuentes de un gran descontento. En 60 finalizó la reconstrucción del templo que Herodes había ordenado construir décadas atrás, y a la tensión creciente se sumaron unos veinte mil trabajadores sin empleo. El procurador romano agravaba la situación con su **gobierno autoritario**: en 66 estalló la insurrección. Aunque los comandantes de la rebelión eran competentes, carecían de liderazgo político, y sus reductos fueron cayendo gradualmente, primero a manos de Vespasiano y después de su hijo, Tito (39–81). En 70, **Jerusalén** fue sitiada, y a finales de agosto caía y el templo era destruido. Pudieron morir hasta 200 000 personas, muchos de los tesoros sagrados judíos fueron llevados a Roma, y miles de judíos fueron esclavizados. La resistencia continuó en **Masada** hasta 74, cuando cayó después de dos años de asedio.

Fresco de Pompeya: muchos de los elaborados frescos pompeyanos han sobrevivido casi dos mil años enterrados bajo la ceniza.

MEDIADA LA DÉCADA DE 70, el levantamiento de Civilis se había malogrado, y el resto del reinado de Vespasiano fue básicamente pacífico. De reputación austera, restableció las finanzas del imperio imponiendo tributos a una serie de provincias, entre ellas Egipto. Para cuando murió, en 79, **la estabilidad se había recuperado** hasta tal punto que la sucesión por su hijo mayor, **Tito** (r. 79–81), no tuvo oposición.

Dos meses después del acceso de Tito al trono, la ciudad de **Pompeya** (cerca de la actual Nápoles) fue destruida por una erupción volcánica. Torrenciales cortinas de ceniza llovieron desde el **Vesubio**, y quienes no escaparon a tiempo fueron arrollados por el flujo piroclástico (una veloz masa de gases, ceniza y escombros) procedente del volcán. Pudo perder la vida una décima parte de una población de veinte mil personas y todavía más en el área vecina, entre ellas el naturalista Plinio el Viejo, que comandaba una unidad naval cercana y pereció en un intento fallido de rescate.

Figura de Pompeya
Los cuerpos de quienes murieron en la erupción del Vesubio quedaron cubiertos de ceniza volcánica que, al solidificar, dejó sus contornos detrás.

En **Britania**, la zona controlada por los romanos seguía expandiéndose: el gobernador Petilio Cerialis ocupó (71–74) el reino septentrional de **Brigantia**; Julio Frontino (74–77) completó la subyugación de Gales al derrotar a los siluros; pero aún quedó en manos de Julio Agrícola (77–*c.* 83) el envío de tropas al interior de Escocia, donde la derrota final de los caledonios en la **batalla del Monte Graupio** (posiblemente cerca de Aberdeen) hacía factible la anexión de toda Escocia. Sin embargo, el emperador **Domiciano** (81–96) estaba teniendo problemas en el Danubio, y la legión fue retirada de Britania *c.* 86, dejando una fuerza insuficiente para defender el norte de Escocia, que fue evacuado.

En 84, Domiciano había conseguido repeler a lo largo del **Danubio** las amenazas de **sármatas, marcomanos y cuados**, pero entonces estalló la guerra con los **dacios** (de la Rumanía actual), que cruzaron el Danubio y mataron al gobernador de la Mesia romana. En 86, Domiciano había derrotado a los dacios y a su nuevo rey, **Decébalo**. Pero los romanos no ocuparon Dacia, y dejar a Decébalo en su trono sería causa de futuros problemas para Roma.

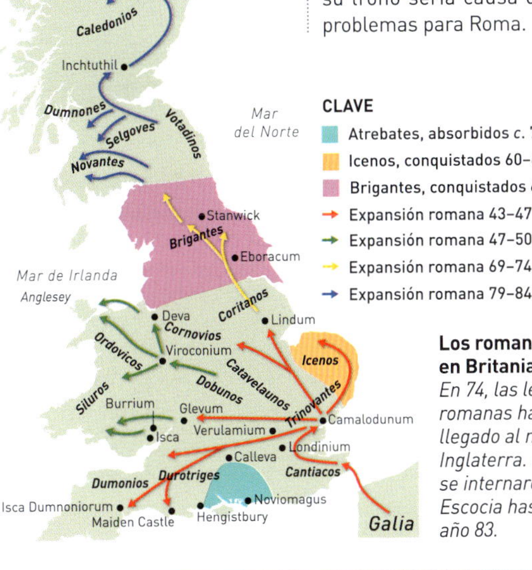

Los romanos en Britania
En 74, las legiones romanas habían llegado al norte de Inglaterra. Luego se internaron en Escocia hasta el año 83.

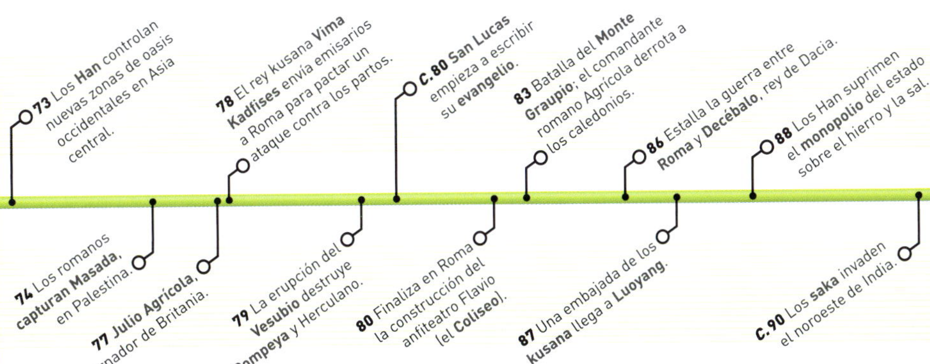

91–100

« [UN EMPERADOR] BAJO EL CUAL SE LE **PERMITIÓ TODO** A **TODO EL MUNDO.** »

Frontón, orador romano, sobre el emperador Nerva, en *Historia de Roma*, de Dion Casio

El emperador Domiciano
El reinado de Domiciano empezó bien, pero su caída en la tiranía resultó excesiva para sus oponentes, que lo asesinaron.

DOMICIANO (51–96) SE CONVIRTIÓ EN EMPERADOR romano tras la inesperada muerte de su hermano Tito (39–81). Domiciano nunca había comandado ejércitos, y no estaba preparado para el ejercicio del poder supremo. Tuvo algunos éxitos en sus primeras campañas, pero se extralimitó frente a los dacios y en la represión de una revuelta legionaria liderada por **Saturnino**, gobernador de la Germania Superior. Esta distracción permitió a **Decébalo, rey de Dacia** (r. 87–106) retomar su guerra contra Roma, y Domiciano se vio obligado a rendir a los dacios un subsidio anual.

La conspiración de Saturnino obsesionó a Domiciano hasta el punto de ordenar la ejecución por traición de muchos senadores. En septiembre de 96 fue asesinado en una conspiración palaciega, y el senado eligió al anciano **Marco Coceyo Nerva** (30–98) para sustituirlo. También votó por destruir todas las estatuas de Domiciano y por el retorno de los exiliados. Pero en 97, Nerva tuvo que enfrentarse a un motín de la guardia pretoriana, que exigía el castigo de los asesinos de Domiciano. Tuvo que acceder, lo cual debilitó su autoridad. La falta de un heredero menoscababa aún más su posición. Para subsanarla, adoptó a Marco Ulpio **Trajano**, gobernador de la Germania Superior y que contaba con un fuerte apoyo militar. Poco tiempo después moría Nerva, y Trajano ascendió al trono de Roma.

En **Asia central**, la confederación xiongnu septentrional (*véanse* 146–131 a. C. y 24–40 d. C.) se derrumbó en 89, lo que facilitó a los Han, dirigidos por el **general Ban Chao** (32–102), grandes avances en la región. Ban Chao asumió el rango de protector general de las regiones occidentales en 91, y recuperó el control sobre oasis claves a lo largo de la **Ruta de la Seda**. Para cuando se retiró, en 102, los Han controlaban gran parte de la cuenca del Tarim. La **organización estatal china** se complicó enormemente bajo los Han: tres oficiales supremos supervisaban grandes y complejos departamentos, subdivididos en nueve ministerios. Los gobernadores administraban cada región, algunas de ellas compuestas por más de mil condados, cada uno supervisado por un magistrado. En la corte Han, los eunucos iban adquiriendo una influencia creciente.

101–117

La columna de Trajano, en Roma, ofrece un relato visual de las campañas de Trajano contra Decébalo en las guerras dacias.

EL EMPERADOR TRAJANO (R. 98–117) ERA DE ASCENDENCIA ROMANA asentada en Hispania: fue el primer emperador nacido en una provincia distinta de Italia. Después de regresar a Roma desde Germania para reclamar su trono en el año 100, en 101 comenzó una nueva **guerra dacia** contra Decébalo. Desde su base en Viminacium (en la actual Serbia) se internó en la Dacia central y libró una importante batalla en Tapae, en la que ambos bandos sufrieron graves pérdidas. Cuando las legiones de Trajano se acercaron a la capital real dacia, **Sarmizegetusa Regia**, pidió un armisticio, aceptando entregar sus armas y equipos de asedio, y derribar sus fuertes restantes. El ejército romano no se retiró por completo: estableció una base junto a las montañas y tendió un puente sobre el Danubio en Drobeta a fin de facilitar el cruce del río. Tres años más tarde, en 105, el senado declaró que Decébalo había violado el tratado, y Trajano se embarcó en su **segunda guerra dacia**. En esta ocasión las legiones alcanzaron y finalmente tomaron Sarmizegetusa Regia (106). Decébalo huyó y después se quitó la vida para evitar ser capturado por el enemigo. Los romanos se hicieron con un inmenso tesoro en Dacia, lo que permitió a Trajano lanzarse a un desenfreno constructor, que incluyó la erección de un **nuevo foro** en Roma. Dacia fue anexionada como primera provincia transdanubiana, y continuó en manos del imperio más de 160 años.

En algún momento en torno al año 106, el gobernador romano de Siria se anexionó el **reino nabateo**, que se convirtió en la provincia de Arabia. No fue la última adquisición de Trajano en el este: en 113 lanzó una campaña contra **Partia**. Empezó por atacar Armenia en 113–114, pero fue el ataque contra la propia Partia lo que le proporcionó más éxitos en Oriente que a ningún otro emperador anterior. A finales de 114, los armenios se habían rendido y Trajano se internó en Mesopotamia y consiguió ha-

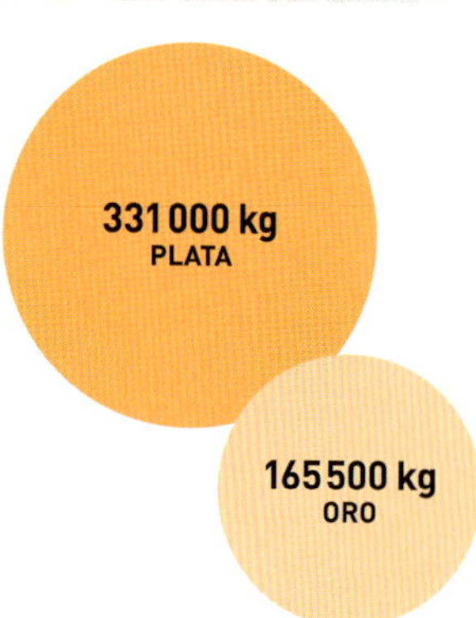

El tesoro dacio
La enorme fortuna adquirida por Trajano en Dacia le permitió construir impresionantes monumentos para conmemorar su victoria en la guerra.

Ciudad sagrada
Este templo en ruinas pertenece a la capital dacia, Sarmizegetusa (en la actual Rumanía). Contenía las reliquias más sagradas del reino.

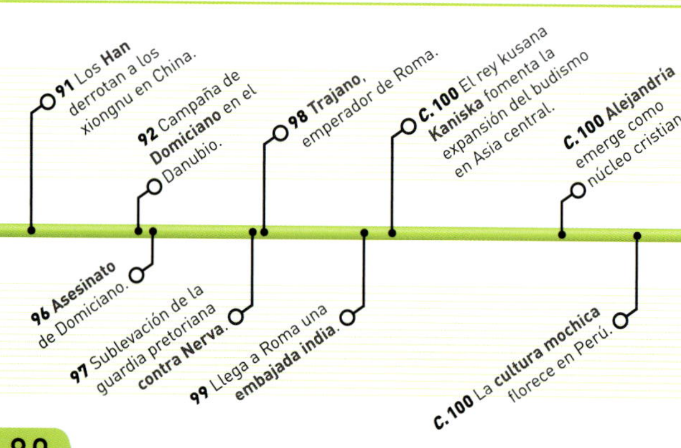

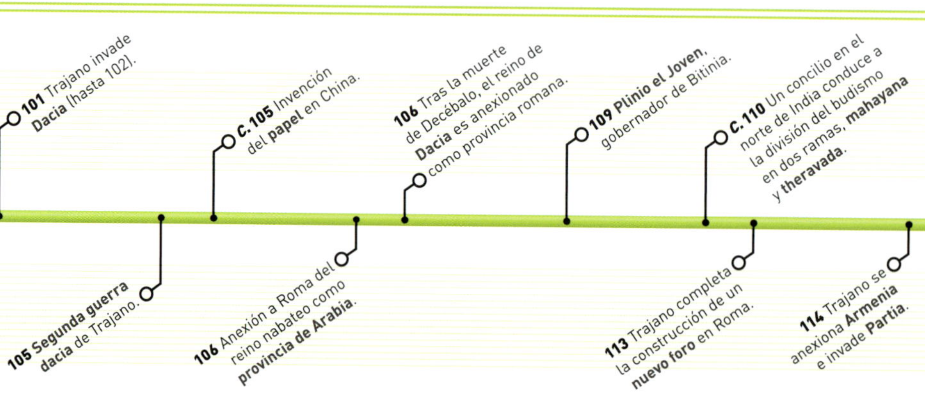

Restos del Muro de Adriano en el norte de Inglaterra. La porción central del muro ocupaba una posición alta que aumentaba enormemente su valor defensivo.

cerse con la capital parta de **Ctesifonte**. A finales de 115 ya había alcanzado el golfo Pérsico a la altura de la actual Basora (Iraq), donde se dice que comentó que, de haber sido más joven, podría haber penetrado en India. Los territorios recién conquistados fueron organizados como las provincias de **Mesopotamia** y **Asiria**, pero ya estaban en rebelión en el momento en que Trajano regresó a Roma en 117. Los partos rechazaron a **Partamaspates, rey cliente de Trajano**, y para cuando este falleció en agosto de 117, casi todas sus conquistas en el este se habían perdido. En su lecho de muerte, Trajano adoptó a Publio Elio **Adriano**, gobernador de Siria, nombrándolo su sucesor de hecho.

En 109, Trajano nombró al historiador **Plinio el Joven** (61–*c.* 112) representante personal para gobernar **Ponto-Bitinia**, en la costa anatolia del mar Negro. Esta decisión generó mucha controversia, ya que Ponto-Bitinia era, en teoría, una provincia senatorial. Las provincias habían sido repartidas entre el emperador y el senado desde que Augusto accedió al trono en 27 a. C., correspondiendo al emperador únicamente aquellas provincias con guarniciones legionarias. Esta división todavía persistía durante la época de Trajano. Plinio permaneció en Ponto-Bitinia al menos dos años, intentando ordenar las finanzas de las ciudades principales, que habían caído en el caos. Las cartas que remitió a Trajano son un testimonio inestimable del gobierno imperial de la época.

ADRIANO (R. 117–135), sucesor de Trajano, rechazó la política de expansión de su antecesor y se concentró en mejorar las defensas de los ***limes* imperiales**. En 122 visitó Britania, donde se desarrollaban conflictos fronterizos; ordenó la construcción de una enorme barrera desde el fiordo de Solway, en el oeste, hasta el río Tyne, en el este. Al gobernador, **Aulo Platorio Nepote**, le llevó dos años completar el **Muro de Adriano** (en parte de piedra y en parte de turba), que recorría 76 millas romanas (113 km) y estaba equipado con una serie de fuertes y fortines para su guarnición. El muro actuó como *limes* septentrional de la Britania romana durante cuarenta años.

El **reino parto** quedó bajo cierto desorden después de las campañas de Trajano. Su rey cliente, Partamaspates, fue expulsado en 117, pero entonces el reino pareció quedar dividido entre **Vologeso III** (r. 105–147) en el este, y en el oeste **Osroes I** (r. 117–129) y más tarde

985
NÚMERO DE **PUEBLOS ARRASADOS** DURANTE LA **REBELIÓN DE BARCOKEBAS**

Mitídrates IV (r. 129–140). Por el momento, no hubo nuevos conflictos entre Partia y Roma.

En India, el **Imperio kusana** se extendió enormemente con **Kaniska** (r. 127–140), quien conquistó Magadha y lanzó campañas contra los chinos en Asia central; se han encontrado inscripciones suyas desde el río Amu Daria en Afganistán hasta Varanasi y Sanchi (India)

por el sur. Gran defensor del budismo, presidió el **cuarto concilio budista** y construyó una gran estupa en su capital, Purushapura (Peshawar).

La prohibición de la circuncisión por parte de **Adriano**, sus planes de convertir Jerusalén en la ciudad romana de Aelia Capitolina y su intento allí de proscribir las prácticas religiosas judías provocaron una enfurecida **rebelión en Jerusalén** en 132, cuando los religiosos judíos se alzaron contra sus reformas. Liderados por **Barcokebas (Simón bar Kosebá)**, los rebeldes tuvieron éxitos iniciales contra Roma: establecieron los rudimentos de un gobierno independiente y acuñaron su propia moneda. En respuesta, Adriano convocó a **Julio Severo**, gobernador de Britania, para emprender una guerra contra los rebeldes. Severo dirigió un ejército formado con destacamentos de doce legiones. Los judíos no tenían grandes ciudades bajo su control, y por ello adoptaron una **táctica de guerrillas**, al mismo tiempo que intentaban mantener sus fortificaciones de menor tamaño. En 135 caía el **último bastión** rebelde, **Betar**, en medio de una sanguinaria matanza; después de ello, la revuelta se extinguió. Adriano procedió con su plan de **proscribir el judaísmo** en Palestina, y muchos de los judíos que habían sobrevivido a la rebelión huyeron.

Vaso valioso
Este hermoso jarro fue encontrado en Kapisa (Bagram), cerca de Kabul, que fue la capital de verano kusana en el siglo I.

ADRIANO (76–138)

De orígenes hispanos, fue adoptado por su predecesor, Trajano. Adriano fue objeto de algunas burlas por su filohelenismo, y fue el primer emperador en dejarse barba: una moda griega. También fue el primer emperador que viajó ampliamente por todo el imperio, lo que le permitió un conocimiento directo de sus provincias, desde Britania hasta el norte de África.

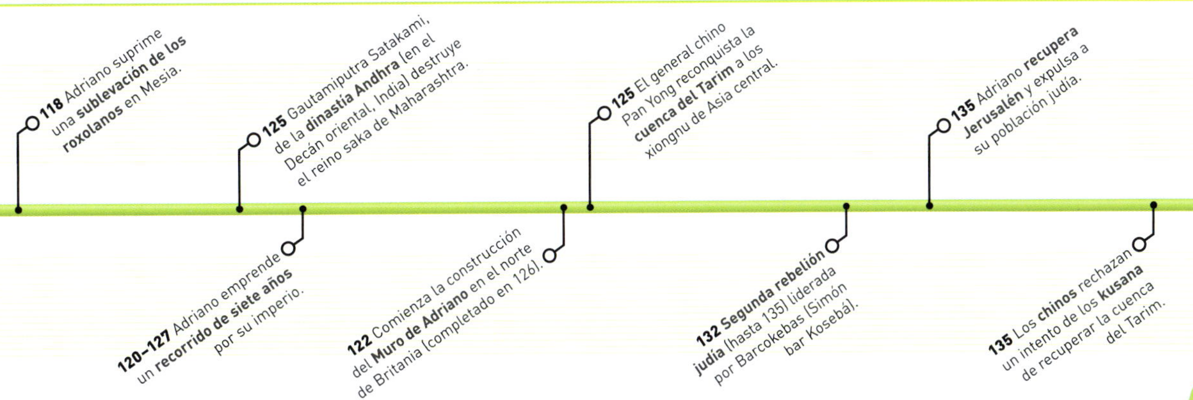

200 000

POBLACIÓN DE **TEOTIHUACÁN** EN SU **PUNTO ÁLGIDO**

La pirámide del Sol en Teotihuacán (México).

Ruinas de Hatra, una ciudad controlada por los partos.

LA CIUDAD DE TEOTIHUACÁN, EN EL VALLE DE MÉXICO, experimentó un **intenso crecimiento** durante los siglos I y II, y antes del año 200 superaba los ochenta mil habitantes. Estaba diseñada en cuadrícula, con **dos enormes pirámides** –del Sol y de la Luna–, una en cada extremo de la calle principal. Durante la fase Teotihuacán II (0–350) se construyó el inmenso **templo de Quetzalcóatl** y se forjó el imperio: la ciudad dominó vastas áreas de México y administró reinos clientes hasta Guatemala por el sur.

Adriano había adoptado a **Antonino Pío** (86–161) como hijo y sucesor, un sustituto temporal hasta que su propio sobrino, Marco Aurelio (121–180), tuviera edad suficiente para reinar; sin embargo, Antonino sobrevivió 23 años a Adriano y se convirtió en emperador romano en 138. Fue famoso por su moderación, y apenas abandonó Roma. Los disturbios en **Dacia** (en la actual Rumanía) *c.* 156 y una sublevación en África en 145 no alteraron en exceso la calma del imperio. Antonino extendió los límites tanto en Caledonia (Escocia) como en Germania Superior. En Caledonia ordenó la construcción de una nueva barrera de turba y tierra a unos 160 km al norte del **Muro de Adriano** (*véase* 118–135). Este Muro de Antonino tenía 63 km de longitud. La guarnición del Muro de Adriano fue desplazada al norte, ocupando una serie de nuevos fuertes, pero su estancia fue breve: Marco Aurelio, sucesor de Antonino, ordenó en torno a 161 la **retirada hacia el Muro de Adriano**, donde el *limes* romano permaneció hasta el siglo V.

A medida que crecía la **cristiandad**, lo hacía también el problema de definir una doctrina única. Entre las doctrinas alternativas surgidas durante el siglo II se encontraba el **marcionismo**, que mantenía que el Dios de los cristianos era distinto del Yahvé judío del Antiguo Testamento y que Cristo no era el mesías de dicho libro. **Justino Mártir** (*c.* 103–165) afirmó que el cristianismo era la culminación de la profecía judía y que los cristianos eran el nuevo pueblo elegido. También escribió a Marco Aurelio, intentando explicarle la doctrina cristiana.

63 **KILÓMETROS** ERA LA LONGITUD DEL **MURO DE ANTONINO**, EN **ESCOCIA**

piezas de mosaico de turquesa

collar de cuentas de coral

Máscara mexica
Esta suntuosa máscara de Teotihuacán muestra los rasgos planos y suaves característicos del arte de la ciudad.

EN 161, MARCO AURELIO ACCEDIÓ AL TRONO DE ROMA junto con **Lucio Vero**, pero fue Lucio el enviado en 162 a salvar la situación en el este cuando el gobernador de Capadocia fue derrotado y muerto por los persas tras una **desastrosa invasión de Armenia**. En los dos años siguientes, Lucio devolvió el control de Armenia a Roma y renombró su capital como Kainepolis («Ciudad Nueva»). Quedó instalado un rey pro romano y después las legiones continuaron avanzando, internándose en territorio persa con el objetivo de tomar Edesa en Mesopotamia, y llegando a la **capital parta, Ctesifonte**, en el año 165. El general **Avidio Casio** (*c.* 130–175) quemó el palacio real y a continuación retrocedió hacia el oeste. Roma incorporó una franja de territorio en el bajo Éufrates que se extendía hasta Dura Europos (en el sureste de Siria). Sin embargo, las celebraciones por la victoria no duraron mucho tiempo, pues las tropas trajeron la **peste** cuando regresaron a Roma, y hacia el año 167 la epidemia ya se

> « SI **NO ES CORRECTO**, NO LO HAGAS; SI **NO ES CIERTO**, NO LO DIGAS. »
>
> **Emperador Marco Aurelio,** *Meditaciones* (161–180)

136–137 Fracasa la **invasión de Capadocia** por los alanos del sureste de Rusia.

138 Adriano es sucedido por su hijo adoptivo **Antonino Pío**.

142 El *limes* romano en Britania es desplazado al norte hasta el **Muro de Antonino**.

147 Se celebra el **900.º aniversario** de la fundación de **Roma**.

C. 150 Los **kusana** son sometidos por los partos.

C. 150 Se restablece el dominio **Han** sobre Asia central.

C. 150 El **cristianismo** se extiende por el norte de África.

C. 150 Auge de la **cultura nok** en Nigeria.

154–155 Revuelta de los **brigantes** del norte de Britania contra el control romano.

155 Tratado de **paz parto-romano** tras el intento parto de conquistar Armenia.

159 Ascenso al poder de la **facción de los eunucos** en la China Han.

160 Roma extiende el ***limes* del Rin** más allá del valle del Neckar (en la Alemania actual).

161 Marco Aurelio, emperador romano, con **Lucio Vero** como coemperador.

C. 161 La Muralla de Antonino es abandonada y el ***limes* en Britania** regresa al Muro de Adriano.

162 Los partos colocan a su candidato en el trono armenio y atacan **Persia**.

162 Revuelta de los **catos** germanos.

Estuco pintado del dios más importante de los mochicas, Ai Apaec, representado a menudo con colmillos de serpiente.

había **extendido por el Mediterráneo**.

Apenas terminada la **guerra** parta comenzó la **marcomana**. A principios de 167, un grupo de guerreros germanos de las tribus de los **longobardos (lombardos)** y **boyos** cruzaron el río Danubio para atacar la provincia romana de Panonia. A pesar de que fueron rechazados con facilidad, en la primavera de 168 Marco Aurelio decidió visitar la región para evaluar la situación. Otras dos tribus germanas, los **marcomanos** y los **cuados**, amenazaban con atravesar el *limes* a la fuerza a menos que se les permitiera establecerse en el imperio, pero la presencia de Aurelio los disuadió. Sin embargo, la expedición fue suspendida por la muerte de Lucio Vero de peste a principios de 169. Marco Aurelio volvió a Italia, pero ese mismo año regresaba a Panonia para lanzar una **ofensiva masiva** al otro lado del Danubio. Fue un completo desastre: los romanos sufrieron unas veinte mil bajas, y marcomanos y cuados se lanzaron hacia Italia, donde sitiaron Aquilea. Lejos de ofrecer una fácil victoria a Aurelio, la guerra se prolongó otros diez años.

En **China**, la **facción de los eunucos** de la corte se había hecho cada vez más poderosa, e incluso maquinó el asesinato del emperador Shaodi en el año 125. Bajo el **emperador Huandi** (r. 146–168), una serie de desastres naturales debilitó la autoridad del gobierno central, por lo que este abandonó el control activo en manos de los eunucos. En 168, un complot de **Duo Xian** –regente del emperador **Lingdi** (r. 168–189), quien a la sazón tenía doce años– para exterminar a los eunucos fue traicionado y fracasó: Duo Xian fue obligado a suicidarse, varios cientos de sus partidarios fueron ejecutados y, con sus enemigos ahora muertos, los eunucos pudieron ejercer el poder prácticamente sin oposición.

Marco Aurelio
Estatua ecuestre de Marco Aurelio en actitud de victoria, algo que afirmó, pero nunca logró del todo, en sus guerras marcomanas.

LA CULTURA MOCHICA SURGIÓ EN LA COSTA NORTE DE PERÚ entre los años 100 y 200. Desde sus bases en los valles peruanos de Moche, Chicama y Virú, estos pueblos se extendieron hasta dominar casi toda la costa septentrional. Eran gentes guerreras, que sacrificaban a los prisioneros a sus dioses, entre ellos **Ai Apaec** («el degollador»). Además, eran hábiles orfebres del oro y su alfarería muestra un realismo extraordinario.

En 170, el **Imperio romano** estaba en **crisis**: marcomanos y cuados habían ocupado zonas del norte de Italia, y **yácigos** y **costobocos** invadieron gran parte de los Balcanes. Los marcomanos fueron atrapados cuando regresaban cruzando el Danubio y muchos perdieron la vida; los **cuados pidieron la paz más adelante**, en 171; sin embargo, los marcomanos, que se mantenían desafiantes, forzaron una **nueva ofensiva en el año 172**. Las tropas de Marco Aurelio nunca consiguieron asestar el golpe definitivo, y en 175 la guerra ya había alcanzado un **punto muerto**. En mayo de ese año, los rumores acerca de la muerte de Aurelio en campaña incitaron la revuelta de **Avidio Casio**, gobernador de Siria. Avidio fue declarado **emperador** en Egipto, y recibió el apoyo de Arabia además del de su propia provincia. Pero fracasó en lograr el respaldo del gobernador de Capadocia, **Marcio Vero**, junto al cual había combatido en la guerra parta.

Ante el acercamiento del ejército de Marcio, la lealtad de las tropas del usurpador se debilitó, y en julio de 175 **Avidio Casio fue asesinado** por un centurión desafecto, poniendo fin a su efímera pero peligrosa rebelión. Hubo rumores sobre la incitación a Casio por parte de **Faustina**, la esposa de Marco Aurelio, debido al temor de esta por la salud de su esposo y a su preocupación de la aptitud para el gobierno de su propio hijo, Cómodo.

Liberado de la distracción de la revuelta de Avidio, Marco Aurelio regresó al Danubio en 177. En el invierno de 179–180, el **ejército romano** ocupó posiciones avanzadas más allá del río, y la impresión era que Aurelio sería capaz de crear dos nuevas provincias romanas: Marcomania y Sarmacia. Sin embargo, Aurelio estaba viejo y cansado: murió en marzo de 180. Su hijo **Cómodo** puso un rápido fin a la guerra para poder regresar a Roma.

Vasija mochica con asa estribo
Esta vasija tiene el típico «estribo» mochica en su parte trasera. El realismo del remero es característico de las cerámicas de esta cultura.

LAS TRIBUS GERMANAS

Los romanos se habían enfrentado a las tribus germanas desde el momento en que alcanzaron el Rin en la época de Julio César. Los grupos asentados a lo largo del Danubio, como cuados y marcomanos, fueron un grave problema en el siglo II, y a finales del siglo III surgieron nuevas y más peligrosas confederaciones de tribus, como francos, alamanes y godos, que mediado el siglo V iban a invadir gran parte del Imperio romano.

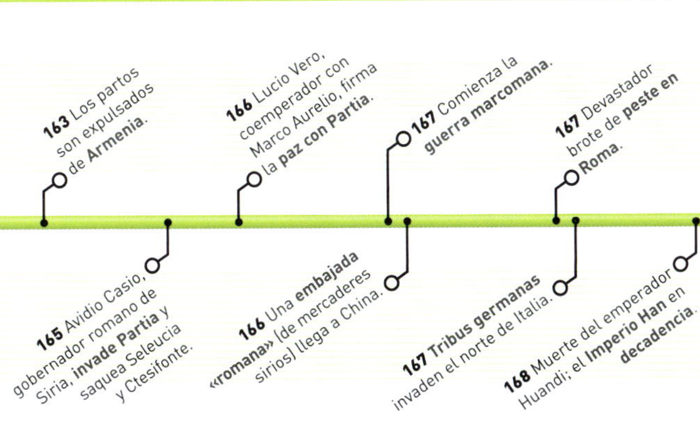

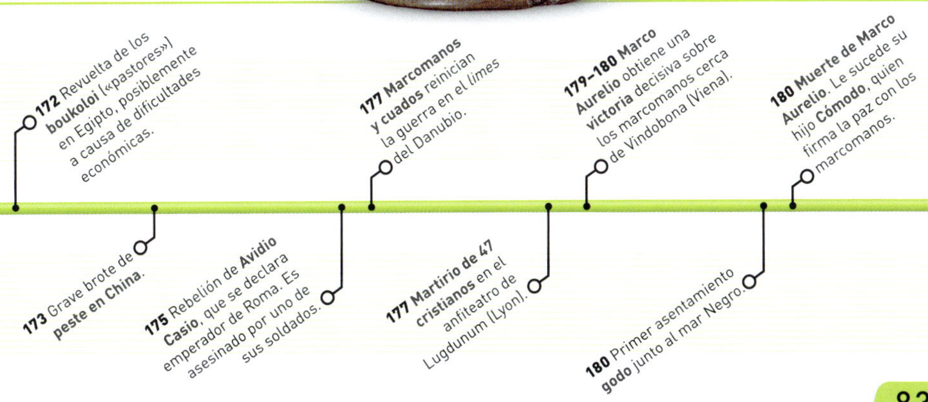

Pendientes con delfines
Los pendientes con motivos animales fueron especialmente populares en el Imperio romano oriental. Estos simbolizan a Neptuno, dios del mar.

Collar de granates
Hecho de oro y piropo (granate rojo), este collar recuerda la forma de un espectacular árbol frutal.

Alfiler de hueso
Esta delgada cuchilla o alfiler plano está rematado con una cabeza femenina, un toque ornamental para una pieza doméstica por lo demás anodina.

Plomada
Esta plomada con pesa de bronce iba unida a una *groma*: un instrumento usado por los romanos para comprobar las alineaciones.

ANTIGUA ROMA

LOS ROMANOS DIFUNDIERON UNA RICA CULTURA MATERIAL A TRAVÉS DE SU VASTO IMPERIO

A medida que el control político de Roma se extendía fuera de Italia, tras él llegaba el modo de vida romano. Los agrimensores trazaban nuevas ciudades, las élites locales absorbían las prácticas romanas y las masas acudían a los espectáculos. También se difundían las modas en el vestido y los complementos.

Aunque muchos territorios conquistados por Roma se resistieron inicialmente, las poblaciones de estas provincias, en especial las antiguas clases dirigentes, adoptaron gradualmente muchas costumbres romanas. Los hombres influyentes se convertían en ciudadanos romanos; los pueblos eran dotados con nuevos edificios públicos, como termas y juzgados; se establecían guarniciones legionarias en puntos estratégicos, y nuevas rutas comerciales llevaban artículos de lujo desde Roma. Como resultado, artefactos romanos similares, datados entre el siglo I a.C. y el V d.C. han sido hallados en toda Europa, Oriente Próximo y norte de África.

Compás y regla de un pie de bronce
El compás permitía escalar planos o modelos a la mitad o al doble de su tamaño: el espacio entre las puntas inferiores es siempre el doble que entre las superiores. La regla, que tiene un pie romano de longitud (29,6 cm), se plegaba para facilitar su transporte.

Termas de Océano
Las termas romanas más importantes estaban adornadas con lujosos mosaicos como este del titán Océano, procedente de Sabratha, en Libia.

Tablilla de madera
Este tipo de tablilla, hecha de madera muy fina, era usado en los ejércitos romanos para las cartas rutinarias y el mantenimiento de registros. Esta procede de Vindolanda (Inglaterra).

El Gran Plato
El relieve intrincado de este plato del siglo IV –parte del tesoro de Mildenhall desenterrado en Suffolk (Inglaterra) en 1942– se refiere a Baco, dios romano del vino.

Rallador antiguo
El queso ocupaba un lugar importante en la dieta romana. Estos ralladores se inventaron para utilizar el queso como cobertura para otros alimentos.

Ánfora
Los romanos transportaban líquidos como aceite y vino en ánforas, una especie de gran tinaja de almacenaje con doble asa.

Enseres de baño
En las termas era común engrasar la piel y después rasparla para eliminar sudor y suciedad. Los útiles se transportaban en una anilla.

Espada corta
La espada militar romana, o *gladius*, tenía una hoja corta, ideal para el combate cuerpo a cuerpo. Era usada por los soldados y por algunos gladiadores.

Jabalina militar
Cada legionario romano llevaba dos de estos *pila*. La punta de hierro de la jabalina estaba diseñada para romperse al impactar, evitando que el oponente la usara de vuelta.

Monedas imperiales
Las monedas mostraban el busto del emperador vigente (aquí, Augusto y Claudio); constituían una poderosa herramienta de propaganda en todo el imperio, pues mostraban a las masas la imagen de su soberano.

Prueba de ciudadanía
Los no ciudadanos que servían 25 años en el ejército romano eran premiados con la ciudadanía; la concesión quedaba grabada en diplomas de bronce como este.

Balas de honda
Normalmente los legionarios se valían de sus espadas, pero la infantería ligera auxiliar usaba otras armas de efecto devastador, como estas *glandis* de metal.

Casco de gladiador
Los gladiadores portaban diversas armas y armaduras. Esta especie de yelmo era usado por un tracio, un tipo de gladiador cuyo equipamiento se basaba en el de los antiguos guerreros tracios.

Escudo de bronce de gladiador
Los gladiadores tracios –una clase de gladiadores con armas ligeras– portaban escudos circulares de poco peso para defenderse y una cimitarra, de hoja corta y curvada, para atacar.

181–192

En este grabado de Giovanni Stradano, el emperador Cómodo lanza una flecha para abatir a un leopardo. Su pasión era luchar en la arena como un gladiador.

EN CHINA, LA DISENSIÓN CRECIENTE causada por la corrupción de los eunucos en la corte del emperador Lingdi de Han (r. 168–189), unida a una sucesión de desastres naturales, condujeron en 184 al estallido de una gran sublevación, llamada **revuelta de los Turbantes Amarillos** por el color de los tocados de sus partidarios. Más de 400 000 rebeldes avanzaron desde el este hacia la capital. Otro levantamiento, azuzar por la secta de los **Cinco Celemines de Arroz**, consiguió tomar el control de Sichuan, en el suroeste. Aunque los turbantes amarillos ya habían sido casi aplastados a principios de 185, la rebelión no se sofocó hasta 204, y el **control de los Han seguía debilitándose**. A su muerte, Lingdi fue sucedido por su hermanastro **Xiandi** (r. 189–220), pero este nunca ejerció un poder real; el control del imperio recayó en el general **Cao Cao**, que combatió durante treinta años contra una serie de **señores de la guerra rivales**, en especial con **Liu Bei** en el suroeste y con **Sun Qan** en el sur.

Cómodo (r. 180-192), hijo de Marco Aurelio, fue el primer emperador romano en noventa años, pero demostró ser una **elección desastrosa**. En 183, tras un intento de asesinarlo, aparentemente organizado por su hermana Lucila, Cómodo fue haciéndose cada vez más **despótico**. Muchos senadores implicados en la conspiración fueron ejecutados, y el gobierno recayó en las manos de **Tigidio Perenne, el prefecto del pretorio** (comandante de la guardia imperial). Hubo escaramuzas en Britania y en Dacia (en la actual Rumanía); en 185, sospechoso de alentar un complot para hacer emperador a su propio hijo, Perenio fue ejecutado por sus tropas.

Cómodo se hizo cada vez más **aficionado a luchar** en el anfiteatro como **gladiador**, mientras **Cleandro**, su chambelán, controlaba el gobierno y vendía cargos públicos al mejor postor, hasta que el encargado del suministro de cereales, **Papirio Dionisio**, provocó su caída culpándolo de una grave situación de escasez. Sin embargo, esto no supuso un gobierno más estable, pues su sustituto fue asesinado poco después. Por su parte, Cómodo se identificaba a sí mismo con **Hércules** (el héroe griego), y renombró Roma con su nombre: *colonia Commodiana*. A finales de 192, el prefecto de pretorio, **Laeto**, convencido de que Cómodo planeaba matarlo, tomó la iniciativa y **envenenó** al emperador en la última noche del año; el intento fracasó, y Cómodo fue **estrangulado** en la mañana de **Año Nuevo de 193**.

18
EDAD DE **CÓMODO** AL CONVERTIRSE EN **ÚNICO EMPERADOR**

193–211

El arco de Septimio Severo en Leptis Magna (en la actual Libia) conmemoraba una visita del emperador norteafricano a su ciudad natal.

« MANTENED LA **CONCORDIA**, **ENRIQUECED** A LOS **SOLDADOS** E IGNORAD A LOS **DEMÁS**. »

Últimas palabras de Septimio Severo según las recoge el historiador Dion Casio en el Libro LXXVII de su *Historia de Roma* (211)

EN 193, TRAS LA MUERTE DE CÓMODO, fue declarado emperador Helvio Pertinax (126–193), prefecto de la ciudad; sin embargo, fue asesinado tres meses después. Los pretendientes rivales al trono se enzarzaron en una subasta junto al campamento pretoriano para decidir quién sería el próximo emperador. Ganó **Didio Juliano** (133–193), pero su mandato fue corto, ya que los ejércitos fronterizos se levantaron casi de inmediato: los del Danubio proclamaron a **Septimio Severo** (*c.* 145–211), mientras que las legiones sirias elevaron a su comandante, **Pescenio Níger** (*c.* 135–194). Septimio Severo llegó antes a Roma y, tras garantizar el título de César (heredero imperial) a **Clodio Albino**, gobernador de Britania, regresó al este donde, en la primavera de 194, sus tropas derrotaron a las de Níger en la **batalla de Issos**, en Siria. Septimio Severo permaneció en Oriente y al año siguiente atacó el Imperio parto. Pero se vio obligado a regresar a Occidente para enfrentarse al ahora rebelado Albino, que fue derrotado y se suicidó en Lugdunum (actual Lyon, en Francia) en 197. Tras ello, volvió a Partia, y ese mismo año ocupó su capital, Ctesifonte: desplazó el *limes* hacia el Tigris y creó la **nueva provincia de Mesopotamia**.

Los **problemas en Britania** llevaron al envejecido emperador a la provincia en 208. Un avance romano a gran escala empujó a caledonios y maetas del norte de la provincia a llegar a un acuerdo en 209, pero no tardaron en romper el tratado, lo que provocó una nueva campaña en 210. Para entonces Septimio Severo ya estaba muy enfermo, y su hijo Caracalla asumió el mando. **Septimio Severo murió** en febrero de 211 en Eboracum (en la actual York, en Inglaterra), y repartió la sucesión conjunta entre sus hijos, Caracalla y Geta. Acabada la guerra caledonia, ambos se apresuraron a regresar a Roma, pero su **reinado conjunto fue efímero**, pues Caracalla asesinó a Geta en diciembre del 211.

cantidad ofrecida a cada pretoriano por Didio Juliano

25 000 SESTERCIOS

20 000 SESTERCIOS

cantidad ofrecida a cada pretoriano por Flavio Sulpiciano

Comprar la lealtad
El mayor soborno ofrecido a las tropas por Didio Juliano supuso su victoria en la subasta para ser emperador.

JULIA DOMNA (170–217)

Hija de un sumo sacerdote sirio, se casó con Septimio Severo en 187. Una profecía había predicho que se casaría con un emperador, y así fue. Enérgica e inteligente, fracasó al intentar conciliar a sus hijos, Caracalla y Geta, a la muerte de su esposo, y en evitar el asesinato de Geta. Julia se dejó morir de hambre como protesta cuando su otro hijo fue asesinado, medida que cohesionó el apoyo hacia los restantes miembros de la familia de los Severos.

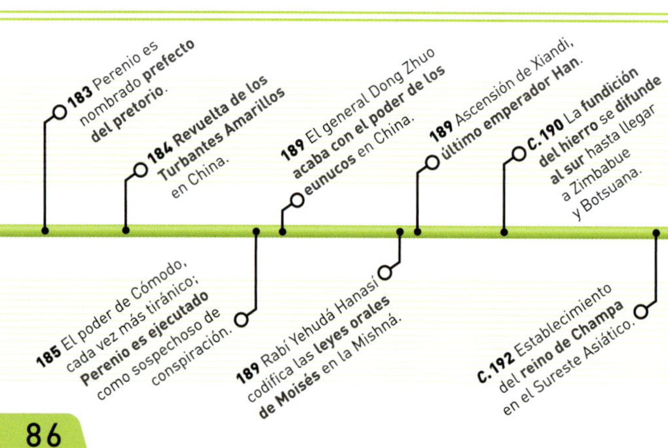

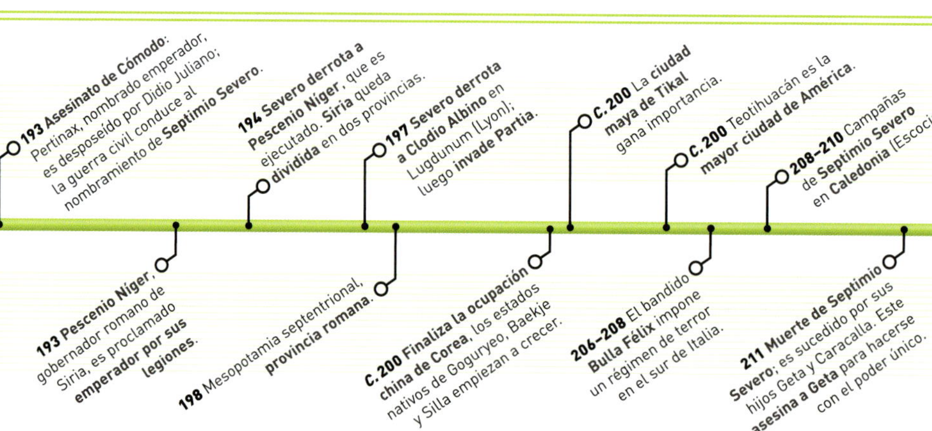

Bajorrelieve de Buda procedente de Sarnath (norte de India), donde floreció una escuela artística budista bajo el Imperio kusana.

EN INDIA, LA EXTENSIÓN DEL IMPERIO KUSANA empezó a reducirse después de la muerte del rey Kaniska en 140, y sufrió importantes pérdidas durante el reinado de Huviska (r. 160–190). El gobierno kusana se hundió por fin bajo Vasudeva (r. 190–225), cuando los invasores persas barrieron el noroeste de India. Aunque los reyes kusanas siguieron gobernando un siglo más sobre un territorio muy menguado, su influencia era puramente local, y sus años de **apogeo habían terminado**.

En Roma, el gobierno de Caracalla era impopular. Entre sus medidas estuvo la **Constitución Antonina** (edicto de Caracalla) de 212, que garantizaba la ciudadanía a casi todos los hombres libres del imperio. Tras una exitosa campaña en el Rin (213), Caracalla se aventuró más lejos aún, llegando a Egipto en 215. Por razones desconocidas, montó en cólera y ordenó la **masacre** de los ciudadanos de **Alejandría**. Al año siguiente lanzó una ofensiva sobre Partia. Su prefecto del pretorio, **Opelio Macrino**, empezó a sospechar que el emperador deseaba su muerte, por lo que convenció a un soldado desafecto para asesinarlo. Después de la muerte de Caracalla, **el ejército declaró emperador a Macrino**, pero aún quedaba mucha lealtad residual hacia la familia de los Severos, y en Siria estalló una sublevación con objeto de poner en el trono a **Heliogábalo** (203–222), nieto de Julia Maesa, la hermana de Julia Domna. Macrino perdió apoyos y en 218 huyó a Capadocia, donde sería asesinado. Heliogábalo **adoptó como heredero** a su primo Alejandro. Cuando ambos se enemistaron en 222, el ejército respaldó a Alejandro, y Heliogábalo fue asesinado. Alejandro iba a convertirse, con trece años de edad, en el **emperador Severo Alejandro**.

2000

BAÑISTAS. CAPACIDAD TOTAL DE LAS **TERMAS DE CARACALLA**

Diploma de bronce
Los diplomas expedidos a los soldados auxiliares del ejército romano garantizaban su ciudadanía. Esta práctica cesó tras la Constitución Antonina.

En Persia, el control parto se había debilitado, tanto por la peste como por las sucesivas invasiones romanas. En 207, el reino se dividió en dos cuando **Artabán IV**, hermano de Vologeso VI, se estableció a sí mismo como rey rival; y en 216 una nueva invasión romana asoló gran parte de la provincia de Media. El desorden reinante fue aprovechado por **Ardasir**, señor de la provincia suroccidental de Fars, para expandir sus dominios y, finalmente, derrotar a Artabán IV *c.* 224. Ardasir I (r. 224–242) iba ser el **primer rey de la dinastía sasánida**. Aunque Persia quedó temporalmente debilitada por una guerra civil, los sasánidas demostraron ser para Roma **adversarios mucho más duros** de lo que nunca habían sido los partos.

En China, Cao Pi, hijo de Cao Cao, **obligó a Xiandi a abdicar** en 220. En el transcurso de dos años se iban a declarar emperadores Cao Pi, Liu Bei y Sun Qan. La **dinastía Han** y la unidad de China habían llegado a su fin.

Arco de Caracalla
Originalmente estaba rematado con una efigie del emperador conduciendo un carro. Se erigió en Volubilis, ciudad principal de la Mauritania Tingitana (actual Marruecos).

El Imperio sasánida en Persia
Tras hacerse rápidamente con el antiguo Imperio parto, los sasánidas libraron varias guerras con los romanos por el control de Mesopotamia.

CLAVE
- Imperio sasánida en su mayor extensión
- Imperio romano de Oriente en el siglo III

212 Caracalla ofrece **la ciudadanía a todos los ciudadanos varones** del imperio.

213–214 Campañas de Caracalla **contra los alamanes**, una nueva confederación germana.

214 Edesa, en Mesopotamia, se convierte en **colonia romana**.

215 Caracalla ordena **masacrar a los ciudadanos de Alejandría**.

216 Los romanos **invaden Partia**.

217 Caracalla es asesinado cerca de Edesa; **Macrino**, prefecto del pretorio, es **declarado emperador**.

218 Derrota de Macrino frente a los oponentes congregados por Julia Maesa, cuyo nieto **Heliogábalo** se convierte en emperador.

c. 220 Colapso de la dinastía Han; es reemplazada por los reinos de **Shu, Wu y Wei**.

222 El papa Calixto I es asesinado durante los **disturbios anticristianos en Roma**.

222 Heliogábalo, asesinado por la guardia pretoriana y sustituido por su primo Severo Alejandro.

224 Ardasir es proclamado **«rey de reyes»** en Persia.

224 Hundimiento del gobierno parto tras la insurrección de **Ardasir**, gobernador de Fars, que funda la **dinastía sasánida**.

225 Muerte del teólogo cristiano **Tertuliano** (n. 160).

226 Muere el emperador chino **Cao Pi** (n. 187).

230 Ardasir I invade Siria.

25 NÚMERO DE **EMPERADORES ROMANOS** QUE REINARON ENTRE LOS AÑOS **235 Y 284**

El emperador romano Gordiano III sucedió a su tío y a su abuelo.

Fresco de san Cipriano, obispo de Cartago durante el apogeo de la persecución deciana. Fue martirizado en 257, durante una campaña de Valeriano.

EN CHINA, EL COLAPSO FINAL DE LA DINASTÍA HAN EN 220 fue seguido por 350 años de inestabilidad. El periodo de los **Tres Reinos** (220–280) supuso la división de China en el reino **Wei** del norte, bajo Wei Wendi (r. 220–226); el **Shu** del oeste, cuyo primer rey fue Shu Han Xuandi (r. 221–223); y el **Wu** del sur, bajo Wu Wudi (r. 222–252). Wendi fue un gobernante capaz, pero sus sucesores tuvieron problemas para repeler a las tribus del norte.

En 235, el emperador romano Severo Alejandro y su madre Julia Mamea fueron asesinados por soldados amotinados, lo que dio fin a la **dinastía de los Severos**. El cabecilla de la sublevación, **Maximino el Tracio** (r. 235–238), un oficial de extracción humilde, fue proclamado emperador, pero pasó la mayor parte de su reinado reuniendo fondos para premiar a las tropas por su apoyo. Esta época marca el inicio del periodo de **«anarquía militar»** durante el cual Roma tuvo docenas de emperadores, la mayoría de ellos efímeros, alzados por las tropas de los *limes*, y desposeídos y muertos con rapidez. En 238, una rebelión en la provincia de África proclamó emperador a su anciano gobernador, **Gordiano I**, pero tanto este como su hijo Gordiano II cayeron rápidamente. El senado, que había desposeído a Maximino, propuso como candidatos a **Pupieno** y **Balbino**. El sentir popular era favorable al nieto de Gordiano I, **Gordiano III** (r. 238–244), por lo que los tres compartieron brevemente el trono: Pupieno y Balbino fueron asesinados poco después, dejando a Gordiano como emperador único. Sus seis años de reinado **devolvieron** cierta apariencia de **estabilidad** al imperio, pero murió mientras dirigía una invasión de Persia en 243–244. Las dificultades en el imperio se agravaron con la aparición de **confederaciones bárbaras** entre los pueblos germanos del Rin y el Danubio; la principal fue la liderada por los **alamanes**: Caracalla había luchado contra ellos en 213, y en 260 ya fueron capaces de **invadir la misma Italia**.

DESIERTO DE GOBI
WEI
Chang'an
Luoyang
Mar Amarillo
Jiankang
Chengdu
SHU
WU
Taiwan
Mar de la China Meridional
Hainán

CLAVE
- Wei (220–225)
- Shu (221–263)
- Wu (222–280)

China bajo los Tres Reinos
Aunque el reino Wei afrontó los mayores desafíos de los tres, finalmente conquistaría Wu y Shu.

Arte de los Tres Reinos
La dinastía Han tardía se caracterizó por su alto nivel artístico, como muestra esta delicada estatuilla. Su colapso en 220 no conllevó un declive equivalente en la producción artística china.

PERSIA LOGRÓ UNA POSICIÓN DE FUERZA RENOVADA bajo el reinado de Sapor I (r. 241–272). En 244 obtuvo una victoria decisiva contra Gordiano III en Misiche, cerca de Ctesifonte. Poco después, Gordiano moría y era reemplazado por su comandante **Filipo el Árabe** (Filipo I), que firmó la paz con Sapor y pagó un abundante rescate para salir de territorio sasánida; sus sucesores rompieron los términos de paz, por lo que en 256 **Sapor invadió Siria** y ocupó las ciudades de Dura Europos y Antioquía. El entonces emperador romano, **Valeriano** (r. 253–260), no tardó en recuperar Antioquía, pero en 260 fue derrotado y **hecho prisionero por Sapor**. Las filas romanas cayeron en la confusión, y las tropas de Sapor avanzaron hasta Iconium (la actual Konya, en Turquía).

La zona occidental del Imperio romano también afrontaba presiones crecientes: desde *c.* 214, Dacia (en la actual Rumanía) sufría invasiones de los carpos que, junto a un nuevo grupo, los **godos**, tomaron parte en una incursión que cruzó el Danubio en 239–240. En 248, el emperador Filipo **suspendió el tributo anual** que había estado pagando a carpos y godos, lo que provocó que se lanzaran sobre Mesia (actual Bulgaria). Filipo envió a **Quinto Decio** para hacerles frente: tuvo tanto éxito que sus tropas lo proclamaron emperador. A principios de 249, Decio marchó hacia Roma y derrotó y mató a Filipo. Enterados de la guerra civil romana, los **godos reanudaron su invasión**, obligando a Decio a regresar a los Balcanes en 250. Al mando de su líder **Cniva**, los godos arrasaron la provincia de Me-

Relieve de Sapor I
En este relieve, Sapor I triunfa sobre los emperadores romanos Gordiano III y Valeriano. Se dice que tras capturar a este último, Sapor lo utilizó como escabel para montar en su caballo.

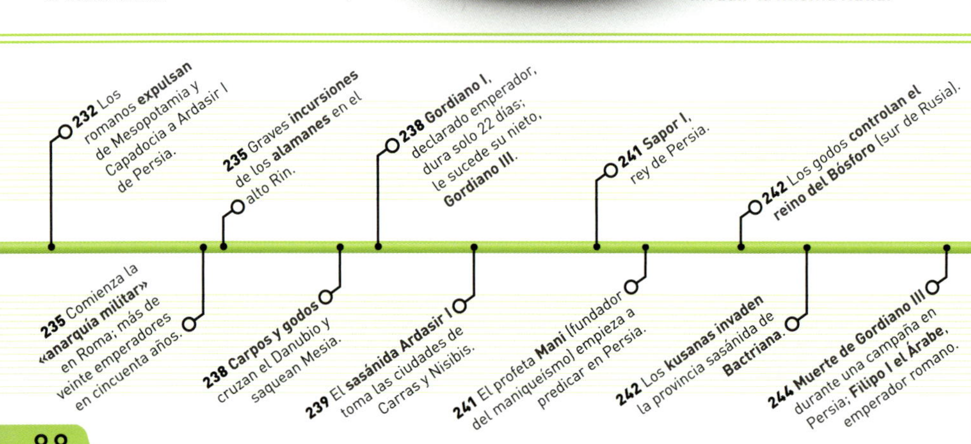

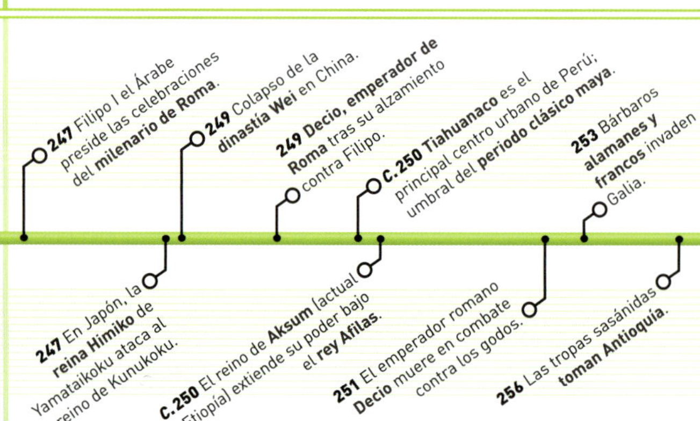

261–275

Columnata principal de Palmira, que obtuvo su riqueza de los aranceles pagados por los mercaderes en tránsito por la ruta del desierto que atravesaba esta ciudad siria.

SAPOR I (m. 272)

Se inició en el liderazgo ayudando a Ardasir I, su padre, a eliminar los apoyos a la dinastía arsácida de los partos. Las victorias logradas sobre Gordiano III (244) y Valeriano (260) supusieron el control temporal de los persas en Siria y Mesopotamia. Usó a los muchos prisioneros romanos capturados en 256 en Antioquía para construir la ciudad de Veh Antiok Shapur («la ciudad de Sapor, mejor que Antioquía»).

sia y pusieron sitio a su ciudad principal, Nicópolis (hoy Nikyup, en Bulgaria). La campaña fue pésima para los romanos: finalizó con su derrota y la muerte de Decio en la **batalla de Abrito** (251).

En el centro de Japón, en la llanura de Nara, surgió *c.* 250 el **reino de Yamato**. Sus soberanos eran enterrados en grandes túmulos y sus ejércitos conquistaron casi todo el Japón central. Gran parte de lo que sabemos de ellos procede de fuentes chinas, que dieron a la reina de Yamataikoku en 238 el nombre de **Himiko**.

LA CAPTURA DE VALERIANO POR LOS PERSAS en 260 resultó desastrosa tanto para la parte occidental como para la oriental del Imperio romano. **Galieno** (r. 260–268), hijo de Valeriano, con problemas para contener una invasión de Italia por los **yutungos** germanos, carecía de recursos para reforzar el *limes* del Rin, horadado por las **incursiones de alamanes y francos**. **Marco Póstumo**, el gobernador de Germania Inferior, se sublevó y mató a Salonio, hijo de Galieno, a quien este había dejado al cargo de Galia y Germania. Póstumo **se declaró emperador** pero, a diferencia de usurpadores anteriores, no marchó hacia Roma, sino que estableció un **Imperio galo** que inicialmente ocupaba Britania, Hispania, Galia y parte del occidente de Germania. Instauró una forma de gobierno que reflejaba la del imperio oficial, incluido su propio senado. Póstumo fue asesinado en 269 por sus tropas y reemplazado por su prefecto del pretorio, Victorino. Galieno –enfrentado a las **invasiones godas** y a la revuelta de **Zenobia de Palmira** en el este– nunca tuvo **poder suficiente** para poner fin al Imperio galo. En 268 fue asesinado por sus hombres y sustituido por Claudio II el Gótico (r. 268–270), que estuvo muy ocupado luchando en los Balcanes como para ocuparse de los galos. Solo con **Aureliano** (r. 270–275) recuperó el Imperio romano poder suficiente, y para entonces el Imperio galo estaba debilitado, con su último rey, Tétrico (r. 271–274), enfrentado a divisiones en el ejército. En 274, Tétrico fue capturado cerca de Duro Catalaunum (Châlons-en-Champagne), y el **Imperio galo fue reabsorbido**.

En el este, después de 260, surgió un **serio desafío al poder romano**: la ciudad de **Palmira** (en Siria) había sido el **único aliado fiable** contra los avances de los persas sasánidas. Su rey, **Septimio Odenato** (*c.* 220–267), recibió diversos títulos romanos, incluido el de *Corrector Totius Orientis* («gobernador de todo Oriente»), e invadió el Imperio sasánida en 262 y 266. Pero murió al año siguiente y su esposa, **Zenobia de Palmira** (r. 267–273), creó un **imperio propio**: en 269, sus ejércitos habían tomado Siria y Egipto, y en 271 nombró emperador a su hijo **Vabalato**. Aureliano marchó al este y no tardó en recuperar las ganancias palmiranas, sitiando Palmira en la primavera de 272. Zenobia fue capturada cuando intentaba escapar, y Palmira fue saqueada en 273, al intentar sacudirse de nuevo el dominio romano.

El Imperio galo
Póstumo instauró su imperio con el control de Galia, Germania, Hispania y Britania. Al hundirse en 274, su último rey, Tétrico, había perdido ya Hispania.

Relieve sepulcral de Palmira
Los palmiranos enterraban a sus muertos en torres funerarias a las afueras de la ciudad, junto con exquisitas y realistas representaciones personales.

En China, **Yuandi** (r. 260–264) recuperó la suerte de Wei al conquistar Shu, pero fue derrocado poco después por uno de sus propios generales, **Sima Yuan**, que fundó la dinastía **Jin Occidental** bajo el nombre de Jin Wudi (r. 265–289). Sus ejércitos asolaron e incorporaron el reino de Wu en 280, con lo que **reunificó brevemente China**.

> **«** EXIGES **MI RENDICIÓN** COMO SI **NO SUPIERAS** QUE **CLEOPATRA** PREFIRIÓ **MORIR COMO REINA** A VIVIR **HUMILLADA**. **»**
>
> **Zenobia,** reina de Palmira, a Aureliano, según la *Historia augusta* (*c.* 375–400)

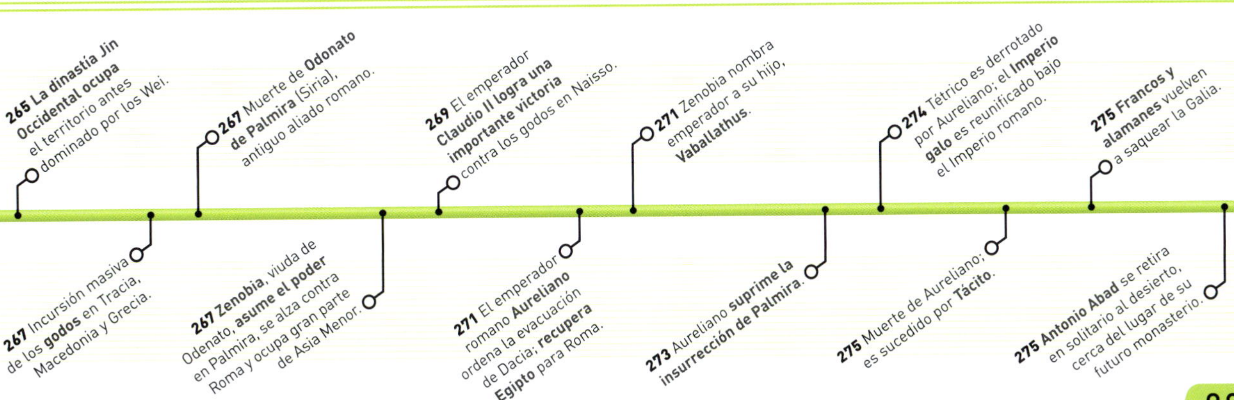

276–283

« **PROBO** FUE CASI UN **SEGUNDO ANÍBAL** POR SU CONOCIMIENTO DEL **ARTE DE LA GUERRA**. »

Aurelius Victor, historiador y político romano, en *Libro de los césares* (*c.* 360)

EN CHINA, EL PRIMER EMPERADOR DE LA DINASTÍA JIN OCCIDENTAL, Wudi (r. 265–289), fue un gobernante enérgico que aseguró las rutas comerciales a Occidente y construyó un puente sobre el río Amarillo para mejorar las comunicaciones. Sin embargo, las **guerras** del **periodo de los Tres Reinos** (*véase* 231–244) habían empobrecido al estado y, a medida que aumentaban los impuestos, muchos campesinos acudieron a los terratenientes en busca de su protección; el resultado fue el auge de los **ejércitos privados**.

En el Imperio romano, Aureliano –asesinado en 275– fue seguido por dos emperadores fugaces, Tácito y Floriano, antes de que Probo asumiera el poder en 276. En dos años, Probo **derrotó a los godos** en el Danubio e **hizo retroceder a los francos** hasta el Rin. Una campaña contra Persia fue frustrada en 281 por el levantamiento de dos usurpadores en Occidente: Bonoso y Próculo. Pese a sus éxitos militares, en 282 **Probo fue asesinado por sus tropas**, resentidas por deber trabajar en proyectos de ingeniería civil en Sirmio (la actual Serbia).

Escultura jin de oso sentado
La primera mitad de la dinastía Jin, bajo Wudi, concedió a China un periodo de cierta paz y estabilidad que permitió el florecimiento del arte.

284–300

La pirámide de la Luna, en Teotihuacán (cerca de Ciudad de México) fue construida en algún momento posterior al año 200 en un extremo de la avenida de los Muertos; junto al extremo opuesto se halla la Ciudadela.

EN 284, LAS TROPAS ROMANAS EN ASIA MENOR PROCLAMARON EMPERADOR A DIOCLECIANO, antiguo comandante de la guardia imperial. En 285, el ya **emperador Diocleciano** (r. 284–305) derrotó a **Carino**, emperador del Imperio occidental, e inició una **reorganización radical del imperio**, reformando el ejército y subdividiendo las provincias. Los desafíos en los *limes* eran demasiado grandes para afrontarlos solo: en 285 nombró a **Maximiano** (250–310) para **gobernar con él**, primero como césar (heredero) y luego como augusto (emperador). Otro problema con la separación de Britania en 286, dirigida por **Carausio**, convenció a Diocleciano de que era necesario introducir más cambios. En 293 nombró, junto a Maximiano, a dos nuevos césares: **Constancio Cloro** (r. 293–306) para ayudarlo en Occidente, y **Galerio** (r. 293–311) para apoyar a Maximiano en Oriente. Esta **tetrarquía** (sistema de cuatro emperadores) consiguió rápidos éxitos militares en Britania (296) y en Egipto (298). En 294, Diocleciano **modificó la moneda**, emitiendo nuevas piezas de bronce y plata, y en 301 promulgó un **edicto sobre los precios máximos** para intentar poner freno a la creciente inflación. A diferencia de otras medidas, esta fracasó.

Friso persa
El friso de Paikuli conmemora las victorias de Narsés en Armenia, así como justifica el derrocamiento de su predecesor, Bahram III.

Tras la muerte de Sapor I en 272, Persia se enfrentó a una **época de inestabilidad política**. En 293 ascendió al trono **Narsés** (r. 293–302). Resuelto a recuperar los territorios perdidos frente a los romanos en Armenia y Mesopotamia, lanzó una gran invasión en 296, y **derrotó** al césar **Galerio** al año siguiente. Pero en 298, Galerio aplastó en Armenia a sus tropas, capturó a su familia y avanzó hasta Ctesifonte, que tomó ese mismo año. Narsés fue obligado a firmar un tratado (**paz de Nisibis**). Persia permaneció en paz con Roma durante cuarenta años.

En el valle de México, la ciudad de **Teotihuacán alcanzó la cima de su poder** en torno a 300. Su calle principal, la calzada de los Muertos, se extendía entre la pirámide de la Luna y la Ciudadela (una gran plaza en torno al templo de Quetzalcoatl), y estaba flanqueada por las residencias de los señores de la ciudad.

30 KILÓMETROS CUADRADOS ERA LA SUPERFICIE DE LA **CIUDAD DE TEOTIHUACÁN** EN SU **APOGEO**

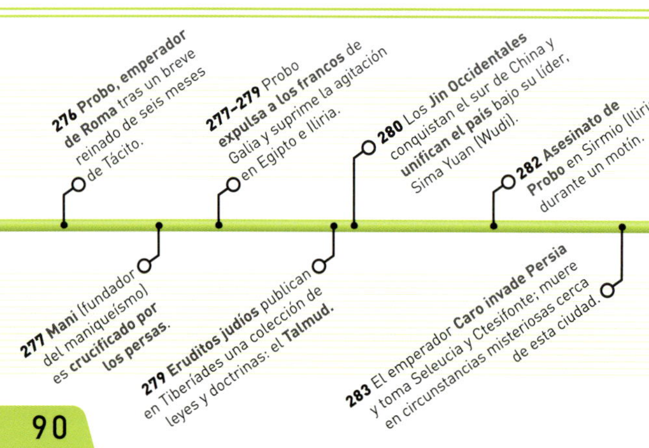

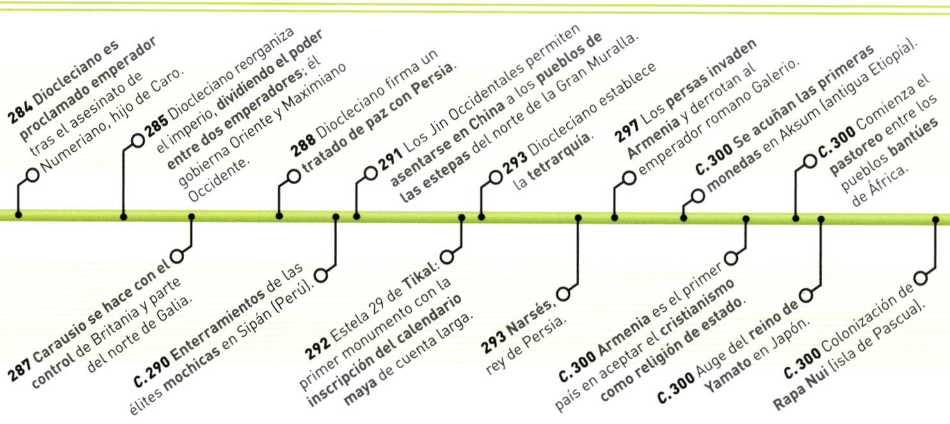

301–319

Este fresco de principios del siglo XVI de la batalla del Puente Milvio está en el palacio apostólico del Vaticano. Se dice que, antes de la batalla, el emperador Constantino vio en sueños un monograma cristiano que predecía su victoria.

DESDE LAS PERSECUCIONES DEL PERIODO 250–260, LA COMUNIDAD CRISTIANA había gozado de unos cuarenta años de tranquilidad en el Imperio romano. Esto cambió en 303, cuando Diocleciano promulgó un **edicto** que ordenaba la **destrucción de las iglesias** y la incautación y **quema de libros cristianos**. A este siguió uno todavía más duro que anunciaba la detención del clero cristiano, y otro en 304 que ordenaba a todos los cristianos ofrecer un sacrificio a los dioses tradicionales. Los cristianos devotos no podían acceder a esa exigencia, y muchos fueron martirizados.

Diocleciano cayó gravemente enfermo en 304, y en 305 anunció que Maximiano y él abdicarían. **Constancio Cloro y Galerio** ascenderían a augustos, y los nuevos césares serían **Maximino y Flavio Severo** (sobrino y compañero de armas de Galieno, respectivamente): la nueva tetrarquía no tardó en deshacerse. **Constancio falleció** en Eboracum (hoy York, en RU) en julio de 306, y sus tropas allí apostadas proclamaron augusto a su hijo **Constantino**. En octubre, **Majencio** (r. 306–312) era coronado emperador en Roma. Severo murió al tratar de arrebatar Roma a Majencio, y Maximiano se restauró a sí mismo como augusto. Para resolver las disputas, en 308 se convocó un encuentro en **Carnuntum** presidido por Diocleciano, que había regresado de su retiro. Constantino aceptó una degradación a césar en Occidente, con **Licinio** (r. 308–324) como augusto, mientras que **Maximino Daya** (r. 310–313) se convertía en el césar de Galerio en Oriente. Este nuevo acuerdo no tuvo más éxito que el anterior.

Galerio murió en 311 y **Maximino, ahora augusto** en Oriente, ordenó **nuevas medidas contra los cristianos**. Mientras, Constantino invadía Italia y, en octubre de 312, derrotaba y mataba a Majencio en la **batalla del Puente Milvio**. Antes de la batalla, se dice que Constantino soñó con el **crismón** (monograma formado por las letras griegas *ji* y *ro*, primeras del nombre de Cristo) y que ordenó a sus tropas marcar con él sus escudos.

Licinio y Constantino se encontraron en Mediolanum (actual Milán) en 313; acordaron compartir el poder y firmaron el **edicto de Milán**, que garantizaba la tolerancia para todos los cultos y legalizaba de hecho **el cristianismo**. Luego Licinio marchó al este y derrotó a Daya, asegurando el control de las provincias orientales. La alianza con Constantino se rompió en 316, aunque al año siguiente acordaron una paz que mantuvo el imperio relativamente estable durante seis años.

En China, la incapacidad mental de **Huidi de Jin** (r. 290–306), sucesor de Wudi, propició que una sucesión de regentes compitieran por el control imperial. El hermano de Wudi, **Huadi** (r. 307–311), invitó a los **xiongnu del norte** a ayudarlo contra las facciones competidoras, pero estos le hicieron prisionero. **Mindi** (r. 313–316), **último emperador de los Jin Occidentales**, fue testigo del saqueo de la capital Chang'an (actual Xi'an) por los xiongnu. Los Jin se desplazaron al sur, donde **Yuandi** (r. 317–323) se convirtió en el **primer emperador de los Jin Orientales** en 317.

75 000
MAJENCIO

50 000
CONSTANTINO

Batalla del Puente Milvio
Las fuerzas de Majencio superaban a las de Constantino, pero su ejército quedó atrapado entre los hombres de Constantino y el río.

Palacio de Diocleciano
Diocleciano construyó el palacio de Spalato (hoy Split, Croacia) para retirarse tras su abdicación en 305. Aquí cuidaba de sus coles.

Monograma de Cristo (crismón)
Compuesto por las primeras dos letras del nombre de Cristo en griego (ji y ro), fue un importante símbolo del cristianismo primitivo.

Difusión temprana del cristianismo
El cristianismo se extendió en los siglos II–III hasta tener comunidades sólidas en Anatolia, sur de Galia, Italia, Egipto y la provincia de África (Túnez).

CLAVE
Zonas con fuerte presencia cristiana en 325

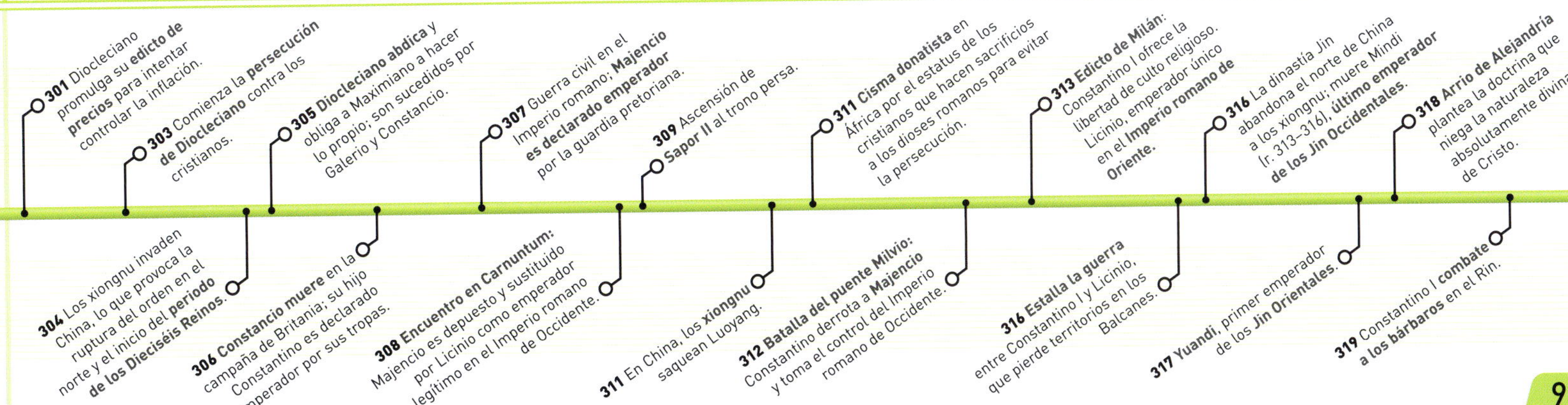

320–330

Casi todos los líderes reunidos en el concilio de Nicea (en la imagen) pertenecían a la Iglesia oriental; solo ocho obispos occidentales viajaron hasta allí.

EN 320 CHANDRAGUPTA I ASCENDIÓ AL TRONO de un pequeño reino en la llanura occidental del Ganges. Gracias a un **ventajoso matrimonio** con la princesa Kumaradevi, de la dinastía Licchachevi, y a las conquistas, **expandió su territorio** hasta incluir gran parte del Ganges central, desde Magadha (en Bihar) en el sur, hasta Prayaga (en Uttar Pradesh). Sus descendientes, los guptas, reinarían en el norte de India casi 150 años.

Columna de Constantino
El único monumento superviviente del foro de Constantino, construido para su nueva ciudad, es esta columna ubicada en el centro de Estambul.

Tras abrazar la **causa del cristianismo** en 313, el emperador Constantino I (r. 306–337) se encontró con que los propios cristianos estaban lejos de la unión **doctrinal u organizativa**. Por ello, en 325 convocó un **concilio** de la Iglesia en **Nicea** (Asia Menor) para establecer (e imponer) la ortodoxia ante la división producida por el arrianismo (la teología de Arrio, que mantenía que Cristo no era Dios, sino que estaba subordinado a Él). Unos trescientos líderes de la Iglesia acudieron a la llamada de Constantino, y la postura de Arrio fue condenada.

14
NÚMERO DE **BARRIOS** DE CONSTANTINOPLA

Una vez que **Licinio** (r. 308–324) fue **derrotado** en 324, Constantino **fundó una nueva capital** para el Imperio romano de Oriente en la antigua ciudad de **Bizancio**, situada entre Europa y Asia. Derribó templos paganos, construyó iglesias como Santa Sofía, y erigió edificios públicos que rivalizaban con los de Roma. La ciudad de **Constantinopla** (actual Estambul) fue inaugurada públicamente el 11 de mayo de 330. Sería la sede de los emperadores orientales durante más de mil años.

331–355

« EN OTROS HOMBRES… EL GUSTO POR LAS **MATANZAS** PIERDE **FUERZA** A VECES… EN **CONSTANCIO** SE HIZO MÁS **VIOLENTO**. »

Amiano Marcelino (m. c. 330) describe el carácter del emperador Constancio II en su *Historias*

8
TIPOS DE **MONEDAS** DE **ORO PURO** EMITIDAS POR **SAMUDRAGUPTA**

SAMUDRAGUPTA (R. 335–375) SUCEDIÓ A SU PADRE, Chandragupta I, como señor de los dominios gupta en el norte de India en 335. En Prayaga perdura una inscripción de su época en que se relatan las **campañas militares** que llevó a cabo en **Uttar Pradesh y Mathura**, territorios ambos incorporados al Imperio gupta. También realizó conquistas en la costa oriental de India, llegando a **Madrás**; sometió **Bengala oriental** y partes del **Rajastán** y el **Punjab**. Otras varias regiones reconocieron su soberanía, con lo que se convirtió en el gobernante **más poderoso de India** desde el Imperio Maurya.

El emperador Constantino I murió en 337, aceptando el bautismo tan solo en su lecho de muerte. No había dejado previsión definitiva alguna para su **sucesión**, por lo que sus tres hijos se repartieron el imperio: **Constantino II** (r. 337–340) obtuvo Hispania, Galia y Britania; **Constante** (r. 337–350), Italia y África; y **Constancio II** (r. 337–361) se quedó Oriente. Estos reinados se iniciaron con una **masacre en Constantinopla**, en la que casi todos los demás familiares varones de su padre fueron asesinados para eliminar cualquier posible rival. Constantino II, el hijo mayor, intentó afirmar su jerarquía de edad, pero **falleció durante una invasión de Italia** en 340. Entonces, Constante tomó el control de todo el Imperio occidental, donde tuvo que hacer frente a una serie de duras campañas para frenar la **invasión de Galia por los francos**, además de a problemas en **Britania** que le hicieron visitar la lejana provincia en 343; de hecho, sería el último emperador romano indiscutido en hacerlo.

Las disputas entre Constante y Constancio, en particular una sobre la situación de **Atanasio, obispo de Alejandría** (a quien Constancio había exiliado y Constante deseaba reponer), cercenaron toda relación entre ambos hermanos.

Moneda gupta de oro
Muchas monedas guptas portaban imágenes de caballos: una posible referencia a los sacrificios equinos realizados por algunos gobernantes.

En 350, un militar de alto rango, **Magnencio**, se sublevó en Augustodunum, en el sur de Galia (actualmente Autun, en Francia), y **Constante fue asesinado**. Distraído por la guerra contra Persia, Constancio II toleró inicialmente al usurpador; sin embargo, en el año 351 avanzó contra él. Puesto que Constancio II carecía de heredero, promovió a césar a su primo Constancio **Galo** –uno de los pocos supervivientes de la masacre de 337– y lo dejó **al mando en Oriente** mientras él combatía a Magnencio en Occidente. El ejército de Magnencio fue **derrotado en Mursa** (en la actual Croacia); Italia y África fueron recuperadas rápidamente, y **Magnencio se quitó la vida** en Galia en 353.

Durante los siete años siguientes, **Constancio gobernó el imperio en solitario**, preocupado principalmente por las incursiones francas en Galia, la sublevación del usurpador Silvano en 355 y una **serie de concilios cristianos** que buscaban resolver disputas doctrinales (Constancio II favoreció al arrianismo sobre la ortodoxia tradicional).

Finalmente, Galo se mostró ambicioso en exceso, y en 354 fue **depuesto y ejecutado**. Constancio II se volvió entonces hacia el hermano de Galo, **Juliano**, un joven estudioso con cierta inclinación hacia la filosofía pagana. En 355, después de la revuelta de Silvano, **Juliano fue enviado como césar a Galia**, donde demostró una sorprendente efectividad a la hora de combatir las incursiones de los francos.

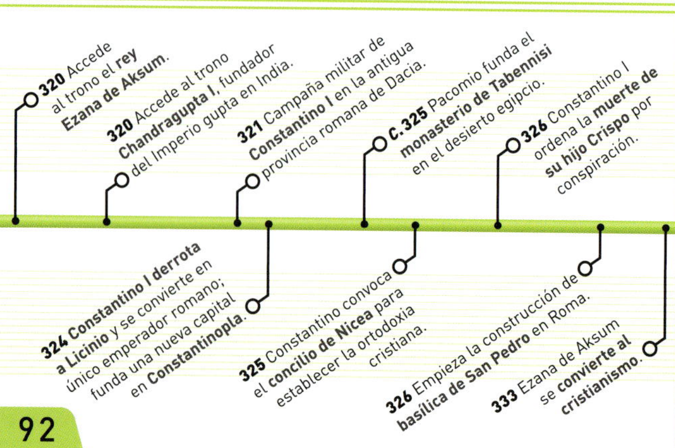

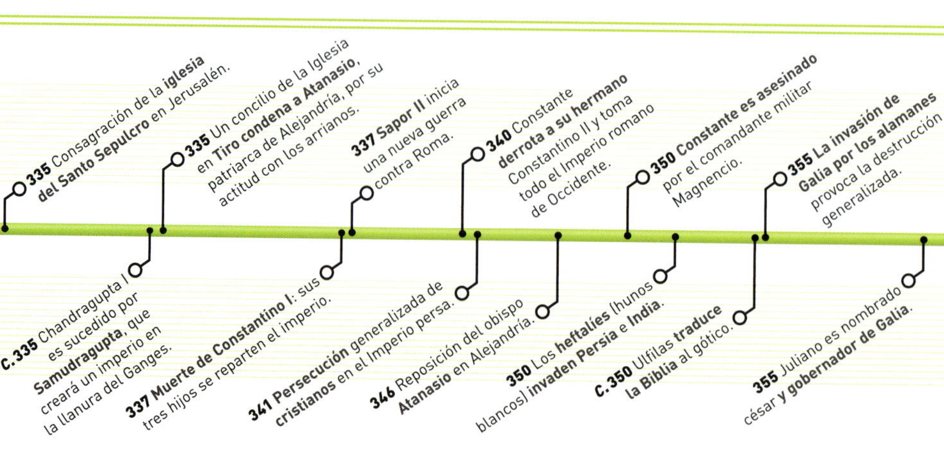

Acrópolis de Tikal: uno de los mayores conjuntos de ruinas supervivientes del mundo maya.

EL REINO DE AKSUM, EN ETIOPÍA, fue uno de los primeros estados en abrazar el **cristianismo** fuera del Imperio romano. El misionero sirio Frumencio convirtió al rey Ezana (r. 320–360) al monofisismo (una doctrina que sostiene una única naturaleza en Cristo, la divina). Ha llegado hasta nosotros una carta de Constantino II a Ezana **en que le urge a cambiar su devoción al arrianismo** y a reemplazar a Frumencio por un obispo arriano, lo cual demuestra la importancia que los emperadores romanos concedían a las lealtades religiosas de sus vecinos. Ezana llevó a cabo campañas militares más allá de sus fronteras: una inscripción da cuenta de sus expediciones contra los colindantes «Gaze, luego Agame y Siguene», y parece que sus tropas pudieron ocupar la **ciudad de Meroe** (en el norte de Sudán). Enriquecido por las conquistas y por el control de las rutas comerciales del África subsahariana y Arabia, **Aksum dominaría la región** hasta el siglo VII.

Los **reinos mayas del periodo preclásico** en Guatemala y México se derrumbaron en algún momento entre los años 200 y 300: sus poblaciones declinaron y cesó la actividad constructora. Sin embargo, la región no tardó en recuperarse con la emergencia de una **nueva fase** de la civilización maya, el periodo clásico (300–900), durante el cual **surgieron una serie de poderosos reinos**. Sus grandes centros urbanos, como los de Tikal (Guatemala) y Palenque (México), se caracterizan por sus **inmensos templos piramidales y sus complejos palaciales** ubicados en una «acrópolis» central. Los mayas desarrollaron un tipo de escritura **jeroglífica** que sobrevive en muchas de las **estelas** (bloques tallados de piedra) que erigieron para conmemorar acontecimientos importantes; la más antigua datada en Tikal procede de 292, y el primer rey nombrado allí es **Siyaj Chan K'awiil I** (c. 305). En el reinado de Chak Tok Ich'aak I (r. 360–378) Tikal ya era, con mucho, la **ciudad más grande y poderosa** del periodo clásico maya.

Sapor II cazando un ciervo
Los señores sasánidas encargaron suntuosas piezas de plata que los mostraban cazando animales salvajes como demostración de su poder real.

El **Imperio romano** se enfrentó a invasiones bárbaras en los *limes* occidentales y orientales durante las décadas de 340 y 350. En el oeste, **los francos** empezaron a presionar a través del Rin, y a principios de la década de 350 superaron parte del *limes* y ocuparon algunas antiguas fortalezas romanas. El **césar Juliano** se embarcó en una serie de **campañas contra los francos** (356–359) y consiguió expulsarlos de buena parte del territorio ocupado. En el este, el **conflicto** entre romanos y persas volvió a estallar cuando **Sapor II** (r. 309–379), aprovechando la agitación política de esa década en el Imperio romano, avanzó en dirección oeste en 359 y **tomó la gran fortaleza romana de Amida** (en la actual Diyarbakir, en Turquía). También ocupó otras ciudades, cuyas poblaciones fueron deportadas a Persia, poniendo de esta manera en peligro la posición romana en Oriente.

16
KILÓMETROS CUADRADOS SUPERFICIE DE LA CIUDAD DE TIKAL *c.* 400

CLAVE
- Mayas del norte
- Mayas del centro
- Mayas del sur
- Asentamiento
- Ruta comercial

Golfo de México
MAYAS DEL NORTE
Península de Yucatán
MAYAS DEL CENTRO
Palenque
Tikal
Petén
Mar Caribe
MAYAS DEL SUR
OCÉANO PACÍFICO

Reinos mayas
La cultura clásica maya surgió en ciudades de tierras bajas, como Uaxactun y Tikal, pero se propagó a las tierras altas y a la península de Yucatán.

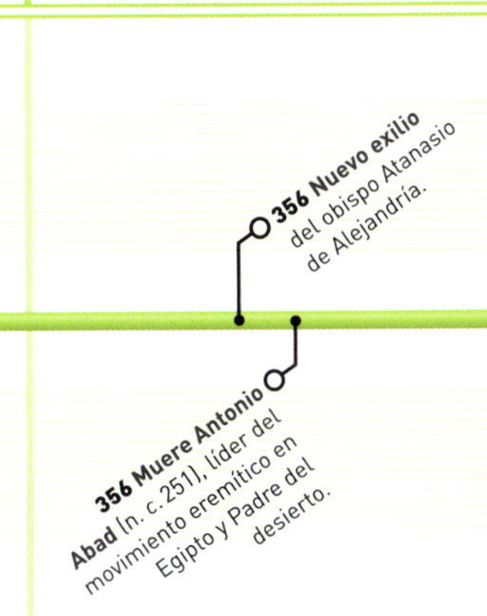

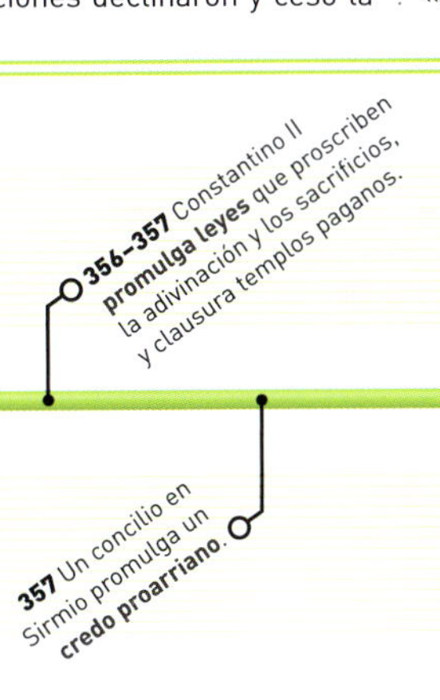

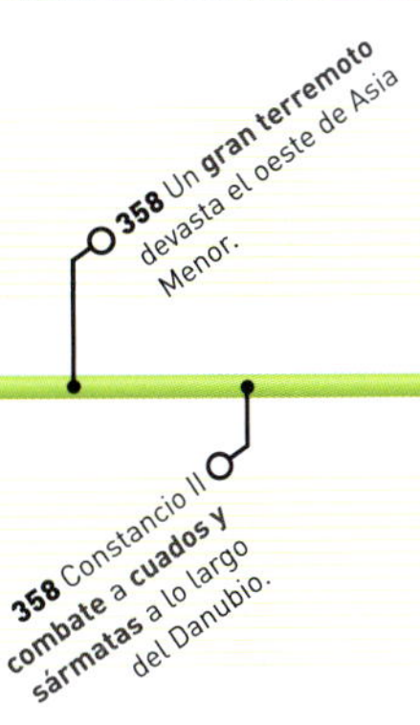

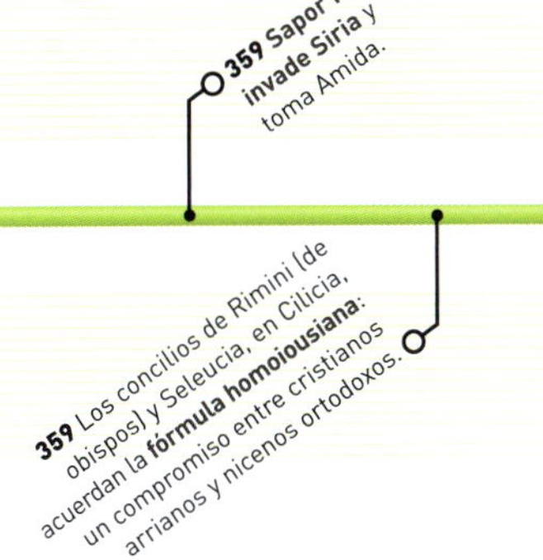

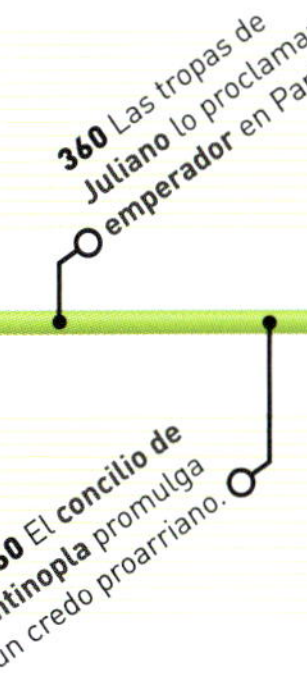

361–375

Pintura que muestra al emperador Juliano en un debate religioso. Intentó crear discordia entre los cristianos decretando el regreso de los que habían sido exiliados por razones religiosas.

EN CHINA, LA DINASTÍA JIN ORIENTAL (317–420) llevó cierta estabilidad al sur del país. Aunque muchos de sus emperadores fueron efímeros, la burocracia en la capital meridional de Nankín funcionaba de forma eficiente y el periodo contempló un **florecimiento cultural**. Entre otros, sobresale el artista Gu Kaizhi (*c.* 345–406), que pintó obras maestras como *Admoniciones de las institutrices del palacio de las Damas*, además de dejar escritos sobre teoría de la pintura. Por el contrario, el **norte de China** sufría una **alta inestabilidad**, dividido entre los Dieciséis Reinos, la mayoría de los cuales eran gobernados por **grupos nómadas**. Los emperadores de los Jin Orientales alternaron entre una postura defensiva frente al norte y campañas agresivas, en especial bajo Mudi (r. 345–361), que retomó Sichuan y Luoyang. Sin embargo, todas estas ganancias serían perdidas por Aidi (r. 362–365). En 383, y bajo Xiaowudi, los Jin se vieron obligados a repeler una gran invasión en el norte del país.

16 REINOS EXISTENTES EN **CHINA** ENTRE **304** Y **439**

En el Imperio romano, **Juliano** fue proclamado **augusto** por sus tropas en 360, por lo que se convirtió en un desafío directo para Constancio II; con todo, la amenaza de los persas, que avanzaban en Asia Menor, era demasiado grande para ignorarla. **Constancio murió** en noviembre de 361, cuando finalmente marchaba hacia Occidente para enfrentarse a la insurrección. Juliano, en este momento emperador único, se aplicó inmediatamente a **restaurar el papel de la religión tradicional** del imperio, intentando establecer una especie de ortodoxia pagana y una jerarquía oficial de sacerdotes para contrarrestar la fortaleza cristiana. Reabrió los antiguos templos y **restableció el derecho a realizar sacrificios**.

Juliano emprendió una **campaña militar contra Persia** en 363 con la que pretendía castigar a Sapor II por sus ataques de 359–360. Llegó a las puertas de Ctesifonte, pero allí fue obligado a retroceder hasta el río Tigris. Escaso de provisiones, el ejército romano sufrió el hostigamiento constante de los persas y, en una de las escaramuzas, **Juliano perdió la vida**: la reacción pagana había terminado.

A la muerte de Juliano, las tropas eligieron emperador a **Joviano** (r. 363–364), pero su cesión a Persia de provincias fronterizas clave le hizo perder popularidad, y murió (asesinado, probablemente) al cabo de unos meses. Entonces fue elevado al trono **Valentiniano** (r. 364–375), un oficial de la guardia imperial, y él a su vez eligió a su hermano **Valente** (r. 364–378) como **corregente**. Valentiniano I pasó gran parte de su reinado repeliendo a los invasores francos y alamanes en el *limes* del Rin. Murió en 375 después de sufrir algún tipo de ataque provocado por su cólera tras una violenta reunión con los enviados cuados.

El Imperio romano de Occidente fue subdividido entonces entre los dos hijos de Valentiniano, **Graciano** (r. 375–383) y **Valentiniano II** (r. 375–392). En el Imperio de Oriente, Valente se vio obligado a pasar casi toda la década de 370 en Siria, conteniendo la amenaza persa; pero más adelante los crecientes problemas con los bárbaros en la línea del Danubio le harían regresar a los Balcanes.

JULIANO EL APÓSTATA (331–363)

Sobrino de Constantino I, Juliano fue educado como cristiano, pero *c.* 351 abrazó el paganismo bajo la influencia de Máximo de Éfeso. Cuando se convirtió en emperador en 363, intentó restaurar el paganismo. Entre otras medidas, prohibió a los cristianos la enseñanza de literatura; por su aparente traición al cristianismo, Juliano empezó a ser conocido como «el Apóstata» entre los autores cristianos.

Daga sármata
La daga de la imagen es de origen sármata, un pueblo de origen iranio que se especializó en el combate a caballo y que fue derrotado por Valentiniano I.

376–382

Constantino I construyó la iglesia de Santa Irene en Constantinopla.

« LOS **BÁRBAROS** [SON] COMO BESTIAS… **LIBERADAS**… SOBRE LA **VASTA EXTENSIÓN**… DEL **PAÍS**. »

Amiano Marcelino, sobre la invasión goda de los Balcanes (*c.* 390)

GRANDES GRUPOS DE GODOS LLEGARON EN 376 AL *LIMES* DEL DANUBIO, que presionaron para ser admitidos en el imperio. Justo detrás venían los **hunos**, un nuevo pueblo nómada de Asia central, y los godos temían verse atrapados entre ellos y la frontera imperial. El emperador Valente no esperó refuerzos, y salió al encuentro del ejército godo, al mando de Fritigerno. **Romanos y godos se encontraron** finalmente el 9 de agosto de 378. Engañado por la ausencia temporal de la caballería goda, Valente atacó; sin embargo, sus tropas se vieron rodeadas por los jinetes bárbaros de regreso, y Valente resultó muerto, y el **ejército oriental quedó destruido**, dejando los Balcanes abiertos a los godos.

Graciano reaccionó acudiendo a **Teodosio**, un comandante hispano al que nombró coaugusto de Oriente. Durante los tres años siguientes, Teodosio negoció con paciencia, sobornó a algunos grupos y golpeó militarmente cuando pudo. En 382, ambos bandos acordaron una tregua según la cual se **per-**

362 Juliano inicia su campaña para **reponer el culto pagano** en el Imperio romano.

363 Juliano **muere cerca de Ctesifonte**.

363 Joviano entrega territorio a los persas.

364 Muere Joviano: **Valentiniano I y Valente**, emperadores.

368 **Invasión a gran escala** de Britania por pictos, escotos y sajones; son derrotados por el comandante Teodosio.

368 Las campañas contra los alamanes finalizan con la **victoria romana**.

369 El rey sasánida **Sapor II** ocupa Armenia.

c. 370 Fuerzas invasoras japonesas establecen una **colonia en Mimana** (sur de Corea).

c. 370 Los **hunos** empiezan a **invadir** el este de Europa.

373 El general romano **Teodosio** aplasta una insurrección en Mauritania.

373 Martín de Tours establece una de las primeras **comunidades monásticas** de Europa occidental.

373 **Fu Jian**, señor de Qin Anterior (uno de los Dieciséis Reinos), ocupa Sichuan, Yunnan y partes de Guizhou.

375 **Valentiniano muere inesperadamente** mientras negocia con embajadores de los cuados.

c. 375 Muerte de Samudragupta; es sucedido por Chandragupta II. El **Imperio gupta controla ahora** el norte y centro de India.

376 **Fu Jian**, de Qin Anterior, **extiende su control** a Asia central.

376 Los **godos** piden a **Valente** que les permita instalarse en el Imperio romano.

378 Los **godos derrotan** al emperador Valente en **Adrianópolis**.

379 Yax Nuun Ayiin, **señor de Tikal**.

mitía a los godos establecerse en el imperio a cambio de proporcionar tropas al ejército romano.

El **Imperio gupta continuó expandiéndose** en el norte de India bajo Chandragupta II (r. 375–415), quien arrebató buena parte del noroeste a los sakas. También estableció una **astuta alianza matrimonial** mediante la cual sus dominios se vieron ampliados hacia el suroeste.

Pilar de hierro en Delhi
Se dice que este pilar de hierro del complejo de Qutb, a las afueras de Delhi, pudo ser erigido por orden de Chandragupta II.

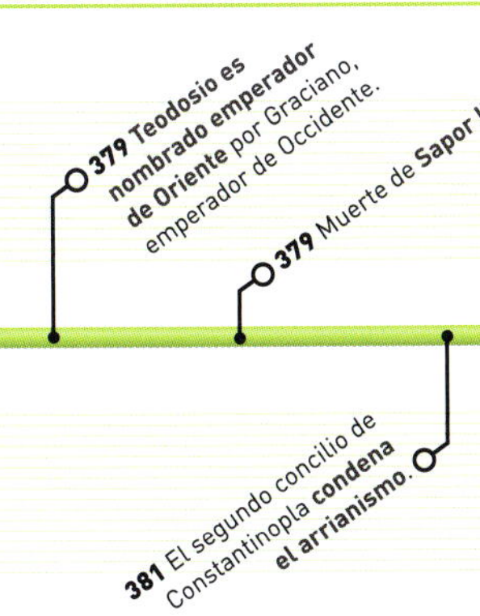

383–391

San Jerónimo (*c.* 347–420) completó la *Vulgata*, primera traducción definitiva de la Biblia al latín, *c.* 405.

EN AMÉRICA CENTRAL, LA CIUDAD MAYA DE TIKAL había alcanzado la cima de su influencia a finales del siglo IV. En 378 llegó a la ciudad, posiblemente desde Teotihuacán, un señor extranjero llamado **Siyaj Kak**. Su llegada, que pudo representar una conquista militar, conllevó la muerte del **gobernante de Tikal**, Chak Tok Ich'aak, y la **destrucción** de gran parte de los **monumentos públicos**. Siyaj Kak instauró una nueva dinastía en el trono de Tikal, posiblemente dirigida desde la casa regente de Teotihuacán, con **Yax Nuun Ayiin I** («Hocico enrollado»: r. 379–404) como primer rey. Los monumentos lo representan con ropajes más típicos del centro de México que propiamente mayas. Bajo su reinado, la influencia directa de Tikal se extendió a unos 50 km de distancia.

En el Imperio romano de Occidente, **Graciano** había pasado gran parte del tiempo posterior a la batalla de Adrianópolis (378) en el norte de Italia, donde **siguió actuando contra los paganos** de Roma, ordenando, en 382, la retirada del Altar de la Victoria de la puerta del senado. En 383 dirigió un ejército al norte para hacer frente a la invasión de Galia por los alamanes, pero luego tuvo que enfrentarse con una **insurrección en Britania**, cuyas legiones proclamaron **emperador a Magno Máximo**, su comandante. Muchos de los jefes militares de Graciano desertaron, y en agosto fue capturado y ejecutado por Máximo, que había cruzado a Galia. **Teodosio**, preocupado por los problemas con Persia o por una posible revuelta goda en los Balcanes si él se desplazaba al oeste, **reconoció a Máximo** como coaugusto. Sin embargo, una paz firmada con Persia en 386 le dejó las manos libres cuando Máximo invadió Italia al año siguiente. En agosto de 388, Teodosio se desplazó velozmente al norte de Italia, **capturando a Máximo** cerca de Aquilea y ordenando su ejecución.

Aparte de las campañas contra los godos y Máximo, Teodosio estaba ocupado con la **imposición de la ortodoxia cristiana**. Actuó contra los arrianos deponiendo al obispo de Constantinopla en 380, y en 381 convocó un concilio en la capital que reafirmó las decisiones antiarrianas tomadas en el concilio de Nicea (*véase* 320–330). Consintió la **destrucción de muchos templos paganos**, entre ellos el de Serapis en Alejandría, y en 391 **prohibió todo sacrifico pagano** en el imperio.

San Ambrosio
Noble romano por nacimiento, Ambrosio fue obispo de Milán entre 374 y 397. Ejerció una poderosa influencia sobre Teodosio I.

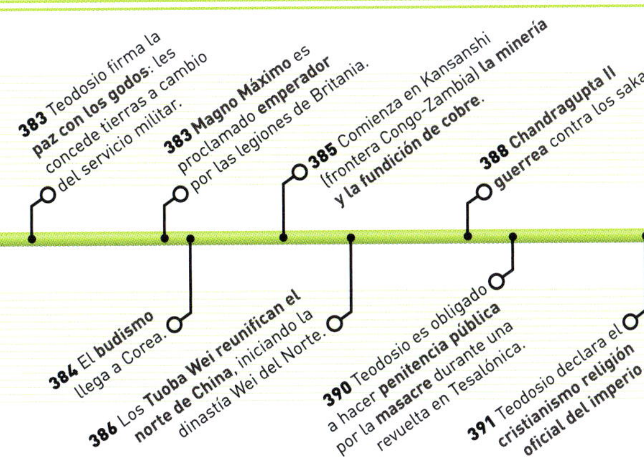

392–400

« CUANTO MÁS **ESPESO** ES EL **HENO**, MÁS **FÁCIL** ES **SEGARLO**. **»**

Alarico I, refiriéndose a sus enemigos (*c.* 400)

EN 392, VALENTINIANO II, QUE HABÍA SEGUIDO REINANDO SOBRE ITALIA, fue encontrado ahorcado. Su comandante Arbogastes –sospechoso del asesinato para algunos– se apresuró a proclamar emperador a **Flavio Eugenio**, un oficial de rango medio. Teodosio se negó a reconocerlo, por lo que en 393 **invadió Italia**. Para ganarse apoyos en el senado, donde el paganismo aún tenía fuerza, el cristiano Flavio Eugenio **revocó** todas las **leyes antipaganas** de Teodosio; pero en agosto de 394 fue derrotado por las tropas de este en el río Frígido, cerca de Aquilea. Teodosio no disfrutó demasiado de su mandato como emperador único, pues murió en enero de 395. El imperio fue dividido entre sus dos hijos: el mayor, Arcadio, tomó la *pars orientalis*, y el pequeño Honorio se quedó la *pars occidentalis*. Aunque la razón de este reparto no está clara, lo cierto es que marcó una división permanente: después de 395, ningún emperador volvería a reinar sobre el imperio completo.

Los godos habían participado junto a Teodosio en la batalla del Frígido, y consideraban que no habían sido suficientemente recompensados por su pérdidas. En 395 se sublevaron, dirigidos por **Alarico** (r. 395–410). A pesar del intento de eliminarlos por parte de **Estilicón** (*c.* 365–408), comandante del ejército occidental de origen vándalo, los godos escaparon y durante el año siguiente ejercieron el pillaje por toda Grecia. Estilicón volvió a avanzar contra Alarico en 397, pero fracasó una vez más. El **desenfreno godo solo tuvo una breve pausa** cuando el gobierno romano oriental nombró a Alarico ***magister militum*** (general en jefe).

Partido en dos
La división en 395 del Imperio romano en Oriente y Occidente fue definitiva. En 476, la parte occidental ya había sido invadida por los bárbaros.

CLAVE
Imperio romano de Oriente
Imperio romano de Occidente

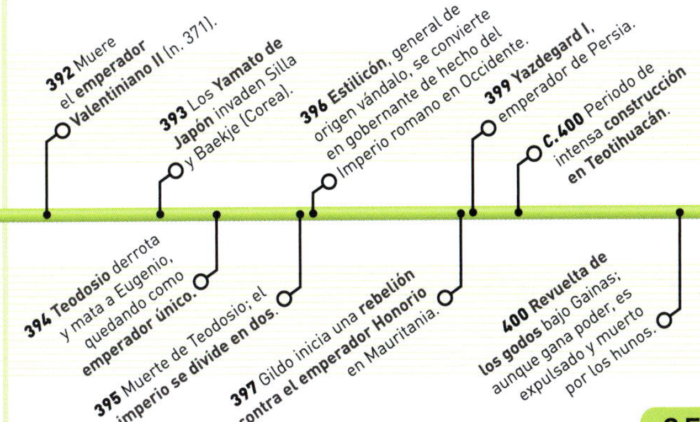

COMERCIO CLÁSICO

FLORECIMIENTO DEL COMERCIO ENTRE CONTINENTES

El crecimiento del poder romano en el Mediterráneo, la unificación de China bajo las dinastías Qin y Han, y el asentamiento del Imperio parto en Irán crearon tres grandes bloques políticos que proporcionaron condiciones estables para el florecimiento de rutas comerciales de muy larga distancia.

La expansión del poder de los Han hacia Occidente en el siglo II a.C. puso a China en contacto con nuevas potencias que ellos llamaron An-hsi (Persia) y Li-chien (Roma). Una embajada china llegó a la corte de Mitrídates II de Partia *c.* 115 a.C. Tras los diplomáticos llegaron los mercaderes, portadores de seda china, por la que tanto Partia como Roma sentían un apetito insaciable. La principal Ruta de la Seda partía de China, atravesaba Asia central, se internaba en Persia y llegaba a los puertos del Mediterráneo a través de Siria, controlada por Roma.

También por el océano Índico se expandió una próspera Ruta de las Especias desde las Indias Orientales y el sur de India hasta puertos de África y del sur de Arabia; desde allí, una ruta terrestre llevaba las mercancías, a través de Petra (actual Jordania) hasta Siria. El control de estas rutas era muy lucrativo, y las ciudades que cruzaban podían imponer fuertes peajes a los comerciantes, usados en la construcción de espectaculares monumentos públicos.

Más al oeste, en el Mediterráneo, artículos de lujo como los vinos de calidad eran transportados por mar; en general, el transporte terrestre resultaba caro y voluminoso: los productos de menor valor eran, por lo general, producidos y consumidos de forma local.

13 000 KILÓMETROS
LONGITUD DE LA RUTA COMERCIAL ENTRE **CHANG'AN** Y **ROMA**

EL COMERCIO ROMANO

La expansión del Imperio romano hasta cubrir la mayor parte de Europa, Asia occidental y norte de África creó condiciones en gran parte pacíficas en las que pudo prosperar tanto el comercio interior como el exterior.

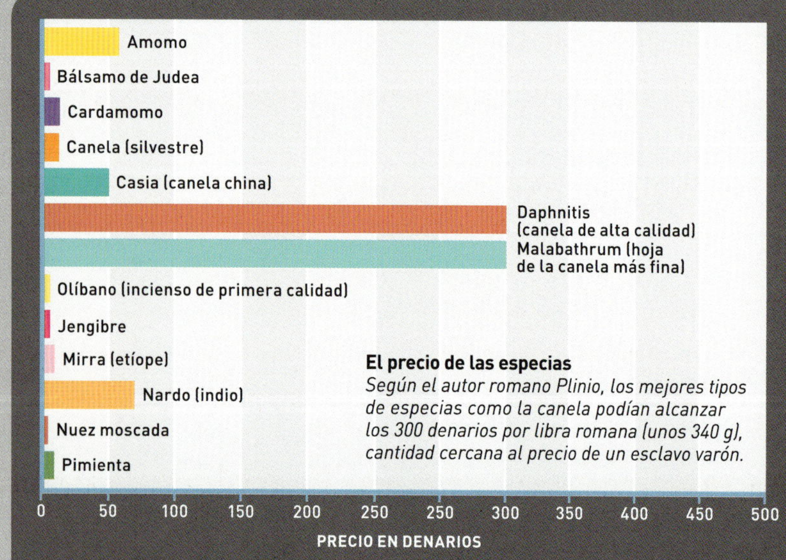

El precio de las especias
Según el autor romano Plinio, los mejores tipos de especias como la canela podían alcanzar los 300 denarios por libra romana (unos 340 g), cantidad cercana al precio de un esclavo varón.

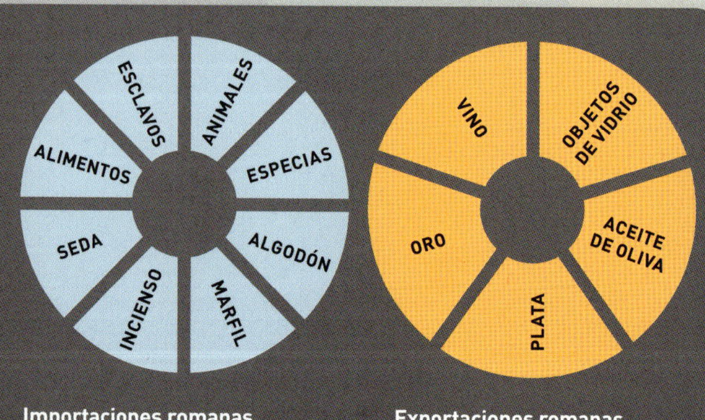

Importaciones romanas
Los romanos importaban cantidades inmensas de materias primas, entre ellas artículos de lujo como oro y marfil, y bienes más baratos, como comida.

Exportaciones romanas
Los romanos pagaban sus importaciones con metales preciosos y moneda, y exportaban productos como vino y cristalería.

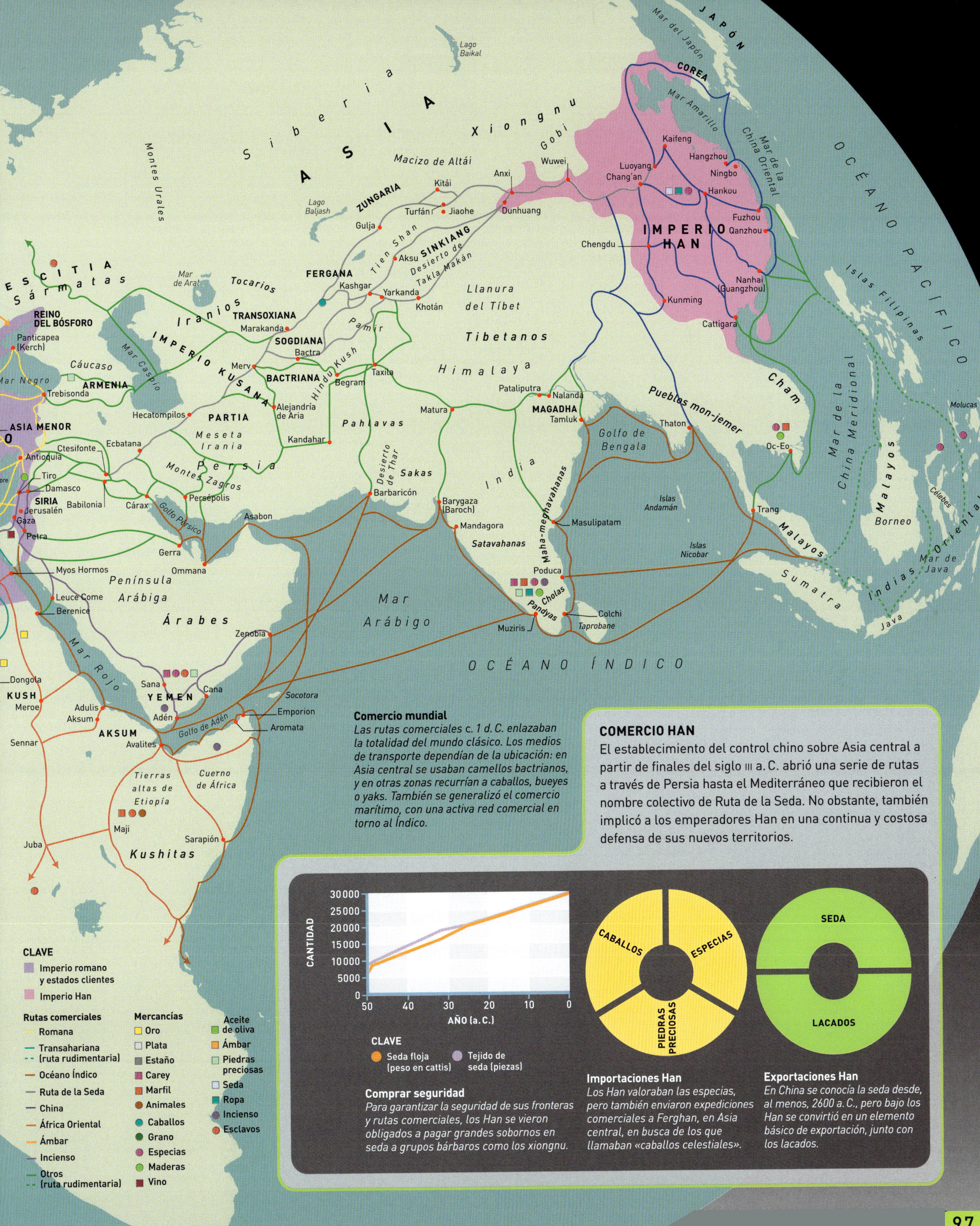

Comercio mundial
Las rutas comerciales c. 1 d. C. enlazaban la totalidad del mundo clásico. Los medios de transporte dependían de la ubicación: en Asia central se usaban camellos bactrianos, y en otras zonas recurrían a caballos, bueyes o yaks. También se generalizó el comercio marítimo, con una activa red comercial en torno al Índico.

COMERCIO HAN

El establecimiento del control chino sobre Asia central a partir de finales del siglo III a. C. abrió una serie de rutas a través de Persia hasta el Mediterráneo que recibieron el nombre colectivo de Ruta de la Seda. No obstante, también implicó a los emperadores Han en una continua y costosa defensa de sus nuevos territorios.

Comprar seguridad
Para garantizar la seguridad de sus fronteras y rutas comerciales, los Han se vieron obligados a pagar grandes sobornos en seda a grupos bárbaros como los xiongnu.

Importaciones Han
Los Han valoraban las especias, pero también enviaron expediciones comerciales a Ferghan, en Asia central, en busca de los que llamaban «caballos celestiales».

Exportaciones Han
En China se conocía la seda desde, al menos, 2600 a. C., pero bajo los Han se convirtió en un elemento básico de exportación, junto con los lacados.

401–423

El templo semisubterráneo de Tiahuanaco está decorado con unas doscientas cabezas de piedra. Pueden representar al grupo que fundó la ciudad: sus tocados planos indican un alto estatus.

A PESAR DE QUE EL IMPERIO ROMANO OCCIDENTAL PARECÍA RELATIVAMENTE SEGURO EN 400, en los diez años siguientes sufrió una serie de catástrofes. Las incursiones godas asolaron el norte de Italia en 401 y 405; en el último día de 406, **hordas de vándalos**, unidos a otros dos grupos bárbaros, **alanos** y **suevos**, cruzaron el Rin helado cerca de Mogontiacum (Maguncia, en Alemania), saquearon Augusta Treverorum (Tréveris) y Reims (en Francia), y se abrieron paso hacia el suroeste hasta alcanzar los Pirineos.

Mientras tanto, las **tropas de Britania** habían elevado a emperador a **varios usurpadores** desde 406. El último de estos, Constantino III (r. 407–411), agrupó a gran parte de las tropas romanas restantes en Britania y **cruzó a Galia** en la primavera de 407 con la idea de arrebatar el trono al entonces emperador de Occidente, Honorio. Aunque fue derrotado y capturado en Arles en 411, los líderes nativos ya habían **expulsado de Britania a los últimos oficiales romanos** en 410, probablemente en venganza por la retirada de las legiones de Constantino. **Britania** era en este momento **independiente de Roma**.

Los visigodos toman Roma
El saqueo de Roma por parte de Alarico (410) fue especialmente traumático: era la primera caída de la ciudad desde que los galos la ocuparan en 390 a. C.

En 408, **Alarico I** (r. *c.* 395–410), rey de los **visigodos**, **invadió Italia** una vez más. El comandante romano Estilicón convenció al senado para **pagar a Alarico un enorme rescate** a cambio de respetar Roma, pero, al parecer, se produjo un golpe de estado: Estilicón fue derrocado y ejecutado. En 409, Alarico declaró emperador al prefecto de la ciudad, Prisco Atalo, en un intento de tomar la iniciativa, pero las negociaciones fracasaron. De esta manera, el 24 de agosto de 410, los **visigodos entraron en Roma** y la sometieron a un intenso **saqueo durante tres días**. El suceso conmocionó a todo el mundo romano; sin embargo, Alarico fue incapaz de asegurar el dominio sobre Italia, ya que falleció ese mismo año.

En América del Sur, la ciudad de **Tiahuanaco**, 25 km al sur del lago Titicaca (en la frontera entre los actuales Perú y Bolivia), **alcanzó su mayor tamaño** durante el siglo v, cubriendo una superficie de unos 8 km². Su zona central contenía abundantes **construcciones y templos ceremoniales**, entre ellas el templo semisubterráneo de **Kalasasaya**, decorado con cabezas de piedra de seres humanos y sobrenaturales; o la inmensa y bellamente decorada **puerta del Sol**. Estas fueron erigidas por una importante cultura precolombina que **dominó el Altiplano** de Perú y Bolivia, y cuya influencia se extendió al norte de Bolivia.

Pimienta
Oro
Plata
0 | 10 000 | 20 000 | 30 000 | 40 000
LIBRAS

Rescate exigido
Al principio, Alarico pidió un inmenso rescate por respetar Roma en 410. Aunque después moderó sus exigencias, estas fueron rechazadas por el senado, y la ciudad fue saqueada.

424–433

« ASÍ, LOS VÁNDALOS, HABIENDO ARREBATADO LIBIA A LOS ROMANOS, LA HICIERON SUYA. »

Procopio, historiador bizantino, de su *Historia de las guerras III*, IV-1

LOS BÁRBAROS, QUE HABÍAN CRUZADO EL RIN EN 406, iban a saquear distintas ciudades antes de internarse en Aquitania, al suroeste, para cruzar los Pirineos y a continuación pasar a Hispania, donde **ocuparon grandes franjas de territorio romano**. Entre los años 416–418, el comandante romano Constantino convenció al **rey visigodo Valia** (r. 415–418) para invadir Hispania, donde derrotó a los alanos y a los vándalos silingos, aunque permitió que algunos de ellos se asentaran en el sur y dejó a los vándalos asdingos y a los suevos en posesión del noroeste. Valia fue recompensado con la posesión oficial de gran parte del suroeste de Hispania.

Más al sur, **Bonifacio**, gobernador romano de la provincia de África en 429, se levantó contra su eterno rival, **Aecio**, y pidió ayuda a los vándalos silingos. El **rey vándalo Genserico** (r. 428–477) cruzó el estrecho de Gibraltar con (según se dice) ochenta mil de los suyos. Pero no prestó ayuda a Bonifacio; en lugar de ello, ocupó rápidamente el norte de África y, en 435, firmó un tratado con Roma por el que se reconocía su **ocupación de Mauritania** (actuales Argelia y Marruecos). Genserico rompería el acuerdo en el año 439: sus tropas **ocuparon Cartago**, capital romana de la provincia, y establecieron un **reino vándalo independiente**.

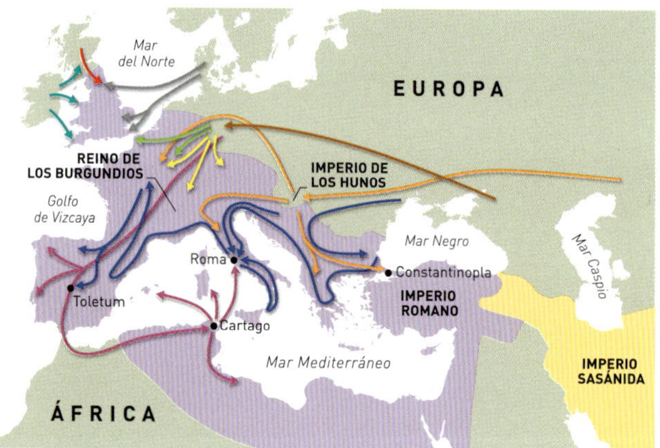

Las invasiones bárbaras
En la primera mitad del siglo v, los grupos de bárbaros ocuparon cada vez más territorio romano, dejando a los emperadores de Occidente impotentes prácticamente.

CLAVE
- Imperio romano
- Imperio sasánida
- Hunos
- Godos
- Alanos
- Vándalos, alanos y suevos
- Burgundios
- Francos
- Jutos, anglos y sajones
- Irlandeses
- Pictos

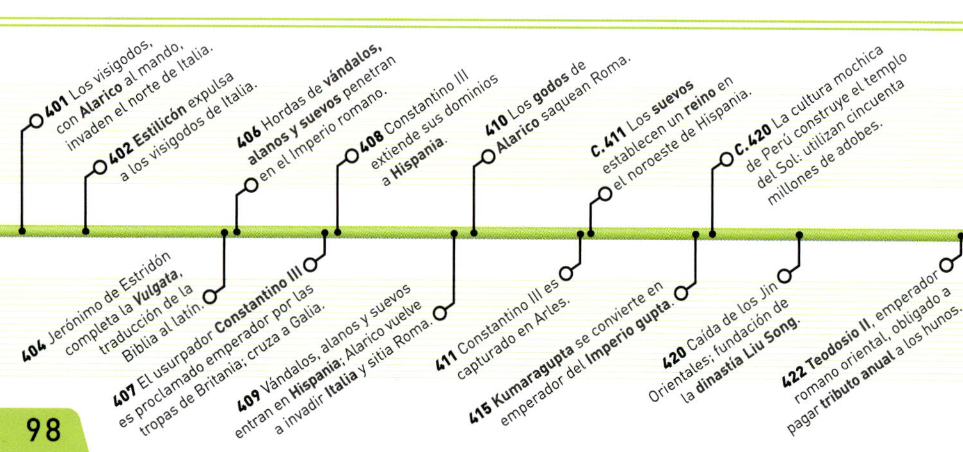

401 Los visigodos, con **Alarico** al mando, invaden el norte de Italia.

402 Estilicón expulsa a los visigodos de Italia.

404 Jerónimo de Estridón completa la **Vulgata**, traducción de la Biblia al latín.

406 Hordas de **vándalos, alanos y suevos** penetran en el Imperio romano.

407 El usurpador **Constantino III** es proclamado emperador por las tropas de Britania; cruza a Galia.

408 Constantino III extiende sus dominios a **Hispania**.

409 Vándalos, alanos y suevos entran en **Hispania**; Alarico vuelve a invadir **Italia** y sitia Roma.

410 Los **godos** de **Alarico** saquean Roma.

411 Constantino III es capturado en Arles.

C. 411 Los **suevos** establecen un **reino** en el noroeste de Hispania.

415 Kumaragupta se convierte en emperador del **Imperio gupta**.

C. 420 La cultura mochica de Perú construye el templo del Sol: utilizan cincuenta millones de adobes.

420 Caída de los Jin Orientales; fundación de la **dinastía Liu Song**.

422 Teodosio II, emperador romano oriental, obligado a pagar **tributo anual** a los hunos.

424 Aecio invade Italia con un ejército de hunos con la intención de apoyar al **usurpador Juan**.

425 Juan es derrotado; **Valentiniano III**, emperador de Occidente.

428 Nestorio, patriarca de Constantinopla, **predica una nueva doctrina** que distingue las naturalezas humana y divina de Cristo: es condenada como herética.

429 Los **vándalos cruzan el estrecho de Gibraltar** hacia el norte de África.

429 El obispo **Germán de Auxerre** visita Britania con la misión de erradicar el pelagianismo.

429–431 La pugna entre **Bonifacio y Aecio** por el control de la corte romana acaba en la muerte de Bonifacio.

C. 431 El papa **Celestino I** envía una misión a **Irlanda** con Paladio.

433 Atila, rey de los hunos.

Colorido mural budista de las grutas de Yungang, iniciadas bajo la dinastía Wei del Norte *c.* 450.

LA DINASTÍA JIN ORIENTAL DE CHINA ACABÓ EN 420 con la abdicación de Gondi; su sucesor, Song Wudi (r. 420–422), un antiguo pescador, ascendió hasta convertirse en general y **fundó la dinastía Liu Song**. Aunque reforzó la frontera septentrional del reino sureño contra las tribus bárbaras, bajo su hijo Wendi (r. 424–453) los norteños ocuparon Luoyang (424) y, unos 25 años después, **asediaron Nankín**, capital de Liu Song. A pesar de que Song Wudi había fortalecido la burocracia central, el creciente poder y riqueza de los **monasterios budistas y taoístas** debilitó las bases económicas del estado. Los sucesores de Wendi fueron débiles, y en 479 los Liu Song fueron derrocados por la efímera **dinastía Qi del Sur** (479–502).

Entre tanto, en el norte de China los **Dieciséis Reinos** habían sido unificados bajo los toba de Wei (un grupo de nómadas turcos), que fundaron la **dinastía Wei del Norte** (386–534). Esta dinastía reinó en China septentrional hasta que se escindió en dos a principios del siglo VI, tras una rebelión contra la imposición del idioma y el vestuario chinos a los nómadas de Wei.

En Europa, el Imperio romano de Occidente seguía perdiendo territorio a manos de los bárbaros. En la década de 420, los **visigodos**, al mando de **Teodorico I** (r. 418–451), ocuparon sectores de la costa mediterránea de Galia antes de ser rechazados hacia el suroeste en 430. Sobre esta época empezó a amenazar al imperio un nuevo grupo de bárbaros: los **hunos**. Estos nómadas de Asia central, cuya presión sobre la retaguardia de los godos había sido causa indirecta de la crisis del año 378 en los Balcanes, habían avanzado desde ese momento hacia el oeste. En 424, el general romano **Aecio reclutó una fuerza de hunos** para apoyar la causa de Juan, un usurpador alzado en Roma tras la muerte de Honorio en 423. Aecio siguió utilizando a los hunos hasta el final de la década para asegurarse una zona de influencia y la designación como patricio (el más alto cargo en el Imperio romano tardío) en 429. **En 435** aún recurrió a ellos para **atacar a los burgundios**, que se habían internado en el bajo Rin; estos fueron derrotados y confinados a una región en el noroeste de Italia.

Todo ello, sin embargo, no fueron sino éxitos temporales, pues la **zona controlada** por los emperadores romanos occidentales **disminuía de forma constante**: entre los años 429 y 439 perdían casi todo el norte de África, y en 440, Sicilia (a manos de los vándalos); pasado 418, el suroeste de Galia (visigodos); para 450, el norte (francos); y en la década de 430, toda Hispania excepto unos pocos puestos avanzados aislados. Esto se tradujo en que los restantes baluartes romanos en Italia y el sureste de Galia **no podían proporcionar ingresos tributarios** suficientes para mantener ejércitos que reconquistaran las provincias perdidas. El largo reinado de **Valentiniano III** (r. 425–455) en el Imperio romano de Occidente **no proporcionó estabilidad alguna**, pues ascendió al trono de niño y nunca logró imponerse; ni siquiera al final, cuando hizo **asesinar a Aecio**, el último general eficaz del imperio en Occidente.

Caballo de Wei del Norte
El arte de los Wei del Norte evocaba a menudo su origen nómada, como en este hermoso caballo de terracota.

« EL **MUNDO PERECE**… ENVEJECE Y **SE AGOTA** CON LA **FATIGA DE LA SENECTUD**. »

Agustín de Hipona, teólogo y filósofo, en *Sermones*, 81, 8

Los **bárbaros** que se asentaban en los antiguos territorios romanos empezaron gradualmente a **establecer reinos propios**; en especial, los francos en el norte de Galia, y los visigodos en el suroeste y en Hispania. En **Britania** la situación era **bastante distinta**, pues la provincia se había rebelado contra Roma y no había sido objeto de conquista por los bárbaros. En épocas anteriores, podría haberse esperado que el ejército romano reafirmara su control; sin embargo, con el imperio cada vez más dependiente de tropas bárbaras que luchaban bajo sus propios comandantes, no quedaba en realidad un ejército que retomara la provincia, por lo que los britanos fueron dejados a su suerte. Parece ser que algunas instituciones sobrevivieron un tiempo: en 429, el obispo Germán de Auxerre visitó la isla y se encontró con hombres que ostentaban títulos romanos. Pero los **asaltantes bárbaros** –atraídos por la debilidad de las defensas britanas y por la ausencia de una autoridad política centralizada que los contrarrestara– **empezaron a llegar en número creciente**. Hacia 446, los hombres principales de Britania dirigieron una carta a Aecio pidiendo su ayuda. No hubo respuesta al grito de ayuda de los britanos, y, al cabo de pocos años, los **invasores anglos, sajones y jutos** empezaron a ocupar partes de la antigua provincia romana.

FLAVIO AECIO
(*c.* 395–454)

Nacido entre la nobleza de Mesia (actual Bulgaria), desde 408 pasó un tiempo en la corte de los hunos. Usó estos contactos para ganar influencia y ascender a los cargos más altos a finales de la década de 420. La muerte de los patricios Félix (430) y Bonifacio (433) le dio un control sin oposición. Apuntaló la posición del imperio y, en 451, logró una gran victoria contra Atila. En 454 fue asesinado por Valentiniano III en persona.

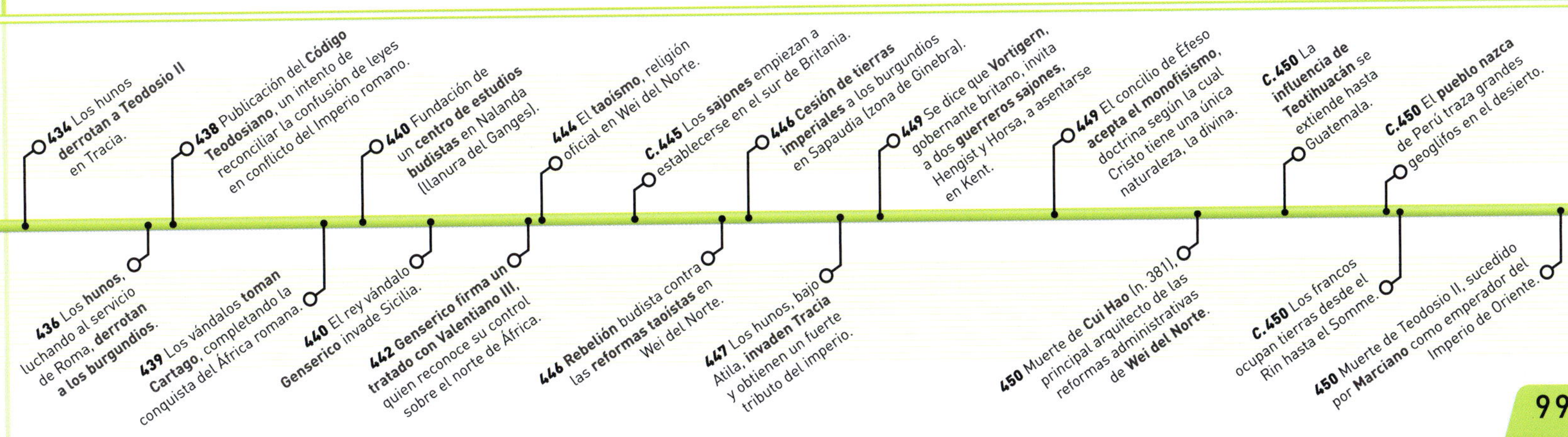

451–465

Pintura no datada que muestra a Atila, rey de los hunos, con su ejército. Según la tradición, se abstuvo de saquear Roma por la súplica del papa León I.

« [LOS HUNOS] **ASALTARON** LAS **IGLESIAS** Y **DEGOLLARON** A **MONJES** Y **DONCELLAS**. **»**

Calínico, discípulo de Hipacio de Bitinia, en su *Vida de Hipacio* (*c.* 450)

EN JAPÓN, EL SIGLO V FUE ÉPOCA DE RÁPIDO DESARROLLO y expansión del **reino de Yamato**. Empezaron a aparecer complejos sistemas de riego, y sus reyes construyeron túmulos funerarios aún mayores, como el de Nintoku, de 486 m de largo. El emperador **Ojin** fundó un nuevo linaje de reyes que ejercieron un control más firme todavía sobre las principales islas de Japón desde su corte en la región Kawachi-Izumi. Los contactos de Yamato con el exterior se ampliaron: entre 421 y 478 enviaron diez misiones diplomáticas a China, y también aumentó su injerencia en las guerras civiles entre los reinos coreanos de Baekje, Silla y Goguryeo.

El papa León I
La ilustración de este manuscrito muestra al papa León I, aristócrata italiano, convenciendo a Atila para que no ataque Roma.

A finales del siglo v, el **Imperio sasánida persa** fue hostigado por grupos de nómadas orientales. Los **hunos heftalíes** ya habían penetrado ese siglo en Bactriana, y fueron una amenaza particular para los sasánidas; pero una hambruna durante el **reinado de Peroz I (457–484)** les hizo volver al oeste. Peroz sufrió una terrible derrota a manos de los heftalíes en 469; capturado, solo fue liberado tras dejar a su hijo como rehén. En 484 buscó venganza lanzando una nueva campaña contra los hunos, que volvieron a derrotarlo y lo mataron.

En 450, **Atila, rey de los hunos** (*véase* 434–450), pidió en matrimonio a Honoria, hermana del emperador romano Valentiniano III. Ante la negativa de este, Atila marchó sobre Galia. Fue derrotado cerca de Châlons-en-Champagne (Campos Cataláunicos) por un ejército combinado de romanos, dirigido por Aecio, y godos al mando de Teodorico. Impávido, invadió Italia en 452, aunque retrocedió en las cercanías de Roma. Atila murió tras su banquete nupcial en 453, y sus hijos iniciaron una guerra civil que conduciría a la destrucción del imperio de los hunos.

Figurilla de oso de arcilla
Las figuras de arcilla haniwa *fueron típicas de los ricos enterramientos en Japón desde tiempos antiguos. Los grandes túmulos de los reyes de Yamato contienen enormes cantidades de ellas.*

Tras el asesinato del general romano Aecio en 454, el **poder real en el Imperio romano de Occidente** fue ejercido por una serie de entronizadores bárbaros como **Ricimero**, líder del ejército romano en Italia. En 457, Ricimero puso en el trono a **Mayoriano**; cuando este empezó a tomar decisiones propias, lo sustituyó por **Libio Severo** (r. 461–465), quien más tarde murió envenenado. Privado de liderazgo efectivo, el imperio perdió aún más territorios en Galia a manos de **visigodos y francos**.

466–500

Bautismo de Clodoveo I: el bautismo convirtió a Clodoveo en un socio diplomático más cómodo para el Imperio romano de Oriente que sus vecinos arrianos.

EN 456, LOS VISIGODOS, alentados por el emperador occidental Avito, habían invadido la península Ibérica. El rey visigodo **Teodorico II** (r. 453–466) derrotó al suevo **Requiario**, que había amenazado la provincia romana de Tarraconensis, y el resto de los suevos se retiraron. Teodorico tomó la mayor parte de Hispania para sí, pero dejó cierto control romano en la costa oriental. Esta política fue revocada por su sucesor **Eurico** (r. 466–484), que invadió los restos de territorios romanos en la década de 470. El reino visigodo durante el reinado de **Alarico II** (r. 487–507) ocupaba casi toda Hispania, así como Aquitania y la Provenza, en el sur de Galia. Esta situación se repitió en otras partes del Imperio romano, y la zona bajo control imperial se redujo a poco más que Italia. **Antemio** (r. 467–472) trató de recuperar terreno, pero una fuerza enviada contra los vándalos del norte de África en 468 acabó en desastre. En el sur de Galia, Eurico había conquistado casi todo el resto del imperio para 475. En 472, Antemio fue destronado por el burgundio **Gundebaldo**, quien colocó en el trono, en rápida sucesión, a **Olibrio** (r. 472) y a **Glicerio** (r. 473–474); pero, desesperado por la fragilidad del imperio, regresó a Burgundia. Los últimos rescoldos del imperio fueron disputados en 475–476 entre **Julio Nepote** y **Rómulo Augústulo**, hijo del general romano **Orestes**. Considerando que los intereses de los bárbaros germanos en el ejército estaban siendo ignorados, su lu-

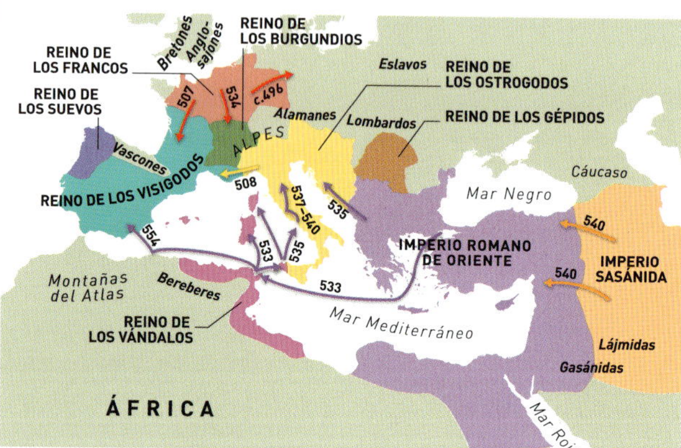

Reinos bárbaros en Europa *c.* **500**
En el año 500, la mayor parte del antiguo Imperio romano de Occidente estaba dividida entre varios estados bárbaros sucesores: vándalos en el norte de África, visigodos en Hispania y sur de Galia, y ostrogodos en Italia.

CLAVE
- Reconquistas bizantinas
- Expansión franca
- Expansión ostrogoda
- Expansión sasánida

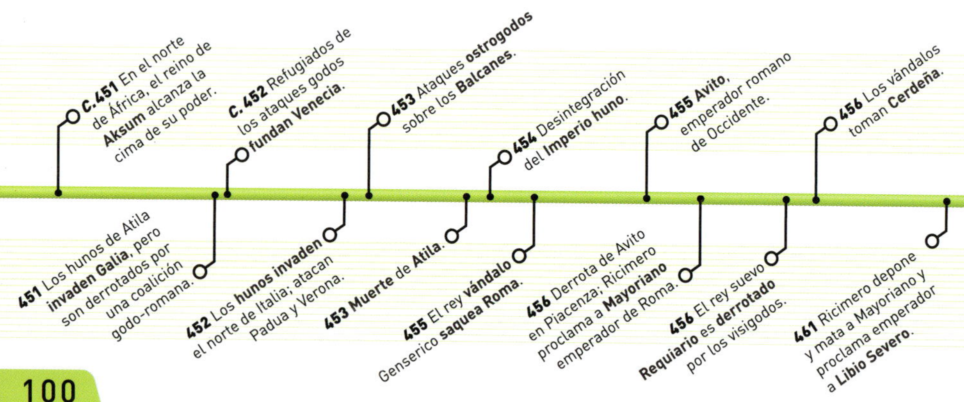

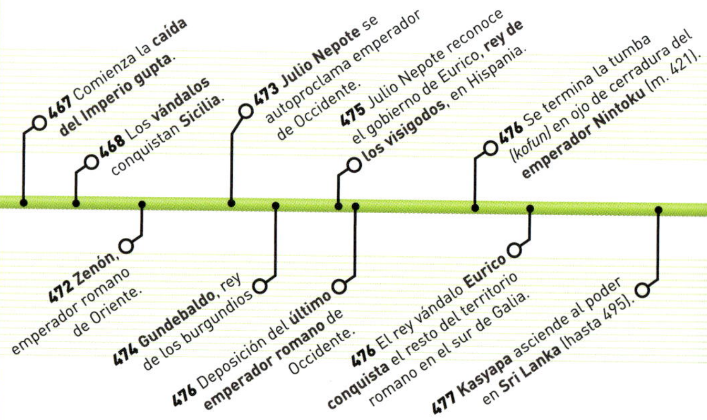

garteniente **Odoacro** se rebeló y depuso a Rómulo en 476. No proclamó un nuevo emperador, sino que declaró que él reinaría en Italia en nombre de **Zenón** (r. 474–491), emperador de Oriente. Este momento marcaría el fin del Imperio romano de Occidente después de quinientos años.

Sin embargo, el Imperio romano sobrevivió en el este. El largo reinado de **Teodosio II** (r. 408–450) había fortalecido su posición y, al cabo de cuatrocientos años, el imperio no había tenido que afrontar amenazas tan directas como las de hunos, godos, vándalos, alamanes, burgundios y francos en Occidente. **Marciano** (r. 450–457) consiguió consolidar las finanzas, dejando a su muerte un superávit de cien mil libras de oro. **León I** (r. 457–474) rechazó la amenaza residual de los godos en los Balcanes, e incluso llevó a cabo un intento por recuperar el norte de África en 468. **Zenón** (r. 474–491) se enfrentó al desafío de los nuevos señores germanos de Italia, dirigidos por Odoacro: lo resolvió encargando a **Teodorico el Grande**, rey de los ostrogodos, el derrocamiento de Odoacro en 489. Para el año 500, el Imperio romano de Oriente, regido por **Anastasio I** (r. 492–518), estaba lejos del peligro de implosión que había borrado a su vecino occidental apenas un cuarto de siglo antes.

El Imperio romano de Occidente fue reemplazado por una serie de **estados germánicos** sucesores. Odoacro ejercía como rey de Italia, pero su legitimidad siempre fue cuestionada. En el año 489, una invasión del ostrogodo Teodorico condujo a un punto muerto de cuatro años, en que Odoacro se protegió aislándose en la capital imperial, Ravena. Teodorico consiguió matarlo en 493, y estableció a continuación un régimen de continuidad de las prácticas administrativas romanas que le granjeó la lealtad de la vieja aristocracia. En 497, el emperador oriental **Anastasio I** reconoció su derecho para gobernar Italia, proporcionándole de esta manera una base segura para consolidar su gobierno y extenderlo a Galia.

Los francos habían aparecido como una amenaza en el noroeste de Galia en el siglo IV, y para la década de 460 se habían labrado un reino propio bajo **Childerico I**. Su sucesor, **Clodoveo I** (r. 481–511), transformó ese reino al lograr derrotar a **Siagrio**, señor del enclave romano de Augusta Suessonum, y extenderlo a lo largo del Rin a costa de los alamanes en la década de 490. En 507 derrotó a los visigodos en la **batalla de Vouillé** y los expulsó de gran parte del suroeste de Galia. A finales de la década de 490 o principio de siglo, **Clodoveo se convirtió** al catolicismo, diferenciándose con ello del resto de los señores bárbaros, en su mayoría arrianos.

Por otro lado, en **Britania**, la expulsión de los oficiales romanos había ido seguida por un periodo en que pequeños reinos rivalizaban por el poder. Estos reinos eran vulnerables a las incursiones por mar y, a finales del siglo V, grupos de bárbaros germanos (**anglos, sajones y jutos**) se establecieron en Britania. La llegada de los sajones ha sido datada en 449, cuando fueron invitados por el señor britano Vortigern. Siete años después se alzaban y establecían un reino en Kent. **Aelle** fundó un reino en **Sussex** *c.* 477; y **Cerdic** lo hizo en **Wessex** (actual Hampshire) *c.* 495. Una victoria britana en Mons Badonicus en torno al año 500 contuvo la marea sajona un tiempo, pero el intervalo fue efímero.

TEODORICO EL GRANDE
(454–526)

Hijo del rey ostrogodo Teodomiro, Teodorico pasó once años como rehén en Roma para garantizar el buen comportamiento de su padre. De regreso a casa fue nombrado rey en 471, y durante los diecisiete años siguientes alternó la alianza con los romanos y los ataques contra sus territorios en los Balcanes. En 493 se convirtió en el primer rey ostrogodo de Italia. Su reinado fue en general pro romano. Fue enterrado en este mausoleo.

Broche sajón
El arte anglosajón del siglo V estimaba los patrones geométricos abstractos, como se aprecia en este prendedor.

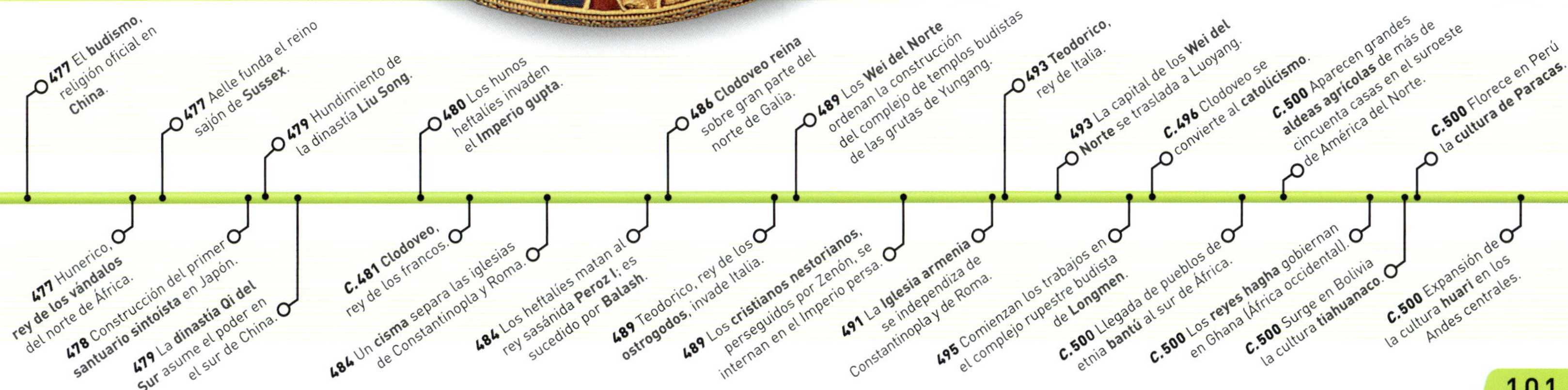

501–526

Paneles de marfil del siglo VI que muestran al emperador Anastasio I. Amasó un inmenso superávit económico que sus sucesores invirtieron en la expansión del Imperio romano de Oriente.

EN EL IMPERIO ROMANO DE ORIENTE (generalmente llamado bizantino a partir de esta fecha), **Anastasio I** (r. 491–518) se enfrentó a dificultades en los Balcanes cuando nuevos grupos, entre ellos los **protobúlgaros**, presionaron hacia el sur a lo largo del Danubio entre 493 y 502. Más graves aún fueron los **problemas en la frontera oriental**, donde los **persas** insistían en exigir una recompensa económica a Bizancio por defender los pasos estratégicos del Cáucaso contra las incursiones bárbaras. En 502, el **rey persa Kavad I** inició una guerra por ello. La lenta reacción bizantina permitió que tomara Amida y varias ciudades más en Armenia. Las fuerzas bizantinas recuperaron Amida en 505, y Kavad –preocupado con la invasión heftalí en el este– acordó una tregua que duró hasta 527.

Anastasio tenía casi sesenta años cuando ascendió al trono en 491, y solo consiguió asegurar su puesto al casarse al año siguiente con Ariadna, la viuda de **Zenón**, su predecesor. Casi de inmediato, **Longino**, hermano de Zenón, se rebeló y a Atanasio le costó seis años someter la región de su hogar natal, en **Isauria** (en el occidente de Asia Menor). Anastasio ganó popularidad aboliendo el **chrysargyron**, un impuesto a los comerciantes y artesanos.

La prosperidad continuó, y a lo largo de su reinado el tesoro acumuló un superávit de 320 000 libras de oro. También impulsó reformas monetarias, en 498 y 512, dirigidas a estabilizar la moneda, que había sufrido devaluaciones sucesivas a lo largo del siglo V. En el aspecto religioso, el reinado de Anastasio no fue tan tranquilo, ya que él era seguidor del **cristianismo monofisita**, el cual mantenía que la única naturaleza de Cristo era la divina, y que esta nunca se combinó en él con la naturaleza humana. En principio, apoyó el **Henotikon** de Zenón, un edicto promulgado en 482 que intentaba mediar entre los partidarios del credo ortodoxo (establecido en el concilio de Calcedonia en 452) y los monofisitas. Sin embargo, más adelante su actitud se hizo más promonofisita, lo que condujo a graves disturbios en 512 y a la rebelión de Vitaliano, un oficial del ejército en Tracia, en 513.

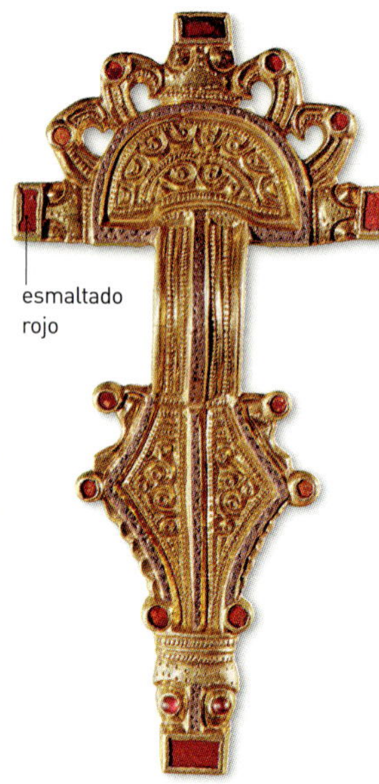

Fíbula franca
Las fíbulas, broches usados para unir prendas, eran prácticas a la vez que decorativas. Esta está adornada con cabezas de aves.

Anastasio no dejó un heredero claro, y a su muerte se hizo con el trono **Justino** (r. 518–527), comandante de la guardia de palacio. Justino I era de origen humilde, y dependía de su sobrino **Justiniano** en gran medida. Restauró el **cristianismo calcedonio** y estableció buenas relaciones con los **ostrogodos** de Italia y con los **vándalos** del norte de África. En el exterior, su reinado fue pacífico en general, a excepción de una campaña menor contra Persia a principios del año 527.

En Galia, **Clodoveo I, rey de los francos**, había derrotado a Siagrio, señor del enclave romano de Soissons, en 486, y luego a alamanes y turingios en 491. Su siguiente objetivo fue el **reino visigodo** del suroeste de Galia, que se hundió tras una victoria franca en Vouillé en 507. Su matrimonio con Clotilde, hermana del rey burgundio Chilperico II, lo llevó a convertirse al **catolicismo** en la década de 490, y a mantener una relación cordial con el emperador Anastasio, que le concedió el título de cónsul *c.* 508. Al final de su reinado, Clodoveo añadió a su reino varios dominios francos previamente independientes, en especial el de los francos ripuarios. A su muerte en 511, su reino fue dividido entre sus cuatro hijos: Teodorico (rey de Reims), Childeberto (rey de París), Clodomiro (rey de Orleans) y Clotario (rey de Soissons). Esta tradición de subdivisiones debilitó a la **dinastía merovingia**, que reinó en Francia hasta el siglo VIII.

527–540

Este mosaico del siglo VI, de la iglesia de San Vitale (Ravena), muestra al emperador Justiniano con su séquito de oficiales, guardias y clérigos.

EL REINADO DEL EMPERADOR BIZANTINO JUSTINIANO I (r. 527–565) se inició con importantes reformas. En 528 encargó un nuevo código legal que reemplazara la confusión existente: el **Codex Justinianeus**, que entró en vigor en 529 (revisado en 534). Entusiasta de la construcción, en 532 ordenó la creación de la gran iglesia de **Santa Sofía**. El mayor reto para su reinado se produjo en 532, cuando las rivalidades entre las facciones de aficionados del hipódromo de Constantinopla, Verdes y Azules, se descontrolaron y dieron paso a la **revuelta Nika**. Los disturbios estuvieron a punto de provocar la huida de Justiniano, y su supresión costó la vida a treinta mil rebeldes.

TEODORA (*c.* 500–548)

Se casó con Justiniano I en 525; había sido prostituta y concubina de Hecébolo, gobernador de la Pentápolis libia. En 524, y tras la muerte de su madre adoptiva, la emperatriz Lupicina (que se había opuesto a su relación), Justiniano cambió las leyes para poder casarse con ella. Resultó una emperatriz enérgica, que reforzó la resolución de Justiniano durante la revuelta de Nika y actuó como protectora de los cristianos monofisitas –ella misma lo era– durante la época de persecución.

Con el trono asegurado, Justiniano dirigió su mirada al exterior. En 533 envió un ejército al mando de **Belisario** al norte de África, controlado por los vándalos, donde **Gelimero** había derrocado al rey Hilderico, aliado de Bizancio. El 13 de septiembre, Belisario derrotó a Gelimero en **Ad Decimum**, a las puertas de Cartago, y la resistencia vándala se hundió: Cartago fue tomada y Gelimero enviado cautivo a Constantinopla.

La rápida conquista del **reino vándalo** animó a Justiniano a intervenir en Italia. La excusa se la proporcionó el asesinato en abril de 535 de su amiga **Amalasunta**, reina ostrogoda. Belisario lanzó una ofensiva sobre Italia en 535, desembarcando en Sicilia con siete mil hombres. La isla fue asegurada hacia finales del año, y Belisario se dirigió al sur de Italia a principios de 536. Tras tres semanas de asedio tomó Nápoles, lo que obligó al rey ostrogodo, **Vitiges**, a retirarse al norte. El 9 de diciembre de 536, el **ejército bizantino ocupaba Roma**, restauración simbólica de las provincias perdidas del imperio; pero Roma no tardó en ser asediada por los godos. Belisario tomó finalmente la capital ostrogoda, **Ravena**, en 540. Ante la sospecha de que tramaba convertirse

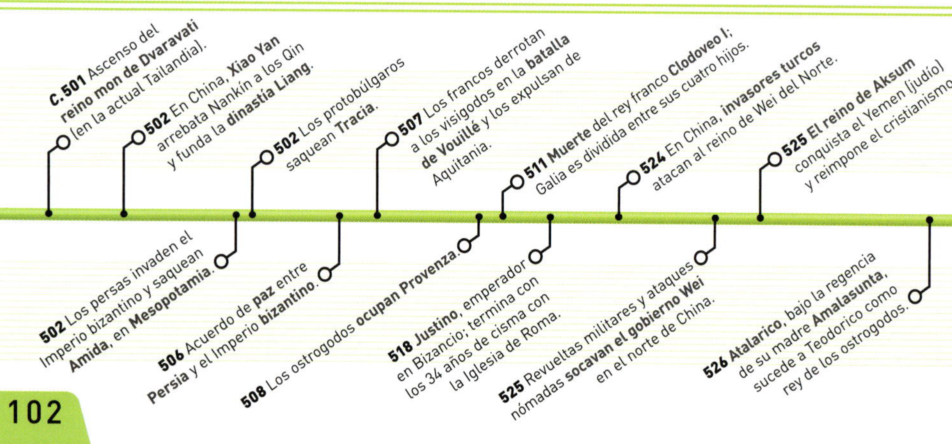

Reconquistas de Justiniano
La Italia vándala cayó ante las tropas bizantinas en 533, pero quedó devastada por los veinte años de guerra necesarios para tomarla. El intento de reconquista de Hispania fracasó, logrando solo unas pocas zonas costeras.

CLAVE
- Imperio bizantino (527)
- Reconquistas justinianas
- → Campañas bizantinas
- ✕ Batalla

en emperador, su presencia fue reclamada en Oriente, lo que estimuló aún más la resistencia ostrogoda.

Persia entró en una época de grandeza bajo **Cosroes I** (r. 531–579), que accedió al trono en un momento en que los mazdaquitas –un movimiento religioso populista– habían causado graves tensiones sociales. **Reformó el sistema de impuestos** y el **ejército**, animando el servicio de los nobles más pobres y sus seguidores a cambio de un salario. Cosroes **tomó Antioquía** en 540, obligando a Justiniano a pagar cinco mil libras de oro para recuperarla. En 544 atacó de nuevo, pero su asedio de Edesa falló y tuvo que pactar una tregua. Una guerra posterior entre Bizancio y Persia (546–561) acabaría en una paz de cincuenta años.

« PARA MÍ, Y PARA MUCHOS OTROS, **ESTOS DOS NO PARECÍAN SERES HUMANOS, SINO** VERDADEROS **DEMONIOS**… **VAMPIROS**. »

Procopio, historiador bizantino, sobre Justiniano y Teodora, en su *Historia secreta* (*c.* 550)

« AUNQUE LA **PESTE** ATACÓ A TODO EL **MUNDO**… ALGUNOS SE **CURARON**… PERO **DE ESTE HOMBRE NI UN ROMANO** LOGRÓ **ESCAPAR**. »

Procopio, sobre Justiniano en su *Historia secreta* (*c.* 550)

LA PARTE FINAL DEL REINADO DE JUSTINIANO careció de los logros de la primera. En 540 se declaró en Egipto un grave brote de **peste** –bubónica probablemente– que causó una mortandad generalizada, privando al imperio de una mano de obra muy necesaria. Los **ingresos por impuestos** cayeron, debilitando más la administración, y **los precios aumentaron**; ello llevó, en 544, a la promulgación de leyes para reducir la inflación. En los siglos VI y VII, nuevos brotes de peste minarían la vitalidad del Imperio bizantino.

Los **ostrogodos** hicieron rápidos avances en Italia tras la partida de **Belisario**. Su rey **Totila** aseguró la zona norte del Po, y en 542 controlaba gran parte de Italia central. Belisario fue reclamado en 544 para solucionar la situación, pero Justiniano lo privó de recursos, y **Roma cayó** en 546. Aunque los bizantinos recuperaron la ciudad en 547, en 550 volvió a pasar a manos de Totila. Justiniano envió dos ejércitos al mando de **Artabanes** y **Narsés** para eliminar a los godos. Artabanes entró en Ravena en junio de 552, y en julio Narsés derrotó a Totila en la **batalla de Busta Gallorum (Taginae)**, en los Apeninos. Totila murió al poco a causa de las heridas de combate, y, aunque aún persistió cierta resistencia ostrogoda, la guerra en Italia había acabado de hecho.

Broche ostrogodo
Este broche de oro y esmalte demuestra el alto grado de destreza del arte ostrogodo en Italia. El empleo de la imagen del águila puede indicar la influencia romana.

533–534 Belisario conquista el **reino vándalo** del norte de África.

534 El **reino burgundio** es absorbido por los francos.

535 La **dinastía Wei** se divide en oriental y occidental.

C. 535 Nubia queda dividida en tres reinos: Nobatia, Alodia y Mukuria.

536 Belisario toma **Roma**.

537 Los **ostrogodos** asedian Roma.

538 Llegada del **budismo** a Japón.

C. 540 Monjes etíopes **traducen la Biblia** a su propia lengua.

540 Los bizantinos capturan **Ravena**, capital ostrogoda.

540 Los **protobúlgaros** llegan a las puertas de Constantinopla.

542 Un brote de **peste** en Constantinopla mata a miles de personas.

543 El reino nubio de **Nobatia** es convertido al cristianismo por misioneros coptos.

544 Establecimiento del **reino de Viet** en Vietnam.

546 El rey ostrogodo **Totila toma Roma**, que es recuperada poco después por Belisario.

547 Estalla una rebelión de **tribus bereberes** en el norte de África; es aplastada por el ejército bizantino.

548 Saqueo de Nankín durante la revuelta de Hou Jing contra la **dinastía Liang**.

550 El general bizantino Belisario es reemplazado por **Narsés**; Roma es tomada de nuevo por los ostrogodos.

C. 550 El reino jemer de **Chenlá** se deshace de la soberanía feudal de Funán.

C. 550 Los pueblos **ávaros** turcos empiezan a migrar hacia el oeste.

C. 550 El reino nubio de **Alodia** es convertido al cristianismo copto.

551–567

La abadía de Iona fue construida en el siglo XIII sobre el enclave del monasterio original fundado por el monje Columbano a su llegada a Iona, en 563.

LA FRANCIA MEROVINGIA HABÍA SIDO DIVIDIDA en reinos separados a la muerte de Clodoveo I en 511 (*véase* 501–526). A pesar de ello, el poder franco siguió creciendo. En 558, **Clotario I** (511–561), que reinaba en la zona de Soissons, ya había absorbido el reino de Reims y la región que rodeaba París a la muerte de sus reyes. Esto dejó a Clotario como **único rey merovingio de Francia** durante tres años, hasta su muerte en 561, momento en que fue dividida de nuevo: Cariberto I recibió París; Gontrán I, Orleans; Sigeberto I, Reims; y Chilperico I, Soissons. El reino de los francos no volvería a unificarse hasta el año 613, bajo **Clotario II** (r. 613–629).

En **Irlanda**, convertida al cristianismo por **Patricio** (m. 461) a mediados del siglo V, se había implantado la **tradición monástica**. Desde el siglo VI, los monjes irlandeses empezaron a llevar a cabo misiones en el exterior. En 563, **san Columbano** (*c.* 520–597) fundó la **abadía de Iona** en una isla frente a la costa occidental de Escocia. Iona se convirtió en centro de monacato de influencia irlandesa, que se extendió al norte de Inglaterra, Escocia y Francia con la fundación del centro monástico de Luxeuil en 590.

El **Imperio gupta se derrumbó** tras el reinado de Vishnugupta (r. 540–550), y el norte de India se dividió en diversos **reinos regionales**. Una rama menor de los guptas gobernó en Magadha, pero fue eliminada por los Maukharis de Kanyakubja (actual Kannauj). La región sería ocupada por el rey vardana **Harsa**, que estableció un imperio a principios del siglo VII.

Arte rupestre de Ajanta
Las grutas de Ajanta, un sitio sagrado budista en Maharashtra (India), experimentaron una segunda fase de uso intenso durante el siglo VI.

568–588

« CUANDO **JUSTINO** OYÓ DE ESTOS SUCESOS… **NO TUVO PENSAMIENTOS SANOS** O SENSATOS… **CAYÓ** EN EL **DESORDEN DE LA MENTE** Y LA **LOCURA**, Y DESDE ENTONCES **PERDIÓ EL ENTENDIMIENTO**. **»**

Evagrio el Escolástico, erudito y asistente de Gregorio de Antioquía, sobre la reacción de Justino II a la caída de Dara en manos persas. De su *Historia eclesiástica* (*c.* 595)

EL CLAN SOGA DE JAPÓN LOGRÓ PREEMINENCIA EN 536, cuando fue nombrado primer ministro **Soga no Iname**. La **muerte del emperador Bidatsu** en 585 llevó a una disputa sucesoria de la que salió victorioso **Yomei**, nieto de Iname. **Sushun** (r. 586–593), el siguiente emperador, era de madre Soga, lo que reforzó el dominio familiar. Cuando Sushun fue asesinado en 593, le sucedió la viuda de Bidatsu, Suiko (r. 593–628), que también era Soga. Durante su reinado se inició el **periodo Asuka**: una época de gran seguridad en las relaciones internacionales, apoyo estatal al budismo y florecimiento de las artes.

En 572, el emperador bizantino **Justino II** (r. 565–578) declaró la **guerra a Persia** al negarse a pagar el tributo debido según el tratado de paz de cincuenta años firmado por Justiniano I (*véase* 527–540). Persia respondió invadiendo Siria y tomando la fortaleza de Dara. Al recibir la noticia, Justino enloqueció; su esposa Sofía, que asumió el poder, tuvo que firmar un humillante tratado con Persia.

7 AÑOS DURÓ EL TRATADO DE **«PAZ ETERNA»** DE 532 **ENTRE** EL **IMPERIO BIZANTINO** Y **PERSIA**

En 567, los **lombardos**, que se habían establecido en la antigua provincia romana de Panonia (Hungría), destruyeron a los gépidos y después, bajo el mando de **Alboíno** (r. 560–572), avanzaron al suroeste hacia Italia, donde la autoridad bizantina estaba demasiado debilitada para resistirlos. En 568–569 **ocuparon el valle del Po**, dejando las ciudades principales al mando de duques. Para cuando tomaron Pavía, en 572, ya habían fundado ducados tan al sur como Benevento.

Los intentos **bizantinos de contraataque** en 575 fueron un desastre. El reino lombardo se consolidó bajo **Agilulfo** (r. 590–616), con los bizantinos limitados a pequeños territorios en torno a Roma, Nápoles y Ravena.

Bajo el **kan Bayan I** (r. *c.* 562–582), los **ávaros** –jinetes nómadas del norte del Cáucaso– explotaron el vacío dejado por la marcha de los lombardos para **hacerse con un vasto territorio** centrado en torno a la actual Austria. Su conquista de varias ciudades bizantinas impulsó al **emperador Mauricio** (r. 582–602) a emprender una exitosa campaña para desalojarlos.

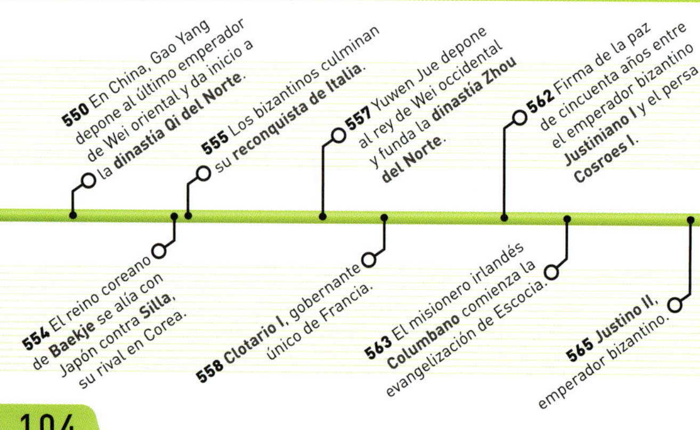

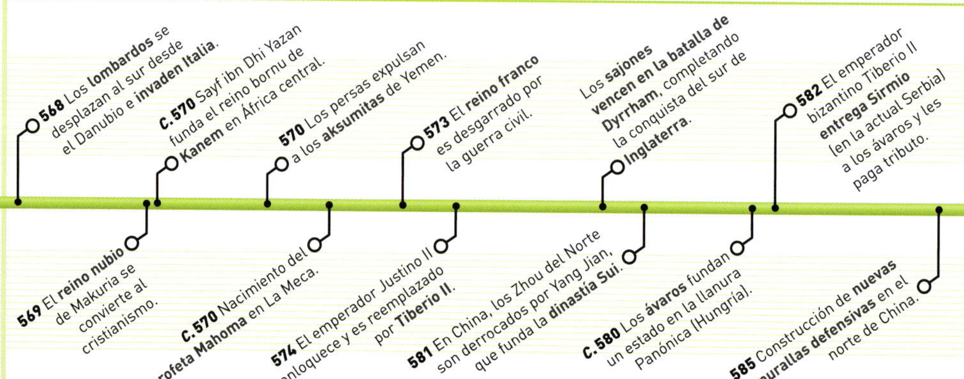

589–599

Fresco pintado *c.* 581–618 en las cuevas de Dunhuang (China), en un oasis estratégicamente situado en la Ruta de la Seda. Las cuevas contienen algunos de los mejores ejemplos de arte budista.

EN 581, YANG JIAN, UN GENERAL DE LOS ZHOU DEL NORTE, se levantó en armas, usurpó el trono y se nombró emperador **Wendi** (r. 581–604). En 589 invadió el sur de China; sus fuerzas vencieron con rapidez a las del último emperador Chen, **How Zhu,** lo que dio a Wendi el gobierno de todo el país y le permitió convertirse en el primer emperador de la **dinastía Sui**. Después de tres siglos de división, **China** volvía a estar **unificada**. Wendi desarmó a los ejércitos privados y estableció colonias agrícolas a lo largo de las fronteras para fortalecer el control central sobre las zonas remotas. Instauró una **gran reforma agraria** que aumentó el número de hogares sujetos a impuestos sobre el suelo, de cuatro millones en 589 a casi nueve millones en 606. También extendió el sistema de canales del país hasta formar un **«Gran Canal»** que permitía a las naves recorrer 2000 km desde Hangzhou, en el sureste, y a través de Luoyang, en la región centroriental de China, hasta las provincias nororientales en torno a Pekín. Austero, estricto y ocasionalmente violento, Wendi parecía haber establecido la dinastía Sui sobre firmes fundamentos; a la postre, solo le sobreviviría catorce años hasta ser reemplazada por los Tang.

« NO SON **ANGLOS**, SINO **ÁNGELES**. »

Papa Gregorio I, al ver a esclavos anglosajones en un mercado de Roma

En 582, el **emperador Mauricio** sucedió a **Tiberio II** (r. 578–582) como emperador bizantino. Mauricio había sido comandante de la guardia y luego en la guerra contra los persas desde 578. Las ineficaces campañas de Tiberio contra persas, lombardos y ávaros habían **vaciado las arcas imperiales**, enfrentando a Mauricio a una crisis económica. Sus consiguientes medidas de ahorro condujeron al **amotinamiento** del ejército oriental en 588 y del balcánico en 593. Mauricio nombró a su padre, Pablo, cabeza del senado, y a su cuñado **Filípico** comandante de la guardia de palacio; este nepotismo aumentó aún más su impopularidad.

En 584 **reinició la guerra contra Persia**, encargando su dirección a Filípico. El nuevo comandante atacó Arzanene; sin embargo, su campaña fue interrumpida por la **deserción de los árabes gasaníes**, antiguos aliados ahora distanciados por la detención de su rey, al-Mundhir III. El amotinamiento de las tropas orientales en 588 aplazó aún más los planes bizantinos, y en 589 perdieron la ciudad de **Martirópolis** (en la actual Turquía). Los bizantinos solo serían salvados por el estallido de una guerra civil en Persia: la intervención de un ejército de Bizancio en la restauración del pretendiente vencedor, **Cosroes II**, condujo a la recuperación de Martirópolis y Dara en 592.

PAPA GREGORIO I (590–604)

Fue prefecto de Roma de 572 a 574, y no se hizo monje hasta la muerte de su padre. Hombre de talento y energía, al inicio de su papado estuvo implicado en la resistencia contra los lombardos en Italia, pero mantuvo buenas relaciones con los merovingios en Francia y con los visigodos hispanos; estas se rompieron con el emperador bizantino Mauricio por el uso del título «patriarca ecuménico» por parte del obispo de Constantinopla, hecho que Gregorio consideró un desafío a su autoridad.

Los **eslavos** –un pueblo no germánico referido en fuentes de la época como *sclaveni*– debieron llegar al norte del Danubio entre principios y mediados del siglo VI. Cuando los ávaros se internaron en la región *c.* 559, los eslavos fueron desplazados al sur de forma que, al acabar el siglo, ya había asentamientos eslavos en todos los Balcanes: norte de Grecia, costa dálmata del Adriático y Macedonia, así como en aquellas zonas de Bulgaria, Bohemia, Moravia, Serbia y Croacia donde más adelante surgirían los grandes reinos eslavos medievales.

El **papa Gregorio I** envió en 596 una misión a Britania para reavivar el cristianismo tras las invasiones de los **paganos anglosajones** en el siglo V y principios del siglo VI. Los misioneros partieron bajo el liderazgo de **Agustín**, antiguo prior de un monasterio en Roma, y llegaron a Kent al año siguiente: la recepción fue razonablemente cálida porque Berta, esposa del **rey Ethelberto de Kent**, ya era cristiana. Ethelberto fue bautizado y Agustín pudo establecer una iglesia en Canterbury. También se convirtieron los reyes **Seberto de Essex** y **Sigeberto de Estanglia** –ambos dependientes de Kent–, pero la naciente Iglesia de Inglaterra aún sufriría una serie de contratiempos antes de que los últimos reinos anglosajones se convirtieran al cristianismo a finales del siglo VII.

Figurilla de la dinastía Sui
Esta figura de un comerciante a camello subraya el interés en China sobre el comercio por la Ruta de la Seda a través de Asia central.

- **589** El **rey visigodo Recaredo** anuncia la conversión de Hispania al catolicismo en el concilio de Toledo.
- **589** Los **turcos azules** establecidos en Zungaria controlan la **Ruta de la Seda.**
- **589** El emperador Wendi de Sui instaura una **reforma agraria** en China.
- **589 Yang Jian** captura la capital de Chen y **reunifica China.**
- **589** Los bizantinos pierden **Martirópolis** a manos de los persas (retomada en 592).
- **590 Cosroes II** es derrocado en Persia por un alzamiento dirigido por Bahram; huye a Constantinopla.
- **590** Los **eslavos** empiezan a penetrar en los **Balcanes.**
- **590 Gregorio I** (Magno) se convierte en papa.
- **591** Los **bizantinos reponen a Cosroes II** en el trono persa.
- **592** El emperador Mauricio lanza un **contraataque bizantino** contra los eslavos en los Balcanes.
- **592** Estalla en China la guerra civil entre los clanes **Soga** (probudistas) y **Mononobe** (antibudistas).
- **593** El ejército bizantino en los Balcanes se **amotina.**
- **595** Los matemáticos indios usan el **sistema decimal.**
- **597** El monje benedictino **Agustín** (de Canterbury) comienza su misión evangelizadora en Inglaterra.
- **598** Tratado entre bizantinos y lombardos que **concede a estos el norte de Italia.**

4

COMERCIO E INVENCIONES 600–1449

600–610

Moneda con la efigie del emperador bizantino Heraclio.

LOS TRASTORNOS EN EL IMPERIO BIZANTINO comenzaron cuando el emperador Mauricio (r. 582–602) envió sus ejércitos al norte de los Balcanes para recuperar el control de la frontera del Danubio, en manos de los ávaros (*véase* 568–588). En 602, las tropas se sublevaron bajo el mando de un oficial, Focas. Mauricio fue asesinado y **Focas fue proclamado emperador**. Sin embargo, **Cosroes II**, emperador de la Persia sasánida, aprovechó la debilidad de la frontera oriental, mientras los ávaros atacaban desde el norte. En 610, el hijo del gobernador de la provincia de África, **Heraclio**, ejecutó a Focas y después se autoproclamó emperador.

En el norte de India, Harsa (c. 590–647) accedió al trono de Thanesar y Kannauj en 606, estableciendo el **último imperio indio nativo** de la Antigüedad.

« EL **EMPERADOR HARSA**, NOBLE DE **NACIMIENTO** Y DE BIEN ELEGIDO **NOMBRE**, SUPERADOR DE **LAS VICTORIAS LOGRADAS** POR TODOS LOS REYES ANTIGUOS. »

Banabhatta, poeta indio, en *Harsacharita* (*Vida de Harsa*) (*c.* 640)

611–620

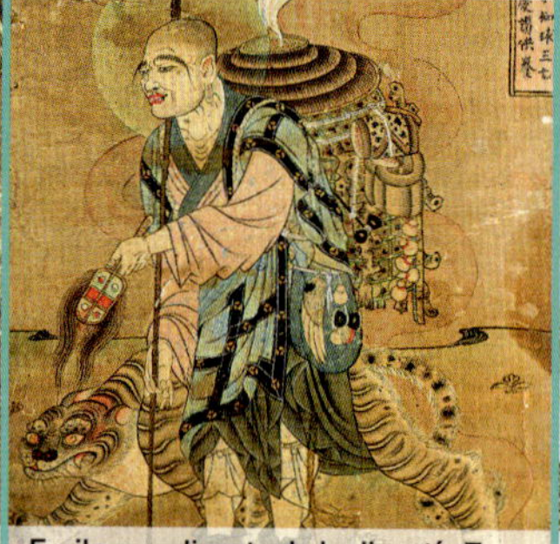
Fraile mendicante de la dinastía Tang, con un inusual compañero de viaje.

Caballo de la dinastía Tang
Los caballos eran símbolos de destreza militar; en especial los de guerra de la frontera occidental del imperio.

CON LA CAÍDA DE JERUSALÉN (614) Y EGIPTO (619), los sasánidas restablecieron el Imperio persa a expensas de Bizancio. En 618, Constantinopla era asediada por los ávaros y sus súbditos eslavos. En 620, Heraclio sobornó a los ávaros con el fin de concentrarse en rechazar a los persas.

En 613, **Clotario II** (584–629) puso fin a la guerra civil y **reunificó el reino franco**. Su Edicto de París (614) introdujo reformas en la Iglesia y en el estado merovingios.

En 616–617, las revueltas contra el gobierno despótico de Yangdi (r. 604–617) provocaron el colapso de la dinastía Sui en China. En el año 618, el gobernador militar Li Yuan, con el nombre de **emperador Gaozu, instauró la dinastía Tang**, que reinó hasta 906.

621–630

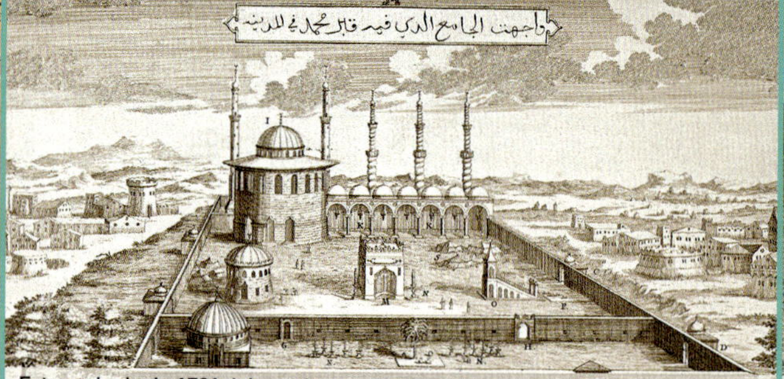
Este grabado de 1721 del arquitecto austriaco Johann Fischer von Erlach muestra la mezquita al-Haram y la Kaaba, en La Meca.

MAHOMA RECIBIÓ SU PRIMERA REVELACIÓN DIVINA en 610 y empezó a predicar en La Meca en 613, pero el inicio de la época islámica lo marca tradicionalmente la hégira (*hiyra*), o **migración a Medina**. La hostilidad de las autoridades de La Meca obligó a Mahoma a huir a Medina con su familia y sus seguidores en 622. Una vez allí, estableció una base de poder político y religioso, y lanzó una serie de ataques contra las tropas de La Meca hasta lograr su rendición final en 630 con la toma de la Kaaba, el santuario más sagrado de la península Arábiga. A partir de ese momento, el gobierno de Mahoma fue incontestable.

Heraclio empezó a recuperar el territorio cedido a los persas, primero en la batalla de Isos (622) y luego en la de Nínive (627). Exhaustos por décadas de guerra e ignorantes de la tormenta que llegaba del sur, los **imperios bizantino y sasánida** firmaron la paz en 628.

En China, el hijo del emperador **Gaozu, Taizong, consolidó el poder de Tang** suprimiendo las revueltas en todo el imperio. En el año 626 obligó a su padre a abdicar e inició una edad dorada de comercio, prosperidad e intercambio cultural.

MAHOMA (570–632)

Nacido en La Meca, Abu l'Qasim Muhammad ibn 'Abd Allāh al-Hashim al-Qurashi trabajó como pastor y mercader antes de retirarse a una vida contemplativa. Recibió la primera de una serie de revelaciones que se convertirían en el Corán en 610. Predicó una fe monoteísta (islam) basada en la completa sumisión a Dios. Unificó a las tribus árabes en el seno de su nueva religión.

631–640

Ruinas de la fortaleza bizantina de Sbeitla, en Túnez (siglo VII).

PARA LA FECHA DE LA MUERTE DE MAHOMA, EN EL AÑO 632, la joven comunidad musulmana –unida por el islam, que trascendía las rivalidades tradicionales– estaba preparada para expandirse. A pesar de que Mahoma no dejó indicaciones en cuanto a su sucesor (califa), cuatro hombres ligados al profeta por enlaces matrimoniales surgieron como **califas** *rashidun* («bien guiados»). El primero, **Abu Bakr** (r. 632–634), suprimió una rebelión árabe, restableció el dominio islámico sobre Arabia e inició la conquista de Siria. Su sucesor, **Omar** (r. 634–644), dirigió la conquista de Siria y derrotó a los bizantinos en Ajnadayn. En 637, Omar ya controlaba Jerusalén y Damasco, y ese mismo año las tropas árabes conquistaban **Persia** (actuales Irán e Iraq), ocupando Ctesifonte, la capital sasánida. **Omar estableció varias prácticas importantes**: la creación de ciudades de guarnición en los territorios conquistados para separar a las fuerzas invasoras árabes de los locales; el reclutamiento de tropas mediante la esclavitud y la filiación tribal (los

« LOS QUE SON **PACIENTES EN LA ADVERSIDAD**... SON LOS QUE ESTÁN EN EL CAMINO RECTO. »

Corán 2: 155–157

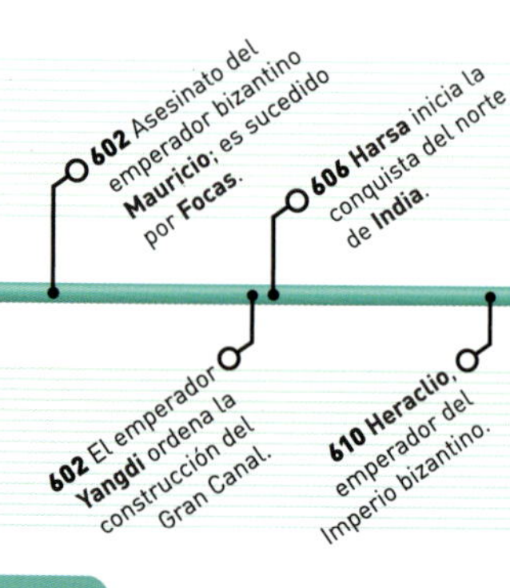

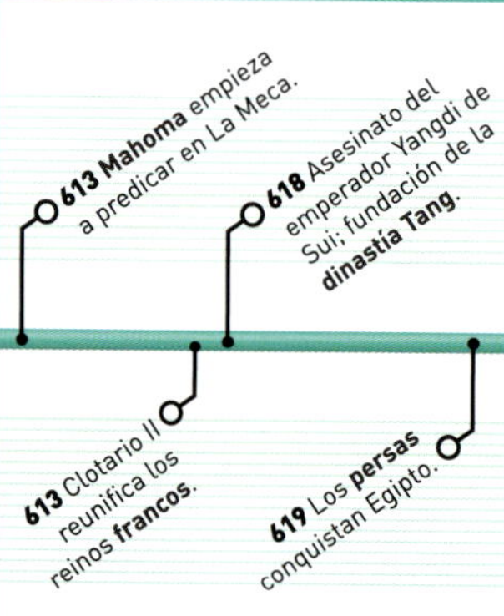

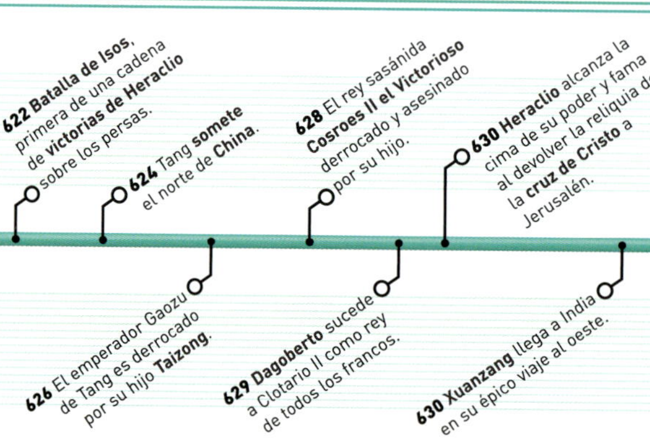

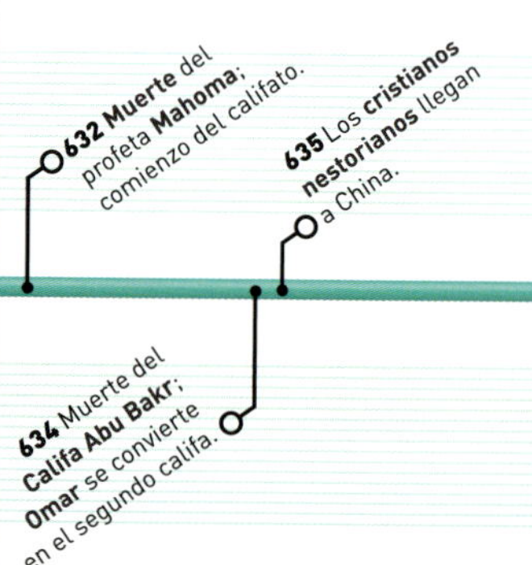

Uno de los veinte túmulos de Sutton Hoo, en Suffolk (Inglaterra), que encierran las tumbas y tesoros funerarios de la dinastía real de Anglia Oriental.

« LAS GRANDES RIQUEZAS QUE HABÍAN TOMADO… A LA TIERRA DIERON. »

De ***Beowulf***, poema épico en inglés antiguo, *c.* finales del siglo x

Los viajes de Xuanzang
El joven monje dejó Chang'an, la capital de Tang, en torno a 630. Cruzó Asia central y llegó a India en 645.

reclutados pasaban a depender de miembros de las tribus); y un sistema de impuestos que favorecía a los musulmanes y que fomentaba la conversión, pero tolerando las creencias de cristianos y judíos.

El **budismo** aumentó su influencia en la China Tang. El monje **Xuanzang** viajó por todas partes en busca de sabiduría; sus viajes, que se hicieron legendarios, anticiparon la creciente movilidad de personas e ideas a través de la **Ruta de la Seda**, favorecida por el poder de los Tang y más adelante por el califato. También utilizaron la Ruta de la Seda los **cristianos nestorianos** que llegaron a **China** desde Persia en el año 635.

LA EXPANSIÓN ISLÁMICA CONTINUÓ cuando los árabes superaron el contraataque persa en la batalla de Nihavand (642), **asestando el golpe final al Imperio sasánida**; Yazdgerd III, su último emperador, murió en 651, por lo que el zoroastrismo dejó de ser la religión dominante de la región. La conversión de la población al **islam** se produjo de forma lenta pero constante a lo largo de los siglos siguientes. Los árabes obtuvieron un éxito similar en Egipto, donde los bizantinos solo ofrecieron una resistencia simbólica. La **caída de Alejandría** llegó en 642, el mismo año en que los musulmanes fundaban el asentamiento militar de Fustat, que luego se convertiría en El Cairo. Al año siguiente, los ejércitos islámicos conquistaron Tripolitania, en el norte de África, mientras su avance continuaba, incontrolable incluso cuando Omar fue asesinado en 644 por un esclavo persa. Su sucesor, **Otmán**, difundió la primera **versión escrita del Corán**, que hasta entonces se había transmitido oralmente.

Después de lanzar exitosos ataques contra tibetanos y mongoles, pero habiendo fracasado en la conquista de Corea, el **emperador Taizong de Tang** (r. 626–649) **murió** en 649, y su hijo, de voluntad débil, empezó a ceder una influencia creciente a la **emperatriz Wu** (624–705). En Japón, el clan **Fujiwara** promulgó las **reformas Taika** en 646, por las que todas las tierras pasaban a propiedad imperial y se establecía un poder centralizado basado en el modelo chino.

En **Inglaterra**, los cristianos conversos combatían con los reyes paganos por el control del territorio y la dirección religiosa y cultural. En 642, por ejemplo, el rey cristiano **Oswaldo de Northumbria**, uno de los reinos más poderosos hasta el momento, murió a manos del rey pagano **Penda de Mercia**. Se cree que el gran barco funerario anglosajón de **Sutton Hoo** –lleno de artefactos, armas y tesoros de maravillosa factura–, en Suffolk, contuvo el cuerpo del **rey anglosajón**. Fue uno de los últimos enterramientos de este tipo en Inglaterra: su contenido es una fusión de elementos cristianos y no cristianos, lo que sugiere una transición en que el **cristianismo** ganaba popularidad y poder.

27 METROS
LONGITUD DEL **BARCO** DE SUTTON HOO

Yelmo de Sutton Hoo
Reconstrucción de hierro con paneles de bronce revestido de estaño sumamente decorados.

637 Batalla de al-Qadisiyya: las fuerzas árabes derrotan a las persas y conquistan Persia hasta Mosul por el norte.

639 Fallece Dagoberto, último de los reyes **merovingios**.

c. 640 Enterramiento de **Sutton Hoo**.

641 Muerte de **Heraclio**.

642 Fin del Imperio sasánida; los **persas son aplastados** en la batalla de Nihavand.

642 Muerte de **Oswaldo de Northumbria**.

644 Asesinato del **califa Omar**; **Otmán** ordena que el Corán se ponga por escrito.

645 Xuanzang regresa a China después de su viaje por Asia.

646 Reformas **Taika** en Japón.

647 Muerte del emperador indio **Harsa**; su imperio se desintegra.

649 Muerte del emperador Taizong de Tang y ascenso de la **emperatriz Wu**.

651–670

Erosionado paisaje de la Anatolia central, un territorio bizantino que sufrió repetidas incursiones de las fuerzas árabes en el siglo VII.

LA DIVISIÓN ENTRE MUSULMANES CHIÍES Y SUNÍES fue resultado de un intenso desacuerdo sobre cómo debía decidirse la sucesión del califato: por selección (como en el caso de los primeros tres califas) o por línea hereditaria. El califa Otmán (r. 644–656) había promocionado a miembros de su propia familia, los **Omeyas**. En 656 fue asesinado por soldados egipcios agraviados por su condición inferior. Alí ibn Abu Talib, primo y yerno de Mahoma, fue elegido **cuarto califa**. Alí contaba con una categoría única en el mundo islámico, pero se enfrentó a muchos desafíos: en la **batalla del Camello** (656), suprimió una revuelta de la viuda del profeta, Aisha, y sus aliados; y en 657, **Muawiyya**, emir omeya de Siria, afirmó su derecho al califato, amenazando con la guerra civil. Tras una batalla indecisa, Alí llegó a un compromiso con Muawiyya que indignó a algunos de sus partidarios, que formaron la secta de los jariyíes. **Alí fue asesinado por un jariyíe** en 661, lo que abrió el camino para que **Muawiyya se autoproclamara califa**, instaurando con ello la dinastía Omeya como monarquía hereditaria. Los partidarios de Alí formaron su propio grupo, que evolucionó en una rama distintiva del islam, los **chiíes**, en oposición a los **suníes**.

El emperador Constante II intentó reasentar las **reclamaciones bizantinas sobre Italia** reubicando su corte en Roma en 663; sin embargo, las profundas incursiones árabes en Anatolia (en la actual Turquía) provocaron un colapso en su autoridad; fue asesinado en 668, y subió al trono **Constantino IV**. Las **incursiones árabes** en Anatolia prosiguieron, y en 670 ya habían alcanzado la capital bizantina, Constantinopla (actual Estambul), y montaban el **primer asedio de la ciudad**, que duraría hasta 677.

En Corea, el **reino unificado de Silla** puso fin al prolongado periodo de los Tres Reinos con la ayuda de la **China Tang**. En 660, los Tang destruyeron el reino de Baejke, y en 668 fuerzas combinadas de Silla y Tang conquistaron Goguryeo, dejando de esta manera toda la península de Corea bajo el control de Silla.

ASIA
Mar de Aral
Transoxiana
Zabulistán
IMPERIO JAZAR
Mar Caspio
Jurasán
IMPERIO SASÁNIDA
Kirmán
Islas británicas
EUROPA
REINOS FRANCOS
Mar Negro
Armenia
Mesopotamia
Juzistán
Fars
Constantinopla
IMPERIO BIZANTINO
Siria
Omán
OCÉANO ATLÁNTICO
Jerusalén
Nayd
Península Arábiga
Mar de Arabia
Mar Mediterráneo
Hiyaz
Magreb
Montañas del Atlas
EGIPTO
Yemen
ÁFRICA

Expansión bajo el califato
La rápida expansión árabe continuó durante la segunda mitad del siglo VII. Los ejércitos musulmanes penetraron en Asia central y norte de África, llegando a un paso de España.

CLAVE
- Tierras musulmanas (656)
- Imperio bizantino (c. 610)
- Imperio sasánida (c. 610)
- Reinos francos (c. 610)

Quemador de incienso de gres
Esta pieza procede del reino de Silla, que estuvo a punto de convertirse en potencia dominante en Corea durante la fase final del periodo de los Tres Reinos.

671–690

Representación actual de la batalla de Karbala; la muerte de Husein ibn Alí es conmemorada en el festividad anual chií de la Ashura.

LA CIUDAD-ESTADO MAYA DE TIKAL EMPEZÓ A RESURGIR después de un siglo de dominación política y cultural por parte de ciudades-estado vecinas, conocido como hiato de Tikal, caracterizado por la ausencia de inscripciones en los petroglifos de la ciudad. Una inscripción datada en 672 registra una campaña militar contra la **ciudad-estado rival de Dos Pilas**, y en las décadas siguientes Tikal recuperó su posición entre los mayas del periodo Clásico Tardío (600–900). Los señores de la ciudad se embarcaron en un plan constructor que se adecuara a sus ambiciones políticas, **construyendo numerosas estructuras**, entre ellas enormes pirámides, canchas para el juego de pelota, calzadas elevadas, observatorios y palacios.

Las tropas árabes que asediaban Constantinopla (*véase* 651–670) fueron incapaces de abrir brecha en sus sólidas murallas y fueron rechazadas con la ayuda de una nueva **arma secreta bizantina**, el fuego griego (*véase* 711–720), cuyo despliegue también pudo ayudar a abatir la flota árabe en la batalla de Silea, en 677, lo que **obligó al califato a aceptar un tregua de treinta años**. Esta paz dio un respiro al agobiado Imperio bizantino, que pugnaba por contener a los búlgaros, quienes en 681 establecieron el **primer Imperio búlgaro** en el territorio arrebatado a los bizantinos al norte de los Balcanes.

CONQUISTAS ÁRABES

Una vez consolidadas las conquistas de Persia y el norte de África bizantino, los ejércitos árabes avanzaron hacia este y oeste. En Asia central cruzaron el río Pamir (Amu Daria) en 667 y siguieron avanzando hasta las cercanías del reino de Bujara, en la Ruta de la Seda. En África aplastaron a los reinos bereberes, alcanzando Tánger en 683.

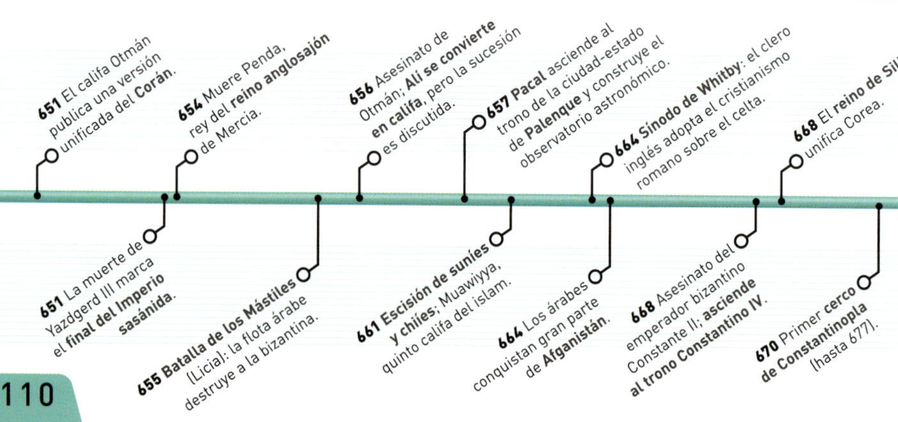

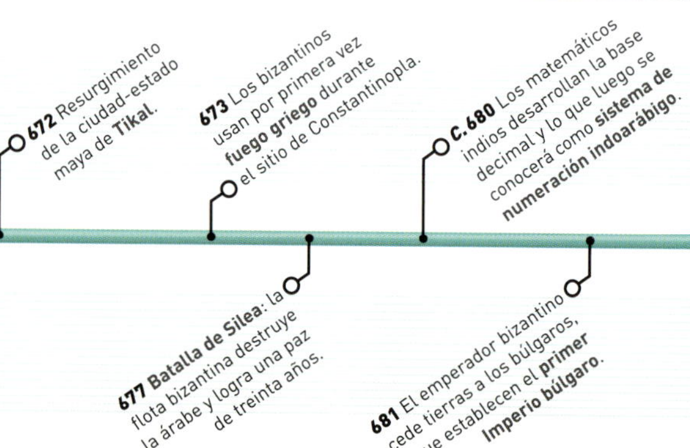

La Cúpula de la Roca de Jerusalén –lugar sagrado para las tres religiones abrahámicas– es de planta octogonal y posee una inmensa cúpula dorada.

En 680, en la **batalla de Karbala**, el líder **Husein ibn Alí**, nieto de Mahoma, fue rodeado por tropas omeyas, privado de agua durante varios días y, finalmente, torturado y asesinado. Su muerte fue proclamada como un **martirio** por los chiíes, que aún la conmemoran en la actualidad.

En China, y después de décadas de controlar el poder a través de su marido y sus hijos, la **emperatriz Wu se hizo finalmente con el trono** en 690: la única mujer en hacerlo en la historia de China. Incluso creó su propia dinastía, la **Zhou**, que encabezó hasta 705.

Templo de Tikal
Flanqueando la Gran Plaza de Tikal, los 38 m del Templo II se irguieron durante el auge constructor del resurgimiento Clásico Tardío.

3000

NÚMERO DE **GRANDES EDIFICIOS DE PIEDRA** CONSTRUIDOS EN EL PERIODO CLÁSICO TARDÍO DE TIKAL

ABD AL-MALIK SE HABÍA CONVERTIDO EN CALIFA EN 685, estableciendo cambios importantes en la forma de gobernar el califato: centralizó el gobierno, insistió en que todos los asuntos de estado fueran tratados en árabe, creó el *barid* (un sistema postal y de espionaje) y, en torno a 697, acuñó nuevas monedas: el dinar y el dírham. También encargó la construcción de un gran santuario en el Monte del Templo de Jerusalén, la **Cúpula de la Roca** (Qubbat as-Sajra, en árabe), terminada en 692.

Los diez crueles años de reinado del **emperador bizantino Justiniano II** habían despertado una oposición generalizada, y en 695 fue derrocado por **Leoncio**, que le cortó la nariz y ocupó el trono. Sin embargo, la **pérdida de Cartago** (698), el último bastión bizantino en el norte de África, a manos de los árabes, condujo a otra revuelta en la que Leoncio sufrió el mismo destino que su predecesor.

En América, el fin de siglo fue una época de cambio y agitación. En América del Norte, la lanza fue sustituida por la **adopción generalizada del arco y la flecha**. En el valle de México, la **gran ciudad-estado de Teotihuacán**, que una vez albergó más de cien mil habitantes, **colapsó** *c.* 700, dando fin a seis siglos de crecimiento y dominancia. La culpa podría achacarse a una combinación de factores sociales, económicos y ambientales.

« NUNCA HE VISTO OTRO IGUAL; NI HE OÍDO HABLAR [DE NADA]… **QUE PUEDA RIVALIZAR EN GRACIA CON ESTA CÚPULA DE LA ROCA. »**

Al-Muqaddasi, geógrafo árabe del siglo x

Máscara teotihuacana
Es probable que esta máscara estuviera unida a una figurilla representativa de un dios. Pudo estar ornada con incrustaciones y adornos en las orejas.

683 Los **árabes** llegan a Tánger.

690 La **emperatriz Wu** ocupa el trono chino y establece la **dinastía Zhou** (hasta 705).

691 Batalla de Sebastópolis: los árabes derrotan al emperador bizantino **Justiniano II** y ocupan Armenia; Justiniano se venga masacrando a los desertores eslavos.

692 Se termina la **Cúpula de la Roca**.

695 Leoncio depone a Justiniano II y le amputa la nariz.

695 El **rey Garra de Jaguar**, de la ciudad-estado maya de Calakmul, es **capturado y sacrificado** por fuerzas de Tikal.

697 Fecha tradicional de elección del semilegendario primer dux de Venecia, **Paolo Lucio Anafesto**.

698 Los **árabes conquistan** y destruyen **Cartago** y fundan Kairuán; la pérdida de Cartago provoca el derrocamiento de Leoncio.

C.700 Surge la **cultura misisipiana** en América del Norte, con asentamientos agrícolas en valles fluviales.

C.700 Colapso de la ciudad de **Teotihuacán** en el valle de México.

C.700 En Perú, el **Imperio huari** conquista el **territorio mochica**.

C.700 Los indígenas norteamericanos adoptan **el arco y las flechas**.

701–710

Detalle del manuscrito iluminado de los *Evangeliario de Lindisfarne*.

EL ARTE ANGLOSAJÓN FUSIONÓ ELEMENTOS GERMANOS Y CELTAS, y, a través de los viajeros y peregrinos cristianos, también reflejó influencias romanas y bizantinas. Producto de esta síntesis única fueron los *Evangeliario de Lindisfarne*, un manuscrito iluminado creado *c.* 701 en el priorato de Lindisfarne, una isla en la costa nororiental de Inglaterra.

En el año 705, y con la ayuda de los búlgaros, el depuesto emperador **Justiniano II regresó del exilio** (*véase* 691–700), recuperó el trono bizantino y se cobró brutal venganza sobre quienes lo habían mutilado.

Ese mismo año, los **refugiados zoroastrianos** huidos de la conquista islámica de Persia que habían **establecido comunidades en India** empezaban a ser conocidos como los parsis; esta emigración prosiguió en los siglos siguientes.

Ruinas de Lindisfarne
El monasterio benedictino fue erigido en el siglo XII sobre la iglesia anterior, fundada por san Aidan en 635.

711–720

Uso del fuego griego según la ilustración del manuscrito *Skylitzes Matritensis* (siglo XII), que relata la historia del Imperio bizantino.

Su concubina favorita
En este rollo de la dinastía Tang, Xuanzong observa cómo Yang Guifei monta a caballo. El amor que sentía el emperador por su concubina inspiró obras dramáticas y poemas.

EN EL AÑO 710, EL REINO VISIGODO DE TOLEDO se hallaba sumido en la guerra civil, lo que representaba una perspectiva tentadora para las tropas islámicas establecidas en el norte de África, separadas solo por la corta distancia del estrecho de Gibraltar. En 711, un ejército musulmán al mando del general **Tariq ibn Ziyad** desembarcó en Gibraltar. Tariq era bereber (nativo del noroeste de África) o, en el lenguaje de la época, moro; y fue una fuerza combinada de árabes y moros la que logró la **conquista de Hispania**, conocida en el mundo islámico como **al-Ándalus**. Según la tradición, Tariq derrotó al rey visigodo Roderico (Rodrigo) en la batalla de Guadalete, y al acabar el año la mayor parte de la península Ibérica estaba bajo control islámico. Solo el noroeste, conocido como **Asturias, consiguió resistir a los invasores**, cuyo avance fue frenado en la batalla de Covadonga, en 718. Ese año es una de las fechas dadas tradicionalmente como inicio del proceso de reconquista de España por los cristianos. No obstante, al final de esa década nuevas expediciones a través de los Pirineos y el éxito de las campañas en Asia central habían **extendido el califato** desde la Provenza hasta las fronteras de China.

A pesar de todo, los árabes sufrieron algunos reveses: en 717, otra incursión en territorio bizantino desencadenó un cambio en la dirección del imperio, que llevó al trono a **León III**, fundador de la dinastía isauria. Aunque fue incapaz de impedir que los árabes llegaran a las murallas de la capital e iniciaran el **segundo sitio de Constantinopla** (717–718), su enérgico mando de la defensa y el empleo de un arma secreta, el **fuego griego**, frenaron el avance árabe en el Mediterráneo oriental. Aprovechando el uso de sifones propulsores de fuego griego, la flota bizantina se hizo con el control del mar, y León pudo empezar a restaurar el imperio.

Xuanzong, el emperador Tang, subió al trono en 712. Sus 43 años de reinado supondrían el **apogeo** económico y cultural **de la China Tang**, con el establecimiento de abundantes escuelas, el patronazgo de las artes y un gran florecimiento literario.

FUEGO GRIEGO

La expansión árabe resultó ser indirectamente la salvación para el Imperio bizantino cuando Calínico, un sirio obligado al exilio por la invasión árabe, llevó a Constantinopla la fórmula de un arma secreta que se conoció como fuego griego. Actualmente se cree que era una mezcla altamente inflamable de nafta, azufre, cal viva y salitre –una especie de napalm medieval–, que era arrojada sobre el enemigo por unos tubos que podían acoplarse a la proa del dromón (barco de guerra bizantino).

721–730

Un icono de Cristo sostenido por Nicéforo, patriarca de Constantinopla.

CASA GRANDE FLORECIÓ HACIA LA DÉCADA DE 720. El éxito de este asentamiento de los hohokam, un antiguo pueblo del desierto de Sonora (en la actual Arizona), se basó en un sistema de regadío que permitía sembrar una amplia variedad de cultivos a pesar de la aridez del entorno. Los hohokam habitaron allí durante más de mil años, y fueron conocidos como los «**constructores de canales**» por sus sofisticadas técnicas de irrigación. Casa Grande estaba en el **centro de una red comercial** que se extendía desde la costa del **Pacífico** a Tucson y el **golfo de México**. Es probable que las primeras construcciones de Casa Grande fueran casas-pozo: la «gran casa» que da nombre al asentamiento llegó mucho después.

En 725, los jazares, un pueblo turco originario de Asia central, **establecieron su capital en Atil**, sobre el delta del Volga, en el extremo noroccidental del mar Caspio. Desde allí controlaron las **rutas comerciales a todos los rincones de Asia** y erigieron un imperio que dominaría durante siglos la zona de Europa oriental y Asia occidental comprendida entre el río Dniéper y el mar de Azov.

En Bizancio, en 726, el emperador León III (*véase* 711–720) instauró una **política de iconoclasia** (destrucción de las imágenes consideradas sacrílegas), basada en la idea de que Dios estaba castigando a los cristianos bizantinos por su pérdida de tierras frente a árabes y eslavos. La controversia estimuló al papado romano a afirmar su independencia de la autoridad imperial bizantina.

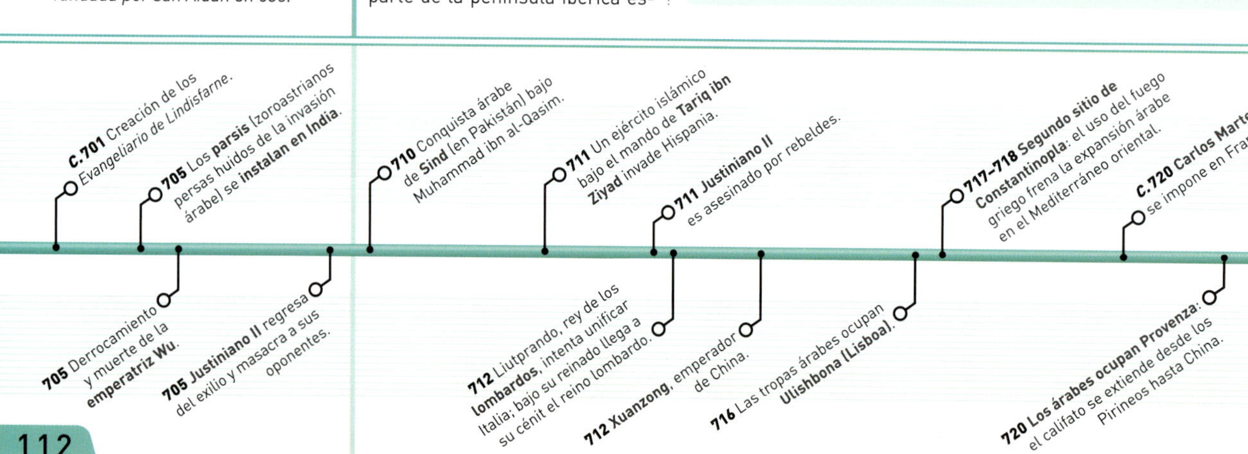

721 Los árabes son rechazados por el duque Eudes en la **batalla de Tolosa**.

C.725 Inicio del asentamiento hohokam de **Casa Grande**, en Arizona.

725 *De temporum ratione*, obra del monje inglés conocido como **Beda el Venerable**, populariza **la datación** a.C./d.C.

726 Iconoclasia en Bizancio: el emperador León III usa esta política para oponerse al creciente poder monástico.

731–740

En 1837, Charles de Steuben pintó la batalla de Poitiers como un choque con el destino de la Europa cristiana en juego. En realidad, los invasores árabes fueron derrotados en una escaramuza menor.

790 PERSONAS POR KM²

DENSIDAD DE POBLACIÓN DE **TIKAL**

DESDE LA CONQUISTA DE HISPANIA, LAS FUERZAS ISLÁMICAS lanzaron ataques habituales a través de los Pirineos, internándose en la actual Francia antes de retirarse a al-Ándalus. En 721, una incursión en Aquitania –un ducado nominalmente vasallo del reino franco– había sido repelida por el **duque Eudes en la batalla de Tolosa**. Pero en 731, Eudes fue incapaz de detener una nueva invasión de tropas árabes bajo el mando de **Abderramán I**, emir de Córdoba. Tras su derrota en la batalla de Arles, Eudes se vio obligado a acudir a **Carlos Martel**, mayordomo de palacio del reino franco, en busca de ayuda. Martel formó un ejército y en 732 se encontró con las tropas islámicas a orillas del Loira, entre Tours y Poitiers: salió victorioso de la **batalla de Poitiers (o de Tours)**, y los historiadores cristianos posteriores describirían su victoria como uno de los choques decisivos de la época: el momento en que la expansión islámica fue frenada y la cristiandad europea salvada. Las fuentes árabes la registraron como una escaramuza menor cuya principal importancia, en realidad, fue demostrar a los reinos francos la necesidad de presentar una defensa unificada.

En América Central, las **ciudades-estado mayas** del periodo Clásico Tardío alcanzaron **la cima de su poder** y sofisticación a mediados del siglo VIII. Por ejemplo, la población de **Tikal** aumentó hasta al menos sesenta mil habitantes en una ciudad que se extendía sobre 76 km². Los señores mayas construyeron templos, palacios, canchas y observatorios, y controlaron una red comercial que se extendía desde California a América del Sur. Pero el auge de la gloria de las ciudades-estado plantó las **semillas de su caída**, ya que sus poblaciones saturaron la capacidad ecológica del entorno y sobrestimaron su capacidad de afrontar las sequías: el colapso estaba a la vuelta de la esquina.

Estatua de Chaac, dios maya
Los mayas buscarían la ayuda de Chaac, dios de la lluvia y el trueno, para sus cultivos. Ocupaban una región de suelos pobres y ecología frágil, por lo que la lluvia era vital.

741–750

La gran mezquita de Samarra (Iraq), erigida por el califato abasí. En el pasado fue la mezquita más grande del mundo, con un minarete de 52 m de altura.

LA FUNDACIÓN DEL CALIFATO ABASÍ EN 750 fue la culminación de la creciente tensión en el mundo islámico. Bajo los Omeyas (*véase* 651–670), la élite árabe mantuvo tercamente sus impuestos especiales y su estatus político, ignorando las quejas de los mawali (musulmanes no árabes), cada vez más intensas. En el año 747 estalló una revuelta en el Jurasán persa, bastión del clan abasí, que trazaba su ascendencia hasta Mahoma a través de su tío, al-Abbas. En 749, **Abu al-Abbas al-Saffah fue proclamado califa** en Kufa (Iraq), y al año siguiente, en 750, derrotaba a Marwan II, el último califa omeya, en la **batalla del Zab**. Marwan huyó a Egipto, pero su cabeza fue devuelta a Damasco, después de lo cual al-Saffah instigó una **masacre contra al clan Omeya** para eliminar toda posible oposición.

En 741 **fallecía Carlos Martel** (*véase* 731–740), al que sucedieron sus dos hijos, **Pipino el Breve** y **Carlomán**. En el año 748, Pipino tuvo un hijo, Carlos (el futuro Carlomagno), que con el tiempo uniría gran parte de Europa occidental bajo un solo cetro (*véase* 761–790).

Tiahuanaco (o Tiwanaku), una ciudad precolombina del Altiplano boliviano, alcanzó su cima *c.* 750. Centro de una cultura que floreció en los siglos III–X (*véase* 951–960), es probable que la propia ciudad fuera un **centro ceremonial y comercial**; su influencia cultural y económica se extendió por América del Sur, y pudo afectar profundamente a civilizaciones posteriores de la región andina. Tiahuanaco prosperó en las duras condiciones del Altiplano gracias a su sofisticado **sistema agrícola de caballones** (campos elevados) y al uso extensivo de **terrazas y canales**, que permitían obtener cosechas incluso superiores a la agricultura convencional petroquímica moderna (abajo) y sustentaron el desarrollo de una cultura compleja. El pueblo tiahuanacota construyó pirámides, templos y estatuas colosales.

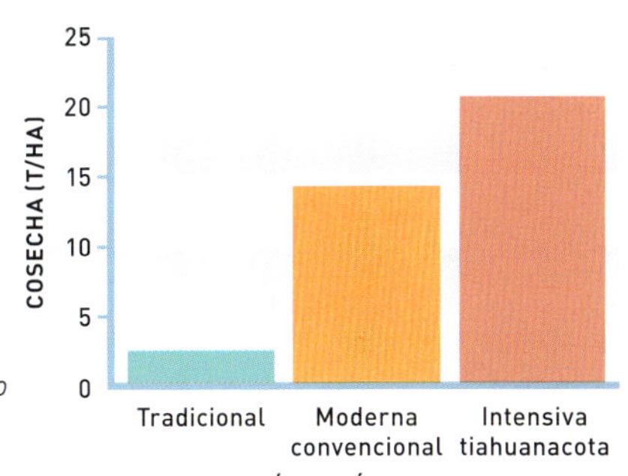

Cosechas de Tiahuanaco
Según reconstrucciones experimentales, los caballones combinados con canales de regadío permitieron a Tiahuanaco obtener cosechas de hasta 21 toneladas por hectárea.

c. 730 La **civilización maya** clásica tardía alcanza su cénit.

c. 731 El monje inglés **Beda** termina su *Historia eclesiástica del pueblo inglés*.

731 Tropas islámicas derrotan a **Eudes**, duque de Aquitania, en Arles.

732 Carlos Martel derrota a las fuerzas árabes y moras en la **batalla de Poitiers**.

733 El Estado Tang emplea a 17 680 **funcionarios**.

737 Carlos Martel recupera Aviñón de manos islámicas.

738 Una **expedición árabe transahariana** regresa con gran cantidad de oro.

739 El reino de **Asturias** se extiende a Portugal.

739 Carlos Martel, aliado con Liutprando, rey de los lombardos, expulsa a los árabes de **Provenza**.

740 Batalla de **Akroinon**: León III derrota a los árabes en Anatolia.

c. 740 Evolución de la **poesía china** con Li Po y Tu Fu, bajo el mecenazgo de los Tang.

741 Muere **León III**, emperador bizantino.

741 Muere Carlos Martel; es sucedido por **Pipino el Breve** y **Carlomán**.

744 Asesinato del califa omeya Walid II; **Marwan II** accede al califato.

745 Fundación del **Imperio uigur** en Asia central.

746 Grave brote de **peste** en el **Imperio bizantino**.

747 Pipino se convierte en rey único de los reinos francos tras la abdicación de su hermano.

749 Al-Saffah es proclamado **califa**.

750 Batalla del Zab, seguida por la masacre general de los Omeyas.

c. 750 Cumbre de la ciudad-estado maya de **Tikal** en América Central y de la preincaica andina de **Tiahuanaco**.

751–760

El interior de la mezquita de Córdoba muestra la arquitectura de su fase más temprana de construcción durante el reinado de Abderramán I.

BAJO LOS NUEVOS CALIFAS ABASÍES (*véase* 741–750) el Imperio islámico continuó creciendo. En 741 se produjo un éxito inicial contra los chinos del reino de Tashkent, en la Ruta de la Seda. Aquel año, los ejércitos islámicos vencieron en la **batalla del río Talas**, cerca de Samarcanda. En 755 comenzó una rebelión dirigida por el general An Lushan que debilitó gravemente el poder de la dinastía Tang en Asia central. Las regiones periféricas del califato afirmaron su autonomía: en el año 756, uno de los últimos supervivientes omeyas, Abderramán I, declaró en al-Ándalus el **emirato de Córdoba**.

En Europa, el carolingio **Pipino III** (*c.* 714–768) **depuso al último rey merovingio**, Childerico III. Pipino fue coronado con el apoyo del papa, favor que no tardó en devolver: cuando los lombardos conquistaron Ravena, el **último territorio bizantino en Italia**, el rey lombardo Astolfo puso sus ojos en Roma. El papa Esteban II recurrió a Pipino en busca de ayuda y, en 755 y 756, este invadió Italia y capturó Ravena. Más adelante el papado reclamaría en un documento, la **Donación de Pipino**, que este había concedido todos los territorios previamente conquistados en el norte de Italia al papa, aunque es casi seguro que no fue así.

Pipino III
También conocido como Pipino el Breve, fue el primer rey carolingio de los francos. Esta escultura de su tumba es del siglo XIII.

761–770

La rotación de cultivos a dos niveles introducida *c.* 760 dividía los campos entre sembrado y barbecho, y luego alternaba, favoreciendo la fertilidad del suelo.

LA MUERTE DE PIPINO III EN 768 supuso la acostumbrada división del reino franco entre sus hijos Carlomán y Carlos.

Mientras tanto, el gran santuario monástico de la **isla de Iona**, en Escocia, ganaba reputación como centro de devoción y erudición. Es posible que uno de los tesoros de la cristiandad celta –el ***Libro de Kells***– fuera elaborado por los monjes de Iona. Espléndidamente decorado e iluminado, este objeto inapreciable sobrevivió a las incursiones vikingas (*véase* 791–800) y luego, por seguridad, fue trasladado al monasterio de Kells (Irlanda).

La **fundación de Bagdad** en 762 marcó la llegada de la primera auténtica ciudad imperial islámica. Situada cerca de Ctesifonte (la antigua capital sasánida), la nueva ciudad fue cuidadosamente dispuesta según un plano circular, y conectada con los ríos Tigris y Éufrates mediante canales. Bagdad se convirtió en un eje comercial que atrajo a mercaderes del norte de Europa, India y China.

CARLOMAGNO (748–814)

Atlético y físicamente imponente, Carlomagno hablaba latín y entendía el griego, pero nunca aprendió a leer. Su intención era extender la hegemonía franca, promover una relación estrecha con el papado y reformar la Iglesia para asegurarse el apoyo divino para el reino franco. Este tapiz del siglo XV da testimonio de su perdurable legado.

771–780

En esta ilustración sobre vitela, Roldán se despide de Carlomagno.

Conquistas europeas de Carlomagno
Carlomagno heredó tierras de su padre, pero luego se embarcó en una guerra tras otra, continuando la obra de su padre y de su abuelo.

CLAVE
- Imperio franco al acceder Carlomagno al trono
- Conquistas de Carlomagno
- Regiones que le reconocieron como señor

LA MUERTE DE CARLOMÁN EN EL AÑO 771 convirtió a Carlomagno en el rey único de los francos. Al año siguiente lanzaba una serie de sangrientas campañas con el objetivo de devolver al dominio franco a los pueblos al este del Rin, que habían sido vasallos de la anterior dinastía merovingia. En esa misma época, las diversas tribus sajonas todavía eran paganas, y Carlomagno estaba decidido a convertirlas al cristianismo para someterlas a la hegemonía del reino franco. Entre los años 773 y 774 consiguió conquistar el reino de los lombardos, **incorporando el norte de Italia a su imperio** y afirmando su dominio sobre Venecia, Dalmacia y Córcega, con lo que su control abarcaba ambas orillas del Adriático y parte del Mediterráneo. A finales de la década de 770, aprovechando las luchas internas entre los gobernantes musulmanes, trató de **proyectar su poder sobre al-Ándalus**: invitado por emires descontentos a intervenir en los asuntos locales, sus tropas cru-

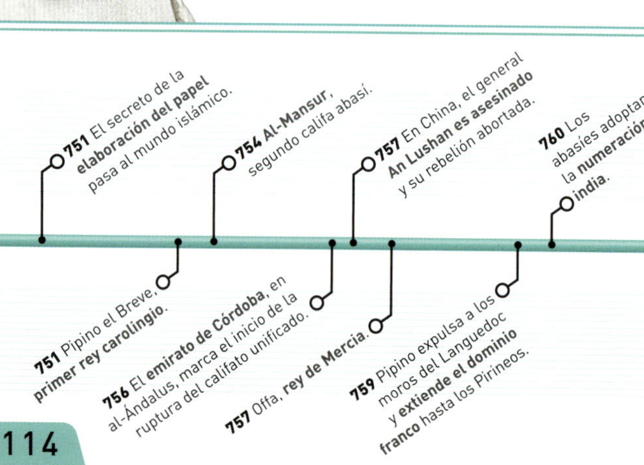

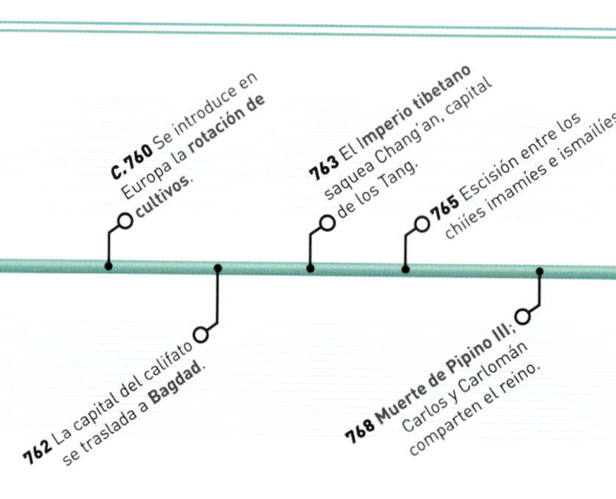

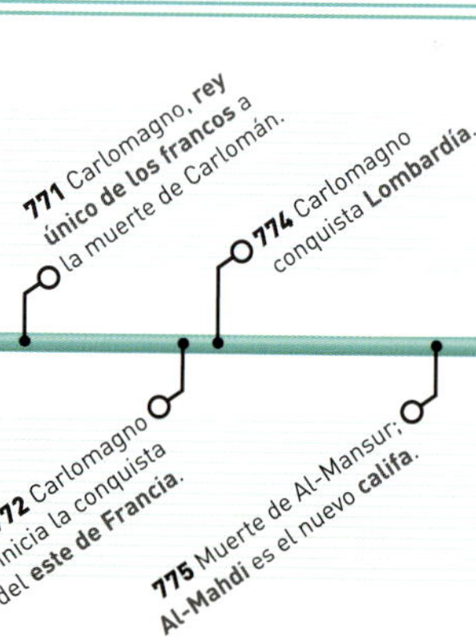

781–790

791–800

La muralla de Offa, en la frontera anglogalesa, fue construida durante el reinado de Offa de Mercia. Aún son visibles tramos de la misma.

El gran Buda de Leshan (China) fue comenzado en 713 y terminado noventa años después.

zaron los Pirineos, pero **fracasaron en la toma de Saraqusta** (Zaragoza) y se vieron obligadas a retirarse.

Esta fallida expedición dio lugar inadvertidamente a uno de los más grandes relatos de la época medieval: la **leyenda de Roldán**. En el año 778, uno de los generales de Carlomagno, Roldán (Roland), resultó muerto cuando llevaba a cabo un ataque contra la retaguardia de las tropas carolingias que se retiraban a través del valle pirenaico de **Roncesvalles**. En realidad, el ataque fue ejecutado por vascones, pero los seguidores bretones de Roldán adoptaron un relato que, a medida que se difundía por Francia en los siglos siguientes, se fue transformando en leyenda con abundancia de elementos ficticios: Roldán se convirtió así en sobrino de Carlomagno y conde de la Marca de Bretaña, y sus atacantes en un ejército de pérfidos sarracenos. En el siglo XI, el ***Cantar de Roldán*** ya aparecía como un cantar de gesta temprano: un relato épico del tiempo de la caballería.

Mientras, en Constantinopla, la **muerte del emperador León IV** llevó al trono a su hijo, **Constantino VI**. Durante su minoría de edad el imperio quedó bajo la regencia de su madre, **Irene**.

LA CONQUISTA POR CARLOMAGNO DE LA SAJONIA OCCIDENTAL en 782 incluyó la sangrienta ejecución de 4500 sajones prisioneros en Werden, suceso del cual se apropiaron los historiadores nazis en la década de 1930 considerándolo una especie de martirio germánico precristiano, mientras que otros han puesto en duda sus detalles o incluso su veracidad. A la vez, preocupado por la ignorancia y el analfabetismo entre el clero, Carlomagno impulsó un renacimiento cultural carolingio.

En 786 accedió al califato en Bagdad **Harún al-Rasid** (r. 768–809). Bajo su reinado tendría gran poder la familia de los Barmakíes, colocados como visires (consejeros de alto rango) y favoritos, y cobraría velocidad el **florecimiento intelectual y cultural del mundo islámico**. El entusiasmo creciente por los libros entre los ricos y poderosos animó a los eruditos a acometer la traducción al árabe de textos antiguos griegos y romanos.

En 785, Offa de Mercia (r. 757–796), soberano de hecho de Britania, comenzó la construcción de la monumental fortificación conocida como Muro de Offa y que se halla en la frontera entre Gales y Mercia. Con sus 27 m de ancho por 8 m de alto originales, su propósito nos es desconocido, y probablemente cayó en desuso poco después de su finalización.

Regalo imperial
Exquisita jarra de agua enviada a Carlomagno por Harún al-Rasid, probablemente c. *800.*

LAS INCURSIONES VIKINGAS sobre las costas de las islas Británicas empezaron en 789 y aumentaron en la década siguiente con el saqueo de los ricos monasterios de Lindisfarne e Iona. Los «vikingos» (palabra posiblemente del nórdico antiguo) procedían de Escandinavia.

En la China Tang, la **influencia del budismo siguió creciendo**, remarcada por monumentos como el **Buda de Leshan**, una gigantesca estatua sedente del Buda tallada en risco junto a la confluencia de varios grandes ríos.

En Constantinopla (actual Estambul), Constantino VI invitó a su **madre Irene a la corregencia** en 792; cinco años después, ella lo dejó ciego y se declaró a sí misma emperatriz. Esta acción espoleó al erudito Alcuino de York a sugerir que el trono imperial estaba vacante de facto, y el 25 de diciembre de 800, **Carlomagno fue coronado emperador de los romanos** por su aliado, el papa León III. Ese mismo año recibió una embajada de Harún al-Rasid, sintomática del cambio de foco del poder en Europa.

Broche funcional y elegante
Este broche vikingo, diestramente trabajado en oro, se usaba para abrochar capas u otras prendas.

En 800, los califas abasíes de Bagdad fueron obligados a reconocer la **pérdida casi total de autoridad en África al oeste de Egipto**. Concedieron al emir de la provincia de Ifriqiya (hoy Túnez y parte de Argelia) el derecho de herencia sobre su cargo. El emir, Ibrahim ibn Aglab, **fundó la dinastía aglabí**, que pagaba tributo a Bagdad y reconocía nominalmente la soberanía abasí, pero que de hecho gobernaba gran parte del norte de África como estado independiente.

> « [CARLOMAGNO] FUE DE CUERPO **ANCHO** Y **ROBUSTO**, DE **ESTATURA**, EMINENTE, SIN EXCEDER LA JUSTA MEDIDA. »
>
> **Eginhardo**, amigo y biógrafo de Carlomagno (*c.* 830)

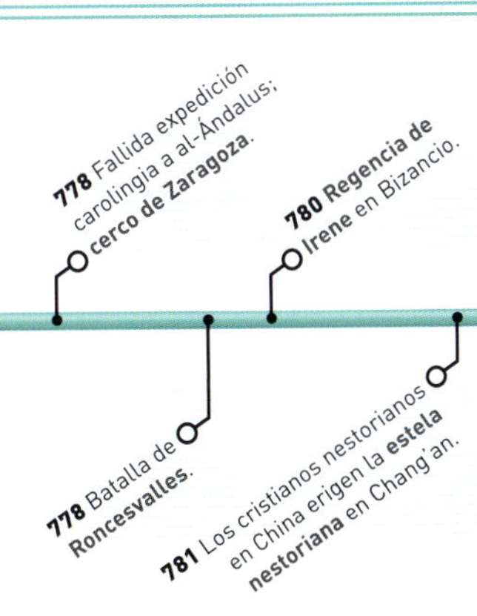

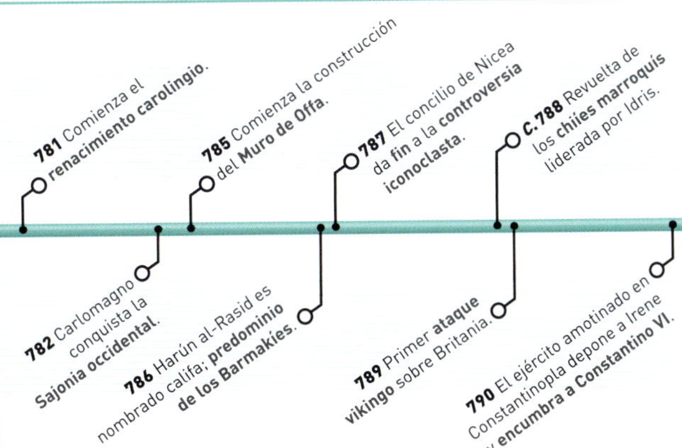

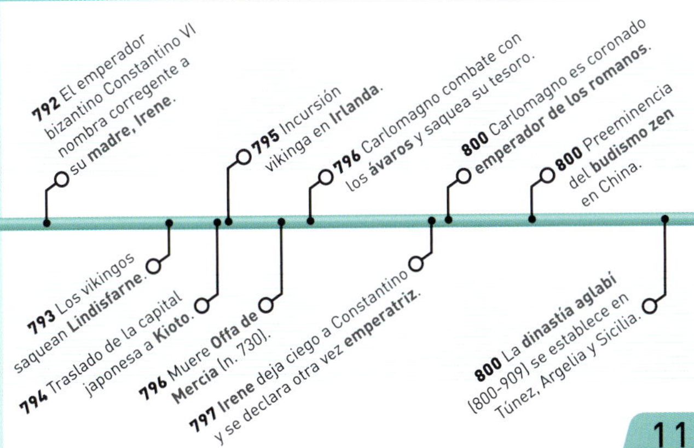

801–810

504 NÚMERO DE ESTATUAS DEL TEMPLO DE BOROBUDUR

EL IMPERIO TIBETANO SE EXPANDIÓ en la primera mitad del siglo IX hasta el golfo de Bengala. Su influencia en Asia central era un indicativo de la debilidad de la **China Tang** en la región. Mientras tanto, en el norte de India, la **dinastía Gurjara-Pratihara**, que había unificado la región y repelido el avance del islam, continuó aumentando su poderío con la conquista de la actual Ka-nauj por parte de **Nagabata II** en torno al año 801.

El **templo de Borobudur**, un **monumento budista** situado en el corazón de la isla de Java, en el Sureste Asiático, se completó en los albores del siglo IX. La colosal estructura, el complejo budista de mayores dimensiones del mundo, está compuesto por más de **dos millones de bloques de piedra** y está cubierto por relieves en una superficie de casi 2000 m². Este templo fue concebido como un *mandala* (o rueda cósmica) tridimensional; el recorrido de su senda, de más de 3 km, representa el viaje hacia el nirvana (iluminación). Su construcción fue toda una proeza épica y un testimonio del poderío del **Imperio de Srivijaya** (*c.* 760–1402), que se había enriquecido merced al extenso comercio marítimo de la región.

Durante gran parte de su era, la **influencia de Srivijaya** llegó al Sureste Asiático peninsular, incluido el **reino de la cuenca del Mekong** anteriormente conocido entre los chinos como Funan. Con todo, en 802, **Jayavarman II**, un soberano vasallo cuya familia había ido ampliando poco a poco sus dominios desde alrededor del año 770, había alcanzado el poder suficiente para establecer un **Imperio jemer** independiente y se autoproclamó *chakravartin*, regente universal o emperador. En sánscrito, este término se traduce como «rey-dios», pues la autoridad de los reyes jemeres estaba basada en el vínculo directo con los dioses, reflejado en los monumentos que erigieron en la ciudad de Angkor varios siglos después (*véase* 1146–1150).

Jayavarman II
Esta estatua de Jayavarman II, fundador del imperio jemer, se encuentra en el templo de Bayon, en Angkor Thom, construido en el siglo XII por orden de su tocayo, Jayavarman VII.

En torno a 801, **Bulan**, kan del Imperio jazar (*véase* 861–870), decidió someter a debate las tres religiones abrahámicas y escogió el **judaísmo**.

811–820

Ludovico Pío en una copia de *De laudibus sanctae crucis*, de Rabano Mauro.

EL CONFLICTO ENTRE BIZANTINOS Y BÚLGAROS (*véase* 671–690) continuó durante la primera parte del siglo IX. A pesar de que el emperador bizantino **Nicéforo I** (r. 802–811) había saqueado la capital búlgara, Pliska, en dos ocasiones (en 809 y 811), el **kan búlgaro Krum** opuso resistencia y se batió con su enemigo en una batalla en 811. Nicéforo fue asesinado, y Krum mandó bañar su calavera en plata para utilizarla como copa para beber. Dos años más tarde, Krum intentó sitiar la capital bizantina, **Constantinopla**, pero no consiguió atravesar sus murallas y se vio obligado a retirarse, no sin antes **devastar Tracia** a su paso.

A la muerte de **Carlomagno** (*véase* 760–800), heredó el trono su último hijo superviviente, **Ludovico Pío** o **Luis el Piadoso** (r. 814–840). Su padre lo había coronado coemperador un año antes.

LA CIENCIA ISLÁMICA

Gracias a la Casa de la Sabiduría y a otros centros de erudición similares, los sabios islámicos superaron en conocimientos a los antiguos griegos y romanos. Los científicos islámicos realizaron grandes avances en campos como la medicina, la alquimia (protoquímica), la toxicología, la metalurgia, las matemáticas y la astronomía. Esta miniatura del *Libro del conocimiento de ingeniosos dispositivos mecánicos* muestra un innovador artilugio para lavar a mano.

821–830

Eruditos en la Casa de la Sabiduría: miniatura de un manuscrito del siglo XIV. Los califas abasíes reclutaron a sabios de todas las religiones y desde Europa a China.

400 000 NÚMERO DE LIBROS DE LA CASA DE LA SABIDURÍA

LA CASA DE LA SABIDURÍA, o *Bait al-Hikma*, era una institución de la **Bagdad abasí** consagrada a la traducción y a la enseñanza de los textos clásicos. Fue el epicentro del renacimiento intelectual islámico, el corazón del movimiento traductológico al árabe y el hogar de grandes sabios, como **Al-Jwarizmi** (*c.* 780–850), de cuyo magnífico tratado matemático de *c.* 830 titulado *Kitab al-Yabr (Libro de la reducción)* procede el nombre de álgebra.

Fue el califa **Al-Mamun** quien consolidó la Casa de la Sabiduría hacia el año 822. Después de la muerte de su padre, **Harún al-Rasid** (*véase* 791–800) y una breve batalla, le sucedió al frente del califato en 813 y continuó la tradición del mecenazgo intelectual mediante la construcción de observatorios y la congregación de los mayores eruditos de todo el mundo. Imitando las prácticas de los **sasánidas**, los predecesores persas de los abasíes, impulsó el **movimiento traductológico** fomentando la búsqueda de manuscritos de otras culturas y tradiciones ancestrales para traducirlos al árabe, gracias a lo cual se conservó gran parte del saber de la Antigüedad que de otro modo se habría perdido. La fundamental obra sobre cosmología de Tolomeo, *Almagesto*, por ejemplo, se tradujo del griego al árabe en torno a 827 y fue esta traducción la que permitió posteriormente a los eruditos europeos acceder al texto antiguo.

Las tensiones entre **Ludovico Pío y sus hijos** por sus herencias generaron conflictos civiles en el **Imperio carolingio** (800–888). Después de la muerte en el año 819 de su primera esposa y madre de sus hijos **Lotario, Pipino y Luis el Germánico**, Ludovico Pío se había casado con la ambiciosa Judit

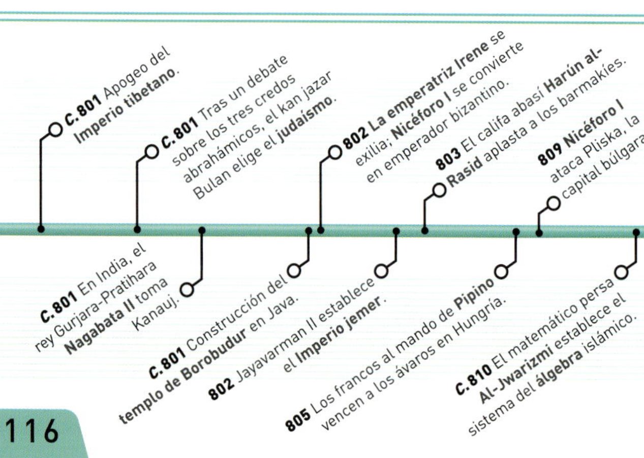

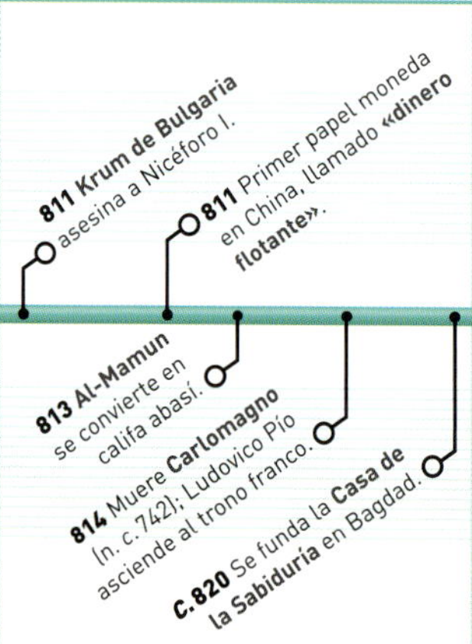

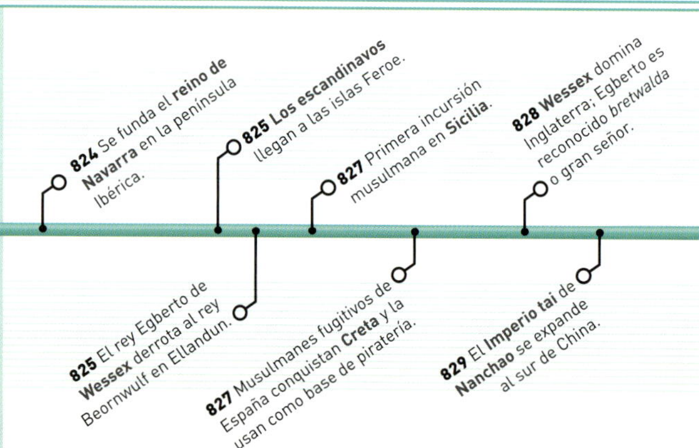

de Baviera, quien lo había convencido para que concediera a su hijo, **Carlos el Calvo** (823–877), tierras que previamente había prometido a **Lotario**. Frustrado, Lotario, coemperador con Ludovico desde 824, incitó a sus hermanos a rebelarse contra su padre. A principios de 830, **Ludovico fue depuesto**. Si bien la ineptitud de Lotario llevó a la restauración de su padre en otoño, la autoridad del anciano soberano se hallaba ya en entredicho y el terreno abonado para futuros conflictos.

El reino anglosajón de **Wessex**, en el sur y el oeste de Inglaterra, se convirtió en la **potencia inglesa dominante** después de la victoria del rey Egberto sobre Beornwulf de Mercia en la batalla de Ellandun (Wiltshire), en 825. Más adelante, Egberto consiguió conquistar los condados del sureste de Inglaterra. En torno al año 828, Wessex era ya el estado más poderoso del territorio, del cual Egberto pretendió ser el *bretwalda*, o gran señor, hasta el momento de su muerte, en 839.

La emergencia de la **Gran Moravia** comenzó alrededor de 830, con la fundación del principado de Mojmir, al oeste de los Cárpatos Blancos, bajo **Mojmir I**. Fue uno de los dos estados eslavos que se establecieron aprovechando el vacío de poder dejado por la caída de los ávaros en 805; el otro, al este de los Cárpatos Blancos, en la actual Eslovaquia, fue Nitra, bajo el **príncipe Pribina**. En 833, Mojmir conquistó Nitra y con ello acabó convirtiéndose en el **Imperio de la Gran Moravia**.

831–840

Vista de los alrededores de Segesta con las ruinas del teatro griego; la zona fue ocupada muy pronto por los aglabíes que invadieron la isla de Sicilia.

LA CONQUISTA ISLÁMICA DE SICILIA comenzó 827 con la llegada de un ejército invasor aglabí desde África del Norte enviado por el **emir Ziyadat Allah I** (r. 817–838) para aprovechar las **divisiones internas** entre los gobernadores **bizantinos** de la isla. Diezmadas por brotes de peste, las tropas musulmanas apenas lograron abrirse paso hasta 831, cuando **Palermo** cayó tras un año de sitio. La ciudad se convirtió en la capital de la Sicilia islámica, si bien la conquista total de la isla no se completó hasta 902.

El llamado **«Campo de la Mentira»**, en Alsacia, fue el escenario del encuentro orquestado por el papa en 833 para mediar entre los **soberanos francos**, cuyo resultado fue la deserción de una parte de los seguidores de Ludovico Pío y Carlos el Calvo, y el posterior encarcelamiento de estos. Este episodio se inscribe en los conflictos que propiciaron el hundimiento de la autoridad central y la vulnerabilidad del territorio franco frente a las incursiones escandinavas al norte y al oeste, de **búlgaros** y **magiares** al este, y de piratas **sarracenos** al sur.

Guerreros sarracenos
«Sarracenos» fue uno de los nombres que dieron los cristianos europeos a los árabes y especialmente a los musulmanes o mahometanos.

841–850

La antigua ciudad de Pagán (Birmania) se convirtió en la capital de un poderoso estado budista que ocupaba un área similar a la región actual.

EL TRATADO DE VERDÚN de 843 supuso la división definitiva del imperio de Carlomagno. Tras la muerte de Ludovico Pío en 840, sus tres hijos supervivientes (*véase* 821–830) se enzarzaron en conflictos territoriales. En 842, Carlos el Calvo y Luis el Germánico aunaron fuerzas y juraron imponer un acuerdo a Lotario por el cual el **Imperio franco quedó dividido** en regiones. A grandes rasgos, las divisiones correspondían a las actuales Francia, al oeste, y Alemania, al este, con un reino intermedio que se conoció como *Lotharii regnum*, el reino de Lotario o Lotaringia (la actual Lorena).

El ascenso de los **Chola**, una dinastía tamil del **sur de India**, puede fecharse en 846, cuando el rey Chola Vijayalaya tomó la ciudad de Thanjavur, en el **reino Pandya**. Mediante la **capitular de Meerssen** (847), el rey franco del oeste, Carlos el Calvo, ordenó a cada hombre libre escoger un señor. Esta medida, que pretendía facilitar el reclutamiento de ejércitos, ponía de manifiesto la creciente incapacidad de los soberanos francos para proteger a sus súbditos. En lugar de en la autoridad central, los campesinos confiaron en los nobles locales, renunciaron a su libertad y se vincularon a una aristocracia feudal a cambio de protección frente a los **vikingos** y otros invasores.

El árbol del café
El cafeto es un árbol originario de las montañas de Etiopía y de Yemen, donde su cultivo se registró por primera vez a mediados del siglo XV.

En torno al año 848 se fundó en el valle del Irawadi la **ciudad-estado birmana de Pagán**. La influencia india se aprecia claramente en la arquitectura de esta zona del Sureste Asiático a causa de los lazos culturales, religiosos y mercantiles.

El legendario **descubrimiento del café** se sitúa alrededor del año 850. Se cuenta que un pastor etíope llamado Kaldi cayó en la cuenta de que, tras comer unas bayas rojas, sus cabras estaban más animadas de lo habitual y llevó una muestra a un santón musulmán local. Este pensó que las bayas eran tóxicas y, en un gesto de desaprobación, las arrojó al fuego, donde se tostaron y exhalaron un delicioso aroma.

830 Luchas internas en el **Imperio carolingio**.

C.830 Se establece el **principado de Mojmir**, que se convertirá en **Imperio de la Gran Moravia**.

831 Continúa la **conquista islámica de Sicilia**; conquista de Palermo.

833 «Campo de la Mentira»: Ludovico Pío es depuesto y Carlos el Calvo encarcelado.

833 Guerra en Decán; el **reino Gurjara** del norte de India se reduce.

833 Al-Mutasim accede al califato abasí y crea un ejército de esclavos turcos.

834 Ludovico Pío es restaurado en el trono franco.

836 Bhoja I restaura el **reino de los Gurjara** en India.

836 Los **vikingos** atacan el interior de Irlanda.

838 Muere Pipino; **división del Imperio franco**.

840 Caída del **Imperio uigur** (Asia central); expulsados por los kirguises, los uigures se instalan en la cuenca de Tarim.

841–842 Guerra civil entre los hijos de Ludovico Pío.

841 Se funda el **reino vikingo de Dublín**.

842 Los vikingos saquean **Londres**.

843 El **tratado de Verdún** pone fin a la guerra civil carolingia.

846 El rey Chola Vijayalaya toma Thanjavur a los Pandya; ascenso al poder de la **dinastía Chola**.

848 Fundación de la ciudad-estado birmana de **Pagán**.

C.850 Primeros **astrolabios árabes**.

C.850 Se usa por primera vez la **pólvora** en China.

C.850 Caída del **Imperio tibetano**.

C.850 Legendario descubrimiento del **café**.

851–860

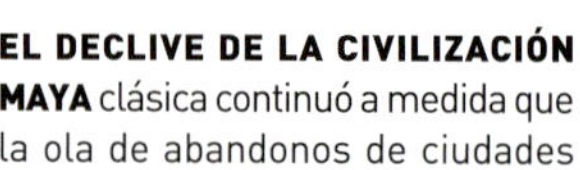
Relieve del patio del palacio de la ciudad maya de Palenque.

EL DECLIVE DE LA CIVILIZACIÓN MAYA clásica continuó a medida que la ola de abandonos de ciudades iniciada en **Palenque** a finales del siglo IX se extendió hacia el sur y el este, hasta el corazón del mundo maya clásico. Las últimas inscripciones registradas en las ciudades de Quiriguá y Copán se remontan a 810 y 822; **en El Caracol a 859**, y en Tikal a 889. La causa pudo ser una combinación de **sequía, hambruna, enfermedades** y disturbios acaecidos cuando la superpoblación de las ciudades y la escasez de recursos alcanzaron un punto álgido.

El primer uso documentado de una **ballesta** tuvo lugar en Francia en 851. Pese a ser más lenta de recargar que un arco, la ballesta (en francés, *arbalette*), requería menos entrenamiento y fuerza.

La **regencia de Fujiwara Yoshifusa** (*c.* 804–872) en nombre de su nieto, el emperador-niño Seiwa, que ascendió al trono en 858, inauguró el dominio del poder japonés por la familia Fujiwara.

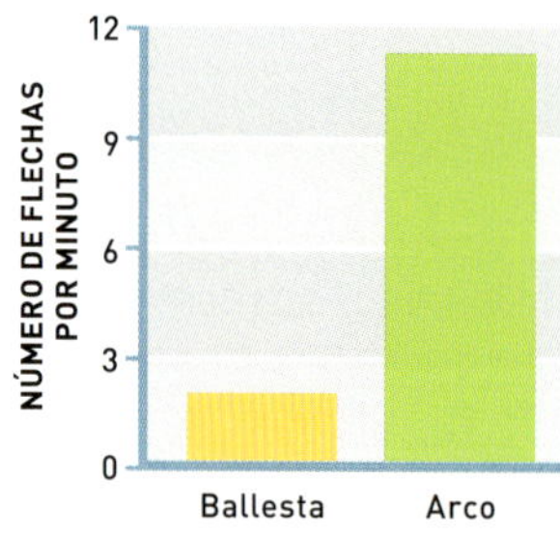

La ballesta y el arco
Pese a que la frecuencia de tiro del arco era mucho mayor, la ballesta tenía mayor alcance y era más fácil de usar.

861–870

El frontispicio del *Sutra del diamante*, la primera obra impresa conocida, muestra a Buda explicando el sutra (sermón) a un discípulo anciano.

EL IMPERIO JAZAR

El mar Caspio sigue conociéndose en la región como mar Jazar por el imperio que dominó la zona entre este y el mar Negro entre los siglos VIII y X. Es posible que una subida de 7 m del nivel del mar contribuyera al declive del imperio.

LA ESCRITURA CIRÍLICA FUE INVENTADA hacia 863 por un misionero bizantino que después fue conocido como **san Cirilo**. Hacia el año 862, el emperador bizantino Miguel III había enviado a Cirilo (cuyo nombre real era Constantino) y a su hermano Metodio a **convertir a los eslavos** de **Moravia**. Para **traducir la Biblia** al eslavo, Cirilo ideó un nuevo alfabeto «glagolítico» (eslavo), que dio origen al cirílico.

Basilio, favorito de Miguel III, depuso a su señor en 867 y ocupó el trono como **Basilio I**. Su reinado marcó el inicio de uno de los periodos más gloriosos de la historia de Bizancio. Basilio reconstruyó el ejército y la flota, y revisó el sistema legal.

El ***Sutra del diamante*** de 868 es el libro impreso más antiguo del mundo que se conoce. Es un texto budista ilustrado y fue hallado en una cueva cerca de Dunhuang, población de la Ruta de la Seda situada en el noroeste de China.

A mediados del siglo IX, los **jazares adoptaron el judaísmo** (*véase* 801–810). Según la tradición, escogieron una **religión abrahámica** para ponerse en pie de igualdad con la cristiandad del Imperio bizantino y el islam del califato.

Escritura cirílica ancestral
Esta tablilla de cera contiene salmos de David escritos a principios del siglo XI. Se cree que es el documento más antiguo escrito en cirílico.

871–880

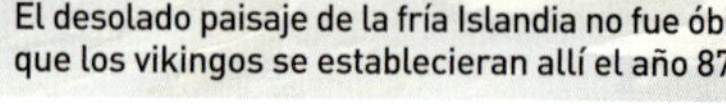
El desolado paisaje de la fría Islandia no fue óbice para que los vikingos se establecieran allí el año 874.

ALFREDO EL GRANDE DE INGLATERRA, un hombre cultivado que había pasado un tiempo en Roma junto al papa, accedió al trono del reino anglosajón de **Wessex** en 871. Durante el reinado de su hermano mayor, Ethelred I (r. 865–871), cuando los **vikingos daneses** invadieron Wessex, Alfredo había ayudado a derrotarlos en la **batalla de Ashdown** en 870. Una vez rey, Alfredo evitó las crisis al derrotar a los daneses en Wilton, en el suroeste de Inglaterra, si bien un nuevo ataque en el año 875 le encontró desprevenido y le obligó a retirarse a las marismas de Somerset. Cuenta una leyenda que allí lo cobijó una campesina, quien, ajena a su identidad, le pidió que vigilara unos pasteles que se estaban haciendo al fuego. Preocupado por los problemas de su reino, Alfredo dejó que los pasteles se quemaran. No obstante, fue capaz de congregar a sus ejércitos para derrotar en 878 al caudillo danés Guthrum en la batalla de Edington. Obligado a firmar la **paz de Wedmore, Guthrum se convirtió al cristianismo** y accedió a dividir el país (*véase* 881–890).

Su **asentamiento en Islandia** demostró que los **vikingos** avanzaban en otros frentes. Es probable que los monjes irlandeses hubieran alcanzado antes la isla del Atlántico Norte y que los navegantes vikingos tuvieran otras pistas de su existencia, como el paso de aves migratorias. Los vikingos ya habían visitado la isla y habían pasado el invierno allí, pero el primer asentamiento permanente, según el *Landnámabók* («Libro de la colonización») medieval islandés, fue el del caudillo noruego Ingólfur Arnarson hacia el año 874. Cuenta la leyenda que eligió el lugar lanzando las columnas de madera de su trono por la borda y siguiéndolas a la deriva.

Alfredo el Grande
En 1901 se erigió una estatua al rey Alfredo en su capital, Winchester. Su espada hace las veces de cruz, símbolo de su fe.

El **duodécimo imán, Muhammad ibn al Hasan** –a quien algunos chiíes consideran **el Mahdi** o sal-

c. Década de 850 Declive de la civilización **maya clásica**.

851 Se introduce la **ballesta** en Francia.

857 Fundación del **reino de Navarra** (España).

857 Intoxicación por cornezuelo en Europa occidental a causa de la ingestión de cereales infectados.

858 Regencia de Fujiwara en Japón; el clan Fujiwara se instala en el poder.

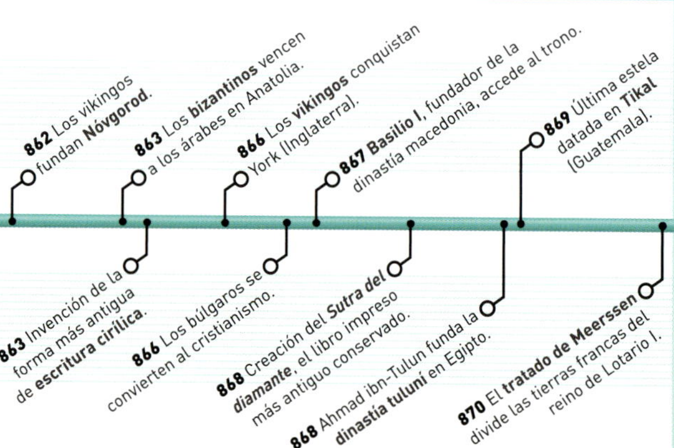

862 Los vikingos fundan **Nóvgorod**.

863 Los **bizantinos** vencen a los árabes en Anatolia.

863 Invención de la forma más antigua de **escritura cirílica**.

866 Los **vikingos** conquistan York (Inglaterra).

866 Los búlgaros se convierten al cristianismo.

867 Basilio I, fundador de la dinastía macedonia, accede al trono.

868 Creación del ***Sutra del diamante***, el libro impreso más antiguo conservado.

868 Ahmad ibn-Tulun funda la **dinastía tuluní** en Egipto.

869 Última estela datada en **Tikal** (Guatemala).

870 El **tratado de Meerssen** divide las tierras francas del reino de Lotario I.

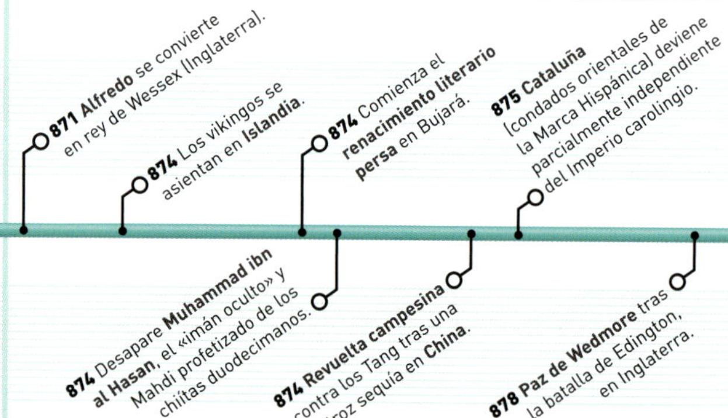

871 Alfredo se convierte en rey de Wessex (Inglaterra).

874 Los vikingos se asientan en **Islandia**.

874 Comienza el **renacimiento literario persa** en Bujará.

874 Desaparece **Muhammad ibn al Hasan**, el «imán oculto» y Mahdi profetizado de los chiitas duodecimanos.

874 Revuelta campesina contra los Tang tras una atroz sequía en **China**.

875 Cataluña (condados orientales de la Marca Hispánica) deviene parcialmente independiente del Imperio carolingio.

878 Paz de Wedmore tras la batalla de Edington, en Inglaterra.

881–890

Fachada del edificio anexo a la Casa de las Monjas, en Chichén Itzá, la principal ciudad-estado maya del periodo Clásico Tardío.

891–900

Simeón de Bulgaria, en el centro, se educó como monje en Constantinopla antes de regresar para asumir el gobierno de los búlgaros en 893.

« PERCIBIMOS A TRAVÉS DE LOS SIGLOS UNA **INTELIGENCIA SUPERIOR** Y **VERSÁTIL**, QUE BLANDE CON IGUAL FUERZA LA ESPADA DE LA **GUERRA** Y LA DE LA **JUSTICIA**. »

Winston Churchill, político británico, sobre Alfredo el Grande (1956–1958)

vador último de la humanidad– desaparece en 874. Según algunos chiíes, cuando el undécimo imán, Hasan al-Askari, falleció en 874, su sucesor, un niño de siete años, vivió en un retiro literal y espiritual, y se dice que desde ese momento permanece «oculto» hasta el día de su **regreso mesiánico**.

La ***Crónica anglosajona***, un testimonio único que describe desde las guerras hasta las condiciones meteorológicas, fue escrita entre 880 y mediados del siglo XII. Es una muestra de la erudición que fomentó el rey Alfredo, quien no solo invitó a sabios a Inglaterra, sino que también tradujo importantes obras clásicas.

LOS VIKINGOS SUECOS, conocidos como **varegos o rus**, utilizaron ríos como el **Volga** y el **Dniéper** para penetrar en el continente desde el Báltico y establecer su dominio sobre los **eslavos orientales** de la región. Tras **fundar el asentamiento de Nóvgorod** en 862 y lanzar audaces ataques contra Constantinopla navegando por ríos hasta el mar Negro, colonizaron territorios más al sur. En 882, el **príncipe ruso Oleg** (r. 882–912) derrotó a sus rivales Askold y Dir, **se apoderó de** su asentamiento en **Kiev** y trasladó allí su capital desde Nóvgorod. La ciudad se convirtió en la capital del **Rus de Kiev**, una federación imprecisa de territorios, hasta 1169.

El **Danelaw**, la zona de Inglaterra regulada por leyes vikingas, se formalizó mediante el **tratado de Alfredo y Guthrum** en 886, tras nuevos ataques del caudillo danés. Alfredo conservó el sur, incluido Londres, mientras que la zona situada al norte de una línea entre los ríos Támesis y Lea correspondió a los daneses, que vivían en ella según sus propias leyes.

En 887, **Carlos el Gordo** (*c.* 839–888), el último carolingio que reinó en los dos territorios francos principales, Francia Occidental y Francia Oriental (las actuales Francia y Alemania), fue **derrocado**. Carlos, rey de los francos orientales desde 879, había sido elegido rey de los francos occidentales en 884. Sin embargo, fue víctima del declive del poder y la autoridad de los monarcas carolingios (*véase* 841–850). Incapaz de hacer frente a los vikingos o reacio a batallar con ellos, sobre todo durante su **asedio de París** de 885 y 886, demostró no ser capaz de proteger a su pueblo. **Eudes**, conde de París (*c.* 860–898), encabezó una defensa heroica contra los vikingos en 885 y fue elegido rey de Francia Occidental en 887. A partir de entonces, la Francia Oriental y la Occidental evolucionaron por separado.

El catastrófico **declive de las ciudades-estado mayas clásicas** de las tierras bajas del sur se prolongó durante todo el siglo IX, y **Tikal fue abandonada** en torno a 889. Las ciudades del norte (la zona de la península de Yucatán de México) prosperaron en el llamado periodo Clásico Tardío. La principal fue **Chichén Itzá**, la primera en aprovechar los cenotes (depósitos naturales de agua subterránea), de trascendental importancia en aquella región propensa a las sequías.

Joyería eslavovikinga
Los invasores vikingos que conquistaron territorios a lo largo de los cauces fluviales de Rusia crearon una cultura híbrida de estilos eslavos y vikingos.

EL PODER DEL KANATO BÚLGARO (*véase* 811–820) inquietaba al emperador bizantino **León VI**, quien en 895 espoleó a los **magiares** contra los búlgaros. Sin embargo, lo único que consiguió fue provocar a **Simeón** (r. 893–927), el nuevo kan, a movilizar a los pechenegos, una tribu recién llegada al Dniéper, para atacar las tierras magiares. Los magiares se vieron forzados a emigrar hacia el oeste y se establecieron en la actual **Hungría**, desde donde lanzaron repetidos ataques a territorios francos en los años posteriores. En el verano de 896, Simeón derrotó a un **ejército bizantino** en Bulgarófigo (en la actual Turquía) y obligó al emperador a pagarle tributo. Simeón gobernó otros treinta años, rivalizando por el trono bizantino, del que lo alejaron en múltiples ocasiones las impenetrables murallas de la capital, **Constantinopla**.

Los **toltecas** (*c.* 800–1000) fueron, probablemente, refugiados que procedían de la **decadente Teotihuacán** (*véase* 690–700) que se asentaron en el valle de México y establecieron su capital en **Tula** (*c.* 900), donde forjaron un imperio militarizado que inspiró a sus descendientes, los aztecas.

Coyote tolteca
El arte tolteca, como esta cabeza de coyote con un ser humano en sus fauces, influyó en otras civilizaciones precolombinas, incluida la azteca.

879 Nepal se independiza del Tíbet.

880 Huang Zhao, un rebelde campesino convertido en general, usurpa el trono imperial Tang.

880 Guerra en India entre los **Pandya** y los **Chola**.

880 Primera ***Crónica anglosajona***.

882 Oleg asedia Kiev y la convierte en capital del **Rus de Kiev**.

884 Huang Zhao es derrotado por los turcos; el poder Tang se tambalea.

887 Coronación de **Eudes** como rey de Francia Occidental.

887 El carolingio **Carlos el Gordo** es depuesto.

889 Tikal es abandonada; **Chichén Itzá** cobra protagonismo.

896 Inicio del apogeo del **Imperio búlgaro** bajo Simeón.

899 Muere **Alfredo el Grande** de Wessex (n. 849).

c. 900 Desarrollo del reino **tolteca** centrado en **Tula**, en el valle de México.

c. 900 Los vikingos descubren **Groenlandia**.

c. 900 Primeras versiones de *Alf-layla wa-layla* (***Las mil y una noches***).

901–910

Este relieve en piedra data del periodo chino de las Cinco Dinastías y los Diez Reinos. La desestructuración de la autoridad central en esta época conllevó un retroceso económico.

LA CHINA DE LOS TANG vivía un declive militar desde su derrota por los árabes en la batalla del río Talas en 751–760, y la **rebelión de Huang Zhao** en la década de 880 señaló el fin de la dinastía. **Zhuwen** (*c.* 852–912) era un señor feudal que había participado en el alzamiento de Huang Zhao y fue decisivo para la derrota rebelde. Recompensado con generosidad, fue afianzando su poder hasta que en 904 estuvo listo para hacerse con las riendas del gobierno, cosa que hizo tras **ejecutar** al **emperador Tang Zhaozong** y a la mayoría de sus hijos e instalar en el trono a uno de ellos, de trece años de edad, como soberano títere. En 907 ocupó él mismo el trono y fundó la **dinastía de los Liang Posteriores**, pero a pesar de controlar el corazón de la China septentrional (la región del valle del río Amarillo o Huang He) no logró evitar que el sur se fragmentara en diez reinos independientes. La dinastía de los Liang Posteriores fue efímera (907–923) y se vio asediada por diversos grupos que fundaron sus propias dinastías en la región del Huang He, si bien fueron incapaces de conservar el poder. El periodo de anarquía conocido como de las Cinco Dinastías y los Diez Reinos se prolongó hasta la instauración de la **dinastía Song del Norte** (*véase* 951–960) y fue una época de grandes adversidades. La autoridad se descompuso, la economía se derrumbó y en muchas zonas el trueque reemplazó al dinero. Como consecuencia del descuido de las defensas frente a las crecidas y de las obras de regadío se produjeron graves inundaciones y una hambruna generalizada.

Al oeste y al norte de la región de las Cinco Dinastías, los **turcos shatuo** y los **mongoles jitán** consolidaron sus propios reinos. Los jitán del sur de Manchuria establecieron su imperio en 905 bajo Yelu Abaoji (872–926). Este se autoproclamó emperador en 916 y fundó la **dinastía Liao**, que perduró hasta 1125, incluido un breve periodo como una de las Cinco Dinastías que controlaron el norte de China.

En 909, Said ibn Husein, un chií ismailí, derrocó a la **dinastía suní aglabí** en Kairuán (actual Túnez), se proclamó **Mahdi** (el último líder mesiánico de los musulmanes antes del fin del mundo) y **fundó la dinastía fatimí**, así llamada en honor de la hija del profeta Mahoma, de la que se declaró descendiente.

La **abadía de Cluny**, en Borgoña, fundada en 910 por el duque de Aquitania Guillermo el Piadoso, se convirtió en el centro de un **«imperio» monástico** europeo (*véase* recuadro).

Rechazados hacia el oeste por los pechenegos (*véase* 891–900), los **magiares** lanzaron una serie de **ataques** devastadores durante toda la década. En 901 saquearon Carintia; en 906 y 907 causaron estragos en Moravia, y en 908 atacaron Baviera, Sajonia y Turingia. Ante la reticencia o la incapacidad del emperador franco para socorrerlos, los francos orientales eligieron «duques» regionales para defenderse de las incursiones.

Manuscrito fatimí
Los fatimíes, así llamados por Fátima, la hija de Mahoma, fueron mecenas del saber mediante su patrocinio de la escuela Al-Azhar de El Cairo.

LA ABADÍA DE CLUNY

En 910, Guillermo el Piadoso donó las tierras a los monjes benedictinos sin imponerles ninguna obligación, de modo que la abadía quedaba al margen de la supervisión secular y solo respondía ante el papa. Cluny se convirtió en el centro de un «imperio» del que dependían unos diez mil monjes. El papa Urbano II, antiguo abad de Cluny, la llamó «la luz del mundo».

Las Cinco Dinastías
Regímenes sucesivos fueron incapaces de consolidar el poder, lo cual permitió a los señores feudales del norte y el sur fundar reinos independientes. La situación geopolítica fragmentada se aprecia en este mapa, que muestra una maraña de fronteras y estados.

GANZHOU
SHAZHOU
Uigures
Jitán
YAN
Mar Amarillo
TANG POSTERIORES
ANTIGUO SHU
Tibetanos
JINGNAN
WU YUE
WU
CHU
MIN
Man
HAN DEL SUR
ANNAM
Mar de la China Meridional

CLAVE
Estados chinos
Estados ocupados por pueblos no chinos

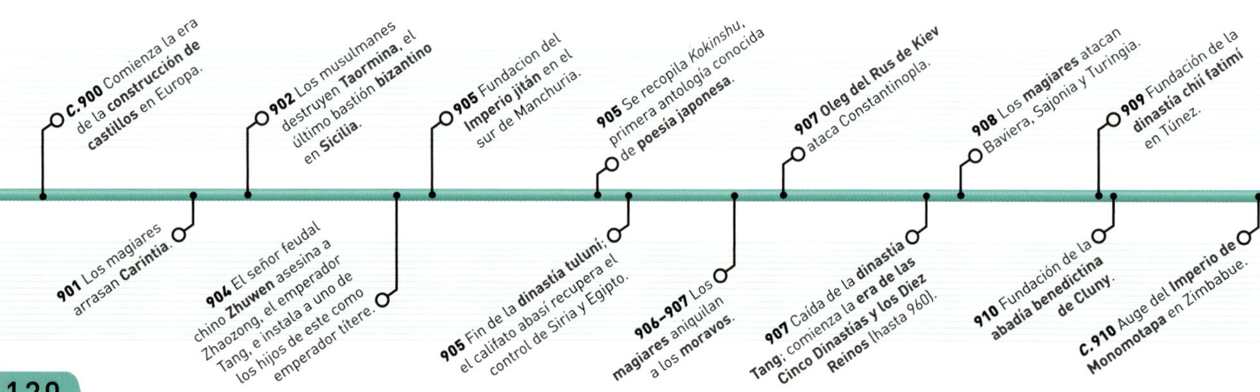

911–920

ABDERRAMÁN III SE CONVIRTIÓ EN EL NUEVO EMIR OMEYA de **Córdoba** a la muerte de su abuelo, Abdallah, en el año 912. Sus territorios habían quedado reducidos por las rebeliones y de inmediato se dispuso a recuperar gran parte de su reino perdido. Durante su reinado y el de sus sucesores, Córdoba alcanzó la cima de su poder (*véase* 921–930).

Según fuentes tradicionales, **el príncipe Igor, soberano del Rus de Kiev** entre 914 y 945, era hijo del legendario Riurik, fundador de Nóvgorod en 862. Bajo su protección, el **Rus de Kiev** (*véase* 881–890) se

Igor I de Kiev
Igor, que reinó desde 914 hasta su muerte en 945, hace un gesto imperioso a su corte en esta ilustración decimonónica.

911 El caudillo escandinavo **Rollón** recibe Normandía.
912 Abderramán III se convierte en emir; llevará a su cénit al emirato **omeya** de Córdoba.
913 El **príncipe Igor** se convierte en gobernante del Rus de Kiev.
914 Los **fatimíes** toman Alejandría.

921–930

931–950

Panel decorativo de Medina Azahara (Madinat al-Zahra), complejo palacial construido por Abderramán III para emular a los califas abasíes de Bagdad.

La Roca de la Ley (Islandia) era el centro del parlamento más antiguo.

« ESTE AÑO, EL **REY ATHELSTAN**, SEÑOR DE GUERREROS, DADOR DE ANILLOS A LOS HOMBRES… GANÓ **GLORIA INMORTAL** CON EL FILO DE LA ESPADA EN LA BATALLA **CERCA DE BRUNABURH**. **»**

Autor desconocido, fragmento de un poema en inglés antiguo sobre la batalla de Brunaburh (937)

convirtió en una potencia regional formidable que se granjeó no solo el respeto de los bizantinos mediante las armas durante la **guerra entre el Rus y Bizancio** de 941, sino también lucrativas concesiones comerciales.

En 911, reconociendo su indefensión frente a los constantes y devastadores **ataques vikingos** (*véase* 881–890), el rey de Francia Occidental **Carlos III**, apodado **el Simple**, cedió una amplia zona en torno a la desembocadura del Sena (gran parte de la futura Normandía) al caudillo noruego **Rollón**, también conocido como Hrolfr, con la condición de que se convirtiera al cristianismo. La posición de Carlos era frágil: la autoridad de los monarcas carolingios había caído en picado y por entonces eran condes locales quienes gobernaban los que a efectos prácticos eran feudos independientes, solo bajo la autoridad nominal del rey (*véase* 841–850). Una poderosa facción de magnates francos occidentales había elegido rey al **conde Eudes** de París en 887, de manera que Carlos pasó gran parte de su reinado enzarzado en una guerra civil con Eudes y sus descendientes.

Uno de los duques regionales que accedieron al poder ante la impotencia de los carolingios frente a la amenaza magiar fue **Enrique I**, elegido rey de los francos orientales en 919 y fundador de la **dinastía sajona**. El último monarca carolingio de Francia Oriental, Luis el Niño, falleció en 911, y Conrado, duque de Franconia, fue elegido rey. A su muerte, este nombró sucesor a su rival más poderoso, Enrique.

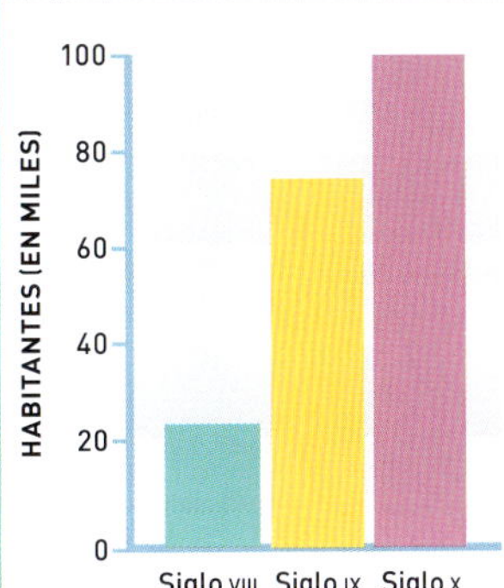

La población de Córdoba
Este cálculo aproximado muestra el rápido crecimiento de Córdoba, una pequeña población convertida en una de las mayores ciudades medievales.

LA MENGUANTE AUTORIDAD DE LOS ABASÍES EN BAGDAD condujo a Abderramán III a declararse el verdadero califa en 929, con lo cual su emirato se convirtió en **califato**. Durante el siglo X, la capital, Córdoba, llegó a ser la ciudad más poblada y desarrollada de Europa occidental.

En 930, los **islandeses** empezaron a reunirse para debatir cuestiones de justicia y legislación en una asamblea al aire libre en las llanuras de **Thingvellir**. Todos los hombres libres que no hubieran sido proscritos podían asistir al **Althing, la asamblea representativa más antigua** del mundo.

Durante el periodo que los arqueólogos denominan **fase Pueblo II**, en América del Norte florecieron los pueblos del Cañón del Chaco, que construyeron unas inmensas estructuras llamadas casas grandes, algunas con cerca de 700 estancias.

EN EL AÑO 932, EL CALIFA OMEYA ABDERRAMÁN III (véase 911–920) volvió a reunir a toda la España musulmana (al-Ándalus) bajo un mismo estandarte con la toma de Toledo. También luchó en sus fronteras septentrionales contra los reinos cristianos de **León** y **Navarra**, a los cuales obligó a reconocer su señorío. En general, judíos y cristianos disfrutaron de tolerancia bajo el califato cordobés, aunque continuaron siendo ciudadanos de segunda clase, por lo que estaban sometidos a cargas fiscales que fueron motivo de muchas conversiones.

El **reino de Silla** (*véase* 651–670) fue conquistado por el **reino de Koryo** en 935, con lo cual **Corea** quedó reunificada bajo el líder de Koryo Wang Kon, conocido como **rey Taejo** (r. 918–943). Wang Kon había accedido al poder en el estado de los Tres Reinos de Koguryo en 918, lo había rebautizado y lo había dirigido en campañas militares victoriosas contra el reino de Paekche, conquistado en 934, antes de apoderarse de Silla. Durante su reinado, Taejo consolidó su poder incorporando a la nobleza de Silla a su nueva administración.

En una de las batallas más sangrientas libradas en suelo británico, el rey **anglosajón** Athelstan (*c*. 893–939) aplastó a una coalición de ejércitos en 937 y con ello cimentó su dominio de Gran Bretaña y su estatus real en el ya unificado reino anglosajón de Inglaterra. El rey de Alba (en la actual Escocia), alarmado por las perspectivas de expansión anglosajona, había aunado fuerzas con los vikingos y otros reinos británicos del norte para contrarrestar la amenaza. Los hechos quedaron inmortalizados en un poema en inglés antiguo recogido en la *Crónica anglosajona* (*véase* 871–880), según el cual cinco reyes y siete condes perdieron la vida en el campo de batalla junto a innumerables soldados. La victoria confinó a galeses y escoceses tras sus fronteras, frenó el expansionismo vikingo y contribuyó a crear la nación de **Inglaterra**.

En 946, los **buyíes** (o buwayíes), persas chiíes, tomaron Bagdad y obligaron al califa a reconocer a Ahmad ibn-Buwayhi como jefe supremo. A pesar de que los **califas abasíes** conservaron su título hasta el año 1258, no eran más que testaferros; el poder real recaía en los sultanes buyíes, que gobernaban desde su capital, **Shiraz** (Persia).

Enrique I (*véase* 911–920) era uno de los duques regionales que tuvieron que enfrentarse a la amenaza magiar. Conocido como Enrique I el Pajarero, amplió su reino e infligió a los magiares (*véase* 901–910) la primera gran derrota que sufrían desde que iniciaran sus incursiones en Europa, en la **batalla de Riade**, en el año 933. Enrique era lo bastante poderoso como para garantizar que su trono fuera hereditario, así que la elección en 936 de su hijo **Otón** como nuevo rey fue una mera formalidad. La ceremonia de coronación de Otón como emperador en 962, celebrada en Aquisgrán, emuló ex profeso la de **Carlomagno** (*véase* 761–770).

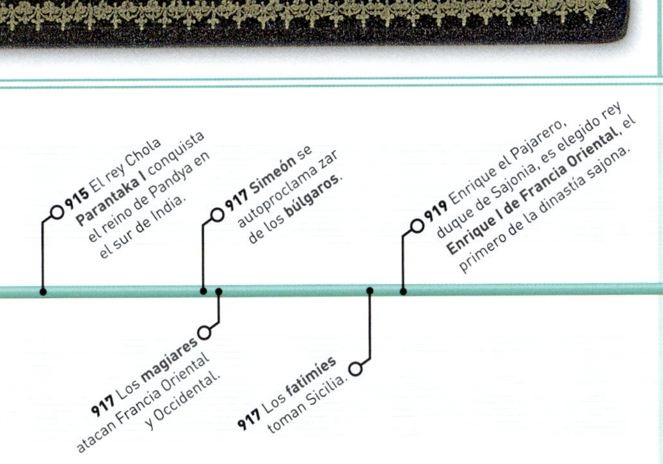

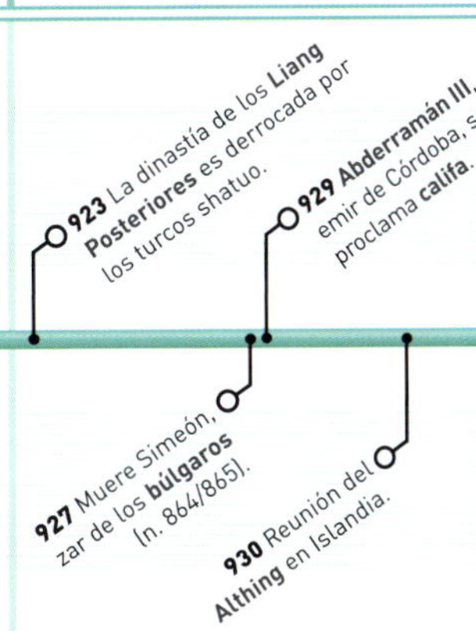

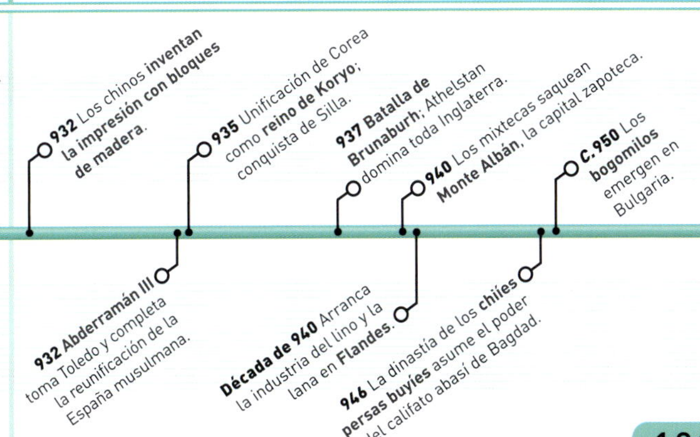

Estatua de Frey
Los vikingos veneraban a Frey, dios escandinavo de la fertilidad. Esta figura procedente de Suecia muestra a Frey tirándose de la barba, símbolo de crecimiento y virilidad.

Colgante con el martillo de Thor
El martillo de Thor, símbolo del poder y de la virilidad, era un motivo recurrente en la joyería. Thor era el dios escandinavo del trueno.

Brazalete de oro
Decorado mediante estampado, filigrana y un minucioso grabado inciso, este brazalete de Räbylille (Dinamarca) presenta cruces y motivos arbóreos.

Caballero de plata
Esta elegante figura metálica procedente de Suecia probablemente representa a un guerrero. Los vikingos eran excelentes jinetes, pero preferían viajar en barco.

extremos del aro con forma de cabeza de gato

LOS VIKINGOS

EL ARTE DE LOS VIKINGOS DESMIENTE SU REPUTACIÓN DE RUDOS SALVAJES

Entre los siglos VIII y XI, el mundo vikingo se extendió por Europa, desde las estepas pónticas al sur y el este hasta las costas de América del Norte al oeste y al norte. Este mundo estaba vinculado por una cultura artesanal.

Los elementos comunes del arte y la artesanía vikingos eran la rica ornamentación, los motivos entrelazados y los animales estilizados. La cultura material vikinga era en gran medida funcional, pero trabajada con maestría. Tanto los objetos cotidianos como los de uso ceremonial y militar se decoraban con profusión mediante técnicas de grabado, estampado, incrustación y filigrana con esferas de oro para crear motivos de zarcillos y bestias con garras y extremidades entrelazadas.

Escudo de madera
Los escudos eran de madera de picea, abeto, pino o tilo, con las abrazaderas (en la parte posterior) y el umbón de hierro. Se pintaban en colores vivos, a menudo con dibujos geométricos.

los colores significaban la intención o la lealtad

Hacha
Los vikingos menos pudientes solían usar hachas, más baratas que las espadas. Esta hacha danesa tiene una hoja metálica enastada en un mango de madera.

hoja de doble filo

Espada
Las espadas escaseaban y eran sumamente valiosas para los vikingos. Esta podía desenvainarse y blandirse fácilmente con una mano.

Fíbula o alfiler
Esta fíbula, o alfiler para sujetar la capa, procedente de Suecia, es de plata bañada en oro realzada con niel, un esmalte metálico negro.

Hebilla
Esta hebilla de metal estaba fijaba a un cinturón de cuero vikingo. Consta de dos placas, una para cada extremo del cinturón.

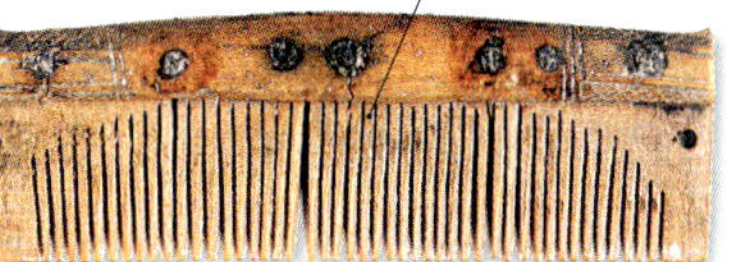

Peine
El equipo de aseo vikingo incluía un peine, unas pinzas y bastoncillos para limpiarse las orejas. El asa de este peine de madera está fijada con remaches de hierro.

Broche
Este broche procedente de Martens, en la isla sueca de Gotland, está decorado con cuatro figuras humanas rechonchas en oro.

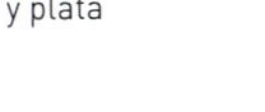

Veleta dorada
Las veletas se instalaban en la proa de los barcos y más tarde también coronaron las iglesias. Esta veleta dorada se halló en Suecia.

Primeras monedas danesas
Al principio, los vikingos usaban monedas procedentes de saqueos, lingotes de plata y el trueque en vez de una moneda propia. El rey Harald Blatand comenzó a acuñar moneda en 975.

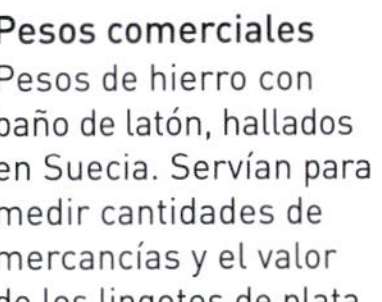

Pesos comerciales
Pesos de hierro con baño de latón, hallados en Suecia. Servían para medir cantidades de mercancías y el valor de los lingotes de plata.

Casco
Confeccionado con placas de hierro soldadas sobre un gorro de cuero, este casco noruego lleva una visera fija con protección para la nariz.

Cuerno para beber
Los vikingos creían que usarían cuernos para beber como este en el Valhalla, el paraíso de los guerreros, si morían en la batalla. Este tipo de vaso se usaba en los banquetes.

Trineo
Este trineo de roble y haya con cabezas de animal talladas en las esquinas de la caja procede de un barco funerario de Oseberg (Noruega).

Ornamento de proa
Algunos elementos de la cultura vikinga muestran influencias o derivan de culturas anteriores. Este adorno de madera de una proa es de época sajona.

951–960

Detalle de la Puerta del Sol de Tiahuanaco, un monumento de andesita, con la figura de una deidad conocida como el dios llorón o de los báculos.

LA CIVILIZACIÓN ANDINA PREINCAICA DE TIAHUANACO declinó bruscamente en la segunda mitad del siglo x. Unas sofisticadas técnicas agrícolas y de regadío (*véase* 741–750) habían permitido a Tiahuanaco alimentar a una **población** de unas 60 000 personas, y hasta **1,4 millones** en una región más amplia, según algunas estimaciones. Se cree que una **sequía prolongada** fue la causa de su **decadencia**. Los hallazgos arqueológicos sugieren que la ciudad principal quedó abandonada cuando sus habitantes se retiraron a asentamientos rurales más reducidos y retomaron un estilo de vida preurbano.

Espejo de bronce
Este espejo ricamente decorado de la dinastía Song ilustra la sofisticación artística de China en este periodo.

La **instauración de la dinastía Song** en China puso fin a la anarquía y al estado de guerra del periodo de las Cinco Dinastías y los Diez Reinos (*véase* 901–910). Conocida como **Song del Norte** en sus inicios por tener la capital en Kaifeng (norte de China), fue fundada por **Zhao Kuangyin** (r. 960–976), general bajo los Zhou Posteriores, la última de las Cinco Dinastías. Zhao combatió contra estados externos como el jitán Liao (*véase* 901–910) y el reino tanguto de Xi Xia, una confederación de tribus tibetanas, y conquistó varios de los Diez Reinos del sur. Zhao empleó el sistema de exámenes para el funcionariado para asegurarse el control del ejército y centralizar el poder.

El **emperador Otón I el Grande** (912–973) derrotó a los **magiares** en la **batalla de Lechfeld** en el año 955. Desde que habían sido desplazados por el **conflicto entre búlgaros y bizantinos** (*véase* 891–900), los magiares habían atacado territorios francos y en 951 habían conseguido llegar a Aquitania. A partir de su coronación en 936, Otón, hijo de Enrique I (*véase* 911–920), impuso con vigor la autoridad real y se hizo con el control de todos los ducados de Francia Oriental. Su poderoso ejército **erradicó la amenaza magiar** y también derrotó a los **vendos**, tribus de la frontera oriental sumidas en una larga lucha de resistencia a la **colonización** franca y a la **cristianización**.

961–970

Este detalle de la corona imperial de Otón I muestra una figura bíblica, el rey Salomón, sosteniendo un pergamino.

Rutas marítimas vikingas
Hacia finales del siglo x, los navegantes vikingos habían penetrado hasta el último rincón de Europa y más allá, hasta llegar a Groenlandia en el norte.

CLAVE
→ Rutas de los vikingos en los siglos VIII-X

LA CORONACIÓN DE OTÓN I COMO EMPERADOR por el papa, en 962, revivió el **Imperio romano carolingio** en Occidente. En 961, Otón lideró una expedición a Italia en respuesta a una demanda de protección del papa Juan XII y asumió la corona italiana en Pavía. Un año después viajó a **Roma** para recibir la corona imperial y afianzar su autoridad sobre el papado rebelde. Su hijo fue coronado coemperador como Otón II en 967.

En 965, el **rey de Dinamarca Harald Blatand** se convirtió al cristianismo, y su **religión** se extendió con rapidez por la región nórdica. Dinamarca se había visto obligada a aceptar misioneros como consecuencia de su derrota por el rey de Francia Oriental, Enrique I, en 933. En otros lugares, los vikingos continuaban prosperando a medida que penetraban en todos los rincones de Europa.

A la **muerte** del emperador bizantino **Constantino VII**, en el año 963, subió al trono su hijo menor de edad, **Basilio II** (958–1025). En la práctica, fue el general **Nicéforo Focas** quien asumió la autoridad. Como **Nicéforo II** (r. 963–969), continuó la restauración del imperio iniciada con la reconquista de Creta en 961, recuperó Chipre y Cilicia en 965, sometió a los búlgaros entre 966 y 969, e invadió el norte de Siria en 969. En este mismo año fue asesinado por su sobrino, **Juan Tzimisces**.

971–980

« UN **HOMBRE TEMERARIO** POR NATURALEZA [QUE]… INTENTÓ HAZAÑAS INSOSPECHADAS. »

León el Diácono, sobre Juan Tzimisces (finales del siglo x)

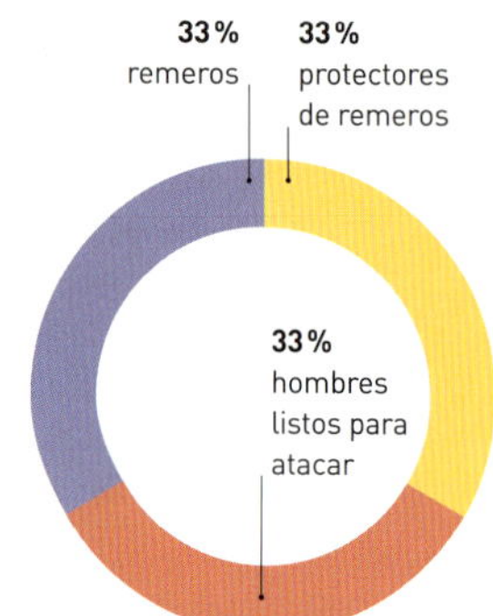

Tripulación de drakar
Manteniendo a parte de la tripulación en los remos, las partidas de asaltantes vikingos gozaban de una posición agresiva sin sacrificar la movilidad.

DURANTE BREVE SU REINADO, Juan I Tzimisces, sobrino de Nicéforo II (*véase* 961–970), se anotó sucesivas victorias. Tras aplastar una revuelta del general Bardas Focas en 971, Tzimisces rechazó una campaña del líder del **Rus de Kiev**, Sviatoslav, y **conquistó Bulgaria** hasta el Danubio. En 972 lanzó una campaña en el este, donde tomó Edesa, Damasco y Beirut, y llegó a las puertas de Jerusalén en 976. Murió repentinamente ese mismo año.

En 980, los **vikingos** reanudaron sus **ataques** a Inglaterra, si bien sufrieron un revés en Irlanda, donde Malaquías II obligó al Dublín vikingo a pagarle tributo.

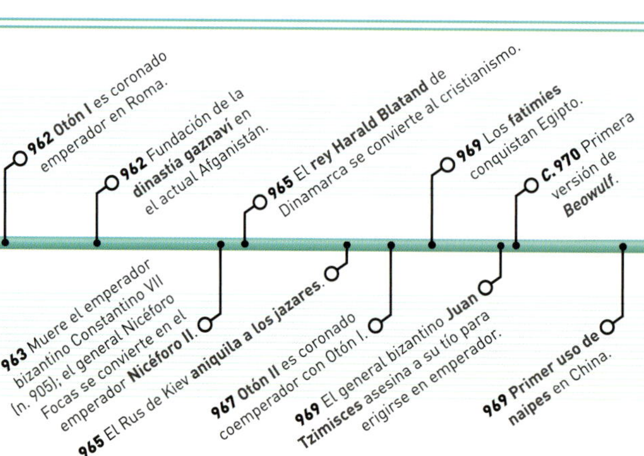

C. 950 Abandono de **Tiahuanaco**.

951 El emperador **Otón I** invade Italia.

951 Los **magiares** llegan hasta Aquitania (suroeste de Francia).

954 Construcción del **templo hindú de Laksmana** en Khajuraho (India central).

955 Batalla de Lechfeld: Otón I derrota a los magiares, que cesan sus ataques y se asientan en Hungría.

957 El general bizantino **Nicéforo Focas** toma la ciudad de Hadath y continúa el avance bizantino en Siria.

958 Victoria bizantina en Raban (Siria).

960 Fundación de la **dinastía Song del Norte (China)**.

962 Otón I es coronado emperador en Roma.

962 Fundación de la **dinastía gaznaví** en el actual Afganistán.

963 Muere el emperador bizantino Constantino VII (n. 905); el general Nicéforo Focas se convierte en el emperador **Nicéforo II**.

965 El Rus de Kiev **aniquila a los jazares.**

965 El rey Harald Blatand de Dinamarca se convierte al cristianismo.

967 Otón II es coronado coemperador con Otón I.

969 Los **fatimíes** conquistan Egipto.

969 El general bizantino **Juan Tzimisces** asesina a su tío para erigirse en emperador.

C. 970 Primera versión de **Beowulf.**

969 Primer uso de naipes en China.

972 El Imperio bizantino se anexiona el **kanato búlgaro.**

973 Muere **Otón I** (n. 912).

973 Taila II derroca a la dinastía Rashtrakuta de India central e instaura la **dinastía Chalukya.**

975 Inicios del estado húngaro bajo el **duque Geisa**, convertido al catolicismo.

980 El **visir Almanzor** ejerce el poder en **Córdoba** tras la muerte de Al Hakam II.

981–990

991–1000

El esplendor de Venecia fue resultado de su dominio de las lucrativas rutas comerciales entre Europa, el Imperio bizantino y Oriente en el siglo x.

EN 981, LAS TROPAS MUSULMANAS de **Almanzor** derrotaron al reino cristiano de **León** en España. «Al-Mansur» (Almanzor) era el título honorífico adoptado por Mohamed ibn Abi Amir, el poderoso y enérgico visir que manejaba en la sombra el verdadero poder del trono **omeya** (*véase* 911–920). Tras sus campañas victoriosas en León, Navarra y Cataluña, a cuyos soberanos subordinó al califato, extendió el control omeya a África mediante campañas en el **Magreb** (Marruecos y parte de Argelia).

En 986, el explorador vikingo **Erik el Rojo** condujo a una partida de colonos islandeses hasta las orillas de la inhóspita tierra que denominó Groenlandia («tierra verde») con la esperanza de atraer nuevos pobladores. Consiguió reclutar 24 barcadas de hombres, mujeres y niños dispuestos a confiar sus vidas a los drakares vikingos y a sobrevivir a la peligrosa travesía. Solo llegaron catorce barcos, pero los supervivientes no tardaron en establecer una floreciente colonia que posiblemente llegó a contar con cinco mil habitantes.

Almanzor
Este óleo del siglo XVII es un supuesto retrato de Al-Mansur, Almanzor para los cristianos. Al-Mansur significa «el Victorioso».

Otón II, emperador y rey de Francia Oriental, murió de malaria en 983, después de una expedición al sur de Italia. Pese a que su hijo, el pequeño **Otón III** (r. 983–1002), consiguió conservar la corona gracias a la firme regencia de su madre, Teófano, los francos del este tuvieron que afrontar también un alzamiento entre los **vendos**, las tribus eslavas convertidas a la fuerza en la frontera oriental. Los vendos restauraron su religión pagana y ofrecieron resistencia a la colonización franca durante casi dos siglos.

En el año 987, los **toltecas** conquistaron el Yucatán maya e hicieron de **Chichén Itzá** la **capital** de un estado maya-tolteca. Según manuscritos históricos hallados en el *Chilam Balam*, Chichén Itzá fue conquistada por toltecas liderados por Kukulkán, nombre maya del dios tolteca Quetzalcóatl o serpiente emplumada, posiblemente el rey tolteca exiliado Topiltzin. A pesar del relato de la crónica, los descubrimientos arqueológicos sugieren que la ciudad se derrumbó en torno a esta época.

Hacia finales del siglo x, las potencias mercantiles de **Venecia** y **Génova** comenzaban a dominar los mares Adriático y Tirreno, respectivamente. Venecia, en particular, gozó de lucrativos vínculos comerciales con el Imperio bizantino.

Drakar vikingo
Considerado por algunos el mayor logro técnico de los inicios de la Edad Media, el drakar vikingo era idóneo para la navegación fluvial, costera (de cabotaje) y oceánica (de altura).

LOS TOLTECAS

Los toltecas, que gobernaron un estado con centro en Tula (en el actual estado mexicano de Hidalgo), destacaban por su militarismo agresivo, que transformó la sociedad en Mesoamérica y abrió el camino a estados guerreros como el azteca. El término «tolteca» llegó a adquirir el sentido de «habitante de ciudad» o «persona culta», si bien su significado literal es «persona de los juncos» o habitante de Tollan («juncal»), la ciudad hoy llamada Tula. El arte tolteca, caracterizado por una arquitectura monumental y por sus estatuas gigantes (atlantes), fue muy influyente en la región.

10 000 KILOGRAMOS
PESO EN PLATA **DEL DANEGELD** RECAUDADO EN 991

EN 991, LOS GUERREROS ANGLOSAJONES plantaron cara a un ejército muy superior de vikingos en la **batalla de Maldon**, en Anglia Oriental (Inglaterra). Fueron masacrados. El rey inglés **Ethelred II el Indeciso** (r. 978–1016), se vio obligado a pagar un impuesto conocido como ***danegeld*** para protegerse de futuras incursiones.

En 996, el emperador bizantino **Basilio II** emprendió la primera de una larga serie de **campañas** contra **el zar búlgaro** Samuel. Basilio se había anotado grandes victorias en Siria un año antes, pero le costó casi veinte años derrotar finalmente a los búlgaros.

A partir del año 1000 aproximadamente, los habitantes de la **isla de Pascua**, o **Rapa Nui**, en el océano Pacífico, empezaron a tallar unas estatuas monumentales conocidas como *moai*. Emplearon técnicas agrícolas sofisticadas y desarrollaron una escritura llamada *rongorongo*. En algún momento pudieron sufrir una pérdida drástica de población; tanto si esto ocurrió como qué lo motivó son algunos de los muchos misterios relacionados con la isla.

981 Almanzor arrasa León (España).

981 Annam rechaza a los Song del Norte.

982 El reino de **Dai Viet** destruye la capital champa.

983 Muere **Otón II** (n. 955).

983 Gran rebelión de los vendos contra la expansión de la Francia Oriental.

983 Los **fatimíes** controlan Palestina.

984 Se fabrica en Isfahán el **astrolabio** más antiguo conservado.

986 Asentamiento escandinavo en **Groenlandia**.

987 El **tolteca Kukulkán** conquista el Yucatán maya y declara a Chichén Itzá su capital.

987 Hugo Capeto funda la **dinastía Capeto** en Francia.

988 Almanzor arrasa de nuevo León.

988 El emperador bizantino Basilio II derrota al general rebelde Bardas Focas con ayuda de los **varegos** (vikingos rusos) enviados por el príncipe Vladímir de Kiev.

c. 990 Prosperan las ciudades-estado comerciales italianas **Génova y Venecia**.

996 Otón III coronado emperador.

c. 1000 Surge Chan Chan como capital del Imperio chimú del norte de Perú.

1000 El norvietnamita **Dai Viet** invade a los champa del sur.

1000 Boleslav coronado primer rey de Polonia.

1001–1010

Estas ruinas de Pueblo Bonito corresponden a una de las trece «casas grandes» construidas por los anasazi en el Cañón del Chaco.

EN TORNO AL AÑO 1000, LA ANTIGUA CIVILIZACIÓN PUEBLO en la región del Cañón del Chaco, en el suroeste de América del Norte, alcanzó su cénit. Los **anasazi** usaron sofisticados sistemas agrícolas de secano e hidrológicos para prosperar en aquel entorno árido y controlaron rutas comerciales que llegaban hasta la costa del Pacífico de la actual California y al Valle de México. Alcanzaron **impresionantes logros arquitectónicos**, en especial la construcción de las llamadas «casas grandes», como la de Pueblo Bonito, uno de los trece edificios de esta índole en el Cañón del Chaco. Pueblo Bonito tenía seis plantas de altura y contenía más de 600 estancias. Probablemente funcionaba como centro ceremonial, almacén y residencia de la élite.

Carreteras bien mantenidas (algunas con bordillos de piedra) conectaban el Cañón del Chaco con miles de asentamientos anasazi de menores dimensiones diseminados por toda la región. Posiblemente el cañón en sí albergara a unas diez mil personas, una población excesiva para la frágil ecología de la región (*véase* 1161–1165).

Mahmud de Gazni (*c.* 971–1030) fue un musulmán decidido a **difundir su fe en India**. En 1001 derrotó en Peshawar a Jaipal, rajá de Punjab, quien se suicidó.

Leif Erikson, probablemente el **primer europeo que pisó suelo norteamericano**, desembarcó en torno a 1002 en una tierra que denominó **Vinland**. Poco después de aquel descubrimiento, los groenlandeses, liderados por Thorfinn Karlsefni, intentaron **establecer allí una colonia**, en la que vivieron durante tres inviernos. Los restos de asentamientos en L'Anse aux Meadows, en el norte de Terranova, atestiguan la presencia de los vikingos en América del Norte.

LEIF ERIKSON (970–1020)

Leif era hijo de Erik el Rojo, fundador de la colonia de Groenlandia (*véase* 981–990). Los relatos difieren en cuanto a los detalles de su descubrimiento de América del Norte. Según uno de ellos, al regresar en 1002 de una visita a Noruega, donde se había convertido al cristianismo, se desvió de su rumbo y desembarcó en un lugar al que llamó Vinland por las vides que allí crecían. Otra versión afirma que se dirigió a unas tierras divisadas al oeste por un comerciante islandés.

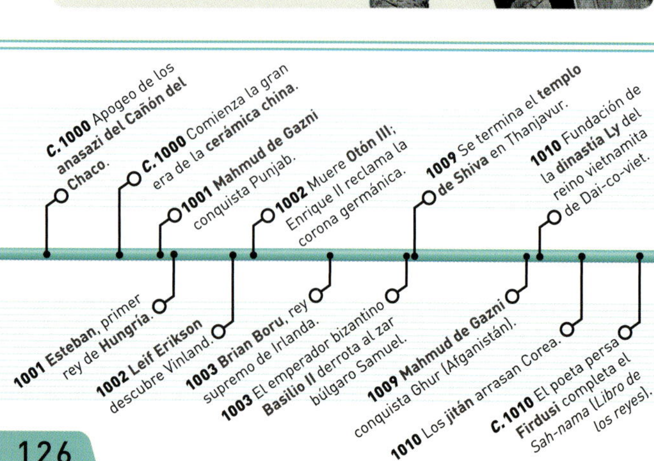

C.1000 Apogeo de los **anasazi del Cañón del Chaco**.

C.1000 Comienza la gran era de la **cerámica china**.

1001 Mahmud de Gazni conquista Punjab.

1001 Esteban, primer rey de **Hungría**.

1002 Leif Erikson descubre Vinland.

1002 Muere **Otón III**; Enrique II reclama la corona germánica.

1003 Brian Boru, rey supremo de Irlanda.

1003 El emperador bizantino **Basilio II** derrota al zar búlgaro Samuel.

1009 Mahmud de Gazni conquista Ghur (Afganistán).

1009 Se termina el **templo de Shiva** en Thanjavur.

1010 Los **jitán** arrasan Corea.

1010 Fundación de la **dinastía Ly** del reino vietnamita de Dai-co-viet.

C.1010 El poeta persa **Firdusi** completa el *Sah-nama* (*Libro de los reyes*).

1011–1020

Basilio II, uno de los emperadores bizantinos más importantes y crueles, fue proclamado emperador en 976 a los 20 años. Gobernó durante casi 50 años.

MURASAKI SHIKIBU («LA DAMA MURASAKI») escribió *Genji monogatari* (*La novela de Genji*) en más de cincuenta rollos, o capítulos, entre 1011 y 1021, considerada la **primera novela japonesa** y posiblemente la primera novela psicológica de la literatura mundial.

En 1014, **Brian Boru, rey supremo de Irlanda** y autoproclamado emperador de los gaélicos, derrotó a una coalición de vikingos de Dublín y soldados de Leinster celtas en Clontarf (Irlanda). Aunque el reino nórdico fue aplastado y las incursiones vikingas en Irlanda repelidas, Brian Boru falleció en el campo de batalla y **su sueño de un reino irlandés** se desvaneció.

En 1014, como colofón de una guerra de 18 años (*véase* 991–1000), el **emperador bizantino Basilio II** derrotó a los ejércitos del zar búlgaro en Belasita. Después de ganarse el apodo de Bulgaróctono («matador de búlgaros»), hizo sacar los ojos a los quince mil guerreros capturados antes de enviarlos de vuelta a sus hogares. Se dijo que el archienemigo de Basilio, Samuel el Búlgaro, murió de la impresión. En las postrimerías de la década, los búlgaros finalmente accedieron a ser **anexionados por Bizancio**.

Murasaki Shikibu
Este rollo vertical del siglo XVI muestra a la dama Murasaki, una escritora de noble cuna que narró los entresijos de la corte Heian.

La sangrienta batalla de Clontarf
Librada entre los mayores ejércitos jamás reunidos en Irlanda, la batalla de Clontarf fue un baño de sangre. En ella murieron unos cuatro mil gaélicos y unos seis mil vikingos y sus aliados.

1013 Boleslao el Valiente de Polonia presta homenaje a Enrique II (**paz de Merseberg**).

1013 Svend I de Dinamarca conquista Inglaterra.

1014 La **batalla de Clontarf** acaba con el dominio vikingo en Irlanda.

1014 Enrique II es coronado emperador.

1014 Canuto el Grande, rey de Inglaterra.

1014 Basilio II ciega al ejército búlgaro.

1016 Canuto es proclamado señor de toda Inglaterra.

1016 Ataque normando en el sur de Italia.

1018 Rajendra I, rey de la dinastía Chola, conquista Sri Lanka.

1018 Se instaura el **celibato** de los sacerdotes católicos romanos.

1019 Yaroslav derrota a su hermano y se proclama gran duque del Rus de Kiev.

1021–1030

Templo de Brihadishvara, construido por los Chola en su capital, Thanjavur.

EL REY CHOLA RAJENDRA I emprendió en 1025 una audaz expedición naval contra el imperio marítimo de Srivijaya en Sumatra y de paso saqueó el reino de Pegu en Birmania. Rajendra había heredado un sólido reino de su padre, Rajaraja I, que había conquistado Sri Lanka y comenzado un programa de **construcción de templos hindúes** centrado en la capital chola de Thanjavur. Bajo Rajendra, los Chola ampliaron su reino hasta incluir Bengala e hicieron añicos el poder de Srivijaya, cosa que les granjeó el control de las **lucrativas rutas comerciales entre India y China**.

Canuto era el hijo de Svend I, rey de Dinamarca y Noruega, que había **invadido Inglaterra** y enviado en 1013 al rey anglosajón Ethelred II al exilio en Normandía. Tras protagonizar su propia invasión victoriosa en 1015, Canuto fue reconocido como señor de toda Inglaterra en 1016 y continuó ampliando su imperio. Hacia 1030, este comprendía ya Noruega, Dinamarca y las islas Feroe, Shetland y Orcadas. Inteligente

Escultura chola de Shiva
Los Chola, hindúes fervorosos, fueron grandes constructores de templos. Aquí, Shiva, una de las principales deidades hindúes, aparece como un hombre joven y apuesto.

1021 Epidemia de baile de san Vito (corea), enfermedad que afecta al sistema nervioso, en Europa.

1022 Supresión de la **herejía de los bogomilos**; la Iglesia romana inicia la práctica de la quema de herejes.

1022 Avicena escribe el *El libro de la curación*.

1024 Boleslao I el Valiente es coronado rey de Polonia; muere un año después.

y capaz, Canuto logró conciliar a sus súbditos daneses y anglosajones, y recaudó el *danegeld* (impuesto danés) para financiar una flota y un ejército permanentes, una importante innovación.

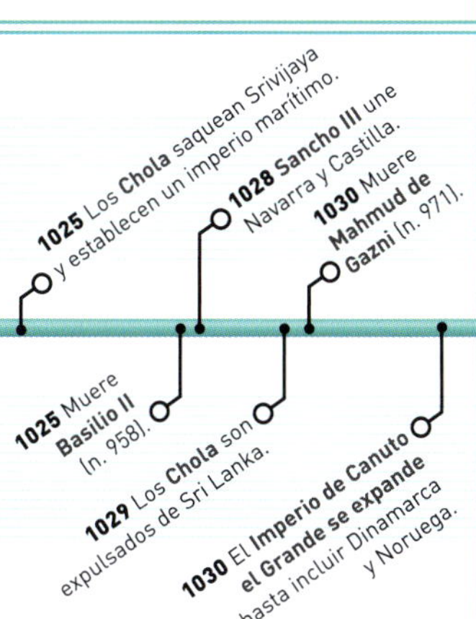

1031–1040

En esta miniatura, los selyúcidas batallan con los bizantinos tras haber conquistado Persia.

EN EL AÑO 1037, LOS SELYÚCIDAS, LIDERADOS POR CHAGRI BEG Y SU HERMANO TUGRIL BEG, invadieron Jurasán (Persia). En 1040 aplastaron a los gaznavíes en la batalla de Dandanqan y se hicieron con el control de la Persia oriental, el primer paso hacia la creación de un **nuevo Imperio islámico**. Los selyúcidas eran turcos uguz, en su origen nómadas del Asia central convertidos al islam y emigrados a Transoxiana, donde sirvieron como mercenarios antes de volver su atención a Jurasán.

En 1031, de las ruinas del **califato de Córdoba** (España) surgieron cuarenta dinastías menores y efímeras. Los llamados reyes de taifas (banderías) asumieron el gobierno de distintas provincias (coras) de Córdoba tras los conflictos que derribaron a los omeyas después de la **ejecución de Abderramán Sanchuelo**, hijo de Almanzor, en el año 1009. Fue el último líder capaz del califato, pero su intento de proclamarse califa conllevó su caída.

Posteriormente, la facción bereber nombró su propio candidato a califa y **Córdoba se sumió en una guerra civil que se prolongó 22 años**. En 1031, la muerte de Hisham III, el último califa omeya, que ya había perdido el control de varias provincias, condujo a la desintegración definitiva del califato: los **abasíes** tomaron Sevilla; los **jariyíes**, Córdoba, y los **hudíes**, Zaragoza. La **desorganización musulmana** impulsó a los reinos cristianos a expandirse hacia el sur.

Rey y emperador
Fernando I fue el primer conde de Castilla que se autoproclamó rey. Después de acceder al trono de León, añadió el título de emperador.

En el año 1035, a la muerte de Sancho III de Navarra, que había incorporado el condado de Castilla y que, además, era el señor más poderoso de la España cristiana, sus reinos quedaron divididos entre sus dos hijos. **Fernando heredó Castilla** y en 1037 sucedió a su cuñado, muerto en la batalla de Tamarón, en el trono de León, reino del cual se declaró emperador en 1039. Recuperó territorios de Navarra enfrentándose a su hermano e impuso parias (tributos) en partes de la España y el Portugal musulmanes.

1041–1050

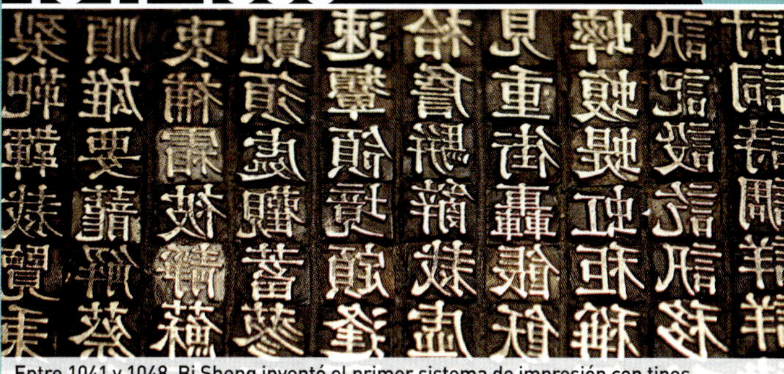
Entre 1041 y 1048, Bi Sheng inventó el primer sistema de impresión con tipos móviles, consistentes en caracteres de arcilla encerados y enmarcados en hierro.

LAS LENGUAS BANTÚES CONSTITUYEN UNA FAMILIA LINGÜÍSTICA originaria de una región correspondiente al sur de Nigeria y al noroeste de Camerún. Los pueblos bantúes se extendieron desde aquí hacia el este y el sur, y las **lenguas bantúes** se convirtieron en la **familia dominante en el África subsahariana**, si bien no está claro si ello respondió a la conquista, la colonización o a la influencia cultural. La expansión bantú comenzó en la Edad de Piedra tardía y se aceleró cuando los pueblos de lengua bantú empezaron a dominar la tecnología del hierro y la ganadería. Hacia mediados del siglo XI, las tribus bantúes se habían convertido en **sofisticadas sociedades dedicadas al pastoreo**, capaces de mantener altas densidades de población y redes socioeconómicas complejas. Ello dio origen a la aparición de jeferías y al dominio del centro y el sur de África por pueblos de lengua bantú.

En 1044, Anawrata se hizo con el poder del **reino de Pagán (Birmania)**. Su talento militar y su hábil utilización del budismo hinayana como fuerza cultural y política convirtieron a Pagán en el centro de la política, la cultura y la religión birmanas. Además de desarrollar el birmano como lengua escrita, inició un programa de construcción y estableció lazos comerciales y culturales con India y China.

En China, en algún momento entre 1041 y 1048, el plebeyo Bi (o Pi) Sheng inventó el **primer sistema de imprenta de tipos móviles**. La impresión con planchas de madera se conocía en China desde hacía siglos y desde la dinastía Tang Posterior (923–936) se usaba para producir libros; la innovación técnica de Bi Sheng consistió en usar **bloques de arcilla** sueltos, uno para cada carácter. Los caracteres se moldeaban en los extremos de finos bastoncillos de arcilla húmeda que se endurecían al fuego. A diferencia de la madera, la arcilla no se deformaba al humedecerse, y los tipos podían usarse repetidas veces.

CLAVE
- ■ Lugar de origen bantú 2000 a. C.
- → Expansión bantú

Expansión bantú
Desde su tierra de origen en la región fronteriza del sur de Nigeria y el noroeste de Camerún, los pueblos de lengua bantú se extendieron hacia el este y el sur, a través de la selva tropical, hasta llegar a todas las zonas del centro y el sur de África.

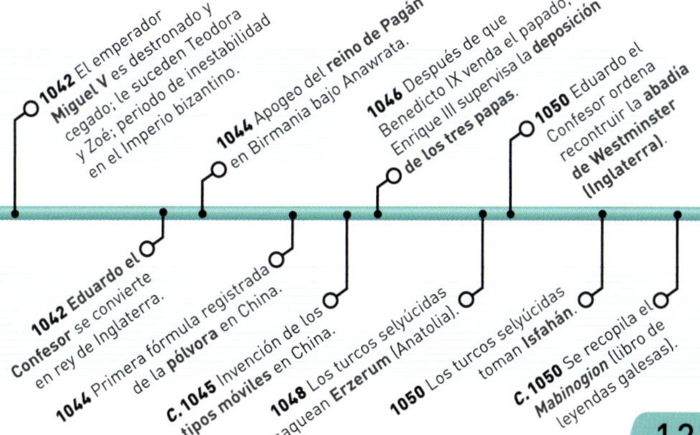

1025 Los **Chola** saquean Srivijaya y establecen un imperio marítimo.

1025 Muere **Basilio II** (n. 958).

1028 Sancho III une Navarra y Castilla.

1029 Los **Chola** son expulsados de Sri Lanka.

1030 Muere **Mahmud de Gazni** (n. 971).

1030 El **Imperio de Canuto el Grande se expande** hasta incluir Dinamarca y Noruega.

1031 Desintegración del **califato de Córdoba**.

1035 Fernando, hijo de Sancho III, se convierte en **conde de Castilla**.

1035 Se funda el **reino de Aragón** con Ramiro I.

1035 Muere **Canuto el Grande** (n. c. 985).

1035 Guillermo el Conquistador, **duque de Normandía**.

1037 Fernando de Castilla, rey de **León**.

1037 Los turcos selyúcidas invaden **Jurasán** (Persia).

1037 Construcción de la **catedral de Ruán**.

1040 El rey Duncan es asesinado por **Macbeth** en Escocia.

1038 Revuelta tibetana contra los Song del Norte.

1039 Enrique III es elegido emperador.

1040 Los **selyúcidas** conquistan la Persia gaznaví.

C. 1040 La **expansión bantú** alcanza su clímax en Sudáfrica.

1042 El emperador **Miguel V** es destronado y cegado; le suceden Teodora y Zoé; periodo de inestabilidad en el Imperio bizantino.

1042 Eduardo el Confesor se convierte en rey de Inglaterra.

1044 Apogeo del **reino de Pagán** en Birmania bajo Anawrata.

1044 Primera fórmula registrada de la **pólvora** en China.

C. 1045 Invención de los **tipos móviles** en China.

1046 Después de que Benedicto IX venda el papado, Enrique III supervisa la **deposición de los tres papas**.

1048 Los turcos selyúcidas saquean **Erzerum** (Anatolia).

1050 Eduardo el Confesor ordena recontruir la **abadía de Westminster (Inglaterra)**.

1050 Los turcos selyúcidas toman **Isfahán**.

C. 1050 Se recopila el ***Mabinogion*** (libro de leyendas galesas).

1051–1060

La mezquita de Labanga en Ghana es, posiblemente, la más antigua del África subsahariana. Los almorávides islamizaron Ghana en el siglo XI.

EN EL AÑO 1054, ABDALÁ BEN YASIN, UN APASIONADO LÍDER ESPIRITUAL, consiguió unificar las tribus del Sáhara. La confederación resultante (los **almorávides**, del árabe «al-murabitun», o pueblos de las guarniciones fronterizas) **construyó un imperio** que acabaría abarcando la mayoría del noroeste africano y de la España musulmana (*véase* 1081–1090). Dos años más tarde, los almorávides iniciaron la **conquista musulmana de África occidental**, donde habían aparecido varios estados, como Ghana.

Los extranjeros llamaban **yoruba** a un grupo de **ciudades-estado en Nigeria** que compartían un mismo lenguaje y cultura. **Ifé** era el reino yoruba más antiguo y prestigioso, y a mediados del siglo XI ya contaba con una **cultura urbana sofisticada** y consolidada. Ifé era el centro espiritual y mítico de los yoruba, pero su mala ubicación le impidió ejercer un gran control político o militar sobre el resto de estados. Ifé es conocido por su producción artística y, sobre todo, por sus **cabezas de terracota y de bronce**.

En 1059, el papa Nicolás II reconoció a **Roberto Guiscardo** el Normando como conde de **Sicilia** y duque de **Apulia** y de **Calabria**, territorios que estaban íntegramente bajo control bizantino y árabe; así legitimó sus intentos de conquista.

Cabeza de bronce de Ifé
Esta cabeza, que data probablemente del siglo XIV, es parte de una tradición artística sofisticada que se remonta al siglo XI. El metal fundido se vertía en un molde hecho con un modelo de cera.

1061–1070

En este detalle del tapiz de Bayeux, terminado en 1080, Guillermo el Conquistador conduce a sus soldados en la batalla.

EN 1066, EN LA BATALLA DE HASTINGS, Guillermo duque de Normandía (*c.* 1028–1087) derrotó a Harold Godwinson (*c.* 1022–1066), el último rey anglosajón de Inglaterra. No era la primera vez que Inglaterra caía en la órbita normanda: **Eduardo el Confesor** había pasado su juventud en el exilio en la corte normanda, mientras Canuto (*véase* 1021–1030) gobernó Inglaterra. Según Guillermo, Eduardo le había prometido la corona inglesa, pero cuando este murió en 1066, **Harold fue coronado rey**. Marchó hacia el norte para repeler una invasión nórdica, antes de correr hacia el sur, a Hastings, donde se enfrentó a Guillermo; **murió y su ejército quedó diezmado**. Guillermo el Conquistador tomó el sureste de Inglaterra, luego el suroeste y reprimió un alzamiento en el norte en 1069.

Bajo **Tugril Beg**, los selyúcidas habían ocupado Bagdad y **puesto fin a la dinastía buyí** (*véase* 931–950). Conservaron al califa abasí como hombre de paja y le concedieron el título de sultán. Tugril Beg murió en 1063 y Alp Arslan, su sucesor, **extendió el poder selyúcida** a Anatolia, Armenia y Siria.

2:1 Batalla de Hastings
Las bajas anglosajonas superaron a las de Normandía en una proporción de dos a uno, en parte por la superioridad táctica normanda.

1071–1080

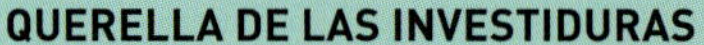

QUERELLA DE LAS INVESTIDURAS

¿Qué autoridad era superior, la secular o la religiosa? Esta era la pregunta que suscitó la querella de las investiduras. Esta iluminación del siglo XII muestra a Enrique IV solicitando la mediación de Matilde de Canossa y de Hugo de Cluny. Matilde fue una de las mujeres más poderosas de toda la Edad Media y Enrique cumplió su penitencia en su fortaleza de Canossa.

DESDE QUE EL PAPA CORONARA A CARLOMAGNO (*véase* 791–800), los emperadores occidentales habían considerado que era su derecho divino designar (o investir) a los obispos. Los emperadores habían obtenido mucho poder e ingresos mediante la **dispensa de nombramientos religiosos**, y el emperador Enrique III (1017–1056) había ido más lejos: en 1046 insistió en que era **derecho del emperador** investir al papa. El **papa Gregorio VII** opinaba lo contrario: correspondía al papa investir a los clérigos. En el sínodo de Pascua de 1075, Gregorio emitió un decreto, el *Dictatus Papae*, que prohibía la investidura laica y que dio lugar a la querella de las investiduras. El emperador, **Enrique IV** (1050–1106), que luchaba por reducir el poder de los prelados alemanes, desafió el decreto. En 1076, Gregorio le **excomulgó** y eximió a sus súbditos de sus juramentos de lealtad, lo que desencadenó una **rebelión de los nobles sajones contra el rey**. En 1077, Enrique IV cruzó los Alpes en pleno invierno y llegó a Canossa, vestido de penitente, para someterse al papa (*véase* recuadro). Fue absuelto, pero la querella estalló de nuevo cuando un rival, **Rodolfo de Suabia**, fue nominado para el trono alemán (previamente franco-oriental). En 1080, Enrique logró que se eligiera a un papa rival, mientras que Gregorio se alió con **Roger I**, conde de Sicilia, contra el bando imperial.

En 1071, los **selyúcidas aplastaron al ejército bizantino** en Mankizert, capturaron al emperador Romano IV, por el que pidieron un rescate, y se dispusieron a conquistar Anatolia (Turquía actual), que así empezó a convertirse en una **región turca musulmana**. Los selyúcidas instauraron el **Sultanato de Rum** en 1077, mientras que obtuvieron Siria y Jerusalén con otras conquistas.

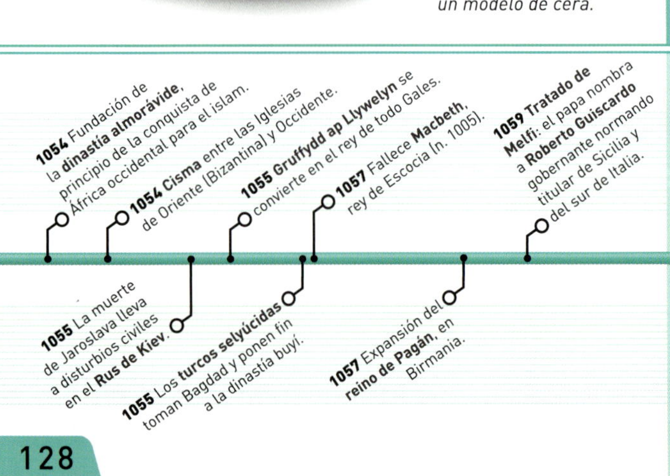

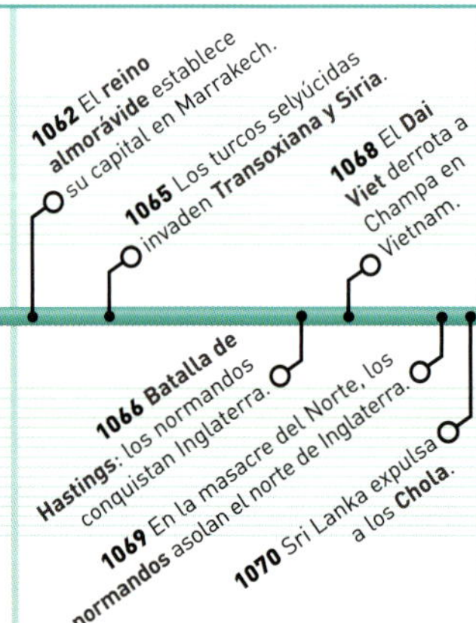

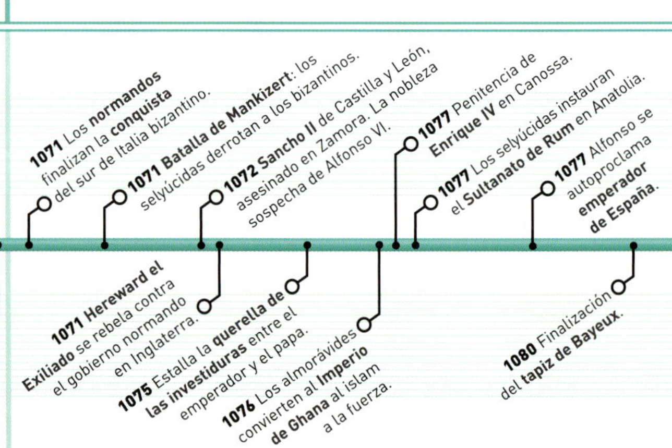

1081–1090

Hassan-i Sabbah lleva a cabo iniciaciones en Alamut, en una ilustración de los *Viajes* de Marco Polo (siglo XIII).

13 000

LUGARES REGISTRADOS EN EL *DOMESDAY BOOK*

EN 1090, UN GRUPO DE CHIÍES ISMAILÍES SE IMPLICÓ EN UNA DISPUTA sobre la sucesión fatimí en El Cairo (*véase* 901–910). Liderado por el carismático **Hassan-i Sabbah**, el grupo legitimó la reclamación de un bebé llamado Nizar, por lo que se les empezó a conocer como **ismailíes nizaríes**. Hassan se vio obligado a huir de El Cairo y llevó a los nizaríes a su región natal, en Persia, donde capturaron la fortaleza de **Alemut**, en la región montañosa de Kazvín, que se convertiría en la base de un **reino nizarí** de facto. Así nació el grupo al que luego se conocería como los **asesinos** (nombre derivado de la palabra *hashashins*, como les apodaban sus enemigos, que afirmaban que utilizaban drogas como el hachís para forzar a sus acólitos a una obediencia ciega).

Alarmados por los avances de **Alfonso VI de Castilla**, los **abasíes** (*véase* 1031) apelaron a los **almorávides** del norte de África para que les ayudaran a defenderse de la amenaza cristiana. Derrotaron a Alfonso en Sagrajas en 1086 y se anexaron la mayor parte de la España musulmana.

En 1085, **Guillermo el Conquistador** (*véase* 1061) encargó un registro censal de su nuevo reino, el ***Domesday Book***, probablemente para regular el servicio militar y evaluar las posibilidades recaudatorias.

El *Domesday Book*
Debe su nombre a la emoción que la gran empresa generó entre los nativos ingleses. El registro de Guillermo se componía de dos manuscritos, el Gran y el Pequeño Domesday.

1091–1100

« QUE QUIENES VAN A **LUCHAR POR LA CRISTIANDAD** PONGAN LA FORMA DE **LA CRUZ** SOBRE SUS VESTIDURAS Y **DEMUESTREN** EXTERNAMENTE SU DEVOCIÓN A LA **FE INTERNA**. »

Papa Urbano II (1095)

EN 1092, EL ERUDITO CHINO SU SUNG DISEÑÓ Y CONSTRUYÓ UN RELOJ astronómico de nueve metros de altura e impulsado por agua, con una esfera armilar que mostraba las posiciones de los objetos celestes.

En 1094, el caballero castellano Rodrigo Díaz de Vivar, que había servido a señores cristianos como musulmanes, y a quien estos últimos llamaban **Cid** (señor), tomó Valencia. Sus gestas inspiraron, entre otros, al desconocido autor del *Cantar de Mío Cid*.

En el **concilio de Clermont** de 1095, el papa Urbano, un cluniacense francés (*véase* 910), se dirigió a una asamblea en la que predominaban los clérigos y los nobles francos y les exhortó a liberar de la «deshonra» musulmana los Santos Lugares. Los bizantinos habían solicitado la ayuda de Urbano para defenderse de los selyúcidas, y el papa vio la oportunidad de canalizar la energía de la nobleza europea y alejarla de las constantes luchas fratricidas hacia una **expansión cristiana** que beneficiaría al papado. Impulsados por el celo religioso y alentados por la promesa del perdón de sus pecados, junto a la esperanza de lograr botín, tierras y control sobre el lucrativo comercio con Oriente, muchos nobles de Francia (antes Francia Occidental) y Lorena se unieron, o «tomaron la cruz». El resto de naciones, o bien estaban enfrentadas al papado, o bien se mostraron indiferentes al conflicto, por lo que la **primera cruzada** fue una cuestión fundamentalmente francesa. Tres grupos de cruzados, liderados por Godofredo y Balduino de Bouillón, el conde Raimundo de Tolosa, y el normando Bohemundo de Otranto, tomaron la capital del Rum selyúcida, **Nicea**, en 1097. Ese año conquistaron **Edesa** y, en 1098, capturaron **Antioquía**. En 1099 marcharon hacia **Jerusalén**. Godofredo fue elegido rey de Jerusalén, pero asumió el título de **Defensor del Santo Sepulcro**; su hermano, Balduino, fue coronado el año siguiente. Bajo el señorío del rey de Jerusalén, los cruzados instauraron **cuatro estados principales**: el reino de Jerusalén, que prosperó gracias al comercio mediado por las potencias comerciales italianas; el condado de Trípoli, fundado por Raimundo; el condado de Edesa, fundado por Balduino; y el principado de Antioquía, fundado por Bohemundo.

Batalla de las cruzadas
Esta ilustración de un manuscrito muestra a caballeros cruzados en batalla con los sarracenos, el término con que los europeos se referían a sus enemigos musulmanes. Unos treinta mil caballeros participaron en la primera cruzada.

75 000
SARRACENOS

15 000
CRUZADOS

El sitio de Antioquía
Las fuerzas musulmanas superaban con mucho a las cristianas en el sitio de Antioquía. De hecho, Antioquía solo cayó porque un traidor abrió la puerta a un grupo de caballeros liderados por Bohemundo de Otranto.

1081 Alejo Comneno accede al trono bizantino.

1084 Fundación de la **orden monástica cartuja**.

1085 Alfonso VI de Castilla toma Toledo y Valencia.

1085 Encargo del ***Domesday Book***.

1085 Fallece el **papa Gregorio VII** (nacido c. 1020).

C. 1085 Los **esquimales thule** controlan el ártico norteamericano.

1086 Batalla de Sagrajas (o Zalaca), en España. Los almorávides derrotan a Alfonso VI.

1089 Los **fatimíes** toman Palestina.

1089 Desarrollo del **románico**.

C. 1090 Los **asesinos** se asientan en Alamut.

1092 Los normandos finalizan la conquista de **Sicilia**.

1092 Su Sung construye **el reloj cósmico** en Pekín.

1092 Fallece el sultán **selyúcida Malik Sah**. El Imperio selyúcida empieza a desmembrarse.

1094 El Cid toma Valencia.

1095 El papa Urbano proclama la **primera cruzada**.

1096 Inicio de la construcción de la **basílica de san Marcos**, en Venecia.

1097 Los cruzados saquean **Constantinopla**.

1098 Antioquía cae ante los cruzados tras un año de sitio.

1098 Fundación de la **orden del Císter**.

1098 Concilio de Bari: intento de reunificar las Iglesias oriental y occidental.

1099 Los cruzados toman Jerusalén. **Fin de la primera cruzada**.

1099 Fundación de la orden de los **caballeros hospitalarios**.

1099 Fallece **el Cid** (n. 1043).

1100 Balduino I se convierte en el primer rey de Jerusalén.

1100 Guillermo II muere en un accidente de caza; **Enrique I** se convierte en rey de Inglaterra.

1100 Adelardo de Bath traduce a Euclides del árabe al latín.

1101–1105

Ilustración de la traducción de Edward Fitzgerald del *Rubaiyat*; de los 600 poemas, se cree que Jayyam no escribió más de 120.

EN ALGÚN MOMENTO A PRINCIPIOS DEL SIGLO XII, OMAR JAYYAM (1048–1131), astrónomo y matemático al servicio de los **sultanes selyúcidas**, escribió una serie de cuartetos, o rubaiyats, que se harían famosos en Occidente gracias a la traducción de **Edward Fitzgerald** en 1859. La carrera de Jayyam es un reflejo de la cultura selyúcida. En **Samarcanda**, a principios de la década de 1070, pudo emprender **estudios matemáticos** gracias al patrocinio de un jurista local y del auspicio del poderoso sultán selyúcida **Malik Sah** (r. 1072–1092). Fue invitado a **Isfahán** en 1073 para **fundar un observatorio** y liderar a un grupo de eruditos. Durante este periodo, llevó a cabo múltiples **descubrimientos matemáticos y astronómicos**, como, por ejemplo, la **medición de la duración del año** más precisa hasta ese momento, con una desviación de un día cada 3770 años. A pesar de que en la actualidad se le conoce fundamentalmente por el ***Rubaiyat***, no se tiene la certeza de que Jayya escribiera la mayoría (o ninguno) de los cuartetos, y en su época no se le conocía como poeta. La reputación de su trabajo procede en gran medida de la traducción, muy libre, de Edward Fitzgerald.

El éxito de la **primera cruzada** (*véase* 1091–1100) se explica en su mayor parte por la desorganización de los regímenes musulmanes que derrocó. El **Califato fatimí** de El Cairo era rico, pero decadente; los **abasíes** de Bagdad eran poco más que hombres de paja; los **turcos selyúcidas** no habían conseguido forjar un imperio unido; por el contrario, los señores feudales y las tribus rivales habían tejido una red de estados enfrentados como **Rum, Danismend y Damasco**. Durante el principio del siglo XII, los cruzados lucharon sin tregua contra estos enemigos. En 1101, **Raimundo IV de Tolosa** (*c.* 1042–1105) lideró un nuevo ejército cruzado desde **Constantinopla** y contra el Sultanato de Rum; en junio tomó **Ankara**, solo para que los turcos de Danismend la destruyeran en agosto. **Balduino I de Jerusalén** (*c.* 1058–1118) mejoró los accesos al Mediterráneo mediante la captura de varias ciudades costeras **fatimíes**; tomó **Jaffa en 1102, Acre** en 1104 y **Ramla** en 1105, pero murió en el intento de tomar **Trípoli**, también en 1105.

Balduino de Bourcq
Moneda en la que aparece Balduino de Bourcq, primo de Balduino I de Jerusalén y al que sucedería, primero como conde de Edesa y después como rey de Jerusalén (véase 1118).

1106–1110

Ruinas monumentales en la ciudad de Gran Zimbabue, capital del Imperio de Monomotapa, que se enriqueció tras asumir el control de la ruta del oro.

CONOCIDA POR SU ARTE, SU ARTESANÍA y la construcción de **túmulos monumentales**, la cultura posmochica, o cultura Sicán o Lambayeque en la costa norte de Perú, llegó a su apogeo en el siglo XI. Sin embargo, una sequía y terribles inundaciones la llevaron al **colapso cultural y político**. A principios del siglo XII, el estado se recuperó de las convulsiones del siglo anterior y se reconstruyó en la nueva capital de **Túcume**. Se construyeron templos y la capital prosperó hasta que los **chimúes** (*véase* 1375) la conquistaron, momento en que contaba con 26 túmulos con sus correspondientes recintos.

En el centro de África del sur, en el actual Zimbabue, el **Imperio de Monomotapa**, también conocido como **Gran Zimbabue**, por lo monumental de su capital, se convirtió en el poder regional más importante. Monomotapa fue un reino de los pueblos **shona** que apareció cerca del año 900 y que, al principio, se basaba en la ganadería; pero a partir de 1100 asumió el control de las lucrativas **rutas comerciales** de los centros productores de oro, hierro y marfil en el interior hacia los **reinos comerciales árabes** en la costa este, que ofrecían productos de lujo procedentes de Asia.

turquesa incrustada

Cuchillo ceremonial
Cuchillo de oro de la cultura Sicán Media de Perú. El principio de la década de 1100 marca el umbral entre la cultura Sicán Media y Tardía.

1111–1115

Catedral de san Nicolás en Nóvgorod (Rusia), del siglo XII.

LA CONSTRUCCIÓN DE CATEDRALES VIVIÓ UN GRAN AUGE en toda Europa durante el siglo XII, a medida que el crecimiento demográfico, el aumento de la riqueza y los **avances en la arquitectura** se combinaban con el celo religioso, el **orgullo civil** y la ambición personal de los potentados. Los estilos **románico y gótico** encontraron su máxima expresión en las grandes catedrales, pero cada uno de ellos desarrolló su lenguaje característico y particular. Por ejemplo, la **catedral de san Nicolás** (iniciada en 1113) en **Nóvgorod**, se construyó con cúpulas abovedadas.

La **querella de las investiduras** entre el papado y los emperadores occidentales continuaba (*véase* 1071–1080). **Enrique IV** no consiguió reconciliarse con el papado, lo que propició su caída: su propia familia, preocupada porque la disputa permanente pudiera socavar la autoridad real, conspiró contra él y le encarceló. Su sucesor, **Enrique V** (1086–1125) envió una potente expedición a **Italia** para forzar una **coronación imperial**. Bajo coacción (era prisionero de Enrique en aquel momento), el **papa Pascual II** hizo grandes concesiones en la cuestión de la investidura en el **tratado de Sutri**, pero las repudió al año siguiente y la cuestión continuó sin dirimirse (*véase* 1122).

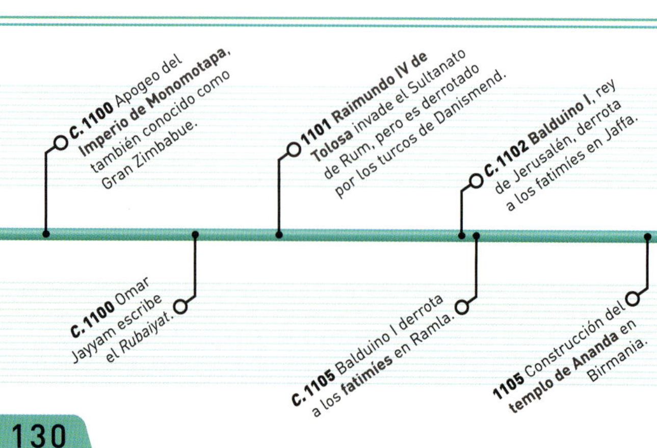

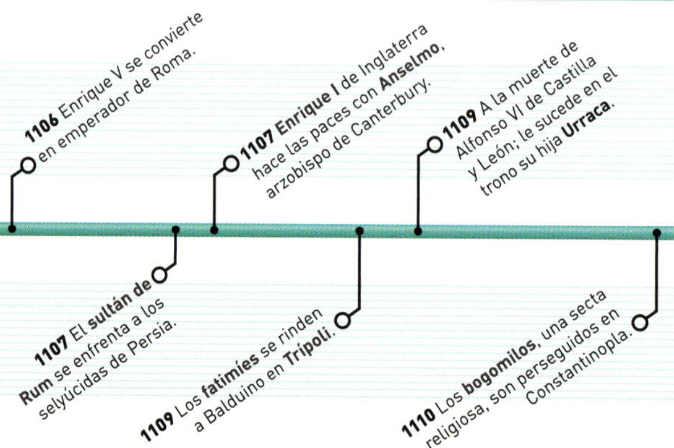

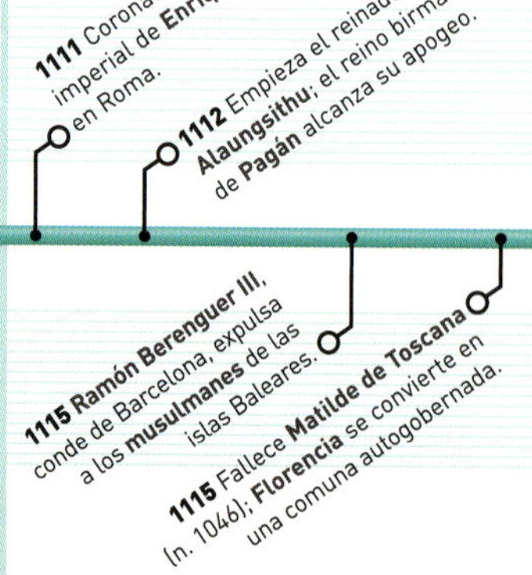

Vitral que muestra a un caballero templario en Warwickshire (Inglaterra).

Güelfos y gibelinos se enfrentan en Italia. Estas facciones, asociadas a las dinastías alemanas de Welf y Hohenstaufen, llegarían a dominar la política italiana.

« EN ESTA **ORDEN RELIGIOSA** HA **FLORECIDO** Y SE HA **REVITALIZADO** LA **ORDEN** DE LA CABALLERÍA. **»**

De la *Regla primitiva de la Orden del Temple*

En **Jerusalén**, en 1119, un grupo de caballeros liderados por el francés **Hugues de Payns** (*c.* 1070–1136) fundó una orden cuyo objetivo era **proteger a los peregrinos** que viajaban por el peligroso camino desde Jaffa, en la costa, a la ciudad santa. El nuevo rey de Jerusalén, **Balduino II** (primo de Balduino I y su sucesor como conde de Edesa) les asignó instalaciones en el lugar donde antes se erigía el **templo de Salomón**. Por este motivo se llamaron a sí mismos los Pobres Soldados de Cristo y el Templo de Salomón, a quienes también se les conoce como **caballeros templarios o caballeros del Temple**.

La **Universidad de Bolonia** fue la primera universidad de Occidente. Se fundó en el año 1119 (o posiblemente antes de esta fecha, según la fuente). Instituciones como la Universidad de Bolonia desarrollaron la base del pensamiento teológico-filosófico que se conoce como **escolasticismo** (*véase* recuadro).

EN 1121, MUHAMMAD IBN TUMART, UN LÍDER BEREBER de la cordillera del Atlas, fue nombrado **al-Mahdi** (el Mesías musulmán, *véase* 874) y lideró a sus fuerzas, los **almohades**, en una **campaña de conquista** contra los territorios almorávides africanos.

Un sínodo en la ciudad alemana de **Worms** en 1122, dirigido por el legado papal, elaboró un concordato (acuerdo) que puso fin a la **querella de las investiduras**, aunque no a la rivalidad entre el papa y el emperador. Se llegó a un compromiso similar al que ya habían adoptado **Enrique I de Inglaterra y Anselmo** (*véase* 1107), por el que el emperador participaría en las investiduras, pero no las controlaría. En definitiva, fue una **victoria para el papado**.

En 1123, **fuerzas francas** de Jerusalén **derrotaron al ejército fatimí** en Ibelín, mientras que la flota veneciana destruyó a la fatimí frente a la costa de Ascalón. Esta batalla marcó el principio del **dominio italiano** sobre las aguas mediterráneas.

El **emperador Enrique V** falleció en 1125 sin dejar heredero varón, por lo que se celebraron elecciones para decidir a su sucesor. El heredero más cercano era **Conrado de Suabia** (1122–1190), de la casa de **Hohenstaufen** (aliada de la dinastía sálica y de sus políticas antipapales); sin embargo, los arzobispos de Maguncia y de Colonia inclinaron la elección a favor de un candidato más favorable a la Iglesia. **Lotario de Sajonia** (1075–1137), de la casa de Welf, fue el elegido y se convirtió en el **emperador Lotario II** (III, según algunas fuentes). Se vio inmerso inmediatamente en una cruenta **guerra civil** con los Hohenstaufen; los dos bandos, uno a favor del papa y otro a favor de los emperadores de Alemania, se conocieron como **güelfos y gibelinos**, respectivamente. Enturbiaron las relaciones en el seno y entre las **ciudades-estado del norte de Italia** hasta bien entrado el siglo XIV, mucho más tarde de que hubieran dejado de dominar la política alemana, ya que se asociaron a las luchas de clases y a **partidos reaccionarios y reformistas**.

Las obras de **Aristóteles** (384–322 a. C.) habían sobrevivido en Bizancio gracias a los árabes, pero los europeos occidentales únicamente habían podido acceder a la traducción que el filósofo **Boecio** había hecho de uno de sus tratados de lógica. La situación empezó a cambiar a principios del siglo XII, cuando la conquista de regiones musulmanas, como **Toledo** y **Sicilia**, permitió a los académicos cristianos acceder a obras árabes. La creciente exposición de los eruditos medievales a las obras de Aristóteles les llevó a considerarle como el «**maestro de los que saben**» y la primera autoridad en las cuestiones de razón.

En el año 1125, el rey francés **Luis VI** (1081–1137) logró reunir a la nobleza francesa para repeler una invasión **anglogermana**. Fue un hito en los intentos de la monarquía francesa por imponer su autoridad y, por lo tanto, en la emergencia de **Francia como un estado-nación**.

ESCOLASTICISMO

La escuela de pensamiento conocida como escolasticismo, porque la enseñaban escolásticos, o escolares, se convirtió en la filosofía de aprendizaje dominante en la Europa medieval, de la mano de las incipientes universidades. El escolasticismo abordaba el aprendizaje como una discusión y un debate formales y se convertiría en la base intelectual para el dogma religioso y filosófico medieval.

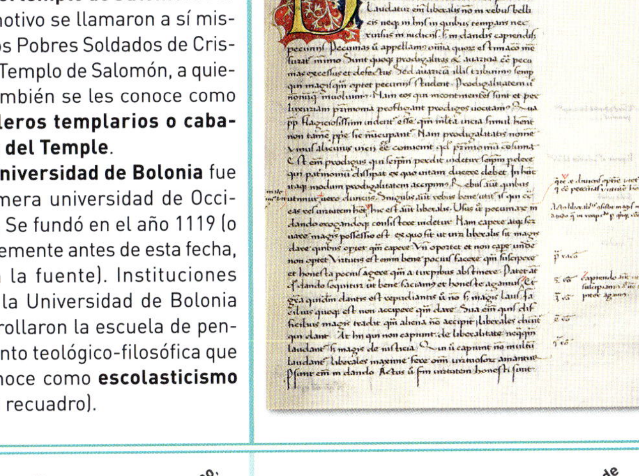

Aristóteles traducido
Página de la traducción de la Ética Nicomaquea de Aristóteles, en vitela (material hecho con piel de ternera, más duradero que el papiro o el papel).

25 % **PROPORCIÓN** DE LA **OBRA DE ARISTÓTELES** QUE HA LLEGADO **A NUESTROS DÍAS**

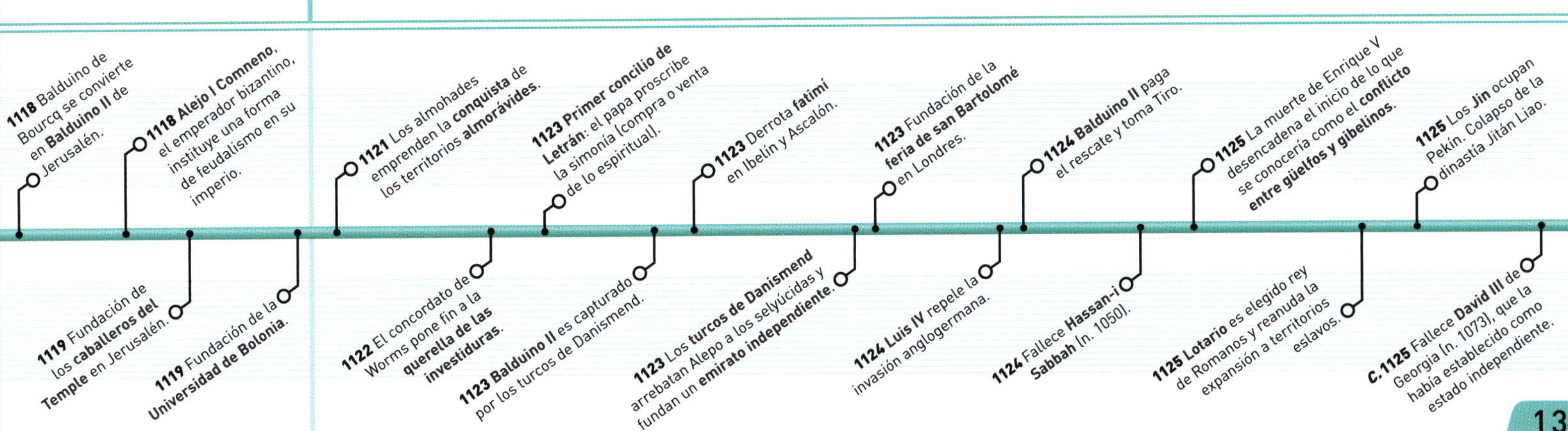

1126–1130

Mosaico donde Jesucristo corona simbólicamente a Roger II.

EN 1126, LOS JIN, la dinastía yurchena fundada por Aguda en Manchuria, se volvieron contra sus hasta entonces aliados chinos, **irrumpieron en el norte de China** y tomaron la capital de los Song del Norte, Kaifeng. Los Jin asumieron el control sobre el norte de China y avanzaron hacia la capital, Pekín. Esto marcó el **fin de los Song del Norte**. Sin embargo, un príncipe Song, **Gaozong**, logró escapar al sur y fundó la dinastía **Song del Sur** en Hangzhou en 1127.

La muerte del **papa Honorio** en 1130 derivó en la elección de dos papas rivales, **Inocencio II** y **Anacleto II**. Durante el cisma papal, **Roger II**, conde de Sicilia, reconoció a Anacleto como papa, lo que le valió el trono de Sicilia en recompensa.

Porcelana de la dinastía Song
El vidriado Qingbai (azul-blanco) de este aguamanil es característico de la porcelana de la dinastía Song, del sureste de China, donde la dinastía sobrevivió a la invasión Jin.

1131–1135

Matilde de Inglaterra sostiene una cédula en la *Crónica* de san Albano.

LA MUERTE DE ENRIQUE I EN EL AÑO 1135 SUMIÓ A INGLATERRA EN UNA DISPUTA DINÁSTICA. Su único heredero varón había fallecido en 1120 mientras cruzaba el Canal de la Mancha. Y aunque Enrique había obligado a los nobles a jurar lealtad a su hija, la **emperatriz Matilde** (1102–1067), esta había pasado poco tiempo en Inglaterra y su segundo marido, **Godofredo de Anjou** era impopular entre la nobleza inglesa. Entre los que habían jurado lealtad a Matilde se encontraba el sobrino y pupilo de Enrique, **Esteban de Blois** (r. 1135–1154). A la muerte de su tío, este se desplazó a Londres, donde obtuvo el apoyo de la mayoría de la nobleza y de la Iglesia, y se autoproclamó rey. Pero Matilde se negó a renunciar a su derecho y la disputa desembocó en un periodo de guerras y de colapso de la autoridad central conocido como periodo de la **anarquía** (*véase* 1136–1140).

En 1133, **Lotario II** (1070–1137) acudió a Italia para intervenir en el **cisma papal** e investir a **Inocencio II**. A cambio, el papa confirmó la **herencia matildina** (los vastos territorios de Matilde de Toscana, que primero había legado al papado y luego al emperador, lo que dio lugar a una disputa que se vería enredada por el conflicto entre güelfos y gibelinos [*véase* 1121–1125]) y **coronó a Lotario como emperador**. Lotario aplacó a sus rivales, **Conrado de Hohenstaufen** y su hermano **Federico de Suabia**, en el año 1135 al prometer la corona alemana a su yerno **Enrique el Soberbio**, duque de Baviera, de la casa de Welf.

1136–1140

Ilustración de un ejemplar del siglo XV de *Historia Regum Britanniae*, de Godofredo de Monmouth, donde Bruto de Troya zarpa hacia la isla de Bretaña.

EN 1137, LOTARIO MURIÓ REPENTINAMENTE mientras regresaba de una exitosa campaña en Italia contra **Roger de Sicilia**. Los planes de Lotario, que quería concentrar los territorios alemanes en manos de los **Welf (Güelfos)** y dejar así una herencia sólida a su yerno, se evaporaron cuando en 1138 se eligió a **Conrado de Hohenstaufen** (1135–1195), de la casa de Waiblinger. Los Waiblinger descendían de los duques de Franconia y los italianos habían corrompido el apellido hasta convertirlo en «gibelino». Conrado se propuso invertir las concesiones de Lotario y arrebató Sajonia a la casa de Welf, lo que desencadenó rápidamente otra guerra civil.

En 1139, Matilde llegó a Inglaterra para reclamar su corona al usurpador Estaban de Blois. Esteban no había logrado consolidar su posición desde que tomara el trono; por un lado, había alienado a gran parte de la nobleza, y, por el otro, a los clérigos más poderosos. Cometió su mayor error al arrestar a su primer ministro, Roger, obispo de Salisbury. De un plumazo perdió a muchos de sus administradores más capaces, por lo que no pudo reinar entre las escaramuzas con los barones y otros propietarios, que se autoproclamaron señores de sí mismos. El país se deterioró y cayó en un estado de anarquía que el autor de la crónica de Peterborough lamentó amargamente. Escribió que, bajo el reinado de Esteban, los ingleses «sufrieron diecinueve largos inviernos... mientras Cristo y todos sus santos dormían».

En algún momento de 1140, el clérigo galés **Godofredo de Monmouth** (*c.* 1100–1155) escribió la *Historia Regum Britanniae*, un ejemplo importante de la literatura anglonormanda temprana, que presentaría la leyenda del **rey Arturo** al público europeo.

Castillo de leyenda
Tintagel (Cornualles), donde aún se yerguen las ruinas de un castillo del siglo XIII, aparece en las leyendas creadas por Godofredo de Monmouth.

1141–1145

Escena del sitio de Damasco, una de las batallas de la segunda cruzada.

EN EL AÑO 1141, JUAN HISPALENSE TRADUJO DEL ÁRABE el *Epitome astrologiae*, y un año más tarde, en 1142, **Adelardo de Bath** tradujo una versión árabe de los *Elementos de geometría* de Euclides, uno de los textos fundacionales de las matemáticas. Esta **transmisión del conocimiento** antiguo y contemporáneo mediante las traducciones del árabe al latín fue un elemento clave en la aparición de un **renacimiento intelectual** europeo y, más adelante, en los avances científicos de la **primera era moderna** (1500–1800).

En 1142, en un intento de poner fin a la guerra civil que asolaba Alemania, una reunión, o dieta, en Frankfurt confirmó a **Enrique el León** (1129–1195), de la casa de Welf, como **duque de Sajonia** (que ya había tomado por la fuerza). Enrique emprendió una vigorosa renovación de la **expansión alemana** hacia el este, donde

Yelmo de una sola pieza
Los caballeros cruzados llevaban este tipo de yelmo. Era de acero y cubría por completo la cabeza, a excepción de dos pequeñas ranuras para los ojos.

1126 Los **Jin yurchenos** derrotan a los Song del Norte y toman el norte de China.

1127 Conrado es elegido rey de Romanos, como rival de Lotario.

1127 Instauración de la **dinastía Song del Sur**.

1127 Imad el-Din Zengi funda la **dinastía zangí** en Mosul.

1127 Esteban II de Hungría arrebata Belgrado y Sofía a los bizantinos.

1130 Roger II se convierte en **rey de Sicilia**.

1131 Fulco de Anjou es coronado rey de Jerusalén.

1133 Lotario II expulsa a Anacleto e inviste a **Inocencio II** como papa y es coronado emperador.

1134 Construcción de una **torre gótica** en Chartres.

1135 Año de pacificación de Lotario. Afirma su poder en Alemania.

1135 Fallece Enrique I de Inglaterra (n. 1068) y **Esteban** usurpa el trono a Matilde.

1137 Owain el Grande asciende al trono de Gales.

1137 El general Yehlü funda el kanato de **Kara-Kitai** en el centro de Asia.

1137 Fallece **Lotario II** (n. 1070).

1138 Conrado III es elegido rey de Romanos en Alemania, lo que lleva a otra **guerra entre güelfos y gibelinos**.

C. 1139 Los **igbo de Níger** desarrollan sofisticadas técnicas de trabajo del bronce.

1139 Matilde llega a Inglaterra para reclamar su corona. Principio del periodo de la **anarquía**.

1140 Finalización de la fachada oeste de la **basílica de Saint-Denis** en París, un hito de la arquitectura gótica.

C. 1140 Godofredo de Monmouth escribe *Historia Regum Britanniae*.

1141 Batalla de Lincoln: Esteban es capturado y Matilde asciende al trono de Inglaterra.

1141 El **partido de la paz** supera al Imperio **Song del Sur**.

1141 Kara-Kitai derrota a los selyúcidas en Samarcanda.

1142 Dieta de Frankfurt: intento de poner fin al conflicto Welf-Waiblinger en Alemania.

1146–1150

El templo de Angkor Wat, en Camboya, se construyó bajo el reinado de Suryavarman II. Cubre casi 200 hectáreas de terreno y la torre central tiene 42 m de altura.

« QUIENES SOIS DE DIOS… **LUCHAD** PARA **OPONEOS** A LA MULTITUD DE **INFIELES** QUE **SE REGOCIJAN** CON LA VICTORIA OBTENIDA SOBRE NOSOTROS, Y **DEFENDED LA IGLESIA ORIENTAL**, QUE LA **SANGRE** DE VUESTROS PADRES LIBRÓ DE LA **TIRANÍA**. »

Papa Eugenio III, en la bula donde llamaba a una segunda cruzada (1145)

sus campañas contra los **eslavos** paganos se elevaron a la categoría de cruzadas.

El *atabeg* (gobernador) de Mosul, **Imad al-Din Zangi** (1084–1146), fundador de la **dinastía zangí**, aprovechó en 1144 las disputas internas existentes entre los principados cruzados y tomó el condado cruzado de Edesa. Fulco, rey de Jerusalén, había fallecido en el año 1143 y su sucesor, **Balduino III** (1130–1163), no era más que un niño bajo la regencia de su madre, **Melisenda de Bouillon**. Carecía de la autoridad necesaria para acabar con las disputas entre Antioquía y Edesa, e Imad al-Din asedió Edesa hasta conseguir que se rindiera. La **pérdida de Edesa** provocó gran alarma e indignación en Europa, lo que permitió emprender la **segunda cruzada** (*véase* 1146–1450). En el año 1145, Eugenio III emitió una llamada a las armas en forma de bula papal.

EN 1146, EL INFLUYENTE MONJE CISTERCENSE BERNARDO DE CLARAVAL (1090–1153), alentado por el papa Eugenio III, predicó una nueva cruzada para liberar a Edesa de las garras de los zangíes. **Conrado III de Alemania** (1093–1152) junto con **Luis VII de Francia** (1120–1180) «tomaron la cruz». Pero la expedición fue un desastre, excepto por una pequeña victoria que un contingente de fuerzas inglesas y flamencas obtuvo en tierras lusas, cuando ayudaron a **Alfonso Enríquez**, conde de Portugal, a arrebatar Lisboa a los **árabes** en 1147. Conrado y Luis llegaron a Tierra Santa por rutas distintas, pero sus ejércitos encontraron un mismo destino fatal en sus intentos de avanzar por Anatolia. En 1148, obligado a pedir asilo en un barco bizantino tras haber perdido a su ejército en la **batalla de Dorilea**, Conrado se reunió con Luis. En vez

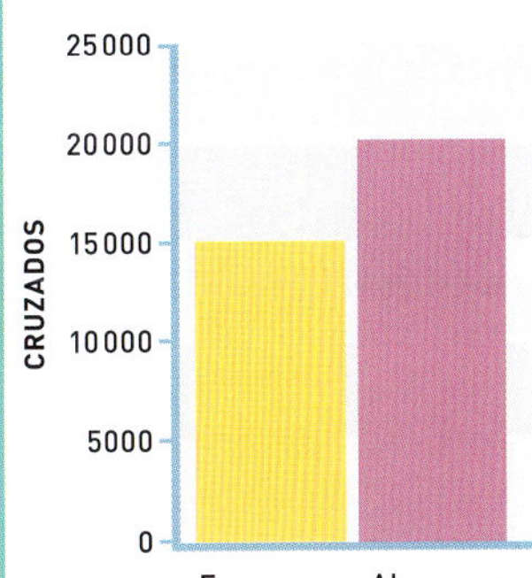

Cruzados franceses y alemanes
Los alemanes superaron en número a los franceses en la segunda cruzada. Ninguno de los dos ejércitos obtuvo victoria alguna: la derrota en Anatolia fue seguida por el fracaso de Damasco.

Mezquita de Kutubiya
Los almohades construyeron la mezquita de Kutubiya (de los libreros), que refleja el éxito comercial del Marrakech almohade, en el que florecieron los zocos de libros y de tejidos, entre otros.

de lanzar a sus diezmadas tropas contra los zangíes, decidieron lanzar un ataque sobre Damasco, el único estado musulmán que mantenía relaciones amistosas con los reinos cruzados. Debilitados por la **falta de víveres** y amenazados por el líder zangí Nur al-Din, también **fracasaron** en el **sitio de Damasco**. La segunda cruzada terminó sin haber conseguido más que una perjudicial ruptura matrimonial. Uno de los generales de Luis inició relaciones con su esposa, **Leonor de Aquitania** (c. 1122–1204), de la que se divorció, con la consiguiente pérdida de los territorios que le pertenecían a ella (*véase* 1151–1555). Los **bizantinos** se vieron obligados a intervenir allá donde la cruzada había fracasado y ocuparon Edesa occidental, pero **Roger de Sicilia** se aprovechó de la distracción bizantina e invadió Grecia en 1147. Los desastres de la segunda cruzada marcaron el inicio del **fin** de los **reinos cruzados francos**.

En 1147, los **almohades**, bajo **Abd al-Mumin** (1094–1163), finalizaron la conquista del Marruecos almorávide y tomaron **Marrakech** antes de invadir la **España musulmana** (aunque hasta 1172 no lograron subyugar a todos los reinos musulmanes).

Suryavarman II (c. 1113–1150) fue el **rey jemer** más belicoso, aunque la mayoría de las aventuras que emprendió en el extranjero fueron infructuosas. Lanzó ataques contra el **Dai Viet** en el norte de Vietnam e hizo intentos repetidos de subyugar el reino de **Champa**. Tuvo más éxito en su campaña de construcción, pues levantó el **templo** de **Angkor Wat**, un vasto complejo compuesto por cinco torres que simbolizan montañas sagradas y una miríada de tallas intrincadas.

200
HECTÁREAS
CUBRE
ANGKOR WAT

1142 Adelardo de Bath traduce del árabe los *Elementos* de Euclides.

1143 Manuel I Comneno se ve obligado a abordar la **rebelión armenia**.

1143 Alfonso VII de Castilla y León reconoce a **Alfonso I** como rey de Portugal.

1144 La muerte de **Guillermo de Norwich** desencadena **pogromos** antisemitas en Inglaterra.

1144 Godofredo Plantagenet, conde de Anjou, completa la **conquista de Normandía**.

1144 El atabeg zangí de Mosul toma **Edesa** y provoca la segunda cruzada.

1145 El emperador jemer **Suryavarman II** invade el reino de Champa.

1145 Inicio de la construcción de la portalada oeste de la **catedral de Chartres**.

1146 Bernardo de Claraval predica la segunda cruzada.

1146 Los normandos de Sicilia toman **Tripolitania**, en el intento de Roger de crear un imperio mediterráneo.

1147 Conrado de Alemania y Luis de Francia parten a la **cruzada**.

1147 Alzamiento de los **vendos** contra los **sajones**.

1147 Los **almohades** finalizan la conquista del Marruecos almorávide e invaden España.

1147 Los **musulmanes** son expulsados de Lisboa.

1147 Roger de Sicilia instaura la **industria de la seda** en Sicilia, después de saquear Bizancio y Grecia.

1148 Clímax de la segunda cruzada con el fallido **sitio a Damasco**.

1149 Las fuerzas de Nur al-Din derrotan a **Raimundo de Antioquía**.

1149 Champa retoma su capital de manos **jemeres**.

c.1150 Construcción del templo de **Angkor Wat**.

Cerámica persa y aguamanil con hojas doradas
1200–1399 • IRÁN
El islam prohibía los recipientes de oro y plata porque los consideraba ostentosos, por lo que los artesanos árabes se volvieron expertos en alternativas como la cerámica, que luego decoraban profusamente.

Jarra de bronce
Siglo XVIII • CHINA
Esta jarra de bronce procede de China y está decorada con una cita del Corán en árabe, aunque la influencia china es evidente.

Azulejo con forma de estrella
1267 • IRÁN
Aunque es claramente islámica en el uso del lustre (técnica cerámica que imita el oro) y de los arabescos (follaje estilizado), el azulejo deja entrever la influencia mogola con la inclusión de animales parecidos a perros.

EL MUNDO ISLÁMICO

LA INNOVACIÓN TECNOLÓGICA Y EL FERVOR RELIGIOSO SE UNEN PARA CREAR UN PATRIMONIO ÚNICO DE ARTE Y ARTESANÍA

La artesanía y el arte musulmanes evolucionaron por las creencias religiosas, el patrimonio cultural adquirido por conquista y la introducción de características únicas como la ornamentación, el color y la caligrafía árabe.

El califato musulmán conquistó un enorme imperio, con lo que se vio expuesto a variedad de estilos y patrimonios culturales, que el arte reflejó al tiempo que mantenía un gran nivel de homogeneidad por la uniformidad religiosa. Las restricciones que imponía el islam convencional, como la prohibición del arte figurativo y el uso de metales preciosos, dieron lugar a respuestas muy creativas, sobre todo en diseños abstractos y estilizados, la ornamentación elaborada, el uso del color y la inclusión de caligrafía árabe y de citas del Corán.

Tijeras quirúrgicas y escalpelo
Siglo X • ORIGEN DESCONOCIDO
Los médicos árabes dieron pasos de gigante en los ámbitos de la medicina y de la cirugía, como en el diseño de instrumentos quirúrgicos como el *mibda* (escalpelo) y las *miqass* (tijeras).

Khanjar
Siglo XIX • INDIA
Aunque procede de India, esta daga curvada de doble filo es una hoja tradicional omaní. Está decorada con follaje intrincado, un motivo musulmán habitual.

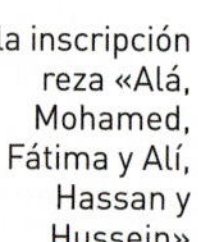

Collar de jade
1875–1925 • ORIGEN DESCONOCIDO
Este collar de jade se compone de cinco piezas de formas distintas y grabadas con versos del Corán. Estos artículos hacían las veces de amuletos con poderes cuasi mágicos.

Colgante
Siglo XVIII • INDIA
Este colgante de oro, del Imperio mogol indio, demuestra que los gobernantes árabes desoían en ocasiones las prohibiciones sobre el arte figurativo y el uso de metales preciosos.

Monedas
720–910 • SIRIA/EGIPTO
Monedas de los califatos omeya y abasí, acuñadas en Damasco y El Cairo, con texto en caligrafía árabe en lugar de imágenes de los cabezas de estado.

la inscripción reza «Alá, Mohamed, Fátima y Alí, Hassan y Hussein»

Estandarte dorado chií
Siglo XVII • IRÁN
Este estandarte (o alam) de latón y oro rememora simbólicamente el estandarte chií plantado en la batalla de Karbala el año 680.

cinta entrelazada en ocre, blanco y negro

Cuenco
1000–1199 • IRÁN/IRAQ
Los llamativos colores de este sencillo cuenco son típicamente árabes, al igual que la cinta entrelazada. El diseño entretejido otorga una cualidad meditativa al dibujo.

la cabeza se une al cuerpo por una bisagra

Incensario felino
Siglos XI–XII • IRÁN/AFGANISTÁN
Las cortes de los reyes musulmanes medievales utilizaban incensarios como este, con forma de gran felino. Los leones y los guepardos simbolizaban el poder.

Candelabro
Siglo XV • EGIPTO MAMELUCO
Para superar la prohibición de usar metales preciosos, los artesanos islámicos se convirtieron en expertos en la combinación de metales básicos, como el latón con incrustaciones de plata y oro.

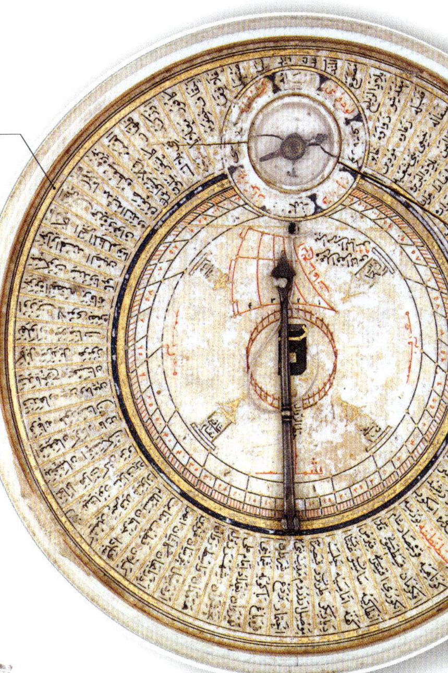

las marcas del borde indican la ciudad o ubicación

Brújula
FECHA Y ORIGEN DESCONOCIDOS
Esta brújula ornamental se utilizaba para indicar la dirección, o *alquibla*, de la oración, para que los creyentes se orientaran correctamente hacia la Kaaba de La Meca.

Tijeras de caligrafía
1700–1799 • IRÁN
Estas tijeras se utilizaban para perfilar plumas y cepillos. Las hojas tienen incrustaciones de oro, en una variedad de damasquinado llamada *koftgari*.

Estuche para plumas
1700–1899 • ORIGEN DESCONOCIDO
Estuche hexagonal con formas geométricas, una característica del diseño musulmán.

Lámpara musulmana
FECHA Y ORIGEN DESCONOCIDOS
Esta lámpara con forma de reloj de arena está adornada con caligrafía árabe. Su tinte azul intenso fue perfeccionado por los ceramistas musulmanes.

colores intensos y pan de oro

no hay espacios vacíos

cuidadosa caligrafía árabe

las iluminaciones se saltan las prohibiciones habituales

Diván iluminado
1800–1899 • INDIA
Un diván es una colección o antología de poemas inspirados en los patrones poéticos de la antigua Persia. La cubierta de este diván iluminado del poeta persa Hafez, de la India del siglo XIX, está decorada con un lacado típico de Cachemira.

1151–1155

Túmulo del Monje, el mayor de Cahokia. Supera los 30 m de altura y se estima que en su construcción se emplearon unos quince millones de cestos de tierra.

LA CIUDAD DE CAHOKIA SURGIÓ EN EL CULMEN de la cultura misisipiense (o de los indios Natchez), que ocupaba una región del valle del río que le dio el nombre. A mediados del siglo XII construyeron más de **cien montículos**, entre ellos uno cuya base es mayor que la de la pirámide de Guiza y con una plaza que, probablemente, sea la **mayor plaza urbana de tierra del mundo**. La característica más asombrosa de Cahokia es la velocidad a la que apareció. Hasta cerca de 1050, los indios **misisipienses** vivieron en pequeñas aldeas y jamás construyeron nada semejante a ese espacio. A mediados de la década de 1150, la ciudad cubría unas **493 hectáreas** y albergaba a **treinta mil habitantes**. Su influencia económica y cultural se extendió por todo el **Medio Oeste**, desde la actual frontera canadiense hasta la costa del Golfo. Quizás fuera precisamente lo excepcional de la vida urbana en la cultura misisipiense lo que llevó al **rápido declive** de Cahokia: en cuestión de un siglo, la población volvió a organizarse en comunidades agrícolas de baja densidad.

Conrado II (n. 1093), rey de Romanos, falleció en 1152, y su sobrino, **Federico de Suabia**, conocido como **Barbarroja** (*véase* recuadro), fue elegido para que le sucediera. De ascendencia Welf y Waiblinger combinada (*véase* 1131–1135), su nombramiento trajo una paz relativa a Alemania. Su coronación como **emperador** en Roma se vio retrasada porque la ciudad había caído en manos de una **comuna revolucionaria** liderada por el reformista radical **Arnoldo de Brescia** (1090–1155). Federico se alió con el papado y contra Arnoldo y la Sicilia normanda, y realizó su primera incursión en Italia en 1154. En 1155 y frente a la hostilidad romana, fue coronado por el nuevo papa, **Adriano IV** (1100–1159), pero tuvo que retirarse a Alemania y abandonar a Adriano, que se vio obligado entonces a aliarse con **los normandos**.

FEDERICO BARBARROJA (1122–1190)

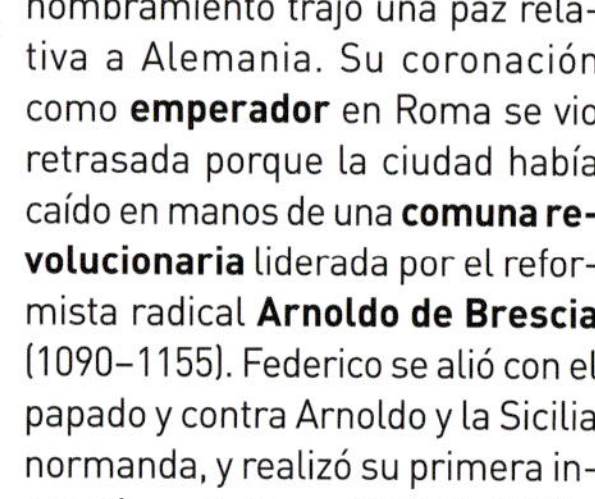

Enérgico y ambicioso, Federico I estaba decidido a convertir a Alemania en el principal estado europeo y a reafirmar su autoridad sobre el territorio imperial italiano. Consciente del contexto de su reinado, intentó devolver a la corona imperial la gloria de la antigua Roma y empezó a llamar a su reino Sacro Imperio Romano. En Alemania, aplacó a los rebeldes y amplió el territorio imperial.

1156–1160

La Universidad de Bolonia fue, en sus orígenes, una facultad para juristas.

CON UNOS ORÍGENES QUE QUIZÁS SE REMONTEN A 1088, LA DE BOLONIA afirma ser la **universidad más antigua** del mundo occidental (*véase* 1116–1120), en el sentido de institución designada específicamente como ***universitas***, en oposición a un *studium generale*, como se llamaba hasta entonces a los centros de enseñanza. En 1158, **el emperador Federico I** (1122–1190), aconsejado por eruditos que probablemente fueron **alumnos de Bolonia**, otorgó a la universidad una cédula que la establecía firmemente como un **centro independiente de estudio**. Las primeras universidades tendían a especializarse en un único campo de estudio, y la de Bolonia se **dedicó al derecho**.

En 1159, **Alejandro III** (c. 1100–1081) fue investido papa a pesar de la oposición del emperador **Federico I**, que había vuelto a invadir Italia, esta vez decidido a recuperar todo su patrimonio imperial. Con la ayuda de la **Liga de Pavía** (Brescia, Parma y otras), había tomado Milán y a sus ciudades asociadas, pero en la **Dieta de Roncaglia**, en 1158, fue demasiado lejos. Se remontó a la era romana e insistió en que el derecho antiguo le otorgaba la posibilidad de nombrar a un ***podestá*** (gobernador local) **imperial** para gobernar cada ciudad. Milán se rebeló y, junto a otras ciudades, formó una **Liga Lombarda** bajo los auspicios del papado. Alejandro II se ganó el título de **el Grande** por su liderazgo al frente de esta rebelión antiimperial.

1161–1165

La torre de Hassan en Rabat (Marruecos) es todo lo que se construyó de lo que iba a ser una macromezquita almohade.

El Guanyin bodhisattva
Esta figura china (siglo XII) representa a la deidad budista Guanyin, que protege a los hogares del peligro, lo que quizás explique su popularidad.

EN 1161, LOS SONG DEL SUR REPELIERON UNA INCURSIÓN de los Jin del Norte (*véase* 1126–1130), con lo que evitaron la invasión del reino. En 1165 se firmó un tratado de paz que establecía una tregua incómoda entre ambas potencias.

El califa **almohade Abd al-Mumin** murió en 1163, tras destruir a los **almorávides** y haber extendido el dominio almohade desde Marruecos hasta Túnez (provincia de Ifriquiya). Otorgó carácter **hereditario** a su cargo y su hijo, **Abu Yakub Yusuf** (1135–1184) le sucedió. Pasó la mayor parte de su reinado repeliendo a la **oposición interna**, aunque también obtuvo victorias militares en la **España musulmana**.

En 1164, el emir zangí **Nur al-Din** (1118–1174) derrotó a los príncipes cruzados en **Arta**. Durante la década de 1160, Nur al-Din se enfrentó a los reinos cruzados, sobre todo porque intentaban obtener el control del **debilitado reino fatimí en Egipto**, liderado por el visir **Shawar**. **Amaury**, rey de Jerusalén desde 1162, fue el primero en ocupar Egipto, pero la **victoria zangí** en Arta le obligó a marchar hacia el norte, dejando el camino expedito para que el general Sirkuh, del ejército de Nur al-Din, y su sobrino **Saladino** invadieran Egipto (*véase* 1167).

A mediados del siglo XII, la densa cultura urbana de las **tribus pueblo** en el **Cañón del Chaco**, en América del Norte, se hundió, probablemente porque su sistema agrícola había explotado el **frágil ecosistema de secano** y les había dejado expuestos a la sequía. El fechado de vigas de los pueblos del Cañón del Chaco ha concluido que las más recientes son de la década de 1160; en otras palabras, no se construyó más a partir de ese momento. En otros enclaves pueblo, o **anasazi**, se han hallado restos de fortificaciones, de destrucción e incluso de canibalismo correspondientes a este periodo, pero también hay pruebas de que se trató, en general, de un abandono ordenado, probablemente porque la población se trasladó a otros lugares.

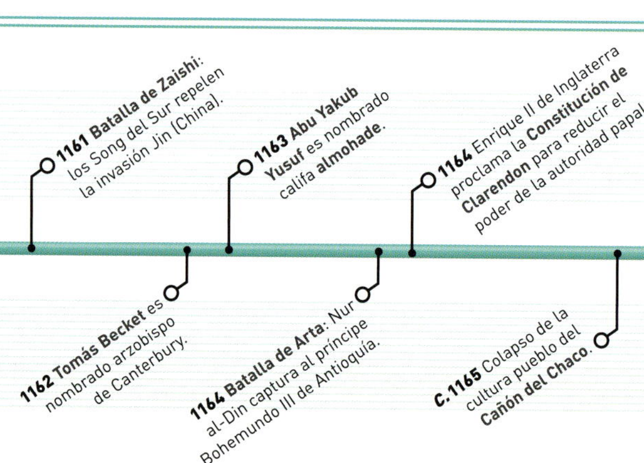

c. 1150 Culmen del asentamiento misisipiense de **Cahokia**, en América del Norte.

1151 Primera utilización de **explosivos de pólvora** con fines bélicos en China.

1152 **Federico I (Barbarroja)** sucede a Conrado como rey de Romanos.

1152 Leonor de Aquitania se casa con Enrique de Anjou y la combinación de sus territorios da lugar al **Imperio angevino**.

1153 Los Jin trasladan su capital de Manchuria a **Pekín**.

1154 Enrique II es coronado rey de Inglaterra.

1155 Federico I es coronado emperador.

c. 1156 Las ciudades-estado **yoruba** prosperan en África occidental.

1158 Federico I otorga una cédula a la **Universidad de Bolonia** (Italia).

1159 Elección del **papa Alejandro III** el Grande; formación de la **Liga Lombarda**, para enfrentarse a Federico en Italia.

1161 **Batalla de Zaishi**: los Song del Sur repelen la invasión Jin (China).

1162 **Tomás Becket** es nombrado arzobispo de Canterbury.

1163 **Abu Yakub Yusuf** es nombrado califa **almohade**.

1164 **Batalla de Arta**: Nur al-Din captura al príncipe Bohemundo III de Antioquía.

1164 Enrique II de Inglaterra proclama la **Constitución de Clarendon** para reducir el poder de la autoridad papal.

c. 1165 Colapso de la cultura pueblo del **Cañón del Chaco**.

1166–1170

« ¿NO HABRÁ QUIÉN ME LIBRE DE ESTE CURA ALBOROTADOR? »

Atribuido a Enrique II (1170)

El asesinato de Tomás Becket ilustra este vitral de la catedral de Canterbury. Canonizado en 1173, santo Tomás Becket se convirtió en uno de los santos más populares de Inglaterra.

EN 1170, TOMÁS BECKET, ARZOBISPO DE CANTERBURY, fue asesinado en la catedral de Canterbury (Inglaterra) a manos de cuatro caballeros de la corte de **Enrique II** (r. 1154–1189). Aunque juró que no había ordenado el crimen y fue absuelto de toda responsabilidad por el **papa Alejandro** en el año 1172, el famoso exabrupto de Enrique (*véase* arriba) provocó la actuación de los caballeros. El motivo de su ira era la disputa permanente sobre el alcance de la autoridad eclesiástica frente a la jurisdicción real. Durante el periodo de anarquía del **reinado de Esteban** (*véase* 1136–1140), los tribunales eclesiásticos se habían apropiado de competencias que antes correspondían a la monarquía. Tras la muerte de Esteban, **Enrique Plantagenet** ascendió al trono de Inglaterra, desde donde también controlaba los territorios de Anjou, Normandía y Aquitania (conocidos como **Imperio angevino**), y se propuso aplicar una muy necesaria reforma del reino. Por ejemplo, las **reformas fiscales** sustituyeron el *danegeld* (un impuesto que recibía el nombre de «oro de los daneses») por tributos nuevos, pero fue la **reforma jurídica** lo que le hizo entrar en conflicto con su amigo y canciller **Tomás Becket**. Becket ya se había visto obligado a exiliarse tras haber sido declarado culpable de violar la **Constitución de Clarendon** (*véase* 1164). A su regreso, ofendió a Enrique al **excomulgar** a los obispos favorecidos por la monarquía.

En su punto álgido, a finales del siglo XII, el **Imperio Srivijaya**, de naturaleza comercial y con sede en Sumatra, controlaba la mayor parte del **archipiélago malayo**. Su autoridad se extendía a colonias en las Indias Orientales, algunas tan remotas como **Sri Lanka** o **Taiwán**. El poder de Srivijaya procedía casi íntegramente de su **fuerza marítima**. Al proteger las aguas de la región de la piratería, permitió y controló el **comercio** entre China, India y el mundo islámico, pero los impuestos que imponía generaron resentimiento y, al final, una rebelión.

La cuarta expedición de **Federico I** a Italia, emprendida en 1166, dio lugar a la renovación de la **Liga Lombarda** (*véase* 1156–1160) y a la construcción de la imponente ciudadela de **Alessandria**, bautizada en honor al papa. Con esta ciudadela protegiendo los pasos entre las montañas, Italia quedó **prácticamente independiente** de la autoridad imperial.

tableta de arcilla con borde trabajado

Tableta votiva (Imperio Srivijaya)
Esta tableta votiva está grabada con budas. La dinastía Sailendra reinante era fervientemente budista.

1171–1175

Muhammad de Gur, a lomos de un elefante, lidera a su ejército en la conquista musulmana de India.

LOS GURÍES FUERON UNA DINASTÍA FUNDADA EN 1151 por Alaudin Husayn, que conquistó gran parte del **Afganistán gaznávida** y fundó un nuevo estado con capital en **Gur**, al oeste de Afganistán, en 1173. **Ghiyas ud-Din** se convirtió en el emir y nombró coemir a su hermano, Muizz ud-Din, más conocido como **Muhammad de Gur**. Juntos, los hermanos consiguieron controlar casi todo Afganistán y, en 1175, Muhammad lideró la **invasión musulmana** del norte de India.

El rabino español **Benjamín de Tudela** (1130–1173) fue el **primer europeo** del que se sabe que llegó a la frontera de **China**, en un viaje épico entre 1159 y 1173. Su *Libro de viajes* de Benjamín de Tudela incluye muchas leyendas exóticas, como la que afirma que el **arca de Noé** descansa en el monte Ararat.

Durante la Edad Media, la ciudad de **Pisa** (Toscana) se convirtió en el centro de una próspera **ciudad-estado**. La catedral se había construido en el siglo XI, pero en 1173 comenzaron las obras de un **campanario** independiente. Los cimientos se hundieron ya durante la construcción y la torre **empezó a inclinarse**, hasta alcanzar una inclinación de 4,5 m respecto a la perpendicular.

Torre inclinada de Pisa
La famosa torre inclinada de Pisa tiene 54,5 m de altura y una base de 17,5 m de diámetro.

Durante la década de 1170 apareció en Lyon un **nuevo movimiento religioso**. También conocidos como los Pobres de Lyon, los **valdenses** estaban liderados por **Pedro Valdo** (c. 1140–1218), un comerciante adinerado que renunció a todas sus propiedades y empezó a predicar un credo radical de **sencillez religiosa** que rechazaba gran parte de las enseñanzas del catolicismo. A pesar de contar con el beneplácito inicial del **papa Alejandro III**, la negativa de los valdenses a acatar su prohibición de predicar, llevó a que se les **denunciara como herejes** en 1179 y a una larga historia de persecución (*véase* 1206–1210).

En 1174, el emir zangí **Nur al-Din** falleció. Su sobrino **Saladino**, que ya había conseguido controlar **Egipto**, marchó rápidamente hacia el norte para tomar **Siria**; el califa de Bagdad le reconoció como **sultán** de Egipto y de Siria y fundó la **dinastía ayubí**.

1166 El **Gran Príncipe Vladislao I** de Bohemia es derrotado por los paganos de Prusia.

1166 La cuarta expedición de Federico I a Italia lleva a la renovación de la **Liga Lombarda**.

1167 Amalrico de Jerusalén se alía con los **fatimíes** contra los **zangíes**.

1168 Amalrico invade Egipto pero **Nur al-Din** le obliga a retirarse.

1169 Casimiro de Polonia invade Rusia.

1169 Saladino se convierte en el visir zangí de Egipto.

1169 Kilij Arslan II, sultán de Rum, toma la ciudad de Ankara durante su conquista de los **turcos de Danismend**.

C.1170 Saqueo de Tula, en que los **toltecas** son destruidos por tribus mexicanas del norte, como los **aztecas**.

C.1170 Auge del reino de **Srivijaya** (Java).

1170 Actividad **anglonormanda** en Irlanda, bajo el liderazgo de Robert Fitz-Stephen, apodado *Strongbow*.

1170 Asesinato de **Tomás Becket** (n. 1118).

1171 Conflicto entre **Bizancio** y **Venecia** por el control del comercio.

1171 Enrique II de Inglaterra llega a Irlanda.

1171 Fallece el último califa **fatimí**. Egipto está completamente bajo control **zangí**.

1172 El emperador bizantino **Manuel I Comneno** captura a Esteban Nemanja, el líder serbio.

1173 Benjamín de Tudela vuelve de Asia y escribe su *Libro de viajes*.

1173 Empieza la construcción de la **torre de Pisa**.

C.1173 Pedro Valdo forma el movimiento cristiano de los **valdenses**.

1174 Fallecen Nur al-Din y Amalrico. **Saladino** toma Damasco (Siria).

1175 Muhammad de Gur invade India.

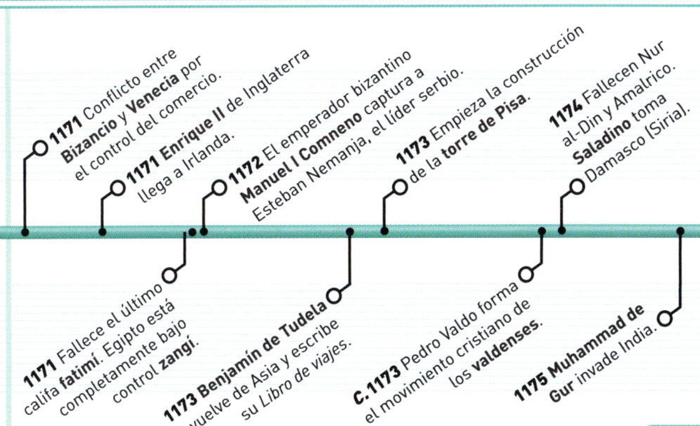

1176–1180

Escena de la batalla de Yashima, durante las guerras Gempei, en la que un Minamoto fuertemente armado acaba de descubrir a la aterrorizada madre del emperador Taira.

LA QUINTA EXPEDICIÓN A ITALIA DEL EMPERADOR FEDERICO BARBARROJA en 1176 (*véase* 1151–1155) fue un desastre para el ejército imperial, que sería aplastado en la **batalla de Legnano**. Fue una de las primeras veces en que la infantería derrotó a la caballería, lo que tenía importantes implicaciones de clase, ya que los caballeros solían pertenecer a la aristocracia feudal, mientras que los piqueros –los soldados que iban a pie armados únicamente con una pica– eran hombres libres pertenecientes a la burguesía en alza. En 1177, Federico se vio obligado a firmar la **paz de Venecia** con el papa, que sería un preludio de la más amplia paz de Constanza de 1183 (*véase* 1181–1185).

Ya reconciliado con el emperador, el **papa Alejandro III** pudo convocar un consejo ecuménico en el palacio de Letrán (Roma) en 1179. El consejo decretó que las **elecciones papales** serían responsabilidad exclusiva de los cardenales y que se necesitaría una mayoría de dos tercios para elegir a un papa. Se esperaba poner fin de esta manera a los años de disputas entre los candidatos papales elegidos por la facción antiimperial y los **«antipapas»**, que eran personas elegidas por el emperador para que se opusieran al papa legítimamente escogido o ya en el cargo.

En el año 1176, los turcos del **Sultanato de Rum** (*véase* 1100–1105) destruyeron al ejército del **emperador bizantino**, Manuel I Comneno, en la **batalla de Miriocéfalo**. Fue la última vez que los bizantinos pudieron enviar infantería para ayudar a los cruzados.

Papa Alejandro III
En este fresco del siglo XIV, el papa Alejandro III ofrece una espada al dogo de Venecia para que la utilice contra el emperador, Federico Barbarroja.

HIERRO Y CARBÓN EN LA EUROPA MEDIEVAL

El aumento de la población, las nuevas herramientas agrícolas y la actividad militar incrementaron la demanda de hierro. El carbón vegetal aún era la principal fuente de energía para las forjas de hierro, pero la deforestación provocó escasez de madera, por lo que la demanda de carbón ascendió, y la búsqueda de carbón marino fue sustituida por la minería. La primera mina de carbón conocida está en Escomb (norte de Inglaterra) y data de 1183.

En Japón, las **guerras Gempei** (1180–1185) marcaron el **fin del dominio de los Taira** y el principio del **sogunado Minamoto**. Las guerras civiles de 1156 y 1159 habían dejado Japón en manos de Taira no Kiyomori (*c.* 1118–1181), que amasó rápidamente un poder comparable al del **clan Fujiwara** (*véase* 851–860). No solo ejerció de primer ministro, sino que casó a sus hijas con miembros de la familia imperial, lo que le permitió colocar a su nieto, aún bebé, en el trono en el año 1180. Sin embargo, su sed de poder y la corrupción percibida alienaron a sus seguidores en las provincias y ese mismo año el **clan Minamoto** se alzó contra el gobierno Taira, lo que supuso el inicio de las guerras Gempei, que duraron cinco años.

1181–1185

« LA ESPERANZA DE **SALADINO** AVANZABA CON FACILIDAD, SUS **HUELLAS** ERAN **FRAGANTES**, SUS **DONES**, **INFINITOS**… SU **PODER** ERA MANIFIESTO Y SU **AUTORIDAD**, **SUPREMA**. **»**

Imad al-Din, secretario de Saladino, en *Relámpago de Siria* (*c.* 1200)

EN LA DÉCADA DE 1180, LOS REINOS CRUZADOS DE ULTRAMAR («más allá del mar», como se conocían en Europa), se encontraban en una situación cada vez más precaria. Europa hacía oídos sordos a la solicitud de **refuerzos** y los bizantinos cristianos estaban ocupados con otros temas, como la guerra contra la Sicilia normanda. Mientras tanto, sus enemigos musulmanes se agrupaban bajo el liderazgo de **Saladino** (*c.* 1137–1193), sultán de Egipto y Siria. En 1183 había sofocado a los rebeldes cristianos de Edesa y Alepo, y, como ambos bandos sufrían los efectos de la sequía, había negociado un tratado de paz con el **rey leproso de Jerusalén, Balduino IV** (*c.* 1161–1185). Pero esta paz inestable se hizo pedazos tras la actuación de Reinaldo de Châtillon, un aventurero que, durante la segunda cruzada, se dedicó a asaltar caravanas desarmadas de peregrinos musulmanes y a financiar una flota pirata que operaba en el mar Rojo. Entonces, Saladino movilizó a su ejército, decidido a castigar a Reinaldo, pero su empeño se vio frenado por las **fortalezas francas** y otra **hambruna** prolongada. En 1185, Balduino murió y su enfermizo sobrino, todavía niño, heredó la corona como **Balduino V** (1177–1186).

En 1183, el tratado de Constanza ratificó la paz entre el emperador Barbarroja y sus enemigos italianos; se reconocía la autoridad imperial sobre Italia, pero las ciudades **lombardas** lograron autonomía.

La **batalla naval de Dannoura**, en 1185, marcó el punto álgido de las **guerras Gempei**. El guerrero Minamoto Yoshitsune, hermano menor de Yoritomo, el fundador del sogunado, acabó con los Taira en esta batalla.

Saladino, sultán de Egipto y Siria
En este grabado del siglo XVIII, Saladino escapa de una batalla a lomos de un camello. Tuvo fama de líder generoso y de principios.

1176 Derrota del ejército bizantino ante los turcos en la **batalla de Miriocéfalo**.

1176 Batalla de Legnano, entre Federico Barbarroja y la Liga Lombarda.

1177 El **reino de Champa** saquea la ciudad jemer de Angkor.

1177 Paz de Venecia entre Federico Barbarroja y el papa.

1179 Tercer concilio de Letrán (Roma).

1180 Felipe II Augusto (r. 1180–1223) es coronado **rey de Francia**.

1180 Guerras Gempei en Japón (hasta 1185).

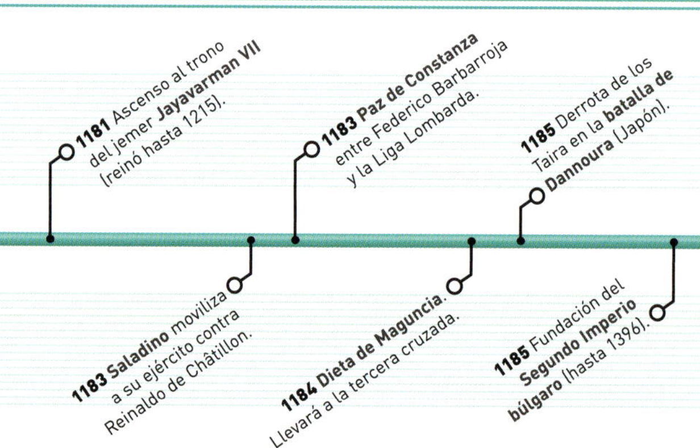

1186–1190

Los Cuernos de Hattin, un volcán extinguido coronado por dos formaciones rocosas, fue el escenario de la batalla de Hattin en 1187.

EL 4 DE JULIO DE 1187, EL EJÉRCITO CRUZADO SUFRIÓ UNA DERROTA a manos de Saladino. Al frente de las fuerzas cruzadas estaba el nuevo rey de Jerusalén, **Gui de Lusignan**, que había tomado el poder tras la muerte de Balduino V en 1186. Los regentes de Balduino habían negociado una tregua con Saladino, pero

3:2 **Batalla de Hattin** *Las huestes de Saladino superaban a los cruzados en treinta mil a veinte mil, pero venció gracias a su estrategia y a la sed desesperada de los cristianos.*

Reinaldo de Châtillon la había roto de nuevo al asaltar una caravana de peregrinos, provocación a la que **Saladino** respondió con una campaña final para librar Tierra Santa de todos los principados cristianos. Incitado por Reinaldo, el rey Gui dirigió una fuerza combinada de caballeros cruzados, **templarios**, hospitalarios y mercenarios ingleses (*véase* 1116–1120) a lo largo de una meseta desierta y bajo un sol ardiente, para que tomaran posiciones en los **Cuernos de Hattin**, un volcán extinguido. Entre ellos y el lago de Tiberíades (la principal fuente de agua fresca para los sedientos cristianos) se hallaba el descansado y bien aprovisionado ejército de Saladino, que usó tácticas de saqueo para sumirles en un estado de confusión desesperada, hasta que los rodeó y los capturó a todos. Más de doscientos caballeros templarios y hospitalarios fueron ejecutados y Saladino decapitó personalmente a Reinaldo. El rey Gui fue liberado después, pero, tras haber aniquilado a su ejército, Saladino consiguió que el resto de enclaves cristianos se rindieran. Tomó **Acre** en julio y **Jerusalén** en octubre. Tiro, Antioquía, Trípoli y algunos castillos desperdigados era todo lo que quedaba de los reinos cruzados.

El reino cruzado de Ultramar había pedido ayuda a Europa durante años y la **caída de Jerusalén** en 1187 indujo por fin al papa Gregorio VIII a predicar una **nueva cruzada**. Las disputas entre Enrique II de Inglaterra y Felipe II de Francia primero, y la muerte de Enrique y la coronación de Ricardo en 1189 después, retrasaron el envío de fuerzas anglofrancesas. Ricardo I y Felipe II zarparon por fin a finales de 1190. Federico Barbarroja había zarpado ya en 1189, pero se ahogó de camino a Tierra Santa al año siguiente.

Armadura samurái
Esta bella armadura japonesa data del siglo XIX, pero los primeros guerreros samurái ya vestían armaduras similares en el siglo XII.

1191–1200

El rey Ricardo I de Inglaterra, también conocido como Ricardo Corazón de León, lidera a los cruzados en la batalla.

LA TERCERA CRUZADA se vio entorpecida por las luchas internas entre las diferentes facciones europeas de los cruzados de Ultramar y, aunque **Ricardo Corazón de León** ganó la mayoría de sus batallas, no pudo cumplir con el juramento de «liberar» Jerusalén. La cruzada había empezado con mal pie (*véase* 1186–1190), y el envío de soldados aún sufrió más retrasos cuando Ricardo se detuvo para conquistar el **Chipre** bizantino. Vendió la isla a los Templarios, que después la cederían a los menguados reinos cruzados; se convirtió en uno de los apoyos principales para la presencia continuada de cristianos en **Tierra Santa**. Cuando por fin llegó a Palestina, Ricardo se unió a Felipe II de Francia en el **sitio de Acre**, que en realidad era un asedio doble: el rey Gui había iniciado el sitio a la ciudad cuando le liberaron (*véase* 1186–1190), pero Saladino había rodeado y bloqueado a su vez a las fuerzas cristianas. Los cruzados tomaron Acre en julio y la mayoría de la población fue masacrada. Felipe II regresó a Francia, pero Ricardo había jurado liberar Jerusalén y marchó a lo largo de la costa; consiguió recuperar varias ciudades y derrotó a Saladino en Arsuf en septiembre. Ricardo logró acabar con las fuerzas musulmanas en toda la franja costera y llegó a acampar frente a Jerusalén, pero se dio cuenta de que no contaba con las fuerzas ne-

ARMADURA CRUZADA

27 kg PESABA LA **ARMADURA**
1,5 kg PESABA LA **ESPADA**
0,4 kg PESABA LA **MAZA**

cesarias para tomar y retener la ciudad santa. Las continuas luchas internas entre los barones cruzados, la muerte de Conrado de Monferrato a manos de los **asesinos** (*véase* 1081–1090), y las malas noticias que llegaban de Inglaterra (donde su hermano Juan conspiraba para arrebatarle la corona) obligaron a Ricardo a firmar un tratado de paz con Saladino en 1192. **Ultramar** quedó reducido a una franja costera de 145 km, desde Tiro a Jaffa, junto a Antioquía y Trípoli.

En 1192, **Minamoto Yoritomo** (*véase* 1181–1185) se autoproclamó Seii tai-sogun («gran general subyugador de bárbaros»). Desde el final de las guerras Gempei, Yoritomo se había deshecho de todos sus rivales, entre ellos de su propio hermano Yoshitsune. Instaurado como dictador militar indiscutible, su *bakufu* (o administración) de Kamakura suplantó a la corte imperial. Japón sería gobernado por **sogunes** (dictadores militares) durante siglos.

En el año 1192, los **guríes de Persia** sofocaron una rebelión hindú en la batalla de Taraori, cerca de Thanesar (India). Al año siguiente consiguieron tomar Delhi, y Muhammad de Gur fundó el **Sultanato de Delhi**.

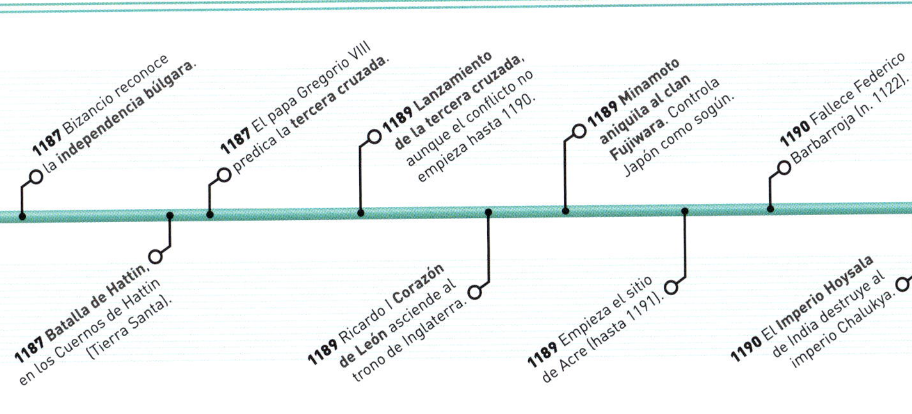

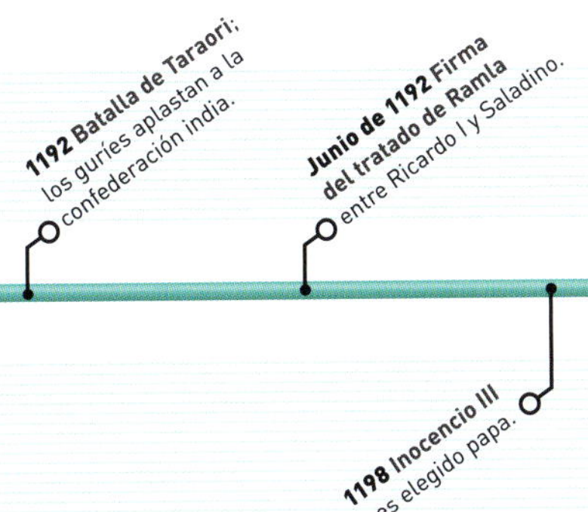

1201–1205

Este cuadro persa muestra a Temuyin, que luego sería conocido como Gengis Kan, luchando contra los tártaros, en lucha constante con los mongoles.

EL PAPA INOCENCIO III HABÍA PROCLAMADO UNA NUEVA CRUZADA en 1199, decidido a recuperar la supervisión papal sobre el movimiento cruzado y con la esperanza de volver a unir a las iglesias griega y latina y hacer así realidad su visión de un **dominio cristiano único** bajo la autoridad del papa. En el año 1201, sus enviados se reunieron con Enrico Dandolo, el dogo de Venecia, para negociar el paso hacia Egipto para la **cuarta cruzada**. Bajo la **paz de Venecia** (*véase* 1176–1180), los venecianos accedieron a transportar a 33 500 hombres y 4500 caballos a cambio de 85 000 marcos. Ofrecieron, además, 50 galeras de guerra a cambio de la mitad de las conquistas cruzadas.

Cuando los cruzados se reunieron en Venecia en 1202, se dieron cuenta de que no eran suficientes y de que no podrían pagar la cantidad acordada. Entonces accedieron a ayudar a Venecia a tomar Zadar (Dalmacia), una rica fuente de madera para las galeras venecianas. El papa Inocencio protestó, pero lo peor estaba aún por venir. En 1204, los cruzados llegaron a **Constantinopla**, donde las relaciones con los bizantinos se deterioraron rápidamente; por primera vez en toda su historia, la ciudad fue tomada y saqueada brutalmente. Se proclamó un nuevo **Imperio latino de Oriente**, con un nuevo emperador, Balduino de Flandes, y Venecia obtuvo la mitad de la ciudad y numerosas islas mediterráneas, entre otros territorios. Aunque los emperadores bizantinos se desplazaron a la **Nicea bizantina**, la cuarta cruzada marcó el fin del Imperio bizantino como potencia real, lo que desacreditó a los cruzados y respaldó a los turcos.

Pese a que, a finales del siglo XII, los nómadas mongoles y turcos de las estepas eran temibles, no estaban unidos. Temuyin, conocido luego como **Gengis Kan** (*c.* 1162–1227) era un líder menor que se convirtió en el *nokhor* (compañero) de Togril, kan de los qarayt, la tribu dominante en **Mongolia** Central. Gracias a su habilidad y carisma, ascendió hasta convertirse en general y aplastó a las tribus **tártaras** vecinas en 1202. Pero el resentimiento entre el resto de los qarayt era tan intenso que en 1203 se enfrentó al propio Togril. Tras la confrontación, se convirtió en el líder dominante de todas las tribus mongolas.

Jayavarman VII
Estatua de bronce del rey Jayavarman VII de estilo budista mahayana, donde el monarca aparece con expresión serena y contemplativa.

CLAVE
- Campañas de Gengis Kan 1206–1227
- Imperio de Gengis Kan 1227
- Ruta de la Seda

Mapa del imperio de Gengis Kan
Temuyin unificó las tribus mongolas y conquistó un imperio gigantesco. Sus sucesores lo ampliaron aún más.

Jayavarman VII (*c.* 1125–1220) había vuelto del exilio para reclamar la corona jemer en 1181. Vengó la destrucción de la capital y depuso al rey de Champa en 1191; aplastó una revuelta en el oeste; recuperó Angkor y consiguió dominar al reino de Champa. Jayavarman hizo del **budismo mahayana** la religión oficial y explotó los recursos del reino para levantar templos, además de hospitales, altares, carreteras y puentes. Uno de sus templos, Preah Khan, era atendido por 98 000 sirvientes.

En torno a 1200 inició su expansión el estado **chimú**, con capital en Chan Chan, en el **valle de Moche** (Perú). Debía su poder al dominio de las técnicas de agricultura intensiva e irrigación. En Chan Chan, los líderes chimúes levantaron ciudadelas, o palacios, unos edificios de paredes muy altas, con salas de audiencias y almacenes. Se cree que cada nuevo gobernante chimú debía erigir y financiar su propia ciudadela, lo que contribuyó a la expansión del imperio.

En 1202, el **matemático** Leonardo de Pisa, más conocido como **Fibonacci** (*c.* 1177–1250), escribió el libro más influyente en las matemáticas europeas hasta la fecha, el *Liber Abaci*, o *Libro del cálculo*. Basado en las matemáticas árabes, introdujo en Europa la numeración hindú (0–9) y la palabra *zephirum* –una versión latinizada de un término árabe que el dialecto veneciano transformó en cero en álgebra–, la suma y la **secuencia de Fibonacci**.

1206–1210

Peterhouse College (Cambridge), fundado en 1284.

EN 1206, TEMUYIN YA HABÍA UNIFICADO todas las tribus de Mongolia en el *Khamag Mongol Uluus* («estado de todos los mongoles») y había reorganizado toda la sociedad tribal en un ejército agrupado mediante un sistema decimal. En Karakórum, capital de Mongolia, adoptó el nombre de Chinggis Kan («señor del mundo») que, por lo general, ahora se transcribe como Gengis Kan.

En 1208, Inocencio III proclamó una **cruzada contra los herejes** del sur de Francia: los **albigenses** (cátaros asentados en los alrededores de Albi) y los **valdenses** (*véase* 1171–1175). Sus enseñanzas criticaban lo mundano de la iglesia institucional, mientras que su anticlericalismo resultaba atractivo a la nobleza, deseosa de hacerse con las propiedades de la Iglesia; los cátaros, por ejemplo, estaban bajo la protección de Raimundo de Tolosa, que gobernaba sobre gran parte del sur de Francia. La declaración del papa permitió que el rey francés, Felipe II (1165–1223), autorizara a sus señores del norte a

« MATADLOS A TODOS; DIOS RECONOCERÁ A LOS SUYOS. »

Obispo Arnoldo Amaury, sobre la cruzada albigense

c. 1200 Emergencia del **Imperio chimú** en Perú, con capital en Chan Chan.

c. 1200 El Imperio jemer alcanza su punto álgido bajo **Jayavarman VII.**

1201 Fundación de **Riga** (en la actual Letonia).

1201 El **tratado de Venecia** prepara la cuarta cruzada.

1202 Fibonacci escribe su *Liber Abaci.*

1202 El **rey Inglaterra, Juan Sin Tierra** se enfrenta a Felipe II por sus tierras en Francia.

1202 Los cruzados toman **Zadar** (Dalmacia).

1203 Temuyin vence a Togril y se convierte en el **principal líder mongol.**

1204 Fundación del **Imperio latino de Oriente** con Balduino I y partición del Imperio bizantino.

1204 Los cruzados saquean **Constantinopla.**

1204 Juan Sin Tierra pierde la mayoría de sus territorios en el Imperio angevino de Francia.

1205 El **Segundo Imperio búlgaro** vence al Imperio latino de Oriente y captura a Balduino I.

1205 Hojo Yoshitoki se convierte en el regente del sogunado de Kamakura; empieza el periodo de gobierno Hojo en Japón.

1206 Temuyin asume el título de **Gengis Kan** y empieza la conquista de Asia.

1206 Qutub-ud-din Aibak, el sultán de Delhi, funda la dinastía de los reyes esclavos en India.

1209 El papa Inocencio III proclama la **cruzada albigense** en el Languedoc (Francia).

1209 Matanza de Béziers (Languedoc) a manos de los cruzados.

LA PERSECUCIÓN DE LOS CÁTAROS

En la ciudad de Béziers (Languedoc) solo vivían unos doscientos cátaros, pero los cruzados mataron a toda la población en 1209. Cuando le preguntaron cómo distinguir entre católicos y herejes, el obispo Amaury, líder de los cruzados, dio su famosa orden de «¡Matadlos a todos. Dios reconocerá a los suyos». Tras la persecución de los cátaros, el papado fundaría la Inquisición (*véase* 1231–1235).

sembrar el caos en las zonas que escapaban a su control, preparando así el terreno para la expansión del poder de la Corona.

En 1209, un grupo de académicos de Oxford fundó la **Universidad de Cambridge**. En 1126 ya había adquirido cierta organización formal.

1211–1215

Óleo del siglo XIX sobre la batalla de las Navas de Tolosa, decisiva en la Reconquista.

PEDRO II DE ARAGÓN (1178–1213) Y ALFONSO VIII DE CASTILLA (1155–1214) derrotaron a los **almohades** (*véase* 1146–1150) en la **batalla de las Navas de Tolosa** en 1212. Alfonso había sido derrotado por los almohades en 1195, pero repelió las invasiones de **otros reinos cristianos españoles** y recompuso su ejército. Expulsaron de España a los almohades, con lo que solo quedaron dinastías musulmanas locales que no pudieron hacer frente al avance cristiano. Esta batalla marcó un momento clave en la toma cristiana, o **Reconquista**, de la España musulmana (*véase* 1241–1245).

El **rey Juan de Inglaterra** (1166–1216) había perdido la mayoría de sus territorios en Francia, por lo que se alió con Otón IV (1178–1215), emperador del Sacro Imperio, para recuperarlos; pero el rey Felipe II de Francia y el emperador alemán rival, Federico II, les derrotaron en la **batalla de Bouvines**, en Flandes. Esto acabó con las esperanzas anglonormandas de recuperar los territorios franceses y los barones del rey Juan se vieron obligados a concentrarse en Inglaterra, donde hallaron varias causas de descontento: tras la disputa con el papa, el rey había sido **excomulgado** temporalmente y, lo que era más importante, además de imponer grandes impuestos a los barones, conculcaba la ley a su conveniencia. Los **barones se rebelaron** y, tras una breve guerra civil, Juan se vio obligado a firmar los Artículos de los Barones, conocidos luego como **Carta Magna**. Aunque concernía sobre todo a los derechos de los barones, fue un hito clave en la historia de los derechos humanos al defender que los monarcas debían acatar la ley. El rey Juan repudió la carta y la guerra civil estalló de nuevo, esta vez con la participación de Francia. Mientras huía de una fuerza invasora francesa en 1216, el rey perdió su equipaje (y tesoro real) mientras cruzaba los pantanos de Wash en Lincolnshire (Inglaterra) y falleció poco después. Su hijo, el niño Enrique III (1207–1272) fue coronado rey.

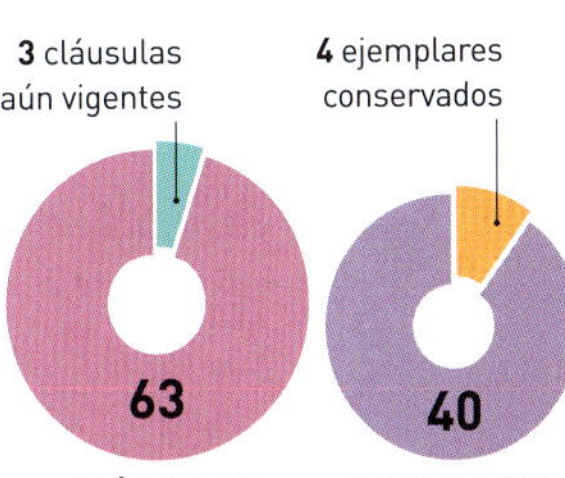

Carta Magna
Solo tres de las 63 cláusulas que contenía la Carta Magna original siguen vigentes en la actualidad. Se hicieron varias copias, que fueron distribuidas por toda Inglaterra. Se conservan cuatro ejemplares.

1216–1220

Detalle de la puerta sur de la gran ciudad jemer de Angkor Thom.

8
METROS
ALTURA DE LA MURALLA DE **ANGKOR THOM**

JAYAVARMAN III MURIÓ HACIA 1220, tras ver cómo tomaba forma su proyecto más ambicioso. Había creado una ciudad nueva, Angkor Thom, en Angkor (Camboya actual) alrededor del gran templo estatal de Bayon. El templo comprende torres decoradas con enormes rostros esculpidos, cuya identidad ha generado gran controversia, aunque es posible que incluyan al propio Jayavarman.

Una vez hubo conquistado la mayor parte de Asia central y del norte de China, Gengis Kan vio cómo su imperio (*véase* 1201–1205) llegaba a la frontera del Imperio persa de Corasmia.

Daga mongola
La temible reputación de los mongoles era bien merecida. Los arqueros diezmaban al enemigo, sobre el que se abalanzaban los soldados con armas de mano.

1221–1225

« SOY EL AZOTE DE DIOS. »

Gengis Kan, caudillo mongol

DOMINGO DE GUZMÁN, UN CLÉRIGO CASTELLANO, MURIÓ EN 1221. En 1203 había ido a Roma para solicitar autorización para emprender una obra de misiones entre los tártaros (*véase* 1201–1210), pero, en vez de eso, le enviaron a Francia para predicar a los **cátaros de Languedoc**. Adoptó la pobreza absoluta, por lo que pudo **hacer frente a los cátaros** y hacer progresos, aunque, al final, su incapacidad para «corregir» a los herejes llevó a la cruzada albigense (*véase* 1206–1210). Al igual que Francisco de Asís (*véase* 1226–1230), había creado una nueva orden (los dominicos), adaptada a la cultura urbana. Los **dominicos** y los **franciscanos** eran frailes mendicantes, procedentes de las clases medias, y se dedicaban a la prédica y a la caridad en pueblos y ciudades, de la que vivían.

La **quinta cruzada** fue ineficaz, fruto de la determinación de Inocencio III de dotar de nuevo impulso al movimiento cruzado. Los cruzados habían puesto sus miras en Egipto, que tomaron, pero perdieron Damieta; además, no previeron la inundación del Nilo, lo que frustró su avance hacia El Cairo. Rechazaron con arrogancia un tratado ofrecido por el sultán y que les hubiera otorgado Jerusalén. Al final, abandonaron Egipto en 1221 sin ninguna conquista.

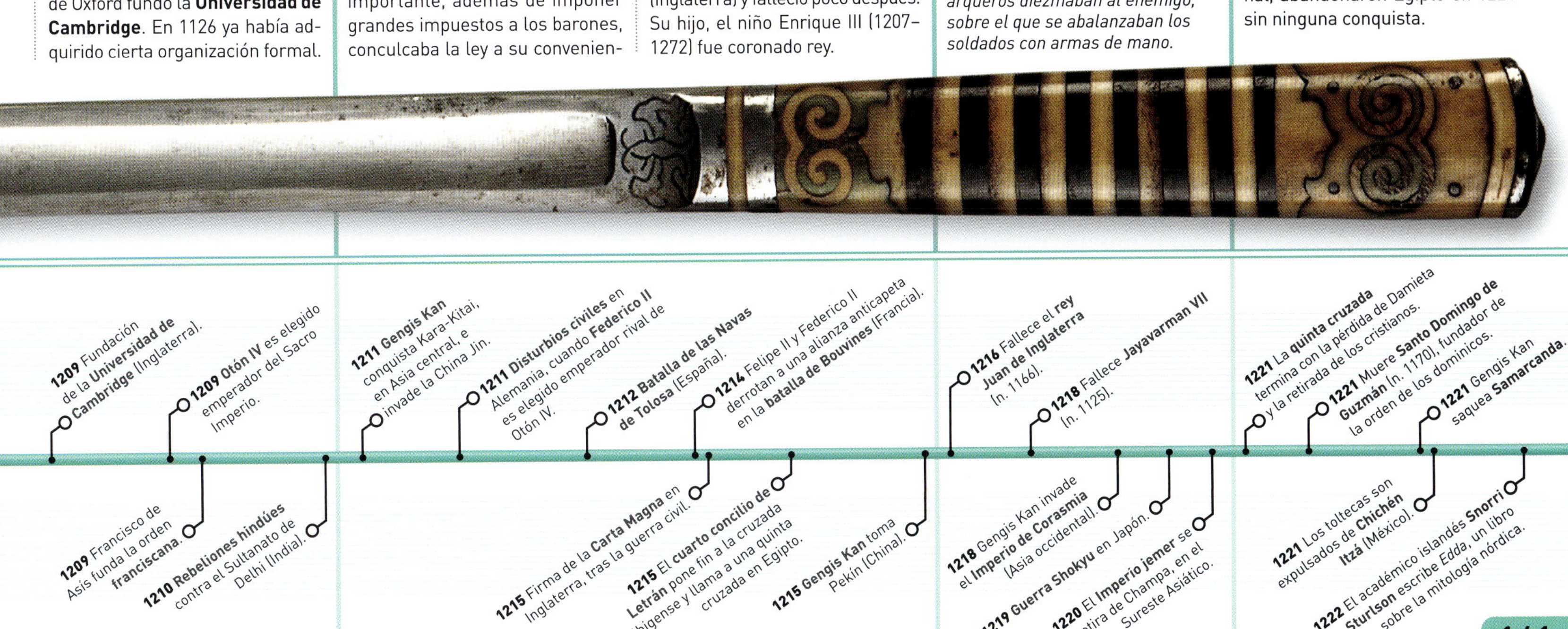

1209 Fundación de la **Universidad de Cambridge** (Inglaterra).

1209 Francisco de Asís funda la orden **franciscana**.

1209 Otón IV es elegido emperador del Sacro Imperio.

1210 Rebeliones hindúes contra el Sultanato de Delhi (India).

1211 Gengis Kan conquista Kara-Kitai, en Asia central, e invade la China Jin.

1211 Disturbios civiles en Alemania, cuando **Federico II** es elegido emperador rival de Otón IV.

1212 Batalla de las Navas de Tolosa (España).

1214 Felipe II y Federico II derrotan a una alianza anticapeta en la **batalla de Bouvines** (Francia).

1215 Firma de la **Carta Magna** en Inglaterra, tras la guerra civil.

1215 El **cuarto concilio de Letrán** pone fin a la cruzada albigense y llama a una quinta cruzada en Egipto.

1215 Gengis Kan toma Pekín (China).

1216 Fallece el **rey Juan de Inglaterra** (n. 1166).

1218 Fallece **Jayavarman VII** (n. 1125).

1218 Gengis Kan invade el **Imperio de Corasmia** (Asia occidental).

1219 Guerra Shokyu en Japón.

1220 El **Imperio jemer** se retira de Champa, en el Sureste Asiático.

1221 La **quinta cruzada** termina con la pérdida de Damieta y la retirada de los cristianos.

1221 Muere **Santo Domingo de Guzmán** (n. 1170), fundador de la orden de los dominicos.

1221 Gengis Kan saquea **Samarcanda**.

1221 Los toltecas son expulsados de **Chichén Itzá** (México).

1222 El académico islandés **Snorri Sturluson** escribe *Edda*, un libro sobre la mitología nórdica.

1226–1230

Este cuadro del siglo XIII, de Giotto de Bondone, muestra a san Francisco predicando a las aves.

1000000

DE **PERSONAS MURIERON** DURANTE LA **CRUZADA ALBIGENSE**

LA REACTIVACIÓN DE LA CRUZADA ALBIGENSE (*véase* 1206–1210) en 1226 se produjo a pesar de que el papa había declarado el fin «oficial» de esta en el cuarto concilio de Letrán en 1215. En realidad, la batalla por el sur de Francia se convirtió en una violenta guerra de guerrillas. Al final, la reanudación de la cruzada terminó con la sumisión de Raimundo VIII, conde de Tolosa (y protector de los cátaros). Bajo el **tratado de Meaux** (también conocido como paz de París) de 1229, la ciudad de Tolosa pasó a la **dinastía Capeto**, la casa gobernante de Francia entre 987 y 1328.

Moneda cruzada
Una de las raras monedas cruzadas del reino de Jerusalén ilustra los efectos de la política de integración: la inscripción está escrita en árabe.

Mientras, el **emperador Federico II de Alemania** se había dado cuenta de que la paz con los musulmanes sería mucho más beneficiosa que las aventuras militares imposibles de ganar. En 1229 cerró un tratado con el sultán de Egipto, que **devolvía Jerusalén** y algunos territorios circundantes a los cristianos. La **sexta cruzada** se zanjó sin derramamiento de sangre, aunque Federico fue muy criticado por este acuerdo diplomático.

Un ex militar, **Francisco de Asís**, había fundado la **orden de los franciscanos** en 1209 (*véase* 1221–1225). En 1224 recibió los estigmas (las heridas de Cristo) y fue canonizado solo dos años después de su muerte, en 1226.

Enclave cátaro
El castillo cátaro de Peyrepertuse, en los Pirineos, fue un enclave estratégico en la frontera entre España y Francia.

1231–1235

El papa Gregorio IX recibe una lista de herejes en esta imagen del siglo XIV.

EN 1231, EL PAPA GREGORIO IX instauró la **Inquisición papal**, una campaña eclesiástica contra la herejía. Antes de 1231, la responsabilidad de investigar la herejía había recaído en los obispos, pero en ese momento correspondía a **inquisidores** especialistas, la mayoría pertenecientes a las órdenes monásticas de franciscanos y dominicos (*véase* 1221–1225). En 1233 se encargó a los dominicos que llevaran la Inquisición al Languedoc, en Francia, donde la herejía **cátara** persistía a pesar de la derrota militar del conde de Tolosa (*véase* 1226–1230).

La expansión mongola prosiguía a pesar de la muerte de Gengis Kan (*véase* 1201–1205) en el año 1227, mientras sofocaba una rebelión en Xia Xia (China). A Gengis Kan le sucedió su segundo hijo, **Ogodei** (*c.* 1186–1241), que era todavía más ambicioso que él. Así pues, Ogodei envió ejércitos al este y al oeste, y además lideró el asalto final contra el **Imperio Jin** de China (*véase* 1126–1130), que conquistó en el año 1234. Los **Song del Sur** habían ayudado a los mongoles en su avance, pero cuando intentaron hacerse con el control de Kaifeng en el norte de China, en 1235, los mongoles se volvieron contra ellos.

En 1235, **Sundiata, rey de la dinastía Keita**, un pueblo mande del Malí subsahariano, derrotó a Sumnaguru, el rey susu, en la **batalla de Kirina**. Los susu habían destruido el antiguo Imperio de Ghana (*c.* 830–1235) y Sundiata construyó un nuevo imperio mande sobre sus ruinas.

1236–1240

El paisaje estepario apenas ha cambiado desde los días del Imperio mongol.

ANTES DE FALLECER, GENGIS KAN había **dividido informalmente su imperio** entre cuatro de sus hijos. Batu Kan (*c.* 1207–1255) obtuvo autoridad sobre el oeste y fundó el kanato de Kipchak, también conocido como **kanato de la Horda de Oro**. Durante el invierno del año 1237 los ríos se congelaron, lo que permitió que la caballería de Batu los pudiera cruzar e **invadiera Rusia**. Durante los siguientes cuatro años, su ejército conquistó los principados rusos y dejó tras de sí un reguero de destrucción hasta Europa central. El liderazgo de Ogodei (*véase* 1231–1235) y la expansión del Imperio mongol tuvieron repercusiones importantes para el comercio paneuropeo. La ***Pax Mongolica***, o paz de los mongoles, sobre las tierras bajo control mongol permitió que el peligroso paso a través de Asia central y la Ruta de la Seda fueran cada vez más viables, lo que, sobre 1240, hizo posible el **primer contacto directo** entre los **europeos** y los **chinos** desde la época romana.

En el año 1236, los **caballeros teutónicos** (orden militar fundada en el año 1198 por mercaderes alemanes que servían en el Hospital de Santa María de Jerusalén) acabaron de subyugar a los **pomeranios**, una tribu pagana de Prusia. Bajo su gran maestre, **Hermann de Salza** (*c.* 1179–1239), los caballeros aseguraron varios enclaves y al año siguiente, en 1237, se unieron a los caballeros portaespadas livonios y se introdujeron en **Livonia** (actuales Estonia y Letonia).

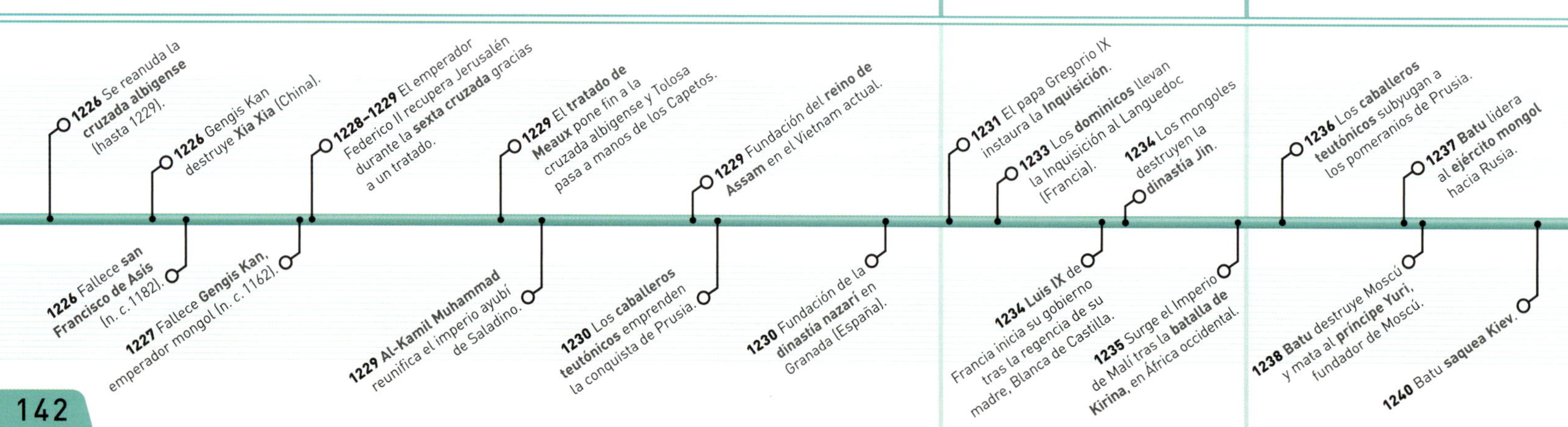

1241–1245

Miniatura de un códice del siglo XVI sobre la batalla del Hielo, librada sobre las aguas congeladas del lago Peipus (Nóvgorod).

EN 1241, LAS CIUDADES COMERCIALES DE LÜBECK Y HAMBURGO forjaron una alianza para proteger las **rutas comerciales del Báltico**. Fue la primera medida tras la formación de la **Liga Hanseática** (del alto alemán *Hanse*, que significa «grupo» o «asociación»). Lübeck se convirtió rápidamente en el centro del próspero comercio alemán en la región báltica, que se extendía a lo largo de los ríos rusos hasta **Nóvgorod** y se unía a los centros comerciales europeos de **Inglaterra y Flandes**.

En 1242, los esfuerzos de los **caballeros teutónicos** (*véase* 1236–1240) por ampliar los territorios de Livonia hacia el este y emprender la conversión de los rusos de la iglesia griega a la católica se vieron frustrados por la derrota en la **batalla del lago Peipus**. Dirigidos por el príncipe de Nóvgorod, **Alejandro Nevski**, los rusos detuvieron el avance de los caballeros y el lago Peipus pasó a ser la frontera oriental de Livonia.

Comercio medieval
Iluminación del puerto de Hamburgo, miembro fundador de la Liga Hanseática, cuyas raíces se hunden en una alianza con Lübeck en 1241.

En una serie espectacular de victorias en Europa oriental y central, los **ejércitos mongoles** destruyeron a todos sus oponentes. A principios de 1241, un ejército de caballería cruzó el congelado río Vístula y penetró en Polonia; en abril saqueó Cracovia y derrotó a una alianza de **polacos, silesios y caballeros teutónicos** en Legnica. Tan solo tres días después, otro ejército dirigido por **Batu** (*véase* 1236–1240) venció al ejército húngaro en Mohi. En diciembre, Batu destruyó Pest, la ciudad húngara más importante. Los mongoles acababan de llegar a las puertas de Viena cuando, en 1242, recibieron la noticia de que el gran kan Ogodei había fallecido. Tal y como mandaba la tradición, Batu retiró a sus fuerzas y volvió a Karakórum, la capital mongola, para **elegir al nuevo líder**. Las fuerzas mongolas también habían llegado al subcontinente indio y habían saqueado Lahore en 1241.

En 1244, los cristianos perdieron definitivamente **Jerusalén**, que había estado parcialmente bajo su control desde que Federico II firmara el tratado con el sultán de Egipto (*véase* 1226–1230). El sultán de Egipto, Ayub, estaba en guerra con la rama siria de los **ayubíes** (*véase* 1117–1175) en Damasco, que se había aliado con los reinos cruzados cristianos. En el año 1244, las fuerzas de Ayub invadieron Jerusalén y **expulsaron a los cristianos**.

LA RECONQUISTA

El concepto de Reconquista es un proyecto único y continuado, un mito con orígenes en la propaganda clerical del siglo XIV. El progreso de los reinos cristianos fue progresivo y estuvo impulsado por la necesidad de tierras, además de verse facilitado por las disputas de los musulmanes y por los avances de la tecnología militar.

1246–1250

En este cuadro del siglo XVI, Fernando III de Castilla y León acepta la rendición de la Sevilla musulmana en 1248.

EN EL AÑO 1247, FERNANDO III DE CASTILLA Y LEÓN (c. 1199–1252) asedió Sevilla, en manos musulmanas. La ciudad se rindió en 1248 y, con ella, el **último reino musulmán en España**, a excepción de Granada, donde Muhammad ibn Yusuf ibn Nasr –Yusuf I– había fundado la dinastía nazarí en 1230. En 1238, los nazaríes habían emprendido la reconstrucción de la **Alhambra**, una antigua fortaleza que se convertiría en una de las maravillas arquitectónicas del mundo a mediados del siglo XIV (*véase* 1350–1355). En 1246, el emir de Granada accedió a convertirse en vasallo de Fernando, pero la última reliquia del al-Ándalus musulmán resistió las presiones cristianas hasta 1492 (*véase* 1490–1492).

Luis IX de Francia (1214–1270) era muy respetado en toda Europa y se había labrado la reputación de ser un monarca justo. Bajo su reinado, el control real llegó al Mediterráneo, y el Languedoc y la Provenza, autónomos hasta entonces, pasaron a formar parte de los territorios **capetos franceses**. En 1244, Luis «tomó la cruz» y partió a una cruzada en 1248. Teobaldo de Navarra había lanzado una cruzada en 1239, pero el fracaso fue de tal envergadura que no suele concedérsele un número ordinal. La cruzada de 1248 de Luis fue la **séptima** y última cruzada de estas magnitudes. Llegó a Egipto y tomó Damieta, pero, en 1250, los **egipcios destruyeron a su ejército** en Fariksur y él fue capturado. Su madre, Blanca de Castilla, reunió un gran rescate para comprar su libertad.

Los **mamelucos** de Egipto eran soldados esclavos capturados en tribus turcas y circasianas (de las estepas pónticas y del Caspio) y componían el mayor contingente del ejército ayubí. Finalmente, los mamelucos adquirieron tal fuerza que pudieron tomar el poder tras **asesinar a Turan Sah**, el último sultán ayubí de Egipto, en 1250. En un primer momento, el comandante mameluco Izad ad-Din Aibak utilizó a la viuda del sultán como gobernante de paja, pero poco tiempo después se casó con ella y fundó la **dinastía mameluca**, la primera dinastía esclava en ocupar el poder con su propio nombre.

LAS CRUZADAS

1096–1099 **PRIMERA** CRUZADA
1145–1149 **SEGUNDA** CRUZADA
1189–1192 **TERCERA** CRUZADA
1202–1204 **CUARTA** CRUZADA
1213–1221 **QUINTA** CRUZADA
1228–1229 **SEXTA** CRUZADA
1248–1254 **SÉPTIMA** CRUZADA

1241 Los **mongoles** asolan **Europa** y saquean Lahore, en el norte de India.

1241 Formación de la **Liga Hanseática**.

1242 Batalla del lago Peipus: Alejandro Nevski derrota a los **caballeros teutónicos**.

1243 Batalla de Köse Dag: los **mongoles derrotan al Rum selyúcida** de Anatolia.

1244 Cae Montsegur, el último gran enclave cátaro.

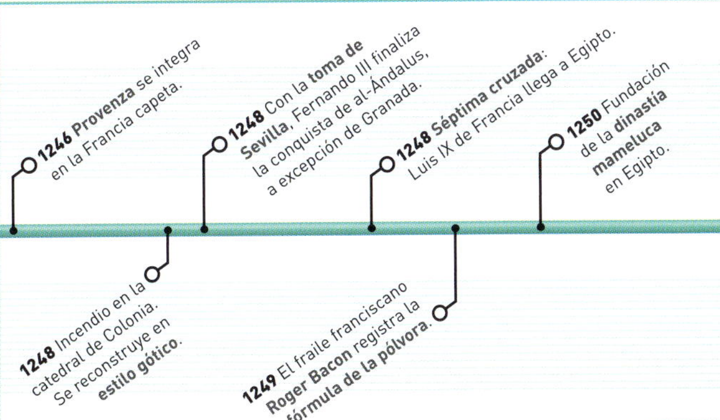

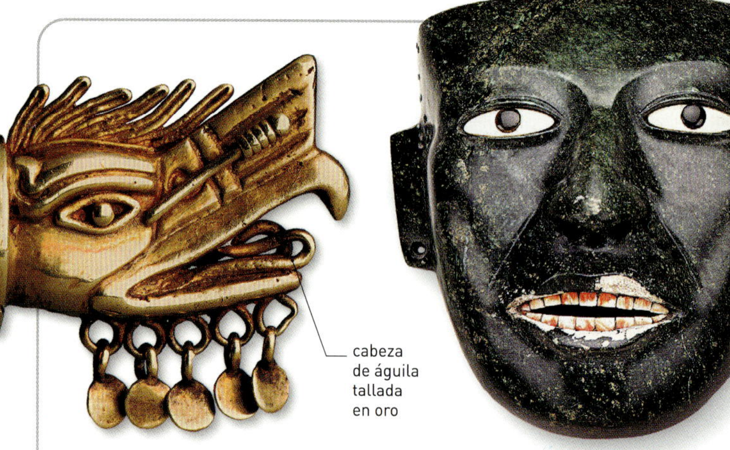

Ornamento labial
MIXTECA
Este bezote en forma de águila pertenecía a un miembro de la élite azteca. Los mixtecas, una tribu conquistada, elaboraban la mayoría de las joyas de oro aztecas.

Máscara
AZTECA
Esta máscara, hallada en el Gran Templo de los aztecas en su capital, Tenochtitlán (Ciudad de México actual), fue una ofrenda votiva.

Guerrero de arcilla
MOCHICA
Este guerrero de arcilla de la cultura mochica (costa norte de Perú), lleva un tocado y está armado con una maza. Las guerras constantes eran un modo de vida.

afilada hoja de obsidiana

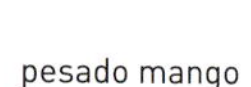
pesado mango de madera

MAYAS, AZTECAS E INCAS

LAS EXTRAORDINARIAS TRADICIONES ARTÍSTICAS MILENARIAS DE LA AMÉRICA PRECOLOMBINA

Las de los mayas, aztecas e incas fueron civilizaciones con un arte, una artesanía y unos sistemas gráficos muy avanzados. Los asombrosos artefactos que crearon son un testimonio valiosísimo de sus creencias, prácticas y tecnologías.

La cultura precolombina de Mesoamérica y los Andes representa el apogeo de unas tradiciones ancestrales que se remontan al IV milenio a. C. Aunque los conquistadores europeos causaron estragos en estos pueblos, los artefactos que han sobrevivido reflejan su rico patrimonio. Buena parte de la cultura inca provenía de estados cliente, como los mochicas; la de mayas y aztecas fue un desarrollo de culturas más antiguas, como la olmeca.

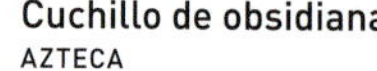
Cuchillo de obsidiana
AZTECA
Los cuchillos de obsidiana, de hoja larga y afiladísimos, eran armas de guerra que también se utilizaban en los sacrificios humanos que practicaban los aztecas.

Maquahuitl
AZTECA
Los precolombinos desconocían el hierro y el acero, y se valían de la obsidiana (vidrio volcánico) para elaborar filos cortantes. El *maquahuitl*, una maza de madera con hojas de obsidiana incrustada, era un arma habitual entre los aztecas.

Piedra solar
AZTECA
Esta piedra solar, o calendario de piedra, es la mayor escultura azteca jamás encontrada. Representa la historia azteca del universo. El Sol, que creían se había formado en la etapa más reciente de la creación, está en el centro.

Xipe Tótec, dios de la primavera
TEOTIHUACANO
El nombre de este dios se traduce como «nuestro señor desollado». Aparece vestido con la piel de una víctima ofrecida en sacrificio, para representar la renovación primaveral de la «piel» de la Tierra.

Corazón de valor incalculable
AZTECA
Para los aztecas, el corazón era el órgano más precioso que podía ofrecerse a los dioses. Esta réplica está tallada en jade, el material más valioso para los aztecas.

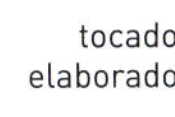

Collar
INCA
La turquesa era un material precioso para los incas (los mayas y los aztecas preferían el jade y otras piedras de color verde). Este collar está hecho con cuentas de oro, turquesa y conchas rojas.

Plato ornamental
MAYA
Este plato, de los mayas del Yucatán, está decorado con escenas de caza: en el centro, un cazador carga un ciervo que acaba de cazar, y los bordes muestran a cazadores con máscaras de ciervo.

Figura de Jaina
MAYA
Esta figura de arcilla de la isla de Jaina representa a un hombre poderoso vestido con sus mejores galas, un gran collar de cuentas, un tocado gigantesco y pendientes.

Figura funeraria
INCA
Esta figura de oro representa a un dios inca y forma parte de los objetos funerarios enterrados en la tumba de una persona notable.

Sikuri
INCA
La zampoña, o flauta de Pan, era uno de los instrumentos tradicionales incas. El de la imagen está hecho con cañones de plumas de cóndor.

Yugo de piedra
AZTECA
Los jugadores de *ulama*, un juego sagrado común a la mayoría de las culturas mesoamericanas, llevaban yugos protectores. Es probable que este, tan ornado, fuera una réplica ceremonial.

Quipus
INCA
Los quipus eran instrumentos utilizados, entre otras cosas, para el cálculo; eran una herramienta muy versátil con que los incas registraban el cobro de tributos y la población del imperio. Los datos se registraban en series de cordeles y nudos.

Códice Troano
MAYA
Este es uno de los cuatro códices mayas que han llegado a nuestros días; recoge instrucciones para la adivinación y los rituales religiosos. Fabricaban papel con corteza de árbol, que cubrían con *gesso* (una pasta de yeso) para poder escribir sobre él.

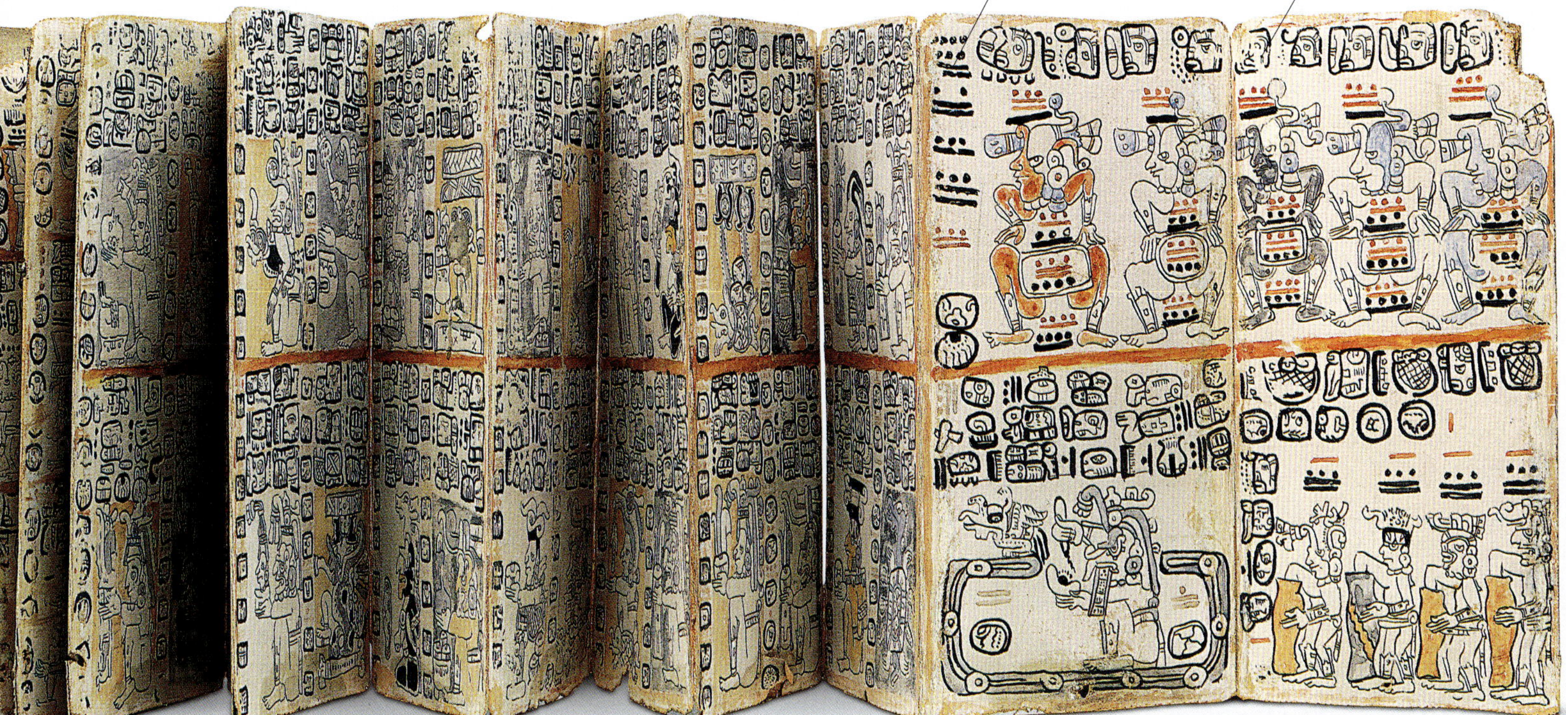

1251–1255

Pictogramas aztecas como los de la imagen eran un sistema de escritura para mantener registros y documentar acontecimientos.

A MEDIADOS DEL SIGLO XIII, LA TRIBU MEXICA, que ahora conocemos mejor como **aztecas**, se asentó en el valle de México. La mitología azteca sugiere que emigraron allí desde las tierras ancestrales de Aztlán a principios del siglo XII. Llegaron a Chapultepec, cerca del lago Texcoco (México) en torno a 1250, pero fueron **expulsados por los tepanecas**, una de las confederaciones tribales que competían por el poder tras el **hundimiento tolteca** a principios del siglo XII.

Sorprendentemente, y a pesar de que los **mongoles** habían conquistado la mayoría de los principados rusos (*véase* 1236–1240) y de que el **kanato de la Horda de Oro** había afirmado su autoridad sobre **Rusia**, la vida había cambiado muy poco para los rusos. A cambio del pago de tributos y de apoyo militar, los príncipes rusos conservaron el poder y la Iglesia rusa no sufrió interferencia alguna. **Alejandro Nevski** (*c.* 1220–1263), príncipe de Nóvgorod y líder de la victoria rusa ante los **caballeros teutónicos** en 1242, se convirtió en el primer noble ruso y fue nombrado gran duque de Vladímir después de que los mongoles expulsaran a su hermano.

Con el apoyo del nuevo **gran kan**, Mongke (r. 1251–1259), sus hermanos Qubilay y Hulagu reanudaron la **expansión mongola**. En 1253, Hulagu dirigió un enorme ejército hacia Asia occidental para conquistar el **gran sultanato selyúcida** (*véase* 1031–1040), mientras Qubilay emprendía campañas contra los **Song del Sur** y el **reino de Nanchao** en China.

Príncipe de Nóvgorod
Esta estatua representa al líder ruso Alejandro Nevski, cuyo nombre procede de la victoria rusa en la batalla del río Neva.

1256–1260

Ilustración de la batalla entre los mongoles y los selyúcidas perteneciente a una crónica de Rashid el-Din, ministro musulmán al servicio del iljanato.

HULAGU KAN (*VÉASE* 1251–1255) PROSIGUIÓ SU CAMPAÑA CONTRA LOS SELYÚCIDAS y otras potencias islámicas. En 1256 aplastó a la orden de los **asesinos** (*véase* 1081–1090) y tomó su enclave de Alamut, en Persia. En 1258 saqueó Bagdad y **ejecutó al califa abasí** (representante del islam) en una de las innumerables atrocidades cometidas por los invasores mongoles, que mataron a cientos de miles de musulmanes durante sus campañas. En 1259, Hulagu llegó al interior de Siria, pero al igual que sucediera con la campaña europea de Batu dieciocho años antes (*véase* 1241–1245), su avance se vio detenido por la notica del **fallecimiento del gran kan**, por lo que retiró a su ejército para volver a la capital mongola y participar en la elección del nuevo líder.

El general **mameluco Baybars** marchó hacia el norte y atacó a las guarniciones mongolas en Siria. Baybars **derrotó a los mongoles** en la **batalla de Ain Yalut**, en Palestina, y les expulsó de Palestina y Siria. A su vuelta a Egipto, asesinó al sultán y ocupó su lugar. Distraído por las disputas dinásticas primero, y por una prolongada guerra en el seno del kanato después, Hulagu no pudo recuperar los territorios sirios y la expansión del Imperio mongol hacia occidente se detuvo. Las **conquistas de Hulagu**, que comprendían Irán, Iraq, la mayoría de Anatolia, Armenia, Azerbaiyán y Georgia, se convirtieron en el **iljanato**, o kanato de Il. Mientras, los mamelucos dieron cobijo a un **príncipe abasí fugitivo** y le nombraron **califa** de El Cairo. Reconocidos como los guardianes de la fe islámica, los **mamelucos** fueron nombrados **sultanes de Egipto, Siria** y **Levante**.

QUBILAY KAN (1215–1294)

Qubilay, nieto de Gengis Kan, pasó ocho años en campaña en el sur de China antes de suceder a su hermano Mongke como gran kan en 1260. Su propio reino, el Gran Kanato, abarcaba Mongolia y China, donde fundó la dinastía Yuan, trasladó la capital a Xanadú e hizo mucho por reforzar el comercio y las relaciones internacionales.

Alfonso X de Castilla (r. 1252–1284) se ganó el sobrenombre de El Sabio gracias a sus conocimientos, su patrocinio de las artes y de la literatura castellanas, el mecenazgo de la filosofía natural, así como sus reformas jurídicas. Además, Alfonso X supervisó la expulsión definitiva de los **almohades** (*véase* 1121–1125) de España, acontecimiento que tuvo lugar en el año 1257.

> « DE HABER ESTADO PRESENTE EN LA **CREACIÓN**, **HABRÍA DADO** VARIOS **CONSEJOS** ÚTILES SOBRE EL **ORDENAMIENTO** DEL **UNIVERSO**. »
>
> **Alfonso X el Sabio,** sobre el sistema ptolemaico

C.1250 Los **aztecas** se asientan en el valle de México.

1252 Alejandro Nevski (1220–1263) se convierte en el príncipe más importante de Rusia.

1252 Formación de ligas de ciudades **pro güelfas y pro gibelinas** en Italia.

1253 Qubilay Kan (1215–1294) conquista Nanchao (China) y provoca la emigración de la población Thai.

1253 Hulagu Kan (c. 1217–1265) emprende la conquista de territorio musulmán.

1254 Guerra civil en los **estados cruzados** de Asia occidental.

1254 Luis IX de Francia parte hacia los reinos cruzados de Acre en Asia occidental.

1254 Los caballeros teutónicos fundan **Königsberg** (Prusia).

1254 Fallece **Conrado IV** de Alemania (n. 1228).

1254 Manfredo de Sicilia emprende una campaña contra el papado después de que el papa Inocencio IV reclame Sicilia.

1256 Hulagu Kan aplasta a los **asesinos** en Alamut (Persia).

1257 Alfonso X el Sabio es designado emperador electo del Sacro Imperio.

1257 Los **almohades**, musulmanes bereberes, son expulsados de España.

1258 Los barones ingleses obligan a Enrique III a aceptar las **Provisiones de Oxford**.

1258 Los mongoles destruyen **Bagdad** y ejecutan al **califa abasí**.

1258 Qubilay Kan invade a los Song del Sur de China y Corea.

1260 Los **mamelucos**, dirigidos por Baybars I, aplastan a los mongoles en **Ayn Yalut** (Palestina).

1260 Los mongoles llegan a **Damasco** (Siria), pero las disputas dinásticas obligan a Hulagu a retirarse.

1260 Los **mamelucos** son reconocidos como sultanes de Siria, Levante y Egipto.

1260 Qubilay Kan es elegido **gran kan**, pero se ve obligado a defender la corona en una guerra civil.

1260 Alzamiento prusiano contra los caballeros teutónicos.

1261–1265

Ejemplo de la arquitectura mameluca durante el cénit del sultanato en la entrada al mausoleo de Qalawun en El Cairo (Egipto).

TOMÁS DE AQUINO, UN NOBLE ITALIANO QUE LUEGO SERÍA MONJE DOMINICO (1225–1274), se convirtió en uno de los filósofos más importantes en la historia del pensamiento occidental. Conocido por su esfuerzo de **unir la fe y la razón**, el periodo de mayor productividad de Aquino se dio entre los años 1258 y 1273, durante el que escribió sus dos obras más conocidas, *Summa contra Gentiles* y *Summa theologica*.

En 1261, Miguel VIII Paleólogo (r. 1259–1261), el emperador bizantino de Nicea, suscribió el **tratado de Nymphaeum** con los genoveses, por el que accedía a cederles todos los privilegios comerciales otrora otorgados a los venecianos (*véase* 981–990). Ya había cerrado una alianza con los búlgaros, y ahora estaba preparándose para hacer realidad su sueño de recuperar Constantinopla de manos del **Imperio latino de Oriente** (Constantinopla y sus alrededores, arrebatados a los bizantinos durante la cuarta cruzada), y reconstituir el Imperio griego de Bizancio. En julio de 1261, un ejército bizantino aprovechó la ausencia de la flota veneciana en el estrecho del Bósforo y tomó Constantinopla. El emperador latino, Balduino II, huyó y así se fundó el **Imperio de los Paleólogos**. Paleólogo fue incansable en su empeño de recuperar las tierras bizantinas.

Tomás de Aquino
En este retablo (siglo XV) aparece Tomás de Aquino, cuya filosofía aún sustenta el dogma católico.

La **segunda guerra de los Barones** en Inglaterra, entre 1264 y 1267, fue resultado de la combinación de una reavivada conciencia nacional y del resentimiento contra la interferencia extranjera. **Enrique III** de Inglaterra (r. 1216–1272) había introducido a un enorme número de funcionarios extranjeros en el gobierno y cobraba fuertes impuestos a los ingleses con el objetivo de financiar sus aventuras en el extranjero y la extorsión papal. Los rebeldes, liderados por **Simón de Montfort**, conde de Leicester, capturaron al rey en Lewes en el año 1265 y constituyeron el primer parlamento europeo con representantes electos.

Mientras tanto, los **mamelucos** habían emprendido una campaña para expulsar a los reinos cruzados de Tierra Santa de una vez y para siempre.

1266–1271

Iglesia de Geneta Mariam en Etiopía, construida en la era salomónida.

El papel frente al pergamino
Tras la introducción de la tecnología de producción del papel en Italia, el coste del papel de origen vegetal se redujo a una sexta parte del coste del pergamino, de origen animal.

LA DINASTÍA SALOMÓNIDA EN ETIOPÍA, FUNDADA EN 1270 por Yekuno Amlak, desplazó a la anterior dinastía Zagwe y afirmaba haber restaurado la sucesión legítima de los antiguos reyes cristianos de Aksum. Amlak afirmaba descender de Salomón, el rey bíblico, posiblemente a través de la etíope reina de Saba.

La ciudad italiana de **Fabriano** se encuentra cerca del puerto de Ancona en el Adriático, que en el siglo XIII era de gran importancia para el comercio con el mundo musulmán. Es posible que esto explique el origen de la industria papelera en este lugar en la década de 1270. El papel de Fabriano era más duradero porque se elaboraba con gelatina animal en lugar de con gelatina vegetal, más degradable. La ciudad se convirtió en el primer centro de manufactura de papel de toda Europa.

En 1270, Luis IX de Francia intentó otra cruzada, pero a petición de Carlos de Anjou, **la octava cruzada** se reorientó a Túnez, donde Luis y su ejército murieron víctimas de una enfermedad.

1272–1275

El krak (fortaleza) de los Caballeros, el antiguo enclave de los caballeros hospitalarios en Siria, cayó ante los mamelucos, que la fortificaron todavía más.

Los viajes de Marco Polo
Para llegar a China, Marco Polo debió atravesar Anatolia, Irán y Afganistán. En el viaje de vuelta, navegó hasta Ormuz (Persia) pasando por Sumatra.

CLAVE
Ruta de Marco Polo 1271–1295
Ruta de la Seda

EN EL AÑO 1271, EL MERCADER Y EXPLORADOR VENECIANO MARCO POLO (c. 1254–1324) viajó a China. Llegó a la corte de Qubilay Kan en 1275, donde el gran kan le contrató para varias misiones. En 1292 escoltó a una princesa mongola a Persia; regresó a Italia tres años después y escribió la **crónica de sus viajes** mientras era prisionero de los genoveses. *Los viajes* de Marco Polo, que los italianos conocen como *Il Milione* porque se cree que contiene un millón de mentiras, constituye un apasionante retrato del Imperio mongol en su cénit. La *Pax Mongolica* (*véase* 1236–1240) garantizaba la libre circulación por tierras del iljanato, y se dijo que incluso una virgen con un caldero de oro sobre la cabeza hubiera podido viajar desde Constantinopla (Estambul actual) a Pekín sin ser molestada.

Eduardo Plantagenet (r. 1272–1307), presunto heredero al trono inglés, regresó en 1272 de Tierra Santa después de haber obligado a los mamelucos a cerrar una tregua de diez años en sus intentos de destruir Acre, el último enclave cruzado en Ultramar. Los mamelucos ya habían arrebatado la supuestamente inexpugnable Krak de los Caballeros a los caballeros hospitalarios en 1271.

22 %
DE LA **SUPERFICIE TERRESTRE**: ÁREA CUBIERTA POR EL **IMPERIO MONGOL** EN SU CÉNIT

1261 Tratado de Nymphaeum entre Génova y Bizancio.

1261 Caída del **Imperio latino de Oriente** y restauración del **Imperio bizantino**.

1262 Guerra civil en el Imperio mongol entre la **Horda de Oro y el Iljanato**.

1263 Los **mamelucos** lanzan una campaña para expulsar a los cruzados de Levante.

1264 Tomás de Aquino finaliza *Summa contra Gentiles*.

1264 Segunda guerra de los Barones en Inglaterra (hasta 1267).

1265 Se convoca el **primer parlamento representativo en Inglaterra**.

1265 Simón de Montfort (n. 1208) muere en la batalla de Evesham (Inglaterra).

1265 Carlos de Anjou, hermano del rey de Francia, acepta la corona de Sicilia.

1266 Roger Bacon (c. 1214–1294) escribe un tratado sobre ciencias naturales, el *Opus Maius*.

1268 Los **mamelucos** toman los estados cruzados de Jaffa y Antioquía.

1269 Jatavarman Sundara, monarca del sur de India y de Ceilán, muere.

1270 Fundación de la **dinastía salomónida** en Etiopía.

1270 Luis IX de Francia fallece durante la octava cruzada (n. 1214).

1271 Marco Polo sale de Venecia en dirección a China.

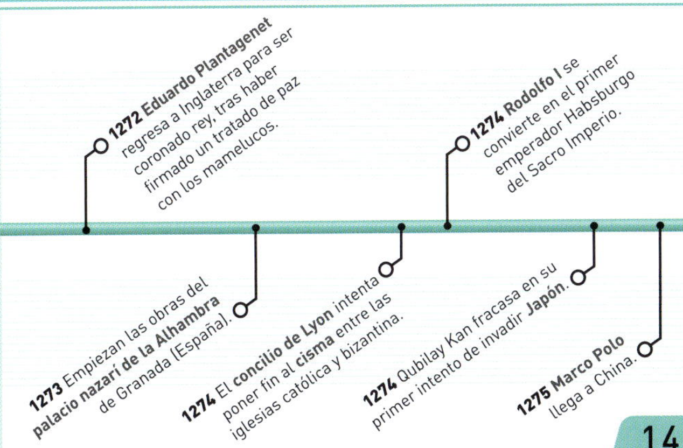

1272 Eduardo Plantagenet regresa a Inglaterra para ser coronado rey, tras haber firmado un tratado de paz con los mamelucos.

1273 Empiezan las obras del **palacio nazarí de la Alhambra** de Granada (España).

1274 El **concilio de Lyon** intenta poner fin al **cisma** entre las iglesias católica y bizantina.

1274 Rodolfo I se convierte en el primer emperador Habsburgo del Sacro Imperio.

1274 Qubilay Kan fracasa en su primer intento de invadir **Japón**.

1275 Marco Polo llega a China.

1276–1285

Estatuas ornamentales en el templo Meenakshi de Madurai (India). Kulasekara Pandya ordenó su construcción, los invasores musulmanes lo destruyeron y posteriormente se reconstruyó.

EN EL SUR DE INDIA, EL REY KULASEKARA I (r. 1268–1308) amplió el Imperio **Pandya** a sus límites máximos. Los Pandya eran un antiguo pueblo **tamil** del sur que durante siglos luchó por la supremacía con los reinos vecinos, como el **Chola** y la isla de **Ceilán** (Sri Lanka). Bajo **Sundara** (r. 1251–1268), el imperio Pandya ya había crecido drásticamente y había sometido a algunos de los estados vecinos, que ahora eran sus vasallos. Su hijo **Kulasekara** conquistó Kerala, Kongu y Ceilán, y en 1279 derrotó al último rey **Chola, Rajendra III**, y se anexó sus territorios. El mercader veneciano **Marco Polo** fue testigo de la grandiosidad de la corte Pandya a su paso por ella en 1293, pero el imperio duró muy poco y a principios del siglo XIV se fragmentó por las disputas familiares y las **invasiones musulmanas**.

A finales del siglo XIII, los **maoríes** ya se habían asentado en **Nueva Zelanda** (a excepción de la Antártida, la última masa terrestre en ser colonizada por el ser humano). Las fechas de la colonización maorí son objeto de controversia; según las estimaciones basadas en la mitología maorí, los primeros **polinesios** visitaron las islas a principios del siglo X, y las oleadas colonizadoras alcanzaron su punto álgido con la **Gran Flota** de canoas capaces de surcar el océano en 1350. Sin embargo, los hallazgos arqueológicos sugieren una historia ligeramente distinta. Aun así, parece probable que los polinesios, con seguridad procedentes de **Haití**, llegaran a Nueva Zelanda en torno a 1280 y dividieran el territorio entre los *hapu* (clanes). Los *hapu* que compartían la misma ascendencia se unieron en *iwi* (tribus), algunas de las cuales podían remontarse hasta una única ***waka houra*** (canoa).

Tras la conquista de Corea y de la mayor parte de China, **Qubilay Kan** (1215–1294) puso a **Japón** en el punto de mira. Ya en 1268 envió a embajadores para exigir su sumisión. Los japoneses, bajo el liderazgo de la **regencia Hojo**, se negaron a someterse. Tras un intento fallido de invasión en 1274, Qubilay envió a **150 000 soldados** en sendas flotas gigantescas en 1281, pero los japoneses lograron retener a la armada invasora hasta que un gran tifón, conocido en Japón como ***kamikaze*** («viento divino»), barrió a la flota mongola.

TALLA MAORÍ

La cultura maorí es conocida por su tradición artesana, cuyo exponente máximo son los *Te Toi Whakairo* (tallas). Se cree que los artesanos canalizan las voces y los espíritus de los antepasados, y que los postes y dinteles tallados que adornaban las estructuras alrededor de los *marae* (espacios sagrados) y las *waka* (canoas) acumulaban y transmitían *mana* (poder espiritual).

Viento divino
Grabado sobre la destrucción de la flota mongola tras el kamikaze *(«viento divino») de 1281.*

1286–1290

Guglielmo Berardi de Narbona murió en la batalla de Campaldino.

EN LA DÉCADA DE 1280, UNA TRIBU DE JINETES NÓMADAS TURCOMANOS del noroeste de Anatolia, sería conocida como los **otomanos**, por el primer jefe al que eligieron, **Osmán**, o Utmán (1258–1354). En ese momento, el mapa político de Anatolia estaba fracturado: la matanza mongol había fragmentado al Rum selyúcida, que se había visto sustituido por varios principados, al tiempo que había atraído a la región a oleadas de refugiados musulmanes. Mientras, el **Imperio bizantino** se había ido **reduciendo** y fragmentando debido al acoso selyúcida y del Imperio latino Oriental. Osmán lideró a su tribu en una campaña de **expansión territorial** y conquistó rápidamente el territorio bizantino.

Florencia, al igual que otras ciudades italianas, se había convertido en una **república prácticamente autónoma**, o comuna. En general, a los emperadores alemanes (los señores feudales nominales) les resultaba más sencillo conceder capacidad de autogobierno a las ciudades que intentar controlarlas directamente. Desde mediados del siglo XIII, Florencia alternaba violentamente entre regímenes **güelfos** y **gibelinos** (*véase* 1221–1225). El conflicto entre **güelfos y gibelinos** había atrapado a las ciudades-estado italianas, porque proporcionaba un vehículo para las **tensiones de clase** locales, además de para la política nacional e internacional. Cuando una facción obtenía el poder en una ciudad, la otra era expulsada. En la década de 1280, los güelfos ostentaban el control y los güelfos exiliados de

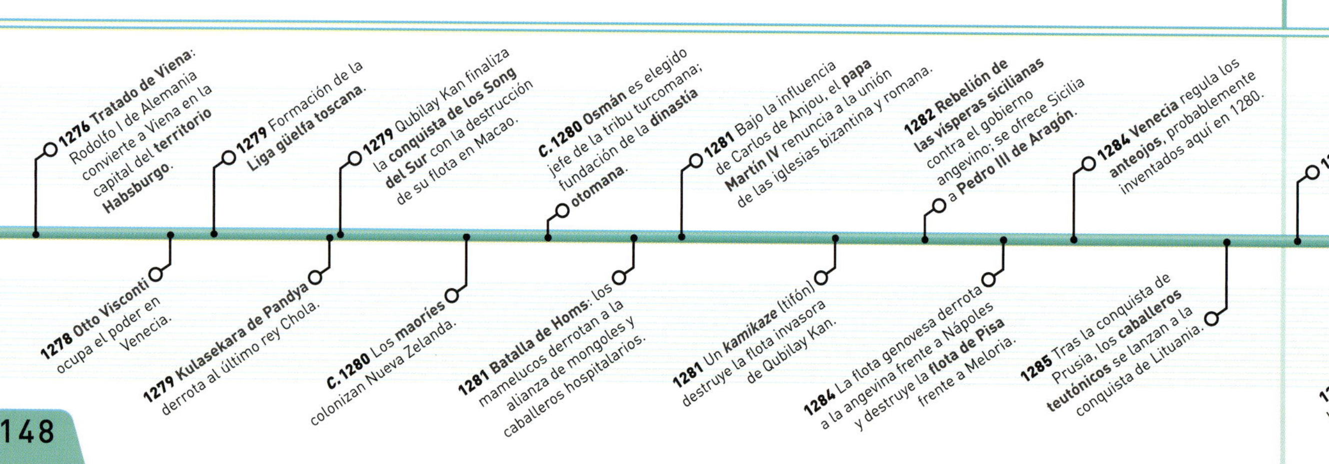

Arezzo les incitaron a enfrentarse a la ciudad rival. Los florentinos derrotaron a Arezzo en la **batalla de Campaldino**, lo que preludió un periodo de **dominio florentino** en la Toscana. Entre los combatientes florentinos se hallaba **Dante Alighieri** (1311–1317).

El linaje de los reyes esclavos de Delhi llegó a su fin en 1290, al tomar el poder uno de los oficiales destacados de la dinastía de los mamelucos, **Firuz** (*c.* 1220–1296). Originario de la tribu de Afganistán de los turcos jalyíes, fundó la **dinastía jalyí**, que gobernaría Delhi hasta 1320.

Celosía mogol ornamentada
Esta celosía de la entrada principal al complejo Qutub de Delhi fue construida por el sultán jalyí Alá al-Din, asesino y sucesor de Firuz.

1291–1295

Cruz de Leonor en Geddington (Inglaterra). Tiene un arco conopial, lo que supuso un hito para el gótico inglés.

EN 1291, TRAS UN DESESPERADO ASEDIO DE SEIS SEMANAS DE DURACIÓN, los **mamelucos** tomaron **Acre**, el último enclave cruzado importante en **Palestina**; unos meses después tomaron Beirut, el último vestigio del reino cruzado de **Ultramar** (*véase* 1181–1185). Tras casi doscientos años, el poder cristiano en Tierra Santa había llegado a su fin. Los mamelucos saquearon la región para desincentivar futuras cruzadas, pero, siguiendo la tradición de tolerancia de otras dinastías musulmanas, permitieron a cristianos y judíos vivir bajo su gobierno.

A fin de reducir el riesgo de incendio, **Venecia** trasladó su **industria de fabricación de vidrio** a Murano en 1291. Los fabricantes de vidrio de Venecia eran los únicos europeos que producían **vidrio transparente**. Su dominio del trabajo del vidrio ya había dado fruto anteriormente con la invención de los **anteojos** (*véase* 1284).

Eduardo I de Inglaterra (r. 1272–1307) se había casado con **Leonor de Castilla** en 1254. Aunque no fue demasiado querida por los ingleses, los monarcas disfrutaron de un matrimonio feliz y Eduardo quedó desolado tras su muerte en 1290. El año siguiente ordenó que se erigieran las doce **cruces de Leonor** para conmemorar la ruta de su cortejo fúnebre a través de Londres.

La pugna entre **Génova y Venecia** por el **control del Mediterráneo** continuaba y la flota genovesa derrotó a la veneciana frente a **Laiazzo** en 1294. Al año siguiente, Génova reunió una **flota enorme** para asestar el golpe definitivo. A pesar de un desafío formal, no llegó a entrar en combate. Por el contrario, en Venecia, la industria de la construcción de barcos avanzaba. Capaz de transportar un cargamento mayor y una tripulación más numerosa, la primera gran galera construida en 1294 anunció una clara ventaja para los venecianos.

Cristal de Murano
Este recipiente de cristal de Murano data de c. 1330. Además de contribuir a la seguridad en caso de incendio, situar la industria en una isla ayudó a regularla y a guardar sus secretos.

165
GALERAS COMPONÍAN LA **FLOTA GENOVESA** DE 1295

1296–1300

Wallace, proscrito tras matar en 1296 a uno de los *sheriffs* de Eduardo, fue uno de los primeros hombres en ser ahorcado, ahogado y descuartizado.

LA DESAPARICIÓN DE LA DINASTÍA CANMORE, seguida por las disputas entre los nobles escoceses, permitió a **Eduardo I** ejercer un control cada vez mayor sobre Escocia y, en 1292, otorgó la corona a **Juan de Baliol**. Sin embargo, Baliol se alió en 1295 con **Francia**, enemiga de Inglaterra. En 1296, Eduardo lanzó una campaña para **someter a los escoceses**; les derrotó en Dunbar y les arrebató la **Piedra del Destino** (la piedra de coronación escocesa), que se llevó a Londres. En 1297, **William Wallace** (*c.* 1272–1305) dirigió una rebelión contra el gobierno inglés y venció a un ejército superior en número en la **batalla del Puente de Stirling**, pero fue derrotado en **Falkirk** en 1298 y se vio obligado a dedicar los años siguientes a una guerra de guerrillas y a buscar financiación extranjera.

1:4 **Batalla del Puente de Stirling**
Se cree que, liderados por William Wallace, 2500 escoceses derrotaron a una fuerza mucho más numerosa de soldados ingleses (hasta 10 000) en la batalla de Stirling Bridge.

El **conflicto naval entre genoveses y venecianos** no se solucionó y se libraron batallas en el mar Negro y en las islas griegas. En la **batalla de Curzola**, en 1298, los genoveses infligieron una **terrible derrota** a los venecianos: destruyeron casi todos sus barcos y mataron a unos siete mil marineros.

Rutas comerciales genovesas
Los genoveses abrieron una lucrativa ruta comercial hacia el mar del Norte y competían con Venecia por el control sobre el comercio con Bizancio y Oriente.

CLAVE
— Rutas comerciales

1287 La invasión mongola del Punjab se detiene en **Lahore**.

1289 Batalla de Campaldino; Florencia domina la Toscana.

1289 Los **mamelucos** toman Trípoli.

1290 Firuz funda la **dinastía kalyí** en el sultanato de Delhi.

1291 Los mamelucos toman **Acre**. Fin de los reinos cruzados en Palestina.

1291 Eduardo I levanta las **cruces de Leonor** en Inglaterra.

1291 La industria del vidrio veneciana se traslada a **Murano**.

1292 Eduardo de Inglaterra nombra a **Juan de Baliol** como rey de Escocia en vista de la oposición escocesa.

1292 Marco Polo viaja a **Java** con la flota de Qubilay Kan.

1294 Fallece **Qubilay Kan** (n. 1215).

1295 Marco Polo regresa a Italia y es capturado por los genoveses.

1295 Ghazan se convierte en Ilkan y declara el **islam** la religión oficial del ilianato.

1295 Los **genoveses** construyen una flota gigantesca.

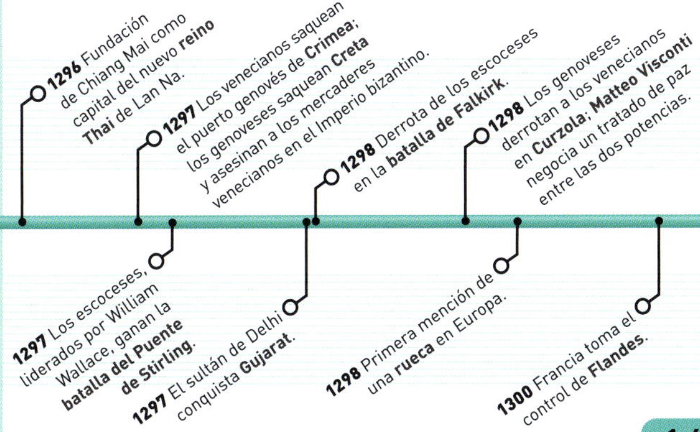

1301–1310

Cuadro de Doménico di Michelino, *La comedia ilumina Florencia*, donde aparecen Dante, la ciudad de Florencia y escenas de la *Divina Comedia*.

PESE A LA EXPULSIÓN DE LOS GIBELINOS DE FLORENCIA (*véase* 1286–1290), la ciudad seguía dividida en la **lucha de poder** entre la antigua nobleza aristocrática, la nueva nobleza comerciante y los poderosos gremios. La **facción güelfa** se escindió en un partido negro (extremista) y otro blanco (moderado). En 1301, los blancos expulsaron a los negros, que regresaron cuando el conde Carlos de Valois llegó a la ciudad. El año siguiente, los güelfos negros dieron a escoger a los blancos entre la muerte o el exilio; entre ellos se encontraba el poeta **Dante Alighieri** (*véase* recuadro).

En el año 1301, el **papa Bonifacio VIII** (*c.* 1235–1303) emitió (supuestamente) una bula en la que afirmaba la **supremacía papal** sobre Francia. En realidad, la bula era una falsificación difundida por el rey francés, **Felipe IV el Hermoso** (r. 1285–1314), con el objetivo de alimentar el descontento hacia el papa. Felipe «respondió» convocando uno de los primeros **Estados Generales** (que incluía a representantes de las ciudades y de la Iglesia), donde consiguió su apoyo. Bonifacio **excomulgó** a Felipe, quien, a su vez, presentó **cargos criminales** contra el papa. En 1303, agentes de Felipe penetraron en los aposentos pontificios de Anagni e intentaron **arrestaron al papa**, que murió poco después. Ante la turbulenta situación en Italia, en 1303 los cardenales escogieron al arzobispo de Burdeos como **papa Clemente V**. Aunque tenía la esperanza de instalarse en Italia una vez hubiera remitido la violencia, Clemente permaneció en el sur de Francia y en 1309 se estableció en **Aviñón**, entonces propiedad del rey de Nápoles. Esta situación temporal duró hasta 1378.

Residencia papal
Situado sobre una formación rocosa, el palacio pontificio de Aviñón es uno de los edificios góticos más grandes e importantes de Europa.

1311–1317

« LA DESGRACIA SE ABATIRÁ PRONTO SOBRE AQUELLOS QUE NOS HAN CONDENADO SIN RAZÓN. DIOS VENGARÁ NUESTRA MUERTE. »

Jaques de Molay, gran maestre de los caballeros templarios, maldice al rey Felipe y al papa Clemente V (1314)

Tortura de Jacques de Molay, gran maestre de los caballeros templarios.

A PARTIR DE UNOS PRINCIPIOS MUY HUMILDES Y DE TANTA POBREZA que dos caballeros se habían visto obligados a compartir un mismo caballo, los **caballeros templarios** habían conseguido encumbrarse hasta alturas extraordinarias. Con el apoyo del obispo cisterciense **Bernardo de Claraval** (1090–1153) y después el del papa, habían quedado exentos de la jurisdicción y la fiscalidad seculares, por lo que prosperaron a medida que iban recibiendo donaciones. Se habían convertido en el siglo XIII en los **banqueros** de gran parte de Europa, con capacidad para dirigir una gran flota y mantener el **ejército cruzado** primario en Ultramar. Los caballeros templarios lograron gran preeminencia en toda Europa, sobre todo en Inglaterra, donde el **maestre del Temple** era el primer barón del reino. Al inicio del siglo XIII, el **maestre William Marshall** gobernaba el país como regente del joven rey **Enrique III** (1207–1272). Sin embargo, tras la **caída de Ultramar**, los templarios empezaron a tener dificultades para mantenerse a flote y se convirtieron en un objetivo fácil para su enemigo, **Felipe IV de Francia**, que deseaba las tierras de los templarios y que urdió la acusación de **herejía** contra ellos. El 13 de octubre de 1307, los oficiales de Felipe arrestaron simultáneamente a **todos los templarios de Francia**. Se les acusó de **varios crímenes**, como perversiones sexuales, ocultismo e idolatría. La **tortura** consiguió confesiones escabrosas y, a lo largo de los años siguientes, se **ejecutó a unos sesenta templarios**. En el resto de Europa también se llevaron a cabo algunos arrestos, pero el deseo de condenar a la orden era mucho menor. En el concilio de Vienne (1311–1312), Felipe obligó a Clemente a disolver a los templarios y, en 1314, su **gran maestre**, Jacques de Molay, murió quemado en la hoguera.

Mapamundi de Hereford
El mundo aparece en forma de disco, con Jerusalén en el centro. Se ilustran algunos lugares de interés, y las rutas comerciales y de peregrinación.

Hereford (Inglaterra) era uno de los principales centros de **comercio de lana** y una de las primeras fuentes de riqueza en la Inglaterra medieval. Los compradores extranjeros acudían para adquirir lana que exportar a la **industria textil** de Flandes y de Italia; su comercio se describía como **«la joya del reino»**. La riqueza de lugares como Hereford se expresaba en la magnificencia de sus **catedrales** y en la riqueza de sus ornamentaciones. En la catedral de Hereford, un **mapamundi**, aproximadamente de 1300 (en función de las fuentes se data entre 1285 y 1314), hace las veces de retablo; es el mapamundi más grande conocido. Estos mapas encapsulaban la visión medieval del mundo, a las puertas de la **era del descubrimiento**.

En la batalla de Bannockburn, en 1314, **Robert I Bruce**, rey de los escoceses (r. 1306–1329), expulsó por fin a los ingleses de Escocia.

DANTE ALIGHIERI
(1265–1321)

A Dante se le suele considerar el más grande de los poetas italianos y una figura muy influyente de la literatura europea. Se le conoce sobre todo por su poema alegórico *Divina Comedia*, y por el trágico amor que profesaba a Beatriz, que se casó con otro y falleció joven. Exiliado de su Florencia natal por motivos políticos, dedicó gran parte de su vida a viajar de una ciudad a otra. Murió en Ravena en 1321.

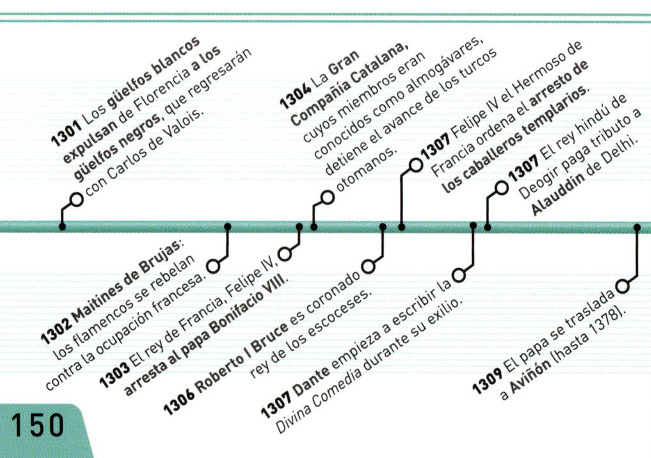

1301 Los **güelfos blancos expulsan** de Florencia **a los güelfos negros**, que regresarán con Carlos de Valois.

1302 Maitines de Brujas: los flamencos se rebelan contra la ocupación francesa.

1303 El rey de Francia, Felipe IV, **arresta al papa Bonifacio VIII**.

1304 La **Gran Compañía Catalana**, cuyos miembros eran conocidos como almogávares, detiene el avance de los turcos otomanos.

1306 Roberto I Bruce es coronado rey de los escoceses.

1307 Felipe IV el Hermoso de Francia ordena el **arresto de los caballeros templarios**.

1307 Dante empieza a escribir la *Divina Comedia* durante su exilio.

1307 El rey hindú de Deogir paga tributo a **Alauddin** de Delhi.

1309 El papa se traslada a **Aviñón** (hasta 1378).

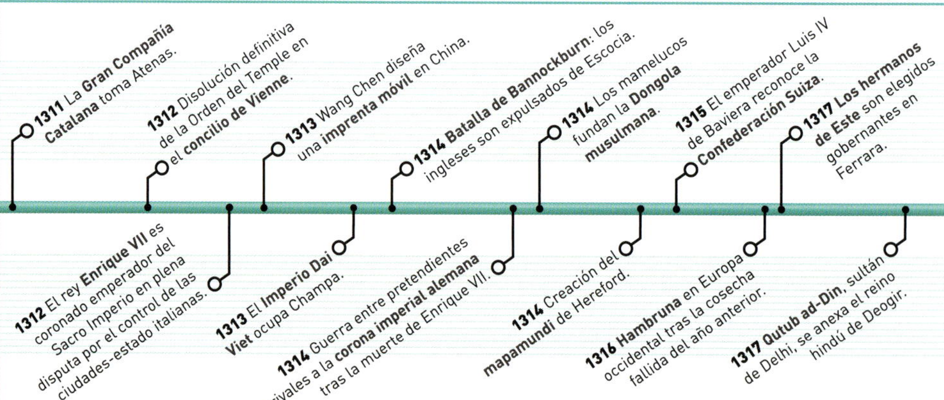

1311 La **Gran Compañía Catalana** toma Atenas.

1312 Disolución definitiva de la Orden del Temple en el **concilio de Vienne**.

1312 El rey **Enrique VII** es coronado emperador del Sacro Imperio en plena disputa por el control de las ciudades-estado italianas.

1313 Wang Chen diseña una **imprenta móvil** en China.

1313 El **Imperio Dai Viet** ocupa Champa.

1314 Batalla de Bannockburn: los ingleses son expulsados de Escocia.

1314 Guerra entre pretendientes rivales a la **corona imperial alemana** tras la muerte de Enrique VII.

1314 Los mamelucos fundan la **Dongola musulmana**.

1314 Creación del **mapamundi** de Hereford.

1315 El emperador Luis IV de Baviera reconoce la **Confederación Suiza**.

1316 Hambruna en Europa occidental tras la cosecha fallida del año anterior.

1317 Los hermanos de Este son elegidos gobernantes en Ferrara.

1317 Qutub ad-Din, sultán de Delhi, se anexa el reino hindú de Deogir.

1318–1325

Mansa Musa, soberano legendario y fabulosamente rico del Imperio de Malí, sostiene un orbe de oro en el *Atlas catalán* de 1375

LA PÓLVORA TRANSFORMABA DE UN MODO LENTO PERO CONSTANTE EL ARTE DE LA GUERRA. Lo más probable es que los árabes y los musulmanes la conocieran por medio de los **chinos**; así, en España ya se utilizaron cañones en 1284. Se cree que los **mamelucos** utilizaron **pistolas** en Ain Yalut, mientras que los mongoles adquirieron la tecnología tras su conquista de China. Probablemente, el resto de Europa la recogió de **España** y del contacto con los **mongoles**. El primer registro del uso de cañones de hierro es en Metz, en 1324; ese mismo año, una fortaleza inglesa en Gascuña fue bombardeada durante un mes.

El **Imperio de Malí**, en África occidental, alcanzó su punto álgido bajo **Mansa Musa** (r. 1312–1337) y llegó a extenderse desde el Atlántico hasta Nigeria y del Sáhara a la selva. Su riqueza procedía del **oro de Malí** y, según la leyenda, cuando viajó a La Meca, dejó tanto oro a su paso por **El Cairo** que desestabilizó la economía local. A su vuelta, contrató a un arquitecto andalusí para que le construyera un nuevo palacio en **Tombuctú**, que se convirtió en un centro de **academia musulmana**. Más adelante, Malí recibiría la visita del académico marroquí **Ibn Battuta** (*c.* 1304–1369), que empezó a viajar en 1325.

25

EL **PORCENTAJE** DE LA **POBLACIÓN** DE **TUMBUKTÚ** EN LA **UNIVERSIDAD SANKORE**

Los viajes de Ibn Battuta
Su primer viaje fue el hayy (peregrinación) a La Meca. Hizo otros siete viajes más, y visitó casi todos los rincones del mundo musulmán.

1326–1339

Andrea Pisano necesitó varios años para completar las puertas de bronce del baptisterio de Florencia, que le encargaron en 1329.

EN LAS DÉCADAS DE 1320 Y 1330, FLORENCIA ALBERGÓ A ARTISTAS como **Giotto di Bondone** (*c.* 1267–1337) o **Andrea Pisano** (*c.* 1290–1349), a quienes se considera precursores del Renacimiento italiano (*véanse* pp. 208–209). Giotto pintó frescos naturalistas en las paredes de la **basílica de la Santa Cruz** aproximadamente en 1325, y en 1334 se le encargó la construcción del **Duomo** (catedral). Muy influido por Giotto, Pisano se encargó de las **puertas de bronce del baptisterio de Florencia**, que terminó en 1336.

La **dinastía tugluquí** del sultanato de Delhi había ampliado el alcance del estado **musulmán**, reducido a los **reinos hindúes** vecinos al estatus de vasallos, y detenido una serie de **incursiones mongolas**. En 1325, **Muhammad Tugluq** (*c.* 1300–1351) asesinó a su padre y tomó la corona; en breve se labró una reputación de gran crueldad. En 1327 trasladó la capital de Delhi a **Dautalabad** por razones defensivas y obligó a la población a trasladarse con él. En 1336, una revuelta liderada por **Harihara I** y su hermano **Bukka**, de la **dinastía Sangama** del sur, llevó al establecimiento del último gran imperio hindú en India, con capital en **Vijayanagar**.

Eduardo II de Inglaterra otorgó gran poder a sus favoritos, especialmente a **Piers Gaveston** (que sería asesinado por barones envidiosos en 1312) y a la **familia Despenser**. También alienó a su esposa, **Isabel de Francia**, a quien envió a Francia en 1325 para negociar el matrimonio de su hijo. Durante su estancia, se hizo amante de **Roger Mortimer** y cuando volvieron en 1326 lideraron una **rebelión contra el rey**. Se ahorcó a todos los Despenser y Eduardo se vio **obligado a abdicar** en favor de su hijo adolescente, mientras **Roger e Isabel actuaban de regentes**. Ocho meses más tarde, Eduardo II fue asesinado de un modo terrible. Los regentes cedieron Gascuña a Francia y reconocieron a **Robert I Bruce** como rey de una Escocia independiente. **Eduardo III** (r. 1327–1377) hizo ahorcar a Mortimer en 1330 y empezó a gobernar por sí solo. La creciente **tensión con Francia** se exacerbó cuando Eduardo decretó el embargo sobre las exportaciones de lana a **Flandes**, lo que **provocó una rebelión** allí contra el control de Francia. En 1337, Felipe VI de Francia declaró que los territorios de Eduardo en Francia pasaban a la corona francesa, mientras que Eduardo reclamó la corona de Francia: había estallado la **guerra de los Cien Años**.

« EL **PRIMER REY** TRAS LA CONQUISTA QUE **NO FUE UN HOMBRE DE NEGOCIOS**. »

William Stubbs, historiador inglés, sobre Eduardo II (1875)

Altorrelieve de Vijayanagar
Hanuman, el dios mono venerado por los hindúes, en un altorrelieve de Vijayanagar, el centro del último gran imperio hindú.

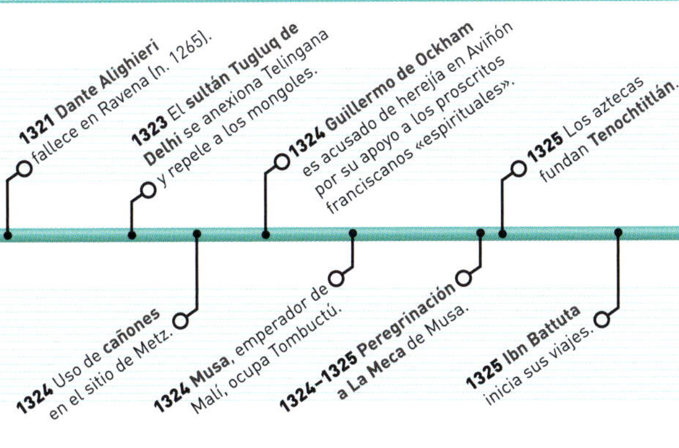

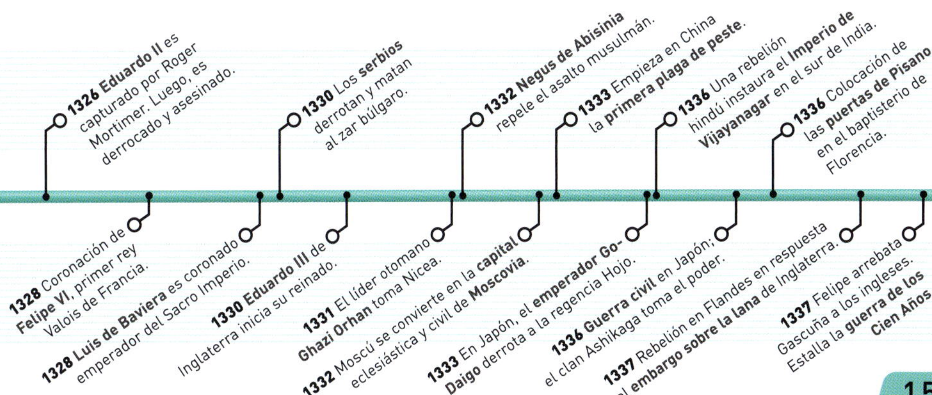

1340–1344

El estrecho de Gibraltar; allí el ejército mariní destruyó a la flota castellana.

LA BATALLA DEL SALADO ES, PARA ALGUNOS, la definitoria de la **Reconquista**, porque puso un fin a la amenaza de las **incursiones musulmanas** desde África hasta la península Ibérica. La **dinastía mariní** de Marruecos, que había derrocado a los **almohades** a mediados del siglo XIII, reunió un gran ejército y destruyó a la flota castellana en el **estrecho de Gibraltar**. Entonces, los mariníes marcharon hacia el interior y hasta el río Salado, donde fueron derrotados por los reyes cristianos **Alfonso XI de Castilla** (r. 1312–1350) y **Alfonso IV de Portugal** (r. 1325–1357).

800 000 FLORINES **DEBÍA EDUARDO III**

Para financiar su costosa guerra en Francia, **Eduardo III** de Inglaterra (r. 1327–1377) había pedido **créditos enormes** a los banqueros florentinos y, especialmente, a la **familia Peruzzi**. Cuando se le acabó el dinero, Eduardo dejó de pagar el préstamo en 1342. El rey de Nápoles tampoco pudo hacer frente a sus pagos, lo que provocó la bancarrota de los Peruzzi y la caída de **Florencia** en el **caos económico**. Se llamó a Walter de Brienne, el mercenario duque de Atenas, para que tomara el poder en Florencia, pero finalmente cayó bajo el control de una **oligarquía comercial**.

1345–1349

Ilustración de la *Crónica* de Froissart de 1346. Representa la batalla de Crécy, donde los ingleses utilizaron por vez primera artillería móvil.

TRAS HABER OBTENIDO EL CONTROL DEL CANAL DE LA MANCHA en la batalla naval de **Sluys** en 1340, **Eduardo III** se vio con libertad para invadir Francia. Llegó a Normandía en 1346 y tomó **Caen**, pero se retiró al encontrarse con un ejército francés enorme. Oculto en los límites del **bosque de Crécy**, Eduardo tomó una posición defensiva e infligió una **derrota aplastante** a las fuerzas de Felipe IV, sobre todo gracias a la indisciplina y la arrogancia de los **caballeros franceses** y también a la efectividad de los **arqueros galeses e ingleses**. A costa de unas cuantas bajas, **los ingleses mataron a decenas de miles**, inclusive al rey de Bohemia, al duque de Lorena, al conde de Flandes, al conde de Blois y a otros ocho condes más, además de a tres arzobispos. El ejército inglés era un **combinado de aristócratas y labradores** que había dado lugar a una nueva forma de ejército de gran potencia. A continuación **asediaron Calais**, que cayó en 1347 tras un largo asedio.

También en 1347, la **peste negra** llegó finalmente a Europa. Se cree que lo hizo a bordo de barcos genoveses que regresaban de **Crimea**, donde los marineros se habrían visto expuestos a la enfermedad e infectado. Se transmitía por **pulgas y la portaban las ratas**, y la epidemia se extendió de puerto a puerto hasta el último rincón de Europa y de Asia occidental. Gran parte de la población murió.

LA MUERTE NEGRA

Sus efectos se registraron mejor en Europa, donde tuvo graves consecuencias. Despobló el territorio, hundió la economía, frenó el avance intelectual y artístico, cambió el orden social y contribuyó al fin del feudalismo, además de provocar campañas antisemitas, pues se acusaba a los judíos de haber traído la peste. Muchos se vieron obligados a huir a Europa oriental.

POBLACIÓN TOTAL

45 %
MUERTOS

Muertos por la peste negra
Se cree que hasta el 45 % de la población europea murió en los diversos brotes de la peste bubónica.

1350–1355

« CUANTO **PLACE** AL MUNDO ES UN **BREVE SUEÑO**. »

Francesco Petrarca, del *Cancionero número I* (*c.* 1352)

EL PAPADO REFORMÓ SU BUROCRACIA y mejoró sus finanzas bajo los papas de Aviñón. En 1348, **Clemente VI** (1291–1352) compró Aviñón a Juana de Nápoles y continuó con la construcción del palacio pontificio. **Académicos y artistas** acudieron a la ciudad pontificia; entre ellos estuvo brevemente el florentino **Francesco Petrarca** (1304–1374), que había sido coronado **poeta laureado** en Roma en 1341. En 1351, Petrarca empezó a componer **sonetos** y **sextinas**. También fue un académico, cuya traducción y popularización de la **literatura clásica** contribuyó a la aparición del **humanismo**, una nueva escuela filosófica que contribuiría a su vez a la aparición del **Renacimiento**.

En 1354, el rey nazarí de Granada, **Yusuf I**, fue asesinado por su hijo **Muhammad V** (1338–1391), que ascendió al trono. Bajo Muhammad, la **Alhambra** (el palacio fortificado de Granada) siguió creciendo hasta convertirse en un **tesoro de la arquitectura musulmana**.

Juan Cantacuceno (*c.* 1292–1383), pretendiente al **trono bizantino**, invitó a los **otomanos a Gallípoli**, en los Dardanelos (el estrecho que separa a Asia de Europa), para que le ayudaran a tomar el poder. Dirigida por Orjan, la **dinastía turca** no tardó en conquistar la península, con lo que se aseguraron un enclave en Europa.

Joya arquitectónica
El Patio de los Leones está en el palacio de la Alhambra, erigido por Muhammad V como la residencia de invierno de la familia real.

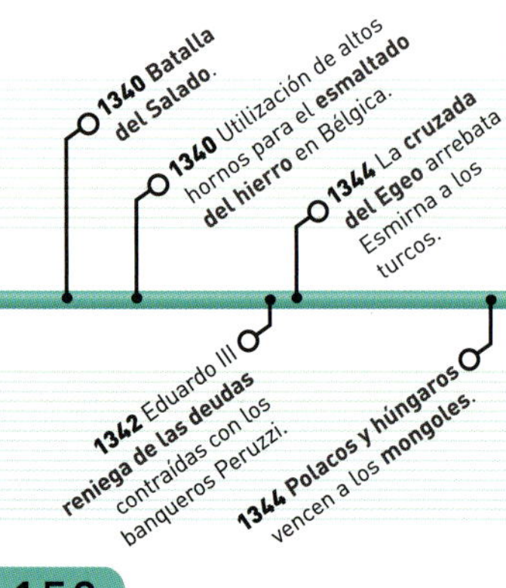

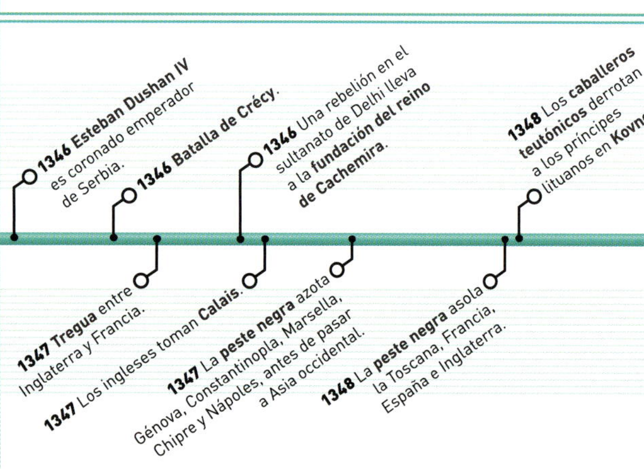

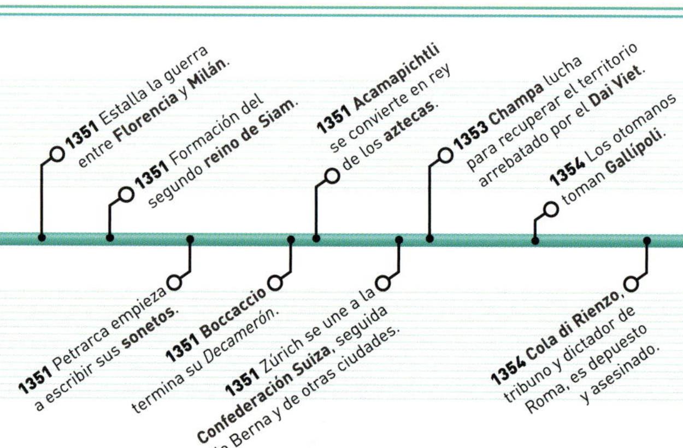

1356–1365

Para muchos, Petrarca es el padre del humanismo.

Mural sobre Tamerlán, que ascendió desde orígenes humildes hasta fundar la dinastía timurí tras superar las conquistas de Gengis Kan.

BOHEMIA SE HABÍA CONVERTIDO EN UN POTENTE ESTADO bajo la dinastía de los Premyslidas en el siglo XIII. Bajo la **dinastía Luxemburgo**, se convirtió en la potencia central de la geopolítica alemana, mientras que su gobernante, **Carlos I** (Carlos IV como emperador del Sacro Imperio), intentaba modernizar la institución imperial y mejorar el futuro de Bohemia. En 1348 había ampliado el reino **concediéndole territorios** como Moravia y Silesia, y refundó **Praga** para que se convirtiera en una de las ciudades más importantes de Europa, con una gran universidad. Carlos IV emitió en 1356 la Bula de Oro, que regularizaba la elección del emperador mediante siete príncipes electores, la mayoría de los cuales eran hereditarios; el papado quedaba sin voz alguna. A su vez, esto permitió que los principados electores desarrollaran **estados soberanos** y sentó las bases constitucionales del Sacro Imperio Romano, hasta su disolución definitiva en 1806. La Bula instauró a Bohemia como elector principal y garantizaba su independencia.

Tamerlán (1336–1405), también conocido como Timur Lang, ascendió desde un origen humilde hasta convertirse en el líder de la **tribu turcomongola yagatay** en Transoxiana (Asia central) en 1362. A pesar de cojear y de carecer de **ascendencia gengísida** (descendencia directa de Gengis Kan; solo los gengísidas podían convertirse en kan) se convirtió en uno de los **mayores conquistadores de la historia**.

Eduardo de Woodstock, el hijo mayor de Eduardo III e históricamente conocido como el **Príncipe Negro** (1330–1376), obtuvo sus espuelas en la **batalla de Crécy**, cuando tan solo tenía dieciséis años de edad. Llegó a ser uno de los comandantes ingleses más efectivos. Cuando las **hostilidades** entre Inglaterra y Francia se **reanudaron** en 1355, invadió Francia y obtuvo una gran victoria cerca de **Poitiers** en 1356, en la que capturó al **rey Juan II de Francia**.

Bula de Oro
Los edictos emitidos con sello de oro se conocían como «bulas de oro». La del emperador Carlos IV tenía el fin de prevenir el conflicto en las futuras elecciones imperiales.

1366–1372

De ladrillo y madera, el campanario de Xian se levantó a principios de la dinastía Ming, durante el reinado de Zhu Yuanzhang, el primer emperador Ming.

EDUARDO DE WOODSTOCK fue nombrado príncipe de Gascuña y de Aquitania en 1362. Se trasladó a Burdeos y se convirtió en un agente importante en las cuestiones continentales. En 1367 intervino en una **disputa dinástica en Castilla**, donde el aliado de los franceses, Enrique de Trastámara (1334–1379), había depuesto a Pedro I, aliado de Inglaterra, lo que puso el **control de la flota castellana en manos francesas**. Eduardo venció a Enrique en **Nájera**, pero enfermó y se vio obligado a retirarse, lo cual permitió a Enrique recuperar el trono de Castilla. En 1372, después de que **Carlos V de Francia** (r. 1364–1380) alentara una **rebelión en Gascuña** que reanudó la **guerra de los Cien Años**, la flota castellana fue clave en la derrota de la flota inglesa en **La Rochelle**.

China se reunificó mediante conquistas desde el sur, cuando una rebelión expulsó a la **dinastía mongola Yuan**. En 1368, los rebeldes bajo **Zhu Yuanzhang** (1328–1398), un agricultor transformado en monje budista y luego en general, atacaron desde su base en Nankín y **expulsaron a los Yuan de Pekín**. Yuanzhang adoptó el nombre imperial de **Hongwu** y fundó la **dinastía Ming**. Estableció un gobierno fuerte y centralizado que reforzó la figura del emperador, pero también fortaleció a la burocracia. En 1372 emitió un edicto por el que prohibía el comercio marítimo y, por lo tanto, **limitaba el contacto con los extranjeros**.

276
AÑOS DURÓ LA **DINASTÍA MING**

Bajo **Murat I** (r. 1362–1389), los turcos otomanos ampliaron su control y llegaron hasta los **Balcanes**. En 1371, Murat derrotó a una alianza de serbios, bizantinos y búlgaros, y tomó el control sobre gran parte de Tracia, Macedonia, Bulgaria y Serbia. También creó el cuerpo de **jenízaros**, una fuerza de esclavos guerreros que se convertiría en el núcleo de los ejércitos otomanos.

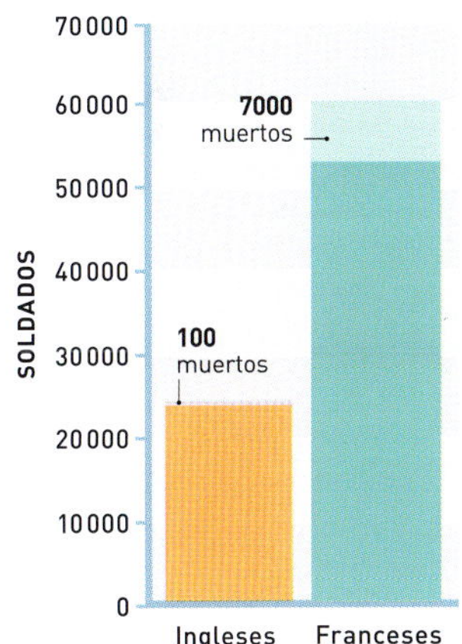

Batalla de Nájera
Superado en número en una proporción de casi tres a uno, el ejército anglogascón derrotó a las fuerzas francocastellanas y solo perdió a un centenar de hombres.

1354 La flota veneciana derrota a la genovesa en **Porto Longo**.

1354 Muhammad V se convierte en rey de Granada y amplía el **palacio de la Alhambra**.

1355 Fallece **Esteban Dushan**, rey de Serbia; su imperio empieza a desintegrarse.

1355 La **rebelión nacionalista** contra el gobierno mongol toma impulso en **China**.

1356 Batalla de Poitiers. El Príncipe Negro captura al rey Juan II de Francia.

1356 Los rebeldes chinos antimongoles toman **Nankín**.

1356 Bula de Oro del emperador Carlos IV.

1359 Guerra civil en la **Horda de Oro** (Europa oriental).

1360 Eduardo III lucha en Francia y acuerda el **tratado de Calais**.

C. 1362 Tamerlán se convierte en líder tribal en Transoxiana (Asia central).

1363 Algirdas de Lituania derrota a los mongoles y extiende sus territorios hasta el mar negro.

1364 Casimiro el Grande de Polonia funda una universidad en Cracovia.

1367 Batalla de Nájera.

1368 Tíbet recupera la **independencia** tras el colapso Yuan.

1368 Zhu Yuanzhang expulsa a la dinastía Yuan y funda la dinastía **Ming**.

1369 Tamerlán conquista Samarcanda.

1369 Se reanuda la **guerra de los Cien Años**.

1369 La **Liga Hanseática** alcanza el cénit de su poder.

1371 Batalla de Chernomen.

1372 Francia vence en **La Rochelle** y recupera Poitiers.

HISTORIA DE LA IMPRENTA

UNA REVOLUCIÓN EN LA COMUNICACIÓN HUMANA QUE CAMBIÓ EL MUNDO PARA SIEMPRE

La imprenta hizo posible comunicar y divulgar la información a una velocidad y a una escala previamente inconcebibles y desencadenó importantes cambios que han llegado hasta hoy, desde la religión hasta las revoluciones científicas y políticas. Ha llegado a transformar el propio lenguaje.

La impresión consiste en dejar marcas sobre un material, normalmente tinta sobre papel. La escritura cuneiforme, la primera que se conoce, era una forma de impresión que consistía en realizar hendiduras con un punzón sobre arcilla blanda. La impresión, en sentido moderno, apareció en el siglo VIII en China, con la imprenta de bloques. Se tallaban bloques de madera en bajorrelieve, que se utilizaban como sellos para reproducir copias de un único texto con imágenes, como el *Sutra del diamante*, el primer libro impreso fechable (*véase* 861–870).

IMPRESIÓN MECÁNICA

La impresión en bloques era laboriosa y lenta, y cada bloque formaba una única página completa. Los tipos móviles supusieron un gran avance (*véase* recuadro). Se inventaron en Asia oriental, pero los perfeccionó el impresor alemán Johannes Gutenberg (*véase* 1454–1455). Su imprenta era muy avanzada; de hecho, a excepción de refinamientos como los tipos de letra, la mecanización de las prensas y la gestión del papel, el proceso básico siguió siendo el mismo hasta el siglo XIX.

En la década de 1880, el desarrollo de la linotipia permitió que un operador compusiera las líneas de tipos con un teclado. La estereotipia permitió duplicar páginas completas para impresiones múltiples. Ya en el siglo XX, la fotocomposición permitió filmar fotolitos a partir de los que se creaban las planchas de impresión. A finales de siglo, los ordenadores asumieron todas las funciones de la imprenta, desde la composición y los gráficos a la impresión y el secado, que ahora hace una única máquina.

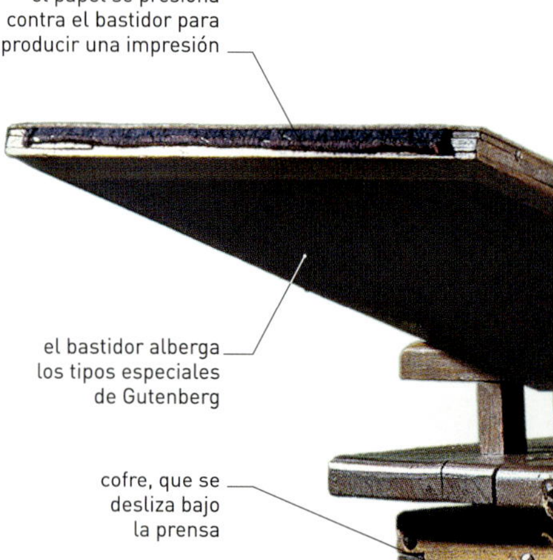

« AQUEL QUE **ACORTÓ** LA **LABOR** DE LOS COPISTAS MEDIANTE UN INSTRUMENTO DE **TIPOS MÓVILES**… CREÓ UN NUEVO **MUNDO DEMOCRÁTICO**; **INVENTÓ** EL ARTE DE LA **IMPRESIÓN**. »

Thomas Carlyle, ensayista e historiador escocés (1759–1881)

C. 2291–2254 a. C.
Escritura sumeria cuneiforme
Esta escritura marca hendiduras en lugar de hacer trazos a mano. Las placas se estampan sobre arcilla blanda que luego se cuece.

Escritura cuneiforme sumeria

Siglo VIII
Imprenta de bloques
La técnica de impresión que usa bloques de madera tallados y tinta se conoce como xilografía. El fragmento xilográfico más antiguo conservado es un rollo budista *dharani* de Corea.

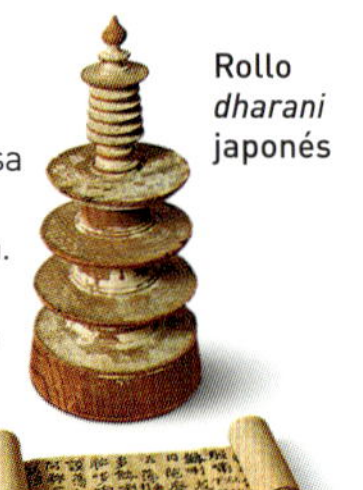
Rollo *dharani* japonés

868
Impreso en bloques
El libro (manuscrito completo) más antiguo que se conoce es el *Sutra del diamante*, un texto budista hallado en una cueva de Dunhuang (China).

Sutra del diamante

C. 1275–1313
Tipos móviles
Se inventaron en China en el siglo XI y fueron perfeccionados por Wang Shen, que utilizó más de sesenta mil tipos de madera en su tratado.

Imprenta de Gutenberg

1377
Tipos móviles de metal
Los primeros tipos de metal se forjaron en bronce en Corea y se usaron para imprimir el *Jikji Simche Yojeol*, un escrito budista.

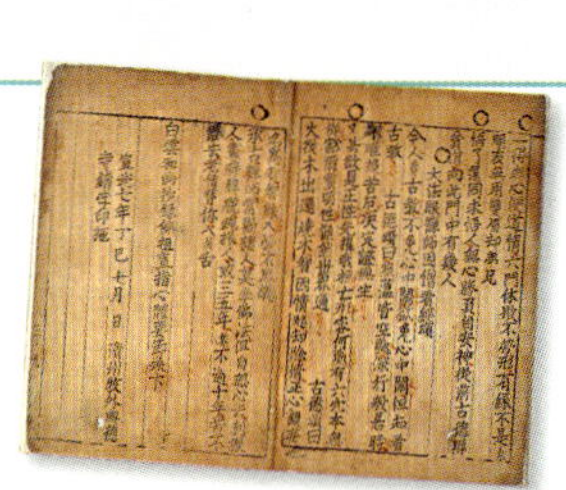
«Incunable» coreano

C. 1455–1456
La imprenta
Gutenberg imprime el primer libro europeo, la Biblia de Gutenberg, o de las 42 líneas (por el número de líneas en cada página).

1790–1820
Imprentas de metal
La imprenta *Columbian*, totalmente metálica, es la primera que sustituye el torno por palancas y pesos.

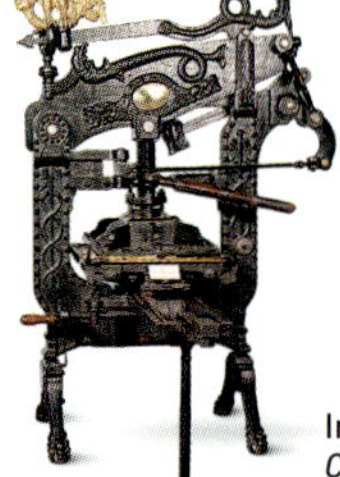
Imprenta metálica *Columbian*

torno, adaptado de una prensa de vino

pieza cuadrada que transfiere la presión a la plancha

plancha de impresión pesada

tampones de tinta de cuero y rellenos con pelo de caballo

construcción sólida para la producción a escala industrial

La imprenta de Gutenberg
Gutenberg creó una imprenta con un torno, que presionaba el tipo impregnado de tinta sobre una hoja de papel. Supuso un avance extraordinario respecto al método tradicional de impresión por fricción.

TIPOS MÓVILES

La tecnología clave en la revolución de la imprenta fue la introducción del tipo móvil, en que cada carácter de un texto tenía un pequeño bloque, o tipo individual. Esto permitía organizar líneas de tipos, que luego podían reordenarse para formar un texto diferente. El primer libro impreso con tipos móviles de bronce se imprimió en Corea a finales del siglo XIV. Gutenberg mejoró la tecnología y desarrolló una técnica que permitía la forja rápida y precisa de los tipos metálicos.

impresión de la tinta sobre el papel

tipo móvil alzado

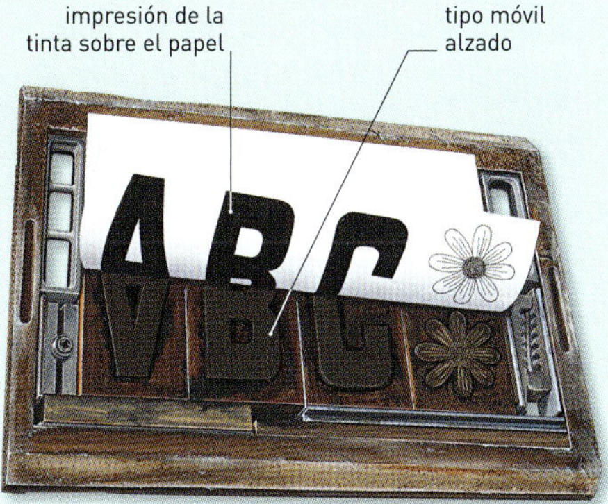

Impresión tipográfica con tipos móviles

Impresora láser

Finales del siglo XX–actualidad
Impresión de sobremesa
La tecnología de una impresora láser hubiera ocupado un taller entero de antaño.

1886
Linotipia
La linotipia permite que el operador componga líneas completas de tipos con un teclado parecido al de una máquina de escribir, en lugar de a mano y letra a letra.

Linotipia

1903
Impresión *offset*
En la impresión *offset*, la imagen impregnada en tinta se transfiere de la plancha de impresión al papel mediante una lámina de goma, para conseguir una impresión precisa y reducir el desgaste de la plancha.

Una de las primeras fotocopiadoras

1949
Fotocopiadoras
Fue un invento de Chester Carlson, de Xerox Corporation. La fotocopiadora utiliza la distribución electrostática de tinta en polvo, o tóner, para crear una copia exacta.

1373–1380

Cuadro del siglo XVI que muestra el regreso del victorioso dogo a Venecia tras haber derrotado a los genoveses.

LA GUERRA DE CHIOGGIA ENTRE VENECIA Y GÉNOVA fue una de las consecuencias de los continuos enfrentamientos por el control sobre las **rutas comerciales a través de los Dardanelos**, por las que fluía el lucrativo comercio con el **Imperio bizantino** y, un poco más allá, la **Ruta de la Seda**. El emperador bizantino **Juan V Paleólogo** (r. 1341–1376) concedió a Venecia en 1376 la isla egea de **Tenedos**, la puerta a los Dardanelos. Al mismo tiempo, su hijo y rival **Andrónico IV** (1348–1385) se la otorgaba a Génova. En la guerra que siguió, los genoveses derrotaron a los venecianos en **Pola**, y en 1379 tomaron **Chioggia**, en Italia, y **bloquearon a Venecia**. Dirigidos por Vittorio Pisano, los venecianos, a su vez, bloquearon a la flota genovesa hasta que consiguieron que se rindiera por hambre. El **poder marítimo de Génova había naufragado** y Venecia controlaba ahora el comercio en el Mediterráneo.

« NUNCA SE CONSIGUE NADA GRANDE SIN MUCHO ESFUERZO. »

Santa Catalina de Siena (1347–1380)

En 1376, la mística y hacedora de milagros **Catalina de Siena** viajó a Aviñón con el objetivo de convencer a **Gregorio XI** (*c.* 1336–1378) para que devolviera el papado a Roma. Unos meses después, Gregorio acudió a Roma para intentar restaurar el orden en los estados pontificios, pero murió poco después. La **turba romana** presionó al cónclave cardenalicio para que escogiera a un **papa italiano** y, al final, se escogió a **Urbano VI** (*c.* 1318–1389). Sin embargo, los cardenales franceses eligieron a **Roberto de Ginebra** (1342–1394) como **antipapa Clemente VII**. El rey francés, Carlos V, apoyó a Clemente, mientras que **Ricardo II de Inglaterra** se alió con el emperador del Sacro Imperio Romano, Carlos IV, en apoyo del candidato romano. Así empezó el **cisma de Occidente**, periodo durante el cual coincidieron papas rivales instalados en Roma y en Aviñón hasta 1417.

El carnicero de Cesena
Se conocía al antipapa Clemente VII como el «carnicero de Cesena», por su brutal represión de una rebelión en los territorios pontificios en sus funciones de legado papal.

1381–1385

Ilustración de la crónica de Froissart sobre la revuelta de los campesinos, la primera gran rebelión en la historia de Inglaterra. Su líder, Wat Tyler, fue ejecutado por el alcalde de Londres.

LA PESTE NEGRA Y LA CONSIGUIENTE ESCASEZ DE MANO DE OBRA contribuyeron al aumento de la tensión social en Inglaterra. En torno a 1362, por ejemplo, el párroco rural William Langland había escrito *Piers Plowman*, un poema en inglés en el que simpatizaba con las tribulaciones de los campesinos pobres. El religioso y académico **John Wycliffe** (o Wiclif) había generado gran agitación con escritos que anticipaban el **protestantismo**. Y una secta bíblica igualitaria, conocida como los **lolardos** e inspirada parcialmente en Wycliffe, cada vez tenía más seguidores. En 1377, el llamado **Parlamento sin piedad**, dominado por el hijo del rey, **Juan de Gante**, conde de Lancaster y muy pronto regente de su sobrino, **Ricardo II** (1367–1400), aprobó un **impuesto censal**; los parlamentos que siguieron lo incrementaron, con lo que generaron un **malestar generalizado**. En 1381, los intentos de reintroducir la servidumbre provocaron una **revuelta campesina**, en la que los labradores se alzaron contra sus señores, quemaron mansiones y destruyeron los registros. Hasta cien mil hombres, liderados por **Jack Straw** y **Wat Tyler**, marcharon hacia Londres y tomaron la Torre, quemaron el palacio de Juan de Gante y **mataron al arzobispo Sudbury**, a quien culpaban de la subida de impuestos. Ricardo II consiguió aplacar a los rebeldes, Tyler fue ejecutado y **la rebelión fue reprimida con brutalidad**.

El **teatro no** japonés apareció a lo largo del siglo XIV, sobre todo de mano de Kanami Kiyotsugo (1333–1384) y de su hijo Zeami Motokiyo (1363–1443), que escribieron cientos de obras no y desarrollaron las representaciones tan estilizadas y simbólicas que caracterizan al género.

La **influencia castellana** en Portugal durante la década de 1380 amenazaba la independencia del reino y generó **resentimiento entre los portugueses**. Una monja provocó un alzamiento que terminó con la toma de poder de **Juan** (1358–1453), el hijo ilegítimo de Pedro I. En 1384, **Juan I de Castilla** (1358–1390) invadió Portugal, pero el parlamento portugués eligió a Juan I de Portugal como rey y, con la ayuda de Inglaterra, derrotó a Castilla en la **batalla de Aljubarrota**, en 1385. Así, libró a Portugal de la influencia castellana y, tras casarse con la hija de Juan de Gante, fundó la **dinastía portuguesa de Avís**.

En 1384, **Felipe el Atrevido, duque de Borgoña**, heredó el condado de Flandes y lo añadió a sus ya vastos territorios. Francia estaba gobernada por **Carlos VI**, que padecía una enfermedad mental, y se vio dominada por la rivalidad entre las casas de **Borgoña** y de **Orleans**.

máscara, normalmente de madera o de arcilla

Máscara no
En el teatro no, que combina música instrumental, canciones, diálogos y mimo, el protagonista y los personajes femeninos o ancianos llevan máscara.

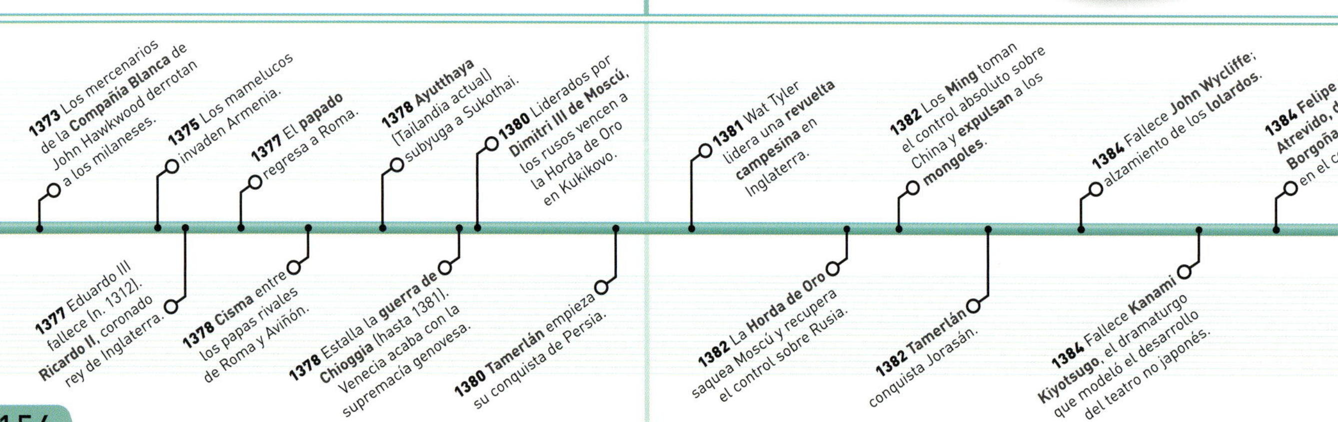

1386–1390

Peregrinos en ruta en esta ilustración de los *Cuentos de Canterbury*. El poema inconcluso de Geoffrey Chaucer, de 17 000 versos de longitud, ilustra la visión del mundo medieval sobre cuestiones sociales, religiosas y morales.

EL ÚLTIMO GOBERNANTE PAGANO DE EUROPA, Jagellón de Lituania (*c.* 1362–1434), fue coronado rey de Polonia y se convirtió al cristianismo en 1386. Su matrimonio con **Eduvigis de Polonia** unió ambos reinos e introdujo Lituania en la Iglesia católica (*véase* 1408–1410).

Tamerlán (*véase* 1356–1365) finalizó en 1386 su **conquista de Persia** y llegó hasta las profundidades del Cáucaso: saqueó **Tblisi** (Georgia) y capturó al rey georgiano. Sin embargo, cuando el ejército de la **Horda de Oro** atacó sus territorios en Asia central en 1387, se vio obligado a retroceder. Tardó nueve años en sofocar la amenaza.

Geoffrey Chaucer (*c.* 1340–1400), militar, académico, escritor, diplomático, funcionario del gobierno y miembro del parlamento, desempeñó un papel crucial en el desarrollo del inglés medio (una combinación de inglés antiguo y de influencias francófonas). Su obra los ***Cuentos de Canterbury***, que empezó a escribir en 1387, está inspirada en el *Decamerón* de Boccaccio, y narra la historia de unos peregrinos que viajan al santuario de **Tomás Becket** (*véase* 1170).

CRISTIANIZACIÓN DE EUROPA

En Europa, la época medieval presenció un fuerte avance de la cristiandad, que llegó a abarcar todo el territorio, con muy pocas excepciones. El espectacular éxito de la conversión europea supuso un enorme reto para la Iglesia, que tenía serias dificultades a la hora de reconciliar el poder temporal y el espiritual. Las fuerzas internas seguirían revolucionando la religión.

En la **batalla de Kosovo** de 1389, los otomanos derrotaron a los serbios y a los bosnios, con lo que **aplastaron al Imperio serbio** y absorbieron la mayoría de sus territorios. El líder otomano, Murat, murió en la batalla, pero su hijo, **Bayaceto I, llamado «el Rayo»** (1360–1403), le sustituyó. Cuando se supo que Murat había muerto, los **vasallos otomanos** en Europa y Anatolia se **rebelaron**, pero Bayaceto redujo deprisa a la mayoría de ellos, que quedaron bajo el **gobierno otomano directo**. Ahora, los otomanos controlaban la mayor parte de Anatolia y de los Balcanes al sur del Danubio. Bayaceto introdujo el **devsirme**, un tributo de niños de familias cristianas a quienes se convertía al islam y se reclutaba para la administración y para el cuerpo de **jenízaros**.

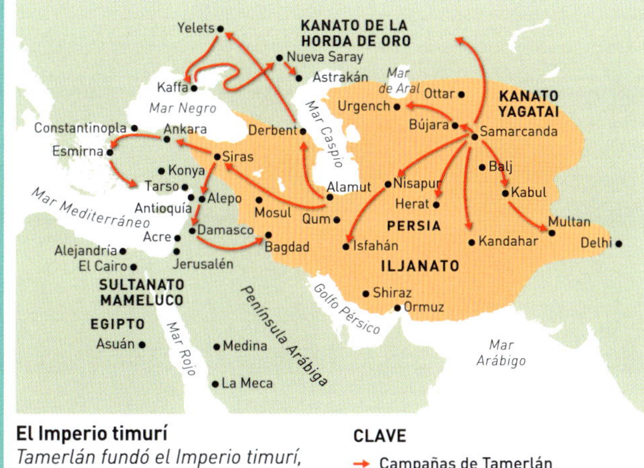

El Imperio timurí
Tamerlán fundó el Imperio timurí, que llegó a abarcar un territorio aún más amplio que el de Gengis Kan, pero que no sobrevivió durante mucho tiempo a su fundador.

CLAVE
- Campañas de Tamerlán
- Alcance del Imperio timurí

1391–1400

Miniatura del Museo Topkapi (Estambul) sobre la batalla de Nicópolis, donde los otomanos destruyeron a las fuerzas invasoras.

EL INICIO DE LA DINASTÍA MING EN CHINA PROVOCÓ CAMBIOS EN COREA, a la que los Ming consideraban un estado tributario. El **Imperio de Koryo** había dado apoyo a la nueva dinastía china, pero esto no impidió a los Ming amenazarles con una invasión. En 1388, Yi Songgye (1335–1408), un importante general que apoyaba a China, tomó el poder en Corea. En el año 1392, como **rey Taejo**, fundó la **dinastía Yi**, también conocida como Choson, nombre que tomaron de un antiguo reino coreano. Taejo reestructuró el gobierno a partir del modelo chino e instituyó **amplias reformas sobre la propiedad de la tierra** para redistribuir los terrenos en manos de la oligarquía, a la que sustituyó por una nueva clase de tecnócratas conocidos como *yangban*. Adoptó el **neoconfucianismo** como religión oficial y fundó una nueva capital en **Hanseong** (Seúl). La dinastía Yi perduró hasta 1910.

En **Japón**, la unión de las cortes imperiales del norte y del sur en 1392 puso fin al **periodo Yoshino** (también conocido como el periodo de las Cortes del Norte y del Sur). Durante este periodo, el linaje del emperador **Go-Daigo** (a quien el sogún Ashikaga Takauji había expulsado de Kioto, la capital) había mantenido una **corte rival** en la montañosa región de Yoshino, al sur de Nara. Japón se vio sumido en una **guerra civil** hasta que el sogún **Ashikaga Yoshimitsu** (1358–1408) negoció una reunificación y llevó el poder Ashikaga a su apogeo.

Durante la **cruzada de Nicópolis** de 1396 (que tenía el objetivo de frenar el avance otomano en los Balcanes), la expedición francohúngara liderada por **Segismundo de Hungría** sufrió una humillante derrota en la ciudad búlgara de Nicópolis, a orillas del Danubio. El enorme ejército, con voluntarios de la mayoría de los **estados cristianos**, dio muestras de una funesta indisciplina y el fracaso de esta aventura demostró la urgente necesidad de reforzar las defensas de la Europa cristiana.

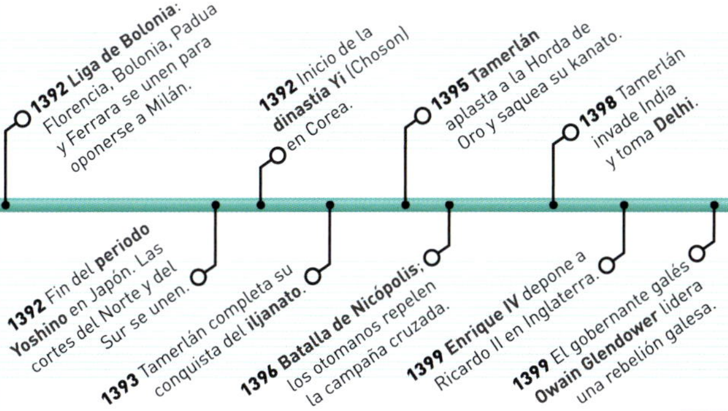

Palacio de Gyeongbokgung
Este colosal palacio, construido por el rey Taejo (Yi Songgye) en 1395, también recibe el nombre de Palacio de la felicidad brillante y de Palacio grandemente bendecido por los cielos.

1386 Jagellón de Lituania, el último monarca pagano europeo, es coronado rey de Polonia (como Ladislao II Jagellón) y se convierte al cristianismo.

1386 Tamerlán completa la conquista de Persia y saquea Georgia.

1387 El escritor inglés **Geoffrey Chaucer** empieza a escribir los *Cuentos de Canterbury*.

1387 Guerra entre Tamerlán y la **Horda de Oro**.

1388 Milán, dirigida por **Gian Galeazzo Visconti**, añade Padua a otras conquistas en el norte de Italia.

1388 Publicación de la traducción de la **Biblia** al inglés de John Wycliffe; una versión posterior se conocerá como la Biblia lolarda.

1389 Venceslao IV, rey de Bohemia y emperador del Sacro Imperio, decreta una **paz general** en Alemania.

1389 Batalla de Kosovo: los otomanos absorben el Imperio serbio.

1392 Liga de Bolonia: Florencia, Bolonia, Padua y Ferrara se unen para oponerse a Milán.

1392 Fin del **periodo Yoshino** en Japón. Las cortes del Norte y del Sur se unen.

1392 Inicio de la **dinastía Yi** (Choson) en Corea.

1393 Tamerlán completa su conquista del **Iljanato**.

1395 Tamerlán aplasta a la Horda de Oro y saquea su kanato.

1396 Batalla de Nicópolis: los otomanos repelen la campaña cruzada.

1398 Tamerlán invade India y toma **Delhi**.

1399 Enrique IV depone a Ricardo II en Inglaterra.

1399 El gobernante galés **Owain Glendower** lidera una rebelión galesa.

1401–1403

El muro de calaveras del Templo Mayor en Ciudad de México está hecho con calaveras esculpidas sobre la piedra y cubiertas de estuco. Los aztecas practicaban sacrificios humanos en los grandes templos en Tenochtitlán.

FUNDADA POR LOS AZTECAS EN EL AÑO 1325, la ciudad de **Tenochtitlán** (erigida sobre una poco prometedora isla pantanosa en un lago parcialmente salobre) alcanzó su máximo esplendor a principios del siglo XV. Tenochtitlán significa «lugar de la fruta del cactus», una referencia a la visión que llevó a la elección del lugar. En la visión, el corazón arrojado de un enemigo caía sobre la isla, donde un águila y una serpiente luchaban sobre un cactus que crecía de una roca, tal y como aparece en la actual bandera mexicana. Los **aztecas** drenaron la isla, reclamaron el territorio circundante y tendieron calzadas elevadas para unirla a tierra firme. Al mismo tiempo, ampliaron su territorio político mediante matrimonios, alianzas y conquistas. Tras una gran inundación, reconstruyeron Tenochtitlán siguiendo una pauta cuadriculada y con barrios dispuestos alrededor de un **distrito sagrado central**, al que consideraban el centro del mundo. Una enorme población de hasta 200 000 habitantes vivía gracias a la **agricultura intensiva**, una extensa **red comercial** y el cobro de tributos.

El **reino africano de Songay** tenía su centro en la ciudad comercial de Gao, a orillas del río Níger (**África occidental**). Gao era una ciudad próspera gracias al comercio interregional y transahariano con el mundo islámico, especialmente de sal, oro, esclavos y marfil. A mediados del siglo XIII, el **Imperio de Malí** (*véase* 1231–1235), atraído por su riqueza, la convirtió en una de sus provincias orientales. No obstante, a principios del siglo XV Malí empezó a declinar y Gao recuperó su independencia, para dar lugar al crecimiento de un Imperio songay que eclipsaría a los otros dos grandes imperios de la Edad de Hierro Tardía en África occidental: Ghana y Malí.

Moneda de oro de Songay
Esa moneda del Imperio songay procede de la ciudad de Gao. Rica y poderosa, la ciudad fue la base a partir de la cual se construyó el imperio.

Mapa de Tenochtitlán
Calzadas elevadas conectaban Tenochtitlán con otros asentamientos en el lago y en tierra firme. La ciudad y su emperador dominaban el valle de México.

CLAVE
- Calle
- Acueducto
- Calzada elevada
- Dique

En 1398, **Tamerlán** (*véase* 1356–1365) había invadido el norte de India y destruido el **sultanato de Delhi** a una velocidad asombrosa y con una crueldad aterradora. Avanzó 260 km en dos días y mató a cien mil fugitivos a las afueras de Delhi, antes de saquear la ciudad, donde supuestamente erigió una pirámide con los cráneos de sus víctimas. En 1401, Tamerlán mató a la población de Bagdad y lanzó una invasión sobre Siria. Entonces, atacó a los **otomanos** (*véase* 1286–1290), ocupó Anatolia y recuperó los antiguos principados turcomanos.

1404–1407

« HEMOS PUESTO LA **MIRADA** EN REGIONES… **MUY LEJANAS.** »

Zheng He, explorador chino

DESPUÉS DE HABER LLEGADO HASTA RUSIA en sus conquistas hacia el este, **Tamerlán** (*véase* 1386–1390) dirigió la mirada al mayor de los imperios: **China**. En 1405 lanzó una campaña pero falleció cuando se dirigía a China y recibió sepultura en la capital de su reino, Samarcanda. A pesar de su posiblemente exagerada reputación de crueldad, Tamerlán era un musulmán devoto y **mecenas del arte** y de la arquitectura. Su enorme imperio no le sobrevivió demasiado tiempo y se fragmentó rápidamente en un estado timurí gobernado por su hijo Sah Ruj (1377–1477).

En 1404, Juan Sin Miedo (1371–1419) se convirtió en el **duque de Borgoña** y lideró la oposición a la regencia de Luis, duque de Orleans (1372–1407) y hermano del demente rey de Francia, Carlos VI (1368–1422). Tres años más tarde, Juan ordenó el asesinato de Luis, lo que desencadenó una **guerra civil** entre los **borgoñones**, que defendían la paz con Inglaterra y dominaban en París y en el norte, y los **armañacs**, contrarios a los ingleses y probélicos, y que contaban con el apoyo de la reina Isabel de Baviera, de los grandes nobles y del sur del país.

En el año 1404, **Zheng He** (1371–1435), un musulmán que había sido capturado cuando era niño en China, castrado y obligado a servir en el ejército, fue nombrado gran eunuco de la corte imperial. Al año siguiente, en 1405, Zheng He emprendió el primero de siete épicos viajes de descubrimiento.

1408–1410

Ladislao II Jagellón de Polonia se prepara para la batalla de Tannenberg.

GRACIAS A SU IMPLACABLE ASCENSO, LA ORDEN DE LOS CABALLEROS TEUTÓNICOS (*véase* 1236–1240) controlaba Prusia y la mayoría de la costa del Báltico, con lo que Polonia perdió su salida al mar. La unión de Polonia y Lituania bajo el rey Ladislao II Jagellón (*c.* 1362–1434) se convirtió en una amenaza para la orden y dio lugar a **una guerra entre los caballeros teutónicos y Polonia y Lituania**. En la **batalla de Tannenberg** de 1410 (uno de los mayores enfrentamientos de caballería de la época), un enorme ejército polacolituano de hasta 16 500 soldados y que comprendía a mercenarios bohemios,

c. 1400 Máximo esplendor de la ciudad azteca de **Tenochtitlán**.

c. 1400 Expansión del **Imperio songay** en África occidental.

1401 Tamerlán (1336–1405) ejecuta a la población de Bagdad.

1402 El arquitecto italiano **Lorenzo Ghiberti** recibe el encargo de diseñar las puertas del **baptisterio de Florencia**.

1402 Batalla de Ankara. **Tamerlán captura al sultán otomano.**

1403 Parmesvara, el monarca malayo, funda el **sultanato de Malaca**.

1405 Los territorios de Visconti se fragmentan. **Venecia toma Padua**, Verona y Vicenza.

1405 Primer viaje del explorador **Zheng He**.

1405 Fallece Tamerlán (n. 1336); **fragmentación del Imperio timurí**.

1407 La **guerra civil en Francia** enfrenta a armañacs y borgoñones.

1409 Donatello (Donato di Niccolò di Betto Bardi) finaliza su obra maestra, *David*.

1409 El **concilio de Pisa** concluye con tres candidatos a papa.

rusos e incluso tártaros (mongoles turcos), derrotó a las fuerzas de los caballeros teutónicos, que contaban con unos 11 000 hombres. La orden fue aplastada, pero Jagellón fue incapaz de mantener la disciplina entre los nobles polacos y no pudo aprovechar la victoria. La **paz de Thorn**, acordada el año siguiente, no consiguió garantizar el acceso de Polonia al Báltico y los caballeros teutónicos pudieron recuperar parte de su ventaja.

Andréi Rubliov (*c.* 1370–1430) fue un monje y pintor ruso, que vivió en el monasterio de la Trinidad y San Sergio de Moscú. Su obra se enmarca en un periodo de revitalización monástica en Rusia, durante el que la Iglesia ortodoxa oriental ofreció consuelo frente a las luchas internas y el odiado **yugo mongol**, el tributo y los servicios exigidos por la Horda de Oro. Aunque se inspiró en el gran pintor de iconos Teófanes el Griego, Rubliov fue celebrado por inaugurar un estilo más sereno y simétrico.

La Santísima Trinidad
Este detalle del mayor icono de Andréi Rubliov, aproximadamente de 1410, muestra a los tres ángeles que visitaron a Abraham. Cada uno representa un aspecto distinto de la Trinidad.

1411–1415

Representación de la batalla de Azincourt, con la caballería en pleno conflicto. Unos diez mil soldados franceses murieron o fueron capturados.

EN 1413, ENRIQUE IV DE INGLATERRA FALLECIÓ y su hijo, Enrique V (1386–1422), ascendió al trono. En 1415 cerró una alianza con Borgoña y reafirmó el **derecho de Inglaterra al trono de Francia**, como pretexto para reanudar la guerra de los Cien Años (*véase* recuadro). En octubre, Enrique infligió una terrible derrota al infinitamente superior ejército francés en **Azincourt**; tomó prisionero al duque de Orleans y conquistó Normandía.

« LOS VIVOS **CAÍAN** SOBRE LOS **MUERTOS**, Y LOS QUE CAÍAN SOBRE LOS **VIVOS** MORÍAN TAMBIÉN. »

De ***Gesta Henrici Quinti*** (*c.* 1416)

Durante su cuarta y mayor expedición en 1413, el **explorador chino Zheng He** visitó Calicut, en India, y llegó a Ormuz, en el golfo Pérsico, desde donde envió a sus barcos para explorar la costa africana hacia el sur, hasta llegar a Malindi (Kenia). La flota se componía de 63 naves de hasta 80 m de eslora.

En 1414, el antipapa **Juan XXIII** (uno de los tres papas que reclamaban el trono de san Pedro), fue expulsado de Roma por el rey Ladislao de Nápoles y buscó refugio en **Segismundo**, el emperador, que le obligó a convocar un concilio ecuménico (el **concilio de Constanza**) para resolver la división de la Iglesia católica conocida como cisma de Occidente (*véase* 1373–1380). En 1415, el concilio depuso a todos los pretendientes y condenó a **Jan Hus**, un párroco de Bohemia, reformista religioso y filósofo. Fue ejecutado ese mismo año.

LA GUERRA DE LOS CIEN AÑOS

Se da este nombre a la serie de conflictos que estallaron entre 1337 y 1453 como consecuencia de varios factores: la situación del ducado de Guyena (Aquitania), que pertenecía a los reyes de Inglaterra, pero que debía rendir vasallaje a la corona francesa; la pretensión de los monarcas ingleses al trono de Francia por su ascendencia capeta; el ansia de poder de ambas partes, y la necesidad de los reyes ingleses de valerse de hazañas en el extranjero para atraer apoyos internos. En teoría, la más pobre y pequeña Inglaterra no debería haber sido rival para la poderosa Francia, pero los ingleses luchaban con nuevas estrategias y armas, como su arco largo. La guerra desangró a ambos países, pero también reforzó su identidad nacional.

1416–1420

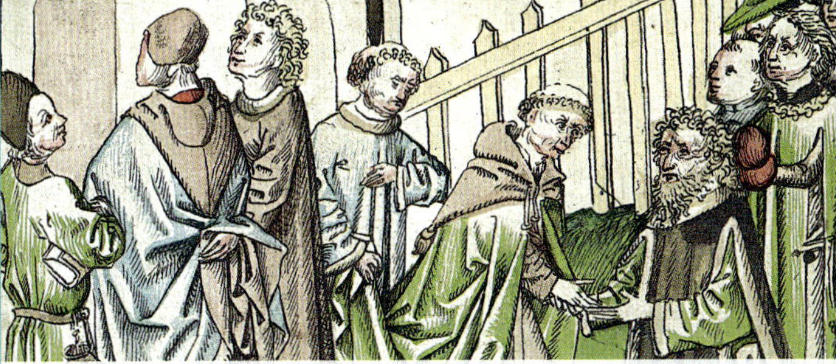

Ilustración de la crónica de Ulrich de Richental, donde los electores papales se despiden del emperador Segismundo en el concilio de Constanza.

EL CONCILIO DE CONSTANZA TERMINÓ CON EL CISMA DE OCCIDENTE en 1417, con el juicio y la democión del último antipapa, Benedicto XIII, y la elección de Martín V (*c.* 1348–1431) como único papa verdadero.

La muerte en la hoguera del reformista religioso bohemio **Jan Hus** (*véase* 1411–1415) y el fallecimiento de Venceslao IV de Bohemia (1361–1419) provocó un **alzamiento husita** en Bohemia que amalgamaba las disputas religiosas entre el papado y quienes se le oponían, además de una lucha nacionalista entre checos (bohemios y moravos) y alemanes. Los husitas, divididos en una facción moderada (utraquistas) y otra extremista (taboritas) se unieron para enfrentarse a una alianza cruzada liderada por el emperador Segismundo, hermano de Venceslao. Los husitas derrotaron a la alianza en las afueras de Praga.

En 1411, **Portugal y Castilla** firmaron la **paz** (*véase* 1381–1385). Portugal empezó a mirar hacia el exterior y consiguió asegurarse un enclave en el norte de África, en Ceuta, en 1415. El explorador **Enrique el Navegante** (1394–1460) se distinguió en esta expedición y su visita a África despertó su interés por la exploración; es posible que fundara la primera escuela de navegación de Europa en la localidad portuguesa de Sagres (*véase* 1434).

45
SESIONES SE CELEBRARON DURANTE EL **CONCILIO DE CONSTANZA**, QUE DURÓ 42 MESES

1410 Fuerzas polacolituanas derrotan a los caballeros teutónicos en la **batalla de Tannenberg**.

1410 Muere **Kanajejdi, rey de Kano** (Nigeria actual).

1410 El antipapa Juan XXIII nombra banco pontificio al **banco Médicis de Florencia**.

1411 La **paz de Thorn** pone fin al conflicto entre los caballeros teutónicos y las fuerzas polacolituanas.

1413 Fallece **Enrique IV de Inglaterra** (n. 1366).

1413 **Batalla de Jamurlu** en Serbia.

1413 Coronación de **Enrique V** de Inglaterra.

1413 Cuarta y mayor expedición de **Zheng He**.

1414 Khizr Kan (r. 1414–1421) funda la **dinastía sayyid** en Delhi.

1415 **Batalla de Azincourt** entre Francia e Inglaterra.

1415 Portugal conquista **Ceuta** en África.

1416 El noble **Amadeo VII** es nombrado duque de Saboya. **Se anexiona el Piamonte** (Italia).

1417 El concilio de Constanza pone fin al **cisma de Occidente**.

1417 El **emperador Ming Yongle** (1360–1424) fija el **canon de Confucio** y reinstaura los exámenes para acceder al funcionariado.

1419 **Enrique el Navegante** (1394–1460) funda, posiblemente, una escuela de navegación en Portugal.

1420 **Guerras husitas**; los husitas, liderados por Jan Zizka derrotan a una cruzada antihusita.

1421–1422

Filipo Maria Visconti, tras ordenar el asesinato de su hermano para convertirse en duque de Milán, recuperó la hegemonía de los Visconti en el norte de Italia.

El sultán Murat II
Murat defendió y amplió el Imperio otomano y fue un mecenas de la poesía y del conocimiento. Hizo de su corte un centro cultural.

EL SULTÁN MEHMET I (1382–1421) había conseguido **recuperar el estado otomano** tras las invasiones timuríes (*véase* 1401–1403), a pesar de que la derrota de su flota ante Venecia en la batalla de Gallípoli en 1416 le había obligado a reconocer las pretensiones venecianas en Albania. En 1421, Mehmet murió y su hijo, **Murat II** (1404–1451), se convirtió en sultán. A escala nacional, volvió a instituir la práctica del *devsirme*, que consistía en entrenar a esclavos cristianos para funciones clave en el gobierno. Internacionalmente, emprendió una política de expansión que empezó con el **primer sitio otomano de Constantinopla**. El sitio fue un fracaso y, además, Murat se distrajo con el alzamiento liderado por un teólogo y predicador sufí, el jeque Badr al-Din. Sofocó el alzamiento y ejecutó al jeque.

La **familia Visconti** había gobernado **Milán** desde que el arzobispo Otto Visconti fuera nombrado su arzobispo en 1277. Sus territorios habían crecido hasta abarcar gran parte del norte de Italia y alcanzó su máximo esplendor bajo **Gian Galeazzo** (1351–1402), que gobernó en solitario a partir de 1385. Forjó alianzas matrimoniales con los principales monarcas europeos; fue nombrado duque hereditario en 1395; conquistó Verona, Vicenza, Padua, Pisa, Siena, Asís y Perugia entre 1386 y 1400; y amenazó a Florencia hasta su muerte en 1402. Las disputas entre sus hijos Gian Maria y Filipo Maria desintegraron su imperio, pero Filipo ordenó asesinar a Gian Maria en 1412 y se propuso reintegrar el legado de su padre. **Recuperó Génova** en 1421. Los Visconti eran mecenas del arte y de la academia y contribuyeron a impulsar el **Renacimiento** (pp. 208–209).

Los franceses habían sufrido grandes pérdidas en **Azincourt** (*véase* 1411–1415), por lo que en 1420, a instancias de los **borgoñones** anglófilos, Carlos VI de Francia aceptó el **tratado de Troyes** y reconoció a Enrique V de Inglaterra como su heredero y regente inmediato. El acuerdo cedía todas las tierras conquistadas hasta el Loira a los ingleses y declaraba ilegítimo a Carlos, el Delfín. Ahora, los **ingleses controlaban todo el norte de Francia**. En 1422 murieron Enrique y Carlos, y bajo los términos del tratado, el niño Enrique VI fue aclamado como rey de Inglaterra y Francia. El Delfín, instalado en Bourges, se negó a aceptarlo y la **guerra de los Cien Años** (*véase* 1411–1415) continuó.

1423–1425

El palacio del Dogo es una obra maestra de la arquitectura gótica del siglo XIV, a la que se añadieron elementos durante los siglos XV, XVI y XVII.

EN LA DÉCADA DE 1420, EL MOVIMIENTO CULTURAL que luego se conocería como **Renacimiento italiano** o **Alto Renacimiento** adquirió impulso, sobre todo en el campo de la **pintura y de las artes visuales**. En 1424, el escultor Lorenzo Ghiberti (1378–1455) terminó las puertas de bronce del **baptisterio de Florencia**, que le habían encargado en 1403; el año siguiente le encomendaron otro par. Toda una hueste de artistas, como Brunelleschi, Jacopo della Quercia, Masaccio, Donatello, Gentile da Fabriano o Jan van Eyck, entre muchos otros, fueron contemporáneos de Ghiberti.

El pago del tributo
Tommaso di Ser Giovanni di Simoni, más conocido como Masaccio, murió cuando solo tenía 27 años, pero creó algunas de las obras de arte más influyentes del Renacimiento.

Aunque **Florencia** fue el centro del Renacimiento en el siglo XV, los otros grandes centros de poder italianos –Milán, Roma y Venecia– también fomentaban los logros artísticos y arquitectónicos. En Venecia, el **palacio del Dogo**, sede del dogo de Venecia, que había evolucionado desde sus orígenes en el siglo IX, incorporaba muchos de los logros arquitectónicos de los seis siglos anteriores. El edificio actual empezó a tomar forma sobre 1340; las obras en la fachada a la Piazzeta no empezaron hasta 1424, bajo el dogo Francesco Foscari (1373–1457).

En 1424, un descendiente de Tamerlán, Ulug Beg (1394–1449), astrónomo y futuro líder mongol, construyó un gran **observatorio** en Samarcanda. Contaba con un sextante de 40 m y su equipo de académicos catalogó más de mil estrellas.

1426–1430

Juana de Arco lidera a su ejército en la batalla, armada con una ballesta.

Puntas de flecha
Estas puntas de flecha son punzones metálicos cuadrados y sencillos; fueron muy utilizadas durante las guerras medievales.

JUANA DE ARCO (1412–1431), HIJA DE UN AGRICULTOR, tenía dieciséis años cuando en 1429 oyó unas voces que le ordenaron acudir en ayuda del Delfín de Francia (*véase* 1421–1422). Los ingleses, dirigidos por Juan de Lancaster, duque de Bedford (1389–1435), habían se-

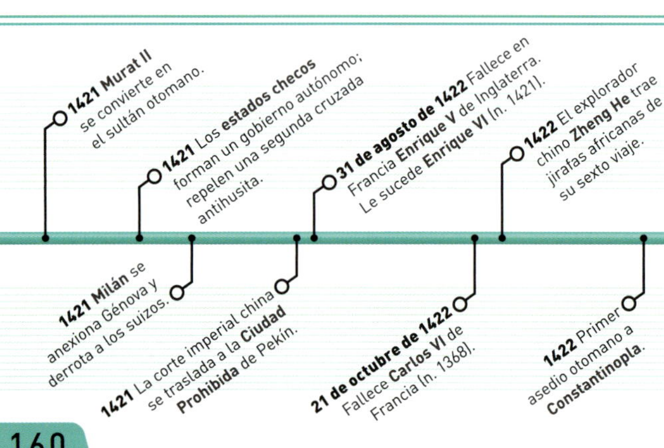

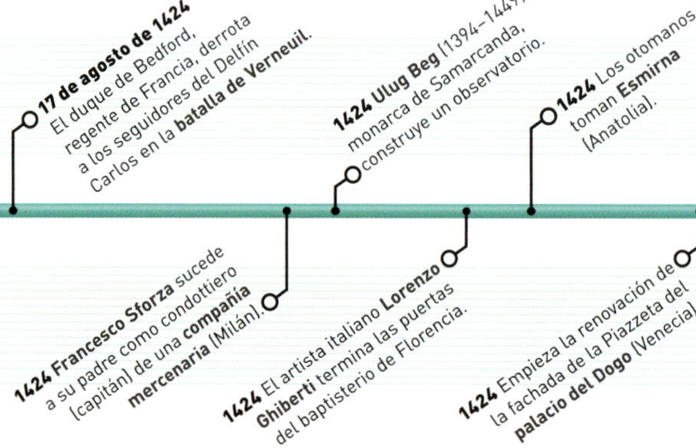

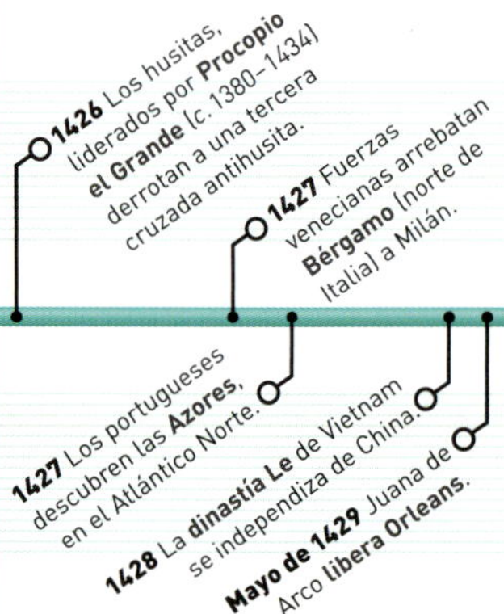

guido obteniendo victorias ante las fuerzas del Delfín y estaban **asediando Orleans**, mientras que Carlos aún no había logrado asegurarse la coronación. Juana consiguió una audiencia con él en Chinon y le convenció para que le proporcionara soldados y la nombrara *chef de guerre*. Consiguió liberar Orleans, **derrotó a los ingleses** dos veces más, y estuvo junto al Delfín durante su coronación como Carlos VII en Reims en 1429. Sin embargo, Juana no consiguió tomar París y el año siguiente fue **capturada** por los borgoñones, que la vendieron a cambio de un rescate a sus aliados ingleses (*véase* 1431–1433).

En 1428, Le Loi, líder de la resistencia vietnamita a la ocupación china, expulsó a los chinos y fundó la **dinastía Le de Dai Viet**. Una vez hubo admitido la autoridad china, los Ming reconocieron la dinastía.

1431–1433

El matrimonio Arnolfini, de Jan van Eyck, es famoso por su detallismo.

ENTRE 1431 Y 1433, ZHENG HE (*véase* 1404–1407) emprendió su séptimo y último viaje de exploración y volvió al **golfo Pérsico**. A pesar de este último viaje, el periodo de exploración chino ya había llegado a su fin con la muerte del **emperador Yongle** en 1424, tras la cual la **dinastía Ming** volvió a su política aislacionista. Ceder el liderazgo de la exploración a Portugal y a los europeos tendría importantes consecuencias para la historia de China y del mundo.

ESLORAS DE LOS BARCOS

22 m BARCO DE **CRISTÓBAL COLÓN**

134 m BARCO DE **ZHENG HE**

No todos los grandes pintores renacentistas fueron italianos. **Jan van Eyck** (*c.* 1390–1441), por ejemplo, era flamenco. Admirado por su dominio del realismo y la perfección de su técnica al óleo, Van Eyck produjo algunas de sus mayores obras maestras durante la década de 1430. En 1432 terminó la mayor de sus obras que ha llegado a nuestros días, el retablo de la catedral de San Bavón en Gante (Bélgica). Ese mismo año pintó el *Retrato de un desconocido* y el *Hombre con turbante rojo*, posiblemente un autorretrato.

En 1431, los ingleses entregaron a **Juana de Arco** a las autoridades eclesiásticas francesas para que la juzgaran. La declararon culpable de herejía y la **quemaron en la hoguera** en Ruán.

1434

« **LEEMOS** QUE DEBEMOS **PERDONAR A NUESTROS ENEMIGOS**; PERO NO LEEMOS QUE DEBERÍAMOS **PERDONAR A NUESTROS AMIGOS**. »

Cosme de Médicis

Retrato de Cosme, el primer gobernante Médicis.

DESDE LA DÉCADA DE 1380, FLORENCIA HABÍA ESTADO DOMINADA por la familia **Albizzi**, que extendió el control de la ciudad a toda la Toscana. Los intentos de los Visconti de Milán (*véase* 1421–1422) por arrebatarles el control sobre esa zona obligaron a Florencia a entrar en una guerra ruinosa, aunque gracias a su alianza con Venecia logró **derrotar a Milán**. El comerciante de lana y banquero Giovanni de Médicis era un defensor de la paz y, posiblemente, el hombre más rico de Europa. Tras su muerte en 1429 y una desastrosa guerra contra los Lucca en la Toscana, los Albizzi lograron que el hijo de Giovanni, Cosme de Médicis, fuera expulsado de Florencia en 1433, pero se le volvió a llamar tras las elecciones de 1434, lo que marcó el principio del **dominio de los Médicis** sobre la ciudad. Cosme combinaba la agudeza empresarial con el genio político, y obtuvo el apoyo popular para sus políticas.

Todos los intentos de las **fuerzas antihusitas**, lideradas por el emperador Segismundo, para derrocarles y recuperar el control sobre los **territorios checos** (*véase* 1416–1420) habían fracasado. La superioridad organizativa y táctica de los husitas, primero bajo Jan Zizka y luego, tras su muerte en 1424, bajo **Andrés Procopio**, les convirtió en una potencia militar. En 1430 invadieron Alemania y llegaron hasta Franconia. Las negociaciones con el **concilio de Basilea** en 1431 condujeron a la *Compactata* de Praga, por la que los husitas moderados (utraquistas) accedían a regresar a la Iglesia católica. Los taboritas, extremistas antipontificios, rechazaron la *Compactata* y así estalló una guerra civil entre ambas facciones, que representaban a clases distintas además de a ideales religiosos diferentes. En 1434, en la **batalla de Lipany**, los utraquistas, de clase alta, aplastaron a los taboritas y mataron a Procopio.

El poder del reino Sukhothai en Tailandia supuso una amenaza cada vez mayor para el **Imperio jemer** (*véase* 1201–1205) durante el siglo XIV. Puede que las repetidas **incursiones thai**, sobre todo una de 1431, contribuyeran al **abandono de Angkor** (*véase* 1146–1150) en 1434 y al traslado de la capital jemer a Phnom Penh, más al sur, aunque también puede que la nueva ubicación ofreciera mejores comunicaciones para el comercio exterior.

Financiados por **Enrique el Navegante** (*véase* 1416–1420), los exploradores portugueses se aventuraron al Atlántico y descubrieron la isla de **Madeira** y las **Azores**. Enrique supervisó la colonización de estos enclaves y consiguió convertirlos en centros de producción agrícola y en avanzadillas para la **exploración portuguesa**. El siguiente objetivo era rodear el cabo Bojador, en la costa de África occidental, el límite más lejano al que habían llegado los portugueses; las leyendas marineras contemporáneas presentaban los mares más allá de ese cabo como un mundo sobrenatural y peligroso. Los portugueses consiguieron rodear el **cabo Bojador** en 1434. Las experiencias de los marineros en estos viajes convencieron a Enrique de que las carracas (o naos) usadas hasta entonces no eran adecuadas, así que trabajó con sus astilleros para diseñar un nuevo tipo de nave: **la carabela**. Era más pequeña, ligera y veloz y permitía maniobras a menor profundidad, cerca de la costa, además de contar con bodegas más espaciosas que permitían trayectos más prolongados.

Rosa de los vientos
El mosaico de la rosa de los vientos en Sagres (Portugal) fue un encargo del príncipe portugués Enrique el Navegante.

17 de julio de 1429 Coronación del Delfín como **Carlos VII** de Francia.

23 de mayo de 1430 Los borgoñones capturan a **Juana de Arco**.

1430 Los otomanos arrebatan **Salónica** (Grecia) a Venecia y demuestran su capacidad naval.

C. 1430 Los caballeros europeos empiezan a usar la **armadura integral**.

30 de mayo de 1431 **Juana de Arco** es quemada en la hoguera (n. 1412).

1431 La capital jemer se traslada de **Angkor** tras el saqueo thai.

1432 El artista flamenco **Jan van Eyck** termina su *Adoración del cordero místico*.

1433 Los tuaregs conquistan **Tombuctú**.

1433 La **Compactata** de Praga pone fin a las guerras husitas.

1433 Último viaje de Zheng He y **aislamiento de China**.

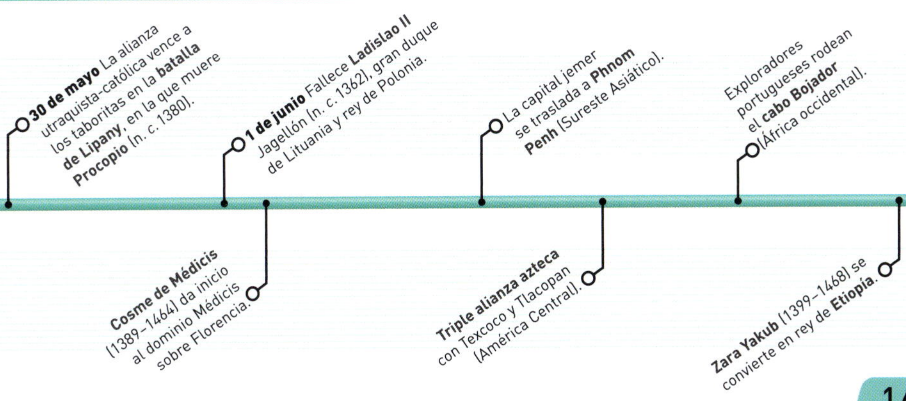

1435–1437

Ilustración de un manuscrito donde Carlos VII entra victorioso en París.

« POR LO TANTO… EL **REINO DE FRANCIA** SERÁ **GOBERNADO** POR EL **REY CARLOS VII**… ENTRARÁ EN PARÍS EN BUENA COMPAÑÍA. **»**

Juana de Arco, visionaria cristiana

A PESAR DE QUE SE HABÍAN ALIADO CON ELLOS DURANTE LA OCUPACIÓN DE FRANCIA, los borgoñones (*véase* 1404–1407) cada vez estaban más preocupados por las victorias inglesas. Con el **tratado de Arras**, los borgoñones hicieron las paces con el rey francés, Carlos VII; sin embargo, los ingleses se negaron a aceptar los términos y se retiraron de las negociaciones. El año siguiente, la alianza francesa arrebató a los ingleses el control sobre París.

La década de 1430 vio cómo aumentaba la **tensión** entre el **papado** y el **movimiento conciliar**, que sostenía que la Iglesia debía estar gobernada por un consejo eclesiástico y no por un solo papa. El papa Eugenio IV convocó un **concilio ecuménico en Basilea** en 1431, pero el sentimiento imperante estaba en su contra y, en 1437, intentó trasladar el concilio a Ferrara. La mayoría de delegados se negaron a abandonar Basilea, lo que dio lugar a **dos concilios simultáneos**.

1435 Tratado de Arras: los borgoñones y Carlos VII de Francia se alían contra los ingleses.

1436 El arquitecto italiano **Filippo Brunelleschi** termina el Duomo de Florencia.

9 de diciembre de 1437 Fallece **Segismundo** (n. 1368).

1437 Guerra civil en Escocia.

1437 Los musulmanes recuperan **Ceuta**.

1438–1440

Fundada por el rey Enrique VI de Inglaterra, la construcción de Eton se detuvo cuando el rey fue depuesto durante la guerra de las Dos Rosas.

EN 1438, PACHACUTI (*C.* 1438–1472) SE CONVIRTIÓ EN EL SÉPTIMO REY INCA, o *Sapa Inca*. Su reinado presagió el principio de una gran expansión del reino inca, que hasta el momento había estado confinado al área inmediata a **Cuzco** (*véase* 1201–1205). Empezó con la invasión de los chancas, sus rivales, que asediaron Cuzco pero fueron aplastados. La **expansión inca** se vio facilitada por la naturaleza sofisticada de la mayoría de reinos y tribus que conquistaban; por la administración precisa y centralizada y orientada al emperador; por su genio organizativo y de registro (empleando los quipus); y por un programa imperial de construcción de carreteras solo comparable al del Imperio romano.

En 1440, el joven rey de Inglaterra fundó una universidad nueva en Eton. El King's College de Nuestra Señora de Eton, cerca de Windsor, al que ahora se conoce como **Eton College**, iba a ser parte de una gran fundación que incluiría una gran iglesia, un hospicio y setenta académicos que recibirían educación gratuita antes de asistir al King's College de Cambridge.

CLAVE

- Expansión en 1400
- Expansión bajo Pachacuti

Expansión inca
El Imperio inca se expandió sobremanera entre 1400 y el fin del reinado de Pachacuti. En el siglo XVI ya había triplicado su tamaño.

Los **otomanos** (*véase* 1286–1290) ya ocupaban territorios a ambos lados de los desperdigados **restos del Imperio bizantino** y amenazaban a la propia Constantinopla, por lo que el atribulado emperador bizantino, Juan VIII Paleólogo (*véase* 1448–1449) se desplazó a Europa para suplicar ayuda al **concilio de Ferrara** en 1438.

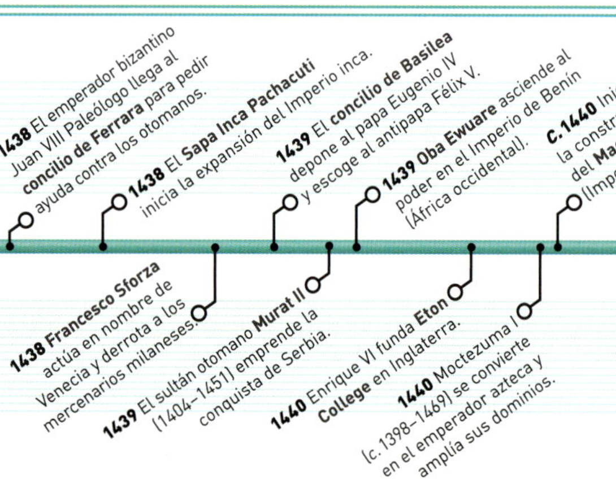

Estatuilla de oro de una llama
La riqueza en oro de los incas era tal que el emperador Atahualpa pudo ofrecer un rescate de 750 toneladas cuando los conquistadores le capturaron en 1532.

1438 El emperador bizantino Juan VIII Paleólogo llega al **concilio de Ferrara** para pedir ayuda contra los otomanos.

1438 Francesco Sforza actúa en nombre de Venecia y derrota a los mercenarios milaneses.

1438 El **Sapa Inca Pachacuti** inicia la expansión del Imperio inca.

1439 El sultán otomano **Murat II** (1404–1451) emprende la conquista de Serbia.

1439 El **concilio de Basilea** depone al papa Eugenio IV y escoge al antipapa Félix V.

1439 Oba Ewuare asciende al poder en el Imperio de Benín (África occidental).

1440 Enrique VI funda **Eton College** en Inglaterra.

1440 Moctezuma I (c. 1398–1469) se convierte en el emperador azteca y amplía sus dominios.

C. 1440 Inicio de la construcción del **Machu Picchu** (Imperio inca).

1441–1444

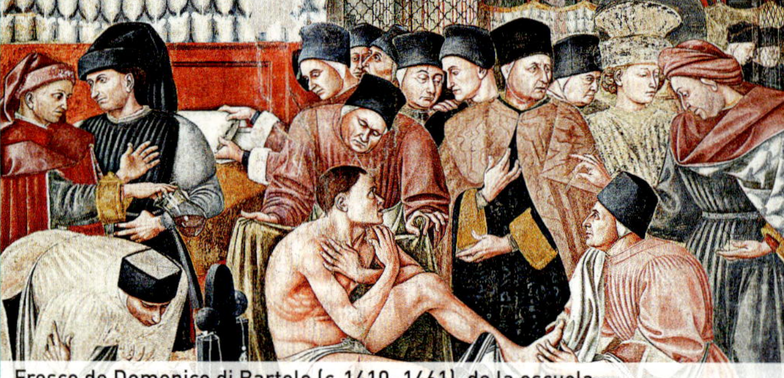

Fresco de Domenico di Bartolo (*c.* 1410–1461), de la escuela de Siena, en el hospital de Santa Maria della Scala de Siena.

MACHU PICCHU («cumbre antigua» en quechua, la lengua de los incas), es una ciudadela en la cumbre de una montaña a unos 70 km al noroeste de Cuzco. Es muy probable que la construcción empezara hacia la década de 1440, bajo los auspicios de **Pachacuti**. Se estima que la población máxima de Machu Picchu no excedió el millar de personas, y se cree que servía de centro ceremonial, además de ser una fortaleza inexpugnable para la élite inca en caso de ataque.

La resistencia a la **ocupación otomana de los Balcanes** se intensificó y, en 1443, un ejército cruzado derrotó a los otomanos en Nis (Bulgaria). El sultán otomano, Murat II (*véase* 1421–1422) se vio obligado a volver de su retiro y sustituir a su hijo, Mehmet II, a quien había intentado confiar la corona.

En Adrianópolis, Murat acordó una tregua de diez años con el líder militar húngaro Hunyadi y otros miembros de la resistencia a los otomanos. Sin embargo, el **papa predicaba la cruzada** y eximió a los cruzados de sus juramentos de paz para que pudieran lanzar un nuevo ataque. Murat aplastó al ejército cruzado dirigido por Hunyadi y Ladislao III de Polonia y Hungría (1424–1444), en lo que fue el

Machu Picchu
En las alturas del valle del Urubamba, en los Andes peruanos, sobre una cordillera inaccesible, descansa Machu Picchu, la ciudadela sagrada de los reyes incas.

1441 Francesco Sforza negocia el **tratado de Cavriana** entre Venecia y Milán.

1441 La ciudad maya de **Mayapán** es destruida durante una rebelión (América Central).

1442 Fallece **Alejandro I el Grande** (n. 1386), reunificador de Georgia.

1445–1447

La rocosa costa norte entre Paul y Ribeira Grande en Santa Ana, en las islas de Cabo Verde.

2:1 **Batalla de Varna**
El ejército cruzado, liderado por Hungría y compuesto por treinta mil hombres sufrió grandes pérdidas a manos del ejército otomano, que sumaba sesenta mil soldados.

último gran intento de expulsar a los otomanos de los Balcanes y ayudar a Constantinopla, en la **batalla de Varna**. Ladislao desapareció en plena batalla y se le dio por muerto, a pesar de los rumores de que había sobrevivido milagrosamente.

EL COSTOSO PROYECTO DE ENRIQUE EL NAVEGANTE, que consistía en acceder a la costa africana (*véase* 1434), fue recibido con gran escepticismo en Portugal, hasta que, en 1441, uno de sus barcos llegó cargado de **polvo de oro y esclavos**, lo que propició una aceleración de la actividad. Entre 1444 y 1446, unos 35 de los barcos de Enrique zarparon hacia la **costa de África occidental**. En 1445, a bordo de una de las nuevas carabelas de Enrique, el explorador **Dinis Dias** avistó la desembocadura del río Senegal, que abría una ruta comercial al interior de África, y rodeó **Cabo Verde**, el punto más occidental del continente africano. Dias regresó al año siguiente, como parte de una flota de carabelas cuya intención era plantar la bandera portuguesa y explorar lo que Enrique creía que podía ser la franja occidental del Nilo; otro de sus capitanes, Nuño Tristão, avistó el río Gambia.

Guillermo de la Pole, consejero jefe del rey y el verdadero poder tras el trono, negoció el matrimonio de **Margarita de Anjou** (*c.* 1430–1482) con Enrique VI de Inglaterra en 1445, para acabar con la guerra en Francia (*véase* 1435–1437). Al principio, tanto el enlace como la novia fueron populares en Inglaterra, pero en 1448, el territorio de Maine en el norte de Francia pasó a manos de Carlos VII y se culpó a la reina de haber influido sobre el débil rey. Sin embargo, Margarita sobrevivió y se convertiría en un elemento importante en la **guerra de las Dos Rosas** (*véase* 1454–1455).

La muerte de **Filipo Maria Visconti** en 1447 señaló el fin de la línea ducal Visconti en Milán (*véase* 1421–1422). Había muchos pretendientes al trono y, deseosos de evitar un gobernante extranjero, los poderes milaneses constituyeron deprisa la *Aurea Republica Ambrosiana* de Milán, o **República Ambrosiana**, aunque se enfrentaron a obstáculos insuperables. Debilitados por las disputas internas y poco dispuestos a perder el control sobre las otras ciudades bajo el gobierno de Milán, pronto se vieron obligados a ceder el control militar a un condottiero (capitán mercenario): el Muzio Attendolo, a quien apodaban Sforza por la fuerza que ejercía.

A mediados del siglo XV, el reino shona de **Monomotapa**, también conocido como Gran Zimbabue (*véase* 1106–1110) se acercaba al fin de sus días de gloria. A estas alturas, las riquezas de los yacimientos de oro ya habían financiado la construcción de la Gran Cerca, un espacio elíptico rodeado de una muralla gigantesca de 244 m de perímetro y de hasta 11 m de altura en algunos puntos, construida con casi un millón de bloques de granito.

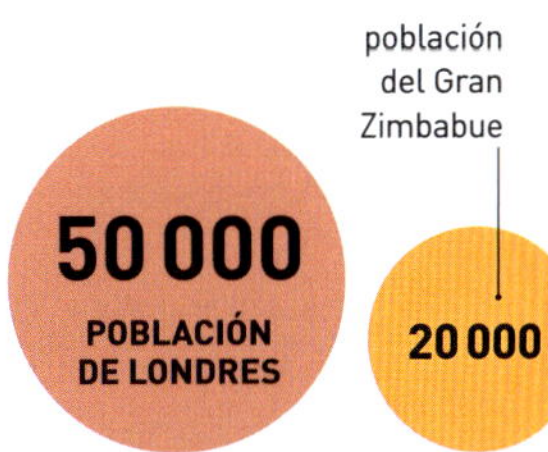

Edad de oro del Gran Zimbabue
A mediados del siglo XV, la población del Gran Zimbabue estaba justo por debajo de la mitad de la de Londres.

1448–1449

Ilustración de un manuscrito del periodo Muromachi. Las artes florecieron en Japón bajo el patrocinio de Ashikaga.

EN 1449, ASHIKAGA YOSHIMASA (1435–1490) SE CONVIRTIÓ EN SOGÚN, o dictador militar, de Japón. A pesar de que su reinado marcó un punto álgido del periodo Ashikaga o Muromachi (1336–1573), también estuvo plagado por los disturbios civiles. Las hambrunas repetidas provocaban alzamientos constantes, mientras que la práctica Ashikaga de conceder *tokuseirei*, o «actos de gracia», para cancelar deudas perjudicó a la economía. A pesar de ello, Ashikaga Yoshimasa gobernó durante un periodo de florecimiento cultural en sus posesiones de Higashiyama.

Nicolás V, el papa elegido en 1447, estaba decidido a poner fin al cisma provocado por el enfrentamiento de su predecesor con el **concilio de Basilea** (*véase* 1435–1437), así como a restaurar la paz en Italia y conseguir unas relaciones armoniosas con otros gobernantes. En el **concordato de Viena** de 1448, realizó concesiones al emperador Federico III, además de a varios príncipes alemanes, quienes a su vez abandonaron el concilio de Basilea y aceptaron el reconocimiento de algunos poderes pontificios. El año siguiente, el concilio de Basilea se disolvió y el antipapa, Félix V, abdicó a cambio de un puesto de cardenal. Esto marcó la **victoria definitiva del papado** sobre el movimiento conciliar.

Después de la muerte del emperador Juan VIII, su hermano Constantino XI Paleólogo (*véase* recuadro), accedió al trono en Constantinopla. Constantino sería el **último emperador bizantino**. Los otomanos habían derrotado a otro ejército cruzado de Juan Hunyadi, que había intentado expulsarles de los Balcanes en la segunda batalla de Kosovo en 1448, y habían recuperado Albania. Era evidente que no habría rescate europeo para los atribulados bizantinos; mientras tanto, los otomanos se acercaban a Constantinopla.

CONSTANTINO XI PALEÓLOGO
(1404–1453)

Fue coronado emperador de los restos de un imperio antaño magnífico, que ahora carecía de recursos para defenderse. Fue el último emperador de Bizancio, un país que perduró durante toda la Edad Media y que hizo de puente entre oriente y occidente. Falleció en las murallas de Constantinopla, tras haber hecho todo lo que estaba en sus manos para garantizar su defensa.

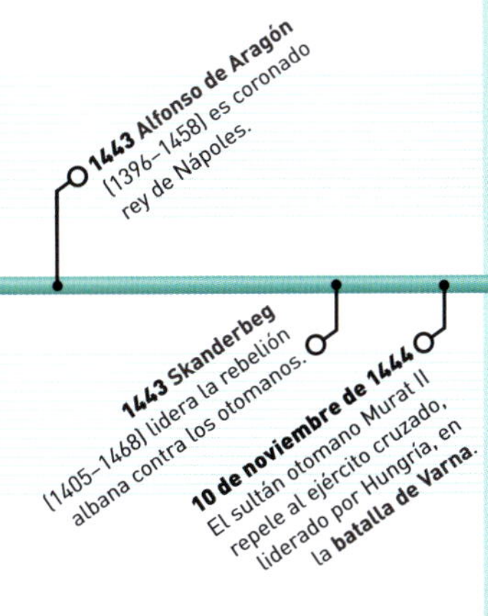

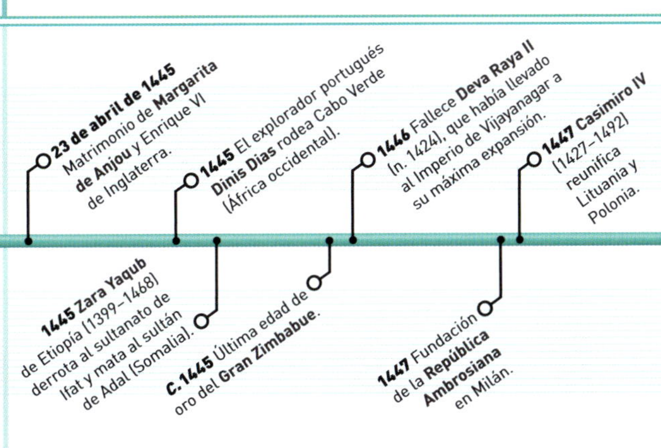

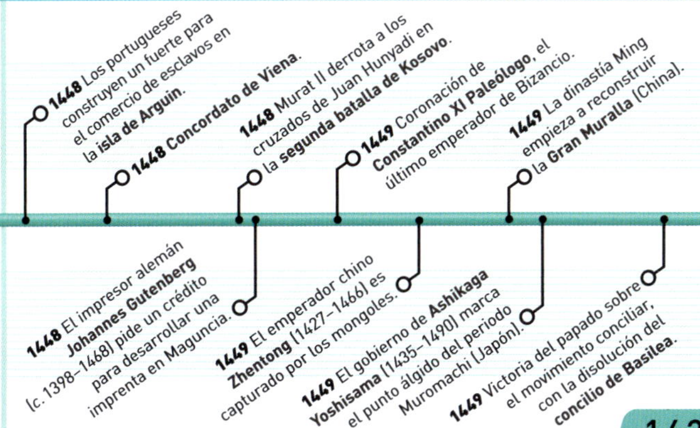

5

REFORMA Y EXPLORACIÓN 1450–1749

Los siglos XVI y XVII se vieron definidos por nuevos horizontes a medida que se exploraban nuevos territorios e ideas. La Reforma y los conflictos religiosos, la exploración del globo y la revolución científica sentaron las bases de nuevos conocimientos.

1450–1452

Detalle de la puerta del Paraíso del baptisterio de la catedral de Florencia, de Ghiberti, decorada con escenas del Antiguo Testamento.

LA CIVILIZACIÓN DEL GRAN ZIMBABUE, que prosperó en África suroriental (*véase* 1106–1110), entró en declive en el siglo xv, coincidiendo con el auge del **reino de Monomotapa** en la región situada entre los ríos Zambeze y Limpopo (en los actuales Zimbabue y Mozambique). Este reino fue la potencia dominante de la región durante más de un siglo, gracias al comercio de cobre, ganado, marfil, esclavos y oro con los asentamientos musulmanes de la costa. Los intentos de invasión portugueses en la década de 1570 acabaron en desastre, y la infiltración colonial no se produjo hasta la década de 1620 (*véase* 1629).

En el subcontinente indio, el **Sultanato de Delhi** quedó fracturado y dividido en poderes regionales enfrentados tras la invasión de Tamerlán en 1398. Sin embargo, en 1451, la nueva **dinastía afgana de los Lodi** recuperó el dominio del sultanato sobre la región, que conservó hasta que el mogol Baber la derrocó en 1526.

En Europa, **Lorenzo Ghiberti**, orfebre y escultor florentino, finalizó los relieves de la segunda puerta de bronce del baptisterio de Florencia en 1452. Tardó 21 años en realizar la primera hoja de la puerta, iniciada en 1403; y 27 en la segunda. Ese mismo año, **Leon Battista Alberti** publicaba *De re aedificatoria* (un tratado de arquitectura). Fueron dos obras maestras, cada una en su campo, que ejemplificaron la confianza y la osadía intelectual del Renacimiento florentino.

« **TODO ARTE**, POR MENOR QUE SEA, **EXIGE DEDICACIÓN ABSOLUTA**. »

Leon Battista Alberti, artista y humanista italiano (1404–1472)

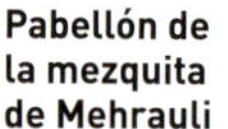

Pabellón de la mezquita de Mehrauli
Restos de la mezquita de Mehrauli (Delhi), construida durante el reinado de los Lodi (1451–1526), miembros de la última dinastía del Sultanato de Delhi.

1453

Fresco del siglo xvi que representa el sitio de Constantinopla, iniciado el 2 de abril de 1453 y concluido el 29 de mayo del mismo año, cuando los turcos otomanos tomaron la ciudad.

Derrota de los ingleses en Castillon
La batalla de Castillon acabó con todas las esperanzas de los reyes Plantagenet, de origen francés, sobre el trono de Francia.

LA GUERRA DE LOS CIEN AÑOS, un conflicto anglo-francés tristemente prolongado (*véase* 1411–1415) finalizó con la victoria absoluta de Francia en 1453. Todas las aspiraciones de los reyes ingleses Plantagenet, de origen francés, al trono de Francia se esfumaron definitivamente en **Castillon**, muy cerca de Burdeos. Dos años antes, la ciudad de Burdeos, que estuvo en manos inglesas durante unos 300 años, había caído en manos francesas. Esto provocó un último y desesperado intento de los ingleses de imponerse a las tropas del rey francés Carlos VII, que iban ganando fuerza en el suroeste de Francia. Los ingleses lograron **recuperar Burdeos**, pero en julio, su intento de salvar Castillon, un enclave inglés asediado por el ejército francés, fue un fracaso desastroso. También fue el primer gran conflicto europeo resuelto por la artillería, y los ingleses perdieron durante la batalla unos 4000 hombres, mientras que Francia apenas sufrió cien bajas. Tres meses más tarde Burdeos ya volvía a ser francesa, lo que dio fin a la **guerra de los Cien Años** y convirtió a **Calais** en la última posesión inglesa en Francia. En Inglaterra, esta derrota provocó el primero de los múltiples ataques de locura que sufrió su desventurado rey Enrique VI. Para Francia, en cambio, la victoria supuso un paso más hacia el objetivo de unificar el reino bajo un único soberano.

Tanto en **Asia occidental** como en las fronteras de la cristiandad, **Constantinopla**, la capital del **Imperio bizantino**, continuaba siendo el centro de la civilización cristiana ortodoxa, pero se enfrentaba a la amenaza del imperio musulmán de los turcos otomanos. Esta amenaza se materializó cuando el **sultán otomano Mehmet II**, apodado el Conquistador, que estaba convencido de que tan solo la conquista implacable podía garantizar una supremacía otomana duradera, consiguió reunir 80 000 hombres para atacar Constantinopla, mientras que los defensores de la ciudad no sumaban más de 7000. Además, Mehmet contaba con la mejor artillería del mundo en aquella época. Las antiguas y ruinosas murallas que protegían la capital bizantina resultaban totalmente inútiles ante una fuerza destructora como aquella, y la ciudad acabó rindiéndose a los otomanos en mayo de 1453.

1:12 **Sitio de Constantinopla**
Mehmed dirigió 80 000 hombres contra solo 7000 defensores regulares en el sitio de Constantinopla, cuyas murallas defendían también 30 000 civiles armados, pero la disparidad hizo casi inevitable la caída de la ciudad.

Conscientes de que su destino de conquistadores del mundo requería una capital imponente que reflejara todo su poder, los otomanos cuidaron y embellecieron la ciudad recién conquistada: la necesitaban como símbolo y estandarte de su nueva grandeza. Las magníficas edificaciones cristianas fueron transformadas en lugares de plegaria musulmana, y la ciudad se convirtió en el espejo de la **potencia militar otomana** durante más de 450 años. La conquista otomana de Constantinopla (que desde entonces pasó a llamarse Estambul) fue una clara señal de que los turcos otomanos eran la fuerza militar y política más poderosa de la región y de que se habían convertido en una amenaza innegable, no solo para lo que quedaba de la cristiandad en Asia occidental, sino para todo el continente europeo.

1451 Se establecen en **Delhi** los **Lodi**, la primera dinastía afgana.

30 de junio de 1451 Los franceses arrebatan **Burdeos** a los ingleses.

1451 Mehmet II asciende al **trono otomano**.

1452 El artista florentino **Lorenzo Ghiberti** termina las puertas del baptisterio de Florencia.

Junio de 1452 El papa Nicolás V publica *Dum diversas*, que da **autoridad religiosa a la trata de esclavos**.

1452 El erudito italiano **Leon Battista Alberti** publica *De re aedificatoria*.

2 de abril Los otomanos inician el **sitio de Constantinopla**, dirigidos por Mehmet II.

29 de mayo Las tropas otomanas de Mehmet II **toman Constantinopla**.

17 de julio Francia derrota a las fuerzas inglesas en la **batalla de Castillon**.

19 de octubre Francia arrebata de nuevo Burdeos a los ingleses y da **fin a la guerra de los Cien Años**.

1454–1455

« CIERTAMENTE **ES UNA IMPRENTA**, PERO UNA IMPRENTA **DE LA QUE FLUIRÁ UN RÍO INAGOTABLE... Y POR LA QUE DIOS DIFUNDIRÁ SU PALABRA.** »

Johannes Gutenberg, inventor e impresor alemán (*c.* 1398–1468)

EL TRATADO DE LODI SIRVIÓ PARA PONER FIN EN 1454 a casi cien años de guerras entre las **ambiciosas ciudades-estado de Italia**. Fue firmado por Milán, Venecia, Florencia, los Estados Pontificios y Nápoles después de que la caída de Constantinopla un año antes hiciera evidente la necesidad de presentar un frente cristiano unido.

Entre 1454 y 1455, el alemán **Johannes Gutenberg** produjo el primer libro de la historia impreso con una **imprenta** de tipos móviles: la Biblia de Gutenberg. Este nuevo y revolucionario método de impresión permitía producir con relativa facilidad miles de copias de libros. El resultado fue una extraordinaria **difusión de las ideas y los conocimientos**, especialmente porque las obras comenzaron a imprimirse también en lenguas vernáculas, y no solo en latín o en griego.

En Inglaterra, los ejércitos del duque de Somerset y del duque de York se enfrentaron el 22 de mayo de 1455 en la batalla de Saint Albans, que dio comienzo a la conocida como **guerra de las Dos Rosas**, una serie de guerras civiles que enfrentaron a dos ramas rivales de la **casa Plantagenet** aspirantes al trono: la de York y la de Lancaster. **Enrique VI**, un Lancaster, ocupaba el trono al principio de la guerra, pero la victoria y la coronación de **Eduardo IV** en 1461 parecieron inclinar la balanza en favor de la casa de York. La guerra continuó hasta 1485, año en que finalmente Enrique Tudor se convirtió en rey (*véase* 1483–1485).

Enrique VI de Inglaterra
Retrato anónimo de un rey con fama de pacífico y piadoso que padeció repetidas y largas crisis de una enfermedad mental grave.

Hacia mediados del siglo XV, **Prusia** (conquistada dos siglos antes por los caballeros teutónicos) estaba descontenta a causa de su bajo estatus dentro de los territorios bálticos de la orden teutónica. En 1454, los estados prusianos decidieron rebelarse y pidieron apoyo militar a Polonia en el conflicto que inició la **guerra de los Trece Años** contra los caballeros teutónicos, y que finalizó en el año 1466 con la división de Prusia en dos territorios: uno al este, aún controlado por la orden, y la llamada Prusia Real, convertida en un estado vasallo de los reyes de Polonia.

Biblia de Gutenberg
Aunque Johannes Gutenberg tan solo imprimió 180 ejemplares de su Biblia, marcó el inicio de la era del libro impreso.

1456–1460

Miniatura turca que muestra a las tropas de Mehmet II durante su infructuoso ataque a Belgrado en 1456.

LA IMPLACABLE EXPANSIÓN OTOMANA CONTINUÓ, tanto en la zona de los Balcanes como en Grecia, a medida que Mehmet II avanzaba en su determinación de conquistar el mundo para el islam. En 1456 intentó tomar **Belgrado**, pero las tropas húngaras consiguieron rechazarlo. Sin embargo, en 1459 el resto de **Serbia** ya se hallaba bajo su control. Simultáneamente los otomanos conquistaban la región del Peloponeso, situada en el sur de Grecia; la ciudad de Atenas cayó en el año 1456. A lo largo de las dos décadas siguientes, los otomanos lucharon por consolidar su dominio sobre los Balcanes, y lo consiguieron gracias a la conquista de **Bosnia** y **Herzegovina**. En la zona del mar Egeo, las islas que aún eran cristianas (principalmente venecianas y genovesas) corrían un peligro evidente.

En 1458, **Matías Corvino**, sobrino de Juan Hunyadi y el hombre que había dirigido la exitosa defensa de la ciudad de Belgrado contra las tropas de Mehmet II en 1456, fue proclamado **rey de Hungría**. Sin duda su reinado prometía mucho: no solo introducir a Hungría en el Renacimiento europeo, sino, además, aumentar el territorio y prestigio del país.

Aunque Corvino se vio sometido a la distracción permanente de tener que defender Hungría de las recurrentes incursiones otomanas, también tenía **ambiciones territoriales** hacia el oeste. Consiguió ampliar el territorio húngaro a expensas de **Bohemia**, contra cuyo soberano husita, Jorge de Podebrady (r. 1458–1471) obtuvo en 1468 una sanción papal que le autorizaba a emprender una cruzada. Durante esta, Corvino consiguió el control de **Moravia**, **Silesia** y **Lusacia**. No obstante, a largo plazo, dichas acciones desestabilizaron tanto a Hungría como a Bohemia y desencadenaron un conflicto con Federico III, entonces emperador del Sacro Imperio. Además, despertaron las suspicacias de la nobleza húngara, que temía perder su poder.

Pese a las primeras ganancias territoriales obtenidas por Corvino, la mayor parte de Hungría terminó cayendo durante la **conquista otomana** de 1526; y tanto Bohemia como lo que quedaba de Hungría quedaron finalmente bajo **dominio directo de los Habsburgo**.

9 de abril de 1454 Firma del **tratado de Lodi** en Lombardía (Italia).

1454 Estalla la **guerra de los Trece Años** entre Polonia y la orden Teutónica.

1454/1455 El impresor alemán Johannes Gutenberg publica la **Biblia de Gutenberg**.

18 de febrero de 1455 Muere el pintor italiano **Fra Angelico** (n. 1395).

8 de abril de 1455 El **papa Calixto III** sucede a Nicolás V.

22 de mayo de 1455 La batalla de **Saint Albans** entre los rivales que se disputan el trono inglés inicia la guerra de las Dos Rosas.

1 de diciembre de 1455 Muere el artista florentino **Lorenzo Ghiberti** (n. 1378).

21–22 de julio de 1456 Victoria húngara sobre los otomanos en la **batalla de Belgrado**.

20 de agosto de 1456 **Vlad III** (el Empalador) accede al **trono de Rumanía**; su crueldad inspira la leyenda de Drácula.

20 de enero de 1458 **Matías Corvino** accede al **trono de Hungría** a los 14 años de edad.

Agosto de 1458 Eneas Silvio Piccolomini se convierte en el **papa Pío II**, el papa humanista más célebre del Renacimiento.

1456 Los otomanos toman **Atenas**.

1459 Los otomanos se anexionan **Serbia**.

1461–1465

El zar Iván III, llamado Iván el Grande, declaró a Moscú libre del yugo tártaro rechazando el pago del tributo al kan.

EL ASCENSO DE LUIS XI, APODADO «la araña universal», al trono de Francia en julio de 1461 marcó un punto de inflexión en la evolución del estado francés. Fuera cual fuera su poder nominal, la **influencia** de los monarcas franceses medievales era **muy restringida**. Tan solo controlaban directamente una zona muy limitada, sobre todo en el norte y el centro del país, en su mayor parte gobernado por señores generalmente hostiles, el más amenazador de los cuales fue el **duque de Borgoña** Carlos el Temerario (*véase* 1472–1476). Al final de la guerra de los Cien Años en 1453, Francia estaba en quiebra, pero en 1481 Luis XI no solamente había conseguido acabar con el último de los duques de Borgoña y obtenido el control de **Artois**, **Picardía y Borgoña**, sino que gracias a herencias y a una hábil diplomacia, también se había anexionado **Rosellón**, **Cerdaña**, **Maine**, **Provenza y Anjou**. Esta ampliación de la **autoridad real** centralizada fue un paso esencial hacia la posterior emergencia de un estado francés unificado y mucho más fuerte. De hecho, las relaciones entre la monarquía francesa y sus súbditos más poderosos fueron delicadas hasta bien entrado el siglo XVII. Al igual que en otros lugares, también fue preciso afirmar la autoridad y negociar con las élites nobles y de provincias. Este proceso dual, fundamental para la construcción de la **primera Francia moderna**, produjo numerosas fricciones y tensiones hasta mucho después del reinado de Luis XI.

Luis XI de Francia
Coronado rey de Francia en 1461, Luis XI fue ampliando su dominio territorial a lo largo de sus 22 años de reinado.

La expansión a una escala todavía mayor también marcó el desarrollo de **Moscovia** (el Gran Ducado de Moscú) después del ascenso al trono de **Iván III el Grande** en **marzo de 1462**. El declive del poder mongol durante los siglos XIV y XV, y la caída de **Constantinopla** (Estambul) en 1453 habían abierto el camino no solo para que Moscovia pudiera reafirmar su liderazgo en el mundo ortodoxo, sino para que desafiara cualquier último intento mongol de dominación. Este mismo proceso impulsó la expansión que caracterizó a **Rusia** hasta bien entrado el siglo XIX.

Sin lugar a dudas, la más notable de las anexiones llevadas a cabo bajo el mandato de Iván III fue la del **territorio de Nóvgorod**, bastante despoblado, de escasa importancia económica y poco conocido, aunque extraordinariamente rico en recursos naturales. En 1478, Iván lo anexionó sin más.

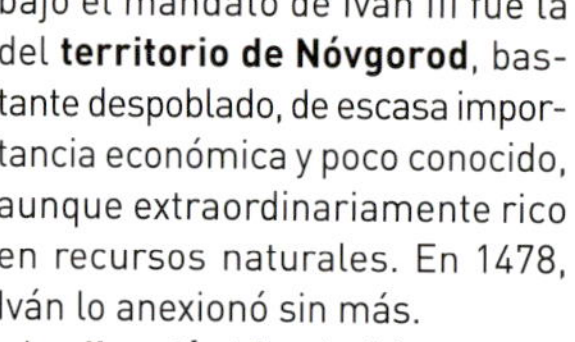

La **dinastía Ming** había aumentado la estabilidad y prosperidad de China, pero se enfrentaba a múltiples amenazas internas a su autoridad, y el conflicto con los **mongoles** del norte todavía no había acabado. La mayoría de las revueltas eran consecuencia del hambre, pero algunas también se debían a la postura cada vez más autocrática y rígida del **imperio Ming**. Todas ellas fueron reprimidas con increíble dureza. En 1464, el mismo año en que el **emperador Chenghua** ascendía al trono se rebelaron los **pueblos nativos miao y yao** en las provincias de Huguang y de Guangxi, en China sur-central; fueron necesarios dos años para sofocar la rebelión. Además de los **160 000 soldados** destinados en el sur, se enviaron 30 000 más a las dos provincias. Resulta imposible calcular la cantidad de muertos. La revuelta se reavivó en 1467 y, de nuevo y a mayor escala, en 1475.

1466–1469

El castillo de Malbork (hoy en Polonia), cuartel general de los caballeros teutónicos, era la fortaleza medieval de ladrillo más grande de Europa.

LA GUERRA DE LOS TREINTA AÑOS entre Polonia-Lituania y los **caballeros teutónicos**, miembros de una orden militar fundada en Palestina, terminó gracias al **segundo tratado de Torun**, firmado en el año 1466. Los caballeros teutónicos, poderosos desde principios del siglo XIII (*véase* 1236–1240), se vieron obligados a entregar la mayor parte de la mitad occidental de su territorio a **Prusia**, que lo cedió a su vez a la corona polaco-lituana por su ayuda durante la guerra.

La **guerra de Onin**, que estalló en 1467 y **duró once años**, puso de manifiesto la gran fragilidad política de **Japón** y la relativa impotencia de los **sogunes Ashikaga**, que gobernaban el país desde 1333. Japón quedó devastado y entró en más de un siglo de turbulencias (*Sengoku jidai* o **periodo de los Estados Guerreros**), durante el cual varios señores feudales, o daimios, trataron de aniquilar a sus rivales. La guerra empezó como una disputa sucesoria para decidir quién debía suceder al anciano sogún **Ashikaga Yoshimasa**, que había decidido retirarse. El clan Hosokawa apoyaba al hermano de Yoshimasa, mientras que el clan Yamana prefería a su hijo, aún en la primera infancia. Duran-

« **LA CAPITAL**, QUE CREÍAMOS **FLORECERÍA** DURANTE **DIEZ MIL AÑOS**, SIRVE AHORA DE **GUARIDA** A **LOS LOBOS**. »

Onin Ki, relato de la guerra de Onin (finales del siglo XV–mediados del siglo XVI)

Espada de samurái
Esta katana del siglo XV, con su vaina, es similar a las que se usaron en la guerra de Onin. Podía cortar de un tajo con un solo movimiento.

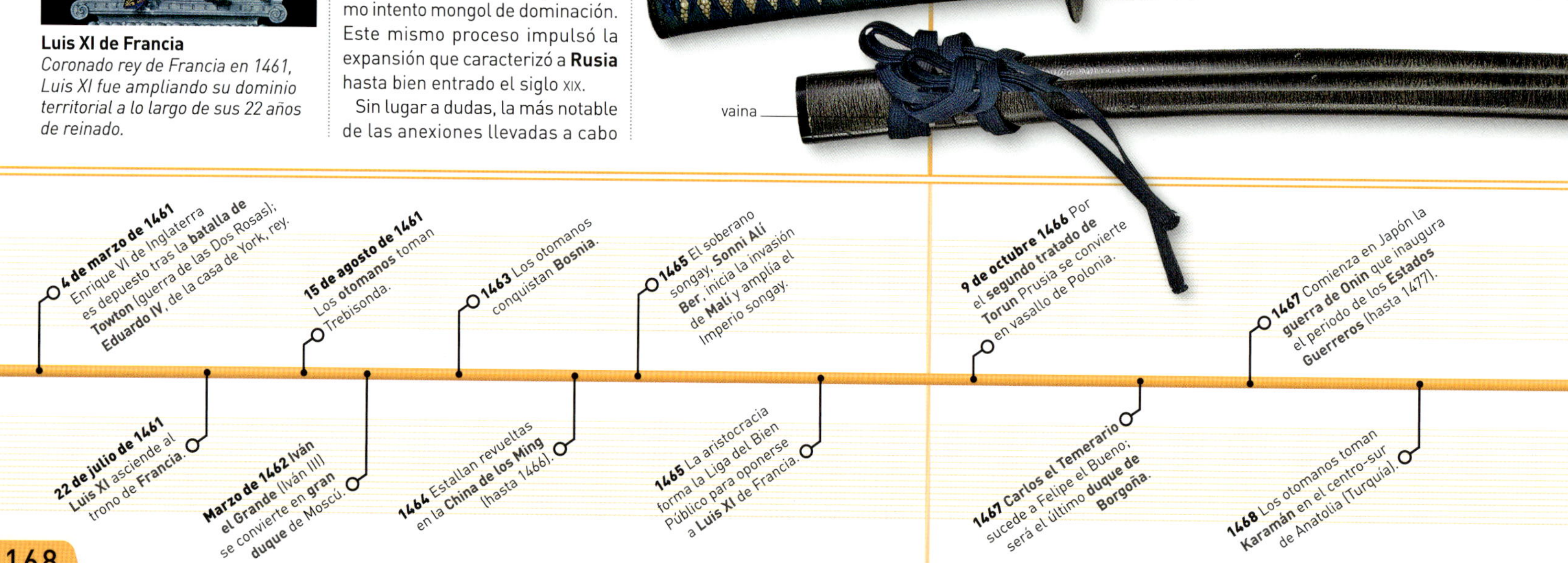

Castilla y Aragón
Los reinos de Castilla y de Aragón se convirtieron en una monarquía conjunta gracias al matrimonio de Isabel y Fernando en 1469.

te el enfrentamiento no solo quedó **completamente destruida** la capital, **Kioto**, sino que los propios clanes Hosokawa y Yamana acabaron perdiendo su poder y prestigio a medida que avanzaba el conflicto, que cada vez fue cobrando tintes más sangrientos.

En 1469, el matrimonio de **Isabel de Castilla** (que accedió al trono castellano en 1474) con **Fernando de Aragón** (que heredó el reino en 1474) condujo a la **unificación de una España decididamente cristiana**, que se convirtió en el estado más poderoso de toda Europa en el siglo XVI. Isabel tenía 17 años cuando se casó con Fernando y, al hacerlo, se arriesgó a incurrir en la ira de su hermanastro mayor, Enrique IV, que la percibía como una amenaza a su propio poder. Sin embargo, la boda, celebrada en Valladolid, supuso el principio de un **periodo fundamental de la historia española**. Al cabo de ocho años, Isabel y Fernando ya gobernaban conjuntamente Castilla y Aragón, aunque ambos reinos seguían estando separados administrativa, política y económicamente, por lo que se vieron abrumados de forma continua por rivalidades y prioridades contradictorias.

No hubo ningún monarca español que fuese capaz de resolver este conflicto de una manera satisfactoria, ni siquiera durante el apogeo del poder español en el siglo XVI y principios del XVII. En cualquier caso, el potencial de España como fuerza dominante en la Europa renacentista fue innegable durante el reinado de Isabel y Fernando, a quienes el papa Alejandro VI dio el nombre de **Reyes Católicos** el 19 de diciembre de 1496. Tanto la tenacidad de Isabel como la habilidad política de Fernando contribuyeron a expandir y transformar sus reinos en una potencia europea y mundial de primer orden.

« EL **MAR CON FIN** SERÁ GRIEGO O **ROMANO**: EL **MAR SIN FIN** ES **PORTUGUÉS**. »

Fernando Pessoa, poeta y escritor portugués (1885-1935)

HACIA 1470, LOS EXPLORADORES PORTUGUESES ya habían recorrido la **costa oeste de África** y habían llegado hasta la actual Sierra Leona. Había sido un proceso complejo, que se vio limitado por las naves de las que disponían, principalmente galeras y cocas, poco adecuadas para la navegación a largas distancias. Los objetivos de dichas exploraciones eran bastante difusos y no iban mucho más allá de la esperanza de encontrar el origen del **comercio transahariano del oro** y de explotar el **comercio de esclavos de África occidental**. La muerte, en 1460, del **príncipe Enrique el Navegante**, el primer adalid de la exploración portuguesa (*véase* 1434), impidió que se avanzara mucho más. Sin embargo, en 1469, el **rey portugués Alfonso V** accedió (a cambio de una renta anual) a que un mercader de Lisboa, **Fernão Gomes**, siguiera impulsando los intereses portugueses a lo largo de la costa occidental africana. Los resultados fueron espectaculares. A los cinco años, Gomes había explorado 3200 km de costa más. Además de reclamar una serie de **enclaves comerciales** que resultaron muy **lucrativos** (*véase* 1480–1482), Portugal llevó a cabo las primeras incursiones en el Atlántico Sur.

4000 KILÓMETROS ALCANCE DEL IMPERIO INCA

El **Imperio inca**, cuya duración fue inferior a la de sus vecinos aztecas del norte, se formó gracias a una serie de conquistas a partir de 1438 desde el corazón de los **Andes**, en el centro de Perú. **Túpac Inca Yupanqui** (Topa Inca), que **subió al trono en 1471**, había sido nombrado **jefe del ejército inca** en 1463 y había aumentado de manera significativa el control de los incas hacia el norte, en el actual Ecuador. El imperio se extendía a lo largo de aproximadamente 4000 km. La principal contribución de Topa Inca a la **expansión inca** fue la conquista del reino peruano de **Chimor**.

Soberano inca
Esta pintura (siglo XVIII) muestra a Túpac Inca Yupanqui (Topa Inca), quinto inca de la dinastía Hanan.

Exploradores portugueses
Fernão Gomes (dcha.) prosiguió las exploraciones impulsadas por Enrique el Navegante (izda.), como refleja el Monumento a los Descubridores (Lisboa).

En el Sureste Asiático, el reino de **Champa** (en el Vietnam actual), que existía desde el siglo VII, **fue destruido en 1471** a manos de las tropas vietnamitas que arrasaron su capital, Vijaya. Lo que quedó pasó a ser un territorio vasallo de los vietnamitas.

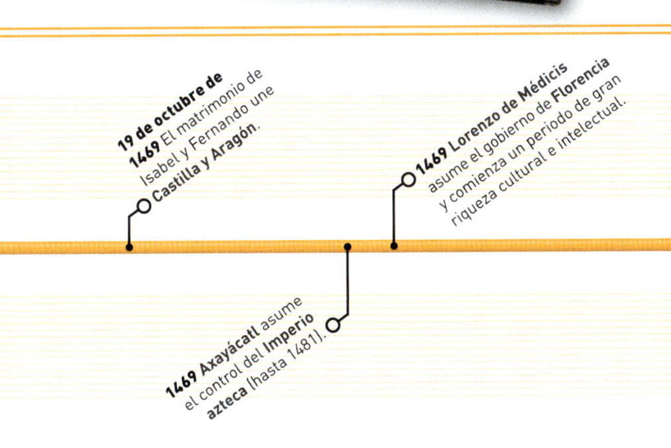

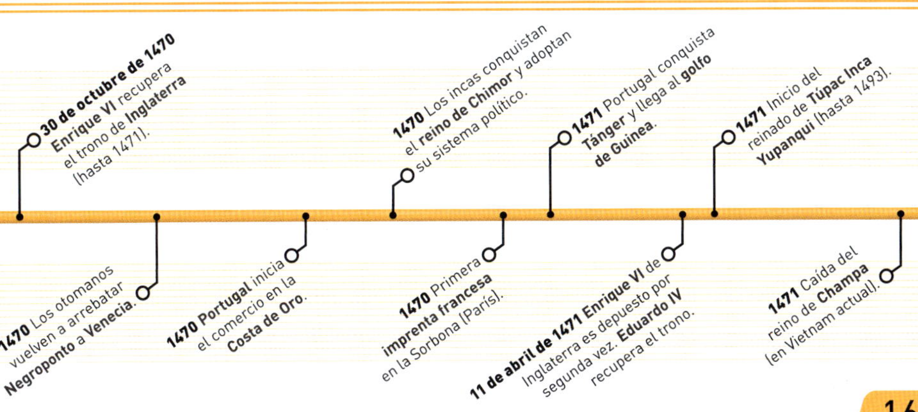

1472–1476

Relieve en madera de la principal deidad azteca, Quetzalcoátl, en Teotihuacán, cerca de la actual Ciudad de México.

TRAS LA TOMA DE CONSTANTINOPLA EN 1453, el conquistador otomano **Mehmet II** se propuso no solo ampliar la dominación otomana en la zona de los Balcanes, sino también reafirmarla en Anatolia, donde se había visto mermada tras la primera invasión de Tamerlán a principios del siglo XV (*véase* 1401–1403). En ese momento, la oposición de los **turcomanos del Carnero Blanco**, dirigidos por **Uzun Hasan**, era todavía más evidente en la región. Varias potencias cristianas, especialmente Venecia, habían intentado, aunque sin demasiado éxito, una unión de las fuerzas cristianas contra la temida expansión otomana. El resultado de los esfuerzos de Uzun Hasan fue una gran derrota en la **batalla de Otlukbeli**, donde la artillería otomana barrió a la caballería ligera turcomana.

Hacia mediados de la década de 1470, la región de Borgoña se encontraba en pleno apogeo. **El condado y el ducado de Borgoña** eran sus territorios principales y fueron concedidos al primer duque de Borgoña, Felipe el Atrevido, hermano del rey **Carlos V de Francia**, en el año 1363. En 1369, el matrimonio entre Felipe y la condesa de Flandes, Margarita, le permitió adquirir **Flandes y Artois**, que actualmente son parte importante de **Bélgica**. Posteriormente, **Felipe el Bueno**, nieto de Felipe el Atrevido, anexionó partes del noreste de Francia y gran parte de la Holanda actual. Pese a su extensión, dichas posesiones distaban mucho de ser un territorio único y continuo. Es más, como muchas de ellas se hallaban en el **Sacro Imperio**, estaban, al menos teóricamente, sometidas al emperador, al igual que las tierras francesas de Borgoña estaban sometidas nominalmente al rey de Francia. Sin embargo, su envergadura y, sobre todo, el hecho de que incluyera a muchos de los más prósperos centros comerciales de **Países Bajos**, hicieron de Borgoña una potencia formidable. El heredero de Felipe el Bueno, **Carlos el Calvo**, recibió este estado entre estados en 1467 y decidió transformarlo no solamente en un territorio continuo (lo que consiguió en 1472, gracias a una audaz combinación de compras y conquistas), sino también reafirmar su independencia como reino. A los borgoñones se opuso inevitablemente el rey de Francia Luis XI, para quien la expansión de Carlos el Temerario era un desafío directo. Luis tenía como aliados a los **ejércitos mercenarios suizos**. En cuatro meses, en lo que hoy es el noroeste de Suiza, los borgoñones sufrieron dos derrotas desastrosas a manos en Grandson y Morat.

Por último, en el continente americano, el rígidamente jerarquizado **Imperio azteca** (1428–1521) llegó a convertirse en una extraordinaria potencia militar y se impuso con enorme brutalidad a sus vecinos en el **centro de México**, desde **Tenochtitlán**, su capital. **Axayácatl**, que subió al trono azteca en 1469, amplió de manera sustancial las fronteras del imperio, sobre todo tras haber conquistado el estado de **Tlatelolco en 1473**.

Expansión de Borgoña
Este mapa muestra los territorios de Carlos el Calvo, que inició una agresiva política de expansión. Los ducados de Bar y de Lorena dieron a Carlos un territorio casi continuo en 1475.

Mar del Norte
Calais
Brujas
Amberes
DUCADO DE BRABANTE
CONDADO DE FLANDES
CONDADO DE HAINAUT
Colonia
SACRO IMPERIO
CONDADO DE VERMANDOIS
DUCADO DE LUXEMBURGO
Luxemburgo
París
FRANCIA
DUCADO DE BAR
DUCADO DE LORENA
DUCADO DE BORGOÑA
CONDADO DE BORGOÑA
CONDADO DE CHAROLAIS
CONDADO DE MÂCON
Zúrich

CLAVE
- Territorios en 1467
- Adquisiciones hasta 1475
- Frontera del Sacro Imperio

Tambores otomanos
Jenízaros del ejército otomano desfilando con los tambores que usaban para animar a los soldados durante la batalla.

1477–1479

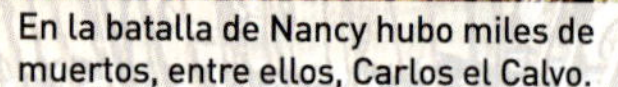
En la batalla de Nancy hubo miles de muertos, entre ellos, Carlos el Calvo.

EN ENERO DE 1477, LAS FUERZAS BORGOÑONAS de Carlos el Calvo se enfrentaron de nuevo contra los suizos en **Nancy** (Lorena). Sufrieron una terrible derrota, y el cadáver del duque fue encontrado boca abajo en un lago congelado. **Luis XI** (*véase* 1461) se apoderó de los territorios borgoñones en Francia, y los de Países Bajos pasaron a los Habsburgo gracias al matrimonio de la única hija de Carlos, Margarita, con Maximiliano I, futuro emperador del Sacro Imperio.

William Caxton (*c.* 1420–1492), un mercader inglés que conoció la imprenta por sus viajes al continente, estableció la **primera imprenta de Inglaterra en 1476** e imprimió el primer libro un año después. Publicó 87 libros, muchos de los cuales también tradujo.

Imprenta de Caxton
La primera imprenta de Inglaterra, fundada por William Caxton en Westminster (Londres), produjo su primer libro en 1477.

1472 Portugal descubre la isla de **Fernando Poo** frente a la costa occidental africana.

1472 Piero della Francesca pinta su *Sacra conversación* o *Pala de Brera*.

1472 Primera edición de las *Etimologías* de san Isidoro de Sevilla, la primera **enciclopedia cristiana**.

1473 Los **aztecas** vencen en **Tlatelolco** y lo anexionan.

1473 Venecia destruye **Esmirna** y toma **Chipre**.

11 de agosto de 1473 Los otomanos vencen a los **turcomanos** en la **batalla de Otlukbeli**.

1474 El **gran ducado de Moscú** incorpora los territorios de **Nóvgorod**.

1474 Los **Habsburgo** austriacos reconocen la independencia de la **Confederación Suiza**.

1474 La **tratado de Utrecht** concede a la **Liga Hanseática** grandes ventajas comerciales en Inglaterra.

1475 Máxima expansión de Borgoña bajo el mandato de **Carlos el Calvo**.

2 de marzo de 1476 Los **suizos** vencen a los **borgoñones** en **Grandson** (Suiza).

1476 Los **incas** conquistan la costa sur de **Perú**.

22 de junio de 1476 Los **suizos** vencen a los **borgoñones** en **Morat** (Suiza).

5 de enero de 1477 Derrota de Borgoña en la **batalla de Nancy**: **muere Carlos el Calvo** (n. 1433).

1477 Luis XI de Francia funda el Servicio Postal Real para acelerar las comunicaciones reales.

Construido en 1482 como San Jorge de la Mina, Elmina fue uno de los primeros fuertes comerciales portugueses en la costa occidental africana (actual Ghana).

« **NO ES NECESARIO TENER ESPERANZAS** PARA **LANZARSE, NI** TENER **ÉXITO** PARA **PERSEVERAR.** »

Carlos el Calvo, duque de Borgoña (1433–1477)

Los otomanos prosiguieron su expansión con el **tratado de Constantinopla** de 1479, que puso fin a una guerra intermitente con Venecia, iniciada en 1463. Confirmaba a los **otomanos** como una **potencia naval** de importancia creciente, además de otorgarles el control de las islas griegas de **Negroponto (Eubea)** y Lemnos, en el norte del Egeo. **Venecia** seguía siendo una gran potencia en la región, pero no quería arriesgar los lucrativos tratos comerciales con los otomanos.

En la península Ibérica, **Juana** de Castilla, llamada la **Beltraneja, esposa de Alfonso V de Portugal** y sobrina de **Isabel I** cuestionó el ascenso al trono de esta en 1474, en parte para desalentar las pretensiones de Castilla a la exploración de la costa atlántica africana. El punto clave de la disputa era qué país reclamaría como suyas las islas atlánticas (Canarias, Azores y Madeira), que tanto Portugal como Castilla habían ido colonizando desde principios del siglo xv. El **tratado de Alcáçovas** confirmó el derecho de Castilla a las Canarias y el de Portugal a las Azores y Madeira, además de al África occidental.

87

SON LOS **LIBROS PUBLICADOS** POR LA **IMPRENTA** DE **CAXTON**

HACIA 1440 SE HABÍAN ESTABLECIDO TRES REINOS MOSSI en África occidental, aproximadamente en lo que hoy es Burkina Faso: Tengkodogo, Yatenga y Uagadugú. A partir de 1480 y gracias a una caballería formidable, explotaron el **gradual declive de Malí** frente a la **expansión songay** y llevaron a cabo varias incursiones en los territorios de Malí. Fueron una presencia importante hasta la colonización francesa, que tuvo lugar unos 400 años más tarde.

Por otro lado, el año 1482 presenció dos hitos cruciales en la historia de la **exploración portuguesa** y la colonización de **África occidental**. El primero fue la construcción de **San Jorge de la Mina**, o de Elmina, en lo que posteriormente se conocería como **Costa de Oro** (en la actual **Ghana**). Se trataba de una factoría fortificada, construida bajo la autoridad real, y el primer asentamiento permanente europeo en el África subsahariana, destinado a garantizar el monopolio portugués del **comercio del oro en África occidental**, inmensamente lucrativo. A principios del siglo xvi pasaban por Elmina 680 kg de oro anuales.

El segundo hito fue la serie de viajes de **Diogo Cão** hacia el sur y a lo largo de la costa oeste de África. **Juan II**, el nuevo rey de Portugal, que **ascendió al trono en 1481** y que comprometió al país en una agresiva política de expansión, financió dichas expediciones. **En su primer viaje, Cão** consiguió llegar hasta la desembocadura del Congo (que reclamó para Portugal). En su segundo viaje, realizado entre 1484 y 1486, avanzó casi **1600 km más al sur**, hasta alcanzar la bahía de Walbis (en la actual Namibia), que también reclamó para el **trono portugués**. Ambos viajes fueron toda una demostración de tenacidad épica frente a las corrientes y los vientos constantemente desfavorables, que fueron un descubrimiento desalentador. Las condiciones de navegación por la **costa occidental de África hasta el golfo de Guinea** eran por lo general benignas, gracias a los vientos alisios del noreste y a la corriente de Guinea; sin embargo, hacia el sur, las condiciones se complicaban mucho más. El logro de Cão fue impresionante, pero no hizo más que subrayar que, de existir una ruta práctica hacia el océano Índico y hacia Oriente, tendrían que ser navegantes portugueses posteriores (sobre todo **Bartolomeu Dias** en 1487) quienes abrieran la nueva ruta en el **Atlántico Sur**.

Cruz de Cão

El explorador portugués Diogo Cão marcó sus paradas en la costa occidental de África con imponentes cruces de piedra.

LA INQUISICIÓN ESPAÑOLA

Fundada por los Reyes Católicos Isabel y Fernando en 1478, su objetivo era el de imponer una identidad cristiana y católica a todos los territorios de España. Los tribunales se encargaban de juzgar a los herejes (en aquella época, tanto judíos como conversos judaizantes), a quienes se castigaba y expulsaba. Tras la caída de Granada en 1492, también se aplicó a los musulmanes. Fue suprimida en 1820.

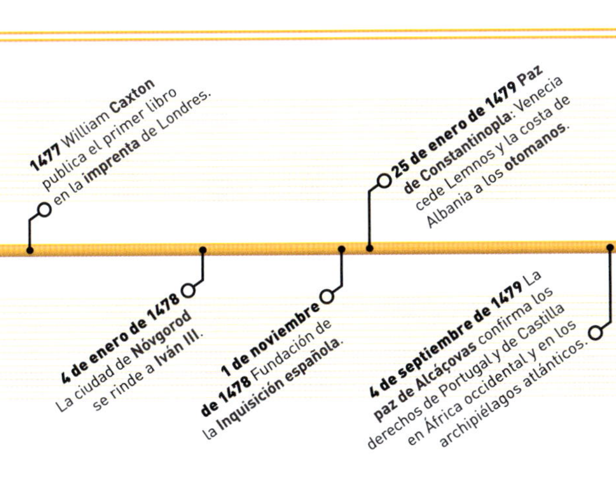

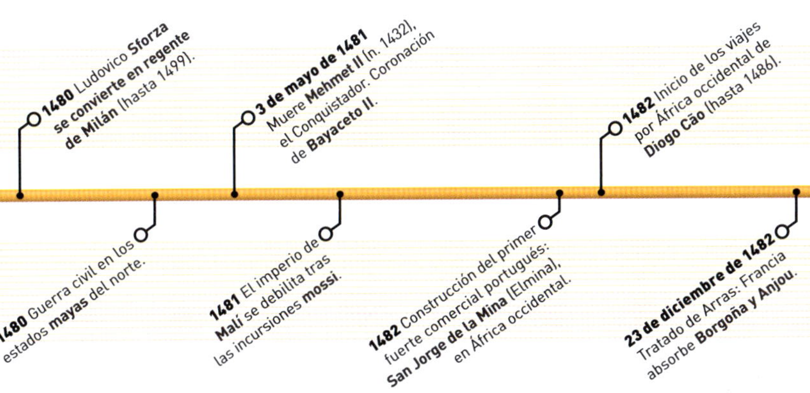

VIAJES DE EXPLORACIÓN

CIRCUNNAVEGACIÓN DEL GLOBO EN LA ERA DE LOS DESCUBRIMIENTOS

El viaje de Cristóbal Colón a través del Atlántico en 1492 impulsó una exploración del mundo sin precedentes, primero por portugueses y españoles, y luego por holandeses, ingleses y franceses. En 1700, los colonizadores europeos ya se habían establecido en todo el mundo.

A los exploradores europeos les motivaban la gloria, el celo cristiano y, sobre todo, el oro, las especias y los esclavos. El objetivo era Oriente, fuente de riquezas legendarias, y las rutas marítimas permitían evitar a los estados musulmanes, que bloqueaban las terrestres. En 1488, Portugal había logrado rodear África; diez años más tarde, llegaron a India y, en 1512, a las islas de las Especias, que luego les disputaron los holandeses. Los españoles zarparon hacia occidente e hicieron un descubrimiento trascendental: América, un continente desconocido. En la década de 1550 ya habían conquistado dos imperios (azteca e inca) y creado uno propio en el Nuevo Mundo. En 1522 también habían completado la primera circunnavegación del globo. Inglaterra y Francia centraron sus primeros esfuerzos en rodear América del Norte: no lo lograron, pero sentaron allí las bases de otros dos imperios europeos.

« MIS COMPAÑEROS Y YO SUFRIMOS UNA **ENFERMEDAD** DEL **CORAZÓN** QUE SOLO PUEDE **CURAR** EL **ORO**. »

Hernán Cortés, explorador español, sobre su conquista del Imperio azteca (1519)

Principales viajes europeos
Este mapa muestra las fechas y rutas de los primeros viajes europeos exploración, desde los de Cristóbal Colón, en 1492, hasta los de Francis Drake en 1577–1580. Los barcos tardaban meses en atravesar los vastos océanos, a menudo con sistemas de navegación rudimentarios.

1:13 **Supervivencia de la expedición de Magallanes**
En septiembre de 1519, Magallanes zarpó de España con 237 hombres. Tres años después, regresaron 18. El propio Magallanes murió en Filipinas en 1521.

5 NAVES EN 1519
1 NAVE EN 1522

Naves al mando de Magallanes
Cinco naves emprendieron la circunnavegación del globo. Dos naufragaron, otra fue abandonada y otra desertó. Solo volvió la Victoria.

25 MILLONES AMÉRICA CENTRAL 1519
población en millones en 1565: 2,5
POBLACIÓN NATIVA ESTIMADA DE AMÉRICA CENTRAL

11 MILLONES PERÚ 1519
población en millones en 1565: 1,5
POBLACIÓN NATIVA ESTIMADA DE PERÚ

Efecto en la población
La conquista española tuvo un efecto devastador sobre la población nativa, a la que sustituyeron esclavos africanos.

INTERCAMBIO COLOMBINO

Alimentos nuevos –y enfermedades– viajaron entre el Nuevo Mundo, Europa, África y Asia como resultado directo de estas expediciones oceánicas, y transformaron culturas y economías. En algunos casos, los resultados fueron beneficiosos, y en otros, fatales. A América llegaron animales domésticos (como caballos, cerdos y vacas) y cultivos (como el trigo, el arroz, el azúcar y el café), mientras cruzaban el Atlántico en sentido inverso plantas como el maíz, las patatas, los tomates, el tabaco y otras. Las enfermedades viajaron en una sola dirección principal: las enfermedades conocidas hacía ya mucho tiempo en Eurasia –como la fiebre tifoidea, las paperas, la viruela y la gripe– resultaron epidémicas entre los indígenas de América.

COSTE E IMPACTO

Las mejoras náuticas permitieron la exploración marítima europea, pero las travesías seguían siendo arduas, y muchas naves desaparecían. El destino de la flota de Magallanes en 1519–1522 dio fe de estos riesgos.

Las relaciones con los pueblos nativos fueron tensas, y muchas acabaron en violencia. Los europeos vieron en los indígenas un recurso a explotar y cristianizar. La destrucción de su modo de vida tradicional y las enfermedades europeas importadas causaron una mortalidad masiva. La mezcla de mundos hasta entonces separados tuvo un impacto enorme (a menudo positivo para los europeos y negativo para los indígenas), con la introducción de animales y plantas en entornos nuevos.

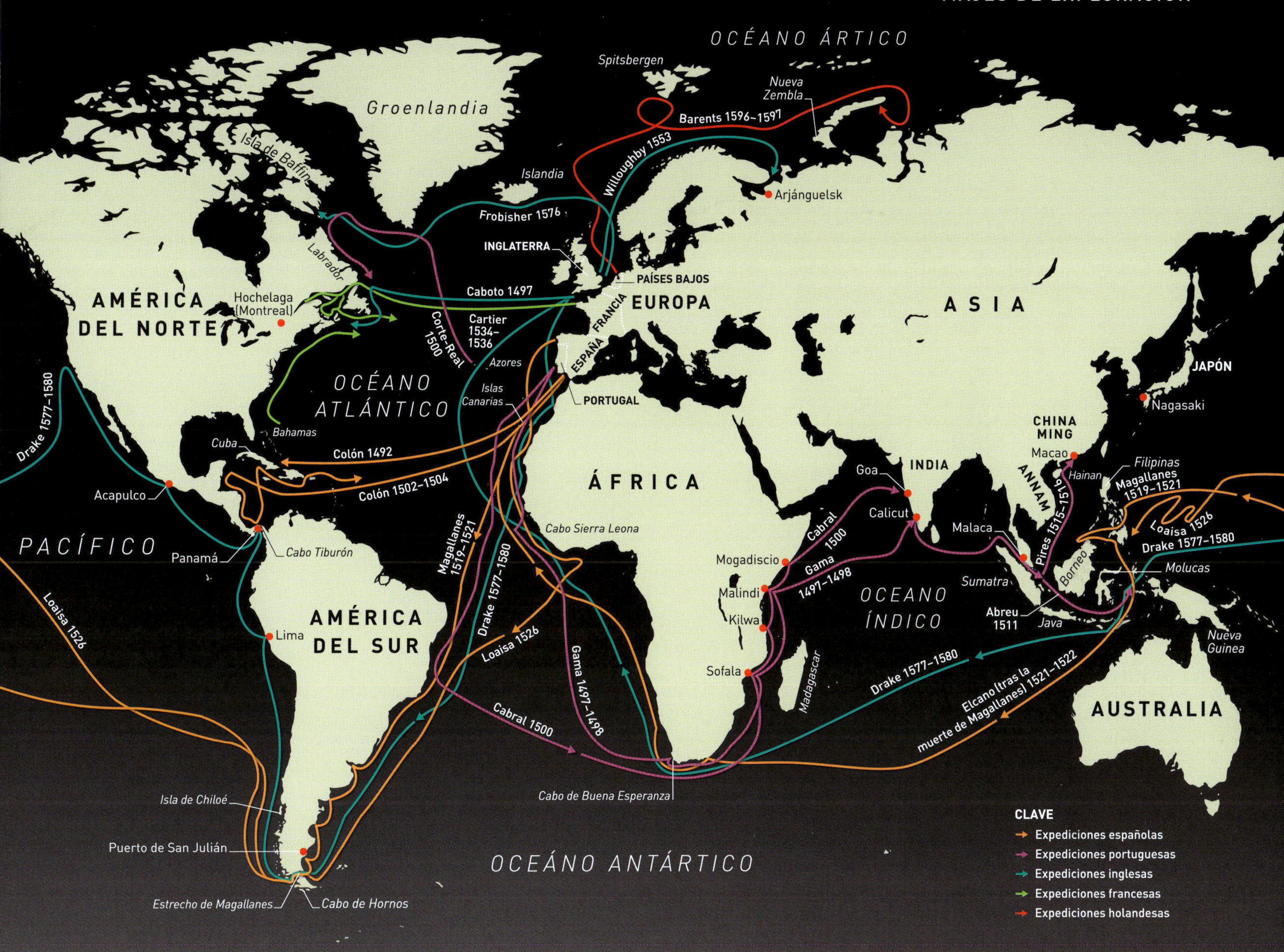

OCÉANO ÁRTICO
Spitsbergen
Nueva Zembla
Groenlandia
Barents 1596–1597
Isla de Baffin
Willoughby 1553
Islandia
Arjánguelsk
Frobisher 1576
INGLATERRA
Labrador
PAÍSES BAJOS
Caboto 1497
AMÉRICA DEL NORTE
Hochelaga (Montreal)
Cartier 1534–1536
Corte-Real 1500
FRANCIA
EUROPA
ASIA
ESPAÑA
Azores
OCÉANO ATLÁNTICO
Islas Canarias
PORTUGAL
JAPÓN
Nagasaki
Drake 1577–1580
Bahamas
Cuba
Colón 1492
CHINA MING
Macao
Colón 1502–1504
ÁFRICA
INDIA
Goa
ANNAM
Hainan
Filipinas
Magallanes 1519–1521
Acapulco
Cabo Sierra Leona
Calicut
Cabral 1500
Malaca
Loaisa 1526
Pires 1515–1516
Drake 1577–1580
PACÍFICO
Panamá
Cabo Tiburón
Magallanes 1519–1521
Mogadiscio
Gama 1497–1498
Borneo
Molucas
Malindi
Sumatra
Kilwa
OCÉANO ÍNDICO
Abreu 1511
Java
Nueva Guinea
Lima
AMÉRICA DEL SUR
Drake 1577–1580
Loaisa 1526
Loaisa 1526
Gama 1497–1498
Sofala
Madagascar
Drake 1577–1580
Elcano (tras la muerte de Magallanes) 1521–1522
Cabral 1500
AUSTRALIA
Cabo de Buena Esperanza
Isla de Chiloé
Puerto de San Julián
OCEÁNO ANTÁRTICO
Estrecho de Magallanes
Cabo de Hornos

CLAVE
- Expediciones españolas
- Expediciones portuguesas
- Expediciones inglesas
- Expediciones francesas
- Expediciones holandesas

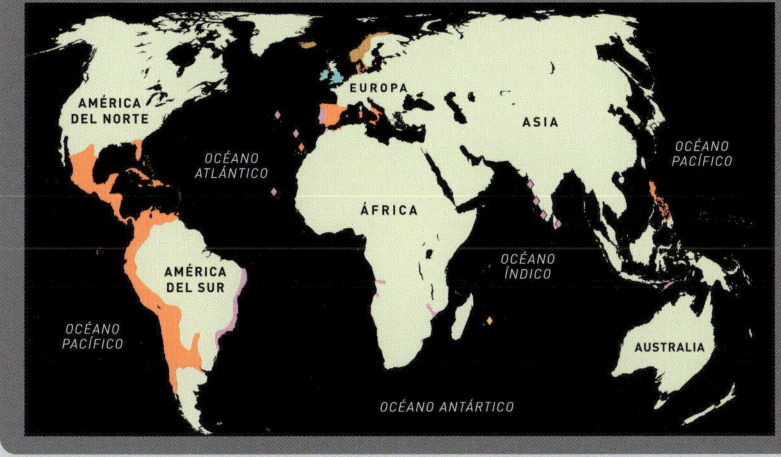

1600 España tomó la iniciativa en la invasión y colonización de nuevos territorios, sobre todo en América Central y del Sur. En 1600 también había reclamado las islas Filipinas. Portugal solo reclamó algunos puertos comerciales en África, India y las islas de las Especias, junto con una franja costera de Brasil.

CLAVE
- España y sus colonias
- Portugal y sus colonias
- Inglaterra y sus colonias
- Dinamarca y sus colonias
- Colonias holandesas (Provincias Unidas)

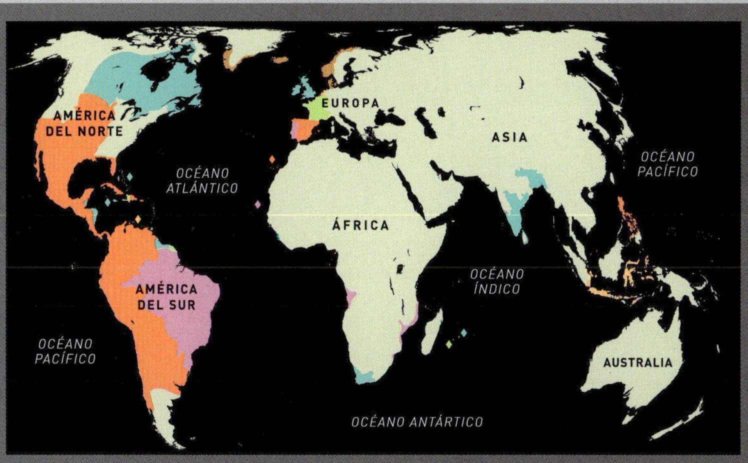

1800 La expansión europea prosiguió en los siglos XVII y XVIII, y en 1800 Europa había colonizado una gran parte del mundo. Gran Bretaña, en concreto, y pese a haber perdido las colonias norteamericanas, iba ampliando su imperio en Canadá, Sudáfrica y, sobre todo, India.

CLAVE
- Gran Bretaña y sus colonias
- Francia y sus colonias
- Dinamarca y sus colonias
- España y sus colonias
- Portugal y sus colonias
- Países Bajos y sus colonias

La mayor parte de lo que se conserva de la Gran Muralla de China se reconstruyó durante la dinastía Ming. Está jalonada de fortificaciones y se extiende a lo largo de 6400 km.

EN EL AÑO 1483 VOLVIÓ A ESTALLAR LA GUERRA DE LAS DOS ROSAS (*véase* 1454–1455) entre las casas de Lancaster y de York (ramas rivales de los **Plantagenet** que se disputaban el trono de Inglaterra), que parecía haber finalizado en 1471. En 1470, **Eduardo IV de York**, que había arrebatado el trono al desventurado **Enrique VI de Lancaster** en 1461, fue derrocado por un grupo de nobles vengativos. En 1471 y con el **apoyo de Carlos el Calvo**, duque de Borgoña (*véase* 1472–1476), Eduardo recuperó el trono. Enrique fue asesinado, probablemente por orden de Eduardo.

Después de la muerte de Eduardo, en 1483, el conflicto se reavivó de inmediato, aunque de distinta forma. El problema residía en que el nuevo rey, **Eduardo V**, solo tenía doce años y que los miembros de su familia materna, los **Woodville**, veían al niño-rey como una oportunidad de autoproclamarse regentes, ocupar el trono y deshacer el legado de Eduardo IV. Al menos esto es lo que sospechaba el defensor más fiel del difunto rey, su hermano el **duque de Gloucester**, capaz, inteligente y leal. Gloucester se adelantó a los Woodville y ocupó el trono él mismo como **Ricardo III**; ordenó la ejecución de los líderes de la familia Woodville y **encarceló a Eduardo V** y a su hermano pequeño en la **Torre de Londres**, donde ambos fueron asesinados. Aunque no hay pruebas de que Ricardo III fuera responsable de la muerte de sus sobrinos, cabe la posibilidad de que **ordenara su asesinato**, puesto que su derecho a la corona era demasiado endeble como para permitir que sobreviviera ningún rival que pudiera destronarle. Posteriormente, la propaganda Tudor envileció la memoria de Ricardo III, pero teniendo en cuenta la vorágine de traiciones de la Inglaterra de finales de la Edad Media, la actuación de Ricardo parece bastante comprensible. En un momento u otro, los Woodville habrían encontrado una razón que les permitiera justificar su muerte.

EL RENACIMIENTO

El Renacimiento, nacido en Italia en las postrimerías de la Edad Media, significó la revalorización del pensamiento europeo a partir de una nueva interpretación de su pasado clásico. Florencia (izda.), fue la cuna de este movimiento que condujo a una revolución artística, cultural y, más tarde, científica. Aunque su impacto inicial fue irregular, acabó extendiéndose lentamente por la mayor parte de Europa.

5:8 **Batalla de Bosworth** *El ejército de Enrique Tudor, con 5000 hombres, superó al de Ricardo III, mucho más numeroso, pero con mandos ineptos.*

Sin embargo, había otro **pretendiente de la casa de Lancaster**, **Enrique Tudor** (1457–1509). Aunque su derecho al trono era tenue en el mejor de los casos, contaba con el apoyo del rey francés, **Carlos VIII** (r. 1483–1498). En agosto de 1485, Enrique dirigió una invasión desde Francia. Al finalizar el mes, Ricardo había fallecido en la **batalla de Bosworth**, donde la incompetencia y traición de muchos de sus comandantes anuló su clara superioridad numérica. Enrique Tudor fue coronado rey en el mismo campo de batalla y se convirtió en **Enrique VII**. La forma en que los Tudor llegaron al trono podría haber desencadenado otra serie de luchas internas desestabilizadoras, pero Enrique VII demostró ser un rey pragmático, capaz y con una gran visión de futuro. Los Tudor reforzaron Inglaterra, controlaron a la nobleza y reformaron completamente el gobierno.

TRAS LAS PRIMERAS EXPEDICIONES PORTUGUESAS (*véase* 1470–1471), en 1487 partieron otras dos con el objetivo de investigar nuevas rutas hacia y a través del océano Índico. **Pêro da Covilhã** fue el encargado de explorar la costa oriental africana y el océano Índico. Desde Adén, adonde llegó por el mar Rojo, zarpó hacia Calicut (India) y llegó al sur hasta Sofala, en **África oriental**, y al norte hasta el estrecho de Ormuz, en el golfo Pérsico; en 1492 informó favorablemente sobre todas estas rutas. La segunda de estas expediciones, que fue dirigida por **Bartolomeu Dias**, tenía la misión específica de hallar un paso navegable alrededor de lo que se suponía el extremo sur de África. En enero de 1488, en lugar de limitarse a seguir la costa africana en dirección sur, como habían hecho Cão y otros antes que él, aproximadamente a 27 °S (varios cientos de kilómetros antes de llegar al extremo sur de África), viró hacia el suroeste, alejándose de la costa. Fue toda una osadía. A kilómetros de tierra, pudo aprovechar los vientos del oeste que soplan en el Atlántico Sur y que le llevaron casi 500 km al este del **cabo de Buena Esperanza**, en la punta sur de África. El viaje de Dias permitió comprender mejor los sistemas de vientos que unen los océanos Atlántico e Índico, un logro que resultó fundamental a la hora de calcular la ruta hacia el cabo de Buena Esperanza y más allá. **Vasco da Gama** y **Pedro Cabral** aprovecharon estos conocimientos en sus viajes.

El **sacrificio humano** es una característica común a muchas so-

Al menos 4000

ES EL NÚMERO ESTIMADO DE **PERSONAS SACRIFICADAS** EN LA **INAUGURACIÓN** DE LA PIRÁMIDE DE **TENOCHTITLÁN**

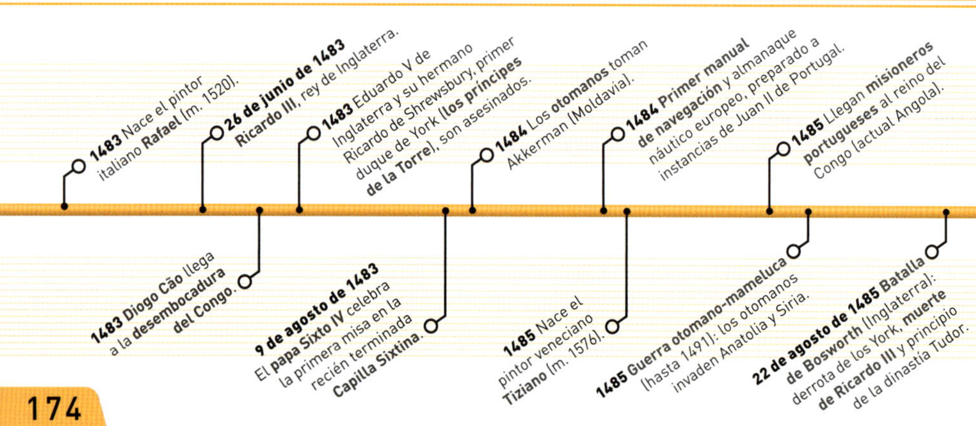

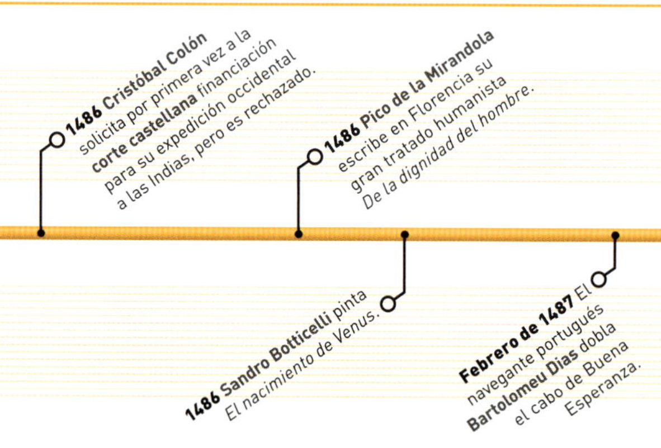

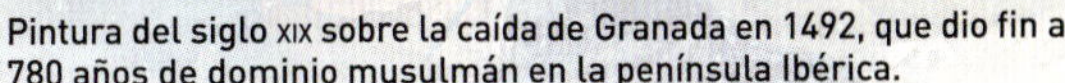

Pintura del siglo XIX sobre la caída de Granada en 1492, que dio fin a 780 años de dominio musulmán en la península Ibérica.

ciedades primitivas. Sin embargo, no se conoce ninguna que lo practicara a la escala de los **aztecas**. Se estima que sacrificaban ritualmente más de **20 000 víctimas anuales** (esclavos, enemigos capturados en combate y personas ofrecidas como tributo). El objetivo era aplacar la ira de los dioses, en especial la del dios de la guerra **Huitzilopochtli**, cuyas batallas diarias contra el sol solo podían mantenerse a base de sangre. En 1487, durante la inauguración del **nuevo gran templo** de la capital azteca, **Tenochtitlán**, fueron ejecutadas ritualmente por lo menos 4000 personas, a las que se extrajo el corazón, en una ceremonia única que pudo haber durado entre cuatro y veinte días.

En el territorio chino, la **dinastía Ming** (1368–1644) proseguía la ambiciosa reconstrucción de la **Gran Muralla**, de 6400 km de longitud, construida en 200 a.C. como símbolo de superioridad y como barrera contra las incursiones de grupos del norte. Bajo los Ming, el tramo oriental, en las montañas, se construyó básicamente con ladrillos y piedra, y el tramo occidental del desierto con arcilla y tierra reforzadas con madera. Su altura media era de unos 8 m, con una anchura de 5,5 m; tenía 25 000 torres y más de 15 000 guarniciones: una obra monumental.

Tenochtitlán
Este mural de la capital azteca del siglo XVI, imaginada en el siglo XX por el artista mexicano Diego Rivera, pone de manifiesto la magnificencia de la ciudad.

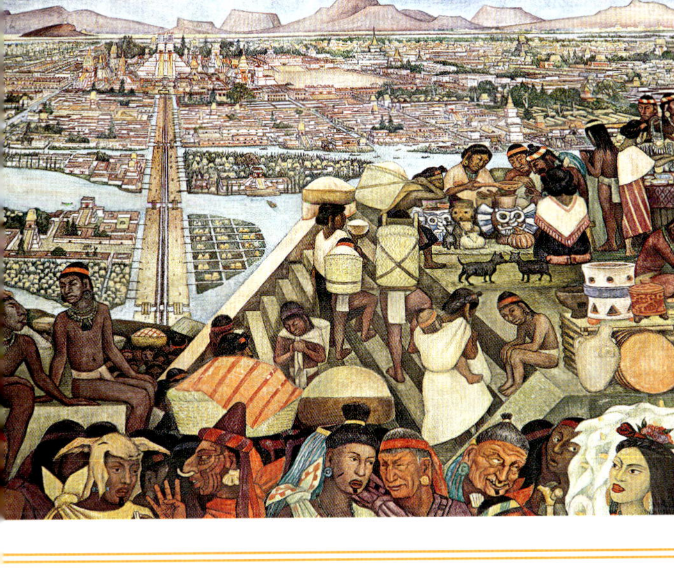

Casco mameluco
Casco de hierro del siglo XV llevado por los soldados mamelucos, y profusamente decorado con finas incrustaciones caligráficas de plata.

EL TRATADO DE PAZ de mayo de 1491 entre los otomanos y los mamelucos puso fin a una guerra iniciada en 1485 por el control de las rutas comerciales de Asia occidental y del mar Rojo. Ninguno de los dos bandos ganó demasiado, pero la contienda agotó económicamente a los mamelucos, que no pudieron evitar la posterior conquista de los otomanos en 1516–1517.

En 1490, **Ladislao II** (1456–1516) reinaba sobre un enorme territorio que abarcaba **Polonia-Lituania**, **Bohemia y Hungría**, cuya corona aceptó ese mismo año. A pesar de sus extensos dominios, apenas ejercía influencia en el conjunto de Europa, de la que Polonia-Lituania, vasta, desolada y empobrecida, se mantenía al margen. Hungría y Bohemia eran más sofisticadas, pero además de ser reinos independientes eran rivales incómodos. Estos amplios territorios nunca pudieron desarrollar su potencial.

El 2 de enero de 1492, los monarcas hispánicos **Isabel y Fernando** (*véase* 1469) consiguieron la **rendición del reino de Granada** como colofón de una campaña de diez años de duración para recuperar los últimos reductos musulmanes en la península Ibérica. Fue el final de un proceso iniciado en el siglo VIII, la **Reconquista**, y subrayó la determinación de España de convertirse en una potencia cristiana agresivamente expansionista.

En 1492, los Reyes Católicos finalmente accedieron a financiar a **Cristóbal Colón** su primera travesía atlántica mediante las **Capitulaciones de Santa Fe**. Colón había hecho una serie de demandas sobre las riquezas que generaría su viaje a las Indias (Asia). La Corona quería igualar las riquezas que llegaban a Portugal gracias a sus expediciones al África occidental y, por otro lado, necesitaba sustituir los ingresos que había perdido en impuestos para la «cruzada», que cesaron tras la caída de Granada. El éxito dependía de la indudable pericia de Colón como navegante y de su insistencia en que Asia se encontraba mucho más al este de lo que se pensaba. Al desembarcar en el **Nuevo Mundo** el 12 de octubre, en una isla de las **Bahamas**, envió de inmediato emisarios a la corte «china». Creía tanto en sí mismo que nunca vio la realidad de lo que acababa de descubrir.

« HOY HEMOS **AVANZADO DIECINUEVE LEGUAS**... (CONTADAS) MENOS QUE LAS VERDADERAS, PARA QUE LA **TRIPULACIÓN** NO SE **DESALIENTE**. »

Cristóbal Colón (1492)

CRISTÓBAL COLÓN
(c. 1451–1506)

Nacido en Génova (Italia), hizo cuatro viajes transatlánticos convencido de poder llegar a las riquezas de Oriente zarpando desde España en dirección oeste. Su primer viaje (1492–1493) fue seguido de otros tres en 1493–1496, 1498–1500 y 1502–1504. Fue el primer europeo en avistar América del Sur, en 1498, y cartografió la mayor parte del Caribe. Murió convencido de haber llegado a Asia.

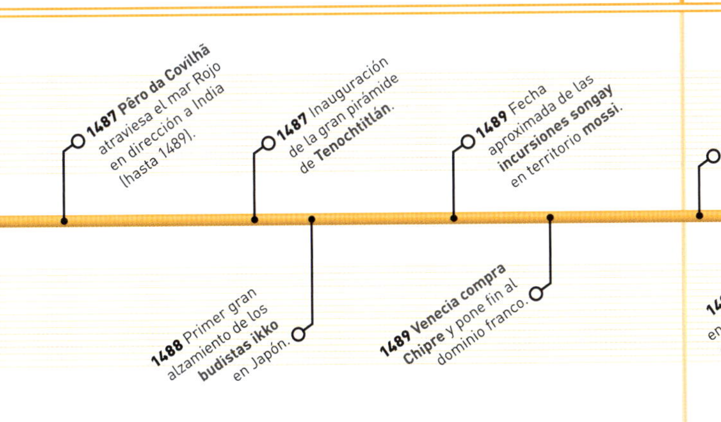

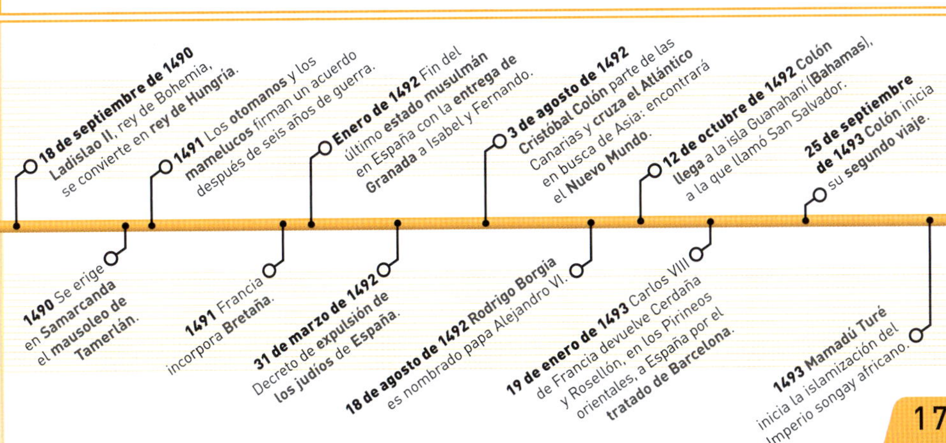

1494–1497

Mapamundi de Alberto Cantino, el primero en plasmar los descubrimientos de Portugal en Oriente y Occidente, y la división entre los territorios españoles y portugueses acordada en Tordesillas.

EN 1494, EL PAPA ALEJANDRO VI redactó el **tratado de Tordesillas**, que repartía los territorios presentes y futuros en el Nuevo Mundo entre **España y Portugal** mediante una línea de norte a sur, a 370 leguas (unos 2000 km) al oeste de las islas de Cabo Verde: los territorios del oeste pertenecerían a España; los del este, a Portugal.

El dominico **Girolamo Savonarola**, aprovechando la crisis política de Florencia tras la **muerte de Lorenzo de Médicis (el Magnífico)** en 1492, impuso una «república cristiana y religiosa» en la ciudad. En 1494 denunció a los tiranos e instituyó la **hoguera de las vanidades**: la destrucción de los bienes pecaminosos. Cuatro años después fue depuesto, torturado y ejecutado.

Las **guerras de Italia**, desencadenadas por el deseo de Carlos VIII de Francia (1470–1498) de **afirmar su derecho** al reino de Nápoles, supusieron una **lucha** intermitente durante **65 años** entre Francia y España por el control de Italia. La salva de apertura, que finalizó en 1499, fue tan destructiva como inconcluyente. La primera fase terminó con la **batalla de Fornovo**, librada cerca de Parma en julio de 1495. Sin embargo, tras su marcha triunfal hacia Nápoles para reclamar el trono, Carlos VIII descubrió que sus antiguos aliados, sobre todo Milán, se habían unido a Venecia, el papado y el Sacro Imperio para oponérsele en una **Santa Liga** que puso fin a sus sueños de conquistar Italia.

LEONARDO DA VINCI
(1452–1519)

Leonardo fue un erudito autodidacta italiano: escultor, pintor, inventor e investigador científico, cuyo genio inquieto le llevó a emprender un gran número de proyectos que no llegó a finalizar. Entre sus obras maestras destacan las pinturas de *La Gioconda* y *La última cena*. Falleció en Francia, estando al servicio de Francisco I.

Hacia 1496 estalló en Italia un brote del llamado **«mal francés»** (porque los primeros casos se detectaron entre los soldados franceses): era sífilis. A mediados del siglo XVI, casi **un millón de personas** habían contraído la enfermedad, seguramente de una cepa muy virulenta, traída por **marineros que regresaban del Nuevo Mundo**.

Desde 1490, el **navegante genovés Giovanni Caboto** había tratado en vano de convencer a Portugal y a España para que le financiaran un viaje en dirección oeste hacia Asia cruzando el Atlántico. Entonces se trasladó a Bristol para centrar sus esfuerzos en la corte inglesa. Fracasó en su primer viaje, pero en mayo de 1497 zarpó de nuevo (con financiación real) y alcanzó el **norte de Terranova**, desde donde se dirigió hacia el sur a lo largo de unos 650 km de costa. Regresó a Inglaterra convencido de haber llegado a China. El año siguiente dirigió una expedición mucho mayor, pero se perdieron cuatro de los cinco barcos, el de Caboto entre ellos. De todos modos, su éxito inicial impulsó **cinco viajes más a Terranova** entre 1501 y 1505, que confirmaron que las tierras alcanzadas no pertenecían en absoluto a Asia. A pesar de la decepción, las expediciones inglesas fueron importantes para demostrar la existencia de un continente hasta entonces desconocido: **América del Norte**, cuya exploración y colonización iba a liderar posteriormente Inglaterra.

1000 000

ES EL NÚMERO APROXIMADO DE **EUROPEOS** QUE **CONTRAJERON** LA **SÍFILIS** ENTRE **1496 Y 1546**

1498–1500

En esta pintura del siglo XX, el rey Manuel I de Portugal bendice a Vasco da Gama y a su expedición durante los preparativos para zarpar de Lisboa.

LA EXPLORACIÓN PORTUGUESA EN DIRECCIÓN SUR por la costa africana durante el siglo XV alcanzó un clímax cuando **Bartolomeu Dias** logró rodear el extremo de África en 1488. En mayo de 1498, **Vasco da Gama** consolidó este logro, se internó en el océano Índico y llegó hasta Calicut, situado en el sureste de India. Había descubierto una **ruta práctica a Oriente**. Su travesía del océano Índico, cruzado por numerosas rutas comerciales árabes y otras desde el siglo IX, dependía de los conocimientos de los musulmanes locales; por el contrario, la ruta hacia el Índico era nueva. Mientras los navegantes portugueses anteriores habían bordeado la cosa africana, Da Gama dio un giro **al oeste, hacia el interior del Atlántico Sur**. No solo fue la mayor travesía oceánica hasta la fecha, sino que inició la ruta

Batalla de Zonchio
Este grabado muestra las naves de la primera batalla de la guerra entre otomanos y venecianos. Fue la primera batalla naval en la que se utilizaron cañones.

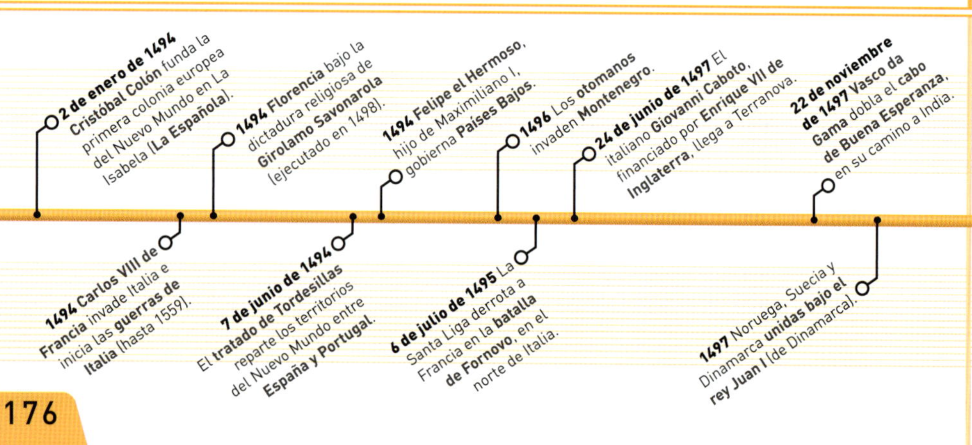

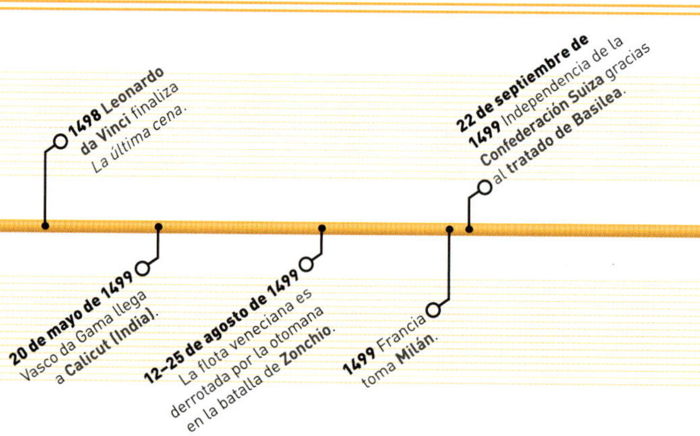

Este detalle de un fresco del palacio de las Cuarenta Columnas de Isfahán (Irán) representa al emperador safaví Ismaíl I luchando con guerreros uzbekos.

utilizada durante la «era de la vela» (pp. 172–173).

La guerra otomano-veneciana de 1499–1503 confirmó la permanente **amenaza marítima otomana** a la cristiandad. A pesar de que ambas partes habían establecido provechosos vínculos comerciales, el poder naval veneciano suponía un obstáculo para las intenciones otomanas en el **Mediterráneo oriental**. La terrible derrota de Venecia en la **batalla de Zonchio**, en agosto de 1499, hizo patente la supremacía otomana en el mar.

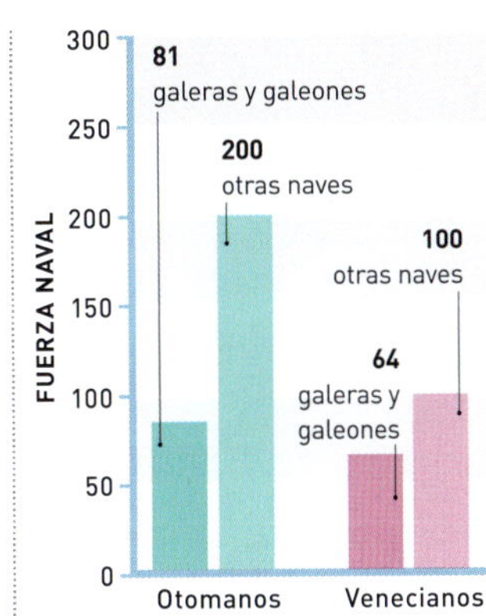

Naves en Zonchio
La disparidad numérica entre las flotas otomana y veneciana se vio agravada por la negativa de algunos comandantes venecianos a luchar.

En el año 1499, Luis XII de Francia (1462–1515) tomó Milán e inauguró otra fase de la **lucha entre Francia y España** por el dominio de Italia. Entonces, el rey francés se alió con Fernando II de Aragón (1452–1516) y accedió a que ambos se repartieran Nápoles. Tras asegurar esta plaza, Luis y Fernando reanudaron sus disputas. **Luis XII firmó reticentemente la paz** en 1504, al sufrir dos derrotas ante su antiguo aliado.

La fiebre de **exploración europea** desatada por Colón siguió en 1500, cuando una **expedición española**, capitaneada por Vicente Pinzón, y **otra portuguesa**, con Pedro Álvares Cabral al frente, llegaron a **Brasil**, camino de India. El avistamiento de este nuevo territorio permitió a Portugal afirmar sus derechos sobre Brasil. Aún más importante fue la creciente convicción de que se trataba de un **Nuevo Mundo**.

SE CONSIDERA QUE 1501 es el año de **fundación del Imperio safaví**. Con el Imperio otomano al oeste y el Mogol al este, el safaví integró el bloque de **imperios musulmanes centralizados, sofisticados y cultos** que dominaron Asia occidental entre los siglos XVI y XVII. Su origen fue una serie de conquistas emprendidas por el **sah Ismaíl I**, cuyas tropas avanzaron hacia el oeste por Persia y pusieron fin tanto al vacío político como a las luchas internas que siguieron a la muerte de Tamerlán (*véase* 1386–1490) en 1405. Ismaíl I se autoproclamó sah de Persia; era musulmán chií y promovió con ardor su fe como religión oficial del estado. El poder militar otomano limitaba sus ambiciones hacia el oeste, por lo que los safavíes dirigieron su atención al este, lo que supuso el desplazamiento hacia oriente de la capital, que acabó estableciéndose en Isfahán.

Por otro lado, los **colonizadores** europeos empezaron a **introducir esclavos africanos** en el Nuevo Mundo a partir de 1502, apenas diez años después de la primera travesía atlántica realizada por Cristóbal Colón. En parte, fue una respuesta a la **alarmante tasa de mortalidad** entre las poblaciones nativas americanas, que también habían sido esclavizadas. Portugal no tardó en seguir el ejemplo de otros grandes países expansionistas de la época. Esta fase inicial del tráfico de esclavos, conocido como **primer sistema atlántico**, perduró aproximadamente hasta 1580.

Imperio safaví
Desde su modesto origen a orillas del Caspio, en 1501 el Imperio safaví se había extendido hasta ocupar una amplia franja de Asia occidental.

El *David* de Miguel Ángel
Miguel Ángel terminó en 1504 esta gigantesca escultura de mármol, de 5,2 m de altura, del héroe bíblico David.

La **expansión del islam** en África oriental se vió reforzada por la instauración en 1504 del **sultanato funj de Sennar**, al norte de Sudán, a expensas de los antiguos dirigentes cristianos de Sennar. Rápidamente el sultanato se consolidó como una importante potencia regional y amenazó tanto a Etiopía como a los otomanos egipcios. En Europa, **dos obras extraordinarias** reforzaron el **papel de Florencia** como capital del Alto Renacimiento (pp. 204–205): el *David* de Miguel Ángel, finalizado en 1504, y *La Gioconda* de Leonardo, terminada entre 1505 y 1507.

« QUIEN HAYA **VISTO EL *DAVID* DE MIGUEL ÁNGEL NO** NECESITA **VER NADA MÁS** DE NINGÚN OTRO ESCULTOR. **»**

Giorgio Vasari, escritor italiano, en *Vidas de los mejores arquitectos, pintores y escultores italianos* (1568)

1499 Da comienzo la **guerra otomano-veneciana** (hasta 1503).

22 de abril de 1500 El explorador portugués **Pedro Álvares Cabral** avista **Brasil**.

Abril de 1500 Francia derrota al ejército de **Ludovico Sforza**, duque de Milán, en **Novara**.

C. 1500 Primer **asentamiento inuit** en el Ártico.

1500 Vicente Yáñez Pinzón llega a las bocas del **Amazonas**.

1501 El ascenso al trono del sah Ismaíl I inaugura la **dinastía safaví** en Persia.

1502 Los españoles llevan al Caribe **esclavos africanos**.

1502 El alemán **Peter Henlein** fabrica el primer **reloj de bolsillo**.

1502 El safaví **Ismaíl I** ejecuta a los disidentes suníes.

1502 Donato Bramante, uno de los grandes **arquitectos renacentistas**, finaliza el templete de San Pietro in Montorio en Roma.

1502 Alberto Cantino traza el **primer mapa** con los territorios del Nuevo Mundo, India, y las divisiones del tratado de Tordesillas.

Abril de 1503 Las tropas españolas vencen a las francesas en **Ceriñola** (Italia).

1 de noviembre de 1503 Giuliano della Rovere se convierte en el papa Julio II e inicia un brillante periodo de **mecenazgo artístico** en Roma.

1503 Moscú logra la **independencia política**.

1504 Miguel Ángel termina la estatua del *David*.

1504 Los **musulmanes funj** derrotan a los cristianos de **Sennar**, entre el Nilo Azul y el Nilo Blanco.

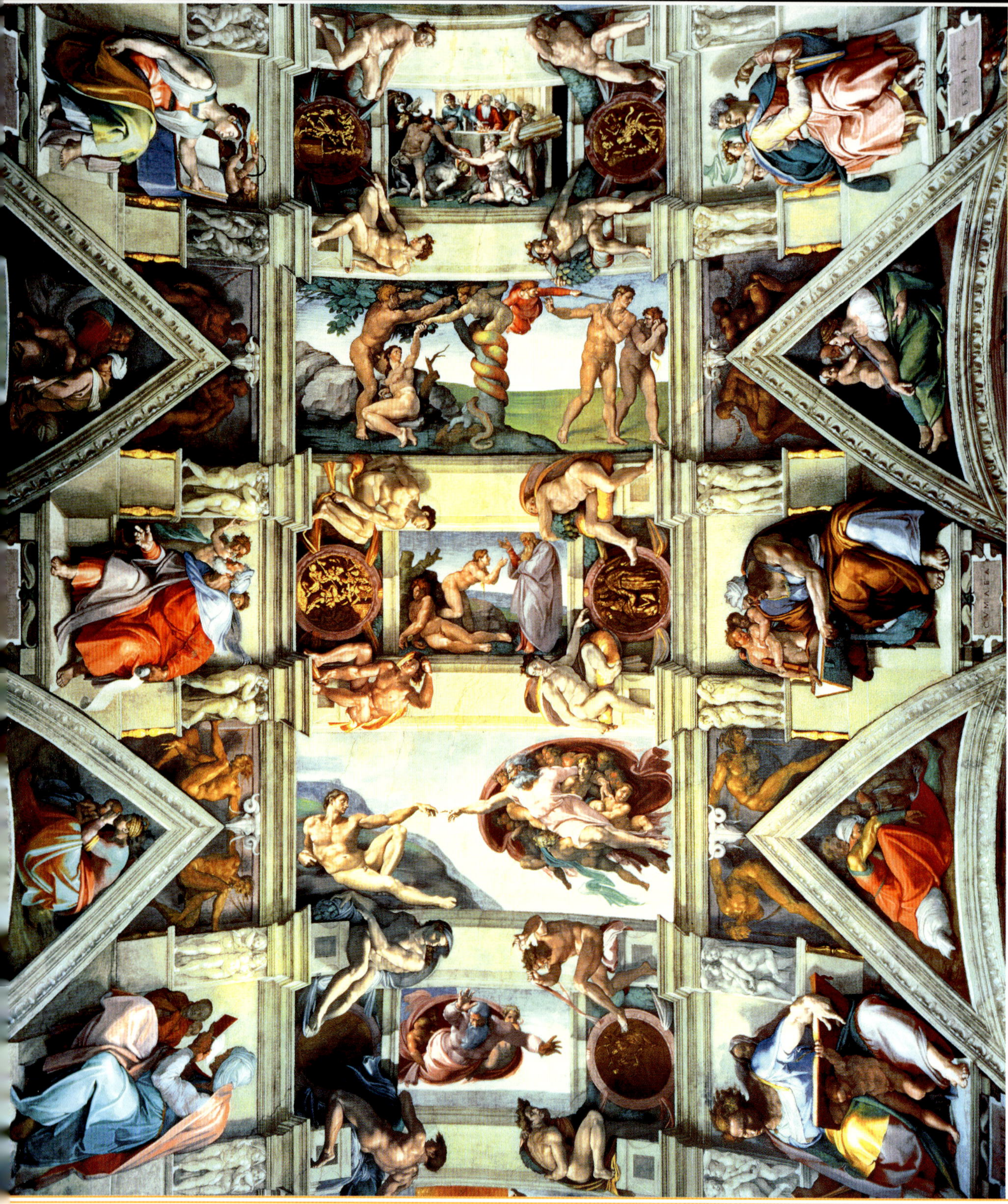

« LA VERDADERA OBRA DE ARTE ES UNA MERA SOMBRA DE LA PERFECCIÓN DIVINA. »

Miguel Ángel Buonarroti,
artista italiano (1475–1564)

EL ARTISTA ITALIANO MIGUEL ÁNGEL BUONARROTI (1475–1564) fue una de las figuras clave del Alto Renacimiento (pp. 204–205). En el año 1505, el papa Julio II le invitó a Roma para que comenzara una tumba monumental, y su asociación perduró 40 años. En 1508 empezó a pintar al fresco el techo de la Capilla Sixtina, que terminó cuatro años después.

A principios del siglo XVI, la **expansión portuguesa** por el océano Índico avanzó a un ritmo trepidante. A partir de 1505, Portugal se estableció en una serie de puertos a lo largo de la **costa oriental africana**. Los portugueses se habían marcado un objetivo sencillo que cumplían implacablemente: dominar el lucrativo comercio de especias con India y Asia oriental. **Alfonso de Albuquerque**, nombrado en 1509 virrey de la creciente colonia portuguesa en India, fue un elemento clave. En 1510 ya había convertido a **Goa** en la principal base portuguesa india y en 1511 había supervisado la fundación del que fue la primera colonia portuguesa en el Sureste Asiático: **Malaca**. También financió la primera expedición portuguesa a las islas de las Especias, las **Molucas**, alcanzadas por vez primera en 1512 por **Francisco Serrão**, que había zarpado junto con **Antonio de Abreu** y **Francisco Rodrigues**. Estos dos últimos se vie-

Techo de la Capilla Sixtina
El techo de la Capilla Sixtina del Vaticano, encargado por el papa Julio II, es una de las obras maestras de Miguel Ángel. Ilustra episodios del Antiguo Testamento.

1505 El papa **Julio II** llama a **Miguel Ángel** a Roma para que realice su tumba.

1505 Los portugueses saquean **Mombasa**, en África oriental.

1505–1507 **Leonardo da Vinci** termina *La Gioconda*.

1506 Los portugueses toman la isla de **Socotora**, en el mar Rojo.

1507 Primera aparición del nombre «América», en el mapamundi de **Waldseemüller**.

1508 Los safavíes toman **Bagdad**.

1508 Los españoles esclavizan a los nativos de **La Española**.

1508 El papa Julio II crea la **liga de Cambrai** contra Venecia.

1508 Miguel Ángel empieza a pintar el techo de la **Capilla Sixtina**.

3 de febrero de 1509 Derrota de la flota otomana por los portugueses en la **batalla de Diu** (océano Índico).

21 de abril de 1509 **Enrique VIII** de Inglaterra asciende al trono.

14 de mayo de 1509 Victoria de Francia sobre Venecia en la **batalla de Agnadello**, cerca de Milán.

1509 El humanista holandés **Erasmo de Rotterdam** escribe el tratado satírico *Elogio de la locura*.

1509 Primeros asentamientos españoles en **América Central** y en **Puerto Rico**.

1510 Portugal toma **Goa**.

1510 Fernando el Católico toma **Trípoli**.

1510 Inicio de los ataques de piratas **japoneses** en la costa sur de China.

1510 Los **safavíes** toman Herat, Bactriana y Jiva.

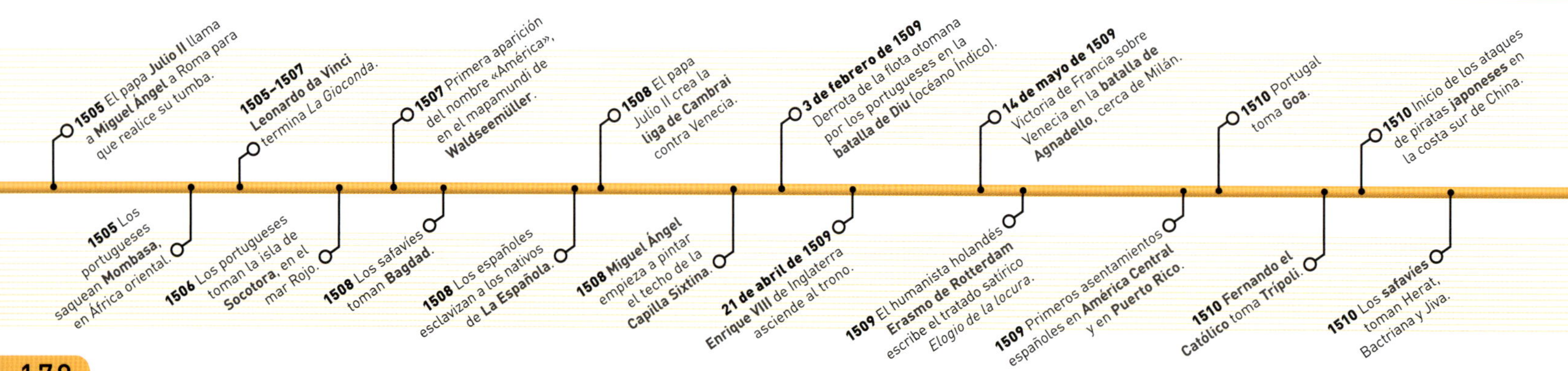

Representación de la batalla de Agnadello, una de las principales batallas de las guerras de Italia, en la tumba de Luis XII de Francia y su esposa Ana de Bretaña.

Detalle de la coronación de Selim I. Durante sus nueve años de reinado, prácticamente triplicó la extensión del imperio.

ron obligados a retroceder en el mar de Banda, pero Serrão pudo seguir hasta llegar a las Molucas en una embarcación nativa.

El hecho de que en 20 años varias **expediciones españolas** hubieran explorado y cartografiado casi todo el **Caribe** es un reflejo del desmedido entusiasmo que generaron los **viajes transatlánticos de Colón** (*véase* 1492). En 1508–1509 se descubrió la **península de Yucatán**, en la costa este de México, lo cual llevaría a la conquista de México por **Hernán Cortés** (*véase* 1519). La codicia fue la motivación fundamental de la colonización europea del Nuevo Mundo, que se logró principalmente mediante la violencia. Sin embargo, se acogía a un imperativo cristiano que contaba con **sanción papal** ya desde 1452, por la que podía esclavizarse a «sarracenos, paganos y cualquier no creyente.» Un fraile dominico, **Antonio de Montesinos**, se opuso enérgicamente a dicha postura en un sermón de 1511, en el que denunció la «crueldad y tiranía» de los colonizadores y que, como era de preveer, provocó la ira de sus conciudadanos.

> **«** ¿ESTOS, **NO SON HOMBRES**? ¿**NO** TIENEN **ALMAS** RACIONALES? **»**
>
> **Antonio de Montesinos,** fraile dominico, en un sermón a colonos españoles en La Española (4 diciembre de 1511)

Españoles y portugueses se mostraron igualmente agresivos en sus intentos de colonizar **Marruecos**, donde conquistaron plazas costeras estratégicas durante el siglo XV y principios del XVI, y contribuyeron en parte a la aparición de una nueva dinastía marroquí (la **sadí**), que ocupó el vacío político que había dejado la caída de la dinastía mariní en la década de 1480.

Cuando en 1508 el papa Julio II creó la **liga de Cambrai**, la **República de Venecia** ya estaba políticamente aislada y enfrentada a la mayor parte de las grandes potencias europeas. La República se derrumbó rápidamente tras su derrota en 1509 frente al ejército francés de Luis XII en la **batalla de Agnadello**, una de las batallas más importantes de las **guerras de Italia** (1494–1559). En 1510, Julio II se alió con Venecia contra Francia porque le preocupaba que las ambiciones territoriales venecianas en el norte de Italia se hubieran visto sustituidas por idénticas ambiciones francesas. El periodo se caracterizó por este tipo de alianzas cambiantes. En 1511 dieron otro giro con la creación de una nueva **Santa Liga** que incluía a Inglaterra y que, esta vez, iba contra Francia. Una de sus consecuencias fue la alianza franco-veneciana.

Pese a la presión de **otomanos** al oeste y a la amenaza de los portugueses desde el sur, los **safavíes** lograron repeler hacia el norte a la **confederación uzbeka** de Asia central. Tras su victoria sobre los uzbekos en las afueras de la ciudad de Merv en diciembre de 1510, extensos territorios, que incluían a Herat, Basora y Kandahar, pasaron a formar parte de **su imperio**.

Hacia las islas de las Especias
El explorador portugués Francisco Serrão llegó a las Molucas (islas de las Especias) después de que otros hubieran desistido.

CLAVE
→ Antonio de Abreu / Francisco Rodrigues (1512)
→ Francisco Serrão (1512)

NO MENOS IMPORTANCIA que la exploración española del Caribe después de la travesía de Colón en 1492 tuvo la llegada a la «isla» de Florida por parte de **Juan Ponce de León** en abril de 1513. Fue el primer contacto de los españoles con tierra firme norteamericana y la base de la posterior reclamación española de la región. En su intento de circunnavegar la isla, Ponce de León hizo otro descubrimiento, casi tan importante para la era de la vela como el del sistema de vientos del Atlántico por Colón: la **corriente del Golfo**.

En 1513, **Nicolás Maquiavelo**, antiguo diplomático en Florencia, escribió el primer manual moderno de ciencia política: *El príncipe* (publicado en 1532). El argumento central (que el ejercicio del poder político requiere violencia y engaños) le proporcionó una notoriedad duradera. La obra contiene consejos sobre cómo gobernar del modo más efectivo que, en esencia, consiste en la determinación pragmática de valerse de cualquier medio disponible.

Una vez finalizada la guerra civil de 1509–1512, en la que **Selim I** fue nombrado sultán en sustitución de su padre, Bayaceto II, que se vio obligado a abdicar, y de su hermano mayor, Ahmed, muerto en combate, la **expansión territorial otomana** recobró nuevo impulso. En 1514, Selim I inició un proceso expansivo (contra los musulmanes del sur y del este, en lugar de contra los cristianos europeos). Los safavíes, superados en número e incapaces de responder a la artillería otomana, cayeron en la batalla de Chaldirán. Una vez asegurado el flanco oriental, Selim atacó a **Siria** y al **Egipto mameluco**, que cayeron inmediatamente. Selim I no solo amplió de manera espectacular el territorio otomano, sino que, al hacerse con casi todos los lugares santos musulmanes de Asia occidental, aumentó en gran manera el prestigio de su imperio (pp. 230–231).

NICOLÁS MAQUIAVELO
(1469–1527)

Filósofo y escritor, también fue funcionario en Florencia, donde tuvo la oportunidad de observar desde primera fila a gobernantes agresivos, como el despiadado César Borgia, hijo ilegítimo del papa, que gobernó entre 1502 y 1503. Se encargó de numerosas misiones diplomáticas, pero en 1513 fue detenido y torturado. Ese mismo año escribió *El príncipe*. Falleció en 1527 en la pobreza, antes de que su libro se hiciera famoso.

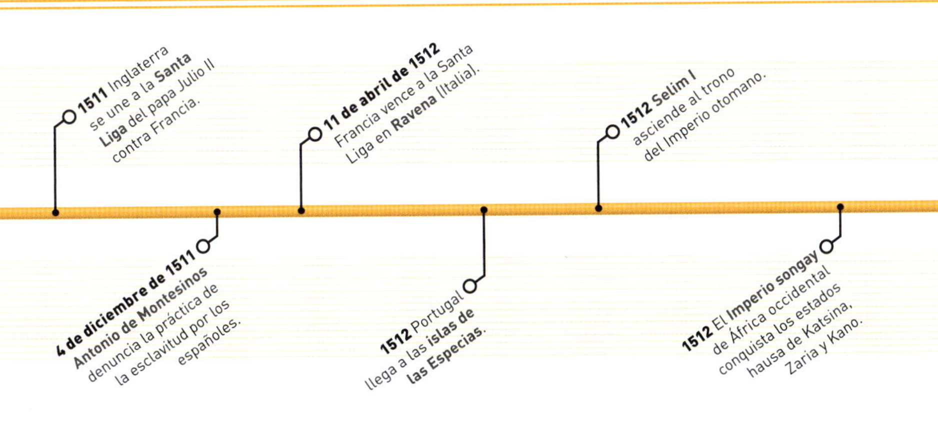

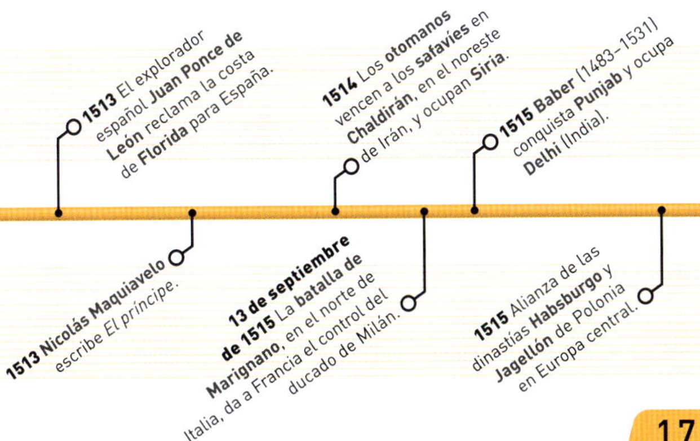

1516–1518

« ¿POR QUÉ NO **CONSTRUYE** EL **PAPA**... **SAN PEDRO** CON **SU PROPIO DINERO**, EN VEZ DE CON EL DINERO... DE LOS **CREYENTES POBRES**? »

Martín Lutero, sacerdote alemán, en las *95 tesis* (1517)

LAS CONQUISTAS OTOMANAS EN ORIENTE MEDIO bajo **Selim I**, que también incluyó a Argelia en la órbita otomana en 1517, transformaron al estado turco otomano en un **imperio**, que estaba desarrollando rápidamente una impresionante potencia naval. El control de Egipto consolidó la presencia otomana en el Mediterráneo oriental, además de proporcionar al imperio un acceso crucial al mar Rojo. Después de hacerse con el control de las rutas comerciales terrestres con Oriente, los otomanos querían dominar la lucrativa «**ruta de las especias**». Esto suponía enfrentarse a los portugueses, que exploraban el mar Rojo desde 1513. Se estaba preparando el terreno para un nuevo conflicto entre el mundo musulmán y el occidente cristiano.

En octubre de 1517, el sacerdote y teólogo alemán **Martín Lutero** (1483–1546) clavó sus *95 tesis* en la puerta de la iglesia de Todos los Santos de Wittenberg (Sajonia), como parte de un creciente movimiento de protesta contra las prácticas y la corrupción de la Iglesia católica. En 1521, después de ser excomulgado por el papa, endureció su postura contra la Iglesia. La rápida respuesta a las enseñanzas de Lutero y la contribución de la imprenta (pp. 154–159) a la difusión de sus ideas condujeron a la **Reforma**, un potente movimiento que buscaba un cambio religioso.

La llegada de una **flota portuguesa** liderada por Tomé Pires a **Cantón (China)**, en agosto de 1517, supuso el clímax de la campaña para abrir nuevas rutas comerciales a través del océano Índico iniciada cuando Vasco da Gama dobló el cabo de Buena Esperanza en 1498. Sin embargo, los resultados de los primeros encuentros no fueron demasiado prometedores, ya que los chinos consideraron a los recién llegados **bárbaros e incultos**. La misión comercial portuguesa a Pekín en 1520 fue recibida con el mismo desdén.

LA REFORMA

La reforma religiosa instigada por Martín Lutero (dcha.) escindió la Iglesia occidental. Las cuestiones políticas interfirieron desde un primer momento a medida que las ideas reformistas se iban extendiendo por Europa. El legado de las disensiones y confrontaciones violentas entre católicos y protestantes fue la división permanente de la cristiandad europea.

1519–1522

Hernán Cortés conquistó Tenochtitlán el 13 de agosto de 1521 no solo gracias a la ferocidad de sus soldados, sino también a los 20 000 nativos que había reclutado.

LA ELECCIÓN DE CARLOS V COMO EMPERADOR DEL SACRO IMPERIO en el año 1519 resultó crucial. Carlos (1500–1558) ya era monarca de varios territorios europeos: España, Italia, Austria y Países Bajos. Al acceder al trono del Sacro Imperio, su poder parecía inigualable. Para el devoto Carlos, los imperativos eran evidentes: presidir una próspera entidad católica paneuropea que, movilizada adecuadamente, pudiera **aplastar la amenaza turca otomana**. La realidad fue dolorosamente distinta. Carlos se enfrentaba sin duda a desafíos formidables dadas las dimensiones de sus dominios, la diversidad política de sus Estados y la hostilidad permanente de sus enemigos, quienes temían que pretendiera una **monarquía universal de los Habsburgo**. Sus ambiciones toparon con reveses graves, pero fue todo un logro en sí mismo su capacidad para movilizar aliados en defensa de la monarquía apelando a la fascinación por el prestigio imperial y al liderazgo personal.

El emperador Carlos V
Pocos monarcas fueron tan diligentes o conscientes de su destino divino como Carlos V. Sin embargo, todos sus esfuerzos resultaron vanos.

La osadía, falta de escrúpulos y determinación con que **Castilla** emprendió su aventura ultramarina dieron fruto cuando **Hernán Cortés** tomó Tenochtitlán, capital del **Imperio azteca**. A partir de 1519 y en menos de cinco años, una fuerza española, con la ayuda de guerreros tlaxcaltecas y otros enemigos de los aztecas, lograron someter gran parte de Mesoamérica, región cuya colonización fue el resultado de la iniciativa de Cortés, noble de rango menor y aventurero autofinanciado.

En 1519, otro hito a la hora de cimentar el papel global de España fue el inicio de la expedición que acabó en la **primera circunnavegación del globo**. Su capitán, el portugués **Fernando de Magallanes** (n. 1480), convenció a Carlos I para que financiara el viaje a las islas de las Especias, en el Pacífico, navegando hacia el oes-

« **CONOCÍA** MEJOR QUE NADIE EL **VERDADERO ARTE** DE LA **NAVEGACIÓN**. »

Antonio Pigafetta, navegante italiano, sobre Fernando de Magallanes (1521)

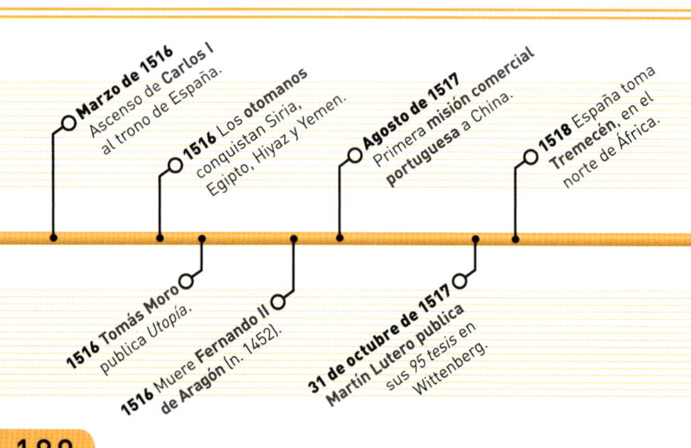

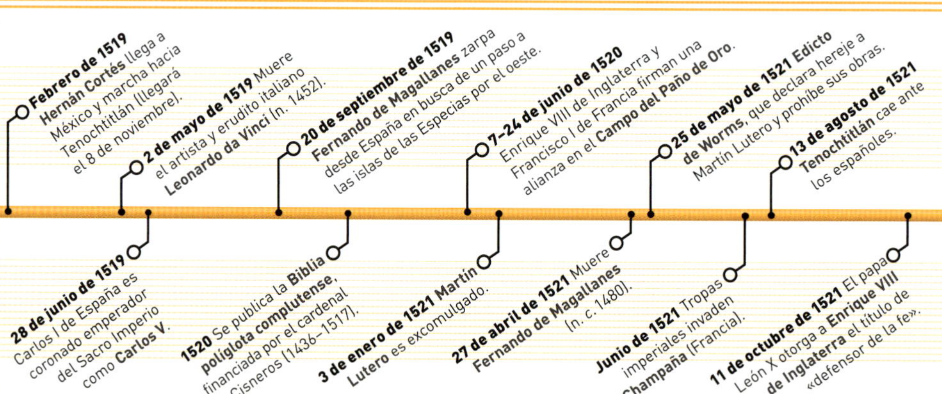

te. Zarparon cinco naves, y tres años después volvió una sola, sin Magallanes, muerto a manos de los nativos de Mactán (Filipinas) en 1521. Con todo, fue quizá la empresa más extraordinaria de la era de la vela, y reveló por primera vez la inmensidad del océano Pacífico.

El año 1521 vio el resurgir de las **guerras de Italia** (1494–1559), esta vez por el temor de Francia a una Europa dominada por los Habsburgo tras la elección de Carlos V como sacro emperador. Francia y, al principio, Venecia, se unieron para enfrentarse a Carlos, a Inglaterra y al papado. Para los franceses, esta contienda resultó tan insatisfactoria como las anteriores y culminó en una serie de derrotas.

Carabela portuguesa
La nave capitana de Magallanes, la Trinidad*, era una carabela como esta. En general, las carabelas medían menos de 30 m de eslora y eran barcos resistentes y marineros.*

1523–1525

En Pavía, en 1525, el ejército español rompió las líneas de asedio francesas, cuyos soldados fueron despedazados por los piqueros y los cañones.

LA CREENCIA DE QUE LAS TIERRAS descubiertas al oeste por exploradores europeos posteriores a Colón eran costas asiáticas desconocidas, y no un nuevo continente, resultó muy persistente. Del mismo modo, se sostenía que debía existir un **paso navegable hacia el este** a través de esa tierra firme. Hasta los viajes de Florida a Nueva Escocia entre 1524 y 1528 de **Giovanni da Verrazzano** (1485–1528), un florentino al servicio del rey francés Francisco I, no se supo de la existencia de una línea de **costa continua**. Aun así, Verrazzano siguió creyendo que el Pacífico estaba muy cerca.

La **guerra de los Campesinos alemana** entre 1524 y 1525 fue un amargo recordatorio de cómo grupos que solían carecer de voz política podían apropiarse del lenguaje de la reforma protestante. Estas revueltas fueron el intento de una multitud que carecía de representación política en Alemania y en Austria (no todos los rebeldes eran campesinos) por acabar con lo que consideraban abusos (impuestos y obligación de trabajar) de la Iglesia y de la nobleza. En el punto más álgido de la guerra, en la primavera de 1525, se habían reunido unos 300 000 en grupos diversos y en ejércitos reunidos apresuradamente. El **alzamiento fue reprimido con brutalidad**, y miles de personas murieron. Lutero y otros líderes de la Reforma «oficial» negaron vehementemente toda relación con los rebeldes, y la revuelta desencadenó la persecución implacable de todas las formas de radicalismo religioso protestante, como el **anabaptismo**, que se consideraban un desafío tanto a la jerarquía social como a la autoridad protestante.

CLAVE
Posesiones de los Habsburgo en 1525
Fronteras del Sacro Imperio

INGLATERRA · PAÍSES BAJOS · SACRO IMPERIO · POLONIA · París · TIERRAS DE LA CORONA BOHEMIA · OCÉANO ATLÁNTICO · FRANCIA · FRANCO CONDADO · AUSTRIA · Viena · ESTIRIA · Buda · TIROL · CARINTIA · HUNGRÍA · DUCADO DE MILÁN · Milán · CARNIOLA · REPÚBLICA DE VENECIA · ESPAÑA · Madrid · Barcelona · ESTADOS PONTIFICIOS · IMPERIO OTOMANO · Islas Baleares · Roma · REINO DE NÁPOLES · REINO DE CERDEÑA · Nápoles · Mar Mediterráneo · ÁFRICA · REINO DE SICILIA

Imperio Habsburgo bajo Carlos V
El tamaño del imperio de Carlos V lo hacía ingobernable. A pesar de su potencial, se vio asolado por luchas religiosas y políticas.

Durante la **batalla de Pavía**, en 1525, **Francisco I** fue **hecho prisionero**. Trasladado a Madrid, el rey francés fue obligado a rendirse y a renunciar a Italia. Sin embargo, no tenía la menor intención de respetar ese compromiso.

8:1 **Batalla de Pavía**
El 24 de febrero de 1525, el ejército francés fue literalmente barrido del mapa. Sufrió 8000 bajas, frente a las mil del ejército imperial.

100 000
REBELDES MUERTOS DURANTE LA **REVUELTA POPULAR** EN **ALEMANIA**

1526

Baber solo pudo crear (y mantener) su Imperio mogol por la fuerza.

> « SI HAY UN **PARAÍSO EN LA TIERRA**, ES ESTE, ES ESTE, ES ESTE. »
>
> **Inscripción en la tumba de Baber** (1530)

DURANTE SU ENFRENTAMIENTO CON CARLOS V (*véase* 1521), Francisco I pidió ayuda a los otomanos en 1525, en el proceso que dio lugar a una **alianza franco-otomana** que se prolongó 250 años. Los otomanos vieron en esta alianza una justificación adicional para renovar su conflicto con Hungría y en agosto de 1526 aplastaron a una fuerza combinada húngara y bohemia en Mohács.

En 1526 se fundó en India el **Imperio mogol**. Fue obra de **Baber** (1483–1530), un descendiente de Gengis Kan (*véase* 1201–1205) procedente de Ferganá, en Asia central, de donde había sido expulsado. Sin embargo, en el año 1522 tomó Kandahar, un importante punto estratégico en la ruta hasta India, y en 1526 derrotó al sultán afgano de Delhi, Ibrahim Lodi, y se autoproclamó emperador. En su punto álgido, que tuvo lugar durante el siglo XVIII, el Imperio mogol abarcaba prácticamente todo el subcontinente. Era sinónimo de vida sofisticada y cortesana, enriquecido por el comercio y por las conquistas y, a pesar de ser islámico, tolerante con otras religiones.

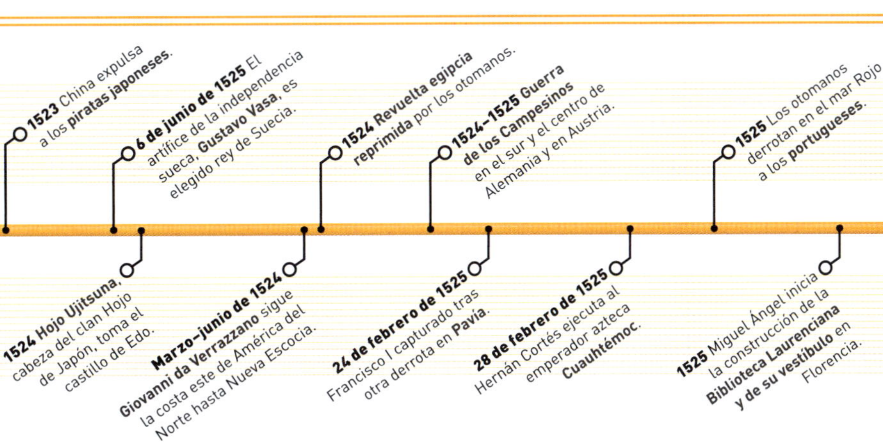

HISTORIA DE LA ASTRONOMÍA

UNA DE LAS CIENCIAS MÁS ANTIGUAS, LA ASTRONOMÍA QUIZÁ ESCONDE LA CLAVE DEL ORIGEN DE TODAS LAS COSAS

Telescopio de Newton (vista frontal)

El desarrollo de la astronomía se vio influenciado por dos factores clave: la invención del telescopio, que reveló objetos celestes antes indetectables, y los avances en matemáticas, física, química y cálculo, que resultaron cruciales para la explicación de las observaciones astronómicas.

En sus orígenes, la astronomía estuvo ligada a la mitología, la religión y la adivinación. Las observaciones celestes se utilizaban para medir el tiempo, elaborar calendarios, fijar las fechas de celebraciones religiosas y hacer predicciones astrológicas. Durante milenios se creyó que la Tierra era el centro del cosmos, pero esto no explicaba los movimientos observables de la Luna, el Sol y los planetas.

LA ASTRONOMÍA MODERNA

En 1543, Nicolás Copérnico publicó su modelo heliocéntrico, que situaba al Sol en el centro del cosmos y que hoy día se considera el punto de partida de la astronomía moderna. A partir de 1609, el recién inventado telescopio reveló una multitud de objetos astronómicos nuevos. También en el siglo XVII, Kepler publicó sus leyes del movimiento planetario e Isaac Newton explicó la fuerza gravitatoria que controla dicho movimiento. En el siglo XIX se midió con precisión la distancia al Sol y a las estrellas cercanas, se desarrolló la espectroscopia y los avances de la física teórica permitieron explicar problemas como la generación de energía en las estrellas (por las reacciones nucleares en sus núcleos). Antes de 1920, muchos pensaban que el universo tan solo consistía en nuestra Vía Láctea; sin embargo, Edwin Hubble midió la velocidad a la que se alejaban nebulosas distantes y se dio cuenta de que esas nebulosas eran galaxias independientes, que no solo se alejaban, sino que la velocidad a que lo hacían aumentaba con la distancia, lo que implicaba que el universo había tenido un principio, en el que todo habría estado junto. Se propuso que la expansión era la consecuencia de una explosión gigantesca (el Big Bang). Los descubrimientos de la astronomía moderna sustentan la teoría del Big Bang, pero también han probado que gran parte del universo consiste en materia y en energía oscuras, cuyos orígenes y naturaleza se desconocen.

Astrolabio persa
Los astrolabios muestran una representación del cielo nocturno; se usaron hasta el siglo XVII para estimar la hora y para la navegación.

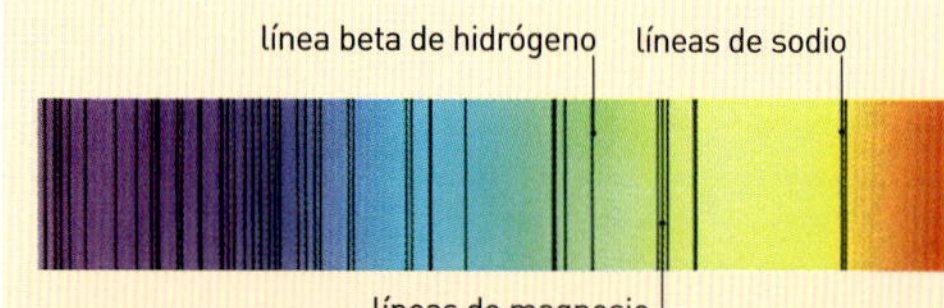

EL ESPECTRO ELECTROMAGNÉTICO

Las estrellas y otros objetos celestes emiten luz y otras formas de energía electromagnética, como rayos X y ondas de radio. El espectroscopio descompone estas emisiones en un espectro cromático. En el espectro de las estrellas aparecen líneas de absorción oscuras, cada una de las cuales corresponde a un elemento químico. El estudio de la intensidad de las líneas revela la composición química de una estrella, y un análisis más detallado, su temperatura y su velocidad relativa, así como la presión y la densidad de su atmósfera.

2000 a. C.
Calendarios solares y lunares
Los babilonios crean el primer calendario, que integra los 365,25 días del año solar con los 29,53 días del mes lunar. En el antiguo Egipto se usaron calendarios similares.

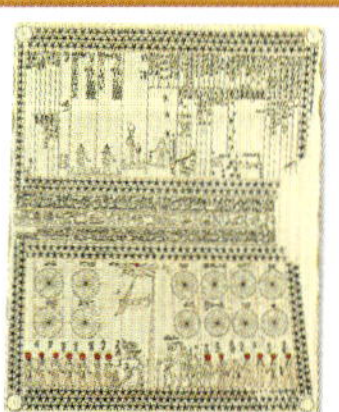
Zodíaco de Senmut

Estela fronteriza babilonia

***C.* 1400 a. C.**
Los dioses y el zodíaco
En Egipto se crea la primera representación conocida del zodíaco (en el techo de la tumba de Senmut), con estrellas, planetas y deidades asociadas. También aparecen zodíacos en artefactos babilonios.

***C.* 90 a. C.–168 d. C.**
Universo de Tolomeo
El erudito griego Claudio Tolomeo propone que la Tierra es el centro del cosmos, una idea que prevaleció hasta el siglo XVI.

Constelaciones de Tolomeo

1420
Ulug Beg
El persa Ulug Beg construye un observatorio en Samarcanda y mide la inclinación del eje de la Tierra hasta 1/100 de grado.

Observatorio de Ulug Beg

1543
Universo heliocéntrico
Nicolás Copérnico sugiere que la Tierra gira en torno al Sol y no a la inversa. Esto implica que la Tierra es uno más de los seis planetas entonces conocidos.

Sistema solar copernicano

1608–1668
Primeros telescopios
Hans Lippershey, fabricante de lentes holandés pero de origen alemán, construye el primer telescopio refractor en 1608. Posteriormente, Isaac Newton construye el primer telescopio reflector en 1668.

Telescopio de Newton

tubo superior, cubierto con papel vitela decorativo

abertura por la que entra la luz en el telescopio

tubo inferior, hecho con capas de papel y de cartón

lente (ocular) de 35 aumentos

la esfera gira para poder apuntar el tubo del telescopio en distintas direcciones

3 CM ES EL DIÁMETRO DEL **ESPEJO PRIMARIO, U OBJETIVO**, DEL TELESCOPIO DE NEWTON. LOS **TELESCOPIOS MODERNOS** TIENEN ESPEJOS DE HASTA **1040 CM DE DIÁMETRO**

tornillo que mantiene el espejo primario en posición

soporte

base de madera

placa conmemorativa de la donación del telescopio a la Royal Society de Londres en enero de 1672

Telescopio de Newton
Isaac Newton construyó su primer telescopio reflector en 1668. Poco después construyó un segundo modelo (en la imagen), de unos 20 cm de altura. Fue el primero en utilizar un espejo primario en lugar de una lente para recoger la luz; un espejo secundario la refleja a través de una lente de aumento para ver la imagen.

Década de 1780
William Herschel
Herschel halla Urano (1781) con un telescopio casero. Fabrica 400 telescopios más, incluido un reflector de 1,26 m.

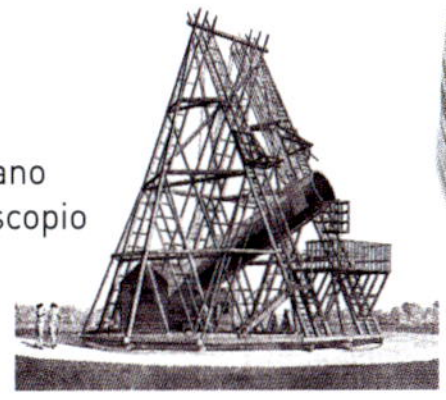

Telescopio de Herschel (1,26 metros)

Telescopio espacial Hubble

1990–actualidad
Telescopios espaciales
Telescopios como el Hubble y el James Webb se sitúan cerca de la Tierra o en su órbita, desde donde observan el cielo sin obstáculos.

Década de 1920
Edwin Hubble
Con el telescopio Hooker de 2,5 m, Hubble demuestra que hay más de 100 000 millones de galaxias en el universo, que está en expansión.

Telescopio Hooker

Década de 1930
Radiotelescopios
La radioastronomía nace cuando los primeros radiotelescopios detectan ondas de radio procedentes del Sol y de galaxias lejanas.

Radiotelescopio de Grote Reber

Década de 1960–actualidad
En busca de otros mundos
El Sistema Solar se explora con naves espaciales que sobrevuelan, se sitúan en órbita y aterrizan en planetas, asteroides, satélites y cometas.

Vehículo todoterreno en Marte

El saco de Roma en 1527 conmocionó a Europa y destrozó a la Iglesia. Aunque también avergonzó profundamente a Carlos V, significó la confirmación de su poder en Italia.

EL EPISODIO MÁS IMPACTANTE DE LAS GUERRAS DE ITALIA fue el **saco** (saqueo) **de Roma** en 1527 por las tropas de Carlos V. Este hecho también subrayó las contradicciones a las que se enfrentaba Carlos V en su intento de imponer el orden en sus vastos territorios. Como emperador del Sacro Imperio era el aliado natural de la Iglesia católica y el enemigo natural del luteranismo (*véase* 1517). Sin embargo, no solo estaba en guerra con la Santa Liga papal (creada para evitar que dominara Italia), sino que parte de las tropas que arrasaron Roma cuando su ejército se descontroló en protesta por las soldadas que se le debían, simpatizaba con la doctrina de Lutero. Pese a ello, mientras el papa Clemente VII se refugiaba en el castillo de Sant'Angelo, iglesias y palacios eran saqueados, las monjas violadas y los sacerdotes asesinados, Carlos V fortaleció su control sobre Italia.

Después de su victoria en Mohács en 1526 y la conquista de gran parte de Hungría en 1529, los **otomanos** temían que los Habsburgo intentaran recuperar los territorios perdidos, por lo que decidieron sitiar **Viena**. Esto resultó una hazaña demasiado ambiciosa incluso para el formidable ejército otomano, ya que el mal tiempo demostró ser tan temible como los austriacos. Un segundo intento de tomar la ciudad en 1532 también fracasó.

Baber, tras su victoria en **Panipat** en 1526, reafirmó su dominio sobre el norte de India al año siguiente, al derrotar al ejército rajputa de Rana Sanga en la **batalla de Khanwa**. El poder mogol logró la consolidación definitiva en 1529, con la destrucción del ejército afgano en Gagra.

En 1531 se formó la **liga de Esmalkalda**, una alianza militar, en origen entre los gobernantes luteranos de Hesse y Sajonia, en el norte de Alemania, por la que se comprometían a ayudarse si Carlos V intentaba reinstaurar el catolicismo por la fuerza. Rápidamente pasó a incluir a otros estados alemanes protestantes, además de ganarse el apoyo de los enemigos exteriores de Carlos: los otomanos y Francia. También representaba una oportunidad para los estados de enriquecerse a costa de las propiedades de la Iglesia.

Sitio de Viena
El asedio otomano de Viena en 1529 fracasó por culpa del tiempo (fuertes lluvias otoñales y nevadas tempranas) y del éxito del avituallamiento vienés.

SOLIMÁN I (1494–1566)

Los 46 años de su reinado estuvieron marcados por una serie de victorias en los Balcanes, Oriente Medio y el norte de África, que hicieron de los otomanos la presencia más dinámica y dominante del hemisferio occidental. En Occidente se le conoce como «el Magnífico», y en el mundo islámico como *Kanuri* o «el Legislador». En su tiempo florecieron la cultura y el arte otomanos.

1532

Atahualpa, último emperador inca, lidera a su ejército en Cajamarca.

TANTO LA EXPLORACIÓN COMO LA COLONIZACIÓN ESPAÑOLAS del Nuevo Mundo, que la conquista de México reforzó en el año 1521, continuaron a una escala todavía más espectacular cuando **Francisco Pizarro** (1476–1541) logró apoderarse del Imperio inca de Perú en 1532. En poco más de un año, un grupo de 188 españoles venció a un estado altamente organizado y con cinco millones de habitantes. Como ocurrió durante la invasión de México por Cortés, su éxito se debió a las divisiones internas del **Imperio inca** y a una combinación de celo religioso, codicia y superioridad militar (acero, pistolas y armaduras contra las piedras afiladas y armaduras de algodón incas), todo ello orquestado por el ambicioso Pizarro.

Al otro lado del continente, la penetración europea en América del Sur proseguía, aunque a una escala menor. En 1532, los portugueses fundaron su primer asentamiento permanente en **Brasil**, en San Vicente, el núcleo de lo que hacia finales de siglo ya se había convertido en una enorme operación colonial basada en la esclavitud y en las plantaciones de caña de azúcar.

En 1532, las hostilidades entre la liga de Esmalkalda alemana y el emperador Carlos V llegaron a su fin gracias a la firma de la **paz de Nuremberg**. Martín Lutero recibió con agrado todas las concesiones hechas a los protestantes, como la libertad de culto, que permitieron a los protestantes alemanes extenderse por todo el país a lo largo de la década siguiente.

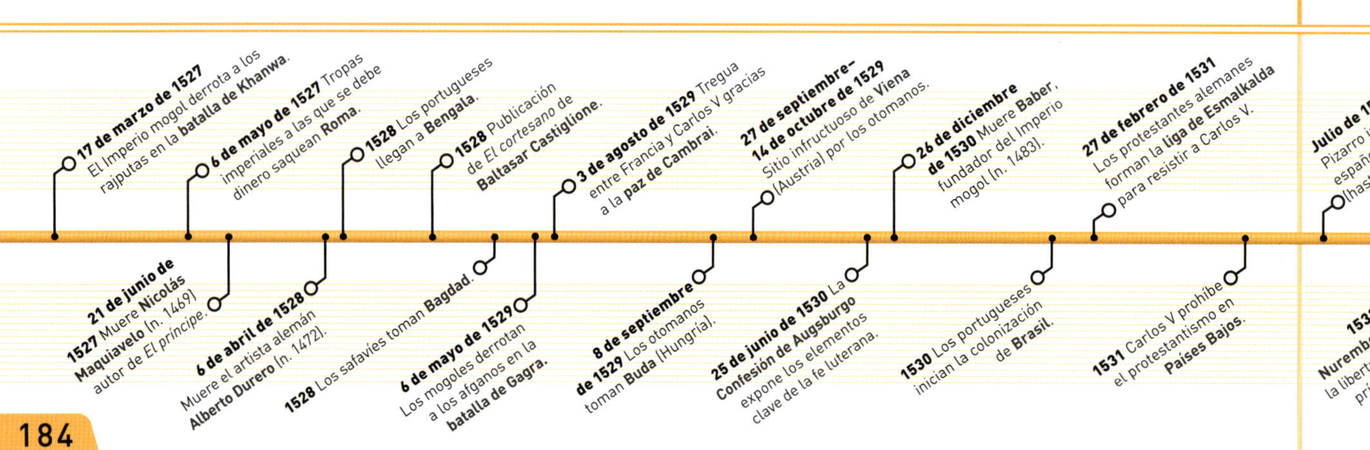

1533–1534

« EL **ESCÁNDALO** DE LA **CRISTIANDAD** Y UNA **VERGÜENZA PARA TI**. »

Catalina de Aragón a Enrique VIII, sobre Ana Bolena (1533)

1535–1537

La toma de Túnez en junio de 1535 fue el único gran éxito de Carlos V en sus campañas contra los otomanos en el Mediterráneo.

ENRIQUE VIII DE INGLATERRA había recibido del papa León X el título de *fidei defensor* (defensor de la fe) en reconocimiento a su férrea defensa de la Iglesia católica contra los ataques protestantes. Enrique siguió siendo hasta su muerte un católico devoto y contrario a cualquier reforma de la práctica católica. No obstante, la Iglesia romana le excomulgó en 1533, y al año siguiente el rey confirmó la ruptura definitiva al instaurar una iglesia nacional, completamente independiente de Roma y de la que él mismo era la cabeza. Los motivos que condujeron al rey a esta inesperada ruptura fueron muy simples. Al principio, Enrique deseaba **divorciarse** de su esposa española ya entrada en años, **Catalina de Aragón**, que después de 24 años de matrimonio no había podido darle ningún hijo varón. Enrique se había convencido a sí mismo de que esto era un castigo divino por haberse casado con la viuda de su hermano mayor, Arturo, fallecido en 1504, solo un año después de su matrimonio con Catalina. Enrique y Catalina se casaron en 1509. El papa, que se vio sometido a las fuertes presiones de Carlos V, sobrino de Catalina, le negó el divorcio; la respuesta de Enrique, formulada a lo largo de varios años, fue convertirse en su propio papa, con total capacidad para autorizar el divorcio. Además, sabía que, como en el resto de Europa, el gobernante que además controlara a la Iglesia de su país aumentaría necesariamente su propia autoridad. Así, en 1534 la Ley de Supremacía legitimó a la **Iglesia de Inglaterra** (o anglicana). El **catolicismo romano fue abolido** para defender los intereses personales de Enrique.

Ana Bolena
Enrique VIII se casó en secreto con ella en enero de 1533, cuatro meses antes de divorciarse de Catalina de Aragón. Ana fue coronada en junio.

LA ORDEN JESUITA

La respuesta católica inicial a la Reforma fue dubitativa y descoordinada, dirigida por personas concretas más que por la propia Iglesia. Ignacio de Loyola (dcha.), un noble vasco, fundó la Compañía de Jesús en el año 1534. El objetivo de san Ignacio era el de formar una generación de sacerdotes eruditos que difundieran una renovada fe católica militante. La orden acabó recibiendo la sanción papal en 1540 e impulsó la Contrarreforma.

TRAS LA RUPTURA CON ROMA, era lógico que el estado confiscara todas las estructuras que la Iglesia católica poseía en Inglaterra. No tan solo se trataba de erradicar la autoridad papal: la Iglesia católica inglesa era inmensamente rica, y Enrique VIII, siempre escaso de dinero, estaba decidido a hacerse con toda aquella fortuna. Durante 1535, el secretario del rey, **Thomas Cromwell** (*c.* 1485–1540) se encargó de la **disolución de los monasterios del país**. Iniciada en 1536, culminó en 1539 y consistió en un vandalismo sistemático que supuso la mayor transferencia de propiedad de tierras en Inglaterra desde la conquista normanda del año 1066. Todos y cada uno de los 560 monasterios ingleses fueron disueltos, lo que supuso un incremento de cerca de 200 000 libras anuales a las arcas de la corona. Sin embargo, todo ese dinero desapareció en solo unos pocos años, derrochado por el rey.

Enrique VIII tuvo que divorciarse de Catalina de Aragón en 1533 para así poder casarse con **Ana Bolena**. No obstante, cuando esta tampoco le dio un hijo varón, decidió ejecutarla **acusándola de adulterio**, en 1536. Ese mismo año, las tensiones por el ritmo y el alcance de los cambios religiosos, y la sincera preocupación que muchos sentían porque la ruptura con Roma supusiera unos cambios mucho más profundos en el tejido de la Iglesia tradicional, alcanzaron un punto álgido en el norte de Inglaterra. La **Peregrinación de Gracia** fue el mayor levantamiento en Inglaterra desde la revuelta de los campesinos de 1381. Los participantes no estaban en absoluto insatisfechos con la Iglesia católica y tampoco estaban dispuestos a ver cómo se rompía con siglos de un culto tradicional. Debido a la magnitud de dicha protesta, Enrique VIII terminó cediendo a sus demandas, pero una vez resuelta la crisis, ejecutó a sus líderes.

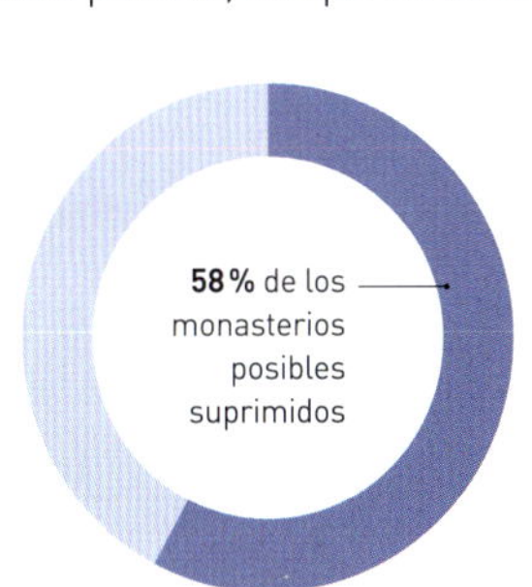

Disolución de los monasterios
Bajo la Ley de Disolución de los Monasterios Menores de 1536 se clausuraron o se suprimieron 243 de los 419 monasterios posibles.

29 590 PENITENCIAS IMPUESTAS

1175 personas quemadas

INQUISICIÓN PORTUGUESA

644 quemadas en efigie

La Inquisición portuguesa
Entre los años 1540 y 1794, los tribunales de Lisboa, Coímbra, Oporto y Évora enviaron a la muerte en la hoguera a 1175 personas, la mayoría de ellas judías.

Distraído por lo que sucedía en Europa, Carlos V apenas pudo dedicarse a su objetivo de rechazar a los otomanos hasta los territorios turcos. Sin embargo, en 1535 obtuvo un éxito aislado gracias a la **conquista de Túnez**, en el norte de África. La victoria resultó muy cara y provocó que los otomanos saquearan Mallorca, donde capturaron a seis mil cristianos, además de animar al monarca francés a estrechar la colaboración con ellos.

Aunque no alcanzó la notoriedad de su equivalente española (*véase* 1480), la **Inquisición portuguesa**, fundada en 1536, fue igualmente enérgica en Portugal y, a partir de 1560, en sus colonias, como Goa. Su principal objetivo eran los judíos, muchos de ellos de origen español, obligados a abrazar el catolicismo.

11 de julio de 1533 Enrique VIII es excomulgado.

7 de septiembre de 1533 Nace Isabel I de Inglaterra (m. 1603).

26 de julio de 1533 Francisco Pizarro asesina al emperador inca **Atahualpa**.

1533 El artista alemán **Hans Holbein el Joven** pinta *Los embajadores*.

Febrero de 1534 Los **anabaptistas** toman Münster (Alemania) y la declaran la «Nueva Jerusalén».

9 de junio de 1534 Jacques Cartier alcanza la orilla del río San Lorenzo.

Agosto de 1534 Ignacio de Loyola funda la Compañía de Jesús **(jesuitas)**.

Noviembre de 1534 La ley de Supremacía funda la **Iglesia de Inglaterra**.

1534 El tratado de Augsburgo alía a Francia con príncipes alemanes protestantes contra Carlos V.

1534 El escritor francés **François Rabelais** escribe *Gargantúa*.

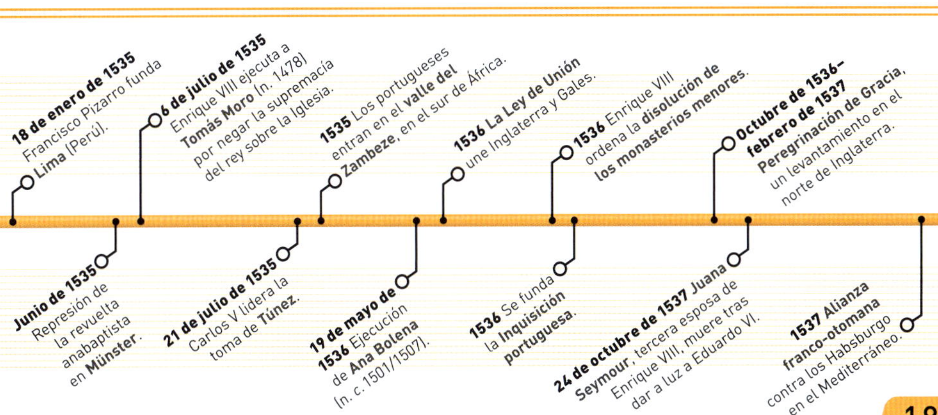

18 de enero de 1535 Francisco Pizarro funda **Lima** (Perú).

Junio de 1535 Represión de la revuelta anabaptista en **Münster**.

6 de julio de 1535 Enrique VIII ejecuta a **Tomás Moro** (n. 1478) por negar la supremacía del rey sobre la Iglesia.

21 de julio de 1535 Carlos V lidera la toma de **Túnez**.

1535 Los portugueses entran en el **valle del Zambeze**, en el sur de África.

19 de mayo de 1536 Ejecución de **Ana Bolena** (n. c. 1501/1507).

1536 La Ley de Unión une Inglaterra y Gales.

1536 Se funda la **Inquisición portuguesa**.

1536 Enrique VIII ordena la **disolución de los monasterios menores**.

24 de octubre de 1537 Juana **Seymour**, tercera esposa de Enrique VIII, muere tras dar a luz a Eduardo VI.

Octubre de 1536–febrero de 1537 Peregrinación de Gracia, un levantamiento en el norte de Inglaterra.

1537 Alianza franco-otomana contra los Habsburgo en el Mediterráneo.

1538–1541

Ilustración del *Atlas Vallard*, de 1547, que representa a Jacques Cartier y miembros de la fallida colonia francocanadiense de 1541–1542.

« ME INCLINO A CREER QUE **ESTA ES LA TIERRA QUE DIOS DIO A CAÍN.** »

Jacques Cartier, explorador francés, sobre Canadá (1536)

LA BATALLA DE PRÉVEZA, librada ante Grecia occidental en septiembre de 1538 puso de manifiesto la potencia naval otomana, enfrentada a la flota conjunta papal, veneciana, genovesa y española, reunida por el papa Paulo III. La **victoria otomana** subrayó la dificultad cristiana de aunar fuerzas dispares en una alianza precaria.

En agosto de 1539, **Gante**, la ciudad natal de Carlos V, **se alzó** contra él en protesta por el impuesto exigido para financiar las guerras de Italia. El conflicto reveló las dificultades a las que se enfrentaba Carlos V a la hora de imponer su autoridad sobre ciudades autónomas decididas a proteger sus «libertades» negándose a sufragar las guerras lejanas de un soberano no igualmente distante. Carlos dirigió personalmente la represión de la revuelta, y obligó a los notables de la ciudad a desfilar descalzos. Sin embargo, la tensión subyacente no desapareció.

A pesar de todos los esfuerzos que se llevaron a cabo, **la exploración española de América del Norte** durante el siglo XVI fue absolutamente desalentadora. Los mitos que la impulsaban (la existencia de una vía marítima entre el Atlántico y el Pacífico, o de las «siete ciudades de oro») resultaron ser justamente eso: mitos. La realidad era que se trataba de unos territorios inmensos, hostiles y pobres. Aun así, en 1539, **Hernando de Soto** inició una expedición de cuatro años a través de los territorios del sur de los actuales EE. UU. De igual modo, en 1540–1542, **Francisco Vázquez de Coronado** condujo una expedición aún mayor desde México hacia el norte y llegó hasta Kansas, y en 1542–1543, **Juan Rodríguez Cabrillo** dirigió una flota en dirección norte a lo largo de la desconocida costa pacífica y recaló en el puerto de San Diego. Sin embargo, ni una sola de dichas expediciones tuvo continuidad hasta finales de siglo.

Batalla de Préveza
A pesar de su gran envergadura, la flota cristiana cayó ante la otomana, liderada por Jair al-Din (Barbarroja), en la batalla de Préveza de septiembre de 1538.

Los intentos franceses de asentarse en América del Norte, motivados en parte por el temor a que España llegase primero (del mismo modo que los españoles querían evitar que Francia se les adelantara), no gozaron de más éxito. **Jacques Cartier** (1491–1557) dirigió las primeras expediciones en 1534 y posteriormente en 1535–1536, durante las cuales descubrió y reclamó para Francia el golfo de San Lorenzo y el río del mismo nombre, en el actual **Canadá**. En 1541, y alarmada por las intenciones españolas, Francia envió una expedición mucho más numerosa a Canadá, con el objetivo explícito de fundar un asentamiento permanente. La dirigió Jean-François de La Rocque de Roberval, asistido por Cartier, y fue un fracaso total. Cartier volvió sin autorización a Francia en 1542, con «oro y diamantes» sin valor, y Roberval abandonó la colonia un año más tarde, tras un invierno de hambruna. Francia tardó medio siglo en reemprender sus esfuerzos en América del Norte.

Por otro lado, san **Francisco Javier** (1506–1552), cofundador de los **jesuitas** en 1534, llevó a cabo su obra misionera entre 1541 y 1552, como parte de la respuesta católica a la Reforma. Concebidas a una escala heroica, las misiones tenían el propósito de llevar el cristianismo a Asia oriental. Francisco Javier viajó a Goa vía Mozambique y siguió hasta las islas de las Especias entre 1545 y 1547; luego llegó hasta Cantón y Japón antes de regresar a China, donde falleció en 1552. Se dice que solo san Pablo convirtió a más personas al cristianismo.

- **28 de septiembre de 1538** Victoria otomana en la **batalla de Préveza**.
- **1538** Portugal somete **Yemen y Adén**.
- **Agosto de 1539** Carlos V reprime la sublevación de **Gante**.
- **1539 Hernando de Soto** explora el sur de Estados Unidos (hasta 1543).
- **6 de enero de 1540** Enrique VIII se casa con **Ana de Clèves** (1515–1557), su cuarta esposa.
- **28 de julio de 1540** Ejecución de **Thomas Cromwell** (n. c. 1485), primer ministro de Enrique VIII.
- **28 de julio de 1540** Enrique VIII se casa con su quinta esposa, **Catalina Howard** (n. c. 1520–1525).
- **27 de septiembre de 1540** Los **jesuitas** reciben autorización papal.
- **1540** Los **afganos** detienen la expansión mogola temporalmente.
- **1540** Portugal forja vínculos comerciales con **Cochinchina** (actual Vietnam).
- **1540 Pedro de Valdivia** cruza el desierto de Atacama (Chile) y amplía las conquistas españolas hacia el sur.
- **1540 Francisco Vázquez de Coronado** explora el suroeste de Estados Unidos (hasta 1542).
- **7 de abril de 1541** La misión jesuita de **Francisco Javier** parte desde Portugal hacia el Lejano Oriente.
- **26 de junio de 1541** Asesinato del conquistador español **Francisco Pizarro** (n. c. 1471/1476).
- **1541** Jacques Cartier funda **Charlesbourg Royal**, colonia francesa en Canadá (abandonada en 1543).
- **1541** El sur de **Hungría** pasa a ser provincia otomana.

1542–1548

EN 1543, EUROPA Y JAPÓN ESTABLECIERON CONTACTO POR PRIMERA VEZ. Según el escritor y explorador portugués **Fernão Mendes Pinto**, tuvo lugar en la isla de Tanegashima, al sur del archipiélago japonés principal. Además de introducir las armas de fuego en el país, los portugueses sirvieron de intermediarios entre China y Japón, cuyos comerciantes tenían prohibidos los tratos con China debido a los persistentes ataques de los piratas japoneses.

En 1543, el astrónomo y matemático polaco **Nicolás Copérnico** (1473–1543) publicó *De las revoluciones de las esferas celestes*, una obra basada no tanto en las observaciones realizadas por el propio Copérnico como en las de astrónomos griegos y árabes. Sin embargo, consiguió demostrar que esas antiguas observaciones podían explicarse mucho mejor por la **órbita de la Tierra alrededor del Sol** que a la inversa. Otros as-

Universo de Copérnico
Grabado de Andreas Cellarius, realizado en 1660, que muestra «El sistema de todo el universo creado según Copérnico».

- **13 de febrero de 1542 Catalina Howard** es ejecutada.
- **6 de mayo de 1542 Francisco Javier** llega a Goa.
- **26 de agosto de 1542** El español **Francisco de Orellana** completa la primera navegación completa del río Amazonas.
- **28 de septiembre de 1542** El portugués **Juan Rodríguez Cabrillo** llega a la actual San Diego en su exploración de la costa californiana.

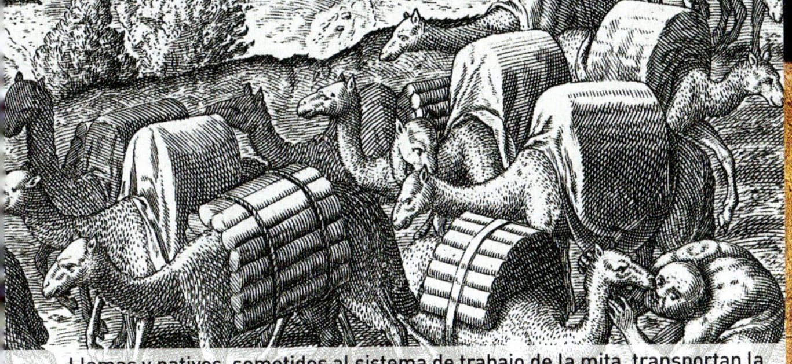

Llamas y nativos, sometidos al sistema de trabajo de la mita, transportan la plata de Potosí. La ciudad minera se convirtió en la mayor del Nuevo Mundo.

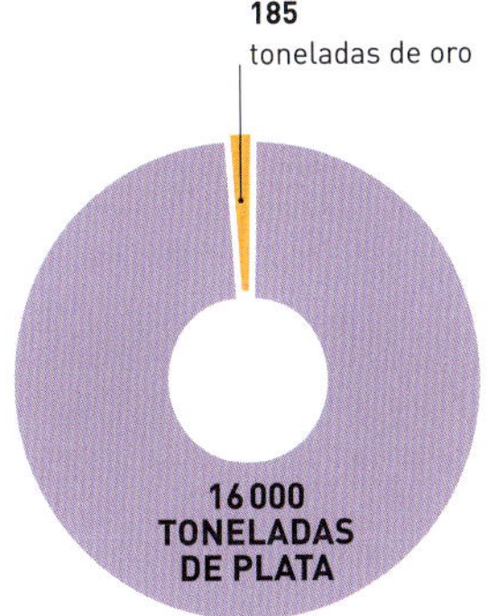

Oro y plata enviados a Sevilla
La montaña de plata de Potosí dominó la exportación de metales preciosos enviados a España desde Chile y México entre 1503 y 1660.

trónomos, sobre todo el danés Tycho Brahe en la década de 1570, tuvieron que hacer numerosas observaciones directas a fin de demostrar que Copérnico estaba en lo cierto. De todos modos, su obra abrió una gran brecha en la teoría geocéntrica del universo.

También en 1534 Vesalio publicó *Sobre la estructura del cuerpo humano*. Al igual que Copérnico, **Andrés Vesalio** (1514–1564) se basó en los conocimientos de la antigua Grecia, pero también llevó a cabo observaciones directas a partir de la disección de varios cuerpos humanos. Quizá sea este el momento inicial de una **revolución científica** en Occidente: la creencia de que la observación empírica posibilita la mejor explicación del mundo que nos rodea.

Desde que se formara la **liga de Esmalkalda** protestante en 1534, Carlos V se vio obligado a controlar esta amenaza a su autoridad como emperador del Sacro Imperio. Distraído en permanencia por Francia y por los otomanos, poco más pudo hacer que aplacar a la liga (*véase* 1532); solo en 1546, tras haber firmado la **paz de Crépy** con Francia en 1544, pudo enfrentarse directamente a ella. El resultado, decidido en la **batalla de Mühlberg** en abril de 1547, fue una abrumadora victoria militar de Carlos V que, no obstante, tuvo consecuencias contradictorias a largo plazo.

En 1545, los colonizadores españoles descubrieron en **Potosí** (en la actual Bolivia) los mayores yacimientos de plata encontrados hasta ese momento: una montaña entera. Junto con la del norte de México, la plata de Potosí se convirtió en el motor del Imperio español, siempre necesitado de dinero, y financió tanto el comercio español con China como los intentos de dominar Europa.

Ese mismo año, la Iglesia católica se propuso enfrentarse a la Reforma protestante reformándose y renovándose en Trento (situado en los Alpes italianos). El **concilio de Trento** quiso erradicar la corrupción, dar una mayor coherencia a las enseñanzas de la Iglesia y proyectarla como una fuerza religiosa competitiva. Este concilio dio origen a **nuevas órdenes católicas** y volvió a reunirse dos veces más, en 1551–1552 y 1559–1563.

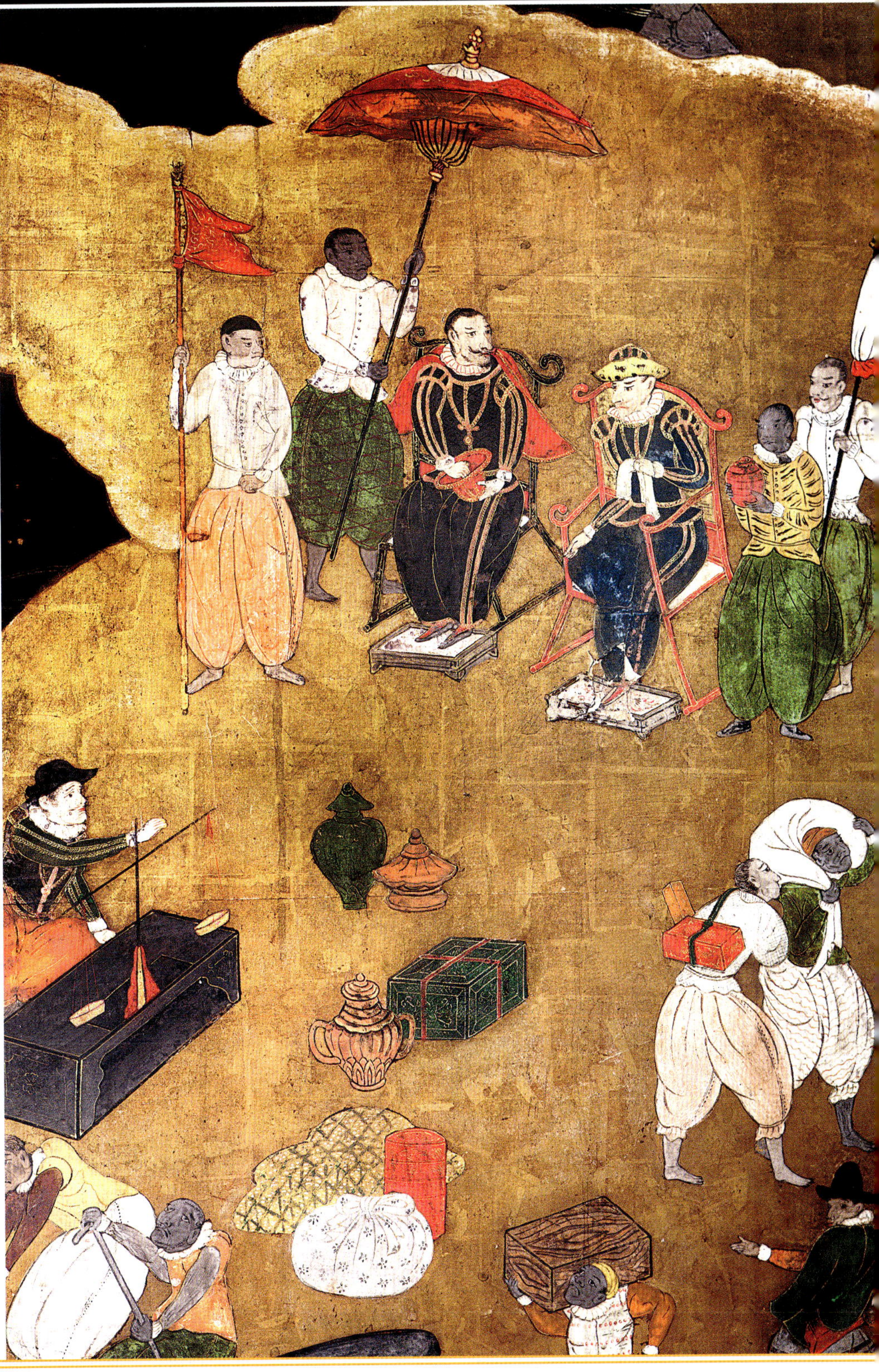

Los portugueses llegan a Japón
Unos comerciantes portugueses muestran algunas de sus mercancías a los curiosos nativos a su llegada a las costas japonesas en 1543.

1542 Nuevas hostilidades entre **Francia y los Habsburgo**.

1542 Se funda la **Inquisición romana**.

3 de enero de 1543 Muerte de **Juan Rodríguez Cabrillo** (n. c. 1499).

1543 Nicolás Copérnico (1473–1543) publica su teoría heliocéntrica.

12 de julio de 1543 Enrique VIII se casa con **Catalina Parr**, su sexta esposa.

1543 Francia ataca Países Bajos, el norte de España y Niza.

1543 Los portugueses llegan a **Japón**.

1543 Andrés Vesalio publica *Sobre la estructura del cuerpo humano*.

1544 Portugal establece puertos comerciales en **Quelimane y la bahía de Maputo**, en el sur de África.

18 de septiembre de 1544 Paz de Crépy entre Francia y los Habsburgo tras la victoria de Francia en Cerisoles (norte de Italia).

1544 Finalización de **la capilla del King's College** (Cambridge).

Abril de 1545 Los españoles descubren un enorme yacimiento de plata en **Potosí** (Perú, hoy Bolivia).

13 de diciembre de 1545 El **concilio de Trento** acuerda iniciar la Contrarreforma católica.

1545 Los mogoles toman **Kandahar** (actual Afganistán).

4 de julio de 1546 Muere el pirata otomano Jair al-Din, más conocido como **Barbarroja** (n. 1478).

1546 Portugal derrota al ejército indio en **Diu** (India).

Julio de 1546 Comienzo de la **guerra de Esmalkalda** entre Carlos V y la liga de Esmalkalda (hasta 1547).

1546 El **Imperio songay** destruye el Imperio de Malí.

28 de enero de 1547 Muere **Enrique VIII** de Inglaterra (n. 1491).

20 de febrero de 1547 Eduardo VI, rey de Inglaterra.

24 de abril de 1547 Los Habsburgo vencen a la liga de Esmalkalda en la **batalla de Mühlberg**.

2 de diciembre de 1547 Muere el conquistador español **Hernán Cortés** (n. 1485).

1547 Los mogoles toman **Kabul** (actual Afganistán).

8 de septiembre de 1548 Muere **Catalina Parr** (n. 1512).

1548 Los **jesuitas** envían una misión al Congo (África central).

1548 El gobierno Ming cierra **China** al comercio exterior para proteger sus costas de los piratas japoneses.

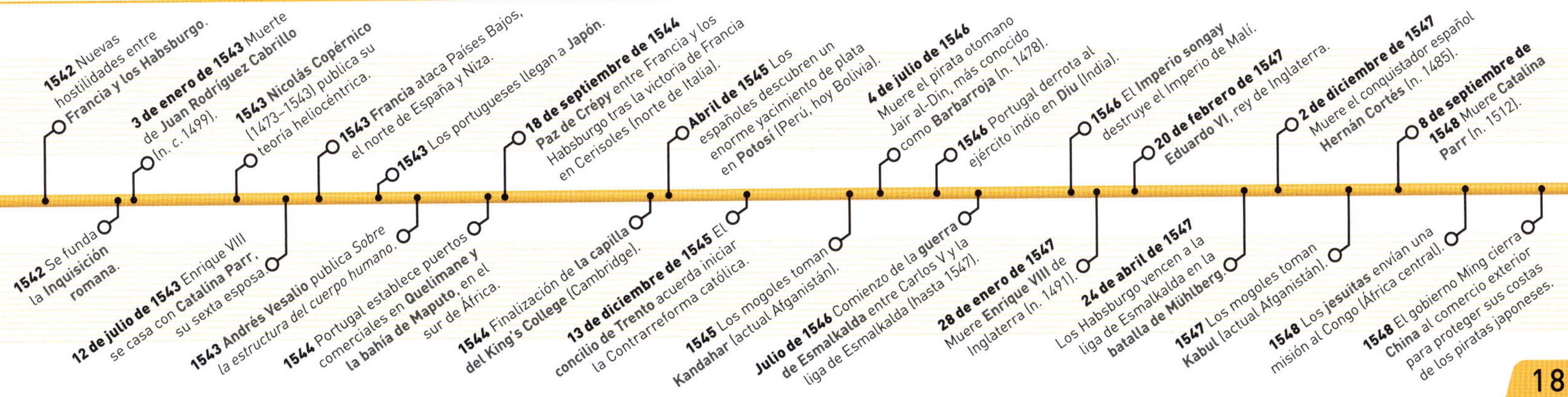

1549–1551

« EL **ARTE DEBE** SU **ORIGEN** A LA **NATURALEZA**... LA BELLA CREACIÓN... FUE **EL PRIMER MODELO**, Y EL **MAESTRO ORIGINAL** FUE **LA INTELIGENCIA DIVINA**. »

Giorgio Vasari, de *Vidas de los mejores arquitectos, pintores y escultores italianos* (1550)

EN EL AÑO 1547, EL ACCESO AL TRONO DE EDUARDO VI de Inglaterra (1537–1553), de solo nueve años de edad, supuso un cambio radical respecto a la postura religiosa de su padre. La Iglesia de Inglaterra de Enrique VIII (*véase* 1534) era protestante solamente por su rechazo

THE booke of the common prayer and adminiſtracion of the Sacramentes, and other rites and ceremonies of the Churche: after the uſe of the Churche of England.

Book of Common Prayer
El Book of Common Prayer *hizo del inglés el idioma de la Iglesia de Inglaterra. También provocó protestas y alzamientos.*

de la autoridad papal; Eduardo VI, guiado por el **duque de Somerset, *lord protector***, que actuaba como jefe de gobierno, y por el arzobispo de Canterbury **Thomas Cranmer** (1489–1556), introdujo una nueva iglesia vehementemente protestante, legitimada en 1549 por la ***Act of Uniformity***, que **prohibía** muchas manifestaciones externas del **culto católico**, como el toque de campanas, y que se vio reforzada por el *Book of Common Prayer* de Cranmer, cuyo uso era obligatorio.

Cuando **Tomé de Sousa**, el primer gobernador general portugués, llegó a **Brasil** en 1549, lo hizo junto con cinco jesuitas liderados por Manuel de Nóbrega (1517–1570), por deseo expreso del rey de Portugal Juan III. En otras palabras, los **jesuitas** (*véase* 1533–1534) fueron cruciales para la colonización portuguesa de Brasil desde el principio. Además de celebrar la primera misa de Brasil en Salvador, la primera capital de la nueva colonia, Nóbrega fundó el **primer colegio jesuita del Nuevo Mundo**. Él y sus compañeros fueron misioneros enérgicos, construyeron **escuelas** y **capillas**, y centraron sus esfuerzos en los niños nativos. Fue un defensor pertinaz de los indios ante la brutalidad de los colonizadores portugueses.

Durante el siglo XVI, la **costa norteafricana** fue uno de los campos de batalla determinantes entre el Occidente cristiano (básicamente España) y el Imperio otomano por el control del Mediterráneo. España necesitaba poner fin a los terribles ataques de los **piratas berberiscos**, alentados por los otomanos, que amenazaban constantemente con cortar las comunicaciones de los Habsburgo con sus territorios italianos. La **toma otomana de Trípoli**, con ayuda naval francesa, asestó un durísimo golpe a las aspiraciones estratégicas de los Habsburgo y supuso una gran **victoria para los turcos**. Posteriormente, la ciudad resistió los repetidos intentos de ser recuperada.

1552–1554

María I, única descendiente de Enrique VIII y Catalina de Aragón que sobrevivió, fue la primera reina de Inglaterra de pleno derecho.

EN 1552 SE ABRIÓ EL ÚLTIMO CAPÍTULO de los más de 60 años de **guerras de Italia** (*véase* 1505–1512). Los franceses se aliaron con los otomanos en el Mediterráneo y también con varios príncipes protestantes, como Mauricio de Sajonia, en Alemania. Inglaterra hizo una última y desastrosa aportación a la causa española en 1557. **María**, hija de Enrique VIII, fue coronada reina en 1553 y en 1554 **se casó** con el hijo de Carlos V, el futuro **Felipe II de España**. Que la reina de una Inglaterra protestante desde 1534 se casara con el hijo del monarca europeo más beligerante a favor del catolicismo tiene fácil explicación. Eduardo VI había sido un rey agresivamente protestante (*véase* 1549–1551), pero María I profesaba un **catolicismo no menos agresivo** y estaba totalmente decidida a restaurar la supremacía católica (y papal). En menos de un año, Inglaterra pasó de

4:1 **Herejes ejecutados**
Durante sus cinco años de reinado, la reina María I envió a la hoguera por herejía a 283 protestantes; de ellos, 227 eran hombres, y 56, mujeres.

un extremo a otro. En 1555 se empezó a **perseguir** sistemáticamente a los **protestantes** más prominentes, 823 de los cuales fueron condenados a morir **quemados en la hoguera**; este es el origen del apodo **«la Sangrienta»** que más se dio a María.

Le ejecución del teólogo y **humanista** español **Miguel Servet**, que murió quemado en la hoguera en Ginebra en octubre de 1553 por orden expresa del reformador francés **Juan Calvino** (1509–1564), marcó un claro punto de inflexión en la **Reforma** (*véase* 1516–1518). Para Calvino, Servet era culpable de «blasfemias execrables», porque negaba su creencia en la predestinación, es decir, que todos los hechos son «voluntad divina» y la salvación eterna tan solo está al alcance de aquellos que se someten a la voluntad de Dios (ampliamente definida por Calvino). Lo más significativo de la ejecución de Servet es que puso de manifiesto que el protestantismo podía ser tan intolerante en lo que respecta a la herejía como lo era el catolicismo. Las implicaciones, sin duda, resultaban inquietantes.

Quemado en la hoguera
Miguel Servet murió en Ginebra con un ejemplar de su libro sujeto a la pierna, exclamando: «¡Jesús, Hijo del Dios eterno, ten compasión de mí!».

1555–1556

Grabado en cobre que representa la paz de Augsburgo de 1555.

LA FASE FINAL DE LAS GUERRAS DE ITALIA evidenció que Carlos V nunca conseguiría imponerse militarmente a los súbditos nominales del Sacro Imperio que habían abrazado el protestantismo. Por lo tanto, y aunque fuera reticente, permitió que su hermano el archiduque Fernando, representante del Sacro Imperio, negociara un acuerdo, la **paz de Augsburgo**, que fue firmada en septiembre de 1555 y que se basaba en el lema *cuius regio eius religio* («a tal rey, tal religión»). Dicho texto permitía a cada gobernante **imponer su propia religión** en sus respectivos territorios. Aunque esta tolerancia supuso un gran avance, la elección únicamente era posible entre catolicismo y luteranismo; el calvinismo (*véase* 1552–1554) y otras formas de protestantismo no estaban incluidos.

En 1556, el ascenso al **trono mogol** de **Akbar**, de solo catorce años de edad, resultó decisivo para el destino de la dinastía. Su padre, Humayun, había presenciado cómo los avances afganos e hindúes erosionaban el Imperio mogol. Akbar consiguió repeler un fuerte ataque hindú durante la **segunda batalla de Panipat**, que tuvo lugar en noviembre de 1556, y amplió enormemente el poder mogol.

Los **zares de Rusia** afirmaban ser los únicos herederos legítimos de Roma y, por lo tanto, los únicos guardianes de la cristiandad; por lo que la expansión rusa por conquista no tan solo era deseable, sino inevitable. **Iván IV**, conocido como **«el Terrible»** (1530–1584), dio un enorme impulso a todas estas ambiciones. Pese a que los

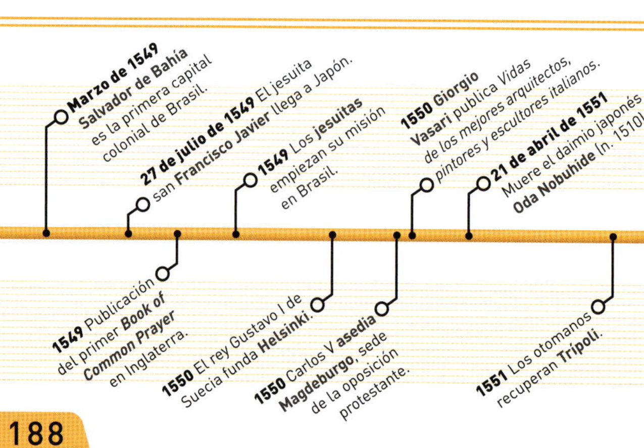

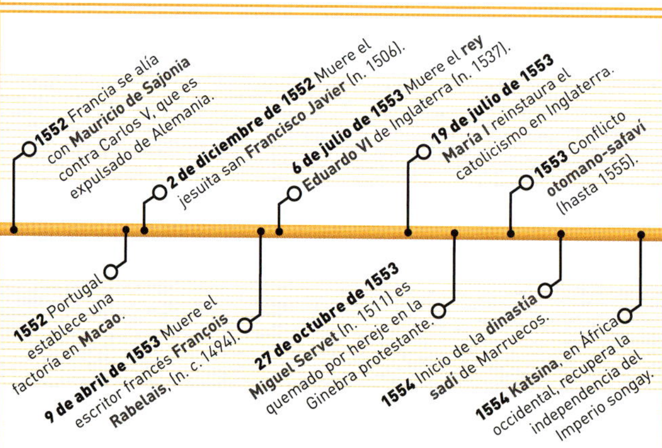

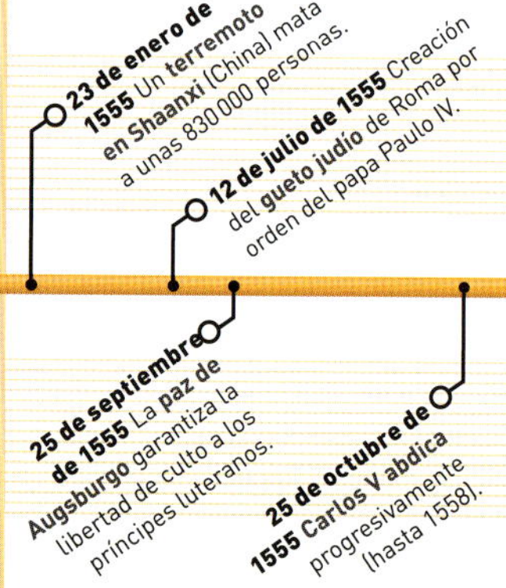

Óleo que representa la reunión de Enrique II de Francia y Felipe II de España en Cateau-Cambrésis el 3 de abril de 1559, para firmar el tratado de paz. En realidad, lo firmaron sus embajadores.

ejércitos lituanos consiguieron frenar sus avances hacia el oeste, obtuvo un gran éxito en aquellas ofensivas dirigidas hacia el sur. En 1552 ya había conquistado el kanato de Kazán y en 1556 realizó una hazaña aún más notable al poner fin al debilitado kanato de Astraján. A partir de ese momento Rusia no solo controlaba las distintas **rutas comerciales hacia Asia central**, sino que además estaba dispuesta a atravesar Siberia hacia el este.

Desfile de Akbar el Grande
Durante los 46 años de reinado de Akbar, la India mogol amplió sus territorios y gozó de prosperidad, tolerancia religiosa y riqueza cultural.

LAS TENSAS RELACIONES ENTRE los portugueses, que desde 1513 intentaban establecer puestos comerciales en China, y los **chinos**, que desconfiaban de las intenciones portuguesas, se relajaron durante la década de 1540, hasta el punto de que en 1552 China accedió a permitir que **Portugal estableciera una factoría en Macao**, en la costa sur de China. Era lo que los portugueses habían estado buscando. En 1557, este enclave temporal ya era permanente y acabó convirtiéndose en un punto crucial para el sistema comercial global de Portugal y, luego, de España. Macao siguió siendo portugués hasta 1999.

En 1557, Felipe II de España persuadió a su esposa, **María I de Inglaterra** (*véase* 1552–1554) para que se uniera a España en su **nueva guerra con Francia**. Fue un terrible desastre que desembocó en la **pérdida de Calais** en enero de 1558. Calais había sido inglesa desde 1360 y era el último enclave que Inglaterra conservaba en el continente europeo. María murió sin hijos en noviembre de 1558; le sucedió su hermanastra Isabel I, hija de Ana Bolena.

Toma de Calais
Placa esmaltada del artista francés Léonard Limosin que conmemora la toma de Calais por las tropas francesas al mando del duque Francisco de Guisa el 7 de enero de 1558.

CLAVE
Territorio de Moscú (1300–1505)
Expansión de Moscú (1505–1584)

Expansión de Moscú
En 1547, Iván IV transformó el Gran Ducado de Moscú en Imperio de Rusia. En la década de 1550 inició la expansión de sus fronteras; durante su reinado, duplicó su población y sus territorios.

La **paz de Cateau-Cambrésis**, firmada en abril de 1559, marcó el **final definitivo de las guerras de Italia**. Sin embargo, resultó ser un éxito muy breve. La España de los Habsburgo había sido la clara vencedora y había establecido su dominio total sobre Italia (a expensas del papado y de Francia). Francia conservó Calais, Metz, Toul y Verdún. Los términos del tratado implicaban de modo tácito que la contribución militar y económica de Países Bajos al conflicto había servido principalmente para que España lograra sus objetivos en Italia. Era prácticamente seguro que estallaría un conflicto entre Países Bajos y España. Una consecuencia impredecible fue la **muerte del rey francés, Enrique II** (n. 1519) tres meses más tarde, durante un torneo que se organizó para celebrar el tratado. La sucesión de niños-rey que se dio a continuación acabó sumiendo a Francia en una guerra civil que duró 40 años (*véase* 1572).

En 1558, el **zar Iván IV** prosiguió su política de **expansión rusa** con los primeros asentamientos en el kanato de Sibir (Siberia occidental). En 1552, la conquista de Kazán había abierto el camino hacia los Urales y Siberia, al este. La colonización fue liderada por mercaderes ricos, como los Strogonov, que obtuvieron a cambio tierras y beneficios fiscales. Durante la década de 1570, los cosacos protegieron la **migración a gran escala** a Siberia, que permitió establecer vínculos comerciales con las tribus nativas. El kanato de Sibir fue conquistado en 1582, lo que aumentó significativamente la extensión de Rusia.

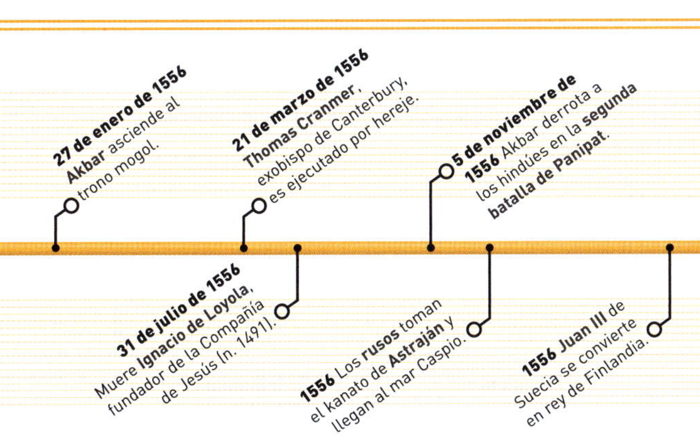

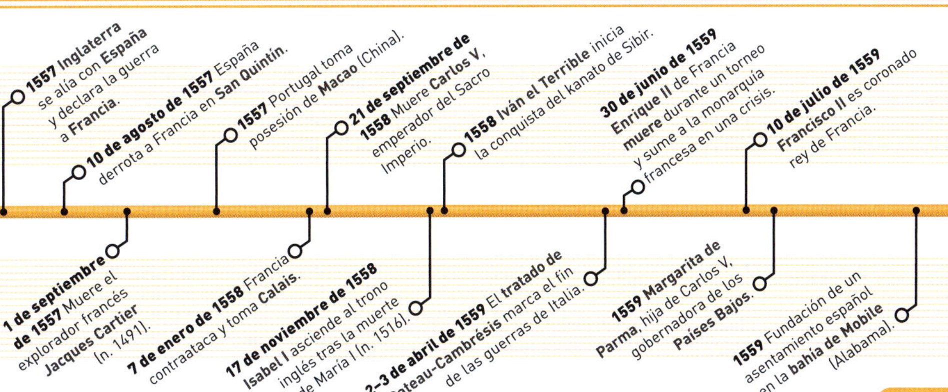

Inro lacado
1750–1799
Los inros eran cajitas que colgaban del cinturón y se ataban con un netsuke. Este ejemplar de laca y oro está decorado con escenas de Kioto.

superficie dorada

el netsuke impide que el inro caiga del cinturón

cordón

Netsuke de luchador
1800–1850
Durante el periodo Edo se elaboraron ingeniosos botones tallados llamados netsuke. Este que representa a un caracol sobre una seta está hecho de madera de boj.

Tetera
Siglo XVII
Esta tetera, que tenía tapa, es de loza de Agano. Su forma, cuerpo negro y vidriado azul imitan a los objetos importados de China para la ceremonia del té.

figura humana

Cuenco de té de porcelana
1700–1750
Utilizado como taza, es un ejemplo de porcelana de Arita azul y blanca, decorada con figuras a imitación de un diseño chino del periodo de Kangxi.

decoración floral característica

Plato de Imari
Periodo Edo
Una gran parte de la porcelana de Imari, nombre de su principal puerto de distribución, presenta la misma paleta que este plato, dominada por los tonos azules, rosas y naranjas.

PERIODO EDO

EL ARTE JAPONÉS FLORECIÓ BAJO EL GOBIERNO DE LOS SOGUNES TOKUGAWA

El periodo Edo (1603–1868) fue pacífico. Los comerciantes ricos eran cultivados y empezaron a disfrutar de artes cuyo disfrute antes estaba reservado a las élites terratenientes y a los guerreros samuráis.

Los artistas y artesanos japoneses se inspiraban en la cultura del *ukiyo* (mundo flotante), que a su vez se basaba en el concepto budista de que todo es ilusión. El Japón Edo, asoció el *ukiyo* a los placeres fugaces, desde flirtear con cortesanas hasta asistir a representaciones de teatro kabuki. Los artesanos buscaban una estética de elegancia sobrenatural. Rodeados de belleza, sus clientes se dedicaban a sus quehaceres, desde escribir a orar, como si también formaran parte del ilusorio mundo flotante.

las varillas de bambú dan rigidez al abanico

monte Fuji

Abanico estampado
1858
Este abanico de finales del periodo Edo, de bambú y papel, está decorado con una escena de Hiroshige II (1826–1869) serigrafiada en cada cara.

superficie lacada

trono de loto

Buda de madera
Siglo XVIII
Las ideas de Tokugawa sobre una sociedad coherente procedían del budismo. Esta pequeña imagen servía para recordar a Buda.

sombrero de paja decorativo

finura de detalles

Figura de marfil
Siglo XVIII
Esta delicada talla de marfil de una anciana con un haz de leña lleva la inscripción de Gyokusen.

la pieza superior aumenta la altura

pieza desmontable

Linterna de latón
Siglo XVIII
Este enorme farol portátil destinado a un uso exterior, probablemente cerca de una entrada, se desmonta en cinco piezas.

decoración con tinta zen

Biombo plegable
Periodo Edo
Los paneles *(fusuma)* y los biombos servían de tabiques móviles durante el periodo Edo.

Estampa de brocado
Siglo XVIII
Esta *nishiki-e* (estampa de brocado) de Suzuki Harunobu (c. 1725–1770), titulada *Verdad-Sinceridad*, fue realizada superponiendo impresiones de tacos de tinta de distintos colores.

Máscara teatral
Periodo Edo
Esta máscara representa a Hannya, personaje femenino del teatro *no* a quien los celos y la ira convirtieron en demonio. El teatro *no* coexistió con otros estilos, como el kabuki.

Utensilios de escritura
1800–1899
La clase acomodada practicaba la caligrafía como actividad de ocio. Los compartimentos de esta caja contienen pinceles y otros útiles necesarios para este arte.

Xilografías encuadernadas
1779
Los grabados monocromos se obtienen mediante una impresión única con un taco de madera tallado. Algunos ejemplos posteriores se coloreaban a mano.

1560–1562

« SIN DESTRUCCIÓN,
NO HAY **CREACIÓN**...
NI HAY **CAMBIO.** »

Oda Nobunaga (1534–1582)

Oda Nobunaga se mostró implacable con los daimios regionales de Japón, en busca de un control que acabó unificando al país.

HACIA 1560, ODA NOBUNAGA, líder del clan Oda en el centro de Japón, se estaba convirtiendo en el mayor de los señores feudales regionales, o daimios. Después de la desastrosa guerra de Onin, iniciada en 1466, **Japón había sido ingobernable**, y los daimios luchaban brutalmente por la supremacía. Los portugueses, que llegaron hacia mediados del XV e introdujeron las armas de fuego, no hicieron más que aumentar el caos; los japoneses demostraron ser alumnos aventajados en los bombardeos de artillería al estilo occidental (*véase* 1574–1577).

A partir de 1561, los **territorios bálticos** de la **orden Portaespadas o livonia** (*véase* 1236–1240), que ya había perdido Prusia oriental en 1525, cuando el gran maestre de los caballeros teutónicos, Alberto de Brandeburgo, se convirtió al protestantismo, **fueron desmembrados progresivamente** por Rusia, Suecia, Polonia y Dinamarca. En origen, Livonia había sido una entidad fronteriza cruzada (es decir, cristiana) y cayó víctima, en parte de la Reforma, pero sobre todo de la rivalidad entre Polonia y Rusia, que no estaban dispuestas a que una creciera a expensas de la otra.

Pocos conflictos resultaron tan desestabilizadores como las **guerras de religión francesas**, que empezaron en 1562 y se prolongaron hasta 1598. En sentido estricto fueron ocho guerras, pero en realidad se trató de un único conflicto muy prolongado. Por un lado se dirimía una cuestión religiosa: ¿Francia debía ser católica o protestante? Inevitablemente, esto significó que los principales **gobernantes católicos y protestantes de Europa** se vieron **arrastrados al conflicto**, ya que ni el papa ni el rey español Felipe II deseaban una victoria protestante, al igual que los líderes protestantes rechazaban a un líder católico. Sin embargo, también se trataba de decidir quién ostentaba la autoridad en Francia, si la corona o los nobles, ya fueran **católicos o hugonotes**. A los protestantes franceses se les conocía como hugonotes, por el término suizo-germano *Eidgenossen*, o «juramento de camaradería». Aunque los católicos eran mayoría, los protestantes estaban bien organizados, y ambos bandos contaban con poderosos líderes aristocráticos para quienes el conflicto también era político. Las minorías monárquicas siempre habían provocado inestabilidad política (*véase* 1557–1559), pero desde 1560 esta se había agravado por la sucesión de tres reyes incapaces de dominar a la nobleza. Ninguno tuvo herederos, por lo que estaba en juego no solo el destino religioso del país, sino la propia autoridad real.

Matanza de hugonotes
El asesinato de 80 hugonotes en Vassy (noreste de Francia), en marzo de 1562, fue el detonante de las guerras de religión francesas.

44 **NÚMERO DE CABALLEROS** QUE EJERCIERON DE **GRAN MAESTRE** DE LOS **PORTAESPADAS**

1563–1564

En 1563 se inició la construcción del austero e inmenso monasterio-palacio de El Escorial, exponente de la piedad y majestad del monarca español Felipe II.

EN 1563, SUECIA Y DINAMARCA COMPETÍAN por obtener la supremacía en el Báltico. Este hecho terminó desembocando en la **primera guerra naval moderna**, es decir, con navíos en lugar de galeras (que todavía eran habituales en el Mediterráneo) y armados con artillería pesada. Ambos países rivalizaban por obtener el control de las rutas de invasión marítimas, y los daneses contaban con el apoyo de la ciudad alemana semiindependiente de Lübeck. Entre 1563 y 1570 se libraron **siete batallas navales importantes**, que terminaron conduciendo a la bancarrota a ambos países. Como descubrirían otras potencias, aunque estos **buques de guerra** eran las **armas más formidables de la época**, también resultaban increíblemente caros. La guerra, por tanto, terminó sin ganancias territoriales para ninguno de los dos bandos.

Un grupo de **colonos hugonotes** huyó y fundó la **colonia del Fuerte de la Carolina en Florida**, situada a orillas del río San Juan, en lo que hoy es Jacksonville. Duró menos de un año, hasta que finalmente fue **destruida por tropas españolas**, decididas a impedir que colonos franceses, en especial protestantes, se asentaran en los territorios controlados por España. Todos sus colonos y los soldados, excepto un pequeño grupo de mujeres y niños, fueron asesinados. Como respuesta, **fuerzas francesas destruyeron en 1568 el Fuerte de Matanzas, una colonia española** creada después de la destrucción del Fuerte de la Carolina.

Batalla de Oland
Los daneses vencieron en la batalla de Oland el 30–31 de mayo de 1564, en la que los suecos perdieron su nuevo buque insignia real Marte.

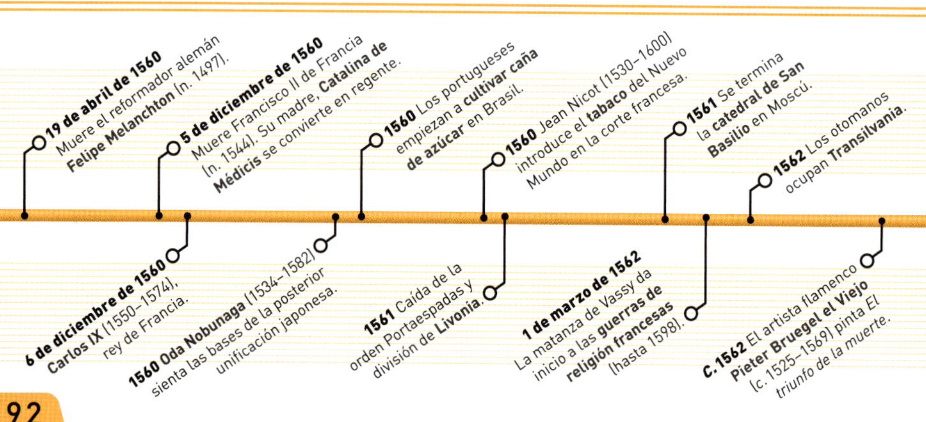

19 de abril de 1560 Muere el reformador alemán **Felipe Melanchton** (n. 1497).

5 de diciembre de 1560 Muere Francisco II de Francia (n. 1544). Su madre, **Catalina de Médicis** se convierte en regente.

6 de diciembre de 1560 **Carlos IX** (1550–1574), rey de Francia.

1560 Oda Nobunaga (1534–1582) sienta las bases de la posterior unificación japonesa.

1560 Los portugueses empiezan a **cultivar caña de azúcar** en Brasil.

1560 Jean Nicot (1530–1600) introduce el **tabaco** del Nuevo Mundo en la corte francesa.

1561 Caída de la orden Portaespadas y división de **Livonia**.

1561 Se termina la **catedral de San Basilio** en Moscú.

1 de marzo de 1562 La matanza de Vassy da inicio a las **guerras de religión francesas** (hasta 1598).

1562 Los otomanos ocupan **Transilvania**.

C. 1562 El artista flamenco **Pieter Bruegel el Viejo** (c. 1525–1569) pinta *El triunfo de la muerte*.

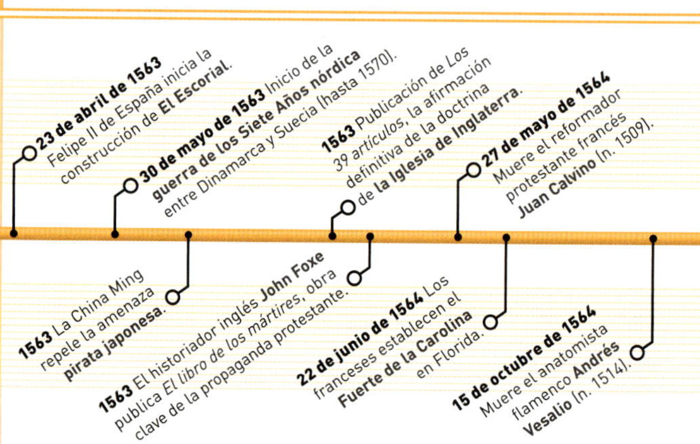

23 de abril de 1563 Felipe II de España inicia la construcción de **El Escorial**.

30 de mayo de 1563 Inicio de la **guerra de los Siete Años nórdica** entre Dinamarca y Suecia (hasta 1570).

1563 La China Ming repele la amenaza **pirata japonesa**.

1563 Publicación de *Los 39 artículos*, la afirmación definitiva de la doctrina de **la Iglesia de Inglaterra**.

1563 El historiador inglés **John Foxe** publica *El libro de los mártires*, obra clave de la propaganda protestante.

27 de mayo de 1564 Muere el reformador protestante francés **Juan Calvino** (n. 1509).

22 de junio de 1564 Los franceses establecen el **Fuerte de la Carolina** en Florida.

15 de octubre de 1564 Muere el anatomista flamenco **Andrés Vesalio** (n. 1514).

1565–1567

El tema de *La matanza de los inocentes* de Bruegel es supuestamente bíblico, pero en realidad se trata de una denuncia de la brutal represión española de la revuelta de Países Bajos.

IVÁN IV INSTAURÓ SU PROPIO absolutismo con sanción divina ortodoxa, por lo que nunca se vio obligado a enfrentarse a los potentes intereses mercantiles, aristocráticos o clericales que frustraban a sus iguales en Europa occidental. Sus enemigos principales eran los cosacos (un pueblo fronterizo independiente) y los boyardos, la nobleza hereditaria.

Asentamiento español
San Agustín (Florida), fundado por los españoles en agosto de 1565, es el asentamiento europeo de ocupación ininterrumpida más antiguo de Estados Unidos.

Reclutó a los cosacos como aliados con la estrategia del soborno, pero a partir de 1565 **desposeyó**, y en la mayoría de casos asesinó, a los **boyardos**, cuyos territorios pasaron a ser los «dominios privados» de Iván, la *opríchnina*, una extensa área en el centro de Rusia que repartió entre una nueva nobleza, los *dvoriane*, leal al zar.

Tras la conquista de México y de Perú (*véase* 1532), el principal **reto marítimo español** era unirlos con las Filipinas y las islas de las Especias en el extremo oeste del Pacífico que, en 1564, España estaba decidida a colonizar. En 1527 se había abierto una ruta pionera a través del océano Pacífico, pero todavía no se conocía ninguna ruta de regreso. Entre junio y octubre del año 1565, el navegante español **Andrés de Urdaneta** dio un paso fundamental cuando navegó hacia el norte hasta encontrar vientos favorables en el que fue el **viaje sin escalas más largo** de la historia hasta ese momento (18 700 km), y que permitió completar una **red comercial vital**.

Del mismo modo que el conflicto religioso y político de las guerras de religión francesas, la **rebelión de Países Bajos**, que empezó en 1566 y que se prolongó hasta el año 1648, también fue consecuencia de una nefasta mezcla de intolerancia religiosa y de un fuerte deseo de lograr un pleno control político. En 1566, **Felipe II, monarca católico de Países Bajos**, afirmó que ni se proponía ni deseaba ser monarca de herejes. Consciente de que la creciente minoría **protestante** cada vez contaba con más apoyo en **Países Bajos**, no podía obviar la obligación divina de erradicar la herejía. Sin embargo, había más problemas. Países Bajos, ya fueran católicos o protestantes, no querían someterse a Felipe II porque ello significaría tener que renunciar a sus «libertades» (entre las que se encontraba su derecho al autogobierno aunque reconocieran la autoridad de Felipe II). Además, tampoco entendían por qué debían pagar impuestos cuya finalidad era financiar las campañas del rey de España en el extranjero. Aunque la solución pacífica de este problema fuera imposible, el conflicto resultante fue de una violencia inusitada incluso para la época (*véase* 1572–1573).

IVÁN EL TERRIBLE
(1530–1584)

Aunque podía ser capaz de sentir arrepentimiento (como cuando acabó con la vida de su primogénito y heredero partiéndole el cráneo con un bastón, en 1581), Iván IV gobernó con crueldad; de ahí su apodo de «el Terrible». Una consecuencia clave fue la huida de Rusia de una gran parte de la población entre 1547 y 1584. El país quedó tan despoblado que la servidumbre fue el único modo de conservar la mano de obra agrícola suficiente.

1568–1569

Un sacerdote bendice a dos soldados durante la sublevación del Norte de 1569, el último intento católico sostenido en Inglaterra en protesta por la Reforma.

EN 1568, OMURA SUMIDATA, un daimio japonés convertido al cristianismo en 1563, permitió a misioneros y comerciantes portugueses establecer un puerto en un pueblo pesquero del extremo sur de Japón: **Nagasaki**. Hasta que el cristianismo se prohibiera en Japón en 1614, Nagasaki, convertida en colonia jesuita, no solo fue casi íntegramente católica (o *kirishitan*), sino también el enclave comercial portugués más importante de toda Asia oriental.

La tarea más urgente a la que se tuvo que enfrentar **Akbar** para consolidar el poder mogol en India (*véase* 1555–1556) fue derrotar a los **rajputas hindúes del noroeste**. La campaña duró una década y culminó en 1569 con la caída de las fortalezas de Mewar y Ranthambore. Una vez asegurada la sumisión de los principales soberanos rajputas, Akbar contrajo matrimonio con una serie de princesas hindúes (tuvo 36 esposas en total), a fin de atar a sus enemigos por medio de alianzas matrimoniales.

En 1659, **Segismundo II**, el último soberano jagellón del Gran Ducado de Lituania y Polonia, todavía no había conseguido tener un heredero, lo que llevó a la unión formal de los dos estados. Esta nueva **confederación polaco-lituana** se convirtió en el **mayor estado territorial de Europa** y se debió al deseo de Segismundo de asegurar la integridad de los territorios de su dinastía y a la necesidad de proteger a Lituania de otomanos y rusos. La nueva disposición constitucional enfrentó a los nobles de ambos territorios, que temían acabar en desventaja. Para los **polacos**, lo más importante era que se **les transfirieran territorios inmensos**, **Ucrania** entre ellos.

La **sublevación del Norte** inglesa, que se inició en noviembre del año 1569, fue la **mayor amenaza al protestantismo pragmático de Isabel I**. Liderada por los condes católicos de Westmorland y Northumberland, arrasó el norte de Inglaterra antes de ser **reprimida con enorme brutalidad**.

En 1569, el cartógrafo flamenco **Gerardo Mercator** (1512–1594) concibió un **mapamundi** con las verdaderas posiciones cardinales de todos los continentes. Hoy en día, la **proyección de Mercator** es aún la representación plana de la Tierra más conocida.

Gerardo Mercator
Fue grabador y matemático, además de un cartógrafo excepcional. Diseñó su mapamundi en 1569 para facilitar la navegación marítima.

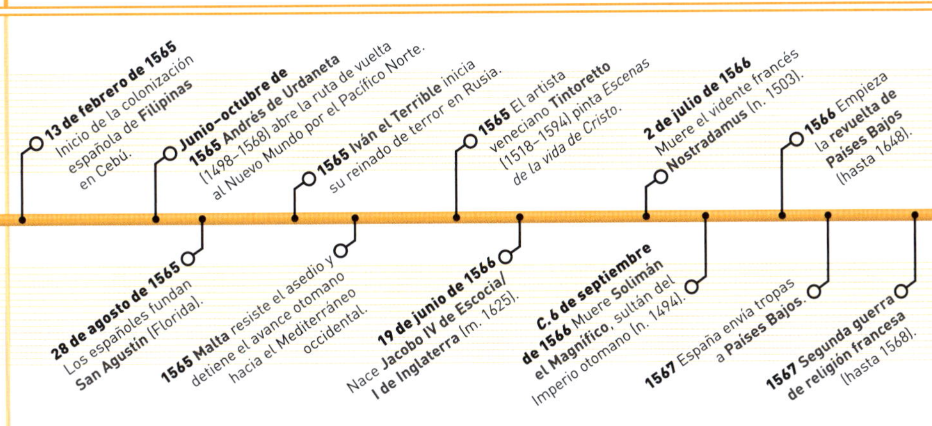

13 de febrero de 1565 Inicio de la colonización española de **Filipinas** en Cebú.

Junio–octubre de 1565 Andrés de Urdaneta (1498–1568) abre la ruta de vuelta al Nuevo Mundo por el Pacífico Norte.

28 de agosto de 1565 Los españoles fundan **San Agustín** (Florida).

1565 Iván el Terrible inicia su reinado de terror en Rusia.

1565 Malta resiste el asedio y detiene el avance otomano hacia el Mediterráneo occidental.

1565 El artista veneciano **Tintoretto** (1518–1594) pinta *Escenas de la vida de Cristo*.

19 de junio de 1566 Nace **Jacobo IV de Escocia/I de Inglaterra** (m. 1625).

2 de julio de 1566 Muere el vidente francés **Nostradamus** (n. 1503).

C. 6 de septiembre de 1566 Muere **Solimán el Magnífico**, sultán del Imperio otomano (n. 1494).

1566 Empieza la **revuelta de Países Bajos** (hasta 1648).

1567 España envía tropas a **Países Bajos**.

1567 Segunda guerra de religión francesa (hasta 1568).

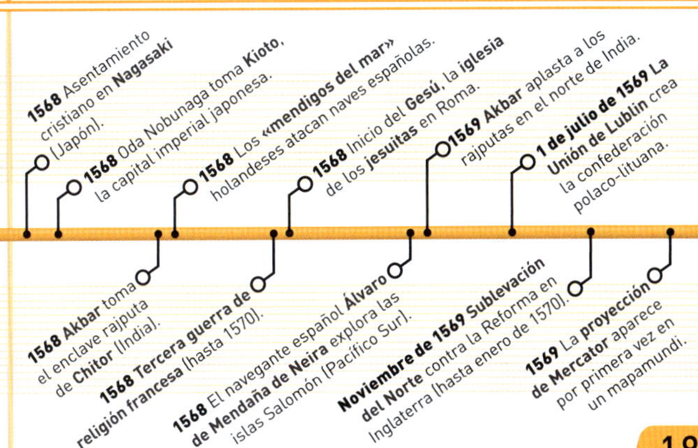

1568 Asentamiento cristiano en **Nagasaki** (Japón).

1568 Oda Nobunaga toma **Kioto**, la capital imperial japonesa.

1568 Akbar toma el enclave rajputa de **Chitor** (India).

1568 Los **«mendigos del mar»** holandeses atacan naves españolas.

1568 Tercera guerra de religión francesa (hasta 1570).

1568 Inicio del **Gesù**, la **iglesia** de los **jesuitas** en Roma.

1568 El navegante español **Álvaro de Mendaña de Neira** explora las islas Salomón (Pacífico Sur).

1569 Akbar aplasta a los rajputas en el norte de India.

1 de julio de 1569 La **Unión de Lublin** crea la confederación polaco-lituana.

Noviembre de 1569 Sublevación del Norte contra la Reforma en Inglaterra (hasta enero de 1570).

1569 La **proyección de Mercator** aparece por primera vez en un mapamundi.

1570–1571

« LA BELLEZA RESULTARÁ DE LA FORMA Y DE LA CORRESPONDENCIA DE LA TOTALIDAD. »

Andrea Palladio, en *Los cuatro libros de arquitectura* (1570)

Andrea Palladio, el arquitecto más influyente del Renacimiento tardío.

EL GALEÓN DE MANILA fue uno de los elementos distintivos del **sistema comercial español** en el Nuevo Mundo. A partir de la década de 1570, tres galeones (dos después de 1593) hacían un viaje circular anual entre Acapulco (México) y Manila (Filipinas). A cambio de la plata del Nuevo Mundo, España importaba seda, especias, porcelana, lacas y marfil. Se estima que en 1600, el valor de un solo cargamento de estas naves (las más grandes del mundo) superaba los ingresos anuales de la corona inglesa.

En 1571, **Portugal intentó colonizar Angola**, pero le fue imposible vencer a los kimbundu, la tierra de la costa era demasiado pobre para el cultivo y no pudo arrebatar el comercio de la sal a los africanos. Los portugueses establecieron puestos comerciales en Luanda y en Benguela en 1575 y 1587, lo que reforzó el comercio de esclavos.

La **batalla de Lepanto**, librada frente a la costa griega en octubre de 1571 fue el último gran enfrentamiento entre galeras (208 cristianas contra 251 otomanas). La artillería fue crucial para la victoria de la flota cristiana al mando de **don Juan de Austria**, hijo ilegítimo de Carlos V. Venecia cedió de inmediato Chipre al Imperio otomano mediante un tratado, pero se puso fin a su expansión en el Mediterráneo occidental.

Batalla de Lepanto
Se estima que 20 000 otomanos y 7500 cristianos murieron en la batalla de Lepanto. Las tácticas de embestida de las galeras turcas resultaron ineficaces.

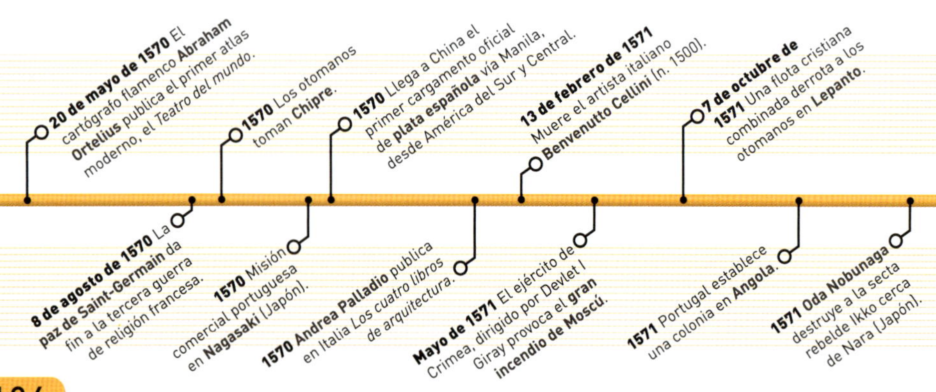

1572–1573

Al fondo de esta pintura del hugonote François Dubois sobre la matanza de San Bartolomé, Catalina de Médicis contempla un montón de cadáveres.

A PESAR DE LA CONQUISTA ESPAÑOLA del **Perú inca** (*véase* 1532), en 1539 se asentó un pequeño estado inca en Vilcabamba, en el Alto Amazonas, liderado por un noble inca menor, Manco Inca Yupanqui. Desde allí, él y sus descendientes lanzaron una campaña intermitente, y por lo general no demasiado efectiva, contra los españoles. En 1572, Vilcabamba cayó, y **el último líder inca, Túpac Amaru, fue ejecutado**.

En 1566, una delegación de nobles holandeses se presentó ante **Margarita de Parma** (1522–1586), hermanastra de Felipe II y gobernadora general de Países Bajos, para declarar su oposición a la campaña antiherética llevada a cabo por Felipe en Países Bajos. Uno de los consejeros de Margarita los calificó despectivamente de «*gueux*» (mendigos). Los protestantes holandeses adoptaron el apodo con entusiasmo, especialmente los **mendigos del mar**, unos piratas cuyos ataques a las naves españolas a partir del año 1568 mermaron de manera significativa los esfuerzos militares españoles. Los mendigos del mar dependían en gran medida de Inglaterra, que, con discreción, hacía cuanto podía para perjudicar a España. No obstante, en la primavera de 1572, **Isabel I** (*véase* 1586–1589), que tampoco deseaba ofender demasiado directamente a los españoles, les cerró los puertos. Como respuesta, el 1 de abril de 1572 los mendigos del mar tomaron Brielle (Holanda). A los tres meses ya habían **tomado prácticamente todas las ciudades en Holanda y Zelanda**, donde purgaron a monárquicos y católicos. Cuando **Guillermo de Orange** (1533–1584), la figura política y militar más importante de dicha revuelta, accedió a tomar el mando, el conflicto derivó en una guerra abierta.

La matanza de la noche de San Bartolomé en París, el 24 de agosto de 1572, fue la peor atrocidad de las **guerras de religión francesas**. Fue el resultado del intento de resolver el conflicto mediante el matrimonio de Enrique de Navarra, un hugonote cercano a la sucesión del trono francés, con Margarita de Valois, hermana de Carlos IX, el joven rey de Francia. El matrimonio fue concertado fundamentalmente por la madre del rey, **Catalina de Médicis** (*véase* recuadro), que temía por el trono de su hijo ante el poder creciente de los hugonotes y había insistido en que ambos bandos llegasen a un acuerdo. El ambiente ya estaba muy caldeado cuando católicos y hugonotes se reunieron en París para asistir a la boda. Sin embargo, existía un **complot para asesinar a Gaspar de Coligny**, una fi-

Población inca
La conquista diezmó a los incas, más por las enfermedades importadas desde Europa que a causa de un genocidio deliberado.

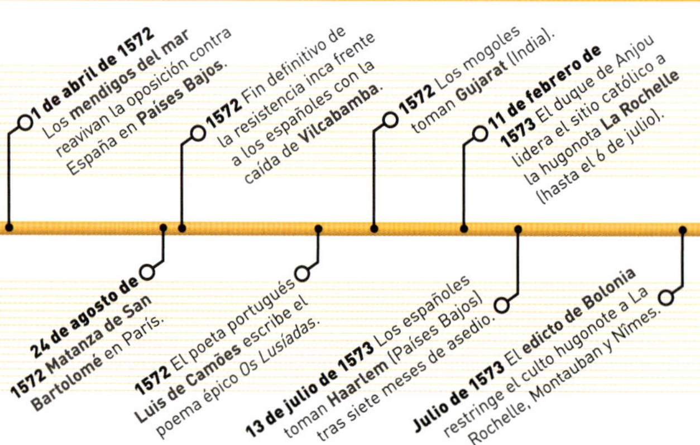

1574–1577

« LA SOBERANÍA ES EL PODER ABSOLUTO Y PERPETUO DE UNA COMUNIDAD… EL MAYOR PODER DE TODOS. »

Jean Bodin, filósofo y político francés (1576)

CATALINA DE MÉDICIS
(1519–1589)

Nació en Italia y se casó con Enrique II de Francia en 1533. Al enviudar en 1559, se convirtió en monarca oficiosa mientras Francia se sumía en el caos, pues Francisco II y Carlos IX, sus dos hijos mayores, eran jóvenes e inexpertos, y Enrique III se enfrentaba a una situación política deteriorada. Todos sus esfuerzos por preservar el trono Valois fracasaron.

gura hugonota clave. No se sabe quién lo organizó, pero en cualquier caso fracasó, ya que Coligny sobrevivió, aunque fue herido. Tal vez Catalina persuadiera entonces al rey de que los hugonotes estaban a punto de destronarle y de que podría evitarlo si asesinaba a los más destacados de la ciudad; parece igualmente posible que la matanza fuera espontánea. Al final, Coligny y **más de 3000 hugonotes fueron asesinados**. En toda Francia pudieron haber muerto otros 3000 durante las semanas siguientes.

EL NORTE DE LA COSTA AFRICANA del Mediterráneo occidental fue un foco clave de la **rivalidad otomano-cristiana**. España, sobre todo, trataba de impedir los ataques musulmanes a sus barcos; sin embargo, fue perdiendo las ciudades norteafricanas que tenía en su poder: Argel en 1529, Trípoli en 1551 y Bujía en 1555. En 1574 solo le quedaba Túnez, cuya caída ese mismo año ante una imponente flota otomana marcó el **final de las ambiciones de los Habsburgo en el norte de África**, que desde entonces permaneció firme en la órbita otomana.

La **batalla de Nagashino**, que libraron en junio de 1575 las fuerzas de **Takeda Katsuyori** (1546–1582) y una alianza liderada por el daimio **Oda Nobunaga** (*véase* 1560–1562) fue un hito decisivo en la evolución bélica japonesa: por primera vez se usaron armas de fuego de manera efectiva. Japón había intentado imitar los arcabuces introducidos por los portugueses en 1540, aunque cargarlos era un proceso muy lento. Nobunaga resolvió el problema dotando a cada tirador con tres armas y un equipo de cargadores. Así generaron un fuego casi continuo que diezmó a las tropas tradicionales del clan Takeda.

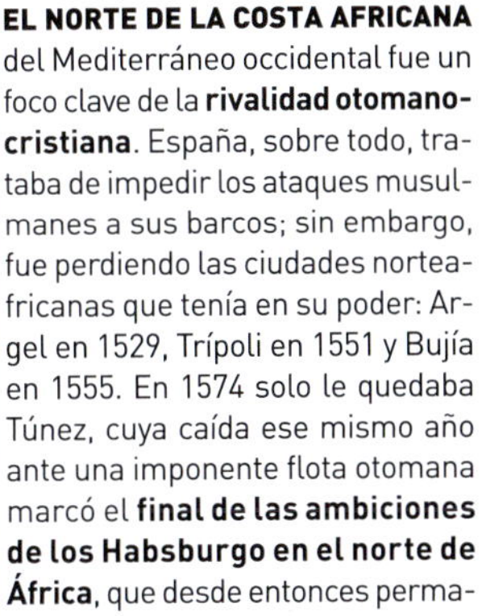

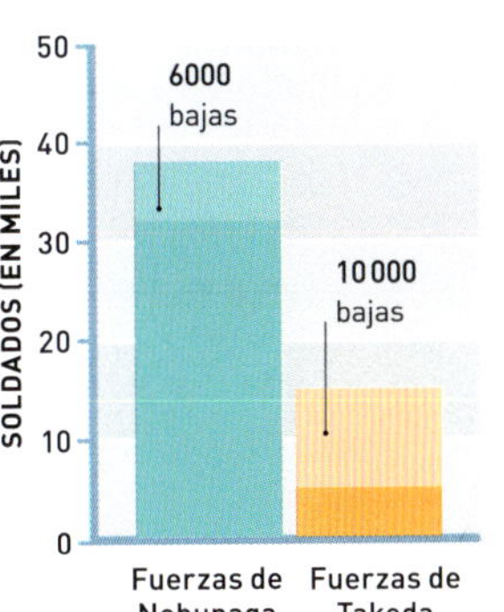

Batalla de Nagashino
Los hombres de Nobunaga superaban a los de Takeda en una proporción de 2:1, pero si vencieron fue gracias al hábil uso de las armas de fuego.

Mezquita Selimiye
Construida por Mimar Sinán para Selim II en Edirne, se terminó en 1575 y es el ejemplo supremo de la arquitectura islámica otomana.

Los esfuerzos de España para **reprimir la revuelta de Países Bajos** (*véase* 1572–1573) fracasaron en 1575. Al no poder cobrar impuestos a Países Bajos, fue incapaz de pagar a sus tropas, que se amotinaron y se entregaron a asesinatos y saqueos indiscriminados. La autoridad de Felipe II en Países Bajos se desmoronó. El vacío fue ocupado por holandeses, monárquicos y católicos o protestantes rebeldes. El acuerdo se selló en la **pacificación de Gante**, firmada en noviembre de 1576.

1578–1579

Los portugueses, muy inferiores en número, fueron exterminados en Alcazarquivir y, además de a su rey, perdieron a casi todos sus nobles.

AL IGUAL QUE LOS INTENTOS DE FELIPE II DE REAFIRMAR SU AUTORIDAD sobre los heréticos Países Bajos se veían entorpecidos por la necesidad simultánea de enfrentarse a los otomanos suníes en el Mediterráneo, los intentos de estos de enfrentarse a los herejes safavíes shiitas de Persia se veían entorpecidos por el conflicto con España. La pausa tras la caída de Túnez en 1574, y que un tratado de paz confirmó en 1580, permitió a ambos estados perseguir sus objetivos en otros lugares. Los beneficios para los **otomanos** fueron inmediatos: **una serie de conquistas en Georgia y Azerbaiyán** que, tras la caída de Tabriz en 1585, se incorporaron al imperio.

En agosto de 1578, el rey Sebastián de Portugal fue asesinado en la **batalla de Alcazarquivir**, en el norte de Marruecos, que tuvo dos importantes consecuencias. La primera fue confirmar a **Ahmad al-Mansur** (1549–1603) como el nuevo sultán de **Marruecos**, con apoyo otomano; la segunda fue una **crisis sucesoria en Portugal**. El heredero de Sebastián fue su tío Enrique, un cardenal de 66 años de edad que murió sin descendencia 17 meses después. Felipe II (*véase* 1580) era uno de los aspirantes al trono.

Después de la pacificación de Gante (*véase* 1576), Felipe II se vio obligado a retirar sus tropas y a reinstaurar los privilegios tradicionales en las provincias de Países Bajos. Sin embargo, permaneció inflexible en la cuestión religiosa: el catolicismo debía reinstaurarse en todas partes. La violencia estalló de nuevo. Don Juan de Austria, el enviado de Felipe, asoló la ciudad de Namur y, en venganza, los calvinistas disidentes tomaron varias ciudades del sur. En enero del año 1579, la nobleza católica del sur reafirmó su lealtad a Felipe con la **Unión de Arras**, y las provincias del norte formaron la **Unión de Utrecht**. La guerra civil se sumó a las desgracias de Países Bajos.

Casco *chichak*
El casco otomano de cuero y con incrustaciones de cobre era tan efectivo que fue imitado en toda Europa durante el siglo XVII.

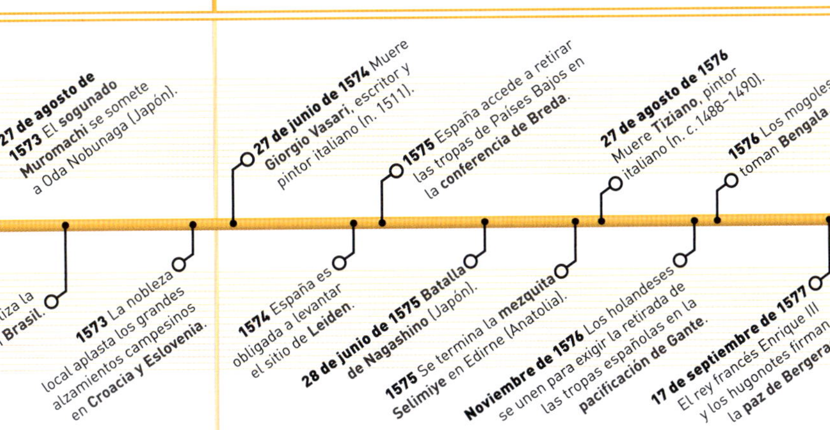

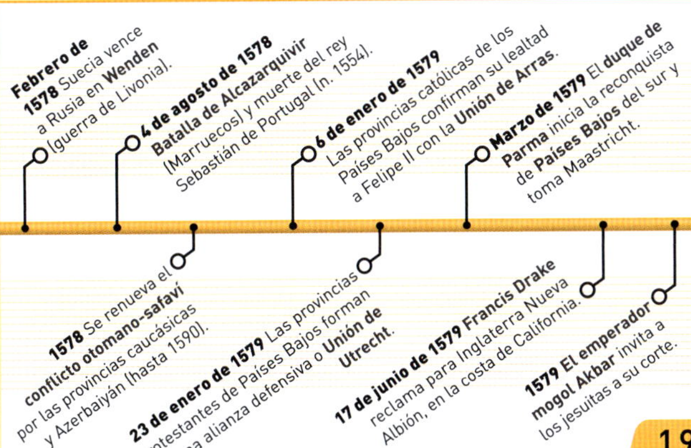

1580–1581

Felipe II no halló mucha resistencia al reclamar el trono portugués en 1580: mientras un ejército marchaba hacia Lisboa, la flota española atacaba por mar.

LA PUBLICACIÓN EN DRESDE del *Libro de la concordia* fue un hito fundamental para el desarrollo del **luteranismo** (*véase* 1516–1518). La obra reafirmaba la importancia suprema de las Sagradas Escrituras (la Biblia), que interpretaba estrictamente como «el consenso unánime y la exposición de nuestra fe cristiana», y aún continúa siendo la base de las creencias luteranas actuales.

El rey **Felipe II de España** consiguió materializar en agosto de 1580 su derecho al **trono portugués** vacante (*véase* 1578–1579) mediante una estratégica combinación de sobornos y de potencia militar.

« NO **SE CREE** TAN **FIRMEMENTE** EN NADA COMO **EN AQUELLO QUE SE DESCONOCE**. **»**

Michel de Montaigne, escritor francés, *Ensayos (Libro I)*

En julio del año 1581, las provincias del norte de Países Bajos (las **Provincias Unidas**) declararon su independencia con el **Acta de Abjuración**, por la que revocaban su juramento de lealtad a Felipe II. Se depuso al rey de España y se creó la corona de Países Bajos, que fue aceptada por el **duque de Anjou** (1555–1584), hermano de Enrique III de Francia. Casi todo el sur continuó siendo leal a Felipe II, pero el Acta afirmaba que un **rey legítimo podía ser legalmente** destronado, lo que tendría consecuencias importantes.

El duque Francisco de Anjou
El apoyo extranjero (inglés o francés) resultó crucial para la derrota de los españoles por los Países Bajos protestantes, que ofrecieron la corona al duque de Anjou en 1581.

La **reforma del «látigo único»** o «regla simple» de 1581 en la **China Ming** tuvo un enorme impacto. No solo establecía que todos los impuestos debían basarse en la propiedad (registrada en un censo universal), sino que obligaba a que se **pagaran en plata**. El objetivo era simplificar el sistema fiscal chino y evitar así los problemas de inflación creados por el papel moneda y por una moneda devaluada, y fue posible gracias a la afluencia de plata española y japonesa. El nuevo sistema fiscal incrementó la demanda de lingotes de plata, lo que elevó su precio todavía más y, a largo plazo, contribuyó a desestabilizar la economía Ming.

1582–1585

Toyotomi Hideyoshi venció en Shizugatake en mayo de 1583 tras un implacable despliegue de fuerzas sobre el enemigo.

EL SUICIDIO RITUAL DE ODA NOBUNAGA (*véase* 1560–1562) llevó al poder a su general más capaz, **Toyotomi Hideyoshi** (*c.* 1536/1537–1598). En tan solo una década, este consiguió **unificar a casi todo Japón**, un gran logro para alguien de cuna campesina. Para que el vulgo no pudiera alzarse en contra de su autoridad, desarmó a todos los que no fueran samuráis, y reorganizó el sistema fiscal y redistribuyó las tierras a fin de asegurarse los ingresos necesarios para proseguir sus conquistas.

Imperio songay
La muerte de Askia Daud en 1582 y la posterior invasión marroquí (véase 1591) resultaron determinantes en el declive del Imperio songay.

SÁHARA
Kumbi Saleh
Tombuctú
Gao
IMPERIO SONGAY
Djenné
OCÉANO ATLÁNTICO

CLAVE
Territorio songay en 1500
Territorio songay en 1625

El 24 de febrero de 1582, el **papa Gregorio XIII** (1502–1585) decretó la **reforma del calendario juliano**, introducido en el año 46 a. C. y que subestimaba la duración de cada año en once minutos. Hacia finales del siglo XVI, la fecha juliana estaba diez días atrasada respecto a la real, de manera que el equinoccio de primavera, a partir del cual se calculaba la Semana Santa, caía el 11 de marzo en lugar del 21 de ese mes. Así pues, fue por motivos doctrinales por lo que el papa introdujo su modesta modificación. El cambio entró en vigor en octubre (al jueves 4 le siguió el viernes 15), pero únicamente afectó a España, Portugal y Polonia-Lituania. El resto de Europa, en especial la protestante, sospechaba un complot papal y tardó más en seguir el ejemplo.

Sir Francis Drake (1540–1596) fue célebre por ser el primer capitán inglés que consiguió circunnavegar el globo (1577–1580), lo que provocó una renovación del interés de Inglaterra por el Nuevo Mundo. **Sir Humphrey Gilbert**, que había viajado a **Terranova** en 1578–1579, regresó allí en 1583 con el apoyo de Isabel I y reclamó el territorio para Inglaterra. En 1584, y una vez más con apoyo real, **sir Walter Raleigh** (*c.* 1552–1618) envió una expedición con el objetivo de fundar la **colonia de Virginia**, así llamada en honor a la «reina virgen», que se estableció al año siguiente en la isla de Roanoke, hoy en Carolina del Norte, y que en 1590 ya había desaparecido.

La **rendición de Amberes**, el 17 de agosto de 1585, fue un momento clave para definir las fronteras de los **Países Bajos Españoles** –lo que acabaría siendo Bélgica– y un **triunfo militar** decisivo para **España**.

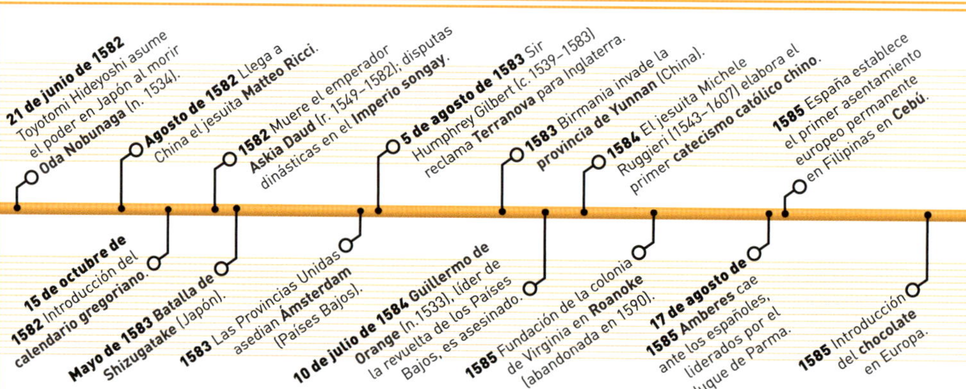
Sitio de Amberes
El sitio redujo la población de 100 000 a 40 000 habitantes y duró trece meses, pero devolvió a España el control del sur de Países Bajos.

31 de enero de 1580 La muerte de **Enrique I de Portugal** (n. 1512) origina una crisis sucesoria.

25 de junio de 1580 Publicación del ***Libro de la concordia*** luterano.

1580 Felipe II reina en España y Portugal (hasta 1640).

1580 Publicación de los *Ensayos* del filósofo renacentista francés **Michel de Montaigne** (1533–1592).

4 de abril de 1581 El corsario inglés **Francis Drake**, nombrado caballero por Isabel I.

26 de julio de 1581 El **Acta de Abjuración** depone a Felipe II como monarca de las Provincias Unidas.

1581 La **reforma del látigo único** en China establece que todos los impuestos sobre la propiedad se deben pagar en plata.

Septiembre de 1581 El asedio **de Pskov** por Polonia-Lituania hace abandonar a Rusia sus pretensiones sobre Livonia (hasta febrero 1582).

21 de junio de 1582 Toyotomi Hideyoshi asume el poder en Japón al morir **Oda Nobunaga** (n. 1534).

Agosto de 1582 Llega a China el jesuita **Matteo Ricci**.

15 de octubre de 1582 Introducción del **calendario gregoriano**.

1582 Muere el emperador **Askia Daud** (r. 1549–1582); disputas dinásticas en el **Imperio songay**.

Mayo de 1583 Batalla de Shizugatake (Japón).

1583 Las Provincias Unidas asedian **Ámsterdam** (Países Bajos).

5 de agosto de 1583 Sir Humphrey Gilbert (c. 1539–1583) reclama **Terranova** para Inglaterra.

1583 Birmania invade la **provincia de Yunnan** (China).

10 de julio de 1584 Guillermo de Orange (n. 1533), líder de la revuelta de los Países Bajos, es asesinado.

1584 El jesuita Michele Ruggieri (1543–1607) elabora el primer **catecismo católico chino**.

1585 Fundación de la colonia de Virginia en **Roanoke** (abandonada en 1590).

17 de agosto de 1585 Amberes cae ante los españoles, liderados por el duque de Parma.

1585 España establece el primer asentamiento europeo permanente en Filipinas en **Cebú**.

1585 Introducción del **chocolate** en Europa.

1586–1587

Tras haberla mantenido bajo custodia 19 años, Isabel I acabó juzgando por traición y ejecutando a María, reina de los escoceses, en febrero de 1587.

LA INTERVENCIÓN DE INGLATERRA EN LA REVUELTA de Países Bajos (*véase* 1572–1573) se vio marcada por la batalla de Zutphen, en septiembre de 1586, donde los españoles lograron vencer al ejército angloholandés. La reina **Isabel I** tuvo más suerte en sus intentos de desestabilizar a España. Mediante una serie de saqueos en el Caribe, **Drake** había demostrado cómo interferir en el lucrativo comercio de los españoles en el Nuevo Mundo, y en abril de 1587, Isabel lo envió en una misión a España, con órdenes de proseguir los saqueos y la destrucción. Aunque como era habitual, la reina cambió de opinión casi de inmediato, a Drake nunca le llegó el mensaje en el que se le ordenaba regresar. Su éxito fue espectacular: atacó con gran audacia naves españolas y portuguesas, y llevó a cabo un **ataque de tres días de duración contra Cádiz**, durante el cual se hundieron 23 naves españolas (según fuentes españolas; Drake afirmó que fueron 33) y se capturaron otras cuatro. Su acción retrasó la Armada de Felipe II más de un año.

El reinado de Isabel I estuvo plagado de complots y rebeliones. En 1587, la reina ordenó ejecutar a su prima católica **María, reina de los escoceses**, pues era una peligrosa rival al trono.

En Japón, el cristianismo prosperó desde su introducción por los portugueses a mediados del siglo XVI. Se estima que hacia 1580 ya había unos 130 000 cristianos japoneses, la mayoría en Nagasaki y sus alrededores. El general **Toyotomi Hideyoshi** (*véase* 1582–1585) veía en ellos a una fuerza armada en torno a la cual podía reunirse la oposición a su autoridad. Muchos daimios se habían convertido básicamente porque ello les facilitaba el acceso a la pólvora, ya que los portugueses seguían controlando la mayor parte del comercio. Al mismo tiempo, Hideyoshi no deseaba poner en peligro los importantes vínculos comerciales que mantenía con los portugueses. Su respuesta fue característica de su determinación: siguió fomentando el comercio, pero prohibió el cristianismo. En julio de 1587 emitió una **orden de purga contra los jesuitas** y asumió el control directo de Nagasaki. Aunque la orden no llegó a aplicarse plenamente durante una década o más, el cristianismo japonés se vio obligado a pasar a la clandestinidad.

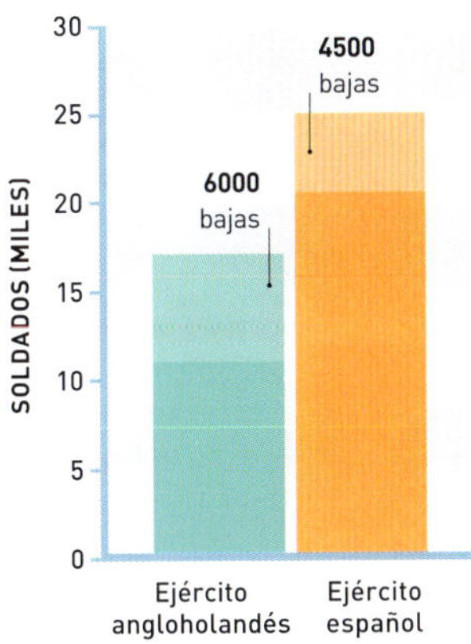

Batalla de Zutphen
Las fuerzas angloholandesas sufrieron grandes pérdidas durante la batalla de Zutphen, en 1586, y la ciudad pasó a manos españolas.

1588–1589

« TENGO EL **CUERPO DE UNA MUJER DÉBIL** Y DELICADA, PERO EL **CORAZÓN Y LAS AGALLAS DE UN REY**. »

Isabel I de Inglaterra, en su arenga a las tropas en Tilbury (19 de agosto de 1588)

LA ARMADA INVENCIBLE fue la mayor apuesta militar de Felipe II: un enorme despliegue de potencia naval española con el objetivo primordial de derrotar a Inglaterra y luego a las provincias protestantes de Países Bajos. Fue un absoluto fracaso. Demostró lo esquivo del éxito militar directo y de las dificultades logísticas a que se enfrentaba toda operación militar de largo alcance. La armada zarpó el 30 de mayo de 1588 y fue víctima de la pericia naval inglesa, la dificultad del aprovisionamiento y el tiempo: destruida por las tormentas, se vio obligada a regresar. Con ella se esfumó toda esperanza española de exterminar las herejías protestantes.

ISABEL I (1533–1603)

Isabel se vio obligada a afrontar múltiples problemas para acceder al trono inglés: desde conflictos religiosos y dificultades económicas hasta amenazas de Escocia, España y Francia. Los superó todos con una combinación de astucia e inteligencia, y logró convertir a Inglaterra en un país protestante seguro de sí mismo.

La muerte de Enrique III apuñalado por un antiguo monje en 1589 llevó al trono francés a **Enrique III de Navarra** (1533–1610). Este suceso sumió a Francia en la crisis. El derecho al trono de Enrique era evidente, pero era protestante. Tanto para la poderosa Liga católica de Francia como para el rey Felipe II de España **era inconcebible que en Francia reinara un protestante**. Enrique IV de Francia no logró acceder al trono hasta el año 1593, después de una serie de guerras extenuantes y de su (oportuna) conversión al catolicismo.

La Armada Invencible
Las tempestades y la flota inglesa causaron graves daños a la Armada española, que contaba con unas 150 naves al zarpar de Lisboa.

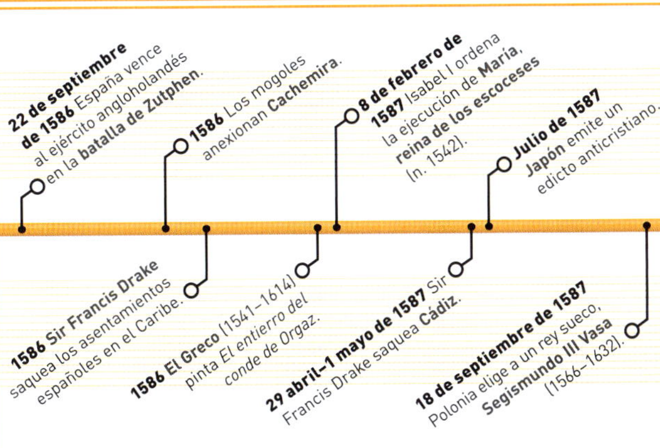

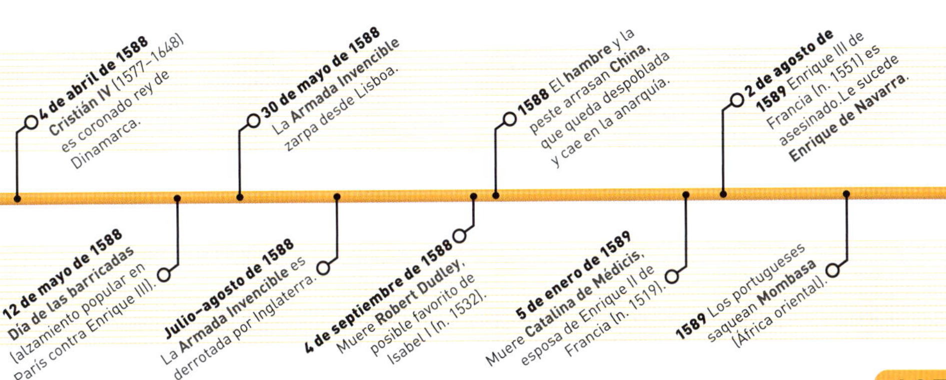

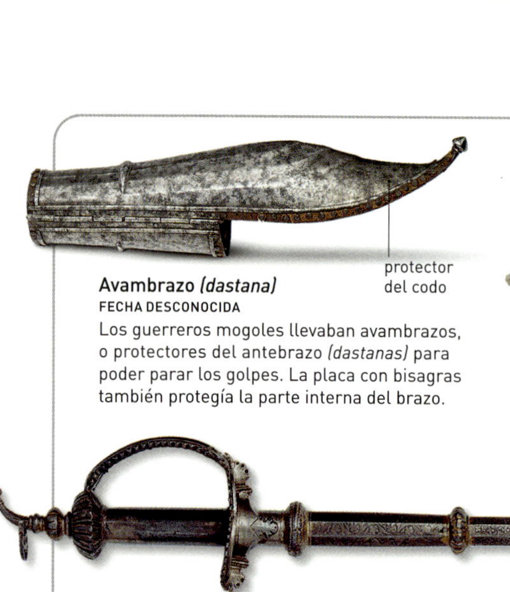

Avambrazo *(dastana)*
FECHA DESCONOCIDA
Los guerreros mogoles llevaban avambrazos, o protectores del antebrazo *(dastanas)* para poder parar los golpes. La placa con bisagras también protegía la parte interna del brazo.

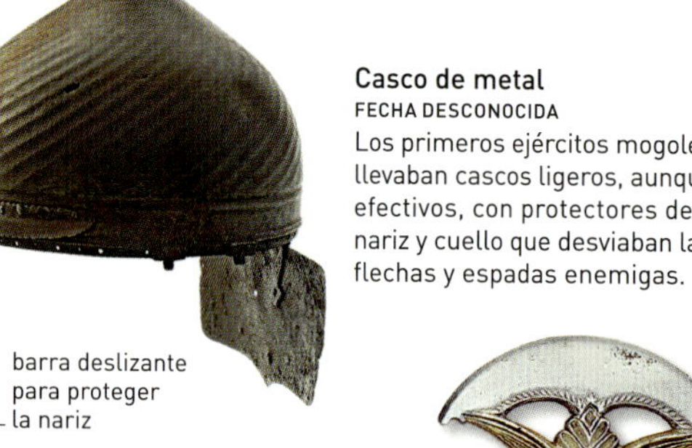

Casco de metal
FECHA DESCONOCIDA
Los primeros ejércitos mogoles llevaban cascos ligeros, aunque efectivos, con protectores de nariz y cuello que desviaban las flechas y espadas enemigas.

Escudo de combate con puntas de lanza
Siglo XVIII
Las cinco puntas y la placa central hacían de este escudo mogol un arma peligrosa e imponente y una protección vital para su portador.

cada hoja
mide 17,7 cm

placa
central

hoja estilizada
con puntas

Hacha de guerra
Siglo XVII
Los ideales estéticos mogoles llegaban a las armas, como esta hacha, tan bella como temible, de la región india de Decán.

Maza de hierro
Siglo XVIII
La infantería mogola utilizaba armas sólidas, como esta maza, que podían romper el cráneo del enemigo aunque llevara casco.

EL IMPERIO MOGOL

UNA SOCIEDAD AVANZADA, PRÓSPERA E INTEGRADA SURGIDA DE UNA LUCHA DE PODER

Los mogoles gobernaron durante más de dos siglos (1523–1761) sobre gran parte de India. Su hegemonía militar y eficacia administrativa integraron a hindúes y musulmanes en una rica cultura de esplendor imperial.

Con raíces en las culturas mongola y turca, siete generaciones de soberanos mogoles, empezando por Baber I (r. 1523–1530), fusionaron las influencias militares y artísticas persas e islámicas con la cultura hindú india nativa. El resultado fue uno de los imperios de la época más extraordinarios que, en su punto álgido (1556–1707), acumulaba grandes riquezas, había asimilado a los hindúes en la élite gobernante y fomentaba el mecenazgo de las artes.

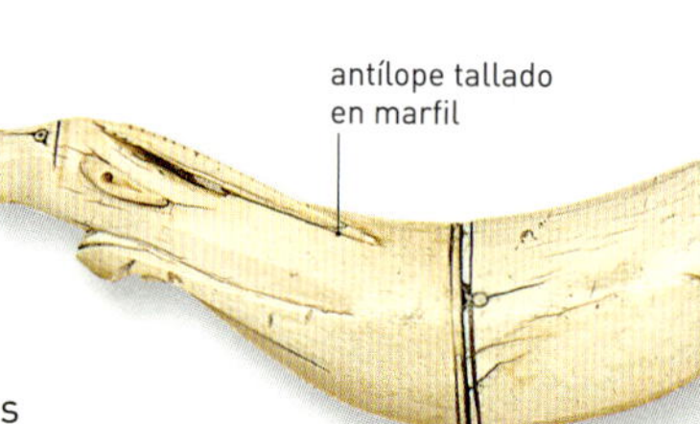

Cuerno para pólvora de marfil
FECHA DESCONOCIDA
La talla del marfil tenía una larga historia en India y fue muy apreciada por las cortes mogolas. Este cuerno de pólvora, utilizado en cacerías, tiene forma de antílope.

Escena de cacería
Siglo XVII
Cazar y montar a caballo eran los pasatiempos favoritos de los dirigentes mogoles. La imagen representa a un príncipe que cabalga junto a un sirviente y un perro de caza.

Chaqueta de caza de satén
Principios del siglo XVII
El deporte real también exigía una vestimenta ornamentada y muy rica. Esta chaqueta sin mangas está bordada con dibujos florales típicos persas.

Miniatura mogola
FECHA DESCONOCIDA
El arte y la literatura florecieron gracias al mecenazgo de soberanos mogoles como Akbar (r. 1542–1605). Las miniaturas con que se ilustraban los manuscritos eran muy apreciadas.

Sarpech
FECHA DESCONOCIDA
La extraordinaria riqueza de los mogoles se hacía patente en su predilección por las joyas. Este *sarpech* de oro con esmeraldas, diamantes, rubíes y una perla adornaba un turbante real.

Collar *hansli*
Siglo XVIII
Hecho de oro y con multitud de piedras preciosas, este tipo de collar rígido se conocía como *hansli* porque estaba diseñado para descansar sobre las clavículas (*hansli* en urdu).

Talismán
FECHA DESCONOCIDA
Este talismán, o *taweez*, decorado con versículos del Corán atestigua el exquisito trabajo que realizaban los orfebres mogoles.

Mortero y mano de mortero
Siglo XVII
El jade solo podía trabajarse con polvo de diamante y era muy apreciado por la sociedad mogola. Este mortero y su mano fueron tallados del mismo bloque.

Cuenco con incrustaciones de jade
Siglo XVIII
El parchîn-kârî, o incrustación (de jade y piedras preciosas en este cuenco), alcanzó su cénit durante el reinado de Sah Yahan (1628–1658).

Copa de vino de oro y esmalte
Siglo XVII
Las narraciones de la vida cortesana mogola describen a los reyes bebiendo vino en copas de oro o plata esmaltadas, y docenas de platos servidos en fuentes de oro y plata.

Escena cortesana mogola
Siglo XVII
El esplendor de la corte mogola es evidente en esta imagen de Sah Yahan (r. 1628–1658) rodeado de nobles, agrupados en estricto orden jerárquico alrededor del trono.

Narguiles
Siglo XVIII
Los mogoles introdujeron en India la tradición persa de fumar en narguiles, que enfrían el humo del tabaco con agua. Los usaban tanto hombres como mujeres.

1590–1591

Se estima que en los cuatro meses de sitio murieron en París entre 40 000 y 50 000 personas hasta la victoria del ejército español del duque de Parma.

EN EL AÑO 1590, TOYOTOMI HIDEYOSHI (*véase* 1582–1587) ya había **logrado unificar Japón** y establecer el singular carácter del régimen que dominó el país durante más de 250 años. Aunque no era la capital, a partir de 1590 Hideyoshi se estableció en **Edo**, donde la nobleza feudal, ya completamente sometida a él, debía residir en años alternos, una medida muy efectiva para impedir las rebeliones. El campesinado, que debía pagar grandes impuestos, sostenía esta elaborada estructura social.

En su intento de imponerse como rey de Francia, **Enrique de Navarra** (*véase* 1588–1589) **sitió París** en mayo de 1590. Las tropas españolas del duque de Parma consiguieron romper el asedio en septiembre de ese mismo año.

En 1591, el **sultán de Marruecos, Ahmad al-Mansur** (*véase* 1578–1579), inició la invasión del atribulado **Imperio songay** (*véase* 1582–1585), con el fin de controlar el **comercio transahariano del oro**. La invasión exigió que una fuerza de 3000 hombres y 8000 camellos realizara la peligrosa travesía del Sáhara, de cuatro meses de duración. En marzo de 1592, un ejército songay de más de 40 000 hombres fue derrotado en la **batalla de Tondibi** por las armas de fuego infinitamente superiores de los marroquíes, que contaban con arcabuces y con ocho cañones ingleses.

Castillo
El castillo Himeji, o de la «garza blanca», es uno de los 200 castillos que Toyotomi Hideyoshi ordenó erigir por todo Japón con el objetivo de asegurar su poder.

1592

500 000 £

EL **MAYOR BOTÍN** OBTENIDO POR **CORSARIOS INGLESES**, DE LA NAVE **MADRE DE DEUS**

Puente de Rialto
Este puente sobre el Gran Canal de Venecia se terminó en 1592. Era el quinto puente que se construía en ese lugar, pero el primero de piedra.

DURANTE LA PRIMAVERA DE 1592, las **fuerzas japonesas** comenzaron una **invasión sostenida de Corea** que dio lugar a la **guerra de los Siete Años**. Aunque en parte era un intento de Toyotomi Hideyoshi de unir a los japoneses en una causa común, perseguía el ambicioso objetivo de su predecesor de **conquistar la China Ming**. La campaña obtuvo resultados contradictorios. Las victorias terrestres de los japoneses en Corea se vieron igualadas por sus derrotas en el mar, donde los barcos tortuga coreanos, armados y protegidos, resultaron decisivos contra las flotas japonesas cada vez más debilitadas. La **intervención de China** a finales de año acabó inclinando la balanza en contra de Japón. En la primavera de 1593, los japoneses se vieron obligados a pedir la paz y hacia mediados de año empezaron a retirarse. En 1597, el ya anciano Hideyoshi reanudó la campaña con un ejército mayor; **Japón volvió a ser derrotado** en 1598, pero las luchas salvajes **arrasaron Corea**. La guerra no finalizó formalmente hasta 1608, pero en 1599 había terminado a efectos prácticos. Paradójicamente, fue Japón quien salió más beneficiado. Esta derrota tuvo una enorme influencia en su posterior aislamiento (nunca absoluto) del resto del mundo. En cambio, Corea tardó varios años en recuperarse, mientras que el inmenso coste de la guerra para la China Ming no solo provocó revueltas contra los impuestos adicionales sino que debilitó su capacidad militar en la vulnerable frontera noreste.

En 1592, **Akbar** (*véase* 1555–1556) inició otra serie de conquistas que **llevaron las fronteras mogolas** a su máxima extensión durante su reinado. En el este logró anexionar Orissa. En 1594 conquistó Baluchistán y la franja costera de Makrán en la frontera persa safaví, y en el año 1596 recuperó la **importante ciudad afgana de Kandahar**, que su padre había perdido.

1593–1594

Mapa portugués de Mombasa con el Fuerte Jesús, a la derecha.

LA FRONTERA OTOMANA-HABSBURGO, por lo general estable después del último ataque turco a Viena en el año 1529, fue un foco de conflicto importante entre otomanos y cristianos. Volvió a reactivarse en 1593 con la llamada **«guerra larga»**, una serie de campañas inconcluyentes que tuvieron lugar en Hungría y en los Balcanes, en las que los vasallos nominales de los otomanos en Transilvania, Valaquia y Moldavia apoyaron a los Habsburgo. El resultado del tratado final **(paz de Zsitvatorok de 1606)** dejó a la frontera en un estado de incertidumbre constante.

El 10 de junio del año 1594, en San Agustín de Florida, uno de los asentamientos españoles, el padre Diego Escobar de Zambrana bautizó a María, hija de Juan Jiménez de la Cueva y de María Meléndez. Este bautismo quedó registrado en el documento público más antiguo de los futuros Estados Unidos: se trata del primer registro auténtico de un **hijo de colonos europeos nacido allí**.

El **Fuerte Jesús de Mombasa**, en África oriental, fue construido por orden de Felipe II y se terminó en 1593. Resultó crucial para las expediciones portuguesas al océano Índico durante el siglo XVII.

> « **PARÍS** BIEN VALE UNA **MISA**. »
>
> **Enrique IV de Francia** (1593)

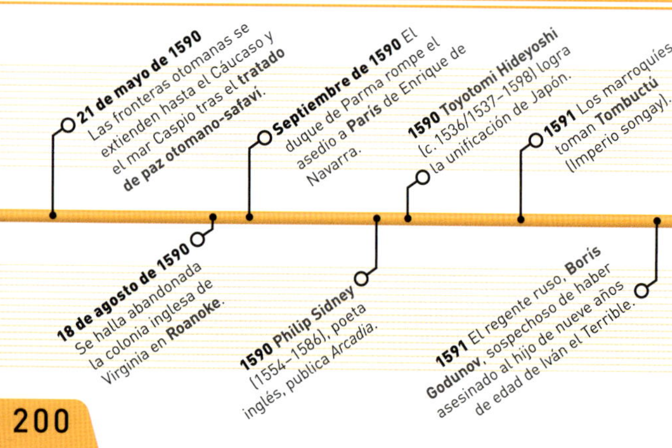

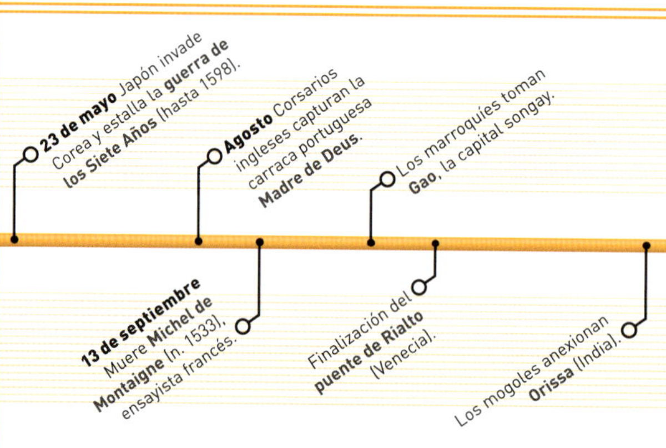

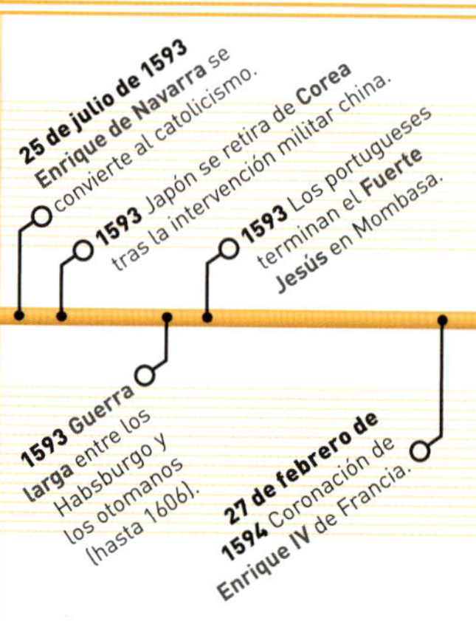

1595–1596

A pesar de lo peligroso de la expedición, las cuatro naves holandesas que zarparon hacia las Indias Orientales en 1595 consiguieron regresar a Amsterdam en 1599 con su cargamento.

LAS GUERRAS DE RELIGIÓN FRANCESAS (1562–1598) remitieron en 1595. La conversión al catolicismo de **Enrique IV** (*véase* 1588–1589) hizo posible que la mayoría le aceptara como rey, pero había levantado las sospechas de los **hugonotes**, que temían que ahora se volviera contra ellos, y no había aplacado las ambiciones de los líderes de la **Liga Católica**, cuyo propósito, además de acabar con el protestantismo en Francia, era ocupar el trono. En enero de 1595, Enrique respondió **declarando la guerra a España**. Su objetivo era tanto erradicar la Liga Católica, apoyada por España, como demostrar a los hugonotes que su condición de católico no le hacía una marioneta de la Monarquía Hispánica. En junio de 1595 obtuvo una victoria temprana contra una fuerza conjunta de España y la Liga Católica en Borgoña, a la que siguió una ofensiva española la primavera siguiente, en la que cayeron Calais y Amiens. Los asedios posteriores de Enrique IV finalizaron con la capitulación de Amiens en septiembre de 1597, su triunfo definitivo.

Hasta el estallido de la **revuelta de Países Bajos** en 1566, estos dominaban el **lucrativo comercio marítimo** entre España y Portugal, y el norte de Europa: eran barcos holandeses los que transportaban especias y otras bienes de lujo del Lejano Oriente y plata del Nuevo Mundo desde la península Ibérica hasta países del norte. Cuando se les prohibió comerciar en los puertos de la península, y conscientes de los fallos que la derrota de la Armada Invencible había puesto de manifiesto, los **holandeses decidieron irrumpir en el comercio de especias**. En 1595, cuatro naves holandesas al mando de Cornelius van Houten zarparon hacia las Indias Orientales. Las tripulaciones padecieron escorbuto y se enfrentaron repetidamente a los gobernantes locales y a los portugueses, y Van Houten fue asesinado en Sumatra. A su regreso a Ámsterdam en 1599, la mermada flota trajo lo que parecía una cantidad de especias ínfima, aunque bastó para obtener beneficios. Los holandeses habían abierto el camino a su dominio del comercio con las Indias Orientales (*véase* 1602–1603).

Uno de los **escasos éxitos de Inglaterra** durante su intervención en la revuelta de Países Bajos fue el **saqueo de Cádiz** en julio de 1596. Al igual que el de Drake en 1587, causó una enorme destrucción en la ciudad y contribuyó a la bancarrota de la corona española en 1597.

La flota angloholandesa en Cádiz
Aunque supuestamente era una operación angloholandesa, 130 de los 150 barcos que componían la flota que atacó Cádiz en el verano de 1596 eran ingleses.

naves angloholandesas: 150
naves españolas: 40
SAQUEO DE CÁDIZ
naves angloholandesas perdidas: 10
naves españolas perdidas: 32

Ataque a Cádiz
España perdió el 80 % de la flota anclada. Muchos barcos fueron incendiados para evitar el saqueo.

1597–1599

Fresco del palacio de las Cuarenta Columnas de Isfahán (Irán); muestra al sah Abbas I sentado a la derecha, como anfitrión del valí Muhammad Kan de Bujará.

AUNQUE LA PROHIBICIÓN DEL CRISTIANISMO EN JAPÓN solo se había aplicado de manera parcial desde 1587, en diciembre de 1596, convencido de que España y Portugal se valían de la penetración cristiana como preludio de una conquista, Toyotomi Hideyoshi ordenó la **ejecución de 26 cristianos**: seis misioneros franciscanos y 20 japoneses fueron atados a cruces y alanceados hasta la muerte el 5 de febrero de 1597 en Nagasaki. Más que intolerancia hacia el cristianismo, estas ejecuciones demostraban que no se permitiría ningún ataque a la autoridad central.

El **edicto de Nantes** de abril de 1598 fue únicamente una prueba de la precariedad del acuerdo que el rey Enrique IV había conseguido en Francia después de 1597. Los protestantes franceses obtuvieron el derecho a organizar un estado casi independiente en el seno de Francia. Además de poder practicar libremente su religión (excepto en París), la corona garantizaba su seguridad y financiaba la guarnición de sus ciudades. Aunque fue pragmático y efectivo a corto plazo, ya que **puso fin a las guerras de religión francesas**, no satisfizo a nadie. Los hugonotes continuaban sintiendo un agravio comparativo respecto a los católicos que, a su vez, estaban horrorizados de que se tolerara a los hugonotes y además se les protegiera.

La coronación en el año 1587 de **Abbas I**, de 16 años de edad, como **sah de la Persia safaví** fue el inicio de una época de gloria. Bajo su padre, el sah Muhammad, Persia había vivido en un estado de cuasi guerra civil, debido a las facciones rivales del ejército kizilbash, y había perdido una enorme cantidad de territorios ante los otomanos y los uzbekos. Abbas acometió una **profunda renovación de su ejército rebelde**, reclutó tropas nuevas –sobre todo soldados esclavos del Cáucaso leales a su persona– y las armó con mosquetes. Parte de estas armas las pudo proporcionar el diplomático inglés Anthony Shirley, quien negociaba un tratado anglopersa contra el Imperio otomano. Entre abril y agosto de 1598, Abbas lanzó una **campaña contra los uzbekos** y los expulsó del noreste de Persia.

WILLIAM SHAKESPEARE
(1564–1616)

La obra de Shakespeare ha ejercido más influencia sobre la literatura inglesa y el teatro europeo que la de ningún otro escritor. Hijo de un comerciante de lana de Stratford-upon-Avon, fue un actor convertido en autor de al menos 37 obras teatrales y 154 sonetos. Se cree que escribió la tragedia *Hamlet* entre 1599 y 1602.

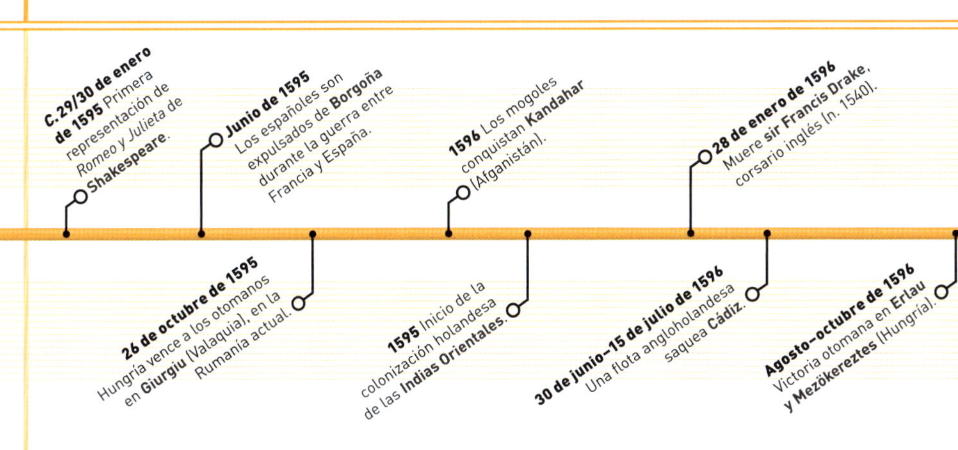

C.29/30 de enero de 1595 Primera representación de *Romeo y Julieta* de **Shakespeare**.

Junio de 1595 Los españoles son expulsados de **Borgoña** durante la guerra entre Francia y España.

26 de octubre de 1595 Hungría vence a los otomanos en **Giurgiu** (Valaquia), en la Rumanía actual.

1596 Los mogoles conquistan **Kandahar** (Afganistán).

1595 Inicio de la colonización holandesa de las **Indias Orientales**.

28 de enero de 1596 Muere **sir Francis Drake**, corsario inglés (n. 1540).

30 de junio–15 de julio de 1596 Una flota angloholandesa saquea **Cádiz**.

Agosto–octubre de 1596 Victoria otomana en **Erlau y Mezőkereztes** (Hungría).

5 de febrero de 1597 Ejecución de 26 cristianos en **Japón**.

25 de septiembre de 1597 Amiens, conquistada por los españoles, cae ante Enrique IV de Francia.

1597 Nueva invasión japonesa de **Corea**.

21 de febrero de 1598 Borís Godunov, zar de Rusia.

13 de abril de 1598 Enrique IV de Francia emite el **edicto de Nantes**.

2 de mayo de 1598 El **tratado de Vervins** pone fin a la guerra franco-española.

1598 Los bambara expulsan al rey de Malí y fundan el **reino de Segu** (África occidental).

1598 El sah **Abbas de Persia** (1571–1629) expulsa a los invasores uzbekos turcos.

1599 Primera actuación registrada en el **teatro The Globe** (Londres).

1599 El artista italiano **Caravaggio** (1571–1610) pinta la *Vocación de san Mateo* en Roma.

1600–1601

La Compañía Inglesa de las Indias Orientales inició tratos con Surat, en el océano Índico, en 1608. En 1615 ya había expulsado a los portugueses.

HACIA 1600, LOS PUEBLOS POLINESIOS DE NUEVA ZELANDA, los maoríes, se habían ido asentando de forma progresiva en sus nuevos territorios (*véase* 1276–1285). A pesar de que todavía no conocían los metales (que fueron introducidos por los europeos) estaban muy bien adaptados a su nuevo entorno. Esta cultura, conocida como **fase maorí clásica**, se distinguía por sus elaboradas tallas de madera, herramientas y armas de hueso muy precisas, e importantes asentamientos.

El 31 de diciembre de 1600 se fundó la **Compañía Inglesa de las Indias Orientales** con autorización real, una señal clara para España y Portugal de que no podían pretender monopolizar el comercio con Asia oriental. Dicho esto, la Compañía de las Indias Orientales fue desde el principio, y a lo sumo, una mera apuesta especulativa. No solo dependía de la capacidad para llegar a aquellas islas lejanas sino que, una vez allí, debía presentarse (tanto militar como diplomáticamente) como una alternativa válida a sus rivales europeos. Es decir, requería una combinación de habilidad naval, intuición comercial y fuerza militar (esta última fue una necesidad permanente). Al final, se estableció casi como una rama del estado inglés y luego británico. Sin embargo, nunca llegó a entenderse como un medio de conquista o colonización: **su único objetivo era lograr el enriquecimiento de sus accionistas**. Su llegada a los nuevos mercados coincidió con la de otro rezagado, Países Bajos. El dominio europeo de las riquezas de las Indias Orientales no se disputó entre Inglaterra y la península Ibérica, sino entre Inglaterra y Países Bajos.

Arma maorí
La wahaika, una maza sujeta por una tira de cuero enrollada a la muñeca y al índice, se utilizaba en los combates cuerpo a cuerpo.

30
KM CÚBICOS
ES EL **VOLUMEN** DEL **MATERIAL EXPULSADO** POR EL **VOLCÁN HUAYNAPUTINA**, EN PERÚ

1602–1603

Tokugawa Ieyasu tenía sesenta años de edad cuando el emperador Go-Yozei le nombró sogún. Gobernó Japón hasta su muerte.

DURANTE UNOS CIEN AÑOS, LA COMPAÑÍA NEERLANDESA DE LAS INDIAS ORIENTALES, fundada en 1602 y equivalente de su rival inglesa, fue la **empresa comercial más exitosa del mundo**. Sus navegantes no solo superaron a los portugueses en el océano Índico (también consiguieron abrir rutas nuevas en el océano Antártico para acceder a las Indias Orientales) sino que, una vez llegaron a sus objetivos, los exploraron con tal determinación que acabaron con sus antecesores.

En 1602, los holandeses reclamaron Guayana en América del Sur y en 1605 ya habían expulsado a los portugueses de las Molucas (islas de las Especias). Así sentaron los cimientos de un imperio comercial en el Asia oriental.

Cuando **Jacobo I** (1566–1625) se convirtió en **rey de Inglaterra** a la muerte de Isabel I, ya había sido **rey de Escocia** como Jacobo VI durante 36 años. Aunque Inglaterra y Escocia seguían siendo dos países distintos que solo compartían monarca, Jacobo consiguió gestionar las leyes mutuamente hostiles. Lo más cerca que estuvo de la unión que tanto deseaba fue la bandera angloescocesa, la **Union Jack**, así conocida por su nombre en francés, Jacques, que él prefería.

El mismo día de la coronación del rey Jacobo I, **Tokugawa Ieyasu** (1543–1616) se convertía en **sogún** e inauguraba una dinastía de **Japón** que gobernó una sociedad rígida, jerárquica y voluntariamente aislada durante 250 años.

Samuel de Champlain reanudó la exploración francesa del Nuevo Mundo en 1603. Durante los doce años siguientes, realizó distintas expediciones pioneras por el río San Lorenzo hacia los Grandes Lagos. En 1605 también fundó una efímera colonia francesa, Port Royal, en Nueva Escocia, y en 1608, una **base francesa permanente en Quebec**. Aunque lo que estaba buscando era un paso fluvial al océano Pacífico, Champlain se dio cuenta de que aquel terreno accidentado era valioso en sí mismo, sobre todo por sus **pieles**. Por lo tanto, financió una serie de exploraciones hacia el oeste, más allá de los Grandes lagos, para explotar el potencial de la *Nouvelle France*.

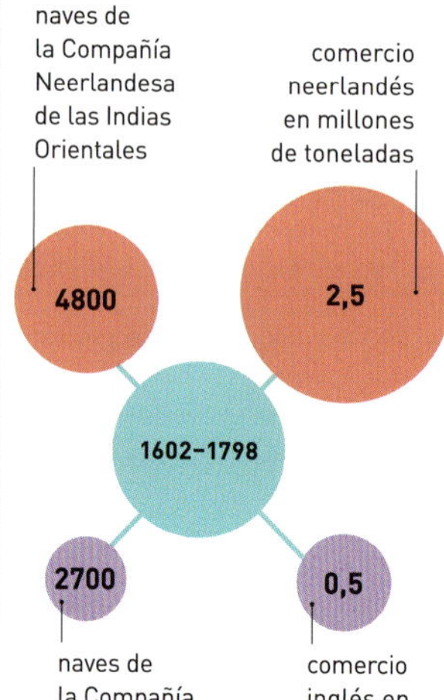

Comercio en Asia oriental
La Compañía Neerlandesa de las Indias Orientales fue cinco veces más rentable que su homóloga inglesa durante los siglos XVII y XVIII.

1604–1605

Guy Fawkes (tercero por la derecha) junto a los conspiradores católicos.

« LOS **ESPAÑOLES ASEDIARON** LO INASEDIABLE, Y LOS **HOLANDESES DEFENDIERON** LO INDEFENDIBLE. »

Anónimo, sitio de Ostende

CUANDO LAS FUERZAS ESPAÑOLAS LIDERADAS POR EL GENERAL SPÍNOLA consiguieron arrebatar Ostende a una fuerza combinada angloholandesa, el 16 de diciembre de 1604, **pusieron fin a un sitio** que había durado tres años, dos meses y 17 días. Fue un suceso de una dureza inaudita incluso para la Europa del siglo XVII, que solamente disfrutó de cuatro años de paz. Los castillos medievales, con sus muros altos y estrechos, eran muy vulnerables a la artillería, por lo que las fortificaciones se volvieron más bajas, gruesas y voluminosas, tanto que algunas ciudades fortificadas quedaban fuera del alcance de las armas contemporáneas, y los asedios se convirtieron en el único modo de tomarlas.

La **muerte del zar Borís Godunov** en el año 1605 desencadenó una **profunda crisis política** en Rusia, agravada por una **hambruna** terrible que entre 1601 y 1603 mató a dos millones de personas, es decir, **un tercio de la población**. Una fuerza **polaco-lituana** oficiosa ya había invadido el país, con la esperanza de aprovecharse de la división rusa y con el apoyo de la nobleza desafecta; el objetivo era,

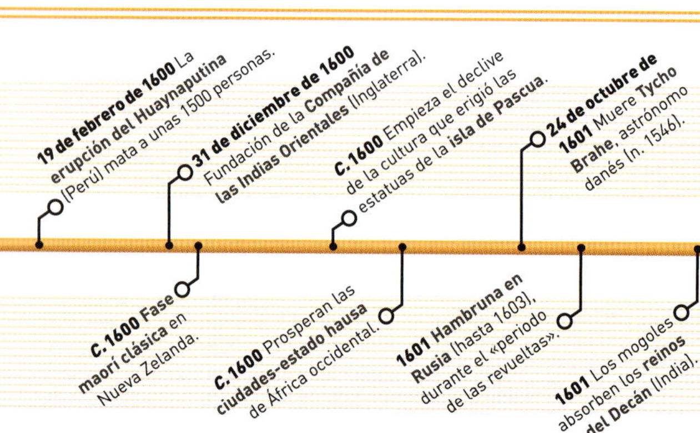

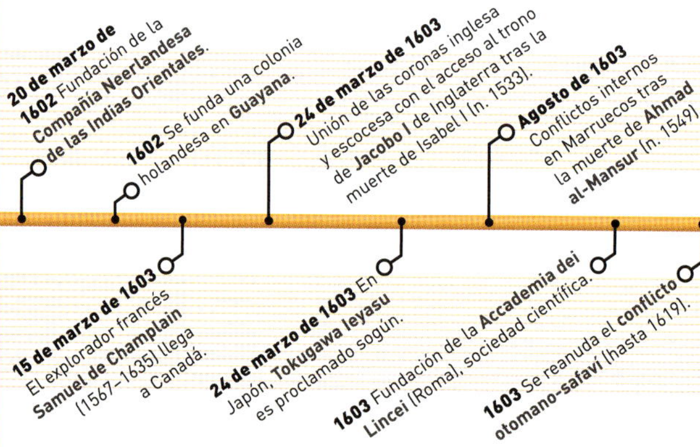

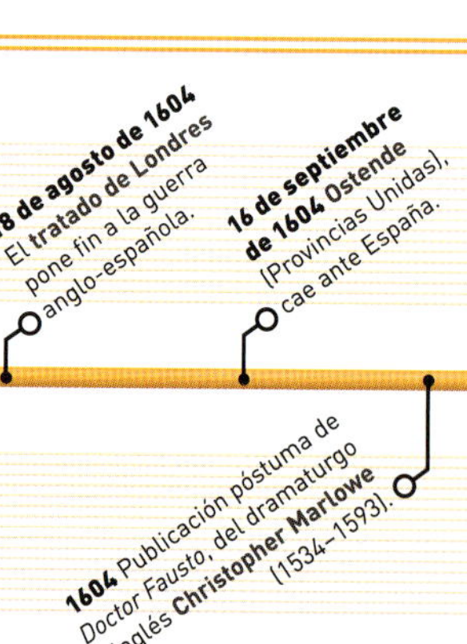

Reconstrucción de Jamestown, el primer asentamiento inglés permanente en América del Norte, establecido junto al río James, en el actual estado de Virginia.

en parte, recuperar a la Rusia ortodoxa para la Iglesia católica. Después de la muerte de Godunov, los invasores instalaron en el trono a su candidato, de quien afirmaron que era el hijo pequeño de Iván el Terrible. Menos de un año después, el falso Dimitri fue derrocado por **Basilio IV** (1552–1612), que masacró a los polacos de Moscú, tal vez cerca de 2000. En 1609, Basilio estableció una alianza con Suecia con el fin de reforzar su posición frente a la continua agitación polaca, lo que provocó que Polonia declarara oficialmente la guerra a Rusia. Un año más tarde, **Polonia había tomado Moscú** y su rey, **Segismundo III**, reclamaba su derecho al trono ruso. Alarmada por la posibilidad de que Polonia-Lituania pudiera tomar Rusia, **Suecia invadió y ocupó Nóvgorod**. En 1612, el príncipe Pozharski lideró una rebelión patriótica que expulsó de la ciudad de Moscú a los polacos y eligió al **primer zar Romanov, Miguel III** (1596–1645). Rusia no pudo expulsar a los suecos, pero en 1617 llegó a un acuerdo con ellos a costa de renunciar a su acceso al Báltico. En 1619, **terminó** el **conflicto polaco-ruso** cuando Rusia cedió territorios sustanciales en su frontera occidental.

En el Estrasburgo del año 1605, **Johann Carolus** (1575–1634) publicó lo que generalmente se considera como el **primer periódico del mundo**: *Relation aller Fürnemmen und gedenckwürdigen Historien* («Relación de todas las noticas distinguidas y memorables»). Carolus ya vendía una hoja de noticias manuscritas, pero pensó que una versión impresa, más barata y dirigida a un público más amplio, sería más rentable. En 1617 había cuatro periódicos más en Alemania.

Las esperanzas de Jacobo I de conseguir la tolerancia religiosa en Inglaterra desaparecieron cuando el 5 de noviembre de 1605 se descubrió un **complot católico para volar el Parlamento** (la «conspiración de la pólvora»). Puede que los confabulados fueran alentados por Robert Cecil, el primer ministro de Jacobo I, con el fin de azuzar el anticatolicismo.

El primer periódico a la venta
La aparición de la Relación *en Europa en 1605 puso de manifiesto la creciente demanda de información en un mundo en constante cambio.*

« EL DÍA QUINCE DE JUNIO LEVANTAMOS Y TERMINAMOS EL FUERTE… ESTE PAÍS ES FÉRTIL Y CRECEN MUCHOS ÁRBOLES BENEFICIOSOS Y NUTRITIVOS. »

George Percy, colono inglés, en *Jamestown Narratives*

EN DICIEMBRE DE 1605, EL NAVEGANTE PORTUGUÉS Pedro Fernández de Quirós obtuvo autorización real para un segundo viaje a través del Pacífico **en busca del supuesto continente del sur**, la Terra Australis Incognita. Consiguió atravesar el archipiélago Tuamotú en febrero de 1606 y llegó a las Nuevas Hébridas en mayo, pero los alisios le empujaron mar adentro y tuvo que regresar a Nueva España. La expedición aún contaba con un segundo barco, capitaneado por **Luis Váez de Torres**, que siguió hacia el oeste y llegó al estrecho que lleva su nombre entre **Nueva Guinea y Australia**, además de avistar este continente. Anotó sus logros meticulosamente, pero nunca los publicó, y los españoles no hicieron nada al respecto. Fueron los holandeses quienes confirmaron la existencia de Australia.

El 4 de mayo de 1607 se estableció **el primer asentamiento permanente inglés** en **América del Norte: Jamestown** (en la actual Virginia), una operación especulativa financiada por la Compañía de Londres (luego Compañía de Virginia). Era un intento de impedir los asentamientos españoles, franceses y holandeses, y principalmente, de encontrar un paso marítimo hacia Asia oriental, además de buscar oro y otros metales preciosos. Los primeros años fueron poco prometedores. El lugar, escogido sobre todo porque parecía fácil de defender, era pantanoso, con malaria endémica y poca tierra cultivable. Los colonos sucumbieron a la enfermedad y al hambre, y las relaciones con los **indios powhatan** eran tensas. Solo en 1612, cuando exportó la **primera cosecha de tabaco**, la colonia empezó a albergar esperanzas de supervivencia.

Máscara de las islas del estrecho de Torres
Los isleños del estrecho de Torres, buenos navegantes, tenían diversas máscaras rituales; muchas de las más elaboradas eran de carey.

23 de abril de 1605 Muere **Boris Godunov**, zar de Rusia (n. 1551).

5 de noviembre de 1605 El conspirador católico **Guy Fawkes** intenta volar el Parlamento inglés.

15 de octubre de 1605 Muere el emperador mogol **Akbar I** (n. 1542).

1605 Polonia-Lituania invade Rusia.

1605 Fundación de **Port Royal** (colonia francesa en Nueva Escocia).

1605 Los holandeses arrebatan las **Molucas** (Asia oriental) a Portugal.

1605 Johann Carolus publica el **primer periódico** en Estrasburgo (Alemania).

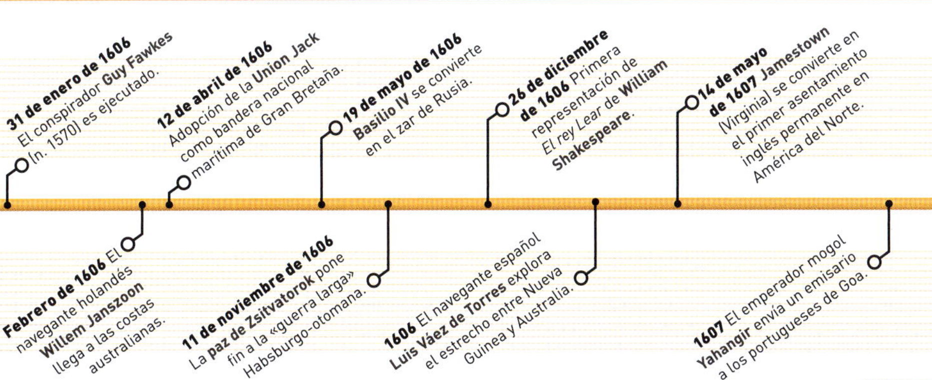

31 de enero de 1606 El conspirador **Guy Fawkes** (n. 1570) es ejecutado.

Febrero de 1606 El navegante holandés **Willem Janszoon** llega a las costas australianas.

12 de abril de 1606 Adopción de la **Union Jack** como bandera nacional marítima de Gran Bretaña.

11 de noviembre de 1606 La **paz de Zsitvatorok** pone fin a la «guerra larga» Habsburgo-otomana.

19 de mayo de 1606 Basilio IV se convierte en el zar de Rusia.

1606 El navegante español **Luis Váez de Torres** explora el estrecho entre Nueva Guinea y Australia.

26 de diciembre de 1606 Primera representación de *El rey Lear* de **William Shakespeare**.

14 de mayo de 1607 Jamestown (Virginia) se convierte en el primer asentamiento inglés permanente en América del Norte.

1607 El emperador mogol **Yahangir** envía un emisario a los portugueses de Goa.

Cruz procesional
Siglo XV • ITALIA
Esta cruz de oro, plata y esmalte, destinada a salir en procesión en las festividades religiosas, evidencia la riqueza de la Iglesia católica italiana.

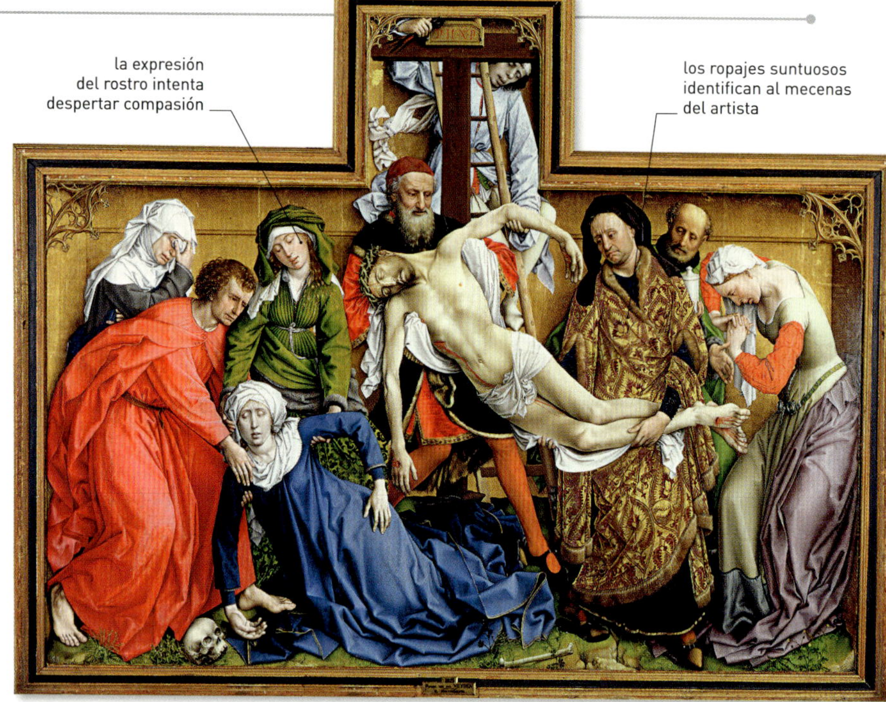

la expresión del rostro intenta despertar compasión

los ropajes suntuosos identifican al mecenas del artista

Descendimiento de la Cruz
C. **1435** • PAÍSES BAJOS
Esta pintura de Roger van der Weyden (*c.* 1399–1464) ejemplifica la asimilación flamenca de la idealización renacentista de los rostros y las figuras.

Ducado de oro veneciano
Siglo XVI • ITALIA
Esta moneda de oro representa al dux de Venecia (dcha.) recibiendo la enseña de la ciudad de un prominente san Marcos Evangelista.

EL RENACIMIENTO

EL RENACER DE LA CULTURA EUROPEA INSPIRADA EN LAS ANTIGUAS GRECIA Y ROMA

Mil años después de la caída del Imperio romano, eruditos de Florencia (Italia) alcanzaron una nueva concepción del arte, la arquitectura y la literatura de la Antigüedad clásica e iniciaron una revolución cultural.

En el siglo XIV se intensificó el comercio entre los estados europeos. En Florencia, convertida en un próspero centro bancario y comercial (al final bajo el control de los Médicis), se desarrolló una clase de personas ricas e instruidas que se convirtieron en mecenas de artistas y pensadores. En un primer momento, Florencia estuvo a la cabeza de los avances artísticos e intelectuales, pero en el siglo XVI, la Roma papal y Venecia habían recogido el testigo.

los cuernos son rayos de luz

la barba demuestra la habilidad del escultor

tamaño mayor que el natural (2,54 m)

Estatua de Moisés
C. **1515** • ITALIA
Esta escultura de Miguel Ángel (1475–1564) para la tumba del papa Julio II está hoy día en la iglesia de San Pietro en Vincoli (Roma).

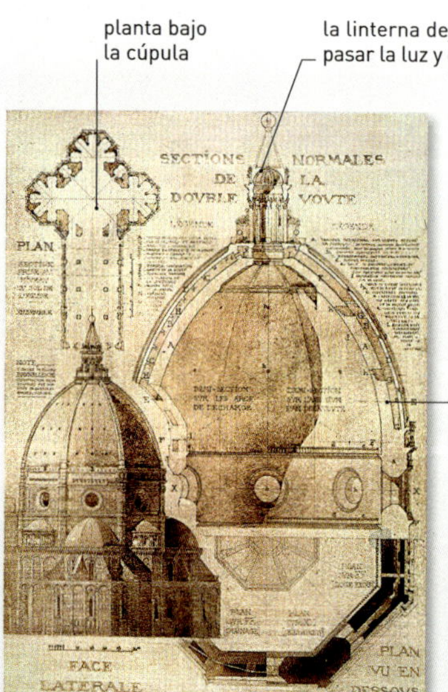

planta bajo la cúpula

la linterna deja pasar la luz y el aire

una cúpula interna de ladrillo soporta el techo, liviano

Cúpula de la catedral de Florencia
Siglo XV • ITALIA
La cúpula sobre tambor octogonal de la catedral de Florencia, obra de Filippo Brunelleschi (1377–1446), se compone de tres partes, como muestra este grabado (siglo XIX).

La Gioconda
1503–1506 • ITALIA
El enigmático retrato de Mona Lisa, realizado por Leonardo da Vinci (1452–1519), es la obra más famosa del Renacimiento y el cuadro más conocido del mundo.

la bola roja representa una píldora

Cerámica de los Médicis
Siglo XV • ITALIA
Este plato de mayólica con el escudo de armas de los Médicis evoca la riqueza y el prestigio de esta familia florentina.

las líneas rectas representan direcciones de brújula

mar Mediterráneo

Mapamundi
1502 • ESPAÑA
Venecia debía su riqueza al dominio de las rutas comerciales. Este mapa muestra el Mediterráneo y los mares adyacentes, que los barcos venecianos cruzaban a menudo para distribuir las mercancías que llegaban a occidente por las rutas terrestres.

la postura de la diosa Venus se basa en una estatua romana

El nacimiento de Venus
C. **1486** • ITALIA
Esta pintura del Renacimiento temprano, realizada por Sandro Botticelli (*c.* 1445–1510), expresa el deseo renacentista de adoptar y renovar los ideales de belleza de la Antigüedad clásica.

riñón

cavidad abdominal sin intestinos, para revelar los órganos que hay detrás

Órganos de la cavidad abdominal
C. **1453** • ITALIA
Extraído de la obra *Sobre la estructura del cuerpo humano*, de Andrés Vesalio (1514–1564), este dibujo anatómico ilustra la determinación renacentista de ampliar el conocimiento científico.

el globo terráqueo simboliza la pericia náutica

el torquetum, un instrumento astronómico, simboliza el conocimiento científico

la alfombra asiática simboliza la exploración

el gabán forrado de piel denota riqueza y prestigio

la calavera distorsionada simboliza la muerte; si se mira de lado, no está distorsionada

el laúd con la cuerda rota sugiere desacuerdo religioso

Los embajadores
1533 • ALEMANIA
Este retrato de Hans Holbein el Joven (*c.* 1497–1543) de dos jóvenes diplomáticos está repleto de símbolos complejos y detalles alusivos a su vida y a sus logros como hombres cultivados del Renacimiento.

estructura basada en un ala de murciélago

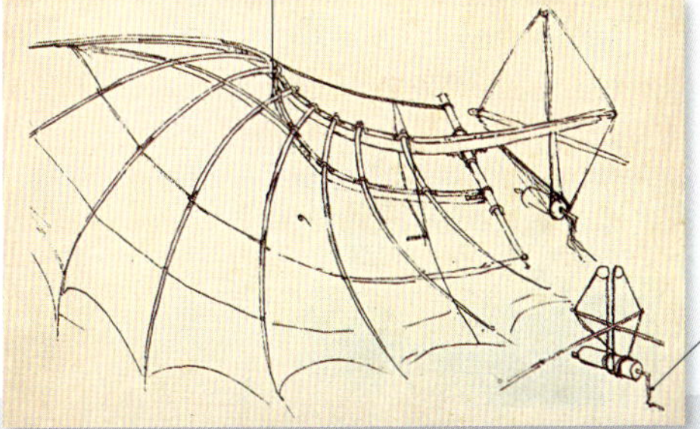

mecanismo de manivela

Ala impulsada a mano
C. **1490** • ITALIA
Leonardo da Vinci propuso varios artefactos voladores movidos por el hombre, como muestra este esbozo de un ala impulsada a mano de su *Codex Atlanticus*, de doce volúmenes.

1608–1609

« MIENTRAS VIVA LA MADRE **IGNORANCIA, NO ES SEGURO** QUE SU HIJA, **LA CIENCIA, DIVULGUE** LA **CAUSA OCULTA** DE LAS COSAS. **»**

Johannes Kepler, astrónomo alemán

EL 2 DE OCTUBRE DE 1608, HANS LIPPERSHEY (1570–1619), un fabricante de lentes de Zelanda (Países Bajos), solicitó una patente para un instrumento «para ver objetos lejanos como si estuvieran cerca» que pronto se conoció como **telescopio**. El instrumento de Lippershey era rudimentario y solo tenía tres aumentos, por lo que no tardó en ser superado. Aun así, fue un hito decisivo para la observación científica en la Europa del siglo XVII.

Desde 1606, **Países Bajos** trataba de negociar una tregua con **España** para acabar con la **contienda que los enfrentaba**. Cuarenta años de guerra habían agotado a los dos bandos, pero también ambos temían que el otro aprovechara el alto el fuego para reagruparse, cosa que ambos pensaban hacer. Pese a ello, en abril de 1609 se firmó la **tregua de los Doce Años**.

En 1526, Carlos V había decretado que todos los musulmanes de España debían convertirse al catolicismo. La minoría **morisca** resultante seguía marginada: era valorada como mano de obra barata, pero vista con recelo por su filiación religiosa. En 1609, Felipe II decidió **expulsar a los moriscos** de España. La medida provocó la partida de comunidades enteras, y sus propiedades fueron confiscadas. También alteró la economía de muchas regiones, que perdieron una valiosa mano de obra. El resentimiento musulmán hacia España aumentó.

En 1609, la Compañía Neerlandesa de las Indias Orientales envió a **Henry Hudson** a explorar la costa este de América de Norte. Hudson recorrió el río que lleva su nombre hasta la Albany actual y reclamó la región para Países Bajos.

Río Hudson
El río del estado de Nueva York lleva el nombre del noble inglés Henry Hudson, que exploró su curso.

1610

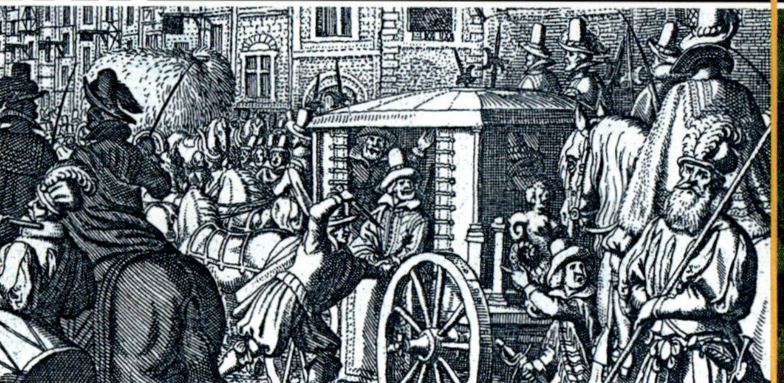

Grabado en cobre sobre el asesinato de Enrique IV de Francia en París. El rey había sobrevivido a 18 intentos de asesinato.

EL ASESINATO DEL REY ENRIQUE IV en París el 14 de mayo del año 1610, que murió apuñalado por el antiguo monje y maestro François Ravaillac, hizo temer la reaparición de las sangrientas divisiones religiosas por cuya eliminación Enrique se había esforzado tanto (y matado a tantos). No obstante, no solo se aceptó de inmediato como nuevo monarca a su hijo de nueve años, **Luis XIII**, sino que también se evitó la amenaza de un nuevo conflicto entre Francia y España. Ambos países competían por el control del ducado de Jülich-Cléveris en Alemania, lo que suponía la amenaza de que estallase un nuevo conflicto religioso paneuropeo. Con la muerte de Enrique, ambos podían retirarse sin deshonra. Enrique IV, el primer Borbón, fue sin lugar a dudas uno de los reyes franceses más extraordinarios: su **reconstrucción** del pestilente y caótico París medieval es una metáfora de la reconstrucción de la propia Francia.

Menos de un año después de que Lippershey afirmara haber inventado el telescopio, **Galileo Galilei** (*véase* recuadro) diseñó un telescopio propio a partir de simples descripciones del de Lippershey. Afirmó haberlo montado en menos de un día, y era diez veces más potente. Con él, en enero de 1610 Galileo comenzó a observar y a estudiar las «tres estrellas fijas» invisibles a simple vista junto al planeta Júpiter y se dio cuenta de que **orbitaban** en torno al planeta. Este descubrimiento contradecía la noción aceptada de que los cuerpos celestes únicamente podían girar alrededor de un punto fijo en el firmamento: la Tierra. Esta revelación explosiva se vio además reforzada ese mismo año cuando Galileo inició una serie de observaciones sistemáticas del planeta Venus. Sus fases (creciente, parcial y llena) solo podían explicarse si también orbitaba en torno a otro cuerpo celeste: el **Sol**. El telescopio hizo posibles las observaciones que causaron una revolución en la manera de comprender las relaciones del ser humano con un universo vasto e impersonal.

GALILEO (1564–1642)

Galileo Galilei, nacido en Pisa, fue un científico italiano que, pese a la obstrucción de la ortodoxia religiosa, aportó una visión totalmente nueva y científica del mundo. La Iglesia consideró que sus ideas eran heréticas, pero como no quería condenar directamente a un científico pionero, hizo lo posible por aceptarlo. Hereje o no, murió con su reputación no solo creciente, sino garantizada.

1611

Pintura que representa la batalla de Kalmar en el mar Báltico.

EN 1604, EL REY JACOBO I DE INGLATERRA autorizó una nueva traducción al inglés de la **Biblia**. Desde la Reforma se habían realizado dos traducciones. La *Gran Biblia* de 1539 y la *Biblia del obispo* de 1568. Sin embargo, se pensaba que ambas versiones contenían algunas **inexactitudes** menores y que, en cualquier caso, ninguna de ellas reflejaba plenamente ni la autoridad doctrinal, ni la estructura de la **Iglesia de Inglaterra**. La nueva traducción, que fue publicada en 1611 como *Santa Biblia*, fue obra de 47 eruditos supervisados por el arzobispo de Canterbury, Richard Bancroft. Aunque los anglicanos la aceptaron con relativa lentitud, en el siglo XVIII todas las iglesias protestantes de habla inglesa la consideraban la Biblia **definitiva** en inglés. Cuando se publicó la edición revisada a finales del siglo XVIII, recibió el nombre de *Biblia del rey Jacobo*, que a principios del siglo XIX se llamó Versión Autorizada del rey Jacobo.

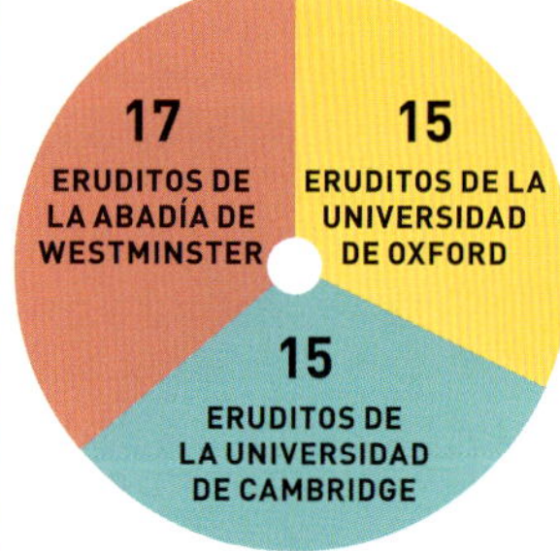

Biblia del rey Jacobo
Varios eruditos de cada institución llevaron a cabo la traducción de la Biblia del griego, el hebreo y el latín al inglés entre 1604 y 1608.

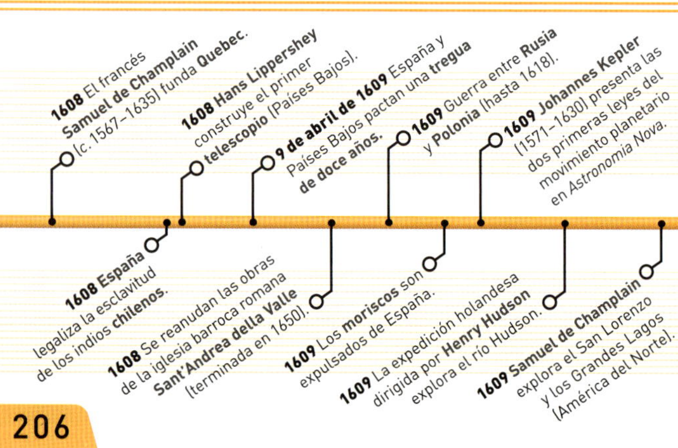

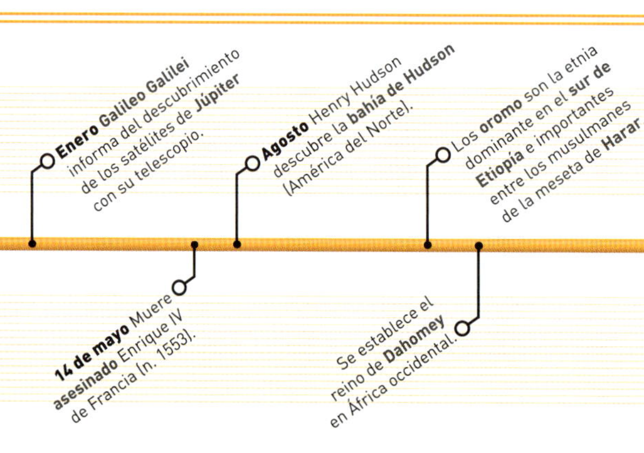

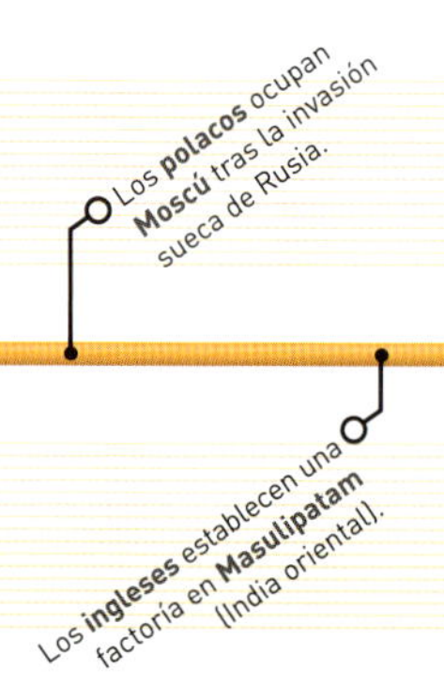

1612–1613

El castillo de Tully, en el condado de Fermanagh (Irlanda del Norte) se construyó en 1619 para sir John Hume, un colono escocés.

1614–1615

Grabado de la portada de *El Quijote*, cuya primera parte se publicó en 1605. La segunda se editó en 1615.

En junio del año 1611, el explorador inglés **Henry Hudson**, que en aquel momento estaba financiado por un grupo de comerciantes ingleses, fue abandonado por su tripulación después de pasar un durísimo invierno en la costa sur de la gran bahía del **noroeste de Canadá** que hoy lleva su nombre. Jamás se le volvió a ver. Hudson buscaba un paso que permitiera llegar hasta Asia por el noroeste. Al igual que el descubierto por Fernando de Magallanes cuando rodeó el extremo de América del Sur, se creía que debía existir un **paso equivalente por el norte**. Su búsqueda dio lugar a uno de los episodios más heroicamente inútiles de la exploración del planeta, una serie de expediciones (casi todas inglesas) llevadas a cabo a partir de 1576 y que únicamente llegaron a puntos sin salida no navegables y congelados.

El **estrecho** paso marítimo que separa **Dinamarca** y **Suecia** a la entrada del Báltico era una de las principales preocupaciones en la continua lucha escandinava por conseguir la supremacía en ese mar. En 1611, Suecia, decidida a terminar con el dominio danés sobre esa importante franja de agua, inició una serie de campañas que se conocen como **guerra de Kalmar**. El resultado, en 1613, no fue definitivo. Países Bajos, e Inglaterra en particular, prestaron su apoyo a Suecia ante la amenaza de una posible victoria danesa, pero solamente consiguieron posponer el conflicto.

una de las 17 perlas

zafiros y esmeraldas

escenas del Antiguo Testamento

Orbe del zar
Orbe incrustado de joyas usado en la coronación de Miguel III Romanov el 22 de julio de 1613.

EN EL INVIERNO DE 1609–1610, la incipiente colonia inglesa de Jamestown (Virginia) sufrió lo que se conoce como la **«época del hambre»**, el intento sistemático de los indios powhatan de que los colonos se rindieran por hambre.

Tan solo sobrevivieron 60 de los 500 colonos, pero el **tabaco** transformó el destino de la colonia. Los indios también cultivaban tabaco, pero la especie nativa, *Nicotiana rustica*, era tan fuerte que resultaba infumable. John Rolfe, que llegó a Jamestown en 1610, llevó semillas de *Nicotiana tabacum*, mucho más suave. Su primera cosecha, en 1612, halló un **mercado inmediato** en Londres. En 1627, su comercio ya reportaba 500 000 libras anuales.

En **Irlanda**, en 1613, había empezado el asentamiento deliberado de **protestantes**, muchos de ellos escoceses. El objetivo era demostrar a los súbditos escoceses de Jacobo I que este no había olvidado sus intereses y «pacificar» y convertir a la rebelde población **católica** de Irlanda. En general, únicamente consiguió inflamar las pasiones religiosas y, con la creación de una clase baja católica, generar tensiones que aún perduran en nuestros días.

100 000 NÚMERO ESTIMADO DE EUNUCOS EMPLEADOS EN CHINA POR LA DINASTÍA MING

EN DRÁSTICO CONTRASTE CON INGLATERRA, donde la autoridad parlamentaria aumentó a lo largo del siglo XVII, la asamblea legislativa de **Francia**, los **Estados Generales**, se había atrofiado casi completamente. Durante las guerras de religión francesas y en los años posteriores, los Estados Generales se habían reunido con bastante regularidad: seis veces entre 1560 y 1614. Sin embargo, no volvieron a reunirse hasta 1789, cuando Francia ya se encontraba al borde de la revolución.

En 1615, **China** se tuvo que enfrentar a una profunda crisis financiera y a la desintegración social. Existían fuertes **tensiones** en el **gobierno** debido al conflicto existente entre los eruditos de la Academia de Donglin (literalmente, «academia de la arboleda del este») en China oriental, y los eunucos de la corte, especialmente el caprichoso y cruel Wei Zhongxian. El emperador Wanli estaba semirretirado, y Wei Zhongxian había asumido el control del gobierno. Los académicos de Donglin, que seguían los imperativos morales del confucianismo, se oponían con rotundidad al autoensalzamiento y la extravagancia de los eunucos. En 1624, Wei Zhongxian ya había ordenado la ejecución de los eruditos de Donglin más prominentes.

Mientras tanto, los **holandeses** empezaban a asentarse en **América del Norte**. En 1615, afianzaron su derecho a la región de la actual Albany gracias a la construcción del Fuerte Nassau. Diez años más tarde, en 1625, levantaron **Nueva Ámsterdam**, un asentamiento situado en la desembocadura del río Hudson. Sin embargo, la colonización holandesa comenzó a declinar hacia finales del siglo XVII.

Los huesos de Napier
Se trata del ábaco que John Napier diseñó en 1615, con unas varillas numeradas que simplificaban la multiplicación.

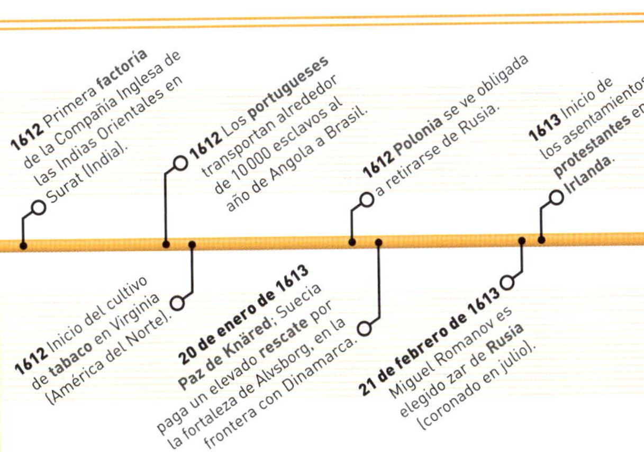

- Se publica la ***Biblia del rey Jacobo*** en Inglaterra.
- **Abril** Inicio de la **guerra de Kalmar**: conflicto entre Suecia y Dinamarca por el control del Báltico (hasta 1613).
- **1612** Primera **factoría** de la Compañía Inglesa de las Indias Orientales en Surat (India).
- **1612** Inicio del cultivo de **tabaco** en Virginia (América del Norte).
- **1612** Los **portugueses** transportan alrededor de 10 000 esclavos al año de Angola a Brasil.
- **20 de enero de 1613** **Paz de Knäred**: Suecia paga un elevado **rescate** por la fortaleza de Alvsborg, en la frontera con Dinamarca.
- **1612 Polonia** se ve obligada a retirarse de Rusia.
- **21 de febrero de 1613** Miguel Romanov es elegido zar de **Rusia** (coronado en julio).
- **1613** Inicio de los asentamientos **protestantes** en **Irlanda**.

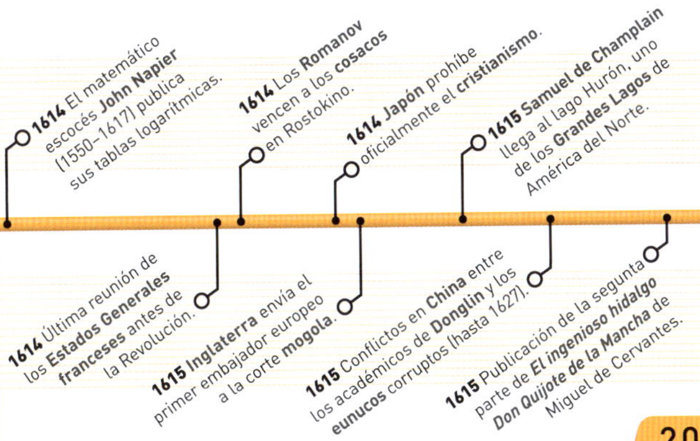

- **1614** El matemático escocés **John Napier** (1550–1617) publica sus tablas logarítmicas.
- **1614** Última reunión de los **Estados Generales franceses** antes de la Revolución.
- **1614** Los **Romanov** vencen a los **cosacos** en Rostokino.
- **1615 Inglaterra** envía el primer embajador europeo a la corte **mogola**.
- **1614 Japón** prohíbe oficialmente el **cristianismo**.
- **1615** Conflictos en **China** entre los académicos de **Donglin** y los **eunucos** corruptos (hasta 1627).
- **1615 Samuel de Champlain** llega al lago Hurón, uno de los **Grandes Lagos** de América del Norte.
- **1615** Publicación de la segunda parte de ***El ingenioso hidalgo Don Quijote de la Mancha*** de Miguel de Cervantes.

1616–1617

« ESPERO QUE A LOS **RUSOS** LES **CUESTE SALTAR** ESTE **RIACHUELO**. **»**

Gustavo Adolfo de Suecia, tratado de Stolbovo (1617)

LAS SEMILLAS DE LA CAÍDA de la dinastía Ming en China (*véase* 1664) se sembraron en el año 1616, cuando el líder tribal manchú Nurhaci (1559–1626) se **autoproclamó Gran Jin** y fundó la dinastía Qing. En 1599 había empezado a unir a otras tribus en el **sistema militar de ocho banderas**, y la guerra contra los Ming estalló en 1618.

20 000

ES EL NÚMERO DE **AZULEJOS DEL TECHO** CUYO COLOR DA NOMBRE A LA **MEZQUITA AZUL**

Aunque el estrecho de Magallanes, donde se encuentran el **Atlántico y el Pacífico** al sur de América del Sur, fue descubierto en 1519, resultaba muy difícil de atravesar. En 1616, la **expedición holandesa** de Willem Schouten y Jakob Le Maire descubrió una ruta nueva por mar y dio el nombre de **cabo de Hornos** a la isla más meridional.

En 1616, y después de unos siete años de construcción, se terminó uno de los **edificios más bellos de la arquitectura islámica**: la mezquita del sultán Ahmed en Estambul, conocida como **mezquita Azul** por los múltiples azulejos de ese color que decoran su interior.

Los holandeses compraron la **isla de Gorea**, situada al sur de Cabo Verde (África), a sus propietarios portugueses en 1617 y la convirtieron en una **gran base del comercio de esclavos**, actividad que continuaron los franceses, que la compraron en 1677.

El **tratado de Stolbovo** puso fin a la guerra entre Rusia y Suecia, que se había prolongado durante siete años, y trazó una **frontera nueva y más segura para Suecia**, a partir de los lagos Ladoga y Peipus.

Base esclavista holandesa
Este grabado coloreado muestra el fuerte de la isla de Gorea bajo control de los holandeses, cuya explotación les resultó muy rentable.

1618

La defenestración de dos regidores por los protestantes en el castillo de Praga (Bohemia) desencadenó la guerra de los Treinta Años.

« AUNQUE ES UNA **MEDICINA AMARGA**, ES EL **REMEDIO** DE **TODAS** LAS **ENFERMEDADES** Y **DESDICHAS**. **»**

Sir Walter Raleigh, últimas palabras antes de ser ejecutado (29 de octubre de 1618)

EL 23 DE MAYO DE 1618, EL CONDE PROTESTANTE THURN ordenó lanzar por la ventana del castillo de Praga (Bohemia) a los dos regidores del rey católico de Bohemia y futuro emperador del Sacro Imperio, Fernando II (1578–1637). La **defenestración de Praga** desató la sangrienta **guerra de los Treinta Años**. Se libró sobre todo en Alemania, muchos de cuyos estados sufrieron una destrucción y unas matanzas a gran escala hasta 1648. Empezó como un conflicto religioso, pero el **objetivo de Fernando de acabar con el protestantismo** en todos sus dominios terminó convirtiéndose en una pugna por el poder en Europa en la que participaron, en un momento u otro, todas las potencias europeas.

El 29 de octubre de 1618, el soldado y explorador inglés **sir Walter Raleigh** (1552–1618) fue **decapitado** en la Torre de Londres. Había sido uno de los primeros colonos ingleses de Virginia (Norte América), pero su incapacidad para encontrar la legendaria ciudad sudamericana de **El Dorado** y su ataque a un asentamiento español contra el deseo expreso del rey Jacobo I sellaron su destino.

Los corsarios ingleses (piratas pagados por el estado) compraban y vendían **esclavos africanos** desde finales del siglo XVI, pero en 1618 Inglaterra intensificó su participación en esta actividad cuando llegó el **primer cargamento de esclavos a sus colonias norteamericanas**, a Jamestown (Virginia), desde África occidental.

TRATA DE ESCLAVOS

Aunque el comercio atlántico de esclavos alcanzó su punto álgido en el siglo XVIII, a inicios del XVII ya crecía rápidamente. Los esclavos eran llevados desde una serie de fuertes esclavistas de la costa oeste africana hacia las prósperas colonias europeas del Nuevo Mundo. Durante la travesía atlántica, a la que el 25 % no sobrevivía, los esclavos varones eran marcados con hierros de ganado (imagen).

1619–1620

La obra del filósofo inglés Francis Bacon tuvo un impacto duradero.

PAÍSES BAJOS, QUE BUSCABA AGRESIVAMENTE suplantar a Portugal en las **Indias Orientales**, habían intentado establecer un **puesto comercial en Java** en 1596. A partir de 1602 también tuvieron que defenderse de los esfuerzos de Inglaterra por infiltrarse en las Indias Orientales. En 1619, los **holandeses respondieron** con decisión y expulsaron a los ingleses y a sus aliados de Java, para establecerse en Jayakarta, a la que rebautizaron como **Batavia** y que no solo se convirtió en la **capital holandesa de las Indias Orientales**, sino en el foco del imperio colonial holandés, que perduró hasta la conquista japonesa de 1942.

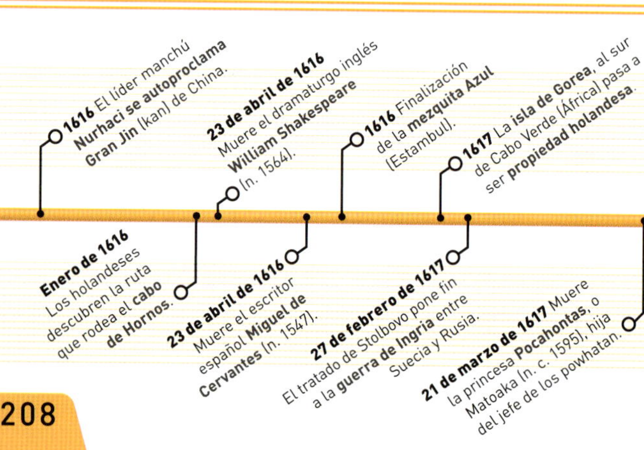

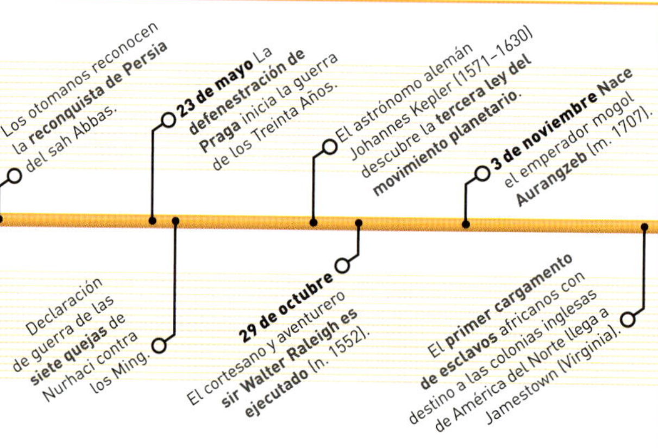

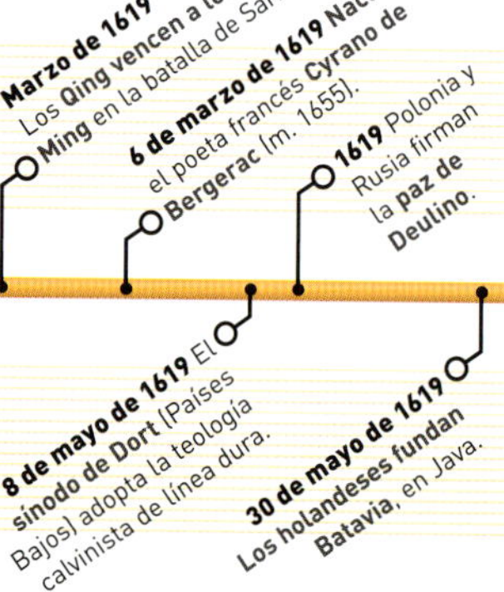

« MUCHOS VIAJARÁN, Y EL CONOCIMIENTO SE AMPLIARÁ. »

Francis Bacon, filósofo inglés, en *Novum organum* (1620)

Los indios powhatan atacan una granja en la colonia inglesa de Virginia en 1622 y matan a todos sus habitantes.

El filósofo y científico inglés Francis Bacon (1561–1626) escribió en 1620 *Novum organum*, obra de gran importancia en el **desarrollo del método científico**.

La fase inicial de la guerra de los Treinta Años culminó en noviembre de 1620 en la **batalla de la Montaña Blanca**, en la cual las tropas imperiales del sacro emperador Fernando II **aplastaron** a las del calvinista Federico V (1596–1632), soberano del Palatinado, en el suroeste de Alemania. A la **victoria de Fernando** siguió la imposición rigurosa de la autoridad católica e imperial en Bohemia y otras partes de Alemania. Esto hizo que la oposición protestante internacional siguiera combatiendo al emperador a lo largo de la década de 1620.

La fundación de Jamestown en 1607, como primera **colonia inglesa** permanente en el Nuevo Mundo, quedaría eclipsada por la llegada del navío ***Mayflower*** cerca de la actual Boston en noviembre de 1620. Sus 102 pasajeros eran **peregrinos puritanos**, protestantes autoexiliados que lo arriesgaron todo por una nueva vida allí.

Batalla de la Montaña Blanca
Esta batalla, que acabaron ganando los católicos, fue librada cerca de Praga y cerró el primer periodo, o periodo bohemio, de la guerra de los Treinta Años.

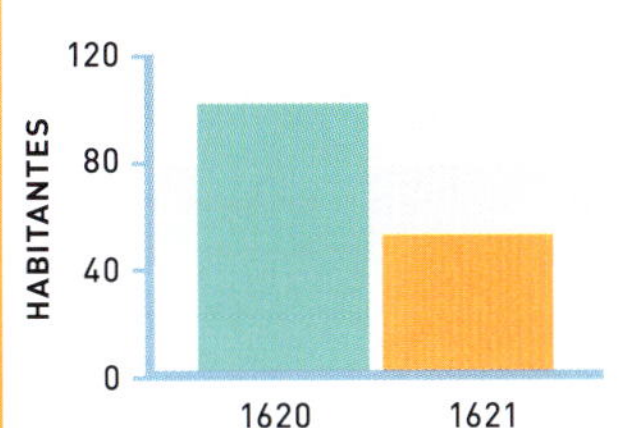

Población de Plymouth
La población de la colonia de Plymouth se redujo drásticamente durante el primer y difícil año tras su fundación.

LOS PEREGRINOS PURITANOS del *Mayflower* que alcanzaron el Nuevo Mundo en 1620 no solo lo hicieron hacia finales de año, en pleno invierno de Nueva Inglaterra, sino en el lugar equivocado, ya que su objetivo original era el río Hudson, varios cientos de kilómetros al sur. Al principio, su **supervivencia** en lo que llamaron colonia de Plymouth fue casi por completo una **cuestión de suerte**, y aquellos que superaron el durísimo invierno lo hicieron, sobre todo, gracias a la ayuda de los indios. Posteriormente llevaron una **vida mísera** que dependía del apoyo incierto de Inglaterra y de su propio esfuerzo.

En **1621 expiró la tregua de los Doce Años** que España y la República de las Provincias Unidas de los Países Bajos habían firmado en 1609, lo que señaló, quizá previsiblemente, la reanudación del **conflicto hispano-holandés**. Ambos bandos habían reforzado tanto sus ejércitos como sus flotas en previsión de una nueva guerra. Además, la ayuda económica (si no militar) holandesa al rey Federico V (exiliado en las Provincias Unidas tras su derrota en la Montaña Blanca el año anterior) proporcionaba a los españoles un motivo evidente para **renovar las hostilidades**. Sin embargo, el conflicto subsiguiente fue menos un intento por parte de España de reconquistar Países Bajos que un esfuerzo por **desestabilizarlos tanto a nivel político como económico**, y el intento de prohibir su actividad mercantil y de bloquear sus puertos principales. España tuvo éxito en el asedio de Jülich y de Steenbergen en 1622, pero se vio obligada a abandonar, con un gran coste, el sitio a Bergen-op-Zoom.

Las **islas Banda**, en las Indias Orientales, eran la única **fuente conocida de nuez moscada y macis**, especias que daban grandes beneficios en Europa, por lo que fueron causa de una **rivalidad a menudo violenta**, primero entre los portugueses y los holandeses, y a principios del siglo XVII, entre estos y los ingleses. En 1621, después de expulsar a los ingleses de las islas y animados por el gobernador general de las Indias Orientales, Jan Pieterszoon Coen, los holandeses **exterminaron a los isleños**. Se ha estimado que de una población de 15 000 tan solo unos mil escaparon a la muerte o la expulsión.

El 22 de marzo de 1622, en la colonia inglesa de Virginia, los **indios powhatan mataron a 347 colonos**, cerca de un 25 % del total. Hacia 1610, las **tensiones** entre los colonos y los indios ya se habían convertido en un **conflicto abierto**, pero en 1622, cuando los indios se dieron cuenta de que, si bien los colonos afirmaban querer mantener unas relaciones pacíficas con los powhatan, lo hacían exclusivamente en sus propios términos, decidieron alzarse contra ellos. La previsible consecuencia fue un **violento contraataque inglés**, que a mediados de siglo había **exterminado prácticamente a los powhatan**.

Decidido a poner fin al **poder de los jenízaros** (la élite militar que componía las tropas nacionales y la escolta del sultán otomano), Osmán II (1604–1622) se buscó unos enemigos muy peligrosos desde que, en 1618, se convirtiera en sultán. Sus intentos de afirmarse como gobernante independiente provocaron un **alzamiento jenízaro** por el que acabó prisionero en su propio palacio. El 20 de mayo de 1622, uno de los captores **asesinó al sultán**, de 17 años de edad, probablemente estrangulándolo.

El sultán Osmán II
Retrato ecuestre a la aguada sobre papel del sultán otomano Osmán II cuyo breve reinado tuvo un final trágico y violento.

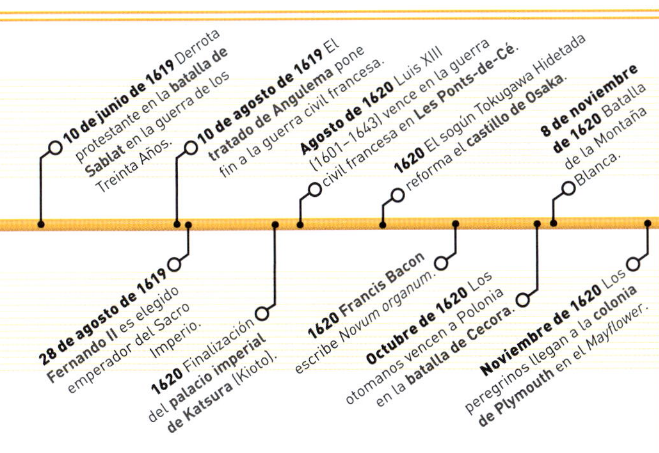

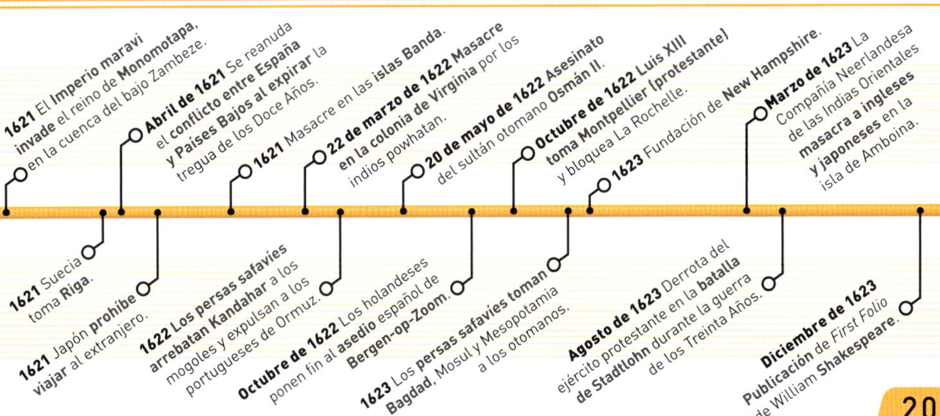

1624–1625

« LA **GUERRA** ES UNO DE LOS **AZOTES** CON QUE **DIOS SE COMPLACE EN CASTIGAR AL HOMBRE.** »

Cardenal Richelieu, primer ministro de Francia (década de 1620)

EN AGOSTO DE 1624, EL CARDENAL RICHELIEU (1585–1642) se convirtió en el primer ministro del rey de Francia, Luis XIII (1601–1643). Sus objetivos eran «destruir el poder militar de los Habsburgo, dar una lección de humildad a los grandes nobles (de Francia) y aumentar el prestigio de la **casa de Borbón** en Europa». Eran objetivos ambiciosos, que exigían alianzas con grupos poco comprometidos con su programa. Al final, el precio de enfrentarse a los enemigos externos y a los protestantes nacionales fue el alzamiento popular contra las cargas económicas y financieras impuestas por el cardenal. También condujeron a la rebelión de las élites, que culminó en la guerra civil de la Fronda (*véase* 1648–1649). Sin embargo, Richelieu impidió que se produjese una fractura política gracias a su **astucia y a su capacidad de manipulación** de las facciones, y a su muerte, Francia iba avanzando posiciones respecto a sus enemigos Habsburgo. El cardenal sabía que el poder militar hugonote en Francia (*véase* 1597–1598) era una amenaza permanente a la estabilidad nacional, pero era consciente de que la persecución del protestantismo generaría una fuerte resistencia interna y pondría en peligro las alianzas establecidas con las potencias protestantes sobre las que descansaba su **estrategia contra los Habsburgo**.

En el año 1625, los complejos conflictos de la **guerra de los Treinta Años** en curso se complicaron todavía más. Tras la tregua de los Doce Años, España aplastó a Países Bajos y **tomó Breda después de un asedio de once meses**, mientras Francia, cuya política dirigía el astuto Richelieu, participaba de manera encubierta en un **conflicto antihabsburgo en el norte de Italia**. Se trataba del intento de Richelieu de bloquear el Camino Español, el tenue aunque vital vínculo entre la Italia de los Habsburgo y Países Bajos. Casi al mismo tiempo, Cristián IV de Dinamarca (1577–1648) decidió implicarse en la guerra, en parte para **defender la causa protestante**, pero sobre todo con el objetivo de contener las ambiciones suecas de controlar el norte de Alemania y el Báltico. Su ejército fue **derrotado**, en agosto de 1626, **en la batalla de Lutter** (dcha.) por un ejército bávaro católico liderado por el conde de Tilly y aliado con el emperador Habsburgo. De momento, parecía que las intrigas francesas y las guerras con Países Bajos no iban a impedir la victoria de los Habsburgo.

La rendición de Breda
La obra del pintor español Diego Velázquez muestra a Justino de Nassau entregando Breda al capitán general Ambrosio Spínola en 1625, tras un largo asedio.

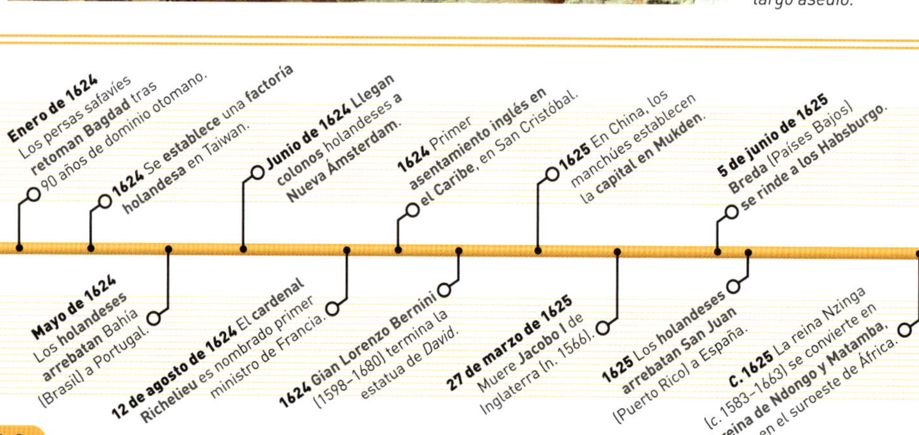

1626–1627

Pierre Minuit «compra» la isla de Manhattan a los indios, probablemente de la tribu lenape, en 1626.

UNA DE LAS TRANSACCIONES MÁS FAMOSAS de la historia tuvo lugar el 26 de mayo de 1626, cuando **Pierre Minuit**, director general de la colonia de los Nuevos Países Bajos de la Compañía Neerlandesa de las Indias Occidentales, **compró la isla de Manhattan** (donde se alzaba el Fuerte Ámsterdam desde 1625) a los nativos por 60 florines holandeses (unos 24 dólares). Ninguna de las partes creyó que el precio fuera poco razonable.

La **guerra de los Treinta Años** fue una **sangría brutal** para la Europa del siglo XVII, pero no solo como consecuencia de los combates. Los ejércitos siempre necesitaban dinero, por lo que decidieron autofinanciarse y **exigieron impuestos directamente** a los campesinos y a las ciudades. Tras pagar a los soldados, los campesinos y los pobres de las ciudades quedaron aún más **vulnerables ante las fluctuaciones de la provisión de alimentos** por las malas cosechas, la actividad militar y los saqueos. En gran parte de Europa, pero sobre todo en Francia, la Austria de los Habsburgo y el sur de Italia español, **los alzamientos campesinos y las revueltas urbanas** amenazaban con arrebatar el control a los gobiernos. El problema se agravó con el inicio de la «pequeña glaciación» a mediados del siglo XVII (*véase* 1645).

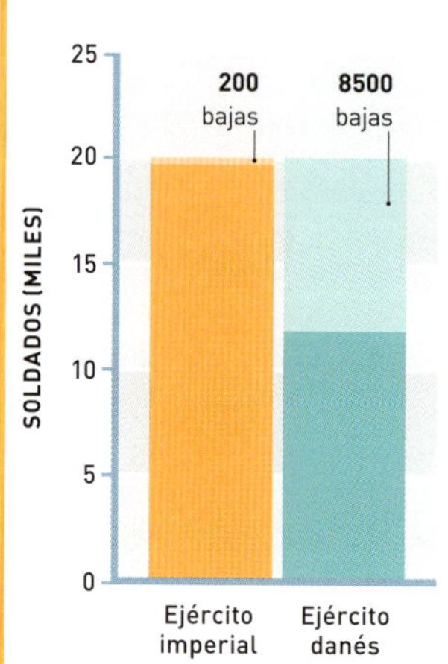

Batalla de Lutter
En 1626, tropas bávaras de la Liga Católica e imperiales derrotaron a un ejército danés de número similar, que perdió unos 8500 hombres.

ARQUITECTURA BARROCA

El barroco romano cobró un fuerte impulso a lo largo del siglo XVII. Fue una potente respuesta de los católicos a la Reforma y, además, sirvió para reafirmar la arquitectura clásica del Renacimiento. La construcción de iglesias suntuosas, y en concreto de la basílica de San Pedro (en la imagen), tenía el propósito de promocionar y glorificar a la Iglesia católica, y dio lugar a edificios nuevos y grandiosos.

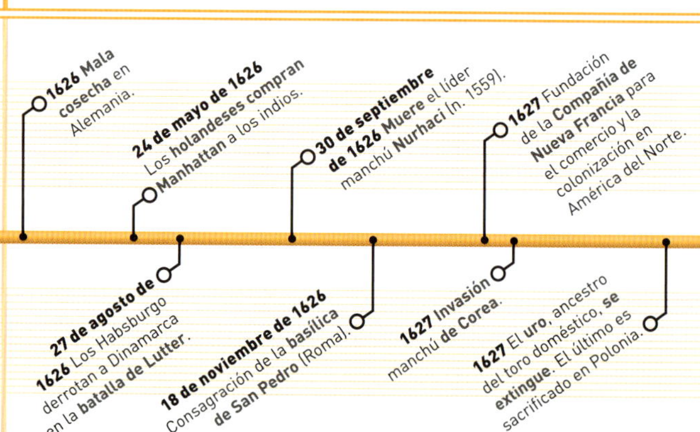

1628–1629

Esta miniatura en tinta y acuarela del siglo XVII muestra a Sah Yahan, el quinto emperador mogol, con una aureola de santidad.

Sitio de La Rochelle
El cardenal Richelieu, primer ministro de Francia, inspecciona las defensas que hizo construir para impedir el socorro por mar a La Rochelle.

TRAS MÁS DE UN AÑO, EL SITIO DE LA ROCHELLE, que era el enclave protestante más fuerte de Francia, terminó en octubre de 1628 con la **derrota de los hugonotes**. El sitio había sido la respuesta del cardenal Richelieu a las persistentes aspiraciones de la oposición hugonota a la corona francesa, con el objetivo de aplastar la resistencia hugonota y desmantelar su todavía formidable ejército. Richelieu reconocía su derecho a la tolerancia religiosa, pero se aseguró de **impedir que pudieran suponer una amenaza para la corona**.

En el año 1628, el médico inglés **William Harvey** (1578–1657) publicó *Sobre el movimiento del corazón y la sangre*, obra donde **explicaba** tanto la circulación sanguínea como el **funcionamiento del corazón** mediante la observación y la experimentación.

Ese mismo año, uno de los grandes líderes del Imperio mogol de India, **Sah Yahan** (1592–1666) fue **coronado emperador**. Sus 30 años de reinado fueron una **edad de oro para la India mogola**, durante la cual el territorio se expandió enormemente y florecieron la arquitectura y la cultura mogolas.

Durante el siglo XVII, los soberanos europeos adoptaron la idea de una **autoridad central potente** como la única garantía de estabilidad. En Inglaterra, Carlos I (1600–1649) consideró que la monarquía absoluta estaba plenamente legitimada por sanción divina. En 1629, irritado por el control parlamentario de su autoridad, decidió **disolver el Parlamento** y con ello provocó un **resentimiento creciente** entre aquellos que buscaban compartir el poder ante lo que entendieron como un intento de imponer impuestos ilegales.

1630–1631

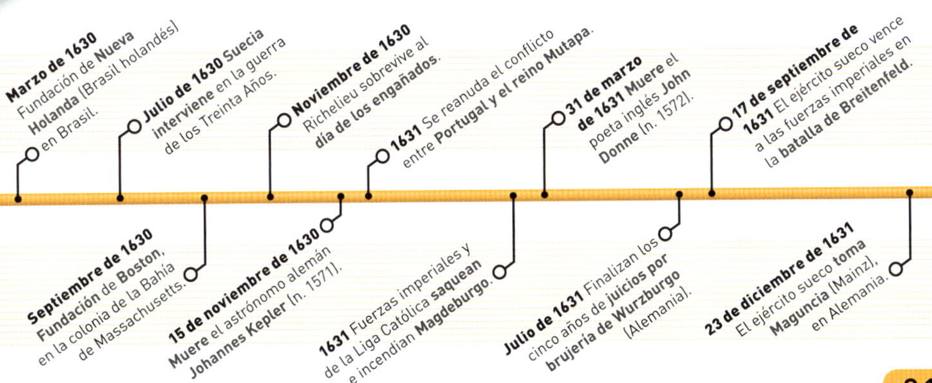

Grabado en madera pintado a mano que representa el sitio del Sacro Imperio a Magdeburgo. La ciudad fue incendiada y 20 000 personas asesinadas.

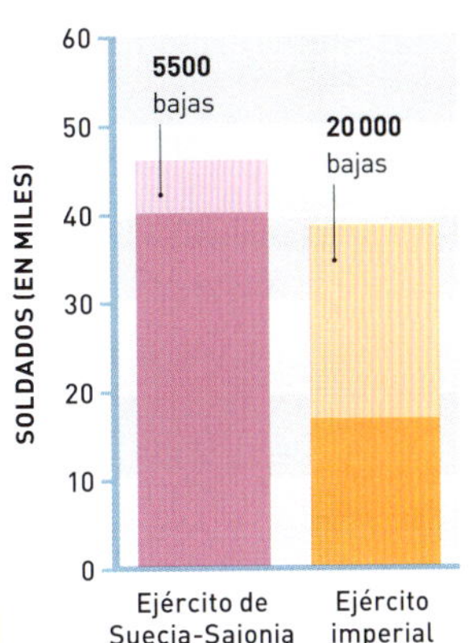

Batalla de Breitenfeld
En 1631, el poderoso ejército de Suecia-Sajonia infligió en Breitenfeld un enorme número de bajas al del Sacro Imperio.

LA ENTRADA DE SUECIA EN LA GUERRA DE LOS TREINTA AÑOS en 1630 dio una nueva dimensión al conflicto. Todavía era una guerra fundamentalmente religiosa, que el emperador católico Fernando II estaba ganando con claridad. **Gustavo II Adolfo** (1594–1632), rey luterano de Suecia, decidió aprovechar dicha situación para presentarse como el **salvador de los príncipes luteranos** del norte de Alemania. Sin embargo, era una amenaza potencial tanto para ellos como para Fernando. Durante los 19 años anteriores ya se había enfrentado a Rusia, Polonia y Dinamarca por el control del Báltico y **esperaba dominar también la costa alemana**. Su intervención podría haber quedado en nada, si los incendios durante el asalto a la plaza fuerte luterana de Magdeburgo por las tropas imperiales en 1631 no hubiera destruido la ciudad y matado a 2000 de sus habitantes, desatando la ira de los príncipes luteranos. Con su apoyo político y la gran ayuda económica de Francia, Gustavo Adolfo infligió una **derrota devastadora** al ejército imperial en **Breitenfeld**, cerca de Leipzig, en septiembre de 1631. En este punto, con su ejército marchando triunfal hacia el sur, el rey Gustavo Adolfo tuvo la visión de un imperio que incluyera a Suecia y Alemania. Sin embargo, los sucesos del año siguiente acabaron con sus esperanzas (*véase* 1632).

Un día de noviembre del año 1630, conocido como **el día de los engañados**, los no pocos enemigos del cardenal Richelieu intentaron deponerle. Exigieron a Luis XIII que lo sustituyera por **María de Médicis** (1575–1642), su madre, y cuando el rey se retiró a fin de meditar su decisión creyeron haberlo conseguido. Sin embargo, **los poderosos amigos del cardenal Richelieu lo salvaron**, y la madre del rey fue exiliada a Compiègne.

Reina de Francia
María de Médicis, segunda esposa de Enrique IV de Francia, que intentó deponer al cardenal Richelieu en 1630, retratada por Rubens.

Cañón sueco
Cañón utilizado por las fuerzas del rey Gustavo II Adolfo. Tiene un calibre (diámetro) de 7 cm y pesa 200 kg.

900 ES EL **NÚMERO** APROXIMADO DE **PERSONAS QUE FUERON QUEMADAS EN LA HOGUERA** TRAS LOS **JUICIOS POR BRUJERÍA DE WURZBURGO**

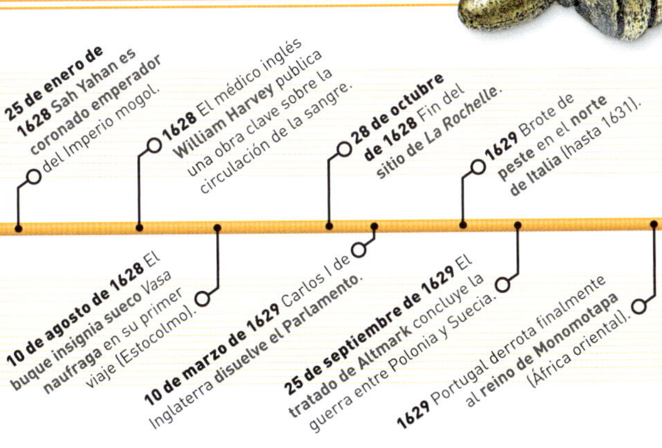

25 de enero de 1628 Sah Yahan es coronado emperador del Imperio mogol.

10 de agosto de 1628 El buque insignia sueco **Vasa naufraga** en su primer viaje (Estocolmo).

1628 El médico inglés **William Harvey** publica una obra clave sobre la circulación de la sangre.

10 de marzo de 1629 Carlos I de Inglaterra **disuelve el Parlamento**.

28 de octubre de 1628 Fin del sitio de *La Rochelle*.

25 de septiembre de 1629 El **tratado de Altmark** concluye la guerra entre Polonia y Suecia.

1629 Brote de **peste en el norte de Italia** (hasta 1631).

1629 Portugal derrota finalmente al **reino de Monomotapa** (África oriental).

Marzo de 1630 Fundación de **Nueva Holanda** (Brasil holandés) en Brasil.

Septiembre de 1630 **Fundación de Boston**, en la colonia de la Bahía de Massachusetts.

Julio de 1630 **Suecia interviene** en la guerra de los Treinta Años.

Noviembre de 1630 Richelieu sobrevive al **día de los engañados**.

15 de noviembre de 1630 Muere el astrónomo alemán **Johannes Kepler** (n. 1571).

1631 Se reanuda el conflicto entre **Portugal y el reino Mutapa**.

1631 Fuerzas imperiales y de la Liga Católica **saquean** e incendian **Magdeburgo**.

31 de marzo de 1631 **Muere** el poeta inglés **John Donne** (n. 1572).

Julio de 1631 Finalizan los cinco años de **juicios por brujería de Wurzburgo** (Alemania).

17 de septiembre de 1631 El ejército sueco vence a las fuerzas imperiales en la **batalla de Breitenfeld**.

23 de diciembre de 1631 El ejército sueco **toma Maguncia** (Mainz), en Alemania.

1632–1633

Este óleo sobre el juicio de Galileo muestra al físico y astrónomo italiano sentado frente a los miembros del tribunal de la Inquisición en Roma.

2 000 000

NÚMERO DE **FALLECIDOS** DURANTE LA **HAMBRUNA DE DECÁN (1630–1632)**

DESEOSA DE RECUPERAR LAS PÉRDIDAS ANTE POLONIA-LITUANIA por la paz de Deulino de 1616, y aprovechando la muerte del rey de Polonia Segismundo III Vasa, **Rusia sitió Smolensk** en octubre de 1632. El ejército polaco no pudo intentar romper el asedio hasta casi un año después, y su **derrota final por los rusos** en 1634 fue absoluta.

En la guerra de los Treinta Años, el éxito de Suecia el año anterior prosiguió con la **derrota del ejército imperial** en abril de 1632, durante la batalla de Rain (Baviera). Un triunfo menor en la **batalla de Lützen**, cerca de Leipzig, pudo haber confirmado las ambiciones territoriales suecas en Alemania si el **rey Gustavo Adolfo no hubiera muerto en combate**. El ímpetu de la campaña protestante se desvaneció, y la **supremacía Habsburgo** parecía nuevamente restaurada.

En Italia, el astrónomo **Galileo Galilei** (1564–1642) fue convocado en 1633 por la **Inquisición romana**. Su delito era defender públicamente la visión heliocéntrica del Sistema Solar, que situaba al Sol, y no a la Tierra, en el centro. **Declarado culpable de herejía**, Galileo fue obligado a retractarse y pasó el resto de su vida bajo arresto domiciliario.

En 1633, en Japón, el **sogunado Tokugawa** decretó la política de *kaikin* («restricción marítima»), un **control estricto del contacto** con el mundo exterior, aunque se permitiera el comercio con Corea y China, y a los neerlandeses conservar una base para comerciar. Se trataba de evitar incursiones en Japón, y esa política se mantuvo como oficial hasta 1853.

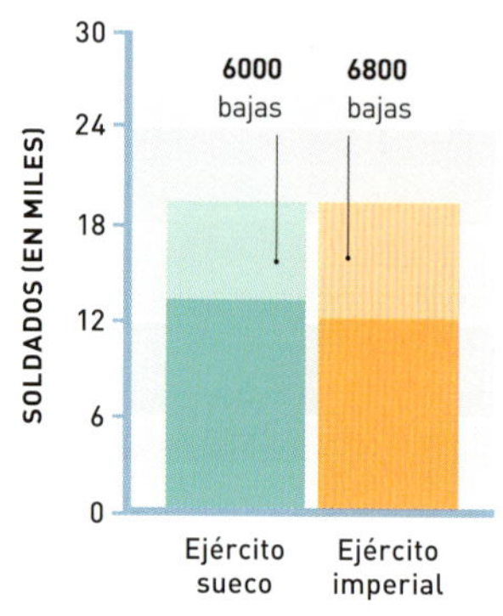

Batalla de Lützen
Aunque los ejércitos, con efectivos similares, sufrieron casi las mismas bajas, los suecos perdieron a su rey, Gustavo II Adolfo.

1634–1635

Asesinato del mariscal de campo Albrecht Wallenstein en la Casa Pachelbel de Eger (Bohemia). Sus propios hombres le despertaron y le asesinaron.

LA DERROTA DE LÜTZEN FUE una de las últimas ocasiones en que **Albrecht Wallenstein** (1583–1634) lideró un ejército imperial. Aunque victorioso en general, casi todo el mundo desconfiaba de él, y se creía que estaba negociando una paz alternativa. El sacro emperador Fernando II le acusó de traición, pero en febrero de 1634 fue **asesinado por algunos de sus oficiales**, con la aprobación tácita de Fernando. Aun así, los suecos no aprovecharon la victoria de Lützen, y las fuerzas imperiales retomaron la iniciativa y aplastaron a los suecos en la **batalla de Nördlingen**, que tuvo lugar en septiembre de 1634. La paz de Praga de 1635 hizo patente el alcance de la **victoria de los Habsburgo y de la derrota sueca**. Los príncipes protestantes pasaron a apoyar a Fernando II, lo que provocó la fase final y más sangrienta de la guerra de los Treinta Años, así como la **intervención directa de Francia**.

Al igual que en el siglo XVI, Francia temía verse rodeada por los Habsburgo. Hasta entonces había intentado protegerse financiando a los estados con más posibilidades de vencer a los Habsburgo, sobre todo a Suecia. Con los suecos a punto de abandonar Alemania, Francia tuvo que salir al campo de batalla. A medida que el **ejército francosueco avanzaba por Alemania** y los suecos recuperaban las pérdidas anteriores, Alemania iba quedando devastada. La lucha **llegó a Francia** en 1636, cuando el ejército español invadió el noreste y amenazó brevemente París, y de nuevo en 1637, cuando España atacó la región del Languedoc, en el sur. En 1639, Francia respondió con la invasión de Cataluña. Esta oleada de violencia **arruinó** a todos los **participantes**. España fue la que más sufrió, y los intentos de obtener financiación generaron un amargo resentimiento en su propio suelo. En 1640, Cataluña y Portugal se alzaron contra la corona española, con el **apoyo de Francia**; ese mismo año no hubo flota de Indias que trajera riquezas del Nuevo Mundo. A estas alturas, las causas originales de la guerra de los Trein-

Batalla de Nördlingen
Se libró en el sur de Alemania y acabó con una arrolladora victoria de los Habsburgo. Sin embargo, no supuso el fin de la guerra.

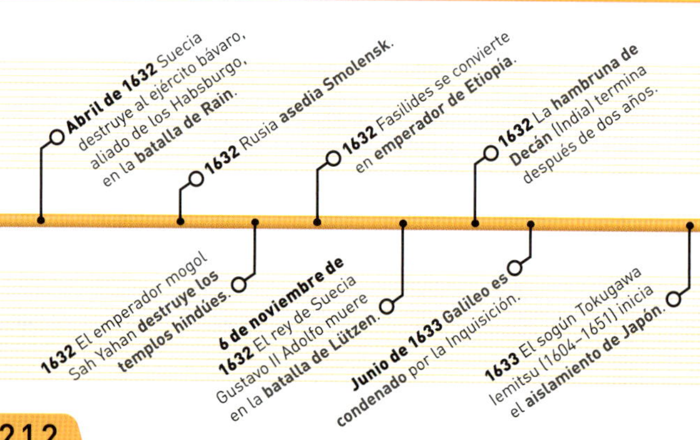

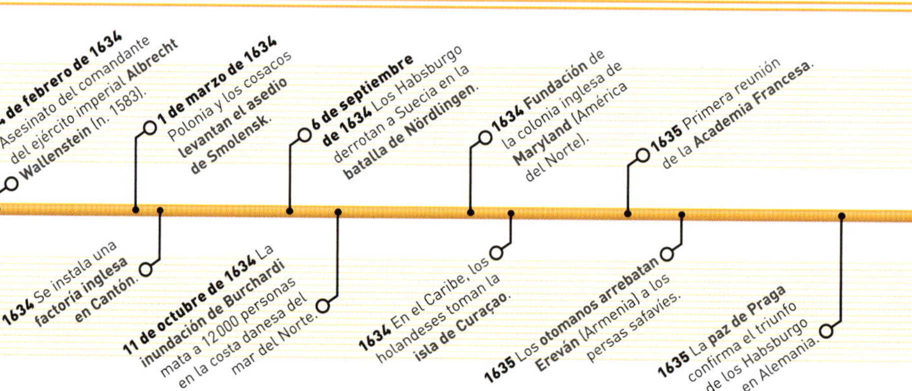

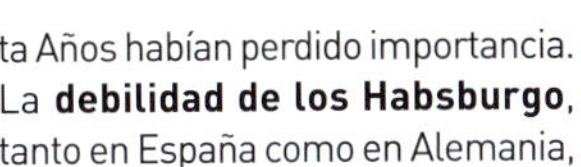

ta Años habían perdido importancia. La **debilidad de los Habsburgo**, tanto en España como en Alemania, **resultaba cada vez más evidente**.

Cuando no conspiraba contra sus enemigos, el **cardenal Richelieu** se esforzaba en promover *la gloire* (el prestigio) de Francia. Además de defender la expansión colonial, **fomentó las artes y el conocimiento**. La **Academia Francesa**, fundada en 1635, fue sin duda una de sus mayores y más duraderas contribuciones. Formaba parte de un movimiento paneuropeo a favor de las instituciones oficiales de enseñanza, pero también estaba **destinada a consolidar** lo que Francia consideraba uno de sus méritos principales: **su lengua**. Sus 40 académicos siguen pronunciándose acerca de los usos lingüísticos del francés en la actualidad.

En **Japón**, en1635 se determinó la **obligatoriedad del sistema de *sankin kotai*** («asistencia alterna»), instaurado por Toyotomi Hideyoshi en la década de 1590. Los daimios (señores feudales) tenían la obligación de residir años alternos en la corte del sogún en Edo para participar en fastuosos rituales; cuando regresaban a sus tierras, que dependían del sogún, sus esposas y herederos permanecían en la corte. El coste de dicha sumisión, más el tiempo que pasaban en la corte, **reducía las probabilidades de rebelión**. Se impusieron **estrictas exigencias** en cuanto a la ropa, el tipo de armas y los soldados que podían acompañar a cada daimio, así como sobre las aportaciones (económicas y militares) que se esperaban de ellos.

1636–1637

« **NO BASTA** CON POSEER UNA **BUENA MENTE**; LO IMPORTANTE ES **USARLA BIEN**. »

René Descartes, en *Discurso del método* (1637)

Castillo de Gonder
Forma parte de Fasil Ghebbi, fundada por Fasilides en Etiopía, y reúne influencias árabes, nubias y barrocas.

EMPERADOR ETÍOPE desde 1632, **Fasilides** (*c.* 1603–1667) fundó una **capital imperial permanente en Gonder** en 1636. Entre los edificios que levantó se halla Fasil Ghebbi, la ciudadela que fue la **residencia de los emperadores etíopes** hasta el siglo XVIII.

Por otro lado, en 1637 **estalló una primera burbuja especulativa** en Países Bajos, cuando el precio de los bulbos de tulipán, considerados como un bien de lujo y una inversión segura, alcanzó máximos para caer en picado de repente, lo que arruinó a muchos inversores. Aunque es difícil conocer con seguridad los precios durante la **«tulipomanía»**, las pruebas anecdóticas sugieren que se alcanzaron máximos importantes.

Uno de los fundadores de la filosofía moderna, el escritor francés **René Descartes** (1596–1650), defensor del racionalismo, escribió en 1637 el *Discurso del método*, una de las obras más influyentes de la filosofía occidental.

En China, **Song Yingxing**, un funcionario de provincias, escribió una nueva **enciclopedia** titulada *La explotación de las obras de la naturaleza*, que fue publicada en mayo de 1637. En ella se recogía abundante información acerca de la tecnología china, a diferencia de obras anteriores tradicionales.

1000 %

PRECIO RELATIVO DE LOS BULBOS DE TULIPÁN EN COMPARACIÓN CON LOS **INGRESOS ANUALES** DE UN **ARTESANO** HOLANDÉS

1638–1639

Grabado del sultán otomano Murat IV a caballo. Su reinado restauró la autoridad interna y aseguró las fronteras con Persia.

EL CONFLICTO INTERMITENTE entre el Imperio otomano y el Imperio persa safaví, iniciado en 1623, culminó en 1638. **Bagdad cayó ante los otomanos** al mando del sultán Murat IV (1612–1640), el último soberano otomano que lideró a sus tropas en la batalla. En 1639 se firmó el **tratado de Zahab**, que confirmó definitivamente la tan disputada frontera otomano-safaví en claro favor de los otomanos. Otorgaba toda **Mesopotamia** (Irak actual) a los otomanos, mientras que Ereván (en la actual Armenia) pasaba a los persas safavíes.

Los problemas que llevaron a la ejecución del rey **Carlos I** de Inglaterra en 1649 tuvieron su origen en la firme convicción del monarca de que siempre podría imponerse sobre sus súbditos. No se trataba de un mero enfrentamiento entre la autoridad real y la parlamentaria; también había un importante elemento de **controversia religiosa**. En 1637, Carlos I, alentado por el entonces arzobispo de Canterbury William Laud, había hecho obligatorio el uso del *Book of Common Prayer* de la **Iglesia de Inglaterra** en Escocia. Tanto Carlos como Laud despreciaban profundamente a la ***scottish Kirk*** (Iglesia escocesa) **calvinista**. Por su parte, los miembros del consejo de la Iglesia escocesa consideraban, del mismo modo que sus equivalentes puritanos en Inglaterra, que los intentos de **imponer la uniformidad religiosa anglicana** eran poco mejores que el papismo. A las violentas protestas que se produjeron durante el año siguiente, conocidas como el ***Great Covenant***, siguió la **invasión de Inglaterra** por un **ejército *covenanter*** («pactista») **escocés**.

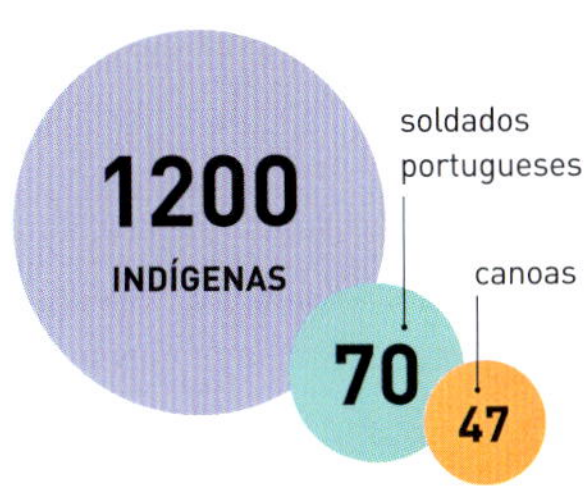

Expedición amazónica de Pedro Teixeira
La expedición de Teixeira fue tan inmensa como cara. Tenía cierto interés político y fue financiada por el gobernador de Maranhão (Brasil).

El **explorador portugués Pedro Teixeira** (m. 1641) llevó a cabo una doble hazaña en 1638, al convertirse en la primera persona en realizar **el viaje de ida y vuelta a lo largo del curso del río Amazonas**. Teixeira llegó hasta Belém, en su desembocadura, más de dos años después de iniciar la expedición; el año anterior había sido el primero en realizar el viaje río arriba. La expedición fue impulsada en parte por la necesidad de saber hasta qué distancia habían conseguido avanzar los **colonos españoles** hacia el este, más allá de los Andes y en la cuenca del Amazonas.

El 24 de noviembre del año 1639, el astrónomo inglés **Jeremiah Horrocks** (1618–1641) fue el primero en predecir y observar el **tránsito de Venus**, que sucede en las raras ocasiones en que este planeta se alinea con el Sol y la Tierra al pasar entre ellos. La observación del tránsito resultó vital para calcular la distancia de la Tierra al Sol.

1635 Se introduce en Japón el sistema *sankin kotai*.

Abril de 1635 Francia declara la guerra a la España de los Habsburgo.

1635 Se funda la colonia inglesa de **Connecticut** (América del Norte).

25 de diciembre de 1635 Muere el explorador francés **Samuel de Champlain** (n. c. 1567).

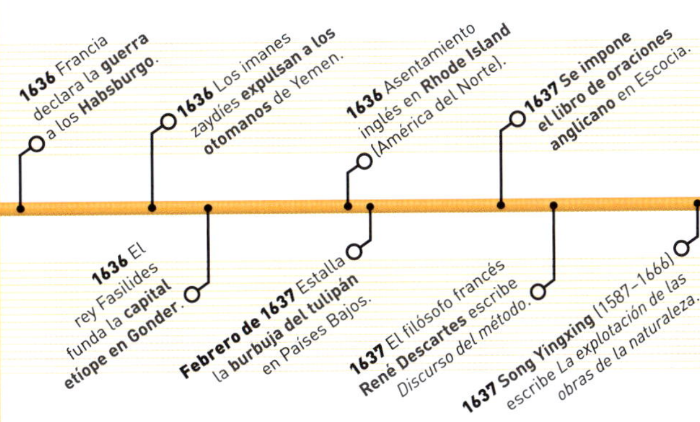

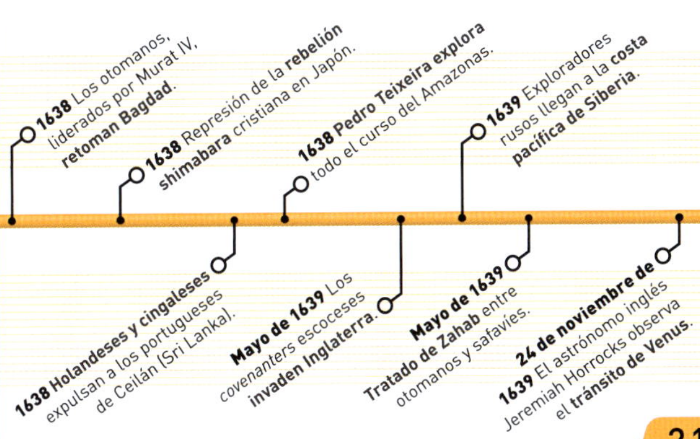

1640–1641

Ilustración de Malaca, que los holandeses arrebataron a Portugal en 1641, tras un intento fallido en 1605.

TRAS LA INVASIÓN ESCOCESA DE INGLATERRA EN 1639, en abril de 1640, Carlos I (1600–1649) **volvió a convocar el Parlamento** que había disuelto once años antes, movido por la necesidad de levantar un impuesto para el ejército. Volvió a disolverlo, pero una segunda invasión en agosto le obligó a convocarlo una vez más. En diciembre de 1641, el Parlamento presentó la ***Grand Remonstrance***, una acusación de abuso de poder al monarca. En enero de 1642, el rey respondió intentando detener a sus adversarios en el Parlamento. En agosto, el **país estaba en guerra**.

El baile de la vida
La danza de la vida humana *de Poussin muestra cuatro bailarinas que encarnan la pobreza, el trabajo, la riqueza y el placer en un ciclo eterno.*

En 1640, el francés **Nicolas Poussin** (1594–1665) terminó *La danza de la vida humana*, **obra clave de la época** que enfatiza la claridad y el orden, y no la emoción y el color, como el estilo barroco dominante.

En 1641, una epidemia devastadora asoló China, lo que **debilitó aún más a la dinastía Ming**, amenazada por los manchúes del norte y por bandas de campesinos, víctimas de las repetidas hambrunas y cada vez más violentos, que saqueaban el país. El resultado fue el **hundimiento casi total del poder central chino**.

Países Bajos siguió acaparando las Indias Orientales. En 1641, el comercio portugués **perdió la importante base comercial de Malaca**, que pasó a ser un enclave fundamental del vasto imperio holandés de las Indias Orientales.

- **Abril de 1640** Carlos I convoca al **Parlamento corto** en Inglaterra.
- **1640 Nicolas Poussin** termina *La danza de la vida humana*.
- **Mayo de 1640 Insurrección catalana** contra las imposiciones militares castellanas.
- **Noviembre de 1640** Se convoca el **Parlamento largo** inglés y termina el gobierno personal de Carlos I.
- **Diciembre de 1640 Fin de la unión ibérica**. Juan IV es proclamado rey de Portugal.
- **1641 Países Bajos** arrebata **Malaca** a Portugal.
- **1641** Alzamientos contra el gobierno Ming en China; **una epidemia asola el país.**
- **22 de noviembre de 1641** *Grand Remonstrance* del Parlamento inglés.

1642–1643

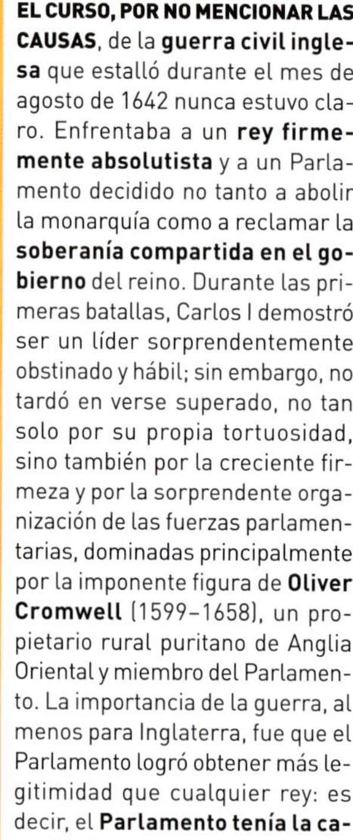

Pintura de la batalla de Rocroi, librada el 19 de mayo de 1643. El ejército francés obtuvo una victoria abrumadora sobre las fuerzas españolas.

EL CURSO, POR NO MENCIONAR LAS CAUSAS, de la **guerra civil inglesa** que estalló durante el mes de agosto de 1642 nunca estuvo claro. Enfrentaba a un **rey firmemente absolutista** y a un Parlamento decidido no tanto a abolir la monarquía como a reclamar la **soberanía compartida en el gobierno** del reino. Durante las primeras batallas, Carlos I demostró ser un líder sorprendentemente obstinado y hábil; sin embargo, no tardó en verse superado, no tan solo por su propia tortuosidad, sino también por la creciente firmeza y por la sorprendente organización de las fuerzas parlamentarias, dominadas principalmente por la imponente figura de **Oliver Cromwell** (1599–1658), un propietario rural puritano de Anglia Oriental y miembro del Parlamento. La importancia de la guerra, al menos para Inglaterra, fue que el Parlamento logró obtener más legitimidad que cualquier rey: es decir, el **Parlamento tenía la capacidad de limitar al rey**, tuviera sanción divina o no, si se consideraba que había perdido la confianza de sus súbditos.

Once años después de que la aldea de Breitenfeld (Sajonia) viera cómo el rey Gustavo II Adolfo de Suecia derrotaba al ejército del Sacro Imperio (*véase* 1631), la **segunda batalla de Breitenfeld**, que tuvo lugar en octubre de 1642, supuso otra victoria decisiva para Suecia en la guerra de los Treinta Años. Por lo tanto, Suecia ocupó Leipzig y el resto de Sajonia, hecho que **reforzó todavía más el protestantismo** en Europa central y predispuso a los católicos del Sacro Imperio a negociar.

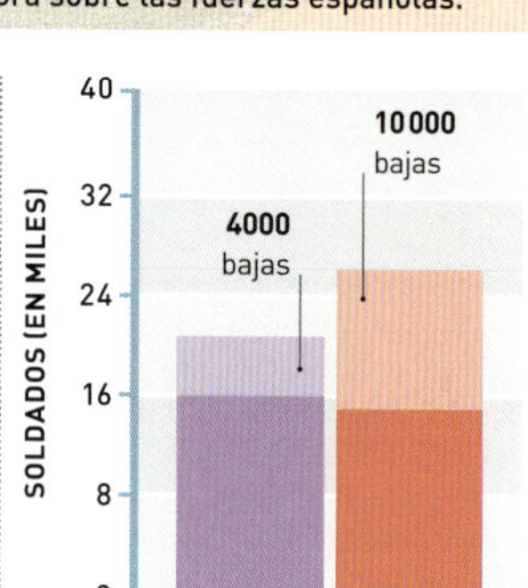

Segunda batalla de Breitenfeld
El ejército del Sacro Imperio sufrió unas pérdidas enormes a manos de los suecos durante la batalla de Breitenfeld (Sajonia).

La abrumadora victoria de Francia sobre España en la **batalla de Rocroi**, en el noreste de Francia, en mayo de 1643 puso fin a las esperanzas españolas de vencer a la República de las Provincias Unidas o a Francia en la guerra de los Treinta Años. **España estaba a la defensiva** ante ambos países. Rocroi marcó el final de sus sueños de dominio imperial sobre Europa. El ejército español de Flandes había sido diezmado y **había perdido a casi toda la infantería más experimentada** durante la batalla. Esto, añadido a las luchas internas que mantenía con portugueses y catalanes, y a la escasez crónica de dinero, había conducido a España al borde de un eclipse permanente. Aunque a corto plazo esta derrota sirvió para aliviar la amenaza de Países Bajos, que temían haber cambiado la posibilidad de un dominio español por la de otro francés; a largo plazo, **el declive español parecía inevitable**.

Por otro lado, en 1643, el físico y matemático italiano **Evangelista Torricelli** (1608–1647) hizo una importantísima contribución al método científico en Europa gracias al **invento del barómetro de mercurio**. Fue fruto de la casualidad: estaba trabajando en una bomba de agua para el duque de Toscana, y al sustituir el mercurio, mucho más pesado, por agua, se dio cuenta de que los **cambios de presión atmosférica** provocaban el ascenso y el descenso de una columna de mercurio en un tubo sellado en un extremo.

Barómetro de Torricelli
Grabado en el que Torricelli demuestra la existencia de la presión atmosférica mediante tubos llenos de mercurio.

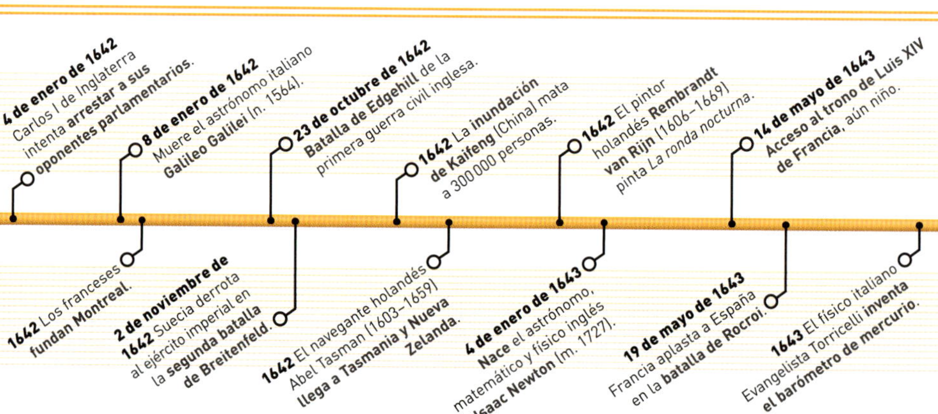

- **4 de enero de 1642** Carlos I de Inglaterra intenta **arrestar a sus oponentes parlamentarios**.
- **1642** Los franceses **fundan Montreal**.
- **8 de enero de 1642** Muere el astrónomo italiano **Galileo Galilei** (n. 1564).
- **2 de noviembre de 1642** Suecia derrota al ejército imperial en la **segunda batalla de Breitenfeld**.
- **23 de octubre de 1642 Batalla de Edgehill** de la primera guerra civil inglesa.
- **1642** El navegante holandés Abel Tasman (1603–1659) **llega a Tasmania y Nueva Zelanda**.
- **1642** La **inundación de Kaifeng** (China) mata a 300 000 personas.
- **4 de enero de 1643 Nace** el astrónomo, matemático y físico inglés **Isaac Newton** (m. 1727).
- **1642** El pintor holandés **Rembrandt van Rijn** (1606–1669) pinta *La ronda nocturna*.
- **19 de mayo de 1643** Francia aplasta a España en la **batalla de Rocroi**.
- **14 de mayo de 1643 Acceso al trono de Luis XIV de Francia**, aún niño.
- **1643** El físico italiano Evangelista Torricelli **inventa el barómetro de mercurio**.

1644–1645

« ESTUDIAMOS LA GLORIA DE DIOS Y EL HONOR Y LA LIBERTAD DEL PARLAMENTO POR EL QUE… LUCHAMOS, SIN INTERÉS PERSONAL ALGUNO. »

Oliver Cromwell, miembro del Parlamento inglés, batalla de Marston Moor (1644)

EL 24 DE ABRIL DE 1644, MIENTRAS UN EJÉRCITO REBELDE MING dirigido por Li Zicheng se disponía a tomar Pekín, el **emperador Chongzeng**, el último soberano de la dinastía Ming, **decidía quitarse la vida**. En febrero, Li había proclamado la efímera dinastía Shun. En mayo, los manchúes, aliados con los restos del ejército Ming, derrotaron al ejército de Li en la batalla del paso de Shanhai. Ese otoño, el **primer emperador Qing manchú**, Shunzi, de solo seis años de edad (1638–1661) se instalaba en Pekín. La resistencia Ming en el sur persistió hasta 1681. Los Qing reinaron hasta su caída en 1911.

Por otro lado, en la **guerra civil inglesa**, la batalla de Marston Moor, librada en julio de 1644, terminó con una **victoria decisiva para el Parlamento**. El verano siguiente, en junio de 1645, los parlamentarios obtuvieron la victoria definitiva en Naseby, donde consiguieron aniquilar al ejército principal del rey Carlos I con su recién formado ejército «nuevo modelo». Dirigido por Oliver Cromwell y sir Thomas Fairfax, el **New Model Army** dio mayor profesionalidad y movilidad al conflicto, además de demostrar la gran superioridad de recursos de la causa parlamentaria.

Palacio del Potala (Tíbet)
Vista desde el sur del palacio del Potala, situado en la cima de la colina Marpo Ri. Se eleva más de 300 m sobre el valle.

A partir de 1645, el hemisferio norte sufrió una serie de **cosechas fallidas** debido a unos inviernos inusualmente fríos, que provocaron una **hambruna** a gran escala y guerras y caídas de las estructuras gubernamentales en todo el globo. Este **cambio climático**, que desde el año 1976 se conoce como mínimo de Maunder, fue consecuencia de una menor actividad solar cuyo resultado directo fue una **pequeña glaciación**, durante la cual las temperaturas de todo el planeta bajaron varios grados.

Finalmente, en el año 1645, el quinto dalai lama, Lozang Gyatso (1617–1682) inició la construcción del **palacio de Potala** moderno en Lhasa (Tíbet), terminado en 1694 y sede del dalai lama hasta 1959.

EXPANSIÓN DEL IMPERIO QING

Una vez asegurada China en 1644, el Imperio Qing continuó expandiéndose durante los siglos XVII y XVIII, en parte como respuesta a la amenaza de la penetración rusa, británica y francesa en Asia. Pocas regiones del imperio estaban bajo el gobierno directo de los manchúes o pobladas por chinos. La mayoría estaban protegidas, con un coste enorme, por guarniciones militares.

1646–1647

Castillo Carisbrooke (isla de Wight), donde Carlos I de Inglaterra permaneció encarcelado catorce meses a partir de 1647, tras su derrota en la guerra civil.

DURANTE LOS PRIMEROS AÑOS DE LA DINASTÍA QING, EL PODER recayó en el tío del emperador-niño, el **príncipe Dorgon** (1612–1650). El peinado era una característica distintiva de los Qing, que se rasuraban la frente y se hacían una trenza detrás. Dorgon ordenó que fuera **obligatoria para todos los varones chinos de la etnia han**. Esto contradecía al confucianismo, según el cual el cabello era un regalo de los padres y por ello nunca debía cortarse; por tanto, llevar la coleta manchú se consideraba una expresión de servilismo, tal y como quería Dorgon. **Ejecutó** a **miles que se negaron** a adoptarla.

El 26 de mayo de 1647, la **colonia de la Bahía de Massachusetts**, un enclave firmemente puritano, **expulsó a los jesuitas**, considerados una manifestación siniestra de papismo. Además, alarmados porque los misioneros jesuitas franceses en Canadá habían logrado convertir a un gran número de indios hurones y algonquinos, los colonos estaban decididos a impedir que un movimiento **«subversivo para la sociedad»** se instalara en la nueva colonia.

Después de escapar del sitio del Parlamento de Oxford en abril 1646, el rey **Carlos I se rindió** al ejército escocés. Fue entregado al Parlamento en 1647 y encarcelado en el **castillo de Carisbrooke**, situado en la isla de Wight, desde donde trató de negociar con las partes. Sin embargo, sus negociaciones secretas con los presbiterianos escoceses para organizar la invasión de Inglaterra llevaron a la **reanudación de la guerra civil inglesa**.

clavija para sostener los tirantes

Armadura de la guerra civil inglesa
La infantería de los dos bandos usó petos de metal con faldones (para protegerse las piernas y el abdomen) durante la guerra civil.

1644 Abel Tasman cartografía las **costas** norte y oeste **de Australia**.

25 de abril de 1644 Suicidio del último emperador Ming de China; inicio de la **dinastía Qing**.

2 de julio de 1644 Batalla de Marston Moor durante la primera guerra civil inglesa.

1644 Guerra civil de Torra en Zimbabue.

1644 El filósofo francés **René Descartes** (1596–1650) escribe *Principios de filosofía*.

1645 Inicio de la **guerra de Creta** entre los otomanos y Venecia (hasta 1669).

1645 Guerra entre **mogoles y marathas hindúes** en India.

14 de junio de 1645 Batalla de Naseby durante la primera guerra civil inglesa.

1645 La **paz de Linz** garantiza la **libertad religiosa** en Hungría.

1645 Revuelta contra los Habsburgo en Nápoles.

1645 Inicio del **mínimo de Maunder**; alteración del clima global.

1645 Se inicia la construcción del **palacio del Potala**, el mayor monasterio budista del Tíbet.

1646 Conquistas mogolas efímeras en el norte de Afganistán.

1646 El control Qing sobre China se amplía a las provincias de Zhejiang, Fujian y Sichuan.

Mayo de 1646 Carlos I se rinde ante el ejército presbiteriano escocés.

1647 Expulsión de los jesuitas de Massachusetts (América del Norte).

1647 Los Qing **extienden su control sobre China** y toman Cantón.

Mayo de 1647 Peter Stuyvesant (1612–1672) llega a Nueva Amsterdam como director general.

1647 Carlos I es **encarcelado** en el castillo de Carisbrooke.

1647 Gian Lorenzo Bernini (1598–1680) esculpe el *Éxtasis de santa Teresa*, en Roma.

HISTORIA DE LAS ARMAS Y ARMADURAS

DE LOS PALOS Y LAS PIEDRAS A UN ARTE MORTÍFERO

Tanto si se usan para la caza y el deporte como en conflictos o competiciones, las armas han sido cruciales para la existencia y el progreso humanos. Las primeras fueron útiles de supervivencia a partir de objetos encontrados, como piedras con las que se abatían presas o se ahuyentaba a depredadores y rivales.

Las mazas y hachas de mano prehistóricas dieron paso a lanzas de madera cuidadosamente talladas para cazar animales o ensartar peces. La inserción de afiladas hojas de sílex en mangos de madera dio lugar a hachas, dagas, lanzas y flechas mucho más efectivas. Cuando el sílex fue sustituido por metales blandos y maleables como el cobre, aparecieron las espadas, dagas, jabalinas y hachas de guerra más resistentes y afiladas de la Edad del Bronce y del Hierro. Hasta la aparición de las armas de fuego, la historia de las armas de mano es una serie de variaciones sobre un mismo tema que culminaron en las sofisticadas espadas de samurái japonesas que, en su cénit (siglo XIV al XVI), consistían en un núcleo de hierro flexible cubierto de acero ultraafilado.

ESCUDOS

Los escudos («armaduras suplementarias»), como las armas y las armaduras, podían ser funcionales, decorativos o ambas cosas. En la Europa medieval, en que los caballeros ocupaban una posición social muy prestigiosa, los escudos se solían decorar con escenas de amor cortés o de valor en la batalla. Se creía que este tipo de decoración protegía a su dueño.

Escudo flamenco del siglo XV

LA EVOLUCIÓN DE LAS ARMADURAS

Las primeras «armaduras» consistían en gruesas capas de tela y un «casco» de cuero rígido. Las tropas de las antiguas Grecia y Roma llevaban cascos y corazas de placas metálicas y escudos de madera, pero en otros lugares dependían de la tela acolchada, el cuero y la suerte. La situación apenas cambió en Europa hasta que en el siglo XI, en Francia, se perfeccionó la cota de malla. Las armaduras completas eran muy caras y un símbolo de estatus.

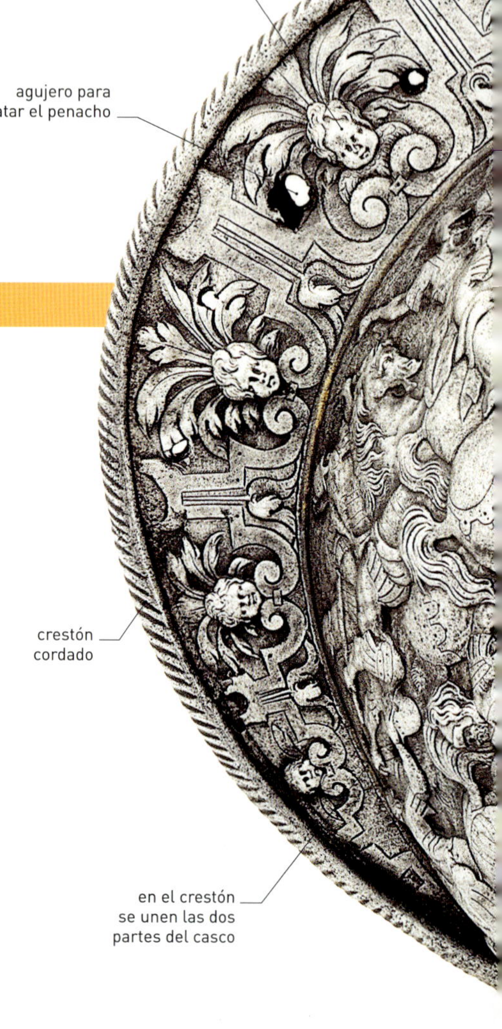

Yelmo repujado francés del siglo XVI
Las armaduras alcanzaron la máxima opulencia decorativa durante el Renacimiento. Los yelmos estaban repujados, grabados y chapados en oro o en plata, sobre todo los de torneo, para dar fe de la riqueza y el estatus del dueño.

750 000–50 000 a. C.
Sílex afilado
Se cazaba y se luchaba con ayuda de dagas, lanzas y hachas de sílex afilado.

Daga de sílex

450 000–400 000 a. C.
Armas de madera
La madera era fácil de encontrar y de trabajar. Se tallaban lanzas para cazar o defenderse.

Lanza de madera

5500–3300 a. C.
Puntas de flecha de sílex
El arco de madera y las puntas de flecha de sílex afilado demostraron ser una combinación mortífera, ya que permitían disparar a distancia.

3700–2300 a. C.
Armas de metal
El empleo del metal produjo hojas efectivas y sofisticadas durante la edad del Bronce y la del Hierro.

Hacha de bronce

2500 a. C.
Cascos
La cabeza fue la primera parte del cuerpo que se protegió. Los primeros cascos eran de metal, pero casi todos los soldados llevaban casquetes de cuero.

Casco ático

C. 1400 a. C.
Aparece la armadura
Las primeras armaduras metálicas eran muy caras y no siempre resultaban prácticas para moverse durante la batalla.

Armadura micénica

Siglo VI a. C.–mediados del siglo V a. C.
Ballesta
La ballesta puede prepararse antes de disparar; por ello fue una de las primeras armas «cargadas».

Ballesta china antigua

Siglos III y IV
Hojas de acero
La aleación de hierro y de carbono produce acero, que permite la producción en masa de armas de hoja afilada, más fuertes y largas.

Gladio romano

El regreso de la armadura *La Primera Guerra Mundial recuperó la armadura. Los ametralladores alemanes llevaban trajes como este cuando disparaban desde puntos descubiertos.*

35 KG ES EL **PESO** APROXIMADO DE UNA **ARMADURA EUROPEA** DE **TORNEO COMPLETA DEL SIGLO XVI**

Siglo XI
Cota de malla perfeccionada
Más ligera y práctica que la armadura, se llevaba sobre el gambesón (jubón acolchado).

1100 en adelante
Las espadas mejoran
Se añaden gavilanes para proteger la mano, el primer gran cambio del diseño de espadas desde la antigua Roma. El borde afilado permite cortar y apuñalar.

Siglo XV
Primeras armaduras articuladas
Mejoran la protección. Los guanteletes tienen dedos articulados y las placas de los hombros (espaldarcetes) dan más libertad de movimiento.

Siglos XV–XVII
Desarrollo de las armas de fuego
Con la invención de las pistolas, la armadura se reduce a la coraza (peto) para poder desenfundar el arma.

Siglo XIX
Armas de carga automática
El cilindro rotatorio del revólver permitía disparar varias veces antes de volver a cargar.

1939–1945
Chalecos antibalas
Basados en la coraza, los de la Segunda Guerra Mundial solo detenían la metralla.

Siglos XX y XXI
Armaduras «líquidas» de kevlar
La fibra de kevlar es cinco veces más fuerte que el acero. Empapada en fluido dilatante puede detener las balas.

1648

Detalle de cañones y artilleros en una pintura del siglo XVII que conmemora las acciones de las fuerzas realistas que derrotaron a la Fronda.

LA MUERTE DE LUIS XIII en mayo de 1643 llevó hasta el trono francés a **Luis XIV, de cinco años de edad**, bajo la regencia de su madre, la española Ana de Austria (en contra de la voluntad de Luis XIII). Pese a los éxitos obtenidos por Francia durante la guerra de los Treinta Años (*véase* 1635) y de su incipiente supremacía sobre España, el país no solo **necesitaba dinero**, sino que se enfrentaba a **alzamientos campesinos**, consecuencia de las cosechas fallidas y de las **exigencias fiscales**. Además, los nobles a los que el cardenal Richelieu (*véase* 1624) había excluido del gobierno, fueron invitados a regresar para contrarrestar a los seguidores de Richelieu, hostiles a Ana y a su nuevo primer ministro, el cardenal Mazarino (1602–1661). El fracaso a la hora de controlar a facciones rivales durante una guerra costosa acabó por desbaratar al gobierno en 1648 con la **Fronda**, iniciada como protesta de abogados y jueces parisinos, y convertida luego en **rebelión aristocrática**. Siguieron cuatro años en los que cayó París, la familia real huyó y Mazarino tuvo que exiliarse dos veces. Al calmarse la situación en 1652, el camino estaba despejado para la mejor gestión de las lealtades aristocráticas del gobierno de Luis XIV a partir de 1661.

«¿SABES, HIJO MÍO, LA **POCA SABIDURÍA** CON QUE SE **GOBIERNA EL MUNDO**?»

Axel Oxenstierna, canciller sueco, Westfalia (1648)

En octubre de 1648, tras cuatro años de negociaciones, los horrores de la **guerra de los Treinta Años** en Alemania terminaron con los tratados de la **paz de Westfalia**. Francia y España siguieron en guerra hasta 1659. Francia logró concesiones vagamente definidas en su frontera oriental; Suecia vio confirmada su posesión de la mitad más rica de Pomerania y los obispados de Bremen y Verden, y recibió una suma enorme de los **Estados alemanes** como pago por su ejército mercenario. De los Estados alemanes, **Prusia-Brandeburgo** fue el más beneficiado. El reconocimiento por la Monarquía Hispánica de la independencia de las Provincias Unidas resultó crucial, y los gobernantes alemanes vieron reforzada su autoridad sobre sus súbditos y confirmados **sus derechos como actores políticos semiindependientes**. Aunque no hubo un cambio decisivo en su relación con el sacro emperador, su autoridad quedó **debilitada**.

sello de una de las 109 partes

Paz de Westfalia
Firmada por el emperador del Sacro Imperio y el rey de Francia, y acordada a lo largo de varios meses, puso fin a treinta años de guerra.

1649–1650

Pintura del artista inglés John Weesop sobre la ejecución del rey Carlos I de Inglaterra junto a la Banqueting House de Londres.

EL 30 DE ENERO DEL AÑO 1649, murió decapitado Carlos I, el único **rey de Inglaterra que fue ejecutado legítimamente**. El tribunal superior de justicia le condenó por «tirano, traidor y asesino», por 68 votos frente a 67. A lo largo de todo el juicio, Carlos negó que un tribunal pudiera juzgar a un rey. «Deberíais saber qué poder os ha traído aquí... soy vuestro rey, vuestro rey legítimo.» En realidad, existen pocas dudas de que tras la victoria del New Model Army parlamentario, **liderado por Oliver Cromwell**, su muerte se había convertido en una de las soluciones posibles de la crisis. La cuestión era si estaban cambiando una tiranía por otra. De todas maneras, lo importante fue que con esta sentencia se confirmó la existencia de un organismo legislativo independiente de la figura del rey que nadie, ni siquiera el propio monarca, podía pasar por alto: **el Parlamento, y no el rey, era el custodio de la ley**.

Oliver Cromwell
Retrato de Oliver Cromwell, principal instigador del juicio y la ejecución del rey, pintado por el artista inglés Robert Walker.

Máscara de Dahomey
Este colgante de Dahomey de bronce, con forma de una estilizada cabeza de pantera, es una muestra de la gran sofisticación cultural del Dahomey del siglo XVII.

A finales de la década de 1640 surgió el **reino de Dahomey** como un **Estado militarizado poderoso** bajo el rey Wegbaja (m. 1685). Muy implicado en el tráfico de esclavos, se caracterizaría durante más de dos siglos por una administración de eficacia creciente y un **ceremonial elaborado**.

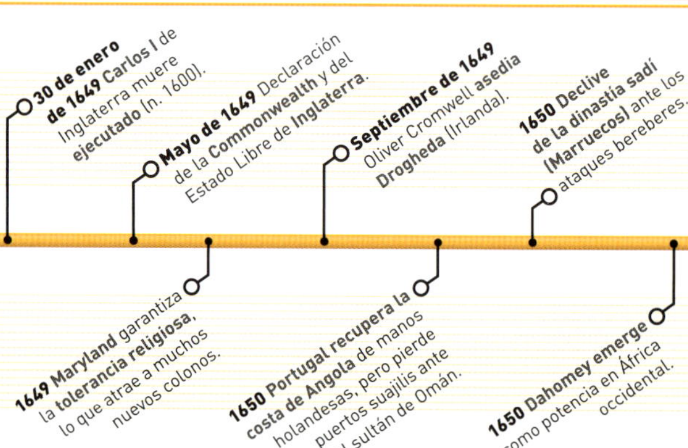

- **Enero Rebelión de Jmelnitski** (hasta 1651); los cosacos ucranianos buscan la independencia de Polonia-Lituania.
- **17 de enero** El Parlamento largo rompe las negociaciones con Carlos I y estalla la **segunda guerra civil inglesa**.
- **30 de enero** Fin de la **guerra de los Ochenta Años** entre los Países Bajos y España.
- **24 de octubre** La **paz de Westfalia** acaba con la guerra de los Treinta Años en Alemania.
- **La Fronda**, rebelión aristocrática francesa en contra del cardenal Mazarino (hasta 1652).
- **Abril** Los **portugueses vencen al ejército holandés** en Brasil.
- Los mogoles **trasladan** a Sahyahanabad (Delhi) **la corte imperial**.
- Los **siervos rusos pierden derechos**; alzamiento en contra de los impuestos en Moscú.
- Los **otomanos asedian** la **Creta** veneciana.
- **12 de septiembre** Batalla de Stirling durante la **guerra civil escocesa**.
- El explorador ruso Semion Dezhnev (1605–1672) **atraviesa el estrecho de Bering**.
- **11 de diciembre** La **purga de Pride** expulsa a la mayoría del Parlamento largo de Inglaterra y **crea el Parlamento rabadilla**.
- **30 de enero de 1649 Carlos I** de Inglaterra muere **ejecutado** (n. 1600).
- **Mayo de 1649** Declaración de la **Commonwealth** y del Estado Libre de **Inglaterra**.
- **1649 Maryland** garantiza la **tolerancia religiosa**, lo que atrae a muchos nuevos colonos.
- **Septiembre de 1649** Oliver Cromwell **asedia Drogheda** (Irlanda).
- **1650 Portugal recupera la costa de Angola** de manos holandesas, pero pierde puertos suajilis ante el sultán de Omán.
- **1650 Declive de la dinastía sadí (Marruecos)** ante los ataques bereberes.
- **1650 Dahomey emerge** como potencia en África occidental.

1651–1652

« LA LEY NO ES CUESTIÓN DE **SABIDURÍA, SINO** DE **AUTORIDAD. »**

Thomas Hobbes, filósofo inglés, en *Leviatán* (1651)

LA EJECUCIÓN DEL REY CARLOS I no supuso el colapso definitivo de la causa monárquica en Inglaterra. Todavía quedaba activo un remanente militar, fundamentalmente escocés. Los monárquicos tenían una **figura obvia a la que apoyar**, el primogénito del rey, también llamado Carlos. Sin embargo, su **derrota en Worcester** en septiembre de 1651 marcó la última batalla de la guerra civil inglesa, y Carlos se vio obligado a vivir en el exilio durante nueve años.

En el año 1651, Thomas Hobbes publicó ***Leviatán***, una de las bases de la **filosofía política occidental** y donde defendía el **absolutismo de una autoridad soberana**. Aunque reconocía la libertad individual, Hobbes opinaba que la única manera de evitar la anarquía era por medio de un gobierno central fuerte. Fue un ejemplo temprano y muy influyente de la **teoría del contrato social** (los miembros de una sociedad se unen por consentimiento mutuo).

En 1648, el **alzamiento de Jmelnitski** dio lugar a una rebelión de los cosacos en contra de la Confederación polaco-lituana en Ucrania, que el tratado de Lublin había cedido a Polonia en 1589. El levantamiento culminó en la **batalla de Berestechko**, la mayor batalla del siglo XVII. Aunque la victoria fue para Polonia-Lituania, el resultado del conflicto fue el **debilitamiento de la Confederación**, que ya se encontraba resquebrajada a causa de las numerosas disputas internas entre los belicosos nobles.

La primera de las tres **guerras** que enfrentaron a **Inglaterra y Países Bajos** estalló en 1652 (seguida de otras dos que tuvieron lugar en 1665–1667 y 1672–1674). Todas ellas fueron contiendas navales por conseguir el control del mar y del **comercio marítimo**. Para Países Bajos, una nación pequeña y con pocos recursos naturales, pero la primera potencia mercantil europea, fueron de suma importancia; para Inglaterra, marcaron la **aparición de una creciente seguridad en sí misma**. La victoria final inglesa en la primera guerra señaló el fin de la hegemonía mercantil holandesa y el comienzo de la **rivalidad anglo-francesa** por la supremacía colonial y comercial.

FUERZAS POLACO-LITUANAS
40 000 caballería
700 bajas
63 000 INFANTERÍA

40 000 caballería
40 000 bajas
100 000 INFANTERÍA
FUERZAS TÁRTARAS COSACO-CRIMEAS

Batalla de Berestechko, 1651
Las fuerzas tártaras cosaco-crimeas sufrieron 40 000 bajas en la batalla de Berestechko, muchas más que sus adversarios polaco-lituanos.

1653–1654

La coronación de Luis XIV, tapiz a partir de una pintura de Charles Le Brun, artista de la corte de Luis XIV, muestra al joven rey a punto de ser coronado.

SIN DUDA UNA DE LAS EDIFICACIONES MÁS CÉLEBRES DEL MUNDO, el **Taj Mahal** (Agra), se terminó en 1653 tras 19 años de construcción. Este mausoleo erigido por Sah Yahan (1592–1666) **en memoria de su tercera esposa, Mumtaz Mahal**, combina estilos arquitectónicos indios, persas e islámicos.

En diciembre del año 1653, **Oliver Cromwell** fue nombrado *lord protector* **de Inglaterra**. Tras una asamblea brevemente dominada por oficiales del ejército, sustituyó el Parlamento rabadilla –cuyos miembros parecían demasiado reacios a las reformas que deseaban el ejército y los radicales religiosos– por el Protectorado. Durante este, Cromwell convocó, y rápidamente disolvió, otros dos parlamentos, y experimentó con un régimen casi militar, pero se resistió a los intentos de nombrarle rey. Con los conflictos que siguieron a su muerte en 1658, quedó claro que solo restaurar al heredero al trono, el futuro Carlos II, podía llenar el vacío de poder.

Debilitada por la lucha contra los cosacos durante el alzamiento de Jmelnitski, fue inevitable el **desmembramiento parcial de la Confederación polaco-lituana** a manos de vecinos ávidos de territorios. La **devastación** que supuso el llamado «Diluvio» redujo su población casi a la mitad y destruyó casi por completo su economía. Rusia invadió Polonia en junio de 1654, en la luego llamada **guerra de los Trece Años**, y al año siguiente lo hizo Suecia. La consecuencia más duradera, además de la **pérdida polaca de Ucrania** en favor de Rusia por el tratado de Andrúsovo de 1667, fue el reforzamiento de la Rusia ortodoxa, que hizo efectiva la aspiración de sus zares a reinar sobre «todas las Rusias».

El 7 de junio de 1654 **fue coronado rey de Francia Luis XIV** a los 15 años. Rey desde los cuatro años, fueron regentes, primero, su madre y, más tarde, el cardenal Mazarino. Su reinado, de 72 años y 110 días, es uno de los más largos de la historia.

Taj Mahal
Esta perspectiva de la cúpula de mármol blanco del Taj Mahal (India) lo ha convertido en uno de los edificios más conocidos y admirados del mundo.

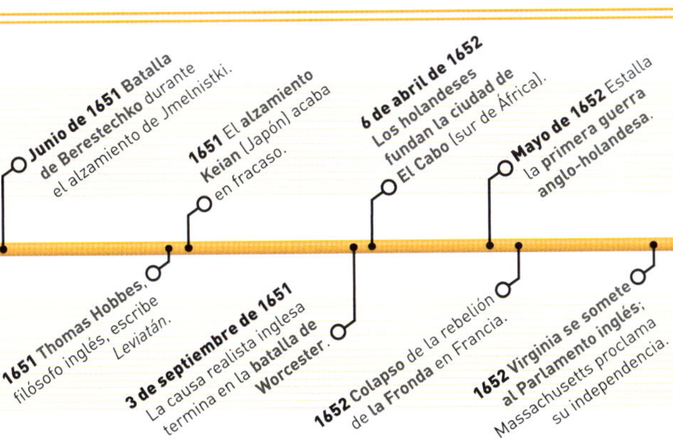

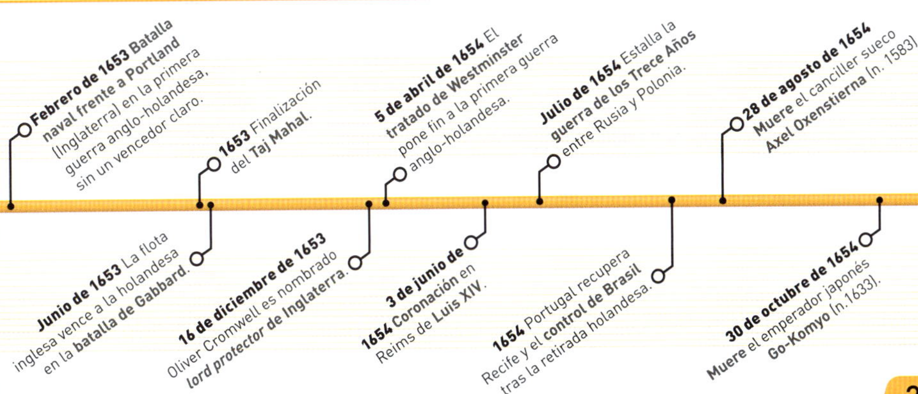

1655–1656

El ejército de Brandeburgo aplasta las posiciones polacas en la batalla de Varsovia de 1656, durante la primera guerra del Norte.

12 000 000 KM²

EXTENSIÓN APROXIMADA DEL IMPERIO RECLAMADO POR PORTUGAL

TEMEROSA DE QUE RUSIA DOMINARA EL BÁLTICO, Suecia entró en la guerra de los Trece Años entre Rusia y Polonia-Lituania en 1655, lo que dio paso a las **guerras del Norte**, a las que otros países se vieron arrastrados y en las que cambiaron las alianzas. En 1656, la capital polaca, Varsovia, fue tomada por una fuerza combinada de Suecia-Brandeburgo, lo que **debilitó aún más al estado de Polonia-Lituania**.

En 1656, el español Diego Velázquez (1599–1660) pintó *Las meninas* (o *La familia de Felipe IV*), **una de las obras cumbre del Siglo de Oro español y de la cultura occidental**, que ha ejercido una gran influencia.

Mehmet (1575–1661) fue nombrado **gran visir** en 1656, y el sultán Mehmet IV le entregó el control del imperio, lo que dio paso a otra fase de esplendor de la **potencia otomana**. Köprülü fue implacable con la oposición y se embarcó en una serie de campañas militares (finalizadas tras su muerte, en 1661) que llevaron al **imperio a su máxima extensión**.

Las meninas
El óleo de Velázquez, centrado en el retrato de Margarita de Austria, hija de Felipe IV de España, es célebre por la complejidad de su composición.

1657

Ilustración que muestra a las tropas otomanas en la isla de Lemnos.

EL 2 DE MARZO DE 1657, estalló el **incendio de Meireki**, en Edo (Tokio). En dos días, y atizado por un viento incesante, el fuego destruyó casi el 70 % de la ciudad; los edificios de madera y papel se consumieron y unas **100 000 personas fallecieron**.

Aunque se iniciaron como parte de la primera guerra del Norte, las **guerras sueco-danesas** que tuvieron lugar entre 1657 y 1658 se convirtieron en un conflicto independiente por el control del Báltico cuando, en junio de 1657, Dinamarca decidió unirse a la coalición que se enfrentaba a Suecia en Polonia. Suecia se había **expandido a costa de Dinamarca** desde mediados del siglo XVI, pero el estrecho del Sund, la entrada al Báltico, de vital importancia estratégica y económica, seguía bajo control danés en 1657. El invierno de 1657–1658, Carlos X de Suecia (1622–1660) superó a las fuerzas danesas, entró en Dinamarca y en febrero, después de lograr atravesar el Báltico helado, en Copenhague. El **tratado de Roskilde** de 1658 confirmó el dominio territorial sueco. Aunque la segunda guerra (1658–1660) no resultó tan favorable para Suecia, también subrayó **la superioridad de Suecia en el Báltico**.

A finales del año 1657, el Imperio otomano, reforzado por el gran visir Mehmet Köprülü, **arrebató** a Venecia **las islas de Lemnos y de Tenedos en el Egeo**. Hasta aquel momento, Venecia había utilizado estas islas, que dominaban la entrada a los Dardanelos, para **bloquear Estambul**, la capital otomana. Ya no podría hacerlo más.

1658–1659

EN JUNIO DE 1658, AURANGZEB (1618–1707) o Alamgir («conquistador del mundo»), como se llamaba a sí mismo, fue **coronado emperador mogol**, lo que dio fin a dos años de guerras internas con sus hermanos por el trono de su padre, Sah Yahan, a pesar de que este aún vivía. Los **tres hermanos fueron ejecutados** (dos de ellos por Aurangzeb). Su reinado resultó paradójico. La India mogola continuaba siendo muy poderosa y rica, y bajo Aurangzeb, ferviente musulmán, llegó a alcanzar su **máxima extensión territorial** (p. 234). Sin embargo, las guerras casi continuas durante sus 49 años de reinado, con campañas inmensas en

Conquistador del mundo
Este retrato del emperador mogol Aurangzeb I rodeado de sus cortesanos se atribuye al artista indio Bhawani Das.

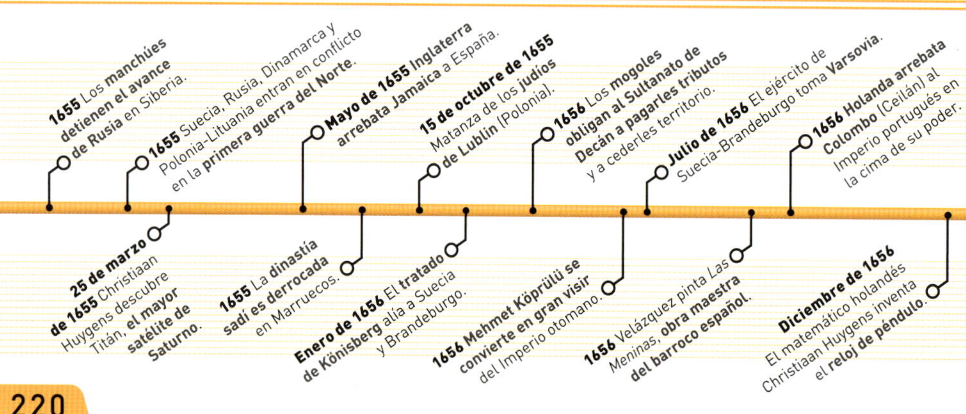

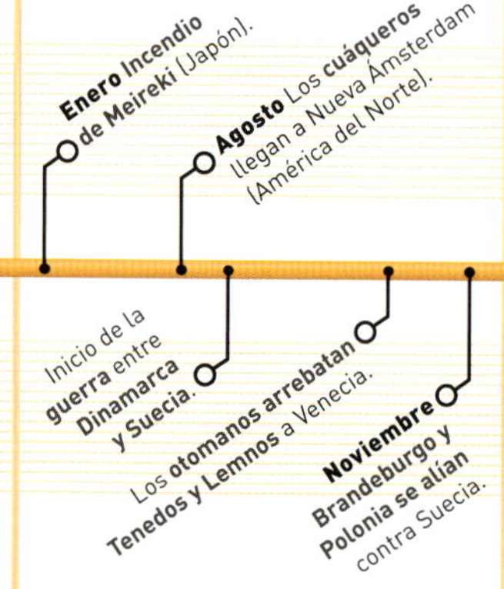

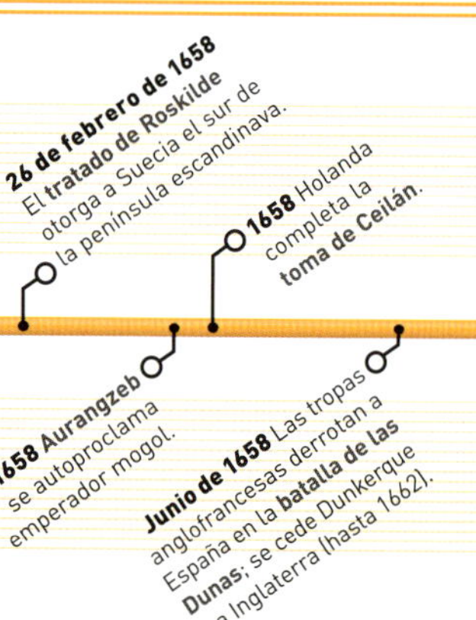

1660–1661

> **«** LO CIERTO ES QUE AHORA **ME CONCEDO MÁS PLACERES**, PORQUE SÉ QUE ES EL **MOMENTO ADECUADO** PARA **HACERLO**. **»**
>
> **Samuel Pepys**, diarista inglés, anotación de su diario (1660)

Luis XIV de Francia (centro izda.) y Felipe IV de España se reunieron para zanjar el conflicto franco-español con la paz de los Pirineos de 1659.

El Imperio sueco
El Imperio sueco alcanzó su cénit en 1658, durante el reinado del rey Carlos X y tras la firma del tratado de Roskilde, pero la necesidad de defender sus nuevas fronteras condujo a una serie de guerras insosteniblemente costosas.

LUIS XIV (1638–1715)

La influencia de Luis XIV, el rey Sol, sobre Francia fue mayor que la de ningún otro monarca. Decidido a ser el gobernante absoluto de sus nobles y de su país, centralizó el estado, libró numerosas batallas y fomentó la cultura. Al final de su reinado, Francia había ampliado su territorio y era la primera potencia europea, admirada e imitada por los demás países.

contra de los sijs y los marathas, **agotaron las arcas del país** y pusieron de manifiesto las debilidades internas de este enorme imperio. A su muerte, en 1707, el declive era evidente.

Cerca de Dunkerque (noreste de Francia), una fuerza anglofrancesa logró derrotar a las tropas españolas el 14 de junio de 1658. Fue el último conflicto decisivo de la **guerra franco-española** iniciada en el año 1635 y, como tal, la última de la guerra de los Treinta Años. También fue la última confrontación de la **guerra anglo-española** iniciada en 1654. Para los franceses, como siempre, el imperativo era el dominio de Europa; para Inglaterra, obtener cualquier ventaja, comercial o territorial, sobre España. De ahí la **alianza pragmática** entre la Inglaterra puritana de Cromwell y la Francia católica de Luis XIV.

El año 1659 marcó el comienzo de uno de los hitos más importantes de la **revolución científica europea**: el hoy conocido como registro de la **Temperatura de Inglaterra Central (CET)**. Fue un experimento científico que se realizó a una escala sin precedentes, un intento de medir las temperaturas casi a escala nacional, aunque en realidad se llevó a cabo en un triángulo delimitado al norte por Manchester, Londres al este y Bristol al oeste. En la actualidad, es el **registro de temperaturas** continuo más antiguo del mundo. Existió un precedente en 1657 en Italia, cuando la Academia del Cimento (academia de la experimentación) de Florencia instituyó lo que se ha llamado «primera red de observación meteorológica del mundo.» Si la revolución científica europea dependía de **la observación y el registro precisos**, el CET fue un precursor determinante.

La **paz de los Pirineos**, firmada en noviembre de 1659, puso fin al conflicto franco-español en Europa. Francia se convirtió en la **primera potencia europea** y España entró en un lento pero implacable declive, a causa de la reducción de los ingresos del Nuevo Mundo, las crecientes tensiones internas y el menor apoyo de Austria. El cambio condujo a los países capaces de medirse con la poderosa Francia a hacer justamente eso; así, Francia se vio obligada a enfrentarse al resto de las **potencias emergentes europeas**: Inglaterra, Holanda y la Austria de los Habsburgo.

400 £
ES EL **VALOR** DEL **PRIMER CHEQUE** QUE SE **CONOCE**

«DI GRACIAS A DIOS [...] FUE OBRA DEL SEÑOR.» El diarista John Evelyn registró con estas palabras la abrumadora recepción a Carlos II (1630–1685) en Londres en mayo de 1660, con motivo de su **restauración como rey de Inglaterra**. Fue una confirmación triunfante tanto de los principios monárquicos como de las limitaciones contradictorias del experimento republicano llevado a cabo por Oliver Cromwell. Carlos II recuperó así su trono en medio del fervor popular. Sofisticado, muy astuto y, en el fondo, indolente, siempre se mostró dispuesto a **pactar** con sus adversarios parlamentarios. Su encanto era legendario. Con todo, su tendencia a la búsqueda del placer junto con su simpatía instintiva por el catolicismo, en especial mientras Luis XIV le mantuvo en Francia, pusieron de manifiesto la **crisis política todavía sin resolver**. Carlos, alternativamente vengativo e indulgente, nunca llegó a resolver este dilema. Fue su sucesor, el menos astuto Jacobo II, quien provocó la crisis que lanzaría a Inglaterra a una **revolución parlamentaria sin igual** (*véase* 1688).

El famoso **diarista inglés Samuel Pepys** (1633–1703) comenzó a escribir sus pensamientos diarios en 1660. Era un oficial naval de alto rango, y su diario, que escribió hasta 1669 pero que no fue publicado hasta el siglo XIX, fue una de las fuentes de información más valiosas sobre la **vida durante la Restauración inglesa**.

La muerte del cardenal Mazarino (*véase* 1648) en 1661 dio paso al **reinado personal de Luis XIV, de 22 años de edad** y que iba a permanecer en el trono francés durante otros 53 años. La división de Francia que había vivido durante su infancia le hizo comprender la necesidad de desarrollar un estilo personal de autoafirmación y de grandeza con el que impresionar a la élite francesa que formaba parte de su gran proyecto de conducir a su reino a la gloria y a la **dominación de Europa**. Unidos bajo un monarca que reconocía sus privilegios y su estatus, los nobles y los funcionarios franceses apoyaron una serie de guerras con el objetivo de afianzar su posición. Sin embargo, estas guerras llevaron a Francia al borde del desastre y sumieron en la miseria a la mayoría de su población. Aun así, el **impacto cultural** del reinado de Luis XIV fue inmenso; ningún otro país europeo estuvo a la altura de Francia durante la segunda mitad del siglo XVII en lo que a proyección e importancia nacional se refiere.

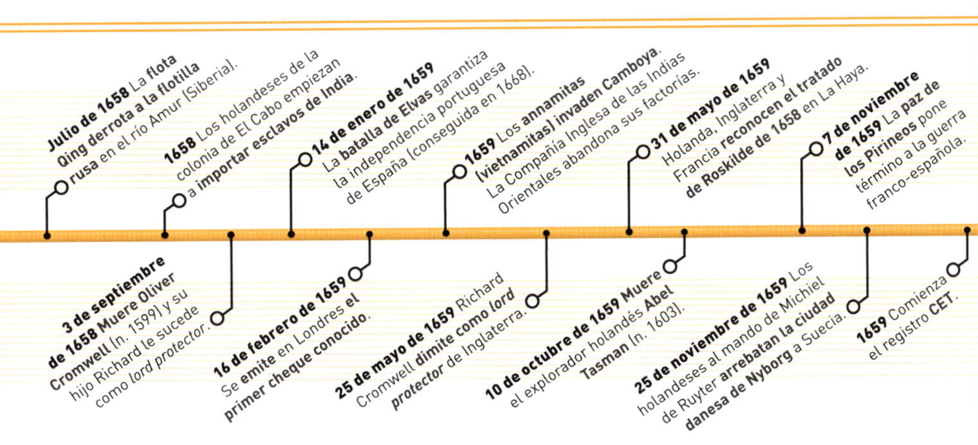

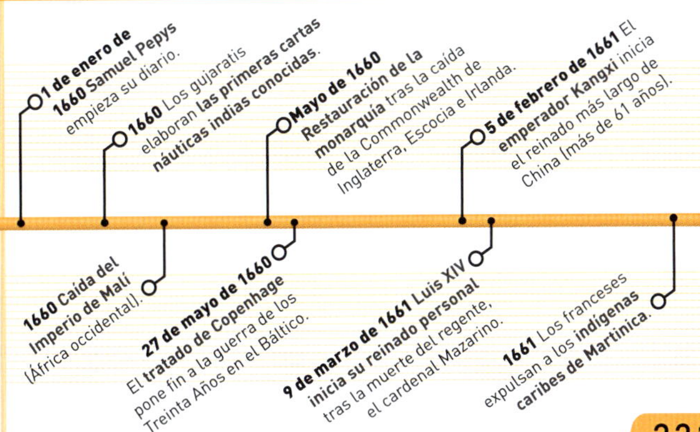

1662–1663

Imagen de Fuerte Zelandia en Tainán (actual Taiwán) en 1635.

EXPLOTANDO LOS CONFLICTOS causados por la caída de la China Ming y el ascenso de los Qing (*véase* 1644–1645), la **Compañía Neerlandesa de las Indias Orientales** se apoderó del oeste de **Formosa** (Taiwán). Presionado por los ejércitos Qing en la China continental, en 1661, el partidario de los Ming Koxinga invadió Formosa y puso sitio a la nueva base militar y comercial neerlandesa, el Fuerte Zelandia, que se rindió en febrero de 1662.

El **progreso de la investigación científica** llevó a los científicos europeos a compartir ideas y a crear organismos dedicados a la ciencia. En 1662 se fundó en Londres la **Royal Society**, la sociedad científica más antigua de la historia. Contaba con sanción real, prueba de que la aplicación práctica de la **ciencia** y la búsqueda del **conocimiento puro** interesaban al estado.

5 MILLONES ES EL **PRECIO EN LIBRAS** QUE PAGÓ **FRANCIA** POR **DUNKERQUE**

1664

La población de Nueva Ámsterdam ruega a su director general, Peter Stuyvesant, que no se resista a los buques ingleses reunidos en el puerto.

LOS MÚLTIPLES SAQUEOS ingleses a las bases navales y comerciales holandesas se debían al **deseo inglés de arrebatarles** cuanta más actividad comercial fuera posible. Obtuvieron su mayor éxito el 27 de agosto, cuando una pequeña flota inglesa llegó a **Nueva Ámsterdam**, la capital colonial holandesa en América del Norte, y exigió su rendición. El director general, Peter Stuyvesant, acabó accediendo. En marzo de 1665 estalló la segunda guerra anglo-holandesa.

La **guerra austro-turca** que había estallado en 1663 alcanzó su clímax en agosto de 1664, cuando el ejército otomano, decidido a tomar Viena, fue vencido en la **batalla de San Gotardo** (Hungría). Aunque los otomanos consiguieron la paz en términos favorables, la **invasión se detuvo**.

« ES FÁCIL SER **ENGAÑADO** POR AQUEL **A QUIEN SE AMA**. »

Molière, en el *Tartufo* (1664)

En 1664 se fundó la **Compañía Francesa de las Indias Orientales** con patrocinio real, como respuesta al dominio holandés e inglés del comercio con Asia. A pesar de su gran financiación, solamente consiguió un asentamiento en la isla Reunión en el océano Índico y algunas **factorías** en India.

Batalla de San Gotardo
Basado en un dibujo de Adolf Ehrhardt, este grabado muestra la carga de la caballería Habsburgo en la derrota de los otomanos durante la batalla de San Gotardo.

1665

Esta representación de la peste de Londres muestra en el centro al ángel de la muerte con un reloj de arena y una lanza.

EN 1665 SE PUBLICÓ *Micrographia*, del naturalista y erudito inglés Robert Hooke (1635–1703), que destaca por ser el primer trabajo **patrocinado por la Royal Society**. Por primera vez, personas ajenas a los cerrados círculos de los especialistas tenían la posibilidad de acceder al insólito mundo que revelaban los **microscopios**, y sus detallados y precisos dibujos de una hormiga, un piojo y una pulga provocaron el asombro general por la complejidad de ese **mundo desconocido hasta entonces**. En palabras del diarista Samuel Pepys, fue «el libro más ingenioso que jamás haya leído». Todavía más importante fue que Hooke **utilizó por primera vez el término «célula»** para aludir a la unidad más pequeña de un organismo; lo eligió porque lo que observó le recordó a las celdas de los monjes.

Los hallazgos de Hooke
Página de la Micrographia *de Hooke de 1665, con la detallada ilustración de una hormiga. Hooke la dibujó después de observarla con su microscopio (dcha.).*

También durante este año se produjo el último brote de **peste bubónica en Inglaterra**, concentrado fundamentalmente en Londres, donde en septiembre fallecían cerca de 7000 personas al día. Al cabo de 18 meses, la terrible **epidemia había asolado la ciudad** y matado a 100 000 personas.

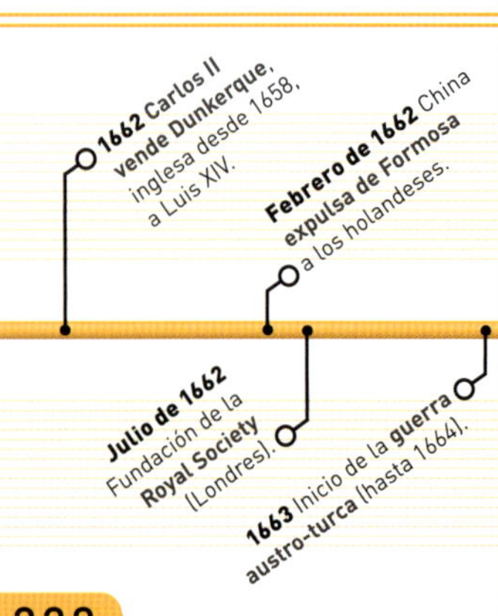

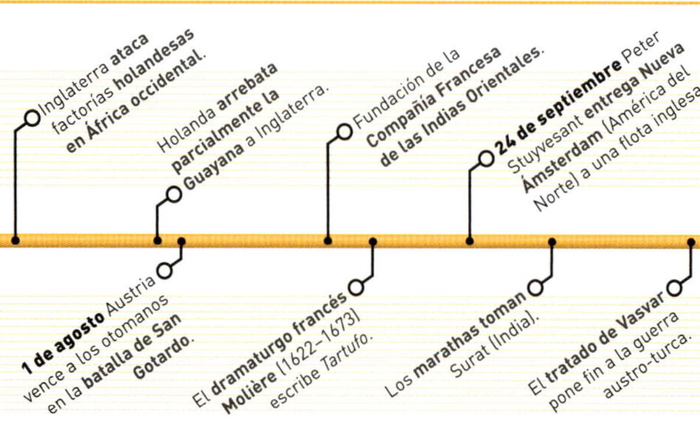

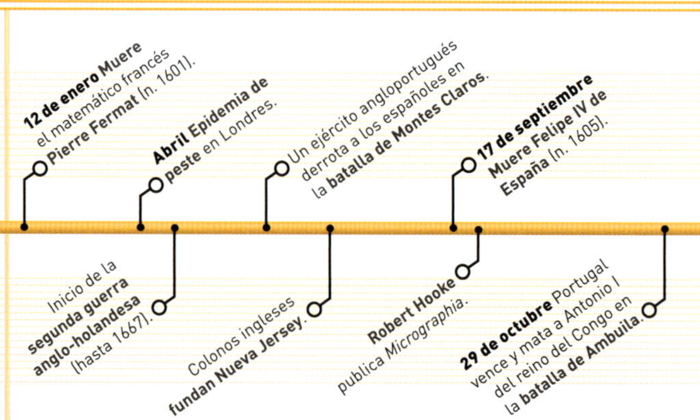

1666

En 1666, un gran incendio arrasó el centro de Londres. Consumió miles de edificios y borró siglos de historia.

79 BARCOS — 10 barcos perdidos — FLOTA INGLESA

84 BARCOS — 4 barcos perdidos — FLOTA HOLANDESA

Batalla de los Cuatro Días
Los holandeses derrotaron a los ingleses en uno de los enfrentamientos navales más largos de la historia, la batalla de los Cuatro Días, librada en junio de 1666.

EL MAYOR ENFRENTAMIENTO DE LA SEGUNDA GUERRA ANGLO-HOLANDESA, que había estallado en 1665, fue la **batalla de los Cuatro Días**, el intento de Inglaterra de destruir la flota holandesa antes de que pudiera suponer un riesgo. Sin embargo, los **ingleses** sufrieron tales **pérdidas** que los **holandeses** tomaron la iniciativa y en junio 1667 **saquearon** el río Medway, en el estuario del Támesis. El descontento nacional hizo que Inglaterra detuviera la guerra.

Tras el fin de la peste, **otro desastre arrasó Londres**: el **gran incendio** entre el 2 y el 5 de septiembre. Londres era aún una ciudad medieval, sucia y sin planificación alguna, sin grandes espacios y con pocos edificios públicos importantes. La City, su núcleo comercial, era especialmente insalubre y estaba superpoblada. El fuego se originó allí; a pesar de que se conocía el fuerte riesgo de incendio, no se habían tomado precauciones. La **sequía y una ola de calor** habían hecho a la ciudad especialmente vulnerable, y un fuerte viento del este también desempeñó un papel crucial. El resultado fue la **total destrucción de la City**, incluida la catedral medieval de San Pablo, otras 87 iglesias y 13 000 viviendas. Las seis muertes oficiales continúan siendo objeto de controversia.

En diciembre de 1666, Luis XIV, decidido a no verse superado por la Royal Society londinense (*véase* 1662), autorizó la fundación de la **Academia de las Ciencias**, que en 1669 se convertiría en Real Academia de las Ciencias, con sede en el palacio del Louvre (París). En la actualidad forma parte del Instituto de Francia. La institución impulsó la **búsqueda de conocimiento científico y verificable** y era un brazo del estado, también interesado en descubrimientos que pudieran enriquecer al país, por ejemplo en los ámbitos de la agricultura o el armamento.

1667

« LA MENTE TIENE SU PROPIO LUGAR Y **PUEDE HACER** DEL **INFIERNO UN CIELO**, Y DEL **CIELO UN INFIERNO. »**

John Milton, poeta inglés, en *El paraíso perdido* (1667)

EL TRATADO DE ANDRÚSOVO, FIRMADO EN ENERO de 1667, puso fin a la calamitosa guerra que enfrentaba a Polonia-Lituania con Rusia desde 1654. También supuso el clímax del Diluvio, el **drástico declive ante la expansión Rusa**. Rusia obtuvo Smolensk y la actual Bielorrusia, lo que le permitió afirmar por primera vez que había **unido a los pueblos eslavos de la región**.

Durante este año, Gian Lorenzo Bernini (1598–1680) finalizó la **Plaza de San Pedro**, el culmen de la planificación urbana de la Roma barroca. Varios arquitectos reformaron diversos espacios públicos de la ciudad con el objetivo de darles una grandiosidad digna del corazón de la Iglesia católica.

En mayo estalló la **guerra de Devolución** a causa de las continuas reclamaciones del rey Luis XIV sobre los **Países Bajos españoles**. Francia logró tomar algunas ciudades de los Habsburgo en Flandes y el Franco Condado al este, pero la Triple Alianza de Inglaterra, Suecia y Holanda obligó al aislado Luis a devolver la mayor parte de los territorios ganados por el **tratado de Aquisgrán** de 1668.

80 000
NÚMERO DE **MUERTOS** EN EL **TERREMOTO DE SAMAKHI** (AZERBAIYÁN)

En 1667, el **poema épico** *El paraíso perdido*, del inglés John Milton (1608–1774), donde narraba la historia bíblica de la pérdida del Edén, supuso uno de los **mayores logros literarios** de la lengua inglesa.

Sitio de Lille
Luis XIV dirige el ejército francés en Lille durante la guerra de Devolución. Esta ciudad fue una de las pocas ganancias que obtuvo Francia en un conflicto frustrante.

1668

Grabado en madera con el retrato del almirante y corsario Henry Morgan.

LA FACTORÍA PORTUGUESA de Bombay (Mumbai) **pasó a la corona inglesa** en 1662 como parte de la dote de Catalina de Braganza, la esposa portuguesa de Carlos II. En 1668, el rey la cedió a la **Compañía de las Indias Orientales** por un alquiler anual de diez libras, lo que la convirtió en el tercer puesto comercial de la Compañía en India junto con Surat y Madrás. En 1675 se terminó el castillo, y a partir de 1687 se convirtió en el centro de todo el comercio de la Compañía en India, que tuvo que resistir ataques de mogoles y holandeses.

En 1668, el **corsario galés Henry Morgan**, famoso por sus ataques a los asentamientos españoles en el Caribe, realizó uno de sus **asaltos más atrevidos**: sus naves se apoderaron de la bien protegida **ciudad comercial española de Portobelo**, situada en Panamá. Con ello consiguió incrementar su fortuna y más apoyo inglés en sus expediciones corsarias.

Así como la incorporación de la corona portuguesa en el año 1580 por el rey Felipe II había sido una demostración del poder de España, el **reconocimiento de la independencia portuguesa en 1668**, por el tratado de Lisboa, que confirmaba a la casa de Braganza en el trono de Portugal, fue una prueba de su declive. Desde 1640, Portugal estaba en rebelión abierta contra España, y en junio de 1665, en la **batalla de Montes Claros**, fuerzas angloportuguesas obtuvieron una victoria aplastante. Al borde de la bancarrota y segura de más hostilidades francesas, España solo pudo ceder.

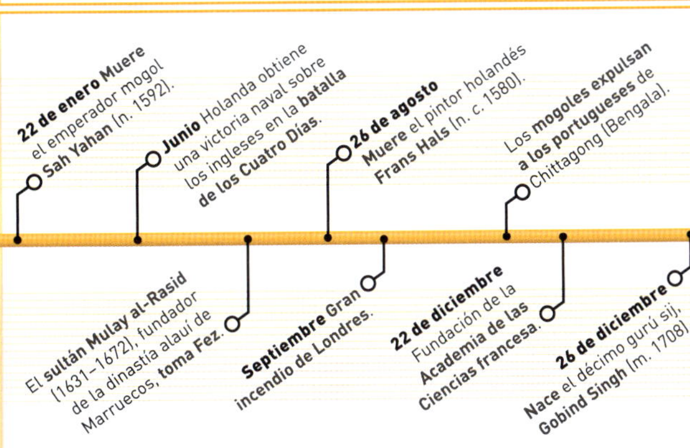

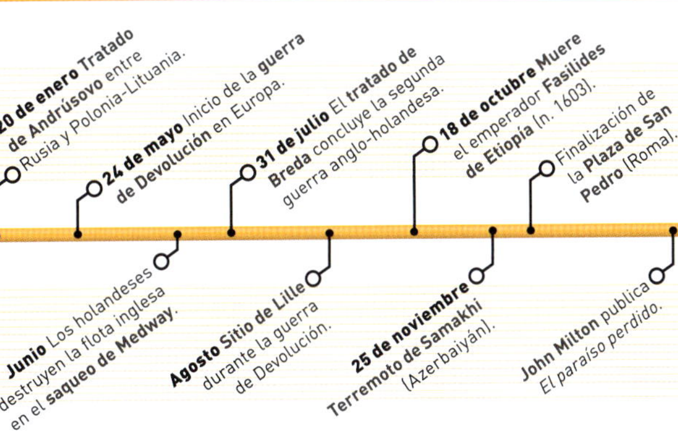

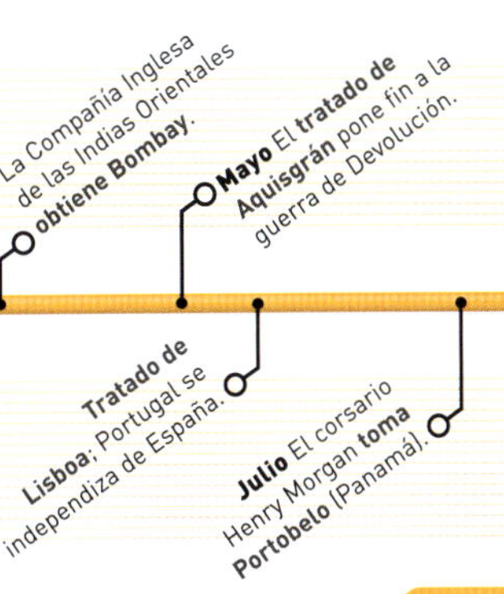

1669

Mezquita del Emperador de Lahore, encargada por Aurangzeb.

UNA DE LAS EXPLICACIONES DE LA DESINTEGRACIÓN del Imperio mogol tras la muerte de **Aurangzeb** en 1707 alude a su supuesta **persecución de los hindúes** y otras minorías. Su predecesor, Akbar I, había aplicado una política de tolerancia religiosa como el medio más efectivo para controlar a sus vasallos hindúes, pero se dice que Aurangzeb (que era musulmán suní) **destruyó sistemáticamente sus templos**. Además, prohibió el uso de la música, básica para la práctica hindú, y emitió un decreto, posiblemente hacia 1669, a tal efecto. También elaboró un **compendio exhaustivo de la ley musulmana**, el *Fatawa-i-Alamgiri*, que al parecer impuso rigurosamente. Sin embargo, se duda de estas afirmaciones; de hecho, el número de templos hindúes supuestamente destruidos oscila entre 80 y 60 000. Lo que sí parece cierto es el **firme anticristianismo** de Aurangzeb.

100
MILLONES DE LIBRAS
RECAUDACIÓN ANUAL DEL **TESORO PÚBLICO** DE **AURANGZEB**

1670

« VENID RÁPIDO, ESTOY **BEBIENDO ESTRELLAS**. »

Atribuido a Dom Pérignon al probar el champán (1670)

Líder cosaco
Stepan Razin, el líder cosaco que se alzó contra la nobleza y la burocracia zarista, en el río Volga (sur de Rusia).

EN MAYO DEL AÑO 1670 SE FUNDÓ LA COMPAÑÍA DE LA BAHÍA DE HUDSON bajo cédula real británica y por iniciativa de dos comerciantes de pieles franceses, Pierre Esprit Radisson y Médard des Groseilliers. Sabiendo que las **mejores pieles** se conseguían en el **territorio de los cree**, al norte del lago Superior, al que era más fácil acceder desde la bahía de Hudson que desde los ríos o lagos del sur, propusieron establecer una base allí. Francia se negó, por lo que **solicitaron el apoyo de Inglaterra**. La compañía se convirtió en una de las grandes empresas comerciales de Inglaterra y en el **origen de su reclamación de Canadá** y de su rivalidad regional con Francia.

La afirmación de que **Dom Pérignon** (1638–1715), un monje de la abadía benedictina de Hautvilliers, ubicada en Champaña, **inventó el vino espumoso** que lleva el nombre de la región ha quedado desmentida. En realidad, lo que se proponía era **eliminar las burbujas** que producían esos vinos porque la presión acumulada tendía a hacer explotar las botellas. Sin embargo, como encargado de la bodega de la abadía, hizo una gran aportación a la **producción de vinos blancos** al empezar a utilizar uvas que también se usaban para el vino tinto. Hasta principios del siglo XVIII no se extendió la **predilección por los vinos espumosos** en Francia e Inglaterra.

En 1670, el zar **reprimió brutalmente** un **alzamiento cosaco** en el sur de Rusia, cuyo líder, Stepan Razin, fue ejecutado al año siguiente. El intento de proteger la independencia cosaca frente al **centralizado estado ruso** se había convertido en una revuelta campesina que saqueó varias ciudades.

1671–1672

Azulejos portugueses decoran la fortaleza de San Miguel en Luanda, un enclave militar crucial para la colonización de Angola a finales del siglo XVII.

EN 1671, PORTUGAL PUSO FIN A LA INDEPENDENCIA del reino de Ndongo, en la actual Angola. Una colonia portuguesa **dominaba a los ndongo** desde el siglo XVI, pero la rebelión de su rey, Felipe, en 1671 condujo a la **toma de la capital** y al control del territorio por los **portugueses**.

Así como el temor a que España dominara Europa había llevado a la alianza de Francia, Inglaterra y Holanda (Provincias Unidas), el dominio de Francia a partir de 1659 unió a España y Holanda en una **alianza antifrancesa**. Luis XIV reclamaba su derecho por matrimonio a los Países Bajos españoles, a lo que España se oponía, mientras que las Provincias Unidas preferían como vecino a una España debilitada que a una Francia potente. En la guerra de Devolución de 1667–1668, Francia terminó perdiendo casi todo lo ganado en los Países Bajos españoles, pero en 1672, Luis, aliado con Inglaterra y Suecia, volvió a intentarlo en la **guerra franco-holandesa**. La guerra terminó con Nueva Amsterdam en manos inglesas, mientras que Francia, pese a haber fracasado en la conquista de Holanda, recuperaba el anterior territorio borgoñón del Franco Condado y una serie de territorios fronterizos en los Países Bajos españoles. No obstante, la paz solo fue una breve pausa en los intentos de Luis de ampliar y proteger Francia.

COMERCIO DE PIELES

La búsqueda de pieles impulsó a los franceses a adentrarse hacia el oeste en Canadá y a los ingleses a fundar la Compañía de la Bahía de Hudson (*véase* 1670), y fue el origen del conflicto anglo-francés en aquellas tierras. Los franceses acompañaban a los indios en las expediciones de caza, mientras que ingleses y holandeses (en la imagen) solían comprar las pieles a los indios. Todos dependían de la ayuda de los indios, quienes a su vez se volvieron dependientes de las armas y herramientas europeas.

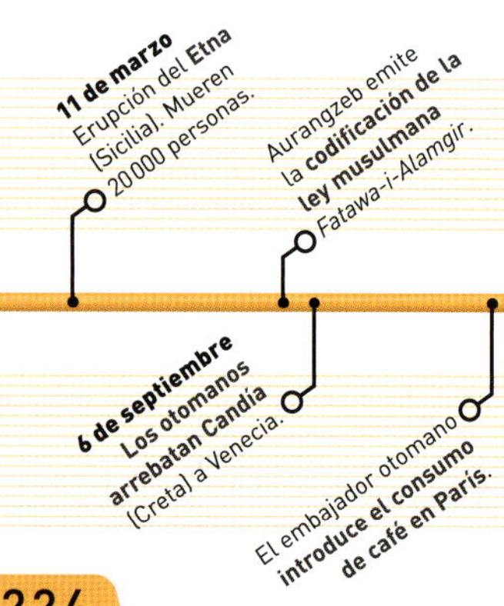

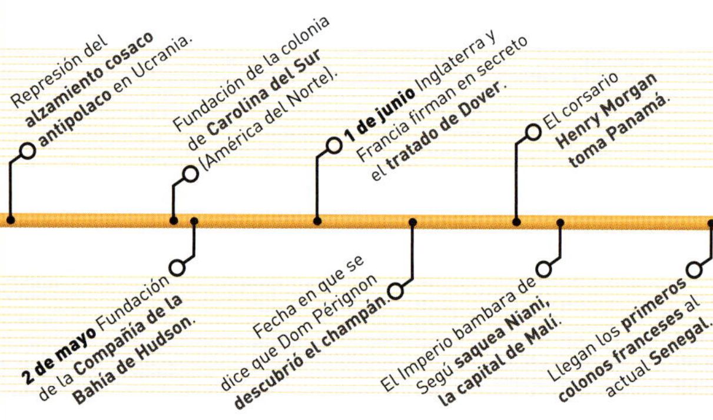

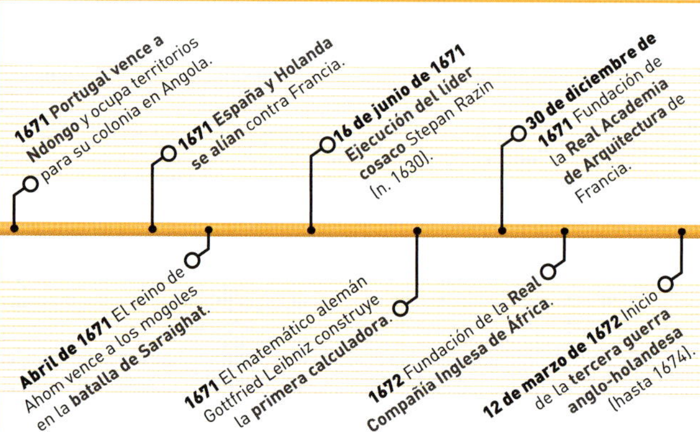

1673

Marquette y Jolliet descienden el río Mississippi con sus guías.

1674

Entrada ceremonial en Pekín de Kangxi, el emperador Qing, que reprimió por completo la rebelión de los Tres Feudatarios.

1675

Federico Guillermo I al frente de sus tropas en la batalla de Fehrbellin.

Calculadora mecánica de Leibniz
Una de las primeras máquinas calculadoras, desarrollada por Leibniz, que multiplica haciendo sumas múltiples.

En 1671, el matemático alemán **Gottfried Leibniz** (1646–1716) presentó una de las **primeras calculadoras mecánicas de la historia**. La suya fue la primera capaz de realizar las cuatro operaciones aritméticas básicas, y Leibniz continuó perfeccionándola, proporcionando así la base para las calculadoras modernas.

Por último, las repetidas **revueltas de los cosacos y los tártaros de Crimea** contra la debilitada Polonia-Lituania en 1672 llevaron a sus aliados otomanos a la **guerra polaco-otomana**, que se prolongó durante cuatro años. La resistencia polaca, dirigida por Juan III Sobieski (1629–1696), se vio muy mermada por el reticente apoyo del parlamento polaco, el Sejm, y apenas podía equipararse al creciente ejército otomano. **Polonia acabó perdiendo el escaso prestigio** que le quedaba además de la mayoría de sus territorios en Ucrania.

LAS EXTENSAS VÍAS FLUVIALES de América del Norte facilitaron el acceso directo a la exploración del interior del continente. En el año 1673, el **explorador francocanadiense** Louis Jolliet, acompañado por el jesuita francés Jacques Marquette, consiguió **descender el río Misisipi** hasta llegar a unos 600 km del golfo de México. Regresaron por temor a despertar la hostilidad de España, pero descubrieron los ríos Missouri y Ohio, además de confirmar que el río desembocaba en el golfo, y no en el Pacífico. Los **ingleses exploraron** el interior desde sus asentamientos costeros, aunque de un modo mucho más dubitativo y rara vez coordinado; además, la **cordillera de los Apalaches** les obstaculizaba el paso. Casi siempre dependían de la ayuda de los nativos. Así, Gabriel Arthur viajó junto a un grupo de indios tomahitan tras haber pasado un año con ellos y, al **cruzar el desfiladero de Cumberland**, topó por casualidad la que en el siglo XVIII fue la ruta principal a Kentucky y al Oeste.

3200 KILÓMETROS LONGITUD DE LOS MONTES APALACHES

TRAS OCUPAR CHINA Y DERRIBAR a la dinastía Ming en 1644, los Qing acogieron a algunos de sus **generales más poderosos**, les nombraron gobernadores generales y les concedieron gran flexibilidad para el gobierno de unos territorios que acabaron siendo prácticamente independientes. Pensaban que si les dejaban **enriquecerse** (cosa que hicieron de una manera espectacular), reducirían las probabilidades de que se rebelaran; el riesgo era que los ingresos crecientes les llevaran a **aspirar al control de China**. En 1674 estalló la **rebelión de los Tres Feudatarios** en las provincias del sur de China, que eran controladas por los tres rebeldes más importantes, Wu Sangui, Geng Jingzhong y Shang Kexi Gungdong, a los que también se unieron gobernadores menores Ming. El emperador Kangxi (1654–1722) lideró la respuesta Qing, que obtuvo la victoria gracias a su clara **superioridad militar**, aunque no hasta 1681. Los rebeldes, además, desconfiaban entre sí tanto como del emperador, por lo que apenas cooperaban; esto **permitió a los Qing capturarlos uno por uno** y ejecutar a los que no se suicidaron.

Después de liberar a los marathas hindúes del sultán de Bijapur, **Sivaji** (1630–1680) fue coronado rey en 1674 y estableció el **Imperio maratha** (p. 242), que luego derrotó a los mogoles y dominó India hasta principios del siglo XIX.

Estatua de Sivaji
Estatua ecuestre de bronce de Sivaji en Maharastra (India), en conmemoración de su liderazgo en la lucha maratha por la independencia.

EN 1675, EL EMPERADOR MOGOL AURANGZEB ORDENÓ la ejecución de Tegh Bahadur, noveno gurú de los sijs, por negarse a convertirse al islam. Esto llevó al trono sij a su hijo de nueve años, **Gobind Singh** (1666–1708). Varios años después, bajo el liderazgo de Singh, los sijs se convirtieron en una **creciente amenaza militar para el dominio mogol** y contribuyeron de manera significativa a su caída. Sin embargo, la pauta de la **oposición religiosa a los mogoles** ya se había instaurado sólidamente en varias partes de India, sobre todo en los Gates Occidentales, donde Sivaji había declarado el Imperio maratha.

El 18 de junio del año 1675, un ejército combinado de Prusia y Brandeburgo, dirigido por Federico Guillermo I, elector de Brandeburgo (1620–1688), se enfrentó y **derrotó al ejército sueco** al mando del conde Von Wrangel cerca de **Fehrbellin**, en Brandeburgo. Esta batalla relativamente insignificante de la **guerra de Escania**, consecuencia de la guerra franco-holandesa, marcó un momento crucial en la larga lucha que Suecia mantenía por imponerse en la zona del Báltico. La derrota por un estado alemán menor **fue un gran golpe para los suecos**, cuyas pretensiones de convertirse en una gran potencia demostraron ser precarias, en el mejor de los casos.

Abril de 1672 Estalla la **guerra franco-holandesa** tras la invasión de Holanda (hasta 1678).

7 de junio de 1672 **Batalla de Solebay**, en la tercera guerra anglo-holandesa, inconcluyente.

4 de julio de 1672 Guillermo III de Orange es nombrado **estatúder de Holanda**.

18 de octubre de 1672 **Tratado de Buczacz** entre el Imperio otomano y Polonia-Lituania.

17 de febrero Muere el dramaturgo y actor **Molière** (n. 1622).

Mayo Jolliet y Marquette inician la **exploración del río Misisipi**.

El explorador inglés Gabriel Arthur **cruza los Apalaches**.

Batallas de Schooneveld entre las flotas inglesa y holandesa.

Estalla la **rebelión de los Tres Feudatarios** (China).

19 de febrero El **tratado de Westminster** pone fin a la tercera guerra anglo-holandesa.

21 de mayo Juan III Sobieski es elegido rey de Polonia-Lituania.

6 de junio Sivaji instaura el **Imperio maratha** hindú.

Pondicherry (sur de India) se convierte en la base de la **Compañía Francesa de las Indias Orientales**.

11 de agosto Francia derrota al ejército de Holanda-España-Austria en la **batalla de Seneffe**.

8 de noviembre Muere el poeta inglés **John Milton** (n. 1608).

10 de noviembre Cesión a Inglaterra de los **Nuevos Países Bajos** (incluida Nueva ámsterdam), en América del Norte.

Los mogoles ejecutan al líder sij **Tegh Bahadur**.

18 de junio Brandeburgo y Prusia derrotan a Suecia en la **batalla de Fehrbellin**.

Desarrollo de la poesía haiku en Japón.

Guerra entre los **colonos ingleses** y las **tribus algonquinas** en América del Norte.

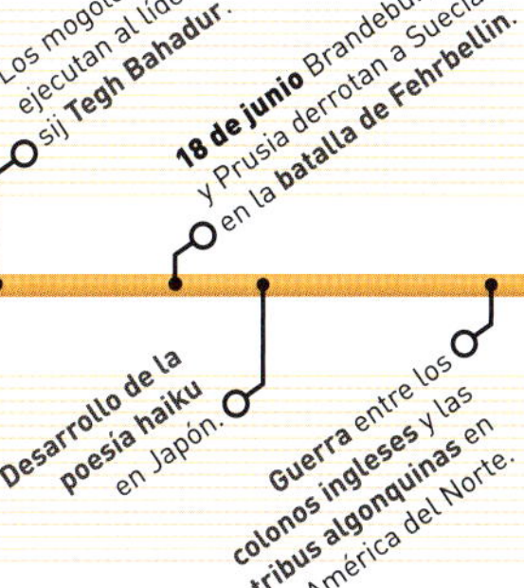

1676–1678

La catarata de la Herradura, en el lado canadiense de las cataratas del Niágara, tiene unos 800 m de anchura. Los europeos contemplaron esta maravilla por primera vez en 1677.

EN FRANCIA, LUIS XIV concentró sus esfuerzos en la remodelación del **inmenso palacio de Versalles**, cerca de París, pero también estaba decidido a continuar la transformación de la capital francesa iniciada por su abuelo, Enrique IV, a principios del siglo XVII. Enrique había querido hacer del París medieval una **capital digna de la primera potencia europea**, con edificios y espacios públicos imponentes que rivalizaran con los de Roma. Como era previsible, se amplió y remodeló el palacio del Louvre, sobre todo su ala este, cuya elegante fachada resume **el gusto francés por el clasicismo** en su vertiente más austera y estricta. Sin embargo, el edificio que mejor refleja la contribución de Luis a París es el **Hotel de los Inválidos**, en parte hospital y en parte casa de retiro para los soldados franceses, terminado en 1676. El arquitecto Libéral Bruant (1635–1697) lo concibió a gran escala, con vastos jardines formales ante su fachada y quince patios posteriores. Su elemento más sobresaliente, la **suntuosa capilla**, ubicada en el extremo sur del complejo y coronada con una cúpula y una aguja majestuosas y decoradas con oro, fue añadida poco después.

El reinado de Luis XIV fue uno de los **periodos más fecundos de la literatura francesa**. En 1677 se estrenó *Fedra*, la tragedia cumbre del dramaturgo francés **Jean Racine** (1639–1699). Autores teatrales como Racine, Pierre Corneille (1606–1684) y **Molière** (1622–1673) prosperaron bajo el mecenazgo real y cautivaron al público cortesano de diversas maneras. Corneille y Racine ilustraban las preocupaciones de la corte mediante el verso formal, los temas clásicos y el énfasis en el honor y la virtud, mientras que las comedias de Molière se burlaban de las pretensiones sociales burguesas. La fundación, con mecenazgo real, de la **Comédie Française** fue consecuencia de esta creciente y rica tradición teatral. Este teatro nacional iba a encargarse de llevar la gloria escénica y cultural francesa lo más lejos posible.

En España, la **incapacidad de la corona** se puso de manifiesto tras el acceso al trono de Carlos II. En 1676 fue nombrado primer ministro **Fernando de Valenzuela**, cuya rápida acumulación de poder y títulos le granjeó la oposición de la alta nobleza. En enero de 1677, el hermanastro del rey, don Juan José de Austria, lideró un **ejército de aristócratas** aragoneses y castellanos que entró en Madrid y consiguió la destitución de Valenzuela, que acabó siendo exiliado a Filipinas. Con él se extinguió la serie de validos de los Austrias (Habsburgo españoles) del siglo XVII.

Los exploradores europeos se comenzaron a percatar de la **inmensidad de América del Norte** a lo largo del siglo XVII. El **descubrimiento de las cataratas del Niágara** en 1677, unas cascadas con más de 170 000 cm³ de caudal por minuto, asombró al Viejo Mundo. No es seguro qué europeo pudo ser el primero en contemplarlas, pero su descubrimiento se atribuye al franciscano francés Louis Hennepin (1626–1701), que exploraba a las órdenes de Luis XIV.

grabado del autor

Obra religiosa
Frontispicio perteneciente a la tercera edición de El progreso del peregrino, *de John Bunyan, una obra enormemente influyente durante el siglo XVII.*

Por último, en febrero de 1678 se publicó una de las **obras religiosas más importantes de la historia de la literatura inglesa**: *El progreso del peregrino*, de **John Bunyan** (1628–1688), que la escribió casi en su totalidad mientras cumplía pena en la cárcel de Bedford. Se trata de una **fábula alegórica** del trayecto del hombre común desde este mundo hasta el cielo y se publicó en dos partes (la segunda en 1684). Es uno de los libros ingleses más traducidos de la historia.

Los Inválidos (París)
El complejo alberga hoy museos y monumentos relacionados con la historia militar de Francia y un hospital para veteranos de guerra.

1679–1681

Ilustración del siglo XIX sobre los ashanti, de África occidental.

EN 1679, EL PARLAMENTO INGLÉS aprobó la **ley del Hábeas Corpus**, que afirmaba que **nadie podía ser detenido sin un motivo legal**. Del mismo modo que la Carta Magna (*véase* 1215), también fue un hito en la historia de las libertades inglesas. Sin embargo, se aprobó por razones pragmáticas, y no por un **principio liberal de justicia**, y tenía el objetivo de impedir que el católico Jacobo, duque de York, hermano y heredero del rey Carlos II, arrestara a sus adversarios protestantes sin ningún tipo de justificación legal, como había comenzado a hacer el conde de Shaftesbury, su adversario en el parlamento. El principio subyacente a la ley, que más tarde se incorporó a la **Constitución estadounidense**, sigue siendo básico en la mayoría de sistemas legales anglosajones como **garantía última de la libertad individual**. Sin embargo, la ley apenas se invoca.

> « QUE **TENGAS EL CUERPO**, SUJETO A **EXAMEN**. »
>
> **Acción de hábeas corpus inglesa** (1679)

En agosto de 1680, los **indios pueblo** de la colonia de Nuevo México **se alzaron en contra de los colonos españoles** y los expulsaron de la región durante doce años.

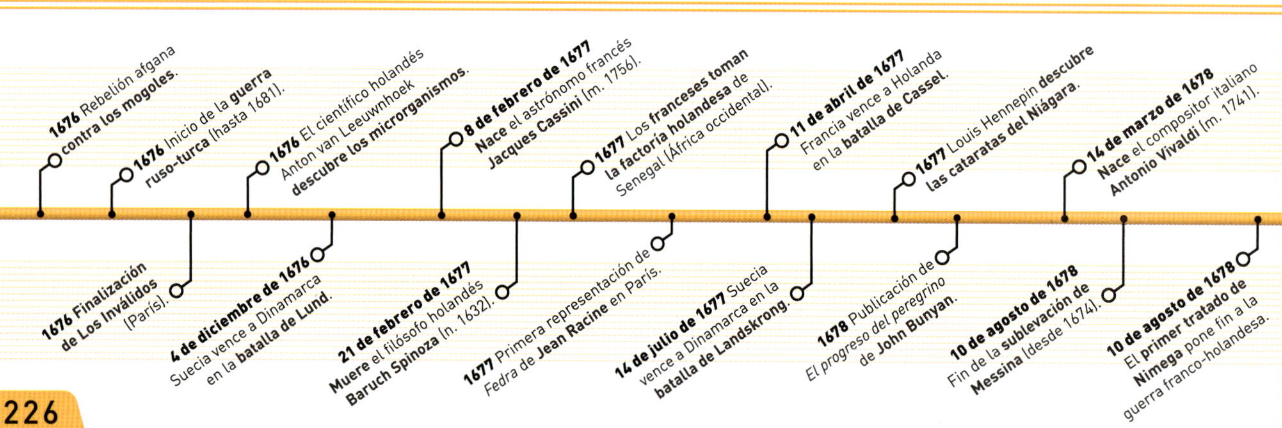

« QUIEN HACE EL BIEN POR EL BIEN **NO BUSCA NI EL PARAÍSO NI RECOMPENSA**, PERO TIENE AMBOS **GARANTIZADOS. »**

William Penn, cuáquero inglés, fundador de Filadelfia (1682)

La reclamación española del territorio de Nuevo México se remontaba a las expediciones llevadas a cabo por Coronado a mediados del siglo XVI, pero nunca habían consistido en mucho más que en exigencias de prioridad y predominio cristiano sobre esta región. Nuevo México era considerada una tierra de valor marginal debido a su **lejanía** y a su **aridez**. La rebelión de los pueblo fue provocada en parte por la sequía y por el sufrimiento que conlleva este fenómeno natural, pero también por la firme determinación española de **acabar con las prácticas religiosas locales**: los chamanes pueblo eran acusados de brujería y ejecutados sistemáticamente. Cuando los españoles regresaron en 1692, lo hicieron en cantidades abrumadoras.

El **reino ashanti**, que fue fundado aproximadamente en 1680, se componía del pueblo akan, que dominaba África occidental. El grupo akan más importante era el de los **oyoko** que, mediante la diplomacia y la guerra, **consolidó a las tribus akan** durante la década de 1670 y las unió contra la amenaza de los vecinos denykira, a quienes conquistaron en 1701 en la batalla de Feyiase (Ghana actual).

Pocos proyectos pueden ilustrar mejor la fuerte voluntad expansionista de la Francia de Luis XIV que la construcción del **Canal du Midi**, una vía navegable interior que permitiría conectar el mar Mediterráneo con el océano Atlántico y cuya construcción era necesaria para evitar una larga y peligrosa travesía marítima sustituyéndola por una ruta canalizada. Los problemas técnicos que comportó su construcción, por no mencionar el coste, fueron colosales. El principal obstáculo era cómo garantizar el caudal de agua suficiente en las partes más elevadas del canal. Sin duda fue la obra de ingeniería más compleja emprendida por un estado europeo del siglo XVII y requirió mano de obra a gran escala, así como soluciones de ingeniería innovadoras. Se **terminó en 1681**, y poseía una longitud de 240 km.

CERÁMICA PUEBLO

Los indios del suroeste de América del Norte a quienes los españoles llamaron pueblo por sus aldeas, eran conocidos por su sofisticada y elaborada cerámica de fondo claro, profusamente decorada con pinturas de animales estilizados y con elaborados dibujos abstractos en tonos ocre, negro y gris.

Penn en América
Detalle de una pintura que muestra al cuáquero William Penn en una reunión con los indios en lo que ahora es el estado de Delaware.

LA CORONACIÓN en 1682 de **Pedro I el Grande** (1672–1725), de nueve años de edad, como zar de Rusia terminó con la vaga influencia imperial de esa extensa nación como semipotencia al margen de Europa. Las rebeliones marcaron la infancia de Pedro, lo que le llevó a castigar a sus enemigos internos y a convertir a **Rusia en una potencia europea occidental**. Durante una vida en que derrochó una energía compulsiva, construyó una nueva capital, **San Petersburgo**, y se impuso implacablemente sobre sus boyardos (nobles). Su versión de Versalles, recreado a orillas del Báltico, no fue más que una declaración de intenciones, pero al final de su reinado, **Rusia** era una gran potencia que se **cernía sobre Europa**.

En 1682, nueve años después de que Jolliet y Marquette se aventuraran curso abajo del **Mississippi** y confirmaran que los territorios no contenían ni nativos ricos a los que poder explotar fácilmente ni fuentes obvias de oro, **Robert de La Salle** (1647–1687), un explorador veterano de América de Norte, decidió seguir el río hasta su desembocadura, que alcanzó el 9 de abril junto con 19 indios. **Proclamó al río** y sus tierras circundantes **propiedad de Francia** y bautizó a la región con el nombre de **Luisiana**, en honor al rey francés: este fue el origen de la reclamación francesa de una gran parte de América del Norte. Sin embargo, una segunda expedición marítima en 1684 no consiguió encontrar el río, y tres de los cuatro barcos que la formaban naufragaron. La Salle fue asesinado por el resto de la expedición.

También fue en este año cuando **William Penn** (1644–1718), un cuáquero y filósofo inglés a quien se había concedido tierras pertenecientes a Jacobo, duque de York, en América del Norte, fundó la colonia que acabó convirtiéndose en la ciudad de **Filadelfia (Pensilvania)**. Penn prometió tanto libertad religiosa como prosperidad económica a todos los europeos que decidieran asentarse allí.

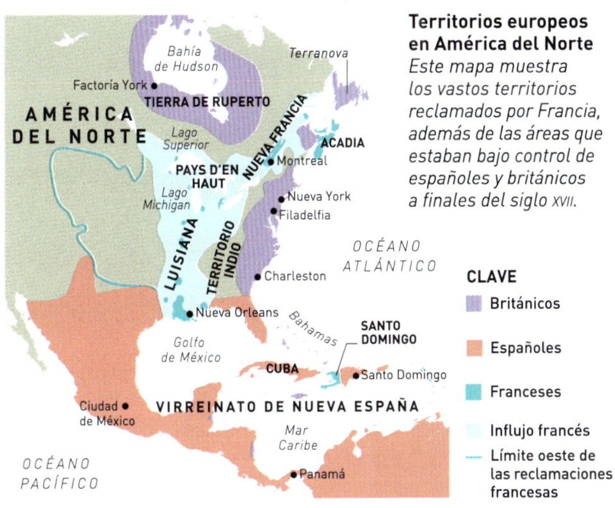

Territorios europeos en América del Norte
Este mapa muestra los vastos territorios reclamados por Francia, además de las áreas que estaban bajo control de españoles y británicos a finales del siglo XVII.

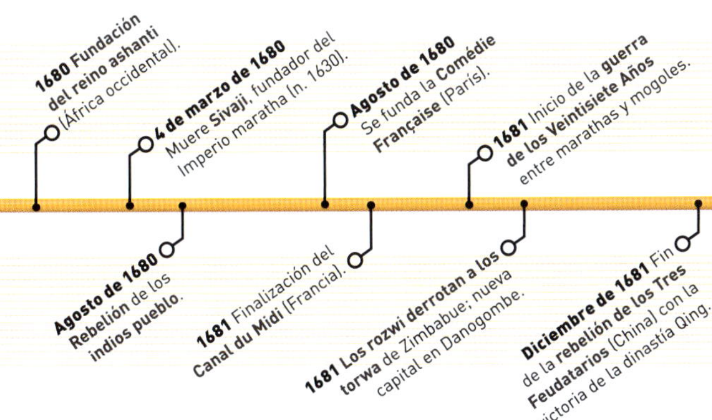

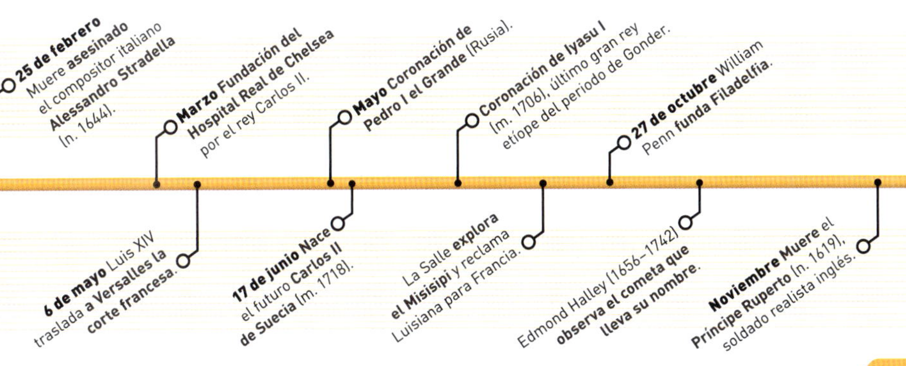

1683–1684

El ejército polaco imperial rompe el sitio de Viena por el Imperio otomano en la batalla de Kahlenberg.

EL 14 DE JULIO DE 1683, UN EJÉRCITO otomano inició el **sitio de Viena**. Al igual que el de 1529, se trataba de un ataque directo contra el Occidente cristiano y también terminó fracasando. Sin embargo, mientras que el de 1529 había sido la culminación de una serie de conquistas que arrasaron Hungría, el sitio de 1683 fue un **último y desesperado intento de recuperar la antigua gloria** otomana y superar así las numerosas debilidades internas. Viena logró resistir una vez más, y en septiembre un ejército imperial liderado por el rey de Polonia, Juan III Sobieski, pudo al fin **romper el sitio en Kahlenberg**. Le siguió el **colapso del dominio otomano en Hungría**: la Santa Liga compuesta por el Sacro Imperio, Polonia y Venecia, y formada en 1684 bajo la autoridad papal, rechazó a los turcos hacia el sur a través de los Balcanes.

El reino Tungning de Taiwán, aliado de los depuestos Ming en China, había apoyado **asaltos militares contra los Qing** desde el año 1661. En 1683, las negociaciones no habían dado ningún fruto, por lo que el emperador Kangxi (1654–1722) arremetió con todo el poder militar Qing y consiguió una gran **victoria naval y terrestre** en la **batalla de Penghu**, gracias a la cual el reino Tungning pasó a formar parte del imperio Qing.

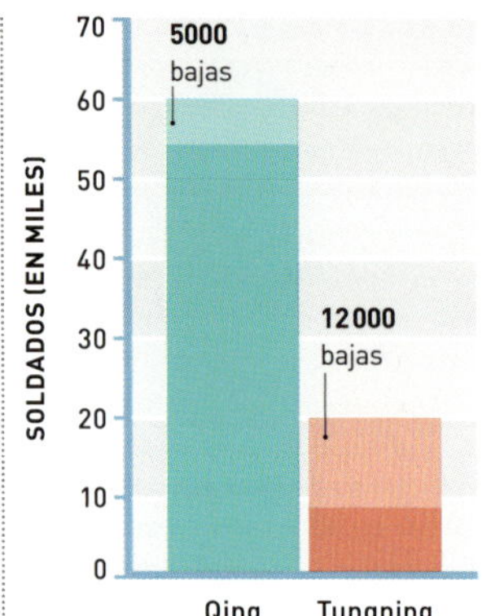
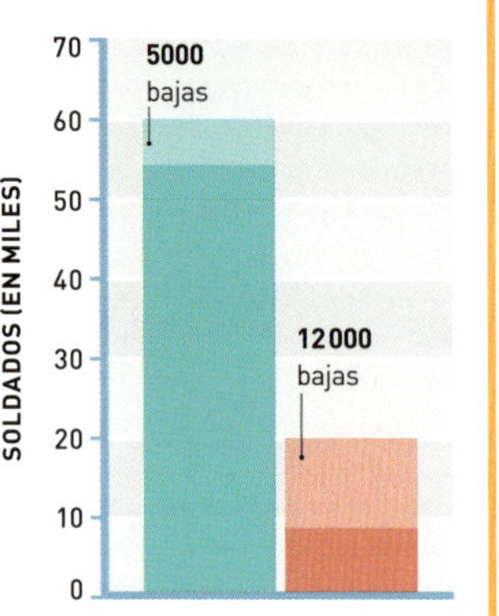

Batalla de Penghu
Los Qing se tomaron muy en serio la amenaza Tungning: con el objetivo de asegurarse la victoria, enviaron un extraordinario ejército terrestre y naval que incluía 200 barcos.

A lo largo de la década de 1680, los cambios climáticos del mínimo de Maunder, que habían empezado en la década de 1640 como resultado de una reducción de la actividad solar, dieron lugar a un periodo especialmente frío en todo el planeta, conocido como la **«pequeña glaciación»**, durante el cual las temperaturas descendieron varios grados y que se prolongó hasta el siglo XIX. Entre los **muchos crudos inviernos** de este periodo, el de 1683–1684 fue considerado el peor.

Insatisfecho con el tratado de Nimega de 1679, el rey Luis XIV trató de **ampliar las fronteras de Francia** a expensas de los estados alemanes y de los Países Bajos españoles en Flandes y en Renania. Mediante amenazas e insistentes reclamaciones legales, obtuvo Alsacia, Luxemburgo y fortalezas clave en Flandes, logros que consolidó el **tratado de Ratisbona** de 1684, al término de la breve guerra de las Reuniones de 1683–1684. Luis había llegado a la cima de su poder y estaba **decidido a imponerse a Europa**, pero lo único que consiguió fue que católicos y protestantes se unieran contra él.

Feria sobre hielo en el Támesis
En Londres, durante los inviernos de la pequeña glaciación, fueron habituales las ferias sobre un río Támesis completamente helado. Se plantaban tenderetes sobre el hielo.

1685–1686

Ilustración del siglo XIX: el elector de Brandeburgo Federico Guillermo I recibe a los hugonotes (protestantes franceses) en Berlín en 1685.

EL EDICTO DE NANTES EMITIDO por el rey Enrique IV en 1598, por el que la importante **minoría hugonota francesa obtuvo tolerancia religiosa** a cambio de aceptar a Enrique como rey, fue un compromiso necesario y crucial para el fin de las guerras de religión francesas. En octubre de 1685, Luis XIV **lo revocó con el edicto de Fontainebleau**. Su decisión era lógica, ya que prácticamente no había ningún otro estado europeo que permitiera la libertad religiosa; por otra parte, el absolutismo de Luis no podía exigir menos que una **religión estatal reconocida oficialmente**, y esta fue el catolicismo romano. Un gran número de los **aproximadamente 200 000 hugonotes que huyeron del país** eran algunos de los habitantes más industriosos de Francia y fueron recibidos con los brazos abiertos por los países a los que emigraron (como Inglaterra, las Provincias Unidas y Prusia). Además, supuso una agresión tan directa contra los protestantes franceses (la política se impuso con gran brutalidad), que no solo despertó la **indignación de la Europa protestante**, sino que sirvió para reforzar la idea de la necesidad de oponerse a la Francia de Luis XIV a toda costa.

La consecuencia de las evidentes intenciones de Luis XIV respecto a Europa fue la fundación, en 1686, de la **Liga de Augsburgo**, que luego se denominó **Gran Alianza**. Fue iniciativa del emperador del Sacro Imperio, Leopoldo I (1640–1705), reforzado tras su victoria sobre los otomanos y alentado por Guillermo III de Orange (1650–1792), estatúder de las Provincias Unidas. Con el tiempo, todos los estados europeos excepto Suiza se **alinearon contra Francia**.

A partir de 1685, el ya anciano **Jacobo II** de Inglaterra (1633–1701), hijo de Carlos I y hermano menor de Carlos II, demostró una **increíble torpeza** durante su breve ocupación de los tronos inglés y escocés. **Decidido a imponer el catolicismo** en una nación ya parlamentaria y protestante, consiguió desbaratar en menos de tres años el delicado y cínico equilibrio político que había conseguido Carlos II.

200 000

NÚMERO DE **HUGONOTES** DE UN TOTAL DE 800 000 QUE **HUYERON DE FRANCIA TRAS EL EDICTO DE FONTAINEBLEAU** DE LUIS XIV

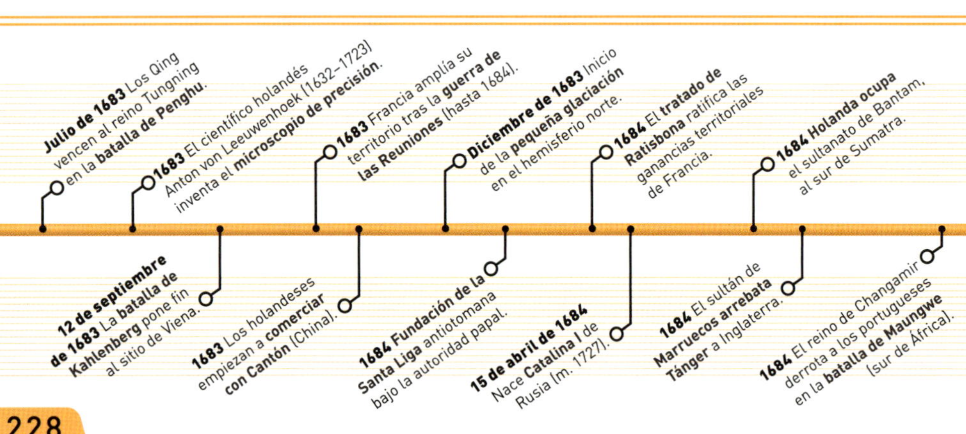

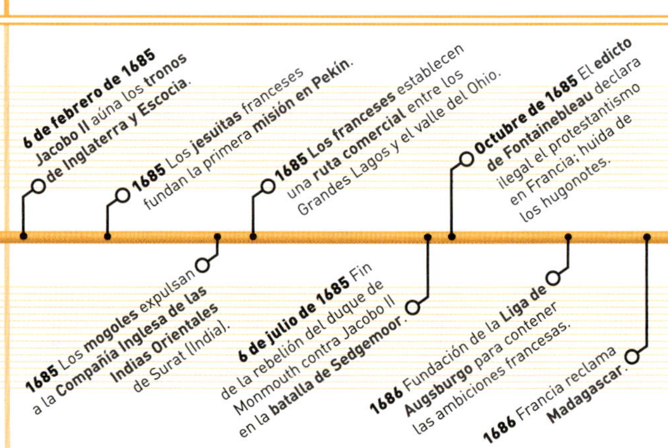

1687–1688

Pintura holandesa que representa la partida de la flota de Guillermo III de Países Bajos hacia Inglaterra al principio de la Revolución Gloriosa de 1688.

EN OCTUBRE DE 1688, Y PESE A LA FALTA de financiación, las tropas de Luis XIV arrasaron Renania-Palatinado (Alemania), iniciando así la **guerra de los Nueve Años**. Su objetivo era el de obligar a Leopoldo I a reconocer el dominio francés en los territorios fronterizos anexionados anteriormente, además de crear una franja de tierra devastada difícil de cruzar por los ejércitos que quisieran invadir Francia. El mes siguiente, **Guillermo III de Orange llegaba a Inglaterra** con un ejército de 15 000 hombres. Estas dos acciones desencadenaron una especie de erupción volcánica en la historia política europea. El barro invernal detuvo casi inmediatamente la invasión de Luis, lo que acabó llevando al **eclipse del poder francés** frente a una Europa unida contra él (*véase* 1685–1686); por el contrario, Guillermo, en tres meses no solo había conseguido convertirse en monarca conjunto de Inglaterra (con su esposa María), sino también en el líder de la **alianza protestante antifrancesa paneuropea**. Estaba en juego la naturaleza del gobierno legítimo.

La monarquía en apariencia absoluta de Luis XIV parecía ser el modelo del ejercicio del poder más eficaz para los príncipes modernos, pero el **acceso de Guillermo III** a los tronos de Inglaterra y de Escocia planteó una alternativa radical: el parlamento como árbitro último sobre quién debía gobernar. Nadie había discutido el derecho al trono de Inglaterra del predecesor de Guillermo, Jacobo II, pero su torpe fomento del catolicismo chocó con las profundas **simpatías protestantes de la élite dirigente**, que ejercía su poder mediante el parlamento. Por ello, un consorcio de magnates ingleses de todos los partidos invitó a Guillermo a subir al trono de Inglaterra en lo que, filigranas legales aparte, fue la deposición de un monarca reinante. La consecuencia, conocida como **Revolución Gloriosa de 1688**, significó el triunfo de la autoridad parlamentaria, e Inglaterra salió inmensamente reforzada.

Sin embargo, Luis XIV no obtuvo el resultado esperado de la **guerra de los Nueve Años**, librada principalmente en las fronteras francesas, pero también en Irlanda, América del Norte e India. **Francia** quedó **exhausta económicamente** y al final se vio obligada a acceder a un acuerdo con la Gran Alianza, cuyas **finanzas también estaban agotadas**. En 1697, aunque Luis conservó Alsacia, tuvo que devolver el ducado de Lorena y todo lo que había ganado en la orilla oriental del Rin, además de aceptar a Guillermo como rey de Inglaterra y una serie de fortalezas holandesas a lo largo de su frontera con los Países Bajos españoles.

ISAAC NEWTON (1642–1727)

El físico inglés Isaac Newton publicó en 1687 *Principios matemáticos de la filosofía natural*, donde explicaba la ley de la gravitación universal: el universo se mantiene unido gracias a una fuerza, llamada gravedad o peso, que ejercen todos los cuerpos celestes. La obra de Newton dominó la visión del universo físico durante casi 300 años.

Moneda de la guerra de los Nueve Años
Esta moneda conmemorativa alemana (una forma de propaganda) muestra la destrucción, a manos de los franceses, de Renania-Palatinado durante la guerra de los Nueve Años.

1689

« **HE CONQUISTADO UN IMPERIO**, PERO **NO** HE PODIDO **CONQUISTARME A MÍ MISMO**. »

Pedro I el Grande, reflexión sobre su reinado (1672–1725)

ANTE LA INVASIÓN DE GUILLERMO III EN 1688, el rey Jacobo II de Inglaterra abandonó al ejército que envió para enfrentarse a él y **huyó a la Francia de Luis XIV**. Ya antes Carlos II había aceptado la financiación de Luis XIV, pero lo había ocultado; ahora, Jacobo II contaba con el activo respaldo francés. En marzo de 1689 **desembarcó en Irlanda con un ejército financiado por Francia** y, gracias al apoyo católico, amenazó brevemente al nuevo monarca, holandés y protestante. Sin embargo, la clara victoria de Guillermo en la batalla del Boyne, en 1690, devolvió a Jacobo a Francia tres días después. A partir de entonces, la reclamación jacobita de los Estuardo de sus tronos en Gran Bretaña (*véanse* 1715 y 1744–1747) complicó la diplomacia francesa, aunque no logró cambiar la realidad política.

La Revolución Gloriosa tuvo un breve eco en **Nueva York**, cuando el calvinista alemán **Jacob Leisler destituyó al gobernador real** en mayo de 1689 en nombre de Guillermo III. En enero de 1691 llegó un ejército inglés para obligarle a rendirse, y Leisler acabó siendo ejecutado por traición.

Reinaba en Rusia **Pedro I** (1672–1725) junto con Iván V, su hermanastro discapacitado, desde 1682, pero era su **hermana y regente, Sofía**, quien ejercía el verdadero poder. En 1689, con apoyo de los guardias reales (los *streltsí*), Pedro la derrocó y la obligó a recluirse en un convento, y él e Iván siguieron gobernando como cozares.

La rebelión de Leisler
Jacob Leisler toma juramento a los voluntarios dispuestos a apoyarle para derrocar al gobernador de Nueva York. Leisler tomó Fort James (Manhattan), rebautizado brevemente como Fort William.

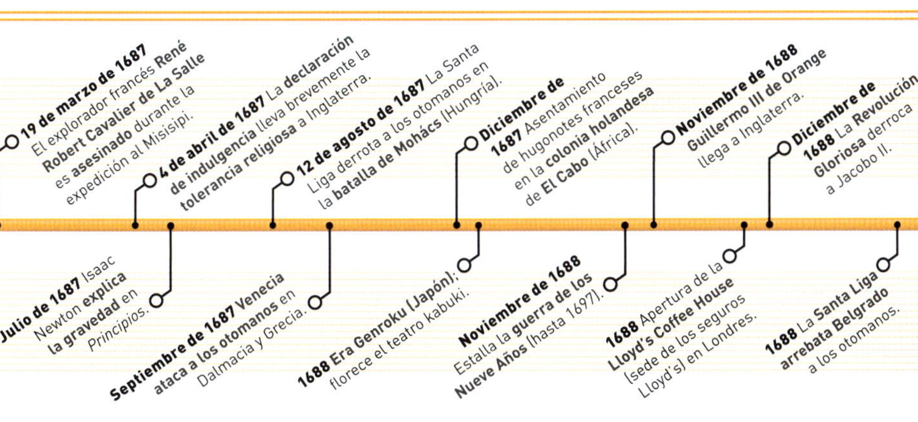

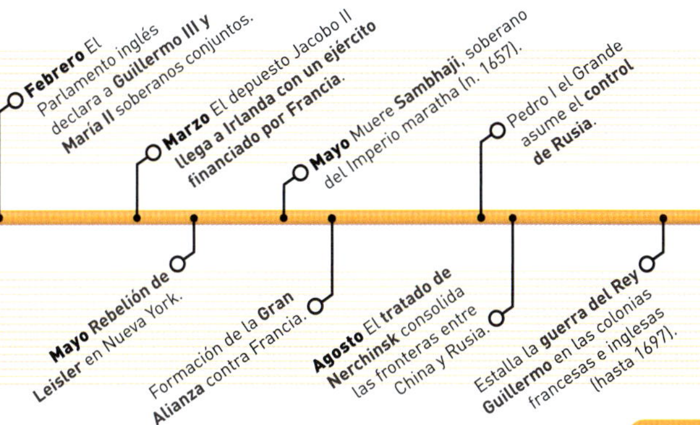

AUGE Y CAÍDA DEL IMPERIO OTOMANO

UNA GRAN POTENCIA QUE DOMINÓ EUROPA Y ORIENTE MEDIO DURANTE CASI 500 AÑOS

El largo declive del Imperio otomano a lo largo del siglo XIX puede hacer olvidar que durante los 450 años posteriores a su aparición, en torno a 1300, no solo fue una de las potencias más dinámicas y sofisticadas del mundo, sino también una de las más grandes, capaz de ensombrecer a sus rivales de Europa y Oriente Medio.

En su máximo esplendor, hacia finales del siglo XVII, el Imperio otomano se extendía desde las puertas de Viena hasta el océano Índico, y de Crimea a Argelia. Aunque el líder mogol Tamerlán había detenido los avances otomanos a inicios del siglo XV, Murat I retomó el programa expansivo tras su coronación en 1413. Su hijo, Mehmet II (r. 1451–1481) llevó la dominación otomana a través de los Balcanes y tomó Constantinopla (Estambul) en una marea conquistadora. Bajo Selim I (r. 1512–1520), el avance de los safavíes fue detenido en Chaldirán y se conquistó gran parte de Oriente Medio y del norte de África. Solimán el Magnífico (r. 1520–1566) amplió los territorios otomanos hasta el interior de Hungría y casi hasta el Atlántico. El Occidente cristiano poco pudo hacer ante tamaña potencia. Inmensamente rico, tecnológicamente avanzado y sostenido por su liderazgo del mundo musulmán, el Imperio otomano parecía irresistible. Su declive tras el fracasado sitio de Viena de 1683 no fue tanto el resultado de sus debilidades internas como de la fuerza creciente de sus rivales europeos.

RIVALES FORMIDABLES

El estado otomano comenzó siendo un pequeño principado fronterizo que atacó al Bizancio cristiano. Durante el siglo XIV, una serie de sultanes guerreros emprendió una serie de conquistas rápidas, sobre todo la de Kosovo en 1389, donde fue derrotado un ejército compuesto de tropas cristianas y balcánicas. Bayaceto I (r. 1389–1402) explotó esta victoria anexionando Bulgaria e invadiendo Hungría. El éxito otomano se basaba en un ejército muy bien entrenado. Sus miembros más temidos, los jenízaros, se reclutaron entre los pueblos conquistados de los Balcanes, que se convirtieron al islam. Además, la artillería otomana de los siglos XV y XVI era una de las más destructoras del mundo.

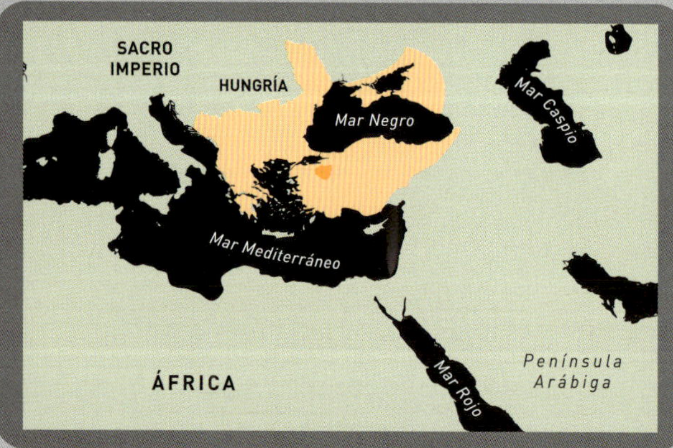

1481 A partir de *c.* 1300 y de un pequeño núcleo, los otomanos conquistaron un enorme territorio, que en 1481 comprendía gran parte de Anatolia y la zona circundante del mar Negro.

CLAVE
- El Imperio en 1300
- El Imperio en 1481

Extensión del Imperio otomano
A principios del siglo XX, el Imperio otomano se había reducido a un tercio del territorio que ocupaba siglos antes. La Turquía actual es solo una pequeña parte.

El Imperio en el siglo XVI
En la cima de su esplendor, el Imperio otomano era más que una potencia terrestre: su flota dominaba todo el Mediterráneo oriental y las rutas marítimas hacia el océano Índico. No solo rivalizaba con las potencias europeas, sino también con las de Oriente Medio: el Egipto mameluco, conquistado en 1517, y la Persia safaví, un estado igualmente dinámico y sofisticado.

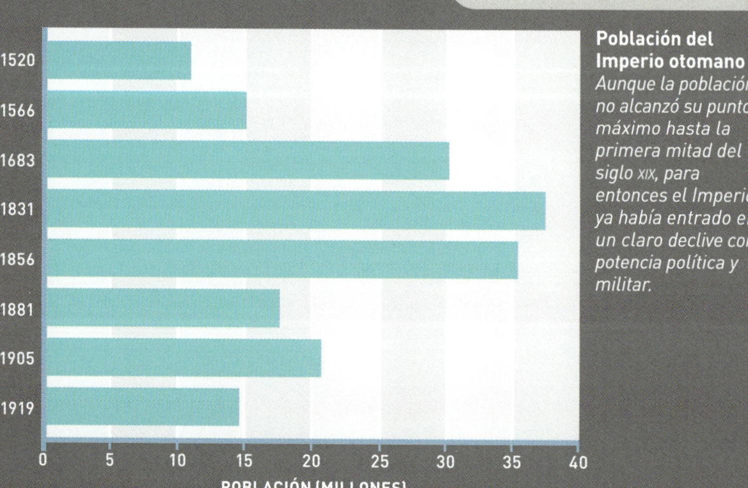

Población del Imperio otomano
Aunque la población no alcanzó su punto máximo hasta la primera mitad del siglo XIX, para entonces el Imperio ya había entrado en un claro declive como potencia política y militar.

« EL TERROR DE NUESTRO MUNDO. »

Atribuido a un embajador europeo (*c.* 1600)

1913 El poder otomano había menguado. Grecia, Serbia, Rumanía y Montenegro ya eran independientes, y otras potencias europeas habían tomado el norte de África y el mar Negro.

1923 Gran Bretaña y Francia se repartieron los territorios árabes otomanos que quedaban. Turquía quedó prácticamente reducida a Anatolia, lo que provocó conflictos con Grecia y Armenia.

1690

Fort William en el siglo XVIII. Se erigió a raíz del traslado de la principal factoría de la Compañía Inglesa de las Indias Orientales de Bengala a Calcuta en 1690.

LA COMPAÑÍA INGLESA DE LAS INDIAS ORIENTALES estaba instalada en Bengala desde principios del siglo XVII. En 1690 instaló una nueva base, **Fort William** (en honor de Guillermo III), en lo que hoy es Calcuta, con el propósito de garantizar **la seguridad de su comercio**. Este fuerte, continuamente ampliado y mejorado, fue crucial para el posterior dominio británico en India.

En 1690, el **filósofo inglés John Locke** (1632–1704) escribió *Ensayo sobre el entendimiento humano*, una obra que le consagró como uno de los **pensadores clave** de la tradición filosófica occidental, sobre todo por afirmar que el conocimiento del mundo procede de la experiencia, y que la base de ese conocimiento es el razonamiento empírico (basado en la observación). Muchas de sus ideas sobre el derecho a la propiedad, la tolerancia religiosa y la monarquía ejercieron una gran influencia en los debates sobre **libertad y razón** en Francia y América del Norte durante el siglo XVIII.

El filósofo John Locke
Locke sostenía que entre un monarca y su pueblo existe un contrato por el que el primero puede ser depuesto si abusa de su poder.

Hacia 1690 se empezó a cultivar en Inglaterra el nabo, una planta de raíz comestible esencial para la revolución agrícola del siglo XVII. Los holandeses habían descubierto la **rotación de cultivos** (cosechas de cereales y leguminosas alternas, en vez de dejar los campos en barbecho) para aprovechar al máximo sus limitadas tierras, lo que no solo mejoraba la fertilidad del suelo, sino que proporcionaba alimento a las ovejas cuyo estiércol aumentaba aún más la productividad.

El día 12 de julio de 1690, la victoria de Guillermo III sobre el depuesto Jacobo II en la **batalla del Boyne** (Irlanda), fue decisiva para el mantenimiento de la **supremacía protestante** establecida por la Revolución Gloriosa en 1688. En Irlanda, la **violencia sectaria** continuó durante siglos.

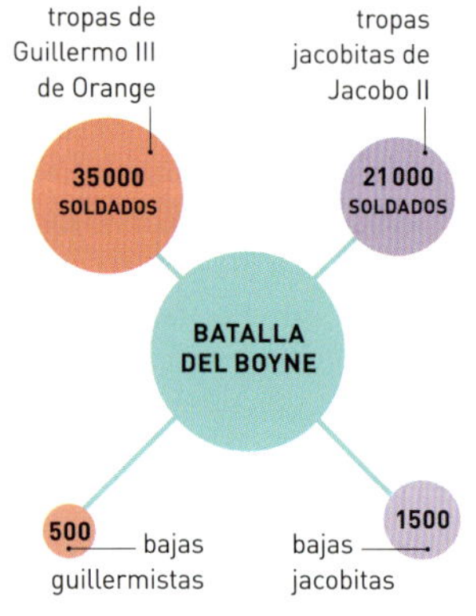

Batalla del Boyne (Irlanda)
La derrota jacobita por el ejército guillermista provocó la «revolución sin sangre» de Guillermo III.

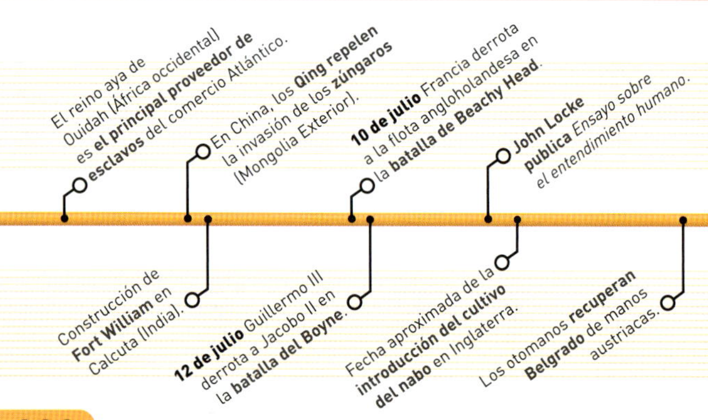

1691–1692

Grabado de la portada de un panfleto que muestra la devastación causada por el terremoto y el tsunami de junio de 1692 en Port Royal (Jamaica).

« LOS **EUROPEOS** SON MUY **TRANQUILOS**; **NO PROVOCAN DISTURBIOS**… **NO PERJUDICAN** A NADIE, **NO COMETEN DELITOS.** **»**

Kangxi, emperador Qing de China, anuncia el edicto de Tolerancia (1692)

LA GUERRA DE LOS NUEVE AÑOS desembocó rápidamente en un empate terrestre que perduró hasta el año 1697, pero en el mar, la Triple Alianza demostró una clara superioridad sobre Francia. La **batalla de La Haya**, que duró seis días entre mayo y junio de 1692, supuso el hundimiento o la destrucción a cañonazos de casi toda la flota francesa y **acabó con las esperanzas de Francia de invadir Inglaterra**.

A las 11.43 del 7 de junio de 1692, un **fuerte terremoto arrasó Port Royal**, capital de la colonia inglesa de Jamaica y uno de sus puertos caribeños más importantes, además de legendario centro de piratería. **Casi toda la ciudad se hundió en el mar**, y tras el tsunami posterior, el número de víctimas mortales ascendió a 5000.

En **Salem** (Massachusetts), a finales de 1691, varias adolescentes sufrieron alucinaciones y afirmaron estar poseídas por el demonio. Esto dio lugar a acusaciones de brujería que en 1692 rozaban ya la histeria. El 10 de junio, una anciana viuda, Bridget Bishop, fue **ahorcada por bruja**; en septiembre, 18 personas más habían sido ejecutadas con la misma acusación y un hombre fue aplastado con piedras hasta morir. Los juicios por brujería ya no eran frecuentes en Inglaterra en esa época, y la **histeria colectiva** de Salem sigue siendo difícil de explicar.

Los misioneros **jesuitas** había llegado a Asia en el siglo XVI. Al contrario que en Japón (*véase* 1597–1599), en China fueron **muy apreciados por una serie de emperadores**, entre otras cosas por su conocimiento de la ciencia occidental. Consiguieron muchas conversiones, y en 1692 el emperador Kangxi emitió un **edicto de tolerancia del cristianismo**.

Juicio de las brujas de Salem
El juicio de George Jacobs fue uno de muchos en una sociedad puritana donde imperaban los celos mutuos y nadie negaba la existencia de Satán.

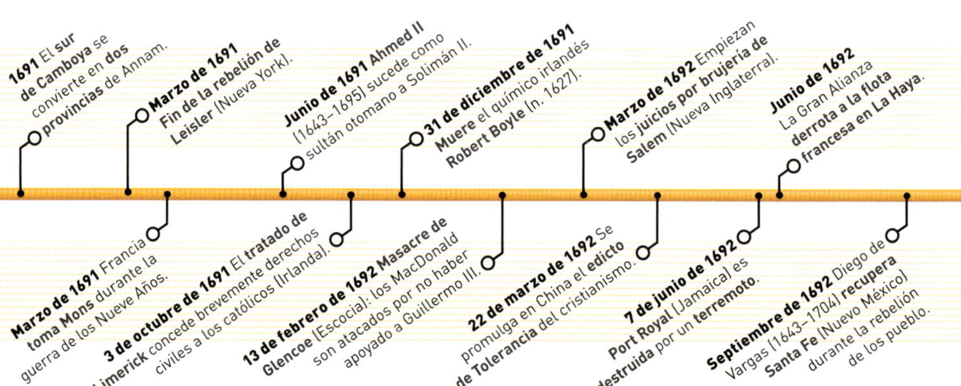

1693

El cráter de la cima del monte Etna, un volcán activo de la costa oriental de Sicilia (Italia), ha vivido varias erupciones destructivas, como la de 1693.

EN EL SUR DE EUROPA, relativamente a salvo de los peores efectos de la pequeña glaciación (*véase* 1683–1684), la erupción del **Etna** (Sicilia) fue un cruel recordatorio del poder de la naturaleza. El **terremoto provocado por la erupción devastó Sicilia** y grandes zonas del sur de Italia y de Malta. En Sicilia perdieron la vida unas 60 000 personas, y la lava y los tsunamis dejaron inhabitables miles de kilómetros cuadrados.

El dodo
Esta ave, incapaz de volar, medía cerca de 1 m de altura y pesaba unos 20 kg. Tenía un pico fuerte y ganchudo, el plumaje grisáceo o marrón, el cuerpo rechoncho y unas alas muy pequeñas.

Durante años después del verano de 1693, varias **hambrunas barrieron Europa occidental**. Solo en Francia murieron unos dos millones de personas. Esta fue una de las **consecuencias más calamitosas de la pequeña glaciación**, cuando unos crudos inviernos dieron paso a veranos tibios y lluviosos durante los cuales las cosechas se pudrían en los campos anegados. Incluso en los años de relativa abundancia, la **gran mayoría de los campesinos europeos**, es decir, la inmensa mayoría de la población del continente, sobrevivía en el mejor de los casos con una dieta básica de raíces, pan y gachas. Si las cosechas fallaban, se morían de hambre. Parecía no haber respuesta a estas calamidades de proporciones casi bíblicas. Al depender casi totalmente de los excedentes de alimentos generados por la población campesina, que soportaba una enorme carga fiscal, incluso un estado tan poderoso como la Francia de finales del siglo XVII apenas podía hacer nada más que sufrir y aceptar su inevitable destino.

En 1598, en la **aislada isla Mauricio** del océano Índico, el almirante holandés Wybrand van Warwijck describió un ave a la que denominó *walghvogel*. Los colonos holandeses posteriores la llamaron *dodaar* en alusión a lo que les parecía un nudo de plumas en la parte posterior, y los marineros portugueses que visitaban la isla le dieron el nombre de *doudo*, que significaba «tonto» o «loco». Hacia 1693, el **dodo, un ave que no volaba**, emparentada con la paloma, **se extinguió**. Fue el primer animal cuya extinción se puede atribuir claramente al hombre: fue víctima de su carácter confiado, de la destrucción de su hábitat de bosque y de la introducción de gatos, ratas, cerdos y perros que lo cazaron hasta acabar con él.

1694–1696

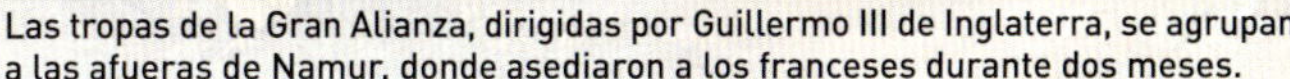

Las tropas de la Gran Alianza, dirigidas por Guillermo III de Inglaterra, se agrupan a las afueras de Namur, donde asediaron a los franceses durante dos meses.

EN JULIO DE 1694, INGLATERRA ENCONTRÓ UNA SOLUCIÓN novedosa a la falta de financiación que afligía a los combatientes de la guerra de los Nueve Años: el **Banco de Inglaterra**, que servía tanto a la Corona como al Gobierno y se basaba en el Banco de Amsterdam, fundado en 1609. Era una empresa privada (hasta 1931) y **prestó inmediatamente al gobierno** 1,2 millones de libras (reunidos por los inversores en doce días) a una tasa de interés anual del 8 % y con una comisión de servicio anual de 4000 libras, a cambio del derecho a imprimir papel moneda. Aunque **generó una deuda nacional**, permitió a Inglaterra financiarse a sí misma, y también a sus aliados, durante la guerra. Es muy posible que este banco fuera el factor más importante de la emergencia posterior de Gran Bretaña como potencia mundial.

El fin del colonialismo europeo de los siglos XVII y XVIII era simplemente enriquecerse. En el Nuevo Mundo, los españoles habían conquistado dos civilizaciones ricas y un suministro de plata aparentemente inagotable. En **Brasil**, los **portugueses** solo habían dado con pueblos indígenas y selvas tropicales, y las plantaciones de caña de azúcar con mano de obra esclava solo daban unos beneficios mínimos. El **descubrimiento de oro** en 1695 en **Minas Gerais**, al sureste, y más tarde de diamantes, transformó el Brasil colonial. Surgieron enormes ciudades sin ley, como Ouro Preto y Diamantia, y la **población de la región** pasó de pequeños grupos diseminados a **320 000 habitantes** (la mitad de ellos esclavos). El resultado fue el casi hundimiento de la industria azucarera, que se quedó sin la mayor parte de su mano de obra.

Uno de los pocos hechos relevantes de la guerra de los Nueve Años fue la **recuperación de la ciudad de Namur por la Gran Alianza** en septiembre de 1695, tras tres años de dominio francés. La pérdida de su plaza más importante en Países Bajos debilitó aún más la posición de Francia, ya a la defensiva.

En 1691, **China inició una expansión** que le llevó a **casi duplicar su territorio** a finales del siglo XVIII. Fue consecuencia de la invasión de Jalja (Mongolia Exterior) en 1690 por los zúngaros nómadas de Asia central, que querían impedir una posible invasión china de la región. La **invasión fracasó**; solo consiguió provocar una serie confusa de campañas lideradas por el soberano zúngaro Galdan, además de una guerra civil. En 1696, el emperador Kangxi, al frente de un ejército compuesto por chinos y por mongoles, aplastó a los zúngaros. Un año más tarde, **Mongolia Exterior** pasó a **formar parte del Imperio chino**.

Rusia lanzó dos campañas entre 1695 y 1696 con el objetivo de tomar la **fortaleza otomana de Azov**. El puerto resultaba crucial para Rusia porque bloqueaba el acceso al mar Negro, lo que en 1687–1689 había contribuido al fracaso de sus campañas en Crimea contra los otomanos. Al final, Pedro I el Grande, único zar de Rusia tras la muerte de su hermanastro Iván, atacó Azov por mar y por tierra, y la tomó en julio de 1696. Rusia comprendió que necesitaba una flota de guerra y emprendió un gigantesco proyecto de construcción naval.

Batalla de Azov
En esta obra de Robert Kerr Porter, Iván I dirige personalmente su flota durante la toma de Azov en 1696.

Pistola caucásica
Pistolas como esta, ricamente decorada, de cañón largo y algo curvada, con empuñadura corta y algo curvada, se utilizaron durante las campañas de Azov.

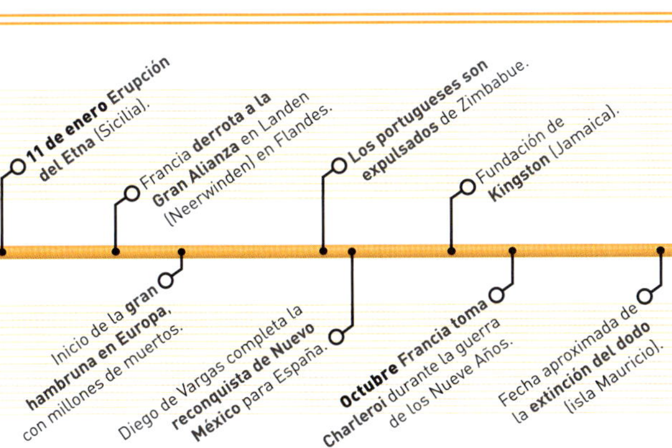

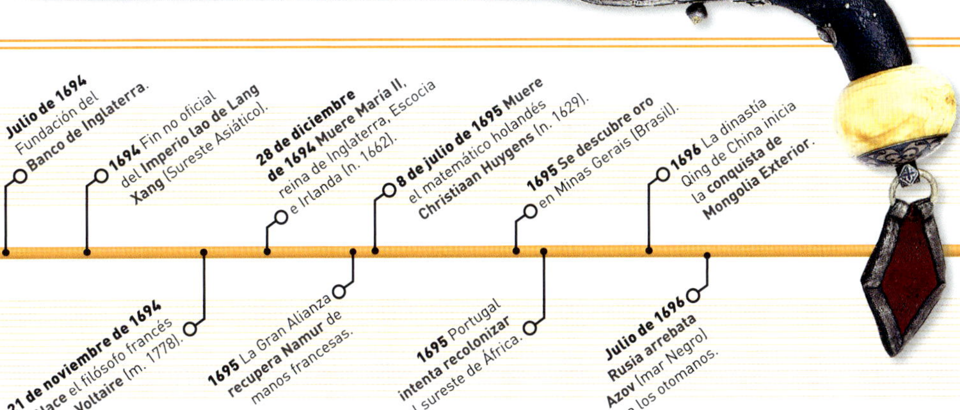

- **11 de enero Erupción del Etna** (Sicilia).
- Inicio de la **gran hambruna en Europa**, con millones de muertos.
- Francia **derrota a la Gran Alianza** en Landen (Neerwinden) en Flandes.
- **Los portugueses son expulsados** de Zimbabue.
- Diego de Vargas completa la **reconquista de Nuevo México** para España.
- Fundación de **Kingston** (Jamaica).
- **Octubre Francia toma Charleroi** durante la guerra de los Nueve Años.
- Fecha aproximada de la **extinción del dodo** (isla Mauricio).
- **Julio de 1694** Fundación del **Banco de Inglaterra**.
- **1694** Fin no oficial del **Imperio lao de Lang Xang** (Sureste Asiático).
- **21 de noviembre de 1694 Nace** el filósofo francés **Voltaire** (m. 1778).
- **28 de diciembre de 1694 Muere María II**, reina de Inglaterra, Escocia e Irlanda (n. 1662).
- **1695** La Gran Alianza **recupera Namur** de manos francesas.
- **8 de julio de 1695 Muere** el matemático holandés **Christiaan Huygens** (n. 1629).
- **1695 Se descubre oro** en Minas Gerais (Brasil).
- **1695** Portugal **intenta recolonizar** el sureste de África.
- **1696** La dinastía Qing de China inicia la **conquista de Mongolia Exterior**.
- **Julio de 1696 Rusia arrebata Azov** (mar Negro) a los otomanos.

1697–1699

« LA **MAYOR COMODIDAD** Y LA **PAZ DURADERA** SE **ALCANZAN** CUANDO SE **ERRADICA EL EGOÍSMO DESDE EL INTERIOR**. »

Gurú Gobind Singh, décimo maestro sij (1697)

LA GUERRA DE LOS NUEVE AÑOS QUE ENFRENTÓ A FRANCIA con la Gran Alianza de Inglaterra, el Sacro Imperio, España y Holanda (Provincias Unidas) **terminó con la firma del tratado de Ryswick** de 1697, que exigía la devolución de todos los territorios conquistados desde 1679.

La derrota otomana en el sitio de Viena de 1683 no solo marcó el inicio del inexorable declive otomano, sino también la **emergencia de la Austria de los Habsburgo** como una gran potencia europea capaz de enfrentarse a Francia, Inglaterra y Holanda. Después de 1683, el ejército imperial austriaco persiguió a los otomanos en su retirada hacia el sur a través de los Balcanes, una persecución que culminó en la **batalla de Zenta** (Serbia) en septiembre de 1697. Lideradas por el príncipe italofrancés Eugenio de Saboya-Carignan (1663–1736), que se estaba convirtiendo rápidamente en uno de los generales más importantes de Europa, las tropas imperiales sorprendieron a los otomanos cuando intentaban cruzar el río Tisa y los masacraron: unos 10 000 perecieron en la batalla o se ahogaron. El **tratado de Karlowitz** de 1699 confirmó las victorias austriacas, inclusive la gradual absorción de Hungría por la Corona austriaca.

Tratado de Ryswick
El tratado se firmó en la Huis ter Nieuwburg, la residencia campestre que Guillermo de Orange poseía en Ryswick (Holanda).

En julio del año 1698, el ingeniero militar inglés **Thomas Savery** (1650–1715) **patentó** «un nuevo invento para bombear agua... de gran utilidad y beneficio para achicar minas». Desde el siglo I d. C. se habían utilizado formas básicas de energía a vapor, aunque nunca se habían traducido en máquinas. La **máquina de vapor** ideada por Savery era muy **sencilla**, tendía a explotar y no podía bombear agua a más de 10 m de profundidad, de modo que su instalación en las minas debía ser subterránea, lo cual resultaba extremadamente peligroso. Años después, en 1721, Thomas Newcomen (1664–1729), socio de Savery, inventó la **máquina atmosférica**, la primera máquina de vapor para la que se encontró un uso comercial viable. Sin embargo, el verdadero potencial del vapor como **motor de la industrialización** no se materializó hasta que el escocés James Watt (1736–1819) inventara en 1769 un condensador independiente y obtuviera la financiación de Matthew Boulton (pp. 274–275).

IMPERIO MOGOL

En 1699, el Imperio mogol alcanzó su cénit tras aplastar una rebelión sij en Punjab. Desde sus orígenes afganos, se había expandido bajo Akbar hasta dominar en el siglo XVII el subcontinente indio, menos el extremo sur. El gobierno de Aurangzeb provocó revueltas y la posterior rebelión de los marathas (*véase* 1720) convirtió a los mogoles en títeres.

CLAVE
- Dominios de Akbar en 1556
- Área controlada por los mogoles a la muerte de Akbar en 1605
- Regiones adquiridas hasta la muerte de Aurangzeb, en 1707

1700

Grabado que muestra a Felipe, duque de Anjou, reconocido como rey Felipe V de España, el 2 de octubre de 1700, a los 16 años de edad.

LA MUERTE DE CARLOS II DE ESPAÑA EN 1700 desató una gran crisis. Carlos no tenía hijos y había designado como sucesor a Felipe de Anjou (1683–1746), nieto de Luis XIV, con la esperanza de que el poder francés preservara el **Imperio español** al estar **gobernado por un Borbón**. El rey Luis XIV aceptó el aumento de prestigio familiar y de la **influencia de Francia** que ello significaba, pero **la oposición** al cambio dinástico y al incremento del poder francés también **creció enormemente**.

Carlos XII (1682–1718) fue coronado rey de Suecia en 1697, a los quince años de edad. La juventud del rey impulsó a los **rivales de Suecia en el Báltico** (Dinamarca, Sajonia, Polonia y, cada vez más, Rusia) a revertir la hegemonía sueca. Sin embargo, en el conflicto que siguió, la **guerra del Norte** de 1700–1721, Carlos, «el meteoro sueco», demostró ser un gran general. En los cuatro meses posteriores a agosto de 1700, derrotó a Dinamarca y luego, en Narva, en la orilla opuesta del Báltico, consiguió **aniquilar al ejército ruso**. En julio de 1701 infligió una derrota igualmente aplastante a un ejército de Polonia y Sajonia en Klissow (Polonia). **Suecia nunca había sido tan poderosa**, y la audaz campaña de Carlos XII fue todo un éxito a pesar de las probabilidades en su contra.

Hacia 1700 comienza un periodo **fundamental de la música europea**. La **música barroca**, en parte cortesana y en parte sacra, evolucionó a partir de la última música renacentista, sobre todo en Italia, hasta alcanzar niveles de polifonía tonal y de **complejidad instrumental** desconocidos hasta ese momento. Se caracterizó por formas musicales nuevas y más elaboradas (concierto, fuga, oratorio, preludio, cantata y ópera), y fue posible gracias a **nuevas versiones de instrumentos ya existentes** (el órgano, el clavicémbalo y, especialmente, el violín), así como al **genio de compositores** como Johann Sebastian Bach (1685–1750) o Georg Friedrich Haendel (1685–1759), Antonio Vivaldi (1678–1741) y Arcangelo Corelli (1653–1713) y al creciente mecenazgo que se dio en los círculos privados y cortesanos.

Violín Stradivarius
Los Stradivarius, fabricados por el italiano Antonio Stradivari, vivieron su edad de oro a principios del siglo XVIII. Eran más grandes que los modelos anteriores.

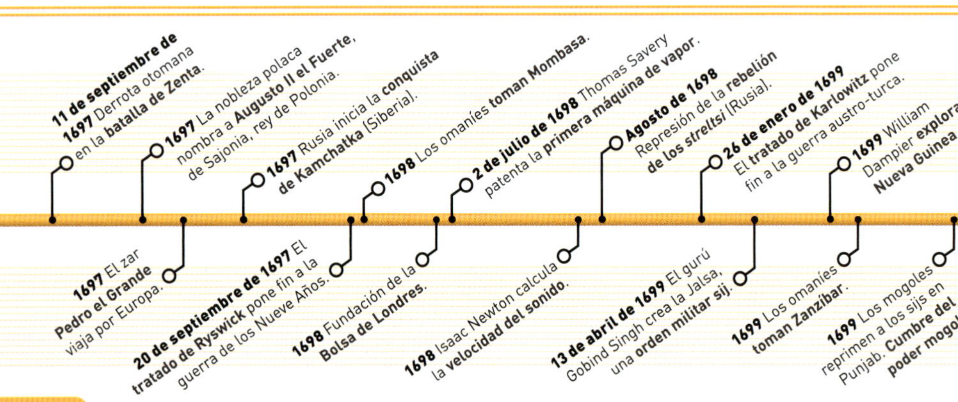

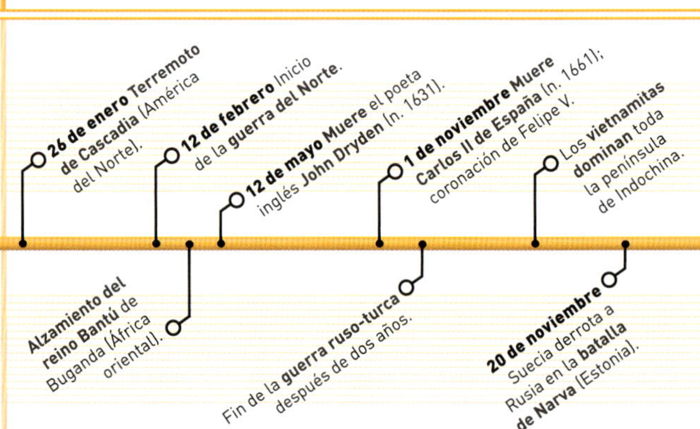

Sembradora de Jethro Tull accionada manualmente. Sembraba las semillas en hileras, una tarea que antes requería varias personas.

EN 1701 EMPEZÓ UNA REVOLUCIÓN AGRÍCOLA cuando el agricultor inglés **Jethro Tull** (1674–1741) inventó la **sembradora** tirada por caballos (pp. 250–251), que permitía un gran ahorro de tiempo y de mano de obra, ya que sembraba gran cantidad de semillas en hileras rectas. Pese a que no se adoptó inmediatamente, acabó haciéndose popular entre los grandes propietarios de tierras y sentó las bases de la **agricultura productiva** moderna.

Apenas concluida la guerra de los Nueve Años, las potencias europeas se enzarzaron en otra guerra tan prolongada como costosa. La inesperada elección de Felipe, duque de Anjou, como Felipe V de España (*véase* 1700) **alteró el equilibrio del poder en toda Europa**. Su abuelo, Luis XIV, no hizo nada por disipar el temor a una alianza militar francoespañola. Asumió operaciones militares en los territorios de Felipe y trasladó tropas a los Países Bajos españoles para defenderlos de los ingleses y los holandeses y luego, con una seguridad renovada en el poder de Francia en Europa, **reconoció a Jacobo III**, hijo del exiliado Jacobo II (1633–1701) como rey de Inglaterra. Inglaterra y Holanda apoyaban la **reclamación austriaca del trono de España** (y a su candidato Carlos, archiduque de Austria), por lo que la oposición militar contra Francia estaba asegurada. La **guerra de Sucesión española** que estalló en 1701 vio el resurgir de una Gran Alianza contra la unificación de los tronos de Francia y España. El conflicto se prolongó hasta 1713–1714 y redefinió el mapa del continente y del mundo.

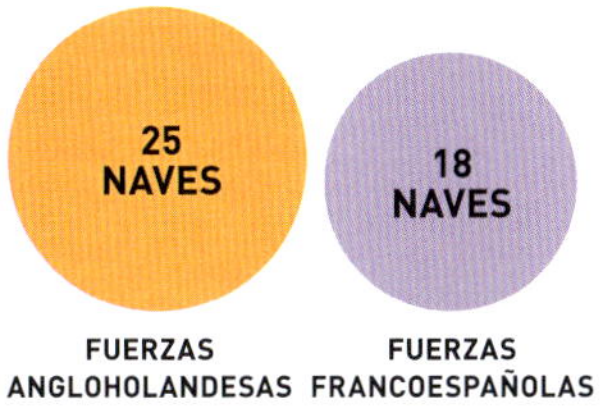

FUERZAS ANGLOHOLANDESAS | FUERZAS FRANCOESPAÑOLAS

Batalla de Rande, octubre de 1702
Fue uno de los primeros combates de la guerra de Sucesión española, librado en la ría de Vigo. Los navíos angloholandeses derrotaron a la flota francoespañola.

Tras las guerras civiles japonesas de los siglos XIV y XV aparecieron los **guerreros samuráis autónomos llamados ronin**, que se rebelaron en 1651 y siguieron **instigando disensiones** hasta el siglo XVIII. En 1701, un señor respetable, Asano Naganori, fue obligado a suicidarse tras haber atacado a un funcionario que le había ofendido. Como venganza, 47 de sus samuráis, convertidos en ronin, mataron al funcionario, acto que se castigaba con la ejecución. Sin embargo, como el confucianismo enseñaba que era honorable vengar la muerte de un señor, se les permitió suicidarse.

Por otro lado, el **reino de Prusia** (precursor del estado alemán) **se proclamó en el año 1701**, cuando Federico I, duque de Prusia y elector de Brandeburgo, fue coronado como primer «rey de Prusia» en el castillo de Konigsberg.

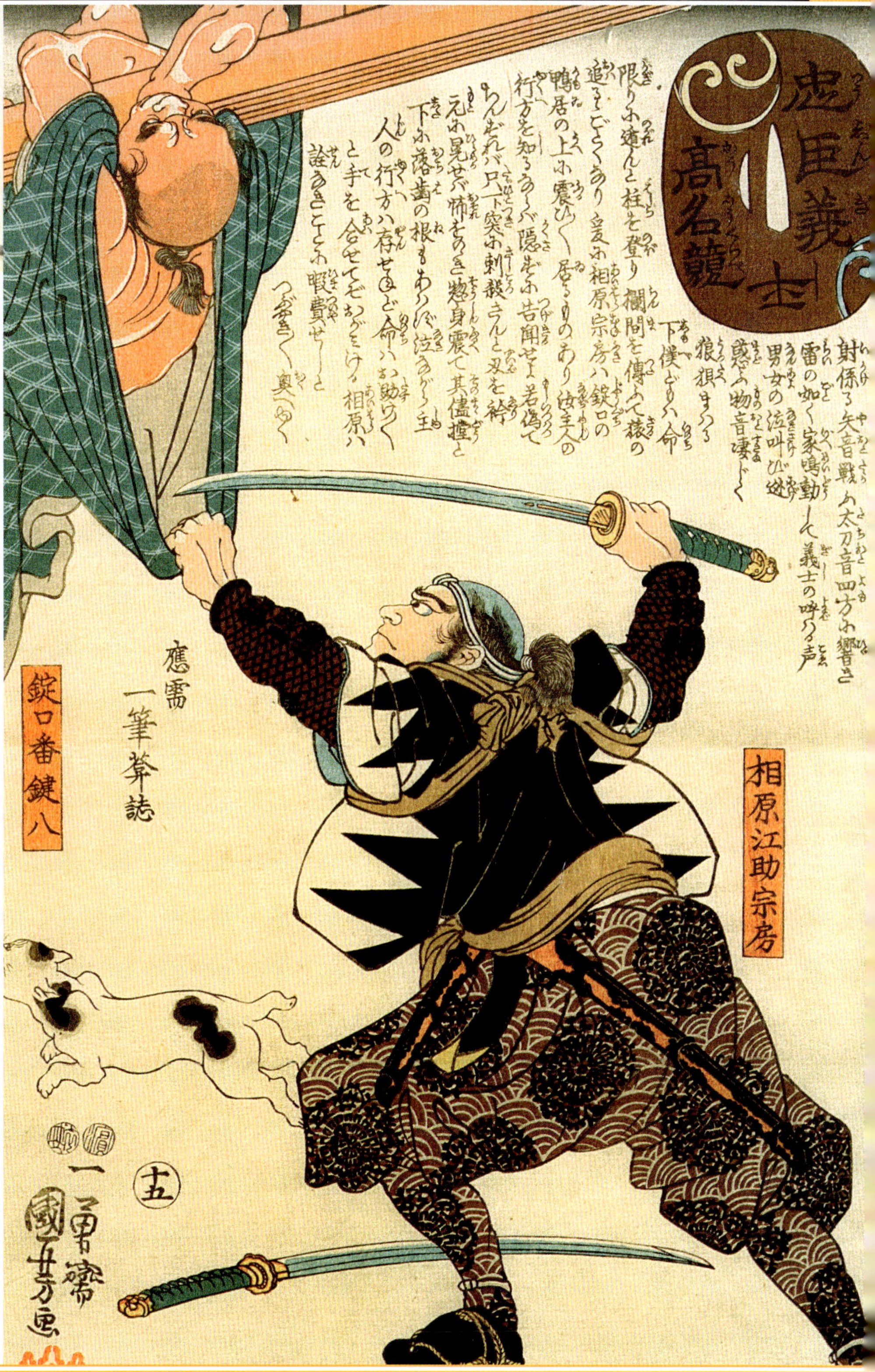

La venganza de los 47 ronin
Grabado en madera coloreado de una serie sobre la rebelión de los 47 ronin, el incidente más famoso del bushido, *el código de honor samurái.*

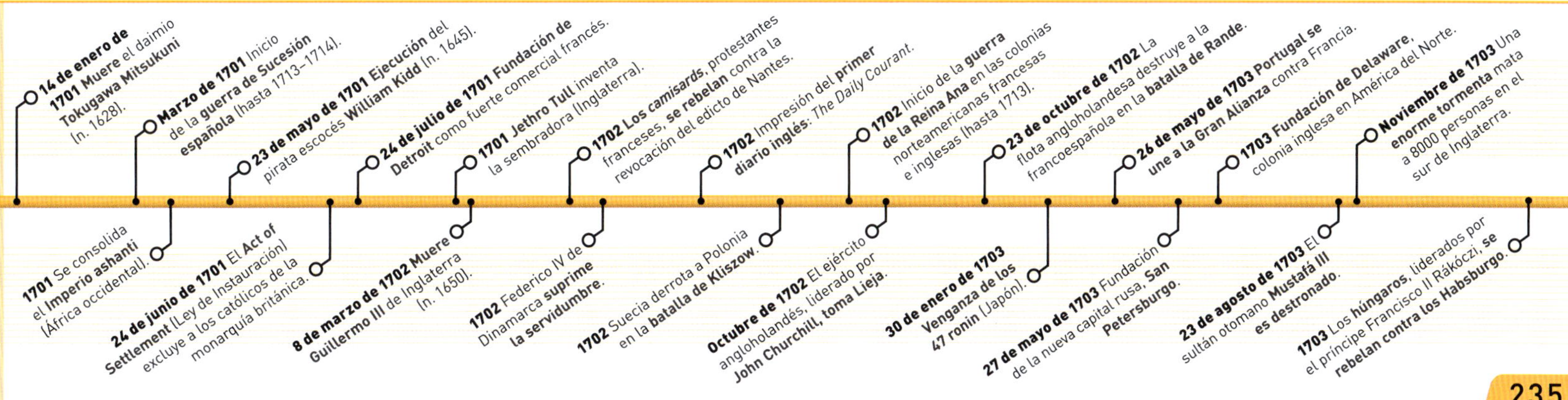

Fotografía del cometa Halley, así llamado en honor al astrónomo británico Edmond Halley, que determinó que regresa periódicamente, cada 76 años.

LA BATALLA DE BLENHEIM, librada en 1704 cerca de la aldea de Blindheim, junto al río Danubio, en Baviera (Alemania), concluyó con la victoria de las tropas del duque de Marlborough y de la Gran Alianza (*véase* 1701), y decantó la **guerra de Sucesión española** a favor de los aliados. La batalla detuvo una marcha francobávara hacia Viena, y la participación de Baviera en el conflicto terminó aquí.

Mientras tanto, las fuerzas angloholandesas tomaban en España el **peñón de Gibraltar**, que finalmente fue cedido a perpetuidad a Gran Bretaña en 1713.

En el sureste de Túnez, se estableció en 1705 la **dinastía husainí,** cuando el sultán otomano reconoció a Husain ibn Alí (1669–1740) como gobernador de la provincia. La dinastía husainí perduró hasta 1957, año en que Túnez obtuvo al fin la independencia.

300

NÚMERO DE **POCUMTUCS** QUE PARTICIPARON EN EL **ATAQUE A DEERFIELD**

En América del Norte, **Deerfield (Massachusetts)** fue el escenario en 1704 de una brutal matanza de colonos ingleses a manos de un grupo de indios y de soldados francocanadienses. También en 1704 aparecía ***The Boston News-Letter***, el primer periódico de América del Norte, con financiación mayoritaria del gobierno británico.

En el año 1706 tuvo lugar el acontecimiento más decisivo de toda la guerra de Sucesión española en el norte de Italia, donde el duque Víctor Amadeo II de Saboya, aliado con Austria y con Gran Bretaña, defendía su territorio de la invasión francesa y del asedio a la capital, Turín. El duque de Saboya y el príncipe Eugenio consiguieron finalmente romper las líneas francesas y diezmaron a su ejército, al que expulsaron del norte de Italia.

El vencedor de Blenheim
El duque de Marlborough (de rojo) a caballo en un tapiz que hoy cuelga en su residencia familiar, el palacio de Blenheim (Inglaterra).

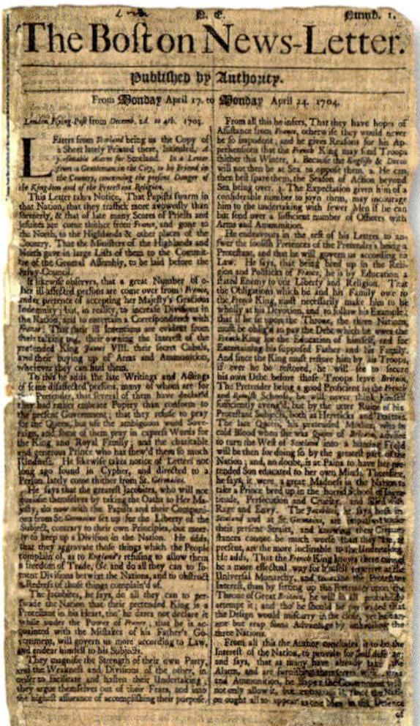
The Boston News-Letter.
Published by Authority.

Noticias de la metrópoli
The Boston News-Letter *era un periódico semanal que ofrecía a los colonos ingleses de América del Norte noticias de la actualidad política y militar de Inglaterra.*

También en 1706, el conquistador español **Juan de Uribarri** reclamó el sureste de Colorado, una región habitada por belicosas tribus indias, y lo anexionó al **Nuevo México español**.

En Inglaterra, **Thomas Newcomen** (1663–1729) y Thomas Savery (*véase* 1698) construyeron en 1704 la **primera máquina de vapor** con piezas móviles. La primera máquina Newcomen funcional se instaló para bombear agua en una mina de Staffordshire en 1712.

El matemático y astrónomo inglés **Edmond Halley** (1656–1742) publicó en 1705 *Sinopsis de la astronomía de los cometas*, obra donde describía con meticulosidad las órbitas parabólicas de 24 cometas. Demostró que tres avistamientos distintos con décadas de diferencia correspondían a un mismo cometa, actualmente conocido como cometa Halley, y calculó que regresa al Sistema Solar cada 76 años.

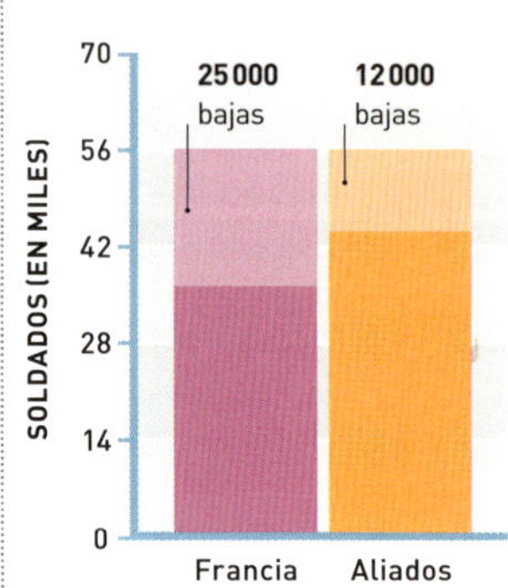

Bajas en la batalla de Blenheim
Lucharon unos 112 000 soldados. Francia tuvo 25 000 bajas, incluidos prisioneros, y Gran Bretaña y sus aliados, casi la mitad.

1707–1708

El emperador mogol Aurangzeb durante una cacería.

ACAECIDA EN 1707, LA MUERTE DE AURANGZEB (n. 1618), el sexto emperador mogol de India, supuso un punto de inflexión y marcó el principio del declive del Imperio mogol. Sus sucesores dilapidaron las riquezas de la dinastía y, además, perdieron el control sobre los gobernadores locales, que comenzaron a levantar sus propios imperios. Aurangzeb había convocado al **gurú sij Gobind Singh**, preocu-

GURÚ GOBIND SINGH
(1666–1708)

Gobind Singh, el décimo y último de los gurú sij, es una figura de enorme relevancia en la historia india. En el año 1699 transformó el sijismo cuando creó una comunidad jalsa (pura), con formación guerrera; en la actualidad, la Jalsa comprende a todos los sijs. Aurangzeb consideró la posibilidad de aliarse con él, pero los rajás de los montes Sivalik continuaban siendo hostiles y finalmente, en 1708, asesinaron al gurú.

29 de febrero de 1704 Matanza de colonos ingleses en Massachusetts y **saqueo de Deerfield**.

13 de agosto de 1704 La Gran Alianza y las tropas francobávaras se enfrentan en la **batalla de Blenheim**.

1704 Thomas Newcomen y Thomas Savery, inventores británicos, construyen la **primera máquina de vapor** con piezas móviles.

1705 El astrónomo británico **Edmond Halley** publica *Sinopsis de la astronomía de los cometas*.

Noviembre de 1705 Finalización del Capitolio de **Williamsburg**, capital de la colonia inglesa de **Virginia**.

17 de enero de 1706 Nace **Benjamin Franklin** (m. 1790), escritor y científico y padre fundador de EE.UU.

7 de septiembre de 1706 Las tropas austriacas y saboyanas derrotan a Francia en la **batalla de Turín**.

1706 El Nuevo México español reclama el **sureste de Colorado**.

17 de marzo de 1707 Muere el emperador mogol **Aurangzeb** (n. 1618).

25 de abril de 1707 Derrota de la Gran Alianza en **Almansa (España)**.

1 de mayo de 1707 Entran en vigor las Leyes de Unión, por las que se unen **Escocia** e **Inglaterra**.

1709–1710

Detalle de una pintura de Ignace Jacques Parrocel donde las tropas del príncipe Eugenio de Saboya se enfrentan a los franceses en la batalla de Malplaquet.

48
AÑOS DE REINADO

27
AÑOS DE GUERRA

El reinado de Aurangzeb
El emperador Aurangzeb reinó durante 48 largos años, desde el año 1658 hasta su muerte en 1707, pero durante 27 de ellos estuvo en guerra con los maratha.

pado por su creciente poder, pero murió antes de poder reunirse con él. Gobind Singh entabló amistad con el nuevo emperador, Bahadur Sah I (r. 1707–1712), pero fue asesinado en 1708 por orden de un líder rival, el nabab Wazir Kan.

Lejos de India, en el continente europeo, **Inglaterra y Escocia** se unieron oficialmente como reino de Gran Bretaña por las **Leyes de Unión** de 1707. A partir de entonces, ambos reinos han sido siempre gobernados por un único monarca y un único parlamento, con sede en Londres.

Gran Bretaña, todavía inmersa en la guerra de Sucesión española, se unió a las fuerzas holandesas con el objetivo de arrebatar **Menorca** y **Sicilia** a Francia en 1708 y usarlas como bases militares. También fue en 1708 cuando los colonos británicos perdieron el control de la costa este canadiense después de su derrota frente a los franceses en **San Juan de Terranova**.

LA BATALLA DE MALPLAQUET, que tuvo lugar en 1709, fue la más sangrienta de todas las libradas en la **guerra de Sucesión española** (*véase* 1701) y probablemente también de todo el siglo XVIII. Las fuerzas de la Gran Alianza, lideradas por el duque de Marlborough, atacaron a las tropas francesas en Malplaquet (Francia) al suroeste de la fortaleza francesa de **Mons**, situada en la frontera belga actual. Durante la contienda, los aliados perdieron a más de 21 000 hombres para hacerse con el campo de batalla, el doble que los franceses, pero estos se retiraron y siguieron constituyendo una amenaza.

Mientras tanto, en la **guerra del Norte** (1700–1721), que se libraba entre los rusos y sus vecinos occidentales (*véase* 1700), el rey Carlos XII de Suecia dirigía a sus tropas en una marcha hacia Rusia. El ejército sueco, compuesto por 17 000 hombres, acometió contra la plaza fuerte de **Poltava**, situada en Ucrania, en julio del año 1709 y se enfrentó a los 80 000 soldados de Pedro el Grande, que lo barrió del mapa. Exiliado en Moldavia, el rey sueco logró persuadir al **Imperio otomano** para que declarase la guerra a Rusia en 1710, pero Pedro I el Grande (1672–1725) consiguió la paz en 1711.

17000 SOLDADOS SUECOS

80000 SOLDADOS RUSOS

BATALLA DE POLTAVA

10000 soldados suecos muertos/capturados

1300 soldados rusos muertos

Soldados de la batalla de Poltava
Durante la batalla de Poltava, el 60% de los soldados suecos murieron o fueron capturados; menos del 2% de los rusos corrieron la misma suerte.

En 1709, los gobernantes persas safavíes del suroeste de **Afganistán** se vieron superados por el **alzamiento** organizado por **Mir Wais Hotak** (1673–1715), jefe tribal de los pastunes gilzai y fundador de la dinastía hotaki (de 1709 a 1738). Enfurecidos por la crueldad safaví y por los intentos de convertirlos del islam suní al chií, los afganos decidieron acabar con la vida de su gobernador safaví, Gurgin Kan, y de muchos persas.

Mientras tanto, en Inglaterra se estaba gestando la revolución industrial. En 1709, **Abraham Darby** (1678–1717), un herrero cuáquero que **fundía hierro con carbón vegetal** fue el primero en producir arrabio de alta calidad con **coque**. Gracias al nuevo proceso, la fundición del hierro ya no dependía de la madera, y el coque, un derivado del carbón, era mucho más abundante. En 1710, Alemania transformó otra industria. Ese año, la fábrica de **Meissen**, ubicada muy cerca de Dresde, produjo la primera **porcelana europea**.

Al norte de Alemania, **Dinamarca** comenzaba a interesarse por la guerra del Norte que mantenía enfrentadas a Suecia y Rusia. Ya había perdido las provincias de **Escania, Halland y Blekinge** ante Suecia en 1700, pero todavía tenía esperanzas de recuperarlas. Asumió que Suecia estaría debilitada tras la batalla de Poltava y buscó un pretexto para declararle la guerra el 18 de octubre de 1709. En noviembre, un gran ejército danés entró en Suecia sin encontrar apenas resistencia; sin embargo, en febrero de 1710 Suecia ya había conseguido reunir a 16 000 hombres y derrotó a los daneses en la **batalla de Helsingborg**. Dinamarca sufrió 7500 bajas y se vio obligada a abandonar toda esperanza de recuperar sus antiguos territorios.

También en 1710, los colonos franceses de la región de **Acadia** (actual Nueva Escocia), situada en la costa este de Canadá, sufrieron un tercer, y esta vez exitoso, intento por parte de los británicos de tomar **Port Royal**. La victoria proporcionó a Gran Bretaña su primera posesión colonial francesa y le ayudó a dificultar la colonización francesa de Canadá durante los años siguientes.

Porcelana chinesca alemana
Tanto la forma como los motivos ornamentales de este jarrón de porcelana de Meissen del siglo XVIII, profusamente decorado con pan de oro, están inspirados en la porcelana china importada.

29 de julio–31 de agosto de 1707 La Gran Alianza vence a la flota francesa en la **batalla de Toulon**.

1708 Británicos y holandeses arrebatan **Menorca y Sicilia** a Francia.

7 de octubre de 1708 **Asesinato** del gurú sij **Gobind Singh**.

1709 El herrero británico Abraham Darby es el primero en usar coque para producir **arrabio**.

8 de julio de 1709 Rusia vence al ejército de Carlos XII de Suecia en la **batalla de Poltava**.

1709 El líder afgano **Mir Wais Hotak** organiza un **alzamiento** contra los gobernantes persas safavíes.

11 de septiembre de 1709 La Gran Alianza vence a los franceses en la **batalla de Malplaquet**, pero sufre numerosas bajas.

1710 La fábrica alemana de **Meissen** produce la primera **porcelana** europea.

28 de febrero de 1710 Suecia vence a los 14 000 invasores daneses en la **batalla de Helsingborg**.

5–13 de octubre de 1710 Los británicos toman Port Royal, en Acadia (Canadá), y llaman **Nueva Escocia** a la provincia.

20 de noviembre de 1710 El Imperio otomano declara la **guerra a Rusia**, instigado por Carlos XII de Suecia.

HISTORIA DE LA NAVEGACIÓN

LA AVENTURA DE EXPLORAR Y CARTOGRAFIAR LOS OCÉANOS Y LOS CONTINENTES DEL MUNDO

Cronómetro H1

Posiblemente lo más sorprendente de la historia de la navegación es que, hasta el siglo XVIII, los exploradores y los navegantes no pudieran determinar su posición exacta. Hoy, los avances de las técnicas de navegación permiten precisar la posición con un error de metros.

El único medio del que disponían los primeros navegantes para orientarse era la vista y dependían de puntos de referencia costeros y de las posiciones del Sol, la Luna y las estrellas para poder calcular la distancia, así como de sencillos instrumentos de medición de profundidad, como unas cuerdas con pesos, para impedir que los barcos encallaran. La aparición de diversos instrumentos, como la brújula magnética, el astrolabio y el sextante, permitió calcular la dirección y la latitud con una precisión razonable (midiendo el ángulo del Sol o de una estrella sobre el horizonte), pero determinar la longitud continuaba siendo un problema.

John Harrison
Este fabricante de relojes inglés fue el primero en crear mecanismos que permitían calcular la longitud con precisión.

NAVEGACIÓN PRECISA

La longitud se mide comparando la hora local con la «universal» (la hora en un lugar acordado, que hoy es Greenwich, en Inglaterra). Cada hora de diferencia equivale a 15° de longitud. Por lo tanto, calcular la longitud requiere instrumentos de medición del tiempo precisos, que no existieron hasta que John Harrison inventó su cronómetro en el siglo XVIII. Hasta el siglo XX no hubo grandes avances en navegación: la brújula giroscópica, el radar y, a partir de la década de 1990, el GPS (Sistema de Posicionamiento Global).

LATITUD Y LONGITUD

LATITUD
Las líneas de latitud (paralelos) son horizontales y se miden en grados al norte o al sur del ecuador. Cada grado equivale a unos 111 km.

línea de latitud

LONGITUD
Las líneas de longitud (meridianos) son verticales y se miden en grados al este o al oeste de Greenwich (en Inglaterra). Su separación máxima se da en el ecuador y se unen en los polos.

línea de longitud

> « UNO DE LOS **MECANISMOS MÁS EXQUISITOS** DE LA HISTORIA. »

William Hogarth, artista inglés, sobre el cronómetro H1 de Harrison, en *Análisis de la belleza* (1753)

manivela para dar cuerda

3000–1500 a. C.
Primeras sondas
Los egipcios usaban pértigas para medir la profundidad del agua y calcular su posición respecto a puntos de referencia costeros.

Barco de la XII dinastía

C. 150 d. C.
Mapas de Tolomeo
Claudio Tolomeo elaboró sus mapas por medio de cuadrícula que influyó en las cartas náuticas hasta el siglo XVII.

Mapa de Tolomeo

Siglo XI
Navegación a estima
Se utilizan relojes de arena para navegar a estima: medir el tiempo y la velocidad del desplazamiento permite calcular la posición del barco.

Reloj de arena

C. 1100
La brújula
Los chinos fueron los primeros en utilizar una brújula magnética (que señala el norte y el sur con una aguja imantada) para la navegación.

Brújula de marinero

1300–1500
Cartas náuticas
Los portulanos o cartas de marear de las costas del mar Mediterráneo permiten navegar de puerto a puerto orientándose con brújula.

Portulano

C. 1480
El astrolabio
Se empieza a usar el astrolabio para estimar la latitud midiendo el ángulo del Sol o de otra estrella concreta sobre el horizonte.

Astrolabio marinero

segundero

minutero

aguja del calendario, que indica el día del mes

horario

Cronómetro H1 de Harrison
El H1 fue el primer «reloj marítimo» de John Harrison, con el que quiso resolver el problema del cálculo de la longitud: cómo medir el tiempo en el mar con la precisión suficiente. Sin embargo, el H1 era demasiado grande, problema que Harrison resolvió en 1759, con el cronómetro H4.

1735–1759
El cronómetro marino
John Harrison construye el primer cronómetro marino (el H1) en 1735 y sigue realizando versiones mejoradas que culminan en el H4, de 1759.

1907
Brújula giroscópica
El estadounidense Elmer Sperry inventa la brújula giroscópica, un importante avance para la navegación porque siempre apunta al norte verdadero y nunca se desvía.

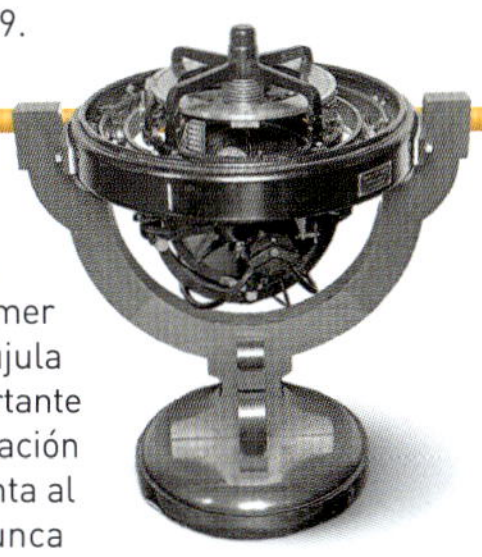

Brújula de barco

Décadas de 1930 y 1940
Radar
La invención del radar hace posible determinar la posición de un objeto aunque no sea visible.

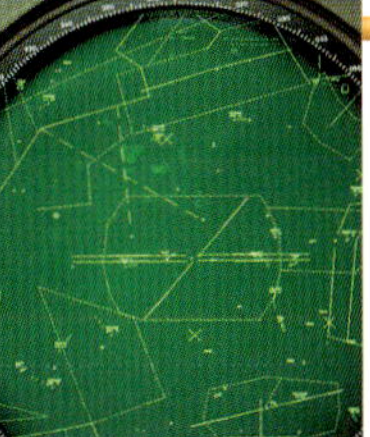

Pantalla de radar

Finales del siglo XX
Sistemas de posicionamiento global
La introducción de los GPS por satélite permite marcar posiciones y navegar hacia ellas con una precisión de metros.

Navegador GPS

1711

La reconstruida catedral de San Pablo dominó la orilla izquierda del Támesis y fue el edificio más alto de Londres hasta 1962.

EN AMÉRICA, UNA CONSECUENCIA DE LA GUERRA DE SUCESIÓN ESPAÑOLA (*véase* 1701–1703) fue el ataque perpetrado por una escuadra francesa a **Río de Janeiro**, en aquel momento posesión de Portugal, que inhabilitó los barcos anclados en el puerto y obligó a la ciudad a pagar un rescate para evitar que sus defensas fueran destruidas. El ánimo de los franceses, en horas bajas desde su retirada en la batalla de Malplaquet (*véase* 1709), se recuperó tras esta prueba de su potencia naval.

En **Carolina del Norte** estalló la **guerra de los tuscarora** contra los colonos británicos, alemanes y holandeses. Los colonos y los indios tuscarora del norte comenzaron a secuestrar y a vender como esclavos a los tuscarora del sur con el objetivo de apropiarse de sus tierras. Los tuscarora del sur respondieron en septiembre con ataques generalizados contra los asentamientos, y cientos de colonos perdieron la vida.

En el continente asiático, los gobernantes persas safavíes de **Afganistán** occidental respondieron al alzamiento organizado por Mir Wais Hotak (*véase* 1709–1710), pero tanto el ejército safaví como Josru Kan, su líder, fueron finalmente aniquilados y la **independencia afgana** quedó asegurada.

Por último, en diciembre de 1711 finalizó la construcción de la **catedral de San Pablo de Londres**. Diseñada por Christopher Wren, se trataba del cuarto templo erigido en el mismo emplazamiento, después de que el anterior quedara gravemente dañado debido al gran incendio de Londres del año 1666. El edificio estaba coronado por la **primera cúpula triple del mundo**: un cascarón exterior ligero con estructura de madera, sostenido por un cono de ladrillo oculto y, finalmente, el cascarón de la bóveda visible desde el interior.

Pérdidas en Río de Janeiro
El ataque naval francés cogió por sorpresa a las naves portuguesas, que intentaron escapar. Tres de ellas encallaron y una fue destruida por la propia tripulación.

Ataque a Río de Janeiro
Los barcos del corsario francés René Duguay-Trouin entran en el puerto de Río de Janeiro en busca de honor para Francia y de botín.

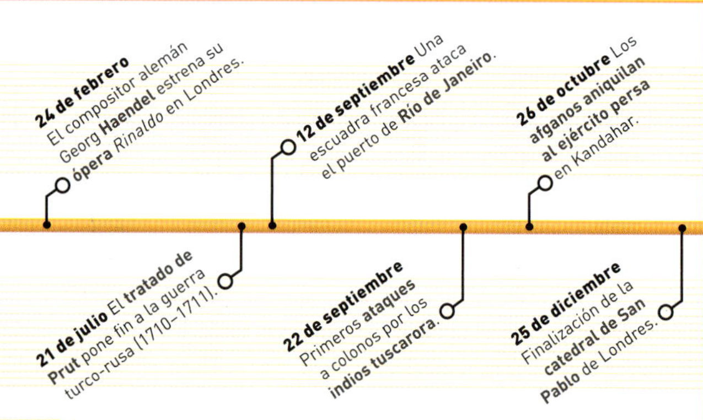

1712–1714

« LO QUE ESTÁ BIEN ESTÁ BIEN, AUNQUE TODOS SE OPONGAN; Y LO QUE ESTÁ MAL ESTÁ MAL, AUNQUE TODOS LO APOYEN. »

William Penn, fundador de Pensilvania (1681)

El fin de la guerra
Este grabado del almanaque real francés de 1714 muestra a los signatarios del tratado de Utrecht, que puso fin a la guerra de Sucesión española.

1:9 **Epidemia de viruela**
La terrible epidemia de viruela que asoló El Cabo, en el sur de África, diezmó a la población koisan nativa: murieron nueve personas por cada superviviente.

EL 7 DE JUNIO DE 1712, PENSILVANIA liberó a todos los esclavos ante la presión de la población cuáquera, en un primer paso hacia la abolición de la esclavitud. Sin embargo, la reina Ana revocó la decisión al año siguiente. El cuáquero William Penn (1644–1718), fundador del estado y tratante de esclavos, tampoco se oponía a la esclavitud.

En la región **sudafricana de El Cabo**, un grupo de marineros infectados de **viruela** diezmó involuntariamente a los **pueblos koisan** nativos en 1713. La enfermedad se propagó con rapidez entre las lavanderas, contagiadas por la ropa sucia de los marineros, y ellas contagiaron al resto de la población, que no estaba inmunizada y carecía

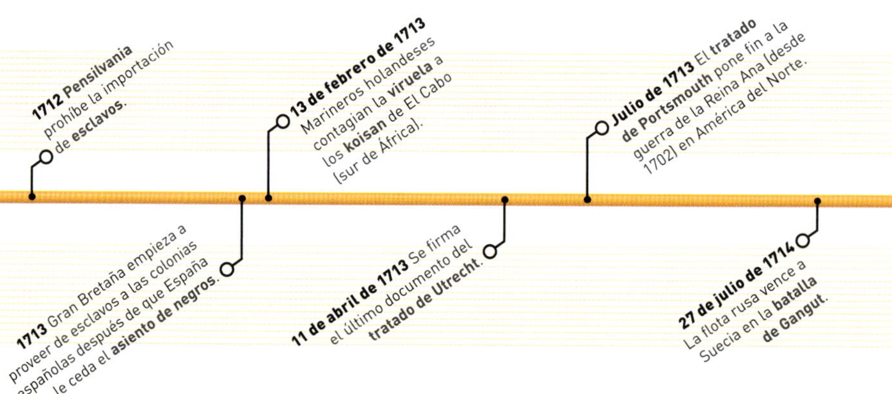

William Penn, líder cuáquero y colono inglés.

La bandera del pirata inglés Edward Teach, conocido como Barbanegra, se hizo famosa en el Caribe entre 1717 y 1718, año de su muerte.

« UNA **FIGURA** TAL QUE **LA IMAGINACIÓN NO BASTA** PARA PENSAR EN UNA **FURIA INFERNAL** MÁS **ESPANTOSA**. »

Capitán Charles Johnson, descripción de Edward Teach en *A General History of the Robberies and Murders of the most notorious Pyrates* (1724)

de medicamentos. La epidemia mató al 90% de los koi del suroeste de El Cabo. Los supervivientes que huyeron hacia el interior fueron asesinados por tribus vecinas para evitar el contagio.

En 1713 se **firmó el tratado de Utrecht** que, junto con el **tratado de Rastadt** de 1714, puso **fin a la guerra de Sucesión española**. El tratado de Utrecht (en realidad, una serie de tratados) se basaba en el principio del equilibrio de poder entre Francia, España y sus vecinos, a fin de impedir que ningún estado pudiera dominar Europa. Las líneas sucesorias de los dos países se separaron para que ningún español pudiera reclamar el trono francés, y viceversa. Saboya ganó Sicilia; Austria recibió los Países Bajos españoles el ducado de Milán y el reino de Nápoles, y Gran Bretaña obtuvo Terranova (Nueva Escocia) y Gibraltar. Además, el **asiento de negros** autorizaba a Gran Bretaña a suministrar esclavos y mercancías a las colonias españolas durante 30 años.

En Gran Bretaña, tras la muerte de la reina Ana (m. 1714), **Jorge I** (1660–1727) se convirtió en el **primer monarca** de la **casa de Hanover** alemana en reinar sobre **Gran Bretaña e Irlanda**, poniendo fin así al reinado de los Estuardo, que habían gobernado Escocia desde 1371 y Gran Bretaña e Irlanda desde 1603.

En 1714, los **otomanos declararon la guerra a la República de Venecia**. Fue el último conflicto entre las dos potencias y terminó cuatro años después, en 1718, con una **victoria otomana** que supuso para Venecia la pérdida del Peloponeso, su mayor posesión en Grecia.

LAS CONSTANTES GUERRAS ENTRE las principales potencias europeas a finales del siglo XVII e inicios del XVIII generaron una profunda sensación de **ausencia de ley**, sobre todo en aquellas regiones donde se libraba una lucha encarnizada por hacerse con el poder colonial. Como las flotas oficiales estaban en guerra, parte de la tarea del mantenimiento del orden en las nuevas colonias recayó en los **corsarios**, que para muchos apenas se diferenciaban de los **piratas**. Uno de los más famosos, el inglés Edward Teach, popularmente conocido como **Barbanegra** (c. 1680–1718), se convirtió en objetivo de las autoridades tras asumir el mando de su propio barco en 1717. Fue asesinado en 1718.

En **América del Norte**, la firma del tratado de Utrecht (*véase* 1713) no había conseguido poner fin a las hostilidades entre las potencias coloniales europeas que, a su vez, intentaban dominar a las tribus indias rivales. En el año 1716, en un intento por detener la expansión francesa hacia el oeste desde Luisiana, los **españoles entraron en el este de Texas**, donde fundaron varias misiones y, en 1718, la ciudad de San Antonio. Esta última se convirtió en objetivo de los apaches, mientras que los españoles alentaron los ataques de los indios yamasee y de otras tribus a cientos de colonos británicos en Carolina del Sur, en un conflicto conocido como **guerra de los yamasee** (1715–1717).

« **NO SE PERMITE A LOS CATÓLICOS CHINOS VENERAR** EN SUS TEMPLOS FAMILIARES **A SUS ANTEPASADOS**. »

Papa Clemente XI, bula *Ex illa die* (1715)

Esmalte Qing
Este elefante decorativo con dos jarrones en miniatura ilustra el alto grado de sofisticación que alcanzó el esmalte cloisonné *durante la dinastía Qing.*

En Asia, los **mongoles zúngaros** invadieron Mongolia Exterior y Tíbet en 1717, **saquearon Lhasa**, la capital tibetana, y profanaron la tumba del quinto dalai lama. Tíbet reclamó ayuda al emperador chino Kangxi (1654–1722). Los zúngaros derrotaron a un ejército invasor Qing en 1718, y el Imperio Qing tardó tres años en liberar Lhasa (*véase* 1720).

Mientras tanto, en China, los **misioneros jesuitas** estaban en grave peligro. El emperador Kangxi, impresionado por sus servicios, había garantizado su seguridad con el edicto de Tolerancia (*véase* 1692), pero en 1715, cuando el papa Clemente XI emitió una bula que zanjaba la **controversia de los ritos chinos** condenando el culto a los antepasados, respondió revocando el edicto y prohibiendo las misiones jesuitas en China.

En Europa, **Luis XIV** de Francia **falleció en 1715** dejando como heredero a su nieto Luis XV, menor de edad. Contraviniendo los términos del tratado de Utrecht, Felipe V de España reclamó el trono de Francia si el niño moría. Para obligar a Felipe a abandonar sus ambiciones expansionistas, Holanda (Provincias Unidas), Francia y Gran Bretaña firmaron en 1717 una **Triple Alianza** que al año siguiente se convirtió en Cuádruple Alianza tras la adhesión de Austria (*véase* 1718–1719).

En Gran Bretaña, la ira que la instauración en el trono de un Hanover (*véase* 1714) había despertado en los jacobitas, partidarios del depuesto rey Estuardo Jacobo VII de Escocia y II de Inglaterra, hizo estallar la **primera rebelión jacobita**. Sobreestimando el apoyo con que contaban en Inglaterra, los jacobitas enviaron un ejército de unos 4000 hombres (casi todos escoceses) a Londres, pero en noviembre fueron brutalmente aplastados por las tropas hanoverianas durante la **batalla de Preston**. Mientras sus soldados repelían la amenaza a su reino en el norte, la vida londinense de Jorge I, el rey Hanover, no parecía verse afectada: el compositor barroco alemán **Georg Friedrich Haendel** (1685–1759), que se había establecido en Londres en 1712, ofreció varias interpretaciones de su *Música acuática* para el monarca y su corte.

LA MÚSICA BARROCA

El barroco musical europeo, que se inició hacia 1600 y perduró hasta cerca de 1750, evolucionó a partir de las misas y los madrigales del Renacimiento. Enfatizaba el ritmo, el contrapunto y la expresión de la emoción, además de conceder mayor relevancia a los solos vocales e instrumentales. También supuso el surgimiento de la ópera, cuyos primeros exponentes fueron Cavalli y Monteverdi. Algunos de los compositores barrocos más notables son Allegri y Peri (barroco temprano); Lully, Pachelbel y Purcell (barroco intermedio); y Bach, Haendel, Vivaldi y Telemann (barroco tardío).

LAÚD BARROCO

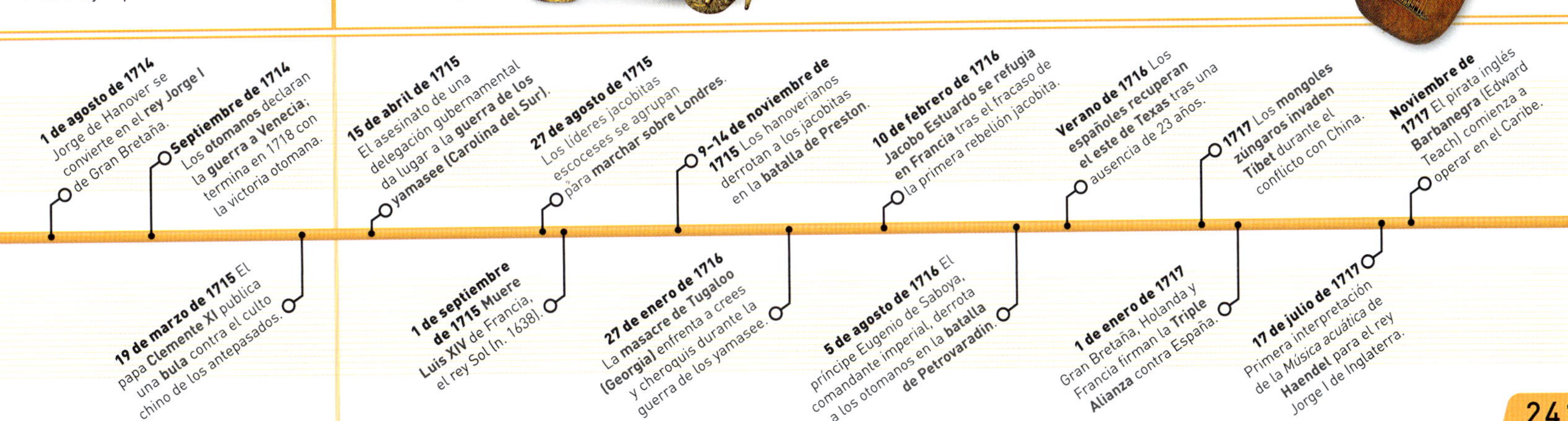

1718–1719

La flota del almirante sir George Byng en el estrecho de Messina antes de la batalla del Cabo Passaro, en una pintura de Richard Vale.

EL TRATADO DE UTRECHT (*véase* 1713) había cedido Sicilia a Saboya, pero el rey Felipe V de España (1683–1746) ignoró el tratado en 1717 y, después de tomar Cerdeña, ordenó la invasión de Sicilia. Se enfrentaba a la **Triple Alianza** (*véase* 1717) de Gran Bretaña, Francia y Holanda (Provincias Unidas), a la que se incorporó Austria el 2 de agosto de 1718 para crear una **Cuádruple Alianza**. El 21 de julio, Austria, bajo el emperador del Sacro Imperio Carlos VI (1684–1740), había firmado el **tratado de Passarowitz**, que supuso el final de la guerra austro-turca (1716–1718). Esto dejó libres a las tropas del emperador para combatir contra España, y la **guerra de la Cuádruple Alianza** se declaró el 17 de diciembre de 1718.

Anteriormente la Triple Alianza había lanzado un ultimátum a las fuerzas invasoras de Felipe V para que se rindieran. Capitaneada por sir George Byng, la flota inglesa, se enfrentó a la española (a la que no se informó del ultimátum) en la **batalla del Cabo Passaro**, el 11 de agosto de 1718. Los navíos españoles más grandes fueron apresados. Más adelante, ese mismo año, un ejército austriaco llegó a Messina (Sicilia) y expulsó a las tropas españolas, pero fue derrotado el 15 de octubre en la **batalla de Milazzo**.

En 1719, la **Cuádruple Alianza**, a quien también se había agregado **Saboya**, reanudó sus ataques contra España. Francia invadió el **País Vasco** español y **Cataluña**, pero las enfermedades obligaron a su ejército a retirarse de ambos territorios. Los austriacos atacaron **Sicilia**, y los ocupantes españoles acabaron capitulando después de que la flota británica bloqueara todas las líneas de avituallamiento. Otro ejemplo de la vulnerabilidad de España ante los ataques desde el mar fue la toma, en octubre, del puerto de **Vigo** por Gran Bretaña.

Bajas
En la guerra de la Cuádruple Alianza, 28 350 hombres resultaron muertos o heridos. Más de 2000 provenían de Cerdeña, invadida por España.

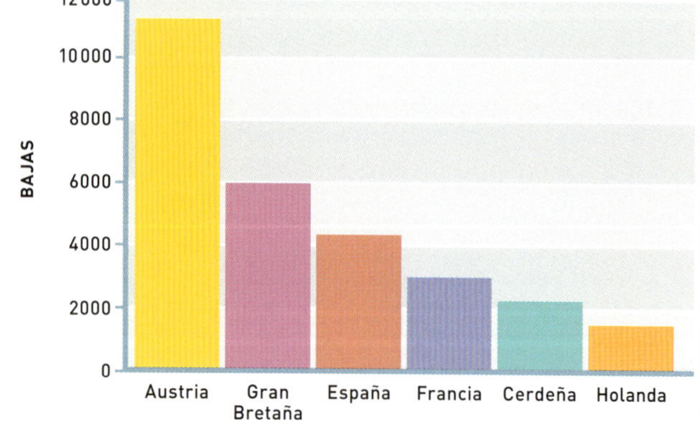

1720

Detalle de un mapa de Willem Blaeu (c. 1650), que muestra la situación de la colonia británica de Honduras en la costa este de la península de Yucatán.

LA COLONIA BRITÁNICA DE HONDURAS (actual Belice), la única posesión británica continental en América Central antes de que lograra independizarse plenamente en el año 1981, fue establecida por **bucaneros británicos** en la costa este de la península de Yucatán. Hacia principios del siglo XVIII, la colonia ya había empezado a explotar el palo de Campeche (*Haematoxylum campechianum*) de la región, del que se obtenía un apreciado tinte para tejidos y papel. En 1720 se importaron por primera vez **esclavos** (muchos de ellos desde Jamaica y otros directamente desde el continente africano) a la llamada costa de los Mosquitos, con el objetivo de utilizarlos como mano de obra para ampliar la explotación maderera en el río Belice.

También en 1720 llegó a su fin la guerra de la Cuádruple Alianza (*véase* 1718) con la firma del **tratado de La Haya**. Felipe accedió a abandonar Sicilia y Cerdeña. La primera pasó a formar parte de Austria, y la segunda recayó en el duque de Saboya, que fue nombrado rey de Cerdeña. En lo concerniente a América del Norte, Francia devolvió **Pensacola** (Florida) a Felipe V, junto con los enclaves ocupados en el norte de España, a cambio de algunas ventajas comerciales. El tratado también confirmó que **Texas** era territorio español.

Mientras tanto, los **marathas**, un grupo subétnico que habitaba en la región de Maharashtra, en India occidental, emprendieron una enorme expansión del imperio que habían reestablecido en 1674. El catalizador de esta expansión, iniciada en 1720, fue el fallecimiento en 1719 de Balaji Vishwanath (n. 1680) y el acceso al trono de su hijo **Bajirao** (1700–1740), que con tan solo veinte años de edad ya era un líder carismático. Consciente de que la debilidad del **Imperio mogol**, con sede en Delhi, radicaba en los estados que le rodeaban, Bajirao ordenó invadir Indostán. Su campaña fue todo un éxito, y el prestigio que le proporcionó le ayudó a negociar tratados de paz con las autoridades mogolas del Decán. Posteriormente, una vez garantizada la seguridad del territorio maratha, Bajirao prosiguió con su política de expansión en 1728, año en que decidió trasladar la capital de Satara a **Pune**.

Expansión maratha
El imperio maratha se extendió hacia el norte, el sur y el este. Su reputación permitió a los marathas cobrar impuestos incluso a regiones ajenas a su administración directa.

CLAVE
Imperio maratha
Campañas marathas

Maza maratha
La cabeza erizada con 118 púas y la aguzada punta cuadrangular de esta maza atestiguan su temible efectividad como arma.

En el noreste, los **mongoles zúngaros** que habían tomado posesión de **Tíbet** (*véase* 1717) fueron expulsados por un ejército de guerreros Qing y tibetanos en 1720. El sexto dalai lama había sido asesinado por los zúngaros acusado de ser un impostor. Las tropas chinas llevaron consigo a Kelsang Gyatso, que fue nombrado **séptimo dalai lama**. Tíbet pasó a ser un protectorado de la China Qing, a la que debía pagar tributos, y la región tibetana de Kham fue incorporada a la provincia china de Sichuan. Sin embargo, las disputas sobre quién debía gobernar bajo el emperador Qing generaron una **dura represión** por los chinos durante los años siguientes.

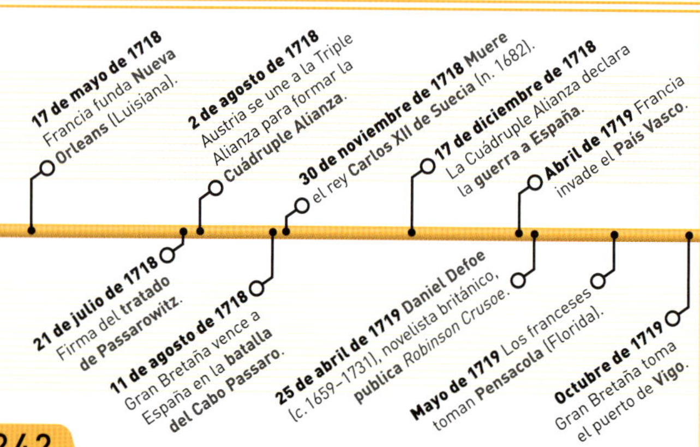

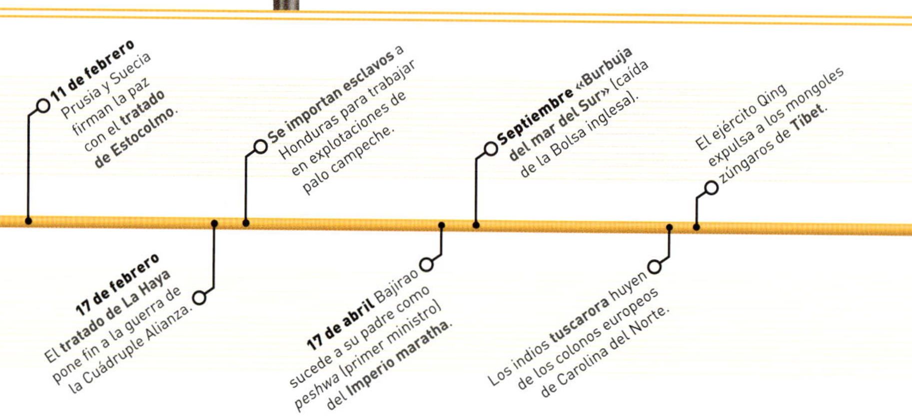

1721–1722

La profusa decoración de brillante colorido es característica de la cerámica persa del siglo XVIII durante la dinastía safaví.

LA GUERRA DEL NORTE (1700–1721) que tuvo lugar entre Suecia y Rusia llegó a su fin con la firma del **tratado de Nystad**. En el año 1719, Rusia había desafiado, con éxito, la supremacía de Suecia en el Báltico cuando atacó las ciudades de la costa oriental sueca; sin embargo, una alianza suecobritánica, que ponía a Suecia bajo la protección de la flota británica, disuadió a Rusia de proseguir sus ataques. El tratado de Nystad devolvió Finlandia a Suecia, pero los **antiguos territorios suecos** del Báltico en Estonia y en otros lugares pasaron a formar parte de Rusia. Es decir, los términos del tratado reducían irrevocablemente el territorio sueco, mientras que Rusia, con la adquisición de sus nuevos puertos bálticos, dominaba Europa oriental.

En uno de los momentos clave de la historia de la exploración holandesa, Jakob Roggeveen (1659–1729) zarpó en 1721 en busca de la **Terra Australis**, el misterioso continente del sur que ya habían cartografiado en parte el español Juan Fernández y el holandés Abel Tasman, entre otros. Roggeveen, un antiguo empleado de la Compañía Holandesa de las Indias Orientales, pero ahora financiado por su equivalente de las Indias Occidentales, navegó hasta las islas Malvinas, Chile y las islas Juan Fernández. Un año más tarde, mientras cruzaban el océano Pacífico, sus tres barcos llegaron por casualidad a la **isla de Pascua** (Rapa Nui), así llamada porque se avistó el domingo de Pascua. Roggeveen también descubrió las **islas de la Sociedad** y **Samoa** antes de regresar.

En 1722, la decadente **dinastía safaví** de Persia fue finalmente depuesta por un grupo de **afganos independientes** del este. Mahmud Hotaki (*c.* 1697–1725), hijo de Mir Wais Hotak (*véase* 1709–1710), entró con su ejército en la capital safaví, Isfahán, la saqueó y se proclamó **sah de Persia**. En 1729, la derrota de la dinastía hotaki a manos de los persas afsharíes, descendientes de los mongoles, en la **batalla de Damghan**, obligó a los afganos a regresar a Kandahar.

Ancestros divinizados
Los imponentes moai de la isla de Pascua fueron erigidos por los clanes con el fin de que vigilaran los campos. Este grupo, en Ahu Akivi, es el más alejado de la costa.

1723–1724

« LOS **ESCLAVOS** SERÁN **MANTENIDOS** POR SUS AMOS CUANDO **YA NO SEAN APTOS** PARA TRABAJAR. **»**

Del *Code Noir* de Luisiana (1724)

EL ÉXITO EUROPEO a la hora de procurarse esclavos en África occidental y transportarlos hasta las nuevas colonias dependía, en gran parte, de la cooperación de algunas tribus. En **Dahomey** (actual República de Benín), bajo el rey Agadja (r. 1708–1740), se practicaban la esclavitud y los sacrificios humanos. Su conquista del vecino reino de Allada en 1723 le proporcionó una **fuente de prisioneros que vender**, y en 1724 Dahomey se había convertido en el principal proveedor de esclavos para los europeos.

En 1724 se introdujo en el territorio francés de Luisiana (América del Norte) el ***Code noir*** (Código negro), una extensa definición de las condiciones de la esclavitud establecidas por el rey Luis XIV de Francia. En parte tenía el propósito de proporcionar una protección básica a los esclavos (sus amos debían proveerles de alimentos y de ropa, por ejemplo), pero también legitimaba **castigos crueles**: los fugitivos serían marcados a fuego, se les cortarían las orejas y, si lo intentaban de nuevo, se les cortarían los ligamentos de la corva con el fin de dejarlos inválidos.

También en 1724, el Imperio mogol en vías de desintegración vio cómo el **estado indio de Oudh** se independizaba bajo Saadat Alí Kan (*c.* 1680–1739), fundador de la **dinastía mogol de Oudh**, que gobernó hasta que los británicos tomaron el poder a principios del siglo XIX.

1721 El compositor alemán Johann Sebastian **Bach** (1685–1750) **compone** los *Conciertos de Brandeburgo*.

4 de abril de 1721 Robert Walpole es nombrado primer ministro, el primero de Gran Bretaña.

1 de agosto de 1721 Jakob Roggeveen zarpa para llegar a la **Terra Australis**.

10 de septiembre de 1721 El tratado de Nystad pone fin a la **guerra del Norte**.

2 de noviembre de 1721 Pedro I el Grande es proclamado zar de todas las Rusias.

8 de marzo de 1722 Los afganos derrotan a las tropas persas en la **batalla de Gulnabad** y toman el control del Imperio persa.

5 de abril de 1722 Jakob Roggeveen llega a la **isla de Pascua**.

Junio de 1722 Jakob Roggeveen es el primero en avistar **Samoa**, aunque no pone pie en tierra.

23 de octubre de 1722 Mahmud Hotaki es reconocido como sah de Persia.

20 de diciembre de 1722 Muere el emperador **Qing Kangxi** (n. 1654), tras el reinado más largo de **China**.

1723 Pedro el Grande de Rusia convierte en **siervos** a los esclavos domésticos.

1 de septiembre de 1723 El **tratado de San Petersburgo** obliga a Persia a ceder territorios a Rusia.

14 de enero de 1724 Abdicación de Felipe V de España.

22 de abril de 1724 Nace el filósofo alemán **Immanuel Kant** (m. 1804).

1724 Asaf Jah arrebata **Hyderabad** a los mogoles y se proclama nizam de Hyderabad.

1724 China expulsa a los **misioneros** extranjeros como represalia por las críticas del papa Clemente XI (*véase* 1715).

La Academia de las Ciencias de San Petersburgo, fundada por Pedro I el Grande en 1725, se trasladó a este edificio de 1783–1785 a orillas del Nevá.

« OS DIRIGÍS AL **PARAÍSO DE LOS ACADÉMICOS.** »

Caspar Wolff, científico alemán, elogio a la Academia de las Ciencias en una carta al matemático Leonhard Euler (*c.* 1779)

Puerta *(torii)* del santuario sintoísta de Itsukushima (Japón).

LA FIRMA DEL TRATADO DE LA HAYA (*véase* 1720) no logró extinguir las fuertes rivalidades entre las grandes potencias europeas. En 1725, el **tratado de Viena** entre España y Austria, reportó a esta última ciertas ventajas comerciales para su Compañía de Ostende en las colonias españolas; a cambio, renunció a reclamar el trono de España, a la que prometió ayudar a recuperar Gibraltar. En 1726, Gran Bretaña trató de bloquear los barcos de la flota de Indias española en Portobelo (Panamá), pero se retiró en 1727 sin éxito, tras haber sufrido numerosas bajas por enfermedad.

Envalentonada por la promesa del apoyo austriaco, negado por un pacto secreto entre Austria y Gran Bretaña, **España decidió sitiar Gibraltar** en 1727, lo que precipitó la **guerra anglo-española**. El sitio se prolongó durante cuatro meses, pero fracasó; los españoles sufrieron 1400 bajas, frente a las 300 de los británicos. La guerra terminó con el tratado de Sevilla en 1729.

Pedro el Grande (1672–1725) fundó en Rusia, en 1725, la **Academia de las Ciencias de San Petersburgo**. Los estudiosos más eminentes de todas las disciplinas fueron invitados a trabajar en ella; así, el embriólogo alemán Caspar Wolff (1733–1794) ofreció al matemático suizo Leonhard Euler un salario de 200 rublos como incentivo, que este aceptó.

CATALINA I (1684–1727)

Huérfana de campesinos lituanos, la futura esposa de Pedro I el Grande se llamaba Marta Skowronska. Contrajo matrimonio en secreto con Pedro en 1707 y, después de enviudar, se convirtió en la primera monarca rusa hasta su fallecimiento. Durante su reinado recibió el respaldo del Consejo Supremo de Privados, que quería negar poder a la aristocracia.

Café en Brasil
Este grabado del siglo XIX muestra una plantación de café brasileña. A partir de unos inicios modestos en 1727, Brasil se convirtió en el primer productor de café del mundo.

En Asia occidental, el sah de Persia afgano, Mahmud Hotaki (*véase* 1721–1722) falleció en 1725. Le sucedió su primo, Ashraf Kan (m. 1730), que probablemente le había asesinado. Por entonces, los **territorios persas** estaban rodeados por **tropas otomanas**, vinculadas al régimen anterior debido a una **alianza otomanosafaví**. Sin embargo, Ashraf Kan derrotó a los otomanos en una batalla que tuvo lugar cerca de Isfahán, en Kirmansah, y en 1727 se firmó la paz en Hamadán (Persia).

Novela satírica
El clérigo y escritor irlandés Jonathan Swift (1667–1745) publicó en 1726 la novela Los viajes de Gulliver, *una sátira sobre la humanidad. Esta edición se publicó en la década de 1860.*

También en 1727, la **Rusia imperial** y el **Imperio chino Qing** firmaron el **tratado de Kiajta**, en el que se basaron las relaciones entre ambos hasta mediados del siglo XIX. Se trazó y acordó la frontera norte de Mongolia y se establecieron rutas comerciales para las pieles y el té.

A finales de la década de 1720 se empezó a **cultivar café** en el Caribe y América del Sur. Las primeras semillas llegaron a Martinica en 1720, y hacia 1727 el rey de Portugal envió a buscar más a la Guinea Francesa a Francisco de Mello Palheta que convenció a la esposa del gobernador para que le proporcionara semillas y plantas de semillero con las que Portugal pudo iniciar una industria cafetera en Brasil.

EN RUSIA, EL ZAR PEDRO I EL GRANDE, que estaba plenamente decidido a descubrir toda **la extensión de sus tierras hacia el este**, encargó al navegante danés Vitus Bering (1681–1741) que recorriera la costa siberiana hacia el norte desde la península de Kamchatka. En 1728, **Bering** atravesó el angosto **estrecho** que hoy lleva su nombre y que **separa Siberia de Alaska**. Continuó hacia el norte y descubrió que Siberia alcanza su límite oriental en el estrecho. Aunque sospechaba que debía de haber más tierras en dirección este, no avistó las costas de Alaska hasta un segundo viaje en 1741.

En el subcontinente indio, los **marathas**, después de casi una década durante la cual Bajirao (*véase* 1720) había consolidado su poder, atacaron la región del Decán, que rodeaba sus territorios. En 1728, en la **batalla de Palkhed**, se enfrentaron al príncipe rival Asaf Jah I de Hyderabad (también conocido como Nizam-ul-Mulk), que aspiraba al liderazgo maratha y se negaba a pagarles el *chauth* (tributo). Con un golpe estratégico magistral, los marathas acorralaron al ejército del nizam en una zona sin agua, en la que este se negó a pelear. El nizam tuvo que abandonar finalmente sus pretensiones de liderazgo y reanudar el pago del *chauth*.

Por otro lado, 1729 fue un año clave para las **relaciones comerciales entre China y Occidente**, pues el emperador Yongzheng prohibió casi por completo la importación de **opio**. Aunque había gran demanda de productos chinos en Europa, a los chinos no les atraían los productos eu-

28 de enero de 1725 Muere Pedro I el Grande (n. 1672). Catalina I continúa con la fundación de la Academia de las Ciencias.

22 de abril de 1725 El sah **de Persia Mahmud Hotaki muere** o es asesinado (n. c. 1697).

30 de abril de 1725 Austria y España firman el **tratado de Viena**.

1726 Impresión con tipos móviles de la vasta **enciclopedia china** *Gujin tushu jicheng*.

11 de febrero de 1727 España inicia el **sitio de Gibraltar** (hasta el 12 de junio).

1727 Portugal introduce el **café en Brasil**.

23 de agosto de 1727 Rusia y China firman el **tratado de Kiajta**, ciudad mongola fronteriza.

18 de noviembre de 1727 Primera piedra de la nueva ciudad de **Jaipur** (India).

28 de febrero de 1728 Los marathas vencen a Asaf Jah I, soberano de Hyderabad, en la **batalla de Palkhed**.

18 de mayo de 1728 Pedro II es coronado **zar de Rusia** y sucede a Catalina I.

Estrecho de Bering
Vista desde satélite del estrecho de Bering, un brazo de mar de 96 km que separa Asia y América del Norte.

ropeos y solo aceptaban pagos en plata, un metal que Europa, y Gran Bretaña en particular, debía obtener a un precio exorbitante. A principios del siglo XVIII, los comerciantes británicos comenzaron a intercambiar opio indio por productos de China y pronto hubo un número creciente de **chinos adictos**, lo cual redujo enormemente la cantidad de plata que necesitaba Europa. Los contrabandistas de opio europeos fueron un gran problema para China hasta bien entrado el siglo XIX.

También en 1729 y tras más de una década sufriendo maltrato, los **indios natchez acabaron con la vida** de más de 200 **colonos franceses en Fort Rosalie** (Misisipi). La respuesta llegó dos años más tarde, en 1731, cuando los franceses, con la ayuda de los choctaw, se vengaron y esclavizaron a muchos natchez, a quienes enviaron a las plantaciones del Caribe.

La breve **Era del Tulipán otomana** (1718–1730) llegó a su fin con una rebelión contra una serie de medidas impopulares, liderada por un jenízaro (soldado), **Patrona Halil**, y que acabó con la sustitución del sultán Ahmed III por Mahmud I. La Era del Tulipán fue un periodo de estabilidad para el Imperio otomano y se caracterizó por un creciente interés por las costumbres de Occidente. Al igual que Europa occidental en el siglo XVII, la corte otomana se obsesionó con el tulipán. La **arquitectura y el arte** otomanos **florecieron**, pero el elevado precio de los tulipanes y de los bulbos de estas flores distorsionó la economía. La coronación de Mahmud I en 1730 puso fin a la Era del Tulipán, pero **Halil murió estrangulado** en presencia del sultán en 1731 por excederse.

En **Japón**, gobernado por el sogunado Tokugawa desde 1603, el **sintoísmo** experimentó un renacimiento que, hacia el año 1730, se vio impulsado gracias a los textos de eruditos como Kada no Azunamaro (1669–1736) y Kamo no Mabuchi (1697–1769). Los eruditos sintoístas rechazaban las influencias chinas y budistas, y deseaban encontrar una **identidad espiritual japonesa** pura. Finalmente, el sintoísmo se reinstauró como religión nacional de Japón más de un siglo después, en 1868.

Mientras tanto, el estado árabe de **Omán** ampliaba sus territorios en el continente africano. Los omaníes habían arrebatado a Portugal la ciudad keniata de **Mombasa** y la isla de Pemba en 1698, y para 1730 habían expulsado a los portugueses de las costas de Kenia y Tanzania, y controlaban la isla de **Zanzíbar** (hoy parte de Tanzania).

MUERTOS
180
150
120
90
60
30
0
Hombres Mujeres Niños

Masacre de Fort Rosalie
El 28 de noviembre del año 1729, los indios natchez asesinaron a 242 colonos franceses en Fort Rosalie (Misisipi) en venganza por años de maltrato.

En **África occidental**, el pueblo musulmán fulbé (o fulani) empezó a organizarse en comunidades más amplias, en un proceso que actualmente se conoce como **revolución fulbé**. El primero de estos estados fue Bondu (Guinea), a finales del siglo XVII. Mas tarde se creó Futa Yallon (centrado en Guinea, pero que abarcaba territorios vecinos), donde los fulbé musulmanes arrebataron el poder a los líderes existentes y a los fulbé no musulmanes. En 1735 se creó formalmente una **confederación de provincias**, cuya capital era Timbo (Guinea). Otra de las áreas que se vio profundamente afectada por la yihad fulbé (como se denominó a la toma de poder) fue el antes en declive **Imperio de Bornu** (en la actual Nigeria), que experimentó un renacimiento.

En 1731, el antaño independiente **Dahomey** de África occidental aceptó finalmente la soberanía del **Imperio yoruba de Oyo** (Nigeria actual). Los yorubas lo habían invadido y derrotado después de una larga y cruenta campaña que tuvo lugar en 1728, pero la resistencia en Dahomey logró persistir hasta el año 1748.

« EN MENOS DE DOS HORAS MATARON A MÁS DE 200 FRANCESES. »

Padre Le Petit, misionero, en una carta al padre D'Avaugour, procurador de las misiones de América del Norte (1730)

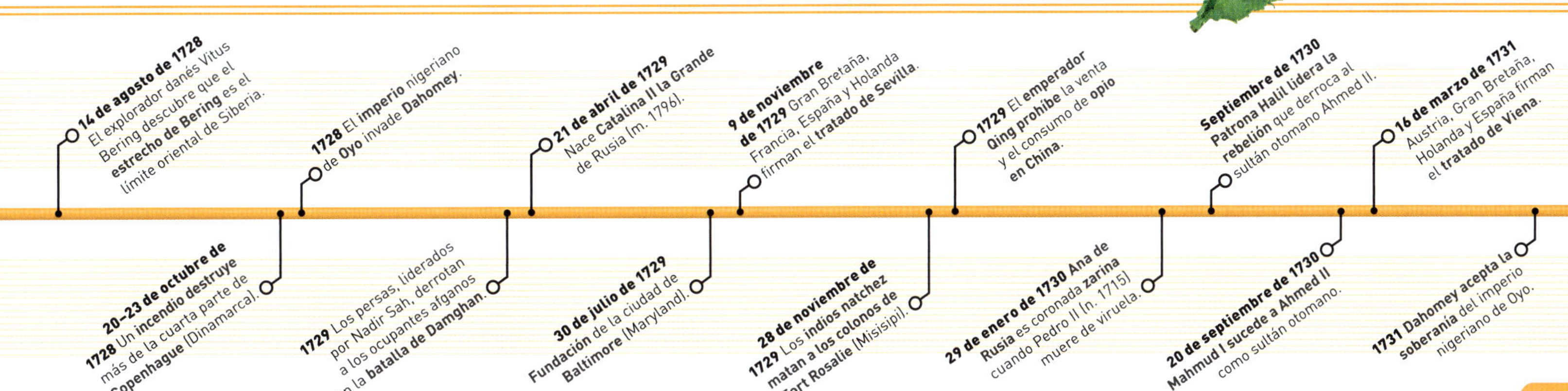

Pipa y adormidera
Pipa de opio tradicional china con una cazoleta en forma de pomo donde la droga (savia seca de la cápsula de la adormidera) se evapora al calentarla.

14 de agosto de 1728 El explorador danés Vitus Bering descubre que el **estrecho de Bering** es el límite oriental de Siberia.

20-23 de octubre de 1728 Un **incendio destruye** más de la cuarta parte de **Copenhague** (Dinamarca).

1728 El **imperio** nigeriano **de Oyo** invade **Dahomey**.

1729 Los persas, liderados por Nadir Sah, derrotan a los ocupantes afganos en la **batalla de Damghan**.

21 de abril de 1729 Nace **Catalina II la Grande** de Rusia (m. 1796).

30 de julio de 1729 **Fundación** de la ciudad de **Baltimore** (Maryland).

9 de noviembre de 1729 Gran Bretaña, Francia, España y Holanda firman el **tratado de Sevilla**.

28 de noviembre de 1729 Los **indios natchez matan a los colonos de Fort Rosalie** (Misisipi).

1729 El **emperador Qing prohíbe** la venta y el consumo de **opio en China**.

29 de enero de 1730 **Ana de Rusia** es coronada **zarina** cuando Pedro II (n. 1715) muere de viruela.

Septiembre de 1730 **Patrona Halil lidera la rebelión** que derroca al sultán otomano Ahmed III.

20 de septiembre de 1730 **Mahmud I sucede a Ahmed III** como sultán otomano.

16 de marzo de 1731 Austria, Gran Bretaña, Holanda y España firman el **tratado de Viena**.

1731 **Dahomey acepta la soberanía** del imperio nigeriano de Oyo.

1732–1734

«Escena de taberna», uno de los ocho cuadros de la serie *La vida de un libertino* (1732–1733), de William Hogarth, que narra la caída del insensato heredero de un rico comerciante.

OBSESIONADO CON LA CREACIÓN de un estado fuerte e independiente, Federico Guillermo I (r. 1713–1740), el «rey soldado» de **Prusia**, instituyó el **servicio militar obligatorio**: todos los jóvenes debían servir en el ejército durante tres meses al año. Fue así como el ejército prusiano pasó a ser el cuarto más numeroso de Europa, con 60 000 soldados, pese a que el país ocupaba el duodécimo lugar por su población.

En **América del Norte** se fundó en 1732 el estado de **Georgia**, la última de las trece colonias establecidas por Gran Bretaña en la costa atlántica. Con el nuevo estado, cuyo nombre rendía homenaje al rey Jorge II, Gran Bretaña pretendía reforzar su presencia en el sur. Los primeros colonos empezaron a llegar en 1733, muchos de ellos liberados de cárceles de morosos.

Azul de Prusia
El ejército de Federico Guillermo I de Prusia llevaba casacas de color azul oscuro con solapas rojas y grandes ojales blancos.

> « ALGUNOS **ESTADOS** TIENEN UN **EJÉRCITO**, EL **EJÉRCITO PRUSIANO** TIENE UN **ESTADO**. »
>
> **Voltaire,** filósofo francés (1694–1778)

También en 1733, el navegante danés Vitus Bering (1681–1741), cuyo nombre lleva el estrecho de Bering (*véase* 1728) inició la **exploración del Gran Norte**. La emperatriz Ana de Rusia (1693–1740) había autorizado una expedición en la que participaron 3000 personas en tres grupos separados: uno iba a cartografiar el norte de Siberia, otro a explorar el norte de Japón, y el de Bering, a descubrir qué había al este del estrecho. Bering no avistó el monte San Elías, en la **costa de Alaska**, hasta junio de 1741, solo cuatro meses antes de morir. Ese mismo mes, algunos hombres de su segundo barco llegaron a la isla del Príncipe de Gales (Alaska).

Mientras tanto, durante el **periodo Kyoho** (julio de 1716 a abril de 1736), el **hambre** provocaba estragos en **Japón**. En 1732, nubes de langostas atacaron los cultivos, especialmente los de arroz, de las comunidades agrícolas costeras. Luego, las intensas lluvias destruyeron los cultivos de invierno de trigo y de cebada, y los insectos diezmaron la cosecha de arroz del año siguiente. La zona que se vio más afectada fue el norte de la isla de Kyushu, donde **perecieron** unas 15 000 personas. En ciudades como Edo (Tokio actual) y Osaka, el precio del arroz se multiplicó por siete, y en 1733, las tiendas de venta de arroz fueron asaltadas durante los **disturbios** provocados **por la escasez de alimentos**.

En 1733 murió Augusto II de Polonia. Estanislao Leszczynski fue elegido rey por 12 000 nobles polacos, pero los 3000 que habían votado por Augusto III se apoyaron en Rusia y Austria para coronarle rey en 1734. La que empezó como una guerra civil acabó convirtiéndose en la **guerra de Sucesión polaca** (1733–1738) cuando los Borbones (Francia y España), los Habsburgo (Austria), Prusia, Sajonia y Rusia entraron en liza para recuperar los territorios perdidos después de la guerra de Sucesión española (*véase* 1701). Estanislao renunció a su derecho legítimo por el **tratado de Viena** de 1738.

Hambruna de Kyoho en Japón
Cerca de un 20 % de la población de Fukuoka, al norte de Kyushu, pereció durante la hambruna de 1733 del periodo Kyoho.

1:4 **Elecciones polacas de 1733**
Estanislao Leszczynski, con 12 000 votos, fue rey de Polonia temporalmente. Augusto III tan solo obtuvo 3000, pero le sucedió en 1734.

En esta época, el ámbito cultural británico se vio dominado por un **humanismo radical**, la convicción de que la identidad, la ética y el conocimiento humanos no necesitaban basarse en la creencia en Dios. Alexander Pope (1688–1744) escribió en su poema *Ensayo sobre el Hombre* (1734): «conócete a ti mismo/no esperes el conocimiento divino/el estudio propio de la humanidad es el hombre». En el ámbito de las artes, dio lugar a una **visión satírica** de la humanidad y a la **crítica social**, en ocasiones muy aguda, de artistas como William Hogarth (1697–1764).

En 1733, John Kay (1704–1780) patentó su **telar de lanzadera volante**, una lanzadera con ruedas que llevaba el hilo y permitía aumentar significativamente la velocidad a la que se tejía. El telar de Kay suponía una **amenaza para la supervivencia de los tejedores**, que intentaron que se prohibiera. Pero fracasaron, y la máquina fue adoptada mayoritariamente.

VOLTAIRE (1694–1778)

François-Marie Arouet, nacido en París, fue un prolífico escritor, historiador, y filósofo de la Ilustración (*véase* 1763). Escribió obras históricas, ensayos, obras de teatro, poemas y novelas. Sus ideas (sobre la reforma social y las libertades civiles, por ejemplo) generaron gran hostilidad, por lo que tuvo que huir en varias ocasiones, pero ejercieron una enorme influencia sobre los ideólogos de la Revolución Francesa y de la independencia de las colonias americanas.

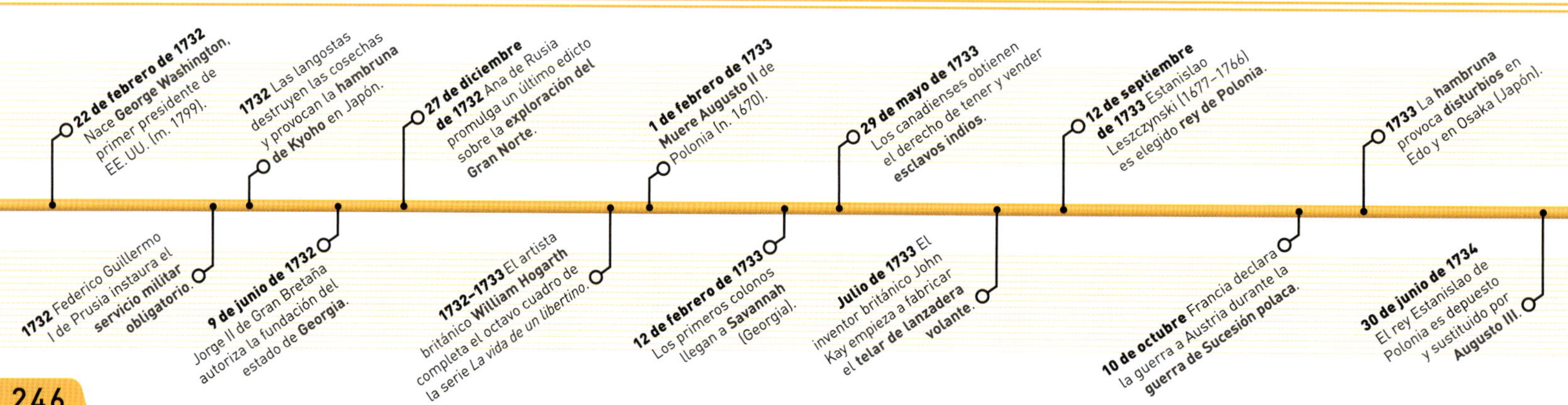

Grabado que ilustra el proceso de producción del azúcar en el Caribe de *Historie des Antilles*, obra del sacerdote y plantador francés Jean-Baptiste Labat.

CHARLES MARIE DE LA CONDAMINE (1701–1774), explorador, científico y matemático francés, se unió a una expedición a Perú en 1735. A causa de una discusión con sus colegas, prosiguió en solitario hasta Quito (Ecuador), desde donde descendió el **Amazonas** hasta llegar a Cayena, en la que fue la primera exploración científica del río. En 1744 regresó a París y en 1751 publicó un diario con sus descubrimientos. Durante su estancia en **Ecuador**, La Condamine descubrió el **caucho** (si bien el pueblo maya llevaba siglos fabricando goma flexible) y en 1736 introdujo el producto en Europa al enviar a París láminas de látex procesado como muestra.

A principios del siglo XVIII, Portugal, España, Francia, Gran Bretaña y Holanda tenían **plantaciones de caña de azúcar con mano de obra esclava** en Brasil y en todo el Caribe. En 1735, la Compañía Francesa de las Indias Orientales empezó a desarrollar plantaciones en las islas de **Ile de France y Borbón** (actuales Mauricio y Reunión). No tardó en instalarse la primera **refinería de azúcar** de Mauricio, en Ville Bague, al norte.

En América del Norte, la presión de las colonias británicas en expansión obligó a Francia a reforzar sus derechos sobre **Indiana** con un **asentamiento permanente**. En 1732 ya había construido un puerto comercial en la actual **Vincennes**, pero en 1735 una oleada de agricultores se unió a los comerciantes. Vincennes creció rápidamente y se convirtió no solo en el núcleo comercial francés más importante de toda Indiana, sino en el **centro cultural francés** de la región.

hoja con incrustaciones caligráficas de plata

Arma de conquista
Esta ornamentada hacha de guerra perteneció a Nadir, coronado sah de Persia en 1736. Tan solo un año después, Nadir dirigió a los persas en la guerra contra Afganistán.

El año 1736 asistió al **fin del gobierno safaví** en Persia. El líder militar persa **Nadir Sah** (1698–1747) había llegado a ser más poderoso que los safavíes a quienes servía (Tahmasp II hasta 1732, y su hijo Abbas III, todavía niño). Cuando Nadir se propuso a sí mismo como **sah**, pocos se le opusieron, y fue coronado en 1736. En 1737, Nadir se enfrentó a los antiguos gobernantes afganos al ocupar el sur de **Afganistán**. La dinastía safaví se extinguió definitivamente en 1740 con el asesinato de Tahmasp y de Abbas.

La **guerra entre Rusia y Turquía** (1735–1739) puso de manifiesto que ningún tratado podría zanjar con facilidad la guerra de Sucesión polaca (*véase* 1733). Además, Rusia, a la que Austria se unió en el año 1737, deseaba apoderarse de **Crimea** para tener acceso al mar Negro y poner así fin a los ataques de los **tártaros crimeos**. Un ejército ruso conquistó parte de Crimea en 1736, pero se vio obligado a retirarse debido a las enfermedades. Otro ejército arrebató **Azov** a los otomanos y avanzó hacia **Jassy** (Iasi), en Moldavia. En 1737, Rusia perdió sus nuevas conquistas debido a la falta de suministros.

En 1737, el **Imperio maratha** de India (*véase* 1728) disfrutaba de su máxima **expansión** hacia el norte, a expensas del Imperio mogol. El peshwa (primer ministro) **Bajirao I** (r. 1721–1740) fue quien planeó dicha expansión, pero casi tan poderosos como el peshwa eran los nobles marathas llamados sardar (entre los cuales estaban los Gaekwad de Baroda, los Shindias de Gwalior y los Holkar de Indore), que fundaron sus propios reinos en las tierras conquistadas.

En 1737, el taxónomo y botánico sueco **Carlos Linneo** (1707–1778) publicó *Genera plantarum*. Esta obra, junto con la posterior *Species plantarum* (1753) y la anterior *Systema naturae* (1735), sentaron las bases del sistema de clasificación biológica que todavía se utiliza en la actualidad.

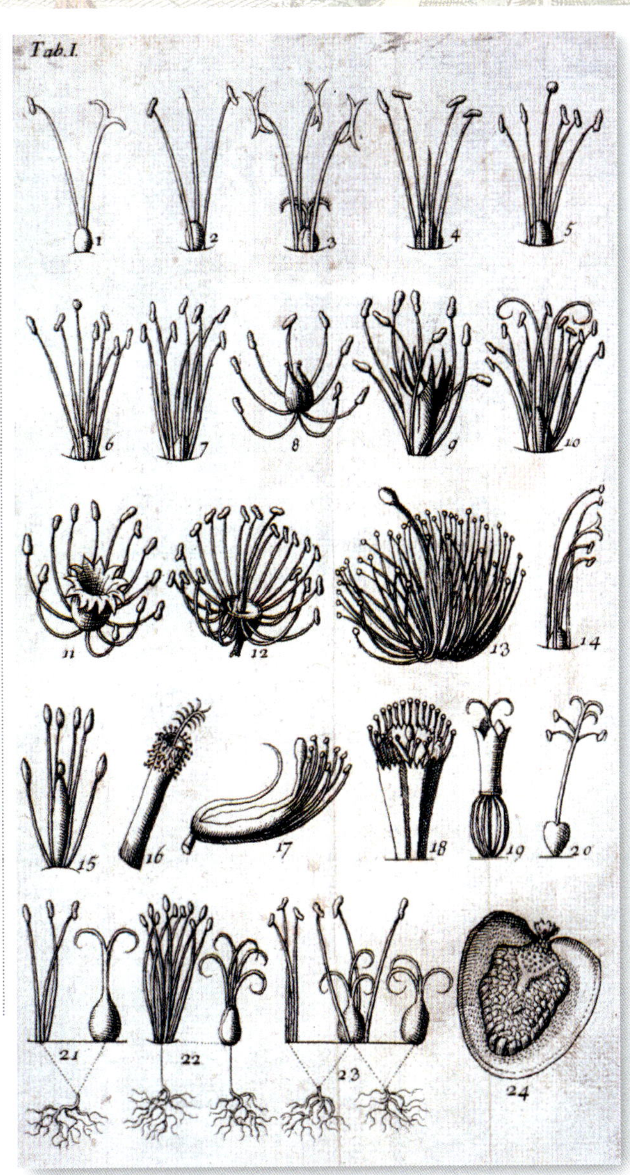

Anatomía de las plantas
En Genera plantarum, *Carlos Linneo clasificó las plantas por sus órganos sexuales (número de estambres y pistilos de las flores).*

1735 Carlos **Linneo** publica la primera edición de *Systema naturae*.

Abril de 1735 El explorador francés La Condamine embarca en una expedición a **Perú**.

1735 Fundación de **Vincennes** (Indiana) junto al río Wabash.

3 de octubre de 1735 La firma de los **Preliminares de Viena** pone fin a las luchas de la guerra de Sucesión polaca.

8 de octubre de 1735 Qianlong sucede a Yongzheng como **emperador Qing de China**.

8 de marzo de 1736 Nadir Sah, fundador de la dinastía afshari, es coronado **sah de Persia**.

19 de junio de 1736 El ejército ruso toma **Azov** (Rumanía) a los otomanos.

1736 La Condamine envía a Europa las primeras muestras de **caucho procesado**.

30 de junio de 1737 El ejército ruso irrumpe en la fortaleza otomana de **Ochakov** (Rumanía).

Julio de 1737 Austria se une a Rusia en la **guerra contra los otomanos**, pero sufre varias derrotas.

Julio de 1737 El ejército ruso derrota al del **kan de Crimea**, pero se retira por falta de víveres.

1737 Carlos **Linneo** publica la primera edición de *Genera plantarum*.

1738–1739

Ruinas de la antigua ciudadela de Kandahar (Afganistán) sobre una colina tras un arco del siglo XII. Durante el asedio persa, Husein Hotaki se refugió en ella, pero se rindió tras el bombardeo de Nadir Sah.

LA DINASTÍA AFGANA HOTAKI HABÍA SIDO EXPULSADA de Persia en 1729 por Nadir Sah (1698–1747), que estaba completamente decidido a eliminar la amenaza que suponía el pueblo afgano **gilzai**. En 1737 había ocupado el sur de Afganistán y en 1738 asedió el enclave hotaki de **Kandahar**. Nadir Sah envió al exilio a Husein, el último de los hotaki, destruyó las ciudades de Kandahar y de Qalat-i-Gilzai y, por último, **acabó con las esperanzas de los gilzais** al apoyar el alzamiento de los **durraníes**, un pueblo afgano rival. Afganistán formaba parte del Imperio mogol, centrado en Delhi, pero el gobernador mogol se había visto totalmente impotente ante el **ejército persa** de Nadir, que arrasó Kabul y **cruzó el Indo** en diciembre de 1738. Después de derrotar a las tropas del mogol Muhammad Sah en la **batalla de Karnal**, en febrero de 1739, a unos 110 km de Delhi, Nadir Sah entró victorioso en la ciudad el 9 de marzo de 1739. Las arcas mogolas estaban vacías, pero el sah se **apoderó de las joyas personales del emperador**, como los famosos diamantes Koh-i-Noor y Darya-i-Noor.

También en el año 1739 concluyó la guerra austro-turca (1737–1739) gracias a la firma del **tratado de Belgrado**. Ese mismo año, el tratado de Niš ponía fin a la **guerra ruso-turca** (1735–1739). Ambos tratados confirmaron las pérdidas de Austria del norte de Serbia y Belgrado en favor de los otomanos, lo que obligó a Rusia a abandonar sus esperanzas de tomar Crimea, pese a que se le permitió construir un puerto no fortificado en Azov y comerciar en el mar Negro.

Las **hostilidades** entre **España** y **Gran Bretaña** volvieron a tomar fuerza en 1739. Gran Bretaña había obtenido derechos limitados al comercio de esclavos y bienes con las colonias españolas (*véase* 1713), y se desarrolló el contrabando. Los españoles se incautaban de cada vez más cargamentos británicos y en 1731 cortaron una oreja al capitán británico Robert Jenkins. Este incidente dio lugar en 1739 al conflicto que Thomas Carlyle, historiador escocés, bautizó como **guerra de la Oreja de Jenkins**. Gran Bretaña empezó a atacar las posesiones españolas en el Nuevo Mundo, como la base naval de Portobelo (Panamá). Tras la **batalla de Portobelo**, los británicos tomaron posesión del enclave en noviembre de 1739. El virreinato de Nueva España, fundado a principios del siglo XVI, respondió aumentando sus defensas en la costa del Caribe.

8:1 **Batalla de Karnal**
Los mogoles perdieron 20 000 hombres en el intento de impedir que el ejército de Nadir Sah llegara a Delhi, mientras que los persas solo perdieron 2500.

Administración imperial
El virreinato de Nueva España, en torno al Caribe y al golfo de México, fue el primero de los cuatro que España creó en sus posesiones del Nuevo Mundo.

Por otro lado, los colonos franceses de **América del Norte**, persistían en su afán **expansionista hacia el oeste**, hasta los territorios españoles. Una de las prioridades era encontrar una ruta que permitiera **unir la cuenca del río Misisipi** con los territorios españoles de **Colorado** y **Santa Fe**. En 1739, los hermanos franceses **Pierre y Paul Mallet abrieron una ruta** tras superar los ríos Missouri y Platte, dirigirse al sur hacia el río Arkansas y seguir a un guía local hasta llegar a Santa Fe. A pesar de que continuaba existiendo un territorio intermedio ocupado por tribus indias que estaban en guerra, finalmente se estableció un vínculo entre los asentamientos franceses y los españoles.

Batalla de Portobelo
Después de esta batalla librada en 1739, durante las primeras fases de la guerra de la Oreja de Jenkins, la base naval de Portobelo pasó de manos españolas a británicas.

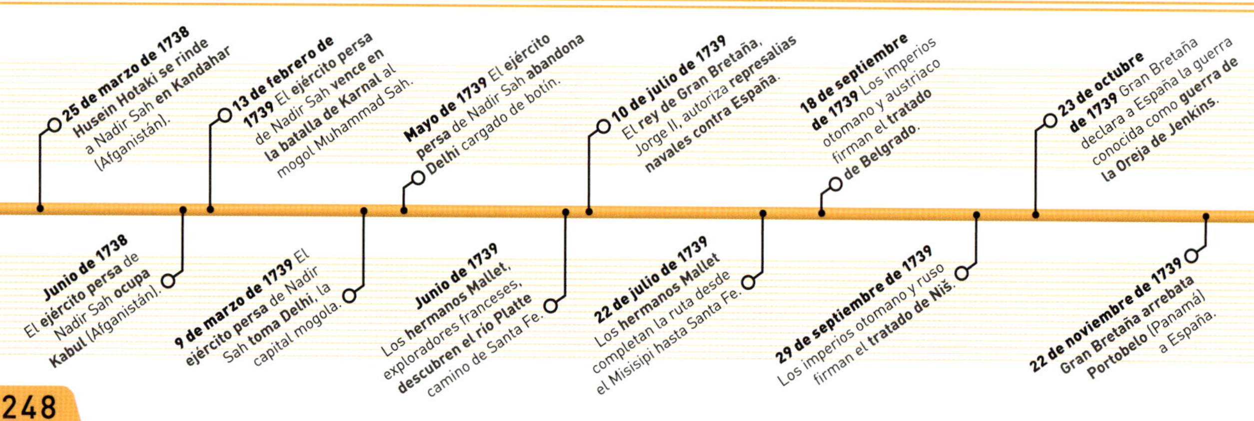

1740–1741

Federico II de Prusia con el marqués de Argens cerca de Sans Souci.

DESPUÉS DE LA MUERTE DE FEDERICO GUILLERMO I DE PRUSIA, en 1740, ascendió al trono su hijo Federico II (1712–1786). En su juventud, Federico había mostrado una gran afición por la música, la poesía y la filosofía. Durante su formación como heredero tuvo la oportunidad de estudiar las obras de Nicolás Maquiavelo (*véase* 1513) y en 1739 escribió en francés una refutación de las ideas del renacentista florentino, *El antimaquiavelo*, que se publicó anónimamente en el año 1740. Su reinado se caracterizó por la tolerancia, la modernización y el mecenazgo de las artes; sin embargo, se le conoce como **el Grande** por las gestas políticas y militares gracias a las cuales consiguió llevar las fronteras de Prusia (hasta 1701 Prusia-Brandeburgo) mucho más allá de sus límites históricos. Más tarde, defendió estas adquisiciones contra enormes coaliciones de poderosos enemigos. Federico tuvo la primera oportunidad de ampliar las fronteras de Prusia poco después de su coronación. El emperador Habsburgo, Carlos VI, falleció en 1740, y le sucedió su hija María Teresa (1717–1780), que iba a reinar en los dominios hereditarios de Austria con su esposo, Francisco de Lorena, como emperador del Sacro Imperio. Tanto Prusia como Francia se opusieron a ello inmediatamente. La mayor parte de Europa tomó partido en el conflicto de la **guerra de Sucesión austriaca** (1740–1748), en la que Gran Bretaña, Holanda, Cerdeña y Sajonia apoyaron a la soberana. Federico, que reclamaba **Silesia** (parte de las actuales Polonia, Alemania y Repú-

« HACIA EL NORTE, DESDE DONDE BRILLABA FEDERICO, LA ESTRELLA POLAR, ALEMANIA, EUROPA Y HASTA EL MUNDO PARECÍAN GIRAR. »

Johann Wolfgang von Goethe (1749–1832), escritor alemán, sobre Federico II el Grande

El palacio de Poppelsdorf (Alemania) es un ejemplo del estilo rococó que floreció en el siglo XVIII sobre todo en Francia, Alemania, Bohemia y Austria.

blica Checa), se apoderó del territorio de los Habsburgo (Austria) y lo convirtió en una provincia prusiana, incorporada al Imperio alemán en 1871.

En el continente asiático, el reino mon de **Pegu**, en Birmania (Myanmar), se rebeló en 1740 contra el de **Toungoo**, en el norte de Birmania, que lo había sometido en 1539. Después de dicha rebelión fue elegido rey de Pegu un monje birmano de ascendencia real toungoo. El reino conservó su independencia hasta 1757.

También en 1740 comenzó a expandirse el **reino de los lunda**, en África central, cuando una expedición cuya misión era la exploración del oeste fundó el reino de **Cazembe**. Durante los cien años siguientes, Cazembe fue incrementando su territorio mediante una agresiva política de anexión que abarcó la mayor parte de Katanga (República del Congo actual).

Mientras tanto, la guerra de Sucesión austriaca tenía repercusiones en el norte de Europa. Suecia, aún resentida por la pérdida de los **territorios bálticos** tras la guerra del Norte (*véase* 1721–1722) desplegó sus tropas en la frontera rusa y declaró la **guerra ruso-sueca** (1741–1743). La amenaza a San Petersburgo propició un golpe de estado en Rusia, pero la nueva zarina, Isabel Petrovna (1709–1762) prefirió continuar la guerra a ceder los territorios bálticos a Suecia, como había prometido.

En Ulster (Irlanda del Norte), la **emigración a América del Norte** aumentó drásticamente. Muchos de los que partían pertenecían a la **iglesia presbiteriana escocesa**, en su mayoría descendientes de las familias que habían colonizado el norte de Irlanda en el siglo XVII. Los señores ingleses desconfiaban de la colonia escocesa irlandesa, que apoyaba intereses escoceses. **Multaban o encarcelaban** a los ministros presbiterianos, y se limitaron las actividades económicas de los miembros de la Iglesia, lo que provocó pobreza y hambre. Hacia principios del siglo XVIII, esta discriminación se recrudeció porque se les obligó a pagar diezmos a la Iglesia de Inglaterra y se les excluyó de los cargos importantes. La gran **hambruna** de 1741–1742 provocó que unas 12 000 personas abandonaran Irlanda cada año con destino al Nuevo Mundo. Estos **emigrantes escoceses-irlandeses**, resentidos por el trato recibido por los ingleses, apoyaron con entusiasmo la causa de la independencia norteamericana en las décadas de 1770 y 1780.

Auge de Prusia-Brandeburgo
A finales de los siglos XVII y XVIII, líderes sucesivos aumentaron el poder y el territorio de Prusia-Brandeburgo por medios militares y políticos.

CLAVE
- Brandeburgo en 1648
- Adquisiciones de 1648 a 1786

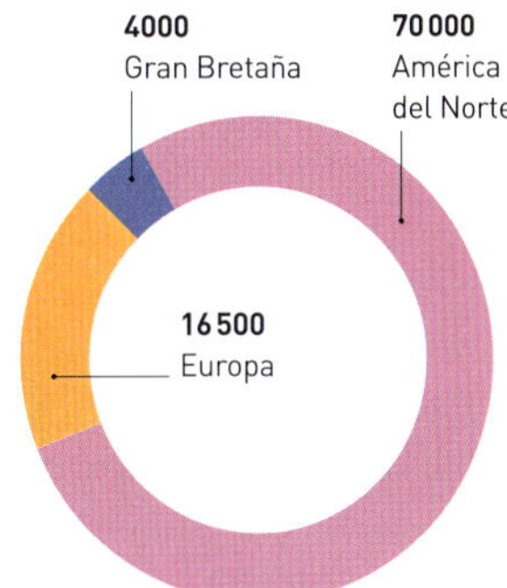

La diáspora del Ulster
Entre 1680 y 1750 salieron del Ulster 70 000 emigrantes irlandeses de origen escocés hacia América del Norte, 4000 hacia Gran Bretaña, y 16 500 hacia el resto de Europa.

LA OPORTUNISTA TOMA DE SILESIA por Federico II de Prusia (*véase* 1740–1741) resultó una apuesta acertada. El ejército austriaco había sido derrotado por el prusiano en 1741, durante la batalla de Mollwitz. En 1742, María Teresa de Austria y los prusianos victoriosos firmaron el **tratado de Berlín**, que concedía a Prusia gran parte de Silesia. El tratado puso **fin a la primera guerra de Silesia** (1740–1742), pero el conflicto europeo más amplio, la guerra de Sucesión austriaca, se prolongó hasta el año 1748.

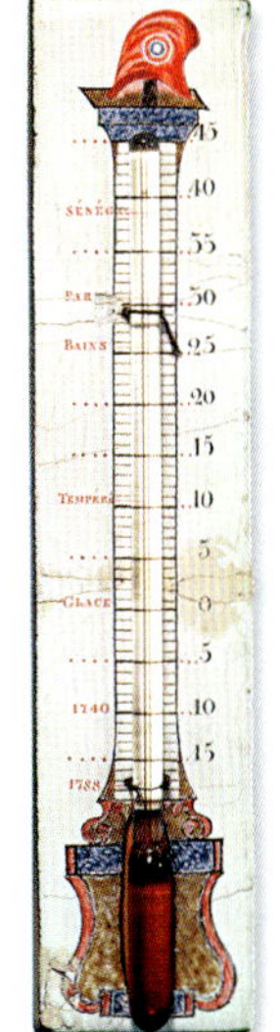

Termómetro Celsius
Este instrumento de origen francés del siglo XVIII para medir la temperatura exterior, está graduado de −15 a 45 °C.

El astrónomo sueco **Anders Celsius** (1701–1744) desarrolló en 1741 el **termómetro** en grados Celsius o centígrados. De hecho, estableció el punto de fusión del hielo en 100 °C y el de ebullición del agua en 0 °C, aunque tres años más tarde, el botánico sueco Carlos Linneo (1707–1778) invirtió esta escala.

En el **Perú español**, **Juan Santos Atahualpa**, un nuevo líder indígena educado por los jesuitas y que afirmaba ser descendiente directo de Atahualpa (1497–1533), el inca asesinado, encabezó la **rebelión de Quisopango** en 1742. Los españoles organizaron de inmediato una campaña contra él y de nuevo en 1743, 1746 y 1750, pero nunca consiguieron vencerle en su territorio natal andino.

En India proseguía la **lucha** por el poder entre los **marathas** (*véase* 1720) y el **nizam de Hyderabad**, representante semiindependiente del Imperio mogol. Después de tomar **Tiruchirapalli**, los marathas nombraron gobernador de la ciudad a Murrarao Ghorpade y se negaron a pagar tributo al nizam. En 1743, este, decidido a recuperar el control de la zona, asedió la ciudad con 80 000 soldados. Derrotado, Murrarao aceptó dinero por cambiar de aliados.

Mientras tanto, en el continente europeo, la firma del **tratado de Abo**, que tuvo lugar en 1743, puso fin a la guerra entre Rusia y Suecia (1741–1743). Con el propósito de librar de la amenaza sueca a la ciudad de San Petersburgo, Rusia había ocupado **Finlandia**, pero el tratado desplazó la frontera sueca de nuevo hacia el norte. Suecia pudo recuperar la mayor parte de Finlandia a cambio de aceptar como heredero del trono sueco a **Adolfo Federico de Holstein-Gottorp** (1710–1771), cliente de la emperatriz Isabel de Rusia.

Por último, en América del Norte, también en 1743, los **europeos comenzaron a explorar Dakota del Sur**, cuando los hermanos franceses La Vérendrye volvieron al oeste tras ser los primeros europeos en ver las **montañas Rocosas** durante su intento de llegar al Pacífico.

16 de diciembre de 1740 Federico II de Prusia invade Silesia.

25 de junio de 1741 María Teresa de Austria es coronada **reina de Hungría**.

1741 El reino de **Cazembe amplía** el reino lunda de África central.

15 de julio de 1741 Uno de los barcos de la expedición rusa de Vitus Bering deja a los **primeros europeos en la costa de Alaska**.

8 de agosto de 1741 Suecia declara la guerra a Rusia: inicio de la **guerra ruso-sueca** (hasta 1743).

1741 Emigración masiva desde el Ulster a causa del hambre.

26 de noviembre de 1741 Los **franceses irrumpen en Praga** durante la guerra de Sucesión austriaca.

6 de diciembre de 1741 **Isabel Petrovna** asciende al trono de Rusia tras un golpe de estado.

9 de diciembre de 1741 Carlos Alberto, elector de Baviera, se proclama **rey de Bohemia** (r. 1741–1743).

24 de enero de 1742 Carlos Alberto, elegido **emperador del Sacro Imperio** como Carlos VII.

28 de julio de 1742 Prusia y Austria ponen fin a la primera guerra de Silesia con el **tratado de Berlín**.

1742 El astrónomo sueco Anders Celsius introduce la **escala Celsius de temperatura**.

1742 Juan Santos Atahualpa inicia la **rebelión contra España en Perú**.

7 de agosto de 1743 Rusia y Suecia firman el **tratado de Abo**, que pone fin a la guerra ruso-sueca.

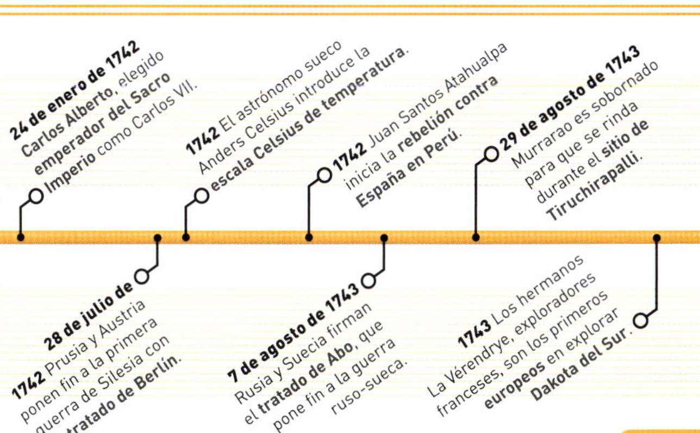

29 de agosto de 1743 Murrarao es sobornado para que se rinda durante el **sitio de Tiruchirapalli**.

1743 Los hermanos La Vérendrye, exploradores franceses, son los primeros **europeos en explorar Dakota del Sur**.

HISTORIA DE LA AGRICULTURA

DE LA CAZA-RECOLECCIÓN Y LA DOMESTICACIÓN AL CULTIVO Y LA MANIPULACIÓN GENÉTICA

Ninguna actividad ha ejercido mayor impacto sobre la sociedad y el medio ambiente que la agricultura. Su descubrimiento y aplicación permitieron que las pequeñas sociedades antes nómadas y cazadoras-recolectoras se hicieran sedentarias, transformaran el entorno natural, formaran comunidades mayores y forjaran civilizaciones.

La mayoría de arqueólogos aceptan que las primeras plantas se cultivaron en la región del Creciente Fértil, en Oriente Próximo y Medio, hacia el año 10 000 a. C. Se cree que los higos fueron el primer alimento cultivado, pero el farro, la cebada, las lentejas, los guisantes y el lino fueron también unos de los primeros cultivos. Los primeros animales domesticados fueron las ovejas y las cabras, seguidas de algunos bovinos.

En el otro lado del mundo, en América Central y del Sur, se plantaban calabazas y maíz, a los que se añadieron las judías. El cultivo conjunto de estas plantas, llamadas más tarde «las tres hermanas», representó un primer conocimiento del proceso de la nutrición, ya que no solo mantenía los nutrientes del suelo, sino que proporcionaba las vitaminas y los minerales esenciales para la salud humana.

HERRAMIENTAS AGRÍCOLAS

Los agricultores neolíticos usaban unos palos largos y planos con la punta redondeada, llamados bastones plantadores, para excavar agujeros poco profundos en los que sembraban. También despejaron con hachas y con fuego zonas boscosas para dejar espacio para los cultivos y recintos para el ganado. Sin embargo, ya en 5000 a. C. se practicaban en Sumer técnicas agrícolas más sofisticadas, como el regadío y el monocultivo a gran escala, mientras que en Egipto los agricultores utilizaban arados y hoces, y contaban con una gran diversidad de cultivos y ganado.

El arado ligero romano utilizado en los países del Mediterráneo dominó la agricultura europea hasta la Edad Media, cuando el arado tirado por caballos y el sistema de rotación de cultivos revolucionaron la agricultura y aumentaron de manera significativa la cantidad de alimentos disponibles. Los viajes a Asia y América en el siglo XV también ejercieron un fuerte impacto en la agricultura mundial gracias al intercambio de plantas y ganado entre Asia, Europa y América. Esto transformó la agricultura a una escala que no se volvería a ver hasta que la maquinaria agrícola y las técnicas de producción intensiva, incluido el uso de abonos y pesticidas químicos, se convirtieran en la norma durante el siglo XX.

C. 10 700–9000 a. C.
Domesticación de plantas
En Oriente Próximo y Medio, la higuera fue una de las primeras plantas cultivadas.

Higos

C. 8000–2000 a. C.
Las tres hermanas
El cultivo conjunto de calabazas, teosinte (variedad primitiva de maíz) y judías en América demuestra el conocimiento de las técnicas de policultivo.

Mazorca de teosinte

C. 5000 a. C.
Sumer desarrolla la agricultura intensiva
El cultivo a gran escala, el monocultivo y el regadío, junto con una mano de obra especializada, permiten el florecimiento y la expansión de la cultura sumeria.

Arado sumerio

2500–1500 a. C.
Egipto cultiva el valle del Nilo
Los egipcios practicaban un sofisticado sistema de plantación y recolección que dependía de la inundación anual del río Nilo.

Segador egipcio

Siglo I
Comercio romano
La agricultura era una actividad económica clave en el Imperio romano; se comerciaba con productos como aceitunas, aceite y vino.

Rueda de molino romana

Arado de madera de Small
El inventor escocés James Small contribuyó significativamente al desarrollo del arado. Hacia mediados de la década de 1700 rediseñó el arado simple de madera tirado por caballos y remodeló la vertedera, que al ser de hierro era más fuerte y más eficiente a la hora de voltear la tierra.

mancera

la vertedera volteaba los terrones hacia un lado

1950
3 400 000

1907
600

Uso del tractor en EE. UU. en el siglo XX
Los tractores se generalizaron a medida que mejoraba su diseño. Eran más pequeños y la producción industrial a gran escala los hizo asequibles.

LA REVOLUCIÓN AGRÍCOLA

Hacia finales del siglo XVI, algunos terratenientes europeos adoptaron una visión más científica de la agricultura. Se aplicaron técnicas como la rotación de cultivos para no agotar el suelo, se usaron aperos más eficientes, como arados mejorados, y se cruzó el ganado con el objetivo de evitar debilidades genéticas. El éxito de estas técnicas produjo más alimentos, aunque tuvo un coste: la necesidad de mano de obra agrícola se redujo de modo drástico, y muchos jornaleros y campesinos se quedaron sin trabajo y sin hogar.

1050–1300
Edad Media
El arado pesado, tirado por yuntas de bueyes o por caballos, transforma los campos, aumenta las cosechas y mejora de manera significativa la alimentación de la Europa medieval.

Arado de madera

Finales del siglo XVIII
Arado de hierro forjado
La vertedera, y después la reja, de hierro forjado mejoran de forma drástica la eficiencia del arado en la agricultura del Viejo Mundo y del Nuevo.

1890–principios del siglo XX
Vehículos de motor
Los tractores agrícolas con motor de combustión interna marcan el fin del laboreo con animales. Ya era un elemento habitual entre la maquinaria agrícola de EE. UU. antes de la Primera Guerra Mundial.

Tractor Ivel

1492
Intercambio colombino
Con la llegada de Colón a América se inicia un intercambio cultural sin precedentes de animales y de plantas, como el tabaco y el maíz.

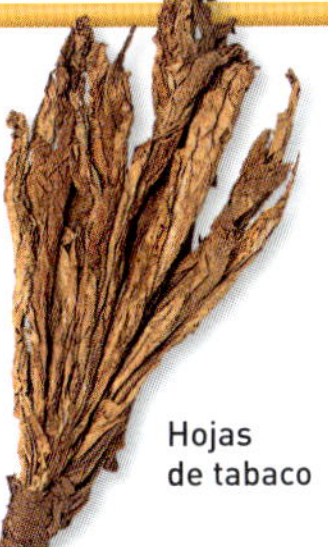
Hojas de tabaco

1800–1840
Cosechadora mecánica
Aún tirada por caballos, la cosechadora mecánica es el primer paso hacia la mecanización de la agricultura, pues permite cosechar en mucho menos tiempo que manualmente.

Cosechadora de McCormick

Década de 1970
Hacia la sostenibilidad
En esta década empiezan a desarrollarse prácticas ecológicas y sostenibles como alternativa al uso de productos químicos de gran impacto y perjudiciales para el medio ambiente.

2000–actualidad
Agricultura urbana
El aumento de la población ha hecho que se intensifique la búsqueda de nuevos modos de alimentar al mundo. En los espacios urbanos, los huertos hidropónicos verticales han sido todo un éxito.

1744–1747

Grabado coloreado a mano en plancha de cobre que muestra a las disciplinadas tropas hanoverianas, con casacas rojas, disparando contra los jacobitas escoceses en la batalla de Culloden, la última de la rebelión jacobita.

EL PUERTO DE MOMBASA, EN ÁFRICA ORIENTAL, estaba dedicado al tráfico de oro, marfil y esclavos en el siglo XVIII. Mombasa perteneció a los portugueses durante casi 200 años, hasta que una rebelión indígena logró expulsarlos en 1729. Después los **árabes de Omán** tomaron el relevo hasta que en 1744, tras la instauración de una nueva dinastía en Omán, el nuevo gobernador de Mombasa les desposeyó del dominio del puerto. En 1745, unos asesinos omaníes acabaron con la vida del gobernador, pero su hermano, Alí Ibn Athman (r. 1746–1755) encabezó una rebelión y los ejecutó. Alí ibn Athman se proclamó **sultán de Mombasa** y aseguró la independencia del puerto respecto a Omán.

Entre tanto, continuaba la guerra entre Prusia y Austria (*véase* 1740). Durante la **segunda guerra de Silesia** (1744–1745), los austriacos intentaron recuperar este territorio, pero Prusia consiguió derrotar a las tropas de la emperatriz María Teresa en las batallas de **Hohenfriedberg**, Soor y Kesseldorf, libradas en 1745. María Teresa se vio finalmente obligada a reconocer la soberanía de Federico II sobre Silesia en el **tratado de Dresde**, firmado a finales de ese mismo año; a cambio, Prusia reconocía a su esposo, Francisco, como emperador del Sacro Imperio. Esto dejaba sola a Francia en la guerra de Sucesión austriaca (1740–1748).

9000
AUSTRIACOS Y SAJONES

5000
PRUSIANOS

Bajas en Hohenfriedberg
Durante esta batalla, los victoriosos prusianos sufrieron menos bajas que los austriacos y sus aliados de Sajonia.

Mortero Coehorn letal
El ejército hanoveriano en Culloden tenía seis morteros Coehorn de cañón corto. Eran fáciles de transportar y mortíferos en el campo de batalla.

En 1744, Francia apoyó el intento de **invasión de Gran Bretaña** por el príncipe Carlos Eduardo Estuardo (1720–1788), nieto del depuesto rey Estuardo Jacobo II y **«joven pretendiente»** al trono de los Hanover de Gran Bretaña. En 1745, el ***«bonnie prince Charlie»***, como también se le conocía popularmente, entró en Escocia y reunió a los **jefes jacobitas** de diversos clanes de las tierras altas escocesas con el objetivo de marchar sobre Inglaterra. Los escoceses derrotaron a un ejército hanoveriano en la **batalla de Prestonpans** y consiguieron llegar hasta Derby, pero decidieron retirarse debido al escaso apoyo que recibieron en Inglaterra y Francia. Aunque obtuvieron más éxitos militares durante su regreso a Escocia, en 1746 fueron derrotados por el ejército hanoveriano en la **batalla de Culloden**. La caza y el asesinato sistemático de los escoceses heridos le valió al comandante hanoveriano William Augustus, duque de Cumberland, el apodo de **«el carnicero de Culloden»**. Esta batalla terminó con la segunda rebelión de los jacobitas y con sus esperanzas de recuperar el poder en Gran Bretaña.

En 1745, un agricultor inglés empezó a experimentar con la cría selectiva de ganado y revolucionó la **ganadería**. Aunque ya se conocía el principio del cruzamiento de animales con las características más interesantes, los métodos empleados por **Robert Bakewell** eran mejores. Su trabajo dio lugar a la raza ovina Leicester y a la vacuna New Longhorn, que siguen siendo importantes en la ganadería actual.

En Japón, el poder de la **dinastía Tokugawa** se iba debilitando. En 1745 fue elegido sogún Tokugawa Ieshige (1712–1761). El primogénito del sogún saliente tenía mala salud, problemas de habla y escaso interés por el gobierno, pero su padre exigió que le sucediera, tal como dictaba la ley de primogenitura. Sus años de reinado se vieron marcados por **desastres naturales y hambrunas**, y a medida que iba en aumento el poder de la clase mercantil, declinaba el suyo como consecuencia de sus malas decisiones y de la **delegación del poder** en subordinados.

Mientras tanto, en el continente europeo, Francia continuaba enfrentada con Austria y sus aliados. En 1746, el entonces gobernador general Joseph François Dupleix (1697–1763), autorizó a un ejército francés para que tomara el puerto británico de **Madrás** (India). En 1747, Dupleix **atacó** el bien defendido **Fort Saint David**, cuartel general británico en el sur de India, a unos 160 km al sur de Madrás, pero esta vez fracasó. Aun así, los franceses conservaron Madrás hasta que el **tratado de Aquisgrán** (*véase* 1748) se lo devolvió a los británicos a cambio de Louisbourg, en Nueva Escocia.

En China, durante el reinado del emperador Qianlong (r. 1736–1799), los **cristianos** padecieron nuevas **persecuciones** entre 1746 y 1748, dentro del marco de la **política imperial**. En 1715, las denuncias del papa Clemente XI sobre las prácticas idólatras chinas alertaron al emperador Qianlong, que se percató de que los cristianos chinos sentían más **lealtad hacia potencias extranjeras** que hacia él. En consecuencia, prohibió la evange-

Cría selectiva de ovejas
Grabado de 1842 que representa un carnero New Leicester, una raza obtenida por Robert Bakewell mediante sus nuevos métodos de cría en su granja de Leicestershire.

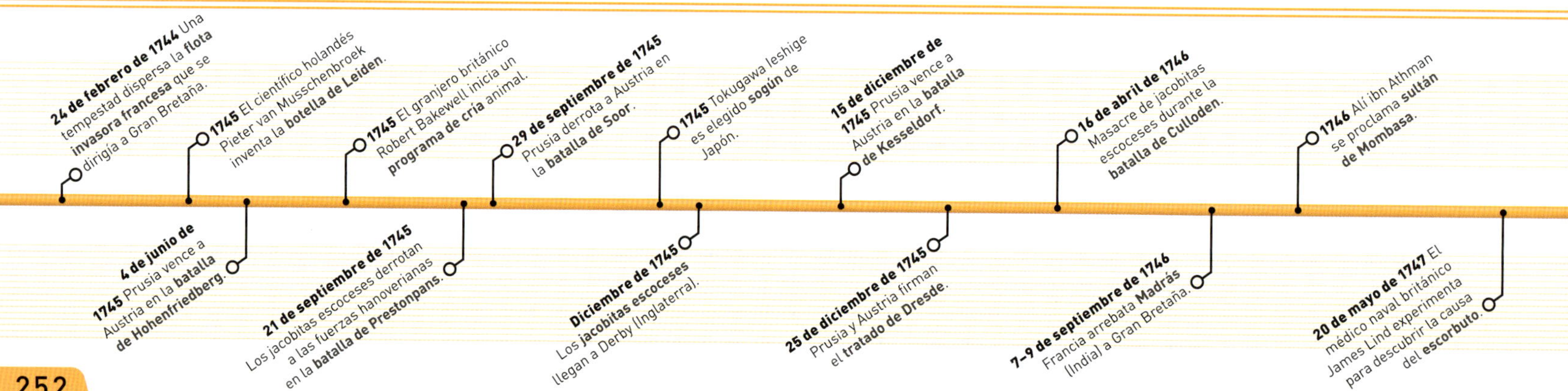

> **«** LAS **NARANJAS** Y LOS **LIMONES**… PRODUJERON LOS **BENEFICIOS** MÁS RÁPIDOS Y EVIDENTES. **»**

James Lind, médico británico, en *Tratado sobre la naturaleza, las causas y la curación del escorbuto* (1753)

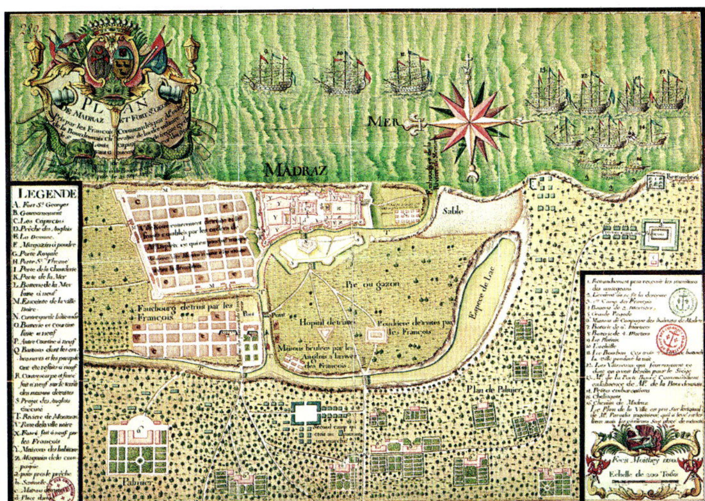

Mapa de Madrás
Grabado de 1750 del puerto de Madrás (India) con el fuerte británico de San Jorge, ambos capturados por una expedición naval francesa en 1746.

lización, y los cristianos chinos tuvieron que ocultarse. Si se descubría a misioneros que infringían la ley y predicaban, se intensificaba la persecución del cristianismo.

En 1747, el científico británico William Watson realizó en Londres una demostración pública del circuito eléctrico utilizando una **botella de Leiden**. Dicho experimento fue probablemente el paso más importante del siglo XVIII hacia la comprensión de la **electricidad**. La botella de Leiden, uno de los primeros **condensadores**, que había sido inventada en 1745 por el científico holandés Pieter van Musschenbroek, de la universidad de Leiden, demostró que la electricidad podía almacenarse. A partir de este dispositivo se desarrolló la idea de la pila eléctrica, en origen un grupo de botellas de Leiden que, combinadas, generaban una carga eléctrica más potente.

Primer condensador
La botella de Leiden podía almacenar la electricidad, creada por un generador electrostático, que la varilla metálica conducía a la botella.

El soberano persa **Nadir Sah** (n. 1688), que se había vuelto paranoide y despiadadamente cruel, murió **asesinado** por sus guardaespaldas en 1747. A su muerte, una gran asamblea en Kandahar (Afganistán) detectó la debilidad del Imperio persa y eligió al lugarteniente afgano de Nadir, **Ahmad Kan Abdalí** (1722–1773) como cabeza y fundador del **moderno estado de Afganistán**. Abdalí unificó el país y lo convirtió en un gran imperio que comprendía parte de los actuales Irán, Pakistán e India.

En África occidental, los **yoruba**, que ocupaban un territorio que se extendía desde el actual Benín hasta el sur de Nigeria, invadió en 1747 el **reino de Dahomey**. Este reino cuya riqueza se debía al comercio de esclavos y productos como el aceite de palma se vio obligado a pagar tributo al **Imperio yoruba de Oyo** hasta 1818.

En 1747, un descubrimiento vino a mejorar la vida de los **marineros**. En un estudio pionero, el médico de la marina británica James Lind demostró que el **escorbuto**, una enfermedad frecuente durante los viajes largos y en ocasiones letal, podía tratarse mediante el consumo de **cítricos**. Sin embargo, la Royal Navy no empezó a utilizar el zumo de cítricos para prevenir y tratar el escorbuto hasta 1795.

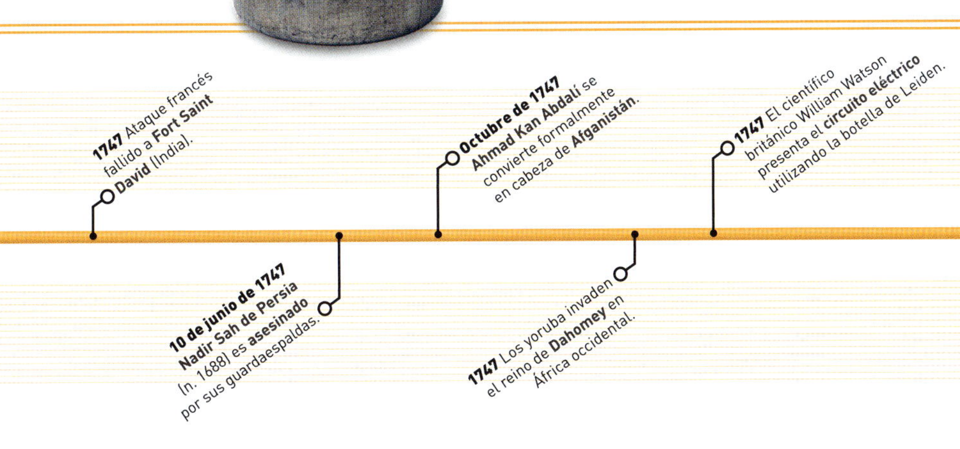

1748–1749

Espectáculo pirotécnico en el río Támesis el 15 de mayo de 1749, organizado por el duque de Richmond para celebrar la firma del tratado de Aquisgrán.

LA GUERRA DE SUCESIÓN AUSTRIACA (*véase* 1740) llegó a su fin con la firma del **tratado de Aquisgrán** (actual Aachen) en 1748. Se reconocía la conquista de Silesia por parte de Prusia; Francia recuperaba parte de sus colonias a cambio de retirarse de Países Bajos; y se renovaba el contrato de **asiento** entre España y Gran Bretaña (*véase* 1713).

El lucrativo **saqueo de Delhi** (*véase* 1739) por Nadir Sah incentivó un segundo ataque, esta vez al **Punjab**, liderado por Ahmad Kan Abdalí (*véase* 1747). Su ejército, formado por 12 000 jinetes, se enfrentó a una fuerza defensiva mogol de 60 000 hombres en la **batalla de Manipur**. Los afganos de Abdalí resistieron hasta que la explosión de un polvorín mató a mil, y los demás huyeron. Mientras tanto, al sur, prosperaba el **reino de Mysore** bajo Haidar Alí (1722–1782), padre del famoso sultán Tipu (1750–1799). Liderado por Haidar Alí, el Imperio de Mysore **ganó territorios** a los marathas, a Hyderabad y a los reinos colindantes.

En **América del Norte**, los británicos consolidaron su presencia en Nueva Escocia mediante la fundación en 1749 de **Halifax**, a donde se trasladó la capital de la región desde Annapolis Royal. Violando un tratado anterior, el teniente general **Edward Cornwallis** (1713–1776), arribó con barcos mercantes que transportaban a **2500 colonos**, lo que provocó una guerra durante la cual los franceses y los indios micmac atacaron sin cesar el asentamiento británico.

Platino en bruto
El platino, descubierto por los conquistadores españoles en América del Sur, debe su nombre a su parecido con la plata.

En Pensilvania, Henry Melchor Mühlenburg (1711–1787) fundó el **primer sínodo luterano**. Los luteranos alemanes habían llegado a Pensilvania en 1683, pero fue la creación del sínodo lo que **unificó a la comunidad luterana**.

Aunque Europa llevaba ya mucho tiempo explotando el oro y la plata sudamericanos, el valor del **platino de América del Sur** no fue reconocido hasta el año 1748, gracias a un informe realizado por el explorador español Antonio de Ulloa (1716–1795). Este metal, caracterizado por su densidad y su enorme resistencia a la corrosión se extraía de las minas de la cordillera Occidental de **Colombia** y del centro de **Perú**.

Por último, otro español, Jacobo Rodríguez Pereira (1715–1780) hizo historia en 1749 cuando llevó a uno de sus alumnos a la Academia de las Ciencias de París para presentar su nuevo **lenguaje de signos** para sordomudos, para el que únicamente se necesitaba una mano.

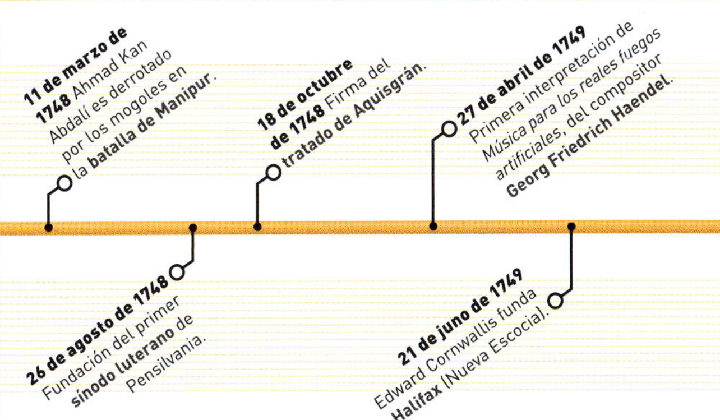

6

LA ERA DE LAS REVOLUCIONES 1750–1913

Este periodo convulso, con frecuencia violento y teñido de sangre, también se caracterizó por importantes avances tecnológicos en los campos de la medicina, las comunicaciones y el transporte que abrieron las puertas al mundo moderno.

1750

Escudo de José I de Portugal en la Universidad de Coímbra.

EL TRATADO DE MADRID, cuya firma tuvo lugar el 13 de enero, estableció los límites coloniales entre España y Portugal en el Nuevo Mundo, lo cual suponía una modificación significativa del **tratado de Tordesillas** (1494), por el cual se estipulaba que el territorio portugués no podía extenderse más allá de 370 leguas al oeste de las Azores (unos 46° oeste). El nuevo tratado tenía en cuenta el alcance de los asentamientos portugueses en Brasil, ya que el Imperio español confiaba en que estas concesiones sirvieran para moderar las ambiciones territoriales de los portugueses en la región.

EL MARQUÉS DE POMBAL
(1699–1782)

Nombrado primer ministro de Portugal en 1750, año en que José I (1714–1777) subió al trono, fue una figura política controvertida. A lo largo de sus 27 años de gobierno llevó a cabo varias reformas tanto sociales como económicas y expulsó a los jesuitas.

1751

Detalle del grabado *Gin Lane*, de William Hogarth, sobre el problema social del alcoholismo callejero provocado por la ginebra barata.

17 VOLÚMENES DE LA *ENCICLOPEDIA* FRANCESA QUE SE **PUBLICARON** ENTRE LOS AÑOS 1751 Y 1765

INGLATERRA PADECÍA UNA GRAVE CRISIS ALCOHÓLICA como consecuencia de la gran popularidad de la ginebra barata, que **William Hogarth** (1697–1764) ilustró en 1751 en su grabado satírico *Gin Lane* (Callejón de la Ginebra). La mejora de los métodos de producción a lo largo de los cincuenta años anteriores había convertido a la ginebra en una bebida muy asequible: el año en que Hogarth realizó el grabado, los británicos bebían más de nueve litros de ginebra al año. El descontento popular por los efectos sociales del abuso de la ginebra llevó a la promulgación de la *Gin Act* (1751) para limitar la cantidad que podía adquirir un consumidor.

En Francia, un grupo de intelectuales dirigido por el filósofo y escritor **Denis Diderot** (1713–1784) comenzó a publicar la ***Enciclopedia*** *(Encyclopédie) o Diccionario razonado de las ciencias, las artes y los oficios*, probablemente la obra que mejor reflejó el espíritu de la **Ilustración** (*véase* 1763). Muchos pensadores franceses de la talla de **Montesquieu** (1689–1755), **Voltaire** (1694–1778), **Jean-Jacques Rousseau** (1712–1778) y **Turgot** (1727–1781) contribuyeron con artículos a una obra que aspiraba a catalogar todos los conocimientos de la época en ciencias, filosofía, política y religión. Su énfasis en la razón le valió el rechazo de diversos sectores vinculados a la **Iglesia católica**, que llegó a incluirla en su Índice de **libros prohibidos**.

Al otro lado del mundo, China extendía su poder hasta **las cuencas de Zungaria y de Tarim** luchando contra las tribus mongolas por el poder sobre esa región clave de las estepas, cuya importancia residía en su proximidad a la **Ruta de la Seda** (pp. 100–101), la principal ruta comercial entre China y Occidente.

1752

Estatua de Buda en el templo Sulamani Pahto de Pagán (Birmania), que fue construido en 1181, pero contiene imágenes y frescos del periodo Konbaung.

BIRMANIA (MYANMAR) ESTUVO MUCHO TIEMPO DIVIDIDA entre facciones rivales hasta que **Alaungpaya**, o Alompra (1714–1760), inició la unificación del país mediante una serie de campañas victoriosas y estableció la **dinastía Konbaung**. Además de unir a grupos muy dispares, Alaungpaya se tuvo que enfrentar a Gran Bretaña y Francia, ansiosas por obtener territorios en Birmania y dispuestas a armar a sus enemigos; sin embargo, consiguió resistir durante siete años y expulsó a los ejércitos de ambas potencias. El reino unificado se fue reforzando bajo reyes sucesivos y a lo largo de varias décadas incluso llegó a realizar incursiones en Siam (Tailandia).

El 14 de junio, **España y los reinos de Hungría y Bohemia y de Cerdeña**, a quienes posteriormente se les añadieron los ducados de Parma y Toscana, suscribieron el **tratado de Aranjuez** con el objetivo de proteger los intereses territoriales que las tres potencias tenían en Italia.

« LA ENERGÍA Y LA PERSEVERANCIA LO **CONSIGUEN TODO**. **»**

Atribuido a Benjamin Franklin, inventor, político y diplomático estadounidense

En Gran Bretaña, la población se fue a dormir el 2 de septiembre y se despertó el 14. El gobierno había decidido sustituir el **calendario juliano** por el **gregoriano**, un cambio que otros países europeos ya habían hecho siglos antes. El papa Gregorio XIII decidió introducir el nuevo calendario en 1582, cuando se hizo evidente que el juliano añadía cerca de once días entre los equinoccios de primavera y adelantaba la Semana Santa cada año.

Mientras tanto, en la América del Norte británica, los avances científicos progresaban a su propio ritmo. El político, diplomático e inventor estadounidense **Benjamin Franklin** (1706–1790) concibió el **pararrayos**. Hasta aquel momento era habitual ver edificios destruidos por incendios provocados por rayos. Franklin supuso que existía una relación entre el rayo y la **electricidad**, y se dice que hizo volar una cometa para demostrarlo. El pararrayos, que desarrolló tras su experimento, atrae el rayo y lo conduce hasta el suelo sin pasar por el edificio, que queda a salvo.

ROCOCÓ

Este fresco, realizado en el siglo XVIII en el techo de una iglesia bávara, ejemplifica el estilo rococó que dominó las artes decorativas, la pintura, la arquitectura y la escultura europeas. Evolucionó a partir del barroco (*véase* 1626), pero sus detalles y adornos eran todavía más elaborados, y, con frecuencia, frívolos. Este periodo artístico suele estar asociado al diseño y al gusto francés durante los reinados de Luis XV (r. 1715–1754) y Luis XVI (r. 1774–1792).

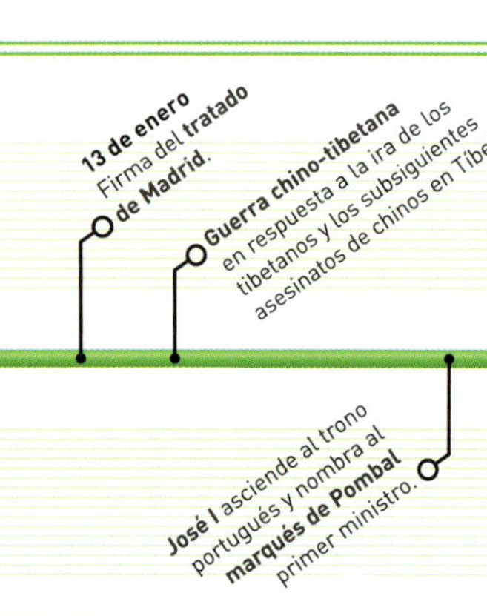

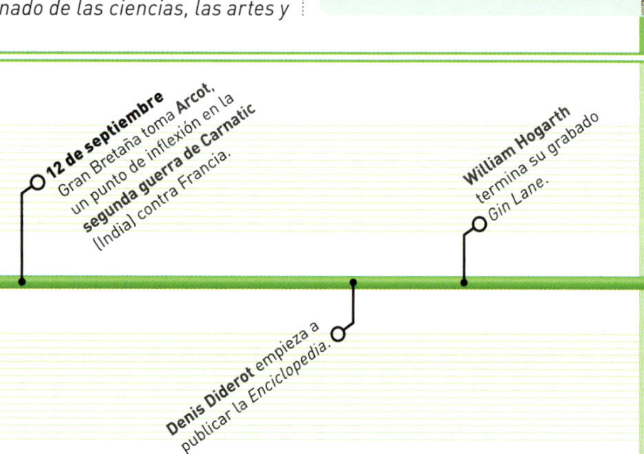

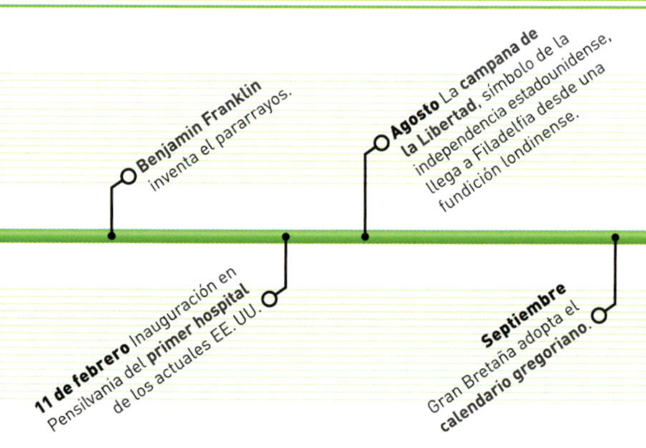

1753

Ilustración botánica de la zarzamora por J. Miller, basada en la obra de Carlos Linneo.

EL MÉDICO Y COLECCIONISTA irlandés Sir Hans Sloane (1660–1753), logró reunir a lo largo de su vida una colección de 71 000 objetos, desde muestras de flora y fauna procedentes de todo el mundo hasta libros y manuscritos que abarcaban una gran variedad de temas. Al igual que otros científicos e intelectuales europeos, formaba parte de corrientes intelectuales ilustradas más amplias y era plenamente consciente del valor académico de su colección, que decidió legar a Gran Bretaña. A cambio, pidió un pago único de 20 000 libras (muy por debajo del valor de la colección). El parlamento aceptó el trato y aprobó la ley por la que se fundó el **Museo Británico**, donde años después se expusieron partes de la colección.

Los contemporáneos europeos de Sloane también se dedicaron al coleccionismo y otras actividades científicas. Ese mismo año, el botánico sueco **Carlos Linneo** (1707–1778) publicó *Species plantarum*, donde clasificaba más de siete mil especies de plantas por género, clase y orden, un sistema que se sigue utilizando en la actualidad.

Colección impagable
Este astrolabio de oro, de la colección de Hans Sloane, se utilizaba para determinar la posición del Sol y de las estrellas.

1754

LA SEGUNDA GUERRA DE CARNATIC (1749–1754) y la **guerra de británicos contra franceses e indios** norteamericanos (1754–1763), fueron precursoras de la **guerra de los Siete Años** (1756–1763). Ninguna de ellas se libró en suelo europeo. La **guerra entre franceses y británicos** se extendió desde Virginia, en el sur de América del Norte, hasta alcanzar Nueva Escocia, en el norte.

Las batallas de la **segunda guerra de Carnatic** se libraron en el sur de India. El **tratado de Pondicherry** detuvo temporalmente las tensiones entre Francia y Gran Bretaña, cuyos ejércitos estaban al servicio de las **Compañías de las Indias Orientales**. El tratado reconocía a Muhammad Alí, que contaba con el apoyo británico, como nuevo **nabab de Carnatic**, un elemento clave de la disputa.

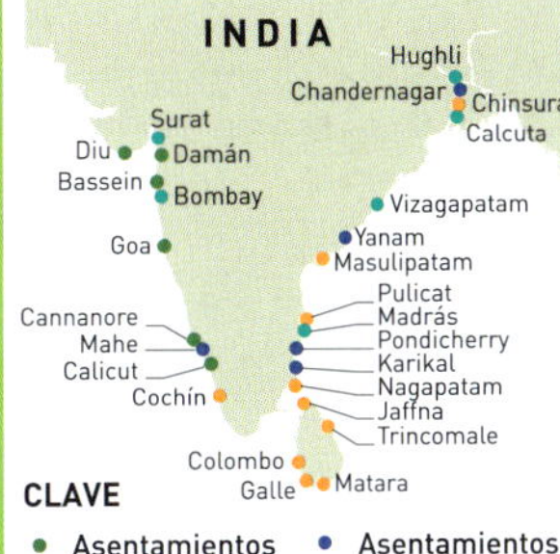

Europa en India
A mediados del siglo XVIII, las potencias europeas tenían asentamientos y territorios consolidados en India.

Soldados montados sobre elefantes durante la guerra de Carnatic.

1755

Búsqueda desesperada de supervivientes en Lisboa tras el terremoto que arrasó la ciudad en noviembre.

> « NO ESTOY TAN **PERDIDO EN LA LEXICOGRAFÍA** COMO PARA OLVIDAR QUE LAS **PALABRAS** SON HIJAS DE LA TIERRA. »
>
> **Samuel Johnson**, escritor inglés, en el prólogo de su *Dictionary of the English Language* (1755)

DECENAS DE MILES DE PERSONAS PERECIERON en Lisboa el 1 de noviembre por la mañana como consecuencia de un terremoto. Los historiadores han estimado que el seísmo llegó a alcanzar 9 grados en la escala de Richter, y se calcula que perdieron la vida entre 10 000 y 100 000 personas de una población de 200 000. El terremoto también provocó un tsunami que destruyó poblaciones más al sur, en el Algarve. Este desastre causó una honda impresión en toda Europa: inspiró a **Voltaire** (1694–1778) su *Poema sobre el desastre de Lisboa*, y el filósofo alemán Immanuel Kant (1724–1804) escribió una serie de ensayos sobre el tema. El **marqués de Pombal** (*véase* recuadro) actuó con gran rapidez y se aseguró de que los incendios se extinguieran y se enterrara a los muertos enseguida. Entonces ordenó la reconstrucción de la ciudad con edificios, esta vez concebidos para resistir nuevos seísmos.

Durante ese mismo año, en Inglaterra, el escritor **Samuel Johnson** (1709–1784) culminó el encargo de un sindicato de impresores de Londres: la elaboración de un **diccionario de la lengua inglesa**. Aunque no fue el primer diccionario inglés, rápidamente se convirtió en el más celebrado y respetado. Algunas de sus definiciones más conocidas son: «mecenas: normalmente, un infeliz que paga con insolencia y es pagado con adulación» o «avena: cereal que en Inglaterra suele ser alimento de caballos, pero que en Escocia consumen las personas».

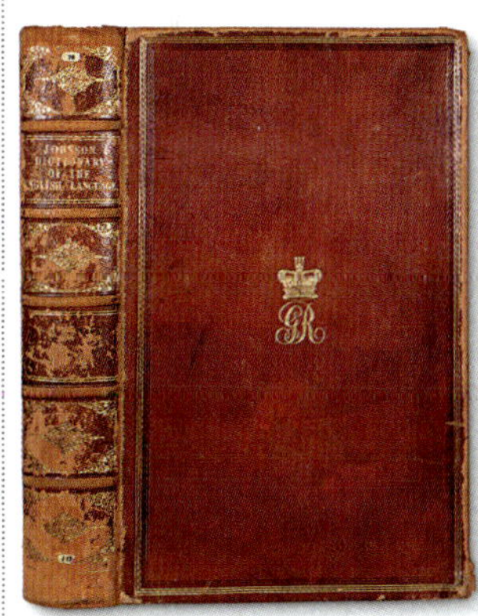

Inglés por definición
Cubierta de la primera edición del Diccionario de la Lengua Inglesa de Samuel Johnson.

- **Marzo** Suecia adopta el **calendario gregoriano**.
- **5 de abril** Acta de fundación del **Museo Británico**.
- Se publica *Species plantarum*, obra de **Carlos Linneo**.
- Empieza la **guerra entre británicos y franceses e indios** en América del Norte.
- El **tratado de Pondicherry** pone fin a la segunda guerra de Carnatic.
- El físico y químico escocés **Joseph Black** (1728–1799) descubre el **dióxido de carbono**.
- Los británicos expulsan de **Acadia** (hoy parte de Canadá) a los colonos franceses.
- **15 de abril Samuel Johnson** publica su innovador diccionario de la lengua inglesa.
- **1 de noviembre** Un violento **terremoto** destruye **Lisboa**.

Detalle de un grabado de Paul Revere sobre la toma del fuerte francés de Louisbourg (Nueva Escocia) por los británicos. El fuerte, construido por Francia para proteger sus intereses en la región, se convirtió en objetivo de los británicos cuando estalló la guerra en 1756. La ciudad fue atacada por tierra y mar, y se rindió en 1758.

LA GUERRA DE LOS SIETE AÑOS (1756–1763) se libró en India, América del Norte y Europa, lo que la convirtió en un verdadero conflicto mundial, aunque sus raíces fueran europeas. La anterior **guerra de Sucesión austriaca** (*véase* 1740) dejó sin resolver numerosas cuestiones territoriales. **El tratado de Aquisgrán** (1748) no solucionó la disputa entre **Prusia** y **Austria** por la provincia de **Silesia**, en el sureste de Prusia y limítrofe con Austria. Al mismo tiempo, las tensiones entre **Gran Bretaña** y **Francia** se intensificaban. Complejas alianzas empeoraron la situación y desencadenaron la que se conoció como guerra de los Siete Años.

En 1756, algunos incidentes clave dejaron claras las líneas de batalla. En abril, **Francia invadió Menorca**, que Gran Bretaña había arrebatado a España en 1708. Los franceses enviaron 15 000 soldados a la isla, donde los británicos solo tenían unos 2500. Gran Bretaña declaró la guerra a Francia. El conflicto terminó arrastrando también al **Electorado de Hanover**, en el noroeste de Alemania, que se mostró dispuesto a enviar soldados para apoyar a las fuerzas británicas.

Federico II de Prusia (1712–1786) recelaba cada vez más de la alianza entre **Francia y Rusia**. En mayo, sus tropas entraron en el **Electorado de Sajonia**, entre Prusia y Rusia. Superaban a las de Sajonia por más de tres a uno, pero **María Teresa** de Austria (1717–1780) envió rápidamente más soldados. Había estallado la guerra.

Gran Bretaña y Prusia se aliaron contra Francia, Rusia, Austria, Suecia, Sajonia y, al final, España. Sin embargo, cada país perseguía también sus propios intereses. Gran Bretaña quería expulsar a Francia de **India** y de **América del Norte**; Austria y Prusia ambicionaban Silesia; y Rusia pretendía compensar el creciente poder de Federico II y ayudar a Austria y Francia.

El conflicto europeo se había visto precedido por escaramuzas en los territorios coloniales: británicos y franceses se habían enfrentado en América del Norte y en India. Las **tensiones anglo-francesas** provocaron disputas con los gobernantes locales en India y llevaron al trágico episodio del **agujero negro de Calcuta**. **Siraj-ud Daula** (1733–1757), **nabab de Bengala,** que contaba con el apoyo de Francia, atacó a los británicos de Calcuta y encerró a muchos de ellos en una pequeña celda de Fort William. Se estima que había entre 60 y 150 cautivos. Por la noche, entre 40 y 123 de ellos murieron como consecuencia del hacinamiento y el calor.

Ejércitos
Este gráfico muestra los efectivos de los ejércitos que combatieron en la guerra de los Siete Años. Aunque algunas batallas importantes se libraron en el mar, la mayoría recayó en la infantería.

RUSIA 333 000
AUSTRIA 201 000
FRANCIA 200 000
PRUSIA 145 000
GRAN BRETAÑA 90 000

FEDERICO II (1712–1786)

Federico II de Prusia, «el Grande», reinó durante 46 años. Aunque le interesaba la cultura y la filosofía, debe su sobrenombre a sus proezas militares, que hicieron del pequeño reino prusiano una gran potencia europea. Su reinado estuvo caracterizado por un espíritu liberal y sus teorías acerca del poder le valieron la reputación de déspota ilustrado.

La guerra de los Siete Años
Los campos de batalla de este conflicto abarcaron todo el globo, desde Canadá a India y Europa, convirtiéndolo así en la primera guerra global. Las cruces identifican a los vencedores de las principales batallas.

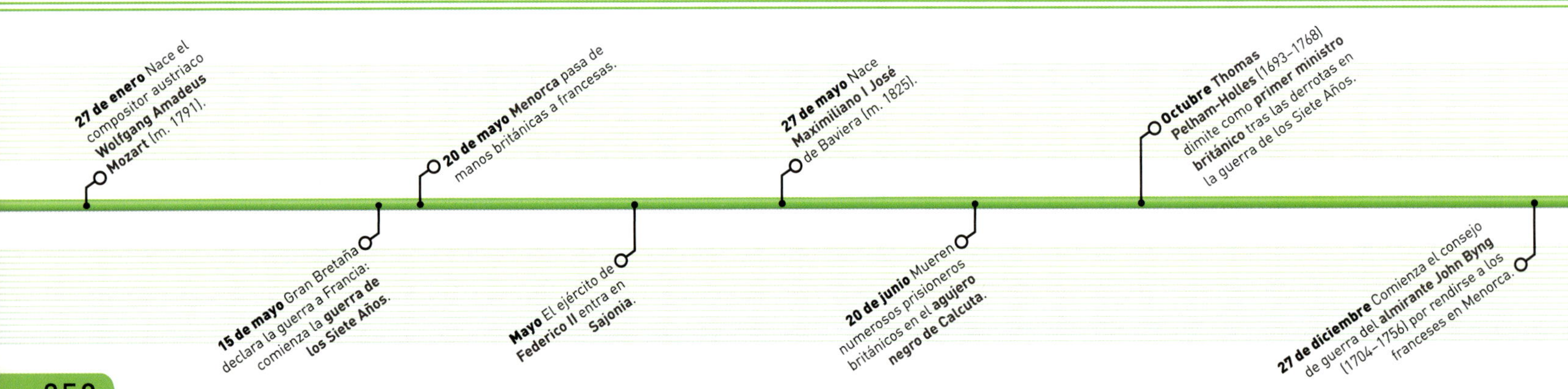

1757

Combate de piratas berberiscos con la flota veneciana.

1758

Federico II conduce a sus soldados a la victoria en la batalla de Zorndorf.

1759

El nuevo rey de España, Carlos III, reinó durante casi treinta años. Luis Paret y Alcázar (1746–1799) ilustró la vida en palacio en el cuadro *Carlos III comiendo ante su corte.*

LA ALIANZA BRITÁNICOPRUSIANA (*véase* 1756) obtuvo varias victorias en 1757. **Robert Clive** (1725–1774) recuperó Calcuta para la Compañía de las Indias Orientales (*véase* 1600) y para Gran Bretaña cuando logró derrotar al nabab de Bengala en la **batalla de Plassey**. El emperador del Sacro Imperio, **Francisco I** (casado con María Teresa de Austria) declaró la guerra a Prusia. El **rey Federico II** de Prusia atacó Bohemia, aunque fue derrotado por el ejército austriaco. Prusia venció al ejército austrofrancés en el mes de noviembre en Rossbach, pero en diciembre perdió ante los austriacos en Leuthan.

En Marruecos, el sultán **Muhammad III** (c. 1710–1790) estabilizó el país después de treinta años de inestabilidad. Se hizo famoso por sus victorias sobre los **piratas berberiscos**, que saqueaban ciudades por todo el Mediterráneo.

Robert Clive
El general Robert Clive recuperó Calcuta para Gran Bretaña en la batalla de Plassey. Esta victoria le aseguró el control de Bengala.

LA GUERRA DE LOS SIETE AÑOS PROSIGUIÓ CON UNA SERIE de victorias británicas sobre Francia que resultaron cruciales: los británicos se apoderaron de **Fort Duquesne** y **Louisbourg** en América del Norte y de **Pondicherry** en India (mapa p. 258), e invadieron **Senegal** en África occidental. En Europa, Gran Bretaña y Prusia consiguieron vencer a las fuerzas francesas cerca del río Rin en **Krefeld**, en junio, y a Rusia en la batalla de **Zorndorf**, en territorio prusiano, en agosto.

Mientras tanto, en India, estallaba otro conflicto armado entre los afganos y los marathas. Las fuertes disputas territoriales finalmente desembocaron en la **guerra afgano-maratha** (que continuó hasta 1861). Tras la muerte de **Nadir Sah** (1688–1747), el Imperio persa había comenzado a desintegrarse y Afganistán se independizó bajo el gobierno de **Ahmad Sah Durrani** (c. 1723–1773), que deseaba controlar los territorios cercanos en **Punjab** y el **Ganges superior**. Durrani había saqueado la ciudad mogola de **Delhi** el año anterior, y los vecinos marathas, que aspiraban a gobernar el territorio, declararon la guerra a los afganos.

En la **península Arábiga** se estaban produciendo cambios políticos de una gran importancia, aunque no violentos: los jefes de la confederación **utub** escogieron a **Sabah bin Jaber (Sabah I)** (c. 1652–1762) como emir del territorio que pronto pasaría a llamarse **Kuwait**. Su familia, la dinastía al-Sabah, continúa gobernando Kuwait en la actualidad.

« TODO SUCEDE PARA BIEN EN EL MEJOR DE LOS MUNDOS POSIBLES. »

Voltaire, escritor francés, en *Cándido* (1759)

PARA LOS BRITÁNICOS, LA GUERRA DE LOS SIETE AÑOS alcanzó un punto de inflexión con la toma de la isla francesa de **Guadalupe**, en las Antillas, en mayo; de territorio canadiense en julio y de Quebec en septiembre. También derrotaron a la flota francesa en la **bahía de Lagos** (Portugal), en agosto, y en la **bahía de Quiberon** (Francia), en noviembre. Un ejército angloprusiano venció a los franceses en la **batalla de Minden** (Alemania) a principios de agosto, pero poco después Prusia sufrió una humillante derrota en **Kunersdorf** (Alemania) seguida de otra por los austriacos en la **batalla de Maxen** (Sajonia).

En España, tras la muerte de Fernando VI heredó el trono su hermanastro **Carlos III** (1716–1788), hasta entonces rey de Nápoles y Sicilia. Máximo representante del despotismo ilustrado en España, destacó por su celo reformista.

Entre tanto, **Portugal** había empezado a desconfiar de las actividades de los **jesuitas** (*véase* 1533) y los expulsó de sus territorios.

Un hito cultural fue la publicación de *Cándido*, de **Voltaire**, una sátira sobre el optimismo infundado.

EL ABOLICIONISMO

La imagen de un esclavo arrodillado con la inscripción «¿Acaso no soy un hombre y un hermano?» fue el símbolo del movimiento abolicionista británico, que luego adoptó la Sociedad Antiesclavista Americana, fundada en el año 1833. Josiah Wedgwood creó el sello para la Sociedad para la Abolición de la Trata de Esclavos. Tras décadas de presiones, en 1807 se abolió el comercio de esclavos en Gran Bretaña. En otros países también se fundaron diversos grupos abolicionistas, como la Sociedad de Amigos de los Negros, en Francia.

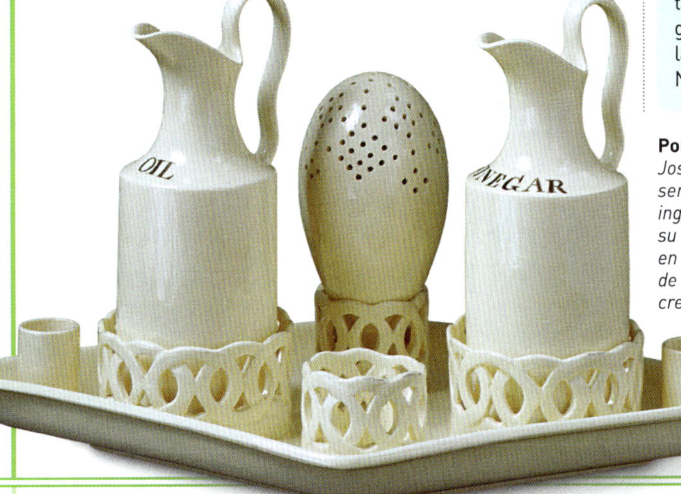

Porcelana Wedgwood
Josiah Wedgwood nació en el seno de una familia de alfareros ingleses y transformó el oficio con su técnica y su estilo. Se estableció en 1759 y se convirtió en proveedor de la reina Carlota. Su loza de color crema alcanzó gran popularidad.

23 de junio Lord Clive (1725–1774) recupera Calcuta y Bengala.

Mustafá III (1717–1774) se convierte en sultán del **Imperio otomano**.

El Sacro Imperio (Austria) declara la guerra a Prusia.

Ahmad Sah Durrani (c. 1723–1773), de Afganistán, saquea Delhi.

Inicio de la **guerra afgano-maratha** por disputas territoriales.

Sabah bin Jaber (1718–1762) es elegido emir por la confederación utub.

25 de agosto Prusia derrota a Rusia en la **batalla de Zorndorf**.

Los **británicos** vencen a los **franceses** en Fort Duquesne (colonias americanas) y en Gorea (Senegal).

El escritor y filósofo francés **Voltaire** (1694–1778) publica *Cándido*.

Mayo Gran Bretaña arrebata a Francia **Guadalupe**.

1 de agosto Tropas angloprusianas vencen a Francia en la **batalla de Minden**.

12 de agosto Derrota de Prusia por tropas francorrusas en la **batalla de Kunersdorf**.

Agosto Carlos III (1716–1788) asciende al **trono de España**.

13 de septiembre Gran Bretaña arrebata **Quebec** a Francia.

El ceramista inglés **Josiah Wedgwood** (1730–1795) se establece por su cuenta.

Inauguración del **Real Jardín Botánico** (*Physick Gardens*) en Kew.

12 de noviembre Austria vence a Prusia en la **batalla de Maxen**.

Portugal expulsa a los **jesuitas** de sus territorios.

1760

Caricatura de Jorge III y de su esposa, la reina Carlota. El rey Jorge III nació en Gran Bretaña y reinó durante casi sesenta años.

EN 1760 ASCENDIÓ AL TRONO DE INGLATERRA Jorge III (1738–1820), el primer monarca de la dinastía alemana Hanover nacido en Gran Bretaña. A diferencia de su abuelo **Jorge II** (1683–1760), cuya lengua materna era el alemán, Jorge III era anglófono. La corona saltó una generación, debido a la muerte de su padre, Federico Luis (1707–1751). Antes de morir, este dejó instrucciones para que cuando Jorge, de solo doce años de edad, accediera al trono, separara el Electorado de Hanover de Inglaterra y redujera la deuda nacional.

Después de la muerte de su padre, Jorge cayó bajo la influencia de **John Stuart, tercer conde de Bute** (1713–1792), su tutor y consejero. La gran influencia de Bute sobre Jorge III durante sus primeros años de reinado se hizo especialmente evidente por el deterioro de las relaciones con **William Pitt el Viejo** (1708–1778) y la coalición Newcastle-Pitt, que gobernó Gran Bretaña durante la **guerra de los Siete Años** (*véase* 1756). El deseo urgente de Jorge III de poner fin a la guerra y distanciar a Gran Bretaña de Prusia quedó de manifiesto cuando nombró primer ministro a Bute en 1762.

Mientras Jorge III se enredaba en la política británica y europea, sus dominios en el **Caribe** se transformaron. Ya no eran enclaves imperiales, sino ricas colonias azucareras, y su riqueza dependía de explotar el trabajo de miles de **esclavos africanos** en plantaciones. En 1760, la población de la América británica había alcanzado los dos millones de habitantes, y más de 300 000 de ellos eran esclavos. De modo similar, la población esclava de las colonias francesas en el Caribe llegaría a las 379 000 personas hacia el final de la década. En la Cuba española había menos de 40 000 esclavos, pero se multiplicarían con la explosión azucarera posterior.

La isla británica de **Jamaica** se había convertido en una gran productora de azúcar, y había crecido el transporte forzoso de esclavos, muchos de los cuales escaparon o se rebelaron. El domingo de Pascua de 1760 estalló una **rebelión liderada por un esclavo** llamado Tacky en la parroquia de St. Mary, desde donde se extendió; participaron unos 30 000 esclavos antes de que fuera reprimida el año siguiente.

Mientras tanto, en la **China Qing**, las **revueltas continuas** de las **tribus mongolas** en la frontera noroeste, iniciadas hacia 1755, habían terminado por fin. El conflicto empezó cuando los mongoles se negaron a pagar el tributo anual que exigía el gobierno chino; de hecho, mataron a los recaudadores de impuestos chinos. Sin embargo, al final China se impuso y en 1760 incorporó el territorio mongol.

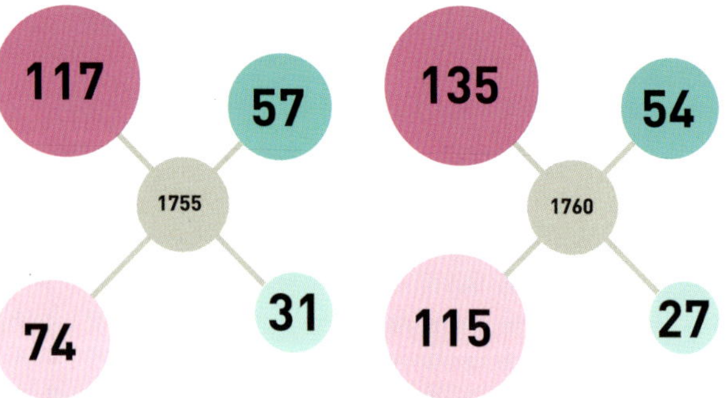

Flotas (guerra de los Siete Años)
Muchas batallas importantes fueron en el mar. La potencia naval británica llegó a superar a la francesa.

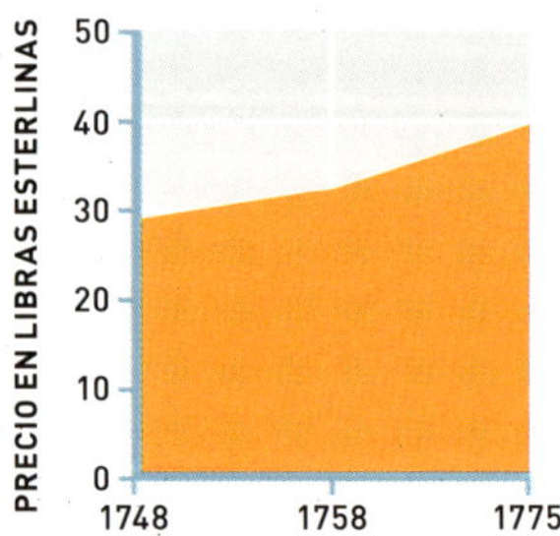

Precio de un esclavo varón
Mientras aumentaba la producción de azúcar en las colonias británicas y francesas del Caribe, importaron más esclavos africanos.

1761

Haidar Alí, sultán de Mysore, se convirtió en enemigo del ejército de la Compañía Británica de las Indias Orientales.

LA GUERRA DE LOS SIETE AÑOS SE INTENSIFICÓ en el continente europeo y también alcanzó un clímax en los territorios coloniales. Gran Bretaña tomó **Pondicherry** (mapa inferior) y consiguió acabar con el poder de Francia en India. La Compañía Francesa de las Indias Orientales había fundado este puerto en el año 1674 y, con el paso del tiempo, lo había convertido en una de sus principales bases de operaciones tanto comerciales como militares en los continuos enfrentamientos que mantenía con la Compañía Británica de las Indias Orientales. Dicha victoria siguió a otra obtenida el año anterior en **Wandiwash** (sureste de India).

Al mismo tiempo, en India, el enfrentamiento entre **afganos y marathas** (*véase* 1758) culminó en la batalla de **Panipat**, al norte, que tuvo lugar el 17 de enero. Fue una batalla muy cruenta, con un gran número de bajas (murieron cerca de 75 000 marathas y aproximadamente 30 000 fueron capturados). Sin embargo, Ahmad Sah Durrani, que en ese momento lideraba a los afganos, fue obligado por su propio ejército a regresar al trono en Afganistán. Esto permitió a marathas y británicos repartirse el anterior territorio mogol. La guerra contribuyó al debilitamiento de la confederación maratha y a una mayor descentralización de su poder que condujo a la desintegración de los reinos y a batallas posteriores con Gran Bretaña por el territorio.

Algo más al sur, en **Mysore**, otro futuro enemigo de Gran Bretaña, **Haidar Alí** (1722–1782) estaba reuniendo un ejército y consolidando su poder con el objetivo de asumir el control del territorio.

En el otro extremo del mundo, las tropas británicas y francesas se enfrentaban en el **Caribe**. Gran Bretaña utilizó la isla de Guadalupe, que había ocupado dos años antes (*véase* mapa 1756), como base para arrebatar Dominica a los franceses. Al año siguiente irrumpieron en Martinica.

Para complicar todavía más las cosas, **España** también se había involucrado en el conflicto, y la flota británica se preparaba para atacar a las naves españolas. Sin embargo, sus planes de ataque iban mucho más allá de unas simples escaramuzas navales: los británicos no solo invadieron y ocuparon el puerto de **La Habana** al año siguiente, sino que utilizaron las naves ancladas en India para atacar **Manila**, la capital de la colonia española de Filipinas.

Conflictos en India
En 1761, India fue escenario de importantes batallas, no tan solo entre Gran Bretaña y Francia, sino también entre marathas y afganos.

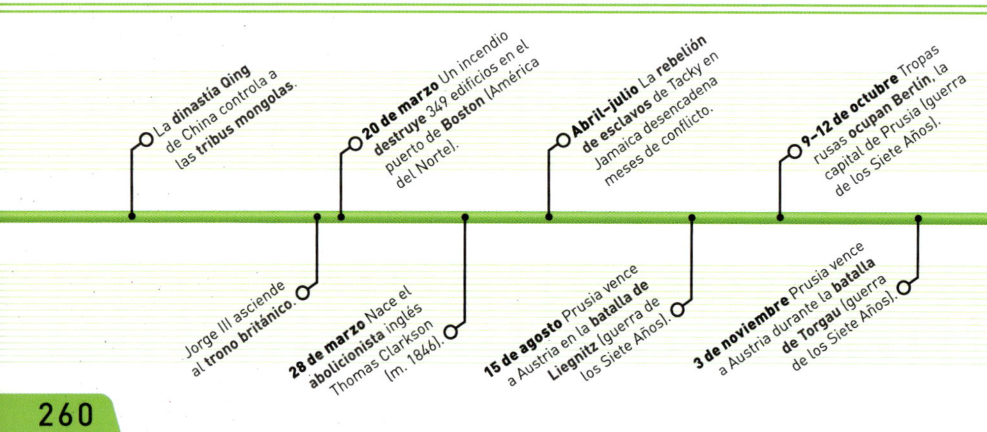

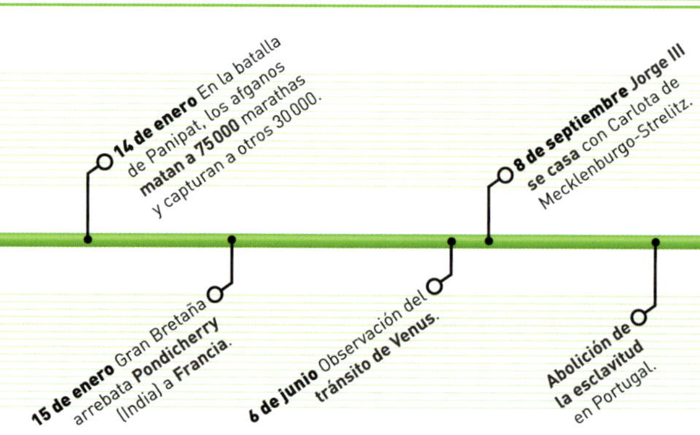

1762

« SERÉ UNA AUTÓCRATA, ES MI OFICIO; Y EL BUEN DIOS ME PERDONARÁ, ES EL SUYO. »

Atribuido a Catalina la Grande, emperatriz de Rusia

RUSIA PRESENCIÓ EL ASCENSO DE DOS MONARCAS durante 1762, primero **Pedro III** (1728–1762) y luego **Catalina II** (1729–1796), posteriormente conocida como Catalina la Grande. Cuando Pedro III se convirtió en emperador, dejó muy claro su apoyo a Prusia en la guerra de los Siete Años, una postura enormemente impopular entre los ministros y la población. No tardó en organizarse una conspiración contra él que acabó con su arresto y la posterior coronación de su esposa, Catalina, como emperatriz de Rusia. Pedro III fue encarcelado y falleció en circunstancias dudosas. El reinado de Catalina la Grande se caracterizó por **la agresividad y la expansión territorial de Rusia**. Además de introducir importantes reformas en la agricultura, la industria y la educación, la zarina relajó la censura rusa y se hizo famosa por su gran amor a la literatura y su especial predilección por los filósofos franceses, como Voltaire, con quien mantuvo correspondencia durante quince años.

La guerra de los Siete Años continuaba avanzando, y **España** se vio mucho más implicada en ella después de que Gran Bretaña tomara el importante puerto caribeño de La Habana. Además, los británicos utilizaron las tropas de India para ocupar Manila (Filipinas), que en aquel momento también era una colonia española. Al mismo tiempo, **España y Francia** firmaban un acuerdo secreto, el **tratado de Fontainebleau**, por el que España recibía el territorio francés de Luisiana (América del Norte), situado al oeste del río Misisipi. Se trataba, en parte, de una recompensa a los Borbones españoles por su apoyo a Francia, pero también se debía al deseo de esta última de librarse de una posible fuga de recursos. España se beneficiaba porque, así, bloqueaba el avance de los británicos hacia territorio español, sobre todo cerca de México.

Catalina la Grande
La emperatriz de Rusia, nacida en Alemania, reinó entre 1762 y 1796, y dirigió la expansión territorial de su país de adopción.

Entre tanto, en Francia, el filósofo y escritor **Jean-Jacques Rousseau** (1712–1778), publicó su influyente tratado *El contrato social o principios de derecho político*, en el que analizaba con minuciosidad la relación entre los gobiernos y los gobernados, y la cuestión de la libertad frente a la autoridad política. Aunque las autoridades francesas lo prohibieron de inmediato, esta obra inspiró la declaración de los derechos del hombre redactada por los revolucionarios franceses en 1789.

1763

Espectáculo pirotécnico en Londres durante la celebración de la paz de París, que puso fin a la guerra de los Siete Años.

LAS POTENCIAS EUROPEAS enfrentadas en la guerra de los Siete Años **pusieron fin al conflicto** con la firma de los tratados de París y Hubertusburg. El coste del conflicto, en cientos de miles de vidas y sumas ingentes de dinero, había sido enorme. La deuda nacional británica pasó de 75 a 133 millones de libras. Prusia elevó los impuestos y devaluó el tálero tres veces. A Austria le costó 392 millones de florines (tras una estimación original de 28 millones), y la deuda nacional francesa pasó de 1360 millones a 2350 millones de libras francesas entre 1753 y 1764.

Por el **tratado de París** entre Gran Bretaña, Francia y España, Francia sufrió las mayores pérdidas: cedió a Gran Bretaña la mayor parte de sus territorios en el actual Canadá; los territorios en los actuales EE. UU. al este del Misisipi; las islas caribeñas de Granada, Dominica, San Vicente y las Granadinas y Tobago; Menorca, en el Mediterráneo; y Senegal, en África occidental. También ratificó la cesión de la **Luisiana** a España, y aceptaron evacuar territorios alemanes en Europa. A cambio, Gran Bretaña devolvió a Francia sus factorías en India, las valiosas islas azucareras caribeñas de Martinica y Guadalupe, la isla Belle (junto a la costa de Bretaña) y la de Gorea (en África occidental). España tuvo que ceder Florida a Gran Bretaña, a cambio de que los británicos retiraran sus tropas de La Habana y Manila.

Con el **tratado de Hubertusburg** se restablecieron las fronteras de 1756: Austria se retiró de Silesia, y Prusia, de Sajonia, volviendo así Europa a sus fronteras anteriores.

Para recompensar a sus aliados indígenas en América del Norte, Gran Bretaña decretó también la proclamación real de 1763 para contener los asentamientos de colonos más allá de los montes Apalaches. En el territorio del valle del Ohio, el acuerdo indignó a Pontiac (1720–1769), un jefe de los **ottawa** cuyas tierras quedaban bajo dominio británico, y en la llamada **rebelión de Pontiac** lanzó varios ataques contra asentamientos hasta llegar a un acuerdo con los británicos en 1766.

LA ILUSTRACIÓN EN EUROPA

La Ilustración cuestionó muchas de las creencias establecidas en Europa, un cambio de mentalidad reflejado en los escritos y otras manifestaciones culturales de mediados del siglo XVIII. También se caracterizó por la curiosidad y el progreso científicos. Esta obra de Luke Howard (1772–1864) ilustra su pasión por la meteorología, que le llevó a clasificar y nombrar muchos tipos de nubes.

1764

Wolfgang Amadeus Mozart visitó Gran Bretaña cuando tenía 8 años.

EN UN INTENTO DE LLENAR LAS ARCAS QUE LA GUERRA HABÍA VACIADO, el gobierno británico aprobó la ***Sugar Act***, que eliminó la exención fiscal sobre la melaza importada de América del Norte, una medida que encolerizó tanto a colonos como a comerciantes.

También en esta época, el genio musical **Wolfgang Amadeus Mozart** (1756–1791) y su familia emprendieron una gira de tres años por toda Europa. Visitaron Munich, Bruselas, París y Londres, donde el padre, Leopoldo, presentaba al pequeño Wolfgang para que tocara ante las cortes reales. En Londres conoció al compositor alemán **Johann Christian Bach** (1735–1782), que se convirtió en su mentor.

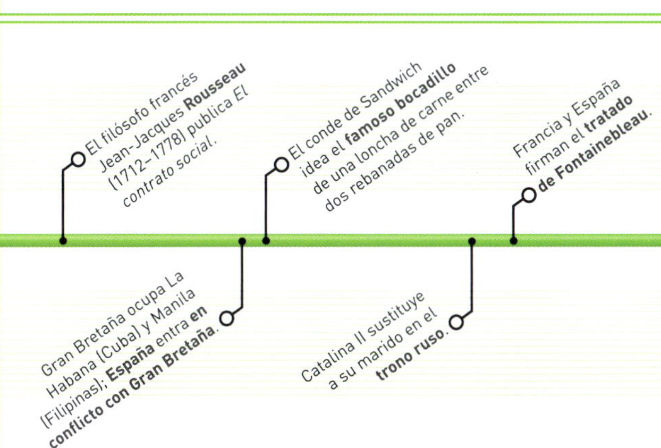

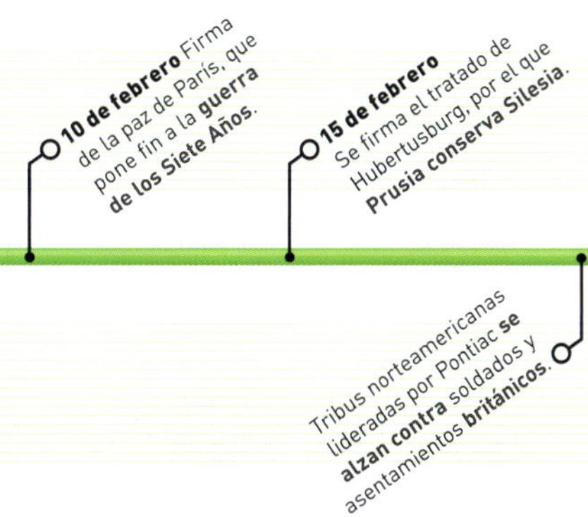

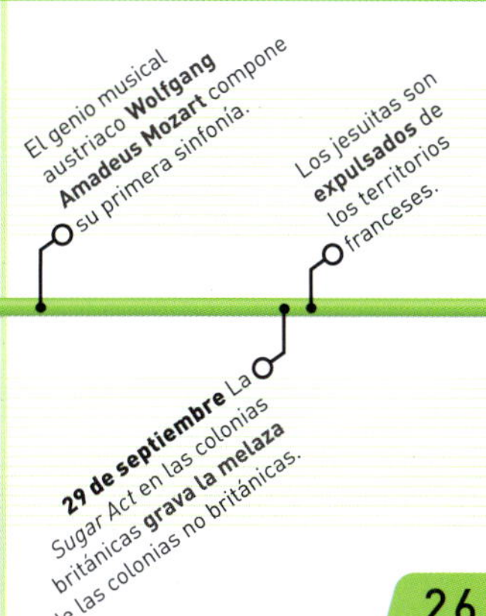

NACIONES Y ESTADOS EUROPEOS

PLANIFICACIÓN DE LA PAZ PARA UN CONTINENTE EN GUERRA

A principios del siglo XIX, Europa se parecía muy poco a la pacífica unidad política de países colaboradores que es en el siglo XXI. Antes de 1815, el equilibrio de poder y las alianzas políticas cambiaban constantemente, lo que provocaba enfrentamientos casi continuos.

Las guerras napoleónicas sumieron a Europa en un ciclo de conflictos durante más de una década y la dejaron en un estado de desequilibrio. En 1814 se celebró un congreso en Viena para decidir cómo reorganizar el continente destrozado por la guerra. Se tomaron decisiones sobre qué hacer con los nuevos estados creados por Napoleón, como el Gran Ducado de Varsovia (mapa, abajo) y las regiones de Alemania, Italia y Países Bajos que se había anexionado Francia. El objetivo final era evitar los conflictos que habían desgarrado Europa, y el espíritu imperante era el de conservación y restauración, aunque no todos los gobernantes depuestos fueron restaurados ni se recuperaron todas las posesiones perdidas.

Las fronteras nacionales resultantes del tratado de Viena de 1815 perduraron más de cuatro décadas. El miedo a una revolución incitó a los estadistas europeos a mantener el *statu quo*. A pesar de las amenazas de elementos liberales y nacionalistas, el sistema de Viena sobrevivió, y la diplomacia permitió resolver la mayoría de disputas.

1815 El Congreso de Viena reorganizó Europa y creó la Confederación Germánica. El auge tanto del liberalismo como del nacionalismo en Europa provocó alzamientos en todo el continente, pero el sistema de Viena llegó a mantenerse hasta las revoluciones de 1848.

CLAVE
- Amenaza al sistema de Viena
- Fronteras internas en 1815
- Confederación Germánica

EL IMPERIO NAPOLEÓNICO

Cuando Napoleón se convirtió en primer cónsul de Francia en 1799 no tardó en dejar claras sus ambiciones imperiales: se coronó a sí mismo como emperador de Francia en 1804 y lanzó campañas militares por toda Europa.

1812 Desde su acceso al poder en 1799, Napoleón se esforzó en extender el de Francia en Europa. Se impuso en Países Bajos, en algunas partes de Alemania e Italia, España y Polonia, pero sus intentos de tomar Rusia acabaron con una humillante derrota en 1812.

CLAVE
- Territorio francés gobernado desde París en 1812
- Estado dependiente en 1812

Prusia
Inglaterra
Imperio Habsburgo
Francia

0 10 20 30 40

POBLACIÓN EN 1800 (MILLONES)

Población
Al principio del gobierno de Napoleón, la población de Francia era muy superior a la de los países que la rodeaban. La gráfica muestra las cifras de población c. 1800.

2 000 000 SOLDADOS FRANCESES NATIVOS 1804–1815

1 000 000 BAJAS 1804–1815

Fuerzas francesas
Durante las guerras napoleónicas, soldados de todo el Imperio francés combatieron, y perdieron la vida, en el ejército de Napoleón, que llegó a contar con casi 600 000 hombres.

200 ES EL NÚMERO DE LOS **ESTADOS REPRESENTADOS** EN EL **CONGRESO DE VIENA**

NORUEGA
1814: Dinamarca es obligada a ceder Noruega a Suecia
SUECIA
Estocolmo
FINLANDIA
1808–1809: Rusia invade y se anexiona Finlandia
Helsinki
San Petersburgo
Riga
Mar del Norte
Copenhague
DINAMARCA
SCHLESWIG-HOLSTEIN
Mar Báltico
Bornholm
Amsterdam
Hamburgo
HANNOVER
Unión personal con Gran Bretaña
1817–1831: protestas estudiantiles alemanas
Hanover
Berlín
PRUSIA ORIENTAL
Danzig
IMPERIO RUSO
PAÍSES BAJOS UNIDOS
Bruselas
PRUSIA
Colonia
1831: Bélgica se independiza de los Países Bajos Unidos
SAJONIA
PRUSIA
Posen
Varsovia
POLONIA
1830–1831: revuelta nacional
Brest-Litovsk
BAVIERA
Praga
Cracovia
REPÚBLICA DE CRACOVIA
1847: a Austria
1847: alzamiento campesino
GALITZIA
PRINCIPADO DE NEUCHÂTEL
Stuttgart
WURTEMBERG
BADEN
BAVIERA
Múnich
Viena
IMPERIO AUSTRIACO
Ginebra
SUIZA
Buda
Pest
MOLDAVIA
Lyon
CERDEÑA
1821: revolución del Piamonte
Milán
LOMBARDÍA-VÉNETO
Venecia
REINO DE ILIRIA
HUNGRÍA
TRANSILVANIA
Marsella
MÓNACO
PARMA
MÓDENA
VALAQUIA
MASSA Y CARRARA
LUCCA
SAN MARINO
TOSCANA
1807–1833: revueltas serbias
Belgrado
Bucarest
1821: revueltas en Valaquia y Moldavia
SERBIA
BOSNIA
Córcega
ESTADOS PONTIFICIOS
MONTENEGRO
BULGARIA
DALMACIA
Roma
IMPERIO OTOMANO
RUMELIA
1820: revolución
TRACIA
CERDEÑA
Nápoles
Salónica
ALBANIA
REINO DE LAS DOS SICILIAS
Corfú
1815: a Gran Bretaña
GRECIA
1821: revolución
Palermo
Islas Jónicas
1815: a Gran Bretaña
Esmirna
Atenas
1821–1833: guerra de la Independencia
Mar Mediterráneo
Malta
1800: a Gran Bretaña
Creta

VUELTA A LA GUERRA

Muchas de las tensiones constantes que surgieron entre los países en el siglo XIX cobraron fuerza en el siglo XX. En 1914, el asesinato del archiduque austriaco Francisco Fernando por nacionalistas serbios marcó el inicio de la Primera Guerra Mundial, un conflicto global que remodeló Europa.

1914 La oleada de nacionalismo que barrió Europa a partir de mediados del siglo XIX acabó con el sistema de Viena. En 1914, con Europa al borde de la guerra, países como Italia y Alemania ya estaban unificados. En 1919, en Versalles, se volvió a dibujar el mapa europeo.

CLAVE

- Imperio alemán
- Imperio austrohúngaro
- Imperio ruso
- Países Bajos
- Francia
- Reino Unido
- Noruega
- España
- Suiza
- Suecia
- Bélgica
- Montenegro
- Portugal
- Rumanía
- Italia
- Grecia
- Imperio otomano
- Albania
- Luxemburgo
- Dinamarca
- Serbia
- Bulgaria

13:6 **Poblaciones rivales**
Al principio de la Primera Guerra Mundial, la población de los países aliados duplicaba con creces a la de las Potencias Centrales.

5,4 millones
3,5 MILLONES

CLAVE
- Fuerzas aliadas: Rusia, Francia, Gran Bretaña, Bélgica y Serbia
- Alemania y Austria-Hungría

Efectivos militares
En 1914, los aliados contaban con muchos más hombres que las Potencias Centrales.

« **ANTE CIRCUNSTANCIAS** EXTREMAS, CUALQUIER **PLAN** CONCEBIDO CON MODERACIÓN **FRACASARÁ**. »

Príncipe Klemens de Metternich (1773–1859), ministro de Asuntos Exteriores austriaco

1765

En este grabado satírico sobre la *Stamp Act*, el secretario del Tesoro, George Grenville, lleva un ataúd infantil con las palabras: «Miss Ame-Stamp, 1765–1766».

DURANTE ESTE AÑO CRECIÓ EL DESCONTENTO con el gobierno colonial en la América británica y española. En el mes de mayo, los habitantes de la ciudad andina de **Quito** (Ecuador actual) protestaron por la imposición de un nuevo sistema de administración fiscal que intentaba incrementar los ingresos de la agotada Hacienda española. Los rebeldes consiguieron expulsar a los funcionarios reales e instauraron un gobierno que controló la ciudad hasta la llegada de un ejército que reinstauró el poder real el año siguiente.

En el norte, los colonos británicos cada vez se mostraban más reacios a aceptar las subidas de impuestos similares. Después de la impopular *Sugar Act* (*véase* 1764) también **se aprobó la *Stamp Act*** (Ley del Timbre), la cual estipulaba que todos los colonos americanos debían pagar un **impuesto sobre cada papel impreso** que utilizaran. Esto suponía gravar productos que iban desde documentos legales hasta periódicos y naipes. Los colonos temieron que dicho impuesto fuera una forma encubierta de censura de prensa. Además, la ley les irritaba no tanto por el importe de la tasa, sino porque la Corona ya no apuntaba solamente al comercio exterior americano en busca de ingresos, sino también al interior, algo que nunca había hecho hasta aquel momento, y por añadidura había actuado prescindiendo del consentimiento de los colonos. Ante las fuertes **protestas**, la ley fue finalmente revocada al año siguiente.

También en 1765, en Lancashire (Inglaterra), el tejedor y carpintero James Hargreaves (1720–1778) había inventado una máquina conocida como **hiladora Jenny**, que mejoraba la rueca porque podía mover varios husos. Se dice que se le ocurrió la idea cuando observó una rueca que había caído al suelo; esto le habría hecho comprender que una máquina horizontal admitiría añadir más husos, y su innovación permitió multiplicar por ocho la producción textil. Posteriormente, otros inventores modificaron su diseño para producir máquinas todavía más eficientes.

En Alemania, **José II** (1741–1790) se convirtió en emperador del Sacro Imperio y en soberano conjunto de las tierras hereditarias de los Habsburgo con su madre María Teresa, hasta que esta falleció en 1780. Posteriormente emprendió un programa de reformas que incluyó la emancipación de los siervos y la mejora del sistema educativo, un reflejo de las obras de la Ilustración que leía. Se le consideró un «déspota ilustrado».

« SI **GRAVAN** EL **COMERCIO**, ¿POR QUÉ NO HABRÍAN DE GRAVAR LA **TIERRA**, LOS **PRODUCTOS**, EN SUMA, TODO AQUELLO QUE **POSEEMOS**? »

Samuel Adams, político norteamericano, sobre la *Sugar Act* (1764)

La era de las máquinas
Mujer trabajando con una hiladora Jenny a inicios del siglo XIX. El invento de James Hargreaves revolucionó la producción textil.

1766

Unos jacobitas brindan por Carlos Estuardo en Edimburgo. Muchos de los partidarios de Carlos eran escoceses.

JACOBO FRANCISCO EDUARDO ESTUARDO FALLECIÓ EN 1766 en el palacio Muti de Roma, tras haber fracasado en su misión de **recuperar el trono británico** como Jacobo III. Su nacimiento en 1688 había dado lugar a la Revolución Gloriosa, que obligó a su padre Jacobo II (1633–1701) a trasladar a toda su familia a Francia, para vivir en el exilio. El origen del conflicto era la fe de los Estuardo: el **catolicismo**. Tras la huida de la familia real, el parlamento inglés aprobó la *Act of Settlement* de 1689, que impedía el acceso al trono de un católico romano. Sin embargo, los Estuardo contaban con un gran número de seguidores en Inglaterra, Escocia e Irlanda, a los que se conocía como jacobitas.

Se llevaron a cabo varios intentos de restaurar a Jacobo III, o el «viejo pretendiente», como se le conocía; los más notables fueron los alzamientos producidos en 1715 y 1745, pero todos fracasaron. Durante el exilio del viejo pretendiente, su hijo, **Carlos Eduardo Estuardo** (1720–1888), llamado «Bonnie Prince Charlie» o el «joven pretendiente», tomó el relevo de la lucha de su padre, también sin resultado. Carlos nunca llegó a recuperarse de la derrota en la batalla de Culloden (el último enfrentamiento armado del alzamiento de 1745; *véase* 1744–1747), aunque intentó obtener el apoyo de Francia y del Sacro Imperio en alzamientos posteriores. Cuando **el viejo pretendiente murió** y Carlos se convirtió en el pretendiente oficial al trono Estuardo, la batalla que había consumido las vidas de ambos ya estaba perdida, aunque la admiración por su causa perduraba.

Estrella y jarretera del «Bonnie Prince Charlie»
Tanto la estrella como la jarretera de Carlos Estuardo indicaban que era hijo de un soberano legítimo. Se le otorgaron mientras la familia vivía en el exilio.

Poco antes de cumplir diecisiete años, **Cristián VII** (1749–1808) **fue coronado** en Dinamarca. Ese mismo año contrajo matrimonio con Carolina Matilde, una de las hermanas de Jorge III de Gran Bretaña. Su reinado se caracterizó por su **inestabilidad mental** y su **libertinaje**. Al principio, el médico alemán **Johann Freidrich Struensee** (1737–1772) se introdujo en la corte y ejerció gran influencia sobre el débil rey; llegó a aplicar políticas e incluso tuvo una aventura con la reina. Al final fue detenido y ejecutado. Los últimos años del reinado de Cristián fueron nominales, y a partir de 1784, su hijo Federico VI (1768–1839) actuó como regente.

Protestas en las colonias británicas americanas por la *Stamp Act*.

22 de mayo Alzamientos en **Quito** por la imposición de un nuevo sistema fiscal.

18 de mayo Un gran **incendio** destruye la cuarta parte de la ciudad de **Quebec**.

El emperador mogol concede a **Bengala** el *diwani* (derecho a recaudar impuestos).

18 de agosto **José II** (1741–1790) se convierte en emperador del Sacro Imperio.

Diciembre Inicio de la **guerra** entre **Birmania y China** (hasta 1769) cuando **China invade Birmania** después de que las tropas birmanas entren en territorio chino.

14 de enero Cristián VII (1749–1808) es coronado **rey de Dinamarca**.

Enero Primera guerra de Mysore (hasta 1769), en India, entre la **Compañía de las Indias Orientales** y **Haidar Alí**.

17 de marzo Se **revoca** la ***Stamp Act*** en las colonias británicas americanas; le sigue la ***Declaratory Act***, que reafirma la autoridad británica.

30 de julio William Pitt el Viejo (1708–1778) es nombrado primer ministro británico (hasta 1768).

1767

Ilustración de la expulsión de los jesuitas del reino de España.

102 NUEVA ESPAÑA

78 PERÚ

42 NUEVA GRANADA

Asentamientos jesuitas en el Nuevo Mundo
La Compañía de Jesús fue crucial para la colonización de América y en 1767 contaba con extensas misiones.

AL IGUAL QUE PORTUGAL CASI UNA DÉCADA ANTES, la Corona española también comenzó a desconfiar de los **jesuitas** y de las actividades que esta orden llevaba a cabo en las colonias americanas. Entre las causas que subyacían a este malestar destacaba la resistencia de los jesuitas a pagar **tributos** a la corona, que era sintomática de conflictos más antiguos entre la orden y el rey. Uno de los problemas fundamentales era la **influencia y la riqueza crecientes** de los jesuitas en las colonias americanas españolas, gracias a sus escuelas y extensas propiedades de tierras, y al éxito de sus cultivos. Carlos III adujo «razones de peso» y decidió expulsarlos de su reino, lo que le permitió confiscar tierras y propiedades muy valiosas. Miles de miembros de la orden se vieron obligados a huir a los Estados Pontificios y a Córcega.

1768

El capitán James Cook y su tripulación se aprovisionan de agua en la bahía del Buen Suceso (Tierra del Fuego).

EL CAPITÁN INGLÉS JAMES COOK (1728–1779) se hizo famoso entre la Marina Real británica gracias a sus excelentes dotes de navegante y por haber cartografiado las aguas canadienses durante la guerra de los Siete Años (1756–1763). Estos logros le abrieron las puertas de su siguiente misión: una expedición al Pacífico Sur organizada por la Royal Society y con un barco del Almirantazgo. El *Endeavour* zarpó de Plymouth el 25 de agosto de 1768 y llegó a Tahití (pasando por Madeira, Río de Janeiro y el cabo de Hornos) el 13 de abril de 1769. Entonces siguió en dirección sur y encontró la isla que más tarde se llamó **Nueva Zelanda**. Desde allí zarpó a la desconocida costa oriental australiana, donde desembarcó en la que, posteriormente, recibió el nombre de **bahía de Botany**. El *Endeavour* regresó a Inglaterra en 1777, y la expedición de Cook fue declarada un éxito.

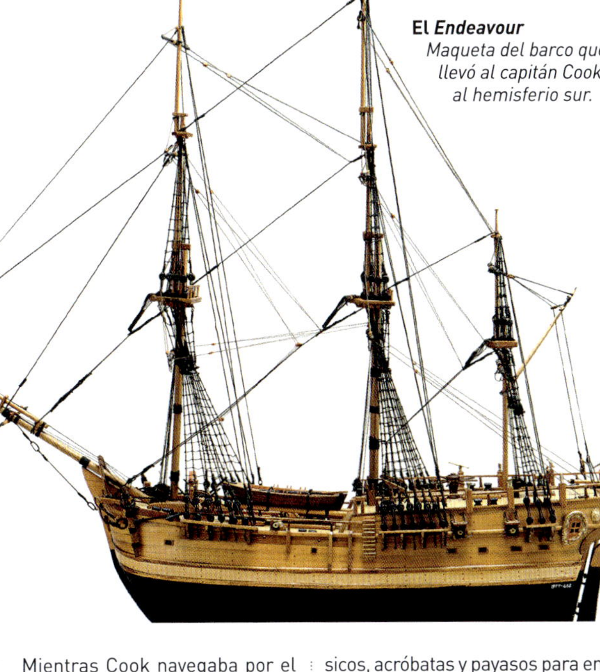

El *Endeavour*
Maqueta del barco que llevó al capitán Cook al hemisferio sur.

96 NÚMERO DE **TRIPULANTES** Y **CIVILES** QUE ZARPARON CON **JAMES COOK**

Mientras Cook navegaba por el Pacífico, en Gran Bretaña se sucedían los cambios. En Edimburgo se publicó el primer volumen de la ***Enciclopedia Británica***, un claro reflejo del creciente deseo de conocimientos de la Ilustración. Se «compiló según un plan nuevo, en el que las distintas ciencias y artes se organizan en tratados o sistemas separados». Se agotó rápidamente y en 1771 se terminó una edición de tres volúmenes.

Mientras tanto, en Londres, el exsoldado **Philip Astley** (1742–1814) inauguraba en 1768 una escuela de equitación llamada **Halfpenny Hatch** y situada en Lambeth. Allí practicaba trucos sobre la pista a lomos de un caballo y añadió músicos, acróbatas y payasos para entretener al público en las pausas: **había nacido el circo moderno**.

En Rusia, la situación se había complicado. Las continuas tensiones con el Imperio otomano habían llevado a ambos países a la **guerra ruso-turca** de 1768–1774, como consecuencia de la negativa de Catalina la Grande a cumplir los términos del tratado que había zanjado la guerra anterior (1736–1739) y de sus intervenciones en Polonia. Los otomanos declararon la guerra después de que Rusia saqueara una ciudad turca.

Más al este, **Prithvi Narayan Sah** (1723–1775) unió los reinos del valle de Katmandú para crear el reino de **Nepal**.

1769

Detalle del campanario de la misión de San Diego de Alcalá (California).

LA COLONIZACIÓN DE AMÉRICA DEL NORTE SEGUÍA ADELANTE, aunque aún se desconocían los extensos territorios del oeste. En 1769, un norteamericano llamado **Daniel Boone** (1734–1820) emprendió una expedición de caza en el actual estado de Kentucky, un área completamente desconocida para los colonos blancos, y descubrió un camino mejor a lo largo del desfiladero de Cumberland, un altiplano en los montes Apalaches. Este se convirtió en parte de la Wilderness Road, la ruta abierta por Boone y la Compañía de Transilvania que luego utilizaron los colonos para cruzar las montañas y llegar hasta Kentucky. En 1775, Boone se trasladó con toda su familia a Kentucky, donde fundó una de las primeras ciudades, Boonesborough, y dedicó el resto de su vida a trabajar como cazador y explorador.

Por su parte, los **españoles** también querían ampliar su territorio en América del Norte. Habían reclamado una región del sur de la actual California, y **Carlos III**, deseoso de poblarla con colonos españoles a raíz de los rumores que afirmaban que Rusia quería establecerse allí, envió a frailes franciscanos para que fundaran misiones. El franciscano español **fray Junípero Serra** (1713–1784) comenzó a establecer y a organizar varias misiones en el territorio español de California. La primera, que fue fundada en 1769, fue **San Diego de Alcalá**, y durante los 54 años siguientes, se crearon 20 más a lo largo de la costa californiana.

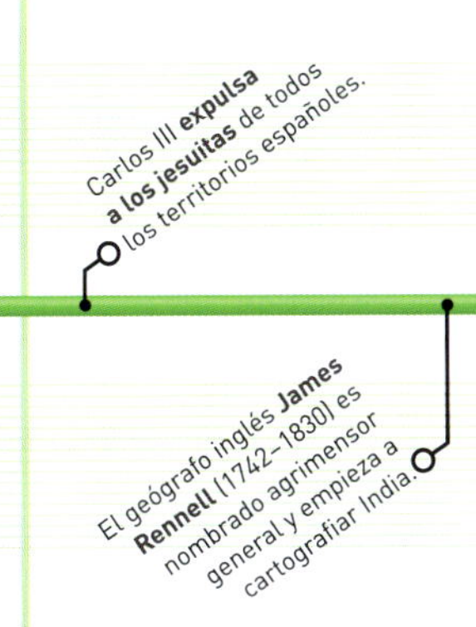

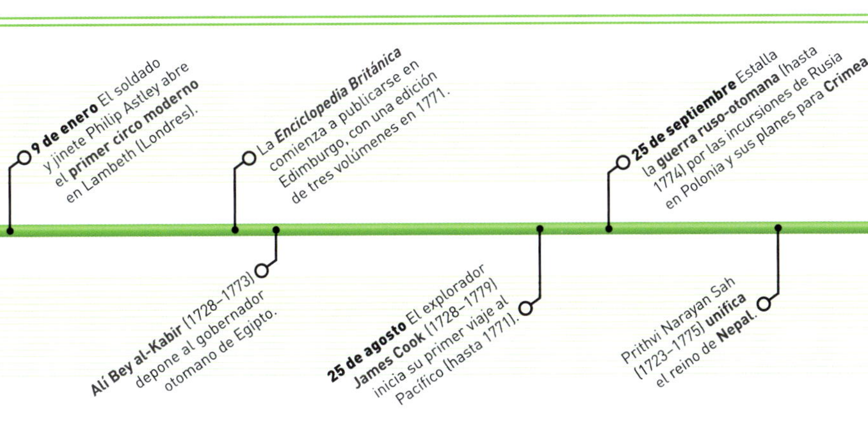

- Carlos III **expulsa a los jesuitas** de todos los territorios españoles.
- El geógrafo inglés **James Rennell** (1742–1830) es nombrado agrimensor general y empieza a cartografiar India.
- **9 de enero** El soldado y jinete Philip Astley abre el **primer circo moderno** en Lambeth (Londres).
- La ***Enciclopedia Británica*** comienza a publicarse en Edimburgo, con una edición de tres volúmenes en 1771.
- **Alí Bey al-Kabir** (1728–1773) depone al gobernador otomano de Egipto.
- **25 de agosto** El explorador **James Cook** (1728–1779) inicia su primer viaje al Pacífico (hasta 1771).
- **25 de septiembre** Estalla la **guerra ruso-otomana** (hasta 1774) por las incursiones de Rusia en Polonia y sus planes para **Crimea**.
- Prithvi Narayan Sah (1723–1775) **unifica** el reino de **Nepal**.
- El exfabricante de pelucas inglés **Richard Arkwright** (1732–1792) inventa la **hiladora hidráulica**.
- El inventor escocés **James Watt** (1736–1819) patenta la **máquina de vapor**.
- Se disuelve la **Compañía Francesa de las Indias Orientales**.

1770

Grabado que ilustra la violencia de la matanza de Boston.

EL FRACASO DE LA *STAMP ACT* (*véase* 1765) hizo que el gobierno británico buscara otro modo de obtener dinero de las colonias y lo halló en una serie de leyes formuladas por el ministro de Hacienda, **Charles Townshend** (1725–1767). La legislación incluía impuestos sobre la pintura, el papel, el vidrio, el plomo y el té importado a las colonias americanas, además de la reorganización de las aduanas para reducir el contrabando. Además, otra ley suspendió la legislatura de Nueva York porque se negaba a cumplir la ***Quartering Act***, que exigía que las asambleas coloniales satisficieran las necesidades básicas de los soldados británicos. El 5 de marzo, un grupo de estibadores empezó a acosar a una patrulla de soldados británicos cerca de las aduanas de Boston, y la multitud se agolpó. Los soldados enviados para sofocar este tumulto abrieron fuego contra los colonos (la mayoría desarmados) y mataron a cinco e hirieron a otros seis. Este episodio, conocido como la **matanza de Boston**, alimentó el resentimiento entre Gran Bretaña y sus colonias norteamericanas.

Miniatura de María Antonieta
Medallón con el retrato de María Antonieta, una de las reinas más tristemente célebres de Francia.

14

AÑOS: EDAD DE **MARÍA ANTONIETA** CUANDO SE CASÓ CON LUIS XVI

En Europa, el delfín de Francia, **Luis XVI** (1754–1793), contrajo matrimonio con la hija de María Teresa de Austria, **María Antonieta**. Tenían 15 y 14 años, respectivamente.

1771

Cromford Mill, factoría textil fundada por Richard Arkwright en Derbyshire.

LA REVOLUCIÓN INDUSTRIAL, DURANTE ESTE AÑO, SE ACERCÓ un paso más cuando el inglés **Richard Arkwright** (1732–1792) colaboró con el relojero John Kay con el objetivo de fabricar una máquina **hiladora**. En 1771, ambos decidieron utilizar un molino de agua para que la impulsara (de ahí su nombre de ***water frame*** en inglés) y construyeron una fábrica (Cromford Mill), situada en el norte de Inglaterra: fue la primera **fábrica de algodón hidráulica**. Posteriormente, su rentabilidad incitó a Arkwright a abrir varias fábricas textiles similares en Inglaterra y en Escocia.

Sin lugar a dudas, la aportación de Richard Arkwright resultó fundamental para la puesta en marcha de la **revolución industrial**, que hizo pasar a Gran Bretaña de la economía agrícola a la manufacturera. Las fábricas permitieron desarrollar el sistema de **producción en masa** que luego se adoptó en todo el mundo.

LA REVOLUCIÓN INDUSTRIAL

La revolución industrial fue la transformación económica que experimentó Europa a finales del siglo XVIII y principios del XIX, cuando las economías rurales y agrícolas fueron sustituidas por las basadas en la producción de bienes manufacturados, que se solían fabricar en las ciudades. Empezó en Inglaterra, impulsada por inventos como la hiladora Jenny (*véase* 1765) y el uso de la energía del vapor (*véase* 1775), que permitieron el desarrollo de industrias como la textil. Las nuevas tecnologías se difundieron pronto por Europa: países como Francia, Alemania y Bélgica pasaron por una transformación económica similar a medida que los campesinos abandonaban la tierra para trabajar en centros urbanos o en las minas que suministraban carbón a las fábricas.

1772

Grabado sobre el asesinato de Gustavo III de Suecia (abajo), cuyas reformas y constitución le valieron la enemistad de la nobleza y le llevaron a la muerte.

Reparto de Polonia
Rusia, Austria y Prusia fueron las beneficiarias del primer reparto de Polonia.

POLONIA SUFRIÓ el primero de los tres **repartos** de su territorio como consecuencia de las **victorias de Rusia sobre los turcos otomanos** durante la guerra ruso-turca (*véase* 1768), que habían alarmado a **Austria** y **Prusia**. Federico II quería que Rusia se expandiera hacia la confederación polaco-lituana, debilitada por la guerra civil, en lugar de hacia territorio turco. El 5 de agosto, Rusia, Prusia y Austria firmaron un **tratado** (ratificado por el Sejm, el parlamento polaco), por el que Polonia perdía una tercera parte de su territorio, que las tres potencias se repartieron.

En Suecia ascendió al trono **Gustavo III** (1746–1792), aunque la monarquía había quedado debilitada por una facción del gobierno que deseaba limitar el poder de la Corona. Gustavo respondió con un golpe de estado y con una nueva constitución. Introdujo reformas legales y reforzó la armada sueca; sin embargo, era impopular entre la nobleza, a la que había criticado y que le reprochaba el gasto de fondos públicos. Fue asesinado en 1792.

En Inglaterra, llegó a los tribunales el caso de un esclavo, **James Somerset**, traído de Jamaica en 1771 y a quien querían devolver allí. Lord Mansfield, presidente del Tribunal Supremo, resolvió que Somerset debía quedar libre, lo que sentó el precedente de que nadie podía ser alejado de Inglaterra contra su voluntad.

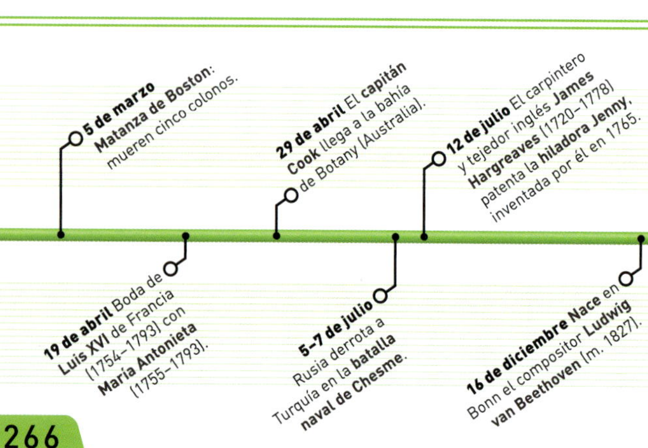

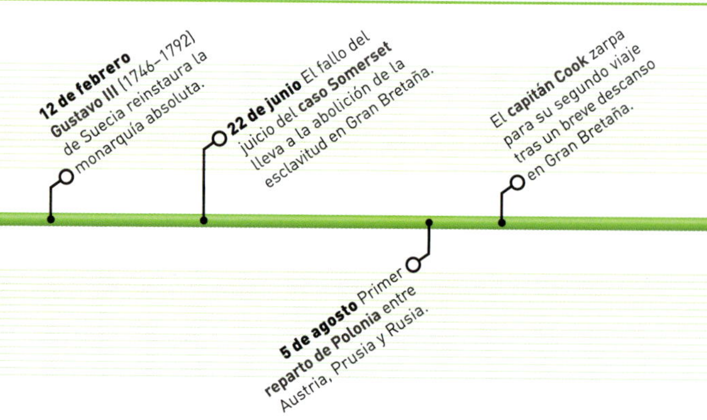

1773

Pintura de Vasili Petrov en la que el líder cosaco Yemelián Pugachev juzga y sentencia a sus enemigos.

LOS COLONOS NORTEAMERICANOS BRITÁNICOS estaban cada vez más irritados a causa de los límites que se les imponían, aunque algunos de ellos llegaran a suponer beneficios inesperados, como la reducción del precio del té. La ***Tea Act*** (Ley del Té) de **1773**, que permitió la importación directa desde India hasta América del Norte, además de gravar el producto en origen y no a la llegada, hizo que los colonos americanos pagaran menos que cualquier británico por su té. Sin embargo, para los muchos comerciantes coloniales que traficaban con té de contrabando el hecho de que el té legal fuera más barato que el suyo significaba la ruina, por lo que presionaron a los barcos de las Indias Orientales para que no amarraran en puertos americanos. Aún así, el ***Dartmouth*** logró atracar en el puerto de Boston. El 16 de diciembre, unos encolerizados comerciantes se hicieron con 342 contenedores de té del *Dartmouth*, por un valor de diez mil libras esterlinas, y los arrojaron al mar. Este fue uno de los momentos clave de la resistencia al gobierno británico.

Rusia también sufría tensiones, lideradas por el cosaco **Yemelián Pugachev** (1742–1775). Pugachev había servido en la guerra de los Siete Años, pero desertó en el año 1762. Tras su deserción, recorrió toda Rusia afirmando ser el depuesto zar Pedro III y, con la promesa de abolir la servidumbre, consiguió reunir 25 000 soldados. A pesar de sus victorias iniciales sobre el ejército de Catalina la Grande, al final fue derrotado y ejecutado el 10 de enero de 1775.

El Imperio otomano se enfrentaba a una revolución en Egipto. **Alí Bey al-Kabir** (1728–1773) había gobernado Egipto de facto, pero en 1769 depuso al gobernador otomano e intentó independizar al país. También envió tropas a los territorios de Palestina y Siria, pero en 1773 fue derrotado por el ejército otomano y murió a causa de sus heridas, encarcelado en El Cairo.

En su travesía del Atlántico Sur, el capitán James Cook cruzó el **círculo polar antártico**. El año anterior había zarpado para otra misión a bordo del *Resolution*, decidido a explorar las vastas regiones desconocidas del hemisferio sur.

Motín del Té de Boston
Los comerciantes lanzan al mar fardos del té de un barco de la Compañía de las Indias Orientales en el puerto de Boston.

1774

Comitiva fúnebre de Luis XV (1710–1774), apodado «el Bienamado». Había gobernado Francia durante casi sesenta años.

EN AMÉRICA DEL NORTE, los representantes de las trece colonias británicas, excepto Georgia, se reunieron en Filadelfia para decidir qué hacer al respecto de un conjunto de leyes, conocidas como **leyes intolerables**, promulgadas en represalia por el incidente del té en el puerto de Boston (*véase* 1773) y por la creciente rebeldía americana. Estipulaban que el puerto de Boston debía permanecer cerrado a todos los barcos excepto los británicos; que los colonos debían albergar al ejército británico si fuera necesario; que los funcionarios británicos no serían juzgados en las colonias, sino en Gran Bretaña, lo que les otorgaba impunidad; y el autogobierno de Boston también se daba por terminado. También se incluía el **Acta de Quebec**, que ampliaba las fronteras de la provincia canadiense, le permitía cierto grado de autogobierno mediante un gobernador y consejeros designados, garantizaba la libertad religiosa para los colonos católicos, y permitía que se aplicara el derecho civil francés junto con el derecho penal británico. Esto suponía un agravio más para muchos colonos americanos, que se oponían a que Quebec se extendiera a un territorio que consideraban suyo y desconfiaban del gobierno que se acababa de formar. El **Congreso Continental** (un grupo de delegados de cada una de las trece colonias) decidió actuar y boicotear los productos y el comercio británico para enviar un mensaje potente a Jorge III.

En Francia, **Luis XVI** fue coronado rey a los 17 años de edad, tras la muerte de su abuelo, Luis XV.

Luis XVI
Luis XVI de Francia en traje de coronación. Tenía solo 17 años cuando empezó a reinar.

Mientras tanto, el enfrentamiento entre **Rusia** y el **Imperio otomano** llegaba a su fin. En julio, firmaron el **tratado de Kuchuk-Kainarzhi**, que daba a Rusia derecho a navegar por el mar Negro y reconocía la independencia de la península de **Crimea**, lo que significaba que la región quedaba finalmente libre del gobierno otomano. No tardó en alinearse con Rusia.

Los otomanos se enfrentaron a más disturbios durante el mes de octubre, después de la muerte del sultán **Mustafá III** (1717–1774), a quien sucedió su hermano, **Abdulhamid I** (r. 1774–1789). El imperio ya había comenzado a declinar en el momento en que Mustafá accedió al trono, como consecuencia del cese de su crecimiento económico. Además, la costosa y desastrosa guerra librada contra Rusia no había hecho más que empeorar dicha situación.

Warren Hastings (1732–1818), nombrado gobernador general de **Bengala** (hasta 1785).

El **capitán Cook** cruza el círculo polar antártico y circunnavega el continente.

Alzamientos de siervos en Rusia, dirigidos por Yemelián Ivánovich **Pugachev** (1726–1775).

16 de diciembre Motín del Té de Boston: los colonos británicos lanzan un cargamento de té al mar en el puerto como protesta.

Abdulhamid I (1725–1789) se convierte en sultán otomano.

Luis XVI es coronado rey de Francia.

21 de julio Rusia y el Imperio otomano firman el **tratado de Kuchuk-Kainarzhi** que otorga a Rusia el control de gran parte de la costa del mar Negro.

El **Acta de Quebec** garantiza mayor libertad religiosa a los católicos de América del Norte, reinstaura el derecho civil francés y amplía Quebec.

Las **leyes intolerables** autorizan medidas de castigo contra las trece colonias.

Disparos de apertura de la guerra entre las tropas británicas (de rojo) y la milicia colonial norteamericana (en primer plano) en Lexington Common (Massachusetts), por el pintor inglés William Barnes Wollen (1857–1936).

« QUE SE HAGA **JUSTICIA** AUNQUE EL **CIELO** SE **DESPLOME**. »

John Adams, político estadounidense (5 de diciembre de 1777)

LA AIRADA ACOGIDA A LA LEGISLACIÓN y el descontento por los **«impuestos sin representación»** en las trece colonias británicas de América del Norte habían empezado a preocupar a los funcionarios británicos, que temían una rebelión armada. El 18 de abril, el general Thomas Gage (1721–1787), que también era gobernador de Massachusetts, decidió enviar a soldados británicos (conocidos como «casacas rojas») a requisar las armas y las municiones almacenadas por los habitantes de Concord, muy cerca de Boston. Los colonos, conscientes de que los británicos podían tomar esta decisión, habían establecido un sistema de alertas, y cuando se supo que el ejército se dirigía hacia Concord, el grabador bostoniano **Paul Revere** (1735–1818) partió para avisar de la inminente llegada de los soldados británicos. Los milicianos prepararon las armas y se dispusieron a esperar a los casacas rojas.

En la mañana del 19 de abril, una «salva que se oyó en el mundo entero» anunció el inicio de una batalla entre el ejército británico y los colonos en **Lexington** y en la cercana **Concord**. Había comenzado la **guerra de la Independencia de Estados Unidos** (o Revolución americana).

La contienda se prolongó durante todo el verano. Las tropas coloniales, lideradas por el **general George Washington** (1732–1799) tomaron puntos clave próximos al **lago Champlain**, pero los británicos las vencieron en la **batalla de Bunker Hill** el 17 de junio, aunque perdieron a la mitad de sus hombres para conseguirlo.

La guerra dividió a las colonias, ya que no todos los colonos querían enfrentarse a Gran Bretaña, y pronto la población se dividió entre **patriotas** y **realistas**. Se estima que un 20% de los habitantes de las trece colonias estaban a favor de la Corona. En este porcentaje estaban incluidos los **indios** y los **esclavos**. En el caso de los primeros, algunas tribus decidieron aliarse con los británicos por los vínculos comerciales que habían establecido con ellos. Muchos también pensaban que sus intereses, así como los límites territoriales, quedarían mucho más protegidos por Gran Bretaña. Para los esclavos, el principal incentivo era la posibilidad de la **emancipación**, ya que se les había dicho que si luchaban por el rey ganarían la libertad. Por último, algunos sectores de la población, como los **cuáqueros**, se oponían a la lucha armada y muchos otros querían evitar participar en el conflicto, fuera del lado que fuera.

En el otro lado del mundo, el ejército de la Compañía Británica de las Indias Orientales tenía problemas con los marathas (*véase* 1758). La **primera guerra anglo-maratha** (1775–1782) fue una consecuencia de la intervención de la Compañía en la Confederación maratha, una unión de cinco clanes que llegó al poder después de la caída del reino de Maharashtra. Esta guerra dejó un gran número de problemas sin resolver, por lo que las tensiones entre británicos y marathas reaparecieron y provocaron dos guerras más (*véase* 1803).

Entre tanto, en Gran Bretaña, el inventor e ingeniero escocés **James Watt** (1736–1819) se había asociado con Matthew Boulton (1728–1809), propietario de una empresa de maquinaria. Watt había mejorado la **máquina de vapor de Newcomen**, inventada a principios de siglo, gracias a una cámara de condensación independiente que conseguía que la máquina perdiera menos vapor y fuera más eficiente. Tras asociarse con Boulton empezó a fabricar su máquina de vapor en 1775. En aquel momento, las máquinas de vapor se utilizaban fundamentalmente para extraer agua de las minas, pero Watt intuyó más usos posibles del vapor y siguió trabajando en estas máquinas durante toda su vida. Sus inventos permitieron a ingenieros posteriores revolucionar el transporte y sentaron las bases de la industria moderna.

Tricornio de soldado continental
Los colonos que combatían en el ejército Continental llevaban este tricornio.

el vapor utilizado escapa por la chimenea

válvula de cuatro vías que controla la admisión y la salida del vapor

Máquina de vapor
El trabajo que James Watt realizó sobre las máquinas de vapor permitió el desarrollo de la locomotora y de los trenes de vapor.

THOMAS PAINE (1737–1809)

Nacido en Norfolk (Inglaterra), emigró a América y apoyó la independencia de las colonias británicas. Tras su regreso a Inglaterra, Paine defendió la Revolución francesa en *Los derechos del hombre*, obra que cimentó su reputación de propagandista radical.

15 de febrero El papa **Pío VI** sucede a Clemente XVI.

19 de abril Inicio de la **guerra de la Independencia de EE. UU.** con batallas en Lexington y en Concord.

30 de julio El capitán **Cook** llega a Portsmouth al final del segundo viaje.

7 de noviembre Se **promete la libertad a los esclavos varones** que luchen por los británicos en la guerra de Independencia de EE. UU.

Primera guerra anglo-maratha (hasta 1782) entre la Confederación maratha y la Compañía Británica de las Indias Orientales.

James Watt patenta su máquina de vapor.

1776

Unos colonos exultantes derriban una estatua del rey Jorge III en Nueva York para celebrar la firma de la Declaración de Independencia.

« SOSTENEMOS QUE ESTAS VERDADES SON EVIDENTES Y QUE TODOS LOS HOMBRES **NACEN IGUALES**; QUE SU CREADOR LES HA CONCEDIDO UNOS **DERECHOS INALIENABLES**; Y QUE ENTRE ESTOS SE ENCUENTRAN **LA VIDA, LA LIBERTAD Y LA BÚSQUEDA DE LA FELICIDAD**. »

Declaración de Independencia de EE. UU. (4 de julio de 1776)

MIENTRAS LA GUERRA POR LA INDEPENDENCIA DE LAS COLONIAS DE AMÉRICA DEL NORTE seguía su curso, el **primer** Congreso Continental emitió el 4 de julio una **declaración de independencia** en la que anunciaba formalmente la separación de las colonias del gobierno británico y las llamaba **Estados Unidos**. El documento señalaba qué había motivado la decisión de separarse de Gran Bretaña al mismo tiempo que afirmaba algunos derechos naturales. Sin embargo, las ideas expuestas en esta declaración (todos los hombres nacían iguales y tenían derecho a la «vida, la libertad y la búsqueda de la felicidad») no se aplicaban por igual. Los esclavos africanos (algunos de los cuales habían luchado junto a los norteamericanos) quedaban excluidos.

En 1776 vieron la luz varias obras influyentes. En enero, el escritor y pensador radical **Thomas Paine** (*véase* recuadro), que había residido algún tiempo en Filadelfia, publicó un panfleto titulado *Sentido común*, en el que defendía la independencia americana y la formación de un gobierno republicano. Este panfleto, anónimo en su primera edición, ejerció una gran influencia tanto a escala nacional como internacional y contribuyó significativamente al movimiento independentista. En Gran Bretaña, el filósofo escocés **Adam Smith** (1723–1790) publicó *La riqueza de las naciones*, donde subrayaba las ventajas del sistema de libre comercio y que cambió el modo de pensar sobre la expansión económica de los políticos y de la población en general.

Durante ese mismo año se publicó también *Historia de la decadencia y caída del Imperio Romano*, del historiador inglés **Edward Gibbon** (1737–1794), que cosechó un gran éxito. La metodología objetiva y meticulosa de Gibbon a la hora de utilizar el material de referencia convirtió a esta obra en un ejemplo para los historiadores futuros. En la década siguiente se publicaron cinco volúmenes más.

1777

Plano de la ciudad de Colonia del Sacramento (Uruguay) en el siglo XVIII.

EN BAVIERA, LA SUCESIÓN AL TRONO GENERABA INQUIETUD. Tras la muerte del elector **Maximiliano III José** (1727–1777), el último Wittlesbach, fue coronado **Carlos Teodoro** (1724–1799), elector palatino. Este carecía de herederos legítimos, pero tenía varios bastardos para los que quería conseguir tierras, y firmó un tratado con José II de Austria, por el que cedía la Baja Baviera a Austria a cambio de los Países Bajos austriacos. Esto irritó a Federico II de Prusia, y en 1778 estalló la **guerra de sucesión de Baviera**, que terminó en 1779.

España y Portugal resolvieron por fin sus disputas sobre la región de **Río de la Plata** con el **primer tratado de San Ildefonso**. España cedió a Portugal varios territorios en la cuenca del Amazonas a cambio de tener el control sobre la Banda Oriental (Uruguay actual).

Carlos Teodoro
El elector palatino Carlos Teodoro no contaba con herederos legítimos, pero sí con varios ilegítimos. Fue un soberano impopular.

1778

Grabado del interior de la Scala de Milán durante una representación.

Mazas usadas contra Cook
Mazas tradicionales hawaianas como estas pudieron ser usadas en el ataque que costó la vida a James Cook.

TRAS DOS VIAJES AFORTUNADOS, EL CAPITÁN JAMES COOK (*véase* 1773) emprendió el tercero en 1776, esta vez en busca del **paso del Noroeste**, un supuesto atajo por el Ártico que conectaba los océanos Atlántico y Pacífico. En 1778, Cook estableció el primer contacto europeo con las **islas Hawái** y prosiguió hacia el círculo polar ártico, aunque no consiguió encontrar el paso. Al regresar a Hawai, una disputa por un bote perdido fue la causa de su muerte a manos de los hawaianos en 1779.

En **Milán** se inauguró el nuevo teatro operístico de **La Scala**, construido bajo el patrocinio de María Teresa de Austria (entonces la ciudad estaba bajo dominio austriaco) para sustituir al anterior, devorado por un incendio. El nuevo se erigió en el lugar de la iglesia de Santa Maria alla Scala con financiación de mecenas acaudalados y se inauguró el 3 de agosto con la representación de la **ópera** *L'Europa riconosciuta* de Antonio Salieri (1750–1825).

1779

Familia xosa según una pintura del naturalista francés Pierre Sonnerat.

EL TRASLADO DE LOS BÓERS (colonos holandeses) a regiones remotas, a cientos de kilómetros al norte de Ciudad de El Cabo, generó problemas con los **xosa**. Estas tribus se habían instalado en el territorio mucho antes que los bóers. Ambos grupos eran ganaderos y competían por los pastos para las reses.

Los intentos de fijar una frontera entre los **ríos Fish y Sundays** fracasaron, ya que ambas partes violaban los acuerdos. La tensión derivó en violencia: los xosa atacaron al ganado bóer y asesinaron a algunos ganaderos, probablemente como represalia por la muerte de uno de los suyos; los bóers atacaron a su vez y se apoderaron de más de cinco mil cabezas de ganado.

Casa bóer
Los colonos holandeses de África de Sur se alejaron de El Cabo hacia zonas rurales para criar ganado.

Estas escaramuzas, que desembocaron en la primera **guerra de los xosa**, no consiguieron resolver la causa primera de las disputas: el acceso a los pastos y al agua. La lucha intermitente se prolongó durante casi un siglo.

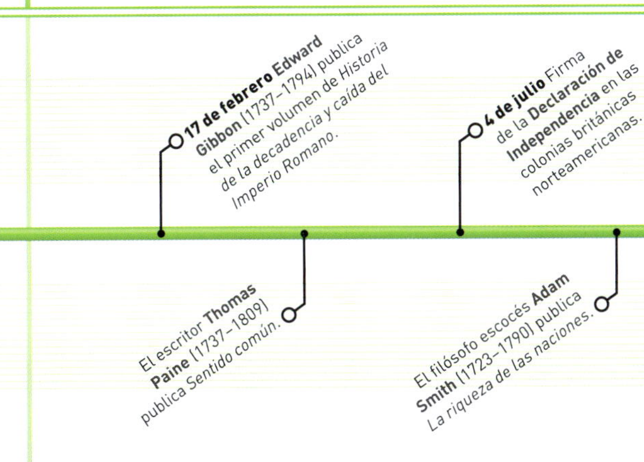

17 de febrero Edward Gibbon (1737–1794) publica el primer volumen de *Historia de la decadencia y caída del Imperio Romano*.

El escritor **Thomas Paine** (1737–1809) publica *Sentido común*.

4 de julio Firma de la **Declaración de Independencia** en las colonias británicas norteamericanas.

El filósofo escocés **Adam Smith** (1723–1790) publica *La riqueza de las naciones*.

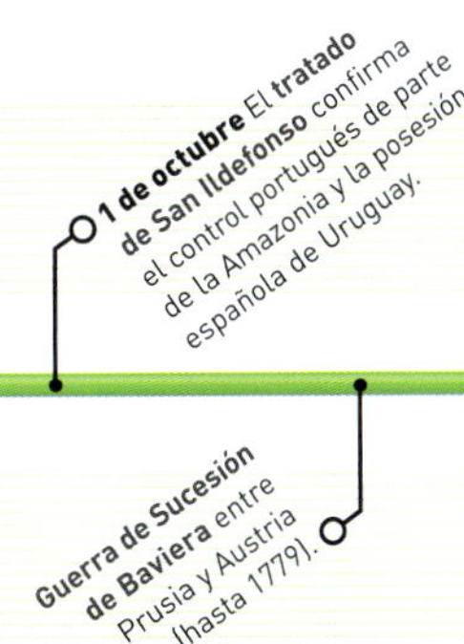

1 de octubre El tratado de **San Ildefonso** confirma el control portugués de parte de la Amazonia y la posesión española de Uruguay.

Guerra de Sucesión de Baviera entre Prusia y Austria (hasta 1779).

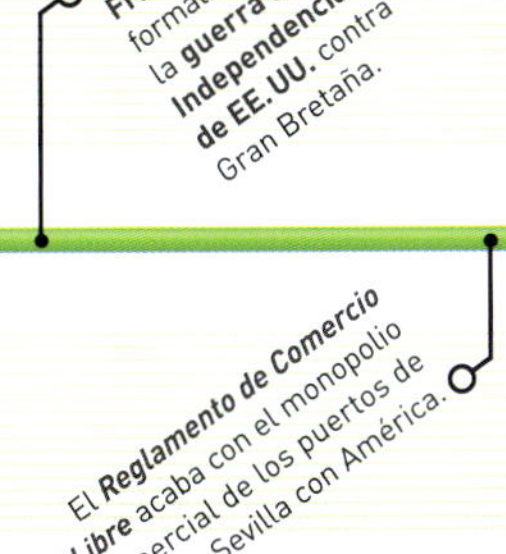

6 de febrero Francia entra formalmente en la **guerra de la Independencia de EE. UU.** contra Gran Bretaña.

El **Reglamento de Comercio Libre** acaba con el monopolio comercial de los puertos de Cádiz y Sevilla con América.

14 de febrero El **capitán Cook** es **asesinado** en las islas Hawái durante su tercer viaje.

Guerras de los xosa contra los colonos británicos y bóers (hasta 1879).

1780

Pintura mural del Daria Daulat Bagh, el palacio de verano de Tipu, sultán de Mysore (suroeste de India) entre 1782 y 1799.

LOS INTENTOS DE LA COMPAÑÍA BRITÁNICA DE LAS INDIAS ORIENTALES de extender su alcance más allá de Bengala chocaron con la resistencia de los estados indios, en particular del reino suroriental de Mysore, gobernado por el poderoso **Haidar Alí** (1722–1782). Las fuertes disputas territoriales habían desencadenado la primera guerra de Mysore (1767–1769), a la que no tardó en seguir la **segunda guerra de Mysore** (1780–1784). Estas guerras no resolvieron totalmente el conflicto, que prosiguió hasta 1799.

Sin embargo, India no era la única preocupación militar para Gran Bretaña, que tenía varios frentes abiertos. Además de sostener la guerra en América del Norte, también había entrado en conflicto con los holandeses. La **cuarta guerra anglo-holandesa** (1780–1784), que se libró sin batallas, fue una consecuencia directa del conflicto norteamericano. Los holandeses proporcionaban armas a los colonos rebeldes, y Gran Bretaña interceptó sus barcos, lo que generó una disputa: los holandeses afirmaban que Gran Bretaña debía respetar su neutralidad, pero los británicos no estaban de acuerdo.

Los colonos norteamericanos no estaban solos en su lucha: al sur, en Perú, estalló la **revuelta de Túpac Amaru** (1780–1782), provocada por la enorme insatisfacción con el régimen colonial español. Cerca de 75 000 rebeldes indios y criollos (nacidos en Perú, pero con ascendencia española), se alzaron en protesta por cómo se les trataba. Su líder, Túpac Amaru (*véase* recuadro), fue capturado y ejecutado en 1781, pero fueron necesarios otro año y sesenta mil soldados españoles para sofocar la rebelión.

En el continente africano, el reino de **Buganda**, en la orilla norte del lago Ukerewe (lago Victoria), emergió como potencia regional a medida que ampliaba su territorio. En la misma época, los **masái**, que ocupaban la orilla sureste del lago, comenzaban también a ser una presencia importante en esta región y avanzaban hacia el sur y el este gracias a su numerosa y organizada clase guerrera.

TÚPAC AMARU II (*c.* 1742–1781)

José Gabriel Condorcanqui, nacido en Cuzco (Perú), adoptó el nombre de Túpac Amaru II, por el último soberano que gobernó el Imperio inca entre 1545 y 1572. Era mestizo y dedicó toda su vida a luchar en contra del régimen colonial con el objetivo de mejorar las condiciones de vida del pueblo indígena peruano.

1781

Lord Cornwallis (izda.) entrega su espada a George Washington (dcha.), tras la derrota británica en la batalla de Yorktown.

LA GUERRA ENTRE GRAN BRETAÑA Y LOS COLONOS NORTEAMERICANOS llegó a un punto de inflexión decisivo en la **batalla de Yorktown** (Virginia), que fue librada el 19 de octubre. El **ejército Continental** había recibido el apoyo de Francia el año anterior, y el **conde de Rochambeau** (1725–1807) dirigió las tropas junto con el **general George Washington** (1732–1799). Dicha combinación de fuerzas supuso que cuando las tropas rebeldes tomaron sus posiciones el 28 de septiembre, las del **general Charles Cornwallis** (1738–1805) se vieran superadas en una proporción superior a dos a uno, y los refuerzos no pudieron llegar a tiempo. Este hecho, sumado al bloqueo naval francés, dejó a Cornwallis sin otra opción que la de rendirse. Aunque esta fue la última gran batalla de la guerra, el reconocimiento oficial de la independencia de EE UU aún se hizo esperar.

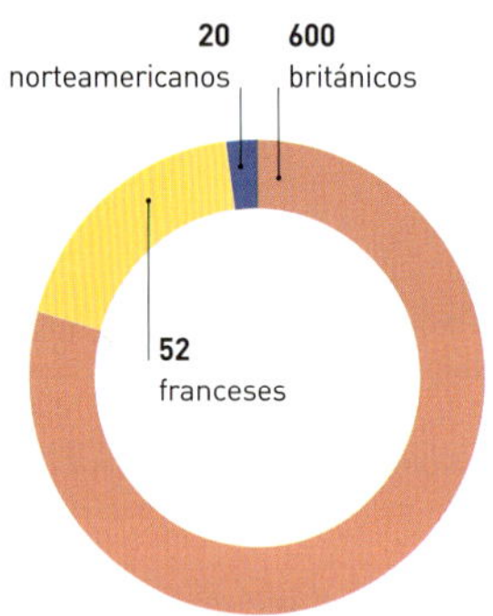

Bajas en la batalla de Yorktown
Gran Bretaña pagó un alto precio en esta batalla, decisiva para el fin de su dominio en América del Norte.

La política de las colonias británicas norteamericanas estaba cambiando. Los **Artículos de la Confederación** se habían aprobado a principios de ese mismo año, el 1 de marzo. El proceso de ratificación había empezado en 1777, bajo el **segundo Congreso Continental**. El acuerdo establecía una «firme alianza de amistad» entre los futuros **Estados Unidos de América**, así como las responsabilidades que tendría el gobierno central. Este documento fue sustituido posteriormente por la Constitución estadounidense (*véase* 1787).

En Europa, las tensiones entre los holandeses y Gran Bretaña indujeron a esta a enviar una flota desde India a **Sumatra** el 9 de agosto, con la orden de destruir los asentamientos holandeses. Cuando llegaron los británicos, la escasa población colonial holandesa se rindió inmediatamente, y todas las factorías y almacenes holandeses de **Padang** pasaron a pertenecer a la Corona británica.

Mientras tanto, crecía también el descontento con el régimen español entre la población local del **Virreinato de Nueva Granada** (que abarcaba los actuales Colombia, Venezuela, Panamá y Ecuador), donde estalló una revuelta contra el aumento de los impuestos sobre el tabaco y el alcohol conocida como **revolución de los Comuneros**. Tras llegar a un acuerdo sobre los impuestos, los rebeldes abandonaron sus planes de marchar sobre Bogotá, pero entonces el virrey español atacó a los revolucionarios y mató a dos de sus líderes.

Fusileros norteamericanos
Esta imagen muestra a un fusilero exhausto y mal equipado, aunque fueron soldados como este los que consiguieron derrotar a las tropas regulares británicas.

En Prusia tenía lugar otra revolución, en esta ocasión intelectual, después de la publicación de *Crítica de la razón pura* del filósofo **Immanuel Kant** (1724–1804). Esta obra era un desafío para la naturaleza del conocimiento según se entendía entonces.

« LA **CIENCIA** ES **CONOCIMIENTO** ORGANIZADO. LA **SABIDURÍA** ES **VIDA** ORGANIZADA. »

Immanuel Kant, filósofo alemán, de *Crítica de la razón pura* (1781)

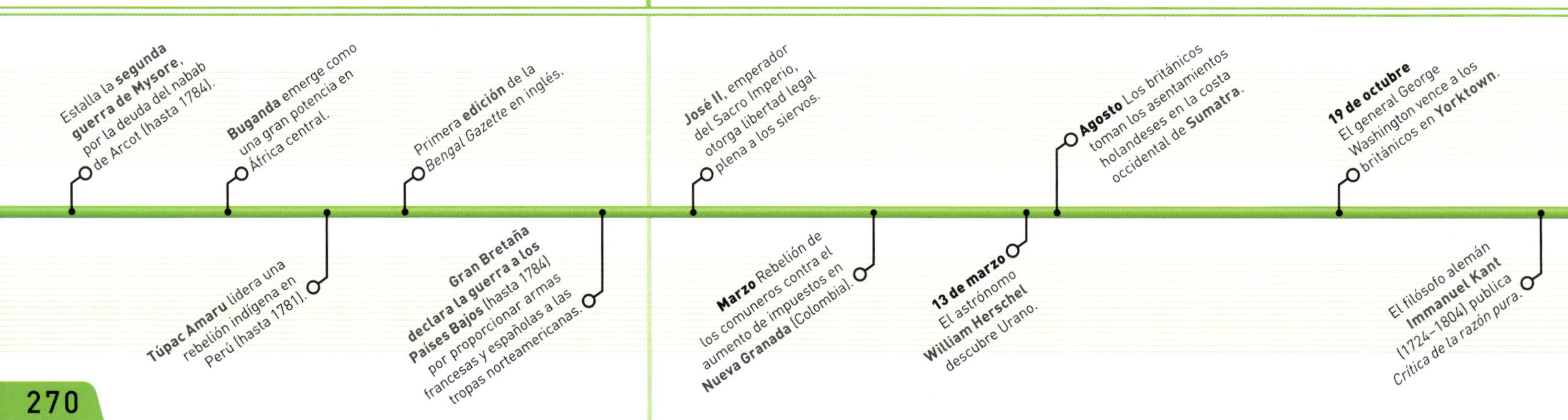

1782

Detalle del Chakri Mahaprasad de Bangkok, construido bajo Rama I.

MIENTRAS LAS VICTORIOSAS EX-COLONIAS NORTEAMERICANAS iniciaban complejas y prolongadas negociaciones con Gran Bretaña acerca de su reconocimiento oficial y de su futuro, **Irlanda** descubría que también se hallaba en posición de establecer un **acuerdo político nuevo** con el gobierno británico. Tanto la *Declaratory Act* de 1720 como la ley de Poyning de 1494, cuyo objetivo había sido subordinar a Irlanda al parlamento inglés, fueron finalmente derogadas. Una vez eliminadas muchas de las restricciones que imponían dichas leyes, Irlanda pudo disponer de cierta **independencia legislativa**. Sin embargo, y a pesar de las nuevas libertades, los únicos que gozaban de participación política eran los **protestantes**, y la fuerte inestabilidad que esto acabó provocando en un territorio mayoritariamente católico hizo que el autogobierno durara muy poco tiempo.

También en 1782, en **Siam (Tailandia)**, se estableció una nueva dinastía (**Chakri**) una vez resuelta la lucha por el poder después de la muerte sin heredero del soberano anterior, el **rey Taksin**. En la actualidad, los Chakri continúan siendo la familia real de Tailandia, fundada por **Rama I** (1737–1809), antiguo general del ejército que consiguió apoyos leales durante las luchas con Birmania. Rama I dedicó gran parte de su reinado a **reconstruir Siam**, devastado por años de guerra. Hizo levantar numerosos edificios, como un palacio real y templos budistas, y fue un líder militar fuerte que logró repeler hasta cinco invasiones birmanas.

1783

Friso de bronce sobre la firma del tratado de París en 1783, por el que Gran Bretaña reconocía la independencia de sus colonias norteamericanas.

CASI DOS AÑOS DESPUÉS DE LA RENDICIÓN DE YORKTOWN, el 3 de septiembre tuvo lugar la firma del **tratado de París** entre Gran Bretaña y Estados Unidos, que concluyó formalmente la **guerra de la Independencia estadounidense**. Gran Bretaña, junto con sus excolonias norteamericanas acordaban «dejar atrás todos los malentendidos y diferencias.» El documento reconocía oficialmente a Estados Unidos y fijaba las fronteras de sus trece estados. No obstante, todavía existía una importante presencia europea en el territorio estadounidense actual, pues España seguía conservando extensos territorios al oeste.

Gran Bretaña, Francia y España firmaron a su vez otro tratado por el que Gran Bretaña entregaba **Tobago** y **Senegal** a Francia y accedía a que España conservara **Menorca** (recuperada el año anterior), así como los territorios que poseía en **Florida**.

Por otro lado, en Annonay, una pequeña población del sureste de Francia, dos hermanos estaban a punto de hacer historia. El 4 de junio, **Joseph** (1740–1810) y **Étienne** (1745–1799) **Montgolfier** llevaron a cabo el primer vuelo público registrado en un **globo aerostático**. Tan solo dos meses después, y después de algunos cambios en su diseño, realizaron otro vuelo en presencia de Luis XVI y María Antonieta en Versalles. En un vuelo posterior, que tuvo lugar el 19 de septiembre, metieron una oveja, un pato y un gallo dentro de la cesta con el objetivo de observar el comportamiento de los animales a gran altura. Finalmente, el primer vuelo libre (sin que el globo estuviera atado al suelo) tripulado fue llevado a cabo el 21 de noviembre del mismo año.

CLAVE
Territorio del Oeste
Estados Unidos

AMÉRICA DEL NORTE BRITÁNICA
NEW HAMPSHIRE
MASSACHUSETTS
NUEVA YORK
RHODE ISLAND
CONNECTICUT
PENSILVANIA
NUEVA JERSEY
DELAWARE
VIRGINIA
MARYLAND
CAROLINA DEL NORTE
CAROLINA DEL SUR
GEORGIA
OCÉANO ATLÁNTICO
Golfo de México

Estados de la Unión
Este mapa muestra los trece estados originales reconocidos por el tratado de París. Las fronteras de EE. UU. llegaban hasta el río Misisipi.

Vuelo en globo
Este grabado muestra un globo Montgolfier posterior, llamado Flesselles, sobrevolando la ciudad de Lyon el 19 de enero de 1784. Uno de sus siete pasajeros era Joseph Montgolfier.

1784

Ilustración satírica sobre la Ley de India y sus implicaciones políticas.

LA PRESENCIA BRITÁNICA EN INDIA HABÍA IDO EN AUMENTO gracias a la Compañía de las Indias Orientales, aunque a lo largo del siglo XVIII se intensificaron las tensiones entre esta y el gobierno británico. La **Ley de India de 1773** había estrechado el control gubernamental sobre la Compañía, pero sus demandas de fondos públicos para poder cubrir con ellos el coste de las múltiples batallas dieron lugar a más acciones. La **Ley de India de 1784**, que fue aprobada bajo el gobierno del primer ministro **William Pitt el Joven** (1759–1806), determinó que la Compañía tenía que someterse a un Consejo de Control sobre cuestiones civiles y militares, además de económicas, del que debían formar parte miembros del gobierno británico. También estipulaba que el comercio y el gobierno territorial eran dos actividades distintas. En el siglo XIX, la legislación fue todavía más lejos: abolió el monopolio de la Compañía y aprobó la apertura del comercio, además de autorizar el establecimiento de las misiones cristianas en la región.

> « **INDIA PIERDE** PARA SIEMPRE **CADA RUPIA** DE **BENEFICIO** QUE LOGRA UN **INGLÉS.** »
>
> **Edmund Burke,** político británico, sobre la Compañía de las Indias Orientales (1783)

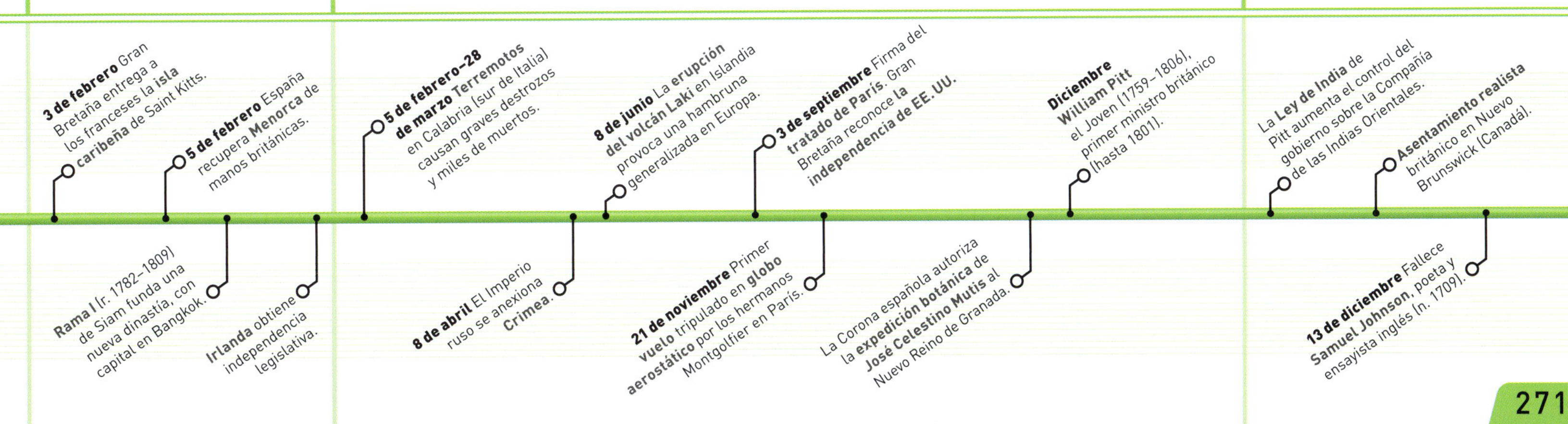

1785

El telar mecánico transformó la industria textil.

EN 1784, EL CLÉRIGO INGLÉS EDMUND CARTWRIGHT (1743–1823), visitó una de las factorías de algodón de Richard Arkwright (*véase* 1771). Lo que allí observó le inspiró la invención de máquinas parecidas, pero esta vez para tejer. En 1785 ya había patentado su primer **telar mecánico**. El telar de Cartwright se convirtió en un elemento esencial para la industria textil británica. El empresario estadounidense **Francis Cabot Lowell** mejoró su diseño después de ver los telares en funcionamiento durante una visita a Gran Bretaña, y hacia 1820 su uso ya se había extendido a ambos lados del Atlántico.

Entre tanto, en Birmania, el **rey Bodawpaya** (1745–1819), de la dinastía Konbaung, había conquistado el reino costero de Arakan el año anterior. Animado por esta victoria, decidió seguir avanzando hacia el este e invadir Siam (Tailandia), pero fue derrotado.

Expedición alrededor del mundo
Jean-François de Galaup, conde de La Pérouse, dirigió una expedición patrocinada por Luis XVI a las aguas del Pacífico aún sin cartografiar.

1786

Federico II de Prusia era admirado y temido en toda Europa por su capacidad militar.

Primer barco de vapor
John Fitch logró aplicar la máquina de vapor a los barcos. Sin embargo, el éxito comercial se hizo esperar.

EE. UU. PASABA POR UNA ÉPOCA DE INNOVACIÓN TECNOLÓGICA. En Filadelfia (Pensilvania), **John Fitch** (1743–1798) había creado la Steamboat Company con el objetivo de diseñar un barco de vapor. Fitch lo consiguió antes que sus rivales, y en agosto de 1787, el ***Perseverance*** navegó con éxito por el río Delaware. En 1790, un incipiente servicio de barcos de vapor hacía la ruta de Filadelfia a Trenton (Nueva Jersey), pero Fitch tenía dificultades para atraer a los inversores. Hubo que esperar a diseños más avanzados y a la mayor visión empresarial de **Robert Fulton** (1765–1815) para que el transporte en barcos de vapor se convirtiera en una actividad comercial viable.

La navegación aún era peligrosa, y los ataques **piratas** continuaban siendo frecuentes. Los estadounidenses que deseaban comerciar en los mercados mediterráneos se arriesgaban a ser abordados. Los **piratas berberiscos** eran particularmente temibles. El 23 de julio, Estados Unidos firmó un tratado con Marruecos que garantizaba la seguridad de los barcos estadounidenses a cambio de un trato comercial equitativo.

En el continente europeo, **Prusia** lloraba la muerte de su soberano **Federico II**, que la había convertido en una potencia formidable y había transformado el equilibrio político de toda Europa.

« UN **PUEBLO EDUCADO** ES **FÁCIL** DE **GOBERNAR**. »

Atribuido a Federico II, rey de Prusia

1787

Este grabado del siglo XIX muestra el asentamiento costero de Sierra Leona, en África occidental.

TRAS EL FALLO DEL CASO SOMERSET (*véase* 1772), que estableció que los esclavos que llegaban a Gran Bretaña quedaban libres, muchos amos abandonaron a sus esclavos, y los **«pobres negros»** de Londres no tuvieron medio alguno de subsistencia. El abolicionista Granville Sharp (1735–1813) organizó un asentamiento libre en **Sierra Leona**, en África occidental, adonde el *Nautilus* llevó a unos 400 antiguos esclavos. Se les unieron más tarde esclavos liberados de **Nueva Escocia** (Canadá), que habían luchado con los británicos en la guerra de la Independencia de EE. UU. Al mismo tiempo, los esclavistas europeos seguían siendo muy activos en África occidental.

En EE. UU. crecía la demanda de un gobierno central fuerte. Entre mayo y septiembre se reunió la **Convención Constitucional**, supuestamente para enmendar los Artículos de la Confederación (*véase* 1781). En lugar de ello, los delegados crearon un nuevo sistema de **gobierno bicameral**, en el que todos los estados tenían la misma representación en el Senado y una representación proporcional a su población en la Cámara de Representantes.

En Europa oriental, las pretensiones de Rusia sobre el territorio otomano desembocaron en la **guerra ruso-turca**, que duró hasta 1792.

Colonia de esclavos
Antes centro de trata de esclavos, Sierra Leona se convirtió en un lugar de asentamiento para esclavos liberados.

LA CONSTITUCIÓN ESTADOUNIDENSE

Es la más antigua del mundo todavía vigente. Se adoptó el 17 de septiembre de 1787 y ha sido modificada 27 veces para abordar cuestiones como la libertad de expresión. George Washington (izda.) presidió la Convención Constitucional de Filadelfia y se convirtió en el primer presidente de EE. UU. en 1789. Durante su mandato se ratificaron las diez primeras enmiendas, conocidas como Carta de Derechos.

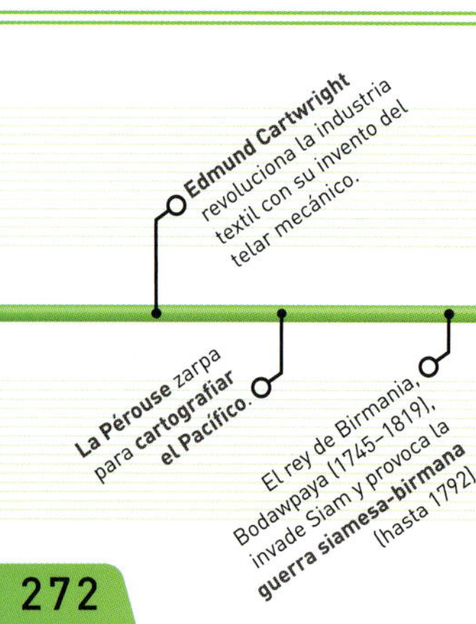

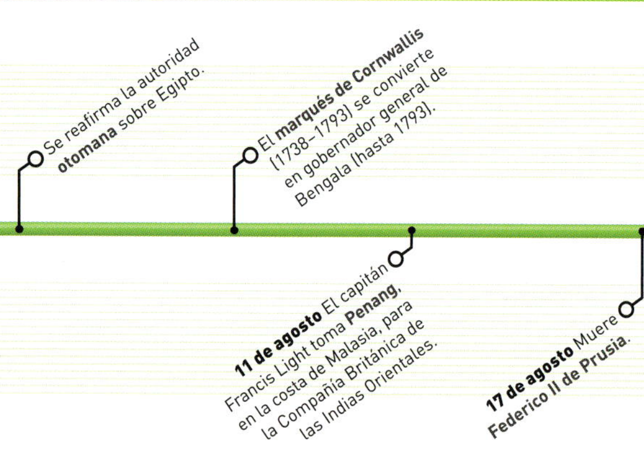

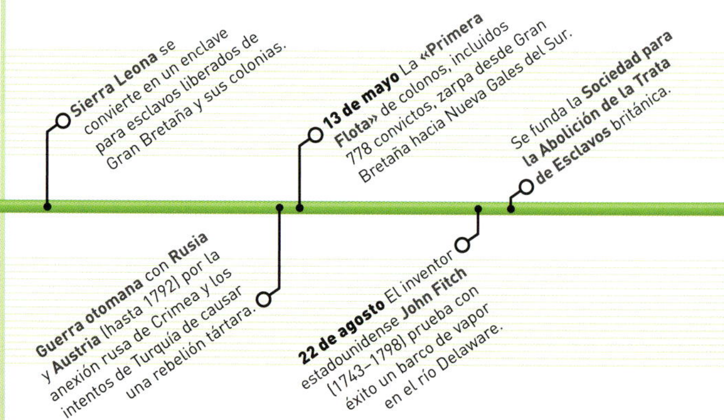

35 MILLONES DE PESOS ES LA CANTIDAD DE **DINERO QUE ESPAÑA RECIBÍA CADA AÑO** DE SUS **COLONIAS** A LA **MUERTE DE CARLOS III**

Detalle del retrato de Carlos IV (centro, dcha.) y su familia, por Francisco de Goya (1746–1828).

DESPUÉS DE CASI TREINTA AÑOS EN EL TRONO ESPAÑOL, murió el déspota ilustrado Carlos III, y su hijo, **Carlos IV** (1748–1819), heredó la corona. A diferencia de su padre, el nuevo rey era de carácter abúlico, y fueron su esposa, **María Luisa de Parma** (1751–1819) y su favorito **Manuel Godoy** (1767–1851), que acabó siendo primer ministro, quienes gobernaron el Imperio español y lo llevaron al desastre. Este periodo estuvo marcado por **guerras constantes con Francia**, que culminaron en 1808 con la invasión por parte de las tropas napoleónicas y la abdicación forzosa de Carlos IV (*véase* 1808).

En Francia, al igual que en Gran Bretaña, la **abolición** de la esclavitud cada vez tenía más partidarios. En mayo de 1787 ya se había establecido en Gran Bretaña el Comité para la Abolición de la Trata de Esclavos con el objetivo de acabar con este comercio inicuo. Poco después, en febrero de 1788, un grupo de parisinos fundó la **Sociedad de Amigos de los Negros** (*Société des Amis des Noirs*), que no solo exigía la abolición del comercio de esclavos y de la esclavitud, sino que también defendía la igualdad de los mestizos y los mulatos, cuyo trato era un problema creciente en las colonias azucareras del Caribe francés.

Mientras tanto, en Suecia, **Gustavo III** intentó materializar sus ambiciones imperialistas declarando la guerra a Rusia sin contar con el beneplácito del parlamento. Esperaba conquistar el territorio **finlandés** mientras los **rusos** se hallaban ocupados en la **guerra contra Turquía**, pero sus esfuerzos iniciales fracasaron como consecuencia de una conspiración de aristócratas y altos funcionarios irritados por el aumento del poder de la corona a expensas del **Riksdag** (parlamento) y de la nobleza. Los funcionarios intentaron negociar con Catalina la Grande de Rusia sin el conocimiento de Gustavo III. Posteriormente, **Dinamarca** se incorporó a la **guerra ruso-sueca** (hasta 1790) como aliada de Rusia y sitió el importante puerto de Gotenburgo, en el suroeste de Suecia.

En el vecino Imperio Habsburgo, los nobles **magiares (húngaros)** estaban descontentos con las reformas llevadas a cabo por José II (*véase* 1765), sobre todo por la introducción del alemán como lengua oficial del gobierno y de la educación secundaria. José también quería reformar el sistema fiscal sobre la tierra y ya había abolido la servidumbre. A su muerte, en 1790, los húngaros se hallaban al borde de la rebelión e incluso habían solicitado el apoyo de Prusia. Sin embargo, el descontento no llegó al conflicto armado gracias a la intervención de Leopoldo II (1747–1792), que sucedió a su hermano y prometió anular las reformas anteriores. Juró tratar a Hungría como a un reino independiente y permitir que se administrara según su propia legislación.

En Gran Bretaña, el capitán Arthur Phillip (1738–1814) había zarpado el 13 de mayo de 1787 con once barcos cargados de convictos con destino a la **bahía de Botany** (Australia), que había descubierto James Cook (*véase* 1768) en 1770 y que el gobierno británico deseaba colonizar. Al mismo tiempo, el envío de convictos a Australia era una sencilla solución para vaciar las superpobladas prisiones británicas. Aquellos barcos, conocidos como la **«Primera Flota»**, transportaban más de 1400 personas, 778 de las cuales eran convictos. Llegaron a la bahía de Botany en 1788, pero Phillip decidió que aquel lugar no era adecuado para un asentamiento permanente, y la colonia se trasladó a Port Jackson, que luego se denominó **Sydney**. Aunque los primeros tiempos fueron difíciles, los barcos continuaron transportando convictos, y en menos de cincuenta años había unos sesenta mil colonos en Australia.

La Primera Flota
Solo algo más de la mitad de los que viajaban en la Primera Flota eran convictos. Los restantes eran soldados, marineros y sus familias.

Llegada a Port Jackson
Los colonos llegan a la bahía australiana en cuyas orillas se desarrolló la ciudad de Sydney. Unas mujeres nativas les observan desde tierra.

18 de enero El barco del capitán Arthur Phillips, HMS Sirius, llega a la **bahía de Botany (Australia)**.

26 de enero La **Primera Flota** zarpa de la bahía de Botany y llega a la futura **Sydney (Australia)**.

9 de febrero Austria entra en la **guerra ruso-turca** (1787–1792).

Inicio del juicio del gobernador general de India, **Warren Hastings**, por delitos cometidos en India.

Suecia entra en guerra con **Rusia** y **Dinamarca** (hasta 1790), tras invadir la Finlandia rusa.

24 de julio El gobernador general lord Dorchester divide **Canadá** en cinco distritos.

Revuelta húngara (hasta 1790) contra José II en el Sacro Imperio.

Los abolicionistas franceses fundan la **Sociedad de Amigos de los Negros**.

14 de diciembre **Carlos IV** (1748–1819) accede al trono español.

Motor de balancín
En el motor diseñado por Thomas Newcomen y mejorado por James Watt, la barra superior (balancín) se desplaza hacia delante y hacia atrás, y transfiere el movimiento del pistón que sube y baja en el interior de un cilindro.

el balancín va hacia delante y hacia atrás

biela

el pistón sube y baja

el vapor se condensa en el cilindro

un gran volante gira

cigüeñal unido al pistón

Siglo I d.C.
Máquina de Herón
El científico griego Herón describe una eolípila, cuya bola gira impulsada por chorros de vapor.

Eolípila

1679
La primera olla a presión
El inventor francés Denis Papin crea un aparato que convierte el líquido en vapor: la primera olla a presión.

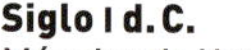

Digestor de vapor de Papin

1698
Máquina de vapor de alta presión
En Inglaterra, Thomas Savery utiliza vapor para construir el «amigo del minero», que extrae agua de las minas de carbón, aunque no tiene éxito.

1712
Máquina de Newcomen
Thomas Savery colabora con Thomas Newcomen y crean la muy mejorada máquina de vapor atmosférica.

Máquina atmosférica de Newcomen

1765
Máquina de James Watt
El inventor escocés James Watt mejora la máquina de Newcomen con un condensador y desarrolla una máquina que hace girar una manivela en lugar de bombear.

1769–1770
Automóvil de vapor
En Francia, Nicolas Cugnot idea un vehículo propulsado por la conversión del vapor en acción de pistones y en movimiento giratorio.

1801–1804
Máquina de Trevithick
Richard Trevithick, ingeniero de minas, desarrolla una máquina de vapor mucho más pequeña y ligera, y le añade ruedas: una «locomotora de carretera».

1802–1807
Barco de vapor
En EE. UU., Robert Fulton aplica la energía del vapor a un barco de pasajeros y consigue navegar a contracorriente.

HISTORIA DE LA ENERGÍA DEL VAPOR

LA FUERZA DEL VAPOR DE AGUA SIRVIÓ PARA PONER EN MARCHA LA REVOLUCIÓN INDUSTRIAL

Aunque hasta el siglo XVII no se aprovechó plenamente la energía del vapor, hacía siglos que los científicos conocían su potencial. En el siglo I a. C., el científico griego Herón de Alejandría describió un aparato (la eolípila) que ilustraba las posibilidades del vapor de agua.

La eolípila funcionaba calentando agua en una esfera hueca montada en dos tubos acodados en ángulo recto; cuando el vapor salía por los tubos, la esfera giraba. Aunque no tuvo aplicación práctica en su época, fue el primer experimento sobre la fuerza del vapor del que se tiene noticia. En el siglo XVII se hicieron avances mucho más radicales: la invención del «digestor», también llamado marmita de Papin, poco más que una olla a presión, abrió el camino a una serie ininterrumpida de innovaciones.

LA INDUSTRIA DEL VAPOR

En el siglo XVIII, los ingenieros ya se habían dado cuenta de la utilidad del vapor para impulsar dispositivos capaces de bombear agua de las minas, una operación cada vez más importante debido a la creciente demanda de carbón en Europa durante la revolución industrial. Pronto vieron que el vapor también podía impulsar motores. Thomas Newcomen inventó una máquina de vapor en 1712 en la que James Watt introdujo mejoras esenciales que la hicieron más eficiente. La aportación clave de Watt fue el condensador del vapor, que evitaba tener que calentar y enfriar el cilindro. Pronto, el vapor empezó a impulsar barcos y locomotoras que permitían viajar más rápido y a mayor distancia. En el siglo XIX se utilizó para generar electricidad, algo que sigue haciéndose hoy en parte gracias a una tecnología desarrollada en los siglos pasados.

Richard Trevithick
Además de desarrollar la primera locomotora de vapor sobre raíles del mundo, el ingeniero inglés Richard Trevithick adaptó su máquina de alta presión para usarla en fundiciones de hierro y en barcazas de vapor.

« SERÍA DIFÍCIL ENCONTRAR **UN AVANCE MAYOR** QUE ESTE EN TODA LA HISTORIA DE LA **TECNOLOGÍA**. »

L. T. C. Rolt, escritor e ingeniero inglés, *Thomas Newcomen: The Prehistory of Steam* (1963)

1819
Travesía atlántica
El barco estadounidense *Savannah* es el primero que cruza el Atlántico usando vapor además de velas. La era de la vela termina poco después.

El vapor *Savannah*

1829
La *Rocket* de Stephenson
El ingeniero inglés George Stephenson aplica el vapor a las locomotoras. Su *Rocket* es un éxito comercial.

La *Rocket* de Stephenson

1867
Caldera de tubos
En EE. UU., George Babcock y Stephen Wilcox inventan una caldera en la que el agua circula por tubos. En 1882 la usan para generar electricidad.

Caldera de vapor de Babcock y Wilcox

1884–1897
Turbina de vapor
Sir Charles Algernon Parsons desarrolla un generador con una turbina de vapor, que produce cantidades enormes de electricidad y que se utiliza para impulsar grandes barcos.

Transatlántico impulsado por la turbina de vapor de Parsons

Principios del siglo XX
Energía geotérmica
Científicos de Lardarello (en Italia) descubren la energía geotérmica o de «vapor seco» y construyen la primera central eléctrica de este tipo en 1911.

Central eléctrica geotérmica

Siglo XX
Turbinas de vapor y energía nuclear
Las reacciones nucleares en cadena controladas generan calor en los reactores, donde el agua hierve y produce vapor que impulsa una turbina que genera electricidad.

1789

Los representantes del tercer estado (el pueblo) de Francia prestan el juramento del Juego de Pelota: no separarse hasta haber instaurado una constitución en Francia.

« LIBERTÉ, EGALITÉ, FRATERNITÉ! »

«¡Libertad, igualdad, fraternidad!»
Divisa de la Revolución francesa

EN 1789, LUIS XVI DE FRANCIA SE ENFRENTABA A MÚLTIPLES CRISIS: el país estaba en bancarrota a consecuencia de las guerras constantes, existía inquietud popular, y el fracaso de la cosecha de cereales de 1788 había provocado alborotos por el pan. Ante esta situación, Luis convocó los Estados Generales, la asamblea de representantes francesa. Esta no se reunía desde 1614, por lo que entre los meses de enero y abril se celebraron elecciones para seleccionar a los diputados.

Los tres estados
Estas figuras simbolizan los tres estados que representaban a Francia: de izda. a dcha., la nobleza, el pueblo y el clero.

Los **Estados Generales** se componían de tres «estados» u órdenes: el primer estado (el clero), el segundo estado (la nobleza) y, por último, el **tercer estado (el pueblo)**. La asamblea se reunió el 5 de mayo en Versalles. La cuestión inmediata fue cuánto poder debía concederse al tercer estado; el primero y el segundo querían que el voto fuera por estado y no por cabeza, para que los representantes del pueblo no les superaran. El 17 de junio, un frustrado tercer estado se autoproclamó **Asamblea Nacional** y decidió continuar sin los nobles ni el clero. Cuando por un error administrativo creyeron que se les impedía entrar en el lugar de reuniones habitual, ocuparon la sala destinada al *jeu de paume* (juego de pelota) de Luis XVI, y el 20 de junio juraron no disolverse hasta haber redactado una constitución para Francia, en el famoso **juramento del Juego de Pelota**, que fue firmado por los 577 diputados, excepto uno: Joseph Martin-Dauch, de Castelnaudary, que se negó a firmar el documento porque carecía de sanción real.

Luis XVI creyó que no le quedaba otra opción que ceder a las exigencias del tercer estado y pidió a la nobleza y al clero que participaran en la que se denominó el 9 de julio **Asamblea Constituyente** (aunque continuara llamándose Asamblea Nacional).

Días después corrió por París el rumor de que el ejército se dirigía a la ciudad para disolver la Asamblea Nacional. En respuesta, unas 600 personas, con armas robadas en el Hotel de los Inválidos, asaltaron la **Bastilla**, una fortaleza medieval utilizada como prisión y que tan solo albergaba a siete prisioneros en aquel momento, pero que simbolizaba el despotismo de la monarquía y contenía munición de la que el pueblo quería apoderarse. El ataque, en el que perdieron la vida 98 asaltantes y toda la guarnición, se convirtió en un hito emblemático de la **Revolución francesa**, que acababa de estallar.

600
ES EL NÚMERO DE **PERSONAS** QUE **TOMARON LA BASTILLA**

Toma de la Bastilla
Una multitud de unas 600 personas se reunió pacíficamente frente a la prisión para pedir que se rindiera, pero la violencia no tardó en estallar.

A finales de julio y principios de agosto, los rumores habían llegado al campo francés, donde la escasez de cereales había generado un gran malestar. Se oían historias de bandidos que recorrían las tierras y quemaban las cosechas. Durante este periodo, conocido como el **Gran Miedo**, el pánico se apoderó de los campesinos, muchos de los cuales se armaron y atacaron a los nobles y sus castillos.

El 4 de agosto, la Asamblea Constituyente trató de controlar esta situación y decretó la **abolición del feudalismo** y del diezmo. A estas medidas siguió el 26 de agosto la ***Declaración de los derechos del hombre y del ciudadano***, que proclamaba que «los hombres **nacen y permanecen libres** e iguales en derechos» y que «el origen de toda soberanía descansa fundamentalmente en la Nación.»

Durante todo este periodo turbulento, periódicos sin censura informaban de lo que sucedía y se organizaban **clubes políticos**, donde el pueblo expresaba su opinión. Pese a la avalancha de nuevas libertades y a la ingente reforma social, la Revolución apenas había hecho más que empezar y el futuro de Francia distaba mucho de estar claro.

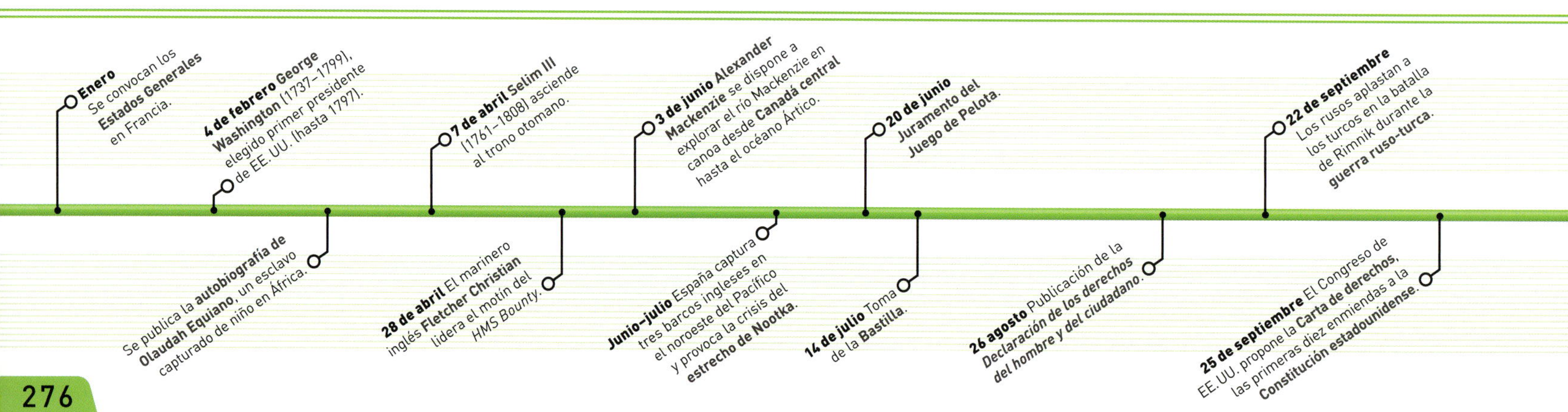

1790

El general Josiah Harmar fue derrotado en su campaña contra una coalición india en el Territorio del Noroeste (EE. UU.).

LAS NOTICIAS DE LO SUCEDIDO EN PARÍS llegaron a las colonias francesas. Como sabía la Asamblea Nacional, ni la **esclavitud** ni la desigualdad que sufrían las **personas libres de color** en Francia y su imperio encajaban con las ideas que defendía la *Declaración de los derechos del hombre*.

Saint Domingue (actual Haití), la mitad occidental de la isla de La Española, era parte del imperio francés. En 1790, estaban en París dos plantadores mulatos ricos de Saint-Domingue, **Vincent Ogé** (1750–1791) y **Julien Raimond** (1744–1801), y reclamaron sus plenos derechos como propietarios. Al volver a Saint-Domingue, Ogé, indignado porque la Asamblea no hacía frente a los plantadores blancos en la cuestión, lideró la revuelta de unos 200 partidarios en Grande-Rivière, rápidamente reprimida.

Mientras la Asamblea Nacional redactaba una **constitución**, prohibió oficialmente la nobleza, suprimió las órdenes religiosas y nacionalizó todas las propiedades eclesiásticas.

En EE. UU., el general Josiah Harmar (1753–1813) cayó en una emboscada organizada por una coalición de tribus indígenas. **Akima Mihškinaahkwa** (el jefe Pequeña Tortuga) (1752–1812) dirigió el ataque, cerca del río Maumee (Indiana), en el **Territorio del Noroeste**. El presidente Washington había encargado a Harmar una expedición contra los indígenas, pero su ejército de 320 soldados y 1100 milicianos tuvo que **retirarse**.

Ilustración revolucionaria
Ilustración con una versión del emblema revolucionario francés y la famosa llamada a la libertad, la igualdad y la fraternidad, o la muerte.

> « LOS HOMBRES **NACEN** Y PERMANECEN **LIBRES** E **IGUALES EN DERECHOS**. LAS **DISTINCIONES SOCIALES** SOLO PUEDEN FUNDARSE EN LA **UTILIDAD COMÚN**. »
>
> **Artículo 1.°, *Declaración de los derechos del hombre y del ciudadano*** (1789)

1791

Plantaciones incendiadas en Le Cap, al norte de Saint-Domingue (Haití), durante la rebelión de los esclavos.

DURANTE EL MES DE ENERO, Vincent Ogé y **Jean-Baptiste Chavannes** (c. 1748–1791), que había ayudado a Ogé a organizar la revuelta de 1790, estaban ocultos en la colonia española de Santo Domingo. Sin embargo, los españoles los devolvieron a Saint-Domingue, donde les rompieron los huesos en un torno, los decapitaron y **empalaron sus cabezas**. Lo sucedido conmocionó a Francia, y en mayo se concedieron derechos políticos a las personas de color libres, siempre que sus dos progenitores hubieran sido libres.

Los esclavos de Saint-Domingue también habían oído una mezcla de noticias y rumores sobre los sucesos de París y empezaron a albergar esperanzas de ver la abolición de la esclavitud. Al final, decidieron no esperar a que Francia les concediera la libertad.

Una cálida tarde de agosto, el líder esclavo **Dutty Boukman** (m. 1791) instó a los esclavos reunidos en una ceremonia vudú en Bois-Caïman a escuchar «la voz de la libertad que habla en todos nosotros». Una semana más tarde, Boukman y sus seguidores iniciaron una **revuelta masiva** en el norte de la isla. Atacaron las plantaciones, asesinaron a los propietarios de esclavos, destruyeron las herramientas y prendieron fuego a los campos. Los números jugaban a su favor, ya que en Saint-Domingue había quince veces más esclavos que europeos. A diferencia de las revueltas anteriores, esta fue **imposible de detener**.

En Francia, Luis XVI y su familia intentaron **refugiarse** en el reducto monárquico de Montmédy, en la frontera oriental, pero cuando llegaron a **Varennes**, en el noreste del país, fueron detenidos y obligados a regresar a París. Después de este intento de huida fallido, Luis perdió toda la credibilidad que le quedaba como monarca.

Esclavos y colonos
El gran número de esclavos traídos para trabajar en la industria azucarera de Saint-Domingue fue una desventaja para los colonos cuando aquellos se rebelaron.

La revolución de Haití
La revuelta de los esclavos de Saint-Domingue se convirtió en un conflicto internacional cuando Gran Bretaña y España entraron en guerra contra Francia.

EL VUDÚ DE HAITÍ Y SAINT-DOMINGUE

El vudú es una religión nacida de la esclavitud. Bebe de tradiciones africanas diversas, en particular las de Benín, lugar de origen de muchos esclavos. También incorpora el catolicismo impuesto por los europeos, y quizás también rasgos de los rituales de los indígenas arawak. Las prácticas católicas sirvieron para ocultar su verdadera religión a los amos, y los santos del catolicismo, para representar a los *loa* (espíritus) venerados en el vudú. El nuevo sistema de creencias sirvió a los esclavos para formar una identidad propia y conformó un medio para organizar la resistencia, como sucedió en Saint-Domingue.

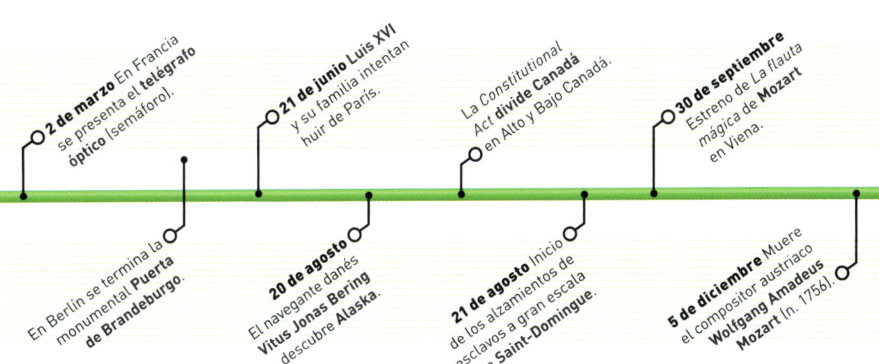

Leopoldo II (1746–1792) es coronado emperador del Sacro Imperio.

La **tercera guerra de Mysore** (hasta 1792) acaba con la derrota del sultán Tipu (1750–1799).

14 de agosto La **guerra sueco-rusa** termina con el tratado de Värälä.

Octubre Vincent Ogé y Jean-Baptiste Chavannes lideran la primera **revuelta** en la colonia francesa de **Saint-Domingue**.

2 de marzo En Francia se presenta el **telégrafo óptico** (semáforo).

En Berlín se termina la monumental **Puerta de Brandeburgo**.

21 de junio Luis XVI y su familia intentan huir de París.

20 de agosto El navegante danés **Vitus Jonas Bering** descubre **Alaska**.

La Constitutional Act **divide Canadá** en Alto y Bajo Canadá.

21 de agosto Inicio de los alzamientos de esclavos a gran escala en **Saint-Domingue**.

30 de septiembre Estreno de *La flauta mágica* de **Mozart** en Viena.

5 de diciembre Muere el compositor austriaco **Wolfgang Amadeus Mozart** (n. 1756).

1792

Detalle de *La batalla de Valmy*, obra del pintor francés Émile Jean Horace Vernet, sobre la derrota de Prusia por los franceses.

LA SITUACIÓN EN FRANCIA ADQUIRIÓ TINTES DRAMÁTICOS el 20 de abril de 1792, al declarar la Asamblea Nacional la guerra al Sacro Imperio para expandir Francia hasta sus «fronteras naturales» (el Rin y los Alpes) y distraer a la población de los conflictos internos. Luis XVI confiaba en que Francia perdiera la guerra para socavar la revolución. En la **Declaración de Pillnitz**, firmada por el emperador Leopoldo II y Federico Guillermo II de Prusia, se acordó defender a Luis XVI junto con otras potencias europeas. Ante la declaración francesa de guerra, las tropas austriacas y prusianas se movilizaron.

Las noticias enfurecieron al pueblo francés, que se creyó traicionado por su monarca y la aristocracia. El 10 de agosto, un grupo de revolucionarios irrumpió en el **palacio de las Tullerías** y encontró a **Luis XVI**, al que encerraron con el resto de la familia real en la **prisión del Temple**.

El temor creciente a un complot contrarrevolucionario de los prisioneros monárquicos movió a un grupo de parisinos armados a atacar y matar a algunos mientras se les trasladaba a otra prisión. Esto desencadenó las **matanzas de septiembre**, en las que multitudes enfurecidas sacaron a presos de las prisiones parisinas y ejecutaron a unas **1200 personas** en cinco días.

Aunque Francia sufrió varios reveses al principio de la guerra, el 20 de septiembre ya había conseguido contener a los prusianos en la **batalla de Valmy**, al noreste del país; luego atacó a los Países Bajos austriacos y venció en **Jemappes** (Bélgica actual). Al día siguiente se reunió en París un nuevo organismo de gobierno, la **Convención Nacional**, que abolió la monarquía constitucional en favor de la **república**, la primera en la historia europea

A esas alturas, el resto de Europa estaba muy preocupada por lo que sucedía en Francia y por su osadía más allá de sus fronteras, así que Holanda, España, Austria, Prusia y Rusia formaron la **Primera Coalición**, a la que se unió Gran Bretaña en 1793, y se enfrentaron a Francia a lo largo de los seis años siguientes durante la **guerra de la Primera Coalición**.

Mientras tanto, en India, la Compañía Británica de las Indias Orientales descubría que era rentable suministrar a los británicos **té de China**, que pagaba con opio producido en Bengala. Las exportaciones se duplicaron en una década, pero los negocios con China eran complicados: la Compañía tenía acceso comercial a un solo puerto, **Cantón** (Guangzhou), pues el gobierno chino mantenía un control estricto de la entrada de extranjeros al resto del país.

MARY WOLLSTONECRAFT (1759–1797)

Esta escritora inglesa fue una de las primeras defensoras de los derechos de las mujeres. En 1792, influenciada por lo sucedido en Francia y los consiguientes debates en Gran Bretaña, publicó *Vindicación de los derechos de la mujer*, obra en la que pedía que el sistema educativo ofreciera a las niñas los mismos privilegios que a los niños y que generó una enorme polémica. Pasaron años antes de que algo cambiara, pero ello no le resta mérito como pionera de la filosofía feminista.

1783–1784
142,5 MILLONES

1792–1793
285 MILLONES

Exportaciones de té
La afición creciente por el té en ámbito anglosajón duplicó las libras exportadas por la Compañía Británica de las Indias Orientales desde China.

1793

Ejecución de Luis XVI en la guillotina, en la plaza de la Revolución (París). Su esposa María Antonieta fue guillotinada unos meses después.

EL 18 DE ENERO, LA CONVENCIÓN NACIONAL FRANCESA CONDENÓ a muerte a Luis XVI. El rey fue guillotinado en la plaza de la Revolución (después llamada de la Concordia) de París el 21 de enero. Su esposa **María Antonieta** permaneció en prisión hasta octubre, cuando compareció ante un tribunal revolucionario, y sufrió el mismo destino que su marido.

María Antonieta murió ejecutada durante el **periodo del Terror**, resultado de un decreto del 5 de septiembre que convirtió al «terror» en una forma de gobierno. Dos semanas más tarde se aprobaba la **Ley de Sospechosos**, que estableció los **tribunales revolucionarios**. Cualquier persona sospechosa de ser enemiga de la revolución era juzgada y podía ser sentenciada a muerte. El **Comité de Salvación Pública**, liderado por **Maximilien Robespierre** (1758–1794) controlaba el gobierno. Los miembros del mismo club político que

Desmotadora de algodón de Eli Whitney
Separaba las semillas del algodón mucho más rápido que a mano, lo cual aumentó significativamente la producción algodonera.

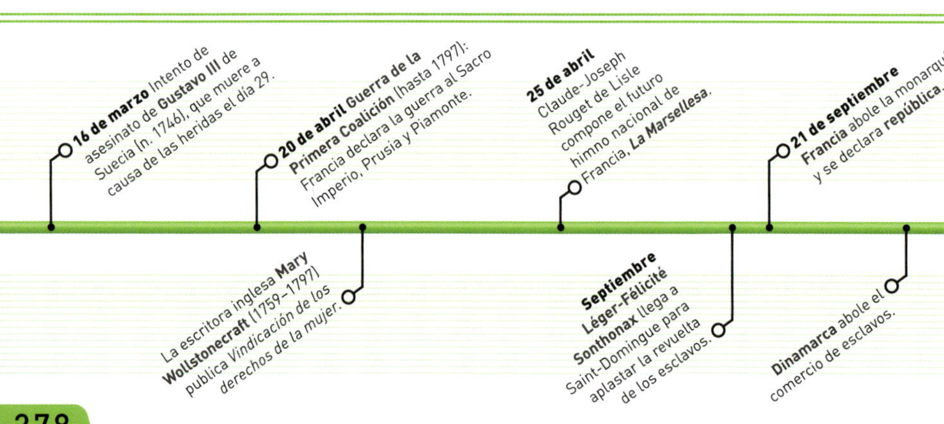

16 de marzo Intento de asesinato de **Gustavo III** de Suecia (n. 1746), que muere a causa de las heridas el día 29.

20 de abril Guerra de la Primera Coalición (hasta 1797): Francia declara la guerra al Sacro Imperio, Prusia y Piamonte.

La escritora inglesa **Mary Wollstonecraft** (1759–1797) publica *Vindicación de los derechos de la mujer*.

25 de abril Claude-Joseph Rouget de Lisle compone el futuro himno nacional de Francia, *La Marsellesa*.

Septiembre Léger-Félicité Sonthonax llega a Saint-Domingue para aplastar la revuelta de los esclavos.

21 de septiembre Francia abole la monarquía y se declara **república**.

Dinamarca abole el comercio de esclavos.

21 de enero Ejecución de **Luis XVI**.

23 de enero Segundo reparto de **Polonia**.

Febrero Gran Bretaña y **España** firman la **segunda convención de Nootka**.

Francia declara la guerra a Gran Bretaña, Holanda y España; Gran Bretaña interviene en la lucha de **Saint-Domingue**.

« ¡PUEBLO MÍO, MUERO INOCENTE! »

Luis XVI de Francia, antes de su ejecución

1794

Detalle de un fresco sobre la batalla de Raclawice, el 4 de abril de 1794, en la que las tropas polacas al mando del general Tadeusz Kosciuszko derrotaron a los rusos.

Robespierre **(jacobinos)** también participaban en la vigilancia de los posibles sospechosos.

En **Saint-Domingue (Haití)**, la lucha se complicó con la llegada del **ejército británico**. Gran Bretaña, a raíz de la declaración de guerra francesa de 1792, aspiraba a tomar la isla y añadirla a sus otras islas azucareras caribeñas, como Jamaica. El conflicto duró cinco años.

En EE. UU., **Eli Whitney** (1765–1825) desarrolló una máquina para **desmotar algodón**, que al año siguiente patentó. Muchos plantadores querían diversificar la producción del algodón, pero la variedad de fibra larga, que produce fibras largas y sedosas, solamente podía cultivarse cerca de la costa. La única opción era el algodón de **fibra corta**, que producía unas fibras cortas pero tenía muchas semillas y retirarlas era una tarea laboriosa y muy lenta. La máquina de Whitney, en cambio, al desmotar el algodón muy rápido, permitió el desarrollo de la industria algodonera en el sur de EE. UU. e hizo aumentar la explotación de la mano de obra esclava.

En Europa, **Polonia** fue víctima de un **segundo reparto**, esta vez entre Prusia y Rusia, que se quedaron con unos 300 000 km². Polonia tan solo conservaba una pequeña parte de su territorio anterior: cedió las provincias orientales, desde Livonia hasta Moldavia, a Rusia, mientras que Prusia se quedó con Gran Polonia, Torun y la ciudad portuaria de Gdansk.

Gran Bretaña y España evitaron entrar en guerra por el **estrecho de Nootka**, en el océano Pacífico, al noroeste del territorio norteamericano, con la firma de la segunda convención del estrecho de Nootka. Un año después firmaron otro acuerdo, por el que España cedía a las exigencias británicas. El conflicto diplomático (que acabó involucrando a los aliados europeos de ambas partes) había comenzado en 1789, cuando España capturó tres barcos británicos que navegaban cerca del estrecho; dicho incidente se convirtió en una disputa verbal sobre quién tenía **derecho a colonizar el territorio**.

17 000
NÚMERO DE **PERSONAS EJECUTADAS** DURANTE **EL TERROR**

En China, el oficial de la Compañía de las Indias Orientales George Macartney (1737–1806), que en 1792 había llegado a Pekín junto con un grupo de 94 personas y con varios productos británicos, consiguió ser recibido por el emperador Qianlong en septiembre de 1793. El gobierno británico y la Compañía de las Indias Orientales deseaban **ampliar el comercio con China**, pero los funcionarios Qing no estaban interesados y se negaron a negociar un tratado.

EN FRANCIA, EL RÉGIMEN DEL TERROR HABÍA CONSEGUIDO acabar con los enemigos del Comité de Salvación Pública en 1794. Sin embargo, el Comité consideró que debía ir aún más lejos y suspendió el derecho de los sospechosos a un juicio público y a la asistencia legal; los jurados tenían la orden de absolver o de condenar a muerte. Esta medida fue aprobada en junio, pero poco más de un mes después, se fraguó una rebelión en el seno de la Convención Nacional que terminó con el poder de Robespierre el 27 de julio de 1794, 9 de termidor del año II según el calendario revolucionario francés. Este calendario, instaurado por la República francesa, se aplicó en 1792 y estuvo vigente hasta 1806. El año empezaba el día del aniversario de la proclamación de la república (21 de septiembre, el equinoccio de otoño) y los meses, que recibieron nombres alusivos a la estación del año y a las tareas agrícolas, tenían todos treinta días y estaban divididos en «décadas» de diez días.

Moneda revolucionaria
Hércules, flanqueado por la Libertad y la Igualdad, sustituyó a la efigie de Luis XVI en las monedas francesas.

Revolucionario y general haitiano
Toussaint Louverture lideró en Haití la lucha por la abolición y la independencia. Su retrato póstumo es el primero de un pintor haitiano.

El 27 de julio, Robespierre fue detenido y, junto con cien de sus partidarios, condenado a morir en la misma **guillotina** que había hecho rodar la cabeza de sus enemigos.

La Revolución francesa llegó a un punto de inflexión. La Convención Nacional había reafirmado su poder, pero el Terror había tenido un coste muy elevado: oficialmente se ejecutó a unas 17 000 personas y cientos de miles fueron detenidas.

En Saint-Domingue, se convenció al antiguo esclavo y líder militar **Toussaint Louverture** (*c.* 1743–1803) de dejar a los españoles y unirse al comisionado francés, Léger-Félicité Sonthonax (1763–1813), para dirigir tropas republicanas francesas, aunque luego rompiera con los franceses (*véase* 1803). Sonthonax había llegado a Saint-Domingue en 1792 para mantenerla bajo control tras la rebelión de los esclavos, y aplicar la decisión de la Convención Nacional que reconocía la igualdad de las personas libres de color. La declaración de guerra de Francia a Gran Bretaña complicó la situación: al luchar España y Gran Bretaña junto a antiguos esclavos, Sonthonax recurrió a los que seguían esclavizados. En 1793 les prometió la **libertad** si luchaban por la causa de Francia, y en agosto decretó la **abolición de la esclavitud**, ratificada por la Convención Nacional el 4 de febrero de 1794.

Mientras tanto, la indignación que había suscitado en **Polonia** el devastador reparto del año anterior impulsó a los patriotas a organizar la **rebelión polaca de 1794**. Pese a una victoria inicial en Varsovia (en poder de Rusia), los polacos fueron aplastados por el ejército ruso.

« NACÍ ESCLAVO, PERO LA NATURALEZA ME DIO EL ALMA DE UN HOMBRE LIBRE. »

Toussaint Louverture, antiguo esclavo y líder militar

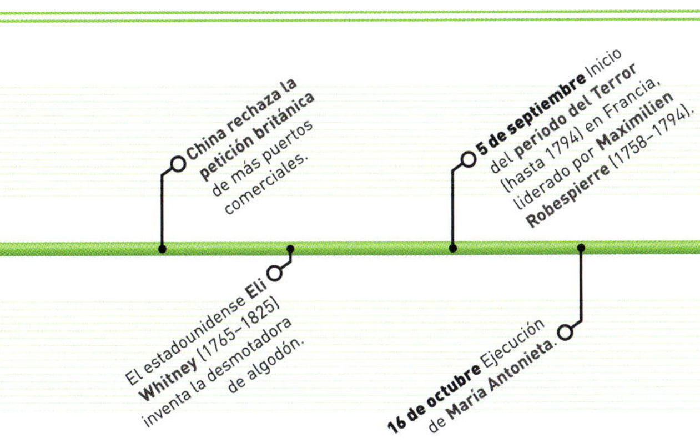

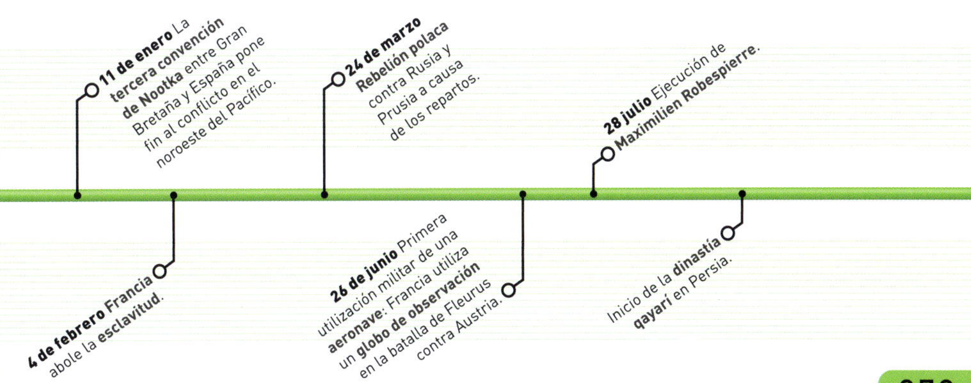

1795

Vista de la isla de Penang, al norte del asentamiento holandés de Malaca. El estrecho de Malaca aún es una importante ruta comercial hacia China.

EL SEGUNDO REPARTO DE POLONIA había provocado un alzamiento en 1794, liderado por el oficial polaco Tadeusz Kosciuszko (1746–1817). En 1795, y después de ocho meses de combates, una alianza rusoprusiana consiguió finalmente derrotar a los polacos y tuvo lugar el **tercer reparto**: Rusia, Prusia y Austria se dividieron lo poco que quedaba del territorio polaco, y Polonia dejó de existir.

Al mismo tiempo, en el resto del continente europeo, la guerra de la Primera Coalición estaba llegando a su fin, negociado parcialmente en tres tratados en la **paz de Basilea**. Los acuerdos cedían a Francia territorios alemanes al oeste del Rin y acababan con la lucha entre Francia y España en los Pirineos con la cesión de Santo Domingo a Francia. Esto significaba que los franceses pasaban a controlar toda la isla de La Española, aunque la lucha iniciada en Saint-Domingue no daba señas de remitir.

300 000 ES EL **NÚMERO DE PERIÓDICOS** QUE SE **VENDÍAN DIARIAMENTE** EN LA **FRANCIA REVOLUCIONARIA** HACIA **1795**

En **Jamaica**, la paz conseguida en el año 1739 entre los británicos y los exesclavos huidos, conocidos como ***maroons*** (cimarrones) llegó a su fin. Al principio, los cimarrones habían invadido y saqueado a los colonos, pero accedieron a firmar un tratado que les concedía tierras y autonomía, y los ataques prácticamente habían cesado. Sin embargo, en 1795, después de que los británicos azotaran cruelmente a dos cimarrones por robar cerdos estalló una revuelta. Temeroso de que la isla pudiera seguir el ejemplo de Saint-Domingue, el gobernador llamó al ejército para que la reprimiera. Tras rendirse, algunos cimarrones fueron enviados a **Nueva Escocia**.

Lejos de allí, los británicos tomaron **El Cabo**, en Sudáfrica, y el puerto de **Malaca**, situado en el estrecho del mismo nombre que conecta los océanos Índico y Pacífico, y que en aquel momento estaba en manos de los holandeses.

Asentamiento cimarrón (Jamaica)
En este antiguo grabado se aprecia un asentamiento de cimarrones, antiguos esclavos huidos que habían conseguido la autonomía.

1796

Uno de la serie de retratos de la familia y el harén del sah de Persia encargados por Fath Alí Sah, el segundo soberano qayarí.

MÁS DE UN AÑO DESPUÉS DE ZARPAR para encontrar el río Níger, el cirujano y explorador escocés **Mungo Park** (1771–1806) logró su objetivo. La Asociación para el Fomento del Descubrimiento del Interior de África le había encomendado la expedición a fin de «determinar el curso» del gran río africano. Partió desde el río Gambia en 1795, y el 20 de julio, después de padecer varias enfermedades y cuatro meses de cautiverio, llegó a Ségou (en el Malí actual), a orillas del río.

El médico británico **Edward Jenner** (1749–1823) realizó la primera vacunación documentada el 14 de mayo. En un intento de prevenir la mortífera **viruela**, que mataba a miles de personas en Europa, experimentó con el virus de la **viruela bovina**, una enfermedad parecida aunque menos letal que solía contraerse al ordeñar vacas infectadas. El experimento consistió en inocular viruela bovina extraída de Sarah Nelmes, una lechera, a James Phipps, de ocho años de edad. El éxito del experimento llevó al desarrollo de las **vacunas modernas**.

En el continente europeo, el comandante del ejército francés **Napoleón Bonaparte** (*véase* recuadro), asumió en marzo el mando del ejército en el norte de Italia con la orden de tomar Lombardía y obtuvo múltiples victorias sobre el ejército austriaco, hasta obligar a Austria a iniciar negociaciones de paz. El resultado fue el **tratado de Campoformio**, firmado el año siguiente, por el que Austria reconocía al estado títere francés de la República Cisalpina y cedía a Francia los Países Bajos austriacos (Bélgica).

En **Persia** se estableció la nueva dinastía **qayarí**. **Agá Muhammad Kan** (1742–1797), su líder, había dedicado la década anterior a afirmar su autoridad sobre territorios tan lejanos como Georgia, en el Cáucaso. En 1796 se proclamó sah (rey), pero murió un año después. Su familia siguió gobernando hasta 1925.

En Extremo Oriente, China estaba a las puertas de una rebelión. El **Loto Blanco**, una secta budista secreta, pretendía derrocar a los gobernantes **manchúes** y restaurar la dinastía **Ming**. Consiguió mucho apoyo, pero fracasó tras ocho años de lucha.

En España, Manuel Godoy firmó el 18 de agosto el **segundo tratado de San Ildefonso**, una alianza militar con la República francesa en caso de guerra, pero solo contra Gran Bretaña. Una vez hecho público, el 6 de octubre, España entró en guerra con Gran Bretaña.

1797

El marqués de Wellesley presencia una lucha de elefantes.

DURANTE ESTE AÑO, EL NOMBRAMIENTO DEL NOBLE IRLANDÉS Richard Wellesley (1760–1842) como **gobernador general de Bengala** señaló el inicio de un periodo de agresiva expansión británica en la región. Wellesley partió hacia Calcuta en noviembre, decidido a ampliar el territorio británico por vía militar y diplomática.

Durante sus ocho años de gobierno (1797–1805), logró vencer a algunos de los soberanos más poderosos de India, como el sultán Tipu, conocido como el Tigre de Mysore (*véase* 1761 y 1799). Este periodo también se caracterizó por los enormes esfuerzos realizados a fin de profesionalizar a la Compañía de las Indias Orientales, como la apertura de un **instituto** donde los funcionarios estudiaban lenguas indias, entre otras materias, aunque algunas de estas medidas generaron una fuerte controversia.

NAPOLEÓN BONAPARTE (1769–1821)

Nació en Córcega y estudió en Francia, donde se convirtió en oficial del ejército en 1785. Su brillante campaña italiana (1796–1797) fue seguida por una serie de nuevas victorias militares y políticas. En 1804 se convirtió en emperador y dirigió al ejército francés en más batallas, aunque con un éxito cada vez menor, lo que acabó agotando los recursos de la nación y provocó su caída. Napoleón murió en el exilio en la remota isla de Santa Elena, situada en el Atlántico Sur.

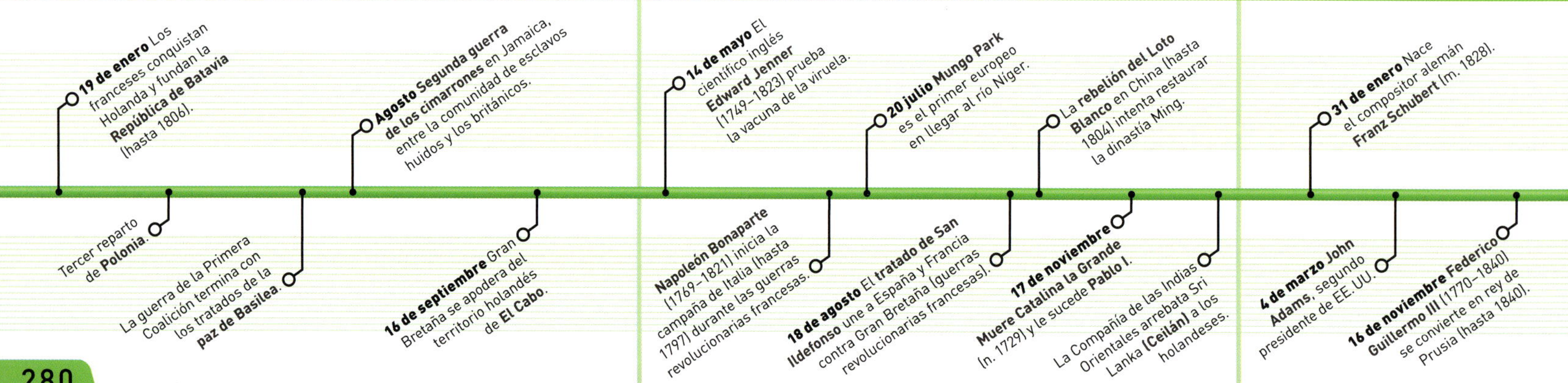

1798

Destrucción del *Orient*, el buque insignia francés, en la primera batalla de Abukir (Egipto), donde la flota británica aniquiló a la francesa.

A PESAR DE QUE LA GUERRA de la Primera Coalición había terminado en 1795, Francia seguía viendo a un enemigo en Gran Bretaña. Los franceses consideraron la posibilidad de una **invasión**, pero la rechazaron debido a la superioridad de la **flota y las defensas navales** británicas. Buscando una ventaja comercial sobre los británicos, Napoleón propuso hacer de **Egipto** una colonia francesa, plan que respaldó el Directorio. Partió de Francia con **35 000 soldados** y, tras tomar la isla mediterránea de Malta, llegó a Alejandría en julio y derrotó rápidamente al ejército **mameluco** en la **batalla de las Pirámides**. Sin embargo, el 1 de agosto, la flota británica al mando de **Horatio Nelson** (1758–1805) aplastó completamente a los franceses en la primera **batalla de Abukir**. Napoleón y sus soldados quedaron abandonados a su suerte en Egipto, pero la derrota y la humillación no menguaron en absoluto las ambiciones imperiales del comandante francés.

10–25 MIL

ES EL NÚMERO ESTIMADO DE **IRLANDESES MUERTOS TRAS** LA **REBELIÓN**

Dos años atrás, los británicos habían aprovechado los conflictos bélicos en Europa para arrebatar a los holandeses la isla de **Sri Lanka**, donde apenas encontraron resistencia. Los británicos llamaron a la isla **Ceilán** y la administraron desde Madrás (India). En 1798 empezaron a darse cuenta de su enorme importancia estratégica, y **Frederick North** (1766–1827) fue nombrado primer gobernador de la colonia. Sin embargo, Gran Bretaña no controlaba toda la isla de Ceilán. El reino de **Kandy**, cuyos súbditos ocupaban el interior, continuaba siendo independiente. Su autonomía terminó siendo motivo de preocupación para los gobernadores británicos de Ceilán.

Entre tanto, en **Irlanda**, el resentimiento contra el gobierno británico se había convertido en una rebelión dirigida por los nacionalistas de la **Sociedad de los Irlandeses Unidos**. Liderado por Theobald Wolfe Tone (1763–1798) y James Napier Tandy (1740–1803), el grupo había intentado obtener el apoyo de la Francia revolucionaria, pero los británicos, conocedores de sus planes, habían obligado a los rebeldes a cambiar de estrategia. A pesar de no contar con refuerzos franceses, decidieron alzarse y lograron controlar el **condado de Wexford**. El ejército británico interceptó a una fuerza expedicionaria francesa que acudía en su ayuda, y la revuelta no tardó en fracasar. Tone se suicidó mientras esperaba la ejecución.

Rebelión irlandesa
En Wexford, nacionalistas irlandeses ejecutaron a aquellos prisioneros protestantes sospechosos de ser leales al gobierno británico.

1799

« LA **REVOLUCIÓN** HA **TERMINADO**. LA **REVOLUCIÓN SOY YO**. »

Napoleón Bonaparte (1799)

UNA VEZ QUE NAPOLEÓN BONAPARTE HUBO REGRESADO de su campaña en Egipto, decidió centrarse en su futuro político y no tardó en preparar un **golpe de estado** para disolver el Directorio, el organismo que gobernaba el país desde 1795. El resultado del **golpe del 18 de brumario** (9 de noviembre) fue la sustitución del Directorio por el Consulado, y Napoleón pasó a tomar las riendas de Francia como **primer cónsul**.

Piedra de Rosetta
La traducción de las tres grafías de este gran fragmento de una estela desveló el mundo de los jeroglíficos y del antiguo Egipto.

Por otro lado, durante la campaña de Egipto, un soldado francés desenterró un objeto que iba a revolucionar los conocimientos sobre el mundo antiguo: se trataba de una placa de **granito** negro (un fragmento de una estela) con inscripciones en tres tipos de escritura a la que dieron el nombre de **piedra de Rosetta**, por la localidad donde se encontró, y que en 1801 pasó a manos británicas. Se necesitaron años de estudio antes de que alguien fuese capaz de **traducirla**; finalmente, los estudiosos lograron establecer una relación entre las tres grafías de la piedra: **jeroglíficos**, escritura demótica (escritura egipcia cotidiana) y griego. Dicho descubrimiento permitió transcribir los jeroglíficos, un tipo de escritura que, desde el siglo IV d. C., no se había vuelto a utilizar. Descifrar la piedra fue como abrir una ventana al antiguo Egipto.

En India, los soldados de la Compañía de las Indias Orientales vencieron al temible **sultán Tipu** (1750–1799), soberano de **Mysore**. Tipu había forjado diversas alianzas con el ejército francés en India, y ello sirvió de pretexto al gobernador general británico, Richard Wellesley (*véase* 1797), para autorizar la **cuarta guerra de Mysore**, decidido a expulsar a los franceses y anexionar el territorio. Tipu murió en la batalla, y la Compañía de las Indias Orientales se quedó con la mitad de su territorio.

Lord Mornington, luego marqués de Wellesley (1760–1842), asume el cargo de gobernador general de Bengala (hasta 1805).

24 de mayo Primera batalla de la **rebelión de Irlanda** contra el gobierno británico.

1 de julio Napoleón invade y ocupa **Egipto** (hasta 1801).

14 de julio Primera ley del **impuesto directo federal** en EE. UU., que introduce el impuesto sobre la propiedad.

21 de julio Napoleón vence a los mamelucos en la **batalla de las Pirámides**.

1 de agosto Napoleón es derrotado por los británicos en la primera **batalla de Abukir**.

El economista inglés **Thomas Malthus** (1766–1834) publica *Ensayo sobre el principio de la población*.

4 de mayo Muere el sultán Tipu (1750–1799) en la **cuarta guerra de Mysore**; los británicos establecen un protectorado en el territorio.

China prohíbe la importación de **opio**.

Guerra de la Segunda Coalición: Rusia, Gran Bretaña, Austria, Nápoles, Portugal y el Imperio otomano luchan contra los franceses.

Julio El naturalista alemán **Alexander von Humboldt** empieza a explorar América del Sur (hasta 1804).

Hallazgo de la **piedra de Rosetta** en Egipto.

El gobierno de Países Bajos asume el control de los territorios de la **Compañía Neerlandesa de las Indias Orientales**.

HISTORIA DE LA MEDICINA

LOS AVANCES CIENTÍFICOS DEJAN ATRÁS A LAS ANTIGUAS CREENCIAS Y TRANSFORMAN EL CONCEPTO DE LA SALUD

Durante los siglos XVIII y XIX, los conocimientos sobre el cuerpo humano y la enfermedad hicieron importantes progresos que sentaron las bases de la atención médica moderna. Las prácticas antiguas, como las sangrías, se sustituyeron por otras basadas en un enfoque científico más riguroso.

La humanidad ha intentado tratar las enfermedades desde la Prehistoria, pero hasta el siglo XVIII la medicina se basaba en la superstición, los curanderos y en teorías acientíficas, como que la salud dependía de cuatro fluidos (humores) corporales. Se había avanzado en anatomía y en cirugía, pero, en general, la ciencia de la medicina aún estaba poco evolucionada.

EL DESARROLLO DE LA MEDICINA MODERNA

En el siglo XVIII, la medicina empezó a adquirir más rigor científico y se lograron avances importantes, como el desarrollo de la vacuna de la viruela en 1796. El siglo XIX presenció la aparición de la teoría de los gérmenes para explicar las enfermedades y la introducción de técnicas antisépticas y anestésicas, además del uso de los rayos X. En torno a 1900, la farmacología avanzó rápidamente, con la aparición de la aspirina en 1897 y del primer fármaco antibacteriano sintético en 1908. El siglo XX trajo muchas vacunas, antibióticos y fármacos contra el cáncer, y los avances en cirugía hicieron habituales los trasplantes de órganos y la cirugía laparoscópica. Además, para el diagnóstico se generalizaron las técnicas de imagen y análisis. A finales del siglo XX comenzó el impacto de la genética sobre la medicina, al descubrirse causas genéticas de enfermedades y desarrollarse el análisis genético.

« EL **ALEJAMIENTO DEL HOMBRE** DEL ESTADO QUE LE OTORGÓ ORIGINALMENTE LA **NATURALEZA** PARECE HABER SIDO **UNA FUENTE PROLÍFICA DE ENFERMEDADES**. »

Edward Jenner, médico inglés, *An Inquiry into the Causes and Effects of the Variolae Vaccinae, or Cow-Pox* (1798)

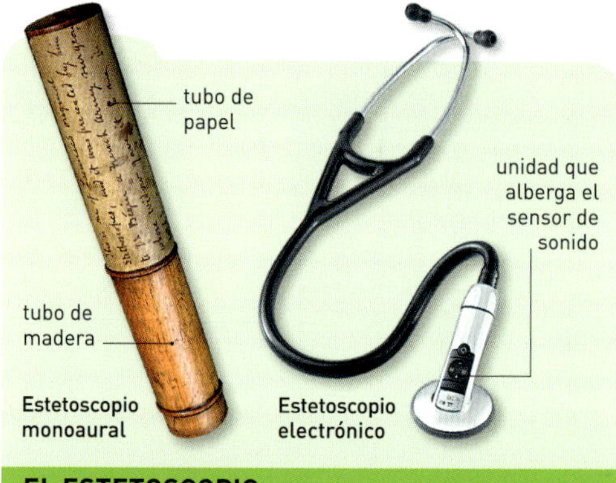

EL ESTETOSCOPIO

El médico francés René Laennec inventó en 1816 el estetoscopio, al utilizar un tubo (estetoscopio monoaural) para auscultar el pecho a una mujer. En 1851, el médico británico Arthur Leared concibió el estetoscopio biaural (fonendoscopio), con un auricular para cada oreja, y en la década de 1940, los estadounidenses Maurice Rappaport y Howard Sprague crearon el estetoscopio acústico moderno, con dos «campanas», una para auscultar el corazón y otra para auscultar los pulmones. El último avance es el estetoscopio electrónico, provisto de un sensor y un amplificador de sonido electrónicos.

C. 5100–4900 a. C.
Trepanación neolítica
La trepanación, que consiste en perforar el cráneo, ya se llevaba a cabo en el Neolítico con el objetivo de tratar diversas dolencias.

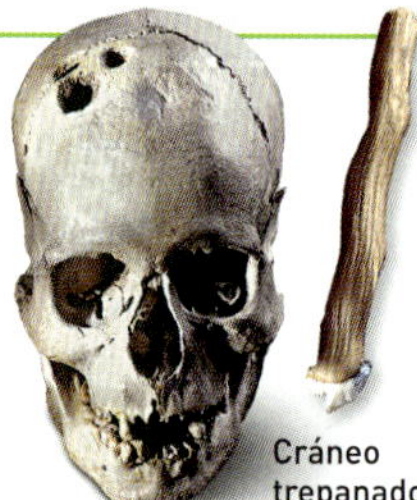
Cráneo trepanado

C. 1550–700 a. C.
Cirugía en el antiguo Egipto
La medicina, y sobre todo la cirugía, avanzan gracias a la práctica de la momificación que da a los médicos acceso a la anatomía.

Lancetas y bisturíes egipcios

C. 420 a. C.
Hipócrates desarrolla la diagnosis
Hipócrates, el médico griego considerado el padre de la medicina moderna, aleja la salud de la religión y la acerca a la ciencia.

C. 1000–1300
Avances de la medicina árabe
El mundo árabe contribuye al progreso médico a través de sus boticarios, que estudian las plantas y las usan para encontrar nuevos remedios.

Manuscrito médico árabe

1543
Andrés Vesalio
Este cirujano nacido en Bruselas escribe su influyente obra acerca de la anatomía humana, con dibujos muy precisos basados en numerosas disecciones y operaciones.

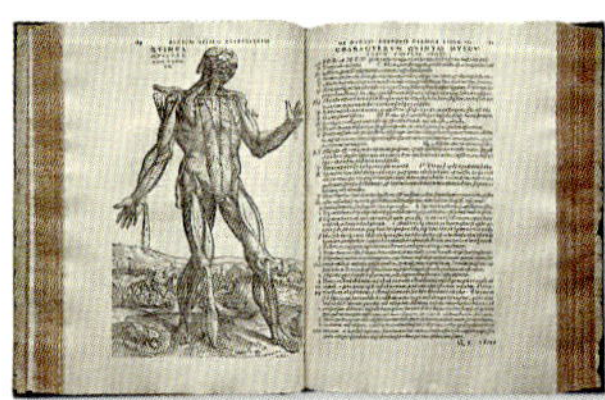
De humani corporis fabrica

1796
La primera vacuna
El científico británico Edward Jenner logra desarrollar una vacuna contra la viruela. Fue la primera de las vacunas, que han permitido salvar innumerables vidas.

Punzón de inoculación de Jenner

1818
Primera transfusión de sangre
El obstetra británico James Blundell realiza la primera transfusión con éxito, usando una jeringa para transfundir la sangre de un paciente a otro.

interruptor del ventilador

motor

engranaje para impulsar el ventilador

rodillo

manivela para dar cuerda al motor

receptáculo del ventilador

salida del espray antiséptico

martillo para golpear el contenedor del polvo antiséptico

contenedor del polvo antiséptico

Máquina antiséptica
El cirujano británico Anthony Bell patentó en 1879 este aparato que servía para eliminar los microorganismos patógenos de los quirófanos. Era un pulverizador que lanzaba una mezcla de polvos antisépticos y de ácido carbólico (fenol) al aire mediante un ventilador mecánico.

1846–1847
Anestesia práctica
En 1846, el dentista estadounidense Henry Morgan usa públicamente éter como anestesia. En 1847, el médico escocés James Simpson decide utilizar cloroformo.

Inhalador de cloroformo

1865–1867
Antisepsia
El cirujano británico Joseph Lister inicia la cirugía antiséptica con una solución de ácido carbólico para matar los organismos infecciosos durante las operaciones.

1881
Medición de la presión arterial
Samuel von Basch idea un método no invasivo para medir la presión o tensión arterial con una pera conectada a un manómetro aneroide.

Tensiómetro

1901
Identificación de los grupos sanguíneos
Karl Landsteiner publica su descubrimiento de los cuatro grupos sanguíneos humanos principales (A, B, AB, 0), que aumenta el éxito de las transfusiones.

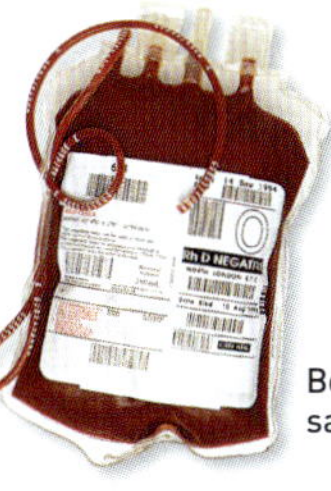
Bolsa de sangre

1954
Trasplante de órganos
El equipo dirigido por Joseph Murray, J. Hartwell Harrison y John P. Merrill lleva a cabo en Boston el primer trasplante de órganos entre pacientes vivos (trasplante de riñón entre gemelos idénticos).

1971 y 1977
TC y RM
El británico Godfrey Hounsfield inventa el primer tomógrafo computarizado (TC) comercial en 1971. La primera IRM se realiza en 1977.

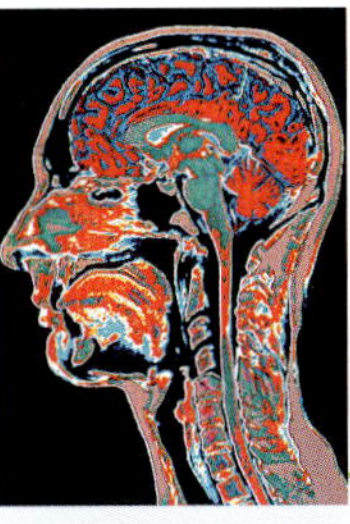
Imagen por resonancia magnética (IRM)

Finales del siglo XX
Cirugía laparoscópica
Después de la primera apendicectomía, que fue realizada mediante laparoscopia con una microcámara en 1981, se extiende la cirugía laparoscópica.

Siglo XXI
Cirugía robótica
Los avances en robótica permiten una cirugía menos invasiva, con una recuperación más rápida y menos dolorosa.

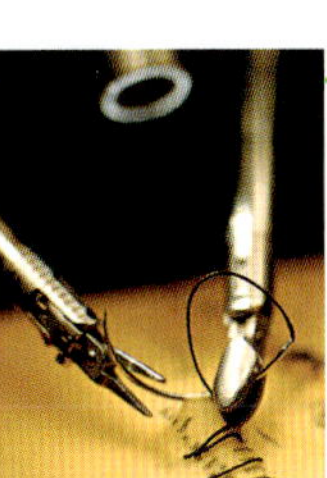
Sutura robótica

1800

En la batalla de Marengo, Francia consiguió derrotar a Austria.

EL NUEVO SIGLO NO PUSO FIN a la inestabilidad en Europa. A pesar de los tratados anteriores, las acciones militares francesas ganaron agresividad. La desconfianza hacia Francia inspiró en 1798 la formación de la **Segunda Coalición**; en 1799, comprendía a Austria, Gran Bretaña, Rusia, Portugal, Nápoles y el Imperio otomano. El 14 de junio, cuando Napoleón obtuvo una gran victoria sobre Austria en la **batalla de Marengo**, el norte de Italia quedó bajo el control de Francia.

Mientras, España, carente de recursos, no había hecho demasiados progresos en Luisiana (América del Norte). Así, cuando Napoleón presionó a Carlos IV para que la devolviera a Francia, el rey español accedió. En un nuevo **tratado de San Ildefonso**, Napoleón acordó no ceder el territorio a una tercera potencia.

Sable de Napoleón en Marengo
En las guerras napoleónicas, tanto la caballería como la infantería combatían con sables.

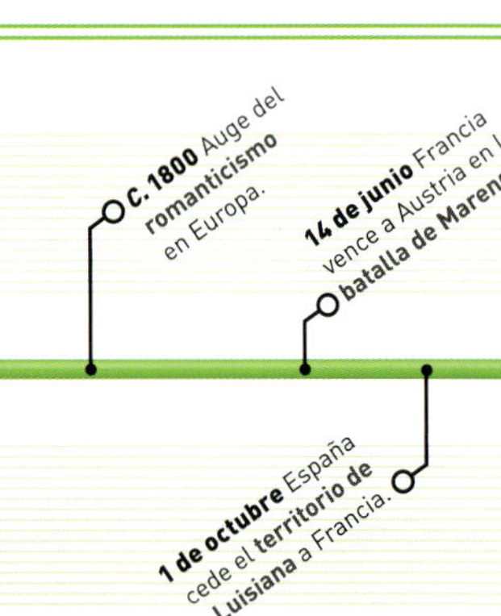

1801

Grabado sobre la celebración de la paz en Milán (Italia), tras el tratado de Lunéville, que obligó a Austria a reconocer las nuevas fronteras de Francia.

TRAS LA REBELIÓN EN IRLANDA (*véase* 1798), el primer ministro británico William Pitt el Joven concluyó que la solución para la «cuestión irlandesa» era la unión política. En 1800 presentó al parlamento irlandés un proyecto de ley que recogía su plan, y tras muchas discusiones, la ley se aprobó. La **Ley de Unión**, aprobada también por el gobierno británico, entró en vigor el 1 de enero de 1801. El parlamento irlandés fue disuelto, y la representación se trasladó a Londres, donde 32 nobles irlandeses se incorporaron a la Cámara de los Lores y cien miembros del parlamento a la Cámara de los Comunes. Pitt esperaba que esto permitiera la aprobación de concesiones a los católicos, pero la ley mantuvo la prohibición de que ocuparan cargos públicos.

En el resto de Europa, la derrota de Marengo en 1800 obligó a Austria a aceptar el **tratado de Lunéville**, por el que reconocía las fronteras de Francia en el Rin, los Alpes y los Pirineos.

Mientras tanto, Rusia proseguía su expansión e invadió los reinos de **Kartalinia-Kajetia** (Georgia oriental actual). En un tratado de 1783, la dinastía Bagration reinante accedió a aceptar la protección de Rusia a cambio de la garantía de que se conservara su integridad territorial. Sin embargo, el zar **Pablo I** (1754–1801), que había sido el sucesor de Catalina la Grande después de su muerte en 1796, decidió anexionarse formalmente este territorio.

THOMAS JEFFERSON
(1743–1826)

Nacido en Virginia, Jefferson tenía una plantación y poseía muchos esclavos. Fue un republicano prominente y también uno de los autores principales de la Declaración de Independencia de EE. UU.. Mantuvo su poder político durante toda la vida y ejerció los cargos de vicepresidente (1797–1801) y de presidente (1801–1809). A pesar de la influencia de sus escritos sobre temas como la libertad, nunca liberó a sus esclavos.

En Viena, el compositor **Ludwig van Beethoven** (1770–1827) acabó de componer su Sonata para piano núm. 14 en do sostenido menor, op. 27 núm. 2, conocida como ***Claro de luna***, que se convirtió en una de sus obras más célebres. Se cree que estaba dedicada a la condesa Giulietta Guicciardi, su alumna, de la que estaba enamorado aunque su amor no fuese correspondido.

También en este año, en EE. UU., **Thomas Jefferson** (*véase* recuadro) fue elegido tercer presidente del país.

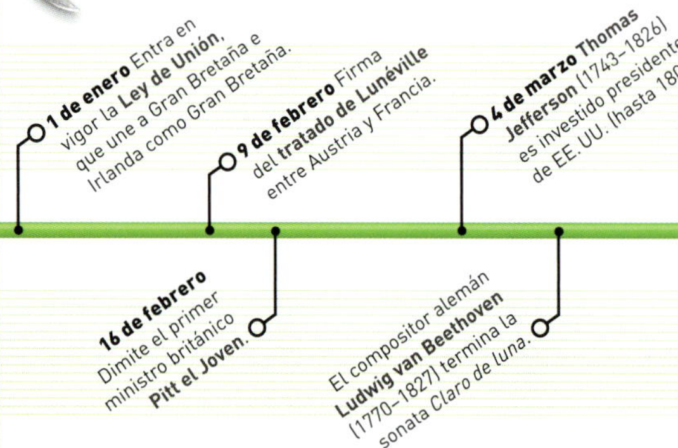

1802

Mausoleo del emperador Gia Long, fundador de la dinastía Nguyen.

DESPUÉS DE TREINTA AÑOS DE GUERRA CIVIL, VIETNAM SE UNIFICÓ bajo el liderazgo de **Nguyen Phuc Anh** (1762–1820), un poderoso general que, con la ayuda de mercenarios franceses, consiguió derrotar a sus rivales de la familia Trinh. Nguyen Anh se autoproclamó emperador con el nombre de **Gia Long** y restauró a la familia Nguyen como dinastía reinante.

Entre tanto, en el continente europeo, el **tratado de Amiens** dio paso a casi cinco años de paz absoluta en Europa. Lo firmaron Gran Bretaña, Francia, España y Países Bajos (llamados República de Batavia entre 1795 y 1806).

El tratado de Amiens establecía que Gran Bretaña podía conservar las colonias de **Trinidad**, que había arrebatado a España, y de **Ceilán**, que había arrebatado a los holandeses. El Imperio otomano pudo recuperar **Egipto**, y Francia accedió a devolver **Malta**. Sin embargo, dicha situación no duró mucho.

Francia y Gran Bretaña a la mesa
Ilustración satírica que muestra al británico William Pitt y al francés Napoleón Bonaparte trinchando el globo por el tratado de Amiens.

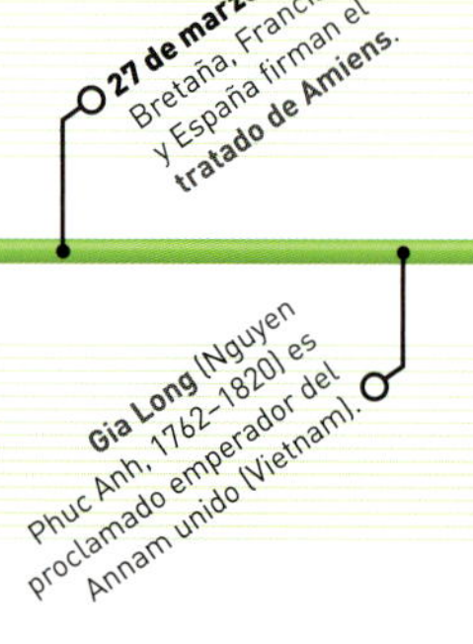

1803

Jean-Jacques Dessalines, que luchó por la independencia de Haití.

EN SAINT-DOMINGUE (HAITÍ), LA GUERRA DIO UN GIRO decisivo con la captura y el exilio del **general Toussaint Louverture** en 1803. Diez años antes se había unido a la causa republicana francesa (*véase* 1793) y había expulsado a las fuerzas británicas que quedaban en la isla antes de asumir el cargo de **gobernador** en 1801. Sin embargo, Napoleón estaba molesto por los éxitos de Louverture y se enfureció cuando le desobedeció y marchó sobre Santo Domingo (en aquel momento bajo control francés) para liberar a los esclavos. En 1802, Napoleón **reinstauró la esclavitud** y envió 25 000 soldados para que recuperaran la isla. Tras meses de enfrentamientos, se invitó a Louverture a negociar un acuerdo, pero fue apresado y enviado al exilio. La lucha por la abolición de la esclavitud recayó en su lugarteniente, **Jean-Jacques Dessalines**.

Casi todos los soldados de Napoleón murieron en el campo de batalla o por la **fiebre amarilla**; los hombres de Dessalines expulsaron a los que quedaban. Los refuerzos quedaron retenidos por el **bloqueo** británico de los puertos franceses a causa de la guerra entre ambos países, y Francia abandonó la isla.

El coste de la lucha en Haití había esquilmado aún más las maltrechas finanzas francesas, y a Napoleón se le ocurrió que podía obtener dinero vendiendo los extensos y, en general, poco desarrollados territorios de Francia en América del Norte. EE. UU. se había interesado por Luisiana, especialmente por el puerto de **Nueva Orleans**, ya que la población se iba despla-

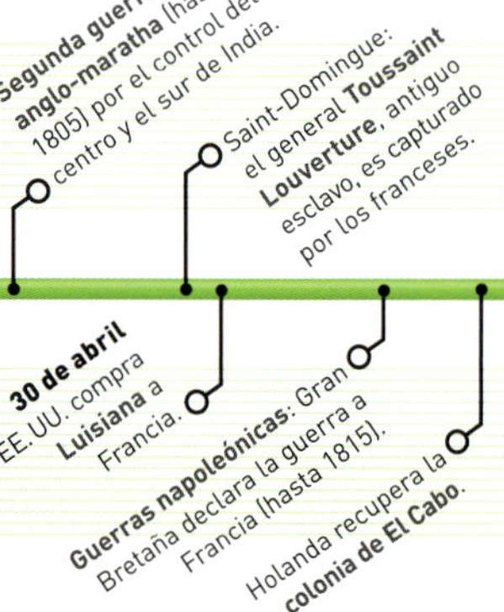

« ¡LIBERTAD O MUERTE! »

Inscripción en la bandera y en el Acta de Independencia de Haití

Territorio ganado por EE. UU.
Gracias al inmenso territorio de Luisiana, EE. UU. casi dobló su tamaño. Un año después se extendió hacia el sur hasta Nueva Orleans.

zando cada vez más hacia el oeste y dependía del comercio a lo largo del río Misisipi. El 2 de mayo se firmó el documento de la **compra de Luisiana**, por el que EE. UU. adquirió un territorio que iba desde el golfo de México hasta las montañas Rocosas (unos 2 147 000 km²). El precio acordado fue de 15 millones de dólares, pero su importe total, incluidos los intereses, se acercó más a los 27 millones.

Napoleón se enfrentaba a nuevos problemas en Europa, ya que Gran Bretaña declaró la guerra a Francia y dio inicio a las **guerras napoleónicas**. Mientras, las tropas de la Compañía Británica de las Indias Orientales y la Confederación maratha emprendían otra guerra: la **segunda guerra anglo-maratha** (hasta 1805). La Compañía trató de obtener el control del territorio en India, pero solo consiguió abonar el campo para conflictos futuros.

1804

Dibujo de una hoja de arbusto perenne del diario de William Clark, que exploró durante años el vasto territorio de Luisiana con Meriwether Lewis.

TRAS EXPULSAR POR FIN A LOS FRANCESES de Saint-Domingue, Jean-Jacques Dessalines declaró la independencia de la **nueva república de Haití** el 1 de enero de 1804. El nombre procedía parcialmente del nombre original indígena de la isla. Fue la primera (y la única) antigua colonia de esclavos que consiguió liberarse tanto del gobierno colonial como de la esclavitud. Su nacimiento tuvo un recibimiento receloso: en EE. UU., algunos esclavistas no querían que Haití sirviera de ejemplo a los estados sureños, preocupación compartida por los británicos, cuya colonia esclavista de Jamaica estaba también cerca.

La derrota en el Caribe no menoscabó el poder de Napoleón en Europa. En 1804, Napoleón convirtió a Francia en un **imperio hereditario**, supuestamente para evitar posibles intentos de asesinato, pero también para demostrar su poder. El 2 de diciembre tuvo lugar la ceremonia de coronación y fue insólita, pues Napoleón no fue coronado por el papa Pío VII (1742–1823), que oficiaba la ceremonia, sino por él mismo, que se puso la corona y se autoproclamó **Napoleón I**. Ese mismo año introdujo drásticas reformas en el sistema legal tanto en Francia como en el resto de los territorios franceses con el Código Civil de los Franceses, que fue conocido como Código de Napoleón (*véase* recuadro).

En EE. UU., los exploradores **Meriwether Lewis** (1774–1809) y **William Clark** (1770–1838), siguiendo instrucciones del presidente Thomas Jefferson exploraron Luisiana (mapa) con la misión de localizar el río Misuri, establecer relaciones con los indígenas de la región y, con la ayuda de Sacagawea, un traductor shoshone, descubrir el **paso del Noroeste**. Tras elaborar mapas detallados y documentar la flora y fauna de la región, regresaron a Saint Louis en 1806.

En África occidental, **Usmán dan Fodio** (1754–1817), erudito y maestro musulmán, emprendió una **yihad** (guerra santa) de cuatro años que finalizó con la creación del **Califato de Sokoto** en 1808 y el **Imperio fulbé** en Hausalandia (norte de la actual Nigeria).

EL CÓDIGO DE NAPOLEÓN

Una de las reformas más ambiciosas de Napoleón fue la codificación del derecho francés. El Código de Napoleón, que entró en vigor en 1804, era un código civil que pretendía romper con las instituciones del pasado. Se basaba en la razón y estaba muy influenciado por el derecho romano; declaraba a todos los hombres iguales y suprimía la nobleza hereditaria. Las mujeres no tuvieron tanta suerte, ya que quedaban bajo el control masculino. Las leyes también abordaban cuestiones como el derecho a la propiedad, el matrimonio y los derechos civiles. El Código de Napoleón se aplicó en todos los territorios franceses (en Europa y fuera de ella) y ejerció gran influencia en otros lugares (en la República Dominicana sigue vigente una versión adaptada). También se adoptó en algunas nuevas repúblicas latinoamericanas, como Bolivia y Chile.

1805

Batalla de Trafalgar, donde Francia y España sufrieron grandes pérdidas frente a la flota británica.

FRANCIA NO TARDÓ EN OLVIDAR LA DERROTA SUFRIDA EN EL CARIBE, en Saint-Domingue, gracias a las victorias obtenidas sobre Rusia y Austria, que se habían visto arrastradas a la guerra. Napoleón también se había declarado rey de Italia, que en aquella época abarcaba Venecia y los reinos italianos del norte. Esta beligerante actitud por parte de Napoleón provocó la formación de una **Tercera Coalición**, en la que participaron Gran Bretaña, Austria, Rusia y Suecia. Napoleón decidió no conquistar Gran Bretaña y envió a su ejército a **Ulm** (Baviera), de donde logró salir vencedor (25 septiembre–20 octubre). Después de la batalla de Ulm, sufrió una humillante derrota naval en la **batalla de Trafalgar** frente a la flota británica, liderada por un antiguo enemigo, **Horatio Nelson** (*véase* 1798). Durante esta batalla, que fue librada cerca del cabo Trafalgar, entre Cádiz y el estrecho de Gibraltar, 18 naves francesas y otras 15 españolas se enfrentaron con 27 naves británicas. Gran Bretaña salió victoriosa y consiguió capturar o destruir 18 barcos, pero Nelson fue herido durante la batalla y falleció antes de que esta finalizara. Napoleón decidió cambiar de estrategia y regresó a Europa, donde dirigió sus tropas para ocupar Viena y derrotar a Rusia y a Austria en la **batalla de Austerlitz**, que tuvo lugar el 2 de diciembre.

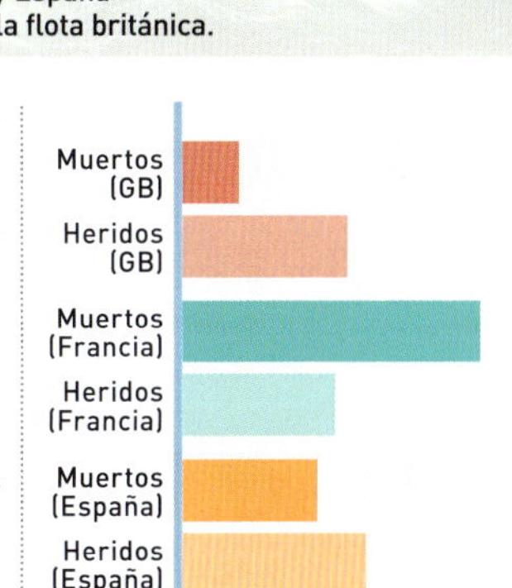

Bajas en Trafalgar
Francia y España sufrieron grandes pérdidas en esta batalla naval, pero Gran Bretaña (GB) perdió a su gran almirante Horatio Nelson.

También durante 1805, en Egipto, **Mehmet Alí** (1769–1849) fue nombrado virrey, o bajá, del sultán otomano. De origen macedonio, había llegado a Egipto en 1801 con un regimiento enviado para expulsar a los franceses.

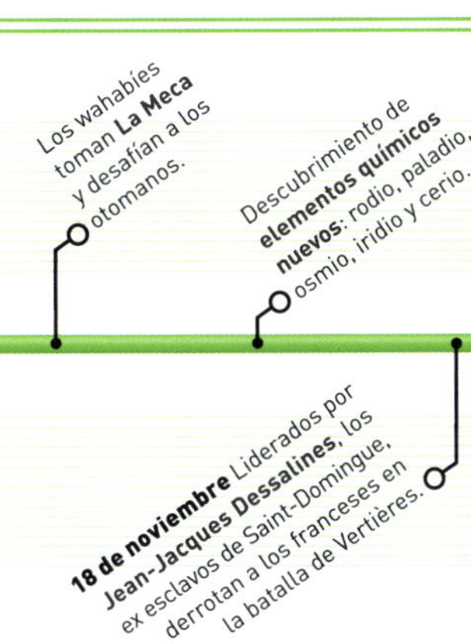

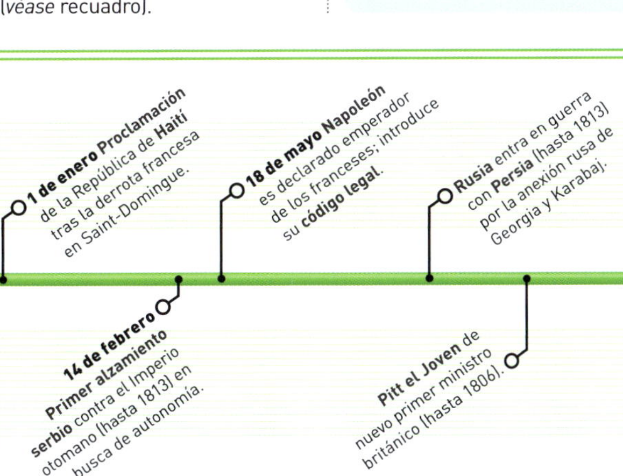

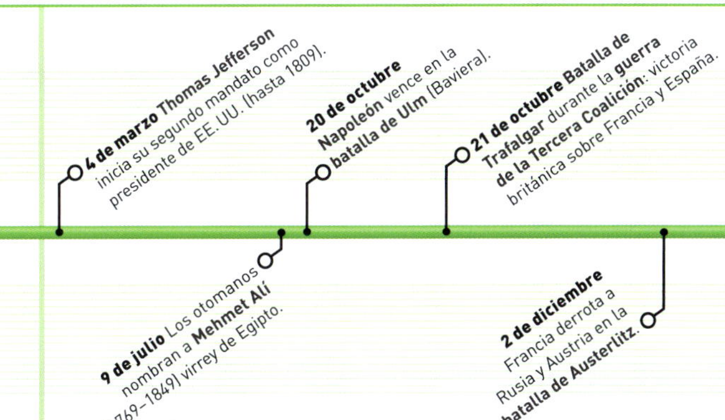

1806

Napoleón tras su victoria en la batalla de Jena (Sajonia).

PRUSIA SUFRIÓ UNA DERROTA devastadora ante Francia en la **batalla de Jena**, el 14 de octubre. Unos 122 000 soldados franceses y 114 000 prusianos se enfrentaron en Jena y Auerstadt, en Sajonia (sureste de Alemania). Federico Guillermo III (1770–1840) decidió que eran necesarias reformas internas para fortalecer el reino, entre ellas la abolición de la **servidumbre**. La medida fue beneficiosa para la agricultura, pero tardó años en hacerse efectiva.

Napoleón quería ampliar sus dominios en Alemania controlando el **Sacro Imperio**. El emperador Francisco II (1768–1835) no estaba en condiciones de enfrentarse a Francia, y **abdicó**. Ante la disolución oficial del imperio, Napoleón estableció la Confederación del Rin a partir de varios Estados alemanes, cuyos príncipes fueron soberanos de unos dominios ampliados.

En Oriente Próximo, **La Meca**, destino de peregrinación islámica, fue invadida por miembros de la dinastía árabe **saudí** de la secta tradicionalista conocida como **wahabí**. por su fundador Muhamad ibn Abd al Wahab (1703–1792). En 1805, los wahabíes tomaron **Medina**, realizaron incursiones en el interior de la península Arábiga, saquearon la ciudad de **Kerbala**, en Irak, y extendieron su influencia hacia el sur, hasta **Yemen**. Como en el caso de La Meca, estos fueron reveses alarmantes para el Imperio otomano, que hasta entonces había controlado estos lugares.

1807

« PUEDEN DECIDIR MIRAR A OTRO LADO, PERO NUNCA PODRÁN VOLVER A DECIR QUE NO LO SABÍAN. »

William Wilberforce, al parlamento inglés antes de la votación sobre la abolición (1789)

Tropas de élite
Un jenízaro (izda.) en El Cairo. Al principio los jenízaros eran los guardias del sultán, pero no tardaron en convertirse en soldados de élite del ejército otomano.

LA LARGA LUCHA DEL abolicionista y político inglés **William Wilberforce** (1759–1833), así como la de los miles de británicos que apoyaban su campaña, dio sus frutos en 1807, cuando se aprobó por abrumadora mayoría la ley que **prohibía el comercio de esclavos**. La prohibición, sin embargo, se limitaba a Gran Bretaña y sus territorios y no acababa con la esclavitud.

Por su parte, Rusia y Prusia habían reanudado las hostilidades contra los franceses en la **batalla de Eylau** (7–8 febrero), en Prusia oriental. La batalla fue inconcluyente y terminó en tablas: ambos bandos perdieron más de veinte mil soldados. Después de la decisiva derrota rusa durante la posterior **batalla de Friedland**, Rusia suscribió uno de los **tratados de Tilsit** el 7 de julio, mientras que Prusia firmó el otro el 9 de julio. A raíz de estos tratados Francia y Rusia establecieron una alianza, mientras que los territorios de Austria y Prusia se vieron reducidos significativamente.

En el Imperio otomano, los **yamaks** (tropas auxiliares) se rebelaron ante los intentos de introducir reformas de estilo europeo en el ejército. Los **jenízaros** (cuerpo de élite) no tardaron en unirse a ellos. La rebelión terminó con el asesinato de Selim III (1761–1808).

1808

El tres de mayo de 1808 en Madrid: los fusilamientos en la montaña del Príncipe Pío, pintura de Francisco de Goya.

NAPOLEÓN YA DOMINABA LA MAYOR PARTE de Europa occidental y central. Entonces dirigió la mirada a la península Ibérica. Ante la negativa de Portugal a secundar un boicot a Gran Bretaña en apoyo de Francia, Napoleón respondió enviando a su ejército por el norte de España. La presencia de soldados franceses y las impopulares concesiones anteriores a Francia hicieron que el pueblo español se alzara y pidiera la abdicación del rey **Carlos IV** a favor de su hijo Fernando en el **motín de Aranjuez**, el 19 de marzo. **Fernando VII** (1784–1833) ascendió al trono, pero durante poco tiempo.

Napoleón se ofreció a mediar entre padre e hijo y citó a Fernando VII en Bayona, donde este fue obligado a abdicar. Carlos IV ya había renunciado al trono antes, así que Napoleón pudo proclamar rey de España a su hermano, José Bonaparte (1768–1844). La evidencia de la invasión francesa desencadenó la **guerra de la Independencia española**, iniciada con el alzamiento del 2 de mayo en Madrid. Cuando esto se supo en las colonias, hubo alzamientos furiosos. En Santo Domingo, los realistas lanzaron la **guerra de la Reconquista** (hasta 1809).

1809

ENEMIGAS HISTÓRICAS, ESPAÑA Y GRAN BRETAÑA LUCHARON UNIDAS contra Francia en suelo español. El 9 de julio de 1808, los españoles habían logrado una sonada victoria en la **batalla de Bailén**. En 1809, el ejército británico sufrió una derrota en la **batalla de La Coruña** por el ejército francés con Napoleón al frente, pero venció en la **batalla de Talavera** (27–28 julio), liderado por Arthur Wellesley (1769–1852), luego **duque de Wellington**.

Durante la guerra, los españoles crearon **juntas** provinciales y regionales que asumieron el poder y la organización de la resistencia. La Junta Central Suprema emitió un decreto que declaraba que los territorios americanos eran más que colonias: formaban parte de la Corona. Al otro lado del Atlántico, la crisis de **legitimidad** del gobierno español resultaba evidente: sin rey, ¿a quién debían lealtad? Mientras se debatía sobre esta cuestión se establecieron juntas también en América, y pronto quedó claro que no todas las colonias mantendrían su lealtad a la Corona.

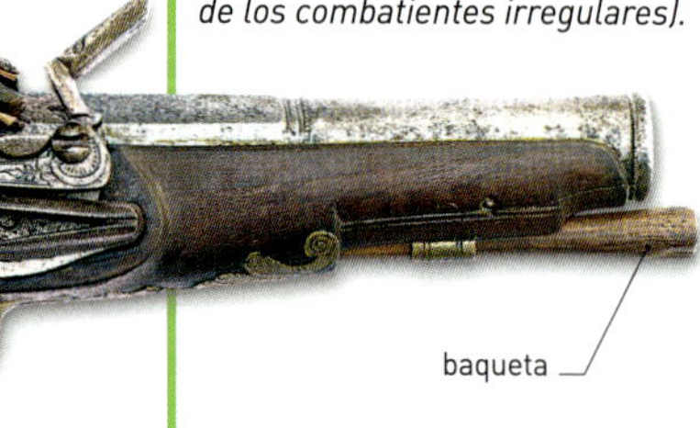

Pistola de la guerra de la Independencia española
Las pistolas de pedernal eran muy habituales en este periodo, cuando se acuñó el término guerrilla (táctica de los combatientes irregulares).

Francia insta a los **otomanos** a declarar la **guerra a Rusia** (hasta 1812).

Gran Bretaña arrebata a los holandeses la **colonia de El Cabo**.

6 de agosto Disolución formal del **Sacro Imperio Romano Germánico**.

14 de octubre Napoleón derrota a Prusia en las batallas de **Jena y Auerstadt**.

7–8 de febrero Napoleón vence a Rusia en la **batalla de Eylau**.

25 de marzo Gran Bretaña **prohíbe el comercio de esclavos** en todos sus territorios.

La **rebelión de los jenízaros** lleva a la caída del sultán otomano **Selim III**, sustituido por **Mustafá IV** (1779–1808).

14 de junio Victoria de Francia sobre Rusia en la **batalla de Friedland**.

Gran Bretaña no consigue tomar **Buenos Aires** en su intento de apoderarse de las colonias de España, aliada de Francia.

Noviembre Francia invade **Portugal** y la familia real portuguesa se refugia en **Brasil**.

2 de mayo Inicio de la **guerra de la Independencia española** (hasta 1814).

6 de junio José I (1768–1844), hermano de Napoleón, coronado rey de España.

Sierra Leona cae bajo dominio británico.

16 de junio Guerra de la Independencia española: Gran Bretaña es derrotada en La Coruña.

8 de febrero Austria declara la guerra a Francia.

17 de septiembre Suecia cede Finlandia a Rusia por el **tratado de Hamina**.

1810

Mural de José Clemente Orozco (1883–1949) que representa al cura Miguel Hidalgo, cuya iniciativa impulsó la guerra de la Independencia mexicana.

América Latina en vísperas de la independencia
Al principio de la guerra de Independencia española, España y Portugal aún controlaban parte de América del Norte y, al sur, la mayoría del continente.

LOS POLÍTICOS ESPAÑOLES vieron en el caos existente una oportunidad para la reforma y la liquidación del antiguo régimen, por lo que convocaron las **Cortes** en Cádiz, sitiada por los franceses. Las sesiones comenzaron el 24 de septiembre. De los 104 diputados, 30 representaban a los territorios coloniales, aunque luego llegaron más. Las Cortes elaboraron una constitución, aunque los españoles estaban divididos sobre el alcance de la reestructuración del gobierno. También estaba la cuestión de la **representación** política que debía concederse a los territorios de ultramar. La población de las colonias hispanoamericanas superaba a la de España, lo que significaba que, en teoría, estas podrían dominar las Cortes. Los políticos peninsulares querían evitarlo, pero también necesitaban el apoyo de las colonias.

Por su parte, algunos habitantes de las colonias decidieron tomar la iniciativa y emprender el camino hacia la emancipación. En el pueblo mexicano de Dolores (hoy Dolores Hidalgo), el cura **Miguel Hidalgo y Costilla** (1753–1811) hizo un llamamiento a la insurrección contra el dominio español conocido como **Grito de Dolores**. Miles de personas respondieron a la llamada y se dirigieron a Ciudad de México, donde fueron derrotadas por las tropas realistas al año siguiente. Sin embargo, las acciones de Hidalgo habían encendido la lucha de México por su libertad.

En otras colonias españolas empezaron a surgir alzamientos parecidos. El 20 de julio, el virreinato de **Nueva Granada** también declaró su independencia, y en Quito y Buenos Aires estallaron disturbios.

Entre tanto, en el océano Pacífico, el **rey Kamehameha I** (1758–1819) se convertía en el primer soberano de un **Hawai** unificado, hecho que ayudó a las islas a resistir las incursiones europeas.

1811

Sátira que compara a los luditas con las turbas de la Revolución francesa.

EL 5 DE JULIO DE ESTE AÑO, EL TERRITORIO SUDAMERICANO de Venezuela se unió a Nueva Granada y México (mapa) y declaró su independencia de España. Uno de los rebeldes que intervinieron en las deliberaciones sobre la independencia era **Simón Bolívar** (*véase* recuadro) que, después de su viaje por el continente europeo, acababa de regresar de Gran Bretaña, donde había intentado en vano recabar apoyo británico para la causa independentista.

Bolívar solamente visitó Londres, pero de haber viajado más al norte se habría encontrado con rebeldes de otro tipo: los llamados **luditas**, obreros textiles británicos que atacaban las fábricas del norte industrial de Inglaterra para destruir la nueva maquinaria. Temían que las máquinas acabaran **reemplazándolos** y les condenaran al desempleo y la pobreza.

SIMÓN BOLÍVAR (1783–1830)

Nació en Caracas, en el seno de una familia acaudalada. A los 16 años viajó por Europa, donde conoció las ideas de la Ilustración sobre la libertad. Poco después de su regreso a América del Sur en 1807 se implicó en conspiraciones para la independencia. Más tarde lideró la lucha por la emancipación en gran parte del norte de América del Sur y fue llamado «el Libertador». También gobernó la Gran Colombia, una unión política que acabó fracasando.

1812

Cuando el ejército de Napoleón llegó a Moscú, la ciudad estaba en llamas, como muestra esta pintura de Jean-Charles Langlois (1789–1870).

AL IGUAL QUE PORTUGAL, RUSIA DECIDIÓ resistirse al **sistema continental** de Napoleón, una serie de medidas destinadas a perjudicar la economía británica. Rusia abandonó el sistema en el año 1810, y Napoleón decidió invadirla como represalia. En junio envió más de **500 000 soldados** que obtuvieron victorias iniciales en las batallas de **Smolensk**, el 17 de agosto, y de **Borodino**, el 7 de septiembre, pero cuando entraron en Moscú el 14 de septiembre se encontraron con una ciudad arrasada y sin habitantes. El ejército ruso contuvo todos los avances posteriores, y con la llegada del crudo invierno ruso, el ejército de Napoleón comenzó a resquebrajarse. La ***Grande Armée*** se estaba quedando sin víveres, y muchos soldados, que no estaban habituados a un frío tan extremo, murieron. A Napoleón no le quedó otra opción que la **retirada** en diciembre. Solo sobrevivieron treinta mil soldados franceses.

En América del Norte, los comerciantes prosperaban gracias a sus tratos con Francia y afirmaban ser neutrales en la disputa entre británicos y franceses. Gran Bretaña se negó a reconocer esta **neutralidad** y comenzó a atacar los barcos americanos, a cuya tripulación capturaba con frecuencia con el fin de obligar a los marineros a servir en la marina británica. Esto provocó la **guerra de 1812** (hasta 1814) durante la cual también hubo batallas en tierra firme, donde Gran Bretaña persuadió a los indios leales a la Corona para que atacaran los asentamientos del Territorio del Noroeste.

En España, las Cortes promulgaron por fin una **constitución** que limitaba el poder de la monarquía (aunque Fernando VII continuaba en el exilio) y no preveía una representación especial en las Cortes para la nobleza o el clero. Estas ideas liberales provocaron una reacción airada de los defensores de la Corona y de la Iglesia, y dio lugar a un enfrentamiento entre liberales y conservadores que se prolongó durante décadas.

También en 1812, en Egipto, se ordenó a Mehmet Alí que lanzase una campaña a fin de restaurar el dominio otomano sobre **La Meca** y expulsar a los wahabíes, que habían ocupado gran parte de Arabia. Su ejército tomó Medina en 1812, y Yidda y La Meca el año siguiente.

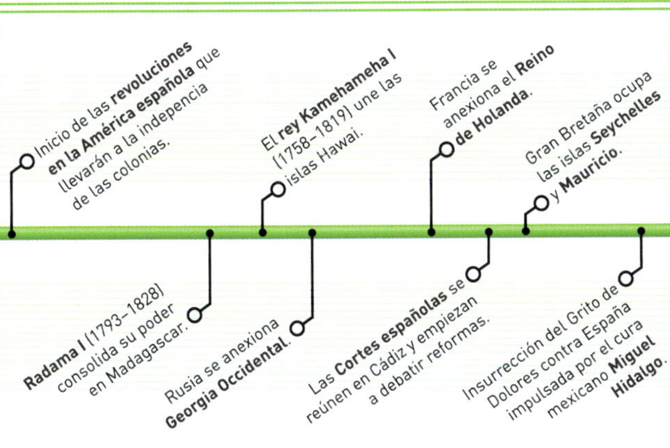

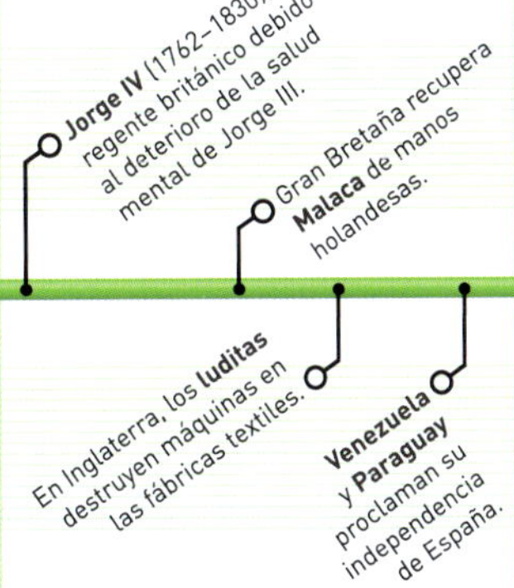

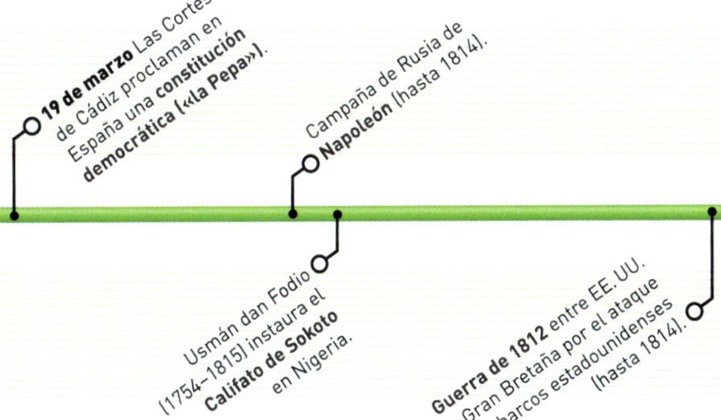

1813

« AÚN NO SE HA FUNDIDO LA BALA QUE HA DE **MATARME. »**

Napoleón Bonaparte, afirmación en Montereau (17 febrero de 1814)

DESPUÉS DE LA HUMILLANTE RETIRADA DE RUSIA, NAPOLEÓN Bonaparte asistió al rápido declive de su potencia militar (*véase* 1812), que se hizo evidente durante la decisiva derrota sufrida en la **batalla de Leipzig** (también conocida como batalla de las Naciones), librada entre el 16 y el 19 de octubre. Francia contaba con casi 185 000 soldados, pero los aliados disponían de 300 0000 soldados de Austria, Rusia, Prusia y Suecia. A pesar de esta terrible derrota, Napoleón siguió negándose a firmar un tratado de paz que obligara a las fronteras de Francia a retroceder hasta el Rin y los Alpes.

Además de participar en las guerras napoleónicas, Rusia también tenía otros conflictos territoriales hacia el este. Rusia y Persia firmaron el **tratado de Gulistán**, por el que Rusia recibía una gran parte del territorio persa en el Cáucaso. Este acuerdo puso fin a la **guerra ruso-persa** (1804–1813), que había estallado a raíz de la anexión por Rusia de **Georgia** y de **Karabaj** (hoy una región de Azerbaiyán). Estos territorios, que anteriormente habían pertenecido a Persia, habían pedido ayuda al sah para resistir ante Rusia.

Entre tanto, en **Venezuela**, Simón Bolívar (*véase* 1811) había conseguido una importante victoria sobre los españoles y había tomado **Caracas**, aunque más tarde fue derrotado por las tropas españolas y obligado a exiliarse durante dos años, periodo durante el cual se fue a Jamaica y Haití para recuperarse y reunir más apoyos antes de volver a Venezuela en 1816.

1814

Nativos llevando un palanquín (litera) en Mauricio.

LAS TROPAS ALIADAS PERSIGUIERON a Napoleón hasta París, donde le capturaron. El emperador abdicó el 6 de abril y fue exiliado a la isla de Elba, frente a la costa toscana. Para sustituirle se colocó en el trono francés a **Luis XVIII** (1755–1824), hermano del decapitado Luis XVI. Acto seguido, las potencias europeas se reunieron en el **Congreso de Viena** (septiembre de 1814–junio de 1815). Gracias al acuerdo resultante, Prusia recibió dos quintas partes de Sajonia; se formó la Confederación Germánica; y Gran Bretaña pudo conservar las islas francesas del océano Índico (**Mauricio** y **Seychelles**), de las que anteriormente se había apoderado.

1815

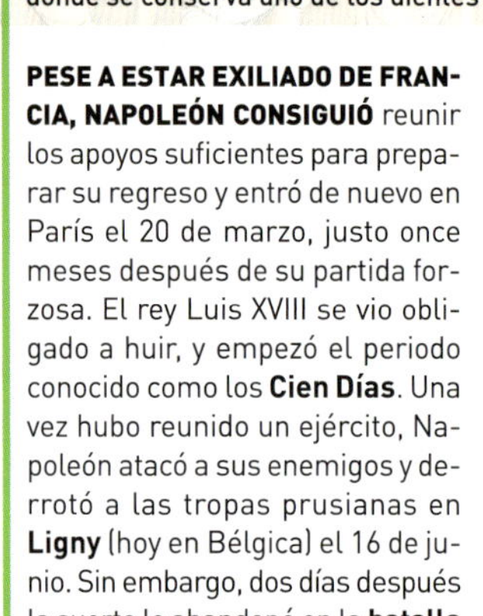

Templo del Diente, del siglo XVII, en el reino de Kandy, donde se conserva uno de los dientes de Buda.

PESE A ESTAR EXILIADO DE FRANCIA, NAPOLEÓN CONSIGUIÓ reunir los apoyos suficientes para preparar su regreso y entró de nuevo en París el 20 de marzo, justo once meses después de su partida forzosa. El rey Luis XVIII se vio obligado a huir, y empezó el periodo conocido como los **Cien Días**. Una vez hubo reunido un ejército, Napoleón atacó a sus enemigos y derrotó a las tropas prusianas en **Ligny** (hoy en Bélgica) el 16 de junio. Sin embargo, dos días después la suerte le abandonó en la **batalla de Waterloo** ante las tropas británicas, bajo el mando del duque de Wellington, que el año anterior había puesto fin a la guerra de la Independencia española (*véase* 1808). Napoleón estuvo a punto de conseguir la victoria, pero la llegada de refuerzos prusianos se lo impidió. Obligado a abdicar de nuevo, fue enviado al exilio mucho más lejos, a la isla de **Santa Elena**, un enclave británico situado en el Atlántico Sur, donde falleció en 1821.

Al mismo tiempo, el ejército británico en **Ceilán** (Sri Lanka) había tomado el reino de **Kandy**, y toda la isla quedó bajo el dominio británico.

Batalla de Waterloo
Este combate supuso la derrota definitiva de Napoleón Bonaparte, que fue obligado una vez más a abdicar y a partir al exilio.

1816

Habitante nativo de Alaska, territorio reclamado por Rusia.

UN SACERDOTE ORTODOXO RUSO, EL PADRE SOKOLOFF, fue enviado a **Sitka** (Alaska) para construir una iglesia como parte del intento de Rusia de colonizar la región. Alaska había sido un puesto avanzado secundario, pero los asentamientos empezaron a crecer a medida que prosperaba el comercio de pieles de foca.

En el sur de África, **Shaka** (*c.* 1787–1828) asumió el gobierno de los **zulúes**. Reorganizó el ejército, condujo a su tribu a la victoria militar e integró en la nación zulú a las tribus conquistadas.

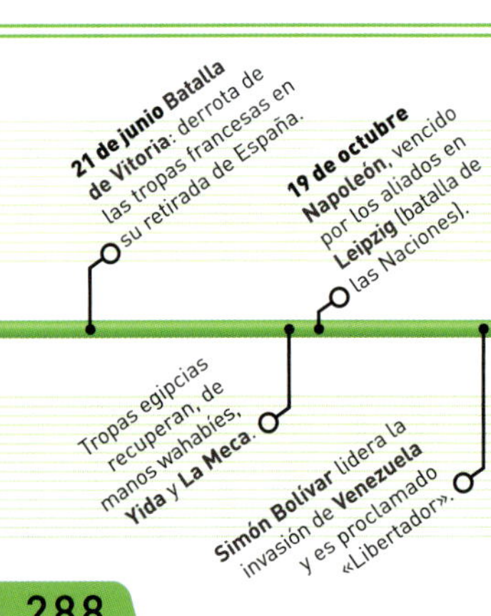

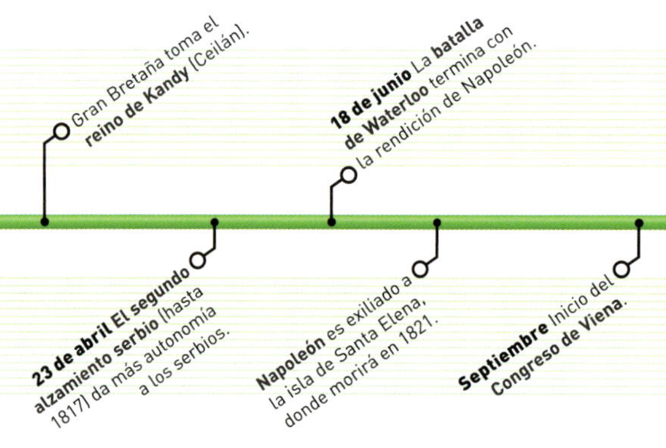

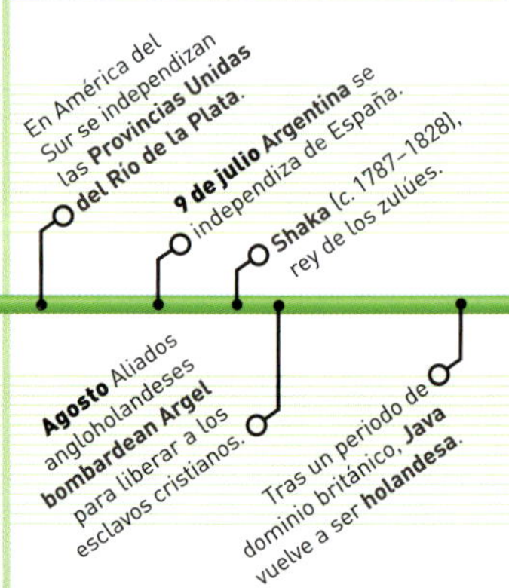

1817

El general argentino José de San Martín junto a su caballo y algunos oficiales.

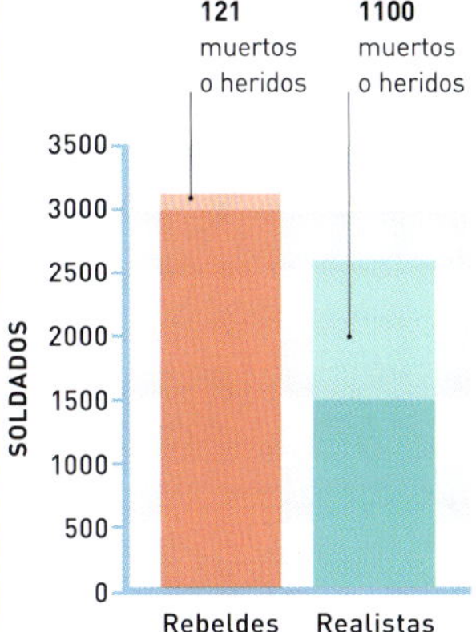

Batalla de Chacabuco
El líder José de San Martín tomó una decisión arriesgada y consiguió emboscar con éxito a los españoles, que sufrieron graves pérdidas.

LA LUCHA CONTRA EL DOMINIO ESPAÑOL DIO UN GIRO DECISIVO cuando el general argentino **José Francisco de San Martín** (1778–1850) condujo a cerca de tres mil soldados argentinos a Chile a través de los traicioneros pasos de los **Andes** y lanzó un ataque sorpresa contra las fuerzas realistas el 12 de febrero en la **batalla de Chacabuco**. A continuación, avanzó hacia Santiago, donde rechazó el cargo de gobernador de Chile, que cedió a su compañero de armas **Bernardo O'Higgins** (*c.* 1776–1842), que se convirtió en «director supremo» de todo el territorio.

Serbia había tenido que luchar una vez más por su independencia tras la invasión turca de 1813. El **segundo alzamiento serbio** tuvo éxito, y en 1817 recuperó la mayoría de sus derechos.

1818

« SEAMOS LIBRES. ¡LO DEMÁS NO IMPORTA! »

José de San Martín, héroe de la independencia latinoamericana

EL CONFLICTO EN ARABIA ENTRE Egipto y la secta islámica wahabí, iniciado en 1811, terminó en 1818, cuando el ejército egipcio al mando de Mehmet Alí, recuperó las ciudades santas de La Meca y Medina. El poder de los **wahabíes** se había extendido rápidamente: desde su base en Arabia se habían asegurado el control de La Meca, Medina y Yidda, y amenazaban a Siria cuando Mehmet Alí recibió la orden de derrotarlos y recuperar las ciudades para los otomanos. Un sitio final a la capital, **Diriyah** (en la Arabia Saudí actual), frenó temporalmente las ambiciones wahabíes.

En América del Sur, el esfuerzo de José de San Martín en la batalla de Maipú, el 5 de abril, aseguró la **independencia de Chile** con la aplastante derrota de las tropas realistas. Con una pequeña flota de siete barcos al mando del mercenario británico lord Thomas Cochrane, los rebeldes también consiguieron terminar con el dominio español sobre la costa.

En París, el inventor alemán Karl von Drais, barón de Sauerbrun, impresionaba al público con su **draisiana**, un vehículo de dos ruedas alineadas precursor de la **bicicleta**. Era de madera y se propulsaba apoyando los pies sobre el suelo, en lugar de con pedales. En alemán se llamó ***Laufmaschine*** (máquina de correr). El año anterior, durante las pruebas de diseño, había logrado recorrer con ella unos 14 km. Esta idea no tardó en ser recogida y modificada por otros inventores, como el británico **Denis Johnson** (*c.* 1759–1833), un fabricante de carruajes, que concibió un «carruaje para peatones», más tarde conocido como ***dandy horse***.

Mary Shelley
La novelista inglesa Mary Shelley publicó en 1818 su primera novela, Frankenstein, *que sigue siendo un clásico en nuestros días.*

Mary Shelley (1797–1851), esposa del poeta Percy Bysshe Shelley (1792–1822) e hija de la escritora Mary Wollstonecraft (*véase* 1792), publicó en Inglaterra *Frankenstein o El moderno Prometeo*. La novela trata de un científico que crea artificialmente a otro ser humano y de las consecuencias que sufren ambos. Su éxito fue inmediato y se considera una obra clásica de la literatura **gótica** o de terror, así como uno de los primeros ejemplos de la narrativa de ciencia ficción.

En España, por iniciativa de Fernando VII, y en particular de su esposa María Isabel de Braganza, se remodeló el edificio destinado a albergar el **Museo del Prado**, inaugurado como pinacoteca el 19 de setiembre de 1819 con parte de la colección real.

1819

Ilustración de la masacre llamada de Peterloo, en Manchester (Inglaterra), donde la caballería cargó contra una manifestación pacífica.

EL 16 DE AGOSTO, una reunión política con unos sesenta mil asistentes en St Peter's Field, en Manchester, se transformó de protesta por el elevado precio de los alimentos y la falta de sufragio popular en la **masacre de Peterloo**. Los magistrados, preocupados por el número de personas congregadas, ordenaron a la caballería voluntaria que detuviera a los oradores, pero esta **atacó** a la multitud, que le cortó el paso. Entonces se envió un regimiento, el 15 de húsares; se estima que murieron 15 personas y más de 500 resultaron heridas.

A su regreso del exilio, el general venezolano **Simón Bolívar** consiguió avances considerables ante las fuerzas realistas. En 1819, condujo a su ejército desde Venezuela a través de los Andes para lanzar un ataque. Tras derrotar a los españoles en la **batalla de Boyacá** el 7 de agosto, marchó al sur, hacia Santa Fé, con lo que obtuvo la independencia de **Nueva Granada** y fue nombrado presidente de la nueva Gran Colombia.

Con la intención de terminar con el dominio holandés sobre las rutas comerciales entre China e India (*véase* 1795), la Compañía Británica de las Indias Orientales se propuso instalar una nueva base en la península de Malaca. **Stamford Raffles** llegó a **Singapur**, que entonces pertenecía al sultanato de Riau-Johore, negoció un acuerdo con el sultán y fundó un puerto.

LAS COMPAÑÍAS DE LAS INDIAS ORIENTALES

Las compañías de las Indias Orientales monopolizaban el comercio entre Europa y el Sureste Asiático, India y Extremo Oriente desde inicios del siglo XVII. Sin embargo, la francesa *(Compagnie française des Indes Orientales)* dejó de operar durante la Revolución (*véase* 1789); los estatutos de la holandesa *(Vereenigde Oost-Indische Compagnie)* fueron revocados en 1799, cuando el gobierno asumió el control sobre ella, y la sueca *(Svenska Ostindiska Companiet)* cerró en 1813. Por el contrario, la británica (imagen) perduró hasta 1874.

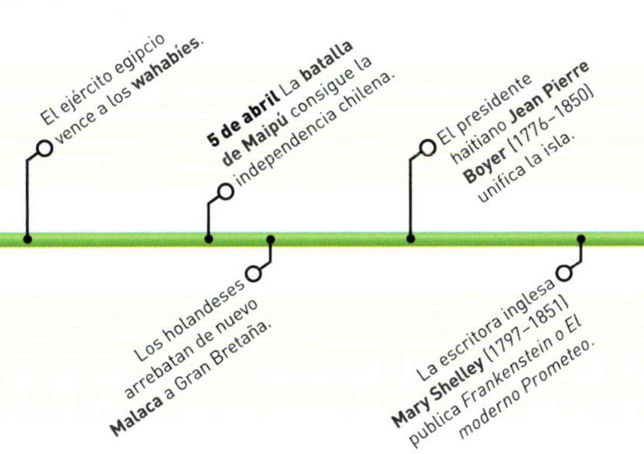

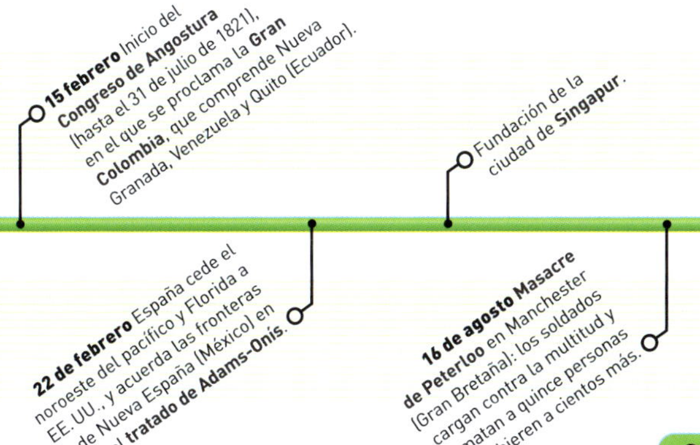

Collar de cuentas europeas
Finales del siglo XIX • ORIGEN DESCONOCIDO
Este collar tiene distintos tipos de cuentas de color azul y amarillo ensartadas. Las cuentas se obtenían de comerciantes europeos, y servían como moneda.

Brazalete de abalorios
Finales del siglo XIX • SARSI
Brazalete de los sarsis, una tribu de los indios de las llanuras, decorado con abalorios azules, rosas, negros y amarillos.

Gorro
***C.* 1860** • IROQUESES
Gorro iroqués de terciopelo negro, con bordado complejo de abalorios y motivos florales tejidos en la parte inferior.

Tocado de plumas de jefe
***C.* 1930** • ARAPAJÓ
Tocado de Ternero Amarillo, el último jefe de los arapajós, confeccionado con plumas de águila real y piel decorada.

INDIOS AMERICANOS

OBJETOS DE LAS DIVERSAS NACIONES QUE VIVEN POR TODA AMÉRICA DEL NORTE

Durante miles de años, millones de indígenas poblaron América del Norte. La llegada de los europeos hizo pedazos su mundo, y sus poblaciones se redujeron drásticamente.

Las diversas culturas y sociedades de América del Norte iban desde el mundo ártico de los aleutianos, ntisinan (innus) y yupik (inuits) al hogar cálido y árido de los hopi en el suroeste. Pueblos como los lakota, dakota y nakota (sioux), niitsitapi (pies negros) y hinanaeina (arapajós) de las Grandes Llanuras, o los anishinaabeg (algonquinos) y haudenosaunee (iroqueses) de los Grandes Lagos, pronto establecieron contactos regulares con colonos europeos.

Utensilio para trabajar el cuero
***C.* 1890** • ALEUTIANO
Desollar y despiezar la carne solía ser tarea de las mujeres. Esta especie de rasqueta servía para descarnar pieles de nutria marina y ballena.

Juego de costura
***C.* 1880** • NTISINAN
Este juego de costura consiste en utensilios de hueso labrado y una bolsa de piel de foca y pelo de animal.

Anzuelo
Siglo XIX • ALEUTIANO
Anzuelo de madera, hueso y fibra. La madera está tallada en forma de «U», y los extremos son de hueso.

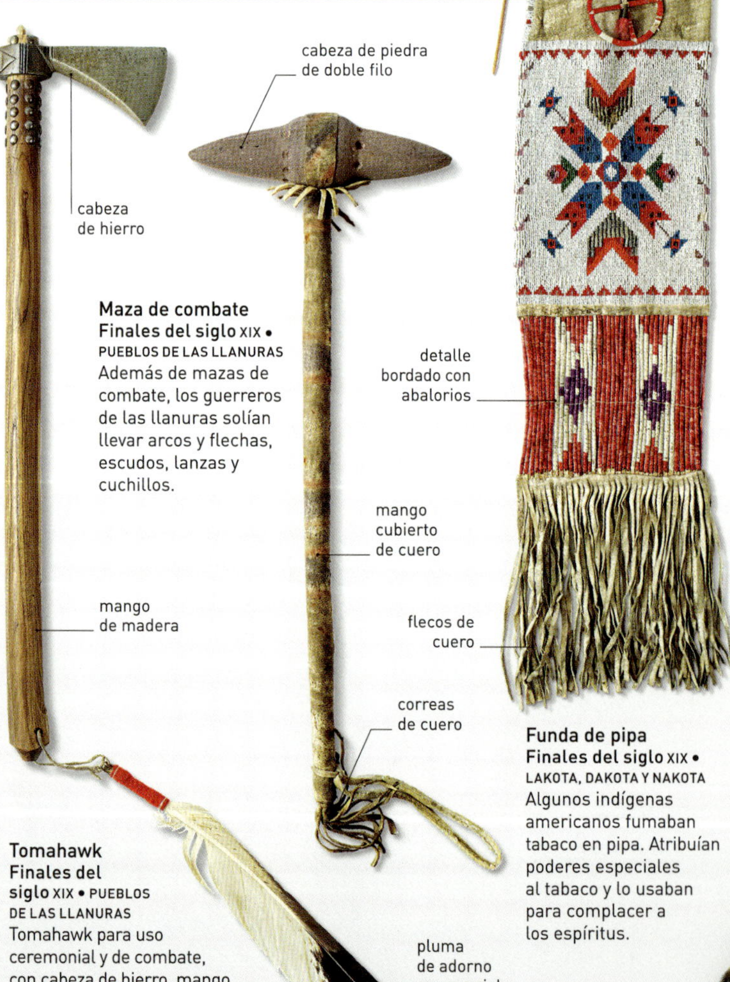

Maza de combate
Finales del siglo XIX • PUEBLOS DE LAS LLANURAS
Además de mazas de combate, los guerreros de las llanuras solían llevar arcos y flechas, escudos, lanzas y cuchillos.

Tomahawk
Finales del siglo XIX • PUEBLOS DE LAS LLANURAS
Tomahawk para uso ceremonial y de combate, con cabeza de hierro, mango de madera y pluma ornamental.

Funda de pipa
Finales del siglo XIX • LAKOTA, DAKOTA Y NAKOTA
Algunos indígenas americanos fumaban tabaco en pipa. Atribuían poderes especiales al tabaco y lo usaban para complacer a los espíritus.

Chaqueta
C. 1890 • LAKOTA, DAKOTA Y NAKOTA
El diseño de esta chaqueta de ante con abalorios refleja la transformación de las culturas y economías de los pueblos indígenas de las Grandes Llanuras después de la llegada de los caballos a América del Norte en el siglo XVII.

Mocasines con abalorios
Finales del siglo XIX • LAKOTA, DAKOTA Y NAKOTA
Mocasines de cuero adornados con abalorios que llevaban cazadores y comerciantes. La suela cubre también los dedos.

Osos polares de madera
Principios del siglo XX • INUIT
Figurillas talladas de osos polares, un animal central en la cultura y la economía de los inuit de las regiones árticas.

Fajines
Mediados del siglo XIX • MOHAWK
Fajines con un trabajo elaborado de abalorios. Muchas tribus creaban arte decorativo con abalorios de cálamo, concha, hueso y piedra antes de que los europeos trajeran cuentas de vidrio como estas.

Muñeca kachina
Siglo XX • HOPI
Los hopis usaban figuritas como esta para instruir a los niños sobre el mundo de los espíritus.

Mukluks
Principios del siglo XX • INUIT
Botas infantiles con exterior de piel de foca o de reno curtida y forradas de pelo por dentro.

Abrigo de invierno
Finales del siglo XIX • NTISINAN
Los anoraks eran abrigos de invierno, por lo general sueltos y amplios por abajo para dejar que entre aire frío si hace falta ventilar.

Dientes tallados y perforados
Siglo XIX • INUIT
Los chamanes, o curanderos empleaban estos dientes, ensartados en un anillo, y algunos tallados en forma de pájaro.

Cráneo de bisonte
Siglo XIX • PIES NEGROS
Este cráneo de bisonte para el ritual de las danzas de sol de los indígenas de las llanuras está decorado con lunares.

1820

Los soldados mamelucos egipcios eran antiguos esclavos. Egipto invadió Sudán con la esperanza de incorporar prisioneros sudaneses a sus filas.

CUANDO EE. UU. comenzó a colonizar los territorios del oeste, la cuestión de la **esclavitud** ya no podía seguir ignorándose. Aunque la mayoría de los estados norteños la habían abolido, los del sur dependían cada vez más del trabajo de los esclavos. Cuando el territorio de Misuri solicitó el estatus de estado en 1817, provocó una crisis política acerca del derecho del gobierno federal a prohibir la esclavitud allí. La solución fue el **Compromiso de Misuri**, que permitía la esclavitud en Misuri, pero en ningún nuevo estado más al norte de la latitud 36° 30'.

Mientras, la mayor parte de Europa estaba sumida en la inestabilidad política, con **revoluciones** liberales en los estados italianos, Portugal, Francia y Países Bajos. En **España**, Fernando VII había revocado la nueva constitución cuando recuperó el trono (*véase* 1812) y arrestado a los líderes liberales. El pronunciamiento de Riego le obligó a aceptar la Constitución de 1812, lo que marcó el inicio del **Trienio Liberal** (tres años de gobierno liberal entre 1820 y 1823). En 1823,

Población esclava
Aunque la población esclava de Misuri era reducida, la disputa sobre la permisión de la esclavitud en el estado provocó una crisis política.

Luis XVIII de Francia (*véase* 1815), envió a un ejército, conocido como los **Cien Mil Hijos de san Luis**, a fin de «liberar» a Fernando. Las tropas depusieron al régimen liberal y devolvieron el poder a Fernando.

Egipto invadió **Sudán**, su vecino del sur. Mehmet Alí ambicionaba el oro sudanés y esclavos para su ejército. En 1821, Sudán había caído en poder de Egipto, que se extendía del Nilo a la actual Uganda.

« ESTA **TRASCENDENTAL CUESTIÓN** ME DESPERTÓ Y ME LLENÓ DE **TERROR**, COMO UNA **CAMPANA QUE TOCARA A FUEGO** EN PLENA NOCHE. »

Thomas Jefferson, tercer presidente de EE. UU., sobre las implicaciones del Compromiso de Misuri, en una carta a John Holmes (22 de abril de 1820)

1821

Grabado sobre la lucha por la independencia de México.

EN GRECIA ESTALLÓ LA LUCHA POR LA INDEPENDENCIA. Resentidas por años de opresión otomana, gentes de toda la sociedad griega, inclusive la **Iglesia ortodoxa**, comenzaron a planear su liberación. Algunos grupos rebeldes se habían organizado gracias a la formación de diversas sociedades patrióticas secretas, como la **Filiki Etería** (Sociedad de Amigos), en la que participaban habitantes de las islas, pero que también contaban con un importante apoyo de la gran **diáspora griega**.

Mientras tanto, en **América Latina** los rebeldes decidieron aprovechar la crisis interna y la debilidad de España para realizar un último **esfuerzo por la independencia**. **México** consiguió la libertad cuando los realistas, tras conocer lo sucedido en España (*véase* 1820), decidieron que el autogobierno era el único medio de **evitar un régimen liberal** como el español. El 24 de agosto se firmó un tratado que reconocía la independencia mexicana y el 19 de mayo de 1822, el antiguo realista Agustín de Iturbide (1783–1824) se coronó a sí mismo emperador como **Agustín I**.

En América del Sur se formó el **Congreso de Cúcuta**, que fundó la **Gran Colombia**, compuesta por los actuales Colombia, Panamá, Venezuela y Ecuador. **Simón Bolívar** fue confirmado como presidente y la capital se instaló en Bogotá.

En Perú, **José de San Martín** dirigió a su ejército hacia Lima y declaró la **independencia de Perú**, aunque los enfrentamientos para asegurar su libertad prosiguieron durante un tiempo.

1822

Coronación de Pedro I como emperador de Brasil. Pedro, hijo del rey de Portugal, proclamó la independencia de la colonia.

LAS RELACIONES ENTRE PORTUGAL Y BRASIL se vieron profundamente afectadas a raíz de la llegada de la corte portuguesa a Brasil en 1808 huyendo de Napoleón Bonaparte. En 1821, **Juan VI** (1769–1826) volvió a Portugal y dejó a su hijo, **don Pedro** (1798–1834), a cargo del reino de Brasil como príncipe regente. Don Pedro, frustrado por el intento de las Cortes portuguesas de reducir a Brasil al estatus colonial anterior a 1808, pronunció el **Grito de Ipiranga**, que proclamaba la libertad de Brasil, y se coronó a sí mismo emperador como Pedro I.

Incluso el realista **Santo Domingo**, en la isla de La Española, se vio arrastrado por el espíritu revolucionario de la época y proclamó su **independencia** en 1821, aunque no consiguió materializar su plan de unirse a la Gran Colombia. El vecino de Santo Domingo, **Haití** (antes Saint-Domingue) estaba cada vez más preocupado por la posibilidad de que Francia o Gran Bretaña pudieran introducirse por los mal vigilados puertos de Santo Domingo y lanzaran un

ÁFRICA
LIBERIA
OCÉANO ATLÁNTICO

Liberia
La American Colonization Society fundó una colonia para esclavos liberados en las proximidades de puertos esclavistas activos.

12 MIL NÚMERO DE **ESCLAVOS LIBERADOS QUE** ENTRE 1822 Y 1862 **SE INSTALARON** EN LIBERIA

ataque para volver a colonizar y **esclavizar** la isla. El presidente de Haití, **Jean-Pierre Boyer** (g. 1818–1850) llegó a Santo Domingo con sus fuerzas para impedir esta posibilidad y poner fin a la esclavitud allí. El gobierno provisional entregó el poder a Boyer, que unificó toda la isla bajo el control de Haití.

En EE. UU., la cuestión de la esclavitud seguía siendo fuente de conflicto y, además, surgió la cuestión de cómo tratar a los **esclavos liberados**. La Sociedad Americana de Colonización, fundada en 1816, defendía que fuesen devueltos a África y cerró acuerdos con gobernantes locales de África occidental, donde se fundó cerca del **cabo Mesurado** un asentamiento que después se llamó **Liberia**.

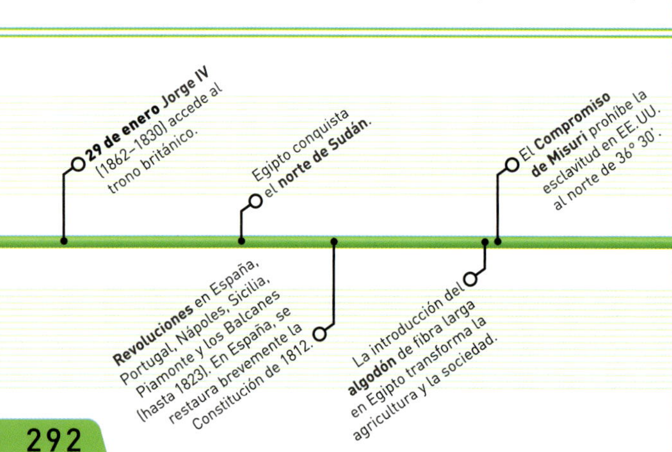

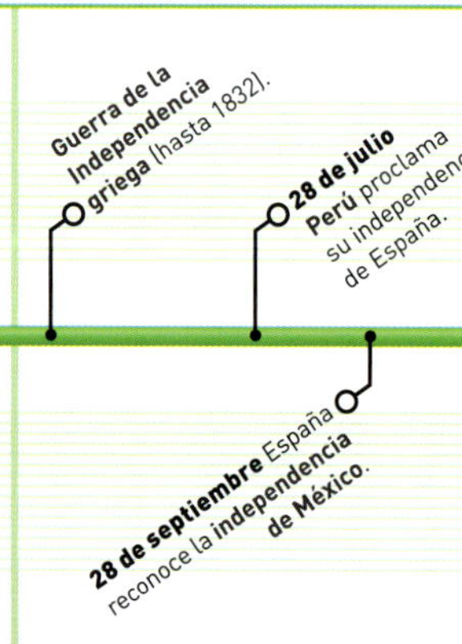

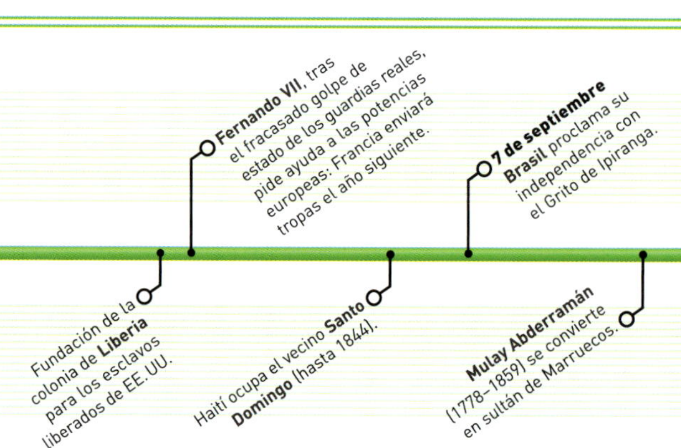

1823

Cuando la dinastía birmana Alaungpaya invadió el norte de India, Gran Bretaña le declaró la guerra y tomó la ciudad de Rangún (en la imagen).

EN SU MENSAJE ANUAL AL CONGRESO DE EE. UU. DEL 2 DE DICIEMBRE, el presidente James Monroe (*véase* recuadro) presentó una nueva política diplomática: la **doctrina Monroe**. Preocupado ante la posibilidad de incursiones europeas en las nuevas repúblicas latinoamericanas, Monroe trató de **marcar límites** entre Europa y América. La doctrina establecía que EE. UU. no interferiría ni en los asuntos internos, ni tampoco en las guerras entre potencias europeas o en las colonias americanas, pero del mismo modo declaraba el hemisferio occidental cerrado a cualquier intento de **colonización** por los europeos. La intromisión en territorio americano se consideraría un acto hostil contra EE. UU.

Hacia principios de año nació una nueva república latinoamericana, que recibió el nombre de **Provincias Unidas de América Central**,

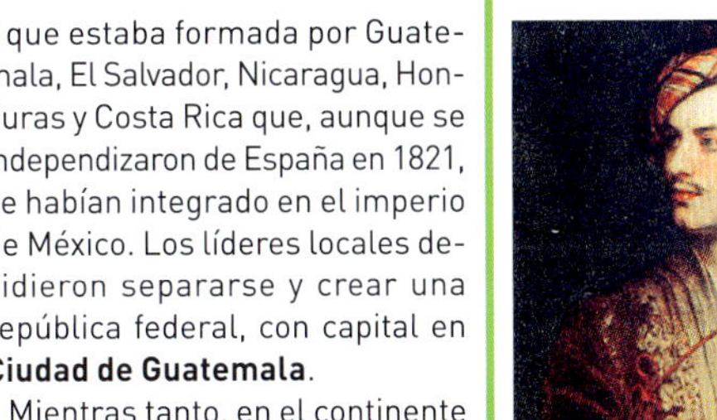

y que estaba formada por Guatemala, El Salvador, Nicaragua, Honduras y Costa Rica que, aunque se independizaron de España en 1821, se habían integrado en el imperio de México. Los líderes locales decidieron separarse y crear una república federal, con capital en **Ciudad de Guatemala**.

Mientras tanto, en el continente asiático, la **dinastía Alaungpaya** de Birmania (actual Myanmar; *véase* 1752), había realizado varias incursiones en el estado de **Assam**, situado en el norte de India, donde había entrado en contacto con los británicos, que entonces ocupaban la región. En un esfuerzo por proteger sus intereses en India, Gran Bretaña inició al año siguiente la **primera guerra anglo-birmana** (1824–1826), que le permitió apoderarse de gran parte del territorio birmano, inclusive **Rangún**, que fue ocupada en 1825.

AISLACIONISMO ESTADOUNIDENSE

James Monroe (1758–1831; dcha.) fue el quinto presidente de EE. UU., entre 1817 y 1825, periodo durante el cual el país empezó a emerger como una gran potencia mundial y que se conoce como «era de los buenos sentimientos», marcada por el crecimiento económico y un optimismo generalizado. Con la aversión a interferir en aquellos asuntos que atañían a otros países, minuciosamente expuesta en la doctrina Monroe, EE. UU. comenzó a aplicar una política aislacionista.

1824

Este grabado muestra el sitio otomano de Missolonghi, donde los griegos establecieron un gobierno provisional durante la guerra por su independencia.

Lord Byron
La lucha del pueblo griego por librarse del yugo otomano inspiró al poeta romántico Lord Byron, que marchó a Grecia con el objetivo de contribuir a la causa.

LA LUCHA POR LA INDEPENDENCIA GRIEGA SE INTENSIFICÓ y atrajo la atención en Europa, en especial de escritores y artistas. Uno de ellos fue el poeta **romántico** inglés **Lord Byron** (1788–1824), célebre por su poema *Don Juan*. Byron había llegado a Grecia el año anterior con el propósito de participar en la lucha; sin embargo, fue víctima de una grave enfermedad y falleció el 19 de abril en **Missolonghi**.

También en 1824, en Perú, la victoria de Antonio José de Sucre en la **batalla de Ayacucho** el 9 de diciembre puso fin a la dominación española, aunque en el territorio conocido como **Alto Perú** las fuerzas monárquicas siguieron resistiendo a los patriotas en uno de sus últimos bastiones.

1825

EL TERRITORIO DEL ALTO PERÚ obtuvo la ayuda que tanto necesitaba gracias a la llegada de Simón Bolívar (*véase* 1811) y de **Antonio José de Sucre** (1785–1830), cuyo ejército ayudó a derrotar a los españoles. Bolívar deseaba incorporar este territorio al resto de Perú, pero Sucre ya había acordado con los líderes rebeldes que su destino sería el de convertirse en una **república independiente**. En agradecimiento a la ayuda de Bolívar, los rebeldes llamaron **Bolivia** a la nueva nación e invitaron a Sucre a ser el primer presidente, a lo que este accedió. Con la creación de Bolivia, todas las colonias españolas (a excepción de Cuba, Puerto Rico y Filipinas) pasaron a ser naciones independientes.

Ese mismo año, en Inglaterra, la inauguración de la línea férrea que conectaba **Stockton y Darlington**, en el norte industrial del país, había suscitado una gran expectación. Las innovaciones tecnológicas del uso del vapor (*véanse* 1775 y 1786) habían hecho posible el desarrollo de las **locomotoras**, como la diseñada por el inventor inglés **John Blenkinsop** en 1812. **George Stephenson** (1781–1848), ingeniero mecánico de minas, introdujo varias mejoras en su diseño y consiguió atraer el interés de un grupo de inversores que querían unir la ciudad de Stockton con Darlington. Darlington se hallaba en el centro de una región **minera**, y los montes Peninos dificultaban el transporte de carbón y de personas. La línea férrea, de 40 km, abrió la vía al desarrollo del ferrocarril.

Atracción popular
La inauguración de la línea férrea atrajo mucho público: por primera vez en el mundo, una locomotora iba a tirar de un tren de pasajeros.

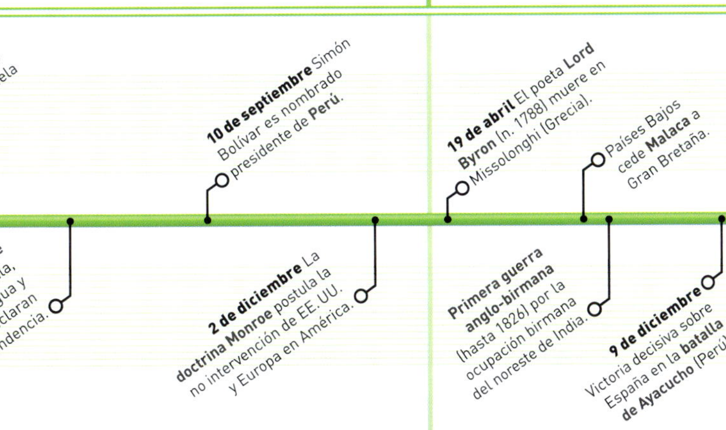

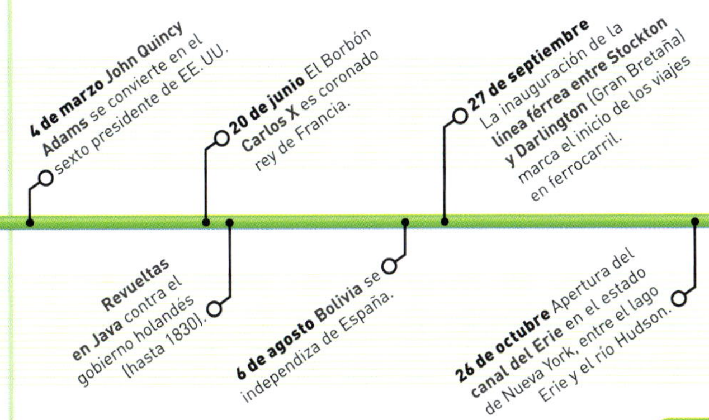

1826

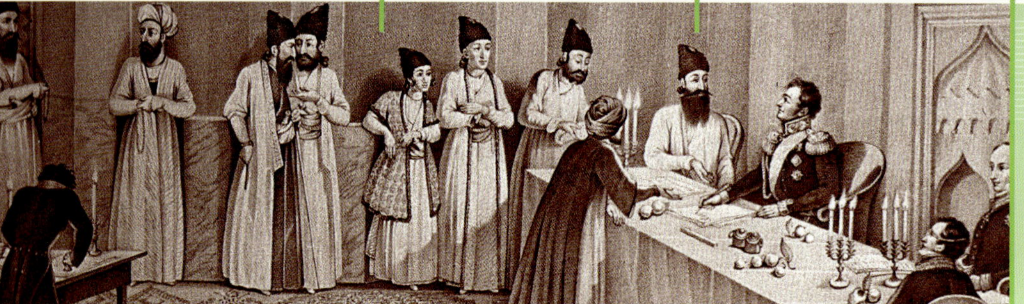
Ceremonia de la firma del tratado de Turkmanchai, por el que Persia renunciaba al disputado territorio del Cáucaso en favor de Rusia.

LOS ENFRENTAMIENTOS ENTRE RUSIA Y PERSIA SE REANUDARON (*véase* 1813) a propósito de la región del Cáucaso, donde los persas trataron de recuperar el territorio de **Georgia** un año antes. El 26 de septiembre de 1826, una derrota abrumadora por los rusos en la **batalla de Ganja** detuvo sus avances. Entonces, el ejército ruso marchó hacia Persia y tomó Teherán. Sin ninguna otra opción que la de aceptar la **derrota**, los persas negociaron el **tratado de Turkmanchai**, que llevaba las fronteras rusas hasta el río Aras y devolvía a Rusia el territorio del Cáucaso.

A **Hawái** estaban afluyendo misioneros estadounidenses, y EE. UU. era ya uno de los principales socios comerciales del reino. Para proteger sus crecientes intereses ante la competencia europea, los estadounidenses convencieron al gobierno regente del **rey Kamehameha III** (1813–1854) para que firmara el **tratado Hawái-EE. UU.** de 1826, que establecía relaciones políticas y comerciales amistosas.

Francia reconoció la **independencia de Haití** a cambio de una indemnización de 1,5 millones de francos que lastró al gobierno y la economía del país durante décadas.

El inventor francés **Joseph-Nicéphore Niépce** (1765–1833) tomó la primera **fotografía** del mundo, una vista desde la ventana de su casa. Su técnica consistía en una exposición de ocho horas sobre una placa de estaño usando una **cámara oscura**: una caja con un orificio diminuto por donde pasaba la luz, precursora de la cámara moderna.

1827

LA GUERRA DE GRECIA CONTRA EL IMPERIO OTOMANO proseguía, y los países vecinos comenzaron a exigir el fin del conflicto. Gran Bretaña, Francia y Rusia se unieron para firmar el **tratado de Londres** del 6 de julio, en el que pedían la formación de un estado griego independiente. Los otomanos se negaron, convencidos de contar con la potencia naval y de infantería suficiente para vencer a los griegos.

En otoño pusieron a prueba sus recursos durante el enfrentamiento entre una flota turcoegipcia y otra compuesta por barcos británicos, franceses y rusos en la **batalla de Navarino**, que tuvo lugar el 20 de octubre. La flota rusoeuropea consiguió hundir a tres cuartas partes de las naves otomanas, y la humillante derrota llevó finalmente a la retirada definitiva de las tropas turcas de Grecia, que consiguió la independencia en 1832.

Batalla desigual
Navío turco incendiado en la batalla de Navarino, donde la flota otomana quedó devastada sin que la flota aliada perdiera ni una sola nave.

1828

José Gervasio Artigas
Artigas fue el padre del movimiento uruguayo por la independencia, pero estuvo exiliado durante varios años antes de ser liberado.

EL TRATADO DE MONTEVIDEO RECONOCIÓ LA INDEPENDENCIA DE URUGUAY en agosto de este año. Brasil y Argentina se disputaban la región en aquel momento conocida como **Banda Oriental**. Aunque había estado bajo control español durante las guerras de independencia de América del Sur, bajo el liderazgo del prócer **José Gervasio Artigas** (1764–1850) consiguió independizarse de España y de Argentina en 1815. Sin embargo, al año siguiente **Brasil la invadió** y la ocupó, hecho que desembocó en una nueva guerra, liderada por **Juan Antonio Lavalleja** (1784–1853) y un grupo conocido como los **Treinta y Tres Orientales**. Lavalleja, que contaba con el apoyo de Argentina, derrotó al ejército brasileño y fundó el Uruguay independiente.

Ese mismo año, las disputas territoriales originaron otro conflicto entre el **Imperio otomano** y **Rusia**, que tomó **Vidin** y **Varna** (en la actual Bulgaria).

1829

29 KILÓMETROS POR HORA
VELOCIDAD PUNTA DE LA **PRIMERA LOCOMOTORA DE VAPOR DE EE. UU.**

EL DEBATE SOBRE IRLANDA no cesó después de la Ley de Unión (*véase* 1801). **Daniel O'Connell**, un abogado católico, solicitó que Inglaterra revocara las **leyes anticatólicas**, argumentando que no podían representar al pueblo de Irlanda. Además, convocó mítines multitudinarios acerca de la **emancipación católica**. En 1828, O'Connell se presentó a las elecciones al parlamento y ganó, pese a que no se le permitió ocupar su escaño por ser católico. Sin embargo, su victoria llamó la atención del primer ministro británico, Arthur Wellesley, **duque de Wellington** (*véase* 1815), también irlandés, aunque no católico. En **1829**, este supervisó la ***Catholic Relief Act***, que permitía a los católicos de Irlanda y de Inglaterra ocupar cargos públicos y escaños en el parlamento.

En Inglaterra, el inventor George Stephenson (*véase* 1825) presentó su nueva locomotora ***Rocket***, que llegaba a alcanzar una velocidad de 58 km por hora, al concurso de la compañía ferroviaria **Liverpool and Manchester Railway**. La *Rocket* fue la clara vencedora.

Este año, el ferrocarril también avanzó en EE. UU., donde se fabricó la primera locomotora de vapor americana, la ***Tom Thumb***. En 1830 se organizó una carrera contra un carro sobre raíles tirado por un caballo para demostrar la **superioridad del vapor**. Aunque el caballo de carne y hueso derrotó al «caballo de hierro» debido a un fallo técnico de la *Tom Thumb*, los propietarios de la **Baltimore and Ohio Railroad** adoptaron las locomotoras de vapor al año siguiente.

1830

Alzamiento que llevó a la independencia de Bélgica.

EUROPA APENAS HABÍA CONSEGUIDO RECUPERARSE de las tensiones de la década anterior (*véase* 1820) cuando Francia se vio inmersa en la llamada **Revolución de Julio**, una insurrección que obligó a abdicar a Carlos X (r. 1824–1830). Le sustituyó **Luis Felipe**, duque de Orleans (r. 1830–1848). La chispa que encendió la rebelión fue el intento de Carlos de imponer medidas represoras, como la suspensión de la libertad de prensa y una modificación de la ley electoral que suponía la pérdida del derecho a votar para muchos ciudadanos.

El ascenso de Luis Felipe al trono francés también supuso la llegada al poder de la **burguesía**, su principal apoyo en lugar de la aristocracia hasta 1848.

Al mismo tiempo estallaron **revoluciones** en los reinos italianos y alemanes, en Países Bajos y en Rusia, donde los **polacos** que vivían bajo el dominio ruso se alzaron contra el gobierno del zar.

Cherokees muertos en el Sendero de las Lágrimas
Miles de indios fueron obligados a salir del sureste de EE. UU. por la ruta llamada Sendero de las Lágrimas.

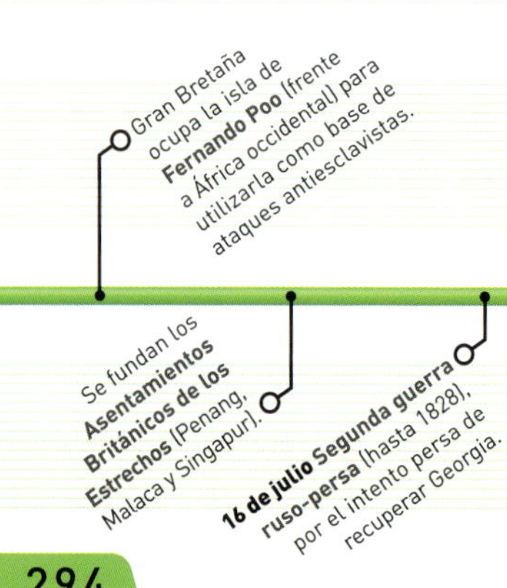

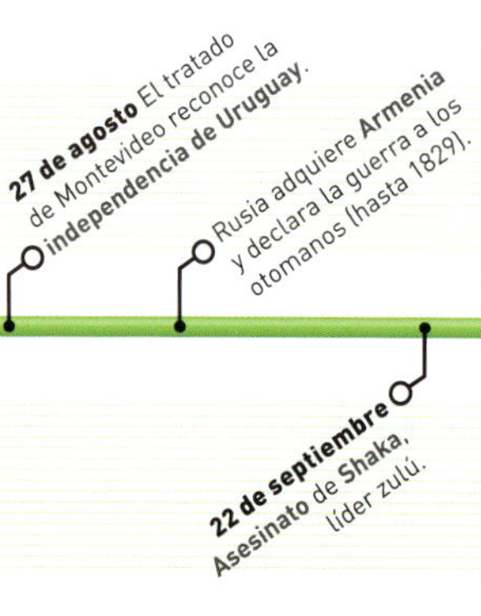

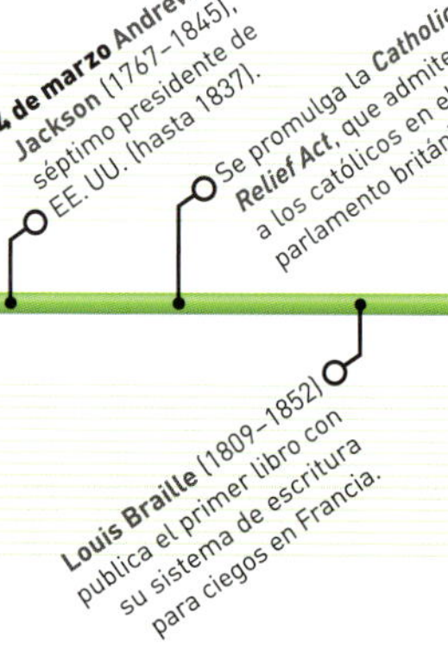

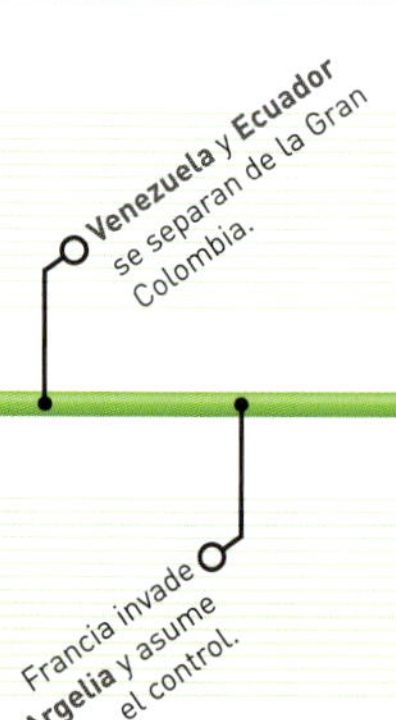

1831

1832

« NINGÚN MINISTRO PUEDE **MANTENERSE** EN **CONTRA** DE **LA OPINIÓN PÚBLICA. »**

Robert Peel, político británico, sobre la *Reform Act* (1834)

También en este periodo, Francia envió a su ejército a **Argelia** con la intención de asumir el control del país. Años antes, en 1827, el gobernador provincial otomano, o dey, Husein (g. 1818–1838) había azotado a un cónsul, lo que sirvió de pretexto a los franceses para entrar en guerra. El origen del conflicto era una deuda pendiente entre Francia y el dey. Cuando Francia bloqueó Argel, la situación se complicó. El 5 de julio, Francia izó su bandera en la kasba de la ciudad, marcando así el inicio del control francés sobre este territorio norteafricano.

En **América del Sur**, las alianzas políticas también estaban revelando su fragilidad. Antes de fallecer en 1830, Simón Bolívar (*véase* 1811) asistió a la separación de **Venezuela y Ecuador** de la Gran Colombia, lo que puso fin a su sueño de **unidad** entre las nuevas repúblicas.

En América del Norte, EE. UU. vivía la que se conoce como **era de las caravanas**. Cada vez más colonos emprendían el camino hacia el oeste en grupos de carretas tiradas generalmente por caballos y cargadas con todas sus pertenencias rumbo a un territorio desconocido para instalar granjas y colonizarlo.

Mientras, para favorecer el asentamiento en el este, el gobierno estadounidense promulgó en 1830 la ***Indian Removal Act*** (Ley de Desplazamiento de los Indios), que privaba a los indios de todos sus derechos legales y les obligaba a abandonar su codiciado territorio del sureste del país para instalarse en tierras escasamente pobladas al oeste del Misisipi. Los desplazamientos provocaron muchas muertes.

La Libertad guiando al pueblo
El pintor francés Eugène Delacroix (1798–1863) se inspiró en los sucesos de la Revolución de Julio de 1830 en París para pintar este famoso cuadro.

EN 1831, EL REINO DE LOS PAÍSES BAJOS SE VIO ARRASTRADO por la vorágine europea. El Congreso de Viena (*véase* 1814) había obligado al territorio belga, que en aquel momento se hallaba bajo control francés, a unirse a los holandeses para crear un estado tampón entre Rusia y Francia. Esta medida resultó enormemente impopular y generó numerosas tensiones que fueron en aumento con los años.

En agosto del año anterior, e inspirada por los recientes acontecimientos que habían tenido lugar en Francia, estalló la **Revolución belga**, que terminó con la escisión del reino de los Países Bajos. Ese mismo año se promulgó una **constitución** que establecía una monarquía constitucional y un sistema parlamentario. El 20 de enero de 1831, Gran Bretaña y Francia, aunque no Países Bajos, reconocieron al nuevo estado de **Bélgica**. Los belgas se vieron entonces obligados a escoger un monarca que no tuviese relación directa con el resto de las grandes potencias europeas y finalmente se decantaron por Leopoldo de Sajonia-Coburgo-Saalfeld (tío de la reina Victoria de Inglaterra), que reinó con el nombre de **Leopoldo I** hasta el año 1865.

Ese mismo año, en el continente africano, Egipto se anexionó Siria. Esta anexión duró solo nueve años, puesto que en 1840 se vio obligado a devolverla a los otomanos.

Ley de reforma electoral inglesa
En este grabado satírico, los reformistas talan el «árbol podrido», símbolo de los municipios corruptos. Exigían una distribución más justa de los escaños parlamentarios.

GRAN BRETAÑA TAMBIÉN VIVIÓ UN PERIODO DE CONVULSIONES Y CAMBIOS SOCIALES durante la década de 1830. El desfasado sistema electoral (*véase* 1819) había suscitado cada vez más malestar entre la población. Se elaboró una ley orientada a transferir los votos y a redistribuir los escaños de los pequeños municipios (llamados «burgos podridos») controlados por la nobleza, a ciudades industriales más pobladas. El primer proyecto de **ley de reforma electoral** no consiguió ser aprobado por el parlamento, lo que dio lugar a graves incidentes en muchas ciudades y a una crisis política cuando el primer ministro, **Charles Grey** (1764–1845), amenazó con dimitir. La ley ***(Reform Act)*** se aprobó finalmente el 4 de junio de 1832: concedía el derecho a votar a más varones de clase media, pero la clase obrera y las mujeres seguían excluidas.

7 de febrero Se reconoce la constitución belga; **Bélgica** proclama su independencia.

26 de mayo El Congreso de EE. UU. aprueba la ***Indian Removal Act.***

26 de junio Guillermo IV (1765–1837) asciende al trono británico.

Primera oleada **revolucionaria** y de turbulencias sociales en Europa a favor de reformas liberales.

9 de agosto Luis Felipe (1773–1850) es coronado rey de Francia tras la Revolución de Julio.

25 de agosto Inicio de la **Revolución belga** (hasta 1831).

10 de octubre Nace en Madrid la reina **Isabel II de España** (m. 1904), hija de Fernando VII y de su cuarta esposa, María Cristina de Borbón.

29 de noviembre Alzamiento polaco contra Rusia.

Egipto ocupa **Siria** (hasta 1840).

26 de mayo Ejecución en Granada (España) de **Mariana Pineda**, acusada de colaborar con los liberales.

21 de agosto Rebelión del esclavo Nat Turner en EE. UU., que deja más de cincuenta muertos blancos en Virginia.

4 de junio El parlamento británico aprueba la ***Reform Act***, que introduce en el sistema electoral cambios importantes.

30 de agosto El **tratado de Londres** crea un **reino independiente en Grecia** e instala una monarquía.

Rusia se anexiona el **Ducado de Varsovia.**

1833–1834

Niños trabajando en una fábrica textil inglesa. El tamaño de las primeras hiladoras de algodón hacía que los niños fueran los operarios más adecuados.

48 **HORAS SEMANALES DE TRABAJO** PERMITIDAS A LOS **NIÑOS** DE ENTRE **NUEVE Y DOCE AÑOS** EN LA **INDUSTRIA TEXTIL INGLESA**

EN GRAN BRETAÑA, DONDE EL DESARROLLO industrial y el crecimiento urbano avanzaban rápidamente, se aprobaron leyes que abordaban la explotación de la mano de obra y el coste creciente de la atención a los pobres. La ***Factory Act* de 1833** nombró inspectores que controlaban las fábricas y limitó las horas que podían trabajar los niños.

En Inglaterra, las parroquias locales proporcionaban asistencia a enfermos, ancianos y pobres. Así se creó un sistema de ***workhouses***, lugares de acogida destinados a dar empleo a las personas que podían trabajar. En **1834**, una **nueva ley** estipuló que los pobres solo podían recibir ayuda en las *workhouses*, que se construyeron en todas las parroquias. Las condiciones en estas instituciones eran deliberadamente duras, y la ley resultó impopular inmediatamente.

En China se **autorizó el comercio** a los particulares británicos cuando la legislación puso fin al monopolio de la Compañía Británica de las Indias Orientales. Ya antes se habían instalado algunos comerciantes en Cantón, pero ahora eran más los que podían vender sus productos y exportar los de China, como el **té**, cuyas importaciones crecieron un 40 % tras el inicio del libre comercio.

En 1832, **Egipto invadió Siria**. El bajá Mehmet Alí, furioso por el incumplimiento de la promesa del sultán otomano de otorgarle el territorio, tomó Gaza y Jerusalén durante la **primera guerra turco-egipcia**. En 1833, el gobierno otomano suplicó a Rusia que le ayudara, y 18 000 soldados fueron enviados a Estambul. Gran Bretaña y Francia intervinieron y exigieron un acuerdo, por el que Siria fue entregada a Egipto, y Rusia se retiró.

Moneda conmemorativa
En casi todo el Imperio británico, la Ley de Emancipación prohibió la compraventa de personas, liberó a los niños y compensó a los plantadores.

1835

Pinzón de cactus de Galápagos, una especie descrita por Charles Darwin.

EN EL OCÉANO PACÍFICO, a casi mil kilómetros de la costa sudamericana, el naturalista inglés **Charles Darwin** (1809–1882) tomaba notas sobre la flora y la fauna de las **islas Galápagos**. Darwin había aceptado un puesto en una expedición científica a bordo del *Beagle*, que zarpó de Inglaterra el 27 de diciembre de 1831 y llegó a las Galápagos en septiembre de 1835 (*véase también* 1839). Fue allí donde pudo observar por primera vez la diferencia entre las especies de aquellas islas y las del continente sudamericano. Este importante descubrimiento sentó las bases de su obra científica posterior acerca de la **evolución** de las especies (*véase* 1859).

En Gran Bretaña se había fundado la **National Colonisation Society** para facilitar el asentamiento de no convictos en Australia. Su fundador, **Edward Gibbon Wakefield** (1796–1862), que estuvo en prisión, ideó un sistema para poblar las colonias basado en la venta de terrenos y en un impuesto sobre su precio con el que se podría costear el transporte hasta la colonia. Una flota zarpó hacia **Australia Meridional**, donde en 1835 se fundó Melbourne, y un año después, Adelaida.

> « PARECE SER UN **PEQUEÑO MUNDO EN SÍ MISMO**. »
>
> **Charles Darwin**, en *Diario de investigaciones* (septiembre de 1835)

1836

El Álamo, escenario de una batalla crucial en la independencia de Texas.

MUCHOS COLONOS ESTADOUNIDENSES que se dirigían hacia el oeste decidieron quedarse en Texas, que pertenecía a México. Sin embargo, las autoridades mexicanas quisieron aumentar su control sobre este vasto territorio, y los colonos se rebelaron en octubre de 1835, iniciando la **guerra de la Independencia de Texas**. Tras meses de conflicto, en febrero del año siguiente, el general mexicano Antonio López de Santa Anna (1794–1876) atacó Texas con cinco mil soldados. Pese a su superioridad numérica, los rebeldes lograron resistir en El Álamo, un fuerte de San Antonio. Al final sucumbieron el 6 de marzo, pero El Álamo pasó a ser punto de reunión de los texanos, decididos a vengarse. Poco después, el general **Samuel Houston** (1793–1863) dirigió un ejército texano con el grito de guerra «¡Recordad El Álamo!» y venció a Santa Anna el 21 de abril en la **batalla de San Jacinto**. México se vio obligado a reconocer a la nueva república de Texas.

Batalla de El Álamo
Los mexicanos superaban con mucho a los texanos durante el sitio, entre el 23 de febrero y el 6 de marzo. Muy pocos texanos sobrevivieron.

1837

Coronación de la reina Victoria en la abadía de Westminster.

Comunicaciones a larga distancia
Telégrafo eléctrico con una única aguja, que más tarde evolucionó en aparatos con dos y cuatro agujas.

HACÍA YA DÉCADAS QUE SE EXPERIMENTABA sobre cómo transmitir la corriente eléctrica a través de cables. En 1837, dos inventores británicos, **Charles Wheatstone** y **William Fothergill Cooke**, dieron un gran paso al patentar un **telégrafo eléctrico** que hacía posible la comunicación por cable y cuyas **agujas podían señalar letras y números concretos**. En esa misma época, en EE. UU., **Samuel Morse** también patentaba un transmisor electromagnético que podía transferir información por medio de puntos y guiones. El telégrafo de Morse, mucho más sencillo

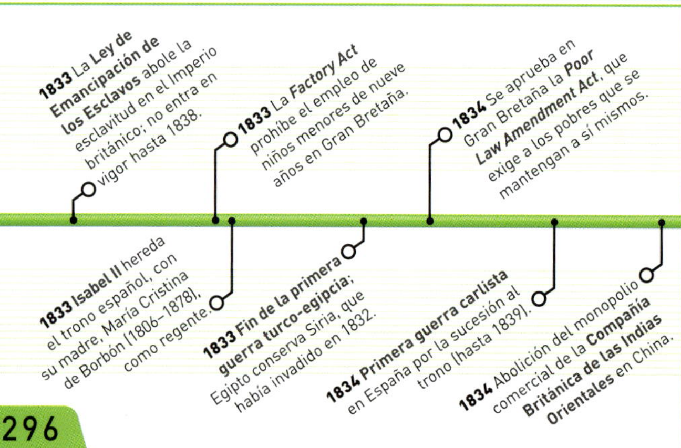

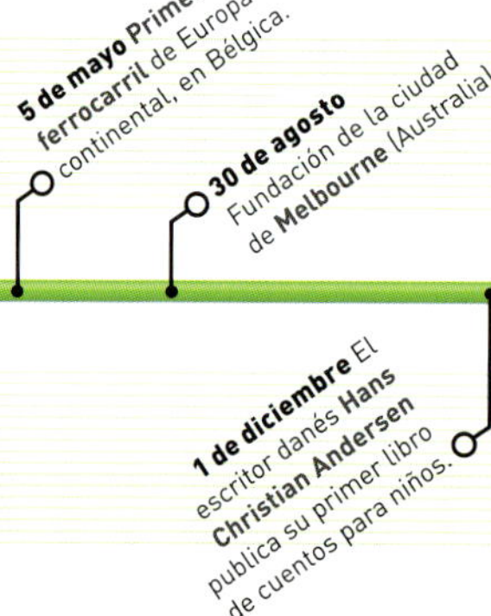

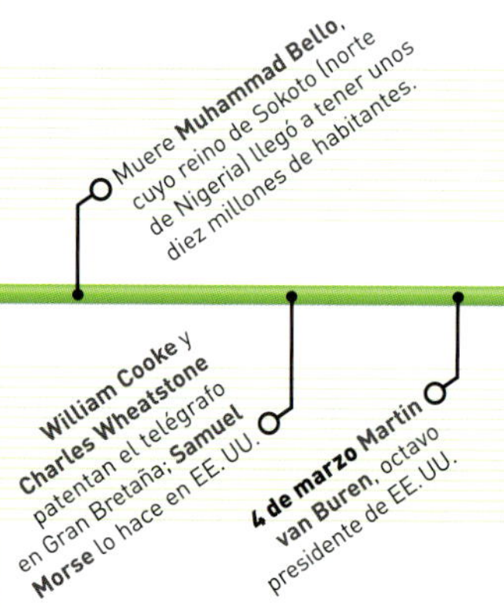

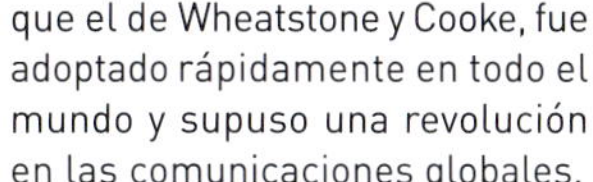

que el de Wheatstone y Cooke, fue adoptado rápidamente en todo el mundo y supuso una revolución en las comunicaciones globales.

En otro orden de cosas, la muerte del rey Guillermo IV de Gran Bretaña, el 20 de junio, sin dejar herederos legítimos supervivientes, planteaba un problema sucesorio que se resolvió cuando la corona pasó a su sobrina **Victoria** (*véase* recuadro), hija de Eduardo, duque de Kent, y nieta de Jorge III. El largo reinado de Victoria I fue una era de innovación tecnológica, de prosperidad creciente y de expansión colonial para Gran Bretaña.

Entre tanto, en **Japón**, **Tokugawa Ieyoshi** (1793–1853) se convirtió en sogún. En aquel momento, el país se encontraba sumido en un declive social y económico. La serie de medidas conocidas como **reformas Tempo**, que introdujo con el fin de limitar la migración a las áreas urbanas y fomentar el control de precios, fracasaron.

VICTORIA I (1819–1901)

El reinado de la reina Victoria fue uno de los más largos de un monarca británico: 63 años y 216 días. En 1840 se casó con su primo, Alberto de Sajonia-Coburgo-Gotha (1819–1861), al que adoraba, y tuvo nueve hijos con él. La era victoriana contrastó drásticamente con los excesos de los anteriores soberanos Hanover, y la vida doméstica de la reina Victoria se consideró un modelo para las familias de la época.

1838

« **CONSEGUIRÁ** LLEVARNOS **HASTA LA LUNA.** »

Director de la Great Western Railway, sobre Isambard Kingdom Brunel

El *Great Western* de Brunel
El barco Great Western *navegando cerca de la costa oeste de Inglaterra. Aunque contaba con velas, estaba impulsado por la fuerza del vapor.*

LA TECNOLOGÍA DEL TRANSPORTE estaba cambiando a toda velocidad. Junto con la expansión del ferrocarril, varias innovaciones habían revolucionado también el transporte por mar. Finalmente se había conseguido aprovechar el vapor de un modo eficiente, hecho que permitía navegar mucho más rápido por mar (*véase* 1786). El 8 de abril de 1838, un vapor con rueda de paletas, que se bautizó con el nombre de ***Great Western*** zarpó desde el puerto de Bristol para su primer viaje transatlántico y arribó a Nueva York quince días después. Había reducido el tiempo del viaje a la mitad y, además, le había sobrado combustible. Su diseñador, el ingeniero civil inglés **Isambard Kingdom Brunel** (1806–1859), que anteriormente ya había participado en otros proyectos de ingeniería, como el del ferrocarril Great Western Railway, sugirió la idea del barco de vapor a los directores de la compañía para que prolongasen la línea de ferrocarril, con un servicio transatlántico regular, hasta Nueva York. Poco después se fundó la **Great Western Steamship Company** para facilitar la construcción del barco.

En América, **Guatemala**, **Honduras** y **Nicaragua** se separaron de las Provincias Unidas de América Central y se convirtieron en naciones independientes.

1839

El vapor *Nemesis*, de la Compañía Británica de las Indias Orientales, ataca a unos juncos chinos en la bahía de Anson, durante la primera guerra del Opio.

EL COMERCIO BRITÁNICO CON CHINA SEGUÍA CRECIENDO, pero también el problema del opio chino. Décadas antes, la Compañía Británica de las Indias Orientales había comenzado a exportar a China la droga (producida a partir de **adormideras** en Bengala) a cambio de té, que expedía a Gran Bretaña. A pesar de los múltiples intentos de prohibir dicha sustancia, los barcos británicos continuaron importándola. El 30 de marzo de 1839, un frustrado inspector chino ordenó la destrucción de los almacenes y de los barcos británicos de Cantón. Como represalia, Gran Bretaña envió barcos de guerra y atacó las costas chinas, en la **primera guerra del Opio**.

Entre tanto, las tensiones entre Egipto y el sultán otomano habían vuelto a estallar, con la **segunda guerra turco-egipcia**. Esta vez el desencadenante fue el intento del Imperio otomano de invadir Siria, que había cedido anteriormente a Egipto (*véase* 1833).

Al mismo tiempo, la intervención británica en Afganistán dio lugar a **la primera guerra afgana** (hasta 1842). Preocupada por la creciente influencia rusa sobre **Dust Muhammad** (1793–1863), el emir afgano, Gran Bretaña intentó sustituirlo por un emir que fuera más afín a los intereses que el Imperio británico tenía en el norte de India, como la protección de las rutas comerciales terrestres que atravesaban la región.

En Inglaterra, el naturalista Charles Darwin (*véase* 1835) publicó el diario que había escrito durante su expedición a bordo del ***Beagle***, con el que había dado la vuelta al mundo. Zarpó de Plymouth en 1831 hacia las islas de Cabo Verde, y luego hacia Brasil, Argentina, Uruguay y Tierra del Fuego. A continuación, se dirigió al norte a lo largo de la costa pacífica sudamericana y recaló en las islas Galápagos antes de seguir rumbo a Tahití, Nueva Zelanda, Australia y Mauricio para finalmente volver a Inglaterra, adonde llegó en octubre de 1836. Su diario le ayudó a alcanzar la fama científica.

VIAJE DE DARWIN
Feb. 1832 → Sep. 1835

El periplo de Darwin a bordo del *Beagle*
El viaje de Darwin en el Beagle *(1831–1836), un barco de guerra con diez cañones, le llevó a conclusiones científicas nuevas y revolucionarias.*

20 de junio Victoria (1819–1901) se convierte en monarca británica.

Louis Daguerre desarrolla la técnica fotográfica del **daguerrotipo**.

Las **rebeliones del Alto y el Bajo Canadá** contra el gobierno británico son reprimidas.

28 de septiembre Muere **Akbar II** (n. 1760), último emperador mogol de India.

Inicio del movimiento **cartista** a favor de reformas sociales en Gran Bretaña.

Guatemala, Honduras y **Nicaragua** se independizan.

8–23 de abril El vapor *Great Western* de Isambard Kingdom Brunel (1806–1859) **cruza el Atlántico en un tiempo récord.**

26 de mayo En EE. UU., traslado forzoso de los **cherokees** por el **Sendero de las Lágrimas.**

10 de junio Matanza de Myall Creek (Australia): 28 aborígenes son asesinados por colonos.

El químico sueco **Jons Jakob Berzelius** (1779–1848) descubre las **proteínas**.

16 de diciembre Victoria de los bóers sobre los zulúes en la batalla del río Blood (Sudáfrica).

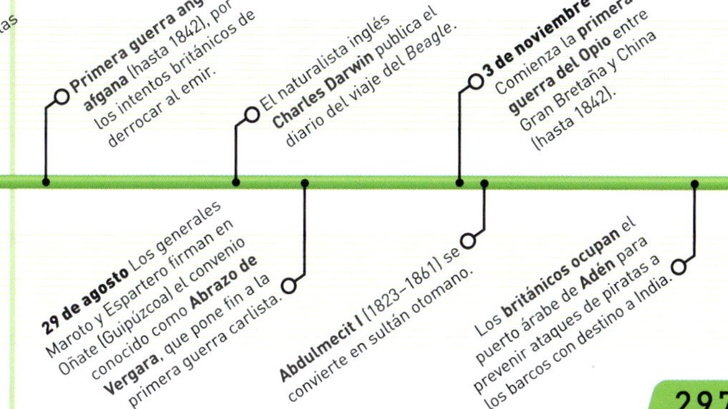

Primera guerra anglo-afgana (hasta 1842), por los intentos británicos de derrocar al emir.

El naturalista inglés **Charles Darwin** publica el diario del viaje del *Beagle*.

29 de agosto Los generales Maroto y Espartero firman en Oñate (Guipúzcoa) el convenio conocido como **Abrazo de Vergara**, que pone fin a la primera guerra carlista.

3 de noviembre Comienza la **primera guerra del Opio** entre Gran Bretaña y China (hasta 1842).

Abdulmecit I (1823–1861) se convierte en sultán otomano.

Los **británicos ocupan** el puerto árabe de **Adén** para prevenir ataques de piratas a los barcos con destino a India.

HISTORIA DE LA ELECTRICIDAD

APROVECHAMIENTO DE LA FUERZA QUE LEVANTÓ EL MUNDO MODERNO

Cuando el matemático y filósofo griego Tales de Mileto experimentó con un fragmento de ámbar (*elektron* en griego) no podía imaginar que sus observaciones iban a ocupar un lugar de honor en la ciencia más de dos mil años después.

Tales observó que si frotaba con pelo de animal un trozo de ámbar, este atraía polvo y plumas próximos; aunque desconocía la causa, había descubierto lo que hoy llamamos electricidad estática. A lo largo de los siglos posteriores, científicos de todo el mundo experimentaron sobre esta forma de electricidad, así como sobre los imanes y el magnetismo. En los siglos XVII y XVIII ya se habían dado grandes pasos tecnológicos, aunque la relación entre la electricidad y los imanes no se hizo evidente hasta el siglo XIX (*véase* recuadro).

ELECTRICIDAD PARA EL PUEBLO

A medida que avanzaba el siglo XIX, mejoraba la comprensión de la electricidad y las innovaciones se sucedían rápidamente. A principios del siglo XX ya habían aparecido muchas de las tecnologías que se siguen usando hoy en día, adaptadas y mejoradas (como las pilas y las bombillas). El reto tecnológico actual es encontrar un sistema no contaminante de generación de electricidad.

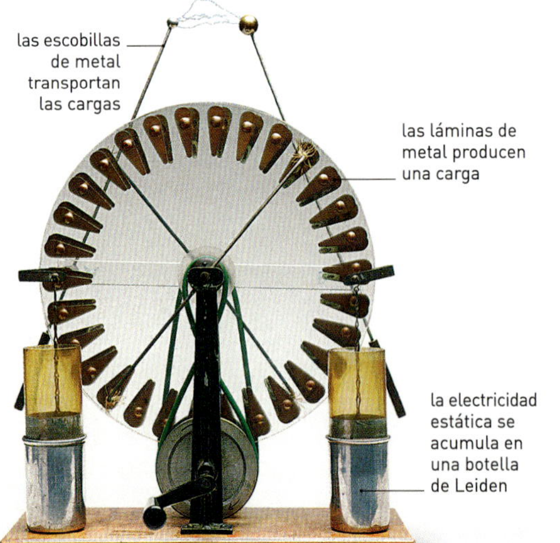

Máquina de Wimshurst
El inglés James Wimshurst desarrolló un dispositivo que generaba electricidad estática y la almacenaba en un recipiente llamado botella de Leiden. Durante muchos años, los científicos que estudiaban la electricidad usaron la máquina de Wimshurst para generar cargas eléctricas.

Bombilla de rosca de Edison
Aunque suele atribuírsele el invento de la bombilla, lo cierto es que Thomas Edison mejoró una idea ya existente (véase cronología, p. 299). Dedicó varios años a dar con un modo de generar luz eléctrica (con bombillas de incandescencia) práctica y segura para su utilización pública.

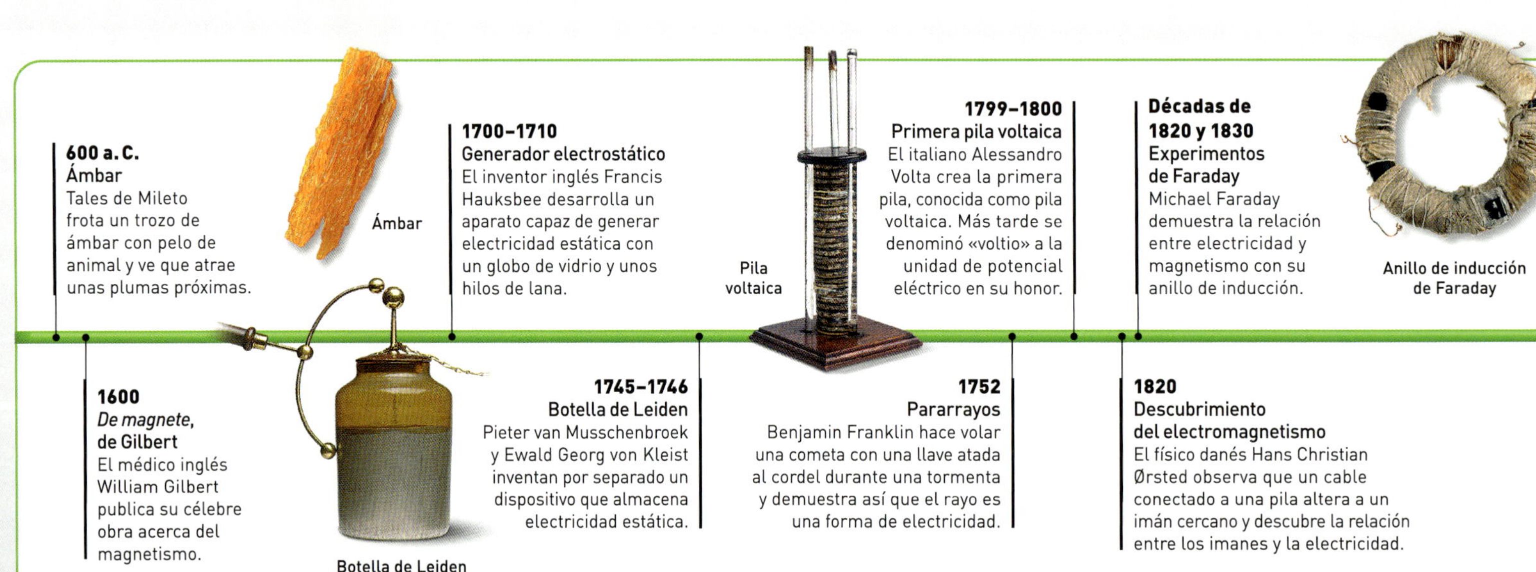

600 a. C.
Ámbar
Tales de Mileto frota un trozo de ámbar con pelo de animal y ve que atrae unas plumas próximas.

1600
***De magnete*, de Gilbert**
El médico inglés William Gilbert publica su célebre obra acerca del magnetismo.

1700-1710
Generador electrostático
El inventor inglés Francis Hauksbee desarrolla un aparato capaz de generar electricidad estática con un globo de vidrio y unos hilos de lana.

1745-1746
Botella de Leiden
Pieter van Musschenbroek y Ewald Georg von Kleist inventan por separado un dispositivo que almacena electricidad estática.

1752
Pararrayos
Benjamin Franklin hace volar una cometa con una llave atada al cordel durante una tormenta y demuestra así que el rayo es una forma de electricidad.

1799-1800
Primera pila voltaica
El italiano Alessandro Volta crea la primera pila, conocida como pila voltaica. Más tarde se denominó «voltio» a la unidad de potencial eléctrico en su honor.

1820
Descubrimiento del electromagnetismo
El físico danés Hans Christian Ørsted observa que un cable conectado a una pila altera a un imán cercano y descubre la relación entre los imanes y la electricidad.

Décadas de 1820 y 1830
Experimentos de Faraday
Michael Faraday demuestra la relación entre electricidad y magnetismo con su anillo de inducción.

« EL GENIO ES SOLO UN UNO POR CIENTO DE INSPIRACIÓN Y UN NOVENTA Y NUEVE POR CIENTO DE TRANSPIRACIÓN. »

Thomas Edison, inventor estadounidense (*c.* 1903)

la bombilla debe contener gas inerte

el vacío parcial en la bombilla permite que los filamentos alcancen temperaturas elevadas sin incendiarse

el alambre conduce la electricidad hacia y desde el filamento

el extremo metálico (casquillo) se enrosca en la lámpara

el contacto transmite la electricidad

un filamento de bambú carbonizado transporta los electrones

el filamento se vuelve incandescente cuando la corriente lo atraviesa

MICHAEL FARADAY (1791–1867)

Este inventor inglés desempeñó un importante papel para el conocimiento de la relación entre los imanes y la electricidad. Su descubrimiento de lo que denominó «rotación electromagnética» resultó crucial para el desarrollo del motor eléctrico. Faraday descubrió que la interacción entre la electricidad y un imán llevaba a la rotación constante de la corriente y lo probó usando un imán, un cable que transportaba electricidad y un recipiente con mercurio.

1878–1879
Bombilla eléctrica
Joseph Swan, inventor británico, concibe una «lámpara eléctrica» incandescente. Más tarde el estadounidense Thomas Edison mejora esta idea y desarrolla la bombilla.

Presa Hoover

1882
Hidroelectricidad
Los científicos se dan cuenta de que la fuerza del agua puede generar electricidad. Para aprovechar esta energía se construyen presas y centrales hidroeléctricas.

Turbina de vapor

1884
Electricidad mediante vapor
También el vapor de agua se aprovecha para producir electricidad mediante dispositivos como la turbina, creada por Charles Patton.

Principios del siglo XXI
Electricidad sostenible
La preocupación por la contaminación causada por los sistemas de generación de energía lleva al desarrollo de tecnologías «verdes», como las turbinas movidas por el viento.

Turbinas eólicas

1825
Electroimán
Este dispositivo de Joseph Henry lleva dos placas metálicas que se sumergen en ácido para formar una célula voltaica.

Electroimán de Henry

1881
Primer alumbrado eléctrico público
La ciudad inglesa de Godalming (Surrey) pone fin a la era de las farolas de gas al iluminar las calles con electricidad.

Bobina de Tesla

1883–1884
La bobina de Tesla
Nikola Tesla desarrolla una bobina que puede transmitir electricidad a larga distancia. Este descubrimiento permite la generalización de la electricidad.

Década de 1950
Energía nuclear
Los científicos descubren cómo usar los átomos (en reacciones nucleares controladas) como fuente de energía para calentar agua, que a su vez genera electricidad. En 1951 se construye la primera central nuclear del mundo en EE. UU., en Arco (Idaho).

1840

Un carruaje abandona una estación de Londres para repartir el correo. La evolución de la diligencia permitió repartir el correo por toda Gran Bretaña.

LA PRESENCIA EUROPEA en Nueva Zelanda llevaba una década aumentando progresivamente, periodo en el que se habían asentado en la región numerosas misiones. Los colonos comerciaban con los **maoríes**, primeros pobladores de la isla, e intercambiaban mosquetes por cereales y otros alimentos. Como consecuencia, ya había tenido lugar la primera carrera armamentística entre tribus rivales durante las **guerras de los Mosquetes** (1820–1835).

Los británicos querían establecer una colonia, por lo que fundaron la **Compañía de Nueva Zelanda**, que vendía tierras para los asentamientos (*véase* 1835). En 1839, un barco de colonos, cuya tripulación sabía que los maoríes podrían mostrarse hostiles, zarpó rumbo a Nueva Zelanda. En 1840, el vicegobernador de Nueva Zelanda, William Hobson (1792–1842), presentó el **tratado de Waitangi** a los jefes maoríes, por el que los británicos les brindaban protección a cambio de la soberanía sobre la isla. Los maoríes conservarían sus tierras; además, podían venderlas, pero solo a la corona británica. Al principio acogieron el tratado con hostilidad, pero algunos jefes maoríes confiaron en que la presencia británica aportaría estabilidad al país; así, pues, el 21 de mayo se proclamó la soberanía británica sobre el territorio.

En Reino Unido se reformó el **sistema postal**. Con las mejoras del transporte se pudo repartir el correo por todo el país, pero los costes aumentaron, puesto que el timbrado se pagaba en destino según la distancia. Se propuso un sistema de **«correo a penique»**, por el cual los envíos se pagaban por adelantado mediante sellos. Este sistema, el primero de este tipo en todo el mundo, entró en vigor en 1840.

Tamati Waka Nene
Nene, caudillo guerrero de la tribu maorí ngatihoa a principios del siglo XIX, apoyó el tratado de Waitangi.

Población de Nueva Zelanda (1840)
La población de origen europeo aún era escasa hacia finales de 1840. El tratado de Waitangi allanaría el camino a nuevos asentamientos.

1841

El puerto de Hong Kong, clave en el comercio británico con Oriente.

LA GUERRA DEL OPIO entre chinos y británicos proseguía. Un contingente de barcos británicos ascendió por el río Perla y fue capturando los fuertes situados alrededor de Cantón y los puertos de Amoy y Ningpo. Los británicos ocuparon también el puerto clave de Hong Kong. En el mes de enero se redactó el borrador de la **Convención de Chuenpee**, un acuerdo preliminar con el que se intentaba poner fin a la guerra y por el que China cedía Hong Kong a los británicos. Sin embargo, el documento fue redactado en un momento de hostilidades y nunca llegó a ratificarse.

Mientras tanto, la **guerra por Siria** que enfrentaba a egipcios y turcos (*véase* 1839) finalizó con la retirada egipcia de Siria.

1842

Caravana de esclavos africanos. El comercio de esclavos prevaleció en muchas partes del mundo a pesar de los crecientes esfuerzos por erradicarlo.

FIN DE LA GUERRA DEL OPIO. Las tropas británicas lograron conquistar más territorio hasta alcanzar Nankín en agosto. Las autoridades chinas se apresuraron a pactar la paz y el 29 de agosto se firmó el **tratado de Nankín**. China aceptó pagar una indemnización de veinte millones de libras y ceder Hong Kong a los británicos; además, debió abrir al comercio los puertos de Cantón, Amoy, Foochow, Ningpo y Shanghai, llamados desde entonces los **«puertos del tratado»**.

La explotación infantil en condiciones laborales antihigiénicas y peligrosas en la industria y la **minería** era habitual. En Gran Bretaña, Anthony Ashley Cooper, sociólogo reformista y séptimo conde de Shaftesbury (1801–1885), fue uno de los defensores de la **Ley de Minas de 1842**, que prohibía que los niños menores de diez años y las mujeres trabajaran en la industria minera. El estado de Massachusetts (EE. UU.) fijó la **jornada laboral infantil máxima** en diez horas. El rey Leopoldo I de Bélgica también intentó regular las condiciones laborales de niños y mujeres, pero sus propuestas fueron rechazadas.

El **comercio de esclavos** aún persistía. Francia había reinstaurado la esclavitud en sus colonias (*véase* 1803). Gran Bretaña había abolido el comercio de esclavos en 1807, pero España no cumplió el tratado de abolición que había firmado en 1817 hasta décadas después. Tampoco se respetaron el tratado entre Gran Bretaña y **Portugal** de 1818 ni otros posteriores. Aunque Portugal no abolió la esclavitud en sus colonias, en 1842 un nuevo tratado permitió que los barcos británicos atacaran a los portugueses que zarparan del este de África con esclavos. La colonia portuguesa de **Mozambique** era un gran puerto esclavista del que entre 1820 y 1830 partieron quince mil esclavos al año.

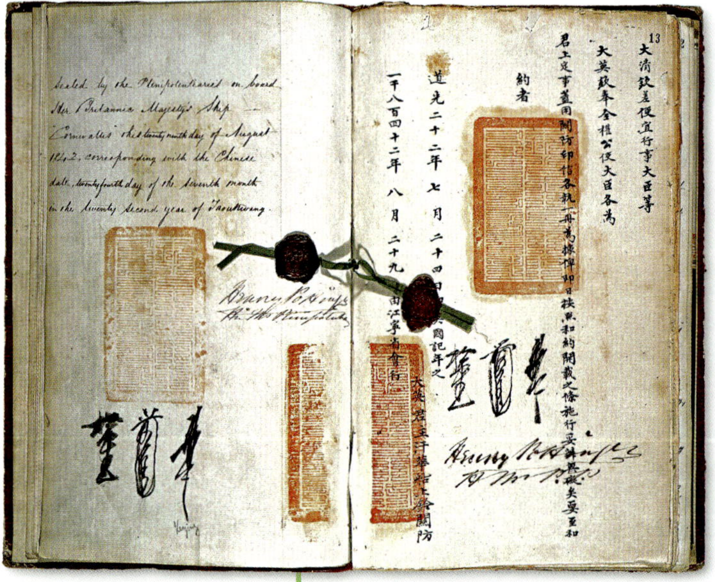

Tratado de Nankín
Puso fin a la guerra del Opio, que duró tres años. China cedió Hong Kong a Gran Bretaña y abrió al comercio los cinco «puertos del tratado».

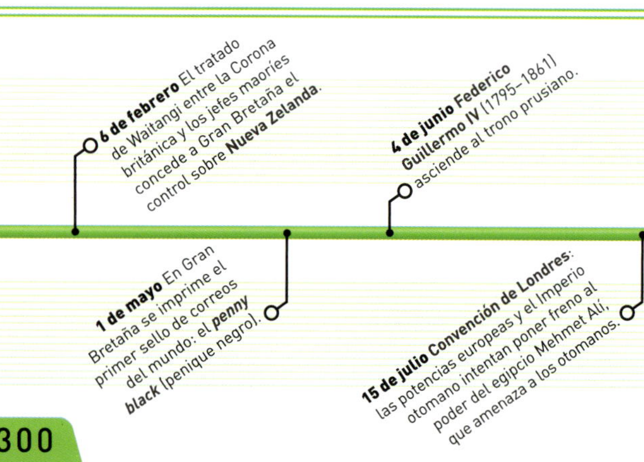

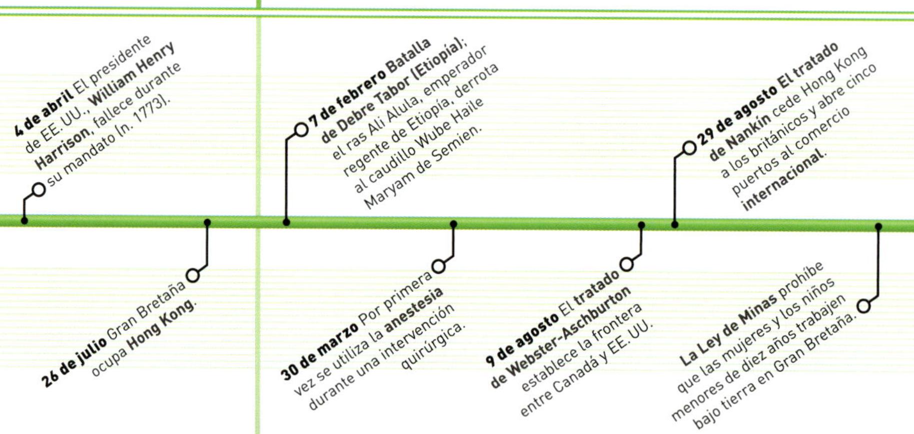

1843

Retrato de Abdul Rahman, cuyo padre, Faisal, resucitó la potencia saudí.

LA DESTRUCCIÓN OTOMANA del primer estado saudí (*véase* 1818), fundado por el movimiento wahabí y la familia **Saud**, no evitó la fundación de un nuevo estado saudí en 1824. Tras las revueltas iniciales, **Faisal al Saud**, segundo líder del segundo estado, retomó el gobierno en 1843 y lo dirigió con éxito hasta 1865.

En Sudáfrica, tras varias derrotas de la tribu zulú, los colonos bóers (*véase* 1880) fundaron la **República de Natal** en el sureste del país, región que los británicos se anexionarían en 1843. Muchos bóers decidieron trasladarse al norte, hacia lo que más tarde se convertiría en el Transvaal y el Estado Libre de Orange, sumándose así a los emigrantes bóers de la colonia de El Cabo, en un movimiento migratorio conocido como el **Gran Trek**.

12 000

ES EL NÚMERO DE BÓERS QUE EMIGRARON DESDE LA COLONIA DE EL CABO

Pese al tratado entre maoríes y británicos en Nueva Zelanda (*véase* 1840), las ventas ilegales de tierras dieron lugar a una escalada de tensiones que culminó con la **masacre de Wairau** el 17 de junio, en que murieron la esposa de uno de los jefes y 22 europeos.

1844

« LO QUE DIOS HA CREADO. »

Mensaje telegrafiado por Samuel Morse, artista e inventor estadounidense

Con el respaldo del gobierno de EE. UU., Samuel Morse logró que se tendieran cables para transmitir mensajes.

Friedrich Engels
El filósofo prusiano escribió sobre las condiciones de vida de la clase obrera inglesa. Su trabajo con Karl Marx le haría famoso.

FRIEDRICH ENGELS (1820–1895) era hijo de un próspero industrial con varias fábricas textiles en Prusia y una fábrica de algodón en Inglaterra. En 1841 empezó a trabajar en la fábrica familiar en Manchester, pero en realidad llevaba una doble vida: en su tiempo libre se reunía con trabajadores y estudiaba los requisitos económicos de los ingleses. El resultado fue ***La situación de la clase obrera en Inglaterra,*** libro en el que Engels describía las condiciones de vida del proletariado. De esta época data también su amistad con el escritor y filósofo **Karl Marx** (1818–1883). Juntos escribirían obras, de históricas repercusiones, sobre el capitalismo y el comunismo.

Entre tanto, en el Caribe, un grupo de conspiradores conocidos como **La Trinitaria**, liderados por Juan Pablo Duarte (1813–1876), emprendieron la lucha por la independencia de la mitad hispanohablante de la isla La Española (*véase* 1822). Mientras la vecina Haití se hallaba inmersa en su propia guerra civil, Duarte y sus seguidores lograron expulsar a los haitianos, y a renglón seguido declararon la independencia de la nueva **República Dominicana** el 27 de febrero.

Mientras, Samuel Morse (*véase* 1837) había logrado obtener financiación del gobierno estadounidense para construir la primera **línea de telégrafo** desde Baltimore hasta Washington, que se completó en 1844. Ese año, en su primera demostración pública del telégrafo, envió un mensaje que se haría famoso: «¡Lo que Dios ha creado!».

Hierro y vidrio
El invernadero de palmeras de los Reales Jardines Botánicos de Kew (Reino Unido) fue edificado en 1844 con placas de vidrio y, por vez primera en una estructura de semejantes dimensiones, con hierro forjado.

1845

Víctimas de la hambruna irlandesa. Un millón de personas murieron al malograrse la cosecha de patata; varios millones más emigraron a América.

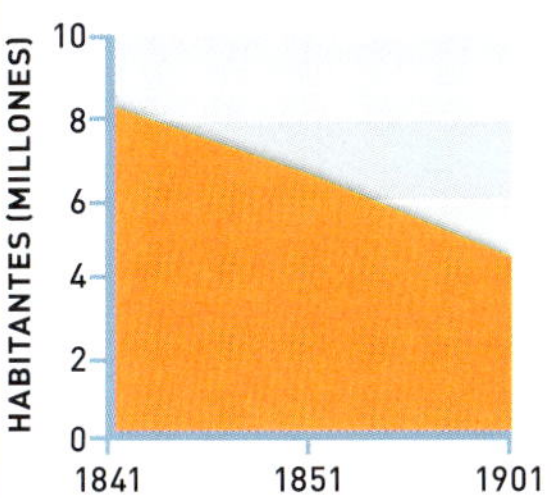

Declive demográfico en Irlanda
A inicios del siglo XX, las muertes, pero sobre todo la emigración masiva para huir de las penurias, redujo la población irlandesa a la mitad.

LAS REPETIDAS PÉRDIDAS de la cosecha de patata en Irlanda por el **tizón tardío** (*véase* recuadro) causaron una hambruna de cinco años y más de un millón de muertos, sobre todo porque la patata era el principal sustento de millones de campesinos. La respuesta del gobierno británico fue insuficiente: no intervino directamente y delegó el asunto en los terratenientes. Dado que muchos agricultores arrendatarios no tenían cosecha que vender, no pagaban los arrendamientos y los terratenientes los echaron de sus tierras. Los terratenientes dejaron de poder asistir a los pobres locales o simplemente se negaron a ello. Además, muchas de las mayores explotaciones agrícolas del país siguieron exportando grano, carne y otros alimentos a Inglaterra, pues en Irlanda no había mercado ni dinero para adquirir estos bienes. El hecho de que no se repartieran estos alimentos a las personas que morían de hambre en Irlanda contribuyó a tensar aún más las relaciones entre los irlandeses y el gobierno británico. Más de dos millones de irlandeses **emigraron** a Inglaterra, EE. UU. o Canadá, lo que contribuyó a que la población se redujera de 8 a 6,5 millones de habitantes entre 1841 y 1851.

Mientras, la república de Texas había intentado pertenecer a EE. UU. sin éxito desde 1836, pero el gobierno estadounidense se oponía. La petición fue aprobada en diciembre, cuando EE. UU. comprendió que Gran Bretaña estaba interesada en que Texas siguiera siendo independiente con el único fin de frenar su expansión hacia el oeste.

PLAGA DE LA PATATA

El tizón tardío que malogró la cosecha de la patata era *Phytophthora infestans*, un moho que pudría el tubérculo en dos semanas. Esta plaga se propaga deprisa cuando la humedad supera el 75 % y la temperatura los 10 °C durante dos días enteros. Ambos factores se dieron en el verano de 1845. Ese otoño, toda la cosecha se perdió y la gente abandonó el campo.

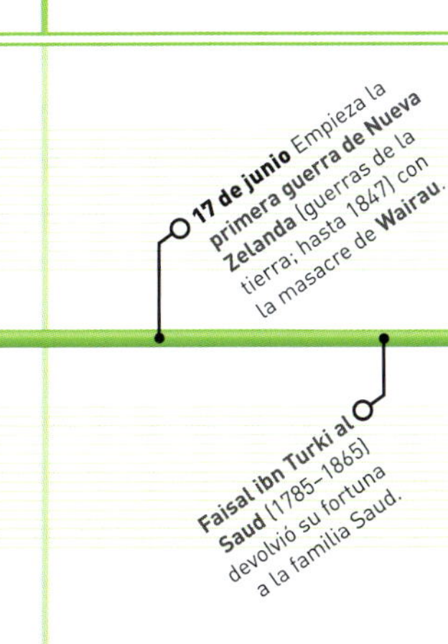

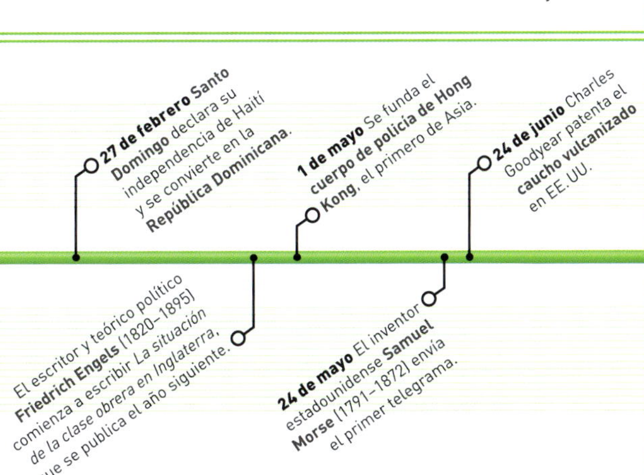

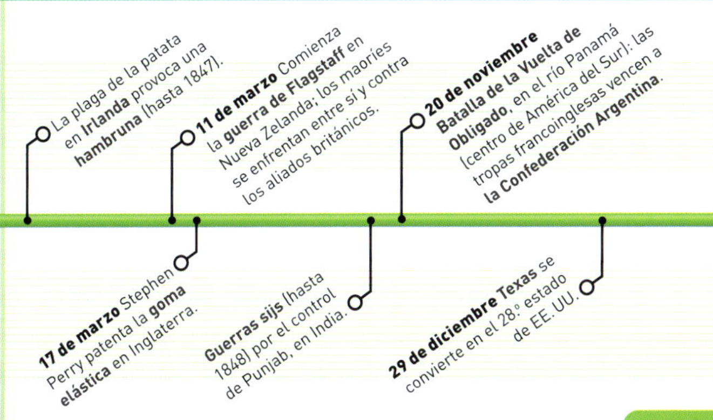

1846

Batalla de Palo Alto cerca de Brownsville (Texas), primera de la guerra entre México y EE. UU., desencadenada por discrepancias sobre las fronteras.

LAS RELACIONES ENTRE MÉXICO Y EE. UU. SE VOLVIERON TENSAS cuando Texas se convirtió en el 28.º estado (*véase* 1845). México era contrario a la anexión; además, EE. UU. declaraba que la frontera sur de Texas corría paralela al río Grande, mientras **México** afirmaba que se hallaba más al norte, en el río Nueces. En 1845, EE. UU. envió una delegación diplomática a Ciudad de México para zanjar la cuestión e intentar comprar Nuevo México y California, pero fue en vano. El 25 de abril de 1846, las tropas mexicanas cruzaron el río Grande y atacaron a los soldados estacionados allí. El presidente de EE. UU., **James K. Polk** (1795–1849), declaró la guerra, que duró hasta la rendición de México en 1847.

EE. UU. mantuvo **disputas fronterizas** también con Gran Bretaña por el territorio de Oregón, entre los 42° N y los 54° 40' N. EE. UU. reclamaba las tierras hasta los 54° 40' N, de ahí el lema de campaña de Polk: «¡Cincuenta y cuatro cuarenta o lucha!». Finalmente, por el **tratado de Oregón** de 1846 la frontera se estableció en los 49° N.

En Gran Bretaña hacía décadas que las **leyes** que controlaban la importación y la exportación **de cereales** provocaban controversias. Las malas cosechas, los bloqueos y las interrupciones del suministro durante la guerra habían dado lugar a la fluctuación de los precios del trigo. La legislación para proteger la agricultura nacional mediante la limitación de la importación de cereal barato y la fijación de precios tuvo una mala acogida y originó la fundación de la Liga contra la **Ley de los Cereales** en 1839. La Liga alegaba que estas leyes impedían el progreso, ya que la restricción de las **importaciones** de cereales provocaba subidas de los precios y aumentos del coste de los salarios. Además, el control de las exportaciones limitaba el mercado exterior para los bienes británicos. La combinación de las presiones de la Liga y la pérdida de la cosecha de patata en Irlanda (*véase* 1845) forzaron la derogación de las leyes.

Japón era una **nación aislacionista**, pero la presión internacional intentaba que abriera sus puertos al comercio exterior. Los holandeses, que eran los únicos europeos autorizados a comerciar en Japón dentro de ciertos límites, enviaron una delegación en 1844 para instar a los gobernantes nipones a que abrieran sus fronteras. Franceses y británicos pidieron derechos mercantiles. En 1846, una delegación de EE. UU. también fracasó, pero los estadounidenses no tardarían en volver a intentar acceder a los puertos japoneses (*véase* 1853).

> « ¡**CINCUENTA** Y CUATRO **CUARENTA O LUCHA**! »
>
> **William Allen**, gobernador de Ohio, durante la campaña electoral

1847

Rebelión de Abd el-Kader
Pese a que las tropas argelinas eran muy inferiores en número a las francesas, Abd el-Kader supo aprovechar la táctica de guerrilla.

DURANTE LOS AÑOS POSTERIORES A LA INVASIÓN Y LA COLONIZACIÓN DE ARGEL (*véase* 1830) por parte de Francia, los argelinos ofrecieron una enorme resistencia. El emir **Abd el-Kader** (1807–1883) consiguió el apoyo de las tribus argelinas en la lucha contra los franceses. Después de varias derrotas fue obligado a **rendirse** en 1847, y aunque cayó prisionero, posteriormente fue puesto en libertad.

Ese mismo año, en Alemania, una empresa propiedad de **Werner Siemens** (1816–1892), quien había desarrollado una técnica para aislar el hilo de cobre a la perfección, instaló una **línea de telégrafo** entre Frankfurt y Berlín.

En Inglaterra, la escritora inglesa **Emily Brontë** (1818–1848) publicó *Cumbres borrascosas*. Si bien la novela no fue muy bien acogida por la crítica, más tarde acabaría convirtiéndose en una de las principales influencias literarias del **romanticismo**.

1848

Cartel de 1848 en el que los parisinos se enfrentan a la guardia municipal durante la revolución de febrero contra el gobierno.

FRIEDRICH ENGELS Y KARL MARX (*véase* 1844) se unieron a un grupo de revolucionarios alemanes conocidos como la Liga de los Justos, aunque pronto cambiarían su nombre por el de la **Liga de los Comunistas**. Engels y Marx se encargaron de desarrollar un programa de acción para el grupo, y el resultado fue el panfleto que se conocería más tarde como ***Manifiesto del Partido Comunista***. En él instaban a derrocar a la burguesía al grito de «¡trabajadores del mundo, uníos!». Marx creía que el abismo entre ricos y pobres en Europa ofrecía las condiciones adecuadas para una revolución socialista.

En febrero, tan solo un par de semanas tras la publicación del manifiesto, la revolución estalló en las calles de París. Aunque fue dramática y violenta, no se trató de un levantamiento socialista. **Francia** llevaba tiempo sufriendo una crisis económica y el ministro **François Guizot** pasó a simbolizar la incapacidad del gobierno para solucionar la situación. La monarquía no estaba mucho mejor valorada, ya que la popularidad del rey Luis Felipe (*véase* 1830) también era muy baja. La lucha estalló el 22 de febrero y pronto se volvió violenta. Los soldados abrieron fuego contra las masas, por lo que al día siguiente

Revueltas en Europa
Los levantamientos republicanos en 1848 pusieron fin a la monarquía en Francia; los revolucionarios tuvieron, en cambio, menos éxito en otros países.

Tras años de protestas, las proteccionistas **leyes de los cereales** son abolidas en Gran Bretaña.

EE. UU. entra en guerra con **México** (hasta 1848) por el territorio de Texas.

Segunda guerra carlista en España entre las fuerzas carlistas y las de Isabel II.

Elias Howe patenta la **máquina de coser** en EE. UU.

Richard March Hoe inventa la **rotativa** en EE. UU.

23 de septiembre Los astrónomos alemanes **Johann Gottfried Galle** y **Heinrich Louis d'Arrest** observan por primera vez el planeta Neptuno.

El **Imperio otomano** cede la isla de **Abadán** en Irán al Imperio persa.

26 de julio **Liberia** declara su independencia.

La **resistencia argelina** se enfrenta a los franceses.

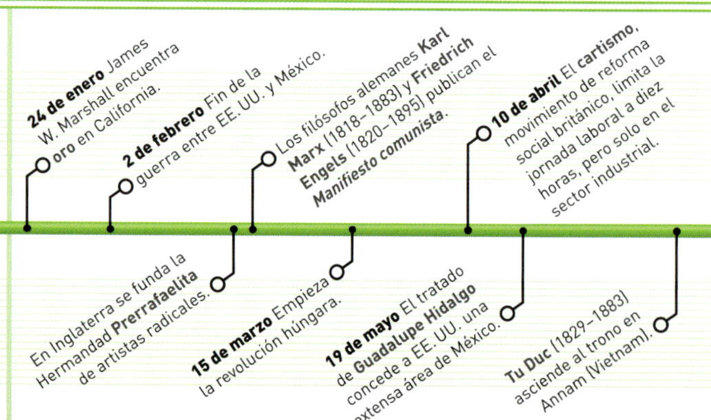

24 de enero James W. Marshall encuentra **oro** en California.

2 de febrero Fin de la guerra entre EE. UU. y México.

En Inglaterra se funda la Hermandad **Prerrafaelita** de artistas radicales.

Los filósofos alemanes **Karl Marx** (1818–1883) y **Friedrich Engels** (1820–1895) publican el ***Manifiesto comunista***.

15 de marzo Empieza la revolución húngara.

10 de abril El **cartismo**, movimiento de reforma social británico, limita la jornada laboral a diez horas, pero solo en el sector industrial.

19 de mayo El tratado **de Guadalupe Hidalgo** concede a EE. UU. una extensa área de México.

Tu Duc (1829–1883) asciende al trono en Annam (Vietnam).

Barcos mercantes en la bahía de San Francisco en los años de la fiebre del oro, cuando decenas de miles de personas llegaron a California en busca de fortuna.

COMUNISMO

Con la publicación del *Manifiesto del Partido Comunista*, Marx y Engels sentaron las bases de un movimiento político que pretendía que los medios de producción, como la tierra o las fábricas, fueran propiedad común. Los comunistas querían crear una sociedad sin clases ni estado, y abolir las trampas capitalistas de la propiedad privada y el trabajo asalariado.

Guizot fue obligado a dimitir y Luis Felipe abdicó. Se estableció un gobierno provisional y empezó la **Segunda República**, que con el tiempo promulgaría una constitución y ampliaría el derecho al voto. Sin embargo, las luchas internas por el poder condujeron a una revuelta de los trabajadores en junio. A finales de año, otro Bonaparte ocupaba el poder, esta vez el sobrino de Napoleón, el **príncipe Luis Napoleón Bonaparte** (1808–1873), quien había sido elegido presidente.

La inestabilidad no se limitaba a Francia. En enero habían empezado revueltas en Sicilia que se propagarían a otros lugares. Los factores que dieron lugar al conflicto fueron los altos precios de los alimentos, la crisis económica, los **movimientos nacionalistas**, el deseo de **reformas constitucionales** y el descontento con las monarquías. Las revoluciones variaron en intensidad y éxito. En algunos lugares, no fueron más que protestas a gran escala, como las manifestaciones del **cartismo** para pedir cambios en el sistema electoral de Gran Bretaña, o la exigencia de reformas institucionales en Bélgica y Países Bajos.

La verdadera tensión se concentraba en Francia, Alemania, el Imperio austrohúngaro y los estados italianos. En el **reino de las Dos Sicilias** (*véase* mapa), el rey se vio obligado a otorgar una constitución. En **Alemania** hubo enfrentamientos callejeros en marzo que forzaron al rey de Prusia a aprobar una constitución alemana. En Viena también hubo enfrentamientos, y se nombró un nuevo gobierno, mientras que muchos de los territorios del imperio (como **Hungría**) reclamaron más autonomía. A pesar de ello, en términos generales las revueltas de 1848 **fracasaron** y la represión social continuó.

> « **DESHONRADO** POR EL **HEDOR** DE LA **REVOLUCIÓN**, ENSUCIADO Y ENFANGADO. »
>
> **Federico Guillermo IV de Prusia**, tras la revolución de 1848

CON EL FIN DE LA GUERRA ENTRE EE. UU. Y MÉXICO en 1847 y la firma del tratado de Guadalupe Hidalgo (1848), EE. UU. obtuvo una extensa área de territorio que incluía **California**. Al año siguiente, un carpintero llamado James Wilson Marshall observó unos pedacitos de metal brillantes en el río junto al actual Sacramento y no tardó en comprender que se trataba de **oro**. La noticia de este hallazgo se propagó por todo el país y más allá, en parte gracias al anuncio del presidente James K. Polk, y en 1849 la **fiebre del oro** ya había empezado: unas cuarenta mil personas llegaron a San Francisco en barco y otras tantas en tren procedentes de todos los rincones de EE. UU. y otros países. La mayoría de los buscadores de oro acabaron con las manos vacías, pero muchos se quedaron en California y convirtieron la costa oeste en una región en plena efervescencia.

En el sur de África, el explorador y misionero escocés **David Livingstone** (1813–1873) cruzó el **desierto del Kalahari** en busca de un lago del que había oído hablar, y dio con el río Botletle. Livingstone había viajado mucho por la región desde que había ido a vivir a la Colonia del Cabo en 1841, y pensó que el río podía ser «la llave al interior».

En el noroeste de **India**, durante los últimos cuatro años, se habían producido dos guerras entre las tropas de la Compañía Británica de las Indias Orientales y los sijs. La **primera guerra sij** (1845–1846) se desató tras la muerte de su regente, Ranjit Singh (1781–1839). Hasta ese momento la Compañía había calculado que los cien mil guerreros khalsa de Singh eran demasiado fuertes. A su muerte, las tropas británicas entraron y tomaron áreas cercanas a la frontera, donde conquistaron la ciudad de **Lahore** en 1845. Los sijs tuvieron que ceder aún más territorio por un tratado. En 1848, una revuelta contra los británicos desencadenó la **segunda guerra sij**, que en el año 1849 se resolvió con la anexión británica de la región del Punjab.

Yemen luchaba contra los avances del **Imperio otomano**, que intentaba consolidar su autoridad en la región. Al sur del país, la Compañía Británica de las Indias Orientales ya había tomado el control sobre el **puerto de Adén** una década antes para establecer un puesto de repostaje de carbón para los barcos británicos rumbo a India.

La brújula de Livingstone
Brújula magnética del misionero David Livingstone, que pasó una gran parte de su vida explorando el interior de África.

La Asamblea de Frankfurt, compuesta por representantes de los Estados alemanes, adoptó una constitución democrática el 28 de marzo, pero el rechazo de Austria y Prusia llevó a la disolución de la Asamblea.

LOS PRERRAFAELITAS

William Holman Hunt, Dante Gabriel Rossetti y John Everett Millais, decepcionados con la pintura británica de la Royal Academy, donde realizaban sus estudios, fundaron un nuevo movimiento cuyo objetivo era el de aportar seriedad moral a la pomposidad y frivolidad del arte de la época. Este grupo, conocido como Hermandad Prerrafaelita, pintó temas medievales, románticos y religiosos con una fuerte carga simbólica, si bien su técnica era realista.

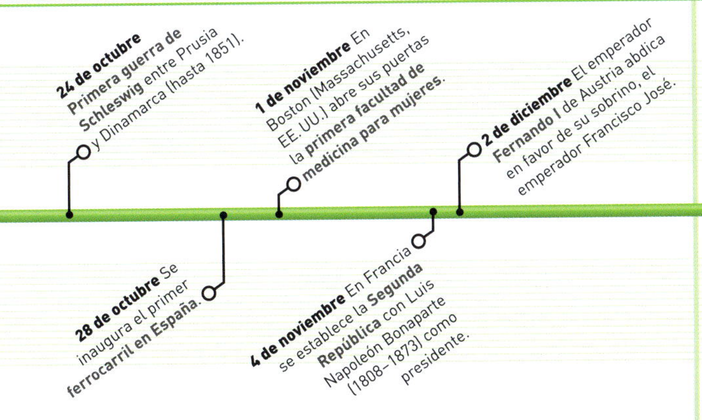

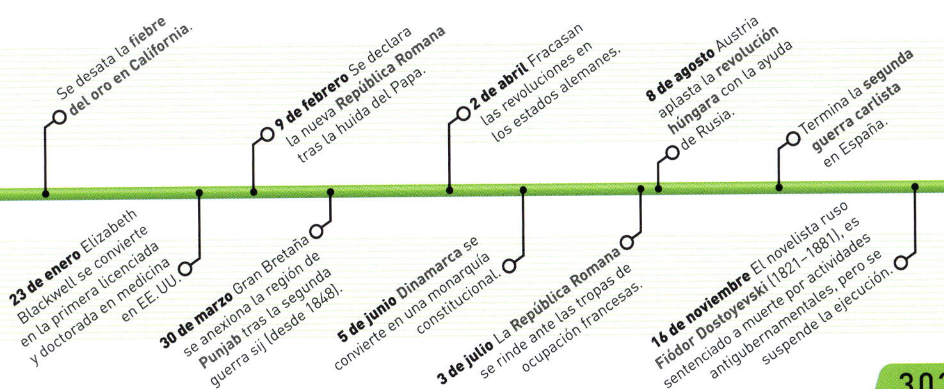

1850

Una de las sangrientas batallas durante la rebelión de los Taiping.

CHINA SE HABÍA CANSADO de intentar mantener los barcos europeos alejados de sus puertos y había tratado de expulsar a los misioneros cristianos para limitar la influencia del **cristianismo**. A pesar de ello, a mediados del siglo XIX unos 200 000 chinos se habían **convertido** y miles más conocían la religión.

En 1850, las autoridades enviaron tropas para dispersar a un grupo religioso cuyas creencias se basaban grosso modo en el **protestantismo**. Esta secta, liderada por **Hong Xiuquan** (1814–1864), que se creía el hermano menor de Jesucristo, inició una revuelta que derivaría en la **rebelión de los Taiping**. Atraídos por su demanda de una propiedad común, un gran número de campesinos hambrientos se sumaron a sus filas, en una lucha que duró catorce años y que se cobró millones de vidas.

MILLONES DE PERSONAS FALLECIERON DURANTE LA REBELIÓN DE LOS TAIPING

1851

Litografía del Palacio de Cristal de la Exposición Universal de 1851, en el Hyde Park de Londres. En seis meses la visitaron unos seis millones de personas.

« ES UN LUGAR MARAVILLOSO: **VASTO, EXTRAÑO, NUEVO E INDESCRIPTIBLE.** »

Charlotte Brontë, novelista inglesa, tras su visita a la Exposición Universal

EL MUNDO ENTERO SE MOSTRABA EN LONDRES. Se había organizado una exposición con el título «**Gran exposición** sobre los avances de la industria mundial», que más tarde se conocería como la «Exposición Universal». Se celebró en el Palacio de Cristal, un pabellón de exposiciones de hierro y vidrio construido expresamente para la ocasión. Unos seis millones de personas visitaron las cien mil muestras allí reunidas entre el 1 de mayo y el 31 de octubre. De los catorce mil expositores, poco más de la mitad eran británicos. Se podían contemplar gran cantidad de artículos agrícolas y manufacturados, desde el **diamante indio Koh-i-Noor** («montaña de luz») hasta tapices persas y maquinaria británica.

Ese mismo año se instaló un **cable de telégrafo** que atravesaba el canal de la Mancha y que permitió por primera vez la comunicación internacional instantánea.

A lo largo de las últimas décadas, Gran Bretaña había experimentado un gran ***boom* demográfico** y se había **urbanizado** a medida que los trabajadores del campo se trasladaban a las ciudades para trabajar en las fábricas, cada vez más numerosas (*véase* 1771). Los censos detallados de la época muestran que de 1801 a 1851 la población de Londres pasó de alrededor de un millón a más de dos millones de habitantes.

En **Australia**, el descubrimiento de oro en Victoria y Nueva Gales del Sur ese mismo año dio lugar a una **fiebre del oro** que haría que la población del país se triplicara a lo largo de los diez años siguientes.

En Siam (Tailandia), el **rey Mongkut** (1804–1868) ascendió al trono. Durante su reinado se intensificaron las relaciones con Occidente. Contrató a una institutriz inglesa, **Anna Leonowens** (1831–1915), cuyas memorias inspirarían el musical *El rey y yo* en el siglo XX.

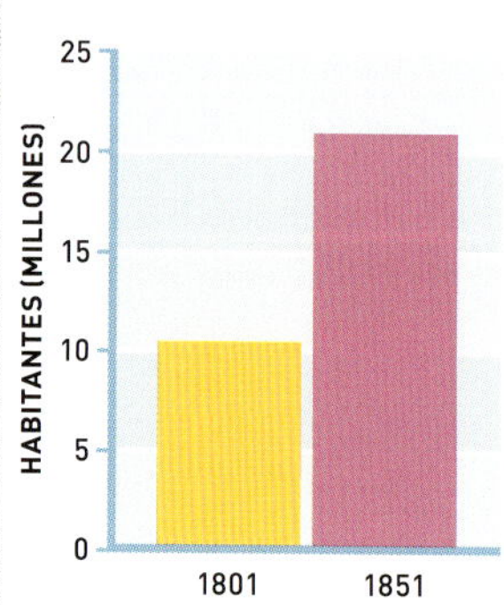

Población británica creciente
La población de Inglaterra, Escocia y Gales prácticamente se duplicó en solo cincuenta años: de 10,6 millones en 1801 a casi 21 millones en 1851.

1852

La Royal Navy desempeñó un papel crucial en la guerra anglo-birmana.

LAS HOSTILIDADES SE HABÍAN DESATADO DE NUEVO entre las tropas británicas y los **birmanos**. Después de haber conquistado un extenso territorio durante la última guerra (*véase* 1823), Gran Bretaña deseaba tener un mayor control para establecer una conexión costera entre Calcuta, en el territorio británico en India, y el puerto británico de Singapur. Además, la Compañía de las Indias Orientales quería acceder a los **bosques de teca** de Birmania. En 1852, los británicos apresaron un barco del rey birmano, razón suficiente para que comenzase la **segunda guerra anglo-birmana**, que duraría tan solo unos meses, pero durante los cuales las tropas británicas ampliaron sus conquistas en el sur, destronaron al rey Pagán Min (1811–1880) y le sustituyeron por su hermano, Mindon Min (1814–1878), que estaba dispuesto a aceptar el dominio británico de la parte sur del reino.

En **África occidental**, en la región ocupada actualmente por Senegal, el jefe toucouleur musulmán **Omar Tall** (1797–1864) sacó partido de las tensiones entre los bambara y los dinguiraye para iniciar una yihad (guerra santa) en el norte de **Senegal** y apoderarse del territorio. Su imperio llegaría hasta **Tombuctú** (en la actual Malí). Bajo su mandato, el islamismo se hizo aún más fuerte en el occidente de África.

En Sudáfrica, el Imperio británico reconoció la independencia del **Transvaal** tras negarse a aceptar la anterior República de Natal de los bóers (*véase* 1843). Dos años después, los colonos aceptarían el nuevo **Estado Libre de Orange**.

1853

El comodoro Perry llevó a Japón un vagón de tren como regalo.

AL COMODORO DE EE. UU. MATTHEW PERRY (1794–1858) se le encargó entablar relaciones comerciales con **Japón**, cuyo gobierno militar aislacionista, el *bakufu* de Edo, llevaba años bajo presión internacional para abrir sus puertos a los comerciantes extranjeros. Los neerlandeses eran los únicos europeos a los que permitía un **acceso comercial** muy limitado, y las anteriores delegaciones de Francia, Reino Unido y EE. UU. habían topado con un rechazo rotundo (*véase* 1846). EE. UU. tenía un gran interés en obtener derechos mercantiles en Asia oriental, y envió a Perry para reanudar las negociaciones. El comodoro arribó a Japón el 8 de julio y se negó a marcharse hasta que hubiera entregado sus cartas. Japón cedió varios días más tarde y aceptó sus documentos, en los que se pedía un tratado mercantil. Con el tiempo llegó a aceptar los términos y al año siguiente se firmaría el **tratado de Kanagawa**.

Mientras **China** estaba inmersa en la lucha contra la rebelión taiping (*véase* 1850), en las provincias centrales y orientales se produjo otro levantamiento. Los rebeldes eran forajidos y campesinos de las regiones afectadas por el hambre. Con el gobierno ocupado en otras batallas, los rebeldes pudieron organizarse militarmente e iniciar la **rebelión de los Nian**. En los quince años posteriores llegaron a controlar gran parte del norte de China, pero al final fueron derrotados.

Nueva Zelanda, a la que la Ley de Constitución de 1852 británica concedió el derecho al autogobierno, eligió su primer parlamento.

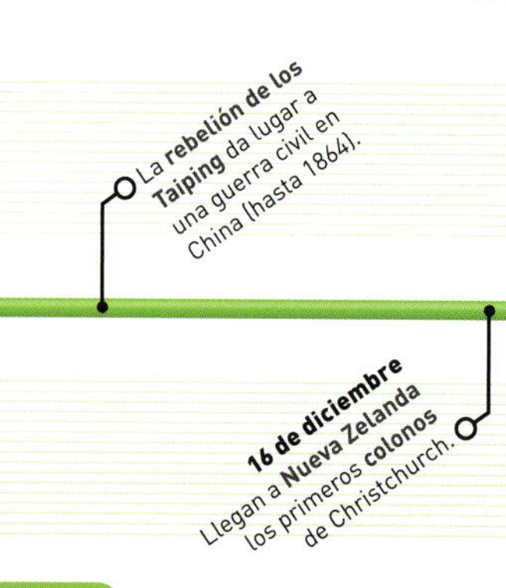

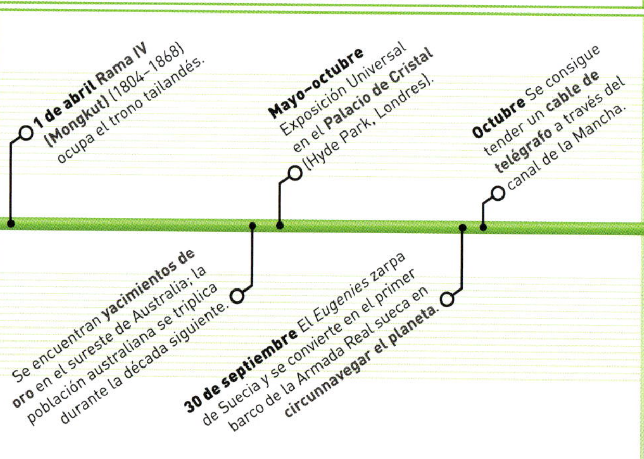

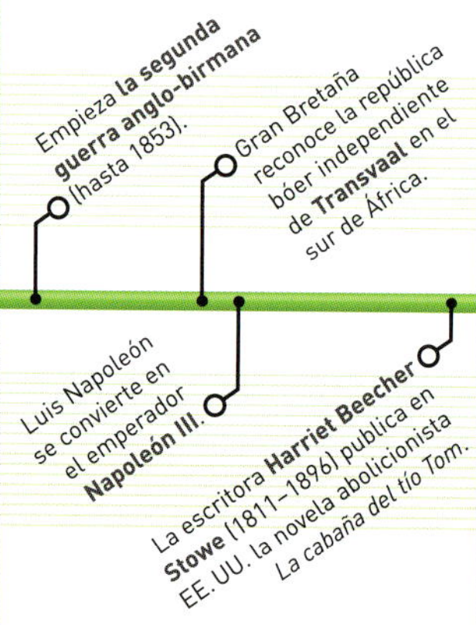

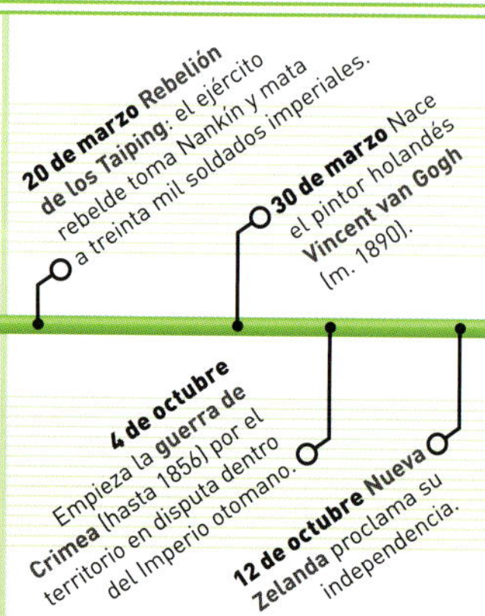

1854

« NO HAY RETIRADA DESDE AQUÍ, SOLDADOS. DEBEN MORIR DONDE SE ENCUENTRAN. »

Colin Campbell, comandante de la brigada de los highlanders, en la batalla de Balaklava (25 de octubre de 1854)

LAS TENSIONES ENTRE RUSIA Y EL IMPERIO OTOMANO durante el año anterior acabaron en guerra, una contienda a la que Gran Bretaña y Francia se sumaron en octubre. El conflicto fue avivado por la decisión del zar Nicolás I (1796–1855) de proclamar su derecho a proteger a los **cristianos ortodoxos** bajo gobierno otomano. Ante la negativa de los otomanos, Nicolás envió tropas a Moldavia y Valaquia, a lo que el Imperio otomano respondió con una declaración de guerra. En marzo de 1854, Gran Bretaña y Francia también habían declarado la guerra a Rusia; en septiembre, sus tropas llegaron al territorio ruso de **Crimea** y dio comienzo el sitio de **Sebastopol**. En octubre, una brigada británica malinterpretó las órdenes durante la **batalla de Balaklava** y descendió un valle en lugar de ascender por él, hecho que permitió a los rusos acribillar a los 673 soldados por los cuatro costados. De no ser por la intervención francesa, el número de muertos hubiera superado el 40%. Este incidente se inmortalizó en el poema de Lord Alfred Tennyson *La carga de la Brigada ligera*.

Austria amenazó con sumarse a la guerra contra Rusia en 1856 y se acordó una paz preliminar el 1 de febrero, que fue seguida del **tratado de París** el 30 de marzo.

La guerra de Crimea fue el primer conflicto cubierto por los periódicos, beneficiados por la nueva tecnología telegráfica y fotográfica. Esta guerra también hizo famosa a la **«dama de la lámpara»**, la enfermera británica Florence Nightingale (1820–1910), cuyas reformas de los hospitales de campaña redujeron drásticamente las muertes por enfermedad durante la guerra. Contribuyó a promover la enfermería como una profesión respetable para las mujeres.

1855

Retrato del rey Mongkut de Siam, conocido también como Rama IV.

EL MISIONERO DAVID LIVINGSTONE se hallaba inmerso en su segunda expedición por África (*véase* 1849). Convencido de que existía una ruta comercial hasta el mar, en noviembre de 1853 remontó en barco el **río Zambeze** en su busca. Dos años después, llegó a una gran cascada, conocida como **Mosi-oa-Tunya** («la humareda atronadora»). Fue el primer europeo que vio estas cataratas, a las que rebautizó con el nombre de **Victoria**.

En el este, en Siam (Tailandia), el rey Mongkut (*véase* 1851), conocido por su interés por Occidente, firmó acuerdos comerciales con EE. UU. y Gran Bretaña en un intento de abrir **Siam** al comercio.

1856

El filibustero William Walker se rinde ante las tropas costarricenses.

EN NICARAGUA, EL ESTADOUNIDENSE WILLIAM WALKER (1824–1860), que llegó al país un año antes con 58 hombres, se autoproclamó **presidente**. En un principio había sido invitado por Francisco Castellón (1815–1855), quien pretendía organizar una revuelta liberal. Fue un periodo de **filibusteros**: mercenarios financiados por intereses privados intentaban conquistar pequeños países para anexionarlos a EE. UU. Walker intentó convertir Nicaragua en un **estado esclavista**, ya que los estados sureños de EE. UU. querían ampliar sus territorios ante el auge abolicionista. Walker fue capturado y fusilado por fuerzas costarricenses invasoras.

La guerra de Crimea
El brigadier Scarlett lidera la brigada pesada británica durante la subida de Balaklava el 25 de octubre de 1854, en la guerra de Crimea contra Rusia.

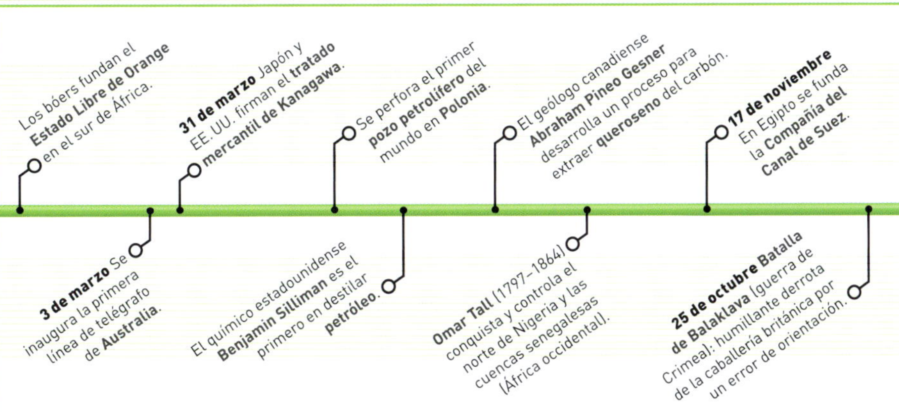

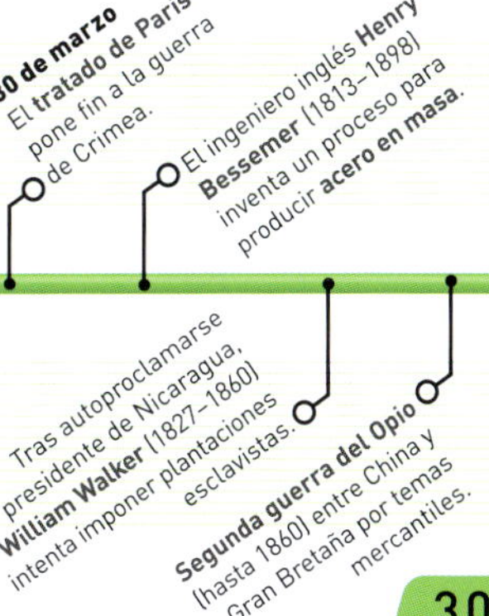

1857

La obra *La liberación de Lucknow*, del pintor inglés Thomas Jones Barker, terminada en 1859, representa a las tropas británicas defendiendo la ciudad colonial tras un largo sitio durante la rebelión de los Cipayos.

EN EL AÑO 1857 SE EXTENDIÓ UN RUMOR ENTRE LAS TROPAS INDIAS (conocidas como **Cipayos**) del ejército bengalí estacionado en Meerut, al norte de India. Se decía que sus nuevos cartuchos para rifles estaban engrasados con grasa de cerdo y de ternera. Los cartuchos eran para un nuevo tipo de rifle, el **Enfield**, y para cargarlos era necesario arrancar los extremos de los cartuchos de papel de un mordisco. Dejar que la grasa de ternera o de cerdo tocara sus labios iba en contra, respectivamente, de las creencias religiosas de los soldados hindúes y musulmanes. A este rumor se sumaron otros agravios y la creciente sospecha de que los británicos estaban intentando destruir la cultura y las tradiciones indias. Los soldados se negaron a usar los cartuchos y la lucha resultante entre las tropas indias y los comandantes británicos derivó en una revuelta conocida como la **rebelión de los Cipayos** (o el **Motín de la India**).

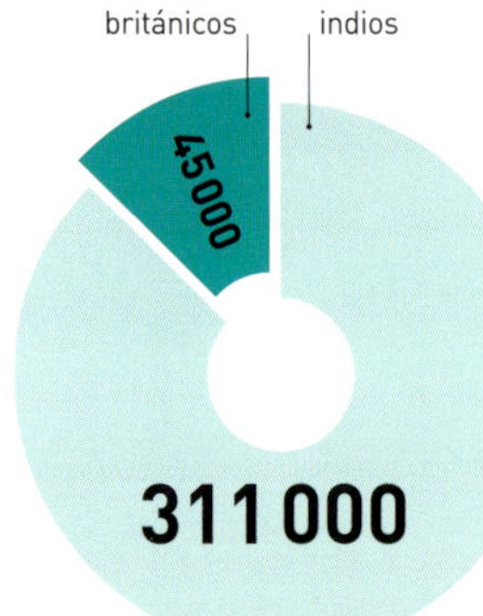

Ejército británico-indio en 1857
El ejército estaba integrado por más indios que británicos, por lo que la insurrección de las tropas indias suponía una seria amenaza.

La inestabilidad duró más de un año, ya que a los amotinados se sumaron campesinos enojados con los terratenientes que los explotaban y población descontenta con la reciente anexión británica de la región de Oudh, al norte de India. Los rebeldes lograron capturar Delhi y «reinstaurar» en el poder a un antiguo emperador mogol, **Bahadur Sah II** (1775–1862), al tiempo que mataron a los británicos en Delhi y en las ciudades cercanas de Kanpur y Lucknow. La represalia del ejército británico fue igual de brutal, y recapturó Delhi en septiembre y Lucknow en marzo de 1858; la revuelta fue aplastada en junio.

Este enfrentamiento supuso el culmen de la frustración por el gobierno de la Compañía de las Indias Orientales y por la discreta **occidentalización** a medida que Gran Bretaña se anexionaba más territorios y enviaba a más oficiales. El levantamiento provocó una enorme inquietud en Gran Bretaña y los poderes de la Compañía de las Indias Orientales para controlar el territorio fueron anulados. A estas alturas, la Compañía era odiada en toda India y el gobierno británico pensó que no podía continuar confiando en ella para mantener la estabilidad (*véase* recuadro, 1858). El motín había demostrado el nivel de descontento y enojo de los indios, que seguiría aumentando bajo el dominio británico, al tiempo que avivaba el movimiento independentista.

> « UN **NEGRO LIBRE**... **NO ES UN "CIUDADANO"** TAL Y COMO SE ENTIENDE EN LA **CONSTITUCIÓN DE EE. UU.** »
>
> **Roger Taney**, presidente del Tribunal Supremo, sobre el caso de Dred Scott vs. Sandford (abril de 1854)

Además del conflicto en India, las tropas británicas habían vuelto a las armas en **China**. Gran Bretaña deseaba más libertad de comercio en China a raíz del tratado de Nankín (*véase* 1842), pero los chinos se resistían. En 1856, Gran Bretaña envió una expedición militar junto con los franceses para atacar los puertos de China, lo que dio lugar a la **segunda guerra del Opio**. Las fuerzas anglofrancesas atacaron Cantón en 1857, y un año más tarde se negociaron los **tratados de Tianjin** entre China, Gran Bretaña y Francia, además de con Rusia y EE. UU. Dichos acuerdos exigían a China que abriera más puertos y legalizara la importación de opio. Además, los diplomáticos extranjeros tendrían derecho a residir en **Pekín**. Los chinos se negaron a ratificar estos acuerdos hasta 1860.

En EE. UU., la causa **abolicionista** sufrió un serio revés cuando el Tribunal Supremo declaró la esclavitud **legal** en todo el país en su sentencia al caso de Dred Scott vs. John F.A. Sandford. **Dred Scott** había interpuesto una demanda a su amo, John Emerson, quien le había llevado del estado esclavista de Misuri (*véase* 1820) al territorio «libre» de Wisconsin para regresar posteriormente a Misuri. Scott, asesorado por los abolicionistas, presentó una demanda reclamando que el traslado de un territorio esclavista a otro libre había roto su yugo de servidumbre. El caso llegó al Tribunal Supremo en 1857, donde los jueces denegaron la liberación de Scott basándose en el hecho de que no tenía derechos como **ciudadano estadounidense**, empezando por el derecho a presentar una demanda judicial. Además, los jueces declararon también inconstitucional el Compromiso de Misuri (*véase* 1820), pues el congreso no podía privar a los ciudadanos de sus propiedades. Si bien los estados eran libres de decidir prohibir la esclavitud, nada podía evitar que los nuevos territorios se convirtieran en estados esclavistas.

Dred Scott
Dred Scott, esclavo estadounidense, demandó a su amo a fin de obtener la libertad. Su caso llegó hasta el Tribunal Supremo de EE. UU., donde finalmente le fue denegada.

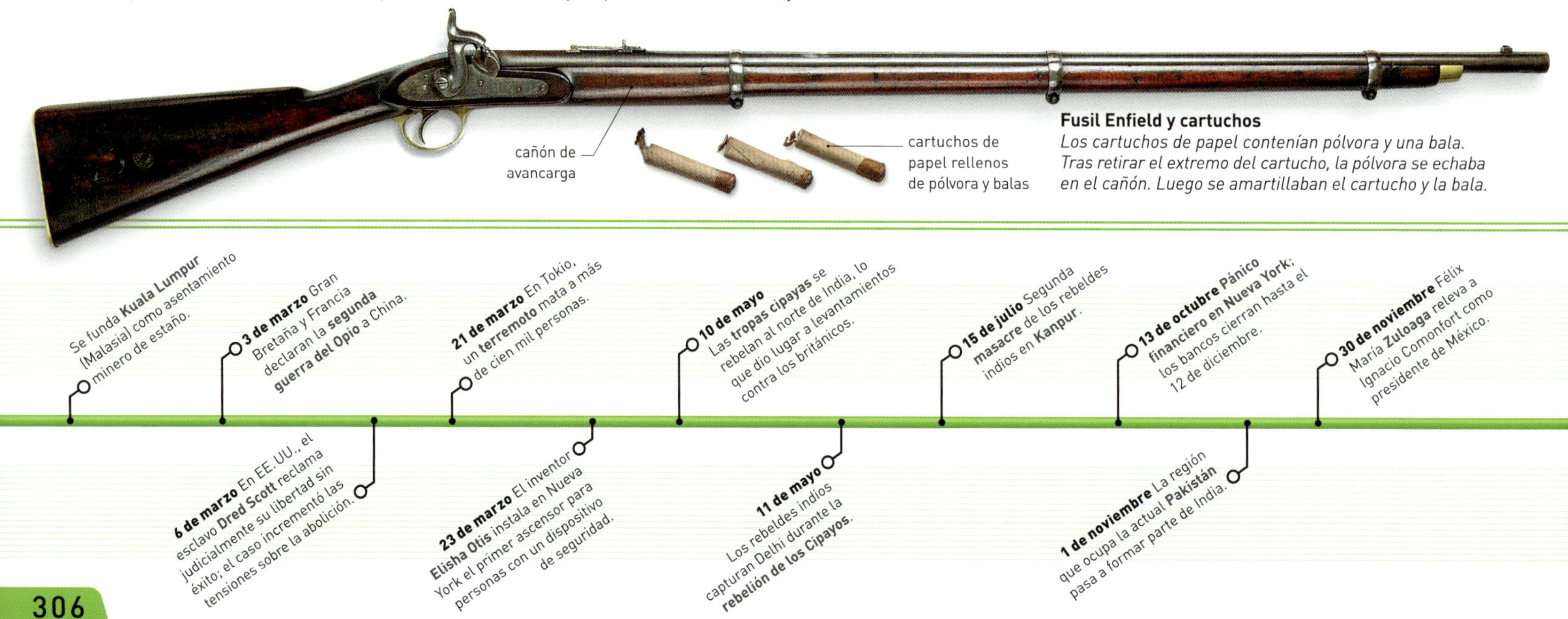

Fusil Enfield y cartuchos
Los cartuchos de papel contenían pólvora y una bala. Tras retirar el extremo del cartucho, la pólvora se echaba en el cañón. Luego se amartillaban el cartucho y la bala.

Se funda **Kuala Lumpur** (Malasia) como asentamiento minero de estaño.

3 de marzo Gran Bretaña y Francia declaran la **segunda guerra del Opio** a China.

6 de marzo En EE. UU., el esclavo **Dred Scott** reclama judicialmente su libertad sin éxito; el caso incrementó las tensiones sobre la abolición.

21 de marzo En Tokio, un **terremoto** mata a más de cien mil personas.

23 de marzo El inventor **Elisha Otis** instala en Nueva York el primer ascensor para personas con un dispositivo de seguridad.

10 de mayo Las **tropas cipayas** se rebelan al norte de India, lo que dio lugar a levantamientos contra los británicos.

11 de mayo Los rebeldes indios capturan Delhi durante la **rebelión de los Cipayos**.

15 de julio Segunda **masacre** de los rebeldes indios en **Kanpur**.

13 de octubre Pánico financiero en Nueva York; los bancos cierran hasta el 12 de diciembre.

1 de noviembre La región que ocupa la actual **Pakistán** pasa a formar parte de India.

30 de noviembre Félix María **Zuloaga** releva a Ignacio Comonfort como presidente de México.

1858

Un óleo contemporáneo ilustra la batalla de Guadalajara de 1860, durante la guerra reformista mexicana entre liberales y conservadores.

DESPUÉS DE LA DERROTA SUFRIDA POR MÉXICO FRENTE A EE. UU. (*véase* 1846), muchos mexicanos estaban a favor de la reforma, incluido el liberal de clase media y ministro de justicia **Benito Juárez** (1806–1872). Juárez, junto con otros liberales, entre los que se encontraba el presidente **Ignacio Comonfort** (1812–1863), redactaron el borrador de una nueva constitución que limitaba los privilegios de la Iglesia y del ejército, como la asignación de tribunales especiales para juicios civiles y algunos derechos de los terratenientes. Esta constitución, que además prohibía la esclavitud y reclamaba una democracia en México, entró en vigor en 1857.

Sin embargo, tanto la Iglesia católica como los militares se negaron a aceptar dichas reformas y los enfrentamientos desembocaron en la **guerra de la Reforma** (1857–1860). Con los conservadores al mando del ejército, los liberales se vieron relegados a Ciudad de México, y con el tiempo tuvieron que trasladar la nueva capital al puerto de **Veracruz** en 1858. EE. UU. decidió intervenir en el conflicto, reconoció el gobierno liberal de Veracruz en 1859 y les envió unas armas muy necesarias. Esto ayudó a los rebeldes a contraatacar y derrotar a las fuerzas conservadoras. El 1 de enero de 1861, Juárez regresó a Ciudad de México como presidente, tomó el control de todo el país y recuperó la constitución.

En el continente europeo, Francia no solo tenía frentes abiertos en China, sino también en otros reinos del este y el Sureste Asiático, donde los franceses intentaban consolidarse comercialmente. Francia estaba preocupada por el aumento del poder siamés y por los continuados ataques contra misionarios franceses en Vietnam. A finales de 1858, una expedición francoespañola tomó la ciudad de Da Nang, en Vietnam, y empezó la **campaña de Cochinchina**. En 1859, la coalición capturó el puerto clave de **Saigón**, donde una guarnición de mil soldados se enfrentaría luego a un año de sitio (de 1860 a 1861). La guerra finalizó en 1863 gracias a un acuerdo con el rey de Vietnam, **Tu Duc** (1829–1883), por el que se cedían tres provincias a Francia.

EL AUGE DEL RAJ

En el año 1857, India pasó del control administrativo de la Compañía de las Indias Orientales al gobierno de un virrey, de acuerdo con la propuesta del primer virrey y gobernador general Charles John Canning (1856–1862). El periodo, conocido como Raj (Imperio Británico de India), duró hasta la independencia de India en 1947.

1859–1860

Marines bajo el mando del coronel Robert E. Lee derriban la puerta de la armería en Harper's Ferry, donde John Brown y sus hombres se habían atrincherado.

« LOS CRÍMENES DE ESTE PAÍS CULPABLE SOLO SE PUEDEN PURGAR CON SANGRE. »

John Brown, abolicionista, antes de su ejecución el 2 de diciembre de 1859

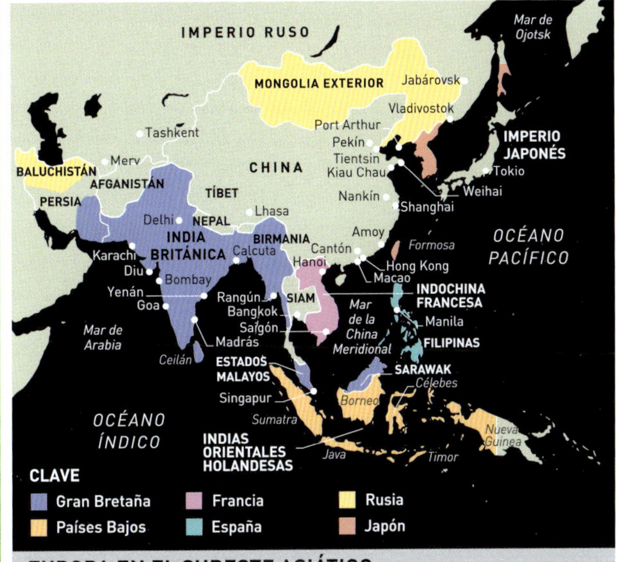

EUROPA EN EL SURESTE ASIÁTICO

Los países europeos rivalizaron en el siglo XIX por controlar las rutas comerciales de China a través del Sureste Asiático. Se enviaban mercancías como especias de las colonias en Asia a Europa, y productos textiles desde Europa hasta Asia. La apertura del canal de Suez en 1869 agilizó y abarató este comercio.

POR FIN EMPEZARON LAS OBRAS de construcción del canal que comunicaría el Mediterráneo con el mar Rojo. Acortaría los viajes entre Europa y Asia en miles de kilómetros, ya que permitiría que los barcos no tuvieran que rodear el cabo de Buena Esperanza. En 1854, el oficial francés **Ferdinand de Lesseps** (1805–1894) consiguió obtener permiso del jedive (virrey) de Egipto, el bajá Mehmet Said (1822–1863), para construir un canal en Suez. En 1856 se había fundado la Compañía del Canal de Suez (*Compagnie universelle du canal maritime de Suez*), que tenía autorización para gestionar el canal durante 99 años una vez finalizada su construcción.

En EE. UU., el abolicionista **John Brown** (1800–1859) atacó una armería federal situada en **Harpers Ferry (Virginia)** la noche del 16 de octubre. Tomó como rehenes a más de sesenta esclavistas con la esperanza de que los esclavos se unieran a su causa. Les atacó la milicia local y la rebelión fue reprimida finalmente por tropas federales encabezadas por el coronel Robert E. Lee. De los 22 hombres que participaron en el ataque, 10 perdieron la vida, incluidos los dos hijos de Brown, quien más tarde fue ajusticiado en la horca.

Por otro lado, en Inglaterra, el naturalista **Charles Darwin** (*véanse* 1835 y 1839) consolidó su reputación gracias a la publicación de *El origen de las especies* (traducida al español en 1877). La obra trataba de la evolución, y en ella Darwin exponía sus ideas sobre la adaptación de las especies y la supervivencia de los más fuertes.

Mientras, en EE. UU. Abraham Lincoln (1809–1865) ganó la carrera a la presidencia como candidato del nuevo partido **republicano**, fundado a fin de contrarrestar el poder de los estados esclavistas existentes y detener la creación de otros. Los demócratas estaban divididos y presentaban dos candidatos.

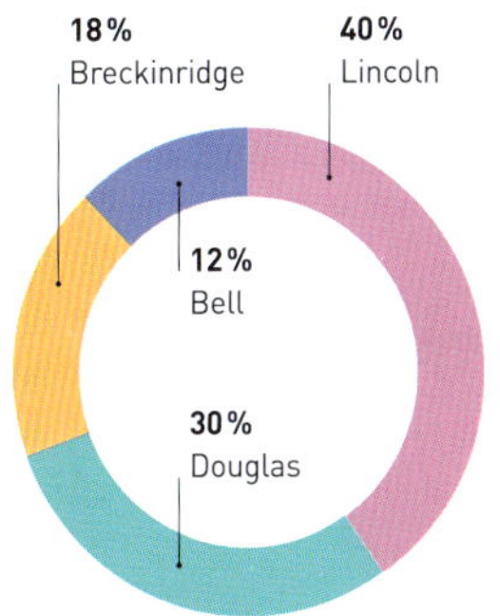

Una clara mayoría
Los candidatos demócratas Douglas y Breckinridge sumaban más apoyos populares, pero Lincoln obtuvo los votos necesarios en las elecciones.

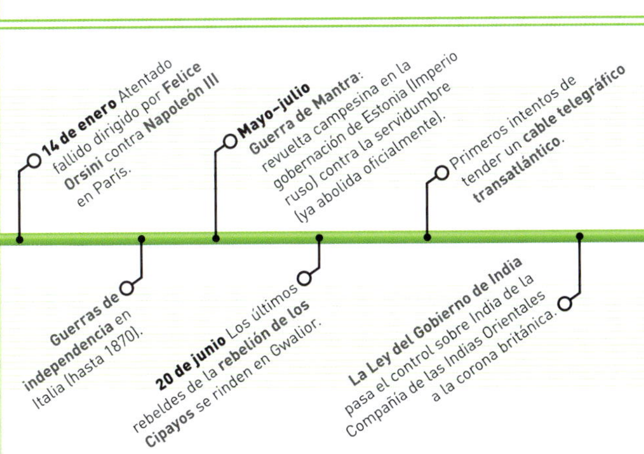

14 de enero Atentado fallido dirigido por **Felice Orsini** contra **Napoleón III** en París.

Guerras de independencia en Italia (hasta 1870).

Mayo-julio Guerra de Mantra: revuelta campesina en la gobernación de Estonia (Imperio ruso) contra la servidumbre (ya abolida oficialmente).

20 de junio Los últimos rebeldes de la **rebelión de los Cipayos** se rinden en Gwalior.

Primeros intentos de tender un **cable telegráfico transatlántico**.

La Ley del Gobierno de India pasa el control sobre India de la Compañía de las Indias Orientales a la corona británica.

1859 Edwin Drake es el primero en perforar un pozo de petróleo con **tuberías** en EE. UU.

1859 Marruecos va a la guerra contra **España** (hasta 1860) por ataques en los enclaves españoles de Ceuta y Melilla.

1859 Francia conquista Saigón (**Vietnam**) durante la campaña de Cochinchina.

25 de abril de 1859 Empieza la construcción del **canal de Suez** en Egipto.

1-2 de septiembre de 1859 Se produce la **tormenta solar** más potente de que se tiene constancia.

1859 Holandeses y portugueses acuerdan repartirse la isla de **Timor**, en el Sureste Asiático, y otras islas próximas.

16 de octubre 1859 El abolicionista **John Brown** lidera una rebelión de esclavos en Virginia (EE. UU.) sin éxito.

C. década de 1860 Movimiento impresionista en Europa.

24 de noviembre de 1859 Charles Darwin publica *El origen de las especies*.

1860 Francia y Gran Bretaña ocupan **Pekín**.

1860 Los rebeldes vencen a 180000 soldados Qing por segunda vez en **Nankín** durante la rebelión taiping.

9 de abril 1860 El tipógrafo francés **Édouard-Léon Scott de Martinville** (1817–1879) realiza la primera grabación conocida en **fonoautógrafo**.

El ataque de la batería confederada del fuerte Moultrie al fuerte Sumter, en el puerto de Charleston, el 12 de abril, inicia la guerra de Secesión, que devastó EE. UU.

LA FRAGMENTACIÓN DEL PARTIDO DEMÓCRATA DE EE. UU. antes de las elecciones de 1860 precipitó una división mucho mayor y peligrosa en 1861: la **secesión** de los estados del Sur, que formaron una confederación. Muchos nordistas, incluido el presidente Lincoln, eran reacios a exigir la abolición en un clima político tan tenso, pero el apoyo a tal medida entre la opinión pública no dejó de crecer durante la década de 1850.

Al principio, EE. UU. estaba fragmentado económicamente, lo cual intensificó la polémica sobre la esclavitud. El Sur era principalmente agrícola y utilizaba esclavos para cultivar algodón, tabaco y arroz. En cambio, los estados del Norte, más urbanos, contaban con muchos trabajadores inmigrantes.

La victoria de Lincoln en las elecciones presidenciales fue el colmo para los propietarios de esclavos sudistas, y Carolina del Sur se escindió de la Unión en diciembre de 1860. Durante los meses siguientes le siguieron Georgia, Alabama, Luisiana, Misisipi, Texas y Florida. Estos estados formaron la **Confederación** y eligieron a Jefferson Davis (1808–1889) como presidente. En primavera se les sumaron Virginia, Arkansas, Tennessee y Carolina del Norte. En cambio, Kentucky, Misuri, Maryland y Delaware, también esclavistas, no se separaron. Uno de los motivos subyacentes a la secesión, además de la postura sobre la esclavitud, fue el problema de los **derechos de los estados** frente al gobierno **federal**. Carolina del Sur y los demás estados confederados argumentaban que los estados tenían derecho a poseer esclavos y a abandonar la Unión.

La situación se fue volviendo más tensa. La presencia continua de las tropas de la Unión (federales) en el **fuerte Sumter**, en el puerto de Charleston (Carolina del Sur), provocaba que mucha gente tuviera la sensación de que su nueva soberanía estaba en entredicho. Así, a las 4.30 horas del 12 de abril, el general de brigada P. G. T. Beauregard dio la orden de disparar contra los soldados allí estacionados. Fueron los **primeros disparos** de la **guerra de Secesión**.

Mientras, la segunda guerra de la Independencia italiana, que había empezado en 1859 como parte del proceso de unificación de los **estados italianos**, llegaba a su fin. Francia se había aliado con el reino de Cerdeña-Piamonte para expulsar a los austriacos de Italia y lo lograron tras varias victorias en 1859. Sin embargo, durante las negociaciones de la **paz de Zúrich**, el emperador francés Napoleón III permitió que Austria conservara el Véneto (básicamente Venecia) para indignación de los partidarios de la independencia de Italia. En el sur, el revolucionario nacionalista italiano y líder militar **Giuseppe Garibaldi** (1807–1882) atacó el reino de las Dos Sicilias y tomó Palermo en 1860. Con revueltas en casi todos los reinos italianos, **Víctor Manuel II** (1820–1878) de Cerdeña-Piamonte fue proclamado rey de Italia. Sin embargo, la lucha aún no había llegado a su fin, ya que Francia ocupó Roma, mientras que Venecia seguía bajo dominio austriaco. El intento de Garibaldi de liberar los Estados Pontificios (Roma) en 1862 acabó con su derrota en la batalla de Aspromonte el 29 de agosto, y el proyecto de unificación no se consumó.

Alejandro II (1818–1881) abolió la **servidumbre** en Rusia. Tras la derrota en la guerra de Crimea (*véase* 1854), el zar quiso reformar el país, empezando por la mano de obra, y proclamó el **Edicto de Emancipación** en 1861 a pesar de la oposición de los terratenientes. En 1818 ya se había intentado abolir la servidumbre, sin éxito. El 19 de febrero se emanciparon unos diez millones de personas con la promesa de recibir tierras propias.

Una guerra civil sangrienta
El conflicto entre el gobierno federal del Norte y los once estados del Sur se saldó con unas cifras de soldados muertos y heridos muy elevadas.

Gorra nordista
Durante la guerra de Secesión, los soldados de la Unión llevaban esta gorra con el distintivo del regimiento. Los confederados iban de gris.

El zar Alejandro II
Alejandro II, emperador de Rusia de 1855 a 1881, liberó a los siervos y llevó a cabo una profunda reforma de los sistemas judicial y educativo.

LA CONFEDERACIÓN SUDISTA

La Confederación Sudista (Estados Confederados de América), necesitaba una bandera. La bandera nacional confederada, conocida como «barras y estrellas», era muy parecida a la de la Unión. Con el fin de evitar confusiones en el campo de batalla, el ejército de Virginia del Norte adoptó una nueva (dcha.), utilizada luego por todas las fuerzas sudistas.

> « ES MEJOR **ABOLIR LA SERVIDUMBRE DESDE ARRIBA** QUE **ESPERAR A QUE ELLA LO HAGA** DESDE ABAJO. »
>
> Zar Alejandro II de Rusia

1862

« LA **POLÍTICA** ES EL **ARTE** DE LO **POSIBLE.** »

Otto von Bismarck a Meyer von Waldeck (11 de agosto de 1867)

UNA EXPEDICIÓN formada por fuerzas británicas, francesas y españolas llegó a **México** dispuesta a cobrar las deudas. Tras la guerra de la Reforma (*véase* 1858), el presidente Benito Juárez había declarado en 1861 una **moratoria** de dos años del pago de los intereses de la **deuda extranjera**. Los países prestamistas no aprobaron dicha decisión y no tardaron en recurrir al **conflicto armado**. Francia envió tropas que pronto fueron derrotadas, pero más tarde llegaron refuerzos a Ciudad de México, y Napoleón III vio la oportunidad de establecer un imperio en México.

Más al norte, durante la **guerra de Secesión estadounidense**, las tropas de la Unión (federales) trataron de tomar Richmond, la capital confederada, avanzando por la península al este de **Yorktown**, pero no lo lograron. Siguió la **segunda batalla de Bull Run** (28–30 agosto; p. 310), en la que 55 000 soldados confederados derrotaron a 70 000 federales. Unas semanas después, el 17 de septiembre, tuvo lugar una de las batallas más sangrientas de la guerra en **Antietam** (Maryland), donde las tropas de la Unión perdieron unos 12 000 hombres y las confederadas cerca de 11 000. Más al oeste, las tropas federales, lideradas por el general **Ulysses S. Grant** (1822–1885), obtuvieron una decisiva victoria en la **batalla de Shiloh** (Tennessee).

En Japón, el **régimen Tokugawa** desconfiaba cada vez más de los **extranjeros** (*véase* 1853) y, entre otras medidas, intentó expulsarlos y aprobó **leyes contra ellos**. Esto precipitó los ataques a barcos de EE. UU., Francia, Gran Bretaña y Holanda. Como represalia, en 1863 los estadounidenses dispararon contra dos barcos japoneses, y buques de guerra franceses atacaron e incendiaron una aldea. Un año después, Francia, Holanda, Gran Bretaña y EE. UU. destruyeron las baterías japonesas a lo largo de toda la costa en el **estrecho de Shimonoseki**. Este ataque les permitió conseguir un tratado que les concedía libertad de tránsito y derecho a comerciar.

OTTO VON BISMARCK
(1815–1898)

Bismarck, uno de los líderes prusianos más influyentes, llegó al poder como primer ministro en el año 1862 y orquestó el plan maestro de la unificación de Alemania (*véase* 1871). Reorganizó el ejército e intentó forjar una identidad nacional alemana; se enfrentó con la Iglesia católica y trató de frenar el avance del socialismo.

1863

Los obreros se apresuran a tomar el tren de la mañana en la estación de Gower Street del ferrocarril metropolitano (subterráneo) de Londres.

30 MIL ES EL **NÚMERO** DE **PASAJEROS** DE LA **LÍNEA METROPOLITANA** DURANTE EL **PRIMER DÍA**

LA SITUACIÓN DE MÉXICO SE COMPLICÓ cuando los conservadores, aún resentidos por su derrota en la guerra de la Reforma (*véase* 1858), aprovecharon las hostilidades entre las tropas francesas y mexicanas (*véase* 1862), y conspiraron con **Napoleón III** para derrocar al gobierno. Entonces se ofreció la corona al archiduque Fernando Maximiliano José de Austria (1832–1867), que aceptó creyendo que había sido elegido por el pueblo y se convirtió en el **emperador Maximiliano I** de México un año después.

En EE. UU., Abraham Lincoln intentó persuadir a los estados confederados para que volvieran a la Unión dándoles la opción de abolir la esclavitud gradualmente en lugar de hacerlo de inmediato. Ningún estado aceptó su oferta, por lo que el 1 de enero decidió seguir con su plan y presentó la **Proclamación de la Emancipación**, que abolía la esclavitud en el Sur.

En el campo de batalla, la Unión encadenaba notables victorias en el sur: en julio, el general Grant tomó el puerto de Vicksburg, a orillas del Misisipi, con lo que las tropas nordistas pasaron a controlar las zonas clave del río. Mientras, la flota de la Unión había tomado el puerto de **Nueva Orleans**, y la ciudad fue ocupada a continuación. Al norte, la derrota de los confederados en la **batalla de Gettysburg**, (Pensilvania), librada del 1 al 3 de julio, supuso un punto de inflexión en la guerra.

En el otro lado del Atlántico, los londinenses estaban entusiasmados con la inauguración del **ferrocarril metropolitano**, que circulaba bajo tierra desde la calle Farringdon hasta Paddington. Este fue el primer tramo del **metro de Londres (*Tube*)**. Más tarde, otras compañías ferroviarias siguieron su ejemplo.

Proclamación de la Emancipación
El presidente Abraham Lincoln lee la Proclamación de la Emancipación ante los miembros de su gabinete. El decreto abolía la esclavitud en el Sur.

1864

Prusia y Dinamarca entraron en guerra por Schleswig y Holstein.

EN EE. UU., LA GUERRA DE SECESIÓN SEGUÍA SU CURSO. Lincoln nombró comandante en jefe de las fuerzas de la Unión al general Grant. Meses después, el general nordista **William T. Sherman** (1820–1891) emprendió la llamada «marcha hacia el mar». Sherman seguía una política de tierra quemada: destruyó las vías férreas e incendió las poblaciones desde Atlanta hasta Savannah, en la costa de Georgia.

Las relaciones entre **Dinamarca** y **Prusia**, integrada en la Confederación Germánica, se habían deteriorado. El resultado de la revuelta alemana en **Schleswig** y **Holstein**, dos ducados bajo gobierno danés, fue una breve guerra. Tropas prusianas ocuparon el territorio, y el 1 de agosto Dinamarca renunció a sus derechos sobre estos ducados, que pasaron a estar bajo el gobierno conjunto de Austria y Prusia, una situación que iba a ser fuente de conflictos en el futuro (*véase* 1866).

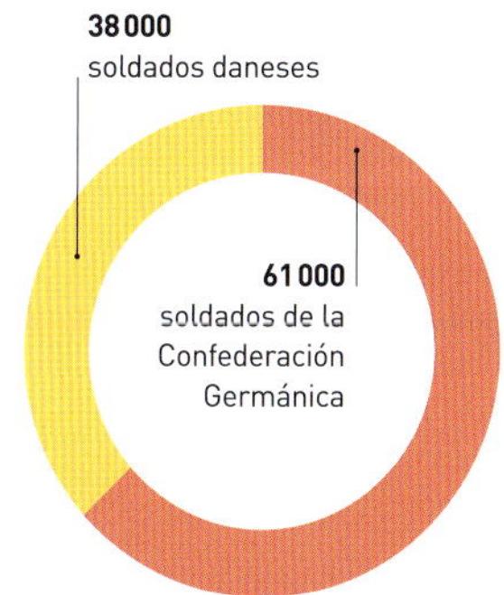

La guerra de los Ducados
La guerra empezó cuando las tropas prusianas cruzaron la frontera de Schleswig, y Dinamarca tuvo que ceder el control del ducado.

9 de marzo Primera **batalla entre dos acorazados**, el *USS Monitor* y el *CSS Virginia*.

Gran Bretaña se anexiona **Lagos**.

Omar Tall conquista Masina, hoy en Malí (África occidental).

Francia, Gran Bretaña y España envían expediciones a **México**: comienzo de la **intervención francesa**.

6–7 de abril Derrota de los confederados en la **batalla de Shiloh**.

28–30 de agosto Segunda batalla de Bull Run (guerra de Secesión).

17 de Septiembre Batalla de Antietam, que acaba con una victoria estratégica para la Unión.

23 de septiembre Otto von Bismarck asume el cargo de primer ministro de Prusia.

1 de enero Abraham Lincoln firma la **Proclamación de la Emancipación**, que libera a todos los esclavos en EE. UU.

10 de enero Inauguración en Londres del **primer metro** del mundo.

22 de enero Empieza la **insurrección de enero** contra el gobierno ruso en la antigua **confederación polaco-lituana**.

26 de mayo Empieza el **sitio de Vicksburg** (guerra de Secesión).

1–3 de julio Batalla de Gettysburg, la más larga de la guerra de Secesión.

Camboya se convierte en protectorado francés.

1 de febrero Guerra de los Ducados (hasta el 30 de octubre), parte de las guerras de unificación de Alemania (hasta 1870).

10 de abril Maximiliano I de Austria (1832–1867), coronado emperador de México.

Omar Tall muere tratando de sofocar la Revolución fulbé en África occidental.

Noviembre–diciembre «Marcha hacia el mar» del general Sherman durante la guerra de Secesión.

ORÍGENES DE LA GUERRA DE SECESIÓN
Al ampliarse EE. UU., la cuestión de qué estados podían tener esclavos fue el principal foco de disensión entre Norte y Sur. En 1860, los 18 estados libres del Norte y los 15 estados esclavistas del Sur estaban al borde de la guerra.
TERRITORIO DE MICHIGAN
VERMONT
MAINE
NEW HAMPSHIRE
PENSILVANIA
MASSACHUSETTS
NUEVA YORK
RHODE ISLAND
CONNECTICUT
ILLINOIS
OHIO
NUEVA JERSEY
INDIANA
DELAWARE
VIRGINIA
MISURI
KENTUCKY
MARYLAND
TERRITORIO DE ARKANSAS
TENNESSEE
CAROLINA DEL NORTE
CAROLINA DEL SUR
MISISIPI
GEORGIA
LUISIANA
Territorio no administrado
ALABAMA
CLAVE
Estado libre
Estado esclavista
Territorio libre
Territorio donde la esclavitud era legal
1820: EL COMPROMISO DE MISURI
El problema de la esclavitud se agravó cuando EE. UU. empezó a extenderse hacia el oeste. Cuando Misuri solicitó en 1817 convertirse en estado, su condición de esclavista provocó una crisis política. La solución fue el Compromiso de Misuri, que permitía la esclavitud en este estado, pero en ningún otro por encima de 36° 30' de latitud.
TERRITORIO DE MINNESOTA
WISCONSIN
MICHIGAN
TERRITORIO DE OREGÓN
TERRITORIO DE UTAH
Territorio indio
IOWA
TERRITORIO DE NUEVO MÉXICO
CALIFORNIA
TEXAS
FLORIDA
ARKANSAS
CLAVE
Estado libre
Estado esclavista
Territorio libre
Territorio donde la esclavitud era legal
1850: NUEVO COMPROMISO
Treinta años después del Compromiso de Misuri, la polémica sobre la esclavitud se agudizó. El senador Henry Clay propuso varios proyectos de ley considerados un compromiso: California fue admitida como un estado libre, pero también se aprobó la Ley de Esclavos Fugitivos, que penalizaba a los oficiales que no arrestaran a los esclavos supuestamente huidos, ante la indignación de los abolicionistas.
OHIO
Antietam
17 sep. 1862
Harpers Ferry
12–15 sep. 1862
NUEVA JERSEY
Bull Run
21 jul. 1861,
29–30 ago. 1862
Gettysburg
1–3 jul. 1863
Washington
Fredericksburg
13 dic. 1862
Spotsylvania Court House
8–12 mayo 1864
Batalla de los Siete Días
25 jun.–1 jul. 1862
Fuerte Monroe
26 jun.–2 jul. 1862
Columbus
Chancellorsville
30 abr.–6 mayo 1863
Territorio virgen
30 abr. 1863
5–6 mayo 1864
ILLINOIS
Indianápolis
Cincinnati
INDIANA
Lexington
Bonneville
17 jun. 1861
Saint Louis
MISURI
Louisville
Frankfort
Richmond
VIRGINIA OCC.
Staunton
8–9 jun. 1862
Richmond
KENTUCKY
Springfield
Perryville
8 oct. 1862
Cold Harbor
3 jun .1864
Norfolk
VIRGINIA
Wilson's Creek
10 ago. 1861
Cairo
Bentonville
Nashville
15–16 dic. 1864
TENNESSEE
CAROLINA DEL NORTE
Columbia
Stones River
31 dic. 1862–
2 ene. 1863
Sitio de Knoxville
17–29 nov. 1863
Fuerte Hatteras
29 ago. 1862
ARKANSAS
Memphis
5 jun. 1862
Franklin
30 nov. 1864
Chattanooga
CAROLINA DEL SUR
Fuerte Macon
23 mar.–26 abr. 1862
Desembarco en Shiloh/Pittsburg
6–7 abr. 1862
Chickamauga
19–20 sep. 1863
Monte Kennesaw
27 jun. 1864
Nov.–dic. 1864:
Las tropas de Sherman saquean e incendian gran parte de Georgia en su «marcha hacia el mar»
Wilmington
TEXAS
Charleston
MISISIPI
Atlanta
20 jul.–2 sep. 1864
Fuerte Sumter
12–14 abr. 1861
1861: LA GUERRA DE SECESIÓN
El bombardeo del fuerte Sumter, en Carolina del Sur, desencadenó un feroz conflicto que arrasó el país durante cuatro años, hasta que la Confederación se vio obligada a rendirse.
LUISIANA
Sitio de Vicksburg
19 mayo–4 jul. 1863
ALABAMA
Fuerte Pulaski
12 abr. 1862
Port Royal
17 feb. 1862
Port Hudson
21 mayo–9 jul. 1863
Mobile
12 abr. 1865
Fuerte Pickens
GEORGIA
Fernandia
2 mar. 1862
Pensacola
9–10 mayo 1862
Baton Rouge
5 ago. 1862
Tallahassee
Jacksonville
11 mar. 1862
Olustee
20 feb. 1864
Saint Augustine
9 mar. 1862
Bahía de Mobile
5 ago. 1864
Nueva Orleans
18–29 abr. 1862
Isla Ship
17 sep. 1861
Fuerte Jackson
Fuerte Saint Philip
Tampa
FLORIDA
Golfo de México
OCEANO ATLÁNTICO
CLAVE
Estados federales en 1861
Estados confederados en 1861
Estados teóricamente neutrales
Frente federal hasta dic. de 1861
Frente federal hasta dic. de 1862
Frente federal hasta dic. de 1864
Movimientos de los federales
Movimientos de los confederados
Fuertes federales
Fuertes confederados
Bloqueo naval por los federales
Victoria federal
Victoria confederada
Batalla sin claro vencedor
Ciudad destruida por los federales

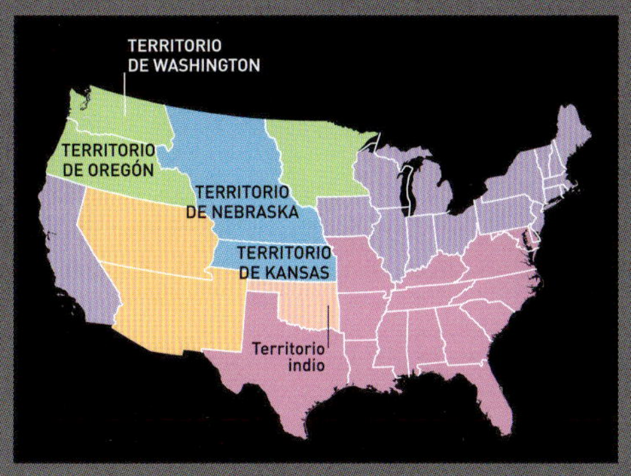

1854: LA LEY DE KANSAS-NEBRASKA
El compromiso de 1850 preveía que los territorios de Utah y de Nuevo México tomaran una decisión sobre la esclavitud al convertirse en estados. La Ley de Kansas-Nebraska aplicó el mismo principio a estos estados y permitió que la población votara sobre la cuestión de los esclavos, pero también generó una gran controversia debido a que anulaba de hecho el Compromiso de Misuri.

CLAVE
- Estado libre
- Territorio libre
- Estado esclavista
- Territorio donde la esclavitud era legal
- Territorio abierto a la esclavitud en 1854
- Territorio no sujeto a las leyes territoriales generales

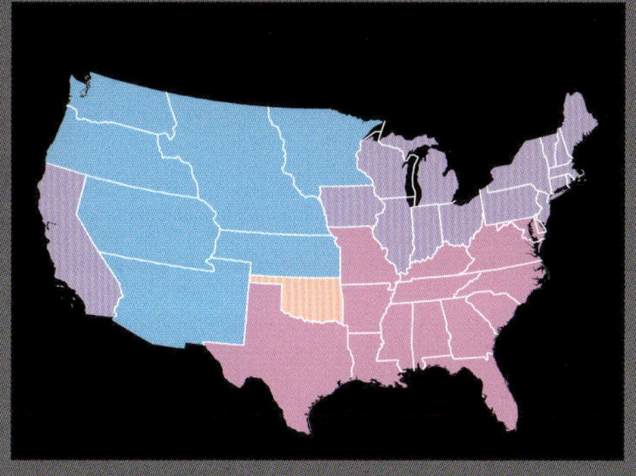

1857: LA SENTENCIA DRED SCOTT
La causa abolicionista recibió un duro revés con la sentencia del Tribunal Supremo en el caso Dred Scott contra John F. A. Sandford (*véase* 1857), según la cual la esclavitud era legal en todos los territorios. Los jueces declararon inconstitucional el Compromiso de Misuri argumentando que, aunque los estados podían prohibir la esclavitud, los territorios no eran estados.

CLAVE
- Estado libre
- Estado esclavista
- Territorio abierto a la esclavitud
- Territorio no sujeto a las leyes territoriales generales

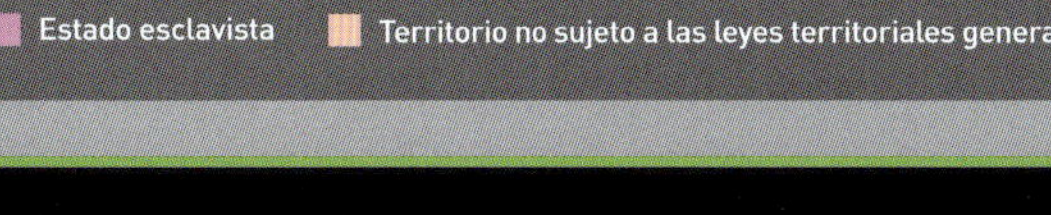

GUERRA DE SECESIÓN DE EE. UU.

EL CONFLICTO CIVIL QUE DESGARRÓ A EE. UU.

Los proyectiles disparados en 1861 en el fuerte Sumter (Carolina del Sur) desataron un combate sangriento entre miembros de una misma familia. Los hermanos del Norte y del Sur se batieron a muerte en el campo de batalla cuando la Confederación Sudista tomó las armas por el esclavismo.

La cuestión no era solo ideológica, sino también económica. Los sudistas creían que la política del gobierno federal amenazaba su modo de vida agrario y rural. El Norte industrial y urbano, presidido por Abraham Lincoln, también tenía otros intereses más allá de la emancipación de los esclavos. Sin los quince estados esclavistas, ¿qué futuro le esperaba a la Unión? La guerra costó miles de millones y destruyó la economía sudista. El bloqueo de los puertos por la flota nordista provocó que los precios se dispararan en el Sur: por ejemplo, una taza de café en un restaurante de Richmond (Virginia) llegó a costar cinco dólares en 1864. Para cuando el Sur admitió la derrota y se rindió, en 1865, ambos bandos estaban bastante maltrechos, pero el país resurgió unificado.

Este conflicto fue, además, precursor de la guerra moderna. Los avances en infraestructuras, como el ferrocarril, y las innovaciones tecnológicas armamentísticas, como los rifles de retrocarga, cambiaron la forma de combatir e incrementaron el número de bajas.

DURANTE LA GUERRA DE SECESIÓN, LA UNIÓN FACILITÓ A SUS SOLDADOS:

1000 MILLONES DE CARTUCHOS

100 MILLONES DE LIBRAS DE CAFÉ

10 MILLONES DE PANTALONES

1 MILLÓN DE CABALLOS Y MULAS

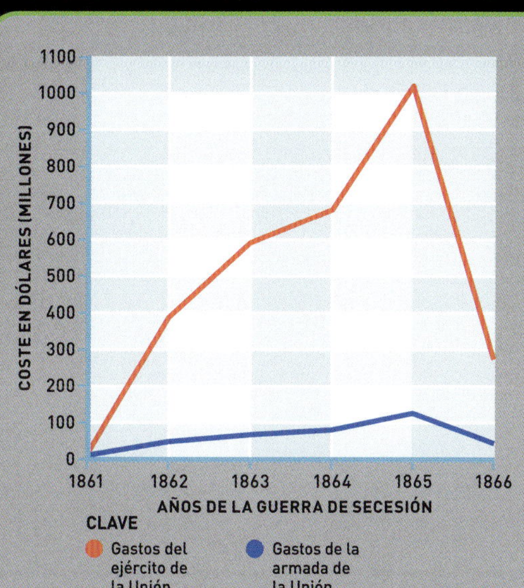

Coste de la guerra
La guerra de Secesión costó miles de millones de dólares. La Unión invirtió en el ejército y la armada cientos de millones. Para la Confederación, el coste aproximado, incluida la emancipación de los esclavos, fue de unos 2100 millones, lo que desbarató la economía sudista.

Población
El Norte industrial estaba mucho más poblado que el Sur, principalmente agrícola.

23 MILLONES POBLACIÓN DE LA UNIÓN

9 MILLONES POBLACIÓN CONFEDERADA

1200 $
ERA EL PRECIO DEL **TONEL DE HARINA** EN VIRGINIA EN 1865

1:3
Superados
A pesar de la clara inferioridad numérica del Sur, la lucha se prolongó durante cuatro años. Hubo unos 600 000 muertos.

1865

La guerra de la Triple Alianza devastó Paraguay. Esta pintura de Cándido López representa la llegada del ejército aliado a Itapirú (Paraguay).

LA GUERRA DE SECESIÓN DE EE. UU. SE ACERCABA A SU FIN. En primavera, las tropas nordistas tomaron Richmond, la capital confederada, y tras varias derrotas más, el general confederado **Robert E. Lee** (1807–1870) no vio otra opción que la de **rendirse** el 9 de abril, fecha que señaló el fin del conflicto más sangriento de la historia de EE. UU. La guerra no había modificado las fronteras estadounidenses, pero más de 600 000 hombres perdieron la vida y medio millón estaban heridos. La nueva paz pronto quedó ensombrecida: tan solo unos días después de la victoria nordista, el presidente Lincoln asistía a una función en el teatro Ford de Washington D. C. cuando el confederado **John Wilkes Booth** se coló en su palco y le disparó. Lincoln murió a la mañana siguiente, el 15 de abril.

La guerra de Secesión había terminado en EE. UU., pero la situación en **México** todavía era delicada. Las tropas estadounidenses se desplegaron en el país cuando el gobierno de EE. UU., presidido por Andrew Johnson (1808–1875), puso objeciones a la intervención francesa en los asuntos mexicanos (*véase* 1863).

En América del Sur había estallado la guerra entre **Paraguay** y sus vecinos Uruguay, Brasil y Argentina. Brasil invadió Uruguay en 1864 con la finalidad de ayudar a derrocar al partido gobernante. En respuesta, el presidente de Paraguay, Francisco Solano López (1827–1870), declaró la guerra a Brasil y poco después a Argentina. Uruguay se alineó con Brasil y comenzó la **guerra de la Triple Alianza** (o guerra de Paraguay). López falleció en el campo de batalla el 1 de marzo de 1870 y se negoció un tratado de paz. Esta guerra devastó Paraguay, cuya población se vio reducida de 525 000 a 221 000 personas.

Tropas en la guerra de la Triple Alianza
Aunque las tropas paraguayas eran mucho más numerosas, no estaban entrenadas ni tenían una jerarquía de mando: López tomaba las decisiones.

En **Jamaica**, unos campesinos a los que se había denegado tierras en las que plantar irrumpieron en el juzgado de **Morant Bay** durante una reunión del consejo parroquial, y en el altercado murieron 19 blancos. En represalia, el gobernador **Edward Eyre** dirigió un ataque despiadado contra la comunidad negra, declaró la ley marcial, encarceló a cientos de personas y mató a cientos más. Cuando las noticias llegaron a Gran Bretaña, toda la opinión pública clamó en su contra y Eyre se vio obligado a regresar a Inglaterra.

Muerte de Lincoln
Esta pintura de Alonzo Chappel representa la muerte de Abraham Lincoln, decimosexto presidente de EE. UU.

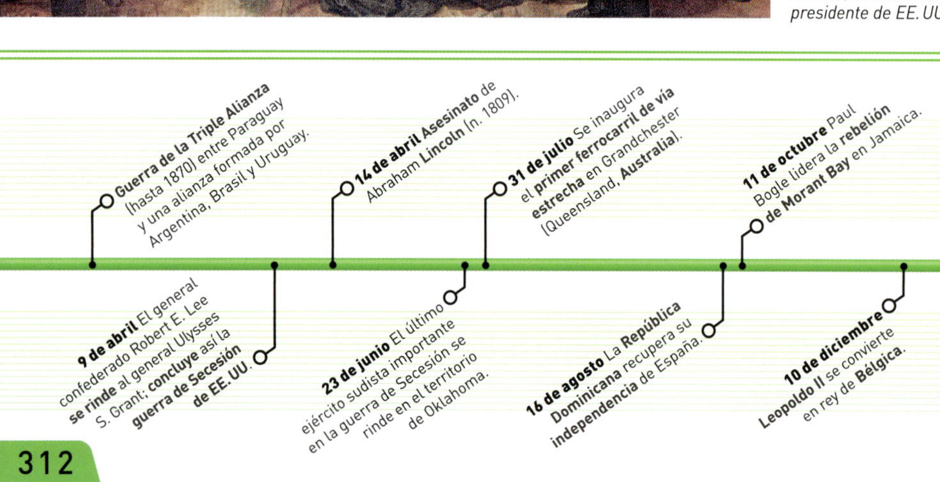

1866

EN 1866, PERÚ Y CHILE DECLARARON LA GUERRA A ESPAÑA. La causa de esta guerra, conocida como **guerra del Pacífico**, se remontaba a un incidente ocurrido en 1862, en la hacienda de Talambo, al norte de **Perú**, donde unos colonos españoles fueron atacados por trabajadores peruanos. España pidió compensaciones, pero su demanda fue ignorada, por lo que en 1864 tomó las **islas Chincha**, muy apreciadas por el **guano**, usado como abono. España pidió tres millones de pesos a cambio de las islas en 1865.

El general peruano Mariano Ignacio Prado declaró la guerra a España en enero de 1866. Chile, temeroso del regreso de los españoles a América del Sur, se unió a Perú. Aunque ambos países trataron de cerrar sus puertos, España consiguió bombardear **Valparaíso** (Chile) el 31 de marzo y **El Callao** (Perú) el 2 de mayo, antes del alto el fuego de la semana siguiente. Este fue el último intento español de reconquista en América del Sur.

Batalla de El Callao
Las tropas peruanas defienden el puerto fortificado de El Callao (Perú) durante el bombardeo de la armada española.

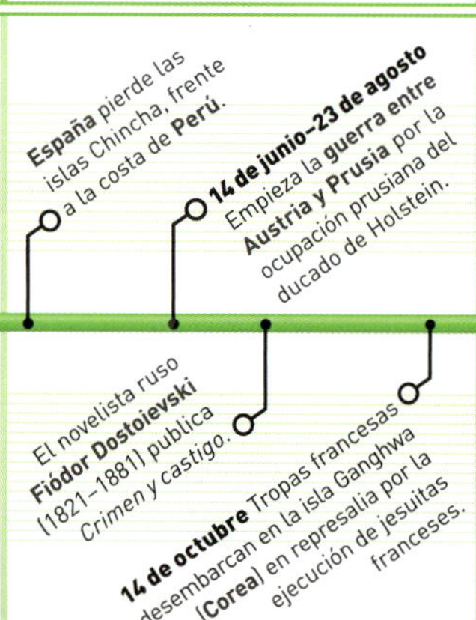

1867

La ejecución del emperador Maximiliano, por Édouard Manet.

« UN **ESPECTRO SE CIERNE SOBRE EUROPA**: EL ESPECTRO **DEL COMUNISMO**. »

Karl Marx, *Manifiesto comunista* (en colaboración con F. Engels, 1848)

EL INTENTO DE FRANCIA DE CONTROLAR MÉXICO (*véase* 1863) parecía destinado al fracaso después de la llegada de refuerzos de EE. UU. Francia decidió entonces abandonar al emperador Maximiliano I, que había sido instalado en el trono a instancias suyas y de los monárquicos mexicanos. Apresado por las fuerzas liberales, Maximiliano I fue juzgado por un consejo de guerra y fusilado el 19 de junio. Tras este suceso, Benito Juárez recuperó su cargo de presidente.

Más al norte, EE. UU. amplió considerablemente su territorio con la **compra de Alaska** a Rusia. EE. UU. recibió 1 717 856 km^2 por 7,2 millones de dólares.

En Europa, Karl Marx (*véase* recuadro) había publicado el primero de los tres volúmenes de su obra más influyente, ***El capital***. Mediante el análisis del sistema capitalista, Marx intentaba abordar diversas cuestiones económicas e históricas de mayor alcance acerca de la naturaleza de las relaciones sociales y de clases.

En **Prusia**, las tensiones con Austria habían dado lugar a la **guerra de las Siete Semanas** el año anterior. Gracias al tratado de Praga,

KARL MARX (1818–1883)

De origen alemán, Karl Marx fue un filósofo, economista, historiador, teórico político, revolucionario comunista y sociólogo, cuyas innovadoras ideas y teorías desempeñaron un papel fundamental en el desarrollo del comunismo y del socialismo modernos. Su crítica del capitalismo en *El capital* continúa teniendo una enorme influencia en la actualidad.

Prusia recibió Schleswig-Holstein, Hannover, Hesse-Kassel, Nassau y Frankfurt, lo que le permitió organizar la **Confederación Alemana del Norte**. Al frente estaba el rey prusiano, **Guillermo I** (1797–1888), respaldado por el primer ministro **Otto von Bismarck** (*véase* 1862). Austria también cedió el control sobre el Véneto (Venecia) y permitió que la región se uniera a Italia.

En España, a finales de este año, **progresistas** y **liberales** se unieron en contra de la reina **Isabel II**: ya nada podía detener la revolución, que estalló al año siguiente.

1868

Buques de guerra durante la guerra de los Diez Años (1868–1878), parte de la larga lucha por la independencia cubana de España.

DESPUÉS DE LA CAÍDA EN 1868 DEL SOGUNADO TOKUGAWA y la subida al trono del emperador Meiji Tenno (1852–1912), Japón invirtió su política aislacionista y emprendió un programa de occidentalización con el objetivo de poder plantar cara a las potencias occidentales que exigían su acceso al país (*véase* 1853). Este periodo, que recibió el nombre de **Restauración Meiji**, se caracterizó por una serie de reformas sociales profundas y duraderas, como el fin del feudalismo, la formación de un ejército nacional y la aplicación de sistemas fiscales, así como por una espectacular modernización en el campo de las infraestructuras, gracias a la llegada del ferrocarril y del telégrafo.

En España, Isabel II (1830–1904) fue destronada por la **Revolución de 1868**, también llamada **Revolución de Septiembre** o la **Gloriosa**, y partió al exilio en Francia tras la victoria revolucionaria en la **batalla de Alcolea**, el 28 de septiembre.

Al otro lado del Atlántico, en **Cuba**, los partidarios de la independencia no desaprovecharon la oportunidad para sublevarse contra los gobernantes españoles. El levantamiento, que fue liderado por Carlos Manuel de Céspedes y conocido como **Grito de Yara**, acabó desembocando en la guerra de los Diez Años (1868–1878), una campaña de guerrillas que concluyó con la derrota de los rebeldes cubanos.

Ese mismo año también tuvo lugar un levantamiento contra el dominio español en Puerto Rico. La insurrección o **Grito de Lares**, duró poco y, al igual que en el caso cubano, acabó fracasando.

En **Sudáfrica**, el control británico se expandía. Los colonizadores bóers se habían alejado de la colonia de El Cabo para ocupar tierras de las tribus locales, incluido el vecino territorio de Basutolandia (actual Lesotho). El jefe de los basutos, **Moshoeshoe I** (*c.* 1786–1870), pidió ayuda a los británicos contra nuevas incursiones en sus territorios, y la consecuencia fue la **anexión del reino** a la corona británica en 1868 como protectorado. A la muerte de Moshoeshoe, en 1870, se incorporó a la colonia de El Cabo sin consultar al pueblo basuto.

Jarrón Meiji
Jarrón japonés de Satsuma del periodo Meiji. En esta época, el gobierno japonés fomentó el arte.

1869

« ME ALEGRO DE HABER VIVIDO PARA VER ESTE DÍA, EN QUE LA GENTE DE COLOR... TIENE LOS MISMOS PRIVILEGIOS QUE LOS MÁS FAVORECIDOS. »

Thomas Garret, abolicionista estadounidense, sobre la aprobación de la 15.ª enmienda de la Constitución de EE. UU.

Ceremonia inaugural
Inauguración del canal de Suez en Port Said (Egipto). La construcción duró diez años, pero su repercusión en el comercio mundial fue inmediata.

MIENTRAS CONTINUABA la reconstrucción del sur tras la devastadora guerra, el Congreso de EE. UU. aprobó una enmienda de la constitución que los estados ratificaron en febrero de 1869 y que ampliaba el derecho al voto a todos los hombres de color, tanto si habían sido esclavos como si no. La **15.ª enmienda** establecía que «ni en EE. UU. ni en ningún estado se denegará o restringirá el derecho al voto a los ciudadanos estadounidenses por motivos de raza, color o condición de servidumbre previa».

La expansión de EE. UU. hacia el oeste se aceleró gracias a la llegada del ferrocarril. En 1869, la línea Central Pacific completó el **primer ferrocarril transcontinental**. El proyecto fue financiado con bonos del gobierno. La vía se comenzó a instalar desde Sacramento (California) en dirección este y se enlazó con las líneas existentes en Promontory (Utah) el 10 de mayo de 1869. Una gran parte del trabajo en este tramo fue realizado por más de diez mil trabajadores inmigrantes chinos. La construcción de esta línea permitió viajar rápidamente de costa a costa de EE. UU. y facilitó aún más la colonización del oeste.

Por esas fechas también se inauguró otra gran obra de ingeniería: el **canal de Suez** (*véase* 1859). Tras una década de trabajo, este canal enlazó los mares Mediterráneo y Rojo, y proporcionó un paso mucho más rápido al océano Índico.

En Sudáfrica, después del descubrimiento en 1866 de **diamantes** en la **provincia de El Cabo Septentrional**, se desató una fiebre entre bóers, británicos y nativos por extraerlos. Los británicos se anexionaron rápidamente este territorio mientras **miles de buscadores** llegaban para probar suerte.

En España, las Cortes proclamaron el 9 de junio una **Constitución** que garantizaba amplios derechos y libertades (de prensa, de culto, de reunión), y el derecho al voto para los hombres mayores de 25 años.

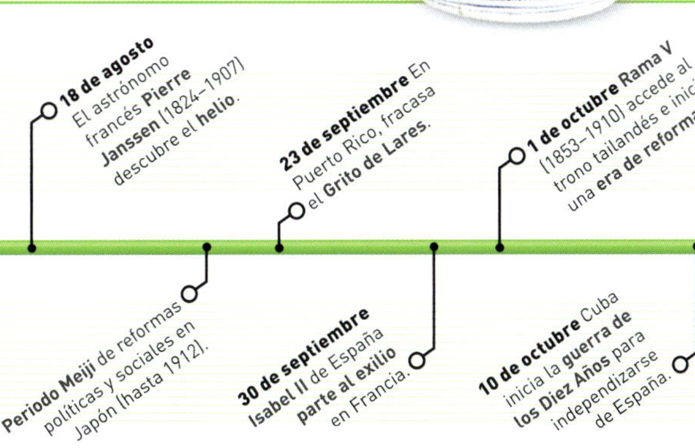

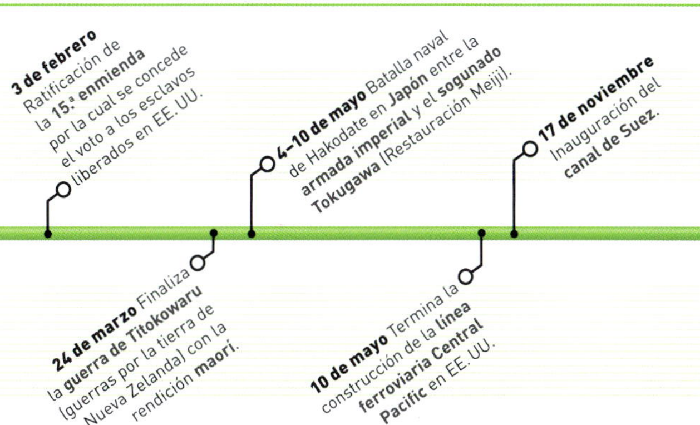

1870

En esta pintura del siglo XIX, los húsares prusianos disparan contra un globo de observación francés durante la guerra franco-prusiana de 1870.

Hombres en una batería durante la lucha entre la Tercera República y la Comuna de París que estalló al final de la guerra franco-prusiana.

« EL **EJÉRCITO ES LA** VERDADERA **NOBLEZA DE FRANCIA. »**

Napoleón III, emperador de los franceses

LA VICTORIA DE PRUSIA EN LA GUERRA DE LAS SIETE SEMANAS (*véase* 1867) sirvió para impulsar la unificación de Alemania, en esta ocasión mediante la incorporación de los estados del sur. Prusia apoyaba la propuesta del general Juan Prim para instalar al príncipe **Leopoldo de Hohenzollern-Sigmaringen** (1835–1905) en el trono de España, vacante tras la partida de Isabel II en 1868 (*véase* recuadro), aunque la presión diplomática del emperador francés Napoleón III lo impidió. Entonces, el primer ministro prusiano Otto von Bismarck, deseoso de provocar la guerra con Francia, publicó el **telegrama de Ems** (como se conoció más tarde) manipulándolo para que pareciera que se había producido un intercambio de insultos entre el embajador francés y el rey Guillermo I de Prusia. A consecuencia de este hecho, Francia declaró la guerra a Prusia el 19 de julio. Prusia ganó las batallas de **Gravelotte** (18 de agosto) y de **Sedán** (1 de septiembre), en la que un enfermo Napoleón III se **rindió** a las tropas alemanas y fue hecho prisionero. Durante el cautiverio de Napoleón, se estableció un gobierno provisional para la defensa nacional en Burdeos que decidió destituirlo y declarar la **Tercera República**. A mediados de septiembre, los prusianos sitiaban París. Privada de alimentos, la ciudad se rindió a principios de 1871. En marzo se acordó un armisticio, y Alemania obtuvo las regiones de **Alsacia** y **Lorena**.

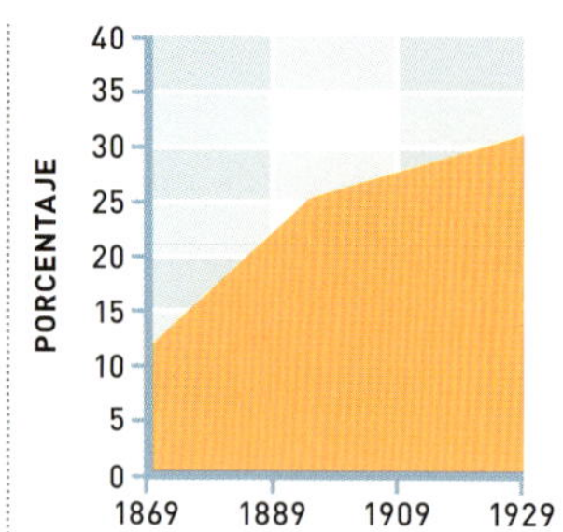

Inmigración en Argentina
En este gráfico se puede ver el aumento constante del porcentaje de inmigrantes españoles e italianos que llegaron a Argentina entre los años 1869 y 1929.

Mientras tanto, un flujo incesante de **inmigrantes** que huían de la pobreza y de las guerras en Europa comenzó a dirigirse hacia América. En EE. UU., la **población** llegó a alcanzar los 40 millones y, a finales de siglo, casi duplicó esta cifra, 76 millones. Algo similar sucedió en **Argentina**, donde de los cerca de 1,8 millones de habitantes registrados en 1870 se pasó a 8 millones en 1914. La mayoría de estos inmigrantes procedían de España e Italia, dos países profundamente castigados por años de guerra.

Sitio de París
El sitio acabó con la toma de la capital francesa por los prusianos, símbolo de la humillante derrota francesa en la guerra franco-prusiana.

1871

Unificación de Alemania
Mapa del recién unificado Imperio alemán después de la victoria de Prusia en la guerra franco-prusiana.

CLAVE
- Ganancias prusianas en 1866
- Otros estados de la Confederación Alemana del Norte en 1867
- Otros estados alemanes en 1866
- Imperio austrohúngaro en 1867
- Invasión prusiana de Francia en la guerra de 1870–1871
- Fronteras del Imperio alemán en 1871

LAS TROPAS ITALIANAS HABÍAN ENTRADO EN ROMA EN SEPTIEMBRE. Un mes más tarde, en octubre, un **plebiscito** convirtió a Roma en la capital de la Italia unida, oficializada en 1871. Sin embargo, el papa, disconforme con las disposiciones que le incumbían, decidió **excomulgar** al rey italiano Víctor Manuel II y se atrincheró en el Vaticano mientras Roma se transformaba en la nueva capital. La tensión entre el Vaticano y el gobierno italiano no se relajó hasta el siglo XX.

Mientras Francia y Prusia estaban negociando el fin de la guerra franco-prusiana en 1871, los parisinos se alzaron contra la rendición y establecieron la **Comuna de París**. Un consejo de ciudadanos que incluía a republicanos, jacobinos, socialistas y anarquistas gobernó la ciudad durante dos meses. Las duras represalias de la Asamblea Nacional, que se había trasladado a Versalles, no se hicieron esperar. El presidente Adolphe Thiers envió tropas a París y perdieron la vida veinte mil personas.

Después de la victoria obtenida sobre Francia, el rey Guillermo I de Prusia se autoproclamó **emperador de Alemania** y nombró **canciller** a Bismarck (*véase* 1862).

En otro orden de cosas, en Sudáfrica, a la fiebre de los diamantes (*véase* 1869) en El Cabo Septentrional siguió el descubrimiento de **oro** en **Transvaal**, que atrajo a miles de buscadores a la región.

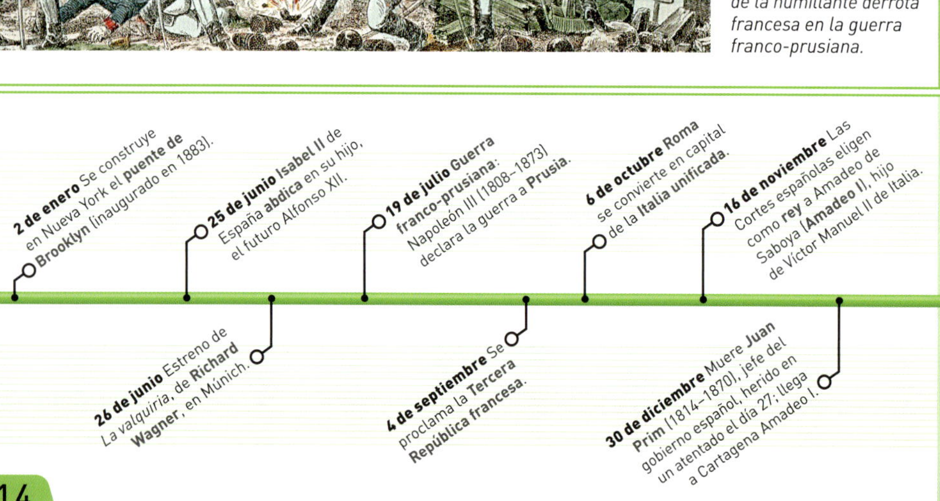

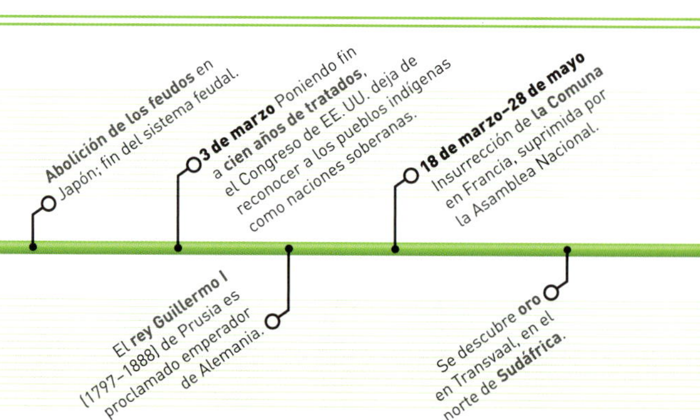

2 de enero Se construye en Nueva York el **puente de Brooklyn** (inaugurado en 1883).

25 de junio Isabel II de España **abdica** en su hijo, el futuro Alfonso XII.

26 de junio Estreno de *La valquiria*, de **Richard Wagner**, en Múnich.

19 de julio Guerra franco-prusiana: Napoleón III (1808–1873) declara la guerra a **Prusia**.

4 de septiembre Se proclama la **Tercera República francesa**.

6 de octubre Roma se convierte en capital de la **Italia unificada**.

16 de noviembre Las Cortes españolas eligen como **rey** a Amadeo de Saboya (**Amadeo I**), hijo de Víctor Manuel II de Italia.

30 de diciembre Muere **Juan Prim** (1814–1870), jefe del gobierno español, herido en un atentado el día 27; llega a Cartagena Amadeo I.

Abolición de los feudos en Japón; fin del sistema feudal.

3 de marzo Poniendo fin a **cien años de tratados**, el Congreso de EE. UU. deja de reconocer a los pueblos indígenas como naciones soberanas.

El rey Guillermo I (1797–1888) de Prusia es proclamado emperador de Alemania.

18 de marzo–28 de mayo Insurrección de la **Comuna** en Francia, suprimida por la Asamblea Nacional.

Se descubre **oro** en Transvaal, en el norte de **Sudáfrica**.

1872

Retrato de la líder de las sufragistas estadounidenses, Susan B. Anthony. En 1872 transgredió la ley y votó para llamar la atención sobre su campaña.

100 DÓLARES ES EL IMPORTE DE LA **MULTA** IMPUESTA A **SUSAN B. ANTHONY POR VOTAR**

EN EL REINO AFRICANO DE ETIOPÍA, Juan (o Johannes) IV (1831–1889) fue coronado emperador. Se le consideraba un gobernante fuerte y capaz de contener las incursiones cada vez más frecuentes de los europeos y de sus vecinos africanos. A finales de la década siguiente, Etiopía había derrotado a las fuerzas **invasoras** egipcias e italianas.

En EE. UU., la presión para que se concediera el **derecho al voto** a las mujeres iba a más. Una de sus principales defensoras era la sufragista **Susan B. Anthony** (1820–1906) quien, durante las elecciones presidenciales de 1872 desafió a la ley y votó en el colegio electoral de Rochester (Nueva York). Fue detenida y multada. Aunque se negó a pagar la multa, la causa contra ella nunca prosperó, y continuó su cruzada.

Entre tanto, el capitán Benjamin Briggs zarpó el 7 de noviembre de Nueva York para cruzar el océano Atlántico en el barco ***Mary Celeste***. El 4 de diciembre, la tripulación del *Dei Gratia* divisó al *Mary Celeste* a la deriva cerca de la costa de Portugal, totalmente **desierto**. Faltaba el bote salvavidas, y el barco se había desviado unos 1110 km respecto a las últimas coordenadas registradas en el cuaderno de bitácora. Su tripulación desapareció para siempre sin dejar rastro, y jamás se resolvió este **misterio**.

En Francia, el físico Louis Ducos du Hauron había intentado obtener una **fotografía en color** con un sistema tricolor. Patentó su procedimiento en 1868 y realizó algunas de las primeras fotografías en color.

En España estalló la **tercera guerra carlista** cuando Carlos de Borbón, duque de Madrid, pretendiente al trono español como Carlos VII, entró en España. El primer alzamiento, en Navarra y el País Vasco, fracasó muy pronto, pero prendió y prosiguió en Cataluña.

LAS GUERRAS CARLISTAS

El siglo XIX en España estuvo marcado por estas tres guerras civiles iniciadas en 1834 tras la muerte de Fernando VII. Los carlistas conservadores se oponían a que reinara la hija del rey, Isabel II (1830–1904) acogiéndose a la ley de 1713, que excluía a las mujeres del trono español, y defendían los derechos del hermano del rey, Carlos María Isidro (1788–1855). La disputa se resolvió en 1876 con la subida al trono del hijo de Isabel, Alfonso XII (1857–1885), en quien la reina había abdicado en 1870 durante su exilio.

1873

« LO PRINCIPAL ES HACER HISTORIA, NO ESCRIBIRLA. »

Otto von Bismarck, estadista alemán del siglo XIX

Real Policía Montada de Canadá
Los «mounties», como se les llamó posteriormente, desfilan con sus característicos uniformes en Regina (Saskatchewan).

BISMARCK, ANSIOSO POR PROTEGER EL CRECIENTE PODER DE ALEMANIA, propuso la **Liga de los Tres Emperadores**, una alianza entre Alemania, el Imperio austrohúngaro y Rusia que excluía expresamente a Francia. Formada en 1873, la liga duró tres años, se restableció luego en secreto en 1881, se reanudó en 1884 y se extinguió por fin en 1887 a causa de los conflictos de intereses entre Rusia y el Imperio austrohúngaro por los Balcanes.

En España, el 11 de febrero el rey **Amadeo I renunció al trono**, abrumado por las dificultades a las que tenía que enfrentarse (la guerra en Cuba (*véase* 1868), la tercera guerra carlista y las disensiones en el seno del gobierno). El mismo día las Cortes proclamaron la **Primera República**, con Estanislao Figueras al frente del gobierno.

En el Caribe, la esclavitud se abolió por fin en la isla de **Puerto Rico**. A pesar de que la trata de esclavos se había suprimido anteriormente, había continuado en la isla y en la vecina Cuba, ambas aún bajo dominio español. El final de la esclavitud se anunció en mayo de 1873, aunque se puso en práctica un sistema de **patronato** que prorrogó las condiciones de la esclavitud para algunas personas hasta 1876.

Mientras, en **Canadá**, se crearon los Fusileros Montados del Noroeste, cuya misión consistía en patrullar las provincias, en gran medida rurales, del inmenso territorio canadiense. Los primeros cientos de oficiales tenían bajo su jurisdicción cerca de 800 000 km^2. Sin embargo, a EE. UU. le inquietaba la idea de que tropas armadas patrullaran la frontera, así que se decidió cambiar su nombre por el de Policía Montada del Noroeste y más tarde por el actual, **Real Policía Montada de Canadá**, cuyos miembros se conocen como *«mounties»*.

1874

Recepción de Garnet Wolseley por el pueblo ashanti.

EN EL MES DE MARZO, EL OFICIAL DEL EJÉRCITO BRITÁNICO Charles George Gordon (1833–1885) llegó a la provincia de **Ecuatoria**, en el sur del Sudán ocupado por Egipto, a fin de asumir el control del territorio con la aprobación del jedive (virrey) de **Egipto**. Se le encomendó la tarea de establecer puestos de control a lo largo del curso del Nilo Blanco e intentar eliminar la **trata de esclavos**. En 1877 se convirtió en gobernador general de Sudán.

Entre tanto, en África occidental, la expedición de **sir Garnet Wolseley** (1833–1913) derrotó al **Imperio ashanti** (actual Ghana) y consolidó el control británico del sur de su territorio (**Costa de Oro**).

En España, a principios de enero, las tropas del general Manuel Pavía (1827–1895) desalojaron las Cortes, que fueron disueltas. En diciembre **se restauró la monarquía**.

Charles George Gordon
General británico y administrador colonial, Gordon fue invitado por el jedive de Egipto a gobernar parte de su territorio en Sudán.

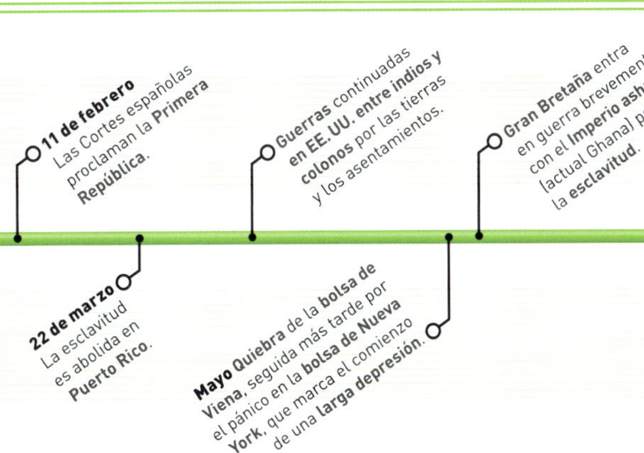

12 de enero Juan IV (1831–1889) es coronado negus de Etiopía.

El físico francés **Louis Ducos du Hauron** (1837–1920) inventa la **fotografía en color**.

1 de marzo Se crea el **primer parque nacional** del mundo en Yellowstone (EE. UU.).

Abril Empieza la **tercera guerra carlista en España** (hasta 1876).

18 de noviembre La sufragista estadounidense **Susan B. Anthony, detenida por votar** en unas elecciones en EE. UU.

4 de diciembre Se encuentra el *Mary Celeste* a la deriva y desierto.

11 de febrero Las Cortes españolas proclaman la **Primera República**.

22 de marzo La esclavitud es abolida en **Puerto Rico**.

Guerras continuadas **en EE. UU. entre indios y colonos** por las tierras y los asentamientos.

Mayo Quiebra de la **bolsa de Viena**, seguida más tarde por el pánico en la **bolsa de Nueva York**, que marca el comienzo de una **larga depresión**.

Gran Bretaña entra en guerra brevemente con el **Imperio ashanti** (actual Ghana) por la **esclavitud**.

3 de enero El **golpe del general Pavía** marca el principio del fin de la Primera República española.

Sudán queda bajo la administración británica.

Gran Bretaña gana la **segunda guerra ashanti** (1873–1874) y se asegura el control de la **Costa de Oro**.

15 de abril Primera exposición en París de un grupo de pintores que se llamarán **impresionistas**.

Silla de olmo
C. 1850
Silla de madera de olmo de estilo Ming, con travesaño en cresta y un listón curvado con tallas caladas enmarcadas en el respaldo.

Armario de olmo
C. 1860
Las puertas de este armario de olmo rectangular lacado en negro están decoradas con pájaros y árboles en flor pintados en vivos colores.

Soporte de jade para cepillo
C. siglo XVIII
En esta pieza de jade se talló la figura del filósofo taoísta Laozi. Los antiguos ritos taoístas, muy populares durante el periodo Ming, cayeron en desuso bajo el gobierno de los Qing.

Lohan de esteatita
1600–1799
Figura de lohan, un ser humano que alcanzó la iluminación meditando sobre las enseñanzas de Buda. El budismo floreció durante el periodo Qing.

LA DINASTÍA QING

OBJETOS DE LA DINASTÍA QUE GOBERNÓ CHINA DURANTE MÁS DE DOS SIGLOS

La dinastía Qing accedió al trono tras el derrocamiento del último emperador Ming en 1644. Los nuevos gobernantes eran manchúes y permanecieron en el poder hasta 1911. En esa época la población de China se triplicó hasta alcanzar los 450 millones de habitantes.

Pese a que los chinos consideraban extranjeros a los manchúes, estos se mantuvieron en el poder tanto tiempo porque siguieron gobernando como lo hiciera la dinastía Ming (1368–1644). Esta continuidad se reflejó también en las artes y la artesanía: las obras creadas en la época Qing, en particular las porcelanas, acusan una profunda influencia de los diseños de la época Ming.

Frasco
1736–1795
Este frasco se apoya sobre un pie circular y tiene un cuello corto recogido y asas en ángulo recto. Los lados están decorados con franjas de flores.

Hoja de hacha
Siglo XIX
Hoja de hacha verde y roja, hecha de calcedonia, con una máscara de taotie y gusanos de seda durmientes tallados en relieve. El filo es plano y redondeado.

Hebilla
Siglo XIX
Hebilla de jade decorada con diseños taoístas: un murciélago y dos dragones en la parte exterior, un ave fénix a un lado y un motivo de gusano de seda en el reverso.

Caja con tapa
1736–1795
En la parte superior de esta cajita con forma de melocotón (símbolo de la vida eterna) se puede ver el carácter *chun* (primavera) con el dios de la longevidad Shou Lao en un círculo y un dragón a cada lado.

Caja para té
Siglo XVIII
Esta caja para té de sencillo diseño es de peltre decorado con unos grabados florales y caligráficos.

Cuenco de té con plato
1850–1899
Parte de un juego de dos, este cuenco de porcelana con tapa y plato está decorado con esmalte de la familia rosa sobre fondo azul.

Cuenco de boda de latón
Siglo XVIII
Este cuenco para la ceremonia del matrimonio forma parte de un juego de dos. Su interior está chapado en plata (el del otro es de plata dorada) y el pie está tallado.

Tetera sancai
1662–1772
Esta tetera de porcelana sancai (tricolor) tiene forma rectangular, con paneles en relieve en cada lado que representan las cuatro estaciones.

Estuche de cubiertos de viaje
1736–1795
El contenido de este estuche incluye dos pares de palillos, un cuchillo, dos tenedores y un mondadientes de marfil.

Collar de marfil para funcionarios
Década de 1900
Los abalorios de marfil están separados en grupos de 27 por cuentas de cerámica pintada con pan de oro más grandes conocidas como cabezas de Buda. El collar lleva también sartas complementarias con diez abalorios azules.

Fundas para uñas de oro
***C.* siglo XIX**
Estas elaboradas piezas de filigrana de oro con un motivo de «hielo agrietado» se usaban para proteger las uñas de los meñiques.

Sello de Xi'an
Siglo XIX
Este sello de Xi'an ovalado tiene una inscripción incisa en los lados largos. En la base pone: «Vivir junto a la Torre Dorada».

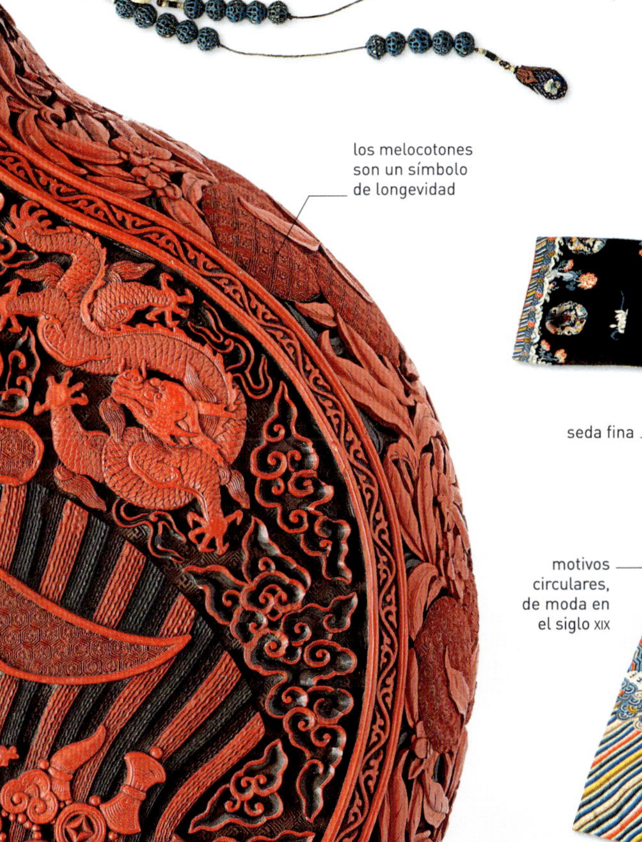

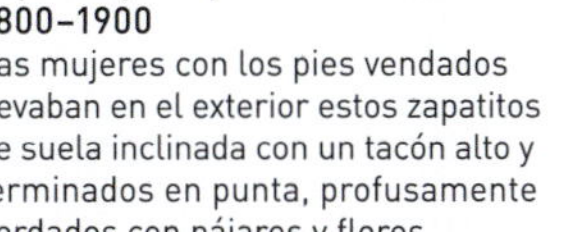

Zapatos para pies vendados
1800–1900
Las mujeres con los pies vendados llevaban en el exterior estos zapatitos de suela inclinada con un tacón alto y terminados en punta, profusamente bordados con pájaros y flores.

Vestido de seda
***C.* siglo XIX**
Este vestido de mujer de seda negra lleva un estampado floral entretejido que incluye también una escena primaveral con flores y mariposas.

1875

1876

1877

Los vencedores, del pintor realista ruso Vasili Vereschaguin (1842–1904), representa a los turcos celebrando una victoria durante la guerra ruso-turca. Las hostilidades entre Rusia y el Imperio otomano venían de lejos: ambos habían batallado en numerosas ocasiones durante los dos siglos precedentes.

LA FISURA ENTRE EL IMPERIO OTOMANO Y SUS SÚBDITOS EN BOSNIA Y HERZEGOVINA se agrandó cuando los **cristianos** de ambos territorios **decidieron rebelarse** contra el gobierno otomano y pidieron ayuda a la vecina **Serbia**, que en aquel momento gozaba de un grado de autonomía muy superior. Animada por las promesas rusas de apoyo e inspirada por el nacionalismo imperante en la región, Serbia también declaró la guerra al Imperio otomano el 30 de junio de 1876. Montenegro le siguió al día siguiente, lo que provocó que el debilitado imperio se viera inmerso en otro conflicto desestabilizador. Al principio, **Montenegro** obtuvo una victoria en Herzegovina, pero el apoyo ruso a Serbia finalmente no se materializó, y los turcos salieron victoriosos de la batalla de Aleksinac, que tuvo lugar el 9 de agosto de 1876. Debido a esta derrota, los serbios se vieron obligados a pedir ayuda a otras naciones.

En otras partes del Imperio otomano, **Egipto** continuó realizando incursiones en **Etiopía** hasta que su rey, Juan IV (*véase* 1872), declaró la guerra a los egipcios. El enfrentamiento surgió porque Ismaíl Bajá (1830–1895), jedive (virrey) de Egipto, deseaba crear asentamientos en puntos estratégicos a lo largo de la costa del **mar Rojo** en territorio etíope (la actual Eritrea). En 1875, Egipto había logrado ocupar muchas poblaciones costeras y la ciudad interior de Harar. La lucha perduró hasta 1877; para entonces, Etiopía había conseguido vencer a los egipcios en dos campañas.

EL RESENTIMIENTO Y LA PREOCUPACIÓN HABÍAN IDO EN AUMENTO entre los indios de EE. UU., muchos de los cuales habían sido obligados a abandonar sus tierras. Esta situación derivó a menudo en conflictos armados con el ejército de EE. UU. Uno de los enfrentamientos más conocido fue la **batalla de Little Bighorn**, donde el teniente coronel George A. Custer (1839–1876) y sus hombres murieron a manos de una coalición de **lakotas** y **cheyenes** (tsitsistas) el 25 de junio. Por entonces, las tropas de EE. UU. estaban luchando contra los **apaches**, que vivían cerca de la frontera con México. Estos también se resistieron a los intentos de trasladarlos a una reserva y atacaron los asentamientos blancos. El conflicto se prolongó durante una década más hasta que **Jerónimo** (1829–1909), su líder, se rindió en 1886.

> « LA NACIÓN QUE CONSIGA **DOMINAR EL AIRE** LLEGARÁ A **DOMINAR EL MUNDO**. »
>
> **Alexander Graham Bell**, inventor escocés

En otro lugar de EE. UU., el inventor de origen escocés **Alexander Graham Bell** (1847–1922) patentó un aparato que permitía «transmitir telegráficamente sonidos vocales o de otro tipo»: el **teléfono**, que había inventado el italiano **Antonio Meucci** y que cambiaría para siempre la comunicación en el mundo.

En México, **Porfirio Díaz** (*véase* recuadro), que había servido como soldado, intentó iniciar una revuelta contra el presidente Sebastián Lerdo de Tejada. Después del fracaso de su primer intento a principios de 1876, huyó a EE. UU., pero regresó en noviembre y derrotó a las tropas del gobierno. En mayo de 1877 fue elegido presidente y gobernó México durante décadas.

Entre tanto, el explorador **Henry Morton Stanley** (1841–1904) trataba de seguir el río Lualaba, en el **Congo**, cuyo curso aún no se había cartografiado, para averiguar dónde desembocaba. Stanley ya era célebre por sus exploraciones en África: previamente había sido enviado por un diario de EE. UU. para buscar a otro explorador: David Livingstone (*véase* 1855). Fue en 1871, a orillas del lago Tanganyika, cuando se cree que pronunció la famosa frase: «El doctor Livingstone, supongo».

PORFIRIO DÍAZ
(1830–1915)

General, político y presidente de México, Díaz descendía de europeos e indígenas. Pese a que sus orígenes eran muy humildes, consiguió hacerse un nombre en el ejército. Una vez obtuvo la presidencia del país, consolidó sus apoyos y estableció una maquinaria política que le mantuvo en el poder y le permitió eliminar toda oposición y controlar la política mexicana a lo largo de sus más de treinta años de mandato (porfiriato).

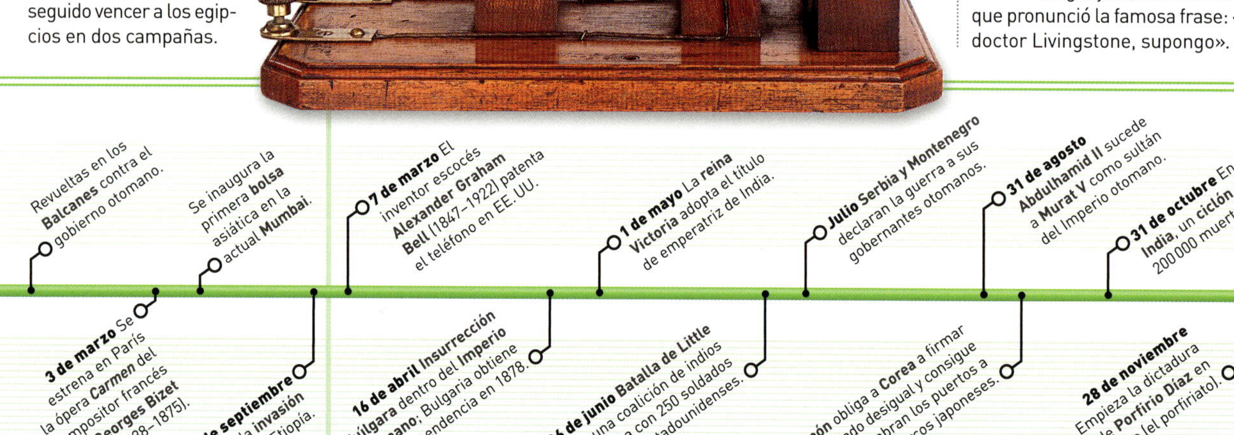

Uno de los primeros teléfonos
Este primitivo modelo de teléfono, llamado teléfono de caja, posee un micrófono con forma de trompetilla; el sonido se transmitía mediante un electroimán.

EN CHINA, LA HAMBRUNA HACÍA ESTRAGOS en las provincias del norte. La sequía había afectado el año anterior al **río Amarillo**, una fuente vital de agua, y en 1877 se agravó por la falta de lluvia y por una plaga de langostas. Cuando volvieron las lluvias a finales del año siguiente, entre 9 y 13 millones de personas habían muerto en una región con 108 millones de habitantes.

En Sudáfrica, el descubrimiento de **oro** (*véase* 1871) había exacerbado las tensiones entre los colonos bóers y británicos, quienes ya gobernaban la mayor parte del país. En 1877, los británicos consiguieron **anexionarse el Transvaal**. Sin embargo, los afrikáners se rebelaron contra este avance y recuperaron su independencia unos años después (*véase* 1881).

Hambre en China
Ilustración de un semanario francés sobre la pobreza durante los años del hambre en China, cuando millones de personas murieron en el norte.

Revueltas en los **Balcanes** contra el gobierno otomano.

3 de marzo Se estrena en París la ópera ***Carmen*** del compositor francés **Georges Bizet** (1838–1875).

Se inaugura la primera **bolsa** asiática en la actual **Mumbai**.

7 de septiembre Fracasa la **invasión egipcia** de Etiopía.

7 de marzo El inventor escocés **Alexander Graham Bell** (1847–1922) patenta el teléfono en EE. UU.

16 de abril Insurrección búlgara dentro del **Imperio otomano**; Bulgaria obtiene la independencia en 1878.

1 de mayo La **reina Victoria** adopta el título de emperatriz de India.

25–26 de junio Batalla de Little Bighorn: una coalición de indios acaba con 250 soldados estadounidenses.

Julio Serbia y Montenegro declaran la guerra a sus gobernantes otomanos.

31 de agosto Abdulhamid II sucede a **Murat V** como sultán del Imperio otomano.

Japón obliga a **Corea** a firmar un tratado desigual y consigue que se abran los puertos a los barcos japoneses.

31 de octubre En **India**, un **ciclón** deja 200 000 muertos.

28 de noviembre Empieza la dictadura de **Porfirio Díaz** en **México** (el porfiriato).

Rusia declara la guerra al **Imperio otomano** (hasta 1878) por el control de Serbia.

6 de mayo Caballo Loco (c. 1840–1877), jefe de los oglalas lakotas, se rinde al ejército de EE. UU.; más tarde es asesinado.

Gran hambruna en el **norte de China** (hasta 1879).

Rumanía declara su independencia del Imperio otomano.

1878

El óleo *Los vencidos. Réquiem por los muertos*, de Vasili Vereschaguin, muestra las dramáticas secuelas de una derrota rusa durante la guerra ruso-turca de 1877–1878.

RUSIA DECIDIÓ DECLARAR LA GUERRA DE NUEVO al Imperio otomano el 24 de abril de 1877 en un intento de ayudar a los serbios en su lucha contra los otomanos (*véase* 1875). Rusia contó con la ayuda de Rumanía (Moldavia y Valaquia unidas). La **guerra ruso-turca de 1877–1878** incluyó un sitio de cinco meses a la ciudad búlgara otomana de Plevna (Pleven), que terminó cayendo ante las fuerzas rusas. Rusia consiguió tomar también algunas fortalezas clave, y se pidió una tregua. El 3 de marzo de 1878 se alcanzó un acuerdo, conocido como **tratado de San Stefano**, por el que Serbia, Rumanía y Montenegro conseguían la independencia, mientras que se concedía cierta autonomía a Bulgaria bajo la autoridad rusa.

Las potencias europeas no vieron con buenos ojos dicho acuerdo, ya que existían muchos intereses encontrados. **Prusia** respaldaba el deseo de Gran Bretaña de frenar la expansión rusa hacia Bulgaria (que en aquella época llegaba hasta el mar Egeo) y se negaba a dejar que Rusia extendiera su poder naval hasta el Mediterráneo. El **Imperio austrohúngaro** quería seguir ocupando Bosnia y Herzegovina para mantener su influencia regional intacta y acabar con el creciente nacionalismo eslavo.

Mientras, Gran Bretaña había firmado la **convención de Chipre** con Turquía. Este acuerdo permitía a los británicos administrar la isla mientras estuviera bajo soberanía turca, de modo que pudieron establecer su presencia y una base naval en la parte oriental del Mediterráneo con el objetivo de frenar posibles incursiones rusas en la región.

Al margen de la mesa de negociaciones diplomáticas europeas, los británicos se vieron envueltos una vez más en una guerra con los afganos. La **segunda guerra afgana** (hasta 1880) estalló cuando agentes británicos descubrieron que existían negociaciones entre el líder afgano, Sher Alí Kan (1825–1879), y Rusia. La negativa de Sher Alí a recibir a una delegación británica complicó la situación. En noviembre de 1878, tropas británicas invadieron la región. Sher Alí pidió ayuda a Rusia, pero se le dijo que firmara la paz con Gran Bretaña. Sher Alí falleció un año más tarde, y su hijo Muhammad Yaqub Kan (1849–1923) **firmó** un tratado por el que cedía a los británicos el **paso de Jaybar**. Poco después fue asesinado un enviado británico y las tropas británicas volvieron a tomar Kabul. Muhammad Yaqub huyó. Le sucedió Abd al-Rahman Kan (*c.* 1844–1901) que puso fin al conflicto y favoreció los intereses británicos.

Combatientes afganos
Fotografía de unos soldados afganos con rifles artesanales en Jalalabad (Afganistán) durante el segundo conflicto anglo-afgano.

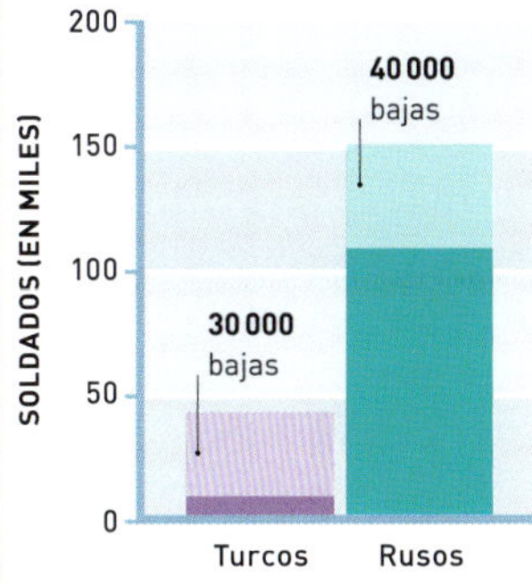

Sitio de Plevna
Aunque vencieron los rusos, las exiguas tropas turcas resistieron heroicamente el avance de Rusia hacia el interior de Bulgaria.

23 de enero En España, **Alfonso XII** se casa con su prima **María de las Mercedes de Orleans**, que muere el 26 de junio.

2 de febrero Grecia declara la guerra al **Imperio otomano**.

3 de marzo El **tratado de San Stefano** declara la independencia de Montenegro, Serbia y Rumanía.

24 de abril Rusia declara la guerra al **Imperio otomano**.

El inventor estadounidense **Thomas Edison** (1847–1931) funda la **Compañía eléctrica Edison**.

Junio–julio Reunión del **Congreso de Berlín** sobre los Balcanes.

21 de noviembre Segunda guerra anglo-afgana (hasta 1880) por las conversaciones de Afganistán con Rusia.

1879

Este óleo muestra la defensa de Rorke's Drift el 22 de enero, donde un puñado de soldados británicos repelió el ataque de cuatro mil soldados zulúes.

EN AMÉRICA DEL SUR, PERÚ, BOLIVIA Y CHILE se disputaron el control sobre la región del **desierto de Atacama**, a lo largo de la frontera entre Perú y Chile. En la década anterior se había descubierto en la región **salitre** (compuesto sobre todo por **nitrato de sodio** y que se llamó **nitrato de Chile**), un valioso mineral que las empresas chilenas habían comenzado a explotar. No tardaron en surgir discrepancias acerca del control de este territorio. Al principio, Chile y Bolivia decidieron fijar su frontera en el paralelo 24, pero Bolivia no estaba satisfecha con el trato, por lo que llegó a un acuerdo secreto con Perú para defender sus intereses en el desierto. Posteriormente, Bolivia expropió a las empresas chilenas, por lo que el presidente de Chile se vio obligado a enviar soldados. El 5 de abril, Chile **declaró la guerra** formalmente **a Bolivia y Perú**. La llamada **guerra del Pacífico** se libró tanto en tierra como en el mar, y no concluyó hasta 1883: Chile conservó el control sobre la región de Antofagasta, muy rica en minerales.

En el sur de África, el ejército británico se enfrentó a los zulúes en la **guerra anglo-zulú**. Los británicos querían entrar en su territorio, pero el rey Cetshwayo (1826–1884) se opuso y consiguió reunir a unos sesenta mil guerreros. Después de su inesperada victoria en Isandlwana, los zulúes atacaron la misión británica de **Rorke's Drift**, donde fueron rechazados por un puñado de soldados que mataron a 550 guerreros. Tras siete meses de conflicto, los británicos obtuvieron la victoria definitiva en la batalla de Ulundi el 4 de julio y se hicieron con el control del territorio.

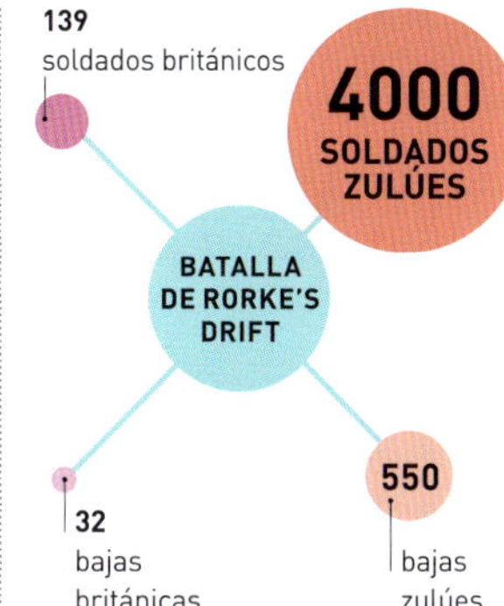

La batalla de Rorke's Drift
Los zulúes tenían pocas armas de fuego efectivas. A pesar de su abrumadora desventaja numérica, los británicos vencieron gracias a la superioridad de sus armas.

Buque hundido en la bahía de Iquique
Buques chilenos y peruanos en la batalla de Iquique, durante la guerra del Pacífico. Bolivia también participó en esta contienda.

14 de enero Inicio de la **guerra del Pacífico** (hasta 1883): Chile declara la guerra a Bolivia y Perú.

22 de enero Los **zulúes** masacran a los **británicos** en la **batalla de Isandlwana**, durante la **guerra anglo-zulú** (entre enero y julio).

3 de febrero Primera **farola eléctrica** en Gran Bretaña.

Junio Se **descubren las pinturas rupestres** de Altamira, en Cantabria (España).

Julio Se funda el **Partido Socialista Obrero Español** (PSOE).

29 de noviembre Boda de **Alfonso XII** de España con **María Cristina de Habsburgo-Lorena**.

31 de diciembre Thomas Edison realiza su primera demostración pública de la **bombilla de incandescencia** en Menlo Park, Nueva Jersey (EE. UU.).

1880

Trabajadores nativos excavando el canal durante el primer y fallido intento de conectar el océano Atlántico y el Pacífico a través del istmo de Panamá.

1881

« LA **PUERTA** QUE **NADIE QUIERE CRUZAR** PARECE ESTAR **SIEMPRE ABIERTA** DE PAR EN PAR **PARA MÍ. »**

Clara Barton, fundadora de la Cruz Roja estadounidense

Clara Barton fue la fundadora de la Cruz Roja estadounidense.

ANIMADO POR EL ÉXITO DEL CANAL DE SUEZ (*véase* 1869), Ferdinand de Lesseps (*véase* 1859) decidió planificar un canal que conectara el océano Pacífico y el Atlántico a través del **istmo de Panamá**. Sin embargo, el proyecto tropezó con dificultades nada más comenzar, en 1881: surgieron desacuerdos sobre los planos del canal, la maquinaria no funcionaba bien sobre el terreno, y muchos trabajadores fallecieron por enfermedades tropicales.

Mientras tanto, el desarrollo de la **refrigeración** comercial comenzó a transformar las relaciones entre consumidores y productores. Por ejemplo, el queso y la carne ya se podían exportar a larga distancia. El 2 de febrero llegó a Londres el primer cargamento de carne congelada que superó intacto la travesía desde Australia. En los años siguientes se produjo un *boom* de **envíos** de carne y otros productos agrícolas de Australia, Nueva Zelanda y Argentina a Europa.

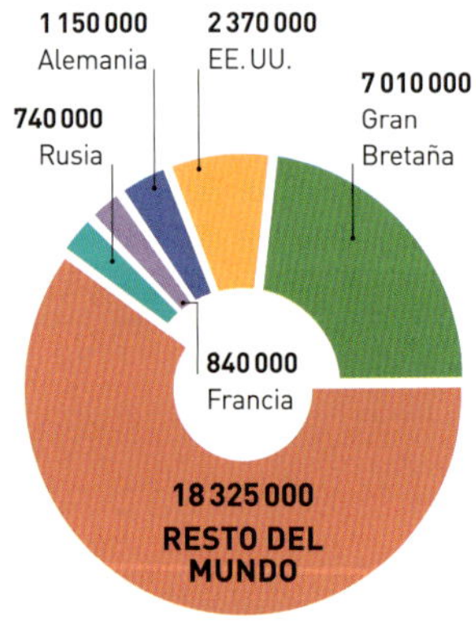

Tonelaje en 1881
Peso total de las mercancías enviadas en barcos de más de cien toneladas. La refrigeración facilitó el transporte de alimentos en grandes cargueros.

LOS BÓERS

Los bóers («granjeros» en holandés) de Sudáfrica eran colonos descendientes de holandeses, alemanes y hugonotes franceses que se trasladaron al norte de la provincia de El Cabo en busca de autonomía. Hablaban afrikáner, una lengua derivada del holandés. Los primeros colonos llegaron al puerto fundado en 1652 por la Compañía Holandesa de las Indias Orientales en el cabo de Buena Esperanza. A menudo entraron en conflicto con zulúes y británicos.

Por esas mismas fechas, **Thomas Edison** (1847–1931), inventor estadounidense, encontró un medio seguro de iluminación artificial. Perfeccionó el diseño de las **bombillas** (pp. 298–299) para evitar que se sobrecalentaran, lo que las hacía mucho más seguras. Inmediatamente empezaron a proliferar los sistemas de alumbrado en calles, empresas, hoteles y viviendas.

En Cuba, una ley sancionada por el rey español Alfonso XII **abolía la esclavitud**, pero al mismo tiempo instauraba el **patronato**, como en Puerto Rico (*véase* 1873), que perduró hasta 1886.

EN EL SUR DE ÁFRICA, LAS TENSIONES ENTRE LOS COLONOS BÓERS (*véase* recuadro) y los británicos por la anexión de Transvaal (*véase* 1877) había degenerado en violencia. Los bóers habían fundado la **República Sudafricana** en el área de Transvaal y comenzaron a proteger con las armas su independencia. Así, en 1880 había estallado la primera guerra de los Bóers. Después de la derrota de las tropas británicas por los bóers en la batalla de Majuba Hill, que se libró el 27 de febrero de 1881, el conflicto llegó a su fin en el mes de marzo gracias a la **paz de Pretoria** que reconocía la independencia de la República Sudafricana, aunque permitía que Gran Bretaña mantuviera una dudosa «soberanía» sobre ella. Esto no contribuyó demasiado a rectificar la situación, y el fuerte resentimiento entre británicos y bóers estalló de nuevo antes del fin de siglo (*véase* 1899).

Mientras, **Francia** intentaba ampliar su influencia en los territorios del norte de África. Con Argelia ya bajo su control, dirigió su mirada al vecino **Túnez**, que se hallaba bajo control otomano. A lo largo del último medio siglo, los gobernadores tunecinos se habían visto atrapados entre las demandas otomanas y los acreedores europeos, especialmente después de la bancarrota del gobierno en 1869, tras la cual se impuso una comisión financiera al territorio formada por británicos, franceses e italianos. Con el pretexto de que los tunecinos habían entrado en territorio argelino, Francia decidió enviar 36 000 soldados en 1881. Ese mismo año, Túnez se convirtió en **protectorado francés** por el **tratado de El Bardo**. Los militares franceses tomaron el territorio y se designó a un ministro francés para que hiciera de enlace con el bey (gobernador) de Túnez, quien solo ejercía un control limitado.

En **Rusia** se produjo un estallido de violencia antisemita que culminó en **pogromos** en el sur del país, incluida la ciudad de Kiev, y que continuaron hasta el año 1884. El detonante fue el **asesinato** del zar reformista **Alejandro II** (1818–1881) a manos de un grupo que se hacía llamar Voluntad del Pueblo. Los rumores falsos de que los judíos habían sido los responsables y de que el gobierno iba a incitar a la población a vengarse de ellos terminaron propiciando los violentos ataques, que provocaron que un gran número de judíos decidiera emigrar a Europa occidental, EE. UU. y Palestina.

En EE. UU., la maestra y enfermera **Clara Barton** (1821–1912) organizó la Cruz Roja estadounidense en el seno de la organización humanitaria Cruz Roja Internacional, fundada en 1863.

Por último, en Nuevo México, el *sheriff* **Pat Garrett** (1850–1908) logró capturar el 30 de abril a uno de los forajidos más célebres de EE. UU., **Billy el Niño** (*c.* 1859–1881), apodo de William H. Bonney Jr., de quien se decía que con solo 21 años ya había asesinado como mínimo a 27 hombres. Tras su detención, fue encarcelado y condenado a muerte, pero consiguió fugarse. Garrett lo encontró de nuevo y lo mató de un tiro el 14 de julio.

El arma de Garrett
Réplica de una pistolera de la época en que Pat Garrett logró capturar a Billy el Niño.

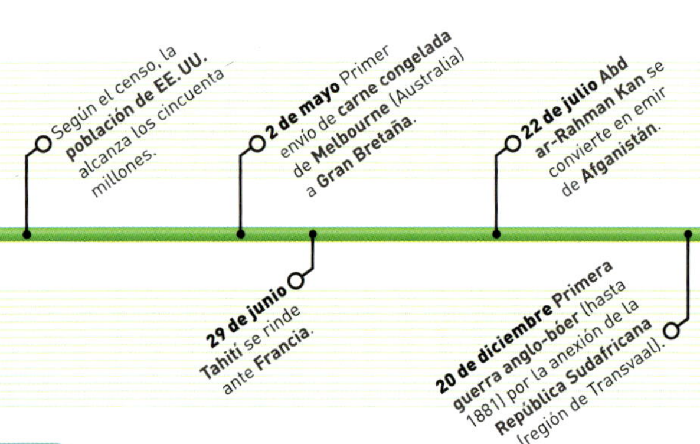

Según el censo, la **población de EE. UU.** alcanza los cincuenta millones.

2 de mayo Primer envío de **carne congelada** de **Melbourne** (Australia) a **Gran Bretaña**.

29 de junio **Tahití** se rinde ante **Francia**.

22 de julio Abd ar-Rahman Kan se convierte en emir de **Afganistán**.

20 de diciembre Primera guerra anglo-bóer (hasta 1881) por la anexión de la **República Sudafricana** (región de Transvaal).

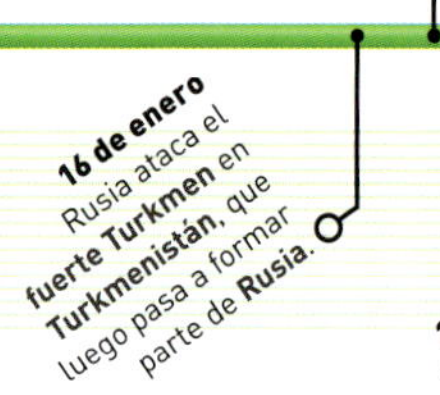

16 de enero Rusia ataca el **fuerte Turkmen** en **Turkmenistán**, que luego pasa a formar parte de **Rusia**.

13 de marzo Alejandro II de Rusia es **asesinado** en un atentado con bomba, lo que desencadena la **violencia antisemita**.

21 de mayo La enfermera **Clara Barton** funda la **Cruz Roja estadounidense**.

Túnez se convierte en **protectorado francés**.

20 de julio Guerras indias: el jefe **Toro Sentado**, jefe de la tribu **sioux** hunkpapa, se rinde a las **tropas de EE. UU.**

23 de julio El **tratado fronterizo** entre **Chile** y **Argentina** fija la frontera entre ambos países.

3 de agosto Fin oficial de la **primera guerra anglo-bóer** por el tratado de paz de Pretoria; se restablece en Transvaal la **República Sudafricana**.

1882

Bombardeo de Alejandría. Los británicos ganaron esta batalla naval y consiguieron destruir las baterías fortificadas del puerto.

DURANTE LOS AÑOS ANTERIORES, los intereses de Francia y de Gran Bretaña en Egipto habían ido en aumento y con ellos la intervención europea en los asuntos egipcios. La intervención se consideraba legítima por la deuda financiera de Egipto con ambos países. En el año 1882, Egipto se hallaba en bancarrota, y el jedive (virrey) tenía serias dificultades para hacer valer su autoridad. Ismaíl Bajá (1830–1895) había sido destituido por el sultán otomano en 1879, presionado por Francia y Gran Bretaña, y sustituido por su hijo, Muhammad Tawfiq (1852–1892). En la época del **doble control** francés y británico de las finanzas egipcias, la agitación interna nacionalista fue en aumento.

Temerosa de lo que un levantamiento nacionalista podría significar para el canal de Suez, en el que tenía grandes intereses, Gran Bretaña decidió lanzar un ataque disuasorio: la Royal Navy bombardeó los fuertes de **Alejandría** el 11 de julio del año 1882. Egipto fue ocupado militarmente y se convirtió en un protectorado británico.

Un poco más al sur, en **Sudán**, las tropas británicas seguían luchando en la **guerra anglo-sudanesa** (1881–1899) contra los secuaces del poderoso **Muhammad Ahmad bin Abd Allah** (1844–1885), que había declarado una guerra santa después de autoproclamarse Mahdi. Su misión era restaurar la justicia en el mundo que, según creía, iba a llegar pronto a su fin.

En Europa se formó una **alianza antifrancesa**, conocida como **Triple Alianza** y constituida por Alemania, Austria-Hungría e Italia. Los dos primeros miembros ya habían establecido alianzas previamente (*véase* 1873) con Rusia. Italia se les sumó tras su disputa con Francia por territorios del norte de África.

Mientras, en Francia, el científico **Louis Pasteur** (1822–1895), ya conocido por haber desarrollado en 1863 el proceso de **pasteurización** para reducir los gérmenes nocivos en alimentos y bebidas, se había dedicado a las vacunas (*véase* 1796). Gracias a sus investigaciones acerca del carbunco, una infección bacteriana que había matado muchas ovejas en Europa y que afecta también a los humanos, en 1881, tras haber realizado con éxito experimentos a gran escala con animales, se empezaron a producir vacunas.

1883–1884

Xilografía coloreada a mano que muestra la isla de Krakatoa (Indonesia) antes de su destrucción por la erupción del volcán en 1883.

AL PRINCIPIO DE LA GUERRA DE SUDÁN, LAS TROPAS BRITÁNICAS sufrieron repetidas derrotas frente al ejército revolucionario del **Mahdi** (*véase* 1882). El 26 de enero, las tropas del Mahdi tomaron la ciudad de El Obeid, en el centro del territorio sudanés, y continuaron avanzando hacia **Jartum**, que había sido puesta bajo control administrativo británico por orden del jedive egipcio (*véase* 1874), y la tomaron después de un sitio de nueve meses.

Mientras, Francia había ido conquistando territorios en torno al **río Níger** (Níger) y había iniciado otra contienda en la isla de Madagascar, frente a la costa africana oriental, con la clara intención de proteger el territorio francés. En 1883, Francia invadió la isla durante la **guerra franco-malgache** contra los hova, el grupo malgache más numeroso, y bombardeó las ciudades costeras de Majunga y de Tamatave desde el mar. En 1885 se llegó a un acuerdo por el que se aceptaba la ocupación francesa de Diego Suarez (Antsiranana), en el norte de la isla; sin embargo, las tensiones persistieron hasta que Francia envió quince mil soldados que desembarcaron en Majunga y tomaron la capital.

En el transcurso de la **conferencia de Berlín sobre África** (*véase* 1885), Alemania reclamó territorios en el suroeste de África (Namibia), Togo, Camerún y parte de la isla de Zanzíbar, situada frente a la costa de Tanzania, en África oriental. **Italia**, por su parte, consiguió el control sobre los pueblos costeros que se hallaban a orillas del mar Rojo, pero no realizó más incursiones en territorio **etíope**.

En el océano **Pacífico**, Gran Bretaña y Alemania se repartieron más territorios. Gran Bretaña, que durante la década de 1870 había establecido varios asentamientos a lo largo de toda la costa de la mitad oriental de **Nueva Guinea** (actual Papúa-Nueva Guinea), se anexionó la isla en 1884, excepto la parte noreste, que pasó a Alemania.

El puente de Brooklyn
El gran puente colgante de Nueva York sobre el East River fue construido entre 1870 y 1883. Su longitud total es de 1825 m.

20 de marzo Gran Bretaña entra en **Liberia** y exige que el territorio sea cedido a **Sierra Leona**, bajo control británico.

20 de mayo Se forma la **Triple Alianza** entre Alemania, el Imperio austrohúngaro e Italia.

11 de junio Revuelta **urabí** contra el jedive y las potencias europeas en **Egipto**.

11 de julio Gran Bretaña ocupa **Egipto**.

Julio Los **bóers** crean la república de **Stellaland** en la actual provincia **Noroeste de Sudáfrica**.

20 agosto Estreno en Moscú de la ***Obertura 1812*** de Piotr Ilich **Tchaikovski**, que commemora la resistencia rusa ante Napoleón.

1 de septiembre Kimberley (Sudáfrica) se convierte en la primera población de África con **alumbrado eléctrico**.

1883 Francia inicia la conquista de **Madagascar**: toma **Níger** y ocupa Agadez (hasta 1904).

26 de agosto de 1883 La erupción del **volcán Krakatoa** mata a unas cuarenta mil personas y destruye la isla. La explosión se oye a 5000 km de distancia.

20 de octubre de 1883 Guerra del Pacífico: **Perú** abandona tras el tratado de Ancón con Chile.

1884 El inventor británico nacido en EE. UU. **Hiram Maxim** (1840–1916) inventa la **ametralladora automática**.

13 de marzo de 1884 Empieza el **sitio de Jartum** (Sudán, hasta el 26 de enero 1885) por las tropas del Mahdi.

5 de julio de 1884 Alemania reclama **Camerún**.

1884 La **conferencia de Berlín sobre África** (hasta 1885) inaugura la **«carrera por el reparto de África»**.

1884 Golpe de estado en Corea con ayuda de Japón, sofocado con ayuda de China.

Octubre de 1884 El **meridiano de Greenwich**, declarado meridiano cero.

1884 Alemania consigue **Togo** y **Camerún**.

Diciembre de 1884 Tras haberse retirado en 1880, **Porfirio Díaz** vuelve a la presidencia de **México**.

1885

Poblado africano del valle del Congo a principios del siglo XIX. El territorio congoleño fue asignado al rey belga Leopoldo II en 1885.

CUANTO MÁS PODER ACUMULABAN ALGUNAS NACIONES EUROPEAS, en especial Alemania e Italia, mayor era su deseo de participar en la creciente colonización de los territorios de ultramar, sobre todo los africanos. Con este fin, entre el 15 de noviembre de 1884 y el 26 de febrero de 1885, se celebró la **conferencia de Berlín sobre África**, considerada luego el desencadenante de la «**carrera por el reparto de África**», en la cual las potencias participantes se disputaron el territorio. No se consultó a ningún líder africano; de hecho, ni siquiera se les invitó. Portugal abrió la sesión, movida por su interés en proteger sus derechos sobre parte del estuario del río Congo (Zaire), una reivindicación que fue desatendida, ya que la cuenca del río se declaró neutral para salvaguardar el comercio en la región. Un grupo de inversores europeos recibió parte de la región del **Congo**, que pasó a estar bajo el control del rey Leopoldo II (1835–1909) de Bélgica con el nombre de **Estado Libre del Congo**.

> « **COMPARADOS CON LEOPOLDO**, NERÓN, CALÍGULA, ATILA, TORQUEMADA, GENGIS KAN Y OTROS **ASESINOS DE SU CALAÑA** SON MEROS **AFICIONADOS**. »
>
> **Mark Twain**, escritor estadounidense, sobre Leopoldo II en el Congo

Entre tanto, en Alemania, el ingeniero **Gottlieb Daimler** (1834–1900) patentó un motor de combustión interna de alta velocidad. Daimler, junto con su socio Wilhelm Maybach (1846–1929) siguieron estudiando más a fondo el motor, montado en bicicletas y carruajes. Otro alemán, **Karl Benz** (1844–1929) produjo en 1885 el **primer automóvil** del mundo. Benz fundó su propia empresa, Benz & Co, que luego se fusionó con Daimler y fabricó los automóviles **Mercedes-Benz**.

En **India**, la creciente conciencia política y el auge del nacionalismo condujeron a la fundación del **Congreso Nacional Indio**, cuya primera reunión se celebró en diciembre.

Primer Benz
Coche Benz de tres ruedas con motor de gasolina. El ingeniero alemán Karl Benz patentó su diseño en 1886: había nacido el automóvil.

1886

Tropas del cuerpo de infantería ligera de Somerset cruzan un río birmano durante la guerra anglo-birmana.

LA EMANCIPACIÓN DE LOS ESCLAVOS EN CUBA llegó finalmente en octubre de 1886, tras una larga lucha. Gran Bretaña había prohibido el comercio de esclavos en 1807, y abolió la práctica de la esclavitud en 1833; pero España y otras potencias coloniales europeas no habían seguido su ejemplo. En 1817, España firmó un tratado con Gran Bretaña para acabar con el comercio de esclavos, pero luego lo ignoró. Tras la pérdida de la mayoría de sus colonias en América, España dependió para llenar sus arcas de las islas azucareras que conservaba, **Cuba** y **Puerto Rico**. Así, aunque las patrullas antiesclavistas británicas interceptaran barcos negreros entre la costa oeste africana y La Habana, la esclavitud no solo continuó, sino que aumentó a lo largo del siglo XIX. En 1840 se transportó a Cuba a cerca de 14 500 esclavos, número que llegó a casi 30 500 en 1859.

En 1866, el transporte forzado de esclavos se había reducido a poco más de mil, y, el año siguiente, España proclamó leyes que ilegalizaban la trata. No obstante, esto no liberó al considerable número de esclavos en la isla, aunque, tras años de abolición progresiva, un real **decreto emancipó a los esclavos** en 1886.

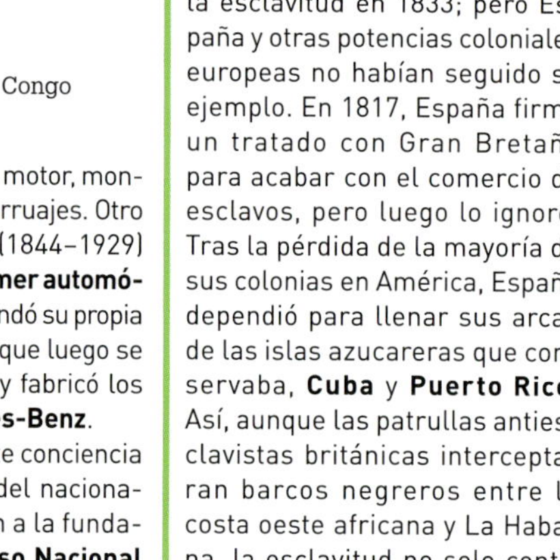

Tercera guerra anglo-birmana
Aunque la guerra solo duró unas semanas, la insurgencia birmana posterior continuó hasta el año 1899 y segó numerosas vidas más, como muestra el gráfico.

El 1 de enero, la anexión de **Birmania** por Gran Bretaña fue el inicio de una larga insurgencia. La anexión fue la culminación de la **tercera guerra anglo-birmana** de 1885, que duró solo unos meses, y se debió a las negociaciones del rey birmano **Thibaw** con Francia para una alianza política y construir una línea de ferrocarril hasta la frontera con India. Thibaw se negó a recibir a un diplomático británico enviado para protestar. Gran Bretaña se había anexionado ya la baja Birmania tras la guerra anterior (véase 1852), y reaccionó ocupando **Mandalay** y el norte de Birmania. Thibaw fue depuesto, y el territorio fue anexionado a India, controlando así los británicos el antiguo reino y poniendo fin a la guerra. A esto siguieron cuatro años de campaña esporádica de guerrilla de los birmanos.

4 de enero Primera apendicectomía con éxito.

Tanganyika se convierte en protectorado alemán.

31 de marzo Bechuanalandia (actual Botswana) se convierte en protectorado británico.

El partido político indio **Congreso Nacional Indio** se reúne por primera vez.

Alemania se anexiona las **islas Marshall**, en el océano Pacífico.

Leopoldo II de Bélgica (1835–1909) establece el **Estado Libre del Congo**.

Derrota de **Serbia** en la guerra contra **Bulgaria**.

Se construye en Chicago el primer **rascacielos** del mundo.

Los ingenieros alemanes **Gottlieb Daimler** (1834–1900) **Karl Benz** (1844–1929) desarrollan los **primeros automóviles**.

18 de septiembre Rumelia Oriental se une a **Bulgaria**.

30 de septiembre Los británicos abolen la república bóer de **Stellaland** y la agregan a Bechuanalandia.

25 de noviembre Muere **Alfonso XII** de España; la reina María Cristina asume la regencia, con Práxedes Mateo Sagasta (1825–1903) al frente del gobierno (hasta 1890).

1 de enero Gran Bretaña se anexiona **Birmania**.

29 de enero Karl Benz patenta el primer **automóvil** de gasolina moderno.

3 de marzo El tratado de Bucarest pone fin oficialmente a la **guerra serbio-búlgara**.

8 de mayo Se vende la primera **Coca-Cola**.

17 de mayo Nace **Alfonso XIII** de España (m. 1941), hijo póstumo de Alfonso XII.

4 de septiembre Guerras indias: **Jerónimo**, jefe de los apaches (diné), se rinde al ejército de EE. UU.

7 de octubre España abole la esclavitud en **Cuba**.

1887

Emblema de Fernando I, príncipe y, desde 1910, zar de Bulgaria

BULGARIA SE VIO ENVUELTA EN LA MAREA NACIONALISTA QUE BARRIÓ TODA EUROPA a principios del siglo XIX (*véase* 1848). La lucha por la independencia de Bulgaria, donde quince mil patriotas búlgaros fueron masacrados por las tropas turcas en 1876, logró despertar el interés del resto de Europa. Dos años después se estableció un pequeño principado búlgaro, y Gran Bretaña y el Imperio austrohúngaro se aseguraron de que Rusia no poseyera influencia sobre él. En 1885, Bulgaria se había fusionado con **Rumelia Oriental**, y tras un golpe de estado, los dos estados se unificaron. Esto alteró el equilibrio de poder en los Balcanes y provocó la declaración de guerra serbia. Este conflicto fue breve y en 1886 se restableció la paz. Al año siguiente, el **príncipe Fernando** de Sajonia-Coburgo-Gotha (1861–1948) fue elegido príncipe de Bulgaria.

El zar Fernando I
Sello de correos de Fernando I, príncipe y luego zar búlgaro. Después de una lucha política interna, el pueblo búlgaro buscó un líder lejos del país.

1888

Esclavos lavando diamantes en una mina brasileña.

Población esclava
Cuando se abolió la esclavitud en Brasil y en Cuba, los esclavos eran muy numerosos. Al principio, la emancipación fue lenta.

EN BRASIL, AL IGUAL QUE EN CUBA, LA ESCLAVITUD perduró después de que fuera abolida en otras antiguas colonias de América del Sur. Como España, **Brasil** también había recibido fuertes presiones por parte de Gran Bretaña para terminar con la trata de esclavos, lo cual ocurrió en 1850. Durante los treinta años posteriores, el **sentimiento abolicionista** fue creciendo progresivamente hasta que el emperador **Pedro II** (1825–1891) se mostró al fin receptivo. Sin embargo, Pedro II deseaba abolir la esclavitud de una manera gradual, puesto que era consciente del riesgo que podía comportar una reacción por parte de los propietarios de esclavos, habida cuenta de lo sucedido tanto en Cuba como durante la guerra de Secesión estadounidense (*véase* 1861). Así, en 1871 se promulgó una medida gradual que fue conocida como **Ley de Rio Branco**, por la que se liberaba a los hijos de madres esclavas; más tarde, en 1885 se emanciparon los esclavos mayores de 65 años, y por fin, **en mayo de 1888 se proclamó la abolición** total.

1889

« SI EXISTIERA UN **DIOS**, CREO QUE **LE GUSTARÍA QUE PINTARA** LA MAYOR PARTE POSIBLE DEL **MAPA DE ÁFRICA CON LOS COLORES BRITÁNICOS**. **»**

Cecil J. Rhodes, colonialista británico

EN PARÍS, EL INGENIERO GUSTAVE EIFFEL (1832–1923) DESLUMBRÓ a la ciudad y a toda Europa con su espléndida **torre metálica**, inaugurada el 31 de marzo. Eiffel había ganado el concurso para construir una torre conmemorativa del centenario de la Revolución francesa con ocasión de la **Exposición Universal de París** de 1889. Con sus 300 m, la torre doblaba la altura de la gran pirámide de Keops de Guiza y atrajo a casi dos millones de visitantes durante los primeros seis meses tras su inauguración.

Mientras, Brasil entraba en una nueva etapa política después de que un golpe militar derrocara a **Pedro II**. Los militares, el clero y la aristocracia estaban disgustados por algunas de sus reformas y, pese a que continuaba siendo querido por el pueblo, el monarca abdicó y se instauró una república.

Torre Eiffel
Criticada al principio por los parisinos, que la consideraban horrenda, la torre se ha convertido en todo un símbolo de París.

Más al norte, en Panamá, el proyecto del canal (*véase* 1880) se enfrentaba a múltiples dificultades, y se detuvieron las obras. La **Compagnie Universelle du Canal Interocéanique** y la opinión pública francesa habían ido perdiendo la fe en la idea a medida que aumentaba la mortalidad entre los trabajadores y los problemas de construcción se sucedían.

En el continente africano, el poder británico se expandió rápidamente cuando **Cecil John Rhodes** (1853–1902), reputado ya gracias a las minas de oro y diamantes sudafricanas, recibió los permisos para su empresa **British South African Company** en 1889. Se esperaba que la compañía respetase las leyes y creencias locales, pero el objetivo de Rhodes era conseguir territorios en el sur de África y seguir extrayendo minerales valiosos. Rhodes pasó a encarnar los excesos de la **codicia colonialista**.

EL IMPERIALISMO

Hacia finales del siglo XIX, las potencias europeas vivieron una época de gran expansión colonialista. Bajo el epígrafe «El coloso de Rhodes» (dcha.), esta ilustración de la revista satírica *Punch* (1892), muestra al británico Cecil J. Rhodes a horcajadas sobre África tras anunciar su proyecto de tender el telégrafo entre Ciudad del Cabo y El Cairo. El periodo se caracterizó por la explotación europea de todos sus recursos naturales y por la indiferencia o la crueldad hacia los nativos.

22 000

NÚMERO DE TRABAJADORES QUE **MURIERON DURANTE** EL **INTENTO FALLIDO DE CONSTRUIR** EL **CANAL DE PANAMÁ**

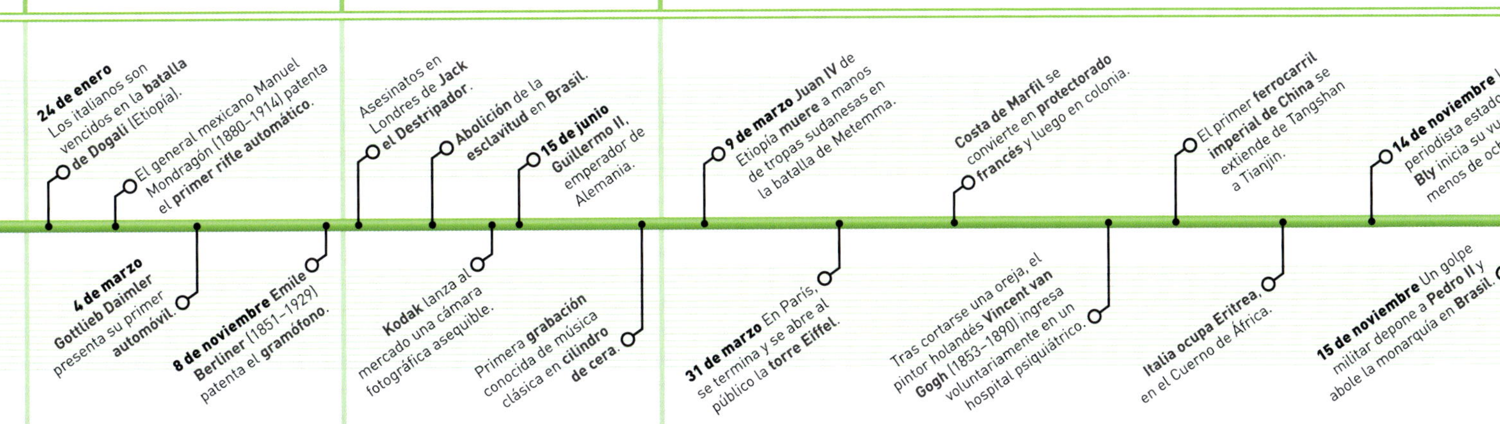

EL MUNDO COLONIAL

LA ERA DE LA EXPANSIÓN COLONIAL EUROPEA POR TODO EL MUNDO

Durante los siglos XVIII y XIX, el mundo fue testigo de un implacable deseo europeo de controlar territorios en todo el globo. Las colonias no eran solo fuentes codiciadas de valiosos recursos naturales, sino también un escenario en el que se dirimían rivalidades europeas.

En la época colonial, España, Gran Bretaña, Francia, Alemania, Holanda, Portugal, Italia y, en menor medida, Dinamarca y Suecia, compitieron por los territorios. Un país podía perder colonias en una guerra para luego reclamarlas en un juego político a mayor escala. Con frecuencia, como en India, las colonias empezaron siendo factorías mercantiles, pero luego, los países europeos fueron tomando el control mediante maniobras políticas y militares. Los pueblos de América, África, India y el Sureste Asiático fueron a menudo víctimas de los prejuicios raciales y la opresión política, así como de la explotación económica: las materias primas se extraían con mano de obra esclava y se exportaban a beneficio de la metrópoli. Esta situación se prolongó hasta después de la Segunda Guerra Mundial, cuando muchas colonias empezaron a exigir su independencia en todo el mundo (pp. 422–423).

« EL SOL NO SE PONE EN EL **IMPERIO BRITÁNICO.** »

Dicho inglés de principios del siglo XIX (una frase similar se atribuye a Carlos V y a Felipe II de España, en el siglo XVI)

CONGO BELGA

Bélgica

Expansión

Siguiendo el ejemplo de Gran Bretaña y Países Bajos, el pequeño estado belga explotó el vasto territorio del Congo, 76 veces mayor que Bélgica.

1037651

5764731

Minoría étnica

Los españoles eran una minoría dentro de las colonias españolas de Nueva España (México y América Central). En 1810, no llegaban al 5 % de la población total.

LONGITUD DE LA LÍNEA (KM)

4000, 3200, 2400, 1600, 800, 0

Rodesia del Norte y del Sur · Sudán · África Oriental Británica y Uganda · Sierra Leona · Costa de Oro · Niasalandia

TERRITORIOS BRITÁNICOS EN ÁFRICA

El ferrocarril

En 1914, miles de km de vías férreas recorrían y mejoraban la comunicación de los extensos territorios de las colonias británicas en África y, gracias a ello, la región se abrió al comercio.

Territorios coloniales

En 1910, el Imperio británico era con mucho el mayor, al ocupar más del doble del globo que la siguiente potencia colonial, Francia.

Población colonial

En 1910, millones de personas en todo el mundo vivían bajo un régimen colonial. Gran Bretaña gobernaba poblaciones repartidas por África, América, Asia y Oceanía.

EE. UU. · PORTUGAL · BÉLGICA · ALEMANIA · FRANCIA · GRAN BRETAÑA

40, 35, 30, 25, 20, 15, 10, 5, 0

EXTENSIÓN DEL IMPERIO (MILLONES DE KM²)

0, 50, 100, 150, 200, 250, 300, 350, 400

POBLACIÓN DE LAS COLONIAS (MILLONES)

LA CONSTRUCCIÓN DE UN IMPERIO

En el siglo XVIII, la mayoría de los asentamientos coloniales se encontraban en zonas costeras de todo el planeta, donde atracaban los barcos. Las factorías comerciales se convirtieron en ciudades, a menudo con una arquitectura de estilo europeo, reflejo de los cambios políticos. Con las mejoras militares, de los transportes y sanitarias (las enfermedades tropicales mataron a miles de europeos), el dominio colonial, en especial el británico y el francés, se expandió durante todo el siglo XIX. En cambio, España, que había empezado a construir un imperio antes y dominaba una gran parte de América Central y del Sur a principios del periodo, había perdido casi todas sus posesiones en la década de 1820.

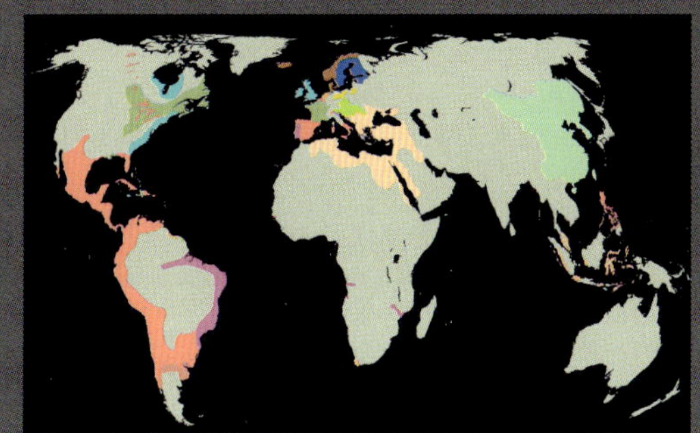

1700 En el siglo XVIII, la expansión europea estaba limitada a ciudades portuarias, a excepción de las colonias españolas en América Central y del Sur. Vastas extensiones del mundo estaban bajo el control de dos antiguos imperios: el otomano y el Qing.

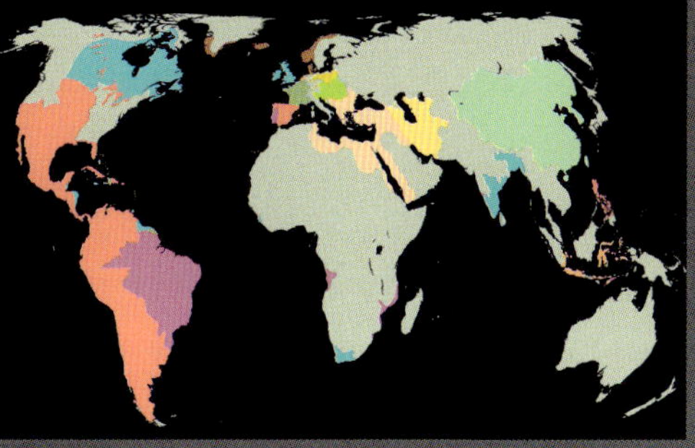

1800 Tan solo un siglo después, España, Francia y Gran Bretaña dominaban ya casi toda América. Los británicos habían realizado además una serie de incursiones en India tras el desmembramiento del Imperio mogol y habían empezado a explorar África.

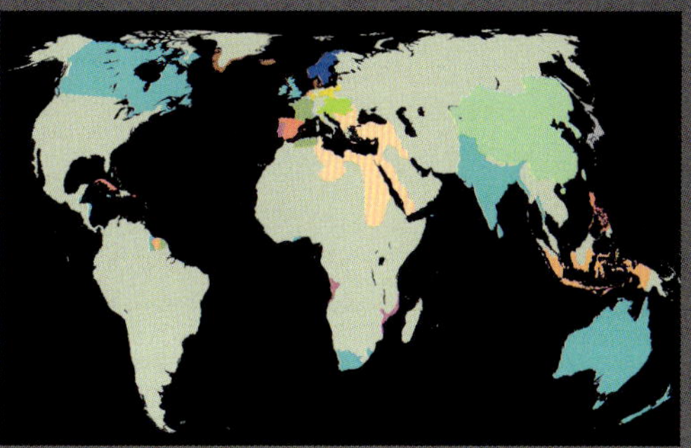

1850 A mediados del siglo XIX, el mapa mundial se había transformado con la independencia de América Latina. Británicos y franceses se habían centrado en África, muy rica en recursos naturales, mientras que los holandeses siguieron expandiéndose por el Sureste Asiático.

1900 Con el cambio de siglo, el colonialismo europeo había llegado a todo el planeta. En la década de 1880, durante la «carrera por el reparto de África», las grandes potencias se disputaron el territorio. EE. UU. se hizo con territorios en el Caribe y en el Sureste Asiático.

CLAVE

- Imperio otomano
- Posesiones británicas
- Posesiones francesas
- Posesiones danesas
- Posesiones españolas
- Posesiones portuguesas
- Imperio sueco
- Posesiones neerlandesas
- Imperio alemán en 1900; de Hohenzollern en 1700; Prusia en 1800 y 1850
- Imperio austriaco en 1850; de los Habsburgo en 1700 y 1800
- Posesiones italianas en 1900; de la República de Venecia en 1700
- Posesiones del Imperio ruso
- Posesiones japonesas
- Imperio Qing
- Posesiones de EE. UU.

1890

Grabado coloreado que representa la matanza de lakotas en Wounded Knee (Dakota del Sur) por soldados del 7.º Regimiento de Caballería de EE. UU.

EN EL OESTE DE ESTADOS UNIDOS, LAS TENSIONES Y LOS ENFRENTAMIENTOS esporádicos entre el ejército y los indios continuaron tras la **batalla de Little Bighorn** (*véase* 1876). Los indios se vieron sometidos a unas condiciones de vida que cada vez eran más duras, abrumados por las enfermedades, la pobreza y la pérdida de sus cosechas. Desde la década de 1880, los **lakota** (sioux) venían practicando un ritual místico conocido como **danza de los espíritus**, que se basaba en la creencia de que en 1891 llegaría un mesías indio que lograría unir a todos los nativos desterrados. Los trances, los bailes y el frenesí colectivo preocupaban a los agentes encargados de vigilar las reservas, que intentaron prohibir estas danzas. Los lakotas se rebelaron, por lo que hacia finales de año tuvo que intervenir el ejército.

La reserva situada a orillas del arroyo **Wounded Knee**, en Dakota del Sur, fue el escenario de una **terrible matanza** que tuvo lugar el 29 de diciembre, cuando tropas estadounidenses asesinaron a unos 150 indios (hombres, mujeres y niños) e hirieron a otros 50. Durante el desarme de los lakotas se produjo una refriega, y en la carnicería resultante perdieron la vida también 25 soldados estadounidenses, muchos de ellos víctimas de fuego amigo. Este fue el último gran conflicto que se dio entre los indios norteamericanos y el ejército de EE. UU., aunque las relaciones entre ambos grupos continuaron siendo malas.

6:1 **Muertos en Wounded Knee** *150 lakotas y 25 soldados estadounidenses perdieron la vida. Otros 50 indios resultaron heridos durante el enfrentamiento.*

Por otro lado, en Europa, la pequeña isla de **Helgoland**, que se halla en el mar del Norte frente a la costa alemana, cerca de Schleswig-Holstein, había pasado a manos británicas en 1814 después de ser conquistada por la Royal Navy siete años antes. Sin embargo, a medida que la expansión de Alemania avanzaba en Europa y África, se alcanzó un acuerdo para que Gran Bretaña la cediera a Alemania a cambio de las islas de **Zanzíbar** y **Pemba**, cerca del puerto de Tanga, en Tanzania, frente a la costa este africana. Alemania convirtió la isla de Helgoland en una enorme base naval.

Zanzíbar pasó entonces a engrosar el ya considerable territorio africano de Gran Bretaña, obtenido por medio de los acuerdos alcanzados con Alemania y de las exigencias formuladas a raíz de la conferencia de Berlín (*véase* 1885). Al año siguiente, Gran Bretaña fundó formalmente el **Protectorado de Nyasalandia**, que pasó a denominarse Protectorado Británico de África Central en el año 1893 y posteriormente, en 1907, Nyasalandia. Parte de este territorio se hallaba a orillas del lago Nyasa (Malawi) y en el valle del río Shire, en el actual Malawi.

Arma lakota
Cuchillo y vaina de cuero bordada con abalorios como los que llevaban los guerreros lakotas del siglo XIX.

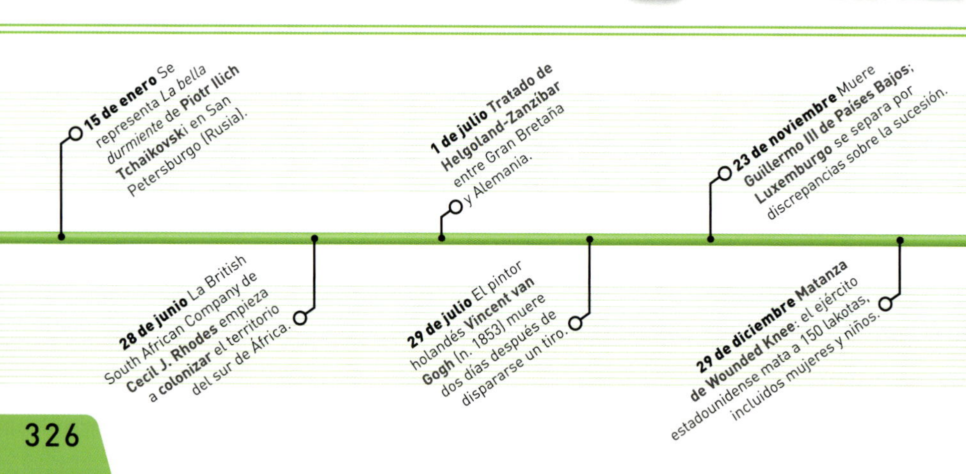

1891

El ferrocarril Transiberiano durante su construcción en Rusia.

9310 KILÓMETROS ES LA **DISTANCIA** QUE **RECORRÍA** EL **FERROCARRIL TRANSIBERIANO** DESDE **MOSCÚ** HASTA EL PUERTO DE **VLADIVOSTOK**

RUSIA HABÍA COMENZADO A CONSTRUIR UN FERROCARRIL a través de su extenso territorio, desde Moscú hasta el puerto de **Vladivostok**, situado 9198 km al este. El proyecto había sido ideado por Alejandro III (1845–1894) y se conocía como el **ferrocarril Transiberiano**. Rusia obtuvo autorización de China para tender las vías por algunas zonas de Manchuria, gracias a lo cual en 1901 se pudo completar la línea del Transmanchuriano. Las obras empezaron en los extremos occidental y oriental, y se unieron en el centro. En 1904, los tramos que comunicaban Moscú y Vladivostok estaban conectados y en funcionamiento. Este ferrocarril facilitó el traslado rápido de personas dentro de Rusia y los posteriores asentamientos en la casi desierta **Siberia**.

En España empezaban a despuntar los nacionalismos regionales. En marzo se presentó durante una reunión de asociaciones catalanistas un sistema de autonomía (**Bases de Manresa**) para Cataluña.

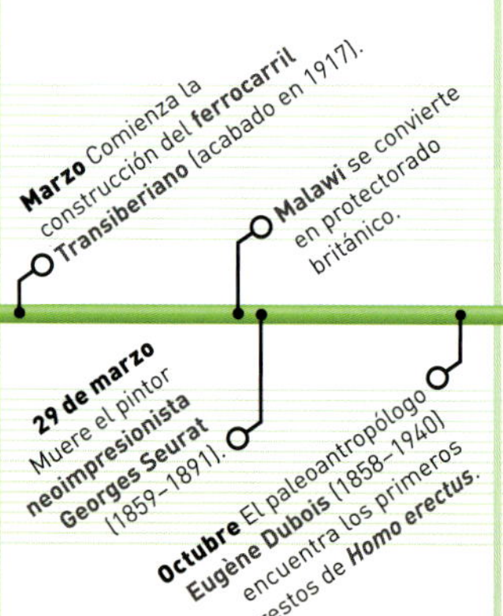

1892

La gran mezquita de Djenné (Malí) fue erigida tras la colonización francesa.

Los franceses en África
Sello de correos del África Occidental Francesa con una máscara nativa. Francia logró dominar gran parte de la región.

GRAN BRETAÑA Y FRANCIA CONTINUABAN SU AVANCE HACIA EL INTERIOR DE ÁFRICA occidental. Los británicos se habían apropiado de los puertos a lo largo de la costa y en 1861 se anexionaron Lagos, un punto clave para controlar la **región yoruba**, que rodeaba la parte inferior del río Níger y correspondía a la mayor parte del territorio suroccidental de la actual Nigeria. Aprovechando las divisiones internas entre gobernantes yoruba, en 1892 derrocaron al gobierno de **Ijebu**, parte del sistema político yoruba.

Del mismo modo, Francia también sacó partido de las divisiones en el seno del **Imperio toucouleur** musulmán, firmó tratados con sus vecinos y construyó fuertes en su territorio. En 1892, los franceses ya controlaban gran parte de la región que rodea el río Senegal.

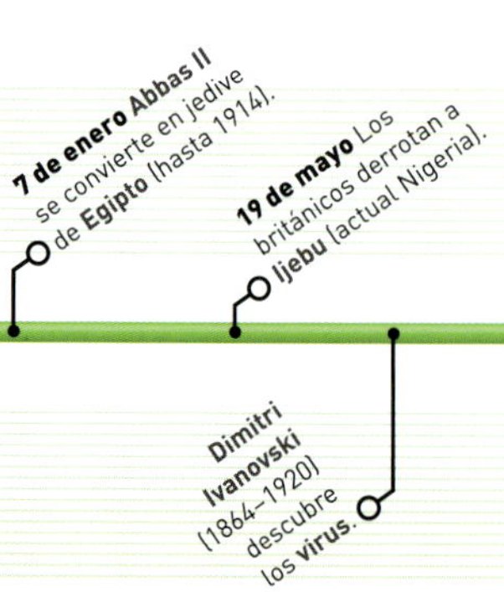

1893

« LA DISCRIMINACIÓN POR... RAZA, CLASE, SEXO O RELIGIÓN ES INHUMANA Y DEBE DESAPARECER. »

Kate Sheppard, sufragista, en el panfleto *Is it Right?* (1892)

AL MARGEN DE LAS CONQUISTAS DE FRANCIA EN EL INTERIOR DE ÁFRICA OCCIDENTAL, los territorios costeros situados alrededor del reino de **Dahomey** (actual Benín) habían logrado resistir. En 1889, el Imperio británico había cedido a los franceses la ciudad costera de **Cotonou**, en Dahomey, sin antes consultar a los dahomeyanos. El resultado de tal agravio fue la primera guerra franco-dahomeyana (1889–1890), que concluyó con la firma de un tratado por el que se cedía Cotonou y Porto Novo a Francia a cambio de pagos al rey de Dahomey. Sin embargo, las tensiones persistieron, y en 1892 comenzó otra guerra, en esta ocasión a causa de la **esclavitud**. El rey Behanzin (1844–1906) continuaba permitiendo las redadas de esclavos a pesar de la abolición. Además, atacó un cañonero francés. Francia respondió contraatacando con un ejército formado por tropas francesas y senegalesas, y conquistó el reino, que pasó a estar bajo dominio francés en 1893.

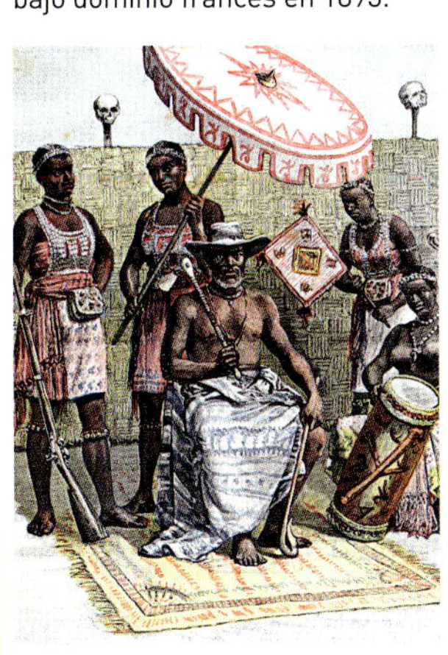

El soberano de Dahomey
El rey Behanzin de Dahomey (actual Benín) con los símbolos reales y rodeado de su séquito.

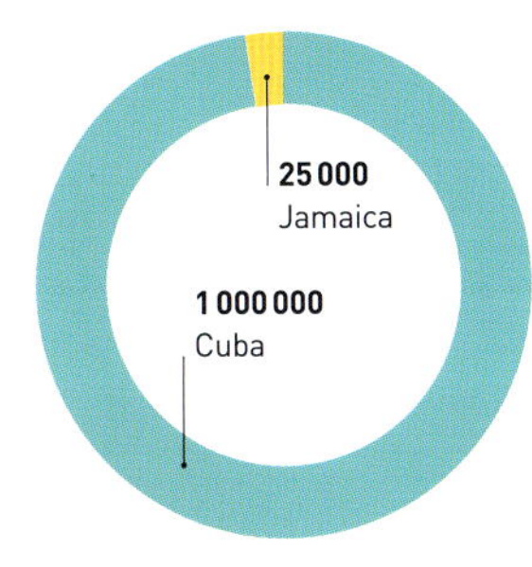

Producción de azúcar en toneladas
Cuba, que por aquel entonces era el principal productor de azúcar del mundo, llegó a producir en 1893 un millón de toneladas, cuarenta veces más que Jamaica.

En el otro extremo del planeta, en la colonia británica de **Nueva Zelanda**, las mujeres consiguieron el derecho a votar. La presión a favor del **sufragio femenino** iba ganando fuerza en muchos lugares, pero estas islas fueron las primeras en conceder este derecho gracias a las contundentes campañas de incansables sufragistas como **Kate Sheppard** (1847–1934). Poco después de que se aprobara la ley, el 65% de las mujeres votó en unas elecciones generales.

Mientras, **Cuba** vivía un auge de la industria azucarera, con beneficios de 64 millones de dólares en 1893. Sin embargo, al año siguiente los estadounidenses impusieron un **arancel** que redujo estos beneficios a 13 millones en 1896.

1894

Ceremonia de coronación del zar Nicolás II y la zarina Alejandra, los últimos monarcas rusos.

EN RUSIA, TRAS LA MUERTE DE ALEJANDRO III accedió al trono su hijo Nicolás II (1868–1918). Fue el último zar: tuvo que gobernar sobre un territorio cada vez más convulso y no pudo superar la **revolución** en que Rusia iba verse inmersa a principios del siglo XX.

China se había involucrado en un conflicto local en **Corea** que dio lugar a la **guerra chino-japonesa**. El enfrentamiento comenzó a raíz de una revuelta interna en Corea, cuyo monarca pidió ayuda a China y Japón. Ambos países enviaron tropas, pero, después de reprimir la rebelión, se negaron a retirarse. Japón se alió con el gobierno coreano, que deseaba modernizar el país, mientras que China respaldaba a la familia real. Las tensiones entre China y Japón fueron en aumento, y el conflicto estalló. Japón declaró la guerra a China el 1 de agosto.

« NO ESTOY PREPARADO PARA SER ZAR. NO SÉ NADA ACERCA DEL ARTE DE GOBERNAR. »

Nicolás II al asumir su cargo de zar de Rusia (1894)

En el Imperio otomano, la población **armenia cristiana** también se vio arrastrada por la marea nacionalista de la época e intentó conseguir su independencia. Sin embargo, todos sus esfuerzos resultaron infructuosos, pues toparon con una **represión** especialmente despiadada ordenada por el entonces sultán Abdulhamid II (1842–1918). Los armenios fueron sistemáticamente masacrados en todo el imperio, por lo que el movimiento independentista acabó extinguiéndose al cabo de unos años. Se calcula que entre 1894 y 1897 murieron 250 000 armenios de un total de 2 millones.

Guerra chino-japonesa
En esta pintura se representa la conquista de Jiuliancheng por las tropas japonesas tras la derrota de los chinos en Pyongyang durante la guerra chino-japonesa.

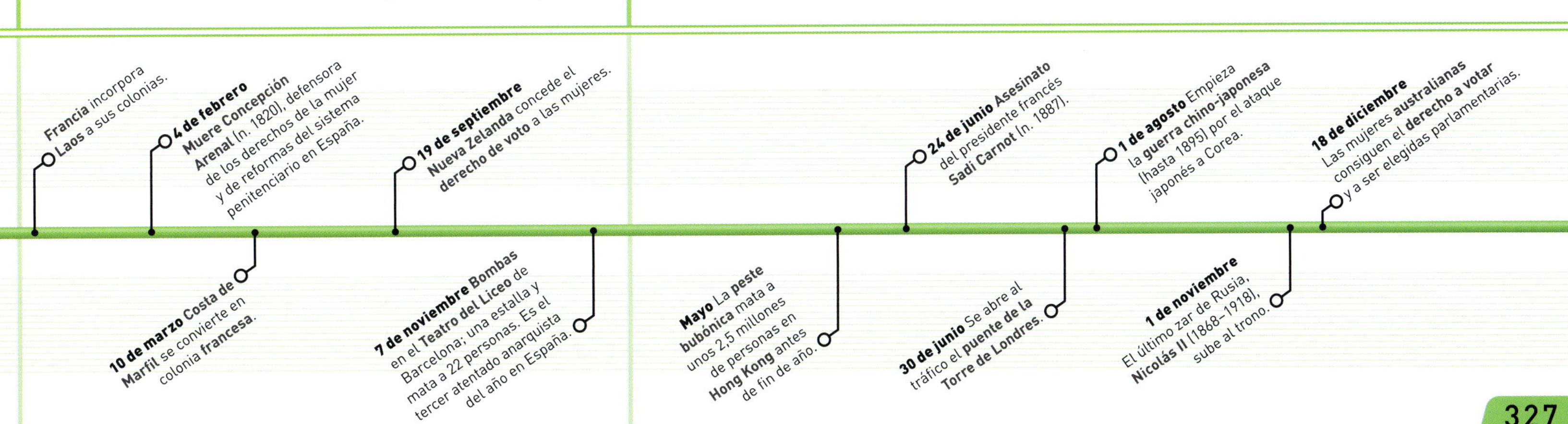

1895

« CADA DÍA, **LA HUMANIDAD SE IMPONE** UN POCO MÁS EN SU LUCHA CONTRA **ESPACIO Y TIEMPO**. **»**

Guglielmo Marconi, inventor italiano

POR TODO EL MUNDO LOS AVANCES TECNOLÓGICOS SE SUCEDÍAN RÁPIDAMENTE. En Italia, el físico **Guglielmo Marconi** (1874–1937) inventó un **telégrafo sin cable**. En sus primeros experimentos utilizó una llave telegráfica para hacer funcionar un **transmisor** y consiguió enviar ondas electromagnéticas en ráfagas según el **código Morse**. A continuación, utilizó un transmisor para hacer sonar un timbre colocado a 9 m de distancia; se centró en la **antena receptora** y hacia finales de año era capaz de transmitir una señal a 2,5 km. Sin embargo, su trabajo no logró despertar demasiado entusiasmo, así que Marconi viajó hasta Gran Bretaña y patentó el aparato al año siguiente. Había sentado las bases de la **transmisión por ondas de radio**. Mientras, el físico alemán **Wilhelm Conrad Roentgen** (1845–1923), que experimentaba con corrientes eléctricas y tubos de rayos catódicos, descubrió un tipo de rayos que permitían ver los objetos en placas fotográficas como si fueran **transparentes**. Roentgen les dio el nombre de **rayos X** y realizó una primera versión de la radiografía actual.

Transmisor inalámbrico
Réplica del telégrafo sin cable inventado por Guglielmo Marconi, que allanó el camino al desarrollo de la radio.

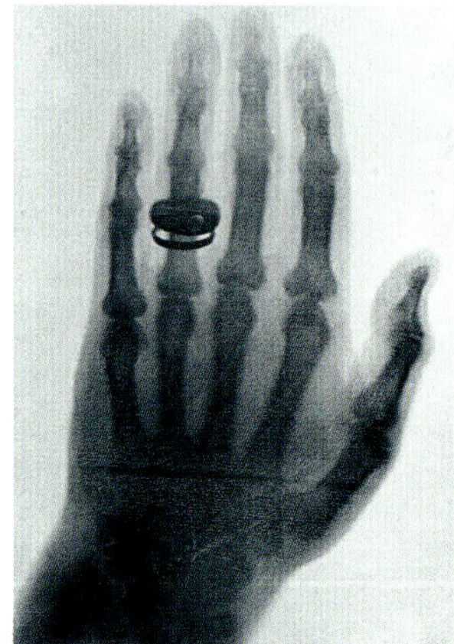

Primeras radiografías
Imagen de la mano de una mujer con anillos tomada por el catedrático alemán Wilhelm Conrad Roentgen (1845–1923).

En otro orden de cosas, el enfrentamiento entre fuerzas japonesas y chinas en **Corea** (*véase* 1894) finalizó después de la **derrota china** en Pyongyang y de las posteriores victorias obtenidas por la **flota japonesa**. China pidió la paz el 12 de febrero, y el **tratado de Shimonoseki** subsiguiente, en el que estuvieron implicadas Rusia, Francia y Alemania, le obligó a entregar a los japoneses la isla de **Formosa** (actual Taiwán), junto con las cercanas islas Pescadores (Penghu). China, además, tuvo que reconocer la **independencia de Corea**, abrir más puertos a los comerciantes japoneses y, por último, pagar una cuantiosa indemnización.

1896

Escena de la invasión italiana de Abisinia en 1896: las fuerzas abisinias derrotan a las italianas.

GRECIA ASISTIÓ AL RENACER DE LOS ANTIGUOS JUEGOS OLÍMPICOS gracias al barón francés **Pierre de Coubertin**, un entusiasta del deporte. Tras entrevistarse en 1890 con **William Penny Brookes**, que había orquestado unos juegos británicos en 1866, Coubertin comenzó a madurar la idea de organizar un festival internacional del deporte moderno. Tras años de negociaciones, logró que se celebraran los **primeros Juegos Olímpicos de la era moderna** en **Atenas**, entre el 6 y el 15 de abril. Fue todo un éxito: participaron **241 competidores** en los deportes de atletismo, gimnasia, levantamiento de peso, tenis, natación, ciclismo, esgrima, tiro y lucha grecorromana, y los animaron **cuarenta mil espectadores**. Luego se decidió que los juegos se celebrarían en diferentes ciudades por todo el mundo y se creó el Comité Olímpico Internacional.

Mientras, **Italia** invadió el **Imperio abisinio** (actual Etiopía) en su empeño de extender su control en África. Su anterior intento de anexionarse este territorio fracasó en 1889 (*véase* 1872). De acuerdo con las condiciones del **tratado de Wichale (o Uccialli)**, Italia se creía con derecho a establecer un protectorado en **Abisinia**, pero se encontró con trabas. En 1895, el desacuerdo entre Italia y el emperador abisinio **Menelik II** (1844–1913) había provocado un conflicto armado. El punto de inflexión se produjo en la **batalla de Adua**, que fue librada el 1 de marzo de 1896 y en la que ochenta mil abisinios derrotaron a veinte mil soldados italianos.

SCRIBNER'S
The Olympic Games and their Revival
Stories
Lord Leighton
Cathode Photography
Quarrel of the English Speaking Peoples
APRIL
Hy. Mayer

El renacimiento olímpico
Ilustración alusiva a la reinstauración de los Juegos Olímpicos en Atenas (Grecia) en la portada del número de abril de 1896 de la revista neoyorquina Scribner's Magazine. *Se organizaron 43 competiciones de nueve deportes.*

JUEGOS OLÍMPICOS DE 1896

- **43** NÚMERO DE **COMPETICIONES**
- **14** NÚMERO DE **PAÍSES PARTICIPANTES**
- **241** NÚMERO DE **ATLETAS**

7000 FUE EL **NÚMERO** DE **ITALIANOS CAÍDOS** EN **ADUA**

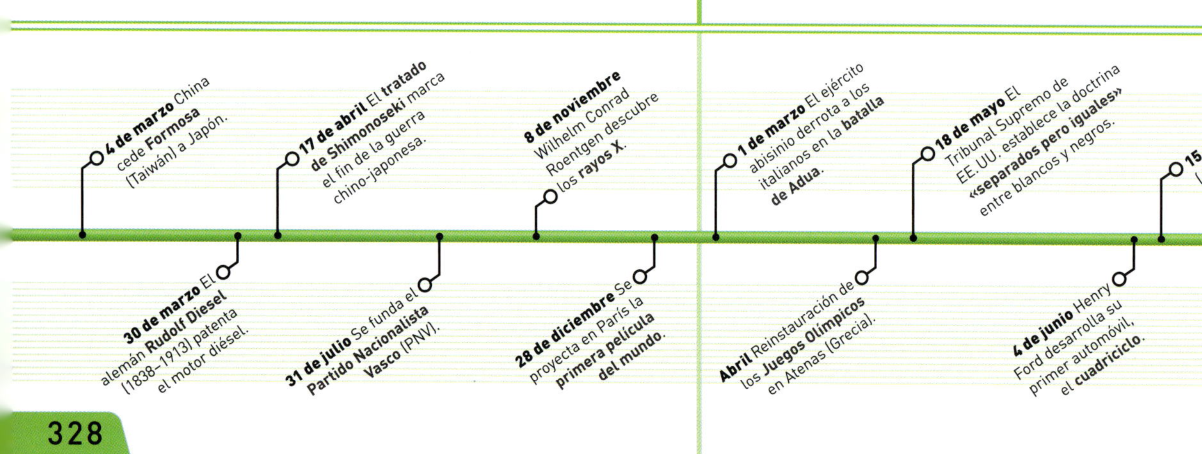

1897

El concierto europeo, sátira de la guerra greco-turca, o de los Treinta Días, en la portada del n.º 338 (9 de mayo de 1897) de *Le Petit Journal illustré*.

A PESAR DEL FRACASO DE LA GUERRA DE LOS DIEZ AÑOS (*véase* 1868), muchos cubanos se resistían a seguir bajo dominio español. El **Partido Revolucionario Cubano** lideró el renovado clamor por la independencia, declaró una república en la provincia de Oriente e inició una guerra de guerrillas («guerra chiquita»), precursora de la **guerra de la Independencia cubana**. Los soldados españoles llegaron a **La Habana** el año siguiente, pero se vieron obligados a retroceder. Al final, Estados Unidos también acabó involucrándose cuando su **acorazado *Maine* voló por los aires** en el puerto de La Habana (*véase* 1898).

Las discrepancias entre **Grecia** y el **Imperio otomano** por la situación de **Creta** estaban llegando al límite. El año anterior se reprimió brutalmente un levantamiento cristiano en la isla, y Grecia estaba decidida a tomar el territorio. No obstante, la **guerra de los Treinta Días** no terminó como Grecia esperaba. Cuando se acordó un armisticio en agosto, se le obligó a pagar una **indemnización** y perdió parte de **Tesalia**. Los turcos retiraron sus tropas de Creta, y la isla se convirtió en un protectorado internacional.

JOSÉ MARTÍ (1853–1895)

Poeta, escritor y político, fue una figura clave de la lucha revolucionaria cubana. Autor de *Versos sencillos* (1891), se le considera precursor del modernismo literario y un héroe nacional de Cuba por sus estrategias y liderazgo en la lucha independentista. Murió en combate en Dos Ríos, al este de la isla.

Mientras, la **minería del carbón** vivía una edad de oro en Gran Bretaña. La extracción del carbón se había duplicado desde la década de 1860. La industria minera era además una importante fuente de empleo: en 1897, el número de **mineros** británicos rondaba los 695 200, cuando en 1851 era de solo 216 200.

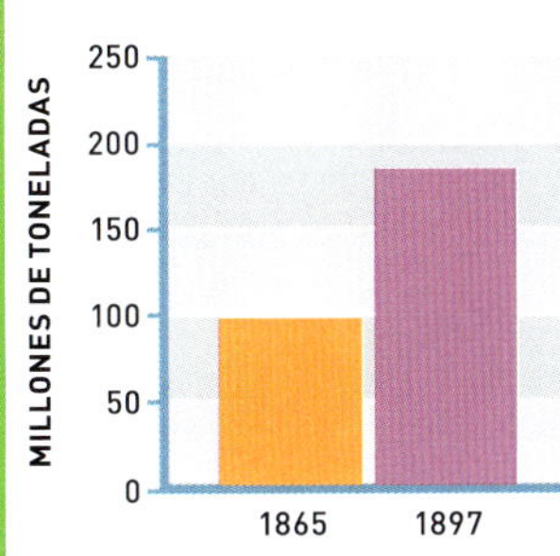

Minería del carbón británica
En 1897, Gran Bretaña produjo 200 millones de toneladas de carbón y se convirtió en líder mundial, por delante de EE. UU. y de Alemania, también grandes productores.

1898

Soldados atrincherados tras unos matorrales en las Lomas de San Juan (Cuba) apuntan con sus rifles durante la guerra hispano-estadounidense.

DESPUÉS DE LA DESTRUCCIÓN DEL *MAINE*, volado mientras se encontraba atracado en el puerto de La Habana, **EE. UU. declaró la guerra a España**. De hecho, la lucha cubana por la independencia tenía numerosos simpatizantes en EE. UU. El gobierno estadounidense culpó a España de la voladura del *Maine*, en la que **murieron 260 tripulantes**. Aunque Cuba y España habían acordado un armisticio, cuya firma tuvo lugar el 9 de abril, EE. UU. inició la **guerra hispano-estadounidense** solo unas semanas después, el día 25. Las batallas se libraron en dos escenarios: el Atlántico y el Pacífico. Los barcos de la armada estadounidense se adentraron en la bahía de Manila, en **Filipinas**, que también era una **colonia española**, mientras otra flota realizaba incursiones en el puerto de **Santiago de Cuba**, donde más tarde desembarcaron sus tropas. **España capituló** el 25 de julio y pagó un altísimo precio por la que el secretario de Estado de EE. UU., John Hay (1838–1905), llamó «espléndida guerrita» en una carta a su amigo y futuro presidente de EE. UU. **Theodore Roosevelt** (1858–1919). Por el **tratado de París** del 10 de diciembre, España se vio obligada a renunciar a las colonias que le quedaban, **reconocer la independencia de Cuba** y ceder Filipinas, Puerto Rico y Guam a EE. UU. Sin embargo, EE. UU. siguió ocupando Cuba y, al año siguiente, intentó excluir a los cubanos del gobierno y desmanteló su ejército. Por aquellas fechas, EE. UU. también consiguió anexionarse las islas **Hawái**.

La anexión de Hawái
En esta ilustración de la época, los Hawáianos reciben la noticia de que EE. UU. se ha anexionado la isla. EE. UU. pasó a controlar también Guam y Filipinas.

Mientras, en **Egipto**, Gran Bretaña y Francia se vieron implicadas en el llamado **incidente de Fachoda**, relacionado con disputas territoriales por sus respectivos intentos de expandirse en África. Los británicos deseaban construir un **ferrocarril que uniera Egipto y Uganda**, mientras que Francia pretendía seguir avanzando hacia el este y entrar en **Sudán**. A pesar de que sus tropas se encontraron en Fachoda el 18 de septiembre, no llegaron a declararse la guerra, ya que ambas partes querían **evitar la batalla**. En su lugar, decidieron que las banderas británica, francesa y egipcia ondearan sobre el fuerte ocupado por los franceses. Finalmente acordaron que las **fronteras** se corresponderían con la bifurcación de los **ríos Nilo y Congo**.

1899

Fusileros de Lancashire en bicicleta, en la segunda guerra de los bóers.

LAS CONTINUAS HOSTILIDADES ENTRE COLONOS BÓERS Y BRITÁNICOS después de la **primera guerra de los Bóers** (*véase* 1880) hacían presagiar un nuevo conflicto. En esta ocasión los bóers reclamaban que las tropas británicas que protegían los intereses mineros se retirasen de **Transvaal**, pero su petición fue desatendida, por lo que tanto la República Sudafricana como el Estado Libre de Orange decidieron **declarar la guerra** a Gran Bretaña en el mes de octubre. Aunque la **segunda guerra de los bóers** duró menos de tres años, para los británicos fue la más larga desde las guerras napoleónicas y en ella llegaron a intervenir más de 500 000 soldados. Los combates fueron librados en un **terreno hostil** que beneficiaba a las tropas bóers, con unos efectivos que no superaban los 90 000. En este conflicto, los **civiles bóers** sufrieron un **tratamiento infame**: sus granjas fueron incendiadas, y cerca de 25 000 mujeres y niños acabaron muriendo en los **campos de concentración**.

Medalla de guerra
La medalla de Sudáfrica, otorgada a personal militar que había servido en la guerra, lleva un busto conmemorativo del jubileo de la reina Victoria.

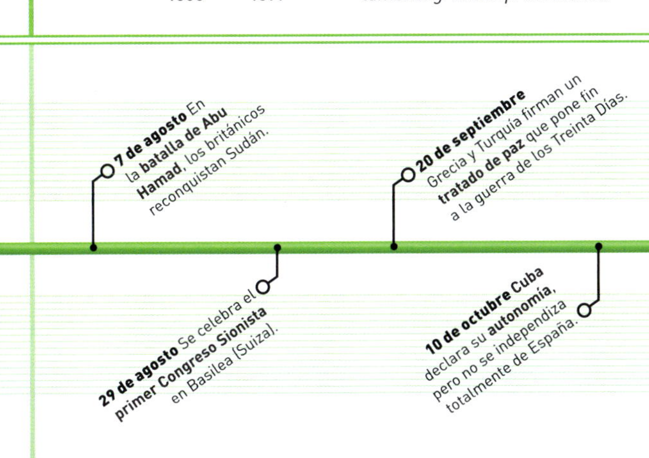

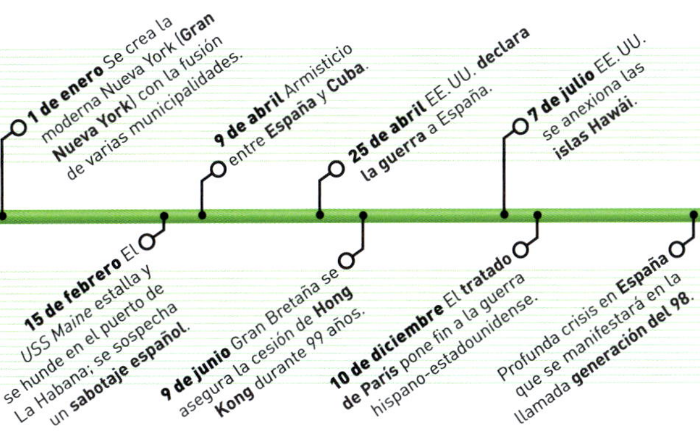

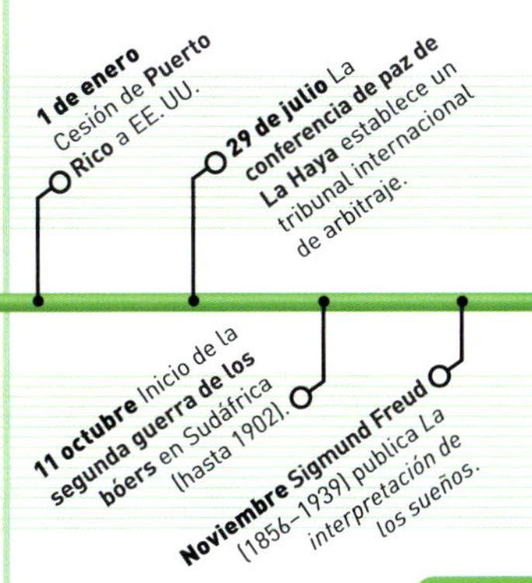

1900

Tropas internacionales asaltan Pekín en represalia por los ataques contra occidentales durante la rebelión de los Bóxers.

LA OPINIÓN PÚBLICA CHINA EMPEZABA A SENTIRSE MOLESTA por la creciente presencia de occidentales, sobre todo misioneros cristianos. Este malestar terminó dando lugar a la **rebelión de los Bóxers**, un levantamiento de campesinos que pretendían expulsar a todos los extranjeros de China. El grupo que inspiró los ataques había fundado anteriormente una sociedad secreta cuyo nombre en chino significaba literalmente «puños rectos y armoniosos», de ahí su sobrenombre de bóxers (boxeadores). Algunos miembros del grupo pertenecían también a la corte Qing, por lo que los violentos ataques contra los extranjeros y contra los chinos conversos al cristianismo contaban con el beneplácito oficial. En el mes de junio de 1900 llegaron al puerto de Tianjin **tropas** internacionales compuestas por soldados británicos, franceses, italianos, rusos, alemanes, japoneses y estadounidenses para socorrer a sus compatriotas, pero los bóxers siguieron incendiando iglesias y asesinando cristianos. Después de que las tropas internacionales se apoderaran de varios fuertes, la emperatriz regente **Cixi** (1835–1908) ordenó matar a cualquier extranjero, y muchos funcionarios y diplomáticos fueron asesinados. Tras la llegada de refuerzos, las tropas internacionales se dirigieron a Pekín y la ocuparon. La emperatriz viuda huyó. En septiembre de 1901, una tregua negociada con los príncipes imperiales terminó con la violencia y estableció compensaciones. Mientras esto sucedía, los **rusos** aprovecharon para tomar el sur de **Manchuria**, limítrofe con el sur de Rusia.

En África se empezaron a explotar minas en **Katanga**, una región al sur de la actual República Democrática del Congo. El descubrimiento de yacimientos ricos en **cobre** y otros minerales, como cinc, cobalto y estaño, dio lugar al rápido establecimiento de una infraestructura minera por los europeos, incluido el ferrocarril, y empezaron a surgir poblaciones a medida que proliferaban las compañías mineras. La región de Katanga muy pronto se convirtió en una de las áreas más industrializadas del Congo; sin embargo, los numerosos trabajadores africanos desempeñaban las tareas más duras y arriesgadas en las minas a cambio de un salario mísero.

Bajo tierra
Señal de metro integrada en una farola de París (Francia). La primera línea de metro parisina se inauguró en 1900.

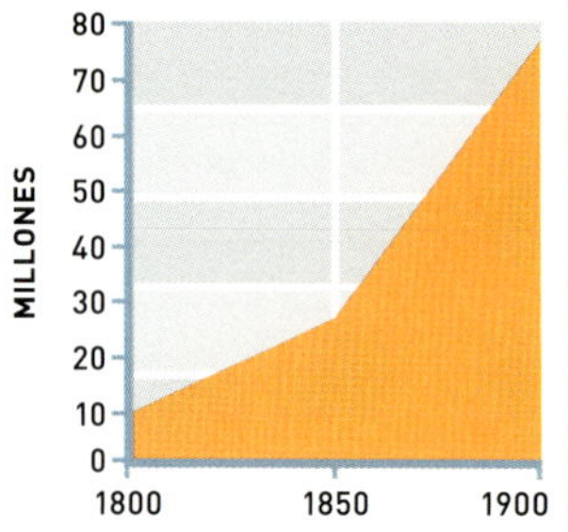

Una nación en crecimiento
Gracias a décadas de inmigración, la población estadounidense había crecido enormemente. En el año 1900 superaba ya los 75 millones.

Entre tanto, en África occidental, las tropas británicas se enfrentaban a una rebelión de los **ashanti** que tardaron ocho meses en sofocar. La inestabilidad en la región de **Costa de Oro** (actual Ghana) persistió durante toda una década, puesto que los africanos seguían resistiéndose al dominio británico.

En EE. UU., la población prácticamente se había duplicado después de varias décadas de **inmigración**, cuya puerta de entrada principal era la aduana de la isla de Ellis (Nueva York). En 1870, EE. UU. ya contaba con 35,5 millones de habitantes, pero en 1900 tenía más de 75 millones. Dicho crecimiento se había producido sobre todo en las **áreas urbanas**: alrededor del 40 % de la población de EE. UU. vivía en ciudades.

1901

Cortejo fúnebre de la reina Victoria en Londres.

LAS NUMEROSAS COLONIAS FUNDADAS EN AUSTRALIA (Victoria, Nueva Gales del Sur, Queensland, Australia Meridional, Australia Occidental y Tasmania) entraron en una nueva era el 1 de enero, tras la redacción y la aprobación del borrador de la **constitución** y el establecimiento oficial de la Commonwealth (Mancomunidad) de Australia.

Unas semanas más tarde, Gran Bretaña y sus colonias estaban de luto por la muerte de la **reina Victoria** el 22 de enero. La soberana había reinado sobre el país y el imperio a lo largo de 63 años, más que ningún otro monarca británico. Le sucedió en el trono su hijo, **Eduardo VII** (1841–1910). Su reinado fue pacífico en gran medida, pero muy estratificado socialmente, y se conoce como **era eduardiana**.

Sello de la Commonwealth
Sello australiano con la efigie de la reina Victoria, fallecida el mismo año en que se fundó la Commonwealth de Australia.

1902

El príncipe Abdelaziz ibn Saud, primer monarca de Arabia Saudí.

EN SUDÁFRICA, LA GUERRA ENTRE BRITÁNICOS Y BÓERS llegó a su fin el 31 de mayo. El final se precipitó cuando los británicos aplicaron una política de tierra quemada consistente en destruir las cosechas y los alimentos para dejar sin suministros a los bóers. Tanto las mujeres como los niños bóers desposeídos fueron encerrados en campos de concentración. El **tratado de Vereeniging** obligó a los bóers a reconocer la soberanía británica, lo cual puso fin a la independencia del Estado Libre de Orange y de la República Sudafricana. Todo el territorio de Sudáfrica quedó bajo dominio británico.

Mientras, **Ibn Saud** (*c.* 1880–1953) recuperó la antigua capital de la dinastía saudí, Riyadh, tras varias décadas de guerra civil (*véase* 1843). En 1901, Saud, que vivía en Kuwait, se puso en marcha para recuperar el territorio que la familia rival Rashid le había obligado a abandonar. Junto con sus hombres, llegó a Riyadh en enero de 1902 y se infiltró entre la población con la intención de capturar al gobernador rashidí a la mañana siguiente en una emboscada. Saud no tardó en tomar la ciudad y el territorio con ayuda de un creciente número de seguidores y lo convirtió en **Arabia Saudí** en 1932. El país continúa bajo el gobierno de la familia Saud en la actualidad.

En la isla de Martinica, una erupción del volcán **Montagne Pelée** el 8 de mayo mató a casi treinta mil personas y destruyó el puerto de Saint Pierre. El volcán ya había entrado en erupción en 1792 y 1851, pero no con tanta intensidad.

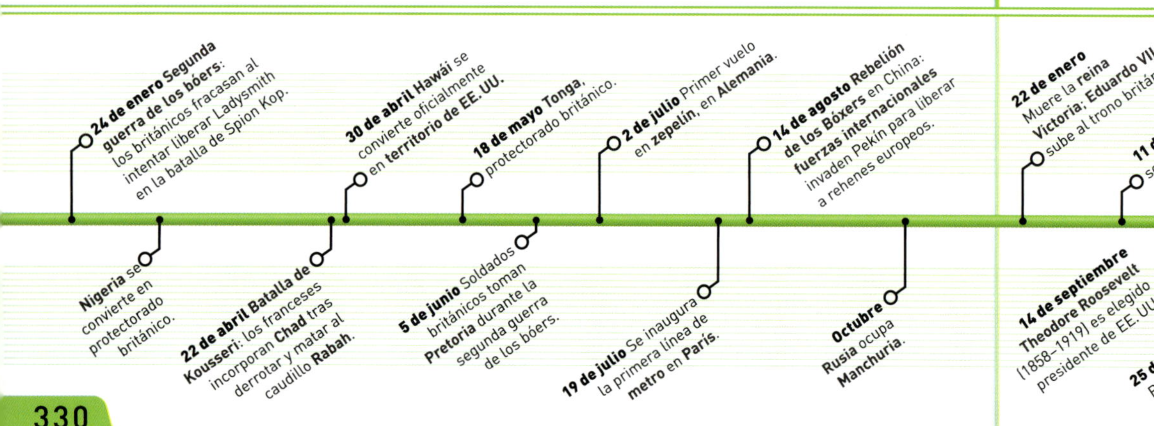

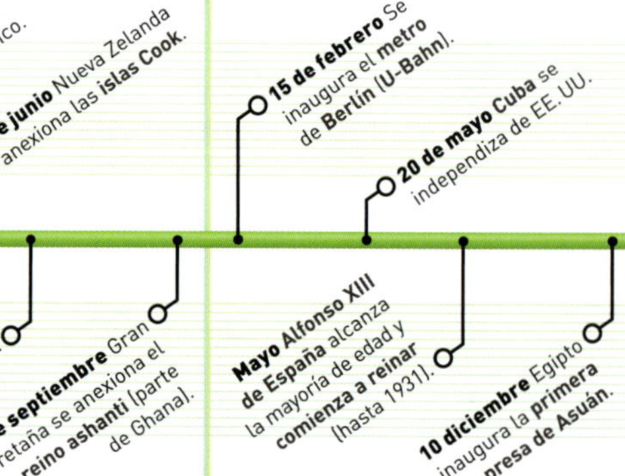

1903

El aeroplano original diseñado por Wilbur y Orville Wright realizó su primer vuelo el 17 de diciembre de 1903 en Kitty Hawk (Carolina del Norte).

EN EE. UU., LOS HERMANOS WILBUR (1867–1912) Y ORVILLE (1871–1948) WRIGHT, obsesionados con la incipiente ciencia de la aviación y decididos a volar, invirtieron todos los beneficios de su tienda de bicicletas de la población de Kitty Hawk, en la costa de Carolina del Norte, para llevar a cabo sus experimentos y construyeron un biplano. Comenzaron a realizar pruebas, y la mañana del 17 de diciembre, sus esfuerzos dieron fruto: Orville realizó el que se considera el **primer vuelo** de un aeroplano en el que el piloto tuvo el control en todo momento (a diferencia de los intentos anteriores con planeadores). Recorrió unos 60 m en 12 segundos. Más tarde, ese mismo día, Wilbur voló 259 m en 59 segundos.

Entre tanto, en **Panamá**, EE. UU. había recuperado la idea de construir un canal entre el Atlántico y el Pacífico tras el fracaso del primer intento más de una década antes (*véase* 1889). EE. UU. quería comprar los activos del antiguo *holding* francés y empezar la construcción, pero las conversaciones con el gobierno **colombiano** (que todavía controlaba el istmo) quedaron interrumpidas. Poco después, en 1903, Panamá declaró su **independencia** con respaldo estadounidense. En 1904, después de que Panamá y EE. UU. alcanzaran un acuerdo acerca de la Zona del Canal por el cual EE. UU. tendría jurisdicción hasta 1979, comenzaron las obras del canal.

También en 1903, en **Francia**, el ciclista y periodista Henri Desgrange (1865–1940) organizó una carrera ciclista que se convertiría en una de las más prestigiosas del mundo: el **Tour de Francia**, cuyos orígenes se entrelazaron con la polémica acerca del **caso Dreyfus**, un escándalo en el que se vio implicado Alfred Dreyfus (1859–1935), un oficial francés acusado de traición. Salieron a la luz varias pruebas de su inocencia, pero se ocultaron. Dreyfus era judío, y la opinión pública se dividió entre las distintas posturas respecto al **antisemitismo**. Durante el escándalo, el periódico deportivo *Le Vélo* respaldó a Dreyfus. Los publicistas, enojados, decidieron fundar un periódico competidor, *L'Auto-Vélo*, que luego pasó a llamarse *L'Auto*. Henri Desgrange fue contratado como director. Sin embargo, las ventas de *L'Auto* eran bajas al principio, y el periodista Géo Lefèvre sugirió que se organizara una carrera con el fin de promoverlo. Desgrange ideó una competición ciclista por etapas de un mes de duración (aunque luego se acortó) que seguía la ruta París-Lyon-Marsella-Toulouse-Burdeos-Nantes-París. El 1 de julio, 60 corredores tomaron la salida, aunque solo 21 completaron la carrera. El primer ganador fue Maurice Garin.

El león en el camino
En esta caricatura de la publicación estadounidense Judge, *el «león en el camino» simboliza el canal de Panamá.*

12 SEGUNDOS DURACIÓN DEL **PRIMER VUELO** DE LOS **HERMANOS WRIGHT**

1904

Ilustración del semanario francés *Le Petit Journal* sobre el traslado de enfermos y heridos rusos sobre esquíes durante la guerra ruso-japonesa.

JAPÓN Y RUSIA habían estado compitiendo por extender su influencia en Manchuria y Corea. Rusia había construido el ferrocarril Transiberiano (*véase* 1891), que ahora contaba con una línea que entraba en **Manchuria**, anexionada durante la rebelión de los Bóxers (*véase* 1900). En esta época **Japón** había empezado a engrosar su ejército y su armada, y en 1903 se aproximó a Rusia; ambos países pretendían dejar entrever que reconocían los intereses del otro en estas regiones. Las conversaciones se interrumpieron el 6 de febrero de 1904 y tres días más tarde Japón atacó buques de guerra rusos, de los cuales hundió dos. Este fue el desencadenante de la **guerra ruso-japonesa**. Japón envió tropas a Manchuria y Corea y, en el transcurso del año, obligó a los rusos a replegarse hacia el norte. El presidente de EE. UU., Theodore Roosevelt (1858–1919), fue intermediario del tratado firmado el 5 de septiembre, por el que Rusia se vio obligada a abandonar Manchuria, ceder parte de la isla de **Sajalín** a Japón y reconocer los intereses de Japón en **Corea**, además de concederle derechos de pesca frente a la costa siberiana. Su victoria sobre Rusia marcó el comienzo de la transformación de Japón en una gran potencia mundial.

En África, el ejército alemán se enfrentaba a la rebelión de sus colonias. En el **África del Suroeste alemana** (Namibia), donde en 1903 se habían rebelado los **koi (hotentotes)**, se levantaron los **herero** en 1904. Muchos africanos fueron capturados y recluidos en campos de concentración, en unas condiciones tan duras que más de la mitad de los prisioneros murieron. En 1908, cuando Alemania sofocó la rebelión, alrededor del 80 % de los herero y del 50 % de los koi habían muerto, en combate o en los campos de concentración.

Guerra ruso-japonesa
Este mapa muestra la evolución del conflicto entre Japón y Rusia. Japón expulsó a Rusia de Manchuria y la obligó a renunciar a su política expansionista en Asia oriental.

11 de junio Asesinato del **rey serbio** Alejandro I (n. 1876) y de la reina Draga (n. 1864).

4 de noviembre **Panamá** declara su **independencia** de Colombia con el respaldo de EE. UU.

29 de septiembre **Prusia**, primer país en exigir **permiso de conducir** a los automovilistas.

18 de noviembre EE. UU. y Colombia firman un acuerdo para construir el **canal de Panamá** (inaugurado en 1914).

17 de diciembre Los hermanos Orville y Wilbur **Wright** realizan el **primer vuelo** controlado en Kitty Hawk (Carolina del Norte).

12 de enero Comienza la **rebelión de los herero** en África del Suroeste, bajo dominio alemán.

8 de febrero Empieza la **guerra ruso-japonesa** (hasta 1905) cuando Japón hunde dos buques de guerra rusos.

8 de abril **Gran Bretaña** y **Francia** firman la *Entente cordiale*, que allana el camino para las **relaciones pacíficas** que han mantenido hasta hoy.

9 de mayo La locomotora *City of Truro* es la primera en **superar los 160 km/h**, en el trayecto Plymouth-Londres (Gran Bretaña).

Octubre **José Echegaray**, premio Nobel de literatura.

21 octubre Guerra ruso-japonesa: incidente del **banco Dogger**, donde la **flota rusa** dispara por error contra pesqueros **británicos** en el mar del Norte.

HISTORIA DEL AUTOMÓVIL

DE LOS FORD T A LOS HÍBRIDOS, LOS AUTOMÓVILES HAN PROPULSADO UN GRAN CAMBIO

Ford Modelo T

Tras miles de años de lento transporte en barcos, caballos o incluso a pie, la invención del automóvil revolucionó la forma en que el mundo entendía las distancias y la velocidad. En vez de invertir años en un viaje, personas y mercancías podían recorrer cientos de kilómetros en unas horas.

Si bien a finales del siglo XIX aparecieron innovaciones tecnológicas importantes en el ámbito del transporte, como los barcos de vapor, ninguna tuvo el alcance y el impacto inmediato de la invención y la producción en serie del automóvil. Reservado al principio a los ricos, cuando en la década de 1920 el inventor estadounidense Henry Ford consiguió aumentar la producción y bajar los precios, el automóvil pasó a estar al alcance de muchos consumidores. Esto cambió drásticamente el paisaje, ya que empezaron a proliferar las carreteras y, en la década de 1950, en EE. UU. empezaron a urbanizarse barrios periféricos partiendo del supuesto de que los residentes se desplazarían en coche.

Salida de la cadena de montaje
Unos obreros montan un modelo T en la cadena de montaje de una factoría de la Ford Motor Company. Las fábricas de Ford permitieron montar millones de coches rápidamente.

LA ERA DEL AUTOMÓVIL

A pesar de la contaminación y de los atascos, la humanidad continúa viviendo una historia de amor con el automóvil. De hecho, cuando en los países en vías de desarrollo aumenta el poder adquisitivo, lo primero que quiere la gente es un coche. El reto es encontrar sistemas de propulsión que consuman menos combustible y contaminen menos, por eso cada vez son más los fabricantes que experimentan con nuevos tipos de coche, como los híbridos (*véase* recuadro). Con todo, el automóvil sigue presente en las redes de transporte en todo el mundo.

COCHES HÍBRIDOS

Hace años que los ingenieros automovilísticos tratan de conseguir que los automóviles funcionen con combustibles distintos al petróleo, como la energía solar y la electricidad. Los híbridos combinan un motor de gasolina y otro eléctrico, consumen menos combustible y son menos contaminantes.

« **CUALQUIER CLIENTE** PUEDE TENER SU COCHE PINTADO EN **EL COLOR QUE DESEE**, **SIEMPRE** QUE SEA **NEGRO**. »

Henry Ford, industrial estadounidense, en su biografía *My Life and Work* (1922)

Siglo XV
El coche de Leonardo da Vinci
El renacentista italiano fue quien diseñó el primer vehículo autopropulsado del mundo.

Reconstrucción del coche de Leonardo

1769–1770
El primer automóvil
El ingeniero francés Nicolas Cugnot construye un vehículo a vapor que puede alcanzar una velocidad de hasta 3 km/h.

Fardier de Cugnot

1801
El coche de vapor
El inventor británico Richard Trevithick monta una versión más ligera y pequeña de la máquina de vapor sobre ruedas: la «locomotora de carretera».

Locomotora de Trevithick

1860
El motor de gas
El belga J.J. Étienne Lenoir crea un motor de combustión interna de dos tiempos (de explosión) con gas de alumbrado.

Motor de gas de Lenoir

1867–1877
El motor Otto de cuatro tiempos
El inventor alemán Nikolaus August Otto patenta su motor de combustión interna de cuatro tiempos.

Motor Otto

1885
La combustión interna mejora
Los alemanes Karl Benz y Gottlieb Daimler conciben por separado coches que utilizan un motor de combustión interna.

Triciclo Benz

1913 El Ford modelo T
El clásico diseño de Henry Ford compartía muchas características con los coches actuales. Además de relativamente barato, era lo bastante robusto y fiable para poder circular por las deficientes carreteras estadounidenses de la época.

parabrisas de dos paneles con marco de latón

retrovisor de latón

soportes del parabrisas de latón

modelo descapotable y sin puertas

bocina de latón con pera de goma

faro lateral de queroseno

faro delantero de acetileno

neumático de caucho macizo

llanta de madera

manivela de arranque

amortiguador

1885–1886
El coche de cuatro ruedas
Gottlieb Daimler mejora el motor y añade una cuarta rueda al chasis: el resultado es el primer coche moderno.

1903–1930
El Ford T
El estadounidense Henry Ford empieza a fabricar el modelo T para el mercado de masas. En 1927 habían salido unos quince millones de coches de las cadenas de montaje de Ford.

Década de 1930
El compacto de Volkswagen
Se desarrolla el «coche del pueblo» alemán, pionero del utilitario asequible y eficiente.

Volkswagen Escarabajo

Dos plazas Panhard-Levassor

1889–1890
Motores delanteros
Los franceses Émile Levassor y René Panhard, primeros en fabricar coches enteros con el motor delante.

1890–principios del siglo XX
Primeros coches eléctricos
No todos los coches tenían motor de gasolina. Hacia 1900, cerca del 28 % funcionaba con electricidad.

Décadas de 1940 y 1950
El auge del coche de lujo
Marcas como Rolls Royce y Cadillac se convierten en sinónimo del automóvil de lujo.

Rolls Royce Silver Dawn

1997–actualidad
Coches híbridos
Los fabricantes buscan sistemas de propulsión más baratos y limpios.

Toyota Prius

1905

« EL ETERNO MISTERIO DEL MUNDO ES SU COMPRENSIBILIDAD. »

Albert Einstein, en el *Franklin Institute Journal* (marzo de 1936)

Albert Einstein, de origen alemán, se convirtió en uno de los científicos más famosos del mundo tras formular su teoría de la relatividad especial.

EN RUSIA, EL DESCONTENTO CON EL ZAR NICOLÁS II IBA EN AUMENTO y cada vez se alzaban más voces a favor de una monarquía constitucional. Dicha situación se complicó después de la humillante derrota en la guerra ruso-japonesa (*véase* 1904). Las **protestas** se propagaron por todo el país. En el mes de febrero, el zar prometió establecer una **asamblea electa**, pero el malestar no cesó. Al final, los militares también se sumaron a la reivindicación, y en junio la tripulación del **acorazado *Potemkin*** se amotinó en la rada de Odesa. En octubre, el zar prometió una constitución y una asamblea legislativa, pero los revolucionarios lo consideraron insuficiente y decidieron organizarse en **sóviets** (consejos revolucionarios). Uno de sus líderes, **León Trotski** (1879–1940), fue encarcelado. Pese a que la agitación continuó, las tropas antirrevolucionarias finalmente aplastaron la denominada **Revolución rusa de 1905**. Al año siguiente, el zar introdujo reformas con las **Leyes Fundamentales**, que incluían la formación de una asamblea legislativa o **duma**.

En **Suiza**, el físico de origen alemán **Albert Einstein** (1879–1955) obtuvo el doctorado y publicó diversos artículos que le valieron el elogio internacional. Su publicación más influyente fue la llamada **teoría de la relatividad especial**, que explicaba la relación entre la masa y la energía por medio de la ecuación **E=mc^2**. En 1921 recibió el premio Nobel gracias a sus innovadoras aportaciones científicas.

En **India**, el virrey británico lord Curzon (1859–1925) se enfrentaba a una creciente oposición nacionalista. Su decisión de **dividir** la provincia de Bengala y de unir **Bengala** Oriental y Assam, con capital en Dacca, se interpretó como un intento de sofocar el **movimiento nacionalista**, que contaba con un amplio respaldo en toda Bengala.

Cartel cinematográfico
La película El acorazado Potemkin *(1925), del director ruso Serguéi Eisenstein, recrea el motín de los marineros de este barco en 1905.*

1906

El ayuntamiento de San Francisco en ruinas tras el terremoto de 1906.

SEÍSMO DE SAN FRANCISCO

25 000 EDIFICIOS **DESTRUIDOS**

450–700 PERSONAS **FALLECIDAS**

350 MILLONES DE DÓLARES EN **DAÑOS**

SAN FRANCISCO SE ENCUENTRA SOBRE LA FALLA DE SAN ANDRÉS y por tanto, en una zona de alto riesgo de **terremotos**. En 1906, la población ya estaba habituada a que la tierra temblara, pues se habían registrado seísmos en 1836, 1865, 1868 y 1892. Sin embargo, aún no se había hecho nada para que la ciudad, de 400 000 habitantes, estuviera mejor preparada. El 18 de abril fue sacudida por un terremoto que alcanzó una **magnitud de 7,8**. El temblor se percibió incluso en Los Ángeles y en Nevada. Aunque duró menos de un minuto, provocó **daños** que se tardaron años en reparar, pues fueron muchos los edificios que se derrumbaron o se incendiaron.

En India se fundó la **Liga Musulmana Panindia** para proteger los derechos de los musulmanes con el beneplácito británico. En 1913 se sumó al creciente clamor por el **autogobierno de India**.

En España, **Alfonso XIII** se casó el 31 de mayo con **Victoria Eugenia de Battenberg**, nieta de la reina Victoria de Gran Bretaña. El cortejo nupcial se vió ensangrentado por el atentado de Mateo Morral, que lanzó una bomba oculta en un ramo de flores. Hubo 23 muertos y más de 100 heridos, pero los soberanos salieron indemnes.

1907

Los campesinos rumanos reclamaban una reforma agraria.

EN RUMANÍA, EL MALESTAR DE LOS CAMPESINOS SE HABÍA IDO EXTENDIENDO de pueblo en pueblo hasta culminar en una **revuelta** en 1907. El origen fue el desacuerdo sobre la distribución de la tierra, ya que los campesinos se veían obligados a firmar unos **contratos abusivos** que les condenaban a vivir en la más absoluta miseria. Antes de que los militares sofocaran definitivamente la revuelta **habían muerto unas diez mil personas**.

En el Sureste Asiático, **Camboya** había recuperado algunas de sus provincias occidentales, bajo dominio tailandés, gracias a la **presión francesa**. En 1863, Francia consolidó su presencia en Camboya hasta restringir los poderes de su rey e instalar un gobernador. Esto facilitó la **colonización**, pero atizó el nacionalismo camboyano. La resistencia fue aplastada en 1907.

Los franceses en Tailandia
Un cañonero francés del siglo XIX, armado con un cañón Hotchkiss, patrulla las aguas del río Chao Phraya en Bangkok (Tailandia).

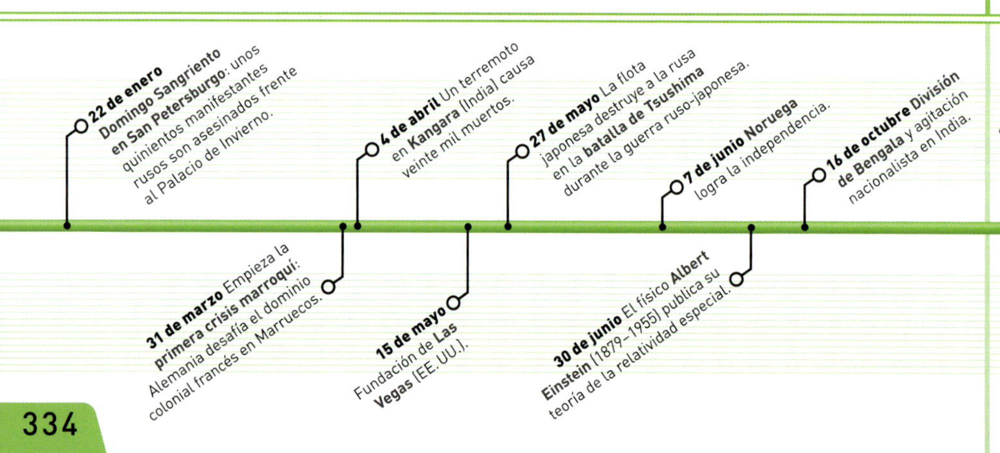

18 de abril La ciudad de **San Francisco** queda prácticamente arrasada por un **terremoto**.

31 de mayo Boda de Alfonso XIII de España con Victoria Eugenia de Battenberg.

23 de agosto Llegan **tropas de EE. UU. a Cuba** a petición del presidente destituido Tomás Estrada Palma (1831–1908).

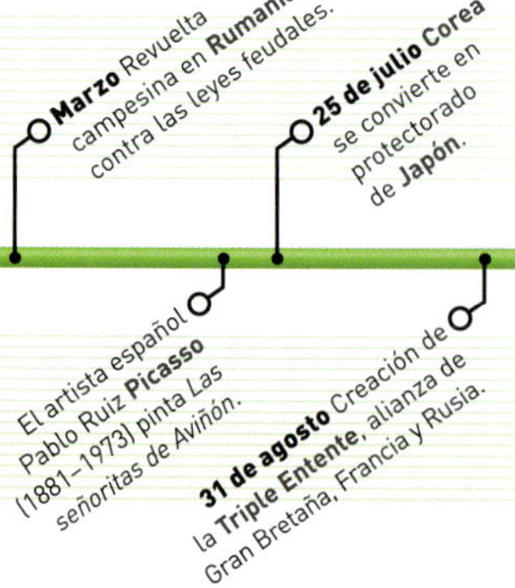

1908

Ilustración publicada en febrero de 1908 en el semanario italiano *La Domenica del Corriere* sobre el asesinato del rey Carlos I de Portugal, que tuvo lugar en un periodo de crecientes demandas de un gobierno republicano.

DESPUÉS DEL ASESINATO DEL REY CARLOS I (1863–1908), en el mes de febrero, Portugal vivió una época convulsa. Carlos I era un monarca muy poco querido y se había granjeado un número mayor de enemigos al nombrar al primer ministro **sin consultar al parlamento**. La violencia estalló definitivamente el 1 de febrero, cuando Carlos y su primogénito, Luis Felipe, fueron asesinados a tiros mientras circulaban por Lisboa en un carruaje. El sucesor del rey Carlos fue su otro hijo **Manuel II** (1889–1932), que acabó siendo destronado tan solo un par de años después (*véase* 1910).

También durante 1908, en el continente africano fue abolido el **Estado Libre del Congo** (*véase* 1884), y el gobierno de Bélgica estableció el **Congo Belga**. El estado libre había sido explotado por una empresa privada controlada directamente por el **rey Leopoldo II** (1835–1909) y que obtenía unos enormes beneficios del **caucho y marfil**, productos de alto valor en el mercado. Sin embargo, los informes acerca de las terribles condiciones laborales en las que se encontraban los trabajadores africanos provocaron un **clamor internacional** en demanda de reformas. La respuesta del estado belga fue convertir el territorio en una **colonia oficial** bajo la administración de Bruselas, asegurándose de esta manera un constante suministro de productos congoleños. No obstante, las brutales condiciones persistieron, y la **población se redujo** de 20–30 millones de personas en el año 1884 a alrededor de 8,5 millones en 1911.

Entre tanto, también se reconfiguraron las relaciones en el seno del **Imperio austrohúngaro**. En el caso de **Bosnia-Herzegovina**, que había ocupado en 1878, el Imperio estaba inquieto por las implicaciones que pudiera tener la **revolución de los Jóvenes Turcos** del vecino Imperio otomano (*véase* 1909). Temía que su poder en los Balcanes pudiera verse debilitado, ya que en rigor Bosnia-Herzegovina seguía bajo soberanía otomana, y uno de los objetivos de los Jóvenes Turcos era reclamar el territorio. Después de asegurarse el respaldo de **Rusia**, Austria-Hungría **se anexionó Bosnia-Herzegovina**. Dicha decisión provocó una reacción inmediata de la vecina **Serbia**, que reclamó una parte de Bosnia-Herzegovina que le permitiera acceder al mar Adriático. Muy pronto Rusia se vio envuelta en lo que posteriormente se denominó **crisis de Bosnia**. Al principio, intentó asegurar algunas concesiones para Serbia, pero más tarde se plegó a las demandas tanto de Austria-Hungría como de sus aliados. El **zar de Bulgaria Fernando I** (*véase* 1887), cuyo papel como líder todavía no había sido reconocido por Rusia y muchos otros países europeos, decidió aprovechar esta crisis para proclamar la **independencia de Bulgaria** del decadente Imperio otomano.

CLAVE
- Reino de Hungría
- Imperio austriaco
- Bosnia-Herzegovina
- Frontera de Austria-Hungría

El Imperio austrohúngaro
En 1908, el Imperio austrohúngaro ansiaba reforzar su control sobre Bosnia-Herzegovina para evitar que el Imperio otomano ganara territorio en los Balcanes.

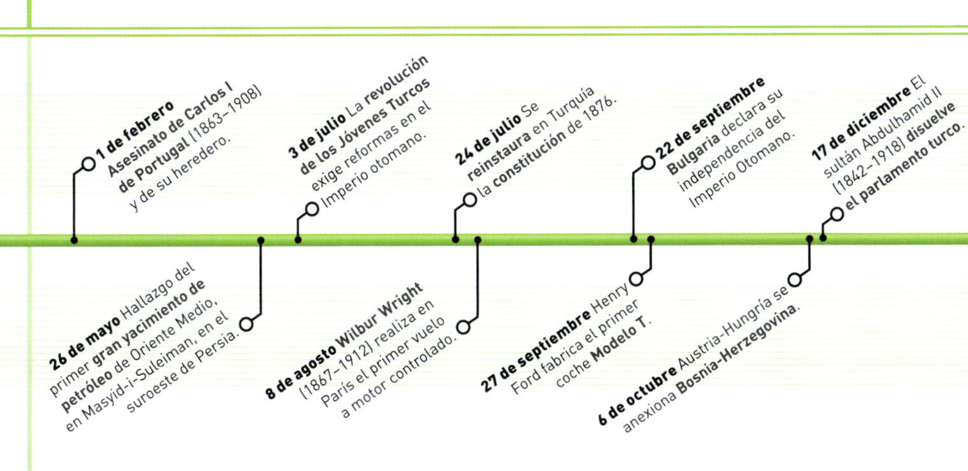

1909

« ALGÚN DÍA **MI CUERPO MORTAL SERÁ POLVO**, PERO **LA REPÚBLICA TURCA** PERSISTIRÁ **PARA SIEMPRE**. »

Mustafá Kemal Ataturk, primer presidente de Turquía (1926)

El sultán Mehmet V
El 35.º sultán otomano, Mehmet V (1844–1918), era en realidad una marioneta del Comité de Unión y Progreso de los Jóvenes Turcos.

TRAS EL TRIUNFO DE LOS JÓVENES TURCOS el año anterior, el **Comité de Unión y Progreso**, el ala política del grupo, tomó el mando del **Imperio otomano** y lo conservó durante los dos años siguientes pese a las disputas internas. Uno de los objetivos de los Jóvenes Turcos era el de obligar al sultán a **restaurar la constitución** y, una vez conseguido, Abdulhamid II (r. 1876–1909) gobernó como monarca constitucional, aunque por poco tiempo, ya que fue destituido el 27 de abril. Su hermano, **Mehmet V** (r. 1909–1918), le sucedió como sultán.

Muchos Jóvenes Turcos fueron estudiantes e intelectuales otomanos que se organizaron mientras vivían en Europa y en Egipto, bajo control británico. A pesar de que al principio se les creía «liberales», muchas de sus políticas se consideraron represivas, en especial en otros puntos del imperio. Gran parte del descontento se debía al **nacionalismo** de los Jóvenes Turcos, que querían potenciar una **identidad turca** en detrimento de los numerosos grupos étnicos del mundo otomano, como los árabes y los eslavos. Sin embargo, introdujeron algunas **reformas progresistas**, como la secularización del sistema legal y la mejora de la educación, incluido el acceso de las mujeres a ella. Además, pretendían limitar la **influencia extranjera** en el imperio, por ejemplo, en áreas como Bosnia-Herzegovina (*véase* 1908).

En el mes de julio, España envió tropas, la mayor parte de Cataluña, para sofocar un levantamiento en su territorio colonial de Marruecos. Esto desató un brote de violencia popular, sobre todo en Barcelona, conocido como **Semana Trágica**.

MUSTAFÁ KEMAL ATATURK (1881–1938)

Después de la revolución de los Jóvenes Turcos de 1908, Kemal lideró el movimiento nacionalista en la guerra de la Independencia turca. Fue el primer presidente de la república (1923) y adoptó el patronímico de Ataturk («padre de los turcos»).

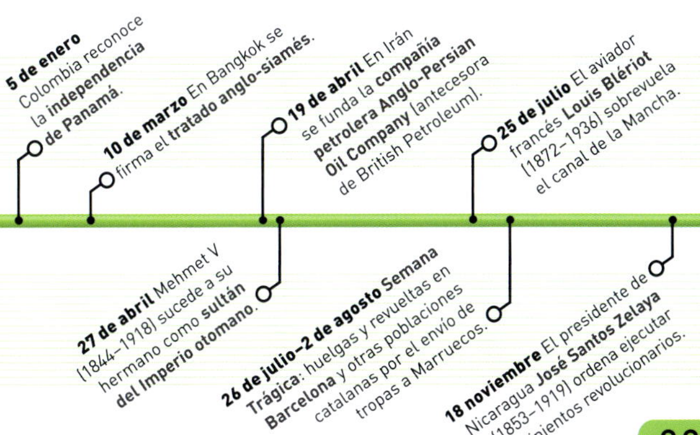

1910

« ES MEJOR MORIR DE PIE QUE VIVIR TODA UNA VIDA ARRODILLADO. »

Emiliano Zapata, líder de la Revolución mexicana

Emiliano Zapata fue uno de los líderes de la lucha para destituir a Porfirio Díaz y sustituirlo por un gobierno revolucionario dirigido por Francisco I. Madero. Zapata fue crucial como organizador de las tropas guerrilleras.

UN SIGLO DESPUÉS DE QUE TUVIESE LUGAR LA INSURRECCIÓN DE HIDALGO (*véase* 1810), México volvía a estar inmerso en convulsos cambios políticos. Los reformistas liberales habían empezado a oponerse al régimen de **Porfirio Díaz** (*véase* 1876) y fundado el **movimiento Regeneración**, cuyos miembros eran con frecuencia encarcelados y cuyo periódico fue vetado. En 1906 publicaron un manifiesto en el que reclamaban una **presidencia de un solo mandato**, así como reformas agrarias (devolución de las tierras que habían sido confiscadas por el régimen porfirista a sus verdaderos propietarios) y educativas. Finalmente Díaz permitió que se formara una oposición, y aparecieron nuevos grupos. Sin embargo, Díaz envió a la cárcel a un candidato a la presidencia muy popular, **Francisco I. Madero** (1873–1913), en vísperas de las elecciones de 1910, incumpliendo con ello su promesa de celebrar unas elecciones justas. Madero huyó a Texas y **organizó un levantamiento** para el 20 de noviembre, aniversario del inicio de la guerra de la Independencia mexicana. No fue una rebelión a gran escala, sino que consistió en ataques a pequeñas poblaciones por **grupúsculos de guerrilleros** que el ejército consiguió reprimir. Un año después, una milicia compuesta en gran medida por campesinos reanudó sus ataques contra el ejército bajo el liderazgo de **Francisco «Pancho» Villa** (1877–1932) y **Emiliano Zapata** (1879–1919). Díaz se rindió y firmó el **tratado de Ciudad Juárez**. En noviembre de 1911, Madero era el nuevo presidente. Sin embargo, pronto se vio acosado por grupos escindidos del movimiento revolucionario. Esta primera fase (etapa maderista) de la **Revolución mexicana** concluyó en 1913 con el asesinato de Madero. El conflicto se prolongó durante décadas.

Mientras tanto, en Asia oriental, **China volvió a invadir el Tíbet** y, una vez más, intentó consolidar su dominio sobre el territorio. Esta invasión se produjo después de los intentos británicos de ocupar Lhasa en 1904, atizados por el temor a que Tíbet cayera bajo influencia rusa. La consecuencia fue el **tratado de 1907 entre China y Gran Bretaña** por el que se reconocía la soberanía de China sobre Tíbet. Sin embargo, los tibetanos no aceptaron la legitimidad de este tratado y aprovecharon la **revolución** que estalló en China al año siguiente (*véase* 1911) para expulsar a los chinos.

En **Corea**, la guerra ruso-japonesa (*véase* 1904) tuvo graves consecuencias, ya que permitió que Japón utilizara la península para sus operaciones militares. Corea se había convertido en **protectorado japonés** por el **tratado de Portsmouth** de 1905, aunque la anexión oficial se produjo en 1910.

Casa Milà
Este edificio barcelonés conocido como La Pedrera, diseñado por el arquitecto catalán Antoni Gaudí i Cornet (1852–1956), fue construido entre 1905 y 1910.

20 de febrero Asesinato del primer ministro egipcio **Butros Ghali** (n. 1846).

Marzo **Levantamiento albano** contra el gobierno otomano.

6 de mayo Jorge V (1865–1936) sube al trono británico.

31 de mayo Se crea la **Unión Sudafricana**.

28 de agosto **Montenegro** se convierte en un reino **independiente** bajo Nicolás I.

5 de octubre La monarquía es derrocada en **Portugal** y se **proclama la república**.

23 de octubre Vajiravudh (1881–1925) es coronado **rey de Siam** como Rama VI.

Noviembre Empieza la **Revolución mexicana**.

Diciembre Una **epidemia mata** a más de **cuarenta mil personas** en el noreste de China.

1911

Los funcionarios imperiales huyen de Tianjín durante la Revolución china, que precipitó el fin de la dinastía Qing, reinante en China desde el siglo XVII.

6000 DIAMANTES ENGASTADOS EN LA CORONA DE JORGE V

EN CHINA, EL CURSO DE LA HISTORIA DIO UN GIRO INESPERADO cuando la dinastía Qing, que llevaba más de 260 años en el poder, se enfrentó a una rebelión. A pesar de su antigüedad en el trono imperial, muchos chinos seguían considerando extranjeros a los gobernantes **manchúes**. También existía resquemor por el **creciente número de occidentales** presentes en el país y por el hecho de que se les hubiera permitido avanzar hacia el interior desde las ciudades portuarias. La gran inestabilidad con la que China había entrado en el siglo XX (*véase* 1900) aumentó a medida que empezaban a formarse **grupos revolucionarios** por todo el país. En octubre se descubrió una trama revolucionaria cuyos miembros fueron detenidos y ejecutados. Los soldados de **Wuchang** que conocían la trama decidieron seguir adelante con la revuelta y el 10 de octubre encabezaron un **motín** que se extendió pronto por todo el país. Los rebeldes **declararon la República de China** sin encontrar apenas resistencia, porque muchos funcionarios daban por hecho que los días de los manchúes estaban contados. En EE. UU., el líder revolucionario exiliado **Sun Yat-sen** (1866–1925) supo de lo ocurrido en China y regresó a su país, donde fue elegido **presidente provisional** aunque la corte imperial ya había otorgado plenos poderes al primer ministro **Yuan Shikai** (1859–1916). Ambos llegaron a un acuerdo, a pesar del cual Yuan Shikai intentó autoproclamarse **emperador** en 1915. Sus esfuerzos fracasaron tres meses antes de su muerte, en 1916.

Entre tanto, en **India**, los británicos quisieron hacer gala de su poder imperial con un enorme **durbar** (asamblea) en Delhi, con ocasión de la visita de **Jorge V y la reina María**, durante la cual el rey anunció el traslado de **la capital colonial de Calcuta a Delhi**. Más o menos en esas fechas, la impopular **división de Bengala** (*véase* 1905) llegó a su fin y el territorio se reunificó.

Sun Yat-sen
Portada de la revista Je sais tout *con la imagen de Sun Yat-sen, presidente de la República de China.*

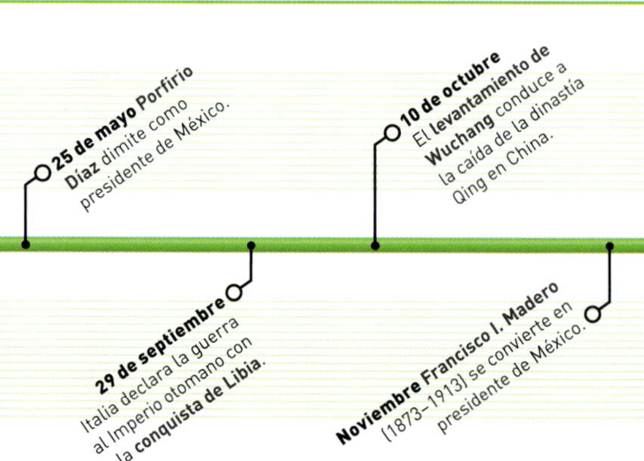

25 de mayo Porfirio **Díaz** dimite como presidente de México.

29 de septiembre Italia declara la guerra al Imperio otomano con la **conquista de Libia**.

10 de octubre El **levantamiento de Wuchang** conduce a la caída de la dinastía Qing en China.

Noviembre Francisco I. Madero (1873–1913) se convierte en presidente de México.

1912

El general Lyautey, gobernador francés de Marruecos.

1913

Fotografía del momento en que la sufragista Emily Davison es arrollada por el caballo que llevaba los colores del rey Jorge V durante el Derby de Epsom.

PRECIO MUNDIAL (LIBRAS/TONELADA)
600
500
400
300
200
100
0
1840 1870 1911

El auge del caucho
Las innovaciones tecnológicas, sobre todo los neumáticos para los cada vez más populares vehículos de motor, dispararon su consumo (y su precio).

En los años siguientes se construyó un nuevo barrio en Delhi con una **residencia del virrey** y edificios gubernamentales diseñados por el arquitecto británico **Edwin Lutyens** (1869–1944). Sin embargo, estas exhibiciones no lograron mitigar el creciente sentimiento nacionalista.

En el continente europeo, la científica francesa de origen polaco **Marie Curie** (1867–1934) recibió su segundo **premio Nobel**, esta vez de química, por su trabajo sobre la **radiactividad**. Ella y su marido, Pierre (1859–1906), ya habían sido galardonados con el premio Nobel de física en 1903.

En 1911, el **precio mundial del caucho** se había disparado por su creciente demanda, especialmente para fabricar **neumáticos**. La materia prima procedía de Brasil, el Sureste Asiático y África occidental, donde crecían los árboles de cuya savia (látex) se obtiene el caucho.

EL IMPERIO OTOMANO SE ENFRENTÓ a nuevas insurrecciones en la **primera guerra de los Balcanes**. El conflicto finalizó con la pérdida de Albania, que se independizó, y Macedonia, que se repartieron los aliados de los Balcanes (*véase* 1913).

En marzo, **Marruecos** pasó a ser **protectorado** francés por el **tratado de Fez**. El año anterior, el nuevo sultán **Mulay Hafiz** (*c.* 1875–1937), sitiado en su palacio, pidió ayuda a Francia para reprimir a los disidentes. El tratado, además, reconocía para España las zonas del Rif, al norte, y de Ifni y Tarfaya, al sur.

EL TRATADO DE LONDRES DE 1913 SEÑALÓ OFICIALMENTE EL FIN de la primera guerra de los Balcanes. Sin embargo, la Liga Balcánica (Serbia, Bulgaria, Montenegro y Grecia), que se había enfrentado al Imperio otomano, no tardó en empezar a desintegrarse. Bulgaria atacó a Serbia en junio por un desacuerdo acerca de la **división de Macedonia**. El enfrentamiento llegó a su fin solo un par de meses después gracias a una **alianza serbio-griega**. Grecia y Serbia se quedaron la mayor parte de Macedonia, mientras que Bulgaria únicamente recibió una pequeña parte. Esta división interna abrió una brecha para los turcos. Así, el **gobierno de los Jóvenes Turcos** que dirigía el Imperio otomano, descontento con las decisiones del **tratado de Londres**, organizó otra invasión y esta vez reconquistó Edirne, el 20 de julio. Sin embargo, para entonces ya había perdido la mayor parte de su territorio en los Balcanes.

En Gran Bretaña, el 4 de junio, la **lucha sufragista** por el derecho al voto femenino (*véase* recuadro) dio un giro completamente inesperado, cuando la sufragista **Emily Davison** (1872–1913) se interpuso en el camino del caballo que defendía los colores de Jorge V durante el Derby de Epsom. El caballo, Anmer, coceó el pecho de Davison, que permaneció inconsciente durante cuatro días hasta que falleció. Se desconoce si su intención era suicidarse. El 14 de junio se celebró un funeral público en Londres.

En 1913, **Henry Ford** (1863–1947), director de la empresa estadounidense Ford Motor Company, fundada en 1903, había vendido casi **250 000 coches modelo T**. Otras empresas también fabricaban automóviles, pero estos resultaban demasiado caros para el consumidor medio. Ford pretendía que fueran más asequibles y comenzó a fabricar el **modelo T** básico. También desarrolló técnicas de producción innovadoras y más eficientes basadas en **cadenas de montaje** móviles, que instaló en su fábrica de Michigan. Esta mejora permitió completar un chasis (la estructura del coche) en poco más de una hora y media, mientras que sus competidores tardaban horas en hacerlo.

Le Petit Journal
SUPPLÉMENT ILLUSTRÉ
UN COUP D'ÉTAT A CONSTANTINOPLE
Meurtre de Nazim Pacha

Golpe de estado
Grabado de Le Petit Journal illustré *sobre el asesinato del ministro otomano de la guerra Nazim Bajá, durante la primera guerra de los Balcanes.*

《 LA HISTORIA ES, EN GENERAL, UNA SIMPLEZA. ES TRADICIÓN. 》

Henry Ford, industrial estadounidense, en una entrevista del *Chicago Tribune* (25 de mayo de 1916)

★VOTES FOR WOMEN★
THE MAP PROVES IT A SUCCESS
Full Suffrage
No Suffrage
Partial Suffrage
PRESIDENTIAL-MUNICIPAL-PARTIAL STATE AND COUNTY SUFFRAGE
ALASKA 1913

EL DERECHO AL VOTO DE LAS MUJERES

A principios del siglo xx, la lucha de las mujeres por conseguir el voto había ido ganando terreno en todo el mundo. Australia siguió el ejemplo de Nueva Zelanda (*véase* 1893) y concedió el sufragio a las mujeres en 1902. Finlandia introdujo el derecho de las mujeres a votar en 1906, y Noruega lo hizo en 1913. Las británicas tuvieron que esperar hasta el fin de la Primera Guerra Mundial. En Rusia y EE. UU. (en el mapa los estados con sufragio universal aparecen en amarillo) también se empezaron a eliminar las restricciones.

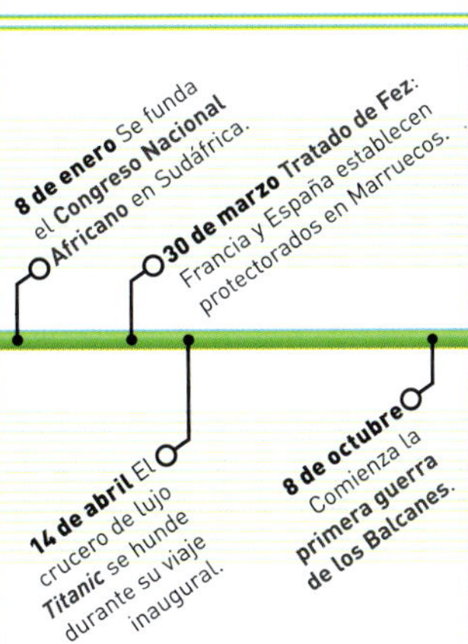

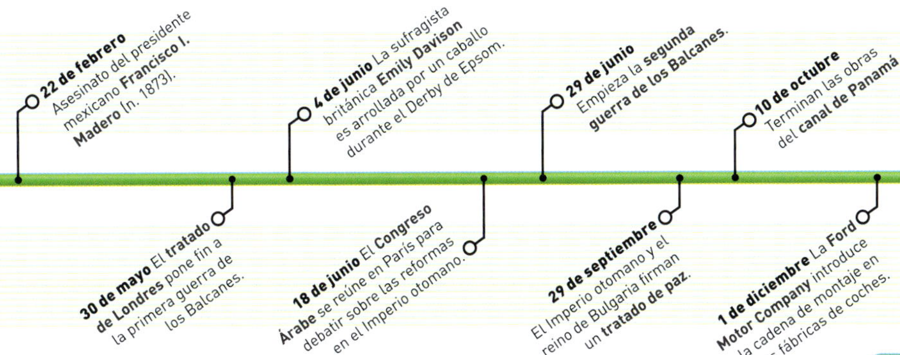

TECNOLOGÍA Y SUPERPOTENCIAS

1914–2023

La tecnología alumbró progresos inimaginables como los vuelos espaciales e Internet, pero los proyectos más osados de transformar la sociedad fracasaron. Pese a las dos guerras mundiales, la población humana se cuadruplicó, lo cual planteó nuevos desafíos económicos y ambientales.

Jóvenes alemanes saludan mientras desfilan por la Pariser Platz de Berlín. Muchos alemanes reaccionaron con entusiasmo al reclutamiento bélico.

Izamiento de la bandera
Soldados de EE. UU. izan la bandera en el puerto de Veracruz. La ocupación costó 17 vidas estadounidenses y duró seis meses.

EL AÑO ARRANCÓ CON LA ATENCIÓN PUESTA EN AMÉRICA CENTRAL. En enero, el primer barco atravesó el **canal de Panamá**. Esta proeza de la ingeniería estadounidense costó 300 millones de dólares y se cobró la vida de unos 4000 obreros.

En abril, EE. UU. intervino en la **guerra civil de México** con el envío de marines para **tomar el puerto de Veracruz**, lo cual impidió al presidente mexicano, Victoriano Huerta, recibir el armamento procedente de Alemania. EE. UU. controló el puerto durante seis meses y contribuyó a la caída de Huerta en julio.

Entre tanto, Europa se sumía en una espiral hacia la guerra. El asesinato del archiduque de Austria y heredero al trono austrohúngaro, Francisco Fernando (1863–1914), y de su esposa, Sophie, **fue el detonante de la Primera Guerra Mundial**. El 28 de junio, durante una visita oficial a Sarajevo en la Bosnia gobernada por Austria, ambos cayeron abatidos por los disparos del serbobosnio Gavrilo Princip, de 19 años. El **gobierno austriaco culpó a Serbia de los asesinatos**. El 23 de julio, con el pleno apoyo de la Alemania del káiser Guillermo II (1859–1941), los austriacos enviaron un ultimátum a Serbia. Sus humillantes exigencias perseguían el rechazo de Serbia, lo cual les brindaría un pretexto para la acción militar. Pese a que Serbia estaba dispuesta a realizar concesiones, Austria-Hungría le declaró la guerra el 28 de julio. En respuesta, Rusia movilizó a su ejército en apoyo de Serbia.

En una semana, **las grandes potencias europeas se hallaban en guerra**. Los mandos militares alemanes descartaron las iniciativas de paz de última hora planteadas por el káiser Guillermo y el zar Nicolás II (1868–1918), e insistieron en que **Alemania declarara la guerra a Rusia**. Puesto que sus planes militares exigían una victoria rápida en el oeste como preludio para derrotar a Rusia en el este, Alemania también **declaró la guerra a Francia**. Alemania no pretendía luchar contra los británicos, pero para invadir Francia su ejército debía atravesar Bélgica, cuya neutralidad garantizaba Gran Bretaña. El 4 de agosto, después de que las tropas alemanas cruzaran la frontera belga, **Gran Bretaña declaró la guerra a Alemania**. Si bien en privado muchos contemplaban el estallido del conflicto con consternación, las multitudes lo recibieron con ovaciones. Incluso el **Partido Socialdemócrata alemán**, de tradición antimilitarista e internacionalista, se sumó al esfuerzo bélico, convencido de que Alemania debía defenderse de la conquista rusa. En Francia, radicales y socialistas hasta entonces antibelicistas se adhirieron a la ***Union sacrée*** (unión sagrada), que planteó una tregua a los partidos belicistas y vetó cualquier conato de huelga. En Reino Unido, los **paramilitares protestantes del Ulster**, que habían estado al borde de una rebelión armada contra los planes del gobierno británico relativos a la autonomía de Irlanda, y sus rivales católicos, los **voluntarios irlandeses**, se alistaron en masa al ejército británico.

En la Europa continental, millones de hombres fueron reclu-

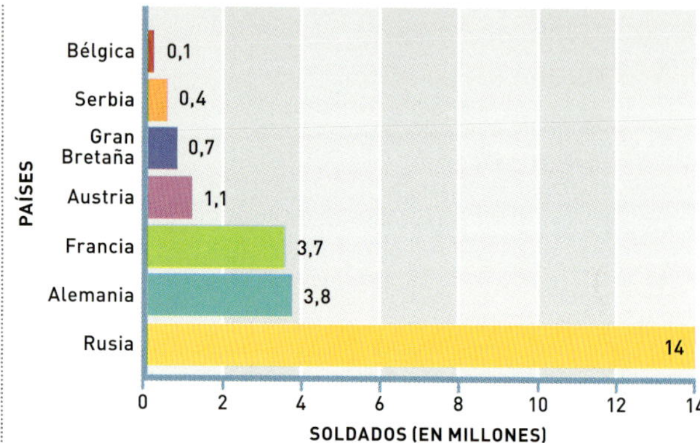

Tamaño de los ejércitos
El ejército ruso era inmenso, pero estaba mal equipado y organizado. Gran Bretaña dependía de su armada para defenderse.

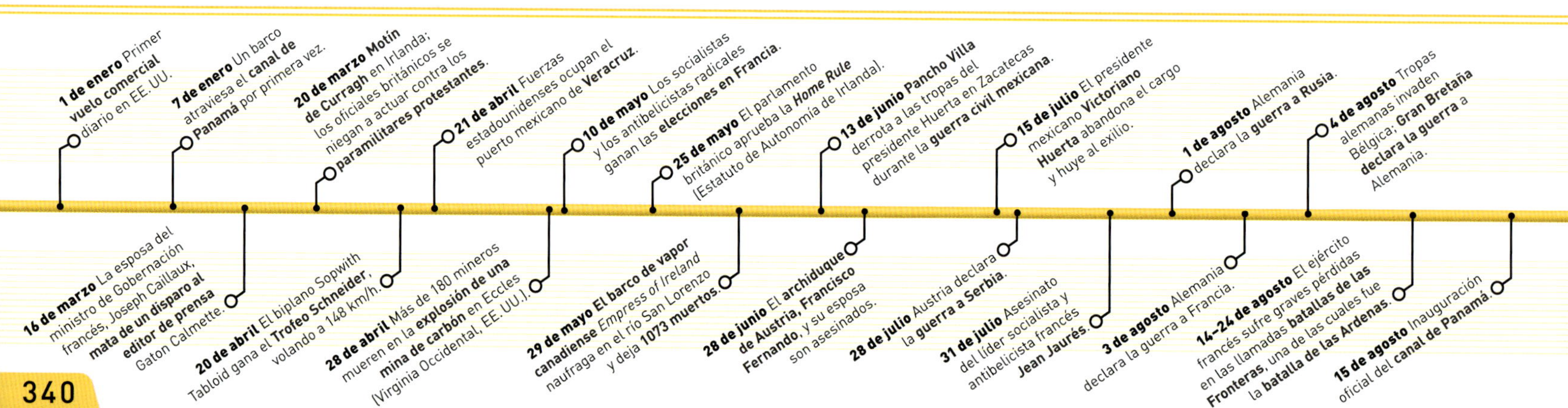

Ciudadanos británicos hacen cola a las puertas de la oficina de reclutamiento del ayuntamiento de Southwark. Miles de hombres de todos los estratos sociales se alistaron voluntarios.

« LA **CAÍDA** DE LA CIVILIZACIÓN EN ESTE **ABISMO DE SANGRE Y OSCURIDAD**... ES DEMASIADO TRÁGICA PARA EXPRESARLA EN PALABRAS. **»**

Henry James, escritor estadounidense (4 de agosto de 1914)

tados y enviados en tren a las fronteras, mientras que en Francia se destacó un ejército de soldados rasos británicos mucho más reducido, las **Fuerzas Expedicionarias Británicas (FEB)**. El secretario de Guerra británico, lord Kitchener (1850–1916), impulsó una campaña para reclutar voluntarios. La respuesta fue abrumadora: más de 750 000 británicos se habían alistado a finales de septiembre. Se preveía una guerra breve con un elevado número de bajas; en aquel momento, dicha previsión parecía verosímil.

Las tropas alemanas invadieron Bélgica bajo la consigna de aplicar la política oficial de ***Schrecklichkeit*** («terror»): cometieron atrocidades contra la población belga (en el peor incidente, 674 civiles fueron masacrados en Dinant) y asolaron la ciudad histórica de Lovaina, donde incendiaron la famosa biblioteca universitaria.

Las **FEB acometieron su primera acción en Mons**. Incapaces de contener el ataque alemán, británicos y franceses **retrocedieron hacia París**. Entre tanto, los franceses lanzaron su propia ofensiva a lo largo de la frontera oriental franco-alemana, que les supuso graves pérdidas en vano. Al despuntar septiembre, la situación de los ejércitos británico y francés era desesperada. Los alemanes también tuvieron que cambiar de estrategia: abandonaron su plan de avanzar hacia el oeste de París y, en su lugar, marcharon hacia el este de la ciudad. El comandante del ejército francés, el general Joseph Joffre (1852 1931), **lanzó un contraataque en el Marne**, mientras que las tropas de París, algunas de las cuales fueron trasladadas al frente en autobuses y taxis, atacaron el flanco alemán. El ejército alemán, forzado a retirarse,

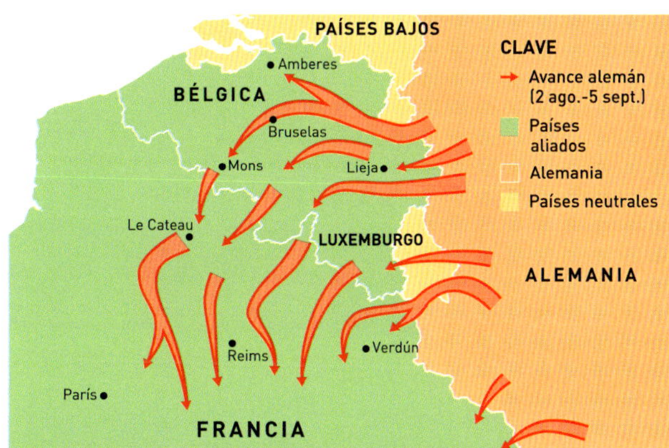

INVASIÓN ALEMANA DE FRANCIA

La estrategia alemana, diseñada en 1905 por el conde Alfred von Schlieffen, consistía en atacar en dos frentes para que Francia concentrara sus tropas en la frontera oriental. El grueso de las tropas alemanas avanzaría por Bélgica y Luxemburgo y rodearía a los soldados franceses. El objetivo era derrotar a los franceses en seis semanas, antes de que los rusos pudieran intervenir.

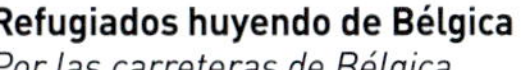

Refugiados huyendo de Bélgica
Por las carreteras de Bélgica transitaban filas de refugiados cargados con sus posesiones huyendo del ejército alemán.

250 000

CIFRA DE BAJAS **BRITÁNICAS, FRANCESAS Y ALEMANAS** EN LA **PRIMERA BATALLA DE YPRES**

vio desvanecerse sus esperanzas de una rápida victoria.

En el Frente Oriental, los rusos se movilizaron con más premura de lo que Alemania había anticipado, pero, al avanzar hacia Prusia Oriental, el 1.er y 2.º Ejércitos rusos fueron aplastados en las **batallas de Tannenberg y de los lagos de Masuria**. Sus victorias valieron al general alemán Paul von Hindenburg (1837–1934) y a su intendente, el general Erich Ludendorff (1883–1918), la consideración de héroes nacionales.

Entre septiembre y noviembre se libraron en el norte del Frente Occidental, cerca de Flandes, varias batallas que culminaron en los combates conocidos como la **primera batalla de Ypres**. Ante la incapacidad de ambos bandos de asestar un golpe decisivo, los ejércitos cavaron trincheras a lo largo de una línea que apenas sufriría modificaciones en tres años.

Mientras tanto, **la guerra se hizo mundial**. La Turquía otomana unió fuerzas con Alemania y declaró la yihad (guerra santa musulmana) contra el Imperio británico. Las tropas británicas de India entraron en Iraq, bajo gobierno turco, y asediaron Basora. Por su parte, Japón se sumó a los aliados y luchó por controlar las posesiones alemanas en China y el Pacífico. En África, el ejército británico invadió el África Oriental Alemana, y las fuerzas sudafricanas atacaron el África del Sudoeste Alemana, además de aplacar una revuelta de los bóers, que respaldaban a los alemanes.

Cartel de reclutamiento
Desde los carteles de reclutamiento, el secretario de Guerra británico, lord Kitchener, instaba a los voluntarios a alistarse y luchar.

En **Navidades, la confraternización** entre las tropas rivales en el Frente Occidental consternó a los generales, quienes temían que sus hombres perdieran las ganas de luchar, pero la guerra prosiguió. Hacia finales de año habían muerto cerca de medio millón de soldados franceses y alemanes, además de un tercio de los británicos llegados a Francia en agosto.

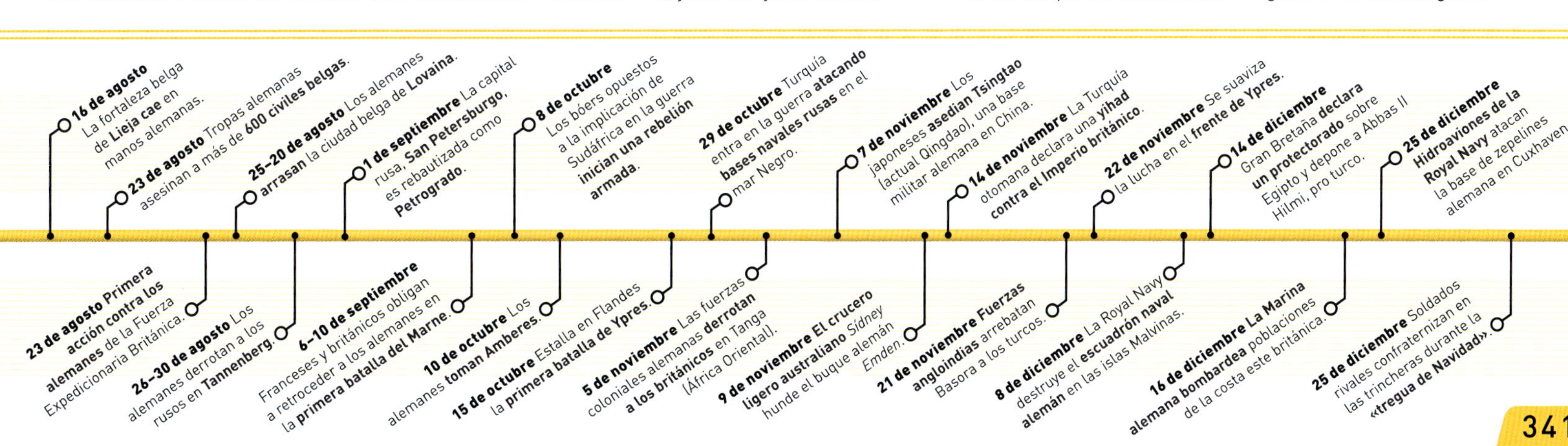

1915

Un submarino emprende una misión en el Atlántico. Los submarinos alemanes desataron el terror al atacar tanto a buques militares como comerciales aliados.

Un dirigible alemán despega de su base para bombardear Londres.

A COMIENZOS DE 1915, LAS GRANDES POTENCIAS DE EUROPA continuaron sumidas en una guerra para la que no estaban preparadas. Las provisiones de munición se agotaron y, para continuar luchando, los países combatientes tuvieron que **ampliar sobremanera su industria armamentística**. Los gobiernos sabían que la guerra se ganaría o perdería tanto en las fábricas como en el frente. Gran Bretaña estableció un nuevo ministerio de Municiones y, en Rusia, el gobierno zarista creó el Comité de Industrias Bélicas. Los franceses, por su parte, tuvieron que recuperar reclutas de las trincheras para trabajar en las fábricas, pues la ocupación alemana de las zonas industriales del noreste de Francia acentuaba sus problemas de producción.

Guerra química
Antes de la invención de la máscara antigás, los soldados, como estos franceses, se protegían de los ataques químicos como podían.

En el **Frente Occidental**, la situación **continuó en tablas** a lo largo de la doble línea de trincheras que se extendía desde el canal de La Mancha hasta la frontera suiza. Los generales creían que con un contingente suficiente de soldados y proyectiles lanzados contra aquellas defensas conseguirían romper la línea del enemigo, pero iban errados.

Los británicos acometieron su primera ofensiva en la guerra de trincheras en **Neuve Chapelle** en marzo, en un asalto liderado por las tropas indias en el que lucharon por primera vez las Fuerzas Expedicionarias Canadienses. Conquistaron unos 2 km de terreno con un coste de once mil bajas. Los alemanes vivieron una experiencia parecida al atacar **Ypres** en abril, y los franceses sufrieron reiteradas ofensivas a lo largo del año. Estas campañas masivas generaron bajas masivas: el choque en Champagne-Loos se cobró **más de 300 000 bajas británicas y francesas** en otoño. En el Frente Oriental, los combates fueron mucho más dinámicos y los **rusos se vieron obligados a retirarse** de Polonia y Lituania.

Para romper el estancamiento en el Frente Occidental, los alemanes **usaron gas venenoso por primera vez en la historia** en Ypres, en abril, que liberaron en forma de cloro letal sobre las trincheras aliadas. Las primeras víctimas fueron las tropas coloniales francesas, el 22 de abril, seguidas dos días después por soldados de la 1.ª División Canadiense. Sin embargo, los alemanes no lograron sacar partido del impacto inicial del gas; por suerte, los soldados aliados hallaron rápidamente medios de protección y adoptaron también el gas como arma contra los alemanes.

MUJERES EN PIE DE GUERRA

La guerra exigió la contratación de mujeres para empleos tradicionalmente masculinos. Hacia 1918, un tercio de los 1,7 millones de obreros de las fábricas de munición francesas eran mujeres (en Alemania la proporción fue del 50 %). Las mujeres también sustituyeron a los hombres como trabajadoras agrícolas, por ejemplo en el Ejército de Tierra Femenino británico.

PORRA FRANCESA

PORRA BRITÁNICA

VARA METÁLICA ALEMANA

Ataques salvajes
Los soldados que atacaban las trincheras enemigas portaban armas primitivas para el combate cuerpo a cuerpo. Además de porras como estas, utilizaban cuchillos, puños de hierro e incluso palas en sus salvajes refriegas.

El 26 de abril, **Italia firmó el tratado de Londres**, por el que se sumaba a la guerra en apoyo de Gran Bretaña y Francia. Antes del conflicto, Italia había sido aliada de Alemania y Austria, de manera que aquel fue un golpe diplomático de los aliados. Italia declaró la guerra a Austria el 23 de mayo, y la lucha en el **frente ítalo-austriaco** pronto llegó al mismo punto muerto que en el Frente Occidental.

Mientras en tierra el conflicto permanecía en punto muerto, **la guerra aérea alcanzó una escala sin precedentes**. Aviones lentos sobrevolaban las trincheras enemigas, tomaban fotografías de reconocimiento y realizaban misiones de bombardeo a pequeña escala, mientras los ágiles cazabombarderos los interceptaban.

Los dirigibles alemanes se embarcaron en la **primera campaña mundial de bombardeos de largo alcance**, con Gran Bretaña como objetivo prioritario. El comandante en jefe de la Fuerza Aérea alemana, Peter Strasser, creía posible «vencer a Gran Bretaña con dirigibles... mediante una destrucción total de sus ciudades, complejos fabriles, muelles...». En realidad, una empresa de tal calibre quedaba fuera del alcance de los dirigibles, pero, a partir del 31 de mayo, los **bombardeos nocturnos** sobre Londres y otras grandes ciudades causaron innumerables bajas civiles y obligaron a Gran Bretaña a destinar efectivos del Frente Occidental a la **defensa del país**.

En el mar, Alemania respondió al bloqueo de sus puertos por parte de la Royal Navy intentando imponer su propio bloqueo a Gran Bretaña mediante sus submarinos. A partir de febrero, los **submarinos alemanes** tenían autorización para atacar buques mercantiles en aguas británicas sin previo aviso. El 7 de mayo, frente a la costa sur de Irlanda, el submarino *U-20* torpedeó al transatlántico ***Lusitania***, que enlazaba Nueva York con Londres y transportaba casi 2000 personas a bordo. Más de 1200 personas murieron ahogadas, incluidos 128 ciudadanos estadounidenses. El ataque provocó disturbios antia-

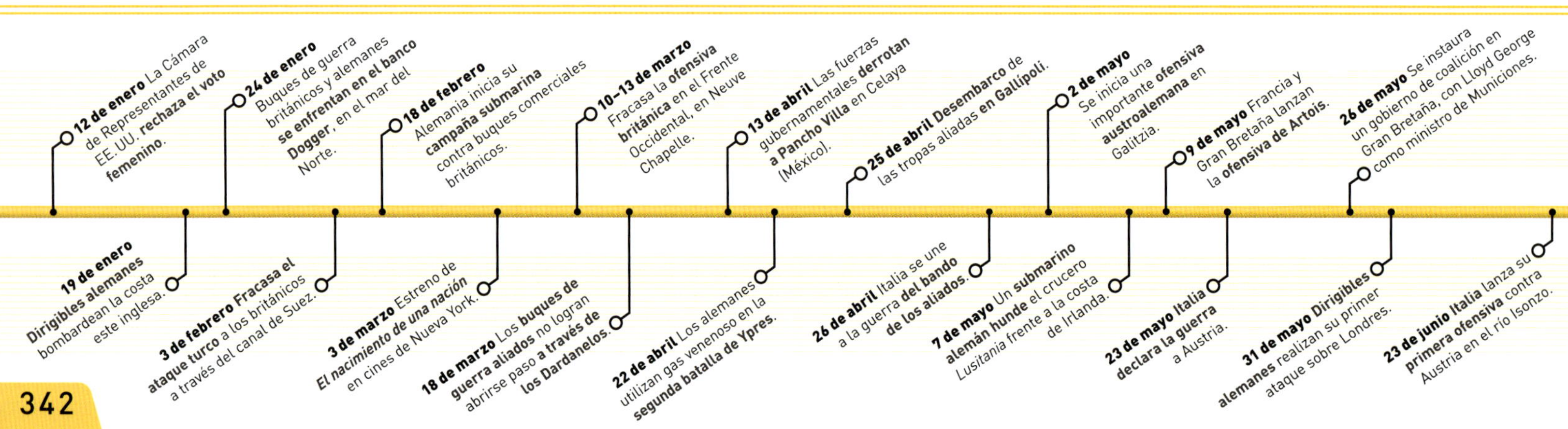

Tropas británicas en el Frente Occidental protegidas con los cascos de acero Brodie, estrenados en octubre de 1915.

lemanes en las ciudades británicas y una respuesta hostil de EE. UU. Tras el hundimiento de otro buque de pasajeros, el *Arabic*, frente a Islandia el 19 de agosto, los **alemanes limitaron sus ataques con submarinos en el Atlántico** para evitar la incorporación de EE. UU. en el conflicto.

Una guerra justa
El cartel de reclutamiento británico recurre al hundimiento del Lusitania *como propaganda para demostrar la justicia de la causa aliada.*

En busca de una alternativa al estancamiento del Frente Occidental, Gran Bretaña y Francia urdieron un plan para **aplastar a Turquía, aliada de Alemania**. Buques de guerra británicos y franceses atravesarían el estrecho de los Dardanelos y entrarían en el mar de Mármara para tomar la capital de Turquía, Estambul. Pero el 18 de marzo, fecha del ataque naval, tres buques resultaron hundidos y se decidió que el estrecho de los Dardanelos debía sitiarse antes de que lo atravesara la Armada.

Las fuerzas aliadas desembarcaron en Gallípoli el 25 de abril, con un gran contingente de soldados australianos y neozelandeses, los **ANZAC**. Ante la dura resistencia turca en un terreno hostil, no lograron sobrepasar las zonas de desembarco, y nuevos desembarcos en la **bahía de Suvla** en agosto también fracasaron. Pronto se extendió otra guerra de trincheras, similar a la de Francia, pero en unas pésimas condiciones exacerbadas por el calor y la enfermedad. En enero de 1916, cuando se abandonó la operación, los aliados habían registrado casi un cuarto de millón de bajas.

El éxito en Gallípoli espoleó la moral de los turcos, cosa que necesitaban después de que los rusos aniquilaran al 3.er Ejército turco en el Cáucaso a principios de año. Con la excusa de que la población armenia del este de Turquía colaboraba con los rusos, los turcos iniciaron una **deportación masiva de armenios** desde la zona de guerra. Tal deportación, que estuvo acompañada por masacres generalizadas, se considera un **genocidio**: se calcula que entre 800 000 y 1,5 millones de armenios murieron como consecuencia de esta campaña.

La segunda mitad de 1915 se caracterizó por las **penurias del ejército y la población civil serbias**. Serbia resistió estoicamente las ofensivas austriacas el primer año de guerra, pero, en octubre de 1915, su ejército cedió ante un ataque combinado de Alemania, Austria y Bulgaria. Gran Bretaña y Francia desembarcaron tropas en **Tesalónica (Grecia)** para acudir en socorro de los serbios, pero llegaron tarde. Serbia fue invadida y unos 200 000 serbios fallecieron al batirse en retirada hacia Albania a través de Kosovo en invierno.

Y mientras en Europa acontecían tales atrocidades, **Hollywood** se establecía como centro de la producción cinematográfica. *El nacimiento de una nación*, la epopeya sobre la guerra civil dirigida por D.W. Griffith, fue un gran éxito de taquilla. Con el racista Ku Klux Klan como protagonista, la obra maestra de Griffith provocó protestas entre los afroamericanos y desencadenó disturbios raciales; con todo, sus tres horas y diez minutos de duración reflejaron una ambición superior a cualquier filme anterior. El actor británico **Charlie Chaplin** fusionó la bufonada con el drama y alcanzó el estrellato con *Charlot, vagabundo*.

« EN LA **PENÍNSULA DE GALLÍPOLI** SE ENCUENTRAN ALGUNAS DE LAS **RUTAS MÁS CORTAS** HACIA EL **TRIUNFO DE LA PAZ**. »

Winston Churchill, primer lord del Almirantazgo, durante su arenga en pro de una nueva ofensiva en Gallípoli (5 de junio de 1915)

Los ANZAC en Gallípoli
Un soldado australiano carga con un compañero herido en Gallípoli. Más de 26 000 australianos fallecieron o fueron heridos en esta campaña.

24 de junio Robert Lansing es elegido **secretario de Estado de EE. UU.** tras la dimisión de William Jennings Bryan.

9 de julio Tropas sudafricanas capturan el **África del Sudoeste Alemana** (actual Namibia).

28 de julio Marines de EE. UU. desembarcan en Port-au-Prince; la ocupación de Haití se prolongará **19 años**.

4 de agosto Los alemanes **ocupan Varsovia** mientras los rusos se retiran de Polonia.

6 de agosto Segunda oleada de **desembarcos en Gallípoli**.

27 de agosto El káiser Guillermo II pone fin a los **ataques indiscriminados con submarinos** en el Atlántico.

5 de septiembre Una **reunión internacional de socialistas** exige el fin de la guerra.

8 de septiembre El zar **Nicolás II asume el mando** del ejército ruso.

19 de septiembre Tropas alemanas arrebatan **Vilna** (Lituania) a los rusos.

25 de septiembre Los aliados lanzan **ofensivas en Champaña y en Loos**.

5 de octubre Soldados aliados desembarcan en **Tesalónica**, en el norte de Grecia.

6 de octubre Fuerzas austroalemanas **atacan Serbia**.

11 de octubre Bulgaria se une a la **invasión de Serbia**.

12 de octubre Los alemanes ejecutan a la enfermera británica **Edith Cavell** en Bélgica por **ayudar a prisioneros aliados huidos**.

28 de octubre Aristide Briand forma el nuevo gobierno francés.

6 de noviembre La **ofensiva francesa en Champaña** se salda con un costoso fracaso.

23 de noviembre Los serbios, derrotados, se retiran de Kosovo.

6 de diciembre Los aliados se reúnen en Chantilly para **coordinar su estrategia**.

7 de diciembre Los turcos sitian a las **fuerzas angloindias en Mesopotamia**, en Kut.

19 de diciembre El general Haig asume el mando de las fuerzas británicas en el Frente Occidental.

19 de diciembre Las tropas aliadas inician la **evacuación de Gallípoli**.

LA GRAN GUERRA

EL CONFLICTO QUE CAMBIÓ LA NATURALEZA DE LA GUERRA PARA SIEMPRE

Pese a tratarse de un conflicto mundial, el epicentro de la Gran Guerra (ago. 1914–nov. 1918) fue Europa, donde las Potencias Centrales (Alemania, Austria-Hungría y Turquía) lucharon contra una alianza encabezada por Francia, Gran Bretaña y Rusia. EE. UU. entró en la guerra del bando anglofrancés en 1917.

Desde el inicio, el terreno de combate decisivo fue el Frente Occidental de Alemania. Los alemanes tomaron Bélgica y Luxemburgo, países neutrales, tras superar la resistencia belga en Lieja y Amberes. Británicos y francesas se replegaron hacia el sur tras enfrentamientos en Mons y Charleroi. En Marne, en cambio, el comandante en jefe francés Joseph Joffre congregó a sus tropas para una contraofensiva que obligó a los alemanes a retroceder.

Tras una batalla desesperada en Ypres en otoño de 1914, los ejércitos rivales cavaron trincheras que se extendían desde el mar del Norte hasta Suiza. Aunque se destinaron ingentes recursos a las ofensivas, no se rompió el estancamiento. Hasta 1918, solo el retroceso voluntario de los alemanes hasta la línea fortificada de Hindenburg cambió de manera significativa la posición de los ejércitos.

A partir de marzo de 1918, una serie de campañas alemanas a gran escala rompieron las defensas aliadas y acercaron la línea del frente a París. Sin embargo, ayudados por la llegada de las tropas de EE. UU., los aliados detuvieron a los alemanes en el Marne. En agosto, el éxito de un ataque británico en Amiens inició el período de los Cien Días, una serie de avances que retrasaron la línea de combate hasta cerca de la frontera alemana.

GRAN BRETAÑA

Londres

El Frente Occidental
Millones de soldados quedaron atrapados en una zona situada al noreste de Francia y al oeste de Bélgica. Allí se libraron las batallas más largas y sangrientas de la guerra.

Canal de la Mancha

GUERRA EN TODOS LOS FRENTES

En el Frente Oriental, Alemania y Austria combatieron al ejército del Imperio ruso. A partir de la batalla de Tannenberg, en agosto de 1914, los alemanes aventajaron a los rusos, si bien los austrohúngaros, con menos recursos bélicos, cayeron en la ofensiva rusa de Brusílov de 1916. La Revolución rusa de 1917 forzó la salida del país de la guerra con la firma de un tratado de paz humillante con Alemania en Brest-Litovsk, en marzo de 1918.

La incorporación del Imperio otomano a la guerra como aliado de Alemania en otoño de 1914 llevó el conflicto a Oriente Medio. La apuesta anglofrancesa de atacar la capital turca, Estambul, fracasó estrepitosamente en Gallípoli.

Bulgaria también se unió a las Potencias Centrales y ayudó a derrotar a Serbia en 1915 y a Rumanía en 1916. Las tropas aliadas establecidas desde 1915 en Tesalónica, en el norte de Grecia, permanecieron en gran medida pasivas hasta los meses finales del conflicto, cuando su avance hacia el norte en septiembre de 1918 ayudó a asestar un golpe decisivo a las Potencias Centrales.

EL FRENTE ORIENTAL La guerra entre Rusia y las Potencias Centrales, librada principalmente en Prusia Oriental, Polonia y Galitzia, hundió a Rusia política y militarmente. La paz de Brest-Litovsk permitió a Alemania ocupar territorio ruso.

CLAVE
- Frente Oriental (1914-1915); límite del avance ruso
- Límite del avance austroalemán (1915-1916)
- Ofensiva de Brusílov (1916)
- Línea del armisticio (dic. 1917)
- Penetración alemana en Rusia hacia 1918
- Batalla importante

LOS BALCANES Serbia rechazó los ataques de Austria, pero no resistió los ataques de Alemania y Bulgaria. Los aliados desembarcaron tropas en Gallípoli y Tesalónica. Muchos serbios huidos se unieron a los aliados en Tesalónica.

CLAVE
- Frente Tesalónica (sept. 1918)
- Avance austriaco, alemán y búlgaro (1915)
- Retirada serbia (1915)
- Ofensiva aliada (sept. 1918)
- Ofensiva rumana (ago.-sept. 1916)

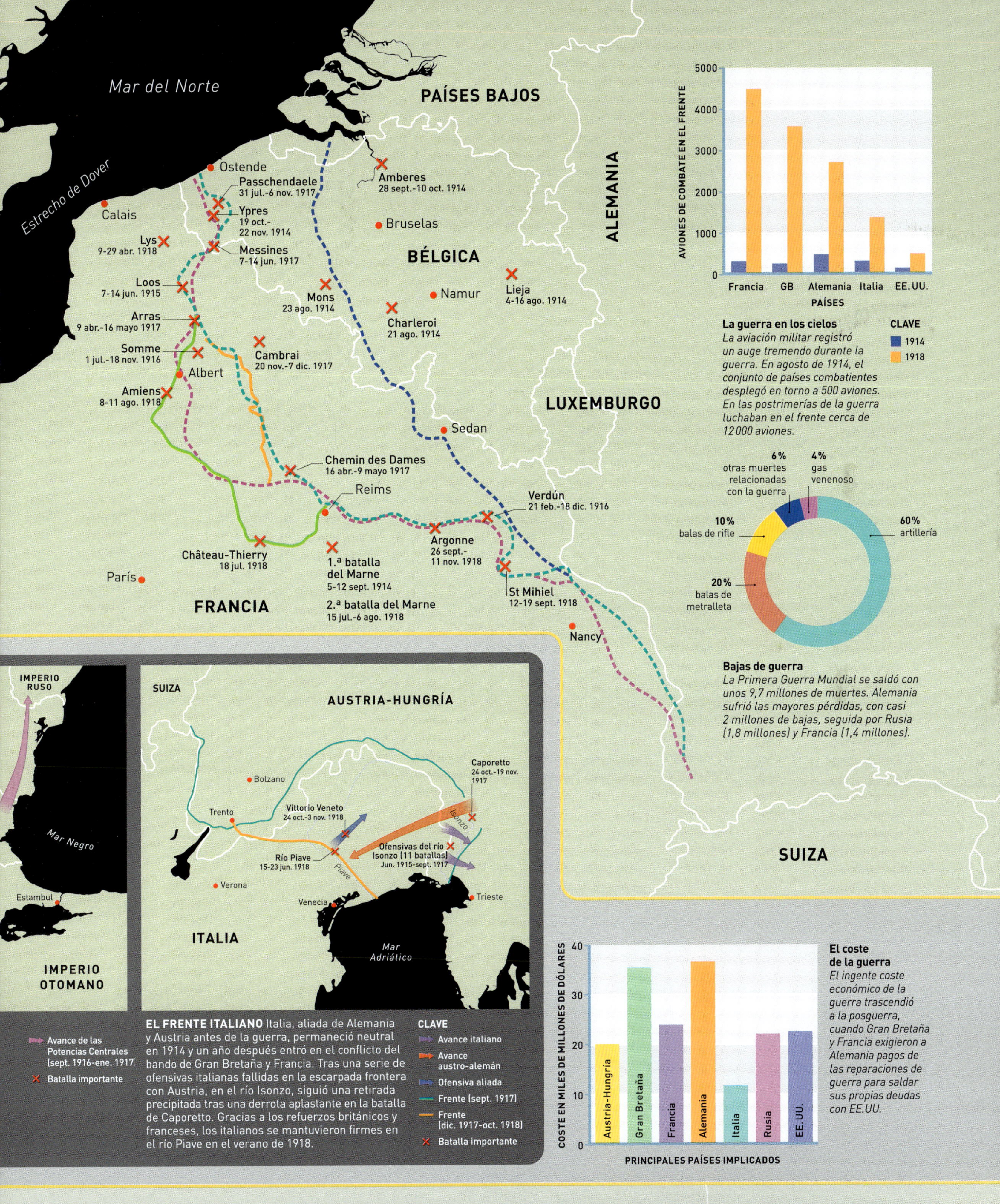

La guerra en los cielos *La aviación militar registró un auge tremendo durante la guerra. En agosto de 1914, el conjunto de países combatientes desplegó en torno a 500 aviones. En las postrimerías de la guerra luchaban en el frente cerca de 12 000 aviones.*

Bajas de guerra *La Primera Guerra Mundial se saldó con unos 9,7 millones de muertes. Alemania sufrió las mayores pérdidas, con casi 2 millones de bajas, seguida por Rusia (1,8 millones) y Francia (1,4 millones).*

EL FRENTE ITALIANO Italia, aliada de Alemania y Austria antes de la guerra, permaneció neutral en 1914 y un año después entró en el conflicto del bando de Gran Bretaña y Francia. Tras una serie de ofensivas italianas fallidas en la escarpada frontera con Austria, en el río Isonzo, siguió una retirada precipitada tras una derrota aplastante en la batalla de Caporetto. Gracias a los refuerzos británicos y franceses, los italianos se mantuvieron firmes en el río Piave en el verano de 1918.

El coste de la guerra *El ingente coste económico de la guerra trascendió a la posguerra, cuando Gran Bretaña y Francia exigieron a Alemania pagos de las reparaciones de guerra para saldar sus propias deudas con EE. UU.*

Los republicanos irlandeses bloquearon la calle Townsend de Dublín durante el alzamiento de Pascua para frenar el avance de las tropas británicas, que intentaban retomar la ciudad.

LA OFENSIVA ALEMANA CONTRA LA CIUDAD FRANCESA DE VERDÚN en febrero (pp. 344–345) inició un año de batallas a una escala sin precedentes. El comandante en jefe alemán, Erich von Falkenhayn (1861–1922), se dispuso a «desangrar al ejército francés» sumiéndolo en un costoso combate. Los franceses reaccionaron tal como él esperaba: enviando refuerzos que los alemanes diezmaron con su armamento pesado. Las bajas alemanas también aumentaron a medida que la resistencia francesa se endureció bajo el inspirador liderazgo del general Philippe Pétain (1856–1951). Los **ataques alemanes** se sucedieron hasta mediados de julio, tras lo cual siguieron **contraofensivas francesas** hasta diciembre. Apenas hubo cambios de manos de territorio y se contabilizaron unas 400 000 bajas.

Mientras, EE. UU. libraba una batalla de una escala bien distinta. En marzo, el general mexicano **Pancho Villa** (1878–1923), el flamante líder de uno de los ejércitos revolucionarios implicados en la guerra civil mexicana en curso, **realizó una incursión en Columbus** (Nuevo México, EE. UU.), repelida por la caballería estadounidense. EE. UU. no podía pasar por alto tamaña provocación, y el presidente Woodrow Wilson (1856–1924) ordenó al general John Pershing (1860–1948) liderar una expedición a México. Unos cinco mil soldados estadounidenses se enfrentaron tanto a partidarios de Villa como al ejército mexicano antes de retirarse en enero de 1917.

Gran Bretaña sufrió un **desastre militar** en primavera en Mesopotamia (Iraq), a la sazón parte del Imperio otomano. Tropas británicas procedentes de India habían ocupado la zona. De diciembre de 1915 en adelante, **el ejército turco** sitió a los soldados angloindios en **Kut-al-Amara**, entre Basora y Bagdad. Los refuerzos no lograron abrirse camino hasta Kut, y, para no morir de inanición, se vieron obligados a rendirse. Los prisioneros padecieron atrocidades; menos de la mitad de ellos lograron sobrevivir.

Líder bandolero
Pancho Villa, jefe de unos bandoleros, se convirtió en figura clave de la Revolución mexicana y del conflicto de México con EE. UU. en 1916.

Casco alemán
El casco alemán acabado en punta, el Pickelhaube*, se sustituyó durante 1916 por el casco de metal* Stahlhelm*, que brindaba mayor protección.*

Este desastre quedó contrarrestado por la **revuelta árabe contra el dominio turco**. Alentado por Gran Bretaña, Hussein bin Ali, jerife de La Meca (1854–1931), lideró un alzamiento en junio. Las fuerzas árabes derrotaron a las guarniciones turcas de La Meca, Medina y otras poblaciones del Hiyaz, y Hussein se autoproclamó sultán de los árabes. Los británicos enviaron a **T. E. Lawrence** (1888–1935), un oficial subalterno de El Cairo, para ejercer como asesor del hijo de Hussein, Faisal, el líder más activo de la revuelta. Entre ambos organizaron una fuerza militar efectiva y desplegaron tácticas de guerrilla para luchar por la liberación de los árabes en la región de Oriente Medio, bajo gobierno turco.

En abril, **Gran Bretaña afrontó una revuelta contra su dominio en Irlanda**. La Hermandad Republicana Irlandesa buscó el apoyo alemán para su levantamiento nacionalista, pero los británicos interceptaron el intento de Alemania de proporcionar rifles a los rebeldes. Aun así, los **republicanos se alzaron el Lunes de Pascua**, ocuparon edificios emblemáticos de Dublín y proclamaron el Gobierno Provisional de la República de Irlanda. Los británicos enviaron tropas a Dublín y, tras cinco días de refriega, los rebeldes se rindieron. Quince líderes republicanos fueron ejecutados tras un juicio sumario realizado ante un tribunal militar británico. Pese a que pocos irlandeses habían defendido la rebelión, las ejecuciones estimularon una oleada de sentimiento pro republicano.

A finales de mayo, la Flota de Alta Mar alemana y la Gran Flota de la Armada Real británica se enfrentaron en la **batalla de Jutlandia**, en el mar del Norte. Los británicos detectaron una misión de combate de la flota alemana y enviaron una fuerza naval muy superior para atacarla. Pese a que el almirante alemán Reinhard Scheer (1863–1928) fue sorprendido con la guardia baja, el almirante británico John Jellicoe (1859–1935) no supo aprovechar la ventaja. Los buques alemanes consiguieron retirarse hasta el puerto e infligieron mayores pérdidas de las que sufrieron. Al margen de aquella actuación decepcionante, la Royal Navy había confirmado su superioridad al forzar la retirada de la flota alemana.

En junio, el general Aleksei Brusílov (1853–1926) urdió la **ofensiva rusa más exitosa** de la Primera Guerra Mundial, que aplastó al ejército austriaco en Galitzia. Tropas alemanas acudieron al rescate de los austriacos. El éxito inicial de Brusílov se basó en tácticas sutiles: ataques por sorpresa y movimiento rápido de tropas de asalto para aprovechar los avances.

Por desgracia, los británicos no aprendieron de sus aliados rusos.

GENERAL DOUGLAS HAIG (1861–1928)

Este oficial de caballería cosechó éxitos como capitán del ejército en el primer año de la Primera Guerra Mundial. Siendo comandante en jefe, sus asaltos a las defensas alemanas en el Somme (1916) y en Passchendaele (1917) se saldaron con un incontable número de bajas. En 1918, se mantuvo firme frente a las ofensivas de los alemanes en primavera y presidió una serie de victorias británicas.

9 de enero Los aliados completan la evacuación de **Gallipoli**.

24 de enero La **Ley del Servicio Militar** introduce el reclutamiento en Gran Bretaña.

16 de febrero La ofensiva rusa en el Cáucaso **arrebata Erzurum** a Turquía.

21 de febrero Alemania lanza una ofensiva contra Francia en **Verdún**.

25 de febrero El general francés **Philippe Pétain** asume el control de la defensa en Verdún.

6 de marzo Newton Baker es designado **secretario de Guerra de EE. UU.**

9 de marzo Alemania **declara la guerra** a Portugal tras el asedio portugués a buques germanos.

9 de marzo El general mexicano **Pancho Villa** ataca Columbus (Nuevo México).

14 de marzo El general estadounidense **John Pershing** lidera una expedición punitiva en México.

24 de abril Los nacionalistas irlandeses **se alzan contra el dominio británico** en Dublín.

29 de abril Los **rebeldes irlandeses se rinden** ante el ejército británico en Dublín.

30 de abril La fuerza angloindia de Kut se rinde a los turcos.

3–12 de mayo Los británicos ejecutan a los cabecillas del **alzamiento de Pascua** aplastado en Dublín.

14 de mayo Austria lanza la **ofensiva de Trentino** contra Italia.

16 de mayo El **acuerdo de Sykes-Picot** contempla el reparto de Oriente Medio entre Gran Bretaña y Francia tras la guerra.

31 de mayo–1 de junio Las flotas británica y alemana se enfrentan en la inconcluyente **batalla de Jutlandia**.

3 de junio El Congreso de EE. UU. aprueba la **Ley de Defensa Nacional**, que amplía el Ejército.

4 de junio Los rusos lanzan en Galitzia la **ofensiva de Brusílov**.

5 de junio El jerife Hussein declara la independencia árabe del dominio turco con una **revuelta árabe**.

7 de junio El bastión francés en Verdún, **Fort Vaux**, cae en manos alemanas.

« EL TRIUNFO SERÁ PARA QUIEN MANTENGA AL ÚLTIMO HOMBRE EN PIE. »

General Philippe Pétain (1916)

Llegada de soldados franceses a Verdún, en el este de Francia. La misión estándar en el frente duraba ocho días, lo máximo que un hombre podía aguantar.

El 1 de julio, el general Douglas Haig lanzó una ofensiva masiva en **el Somme** (pp. 344–345). Más que destruir las defensas enemigas, los ocho días de bombardeos con artillería alertaron a los alemanes de un ataque inminente. Las soldados británicos marcharon hacia el frente formando líneas, ya que sus generales los creían incapaces de ejecutar estrategias más inteligentes, y cayeron abatidos por las metralletas alemanas. Perecieron casi 20 000 hombres, las **mayores pérdidas registradas por el ejército británico** en un día de combate en toda su historia. Haig mantuvo a los hombres luchando durante cinco meses y usó tanques tan pronto como aquella nueva arma estuvo disponible, además de permitir a sus subordinados experimentar con estrategias variadas, incluidos los ataques nocturnos. Sin embargo, no se logró ningún avance significativo y el único resultado fue una guerra de desgaste para ambos ejércitos.

Hacia la segunda mitad de 1916, el peso de dos años de guerra planteaba un dilema a los países: aumentar su esfuerzo bélico o buscar un camino hacia la paz. En agosto, Alemania cambió su liderazgo. Se asignó al general Paul von Hindenburg (1847–1934) y a su intendente, el general Erich Ludendorff (1865–1937), el mando supremo del ejército y el control sobre todo el esfuerzo bélico del país. Con vistas a incrementar la productividad de la industria alemana, crearon una economía estatal, el **«socialismo de guerra»**. En contraste, los aliados austriacos perdían su voluntad de luchar. La muerte del emperador Francisco José I (1830–1916) en noviembre señaló el principio del **fin del Imperio Austriaco**. Su sucesor al trono, Carlos I (1887–1922), buscaba una salida desesperada de la guerra.

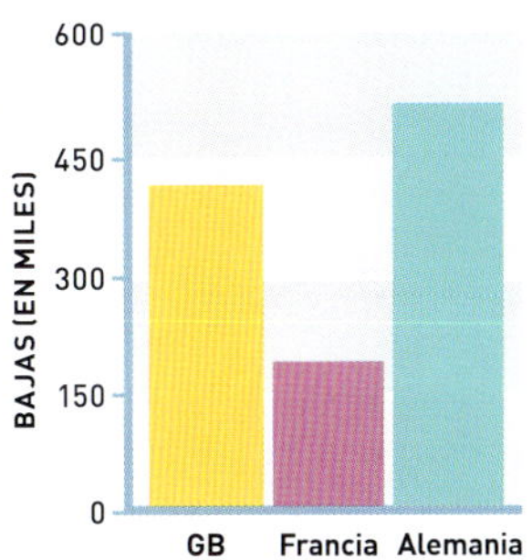

La batalla del Somme
Fue una de las más sangrientas de la guerra. Entre el 1 de julio y el 18 de noviembre cerca de un millón de hombres cayeron muertos o heridos.

La locura colectiva del campo de batalla provocó un **influyente movimiento artístico** que se dotó de un nombre sin sentido, **dadá**. Los dadaístas, como Hugo Ball y Hans Arp, se reunían en el Cabaret Voltaire de Zúrich, en la Suiza neutral, y abogaban por un antiarte alocado que satirizaba un mundo afligido por las masacres a gran escala. Sus obras anárquicas rechazaban el orden social que legitimaba la guerra.

Un portavoz más cabal de la paz fue el **presidente Woodrow Wilson, elegido para un segundo mandato** en noviembre. En tanto que hombre que había mantenido a EE. UU. lejos de la guerra en Europa, Wilson se postuló como pacificador. Emitió una **«nota de paz»** que solicitaba a los países combatientes que declararan sus objetivos bélicos como preludio para la negociación del alto el fuego. El gobierno civil alemán planteó su propia «oferta de paz», pero los líderes militares del país no estaban dispuestos a permitir ninguna concesión que convirtiera la paz en una posibilidad verosímil.

El **Imperio ruso** estaba desesperado por poner fin a la contienda y el régimen zarista perdía la afección popular. En diciembre, conspiradores de la corte asesinaron a Grigori **Rasputín** (1869–1916), un «hombre santo» hirsuto cuya influencia sobre la zarina había degenerado en un escándalo público. El pueblo acogió su asesinato con satisfacción, pero ello no detuvo el **lento derrumbe del gobierno zarista**.

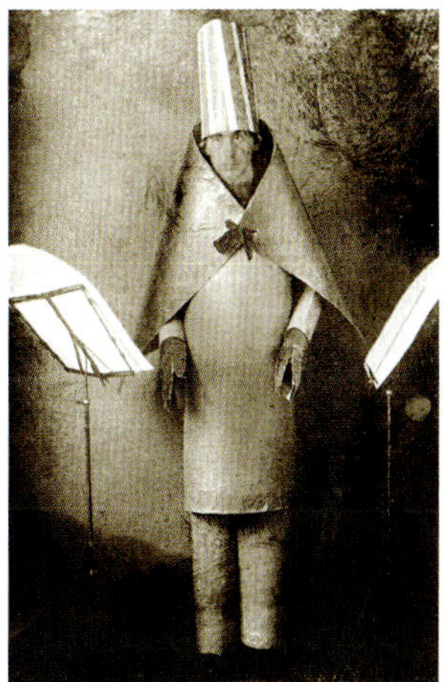

Artistas del la performance
Hugo Ball, uno de los principales artistas dadaístas, en una actuación en el Cabaret Voltaire, que él mismo fundó en 1916.

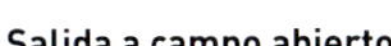

Salida a campo abierto
Soldados británicos dejan atrás el relativo cobijo de las trincheras y se preparan para salir a campo abierto durante la batalla del Somme.

21 de junio La caballería de EE. UU. se enfrenta a tropas federales mexicanas en la **batalla de Carrizal**.

1 de julio Casi **20 000 soldados británicos mueren** el primer día de la ofensiva del Somme.

12 de julio Fracasa la última **ofensiva alemana** en Verdún.

27 de agosto Rumanía **declara la guerra** a las Potencias Centrales.

29 de agosto Hindenburg es designado **comandante supremo** alemán, con un poder casi dictatorial.

30 de agosto Rescate del equipo de exploradores de **Ernest Shackleton** en isla Elefante, en la Antártida.

15 de septiembre Los británicos **usan tanques por primera vez en la historia** en Flers-Courcelette, en el Somme.

20 de septiembre Fin de la **ofensiva de Brusílov**.

26 de septiembre Los británicos **capturan Thiepval**, en el Somme.

16 de octubre Margaret Sanger abre la primera clínica de control de la natalidad en EE. UU.

24 de octubre La ofensiva francesa en Verdún retoma **Fort Douaumont**.

5 de noviembre Alemania crea el **Reino de Polonia** como estado marioneta.

7 de noviembre Woodrow Wilson es reelegido presidente de EE. UU.

18 de noviembre Concluye la **ofensiva del Somme**.

21 de noviembre Fallece el emperador austriaco **Francisco José**; lo sucede su sobrino-nieto Carlos.

3 de diciembre Nivelle sustituye a **Joffre** como comandante en jefe francés.

6 de diciembre Los alemanes entran en la capital rumana, **Bucarest**.

7 de diciembre Lloyd George sustituye a Asquith como primer ministro británico.

18 de diciembre La **«nota de paz»** del presidente Wilson solicita a los combatientes que declaren sus objetivos bélicos.

29 de diciembre Grigori **Rasputín es asesinado** en Petrogrado.

Obreros armados y soldados participan en el derrocamiento del gobierno provisional ruso por parte de los bolcheviques en Petrogrado. Los bolcheviques establecieron un régimen revolucionario comunista.

EL 9 DE ENERO, EL KÁISER ALEMÁN, GUILLERMO II (1859–1941) aprobó la decisión de sus comandantes militares de iniciar una **guerra submarina total**. Los alemanes sabían que ello implicaría hundir buques comerciales estadounidenses y que podría arrastrar a EE. UU., hasta entonces neutral, a la guerra pero estimaron posible hundir suficientes barcos para forzar a Gran Bretaña a solicitar la paz, lo cual haría innecesaria la intervención de EE. UU. El 3 de febrero, un submarino hundió el carguero estadounidense *Housatonic* frente a las islas Sorlingas y EE. UU. rompió las relaciones diplomáticas con Alemania. Previendo la entrada de EE. UU. en la guerra, el ministro de Asuntos Exteriores alemán, Arthur Zimmermann, decidió ofrecer a México una alianza en la lucha contra EE. UU. para recuperar Texas, Nuevo México y Arizona. El servicio de inteligencia británico interceptó, descodificó y transmitió al gobierno estadounidense un **telegrama de Zimmermann** donde se detallaban tales planes. La prensa de EE. UU. publicó la nota, que alimentó el sentimiento antialemán desencadenado con la campaña de submarinos.

Cartel propagandístico
La Comisión de Defensa Nacional del alcalde de Nueva York declaró el 19 de abril «Día de "América, ¡despierta!"» y lo anunció con este cartel.

VLADÍMIR ÍLICH LENIN
(1870–1924)

Nacido en el seno de la pequeña nobleza rusa, Vladímir Ílich Uliánov se convirtió en activista marxista y adoptó el nombre de Lenin. Desde su exilio en la Europa occidental, dirigió a los bolcheviques a partir de 1903. A su regreso a Rusia en 1917, radicalizó la revolución tomando el poder para los bolcheviques. Una vez al mando, aniquiló sin piedad a la oposición y fundó el primer estado comunista del mundo.

El 2 de abril, Woodrow Wilson (1856–1924), presidente de EE. UU., solicitó al Congreso que votara intervenir en el conflicto «para salvaguardar la democracia en el mundo». Cuatro días después, **EE. UU. declaró la guerra a Alemania**, si bien retuvo su libertad de acción al no aliarse formalmente con Gran Bretaña y Francia. Dio comienzo así un lento proceso de construir y formar un ejército de reclutas.

Mientras EE. UU. entraba en la guerra, Rusia quedó atrapada en un levantamiento revolucionario. Los disturbios vividos en torno a los alimentos, las huelgas y un motín de soldados en Petrogrado (San Petersburgo) desencadenaron una secuencia memorable de acontecimientos. El 15 de marzo, el **zar Nicolás II (1868–1918) abdicó** y se instituyó un gobierno provisional con políticos de la Duma (el parlamento ruso). Comités fundados por obreros y soldados, los sóviets, crearon un foco que competía por el poder político. El 16 de abril, **Vladímir Ílich Lenin** (*véase* recuadro), líder del Partido Bolchevique marxista, regresó a Petrogrado de su exilio en Suiza. El propósito de Lenin era radicalizar la revolución proponiendo un fin a la guerra y asignar «todo el poder a los sóviets».

La figura dominante del gobierno provisional, el socialista moderado **Alexandr Kerenski** (1881–1970), estaba resuelto a continuar en guerra. Al fracaso de la campaña que lanzó el 1 de julio, conocida como la **ofensiva de Kerenski**, le siguieron motines generalizados y deserciones en el ejército y en el frente. Los conatos de aplastar a los bolcheviques fracasaron. El gobierno provisional sobrevivió a un intento de golpe de estado, pero el 7 de noviembre sucumbió a un golpe militar organizado por un camarada de Lenin, **León Trotski** (1879–1940). Lenin fundó un **gobierno revolucionario** de los Comisarios del Pueblo y proclamó un armisticio unilateral.

Entre tanto, en el Frente Occidental, el estancamiento y las masacres continuaban. A comienzos del año, el recién proclamado comandante en jefe francés, Robert Nivelle (1856–1924), prometió un ataque implacable que pondría fin a la guerra en días. Sin embargo, la **ofensiva de Nivelle**, lanzada a mediados de abril, no logró más éxitos que las anteriores. La decepción fue amarga. Se produjeron amotinamientos generalizados y el ejército francés amenazaba con desintegrarse. El general Philippe Pétain (1856–1951), designado a toda prisa para sustituir a Nivelle, restauró el orden con una mezcla de concesiones y castigos, y descartó cualquier otra ofensiva por parte de Francia.

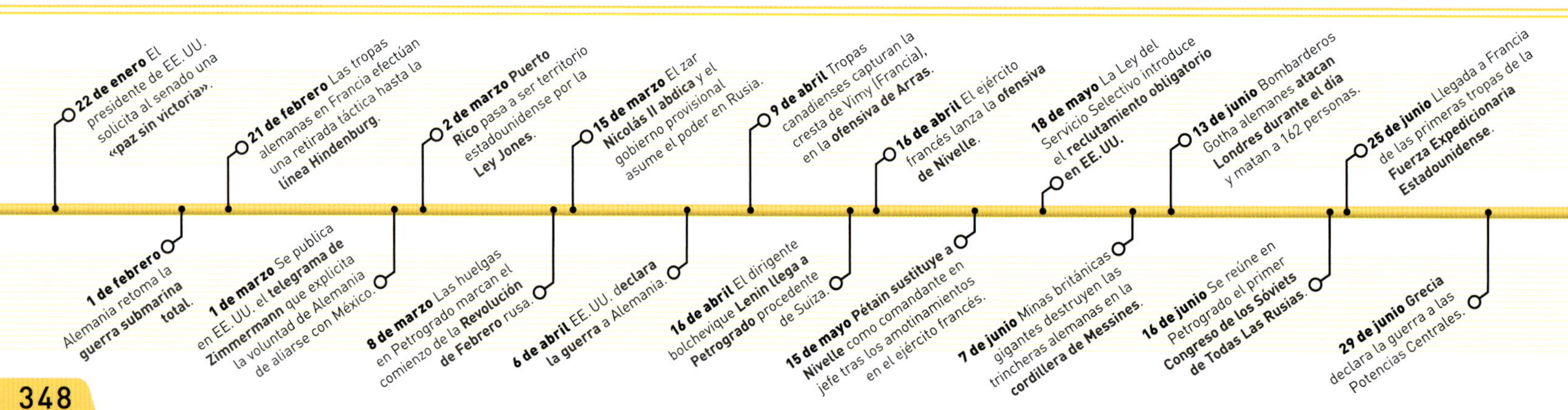

« EL GOBIERNO DE LOS **OBREROS** Y LOS **CAMPESINOS**… **PROPONE** A TODOS LOS **PUEBLOS EN GUERRA**… **NEGOCIACIONES** QUE CONDUZCAN A UNA **PAZ JUSTA Y DEMOCRÁTICA**. **»**

Lenin (8 de noviembre de 1917)

Tanques Mark IV británicos rumbo a la ofensiva de Cambrai. Los tanques portan fajos de maderas para rellenar las trincheras y poder conducir por encima de ellas.

El ejército británico continuó desplegando una estrategia de ofensivas. En la segunda mitad del año, el general Douglas Haig (1861–1928) inició **una nueva campaña de Ypres** (pp. 344–345), con la esperanza de poder atravesar los puertos donde fondeaban los submarinos alemanes. La campaña de Haig topó con un clima adverso constante que redujo el campo de batalla a un mar de fango. La ofensiva se prolongó hasta noviembre, cuando las tropas canadienses y británicas llegaron a **Passchendaele**, la población que finalmente dio nombre a la batalla.

En Flandes, los barrizales impedían utilizar los tanques, un arma-

3 **TRIPULANTES** PILOTABAN Y OPERABAN **UN BOMBARDERO GOTHA ALEMÁN**

mento cada vez más importante para los británicos. En noviembre, en **Cambrai**, sobre un terreno más firme, una dotación de tanques ayudó a las tropas británicas a avanzar 6 km en un solo día, el triple de la distancia recorrida en Passchendaele en tres meses. No obstante, era demasiado temprano para celebraciones, pues los alemanes no tardaron en contraatacar y recuperar gran parte del territorio perdido.

El punto muerto entre Italia y Austria finalizó cuando las tropas alemanas fueron transferidas al frente italiano en octubre. En la **batalla de Caporetto**, una ofensiva austroalemana obligó al ejército italiano a retirarse. En noviembre se estabilizó una línea de frente tras el río Piave, a solo 30 km de Venecia (p. 345).

A partir del mes de junio, la población civil de París y Londres se vio sometida a **ataques aéreos esporádicos por parte de bombarderos Gotha alemanes** y aviones incluso más grandes. Estos aviones de ala fija eran más rápidos y más difíciles de derribar que los dirigibles alemanes (*véase* 1915), si bien las defensas con armas antiaéreas y cazabombarderos les obligaron muy pronto a atacar exclusivamente de noche. Los desperfectos físicos y las bajas no fueron enormes, pero el impacto psicológico de aquellos ataques sorpresa fue considerable, pues obligaban a la población a refugiarse bajo tierra, en sótanos y estaciones de metro.

En todos los países combatientes, el cansancio por la guerra y el empeoramiento de las condiciones de vida dificultaban a los gobiernos mantener la solidaridad. La escasez de alimentos y los sentimientos socialistas, espoleados por el alzamiento revolucionario en Rusia, condujeron a **huelgas generalizadas en las fábricas alemanas**. El Reichstag (parlamento) alemán aprobó iniciar negociaciones de paz en julio, pero carecía de control sobre el gobierno alemán, en manos del ejército.

En Francia, los escándalos y las huelgas agitaron el sistema político en verano y otoño, pero la designación de Georges Clemenceau (1841–1929), pro belicista declarado, como primer ministro en noviembre aplacó las turbulencias.

Por su parte, la familia real británica consideró prudente cambiar su apellido, y pasó del germánico Sajonia-Coburgo-Gotha al de Windsor.

El público británico estalló en júbilo en diciembre cuando **Jerusalén fue arrebatada a Turquía**. Tal éxito imprimió importancia práctica a la **Declaración Balfour** del mes anterior, que expresaba el apoyo del gobierno británico a las aspiraciones sionistas de crear «una patria nacional para los judíos en Palestina». Nadie consultó a los aliados árabes de Gran Bretaña, que lucharon junto con el ejército británico contra los turcos.

Amanece en Passchendaele
Soldados muertos y heridos yacen en el fango del desolado campo de batalla del saliente de Ypres, donde tuvo lugar la batalla de Passchendaele.

amortiguador hidráulico

cureña

Howitzer Mark I
Usado por el ejército británico en la Primera Guerra Mundial, este cañón disparaba dos ráfagas de proyectiles de 132 kg por minuto.

MERCANCÍAS HUNDIDAS (EN TONELADAS)
600
450
300
150
0
Ene. Feb. Mar. Abr. Mayo Jun. Jul. Ago. Sep. Oct. Nov. Dic.
MESES

Pérdidas de buques de mercancías provocadas por submarinos
La guerra submarina total declarada por Alemania aumentó los ataques contra los buques de mercancías entre febrero y abril. La adopción de un sistema de convoyes en mayo redujo los hundimientos a un nivel sostenible.

1 de julio Rusia lanza la **ofensiva de Kerenski** en Galitzia.

16-20 de julio El gobierno ruso **toma medidas enérgicas contra los bolcheviques** tras los disturbios en Petrogrado.

17 de julio La familia real británica se cambia el nombre por **Windsor**.

19 de julio El Reichstag alemán aprueba la **«resolución de la paz»**.

20 de julio Kerenski es nombrado presidente del **gobierno provisional ruso**.

20 de julio Declaración de Corfú: serbios, croatas y eslovenos acuerdan formar **Yugoslavia**.

31 de julio Gran Bretaña lanza una ofensiva en el **sector de Ypres**.

14 de agosto China declara la guerra a las **Potencias centrales**.

1 de septiembre Alemania lanza con éxito una ofensiva en **Riga**.

9 de septiembre Fracasa el **intento de golpe de estado** del comandante en jefe ruso Kornilov.

15 de octubre Ejecutan en Francia a Margarethe Zelle, la espía alemana apodada **Mata Hari**.

24 de octubre El ejército italiano sufre una derrota aplastante en **Caporetto**.

2 de noviembre En la **Declaración Balfour**, Gran Bretaña se compromete a crear una patria para los judíos en Palestina.

6 de noviembre Tropas británicas y canadienses toman **Passchendaele**, en la **tercera batalla de Ypres**.

7 de noviembre Los **bolcheviques de Lenin toman el poder** en Petrogrado.

20 de noviembre Una dotación de tanques posibilita un avance efímero de los británicos en **Cambrai**.

5 de diciembre El general **Sidonio Pais** asume el poder en **Portugal** con un golpe militar.

6 de diciembre Más de dos mil personas mueren al hacer **explotar un barco** cargado de munición en el puerto de Halifax (Nueva Escocia).

9 de diciembre Gran Bretaña arrebata **Jerusalén** a Turquía.

20 de diciembre El gobierno bolchevique crea la **checa, la policía secreta soviética**.

22 de diciembre Los bolcheviques inauguran **negociaciones de paz con Alemania** en **Brest-Litovsk**.

buque
de guerra
Aurora

Héroe revolucionario
FECHA DESCONOCIDA
En esta pintura para un cartel del periodo de la Revolución de 1917, Lenin aparece delante del buque de guerra *Aurora* que los bolcheviques usaron para tomar el poder.

Caballeros rojos
C. 1920
Tras la Revolución de 1917 se desató una guerra civil rusa entre los ejércitos bolchevique y «Blanco», dirigido por oficiales zaristas. Este cartel está dedicado a «los pueblos del Cáucaso del Ejército Rojo».

la caballería
desempeñó un papel
importante en la
victoria comunista

PROPAGANDA SOVIÉTICA

ARTE PROMOCIONAL DE LA IDEOLOGÍA POLÍTICA COMUNISTA Y DE LOS IDEALES REVOLUCIONARIOS

Para los comunistas que tomaron el poder en Rusia en noviembre de 1917, el arte debía estar al servicio de la revolución socialista y difundir su ideología. La propaganda movilizaba al pueblo en apoyo del régimen y ridiculizaba a sus enemigos.

En la fase inicial del gobierno comunista, muchos artistas vanguardistas creían que sus modos revolucionarios de crear arte concordaban con la revolución política. Pero a partir de finales de la década de 1920, bajo la dictadura de Stalin, se requirió a los artistas soviéticos que ilustraran a obreros y campesinos en un estilo realista heroico y que sus imágenes reflejaran la supuesta felicidad y el progreso de la vida comunista.

Cartel modernista
1919
El artista vanguardista El Lissitzky produjo este cartel de la guerra civil. El triángulo rojo representa al Ejército Rojo comunista batiendo a las tropas blancas anticomunistas.

La Revolución te necesita
1928
La mano de obra sufrió una reorganización radical bajo los comunistas. Este cartel urge a los soviéticos a alistarse en cooperativas obreras.

Industrialización acelerada
1928
El gobierno comunista impulsó la industrialización a finales de la década de 1920. Este cartel impone a los obreros aumentar la producción.

Colectivización
1930
Un conductor de tractor y una campesina llaman a sus camaradas a unirse a una granja colectiva durante la brutal campaña de Stalin para abolir las granjas privadas.

la Segunda Guerra Mundial desbarató los planes monumentales de reconstruir Moscú

La vida bajo Stalin
Década de 1930
Este cartel, que celebra la unidad y la fortaleza del pueblo soviético bajo el estandarte de Stalin, proclama: «Hacia las cumbres del júbilo y la felicidad de la humanidad».

Poderío militar
Década de 1940
Este cartel de la Segunda Guerra Mundial ilustra un cazabombardero y a un piloto soviético que refleja el optimismo obligatorio de todo ciudadano comunista retratado en el arte estalinista.

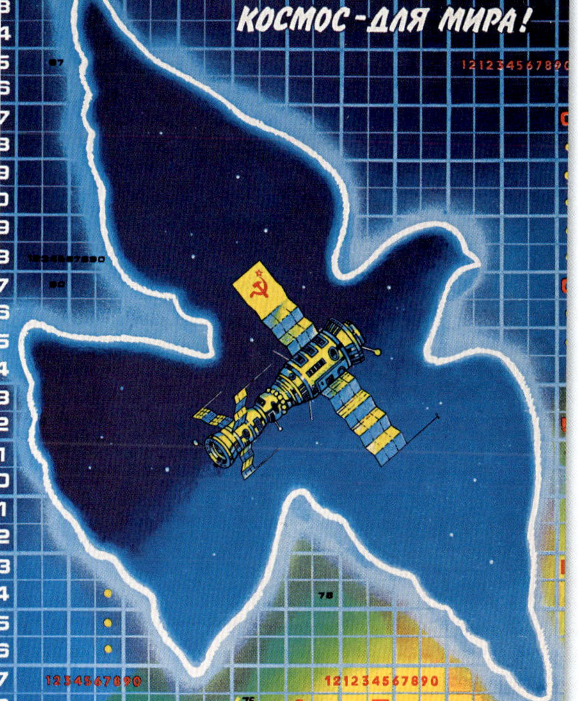

Celebración de la victoria
Década de 1940
El eslogan de este cartel celebra la victoria soviética en la Segunda Guerra Mundial: «Tras ganar la guerra, el soldado trae la primavera».

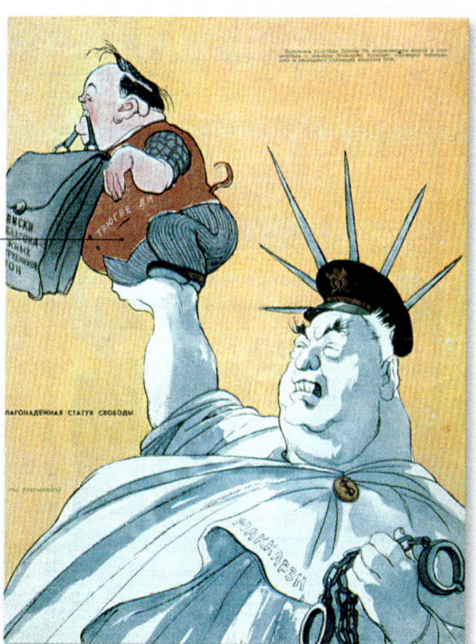

capitalista con aspecto porcino

Propaganda de la Guerra Fría
Década de 1950
Este cartel de la Guerra Fría caricaturiza la Estatua de la Libertad y retrata a EE. UU. como un gordinflón capitalista y militarista.

Paz y progreso
Década de 1970
Una estación espacial Salyut se superpone a una paloma de la paz en este cartel de la era de «convivencia pacífica» con el mundo capitalista.

1918

Prisioneros de guerra alemanes en Francia; en los últimos tres meses de guerra, 363 000 soldados alemanes fueron capturados por los aliados.

A PESAR DE QUE EE. UU. ENTRÓ EN LA GUERRA EN ABRIL DE 1917, a principios de 1918 su Fuerza Expedicionaria desplegada en Europa aún no estaba lista para el combate. Al margen de ello, y anticipando una victoria, el presidente de EE. UU., Woodrow Wilson, anunció un **programa de catorce puntos** para una paz justa y duradera. Sus propuestas incluían la libertad de los mares y el libre comercio, un desarme general, la autodeterminación de los pueblos europeos que carecían de nación-estado propia y una organización internacional que protegiera las nuevas fronteras. Alemania debía devolver el territorio que había ocupado durante la guerra, además de Alsacia-Lorena, arrebatada a Francia en 1871.

Sin embargo, los alemanes tenían ideas distintas. En marzo usaron su dominio militar sobre el recién instalado gobierno bolchevique (*véase* 1917) para imponer unos términos de paz punitivos a Rusia con el **Tratado de Brest-Litovsk**, el cual marcó la salida de Rusia de la Primera Guerra Mundial. Con Polonia, Ucrania, Bielorrusia, Finlandia y los estados bálticos nominalmente independientes como estados satélite de Alemania, el tratado desposeía a Rusia de un tercio de su población previa a la guerra. Las autoridades militares alemanas se dispusieron entonces a explotar sin piedad los recursos de las regiones orientales ahora bajo su control.

El humillante tratado no llevó la paz a Rusia, que se encaminaba a una guerra civil. Decidido a concentrar todo el poder en manos bolcheviques, en enero **Lenin disolvió por la fuerza la asamblea constituyente elegida democráticamente**, al obtener los bolcheviques solo un 25 % de los votos. El régimen de Lenin afrontaba la oposición de grupos tan dispares como los revolucionarios socialistas rivales, los generales zaristas, los anarquistas ucranianos y los cosacos del Don. Aunque Lenin sobrevivió a un atentado en agosto, a lo largo de aquel año zonas aún más extensas de Rusia quedaron fuera de su control.

Mientras, aliviada de la necesidad de luchar una guerra en dos frentes, Alemania intentó lograr una victoria decisiva en el Frente Occidental antes de que los soldados estadounidenses invirtieran la balanza irreversiblemente. El 21 de marzo, la **ofensiva de Primavera, o *Kaiserschlacht***, golpeó la línea británica en el frente del Somme.

El bombardeo inicial con nueve mil metralletas y morteros y munición que incluía dos millones de granadas de gas allanó el terreno para un ataque de la infantería encabezado por las tropas de asalto alemanas, muchas armadas con lanzallamas. Más de veinte mil soldados británicos se rindieron el primer día de la ofensiva y, para el 25 de marzo, las unidades alemanas a la cabeza habían avanzado 65 km. **El punto muerto al que se había llegado en el Frente Occidental desde 1914 tocaba a su fin.**

A principios de abril, los alemanes lanzaron una nueva campaña en Lys (Flandes). En una emotiva arenga a sus soldados, el comandante general británico Douglas Haig (1861–1928) declaró: «Aun con la espalda contra la pared, la justicia de nuestra causa debe impulsarnos a cada uno de nosotros a luchar hasta el final». En términos más prácticos, el general francés **Ferdinand Foch (1851–1929) fue designado comandante supremo** para coordinar las operaciones de los ejércitos aliados, incluidas las tropas de EE. UU. Pese a que los aliados protagonizaron nuevas retiradas y permanecieron a la defensiva hasta julio, los alemanes no lograron alcanzar el éxito decisivo que precisaban.

El famoso as de la aviación alemán Manfred von Richthofen (1892–1918), **«el «Barón Rojo»**, al que se le atribuían 80 aviones derribados, murió en abril, abatido desde tierra sobre las líneas aliadas durante un combate con el piloto canadiense Roy Brown. Su muerte simbolizó el agotamiento del esfuerzo bélico alemán, con los pilotos alemanes abrumados por la ingente cantidad de aviones aliados: las fábricas británicas y francesas construyeron 55 000 solo en 1918.

En junio, más de un **millón de soldados estadounidenses se hallaban en Francia** bajo las órdenes del general John Pershing (1860–1948). Su colaboración era clave para estabilizar la línea aliada frente a las ofensivas alemanas. La destreza para la lucha de los

MAGNICIDIO DE LA FAMILIA REAL RUSA

Tras abdicar en 1917, el zar Nicolás II, su esposa e hijos fueron enviados a Siberia, donde vivieron con una comodidad razonable. En abril de 1918, fueron trasladados a Ekaterimburgo, en los Urales, y sometidos a la estrecha vigilancia de los bolcheviques locales. La noche del 16 al 17 de julio, la policía secreta bolchevique los mandó fusilar en un sótano, junto con su médico y sus criados. Sus cuerpos fueron enterrados y no se descubrieron hasta 1991.

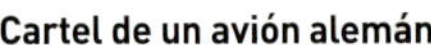

Cartel de un avión alemán

Cartel alemán anunciando una exposición de artículos capturados en la guerra aérea. La mayoría de los aviones de la guerra estaban fabricados con lienzo y madera.

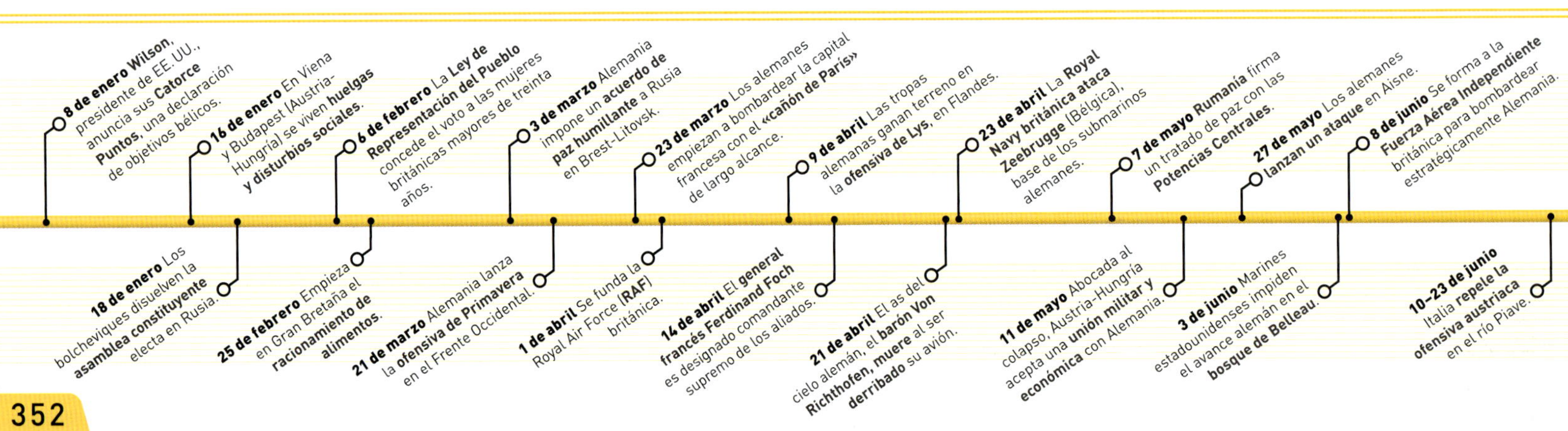

« ESPERO QUE TODOS PODAMOS DECIR QUE **AL FIN**, EN ESTA MAÑANA FATÍDICA, **LA GUERRA DE TODAS LAS GUERRAS HA TOCADO SU FIN**. »

David Lloyd George, primer ministro británico (11 de noviembre de 1918)

Soldados británicos, un marine estadounidense y una enfermera de la Cruz Roja celebran la firma del armisticio el 11 de noviembre, el cual ponía fin a cuatro años de masacres.

marines estadounidenses impresionó a los enemigos alemanes; de hecho, la alusión de los alemanes a los marines como *devil dogs* («perros del diablo») se adoptó como apodo del cuerpo militar.

El **punto de inflexión** llegó con un **ataque en Amiens** el 8 de agosto liderado por la infantería australiana y canadiense, y respaldado por multitud de tanques británicos y franceses. Calificado por el general alemán Erich Ludendorff (1865–1937) como «el día más negro del ejército alemán», dio comienzo a los «Cien Días» de ofensivas aliadas implacables, con un uso a gran escala de tanques y aviones.

En septiembre, Pershing logró su ambición de comandar una operación estadounidense independiente, la captura del **saliente de Saint-Mihiel**. A ella siguió una ofensiva combinada de EE. UU. y Francia en el **bosque Argonne**, la batalla más costosa en vidas de la historia para EE. UU., con 117 000 bajas.

El 29 de septiembre, con las defensas de la línea Hindenburg mermadas y su aliada, Bulgaria, al borde de la rendición, los **alemanes solicitaron un armisticio**. Se dirigieron al presidente Wilson (1856–1924) con la esperanza de cerrar un trato con EE. UU., pero Wilson se alineó con británicos y franceses, quienes insistían en que Alemania debía rendirse. Aunque las tropas alemanas seguían defendiéndose y aún no había soldados aliados en suelo alemán, el país era un polvorín. Un amotinamiento de marines alemanes a finales de octubre estuvo seguido por huelgas y levantamientos socialistas en las principales ciudades, donde la escasez de alimentos había espoleado el descontento político.

Turquía y Austria, principales aliados de Alemania, se retiraron de la lucha. El 9 de noviembre, el socialdemócrata Philipp Scheidemann convirtió Alemania en una república y el káiser Guillermo II (1859–1941) huyó a Países Bajos. Dos días después, una delegación alemana **firmó un armisticio** en un vagón de tren en el bosque de Compiègne. Las armas enmudecieron a las 11.00 h del 11 de noviembre.

15
12
9
6
3
0
TROPAS (EN MILLONES)
Rusia
Francia
Imperio Británico
Italia
EE. UU.
Alemania
Austria-Hungría
Turquía
Bulgaria
Potencias aliadas
Potencias Centrales

Cifras de soldados y muertes
En la Gran Guerra lucharon unos 65 millones de hombres, de los que 8,5 millones murieron. El país que sufrió el mayor número de bajas fue Alemania.

CLAVE
Poderío militar
Bajas

50 MILLONES DE PERSONAS MURIERON EN LA PANDEMIA DE GRIPE DE 1918–1919

En Londres, París y otras ciudades aliadas se desataron **celebraciones por la paz**, pero incluso en los países vencedores la victoria quedó silenciada por la memoria de los millones de fallecidos. No hubo celebraciones en los imperios devastados por el conflicto (Alemania, Austria, Rusia y Turquía), los cuales afrontaban un futuro incierto rodeado de agitación política.

Entre tanto, una pandemia global conocida en EE. UU. y Europa como la **«gripe española»** (por creerse erróneamente que su origen era España) llegó a sus peores cotas. Una de las peores catástrofes naturales de la historia de la humanidad, la propagación de la gripe pudo verse ayudada por los desplazamientos a gran escala de soldados y por los debilitados sistemas inmunitarios de las poblaciones que sufrían malnutrición. La enfermedad se cobró más de cincuenta millones de vidas.

La firma del armisticio
La delegación aliada, encabezada por el mariscal Foch, fotografiada junto al vagón de tren de Compiègne donde se firmó el armisticio.

15 de julio–3 de agosto Los aliados **ponen en jaque la ofensiva alemana** en Marne.

17 de julio El antiguo **zar Nicolás II** y su familia son asesinados en **Ekaterimburgo**.

31 de julio Fuerzas anglofrancesas **ocupan Arjánguelsk**, en el norte de Rusia.

8 de agosto Los británicos imponen una **severa derrota a los alemanes** en Amiens.

30 de agosto Lenin sobrevive a un atentado perpetrado por la socialista revolucionaria **Dora Kaplan**.

15 de septiembre Tropas aliadas avanzan desde Tesalónica e **inician una campaña devastadora** contra Bulgaria.

19–26 de septiembre Gran Bretaña derrota a las tropas turcas en **Meggido** (Palestina).

26 de septiembre EE. UU. lanza la ofensiva de Meuse-Argonne en el este de Francia.

29 de septiembre La victoria aliada en el **canal de San Quintín** rompe la línea Hindenburg.

23 de octubre Italia lanza una ofensiva contra Austria en **Vittorio Veneto**.

29 de octubre Un motín en la flota alemana desencadena levantamientos generalizados en Alemania.

30 de octubre Turquía firma un armisticio.

30 de octubre Checoslovaquia se declara **república independiente**.

3 de noviembre Austria firma un armisticio.

9 de noviembre El káiser Guillermo II abdica y **Alemania se convierte en una república**.

11 de noviembre Alemania acepta los términos de un armisticio.

12 de noviembre Carlos I abdica y pone fin al Imperio austriaco.

14 de noviembre Tomáš Masaryk es elegido presidente de **Checoslovaquia**.

22 de noviembre Pilsudski se convierte en jefe provisional de la **recién independizada Polonia**.

1 de diciembre Fundación del reino de los serbios, croatas y eslovenos: **Yugoslavia**.

10 de diciembre Max Planck gana el **premio Nobel de física** por la creación de la **mecánica cuántica**.

14 de diciembre Las elecciones generales en Reino Unido otorgan una amplia mayoría a la coalición gobernante de Lloyd George.

14 de diciembre El presidente autoritario de Portugal, **Sidonio Pais, es asesinado**.

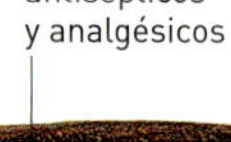

Fusil con bayoneta
ITALIA
Los fusiles de cerrojo M91 y las carabinas fueron las armas de la infantería italiana en la Primera Guerra Mundial. Esta carabina se utilizaba en las trincheras, en el combate cuerpo a cuerpo.

bayoneta plegable

Ametralladora Lewis
GRAN BRETAÑA
De diseño original estadounidense, el ejército británico adoptó la Lewis como ametralladora ligera estándar en 1915. Sirvió para armar aviones y tanques, además de a la infantería.

Ametralladora Maxim
ALEMANIA
La pesada ametralladora del ejército alemán, la Maschinengewehr '08, era una versión de la ametralladora inventada por el estadounidense Hiram Maxim en 1884. Disparaba 400 balas por minuto.

Botiquín de primeros auxilios
ALEMANIA
Los camilleros médicos alemanes llevaban un botiquín con analgésicos y antisépticos básicos, como yodo, para tratar a los heridos antes de enviarlos al hospital de campaña.

I GUERRA MUNDIAL

LA FABRICACIÓN EN SERIE DE ARMAS PERMITE MASACRAR MILLONES DE VIDAS

La Gran Guerra se ha descrito como una «guerra industrial» porque los países industrializados movilizaron tanto a su mano de obra como sus recursos económicos. Las armas de fuego proporcionaron una cadencia de tiro sin precedentes.

Formidables sistemas defensivos de trincheras, alambre de espino y puestos con metralletas convirtieron las ofensivas en operaciones costosas y, a menudo, derivaron en puntos muertos. Las armas usadas en las trincheras iban desde granadas hasta lanzallamas, cachiporras de fabricación casera y cuchillos. En 1916 aparecieron los primeros tanques, lentos y poco fiables. La aviación añadió una nueva dimensión a la guerra: permitía realizar misiones de reconocimiento y bombardear objetivos en tierra.

cañón

freno

cureña

Obuses de artillería
FRANCIA
La munición de artillería en la Primera Guerra Mundial incluía desde metralla hasta obuses de gas altamente explosivos. Estos proyectiles se disparaban con una metralleta de campo francesa de 75 mm.

Howitzer
GRAN BRETAÑA
Los obuses Howitzer, como este de seis pulgadas de calibre, resultaban efectivos en las trincheras, porque disparaban los proyectiles con una trayectoria alta y estos caían sobre el enemigo oculto.

Brújula de oficial

GRAN BRETAÑA

Disponer de una brújula era esencial para las patrullas y en los ataques nocturnos. Sin ella, los soldados podían adentrarse en la tierra de nadie, asolada por los obuses, que se extendía entre las trincheras.

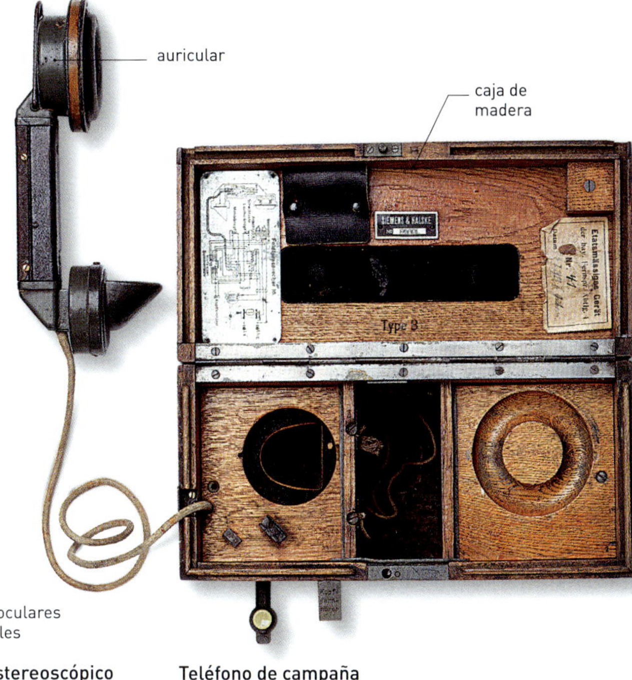

Periscopio estereoscópico

ALEMANIA

En las trincheras, los soldados utilizaban periscopios para vigilar la línea del enemigo. Los francotiradores eran prestos en detectar a quienes asomaban la cabeza por encima del parapeto.

Teléfono de campaña

ALEMANIA

Si bien también se usaban radios, los teléfonos de campaña eran el principal medio de comunicación en la guerra de trincheras. Cuando los cables de telefonía quedaron destrozados por los bombardeos, hubo que recurrir a mensajeros que transportaran los mensajes a la línea de frente en persona.

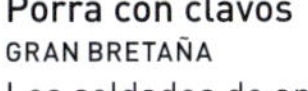

Máscara de gas

ALEMANIA

Evitaba que los ojos y el rostro entraran en contacto con los gases venenosos y, mediante un respirador con filtro, neutralizaba el gas que se respiraba.

Pala plegable

ITALIA

La pala era un instrumento esencial para los soldados de infantería, necesaria para cavar trincheras o refugios temporales. Esta pala plegable correspondía a las tropas alpinas italianas.

Porra con clavos

GRAN BRETAÑA

Los soldados de ambos bandos usaban cachiporras de madera primitivas, con clavos u otros objetos metálicos en la maza, a modo de arma sigilosa y mortal en los ataques a las trincheras.

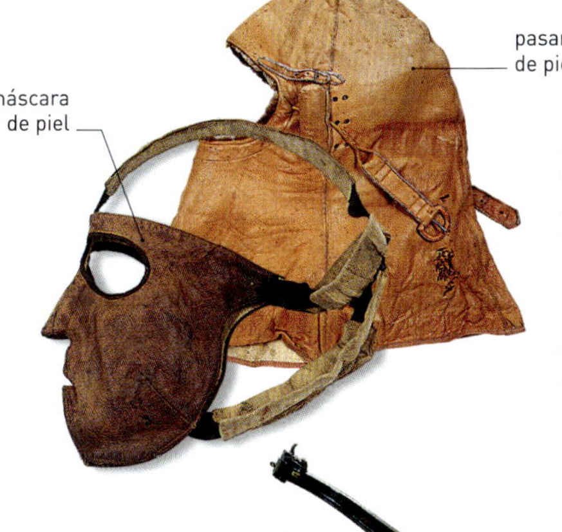

Pasamontañas de aviador

GRAN BRETAÑA

Al volar en aviones con la cabina de mandos abierta, muchos aviadores de la Primera Guerra Mundial llevaban pasamontañas y máscaras para protegerse del frío y del viento.

Bayoneta y granada turcas

TURQUÍA

En la Primera Guerra Mundial, el ejército turco contaba con un equipamiento obsoleto, como espadas y bayonetas, pero también con armamento de última generación suministrado por los alemanes, como granadas de fragmentación.

contenedor de acero

el cañón permitía disparar un obús de medio kilo

Metralleta antiaérea

GRAN BRETAÑA

Los ejércitos adaptaron armas existentes para disparar proyectiles explosivos con mecanismos de relojería y protegerse de los ataques aéreos. Esta metralleta británica, llamada «pom-pom», iba montada sobre un pedestal y sirvió para defender Londres de los ataques aéreos.

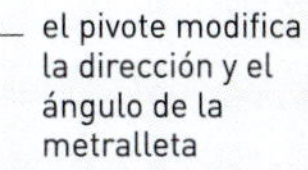

el pivote modifica la dirección y el ángulo de la metralleta

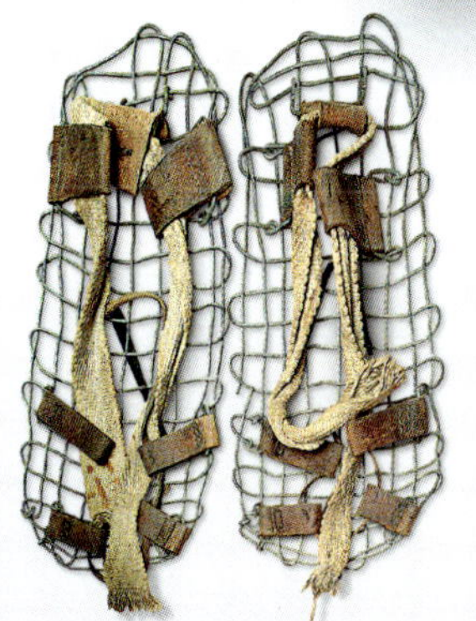

Calzado para el desierto

GRAN BRETAÑA

Las tropas británicas que combatieron contra los turcos en la campaña palestina se calzaban fundas de alambre sobre las botas militares para facilitar la marcha sobre la arena del desierto.

Casco para tanque

GRAN BRETAÑA

Los tripulantes de los tanques británicos descubrieron que cuando las balas alcanzaban sus vehículos armados, algunos fragmentos se colaban en el compartimento interior. Ello llevó a adoptar rápidamente cascos para evitar lesiones en la cabeza y el rostro.

1919

Los «Cuatro Grandes» –David Lloyd George, Vittorio Orlando, Georges Clemenceau y Woodrow Wilson– se reúnen amistosamente en la conferencia de paz de París.

EN ENERO DE 1919, LOS DIRIGENTES DE LOS PAÍSES VENCEDORES de la Primera Guerra Mundial se reunieron en una conferencia de paz en París. El idealismo liberal del presidente estadounidense, Woodrow Wilson, avivó la esperanza popular de construir un mundo nuevo y mejor sobre las cenizas del antiguo. Wilson fue uno de los **«Cuatro Grandes»** que dirigieron las diligencias de París, junto con el primer ministro francés, Georges Clemenceau (1841–1929); el primer ministro británico, David Lloyd George (1863–1945); y el primer ministro italiano, Vittorio Orlando (1860–1952). Cada dirigente europeo tenía su propio programa, dominado lógicamente por temas de interés nacional. El idealismo del estadounidense se fraguó en el acuerdo de fundar la **Sociedad de Naciones**, cuyo objetivo era velar por la «seguridad colectiva» y sustituir la guerra por acuerdos negociados en caso de disputa. Clemenceau, no obstante, consideraba que la mejor garantía para la paz futura de Francia consistía en un debilitamiento permanente de Alemania.

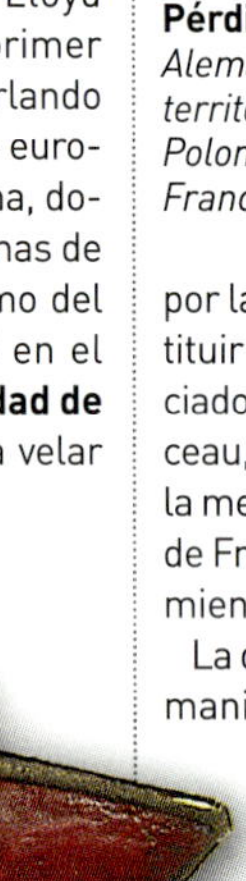

Insignia del Ejército Rojo
La insignia del arado y el martillo simboliza la unión de los obreros industriales y el campesinado en la causa revolucionaria.

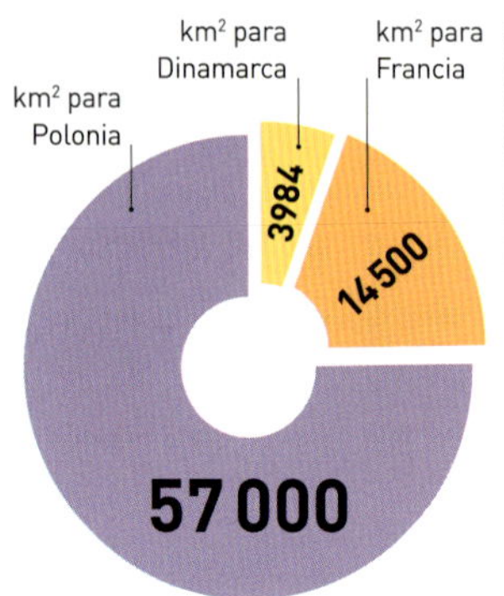

Pérdidas tras la guerra
Alemania perdió el 13 % de su territorio. La mayoría fue a parar a Polonia, un nuevo país, mientras que Francia recuperó Alsacia-Lorena.

La derrota había conducido a Alemania a un colapso económico y social. En enero, unos revolucionarios comunistas, los **espartaquistas** trataron de emular el éxito de los bolcheviques en Rusia (*véase* 1917) protagonizando un alzamiento en Berlín. El **conato de revolución** fue aplastado por el ejército y los *Freikorps* paramilitares de ala derechista; Karl Liebknecht y Rosa Luxembourg, los dos líderes espartaquistas más destacados, fueron apresados y asesinados. En febrero, una asamblea electa reunida en la ciudad de Weimar se dispuso a elaborar una constitución para una república democrática impecable, pero en las calles de Alemania seguía floreciendo **el extremismo, tanto de izquierdas como de derechas**. En el estado sureño alemán de Baviera, los comunistas proclamaron un régimen soviético en abril, que fue desmantelado por el ejército y los *Freikorps* en mayo.

No estando Alemania en posición de retomar las hostilidades, la victoria brindó a los aliados la posibilidad de imponer, sin negociar, los términos para la paz en el **tratado de Versalles**. Alemania perdió todas sus colonias y un territorio sustancial en Europa. Las pérdidas territoriales en el Viejo Continente consistieron principalmente en zonas necesarias para formar el **nuevo estado de Polonia**, además de Alsacia-Lorena, que Alemania había arrebatado a Francia en la guerra franco-prusiana (*véase* 1870). Asimismo, se impusieron restricciones a las fuerzas armadas alemanas y se desmilitarizó Renania. Además, se exigió a Alemania que realizara pagos reparadores, por ser la culpable de haber iniciado la guerra. La **cláusula de la «culpa de la guerra»** indignó a los alemanes más que ninguna otra del tratado. La tripulación de la flota de los Altos Mares alemana, atrapada desde el armisticio en **Scapa Flow**, en las islas Orcadas, al norte de Escocia, hundió sus barcos como acto de desafío. Con todo, los delegados alemanes no tuvieron más alternativa que rubricar el tratado, cosa que hicieron en la Galería de los Espejos de Versalles el 28 de junio.

Mientras la paz se formalizaba en la Europa occidental, **la guerra civil causaba estragos en Rusia**, donde el gobierno bolchevique de Lenin luchaba por la supervivencia contra varios ejércitos contrarrevolucionarios «blancos». El Ejército Blanco contaba con el respaldo de las potencias extranjeras, que desembarcaron fuerzas de intervención en puertos de toda Rusia: Japón y EE. UU. en Vladivostok, Francia en Odesa, y Gran Bretaña en Múrmansk y Arjánguelsk, si bien tales intervenciones foráneas fueron poco entusiastas y en su mayoría efímeras. El comisario de Guerra del Pueblo Bolchevique, **León Trotski** (1879–1940), creó un ingen-

Dirigente revolucionario
Las habilidades organizativas y de liderazgo de Trotski fueron esenciales para el éxito bolchevique en Rusia. Aquí lo vemos dirigiéndose a las tropas del Ejército Rojo.

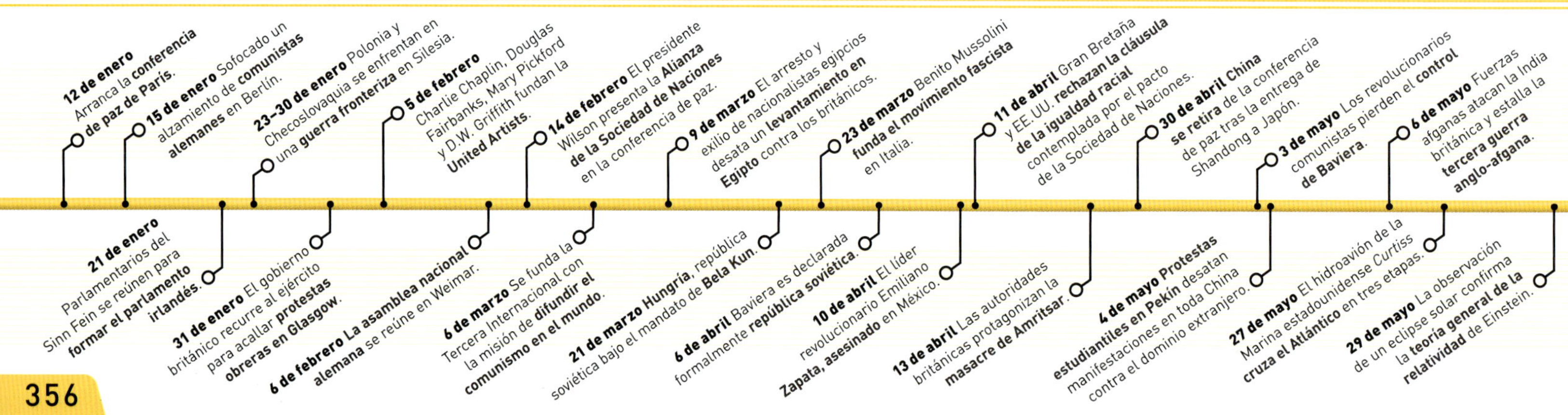

« HEMOS TENIDO **UN VIAJE TERRIBLE**... LO **INCREÍBLE** ES QUE **ESTEMOS AQUÍ**. »

John Alcock, oficial de la RAF británica, tras sobrevolar el Atlántico sin efectuar paradas (15 de junio de 1919)

John Alcock y Arthur Whitten Brown en el avión con el que realizaron el primer vuelo transatlántico sin paradas entre Terranova (Canadá) e Irlanda.

te Ejército Rojo reclutando a campesinos a punta de pistola y sometiéndolos a una férrea disciplina. Los enfrentamientos entre ambos ejércitos fueron sanguinarios y estuvieron acompañados de masacres y atrocidades generalizadas. En medio de tal tumulto, Rusia acogió un congreso en Moscú para fundar la **Tercera Internacional**, conocida como el Komintern. Su fin era difundir la revolución comunista a todo el mundo; su consecuencia fue la escisión del movimiento socialista internacional en dos, lo que obligó a los ciudadanos de izquierdas a escoger entre la socialdemocracia y el comunismo revolucionario. La perspectiva de una revolución mundial inminente gozó de cierta credibilidad en una época en la que los movimientos obreros y anticolonialistas radicales desafiaban a la autoridad establecida en muchos países.

Fuera de Rusia, los **comunistas** solo consiguieron formar un gobierno nacional en **Hungría**, en 1919. La caída del Imperio austrohúngaro fue catastrófica para Hungría, que afrontaba la pérdida de dos tercios de su territorio de preguerra a manos de Checoslovaquia, Rumanía y Yugoslavia. El comunista **Bela Kun** (1886–1938) ascendió al poder en marzo y lanzó ofensivas militares contra Checoslovaquia y Rumanía. Siguió el ejemplo bolchevique formando un Ejército Rojo y sometiendo al imperio del terror a sus oponentes, pero tras 133 días de mandato fue derrotado por los rumanos. El ejército nacional contrarrevolucionario del almirante Miklós Horthy entró en Budapest y derrocó a los comunistas para imponer un nuevo reino del terror. En 1920, Horthy se alzó con el poder en Hungría en calidad de «regente».

En **Italia**, gentes de toda condición política afrontaban con disgusto la limitada participación de su país en los espolios de la victoria. Orlando debió renunciar como primer ministro a su regreso de la conferencia de paz de París, tras no lograr Dalmacia ni el puerto de Fiume (Rijeka) para Italia. En septiembre, Gabriele D'Annunzio (1863–1938), un extravagante poeta y aviador de derechas, asedió Fiume con una banda de seguidores armados. Retuvo la ciudad portuaria y la gobernó en calidad de dictador de la Regencia de Carnaro hasta que la Marina italiana, tras la firma de un acuerdo de paz entre Italia y Yugoslavia en noviembre de 1920, lo expulsó y declaró Fiume un estado libre.

Entrada en Fiume *Los legionarios nacionalistas de Gabriele D'Annunzio saludan la bandera de la efímera Regencia de Carnaro en Fiume, la actual ciudad croata de Rijeka.*

Gran Bretaña afrontaba la oposición a su mandato en India. Durante la Primera Guerra Mundial, los británicos habían prometido un cierto grado de autogobierno a los indios, si bien suspendieron las libertades civiles como parte de una campaña de lo que describieron como «crímenes anárquicos y revolucionarios». El 13 de abril, un oficial británico, el general Reginald Dyer (1864–1927), ordenó a las tropas abrir fuego sobre una muchedumbre desarmada de manifestantes en el Jallianwalla Bagh, un jardín público en Amritsar (Punjab). Fueron asesinadas al menos 379 personas. Pese a que el gobierno británico condenó los asesinatos y destituyó al general Dyer, la **masacre de Amritsar** causó un descontento generalizado en India e incrementó las reclamaciones de independencia.

Al margen de los problemas mundiales, el progreso tecnológico y científico siguió su curso. El 14 de junio, un piloto británico, el capitán John Alcock (1892–1919), y su copiloto, el teniente Arthur Whitten Brown (1886–1948), despegaron en San Juan de Terranova para intentar el **primer vuelo sin paradas sobre el Atlántico**. Tras unas peligrosas 16 horas y 27 minutos, su bombardero Vickers Vimy aterrizó en picado en una ciénaga de Galway (Irlanda). Su hazaña les mereció una recepción como héroes en Londres, si bien el triunfo de Alcock fue efímero, pues falleció en un accidente aéreo seis meses después.

Mientras tanto, los científicos británicos analizaban los resultados de una expedición enviada a la isla africana de Príncipe para observar un eclipse solar. La expedición tenía la misión de comprobar la validez de la **teoría general de la relatividad**, un concepto físico revolucionario formulado por Albert Einstein (1879–1955) durante la Primera Guerra Mundial. En septiembre se anunció que las observaciones habían confirmado la teoría de Einstein, que modificaba los fundamentos de la concepción del tiempo y del espacio definidos por la concepción del universo de Isaac Newton.

ALBERT EINSTEIN
(1879–1955)

Nació en el sur de Alemania, en el seno de una familia judía. Publicó su teoría especial de la relatividad en 1905, a la cual siguió la teoría general de la relatividad en 1915. Sus teorías revolucionaron la comprensión de la relación entre tiempo, espacio, materia y energía. A partir de la década de 1920, Einstein, alabado en todo el mundo, escogió exiliarse en EE. UU., lejos de la Alemania de Hitler.

2 de junio Unos anarquistas hacen estallar bombas en ocho ciudades de EE. UU.

14–15 de junio Los aviadores británicos Alcock y Brown realizan el **primer vuelo transatlántico sin paradas**.

21 de junio La **tripulación de la flota alemana**, confinada en Scapa Flow (islas Orcadas) **hunde sus propios barcos**.

28 de junio Alemania firma el **tratado de paz** en la Galería de los Espejos de **Versalles**.

23 de julio Los nacionalistas turcos se reúnen en Erzurum para oponerse a los **planes aliados de dividir Turquía**.

27–30 de julio Disturbios raciales en Chicago dejan 38 muertos y miles de personas sin hogar.

8 de agosto Gran Bretaña llega a un acuerdo de paz con **Afganistán**.

11 de agosto La nueva Constitución alemana establece la **República de Weimar**.

16 de agosto Los polacos de Silesia protagonizan un **alzamiento frustrado** contra el gobierno alemán.

9–12 de septiembre El gobernador de Massachusetts, Calvin Coolidge, **manda aplacar la huelga de la policía** de Boston.

10 de septiembre El **tratado de Saint Germain** reconoce oficialmente la disolución del Imperio austrohúngaro.

12 de septiembre Soldados irregulares italianos dirigidos por **Gabrielle D'Annunzio toman Fiume**.

27 de septiembre La fuerza de intervención británica se retira de Arjánguelsk (Rusia).

2 de octubre El presidente de EE. UU., Wilson, inhabilitado por un infarto.

19 de octubre El **Ejército Rojo de Trotski defiende Petrogrado** del Ejército Blanco de Yudénich.

28 de octubre Se aprueba la **Ley de Volstead (Ley seca)** en EE. UU.

7 de noviembre Arresto de miles de **activistas izquierdistas** en EE. UU.

19 de noviembre El senado estadounidense rehúsa ratificar el **tratado de Versalles**.

28 de noviembre Nancy Astor se convierte en la primera mujer en ocupar un escaño en la Cámara de los Comunes británica.

21 de diciembre EE. UU. deporta a cientos de socialistas y anarquistas a Rusia.

28 de diciembre La Ley del Gobierno de India permite una participación limitada a los indios en el gobierno de su país.

«¿QUÉ OFREZCO A IRLANDA? ALGO QUE HA DESEADO ESTOS ÚLTIMOS 700 AÑOS.»

Michael Collins, líder revolucionario irlandés (1921)

Mientras la agitación por la independencia de Irlanda aumenta, una muchedumbre enojada de manifestantes en Dublín intenta traspasar una barricada en una calle protegida por soldados británicos.

ALEMANIA QUEDÓ INMERSA en la agitación que siguió a la Gran Guerra (*véase* 1919). Unidades de las tropas paramilitares de los *Freikorps* nacionalistas ocuparon Berlín en marzo y derrocaron la República de Weimar. El político conservador Wolfgang Kapp intentaba formar gobierno, los ministros de Weimar convocaron una **huelga general** para oponerse al golpe de estado de los *Freikorps*. Los obreros dejaron sus puestos de trabajo, las fábricas y el transporte cerraron, y, en cuestión de días, el régimen de Kapp se había desmoronado. El gobierno de Weimar inició a regañadientes conversaciones con los aliados, los vencedores de la guerra, para la **aplicación del tratado de Versalles** (*véase* 1919). Alemania comenzó a disolver gran parte de sus fuerzas armadas y a pagar las reparaciones de la guerra en especies (suministros de carbón a Francia; vacas, ovejas y caballos a Francia y Bélgica).

5 % Serbia
3 % otros
8 % Bélgica
10 % Italia
22 % Gran Bretaña
52 % Francia

Reparto de las reparaciones
Los aliados acordaron repartirse las compensaciones alemanas tras un complejo cálculo de las pérdidas sufridas durante la Gran Guerra.

Más hacia el este, la guerra seguía rugiendo con fuerza. Los bolcheviques derrotaron a los generales blancos en la guerra civil rusa. La toma del poder en Ucrania y Bielorrusia por parte de los bolcheviques hizo que estallara un conflicto entre el Ejército Rojo y los polacos. Tras varios éxitos tempranos contra el ejército polaco, el **Ejército Rojo invadió Polonia**. Liderados por el general Józef Piłsudski (1867–1935), los polacos urdieron una contraofensiva a las puertas de Varsovia que aplastó al Ejército Rojo. Lenin (*véase* 1917) tuvo que aceptar las condiciones de Polonia para poner fin a la guerra.

Los términos impuestos por los aliados al sultán otomano en el tratado de Sèvres después de ganar la guerra conllevaban la **división del Imperio turco**. En abril, el general Mustafá Kemal (1881–1938), el héroe turco de Gallípoli (*véase* 1915), lideró un parlamento nacionalista en oposición al sultán e inició una guerra para tomar el control de lo que él consideraba territorio nacional turco, gran parte del cual había sido cedido a Grecia por los aliados.

Este mismo año comenzó la Ley seca en EE. UU. La **decimoctava enmienda** a la Constitución prohibía la elaboración y venta de bebidas alcohólicas, medida que influyó poco en el consumo de alcohol, pero sí estimuló el surgimiento de las mafias. La **decimonovena enmienda**, más trascendental y ratificada en agosto, garantizaba a las mujeres estadounidenses el derecho a voto en idénticas condiciones que los hombres.

EE. UU. no participó en la fundación de la **Sociedad de Naciones**. Este organismo internacional, consagrado a la resolución pacífica de las disputas y a la disuasión colectiva de la agresión, fue un invento del presidente estadounidense Woodrow Wilson, pero el Congreso de EE. UU. rehusó ratificarlo. Repre-

Victoria del sufragio
Esta portada de revista celebra la aprobación de la decimonovena enmienda a la Constitución de EE. UU., que concedió el derecho a voto a las mujeres.

Cruz al valor polaca
Polonia introdujo esta condecoración militar en 1920 durante la guerra con la Rusia bolchevique, en reconocimiento a los actos heroicos de los polacos.

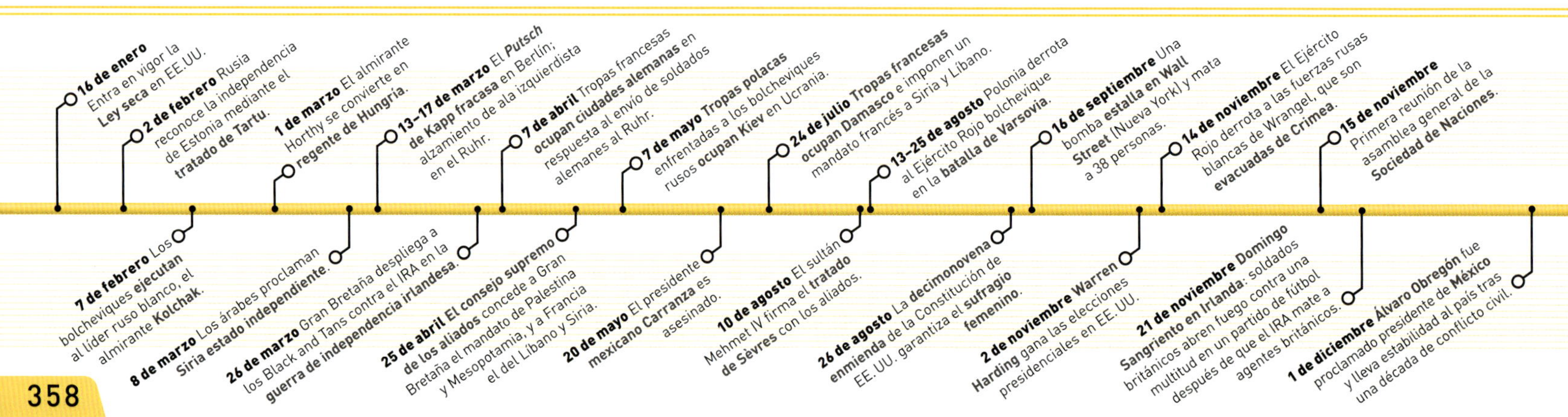

5 MILLONES ES LA CIFRA APROXIMADA DE MUERTES QUE DEJÓ LA HAMBRUNA RUSA DE 1921

Víctimas de la hambruna rusa reciben comida de un tren de auxilio. EE. UU. desempeñó un papel clave en el esfuerzo internacional por repartir alimentos.

sentantes de 41 países acudieron a la primera asamblea general en Ginebra en noviembre. Ni Alemania ni Rusia participaron.

Entre tanto, **la guerra había estallado en Irlanda**, donde Gran Bretaña se resistía a declarar la República Irlandesa. Se reclutó a los veteranos británicos de la Primera Guerra Mundial en dos nuevas unidades, los Black and Tans y los Auxiliares, para combatir contra el Ejército Republicano Irlandés (IRA). El 21 de noviembre, en una operación planeada por el jefe de la inteligencia del IRA, **Michael Collins** (1890–1922), el IRA asesinó a trece personas en Dublín. Los Auxiliares respondieron aquella misma tarde abriendo fuego contra los asistentes a un partido de fútbol gaélico; mataron a catorce personas.

Aquel mes, en el segundo aniversario del armisticio que puso fin a la Gran Guerra, Francia y Gran Bretaña **enterraron a un «soldado desconocido»**. El soldado francés fue sepultado en el Arco de Triunfo de París; el británico en la abadía de Westminster de Londres. Aquel gesto conmemoraba a los combatientes muertos en el conflicto, al margen de su rango o clase social.

Este año el **general Álvaro Obregón** (1880–1928) fue elegido presidente de **México**. Obregón había sido uno de los principales agentes en los conflictos civiles que habían despedazado el país desde la Revolución mexicana (*véase* 1910). La defenestración del presidente Venustiano Carranza (1859–1920) concedió a Obregón la oportunidad de establecer un gobierno relativamente estable.

EN 1921, RUSIA padeció una de las **hambrunas más letales** del siglo. Años de conflictos habían causado estragos en el entorno rural, a los que se sumó una sequía que azotó la región del Volga. Mientras centenares de miles de personas fallecían de desnutrición y enfermedad, el gobierno bolchevique de Lenin solicitaba a regañadientes ayuda al extranjero. El principal participante en aquel **esfuerzo humanitario internacional** fue la American Relief Administration, encabezada por el futuro presidente de EE. UU. Herbert Hoover (1874–1964). La distribución de alimentos entre diez millones de personas no evitó que muchos otros millones hubieran fallecido para cuando la hambruna remitió un año después. Los **bolcheviques** siguieron imponiendo la voluntad de su partido a un país asolado. En marzo, obreros, soldados y marineros se rebelaron en la fortaleza naval de Kronstadt solicitando elecciones libres, libertad de expresión y el derecho del campesinado a la posesión de sus tierras y ganado. La **rebelión** fue aplastada por fuerzas bolcheviques, si bien, ante el descontento popular y la devastación económica, los bolcheviques debieron derogar algunas medidas comunistas. La **Nueva Política Económica** (NEP) de **Lenin** aprobaba una economía de mercado capitalista limitada. Una vez se permitió a los campesinos vender sus productos y obtener beneficios, la economía rural se recuperó pronto y se garantizó la provisión de alimentos. Pese a las tribulaciones del gobierno bolchevique, su ejemplo siguió estimulando la fundación de partidos comunistas en el mundo. Entre ellos figuraba el **Partido Comunista de China**, que celebró su congreso fundador en Shanghai en julio.

División de Irlanda
Irlanda del Norte, de mayoría protestante, se escindió del sur del país, que se convirtió en el Estado Libre Irlandés.

En Irlanda, Gran Bretaña intentó cumplir su compromiso de la Primera Guerra Mundial con el **autogobierno irlandés** (*véase* 1914). Para apaciguar a los protestantes irlandeses, el país se dividió. Se establecieron parlamentos autonómicos en Dublín y Belfast, y ambas partes permanecieron dentro de Reino Unido. Tal situación contó con la aceptación de los protestantes y el rechazo de los republicanos irlandeses. Se abrieron **negociaciones** en Londres y, el 6 de diciembre, la delegación irlandesa aceptó la **división de Irlanda** a cambio de la independencia en el seno de la Commonwealth británica. Irlanda del Sur se convirtió así en el **Estado Libre Irlandés**, si bien muchos republicanos irlandeses se sintieron ultrajados por los compromisos del tratado anglo-irlandés, lo cual condujo a una guerra civil (*véase* 1922).

MAO ZEDONG (1893–1976)

Hijo de un granjero, Mao ayudó a fundar el Partido Comunista chino en 1921. Ideó basar la revolución en el apoyo de los campesinos, en lugar de los obreros industriales. Gobernó la China comunista como presidente del partido a partir de 1949. Sus políticas radicales, como el Gran Salto Adelante de 1958 y la Revolución Cultural de la década de 1960, causaron incontables muertes y un malestar generalizado.

Gran Bretaña vivía también **conflictos internos**. El breve auge económico de la posguerra estuvo seguido por un colapso en la demanda de productos a muchas industrias tradicionales del país, como la minería del carbón y la construcción naval. En junio, la cifra de **parados ascendía a dos millones de personas**. A los veteranos de la Primera Guerra Mundial se les antojaba una ironía hallarse haciendo cola para cobrar el subsidio de desempleo.

En EE. UU. cundían el racismo y la preocupación por la subversión política. En **Tulsa** (Oklahoma), el **disturbio racial** más destructivo de la historia del país se saldó con la práctica destrucción de la sección afroamericana de la ciudad por parte de la población blanca. El apoyo al grupo supremacista blanco Ku Klux Klan ascendió deprisa, y la inquietud por la composición racial de la población estadounidense se hizo eco en el endurecimiento de las condiciones para la inmigración extranjera. **La Ley de Cuotas de Emergencia** vinculaba el derecho a entrada con el país de origen y bloqueaba la inmigración masiva procedente del sur y del este de Europa. Los asiáticos también quedaban excluidos.

La presunción de la superioridad racial blanca sufrió un duro revés en **Marruecos**, país que **Francia y España** habían dividido sin miramientos en «esferas de influencia». Las tropas españolas que intentaban controlar la montañosa región del Rif fueron rodeadas y masacradas por los **bereberes** autóctonos en la batalla de Annual en julio. El líder bereber Abd el-Krim proclamó la **República del Rif independiente**, si bien sucumbió a un contraataque combinado de Francia y España cuatro años después.

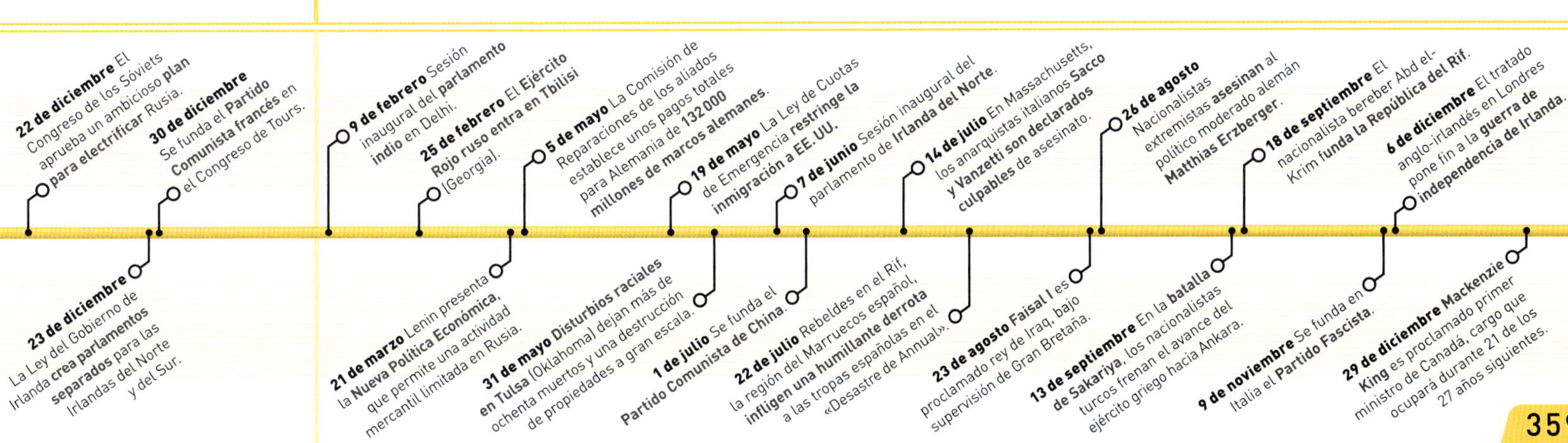

1922

Manifestantes se reúnen en las calles de Delhi para protestar contra el arresto del líder nacionalista indio Mohandas Gandhi.

> « DEBERÍAMOS SER **LIBRES DE EXPRESAR** PLENAMENTE **NUESTRA DESAFECCIÓN** SIEMPRE QUE ELLO **NO CONTEMPLE**, FOMENTE O **INCITE LA VIOLENCIA**. »
>
> **Mohandas (Mahatma) Gandhi,** en una declaración efectuada durante su juicio (18 de marzo de 1922)

CUATRO AÑOS DESPUÉS DEL FIN DE LA «GUERRA QUE DEBÍA PONER FIN A LA GUERRA» se hicieron grandes avances hacia un futuro más pacífico. En una reunión mantenida en EE. UU. en febrero, las cinco principales potencias navales del mundo –Gran Bretaña, Francia, Italia, Japón y EE. UU.– firmaron el **tratado de Washington**, que limitaba el tamaño de sus flotas. Se solicitaba poner fin al uso militar de gas venenoso y se prohibían los ataques submarinos contra buques comerciales. Fue el primer acuerdo efectivo de limitación armamentística entre grandes potencias. Gran Bretaña fue la que más sacrificios asumió, al aceptar la paridad naval con EE. UU. después de un largo dominio de los océanos, si bien donde más polémica suscitó el tratado fue en Japón, donde los nacionalistas rechazaban su inferioridad naval en comparación con Gran Bretaña y EE. UU.

Otro signo esperanzador fue la **aparición de los viajes aéreos internacionales en Europa**. Aviones pequeños, ruidosos e incómodos empezaron a cubrir vuelos regulares entre ciudades europeas, aprovechando el excedente de pilotos entrenados y la capacidad de fabricación aeronáutica legada por la guerra. La navegación era primitiva y muchos pilotos simplemente seguían carreteras o vías de tren. Ello conllevó la **primera catástrofe aérea comercial** en abril, cuando un avión de pasajeros entre Londres y París chocó con un avión que hacía la misma ruta en sentido contrario.

En **Oriente Próximo**, Gran Bretaña lidiaba con problemas inextricables a la hora de reorganizar los territorios que había heredado del Imperio otomano. La inmigración de judíos a Palestina (*véase* recuadro), que Gran Bretaña se había comprometido a permitir, derivó en **enfrentamientos entre judíos y árabes** que escapaban al control de los británicos.

En **Egipto**, otrora territorio otomano, Gran Bretaña afrontaba una oposición nacionalista férrea al protectorado establecido en 1914. Incapaz de llegar a un acuerdo, en febrero Gran Bretaña **declaró unilateralmente la independencia de Egipto**, si bien conservó el derecho a apostar tropas en su territorio.

Un efecto secundario más positivo de la presencia británica en Egipto fue el descubrimiento por parte de arqueólogos británicos de la **tumba de Tutankamón**. El conde de Carnavon (1866–1923) y el egiptólogo Howard Carter (1874–1939) accedieron al sepulcro, donde hallaron un tesoro sin parangón que incluía una máscara de oro y carros con joyas engastadas. El deceso de Carnavon un año más tarde inspiró una leyenda –«la maldición de la tumba»– que magnificó la repercusión de aquel hallazgo.

En India, la oposición nacionalista al mandato británico había hallado un líder en **Mohandas Gandhi** (1869–1948). Gandhi, que había garantizado el apoyo del campesinado al movimiento independentista del Congreso Nacional Indio, organizó una campaña nacional de desobediencia civil, la cual incluía el boicot a los productos británicos. Si bien Gandhi abogaba por una no violencia estricta, su campaña causó numerosos disturbios, incluida la masacre de 23 policías en Chauri Chaura en febrero. Las autoridades británicas arrestaron a **Gandhi** en marzo y lo sentenciaron a seis años de prisión, de los que cumplió dos.

La implantación del **tratado anglo-irlandés** en Irlanda del Sur (*véase* 1921) condujo a una **guerra civil**. Michael Collins (1890–1922), jefe del gobierno del Estado Libre Irlandés en Dublín, se enfrentó a los republicanos, contrarios al tratado. En abril, el Ejército Republicano Irlandés, el **IRA**, ocupó el edificio dublinés Four Courts. Tras un largo punto muerto, en junio Collins usó artillería cedida por Gran Bretaña para bombardear el Four Courts y retomar el edificio. El 22 de agosto, Collins fue asesinado en una emboscada en una carretera del condado de Cork. Los soldados del Estado Libre habían aplastado a gran parte de la oposición para cuando el tratado entró en vigor el 6 de diciembre. La provincia septentrional protestante del Ulster continuó adherida al Reino Unido.

En **Turquía**, los nacionalistas liderados por **Mustafá Kemal** (1881–1938) se hallaban en **guerra con Grecia**, que aspiraba a ampliar sus territorios con la inclusión de Constantinopla y gran parte de la Anatolia occidental. En agosto, la ofensiva turca en Dumlupinar obligó a los griegos a retirarse. La ciudad predominantemente griega de Esmirna fue ocupada por fuerzas tur-

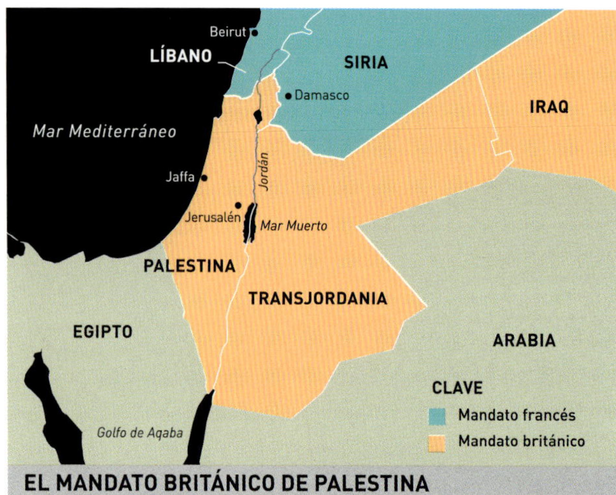

EL MANDATO BRITÁNICO DE PALESTINA

La Sociedad de Naciones autorizó el reparto de los antiguos territorios del Imperio otomano entre Gran Bretaña y Francia. De acuerdo con la Declaración Balfour (*véase* 1917), Gran Bretaña había permitido asentamientos judíos en Palestina, pero durante la guerra también había realizado promesas a los árabes. En 1922 dividió el territorio de su mandato palestino a lo largo de la línea del río Jordán. Se autorizaron asentamientos judíos en la ribera oeste, mientras que Transjordania, en la zona este, seguiría siendo territorio árabe.

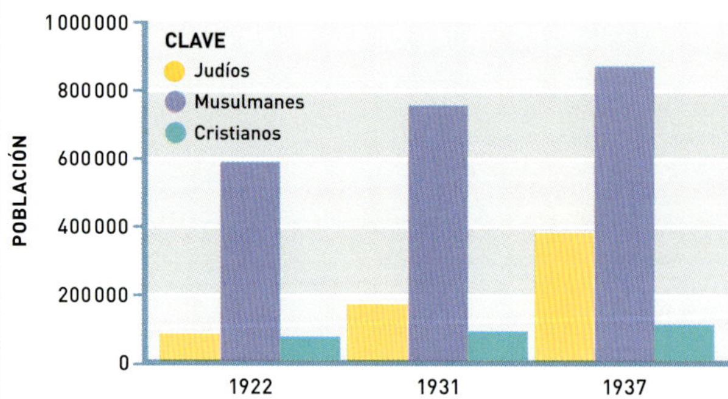

Crecimiento de la población en Palestina
A causa de la inmigración, la proporción de judíos en Palestina aumentó rápidamente. Ello provocó una violenta reacción por parte de la mayoría musulmana.

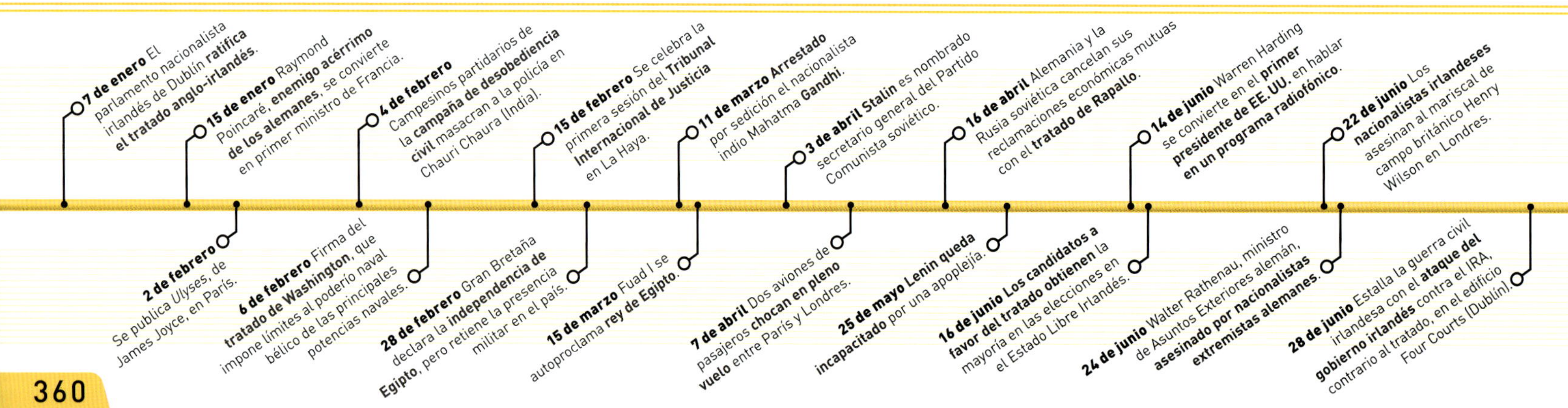

Benito Mussolini se mezcla con los paramilitares fascistas conocidos como «camisas negras» en Roma tras ser designado primer ministro por el rey de Italia en octubre.

> **« O EL GOBIERNO** SE NOS ENTREGA POR LAS BUENAS O **LO TOMAREMOS** MARCHANDO SOBRE ROMA. **»**
>
> **Benito Mussolini** (24 de octubre de 1922)

cas y quedó arrasada por el fuego. Gran Bretaña contempló intervenir contra los turcos, pero, en un **armisticio** firmado en **Mudanya** en octubre, tanto las potencias europeas como Grecia aceptaron la victoria militar de Turquía. De acuerdo con los términos de la paz acordada, se produjo un intercambio de personas a gran escala: más de un millón de griegos fueron expulsados de Turquía y medio millón de turcos tuvieron que abandonar Grecia. Todavía hoy, las poblaciones griegas olvidadas en el oeste de Turquía atestiguan aquella tragedia humana. Un año más tarde **se fundó la República de Turquía** y Mustafá Kemal fue designado su primer presidente.

En 1922, **Benito Mussolini** (1883–1945) tomó el poder de Italia. Desde el final de la Primera Guerra Mundial, la clase gobernante italiana se había visto intimidada por disturbios sociales, como ocupaciones de fábricas por parte de obreros socialistas y la toma de fincas por parte de los campesinos. En medio de tales tribulaciones, Mussolini fundó las *fasci di combattimento*, unas **milicias nacionalistas** que atacaron a los socialistas y asumieron el poder a la fuerza en algunas poblaciones italianas. En octubre, Mussolini amenazó con dirigir a sus partidarios **fascistas** en una «marcha sobre Roma», a menos que lo proclamaran jefe del gobierno. El rey de Italia, Víctor Manuel III (1869–1947), acabó por ceder y Mussolini asumió el cargo de primer ministro; una vez se hizo con el control, comenzó a desmantelar el sistema democrático parlamentario de Italia. Mientras Mussolini se abría camino a la fuerza hacia el poder, en Gran Bretaña se estableció la **primera empresa de radiocomunicaciones nacional**. Como las primeras emisoras de radio que surgían en los EE. UU., la BBC (British Broadcasting Company, luego Corporation) estuvo financiada por fabricantes de aparatos de radio ansiosos por crear un mercado para sus productos. Y funcionó. En torno a marzo de 1923, las retransmisiones diarias de conciertos, noticias y tertulias habían atraído a 125 000 hogares a comprar licencias en las oficinas de correos para sus aparatos «inalámbricos». EE. UU. no contaría con una red de comunicaciones importante hasta la instauración de la NBC (National Broadcasting Company) en 1926.

En 1922 afloraron **nuevas tendencias literarias** que dieron lugar al modernismo anglosajón. *Ulises*, la novela del irlandés James Joyce publicada en París en febrero, rompía todas las convenciones literarias, pero su vocabulario y su temática garantizaron su prohibición por obscena en los países con una censura más estricta que Francia. El poeta expatriado estadounidense T.S. Eliot causó sensación con su largo y sombrío poema *La tierra baldía*, en el que se incluían notas para ayudar al lector a entender sus alusiones literarias. También se experimentó en el cine, con ejemplos como *Nosferatu*, la película de terror expresionista del alemán F.W. Murnau, o el rompedor documental del estadounidense Robert Flaherty, *Nanuk, el esquimal*.

Rusia iniciaba una época de relativa tranquilidad. A finales de año, el antiguo Imperio ruso se reconstituyó como la **Unión de Repúblicas Socialistas Soviéticas** (URSS), pero para entonces el fundador del primer estado comunista del mundo, **Vladímir Lenin** (*véase* 1917) había quedado incapacitado por una apoplejía. Ello no obstó para que dictara un documento, conocido después como **«el testamento de Lenin»**, en el que criticaba a varios de sus colegas. En particular advertía contra la ordinariez e intolerancia de **Stalin** (1878–1953), recién designado secretario general del Partido Comunista soviético, y proponía que lo destituyeran de su cargo. Tras la muerte de Lenin, el conocimiento de aquel documento quedó restringido a un reducido círculo comunista y jamás se adoptaron medidas contra Stalin.

Las primeras ondas aéreas
Las primeras radios eran aparatos de aspecto impresionante. Esta, que data de 1925, posee una inusitada antena con forma de estrella.

«Padre de los turcos»
Mustafá Kemal departe con camelleros durante la guerra entre Turquía y Grecia. Posteriormente adoptó el nombre de Ataturk.

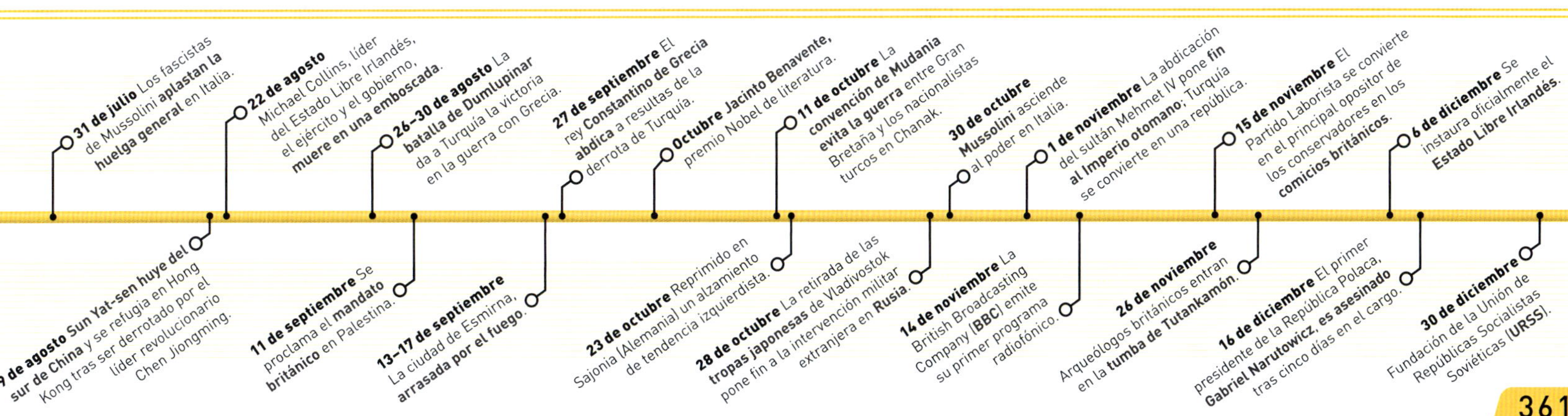

1923

Guardias civiles españoles junto a las ruinas causadas por el estallido de una bomba en Barcelona durante los disturbios que precedieron a la toma del poder por parte de Rivera.

« TENEMOS LA **RAZÓN**, Y **POR ESO TENEMOS LA FUERZA**, QUE HEMOS **EMPLEADO CON MODERACIÓN HASTA AHORA**. **»**

Miguel Primo de Rivera, dictador español (septiembre de 1923)

EN 1922, EL GOBIERNO ALEMÁN se había declarado incapaz de pagar las reparaciones de guerra que debía satisfacer a los aliados. Los franceses, gobernados por el primer ministro antialemán Raymond Poincaré (1860–1934), estaban decididos a tomar represalias. En enero de 1923, **tropas francesas y belgas ocuparon el Ruhr**, el corazón industrial de Alemania. El gobierno alemán respondió alentando una resistencia pasiva: las huelgas detuvieron la producción en minas y fábricas.

La ocupación desató una **hiperinflación** y el colapso del marco alemán. La inflación se hallaba ya descontrolada antes de la ocupación franco-belga, pero la decisión del gobierno alemán de imprimir billetes para pagar a los obreros del Ruhr en huelga fue nefasta. En verano, el marco apenas tenía valor. En su momento álgido, unos ahorros de 68 000 marcos únicamente servían para comprar sellos. En contraste, quienes debían dinero vieron cómo sus deudas desaparecían. En agosto, **Gustav Stresemann** (1878–1929), un reputado político alemán, formó un **gobierno de coalición**, y un mes después desconvocó la resistencia pasiva en el Ruhr. En noviembre, el marco fue reemplazado por el ***Rentenmark***, que suprimió doce ceros a la vieja moneda y restauró la confianza pública.

El caótico estado en el que se encontraba Alemania tentó a un extremista político menor, **Adolf Hitler** (*véase* recuadro) a intentar asir el poder en el ***Putsch* de Múnich**, entre el 8 y el 9 de noviembre. Hitler se había proclamado líder del Partido Nacionalsocialista (los nazis). También contaba con poderosos aliados, incluido un héroe de guerra, el general Erich Ludendorff (1865–1937). Hitler planeó una «marcha sobre Berlín» desde la capital bávara, Múnich, a imitación de la «marcha sobre Roma» de Mussolini (*véase* 1922). En el último momento, los líderes bávaros se opusieron al golpe de Estado. Tras una breve refriega con la policía y el ejército en las calles de Múnich, el conato de revuelta se desintegró. Hitler fue detenido a los dos días y acusado de alta traición (*véase* 1924).

Papel moneda sin valor
El colapso de la divisa alemana llevó a la impresión de billetes de 500 millones de marcos. Los billetes de menor cuantía tenían tan poco valor que se usaban para prender el fuego.

VALOR DEL MARCO FRENTE AL DÓLAR: 0; 10; 100; 1000; 10 000; 100 000; 1 000 000; 10 000 000; 100 000 000; 1 000 000 000; 10 000 000 000; 100 000 000 000; 1 000 000 000 000; 10 000 000 000 000

Ene. 1922; Mar. 1922; Ago. 1922; Dic. 1922; Ene. 1923; Dic. 1923

CLAVE
Tasa de cambio del marco alemán

Hiperinflación en Alemania
El valor del marco frente al dólar refleja la aceleración de la inflación en Alemania. Diez años antes un dólar equivalía a 2,3 marcos.

Mientras el *Putsch* de Hitler fracasaba, **en España, el general Primo de Rivera** (1870–1930) logró hacerse con el poder. Tras el Desastre de Annual (*véase* 1921), el parlamento español había abierto sendas investigaciones al ejército y al rey de España, Alfonso XIII (1886–1941), a quienes responsabilizaba de la derrota. Primo de Rivera disolvió el parlamento y estableció una **dictadura militar** bajo el rey. Su nuevo gobierno fue incapaz de resolver los problemas económicos y la amarga división política de España.

Un militar con más éxito fue el turco Mustafá Kemal (1881–1938), posteriormente llamado Ataturk. Tras vencer en la guerra contra Grecia (*véase* 1922), **Kemal fundó formalmente la República de Turquía** en octubre. Se embarcó entonces en una serie de reformas radicales destinadas a transformar Turquía en un estado secular moderno. Prohibió el atuendo tradicional, abolió el sistema gubernamental musulmán de califatos y sustituyó la escritura árabe por el alfabeto romano.

ADOLF HITLER
(1889–1945)

Austriaco de cuna, Hitler luchó en el ejército alemán en la Primera Guerra Mundial. Orador inspirado, obtuvo un amplio apoyo para su Partido Nacionalsocialista a finales de la década de 1920. A partir de 1933, estableció una dictadura que derivó en el Holocausto (*véase* 1942). Sus políticas expansionistas provocaron una guerra en 1939 que se saldó con la destrucción de su Reich.

El 1 de septiembre, **Japón** se vio sacudido por una de las catástrofes naturales del siglo. Conocido como el **gran terremoto de Kanto**, un seísmo de 7,9 grados en la escala de Richter **devastó Tokio** y los alrededores. El temblor desató incendios que los fuertes vientos avivaron hasta convertir en una tormenta de fuego. Un tsunami de diez metros de altura golpeó los distritos litorales, incluido el puerto de Yokohama. El número de víctimas se estimó en 150 000.

A la sazón, EE. UU. se presentaba como un faro de prosperidad en medio del sombrío mundo. El presidente Warren Harding (1865–

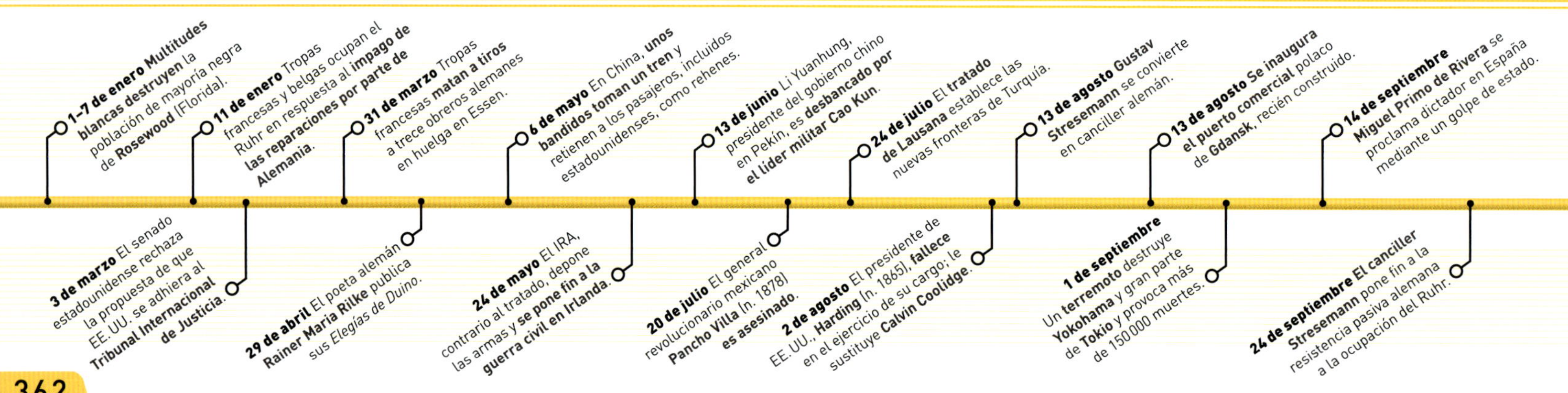

Tokio en ruinas tras el terremoto de 1923. Más de 150 000 personas murieron en la catástrofe, que destruyó además medio millón de edificios.

La reina María, esposa del rey Jorge V, visita la Exposición del Imperio Británico en Wembley, destinada a inspirar entusiasmo por la gloria imperial británica.

1923) falleció en el ejercicio de su cargo y fue reemplazado por su vicepresidente, **Calvin Coolidge** (1872–1933), quien se hizo célebre por su autocomplacencia cuando dijo que EE. UU. disfrutaba de «un estado de satisfacción jamás conocido». Ciertamente, EE. UU. se estaba convirtiendo en la **primera sociedad consumista moderna** y producía nueve de cada diez automóviles mundiales.

Músicos de **jazz afroamericanos** proporcionaron la banda sonora a esta era de prosperidad. Concentrado en las ciudades del norte, como Chicago y Nueva York, el jazz se popularizó a través del nuevo medio de comunicación, la radio.

El barrio neoyorquino de Harlem se convirtió en el epicentro de la explosión cultural afroamericana, literaria y musical. Allí se **inauguró el Cotton Club** en 1923, el cual devino una de las salas más célebres de jazz en directo, si bien solo aceptaba negros como intérpretes, no como público.

El arquitecto Walter Gropius (1883–1969) fundó la escuela de artes y diseño **Bauhaus** en Alemania en 1919, y entre julio y septiembre se celebró su primera exposición. Rechazando la hostilidad del arte tradicional a la tecnología moderna y la producción en serie, la Bauhaus se especializó en el diseño moderno y funcional.

VLADÍMIR ÍLICH LENIN (1870–1924), fundador de la Unión Soviética, murió de una apoplejía el 21 de enero. Cientos de miles de personas visitaron su cadáver en la Sala de las Columnas de Moscú. Por insistencia de Stalin, el cuerpo de Lenin se embalsamó y expuso de modo permanente; se le extirpó el cerebro para su estudio por parte de científicos soviéticos, cuya misión consistía en hallar «la esencia de su genialidad». Se erigieron estatuas a Lenin en toda la Unión soviética y la ciudad de Petrogrado se rebautizó como Leningrado en su honor.

En **Gran Bretaña**, el **Partido Laborista**, liderado por Ramsay Macdonald (1866–1937), disfrutó de su primera **breve temporada en el gobierno**. Pese a la moderación de Macdonald, la presencia de socialistas en el gobierno conmocionó a la clase acomodada británica. Al convocarse comicios en octubre, se filtró a la prensa una carta, supuestamente enviada por el jefe del Komintern soviético Grigori Zinóviev, que sirvió para promover la imagen de unos laboristas timoratos con el comunismo, lo cual contribuyó a su derrota electoral.

La **Exposición del Imperio británico**, celebrada a partir de abril en Wembley (Londres), supuso un intento de fomentar la idea imperial en tanto que fuente de fortaleza y seguridad en un mundo atribulado. Su inauguración supuso la primera ocasión en que un monarca británico, Jorge V (1865–1936), realizó un discurso radiofónico.

La situación política y económica en Alemania empezó a recuperarse del caos de la posguerra con ayuda de EE. UU. El **plan Dawes**, bautizado en honor al banquero y político Charles G. Dawes, dispuso la retirada de las tropas francesas y belgas del Ruhr (*véase* 1923) y el pago de las reparaciones por parte de Alemania con la ayuda de préstamos concedidos por EE. UU.

Mientras, el líder nazi **Adolf Hitler fue juzgado** por su fallido golpe de estado, el ***Putsch* de Múnich** (*véase* 1923). Aprovechando la oportunidad de realizar discursos políticos en los tribunales, se convirtió en una celebridad nacional. Fue declarado culpable de alta traición, pero condenado a una sentencia indulgente de cinco años de cárcel, de los cuales cumplió menos de uno. Durante su estancia en la prisión de Landsberg, dictó el primer volumen de *Mein Kampf (Mi lucha)*, una exposición de sus creencias políticas.

En Italia, el asesinato del diputado parlamentario socialista Giacomo Matteotti (1885–1924) atrajo la atención sobre la violencia subyacente al gobierno de **Mussolini** (*véase* 1922). Supuestamente, Matteotti murió a manos de los **camisas negras fascistas**. Los diputados de la oposición se retiraron del parlamento en señal de protesta, y así le franquearon el camino a Mussolini para avanzar a marchas forzadas hacia una dictadura unipartidista.

Creole Jazz Band (1923)
La banda de Chicago de King Oliver contó con Louis Armstrong, una de las figuras más destacadas del jazz.

900 000

PERSONAS **VISITARON LA CAPILLA ARDIENTE DE LENIN** DURANTE **CUATRO DÍAS**

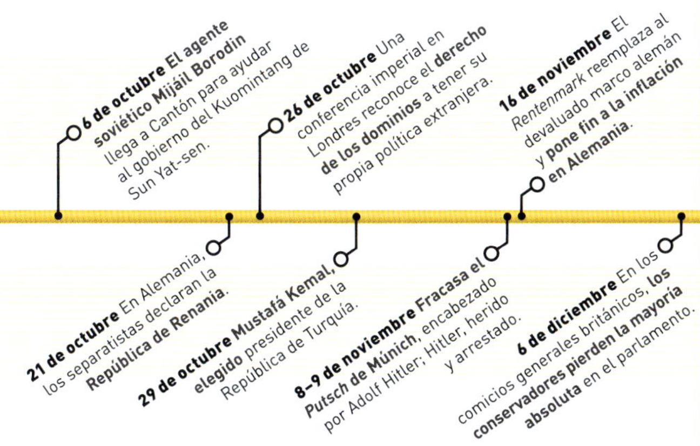

HISTORIA DE LA AVIACIÓN

EN POCO MÁS DE CIEN AÑOS LA AVIACIÓN HA EXPERIMENTADO AVANCES INCREÍBLES

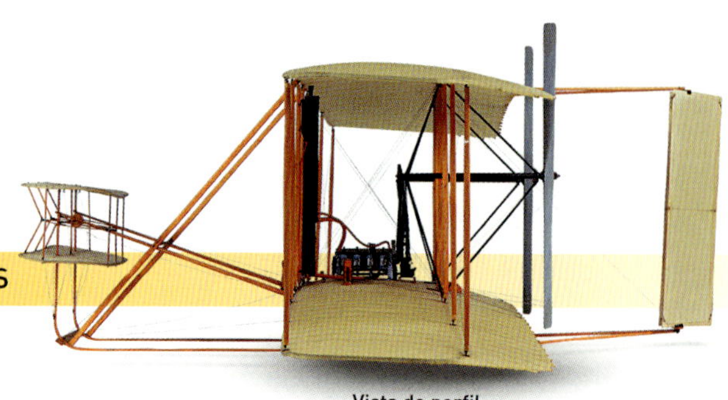

Vista de perfil

Hasta el siglo XX, el sueño del ser humano de volar era un ámbito de experimentación para entusiastas. Los ascensos en globo desencadenaron la primera fiebre del vuelo, si bien su efecto práctico fue escaso. En el siglo XIX, la ingeniería permitió calcular las fuerzas implicadas en un vuelo con alas y se experimentó con planeadores, pero fue la aparición de los motores de gasolina lo que de veras permitió volar.

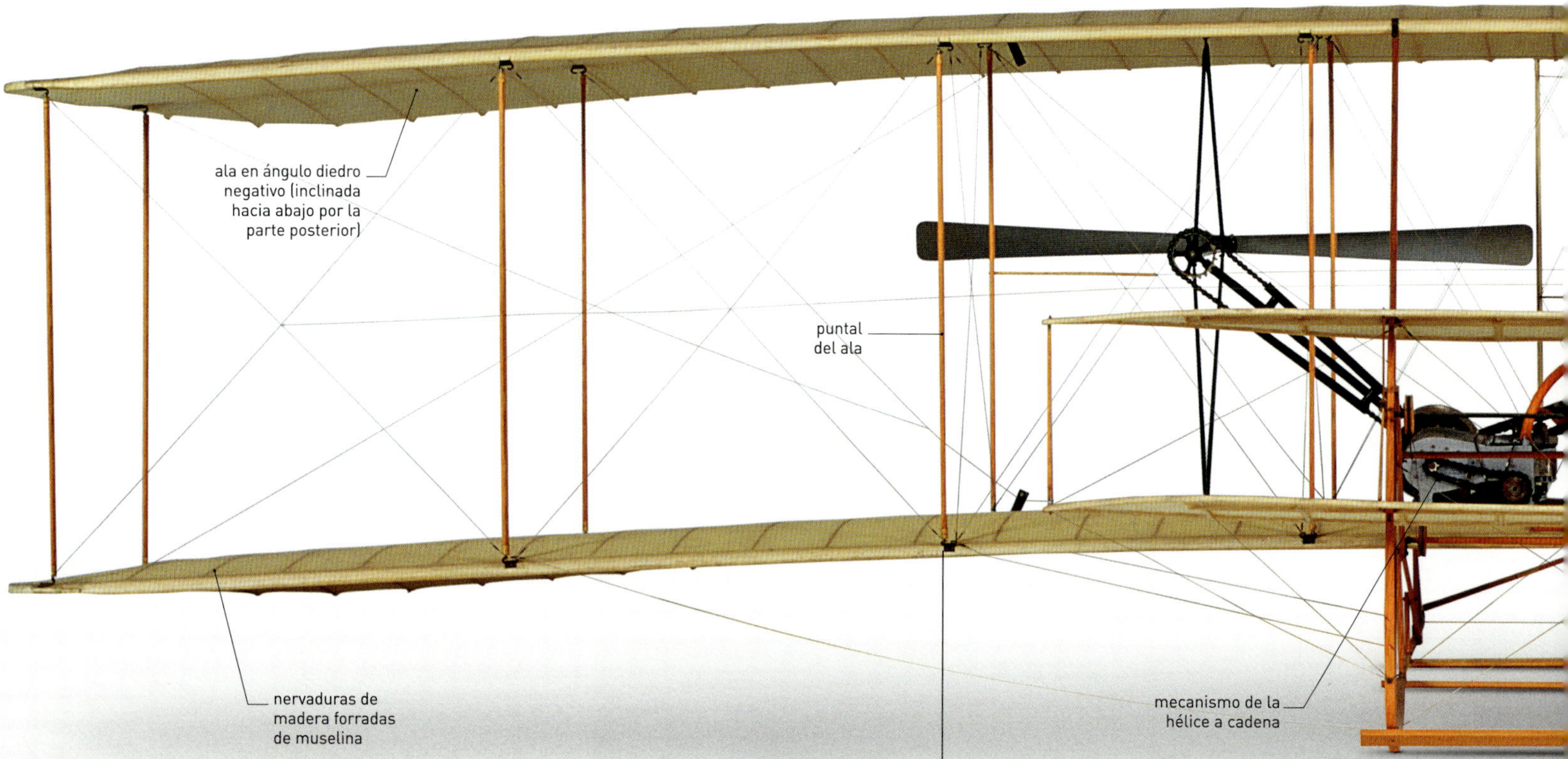

ala en ángulo diedro negativo (inclinada hacia abajo por la parte posterior)

puntal del ala

nervaduras de madera forradas de muselina

mecanismo de la hélice a cadena

C. 1485–1510
La máquina voladora de Leonardo da Vinci
Los primeros conceptos de vuelos humanos, como los esbozados por Da Vinci, se basan en el vuelo de las aves, pero técnicamente son impracticables.

Ornitóptero de Da Vinci

1783
Globo aerostático
Los hermanos franceses Joseph y Étienne Montgolfier realizan el primer vuelo tripulado en un globo de aire caliente.

Globo de los Montgolfier

1852
Primer vuelo a motor
El francés Henri Giffard acopla una máquina de vapor a un globo relleno de gas de carbón, con lo que comienza la aviación a motor.

Aeronave de Giffard

1900
Primer vuelo en zepelín
El 2 de julio, el dirigible LZ-1 del pionero alemán Ferdinand von Zeppelin ascendió con éxito a los cielos.

Zepelín

1903
El Wright Flyer
El 17 de diciembre, los hermanos Wright completaron su primer vuelo sostenido y controlado en una máquina a motor más pesada que el aire en Kill Devil Hills (Carolina del Norte, EE. UU.).

1909
Vuelo de larga distancia
El 25 de julio, el francés Louis Blériot sobrevuela el canal de la Mancha, entre Francia e Inglaterra.

Louis Blériot

1914
Aviación bélica
El uso de aviones para el combate transforma la aviación; por primera vez en la historia se producen decenas de miles de aviones en serie.

1919
Avances en la aviación
Se inaugura el primer servicio aéreo de pasajeros internacional programado entre Londres y París; nacen las primeras aerolíneas.

« NO ENTENDÍAMOS QUE **UN PÁJARO PUDIERA TENER ALGO IMPOSIBLE DE CONSTRUIR** A MAYOR ESCALA. »

Orville Wright (1873–1948), estadounidense pionero de la aviación

En 1903, los estadounidenses Orville y Wilbur Wright construyeron el primer avión con alas viable acoplando un motor a un planeador. Solventaron el problema de controlar el avión en pleno vuelo y, hacia 1905, tenían una máquina que permanecía en el aire hasta agotar el combustible. Los dirigibles ofrecían al principio un mayor rendimiento que los aviones, pero eran lentos y propensos a sufrir accidentes. Los hermanos Wright demostraron que los aviones con alas tenían un potencial asombroso para crecer en tamaño, alcance y velocidad. Hacia la década de 1930, los aviones de alto rendimiento superaban ya los 640 km/h y la evolución de los instrumentos de navegación mejoraba su seguridad. En las décadas de 1920 y 1930 las hazañas de los vuelos de larga distancia ensalzaron a los pilotos. Una década más tarde, aquellos vuelos se hicieron accesibles para los pasajeros que podían costearse un pasaje en la comodidad de cabinas presurizadas. Los motores de reacción permitieron a los aviones alcanzar velocidades supersónicas y bordear el espacio. Más adelante, la tecnología de los cohetes espaciales propulsó a los humanos al espacio. A partir de la década de 1970, el descenso de los precios convirtió la aviación en un sistema de transporte popular y accesible en todo el planeta. Los viajes en avión han acortado las distancias y encogido el mundo.

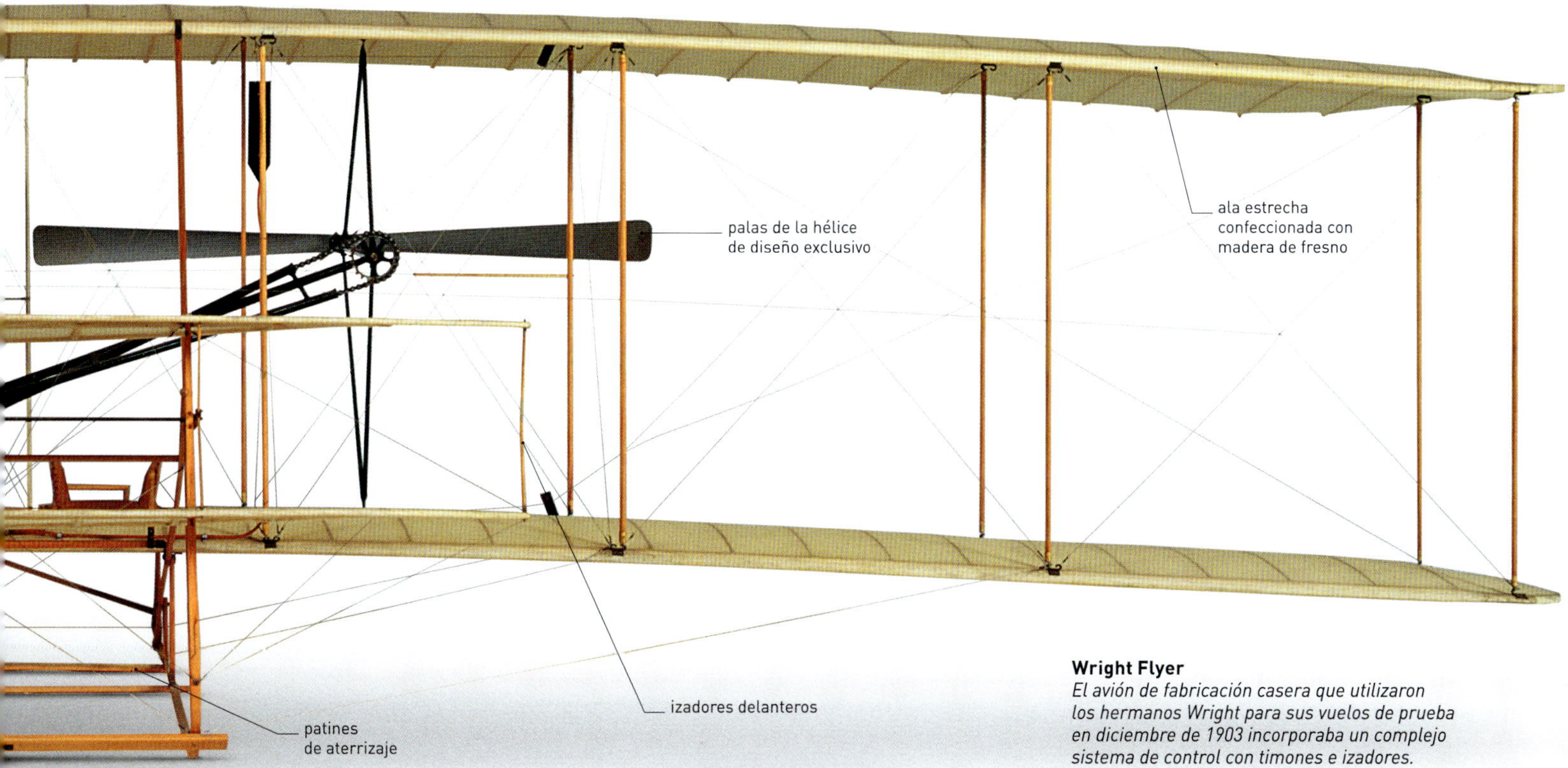

palas de la hélice de diseño exclusivo

ala estrecha confeccionada con madera de fresno

patines de aterrizaje

izadores delanteros

Wright Flyer
El avión de fabricación casera que utilizaron los hermanos Wright para sus vuelos de prueba en diciembre de 1903 incorporaba un complejo sistema de control con timones e izadores.

1927
Primer vuelo transatlántico sin paradas
Entre el 20 y el 21 de mayo, el estadounidense Charles Lindbergh voló en solitario y sin hacer escalas de Nueva York a París en un monoplano de un solo motor.

Spirit of St Louis

Sikorsky VS-300

Década de 1930
Aparición de los helicópteros
Louis Breguet fabrica los primeros helicópteros en Francia, la empresa Focke-Wulf lo hace en Alemania e Igor Sikorsky en EE. UU.

1935
El transporte aéreo se abarata
El avión de pasajeros Douglas DC-3 abarata y hace más viables los vuelos de pasajeros.

1939
Avión a reacción
El inglés Frank Whittle inventa el primer motor a reacción. El primer avión a reacción, el Heinkel He 178, supera con éxito el vuelo de prueba.

1947
Vuelo supersónico
El aviador estadounidense Chuck Yeager se convierte en el primer piloto del Bell X-1, el primer avión que rompió la barrera del sonido.

De Havilland Comet

1952
Primer avión comercial
Despega el prototipo del primer avión comercial, el De Havilland Comet. El transporte de pasajeros se incorpora en la historia de la aviación.

1961
Vuelos espaciales tripulados
El soviético Yuri Gagarin, el primer hombre en llegar al espacio. Orbita alrededor de la Tierra en su nave espacial, la *Vostok*.

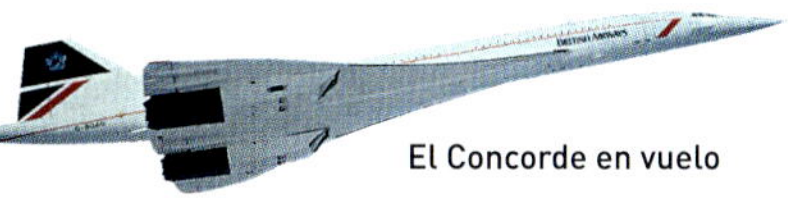

El Concorde en vuelo

1976
El Concorde entra en servicio
El Concorde, el primer avión supersónico de pasajeros, inicia su servicio comercial.

Lanzadera espacial *Columbia*

1981
Lanzaderas reutilizables
El *Columbia* se convierte en la primera lanzadera espacial enviada a la órbita de la Tierra, el 12 de abril.

1925

« LO MEJOR DE AMÉRICA EMIGRA **A PARÍS. »**

F. Scott Fitzgerald,
escritor estadounidense

Ernest Hemingway describió a la bailarina y cantante Josephine Baker como «la mujer más sensacional jamás vista».

PARÍS CONSOLIDÓ SU REPUTACIÓN como líder mundial en gusto y estilo con la **Exposición Internacional de Artes Industriales y Decorativas Modernas**. La muestra dio un nombre, ***Art Déco***, a la tendencia de diseño caracterizada por las formas angulosas, los estampados abstractos, los motivos africanos, aztecas y egipcios exuberantes, y materiales como el cromo y el marfil. El *Art Déco* pronto se convirtió en el estilo de toda suerte de cosas, desde perfumes hasta rascacielos, transatlánticos y cines.

Más desapercibida pasó una modesta muestra en una galería parisiense de obras de artistas **«surrealistas»**. El grupo, que incluía al catalán **Joan Miró** (1893–1983) y al estadounidense **Man Ray** (1890–1976), exploraba los sueños y los impulsos del subconsciente para subvertir la realidad cotidiana. Durante la década siguiente, el surrealismo devino un importante movimiento artístico internacional.

Man Ray formó parte del **ejército de expatriados estadounidenses que viajaron en masa a París** mediada la década de 1920 atraídos por la efervescente escena cultural y una tasa de cambio favorable. Entre los escritores estadounidenses residentes en París figuraban Gertrude Stein (1874–1976), Ernest Hemingway (1899–1961) y F. Scott Fitzgerald (1896–1940), quien publicó su obra clásica, *El gran Gatsby*, en 1925. La bailarina erótica afroamericana **Josephine Baker** (1906–1975) se convirtió en una estrella de la vida nocturna parisiense con sus actuaciones en el Theatre des Champs-Elyseés. Por su parte, los franceses se deleitaron con el jazz estadounidense.

Estilo surrealista
La obra Carnaval del arlequín *ejemplifica el estilo lúdico y anárquico concebido en la década de 1920 por Joan Miró, artista catalán afincado en París.*

En EE. UU., en Dayton (Tennessee), el maestro de biología **John Scopes fue enjuiciado** por enseñar la teoría de la evolución de Darwin. Scopes contó con el apoyo del Sindicato pro Libertades Civiles de EE. UU. para oponerse a la Ley Butler, recién aprobada en Tennessee, que prohibía impartir la evolución. Los fundamentalistas cristianos contrataron al ex secretario de Estado estadounidense William Jennings Bryan para la fiscalía y, tras un juicio que embelesó a EE. UU., Scopes fue **declarado culpable**, si bien el veredicto fue revocado más adelante.

El mundo vivía la mejor **coyuntura política y económica** desde la Primera Guerra Mundial. En abril, el canciller del Tesoro Público de Gran Bretaña, Winston Churchill, devolvió la divisa de su país al **patrón oro** de la preguerra. Con ello incrementó el valor de la libra esterlina a niveles artificiales, lo cual acarreó problemas a los exportadores británicos, si bien supuso un gesto importante hacia la restauración de la estabilidad financiera internacional.

En diciembre **se firmó el pacto de Locarno**, una serie de tratados diseñados para restaurar las relaciones de los tiempos de paz entre Alemania y los vencedores europeos de la Primera Guerra Mundial. El acuerdo dependió de la relación establecida entre los ministros de Exteriores alemán y francés, Gustav Stresemann y Aristide Briand, y alumbró el camino hacia la admisión de Alemania en la Sociedad de Naciones en 1926.

1926

Reza Kan Pahlavi en su trono tras ser designado sah de Irán. Su meta era modernizar el país en la línea laica de Occidente.

La primera cámara de televisión
Logie Baird ofreció la primera demostración de la televisión usando un sistema mecánico con un disco giratorio a modo de escáner.

EN ENERO DE 1926, EL INGENIERO ESCOCÉS JOHN LOGIE BAIRD (1888–1946) realizó la **primera** demostración de una **transmisión televisiva** en una buhardilla en el barrio londinense del Soho. Cincuenta miembros de la Royal Institution contemplaron la imagen en movimiento de una cara, poco definida, aunque reconocible.

En mayo, Gran Bretaña vivió su única **huelga general**. La parada industrial en todo el país en apoyo a los mineros del carbón paralizó las redes de transportes y los muelles, y cerró diarios y fábricas. El gobierno británico movilizó al ejército y reclutó voluntarios para mantener unos servicios mínimos. Tras nueve días, los sindicatos cedieron y ordenaron regresar al trabajo.

En **Polonia**, ante la inestabilidad del gobierno parlamentario, el héroe militar de la nación, el **mariscal Jozef Pilsudski** (1867–1935) **protagonizó un golpe de estado** en mayo. Pilsudski declinó la presidencia, si bien, a efectos prácticos, asumió poderes dictatoriales.

En Irán, otro hombre fuerte del cuerpo militar, **Reza Kan Pahlavi** (1878–1944), **fundó una nueva dinastía** al coronarse sah el 25 de abril; su intención era modernizar el país. La dinastía Pahlavi gobernó Irán hasta la década de 1970.

160 MILLONES DE JORNADAS LABORALES SE PERDIERON EN LAS HUELGAS DE **REINO UNIDO** EN **1926**

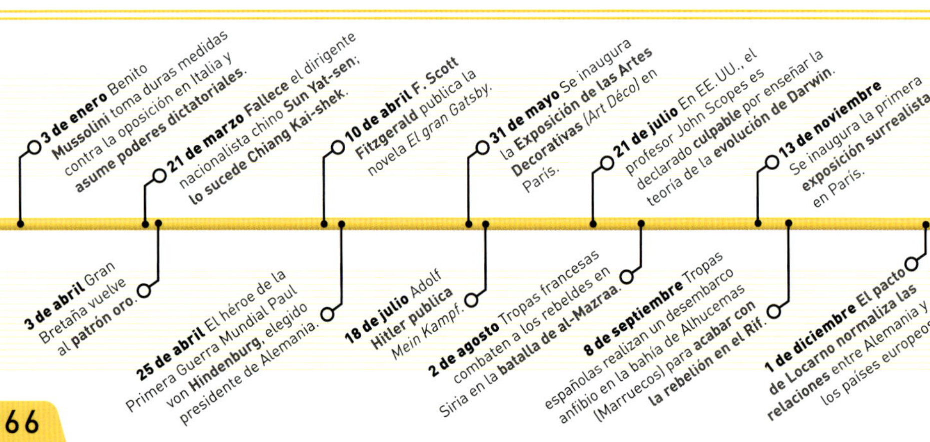

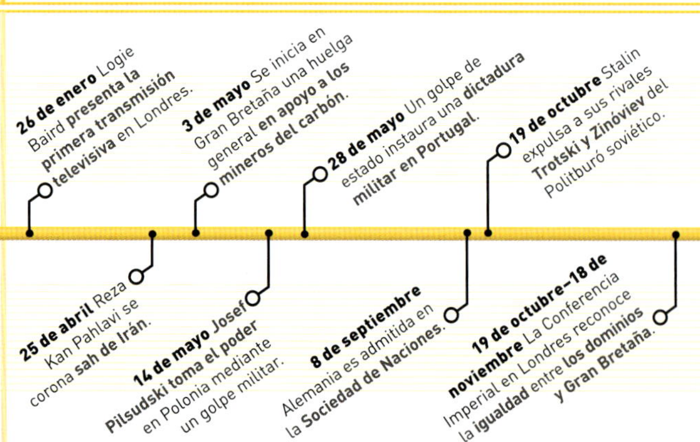

« EL MUNDO FUE MÍO DURANTE LA HORA QUE LO SOBREVOLÉ. »

Charles Lindbergh, aviador estadounidense

El aviador Charles Lindbergh posa ante el *Spirit of St Louis*, el avión en que realizó el primer vuelo sin escalas en solitario entre Nueva York y París.

EN MAYO DE 1927, A LOS 25 AÑOS, CHARLES LINDBERGH (1902–1974) **sobrevoló en solitario el Atlántico,** hazaña que le convirtió en el estadounidense vivo más famoso. La recompensa en metálico ofrecida a quien realizara el primer vuelo sin escalas entre Nueva York y París había estimulado una competición febril. El 8 de mayo, los célebres héroes de guerra franceses Charles Nungesser y François Coli intentaron realizar el vuelo desde París, pero se desviaron al oeste sobre el Atlántico y desaparecieron para siempre. Tales dramas habían alimentado la emoción cuando un tal Lindbergh, un piloto del correo aéreo, despegó del aeródromo de Roosevelt el día 20 de mayo a bordo de un monoplano de construcción propia. No solo logró aterrizar en **París al cabo de 33 horas y 30 minutos**, sino que realizó aquella proeza en solitario. Lindbergh fue asediado al aterrizar en Francia y las mieles de la fama lo acompañaron el resto de su vida. Su hazaña estimuló el crecimiento acelerado de la aviación comercial en EE. UU.

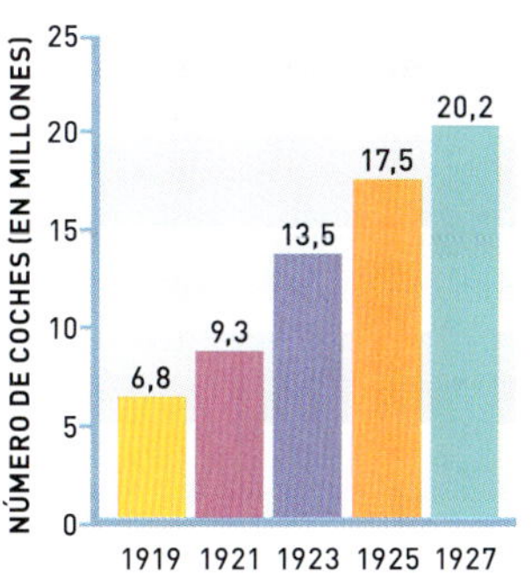

Vehículos en propiedad en EE. UU.
Entre 1919 y 1927, se triplicó la cifra de automóviles en las carreteras estadounidenses. En el mundo, cinco de cada seis estaban en EE. UU.

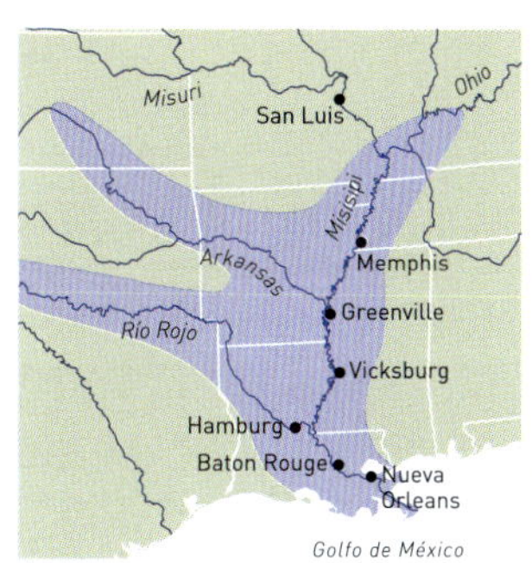

La gran inundación del Misisipi
Tras meses de fuertes precipitaciones, el río Misisipi rompió los diques de contención en la primavera de 1927, inundó una extensa zona (en morado) y cercenó 246 vidas.

El optimismo que vivía EE. UU. propició el **primer *boom* consumista moderno**, materializado en la compra de automóviles y electrodomésticos. Hacia 1927, uno de cada seis estadounidenses tenía coche, una cifra suficiente como para garantizar que incluso las familias modestas podían aspirar a un Ford Modelo T. El nivel de ahorro era elevado y muchos escogieron invertir en el mercado bursátil, en pleno auge.

Pero no todo eran buenas noticias. La **caída de los precios de productos agrícolas** azotaba las zonas rurales de todo el mundo y EE. UU., con la mitad de su población empleada en el campo, no era inmune a la crisis de precios. Los granjeros habían contraído fuertes deudas y pagaban mal a sus asalariados. Las deplorables condiciones experimentadas por muchos jornaleros se vieron exacerbadas en abril de 1927 por la **gran inundación del Misisipi**, la peor riada de la historia del país. Muchas de sus víctimas fueron negros paupérrimos; abandonados en campos de refugiados tras la catástrofe, muchos miles de ellos se sumaron a la emigración de afroamericanos desde el sur del país hacia las ciudades del norte en busca de una nueva y mejor vida.

Dos de las grandes cintas de la historia del cine se estrenaron en 1927: la futurista *Metrópolis*, de Fritz Lang, y la epopeya histórica de Abel Gance, *Napoleón*. Sin embargo, aquellas películas mudas inmensamente ambiciosas quedaron eclipsadas por el éxito de Al Jolson (1886–1950) en un filme sonoro, *El cantor de jazz*. Había nacido la nueva era de las **«películas habladas»**.

Tras el vuelo de Lindbergh en 1927, la segunda noticia más seguida fue la **ejecución de los anarquistas** Ferdinando **Sacco** y Bartolomeo **Vanzetti**. El caso de estos dos inmigrantes italianos dudosamente condenados por un asesinato en Massachusetts en 1920 se convirtió en un foco de protesta entre liberales y socialistas, y su ejecución en la silla eléctrica el 23 de agosto causó disturbios en ciudades de todo el mundo.

En la Unión Soviética, **León Trotski** (1879–1940) era expulsado del Comité Central del Partido Comunista gobernante en noviembre, junto con sus aliados Grigori Zinóviev y Lev Kámenev. Con maniobras arteras, el secretario general Stalin (1878–1953) consiguió desarticular a Trotski, antaño favorito para suceder a Lenin (1870–1924). Acusado de «faccionalismo», Trotski fue enviado en exilio interior a Kazajstán en enero del año siguiente, y finalmente **expulsado de la Unión Soviética** en febrero de 1929. Zinóviev y Kámenev se subordinaron a Stalin, pero este ordenó ejecutarlos en 1936.

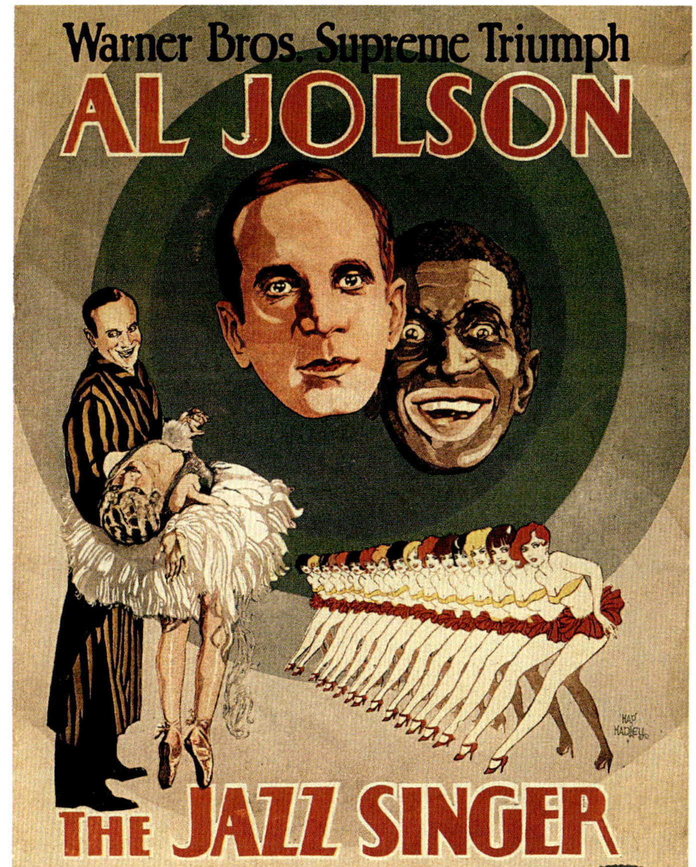

Primer largometraje sonoro
El primer largometraje sonoro que alcanzó el éxito, El cantor de jazz, *dejó 2,6 millones de dólares en las taquillas de EE. UU. e hizo famoso a Jolson.*

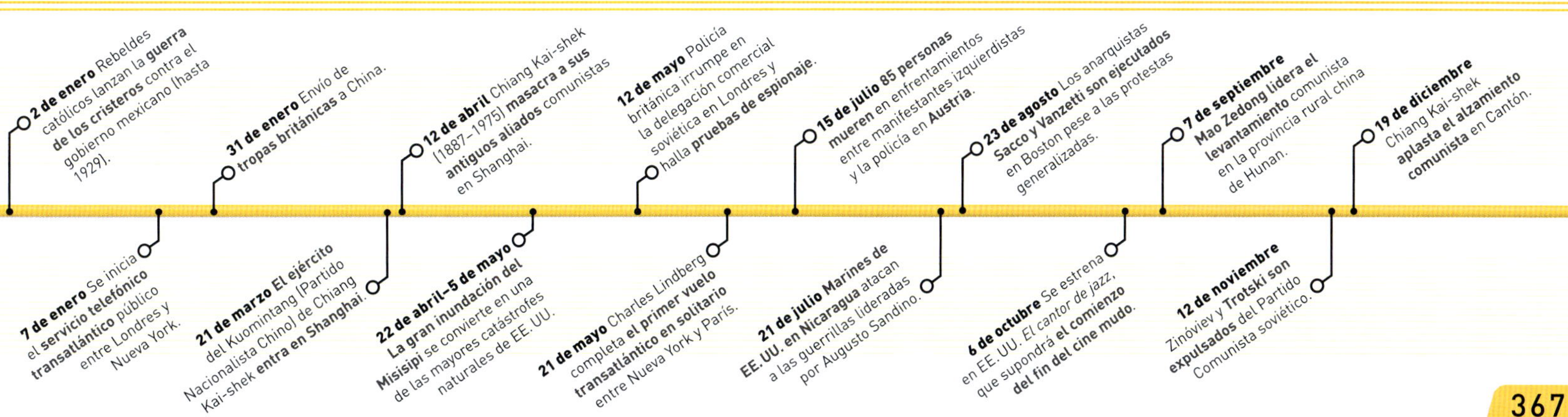

1928

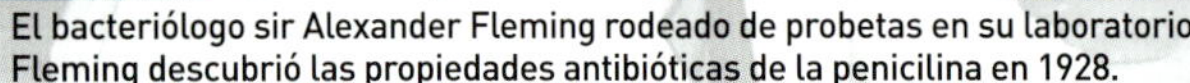

El bacteriólogo sir Alexander Fleming rodeado de probetas en su laboratorio. Fleming descubrió las propiedades antibióticas de la penicilina en 1928.

EN LA UNIÓN SOVIÉTICA, STALIN (1878–1953) inició una **reforma socioeconómica** radical. Abandonando el compromiso de Vladímir Lenin con la Nueva Política Económica (*véase* 1921), Stalin lanzó un **plan quinquenal** para transformar la URSS en un gran país industrializado. Tomó medidas enérgicas contra los empresarios y los campesinos prósperos que se habían beneficiado económicamente gracias a la revolución. Cientos de «expertos burgueses», gentes como ingenieros más valorados por sus habilidades que por su implicación en la revolución, fueron arrestados y **condenados por sabotaje**.

En China, el nacionalista Chiang Kai-shek (1887–1975), líder del **Kuomintang** (Partido Popular Nacional), estaba cerca de establecer su dominio en todo el país. Los caudillos militares que gobernaban las distintas zonas de China o bien se convirtieron en sus aliados o fueron derrotados por su ejército. En junio, fuerzas del Kuomintang tomaron Pekín y, en octubre, Chiang Kai-shek fundó formalmente un gobierno nacional, si bien aún afrontaba resistencia. Los **comunistas**, antiguos aliados del Kuomintang, sufrieron graves pérdidas cuando Chiang Kai-shek les dio la espalda en 1927. Expulsados de las ciudades, continuaron su lucha en las zonas rurales remotas; una extensa zona de las montañosas provincias de Jiangxi y Fujian quedó bajo el control del líder comunista Mao Zedong (*véase* 1921).

La violencia política también fue generalizada en el resto del mundo. En Yugoslavia, las hostilidades entre croatas y serbios se saldaron con el **asesinato del líder del Partido Campesino Croata, Stjepan Radić (1871–1928)**. Tiroteado por un oponente político serbomontenegrino en el parlamento yugoslavo el 20 de junio, falleció a causa de las heridas. Con su reino despedazado por las pulsiones nacionalistas, un año más tarde el rey de Yugoslavia, Alejandro I (1888–1934), ilegalizó los partidos políticos y asumió poderes dictatoriales.

En México, el **general Álvaro Obregón** (1880–1928), figura dominante de la política del país desde 1920, fue **asesinado** tras ser elegido presidente para un segundo mandato. Su asesino, José de León Toral, pertenecía al movimiento **cristero católico**, que había iniciado una rebelión armada en respuesta a las políticas anticlericales del gobierno mexicano. El deseo de estabilidad tras la conmoción por el asesinato de Obregón indujo a formar el **Partido Revolucionario Nacional**, el cual, bajo diversos nombres, dominó la política mexicana durante más de setenta años.

En Alemania parecía haberse alcanzado por fin la estabilidad tras el caótico periodo posterior a la Primera Guerra Mundial. En las elecciones al Reichstag de mayo, el **Partido Nazi** extremista de Adolf Hitler **consiguió menos de un 3% del voto popular**, comparado con el cerca de 30% de los socialdemócratas moderados. Bajo el riguroso sistema de representación proporcional de la República alemana, el apoyo mínimo a los nazis les otorgó doce escaños en el parlamento.

En agosto, Alemania fue uno de los signatarios originales de un acuerdo para «la renuncia a la guerra como instrumento de política nacional». El documento, muy optimista y popularmente conocido como el **pacto Kellogg-Briand**, en honor al secretario de Estado estadounidense Frank B. Kellogg (1856–1937) y al ministro de Asuntos Exteriores francés Aristide Briand (1862–1932), obligaba a los estados a recurrir a la guerra solo en caso de autodefensa. En menos de un año lo habían rubricado todas las grandes potencias mundiales.

Consecuencias más prácticas tuvo el **descubrimiento de la penicilina**. El científico escocés Alexander Fleming (1881–1955) descubrió por casualidad el moho antibiótico en platos de muestras contaminados, si bien fueron otros científicos quienes, en la década de 1940, desarrollaron la penicilina para uso médico.

IÓSIV STALIN
(1878–1953)

Nacido Iósiv Dzhugachvili en Georgia, Stalin se unió a los bolcheviques de Lenin en 1903. Tras el deceso de Lenin, desbancó a otros líderes bolcheviques y, en 1929, se alzó con el poder dictatorial. Lideró un estado policial despiadado, si bien también presidió la transformación de su país en una importante potencia industrial y lo condujo a una victoria sobre la Alemania nazi en 1945.

Sufrimiento en China
Prisioneros arrestados durante los enfrentamientos entre las fuerzas nacionalistas chinas y las del líder militar del norte Zhang Zuolin.

1929

Arma de la Ley seca
Una escopeta de doble cañón recortado oculto en una funda de violín era un arma típica de un gánster de esta década en EE. UU.

EL DÍA 14 DE FEBRERO, SIETE PERSONAS FUERON TIROTEADAS en un garaje de Chicago. Los perpetradores de la **masacre del Día de San Valentín** probablemente fueran miembros de la banda de **Al Capone** (1899–1947), figura destacada del crimen organizado. Las víctimas pertenecían a la banda rival de Bugs Moran. La principal fuente de ingresos de ambas bandas era el contrabando de bebidas alcohólicas que floreció bajo la Ley seca (*véase* 1920). Aquel crimen concentró la indignación ciudadana en la delincuencia y la violencia generalizadas de las ciudades estadounidenses. Las autoridades tuvieron que tomar medidas, como el arresto y encarcelamiento de Al Capone, acusado de evasión de impuestos, en 1931.

El 4 de marzo, el republicano **Herbert Hoover** (1874–1964) alcanzó la presidencia de EE. UU., lo cual coincidió con un punto álgido de auto-complacencia en torno al progreso económico del país. En la década de 1920, EE. UU. era el país con más automóviles en propiedad. El optimismo y la concesión fácil de créditos parecía hacer ascender los precios de las acciones en Wall Street dibujando una curva infinita (unos treinta millones de estadou-

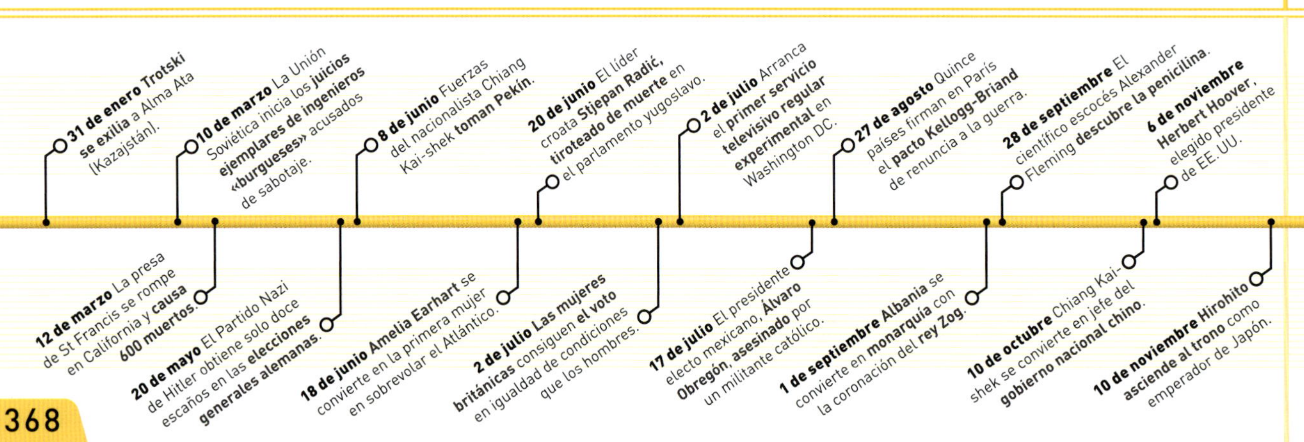

Herbert Hoover jura el cargo como presidente de EE. UU. Su discurso inaugural anticipó «el día en que la pobreza se desvanecerá de esta nación».

« CUALQUIER FALTA DE **CONFIANZA** EN EL **FUTURO ECONÓMICO** DE **ESTADOS UNIDOS** ES UNA **ESTUPIDEZ**. **»**

Herbert Hoover, en una alocución tras el hundimiento de la bolsa (15 de noviembre de 1929)

nidenses tenían inversiones en bolsa). En medio de este entusiasmo, era fácil que el presidente percibiera los problemas económicos –como la ruina de los pequeños granjeros por la caída de los precios de las cosechas, o los salarios por debajo de la línea de la pobreza que percibían muchos obreros urbanos– como baches superables.

El cine era un sector al alza de la economía estadounidense. **Hollywood** se había convertido en el corazón de la producción cinematográfica y sus *Big Five* (los cinco mayores estudios) producían como churros cientos de películas al año. La **industria del cine** vivía una revolución tecnológica, con la transición del cine mudo al cine sonoro. Cada vez más consciente de su situación e imagen, la Academia del Cine y de las Ciencias celebró los primeros **premios Oscar anuales** en 1929, y entregó el galardón a la mejor película a *Wings*, el primer filme mudo premiado con tal reconocimiento (el segundo no llegó hasta 2012 con *The Artist*).

Película ganadora
Wings, una cinta muda sobre los pilotos de bombarderos de la Primera Guerra Mundial, fue el primer filme que logró el Oscar a la mejor película.

En Italia, el régimen fascista de **Mussolini** (1883–1945) logró un triunfo diplomático al firmar el **tratado de Letrán** con el papa Pío XI. Desde la unificación de Italia en 1871 pervivía una disputa irresuelta entre el estado italiano y el papado, como parte de la cual los pontífices se consideraban «prisioneros» en el Vaticano. El tratado de Letrán reconoció la **Ciudad del Vaticano** como **estado independiente** y el catolicismo como la religión oficial de Italia. Extraoficialmente garantizó al régimen fascista el apoyo de la Iglesia católica.

Con la constitución por parte de los aliados de una comisión encabezada por el industrial Owen Young para reconsiderar **los pagos en reparación de Alemania** se realizó un nuevo intento de poner fin definitivo a la Primera Guerra Mundial. El **Plan Young**, que aceptaba que el Plan Dawes (*véase* 1924) había fijado unos pagos demasiado elevados, proponía a Alemania pagar una suma anual reducida hasta 1988. El gobierno alemán aceptó el acuerdo, pero se topó con el rechazo de los nacionalistas conservadores y de los nazis, quienes forzaron un referéndum sobre las reparaciones, que describían como «la esclavización del pueblo alemán». Y aunque solo un 14% de los votantes la respaldaron, aquella campaña por el referéndum subrayó el perfil político de Hitler en Alemania.

La larga sombra de la Primera Guerra Mundial se proyectó también en una **ola de libros antibelicistas**. Entre ellos figuraban *Adiós a las armas*, del estadounidense Ernest Hemingway; la memoria de la guerra del británico Robert Graves (1895–1985) *Adiós a todo esto*, y *Sin novedad en el frente*, del alemán Erich Maria Remarque (1898–1970). Estas obras, que presentaban la guerra como un desperdicio fútil de vidas humanas, capturaron el sentir popular de los tiempos.

No obstante, el hecho más destacado del año fue la **caída de Wall Street**. En septiembre, el alza de los valores bursátiles había titubeado. El 23 de octubre, los precios estaban en descenso y un día más tarde, el «Martes Negro», el **mercado se desplomó** por la estampida de ventas. En vano, el presidente Hoover aseguró a la ciudadanía que «el negocio fundamental del país se sustentaba en una base sólida y próspera». Las ventas de acciones siguieron y también lo hicieron las caídas pronunciadas. Los especuladores que habían comprado valores a crédito se arruinaron, como también ocurrió en el caso de miles de ciudadanos modestos que habían confiado los ahorros de su vida al parqué bursátil. Los expertos hablaban de «corrección del mercado» temporal, y Hoover emprendió medidas para estimular la economía y generar empleo, pero aquel desplome marcó el inicio de un largo derrumbe en los precios de las acciones y señaló el comienzo de una **depresión mundial**.

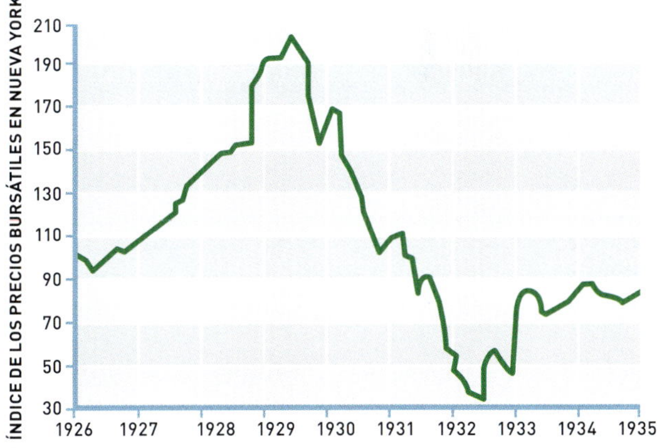

Índice de Wall Street
Los precios de las acciones en el mercado bursátil neoyorquino experimentaron un auge especulador en la década de 1920, seguido por un derrumbe irrefrenable.

14 de febrero Siete muertos en la **masacre del Día de San Valentín** a resultas de la guerra entre mafias en Chicago.

4 de marzo Herbert **Hoover se estrena** como presidente de EE. UU.

8 de abril Revolucionarios indios detonan una bomba en los pasillos de la **asamblea legislativa en Delhi**.

16 de mayo Se celebra la primera ceremonia de entrega de premios de la Academia (los **Oscar**).

8 de junio El gobierno laborista asume el poder en Gran Bretaña bajo **Ramsay Macdonald**.

21 de junio Una tregua mediada por EE. UU. pone fin a la **guerra de los cristeros** en México.

16 de agosto Disturbios en Palestina enfrentan a árabes y judíos.

8–29 de agosto El dirigible alemán *Graf Zeppelin* **da la vuelta al mundo**.

31 de agosto Se paraliza el **Plan Young** de pagos de reparación por parte de Alemania.

5 de septiembre El primer ministro francés Aristide Briand propone crear unos **Estados Unidos de Europa**.

24 de septiembre James Doolittle, piloto del ejército de EE. UU., realiza el **primer «vuelo a ciegas»** usando solo instrumentos de navegación.

28 de septiembre La **ley sarda** prohíbe en **India el matrimonio** de niñas menores catorce años.

3 de octubre Muere Gustav Stresemann, arquitecto de la mejoría en las relaciones de Alemania con Francia (n. 1878).

24–29 de octubre Los precios de las acciones se desploman en la **caída de Wall Street**.

31 de octubre Lord Irwin, el virrey británico de India, declara que India recibirá al fin el estado de dominio.

7 de noviembre Se inaugura el **Museo de Arte Moderno** (MoMA) en Manhattan.

17 de noviembre Nikolái **Bujarin**, el último rival de Stalin en el gobierno soviético, **es expulsado del Politburó**.

29 de diciembre El Congreso Nacional Indio **exige la independencia inmediata** de Gran Bretaña.

1930

« LLEVAMOS **CINCUENTA O CIEN AÑOS DE RETRASO** CON RESPECTO A LOS **PAÍSES AVANZADOS**. DEBEMOS **ACORTAR** ESTA **DISTANCIA** EN **DIEZ AÑOS**. **»**

Stalin, en un discurso pronunciado en la primera Conferencia de la URSS ante los máximos dirigentes de la industria socialista (4 de febrero de 1931)

Parados esperando el reparto de alimentos en Nueva York durante la Gran Depresión. En EE. UU. no existían subsidios por desempleo.

EN LOS PRIMEROS MESES DE 1930, LA UNIÓN SOVIÉTICA vivió una gran agitación debido a la **colectivización masiva de la agricultura**, es decir, la sustitución de las pequeñas granjas de propiedad privada por grandes industrias agrícolas estatales. A ojos del dictador Stalin (*véase* 1928), cuya voluntad era transformar la Unión Soviética en un estado industrial moderno, la agricultura campesina a pequeña escala era un obstáculo que debía erradicarse, pues, además de ser ineficaz, estaba teñida de intereses personales antisocialistas. Pero los campesinos estaban muy apegados a sus tierras y animales, y cuando se enviaba a los oficiales a las poblaciones a organizar las granjas colectivas, los recibían oponiendo **resistencia**. Los granjeros sacrificaban a sus animales antes de entregárselos al estado y atacaban a los comunistas con piedras y cachiporras. Se produjeron entonces **arrestos masivos de *kulaks*** (campesinos en buena posición económica) y alborotadores. En marzo se anunció que catorce millones de granjas soviéticas habían sido colectivizadas, pero el caos interrumpió la producción de alimentos y Stalin tuvo que ordenar una pausa en la campaña. No fue coincidencia que un mes después se **fundara el Gulag**, un organismo creado para dirigir un sistema de campos de trabajos forzados repartidos por la Unión Soviética. Del millón de campesinos arrestados a principios de los años treinta, cientos de miles acabaron en gulags (los campos del Gulag) y trabajaron como esclavos para impulsar el desarrollo de la economía soviética.

La colectivización fracasó en su intento de aumentar la producción agrícola y la imagen de las extensas praderas soviéticas aradas por tractores y cosechadoras mecánicas siguió siendo, en gran medida, una fantasía; lo que imperó fue una hambruna (*véase* 1933). Sí se estimuló, no obstante, una emigración masiva de campesinos a las ciudades, donde hallaron trabajo en obras de construcción y en fábricas. Los **proyectos industriales soviéticos**, muchos de los cuales empleaban mano de obra prisionera de los gulags, avanzaron mucho, mientras el resto del mundo se hundía en una recesión económica.

En **India**, Mahatma Gandhi (*véase* recuadro) organizó una campaña de **desobediencia civil** contra el mandato británico. Gandhi encarnó su oposición al monopolio sobre la sal del gobierno liderando una marcha desde Ahmedabad hasta el océano Índico. La inició el 12 de marzo, llegó al mar el 6 de abril y tomó con las manos un puñado de agua salada, en un desafío público a la prohibición de recoger sal sin licencia. Pese a que Gandhi abogaba por una no violencia estricta, la **Marcha de la Sal desencadenó disturbios** que se redoblaron tras su arresto el 5 de mayo. Con todo, los británicos mantuvieron su compromiso de ampliar gradualmente el limitado autogobierno de India.

Las hazañas de **aviadores** intrépidos siguieron fascinando al público, igual que en la década de 1920. Los pilotos se convirtieron en héroes al realizar por vez primera **vuelos de larga distancia**. Jean Mermoz (1901–1936), empleada de la empresa de correo postal francesa Aéropostale, efectuó en mayo el primer **vuelo postal al otro lado del Atlántico Sur**, pilotando un hidroavión sin hacer escalas entre Dakar (África Occidental) y Natal (Brasil), y estableció una línea de correo aéreo ininterrumpido entre Francia y Chile. Mientras, los británicos celebraban el vuelo en solitario de **la piloto aficionada Amy Johnson** (1903–1941) entre Croydon (Inglaterra) y Darwin (Australia) en un biplano De Havilland Gipsy Moth de segunda mano. El viaje, de 19 días, fue excepcional porque Johnson jamás había sobrevolado siquiera el Canal de la Mancha.

Aquel triunfo *amateur* de la aviación británica contrastó con el mal fario de un costoso proyecto gubernamental, el **dirigible *R101***. En su

MOHANDAS GANDHI
(1869–1948)

Conocido como Mahatma («gran alma»), Gandhi nació en el seno de una familia india privilegiada y estudió derecho en Londres. Sus primeras campañas de desobediencia civil tuvieron lugar en Sudáfrica. A su regreso a India en 1915 lideró la oposición al mandato británico, si bien muchos nacionalistas rechazaban su no violencia. Fue asesinado en 1948 por extremistas hindúes por su actitud conciliatoria hacia los musulmanes.

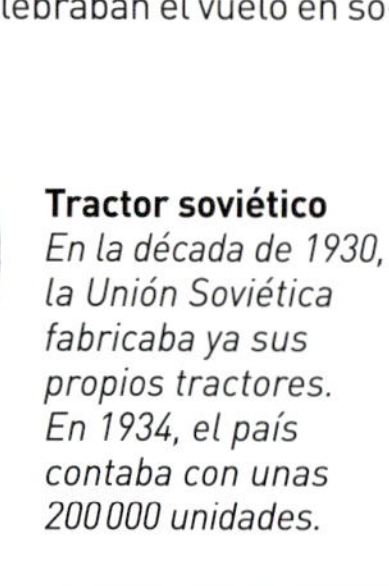

Tractor soviético
En la década de 1930, la Unión Soviética fabricaba ya sus propios tractores. En 1934, el país contaba con unas 200 000 unidades.

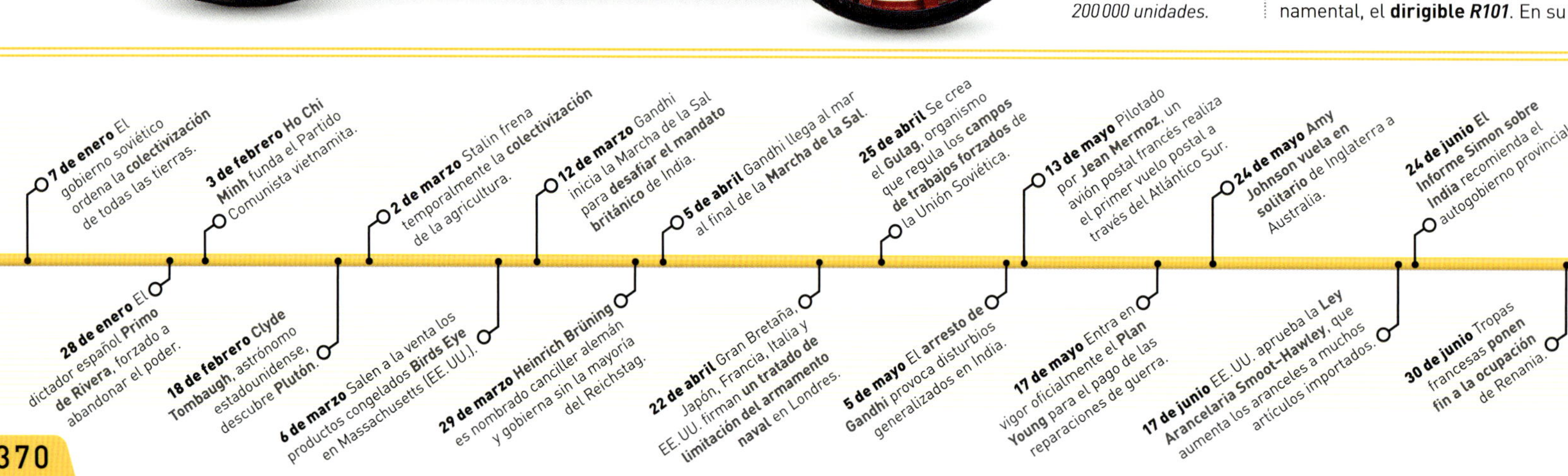

Los restos incinerados del dirigible británico *R101* yacen en un campo a las afueras de Beauvais, en el norte de Francia. El secretario del Aire británico falleció en el accidente.

Vuelo famoso
La aviadora británica Amy Johnson tras su vuelo en solitario desde Inglaterra hasta Australia.

viaje inaugural, en octubre, el *R101* debía transportar al secretario de Estado para el Aire británico y a otros dignatarios de Inglaterra a India. El avión, mal diseñado, no pasó de Francia, donde se estrelló a causa del mal tiempo y se cobró la vida de 48 de sus 54 pasajeros.

Pero el peor desastre de la década lo protagonizó el desplome de la **economía mundial**. En EE. UU., a principios de año, la mayoría de los comentaristas opinaban que, en la estela de la caída bursátil (*véase* 1929), el país afrontaba una recesión económica modesta y efímera. En mayo, el **presidente Herbert Hoover** (1874–1964) tranquilizó a la ciudadanía afirmando que «lo peor había pasado». Sin embargo, el desempleo siguió aumentando, las colas para recibir comida gratis se convirtieron en una imagen habitual, numerosos granjeros se declaraban en bancarrota y más de 1300 **bancos** estadounidenses **quebraron** ese año. EE. UU. cometió el error de aliviar a sus granjeros y desempleados bloqueando las importaciones. La **Ley Arancelaria Smoot-Hawley**, que entró en vigor en junio, gravó fuertes aranceles a miles de artículos importados. Cuando los socios comerciales de EE. UU. tomaron represalias, el mundo entero se abocaba a una reducción desastrosa de los niveles comerciales generales.

En **Alemania**, la crisis económica alimentó el extremismo político y el **hundimiento del gobierno democrático**. En marzo, la coalición gobernante se desmembró al negarse los socialdemócratas a recortar el subsidio por desempleo. Heinrich Brüning (1855–1970), líder del Partido de Centro, formó un gobierno sin el apoyo mayoritario del Reichstag. En julio disolvió el parlamento y convocó elecciones generales con un desempleo generalizado como telón de fondo. El Partido Nazi de Adolf Hitler orquestó una campaña electoral espectacular, en la que culpó de todos los problemas de Alemania al tratado de Versalles (*véase* 1919). Los **nazis aumentaron sus escaños** en el Reichstag de 12 a 107, convirtiéndose en el segundo partido más importante del país. Brüning respondió ante un Reichstag polarizado ignorándolo y aferrándose al poder, gobernando por un decreto de emergencia.

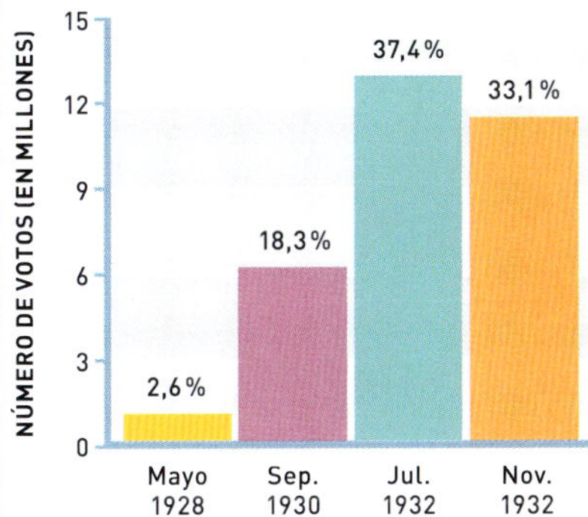

Voto nazi en las elecciones federales (1928–1932)
El Partido Nazi, que en 1928 era un partido extremista minoritario, se convirtió en el partido más votado en verano de 1932, con un 37,4 % de los votos.

Fuera de Alemania se observaba con inquietud el respaldo creciente al extremismo nacionalista y agresivo de Hitler. Francia mostró su desconfianza en un futuro pacífico construyendo fortificaciones defensivas a lo largo de su frontera con Alemania. Con el fin de garantizar la seguridad, **la línea Maginot** consumió gran parte del presupuesto de defensa de Francia en la década de 1930.

América del Sur fue especialmente vulnerable a la depresión económica internacional por su papel como proveedora de alimentos y materias primas a EE. UU. y Europa. Muchos países experimentaron **turbulencias políticas** al agravarse la situación económica. En **Brasil**, una revuelta del ejército encumbró a Getúlio Vargas (1882–1954) en el poder en noviembre. Vargas instauró una dictadura populista que impulsó la industrialización de Brasil y erradicó la disidencia política, al tiempo que introdujo medidas de bienestar social para los pobres. En **Argentina**, un golpe de estado militar desencadenó una década de conflicto político y corrupción gubernamental.

Mientras, en Japón, los nacionalistas radicales, incluidos oficiales del ejército y la Marina, creyeron que la respuesta a los **problemas económicos** estribaba en la conquista militar. El gobierno civil del primer ministro, **Osachi Hamaguchi** (1870–1931), los indignó aún más al proponer recortes en el gasto militar para compensar el déficit presupuestario. El 14 de noviembre, Hamaguchi fue tiroteado en la estación de Tokio por un miembro de una sociedad secreta nacionalista. Jamás se recuperó: falleció nueve meses más tarde. Fue un mal presagio de la determinación de los militaristas japoneses de llevar a la práctica sus agresivas políticas expansionistas.

Asesinato en Japón
El primer ministro Hamaguchi tras ser tiroteado por un extremista nacionalista en la estación de Tokio. Falleció menos de un año después.

18 de julio El canciller alemán Brüning **disuelve el Reichstag** y gobierna mediante un decreto de emergencia.

28 de julio En **Canadá**, los conservadores derrotan al Partido Liberal en el gobierno en los **comicios federales**.

30 de julio Uruguay derrota a Argentina en la **primera final de la Copa del Mundo de fútbol**.

5 de agosto El censo de EE. UU. establece la población de EE. UU. en **122,7 millones de personas**.

22 de agosto El presidente peruano **Augusto Leguía**, destituido por un golpe militar.

6 de septiembre José Félix Uriburu toma el poder mediante un golpe de estado en Argentina.

8 de septiembre El parlamento **canadiense** convoca una sesión especial para responder al **desempleo creciente**.

14 de septiembre El **Partido Nazi** de Hitler **obtiene** 107 escaños en las elecciones al Reichstag alemán.

5 de octubre El **dirigible** británico *R101* **se estrella** en Francia en su viaje inaugural.

17 de octubre El Presidente de EE. UU., Herbert Hoover, funda el **Comité para la Ayuda al Desempleo**.

2 de noviembre Haile **Selassie es coronado** emperador de Etiopía.

3 de noviembre Getúlio Vargas asume el poder en **Brasil** tras la revuelta militar.

4 de noviembre Chiang Kai-shek se impone a los generales chinos rivales en la **guerra de las Planicies Centrales**.

12 de noviembre Se inaugura en Londres la primera conferencia sobre el **futuro de India**.

14 de noviembre El primer ministro japonés, **Hamaguchi, tiroteado** por nacionalistas extremistas.

2 de diciembre El presidente de EE. UU., Hoover, solicita al congreso 150 millones de dólares para proyectos para **estimular el empleo**.

8 de diciembre Nacionalistas indios asesinan al inspector general de prisiones británico en Calcuta.

16 de diciembre Los sindicatos declaran la **huelga general** en España.

« LA **CADENA CAPITALISTA AMENAZA CON ROMPERSE** DE NUEVO POR EL PUNTO MÁS DÉBIL. **ESPAÑA** ES **LA SIGUIENTE EN LA COLA. »**

León Trotski, revolucionario ruso, hablando sobre la revolución en España (enero de 1931)

Manifestantes en Madrid celebran la revolución de abril de 1931 que derrocó a la monarquía española. Entre las nuevas reformas figuró el sufragio femenino.

Riesgos de altura
El fotógrafo Lewis Hine documentó los riesgos que corrieron los obreros en la construcción del Empire State.

EL 14 DE ABRIL DE 1931, EL REY ALFONSO XIII DE BORBÓN (1886–1941) abdicó y huyó al exilio cuando sus partidarios fueron derrotados en las elecciones municipales. Los vencedores de aquella revolución sin derramamiento de sangre, una coalición de republicanos moderados y socialistas, establecieron un gobierno provisional encabezado por Niceto Alcalá-Zamora (1877–1949). La partida del rey y la **fundación de la Segunda República española** infundió esperanza a los pobres del entorno urbano y rural, así como a los nacionalistas del País Vasco y Cataluña, pero los oficiales del ejército, los terratenientes, los industriales y la jerarquía católica se oponían categóricamente al cambio. España se adentraba en la senda de una guerra civil.

En Nueva York, el **Empire State se inauguró oficialmente** el 1 de mayo. Con sus 443 m de altura hasta su aguja, sobrepasó al edificio Chrysler, de estilo *Art Déco*, que había sido el **más alto del mundo** durante apenas once meses. Iniciado en 1929, en el punto álgido del mercado bursátil en EE. UU., el Empire State reflejaba el optimismo ilimitado de la época. Sin embargo, su finalización se produjo sobre un trasfondo de granjeros arruinados y un desempleo galopante.

Entre tanto, la recesión económica mundial se acentuó a resultas de una grave **crisis bancaria europea**. En mayo, el principal banco austriaco, el Creditanstalt, quebró y, para julio, muchos grandes bancos alemanes amenazaban con cerrar. El canciller alemán Heinrich Brüning propuso una unión fronteriza entre Alemania y Austria, y sugirió que Alemania podía incumplir su promesa de pagar las reparaciones por la guerra. La respuesta hostil de Francia consistió en negarse a ayudar a apuntalar el sistema financiero alemán. Alemania y Francia se vieron obligadas a adoptar medidas de emergencia para impedir que los inversores extranjeros retiraran sus fondos.

Gran Bretaña había realizado cuantiosos préstamos a bancos alemanes, capital que quedó congelado. Con la **amenaza de una crisis cerniéndose sobre sus cabezas**, expertos financieros aconsejaron al **gobierno laborista de Ramsay Macdonald** (1886–1937) que recortara gastos para equilibrar los presupuestos. En agosto, la propuesta de reducir los subsidios por desempleo y las pagas de los funcionarios públicos provocó la dimisión en bloque de los ministros laboristas. Macdonald continuó como primer ministro tras formar un gobierno nacional de coalición con los otros dos grandes partidos, los conservadores y los liberales. Una huelga en la Royal Navy por las pagas en Invergordon asustó a los inversores extranjeros y devaluó la libra esterlina en un cuarto de su valor.

El acontecimiento más agorero del año fue **la agresión de Japón a China**. El 18 de septiembre, oficiales del ejército japonés que protegían la línea de ferrocarril del sur de Manchuria sabotearon las vías y culparon a los chinos del suceso. El llamado **incidente de Mukden** dio a los japoneses el pretexto para **ocupar militarmente Manchuria**. La Sociedad de Naciones condenó la ocupación, pero Japón se negó a retirarse. Un año después, Japón instauró un gobierno títere en Manchuria bajo **Pu Yi** (1906–1967), el último emperador chino, que había sido destronado en 1912.

Entre septiembre y diciembre se celebró en Londres una **mesa redonda en torno al futuro de India**. **Mahatma Gandhi** (1869–1948) representaba al Congreso Nacional indio, el principal movimiento na-

Ocupación de Manchuria
Corea pasó a ser colonia japonesa en 1910. En 1931, los japoneses extendieron su dominio a Manchuria, que se convirtió en el estado títere de Manchukuo.

CLAVE
- Imperio japonés (1930)
- Ámbito de influencia japonesa (1930)
- Conquistas japonesas (1931–1933)

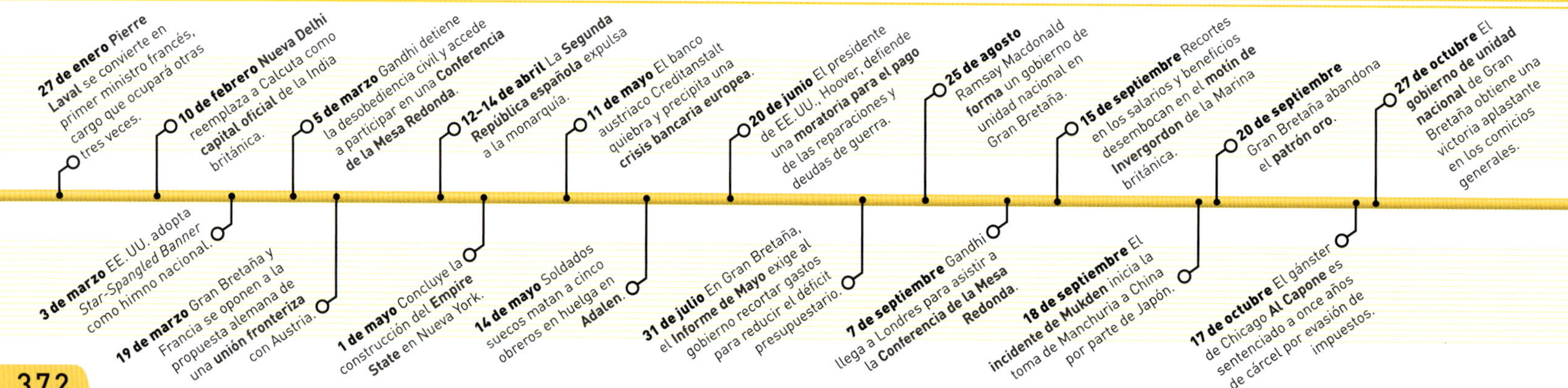

La piloto estadounidense Amelia Earhart aterriza en Inglaterra tras su legendario vuelo transatlántico en solitario en un monoplano Lockheed Vega.

Soldados japoneses en Manchuria
La ocupación japonesa de la provincia septentrional china de Manchuria puede leerse como el primer paso hacia la Segunda Guerra Mundial.

cionalista del país. Había negociado con el virrey británico de India, lord Irwin, la suspensión de la campaña de desobediencia civil (*véase* 1930). Pero la Conferencia de la Mesa Redonda fracasó y, a su regreso a India, Gandhi retomó su campaña pacífica contra los británicos.

En contraste con el tratamiento que los británicos dispensaban a India, el parlamento británico aprobó el **Estatuto de Westminster** en diciembre, por el cual se **reconocía la igualdad plena** entre Gran Bretaña y sus dominios: Australia, Nueva Zelanda, Canadá, Sudáfrica, el Estado Libre Irlandés y Terranova. Para ellos, el Imperio británico se había convertido en una verdadera Commonwealth («comunidad») de naciones.

42 FUERON LOS **ESTADOS DONDE ROOSEVELT SE IMPUSO** EN LOS **COMICIOS DE 1932 EN EE. UU.**

EN EL AÑO ÁLGIDO DE LA GRAN DEPRESIÓN, el declive de la producción y el pronunciado descenso del comercio comportaron un **desempleo generalizado** en los principales países industrializados del mundo. Al menos trece millones de estadounidenses, unos tres millones de británicos y más cinco millones de alemanes se quedaron en paro. En Europa, los programas de subsidios de desempleo nacionales ayudaron a los parados a sobrevivir, pero, en EE. UU., donde solo existían programas de bienestar locales y poco sistemáticos, el desempleo condujo a una pobreza atroz. Miles de personas perdieron sus hogares y acabaron viviendo en barrios de chabolas apodados irónicamente ***Hoovervilles***, en alusión al presidente de EE. UU.

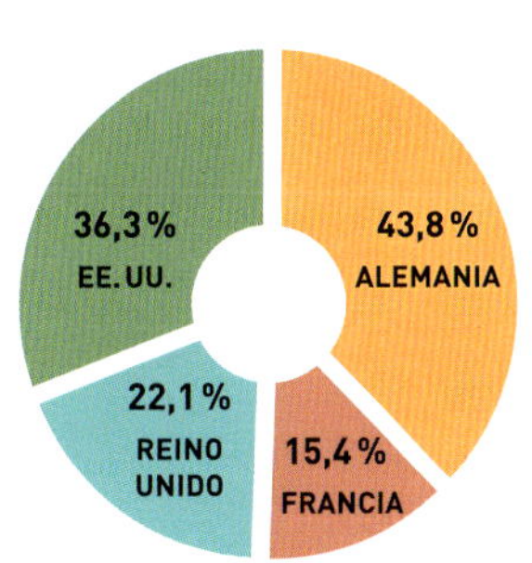

Desempleo industrial
En Alemania, la tasa máxima en el sector industrial se alcanzó en el momento culminante de la depresión, seguida de cerca por EE. UU.

En Irlanda, **Éamon de Valera** (1882–1975) se alzó con la presidencia tras lograr la victoria con el partido Fianna Fàil en marzo. De Valera, un republicano que había participado en el alzamiento de Pascua (*véase* 1916) y dirigido el Ejército Republicano Irlandés (IRA) en la guerra civil de Irlanda (*véase* 1922), era célebre por sus sentimientos antibritánicos. Revocó el juramento de lealtad a la corona británica y declaró una **guerra comercial a Gran Bretaña** que dañó a ambos países.

En Alemania, Adolf Hitler (1889–1945) vio frustrada su campaña de acceder al poder mediante el proceso democrático. Se postuló como presidente en las elecciones de primavera, pero fue derrotado por Paul von Hindenburg (1845–1934), titular del cargo. Pese a que en los comicios al Reichstag **los nazis fueron el partido único más votado**, siguieron quedando excluidos del gobierno. Ignorando el Reichstag, Hindenburg instaló una camarilla conservadora en el poder.

La noticia alegre la aportó la piloto estadounidense Amelia Earhart (1897–1937) al convertirse en la **primera mujer en sobrevolar el Atlántico en solitario**. Tras despegar de Terranova (Canadá) la mañana del 20 de mayo, en el quinto aniversario del famoso vuelo de Charles Lindbergh (*véase* 1927), aterrizó en un campo en Irlanda del Norte 14 horas y 56 minutos después.

En noviembre se celebraron elecciones presidenciales en EE. UU. sobre un trasfondo de desempleo en ascenso, cierres bancarios y granjas en bancarrota. La incapacidad de Herbert Hoover para detener la caída de su país durante la Gran Depresión le daba pocas esperanzas de vencer a su rival demócrata y ex gobernador de Nueva York, **Franklin D. Roosevelt** (*véase* 1933). Durante su campaña, Roosevelt prometió un «nuevo pacto para el pueblo estadounidense». Ganó con un 57,4 % del voto popular, si bien no estaba claro cuál era la estrategia de Roosevelt para detener la crisis.

EL «BONUS ARMY»

En el verano de 1932, más de veinte mil veteranos de la Primera Guerra Mundial en el paro se congregaron en Washington para exigir al gobierno el pago de una «bonificación» en reconocimiento por su servicio militar. Establecieron un barrio de chabolas a pocos metros del Capitolio y se negaron a abandonarlo hasta que les pagaran. Su protesta despertó la simpatía de los estadounidenses, acuciados por el desempleo, pero el presidente Hoover se negó a pagarles. El 28 de julio se desplegó a la infantería, a la caballería y a los tanques para desmantelar el campamento y al «Bonus Army».

- **7 de noviembre** Se proclama la **República Soviética China** en el Primer Congreso Soviético de China.
- **10 de diciembre Alcalá-Zamora** se convierte en presidente de la República Española.
- **31 de diciembre** El **Estatuto de Westminster** crea la Commonwealth de Naciones británica.
- **28 de enero** Tropas japonesas **atacan Shanghái** (China).
- **2 de febrero** El presidente de EE. UU., Hoover, funda la **Corporación Financiera de Reconstrucción** para combatir el desempleo.
- **18 de febrero** Japón proclama la **república títere de Manchukuo** en Manchuria.
- **19 de marzo** Inauguración **del puente de Sidney.**
- **10 de abril Hindenburg es reelegido** presidente de Alemania, superando el desafío de Hitler.
- **15 de mayo** El primer ministro japonés, Tsuyoshi **Inukai, es asesinado** por oficiales de la Marina.
- **20–21 de mayo Amelia Earhart**, la primera mujer **en sobrevolar en solitario** el océano Atlántico.
- **15 de junio** Estalla la **guerra del Chaco** entre Paraguay y Bolivia.
- **5 de julio Oliveira Salazar** es designado primer ministro de Portugal.
- **8 de julio** El índice selectivo **Dow Jones** cae a su nivel más bajo.
- **29 de julio** En Washington, el **«Bonus Army»** de desempleados es dispersado por la fuerza.
- **30 de julio** Se inauguran los **Juegos Olímpicos** en Los Ángeles.
- **31 de julio** El Partido Nazi obtiene 230 escaños en el **Reichstag alemán** y se convierte en el partido mayoritario.
- **1 de octubre** Oswald Mosley forma la **Unión Británica de Fascistas.**
- **3 de octubre** Declaración oficial de la independencia del **Reino de Iraq** de Gran Bretaña.
- **6 de noviembre** El apoyo a los nazis cae y logran solo 192 escaños en las nuevas **elecciones al Reichstag.**
- **8 de noviembre** Franklin D. Roosevelt gana por mayoría aplastante las **elecciones presidenciales de EE. UU.**

HISTORIA DE LA COMUNICACIÓN

LA ELECTRICIDAD ALUMBRÓ UNA REVOLUCIÓN EN LOS MEDIOS DE COMUNICACIÓN MASIVOS Y PERSONALES

receptor

La comunicación mundial instantánea se ha convertido en un rasgo definidor del mundo moderno. Hasta hace 200 años, la mayoría de los mensajes a larga distancia viajaban tan rápido como el caballo o el barco que los transportaba. La invención de la electricidad en el siglo XIX transformó las comunicaciones.

En el siglo XVIII, la Marina francesa ingenió un sistema para transmitir órdenes entre buques utilizando un código de señales. A partir de 1790, dicho código se usó también en tierra, donde cadenas de estaciones transmitían mensajes cifrados mediante grandes dispositivos de señalización, cada uno visible por la estación siguiente. De 1830 en adelante, el telégrafo eléctrico sustituyó este medio. El estadounidense Samuel Morse inventó un sistema robusto y práctico, una simple clave de activación y desactivación que generaba un código transmitido a través de un cable. En la década de 1860, el telégrafo unía continentes y el cableado subacuático permitía comunicaciones transoceánicas casi instantáneas. A finales del siglo XIX y principios del XX, la invención del teléfono permitió la transmisión electrónica de la voz. El hallazgo de que las ondas de radio podían transmitir sonido abrió un nuevo mundo de posibilidades para la retransmisión. A partir de la década de 1920, la radio se generalizó en los hogares. La televisión, por el contrario, no se convirtió en un medio de comunicación de masas hasta la década de 1950.

El auge de Internet y las redes sociales
Con el acceso de la mitad de la población mundial a Internet y más del 30 % empleando alguna red social, ambos son parte integral de la vida cotidiana.

LA ERA DE LA INFORMACIÓN

Varias líneas de desarrollo revolucionaron las comunicaciones tras la Segunda Guerra Mundial y dieron lugar a la «era de la información». La aparición de los transistores abarató los electrodomésticos y redujo su tamaño, y la tecnología espacial permitió colocar satélites en el espacio y proporcionar redes de comunicación mundiales. El triunfo de la tecnología digital y de los microprocesadores a partir de la década de 1980 prácticamente universalizó los ordenadores. Así, el flujo potencial de información mundial se volvió ilimitado.

Llamada de larga distancia
Alexander Graham Bell inaugura la primera línea telefónica entre Nueva York y Chicago en 1892. Para entonces, Nueva York ya estaba conectado con Boston y Filadelfia.

Prehistoria
Señales de humo
El fuego permite enviar señales de humo a distancias considerables. El inconveniente de este método es que se limita a un conjunto limitado de mensajes predefinidos.

Tablilla sumeria

3100–2500 a. C.
Escritura cuneiforme
La escritura supuso un gran avance en la comunicación. La escritura cuneiforme mesopotámica se grababa en tablillas de arcilla sumerias.

2900–2350 a. C.
Palomas mensajeras
En el antiguo Egipto y Persia se adiestran palomas mensajeras. Los ejércitos seguirán usándolas en las guerras mundiales.

Siglos I y II
Cartas por mensajero
En el Imperio romano, las cartas se escribían en papiro o madera. Las tablillas de Vindolanda de la Bretaña romana incluyen una invitación a un cumpleaños.

Tablilla de Vindolanda

Siglo XVII
Periódicos
Los periódicos, que difunden la información entre el gran público, aparecieron en Europa en el siglo XVII. La invención de la imprenta estimuló su desarrollo.

The London Post

1784
Diligencias de correos
Gran Bretaña introduce diligencias de cuatro caballos, más veloces que los carruajes con pasajeros, para el transporte del correo entre las grandes ciudades.

1791–1795
Telegrafía visual
El francés Claude Chappe es el primero en aplicar un código de señales que permite transmitir mensajes cifrados mediante cadenas de estaciones repetidoras.

Telégrafo de Chappe

Receptor de Morse

1837
Telegrafía eléctrica
El inventor Samuel Morse inventa el telégrafo eléctrico en EE. UU. El ferrocarril británico usa el telégrafo eléctrico.

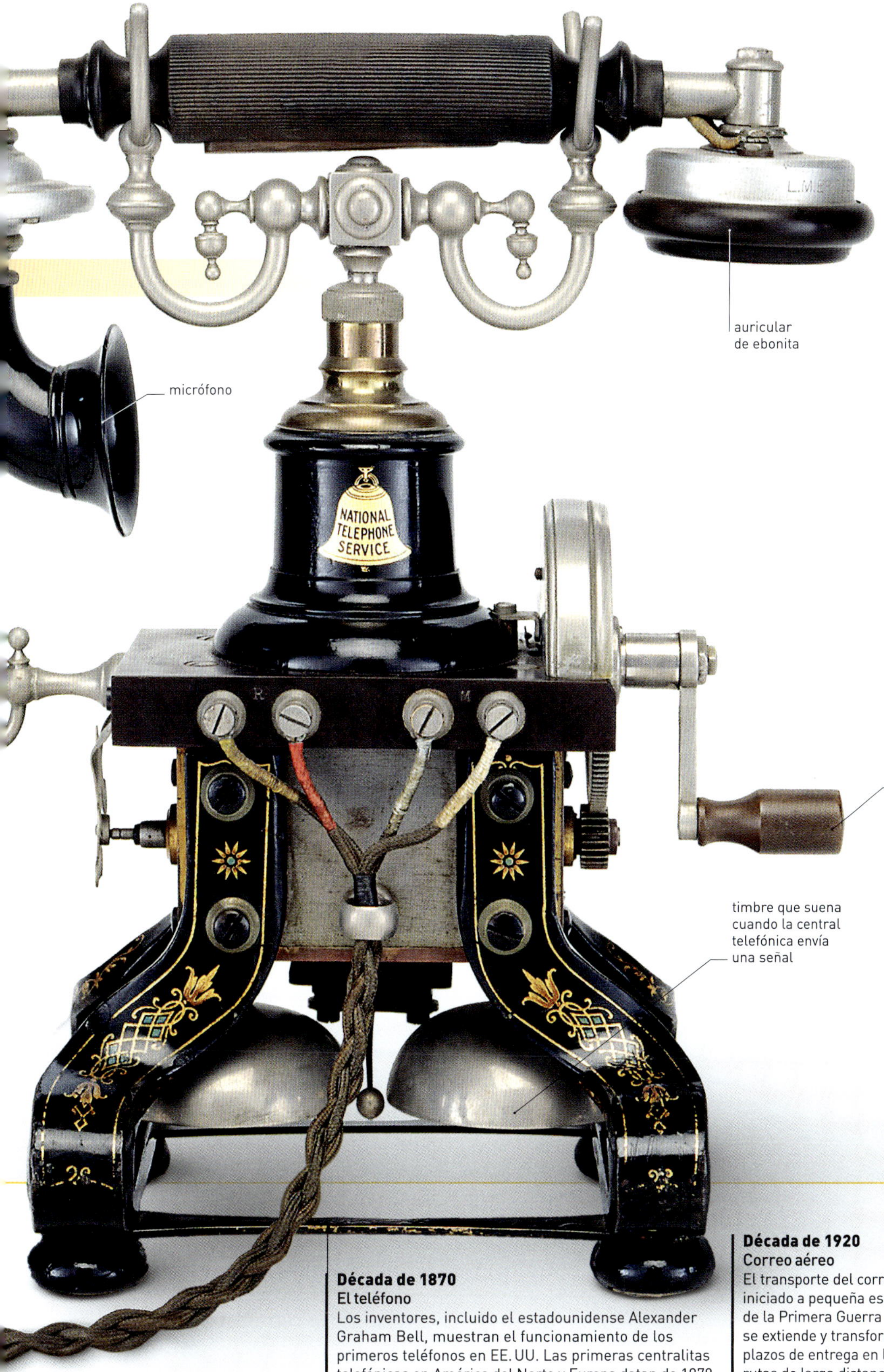

« ES UN **INVENTO ASOMBROSO**, PERO ¿QUIÉN VA A QUERER USARLO? »

Rutherford B. Hayes, presidente de EE. UU., a Alexander Graham Bell tras una demostración del funcionamiento del teléfono (1876)

Teléfono de sobremesa antiguo
Fabricado en metal, el teléfono de sobremesa Ericsson data de 1890. Combinaba un transmisor y un receptor en un mismo auricular. La manivela activaba un generador que hacía sonar una campana en la central telefónica para contactar con la operadora.

Década de 1870
El teléfono
Los inventores, incluido el estadounidense Alexander Graham Bell, muestran el funcionamiento de los primeros teléfonos en EE. UU. Las primeras centralitas telefónicas en América del Norte y Europa datan en 1878.

Década de 1920
Correo aéreo
El transporte del correo en avión, iniciado a pequeña escala antes de la Primera Guerra Mundial, se extiende y transforma los plazos de entrega en las rutas de larga distancia.

iPhone de Apple

Principios del siglo XXI
Comunicaciones móviles
El uso del teléfono móvil deviene un fenómeno masivo en la primera década del siglo XXI.

El Penny Black («penique negro»)

1837–1840
Sello postal
Gran Bretaña introduce una tarifa baja y uniforme para el envío postal, que se paga comprando un sello.

Décadas de 1850 y 1860
Cableado transatlántico
Los cables de telégrafos extendidos por el lecho del Atlántico permiten el intercambio de mensajes entre Europa y América del Norte.

Principios del siglo XX
Radio
La telegrafía inalámbrica y la transmisión del sonido permiten las emisiones radiofónicas.

Radio

Décadas de 1920 y 1930
Televisión
La transmisión de imágenes en movimiento da lugar a la televisión pública, si bien hasta la década de 1950 no fue un medio de masas.

Década de 1960
Satélites de comunicación
El Telstar ofrece la primera retransmisión televisiva transatlántica en directo en 1962.

Telstar

Finales del siglo XX
Internet
Las redes informáticas mundiales permiten una comunicación instantánea por correo electrónico.

« CON LA AYUDA DE DIOS, VOLVEMOS A SER VERDADEROS ALEMANES. »

Adolf Hitler, canciller alemán (1933)

Adolf Hitler ovacionado por sus seguidores en el mitin anual del Partido Nazi en Nuremberg en septiembre de 1933, en la celebración de su ascenso al poder.

Incendio en el Reichstag
Un comunista holandés fue ejecutado por causar un incendio en el edificio del parlamento alemán, si bien muchos atribuyen la responsabilidad a los nazis.

EN ALEMANIA, A FINALES DE ENERO, tras negociaciones en secreto con la camarilla conservadora de políticos y oficiales del ejército próximos al presidente Paul von Hindenburg (1847–1934), **Adolf Hitler (1889–1945)** fue invitado a convertirse en **canciller** (jefe del gobierno). Los conservadores creían que tendrían a Hitler bajo control, pues solo tres miembros del gobierno de coalición eran nazis. Hitler, en cambio, celebró su nombramiento como si se tratara de una toma del poder revolucionaria.

El 28 de febrero, un **incendio devastó el Reichstag en Berlín**. Se culpó del atentado al comunista holandés Marinus van der Lubbe. El hecho sirvió de pretexto para emitir un **decreto de emergencia** que otorgaba al gobierno y a su policía poderes prácticamente ilimitados. Cinco días después, los nazis no lograron una mayoría en los comicios, pero el 23 de marzo, con la ayuda del los partidos nacionalista y católico, el parlamento aprobó a instancias de Hitler una **ley habilitante** que **transfería toda la autoridad** del Reichstag a su gobierno. El parlamento alemán había votado su propia destrucción; al poco, Hitler prohibió los demás partidos políticos y creó un **estado unipartidista**.

Las consecuencias del mandato nazi pronto fueron evidentes. Los primeros **campos de concentración** improvisados se inauguraron en marzo; en abril se forzó un **boicot nacional** durante un día **a los negocios judíos**, y en mayo la Asociación de Estudiantes Alemanes organizó la **quema de libros** calificados de «antialemanes». Aquellos eventos, muy publicitados, fueron solo el principio. Al retirarse la protección legal a comunistas, socialistas y judíos, cientos de **opositores** al régimen fueron **asesinados** y miles de ellos torturados y golpeados.

La violencia nazi preocupaba a muchos alemanes, pero el régimen se granjeó su apoyo gracias a una repentina recuperación de la economía y a la desaparición del desempleo generalizado. Esto se logró, en parte, mediante ambiciosos programas de obras públicas, entre los que destacó la construcción de una red de *Autobahns* (autopistas), que generaron puestos de trabajo. Se **restableció así la confianza** a través de la imagen proyectada por los nazis de una Alemania unida, poderosa y dinámica.

Boicot judío
Un soldado de las tropas de asalto nazis y un soldado de élite de las Schutzstaffeln (SS) cuelgan un cartel en un escaparate judío: «¡No compren a los judíos!».

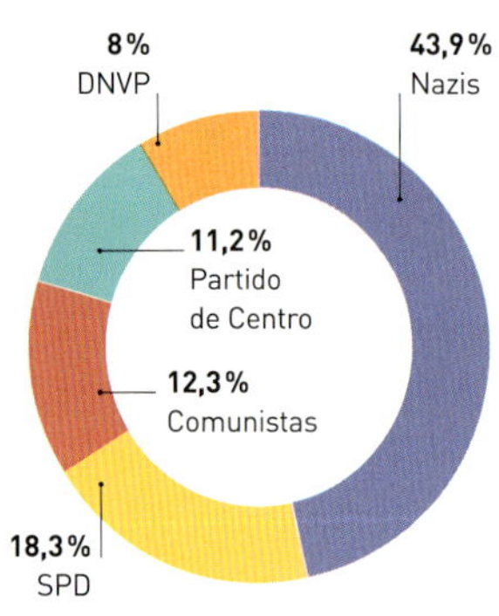

Elecciones alemanas
Las elecciones del Reichstag de marzo de 1933 mostraron el amplio apoyo a los comunistas y a los socialistas socialdemócratas.

EE. UU. también halló un presidente sólido en la figura de **Franklin D. Roosevelt** (*véase* recuadro). En su discurso inaugural del 4 de marzo, Roosevelt aseguró a los estadounidenses que «lo único que debemos temer es al miedo». Y aplicó tal consejo al tambaleante sistema bancario estadounidense. **El día 6 de marzo se cerraron todos los bancos en EE. UU.** El presidente anunció que los bancos no reabrirían hasta que las autoridades federales determinaran su solvencia. Los es-

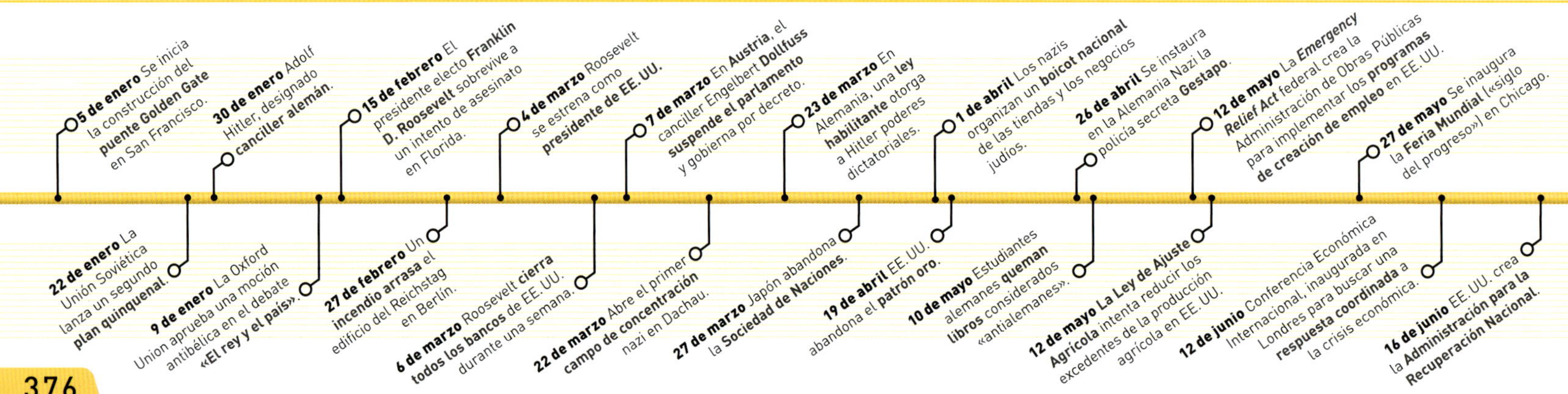

« ME COMPROMETO A TRAZAR UN NUEVO PACTO PARA EL PUEBLO ESTADOUNIDENSE. »

Franklin D. Roosevelt, en su discurso de aceptación a la presidencia (1932)

Muchachas en Florida con el Águila Azul de la Administración para la Recuperación Nacional, símbolo de las empresas adheridas al *New Deal* de Roosevelt, pintada en la espalda.

tadounidenses aceptaron la garantía de Roosevelt de que los bancos volvían a ser seguros y acudieron a ellos a depositar sus ahorros, un truco de confianza que funcionó.

En los frenéticos primeros cien días de su administración, Roosevelt aprobó una plataforma legislativa para cumplir su promesa de un nuevo pacto, el ***New Deal***. Las medidas no eran enteramente coherentes ni cosecharon un éxito uniforme. Los salarios de los funcionarios se recortaron. Se pagó a los granjeros por dejar las tierras en barbecho y sacrificar sus ganados con el único fin de aumentar los precios de los productos ganaderos y agrícolas. La **Administración para la Recuperación Nacional** presionó a las empresas para que aumentaran sus salarios y precios con la intención de incrementar los beneficios y el consumo. Y la Tennessee Valley Authority llevó la electricidad y la modernización a una de las regiones económicamente más atrasadas del país. Las medidas más populares fueron los programas de creación de empleos directos, como los organizados por la **Administración de Obras Públicas**, que incluían desde proyectos de construcción importantes hasta empleos triviales para mantener a los hombres ocupados. Por encima de todo, el carisma de Roosevelt influyó en los ánimos generales. Sus cálidos discursos radiofónicos, conocidos como **«charlas informales»**, convencieron a muchos ciudadanos de que tenían un amigo en la Casa Blanca.

Entre tanto, Gran Bretaña desesperaba por restablecer el comercio libre internacional y poner fin a su campaña de proteccionismo y a la devaluación de su moneda. Sin embargo, cuando la **Conferencia Económica Internacional** se reunió en Londres, Roosevelt insistió en el derecho de EE. UU. a manipular su tasa de cambio y a aplicar aranceles en su interés nacional. La conferencia fracasó y, ante la falta de cooperación internacional, todos los países asistentes siguieron aplicando políticas nacionalistas agresivas, lo cual frenó la recuperación de la economía mundial.

4,4 AÑOS

ESPERANZA DE VIDA DE UN **NIÑO VARÓN NACIDO EN UCRANIA** EN 1933

Mientras los países capitalistas lidiaban con la depresión económica mundial, la **Unión Soviética**, comunista, parecía inmune a estas tribulaciones. Su población padecía una catástrofe distinta. Si bien la propaganda soviética celebraba el aumento de la producción, entre 1932 y 1933 una terrible **hambruna causó estragos en Ucrania** y otras regiones productoras de grano y cercenó millones de vidas entre la población rural. Dicha hambruna fue el resultado de la colectivización de la agricultura (*véase* 1930). La magnitud de la catástrofe se vio exacerbada por la insistencia de Stalin en privar del grano a las zonas rurales para alimentar a las ciudades.

En una época de agitación generalizada, quizá fuera irónico que se inaugurara la **Feria Mundial de Chicago** para celebrar un «siglo de progreso». El público estadounidense acogió con entusiasmo aquella feria que aplaudía el avance de la tecnología. Pero no todo se limitó al «progreso». La bailarina de varietés Sally Rand alcanzó el éxito con su «baile del abanico» y también fueron famosas la llegada de 24 hidroaviones italianos dirigida por el mariscal de las Fuerzas Aéreas italianas Italo Balbo y la visita del dirigible alemán *Graf Zeppelin*.

El énfasis de la Feria de Chicago en las hazañas aéreas fue oportuno, pues ese mismo año la tecnología de los **viajes aéreos** alcanzó un punto de inflexión determinante. La presentación del avión comercial monoplano **Boeing 247**, fabricado en metal, de líneas aerodinámicas y con una velocidad de crucero de 241 km/h, transformó la duración de los viajes. El 247 podía transportar a diez pasajeros de costa a costa de EE. UU. en veinte horas. La Douglas Aircraft Company respondió con los **DC-1** y **DC-2**, que recortaron un vuelo transcontinental en otras dos horas. Los vuelos comerciales seguían siendo caros y un medio de transporte solo para ricos.

Un **extraño incidente** tuvo lugar en enero de 1933. El **cricket**, un juego que tendía lazos rituales entre la Commonwealth británica, **provocó una crisis diplomática**. El equipo inglés, en su gira por **Australia**, adoptó una estrategia intimidatoria en la ***«body line»***, de modo que su lanzador más rápido, Harold Larwood, lanzaba las pelotas contra el pecho y la cabeza de los bateadores australianos. Después de que dos jugadores australianos resultaran heridos en Adelaida, las protestas de los australianos llegaron a instancias gubernamentales. La intervención por parte del **ministerio de Asuntos Exteriores británico**, movido por el deseo de mantener buenas relaciones con un estado firme de la Commonwealth, garantizó que Larwood, que jamás se disculpó, no volvería a jugar en Australia nunca más.

Programa de la feria
La Feria Mundial de Chicago de 1933, celebrada a orillas del lago Michigan, giraba en torno a la ciencia, la tecnología y la industria.

FRANKLIN DELANO ROOSEVELT (1882–1945)

Roosevelt entró en política como demócrata antes de la guerra. Gobernador de Nueva York a partir de 1928, intentó aliviar la situación de los desempleados. Presidente electo cuatro veces, desde su primera campaña en 1932 transformó la política de su país atrayendo el voto de los sindicatos, de las minorías étnicas y de los afroamericanos. Sus políticas del *New Deal* le confirieron una popularidad duradera, reforzada por su liderazgo durante la Segunda Guerra Mundial.

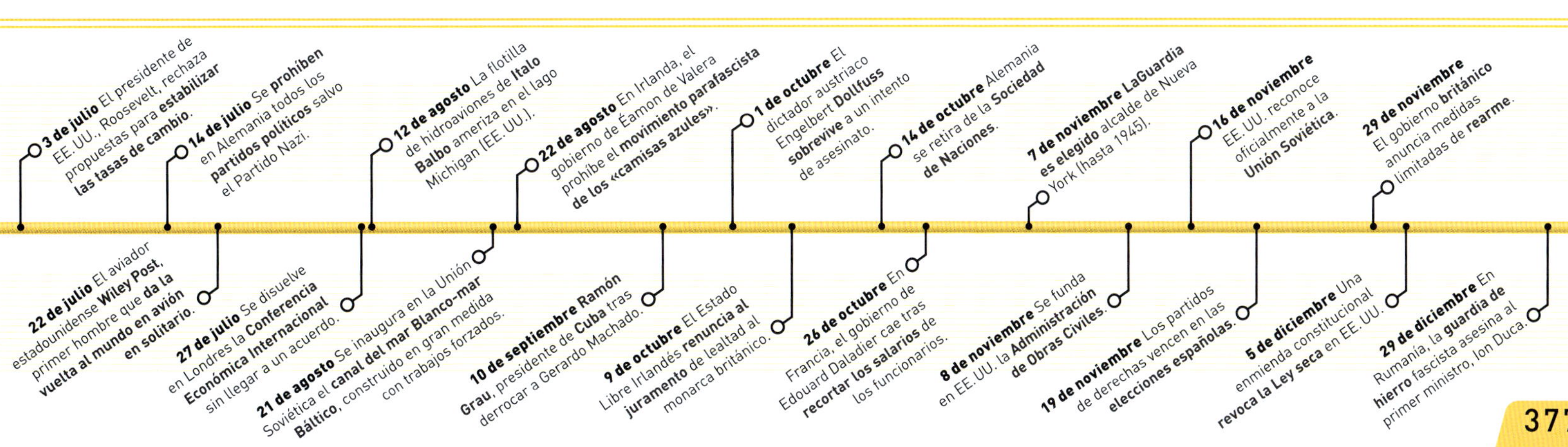

1934

Paramilitares camisas negras de la Unión de Fascistas Británicos de Oswald Mosley realizan el saludo nazi. Mosley se inspiró en los ejemplos de Mussolini y Hitler.

> « MUY **POCOS** DE QUIENES **SIEMBRAN EL PÁNICO** TIENEN ALGÚN **CONOCIMIENTO** PERSONAL DE LOS **PAÍSES** QUE YA SE ENCUENTRAN **BAJO EL PODER DE LOS CAMISAS NEGRAS**. »
>
> **Lord Rothermere,** *Daily Mirror* (22 de enero de 1934)

EN UN AÑO DOMINADO POR LOS ASESINATOS POLÍTICOS, la **Tercera República francesa** se vio sacudida por el **caso Stavisky**. Alexandre Stavisky, un financiero corrupto, se quitó la vida el 8 de enero tras el desplome de su programa de inversiones fraudulento. La prensa de derechas acusó a los dirigentes políticos franceses de aprovecharse de los tratos deshonestos de Stavisky. El 6 de febrero, grupos nacionalistas y antisemitas se congregaron en París con la intención de entrar en la Cámara de Diputados y derrocar la supuestamente corrupta República. En una noche de **combates en las calles** entre miles de manifestantes y la policía, hubo quince muertos y muchos heridos. El intento de forzar la dimisión del gobierno fracasó y la **República sobrevivió**.

En EE. UU., el público se distrajo de las tribulaciones de la **Gran Depresión** con las historias de forajidos y gánsteres. **Bonnie Parker** y **Clyde Barrow** lideraron una banda que robaba bancos, comercios y gasolineras entre Texas y Minnesota. La prensa retrató sus fuegos cruzados con la policía. Parker y Barrow fueron **abatidos** a tiros el 23 de mayo de 1934 en una **emboscada** de la policía en Bienville Parish (Luisiana). Otro criminal buscado era **John Dillinger**. El gánster fue arrestado en enero, pero escapó de la custodia. Logró seguirle la pista J. Edgar Hoover, jefe de una investigación federal. El 22 de julio, Dillinger fue derribado a tiros por agentes federales cuando salía de un cine en Chicago.

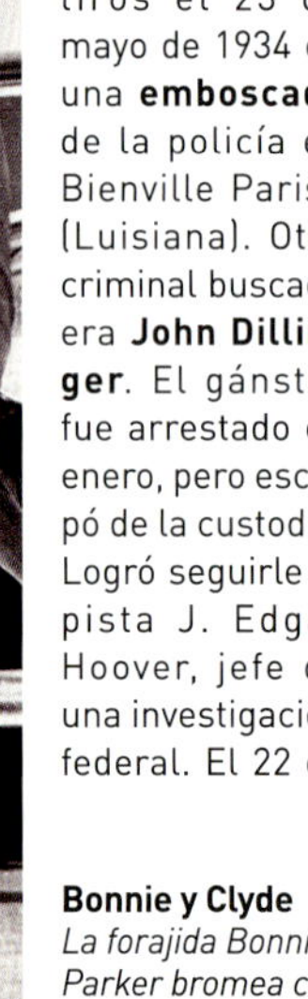

Bonnie y Clyde
La forajida Bonnie Parker bromea con su compinche, Clyde Barrow. Esta foto se encontraba en un carrete hallado por la policía en 1933.

Otro hombre que cayó de un balazo en 1934 fue **Serguéi Kírov**, líder del Partido Comunista de Leningrado y estrecho colaborador del dictador soviético **Stalin**. El 1 de diciembre, un hombre siguió a Kírov por el pasillo frente a su despacho y le descerrajó un tiro en la nuca. El **asesinato** se achacó a Leonid Nikoláyev, un miembro expulsado del partido con rencillas pendientes, si bien persisten las sospechas de que pudo ser el propio Stalin quien ordenó su muerte. El dictador soviético utilizó la muerte de Serguéi Kírov para aprobar una **nueva ley antiterrorista**, que luego se usó para justificar **el arresto y la ejecución** de centenares de personas.

En Alemania, la noche del 30 de junio al 1 de julio, Adolf Hitler confirmó su mano dura en el poder perpetrando la masacre de la **Noche de los Cuchillos Largos**. El objetivo último de esos asesinatos eran los cabecillas de las SA (*Sturmabteilung* o *Stormtroopers*). Los paramilitares habían ayudado a Hitler a ascender al poder, pero sus escaramuzas callejeras se habían convertido en un asunto bochornoso. El jefe de las SA, **Ernst Röhm**, fue uno de los cientos de fallecidos. El propio Hitler, acompañado de guardias de la SS, lo **arrestó** a primera hora de la mañana del 1 de julio. Ordenaron a Röhm que se suicidase, pero, ante su negativa, dos oficiales de las SS **le dispararon sin juicio previo**. Además de los dirigentes de las SA, también se asesinó a muchos ciudadanos críticos con el régimen nazi, incluido Kurt von Schleicher, ex canciller alemán.

En **Austria**, el intento de los nazis de hacerse con el poder fracasó. El canciller austriaco, **Engelbert Doll-fuss**, había instaurado un estado unipartidista autoritario. En febrero, Dollfuss suprimió un levantamiento de izquierdas en Viena desplegando la artillería contra el bastión socialista de la urbanización Karl Marx Hof. Asimismo, prohibió el Partido Nazi austriaco. En julio, los nazis protagonizaron un intento de golpe de estado, probablemente con la intención de anexionar Austria a la Alemania nazi. Pese a que Dollfuss fue asesinado, el golpe fracasó. **Kurt Schuschnigg**, miembro del partido de Dollfuss, le sucedió en la cancillería.

El **fascismo** proliferaba, incluso en Gran Bretaña. El ex ministro de Trabajo, Oswald Mosley, había fundado la **Unión de Fascistas Británicos** (BUF) en 1932, con el anhelo de convertir Gran Bretaña en un estado autoritario bajo su mando. En junio de 1934, Mosley dictó un discurso en el Olympia de Londres que degeneró en una reyerta cuando los paramilitares de la BUF se enfrentaron a manifestantes antifascistas. Tal violencia política tenía poco atractivo para los británicos, quienes rechazaban de plano los lazos de los fascistas con los nazis. Pese a disfrutar de cierto respaldo por parte de algunos diarios nacionales, la BUF fue un partido minoritario sin un apoyo electoral significativo.

1935

Guerreros tribales etíopes preparados para luchar por su emperador, Selassie.

EN LA PRIMERA MITAD DE LA DÉCADA DE 1930, regiones de EE. UU. y de Canadá quedaron asoladas por inmensas tormentas de polvo, cuando el viento azotó unas tierras arruinadas por la combinación de una sequía persistente y un cultivo intensivo y arrancó la capa superior del suelo. La peor de aquellas **«ventiscas negras»** tuvo lugar en abril de 1935 y afectó a una extensa zona de las llanuras de Kansas, Oklahoma, Texas, Nuevo México y Colorado. En medio del ***Dust Bowl*** («cuenca de polvo») generado por aquella **catástrofe ecológica**, los pequeños granjeros no podían sobrevivir y se vieron obligados a emigrar por miles. Muchos de ellos se dirigieron a los campamentos migratorios de California, donde se los utilizó como mano de obra barata.

> **850**
> **MILLONES DE TONELADAS**
> ES LA **CANTIDAD APROXIMADA DE SUELO** QUE **HABÍA VOLADO** DE LAS **LLANURAS MERIDIONALES** DE **EE. UU.** EN DICIEMBRE DE **1935**

Entre tanto, el gobierno de Roosevelt seguía adelante con

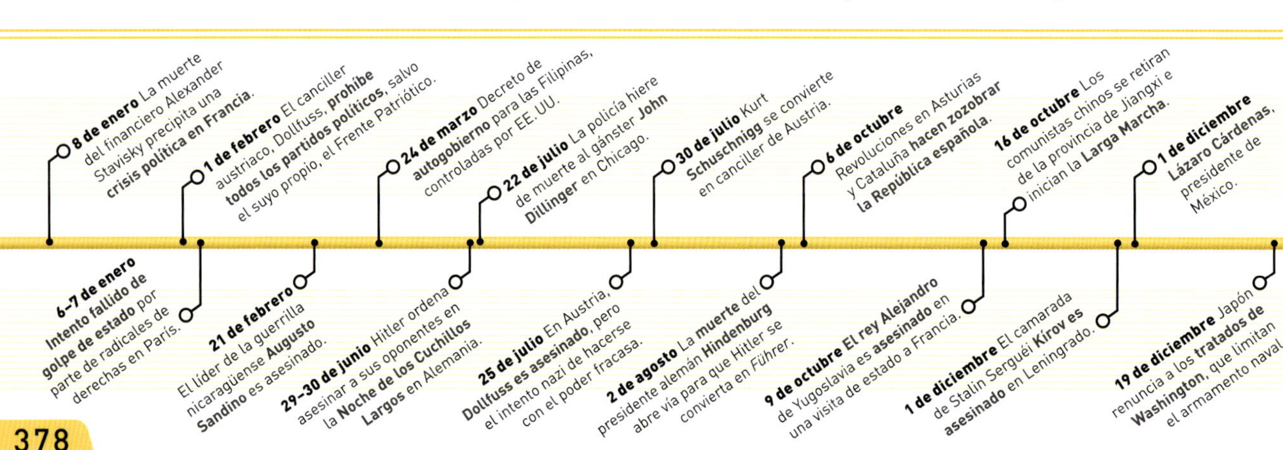

1345

OFICIALES Y TRIPULANTES VIAJABAN EN EL BARCO DE VAPOR *NORMANDIE*

BENITO MUSSOLINI (1883–1945)

Impuso su mandato autoritario y militarista en Italia entre 1922 y 1943. Su estado fascista era muy admirado, pero los sueños de conquista le condujeron a aventuras militares y a aliarse con Hitler. Al encauzar a su país imprudentemente hacia la Segunda Guerra Mundial, fue depuesto cuando los aliados invadieron Italia y asesinado por miembros de la resistencia.

una batería de reformas, popularmente conocidas como el **segundo *New Deal***. Dichas políticas eran más radicales que el *New Deal* original (*véase* 1933): favorecían a los sindicatos frente a las grandes empresas, y a los pobres frente a los ricos. La **Ley de Relaciones Laborales Wagner** situaba al gobierno del lado de los obreros en huelga, que solicitaban su derecho a sindicarse. La **Ley de la Seguridad Social** proporcionaba pensiones federales a los ancianos, subsidios para el desempleo y bajas por enfermedad. Pese a que la mayoría de los diarios de EE. UU. y sus millonarios propietarios las tachaban de socialistas, aquellas medidas financiadas por los elevados impuestos que pagaban las clases pudientes **consolidaron la popularidad de Roosevelt**.

En la **guerra civil** que azotaba **China**, las guerrillas comunistas escaparon de la ofensiva de las fuerzas del gobierno nacionalista de Chiang Kai-shek mediante una serie de **retiradas estratégicas** a regiones remotas del norte y del oeste. Durante la **Larga Marcha** de Jiangxi a Shaanxi, un viaje de unos 10 000 km, **Mao Zedong** se consolidó como el líder comunista más destacado. En diciembre de 1935, Mao declaró que la Larga Marcha había sido «un manifiesto, una fuerza propagandística... que proclamaba al mundo que el Ejército Rojo es un ejército de héroes». Pero, por el momento, aquellos «héroes» seguían siendo rebeldes perseguidos.

Supervivientes de la Larga Marcha *Comunistas chinos del Primer Ejército Rojo llegan a Yan'an, en Shaanxi, tras el fin de una retirada estratégica conocida como la Larga Marcha.*

En Alemania, el régimen nazi formalizó su antisemitismo con la aprobación de las **Leyes de Nuremberg** en septiembre. Se privó a los judíos de la ciudadanía alemana y, mediante la **Ley para la Protección de la Sangre y el Honor Alemanes**, también se prohibieron el matrimonio y las relaciones extramatrimoniales entre judíos y no judíos. Un problema a la hora de aplicar la **legislación antisemita** era identificar a quién atañía, pues los alemanes judíos llevaban generaciones desposando a alemanes no judíos. Estas leyes definieron formalmente a un judío como una persona con tres o cuatro abuelos judíos.

Preocupadas por los planes de Hitler de ampliar el ejército alemán, Gran Bretaña y Francia buscaron aliarse con el dictador fascista italiano **Benito Mussolini** en contra de Alemania. sin embargo, tal política naufragó por las ambiciones imperialistas que Mussolini albergaba con respecto a África. En octubre, tropas procedentes de las colonias africanas orientales de Italia, Eritrea y la Somalia Italiana **invadieron** el estado africano independiente de **Etiopía**. El emperador etíope **Haile Selassie** logró convocar a un gran ejército y, aunque sus soldados estaban mal equipados, ofrecieron una férrea resistencia. Etiopía pertenecía a la Sociedad de Naciones (*véase* 1919), que denunció la agresión de Italia y exigió aplicar sanciones económicas. Gran Bretaña y Francia diseñaron un plan de paz que habría dado a Mussolini una amplia porción de Etiopía. Cuando tal noticia se filtró, la opinión pública de las democracias mostró su indignación. El secretario de Asuntos Exteriores británico, Samuel **Hoare**, y el primer ministro francés, Pierre **Laval**, se vieron forzados a dimitir; las sanciones económicas contra Italia siguieron adelante, y **Mussolini se echó a los brazos de Hitler**.

Al margen de estos acontecimientos, se registraron muchos **signos de progreso tecnológico**. La presa de Hoover fue el más espectacular de una serie de proyectos hidráulicos que debían abastecer de electricidad y agua para regadío a grandes zonas de EE. UU. Para quienes podían permitírselo, los **viajes de lujo** en transatlánticos y aviones intercontinentales **florecían**, y a los que no podían costeárselos siempre les quedaba el cine. La película *Sombrero de copa* marcó la cúspide de los musicales de Hollywood: Fred Astaire y Ginger Rogers llevaron al espectador al mundo de la riqueza y el glamur.

Crucero de lujo *Decorado con un suntuoso estilo Art Déco, era el transatlántico de mayores dimensiones, más veloz y más lujoso que surcaba el Atlántico.*

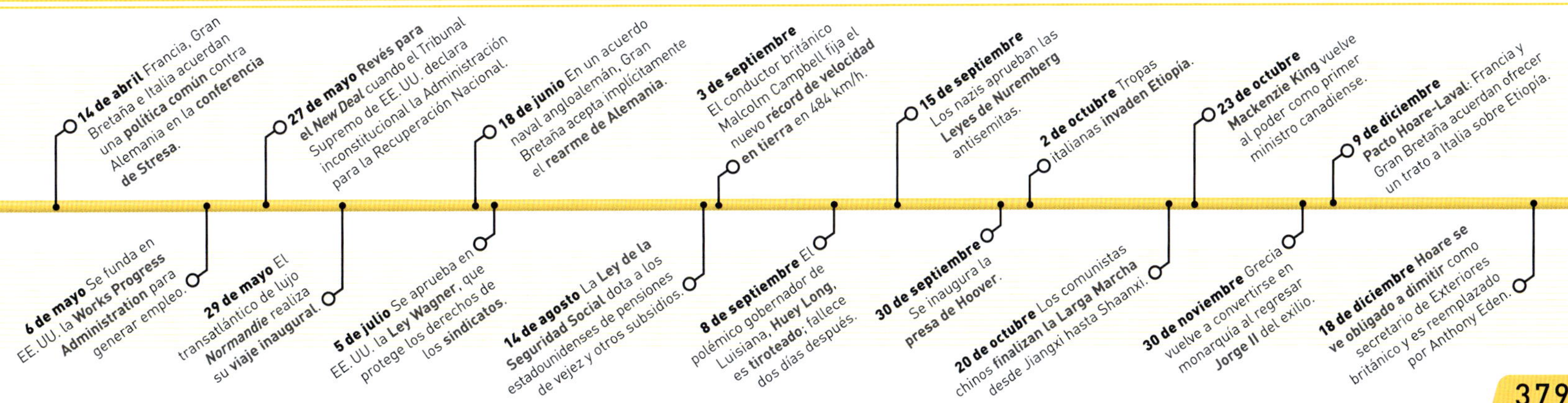

22 MIL SOLDADOS ALEMANES ENTRARON EN RENANIA

Soldados alemanes atraviesan un puente que conduce a Renania, desmilitarizada. Hitler temía una respuesta militar de las democracias occidentales que nunca llegó.

EUROPA DE PRECIPITABA inexorablemente hacia una **gran guerra**. El 7 de marzo, Hitler envió tropas a Renania, una parte de Alemania desmilitarizada bajo los términos del tratado de Versalles (*véase* 1925). La operación se interpretó a la perfección: los soldados ocupantes fueron recibidos con ovaciones y las mujeres les arrojaban flores. Pero, entre bambalinas, la tensión devoraba a Hitler y a sus generales. El **rearme alemán** se hallaba aún en una fase inicial y el ejército no habría resistido si Francia hubiera optado por una respuesta militar, pero asuntos internos y el peso de la opinión pública inhibieron una reacción más contundente. Con su pasividad, los aliados occidentales demostraron que no actuarían para imponer el cumplimiento de los acuerdos internacionales.

Aun así, **Gran Bretaña y Francia** comenzaron a **ampliar sus fuerzas armadas** en respuesta a los avances de Alemania. En Gran Bretaña, el líder conservador Stanley Baldwin había ganado los comicios generales en 1935, en parte debido a su promesa de limitar el rearme. Pese a una resolución para la expansión militar, Baldwin continuó actuando con precaución.

Su principal cometido era lograr una defensa efectiva de Gran Bretaña frente a un ataque de la **Luftwaffe alemana** (la fuerza aérea). Dos días antes de que Hitler ocupara Renania, un nuevo bombardero, el **Supermarine Spitfire**, realizó su vuelo inaugural. El 1 de mayo se creó el RAF Fighter Command, responsable de la defensa aérea. Debía equiparse con el Spitfire y el Hawker Hurricane, a la sazón en fase de desarrollo.

La importancia del poderío aéreo quedó demostrada en la **conquista de Etiopía** por parte de la Italia fascista (*véase* 1935). Aviones italianos rociaron con gas venenoso a las tropas etíopes, lo cual ayudó a derrotar al emperador Haile Selassie y a ocupar Addis Abeba en mayo. **Selassie se exilió** en Gran Bretaña. Un mes después pronunció un discurso memorable ante la Sociedad de Naciones, concluyendo con una certera profecía: «Hoy somos nosotros; mañana serán ustedes».

Frente a los éxitos del fascismo y del nazismo, el **Komintern** (la Internacional Comunista) liderada por los soviéticos había decidido que los partidos comunistas formaran alianzas en un **«Frente Popular»** con los partidos socialdemócratas y de centro. Dicha política obtuvo frutos en Francia en mayo, cuando el Frente Popular, liderado por el socialista **Léon Blum**, obtuvo una amplia mayoría en las elecciones parlamentarias. Simultáneamente, un huelga obrera condujo a la ocupación de fábricas y centros comerciales en toda Francia. La primera actuación de Blum como primer ministro fue acordar el fin de la huelga negociando los **acuerdos de Matignon**, que mejoraron las condiciones de los trabajadores con la imposición de la semana laboral de 40 horas y vacaciones remuneradas. Sin embargo, en su esfuerzo por mantener el apoyo de los comunistas por un lado, y de los radicales centristas por el otro, el gobierno de Léon Blum no tardó en quedar anegado de problemas económicos, a lo que se sumó el dilema diplomático que planteaba el estallido de la Guerra Civil en España.

Cartel de la Guerra Civil española
Obreros armados pisotean símbolos nazis y fascistas en este cartel. Al principio, los comunistas eran minoría en el bando republicano.

Un Frente Popular de comunistas, socialistas, republicanos y anarquistas ganó las **elecciones españolas** en febrero. El gobierno del Frente Popular prometió reformas agrarias y la autonomía a **Cataluña**, pero los acontecimientos pronto escaparon a su control, con los campesinos apoderándose de grandes fincas y ataques a conventos e iglesias. José Calvo Sotelo, líder político contrario al Frente Popular, fue asesinado por militantes socialistas el 13 de julio. Cuatro días más tarde, oficiales del **ejército de los nacionales** desplegados en el Marruecos español protagonizaron un **alzamiento militar**. Milicias socialistas y anarquistas armadas y una amplia porción del ejército español resistieron la revuelta, que fracasó en gran parte de España: Madrid, el País Vasco y Cataluña permanecieron en manos republicanas. Cuando los aviones alemanes e italianos comenzaron a transportar al **ejército de África** del general Francisco Franco desde Marruecos al sur de España, la revuelta militar desencadenó una guerra civil. Al principio parecía probable una rápida victoria de los golpistas. Ale-

La Guerra Civil española
Procedentes del Marruecos español, las tropas nacionales avanzaron hacia el norte. Los republicanos retuvieron Madrid en una lucha desesperada.

CLAVE
- Zona republicana
- Conquistas de los nacionales
- Zona inicial de los nacionales

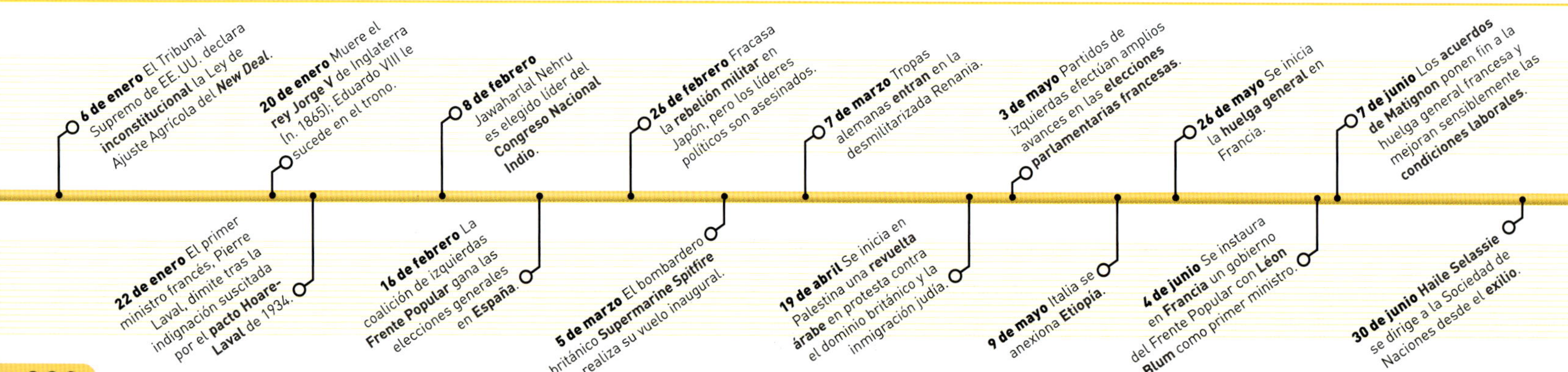

« SI NO COMPITES PARA GANAR PODRÍAS CELEBRAR LAS **OLIMPIADAS EN EL PATIO TRASERO DE TU CASA. »**

Jesse Owens, atleta estadounidense, en los Juegos Olímpicos de 1936

El atleta estadounidense Jesse Owens se alza en el podio tras ganar el salto de longitud en las Olimpiadas de Berlín. El ganador de la medalla de plata, el alemán Lutz Long, realiza el saludo nazi.

mania e Italia proporcionaban soldados, tanques y aviones en apoyo de los rebeldes, mientras que Francia y Gran Bretaña mantuvieron una postura neutral y dejaron a la Unión Soviética sola en su respaldo a la República. El ejército de África de Franco avanzaba sobre Madrid, perpetrando masacres en su camino.

Mientras, el Komintern reclutaba voluntarios en países europeos y en

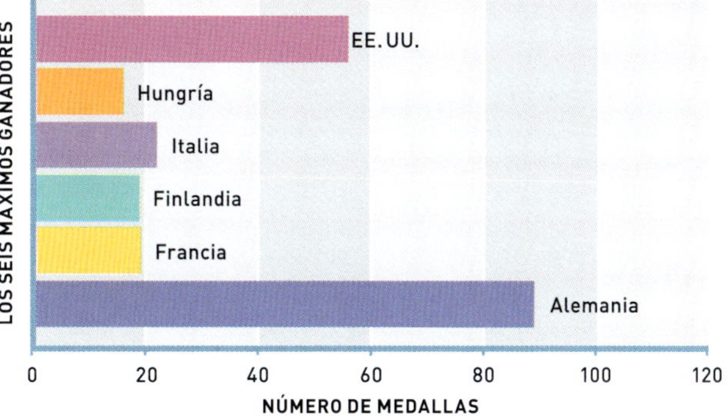

Medallero de los Juegos Olímpicos de 1936
Los países más exitosos en los Juegos Olímpicos de verano celebrados en Berlín en 1936 fueron Alemania y EE. UU. La URSS y España figuraron entre los países que no participaron.

América del Norte para luchar en España. La primera de aquellas **Brigadas Internacionales** desempeñó un papel vital en la defensa de Madrid en noviembre. Se detuvo el avance de los sublevados y Madrid continuó siendo republicano.

En medio del ambiente políticamente revuelto de 1936, la celebración de los **Juegos Olímpicos** de verano en **Berlín**, acordada antes de que los nazis ascendieran al poder, supuso un inevitable golpe propagandístico para Hitler, quien aprovechó para presentar el Tercer Reich bajo una luz favorable. Las Olimpiadas se escenificaron con un despilfarro sin precedentes y con una eficacia impecable. Alemania logró las máximas medallas, pero el atleta estadounidense negro **Jesse Owens** fue quien atrajo la máxima atención al ganar cuatro medallas en atletismo y el salto de longitud. Se acusó a Hitler de desairar a Owens porque los éxitos de este contradecían las teorías nazis de la superioridad de la raza aria. Sin embargo, a Owens le ofendió más el hecho de que Roosevelt no le felicitara.

Durante las Olimpiadas de Berlín tuvieron lugar las **primeras retransmisiones televisivas en directo**. Setenta horas de borrosa cobertura en blanco y negro se proyectaron en salas de visionado especialmente habilitadas en la ciudad, además de ser capturadas por un puñado de televisores privados. Ese mismo año, la BBC inició el primer servicio televisivo regular de alta definición, transmitido desde el Alexandra Palace, en Londres.

En otoño, dos sucesos se incorporaron a la historia política británica: uno fue la **Cruzada de Jarrow**, una marcha realizada por 200 obreros en paro con boinas y capas desde Jarrow, una población de astilleros arruinada por la Gran Depresión a orillas del río Tyne. El porcentaje de desempleo en Jarrow era del 70 %. Los obreros pretendían comunicar su situación presentando una petición ante el parlamento de Westminster. Su periplo de 450 km les llevó casi un mes y atrajo a la prensa. Aunque las consecuencias fueron nulas, para los británicos se convirtió en símbolo de una era de desempleo generalizado. El segundo suceso ocurrió el 4 de octubre, cuando la **Unión de Fascistas Británicos** (BUF) realizó una marcha por una zona predominantemente judía del este de Londres, donde se enfrentaron a antifascistas en lo que se conoció como la **batalla de Cable Street**, pero la marcha se disolvió. A la humillación que esto supuso para la BUF, le siguió la prohibición gubernamental de vestir uniformes políticos. El fascismo británico jamás recobró su impulso.

Televisor Marconiphone
Los primeros televisores, como este fabricado por Marconi, eran productos de lujo: el Marconiphone se vendía en Gran Bretaña por 60 guineas, unos 4500 €.

325
DÍAS REINÓ EDUARDO VIII ANTES DE ABDICAR

En EE. UU., **Roosevelt** (*véase* 1933) obtuvo una gran victoria en las elecciones presidenciales de noviembre, que le garantizó un segundo mandato y confirmó la popularidad de sus políticas del *New Deal*.

Tres semanas después de la reelección de Roosevelt, se dio un paso decisivo hacia una nueva guerra mundial con la firma de Alemania y Japón del **pacto Antikomintern**. Acuerdo explícito para impedir la subversión comunista, el pacto iba dirigido contra la Unión Soviética, y estableció un vínculo ideológico entre los nazis y un Japón cada vez más militarizado.

El 16 de noviembre, el rey **Eduardo VIII** (1894–1972) de Inglaterra informó al primer ministro Stanley Baldwin de su futuro matrimonio con **Wallis Simpson**, divorciada estadounidense. La opinión política respaldó a Baldwin, quien planteó al rey que escogiera entre Simpson y el trono. **Eduardo VIII abdicó** y su hermano, Albert, heredó el trono como Jorge VI (1895–1952).

GENERAL FRANCISCO FRANCO (1892–1975)

Francisco Franco era un oficial de carrera al mando de la Legión Extranjera española en Marruecos en la década de 1920. Monárquico y católico, se unió al alzamiento popular contra la República en julio de 1936, y fue reconocido como el único líder de los rebeldes nacionales en septiembre. Tras su victoria en la Guerra Civil en 1939, impuso una dictadura que permanecería hasta 1975. Declaró a España neutral durante la Segunda Guerra Mundial.

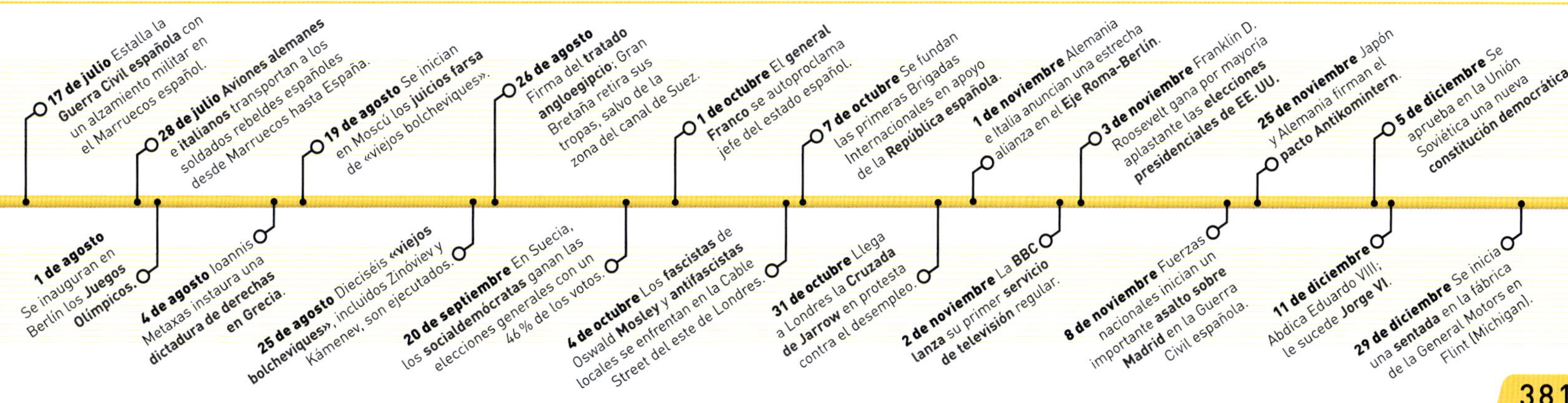

1937

Jorge VI en su coronación en la abadía de Westminster, el 12 de mayo. Ascendió al trono tras la abdicación de su hermano, Eduardo VIII.

« VEO A **UN TERCIO** DEL PAÍS **MAL COBIJADO, MAL VESTIDO Y MAL ALIMENTADO**. »

Franklin D. Roosevelt, presidente de EE. UU., en su discurso inaugural (20 de enero de 1937)

EL AÑO ARRANCÓ CON ROOSEVELT comenzando su segundo mandato como presidente de EE. UU. En su discurso inaugural del 20 de enero, Roosevelt destacó la **pobreza persistente** del país. Prometió poner fin a tal injusticia denunciando los «intereses personales irresponsables» como la amoralidad y la economía nociva. Las **radicales políticas** del presidente lo enemistaron con el Tribunal Supremo, mientras que en todo EE. UU. una oleada de **sentadas** enfrentaron a los trabajadores con sus empleadores. Cuando el desempleo se duplicó entre 1936 y 1938, quedó claro que el enfoque de Roosevelt no funcionaba. Aquel periodo se apodó irónicamente «la Gran Depresión de Roosevelt».

Para Gran Bretaña y su imperio, fue el año del cambio. En mayo, el país vio **coronar a un nuevo rey**, Jorge VI (1895–1952), y a un nuevo primer ministro, Neville Chamberlain (1869–1940), ocupar Downing Street. En Irlanda, en julio se aprobó por referéndum la propuesta de una nueva constitución. El **Estado Libre Irlandés se convirtió en Irlanda** (Eire en gaélico) y en un país independiente, si bien oficialmente sigue siendo un dominio de la Commonwealth británica. La India británica dio un paso más hacia el autogobierno con la entrada en vigor de la **Ley de las Indias**, pero los nacionalistas indios seguían considerando demasiado limitados los poderes de su asamblea electa. Los británicos tampoco hallaron una solución al problema en **Palestina**, y su propuesta de dividirla entre judíos y árabes fue rechazada por ambas partes.

En España, la Guerra Civil en curso (*véase* 1936) progresaba adversamente para los republicanos. Las divisiones políticas, con los comunistas decididos a suprimir a los anarquistas y trotskistas, anularon el valor y la determinación de sus esfuerzos militares. Los rebeldes nacionales continuaron disfrutando del refuerzo alemán e italiano, sobre todo por aire. El 26 de abril, la población vasca de **Guernica** se hizo internacionalmente famosa cuando, en un bullicioso día de mercado, fue arrasada por aviones de la Legión Cóndor alemana. Se calcula que fallecieron entre 300 y 1700 personas. Descrito vívidamente por los periodistas que visitaron la ciudad asolada, aquel episodio centró el **miedo en los bombardeos aéreos** y especialmente en el impacto que la Luftwaffe alemana podía tener en cualquier guerra futura entre grandes potencias.

En un mundo cada vez más dividido, el arte y la literatura se politizaron. **Destacados escritores viajaron a España**, fuera para luchar en la Guerra Civil (casi todos del bando republicano), fuera como turistas o reporteros de guerra. Entre ellos figuraban los británicos George Orwell y W.H. Auden, el estadounidense Ernest Hemingway y el francés André Malraux. La respuesta más célebre al bombardeo de Guernica fue un lienzo de Pablo Picasso expuesto por vez primera en el pabellón de la República española para la Exposición Internacional de París del verano de 1937.

La **Exposición de París** también incorporó grandiosos pabellones de la Alemania nazi y la Rusia soviética. Ambos utilizaban esculturas monumentales para pregonar las glorias de sus sistemas políticos rivales. Además, los nazis tomaron la decisión extraordinaria de incluir una muestra del arte que despreciaban, y exhibieron pinturas confiscadas realizadas por representantes de la modernidad y judíos en

La visión de la guerra de Picasso
En respuesta al bombardeo alemán de la población vasca de Guernica, Pablo Picasso pintó este mural en apoyo a los republicanos españoles. Se exhibió en la Exposición de París de 1937.

« A LAS 2.00 H DE **HOY**, CUANDO VISITÉ LA **CIUDAD**; LA IMAGEN ERA **ESPANTOSA**, **ARDÍA DE PUNTA A PUNTA**. »

George Steer, periodista británico, informando sobre el bombardeo de Guernica para *The Times* (27 de abril de 1937)

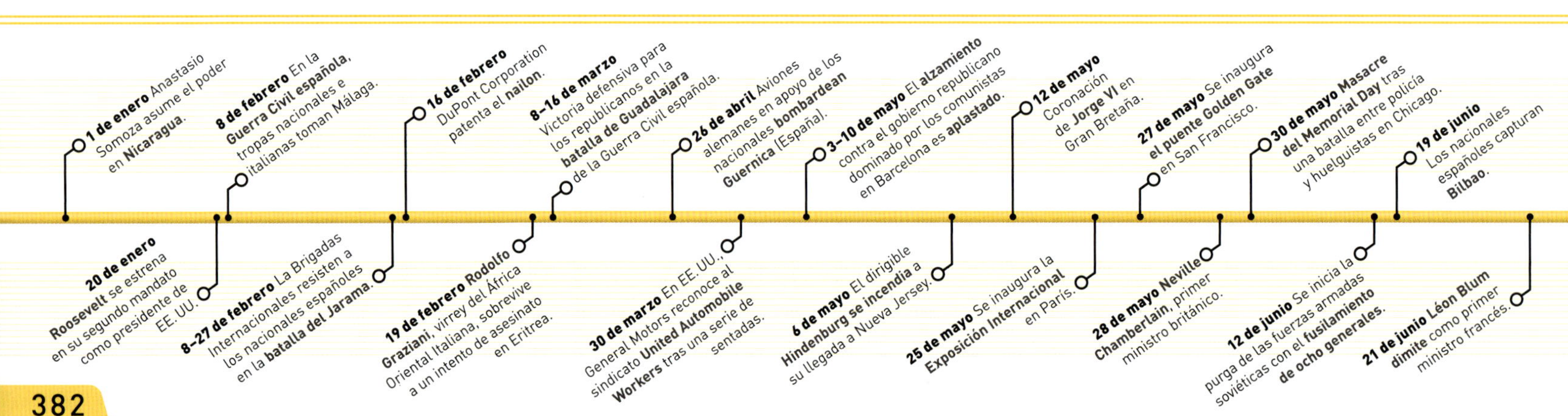

« HAY **LLAMAS** Y AHORA EL **BASTIDOR HA COLISIONADO CONTRA EL SUELO**... ¡OH, LA HUMANIDAD! **»**

Herbert Morrison, reportero de Chicago, mientras observaba el accidente del *Hindenburg* (6 de mayo de 1937)

El zepelín alemán *Hindenburg* se convierte en una bola de fuego al atracar en Lakehurst (Nueva Jersey). La causa del accidente sigue siendo incierta.

una exposición de **«arte degenerado»** en Múnich para regocijo del público alemán.

Entre tanto, bajo la dictadura de Stalin (1878–1953), la Unión Soviética vivía el **terror estalinista**. El régimen soviético siempre había sido despiadado contra quienes consideraba sus enemigos, como, por ejemplo, los campesinos que se oponían a la colectivización de las tierras (*véase* 1930), pero ahora el poder desenfrenado de la policía secreta se había vuelto en contra de las fuerzas armadas soviéticas y del propio partido gobernante. Aquel proceso se inició en 1936, con el arresto, el juicio y la ejecución de **«viejos bolcheviques»**, hombres que habían participado en la Revolución de 1917. Si bien los arrestos de viejos bolcheviques continuaron durante 1937, otras personas también pasaron a ser sospechosas. Entre 1937 y 1939, prácticamente la mitad de los comandantes del ejército de alto rango fueron ejecutados, encarcelados o destituidos. Y si bien el destino trágico de la élite soviética fue lo que más llamó la atención, el reino del terror de Stalin se extendió a toda la población. Al menos 680 000 personas fueron exterminadas durante las **purgas**, y algunos historiadores estiman que la cifra real podría rondar los dos millones.

En verano de 1937, la gradual **invasión japonesa de territorio chino** desencadenó una guerra a gran escala. En julio, China y Japón se enfrentaron en el puente de Marco Polo, a las afueras de Pekín, y un mes más tarde aquella lucha alcanzó Shanghái. Las tropas nacionalistas chinas de **Chiang Kai-shek** ofrecieron una resistencia más férrea de la prevista por los japoneses, a quienes infligieron unas 50 000 bajas, pero se vieron obligadas a abandonar la ciudad. Los japoneses avanzaron entonces sobre la capital nacionalista china, **Nankín**, que tomaron en diciembre. La población civil de Nankín fue sometida a un ataque brutal por parte de las tropas japonesas y miles de soldados chinos rendidos fueron ejecutados. Aquella masacre, presenciada por misioneros cristianos y otros observadores occidentales, conmocionó a la opinión pública de EE. UU.

Obrero y koljosiana
Esta escultura gigante, obra de Vera Mújina, dominó el pabellón soviético de la Feria Mundial de 1937. Es un ejemplo del estilo realista socialista.

y consolidó la simpatía del gobierno estadounidense por los chinos. La hostilidad de EE. UU. hacia las acciones de Japón en China fue el **primer paso en la senda de la guerra del Pacífico** (*véase* 1941).

En el resto del mundo, el año estuvo marcado por los **desastres aéreos**. Los dirigibles alemanes habían iniciado vuelos de pasajeros transatlánticos regulares. El 6 de mayo, el zepelín ***Hindenburg***, con 97 pasajeros y la tripulación a bordo, se incendió al atracar en Lakehurst (Nueva Jersey). En cuestión de segundos, el fuego alcanzó su cámara de gas llena de hidrógeno. Milagrosamente, solo hubo 35 víctimas, pero el accidente puso fin a la breve era de los viajes de lujo en dirigible. Dos meses después, la piloto más famosa de EE. UU., **Amelia Earhart** (1887–1937), despegó de Nueva Guinea con el copiloto Fred Noonan para la etapa del Pacífico de su intento de **vuelta al mundo**. Su avión no volvió a ser visto.

La tecnología continuó progresando durante el año y culminó en la competición por diseñar el primer **motor turborreactor** operativo entre el británico Frank Whittle y el alemán Hans von Ohain. El vencedor fue Whittle, pero los alemanes se avanzaron en la creación de un avión a reacción: el motor de Ohain propulsó el primer vuelo a reacción en agosto de 1939.

Otro hito del progreso fue la inauguración del **puente Golden Gate** en San Francisco. El vano del puente, de 1280 m de longitud, le convirtió en el puente colgante más largo del mundo, récord que conservó hasta que lo superó el puente Verrazano-Narrows de Nueva York en 1964.

27 125 000 $ construcción
4 068 000 $ financiación
1 334 000 $ superávit
423 000 $ administración y preliminares
2 050 000 $ ingeniería e inspección

Construcción del Golden Gate
El presupuesto original para construir el puente Golden Gate de San Francisco fue de 27 millones de dólares, que al final ascendieron a 35 millones.

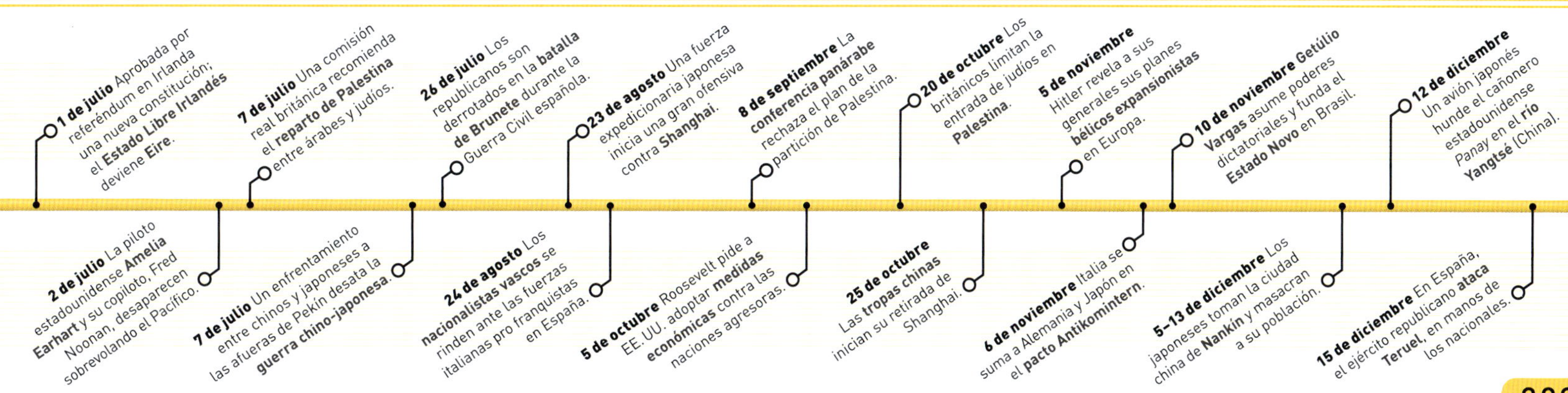

El primer ministro británico, Neville Chamberlain (dcha.), visitó la Alemania nazi durante la conferencia de Múnich el 28 de septiembre.

LA ADAPTACIÓN QUE WALT DISNEY HIZO DEL CUENTO DE *Blancanieves y los siete enanitos* convirtió las películas de dibujos animados en una importante rama de la cultura cinematográfica. Denostada anticipadamente como «una locura de Disney», *Blancanieves* se convirtió en un éxito inmediato y durante un breve lapso retuvo el récord de la **película más taquillera** de todos los tiempos, antes de ser superada por *Lo que el viento se llevó* (*véase* 1939). La capacidad de Hollywood para fabricar películas dirigidas al público universal, junto con la influencia de la música de las ***big bands*** de swing asentaron los cimientos de una **cultura popular internacional** dominada por EE. UU.

La **economía de EE. UU.**, sin embargo, distaba mucho de ir viento en popa. El pronunciado **aumento del desempleo** en 1938 reveló que el *New Deal* de Roosevelt (*véase* 1933) no había logrado solucionar los problemas económicos de la Gran Depresión.

Largometraje musical
La banda de Alexandrer (Alexanders's Ragtime Band), *de la 20th Century Fox, se estrenó en 1938, y fue la película más taquillera de la década de 1930.*

En Gran Bretaña, si bien existían zonas con un alto paro, la **economía** avanzaba a buen ritmo a finales de la década de 1930, con altos niveles de construcción de viviendas, una floreciente producción de bienes de consumo (desde automóviles hasta aspiradores), la electrificación de todo el país y el desarrollo de industrias de alta tecnología, como la aeronáutica. Un símbolo del **éxito tecnológico** del país fue la fabricación de la locomotora de vapor clase A4 *Mallard*. El 3 de julio alcanzó los 203 km/h y estableció un **récord mundial de velocidad** para un motor de vapor jamás superado.

La primera gran crisis internacional del año se produjo en marzo, con la **anexión de Austria** por parte de Alemania, la ***Anschluss*** («unificación»). Hitler había estado presionando al gobierno del canciller austriaco Kurt Schuschnigg (1897–1977) para que respaldara el movimiento nazi dentro de Austria.

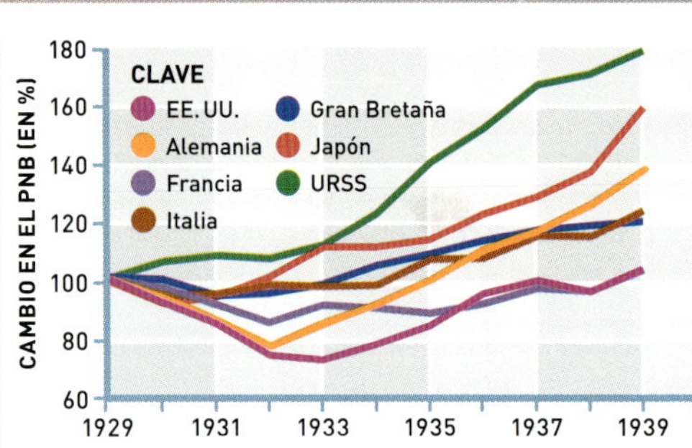

Crecimiento económico
La URSS prosperó en la década de 1930. Japón y Alemania también se recuperaron bien de la Gran Depresión.

Cuando Schuschnigg intentó celebrar un **referéndum sobre la independencia de Austria**, Hitler forzó su dimisión y lanzó una **invasión**. Tropas alemanas atravesaron la frontera sin hallar oposición, y Hitler fue recibido en Viena con ovaciones. La anexión estuvo acompañada por ataques generalizados por parte de los nazis sobre la amplia población judía de Austria.

Pese a que la unificación de Alemania y Austria suponía una importante **infracción del tratado de Versalles** (*véase* 1919), Gran Bretaña y Francia no intervinieron. En su lugar, el primer ministro británico, **Neville Chamberlain**, se embarcó en una política activa de **«apaciguamiento»**, basada en la creencia de que podía asegurarse una paz duradera negociando las

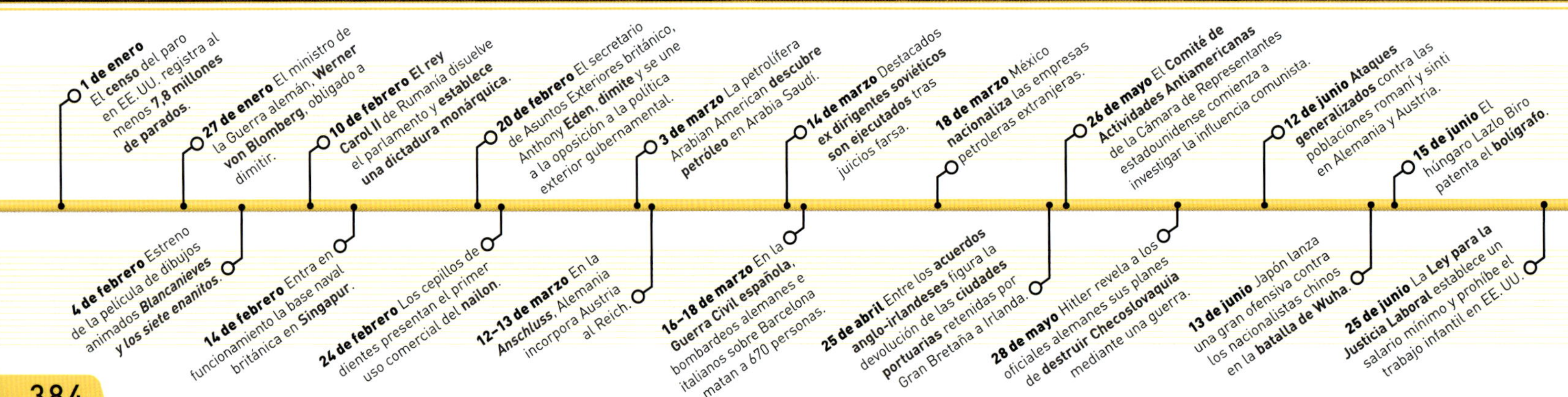

1 de enero El **censo** del paro en EE. UU. registra al menos **7,8 millones de parados**.

27 de enero El ministro de la Guerra alemán, **Werner von Blomberg**, obligado a dimitir.

4 de febrero Estreno de la película de dibujos animados ***Blancanieves y los siete enanitos***.

10 de febrero El rey Carol II de Rumanía disuelve el parlamento y **establece una dictadura monárquica**.

14 de febrero Entra en funcionamiento la base naval británica en **Singapur**.

20 de febrero El secretario de Asuntos Exteriores británico, Anthony **Eden**, **dimite** y se une a la oposición a la política exterior gubernamental.

24 de febrero Los cepillos de dientes presentan el primer uso comercial del **nailon**.

3 de marzo La petrolífera Arabian American **descubre petróleo** en Arabia Saudí.

12–13 de marzo En la ***Anschluss***, Alemania incorpora Austria al Reich.

14 de marzo Destacados **ex dirigentes soviéticos son ejecutados** tras juicios farsa.

16–18 de marzo En la **Guerra Civil española**, bombardeos alemanes e italianos sobre Barcelona matan a 670 personas.

18 de marzo México **nacionaliza** las empresas petroleras extranjeras.

25 de abril Entre los **acuerdos anglo-irlandeses** figura la devolución de las **ciudades portuarias** retenidas por Gran Bretaña a Irlanda.

26 de mayo El **Comité de Actividades Antiamericanas** de la Cámara de Representantes estadounidense comienza a investigar la influencia comunista.

28 de mayo Hitler revela a los oficiales alemanes sus planes de **destruir Checoslovaquia** mediante una guerra.

12 de junio Ataques generalizados contra las poblaciones romaní y sinti en Alemania y Austria.

13 de junio Japón lanza una gran ofensiva contra los nacionalistas chinos en la **batalla de Wuha**.

15 de junio El húngaro Lazlo Biro patenta el **bolígrafo**.

25 de junio La **Ley para la Justicia Laboral** establece un salario mínimo y prohíbe el trabajo infantil en EE. UU.

« SE ACERCAN **TIEMPOS DE PAZ.** »

Neville Chamberlain, primer ministro británico, a su regreso a Londres de la conferencia de Múnich (30 de septiembre de 1938)

Un soldado británico vigila a prisioneros árabes en la Ciudad Vieja de Jerusalén durante la supresión de la revuelta contra el dominio británico de Palestina.

«reclamaciones legítimas» de Alemania. La atención se centró en la minoría alemana de Checoslovaquia, concentrada en la zona de los **Sudetes**. Hitler agitó el descontento entre los alemanes de la región al tiempo que ordenó a sus generales que se prepararan para invadir Checoslovaquia. Los gobiernos británico y francés desesperaban por evitar la guerra, pero Francia estaba comprometida a defender a los checos. En septiembre, Chamberlain lanzó una iniciativa diplomática sin precedentes al volar en dos ocasiones a Alemania para mantener **conversaciones cara a cara con Hitler**. A pesar de que Gran Bretaña presionó al gobierno checo para que llevase a cabo importantes concesiones, aquello no hizo más que incrementar las exigencias de Hitler.

10 000 000

DE HABITANTES **SUMÓ LA POBLACIÓN ALEMANA** CON LAS **ANEXIONES** DE **AUSTRIA** Y LOS **SUDETES**

La guerra parecía inevitable; Francia y Gran Bretaña habían iniciado los preparativos militares cuando, el 28 de septiembre, **Benito Mussolini** propuso una **conferencia de cuatro naciones**. Hitler aceptó reunirse con el primer ministro francés, Édouard Daladier (1884–1970), Chamberlain y Mussolini en Múnich. Se llegó a un acuerdo para conservar la paz a expensas de Checoslovaquia, que tuvo que **entregar los Sudetes** a Alemania. Chamberlain y Daladier fueron recibidos como héroes a su regreso a casa: los británicos y los franceses respiraron aliviados por haber evitado la guerra. El parlamentario conservador Churchill (1874–1965) se contaba entre la minoría que **denunció los acuerdos de Múnich**, a los que clasificó de «una derrota sin guerra».

El optimismo posterior a Múnich perduró hasta noviembre, cuando la ***Kristallnacht*** («Noche de los Cristales Rotos») aportó evidencias gráficas de la naturaleza extremista del régimen nazi. El asesinato de un diplomático alemán por parte de un judío en París sirvió de pretexto a los nazis para llevar a cabo ataques contra hogares y negocios judíos en toda Alemania y Austria. Se incendiaron sinagogas y se desacralizaron objetos sagrados; treinta mil hombres judíos fueron reunidos y enviados a campos de concentración, donde las palizas y las torturas eran moneda corriente.

Locomotora de récord
La locomotora a vapor Mallard, *diseñada por Nigel Gresley, fue una magistral fusión de forma y función. Logró un récord mundial de velocidad imbatido.*

La Noche de los Cristales Rotos
Un comerciante recoge los vidrios del escaparate de un comercio judío saqueado después de los ataques contra los judíos alemanes y austriacos de noviembre.

Los países aún comprometidos con la democracia y la libertad expresaron su **indignación por el antisemitismo nazi**, pero no estaban abiertos a acoger a los judíos que, desesperados, intentaban huir de la persecución nazi. En una **conferencia internacional** sobre la materia celebrada en Evian en julio, el representante australiano, T. W. White, espetó: «No tenemos ningún problema racial, y no nos apetece importar ninguno». Gran Bretaña accedió a aceptar a un número limitado de niños judíos, pero sin sus padres, y EE. UU. mantuvo sus barreras existentes a la inmigración. Los **judíos estaban atrapados** porque, si bien los nazis estaban dispuestos a dejarlos marchar, no tenían dónde ir. Un destino potencial para los judíos procedentes de Europa era **Palestina**, reconocida por los británicos como **tierra natal de los judíos** (*véase* 1917). Pero los británicos lidiaban con un alzamiento armado por parte de los **árabes palestinos,** quienes **se oponían radicalmente** a la expansión del asentamiento judío. En un intento por calmar la situación, Gran Bretaña impuso duros límites a la inmigración judía.

El nerviosismo que afectaba a todo el mundo se hizo evidente cuando una emisión radiofónica indujo en EE. UU. un **pánico generalizado**. En Halloween, la CBS emitió la versión radiofónica de Orson Welles del clásico ***La guerra de los mundos*** sobre una invasión alienígena. El formato de boletín informativo empleado convenció a millones de estadounidenses de estar siendo invadidos por los marcianos. Cuando los oyentes atemorizados se percataron de su error, la indignación fue generalizada.

3 de julio La locomotora británica *Mallard* establece el **récord mundial de velocidad**.

6 de julio La **conferencia de Evian** sobre los **refugiados** revela que nadie quiere abrir sus puertas a los judíos huidos del nazismo.

15 de julio El empresario estadounidense Howard Hughes completa **la vuelta al mundo en avión** en 91 horas.

25 de julio Fuerzas republicanas españolas lanzan una ofensiva en el **Ebro**.

4 de agosto Una misión británica llega a Praga para buscar una solución a la crisis con los **alemanes** de los **Sudetes**.

15 de septiembre El primer ministro británico, **Chamberlain**, vuela para reunirse con **Hitler** en **Berchtesgaden** en relación con la crisis de los Sudetes.

22 de septiembre Chamberlain vuela a Alemania por segunda vez al **endurecer Hitler** sus **exigencias**.

29–30 de septiembre La **conferencia de Múnich** garantiza la paz en Europa a expensas de Checoslovaquia.

4 de octubre En Francia se rompe la **alianza del Frente Popular** de la izquierda y el centro.

19 de octubre El gobierno británico **abandona** sus planes de dividir **Palestina**.

21 de octubre Tropas japonesas **ocupan Cantón** (China).

27 de octubre Chiang Kai-shek retira a sus fuerzas a Chongqing, en el sudoeste de China.

30 de octubre La retransmisión radiofónica de *La guerra de los mundos* de **Orson Welles** provoca una **histeria generalizada**.

9–10 de noviembre En la ***Kristallnacht***, los nazis atacan a judíos en **Alemania y Austria**.

16 de noviembre En España, la batalla del **Ebro se salda con una derrota** republicana.

1 de diciembre Eslovaquia se convierte en un estado autónomo.

2 de diciembre Llega a Gran Bretaña el primer ***Kindertransport*** de niños judíos procedente de Alemania.

15 de diciembre EE. UU. **respalda económicamente** la guerra de **Chiang Kai-shek** contra Japón.

1939

Españolas en Madrid celebran la victoria de los nacionales de Franco en la Guerra Civil. El bando derrotado fue sometido a una dura opresión.

EN 1939, LAS DICTADURAS MILITARES SE PROPAGABAN POR EUROPA. Tan solo un puñado de países, encabezados por Gran Bretaña y Francia, conservaban un sistema liberal democrático. En la primavera, los **nacionales** del general Francisco Franco **se proclamaron vencedores en la Guerra Civil española** al ocupar los bastiones republicanos supervivientes de Barcelona y Madrid. Decenas de miles de enemigos de Franco fueron ejecutados. Otros huyeron al exilio y otros muchos fueron internados en campos en Francia. Mientras tanto, el dictador italiano Benito **Mussolini** (1883–1945) se había **anexionado Albania** y había expulsado a su monarca, el rey Zog (1895–1961).

Mayor amenaza para la paz en Europa suponía la **ocupación de Praga** por parte del *Führer* alemán, Adolf Hitler. Los acuerdos de Múnich (*véase* 1938) habían convertido a Checoslovaquia en un país indefenso y los alemanes alentaron a los nacionalistas eslovacos, resentidos por la dominación checa, a declarar la independencia. En marzo, las **tropas de Hitler entraron en Praga sin encontrar resistencia** y convirtieron los territorios checos de Bohemia y Moravia en un «protectorado» alemán. Después de que Hungría y Polonia se anexionara partes del territorio, Checoslovaquia desapareció como país.

La ocupación alemana de Praga forzó a los dirigentes de las democracias occidentales a reconocer la implacabilidad del expansionismo nazi. Era evidente que **Polonia sería el siguiente objetivo**. Convencidos de que una amenaza de guerra disuadiría a Hitler, Gran Bretaña y Francia garantizaron a los polacos su apoyo militar, pero Hitler no se dejó amedrentar. En abril empezó a urdir la invasión militar de Polonia.

Los judíos, desesperados, intentaban huir de la zona cada vez más amplia bajo control nazi, pero muchos países rehusaron aceptarlos. Entre los más afortunados figuraron los rescatados por el programa *Kindertransport*, el cual permitió a unos diez mil **niños judíos refugiarse** en Gran Bretaña. No se permitió a los adultos acompañarlos, y muchos de aquellos críos no volvieron a ver a sus padres.

Mientras todos los ojos se posaban en Europa, la **Unión Soviética luchaba una guerra no declarada con Japón** en Asia. Durante todo el verano se produjeron enfrentamientos a lo largo de la frontera entre Mongolia, un estado satélite soviético, y Manchuria, ocupada por los británicos. La difícil victoria del general soviético Gueorgui Zhúkov en la batalla de Jaljin Gol fue decisiva. Aquella derrota impulsó a los japoneses a iniciar una expansión naval por el Pacífico y el Sureste Asiático en lugar de expandirse hacia el este de Asia.

Anticipando una guerra con Alemania, Gran Bretaña y Francia fra-

> « CUANDO SE INICIA Y SE LIBRA UNA **GUERRA NO ES EL DERECHO LO QUE IMPORTA, SINO LA VICTORIA**. »
>
> **Adolf Hitler**, líder político y militar de Alemania (30 de enero de 1939)

EVACUACIÓN DE LAS CIUDADES

Gran Bretaña y Francia empezaron a evacuar civiles de las zonas de peligro a principios de septiembre. Los británicos evacuaron a 1,5 millones de niños de las grandes ciudades en previsión de ataques aéreos. Francia, por su parte, evacuó las provincias fronterizas de Alsacia y Lorena. Alemania no realizó evacuaciones a gran escala hasta que se iniciaron los bombardeos en 1942.

Invasión de Polonia
Tropas alemanas invadieron Polonia desde Prusia Oriental, Alemania y Eslovaquia el 1 de septiembre. Según lo pactado con los nazis, los soviéticos ocuparon el este de Polonia.

CLAVE
- → Avance/campaña alemana
- → Avance soviético
- — División germano-soviética en Polonia

Máscara de gas británica
Se abasteció a todos los civiles británicos de máscaras de gas para protegerse de los ataques aéreos con gas venenoso. Esta máscara de colores vivos es para niños.

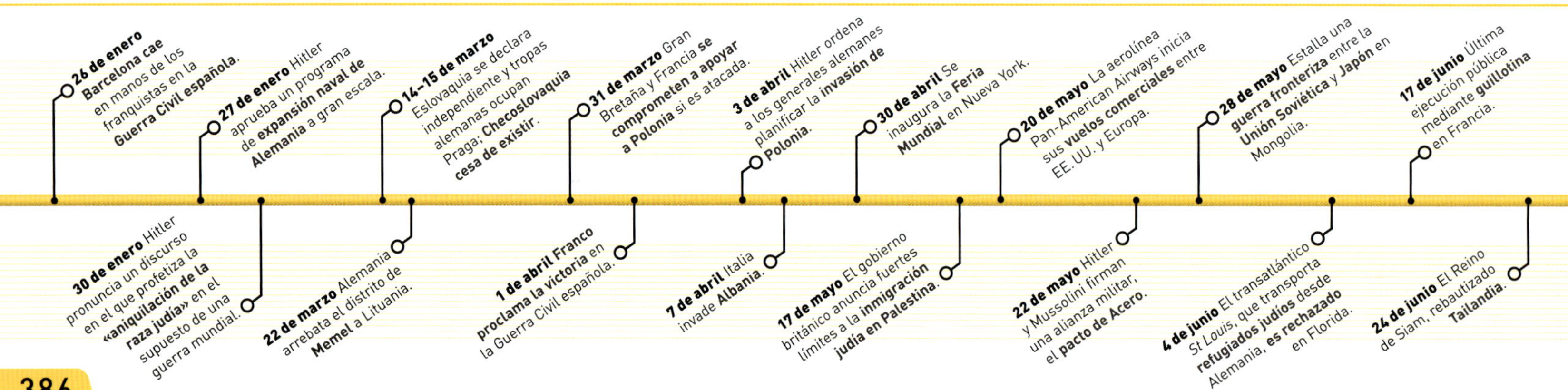

Durante la llamada «falsa guerra», los preparativos para el conflicto en las zonas residenciales de Gran Bretaña solían antojarse extraños, al no existir ningún enemigo real contra quien disparar.

guaron una alianza militar poco entusiasta con la Unión Soviética, de la cual recelaban. Nadie preveía un pacto entre Hitler y el líder soviético Stalin, pero el día 23 de agosto, los ministros de Exteriores soviético y alemán, Vyacheslav Molotov (1890–1986) y Joachim von Ribbentrop (1893–1946), firmaron un tratado de no agresión conocido como el **pacto Molotov-Ribbentrop**, que incluía, además, un acuerdo secreto para repartirse Polonia.

El 1 de septiembre, soldados alemanes invadieron Polonia. Dos días después, incapaces de rehuir su compromiso con los polacos, los **gobiernos británico y francés declararon la guerra a Alemania**. Les siguieron Australia, Nueva Zelanda, Canadá y Sudáfrica. Gran Bretaña implicó a India en la guerra sin consultarlo con sus representantes electos, mientras que **Irlanda** y **EE. UU.** se declararon **neutrales**. Para desagrado de Hitler, Italia también se declaró neutral. La guerra fue recibida por todos los países con miedo y resignación. No hubo multitudes ni ovaciones en Berlín, Londres ni París.

36

DÍAS TARDÓ **ALEMANIA** EN **INVADIR POLONIA**

cargador

apoyo para la cara

Fusil finés
El fusil finés antitanque Lahti *se usó contra los soviéticos durante la guerra de Invierno, iniciada con la invasión rusa de Finlandia.*

La **conquista de Polonia** se logró con una celeridad abrumadora. Las tropas alemanas alcanzaron las afueras de Varsovia en menos de una semana. Los polacos lucharon con valor y tenacidad (Alemania sufrió más de cuarenta mil bajas), pero una vez entraron las tropas soviéticas desde el este, la causa polaca se vio desvalida. **Varsovia se rindió** el 28 de septiembre y la lucha se detuvo una semana después. Soviéticos y nazis se dividieron el país y encarcelaron y masacraron a un gran número de polacos.

Durante el otoño, los alemanes confinaron a los judíos polacos en **guetos**, un importante paso hacia el Holocausto (*véase* 1942). Hitler ya había firmado una orden en Alemania al comienzo de la guerra para matar a las personas con discapacidades mentales incurables. Más de **setenta mil pacientes mentales alemanes murieron** a causa de inyecciones letales o gaseados antes de que la operación se detuviera en agosto de 1941.

Con Polonia aplastada, las democracias occidentales se internaron en una época conocida como la **«falsa guerra»** (*phony war* para los británicos; para los franceses, *drôle de guerre*). Tras la caída de Polonia, Francia y Gran Bretaña rechazaron una oferta de paz de Hitler, pero las tropas congregadas en Francia permanecieron inactivas. La falta de acción militar fue un alivio para los gobiernos francés y británico. Se habían anticipado ataques aéreos alemanes y bajas civiles masivas, que por el momento no ocurrieron.

La única acción dramática en la guerra de Gran Bretaña contra Alemania fue por mar. En octubre, el submarino de la Marina alemana *U-47* rompió las defensas de la principal base naval de Gran Bretaña en Scapa Flow, en las islas Orcadas, frente a la costa de Escocia, y **hundió el buque de guerra *Royal Oak***. La moral británica se recuperó dos meses después cuando barcos británicos obligaron al buque de guerra alemán ***Graf Spee*** a refugiarse en el puerto neutral de Montevideo (Uruguay), donde los alemanes lo hundieron.

A finales de noviembre, la **Unión Soviética atacó Finlandia**. **La guerra de Invierno** reveló graves deficiencias en la organización, el equipamiento y el liderazgo del Ejército Rojo soviético. A finales de año, los fineses seguían manteniendo sus defensas en la línea de Mannerheim y los soviéticos habían sufrido graves pérdidas.

Al permanecer neutral, EE. UU. parecía un mundo ajeno a las ciudades ennegrecidas europeas. La **Feria Mundial de Nueva York** se inauguró en abril bajo el lema «El mundo del mañana». Unos 44 millones de visitantes acudieron a contemplar novedades como las medias de nailon y la fotografía a color.

Hollywood vivía una **edad de oro**, con estrenos clásicos como *Lo que el viento se llevó*, *El mago de Oz* y *La diligencia*. Cines majestuosos, algunos de los cuales con capacidad para cuatro mil espectadores, se llenaban a reventar. La economía estadounidense estaba lista para vivir un repunte decisivo cuando una **enmienda a la Ley de Neutralidad** permitió a las fábricas estadounidenses suministrar equipo militar a Gran Bretaña y Francia.

Asistencia a los cines
Las películas de finales de la década de 1930 fueron auténticos éxitos de taquilla. En EE. UU. se vendían unos 80 millones de entradas de cine cada semana.

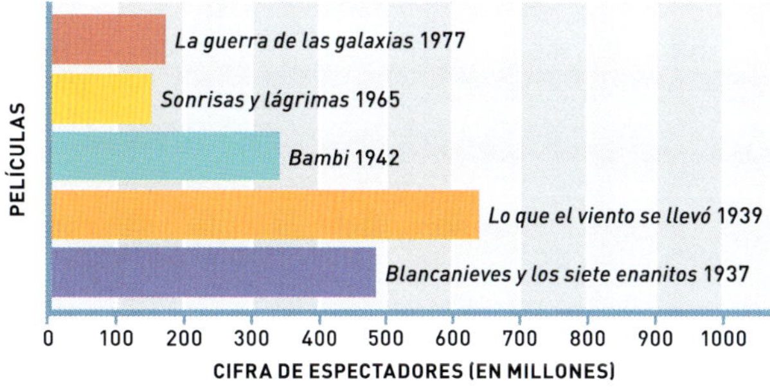

De camino a ver al mago
Judy Garland interpretó a Dorothy en la película de 1939 El mago de Oz, *una fantasía ideal para unos tiempos difíciles y peligrosos.*

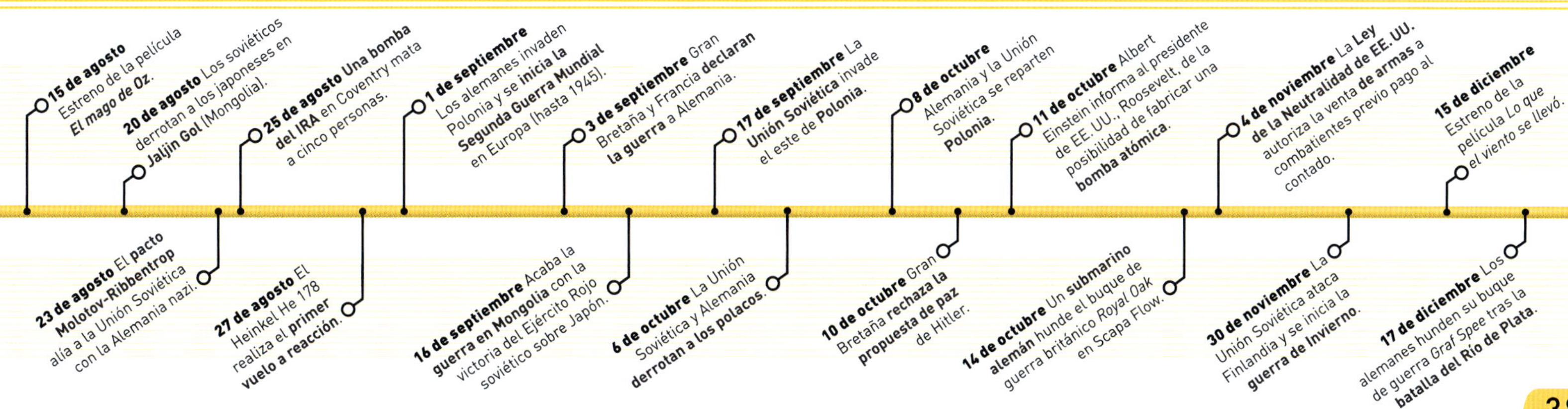

Expansión alemana
Entre septiembre de 1939 y agosto de 1942, las fuerzas de la Alemania nazi conquistaron gran parte de la Europa peninsular, donde tomaron una zona que abarcaba de Noruega a Creta y de Francia al mar Negro. Gran Bretaña no cayó bajo su dominación, pero fue sometida a sus ataques aéreos. Los submarinos nazis también asaltaron las rutas comerciales británicas.

CLAVE
- Avance alemán
- Batalla importante
- Ataque aéreo alemán
- Ataque aéreo aliado

LA GUERRA EN EUROPA

LA BATALLA ALIADA PARA REVERTIR LA MAREA DEL CONTROL NAZI

La invasión alemana de Polonia en septiembre de 1939 condujo a Gran Bretaña y Francia a declararle la guerra a Alemania. Al principio, los alemanes se anotaron una serie asombrosa de victorias, pero a partir de 1942 quedaron sobrepasados por el poderío combinado de EE. UU., la Unión Soviética y Gran Bretaña.

Tras la fulminante derrota de Polonia en abril de 1940, Alemania invadió Dinamarca y Noruega. Su devastadora campaña arrasó muy pronto Países Bajos, Bélgica y Francia. Las tropas británicas se evacuaron de Europa desde Dunkerque (Francia). La Luftwaffe alemana no consiguió superar a la RAF en la batalla de Inglaterra del verano de 1940, pero las ciudades británicas fueron sometidas a bombardeos aéreos nocturnos durante el *Blitz*.

La entrada de Italia en la guerra en junio de 1940 amplió la lucha al Mediterráneo y África del Norte. El ejército alemán, al rescate de las tropas italianas, arrolló Creta e intervino también en territorio africano. La invasión hitleriana de la URSS en junio de 1941 condujo a las tropas alemanas a las puertas de Moscú y Leningrado. No obstante, el avance alemán hacia el este encontró un fin catastrófico en Estalingrado a finales de 1942.

Derrotados en África del Norte, los alemanes afrontaron la invasión aliada de Italia. En enero de 1944, los aliados desembarcaron en Normandía y liberaron Francia y Bélgica. El último contraataque alemán en las Ardenas fue repelido, y finalmente se invadió Alemania desde el este y el oeste.

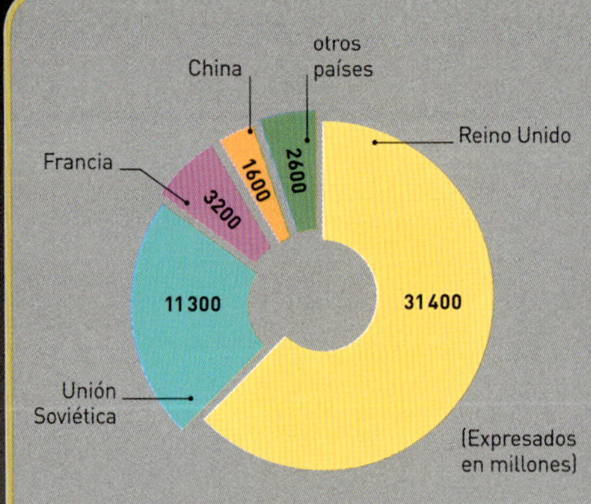

Préstamo y arriendo de EE. UU.
EE. UU. suministró a los aliados inmensas cantidades de provisiones y equipamiento bélico como parte de su programa de préstamo y arriendo. Gran Bretaña y la Unión Soviética fueron las máximas beneficiarias.

EUROPA EN 1942 Hacia 1942, la Alemania nazi dominaba la Europa continental. Sus aliados y satélites incluían Italia, Hungría, Bulgaria, Croacia, Eslovaquia y el gobierno de Vichy francés. Alemania se expandió aún más antes y durante la guerra hasta abarcar Austria, la Alsacia-Lorena francesa y gran parte de Polonia (que cesó de existir como estado en octubre de 1939). A pesar de que los nazis encontraron colaboradores, su ambición de instaurar un «nuevo orden» en Europa acabó en nada.

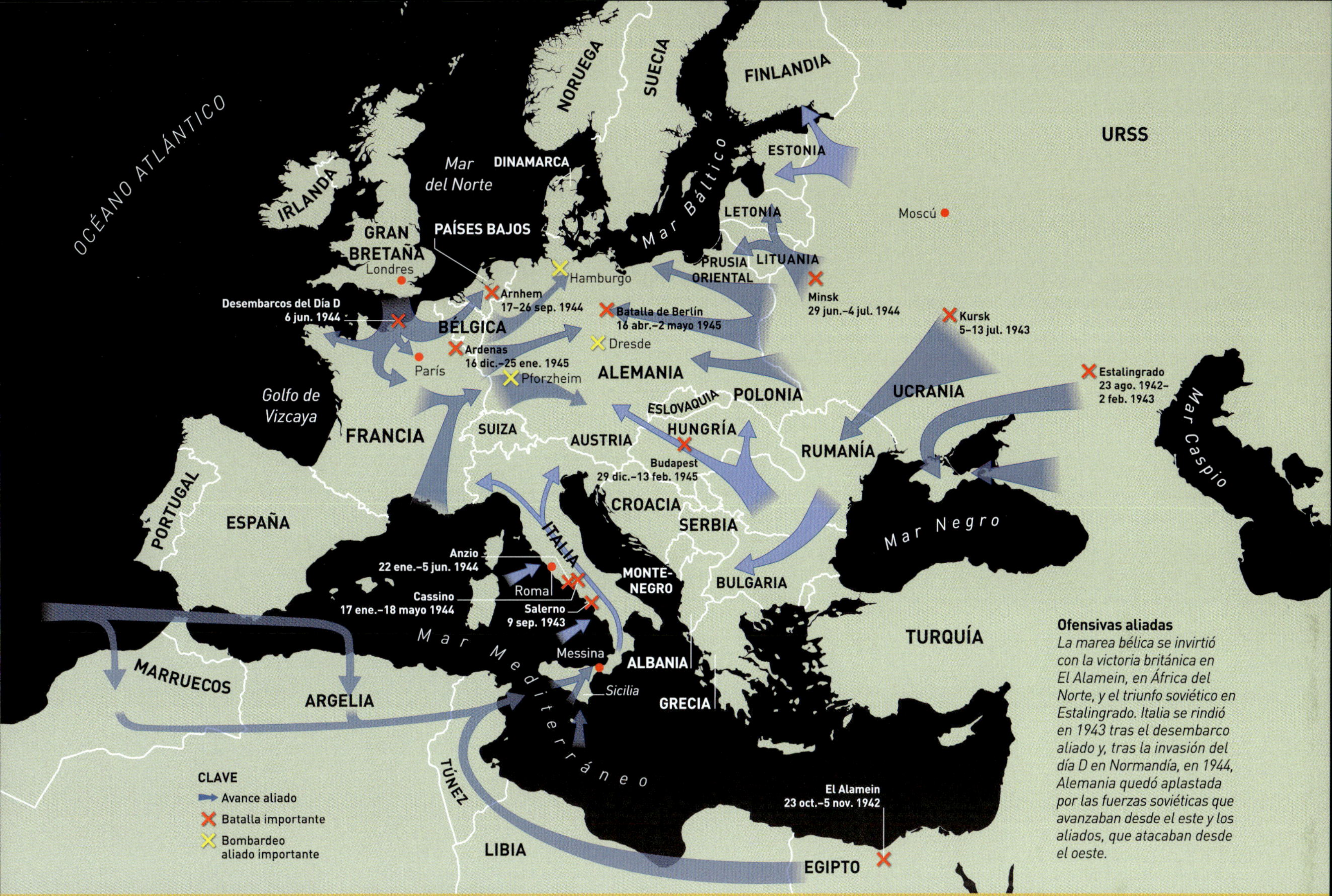

OCÉANO ATLÁNTICO
IRLANDA
GRAN BRETAÑA
Londres
Mar del Norte
DINAMARCA
NORUEGA
SUECIA
FINLANDIA
ESTONIA
Mar Báltico
LETONIA
LITUANIA
PRUSIA ORIENTAL
URSS
Moscú
PAÍSES BAJOS
Hamburgo
Arnhem
17–26 sep. 1944
Desembarcos del Día D
6 jun. 1944
BÉLGICA
Batalla de Berlín
16 abr.–2 mayo 1945
Minsk
29 jun.–4 jul. 1944
Kursk
5–13 jul. 1943
Ardenas
16 dic.–25 ene. 1945
Dresde
París
Pforzheim
ALEMANIA
Estalingrado
23 ago. 1942–
2 feb. 1943
Golfo de Vizcaya
FRANCIA
ESLOVAQUIA
POLONIA
UCRANIA
Mar Caspio
SUIZA
AUSTRIA
HUNGRÍA
RUMANÍA
Budapest
29 dic.–13 feb. 1945
PORTUGAL
ESPAÑA
CROACIA
SERBIA
ITALIA
Mar Negro
Anzio
22 ene.–5 jun. 1944
Roma
MONTE-NEGRO
BULGARIA
Cassino
17 ene.–18 mayo 1944
Salerno
9 sep. 1943
TURQUÍA
Messina
ALBANIA
MARRUECOS
Mar Mediterráneo
Sicilia
ARGELIA
GRECIA
TÚNEZ
LIBIA
El Alamein
23 oct.–5 nov. 1942
EGIPTO
CLAVE
Avance aliado
Batalla importante
Bombardeo aliado importante

Ofensivas aliadas
La marea bélica se invirtió con la victoria británica en El Alamein, en África del Norte, y el triunfo soviético en Estalingrado. Italia se rindió en 1943 tras el desembarco aliado y, tras la invasión del día D en Normandía, en 1944, Alemania quedó aplastada por las fuerzas soviéticas que avanzaban desde el este y los aliados, que atacaban desde el oeste.

GRAN BRETAÑA
IRLANDA
Mar del Norte
NORUEGA
SUECIA
FINLANDIA
URSS
DINAMARCA
PAÍSES BAJOS
OCÉANO ATLÁNTICO
BÉLGICA
ALEMANIA
POLONIA
FRANCIA
SUIZA
ESLOVAQUIA
FRANCIA VICHY
AUSTRIA
HUNGRÍA
RUMANÍA
CROACIA
SERBIA
PORTUGAL
ESPAÑA
ITALIA
BULGARIA
Mar Negro
TURQUÍA
Mar Mediterráneo
ALBANIA
GRECIA
MARRUECOS
ARGELIA
TÚNEZ

CLAVE
- Fronteras (1937)
- Fronteras (nov. 1942)
- Gran Reich alemán
- Ocupación alemana
- País satélite del Eje
- Italia y territorios de la ocupación italiana
- Finlandia
- Países neutrales
- Territorio de los aliados

CLAVE
RAF
USAAF
BOMBAS LANZADAS SOBRE EUROPA (EN CIEN MIL TONELADAS)
0
1
2
3
4
5
6
1939
1940
1941
1942
1943
1944
1945
AÑO

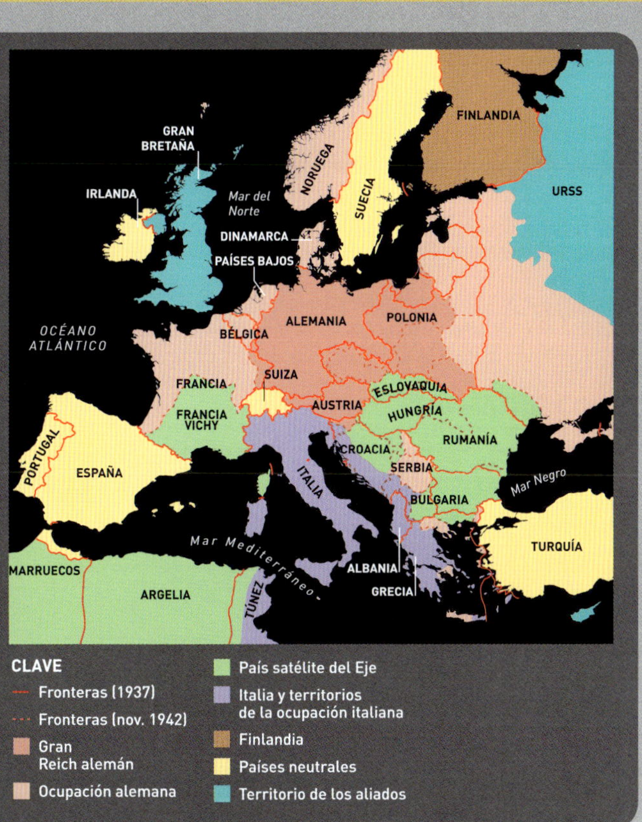

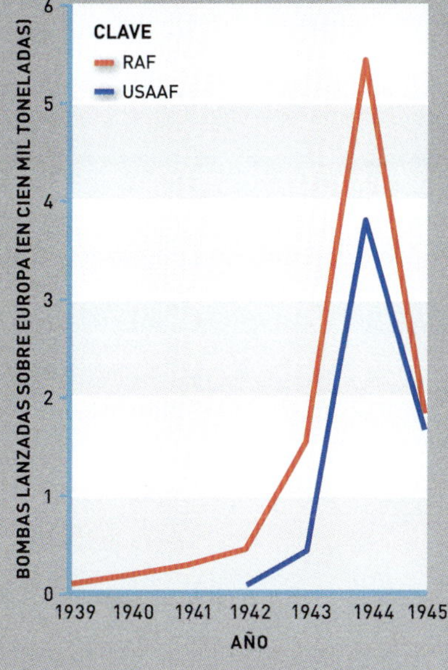

Bombardeo aliado estratégico en Europa
La RAF y las fuerzas aéreas de EE. UU. desarrollaron una campaña de bombardeos a gran escala sobre la Europa peninsular. Los aliados lanzaron 2,7 millones de toneladas de bombas y mataron a medio millón de personas. EE. UU. bombardeaba objetivos industriales de día, mientras que la RAF atacaba las ciudades de noche.

GRAN BRETAÑA
NORUEGA
SUECIA
FINLANDIA
Mar Báltico
ESTONIA
LETONIA
DINAMARCA
PAÍSES BAJOS
LITUANIA
URSS
Berlín
POLONIA
BIELORRUSIA
IRLANDA
ALEMANIA ORIENTAL
BÉL.
ALEMANIA OCC.
CHEC.
LUX.
Viena
UCRANIA
OCÉANO ATLÁNTICO
FRANCIA
SUIZA
AUSTRIA
HUNGRÍA
RUMANÍA
YUGOSLAVIA
Mar Negro
BULGARIA
ITALIA
PORTUGAL
ESPAÑA
TURQUÍA
Mar Mediterráneo
ALBANIA
GRECIA

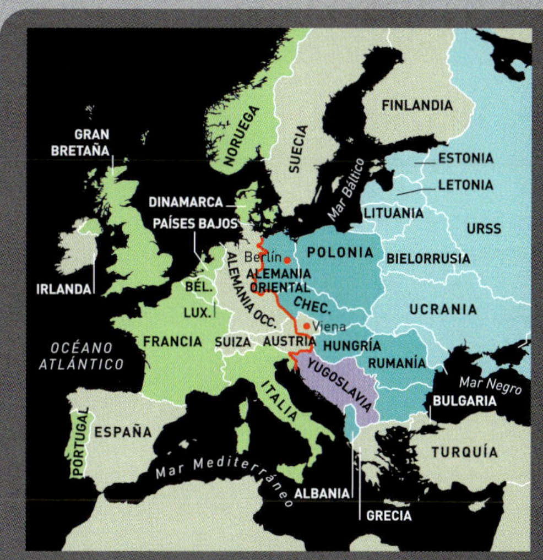

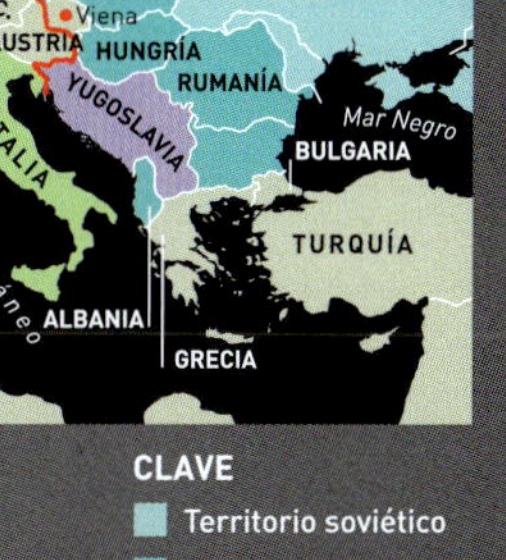

EL TELÓN DE ACERO
Tras la Segunda Guerra Mundial, en los países de la Europa del Este ocupados por los soviéticos se instauró el comunismo. El régimen comunista independiente de Yugoslavia rechazó la tutela soviética. La escisión entre el este comunista y el oeste capitalista, que partía Alemania, dio lugar al Telón de Acero.

CLAVE
- Territorio soviético
- Estados comunistas bajo dominio soviético en 1949
- Miembros de la OTAN en 1949
- Estado comunista independiente
- Telón de Acero en 1949
- Ciudades divididas en zonas de ocupación

1940

Soldados aliados forman cola en la playa de Dunkerque (Francia), a la espera de barcos que los transporten a Inglaterra. Los ataques aéreos alemanes hostigaron la evacuación.

« **LUCHAREMOS CONTRA ELLOS** EN LAS **PLAYAS**, EN LOS **CAMPOS**, EN LAS **CALLES** Y EN LAS **MONTAÑAS**; NO NOS **RENDIREMOS NUNCA**. »

Winston Churchill, primer ministro británico, en un discurso pronunciado ante el parlamento el 4 de junio de 1940

La Commonwealth *Este cartel británico muestra a hombres de los dominios y las colonias unidos en el esfuerzo bélico.*

AUNQUE GRAN BRETAÑA Y FRANCIA se hallaban en guerra con Alemania, la única lucha en Europa a principios de 1940 la libraban la **Unión Soviética** y **Finlandia** (*véase* 1939). Los gobiernos británico y francés, ambos declaradamente anticomunistas, planeaban enviar una fuerza expedicionaria en auxilio de los finlandeses. Aunque se llegaron a reunir tropas, los éxitos militares soviéticos impulsaron a Finlandia a pedir la paz en marzo. En Francia, el fracaso de aquella ayuda provocó la caída del gobierno de **Édouard Daladier**, a quien **Paul Reynaud** (1878–1966) sustituyó como primer ministro. También en marzo, el dictador soviético **Stalin** (*véase* 1928) **aprobó el asesinato** de los oficiales polacos caídos en manos soviéticas en la ocupación de la Polonia oriental (*véase* 1939). Gran parte de la élite cultivada de la región (médicos, abogados y maestros) también fue asesinada. Unas 22 000 víctimas fueron enterradas en **fosas comunes** en el bosque de Katyn y otros puntos. En junio, cuando la Unión Soviética ocupó los estados bálticos de Estonia, Letonia y Lituania, decenas de miles de personas fueron ejecutadas o deportadas a campos de trabajo. La mano despiadada de Stalin llegó hasta México, donde se había exiliado su rival **Trotski**: fue asesinado en agosto por Ramón Mercader, agente de la policía secreta de Stalin.

El 4 de abril, el primer ministro británico, **Neville Chamberlain**, anunció que Hitler había «perdido el tren» al no lograr lanzar una gran ofensiva mientras **Gran Bretaña aceleraba su rearme**. Cinco días después de su complaciente discurso, Alemania **ocupó Dinamarca** e **invadió Noruega**. Gran Bretaña y Francia enviaron tropas y buques de guerra en apoyo de los noruegos, pero no pudieron impedir una victoria alemana. El rey de Noruega, Haakon VII, fue evacuado a Gran Bretaña junto con su gobierno para continuar la lucha desde el exilio.

En Gran Bretaña, la desastrosa campaña en Noruega arrasó la confianza en el gobierno de Chamberlain. El 10 de mayo, Winston Churchill fue proclamado primer ministro al frente de una amplia coalición.

Ese mismo día, **tropas alemanas** invadieron **Países Bajos**, **Bélgica** y **Luxemburgo**. Tras el bombardeo de Róterdam, el ejército holandés se rindió para evitar una devastación innecesaria. La reina holandesa, Guillermina, formó un gobierno en el exilio en Londres.

Tropas aliadas en el norte de Francia entraron en Bélgica para detener la ofensiva alemana. Alemania lanzó un ataque imprevisto **a través de la región de las Ardenas**, entró en Francia y traspasó las defensas francesas en Sedán. Rápidas formaciones de tanques e infantería motorizada alemanas apoyadas por bombarderos Stuka siguieron hacia el norte en dirección a la costa del Canal de la Mancha y bloquearon a las tropas aliadas en Bélgica y el norte de Francia. Los aliados establecieron un perímetro defensivo alrededor del **puerto de Dunkerque** y organizaron una evacuación. Entre el 26 de mayo y el 4 de junio, 338 000 soldados aliados fueron evacuados por mar antes de que Dunkerque cayera en manos alemanas.

El **rey belga Leopoldo III** (1901–1983) **presentó la rendición** el día 28 de mayo, desoyendo el deseo de su gobierno de continuar luchando.

El ejército francés se batió en retirada, cosa que permitió a los alemanes **ocupar París** el 14 de junio. También Italia atacó Francia, en una entrada tardía de Mussolini en la guerra para recoger algunas sobras de la victoria alemana. El gobierno francés, junto con gran parte de su población, huyó al suroeste. En Burdeos se formó un nuevo gobierno bajo el derrotista mariscal Pétain (1856–1951). El **general Charles de Gaulle**, joven ministro bajo Reynaud y oficial del ejército en servicio, huyó a Gran Bretaña y abogó emocionado por la resistencia continuada,

WINSTON CHURCHILL (1874–1965)

Fue soldado y corresponsal de guerra antes de entrar en política. Primer lord del Almirantazgo en la Gran Guerra, fue culpado del desastre de Gallípoli. Durante la década de 1930, se opuso al apaciguamiento de Hitler. En 1939 regresó al Almirantazgo antes de convertirse en primer ministro, en mayo de 1940. Guió a Gran Bretaña a través de la guerra, pero perdió las elecciones en 1945.

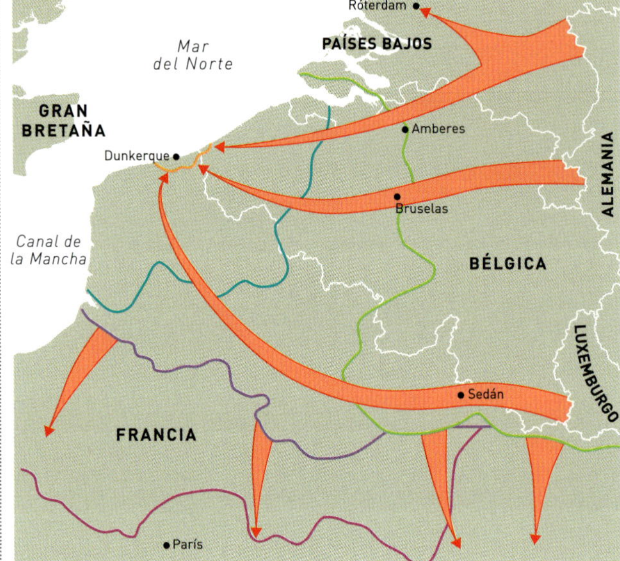

La batalla de Francia *Tras la evacuación de las fuerzas aliadas desde Dunkerque, las tropas alemanas avanzaron a la Francia central y occidental.*

CLAVE
- Avance alemán
- Frente aliado (16 de mayo)
- Frente aliado (21 de mayo)
- Línea de defensa aliada (28 de mayo
- Frente aliado (4 de junio)
- Frente aliado (12 de junio)

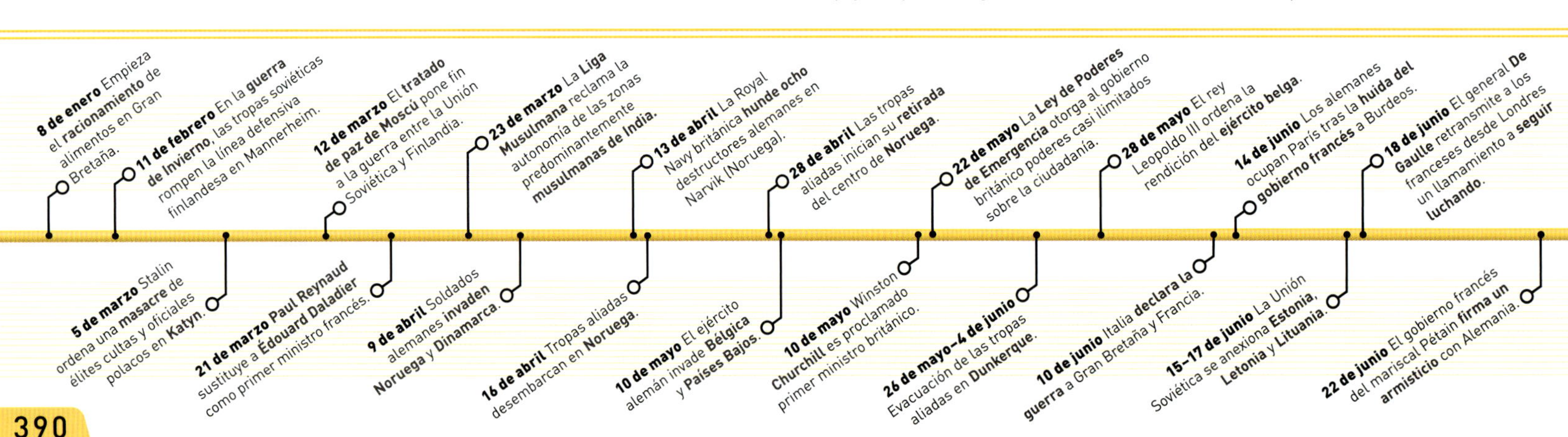

Tropas alemanas avanzan por los Campos Elíseos tras la ocupación de París en junio de 1940. La capital de Francia era una ciudad abierta y se tomó sin armas.

« FRANCIA HA **PERDIDO UNA BATALLA**, PERO **NO LA GUERRA**. »

Charles de Gaulle, general francés (18 de junio de 1940)

pero pocos secundaron su llamamiento. Pétain buscó un **armisticio**, que se **acordó el 22 de junio** y, por insistencia de Hitler, se firmó en el mismo vagón de tren donde se había ratificado el armisticio de 1918.

Soldados alemanes ocuparon el norte y el oeste de Francia. Pétain instauró un régimen en la población de **Vichy** que asumió la administración de toda Francia, si bien la política en la zona ocupada se había acordado en gran medida con los alemanes. Asumiendo poderes casi dictatoriales como jefe del estado, afirmó los principios conservadores de la religión, el patriotismo y la familia. Los **franceses de Vichy colaboraron** en algunos temas con los nazis y aprobaron sus propias leyes antisemitas.

En **Gran Bretaña**, Churchill rechazó el derrotismo. Alentó un **sentimiento popular de desafío** en sus discursos radiofónicos e impulsó medidas radicales para endurecer la resistencia, como el internamiento de extranjeros en la creación de la **Home Guard** miliciana para oponer resistencia a la invasión alemana.

Ante la negativa británica a negociar la paz, Hitler empezó a preparar una invasión a través del Canal de la Mancha, campaña cuyo nombre en clave era *Seelöwe* («león marino»). En

449

BOMBARDEROS ALEMANES PARTICIPARON DURANTE DIEZ HORAS EN EL **ATAQUE** SOBRE **COVENTRY (RU)**

agosto, la Luftwaffe inició una campaña aérea sostenida sobre el sur de Inglaterra que desató la **batalla de Inglaterra**. Las defensas aéreas británicas estaban dotadas con las primeras emisoras de alerta por radar, las cuales les permitían conectar con los centros de mandos y coordinar su respuesta con bombarderos Spitfire y Hurricane. Pese a ello, la RAF sufrió la presión de los escuadrones de bombarderos alemanes escoltados por cazas que atacaban los aeródromos, las emisoras de radar y las fábricas de aviones. Para la RAF fue un alivio que la Luftwaffe empezara a **bombardear Londres** a partir de principios de septiembre. El 15 de septiembre, atacados por más de mil aviones alemanes, los británicos derribaron 60 unidades frente a las 28 pérdidas que sufrieron. Tales cifras significaban que Alemania no podía obtener la victoria aérea necesaria para lanzar una invasión.

En octubre, Alemania abandonó sus planes de invasión, pero entre otoño de 1940 y mayo de 1941, las ciudades británicas **padecieron el *Blitz***, ataques nocturnos por sorpresa realizados por bombarderos Luftwaffe que mataron a más de cuarenta mil civiles y produjeron una destrucción generalizada. Sin embargo, aquellos bombardeos no conllevaron un desmembramiento social ni un derrumbe de la moral. El estoicismo de los británicos bajo el fuego les valió una gran admiración en EE. UU., que permanecía neutral.

Refugios subterráneos
Durante el Blitz, *miles de londinenses pernoctaron en las estaciones del metro para escapar de los bombardeos.*

En 1940, **Franklin D. Roosevelt** fue reelegido para un tercer mandato. Roosevelt había dejado clara su hostilidad a la Alemania nazi y a Japón antes de las elecciones. Había iniciado el rearme del país e introducido el reclutamiento obligatorio, pero era consciente del sentir antibelicista de la población estadounidense. En una «conversación hogareña» por la radio, Roosevelt aseguró a sus conciudadanos que su país se convertiría en un **«arsenal de democracia»** y que sus fábricas suministrarían armas a Gran Bretaña para combatir a las potencias del Eje.

Spitfire supermarino
El Spitfire, el bombardero más famoso de la RAF en la Segunda Guerra Mundial, presentaba un rendimiento equiparable al Messerschmitt 109 alemán.

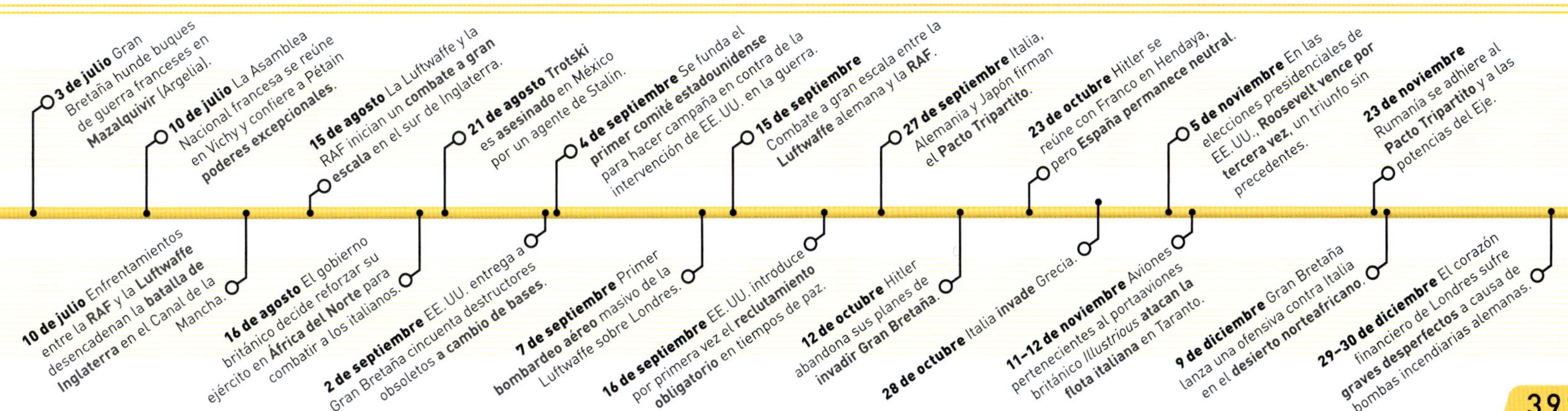

1941

Infantería y tanques alemanes del Afrika Korps de Erwin Rommel avanzan a través de Libia durante la dura campaña en África del Norte.

> **« NO LIBRES** UNA **BATALLA SI** NO **VAS A OBTENER NADA CON LA VICTORIA. »**
>
> **Erwin Rommel,** mariscal de campo alemán y comandante del Afrika Korps, en sus diarios de guerra *Infanterie Greift An* (1937)

LA ENTRADA DE LA ITALIA FASCISTA EN LA SEGUNDA GUERRA MUNDIAL en junio de 1940 amplió la guerra al Mediterráneo y África del Norte, donde Italia tenía colonias, como por ejemplo Libia. A principios de 1941, tropas de la Commonwealth británica avanzaron a través de Egipto y apresaron el puerto libio de Tobruk, donde tomaron 130 000 prisioneros italianos. En represalia, Hitler envió al general (posterior mariscal de campo) Erwin Rommel (1891–1944) a África del Norte con una fuerza armada, el Afrika Korps, en socorro de su aliado. Rommel pronto hizo retroceder a los británicos y declaró el sitio de Tobruk, mientras aviones alemanes apostados en Sicilia atacaban los buques británicos y bombardeaban la isla de Malta, una base naval de gran importancia para Gran Bretaña.

El ejército italiano intentó **invadir Grecia** en 1940, pero de nuevo los alemanes tuvieron que salir en su defensa. Fuerzas del Eje invadieron **Yugoslavia** en abril, a la que derrotaron y desmembraron rápidamente. Se creó entonces una **Croacia independiente** bajo el dominio del **movimiento fascista Ustaša**.

Las tropas alemanas continuaron su avance hacia el sur en Grecia, que fue rápidamente conquistada. Soldados de la Commonwealth británica intentaron defender la **isla griega de Creta**, pero fue tomada por los alemanes tras un asalto inicial con paracaidistas.

Para Hitler, la campaña en el Mediterráneo era secundaria. Ya había iniciado los preparativos para **invadir la URSS**, con el nombre en código de **Operación Barbarroja**. Los nazis tenían intenciones genocidas, por lo que Hitler encargó a sus generales planificar una «guerra de aniquilación». Escuadrones de la muerte especiales de las SS, conocidos como ***Einsatzgruppen***, debían acompañar a los ejércitos y exterminar a los comunistas y judíos en las zonas ocupadas. Los administradores nazis preveían exterminar a treinta millones de ciudadanos soviéticos para disponer de provisiones de alimentos para Alemania.

Lanzada el 22 de junio, la Operación Barbarroja fue una guerra a gran escala. Hitler había congregado a más de **cuatro millones de soldados**, incluidos un millón de sus aliados del Eje. Al principio, la invasión fue un gran éxito. En una serie de circunvalaciones, unos tres millones de soldados soviéticos fueron hechos prisioneros. Los invasores llegaron a las puertas de Leningrado y siguieron hacia Moscú, pero su avance se vio ralentizado por las lluvias otoñales y luego, **detenido por las nieves**. Los soviéticos lanzaron contraataques furiosos, a veces suicidas, para hacer retroceder al enemigo a las afueras de Moscú. Por primera vez, Alemania no logró una victoria aplastante.

En las repúblicas bálticas (Estonia, Letonia y Lituania), además de en Bielorrusia y Ucrania, gran parte de la población **recibió a los alemanes** como libertadores del yugo estalinista. Sin embargo, su entusiasmo se desvaneció al experimentar la brutalidad del dominio nazi. En Leningrado, sitiado por fuerzas alemanas y finlandesas, millones de personas fallecían a diario de inanición. Casi todos los **prisioneros de guerra** capturados por el Eje fueron **ejecutados o murieron** presa del hambre y el olvido.

Los judíos fueron quienes más sufrieron. En **Babi Yar**, fuera de la capital ucraniana de Kiev, más de treinta mil judíos fueron asesinados en dos días. Los nazis también iniciaron una matanza sistemática en Polonia utilizando furgonetas en las que se gaseaba a las víctimas en un centro de exterminio en Chelmno.

Operación aerotransportada
Los alemanes utilizaron con éxito a sus paracaidistas para la invasión de Grecia en Corinto y el posterior ataque de Creta.

Emblema alemán
Los paracaidistas alemanes, como las fuerzas aerotransportadas de todo el mundo, se consideraban una élite, un estatus que se reflejaba en su elegante emblema.

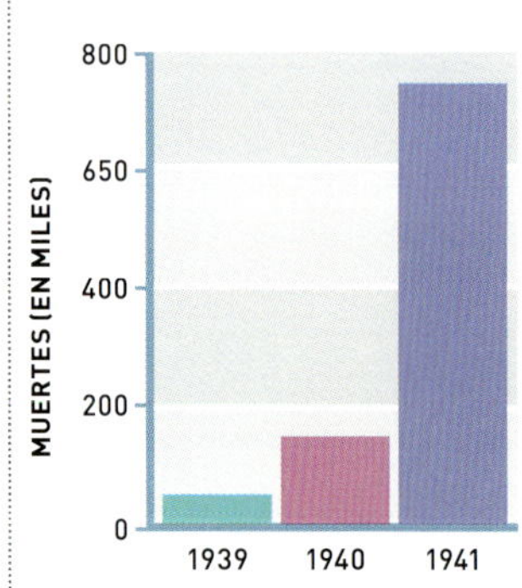

Bajas del Eje durante la guerra
Las bajas sufridas por Alemania y sus aliados del Eje aumentaron de modo drástico entre 1939 y 1941, cuando la guerra se extendió por Europa.

Operación Barbarroja
La invasión de la URSS registró un gran avance en la primera mitad de 1941. Causó graves pérdidas al ejército soviético, pero no logró la victoria rápida que Hitler necesitaba.

CLAVE
- Avance alemán y del Eje
- Frente (21 de junio de 1941)
- Frente (1 de septiembre de 1941)
- Frente (15 de noviembre de 1941)
- Frente (5 de diciembre de 1941)

20 de enero Roosevelt estrena su **tercer mandato** como presidente de EE. UU.

22 de enero Tropas británicas arrebatan el **puerto libio de Tobruk** a los italianos.

7 de febrero Gran Bretaña derrota a Italia en **Beda Fomm (Libia)**.

12 de febrero Rommel llega a África del Norte para **asumir el mando del Afrika Korps**.

1 de marzo Bulgaria se une a las Potencias del Eje.

11 de marzo Roosevelt firma la **Ley de préstamo y arriendo** para proporcionar armamento a Gran Bretaña.

6 de abril Tropas alemanas, italianas y búlgaras **invaden Yugoslavia y Grecia**.

10 de abril Rommel asedia a las **tropas de la Commonwealth británica** en Tobruk.

17 de abril Yugoslavia se rinde a las Potencias del Eje.

27 de abril Grecia se rinde a las fuerzas del Eje.

1 de mayo Estreno de la **película de Orson Welles** *Ciudadano Kane* en Nueva York.

2 de mayo Gran Bretaña invade Iraq para derrocar el gobierno favorable al Eje.

5 de mayo Italia libera al **emperador Haile Selassie**, quien regresa a Etiopía.

10 de mayo El secretario de Hitler, **Rudolph Hess, vuela a Escocia**.

20 de mayo Tropas alemanas **invaden Creta** por aire.

27 de mayo El buque de guerra alemán *Bismarck*, **hundido en el Atlántico**.

8 de junio Fuerzas aliadas **invaden Siria y el Líbano**, en manos del gobierno de Vichy.

22 de junio Alemania y sus aliados invaden la Unión Soviética en la **Operación Barbarroja**.

29 de junio El ejército soviético sufre una **derrota en Minsk** y pierde más de 400 000 hombres.

Los buques de guerra *USS West Virginia* y *USS Tennessee* inmersos en humo y llamas durante el ataque japonés por sorpresa a Pearl Harbor.

« QUE EL **ATAQUE SOBRE PEARL HARBOR** SE HAYA REALIZADO **POR SORPRESA ES UNA BENDICIÓN DEL CIELO. »**

Hideki Tojo, primer ministro japonés

Durante 1941, Gran Bretaña luchó contra los nazis, haciendo caso omiso de la extraña **iniciativa de paz** planteada por **Rudolf Hess** (1894–1987), el **secretario de Hitler**. El 10 de mayo, Hess se lanzó en paracaídas en la Escocia rural, convencido de poder persuadir al gobierno británico de aliarse con Alemania. En lugar de eso, fue arrestado y pasó en la cárcel el resto de su vida.

La principal amenaza para Gran Bretaña en aquel momento era la **batalla del Atlántico**: los intentos alemanes de interrumpir el suministro por mar de alimentos y material bélico. En mayo, el buque de guerra alemán *Bismarck* zarpó hacia el Atlántico en misión de combate. Tras hundir el crucero de batalla de la marina británica *HMS Hood*, el *Bismarck* fue perseguido, detenido por los torpedos lanzados desde aviones Swordfish y finalmente hundido por buques de guerra británicos. Las marinas británica y canadiense no consiguieron proteger tan eficazmente de los **submarinos alemanes** a los convoyes comerciales y las pérdidas se acrecentaron por momentos. La población británica notó las repercusiones en el racionamiento de alimentos.

1 000 000

DE PERSONAS **FALLECIERON** DURANTE **EL SITIO DE LENINGRADO**

Pese a la aversión del primer ministro Winston Churchill (*véase* 1940) por el comunismo soviético, **Gran Bretaña** no dudó en aliarse con la **Unión Soviética**. Con todo, lo que verdaderamente necesitaba era que EE. UU. entrara en la guerra.

Roosevelt (*véase* 1933) no fingió neutralidad. En marzo introdujo la **Ley de préstamo y arriendo** para suministrar a Gran Bretaña material bélico pagado por el gobierno estadounidense. Los astilleros y las fábricas de EE. UU. se beneficiaron enormemente de tal ley, al igual que los trabajadores, pues se generaron multitud de empleos bien pagados. Ese mismo año, la ayuda militar gratuita de EE. UU. se había ampliado a la Unión Soviética.

En agosto, Roosevelt y Churchill se reunieron en la bahía de Placentia, en Terranova (Canadá), donde firmaron la **Carta del Atlántico**, un acuerdo de objetivos bélicos comunes que encarnaba los principios de la liberaldemocracia. Aunque los buques de guerra de EE. UU. ya escoltaban convoyes hacia el este del Atlántico, en octubre un torpedo alemán hundió un destructor estadounidense, pero Roosevelt pensó que carecía del apoyo popular necesario para declarar la guerra.

El dilema de Roosevelt lo resolvió Japón. EE. UU. se oponía a la expansión de Japón en Asia y, cuando las tropas japonesas penetraron en la Indochina francesa, en julio, **Roosevelt impuso un embargo petrolífero**. Como Japón dependía del petróleo importado, a su gobierno no le quedaba más opción que abandonar sus ambiciones militares o batirse en guerra con EE. UU. Siguiendo un plan urdido por el almirante Isoroku Yamamoto, el 7 de diciembre aviones transportados en portaaviones **atacaron por sorpresa** la base naval estadounidense de Pearl Harbor (Hawái). El ataque hundió o dañó 18 buques de guerra y destruyó unos 300 aviones, mermando gravemente la flota de EE. UU. en el Pacífico. Otra sección del ejército japonés invadió Filipinas y la colonia británica de Malasia. La conmoción por el ataque garantizó el apoyo de la población estadounidense a la guerra contra Japón, pero no contra Alemania. Para alivio de Churchill y Roosevelt, Hitler decidió declarar la guerra a EE. UU. en apoyo a sus aliados japoneses. En la **conferencia de Arcadia** celebrada en Washington a finales de año, **Gran Bretaña** y **EE. UU.** acordaron una **estrategia militar** que priorizaba derrotar a los alemanes. Ambos países acordaron asimismo unificar sus mandos militares bajo el Comité de Jefes del Estado Mayor Combinado.

Insignia conmemorativa
El eslogan «Recuerda Pearl Harbor» se usó en EE. UU. para alentar el apoyo patriota a la guerra contra Japón.

ISOROKU YAMAMOTO
(1884–1943)

En la década de 1930, el almirante japonés Yamamoto se convirtió en un destacado defensor del poderío aeronaval. Como comandante en jefe, fue el arquitecto del ataque sobre Pearl Harbor de 1941. Falleció en abril de 1943, cuando los servicios de inteligencia de EE. UU. identificaron su avión y lo derribaron sobre la isla Bougainville, en el Pacífico.

Combates en la nieve
Un soldado alemán padece los rigores del invierno ruso durante la invasión de la URSS. Las fuerzas del Eje estaban mal equipadas para hacer frente a la situación.

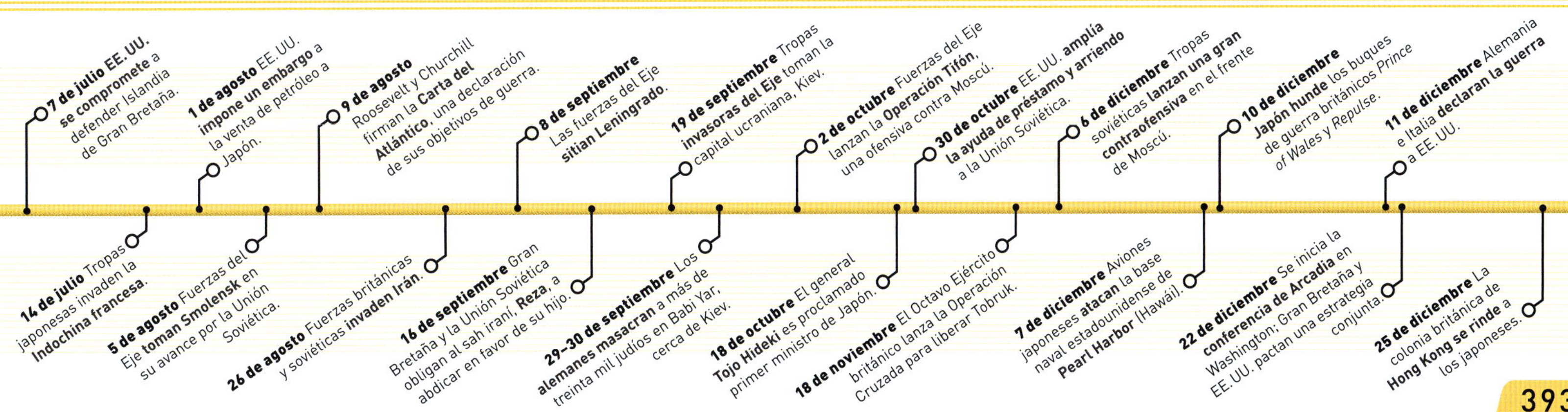

LA GUERRA EN EL PACÍFICO

LOS ALIADOS DERROTAN AL JAPÓN IMPERIAL EN EL PACÍFICO

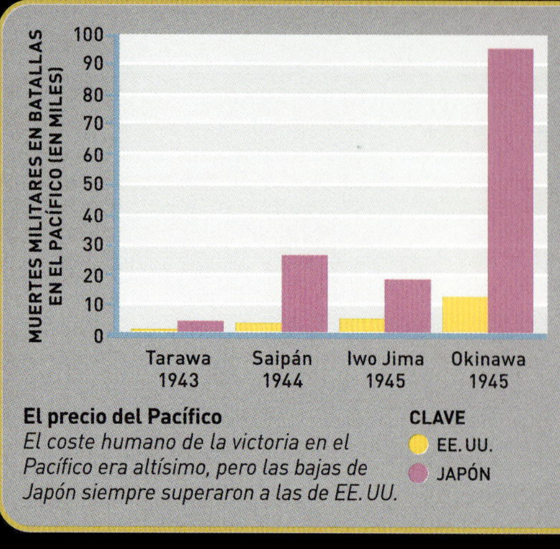

El precio del Pacífico
El coste humano de la victoria en el Pacífico era altísimo, pero las bajas de Japón siempre superaron a las de EE. UU.

En guerra con China desde 1937, Japón hizo una apuesta en 1941 que, en caso de resultar un éxito, le garantizaría un imperio en Asia y el Pacífico. El 7 de diciembre atacó la base estadounidense de Pearl Harbor en Hawái y lanzó una invasión de Filipinas y las colonias europeas en el Sureste Asiático.

Las colonias europeas del Sureste Asiático fueron presas fáciles para Japón: la base británica en Singapur cayó sin apenas oponer resistencia. En cinco meses, los japoneses habían alcanzado la frontera en Birmania. Australia parecía amenazada, pero el avance hacia el sur de Japón quedó en jaque a causa del enfrentamiento en la batalla del Mar del Coral. Se inició entonces una nueva fase de la guerra con el ataque de la marina japonesa contra la isla de Midway. A partir de agosto de 1942, la lucha más intensa se concentró en torno a Guadalcanal, tomado por EE. UU. No fue hasta 1944 cuando EE. UU. logró reunir la fuerza suficiente para acometer un avance sostenido. La marina japonesa fue encauzada hacia las batallas del Mar de las Filipinas y el golfo de Leyte, mientras que el asedio de las Marianas colocó a los japoneses al alcance de los bombarderos estadounidenses. En agosto de 1945, derrotado en Birmania y Okinawa, y ante una posible invasión soviética de Manchuria y la destrucción de ciudades con bombas atómicas, Japón se rindió.

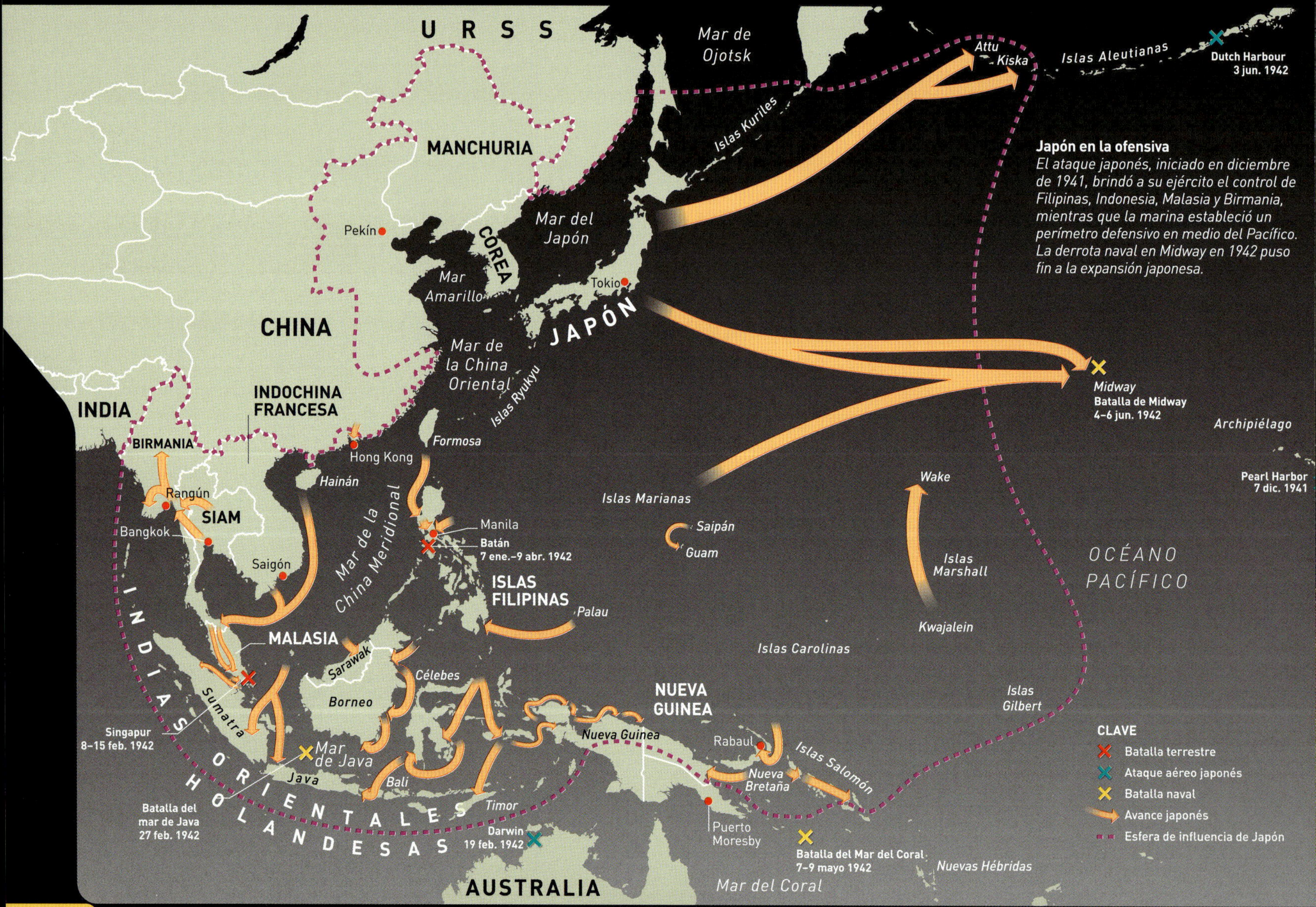

Japón en la ofensiva
El ataque japonés, iniciado en diciembre de 1941, brindó a su ejército el control de Filipinas, Indonesia, Malasia y Birmania, mientras que la marina estableció un perímetro defensivo en medio del Pacífico. La derrota naval en Midway en 1942 puso fin a la expansión japonesa.

CLAVE
- Batalla terrestre
- Ataque aéreo japonés
- Batalla naval
- Avance japonés
- Esfera de influencia de Japón

Ciudad	Número de bombardeos aéreos	Porcentaje destruido de la ciudad
Tokio	5	50 %
Nagoya	4	31 %
Kobe	2	56 %
Osaka	4	26 %
Yokohama	2	44 %
Kawasaki	1	33 %

Las Seis Grandes
Entre el 10 de marzo y el 15 de junio de 1945, seis grandes ciudades japonesas, incluidas Tokio y Kobe, quedaron diezmadas por los bombardeos de EE. UU.

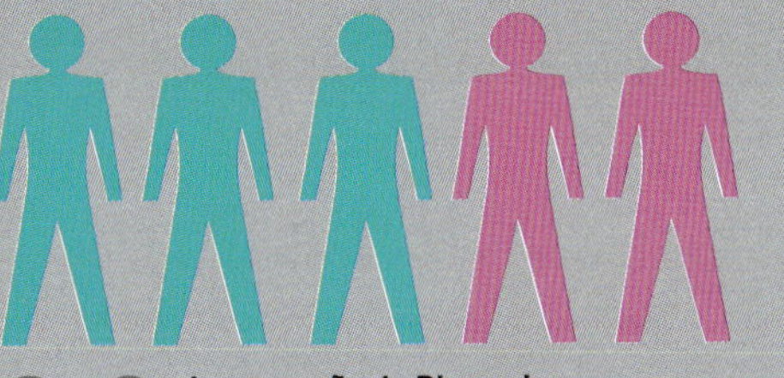

3:2

La campaña de Birmania
El 60 % (tres de cada cinco) de los soldados japoneses que lucharon en la campaña de Birmania entre 1942–1945 perdió la vida. Las bajas totales para Japón rondaron los 200 000 hombres, en comparación con los 71 000 británicos e indios británicos muertos y heridos.

Mar del Japón (Mar de Oriente)
COREA
Tokio
Kawasaki
Nagoya
Hiroshima
Kobe
Osaka
Yokohama
Nagasaki
OCÉANO PACÍFICO
CLAVE
Ataques a las «Seis Grandes»
Objetivo de bomba atómica

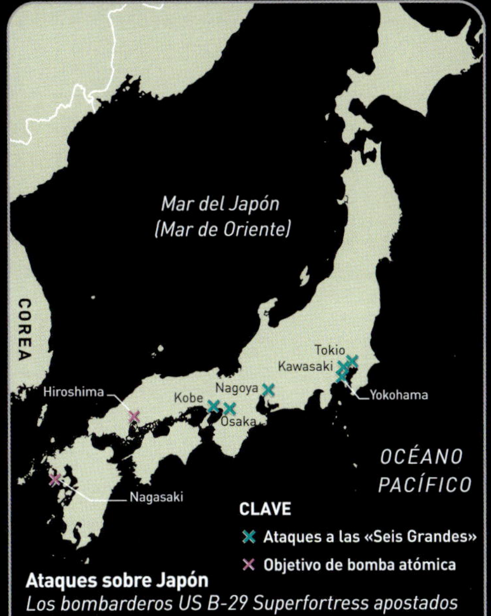

Ataques sobre Japón
Los bombarderos US B-29 Superfortress apostados en las Marianas devastaron las ciudades japonesas con dispositivos incendiarios a partir de marzo de 1945. El lanzamiento de bombas atómicas sobre Hiroshima y Nagasaki impulsó a Japón a rendirse.

« SOY CONSCIENTE DE LA **TRÁGICA REPERCUSIÓN** DE LA **BOMBA ATÓMICA**... **AGRADEZCO** A DIOS **QUE SEA NUESTRA** Y NO DE NUESTROS **ENEMIGOS**. »

Harry S. Truman, presidente de EE. UU.
(9 de agosto de 1945)

URSS
Mar de Ojotsk
Attu
Kiska
Islas Aleutianas
Dutch Harbour
Manchuria
8–21 ago. 1945
MANCHURIA
Islas Kuriles
Pekín
CHINA
COREA
Mar del Japón
JAPÓN
Tokio
Mar Amarillo
Mar de la China Oriental
Islas Ryukyu
Okinawa
1 abr.–22 jun. 1945
INDIA
Kohima
7 mar.–18 jul. 1944
BIRMANIA
Hong Kong
Formosa
Iwo Jima
19 feb.–26 mar. 1945
Midway
OCÉANO PACÍFICO
Archipiélago de Hawái
Pearl Harbor
Batalla del Mar de las Filipinas
19–20 jun. 1944
Islas Marianas
Rangún
Hainán
Manila
3 feb.–3 mar. 1945
SIAM
Bangkok
ISLAS FILIPINAS
Saipán
15 de jun.–9 jul. 1944
Islas Marshall
INDOCHINA FRANCESA
Saigón
Mar de la China Meridional
Batalla de Leyte
23–25 oct. 1944
Guam
21 jul.–8 ago. 1944
Kwajalein
MALASIA
Sarawak
Mindanao
Célebes
Halmahera
Sumatra
Borneo
Balikpapan
Archipiélago de Bismarck
Islas Gilbert
Tarawa
20–23 nov. 1943
Rabaul
4–23 ene. 1942
Hollandia
Mar de Java
Nueva Guinea
Islas Salomón
Java
Bali
Timor
Puerto Moresby
Guadalcanal
7 ago. 1942–9 feb. 1943
Islas Santa Cruz
Darwin
INDIAS ORIENTALES HOLANDESAS
Nuevas Hébridas
AUSTRALIA
Mar del Coral
CLAVE
Batalla terrestre
Batalla naval
Avance aliado

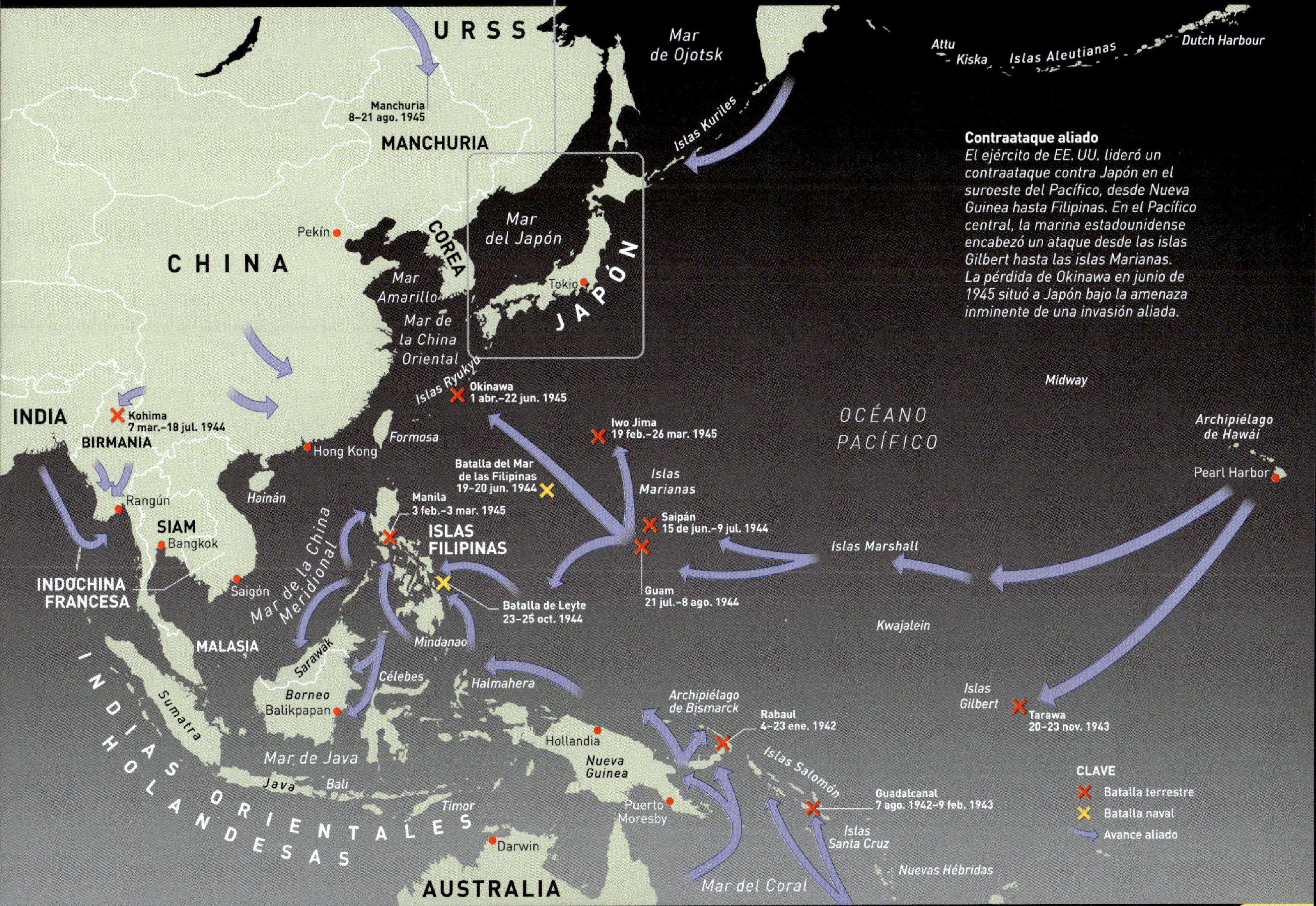

Contraataque aliado
El ejército de EE. UU. lideró un contraataque contra Japón en el suroeste del Pacífico, desde Nueva Guinea hasta Filipinas. En el Pacífico central, la marina estadounidense encabezó un ataque desde las islas Gilbert hasta las islas Marianas. La pérdida de Okinawa en junio de 1945 situó a Japón bajo la amenaza inminente de una invasión aliada.

Habitantes de Nueva Guinea transportan a través de la selva a soldados aliados heridos. El entorno hostil era un enemigo tan mortal como los japoneses.

EL DÍA 20 DE ENERO DE 1942, EL GENERAL DE LAS SS REINHARD HEYDRICH (1904–1942) presidió una conferencia en Wannsee, una zona residencial de Berlín. El objetivo era comunicar a los funcionarios alemanes y a los oficiales del ministerio de Asuntos Exteriores los planes de **deportar sistemáticamente a los judíos** de cada país europeo. Serían transportados a campos, principalmente ubicados en Polonia, desde los cuales, se dejó claro, no debía regresar ningún prisionero.

Entre tanto, una ola japonesa de conquistas avanzaba por el Sureste Asiático. **La caída de Singapur**, importante base británica que se rindió a los japoneses en febrero sin ofrecer apenas resistencia, supuso un mazazo para el prestigio del Imperio británico. Unos 120 000 soldados británicos, australianos e indios fueron hechos prisioneros.

La tenaz resistencia de los soldados estadounidenses y filipinos en la península de Batán (**Filipinas**) concluyó en abril. Muchos prisioneros de guerra fallecieron a manos de los japoneses en la brutal **Marcha de la Muerte de Batán**, un trayecto de 100 km que hombres desnutridos y enfermos se vieron obligados a recorrer.

EL HOLOCAUSTO

Los nazis asesinaron a personas de muchos grupos, como eslavos, homosexuales y gitanos, pero el trato que propinaron a los judíos no tuvo parangón. Hacia 1942 se habían embarcado en el exterminio total de los judíos europeos. Para lograr su «solución final», los llevaron a campos construidos y equipados con cámaras de gas. La mayoría murieron al poco de llegar, pero a algunos se los mantuvo con vida y se los empleó como mano de obra esclava. Murieron unos seis millones de judíos, dos tercios de la población judía europea.

A medida que el avance japonés barría la Indonesia holandesa y Birmania, gobernada por Gran Bretaña, los australianos comenzaron a temer que su país fuera el siguiente objetivo. En febrero, un **ataque** perpetrado por aviones japoneses en el **puerto de Darwin**, en el norte de Australia, provocó más de 500 bajas, y minúsculos submarinos japoneses penetraron en el puerto de Sídney a comienzos de junio. En un abrupto cambio de actitud, Australia posó la vista en EE. UU., en lugar de en Gran Bretaña, como aliado militar principal.

En febrero, con un intenso sentimiento antijaponés en auge, el presidente Roosevelt firmó la **orden ejecutiva 9066**, que permitía deportar a **campos de internamiento** a los estadounidenses de origen japonés residentes en EE. UU. Unas 120 000 personas de etnia japonesa fueron internadas durante la guerra.

Mientras EE. UU. se preparaba para una guerra total, **Japón inició su contraataque**. Las batallas navales en el mar del Coral (mayo) y Midway (junio) fueron duelos entre portaaviones dirimidos sin que las flotas japonesas y estadounidenses llegaran a verse. El encuentro en el **mar del Coral** no concedió una ventaja decisiva a ningún bando, pero **Midway** fue un desastre para la marina japonesa, que perdió cuatro portaaviones a manos de bombarderos en picado y aviones cargados con torpedos estadounidenses.

La victoria en Midway supuso un punto de inflexión, pero no decisivo. Cuando las **tropas estadounidenses desembarcaron en Guadalcanal** (islas Salomón) en agosto, los japoneses respondieron con una determinación feroz y desembarcaron a sus propias tropas para contraatacar, al tiempo que iniciaban una serie de batallas navales en las que ambos bandos sufrieron graves pérdidas. En **Nueva Guinea, las tropas australianas** lideraron la lucha en terreno selvático hostil.

> **« HUÍ** DE BATÁN, PERO **REGRESARÉ. »**
>
> **El general Douglas MacArthur**, oficial al mando estadounidense, tras su huida a Australia posterior a la derrota de Batán (20 de marzo de 1942)

En **India**, los británicos afrontaron un desafío político y militar. Con la amenaza japonesa de invadir Birmania, en agosto, Mahatma Gan-dhi (1869–1948) y otros dirigentes del Congreso Nacional lanzaron el **movimiento *Quit India* (Salgan de India)** para exigir plena independencia. Su campaña de desobediencia civil fue reprimida sin piedad por las autoridades británicas y más de cien mil indios fueron arrestados, Gandhi incluido. Algunos nacionalistas indios se alistaron al **Ejército Nacional Indio de Subhas Chandra Bose**, que luchó del bando japonés, pero fueron muchos más quienes ayudaron a los británicos: unos 2,5 millones de

Campos de la muerte nazis
Los alemanes construyeron campos de la muerte, sobre todo en la Polonia ocupada, para exterminar a los judíos. Hubo muchos otros campos de concentración en los que murieron decenas de miles de presos.

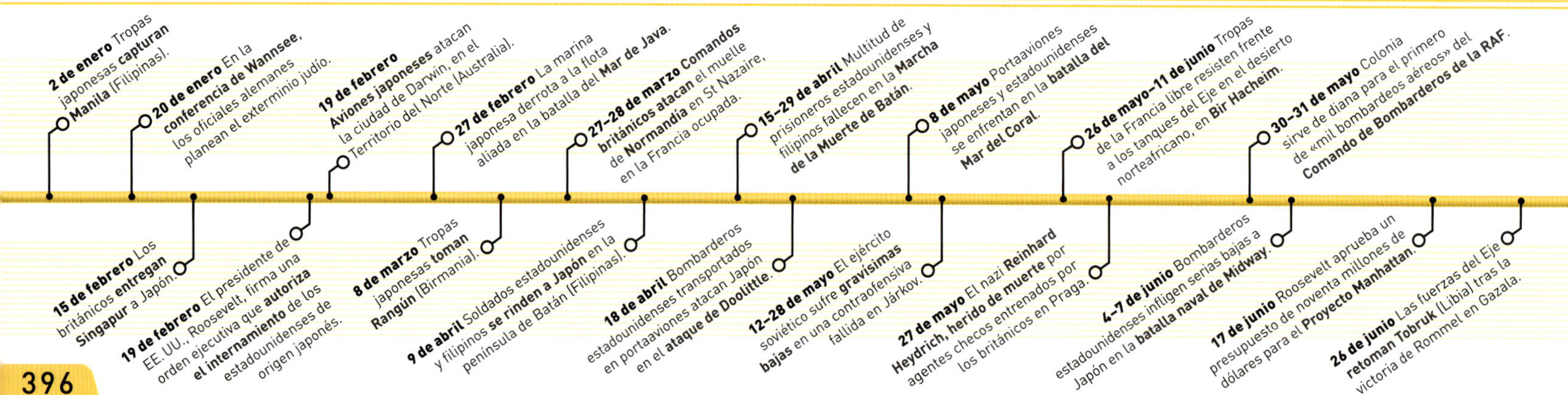

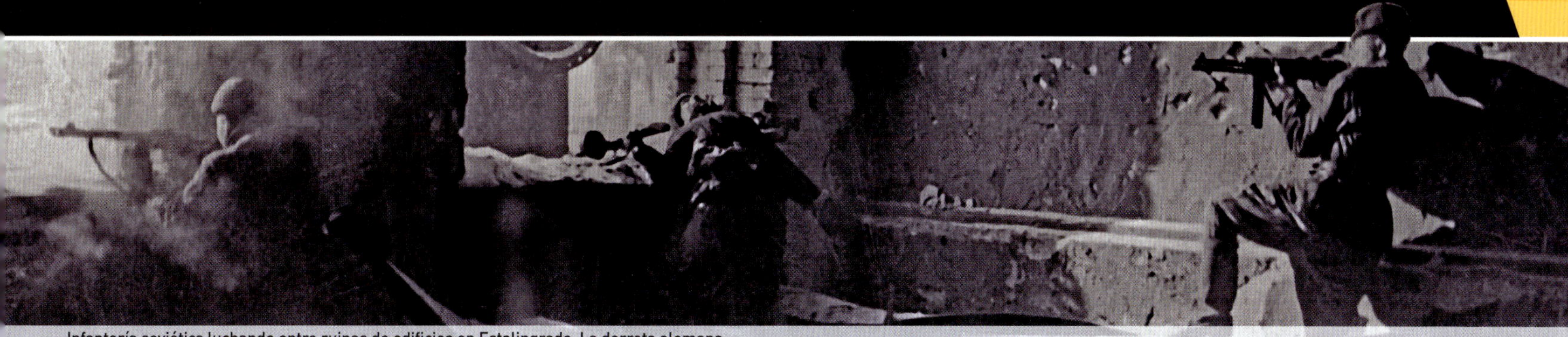

Infantería soviética luchando entre ruinas de edificios en Estalingrado. La derrota alemana en la ciudad supuso un punto de inflexión decisivo en la Segunda Guerra Mundial.

Poderío naval
Bombarderos en picado de la marina estadounidense sobrevuelan la isla de Midway, en el Pacífico. Aquí se libró un duelo decisivo entre portaaviones de EE. UU. y Japón en junio de 1942.

indios se alistaron voluntarios al ejército indio.

En la **guerra en África del Norte**, tras repetidas derrotas a manos del mariscal de campo Erwin Rommel (1891–1944), el Octavo Ejército británico, liderado por el general Bernard Montgomery (1887–1976), se anotó una victoria en una gran ofensiva en **El Alamein** entre octubre y noviembre.

Mientras el ejército del Eje de Rommel retrocedía hacia el oeste a través de Libia, fuerzas aliadas, incluido un numeroso contingente de soldados estadounidenses bajo el mando del general Dwight D. Eisenhower (1890–1969), desembarcaron en el África del Norte francesa durante la **Operación Antorcha**. La oposición de las fuerzas coloniales francesas leales al gobierno de Vichy (*véase* 1940) se superó fácilmente, cosa que dejó a Rommel atrapado entre ejércitos a este y oeste. Los alemanes respondieron ampliando su ocupación militar de Francia hasta la zona gobernada por Vichy.

La guerra que se libraba en la **Unión Soviética** (*véase* 1941) alcanzó su punto álgido en la **batalla de Estalingrado**. Las fuerzas del Eje habían continuado hacia el este durante todo el año y en julio estaban cerca del Cáucaso, con lo que amenazaban los yacimientos petrolíferos vitales de Azerbaiyán. Hitler insistió en que el ejército tomara Estalingrado, de importancia simbólica por su nombre. Soldados alemanes entraron en la ciudad en septiembre, pero los soviéticos la defendieron calle a calle, en medio de edificios en ruinas. En noviembre, el general soviético Gueorgui Zhúkov (1896–1974) planificó un contraataque. Sus ejércitos, que avanzaban desde el norte y el sur, rodearon a las fuerzas del Eje y atraparon a un millón de hombres en el interior de Estalingrado. Hitler les ordenó seguir luchando y, hacia finales de año, morían de hambre, frío y falta de munición. El mariscal de campo alemán Friedrich Paulus figuraba entre los noventa mil hombres que resistieron hasta su rendición en febrero de 1943, y fue uno de los pocos que sobrevivieron al encarcelamiento ruso.

Tanques estadounidenses
EE. UU. suministró tanques Grant al ejército británico desplegado en África del Norte. El de la imagen lo utilizó el general Montgomery como puesto de observación.

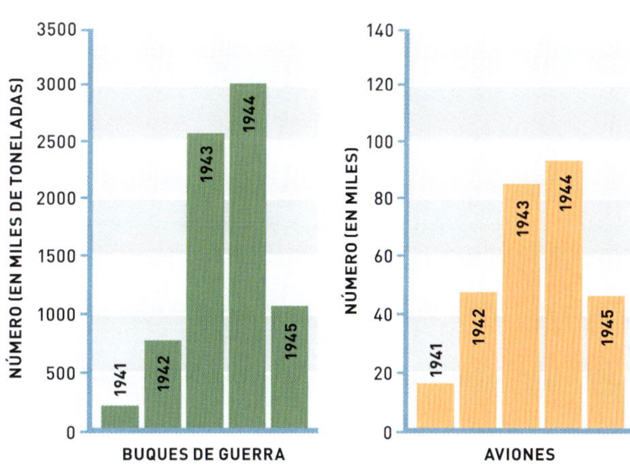

El milagro industrial estadounidense
La producción de las fábricas y los astilleros de EE. UU. aumentó sobremanera durante la Segunda Guerra Mundial. El número de empleados en los astilleros se incrementó de unos 100 000 en 1940 a 1,7 millones durante la guerra.

4 de julio El puerto soviético de Sebastopol, en la península de Crimea, cae en manos alemanas **tras ocho meses de sitio.**

16 de julio Francia agrupa a trece mil judíos para su **deportación a Auschwitz.**

27 de julio El Octavo Ejército británico **frena el avance** por Egipto de las fuerzas del Eje en **El Alamein.**

31 de julio Fundación del Oxford Committee for Famine Relief **(Oxfam).**

7 de agosto Marines de EE. UU. desembarcan en **Guadalcanal.**

8 de agosto Gandhi es detenido tras llamar a la desobediencia civil masiva en India.

13 de agosto El general **Montgomery** asume el mando del Octavo Ejército británico.

19 de agosto El ejército canadiense sufre graves pérdidas en un **bombardeo aéreo sobre Dieppe.**

31 de agosto–25 de septiembre Los británicos **repelen al ejército de Rommel** en Alam el Halfa.

25 de agosto–5 de septiembre El ejército australiano **derrota al japonés** en la bahía de Milne (Nueva Guinea).

13 de septiembre Las fuerzas del Eje atacan el perímetro defensivo de **Estalingrado.**

3 de octubre El **misil balístico alemán A4** supera con éxito su lanzamiento de prueba.

23 de octubre–4 de noviembre El Octavo Ejército británico derrota a las fuerzas del Eje de Rommel en la **segunda batalla de El Alamein.**

7–8 de noviembre Las tropas aliadas lanzan la **Operación Antorcha** y desembarcan en África del Norte.

11 de noviembre Tropas alemanas **ocupan la Francia de Vichy.**

12–15 de noviembre La marina de EE. UU. **causa graves pérdidas** a la flota japonesa estacionada frente a la costa de Guadalcanal.

16 de noviembre Los Álamos (Nuevo México), elegido para la **investigación de la bomba atómica.**

19 de noviembre El general soviético Zhúkov lanza una **contraofensiva para atrapar a los alemanes** en Estalingrado.

2 de diciembre Se consigue una «reacción en cadena» atómica en el **primer reactor nuclear del mundo,** en Chicago.

2 de diciembre El Informe Beveridge propone un **estado del bienestar** en la **Gran Bretaña** de la posguerra.

24 de diciembre El ex primer ministro de Vichy, el **almirante Darlan, asesinado** en Argel.

1943

En enero, el presidente de EE. UU., Roosevelt, y el primer ministro británico, Churchill, se reunieron en Casablanca para discutir la estrategia bélica.

Combatientes de la Resistencia francesa posan para un retrato de grupo. La Resistencia llevó a cabo actos de sabotaje y espionaje y montó operaciones de guerrilla.

EN ENERO DE 1943, Roosevelt se reunió con el primer ministro británico, **Winston Churchill**, en una conferencia en **Casablanca** (Marruecos) que definió el curso futuro de la Segunda Guerra Mundial en Europa. Gran Bretaña convenció a EE. UU. de **planear una invasión de Sicilia**, consciente de que ello obligaba a posponer la invasión del norte de Francia hasta 1944. Los aliados acordaron también que sus fuerzas aéreas lanzaran una ofensiva combinada con bombarderos contra Alemania. Al final de la conferencia, Roosevelt anunció que **solo aceptarían una «rendición incondicional»** de sus enemigos.

La rendición de las fuerzas del Eje en Estalingrado (*véase* 1942) en febrero supuso un fuerte revés para Alemania, si bien continuó ocupando gran parte de Europa. En muchos lugares, **movimientos de resistencia armada** respondieron a la ocupación. La decisión de 1943 de reclutar obligatoriamente a hombres franceses para trabajar en fábricas alemanas supuso un punto de inflexión para la **Resistencia en Francia**. Para evitar los trabajos forzados, miles de jóvenes huyeron y formaron guerrillas en regiones rurales remotas.

Casablanca
El estreno de la película Casablanca *se programó para aprovechar la famosa conferencia de Casablanca.*

Entre los movimientos de resistencia había grandes diferencias políticas. En los **Balcanes**, los partisanos liderados por el comunista **Tito** (*véase* recuadro) lucharon contra los alemanes, pero también contra las guerrillas de los chetniks, encabezadas por el serbio nacionalista y monárquico **Draza Mihailovic**. En Francia, el líder de la Resistencia **Jean Moulin** se esforzó por unir a las facciones rivales, pero en mayo fue arrestado y torturado por el jefe de la Gestapo Klaus Barbie y murió en cautiverio.

La primavera de 1943 trajo el clímax de la lucha contra los submarinos alemanes conocida como la **batalla del Atlántico**. En marzo, los aliados perdieron 260 000 toneladas de envíos comerciales a causa de ataques submarinos alemanes, y se temía que la línea de aprovisionamiento por mar de Gran Bretaña quedara cercenada. Los submarinos alemanes operaban en grupos conocidos como «manadas de lobos», coordinados por radio. Sin embargo, una combinación de factores, incluidos el incremento en el empleo de aviones en patrullas oceánicas, los mensajes navales alemanes descifrados por los servicios de inteligencia y el equipamiento de escoltas de convoyes con equipos de orientación por radar y radio, inclinó la balanza en contra de los submarinos. En torno a mayo, **las pérdidas de submarinos** eran tan elevadas que el almirante al mando, Karl Dönitz, tuvo que retirar a sus fuerzas del Atlántico. La ofensiva con submarinos jamás volvió a recobrar su vigor.

JOSIP BROZ TITO (1892–1980)

Nacido en Croacia, Josip Broz adoptó el nombre de Tito como activista comunista en la década de 1930. Tras la ocupación alemana de Yugoslavia en 1941, Tito lideró una guerrilla que asumió el control del país en 1945. Convirtió Yugoslavia en un estado comunista, pero se opuso al dominio de la Unión Soviética. Fue el presidente de Yugoslavia hasta su muerte.

> **« ALEMANIA** ES UNA FORTALEZA, PERO **UNA FORTALEZA SIN TEJADO**. »
>
> **Franklin D. Roosevelt**, presidente de EE. UU. (1944)

Con diferencia, el combate terrestre más duro de 1943 se libró en el **Frente Oriental de Alemania**. Pese al desastre de Estalingrado, el ejército del Eje logró organizar una contraofensiva con éxito en **Járkov** en primavera. Los soviéticos quedaron cercados en un territorio expuesto, un saliente, en **Kursk**. Los generales alemanes planeaban atacar desde el norte y el sur para atrapar a las fuerzas soviéticas en el saliente y destruirlas. Pero el subcomandante supremo, **Gueorgui Zhúkov**, anticipó la ofensiva alemana y preparó un formidable sistema defensivo. Los ejércitos reunidos en Kursk eran inmensos: en total, ambos bandos englobaban a más de dos millones de hombres, más de seis mil tanques y cinco mil aviones. El ataque del Eje comenzó el 5 de julio e inició la **mayor batalla con tanques de la historia**. Las pérdidas soviéticas fueron muchas, pero tras cuatro días, la ofensiva del Eje se había encallado y el Ejército Rojo lanzó un contraataque. Los alemanes organizaron una retirada combativa, pero la oleada bélica en el este había acabado para siempre.

Insignia soviética
Esta insignia se concedió a la tripulación de los tanques soviéticos durante la Segunda Guerra Mundial. La URSS perdió unos cinco mil tanques en Kursk en el verano de 1943.

Mientras los aliados occidentales montaron una **invasión de Sicilia a gran escala**. Los ejércitos de Gran Bretaña y EE. UU. desembarcaron en la costa y avanzaron rodeando la isla por caras opuestas ante la escasa oposición de las fuerzas italianas, que pronto se rindieron. La campaña devino un pulso entre el general de EE. UU. **George S. Patton** y el británico **Bernard Montgomery**. Patton fue el primero en llegar a Messina, pero el desentendimiento entre ambos generales permitió que la mayoría de las tropas del Eje escaparan a la Italia peninsular.

La pérdida de Sicilia fue todo un contratiempo para Mussolini. Tras una **moción de desconfianza** por parte del **Gran Consejo Fascista**, Mussolini fue depuesto por el rey Víctor Manuel III (1869–1947) y

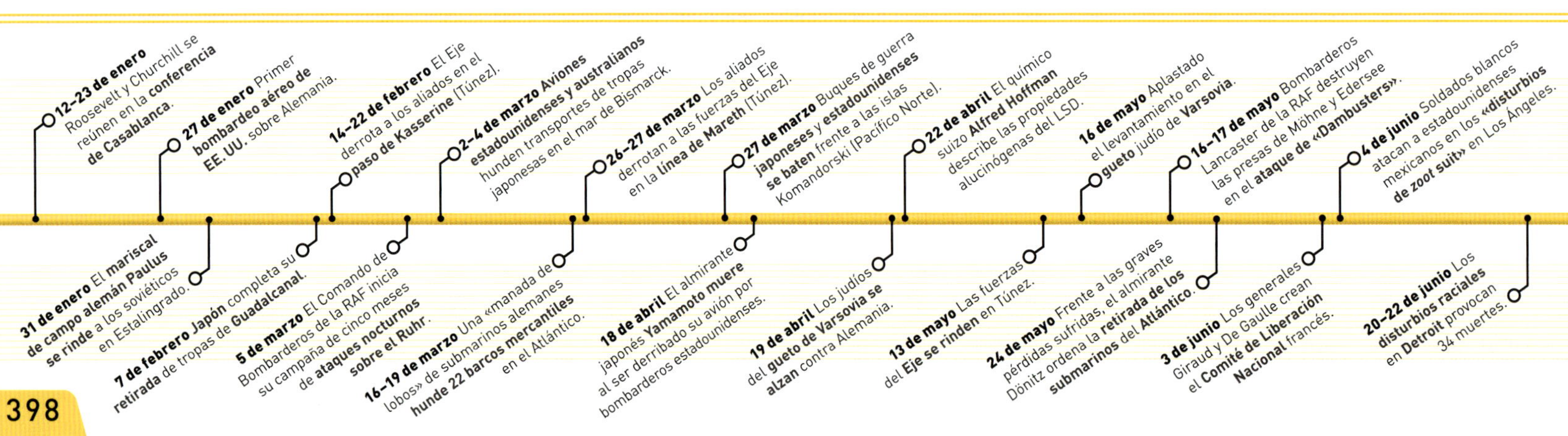

Soldados de la lancha de la Guardia Costera estadounidense *Spencer* observan la explosión de una carga de profundidad que hundió un submarino alemán en el Atlántico el 17 de abril.

Cartel estadounidense
Este cartel sugiere que trabajar en fábricas de munición puede ser tan glamuroso como unirse a los diversos servicios femeninos uniformados.

arrestado. Su sustituto, el **mariscal Pietro Badoglio** (1871–1956), firmó un armisticio con los aliados a principios de septiembre. Con todo, los alemanes tuvieron tiempo de tomar posiciones clave en Italia y defendieron la península de las fuerzas aliadas. Paracaidistas alemanes rescataron a Mussolini y le nombraron gobernante de una **República Social Italiana** títere fundada en la ciudad de Saló. Cuando las tropas aliadas se abrían camino desde Nápoles rumbo a Roma, el **gobierno de Badoglio se sumó a los aliados** y declaró la guerra a Alemania.

Alemania fue **bombardeada por aire** durante 1943. El Comando de Bombarderos de la RAF, equipado con el nuevo bombardero Lancaster, logró un gran éxito en el ataque de **«Dambusters»** de mayo. Con «bombas de rebote», los Lancaster realizaron ataques nocturnos a baja altura sobre cuatro presas del Ruhr y quebraron dos de ellas. En julio, los bombarderos saturaron **Hamburgo** con dispositivos incendiarios. En el ambiente cálido y seco, los fuegos dispersos se fusionaron en una única tormenta de fuego colosal. Más de 37 000 personas fallecieron, en su mayoría civiles. Al mismo tiempo, la **fuerza aérea de EE. UU.** inició una **campaña de bombardeos diurnos**. Los bombarderos estadounidenses debían repeler los ataques de los aviones alemanes y lanzar bombas sobre objetivos usando visores de tecnología avanzada. Los B-17 y B-24 sufrieron unas pérdidas alarmantes, y los bombardeos de precisión resultaron difíciles de conseguir en situación de combate.

El **impacto de los bombardeos** sobre la población alemana fue inmenso: bajas, cientos de miles de personas sin hogar y hambre. Más de **dos millones de niños** fueron **evacuados** de las ciudades. Muchas fábricas se reubicaron bajo tierra para evitar los bombardeos.

Las penurias vividas por los civiles alemanes fueron parecidas, en mayor o menor grado, a las vividas en todos los países europeos, España incluida, pese a su neutralidad. La escasez de mano de obra en Gran Bretaña condujo al **reclutamiento de mujeres para trabajar** en la defensa civil, en servicios militares auxiliares, en las fábricas y en la agricultura. En EE. UU., las mujeres asumieron empleos en la industria pesada tradicionalmente reservados a los hombres.

Los obreros negros también accedieron a puestos que en tiempos de paz se reservaban para los blancos. Ello provocó **tensiones raciales**. En junio se produjo en Detroit un enfrentamiento entre blancos y negros que acabó con 34 fallecidos.

Una de las peores tragedias de 1943 fue la **hambruna de Bengala** que segó la vida a más de un millón de personas en la India británica. La responsabilidad de esta catástrofe aún es objeto de disputa, pero Churchill rechazó reservar espacio en los buques destinados al esfuerzo bélico, lo cual impidió que los alimentos llegaran a la población.

«Fortaleza voladora»
La tripulación de un B-17 Flying Fortress de la Octava Fuerza Aérea se prepara en una base de Inglaterra para un bombardeo sobre Alemania. La Octava Fuerza Aérea perdió a 26 000 hombres entre 1942 y 1945.

En Asia, 60 000 prisioneros de guerra aliados y casi 200 000 trabajadores forzados **construyeron un ferrocarril** desde **Tailandia** para aprovisionar a las tropas japonesas en **Birmania**. En torno a 16 000 de esos prisioneros y 90 000 obreros asiáticos fallecieron durante su construcción.

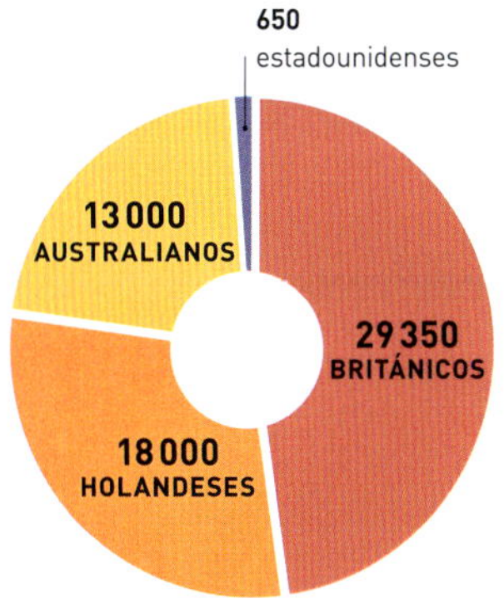

Ferrocarril en Birmania
Junto con mano de obra forzosa asiática, los japoneses usaron a sus prisioneros británicos, australianos y holandeses para construir el ferrocarril.

5–13 de julio Una **batalla a gran escala con tanques en Kursk** concluye con la victoria decisiva del ejército soviético.

8 de julio Fallece **Jean Moulin,** líder de la Resistencia francesa (n. 1899) bajo custodia de la Gestapo.

10 de julio Las fuerzas aliadas invaden Sicilia en la **Operación Husky**.

25 de julio Mussolini es destituido y **arrestado**.

27–28 de julio Un bombardeo aéreo de la RAF provoca una **tormenta de fuego** que **arrasa** la ciudad alemana de **Hamburgo**.

1 de agosto Bombarderos estadounidenses B-24 atacan por aire los **yacimientos petrolíferos de Ploesti (Rumania)** y pierden 53 aviones.

17 de agosto Bombarderos estadounidenses **sufren graves pérdidas** al atacar fábricas en Schweinfurt y Regensburgo (Alemania).

17 de agosto Los aliados completan la **conquista de Sicilia**.

3 de septiembre Tiene lugar el primer **desembarco aliado** en la **Italia** peninsular.

8 de septiembre Italia anuncia su **rendición**.

12 de septiembre Los alemanes **rescatan a Mussolini** del cautiverio.

25 de septiembre Mussolini funda la **República de Saló** en el norte de Italia.

1 de octubre Fuerzas aliadas **entran en Nápoles**.

13 de octubre El **gobierno italiano** del general Badoglio **declara la guerra** a Alemania.

17 de octubre Concluido el **ferrocarril** japonés **de Birmania**, construido por prisioneros de guerra.

1 de noviembre Marines estadounidenses desembarcan en Bougainville (**islas Salomón**).

6 de noviembre Las fuerzas soviéticas **liberan** la ciudad ucraniana de **Kiev**.

18 de noviembre Se inicia el **bombardeo** aliado **sistemático** de Berlín.

20–23 de noviembre Marines de EE. UU. toman el **atolón de Tarawa** tras una intensa lucha en el Pacífico.

28 de noviembre–1 de diciembre Churchill, Roosevelt y Stalin se reúnen en la conferencia de Teherán.

24 de diciembre Eisenhower es designado **comandante supremo aliado** de Europa.

1944

150 000 **SOLDADOS ALIADOS** DESEMBARCARON EN LAS **PLAYAS DE NORMANDÍA**

9000 SOLDADOS **ALIADOS FALLECIERON** EN EL DESEMBARCO

Soldados aliados caminan hacia la orilla como parte de la invasión de Normandía, el 6 de junio. Los desembarcos iniciaron la liberación de la Francia ocupada.

A PRINCIPIOS DE 1944, ITALIA VIVIÓ COMBATES INTENSOS al bloquear las tropas alemanas el avance aliado sobre Roma. En enero, un desembarco aliado por mar en **Anzio**, detrás de la línea defensiva alemana de Gustav, no logró romper el punto muerto. Los comandantes aliados decidieron bombardear en febrero la abadía medieval de la línea de Gustav, pero aquel acto de desacralización, aparte de ser muy criticado, fue ineficaz. **Montecassino acabó cediendo a la infantería polaca** en mayo, lo cual permitió liberar Roma un mes más tarde.

En primavera, soldados indios británicos frenaron el intento japonés de invadir el noreste de India desde Birmania. La **ofensiva japonesa** fue repelida con tal éxito que las tropas aliadas lograron organizar su propia ofensiva y retomar gran parte de Birmania ese mismo año. Con la supresión del movimiento *Quit India* (Salgan de India), los británicos habían corroborado su autoridad en el subcontinente.

Mientras, los preparativos aliados para **invadir la Francia ocupada** convirtieron el sur de Inglaterra en un campamento armado. El general Dwight D. Eisenhower (1890–1969) dirigió la **Operación Overlord**. Los aliados escogieron Normandía como objetivo para su invasión. Pospuestos a causa del mal tiempo, los **desembarcos en Normandía** se produjeron el 6 de junio, conocido como el **Día D**.

Por la noche, 18 000 soldados aerotransportados aterrizaron en paracaídas o planeadores detrás de las defensas litorales alemanas. Al alba, una flota de 5000 barcos con más de 130 000 soldados a bordo llegaron a la costa. Fue la **mayor operación anfibia de la historia**. Tres de las cinco playas donde se realizaron los desembarcos, cuyos nombres en código eran **Sword**, **Juno** y **Utah**, fueron tomadas con relativa facilidad por tropas británicas, canadienses y estadounidenses, mientras que los británicos en la playa de **Gold**, y en especial los estadounidenses en la playa de **Omaha**, sufrieron graves pérdidas antes de asegurarse el terreno.

Estrella de Birmania
Esta condecoración militar se entregó a soldados británicos y de la Commonwealth por su servicio en la campaña de Birmania (1941–1945).

Dos innovaciones ingeniosas, el **puerto flotante Mulberry** y el oleoducto submarino Pluto, permitieron a los aliados aprovisionar a sus fuerzas una vez en tierra firme. Siguió una batalla atroz para tomar Normandía, y hasta agosto no fue posible doblegar la resistencia alemana.

Mientras, el dictador **Adolf Hitler** (1889–1945) había sobrevivido a un **intento de asesinato**. Altos cargos alemanes conspiraron para derrocar al *Führer* y buscar la paz con los aliados occidentales. El 20 de julio, el coronel Claus Schenk von Stauffenberg (1907–1944) transportó una bomba en su maletín a una reunión en el cuartel general de Hitler en Rastenburg (Prusia Oriental). La colocó bajo la mesa en la que Hitler estaba sentado. Cuando explotó, mató a cuatro personas, pero **el dictador salió ileso**. Stauffenberg y los principales conspiradores fueron asesinados por un escuadrón de fusilamiento; otros miles fueron arrestados y torturados, y muchos fallecieron lentamente. Al mariscal de campo Erwin Rommel (1891–1944), también implicado en el complot, le permitieron suicidarse.

Una vez traspasada Normandía en agosto (*véase* p. 389), los aliados avanzaron hacia la **liberación de París**. Después de que los combatientes de la Resistencia francesa iniciaran un alzamiento en la ciudad el 19 de agosto, las Fuerzas Francesas Libres del general Charles de Gaulle, integradas en los ejércitos aliados de Eisenhower, se apresuraron en llegar a París. Una columna de tanques franceses entró en el centro de París el 25 de agosto.

Al mismo tiempo que los alemanes se retiraban, en París comen-

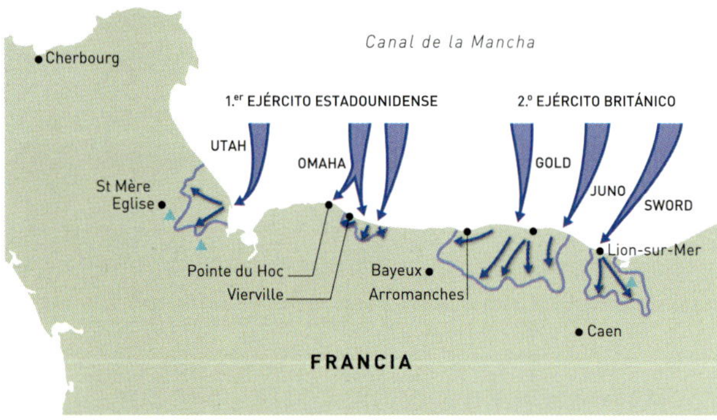

Desembarco de Normandía
Los aliados desembarcaron en cinco playas: Sword, Juno, Gold, Utah y Omaha. Otros soldados se lanzaron en paracaídas tras las líneas enemigas.

CLAVE
- Avance aliado/desembarco
- Paracaidistas aliados
- Frente aliado (7 junio 1944)

22 de enero Fuerzas aliadas **desembarcan en Anzio**, tras la línea de Gustav (Italia).

27 de enero Soldados de la URSS **recuperan Leningrado**.

15 de febrero Bombarderos estadounidenses destruyen la abadía de **Monte Cassino** en la línea de Gustav.

17 de febrero Marines estadounidenses desembarcan en Eniwetok (**islas Marshall**).

20–25 de febrero Bombarderos de EE. UU. y Gran Bretaña atacan fábricas de aviones alemanas en la Gran Semana.

23 de febrero Stalin ordena la **deportación masiva** de chechenos e ingusetios hacia **Asia central**.

7 de marzo Japón lanza una ofensiva desde **Birmania** sobre el noroeste de India.

19 de marzo Tropas alemanas ocupan Hungría para detener las **negociaciones de paz húngaras** con los aliados.

4 de abril Tropas indias británicas resisten a los japoneses en **Kohima**.

18 de abril Japón lanza una gran ofensiva en China, la **Operación Ichi-Go**.

21 de abril El Gobierno Provisional francés reconoce el **derecho femenino al voto**.

28 de abril Más de 700 estadounidenses **fallecen en el ensayo** del desembarco de Normandía.

5 de mayo Gandhi sale de la cárcel por su débil salud.

9 de mayo El ejército soviético retoma el puerto de **Sebastopol**, en el mar Negro.

15 de mayo Alemania inicia la **deportación** de judíos húngaros a **Auschwitz**.

17 de mayo Tropas polacas expulsan a los alemanes de Monte Cassino.

4 de junio Roma cae en manos aliadas.

6 de junio Se inicia la invasión de Normandía con los **desembarcos del Día D**.

13 de junio Alemania lanza las **primeras bombas volantes V-1** contra Inglaterra.

15 de junio La infantería y marines de EE. UU. empiezan el desembarco en Saipán (**islas Marianas**).

19 de junio La aviación naval japonesa sufre gravísimas pérdidas en la **batalla del Mar de las Filipinas**.

22 de junio El ejército soviético lanza la **Operación Bagration** para expulsar a las fuerzas del Eje de Bielorrusia.

Soldados de la 7.ª División Armada de EE. UU. patrullan por la población belga de St. Vith, sometida a duros enfrentamientos durante la ofensiva alemana de las Ardenas, en diciembre.

« UNA OPERACIÓN **EXTREMADAMENTE OSADA.** »

General Alfred Jodl, jefe de operaciones, acerca de la contraofensiva de Hitler

zaron las celebraciones y también las **represalias contra los supuestos colaboradores**. Unos nueve mil franceses fueron ejecutados y decenas de miles sometidos al escarnio público (por ejemplo, se hizo desfilar a las mujeres con la cabeza afeitada) antes de que **De Gaulle instituyera un gobierno provisional** y restableciera el orden.

A principios de agosto, el **movimiento de la resistencia polaca** se alzó contra los alemanes en Varsovia. El Ejército Rojo soviético se hallaba a las puertas de la ciudad, tras avanzar hacia el oeste durante el verano, pero Stalin no deseaba ayudar a los polacos, que, en su gran mayoría, eran antirrusos y anticomunistas. El Ejército Rojo se detuvo a escasa distancia de Varsovia y durante dos meses, mientras el levantamiento polaco era aplastado por tropas nazis, se mantuvo prácticamente inactivo. Varios cientos de miles de polacos fueron asesinados. Cuando los supervivientes se rindieron, a principios de octubre, Alemania destruyó Varsovia.

Liberación de París
Los parisinos celebran la liberación de su ciudad y el retorno del general De Gaulle a Francia como líder de los franceses libres.

En septiembre, con gran parte de Bélgica bajo control aliado, el general británico Bernard Montgomery (1887–1976) urdió un plan para poner fin a la guerra mediante una **invasión aerotransportada de los Países Bajos ocupados**. Paracaidistas británicos, estadounidenses y polacos intentaron asediar y apresar una serie de puentes que permitirían a los tanques aliados avanzar hacia el norte de Alemania. Sin embargo, no lograron tomar el último puente, en **Arnhem**, y la operación fracasó, lo cual obligó a los holandeses a padecer un crudo invierno bajo los nazis.

La **ofensiva de EE. UU. en el Pacífico** cobró impulso a lo largo del año (*véanse* pp. 394–395). Superados en número y en poderío militar, los japoneses lucharon con una determinación suicida. En la batalla por la **isla de Saipán**, entre el 15 de junio y el 9 de julio, casi toda la guarnición japonesa de treinta mil soldados murió. La marina japonesa quedó prácticamente arrasada en dos batallas: en el **mar de las Filipinas** en junio, y en el **golfo de Leyte** en octubre.

Ante una muerte casi certera en un combate desigual con el ejército de EE. UU., algunos pilotos japoneses orquestaron ataques ***kamikazes*** y estrellaron deliberadamente sus aviones contra buques de guerra estadounidenses. Su táctica resultó tan efectiva que se adoptó incluso como forma de ataque masivo, usando a cientos de pilotos suicidas sin apenas formación.

Plegaria por el retorno
Algunos soldados japoneses llevaban su bandera nacional con una plegaria en la que rogaban por su retorno a casa.

Con la derrota perfilándose en el horizonte, Hitler puso toda su fe en las armas secretas. El **Messerschmitt 262**, el primer avión a reacción, entró en el conflicto, pero no logró invertir el dominio creciente de las tropas aéreas aliadas. Las **bombas volantes V-1** arrojadas sobre Londres causaron graves bajas, pero no tuvieron una repercusión decisiva, al igual que los V-2, los primeros misiles balísticos del mundo. Se lanzaron unos tres mil **V-2**, la mayoría sobre Londres y Amberes. Llegaban sin advertencia y era imposible defenderse de ellos, pero eran poco precisos y no inclinaron la balanza como Hitler ansiaba.

Bomba volante alemana
La V-1 se impulsaba mediante un motor a reacción primitivo e iba cargada de explosivos. En verano de 1944 se lanzaron más de cien al día sobre Londres.

En diciembre, el *Führer* lanzó su última campaña con una ofensiva sorpresa en las Ardenas que pasaría a conocerse como la **batalla las Ardenas**. Tanques alemanes atravesaron la línea de frente de EE. UU. y se dirigieron a Amberes. El refuerzo de la resistencia, sobre todo con tropas aerotransportadas estadounidenses en Bastogne, estuvo seguido por un contraataque aliado bien organizado. Los tanques alemanes se quedaron sin combustible y el clima favorable permitió a los aviones aliados acudir en auxilio de sus tropas terrestres. El último lanzamiento de dados de Hitler había fracasado.

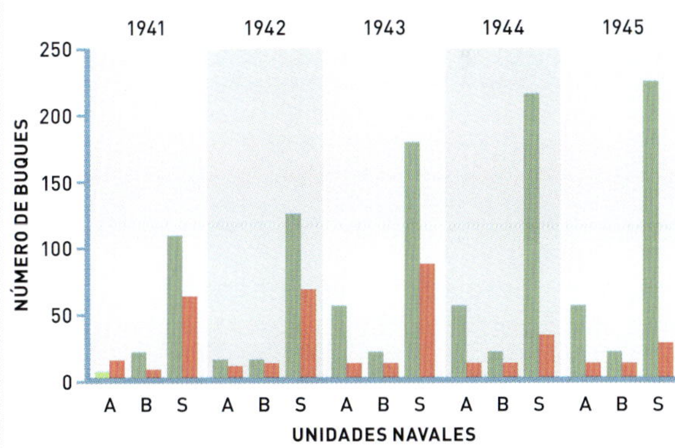

Poderío naval de EE. UU. y Japón
La combinación de unos astilleros muy productivos y de contundentes bajas japonesas permitió a EE. UU. hacerse con el dominio naval del Pacífico.

CLAVE
- EE. UU.
- Japón

A Portaaviones
B Buques de guerra
S Submarinos

1–22 de julio En la conferencia de Bretton Woods, los países aliados acuerdan un **sistema financiero para el mundo de la posguerra**.

18 de julio El **general Tojo dimite** como primer ministro japonés.

20 de julio Hitler escapa por los pelos de un **complot de asesinato** orquestado por oficiales y altos mandos.

22 de julio Los soviéticos liberan el campo de la muerte nazi en **Majdanek** (Polonia).

26 de julio El Me262 alemán es el **primer caza a reacción** que participa en combate.

1 de agosto El Ejército Doméstico Polaco se alza en Varsovia.

12–21 de agosto Las divisiones Panzer (tanques) alemanas sufren graves pérdidas en la **Bolsa de Falaise**.

15 de agosto Tropas aliadas desembarcan en la costa mediterránea francesa.

25 de agosto Unidades armadas francesas y combatientes de la Resistencia **liberan París**.

3 de septiembre Tropas británicas **liberan Bruselas**.

8 de septiembre Se disparan los primeros **misiles balísticos V-2** sobre Londres.

17 de septiembre Tropas aliadas aerotransportadas se lanzan sobre Países Bajos en la **Operación Market Garden**.

21 de octubre La ciudad alemana de **Aquisgrán** cae en manos estadounidenses.

23–26 de octubre La marina japonesa sufre una derrota decisiva en la **batalla de Leyte**.

25 de octubre El buque escolta estadounidense *St Lo* es el primero en hundirse por un **ataque suicida *kamikaze*** japonés.

7 de noviembre Roosevelt gana sus cuartas elecciones presidenciales de EE. UU.

12 de noviembre Bombarderos de la RAF hunden el buque de guerra alemán *Tirpitz* en los fiordos noruegos.

3 de diciembre Enfrentamientos en Atenas entre los combatientes de la resistencia comunista griega y las tropas **británicas.**

16 de diciembre La ofensiva alemana en Bastogne inicia la **batalla de las Ardenas**.

22 de diciembre La guarnición estadounidense en **Bastogne** rechaza la llamada a la rendición alemana.

Afiliación al partido
ALEMANIA
Este carnet de afiliación, fechado el 15 de julio de 1937, certificaba que su propietario era miembro del partido nazi, el partido gobernante en Alemania durante la Segunda Guerra Mundial.

Estrella amarilla
ALEMANIA
Desde septiembre de 1941, los judíos del Reich alemán estaban obligados a llevar una estrella amarilla con la palabra *Jude* («judío») escrita.

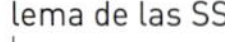

Arma antisubmarinos
GRAN BRETAÑA
Los buques de la marina británica llevaban lanzaderas de cargas de profundidad para responder a los ataques de los submarinos alemanes. La carga hacía explosión a una profundidad predeterminada.

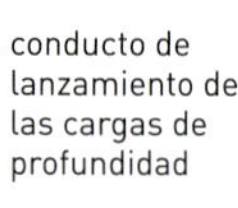

Cartel del Canadá francés
CANADÁ
Ester cartel, dirigido a la población canadiense francófona, insta a los marines voluntarios a unirse en la lucha contra los submarinos alemanes.

Daga de las SS
ALEMANIA
Todos los miembros de las SS de élite nazis recibían una daga ceremonial. La cuchilla luce el lema de las SS, *Meine Ehre heisst Treue* («Mi honor es la lealtad»).

II GUERRA MUNDIAL

UN CONFLICTO MUNDIAL QUE AFECTÓ A LOS COMBATIENTES Y A LA POBLACIÓN CIVIL

La Segunda Guerra Mundial causó más víctimas que ningún otro conflicto de la historia de la humanidad. Se libraron batallas por tierra, mar y aire, con armas que englobaban desde rifles de cerrojo hasta bombas atómicas.

En el conflicto participaron más de cien millones de soldados y la mayoría de los países del mundo. Además de ser la guerra de mayor alcance territorial de la historia, se caracterizó por las enormes bajas entre la población civil, sometida a bombardeos aéreos a gran escala y masacrada por los ejércitos alemán y japonés y por el lanzamiento de las bombas atómicas en Japón.

Máquina encriptadora
EE.UU.
La M-209 era una encriptadora mecánica que proporcionaba una codificación rápida y básica y una seguridad suficiente para su uso en el campo de batalla.

Fusil de cerrojo Lee Enfield
GRAN BRETAÑA
Este fusil, que disparaba cartuchos del calibre 303 alojados en una recámara de diez cartuchos, fue el utilizado por la infantería británica y de la Commonwealth en ambas guerras mundiales.

Teléfono de campaña
EE.UU.
Los teléfonos portátiles, como el estadounidense EE8 de la imagen, se usaban para las comunicaciones a distancias relativamente cortas en el campo de batalla.

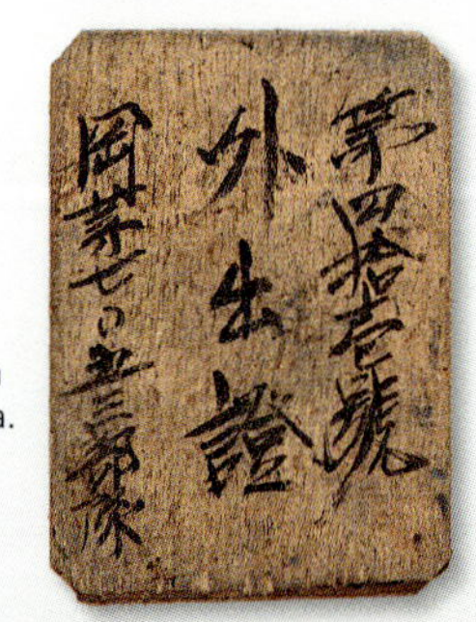

Oración escrita
JAPÓN
Esta oración escrita sobre madera perteneció a un soldado japonés budista. Soldados de todas las nacionalidades buscaban consuelo en la religión y en la superstición.

Sextante naval
JAPÓN
Empleado para calcular la posición de los barcos, el sextante naval se remonta a la época de la navegación a vela, pero aún se usaba en la Segunda Guerra Mundial.

Píldora para el suicidio
GRAN BRETAÑA
Los británicos enviaban a agentes a la Europa ocupada por los nazis para establecer relaciones con combatientes de la resistencia local. Cada agente portaba una píldora para el suicidio que debía tragarse si era capturado.

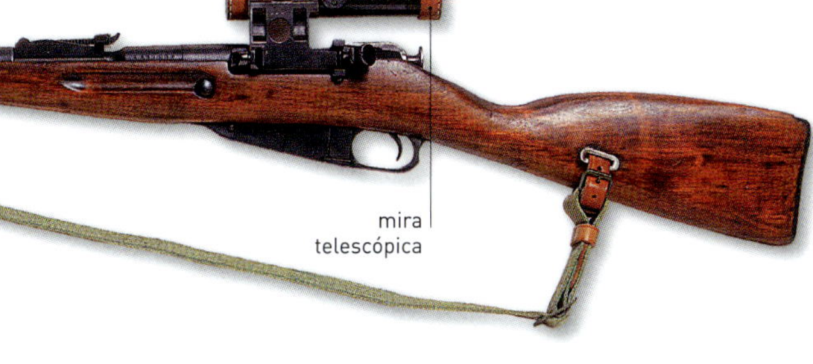

mira telescópica

Fusil de francotirador
URSS
El Ejército Rojo soviético hizo un amplio uso de francotiradores, sobre todo en la batalla de Estalingrado. Utilizaban un fusil de infantería Mosin-Nagant estándar con un visor telescópico.

una ventanilla permite ver las letras en código

rotor del teclado: este ajuste puede modificarse para cambiar el código de cifrado

Calzado improvisado
ALEMANIA
Las tropas alemanas que invadieron la URSS en 1941 no estaban equipadas para afrontar el invierno ruso. Algunos soldados se confeccionaron botas de paja para evitar que se les congelaran los pies.

Gültig vom 24.7. bis 20.8.1944
Reichsfleischkarte
65

Cartilla de racionamiento para civiles
ALEMANIA
La escasez de alimentos, combustible y otros productos básicos condujo a la mayoría de países a aprobar el racionamiento. Esta cartilla alemana es para la carne.

Cartel sobre los apagones
ALEMANIA
Este cartel reclama a los ciudadanos alemanes que cumplan la normativa de apagar la luz durante los bombardeos aéreos. El eslogan dice: «¡El enemigo ve tu luz! ¡Déjalo a oscuras!».

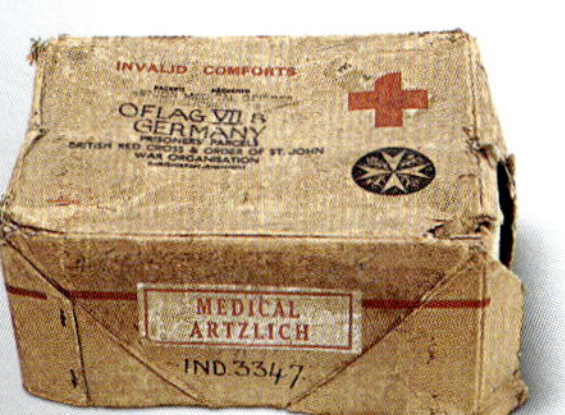

Paquete de la Cruz Roja
GRAN BRETAÑA
Los prisioneros recibían paquetes de comida de la Cruz Roja. Gracias a ello, a finales de la contienda, los prisioneros de guerra aliados estaban mejor alimentados que sus captores.

broche del escorpión del Long Range Desert Group

Turbante para el desierto
NUEVA ZELANDA
El Long Range Desert Group, establecido por los británicos, en un principio estaba integrado por neozelandeses. Descubrieron que el turbante al estilo árabe los protegía de las inclemencias del desierto.

placa de activación por presión

Mina antitanques
ALEMANIA
Esta mina Teller tenía un fusible que se activaba con la presión de las ruedas de los tanques. Durante la guerra se fabricaron más de tres millones de unidades.

Máquina encriptadora Enigma
ALEMANIA
Los alemanes creían que los mensajes encriptados con la Enigma eran seguros, pero, con la ayuda de un protoordenador electromecánico, los aliados lograron descifrar el código.

Reliquia nuclear
JAPÓN
Esta botella de vidrio fundido demuestra el calor extremo generado por la bomba atómica estadounidense que destruyó Hiroshima el 6 de agosto de 1945.

Londinenses eufóricos celebran el Día de la Victoria en Europa (VE), el 8 de mayo, tras el anuncio de la rendición incondicional definitiva de las tropas alemanas.

« ¡LA **VICTORIA ES VUESTRA**! ¡ES LA **VICTORIA** DE LA CAUSA DE **LA LIBERTAD EN CADA PAÍS**! »

Winston Churchill, en un discurso a las multitudes en Londres (8 de mayo de 1945)

EN FEBRERO DE 1945, IÓSIV STALIN, FRANKLIN ROOSEVELT Y WINSTON CHURCHILL se reunieron por última vez en la conferencia de **Yalta** (Crimea). Stalin accedió a celebrar elecciones democráticas en Polonia, promesa que no pretendía cumplir. Para socorrer a las tropas soviéticas que invadían Alemania desde el este, los dirigentes occidentales acordaron aumentar los bombardeos sobre los centros ferroviarios alemanes, incluido **Dresde**. La noche del 13 al 14 de febrero, la RAF británica lanzó bombas explosivas e incendiarias sobre Dresde y provocó una tormenta de fuego que destruyó el centro histórico de la ciudad y mató a 25 000 personas.

No hubo piedad con los alemanes cuando la **liberación de los campos de la muerte** reveló los crímenes nazis. El Ejército Rojo soviético liberó los principales centros de exterminio, incluido **Auschwitz**. Los aliados occidentales vivieron su experiencia más gráfica de la barbarie nazi en **Belsen**, un campo de concentración de Sajonia. Las tropas británicas que liberaron el campo a mediados de abril hallaron a miles de prisioneros inanes, maltratados y enfermos, y cadáveres arrojados a fosas comunes o insepultos. El metraje de lo sucedido en Belsen convenció a la población de que la guerra contra Alemania había sido justificada.

Desembarco en Iwo Jima
Marines estadounidenses inmovilizados por los japoneses en una playa de la isla volcánica de Iwo Jima durante los desembarcos del 19 de febrero.

El **coste humano** de la guerra con Japón **continuó en ascenso**. Entre febrero y marzo, la marina estadounidense sufrió 26 000 bajas durante la captura de la isla de **Iwo Jima**, un peñón volcánico en el Pacífico defendido a muerte por una guarnición japonesa de 18 000 hombres.

La **invasión estadounidense** de la **isla de Okinawa**, lanzada en abril, acabó en un baño de sangre. Como de costumbre, los soldados japoneses se batieron a muerte y decenas de miles de isleños murieron también, de entre los cuales muchos se suicidaron. La flota aliada apostada frente a la costa quedó hecha añicos por **ataques *kamikazes* masivos** (*véase* 1944).

Entre tanto, los bombarderos B-29 estadounidenses iniciaron la **destrucción sistemática de ciudades japonesas**. Entre el 9 y el 10 de marzo, un bombardeo incendiario sobre Tokio mató al menos a ochenta mil personas.

El **presidente Roosevelt** no vivió para ver la derrota de Alemania y Japón. La noticia de su **muerte** el 12 de abril conmocionó al pueblo estadounidense. El inexperto **Harry S. Truman**, que llevaba menos de tres meses como vicepresidente, asumió el poder de la Casa Blanca afrontando responsabilidades de hondo calado.

La Unión Soviética tuvo el honor de **capturar Berlín**, si bien esta padeció las enormes bajas consiguientes. Hitler estaba decidido a luchar hasta el final, aunque gran parte de la defensa de Alemania había recaído en adolescentes y ancianos. Las tropas estadounidenses y soviéticas peinaron Alemania desde el oeste y el este y se reunieron en el río Elba, pero el Ejército Rojo tuvo que luchar calle a calle para tomar Berlín. El 30 de abril, cuando los soviéticos se aproximaban a su búnker, **Hitler se disparó un tiro**. Para entonces, **Benito Mussolini** había muerto también, **ejecutado** por partisanos comunistas. Su cadáver y el de su amante, Clara Petacci, aparecie-

Dresde en ruinas
Los habitantes de la ciudad alemana de Dresde intentan sobreponerse al bombardeo aliado que produjo una tormenta de fuego en la ciudad.

11,5 MILLONES DE **«PERSONAS DESPLAZADAS»** REGISTRÓ **EUROPA** EN 1945

12 de enero Tropas soviéticas **retoman la ofensiva** en Polonia y en la Alemania Oriental.

22 de enero Roosevelt inaugura su **cuarto mandato** como presidente de EE. UU.

27 de enero El Ejército Rojo soviético **libera el campo de la muerte** Auschwitz-Birkenau.

30 de enero Un submarino soviético **hunde** el ***Wilhelm Gustloff*** en el Báltico y mueren 9400 refugiados alemanes.

3 de febrero Tropas de EE. UU. empiezan a **luchar por reconquistar** la capital de las Filipinas, Manila.

4–11 de febrero Roosevelt, Churchill y Stalin se reúnen en **Yalta**.

13–14 de febrero Bombardeos aliados **destruyen Dresde**.

19 de febrero Marines de EE. UU. desembarcan en la isla de **Iwo Jima**.

7 de marzo Tropas de EE. UU. sitian el puente sobre el Rin en Remagen.

8 de marzo Josip Broz **Tito** establece un gobierno provisional en **Yugoslavia**.

9–10 de marzo Un bombardeo aéreo de EE. UU. sobre **Tokio** provoca una **tormenta de fuego** que mata a unas ochenta mil personas.

1 de abril Tropas estadounidenses desembarcan en **Okinawa**.

12 de abril Muere el presidente de EE. UU., **Roosevelt**; le sucede **Harry S. Truman**.

15 de abril Tropas aliadas liberan los campos de concentración de **Belsen** y **Buchenwald**.

25 de abril Tropas soviéticas y estadounidenses se reúnen en el **río Elba**.

28 de abril Miembros de la resistencia italiana **asesinan** a Benito **Mussolini** y a su amante.

30 de abril Hitler se suicida en Berlín.

2 de mayo Fuerzas soviéticas completan la **victoria** en la batalla por **Berlín**.

7–8 de mayo La **rendición** definitiva de **Alemania** pone fin a la guerra en Europa.

5 de junio El **Consejo de Control Aliado** asume formalmente el **poder en Alemania**.

26 de junio Representantes de cincuenta países firman la **Carta de las Naciones Unidas**.

Una delegación japonesa con atuendo formal se prepara para firmar la rendición a bordo del buque de guerra estadounidense *USS Misuri* en la bahía de Tokio, el 2 de septiembre.

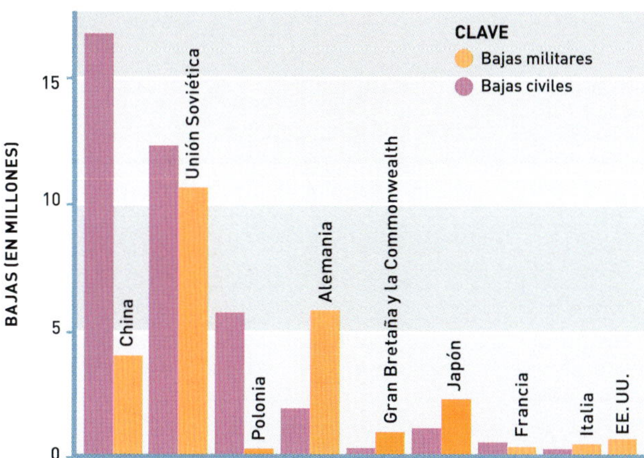

Bajas de la Segunda Guerra Mundial
En la Segunda Guerra Mundial murieron más civiles que soldados. La Unión Soviética y Alemania fueron quienes más bajas militares sufrieron. Polonia perdió a uno de cada cinco habitantes, incluidos la mayoría de judíos polacos.

ron colgados cabeza abajo de ganchos de carne en una gasolinera de Milán.

La **rendición del ejército alemán** se completó el **8 de mayo** y desató sentidas celebraciones de la victoria en los países aliados. Pese a que la guerra con Japón continuaba, el Partido Laborista británico se retiró de la coalición de la guerra para enfrentarse en los comicios generales a los conservadores liderados por Churchill. Para asombro general, los **laboristas** ganaron con una **victoria aplastante**, gracias a que su promesa de un estado del bienestar y una socialdemocracia superó el atractivo para la población del papel de Churchill en la guerra.

El 16 de julio, el desierto de Nuevo México se iluminó con la **primera explosión atómica mundial**. Así culminó el **Proyecto Manhattan** de alto secreto, un hito de la ciencia y la ingeniería que había costado a EE. UU. dos mil millones de dólares gastados con la autoridad del presidente, pero sin la aprobación del Congreso. La explosión generó temperaturas más altas que las registradas en el núcleo del Sol.

El éxito de la prueba atómica coincidió con la reunión de los líderes aliados en una conferencia en Potsdam, un barrio periférico de Berlín. A pesar de que las discrepancias entre la Unión Soviética y los aliados occidentales se acrecentaban, Stalin accedió a unirse a la guerra contra Japón. Al final de la conferencia, los aliados emitieron la **declaración de Potsdam**, que exigía a Japón la rendición incondicional o afrontar una «destrucción rápida y total». El **gobierno japonés descalificó el llamamiento a rendirse** como «sin valor significativo».

Los preparativos para lanzar las bombas atómicas sobre ciudades japonesas estaban avanzados incluso antes del primer ensayo atómico. La primera bomba impactó sobre **Hiroshima** en cuanto estuvo lista y las condiciones climáticas lo permitieron (*véase* recuadro). Tres días después, el 9 de agosto, una segunda bomba devastó la ciudad de **Nagasaki** y mató al menos a 35 000 personas. La **invasión soviética de Manchuria** supuso un nuevo golpe para Japón.

Desde junio, Japón había estado dividido entre los partidarios de una paz negociada y los militaristas, que insistían en luchar hasta la muerte. El 10 de agosto, el **emperador Hirohito intervino** de modo decisivo **a favor de la facción pacifista**. Los japoneses acordaron **rendirse** si se garantizaba el estatus del emperador. Pese a que Truman rehusó ofrecer tal seguridad, el 15 de agosto Hirohito anunció a su pueblo que la guerra no «progresaba del bando de Japón» y que pretendía firmar la paz.

La **guerra finalizó** con una celeridad repentina. Afrontar la **estela** de ciudades devastadas, economías rotas, países enemigos ocupados, refugiados («personas desplazadas») y criminales de guerra se antojaba un desafío equiparable a la propia guerra.

Izando la bandera roja
Tomada por un fotógrafo del Ejército Rojo, esta foto reconstruye el momento en que los soldados izaron la bandera soviética sobre el edificio del Reichstag en Berlín.

La hora de la muerte
Este reloj recuperado del cadáver de un ciudadano de Hiroshima inmortaliza el momento exacto en que se detonó la bomba sobre la ciudad.

HIROSHIMA

El bombardero de EE. UU. B-29 *(Enola Gay)*, pilotado por el coronel Paul Tibbets, despegó de la isla Tinian, en las Marianas, a las 2.45 de la madrugada del 6 de agosto cargado con una bomba atómica. La liberó sobre Hiroshima a las 8.15. El calor, la luz y la explosión mataron al instante a unas 70 000 personas, que llegaron a 140 000 por los efectos persistentes de la radiación.

28 de junio Un gobierno provisional con mayoría **comunista** asume el poder en **Polonia**.

3 de julio Las fuerzas aliadas **ocupan Berlín**.

16 de julio Primera detonación de un **dispositivo atómico** en Nuevo México.

17 de julio Arranca la conferencia de **Potsdam**.

26 de julio Clement Attlee se proclama primer ministro británico al derrotar a Churchill.

6 de agosto Lanzamiento de la bomba atómica sobre **Hiroshima**.

9 de agosto Nagasaki devastada por la bomba atómica; fuerzas **soviéticas invaden Manchuria**.

15 de agosto El emperador Hirohito anuncia por radio a los **japoneses** la rendición del país.

17 de agosto George Orwell publica la fábula política *Rebelión en la granja*.

2 de septiembre El líder del vietminh, Ho Chi Minh, declara **Vietnam** una **república** independiente.

2 de septiembre Japón firma su **rendición** formal a bordo del *USS Misuri*.

8 de septiembre Soldados soviéticos y estadounidenses ocupan **Corea**.

20 de septiembre El **Congreso Nacional Indio**, liderado por Gandhi y Nehru, exige la plena **independencia** de Gran Bretaña.

Octubre Gabriela Mistral es galardonada con el premio Nobel de literatura.

15 de octubre Pierre Laval, ex primer ministro del Vichy francés, es considerado culpable de traición y **ejecutado**.

21 de octubre Los **comunistas franceses ganan** más **votos** que ningún otro partido en las elecciones a la asamblea constituyente.

29 de octubre Getúlio **Vargas dimite** como presidente de Brasil.

20 de noviembre Empiezan los **juicios de Núremberg** contra los principales criminales de guerra nazis.

29 de noviembre Tito se proclama **presidente** de una **Yugoslavia** federal y socialista.

5 de diciembre EE. UU. concede un **préstamo** de cuatro mil millones a **Gran Bretaña** con condiciones estrictas; la devolución del préstamo finaliza en 2006.

1946

Refugiados judíos se dirigen a Palestina. Miles de ellos intentaron este viaje antes de que Gran Bretaña frenara la inmigración ilegal en Palestina.

REPRESENTANTES DE 51 PAÍSES COMENZARON EL AÑO FUNDANDO la **Asamblea General de las Naciones Unidas (ONU)**, sucesora de la Sociedad de Naciones (*véase* 1919). Sus objetivos eran proporcionar un foro para los países del mundo y mantener la paz.

La paz tras la Segunda Guerra Mundial fue efímera, a medida que las relaciones entre los **aliados occidentales** y la **Unión Soviética** continuaron enfriándose. En marzo, **Winston Churchill** resumió la amenaza del comunismo en un discurso en que describió un **«telón de acero»** que dividía Europa. La Unión Soviética atenazó más a Europa al crear **«estados satélites»**. Se instauraron **gobiernos comunistas** en Checoslovaquia, Bulgaria, Albania, Polonia, Rumanía y Hungría. En Francia e Italia, los partidos comunistas no se hicieron con el control por poco.

Las tensiones en **India** aumentaban tras la promesa de Gran Bretaña de concederle la **independencia** tras la guerra. El líder de la Liga Musulmana, **Mohamed Alí Jinnah** (1876–1948), exigía un **estado musulmán separado**, al que los hindúes se oponían. El 16 de agosto, Jinnah declaró un **Día de Acción Directa**, una manifestación masiva contra la propuesta británica de un gobierno indio único. Hubo altercados y miles de muertos. En respuesta, **Gandhi** (1869–1948) inició una campaña de reconciliación entre hindúes y musulmanes.

La división de la Europa de posguerra
Tras la guerra, Gran Bretaña, Francia y EE. UU. ocuparon Alemania Occidental, mientras que la Unión Soviética controlaba Alemania Oriental. Lituania, Letonia, Moldavia y Estonia fueron absorbidas por la URSS.

> « UN **TELÓN DE ACERO** HA **DESCENDIDO** SOBRE EL **CONTINENTE**. »
>
> **Winston Churchill**, político británico (5 de marzo de 1946)

EE. UU. concedió la **independencia** a **Filipinas** en julio, pero esta era una independencia con condiciones: **EE. UU. conservaba la soberanía** sobre varias bases militares, la economía filipina dependía de los mercados de EE. UU. y una cláusula de «paridad» concedía a los estadounidenses derechos económicos iguales a los de los filipinos.

El impulso para la liberación de **África** continuó con la aparición de la **Federación Panafricana** de **Kwame Nkrumah**, de Ghana, y de **Jomo Kenyatta**, de Kenia. El fin era promover la unidad africana y poner fin a la discriminación racial.

En **Palestina** se celebraron conferencias para resolver el conflicto de admitir a **refugiados judíos en el país**, pero no se llegó a ningún acuerdo. El problema se agravó en agosto, cuando **buques de guerra británicos** bloquearon el paso a los barcos que transportaban a los refugiados. Gran Bretaña informó a EE. UU. de que no permitiría más inmigrantes ilegales en Palestina y se inició así una guerra diplomática.

En China se retomó la guerra civil, suspendida durante la guerra mundial. El dirigente comunista **Mao Zedong** (1893–1976) declaró la guerra al partido nacionalista gobernante, el Kuomintang, liderado por **Chiang Kai-shek** (1887–1975).

Francia siguió decidida a retener sus colonias en Indochina, lo cual la sumió en una de las **guerras de guerrilla** más largas de la historia. En noviembre, los enfrentamientos entre el Vietminh, liderado por **Ho Chi Minh** (1890–1969), y los Cuerpos Expedicionarios del Lejano Oriente, liderados por Francia, se intensificaron. El 19 de diciembre (*véase* 1954) se declaró la **primera guerra de Indochina**, que implicó la rebelión de Vietnam, Camboya y Laos contra Francia.

Juan Perón
Ferozmente nacionalista, antiamericano y anticomunista, Perón prometió una «tercera vía» entre el capitalismo y el comunismo.

Rollos del mar Muerto
El descubrimiento de los rollos del mar Muerto fue uno de los hallazgos arqueológicos más relevantes del siglo. Los rollos son fragmentos de manuscritos del Antiguo Testamento.

El **general Juan Domingo Perón** (1895–1974), ex secretario de Trabajo argentino, fue proclamado presidente de Argentina el 4 de junio. Con el apoyo de la clase obrera y del ejército, prometió **seguridad social** y **salarios más altos**.

Técnicos de la Universidad de Pensilvania comenzaron a utilizar el **primer ordenador digital electrónico práctico**. La máquina se usó inicialmente para fines militares. Ocupaba 167 m², tenía 18 000 tubos de ventilación y pesaba casi 50 toneladas.

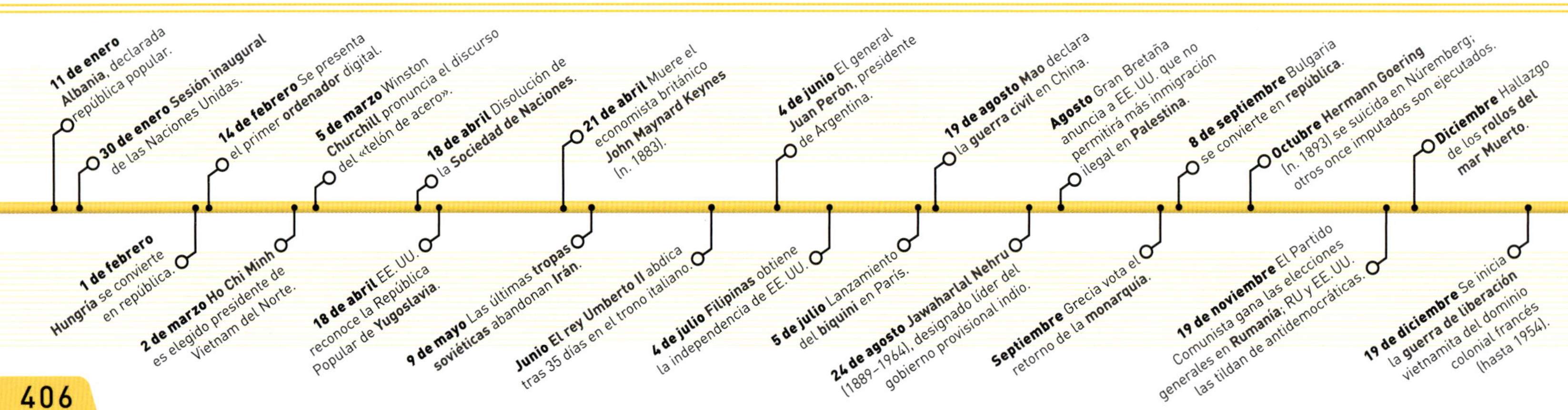

1947

La Asamblea General de la ONU se reúne en Londres. La Asamblea General es el único órgano de la ONU donde todos los miembros tienen la misma representación.

EN 1947, LORD LOUIS MOUNTBATTEN FUE PROCLAMADO EL ÚLTIMO VIRREY de India con objeto de supervisar el **fin del gobierno imperial británico**. Mountbatten consideraba que la única salida viable para el país era su **partición** en dos zonas, en función de la religión imperante. En julio, Gran Bretaña aprobó la **Ley de la independencia de India**, que dividía el Raj en **India** (hindúes y sijs) y **Pakistán** (musulmanes), y permitía a Cachemira determinar su propia fe. Pakistán se dividió en **Pakistán Oriental** y **Pakistán Occidental**, con India escindiendo ambas partes. El 14 de agosto, Pakistán obtuvo la independencia y **Mohamed Alí Jinnah** se convirtió en su primer gobernador general. Un día después nació la **India independiente**. La partición desató oleadas de violencia y desplazó a millones de hindúes y sijs fuera del nuevo territorio pakistaní y a musulmanes fuera del nuevo territorio indio.

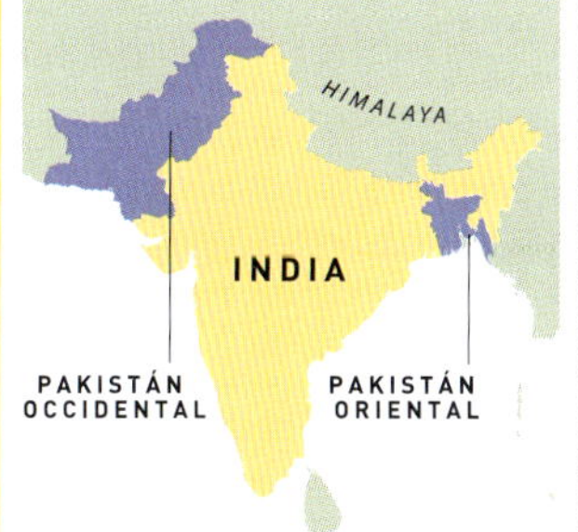

La partición de India
La partición dividió el antiguo Raj británico en dos espacios diferenciados: India y Pakistán. Pakistán estaba integrado por dos territorios a 1700 km de distancia.

Los gobernantes de **Cachemira** tuvieron que tomar una decisión trascendental: independizarse o unirse a India o a Pakistán. En octubre **estalló la guerra entre India y Pakistán** después de que Pakistán respaldase una insurgencia musulmana en Cachemira. India accedió a la petición del **marajá** de Cachemira, a cambio de la anexión de Cachemira una vez cesasen las hostilidades entre Pakistán e India (*véase* 1949).

Después de seis años de guerra, **Gran Bretaña** había perdido peso y **EE. UU.** emergió como la única potencia capaz de rivalizar con la **Unión Soviética**. El 12 de marzo se estableció la **«doctrina Truman»**, cuando Winston Churchill solicitó a EE. UU. ayuda en **Grecia**, donde había estallado una **guerra civil** entre los comunistas y el gobierno monárquico. En respuesta, se enviaron 400 millones de dólares a Grecia para ayudar a atajar la **amenaza comunista**. La doctrina del presidente Truman prometía ayudar a todos los estados que lucharan por mantener la democracia frente a la amenaza del comunismo.

Ante el temor de que toda Europa instaurara regímenes comunistas, **George Marshall** (1880–1959), secretario de Estado de EE. UU., presentó un plan para ayudar a las maltrechas economías europeas a recuperarse de la guerra, destinado a vencedores y vencidos por igual. El Programa de Recuperación Europeo, es decir, el **Plan Marshall**, proveía petróleo, materias primas, préstamos, alimentos y maquinaria para reactivar rápidamente la economía.

Diario de Ana Frank
La publicación de Het Achterhuis (El anexo secreto) *el 5 de junio dio a conocer a Ana Frank, una muchacha judía que glosó en su diario los años que pasó ocultándose de los nazis en Ámsterdam durante la Segunda Guerra Mundial.*

La **crisis en Palestina** (*véase* 1946) continuó agravándose cuando Gran Bretaña delegó la resolución del conflicto en la ONU. Se diseñó un plan para dividir la zona en dos **estados** separados, **árabe y judío**. La Asamblea General de la ONU acordó esta resolución el 29 de noviembre, si bien los árabes la acogieron con desagrado. Mientras los británicos organizaban su retirada de la región, las comunidades árabe y judía se enfrentaron y se intensificaron los **ataques terroristas** (*véase* 1948).

Desarraigo a causa de la partición
La partición provocó la mayor migración masiva de la historia, con el desplazamiento de unos diez millones de personas. Refugiados sij abandonan la sección musulmana del Punjab.

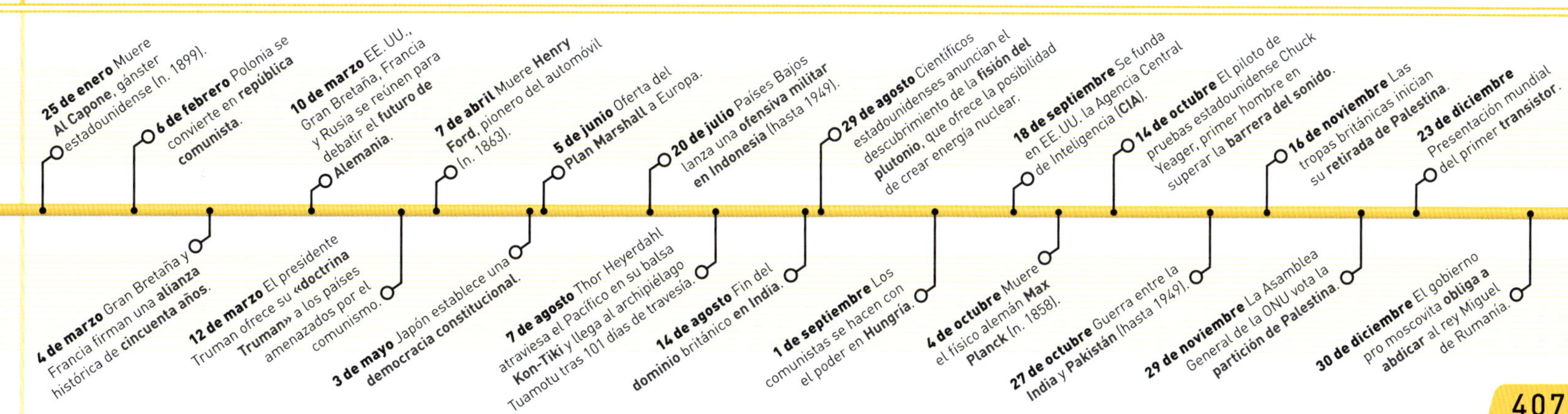

1948

Mahatma Gandhi yace en la capilla ardiente tras ser asesinado por un fanático hindú que lo culpaba de la partición de India.

MAHATMA GANDHI LOGRÓ SU OBJETIVO cuando **India obtuvo la independencia** en 1947. No obstante, la concesiones que realizó a los musulmanes condujeron a su asesinato a manos de un **fanático hindú** que lo culpaba de la partición de India, pese a que Gandhi (n. 1868) se había opuesto amargamente a la escisión del subcontinente. La noticia del **asesinato de Gandhi** conmocionó al mundo e India declaró un luto oficial.

Sudáfrica celebró elecciones en mayo, en las cuales el **Partido Nacional** arrebató el poder al Partido Unido de Jan Smuts. El **doctor D.F. Malan** (1874–1959) se convirtió en primer ministro y formó el primer gobierno con mayoría **afrikáner**. Tras su elección, el gobierno empezó a institucionalizar la **segregación**. Malan creía que los africanos amenazaban la prosperidad y la pureza de la cultura afrikáner. Basó su política en un sistema que pasó a ser conocido como ***apartheid*** e instauró una jerarquía racial que privilegiaba a los sudafricanos blancos (*véase* 1994).

Cartel de la segregación
Bajo el apartheid *se crearon zonas residenciales segregadas y el contacto social entre las distintas razas quedó prohibido.*

En la **península de Malaca** cuajó un sentimiento anticolonial tras la Segunda Guerra Mundial. Grupos de guerrillas se ocultaron en la selva, con el líder insurgente **Chin Peng** (n. 1924) a la cabeza. En febrero se produjeron ataques terroristas contra colonos europeos y poco después se declaró un «estado de emergencia».

En 1948 se habían convocado **elecciones en las dos Coreas**, pero, creyendo que no tenía posibilidad de ganar unos comicios libres, **Kim Il Sung** (1912–1994), el dirigente de Corea del Norte, convenció a los **soviéticos** para no permitir que la ONU se estableciera al norte del **paralelo 38** (la frontera entre la zona norte de la península coreana, ocupada por la URSS, y la zona sur, controlada por EE.UU.). Como resultado, un mes después de que el sur se independizara como la **República de Corea**, el 15 de agosto se proclamó la **República Popular Democrática de Corea**, con Kim Il Sung como su presidente. El 12 de octubre, la Unión Soviética declaró el régimen de Kim Il Sung como el único gobierno legítimo de la península. Hacia 1949, **Corea del Norte** vivía ya bajo una **dictadura comunista** plena.

La ONU había diseñado un plan para dividir **Palestina** en dos países, uno judío y otro árabe, pero no hubo tiempo de implementarlo: el 14 de mayo, **David Ben Gurion** proclamó el **estado de Israel** y se convirtió en su primer ministro. Las últimas tropas británicas se retiraron el 15 de mayo. Cinco **ejércitos árabes** procedentes de Jordania, Egipto, Siria, el Líbano e Iraq invadieron inmediatamente el nuevo estado judío, pero fueron repelidos. El ejército israelí aplastó los reductos de resistencia y amplió sus fronteras en la que se llamó la **primera guerra árabe-israelí** (*véase* 1949). La idea de que pudiera sobrevivir una nación israelí avivó el sentimiento antiisraelí y antisemita en todo el mundo árabe.

Plan para Palestina
La Asamblea General de la ONU propuso dividir el país en dos estados, uno árabe y otro judío, con Jerusalén bajo administración internacional.

El 30 de abril se fundó la **Organización de Estados Americanos** (OEA). Sus integrantes eran los países independientes del continente americano, los cuales se comprometieron a **combatir el comunismo**, aumentar la seguridad y contribuir al crecimiento económico.

Harry Truman (1884–1972) había conducido a EE.UU. hacia el fin de la Segunda Guerra Mundial y el principio de la Guerra Fría. Pero nadie esperaba que ganara las **elecciones de 1948** frente al republicano Thomas E. Dewey, por sus políticas a favor de los derechos civiles, que habían alienado a muchos demócratas sureños. A medida que la campaña progresó, Truman se ganó a la población y fue elegido en uno de los mayores **reveses electorales** de la historia.

En **Gran Bretaña**, el debate en torno a la salud pública libre se prolongaba desde el siglo XIX. Tras la victoria laborista en las elecciones de 1945, **Aneurin Bevan** (1897–1960) presentó un plan para proporcionar asistencia médica gratuita universal por primera vez. Bevan lanzó formalmente el **National Health Service** (NHS) el 5 de julio.

Concluida la Segunda Guerra Mundial, el Comité Olímpico Internacional (COI) pudo seleccionar de nuevo una ciudad para albergar los **Juegos Olímpicos**. Se escogió Londres, pero, tras seis años de guerra, Gran Bretaña padecía escasez de alimentos y ropa, y las celebraciones de 1948 pasaron a ser conocidas como las **«Olimpiadas de la austeridad»**. Aquellos Juegos testimoniaron la **primera deserción** del este comunista a Occidente cuando la entrenadora del equipo de gimnastas checoslovacos, **Marie Provaznikova**, se negó a regresar a casa.

Checoslovaquia había avanzado hacia la democracia tras la Segunda Guerra Mundial, pero los soviéticos no iban a permitir que ningún estado bajo su esfera de influencia se convirtiera en una democracia. Los **comunistas**, con el respaldo soviético, perpetraron un **golpe de estado en Praga** en febrero. **Edvard Beneš** (1884–1948), presidente checo, fue destituido del poder y

DAVID BEN GURION (1886–1973)

Ben Gurion, fundador del estado de Israel, nació en Polonia y emigró a Palestina en 1906. Se convirtió en un defensor activo de la lucha por un estado judío independiente y en 1915 fue expulsado de Palestina por sus actividades nacionalistas. Durante la Segunda Guerra Mundial, ayudó a los judíos a huir del Holocausto nazi. Ben Gurion se retiró de la política en 1970.

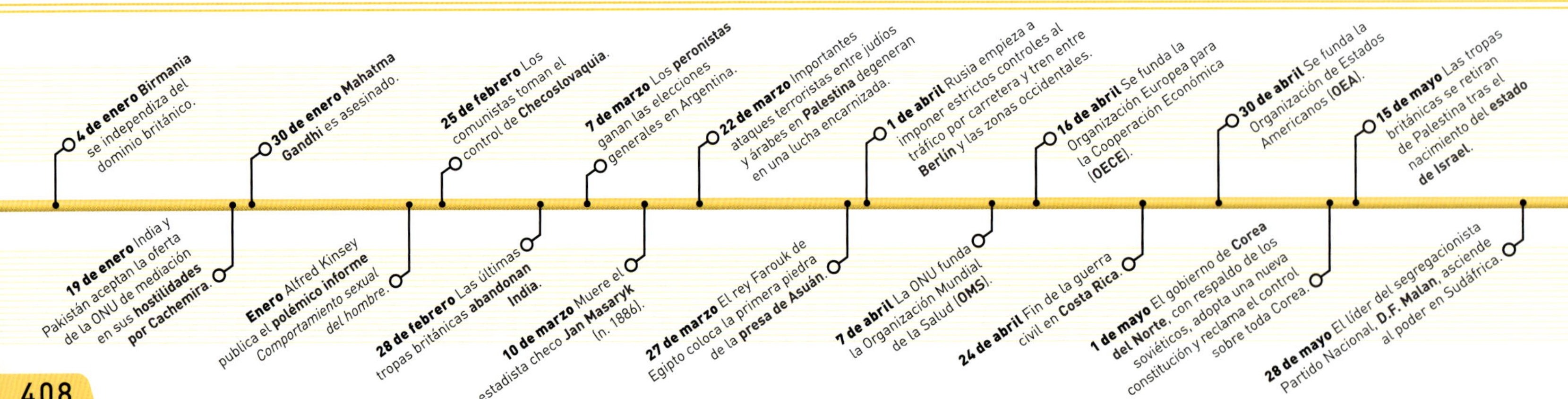

« NO CONOZCO A **NINGÚN OTRO HOMBRE** DE NUESTRO TIEMPO, NI DE **LA HISTORIA RECIENTE**, QUE HAYA DEMOSTRADO TAN CONVINCENTEMENTE EL PODER DEL **ESPÍRITU** POR ENCIMA DE **LAS COSAS MATERIALES**. **»**

Sir Stafford Cripps, estadista británico, sobre Gandhi (1948)

Truman sostiene un diario que había anunciado de modo prematuro la victoria de Thomas Dewey en las elecciones.

sustituido por el líder del partido comunista checo, **Klement Gottwald** (1896–1953; *véase* 1989). Fue un periodo tenso en Checoslovaquia. **Jan Masaryk**, el ministro de Exteriores checo, había intentado asegurar a los soviéticos que una Checoslovaquia democrática no suponía ninguna amenaza a la seguridad. No obstante, se había inclinado a favor de aceptar ayuda del **Plan Marshall** (*véase* 1947), cosa que Stalin desaprobaba. El 10 de marzo, el gobierno checo anunció que Masaryk se había suicidado. Pese a la sospecha de que los comunistas lo habían asesinado, no pudo demostrarse nada.

Berlín se dividió en **cuatro zonas** tras la guerra, bajo un acuerdo entre Gran Bretaña, Francia, EE. UU. y Rusia (*véase* 1961). En su conjunto, Berlín era un enclave en el seno de Alemania Oriental, ocupada por los soviéticos. Estos, decididos a expulsar de Berlín a las potencias occidentales, en la **primera crisis de la Guerra Fría**, cortaron las comunicaciones por carretera y tren entre la ciudad y Occidente en junio. Los aliados respondieron al **«bloqueo de Berlín»** organizando un **puente aéreo** masivo para aprovisionar a los berlineses. El bloqueo se levantó en mayo de 1949.

El final de la Segunda Guerra Mundial conllevó **desplazamientos de refugiados** cuando millones de personas huían o eran expulsadas de la Europa del Este. Muchas de ellas fueron tratadas incomprensiblemente con brutalidad. En respuesta, la ONU adoptó la **Declaración Universal de los Derechos Humanos**, que garantizaba que «en caso de persecución toda persona tiene derecho a buscar asilo, y a disfrutar de él», así como la Convención para la Prevención y la Sanción del Delito de Genocidio.

El puente aéreo de Berlín
Berlineses observan un avión Douglas C-54 Skymaster transportando las provisiones vitales para los sectores aliados de la ciudad.

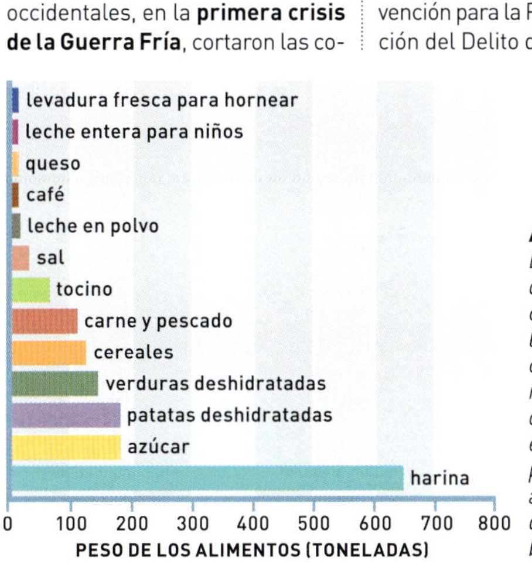

Alimentar a Berlín
En el punto álgido del bloqueo de Berlín, cada treinta segundos llegaba un avión a la ciudad. Este gráfico muestra la cantidad de comida que se enviaba diariamente para aprovisionar a los dos millones de ciudadanos berlineses.

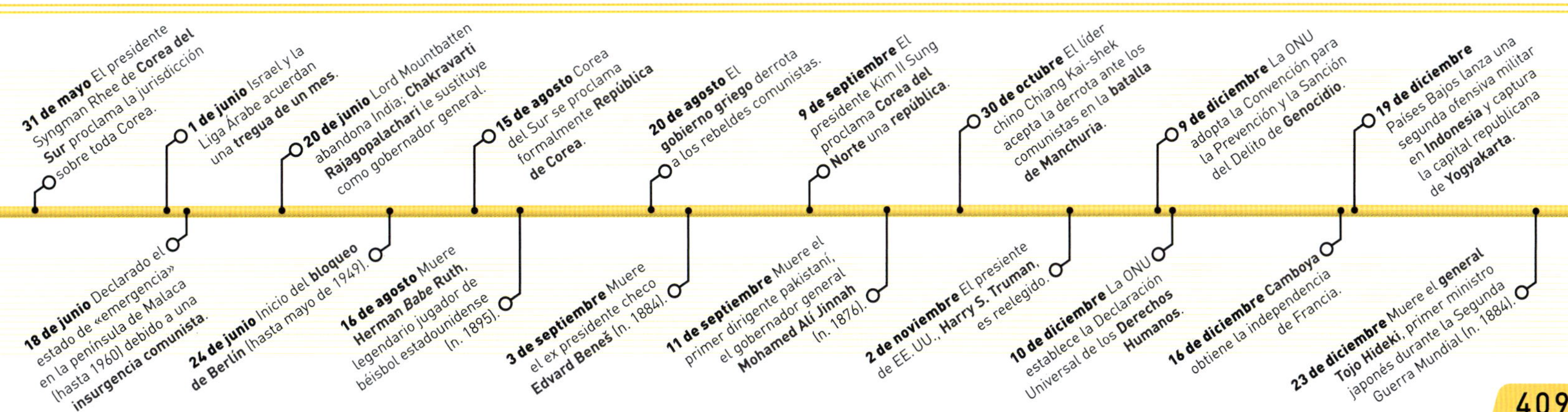

« UN **TEJADO** QUE CUBRE TODO EL **OCÉANO ATLÁNTICO**. »

Ernest Bevin, ministro de Exteriores británico, describiendo la Organización del Tratado del Atlántico Norte

En la firma del tratado del Atlántico Norte en Washington DC, el 4 de abril, Harry S. Truman, presidente de EE. UU., pronunció un discurso sobre su importancia.

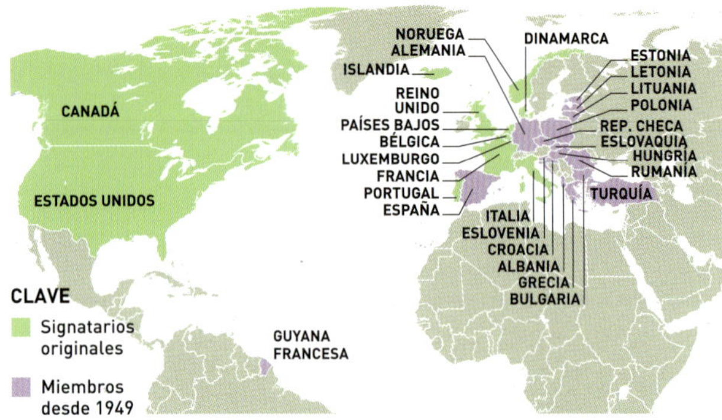

Alianza de la OTAN
Este mapa ilustra los doce países que integraban la OTAN en su fundación, en 1949. La alianza permitía a EE. UU. mantener bases militares en Europa.

EN LA GUERRA ÁRABE-ISRAELÍ SE ACORDÓ UNA TREGUA (*véase* 1948) que puso fin a ocho meses de hostilidades. Los israelíes la denominaron **«guerra de Independencia»**, mientras que los árabes la llamaron *Al Naqba* o **«la Catástrofe»**. Los estados árabes negociaron acuerdos de armisticio por separado. Egipto fue el primero en hacerlo, el 24 de febrero, seguido por Líbano, Jordania y Siria. El acuerdo establecía una línea entre Israel y Cisjordania, en posesión de Jordania, que pasó a ser conocida como la **Línea Verde**.

Representantes de Bélgica, Reino Unido, Canadá, Dinamarca, Francia, Islandia, Italia, Luxemburgo, Países Bajos, Noruega, Portugal y EE. UU. se reunieron en Washington DC en abril para firmar un tratado histórico que estableció la **Organización del Tratado del Atlántico Norte (OTAN)**. La alianza planteaba la **defensa mutua**; los países se comprometieron a desarrollar su capacidad para resistir los ataques armados y a consultarse si alguno de ellos era amenazado. El tratado también recogía que los estados miembros intentarían **solucionar las disputas por medios pacíficos**.

La **Unión Soviética** asombró al mundo al detonar su **primera bomba atómica** el 29 de agosto en una localización de pruebas remota en Kazajstán. Denominada **«primer rayo»**, su creación la facilitaron espías estadounidenses, como Julius y Ethel Rosenberg, y el espía británico Donald Maclean, que había transferido secretos tecnológicos a los soviéticos (*véase* 1951). La pérdida de la supremacía nuclear condujo a Harry Truman, presidente de EE. UU., a encargar el desarrollo de una **bomba de hidrógeno** mucho más potente.

El **puente aéreo de Berlín** (*véase* 1948) realizado por los aliados occidentales había fomentado la solidaridad entre los líderes de Alemania Occidental. El 23 de mayo, las zonas ocupadas occidentales se unieron para formar la **República Federal de Alemania**. La RFA celebró las primeras elecciones libres desde 1932, en las que vencieron los democratacristianos de **Konrad Adenauer** (1876–1967) por una ajustada mayoría.

El Vaticano emitió el ***Acta Apostolicae Sedis*** bajo el papa Pío XII, que **excomulgaba *de facto* a los católicos** que colaboraran o apoyaran al Partido Comunista. El decreto representaba una contraofensiva de la Santa Sede a la **guerra fría religiosa** contra el régimen comunista, tras la persecución de los católicos en los estados comunistas.

El 18 de abril, Eire se convirtió en la **República de Irlanda**, según el proyecto de ley de 1938. Así, Irlanda quedaba liberada de la lealtad a la Corona británica. En mayo, el parlamento británico aprobó un proyecto de ley que mantenía a Irlanda del Norte como parte de Gran Bretaña; seis condados del norte de Irlanda votaron por mayoría permanecer unidos a los británicos en las **elecciones generales de Irlanda del Norte** celebradas el 19 de febrero.

En agosto se adoptó la **IV Convención de Ginebra**, que aunaba los elementos de las tres convenciones previas de 1864, 1906 y 1929, y añadía reglas para proteger a los civiles durante la guerra. Respondía a las **atrocidades nazis** de la Segunda Guerra Mundial y a la práctica de la «guerra total». El tratado internacional regulaba el **trato de los civiles en tiempos de guerra**, incluidos rehenes, diplomáticos, espías, testigos y civiles en territorio bajo ocupación militar.

En **China, la guerra civil** (*véase* 1946) tocó su fin en 1949. Beiping fue tomado por los comunistas y rebautizado **Pekín** de nuevo y, entre abril y noviembre, la mayoría de las grandes ciudades quedaron sometidas a un control comunista con resistencia mínima. **Mao Zedong** (*véase* 1921) proclamó la fundación de la **República Popular de China** el 1 de octubre, y en diciembre, Chiang Kai-shek y sus tropas nacionalistas huyeron de la península a la isla de Formosa (Taiwán), y nombraron **Taipéi** la **capital temporal de China**.

Los holandeses abandonaron finalmente la lucha por **Indonesia** en diciembre y le concedieron la independencia tras cuatro años de guerra. El **presidente Ahmed Sukarno** (1901–1970), que había colaborado con los japoneses durante la guerra y había emergido como el líder nacional más sólido, afrontó la tarea de reunir las distintas regiones en un **país unido** bajo una nueva constitución y con **Yakarta** como capital de la república. El 26 de septiembre de 1950, Indonesia fue **admitida en la ONU** (*véase* 1965).

El 10 de enero, la discográfica RCA presentó los **discos de vinilo de 7 pulgadas** (también llamados «de 45 revoluciones») en EE. UU. El **«sencillo»**, con su formato de una canción por cara, era ideal para el rock and roll y revolucionó la **industria de la música popular**. En su primer año de producción, la RCA imprimió más de **25 millones** de discos de 45 r.p.m.

República Popular
Después de la proclamación de la República Popular de China, carteles propagandísticos mostraban a su presidente, Mao Zedong, sonriente y alentando al pueblo a construir un nuevo y próspero país.

- **1 de enero Java (Indonesia)** queda bajo control de Países Bajos.
- **1 de enero Acaba la guerra indo-pakistaní** por Cachemira con un alto el fuego acordado por la ONU.
- **10 de enero** Los **discos de 45 rpm** se lanzan al mercado en EE. UU.
- **20 de enero** La **toma de posesión** del presidente Truman es la primera en **televisarse** para todo EE. UU.
- **1 de febrero Hungría**, declarada república popular.
- **18 de febrero** En Argentina, altos cargos militares tratan de expulsar a **Eva Perón** del gobierno (mandato de 1946 a 1952).
- **24 de febrero** Israel y Egipto firman una **tregua**.
- **4 de abril** Doce países firman el **tratado del Atlántico Norte**.
- **8 de abril** EE. UU., Gran Bretaña y Francia llegan a un acuerdo sobre el futuro de **Alemania Occidental**.
- **18 de abril** Eire se proclama la **República de Irlanda**.
- **12 de mayo Stalin levanta el bloqueo** de Berlín.
- **23 de mayo** Nace la Alemania Occidental **democrática**.
- **26 de mayo Shanghai** cae en manos de tropas comunistas.
- **28 de junio** Los últimos soldados de combate de EE. UU. abandonan **Corea**.
- **29 de junio** El ejército holandés abandona **Yakarta**.
- **19 de julio Laos** obtiene la independencia.
- **27 de julio** El Havilland Comet, el **primer avión de reacción comercial**, realiza su vuelo inaugural.
- **1 de agosto** Los holandeses acuerdan un **alto el fuego en Indonesia**.
- **29 de agosto** La URSS prueba su primera **bomba atómica**.
- **2 de septiembre** Inauguración del **Festival de Cine de Cannes**.
- **1 de octubre** Mao Zedong proclama China una **República Comunista**.
- **7 de octubre** Stalin establece la **República Democrática Alemana** en Alemania Oriental.
- **Noviembre** Gran Bretaña lanza una gran ofensiva en **Malasia** para expulsar a los rebeldes comunistas.
- **19 de noviembre** Coronación de **Rainiero III**, 30.º príncipe regente de **Mónaco**.
- **8 de diciembre** El **gobierno nacionalista de China** traslada su capital a **Taipéi, en la isla de Formosa** (Taiwán).
- **13 de diciembre** La capital de Israel se traslada de Tel Aviv a **Jerusalén**.
- **16 de diciembre Ahmed Sukarno**, primer presidente de la **República de Indonesia**.

1950

« DESEMBARCAREMOS EN **INCHEON Y LOS APLASTARÉ**. »

Douglas MacArthur,
general estadounidense (1950)

La guerra civil en Corea se agravó y atrajo tropas del todo el mundo bajo el mando de la ONU, incluidos estos operadores de metralleta británicos.

TRAS CERCA DE CIEN AÑOS DE DOMINIO BRITÁNICO, India se convirtió en una **república** el 26 de enero. Desde la partición, en 1947, se había ocupado de sus propios asuntos, pero aquel día marcó el corte oficial de todos sus lazos. En una ceremonia formal, el **presidente Rajendra Prasad** (1884–1963) juró el cargo y se aprobó una nueva constitución.

Emblema
Tras proclamarse república, India adoptó este emblema, tomado de una escultura titulada La capital del león de Ashoka. *Lleva inscrito el lema «Solo la verdad triunfa» en devanagari.*

Desde su creación como **Transjordania** tras la Primera Guerra Mundial, el **Reino Hachemita de Jordania** afrontaba problemas a causa de su estatus disputado, su débil economía y sus fronteras artificiales. El 24 de abril, el rey Abdalá de Jordania (1882–1951) **se anexionó la Palestina árabe** para ampliar su reino y suscitó la furia de sus vecinos árabes. El territorio anexionado incluía el este de Jerusalén y **duplicaba la población de Jordania**.

Sudáfrica, con sus opresivas leyes del *apartheid* (véase 1948), empezó a registrar una **tensión racial creciente**. Blancos y negros se segregaron a gran escala y se introdujo un **carnet de identidad** que indicaba la raza de la persona. El 1 de mayo se celebró una **huelga general** en protesta contra las leyes discriminatorias. La **policía abrió fuego** en Alexandra y mató a dieciocho personas e hirió a otras treinta.

« EL COMUNISMO ES **EL MARTILLO** QUE UTILIZAMOS PARA **APLASTAR AL ENEMIGO**. »

Mao Zedong (1950)

Un año después de que los comunistas asumieran el poder en **China**, invadieron el vecino **Tíbet**. El asalto militar tuvo lugar en octubre y, hacia abril de 1951, los líderes del Tíbet declararon haber sido forzados a punta de pistola a firmar un tratado conocido como el **acuerdo de los 17 puntos**, que otorgaba a China el control sobre los asuntos exteriores tibetanos y permitía la **ocupación militar china**.

El 9 de febrero, en EE. UU., el **senador Joseph McCarthy** lanzó una caza de brujas anticomunista, una especie de cruzada para «asustar a los rojos», afirmando que el Departamento de Estado albergaba a 205 comunistas. Sus afirmaciones jamás se demostraron, pero muchas personas perdieron sus empleos y su reputación (véase 1954).

En junio, una **nueva crisis** dividió a los antiguos aliados de guerra en **Corea**. Escindida en una zona norte ocupada por la URSS y una zona sur ocupada por EE. UU., una vez ambas superpotencias se retiraron, el **norte**, con el apoyo de la URSS, **invadió el sur**. EE. UU., resuelto a no apaciguar a los rusos, aportó el mayor contingente del **ejército de la ONU**, que acudió en auxilio de los surcoreanos. En cuatro meses, la fuerza de la ONU había entrado en Corea del Norte y solo la intervención de **China** evitó el derrumbe de Corea del Norte (véase 1953).

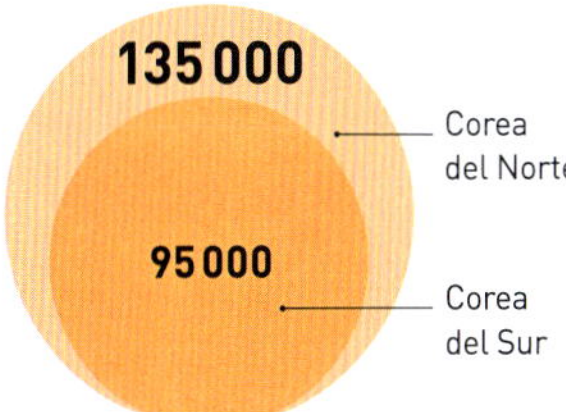

Población y ejército en Corea
Pese a contar con menos de la mitad de la población que Corea del Sur en 1950, el ejército de Corea del Norte era más numeroso y estaba mucho mejor equipado.

MACCARTHISMO

Bautizado en alusión al senador Joseph McCarthy (1908–1957), el maccarthismo se convirtió en sinónimo de la caza de comunistas en la esfera pública de EE. UU. en la década de 1950. El triunfo del comunismo en la Europa del Este y China provocó una grave crisis en EE. UU. El temor a una conspiración mundial derivó en una campaña contra personas sospechosas de inclinaciones comunistas. McCarthy realizó audiencias en el senado para «expulsarlos» y los libros «antiamericanos» se eliminaron de las bibliotecas públicas.

El **primer trasplante de órgano humano** tuvo lugar el 17 de junio en el Little Company of Mary Hospital de Illinois (EE. UU.). Se sustituyó un riñón dañado por el riñón de un cadáver. Pese al posterior rechazo, el trasplante ofreció al otro riñón del paciente el tiempo necesario para recuperarse.

El físico alemán **Albert Einstein** (véase 1919), defensor activo del desarme nuclear y de los derechos civiles, publicó su ***Teoría general de la relatividad*** en la edición de abril del *Scientific American*. En el artículo intentó unificar la **gravedad** y el electromagnetismo de un modo que condujera a un nuevo entendimiento de la **mecánica cuántica**.

El 8 de febrero, Diners Club lanzó la primera **tarjeta de crédito moderna**, que podía utilizarse en diversos comercios. Se estableció principalmente para que los empresarios pagasen sus dietas de viaje y para gastos en ocio. Los propietarios tenían sesenta días para abonar los pagos. Los comerciantes aceptaron rápidamente la tarjeta porque detectaron que los **clientes** que la utilizaban **solían gastar más** si podían «cargarlo a crédito».

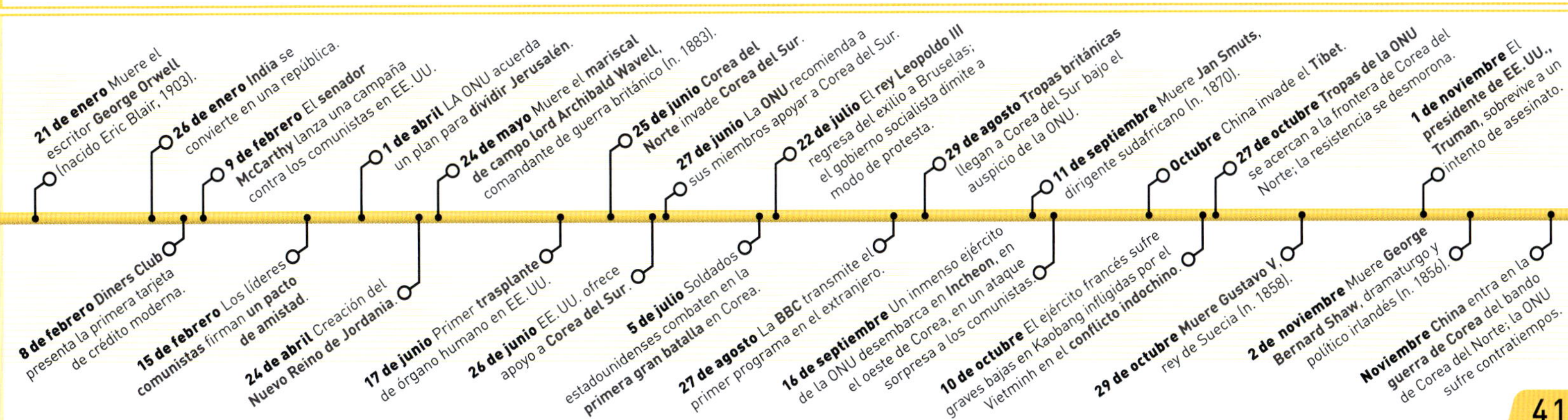

Sputnik 1
1957 • URSS
El primer satélite artificial, anterior a la versión estadounidense, contenía un radiotransmisor. Orbitaba a cientos de kilómetros sobre la superficie de la Tierra y contribuyó a una mejor comprensión de la atmósfera terrestre.

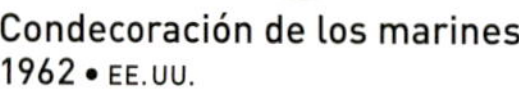
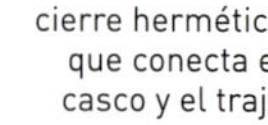

Condecoración de los marines
1962 • EE. UU.
John Glenn fue el primer estadounidense en orbitar la Tierra y recibió una condecoración del Cuerpo de Marines para conmemorarlo. El año anterior, Alan Shephard había sido el primer estadounidense en viajar al espacio.

Cartel de Gagarin
1961 • URSS
Este cartel soviético muestra a un sonriente Yuri Gagarin, que hizo historia al convertirse en el primer hombre en viajar al espacio, a bordo del Vostok I.

Traje de astronauta
1965 • URSS
Alexéi Leonov fue el primero en realizar una caminata espacial, en marzo de 1965. Su traje llevaba una mochila con un sistema de soporte vital.

cierre hermético que conecta el casco y el traje

el traje tiene una capa de aislamiento hermético

válvula de presión

guantes aislantes con huellas de goma que mejoran el agarre

HACIA EL ESPACIO

LA CARRERA DE DOS SUPERPOTENCIAS PARA DEMOSTRAR SU CAPACIDAD TECNOLÓGICA

Durante la década de 1960, EE. UU. y la URSS dominaron la carrera espacial. Lo que empezó con el fin de desarrollar misiles de largo alcance se convirtió en una batalla por el prestigio internacional que nadie quería perder.

En 1957, la URSS asombró a EE. UU. al poner en órbita el Sputnik 1. En 1961, el astronauta soviético Yuri Gagarin se convirtió en el primer ser humano en completar la órbita alrededor de la Tierra. Parecía que EE. UU. se estaba quedando atrás. No obstante, tras la creación del programa Apolo, EE. UU. consiguió el premio definitivo: Neil Armstrong y Buzz Aldrin pisaron la Luna el 21 de julio de 1969 e inauguraron una nueva era en la exploración espacial.

Roca lunar
1969
Los astronautas del Apolo 11 recogieron esta roca lunar; se parece a la lava volcánica terrestre, lo que sugiere que la Luna estuvo fundida.

pala

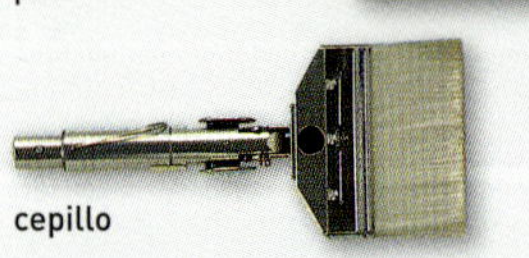
cepillo

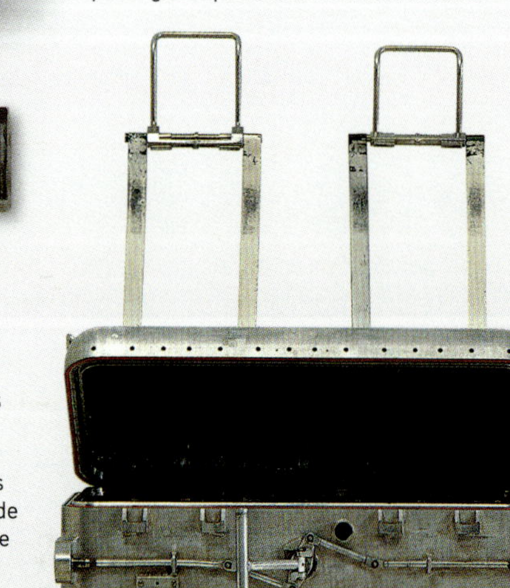

Equipo de recogida de muestras
1969 • EE. UU.
La tripulación del Apolo 11 tenía herramientas y contenedores especiales para recoger muestras de rocas, tierra y polvo de la superficie lunar.

Revista *Life*
20 de enero de 1969 • EE. UU.
El gran interés por la exploración espacial explica que la misión del Apolo 8 apareciera en la portada de la revista *Life*. La tripulación del Apolo 8 fue la primera en orbitar la Luna.

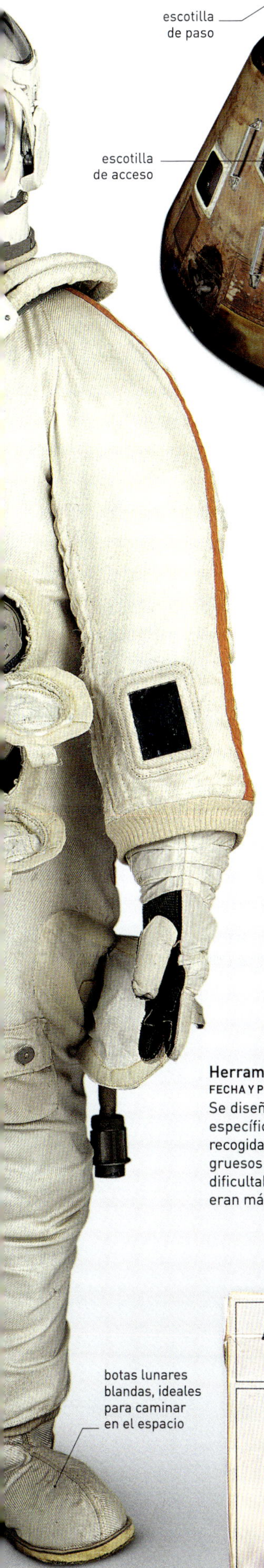

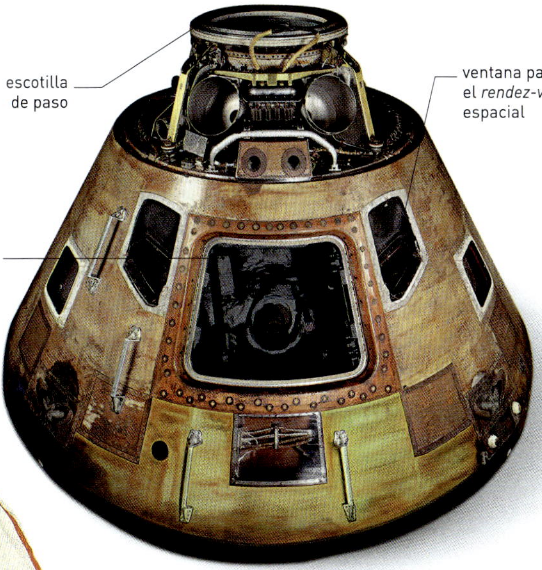

botas lunares blandas, ideales para caminar en el espacio

escotilla de paso
escotilla de acceso
ventana para el *rendez-vous* espacial

Módulo de mando del Apolo 10
1969 • EE. UU.
Este módulo albergaba a tres tripulantes y orbitó alrededor de la Luna, como ensayo de la misión del Apolo 11, que alunizó dos meses después.

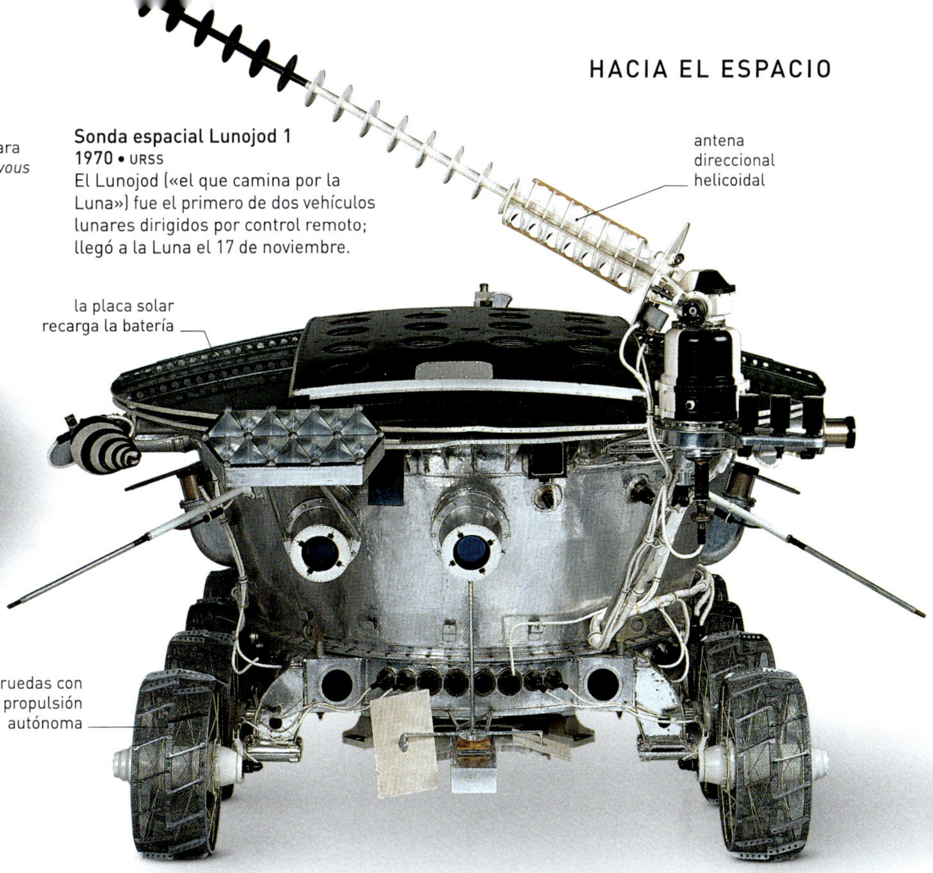

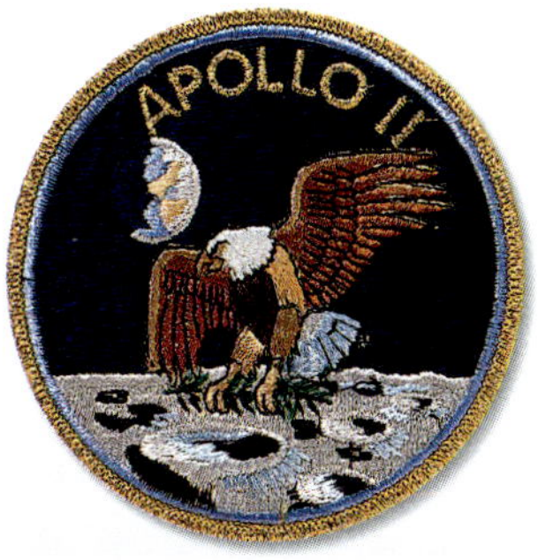

antena direccional helicoidal
la placa solar recarga la batería
ruedas con propulsión autónoma

Sonda espacial Lunojod 1
1970 • URSS
El Lunojod («el que camina por la Luna») fue el primero de dos vehículos lunares dirigidos por control remoto; llegó a la Luna el 17 de noviembre.

APOLLO 11

Insignia del Apolo
1969 • EE. UU.
La tripulación del Apolo 11 diseñó su propia insignia: un águila con una rama de olivo posada en la superficie de la Luna.

МИР

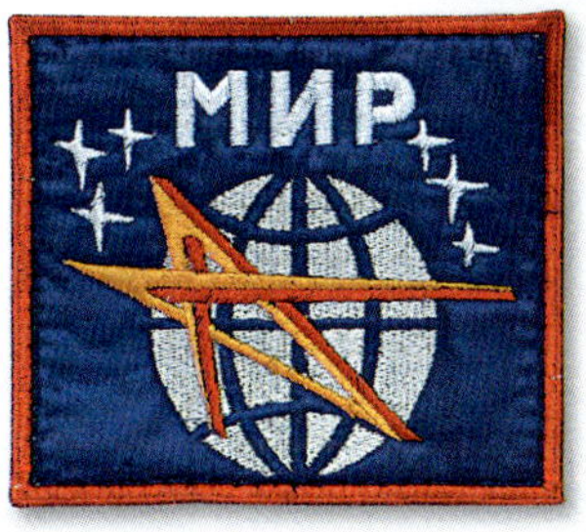

Insignia de la Mir
FECHA DESCONOCIDA • URSS
Insignia oficial de la estación espacial rusa del programa Mir. La palabra «Mir» aparece en cirílico.

Bandeja espacial
FECHA Y PROGRAMA DESCONOCIDOS
Bandeja magnética, para contrarrestar la gravedad reducida; cubiertos metálicos, y sujeciones de velcro para fijar los alimentos y fluidos envasados.

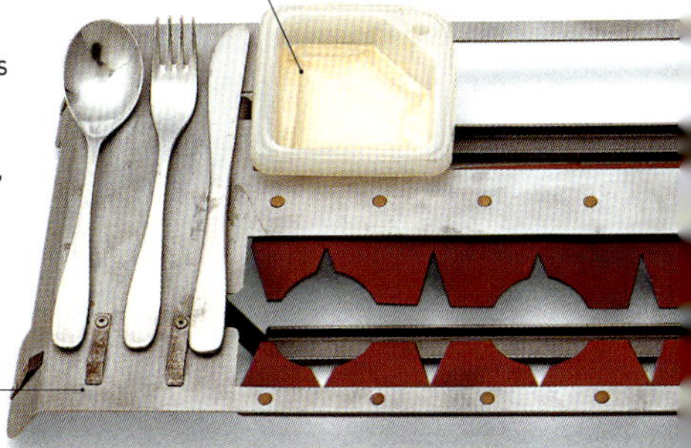

envase de comida liofilizada congelada
superficie magnética

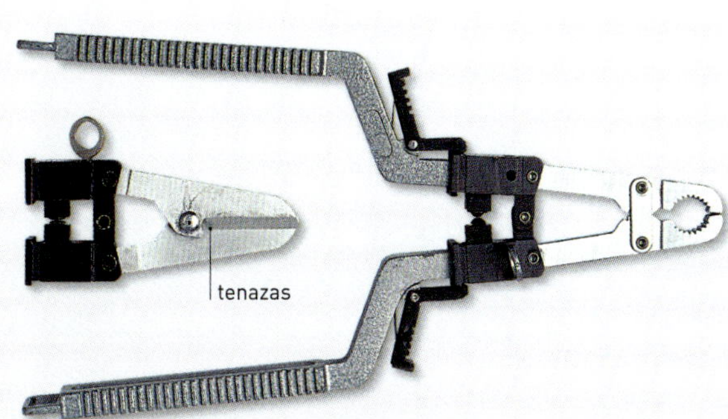

Herramientas espaciales
FECHA Y PROGRAMA DESCONOCIDOS
Se diseñaron herramientas específicas para facilitar la recogida de muestras. Como los gruesos guantes de astronauta dificultaban el agarre, las asas eran más gruesas de lo normal.

tenazas

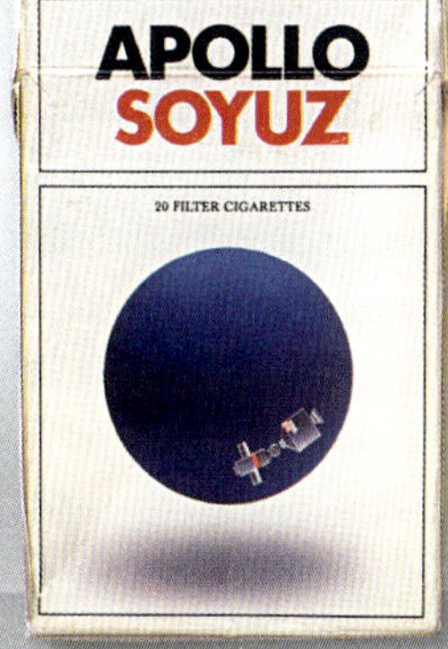

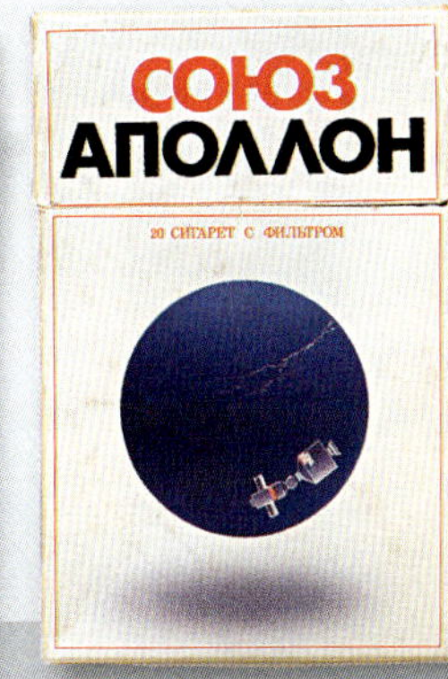

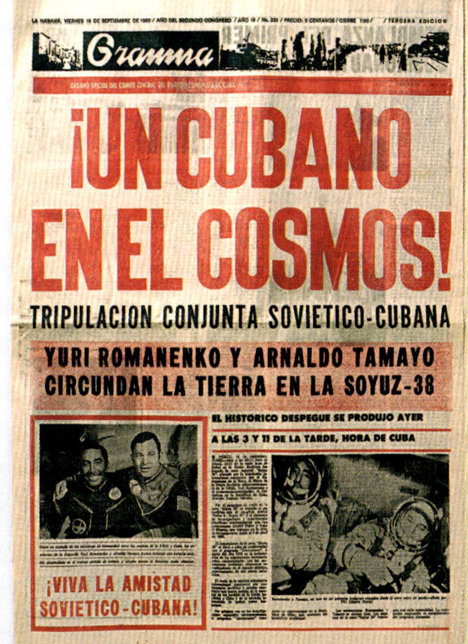

Granma

¡UN CUBANO EN EL COSMOS!

TRIPULACION CONJUNTA SOVIETICO-CUBANA

YURI ROMANENKO Y ARNALDO TAMAYO CIRCUNDAN LA TIERRA EN LA SOYUZ-38

EL HISTORICO DESPEGUE SE PRODUJO AYER

A LAS 3 Y 11 DE LA TARDE, HORA DE CUBA

¡VIVA LA AMISTAD SOVIETICO-CUBANA!

Periódico cubano
1980 • CUBA
Durante la carrera espacial, astronautas de muchos países comunistas, como Cuba, participaron en misiones espaciales soviéticas.

APOLLO SOYUZ
20 FILTER CIGARETTES
СОЮЗ АПОЛЛОН
20 СИГАРЕТ С ФИЛЬТРОМ

Cigarrillos conmemorativos
1975 • EE. UU. Y URSS
Estos cigarrillos se fabricaron para celebrar la misión Apolo-Soyuz de 1974, cuando naves de EE. UU. y la URSS se acoplaron *(rendez-vous)* en el espacio. Las cajetillas se imprimieron en inglés y en ruso.

1951

1952

1953

« TENÍA QUE **PASAR.** »

Julius Rosenberg, espía detenido, sobre su condena a muerte (1951)

Tras la rebelión contra los británicos, se arrestó a miles de keniatas sospechosos de ser activistas Mau Mau.

EGIPTO DIO POR FINALIZADO EL TRATADO DE 1936 QUE OTORGABA A GRAN BRETAÑA el uso de la base de Suez. En octubre, los británicos se negaron a retirarse y estalló una guerra en el **Canal de Suez**.

En marzo, el gobierno iraní nacionalizó su industria petrolera, que había estado dominada por la **Anglo-Iranian Oil Company**. Gran Bretaña respondió con un **embargo mundial** sobre el petróleo iraní.

La primera central nuclear, en Idaho, produjo unos 100 kW de electricidad (suficiente para encender cuatro bombillas de 100 W), lo que inauguró una nueva era para la **energía nuclear**.

El temor a la **propagación del comunismo** se intensificó cuando se acusó a **Julius** y a **Ethel Rosenberg** de pasar a la URSS información sobre EE. UU. El 28 de mayo desaparecieron dos oficiales del Foreign Office británico, **Guy Burgess** y **Donald Maclean**; luego se supo que habían **desertado** a la URSS.

Los Rosenberg esperan el veredicto
Julius y Ethel Rosenberg fueron declarados culpables de pasar secretos atómicos a la URSS.

INDOCHINA ESTUVO SUMIDA EN LA INESTABILIDAD DURANTE TODO EL AÑO. En abril, los franceses lanzaron una gran ofensiva para acabar con la **resistencia del Vietminh**, al noroeste de Saigón. En octubre, otra ofensiva francesa atacó sus fuentes de aprovisionamiento.

El 28 de abril entró en vigor el **tratado de paz** que **Japón** había firmado en San Francisco (EE. UU.) en 1951 y que le devolvía la **independencia**.

El 27 de mayo, **Alemania Oriental** cerró su frontera con **Alemania Occidental**. Se levantó una **«franja de control»** de 10 m de anchura a lo largo de toda la frontera.

El **rey Jorge VI** de Gran Bretaña murió el 6 de febrero. Su hija, **Isabel**, fue proclamada reina dos días después.

En **Kenia**, la oposición al gobierno británico llevó a la **rebelión de los Mau Mau**, un ejército insurgente anticolonialista. Empezaron con ataques a las granjas de los colonos blancos y, a finales de año, los británicos habían declarado el estado de emergencia.

En julio se fundó la **Comunidad Europea del Carbón y del Acero**, que comprendía a seis naciones; creaba un **«mercado común»** para el carbón y el acero y sentó las bases de la futura Unión Europea.

50 000 AFRICANOS FALLECIERON DURANTE LA **REBELIÓN DE LOS MAU MAU**

EVA PERÓN (1919–1952)

María Eva Duarte de Perón, «Evita», desempeñó un papel fundamental en la elección de su marido, Juan Perón, como presidente de Argentina. Las clases pobres la idolatraban e impulsó muchos programas de bienestar y de reforma social. Murió de cáncer a los 32 años.

El **comité de oficiales libres** del coronel Gamal Abdel Nasser lideró un golpe de estado en Egipto y tomó el poder en julio. En 1953, Egipto se convertía en una república.

Las primeras bombas atómicas habían caído sobre Hiroshima y Nagasaki en 1945. EE. UU. probó la **bomba de hidrógeno** (o bomba H), mucho más potente, el 1 de noviembre.

El 3 de julio, EE. UU. anunció que había logrado utilizar con éxito un **corazón artificial**. La máquina **Dodrill-GMR** había conseguido mantener la circulación de la sangre durante los cincuenta minutos que duró la operación.

LAS POLÍTICAS DE STALIN ADOPTABAN UN CARIZ CADA VEZ MÁS ANTISEMITA. A finales de 1952 afirmó ante su Politburó que todos los judíos simpatizaban con EE. UU. El 13 de enero, nueve médicos fueron arrestados, acusados de conspirar para asesinar a personalidades de las fuerzas armadas soviéticas. Seis de ellos eran judíos. Europa occidental respondió con aprensión. Los médicos fueron liberados y **Stalin murió** de una embolia en marzo.

La muerte de Stalin provocó una **lucha de poder** en el Kremlin, donde una coalición moderada liderada por **Gueorgui Malenkov** (1902–1988) asumió el control. Sus políticas moderadas resultaron impopulares y **Lavrenti Beria** (1899–1953), que había dirigido la policía secreta de Stalin, intentó arrebatarle el poder. Beria fue **acusado de traición** y murió acribillado en el remolque de un camión, en lo que parece haber sido un **asesinato** sumario.

Hillary y Norgay
Edmund Hillary y el sherpa Tenzing Norgay fueron los primeros alpinistas documentados en llegar a la cima del Everest, en la expedición británica de 1953.

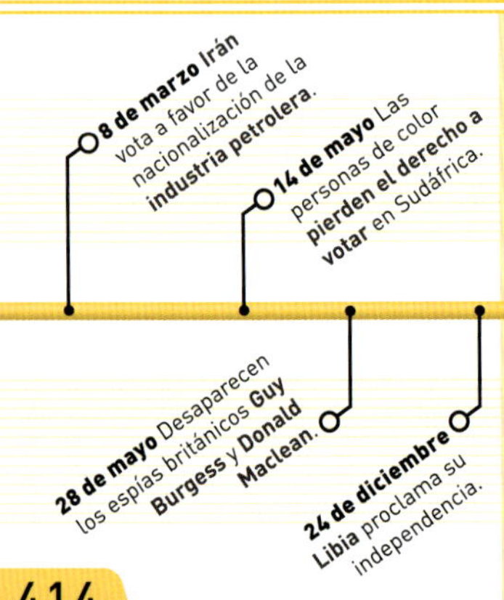

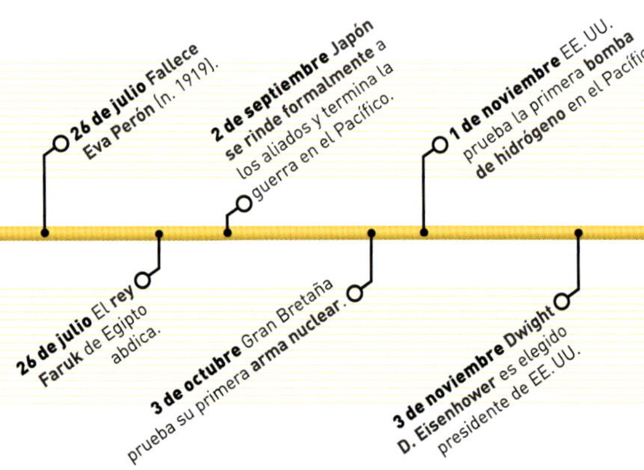

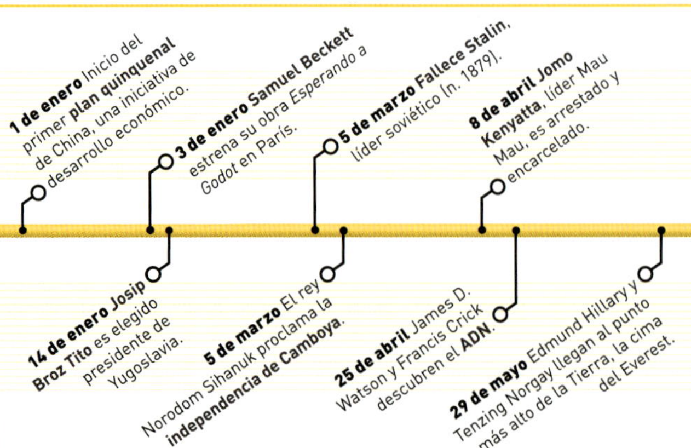

El conflicto en Indochina duró ocho años y terminó en 1954. En la imagen, el ejército francés evacua Hanoi.

ADN

En 1953, un descubrimiento científico revolucionó la ciencia: James Watson y Frances Crick descifraron el ADN (ácido desoxirribonucleico), el material hereditario que contiene la información codificada necesaria para desarrollar y mantener todos los organismos vivos. Watson y Crick propusieron un modelo de ADN de doble hélice. Explicaba la herencia y llevó al desarrollo de toda una industria de biotecnología.

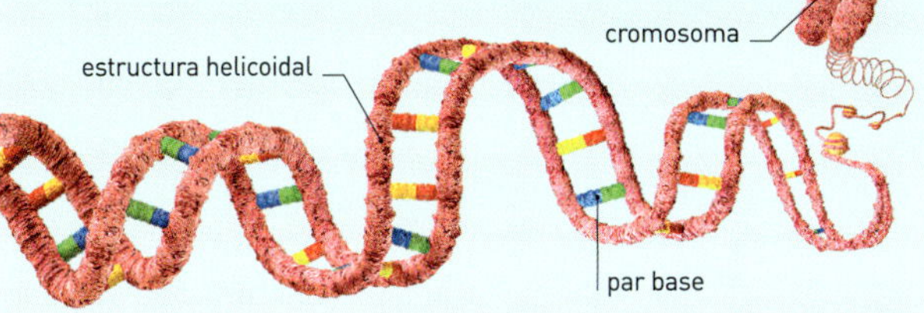

La **guerra de Corea** (*véase* 1950) terminó con la firma de un **armisticio** el 27 de julio. Sin embargo, la hostilidad permaneció en el aire. La **República de Corea** (Sur) y la **República Popular Democrática de Corea** (Norte) decidieron no firmar el tratado de paz.

El 29 de mayo, el neozelandés **Edmund Hillary** (1919–2008) y el sherpa nepalí **Tenzing Norgay** (1914–1986) coronaron por primera vez el **monte Everest**, que con sus 8848 m es el pico más alto del mundo. A causa de la escasez de oxígeno, Hillary y Norgay únicamente pudieron permanecer en la cima quince minutos.

El 5 de enero se estrenó una nueva obra del teatro del absurdo, *Esperando a Godot*, del dramaturgo irlandés **Samuel Beckett**, en el Théatre de Babylone (París). La crítica fue incapaz de ponerse de acuerdo.

EL DOMINIO FRANCÉS EN INDOCHINA FINALIZÓ EL 21 DE JULIO. Laos y **Camboya** se independizaron y Vietnam quedó dividido en **Vietnam del Sur** y **Vietnam del Norte** (comunista). En los tres estados no comunistas aparecieron movimientos de guerrilla comunistas.

Joseph McCarthy intensificó su campaña contra el comunismo (*véase* 1950). Apuntó al ejército estadounidense y formuló diversas acusaciones infundadas contra el mismo, lo que llevó al senado a emitir una moción de censura contra él el 2 de diciembre. El apoyo del público se desvaneció y así llegó a su fin la caza de brujas de McCarthy.

En EE. UU. se llevó a cabo un ensayo clínico de grandes proporciones para probar una **vacuna contra la poliomielitis**. El ensayo tuvo éxito y el año siguiente se implantó un programa de vacunación nacional.

ISRAEL ATACÓ LA FRANJA DE GAZA en febrero. Fue el primer ataque de este tipo contra fuerzas árabes desde la primera guerra árabe-israelí de 1949 (*véase* 1956).

Bajo la legislación del ***apartheid***, el gobierno sudafricano expulsó a sesenta mil personas de color de **Sophiatown** en febrero, para convertirla en una población blanca. El **Congreso Nacional Africano** (CNA), una organización contraria al *apartheid*, respondió con una jornada de plegarias.

El Tratado de Amistad, Colaboración y Asistencia Mutua o **Pacto de Varsovia** se firmó el 14 de mayo. Establecía una alianza militar de estados comunistas como **contrapeso de la OTAN** en Occidente.

La **Unión Soviética** puso fin a la ocupación de **Austria**, que perduraba desde el fin de la Segunda Guerra Mundial, con la condición de que Austria permaneciera neutral.

ROSA PARKS (1913–2005)

Hizo historia cuando se negó a ceder su asiento en el autobús a un hombre blanco. Su arresto provocó el boicot a la compañía de autobuses, que puso fin a la segregación en sus vehículos. El boicot también atrajo la atención internacional a la causa de los derechos civiles, con la que Parks continuó comprometida. Se convirtió en un símbolo de la lucha por los derechos civiles hasta su muerte, en 2005.

El 15 de mayo se firmó el **tratado del Estado Austriaco**, que restablecía la soberanía de Austria. Se unió a la ONU al año siguiente.

La posición de **Juan Perón** como presidente de Argentina se debilitó tras la muerte de su esposa y las desavenencias con la Iglesia. Un golpe de estado le **depuso** el 19 de septiembre; se exilió a Paraguay.

El 1 de diciembre fue un punto de inflexión para el **movimiento por los derechos civiles**. **Rosa Parks** fue detenida por negarse a sentarse en la parte trasera de un autobús en Alabama. Miles de personas boicotearon a la compañía de autobuses como protesta.

En Occidente, a mediados de la década de 1950, los **adolescentes** se diferenciaron como grupo con intereses musicales y estéticos propios; los adultos lo desaprobaron por temor a un incremento de la **delincuencia juvenil**. Se criticó el uso del argot juvenil, se cerraron salas de baile y algunas instituciones prohibieron la entrada con vaqueros.

El Pacto de Varsovia

Unió al Bloque Oriental en una alianza parecida a la OTAN. Los signatarios fueron Albania, Bulgaria, Rumanía, Checoslovaquia, Alemania Oriental, Hungría, Polonia y la URSS.

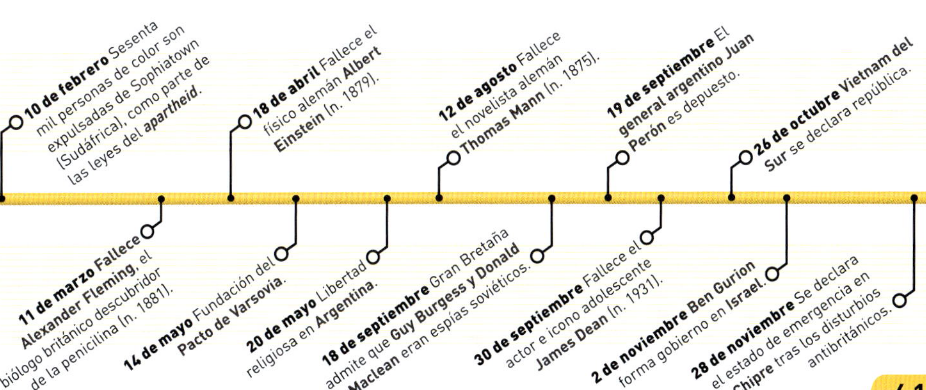

1956

« ¿QUÉ OTRA OPCIÓN TENÍAMOS ANTE UN **REINADO DE TERROR**? »

Nikita Jruschov, sobre Stalin (25 de febrero de 1956)

Nikita Jruschov, fotografiado durante una visita de ocho días a Londres. Su «desestalinización» de la URSS atemperó la Guerra Fría.

1957

Los soviéticos iniciaron la «carrera espacial» con los dos primeros satélites artificiales, el Sputnik 1 y el Sputnik 2, logro que conmemora este cartel.

Chevrolet Bel Air descapotable
El Chevrolet de 1956, rápido, grande y asequible, era justo lo que querían los estadounidenses. Se convirtió en el símbolo del «sueño americano».

FUE UN AÑO TURBULENTO para el movimiento por los derechos civiles estadounidense: un alumno de color empezó a asistir a la Universidad de Alabama; miembros de la comunidad blanca atacaron a afroamericanos, y las actividades del **Ku Klux Klan**, una organización de supremacistas blancos, aumentaron.

Marruecos declaró su **independencia** el 2 de marzo, aunque España conservó el control de Ceuta y Melilla. Las disputas fronterizas con Argelia desembocaron en una breve guerra en 1963.

CLAVE
Áreas afectadas por la crisis de Suez

La crisis de Suez
El Canal de Suez era una ruta comercial básica entre el mar Mediterráneo y el mar Rojo, sobre todo para el transporte de petróleo.

En **Chipre** estallaron revueltas en marzo, después de que las autoridades británicas deportaran al **arzobispo Makarios**, que lideraba la **campaña de unificación de Chipre y Grecia**. Le acusaban de alentar el terrorismo.

El 26 de julio, **Nasser, presidente** de Egipto, nacionalizó el **Canal de Suez**. Gran Bretaña y Francia tenían acciones en la Compañía del Canal de Suez y en octubre llegaron a un acuerdo secreto con Israel para que atacara Egipto. **Israel invadió la península del Sinaí** el 29 de octubre. EE.UU. presionó a Israel para que se retirara, y la ONU envió a sus fuerzas a la frontera entre Egipto e Israel. El 5 de noviembre dio inicio el asalto anglofrancés. La amenaza de EE.UU. de retener préstamos y una posible intervención de la URSS, sin embargo, lograron el alto el fuego y la retirada. Las tensiones continuaron entre Egipto e Israel tras la crisis de Suez, luego llamada **segunda guerra árabe-israelí**.

Nikita Jruschov, primer secretario del Partido Comunista, **llamó a Stalin** «déspota brutal», lo cual enfureció a los estalinistas, pero abrió la posibilidad de que **las relaciones con EE.UU. mejoraran**. Este nuevo escenario despertó la esperanza de un cambio en Europa Oriental.

En octubre, la **Revolución húngara** llevó a la formación de un gobierno liberal y el moderado **Imre Nagy** fue nombrado primer ministro. El 3 de noviembre anunció sus planes de retirarse del Pacto de Varsovia (*véase* 1955). Tras una disposición inicial a retirarse, tropas del Pacto de Varsovia invadieron Budapest y aplastaron la rebelión al día siguiente.

CACHEMIRA SE INCORPORÓ FORMALMENTE A INDIA el 26 de enero, contradiciendo así una resolución de la ONU. La constitución india le concedió un **estatus especial** que garantizaba, entre otras cosas, que los indios no oriundos de Cachemira no podrían adquirir propiedades allí. Pakistán se opuso vehementemente (*véanse* 1917 y 1965).

El 6 de marzo, **Ghana** se convirtió en el primer país del África negra que se **independizó** del gobierno colonial. El primer ministro, el doctor **Kwame Nkrumah** (1909–1972) impulsó ambiciosos programas de desarrollo y alentó el desarrollo político de África.

El 25 de marzo se firmó el **tratado de Roma**, que establecía la **CEE** (Comunidad Económica Europea) y sustentaba los programas sociales y económicos de los países miembro. Además, concedía a las antiguas colonias libre comercio y programas de apoyo.

Acabar con las guerrillas comunistas en **Malasia** había sido una preocupación para los británicos (*véase* 1948). Al final, comprendieron que no podrían resolver la situación por medios militares, por lo que accedieron a cambios constitucionales que culminaron con la **independencia de la Federación de Malasia** el 31 de agosto.

El **presidente Sukarno de Indonesia** había tenido dificultades para mantener la democracia parlamentaria desde la independencia en 1945. El 14 de marzo decidió disolver el parlamento e imponer la **ley marcial**. El 3 de diciembre, Sukarno nacionalizó las empresas holandesas y dos días después expulsó a todos los nacionales holandeses.

La **era espacial** empezó el 4 de octubre, cuando Rusia puso en órbita el **Sputnik 1**. Un mes después, le seguía el Sputnik 2, en el que viajó la perra **Laika**.

Comunidad Económica Europea
Composición de la CEE original en 1957, cuando seis países firmaron el tratado de Roma.

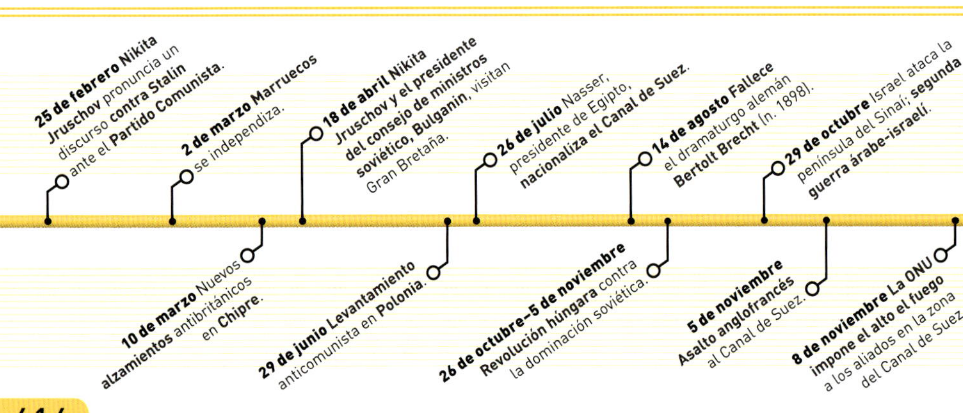

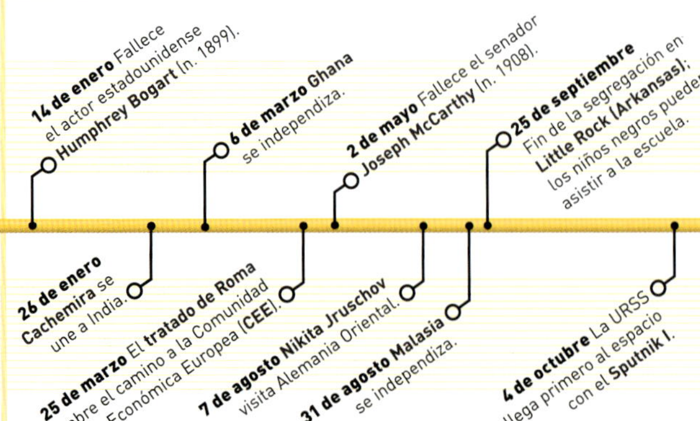

Elvis Presley actúa ante una multitud de jóvenes que le idolatran. Fue llamado a filas y zarpó hacia Alemania, en lo que supuso una pausa en su extraordinaria carrera.

MAO ZEDONG, FUNDADOR DE LA REPÚBLICA POPULAR CHINA, lanzó un programa de reforma que supuso la muerte de millones de personas. El Gran Salto Adelante tenía como objetivo industrializar rápidamente la economía rural china. Sin embargo, el programa de Mao sumió al país en una de las peores hambrunas de su historia. Durante los cuatro años siguientes, al menos 35 millones de personas murieron de hambre, de agotamiento o apaleadas.

35 MILLONES DE MUERTOS DURANTE **EL GRAN SALTO ADELANTE**

Oriente Medio sufrió este año las repercusiones de la **crisis del Canal de Suez** (*véase* 1956). En febrero, Egipto y Siria se unieron para formar la **República Árabe Unida**. Los regímenes pro occidentales de Oriente Medio entendieron que la unión suponía una amenaza para su seguridad, e Iraq y Jordania se aliaron. En julio estalló una **guerra civil** entre el régimen del presidente **Camille Chamoun**, mayoritariamente cristiano y pro occidental, y el **Frente Nacional Socialista Musulmán**. El 14 de julio, un grupo de oficiales libres iraquíes, liderados por el general de brigada Abdul Karim Qasim, tomó el poder en Bagdad tras un salvaje **golpe de estado militar**. El rey Faisal II, el regente Abdul Illah y el primer ministro Nuri al-Said fueron asesinados.

El golpe iraquí amenazaba con **desequilibrar el control de Occidente** sobre Oriente Medio y sus recursos petrolíferos. Para compensarlo, a las 48 horas del golpe de Bagdad, EE. UU. envió a un batallón de marines a Líbano en la **operación Blue Bat**, para apoyar al precario régimen del presidente Chamoun. Las tensiones se redujeron y EE. UU. retiró a sus hombres el 25 de octubre sin haber realizado ni un solo disparo.

Las guerras de Francia en Indochina, la guerra civil en Argelia y una serie de gobiernos inestables llevaron a solicitar al **general Charles de Gaulle** (*véase* recuadro) que se reincorporara a la política francesa. Exigió poderes especiales durante seis meses para reinstaurar el orden y que se redactara el borrador de una nueva constitución para una **Quinta República**, que la población francesa votó en referéndum el 28 de septiembre. De Gaulle consiguió una **amplia victoria y fue elegido presidente** el 21 de diciembre, doce años después de haberse retirado del poder.

El **éxito de Rusia en el lanzamiento de sus satélites** en 1957 impulsó a EE. UU. a fundar la National Aeronautic and Space Administration (**NASA**), es decir, la agencia espacial estadounidense. El 29 de julio, el presidente Eisenhower firmó la **Ley Nacional sobre Aeronáutica y el Espacio**.

Elvis Presley se había convertido en una gran estrella gracias a una serie de éxitos y este año resultó crucial para su carrera. Empezó a rodar su cuarto largometraje, *King Creole*, el 20 de enero. Entonces, en lo que parecía el cénit de una carrera prometedora, **fue llamado a filas** y en septiembre zarpó hacia Alemania. Las ventas de sus álbumes cayeron y los años en el ejército marcaron una clara división entre el Elvis anterior y el posterior.

CHARLES DE GAULLE (1890–1970)

Charles de Gaulle fue militar, político y estadista, y encabezó el gobierno provisional de Francia en 1944. En 1945 fue elegido presidente y en 1946 dimitió; regresó al poder en 1958 para resolver la crisis provocada por la guerra de Argelia. Volvió a dimitir en 1969, tras ser derrotado en un referéndum sobre la reforma constitucional.

El Gran Salto Adelante
Este cartel insta a los obreros a fabricar más acero como parte del Gran Salto Adelante de Mao Zedong, que intentaba modernizar China.

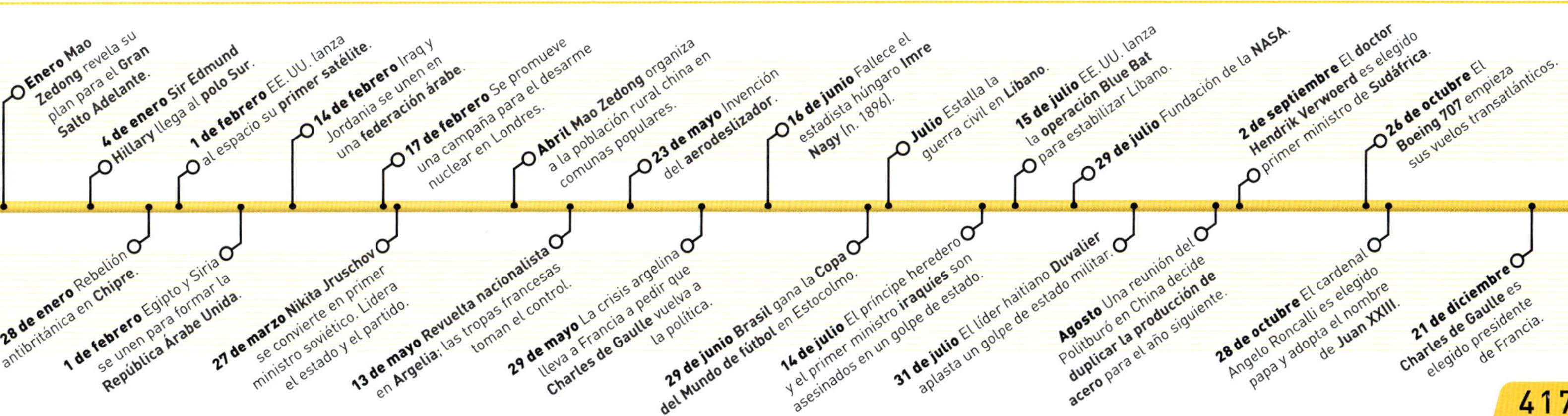

1959

« UNA **REVOLUCIÓN NO** ES **UN CAMINO DE ROSAS.** »

Fidel Castro, primer ministro de Cuba entre 1959–1976

LA CARRERA ENTRE EE. UU. Y LA URSS PARA ENVIAR A UN HOMBRE AL ESPACIO se aceleró en 1959. El 2 de enero, los soviéticos lanzaron la primera nave que logró salir de la órbita terrestre y llegar a la Luna: **Luna 1**. EE. UU. también consiguió su primer éxito ese año, cuando el cohete **Juno 2** lanzó la sonda **Pioneer 4** a la Luna. El 12 de septiembre se lanzó el **Luna 2**, y el 7 de octubre, la humanidad pudo ver por primera vez la **cara oculta de la Luna** gracias a las imágenes tomadas por el **Luna 3**.

Cuba había estado gobernada por una **sucesión de dictadores** que culminó con el gobierno corrupto de **Fulgencio Batista** (g. 1940–1944 y 1952–1959). Un grupo de revolucionarios, liderados por el estudiante de derecho **Fidel Castro**, tomó las armas y se estableció en las montañas de Sierra Maestra, lo que provocó que Batista emprendiera una campaña de represión indiscriminada. Su régimen se hundió y **Castro asumió el poder**; juró como primer ministro el 16 de febrero. La luna de miel con EE. UU. fue muy breve, ya que Cuba se convirtió en un **estado totalmente socialista**.

FIDEL CASTRO (n. 1926)

Encarcelado en 1953 por sus actividades revolucionarias en Cuba, se exilió tras su liberación, pero volvió en 1956. Fue el primer ministro cubano y el primer cabeza de estado comunista de las Américas entre 1959 y 1976. La relación con EE. UU. fue cordial al principio, pero no tardó en deteriorarse. Sigue siendo una figura importante, pero se retiró de la presidencia en 2006.

En **Vietnam**, las guerrillas del norte, bajo **Ho Chi Minh** (1890–1969), atacaron al ejército del sur en marzo. Ho Chi Minh quería unir Vietnam bajo un gobierno comunista. Con el fin de detener la propagación del comunismo, EE. UU. entrenó al **Ejército de la República de Vietnam** (ARVN) y asesoró a Vietnam del Sur. El 8 de julio, soldados del Vietminh mataron a dos estadounidenses: estas fueron las dos primeras bajas de EE. UU. en la **guerra de Vietnam**.

El **dalai lama**, líder espiritual de Tíbet, huyó del país el 31 de marzo y **escapó a India** junto con sus ministros tras la **rebelión abierta contra el gobierno chino** en Tíbet, que había culminado en un alzamiento total. Miles de tibetanos murieron por la **represión china**. Durante los meses siguientes, ochenta mil huyeron a India.

En Sudáfrica, continuaban las **protestas anti *apartheid***. Durante las de la ciudad de **Sharpeville** murieron unos setenta manifestantes, y se prohibió el **Congreso Nacional Africano** (ANC, *véase* 1994). Ambos sucesos provocaron la **condena internacional** de las políticas de *apartheid* sudafricanas. Durante su visita en febrero de 1960 al parlamento sudafricano, el primer ministro británico, **Harold Macmillan**, pronunció un discurso en el que subrayaba los **vientos de cambio** que creía que traerían la independencia a los africanos de color.

El escarabajo de Volkswagen
El «escarabajo» sobrevivió a la guerra, y los escarabajos decorados se convirtieron en un símbolo de paz en todo el mundo.

1960

John F. Kennedy y su esposa, Jacqueline, sonríen desde un descapotable durante las celebraciones de la investidura de Kennedy.

LA TIRANTEZ DE LAS RELACIONES DIPLOMÁTICAS ENTRE CHINA Y LA URSS se hizo patente en junio, durante el congreso del Partido Comunista Rumano, en el que **Nikita Jruschov** y **Peng Zhen**, de China, se enfrentaron abiertamente. Los soviéticos estaban alarmados por el **Gran Salto Adelante** de China (*véase* 1958); además, habían renegado de su acuerdo anterior de ayudar a China a desarrollar armamento nuclear y se les consideraba demasiado conciliadores con Occidente. En una reunión en noviembre, las delegaciones china y soviética volvieron a enfrentarse, pero consiguieron llegar a un acuerdo para impedir una división formal.

El **Congo Belga** se independizó el 30 de junio y entró en una etapa turbulenta. Se denominó **República Federal del Congo**, con Joseph Kasavubu como presidente y Patrice Lumumba (socialista) como primer ministro. En julio, la provincia de Katanga declaró su independencia y solicitó ayuda a Bélgica, que respondió con una invasión y llevó a Kasavubu a **apelar a la ONU**. En septiembre, Kasavubu destituyó a Lumumba como primer ministro y le arrestó en diciembre. El año siguiente, **Lumumba fue asesinado**.

La Organización de los Países Exportadores de Petróleo (**OPEP**) fue fundada en septiembre por los principales exportadores de petróleo fuera del bloque comunista. Se aliaron para fijar los precios del petróleo mediante el control de la oferta (*véase* 1973).

El 16 de mayo se usó el **láser** por primera vez. **Theodore Maiman** (1927–2007), físico estadounidense, se inventó este aparato que emite un intenso haz de luz y que llamó la atención de científicos de todo el mundo, lo que llevó a grandes **avances** en ingeniería, medicina y tecnología.

Martin Luther King (1929–1968), el influyente activista y defensor de los derechos civiles, obtuvo fama internacional a principios de la década de 1960. Le arrestaron en Atlanta (Georgia) durante una sentada el día 19 de octubre. Le sentenciaron a cuatro meses de prisión, pero **John F. Kennedy** (1917–1963), candidato a la presidencia, intervino para que le liberaran tras ocho días de cárcel.

John Fitzgerald Kennedy fue elegido el 35.º presidente de EE. UU. en noviembre. Venció por escaso margen a Richard Nixon, candidato republicano, tras unos disputadísimos debates televisivos.

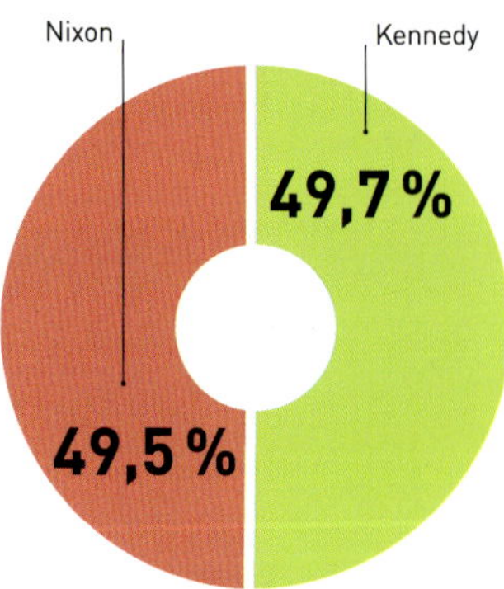

Carrera hacia la Casa Blanca
La carrera presidencial entre Nixon y Kennedy casi terminó en empate. Kennedy derrotó a Nixon por menos de un 1 %: 118 574 votos.

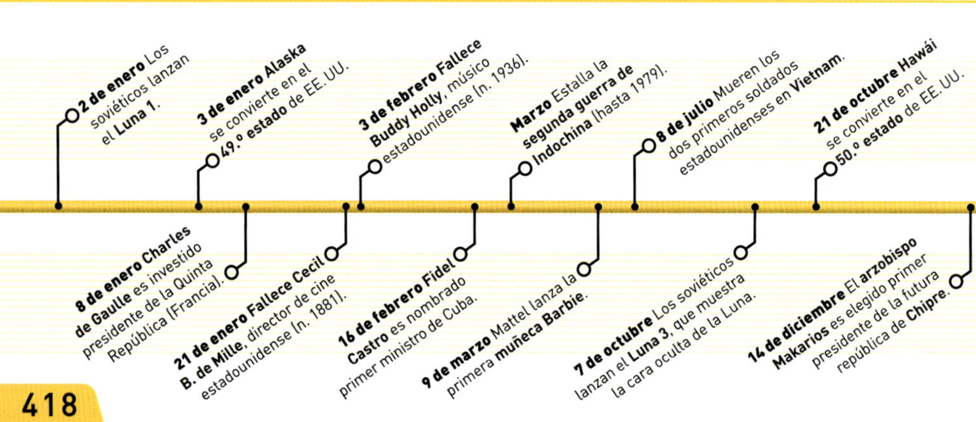

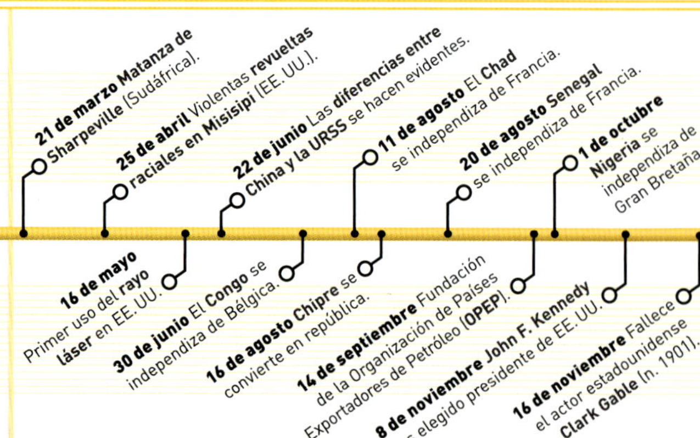

Los paracaidistas contienen a manifestantes franceses, airados por las noticias sobre la autodeterminación de Argelia.

El primer hombre en el espacio
Yuri Gagarin en la cabina de su nave, el Vostok 1. El vuelo de este pionero del espacio duró 1 hora y 45 minutos.

EL *SANTA MARÍA*, UN CRUCERO PORTUGUÉS DE LUJO, fue secuestrado en enero mientras navegaba en aguas de las Indias Occidentales. Los secuestradores eran **revolucionarios portugueses y españoles**, que se oponían al gobierno portugués y al régimen fascista español. Las novecientas personas a bordo fueron liberadas once días después.

La Unión Soviética obtuvo una victoria en la **carrera espacial** cuando **Yuri Gagarin** (1934–1968) se convirtió en el primer hombre en ser lanzado al espacio. **Completó la órbita terrestre** una vez, el 12 de abril, y viajó a más de 27 000 km/h en la nave **Vostok 1**.

En 1960, los rusos habían conseguido aliarse con **Fidel Castro**, el recién instalado dictador de Cuba (*véase* recuadro, p. 418). Washington respondió en abril y financió a 1500 anticomunistas en el desdichado desembarco de la **bahía de Cochinos**. El mal pergeñado intento de invasión de la costa sur fue aplastado inmediatamente (*véase* 1962).

Una de las primeras propuestas de **Kennedy** como presidente de EE. UU. fue la fundación de un **Cuerpo de Paz** que ayudara a los países en vías de desarrollo y que estaría compuesto por personas jóvenes que trabajarían como maestros, profesionales sanitarios o asesores en África, Asia y América del Sur.

El 29 de abril, en Suiza, se lanzó una iniciativa mundial para proteger el **medio ambiente**. El **Manifiesto Morges** sería la base de la primera organización ecologista global, el World Wildlife Fund (**WWF**), cuyas oficinas centrales estaban en Suiza y que abrió gradualmente delegaciones nacionales en todo el mundo, empezando por Gran Bretaña, en noviembre. Ese mismo año se inauguró el primer **parque nacional** de América del Sur, en Brasil. El gobierno creó el **Parque Nacional del Xingú**, de 2,3 millones de hectáreas, para reubicar a la población indígena brasileña, cuyas tierras habían sido expropiadas.

Sudáfrica se centró en sus políticas antibritánicas y el 31 de mayo ganó el referéndum por la **independencia**. Se convirtió en república y abandonó la Commonwealth. **Nelson Mandela** (n. 1918) dirigió ese año la nueva ala militar del ANC y lanzó una campaña de sabotaje.

El presidente Charles de Gaulle defendió la **autodeterminación de Argelia** (*véase* 1954), pero las relaciones entre Francia y Argelia permanecieron enrarecidas. Los colonos franceses residentes en Argelia reaccionaron con ira y Francia se preparó para una guerra civil. Miles de **argelinos se reunieron** en París el 17 de octubre para protestar contra las medidas represivas que se habían tomado en su contra. Unas diez mil personas fueron arrestadas y **cientos murieron durante las protestas**.

El 13 de agosto, los **berlineses** se encontraron con que vivían en una ciudad separada físicamente, ya que el ejército de Alemania Oriental había cerrado la frontera entre **Berlín Oriental y Berlín Occidental**. Se levantaron vallas de alambre de espino de hasta 2 m de altura, que en unos días habían sido sustituidas por bloques de hormigón. El **Muro pasó a ser permanente** (*véase* 1989).

Muro divisorio
El Muro de Berlín comprendía los tres sectores de Berlín Occidental y los separaba del Berlín y la Alemania orientales.

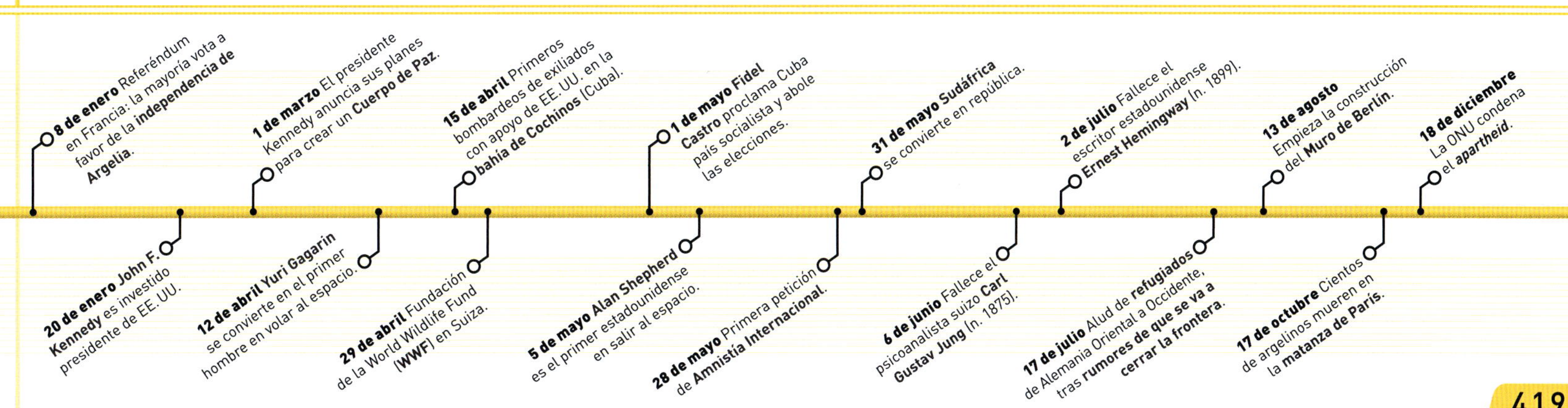

Exhibición de misiles en un desfile en La Habana. EE. UU. estuvo a punto de entrar en guerra con la URSS por haber realizado instalaciones nucleares en Cuba.

Luther King Jr. saluda a la multitud frente al monumento a Lincoln.

« NOS MIRÁBAMOS FIJAMENTE Y EL OTRO ACABÓ POR PESTAÑEAR. »

Dean Rusk, secretario de Estado de EE. UU., sobre la crisis cubana en 1962

EN MARZO, CHARLES DE GAULLE, presidente de Francia, acordó la independencia de Argelia con nacionalistas argelinos. La **Organización del Ejército Secreto** (OAS), formada por oficiales partidarios de que Argelia siguiera siendo una colonia francesa, lanzaron una oleada de atentados con bomba en París e intentaron atentar contra la vida de De Gaulle en repetidas ocasiones. **Argelia se independizó** de Francia el 3 de julio, después de que un referéndum en enero lo aprobara. Así se puso fin a ocho años de tensiones civiles y de guerra de guerrillas. Los funcionarios franceses estimaron que se perdieron unas 350 000 vidas. Fuentes argelinas elevan la cifra a 1,5 millones.

Gable Monroe Clift
in The John Huston Production
the Misfits
Thelma Ritter Eli Wallach
Arthur Miller Frank E. Taylor John Huston

El 10 de julio se lanzó desde Cabo Cañaveral el **Telstar**, el primer satélite de comunicaciones del mundo. A primeras horas del día 11 de julio empezaron a enviarse imágenes televisadas transatlánticas en directo desde Maine (EE. UU.) a Goonhilly (Cornualles, Inglaterra).

EE. UU. volvió a ocupar las portadas de la prensa cuando el 5 de agosto se encontró el cadáver de **Marilyn Monroe**, en su apartamento de Los Ángeles; tenía 36 años de edad. Se especuló mucho sobre la causa de la muerte y el forense declaró que se trataba de un «probable suicidio», pero muchos creyeron que había sido una muerte accidental por sobredosis de somníferos.

Marilyn Monroe
En el momento de su muerte, Marilyn era una gran estrella y había protagonizado 29 películas. Vidas rebeldes *fue la última.*

Mientras tanto, **Nelson Mandela**, líder del Umkhonto we Siwze, el brazo armado del Congreso Nacional Africano (ANC), fue arrestado el 5 de agosto tras 17 días de huida. Le acusaron de sabotaje y el 7 de noviembre le **condenaron a cinco años de prisión**.

El 6 de agosto, **Jamaica** se **independizó** con **Alexander Bustamante** (1884–1977), del Partido Laborista de Jamaica, como primer ministro. El país, que permaneció en la Commonwealth británica, experimentó varios años de crecimiento bajo su gobierno moderadamente conservador.

La población de Berlín no podía celebrar su libertad tras la construcción del **Muro de Berlín** (*véase* 1961). **Peter Fechter**, un peón de la construcción de 18 años de edad, fue una de las primeras víctimas de los guardas fronterizos del Muro, cuando intentaba cruzar de Berlín Oriental a Berlín Occidental.

En Gran Bretaña, **los Beatles**, un grupo de Liverpool, lograba firmar con la discográfica EMI el 4 de junio. Se habían presentado a audiciones de varias discográficas, pero, pese al entusiasmo de su mánager, Brian Epstein, habían sido rechazados. ***Love Me Do***, su primer sencillo, se publicó el 5 de octubre y permaneció 18 semanas en las listas de los superventas.

En EE. UU. crecía la preocupación por la alianza entre **Cuba** y la **URSS**. La instalación de misiles soviéticos en Cuba había reducido el margen de reacción ante un hipotético ataque nuclear a EE. UU. de quince a dos minutos. En octubre, **Kennedy** decretó un bloqueo sobre la isla para impedir la entrada de más misiles, y transmitió un ultimátum al líder ruso, **Nikita Jruschov**, para que retirara los que había instalado. El mundo estuvo al borde de una guerra nuclear, pero Jruschov acabó por claudicar, poniendo fin a un conflicto conocido como la **crisis de los misiles de Cuba**.

India y **China** libraron su propia batalla en una **guerra fronteriza** tan breve como cruenta por la meseta de Aksai Chin, en la frontera nororiental de India. El ejército chino llegó a India el 20 de octubre y decretó un alto el fuego el 21 de noviembre.

5000 intentaron cruzar el Muro

unos **150** murieron en el intento

Cruzar el Muro de Berlín
Fueron muchos los que hicieron intentos desesperados para cruzar el Muro y llegar a Berlín Occidental entre 1961 y 1989.

LA DÉCADA DE 1960 presenció el renacer del movimiento de liberación de la mujer. **Betty Friedan** (1921–2006) plasmó algunas de las frustraciones de las amas de casa estadounidenses en *La mística de la feminidad*. Se publicó en febrero y contribuyó a iniciar una **segunda ola de feminismo** en EE. UU.

En otra demostración de unidad, los cabezas de estado de 32 países africanos firmaron el 25 de mayo los estatutos fundacionales de la **Organización de la Unidad Africana** (OUA), con el objetivo de promover la solidaridad africana, poner fin al colonialismo y coordinar los programas políticos, económicos, sanitarios, científicos, militares y culturales de los países miembro. La cumbre, cuyo anfitrión era **Haile Selassie**, emperador de Etiopía, también apoyaba a quienes luchaban por la libertad de África, proporcionándoles armas, entrenamiento y bases militares.

Kenia, uno de los primeros miembros de la OUA, fue el 34.º país africano en lograr la independencia. **Jomo Kenyatta** (1894–1978) fue elegido líder de la Unión Nacional Africana de Kenia tras haber permanecido nueve años en prisión, y ganó las elecciones nacionales en mayo. Kenyatta fue nombrado primer ministro y dirigió a Kenia desde el autogobierno a la **independencia plena** el 12 de diciembre.

El **presidente de EE. UU. John F. Kennedy** pronunció un **discurso** en **Berlín** el 26 de junio que elevó la moral de los berlineses. Ofrecía su solidaridad a los ciudadanos de Berlín Occidental, alarmados por la construcción del Muro. Miles de

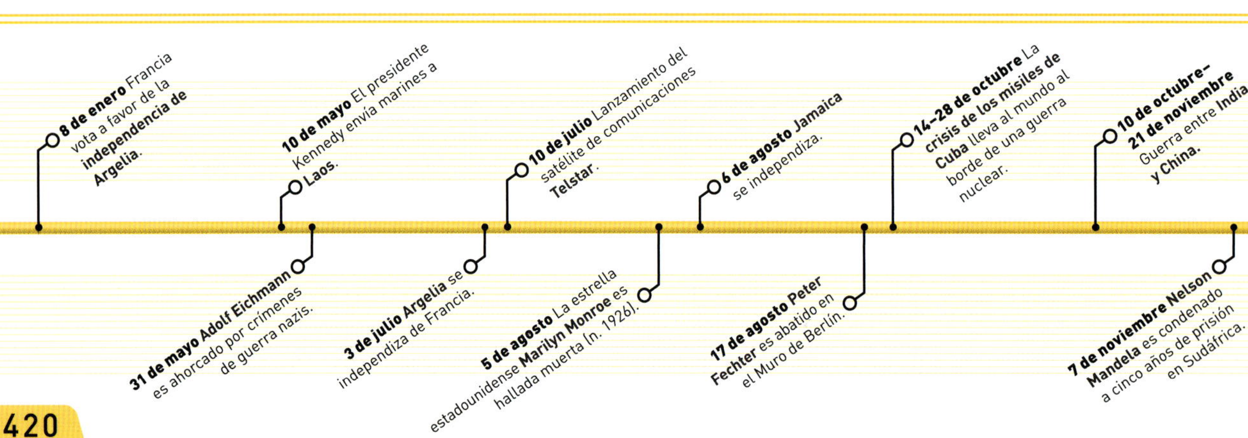

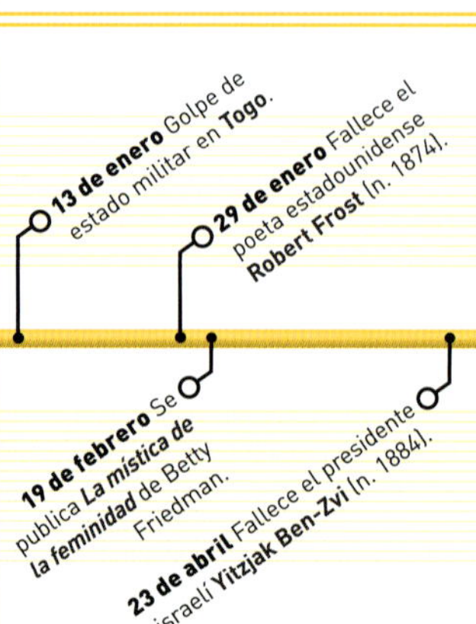

« NO PODEMOS CAMINAR SOLOS... NO PODEMOS **VOLVER ATRÁS**... **TENGO UN SUEÑO**. **»**

Martin Luther King Jr.
en un mitin de 1963

SEGUNDA OLA DE FEMINISMO

La primera ola de feminismo abordó los obstáculos legales, como el voto para la mujer; la segunda se centró en la familia y la sexualidad. Simone de Beauvoir definió en *El segundo sexo* el movimiento de la mujer y acabó con el mito de que las mujeres eran ciudadanas de segunda clase.

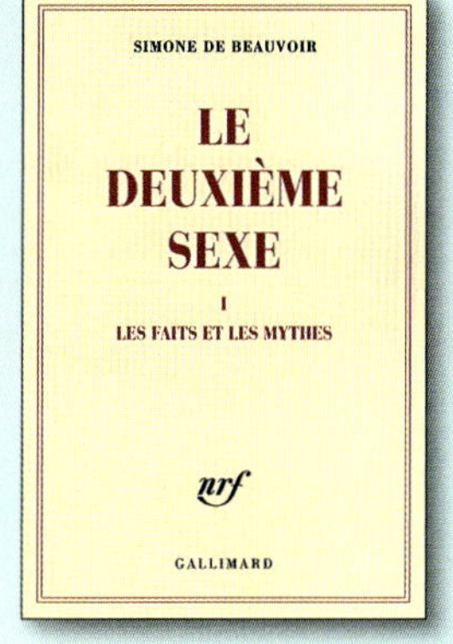

ellos se concentraron frente al ayuntamiento para escucharle un discurso que desafiaba abiertamente a los soviéticos y que presentaba a Berlín Occidental como un símbolo de libertad. Acabó con toda esperanza rusa de que los aliados abandonaran Berlín Occidental.

La **crisis de los misiles de Cuba** (*véase* 1962) complicó la relación entre los países capitalistas y comunistas. El incidente había levantado temores acerca de la contaminación nuclear y abrió la posibilidad de un tratado que prohibiera las **pruebas nucleares** en la atmósfera, el espacio y bajo el agua. El **tratado de prohibición de ensayos nucleares** se firmó en Moscú, con la participación de la Unión Soviética, EE. UU. y Reino Unido. El 24 de septiembre el senado estadounidense lo ratificó y entró en vigor el 11 de octubre.

El 28 de agosto la **campaña por la igualdad racial** en EE. UU. dio un paso al frente hacia la victoria. Una multitud de más de 250 000 defensores de los derechos civiles se congregó ante el monumento a Lincoln para iniciar una **Marcha sobre Washington** por el empleo y la libertad. Hablaron personalidades destacadas, como **Martin Luther King Jr.**, que pronunció su famoso discurso que arrancaba diciendo **«tengo un sueño»**: el día en que la promesa de libertad e igualdad para todos se hiciera realidad en EE. UU.

El 22 de noviembre fue otro día histórico para EE. UU.: el presidente **John F. Kennedy fue asesinado** mientras atravesaba la Plaza Dealey (Dallas) en un descapotable. El gobernador de Texas, John Connally, resultó herido. Las esposas de ambos, que viajaban con ellos, salieron ilesas. Agentes del servicio secreto irrumpieron inmediatamente en el edificio del Depósito de libros escolares de Texas, donde se habían oído disparos, y encontraron un rifle con mira telescópica. Menos de una hora después, un policía se acercó a **Lee Harvey Oswald**, que le disparó y le mató. Oswald fue arrestado y acusado del asesinato del policía y de Kennedy.

El vicepresidente, **Lyndon B. Johnson**, que volaba de vuelta a Washington DC en el avión presidencial, el *Air Force I*, fue nombrado 36.º presidente de EE. UU. El **funeral** de Kennedy se celebró el 25 de noviembre. La reacción de asombro e incredulidad ante lo ocurrido fue universal.

Dos días después del asesinato de Kennedy, Lee Harvey Oswald, el hombre acusado del mismo, también fue asesinado. Oswald, un ex marine, estaba siendo trasladado desde la comisaría a la prisión. Estaba rodeado de policías y de periodistas y, en medio de la confusión, **Jack Ruby**, el propietario de una discoteca de Dallas, avanzó y disparó a Oswald. Posteriormente, afirmó que lo había hecho «por Jackie Kennedy». El asesinato fue filmado y retransmitido en directo por televisión a todo EE. UU. Oswald había negado ser el responsable de la muerte de Kennedy, lo que alentó las teorías de la conspiración. En un intento de esclarecer la verdad, el 29 de noviembre se abrió la **comisión Warren** para que investigara lo sucedido.

El funeral de Kennedy
Más de un millón de personas acompañaron a la procesión fúnebre de Kennedy, que terminó en el cementerio de Arlington. Millones de personas lo siguieron por televisión.

« TODOS LOS **HOMBRES LIBRES**... SON **CIUDADANOS DE BERLÍN**. **»**

John F. Kennedy (26 de junio de 1963)

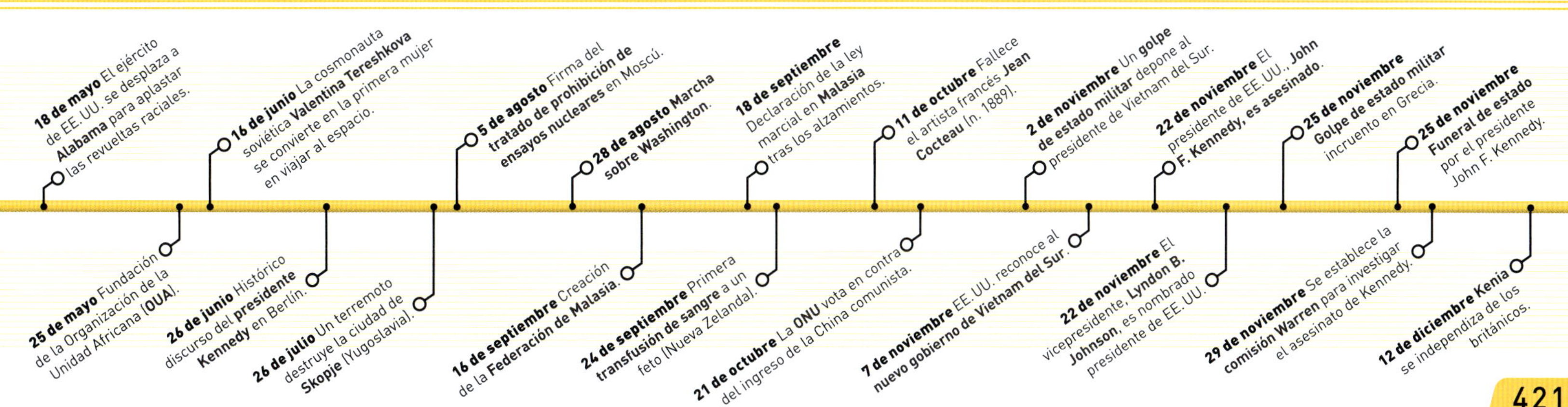

El imperio en 1938
El imperialismo aún imperaba antes de la Segunda Guerra Mundial. Los mayores territorios en manos extranjeras estaban en África, como resultado del reparto de este continente durante el siglo XIX. *Francia y Gran Bretaña eran las primeras potencias coloniales.*

FIN DEL IMPERIALISMO

EL COLONIALISMO SE DERRUMBA ANTE LOS MOVIMIENTOS INDEPENDENTISTAS

Los imperios de Gran Bretaña, Francia, Bélgica, Portugal y Países Bajos se remontaban a varios siglos atrás cuando estalló la Segunda Guerra Mundial; una vez acabada, el paisaje político había cambiado significativamente y el imperialismo se enfrentaba a una creciente oposición. En el mundo moderno, los últimos vestigios de los imperios europeos se limitan a unas cuantas islas.

En 1945, los imperios de Italia, Alemania y Japón ya se habían derrumbado. El Imperio británico había logrado salir de la guerra relativamente incólume, pero dio el primer paso hacia el fin del colonialismo al conceder la independencia a India en 1947. El cambio fue lento. A mediados de la década de 1950, el globo aún estaba repleto de posesiones británicas.

A pesar de la creencia generalizada de que las naciones imperialistas tenían la responsabilidad de proteger a sus pueblos del comunismo, muchas quedaron agotadas por la austeridad de la posguerra y la población cada vez estaba más descontenta. Los nacionalismos prosperaron con apoyo de la Rusia soviética y alentados por EE. UU. El choque ideológico complicó la transición a la independencia y las guerras civiles ocuparon con frecuencia ese vacío.

El imperialismo de Francia y Gran Bretaña sufrió un golpe definitivo con la crisis de Suez en 1956. Los franceses estaban siendo derrotados en Indochina y libraban una guerra civil feroz en Argelia, mientras que Gran Bretaña intentaba sofocar rebeliones en Chipre, Kenia y Malasia. El presidente de Egipto, Nasser, nacionalizó el Canal de Suez y asestó otro golpe al imperialismo británico. Gran Bretaña y Francia invadieron Egipto, pero sufrieron una derrota humillante (*véase* 1956). El siguiente paso fue el desmantelamiento de las colonias africanas: Francia tuvo que renunciar a Argelia y Bélgica, al Congo. Sin embargo, las nuevas naciones no heredaron la riqueza de sus anteriores gobernantes y muchas antiguas colonias sufrieron pobreza, intervenciones extranjeras y corrupción.

TERRITORIOS DEPENDIENTES ACTUALES

Los territorios dependientes son países que, en general, tienen cierto grado de autonomía, pero que carecen de independencia política plena o de soberanía como estados. Después de la Segunda Guerra Mundial muchas colonias lucharon por lograr la autonomía, pero varias rechazaron la independencia. Por ejemplo, algunos territorios son muy pequeños y carecen de los recursos para sobrevivir. Otros, como la Guayana Francesa en el Caribe, bajo gobierno francés, o las islas Malvinas, en el Atlántico Sur y bajo gobierno británico, tienen una importancia económica o estratégica especial para los países que los controlan, por lo que no los ceden con facilidad.

AUSTRALIA	Islas Ashmore y Cartier
	Islas Heard y McDonald
	Isla de Navidad
	Islas del mar del Coral
	Islas Cocos
	Isla Norfolk

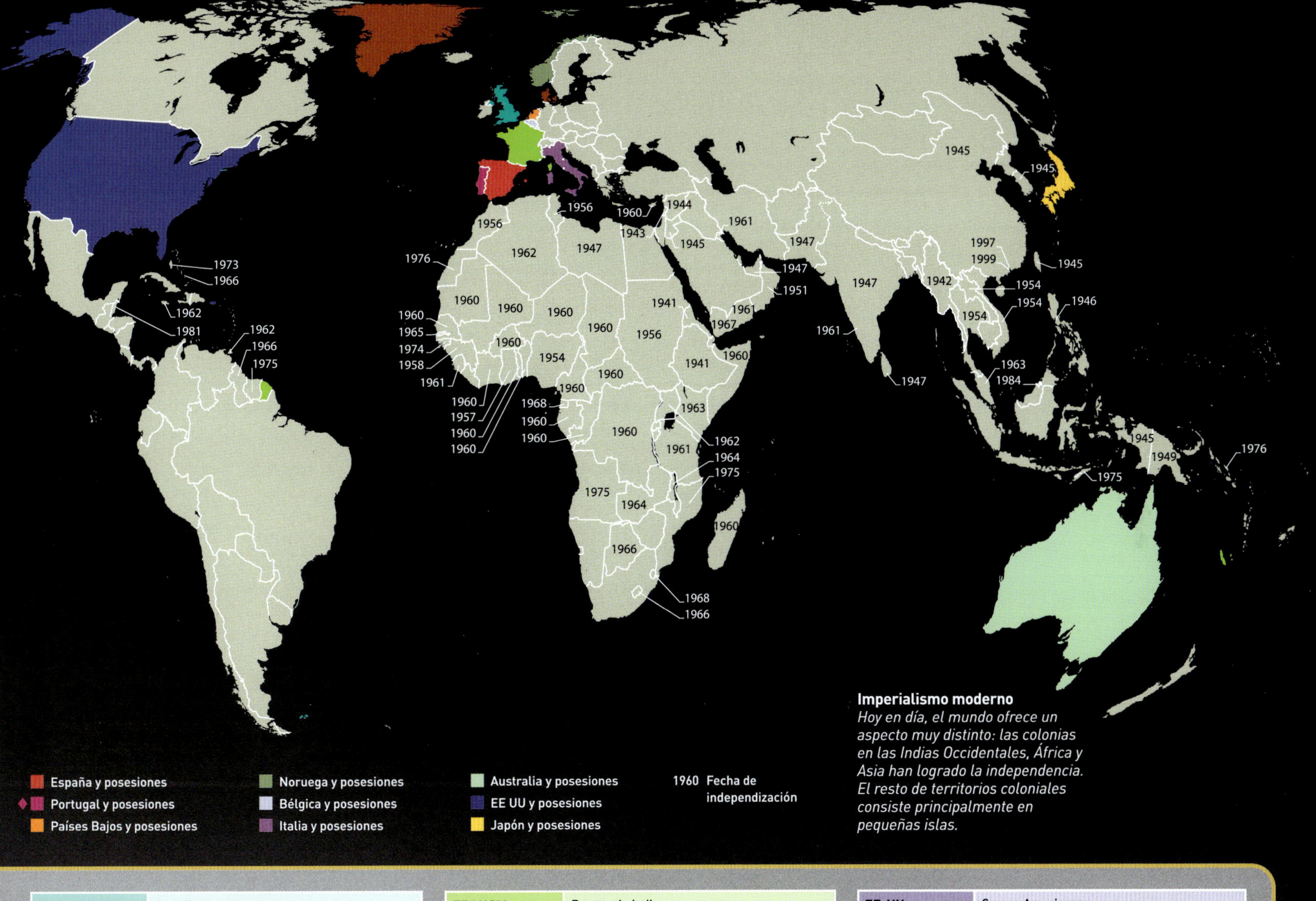

Imperialismo moderno
Hoy en día, el mundo ofrece un aspecto muy distinto: las colonias en las Indias Occidentales, África y Asia han logrado la independencia. El resto de territorios coloniales consiste principalmente en pequeñas islas.

REINO UNIDO	
	Anguila
	Bermudas
	Territorio británico en el océano Índico
	Islas Vírgenes Británicas
	Islas Caimán
	Islas Malvinas
	Gibraltar
	Guernesey
	Jersey
	Isla de Man
	Montserrat
	Islas Pitcairn
	Santa Elena
	Islas Georgias del Sur y Sandwich del Sur
	Islas Turcas y Caicos

FRANCIA	
	Bassas da India
	Isla de la Pasión (o Clipperton)
	Isla Europa
	Guayana Francesa
	Polinesia Francesa
	Tierras Australes y Antárticas Francesas
	Islas Gloriosas
	Guadalupe
	Isla Juan de Nova
	Martinica
	Mayotte
	Nueva Caledonia
	Reunión
	San Pedro y Miguelón
	Isla Tromelin
	Wallis y Futuna

EE. UU.	
	Samoa Americana
	Isla Baker
	Guam
	Isla Howland
	Isla Jarvis
	Atolón Johnston
	Arrecife Kingman
	Islas Midway
	Isla Navaza
	Islas Marianas del Norte
	Atolón Palmira
	Puerto Rico
	Islas Vírgenes
	Isla Wake

DINAMARCA	
	Islas Feroe
	Groenlandia

PAÍSES BAJOS	
	Aruba
	Antillas holandesas

NUEVA ZELANDA	
	Islas Cook
	Niue
	Tokelau

NORUEGA	
	Isla de Bouvet
	Jan Mayen
	Svalbard

TERRITORIOS DISPUTADOS	
	Antártida
	Franja de Gaza
	Islas Paracelso
	Islas Spratly
	Cisjordania
	Sáhara Occidental

1964

Mandela fue uno de los hombres sentenciados a cadena perpetua en el proceso de Rivonia; salieron del tribunal con los puños en alto, en señal de desafío.

EL AÑO EMPEZÓ CON EL AUMENTO DE LA TENSIÓN entre griegos y turcos de **Chipre**. En marzo, la ONU envió a siete mil soldados a la isla en un intento por mantener la paz. La presión diplomática logró poner fin a la violencia el 10 de agosto.

El 27 de mayo fallecía **Jawaharlal Nehru** (el primero en ser primer ministro indio tras la independencia de Gran Bretaña, y considerado por muchos el fundador de la India moderna). Más de 250 000 personas hicieron cola para despedirle.

En Sudáfrica, **Nelson Mandela** (1918–2013), una de las figuras clave en la lucha **contra el *apartheid***, fue condenado a cadena perpetua el 12 de junio. En el juicio, Mandela y otros miembros del **Congreso Nacional Africano** (CNA, *véase* 1994) afirmaron que habían intentado derrocar al gobierno.

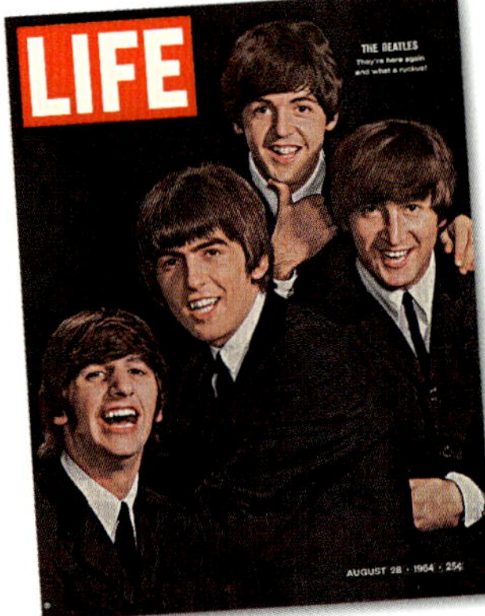

Estalla la *Beatlemania*
Los Beatles tomaron EE. UU. por asalto en 1964. Sus rostros ocupaban revistas y periódicos, y se agotaron todas las entradas para su gira por 23 ciudades.

Mientras, la lucha por la igualdad racial en EE. UU. dio un paso más el 2 de julio, día en que se promulgó la **Ley de Derechos Civiles**. Esta decretaba la igualdad de derechos para todos, con independencia de la raza, la religión o el color de piel. **Martin Luther King Jr.**, el activista que se había convertido en el líder simbólico de la lucha por los derechos civiles en todo el mundo, fue uno de los signatarios. Su labor le convirtió en el hombre más joven en recibir el **Nobel de la paz**.

EE. UU. quería impedir que **Vietnam del Sur** fuera comunistas. El 7 de agosto, el presidente Johnson recibió la aprobación del senado para «emprender las acciones necesarias» contra el régimen comunista en Vietnam del Norte. La guerra se intensificó, lo que se ocultó a la población. En noviembre, Johnson ganó las elecciones con una mayoría aplastante (*véase* 1965).

El 28 de septiembre se hizo público el **informe Warren** sobre el asesinato de Kennedy (*véase* 1963), que cautivó la atención del público. Concluía que no había habido conspiración alguna y que Lee Harvey Oswald había actuado en solitario.

En el Este, Nikita **Jruschov**, líder de la URSS, se «jubiló» en octubre, tras haber permanecido en el poder desde 1958. Sus políticas se habían vuelto cada vez más impopulares y se votó su remoción.

Los **Beatles** desatan una histeria conocida como *Beatlemania*. Aparecieron en la televisión estadounidense en febrero y, en abril, sus *singles* ya ocupaban los cinco primeros puestos de la lista de los cien más vendidos.

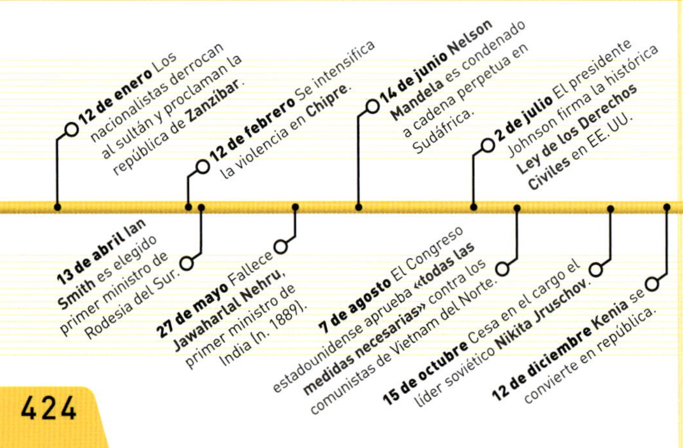

1965

« NADA ES MÁS IMPORTANTE QUE LA INDEPENDENCIA Y LA LIBERTAD. »

Ho Chi Minh, presidente de Vietnam del Norte, en un cartel de propaganda durante la guerra de Vietnam

Terreno hostil
El ejército de EE. UU. era superior tecnológicamente al vietnamita, pero no estaba acostumbrado al terreno del país.

GAMBIA SE INDEPENDIZÓ de Gran Bretaña el 18 de febrero. Dawda Karaiba Jawara fue el primero en ocupar el cargo de primer ministro y fue nombrado caballero al año siguiente. Por su parte, **Rodesia del Sur**, liderada por el primer ministro Ian Smith, anunció el 11 de noviembre una **declaración unilateral de independencia**. Gran Bretaña afirmó que esta era una actuación ilegal y la mayoría de países de la ONU le aplicaron **sanciones económicas**.

En **Vietnam**, el conflicto seguía agravándose. El presidente Johnson ordenó la Operación Rolling Thunder («trueno arrollador»), una **campaña de bombardeos intensivos contra Vietnam del Norte**; en marzo llegaron a Vietnam del Sur los primeros soldados de infantería estadounidenses. En junio ya luchaban junto a las fuerzas vietnamitas del sur contra el **Vietcong**.

En EE. UU., las tensiones raciales habían alcanzado un punto álgido. Tras el arresto de un hombre de color por conducir bebido, estallaron violentos **disturbios raciales** en Watts, un suburbio de Los Ángeles. Hubo quien culpó a la ola de calor, mientras que otros apuntaron a la brutalidad policial.

En septiembre, **India invadió Pakistán Occidental** como represalia a operaciones encubiertas de Pakistán más allá de la línea de alto el fuego. Después de que se estableciera esa línea en 1949, ambos países persistían en sus aspiraciones sobre **Cachemira**. Tras tres semanas de lucha, accedieron a un **alto el fuego a instancias de la ONU**.

Sukarno, presidente de Indonesia, sobrevivió a un intento de golpe de estado en noviembre. El **general Suharto**, comandante de la reserva estratégica del ejército, salió victorioso de la lucha por el poder.

El 9 de noviembre EE. UU. sufrió el mayor **apagón** de toda su historia. Más de treinta millones de personas en el noroeste del país se quedaron sin suministro eléctrico como consecuencia de un error humano.

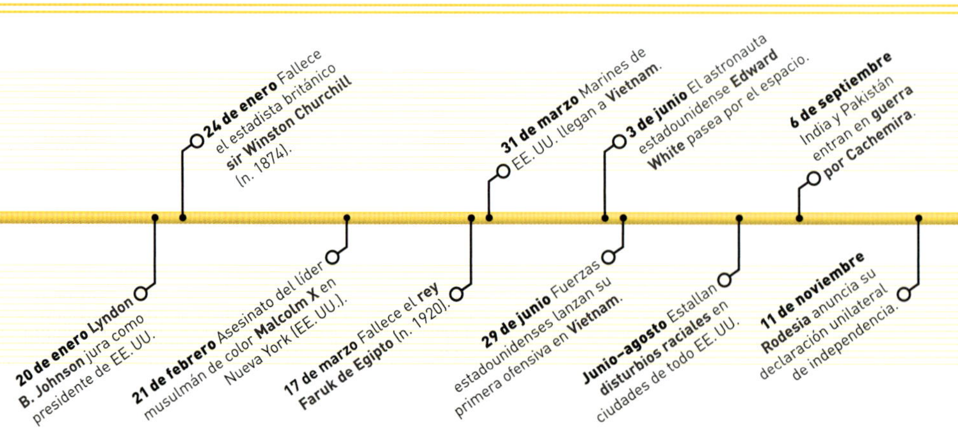

1966

Los Panteras Negras, un grupo nacionalista negro con sede en Oakland (California), defendía la unidad de la clase obrera. En la imagen sostienen ejemplares del *Pequeño libro rojo* de Mao Zedong.

EL CONFLICTO EN VIETNAM CONTINUABA INTENSIFICÁNDOSE Y, EN 1966, EE. UU. lanzó su mayor ofensiva con su Operación Crimp («rizo»), cuyo objetivo era tomar el cuartel general del Vietcong en Saigón. A finales de 1966, ya había 385 000 soldados estadounidenses en Vietnam, por lo que las **protestas de la población** en contra de la guerra no dejaban de aumentar.

En enero, los líderes **pakistaníes** e **indios** celebraron un encuentro en Tashkent (Uzbekistán) para firmar una declaración por la que accedían a resolver su enfrentamiento (*véase* 1965) por **medios pacíficos**. Poco después, Lal Bahadur Shastri, primer ministro de India, falleció de un ataque al corazón. Le sustituyó Indira Gandhi, hija de Nehru.

En **Irlanda del Norte**, estalló la violencia tras el cincuenta aniversario de la batalla del Somme y del alzamiento de Pascua, fechas simbólicas para protestantes y católicos, respectivamente. El asesinato de dos católicos a manos de un grupo terrorista «lealista» llamado **Fuerza de Voluntarios del Ulster** (UVF) provocó más disturbios en mayo y en junio. Tras la ilegalización de la UVF, empezó el ciclo de asesinatos sectarios conocido como **«los disturbios»**.

El asesinato del primer ministro de Sudáfrica, **Hendrik Verwoerd**, planteó dudas sobre el futuro del país. El 6 de septiembre había sido apuñalado por Dimitri Tsafendas, quien afirmaba que Verwoerd no hacía lo suficiente por los blancos.

Los conflictos raciales continuaban en EE. UU. y, a mediados de la década, los **disturbios** se habían extendido a muchas ciudades. Los estudiantes radicales cada vez se mostraban más impacientes con la estrategia de no violencia de Martin Luther King y, en junio, el activista Stokely Carmichael popularizó la expresión ***Black Power*** («poder negro»). En octubre fundó el **partido de los Panteras Negras**, que combinaba los eslóganes tradicionales en defensa de los derechos civiles con el lenguaje marxista y la retórica del separatismo negro.

Estado de la cuestión en Vietnam
Mapa de Vietnam del Norte y del Sur en 1964, separados por una zona desmilitarizada. En 1966, el ejército del norte cruzó la zona y estalló una de las mayores batallas hasta la fecha cerca de Dong Ha.

El *Pequeño libro rojo*
Este libro de citas de Mao contribuyó a su culto y ejerció un profundo impacto sobre las masas durante la Revolución Cultural china.

En agosto, el líder comunista chino Mao Zedong lanzó la **Revolución Cultural** con el objetivo de purgar al país de elementos «impuros». Murieron un millón y medio de personas, y gran parte de la herencia cultural del país fue destruida. En septiembre de 1967, muchas ciudades chinas estaban al borde de la anarquía y Mao envió al ejército para que reinstaurara el orden.

A finales de 1966, la década conocida como los ***Swinging Sixties*** (por el derrumbe de tabúes sociales en cuanto a la raza, el sexo y el género) estaba en pleno apogeo. Sus símbolos eran la música rock, la fotografía y la moda, con la cosmopolita Londres y la cultura de la juventud como epicentro.

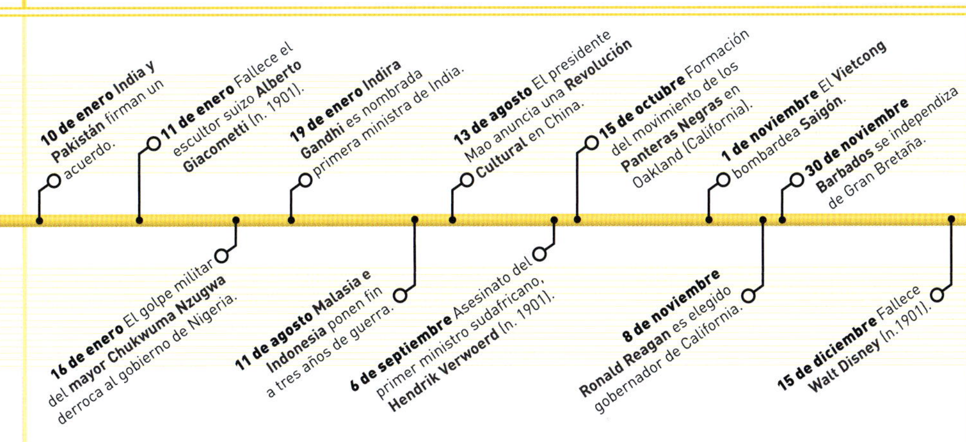

1967

Donald Campbell intentaba romper su propio récord mundial de velocidad cuando su Bluebird estalló y le mató instantáneamente.

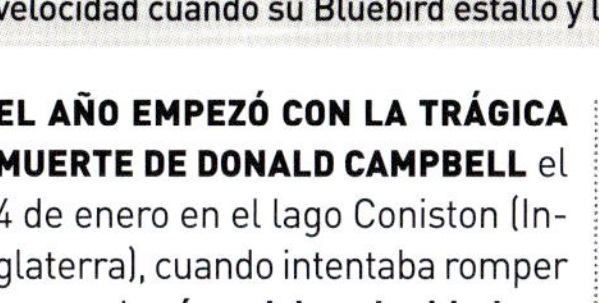

EL AÑO EMPEZÓ CON LA TRÁGICA MUERTE DE DONALD CAMPBELL el 4 de enero en el lago Coniston (Inglaterra), cuando intentaba romper su propio **récord de velocidad sobre el agua**. Se desplazaba a más de 480 km/h cuando la lancha se levantó de la proa y estalló.

En Oriente Medio, la tensión había aumentado después de que Egipto solicitara que las fuerzas de la ONU abandonaran el Sinaí. Los israelíes respondieron con un **ataque preventivo** que duró seis días y con el que obtuvieron el control del Sinaí, Gaza y Cisjordania, los altos del Golán y Jerusalén, en lo que se conoce como la **guerra de los Seis Días**.

En Bolivia, **Ernesto «Che» Guevara** fue capturado y asesinado el 9 de junio por orden del presidente del país. Estaba en América del Sur para ayudar a las guerrillas.

El 3 de diciembre, el cirujano sudafricano Christiaan Barnard llevó a cabo el **primer trasplante de corazón**. Aunque el paciente falleció luego por una neumonía, la operación supuso un gran paso adelante para la medicina.

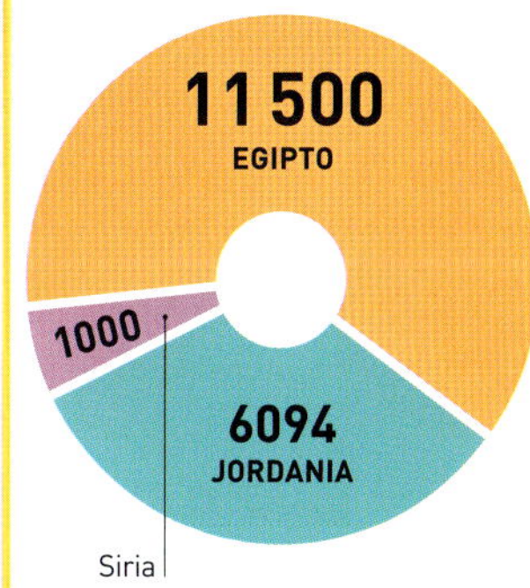

Bajas en la guerra de los Seis Días
Israel obtuvo una victoria decisiva en esta guerra entre Israel, Egipto, Siria y Jordania, y sufrió 759 bajas. Las del frente árabe fueron muy elevadas.

CHE GUEVARA (1928–1967)

Ernesto «Che» Guevara nació en Argentina en 1928 y participó en la oposición a Juan Perón. Viajó por toda Latinoamérica, y la pobreza y la injusticia social que presenció contribuyeron a sus ideas políticas radicales. Colaboró con Fidel Castro y su papel fue clave en la lucha por Cuba. Abandonó el país para ayudar a revolucionarios en otros países. Finalmente, fue ejecutado en Bolivia.

Nicolae Ceausescu se convirtió en el primer ministro de Rumanía el 9 de diciembre y desafió a los soviéticos al entablar relaciones diplomáticas con Alemania.

En **Grecia**, después de que los militares tomaran el poder el 21 de abril, el rey Constantino II impulsó un contragolpe fallido y huyó a Roma.

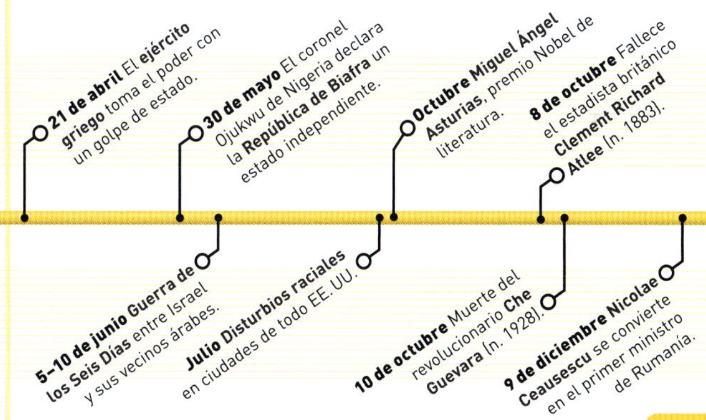

1968

Durante la primera misión tripulada a la Luna, los tres astronautas a bordo del Apolo 8 enviaron imágenes de la Tierra vista desde el espacio.

LA MATANZA DE MY LAI EN VIETNAM sacudió los cimientos del estamento político estadounidense. My Lai se encuentra en el distrito Son My de Vietnam del Sur, en una zona donde el **Vietcong** estaba firmemente atrincherado. El 16 de marzo, **soldados estadounidenses**, que habían emprendido una misión de «búsqueda y destrucción» para acabar con los soldados comunistas, **mataron a sangre fría a 500 civiles vietnamitas**, entre ellos mujeres y niños. La matanza contribuyó a que la **opinión pública se opusiera** a la guerra, pese a que no se conoció lo sucedido hasta el año siguiente.

En 1968, la guerra de Vietnam costaba 66 millones de dólares diarios a EE. UU. Las **protestas contra la guerra se intensificaban** a medida que la población cuestionaba el papel de EE. UU. en el conflicto. Las televisiones retransmitían terribles imágenes de las bajas civiles. El 28 de agosto, durante la convención nacional demócrata en Chicago, **se concentraron unos 10 000 manifestantes en contra de la guerra**, que se enfrentaron a 26 000 policías y miembros de la guardia nacional. La televisión retransmitió en directo lo que sucedía.

Parafernalia bélica
Una brújula china, una cartera de mapas y un mapa donde aparecían las bases enemigas. Este era el equipo básico de la milicia del Vietcong en la guerra de Vietnam.

El 4 de abril, **Martin Luther King Jr.**, líder afroamericano de la defensa de los derechos civiles, fue asesinado en Memphis (Tennessee). Le dispararon en el balcón de su hotel, mientras se preparaba para liderar una marcha de los trabajadores del servicio de recogida de basuras, que **protestaban por sus bajos salarios**. El día antes, también en Memphis, había pronunciado su famoso discurso: «He estado en la cima de la montaña», donde pareció predecir su final: «**He visto la tierra prometida**. Puede que no llegue allí con ustedes». Su muerte desencadenó **disturbios raciales en todo EE. UU.**, que costaron docenas de vidas y causaron daños económicos por valor de millones de dólares. Aceleró el proceso de la **«huida blanca»** del centro de las ciudades, muchas de las cuales quedaron prácticamente abandonadas. **James Earl Ray**, un delincuente común, fue condenado por el asesinato de King y sentenciado a 99 años de prisión.

Cada vez más opuesto a la guerra de Vietnam, el **senador Robert Kennedy** (1925–1968) no se decidía a enfrentarse al actual presidente demócrata, **Lyndon Johnson**. Su hermano pequeño, Edward (Teddy), se oponía, mientras que Ethel, su esposa, le alentaba a que lo hiciera. Muchos temían que siguiera el mismo destino que su hermano John, asesinado en 1963. El 16 de marzo **anunció su candidatura** y dos semanas después, Johnson abandonaba la carrera presidencial. EE. UU. era una nación herida y desangrada por la guerra y los disturbios en las ciudades. Kennedy basó su campaña presidencial en la **desigualdad y en la justicia social**.

El 5 de junio, **Robert Kennedy recibió un disparo** en un hotel de Los Ángeles, tras celebrar su victoria en las primarias de California. Un **emigrante palestino, Sirhan Sirhan**, le disparó mientras era escoltado a través de la cocina del hotel Ambassador. Se cree que el **apoyo de Kennedy a Israel** pudo haber motivado el ataque. Falleció al día siguiente y su muerte, 63 días después de la de Martin Luther King Jr., convirtió a 1968 en uno de los años más **inestables y traumáticos** en la historia de EE. UU.

El 6 de noviembre, el republicano **Richard Nixon** (1913–1994) ganó las **elecciones** de EE. UU. Había basado su campaña en la lucha contra la delincuencia y en la promesa de devolver la ley y el orden al país. Fue un retorno muy significativo: Nixon había sido el vicepresidente de Dwight D. Eisenhower y había perdido las elecciones presidenciales ante John F. Kennedy en 1960.

Enoch Powell (1912–1998), un político conservador británico, pronunció un **discurso muy controvertido** el 20 de abril; advertía al gobierno de que no debía abrir las «compuertas» a los **inmigrantes de color**. Exigía que se redujera la inmigración y veía el futuro con temor. Citó a Virgilio, el poeta romano, y dijo que «como los romanos, veo el río Tíber lleno de espuma ensangrentada». El discurso provocó una **oleada de protestas** y acabó con las ambiciones políticas de Powell.

Lejos de EE. UU., **Francia** vivió **disturbios estudiantiles, manifestaciones** masivas y **huelgas** durante todo el mes de mayo, hasta que el país se vio doblegado. Todo empezó con una serie de protestas estudiantiles que estallaron en las universidades de París, tras enfrentamientos con los administradores y la policía. La actuación policial

200 000

SOLDADOS **DEL PACTO DE VARSOVIA** INVADIERON **CHECOSLOVAQUIA**

MARTIN LUTHER KING JR.
(1929–1968)

Fue uno de los principales defensores de los derechos civiles en EE. UU. Se hizo famoso en 1955, cuando lideró un boicot a los autobuses Montgomery (Alabama) en protesta por las leyes de segregación en el transporte público estatal. Tanto en esta como en las campañas que siguieron, insistió en la no violencia. Le concedieron el Nobel de la paz en 1964. Fue abatido por un blanco en Memphis (Tennessee) en 1968.

5 de enero Alexander Dubcek emerge como **líder** en Checoslovaquia.

5 de enero El **doctor Benjamin Spock** es acusado de actividades contra la ley de reclutamiento en EE. UU.

26 de enero Terremoto en **Sicilia**.

31 de enero Mauricio se independiza de Gran Bretaña.

31 de enero El Vietcong lanza la **ofensiva del Tet**, que resultó crucial para convencer a EE. UU. de que jamás ganaría la guerra de Vietnam.

16 de marzo Robert Kennedy anuncia su **candidatura a la presidencia de EE. UU.**

16 de marzo Matanza de My Lai en Vietnam del Sur.

27 de marzo Fallece Yuri Gagarin, el primer hombre en volar al espacio.

31 de marzo Lyndon Johnson anuncia que no se presentará a las elecciones presidenciales de EE. UU.

4 de abril Asesinato de **Martin Luther King Jr.**

20 de abril El político británico **Enoch Powell** pronuncia su discurso *Los ríos de sangre*.

20 de abril Pierre Trudeau se convierte en primer ministro de Canadá.

23 de abril Las **primeras monedas decimales** entran en circulación en Gran Bretaña.

Mayo Huelgas y **protestas** en Francia.

3 de mayo Primer **trasplante de corazón** exitoso en Gran Bretaña.

8 de mayo Los hermanos Kay, que dirigían una de las mayores organizaciones criminales de Londres, son **arrestados**.

13 de mayo Diplomáticos de **EE. UU.** y de **Vietnam del Norte** se reúnen en unas **conferencias de paz**.

5 de junio Atentado contra el senador estadounidense **Robert Kennedy**.

« GRACIAS **APOLO 8**. HABÉIS **SALVADO 1968**. »

Telegrama anónimo recibido por Frank Borman, tras el éxito de la misión del Apolo 8

posterior empeoró la situación, que desembocó en una **huelga general** seguida por más de diez millones de trabajadores en toda Francia (aproximadamente dos tercios de todos los trabajadores en activo). El gobierno estuvo a punto de caer, y el presidente De Gaulle (1890–1970) convocó elecciones parlamentarias para el 23 de junio. De Gaulle ganó las elecciones, pero los disturbios de París se consideraron toda una **revolución cultural y social**.

El 20 de agosto, soldados de cinco **países del Pacto de Varsovia** (*véase* 1955) irrumpieron en **Checoslovaquia** para tomar el control del país y reinstaurar el comunismo. Durante ocho meses, periodo que se conocería como la **Primavera de Praga**, el primer ministro Alexander Dubcek había aplicado **reformas importantes**, como la libertad de expresión, por lo que fue arrestado, mientras que su gobierno fue reemplazado por un **régimen represivo** (*véase* 1989). La invasión provocó la condena internacional. Jan Palach, un estudiante checo, **se quemó a lo bonzo** como protesta ante la ocupación soviética. Se estima que unas 500 000 personas asistieron a su cortejo fúnebre.

El 7 de septiembre, un numeroso grupo de mujeres interrumpió la celebración del concurso de **Miss America**, un **concurso de belleza** que se llevaba celebrando desde hacía muchos años, en el centro de convenciones de Atlantic City. La protesta había sido organizada por el grupo **New York Radical Women** (NYRW), muy activo en los movimientos de defensa de los derechos civiles y pacifistas. Afirmaron que los criterios del concurso eran racistas, porque ninguna mujer de color había llegado jamás a la final. Las manifestantes llevaban pancartas que defendían la **«liberación de la mujer»** y tiraron sus sujetadores a la basura, en señal de protesta; y así comenzó el mito de que las feministas «queman sujetadores».

Por fin, los estadounidenses tuvieron algo que celebrar a finales de año, cuando el **Apolo 8**, la primera nave tripulada que **orbitó en torno a la Luna**, fue lanzada al espacio el 21 de diciembre y empezó a enviar a la Tierra imágenes de la superficie lunar. Los tripulantes (Frank Borman, James Lovell y William Anders) volvieron el 27 de diciembre convertidos en **héroes nacionales**.

Mayo de 1968
Cuando los huelguistas franceses tomaron las calles en mayo, el país estaba al borde de la revolución. Las manifestaciones más numerosas se vieron en París.

150
MUJERES MANIFESTANTES

52
PARTICIPANTES EN EL CONCURSO

Las bellas y las manifestantes
Las manifestantes superaban tres a una a las glamurosas aspirantes a Miss America, que se celebraba en Atlantic City.

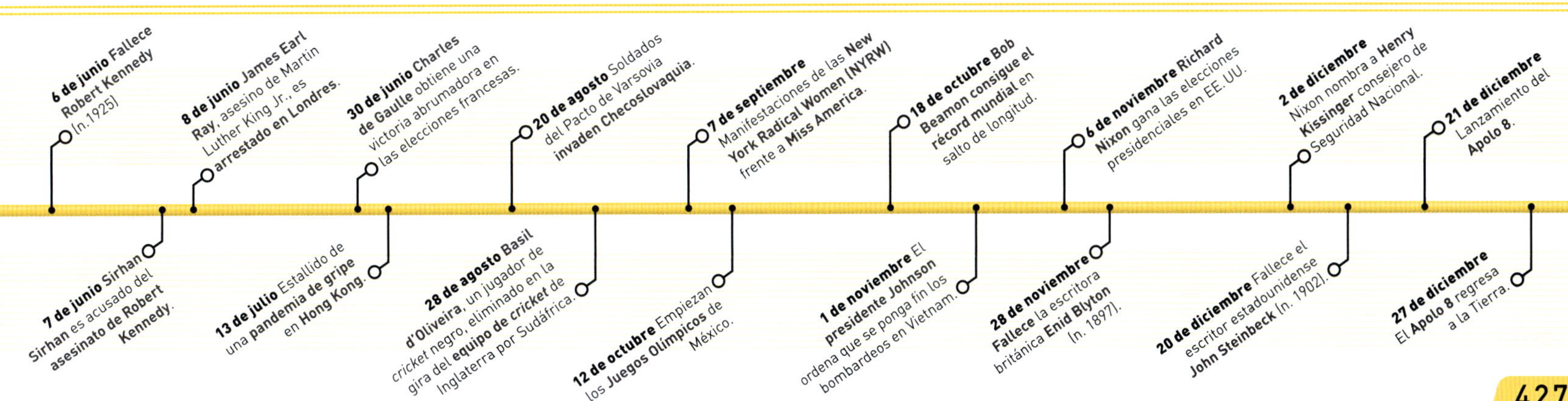

HISTORIA DE LA GENÉTICA

LA BÚSQUEDA DEL CÓDIGO DE LA VIDA Y DEL MECANISMO DE LA HERENCIA GENÉTICA

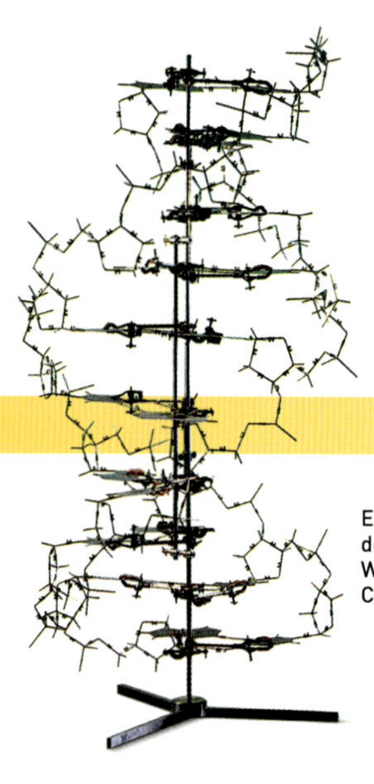

El modelo de ADN de Watson y Crick

La humanidad se ha preguntado durante miles de años cómo se transmitían las características biológicas, pero hasta el siglo XIX no se empezó a entender el mecanismo fundamental de la herencia. Ahora sabemos que el ADN contiene información genética, lo que nos ha permitido entender mejor el origen la vida.

Una de las primeras teorías sobre la herencia, la del griego antiguo Hipócrates, era que los elementos del cuerpo estaban concentrados en el semen y conformaban un ser humano en el útero, con características de ambos progenitores. Más tarde, Charles Darwin denominó «pangénesis» a este mecanismo de herencia.

En el siglo XIX, el monje Gregor Mendel descubrió las reglas básicas de la herencia genética. Al mismo tiempo, el científico Friedrich Miescher extrajo «nucleína» (hoy conocida como ADN) del núcleo celular. A principios del siglo XX, los experimentos del biólogo estadounidense Thomas Hunt Morgan con moscas de la fruta confirmaron que los genes residen en los cromosomas. Sin embargo, aún se creía que eran las proteínas, y no el ADN, las que transmitían los rasgos heredados.

LA IMPORTANCIA DEL ADN

En la década de 1940, Oswald Avery, Colin McLeod y Maclyn McCarty descubrieron que el ADN es la molécula hereditaria en la mayoría de organismos y que constituye la base química de la información genética. A principios de la década de 1950, Maurice Wilkins y Rosalind Franklin descubrieron que el ADN es helicoidal y, en 1953, Francis Crick y James Watson unieron todas estas piezas en su modelo de doble hélice del ADN. El Proyecto Genoma Humano fue más allá, y en 2003 había cartografiado el 93 % del genoma, tarea que no se completó hasta 2022.

CÓDIGO GENÉTICO

Un gen es un fragmento de ADN que contiene la información necesaria para formar una proteína específica (que contiene una secuencia específica de aminoácidos). Se codifica como un «alfabeto» de bases: A (adenina), C (citosina), G (guanina) y T (timina). Las bases se organizan en «palabras» (codones) de tres letras; cada codón se corresponde con un aminoácido concreto. En una célula, la secuencia de codones se traduce en una secuencia concreta de aminoácidos, que se convierte en la proteína concreta que codificaba ese gen.

« **USTED**, SUS ALEGRÍAS Y SUS PENAS, SUS RECUERDOS Y SUS AMBICIONES, SU PROPIO SENTIDO DE LA IDENTIDAD PERSONAL Y SU LIBRE ALBEDRÍO, **NO SON**... **MÁS QUE EL COMPORTAMIENTO DE**... **CÉLULAS NERVIOSAS Y DE MOLÉCULAS**. »

Francis Crick, *La búsqueda científica del alma* (1994)

C. 460–375 a. C.
Hipócrates y la teoría de la pangénesis
Hipócrates formula la hipótesis de que el material genético se recoge de todo el cuerpo y se reorganiza en el útero para formar la vida humana.

Hipócrates

1663–1665
Primera descripción de las células
El científico inglés Robert Hooke acuña el término «célula» para describir las unidades microscópicas que observa al examinar un trozo de corcho a través de uno de los primeros microscopios.

Microscopio de Robert Hooke

1859
Teoría de la selección natural
Darwin publica *El origen de las especies*, donde presenta su teoría de que los organismos mejor adaptados sobreviven y transmiten sus rasgos.

El origen de las especies

1863
Gregor Mendel
El monje austriaco Gregor Mendel experimenta con guisantes y descubre que son lisos o arrugados en función de unas unidades independientes, a las que luego se llamaría genes.

Guisantes redondos y arrugados

C. 1868–1869
La nucleína
El científico suizo Friedrich Miescher descubre una sustancia a la que llama «nucleína» en el núcleo de los leucocitos. Luego se llamaría ácido nucleico y hoy lo conocemos como ADN.

Leucocito

Década de 1880
Descubrimiento de la meiosis
La meiosis es el proceso de división celular que produce gametos (células sexuales) y se describió por primera vez a principios de la década de 1880. El biólogo alemán August Weismann descubrió hacia 1890 su importancia para la herencia.

1888
Los cromosomas
El anatomista alemán Heinrich Waldeyer descubre que la parte central de la célula (el núcleo) a veces contiene unos cuerpos con forma de hilo, a los que llama «cromosomas».

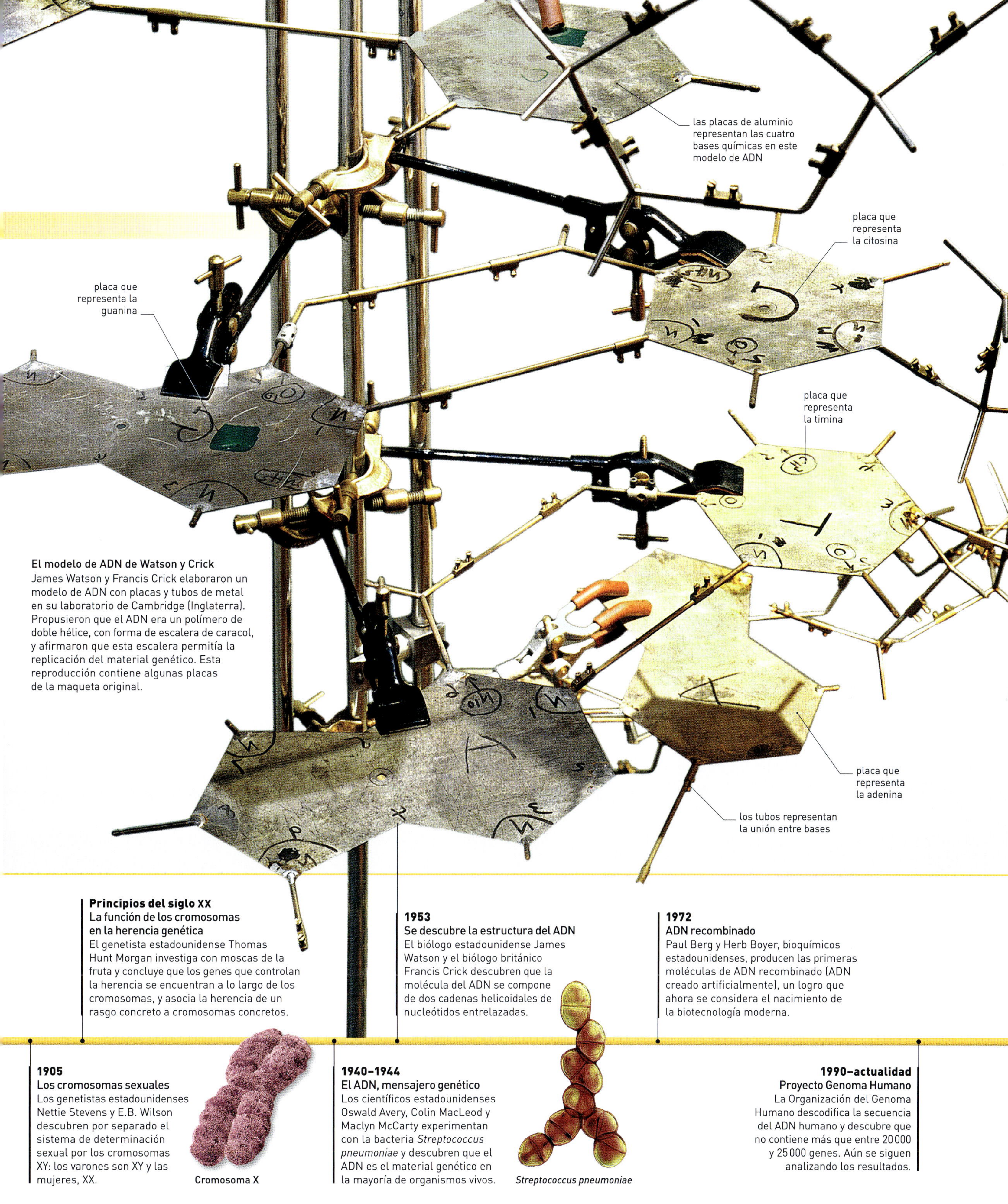

El modelo de ADN de Watson y Crick
James Watson y Francis Crick elaboraron un modelo de ADN con placas y tubos de metal en su laboratorio de Cambridge (Inglaterra). Propusieron que el ADN era un polímero de doble hélice, con forma de escalera de caracol, y afirmaron que esta escalera permitía la replicación del material genético. Esta reproducción contiene algunas placas de la maqueta original.

1905
Los cromosomas sexuales
Los genetistas estadounidenses Nettie Stevens y E.B. Wilson descubren por separado el sistema de determinación sexual por los cromosomas XY: los varones son XY y las mujeres, XX.

Cromosoma X

Principios del siglo XX
La función de los cromosomas en la herencia genética
El genetista estadounidense Thomas Hunt Morgan investiga con moscas de la fruta y concluye que los genes que controlan la herencia se encuentran a lo largo de los cromosomas, y asocia la herencia de un rasgo concreto a cromosomas concretos.

1940–1944
El ADN, mensajero genético
Los científicos estadounidenses Oswald Avery, Colin MacLeod y Maclyn McCarty experimentan con la bacteria *Streptococcus pneumoniae* y descubren que el ADN es el material genético en la mayoría de organismos vivos.

1953
Se descubre la estructura del ADN
El biólogo estadounidense James Watson y el biólogo británico Francis Crick descubren que la molécula del ADN se compone de dos cadenas helicoidales de nucleótidos entrelazadas.

Streptococcus pneumoniae

1972
ADN recombinado
Paul Berg y Herb Boyer, bioquímicos estadounidenses, producen las primeras moléculas de ADN recombinado (ADN creado artificialmente), un logro que ahora se considera el nacimiento de la biotecnología moderna.

1990–actualidad
Proyecto Genoma Humano
La Organización del Genoma Humano descodifica la secuencia del ADN humano y descubre que no contiene más que entre 20 000 y 25 000 genes. Aún se siguen analizando los resultados.

1969

2 de enero Estalla la **violencia** en las calles de **Londonderry** (Irlanda del Norte).

3 de febrero **Yasser Arafat** (1929–2004) es elegido líder de la **Organización para la Liberación de Palestina (OLP)**.

13 de febrero **Robert Edwards** fecunda por primera vez un óvulo humano en una probeta.

2 de marzo El avión anglofrancés **Concorde** realiza su **vuelo inaugural**.

10 de marzo **James Earl Ray** se declara culpable del asesinato de **Martin Luther King** y es condenado a cadena perpetua.

17 de marzo **Golda Meir** es nombrada primera ministra de Israel.

19 de marzo El ejército británico invade la isla caribeña de **Anguila**.

28 de marzo Fallece el **general Dwight Eisenhower** (n. 1890), militar y ex presidente estadounidense.

28 de abril **Charles De Gaulle** (1890–1970) dimite como presidente de Francia.

1 de mayo **James Dawson Chichester-Clark** se convierte en el nuevo primer ministro de Irlanda del Norte.

8 de junio España cierra sus fronteras terrestres con **Gibraltar** (hasta 1985).

30 de junio **Nigeria prohíbe la llegada de ayuda humanitaria a Biafra** durante la guerra civil.

1 de julio El príncipe Carlos es investido como **príncipe de Gales**.

« ES UN **PEQUEÑO PASO** PARA UN **HOMBRE**, PERO UN **GRAN SALTO** PARA LA **HUMANIDAD**. »

Neil Armstrong, al pisar la Luna en 1969

YASSER ARAFAT (1929–2004), COMBATIENTE POR LA LIBERTAD DE PALESTINA, se convirtió en el líder de la **Organización para la Liberación de Palestina (OLP)** en febrero. A finales de la década de 1950 había fundado el grupo radical **Al-Fatah**, que se unió al Frente Popular para la Liberación de Palestina (FPLP) para formar la OLP.

El 1 de septiembre, en Libia, **Muamar al Gadafi** (1942–2011) lideró al grupo de oficiales que derrocó al rey Idris (1890–1983), gracias a un golpe de estado sin derramamiento de sangre, y estableció la **República Árabe Libia**.

Nigeria prohibió que la Cruz Roja llevara alimentos al estado independentista de **Biafra**, lo que condujo a millones de personas al borde de la **inanición**. Biafra acusó a Nigeria de emplear el genocidio y el hambre para ganar la guerra civil (1967–1970) y suplicó ayuda internacional.

El 14 de agosto, **Gran Bretaña envió a su ejército a Irlanda del Norte** tras tres días de violencia en la zona de **Londonderry**, predominantemente católica. Se planteó como una intervención breve, pero la **violencia se intensificó** y el ejército tuvo que permanecer apostado.

Willy Brandt (1913–1992) fue nombrado **canciller de Alemania Occidental** el 21 de octubre y se convirtió en el primer político socialista en liderar un gobierno alemán desde 1930.

El regreso del *Eagle*
El Eagle, *módulo lunar del Apolo 11, regresa al módulo de control con Neil Armstrong y Buzz Aldrin a bordo.*

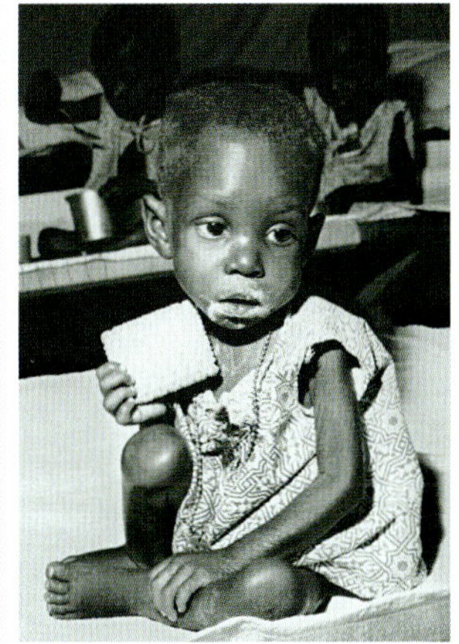

Biafra se muere de hambre
Un niño sufre las consecuencias del hambre durante el bloqueo de Biafra. Las imágenes de la hambruna despertaron la simpatía internacional.

El **Concorde**, un avión supersónico, realizó su **vuelo inaugural** en marzo. Lo pilotó André Turcot y despegó en **Toulouse** (Francia). Alcanzó los 3050 metros de altitud y permaneció durante 27 minutos en el aire.

También en Europa, el **Beatle** John Lennon (1940–1980) y su esposa **Yoko Ono** pasaron **dos semanas en la cama** como protesta para llamar la atención del mundo sobre la paz. Pasaron la primera semana en el Hilton Amsterdam, y la segunda en el hotel Queen Elizabeth de Montreal, donde en mayo grabaron la canción *Give Peace a Chance*.

En Europa y EE. UU. se organizaron **festivales de música**, en un verano que pasó a simbolizar el **movimiento *hippy***. Los Rolling Stones celebraron un concierto gratuito en Hyde Park (Londres); Bob Dylan (n. 1941) fue la estrella principal en el **Festival de la isla de Wight** (Inglaterra), y más de 400 000 personas acudieron a **Woodstock** (Nueva York).

En EE. UU., **millones de personas** participaron en **marchas** para protestar contra la **guerra de Vietnam**. En Washington DC, unos 250 000 manifestantes se reunieron para participar en **mítines pacifistas** y para escuchar a los activistas.

Neil Armstrong (n. 1930) y **Edwin Aldrin** (n. 1930) dieron los **primeros pasos sobre la Luna** el 21 de julio tras viajar en el Apolo 11. Millones de telespectadores presenciaron la escena, que **simbolizó la victoria** de EE. UU. sobre la URSS durante la Guerra Fría.

Tiempo pasado en la luna: **21** horas, **31** minutos y **20** segundos

Duración de la misión: **8** días, **3** horas, **18** minutos y **35** segundos

Misión a la Luna
El objetivo primordial del Apolo 11 era sencillo: «realizar un alunizaje tripulado y regresar».

1970

Aviones secuestrados e incendiados por milicianos palestinos pertenecientes al Frente Popular para la Liberación de Palestina (FPLP).

EN CAMBOYA, EL JEFE DE ESTADO, EL PRÍNCIPE NORODOM SIHANUK (n. 1922) fue depuesto el 18 de marzo, tras el **golpe** del **general Lon Nol**, que afirmaba contar con el apoyo de EE. UU.; en abril, el **presidente Richard Nixon** (1913–1994) envió tropas y bombarderos B-52 a **Camboya** para que destruyeran los santuarios y las líneas de avituallamiento de Vietnam del Norte y del Vietcong.

A principios de septiembre, **milicianos palestinos** obligaron a dos aviones a desviarse al desierto de Jordania, donde los hicieron **estallar** tras haber liberado a la mayoría de rehenes. Un tercer avión fue desviado a **El Cairo**, donde también lo hicieron estallar. El 16 de septiembre hubo enfrentamientos entre el ejército jordano y la guerrilla de la OLP. El presidente egipcio, **Gamal Abdel Nasser** (n. 1918) **negoció un acuerdo** el 27 de septiembre. Sin embargo, **Nasser murió** de un ataque al corazón al día siguiente. Sus negociaciones para **intentar unir a las naciones** árabes le habían convertido en la figura más influyente de Oriente Medio.

Un **ciclón arrasó** Pakistán Oriental (actual Bangladesh) el 12 de noviembre. Con más de medio millón de víctimas, el **ciclón Bhola** fue el **más mortífero jamás registrado**. Los bengalíes afirmaron que Pakistán Occidental no les había ayudado y que les había abandonado a su suerte, por lo que en las siguientes elecciones (*véase* 1971) votaron a la **Liga Awami** de Sheikh Mujibur Rahman, que exigía la autonomía de Pakistán Occidental.

En las elecciones chilenas celebradas el 4 de septiembre, la **coalición marxista liderada por Allende** resultó vencedora. Allende emprendió un paquete de profundas **reformas sociales**, incluida la **nacionalización** de empresas.

En abril, la empresa farmacéutica alemana **Grünenthal** se comprometió a pagar cien millones de marcos alemanes a las **víctimas de la talidomida**, un fármaco que se había administrado a embarazadas para controlar las náuseas y que se retiró del mercado después de que diez mil bebés nacieran con **discapacidades graves**.

Charles de Gaulle (n. 1890), líder de la resistencia francesa durante la ocupación nazi y presidente de la Francia liberada, **murió** el 9 de noviembre. El funeral se celebró dos días después, el Día del Armisticio.

Los Beatles se separaron cuando Paul McCartney (n. 1942) anunció su intención de abandonar el grupo. El **grupo musical se disolvió oficialmente** el 31 de diciembre.

500 MIL **MUERTOS** TRAS EL **CICLÓN DE BANGLADESH**

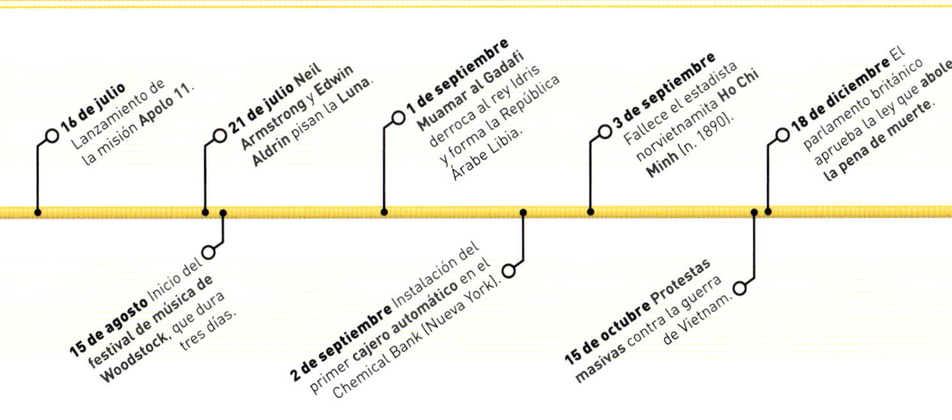

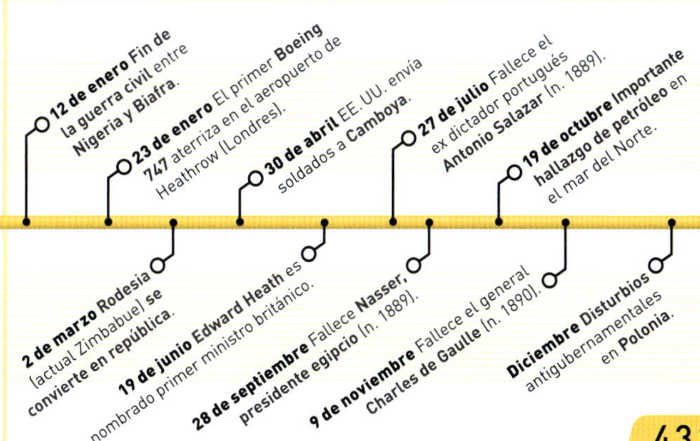

1971

« **NO** SOY **POLÍTICO**, SINO **SOLDADO**. »

Idi Amin, en su primer discurso a la nación de Uganda (enero de 1971)

EL 25 DE ENERO, EN UGANDA, EL GENERAL IDI AMIN ARREBATÓ EL PODER a Milton Obote tras un **golpe militar**, mientras el presidente asistía a una cumbre de la Commonwealth en Singapur (*véase* 1979).

Sierra Leona, en África occidental, y **Qatar**, en Oriente Medio, se independizaron formalmente de Gran Bretaña en este año.

En marzo estalló una **guerra civil** entre **Pakistán** y su territorio de **Pakistán Oriental** (actual Bangladesh). Casi nueve millones de refugiados huyeron a India. En diciembre, el ejército indio irrumpió en Pakistán Oriental, tras un **ataque sorpresa contra campos de aviación indios**. En **Cachemira**, los enfrentamientos también fueron intensos. En una campaña que duró apenas trece días, el ejército indio aplastó al pakistaní en el este. El 20 de diciembre nacía el estado independiente de **Bangladesh** (*véase* 1972).

En **Irlanda del Norte**, el **IRA Provisional** intensificó su campaña contra las fuerzas de seguridad británicas (*véase* 1969). En agosto, el gobierno norirlandés aprobó el ingreso en **prisión sin juicio previo** para detener la creciente violencia.

El 15 de septiembre, un pequeño grupo de activistas zarpó desde Vancouver (Canadá) en el *Phyllis Cormack* para protestar contra los ensayos nucleares de EE. UU. en **Alaska**. Posteriormente adoptaron el nombre de **Greenpeace**.

El 1 de octubre, el centro de ocio **Walt Disney World** abrió oficialmente sus puertas cerca de Orlando (Florida). Contenía Adventureland, Fantasyland, Frontierland, Liberty Square y Tomorrowland.

El 25 de octubre, la **admisión de China en la ONU** catapultó el prestigio internacional del país. El presidente Nixon (1913–1994) envió al consejero de Seguridad Nacional, **Henry Kissinger** (n. 1923) para unas conversaciones secretas. Kissinger también entabló conversaciones con la **URSS**, lo que llevó a varios acuerdos formales, como el que abordaba el **acceso a Berlín**.

IDI AMIN (1925–2003)

Conocido como el Carnicero de Uganda, Amin tomó el poder en 1971 y ejerció un reinado de terror, durante el que se estima que murieron unas 300 000 personas. La conducta de Amin era tan sanguinaria como excéntrica: se autoproclamó «rey de Escocia». Su mandato acabó en 1979, cuando el ejército de la vecina Tanzania le depuso y se vio obligado a abandonar el país.

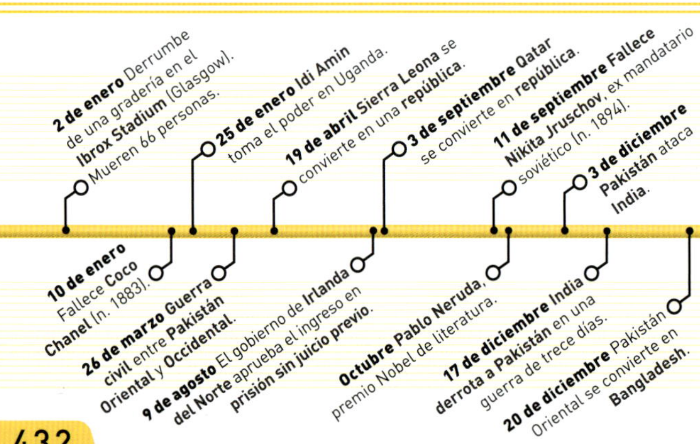

1972

Soldados británicos expulsan a los defensores de los derechos civiles en Londonderry (Irlanda del Norte), después de abrir fuego contra los manifestantes en el Domingo Sangriento. Entre los trece civiles fallecidos había siete adolescentes.

LOS MINEROS BRITÁNICOS CONVOCARON UNA HUELGA GENERAL para el 9 de enero, tras haber rechazado la oferta salarial del gobierno. Se cerraron los 289 pozos del país. El 19 de febrero aceptaron una **oferta salarial nueva** y regresaron a las minas el 25 de ese mismo mes.

El 30 de enero, el ejército británico abrió fuego contra manifestantes en **Londonderry** (Irlanda del Norte); **mataron a trece personas** e hirieron a otras catorce. Ese día se conoce ahora como el **Domingo Sangriento**.

El **IRA** bombardeó el cuartel del 16.º batallón de paracaidistas en Aldershot (Hampshire) el 22 de febrero y mató a siete civiles, en lo que fue el mayor ataque contra la isla de Gran Bretaña desde los disturbios de 1966.

El **presidente Nixon** voló a China en febrero y se reunió con **Mao Zedong** (1893–1976), lo que supuso el principio de una nueva **cordialidad en las relaciones entre EE. UU. y China**. En mayo, Nixon realizó un viaje oficial a **Moscú** para firmar diez acuerdos; los más importantes limitaban el armamento nuclear y se conocen como SALT I.

El 8 de junio, aviones de Vietnam del Sur lanzaron una **bomba de napalm** sobre **Trang Bang**, ocupado por Vietnam del Norte. Las imágenes de **civiles quemados** fueron retransmitidas a todo el mundo y la presión para que EE. UU. abandonara Vietnam creció todavía más.

Los primeros ministros de India y Pakistán, **Indira Gandhi** (1917–1984) y **Zulfikar Alí Bhutto** (1954–1979), firmaron el **acuerdo de Simla** en julio, tras la guerra de 1971. El acuerdo reiteraba las promesas de negociaciones pacíficas acordadas en **Tashkent** (*véase* 1966).

El grupo terrorista **Septiembre Negro**, una facción de la Organización para la Liberación de Palestina (OLP), secuestró a miembros del **equipo israelí** durante los **Juegos Olímpicos** de Múnich (Alemania Occidental). **Asesinaron a once atletas** e inauguraron así una nueva era de terrorismo internacional.

Nuevos horizontes
Artistas de renombre diseñaron 35 carteles para las olimpiadas de Múnich, como el de la imagen. Querían borrar el recuerdo de los juegos de 1936, bajo el gobierno de Hitler.

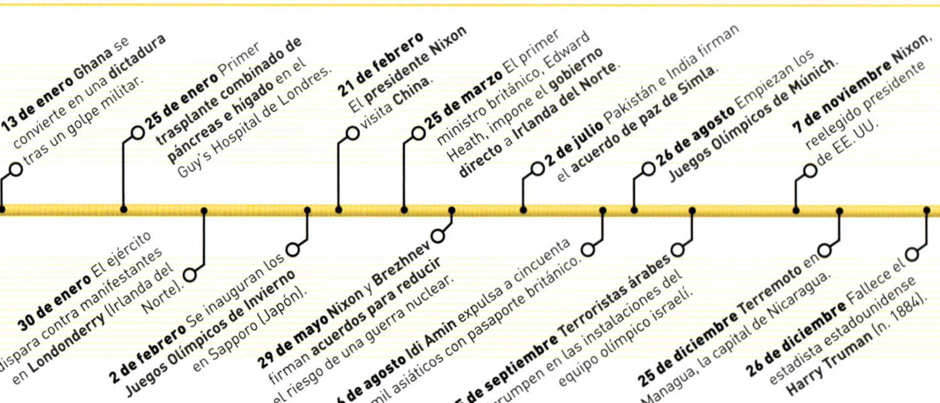

1973

« EN LA **CASA BLANCA** NO BLANQUEAMOS **NADA**. »

Richard Nixon, presidente de EE. UU., durante un discurso televisado sobre el escándalo Watergate (30 de abril de 1973)

La Casa Blanca, residencia oficial del presidente de EE. UU., se vio sacudida durante el escándalo Watergate y la consiguiente dimisión del presidente Nixon.

SIETE HOMBRES fueron condenados el 30 de enero por forzar la puerta de la sede del Partido Demócrata en el edificio **Watergate** (Washington DC), donde instalaron **micrófonos**. **Nixon**, que acababa de ser reelegido, negó toda relación entre el caso Watergate y la **Casa Blanca**, pero dos reporteros del *Washington Post*, **Bob Woodward** y **Carl Bernstein**, sacaron a la luz la implicación de Nixon en el espionaje telefónico, lo que condujo a una **moción de censura** y forzó su **dimisión** (*véase* 1974). La investigación del **escándalo Watergate** le valió el **premio Pulitzer** al periódico, cuyos reporteros habían recibido información clave de un informador misterioso, conocido como Garganta Profunda.

Un inédito fallo del tribunal supremo **legalizó el aborto** en EE. UU., tras lo que se conoce como el caso de **Roe contra Wade**. Norma McCorvey, bajo el pseudónimo de Jane Roe, había presentado una demanda contra las leyes que criminalizaban el aborto en Texas.

Las reformas de Allende
Las reformas y nacionalizaciones del presidente chileno desembocaron en programas sociales muy costosos y llevaron al país al caos económico.

La **guerra de Vietnam** terminó oficialmente para EE. UU. con la firma de un **acuerdo de alto el fuego** en enero, tras meses de conversaciones de paz en París.

Gran Bretaña, Irlanda y Dinamarca se convirtieron en miembros de pleno derecho de la **Comunidad Económica Europea** (CEE) en enero, lo que elevó a nueve el número de estados miembro. Fue la primera ampliación de la organización desde que se fundara en 1957.

El **IRA** llevó su **campaña terrorista** a la isla de Gran Bretaña. El 8 de septiembre estallaron bombas en el centro de Manchester y en la estación de Victoria, en Londres. Dos días después, las explosiones destrozaron las estaciones de King's Cross y de Euston. El 14 de noviembre se **condenó** a un comando del IRA por los **atentados**.

El presidente de Chile, **Salvador Allende** (1908–1973), murió en septiembre en un golpe de estado dirigido por su aliado de confianza, el **general Augusto Pinochet** (1915–2006), quien contaba con el apoyo de **EE. UU.** Pinochet mató a tres mil defensores del régimen de Allende, **disolvió el parlamento** y prohibió cualquier actividad política. En 1974 se autoproclamó presidente (*véase* 1998).

En diciembre, el grupo terrorista vasco **ETA** mató al presidente del consejo de ministros español, el almirante **Carrero Blanco**, en Madrid, conspicuo representante de la dictadura franquista.

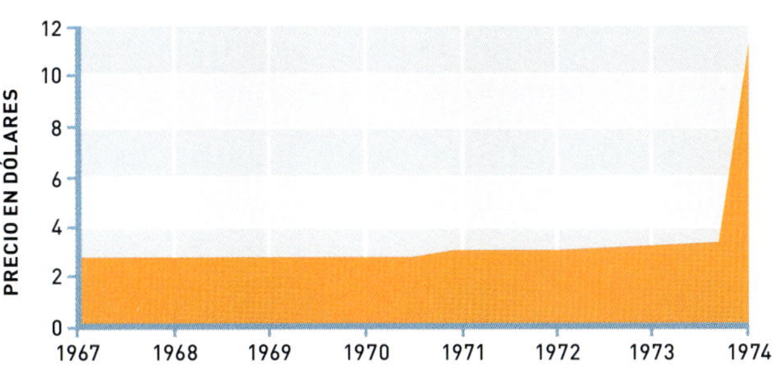

El precio del petróleo
Cuando la OPEP interrumpió el suministro de petróleo a los países occidentales que habían apoyado a Israel, los precios se dispararon desde menos de tres hasta once dólares el barril en cuestión de semanas.

En octubre estallaron enfrentamientos entre **los ejércitos árabes e israelí** en lo que se conocería como la **guerra del Yom Kippur**. El ejército egipcio traspasó la frontera israelí en la orilla oriental del canal de Suez y, en el norte, el ejército sirio se enfrentó al israelí junto a los **altos del Golán**, que Israel había arrebatado a Siria en 1967. El 11 de noviembre, Egipto e Israel firmaron un acuerdo de paz. Tras la guerra, los países árabes impusieron un **embargo petrolífero** contra los países que habían apoyado a Israel. En octubre, el **precio del petróleo** se había disparado en todo el mundo (de tres a once dólares el barril).

LA POLÍTICA DEL PETRÓLEO

El embargo del petróleo por parte de los países árabes provocó un caos mundial. La Organización de Países Exportadores de Petróleo (OPEP) cerró el grifo en un momento en que los mercados ya empezaban a sufrir la escasez del combustible. La crisis reveló el poder del petróleo como arma política. Los países de Oriente Medio parecían haber logrado el control de un producto vital, reflejando la vulnerabilidad de Occidente por su dependencia de las importaciones de petróleo.

1974

El emperador de Etiopía, Haile Selassie, se había proclamado Rey de reyes.

EL EMBARGO DE PETRÓLEO DE 1973 tuvo consecuencias dramáticas para el mundo desarrollado y dio lugar a una prolongada recesión. El desempleo y la inflación se dispararon, y los **mercados de valores se derrumbaron** en todo el mundo.

En Portugal, el **general Antonio de Spínola** lideró un golpe de estado no violento que puso fin a veinte años de dictadura. La **Revolución de los Claveles** abrió las puertas a una nueva era de democracia.

El **IRA** atacó el parlamento británico el 17 de junio, la torre de Londres en julio, y un *pub* de Guildford en octubre.

En julio, el **ejército turco** invadió el norte de **Chipre** tras un golpe que derrocó al **presidente** grecochipriota, **el arzobispo Makarios**. La isla se dividió en dos; los grecochipriotas huyeron al sur, y la comunidad turca se desplazó hacia el norte.

Tras años de guerras en Etiopía, un golpe de estado derrocó al **emperador Haile Selassie** (1892–1975) el 12 de septiembre. El general **Tafari Benti** (1921–1977) pasó a ser el cabeza de estado.

En EE. UU., la investigación sobre el espionaje del **Watergate** (*véase* 1973) desveló un vínculo con el equipo de Nixon. En julio, el tribunal supremo ordenó a Nixon que entregara las **grabaciones** relativas al escándalo. Se presentó una moción de censura y **dimitió** en agosto.

A finales de la década de 1960 se empezó a escuchar música **disco** en las discotecas de Nueva York; en 1974 este estilo llegó a su apogeo con música nueva, trajes de poliéster y películas como *Fiebre del sábado noche.*

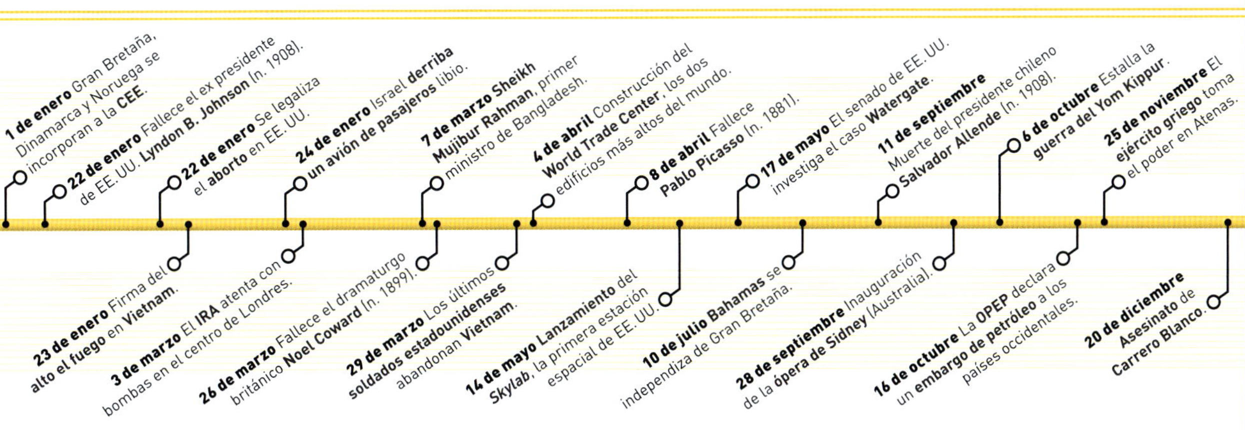

1975

« VIETNAM SE PERDIÓ EN LOS **HOGARES ESTADOUNIDENSES**, NO EN LOS **CAMPOS DE BATALLA VIETNAMITAS**. »

Marshall McLuhan, comentarista periodístico, en un artículo sobre el fin de la guerra de Vietnam

MARGARET THATCHER SE CONVIRTIÓ EN LA PRIMERA MUJER en liderar un partido político en Gran Bretaña el 11 de febrero.

En Oriente Medio, el **rey Faisal** (1906–1975) de **Arabia Saudí** fue asesinado por su sobrino, el príncipe Faisal bin Musaid.

El **príncipe Juan Carlos** fue coronado rey de España dos días después de la muerte de Francisco Franco el 20 de noviembre.

En abril, la capital de Camboya, **Phnom Penh**, cayó en manos del grupo comunista radical de los **Jemeres Rojos**, liderados por **Pol Pot**. Transformaron Camboya en una sociedad comunista y rural. Se expulsó de las ciudades a todos los habitantes, que tuvieron que desplazarse a comunas agrícolas.

Tras casi dos décadas de luchas, la **guerra de Vietnam** por fin terminó el 30 de abril, cuando el gobierno de Saigón se rindió a las fuerzas de **Vietnam del Norte**. Saigón fue rebautizada como **Ciudad Ho Chi Minh** en 1976. El norte y el sur estaban unidos de nuevo.

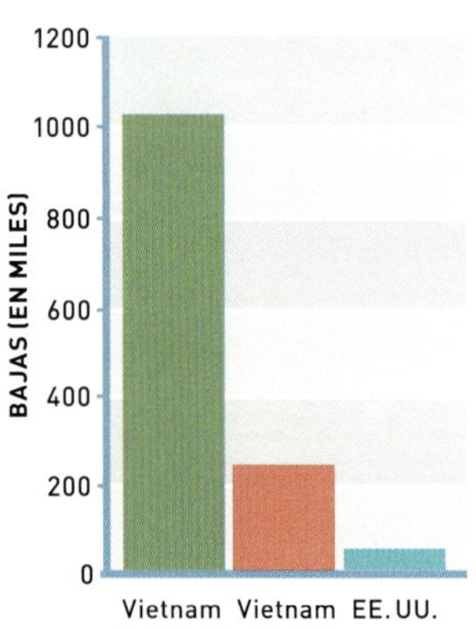

Bajas de la guerra de Vietnam
Más de un millón de soldados de Vietnam del Norte murieron, frente a unos 220 000 de Vietnam del Sur y unos 58 000 estadounidenses.

La caída de Saigón
Las fuerzas de Vietnam del Norte encontraron escasa resistencia en Saigón, pero las últimas horas de la presencia estadounidense estuvieron marcadas por el caos.

Mozambique se independizó el 25 de junio, después de que el golpe en Portugal pusiera fin al colonialismo (*véase* 1974). Cuatro meses después, **Angola** se independizó también (*véase* 1976).

Iraq intensificó la presión militar contra los **rebeldes kurdos** en el norte. Los **kurdos** fueron **aplastados** en Zakho y Qala Diza.

En **Líbano**, la milicia cristiana atacó un autobús en Beirut lleno de pasajeros palestinos. Así comenzó una guerra que duraría quince años (*véase* 1990).

Fue un año de **terrorismo global**: terroristas árabes tomaron **rehenes** en el aeropuerto de Orly (París); un grupo de izquierdas alemán tomó la **embajada alemana** en Estocolmo (Suecia), y terroristas de las islas Molucas del Sur atacaron la **embajada de Indonesia** en Ámsterdam (Países Bajos).

En noviembre, el **petróleo** empezó a fluir en el **mar del Norte**, en yacimientos que British Petroleum (BP) había hallado seis años antes.

Bill Gates (n. 1955) y **Paul Allen** (n. 1953) fundaron Microsoft el 4 de abril, iniciando el mundo de los ordenadores personales.

Corazón púrpura de EE. UU.
Condecoración de las Fuerzas Armadas de EE. UU. que se concedió a los 351 000 soldados que murieron o fueron heridos en la guerra de Vietnam.

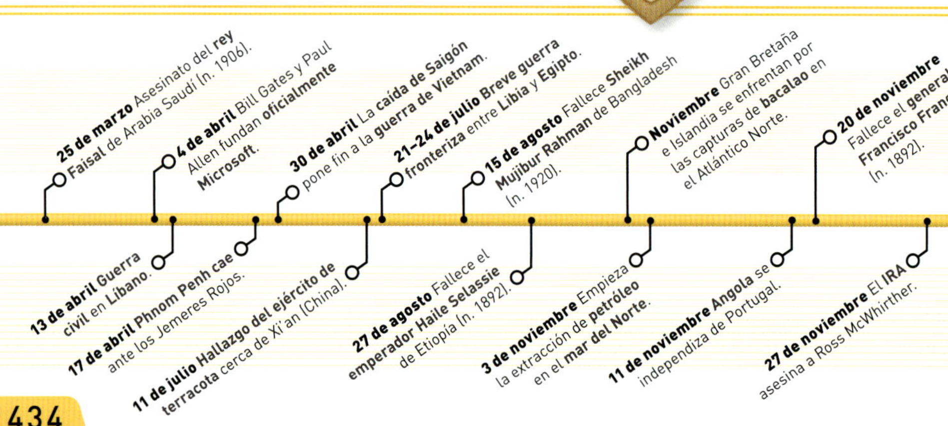

1976

Dos punks se besan en Kings Road (Londres). El punk apareció a mediados de la década de 1970, como una expresión de desdén hacia la política y la sociedad.

EL MOVIMIENTO MARXISTA POPULAR DE LIBERACIÓN DE ANGOLA (MPLA) asumió el control nominal del país en febrero y proclamó la **República Popular de Angola**. Esto vino precedido de luchas en las que también participaron el Frente Nacional para la Liberación de Angola (FNLA) y la Unión Nacional para la Independencia Total de Angola (UNITA).

Las **protestas contra el *apartheid*** en Soweto (**Sudáfrica**) se volvieron violentas el 16 de junio. Los manifestantes se enfrentaron a la policía y más de 300 personas murieron.

40–70 MILLONES DE **MUERTES** DURANTE EL **RÉGIMEN DE MAO**

Mao Zedong (n. 1893), el fundador de la República Popular China, falleció el 9 de septiembre de un ataque al corazón.

Las **fuerzas de paz sirias** llegaron a **Líbano** el 9 de junio. En diciembre, tras la violación de más de cincuenta altos el fuego, prevaleció una paz inestable.

Las **Seychelles se independizaron** de Gran Bretaña el 29 de junio. James Mancham fue nombrado presidente, mientras que France-Albert René ocupó el cargo de primer ministro de la coalición.

1977

EL ARZOBISPO DE UGANDA, EL DOCTOR JANANI LUWUM (n. 1922), fue asesinado el 16 de febrero por su pertenencia a la Iglesia anglicana y por protestar contra los excesos del **régimen de Idi Amin** (*véase* 1971).

Steven Biko (*véase* recuadro), uno de los líderes del movimiento en defensa de los derechos de las personas de color en Sudáfrica, murió en prisión el 12 de septiembre. Se le había detenido sobre la base de la ley antiterrorista y su muerte provocó **indignación internacional**, pero la investigación posterior eximió a la policía de la responsabilidad.

En Pakistán, el **Partido del Pueblo Pakistaní** (PPP) de Zulfikar Alí Bhutto fue acusado de **fraude electoral**. El general Muhammad Zia-ul-Haq se alzó en un **golpe militar** que derrocó a Bhutto el 4 de julio.

El conservador **Menachem Begin** (1913–1992) obtuvo una victoria sorpresiva en las elecciones israelíes en mayo, y puso fin a casi treinta

La fruta de la sabiduría
Los ordenadores de Apple Inc. salieron a la venta este año. El logo, una manzana mordida con los colores del arcoíris, simbolizaba el conocimiento.

1978

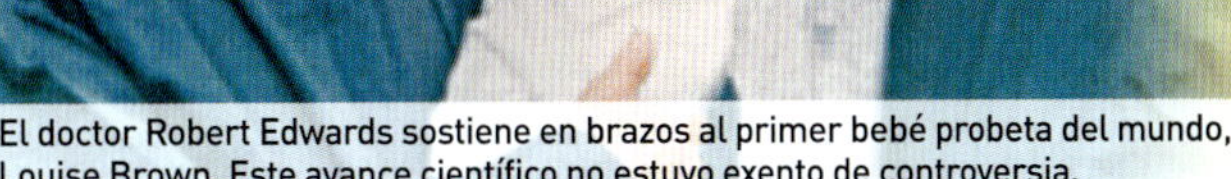

El doctor Robert Edwards sostiene en brazos al primer bebé probeta del mundo, Louise Brown. Este avance científico no estuvo exento de controversia.

«TODAS LAS PRUEBAS INDICAN QUE EL BEBÉ ES **NORMAL.»**

El obstetra Patrick Steptoe, tras el nacimiento de Louise Brown

STEVE BIKO (1946–1977)

En 1968 se convirtió en el primer presidente y fundador de la SASO (Asociación de Estudiantes Sudafricanos), íntegramente negra, destinada a concienciar a la población de color. El gobierno le sometió a arresto domiciliario, pero Biko prosiguió con su labor. El 18 de agosto de 1977 lo detuvo la policía: le retuvieron durante 24 días y le torturaron hasta matarle. El *Rand Daily Mail* denunció la brutalidad policial.

años de gobierno laborista. Ya como primer ministro, inició el **proceso de paz** con Egipto (*véase* 1979).

La organización en defensa de los derechos humanos **Amnistía Internacional** obtuvo el **Nobel de la paz** por «contribuir a garantizar las bases de la libertad, la justicia y, por tanto, la paz en el mundo». El movimiento proclamó 1977 **«Año de los presos de conciencia»**.

EL 14 DE MARZO, SOLDADOS ISRAELÍES cruzaron la frontera libanesa en la Operación Litani. Miles de **palestinos huyeron** de la zona y cientos murieron. Israel afirmó que los combatientes palestinos organizaban los ataques contra objetivos civiles y militares en Israel desde el sur de Líbano.

Los manifestantes en las calles de **Teherán** (Irán) habían hecho visible su descontento durante todo el año, pero en septiembre **se intensificaron las protestas** en contra de las políticas del **sah Mohamed Reza Pahlavi** (1919–1980). La intensidad del desafío sorprendió tanto al sah como a sus generales, que atacaron a los manifestantes. Muchos murieron y se impuso la **ley marcial** en las ciudades más importantes.

El presidente egipcio, **Anuar el Sadat** (1918–1981), viajó a Washington DC en febrero para entablar conversaciones con el **presidente Jimmy Carter** (n. 1924). Su visita supuso un giro en la **política exterior egipcia**, que hasta entonces había buscado el favor de la **URSS**. Poco después, **Menachem Begin**, primer ministro israelí, se reunió con el presidente Carter. Estas reuniones allanaron el camino para unas negociaciones conjuntas en Camp David (Maryland), entre el 5 y el 17 de septiembre. Ambas partes firmaron los **acuerdos de Camp David** para la paz en Oriente Medio. Más tarde, Sadat y Begin recibieron el premio Nobel de la paz.

El 25 de diciembre, **Vietnam invadió Camboya** en un ataque relámpago. Los vietnamitas acabaron con el régimen de los **Jemeres Rojos de Pol Pot**, pero la guerra subsiguiente siguió siendo fuente de tensiones internacionales. El ejército de Pol Pot no había sido derrotado por completo, y miles de sus soldados huyeron a la **frontera de Camboya con Tailandia**, donde pudieron reorganizarse y, a base de escaramuzas, obligaron al ejército vietnamita a permanecer en Camboya durante diez años (*véase* 1991).

Aldo Moro, ex primer ministro italiano, fue **secuestrado** en Roma el 16 de marzo. Las **Brigadas Rojas**, grupo de extrema izquierda que deseaba una transformación revolucionaria de la sociedad italiana, asumieron la autoría del secuestro y exigieron que se detuviera el juicio contra su líder, Renato Curcio. El gobierno se negó y ocho semanas después se halló el **cadáver** de **Moro** en el maletero de un coche en Roma.

El petrolero ***Amoco Cadiz*** encalló en Porstall Rocks, a unas tres millas frente a la costa de Bretaña, tras un fallo del timón. Toda la carga (1,6 millones de barriles) cayó al mar y provocó una **marea negra** de 30 km de anchura y 130 de longitud. Decenas de playas bretonas quedaron **contaminadas**.

En Oldham (Inglaterra), nació **Louise Brown, primer bebé probeta**, con la ayuda del ginecólogo **Patrick Steptoe**, pionero de la técnica *in vitro*, junto al doctor **Robert Edwards** (*véase* 1969).

Jemer rojo
Bajo Pol Pot, los Jemeres Rojos, a menudo adolescentes, controlaron Camboya. Fueron responsables del asesinato de más de un millón de personas.

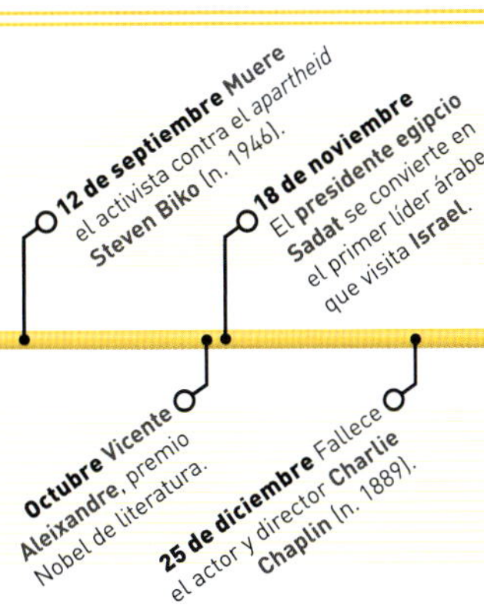

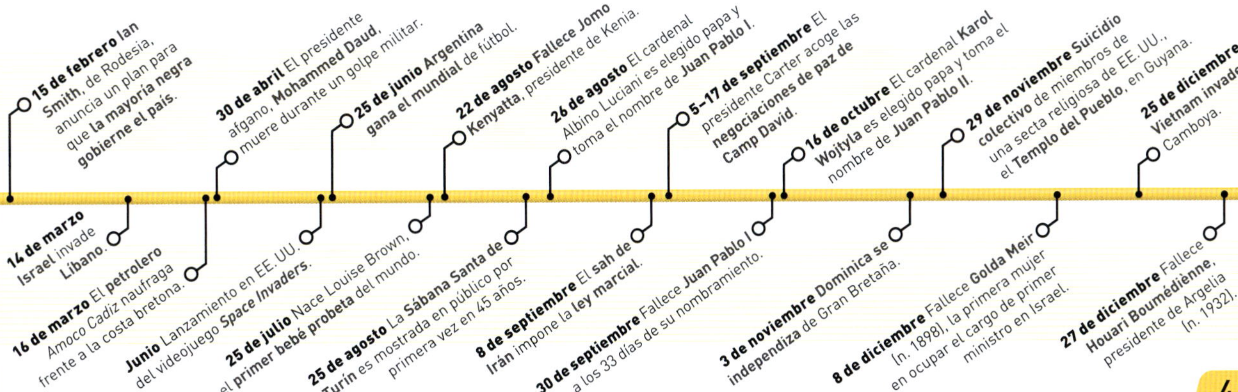

1979

« EN EL ISLAM, EL PODER LEGISLATIVO Y LA COMPETENCIA PARA APLICAR LA LEY CORRESPONDEN ÚNICAMENTE A DIOS. »

Ayatolá Jomeini, en sus conferencias sobre el gobierno islámico

Mujeres iraníes sostienen fotografías del ayatolá Jomeini en apoyo de la Revolución Islámica.

20:1 **Bajas en la guerra** *La invasión soviética tuvo un alto coste para los afganos. Por cada soldado soviético muerto o herido, veinte soldados afganos perdieron la vida.*

EN 1978, EL EJÉRCITO VIETNAMITA ENTRÓ EN CAMBOYA tras repetidos ataques fronterizos por parte de los **Jemeres Rojos** (*véase* 1978). El 7 de enero de 1979 tomaron **Phnom Penh**, la capital, y expulsaron del poder a los Jemeres Rojos, cuyo líder, Pol Pot, huyó a la jungla de Tailandia, desde donde inició una **guerra de guerrillas** contra toda una serie de gobiernos camboyanos. El 2 de abril, soldados vietnamitas descubrieron una **fosa común** en el noreste del país; fue la primera de las muchas fosas comunes de la era de Pol Pot que se descubrirían y que hicieron evidente que había sido responsable de la muerte de más de un millón de personas entre 1975 y 1979.

China consideró el ataque de Vietnam a Camboya como una provocación grave y, el 17 de febrero, **invadió Vietnam**. Ambos bandos sufrieron muchas bajas y ambos afirmaron haber ganado la guerra.

Cuando los **comunistas afganos** tomaron el poder tras el golpe de 1978, se hallaron con presiones a tres bandas: los **soviéticos**, los **estadounidenses** y el régimen islamista en **Irán**. En marzo, un grupo de la resistencia declaró la guerra santa al gobierno marxista «infiel» y mató a ciudadanos soviéticos en Herat, al oeste de Afganistán. En las zonas rurales, la oposición a las iniciativas gubernamentales no hacía más que crecer y el ejército afgano llegó al borde del colapso. La Unión Soviética temía el estallido de una **revolución islámica** como la iraní y, alegando el tratado de amistad de 1978, el **ejército soviético invadió Afganistán** el 24 de diciembre, convencido de su superioridad militar. Sin embargo, ignoraban que EE. UU. había entrenado en secreto a las fuerzas antigubernamentales, los **muyahidines** (guerreros), y se encontraron con una resistencia feroz cuando llegaron a Kabul.

La situación política en **Irán** se deterioraba (*véase* 1978) y el sah se vio obligado a exiliarse. El **ayatolá Ruhollah Jomeini** (1902–1989), un clérigo musulmán chií, volvió tras quince años en el exilio y fue recibido por multitudes jubilosas. El 1 de abril se proclamaba la **República Islámica de Irán**. Se prohibió toda influencia occidental y muchos de los que se habían educado en Occidente huyeron del país. Los seguidores del ayatolá Jomeini, airados por el prolongado apoyo de EE. UU. al sah, ocuparon la embajada estadounidense en **Teherán**. Tomaron 63 rehenes y juraron que no les liberarían hasta que EE. UU. devolviera al sah, para ser juzgado en Irán. El **presidente Carter respondió con un embargo al petróleo iraní**. Entonces, liberaron a las mujeres y a los rehenes no estadounidenses, y luego a un varón que había caído gravemente enfermo en 1980; 52 estadounidenses permanecieron retenidos hasta 1981.

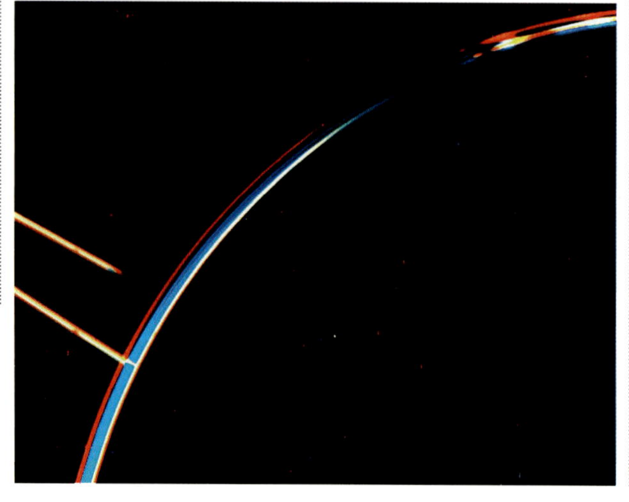

Los anillos de Júpiter
La nave espacial Voyager 2 *de la NASA tomó esta imagen que captó meteoritos bombardeando el sistema de anillos de Júpiter, algo inédito hasta la fecha.*

punto de mira

cañón

cargador extraíble

Fusil de asalto Kalashnikov AK-47
El AK-47 se convirtió en un arma icónica durante la guerra soviética en Afganistán. Eran baratos y fáciles de adquirir, por lo que ambos bandos los usaban.

El **Frente Sandinista de Liberación Nacional**, de izquierdas, consiguió derrocar al gobierno **nicaragüense**, que contaba con el apoyo de EE. UU., y tomar Managua, la capital del país. Así se puso fin a siete años de guerra civil contra el gobierno de **Somoza**. Los sandinistas instauraron un gobierno revolucionario el 20 de julio, liderado por **Daniel y Humberto Ortega**.

Ese año fueron muy activos tanto el Ejército Republicano Irlandés (**IRA**) como el Ejército de Liberación Nacional Irlandés (**INLA**). El 30 de marzo, **Airey Neave**, el secretario de Estado para el Norte de Irlanda, murió en un atentado con coche bomba del INLA. El 27 de agosto, **lord Louis Mountbatten** (miembro de la familia real) murió en un atentado del IRA. Horas después, dieciocho soldados morían en un ataque con bombas trampa cerca de la frontera con la República de Irlanda. Las muertes desencadenaron una oleada de asesinatos sectarios.

El 11 de abril, con la llegada del ejército de Tanzania, el ugandés **Idi Amin** (1925–2003) tuvo que huir de la capital, Kampala, junto a exiliados y el **Frente de Liberación Nacional de Uganda**. Dos días después, Kampala cayó y un gobierno de coalición tomó el poder. **Yusufu Lule** (1912–1985), que se había exiliado bajo Idi Amin, fue elegido presidente. Amin huyó a Libia y dejó tras de sí un país cuya economía se tambaleaba.

Sony lanzó su ***walkman*** en **Japón** el 22 de junio. El primer *walkman* tenía un reproductor de cintas de casete y los primeros auriculares ligeros del mundo. Costaba 200 dólares estadounidenses y se agotó en un mes.

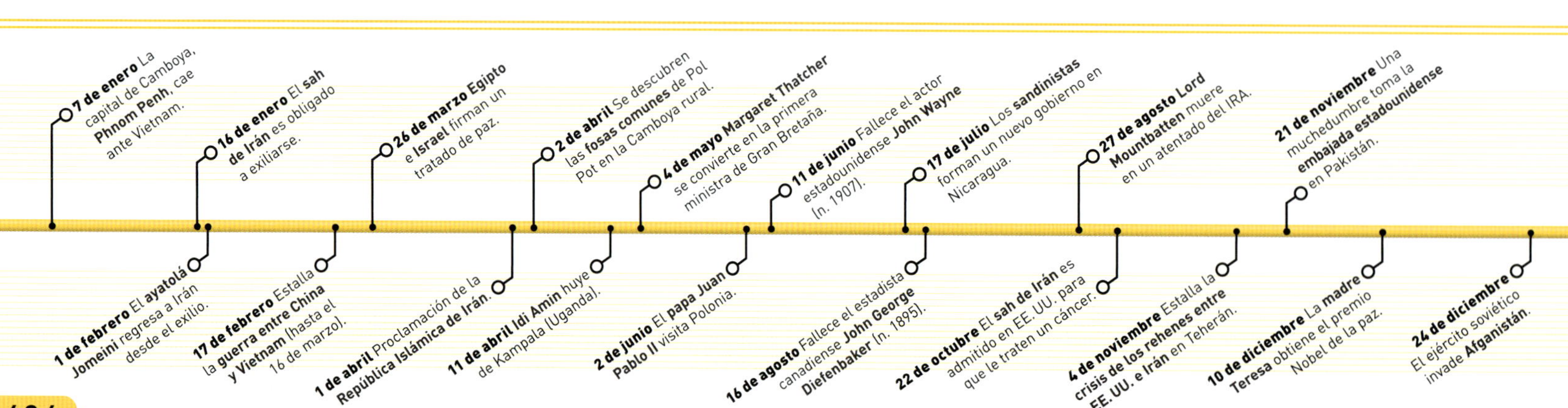

1980

24 KILÓMETROS

ALTURA DE LA **COLUMNA DE HUMO** EN LA GRAN EXPLOSIÓN DEL **MONTE SAINT HELENS**

La erupción, en mayo, del monte Saint Helens, en el estado de Washington, desencadenó una enorme avalancha y una nube de ceniza que ocultó la luz del sol en un perímetro de 400 km.

ROBERT MUGABE OBTUVO UNA VICTORIA ABRUMADORA el 4 de marzo y se convirtió en el primer ministro de **Rodesia**. Había sido guerrillero marxista y el régimen de la minoría blanca de Ian Smith le odiaba. Rodesia se convirtió en **Zimbabue** el 18 de abril.

Varias zonas de **África** sufrieron una **hambruna** extrema en 1980. La sequía, los robos de ganado y los disturbios sociales provocaron una grave escasez de alimentos. La **hambruna de Uganda**, durante la que falleció el 21 % de la población, se considera la peor de la historia.

La Organización Mundial de la Salud declaró la viruela **erradicada**, 21 años después de haber lanzado un programa de erradicación de alcance mundial. El último caso natural de viruela se dio en Somalia en octubre de 1977. Solo durante el siglo XX murieron de viruela unos **300 millones** de personas.

La **embajada iraní** de **Londres** se convirtió en el fin de un dramático asedio el 30 de abril, cuando seis pistoleros de un grupo que se oponía al **ayatolá Jomeini** tomaron el edificio para exigir la liberación de 91 prisioneros políticos iraníes. La SAS asaltó el edificio y puso fin al sitio. Diecinueve rehenes fueron liberados, pero uno murió y otros dos resultaron heridos en el tiroteo.

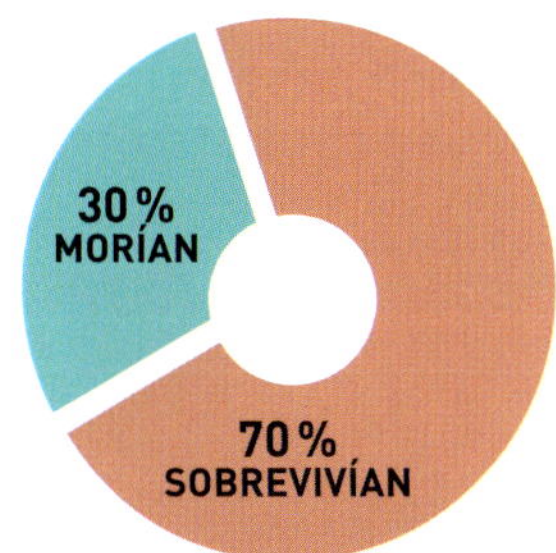

Erradicación de la viruela
Tras una campaña de erradicación en todo el mundo, la OMS declaró en 1980 que la viruela estaba erradicada. Tenía una tasa de mortalidad del 30 %.

El 22 de septiembre, **Iraq** invadió **Irán** y dio inicio a una cruenta guerra que duró ocho años y que desestabilizó toda la región. A finales de octubre, **Jorramshar**, el principal puerto de Irán, cayó ante las fuerzas iraquíes.

Yugoslavia había conseguido la paz interna bajo el yugo del presidente **Tito** (*véase* 1943), cuya **muerte**, el 4 de mayo, combinada con el declive de la ideología comunista, debilitó los elementos que unían a Yugoslavia. Las diferencias étnicas y nacionalistas resurgieron y distintas repúblicas empezaron a exigir la **independencia**.

Una potente bomba estalló en la estación de **Bolonia** (Italia) el 2 de agosto; murieron 85 personas y varios cientos resultaron heridas, en lo que fue el peor atentado terrorista de la historia de Italia. Se **atribuyó la responsabilidad a grupos de extrema derecha**.

La **huelga de los astilleros de Gdansk** fue un punto de inflexión en **Polonia**: fue el primer movimiento político en masa en el bloque soviético. El 30 de agosto, el gobierno polaco llegó a un acuerdo con los trabajadores en huelga, liderados por **Lech Walesa**. Autorizó la creación de **Solidaridad**, un sindicato que no estaría sometido al control comunista y que reunió a más de diez millones de afiliados.

El **monte Saint Helens**, un volcán del estado de Washington (noroeste de EE. UU.) **entró en erupción** el 18 de mayo. Desencadenó un terremoto que alcanzó los 5,2 grados en la escala de Richter, lo cual provocó el hundimiento de la cara norte del volcán. Murieron 52 personas.

Ronald Reagan, ex actor y gobernador republicano de California, ganó las **elecciones de EE. UU.** el 4 de noviembre, en las que obtuvo una victoria avasalladora sobre **Jimmy Carter.**

Guerra de Irán-Iraq
Un soldado iraquí observa cómo arde una refinería de petróleo durante la guerra. Los campos petrolíferos y las refinerías fueron objetivos estratégicos.

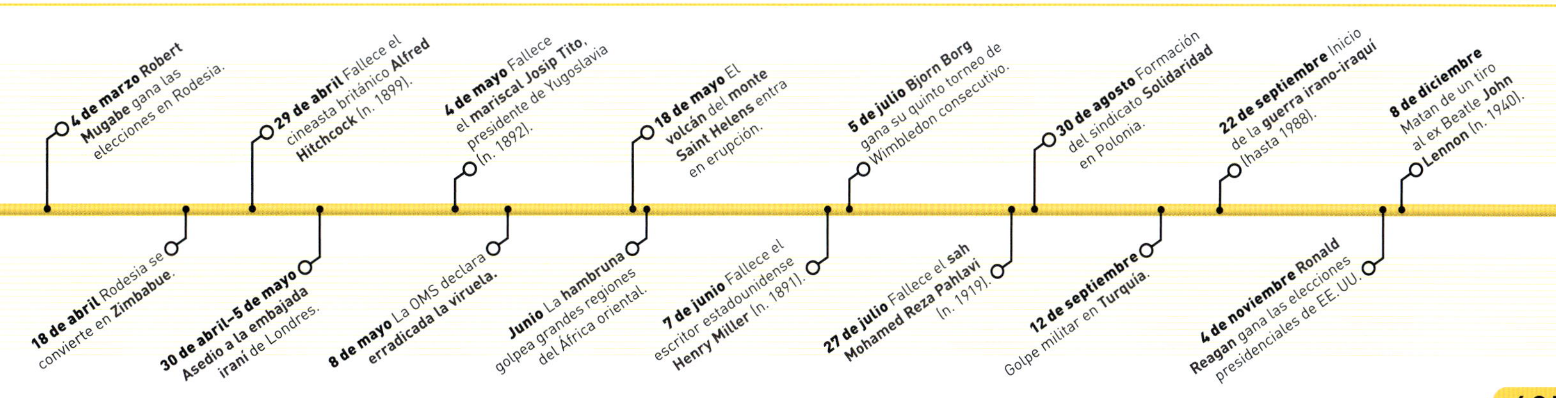

1981

Los manifestantes muestran una bandera donde se lee *Solidarność*, o «Solidaridad», el nombre del primer sindicato no comunista en Polonia.

RONALD REAGAN SE CONVIRTIÓ en el 40.º presidente de EE. UU. el 20 de enero. Dos meses después sobrevivió a un intento de asesinato por parte de **John Hickley**, que estaba obsesionado con la actriz Jodie Foster y creía que la impresionaría si asesinaba al presidente.

El **papa Juan Pablo II** sobrevivió a **cuatro disparos de bala** en la plaza de San Pedro de Roma, el 13 de mayo, mientras se desplazaba entre la multitud en el papamóvil. La policía arrestó al ciudadano turco Mehmet Alí Agca, que fue condenado a cadena perpetua en julio.

En **Egipto** se declaró el **estado de emergencia** tras el asesinato del **presidente Anuar el Sadat**. Un grupo que se llamaba a sí mismo **Organización Independiente para la Liberación de Egipto** asumió la autoría y el vicepresidente, Hosni Mubarak, sucedió a El Sadat como jefe de estado.

El 20 de enero, **Irán** accedió por fin a **liberar a 52 rehenes estadounidenses**, que llevaban 444 días retenidos. EE. UU. había garantizado que liberaría activos iraníes que estaban congelados en bancos estadounidenses desde que se tomó la embajada de EE. UU. en Teherán.

> « SI NOS RENDIMOS HOY, NUESTRA **ESPERANZA DE LIBERTAD** QUEDARÁ ENTERRADA DURANTE MUCHOS AÑOS. UNOS MILES DE PERSONAS **NO PUEDEN IMPONERSE A DIEZ MILLONES**. »
>
> **Solidaridad**, sindicato, mensaje a la población de Polonia (diciembre de 1981)

En Irán, los **muyahidines**, un grupo de combatientes islámicos, orquestaron una serie de asesinatos y atentados con bomba. En agosto, el nuevo presidente, **Mohamed Alí Rajai**, y el primer ministro, **Javad Bahonar**, fueron asesinados. En octubre, **Alí Jamenei** ganó las elecciones presidenciales.

En **España** se produjo un intento de **golpe de estado derechista** liderado por el coronel Antonio Tejero Molina (n. 1932), quien irrumpió en el parlamento con doscientos guardias civiles. Las fuerzas armadas aplastaron a los golpistas el 23 de febrero.

23-F
El coronel Antonio Tejero irrumpió en el parlamento, mientras disparaba al aire y anunciaba un golpe militar; fracasó en cuestión de horas.

Israel sorprendió al mundo al bombardear una **planta nuclear** cerca de Bagdad (**Iraq**) el 7 de junio, alegando que tenía capacidad para fabricar armas nucleares que podrían alcanzar Israel. Iraq lo negó.

El 13 de diciembre, el **gobierno polaco** declaró el **estado de emergencia** en respuesta a las protestas de los sindicatos, y encarceló a los líderes del sindicato **Solidaridad**, a lo que los miembros del sindicato respondieron con la convocatoria de una **huelga nacional** (*véase* 1982).

En **Brixton** (sur de Londres), estallaron **disturbios** el 11 de abril, después de que la policía arrestara a un hombre de color. La violencia se extendió a otras ciudades donde las deterioradas relaciones entre la comunidad de color y la policía también provocaban malestar social.

El ***Columbia*** se convirtió en el primer **transbordador** en volar al espacio el 12 de abril. En su primer vuelo fue pilotado por los veteranos astronautas estadounidenses **John Young** (n. 1930) y **Robert Crippen** (n. 1937). Se había abierto una nueva era en la exploración espacial.

Bob Marley (n. 1945), el rostro internacional de la música reggae, murió de cáncer el 11 de mayo a los 36 años de edad. Bob Marley and the Wailers fueron el **grupo de reggae** más famoso del mundo.

El **sida** (*véase* recuadro) saltó a la palestra en junio, tras la muerte de cinco hombres en Los Ángeles. Era la primera vez que se informaba de casos ajenos a la comunidad homosexual, por lo que se hizo evidente que la enfermedad afectaba también a otros grupos. La enfermedad desconocida recibió el nombre de **síndrome de inmunodeficiencia adquirida** (sida).

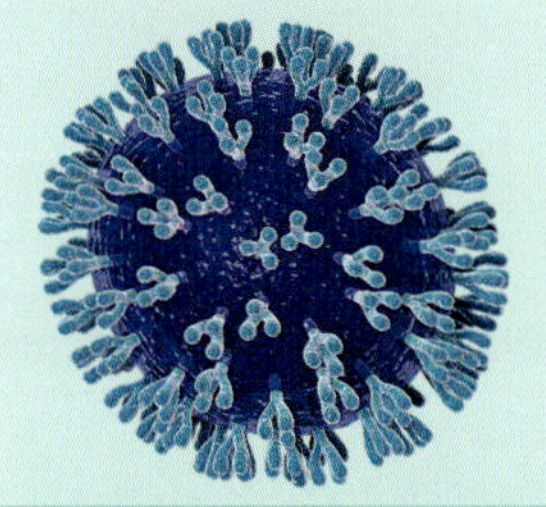

EL VIH

El VIH es el virus que causa el síndrome de inmunodeficiencia adquirida (sida), una enfermedad del sistema inmunitario. Los médicos del Instituto Pasteur de Francia lo descubrieron en mayo de 1983. Aislar el virus permitió el desarrollo de fármacos para alargar la esperanza de vida de los enfermos, aunque aún no se ha hallado una vacuna. Al menos 40,4 millones de personas en el mundo han muerto como consecuencia del sida; África ha sido la región más afectada.

1982

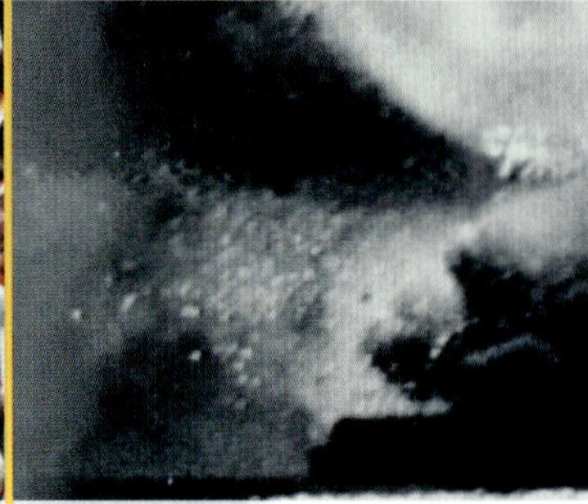

Explosión de la fragata *HMS Antelope* durante la guerra de las Malvinas.

ARGENTINA INVADIÓ EL TERRITORIO BRITÁNICO de las **Malvinas**, en el Atlántico sur, el 2 de abril. Ambos países se disputaban la soberanía de las islas desde hacía mucho tiempo. La primera ministra británica, **Margaret Thatcher** (n. 1925), envió un destacamento naval para liberar las islas. El conflicto resultante costó la vida a cientos de soldados argentinos y británicos, muchos por **ataques de misiles sobre los barcos de guerra**. El conflicto terminó el 14 de junio, cuando el comandante de la guarnición argentina en **Puerto Argentino (Port Stanley)** se rindió a los británicos.

Irán lanzó la Operación Victoria Innegable en marzo, como parte de la guerra contra Iraq (*véase* 1980) y a la que consiguió dar un giro al obligar a Iraq a retirarse. En una semana, Irán había logrado acabar

20 de enero Ronald Reagan (1911–2004) es investido presidente de EE. UU.

20 de enero Irán libera a los **rehenes** de la embajada estadounidense tras 444 días.

4 de febrero La **primera ministra Thatcher** anuncia más planes de **privatización** de empresas públicas británicas.

23 de febrero El rey Juan Carlos de **España** supera un golpe de estado.

30 de marzo El presidente **Reagan** sobrevive a un intento de asesinato.

12 de abril Lanzamiento del **transbordador espacial estadounidense *Columbia***.

5 de mayo El preso del IRA **Bobby Sands** muere estando en huelga de hambre.

10 de mayo François Mitterrand (1916–1996) se convierte en el presidente de Francia.

30 de mayo El presidente **Ziaur Rahman** de Bangladesh es asesinado (n. 1936).

Junio Los científicos identifican el virus del **sida**.

29 de julio El **príncipe Carlos y lady Diana Spencer** se casan en la catedral de San Pablo de Londres.

1 de agosto Inauguración de la **MTV** (Music Television) en EE. UU.

5 de agosto El presidente y el primer ministro de **Irán** son **asesinados**.

6 de octubre El presidente **Anuar el Sadat** de Egipto es asesinado (n. 1918).

1 de noviembre Independencia de **Antigua y Barbuda**.

10 de noviembre Hosni Mubarak (n. 1928), nuevo presidente de Egipto.

8 de enero España pone fin al sitio de **Gibraltar**.

25 de marzo Nicaragua declara el estado de emergencia.

2 de abril Inicio de la **guerra de las Malvinas** entre Gran Bretaña y Argentina

« ES UNA VIOLACIÓN FLAGRANTE DEL DERECHO INTERNACIONAL. »

Consejo de Seguridad de la ONU, sobre la invasión estadounidense de Granada en 1983

2:5 **Bajas en las Malvinas** *La guerra de las Malvinas duró 74 días, durante los que murieron 255 soldados británicos y 649 argentinos. Más de 11 000 soldados argentinos cayeron prisioneros.*

con gran parte de las divisiones iraquíes. El presidente iraní, **Alí Jamenei** (n. 1939), rechazó la oferta iraquí de alto el fuego y envió a miles de jóvenes iraníes a una muerte segura en una serie de **ataques de «mareas humanas»** para allanar el camino para los tanques iraníes. Sin embargo, a finales de año, Iraq había conseguido rearmarse con **armas soviéticas** y la guerra terrestre entró en una nueva fase (*véase* 1983).

Israel invadió el **Líbano** el 6 de junio, en un intento de **arrasar los puestos de la guerrilla** en la frontera del norte de Israel. El 15 de septiembre, el ejército israelí ocupaba Beirut Occidental. Entre el 16 y el 18 de septiembre, los **falangistas**, leales a Israel, asesinaron a cientos de palestinos en un campo de refugiados. El ministro de defensa israelí, **Ariel Sharon, dimitió**, después de que la investigación israelí concluyera que no había hecho nada para impedir la masacre.

El **IRA** proseguía con su campaña contra el gobierno británico en Irlanda del Norte e hizo explotar **dos bombas** en sendos parques londinenses: la primera, en **Hyde Park**, mató a cuatro soldados de caballería y a sus caballos; la otra, colocada bajo el pabellón de música de **Regents Park**, mató a siete soldados.

El **gobierno de Polonia** prohibió **Solidaridad** (*véase* 1981), el sindicato polaco, el 8 de octubre, lo que fue condenado por la **comunidad internacional**. Ronald Reagan, presidente de EE. UU., impuso sanciones económicas a Polonia para presionar al gobierno. **Lech Walesa** (n. 1943), el líder de Solidaridad, fue liberado el 12 de noviembre, tras permanecer once meses encarcelado.

El 10 de noviembre murió **Leonid Brézhnev** (n. 1906), líder de la Unión Soviética, tras haber ejercido de secretario general durante dieciocho años. Le sucedió **Yuri Andropov** (1914–1984). Durante su mandato, Brézhnev había intentado mejorar las relaciones con Occidente y aumentar la potencia militar e industrial soviética, pero el nivel de vida seguía siendo bajo.

El 28 de abril nacieron en Manchester (Inglaterra) los **primeros gemelos probeta** del mundo. Fueron concebidos fuera del útero, después de que su madre fuera sometida a una fecundación in vitro (**FIV**).

Israel ataca el Líbano
Muchas ciudades sufrieron ataques de artillería pesada durante la invasión israelí del Líbano, en un intento de expulsar a la OLP.

El rey del pop
Michael Jackson, la incuestionable estrella del pop de la década de 1980, lanzó el álbum Thriller *en 1982. Fue, y sigue siendo, el álbum más vendido de todos los tiempos.*

EL 17 DE ENERO, NIGERIA ANUNCIÓ su intención de **expulsar a todos los residentes extranjeros**. Más de un millón debieron marcharse. La decisión, condenada en el extranjero, fue bien recibida en el interior del país.

Etiopía se vio azotada por la sequía. Unas pingües cosechas provocaron una enorme escasez de alimentos. El gasto militar del gobierno comunista y la ocultación de la crisis exacerbaron la situación.

La **embajada de EE. UU. en Beirut** fue atacada por un terrorista suicida el 19 de abril. EE. UU. atribuyó el ataque a **Hizbulá**, un grupo militante islámico. Más adelante ese mismo año, los terroristas bombardearon a las fuerzas francesas y estadounidenses de mantenimiento de la paz en Beirut y causaron gran cantidad de muertes.

Iraq había empezado a usar **armas químicas** en su **guerra con Irán**. Desarrolló el gas mostaza, que provoca ampollas en la piel, para repeler las mareas humanas iraníes.

El 23 de julio, miembros de la etnia **tamil**, de **Sri Lanka**, fueron **atacados**, como represalia por una emboscada de los **Tigres Tamiles** en la que habían muerto trece soldados de Sri Lanka. Ese año marcó el inicio de la **guerra civil**.

Los **soviéticos** fueron acusados de **derribar un avión de pasajeros de Corea del Sur** el 1 de septiembre. Alegaron que el avión había invadido su espacio aéreo y no había respondido a los intentos de comunicación.

Reagan impulsó una estrategia de apoyo a la **insurgencia anticomunista** decidida a derrocar los regímenes marxistas. En mayo, el presidente declaró abiertamente su apoyo a la **Contra nicaragüense**, que se oponía al **gobierno sandinista**. En octubre, EE. UU. derrocó al gobierno marxista de **Granada**.

El 23 de marzo, Reagan lanzó su **Iniciativa de Defensa Estratégica** (IDE), un programa para combatir las armas nucleares espaciales. El IDE de Reagan llegó a conocerse como «la guerra de las galaxias».

20 000 MILLONES DE DÓLARES DE PRESUPUESTO PARA LA «GUERRA DE LAS GALAXIAS»

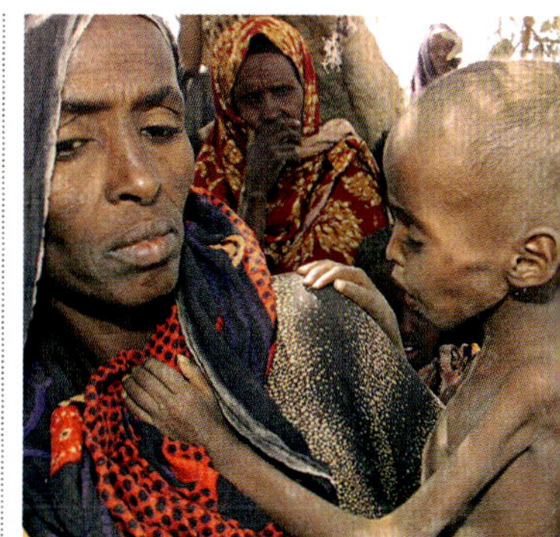

Hambruna secreta
Una madre sostiene en brazos a su hijo durante la hambruna en Etiopía, que el gobierno etíope trató de ocultar al resto del mundo.

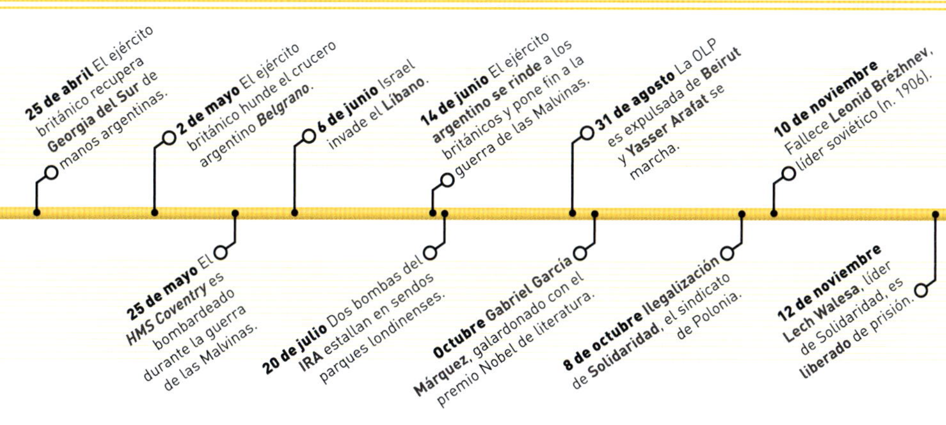

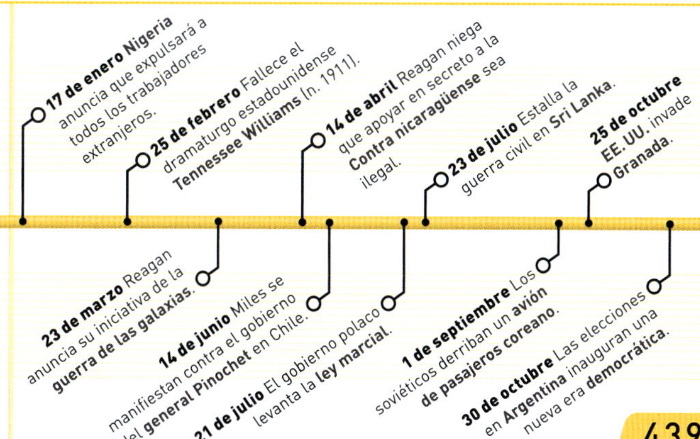

1984

Arthur Scargill, líder del Sindicato Nacional de Mineros (NUM) de Gran Bretaña, se enfrenta a un escuadrón de policías durante la guerra de los mineros británicos, que duró un año.

LOS MINEROS DEL CARBÓN BRITÁNICOS INICIARON UNA HUELGA el día 12 de marzo para protestar por los salarios y por la clausura de pozos. El conflicto duró un año.

La policía Yvonne Fletcher murió frente a la **embajada de Libia** en Londres durante una manifestación el 17 de abril. Su muerte provocó un **asedio policial** al edificio, tras el que Gran Bretaña expulsó del país a los diplomáticos libios.

El 19 de diciembre, **China** y **Gran Bretaña** firmaron un tratado por el que **Hong Kong**, una colonia británica, sería transferida al gobierno chino en 1997.

55 000
HERIDOS

15 000
han muerto desde entonces

3000
murieron en cuestión de semanas

Víctimas de Bhopal
Esta catástrofe afectó a miles de personas y mató a unas tres mil en semanas. Se cree que quince mil más han muerto desde entonces.

Vuelo libre en el espacio
El astronauta estadounidense Bruce McCandless flota en el espacio. Usó una mochila propulsora para alejarse 91 m del transbordador Challenger.

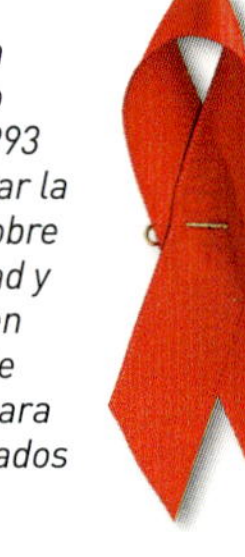

Lazo rojo
La Fundación del Lazo Rojo se creó en 1993 para aumentar la conciencia sobre la enfermedad y se convirtió en un símbolo de solidaridad para con los afectados por el sida.

El 12 de octubre estalló una **bomba del IRA** en el Grand Hotel de **Brighton**, donde se había reunido el **congreso del Partido Conservador**. Margaret Thatcher (1925–2013) escapó por poco.

En Nigeria, el **general Mohamed Buhari** (n. 1942) tomó el poder tras un **golpe militar** incruento, el 1 de enero, que justificó por la historia de corrupción del gobierno.

Indira Gandhi (n. 1917), la primera ministra de India, fue **asesinada** el 31 de octubre por **extremistas sijs**, en respuesta a un ataque a uno de sus lugares de culto, el **Templo Dorado de Amritsar**. Gandhi había ordenado el ataque, conocido como **Operación Estrella Azul**, para expulsar a los separatistas sijs, de quienes se sospechaba que almacenaban armas en el templo. La operación se cobró unas **mil vidas**.

El 3 de diciembre, la **fuga de un gas venenoso** en la planta de pesticidas de la estadounidense Union Carbide en **Bhopal** (India) se convirtió en uno de los peores accidentes industriales de la historia.

Reagan (1911–2004) ordenó la retirada de las tropas de paz de **Beirut** el 7 de febrero ante el aumento de los ataques terroristas.

1985

Dos mil millones de personas vieron la retransmisión de los conciertos *Live Aid*.

TANCREDO NEVES (1910–1985) fue escogido presidente de Brasil el 15 de enero, tras 21 años de gobierno militar. Ese año la democracia también regresó a **Uruguay** y **Bolivia**.

El 25 de mayo, cientos de personas murieron en los ataques de **soldados chiíes** (que contaban con el apoyo de Siria) a enclaves palestinos en **Beirut**. El primer ministro, **Simón Peres** (n. 1923), retiró del Líbano al ejército israelí, pero mantuvo una **zona de seguridad** de 19 km de anchura en el sur. El día 7 de octubre de ese mismo año, milicianos de la Organización para la Liberación de Palestina (**OLP**) secuestraron un crucero italiano, el *Achille Lauro*, para exigir la liberación de **cincuenta presos palestinos** en Israel. La crisis terminó el

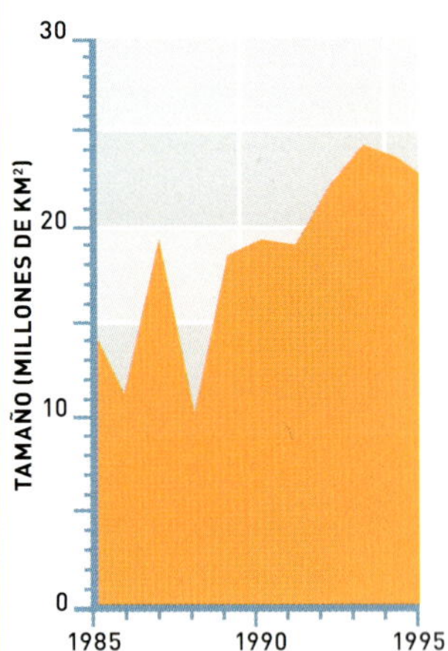

Agujero en la capa de ozono
La gráfica muestra el tamaño medio del agujero de la capa de ozono año a año entre 1985 y 1995. Como orientación, Europa ocupa unos diez millones de kilómetros cuadrados.

1 de enero Golpe de estado sin derramamiento de sangre en **Nigeria**.

9 de febrero Fallece el político soviético **Yuri Andropov** (n. 1914).

12 de marzo Inicio de la **huelga de los mineros** en Gran Bretaña.

17–27 de abril Sitio a la **embajada de Libia** en Londres.

23 de abril Se anuncia en Washington (EE. UU.) el descubrimiento del **virus del sida**.

6 de junio El ejército indio asalta el **Templo Dorado** sij en Amritsar.

28 de julio–12 de agosto Los Ángeles (EE. UU.) acoge los **Juegos Olímpicos**.

12 de octubre Una **bomba del IRA** explota en un hotel de Brighton.

21 de octubre Fallece el cineasta francés **François Truffaut** (n. 1932).

30 de octubre Fallece el **padre Jerzy Popieluszko**, un sacerdote polaco (n. 1947).

31 de octubre Indira Gandhi, primera ministra de India, es **asesinada**.

6 de noviembre Ronald Reagan gana sus segundas elecciones presidenciales.

25 de noviembre Band Aid canta por la causa etíope.

3 de diciembre Desastre químico en **Bhopal** (India).

15 de enero Brasil elige a su primer presidente civil en 21 años.

4 de febrero Fin del **asedio a Gibraltar**.

5 de febrero Terry Waite negocia la liberación de los rehenes británicos en Libia.

11 de marzo Mijaíl Gorbachov (n. 1931) se convierte en el líder soviético.

Mayo Los científicos revelan la disminución de la **capa de ozono**.

La estación espacial rusa Mir («paz») acoge a los astronautas de paso. La primera tripulación llegó el 15 de marzo.

10 de octubre, cuando los secuestradores abandonaron el crucero a cambio de un salvoconducto.

El **asedio de Gibraltar**, que ya duraba dieciséis años, terminó el 4 de febrero, cuando España abrió la frontera, aunque las disputas por la soberanía de la isla prosiguen.

Científicos británicos hallaron un **agujero en la capa de ozono** sobre la Antártida. El artículo que recogía el estudio, publicado en la revista *Nature*, movilizó a los ecologistas.

Live Aid emocionó al mundo en julio, con dos conciertos simultáneos en Londres y en Filadelfia, para recaudar fondos para **aliviar la hambruna en Etiopía**.

MIJAÍL GORBACHOV
(n. 1931)

Se convirtió en el líder de la URSS el 11 de marzo de 985. Fue el artífice de la *Glasnost* y la *Perestroika*. Tendió puentes a Occidente y renunció al ideario estalinista. Obtuvo el premio Nobel de la paz en 1990, pero sus políticas desencadenaron el hundimiento de la Unión Soviética.

CLAVE
Área muy contaminada
Alcance de la radiación

Reikiavik
Oslo
Helsinki
Moscú
Londres
París
Varsovia
Chernóbil
Múnich
Madrid
Roma
Estambul
Ankara
Atenas

Desastre nuclear
Tras el accidente de la planta nuclear de Chernóbil, la radiación se extendió por toda Europa y llegó hasta París.

LA GUERRA IRANO-IRAQUÍ llegó a su octavo año e Irán lanzó un asalto sorpresa y **capturó** el **puerto petrolero abandonado iraquí** de Al-Faw. Se acusó a Iraq de usar gas mostaza para repeler el ataque.

El **Irangate**, escándalo en el que se vio implicado el **presidente Ronald Reagan**, estalló en octubre en EE. UU. La administración Reagan había vendido **armas a Irán** para garantizar la liberación de los rehenes estadounidenses en el Líbano, y había invertido los beneficios de la operación en la financiación de la **Contra nicaragüense**. Reagan sobrevivió, pero su consejero de Seguridad Nacional, **John Poindexter**, dimitió.

Aviones estadounidenses bombardearon **Trípoli** (Libia) el 15 de abril. El presidente Reagan lo justificó como un acto de autodefensa. Días antes, soldados estadounidenses habían muerto en un **atentado con bomba**, atribuido a Libia, en la discoteca La Belle, en Berlín Occidental.

John McCarthy (n. 1956), periodista británico, fue **secuestrado** el 17 de abril por terroristas islámicos en Beirut. Ese mismo día, rehenes británicos fueron asesinados en represalia por el apoyo británico al bombardeo de Libia por parte de EE. UU. (*véase* 1991).

En enero también se desestabilizó Yemen, cuando la lucha de poder en el seno del **Partido Socialista de Yemen** (YSP) condujo a una **guerra brutal** entre el norte y el sur. El *Britannia*, el yate real británico, ayudó a evacuar a los ciudadanos británicos.

Insignia del *Challenger*
El 28 de enero, el transbordador espacial Challenger *explotó 72 segundos después del lanzamiento. Murieron los siete tripulantes.*

La **Unión Soviética** admitió un accidente en la planta nuclear de **Chernóbil** (Ucrania) el 26 de abril. Es aún el peor desastre en la historia de la energía nuclear. Liberó un nivel de **contaminación radiactiva** que se extendió por toda Europa.

Mir, la estación espacial soviética, se lanzó el 20 de febrero para que formara parte de una **ciudad espacial** que alojaría a astronautas. El 15 de marzo subió a bordo la primera tripulación.

El 12 de junio, **Sudáfrica** declaró el **estado de emergencia** ante el décimo aniversario del alzamiento estudiantil negro en **Soweto**. El gobierno impuso toques de queda y prohibió que las cámaras de televisión grabaran los «desórdenes».

Ferdinand Marcos (1917–1989) fue obligado a renunciar como **dictador de Filipinas** el 25 de febrero; tenía en su contra al ejército y a la opinión pública. **Corazón Aquino** (1933–2009) juró como su sucesora y se convirtió en la primera mujer en liderar el país.

El 21 de diciembre, casi **cincuenta mil estudiantes** se reunieron en la **plaza del Pueblo** de Shanghai para pedir más libertades sociales. En toda China, los estudiantes celebraron manifestaciones y exigieron **reformas democráticas**.

50 000
ESTUDIANTES SE MANIFESTARON POR LA **DEMOCRACIA** EN SHANGHAI

DEMÓCRATAS SUECOS

Olof Palme lideraba el Partido Socialdemócrata Sueco desde 1969. Como primer ministro, impulsó grandes reformas y apoyó los derechos de las mujeres, la asistencia sanitaria y el estado de bienestar. Fue de los primeros en impulsar políticas en defensa del medio ambiente. Se le acusaba de ser pro soviético; tal vez eso provocó su asesinato en 1986.

España y **Portugal** se integraron en la **Unión Europea** (UE) el día 1 de enero, lo que elevó a doce el número de países miembro. Se adoptó una nueva bandera como símbolo de Europa.

La **Australia Act**, firmada el 3 de marzo, **independizó** el derecho australiano del sistema legal británico. También transfería a Australia el control sobre los documentos constitucionales australianos.

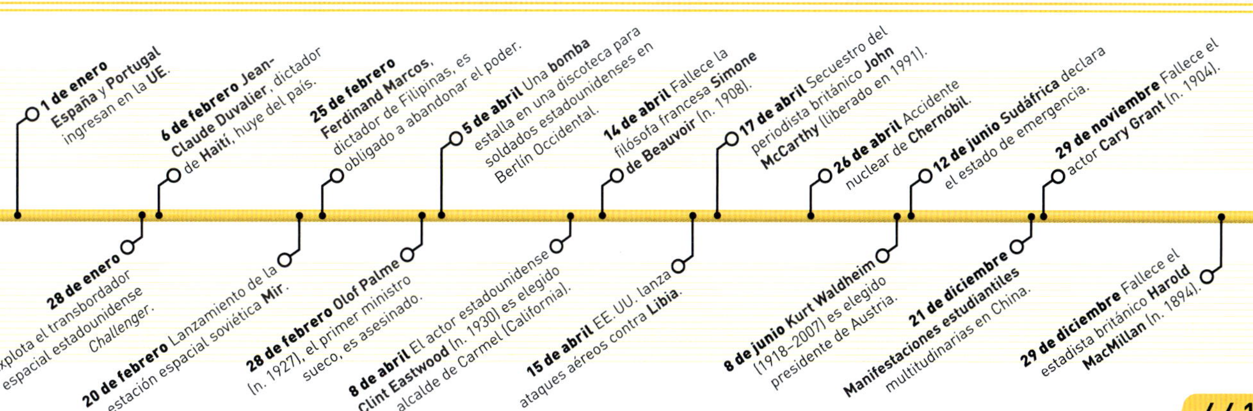

NORUEGA
SUECIA
FINLANDIA
Mar de Barents
Mar de Láptiev
Mar de Kara
Tallin
San Petersburgo (Leningrado)
Riga
Kaliningrado
LITUANIA
Vilnius
ESTONIA
LETONIA
Arjánguelsk
Plesetsk
Minsk
BIELORRUSIA
Moscú
Montes Urales
Siberia
FEDERACIÓN RUSA
Chernóbil
Kiev
Tula
Riazán
Nizni-Nóvgorod
Yoshkar-Ola
Kazán
Perm
MOLDAVIA
UCRANIA
Llanura de Siberia Oriental
Odesa
Vorónezh
Dniepropetrovsk
Samara
Ufá
Ekaterimburgo
Tiumen
Donetsk
Cheliabinsk
Rostov
Volgogrado (Stalingrado)
Tomsk
Mar Negro
Omsk
Novosibirsk
Krasnoiarsk
Lago Baikal
Irkutsk
Grozni
Mar Caspio
KAZAJSTÁN
Akmola
Karaganda
GEORGIA
Tbilisi
Ereván
Mar de Aral
Montes Altai
ARMENIA
Bakú
UZBEKISTÁN
Lago Baljash
MONGOLIA
AZERBAIYÁN
Dashovuz
TURKMENISTÁN
Biskek
Almati
Tashkent
Bujará
Ashgabad
Samarcanda
Dusambé
KIRGUIZISTÁN
IRÁN
TAYIKISTÁN
AFGANISTÁN

CLAVE
Federación Rusa
Antigua URSS

Colapso de la URSS
Tras el colapso de la URSS, el antiguo imperio se dividió en quince estados nuevos. Los gobiernos independientes forjaron una alianza flexible: la Comunidad de Estados Independientes (CEI).

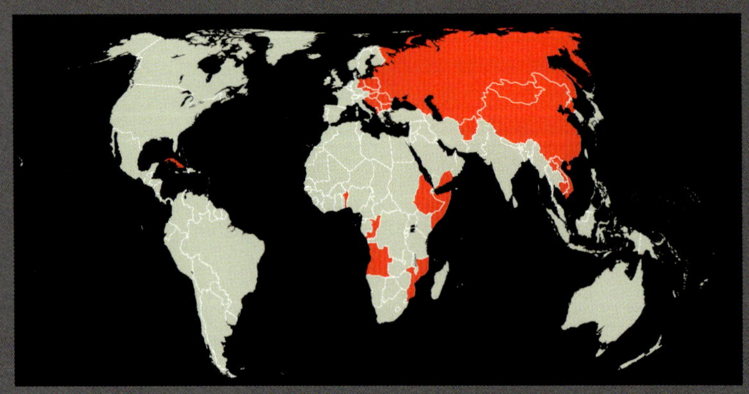

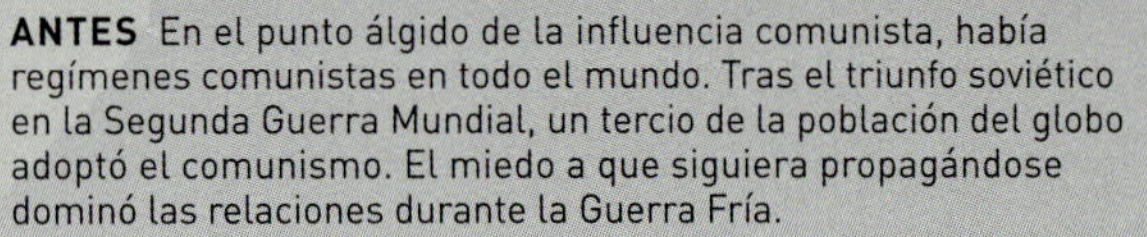

ANTES En el punto álgido de la influencia comunista, había regímenes comunistas en todo el mundo. Tras el triunfo soviético en la Segunda Guerra Mundial, un tercio de la población del globo adoptó el comunismo. El miedo a que siguiera propagándose dominó las relaciones durante la Guerra Fría.

DESPUÉS En la actualidad, solo hay cinco regímenes comunistas en el mundo. China sigue siendo el más importante, y Laos, Vietnam, Corea del Norte y Cuba son regímenes comunistas también. Muchos países democráticos cuentan con un partido comunista.

EL COLAPSO DE LA UNIÓN SOVIÉTICA

LA RÁPIDA DESINTEGRACIÓN DEL ESTADO SOVIÉTICO IMPRESIONÓ AL MUNDO

En marzo de 1985, Mijaíl Gorbachov se convirtió en el líder de la URSS. Se dio cuenta de que el Bloque Soviético necesitaba reformas drásticas e intentó modernizar el socialismo. Pero el resultado fue la desintegración total de la URSS, que cambió el mapa de Europa y trajo consigo un nuevo orden mundial.

Mijaíl Gorbachov fue un líder popular. Introdujo conceptos nuevos, como la *Glasnost* y la *Perestroika* («aperturismo» y «reestructuración»), y defendió una sociedad más liberal y dinámica. Su popularidad aumentó aún más cuando retiró al ejército ruso de Afganistán, pero los grupos minoritarios no rusos de toda la URSS empezaron a rebelarse en busca de independencia. En julio de 1989, Gorbachov anunció que los países del Pacto de Varsovia (*véase* 1955) podrían decidir su futuro en elecciones abiertas.

Europa Central y Europa del Este respondieron a la libertad otorgada por Gorbachov: Hungría abrió sus fronteras a Occidente y el Muro de Berlín fue derruido. Cuando Gorbachov no respondió con la fuerza, Checoslovaquia y Rumanía también se separaron, seguidas de Ucrania y de Armenia en 1990, y de Turkmenistán y Tayikistán en 1991.

Desde fuera fue visto como un héroe; ganó el premio Nobel de la paz y era agasajado por los líderes extranjeros. Sin embargo, el nivel de vida en el país se derrumbó y aparecieron graves problemas económicos. Gorbachov intentó mantener la federación unida a medida que sus ministros le abandonaban y el clamor por la independencia de los países bálticos alcanzaba un nivel atronador. En julio de 1991, Boris Yeltsin fue elegido presidente de Rusia y se presentó como campeón de la reforma tras salvar a Gorbachov de un golpe de estado en agosto, por parte de los opositores de la línea dura. Ese mismo mes, Yeltsin ordenó que el Partido Comunista Soviético cesara toda actividad en Rusia. La URSS se vio abocada a la desintegración cuando Ucrania, Rusia y Bielorrusia planearon en secreto formar una unión nueva. La situación era insostenible, y el día 25 de diciembre de 1991 Gorbachov dimitió como presidente de la Unión Soviética. De las quince repúblicas soviéticas que quedaban, doce se convirtieron en estados soberanos, por lo que la URSS pasó a la historia.

AUGE Y CAÍDA DEL COMUNISMO

El comunismo ha sido uno de los movimientos políticos más importantes del mundo moderno y ha inspirado a grandes filósofos y a guerrilleros por igual. Pretendía liberar a los oprimidos y unió a los que se oponían al capitalismo en Occidente.

El gran experimento que empezó con la toma del palacio de invierno de Petrogrado en 1917 terminó en 1989–1991 con la caída del Muro de Berlín y la desintegración de la Unión Soviética. China, Cuba, Vietnam y Corea del Norte se siguen considerando comunistas, pero el consenso general es que, sin la Unión Soviética como factor de integración, el comunismo se encuentra en un callejón sin salida.

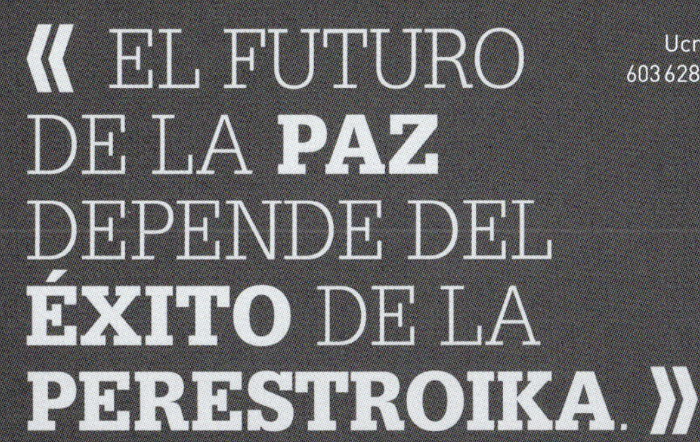

« EL FUTURO DE LA **PAZ** DEPENDE DEL **ÉXITO** DE LA **PERESTROIKA**. »

Mijaíl Gorbachov, estadista soviético (1987)

Lituania 65 200 km²
Estonia 45 228 km²
Azerbaiyán 86 600 km²
Armenia 29 743 km²
Moldavia 33 846 km²
Letonia 64 589 km²
Georgia 69 700 km²
Ucrania 603 628 km²
KAZAJSTÁN 2 734 900 km²
Bielorrusia 207 595 km²
Turkmenistán 488 100 km²
Tayikistán 143 100 km²
Uzbekistán 447 400 km²
Kirguizistán 199 900 km²
FEDERACIÓN RUSA 17 075 400 km²

Desintegración de la Unión Soviética
El territorio que antaño formaba la Unión Soviética se ha convertido en varios estados nuevos. La Federación Rusa es, con diferencia, el mayor de ellos.

1987

Durante el desplome del mercado de valores de Nueva York el «lunes negro», el Dow Jones cayó más de 500 puntos.

50 000
MILLONES DE DÓLARES
CAÍDA DEL **VALOR** DE LAS **ACCIONES** DURANTE EL **LUNES NEGRO**

5000
MILLONES
POBLACIÓN MUNDIAL EN **1987**

EN JULIO, LA POBLACIÓN MUNDIAL alcanzó los cinco mil millones de habitantes, el doble que en 1950 y **mil millones superior** a la de 1974. Crecía a un ritmo de **220 000 personas diarias**. Gran parte del crecimiento se daba en las partes del mundo menos capaces de sostenerlo. La preocupación por el impacto socioeconómico del aumento demográfico llevó a que el 11 de julio se conociera como el **día de los cinco mil millones**. Y, desde entontes, el 11 de julio es el **día de la población mundial**.

Terry Waite (n. 1939), enviado especial del arzobispo de Canterbury, se desplazó al Líbano en enero para negociar la **liberación de los rehenes occidentales**, como el periodista **John McCarthy** (*véase* 1986). Sin embargo, él también fue **capturado por milicianos** y retenido en **Beirut** (*véase* 1991).

En mayo, **Francia** tuvo que pagar 8,6 millones de dólares a **Greenpeace** por el hundimiento del ***Rainbow Warrior***. La nave, que iba a liderar una flotilla de Greenpeace que protestaba contra las **pruebas nucleares de Francia** en el océano Pacífico, se hundió tras una explosión el 10 de julio de 1985 en el **puerto de Auckland** (Nueva Zelanda) y en la que murió el fotógrafo Fernando Pereira. El incidente provocó un **escándalo internacional** y enfrió las relaciones entre Nueva Zelanda y Francia. Dos **agentes secretos franceses** implicados en el ataque fueron encarcelados y Francia pagó 6,5 millones de dólares a Nueva Zelanda como **compensación** y para que devolviera a los agentes a la jurisdicción francesa.

El 20 de marzo, la FDA (Food and Drug Administration, de EE. UU.) aprobó la azidotimidina (**AZT**). Fue el primer fármaco antirretroviral diseñado específicamente para combatir el **VIH**. El AZT no curaba el sida, pero demostró que era tratable y que no equivalía a una sentencia de muerte.

El 19 de octubre, el **índice Dow Jones** estadounidense se desplomó un 22,6 %, el **mayor desplome porcentual** en un solo día en toda su historia. Al día siguiente, la bolsa londinense sufrió un descenso de cincuenta mil millones de libras en el valor de sus acciones. Los **mercados de valores** de todo el mundo **cayeron** también, como consecuencia de los temores sobre la debilidad del dólar y el **déficit comercial estadounidense**. La situación se agravó aún más cuando se supo que EE. UU. había respondido a los ataques iraníes en el golfo Pérsico con el bombardeo de un pozo de petróleo. El **«lunes negro»**, como se le conocería luego, fue casi dos veces peor que el *crash* del 29 de octubre de 1929.

Margaret Thatcher (1925–2013)) **visitó Moscú** en marzo. Fue la primera visita oficial de un primer ministro británico en doce años, y simbolizó la normalización de las relaciones entre **Gran Bretaña y la Unión Soviética**. Durante los encuentros, el primer ministro soviético **Mijaíl Gorbachov** (n. 1931) criticó la doctrina Brézhnev y declaró obsoleto el **Telón de Acero**, además de sugerir políticas más liberales en Europa del Este. Al mes siguiente, Gorbachov visitó Checoslovaquia y dejó entrever la posibilidad de que el Bloque Oriental pudiera **independizarse**.

En diciembre, los líderes de la **URSS** y de **EE. UU. firmaron el tratado sobre las armas nucleares de medio alcance** para reducir el tamaño de sus arsenales nucleares. Su fin era revertir la carrera nuclear mediante la destrucción de todas las armas nucleares de corto y medio alcance en Europa, que hubieran podido alcanzar objetivos a entre 500 y 5500 km de distancia. Fue la primera vez que las superpotencias acordaban **reducir** sus enormes **arsenales nucleares**.

6,5 MILLONES — pago para recuperar a los agentes — 1986

8,6 MILLONES — pago a Greenpeace — 1987

Compensación francesa
Francia pagó a Nueva Zelanda 6,5 millones de dólares para recuperar a sus agentes. Pagó 8,6 millones de dólares también a Greenpeace por el hundimiento de su buque, el Rainbow Warrior.

Negociar la libertad
Terry Waite se convirtió en una presencia habitual en el Líbano. Como enviado eclesiástico, participó en varias misiones para negociar la liberación de rehenes en manos de organizaciones terroristas islámicas.

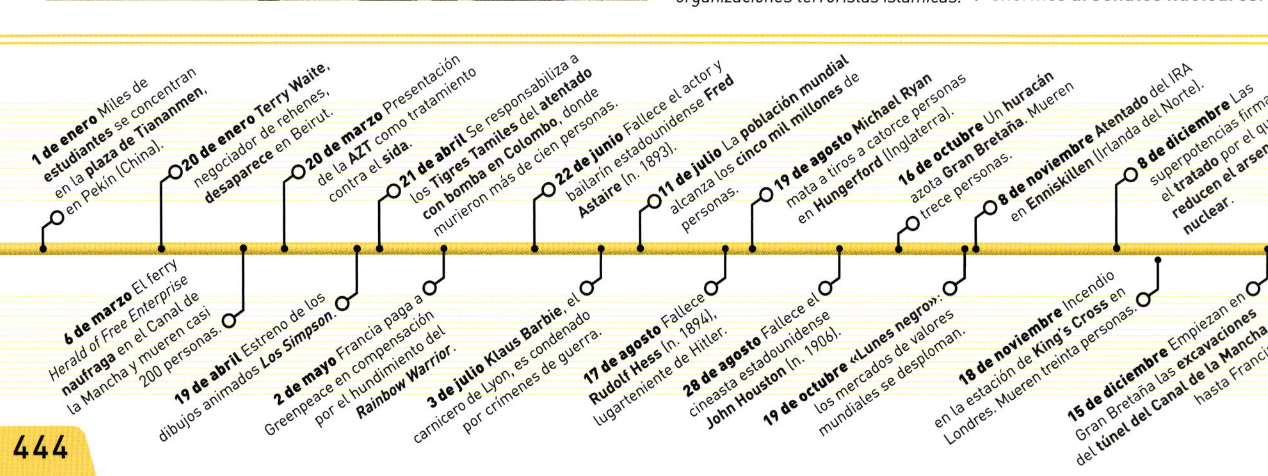

« LEAN MIS LABIOS. NO MÁS IMPUESTOS. »

George Bush, durante la aceptación de la nominación republicana en Nueva Orleans (18 de agosto de 1988)

TRES MIEMBROS DEL EJÉRCITO REPUBLICANO IRLANDÉS (IRA) murieron a manos del Servicio Secreto británico (**SAS**) en Gibraltar, el 6 de marzo. El IRA planeaba hacer **detonar una bomba** en la ceremonia del cambio de guardia en el territorio británico, en el que iba a participar el 1.er batallón del regimiento Royal Anglia, que venía de Irlanda del Norte. El incidente desencadenó una **oleada de violencia** en Belfast.

En ese año tuvo lugar el primer uso documentado de **armas químicas** en la guerra irano-iraquí: Iraq lanzó bombas de **gas mostaza y agentes neurológicos** sobre la ciudad kurda de **Halabja** en Iraq en marzo. Murieron entre tres mil y cinco mil civiles y muchos más sufrieron secuelas a largo plazo. La matanza fue conocida como **«viernes sangriento»** (*véase* 2010).

El 8 de agosto, un **alto el fuego** negociado por la ONU puso fin a la guerra entre Irán e Iraq (*véase* 1980), que duró ocho años y que costó más de **un millón de vidas**.

Los árabes palestinos de la **franja de Gaza** y de **Cisjordania** protagonizaron un alzamiento masivo contra la ocupación israelí de territorios palestinos. El movimiento, conocido como **Intifada**, consistió en huelgas generales, boicot a los productos israelíes, manifestaciones y ataques con **cócteles Molotov**. El 14 de noviembre, la Organización para la Liberación de Palestina (**OLP**) aceptó la **«solución de los dos estados»** (*véase* 1947), con lo que reconoció oficialmente el derecho de Israel a existir como país.

El 2 de diciembre, **Benazir Bhutto** (*véase* recuadro) juró el cargo de **primera ministra de Pakistán**. Además de ser la primera mujer en ocupar el cargo en Pakistán, se convirtió en la cabeza de estado más joven del mundo (*véase* 2007).

La ***Perestroika*** («reestructuración») y la ***Glasnost*** («aperturismo») de Gorbachov fueron clave para poner fin a la Guerra Fría (*véase* 1948). En un discurso ante la ONU, Gorbachov anunció **reducciones unilaterales de armamento y de fuerzas armadas**, y la retirada de fuerzas soviéticas de Europa del Este.

El 21 de diciembre, el vuelo **103 de Pan Am** se estrelló en **Lockerbie** (Escocia). Murieron los 259 pasajeros, toda la tripulación y 11 personas en tierra. Se hallaron restos de una **bomba** y se emprendió una investigación. Se vinculó a **dos agentes de inteligencia libios** con el atentado, pero hicieron falta más de once años para llevarlos a juicio.

George Bush (n. 1924) se convirtió en el primer vicepresidente en ganar las **elecciones presidenciales** desde 1836. El 8 de noviembre obtuvo una cómoda victoria sobre el demócrata **Michael Dukakis**.

La **guerra fronteriza entre** Sudáfrica, Namibia y Angola había empezado en 1966. La comunidad internacional presionaba a Sudáfrica para que **concediera la independencia** a Namibia. Accedieron, pero solo si **Cuba** retiraba a sus tropas de **Angola**. Al principio, la ONU rechazó la propuesta, pero el 22 de diciembre los interesados se reunieron en Nueva York, y Cuba y Angola firmaron un **acuerdo bilateral**; Angola, Cuba y Sudáfrica firmaron un **acuerdo tripartito**.

Stephen Hawking (n. 1942) publicó ***Breve historia del tiempo***, que narraba la historia del universo desde el **Big Bang**. Sigue siendo la obra científica más popular de la historia.

Nebulosa Cabeza de caballo
La NASA reanudó el programa de transbordadores espaciales en 1988 y, con él, el del telescopio espacial Hubble, que proporcionó imágenes asombrosas del universo.

BENAZIR BHUTTO (1953–2007)

Fundó el Partido del Pueblo Pakistaní (PPP) en Londres, después del asesinato de su padre, Zulfikar Bhutto, en 1979. Regresó a Pakistán en 1986, donde fue primera ministra entre 1988–1990 y 1993–1996. En 1999 se exilió después de ser acusada de corrupción, pero regresó en 2007 para presentarse a las elecciones. Fue asesinada en un ataque suicida dos meses después.

10 de mayo François Mitterrand es reelegido presidente de Francia.

11 de mayo Muere **Kim Philby**, doble agente y espía de los soviéticos.

31 de mayo El presidente estadounidense **Reagan** hace su primer viaje a **Moscú**.

6 de julio Desastre de la plataforma petrolífera **Piper Alpha**. Fallecen 167 personas.

8 de agosto Alto el fuego entre **Irán e Iraq**.

17 de agosto El **general Zia ul-Haq**, presidente de Pakistán, muere en un **accidente de aviación**.

Agosto 350 observadores de la ONU supervisan el **alto el fuego irano-iraquí**.

Agosto–septiembre Inundaciones gigantescas cubren dos tercios de **Bangladesh**.

24 de septiembre Los anglicanos estadounidenses escogen a la **primera mujer obispo**.

29 de septiembre El **programa espacial estadounidense** se reanuda con el lanzamiento del ***Discovery***.

30 de septiembre Ben Johnson es despojado del oro olímpico de Seúl.

1 de octubre Mijaíl Gorbachov es elegido presidente de la URSS.

13 de octubre Las pruebas de carbono-14 concluyen que la **Sábana Santa de Turín** es falsa.

8 de noviembre George Bush es elegido presidente de EE. UU.

9 de noviembre Las fuerzas aéreas de EE. UU. presentan sus **bombarderos furtivos**.

14 de noviembre La **OLP** reconoce el derecho a la **existencia** de **Israel**.

16 de noviembre Estonia exige la independencia de la URSS.

19 de noviembre En **Serbia** se celebran manifestaciones en favor de la independencia.

2 de diciembre Benazir Bhutto jura como **primera ministra de Pakistán**.

7 de diciembre Un **terremoto en Armenia** provoca grandes pérdidas humanas.

12 de diciembre Desastre ferroviario de Clapham en Gran Bretaña; mueren 35 personas.

14 de diciembre EE. UU. manifiesta su disposición a entablar un diálogo con la **OLP**.

21 de diciembre Bomba de Lockerbie; el vuelo 103 de Pan Am explota y mata a 270 personas.

22 de diciembre Sudáfrica firma un **acuerdo tripartito** con Angola y Cuba.

31 de diciembre India y Pakistán firman un compromiso de no agresión de las **instalaciones nucleares respectivas.**

Miles de manifestantes se reunieron durante la Revolución de Terciopelo en Checoslovaquia, un alzamiento pacífico que consiguió derrocar el régimen comunista el 29 de diciembre.

F.W. DE KLERK (N. 1936) FUE ELEGIDO LÍDER EN SUDÁFRICA del Partido Nacional el 2 de febrero. El partido gobernaba el país desde 1948 bajo el principio del ***apartheid***, pero De Klerk parecía más dispuesto que sus predecesores a modernizar el sistema político. El 15 de agosto, el presidente, P.W. Botha (1916–2006), sufrió un ictus y **De Klerk** le sustituyó. De Klerk empezó a **liberar a líderes negros importantes**, como Walter Sisulu, un buen amigo de Nelson Mandela (1918–2013), uno de los líderes del Consejo Nacional Africano (ANC).

El 14 de febrero, el **ayatolá Jomeini** (1902–1989), líder espiritual de Irán, emitió una fatua en la que condenaba a muerte a **Salman Rushdie** (n. 1947) y a los editores de su libro, *Versos satánicos*, al que se consideraba una **blasfemia contra el islam**. Rushdie se vio obligado a ocultarse y a llevar escolta armada para proteger su vida (*véase* 1998).

El 3 de junio de ese año **Jomeini falleció** en Teherán. Le **lloraron millones de personas**. Ocho murieron y cientos resultaron heridas durante una avalancha humana mientras se aproximaban al féretro a presentar sus respetos. El presidente, Alí Jamenei, se convirtió en líder supremo de Irán.

Vietnam prometió retirarse de Camboya a finales de septiembre, una década después de haber invadido el país (*véase* 1979). En una declaración del 5 de abril, también instaba al mundo a asegurarse de que la **guerra civil de Camboya** hubiera finalizado realmente y que **Pol Pot** (*véase* 1973), el líder de los jemeres rojos, no recuperara nunca el poder.

Hacer frente
La figura de este hombre, solo frente a los tanques militares en la plaza de Tiananmen (China) se convirtió en el símbolo de las protestas.

En China, una **manifestación** en la **plaza de Tiananmen** de Pekín, el 4 de junio, acabó convirtiéndose en un baño de sangre cuando el Ejército Popular de Liberación atacó a los civiles. Los tanques ocupaban las calles para enfrentarse a los manifestantes, estudiantes en su mayoría, que llevaban semanas acampados allí. La multitud, que superaba las cien mil personas, exigía reformas económicas y políticas para el país.

En febrero, casi una década después de haber invadido el país, el **ejército soviético se retiró** de Afganistán. Dejaron la economía en ruinas. Muchos afganos huyeron y la **guerra civil prosiguió**, en el intento de los **muyahidines** («guerreros», en persa) por derrocar al gobierno del presidente Nayibulah (*véase* 1992), que contaba con el apoyo soviético.

El 17 de abril, **Solidaridad**, el sindicato libre de Polonia, **fue legalizado** tras siete años de clandestinidad. Se transformó en partido político y ganó por una **mayoría abrumadora** en las elecciones siguientes, celebradas el 5 de junio. Tras 45 años, **el gobierno comunista en Polonia había llegado a su fin**. Solidaridad formó un nuevo gobierno no comunista en el antiguo Bloque Oriental. El 12 de septiembre, Tadeusz Mazowiecki fue nombrado primer ministro.

100 000
MANIFESTANTES

3000 muertos

Matanza en Tiananmen
El ejército chino mató a casi tres mil de los cien mil manifestantes que protestaban en la plaza de Tiananmen de Pekín.

A principios del año 1989, los regímenes comunistas llevaban unos 45 años gobernando en Europa del Este. A finales de ese mismo año habían sido derrocados por **alzamientos públicos** extraordinarios. Tras la elección de Solidaridad en Polonia, los dirigentes de Hungría publicaron un **plan para la independencia**. En **Bulgaria**, un golpe derrocó al líder del partido, Todor Zhivkov. El 28 de noviembre, el **régimen comunista** checoslovaco se rindió a la población. Un mes más tarde, Václav Havel se convirtió en el presidente de la República de Checoslovaquia, mediante la pacífica **Revolución de Terciopelo**. En Rumanía, el presidente, **Nicolae Ceaucescu** fue derrocado y **ejecutado de un disparo** en diciembre.

Erich Honecker, líder de la República Democrática Alemana, inició el año convencido de que las reformas en los países vecinos no afectarían al suyo, pero las protestas crecían sin cesar. El gobierno húngaro derribó la valla electrificada a lo largo de la frontera austríaca, parte del **Telón de Acero** (la custodiadísima frontera entre los países del Bloque Oriental y el resto de Europa). En septiembre, los **controles fronterizos se suspendieron** y sesenta mil alemanes de la RDA pasaron a Hungría con la intención de llegar a Occidente. Una **enorme manifestación que exigía**

ESPIONAJE EN LA GUERRA FRÍA

El espionaje se convirtió en uno de los símbolos de la Guerra Fría. La inteligencia, obtenida mediante aparatos electrónicos, satélites y espías se usaba con fines militares y tecnológicos. La CIA (Agencia Central de Inteligencia) de EE. UU., el KGB soviético y la policía secreta de Alemania Oriental, o Stasi (*véase* insignia), dedicaron décadas a espiar al enemigo y a socavarle con acciones encubiertas.

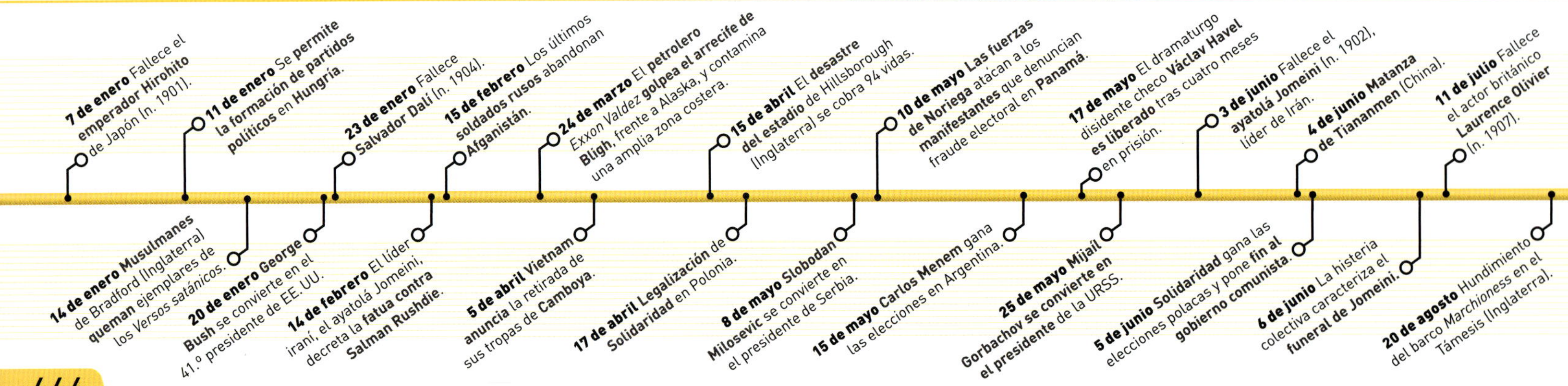

« HEMOS PERMANECIDO EN LA OSCURIDAD DURANTE DEMASIADO TIEMPO. HEMOS VISTO LA LUZ UNA VEZ, Y QUEREMOS VERLA DE NUEVO. »

Alexander Dubcek, líder checoslovaco (1989)

Manifestación multitudinaria por el fin del gobierno comunista en Hungría. El 23 de octubre se proclamó la República de Hungría, lo que marcó una nueva era en Europa.

La caída del Muro
Un guarda fronterizo de Alemania del Este atisba por una brecha del Muro de Berlín, cuyo derribo en 1989 se convirtió en un potente símbolo del fin del comunismo.

una reforma se reunió el 2 de octubre en Leipzig y decidió seguir reuniéndose hasta que sus exigencias se vieran satisfechas. El 9 de octubre, el ejército se negó a disparar a la multitud. Honecker abandonó el cargo el 18 de octubre.

Después de la caída del régimen de Honecker, Günter Schabowski, el líder del partido comunista de Berlín Oriental, anunció el 9 de noviembre que la **frontera con Berlín Occidental se abriría** para «viajes privados al extranjero». Esa misma noche, cincuenta mil berlineses acudieron al Muro de Berlín (*véase* 1961). Los guardias les dejaron pasar y, al otro lado, fueron recibidos por una multitud de berlineses occidentales exultantes de alegría. Por la mañana, empezaron a **derribar el Muro**.

El 3 de diciembre, EE. UU. y la URSS se reunieron en Malta y declararon el **fin de la Guerra Fría**. En una conferencia de prensa conjunta, a bordo del crucero ruso *Maxim Gorky*, el presidente George Bush (n. 1924) y el presidente Mijaíl Gorbachov (n. 1931) anunciaron sus planes para **reducir sustancialmente las armas** en Europa. Aunque fue aclamado internacionalmente, el paso supuso el debilitamiento de la postura de Gorbachov como líder soviético (*véanse* pp. 442–443).

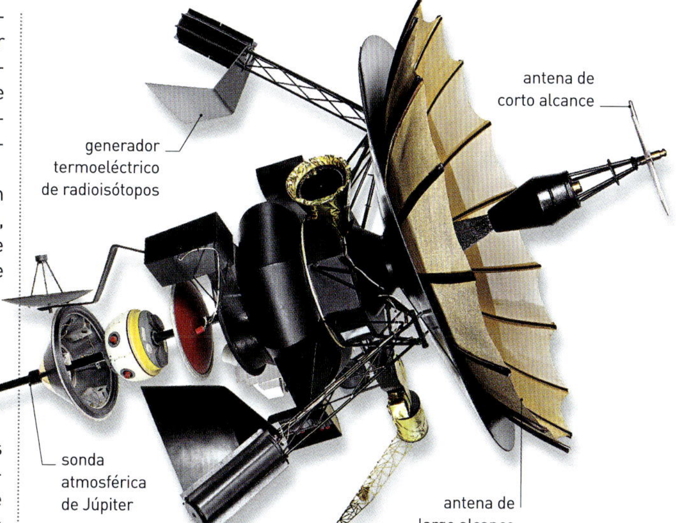

Sonda espacial *Galileo*
Bautizada en honor al astrónomo Galileo Galilei, la sonda se desplazó a más de 4500 millones de distancia y orbitó Júpiter 34 veces.

Kosovo, una provincia autónoma de Serbia, había empezado a exigir la independencia desde la muerte de Josip Tito (*véase* 1980). Cada vez **había más tensiones étnicas entre los serbios y los albanokosovares**, que querían controlar la provincia. Los serbios afirmaban ser perseguidos por la mayoría albanesa. Cuando **Slobodan Milosevic** llegó al poder el 8 de mayo, se escudó en esta supuesta persecución para **arrebatar la autonomía a Kosovo** y proclamarse adalid del nacionalismo serbio.

El 20 de diciembre, el **ejército estadounidense invadió Panamá** para intentar derribar al dictador Noriega. Más de doscientos civiles perdieron la vida durante el enfrentamiento, después del cual Guillermo Endara formó un nuevo gobierno.

En Nueva York, **Wall Street sufrió una caída** el viernes 13 de octubre, cuando el fallido intento de adquisición de American Airlines provocó el hundimiento de las acciones. Fue la segunda mayor caída del índice Dow Jones en toda la historia, y se le conoce como el **mini *crash* del viernes 13**.

EE. UU. lanzó *Galileo*, una **sonda no tripulada a Júpiter** y a sus lunas, a bordo del transbordador *Atlantis* el 18 de octubre. Con un coste de 1500 millones de dólares, *Galileo* llegó a su destino final en 1994, después de haber tomado imágenes detalladas de Venus por el camino.

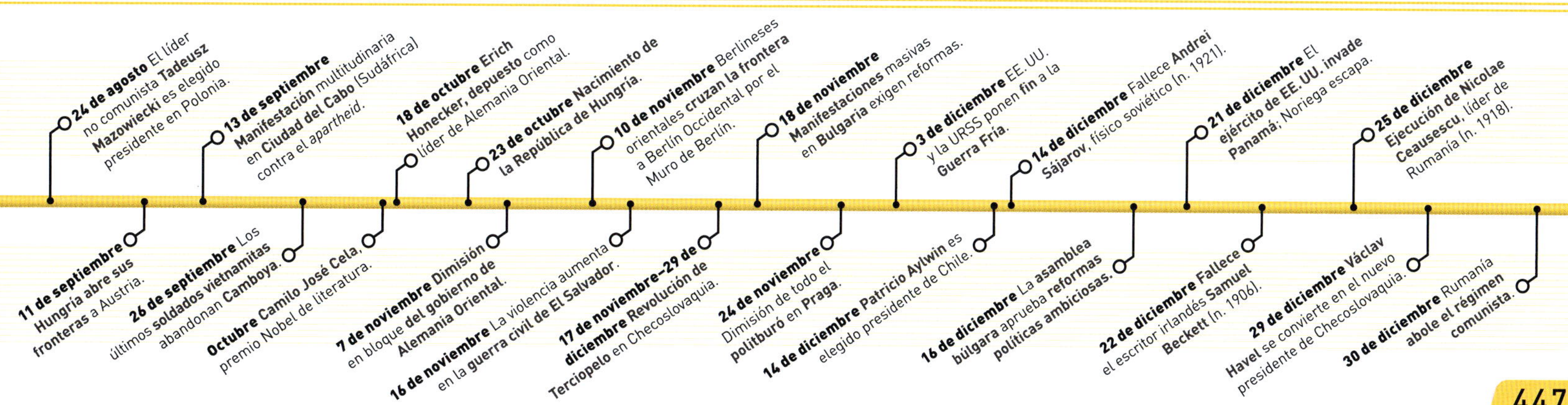

1990

« OS SALUDO EN NOMBRE DE LA PAZ, LA DEMOCRACIA Y LA LIBERTAD. »

Nelson Mandela, líder del ANC

Nelson Mandela y su esposa Winnie saludan victoriosos tras su liberación de la prisión Victor Verster, donde había permanecido prisionero durante 27 años.

EL 2 DE FEBRERO, EL PRESIDENTE DE KLERK LEVANTÓ LA PROHIBICIÓN sobre el Congreso Nacional Africano (ANC). Así empezó el largo proceso de **desmantelamiento del sistema del *apartheid***. De Klerk prosiguió con sus drásticas reformas y anunció que los proscritos Partido Comunista Sudafricano y Congreso Panafricanista podrían reanudar sus actividades políticas legales.

Nueve días más tarde, **Nelson Mandela** (1918–2013), el líder del ANC, **fue liberado** después de 27 años en prisión.

La vecina **Namibia** se convirtió en el 47.º país africano en **obtener la independencia** tras 25 años de gobierno sudafricano.

En América Central, se celebraron **elecciones libres en Nicaragua** el 25 de febrero. La Unión Nacional Opositora, una coalición de partidos políticos financiada por EE. UU., derrotó a los sandinistas, de izquierdas. Violeta Chamorro (n. 1929) se convirtió en la primera presidenta de Nicaragua.

En el golfo Pérsico, **Iraq invadió Kuwait** el 2 de agosto. La invasión llegó tras unas disputas fronterizas entre los dos países y ante la imposibilidad de Iraq de devolver a Kuwait el dinero que le había pedido prestado durante la guerra con Irán (*véase* 1980–1988). **Saddam Hussein** (1937–2006), líder iraquí, anunció que **Kuwait pasaba a formar parte de Iraq**. Los líderes mundiales condenaron la invasión y los países aliados, liderados por EE. UU., enviaron un ejército al golfo (*véase* 1991).

El 23 de agosto de este mismo año, Saddam Hussein apareció en televisión con **rehenes occidentales**, fundamentalmente de origen británico, que habían sido capturados en Iraq. Negó las acusaciones de estar utilizándoles como «escudo humano» ante un posible ataque liderado por EE. UU.

Más al norte, el ejército soviético llegó a Bakú (Azerbaiyán) la tarde del 19 de enero para reducir a un grupo separatista de **nacionalistas azerbaiyanos**. Al día siguiente, miles de azerbaiyanos quemaban sus carnés de pertenencia al Partido Comunista.

LECH WALESA (n. 1943)

Lech Walesa fue uno de los fundadores del sindicato Solidaridad, en Polonia, y le concedieron el premio Nobel de la paz en 1983. En 1990 se convirtió en el primer presidente de la Polonia poscomunista. No logró ser reelegido, pues su errático estilo de liderazgo molestó a sus votantes.

Alemania se reunificó el 3 de octubre, casi un año después de la caída del Muro de Berlín (*véase* 1989), y Helmut Kohl (n. 1930) fue elegido primer canciller del país reunificado.

El 1 de diciembre, bajo **el Canal de la Mancha**, el túnel ferroviario submarino más largo del mundo, que unía Gran Bretaña y Francia, dio un paso más hacia su finalización. Los trabajadores perforaron el último tramo de roca que unía las dos mitades del túnel.

Zona de guerra *Iraq invadió a la vecina Kuwait, una pequeña nación árabe rica en petróleo. La ocupación, que duró siete meses, terminó tras la intervención militar liderada por EE. UU., en la Operación Tormenta del Desierto, fundamentalmente una ofensiva aérea.*

1991

Un hombre intenta sofocar el incendio de un pozo de petróleo en Burhan (Kuwait). El ejército iraquí incendió más de 600 campos de petróleo durante su ocupación.

EL EJÉRCITO SOVIÉTICO IRRUMPIÓ EN LITUANIA para reprimir a los nacionalistas disidentes el 13 de enero. Murieron catorce personas y más de quinientas resultaron heridas en la operación. Los manifestantes se habían reunido para proteger una emisora de televisión, tras un programa en que se había llamado al pueblo a defender los edificios públicos de los soldados soviéticos.

El 13 de junio, **Boris Yeltsin** (1931–2007) se convirtió en el primer presidente de Rusia elegido por el pueblo, lo que supuso una gran derrota para el Partido Comunista. La victoria le permitió enfrentarse al líder de la Unión Soviética, Mijaíl Gorbachov (n. 1931).

Un **golpe militar** intentó deponer a Gorbachov mientras estaba de vacaciones en agosto. Yeltsin organizó la resistencia y los golpistas se rindieron el 21 de agosto. Entonces, Yeltsin ordenó al **Partido Comunista de la Unión Soviética que cesara toda actividad** en Rusia.

Bajas de la guerra (Iraq-Kuwait) *La superioridad de las fuerzas de la coalición se refleja en la gran desproporción de las bajas sufridas por el ejército iraquí.*

El mundo presenció con incredulidad la **desintegración de la URSS** en **quince países diferentes**. El 8 de diciembre, los dirigentes de tres de las quince repúblicas de la Unión Soviética (Rusia, Ucrania y Bielorrusia) se reunieron para disolver la Unión Soviética y formar una nueva unión, la **Comunidad de Estados Independientes**, a la que el 21 de diciembre se unieron otras ocho. Cuatro días después, Mijaíl Gorbachov anunciaba su dimisión como presidente soviético; **la URSS había dejado de existir**.

Yugoslavia también se desmembraba: **Eslovenia y Croacia declararon su independencia** en junio. Slobodan Milosevic, el presidente serbio, envió al ejército a ambas zonas para impedir la secesión. La ciudad de Vukovar quedó asolada tras el sitio serbio, de tres meses de duración y que terminó en diciembre.

En **Irlanda del Norte**, los principales partidos políticos celebraron una **reunión histórica** el 18 de junio para debatir el futuro de la provincia tras años de violencia sectaria; el deseo de la población de que el baño de sangre finalizara era abrumador.

El 30 de octubre también se celebraron **conversaciones de paz** para **Oriente Medio**, entre árabes e israelíes, en España. Era la primera vez en cuarenta años que Israel se sentaba con todos sus vecinos árabes para hablar de paz.

La ONU lanzó un ultimátum a Saddam Hussein para que retirara

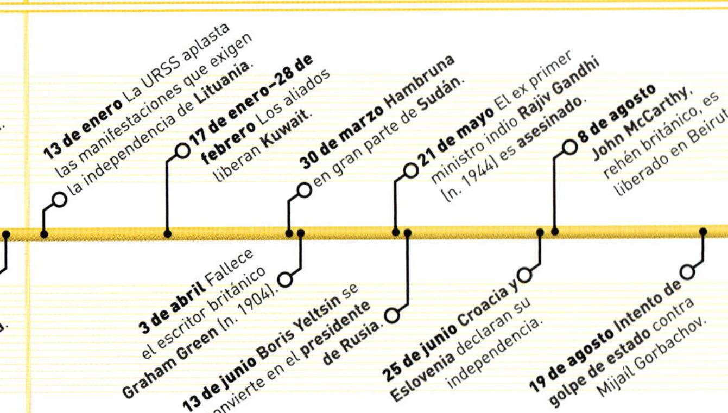

- **19 de enero** El **ejército soviético aplasta a los manifestantes** que reclaman la independencia de Azerbaiyán.
- **11 de febrero** Liberación de **Nelson Mandela**, líder del ANC.
- **2 de febrero Sudáfrica** legaliza el **Congreso Nacional Africano** (ANC).
- **25 de febrero Elecciones libres** en **Nicaragua**.
- **21 de marzo Namibia** consigue la independencia.
- **31 de marzo** Disturbios en Londres en contra de la *poll tax* (impuesto sobre el sufragio).
- **2 de agosto** Iraq invade **Kuwait**.
- **Octubre Octavio Paz** recibe el premio Nobel de literatura.
- **24 de agosto** Los extremistas islámicos **liberan** al rehén irlandés **Brian Keenan** en el Líbano.
- **27 de noviembre John Major sucede a Margaret Thatcher** como primer ministro británico.
- **3 de octubre** Reunificación de **Alemania**.
- **9 de diciembre Lech Walesa** se convierte en el **presidente de Polonia**.
- **13 de enero** La URSS aplasta las manifestaciones que exigen la independencia de **Lituania**.
- **17 de enero–28 de febrero** Los aliados liberan **Kuwait**.
- **3 de abril** Fallece el escritor británico **Graham Green** (n. 1904).
- **30 de marzo Hambruna** en gran parte de **Sudán**.
- **13 de junio Boris Yeltsin** se convierte en el **presidente de Rusia**.
- **21 de mayo** El ex primer ministro indio **Rajiv Gandhi** (n. 1944) es **asesinado**.
- **25 de junio Croacia y Eslovenia** declaran su independencia.
- **8 de agosto John McCarthy**, rehén británico, es liberado en Beirut.
- **19 de agosto Intento de golpe de estado** contra Mijaíl Gorbachov.

AUSTRIA
HUNGRÍA
Liubliana
ESLOVENIA
Zagreb
CROACIA
Voivodina
Novi Sad
RUMANÍA
Belgrado
BOSNIA-HERZEGOVINA
Sarajevo
SERBIA
Mar Adriático
MONTENEGRO
Prístina
BULGARIA
Titogrado
Kosovo
Skopje
MACEDONIA
ITALIA
ALBANIA
GRECIA

La división de Yugoslavia
Tras 72 años de existencia, Yugoslavia desapareció del mapa después de que la guerra y los disturbios políticos llevaran a la formación de seis países independientes.

CLAVE
Nuevos países

a su ejército de Kuwait el 15 de enero. Ante su negativa, el 17 de enero EE. UU. y las fuerzas de coalición lanzaron la **Operación Tormenta del Desierto**, también conocida como **primera guerra del Golfo** (1990–1991). Kuwait fue liberada en cinco semanas.

La primera guerra del Golfo dejó a Saddam Hussein en una posición vulnerable en Iraq. Los **musulmanes chiíes** se alzaron **contra el gobierno** en el sur y los **kurdos** se levantaron en el norte. Miles de personas murieron en la represión de las revueltas en marzo y abril.

En India, **Rajiv Gandhi** (n. 1944), el ex primer ministro del país, fue **asesinado** el 21 de mayo. Murió en un atentado con bomba en Sriperumbudur, durante la campaña de su partido para las próximas elecciones. Más adelante se atribuyó el atentado a una terrorista suicida de los Tigres de Liberación del Eelam Tamil (LTTE), también conocidos como los **Tigres Tamiles**.

El 8 de agosto, **John McCarthy**, periodista británico que un grupo islámico extremista retenía en el Líbano, fue liberado tras **cinco años en cautividad** (*véase* 1986). Más tarde ese mismo año, también se liberó al británico Terry Waite y a los estadounidenses Terry Anderson y Tom Sutherland.

1992

Residentes de Sarajevo (Bosnia) se protegen de los tiros de francotiradores durante una manifestación pacífica contra la guerra de Bosnia, en la que los serbios radicales abrieron fuego contra los manifestantes.

LA IDEA DE UNA EUROPA UNIDA SE ACERCÓ A LA REALIDAD cuando los líderes de doce países europeos firmaron el **tratado de la Unión Europea** y el **tratado de Maastricht** el 7 de febrero. Anunciaba la libre circulación de personas, así como políticas económicas y de defensa comunes.

La división de Yugoslavia prosiguió y **Bosnia-Herzegovina declaró su independencia** el 3 de marzo. Pero los serbios residentes en Bosnia se resistieron y **estalló la guerra**; el ejército yugoslavo, a las órdenes de Slobodan Milosevic, atacó a la población musulmana de Bosnia. Los serbobosnios asediaron la capital, Sarajevo. Los víveres empezaron a escasear y la población tuvo dificultades para subsistir (*véase* 1996). En agosto, las imágenes de los **campos de concentración serbios**, en las que se veía a personas muriendo de hambre tras las alambradas, provocaron la repulsa internacional. Los campos, mayoritariamente en Bosnia, formaban parte de la **«política de limpieza étnica»** de Serbia, cuyo objetivo era eliminar al resto de grupos étnicos de las comunidades mayoritariamente serbias. El 20 de diciembre, **Slobodan Milosevic fue reelegido** como presidente serbio. El primer ministro, Milan Panic, denunció un fraude electoral y pidió que se repitieran las elecciones, pero al cabo de nueve días perdió una moción de censura parlamentaria.

El presidente argelino, **Mohamed Budiaf**, fue **asesinado** el 29 de junio durante un mitin en Annaba. Budiaf había ejercido un papel crucial en la rebelión contra Francia (*véase* 1958), y había vuelto recientemente del exilio para ayudar al gobierno a combatir al Frente de Salvación Islámico, partido fundamentalista a quienes muchos atribuyeron su asesinato.

Marines de EE. UU. llegaron el 9 de diciembre a las costas de **Somalia**, que estaba **asolada por la hambruna**, pero que no podía acceder a la ayuda exterior por la extorsión y el pillaje. La operación liderada por EE. UU. tenía el objetivo de tomar el aeropuerto de Mogadiscio para permitir el transporte de víveres a la población hambrienta.

El departamento de **policía de Los Ángeles** fue acusado de **racismo y violencia** tras la difusión de un video en el que se veía a cuatro policías apaleando a un hombre de color, **Rodney King**, en 1991. Los policías fueron exonerados tras el juicio, lo que provocó **disturbios raciales** el 29 de abril, que se saldaron con 55 víctimas mortales.

El 4 de noviembre, el demócrata **Bill Clinton** (n. 1946) **derrotó** a **George Bush** (n. 1924) en las elecciones de EE. UU. Clinton prometió reactivar la economía de EE. UU.

6000
BOSNIOS Y CROATAS RETENIDOS EN EL CAMPO DE EXTERMINIO DE OMARSKA

CASCOS AZULES

Las fuerzas de paz de la ONU se crearon tras la Segunda Guerra Mundial para que se interpusieran entre países o comunidades en guerra y detuvieran la lucha. En 1948 ejercieron por primera vez de observadores, en el armisticio entre Israel y los estados árabes. Sus funciones se han visto muy ampliadas: comprueban el cumplimiento de los derechos humanos, desactivan minas terrestres, supervisan elecciones e intervienen en estados fallidos. En 1992 habían realizado 26 intervenciones en el mundo.

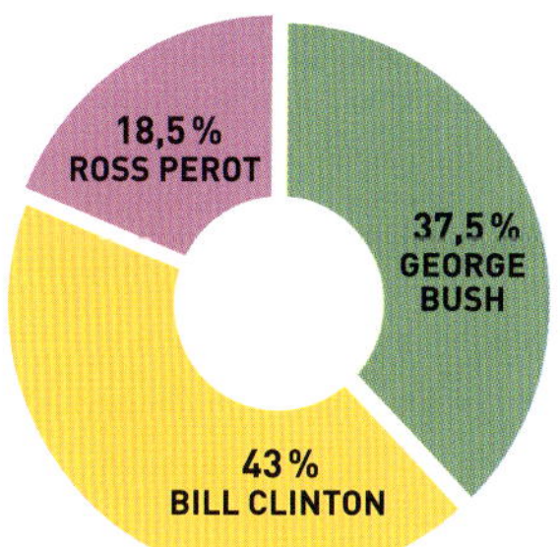

La victoria de Clinton
Bill Clinton se convirtió en el 42.º presidente de EE. UU., tras derrotar a sus oponentes, Ross Perot y George Bush.

20 de agosto **Estonia vota** a favor de la independencia.
26 de agosto El ejército serbio **destruye Vukovar** (Croacia).
29 de agosto El parlamento soviético **suspende todas las actividades comunistas.**
8 de septiembre **Macedonia** declara su independencia.
26 de octubre El ejército serbio bombardea **Dubrovnik.**
30 de octubre España acoge las históricas **conversaciones de paz de Oriente Medio.**
5 de noviembre Fallece el ex parlamentario y magnate de los medios de comunicación británico **Robert Maxwell** (n. 1923).
19 de noviembre El rehén **Terry Waite es liberado** en Beirut.
23 de noviembre **Vukovar se rinde** al ejército de Yugoslavia.
2 de diciembre **Ucrania** vota su independencia.
25 de diciembre **Mijaíl Gorbachov dimite** como presidente soviético.

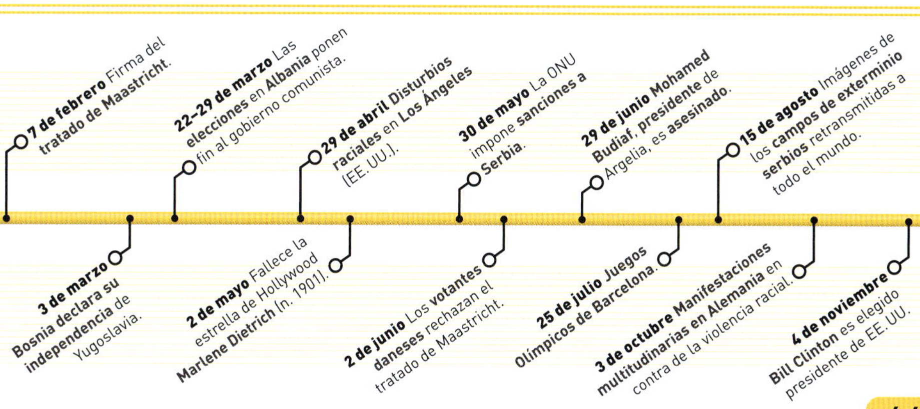

1993

Praga, en la imagen, famosa por la riqueza arquitectónica de su casco antiguo, se convirtió en la capital de la recién formada república Checa. El castillo es la residencia oficial del jefe de estado checo.

EL MERCADO ÚNICO ENTRÓ EN VIGOR en los países miembro de la Unión Europea (UE) en enero. Permitía a sus ciudadanos vivir y trabajar en otros países de la UE y allanaba el camino a la moneda única, el **euro**.

El 1 de enero, **Checoslovaquia se escindió en Eslovaquia y la República Checa**, lo que puso fin a los 74 años de la federación. La creación de la República Checa, con capital en Praga, y de Eslovaquia, con capital en Bratislava, llegó a conocerse como el Divorcio de Terciopelo, en alusión a la Revolución de Terciopelo (*véase* 1989).

La oposición a la **terapia de choque** del presidente ruso, **Boris Yeltsin** (1931–2007), consistente en un programa de reformas iniciado en 1992, era cada vez mayor. Las medidas tenían el fin de flexibilizar el control del estado sobre la economía y facilitar el avance hacia una economía de mercado, pero se criticaron por capitalistas y occidentalizantes. El parlamento ruso trató de presentar una moción de censura contra Yeltsin, pero este respondió con un decreto que **disolvió el parlamento** el 21 de septiembre. Ante la creciente presión de sus oponentes políticos, Yeltsin ordenó a los parlamentarios que abandonaran el edificio del parlamento y, cuando se negaron, envió al ejército para que lo tomara.

Varias **explosiones en cadena** hicieron temblar Bombay, la capital económica de India, el 12 de marzo. Se produjeron 257 muertos y 713 heridos. Los atentados se atribuyeron a grupos del crimen organizado.

El **Ejército Republicano Irlandés** (IRA) colocó una **bomba de gran potencia** en la **City londinense**, el 24 de abril, un mes después de que otra explosión en Warrington matara a dos niños. Ese mismo año, el 15 de diciembre, los líderes de Irlanda del Norte y de Gran Bretaña se reunieron y firmaron una declaración de paz con el objetivo de poner fin a la violencia en la provincia.

Israel y la **Organización para la Liberación de Palestina** (OLP) también dieron pasos hacia la paz con la firma de los **acuerdos de Oslo** en Washington DC, en presencia del presidente estadounidense Bill Clinton (n. 1946), en septiembre. Los acuerdos suponían un reconocimiento mutuo y fueron la culminación de unas reuniones secretas entre ambas partes, a instancias del gobierno noruego.

El 19 de abril, el **sitio** a la sede de una secta religiosa estadounidense, los davidianos, terminó con un incendio en el que murieron al menos setenta personas, inclusive el líder de la secta, **David Koresh**. El FBI rodeaba el edificio desde febrero, cuando cuatro agentes de la Agencia de Alcohol, Tabaco, Armas de Fuego y Explosivos (ATF) habían muerto al intentar arrestar a Koresh por tenencia ilícita de armas.

187 MUERTOS

437 HERIDOS

Bajas del golpe
El presidente ruso Boris Yeltsin asumió la autoridad absoluta cuando irrumpió en el parlamento de Moscú para poner fin a la rebelión de los opositores de línea dura.

Puente de Mostar
Un puente del siglo XVI cruzó el río Neretva durante 427 años, hasta que quedó destruido por las batallas entre croatas y musulmanes.

1994

La guerra en Ruanda provocó una huida de refugiados a Zaire.

EN SUDÁFRICA, LOS ZULÚES Y LOS MIEMBROS DEL CONGRESO NACIONAL AFRICANO (ANC) se enfrentaron el 28 de marzo, y más de dieciocho personas murieron. Los zulúes habían respondido a sus líderes, que les habían llamado a boicotear las elecciones nacionales, que, al final, se celebraron el 10 de mayo. **Nelson Mandela** se convirtió en el **primer presidente negro de Sudáfrica**, tras más de tres siglos de gobierno blanco. Su partido, el ANC (*véase* recuadro), obtuvo 252 de los 400 escaños en las **primeras elecciones democráticas** en la historia de Sudáfrica.

El presidente de Ruanda, **Juvenal Habyarimana** (n. 1937), de etnia hutu, murió cuando su **avión** se estrelló tras ser **atacado** mientras sobrevolaba el aeropuerto de Kigali. El incidente desencadenó un **genocidio en masa**. Entre abril y junio, **murieron unos 800 000 ruandeses**, la mayoría de ellos de etnia tutsi, a mano de hutus.

El 1 de julio, el presidente de la OLP, **Yasser Arafat** (1929–2004), regresó a la **franja de Gaza** tras haber pasado **27 años en el exilio**. Este gesto marcó el principio de la aplicación de los principios acordados en Oslo y firmados en Washington DC, el año anterior (*véase* 1993).

Israel y **Jordania** firmaron un tratado el 26 de octubre y pusieron **fin a 46 años de guerra**. Bill Clinton, presidente de EE. UU., fue testigo del tratado entre el primer ministro israelí, Isaac Rabin (1922–1995) y el rey Husein en una ceremonia en Aravá, en la frontera jordano-israelí.

El 31 de agosto, el **IRA declaró un alto el fuego** tras 25 años de lucha

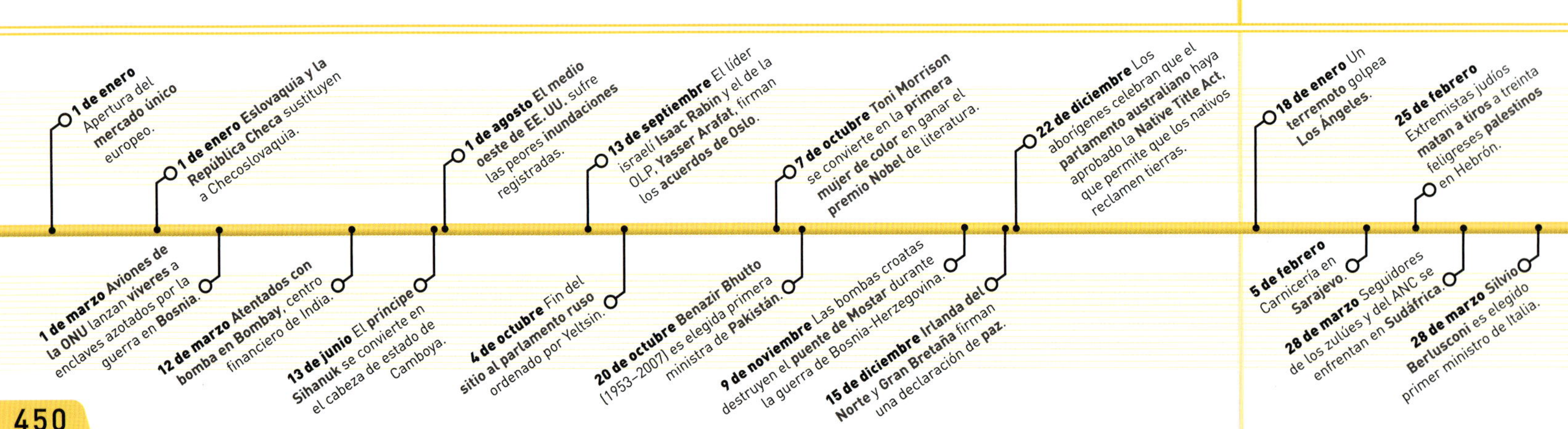

armada contra el gobierno británico en Irlanda del Norte. Con este gesto, el IRA deseaba mostrar su disposición a iniciar **conversaciones de paz** sobre el futuro de la provincia. El primer ministro irlandés, Albert Reynolds, pidió a los paramilitares lealistas que emprendieran la misma senda. Pero los lealistas desconfiaban de la declaración y temían que la pertenencia de Irlanda del Norte a Gran Bretaña se viera amenazada; al final, el 13 de octubre anunciaron su propio alto el fuego.

La guerra proseguía en Bosnia-Herzegovina y, el 5 de febrero, un mercado en el centro de **Sarajevo quedó muy dañado** por una bomba de mortero que mató a 68 personas e hirió a otras 200. La comunidad internacional condenó la atrocidad, atribuida a los serbios.

Mundial para Brasil
Marcio Santos, de Brasil, sostiene el trofeo de la Copa del Mundo de la FIFA para celebrar la victoria. Brasil derrotó a Italia en la final.

Viaje inaugural del Eurostar
El tren de alta velocidad que atraviesa el túnel del Canal de la Mancha hizo su viaje inaugural en 1994.

El 11 de diciembre, el ruso Boris Yeltsin envió al ejército a la **región rebelde de Chechenia** para impedir que se separara del país. La región, de mayoría musulmana, había **declarado su independencia de Moscú** tres años antes, bajo el liderazgo del general Dzyojar Dudayev.

El 19 de septiembre, **EE.UU. lideró una fuerza de invasión en Haití** para poner fin a la junta militar y reinstaurar la democracia con el presidente Aristide, exiliado tres años antes. No se disparó ni un solo tiro.

La **reina Isabel** (n. 1926) de Inglaterra y el **presidente François Mitterrand** (1916–1996) de Francia, **inauguraron** formalmente el **túnel del Canal de la Mancha** el 6 de mayo. Se había tardado ocho años en construir este túnel, que comunicaba Inglaterra con Francia.

El ***MS Estonia***, un *ferry* de automóviles y pasajeros, **se hundió en el mar Báltico** el 28 de septiembre. Murieron 852 pasajeros, la mitad de los cuales eran suecos. La investigación del accidente reveló que la mala mar, la falta de mantenimiento y la elevada velocidad se habían conjurado para causar el desastre.

Millones de espectadores presenciaron horrorizados cómo el campeón del mundo de Fórmula 1, **Ayrton Senna**, se salía de la pista en el Gran Premio de San Marino el 1 de mayo en un **accidente mortal**. Se celebró un funeral de estado en su ciudad natal, São Paulo. Senna era un héroe nacional en Brasil y había donado millones para ayudar a los niños desfavorecidos del país.

CONGRESO NACIONAL AFRICANO (ANC)

Fundado en 1912 con el fin de fomentar los derechos de la población sudafricana de color, el ANC llegó al poder en 1994, cuando Mandela fue elegido presidente del país. El ANC sigue contando con un apoyo mayoritario, pero le han afectado luchas internas de poder entre los sucesores de Mandela, escándalos de corrupción y los desafíos que plantean la pobreza y el sida en el país.

1995

« EL **MAYOR FRACASO DE OCCIDENTE DESDE** LA DÉCADA DE **1930**. »

Richard Holbrooke, subsecretario de Estado de EE. UU., sobre la crisis de Bosnia

UN TERREMOTO DESTROZÓ LA CIUDAD DE KOBE (JAPÓN) el 17 de enero. Con una magnitud de 7,2 grados en la escala de Richter, dejó cientos de muertos y miles de heridos.

Barings, un banco de inversiones inglés, se **declaró en bancarrota** después de que un empleado, Nick Leeson, hubiera arriesgado enormes cantidades de dinero en el mercado de valores japonés, pues el índice Nikkei se hundió tras el terremoto de Kobe.

El 20 de marzo, **Turquía lanzó una importante campaña militar** con más de 35 000 soldados contra los **kurdos**, en el norte de Iraq. Se trataba de un intento de perseguir a los kurdos turcos rebeldes, que habían huido a la región, y de impedir así que se instalaran en bases permanentes. Los kurdos habían emprendido una lucha armada en 1984, en busca de un territorio independiente, y se quejaban de la falta de derechos de los kurdos en

La crisis del ébola (1995)
En Zaire hubo un brote de ébola. De los 315 casos detectados, 254 acabaron en muerte, lo que supone una tasa de mortalidad del 81 %.

Bomba en Oklahoma
Un camión bomba estalló frente al edificio federal Alfred P. Murrah, en Oklahoma (EE. UU.) el 19 de abril. Se percibió a 48 km de distancia.

Turquía. El gobierno turco responsabiliza al **Partido Obrero de Kurdistán (PKK)** de más de treinta mil muertes durante el conflicto. Las repetidas operaciones militares turcas contra el PKK no han sido efectivas, y el conflicto aún perdura.

Una potente **bomba explotó en la ciudad de Oklahoma** (EE. UU.) el 19 de abril y 168 personas murieron. Timothy McVeigh, veterano de la guerra del Golfo, fue encarcelado por el ataque, una reacción a cómo había gestionado el gobierno el **sitio de Waco** (*véase* 1993).

Srebrenica, enclave musulmán declarado lugar seguro por la ONU, fue **invadido por serbobosnios** el 10 de julio, quienes efectuaron una «limpieza étnica» de la ciudad. En diciembre, los líderes de Bosnia, Serbia y Croacia firmaron los **acuerdos de paz de Dayton**, en París, y pusieron fin a tres años de guerra en Bosnia.

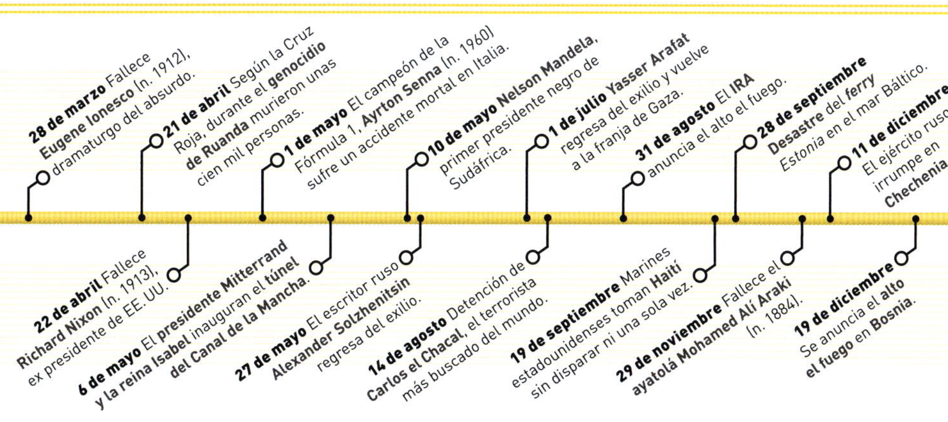

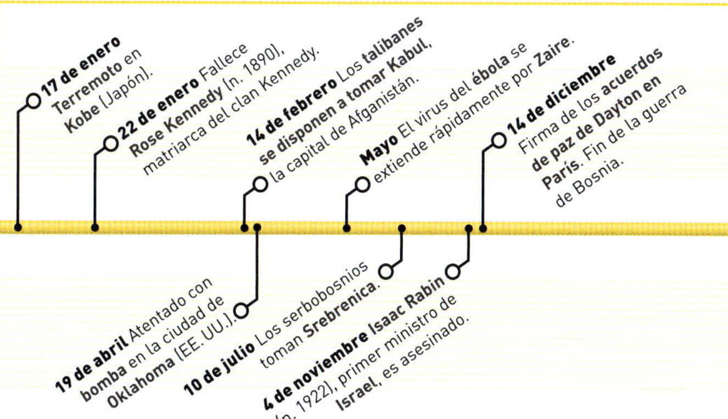

AMPLIACIONES DE LA UNIÓN EUROPEA

1957 Se firma el tratado de Roma, por el que se crea la Comunidad Económica Europea (CEE), con seis miembros.

1973 Acta de adhesión: Reino Unido, Dinamarca e Irlanda se incorporan a la UE, ahora con nueve estados miembro.

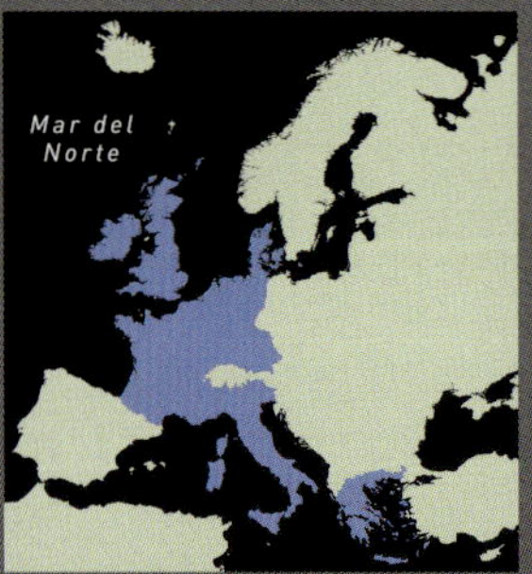

1981 Grecia se convierte en el décimo miembro de la UE. Solicitó el ingreso en 1979, tras la restauración de la democracia.

1986 España y Portugal se integran en la UE. El Acta Única Europea se firma en 1987, con el fin de crear un mercado único.

1995 Austria, Finlandia y Suecia se unen a la UE, que ahora se compone de quince países.

LA UNIÓN EUROPEA

DE LAS RUINAS DE UNA GUERRA SURGE UN CONTINENTE UNIDO

Tras la Segunda Guerra Mundial, Europa quedó empobrecida, temerosa de más guerras y muy inestable. Impulsadas por el deseo de una paz y una unidad que hicieran imposible otra guerra, seis naciones se unieron económicamente en 1957. Desde entonces, la Unión Europea ha crecido sustancialmente.

La era moderna de la Unión Europea (UE) empezó en 1987, con la firma del Acta Única Europea, un intento de reforzar la unión de Europa y de crear un «mercado único». La UE fomenta la cooperación en el medio ambiente, el transporte y el empleo. La ciudadanía europea y la introducción del euro han facilitado el trabajo, los desplazamientos y los negocios, y la UE se ha convertido en la mayor economía del mundo. Los partidarios de ampliar la UE subrayan esto, junto con los beneficios de la estabilidad política. A los críticos les preocupa la pérdida de soberanía, la inmigración, la enorme burocracia y el coste de gestionar la organización.

20 PAÍSES CON EL **EURO COMO** MONEDA OFICIAL

Irlanda
PIB: 529 700 millones de dólares
Población: 5 194 336

Portugal
PIB: 252 400 millones de dólares
Población: 10 467 366

La población de la UE
La UE tiene más de 448 millones de habitantes, lo que equivale a un 5,7 % de la población mundial. Con menos de la mitad del territorio de EE. UU., su población es un 35 % mayor.

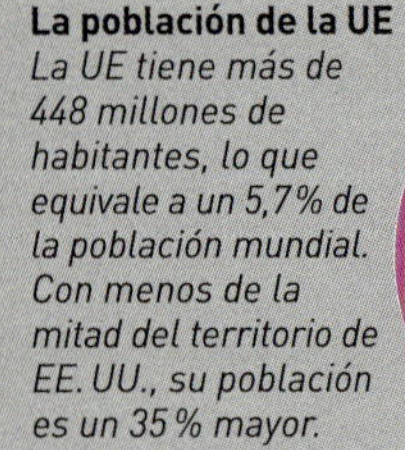
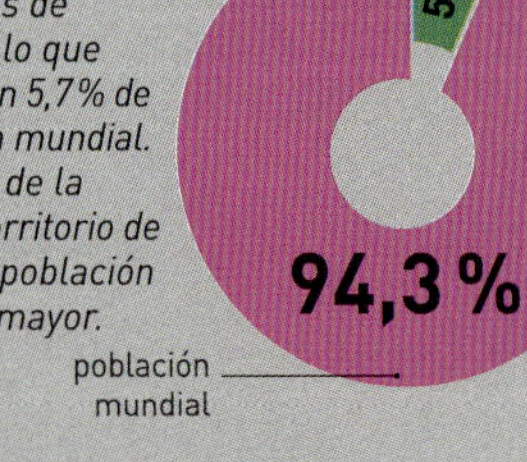

3:4 **Vida urbana**
La población de la UE es fundamentalmente urbana: el 75 % de sus habitantes viven en ciudades y no en áreas rurales. En comparación, solo el 45 % de la población africana es urbanita.

Comparación demográfica
La población de la UE es la tercera más grande del mundo, por detrás de India y China.

INDIA 1 429 000 000
CHINA 1 426 000 000
UE 448 000 000

« **EUROPA** ES LA FUERZA QUE IMPIDE QUE EL ODIO **SEA ETERNO**. DEBEMOS ABRIR NUESTROS **CORAZONES** A ESTA NUEVA **EUROPA**. »

Jean-Pierre Raffarin, primer ministro francés (2004)

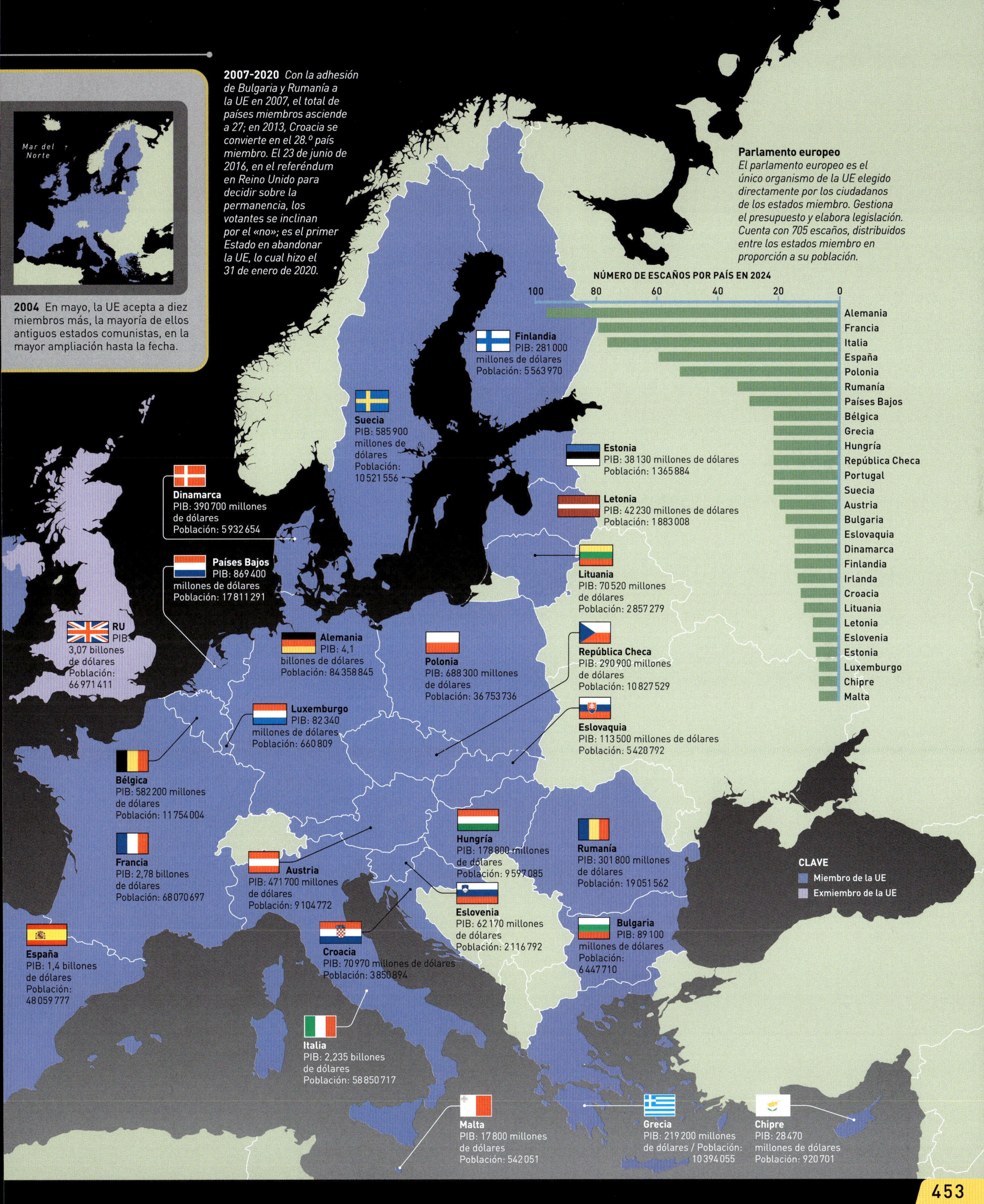

2007-2020 Con la adhesión de Bulgaria y Rumanía a la UE en 2007, el total de países miembros asciende a 27; en 2013, Croacia se convierte en el 28.º país miembro. El 23 de junio de 2016, en el referéndum en Reino Unido para decidir sobre la permanencia, los votantes se inclinan por el «no»; es el primer Estado en abandonar la UE, lo cual hizo el 31 de enero de 2020.
Mar del Norte
2004 En mayo, la UE acepta a diez miembros más, la mayoría de ellos antiguos estados comunistas, en la mayor ampliación hasta la fecha.
Parlamento europeo
El parlamento europeo es el único organismo de la UE elegido directamente por los ciudadanos de los estados miembro. Gestiona el presupuesto y elabora legislación. Cuenta con 705 escaños, distribuidos entre los estados miembro en proporción a su población.
NÚMERO DE ESCAÑOS POR PAÍS EN 2024
100
80
60
40
20
0
Alemania
Francia
Italia
España
Polonia
Rumanía
Países Bajos
Bélgica
Grecia
Hungría
República Checa
Portugal
Suecia
Austria
Bulgaria
Eslovaquia
Dinamarca
Finlandia
Irlanda
Croacia
Lituania
Letonia
Eslovenia
Estonia
Luxemburgo
Chipre
Malta
Finlandia PIB: 281 000 millones de dólares Población: 5 563 970
Suecia PIB: 585 900 millones de dólares Población: 10 521 556
Estonia PIB: 38 130 millones de dólares Población: 1 365 884
Letonia PIB: 42 230 millones de dólares Población: 1 883 008
Dinamarca PIB: 390 700 millones de dólares Población: 5 932 654
Países Bajos PIB: 869 400 millones de dólares Población: 17 811 291
Lituania PIB: 70 520 millones de dólares Población: 2 857 279
RU PIB: 3,07 billones de dólares Población: 66 971 411
Alemania PIB: 4,1 billones de dólares Población: 84 358 845
Polonia PIB: 688 300 millones de dólares Población: 36 753 736
República Checa PIB: 290 900 millones de dólares Población: 10 827 529
Luxemburgo PIB: 82 340 millones de dólares Población: 660 809
Eslovaquia PIB: 113 500 millones de dólares Población: 5 428 792
Bélgica PIB: 582 200 millones de dólares Población: 11 754 004
Hungría PIB: 178 800 millones de dólares Población: 9 597 085
Rumanía PIB: 301 800 millones de dólares Población: 19 051 562
Francia PIB: 2,78 billones de dólares Población: 68 070 697
Austria PIB: 471 700 millones de dólares Población: 9 104 772
CLAVE
Miembro de la UE
Exmiembro de la UE
Eslovenia PIB: 62 170 millones de dólares Población: 2 116 792
Bulgaria PIB: 89 100 millones de dólares Población: 6 447 710
España PIB: 1,4 billones de dólares Población: 48 059 777
Croacia PIB: 70 970 millones de dólares Población: 3 850 894
Italia PIB: 2,235 billones de dólares Población: 58 850 717
Malta PIB: 17 800 millones de dólares Población: 542 051
Grecia PIB: 219 200 millones de dólares / Población: 10 394 055
Chipre PIB: 28 470 millones de dólares Población: 920 701

1996

La oveja Dolly, el primer mamífero clonado a partir del ADN de un ejemplar adulto, en su establo del Instituto Roslin, en Edimburgo (Escocia).

EL LÍDER CHECHENO Salmán Radúyev recibió un disparo el 6 de marzo y se le dio por muerto (en realidad estaba en el extranjero, donde recibía tratamiento médico). Rusia y Chechenia firmaron un **alto el fuego** (*véase* 1994) el 31 de agosto.

En **Rumanía**, la Convención Democrática de Rumanía ganó las elecciones y puso fin a 48 años de gobierno comunista.

En **Afganistán**, los rebeldes talibanes tomaron Kabul el 27 de septiembre: había estallado la guerra civil.

La guerra civil kurda proseguía y, el 31 de agosto, Iraq tomó una ciudad situada dentro del perímetro de seguridad protegido por el ejército de la ONU. En respuesta, EE. UU. lanzó la **Operación Desert Strike** y atacó con misiles varios objetivos militares iraquíes.

17 **MESES** DURÓ EL **ALTO EL FUEGO** DEL **IRA**

El **IRA** (Ejército Republicano Irlandés) hizo explotar una bomba en los Docklands de Londres el 10 de febrero, con lo que puso fin a diecisiete meses de alto el fuego (*véase* 1994), periodo durante el cual ambas partes habían intentado encontrar una solución a los problemas políticos de Irlanda del Norte.

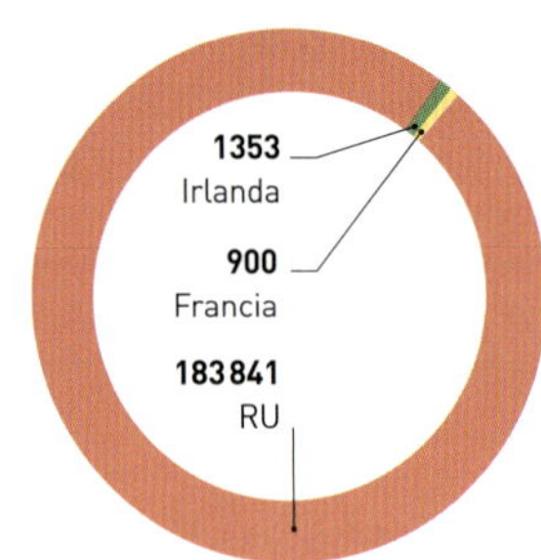

Casos de EEB
La encefalopatía espongiforme bovina (EEB), o enfermedad de las vacas locas, generó una gran alarma en Europa. La mayoría de los casos de EEB se detectaron en Reino Unido.

El presidente de EE. UU., **Bill Clinton**, volvió a ganar las elecciones el 6 de noviembre. El 12 de diciembre reformó su gabinete y **Madeleine Albright** se convirtió en la primera mujer en ocupar el cargo de secretaria de Estado en EE. UU.

La ciencia real y la ciencia ficción se dieron la mano con el nacimiento de la oveja **Dolly** el 5 de julio en Edimburgo (Escocia). Fue el primer mamífero **clonado** a partir de una célula adulta.

Compras por Internet
En 1996, eBay, la página de subastas online, creció mucho gracias a una ingeniosa tecnología y a un foro para puntuar a compradores y vendedores.

1997

1 835 300 000

DE DÓLARES FUE LA RECAUDACIÓN BRUTA EN **TAQUILLA** DE LA PELÍCULA *TITANIC*

LA VIOLENCIA EN ZAIRE SE INTENSIFICÓ en febrero, lo que no hizo más que aumentar la desventura de los refugiados hutu de Ruanda, que habían huido hasta allí para escapar de la guerra civil en Ruanda. En abril, soldados rebeldes, sobre todo tutsis, cerraron los campos en Zaire oriental, donde los refugiados quedaron atrapados en condiciones espantosas. Miles de ellos fueron asesinados. El gobierno de Zaire se disolvió el 3 de abril, y **Étienne Tshisekedi** (n. 1932) se convirtió en el primer ministro del nuevo gobierno. La violencia siguió agravándose y 56 000 zaireños huyeron a Tanzania.

En **Albania** estalló una breve guerra civil en marzo y abril, al atacar manifestantes e insurgentes edificios gubernamentales y asaltar comercios de armas. Los insurgentes del sur del país exigían la autonomía, y se apoderaron de ciudades y puertos. No se restauró el orden hasta la llegada de 7000 militares, italianos en su mayoría, de la ONU.

Hong Kong fue devuelto a las autoridades chinas el 1 de julio, tras 150 años de gobierno británico. El nuevo jefe ejecutivo, **Tung Chee Hwa**, formuló una política basada en «un país, dos sistemas» para proteger la función de Hong Kong como centro capitalista de Asia.

Diana, princesa de Gales, murió en un accidente de tráfico el 31 de agosto en París. Su muerte desencadenó una oleada histórica de escenas de duelo en todo el mundo.

Iraq se negó a permitir la entrada de **inspectores de armas** de la ONU en octubre. Dichos inspectores fueron enviados al país tras la guerra del Golfo de 1991, con instrucciones de destruir el arsenal iraquí de armas nucleares, biológicas y químicas. La **crisis diplomática** subsiguiente remitió gracias a un acuerdo gestionado por Rusia.

El 11 de diciembre se firmó en Japón el **Protocolo de Kioto**. Los países industrializados se comprometían a reducir las emisiones de gases de efecto invernadero, fundamentalmente dióxido de carbono, en un intento de combatir el **calentamiento global**.

Titanic, la película sobre el desdichado viaje del famoso crucero que naufragó en 1912, se estrenó en diciembre. En aquel momento fue la película más cara jamás filmada, pero también la más taquillera: recaudó más de 1800 millones de dólares y fue galardonada con once premios Oscar.

Museo Guggenheim
El arquitecto estadounidense Frank Ehry diseñó este museo de Bilbao, inaugurado el 18 de octubre.

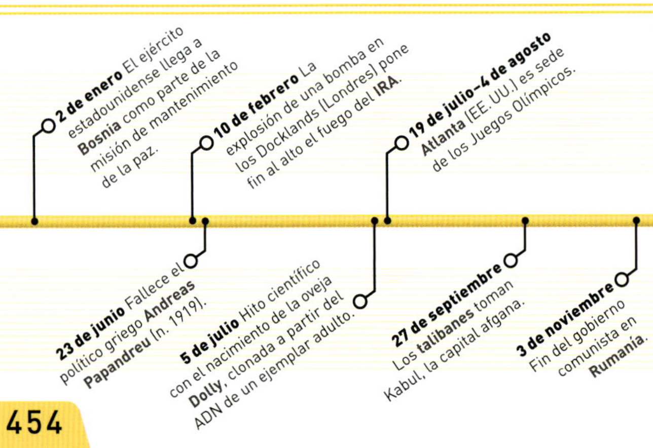

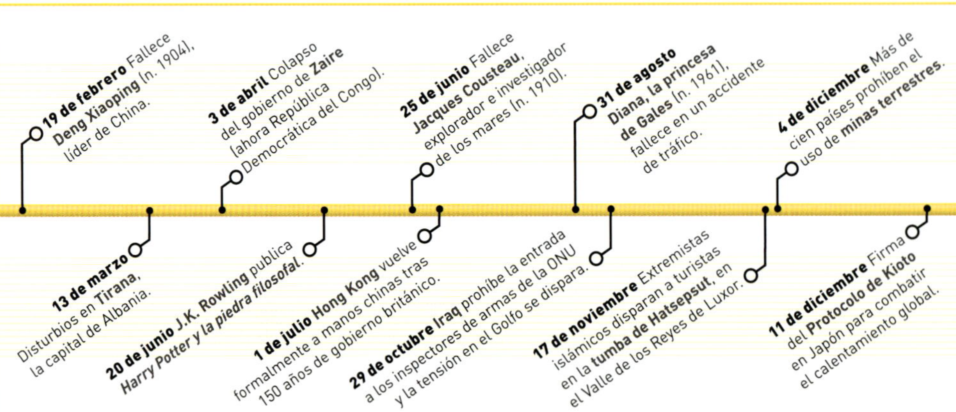

1998

Bill Clinton abraza a Monica Lewinsky, becaria de la Casa Blanca, el día después de su reelección en 1996. Posteriormente, se dijo que esta imagen era una prueba de la relación existente ente ambos.

EN ENERO, BILL CLINTON se vio inmerso en un escándalo por su relación con **Monica Lewinsky**, ex becaria de la Casa Blanca. Clinton, que se había visto implicado en un caso de acoso sexual y estaba siendo investigado por el asesor independiente Kenneth Starr, negó la relación y en diciembre se convirtió en el segundo presidente en toda la historia de EE.UU. (el primero fue Andrew Johnson, en 1868) en enfrentarse a una moción de censura. Se le acusó de cometer perjurio frente al Gran Jurado, pero fue absuelto al año siguiente.

6,1

MAGNITUD DEL **TERREMOTO EN AFGANISTÁN**

El 4 de febrero, un **terremoto** sacudió el norte de **Afganistán**. Murieron unas cuatro mil personas y unas treinta mil perdieron su hogar.

El 10 de abril se firmó el **acuerdo de Viernes Santo**, que marcó un punto de inflexión en el **proceso de paz** de Irlanda del Norte. El 22 de mayo se celebraron sendos referendos en la República de Irlanda y en Irlanda del Norte.

Pol Pot, ex cabeza de estado y jemer rojo en Camboya (*véase* 1978), murió el 15 de abril. En 1997, los Jemeres Rojos le habían destituido como líder y le habían condenado a cadena perpetua.

Los choques fronterizos entre **Eritrea** y **Etiopía** desembocaron en una guerra en mayo. Ambos países, entre los más pobres del mundo, invirtieron millones en armamento.

India y Pakistán se armaron nuclearmente ese año e India llevó a cabo el 12 de mayo ensayos nucleares subterráneos cerca de la frontera con Pakistán, a los que Pakistán respondió con sus propios ensayos el 28 de mayo.

Japón entró oficialmente en **recesión** el 12 de junio. Era la primera vez que la economía japonesa retrocedía en doce años; la noticia provocó la caída de los mercados de valores en todo el mundo.

El 20 de agosto, misiles estadounidenses cayeron sobre objetivos de **Afganistán** y **Sudán**, en represalia por el bombardeo de las embajadas de EE.UU. en Tanzania y en Kenia a principios de mes. EE.UU. afirmó que uno de los objetivos era el cuartel general de **Osama Bin Laden**, fundador de la organización islámica extremista **Al Qaeda**.

El **general Pinochet**, ex dictador de Chile (*véase* 1973), fue arrestado en Londres el 16 de julio a instancias de la justicia española, que le acusaba de cometer atrocidades contra ciudadanos españoles. Se decidió que Pinochet estaba demasiado enfermo para ser extraditado y fue puesto en libertad en 2000.

El 1 de mayo, Saddam Hussein escribió una carta abierta al Consejo de Seguridad de la ONU, en la que amenazaba con «graves consecuencias» si no se levantaban las sanciones contra Iraq. El 16 de diciembre, los **inspectores de armas de la ONU** cesaron en su intento de verificar el arsenal armamentístico de Iraq, cuando los iraquíes se negaron de nuevo a cooperar. Horas después empezó la **Operación Zorro del Desierto**, con ataques de la aviación británica y estadounidense sobre objetivos iraquíes.

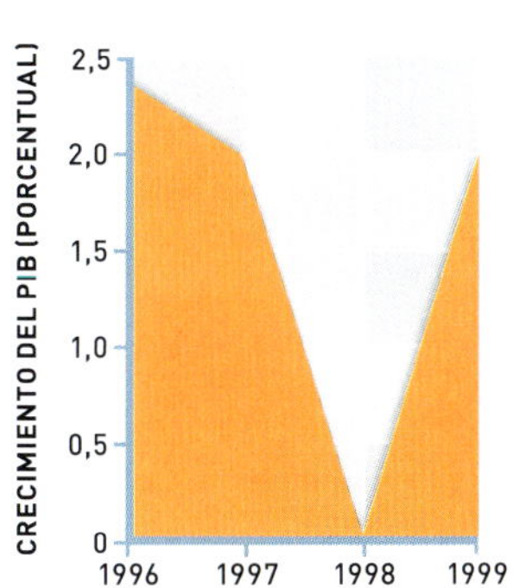

La recesión japonesa
Llegó a su peor momento en 1998 por la caída de las exportaciones, una demanda interna insuficiente y la caída de los precios inmobiliarios.

1999

Policías y manifestantes en la cumbre de la OMC en Seattle (EE.UU.). Los manifestantes protestaban contra las grandes corporaciones y la globalización.

LA MONEDA ÚNICA EUROPEA, el **euro**, entró en vigor el 1 de enero. Once estados de la Unión Europea decidieron adoptarlo y se convirtió en moneda de pleno derecho el año 2002.

La comunidad internacional acusó a Slobodan Milosevic de perpetrar **«limpiezas étnicas»** cuando se hallaron los cuerpos de 45 albanokosovares, aparentemente ejecutados por serbios. Las conversaciones de paz de Kosovo finalizaron sin acuerdo el 23 de febrero y, una semana más tarde, las fuerzas de la OTAN anunciaron sus planes de **intensificar el bombardeo sobre Yugoslavia**. El ejército serbio intensificó, a su vez, la purga de la población albanokosovar y medio millón de personas huyeron de Kosovo. Milosevic accedió a retirar su ejército el 9 de junio, tras los implacables bombardeos de la ONU.

Thabo Mbeki ganó las elecciones presidenciales de Sudáfrica el 2 de junio y sucedió a Nelson Mandela en el cargo. Se enfrentaba a retos económicos y sociales gigantescos, como el terrible impacto del sida.

Timor Oriental, en el Sureste Asiático, solicitó la intervención de las fuerzas internacionales tras el colapso absoluto del orden social en septiembre, tras un referendo que aprobó la independencia respecto a Indonesia. Los rebeldes timorenses contrarios a la independencia, que contaban con el apoyo del ejército tailandés, mataron a unos 1400 ciudadanos y 300 000 huyeron al vecino Timor Occidental.

Un golpe de estado el 12 de octubre en **Pakistán** llevó al poder al **general Pervez Musarraf** (n. 1943), que adoptó el título de «jefe ejecutivo». La comunidad internacional condenó el golpe y varias naciones impusieron sanciones económicas a Afganistán.

Eclipse solar
El 11 de agosto de 1999 hubo un eclipse solar total. Más de 350 millones de personas en Asia y Europa pudieron verlo.

A finales de año, la **Organización Mundial del Comercio** (OMC) celebró una cumbre en la ciudad de Seattle (EE.UU.), que se vio retrasada por las protestas de activistas en defensa del medio ambiente y contra la globalización. Los manifestantes se enfrentaron a la policía antes de ser dispersados.

La **NASA** perdió el contacto con la sonda espacial **Mars Polar Lander** poco antes de su llegada programada a la atmósfera marciana. Se atribuyó el fracaso de la misión a un error informático.

China recuperó la soberanía sobre **Macao** el 20 de diciembre, tras 442 años de control portugués. Macao era el último estado colonial de Asia y **Edmund Ho Hau Wah** (n. 1955), banquero, se convirtió en el líder del nuevo gobierno.

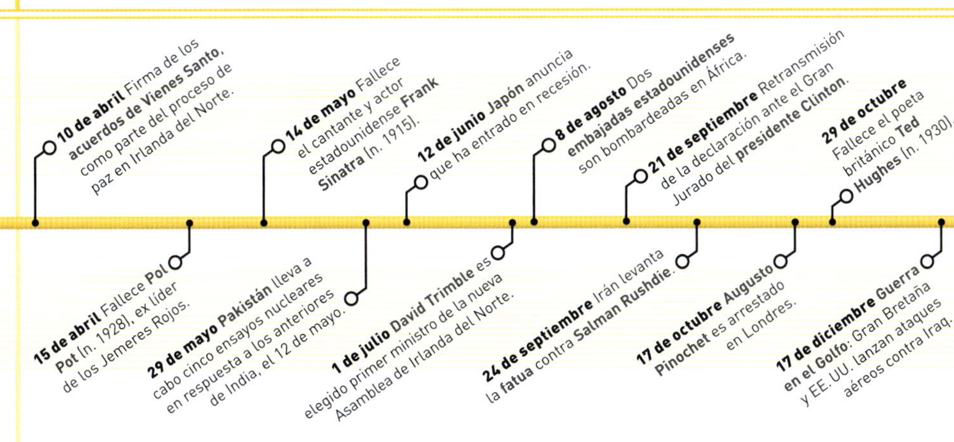

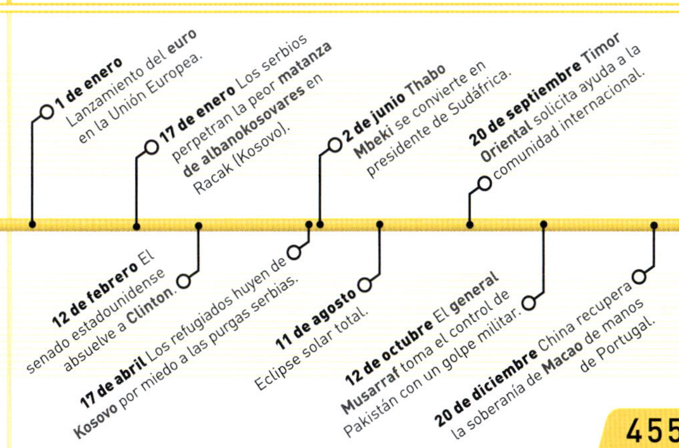

2000

Un agente de bolsa desesperado al caer el mercado de valores Nasdaq y la bolsa de Nueva York cuando estalló la burbuja de las puntocom.

Celebración del milenio
Espectáculo pirotécnico sobre el puente del puerto y la ópera de Sídney, al dar Australia la bienvenida al nuevo milenio.

EN ENERO, EL TRIBUNAL PENAL INTERNACIONAL (TPI) de La Haya sentenció a 25 años de prisión a cinco milicianos bosniocroatas por los asesinatos en 1993 de todos los habitantes musulmanes de un pueblo bosnio durante la guerra de Bosnia (1992–1995).

El 5 de octubre, partidarios de la oposición serbia irrumpieron con un **buldócer** en el Parlamento yugoslavo en Belgrado, y proclamaron a **Vojislav Kostunica** nuevo presidente de Yugoslavia, indignados por las irregularidades en las elecciones de septiembre. El presidente **Milosevic** anunció su dimisión al día siguiente.

En marzo, mercados de valores de todo el mundo se hundieron al caer las empresas tecnológicas, y estalló la burbuja de las puntocom, debido a la **especulación** en empresas basadas en internet.

En noviembre llegó a la **Estación Espacial Internacional** la primera tripulación, con el astronauta de la NASA Bill Shepherd como comandante.

Ante la presión del electorado, **Israel** anuncia su retirada del sur del Líbano en mayo, 22 años después de ocupar la zona.

Corea del Norte y **del Sur** celebraron una cumbre en junio, la primera desde la división de la península en 1945. El presidente surcoreano Kim Dae Jung obtuvo el **Nobel de la Paz**.

Más de 800 seguidores del **culto ugandés** Restauración de los Diez Mandamientos de Dios mueren en marzo en sus iglesias. No está claro si fue un suicidio en masa o un asesinato a manos de los líderes del culto.

El 30 de diciembre se comete una serie de atentados terroristas con bomba en **Filipinas**, llamados **bombardeos del día de Rizal** por la fiesta nacional celebrada ese día.

2001

George W. Bush fue elegido presidente de EE. UU. en 2001. En la imagen, saluda a Al Gore, el candidato demócrata al que derrotó, frente al Capitolio (Washington).

« EL TRASPASO **PACÍFICO** DE PODERES ES **RARO** EN LA HISTORIA, PERO **COMÚN** EN NUESTRO PAÍS. CON UN **JURAMENTO SIMPLE,** AFIRMAMOS VIEJAS TRADICIONES Y EMPRENDEMOS **NUEVOS COMIENZOS.** »

George W. Bush, inicio de su discurso inaugural (20 de enero de 2001)

EN INDIA, un **terremoto** de magnitud 7,9 en la escala de Richter sacudió el estado de **Gujarat** el 26 de enero. Murieron más de 20 000 personas y fueron destruidos 400 000 hogares.

La República de Macedonia estaba al borde de la guerra en marzo, al enfrentarse rebeldes albaneses a fuerzas gubernamentales para exigir la igualdad de derechos. En agosto, la OTAN anunció el envío de **fuerzas de paz** a la antigua república socialista yugoslava.

EE. UU. sufrió un día de terror sin precedentes el **11 de septiembre**, cuando diecinueve terroristas de Al Qaeda secuestraron cuatro aviones comerciales. Estrellaron dos de ellos contra las Torres Gemelas del **World Trade Center** de Nueva York y otro contra el **Pentágono**. El cuarto se estrelló en un campo cerca de Pittsburgh, desviado al rebelarse los pasajeros. Murieron casi tres mil personas. El impacto devastador del hoy llamado **11-S** movió al presidente Bush a declarar una «**guerra al terror**». La OTAN se reunió al día siguiente, ofreció su pleno apoyo e invocó la cláusula de la época de la Guerra Fría, por la que el ataque a un país miembro lo es a todos.

Una semana después del 11-S, varias agencias de noticias y dos senadores demócratas estadounidenses recibieron cartas con esporas de la bacteria causante del **carbunco** *(Bacillus anthracis)*. Cinco personas murieron y otras diecisiete resultaron infectadas. El sospechoso de haberlas enviado se suicidó.

En octubre, EE. UU. y Reino Unido atacaron objetivos en Afganistán, donde se creía que se ocultaba **Osama Bin Laden** (1957–2011), líder de la organización terrorista Al Qaeda. El objetivo de la **Operación Libertad Duradera** era derrocar al régimen talibán y reemplazarlo por un gobierno democrático.

Tras los ataques del 11-S hubo una **recesión** en gran parte del mundo. Los problemas económicos empeoraron en diciembre con la bancarrota de la empresa energética **Enron**, el mayor colapso empresarial del mundo.

En diciembre, **Argentina** se enfrentaba a la ruina económica. El gobierno anunció que no podía pagar la deuda exterior y aprobó medidas de austeridad.

También en diciembre, **Richard Reid**, pasajero británico seguidor de Al Qaeda, fue sorprendido al tratar de cometer un atentado.

Mientras la amenaza terrorista de Al Qaeda acaparaba la atención, el **Ejército Republicano Irlandés** (IRA) declaró el inicio del desarme y haber inutilizado parte de sus armas.

Ataques del 11-S
Monumento a las víctimas del 11-S inaugurado en Nueva York en 2016. Hay dos cascadas en el lugar de las huellas de las Torres Gemelas.

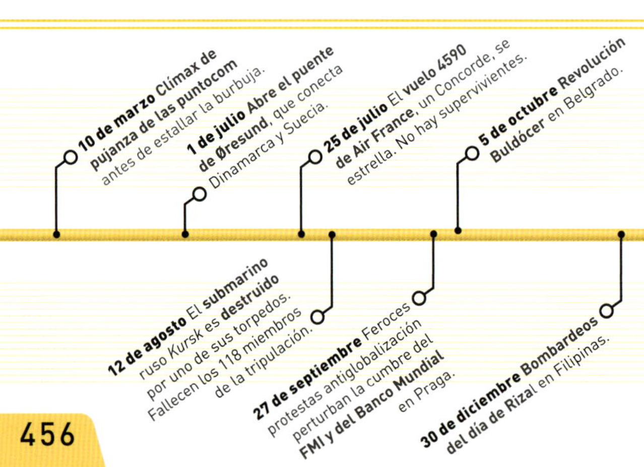

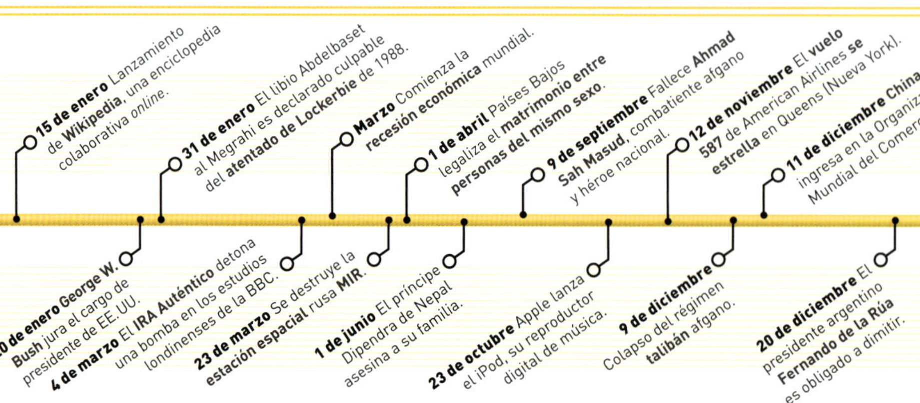

2002

En 2002 se desprendió un trozo inmenso de la plataforma de hielo Larsen, en la Antártida, que perdió unos 3250 km² de superficie.

EL EURO SE CONVIRTIÓ EN MONEDA DE CURSO LEGAL desde principios de año, y sustituyó a las divisas nacionales de doce países de la **eurozona** (*véase* 1999).

Slobodan Milosevic, expresidente yugoslavo, fue a **juicio** el 12 de febrero acusado de **crímenes contra la humanidad**. Murió en 2006, antes de que el juicio hubiera terminado.

Los presidentes George W. Bush y Vladímir Putin acuerdan reducir en dos tercios las armas nucleares de EE. UU. y Rusia en el **Tratado de Moscú**, firmado el 24 de mayo.

Combatientes chechenos asaltaron un teatro en Moscú el 23 de octubre y amenazaron con matar a los rehenes si Rusia no se retiraba de Chechenia. Fuerzas especiales rusas se enfrentaron a los rebeldes en un tiroteo que causó 118 muertos.

Una **discoteca** en **Bali** (Indonesia) fue el objetivo de un ataque terrorista en el que murieron más de 200 personas. Miembros de un grupo islamista violento, **Yamaa Islamiya**, fueron condenados por ello.

« NOSOTROS ... LOS LEGÍTIMOS PROPIETARIOS DE ESTA TIERRA **NO NOS MOVEREMOS. »**

Robert Mugabe, presidente de Zimbabue (diciembre de 2002)

Moneda común
El euro, la nueva moneda para doce países de la Unión Europea, entró en vigor en enero de 2002. Desde entonces se ha convertido en una divisa global sólida.

El periodista **Daniel Pearl** fue secuestrado en enero en Pakistán, mientras investigaba a grupos extremistas musulmanes. Para su rescate se exigió liberar a presos de Guantánamo. El cuerpo de Pearl fue hallado en mayo.

India y **Pakistán** estuvieron al borde de la guerra en mayo tras un ataque terrorista contra el Parlamento indio en 2001, atentado que India atribuyó a grupos armados con base en Pakistán y que reivindicaban la disputada **Cachemira**.

En **Sierra Leona**, en África occidental, acabó una década de guerra civil en enero, mientras un **alto el fuego** firmado en abril ponía fin a los 26 años de guerra civil en **Angola** tras la independencia de Portugal.

Robert Mugabe, presidente de Zimbabue, ordenó marcharse a los granjeros blancos como parte de la redistribución de las tierras a la población negra. Muchos se negaron a acatar la orden.

2003

« HEMOS CONTENIDO LA EPIDEMIA DE SARS EN 2003. »

Wen Jiabao, primer ministro chino

EL NUEVO AÑO COMENZÓ CON la tragedia de la **desintegración** del transbordador espacial estadounidense ***Columbia*** en su reentrada a la atmósfera terrestre. Murieron los siete miembros de la tripulación, y la investigación posterior confirmó el fallo de un escudo térmico que se desprendió en el despegue.

En octubre, tras 27 años operativo, el avión supersónico **Concorde** realizó su último vuelo comercial desde el aeropuerto de Heathrow (Londres). El coste excesivo y la escasa venta de billetes llevaron a cancelar sus vuelos.

Yugoslavia votó poner fin a su existencia como país en febrero, y pasó a convertirse en **Serbia y Montenegro**. La Federación Yugoslava había existido durante 74 años, pero sin sus otras cuatro repúblicas desde los sangrientos conflictos de la década de 1990.

En junio se aprobó el tratado por el que se establece una **Constitución para Europa**, con el fin de reunir los tratados de la Unión Europea (UE) existentes en un texto único e instituir un presidente y un ministro de exteriores de la UE.

Arnold Schwarzenegger, actor famoso por su papel como Terminator en películas de Hollywood, fue elegido gobernador de California (EE. UU.) en octubre.

Dos **bombas** estallaron en **Estambul** el 20 de noviembre, en el consulado británico y la sede del banco británico HSBC. Las explosiones, vinculadas a **Al Qaeda**, se cobraron 60 vidas.

Caída en desgracia
Civiles iraquíes, con la ayuda de marines de EE. UU., derriban una estatua de Sadam Huseín en Bagdad (Iraq).

El régimen de **Iraq** se desplomó el 20 de marzo, cuando fuerzas lideradas por EE. UU. invadieron y derrocaron al gobierno de Sadam Huseín, con el pretexto falso de que Iraq ocultaba **armas de destrucción masiva**. Muchos cuestionaron la legalidad de tal guerra, y, mientras crecía el número de bajas occidentales, la amplia cobertura mediática indignó a la opinión pública. Hubo **protestas masivas** en todo el mundo, y en Iraq la guerra desencadenó años de conflicto civil entre las facciones religiosas.

Para el vecino Irán, el año terminó con un **terremoto** que devastó la antigua ciudad de **Bam**, patrimonio mundial de la Unesco con más de dos mil años de historia. Murieron más de 26 000 personas. La ayuda ofrecida por EE. UU. contribuyó a mejorar las relaciones entre ambos países.

En la región occidental de **Darfur** (Sudán) estalló la **guerra civil**; los rebeldes se alzaron contra el gobierno denunciando desatención a la región por parte de las autoridades de la capital, Jartum. Hasta la fecha, en este conflicto han muerto 200 000 personas, y 2,5 millones han huido a campos de refugiados.

Un virus fue noticia en todo el mundo y causó un pánico considerable, el **síndrome respiratorio agudo severo** (SARS), una enfermedad humana muy infecciosa y, a veces, mortal. En 2003 hubo un brote en China que se propagó a otros 37 países. Los gobiernos tomaron medidas rigurosas para controlar el virus.

En este año proliferaron los **teléfonos móviles** con cámara, que tuvieron un impacto social profundo. Sirvieron para la vigilancia y obtener noticias, pero también para el voyeurismo, y generaron debates sobre la privacidad.

Poder estelar
El actor Arnold Schwarzenegger saluda a sus seguidores durante la campaña de las elecciones a gobernador de California en 2003.

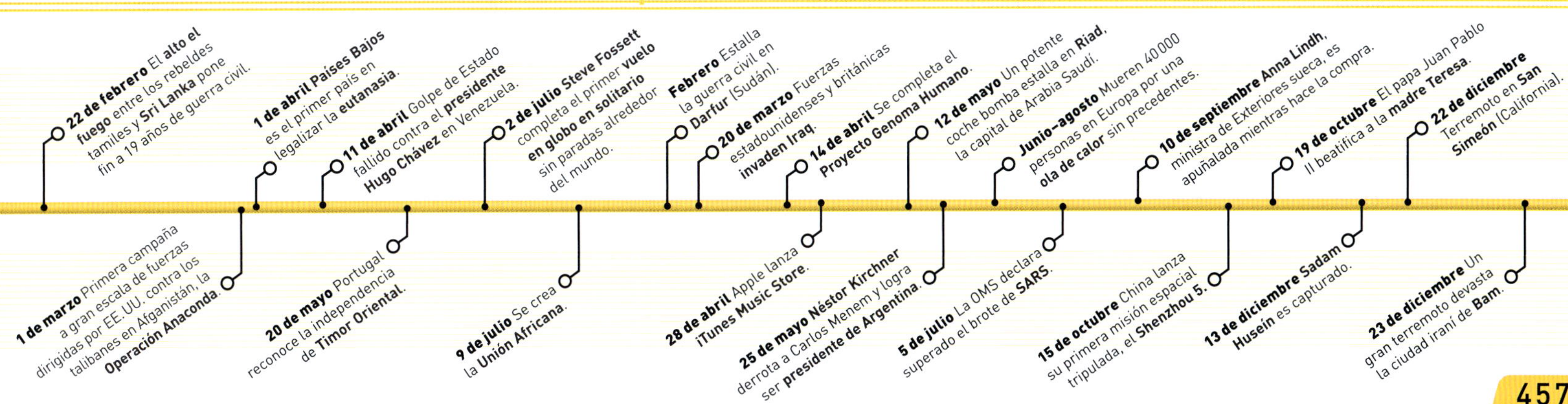

2004

Ciudadanas afganas en Kabul esperan a votar en la mezquita Jaffaria, en las primeras elecciones presidenciales desde el derrocamiento del gobierno talibán.

LA NUEVA CONSTITUCIÓN AFGANA se firmó el 26 de enero en la capital, Kabul. Tras investigarse irregularidades en las elecciones, **Hamid Karzai** fue declarado oficialmente presidente de Afganistán el 3 de noviembre.

En abril, en EE. UU. se emitieron imágenes de maltrato a presos en la prisión de **Abu Ghraib** (Iraq) a manos de la policía militar estadounidense. **George W. Bush** se disculpó, y **fue reelegido** para un segundo mandato presidencial el 2 de noviembre.

El 29 de octubre, la cadena árabe **Al Jazeera** emitió un vídeo en el que **Osama Bin Laden** amenazaba a EE. UU. con nuevos ataques; era la reivindicación más clara de los atentados del 11-S.

Fuerzas de **EE. UU. e Iraq** asaltaron Faluya (Iraq) el 8 de noviembre para arrebatar el control de la ciudad suní a la guerrilla.

El 1 de mayo tuvo lugar la mayor ampliación de la **Unión Europea** (UE), al ingresar diez países, muchos de ellos miembros del antiguo bloque soviético.

El presidente checheno **Ajmad Kadírov** murió en la explosión atribuida a militantes islámicos el 9 de mayo. El conflicto continuó en Chechenia con el asalto por **separatistas** a una escuela en **Beslán** (Osetia del Norte) el 1 de septiembre. En el tiroteo que siguió murieron cientos de los rehenes, niños y personal docente.

1100 REHENES

331 MUERTOS

Crisis de Beslán
Un grupo de separatistas chechenos armados retuvo a más de mil rehenes en una escuela rusa. Hubo 331 muertos, y 186 de ellos eran niños.

Los **Juegos Olímpicos** se celebraron en **Atenas**, en su patria original, por primera vez desde 1896. EE. UU. logró el mayor número de medallas, 103 en total.

El 26 de diciembre, un **terremoto** bajo el océano Índico y cerca de Sumatra desencadenó una serie de olas gigantes, o **tsunamis**, en el mar. Murieron más de 200 000 personas, y millones se quedaron sin hogar en once países; fue el tsunami más destructivo de la historia.

Ola de destrucción
Las olas del tsunami recorrieron 1600 km por el océano Índico en solo 90 minutos. Los daños causados fueron inmensos.

2005

Vista aérea de Nueva Orleans tras el paso del huracán Katrina, que dejó inundado un 80 % de la ciudad.

YASSIR ARAFAT FALLECIÓ EN 2004, y **Mahmud Abás** fue el nuevo presidente de Palestina desde el 6 de enero. Abás y el primer ministro israelí **Ariel Sharon** anunciaron pronto un **alto el fuego**, visto como la mejor oportunidad para alcanzar la paz en la región en muchos años.

El ex primer ministro libanés **Rafik Hariri** fue asesinado por un terrorista suicida en Beirut el 14 de febrero. Planeaba volver a la política, y había pedido públicamente a Siria que retirase sus tropas de **Líbano**. **Siria** negó toda implicación en su asesinato, pero se vio obligada a anunciar la retirada el 26 de abril. Este se considera un día histórico en Oriente Próximo.

« ESTÁ COMPLETAMENTE **BORRADA.** »

George W. Bush, presidente de EE. UU., al supervisar los daños en Nueva Orleans (31 de agosto de 2005)

El antiguo líder de Iraq **Sadam Huseín** fue **juzgado** en octubre. Declarado culpable de las atrocidades cometidas durante su gobierno, fue ejecutado en 2006.

El 7 de julio, cuatro **ataques terroristas** suicidas coordinados (todos hombres británicos con apoyo de **Al Qaeda**) contra tres convoyes de metro y un autobús de dos pisos en **Londres** mataron a 52 personas e hirieron a cientos más. El **huracán Katrina** alcanzó las costas de Luisiana y Misisipi (EE. UU.) el 29 de agosto, causando una destrucción sin precedentes en Nueva Orleans y dejando a la deriva dos plataformas petrolíferas en el golfo de México. Los daños se estimaron en 26 400 millones de dólares.

CLIMATOLOGÍA EXTREMA

El tiempo pareció cada vez más descontrolado en la década de 2000. En 2005, el huracán Katrina (en la imagen) fue uno más de varios huracanes y varias tormentas tropicales sin precedentes. También hubo récords de lluvias, deshielo de los casquetes polares y sequías graves, alimentando todo ello la preocupación sobre el calentamiento global. Se espera más climatología extrema, que perturbará modos de vida, extinguirá especies animales y amenazará las vidas humanas.

2006

« LAS **GENERACIONES FUTURAS** BIEN PODRÁN PREGUNTARSE **EN QUÉ PENSABAN SUS PADRES.** »

Al Gore en *Una verdad incómoda*

EL GRUPO SEPARATISTA VASCO ETA declaró un **alto el fuego** permanente el 22 de marzo, aspirando a luchar por la independencia del pueblo vasco por **medios democráticos**.

Montenegro fue un Estado soberano desde el 3 de junio, tras un **referéndum** en el que solo el 55 % de los votos fueron a favor de la **independencia**. Fue el fin de la Unión de Serbia y Montenegro, creada solo tres años antes a partir de la antigua Yugoslavia (*véase* 2003).

Irán anunció haber producido **uranio enriquecido**, e insistió en que estaba destinado a generar energía nuclear, pero en Occidente se temía que Irán fabricase armamento nuclear.

Corea del Norte, anunció haber realizado un **ensayo nuclear** el 9 de octubre, lo cual provocó una firme condena internacional.

Siete **bombas** estallaron en el metro de **Bombay** (India) el 11 de julio. Murieron más de 200 personas. La tensión entre India y Pakistán se intensificó al apuntar las pruebas a la implicación de la agencia de inteligencia pakistaní en los ataques.

El 20 de mayo se completó la **presa de las Tres Gargantas**, en China. Con una longitud de 2,3 km, es una de las presas más largas y la mayor infraestructura hidráulica del mundo. También fue una de las obras públicas más controvertidas: su objetivo era impedir las inundaciones a lo largo del **río Yangtsé**, pero el impacto social y ecológico fue enorme.

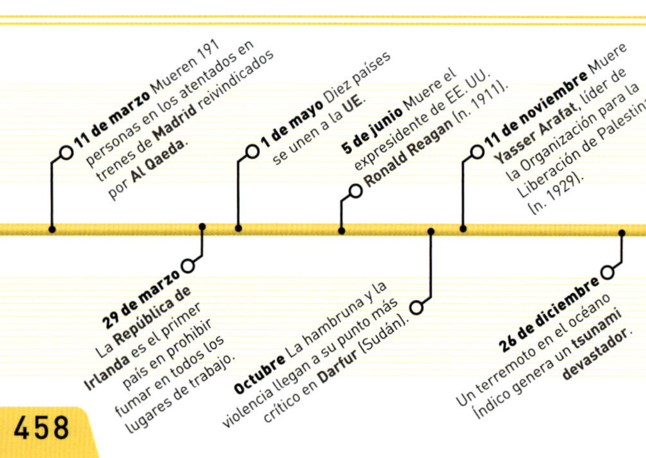

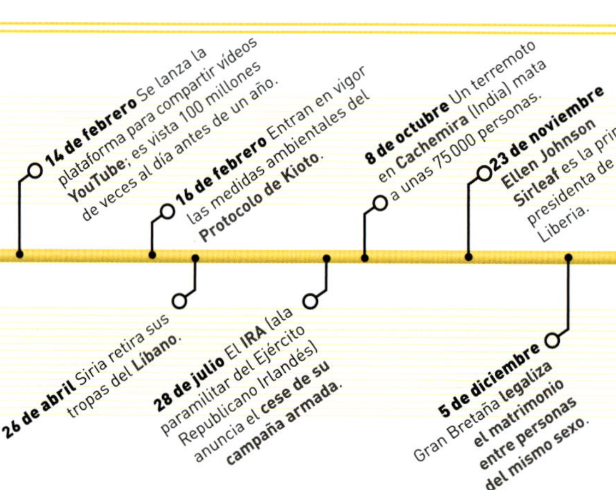

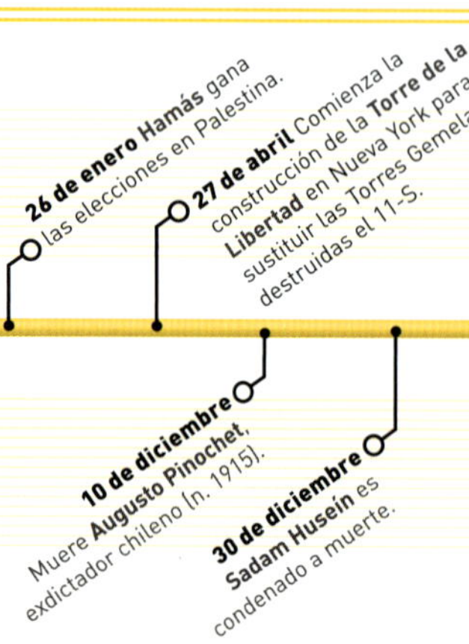

2007

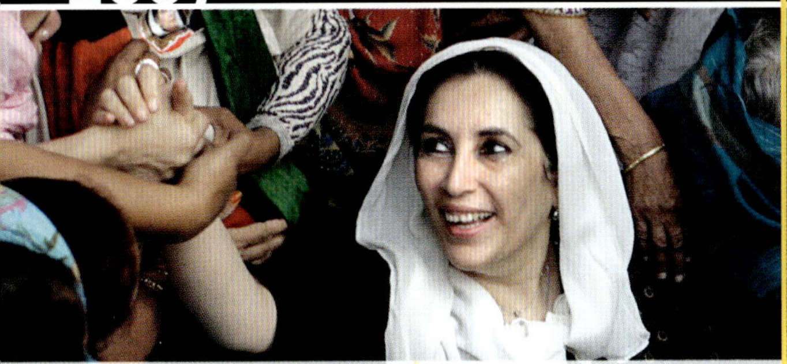
Benazir Bhutto, ex primera ministra de Pakistán, durante la campaña electoral en Karachi.

BULGARIA Y RUMANÍA ingresaron en la **Unión Europea** el 1 de enero, elevando a 27 el número de países miembros.

El gobierno directo de Londres sobre **Irlanda del Norte** finalizó oficialmente el 8 de mayo. El líder del Partido Unionista Democrático, **Ian Paisley**, y **Martin McGuinnes**, del Sinn Fein, juraron respectivamente como primer y vice primer ministro del nuevo ejecutivo.

El 23 de marzo, el ejército iraní capturó a quince marineros británicos. Fueron acusados de invadir aguas iraníes, y pasaron once días retenidos.

Nawaz Sharif, ex primer ministro de Pakistán, regresó del exilio en agosto y se comprometió a poner fin a la «dictadura» del presidente Musharraf. Fue deportado a Arabia Saudí en cuestión de semanas.

iPhone
La empresa tecnológica Apple lanzó un nuevo tipo de teléfono multimedia, el iPhone, que se conecta a internet por pantalla táctil.

Benazir Bhutto, también antigua dirigente pakistaní, fue asesinada el 27 de diciembre durante un mitin político. Se atribuyó el asesinato a militantes islamistas.

El 24 de diciembre, **Nepal** anunció que aboliría la monarquía tras las elecciones de 2008. Algunos partidos se habían negado a participar en el gobierno hasta que Nepal fuera una república.

La ciencia dio un gran paso adelante en abril con el primer **esperma artificial**, creado de muestras de células de médula ósea en un laboratorio de Newcastle (Inglaterra).

La misteriosa **materia oscura** que conforma una cuarta parte del universo se reveló en mayo en un mapa 3D del **telescopio Hubble**, ayudando a comprender cómo se formó el universo.

El 21 de julio se publicó el último volumen de la saga **Harry Potter** de J. K. Rowling, *Harry Potter y las reliquias de la muerte*. Fue el libro más rápidamente vendido de la historia.

« HE PUESTO **MI VIDA EN JUEGO** PORQUE **CREO QUE MI PAÍS** CORRE PELIGRO. »

Benazir Bhutto, política pakistaní, durante un discurso poco antes de ser asesinada

2008

En Pekín, Usain Bolt se convirtió en el hombre más rápido del mundo al correr los 100 m en solo 9,69 segundos, un nuevo récord mundial.

Colisionador de hadrones del CERN
Se espera de la máquina más compleja jamás construida que ayude a desvelar el misterio de cómo comenzó a existir el universo.

LA PEOR CRISIS FINANCIERA DESDE LA GRAN DEPRESIÓN de la década de 1930 llevó a la economía mundial peligrosamente cerca del colapso, y requirió la intervención estatal para mantener a flote el sistema capitalista. Préstamos imprudentes a escala masiva habían **arruinado bancos** y otras instituciones financieras, entre ellas, las de los prestamistas hipotecarios estadounidenses Fannie Mae y Freddie Mac, los bancos británicos Northern Rock y Royal Bank of Scotland y el sector bancario de Islandia. Una rápida y costosa intervención estatal salvó a algunos, pero otros, entre ellos la banca de inversiones **Lehman Brothers**, se hundieron. La crisis tuvo efectos globales, al cerrar empresas y crecer el desempleo. En el mundo en vías de desarrollo hubo motines por alimentos.

En este contexto, el demócrata **Barack Obama** fue elegido presidente de EE. UU. en noviembre con una victoria clara sobre el republicano **John McCain**.

También hubo un cambio de liderazgo en Cuba, donde **Fidel Castro** (*véase* 1959), se retiró tras casi medio siglo en el poder, que cedió a su hermano **Raúl Castro** (n. 1931).

En agosto, **Osetia del Sur** fue causa de una guerra entre Rusia y Georgia al tratar de separarse de esta el territorio prorruso. Un rápido alto el fuego evitó una crisis más grave.

En noviembre murieron 167 personas en ataques **terroristas** en **Bombay** (India), que dañaron las relaciones del país con Pakistán, a cuyos servicios de inteligencia se acusó de estar implicados.

Los **Juegos Olímpicos** se celebraron en **Pekín** en agosto. Tras el despliegue inaugural más espléndido nunca visto, fueron un gran éxito, con actuaciones extraordinarias del velocista Usain Bolt y el nadador Michael Phelps.

BARACK OBAMA (n. 1961)

El demócrata Barack Hussein Obama hizo historia al ser elegido 44.º presidente de EE. UU. Nacido en Hawái, fue el primer afroestadounidense en acceder al cargo. Su encanto relajado y oratoria conmovedora le ganaron admiradores en todo el mundo, pero en su primer año se enfrentó a una oposición feroz en sus intentos de modificar el sistema sanitario de EE. UU., abordar el cambio climático y lograr nuevos acuerdos de desarme nuclear.

2009

173 FALLECIDOS A CAUSA DE LOS **INCENDIOS FORESTALES** EN VICTORIA

LA ECONOMÍA MUNDIAL ENTRÓ EN RECESIÓN, y se contrajo por primera vez en 60 años. Entre las víctimas de la crisis se contaron los gigantes automovilísticos de EE. UU. **General Motors** y **Chrysler**, declarando ambos la bancarrota en este año.

El 7 de febrero, **Australia** sufrió el que pudo ser el peor desastre natural de su historia debido a **incendios forestales** que destruyeron comunidades de todo el estado de Victoria; sucedió tras una larga e intensa sequía que muchos relacionaron con el calentamiento global.

En la cumbre del clima celebrada en Copenhague solo se alcanzó un limitado acuerdo internacional entre China, EE. UU., India, Brasil y Sudáfrica para combatir el **cambio climático**.

En el tenis, la victoria de **Roger Federer** en la final masculina del torneo de Wimbledon le convirtió en el tenista de mayor éxito de la historia, con **15 títulos del Grand Slam**.

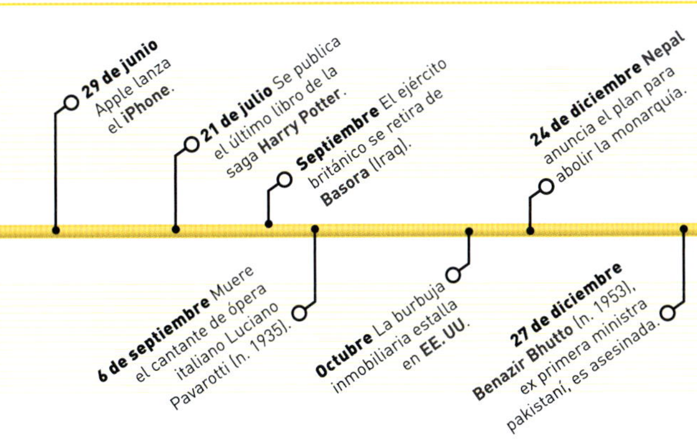

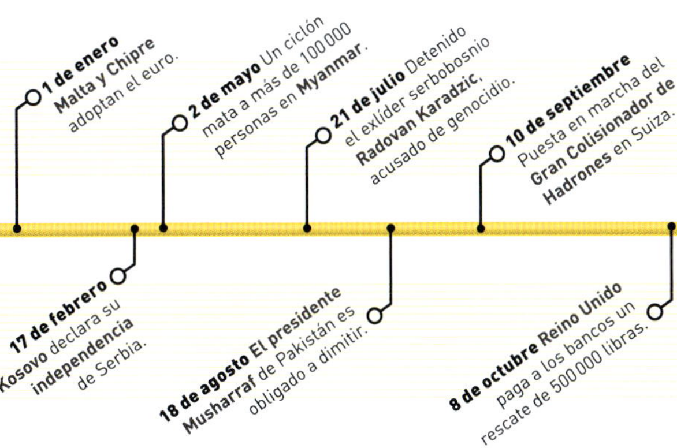

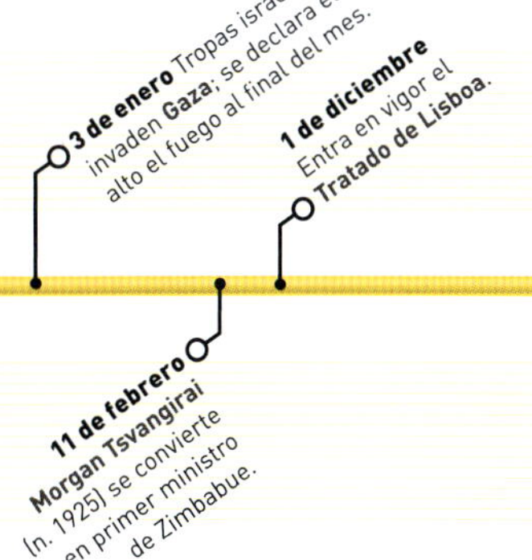

2010

Barrera para limitar los daños del vertido de la plataforma petrolífera Deepwater Horizon.

«EL **PEOR** DESASTRE AMBIENTAL AL QUE SE HA ENFRENTADO **EE.UU.**»

El presidente Obama, sobre el vertido de la Deepwater Horizon (15 de junio de 2010)

UN TERREMOTO DEVASTÓ EL 12 DE ENERO un área densamente poblada en la **República de Haití**, uno de los países más pobres del mundo y que, además, estaba muy mal equipado para reaccionar ante tal destrucción. Hubo una iniciativa internacional de ayuda, pero se estimaron en al menos 100 000 las personas que murieron en el desastre.

La vulnerabilidad humana ante las fuerzas de la naturaleza se puso de relieve de nuevo en abril, cuando la **erupción** del **volcán islandés** Eyjafjallajökull expulsó una **nube de ceniza** a la atmósfera que afectó al tráfico aéreo alrededor de las islas británicas y del norte de Europa.

El peor desastre del año en EE.UU. fue de origen humano: el 20 de abril, una **explosión** en la **plataforma petrolífera Deepwater Horizon**, ubicada en el golfo de México, mató a once personas y vertió petróleo al océano, contaminando las costas de Florida, Luisiana y Misisipi.

Sin embargo, un desastre sí tuvo un final feliz: en **Chile** pudieron ser rescatados **33 mineros** tras pasar más de dos meses atrapados a 700 m de profundidad en una mina en el desierto de Atacama.

Rescate en Chile
Un minero sale a la superficie tras pasar diez semanas atrapado bajo tierra, después del derrumbe de la mina de San José.

Las consecuencias de la **crisis económica** continuaron. La economía de algunos Estados europeos, como Irlanda y Grecia, se volvió precaria, y tuvieron que ser rescatados por el Fondo Monetario Internacional (FMI).

En Asia, las últimas tropas de EE.UU. se retiraron de **Iraq**, pero la seguridad empeoró en **Afganistán**, donde las bajas occidentales se dispararon de nuevo. Un total de 496 soldados estadounidenses murieron allí en 2010.

En **Myanmar**, la líder por la democracia **Aung San Suu Kyi** (n. 1945) fue liberada tras 21 años de arresto domiciliario intermitente.

En junio, Sudáfrica fue el primer país africano anfitrión de la **Copa Mundial** de fútbol, que ganó España por primera vez.

2011

El príncipe Guillermo besa a su esposa, Catherine Middleton, en la terraza del palacio de Buckingham tras su boda en la abadía de Westminster el 29 de abril.

UNA SERIE DE LEVANTAMIENTOS POPULARES sacudieron el mundo árabe a principios de año, y desestabilizaron o derrocaron regímenes políticos autoritarios en el poder desde hacía décadas. La llamada **Primavera Árabe** se propagó desde Túnez por el norte de África y Oriente Próximo. En Egipto, el **presidente Hosni Mubarak** (1928–2020) tuvo que dimitir y se celebraron elecciones democráticas. En Libia, en cambio, **Muamar al Gadafi** (1942–2011) se negó a dimitir, y se desencadenó la guerra civil. Con apoyo aéreo de la OTAN, los rebeldes derrotaron y **mataron a Gadafi** en octubre, pero la situación del país siguió siendo convulsa.

En **Siria**, los que **protestaban pidiendo democracia** no lograron el cambio de régimen, y en julio el país estaba envuelto en un conflicto armado entre partidarios y oponentes del **presidente Bashar al Asad** (n. 1965).

En comparación, las protestas anticapitalistas del radical **movimiento Occupy** en ciudades de Occidente atrajeron un apoyo considerable, pero fueron relativamente menores.

En **Japón**, el 11 de marzo, un **terremoto** submarino generó un **tsunami** devastador. Murieron más de 16 000 personas, y en la planta nuclear de **Fukushima** hubo fusión del núcleo en tres reactores. Aunque se evitó un desastre nuclear grave, las autoridades anunciaron la parada fría completa de la planta a finales de año.

El 22 de febrero, otro **terremoto** causó unas 185 muertes en **Christchurch** (Nueva Zelanda), en el **peor desastre natural** del país en 80 años.

En Pakistán, **fuerzas especiales de EE.UU.** localizaron y mataron en mayo a **Osama Bin Laden** (1957–2011), líder de Al Qaeda, tras una década de búsqueda.

Un mundo sacudido
El terremoto de Japón fue el quinto más potente desde que hay registros. La gráfica muestra la magnitud de los diez mayores de la historia.

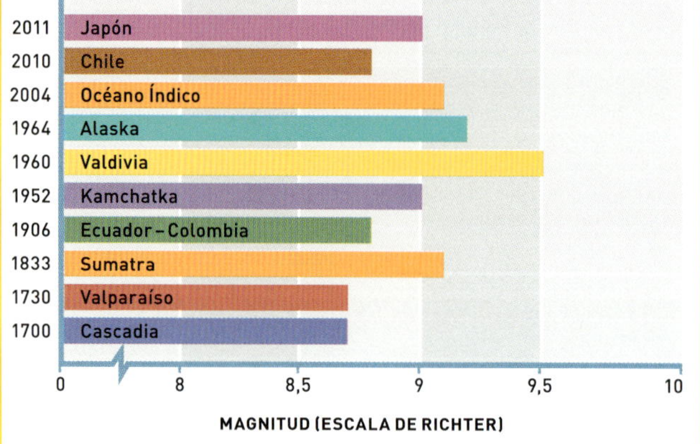

2012

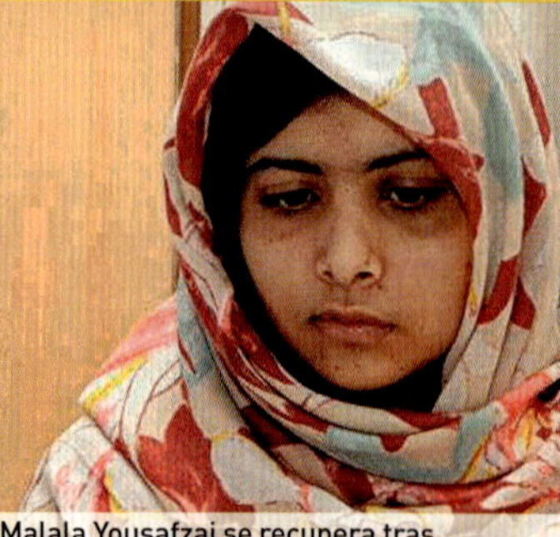

Malala Yousafzai se recupera tras sobrevivir a un intento de asesinato.

LOS CONFLICTOS DEL MUNDO ISLÁMICO siguieron acaparando titulares. En Siria, la escalada de la rebelión armada acabó en **guerra civil**. En Libia reinó el caos en la lucha por el poder de grupos armados rivales, y el 11 de septiembre, durante el ataque de milicianos islamistas a la embajada de EE.UU. en Bengasi, **murió** el embajador estadounidense **John Christopher Stevens**.

Mientras tanto, en Egipto ganó las elecciones **Mohamed Morsi** (1951–2019), candidato de los islamistas **Hermanos Musulmanes**. El resultado fue muy impopular entre los liberales egipcios, que habían agitado en favor de la democracia durante la Primavera Árabe en 2011, y las protestas no tardaron en volver a las calles de El Cairo.

En febrero, la **quema de copias del Corán** por personal estadounidense en la **base aérea de Bagram**, en Afganistán, ofendió a musulmanes de todas las tendencias políticas y desencadenó protestas generalizadas y violentas.

2083

MILITARES DE EE.UU. HABÍAN **MUERTO** EN **AFGANISTÁN** AL TERMINAR **2012**

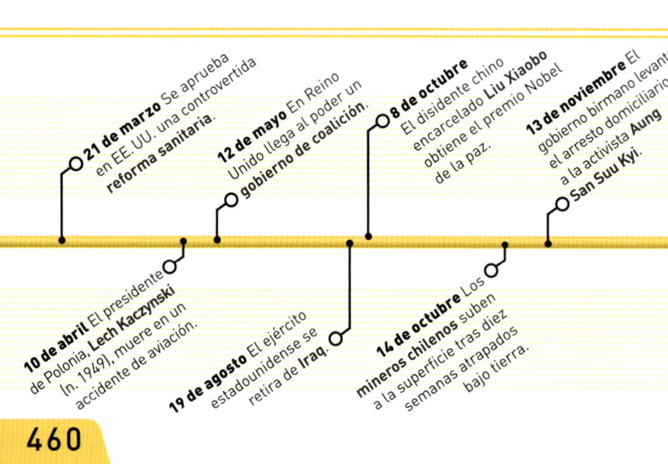

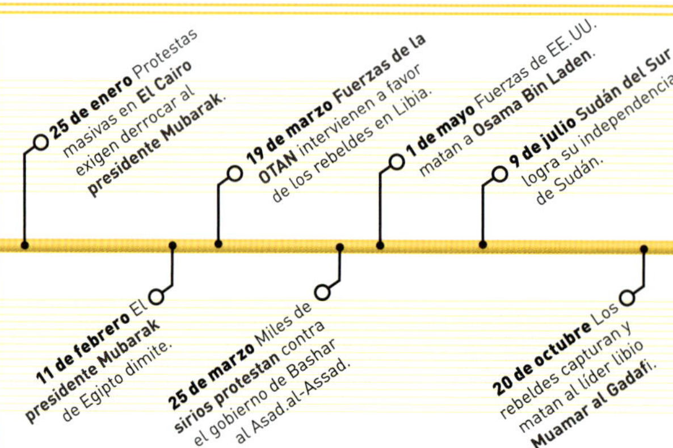

« AUNQUE VENGAN A MATARME, **LES DIRÉ** QUE LO QUE TRATAN DE HACER ESTÁ MAL, QUE **LA EDUCACIÓN ES NUESTRO DERECHO FUNDAMENTAL.** »

Malala Yousafzai (2012)

Particularmente desgarrador fue el atentado de octubre en el que un **talibán disparó** contra la activista **Malala Yousafzai** (n.1997), en Pakistán. Su delito fue hacer campaña por la educación de las mujeres. Afortunadamente, sobrevivió, y se recuperó en un hospital británico.

En EE. UU. y Rusia, **Barack Obama** y **Vladímir Putin** fueron reelegidos en sus respectivas elecciones presidenciales.

Jueces británicos dictaminaron que **Julian Assange**, fundador de la controvertida organización **Wikileaks** dedicada a publicar secretos de Estado, debía ser **extraditado** a Suecia para responder a alegaciones de violación. Para evitarlo, Assange se refugió en la embajada de Ecuador en Londres.

El 14 de octubre tuvo lugar la que fue probablemente la hazaña más extraordinaria del año, al **romper la barrera del sonido** el austriaco **Felix Baumgartner**, en caída libre desde la estratosfera.

2013

El papa Francisco saluda a la multitud durante su visita a Florencia (Italia).

EL 28 DE FEBRERO, EL PAPA BENEDICTO XVI RENUNCIÓ a su pontificado. Elegido en marzo, el cardenal argentino Jorge Mario Bergoglio se convirtió en el **papa Francisco**, quien abrió la puerta a un **catolicismo** más **liberal**, más atento a la desigualdad social y el cambio climático.

En Egipto, un **golpe** militar derrocó en julio al **presidente Morsi** y restauró el poder del ejército. Las protestas en favor de Morsi fueron reprimidas, y hubo atentados terroristas islamistas contra las fuerzas gubernamentales.

Se produjeron atentados terroristas islamistas en Malí y Kenia, en África; y, en abril, en EE. UU. hubo un ataque con bombas caseras contra los asistentes a la **maratón de Boston**.

En agosto, el empleo de gas neurotóxico **sarín** en la región de Guta, en los alrededores de **Damasco** (Siria), en manos rebeldes, estuvo cerca de provocar una campaña de bombardeo occidental contra el gobierno sirio.

El consultor del gobierno de EE. UU. **Edward Snowden** publicó documentos clasificados que revelaban la existencia de programas globales de vigilancia de su gobierno. Acusado de espionaje, huyó a Rusia en junio.

En febrero, la **explosión** de un **meteoroide** cerca de Cheliábinsk (Rusia), llamó la atención sobre el riesgo de **impactos desde el espacio**, aunque no hubo muertes.

El **fallecimiento** de **Nelson Mandela** reunió a jefes de Estado y miembros de la realeza en un acto **conmemorativo** en diciembre.

2014

5 VECES MÁS

EL NÚMERO DE **MUERTES POR ÉBOLA EN 2014** COMPARADO CON TODOS LOS DEMÁS **BROTES** CONOCIDOS

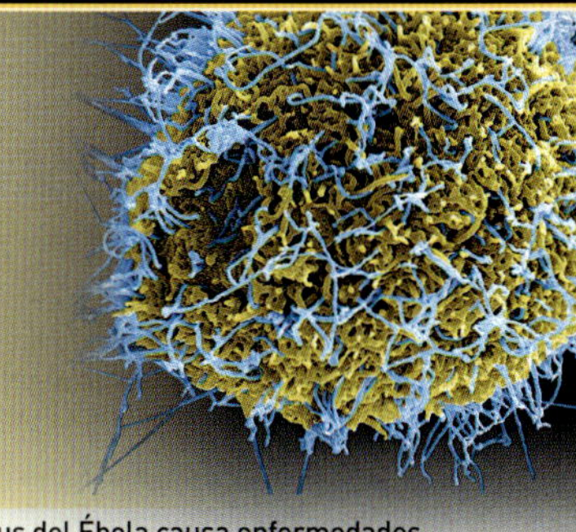

El virus del Ébola causa enfermedades graves, a menudo mortales, en humanos.

EL VUELO 17 DE MALAYSIA AIRLINES, en ruta hacia Kuala Lumpur, fue **abatido** por un **misil** sobre el este de Ucrania el 17 de julio, y sus **298 pasajeros** murieron. Fueron víctimas inocentes del conflicto entre Rusia y Ucrania. Al **derrocamiento** del presidente ucraniano **prorruso Víktor Yanukóvich** (n. 1950) en febrero, después de protestas masivas de ucranianos prooccidentales siguió la anexión rusa de **Crimea** y la toma de zonas del este de Ucrania por milicias prorrusas respaldadas por Moscú, a las que se enfrentaron fuerzas ucranianas.

En Iraq, el movimiento armado del **Estado Islámico de Iraq y el Levante** (EIIL, o EI), o Dáesh, lanzó una ofensiva y tomó la ciudad de **Mosul**. Los combatientes del Dáesh amenazaron Siria y Iraq, y fuerzas aéreas occidentales trataron de detener sin éxito su avance.

Otras muestras de la propagación del extremismo islamista se vieron en Nigeria, donde la rebelión de **Boko Haram** contra el gobierno atrajo la atención mundial por el **secuestro** de más de 200 niñas escolares cristianas en Chibok. África occidental padeció la mayor epidemia de **ébola** de la historia en febrero. Afectó gravemente a Guinea, Liberia y Sierra Leona. El misterio envolvió la suerte del **vuelo 370** de **Malaysia Airlines**, que **desapareció** sin dejar rastro en marzo tras desviarse de su ruta planeada a China.

En EE. UU., un agente de policía disparó al afroestadounidense de 18 años **Michael Brown** el 9 de agosto en San Luis (Misuri), lo cual desencadenó protestas violentas que popularizaron el lema **«Black Lives Matter»**.

La **Copa del Mundo de la FIFA** se celebró de junio a julio en **Brasil**. Protestas contra la corrupción del gobierno acompañaron el evento futbolístico.

En noviembre, la **misión Rosetta** fue la primera en posar con éxito una sonda sobre un cometa. Emprendió un viaje de diez años tras su lanzamiento en 2004.

El auge del Estado Islámico (EI)
Los combatientes del Estado Islámico (o Dáesh) usaron equipo militar pesado al ocupar Iraq.

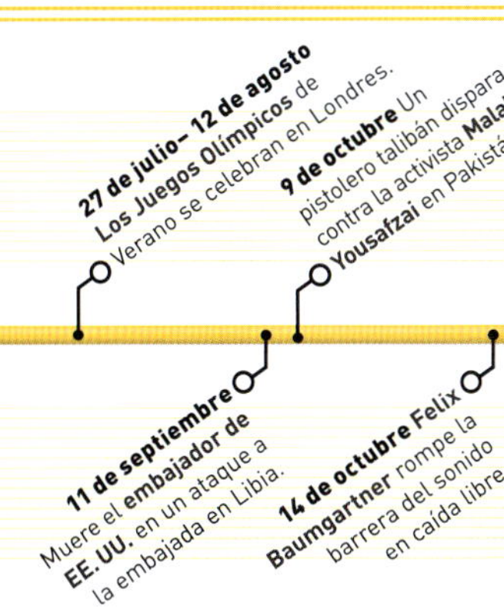

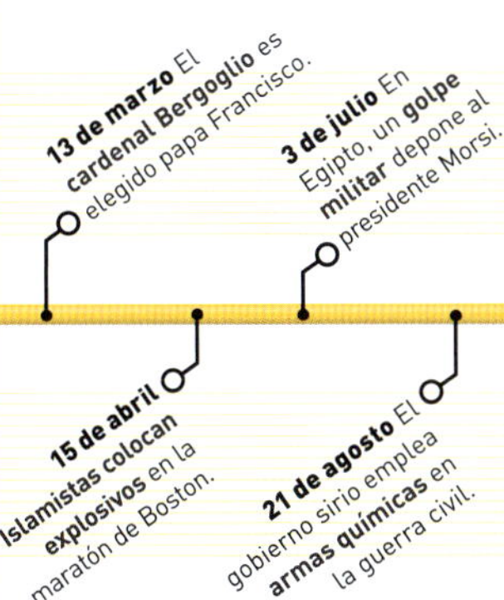

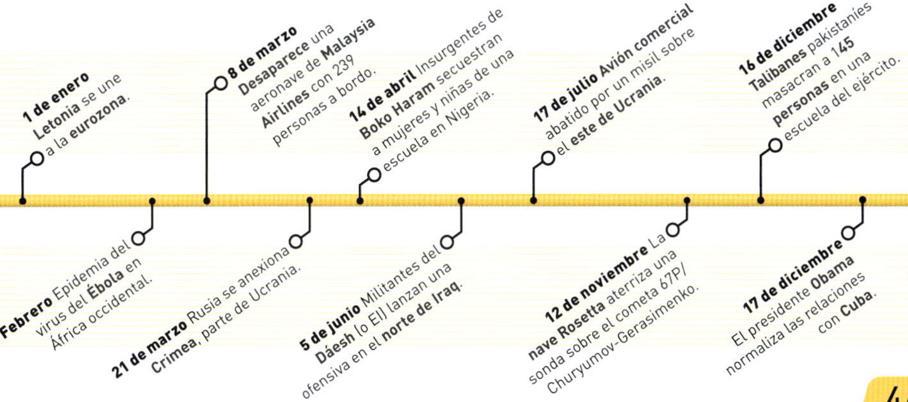

2015

Refugiados sirios llegan a Grecia en balsa.

EL ÁREA MEDITERRÁNEA VIVIÓ UNA CRISIS DE REFUGIADOS MASIVA al huir de la guerra y llegar por mar a Grecia e Italia gran número de migrantes, en su mayoría musulmanes. Muchos, desesperados, se dirigieron al norte y encontraron refugio en **Alemania**. Miles de ellos se ahogaron en naufragios, y la respuesta humanitaria fue escasa, por temor a que se **infiltraran en Europa** terroristas islamistas haciéndose pasar por refugiados.

Francia sufrió **atentados islamistas**. El 7 de enero, en el ataque a la sede del semanario satírico *Charlie Hebdo*, por publicar caricaturas controvertidas del profeta Mahoma murieron doce personas. El 13 de noviembre **murieron 130 personas** en una serie de ataques terroristas en **París**, incluida la sala de conciertos de rock **Bataclan**.

Otros actos terroristas islamistas fueron un **tiroteo** en San Bernardino, en California (EE.UU.), un avión comercial ruso abatido sobre el Sinaí en Egipto y una matanza de turistas en una playa de Túnez. Se **condenó** al Dáesh (o EI) por destruir monumentos, maltratar a comunidades cristianas y realizar matanzas sádicas de prisioneros en zonas de Iraq y Siria.

Aparte de la crisis migratoria, la política europea se caracterizó por la reacción **contra la austeridad**, que llevó al poder en enero al partido de izquierda **Syriza** en Grecia y convirtió en un partido importante a **Podemos** en España.

En junio, las revelaciones sobre corrupción obligaron a **dimitir** al presidente de la **FIFA Sepp Blatter**.

873 000

ES EL NÚMERO DE **REFUGIADOS** QUE LLEGARON A **GRECIA** POR MAR EN **2015**

JUSTIN TRUDEAU (n. 1971)

Elegido primer ministro de Canadá en 2015, Justin Trudeau, líder del Partido Liberal de Canadá, despertó el entusiasmo popular con una imagen glamurosa y un mensaje de esperanza e inclusividad social. Derrotó al conservador Stephen Harper, y el número de escaños del Partido Liberal de Canadá en el Parlamento pasó de 36 a 184. Justin es hijo de Pierre Trudeau, primer ministro de Canadá durante quince años entre las décadas de 1960 y 1980.

2016

« YA NO PODEMOS PERMITIRNOS SER TAN **POLÍTICAMENTE CORRECTOS. »**

Donald Trump, Convención Nacional Republicana (21 de julio de 2016)

ESTE FUE UN AÑO EN QUE LOS ELECTORADOS DESAFIARON LAS PREDICCIONES de los expertos. En EE.UU., los comentaristas habían anunciado que las elecciones de noviembre darían al país su primera mujer presidenta, **Hillary Clinton** (n. 1947) pero el vencedor por un margen estrecho fue el multimillonario candidato republicano **Donald Trump** (n. 1946), pese a la oposición de gran parte de su propio partido y una campaña manchada por declaraciones desaforadas y revelaciones dañinas sobre su actitud hacia las mujeres.

En Gran Bretaña, el primer ministro **David Cameron** (n. 1966) convocó un **referéndum** sobre la pertenencia del país a la **Unión Europea** (UE), confiando en que el voto la confirmara, pero, por una pequeña mayoría, los británicos eligieron abandonarla tras una virulenta campaña de los partidarios de salir de la UE (el llamado *brexit*). La decisión llevó a cambios en el gobierno, con **Theresa May** (n. 1956) como primera ministra y puestos clave del gabinete en manos de partidarios del *brexit*.

El 11 de junio, **Omar Mateen** mató a 49 personas con un fusil semiautomático en la **discoteca gay Pulse** en Orlando (Florida, EE.UU.). En Francia, el 14 de julio, un camión arrolló a familias que celebraban el **Día de la Bastilla** en Niza, **matando a 86 personas**. Los autores de este y otros ataques dijeron ser seguidores del **movimiento del Dáesh** (o Estado Islámico, EI), que empleaba **internet** para incitar a la violencia a los musulmanes. El Dáesh estaba implicado también en la **guerra civil** siria (*véase* 2012), en la que continuaban los combates. La toma de **Alepo** por tropas gubernamentales con respaldo ruso en diciembre fue un gran revés para las fuerzas antigubernamentales y para el Dáesh. Se estimó en medio millón el número de muertos por el conflicto.

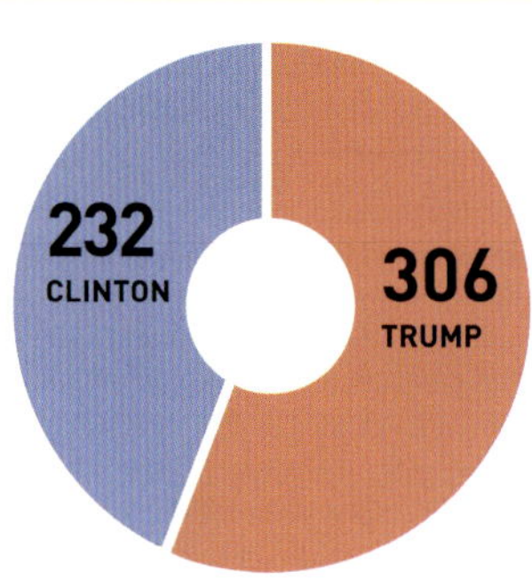

Recuento electoral en EE.UU. (2016)
Hillary Clinton obtuvo más votos a nivel nacional, pero Donald Trump tuvo la mayoría del Colegio Electoral por estados.

En Colombia, un alto el fuego en junio puso fin a la larga campaña guerrillera de las Fuerzas Armadas **Revolucionarias de Colombia (FARC)**, iniciada en 1964. El 24 de noviembre se firmó la paz entre las FARC y el gobierno colombiano.

Los Juegos Olímpicos de Verano se celebraron en **Río de Janeiro**, pese a la epidemia del virus del **Zika** y la crisis política brasileña.

Este también fue el año de la muerte de tres gigantes de la música popular, **Leonard Cohen**, **Prince** y **David Bowie**.

2017

Irma fue el huracán más potente registrado en la cuenca atlántica.

EL INICIO DEL MANDATO DE DONALD TRUMP como presidente de EE.UU. fue **controvertido**. Fue acusado de obtener ayuda rusa encubierta en las elecciones, y los tribunales declararon discriminatoria la orden de **impedir la entrada a visitantes** de determinados países. Abandonó el Acuerdo de París de 2015 sobre Cambio Climático en junio, y estados individuales respondieron con una alianza para lograr sus objetivos.

Los gestos del líder norcoreano **Kim Jong-un** fueron cada vez más agresivos: amenazó con lanzar **misiles nucleares** sobre EE.UU. y realizó una prueba con un misil balístico intercontinental el 4 de julio. **Trump** respondió amenazando con «**destruir totalmente**» Corea del Norte.

Confirmando las predicciones científicas sobre gases de efecto invernadero y clima, la temporada de **huracanes en el Atlántico** en 2017 fue terrible. Había causado una destrucción generalizada en las **islas del Caribe**.

En Europa, los movimientos contrarios a la UE perdieron las elecciones en 2017, destacando la derrota del candidato de la derecha en Francia ante el centrista **Emmanuel Macron** (n. 1977). En Reino Unido, la primera ministra **Theresa May** perdió la mayoría parlamentaria tras prometer hacer efectivo el *brexit* en su campaña.

En España, el **Gobierno de Cataluña** convocó un referéndum ilegal sobre la independencia, y el gobierno central respondió asumiendo el control directo de la comunidad en octubre.

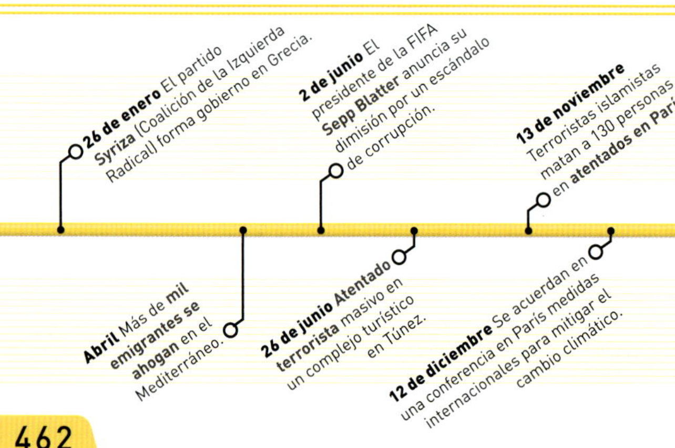

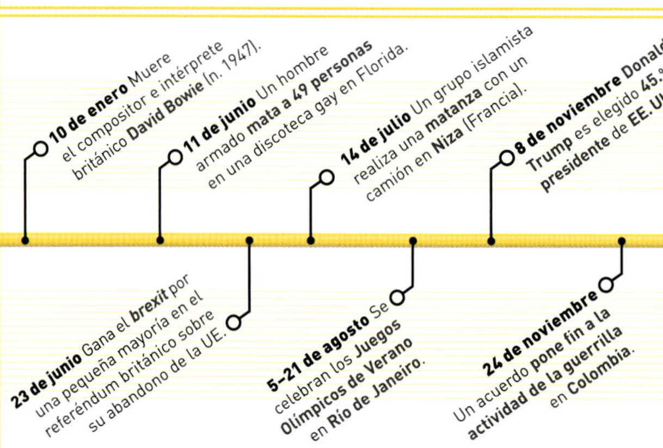

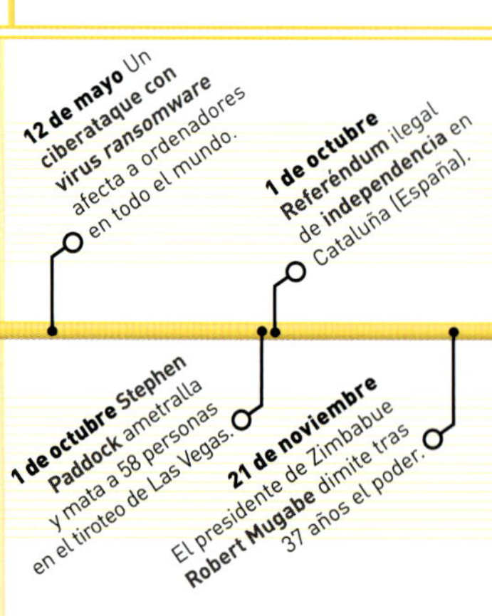

2018

La huelga escolar de Greta Thunberg comenzó como protesta en solitario, pero desencadenó un movimiento juvenil global de activismo contra la crisis climática.

EL 21 DE MARZO, 44 PAÍSES AFRICANOS FORMARON la **Zona de Libre Comercio Continental Africana (AfCFTA)**, la mayor área de libre comercio del mundo después de la OMC. Aunque tardaría años en tener pleno efecto, el acuerdo buscaba eliminar barreras al comercio y estimular la prosperidad para 1300 millones de personas en 55 países.

El físico teórico británico **Stephen Hawking**, brillante científicos de su tiempo, falleció en marzo, a los 76 años de edad.

En abril, **Kim Jong-un** fue el primer líder norcoreano en pisar Corea del Sur y, dos meses después, en reunirse con **Donald Trump** en Singapur.

El productor cinematográfico **Harvey Weinstein** fue detenido en mayo en Nueva York, acusado de delitos sexuales contra dos mujeres. La cobertura mediática de sus abusos contra muy numerosas actrices y trabajadoras revitalizó el movimiento **#MeToo** de 2006, y animó a miles de mujeres a compartir sus experiencias de acoso y abusos en las redes sociales y a exigir el cambio.

El año 2018 trajo victorias sociales progresistas: **Irlanda** votó para derogar la prohibición del aborto en mayo; en junio, en **Arabia Saudí** se abolió al fin la prohibición de conducir a las mujeres; en septiembre, el **Tribunal Supremo de India despenalizó** la **homosexualidad**.

En julio, graves inundaciones en **Japón** mataron a 225 personas, el primero de una serie de **desastres** ambientales, desde inundaciones fatales en el estado indio de Kerala hasta incendios devastadores en Grecia y California. El 20 de agosto, la escolar de quince años **Greta Thunberg** inició la «huelga escolar por el clima» ante el Parlamento sueco, inspirando a cientos de miles en todo el mundo a hacer igual y situándose en el primer plano del debate climático.

En octubre, el candidato de extrema derecha **Jair Bolsonaro** (n. 1955) ganó las elecciones presidenciales en Brasil.

> « SI HAS SUFRIDO **ACOSO O ABUSOS SEXUALES**, ESCRIBE **"ME TOO"** COMO RESPUESTA A ESTE TUIT. »
>
> **Alyssa Milano**, actriz

JACINDA ARDERN (n. 1980)

Elegida primera ministra de Nueva Zelanda en 2017, con 37 años de edad, gobernó primero como parte de una coalición en minoría, antes de llevar al Partido Laborista a la mayoría en 2020. Segunda jefe de gobierno en ser madre ejerciendo el cargo (después de Benazir Bhutto, de Pakistán), fue muy alabada por su liderazgo tras la masacre de Christchurch en 2019 y por su hábil gestión de la pandemia de la COVID-19. Dejó el cargo en enero de 2023.

2019

840 MILLONES DE EUROS ES LA CANTIDAD APORTADA POR **DONANTES PRIVADOS** PARA **RECONSTRUIR NOTRE DAME** EN SEPTIEMBRE DE 2021

Aunque las obras continúan, restaurar los daños del incendio en Notre Dame puede llevar décadas.

UN SUPREMACISTA BLANCO MATÓ A 51 PERSONAS al abrir fuego el 15 de marzo en dos mezquitas en **Christchurch** (Nueva Zelanda). El australiano Brenton Tarrant, de 29 años de edad, emitió en directo en redes sociales en *streaming* la matanza –la más sangrienta en la historia del país–, y pronto fue detenido por la policía. La primera ministra **Jacinda Ardern** (n. 1980) hizo aprobar leyes más estrictas sobre armas de fuego.

Después de muchos años en el poder, el presidente de Sudán **Omar al Bashir** (n. 1944) fue **derrocado en abril** tras meses de **protestas** por la crisis económica. Pero el golpe militar no frenó los disturbios, y en la represión en **Jartum** murieron 100 personas antes de lograrse un acuerdo para la transición a la democracia.

Se difundió la **primera imagen de un agujero negro** en la galaxia Messier 87, a más de 50 millones de años luz.

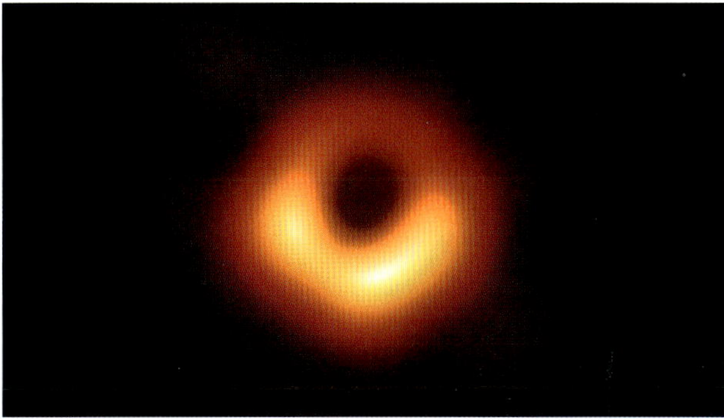

TELESCOPIO EVENT HORIZON
La primera imagen obtenida de un agujero negro se compuso con los datos de una red de telescopios global.

Un incendio devastador en la **catedral de Notre Dame, en París**, destruyó dos tercios del tejado y la aguja principal. Al día siguiente, el 16 de abril, el presidente francés Emmanuel Macron se comprometió a reconstruir el edificio de 850 años de antigüedad.

Por motivos de salud, a sus 85 años, el **emperador Akihito** (n. 1933) abdicó en abril en favor de su hijo el **príncipe heredero Naruhito** (n. 1960). Fue el primer emperador de Japón en **abdicar** en 200 años.

En mayo, el primer ministro indio **Narendra Modi** (n. 1950) logró un segundo mandato con la victoria electoral decisiva del Partido Popular Indio (BJP), nacionalista hindú. La primera ministra británica **Theresa May** tuvo que dimitir en septiembre, tras rechazar repetidamente el Parlamento su acuerdo de retirada del *brexit*. Su sucesor fue **Boris Johnson** (n. 1964), quien logró aplicar un acuerdo revisado tras ganar las elecciones anticipadas de diciembre. En **Hong Kong** **comenzaron** en marzo las **protestas antigubernamentales** contra una propuesta de ley para permitir las extradiciones a **China**. Se temía que acabara con el acuerdo «un país, dos sistemas» de la antigua colonia británica, vigente desde su entrega a China en 1997. La propuesta se retiró en septiembre, pero las **manifestaciones** se volvieron más violentas con las nuevas exigencias de los manifestantes y la represión de las autoridades, que causaron un éxodo de la ciudad.

En junio, **Ecuador** votó para **legalizar el matrimonio** de personas del **mismo sexo**, un triunfo para los derechos LGBTQ+ en América del Sur.

En **Australia**, los incendios destruyeron millones de hectáreas durante el verano en el **peor desastre natural** del país hasta la fecha.

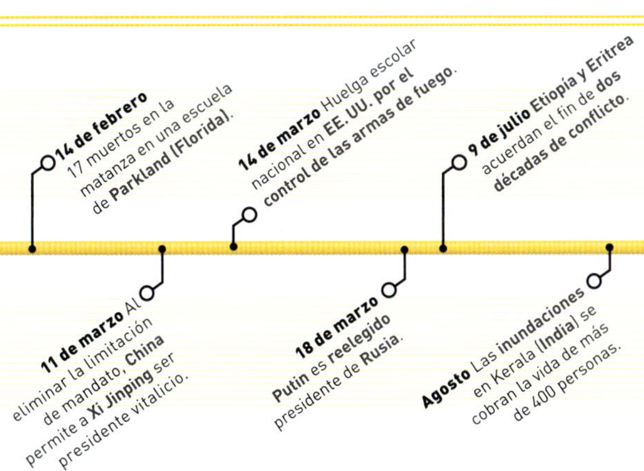

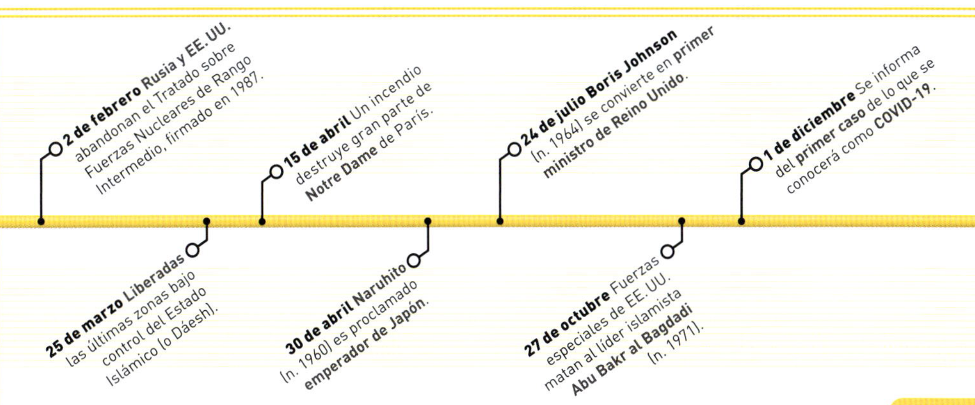

2020

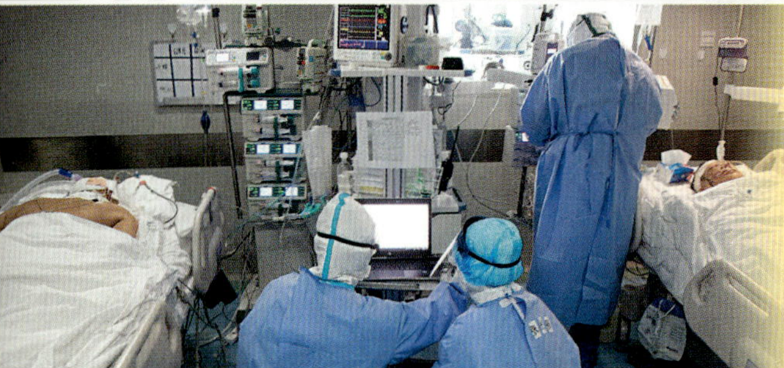
Pacientes con COVID-19 en un hospital de Wuhan (China), donde se produjo el primer brote viral de la pandemia del SARS-CoV-2.

6 960 000

ES LA CIFRA DE MUERTES CONFIRMADAS POR **COVID-19** EN EL MUNDO EN 2023

EL AÑO 2020 ESTUVO DOMINADO POR LA PANDEMIA DE LA COVID-19. Se informó de que los primeros casos de infecciones se produjeron en **Wuhan (China)** en diciembre de 2019. Aunque leves en su mayoría (con fiebre, dolores y tos entre los síntomas más comunes), la **primera muerte** se confirmó el **11 de enero**. Se decretó la cuarentena en la ciudad el 23 de enero, demasiado tarde para detener la propagación. El 11 de marzo, la OMS declaró la **pandemia**.

Italia fue el primer país en introducir el **confinamiento nacional** en marzo. Se detuvo la actividad comercial y se restringieron los viajes, y se instó a la población a permanecer en sus casas y adoptar **medidas preventivas**, como la distancia de seguridad, lavarse regularmente las manos y usar mascarilla para reducir el contagio. El **impacto económico** fue enorme: las bolsas se desplomaron entre febrero y abril, y las **economías entraron en recesión**. Cerraron negocios –sobre todo turísticos y hosteleros– y dieron de baja a sus empleados, mientras se posponían o cancelaban muchos eventos culturales y deportivos. Quienes pudieron trabajaron y estudiaron desde sus casas.

Los precios del petróleo se desplomaron en abril, y se ralentizaron las cadenas de suministro globales. Los gobiernos aprobaron una serie de medidas de apoyo y estímulo, incurriendo con ello en una **deuda enorme**. Con las redes sociales repletas de teorías conspirativas sobre el virus, estallaron **protestas** contra el **confinamiento y la obligación de llevar mascarilla**.

Pandemia global
En India siguen el protocolo de la COVID-19. La pandemia paralizó muchos países, y costó 76 billones de euros a la economía mundial.

Pese a los temores, las tasas de infección se mantuvieron relativamente bajas en **África**, y se alabó a líderes de todo el continente por su **eficaz respuesta**. Mientras tanto, empresas farmacéuticas y gobiernos colaboraron para desarrollar **vacunas** en tiempo récord, consiguiendo realizar en meses un proceso que antes llevaba años. Las primeras vacunas estuvieron disponibles en diciembre.

Más allá de la pandemia, el año comenzó con el proceso de destitución del **presidente de EE. UU. Donald Trump** el 16 de enero por abuso de poder y obstrucción del Congreso. Fue absuelto más tarde.

En mayo, el asesinato del afroestadounidense **George Floyd** a manos de la policía en **Mineápolis** sacó a millones de personas a las calles en apoyo del movimiento **Black Lives Matter** en EE. UU. y unos sesenta países más.

En agosto, la **enorme explosión** en el **puerto de Beirut** (Líbano) de una gran cantidad de nitrato de amonio volátil almacenado mató al menos a 218 personas, hirió a 7000 y causó daños por unos 14 000 millones de euros.

En noviembre, el laboratorio **DeepMind** resolvió uno de los mayores misterios, el plegamiento de proteínas. La capacidad del programa **AlphaFold** para predecir su estructura 3D ayudó a comprender mejor ciertas enfermedades, crear medicamentos nuevos e inventar nuevas maneras de descomponer plásticos contaminantes.

Argentina despenalizó el aborto, siendo el mayor país de América del Sur en hacerlo.

Manifestantes contrarios al resultado electoral ocupan el Capitolio.

LA PRESIDENCIA DE DONALD TRUMP ACABÓ de forma convulsa, con el asalto de más de dos mil **manifestantes al Capitolio** en Washington D. C., el 6 de enero, con el objetivo de detener la certificación del resultado de las elecciones de noviembre. Haciéndose eco de las infundadas acusaciones de fraude electoral, los asaltantes saquearon el edificio durante horas hasta que la policía recuperó el control; finalmente, el vicepresidente Mike Pence (n. 1959) pudo declarar formalmente ganador al presidente electo demócrata **Joe Biden** (n. 1942). Hubo cinco muertos y cientos de heridos. Se inició **un segundo proceso de destitución de Trump** por incitar a la insurrección, pero fue absuelto por el Senado.

En febrero, en **Myanmar**, la líder electa **Aung San Suu Kyi** (n. 1945) fue destituida por militares por un supuesto fraude electoral, y las protestas generalizadas fueron reprimidas.

7,5 MILLONES

43 300

Asistencia a las Olimpiadas de 2016 y 2020
Tras el retraso debido a la pandemia, los Juegos Olímpicos de Tokio de 2020 se celebraron en 2021, pero con la asistencia muy restringida.

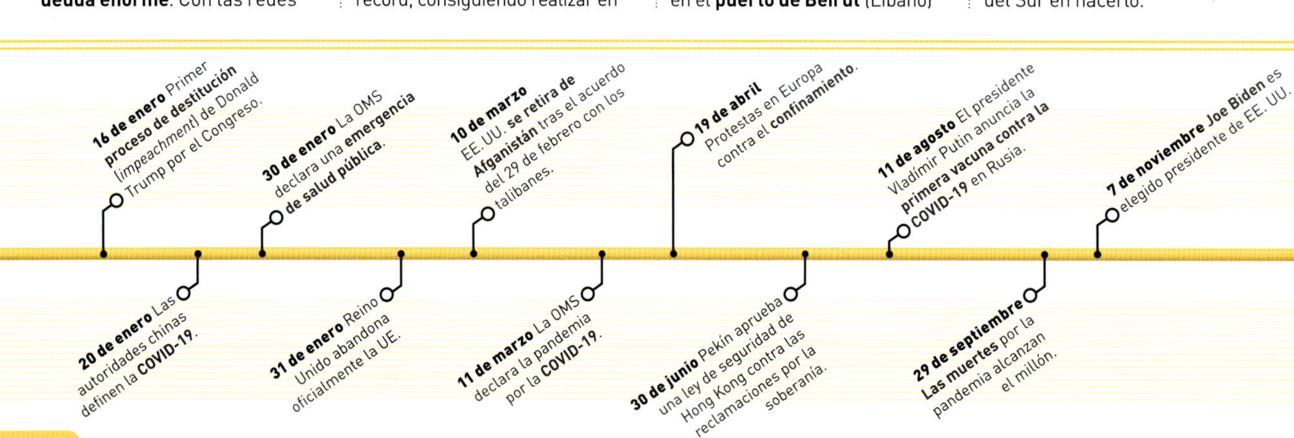

« UN **DÍA SOMBRÍO** EN LA **HISTORIA DEL CAPITOLIO DE ESTADOS UNIDOS**. »

El vicepresidente de EE. UU. Mike Pence, sobre el asalto al Congreso

El presidente de **Chad Idriss Déby** (n. 1952), en el poder desde 1990, fue asesinado en abril durante una visita a las tropas que combatían a los rebeldes en el norte.

En mayo, **Malí** sufrió el **segundo golpe de Estado** en nueve meses, y el **coronel Assimi Goïta** fue objeto de condena internacional por tomar de nuevo el poder.

El 7 de julio, el asesinato del presidente de **Haití Jovenel Moiseis** desestabilizó al país.

Tras la retirada en mayo de tropas de EE. UU., los **talibanes tomaron Kabul** el 15 de agosto, mucho antes de lo esperado, reinstauraron el **Emirato Islámico de Afganistán** y pusieron fin a veinte años de guerra. Durante las dos semanas siguientes, una operación aérea de EE. UU. y sus aliados evacuó a más de 120 000 personas.

Pese al **rápido despliegue** de las **vacunas** (con unos mil millones administradas antes de la primavera), la COVID-19 continuó con la más contagiosa variante del SARS-CoV-2 llamada ómicron. Con todo, la **Olimpiada** pospuesta de **2020** se celebró en **Tokio** en julio y agosto.

2022

« **LA LUCHA ESTÁ AQUÍ**; NECESITO **MUNICIÓN**, NO UN VIAJE. »

Volodímir Zelenski, presidente de Ucrania, en respuesta a la oferta de EE. UU. de evacuarle del país

Elegido presidente de Ucrania en 2019, Volodímir Zelenski se convirtió en una figura internacional, reconocible por la ropa de campaña verde en apoyo a sus fuerzas armadas.

RUSIA INVADIÓ UCRANIA el 24 de febrero. El presidente ruso expuso como objetivo «desmilitarizar» y «desnazificar» **Ucrania**, a la que acusó de perseguir a la población rusa. Su ataque encontró una **resistencia** inesperadamente **feroz**, que impidió a **Putin** una victoria rápida e intensificó el riesgo de represalia nuclear. El presidente de Ucrania **Volodímir Zelenski** (n. 1978), actor retirado, fue alabado por su liderazgo durante el conflicto, que desató la mayor **crisis de refugiados** en Europa desde la Segunda Guerra Mundial. Muchos países **impusieron sanciones a Rusia** y suministraron a Ucrania armas y ayuda. Las repercusiones de la guerra fueron globales: en marzo, el Índice de Precios de los Alimentos (de la FAO) alcanzó su máximo desde que existe, y se dispararon también los precios del petróleo y del gas.

En **Australia**, el líder del Partido Laborista **Anthony Albanese** (n. 1963) derrotó al primer ministro **Scott Morrison** (n. 1968) del Partido Liberal en las elecciones federales de mayo.

En junio, el **Tribunal Supremo** de EE. UU. derogó el fallo del **caso Roe contra Wade**, que consagraba el derecho constitucional al aborto, y de ceder a los estados la potestad de prohibirlo.

Varios museos, como el **Humboldt Forum**, en Berlín (en agosto) y el **Museo Horniman**, en Londres (en noviembre), transfirieron a **Nigeria** la propiedad de los llamados **bronces de Benín**, piezas artísticas (en realidad de latón) que fueron saqueadas del palacio real del **reino de Benín** en el siglo XIX. En **Japón**, el 8 de julio, durante un discurso de campaña por un candidato del Partido Liberal Democrático en Nara, el ex primer ministro **Shinzo Abe** (n. 1954) fue asesinado por un hombre armado con un arma de fabricación casera.

Tras haber celebrado sus 70 años en el trono el mismo año, la **reina Isabel II** de Reino Unido murió el 8 de septiembre a los 96 años en el **Castillo de Balmoral** (Escocia). Se declararon diez días de luto nacional antes de su funeral de Estado. Nombrada dos días antes de la muerte de la monarca, la sucesora de Boris Johnson, **Liz Truss**, fue la **primera ministra más breve de Reino Unido**, al verse obligada a dimitir tras 45 días en el cargo.

En septiembre, en **Irán**, la muerte de **Mahsa Amini**, de 22 años, bajo custodia policial tras ser detenida por no usar correctamente el pañuelo (hiyab) que cubre la cabeza y el pecho, desató **protestas por todo el país**. En la represión del gobierno murieron varios cientos de jóvenes más.

Mientras la población mundial superaba los 8000 millones en noviembre, el lanzamiento del ***chatbot* de inteligencia artificial (IA)** de **ChatGPT** por el laboratorio OpenAI de San Francisco ofreció un atisbo del increíble potencial de la IA.

Funeral de Estado
El 19 de septiembre, un millón de personas vieron el funeral de Estado de Isabel II en Londres.

2023

Xi Jinping jura el cargo tras ser reelegido presidente de China.

EN UN ECO DEL ASALTO AL CAPITOLIO DE EE. UU. EN 2021, partidarios del expresidente de extrema derecha de Brasil **Jair Bolsonaro** asaltaron edificios gubernamentales en la capital, Brasilia, a la semana de asumir el cargo el candidato de izquierda **Lula da Silva** (n. 1945) en enero. En febrero, un **gran terremoto** en **Turquía y Siria** mató a 60 000 personas y causó daños por valor de decenas de miles de millones de euros.

Al obtener un **tercer mandato** sin precedentes en marzo, el jefe del Partido Comunista Chino **Xi Jinping** fue el líder más poderoso del país desde Mao Zedong.

En abril, las tensiones entre facciones militares rivales en **Sudán** estallaron como **conflicto armado** en Jartum y otras ciudades, amenazando con llevar al país a una nueva guerra civil.

El primogénito de Isabel II, **Carlos III**, y su esposa **Camila** fueron coronados **rey y reina de Reino Unido** en la abadía de Westminster el 6 de mayo.

Tras meses de estancamiento en la **guerra entre Rusia y Ucrania**, Ucrania lanzó una ofensiva en junio.

160 000 EDIFICIOS RESULTARON **DESTRUIDOS** EN EL **TERREMOTO DE TURQUÍA Y SIRIA**

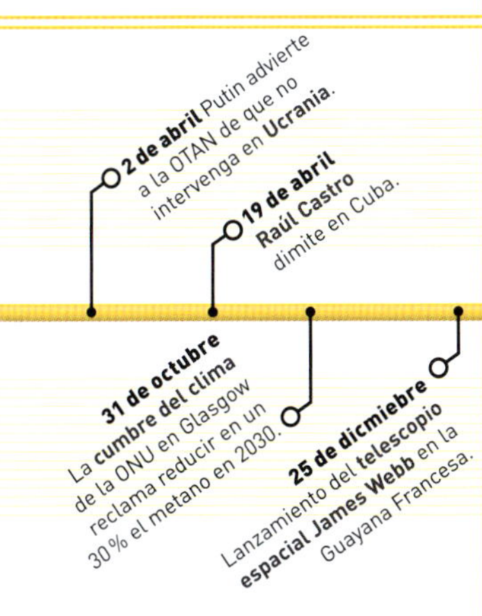

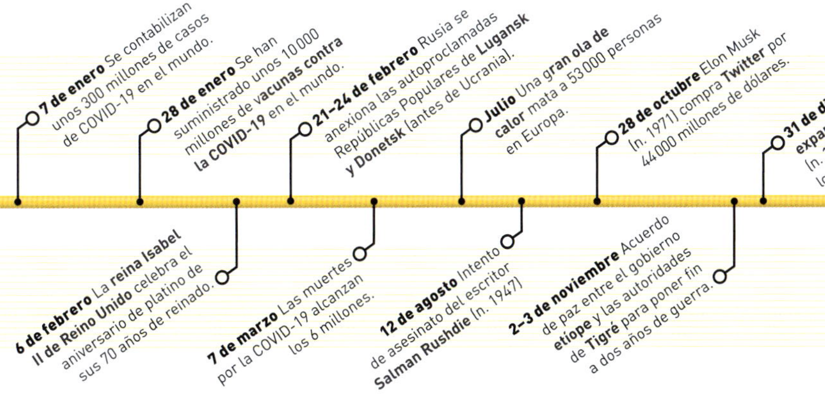

17 de marzo El TPI emite una **orden de detención** contra **Putin**.

4 de abril Finlandia se convierte en el 31.º miembro de la **OTAN**.

4 de mayo Unas **inundaciones** en la **R. D. del Congo** matan a más de 400 personas.

20 de julio Final de la **Copa Mundial Femenina de la FIFA** en Australia y Nueva Zelanda, con victoria de España.

LA ECONOMÍA GLOBAL

LA BRECHA ENTRE RICOS Y POBRES SE ENSANCHA CADA VEZ MÁS

El mundo es más rico que nunca gracias a las alianzas internacionales y a la tecnología. No obstante, prosiguen las guerras, existen muchas bolsas de pobreza y los desastres naturales devastan incluso a las naciones más desarrolladas.

La población mundial es de unos ocho mil millones de personas, el triple que en 1900. El porvenir de las personas depende de su lugar de nacimiento y la distribución de la riqueza no ha cambiado mucho desde el fin de la Segunda Guerra Mundial. Muchos de los países con rentas altas se hallan en el hemisferio norte, mientras que los más pobres están en África. Los cinco países más ricos acumulan más de la mitad del PIB mundial, mientras que casi la mitad de la población del planeta sobrevive con menos de 6,85 dólares diarios.

Los países de Europa occidental, América del Norte y la cuenca del Pacífico cuentan con sectores empresariales consolidados y con multinacionales cuyos productos se venden en todo el mundo. Las naciones de África y América Central tienen una gama más reducida de industrias, y muchas dependen del comercio de una sola mercancía. Las economías de países como México, Brasil e India están creciendo rápidamente.

EE. UU.

Aunque EE. UU. es el país más rico del mundo, solo alberga al 4,2 % de la población mundial. El 39 % de los millonarios del mundo viven en EE. UU., que también presenta el nivel más elevado de deuda privada.

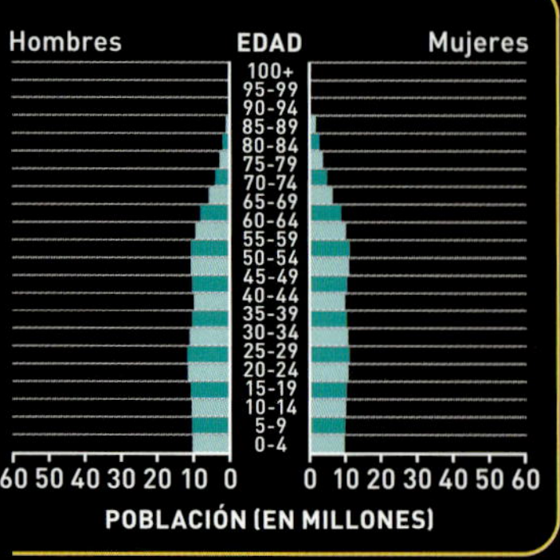

AMÉRICA DEL NORTE

OCÉANO ATLÁNTICO

Mundo interdependiente

Las economías mundiales se basan en un amplio abanico de sectores e industrias y las poblaciones varían entre los ochocientos habitantes (Ciudad del Vaticano) y los más de mil millones (China e India). Sin embargo, no hay ningún país autosuficiente y todos dependen del comercio con otros países para satisfacer plenamente sus necesidades.

AMÉRICA DEL SUR

OCÉANO PACÍFICO

OCÉANO ATLÁNTICO

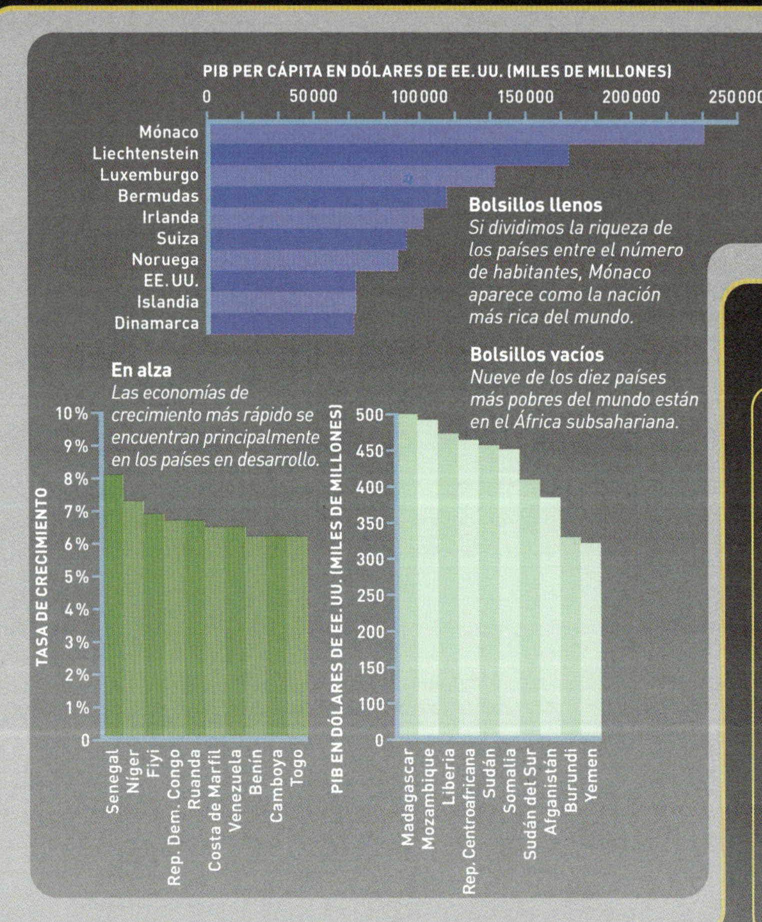

Bolsillos llenos
Si dividimos la riqueza de los países entre el número de habitantes, Mónaco aparece como la nación más rica del mundo.

En alza
Las economías de crecimiento más rápido se encuentran principalmente en los países en desarrollo.

Bolsillos vacíos
Nueve de los diez países más pobres del mundo están en el África subsahariana.

BRASIL

Brasil es la mayor economía de América del Sur y la octava del mundo. Los sectores agrícola, minero y de servicios están muy consolidados y han contribuido a crear una economía saludable. Aun así, sigue habiendo una diferencia gigantesca entre ricos y pobres.

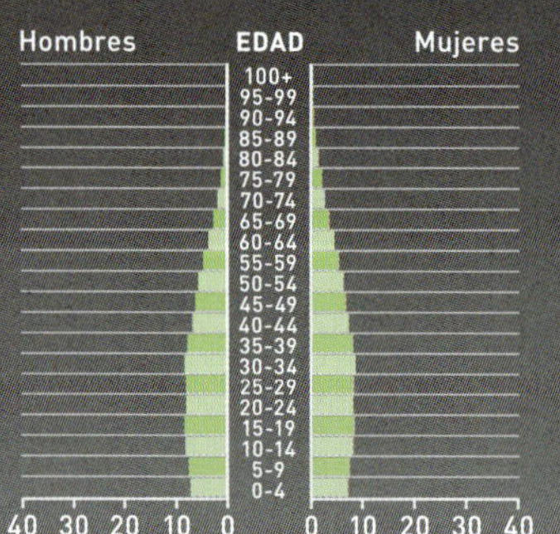

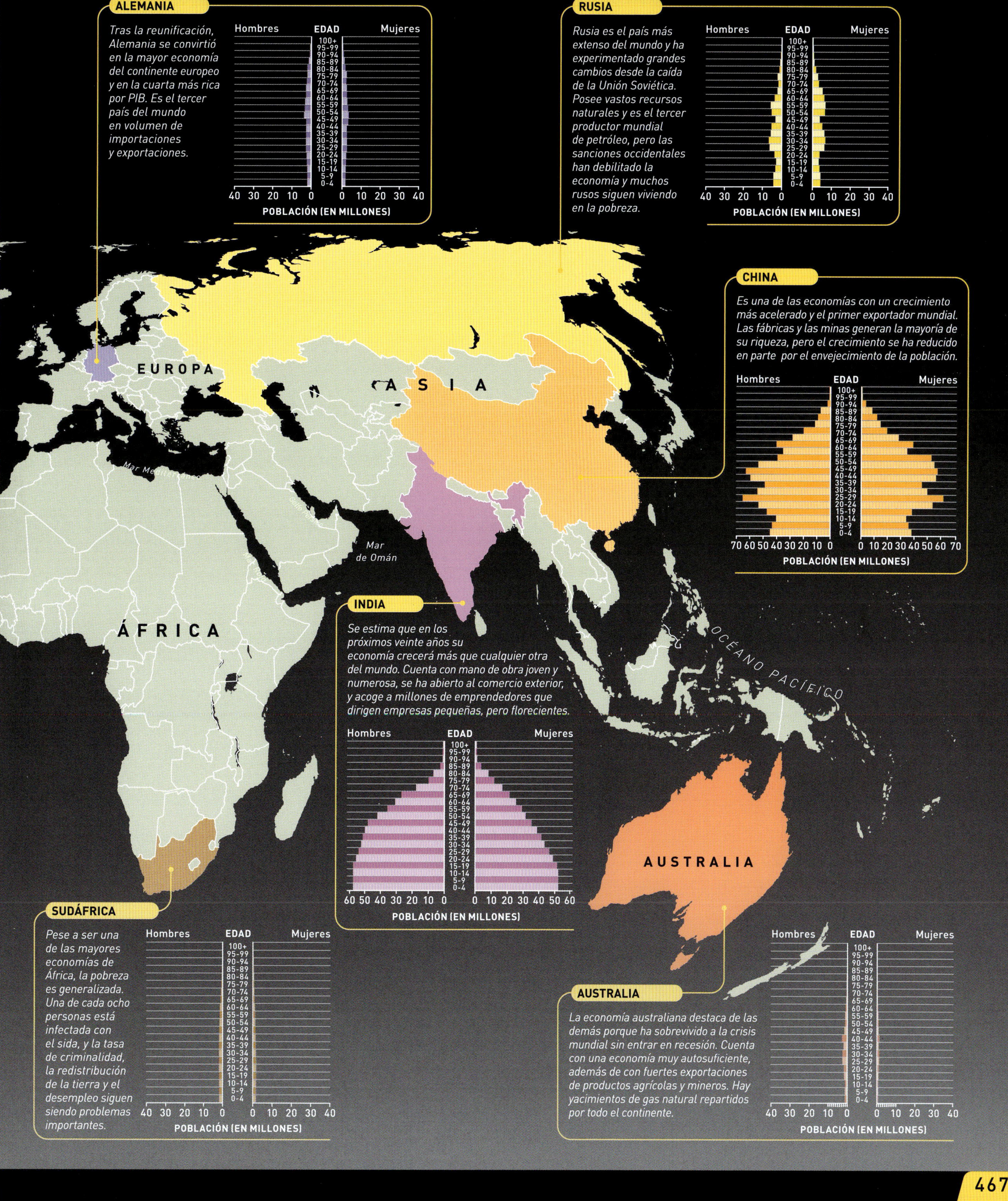
ALEMANIA
Tras la reunificación, Alemania se convirtió en la mayor economía del continente europeo y en la cuarta más rica por PIB. Es el tercer país del mundo en volumen de importaciones y exportaciones.
Hombres
EDAD
Mujeres
POBLACIÓN (EN MILLONES)
RUSIA
Rusia es el país más extenso del mundo y ha experimentado grandes cambios desde la caída de la Unión Soviética. Posee vastos recursos naturales y es el tercer productor mundial de petróleo, pero las sanciones occidentales han debilitado la economía y muchos rusos siguen viviendo en la pobreza.
Hombres
EDAD
Mujeres
POBLACIÓN (EN MILLONES)
CHINA
Es una de las economías con un crecimiento más acelerado y el primer exportador mundial. Las fábricas y las minas generan la mayoría de su riqueza, pero el crecimiento se ha reducido en parte por el envejecimiento de la población.
Hombres
EDAD
Mujeres
POBLACIÓN (EN MILLONES)
EUROPA
ASIA
ÁFRICA
Mar de Omán
OCÉANO PACÍFICO
INDIA
Se estima que en los próximos veinte años su economía crecerá más que cualquier otra del mundo. Cuenta con mano de obra joven y numerosa, se ha abierto al comercio exterior, y acoge a millones de emprendedores que dirigen empresas pequeñas, pero florecientes.
Hombres
EDAD
Mujeres
POBLACIÓN (EN MILLONES)
AUSTRALIA
SUDÁFRICA
Pese a ser una de las mayores economías de África, la pobreza es generalizada. Una de cada ocho personas está infectada con el sida, y la tasa de criminalidad, la redistribución de la tierra y el desempleo siguen siendo problemas importantes.
Hombres
EDAD
Mujeres
POBLACIÓN (EN MILLONES)
AUSTRALIA
La economía australiana destaca de las demás porque ha sobrevivido a la crisis mundial sin entrar en recesión. Cuenta con una economía muy autosuficiente, además de con fuertes exportaciones de productos agrícolas y mineros. Hay yacimientos de gas natural repartidos por todo el continente.
Hombres
EDAD
Mujeres
POBLACIÓN (EN MILLONES)

APÉNDICE

REYES Y GOBERNANTES

Tanto si acceden al poder por herencia como por elección democrática o por la fuerza, los gobernantes toman decisiones que pesarán en el juicio de la historia sobre su mandato. Algunos poderosos líderes fueron la salvación de su pueblo, mientras que los débiles llevaron a la ruina y la humillación a grandes imperios.

FARAONES EGIPCIOS

La historia del antiguo Egipto se divide en varios grandes periodos: el Imperio Antiguo (2686–2181 a.C.); el Imperio Medio (2040–1650 a.C.) y el Imperio Nuevo (1550–1070 a.C.), separados por periodos intermedios, mas un periodo tardío (747–332 a.C.). Durante este tiempo gobernaron Egipto numerosas dinastías, desde la I (3100–2890 a.C.), anterior al Imperio Antiguo, hasta la XXVI (664–525 a.C.), que terminó a raíz de la conquista de Egipto por el rey persa Cambises. Excepto durante un breve periodo en que soberanos nativos recuperaron el poder, Egipto quedó bajo dominio persa hasta 332 a.C., cuando fue conquistado por Alejandro Magno. En el año 30 a.C. pasó a formar parte del Imperio romano.

PERIODO	DINASTÍA	PRINCIPALES FARAONES
Periodo protodinástico (3100–2686 a.C.)	Dinastía I (3100–2890 a.C.)	Narmer (*c.* 3100 a.C.) Menes (*c.* 3000 a.C.) Den (*c.* 2950 a.C.)
	Dinastía II (2890–2686 a.C.)	Peribsen (*c.* 2700 a.C.)
Imperio Antiguo (2686–2181 a.C.)	Dinastía III (2686–2613 a.C.)	Zoser (2667–2648 a.C.)
	Dinastía IV (2613–2494 a.C.)	Snefru (2613–2589 a.C.) Keops (Jufu) (2589–2566 a.C.) Micerino (Menkaura) (2532–2503 a.C.) Sepseskaf (2503–2498 a.C.)
	Dinastía V (2494–2345 a.C.)	Userkaf (2494–2487 a.C.) Sahura (2487–2475 a.C.) Niuserra (2445–2421 a.C.) Dyedkara (2414–2375 a.C.) Unas (2375–2345 a.C.)
	Dinastía VI (2345–2181 a.C.)	Teti (2345–2323 a.C.) Pepi I (2321–2287 a.C.) Menenra (2287–2278 a.C.) Pepi II (2278–2184 a.C.)
Primer Periodo Intermedio (2181–2040 a.C.)	Dinastías VII y VIII (2181–2125 a.C.)	Numerosos soberanos efímeros al decaer la autoridad central
	Dinastías IX y X (de Heracleópolis [Henensu]) (2160–2025 a.C.)	Lucha por el poder entre soberanos menores del Alto y el Bajo Egipto
	Dinastía XI (tebana) (2125–2040 a.C.)	Antef II (2112–2063 a.C.)
Imperio Medio (2040–1650 a.C.)	Dinastía XI (todo Egipto) (2040–1985 a.C.)	Mentuhotep II (2040–2004 a.C.) Mentuhotep III (2004–1992 a.C.) Mentuhotep IV (1992–1985 a.C.)
	Dinastía XII (1985–1795 a.C.)	Amenemes (Amenemhat) I (1985–1955 a.C.) Senusret (Sesostris) I (1965–1920 a.C.) Amenemes II (1922–1878 a.C.) Senusret III (1874–1855 a.C.) Amenemes IV (1808–1799 a.C.)
	Dinastía XIII (1795–*c.* 1650 a.C.)	Soberanos menores
	Dinastía XIV (*c.* 1750–*c.* 1650 a.C.)	Soberanos menores
Segundo Periodo Intermedio (1650–1550 a.C.)	Dinastía XV (hicsa) (1650–1550 a.C.)	Apofis (*c.* 1585–*c.* 1542 a.C.)
	Dinastía XVI (1650–1550 a.C.)	Reyes hicsos menores, coetáneos de la dinastía XV
	Dinastía XVII (tebana) (1650–1550 a.C.)	Kamosis (1555–1550 a.C.)
Imperio Nuevo (1550–1069 a.C.)	Dinastía XVIII (1550–1295 a.C.)	Amosis I (1550–1525 a.C.) Amenofis (Amenhotep) I (1525–1504 a.C.) Tutmés I (1504–1492 a.C.) Tutmés II (1492–1479 a.C.) Tutmés III (1479–1425 a.C.) Hatsepsut (1473–1458 a.C.) Amenofis II (1427–1400 a.C.) Tutmés IV (1400–1390 a.C.) Amenofis III (1390–1352 a.C.) Amenofis IV/Ajnatón (*c.* 1352–1336 a.C.) Semenejkara (1338–1336 a.C.) Tutankamón (1336–1327 a.C.) Ay (1327–1323 a.C.) Horemheb (1323–1295 a.C.)
	Dinastía XIX (1295–1186 a.C.)	Ramsés I (1295–1294 a.C.) Seti I (1294–1279 a.C.) Ramsés II (1279–1213 a.C.) Menefta (1213–1203 a.C.)
	Dinastía XX (1186–1070 a.C.)	Ramsés III (1184–1153 a.C.) Ramsés V (1147–1143 a.C.) Ramsés XI (1099–1069 a.C.)
Tercer Periodo Intermedio (1069–747 a.C.) (inicio de la Baja Época)	Dinastía XXI (1069–945 a.C.)	Smendés (1069–1043 a.C.) Psusenas I (1039–991 a.C.) Osorkon I (984–978 a.C.) Psusenas II (959–945 a.C.)
	Dinastía XXII (945–715 a.C.)	Sesonq I (945–924 a.C.) Osorkon II (874–850 a.C.) Sesonq III (825–773 a.C.) Osorkon V (730–715 a.C.)
	Dinastía XXIII (*c.* 818–715 a.C.) Dinastía XXIV (727–715 a.C.)	Linajes de gobernantes menores rivales en Hermópolis, Leontópolis y Tanis
Periodo tardío (747–332 a.C.)	Dinastía XXV (Nubia y Egipto) (747–656 a.C.)	Piye (747–716 a.C.) Sabaka (716–702 a.C.) Taharka (690–664 a.C.)
	Dinastía XXVI (664–525 a.C.)	Samético I (664–610 a.C.) Apries (589–570 a.C.) Amosis II (570–526 a.C.) Samético III (526–525 a.C.)

EMPERADORES ROMANOS

En 27 a.C., cuando Octavio se convirtió en el primer emperador de Roma, adoptó el nombre de Cayo Julio César Augusto. A partir de entonces, los emperadores llevaron el título honorífico de augusto. Hasta el año 286 este título fue individual, pese a que hubo momentos de gobierno conjunto, en periodos de disputas sucesorias o cuando el heredero era demasiado joven para gobernar en solitario. Sin embargo, el emperador Diocleciano instauró un nuevo sistema, la tetrarquía, de cuatro gobernantes, dos con el título de augusto y dos con el de césar (emperador joven). Este sistema perduró con variantes hasta 395, cuando las partes oriental y occidental del Imperio romano se separaron definitivamente.

NOMBRE	REINADO	NOMBRE	REINADO
Augusto	27 a.C.–14 d.C.	**Trajano**	98–117
Tiberio	14–37	**Adriano**	117–138
Calígula	37–41	**Antonino Pío**	138–161
Claudio I	41–54	**Marco Aurelio**	161–180
Nerón	54–68	**Vero, Lucio Elio (coaugusto)**	161–169
Galba	68–69	**Cómodo**	180–192
Otón	69	**Pertinax**	193
Vitelio	69	**Juliano, Didio**	193
Vespasiano	69–79	**Septimio Severo**	193–211
Tito	79–81	**Caracalla (coaugusto 198–211)**	198–217
Domiciano	81–96		
Nerva	96–98	**Geta (coaugusto)**	209–211

NOMBRE	REINADO
Macrino	217–218
Diadumediano (coaugusto)	218
Heliogábalo	218–222
Severo Alejandro	222–235
Maximino el Tracio	235–238
Gordiano I y Gordiano II	238
Pupieno y Balbino	238
Gordiano III	238–244
Filipo I el Árabe	244–249
Filipo II (coaugusto)	247–249
Decio	249–251
Herenio Etrusco (coaugusto)	251
Treboniano Galo	251–253
Hostiliano (coaugusto)	251
Volusiano (coaugusto)	251–253
Emiliano	253
Valeriano	253–260
Galieno (coaugusto 253–260)	253–268
Claudio II el Gótico	268–270
Quintilio	270
Aureliano	270–275
Tácito	275–276
Floriano	276
Probo	276–282
Caro	282–283
Numeriano	283–284
Carino (coaugusto 283–284)	283–285
Diocleciano	284–305

NOMBRE	REINADO
Maximiano (césar 285–286, coaugusto 286–305)	286–305
Constancio Cloro (césar 293–305, coaugusto 305–306)	305–306
Galerio (césar 293–305, coaugusto 305–311)	305–311
Severo (césar 305–306, coaugusto 306–307)	306–307
Licinio	308–324
Maximino Daya (césar 305–10, coaugusto 310–313)	310–313
Constantino I (augusto 306, césar 306–307, coaugusto 307–324)	306–337
Constantino II (césar 317–337, coaugusto 337–340)	337–340
Constancio II (césar 324–337, coaugusto 337–350)	337–361
Constante (césar 333–337, coaugusto 337–350)	337–350
Juliano el Apóstata (césar 355–360)	360–363
Joviano	363–364
Valentiniano I (coaugusto)	364–375
Valente (coaugusto)	364–378
Graciano (coaugusto)	367–383
Valentiniano II (coaugusto)	375–392
Teodosio I (coaugusto 379–392)	379–395

IMPERIO DE OCCIDENTE

NOMBRE	REINADO
Honorio	395–423
Constancio III (coaugusto)	421
Valentiniano III	424–455
Máximo, Petronio	455
Avito	455–456
Mayoriano	457–461
Severo, Libio	461–465
Antemio	467–472
Olibrio	472
Glicerio	473–474
Julio Nepote	474–475
Rómulo Augústulo	475–476

IMPERIO DE ORIENTE

NOMBRE	REINADO
Arcadio	395–408
Teodosio II (coaugusto 405–408)	405–450
Marciano	450–457
León I	457–474
Zenón (depuesto)	474–475
Basilisco	475–477

EMPERADORES BIZANTINOS

A partir de 395, la mitad oriental del imperio no volvió a estar regida por el mismo emperador que la occidental. Tras la caída del Imperio romano de Occidente en 476, los emperadores de Oriente siguieron reinando desde Constantinopla, la antigua Bizancio griega, y por ello se conocen como emperadores bizantinos a partir de esa fecha.

NOMBRE	REINADO
Zenón	477–491
Anastasio	491–518
Justino	518–527
Justiniano	527–565
Justino II	565–578
Tiberio II	578–582
Mauricio	582–602
Focas	602–610
Heraclio I	610–641
Heraclio II Heraclonas	641
Constantino III	641
Constante II	641–668
Constantino IV	668–685
Justiniano II (depuesto)	685–695
Leoncio	695–698
Tiberio III	698–705
Justiniano II (repuesto)	705–711
Filípico	711–713
Anastasio II	713–715
Teodosio III	715–717
León III el Isaurio	717–741
Constantino V el Coprónimo	741–775
León IV	775–780
Constantino VI	780–797
Irene (emperatriz)	797–802
Nicéforo I	802–811

NOMBRE	REINADO
Estauracios	811
Miguel I	811–813
León V el Armenio	813–820
Miguel II	820–829
Teófilo	829–842
Miguel III	842–867
Dinastía macedonia	
Basilio I el Macedonio	867–886
León VI el Sabio	887–912
Alejandro	912–913
Constantino VII el Porfirogéneta	912–959
Romano I Lecapeno (coemperador)	919–944
Romano II	959–963
Nicéforo II Focas	963–969
Juan I Tzimisces	969–976
Basilio I el Bulgaróctono	976–1025
Constanino VIII (coemperador hasta 1025)	976–1028
Romano III Argiro	1028–1034
Miguel IV el Paflagonio	1034–1041
Miguel V el Calafates	1041–1042
Constantino IX Monómaco	1042–1055
Zoé (emperatriz correinante)	1042–1050

NOMBRE	REINADO
Teodora (emperatriz correinante)	1055–1056
Miguel VI el Estratioticós	1056–1057
Familia Comneno	
Isaac I Comneno	1057–1059
Familia Ducas	
Constantino X Ducas	1059–1067
Romano IV Diógenes	1068–1071
Miguel VII Ducas	1071–1078
Nicéforo III Botaniates	1078–1081
Familia Comneno	
Alejo I Comneno	1081–1118
Juan II	1118–1143
Manuel I	1143–1180
Alejo II	1180–1183
Andrónico I	1183–1185
Familia Ángelo	
Isaac II Ángelo	1185–1195
Alejo III	1195–1203
Isaac II (repuesto)	1203–1204

NOMBRE	REINADO
Alejo IV (coemperador)	1203–1204
Alejo V Ducas el Marzuflo	1204
Familia Láscaris	
Teodoro I Láscaris	1204–1222
Juan III Ducas Vatatzes	1222–1254
Teodoro II	1254–1258
Juan IV	1258–1261
Familia Paleólogo	
Miguel VIII (hasta 1261 como emperador de Nicea)	1259–1282
Andrónico II	1282–1328
Miguel IX (coemperador)	1293–1320
Andrónico III	1328–1341
Juan V	1341–1376
Juan VI (coemperador)	1347–1354
Andrónico IV	1376–1379
Juan V (repuesto)	1379–1391
Manuel II	1391–1425
Juan VII (regente)	1399–1402
Juan VIII	1425–1448
Constantino XI	1448–1453

SULTANES OTOMANOS

NOMBRE	REINADO
Osmán (Utman) I	1299–1326
Orján	1326–1359
Murat I	1359–1389
Bayaceto I	1389–1403
Solimán (pretendiente rival)	1403–1410
Mehmet (pretendiente rival hasta 1410)	1403–1421
Murat II	1421–1444
Mehmet II	1444
Murat (repuesto)	1444–1451
Mehmet II (repuesto)	1451–1481
Bayaceto II	1481–1512
Selim I el Cruel	1512–1520
Solimán I el Magnífico	1520–1566
Selim II	1566–1574
Murat III	1574–1595
Mehmet III	1595–1603
Ahmed I	1603–1617
Mustafá I	1617–1618
Osmán II	1618–1622
Mustafá I (repuesto)	1622–1623

NOMBRE	REINADO
Murat IV	1623–1640
Ibrahim	1640–1648
Mehmet IV	1648–1687
Solimán II	1687–1691
Ahmed II	1691–1695
Mustafá II	1695–1703
Ahmed III	1703–1730
Mahmut I	1730–1754
Osmán III	1754–1757
Mustafá III	1757–1774
Abdulhamid I	1774–1789
Selim III	1789–1807
Mustafá IV	1807–1808
Mahmut II	1808–1839
Abdulmecit I	1839–1861
Abdulaziz	1861–1876
Murat V	1876
Abdulhamid II	1876–1909
Mehmet V	1909–1918
Mehmet VI	1918–1922
Abdulmecit II (califa)	1922–1924

SOBERANOS DEL SACRO IMPERIO

NOMBRE	REINADO
Carlomagno	800–814
Ludovico Pío/Luis el Piadoso	814–840
Lotario I	840–855
Luis II	855–875
Carlos II	875–877
Carlos III el Gordo	881–887
Guido de Spoleto	891–894
Lamberto de Spoleto	894–896
Arnulfo	896–899
Luis III	899–911
Berengario I	915–924
Dinastía sajona u otónica	
Conrado I de Franconia	911–918
Enrique I el Pajarero	919–936
Otón I el Grande	962–973
Otón II	973–983
Otón III	996–1002
Enrique II de Sajonia	1014–1024
Dinastía franca o salia	
Conrado II de Franconia	1027–1039
Enrique III	1046–1056
Enrique IV	1084–1105
Enrique V	1111–1125

NOMBRE	REINADO
Dinastía de Supplinburg	
Lotario III	1133–1137
Dinastía Hohenstauffen	
Conrado III	1138–1152
Federico I Barbarroja	1155–1190
Enrique VI	1191–1197
Felipe de Suabia	1198–1208
Dinastía guelfa	
Otón IV de Brunswick	1209–1215
Dinastía Hohenstauffen	
Federico II	1215–1250
Conrado IV	1250–1254
Guillermo de Holanda	1254–1256
Alfonso X de Castilla y de León	1267–1273
Rodolfo I de Habsburgo	1273–1291
Adolfo de Nassau	1292–1298
Alberto I de Austria	1298–1308
Enrique VII	1312–1313
Luis IV de Wittelsbach	1328–1347
Carlos IV de Luxemburgo	1347–1378
Wenceslao de Luxemburgo	1378–1400
Roberto II del Palatinado	1400–1410
Segismundo de Luxemburgo	1433–1437

SOBERANOS DEL SACRO IMPERIO (CONTINUACIÓN)

NOMBRE	REINADO
Dinastía de Habsburgo	
Alberto II	1437–1439
Federico II de Estiria	1440–1493
Maximiliano I	1493–1519
Carlos V (I de España)	1519–1556
Fernando I	1556–1564
Maximiliano II	1564–1576
Rodolfo II	1576–1612
Matías	1612–1619
Fernando II de Estiria	1619–1637
Fernando III	1637–1658
Leopoldo I	1658–1705
Carlos VI	1711–1740
Dinastía de Wittelsbach	
Carlos VII de Baviera	1742–1745
Dinastía de Habsburgo-Lorena	
Francisco I	1745–1765
José II	1765–1790
Leopoldo II	1790–1792
Francisco II	1792–1806

EMPERADORES DE AUSTRIA

NOMBRE	REINADO
Francisco (II del Sacro Imperio)	1804–1835
Fernando I	1835–1848
Francisco José I	1848–1916
Carlos	1916–1918

REYES DE PRUSIA

NOMBRE	REINADO
Federico I	1701–1713
Federico Guillermo I	1714–1740
Federico II el Grande	1740–1786
Federico Guillermo II	1786–1797
Federico Guillermo III	1797–1840
Federico Guillermo IV	1840–1861
Guillermo I (desde 1871, emperador de Alemania)	1861–1871

EMPERADORES DE ALEMANIA

NOMBRE	REINADO
Guillermo I (rey de Prusia)	1871–1888
Federico	1888
Guillermo II (káiser)	1888–1918

PRESIDENTES Y CANCILLERES DE ALEMANIA

CDU: Unión Democratacristiana, **DVP**: Partido Popular Alemán, **FPD**: Partido Liberal Demócrata, **MSP**: Partido Socialista Mayoritario, **NSP**: Partido Nacionalsocialista (nazi), **SDP**: Partido Socialdemócrata, **Z**: Zentrum (Partido del Centro).

ALEMANIA UNIDA (1919–1945)

NOMBRE	MANDATO
PRESIDENTES (DESDE 1919)	
Friedrich Ebert (MSP)	1919–1925
Walter Simons	1925
Paul von Hindenburg	1925–1934
(Führer) Adolf Hitler (NSP)	1934–1945
(Führer) Karl Dönitz (NSP)	1945
CANCILLERES	
Otto von Bismarck	1871–1890
Leo von Caprivi	1890–1892
Chlodwig Hohenlohe-Schillingfurst	1894–1900
Bernhard von Bülow	1900–1909
Theobald von Bethman-Hollweg	1909–1917
Georg Michaelis	1917
Georg von Hertling	1917–1918
(Príncipe) Max von Baden	1918
Friedrich Ebert (MSP)	1918–1919
Philipp Scheidemann (MSP)	1919
Gustav Bauer (MSP)	1919–1920
Hermann Müller (MSP)	1920
Konstantin Fehrenbach (Z)	1920–1921
Karl Wirth (Z)	1921–1922
Wilhelm Cunto	1922–1923
Gustav Streseman (DVP)	1923
Wilhelm Marx (Z)	1923–1925
Hans Luther	1925–1926
Wilhelm Marx (Z)	1926–1928
Hermann Müller (SDP)	1928–1930
Heinrich Brüning (Z)	1930–1932
Franz von Papen (Z)	1932
Kurt von Schleicher	1932–1933
Adolf Hitler (NSP)	1933–1945
Joseph Goebbels (NSP)	1945

REPÚBLICA DEMOCRÁTICA ALEMANA (RDA, 1949–1990)

NOMBRE	MANDATO
PRESIDENTES	
Wilhelm Pieck	1949–1960
Walter Ulbricht	1960–1973
Willi Stoph	1973–1976
Erich Honecker	1976–1989
Egon Krenz	1989
Manfred Gerlach	1989–1990
Sabine Bergmann-Pohl	1990
PRIMEROS MINISTROS	
Otto Grotewohl	1949–1964
Willi Stoph	1964–1973
Horst Sindermann	1973–1976
Willi Stoph	1976–1989
Hans Modrow	1989–1990
Lothar de Maizière (CDU)	1990
SECRETARIOS GENERALES DEL PARTIDO SOCIALISTA UNIFICADO (SED)	
Walter Ulbricht	1950–1971
Erich Honecker	1971–1989
Egon Krenz	1989

REPÚBLICA FEDERAL DE ALEMANIA (RFA, 1945–1990, CON LA RDA DESDE 1990)

NOMBRE	MANDATO
PRESIDENTES	
Theodor Heuss (FDP)	1949–1959
Heinrich Lübke (CDU)	1959–1969
Gustav Heinemann (SDP)	1969–1974
Walter Scheel (FDP)	1974–1979
Karl Carstens (CDU)	1979–1984
Richard von Weizsäcker (CDU)	1984–1994
Roman Herzog (CDU)	1994–1999
Johannes Rau (SDP)	1999–2004
Horst Köhler (CDU)	2004–2010
Christian Wulff (CDU)	2010–2012
Joachim Gauck (independiente)	2012–2017
Frank-Walter Steinmeir (SDP)	2017–
CANCILLERES	
Konrad Adenauer (CDU)	1949–1963
Ludwig Erhard (CDU)	1963–1966
Kurt-Georg Kiesinger (CDU)	1966–1969
Willy Brandt (SDP)	1969–1974
Walter Scheel (FDP)	1974
Helmut Schmidt (SDP)	1974–1982
Helmut Kohl (CDU)	1982–1998
Gerhard Schröder (SDP)	1998–2005
Angela Merkel (CDU)	2005–2021
Olaf Scholz (SDP)	2021–

REYES DE FRANCIA

Tras la caída de Roma, varios pueblos bárbaros se disputaron el poder en Galia. Los vencedores fueron los francos, liderados por el merovingio Childerico, cuyo hijo Clodoveo unificó el territorio. Tras la muerte de Clodoveo, el reino se dividió entre sus cuatro hijos y sus descendientes hasta que Pipino, el primer carolingio, fue reconocido rey de todos los francos por el papa Zacarías en 751.

NOMBRE	REINADO
Dinastía merovingia	
Childerico I	*c.* 457–481
Clodoveo I	481–511
Teodorico I (Reims)	511–534
Clodomiro (Orleans)	511–524
Childeberto (París)	511–558
Clotario I (Soissons)	511–561
Teudeberto I (Austrasia)	534–548
Teodebaldo (Austrasia)	548–555
Cariberto I (París)	561–567
Gontrán (Borgoña)	561–592
Sigeberto (Metz)	561–575
Chilperico I (Soissons)	561–584
Childeberto II (Austrasia)	575–595
Clotario II (Soissons; único rey, 613–623)	584–629
Teudeberto II (Austrasia)	595–612
Teodorico II (Borgoña; Austrasia, 612–613)	595–613
Dagoberto I (Austrasia, 623–634; Neustria, 629–639)	623–639
Cariberto II (Aquitania)	629–632
Sigeberto II (Austrasia)	634–659
Clodoveo II (Neustria; Borgoña)	639–657
Dagoberto II (Austrasia)	659–661
Clotario III (Neustria)	657–673
Childerico II (Austrasia)	661–675
Teodorico III (Neustria; Austrasia)	673–690
Dagoberto II (Austrasia)	676–679
Clodoveo III	691–695
Childeberto III	695–711
Dagoberto III	711–715
Chilperico II (Neustria)	715–721
Clotario IV (Austrasia)	718–719
Teodorico IV	721–737
Childerico III	743–751
Dinastía carolingia	
Pipino el Breve	751–768
Carlomagno (Carlos I)	768–814
Carlomán (correinante)	768–771
Luis I el Piadoso (Ludovico Pío)	814–840
Carlos II el Calvo	840–877
Luis II el Tartamudo	877–879
Luis III	879–882
Carlomán II	879–884
Carlos el Gordo	884–887
Eudes	887–898
Carlos III el Simple	898–923
Roberto I	922–923
Raúl	923–936
Luis IV	936–954
Lotario	954–986
Luis V	986–987
Dinastía Capeto	
Hugo Capeto	987–996
Roberto II el Piadoso	996–1031
Enrique I	1031–1060
Felipe I	1060–1108
Luis VI el Gordo	1108–1137
Luis VII el Joven	1137–1180
Felipe II Augusto	1180–1223
Luis VIII el León	1223–1226
Luis IX (san Luis)	1226–1270
Felipe III el Atrevido	1270–1285
Felipe IV el Hermoso	1285–1314
Luis X	1314–1316
Juan I	1316
Felipe V el Largo	1316–1322
Carlos IV el Hermoso	1322–1328
Casa de Valois	
Felipe VI	1328–1350
Juan II el Bueno	1350–1364
Carlos V el Sabio	1364–1380
Carlos VI el Bienamado	1380–1422
Carlos VII	1422–1461
Luis XI	1461–1483
Carlos VIII	1483–1498
Casa de Valois-Orleans	
Luis XII	1498–1515
Casa de Valois-Angulema	
Francisco I	1515–1547
Enrique II	1547–1559
Francisco II	1559–1560
Carlos IX	1560–1574
Enrique III	1574–1589
Casa de Borbón	
Enrique IV (III de Navarra)	1589–1610
Luis XIII	1610–1643
Luis XIV	1643–1715
Luis XV	1715–1774
Luis XVI	1774–1792
República Francesa	1792–1804
Primer Imperio	
Napoleón I (Bonaparte)	1804–1814
Casa de Borbón	
Luis XVII	1814–1815, 1815–1824
Carlos X	1824–1830
Casa de Borbón-Orleans	
Luis Felipe	1830–1848
Segunda República Francesa	1848–1852
Segundo Imperio	
Napoleón III	1852–1870

DUQUES DE NORMANDÍA

Desde el siglo IX, gran parte de Francia estuvo regida por soberanos independientes del rey: destacan los duques de Normandía, que dominaron una amplia zona del noroeste desde el año 911 hasta el siglo XIII.

NOMBRE	REINADO
Rollón	911–932
Guillermo I	932–942
Ricardo I	942–996
Ricardo II	996–1027
Ricardo III	1027–1028
Roberto I	1028–1035
Guillermo II (I de Inglaterra)	1035–1087
Roberto II	1087–1106
Enrique I (de Inglaterra)	1106–1135
Esteban	1135–1144
Godofredo de Anjou	1144–1150
Enrique II (de Inglaterra)	1150–1189
Ricardo IV (de Inglaterra)	1189–1199
Juan (rey de Inglaterra)	1199–1204

PRESIDENTES Y PRIMEROS MINISTROS DE FRANCIA

AD: Alianza Democrática, **AR**: Alianza Republicana, **LREM**: La República en Marcha, **MRP**: Movimiento Republicano Popular, **PRS**: Partido Radical Socialista, **PS**: Partido Socialista, **RPR**: Reagrupamiento para la República, **RE**: Renaissance, **RI**: Republicanos Independientes, **UC**: Unión Centrista, **UDR**: Unión para la Defensa de la República, **UDSR**: Unión Democrática y Socialista de la Resistencia, **UMP**: Unión por un Movimiento Popular, **UNR**: Unión para la Nueva República, **URS**: Unión Radical Socialista.

PRESIDENTES (DESDE 1871)

NOMBRE	MANDATO
Adolphe Thiers	1871–1873
Patrice MacMahon	1873–1879
Jules Grévy	1879–1887
François Sadi-Carnot	1887–1894
Jean Casimir-Périer	1894–1895
François Faure	1895–1899
Émile Loubet	1899–1906
Armand Fallières	1906–1913
Raymond Poincaré	1913–1920
Paul Deschanel	1920
Alexandre Millerand	1920–1924
Gaston Doumergue	1924–1931
Paul Doumer	1931–1932
Albert Le Brun	1932–1940
Philippe Pétain	1940–1944
Vincent Auriol (PS)	1947–1954
René Coty (RI)	1954–1959
Charles de Gaulle (UNR, UDR)	1959–1969
Alain Poher (UC)	1969
Georges Pompidou (UDR)	1969–1974
Valéry Giscard d'Estaing (RI)	1974–1981
François Mitterrand (PS)	1981–1995
Jacques Chirac (RPR/UMP)	1995–2007
Nicolas Sarkozy (UMP)	2007–2012
François Hollande (SP)	2012–2017
Emmanuel Macron (LREM/RE)	2017–

PRIMEROS MINISTROS

NOMBRE	MANDATO
Adolphe Thiers	1871–1873
Patrice MacMahon	1873–1874
Ernest de Cissey	1874–1875
Louis Buffet	1875–1876
Jules Dufaure	1876
Jules Simon	1876–1877
Albert de Broglie	1877
Gaëtan de Rochebouet	1877
Jules Dufaure	1877–1879
William Waddington	1879
Charles de Freycinet	1879–1880
Jules Ferry	1880–1881
Léon Gambetta	1881–1882
Charles de Freycinet	1882
Charles Duclerc	1882–1883
Armand Fallières	1883
Jules Ferry	1883–1885
Henri Brisson	1885–1886
Charles de Freycinet	1886
René Goblet	1886–1887
Maurice Rouvier	1887
Pierre Tirard	1887–1888
Charles Floquet	1888–1889
Pierre Tirard	1889–1890
Charles de Freycinet	1890–1892
Émile Loubet	1892
Alexandre Ribot	1892–1893
Charles Dupuy	1893
Jean Casimir-Périer	1893–1894
Charles Dupuy	1894–1895
Alexandre Ribot	1895
Léon Bourgeois	1895–1896
Jules Meline	1896–1898
Henri Brisson	1898
Charles Dupuy	1898–1899
René Waldeck-Rousseau	1899–1902
Émile Combes	1902–1905
Maurice Rouvier	1905–1906
Ferdinand Sarrien	1906
Georges Clemenceau	1906–1909
Aristide Briand (PS)	1909–1911
Ernest Monis	1911
Joseph Caillaux	1911–1912
Raymond Poincaré	1912–1913
Aristide Briand (PS)	1913
Louis Barthou	1913
Gaston Doumergue (PRS)	1913–1914
René Viviani	1914–1915
Aristide Briand (PS)	1915–1917
Alexandre Ribot	1917
Paul Painlevé	1917
Georges Clemenceau	1917–1920
Alexandre Millerand	1920
Georges Leygues	1920–1921
Aristide Briand (PS)	1921–1922
Raymond Poincaré	1922–1924
Frédéric François-Marsal	1924
Édouard Herriot (PRS)	1924–1925
Paul Painlevé	1925
Aristide Briand (PS)	1925–1926
Édouard Herriot (PRS)	1926
Raymond Poincaré	1926–1929
Aristide Briand (PS)	1929
André Tardieu	1929–1930
Camille Chautemps (PRS)	1930
André Tardieu	1930
Théodore Steeg (PRS)	1930–1931
Pierre Laval	1931–1932
André Tardieu	1932
Édouard Herriot (PRS)	1932
Joseph Paul-Boncour (URS)	1932–1933
Édouard Daladier (PRS)	1933
Albert Sarraut (PRS)	1933
Camille Chautemps (PRS)	1933–1934
Édouard Daladier (PRS)	1934
Gaston Doumergue (PRS)	1934
Pierre Étienne Flandin (AD)	1934–1935
Ferdinand Bouisson (PS)	1935
Pierre Laval	1935–1936
Albert Sarraut (PRS)	1936
Léon Blum (PS)	1936–1937
Camille Chautemps (PRS)	1937–1938
Léon Blum (PS)	1938
Édouard Daladier (PRS)	1938–1940
Paul Reynaud (AR)	1940
Philippe Pétain	1940–1942
Pierre Laval	1942–1944
Charles de Gaulle	1944–1946
Félix Gouin (PS)	1946
Georges Bidault (MRP)	1946
Léon Blum (PS)	1946–1947
Paul Ramadier (PS)	1947
Robert Schuman (MRP)	1947–1948
André Marie (PRS)	1948
Robert Schuman (MRP)	1948
Henry Queuille (PRS)	1948
Georges Bidault (MRP)	1948–1950
Henri Queuille (PRS)	1950
René Pleven (UDSR)	1950–1951
Henri Queuille (PRS)	1951
René Pleven (UDSR)	1951–1952
Edgar Faure (PRS)	1952
Antoine Pinay (RI)	1952–1953
René Mayer (PRS)	1953
Joseph Laniel (RI)	1953–1954
Pierre Mendès-France (PRS)	1954–1955
Christian Pineau (PS)	1955
Edgar Faure (PRS)	1955–1956
Guy Mollet (PS)	1956–1957
Maurice Bourgès-Maunoury (PRS)	1957
Félix Gaillard (PRS)	1957–1958
Pierre Pflimlin (MRP)	1958
Charles de Gaulle (UNR)	1958–1959
Michel Debré (UNR)	1959–1962
Georges Pompidou (UNR)	1962–1968
Maurice Couve de Murville (UNR)	1968–1969
Jacques Chaban-Delmas (UDR)	1969–1972
Pierre Messmer (UDR)	1972–1974
Jacques Chirac (UDR)	1974–1976
Raymond Barre	1976–1981
Pierre Mauroy (PS)	1981–1984
Laurent Fabius (PS)	1984–1986
Jacques Chirac (RPR)	1986–1988
Michel Rocard (PS)	1988–1991
Edith Cresson (PS)	1991–1992
Pierre Bérégovoy (PS)	1992–1993
Édouard Balladur (RPR)	1993–1995
Alain Juppé (RPR)	1995–1997
Lionel Jospin (PS)	1997–2002
Jean-Pierre Raffarin (UMP)	2002–2005
Dominique de Villepin (UMP)	2005–2007
François Fillon (UMP)	2007–2012
Jean-Marc Ayrault (PS)	2012–2014
Manuel Valls (PS)	2014–2016
Bernard Cazeneuve (PD)	2016–2017
Édouard Phillippe (UMP)	2017–2020
Jean Castex (REM)	2020–2022
Elisabeth Borne (RE)	2022–

REYES Y REINAS DE ESPAÑA

Los reinos cristianos de Castilla y León se unieron por matrimonio en 1037 y formalmente en 1230. Isabel de Castilla y Fernando de Aragón se casaron en 1469, y cuando heredaron sus respectivos tronos, unieron sus reinos para dar lugar a la Monarquía Hispánica.

REYES Y REINAS DE CASTILLA Y LEÓN

NOMBRE	REINADO
Fernando I	1037–1065
Sancho II el Fuerte	1065–1072
Alfonso VI	1065–1109
Urraca	1109–1126
Alfonso VII	1126–1157
Sancho III (Castilla)	1157–1158
Fernando II (León)	1157–1188
Alfonso VIII (Castilla)	1158–1214
Alfonso IX (León)	1188–1230
Enrique I (Castilla)	1214–1217
Fernando III el Santo (Castilla; León desde 1230)	1217–1252
Alfonso X el Sabio	1252–1284
Sancho IV el Bravo	1284–1295
Fernando IV el Emplazado	1295–1312
Alfonso XI	1312–1350
Pedro I el Cruel	1350–1366
Enrique II	1366–1367
Pedro I el Cruel (repuesto)	1367–1369
Enrique II (repuesto)	1369–1379
Juan I	1379–1390
Enrique III	1390–1406
Juan II	1406–1454
Enrique IV	1454–1474
Isabel I	1474–1504
Juana I la Loca	1504–1516
Felipe I el Hermoso	1504–1506
Fernando V (II de Aragón)	1506–1516

REYES DE ARAGÓN

NOMBRE	REINADO
Ramiro I	1035–1063
Sancho I Ramírez	1063–1094
Pedro I	1094–1104
Alfonso I	1104–1134
Ramiro II	1134–1137
Petronila	1137–1162
Alfonso II	1162–1196
Pedro II	1196–1213
Jaime I el Conquistador	1213–1276
Pedro III	1276–1285
Alfonso III	1285–1291
Jaime II	1291–1327
Alfonso IV	1327–1336
Pedro IV el Ceremonioso	1336–1387
Juan I	1387–1395
Martín I el Humano	1395–1410
Fernando I de Antequera	1412–1416
Alfonso V	1416–1458
Juan II	1458–1479
Fernando II (V de Castilla)	1479–1516

REYES Y REINAS DE ESPAÑA

NOMBRE	REINADO
Casa de Austria (Habsburgo)	
Carlos I	1516–1556
Felipe II	1556–1598
Felipe III	1598–1621
Felipe IV	1621–1665
Carlos II	1665–1700
Casa de Borbón	
Felipe V	1700–1724
Luis I	1724
Felipe V (repuesto)	1724–1746
Fernando VI	1746–1759
Carlos III (VII de Nápoles)	1759–1788
Carlos IV	1788–1808
Fernando VII	1808
Familia Bonaparte	
José I	1808–1813
Casa de Borbón	
Fernando VII (repuesto)	1813–1833
Isabel II	1833–1868
Casa de Saboya	
Amadeo I	1870–1873
Primera República	1873–1874

REYES Y REINAS DE ESPAÑA (CONTINUACIÓN)

NOMBRE	REINADO
Casa de Borbón	
Alfonso XII	1874–1885
Alfonso XIII	1886–1931
Segunda República	1931–1939

NOMBRE	REINADO
Periodo franquista	1939–1975
Casa de Borbón	
Juan Carlos I	1975–2014
Felipe VI	2014–

JEFES DE GOBIERNO DE ESPAÑA

IR: Izquierda Republicana, **PC**: P. Conservador, **PL**: P. Liberal, **PP**: Partido Popular, **PRR**: Partido Republicano Radical, **PS**: Partido Socialista, **PSOE**: Partido Socialista Obrero Español, **UCD**: Unión de Centro Democrático.

NOMBRE	MANDATO
Francisco Cea Bermúdez	1833–1834
Francisco Martínez de la Rosa	1834–1835
Conde de Toreno (José María Queipo de Llano)	1835
Juan Álvarez Méndez (Mendizábal)	1835–1836
Manuel Istúriz Montero	1836
José María Calatrava	1836–1837
Eusebio Bardají y Azara	1837
Conde de Ofalia (Narciso Heredia)	1837–1838
Duque de Frías (Bernardino Fernández de Velasco)	1838
Evaristo Pérez de Castro	1838
Isidro Alaix	1838–1840
Antonio González y González	1840
Valentín Ferraz	1840
Modesto Cortázar	1840
Baldomero Fernández Espartero	1840–1841
Antonio González y González	1841–1842
José Rodil y Gallaso	1842–1843
Joaquín López	1843
Álvaro Gómez Becera	1843
Joaquín López	1843
Salustiano de Olózaga	1843
Luis González Bravo	1843–1844
Ramón María Narváez	1844–1846
Marqués de Miraflores (Manuel Pando)	1846
Francisco Istúriz Montero	1846–1847
Duque de Sotomayor (Carlos Martínez de Irujo y McKean)	1847
Joaquín Pacheco y Gutiérrez	1847
Florencio García Gómez	1847
Ramón María Narváez	1847–1850
Juan Bravo Murillo	1850–1852
Federico Roncali	1852–1853
Francisco de Lersundi	1853
Luis Sartorius	1853–1854
Fernando Fernández de Córdoba	1854
Duque de Rivas (Ángel de Saavedra)	1854–1855
Baldomero Fernández Espartero	1855–1856
Leopoldo O'Donnell	1856
Ramón María Narváez	1856–1857
Francisco Armero y Peñaranda	1857–1858
Francisco Istúriz Montero	1858
Leopoldo O'Donnell	1858–1863
Marqués de Miraflores	1863–1864
Lorenzo Arrazola	1864
Alejandro Mon	1864
Ramón María Narváez	1864–1865
Leopoldo O'Donnell	1865–1866
Ramón María Narváez	1866–1868
Luis González Bravo	1868
José Gutiérrez de la Concha	1868
Francisco Serrano y Domínguez	1868–1869
Juan Prim y Prats	1869–1870
Juan Bautista Topete	1870–1871
Francisco Serrano y Domínguez	1871
Manuel Ruiz Zorrilla	1871
José Malcampo y Monge	1871
Práxedes Mateo Sagasta	1871–1872
Juan Bautista Topete	1872
Manuel Ruiz Zorrilla	1872–1873
Marqués de Sierra Bullones (Juan Zabala de la Puente)	1874
Práxedes Mateo Sagasta	1874
Antonio Cánovas del Castillo	1874–1875
Joaquín Jovellar	1875

NOMBRE	MANDATO
Antonio Cánovas del Castillo	1875–1879
Arsenio Martínez Campos	1879
Antonio Cánovas del Castillo	1879–1881
Práxedes Mateo Sagasta	1881–1883
José Posada Herrera	1883–1884
Antonio Cánovas del Castillo	1884–1885
Práxedes Mateo Sagasta	1885–1890
Antonio Cánovas del Castillo	1890–1892
Práxedes Mateo Sagasta	1892–1895
Antonio Cánovas del Castillo	1895–1897
Marcelo Azcárraga	1897
Práxedes Mateo Sagasta	1897–1899
Francisco Silvela	1899–1900
Marcelo Azcárraga	1900–1901
Práxedes Mateo Sagasta	1901–1902
Francisco Silvela	1902–1903
Raimundo Fernández de Villaverde (PC)	1903
Antonio Maura y Montaner (PC)	1903–1904
Marcelo Azcárraga (PC)	1904–1905
Raimundo Fernández de Villaverde (PC)	1905
Eugenio Montero Ríos	1905
Segismundo Moret (PC)	1905–1906
José López Dominguez (PL)	1906
Segismundo Moret (PL)	1906
Marqués de la Vega de Armijo (Antonio Aguilar y Correa) (PL)	1906–1907
Antonio Maura y Montaner (PC)	1907–1909
Segismundo Moret (PL)	1909–1910
José Canalejas Méndez (PL)	1910–1912
Conde de Romanones (Álvaro de Figueroa) (PL)	1912
Marqués de Alhucemas (Manuel García Prieto) (PL)	1912–1913
Eduardo Dato e Iradier (PC)	1913–1915
Conde de Romanones (PL)	1915–1916
Marqués de Alhucemas (PL)	1916–1917
Eduardo Dato e Iradier (PC)	1917
Marqués de Alhucemas (PL)	1917–1918
Antonio Maura y Montaner (PC)	1918
Marqués de Alhucemas (PL)	1918
Conde de Romanones (PL)	1918–1919
Antonio Maura y Montaner (PC)	1919
Joaquín Sánchez de Toca	1919
Manuel Allende Salazar	1919–1920
Eduardo Dato e Iradier (PC)	1920–1921
Gabino Bugallal Araújo	1921
Manuel Allende Salazar	1921
Antonio Maura y Montaner (PC)	1921–1922
José Sánchez Guerra (PC)	1922
Marqués de Alhucemas (PL)	1922–1923
Miguel Primo de Rivera	1923–1930
Dámaso Berenguer y Fusté	1920–1931
Juan Bautista Aznar y Cabañas	1931
Niceto Alcalá Zamora	1931
Manuel Azaña Díaz (IR)	1931–1933
Alejandro Lerroux García (PRR)	1933
Diego Martínez Barrio (PRR)	1933
Alejandro Lerroux García (PRR)	1933–1934
Ricardo Samper Ibáñez	1934
Alejandro Lerroux García (PRR)	1934–1935
Joaquín Chapaprieta	1935
Manuel Portela Valladares	1935–1936
Manuel Azaña Díaz (IR)	1936
Santiago Casares Quiroga	1936
Diego Martínez Barrio	1936
José Giral y Pereira	1936
Francisco Largo Caballero (PS)	1936–1937

NOMBRE	MANDATO
Juan Negrín (PS)	1937–1939
Francisco Franco Bahamonde	1939–1973
Luis Carrero Blanco	1973
Torcuatro Fernández Miranda	1973–1974
Carlos Arias Navarro	1974–1976
Fernando de Santiago	1976
Adolfo Suárez (UCD)	1976–1981
Leopoldo Calvo Sotelo (UCD)	1981–1982

NOMBRE	MANDATO
Felipe González Márquez (PSOE)	1982–1996
José María Aznar López (PP)	
José Luis Rodríguez Zapatero	1996–2004
(PSOE)	2004–2011
Mariano Rajoy (PP)	
Pedro Sánchez Pérez-Castejón	2011–2018
(PSOE)	2018–

REYES DE CERDEÑA

NOMBRE	REINADO
Víctor Amadeo II	1718–1730
Carlos Manuel III	1730–1773
Víctor Amadeo III	1773–1796
Carlos Manuel IV	1796–1802
Víctor Manuel I	1802–1821

NOMBRE	REINADO
Carlos Félix	1821–1831
Carlos Alberto	1831–1849
Víctor Manuel II (rey de Italia desde 1861)	1849–1861

REYES DE ITALIA

NOMBRE	REINADO
Víctor Manuel II (de Cerdeña)	1861–1878
Humberto I	1878–1900

NOMBRE	REINADO
Víctor Manuel III	1900–1946
Humberto II	1946

PRESIDENTES Y PRIMEROS MINISTROS DE ITALIA

DC: Democracia Cristiana, **DS**: Demócratas de Izquierda, **FDI**: Hermanos de Italia, **FI**: Forza Italia, **I**: Independiente, **L'Ulivo**: Olivo, **PA**: Partido de Acción, **PD**: Partido Democrático, **PdL**: Pueblo de la Libertad, **PLI**: Partido Liberal Italiano, **PPI**: Partido Popular Italiano, **PRI**: Partido Republicano Italiano, **PSI**: Partido Socialista Italiano.

PRESIDENTES

NOMBRE	MANDATO
Enrico de Nicola	1947–1948
Luigi Einaudi	1948–1955
Giovanni Gronchi (DC)	1955–1962
Antonio Segni (DC)	1962–1964
Cesare Merzagora	1964
Giuseppe Saragat (DC)	1964–1971
Giovanni Leone (DC)	1971–1978

NOMBRE	MANDATO
Amintore Fanfani	1978
Alessandro Pertini (DC)	1978–1985
Francesco Cossiga (DC)	1985–1992
Oscar Luigi Scalfaro (DC, PPI)	1992–1999
Nicola Mancino	1999
Carlo Azeglio Ciampi	1999–2006
Giorgio Napolitano (DS)/(I)	2006–2015
Sergio Mattarella (I)	2015–

PRIMEROS MINISTROS

NOMBRE	MANDATO
Camille Cavour	1861
Bettino Ricasoli	1861–1862
Urbano Rattazzi	1862
Luigi Farina	1862–1863
Marco Minghetti	1863–1864
Alfonso la Marmora	1864–1866
Bettino Ricasoli	1866–1867
Urbano Rattazzi	1867
Luigi Menabrea	1867–1869
Giovanni Lanza	1869–1873
Marco Minghetti	1873–1876
Agostino Depretis	1876–1878
Benedetto Cairoli	1878
Agostino Depretis	1878–1879
Benedetto Cairoli	1879–1881
Agostino Depretis	1881–1887
Francesco Crispi	1887–1891
Marqués de Rudini (Antonio Starabba)	1891–1892
Giovanni Giolitti	1892–1893
Francesco Crispi	1893–1896
Marqués de Rudini	1896–1898
Luigi Pelloux	1898–1900
Giuseppe Saracco	1900–1901
Giuseppe Zanardelli	1901–1903
Giovanni Giolitti	1903–1905
Alessandro Fortis	1905–1906
Sidney Sonnino	1906
Giovanni Giolitti	1906–1909
Sidney Sonnino	1909–1910
Luigi Luzzatti	1910–1911
Giovanni Giolitti	1911–1914
Antonio Salandra	1914–1916
Paolo Boselli	1916–1917
Vittorio Orlando	1917–1919
Francesco Nitti	1919–1920

NOMBRE	MANDATO
Giovanni Giolitti	1920–1921
Ivanoe Bonomi	1921–1922
Luigi Facta	1922
Benito Mussolini	1922–1943
Pietro Badoglio	1943–1944
Ivanoe Bonomi (PLI)	1944–1945
Ferrucio Parri (PA)	1945
Alfredo de Gasperi (DC)	1945–1953
Giuseppe Pella (DC)	1953–1954
Amintore Fanfani (DC)	1954
Mario Scelba (DC)	1954–1955
Antonio Segni (DC)	1955–1957
Adone Zoli (DC)	1957–1958
Amintore Fanfani (DC)	1958–1959
Antonio Segni (DC)	1959–1960
Fernando Tambroni (DC)	1960
Amintore Fanfani (DC)	1960–1963
Giovanni Leone (DC)	1963
Aldo Moro (DC)	1963–1968
Giovanni Leone (DC)	1968
Mariano Rumor (DC)	1968–1970
Emilio Colombo (DC)	1970–1972
Giulio Andreotti (DC)	1972–1973
Mariano Rumor (DC)	1973–1974
Aldo Moro (DC)	1974–1976
Giulio Andreotti (DC)	1976–1979
Francesco Cossiga (DC)	1979–1980
Arnaldo Forlani (DC)	1980–1981
Giovanni Spadolini (DC)	1981–1982
Amintore Fanfani (DC)	1982–1983
Benedetto Craxi (PSI)	1983–1987
Amintore Fanfani (DC)	1987
Giovanni Goria (DC)	1987–1988
Ciriaco de Mita (DC)	1988–1989
Giulio Andreotti (DC)	1989–1992
Giuliano Amato (PSI)	1992–1993

NOMBRE	MANDATO
Carlo Azeglio Ciampi	1993–1994
Silvio Berlusconi (FI)	1994–1995
Lamberto Dini	1995–1996
Romano Prodi (PPI)	1996–1998
Massimo D'Alema (DS)	1998–2000
Giuliano Amato (L'Ulivo)	2000–2001
Silvio Berlusconi (FI)	2001–2006
Romano Prodi (L'Ulivo)	2006–2008
Silvio Berlusconi (PdL)	2008–2011
Mario Monti (I)	2011–2013
Enrico Letta (PD)	2013–2014
Matteo Renzi (PD)	2014–2016
Paolo Gentiloni (PD)	2016–2018
Giuseppe Conte (I)	2018–2021
Mario Draghi (I)	2021–2022
Giorgia Meloni (FDI)	2022–

REYES Y REINAS DE INGLATERRA

NOMBRE	REINADO
Casa de Wessex	
Egberto	802–839
Ethelwulf	839–855
Ethelbaldo	855–860
Ethelberto	860–866
Ethelred I	866–871
Alfredo el Grande	871–899
Eduardo el Viejo	899–925
Athelstan	925–939
Edmundo I	939–946
Edred	946–955
Edwy	955–959
Edgar	959–975
Eduardo el Mártir	975–978
Ethelred II el Indeciso	978–1013
Casa de Dinamarca	
Sweyn (Sven) Barba Bifurcada	1013–1014
Casa de Wessex	
Ethelred II (repuesto)	1014–1016
Edmundo II Ironside	1016
Casa de Dinamarca	
Canuto	1016–1035
Haroldo I Harefoot	1035–1040
Harthacnut (Hardeknud)	1040–1042
Casa de Wessex	
Eduardo II el Confesor	1042–1066
Haroldo II Godwinson	1066
Casa de Normandía	
Guillermo I el Conquistador	1066–1087
Guillermo II el Rojo	1087–1100
Enrique I	1100–1135
Esteban	1135–1141
Matilde	1141
Esteban (repuesto)	1141–1154
Casa de Plantagenet	
Enrique II de Anjou	1154–1189
Ricardo I Corazón de León	1189–1199
Juan sin Tierra	1199–1216
Enrique III	1216–1272
Eduardo I	1272–1307
Eduardo II	1307–1327
Eduardo III	1327–1377
Ricardo II	1377–1399
Casa de Lancaster	
Enrique IV	1399–1413
Enrique V	1413–1422
Enrique VI	1422–1461
Casa de York	
Eduardo IV	1461–1470
Casa de Lancaster	
Enrique VI (repuesto)	1470–1471
Casa de York	
Eduardo IV (repuesto)	1471–1483
Eduardo V	1483
Ricardo III	1483–1485
Casa Tudor	
Enrique VII	1485–1509
Enrique VIII	1509–1547
Eduardo VI	1547–1553
María I	1553–1558
Isabel I	1558–1603
Casa Estuardo	
Jacobo I (VI de Escocia)	1603–1625
Carlos I	1625–1649
Commonwealth (República)	1649–1660
Casa Estuardo	
Carlos II	1660–1685
Jacobo II	1685–1688
Guillermo III	1689–1702
María II (correinante)	1689–1694
Ana (de Gran Bretaña desde 1707)	1702–1714

REYES Y REINAS DE ESCOCIA

NOMBRE	REINADO
Casa de Alpin	
Kenneth MacAlpin (de Dalriada)	843–858
Donald I	858–862
Constantino I	862–877
Aed	877–878
Eochaid	878–889
Donald II	889–900
Constantino II	900–942
Malcolm I	942–954
Indulf	954–962
Dubh	962–966
Culen	966–971
Kenneth II	971–995
Constantino III	995–997
Kenneth III	997–1005
Malcolm II	1005–1034
Casa de Dunkeld	
Duncan I	1034–1040
Macbeth	1040–1057
Lulach	1057–1058
Malcolm III Canmore	1058–1093
Donald III Bane	1093–1094
Duncan II	1094
Donald III Bane (repuesto)	1094–1097
Edgar	1097–1107
Alejandro I	1107–1124
David I	1124–1153
Malcolm IV	1153–1165
Guillermo el León	1165–1214
Alejandro II	1214–1249
Alejandro III	1249–1286
Margarita de Noruega	1286–1290
Casa de Baliol	
Juan de Baliol	1292–1296
Casa de Bruce	
Roberto I Bruce	1306–1329
David II	1329–1371
Casa Estuardo	
Roberto II	1371–1390
Roberto III	1390–1406
Jacobo I	1406–1437
Jacobo II	1437–1460
Jacobo III	1460–1488
Jacobo IV	1488–1513
Jacobo V	1513–1542
María I (reina de los escoceses)	1542–1567
Jacobo VI (I de Inglaterra desde 1603)	1567–1625

REYES Y REINAS DE GRAN BRETAÑA

NOMBRE	REINADO
Casa de Hannover	
Jorge I	1714–1727
Jorge II	1727–1760
Jorge III	1760–1820
Jorge IV	1820–1830
Guillermo IV	1830–1837
Victoria I	1837–1901
Casa de Sajonia-Coburgo-Gotha	
Eduardo VII	1901–1910
Casa de Windsor	
Jorge V	1910–1936
Eduardo VIII	1936
Jorge VI	1936–1952
Isabel II	1952–2022
Carlos III	2022–

PRIMEROS MINISTROS DE REINO UNIDO

C: Conservador, **Lab**: Laborista, **Lib**: Liberal, **W**: Whig.

NOMBRE	MANDATO
Robert Walpole	1721–1742
Conde de Wilmington (Spencer Compton)	1742–1743
Henry Pelham	1743–1746
Conde de Bath (William Pulteney)	1746
Henry Pelham	1746–1754
Duque de Newcastle (Thomas Pelham-Holles)	1754–1756
Duque de Devonshire (William Cavendish)	1756–1757
Conde de Waldegrave (James Waldegrave)	1757
Duque de Newcastle	1757–1762
Conde de Bute (John Stuart)	1762–1763
George Grenville	1763–1765
Marqués de Rockingham (Charles Wentworth)	1765–1766
Conde de Chatham (William Pitt el Viejo)	1766–1768
Duque de Grafton (Augustus Fitzroy)	1768–1770
Barón North (Frederick North)	1770–1782
Marqués de Rockingham	1782
Conde de Shelburne (William Petty-Fitzmaurice)	1782–1783
Duque de Portland (William Cavendish-Bentinck)	1783
William Pitt (el Joven)	1783–1801
Henry Addington	1801–1804
William Pitt (el Joven)	1804–1806
Lord Grenville (William Grenville)	1806–1807
Duque de Portland	1807–1809
Spencer Perceval	1809–1812
Conde de Liverpool (Robert Jenkinson)	1812–1827
George Canning	1827
Vizconde de Goderich (Frederick Robinson)	1827–1828
Duque de Wellington (Arthur Wellesley) (C)	1828–1830
Lord Grey (Charles Grey) (W)	1830–1834
Vizconde de Melbourne (William Lamb) (W)	1834
Duque de Wellington (C)	1834
Robert Peel (C)	1834–1835
Vizconde de Melbourne (W)	1835–1841
Robert Peel (C)	1841–1846
Lord John Russell (W)	1846–1852
Conde de Derby (Edward Stanley) (C)	1852
Conde de Aberdeen (George Hamilton-Gordon) (W)	1852–1855
Vizconde de Palmerston (Henry Temple) (W)	1855–1858
Conde de Derby (C)	1858–1859
Vizconde de Palmerston (W)	1859–1865
Lord John Russell (W)	1865–1866
Conde Derby (C)	1866–1868
Benjamin Disraeli (C)	1868
William Gladstone (Lib)	1868–1874
Benjamin Disraeli (C)	1874–1880
William Gladstone (Lib)	1880–1885
Marqués de Salisbury (Robert Cecil) (C)	1885–1886
William Gladstone (Lib)	1886
Marqués de Salisbury (C)	1886–1892
William Gladstone (Lib)	1892–1894
Conde de Rosebery (Archibald Primrose) (Lib)	1894–1895
Marqués de Salisbury (C)	1895–1902
Arthur Balfour (C)	1902–1905
Henry Campbell-Bannerman (Lib)	1905–1908
Herbert Asquith (Lib)	1908–1916
David Lloyd George (Lib)	1916–1922
Andrew Bonar Law (C)	1922–1923
Stanley Baldwin (C)	1923–1924
Ramsay MacDonald (Lab)	1924
Stanley Baldwin (C)	1924–1929
Ramsay MacDonald (Lab)	1929–1935
Stanley Baldwin (C)	1935–1937
Neville Chamberlain (C)	1937–1940
Winston Churchill (C)	1940–1945
Clement Attlee (Lab)	1945–1951
Winston Churchill (C)	1951–1955
Anthony Eden (C)	1955–1957
Harold MacMillan (C)	1957–1963
Alexander Douglas-Home (C)	1963–1964
Harold Wilson (Lab)	1964–1970
Edward Heath (C)	1970–1974
Harold Wilson (Lab)	1974–1976
James Callaghan (Lab)	1976–1979
Margaret Thatcher (C)	1979–1990
John Major (C)	1990–1997
Anthony Blair (Lab)	1997–2007
Gordon Brown (Lab)	2007–2010
David Cameron (C)	2010–2016
Theresa May (C)	2016–2019
Boris Johnson (C)	2019–2022
Liz Truss (C)	2022
Rishi Sunak (C)	2022–

SOBERANOS DE RUSIA

NOMBRE	REINADO
DINASTÍA DE RIÚRIK	
Príncipes de Moscú	
Daniel	1283–1303
Yuri	1303–1325
Iván I	1325–1340
Simeón el Soberbio	1340–1353
Iván II	1353–1359
Grandes príncipes de Moscú-Vladímir	
Demetrio Donskói	1359–1389
Basilio I	1389–1425
Basilio II el Ciego	1425–1462
Iván III el Grande	1462–1505
Basilio III	1505–1533
Zares de Rusia	
Iván IV el Terrible (zar desde 1547)	1533–1584
Fiódor I	1584–1598
DINASTÍA GODUNOV	
Borís Godunov	1598–1605
Fiódor II	1605
Demetrio II	1605–1606

NOMBRE	REINADO
DINASTÍA SHUISKI	
Basilio IV	1606–1610
DINASTÍA ROMANOV	
Miguel	1613–1645
Alejo Mijáilovich	1645–1676
Fiódor III	1676–1682
Iván V	1682–1696
Pedro I el Grande (emperador desde 1721)	1696–1725
Catalina I	1725–1727
Pedro II	1727–1730
Ana	1730–1740
Iván VI	1740–1741
Isabel	1741–1762
Pedro III	1762
Catalina II la Grande	1762–1796
Pablo I	1796–1801
Alejandro I	1801–1825
Nicolás I	1825–1855
Alejandro II	1855–1881
Alejandro III	1881–1894
Nicolás II	1894–1917

LÍDERES DE LA URSS Y DE LA FEDERACIÓN RUSA

Tras la instauración de la Unión de Repúblicas Socialistas Soviéticas (URSS), en 1923, el país estuvo gobernado por jefes de estado y de gobierno, pero el poder efectivo residía en la jefatura del Partido Comunista Soviético. Algunos líderes asumieron varios cargos, pero la base del poder siempre era el Partido Comunista.

NCR: Nuestra casa Rusia, **RU**: Rusia unida.

UNIÓN SOVIÉTICA (URSS, 1923–1991)

JEFES DE ESTADO

NOMBRE	MANDATO
Mijaíl Kalinin	1922–1946
Nikolái Svernik	1946–1953
Kliment Voroshílov	1953–1960
Leonid Brézhnev	1960–1964
Anastas Mikoyán	1964–1965
Nikolái Podgorni	1965–1977
Leonid Brézhnev	1977–1982
Vasili Kuznetsov	1982–1983
Yuri Andrópov	1983–1984
Konstantín Chernenko	1984–1985
Vasili Kuznetsov	1985
Andréi Gromiko	1985–1988
Mijaíl Gorbachov	1988–1991

DIRIGENTES DEL PARTIDO COMUNISTA

NOMBRE	MANDATO
Vladímir Lenin	1923–1924
Stalin	1924–1953
Gueorgui Malenkov	1953
Nikita Jruschov	1953–1964
Leonid Brézhnev	1964–1982
Yuri Andrópov	1982–1984
Konstantín Chernenko	1984–1985
Mijaíl Gorbachov	1985–1991

JEFES DE GOBIERNO

NOMBRE	MANDATO
Vladímir Lenin	1923–1924
Alexéi Ríkov	1924–1930
Viacheslav Molotov	1930–1941
Stalin	1941–1953
Gueorgui Malenkov	1953–1955
Nikolái Bulganin	1955–1958
Nikita Jruschov	1958–1964
Alexéi Kosiguin	1964–1980
Nikolái Tijonov	1980–1985
Nikolái Rískov	1985–1991
Valentin Pavlov	1991

FEDERACIÓN RUSA (DESDE 1991)

PRESIDENTES

NOMBRE	MANDATO
Borís Yelstsin	1990–1999
Vladímir Putin	1999–2008
Dimitri Medvédev	2008–2012
Vladímir Putin	2012–

PRIMEROS MINISTROS

NOMBRE	MANDATO
Iván Siláyev	1990–1991
Borís Yeltsin	1991–1992
Ígor Gaidar	1992
Víktor Chernomirdin (NCR)	1992–1998
Serguéi Kiriyenko	1998
Víktor Chernomirdin (NCR)	1998
Yevgeni Primakov	1998–1999
Serguéi Stepashin	1999
Vladímir Putin	1999–2000
Mijaíl Kasyanov	2000–2004
Víktor Jrislenko	2004
Mijáil Fradkov	2004–2007
Víktor Zubkov	2007–2008
Vladímir Putin (RU)	2008–2012
Víktor Zubkov	2012
Dimitri Medvédev	2012–2020
Mijáil Mishustin	2020–

EMPERADORES DE CHINA

China fue unificada bajo Shi Huangdi, el primer emperador, en 221 a. C. Sin embargo, la caída de la dinastía Han en 220 d. C. fue seguida de tres siglos de fraccionamiento político durante los cuales el país estuvo dividido en algunos momentos en hasta 17 reinos. Los Sui lo reunificaron en 589, pero a la caída de sus sucesores, los Tang, en 907, el país volvió a dividirse durante los periodos de las Cinco Dinastías y de los Diez Reinos (907–960). Los Song rehicieron la unidad de nuevo en 960, pero perdieron el dominio del norte en 1126. La reunificación definitiva fue obra de la dinastía mongola Yuan, en 1279.

NOMBRE	REINADO
Dinastía Qin	
Shi Huangdi	221–210 a. C.
Er Shi	210–207 a. C.
Dinastía de los Han Occidentales	
Gaodi	206–195 a. C.
Huidi	195–188 a. C.
Lu Hou (regente)	188–180 a. C.
Wendi	180–157 a. C.
Jingdi	157–141 a. C.
Wudi	141–87 a. C.
Zhaodi	87–74 a. C.
Xuandi	74–49 a. C.
Yuandi	49–33 a. C.
Chengdi	33–7 a. C.
Aidi	7–1 a. C.
Pingdi	1 a. C.–6 d. C.
Ruzi	7–9
Dinastía Xin	
Wang Mang	9–23
Dinastía de los Han Orientales	
Guang Wudi	25–57
Mingdi	57–75
Zhangdi	75–88
Hedi	88–106
Shangdi	106
Andi	106–125
Shundi	125–144
Chongdi	144–145
Zhidi	145–146
Huandi	146–168
Lingdi	169–189
Xiandi	189–220
Periodo de desunión	220–581
Dinastía Sui	
Wendi	581–604
Yangdi	604–617
Gongdi	617–618
Dinastía Tang	
Gaozu	618–626
Taizong	626–649
Gaozong	649–683
Zhongzong	684
Ruizong	684–690
Wu Zetian	690–705
Zhongzong (repuesto)	705–710
Ruizong (repuesto)	710–712
Xuanzong	712–756
Suzong	756–762
Daizong	762–779
Dezong	779–805
Shunzong	805
Xianzong	805–820
Muzong	820–824
Jingzong	824–827
Wenzong	827–840
Wuzong	840–846
Xuanzong	846–859
Yizong	859–873
Xizong	873–888
Zhaozong	888–904
Aidi	904–907
Periodo de las Cinco Dinastías y los Diez Reinos	907–960
Dinastía de los Song del Norte	
Taizu	960–976
Taizong	976–997
Zhenzong	998–1022
Renzong	1022–1063
Yingzong	1064–1067
Shenzong	1068–1085
Zhezong	1086–1101
Huizong	1101–1125
Qinzong	1126
Dinastía de los Song del Sur	
Gaozong	1127–1162
Xiazong	1163–1190
Guangzong	1190–1194
Ningzong	1195–1224
Lizong	1225–1264
Duzong	1265–1274
Gongzong	1275
Duanzong	1276–1278
Bing Di	1279
Dinastía Yuan	
Shizu (Qubilay Kan)	1279–1294
Chengzong (Timur Ulyaitu)	1294–1307
Wuzong (Qaishan)	1308–1311
Renzong (Ayurparibhadra)	1311–1320
Yingzong (Suddhipala)	1321–1323
Taiding (Yesun Timur)	1323–1328
Wenzong (Togh Timur)	1328–1329
Minzong (Qosila)	1329
Wenzong (repuesto)	1329–1332
Shundi (Toghan Timur)	1332–1368
Dinastía Ming	
Hongwu	1368–1398
Jianwen	1399–1402
Yongle	1403–1424
Hongxi	1425
Xuande	1426–1435
Zhengtong	1436–1449
Jingtai	1449–1457
Zhengtong (repuesto)	1457–1464
Chenghua	1464–1487
Hongzhi	1487–1505
Zhengde	1505–1521
Jiajing	1521–1567

NOMBRE	REINADO
Longqing	1567–1572
Wanli	1572–1620
Taichang	1620
Tiangqi	1620–1627
Chongzhen	1628–1644
Dinastía Qing	
Shunzhi	1644–1661
Kangxi	1661–1722
Yongzheng	1722–1735
Qianlong	1735–1796
Jiajing	1796–1820
Daoguang	1820–1850
Xianfeng	1850–1861
Tongzhi	1861–1875
Guangxu	1875–1908
Pu Yi	1908–1911

LÍDERES DE LA REPÚBLICA POPULAR DE CHINA

Tras la victoria del Partido Comunista de Mao Zedong en la guerra civil china, en 1949, el líder del partido desempeñó un papel preeminente en el gobierno chino. China conservó un presidente con funciones en gran parte representativas y un primer ministro que en teoría estaba al frente del gobierno, pero estos funcionarios estaban subordinados al dictado del Partido Comunista.

JEFES DE ESTADO

NOMBRE	MANDATO
Mao Zedong	1949–1959
Liu Shaoqi	1959–1968
Dong Biwu	1968–1975
(Cargo vacante)	1975–1983
Li Xiannian	1983–1987
Yang Shangkun	1987–1993
Jiang Zemin	1992–2003
Hu Jintao	2003–2013
Xi Jinping	2013–

LÍDERES DEL PARTIDO COMUNISTA

NOMBRE	MANDATO
Mao Zedong	1945–1979
Hua Guofeng	1979–1981
Hu Yaobang	1981–1987
Zhao Ziyang	1987–1989
Jiang Zemin	1989–2002
Hu Jintao	2002–2012
Xi Jinping	2012–

PRIMEROS MINISTROS

NOMBRE	MANDATO
Zhou Enlai	1949–1976
Hua Guofeng	1976–1980
Zhao Ziyang	1980–1987
Li Peng	1987–1998
Zhu Rongji	1998–2003
Wen Jiaobao	2003–2013
Li Keqiang	2013–2023
Li Qiang	2023–

GOBERNANTES DE INDIA

El subcontinente indio ha visto el ascenso y declive de numerosos reinos e imperios. El Imperio Maurya abarcaba casi toda Asia meridional; el Imperio gupta ocupaba una amplia franja en India septentrional y el de los Chola se extendía por el Sureste Asiático. En su apogeo, el Sultanato de Dehli y el Imperio mogol (Gran Mogol) musulmanes dominaban prácticamente toda la India y el Pakistán actuales.

IMPERIO MAURYA (321–180 a. C.)

NOMBRE	REINADO
Chandragupta Maurya	321–297 a. C.
Bindusara	297–272 a. C.
Asoka	272–232 a. C.
Dasaratha	232–224 a. C.
Samprati	224–215 a. C.
Salisuka	215–202 a. C.
Devadharma	202–195 a. C.
Satamdhanu	195–187 a. C.
Brihadratha	187–180 a. C.

INDIA GUPTA (*c.* 275–550)

NOMBRE	REINADO
Gupta	*c.* 275–300
Ghatotkacha	*c.* 300–320
Chandragupta I	*c.* 320–350
Samudragupta	*c.* 350–376
Chandragupta II	*c.* 376–415
Kumaragupta	*c.* 415–455
Skandagupta	*c.* 455–467
Kumaragupta II	*c.* 467–477
Budhagupta	*c.* 477–495
Chandragupta III	*c.* 495–500
Vainyagupta	*c.* 500–515
Narasimhagupta	*c.* 515–530
Kumaragupta III	*c.* 530–540
Visnugupta	*c.* 540–550

INDIA CHOLA (*c.* 846–1279)

NOMBRE	REINADO
Viyayalaya	*c.* 846–871
Aditya I	*c.* 871–907
Parantaka I	907–953
Rajaditya (correinante)	947–949
Gandaraditya	953–957
Arinjaya (correinante)	956–957
Parantaka II	957–973
Aditya II (correinante)	957–969
Madurantaka Uttama	973–985
Rajaraja I	985–1016
Rajendra I	1016–1044
Rajadhiraja I	1044–1054
Rajendra II	1054–1064
Raja Mahendra (correinante)	1060–1063
Virarajendra	1064–1069
Adirajendra	1069–1070
Rajendra III Kulottunga Chola	1070–1122
Vikrama Chola	1122–1135
Kulottunga Chola II	1135–1150
Rajaraja II	1150–1173
Rajadhiraja II	1173–1179
Kulottunga III	1179–1218
Rajaraja III	1218–1246
Rajendra IV	1246–1279

SULTANATO DE DELHI (1206–1526)

NOMBRE	REINADO
Dinastía de los Esclavos (mamelucos)	
Aybak	1206–1210
Aram Sah	1210–1211
Iltutmis	1211–1236
Firuz Sah	1236
Radiyya Begum	1236–1240
Bahram Sah	1240–1242
Masud Sah	1242–1246
Mahmud Sah	1246–1266
Balban	1266–1287
Kai-Qubadh	1287–1290
Kayumarth	1290
Dinastía jalyí	
Firuz Sah II	1290–1296
Ibrahim I	1296
Muhammad I	1296–1316
Umar	1316
Mubarak I	1316–1320
Jusraw	1320
Dinastía tugluquí	
Tugluq I	1321–1325
Muhammad II	1325–1351
Firuz Sah III	1351–1388
Tugluq II	1388–1389
Abu Bakr	1389–1390
Muhammad III	1390–1394
Sikandar I	1394
Mahmud II	1394–1413
Daulat Khan Lodi	1413–1414
Dinastía sayí	
Khidr Khan	1414–1421
Mubarak II	1421–1434
Muhammad IV	1434–1445
Alam Sah	1445–1451
Dinastía de los Lodi	
Bahlul Lodi	1451–1489
Sikandar II	1489–1517
Ibrahim II	1517–1526
Dinastía mogola	
Baber	1526–1530
Humayun	1530–1540
Dinastía surí	
Sir Sah Sur	1540–1545
Islam Sah	1545–1553
Muhammad Adil	1553–1555
Ibrahim III	1555
Sikandar III	1555–1556
Emperadores mogoles	
Humayun (repuesto)	1555–1556
Akbar I el Grande	1556–1605
Yahangir	1605–1627
Sah Yahan I	1628–1658
Aurangzeb	1658–1707
Azam	1707
Bahadur I	1707–1712
Azim-ush-Sha'n	1712
Yahandar	1712–1713
Farrukhsiyar	1713–1719
Rafi ud-Darajat	1719
Sah Yahan II	1719
Nikusiyar	1719
Muhammad Ibrahim	1719–1748
Ahmad	1748–1754
Alamgir II	1754–1759
Sah Alam II	1759–1788
Baidar Bajt	1788
Sah Alam II (repuesto)	1788–1806
Akbar II	1806–1837
Bahadur II	1837–1858

PRESIDENTES Y PRIMEROS MINISTROS DE INDIA

JD: Janata Dal, **JDS**: Janata Dal (secular), **LD**: Lok Dal, **PBJ**: Partido Bharatiya Janata, **PC**: Partido del Congreso, **PCI**: Partido del Congreso indio, **PJ**: Partido Janata, **PJS**: Partido Janata secular.

PRESIDENTES

NOMBRE	MANDATO
Rajendra Prasad	1950–1962
Sarvapali Radhakrishnan	1962–1967
Zakir Husain	1967–1969
Vaharagiri Venkata Giri	1969
Muhammad Hidayat Ullah	1969
Vaharagiri Venkata Giri	1969–1974
Fakhruddin Alí Ahmad	1974–1977
Basappa Danappa Jatti	1977
Neelam Sanjiva Reddy	1977–1982
Gian Zail Singh	1982–1987
Rameswar Venkataraman	1987–1992
Shankar Dayal Sharma	1992–1997
Kocheril Raman Narayanan	1997–2002
Awul Abdul Kalam	2002–2007
Pratibha Patil	2007–2012
Pranab Mukherjee	2012–2017
Ram Nath Kovind	2017–2022
Droupadi Murmu	2022–

PRIMEROS MINISTROS

NOMBRE	MANDATO
Jawaharlal Nehru (PC)	1947–1964
Gulzarilal Nanda (PC)	1964
Lal Bahadur Shastri (PC)	1964–1966
Gulzarilal Nanda (PC)	1966
Indira Gandhi (PC)	1966–1977
Morarji Desai (PJ)	1977–1979
Charan Singh (PJS)	1979–1980
Indira Gandhi (PCI)	1980–1984
Rajiv Gandhi (PCI)	1984–1989
Vishvant Pratap Singh (JD)	1989–1990
Sadanand Singh Shekhar (JDS)	1990–1991
Pamulaparpi Narasimha Rao (PCI)	1991–1996
Atal Bihari Vajpayee (PBJ)	1996
Haradanhalli Dewe Gowda (JD)	1996–1997
Inder Kumar Gujral(JD)	1997–1998
Atal Bihari Vajpayee (PBJ)	1998–2004
Manmohan Singh (PCI)	2004–14
Narendra Modi (PBJ)	2014–

GOBERNANTES DE JAPÓN

Según la tradición japonesa, el primer emperador, Jimmu Tenno, fue entronizado en 660 a. C., pero los hallazgos arqueológicos indican que debió de reinar en torno al año 40 d. C. Con el tiempo, los emperadores de Japón perdieron poder frente a poderosas familias de guerreros, y desde 1185 hasta el siglo XIX el poder efectivo estuvo en manos de señores feudales (sogunes), entre los que destacan los Tokugawa, que ostentaron el título de sogún durante más de 250 años, hasta la restauración del poder imperial en 1867.

EMPERADORES

NOMBRE	REINADO
Periodo Yamato (*c.* 40 a. C.–710 a. C.)	
Jimmu	40–10
Suizei	10 a. C.–20 d. C.
Annei	20–50
Itoki	50–80
Kosho	80–110
Koan	110–140
Korei	140–170
Kogen	170–200
Kaika	200–230
Sujin	230–258
Suinin	258–290
Keiko	290–322
Seimu	322–355
Chuai	355–362
Ojin	362–394
Nintoku	394–427
Richu	427–432
Hanzei	432–437
Ingyo	437–454
Anko	454–457
Yuryaku	457–489
Seinei	489–494
Kenzo	494–497
Ninken	497–504
Buretsu	504–510
Keitai	510–527
Ankan	527–535
Senka	535–539
Kimmei	539–571
Bidatsu	572–585
Yomei	585–587
Sushun	587–592
Suiko (emperatriz)	593–628
Jomei	629–641
Kogokyu (emperatriz)	642–645
Kotoku	645–654
Saimei (Kogokyu repuesta)	655–661
Tenji	661–672
Kobun	672
Temmu	672–686
Jito (emperatriz)	686–697
Mommu	697–707
Periodo Nara (710–784)	
Gemmei (emperatriz)	707–715
Gensho (emperatriz)	715–724
Shomu	724–749
Koken (emperatriz)	749–758
Junnin	758–764
Shotoku (Koken repuesta)	764–770
Konin	770–781
Periodo Heian (784–1185)	
Kammu	781–806
Heizei	806–809
Saga	809–823
Junna	823–833
Nimmyo	833–850
Montoku	850–858
Seiwa	858–876
Yozei	876–884
Koko	884–887
Uda	887–897
Daigo	897–930
Suzaku	930–946
Murakami	946–967
Reizei	967–969
En'yu	969–984
Kazan	984–986
Ichijo	986–1011
Sanjo	1011–1016
Go-Ichijo	1016–1036
Go-Suzaku	1036–1045
Go-Reizei	1045–1068
Go-Sanjo	1068–1073
Shlraqawa	1073–1087
Horikawa	1087–1107
Toba	1107–1123
Sutoku	1123–1142
Konoe	1142–1155
Go-Shlraqawa	1155–1158
Nijo	1158–1165
Rokujo	1165–1168
Takakura	1168–1180
Antoku	1180–1185
Periodo Kamakura (1186–1333)	
Go-Toba	1183–1198
Tsuchimikado	1198–1210
Juntoku	1210–1221
Chukyo	1221
Go-Horikawa	1221–1232
Shijo	1232–1242
Go-Saga	1242–1246
Go-Fukakusa	1246–1260
Kameyama	1260–1274
Go-Uda	1274–1287
Fushimi	1287–1298
Go-Fushimi	1298–1301
Go-Nijo	1301–1308
Hanazono	1308–1318
Corte del Sur (1336–1392)	
Go-Daigo	1318–1339
Go-Murakami	1339–1368
Chokei	1368–1383
Go-Kameyama	1383–1392
Corte del Norte (1336–1392)	
Kogon	1331–1333
Komyo	1336–1348
Suko	1348–1351
Go-Kogon	1352–1371
Go-En'yu	1371–1382
Periodo Muromachi (1392–1573)	
Go-Komatsu	1382–1412
Shoko	1412–1428
Go-Hanazono	1428–1464
Go-Tsuchimikado	1464–1500
Go-Kashiwabara	1500–1526
Go-Nara	1526–1557
Ogimachi	1557–1586
Periodo Tokugawa (1603–1867)	
Go-Yozei	1586–1611
Go-Mizunoo	1611–1629
Meisho	1629–1643
Go-Komyo	1643–1654
Go-Sai	1655–1663
Reigen	1663–1687
Higashiyama	1687–1709
Nakamikado	1709–1735
Sakuramachi	1735–1747
Momozono	1747–1762
Go-Sakuramachi (emperatriz)	1735–1747
Go-Momozono	1771–1779
Kokaku	1780–1817
Ninko	1817–1846
Komei	1846–1867
Japón moderno (1867–)	
Meiji	1867–1912
Taisho	1912–1926
Showa (Hirohito)	1926–1989
Akihito	1989–2019
Naruhito	2019–

SOGUNES

NOMBRE	REINADO
Sogunado Kamakura	
Minamoto Yoritomo	1192–1195
Yoriie	1202–1203
Sanemoto	1203–1219
Kujo Yoritsune	1226–1244
Yoritsugu	1244–1252
Munetaka	1252–1266
Koreyasu	1266–1289
Hisaaki	1289–1308
Morikuni	1308–1333
Sogunado Ashikaga	
Ashikaga Takauji	1338–1358
Yoshiakira	1359–1367
Yoshimitsu	1369–1395
Yoshimochi	1395–1423
Yoshikazu	1423–1425
Yoshinori	1429–1441
Yoshikatsu	1442–1443
Yoshimasa	1449–1474
Yoshihisa	1474–1489
Yoshitane	1490–1493
Yoshizumi	1495–1508
Yoshitane (repuesto)	1508–1522
Yoshiharu	1522–1547
Yoshiteru	1547–1565
Yoshihide	1568
Yoshiaki	1568–1573
Sogunado Tokugawa	
Tokugawa Ieyasu	1603–1605
Hidetada	1605–1623
Iemitsu	1623–1651
Ietsuna	1651–1680
Tsunayoshi	1680–1709
Ienobu	1709–1712
Ietsugu	1713–1716
Yoshimune	1716–1745
Ieshige	1745–1760
Ieharu	1760–1786
Ienari	1787–1837
Ieyoshi	1837–1853
Iesada	1853–1858
Iemochi	1858–1866
Yoshinobi	1867–1868

PRIMEROS MINISTROS DE JAPÓN

NPJ: Nuevo Partido de Japón, **PDJ**: Partido Democrático de Japón, **PL**: Partido Liberal, **PLD**: Partido Liberal Democrático, **PRJ**: Partido de la Renovación de Japón, **PS**: Partido Socialista.

NOMBRE	MANDATO
Ito Hirobumi	1885–1888
Kuroda Kiyotaka	1888–1889
Yamagata Aritomo	1889–1891
Matsukata Masayoshi	1891–1892
Ito Hirobumi	1892–1896
Matsukata Masayoshi	1896–1897
Kuroda Kiyotaka	1897
Matsukata Masayoshi	1897–1898
Ito Hirobumi	1898
Okuma Shigenobu	1898
Yamagata Aritomo	1898–1900
Ito Hirobumi	1900–1901
Saionji Kimmochi	1901
Katsura Taro	1901–1906
Saionji Kimmochi	1906–1908
Katsura Taro	1908–1911
Saionji Kimmochi	1911–1912
Katsura Taro	1912–1913
Yamamoto Gonnohyoe	1913–1914
Okuma Shigenobu	1914–1916
Terauchi Matsakate	1916–1918
Hara Takashi	1918–1921
Uchida Yasuya	1921
Takahashi Korekiyo	1921–1922
Kato Tomosabura	1922–1923
Yamamoto Gonnohyoe	1923–1924
Kiyoura Keigo	1924
Kato Takaaki	1924–1926
Wakatsuki Reijiro	1926–1927
Tanaka Giichi	1927–1929
Hamaguchi Osachi	1929–1931
Wakatsuki Reijiro	1931
Inukai Takashi	1931–1932
Takahashi Korekiyo	1932
Saito Makoto	1932–1934
Okada Keisuke	1934–1936
Goto Fumio	1936
Hirota Koki	1936–1937
Hayashi Senjuro	1937
Konoye Fumimaro	1937–1939
Hironuma Kiichiro	1939
Abe Nobyaki	1939–1940
Yonai Mitsumasa	1940
Konoye Fumimaro	1940–1941
Tojo Hideki	1941–1944
Koiso Kuniaki	1944–1945
Suzuki Kantaro	1945
Naruhiko Higashikini	1945
Shidehara Kiuro	1945
Yoshida Shigeru (PL)	1946–1947
Katayama Tetsu (PS)	1947–1948
Ashida Hitoshi (PDJ)	1948
Yoshida Shigeru (PL)	1948–1954
Hatoyama Ichiro (PLD)	1954–1956
Ishibashi Tanzan (PLD)	1956–1957
Kishi Nobusuke (PLD)	1957–1960
Ikeda Hayato (PLD)	1960–1964
Sato Eisaku (PLD)	1964–1972
Tanaka Kakuei (PLD)	1972–1974
Miki Takeo (PLD)	1974–1976
Fukuda Takeo (PLD)	1976–1978
Ohira Masayoshi (PLD)	1978–1980
Ito Masayoshi (PLD)	1980
Suzuki Zenko (PLD)	1980–1982
Nakasone Yasuhiro (PLD)	1982–1987
Takeshita Nobaru (PLD)	1987–1989
Uno Sosuke (PLD)	1989
Kaifu Toshiki (PLD)	1989–1991
Miyazawa Kiichi (PLD)	1991–1993
Hata Tsutomu (NPJ)	1993–1994
Murayama Tomiichi (NPJ)	1994–1996
Hashimoto Ryutaro (PLD)	1996–1998
Obuchi Keizo (PLD)	1998–2000
Mori Yoshiro (PLD)	2000–2001
Koizumi Junichiro (PLD)	2001–2006
Abe Shinzo (PLD)	2006–2007

»

NOMBRE	MANDATO	NOMBRE	MANDATO
Fukuda Yasuo (PLD)	2007–2008	Noda Yoshihiko (PDJ)	2011–2012
Aso Taro (PLD)	2008–2009	Shinzo Abe (PLD)	2012–2020
Hatoyama Yukio (PDJ)	2009–2010	Yoshihide Suga (PLD)	2020–2021
Kan Naoto (PDJ)	2010–2011	Fumio Kishida (PLD)	2021–

EMPERADORES INCAS

NOMBRE	REINADO	NOMBRE	REINADO
Manco Cápac	*c.* 1100	Túpac Inca Yupanqui (Topa Inca)	1471–1493
Sinchi Roca	desconocido	Huayna Cápac	1493–1526
Lloque Yupanqui	desconocido	Huáscar	1526–1532
Mayta Cápac	desconocido	Atahualpa	1530–1533
Cápac Yupanqui	*c.* 1200	Túpac Hualpa	1533
Inca Roca	desconocido	Manco Inca Yupanqui (Manco Cápac II)	1533–1545
Inca Yupanqui	desconocido	Sayri Túpac	1545–1560
Viracocha	desconocido	Titu Cusi Yupanqui	1560–1571
Inca Urco	1438	Túpac Amaru	1571–1572
Pachacuti	1438–1471		

EMPERADORES AZTECAS

NOMBRE	REINADO	NOMBRE	REINADO
Acamapichtli	1372–1391	Tizoc	1481–1486
Huitzilihuitl	1391–1415	Ahuízotl	1486–1502
Chimalpopoca	1415–1426	Moctezuma II Xocoyotzin	1502–1520
Itzcóatl	1426–1440	Cuitláhuac	1520
Moctezuma I Ilhuicamina	1440–1468	Cuauhtémoc	1520–1521
Axayácatl	1468–1481		

PRESIDENTES DE ESTADOS UNIDOS

D: Demócrata, **DR**: Demócrata republicano, **F**: Federal, **R**: Republicano, **UN**: Unión Nacional, **W**: Whig.

NOMBRE	MANDATO	NOMBRE	MANDATO
George Washington	1789–1797	Grover Cleveland (D)	1893–1897
John Adams (F)	1797–1801	William McKinley (R)	1897–1901
Thomas Jefferson (DR)	1801–1809	Theodore Roosevelt (R)	1901–1909
James Madison (DR)	1809–1817	William Howard Taft (R)	1909–1913
James Monroe (DR)	1817–1825	Woodrow Wilson (D)	1913–1921
John Quincy Adams (DR)	1825–1829	Warren G. Harding (R)	1921–1923
Andrew Jackson (D)	1829–1837	Calvin Coolidge (R)	1923–1929
Martin Van Buren (D)	1837–1841	Herbert Hoover (R)	1929–1933
William Henry Harrison (W)	1841	Franklin D. Roosevelt (D)	1933–1945
John Tyler (W)	1841–1845	Harry S. Truman (D)	1945–1953
James Knox Polk (D)	1845–1849	Dwight D. Eisenhower (R)	1953–1961
Zachary Taylor (W)	1849–1850	John F. Kennedy (D)	1961–1963
Millard Fillmore (W)	1850–1853	Lyndon B. Johnson (D)	1963–1969
Franklin Pierce (D)	1853–1857	Richard Nixon (R)	1969–1974
James Buchanan (D)	1857–1861	Gerald Ford (R)	1974–1977
Abraham Lincoln (R)	1861–1865	James («Jimmy») Carter (D)	1977–1981
Andrew Johnson (D/UN)	1865–1869	Ronald Reagan (R)	1981–1989
Ulysses S. Grant (R)	1869–1877	George H. W. Bush (R)	1989–1993
Rutherford B. Hayes (R)	1877–1881	William («Bill») Clinton (D)	1993–2001
James A. Garfield (R)	1881	George W. Bush (R)	2001–2009
Chester A. Arthur (R)	1881–1885	Barack Obama (D)	2009–2017
Grover Cleveland (D)	1885–1889	Donald Trump (R)	2017–2021
Benjamin Harrison (R)	1889–1893	Joe Biden (D)	2021–

PRIMEROS MINISTROS DE CANADÁ

PC: Partido Conservador, **PCP**: Partido Conservador Progresista, **PL**: Partido Liberal, **PU**: Partido Unionista.

NOMBRE	MANDATO	NOMBRE	MANDATO
John Alexander MacDonald (PL)	1867–1873	W. MacKenzie King (PL)	1935–1948
Alexander MacKenzie (PL)	1873–1878	Louis Saint Laurent (PL)	1948–1957
John Alexander MacDonald (PC)	1878–1891	John Diefenbaker (PCP)	1957–1963
John Abbott (PC)	1891–1892	Lester Pearson (PL)	1963–1968
John Thompson (PC)	1892–1894	Pierre Trudeau (PL)	1968–1979
MacKenzie Bowell (PC)	1894–1896	Joseph Clark (PCP)	1979–1980
Charles Tupper (PC)	1896	Pierre Trudeau (PL)	1980–1984
Wilfred Laurier (PL)	1896–1911	John Turner (PL)	1984
Robert Borden (PC, PU)	1911–1920	Brian Mulroney (PCP)	1984–1993
Arthur Meighen (PU)	1920–1921	Kim Campbell (PCP)	1993
W. Mackenzie King (PL)	1921–1926	Jean Chrétien (PL)	1993–2003
Arthur Meighen (PU)	1926	Paul Martin (PL)	2003–2006
W. MacKenzie King (PL)	1926–1930	Stephen Harper (PC)	2006–2015
Richard Bennett (PC)	1930–1935	Justin Trudeau (PL)	2015–

PRESIDENTES Y PRIMEROS MINISTROS DE SUDÁFRICA

CNA: Congreso Nacional Africano, **PL**: Partido Laborista, **PN**: Partido Nacional, **PNP**: Partido Nacional del Pueblo, **PSA**: Partido Sudafricano, **PU**: Partido Unido, **S**: Solidaridad.

PRESIDENTES

NOMBRE	MANDATO	NOMBRE	MANDATO
Charles Swart	1961–1967	Marais Viljoen	1979–1984
Jozua Naudé	1967–1968	Pieter Botha	1984–1989
Jacobus Fouché	1968–1975	Frederik de Klerk	1989–1994
Jan de Clerk	1975	Nelson Mandela (CNA)	1994–1999
Nicolaas Diederich	1975–1978	Thabo Mbeki (CNA)	1999–2008
Marais Viljoen	1978	Kgalema Motlanthe (CNA)	2008–2009
B. Johannes Vorster	1978–1979	Jacob Zuma (CNA)	2009–2018
		Cyril Ramaphosa (CNA)	2018–

PRIMEROS MINISTROS

NOMBRE	MANDATO	NOMBRE	MANDATO
Louis Botha (PSA)	1910–1919	Charles Swart	1958
Jan Smuts (PSA)	1919–1924	Hendrik Verwoerd (PN)	1958–1966
James Barry Herzog (PN/PU)	1924–1939	Ebenhezer Dönges	1966
Jan Smuts (PU)	1939–1948	B. Johannes Vorster (PN)	1966–1978
Daniel Malan (PN)	1948–1954	Pieter Botha (PN)	1978–1984
Johannes Strijdom (PN)	1954–1958		

PRIMEROS MINISTROS DE AUSTRALIA (DESDE 1901)

PAU: Partido Australia Unida, **PC**: Partido del Campo, **PL**: Partido Liberal, **PLA**: Partido Laborista Australiano, **PN**: Partido Nacional.

NOMBRE	MANDATO	NOMBRE	MANDATO
Edmund Barton	1901–1903	Joseph Chifley (PLA)	1945–1949
Alfred Deakin (PL)	1903–1904	Robert Menzies (PL)	1949–1966
John Watson	1904	Harold Holt (PL)	1966–1967
George Reid	1904–1905	John McEwan (PC)	1967–1968
Alfred Deakin (PL)	1905–1908	John Gorton (PL)	1968–1971
Andrew Fisher (PLA)	1908–1909	William MacMahon (PL)	1971–1972
Alfred Deakin (PL)	1909–1910	E. Gough Whitlam (PLA)	1972–1975
Andrew Fisher (PLA)	1910–1913	Malcolm Fraser (PL)	1975–1983
Joseph Cook	1913–1914	Robert Hawke (PLA)	1983–1991
Andrew Fisher (PLA)	1914–1915	Paul Keating (PLA)	1991–1996
William Hughes (PLA, PN)	1915–1923	John Howard (PL)	1996–2007
Stanley Bruce (PN)	1923–1929	Kevin Rudd (PLA)	2007–2010
James Scullin (PLA)	1929–1932	Julia Gillard (PLA)	2010–2013
Joseph Lyons (PAU)	1932–1939	Kevin Rudd (PLA)	2013
Earl Page (PC)	1939	Tony Abbott (PL)	2013–2015
Robert Menzies (PAU)	1939–1941	Malcolm Turnbull (PL)	2015–2018
Arthur Fadden (PC)	1941	Scott Morrison (PL)	2018–2022
John Curtin (PLA)	1941–1945	Anthony Albanese (PLA)	2022–
Francis Forde	1945		

PRIMEROS MINISTROS DE NUEVA ZELANDA

Lab: Laboristas, **Lib**: Liberales, **PN**: Partido Nacional, **PR**: Partido de la Reforma, **PU**: Partido Unido.

NOMBRE	MANDATO	NOMBRE	MANDATO
Henry Sewell	1856	Thomas MacKenzie (Lib)	1912
William Fox	1856	William Massey (PR)	1912–1925
Edward Stafford	1856–1861	Francis Bell (PR)	1925
William Fox	1861–1862	Joseph Coates (PR)	1925–1928
Alfred Domett	1862–1863	Joseph Ward (PU)	1928–1930
Frederick Whitaker	1863–1864	George Forbes (PU)	1930–1935
Frederick Weld	1864–1865	Michael Savage (Lab)	1935–1940
Edward Stafford	1865–1869	Peter Fraser (Lab)	1940–1949
William Fox	1869–1872	Sidney Holland (PN)	1949–1957
Edward Stafford	1872	Keith Holyoake (PN)	1957
George Waterhouse	1872–1873	Walter Nash (Lab)	1957–1960
William Fox	1873	Keith Holyoake (PN)	1960–1972
Julius Vogel	1873–1875	John Marshall (PN)	1972
Daniel Pollen	1875–1876	Norman Kirk (Lab)	1972–1974
Julius Vogel	1876	Hugh Watt (Lab)	1974
Harry Atkinson	1876–1877	Wallace Rowling (Lab)	1974–1975
George Grey	1877–1879	Robert Muldoon (PN)	1975–1984
John Hall	1879–1882	David Lange (Lab)	1984–1989
Frederick Whitaker	1882–1883	Geoffrey Palmer (Lab)	1989–1990
Harry Atkinson	1883–1884	Michael Moore (Lab)	1990
Robert Stout	1884	James Bolger (PN)	1990–1997
Harry Atkinson	1884	Jenny Shipley (PN)	1997–1999
Robert Stout	1884–1887	Helen Clark (Lab)	1999–2008
Harry Atkinson	1887–1891	John Key (PN)	2008–2016
John Balance (Lib)	1891–1893	Bill English (PN)	2016–2017
Richard Seddon (Lib)	1893–1906	Jacinda Ardern (Lab)	2017–2023
William Hall-Jones (Lib)	1906	Chris Hipkins (Lab)	2023–
Joseph Ward (Lib)	1906–1912		

LA HISTORIA EN CIFRAS

HOMININOS

Los antepasados más lejanos de los humanos modernos fueron animales de aspecto simiesco que vivieron en África hace millones de años. Nuestra especie, Homo sapiens, solo tiene entre 300 000 y 200 000 años.

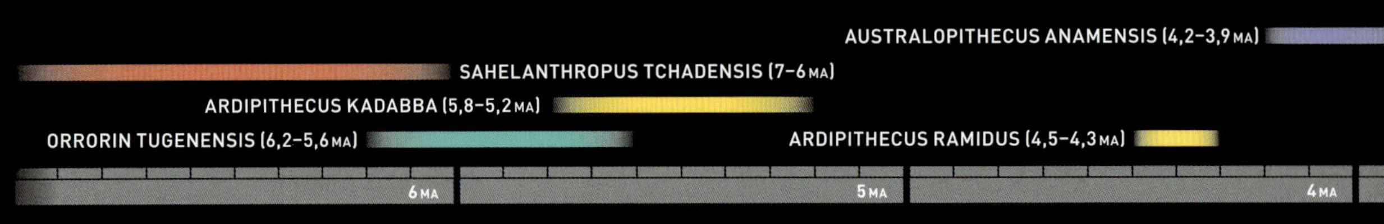

LAS MAYORES CIUDADES

Las grandes ciudades de la Antigüedad estaban relativamente poco pobladas. Con el tiempo, el desarrollo de sistemas de cloacas permitió a ciudades como Roma convertirse en aglomeraciones de 500 000 habitantes en el siglo I a. C., una cifra apenas igualada hasta la revolución industrial del siglo XIX.

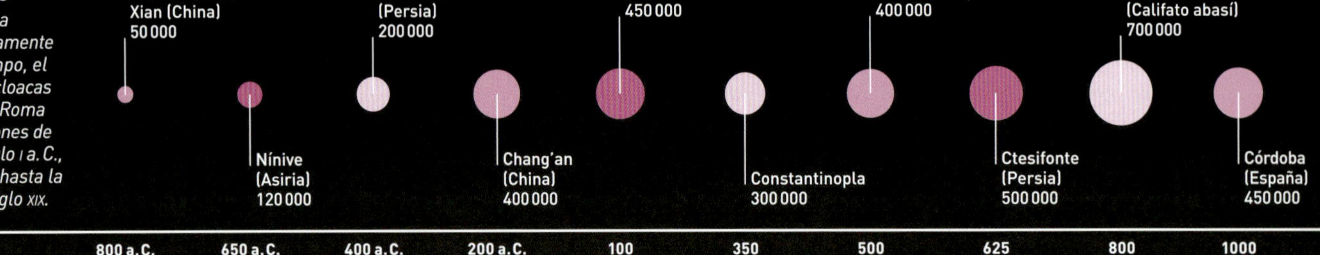

GUERRAS MÁS MORTÍFERAS

Aunque la Segunda Guerra Mundial está a la cabeza por el número de muertes, hubo otros conflictos armados sumamente cruentos, habida cuenta de los menores efectivos de los ejércitos de la época, así como de la menor población de los países implicados.

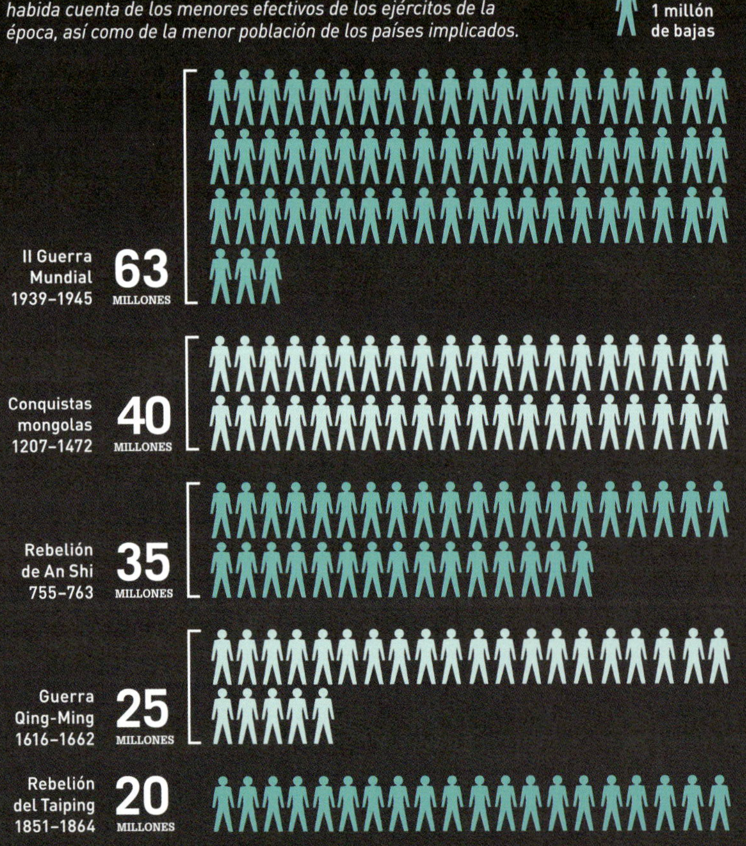

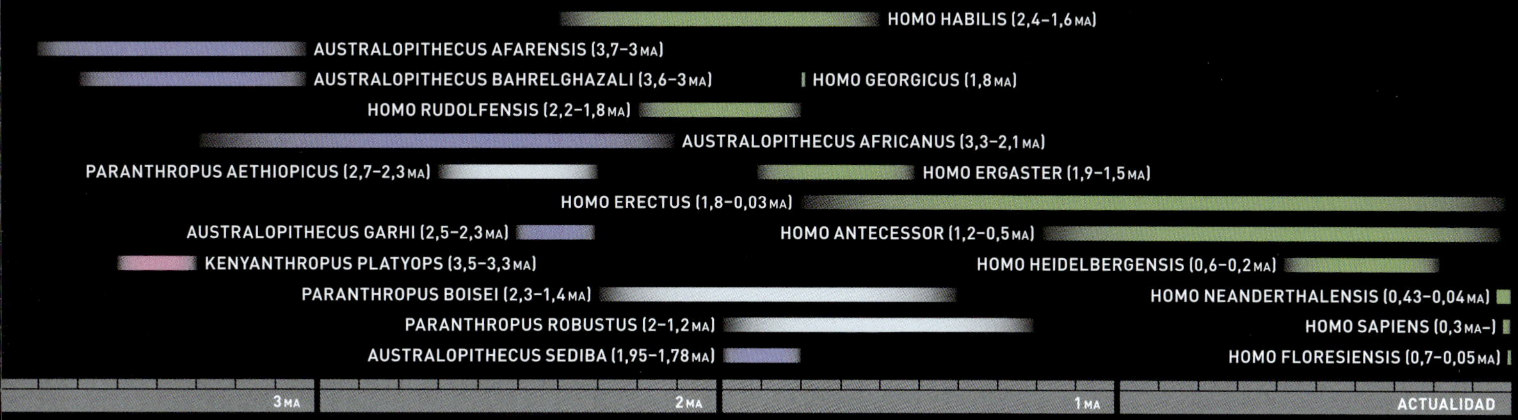

HOMO HABILIS (2,4–1,6 MA)
AUSTRALOPITHECUS AFARENSIS (3,7–3 MA)
AUSTRALOPITHECUS BAHRELGHAZALI (3,6–3 MA)
HOMO GEORGICUS (1,8 MA)
HOMO RUDOLFENSIS (2,2–1,8 MA)
AUSTRALOPITHECUS AFRICANUS (3,3–2,1 MA)
PARANTHROPUS AETHIOPICUS (2,7–2,3 MA)
HOMO ERGASTER (1,9–1,5 MA)
HOMO ERECTUS (1,8–0,03 MA)
AUSTRALOPITHECUS GARHI (2,5–2,3 MA)
HOMO ANTECESSOR (1,2–0,5 MA)
KENYANTHROPUS PLATYOPS (3,5–3,3 MA)
HOMO HEIDELBERGENSIS (0,6–0,2 MA)
PARANTHROPUS BOISEI (2,3–1,4 MA)
HOMO NEANDERTHALENSIS (0,43–0,04 MA)
PARANTHROPUS ROBUSTUS (2–1,2 MA)
HOMO SAPIENS (0,3 MA–)
AUSTRALOPITHECUS SEDIBA (1,95–1,78 MA)
HOMO FLORESIENSIS (0,7–0,05 MA)
3 MA
2 MA
1 MA
ACTUALIDAD

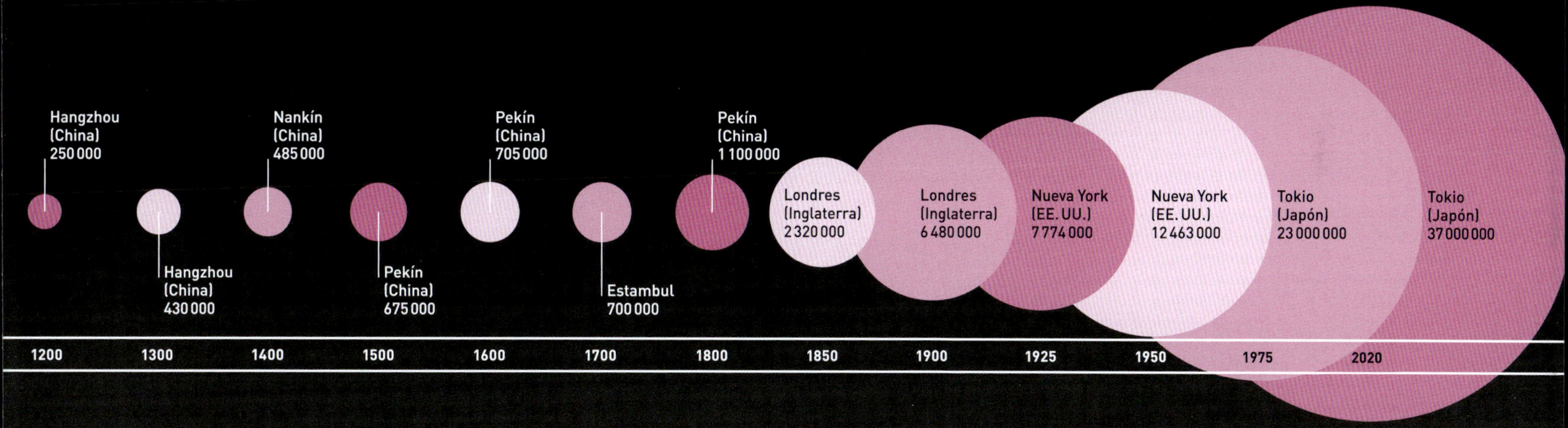

Hangzhou (China) 250 000
Hangzhou (China) 430 000
Nankín (China) 485 000
Pekín (China) 675 000
Pekín (China) 705 000
Estambul 700 000
Pekín (China) 1 100 000
Londres (Inglaterra) 2 320 000
Londres (Inglaterra) 6 480 000
Nueva York (EE. UU.) 7 774 000
Nueva York (EE. UU.) 12 463 000
Tokio (Japón) 23 000 000
Tokio (Japón) 37 000 000
1200
1300
1400
1500
1600
1700
1800
1850
1900
1925
1950
1975
2020

DINASTÍAS MÁS DURADERAS

No es frecuente que una dinastía reinante perdure más de algunos siglos, pero existen casos excepcionales de familias reales que han ejercido el poder a lo largo de más de un milenio. En Japón, la dinastía Yamato ha sobrevivido durante más de 2500 años y aún es la casa reinante.

Yamato (Japón) 660 a. C.–actualidad (2682 años)
Hong Bang (Vietnam) 2897–258 a. C. (2639 años)
Gojoseon (Corea) 2333–108 a. C. (2225 años)
Pandya (Sur de India) C. 350 a. C.–c. 1550 d. C. (1900 años)
Sisodia (India) 191–actualidad (1831 años)
Cham (Vietnam) 192–1832 (1640 años)
Bagration (Georgia) 813–1810 (997 años)
Tu'i Tonga (Tonga) C. 900–1865 (965 años)
Silla (Corea) 57 a. C.–935 d. C. (878 años)
Zhou (China) 1046–256 a. C. (790 años)
Grimaldi (Mónaco) 1297–actualidad (725 años)
0
500
1000
1500
2000
2500
AÑOS

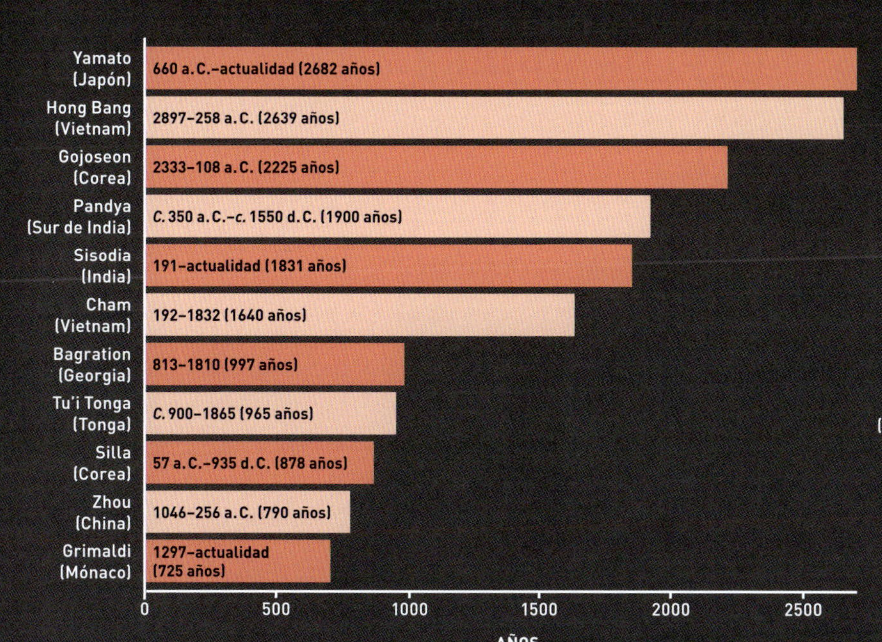

SOBERANOS DE REINADO MÁS LARGO

Algunos monarcas reinaron durante largo tiempo. Aunque esto significa a menudo que subieron al trono siendo niños y que hasta la mayoría de edad no ejercieron el poder, sus años de gobierno suelen coincidir con el auge y la prosperidad de su país.

Min Hti (Birmania) 1279–1374 (95 años)
Pepi II (Egipto) C. 2278–c. 2184 a. C. (94 años)
Taejo (Goguryeo, Corea) 53–146 (93 años)
Sobhuza II (Swazilandia) 1899–1982 (82 años)
Jangsu (Goguryeo, Corea) 413–492 (79 años)
Enrique XI (Reuss-Greiz, Alemania) 1723–1800 (77 años)
Cristián Augusto (Sulzbach, Alemania) 1632–1708 (76 años)
Jorge Guillermo (Schaumburg-Lippe, Alemania) 1787–1860 (73 años)
Carlos Federico (Baden, Alemania) 1738–1811 (73 años)
Luis XIV (Francia) 1643–1715 (72 años)
Trieu Vieu Vuong (Nanyueh, Vietnam) 207–136 a. C. (71 años)
0
25
50
75
100
AÑOS

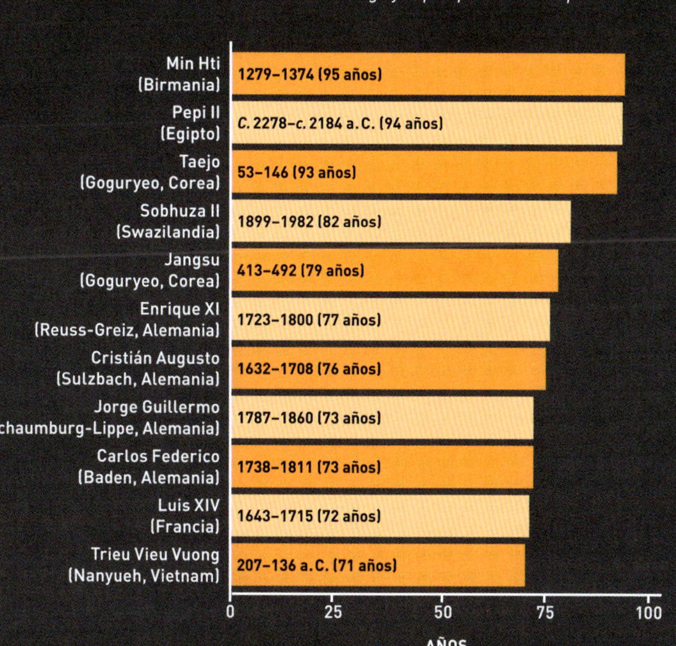

GUERRAS

La historia de la humanidad está plagada de conflictos. A lo largo del tiempo, las disputas por el territorio, la religión y el poder han llevado a la guerra, cuyas trágicas consecuencias no deben quedar ensombrecidas por los apasionantes relatos sobre grandes batallas y caudillos heroicos.

PRINCIPALES GUERRAS

GUERRAS	FECHA	CONTENDIENTES
Guerras médicas	490–448 a. C.	Coalición de ciudades-estado griegas, incluidas Atenas y Esparta, vs. Persia.
Guerra del Peloponeso	431–404 a. C.	Atenas y aliados vs. Esparta y aliados.
Conquistas de Alejandro Magno	334–323 a. C.	Macedonia vs. Imperio persa.
Primera guerra púnica	264–241 a. C.	Roma vs. Cartago.
Segunda guerra púnica	218–202 a. C.	Roma vs. Cartago.
Tercera guerra púnica	149–146 a. C.	Roma vs. Cartago.
Guerras civiles romanas	49–44 a. C. 33–31 a. C.	Julio César vs. Pompeyo. Octavio (Augusto) vs. Marco Antonio.
Guerras bizantino-selyúcidas	1064–1071, 1110–1117, 1158–1176	Bizantinos vs. turcos selyúcidas.
Cruzadas	1095–1272	Varios ejércitos europeos cristianos vs. estados musulmanes del Levante mediterráneo y Egipto.
Conquistas mongolas	1206–1405	Mongoles vs. varios pueblos europeos y asiáticos.
Guerra de los Cien Años	1337–1453	Ingleses (y borgoñones) vs. franceses.
Guerra de Onin	1467–1477	El clan Yamana vs. el clan Hosokawa.
Guerras de Italia	1494–1544 (con intervalos)	Ciudades italianas y Sacro Imperio vs. Francia y sus aliados italianos.
Guerras de unificación japonesas	1560–1603	Oda Nobunaga, Toyotomi Hideyoshi, Tokugawa Ieyasu y aliados vs. clanes de daimios (señores feudales) rivales.
Revuelta de Países Bajos (Guerra de los Ochenta Años)	1568–1648	Los Países Bajos del norte vs. Felipe II y sus aliados de los Países Bajos del sur.
Guerras civiles inglesas (Guerra de los Tres Reinos)	1642–1651	Carlos I de Inglaterra y realistas vs. parlamentaristas.
Guerra de los Treinta Años	1618–1648	Alianza imperial católica vs. estados mayoritariamente protestantes y Francia.
Guerra del Norte	1700–1721	Suecia vs. Dinamarca, Sajonia, Polonia-Lituania y Rusia.
Guerra de los Siete Años	1756–1763	RU y Prusia vs. Francia, Austria, Rusia, Sajonia y Suecia.
Guerra de la Independencia de Estados Unidos	1775–1783	RU vs. colonos norteamericanos (y aliados franceses).
Guerras revolucionarias francesas	1792–1802	Francia vs. coaliciones que incluían a RU, Austria, Prusia y Rusia.
Guerras napoleónicas	1803–1815	Francia vs. coaliciones que incluían a RU, Austria, Prusia y Rusia.
Guerra de Crimea	1853–1856	Rusia vs. Imperio otomano, RU y Francia.
Rebelión de los cipayos	1857–1858	Británicos vs. tropas nativas de India.
Guerra de Secesión (EE. UU.)	1861–1865	La Unión vs. la Confederación.
Guerra franco-prusiana	1870–1871	Francia vs. Prusia.
Rebelión del Taiping	1850–1864	El gobierno central chino (Qing) vs. rebeldes del Taiping.
Guerras de los Bóers	1880–1881, 1899–1902	Británicos vs. bóers (afrikáners).
Guerras de los Balcanes	1912–1913	(Primera) Bulgaria, Grecia, Serbia y Montenegro vs. Imperio otomano. (Segunda) Bulgaria vs. Turquía, Serbia, Grecia y Rumanía.
Primera Guerra Mundial	1914–1918	Entente (RU, Francia, Italia, Rusia, EE. UU. y otros) vs. Potencias Centrales (Alemania, Austria-Hungría, otomanos y otros).
Guerra Civil rusa	1918–1921	Bolcheviques vs. rusos «blancos».
Guerra Civil española	1936–1939	Nacionales vs. republicanos.
Segunda Guerra Mundial	1939–1945	Los aliados (británicos, franceses y otros) vs. el Eje (alemanes, japoneses, italianos hasta 1943, y otros).
Guerra Civil china	1945–1949	Comunistas vs. nacionalistas (Kuomintang).
Guerra de Corea	1950–1953	Norcoreanos y chinos vs. surcoreanos y tropas de la ONU (estadounidenses, australianas y británicas, entre otras).
Guerra de Indochina	1946–1954	Franceses vs. nacionalistas vietnamitas (Vietminh).
Guerras árabe-israelíes	1948–1973	Israel vs. Egipto, Siria, Jordania, Líbano, Iraq y palestinos.
Guerra del Vietnam	1961–1975	Survietnamitas, estadounidenses y australianos vs. norvietnamitas (Vietcong).
Guerra irano-iraquí	1980–1988	Iraq vs. Irán.
Guerras del Golfo	1990–1991, 2003	Iraq vs. una coalición internacional liderada por EE. UU.
Guerra de Afganistán	2001–2021	Coalición liderada por EE. UU. vs. talibanes.
Insurgencia de Boko Haram	Inicio 2009	Gobierno nigeriano vs.Boko Haram
Guerra civil siria	Inicio 2011	El gobierno del presidente Bashar al-Assad vs. fuerzas que se oponen al gobierno
Guerra ruso-ucraniana	Inicio 2014	Comenzando con una invasión encubierta de Crimea, se lanzó una invasión en 2022

EXPLORADORES

Los «descubrimientos» de muchos exploradores eran en realidad tierras habitadas por sociedades indígenas prósperas en las que tuvieron efectos desastrosos para la población nativa. Aun así, sus viajes siguen siendo hitos históricos que dieron forma al mundo tal y como lo conocemos.

EXPLORADORES CÉLEBRES

NOMBRE	VIDA	ORIGEN	EXPEDICIÓN/DESCUBRIMIENTO
Hannón	Activo en el siglo V a. C.	Cartago	Navegó a lo largo de la costa africana occidental (*c.* 470 a. C.).
Erik el Rojo	*C.* 950–1002	Noruega	Exploró la costa de Groenlandia (985).
Leif Eriksson	Activo en el siglo XI	Noruega	Llega a Vinland, en América del Norte (*c.* 1000).
Marco Polo	1254–1324	Italia	Viajó ampliamente por China y a lo largo de la Ruta de la Seda (1275–1292).
Ibn Battuta	*C.* 1304–1368	Marruecos	Exploró el Sáhara, Arabia, India, Asia central, China y el Sureste Asiático.
Dinis Dias	Activo a mediados del siglo XV	Portugal	Viaja a las islas de Cabo Verde, frente a la costa oeste africana (1445).

NOMBRE	VIDA	ORIGEN	EXPEDICIÓN/DESCUBRIMIENTO
Bartolomeu Dias	*C.* 1450–1500	Portugal	Dobló el cabo de Buena Esperanza, en el extremo sur de África (1488).
Vasco da Gama	*C.* 1469–1524	Portugal	Rodeó el cabo de Buena Esperanza y navegó hasta India (1497–1498).
Cristóbal Colón	1451–1506	Italia	Navegó hasta América: desembarcó en una isla de las Bahamas (1492) y después llegó al continente sudamericano (1498).
Giovanni Caboto	*C.* 1450–1499	Italia	Exploró el continente de América del Norte (1497).
Pedro Álvarez Cabral	*C.* 1467–1520	Portugal	Navegó hasta Brasil (1500).
Amerigo Vespucci	1454–1512	Italia	Exploró la costa de América del Sur (1501).
Alfonso de Albuquerque	1453–1515	Portugal	Llegó a India por Zanzíbar (1503–1504).
Vasco Núñez de Balboa	1475–1519	España	Primer europeo que navegó por el océano Pacífico, desde Panamá (1513).
Juan Ponce de León	*C.* 1460–1521	España	Descubrió Florida (1513).
Hernán Cortés	1485–1547	España	Lideró la conquista del Imperio azteca, en México (1518–1522).
Fernando de Magallanes	*C.* 1480–1521	Portugal	Exploró las Filipinas y circunnavegó en parte el globo (1520–1521).
Juan Sebastián Elcano	*C.* 1476–1526	España	Completó la primera circunnavegación del globo (1520–1523).
Francisco Pizarro	1475–1541	España	Lideró la conquista del Imperio inca, en Perú (1530–1533).
Álvar Núñez Cabeza de Vaca	1507–1549	España	Exploró las cataratas de Iguazú y Paraguay (1542).
Jacques Cartier	1491–1557	Francia	Exploró el golfo de San Lorenzo y el río San Lorenzo (1535–1536).
Francisco Vázquez de Coronado	1510–1554	España	Lideró la primera gran expedición al suroeste de los actuales EE. UU. (1540–1542).
García López de Cárdenas	Activo en la década de 1540	España	Llegó al Gran Cañón del Colorado en 1540.
John Davis	*C.* 1550–1605	Inglaterra	Exploró Groenlandia y descubrió el estrecho de Davis (1585) en busca del paso del Noroeste.
Willem Barents	1550–1597	Países Bajos	Dirigió dos expediciones en busca del paso de Noreste (1594–1597).
Walter Raleigh	1552–1618	Inglaterra	Realizó numerosos viajes a América e intentó, sin éxito, fundar una colonia en Virginia (1584).
Cornelis de Houtman	1565–1599	Países Bajos	Dirigió la primera expedición holandesa a las Indias Orientales; navegó a lo largo de la costa sur de Java (1598).
Samuel de Champlain	1567–1635	Francia	Exploró el río San Lorenzo (1603) y fundó Quebec (1608).
Henry Hudson	*C.* 1565–1611	Inglaterra	Exploró la bahía de Hudson (Canadá) en 1610.
William Baffin	1584–1622	Inglaterra	Exploró la bahía de Baffin, parte del paso del Noroeste (1616).
Abel Tasman	1603–*c.* 1659	Países Bajos	Llegó a Nueva Zelanda y Tasmania (1642).
William Dampier	1651–1715	Inglaterra	Cruzó el océano Pacífico (1683).
Vitus Bering	1681–1741	Dinamarca	Exploró Siberia (1733–1741).
James Bruce	1730–1794	RU	Exploró el Nilo Azul y afirmó haber hallado las fuentes del Nilo (1768–1774).
James Cook	1728–1779	RU	Cartografió las costas de Nueva Zelanda y australianas (1769); avistó por primera vez Australia, en la bahía de Botany (Nueva Gales del Sur) (1770).
Antoine (de Bruni) d'Entrecasteaux	1739–1793	Francia	Recorrió el Pacífico Sur (1791–1793).
Mungo Park	1771–1806	RU	Exploró el río Níger (1795–1796).

NOMBRE	VIDA	ORIGEN	EXPEDICIÓN/DESCUBRIMIENTO
George Bass	1771–1803	RU	Exploró la costa de Australia suroriental (1795–1798).
Alexander von Humboldt	1769–1859	Alemania	Exploró la actual Venezuela y el río Orinoco (1799–1800).
Matthew Flinders	1774–1814	RU	Circunnavegó Australia (1801–1803).
Meriwether Lewis	1774–1809	EE. UU.	Dirigió la primera expedición transcontinental de EE. UU. (1804–1805), con William Clark.
Fabian von Bellingshausen	1778–1852	Estonia	Explorador pionero de la Antártida (1819–1821).
Alexander Gordon Laing	1793–1826	RU	Primer europeo en llegar a Tombuctú, en Malí (1826).
James Clark Ross	1800–1862	EE. UU.	Exploró extensamente la Antártida y descubrió el mar de Ross y la plataforma del mismo nombre (1841).
Richard Francis Burton	1821–1890	RU	Viajó por Arabia y llegó a Medina y La Meca (1853).
David Livingstone	1813–1873	RU	Exploró las cataratas Victoria en el río Zambeze (1855).
Robert O'Hara Burke	1820–1861	Irlanda	Dirigió una desafortunada expedición para explorar el interior de Australia (1860–1861).
Henry Morton Stanley	1841–1904	RU	Emprendió varios viajes por el Congo (1874).
Sven Hedin	1865–1962	Suecia	Exploró Asia central y descubrió ciudades perdidas en el Taklamakán (1893–1897).
Otto Nordenskjold	1869–1928	Suecia	Pasó el invierno en la Antártida (1901–1903).
Francis Younghusband	1863–1942	RU	Dirigió una expedición que llegó a Lhasa, en Tíbet (1903–1904).
Aurel Stein	1862–1943	Hungría	Exploró Asia central y localizó el complejo de templos de Dunhuang (1906–1908).
Robert Peary	1856–1920	EE. UU.	Afirmó haber llegado al polo Norte (1909).
Roald Amundsen	1872–1928	Noruega	Fue el primero en llegar al polo Sur (1911).
Robert Falcon Scott	1868–1912	RU	Fue superado por Admundsen en la carrera hacia el polo Sur (1911–1912).
Ernest Shackleton	1874–1922	RU	Dirigió una expedición para cruzar la Antártida, pero quedó atrapado cuatro meses en el hielo de la isla Elefante (1914).
Richard Byrd	1888–1957	EE. UU.	Sobrevoló por primera vez el polo Norte (1926).
Vivian Fuchs	1908–1999	RU	Realizó la primera travesía terrestre del continente antártico (1958).
Wilfred Thesiger	1910–2003	RU	Intrépido viajero que cruzó dos veces el Rub al Jali de Arabia.
Jacques-Yves Cousteau	1910–1997	Francia	Ecologista marino que exploró las profundidades del océano.
Thor Heyerdahl	1914–2002	Noruega	Mediante viajes en balsas de materiales naturales, intentó probar las teorías sobre las migraciones prehistóricas por mar.
Edmund Hillary	1919–2008	Nueva Zelanda	Completó el primer ascenso al Everest, en el Himalaya (1953).
Yuri Gagarin	1934–1968	URSS	**Vostok 1** (12 de abril de 1961); primer hombre lanzado al espacio y en viajar en órbita alrededor de la Tierra.
Alan Shepard	1923–1998	EE. UU.	**Freedom 7** (5 de mayo de 1961); primer estadounidense lanzado al espacio y, después, quinto hombre en pisar la Luna.
Guerman Titov	1935–2000	URSS	**Vostok 2** (6 de agosto de 1961); la persona más joven (25 años) lanzada al espacio y el segundo hombre que viajó en órbita alrededor de la Tierra.
Valentina Tereshkova	n. 1937	URSS	**Vostok 6** (16 de junio de 1963); primera mujer en viajar al espacio.
Alexéi Leónov	1943–2019	URSS	**Vosjod 2** (18 de marzo de 1965); primer paseo espacial unido a la nave por un cable.

EXPLORADORES ESPACIALES (CONTINUACIÓN)

NOMBRE	VIDA	ORIGEN	MISIÓN/LOGRO
Neil Armstrong	1930–2012	EE. UU.	**Apolo 11** (20 de julio de 1969); primer hombre que caminó sobre la Luna.
Vladímir Remek	n. 1948	Checoslovaquia	**Soyuz 28** (2 de marzo de 1978); primer no estadounidense ni soviético en viajar al espacio.
Sigmund Jahn	1937–2019	RDA	**Soyuz 31** (26 de agosto de 1978); primer alemán en viajar al espacio.
Jean-Loup Chrétien	n. 1938	Francia	**Soyuz T-11** (24 de junio de 1982); primer francés en viajar al espacio.
Ulf Merbold	n. 1941	RFA	**STS-9** (28 de noviembre de 1983); primer astronauta de la ESA y segundo alemán en viajar al espacio.
Rakesh Sharma	n. 1949	India	**Soyuz T-11** (13 de abril de 1984); primer indio en viajar al espacio.
Sultan bin Salman al Saud	n. 1956	Arabia Saudí	**STS-56** (17 de junio de 1985); primer árabe (y primer musulmán) en viajar al espacio.
Mamoru Mori	n. 1948	Japón	**STS-47** (12 de septiembre de 1992); primer japonés en viajar al espacio.
Valeri Poliakov	1942–2022	Rusia	**Soyuz TM-18** (8 de enero de 1998); viaje espacial más largo (437 días).
Pedro Duque	n. 1963	España	**STS-95** (29 de octubre de 1998); primer español en viajar al espacio.
Dennis Tito	n. 1940	EE. UU.	**Soyuz TM 32** (28 de abril de 2001); primer «turista espacial».
Yang Liwei	n. 1965	China	**Shenzou 5** (15 de octubre de 2003); primer chino en viajar al espacio.
Serguéi Krikaliov	n. 1958	Rusia	**Soyuz TMA-6** (11 de octubre de 2005); batió el récord de estancia en el espacio (803 días, 9 horas y 39 minutos).
Wally Funk	n. 1939	EE. UU.	**New Shephard** (20 de julio de 2021); mujer de mayor edad en viajar al espacio.

INVENTOS Y DESCUBRIMIENTOS

El mundo actual es muy distinto del que conocieron nuestros antepasados. A lo largo de la existencia de la humanidad, la satisfacción de necesidades básicas –desde la mera supervivencia hasta el deseo de saber– ha dado lugar a miles de inventos y descubrimientos que han ido transformando la manera de vivir y de pensar, y han hecho única a la especie humana dentro del reino animal.

GRANDES INVENTOS Y DESCUBRIMIENTOS

INVENTO/DESCUBRIMIENTO	FECHA	CREADOR	ORIGEN
Útiles líticos (de piedra)	*C.* 2,75 MA	Primeros humanos	África
Dominio del fuego	*C.* 400 000 años	Primeros humanos	África
Barco	*C.* 50 000 años	Primeros migradores	Australasia
Minería	*C.* 40 000 años	Humanos paleolíticos	Europa
Abrigos permanentes	*C.* 28 000 años	Humanos paleolíticos	Este de Europa
Cerámica (alfarería)	*C.* 14 000 años	Cultura jomon	Japón
Agricultura	*C.* 10 000 a. C.	Pueblos de Asia occidental	Mesopotamia
Regadío	*C.* 5000 a. C.	Pueblos de Asia occidental	Mesopotamia
Domesticación del caballo	*C.* 4500 a. C.	Cultura de Andrónovo	Europa/Asia
Arado	*C.* 4000 a. C.	Sumerios	Mesopotamia
Transporte sobre ruedas	*C.* 3500 a. C.	Sumerios	Sumer
Tejido de la seda	*C.* 3500 a. C.	Pueblos chinos	China
Escritura	*C.* 3300 a. C.	Sumerios	Sumer/Egipto
Calendario	*C.* 3000 a. C.	Babilonios	Babilonia
Rollo de papiro	*C.* 2600 a. C.	Imhotep (atribuido)	Egipto
Red de agua corriente	*C.* 2500 a. C.	Civilización del Valle del Indo	Indo (Pakistán)
Código legal	*C.* 1755 a. C.	Hammurabi	Babilonia
Alfabeto	Siglo XIV a. C.	Pueblos semíticos (esclavos de Egipto)	Egipto
Magnetismo	*C.* 1000 a. C.	Tales de Mileto (atribuido)	Grecia
Acuñación de moneda	*C.* 600 a. C.	Lidios	Turquía
Mapamundi	Siglo VI a. C.	Babilonios	Babilonia
Modelos planetarios	*C.* 360 a. C.	Eudoxo de Cnido	Grecia
Rotación de la Tierra	*C.* 350 a. C.	Heráclides Póntico	Grecia
Producción de acero	*C.* 200 a. C.	Dinastía Han	India/China
Polea compuesta	*C.* 200 a. C.	Arquímedes	Grecia
Enciclopedia	77	Plinio el Viejo	Imperio romano
Papel	*C.* 105	Cai Lun	China
Brújula	250	Chinos	China
Concepto de cero/sistema decimal	*C.* 590–650	Brahmagupta	India
Astrolabio	*C.* 800	Muhammad al-Fazari	Persia
Universidad	859	Fátima al-Fihri	Marruecos
Mapa celeste	*C.* 1000–1050	Abul-Rayhan Biruni	Persia
Péndulo	*C.* 1000	Ibn Yunus	Egipto
Lente de aumento	*C.* 1021	Alhazen	Persia
Tipos móviles	*C.* 1045	Bi Sheng	China
Reloj mecánico	1088	Su Song	China
Desarrollo del álgebra	1202	Leonardo Fibonacci	Italia
Método científico	*C.* 1220–1235	Robert Grosseteste	Inglaterra
Imprenta	*C.* 1445	Johannes Gutenberg	Alemania
Globo terráqueo	*C.* 1490	Martin Behaim	Bohemia
Universo heliocéntrico	1503–1543	Nicolás Copérnico	Italia
Microscopio compuesto	*C.* 1595	Hans Lippershey y Zacharias Janssen	Países Bajos
Leyes del movimiento planetario	1609–1619	Johannes Kepler	Alemania
Periódico	1609	Johann Carolus	Alemania
Telescopio refractor	1609	Galileo Galilei	Italia
Calculadora mecánica	1642	Wilhelm Schickard	Alemania
Barómetro	1643	Evangelista Torricelli	Italia
Presión atmosférica	1647–1648	Blaise Pascal	Francia
Vida microscópica	1673	Antoni van Leeuwenhoek	Países Bajos
Leyes del movimiento	1687	Isaac Newton	Inglaterra
Sembradora	1701	Jethro Tull	Inglaterra
Máquina atmosférica de pistón	1712	Thomas Newcomen	RU
Cronómetro marino	1735	John Harrison	RU
Pararrayos	1752	Benjamin Franklin	EE. UU.
Máquina de vapor	1776	James Watt	RU
Oxígeno	1777	Antoine de Lavoisier	Francia
Globo aerostático	1783	Hermanos Montgolfier	Francia
Trilladora	1786	Andrew Meikle	RU
Pila eléctrica	1800	Alessandro Volta	Italia
Bicicleta	1818	Karl Drais	Alemania
Fotografía permanente	*C.* 1820	Joseph Nicéphore Niepce	Francia
Alfabeto braille	1821	Louis Braille	Francia
Motor eléctrico	1821	Michael Faraday	RU

INVENTO/DESCUBRIMIENTO	FECHA	CREADOR	ORIGEN
Computadora programable	1822	Charles Babbage	RU
Electroimán	1823	William Sturgeon	RU
Motor de combustión interna	1826	Samuel Morey	EE. UU.
Turbina hidráulica	1827	Claude Burdin y Benoît Fourneyron	Francia
Locomotora de vapor	1829	George Stephenson	RU
Generador eléctrico	1831	Michael Faraday	RU
Frigorífico	1834	Jacob Perkins	EE. UU./RU
Vulcanización del caucho	1837	Charles Goodyear	EE. UU.
Poliestireno	1839	Eduard Simon	Alemania
Programación informática	1843	Ada Lovelace	RU
Telégrafo submarino	1858	Charles Wheatstone	RU
Teoría de la evolución	1859	Charles Darwin	RU
Pasteurización	1862	Louis Pasteur y Claude Bernard	Francia
Leyes de la herencia	1866	Gregor Mendel	Austria
Dinamita	1867	Alfred Nobel	Suecia
Tabla periódica	1869	Dimitri Mendeléiev	Rusia
Teléfono	1876	Alexander Graham Bell	EE. UU./RU
Fonógrafo	1876	Thomas Edison	EE. UU.
Bombilla de incandescencia	1878	Joseph Wilson Swan	RU
Automóvil	1885	Karl Benz	Alemania
Motor de gasolina	1886	Gottlieb Daimler	Alemania
Teoría neuronal (contigüidad de las neuronas)	*C.* 1888	Santiago Ramón y Cajal	España
Comunicación inalámbrica	1893	Nikola Tesla	Austria-Hungría
Radiotelégrafo	1895	Guglielmo Marconi	Italia
Cinematógrafo	1895	Auguste y Louis Lumière	Francia
Radio (metal)	1898	Marie y Pierre Curie	Polonia/Francia
Teoría cuántica	1900	Max Planck	Alemania
Dirigible	1900	Ferdinand Graf von Zeppelin	Alemania
Aeroplano (autopropulsado)	1903	Hermanos Wright	EE. UU.
Reflejos condicionados	1904	Iván Pavlov	Rusia
Teoría de la relatividad	1905	Albert Einstein	Suiza
Baquelita	1909	Leo Baekeland	Bélgica
Acero inoxidable	1913	Harry Brearley	RU
Estructura del átomo	1913	Niels Bohr	Dinamarca
Televisión	1925	John Logie Baird	RU
Ley de la expansión del universo	1929	Edwin Hubble	EE. UU.
Nailon	1935	Wallace Carothers	EE. UU.
Radar	1935	Robert Watson-Watt	RU
Motor de reacción	1937	Frank Whittle	RU
Bolígrafo	1938	Lazslo Biro	Hungría
Reactor nuclear	1942	Enrico Fermi	Italia/EE. UU.
Escafandra autónoma	1943	Jacques-Yves Cousteau y Émile Gagnan	Francia
Bomba atómica	1945	J. Robert Oppenheimer	EE. UU.
Fotosíntesis	1946	Melvin Calvin	EE. UU.
Avión a reacción comercial	1948	Vickers Limited	RU
Datación por radiocarbono	1949	Willard Libby	EE. UU.
Teoría del Big Bang	1949	George Gamow, Ralph Alpher y Robert Herman	EE. UU.
Estructura del ADN	1953	Rosalind Franklin, Francis Crick y James D. Watson	RU/ EE. UU.
Satélite de comunicaciones	1958	Kenneth Masterman-Smith	EE. UU.
Láser	1960	Theodore H. Maiman	EE. UU.
Tren bala	1964	Hideo Shima	Japón
Tectónica de placas	1967	Dan McKenzie	RU
Púlsar	1967	Jocelyn Bell Burnell	RU
Microprocesador	1969	Intel	EE. UU.
Correo electrónico	1971	Ray Tomlinson	EE. UU.
Modificación genética	1973	Stanley Norman Cohen y Herbert Boyer	EE. UU.
Ordenador personal	1973	Xerox PARC	EE. UU.
Teléfono móvil	1973	Martin Cooper (Motorola)	EE. UU.
Disco compacto	1980	Philips Electronic/ Sony Corporation	Países Bajos/ Japón
World Wide Web	1990	Tim Berners-Lee	RU
GPS (Sistema de Posicionamiento Global)	1995	Departamento de Defensa	EE. UU.
Clonación genética	1996	Ian Wilmut y Keith Campbell	RU
iPod	2001	Apple	EE. UU.
Tecnología blockchain	2008	«Satoshi Nakamoto»	Desconocido
Bosón de Higgs	2012	CERN	Suiza
Onda gravitatoria (observada)	2015L	LIGO	EE. UU.

FILOSOFÍA Y RELIGIÓN

Las primeras respuestas a los interrogantes acerca de la naturaleza y del sentido de la vida proceden de los fundadores de las grandes religiones orientales. Desde entonces, los filósofos occidentales han recorrido un largo camino hasta los confines del pensamiento y el conocimiento, planteando cuestiones que desafían las ideas más arraigadas.

Los sistemas de creencias religiosas son casi tan diversos como las culturas. Algunos surgieron en épocas prehistóricas, pero el siglo XX aún asistió al nacimiento de nuevas religiones cuyos adeptos se cuentan por millones.

GRANDES PENSADORES

NOMBRE	VIDA	ORIGEN	IDEAS/OBRA CLAVE
Siddhartha Gautama (Buda)	*C.* 563–483 a. C.	India	Fundador del budismo como vía para alcanzar el nirvana (iluminación espiritual).
Laozi	Activo en el siglo VI a. C.	China	Fundador del taoísmo, interesado por la actitud vital del individuo. *Tao Te King*.
Confucio	551–479 a. C.	China	Fundador del confucianismo, que promueve la armonía social mediante tradiciones y normas inmutables.
Pitágoras	*C.* 550–*c.* 500 a. C.	Grecia	Fundador de una escuela basada en el poder místico de los números.
Sócrates	*C.* 469–399 a. C.	Grecia	Uno de los fundadores de la filosofía occidental. No dejó escritos.
Platón	*C.* 427–347 a. C.	Grecia	Discípulo de Sócrates, afirmó que todo lo que percibimos es una sombra de su forma ideal, abstracta. *La república* (*c.* 360 a. C.).
Aristóteles	384–322 a. C.	Grecia	Filósofo de obra muy amplia, con un interés especial en la clasificación lógica. *Metafísica* (350 a. C.).
Mencio	372–289 a. C.	China	Filósofo confuciano defensor de la bondad de la naturaleza humana.
Plotino	205–270	Grecia/Imperio romano	Fundador del neoplatonismo, derivado de las ideas de Platón. *Enéadas* (*c.* 253–270).
San Agustín de Hipona	354–430	Norte de África/ Imperio romano	Transmisor del platonismo a través de la teología cristiana. *La ciudad de Dios*.

GRANDES PENSADORES (CONTINUACIÓN)

NOMBRE	VIDA	ORIGEN	IDEAS/OBRA CLAVE
Al-Farabi	c. 878–950	Iraq	Influyente filósofo musulmán. *Gran libro de la música.*
Ramanuja	1017–1137	India	Influyente pensador del hinduismo.
Santo Tomás de Aquino	1225–1274	Italia	El mayor teólogo medieval. *Suma teológica* (1259–1269).
Ibn Jaldún	1332–1406	Egipto	Pensador islámico que sentó las bases de las ciencias sociales. Muqaddimah (1377).
Nicolás Maquiavelo	1469–1527	Italia	Afirmó que el estado debe procurar el bien común sin considerar la evaluación moral de sus actos. *El príncipe* (1413).
Francis Bacon	1561–1626	Inglaterra	Sostuvo que el conocimiento científico permite controlar la naturaleza. *Novum organum* (1620).
Thomas Hobbes	1588–1679	Inglaterra	Padre de la filosofía política inglesa, el estudio de la organización de la sociedad. *Leviatán* (1651).
René Descartes	1596–1650	Francia	Subvirtió el escolasticismo medieval y renacentista. *Meditaciones metafísicas* (1641).
Baruch Spinoza	1632–1677	Países Bajos	Filósofo racionalista; afirmó que el conocimiento del mundo se puede alcanzar mediante la razón. *Tratado teológico-político* (1670).
John Locke	1632–1704	Inglaterra	Defensor del empirismo:el conocimiento debe proceder de la experiencia. *Tratados sobre el gobierno civil* (1690).
Gotfried Wilhelm Leibniz	1646–1716	Alemania	Matemático y filósofo racionalista. *Monadología* (1714).
George Berkeley	1685–1753	Inglaterra	Filósofo metafísico idealista. *Tratado sobre los principios del conocimiento humano* (1710).
David Hume	1711–1776	RU	Principal exponente del idealismo metafísicoe. *Tratado sobre la naturaleza humana* (1734–1737).
Jean-Jacques Rousseau	1712–1778	Suiza	Defensor de la soberanía del cuerpo social de los ciudadanos (el pueblo). *El contrato social* (1762).
Immanuel Kant	1724–1804	Alemania	Buscó establecer la autoridad de la razón a través del examen crítico. *Crítica de la razón pura* (1781).
Thomas Paine	1737–1809	RU	Afirmó que los gobiernos deben respetar los derechos naturales de los ciudadanos. *Los derechos del hombre* (1791–1792).
G. W. F. Hegel	1770–1831	Alemania	El idealista alemán más influyente. *La fenomenología del espíritu* (1807).
Arthur Schopenhauer	1788–1860	Alemania	Idealismo transcendental. *El mundo como voluntad y representación* (1818).
Søren Kierkegaard	1813–1855	Dinamarca	Precursor del existencialismo. *Apostilla conclusiva no científica a las «Migajas filosóficas»* (1846).
Karl Marx	1818–1883	Alemania	Teórico social radical y filósofo del comunismo. *El capital* (1867).
Friedrich Nietzsche	1844–1900	Alemania	Rechazó las interpretaciones religiosas y metafísicas de la condición humana a través del concepto del «superhombre». *Así habló Zaratustra* (1883–1885).
Bertrand Russell	1872–1970	RU	Fundador de la filosofía analítica. *Los principios de la matemática* 1910–1913).
Hannah Arendt	1889-1951	Alemania/ EE. UU.	Teórica política sobre el totalitarismo. *La condición humana* (1958).
Ludwig Wittgenstein	1889–1951	Austria	El filósofo analítico más prominente. *Tractatus logico-philosophicus* (1921).
Jean-Paul Sartre	1905–1975	Francia	Líder del existencialismo. *El ser y la nada* (1943).
Franz Fanon	1925–1961	Martinica	Pensador poscolonialista. *Piel negra, máscaras blancas* (1952).

PRINCIPALES RELIGIONES

NOMBRE	LUGAR/ÉPOCA	FIELES	FUNDADOR	TEXTOS
Religión tradicional china	Desconocido/ Prehistoria	400 millones	Indígena	–
Hinduismo	India/ Prehistoria	900 millones	Indígena	Veda, Upanishad y epopeyas sánscritas
Sintoísmo	Japón/ Prehistoria	3–4 millones	Indígena	*Kojiki* y *Nihongi*
Vudú	África occidental/ Prehistoria	8 millones	Indígena	–
Judaísmo	Israel/ c. 1300 a. C.	15 millones	Abraham/Moisés	Biblia hebrea y Talmud
Zoroastrismo	Irán/ siglo VI a. C.	200 000	Zoroastro	Avesta
Taoísmo	China/ c. 550 a. C.	20 millones	Laozi	*Tao Te King*
Jainismo	India/ c. 550 a. C.	4 millones	Mahavira	Enseñanzas de Mahavira
Budismo	Noreste de India/ c. 520 a. C.	375 millones	Siddhartha Gautama (Buda)	Canon pali y sutras mahayana
Confucianismo	China/ siglos VI–V a. C.	5–6 millones	Confucio	Los Cuatro Libros y los Cinco Clásicos
Cristianismo	Israel/ c. 30	2000 millones	Jesucristo	Biblia
Islam	Arabia Saudí/ siglo VII	1500 millones	Mahoma	Corán (escritura); hadiz (tradición)
Sijismo	Punjab (India)/ c. 1500	23 millones	Gurú Nanak	Adi Granth (Guru Granth Sahib)
Iglesia de Jesucristo de los santos del último día (mormones)	Nueva York (EE. UU.)/ 1830	13 millones	Joseph Smith	Biblia y *Libro del mormón*
Tenrikyo	Japón/ 1838	1 millón	Nakayama Miki	*Mikigaurata*, *Ofudesaki* y *Osashizu*
Bahaísmo	Teherán (Irán)/ 1863	5–7 millones	Baha Allah	*Kitab-i-Iqan* y *Kitab-i-Aqdas*
Iglesia de Cristo, Científico (Ciencia Cristiana)	Nueva York (EE. UU.)/ 1879	Más de 400 000	Mary Baker Eddy	Biblia y *Ciencia y salud con la llave de las Escrituras*
Cao Dai	Vietnam/ 1926	8 millones	Ngo Van Chieu	Canon Cao Dai
Rastafari	Jamaica/ década de 1930	1 millón	Haile Selassie I	*Holy Piby*
Federación de familias para la unificación y la paz mundial	Corea del Sur/ 1954	3 millones (cifra oficial)	Sun Myung Moon	El Principio Divino
Wicca	Década de 1950, pero basada en creencias antiguas	1–3 millones	Gerald Gardner	–
Falun Gong	China/ 1992	10 millones	Li Hongzhi	Escritos del maestro Li, entre ellos *Zhuan Falun*

CULTURA

La obra de escritores y artistas, desde los poetas, pintores y escultores de la Antigüedad hasta los artistas de las últimas tendencias del siglo XXI, aporta una visión de incalculable valor sobre el pensamiento y la vida de las grandes civilizaciones de todos los tiempos. En Europa a partir del siglo XI, y a lo largo de los siglos siguientes en otros continentes, el talento de muchas de estas personas se nutrió en las universidades que florecieron como centros transmisores del saber.

POETAS, DRAMATURGOS Y NOVELISTAS

La literatura es un fiel espejo del pasado. Aunque la trama sea imaginaria, el lenguaje y el comportamiento de los personajes de novelas y obras teatrales reflejan las inquietudes, costumbres e ideales artísticos de su tiempo, y en muchas obras, la cadena de acontecimientos ficticios transcurre sobre un rico trasfondo de hechos históricos verificables.

NOMBRE	VIDA	ORIGEN	GÉNERO	OBRAS DESTACADAS
Homero	Siglo VIII a. C.	Grecia	Poesía	*Odisea* (siglo VIII a. C.)
Esquilo	*C.* 525–456 a. C.	Grecia	Teatro	*Los siete contra Tebas* (*c.* 467 a. C.)
Sófocles	*C.* 496–406 a. C.	Grecia	Teatro	*Antígona* (*c.* 442 a. C.)
Eurípides	*C.* 484–406 a. C.	Grecia	Teatro	*Medea* (*c.* 431 a. C.)
Aristófanes	*C.* 448–388 a. C.	Grecia	Teatro	*Las ranas* (*c.* 405 a. C.)
Valmiki	*C.* 400–200 a. C.	India	Poesía	*Ramayana* (*c.* 400–200 a. C.)
Virgilio	70–19 a. C.	Imperio romano	Poesía	*Eneida* (*c.* 29–19 a. C.)
Ovidio	43 a. C.–*c.* 17 d. C.	Imperio romano	Poesía	*Metamorfosis* (8 d. C.)
Murasaki Shikibu	*C.* 978–1014	Japón	Novela	*La historia de Genji* (*c.* 1001–1010)
Dante Alighieri	1265–1321	Italia	Poesía	*Divina comedia* (*c.* 1321)
Petrarca	1304–1374	Italia	Poesía	*Cancionero* (1327–1368)
Geoffrey Chaucer	1343–1400	Inglaterra	Poesía	*Cuentos de Canterbury* (1387–1400)
Miguel de Cervantes	1547–1616	España	Novela/ poesía/ teatro	*El ingenioso hidalgo don Quijote de la Mancha* (1605)
William Shakespeare	1564–1616	Inglaterra	Teatro/ poesía	*Romeo y Julieta* (*c.* 1591–1595)
Pedro Calderón de la Barca	1600–1681	España	Teatro	*La vida es sueño* (1632–1635)
John Milton	1608–1674	Inglaterra	Poesía	*El paraíso perdido* (1667)
Molière	1622–1673	Francia	Teatro	*El misántropo* (1666)
Jean Racine	1639–1699	Francia	Teatro	*Fedra* (1677)
Jonathan Swift	1667–1745	Irlanda	Novela	*Los viajes de Gulliver* (1726)
Xueqin Cao	*C.* 1715–1763	China	Novela	*Sueño en el pabellón rojo* (1791)
Johann Wolfgang von Goethe	1749–1832	Alemania	Novela/ teatro	*Fausto* (1808)
William Wordsworth	1770–1850	Inglaterra	Poesía	*El preludio* (1799)
Jane Austen	1775–1817	RU	Novela	*Orgullo y prejuicio* (1813)
John Keats	1795–1821	RU	Poesía	*Endimión* (1818)
Mary Shelley	1797–1851	RU	Novela	*Frankenstein* (1818)
Aleksandr Pushkin	1799–1837	Rusia	Poesía/ novela	*Eugenio Oneguín* (1828)
Honoré de Balzac	1799–1850	Francia	Novela	*La comedia humana* (1827–1847)
Alexandre Dumas	1802–1870	Francia	Novela	*Los tres mosqueteros* (1844)
Victor Hugo	1802–1885	Francia	Novela/ poesía	*Los miserables* (1862)
Ralph Waldo Emerson	1803–1882	EE. UU.	Ensayo/ poesía	*La conducta de la vida* (1860)
Hans Christian Andersen	1805–1875	Dinamarca	Relatos	*Cuentos* (1835–1837)
Henry Longfellow	1807–1882	EE. UU.	Poesía	*Hiawatha* (1855)
Charles Dickens	1812–1870	RU	Novela	*Oliver Twist* (1837–1838)
Charlotte Brontë	1816–1855	RU	Novela	*Jane Eyre* (1847)
Iván Turguéniev	1818–1883	Rusia	Novela	*Padres e hijos* (1862)
Emily Brontë	1818–1848	RU	Novela	*Cumbres borrascosas* (1847)
George Eliot	1819–1880	RU	Novela	*El molino del Floss* (1860)
Anne Brontë	1820–1849	RU	Novela	*Agnes Grey* (1847)
Fiódor Dostoiewski	1821–1881	Rusia	Novela	*Crimen y castigo* (1866)
Walt Whitman	1819–1892	EE. UU.	Poesía	*Hojas de hierba* (1855–1889)
Gustave Flaubert	1821–1880	Francia	Novela	*Madame Bovary* (1857)
Henrik Ibsen	1828–1906	Noruega	Teatro	*Casa de muñecas* (1879)
León Tolstói	1828–1910	Rusia	Novela	*Guerra y paz* (1865–1869)
Mark Twain	1835–1910	EE. UU.	Novela	*Huckleberry Finn* (1885)
Henry James	1843–1916	EE. UU.	Novela	*Las bostonianas* (1886)
Benito Pérez Galdós	1843–1920	España	Novela	*Fortunata y Jacinta* (1887)
August Strindberg	1849–1912	Suecia	Teatro	*La danza de la muerte* (1901)
George Bernard Shaw	1856–1950	Irlanda	Teatro	*Pigmalión* (1912)
Joseph Conrad	1857–1924	Polonia	Novela	*El corazón de las tinieblas* (1902)
Antón Chéjov	1860–1904	Rusia	Teatro/ relatos	*El jardín de los cerezos* (1904)
Rabindranath Tagore	1861–1941	India	Poesía/ teatro	*Gitanjali* (1912)
Edith Warton	1862–1937	EE. UU.	Novela	*La edad de la inocencia* (1920)
William Butler Yeats	1865–1939	Irlanda	Poesía	*Los cisnes salvajes de Coole* (1917)
Rubén Darío	1867–1916	Nicaragua	Poesía	*Prosas profanas* (1896)
Marcel Proust	1871–1922	Francia	Novela	*En busca del tiempo perdido* (1912–1927)
Thomas Mann	1875–1955	Alemania	Novela	*La muerte en Venecia* (1913)
Herman Hesse	1877–1962	Alemania	Novela	*El lobo estepario* (1927)
Lu Xun	1881–1936	China	Novela	*Diario de un loco* (1918)
James Joyce	1882–1941	Irlanda	Novela	*Ulises* (1922)
Virginia Wolf	1882–1941	RU	Novela	*La señora Dalloway* (1925)
Franz Kafka	1883–1924	Rep. Checa	Novela	*La metamorfosis* (1916)
D. H. Lawrence	1885–1930	RU	Novela/ poesía	*Hijos y amantes* (1913)
Ezra Pound	1885–1972	EE. UU.	Poesía	*Cantos* (1915–1962)
T. S. Eliot	1888–1965	EE. UU./ RU	Poesía/ teatro	*La tierra baldía* (1922)
Borís Pasternak	1890–1960	Rusia	Novela	*Doctor Zhivago* (1957)
Mijaíl Bulgakov	1891–1940	Rusia	Novela	*El maestro y Margarita* (1928)
William Faulkner	1897–1962	EE. UU.	Novela	*El ruido y la furia* (1929)
Bertolt Brecht	1898–1956	Alemania	Teatro	*Madre Coraje y sus hijos* (1938)
Federico García Lorca	1898–1936	España	Poesía/ teatro	*La casa de Bernarda Alba* (1936)
Ernest Hemingway	1899–1961	EE. UU.	Novela	*El viejo y el mar* (1952)
Jorge Luis Borges	1899–1986	Argentina	Novela	*El Aleph* (1949)
Vladimir Nabokov	1899–1977	Rusia/EE. UU.	Novela	*Lolita* (1958)
John Steinbeck	1902–1968	EE. UU.	Novela	*Las uvas de la ira* (1939)
George Orwell	1903–1950	RU	Novela	*1984* (1949)
Pablo Neruda	1904–1973	Chile	Poesía	*Veinte poemas de amor y una canción desesperada* (1924)
Samuel Beckett	1906–1989	Irlanda	Teatro/ novela	*Esperando a Godot* (1954)
W. H. Auden	1907–1973	RU	Poesía	*El mar y el espejo* (1944)
Naguib Mahfouz	1911–2006	Egipto	Novela	*Trilogía de El Cairo* (1956–1957)
Albert Camus	1913–1960	Francia	Novela	*La peste* (1947)
Saul Bellow	1915–2005	Canadá	Novela	*El legado de Humboldt* (1975)
Arthur Miller	1915–2005	EE. UU.	Teatro	*Muerte de un viajante* (1946)
Aleksandr Solzhenitsin	1918–2008	Rusia	Novela	*Un día de la vida de Iván Denísovich* (1962)
Iris Murdoch	1919–1999	RU	Novela	*El mar, el mar* (1978)
Nadime Gordimer	1923–2014	Sudáfrica	Novela	*El conservador* (1974)
Yukio Mishima	1925–1970	Japón	Novela	*El mar de la fertilidad* (1965–1970)
Dario Fo	1926–2016	Italia	Teatro	*Muerte accidental de un anarquista* (1970)
Gabriel García Márquez	1928–2014	Colombia	Novela	*Cien años de soledad* (1967)
Milan Kundera	1929–2023	Rep. Checa	Novela	*La insoportable levedad del ser* (1984)

POETAS, DRAMATURGOS Y NOVELISTAS (CONTINUACIÓN)

NOMBRE	VIDA	ORIGEN	GÉNERO	OBRAS DESTACADAS
Derek Walcott	1930–2017	Santa Lucía	Teatro/ poesía	*Omeros* (1990)
Harold Pinter	1930–2008	RU	Teatro	*El amante* (1963)
Chinua Achebe	1930–2013	Nigeria	Novela/ poesía	*Todo se desmorona* (1958)
V. S. Naipaul	1932–2018	Trinidad	Novela	*Una casa para Mr. Biswas* (1971)
Sylvia Plath	1932–1963	EE. UU.	Novela/ poesía	*La campana de cristal* (1963)
Philip Roth	1933–2018	EE. UU.	Novela	*El lamento de Portnoy* (1972)
Assia Djebar	1936–2015	Argelia	Novela	*El amor, la fantasía* (1985)
Caryl Churchill	1938–	RU	Teatro	*Top Girls* (1982)
Ngũgĩ wa Thiong'o	1938–	Kenia	Novela	*Un grano de trigo* (1967)
Wole Soyinka	n. 1934	Nigeria	Teatro/ poesía	*La danza del bosque* (1960)
Mario Vargas Llosa	n. 1936	Perú	Novela	*Conversación en la catedral* (1969)
Seamus Heaney	1939–2013	Irlanda	Poesía	*Puerta a las tinieblas* (1969)
Margaret Atwood	n. 1939	Canadá	Novela/ poesía	*El cuento de la criada* (1985)
J.M. Coetzee	n. 1940	Sudáfrica	Novela	*Foe* (1986)
Annie Ernaux	n. 1940	Francia	Novela	*La mujer helada* (1981)
Ama Ata Aidoo	1942–2023	Ghana	Teatro/ poesía	*Nuestra hermana Aguafiestas* (1977)
Paul Auster	1947–2024	EE. UU.	Novela	*La trilogía de Nueva York* (1985–1987)
Alice Walker	n. 1944	EE. UU.	Novela	*El color púrpura* (1982)
Javier Marías	1951–2022	España	Novela	*Corazón tan blanco* (1992)
Ohran Pamuk	1952	Turquía	Novela	*Me llamo Rojo* (1998)
Mo Yan	n. 1955	China	Novela	*Sorgo rojo* (1986)
Arundati Roy	n. 1961	India	Novela	*El dios de las pequeñas cosas* (1997)

PINTORES Y ESCULTORES

Todas las grandes civilizaciones, pero hasta alrededor del siglo IX d. C. solo se conocen los nombres de algunos artistas. En casi todas partes, los temas predilectos eran los religiosos y los retratos de reyes y personajes notables. También los paisajes y las escenas bucólicas gozaron del aprecio de los mecenas. Ya en la era moderna, los artistas, libres de patronazgos, pudieron dejarse llevar de su inspiración con una audacia a veces provocadora.

NOMBRE	VIDA	ORIGEN	PRINCIPALES OBRAS
Exekias	C. 550–525 a. C.	Grecia	*Aquiles y Áyax jugando a los dados*
Fidias	C. 480–420 a. C.	Grecia	Friso del Partenón
Praxíteles	Activo c. 350 a. C.	Grecia	*Afrodita de Cnido*
Gu Kaizhi	C. 345–406	China	*Amonestaciones de la institutriz a las damas de la corte*
Yan Liben	C. 600–673	China	*Palanquín imperial*
Wu Daozi	C. 710–c. 760	China	*Genio volador*
Han Gan	C. 720–c. 780	China	*El corcel blanco del emperador*
Lu Hong	Activo a principios del siglo VIII	China	*Diez vistas de una posada con techo de paja*
Zhang Xuan	Activo en 714–742	China	*Damas aprestando seda recién tejida*
Huang Quan	903–965	China	*Pinturas de aves e insectos*
Li Cheng	919–967	China	*Templo solitario entre picos desnudos*
Huang Jucai	933–c. 993	China	*Faisán y pájaros en un azufaifo*
Dong Yuan	m. 962	China	*Montañas en verano*
Juran	Activo c. 960–985	China	*Bosques en las montañas lejanas*
Zhang Zeduan	Mediados del siglo XI	China	*Fiesta de primavera junto al río* (rollo Qingming)
Guo Xi	C. 1020–1090	China	*Primavera temprana*
Li Gonglin	1049–1106	China	*Caballos pastando*
Wang Shen	Finales del siglo XII	China	*Colinas apiñadas entre la niebla sobre el río*
Li Di	C. 1100–c. 1197	China	*Santuario sobre un árbol en invierno*
Ma Yuan	C. 1190–1224	China	*Sauces desnudos y montañas distantes*
Lian Kai	Siglo XIII	China	*El sexto patriarca chan cortando bambú*
Qian Xuan	C. 1235–1307	China	*Viviendo en las montañas de jade flotante*
Cimabue	C. 1250–1302	Italia	*Virgen en majestad con ángeles y santos*
Zhao Mengfu	1254–1322	China	*Colores de otoño en las montañas Qiao y Hua*
Nicola Pisano	C. 1258–1284	Italia	Púlpito del baptisterio de la catedral de Pisa
Giotto di Bondone	C. 1267–1337	Italia	*Vida de san Francisco*
Huang Gongwang	1269–1354	China	*Viviendo en las montañas Fushun*
Wu Zhen	1280–1354	China	*Tallos de bambú junto a una roca*
Ni Zan	1301–1374	China	*Los seis sabios (o caballeros)*
Wang Meng	1308–1374	China	*Viviendo en las montañas de Qinghai*
Donatello	1386–1466	Italia	*David*
Fray Angélico	1387–1455	Italia	*La Anunciación*
Jan van Eyck	C. 1395–1441	Flandes	*Retrato de Arnolfini y su esposa*
Paolo Uccello	1397–1475	Italia	*La batalla de San Romano*
Rogier van der Weyden	C. 1400–1464	Flandes	*El Descendimiento*
Fra Filippo Lippi	C. 1406–1469	Italia	*Virgen con el Niño y dos ángeles*
Piero della Francesca	C. 1415–1492	Italia	*La Resurrección*
Sesshu Toyo	1420–1506	Japón	*Paisaje otoñal*
Giovanni Bellini	C. 1430–1516	Italia	*La oración del huerto*
Hans Memling	C. 1430–1494	Países Bajos	*Los desposorios místicos de santa Catalina de Alejandría*
Andrea Mantegna	C. 1431–1506	Italia	*Cristo muerto*
Bartolomé Bermejo	C. 1440–c. 1498	España	*Piedad Desplá*
Sandro Botticelli	1445–1510	Italia	*El nacimiento de Venus*
El Bosco	C. 1450–1516	Países Bajos	*El jardín de las delicias*
Leonardo da Vinci	1452–1519	Italia	*La Gioconda*
Lu Ji	Activo c. 1500	China	*Grulla, águila y flores de loto caídas*
Matthias Grünewald	C. 1460–1528	Alemania	Retablo de Isenheim
Wen Zhenming	1470–1559	China	*Viejos cipreses y rocas*
Alberto Durero	1471–1528	Alemania	*Los cuatro apóstoles*
Miguel Ángel	1475–1564	Italia	*David*; frescos de la Capilla Sixtina
Lucas Cranach el Viejo	1472–1553	Alemania	*Descanso en la huida a Egipto*
Jan Gossaert (Mabuse)	C. 1478–1533	Flandes	*La adoración de los Magos*
Kano Motonobu	1476–1559	Japón	*Paisaje con cascada y grulla*
Rafael	1483–1520	Italia	*Madonna Sixtina*; *La escuela de Atenas*
Tiziano Vecellio	C. 1487–1576	Italia	*Venus de Urbino*
Hans Holbein el Joven	C. 1497–1543	Alemania	*Los embajadores*
Tintoretto	C. 1487–1576	Italia	*La Última Cena*
Sesson	C. 1504–1589	Japón	*Tempestad en el lago*
Pieter Bruegel el Viejo	C. 1525–1569	Flandes	*El banquete de bodas*
Kaiho Yushio	1533–1615	Japón	*Peonías*
Pedro Pablo Rubens	1577–1640	Flandes	*Las tres Gracias*
Hasegawa Tohaku	1539–1610	Japón	*Pinos*

NOMBRE	VIDA	ORIGEN	PRINCIPALES OBRAS
El Greco	1541–1614	Grecia/ España	*El entierro del conde de Orgaz*
Kano Eitoku	1543–1590	Japón	*Grulla y pino*
Dong Qichang	1555–1636	China	*Montañas en otoño*
Hon-ami Koetsu	1558–1637	Japón	*Flores de las cuatro estaciones*
Kano Sanraku	1559–1635	Japón	*Ciruelo y faisán*
Juan Sánchez Cotán	1560–1627	España	*Bodegón del cardo*
Caravaggio	1573–1610	Italia	*La cena de Emaús*
Tawaraya Sotatsu	1576–1643	Japón	*Ciervo y caligrafía*
Frans Hals	1580–1666	Países Bajos	*Caballero sonriendo*
José de Ribera	1591–1652	España	*Martirio de san Felipe*
Nicolas Poussin	1593–1665	Francia	*Los pastores de Arcadia*
Francisco de Zurbarán	1598–1664	España	*La visión de san Pedro Nolasco*; bodegones
Gianlorenzo Bernini	1598–1680	Italia	*El éxtasis de santa Teresa*
Diego Velázquez	1599–1660	España	*Las meninas*; *El aguador de Sevilla*
Antoon van Dyck	1599–1641	Flandes	*Carlos I de Inglaterra*
Claudio de Lorena (Claude Gellée)	1600–1682	Francia	*Embarque de santa Úsula*
Rembrandt van Rijn	1606–1669	Países Bajos	*La ronda nocturna*; *La lección de anatomía del doctor Tulp*
Hongren	1610–1664	China	*Paisaje monumental*
Bartolomé Esteban Murillo	1617–1682	España	*Muchachos comiendo melones y uvas*; *Inmaculada Soult*
Jan Vermeer	1632–1675	Países Bajos	*El arte de la pintura*
Wang Hui	1632–1717	China	*El viaje al sur del emperador Kangxi*
Ogata Korin	1658–1716	Japón	*Ciruelos en flor junto a un río*
Antoine Watteau	1684–1721	Francia	*Embarque para la isla de Citera*
Giambattista Tiepolo	1696–1770	Italia	*Abraham y los tres ángeles*
William Hogarth	1697–1764	RU	*La vida de un libertino* (serie)
Canaletto	1697–1768	Italia	*Regreso del Bucentauro al muelle el día de la Ascensión*
Joshua Reynolds	1723–1792	RU	*Las tres Gracias*
Thomas Gainsborough	1727–1788	RU	*Niño azul*
Maruyama Okyo	1733–1795	Japón	Estudios de la naturaleza
Francisco de Goya	1746–1828	España	*La maja desnuda*; *Los fusilamientos en la montaña del Príncipe Pío*
Jacques-Louis David	1748–1825	Francia	*Las sabinas*
Utamaro Kitagawa	1753–1806	Japón	*El libro de los insectos*
William Blake	1757–1827	RU	*La Divina Comedia*
Katsuhika Hokusai	1760–1849	Japón	*La gran ola en Kanagawa*
Caspar David Friedrich	1774–1840	Alemania	*El caminante frente al mar de niebla*
Joseph Mallord William Turner	1775–1851	RU	*El Temerario remolcado a dique seco, 1838*
John Constable	1776–1837	RU	*El carro de heno*
Jean August Dominique Ingres	1780–1867	Francia	*La gran odalisca*
Théodore Géricault	1791–1824	Francia	*La balsa de la Medusa*
Ando (Ichiyusai) Hiroshige	1797–1858	Japón	*Paisaje en Shono*
Eugène Delacroix	1798–1863	Francia	*La Libertad guiando al pueblo*

NOMBRE	VIDA	ORIGEN	PRINCIPALES OBRAS
Edwin Landseer	1802–1873	RU	*El monarca de la cañada*
Gustave Courbet	1819–1877	Francia	*Un entierro en Ornans*
Édouard Manet	1823–1883	Francia	*Olympia*
William Holman Hunt	1827–1910	RU	*Luz del mundo*
Dante Gabriel Rosetti	1828–1882	RU	*Beata Beatrix*
John Everett Millais	1829–1896	RU	*Ofelia*
Camille Pissarro	1830–1903	Francia	*El jardín de Pontoise*
James Abbott McNeill Whistler	1834–1903	EE. UU.	*Arreglo en gris y negro n.º 1 (Retrato de la madre del artista)*
Edgar Degas	1834–1917	Francia	*La clase de danza*
Mariano Fortuny	1838–1874	España	*La vicaría*
Alfred Sisley	1839–1899	RU	*La inundación en Port-Marly*
Paul Cézanne	1839–1906	Francia	*Los jugadores de cartas*
Auguste Rodin	1840–1917	Francia	*El beso*
Claude Monet	1840–1926	Francia	*Impresión, amanecer*
Auguste Renoir	1841–1919	Francia	*El almuerzo de los remeros*
Mary Cassatt	1844–1926	EE. UU.	*Niña en un sillón azul*
Paul Gauguin	1848–1903	Francia	*Arearea*
Vincent van Gogh	1853–1890	Países Bajos	*La noche estrellada*
John Singer Sargent	1856–1925	EE. UU.	*Clavel, lirio, lirio, rosa*
Georges Seurat	1859–1891	Francia	*Tarde de domingo en la Grande Jatte*
Gustav Klimt	1862–1928	Austria	*Dánae*
Joaquín Sorolla	1863–1923	España	*Paseo a orillas del mar*
Edvard Munch	1863–1944	Noruega	*El grito*
Henri de Toulouse-Lautrec	1864–1901	Francia	*Baile en el Moulin Rouge*
Akseli Gallen-Kallela	1865–1931	Finlandia	*Lago Keitele*
Vasili Kandinsky	1866–1944	Rusia	*Primera acuarela abstracta*
Henri Matisse	1869–1954	Francia	*La danza*
Piet Mondrian	1872–1944	Países Bajos	*Broadway boogie boogie*
Olowe de Ise	c. 1873–1938	Nigeria	Puerta del palacio de Yoruba
Paul Klee	1879–1940	Suiza	*El pez dorado*
Jacob Epstein	1880–1959	RU	Monumento funerario de Oscar Wilde
Ernst Ludwig Kirchner	1880–1938	Alemania	*Cinco mujeres en la calle*
Pablo Picasso	1881–1973	España	*Las señoritas de Aviñón*; *Guernica*
Georges Braque	1882–1963	Francia	*El portugués*
Edward Hopper	1882–1967	EE. UU.	*Noctámbulos*
Max Beckman	1884–1905	Alemania	*La noche*
Amedeo Modigliani	1884–1920	Italia	*Retrato de Madame Zborowski*
Diego Rivera	1886–1957	México	*La Creación*
Oskar Kokoschka	1886–1980	Austria	*Vista del Támesis*
Juan Gris	1887–1927	España	*Guitarra y pipa*
Georgia O'Keeffe	1887–1986	EE. UU.	*Lirio negro III*
Marcel Duchamp	1887–1968	Francia	*Fuente*
Marc Chagall	1887–1985	Francia	*Gólgota*
Giorgio de Chirico	1888–1978	Italia	*La nostalgia del infinito*
Paul Nash	1889–1946	RU	*Mar Muerto*
Egon Schiele	1890–1918	Austria	*La madre del artista durmiendo*
Giorgio Morandi	1890–1964	Italia	*Naturaleza muerta*
Man Ray	1890–1978	EE. UU.	*La equilibrista se acompaña de sus sombras*

PINTORES Y ESCULTORES (CONTINUACIÓN)

NOMBRE	VIDA	ORIGEN	PRINCIPALES OBRAS
Max Ernst	1891–1976	Alemania/ Francia	*El elefante de las Célebes*
George Grosz	1893–1959	Alemania	*Suicidio*
Joan Miró	1893–1983	España	*El carnaval del arlequín*
Henry Moore	1898–1986	RU	*Figura reclinada*
René Magritte	1898–1967	Bélgica	*Esto no es una pipa*
Alberto Giacometti	1901–1966	Suiza	*El hombre que camina*
Barbara Hepworth	1903–1975	RU	*Forma única*
Mark Rothko	1903–1970	EE. UU.	*Verde sobre azul*
Salvador Dalí	1904–1989	España	*La persistencia de la memoria*
Willem de Kooning	1904–1997	EE. UU.	Serie *Mujer*
Frida Kahlo	1907–1954	México	*La columna rota*
Francis Bacon	1909–1992	RU	*Tres estudios de figuras en la base de una crucifixión*
Emily Kame Kngwarreye	1910–1996	Australia	*Sueño ntange*
Jackson Pollock	1912–1956	EE. UU.	*Ritmo de otoño (n.º 30)*
Sidney Nolan	1917–1992	Australia	Serie de la historia de Ned Kelly
Roy Lichtenstein	1923–1997	EE. UU.	*Whaam!*
Luz Donoso	1926–2008	Chile	*Señalamientos*
Yayoi Kusama	n. 1929	Japón	*Habitaciones infinitas*
Andy Warhol	1930–1987	EE. UU.	*Lata de sopa Campbell*
Magdalena Abakanowicz	1930–2017	Polonia	*Cuatro figuras sentadas*
Antonio López	n. 1936	España	*Gran Vía*
David Hockney	n. 1937	RU	*Sr. y la Sra. Clark y Percy*
El Anatsui	n. 1944	Ghana	*Buscando conexión*
Marina Abramović	n. 1946	Serbia	*Ritmo 0*
Jaume Plensa	n. 1955	España	*Awilda*
Ai Weiwei	n. 1957	China	*Semillas de girasol*
Shirin Neshat	n. 1957	Irán	*Turbulento*
Jean-Michel Basquiat	1960–1988	EE. UU.	*En este caso*
Liu Xiaodong	n. 1963	China	*Las Tres Gargantas* (serie)

UNIVERSIDADES MÁS ANTIGUAS

UNIVERSIDAD	PAÍS	FECHA DE FUNDACIÓN
Qarawiyyin	Marruecos	*c.* 859
Al-Azhar	Egipto	970
Bolonia	Italia	1088
Oxford	Inglaterra	*C.* 1167
Módena	Italia	1175
Vicenza	Italia	1204
Cambridge	Inglaterra	1209
Salamanca	España	1218
Padua	Italia	1222
Nápoles	Italia	1224
Valladolid	España	1241
Siena	Italia	1246
Lisboa	Portugal	1290
Sorbona	París (Francia)	1297
Lérida	España	1297
La Sapienza	Roma (Italia)	1303
Coimbra	Portugal	1308
Perugia	Italia	1308
Pisa	Italia	1343
Carolina	Praga (Rep. Checa)	1347
Perpiñán	Francia	1350
Pavía	Italia	1361
Jagellónica	Cracovia (Polonia)	1364
Viena	Austria	1365
Heidelberg	Alemania	1385
Santo Domingo	Rep. Dominicana	1530
San Marcos	Lima (Perú)	1551
Harvard	Massachusetts (EE. UU.)	1636
Sídney	Australia	1850
Calcuta	India	1857

CATÁSTROFES

Pocas civilizaciones se han librado de catástrofes naturales que han segado cientos de miles, e incluso, en el caso de las epidemias, millones de vidas. Desastres como la erupción que sepultó Pompeya o la peste del siglo XIV fueron muy mortíferos, pero el mundo actual no es menos vulnerable, como prueba el número de víctimas de los tsunamis del Índico (2004) y Japón (2011), el terremoto en Haití de 2010 y la pandemia de la COVID-19.

TERREMOTOS

LUGAR	FECHA	MAGNITUD	MUERTOS	EFECTOS
Esparta (Grecia)	464 a. C.	7,2	*C.* 20 000	Condujo a la revuelta de los ilotas y contribuyó al estallido de la guerra del Peloponeso.
Rodas (Grecia)	226 a. C.	—	—	Destruyó el coloso de Rodas.
Creta y el este del Mediterráneo	365	9	—	Extensa destrucción en Creta y el norte de África.
Antioquía (Turquía)	526	8	250 000	Destrucción parcial de la ciudad.
Costa libanesa	551	7,5	30 000–50 000	Amplia destrucción en Beirut, Tiro, Trípoli y otras ciudades costeras.
Alepo (Siria)	1138	9	200 000–250 000	Destrucción parcial de la ciudad.
Mediterráneo oriental	1201	7,6	—	Causó hambrunas que mataron a más de un millón de personas.
Shaanxi (China)	1556	8,3	830 000	Fue el terremoto más destructivo de la historia china.
Perú	1687	8,7	5000	Causó graves daños en Lima y destruyó el puerto de Pisco.
Lisboa (Portugal)	1755	8,7 (y tsunami)	80 000	Arrasó gran parte de la ciudad.
Ecuador y Perú	1797	7,3	40 000	Destrucción generalizada en Quito y Cuzco.
Arica (Chile)	1868	8,5	25 000	Destruyó varias ciudades, incluidas Arica y Arequipa.
San Francisco (EE. UU.)	1906	7,9	3000	Destrucción general de la ciudad, en parte a causa del fuego.
Valparaíso (Chile)	1906	8,2	4000	Destrucción de casi toda la ciudad.
Ningxia (China)	1920	7,8	250 000	Destrucción total en Haiyuan.
Kanto (Japón)	1923	7,9	125 000	El terremoto más letal de Japón.
Ancash (Perú)	1970	7,9	75 000	La peor catástrofe natural de Perú.
Tangshan (China)	1976	7,5	240 000–255 000	El mayor terremoto del siglo XX por el número de muertos.
Armenia	1988	6,9	25 000	Destrucción de la ciudad de Spitak (muchas muertes se debieron a la baja calidad de los edificios).
Turquía occidental	1999	7,6	18 000	Destrucción parcial de la ciudad de Izmit; muchos edificios de baja calidad se derrumbaron.
Bam (Irán)	2003	6,6	27 000	La antigua ciudad quedó arrasada.
Océano Índico	2004	9,2 (y tsunami)	230 000	Amplia devastación a lo largo de las costas del océano Índico.
Cachemira (Pakistán)	2005	7,6	75 000	Destrucción generalizada en torno a Muzaffarabad.
Sichuan (China)	2008	8	70 000	El terremoto más letal de China desde el de Tangshan (1976).
Haití	2010	7	316 000	Graves daños en Puerto Príncipe; la mayor cifra de muertos del hemisferio norte.
Noreste de Japón	2011	9 (y tsunami)	*C.* 18 000	Daños en torno a Sendai; alarma nuclear en la central de Fukushima
Turquía/Siria	2023	7,8		Más de 200 000 edificios derruidos; 2,5 millones de personas desplazadas.

ERUPCIONES VOLCÁNICAS

VOLCÁN	FECHA	EFECTOS
Vesubio (sur de Italia)	79	Destrucción de Pompeya y Herculano.
Oraefajökull (Islandia)	1362	La «colada glaciar» devastó poblaciones costeras y cubrió de ceniza el norte de Islandia.
Etna (Sicilia)	1669	Fue su peor erupción de la era moderna: destruyó varias localidades.
Timanfaya (Lanzarote, Canarias)	1730–1736	La erupción más larga registrada en las islas Canarias; sepultó varias poblaciones.
Laki (Islandia)	1783	Originó la mayor colada de lava registrada jamás.
Tambora (Sumbawa, Indonesia)	1815	El efecto aerosol de la ceniza volcánica causó el «año sin verano» y pérdida de cosechas, con la hambruna consiguiente, en muchos países.
Krakatoa (Indonesia)	1883	Provocó el hundimiento de gran parte de la isla de Krakatoa y la muerte de 35 000 personas. Las partículas volcánicas en suspensión originaron bellas puestas de sol en todo el mundo durante varios meses.
Montagne Pelée (Martinica)	1902	Destruyó la ciudad de Saint Pierre.
Monte Saint Helens (Washington, EE. UU.)	1980	Destruyó 300 km de carreteras.
Nevado del Ruiz (Colombia)	1985	La colada de barro destruyó la ciudad de Magdalena y mató a 23 000 personas.
Pinatubo (Filipinas)	1991	Arrojó diez veces más materiales que el Saint Helens, pero la evacuación masiva hizo que la cifra de muertos se elevara tan solo a 200–300.
Monte Nyiragongo (Rep. Dem. del Congo)		Destruyó una tercera parte de la ciudad de Goma; 245 muertos.
Puyehue (Chile)	2011	La nube de cenizas volcánicas obligó a interrumpir el tráfico aéreo en el hemisferio sur.

INUNDACIONES

LUGAR	FECHA	EFECTOS
Inglaterra	48	El desbordamiento del río Támesis provocó la muerte de 10 000 personas.
Inglaterra y costa de Países Bajos	1099	Una gran tormenta invernal causó inundaciones que mataron a 100 000 personas y crearon el banco de Godwin Sands en Kent.
Países Bajos y Alemania	1218	Un temporal del mar de Norte mató a cerca de 100 000 personas.
Bélgica, Países Bajos y Dinamarca	1287	Las inundaciones por fuertes tormentas provocaron entre 50 000 y 80 000 muertos.
Dinamarca, Países Bajos y norte de Alemania	1362	Extensas inundaciones costeras causaron la muerte de 100 000 personas.
China	1887	Las inundaciones a lo largo del río Amarillo rompieron los diques: perecieron ahogadas 900 000 personas.
China central	1931	El desbordamiento de los ríos Amarillo, Yangtsé y Huai mató a unos 3 millones de personas.
Guatemala	1949	Un huracán provocó inundaciones que mataron a 40 000 personas.
Bangladesh	1974	Las inundaciones por las lluvias monzónicas causaron 29 000 muertos.
China	1975	La rotura de la presa de Banqiao (provincia de Henan) fue la peor catástrofe de este tipo de la historia: las inundaciones causaron la muerte de 86 000 personas.
Pakistán	2010	Las inundaciones cubrieron la quinta parte del país y provocan 2000 muertes.
Australia	2010–2011	Las riadas mataron a 35 personas y devastaron varias ciudades en Queensland.
Sureste Asiático	2011	Inundación generalizada en varios países que causó la muerte de casi 3000 personas.
Uttarakhand (norte de India)	2013	Las inundaciones y los corrimientos de tierras provocaron 5700 víctimas mortales.
Pakistán	2022	Las inundaciones causaron 1739 muertes, el peor desastre natural del pási hasta la fecha.

HAMBRUNAS

LUGAR	FECHA	EFECTOS
Mesoamérica	*C.* 800–900	La sequía y el hambre condujeron al hundimiento de la civilización maya clásica.
China	875–884	El hambre desencadena la rebelión de Huang Zhao, que socava fatalmente a la dinastía Tang.
Japón	1229–1232	La hambruna de Kangi fue la peor de la historia de Japón.
Norte de Europa	1315–1317	La «gran hambruna» mató al 10 % de la población (en parte a causa de enfermedades que se cebaron en las personas ya debilitadas).
India	1406–1417	El hambre de Durga Devi, en Maharasthra, causó miles de muertos en un periodo de 12 años.
Rusia	1601–1603	La peor hambruna de la historia rusa: hasta 2 millones de muertos (un tercio de la población).
India	1630–1632	Una grave hambruna en el Decán llevó a la muerte a unos 2 millones de personas.
Prusia	1708–1711	El hambre mató a unas 250 000 personas (dos quintos de la población).
Bengala (India)	1769–1773	La peor hambruna de la historia en India: 10 millones de muertos.
Irlanda	1845–1849	La plaga de la patata causó una grave hambruna y la muerte de 1 millón de personas.
Irán	1870–1871	El hambre mató a 1,5 millones de personas e hizo que muchas tribus nómadas se sedentarizaran.
Etiopía	1888–1892	Una gran hambruna siguió a una epidemia que mató al 90 % del ganado y a las plagas de langostas y orugas que devoraron la mayor parte de los cultivos: pereció un tercio de la población.
Ucrania	1932–1933	El genocidio ucraniano *(Holodomor)*: la política soviética agraria provocó una hambruna que llevó a la muerte a 4 millones de personas.
China	1959–1961	La peor hambruna de la historia china: 30 millones de muertos.
Etiopía	1984–1985	La falta de lluvias causó una hambruna que mató a 1 millón de personas.
Nigeria	2005	Los daños causados por la langosta, la pobreza aguda y los precios de los alimentos provocaron una crisis alimentaria generalizada en la zona, que afectó a casi 3,6 millones de personas.
Somalia	2011	La sequía precipitó una crisis alimentaria que afectó a más de 6,2 millones de personas.
Sudán del Sur	2017	La crisis alimentaria causada por la guerra y la sequía provocó la muerte por inanición de casi 100 000 personas.
Yemen	2017	El cólera y una grave crisis alimentaria afectaron a más de 7 millones de personas.

EPIDEMIAS

LUGAR	FECHA	EFECTOS
Grecia	430–427 a. C.	Primera descripción de síntomas de peste durante una epidemia en Atenas.
Área del Mediterráneo	165–180	La peste antonina mató hasta 5 millones de personas, un tercio de la población del Imperio romano. Esto debilitó gravemente el poder militar del ejército romano.
Área del Mediterráneo	541–542	La peste de Justiniano se llevó al 40 % o más de la población.
Todo el mundo	1348–1350	La peste llamada «muerte negra» segó la vida de unos 30 millones de personas.
India	1817	Primer brote de cólera registrado en Bengala.
India	1907	Un brote de peste bubónica mata a 1,5 millones de personas.
Todo el mundo	1918–1919	La llamada «gripe española» provoca la muerte de 50 millones de personas, el peor desastre natural jamás registrado.
Todo el mundo	2020–2023	La pandemia de la COVID-19 provoca la muerte de al menos 6 960 000 personas.

GLOSARIO

Los términos que aparecen en *cursiva* están definidos en otra entrada del glosario.

abolicionismo
Actitud favorable a la abolición (supresión) de la esclavitud.

absolutismo
Teoría de gobierno según la cual el rey o el soberano se considera poseedor de la **autoridad absoluta**, es decir, no es dependiente del consentimiento del pueblo.

acceso (al trono) o **advenimiento**
Momento en que comienza a reinar un soberano.

agrario, ria
Perteneciente o relativo a la tierra de cultivo o al cultivo.

agrarista
Relativo a un movimiento político cuyo fin es promover los intereses de la agricultura y del mundo rural.

aislacionismo
Política consistente en mantener a un país apartado de las disputas internacionales, especialmente no participando en las alianzas. Se asocia sobre todo a ciertos periodos de la historia de China, Japón y EE. UU.

aliados
Pueblos o países que actúan conjuntamente; en las dos guerras mundiales, los aliados fueron aquellos países que lucharon contra Alemania.

anarquía
Ausencia de gobierno; también se utiliza este término para definir una situación de desorden público. En *política*, movimiento o ideología que preconiza la abolición del gobierno como un ideal para la sociedad.

anticlericalismo
Oposición a la influencia de las iglesias u otras organizaciones religiosas en la sociedad.

antisemitismo
Oposición y hostilidad hacia el pueblo judío.

apartheid
Política de *segregación* racial que estuvo vigente en la *República* de Sudáfrica, y por extensión, *política* similar practicada en cualquier otro lugar.

armisticio
Pacto para el cese de hostilidades entre países en guerra.

autocracia
Régimen político en el que una sola persona **(autócrata)** concentra todo el poder. A diferencia del término *dictador*, el de autócrata se suele aplicar a reyes o emperadores.

autodeterminación
Situación de un pueblo o de una *nación* que puede escoger su propio gobierno, o bien que posee plena capacidad de autogobierno.

autoritario, ria
Se dice de los líderes o los gobiernos que ejercen el poder con un desprecio total o parcial de la *democracia* o con otras restricciones.

bloque
Grupo de países que actúan de manera conjunta en los asuntos concernientes a las relaciones internacionales. Durante la *Guerra Fría*, se dio el nombre de **Bloque Oriental** o **Bloque Soviético** al conjunto de los países comunistas (véase *comunismo*) de Europa oriental.

bolsa
Organismo que permite comerciar con acciones de empresas, bonos del *estado* y otros valores financieros.

bula (pontificia)
Documento sobre una cuestión de fe, de concesión de privilegios o cualquier otro asunto importante para la Iglesia emitido o autorizado por un papa con su sello (que antiguamente tenía forma de bola, o *bulla*).

burgués, esa
En origen, habitante de un burgo, población medieval de la que derivan la mayoría de las ciudades. Más tarde se denominaron burgueses los miembros de la clase media; en la actualidad, este término se aplica a menudo con sentido despectivo a las personas partidarias del *capitalismo*, o sencillamente a aquellos ciudadanos de ideas convencionales y caracterizados por un cierto conformismo social. En la teoría *marxista*, la **burguesía** es la clase capitalista.

caballero
(1) Combatiente a caballo. (2) Durante la *Edad Media*, miembro de una orden de caballería o de una orden militar. (3) Rango feudal (véase *feudalismo*) que combinaba un alto estatus social con las obligaciones de prestar servicios militares.

califato
Dentro de la cultura islámica (véase *islam*), institución de carácter político y religioso en que la máxima autoridad es un individuo elegido, el **califa**, que se considera sucesor del profeta Mahoma, y por consiguiente, otorga plena legitimidad *política* a los gobernantes de todo el mundo islámico. Los califas, en otro tiempo muy poderosos, terminaron siendo unas figuras sin ningún tipo de poder efectivo, si bien los gobernantes otomanos de Turquía siguieron reclamando el título hasta el siglo XX. También se llama así el territorio gobernado por un califa y el tiempo que duraba su *mandato*.

calvinismo
Rama estricta del *protestantismo* cuyo nombre procede del reformador del siglo XVI Juan Calvino. Las **iglesias calvinistas** acostumbran a tener una organización *presbiteriana*.

capitalismo
Sistema social que se caracteriza por favorecer la actividad de los **capitalistas**: particulares u organizaciones privadas que acumulan riqueza **(capital)**, sobre todo en forma de edificios y de equipo, necesarios para la producción de bienes y servicios. Esta actividad genera empleos y a su vez proporciona beneficios a los capitalistas.

carta
(1) Garantía de derechos por escrito o documento legal similar. (2) Mapa.

católico, ca
En origen significa universal, «que comprende a todos», de ahí que en un principio la Iglesia cristiana recibiese el nombre de **Iglesia católica**. Después de las sucesivas divisiones a lo largo de los siglos, el término ha pasado a aplicarse exclusivamente a la iglesia que es fiel al papa de Roma, también llamada **Iglesia católica romana**.

ciudad-estado
Ciudad independiente, dotada de autogobierno.

clásico, ca
Relativo a las antiguas Grecia y Roma, así como a los movimientos artísticos y culturales posteriores que imitaban sus obras y su estilo. El término clásico también se aplica al momento culminante de cualquier civilización o cultura, y en general suele utilizarse con otros matices significativos como «típico» o «poseedor de valores intemporales».

coalición
Acuerdo formal entre dos o más grupos distintos con el objetivo de actuar unidos, por ejemplo, los partidos políticos para formar gobierno.

colonialismo
Práctica y *política* de adquisición de territorios en el extranjero en régimen de colonia, que con frecuencia implica también *dominio* cultural y explotación de sus recursos.

Commonwealth
Sistema de gobierno establecido en Gran Bretaña en los años posteriores a la ejecución de Carlos I; también se dio este nombre a la asociación de países del antiguo Imperio británico para mantener sus vínculos y perseguir el beneficio económico común.

comuna
Grupo de personas que viven juntas, compartiendo todo.

comunismo
(1) Doctrina que propugna y defiende una organización social fundamentada en los principios de cooperación y de supresión de la propiedad individual a favor de la común. (2) Movimiento político o sistema de gobierno derivados de las teorías filosóficas y políticas de Karl Marx (véase *marxista*).

confesión
Conjunto de personas que comparten un mismo credo y una organización, con una denominación reconocida; por ejemplo el cristianismo, el baptismo o el metodismo.

congreso / Congreso
Asamblea representativa electa con funciones legislativas. En España, el **Congreso de los Diputados** es la cámara baja que integra las Cortes Generales junto con el *Senado*. En Estados Unidos, el Congreso es el cuerpo legislativo del gobierno *federal* integrado por la Cámara de Representantes (cámara baja) y el *Senado* (cámara alta).

conservador, ra
Término con diversos significados sociales y políticos: poco dispuesto a aceptar cambios; respetuoso tanto de los valores como de la autoridad tradicionales; persona partidaria del *capitalismo* de libre mercado y opuesta a una intervención económica por parte del *estado*; y perteneciente a un partido político concreto, como el Partido Conservador de Reino Unido.

cónsul
Cada uno de los dos altos magistrados de la *República* romana que ejercían el cargo solo durante un año.

Contrarreforma
Movimiento de reacción de la Iglesia *católica* en el periodo subsiguiente a la *Reforma* que se concretó en reformas internas y una oposición activa contra el *protestantismo*.

cruzadas
Expediciones militares organizadas por el papado durante la *Edad Media* cuyo propósito inicial era dominar Tierra Santa (Palestina), que en aquel momento se encontraba bajo poder musulmán (véase *islam*).

danegeld
Literalmente «oro danés», impuesto recaudado en la Inglaterra anglosajona a fin de pagar tributo a los invasores daneses (vikingos) y evitar de este modo sus ataques. Posteriormente, se convirtió en un impuesto general sobre la tierra.

decimal, sistema (militar)
Principio organizativo del ejército de Gengis Kan en unidades de entre diez y diez mil hombres.

demagogo
Político cuyo poder se basa en excitar los sentimientos del pueblo por medio de discursos carismáticos y emotivos, a veces en contra de la autoridad establecida.

democracia
Sistema político en que el pueblo elige y controla al gobierno. La **democracia directa**, vigente en la antigua Atenas, permitía a los ciudadanos participar en las decisiones mediante el voto directo. La mayoría de regímenes democráticos se basan en una **democracia indirecta o representativa**, en la que el pueblo elige a políticos para que le represente. En ocasiones, la democracia excluía del derecho a votar a ciertos grupos como las mujeres y los que no poseían tierras.

dependencia
Territorio subordinado que no es una parte integrante del país que tiene pleno control sobre él.

despotismo
Autocracia, en especial de un rey o de un emperador. Un **déspota ilustrado** es un monarca absoluto que gobierna procurando el bien de su pueblo en lugar del suyo propio.

devaluación
Reducción del valor de la moneda de un país respecto a otras divisas.

diáspora
Dispersión de los miembros de un grupo étnico (véase *etnicidad*) que abandonan su tierra de origen. Originalmente se refería a los judíos.

dictador
En la antigua Roma, magistrado supremo al que, por un breve periodo de tiempo, se otorgaban poderes extraordinarios en momentos de grave peligro para la *nación*. En la actualidad, persona que gobierna un país en solitario y sin ningún tipo de restricción efectiva a su poder individual. Este término no se aplica a reyes o emperadores hereditarios, al contrario que los términos similares autócrata y déspota (véase *autocracia* y *despotismo*).

diezmo
Impuesto para el sostenimiento de la iglesia, especialmente en la *Edad Media*, que consistía en la décima parte de los productos de una propiedad agrícola.

dinastía
Familia que gobierna un país durante varias generaciones.

disolución
En general, proceso de disolver o separar algo en sus partes constituyentes. En *política* es la acción de poner fin a los poderes de una asamblea antes del plazo legal; por ejemplo, la **disolución de las Cortes** o del parlamento, antes de unas elecciones generales para escoger a los nuevos representantes. En la Inglaterra del siglo XVI, la **Disolución de los monasterios** supuso la dispersión de los monjes y la confiscación de los bienes conventuales durante el reinado de Enrique VIII.

distensión
Relajación de la tensión entre dos países. Este término se utilizó en particular durante el periodo en que disminuía la tirantez de las relaciones entre EE. UU. y la antigua URSS.

dominio
(1) Poder que se tiene o se ejerce sobre alguien o algo. (2) Territorio sujeto a un soberano o gobernante. (3) Nombre de los territorios que gozaban de una amplia autonomía dentro del Imperio británico, en especial Canadá y Australia.

eclesiástico, ca
Perteneciente o relativo a la Iglesia o a los miembros del clero.

ecuménico, ca
Relativo a: (1) la totalidad de las Iglesias cristianas; (2) los movimientos a favor de la unión de las diferentes ramas de la Iglesia.

Edad Media
Periodo de la historia europea que abarca desde la caída del Imperio romano de Occidente hasta mediados o finales del siglo XV.

Eje
Alianza que tuvo lugar entre Alemania e Italia (y posteriormente, también Japón) antes de y durante la Segunda Guerra Mundial; también, denominación de estos tres países en conjunto (*dominio* del Eje o tropas del Eje).

escolasticismo
Escolástica, enfoque cristiano del razonamiento y el conocimiento característico de las escuelas y de las universidades durante la *Edad Media*.

especulación
En economía, compra y venta de acciones u otros efectos negociables con el fin de obtener beneficios si los precios suben o bajan de acuerdo con las previsiones del especulador.

estado
(1) País independiente. (2) Región con autogobierno dentro de un estado. (3) Aparato gubernamental de un estado.

estado cliente
País que depende de otro mayor en lo que respecta al comercio, la protección, etc.

estado tampón
Pequeño país situado entre estados más poderosos y rivales. Su presencia se considera útil para reducir la tensión entre estos.

estado títere
País independiente que está de hecho bajo el control de otro país.

estela
Piedra con inscripciones o relieves que se erigía sobre el suelo con fines por lo general **conmemorativos** o **funerarios**. Las estelas son típicas de un gran número de culturas antiguas, desde Mesopotamia, Egipto, Grecia y Roma hasta la América *precolombina*.

evangélico, ca
Perteneciente o relativo a: (1) los Evangelios; (2) las doctrinas protestantes (véase *protestantismo*) que propugnan la salvación personal a través de la fe; (3) aquellos movimientos cristianos que tienen por objetivo predicar y convertir a otros **(evangelizar)**.

excomunión
Acción de excluir de una organización religiosa a un individuo y/o negarle la participación en los sacramentos y en los ritos.

faraón
Título del soberano en el antiguo Egipto, considerado rey y dios.

fascismo
En origen, ideología del movimiento político liderado por Benito Mussolini, que ejerció el poder en Italia entre los años 1922 y 1943. Las doctrinas fascistas se caracterizaban por ser totalitarias, antidemocráticas (véase *democracia*) y anticomunistas (véase *comunismo*), resaltaban el sometimiento del individuo al *estado* y tendían a glorificar la guerra y el *nacionalismo*. Actualmente, el término **fascista** se usa también para referirse a cualquier ideología o actitud considerada totalitaria o intolerante.

federal
Se dice del sistema político con un gobierno central **(gobierno federal)**, pero en el que muchas de sus áreas de decisión son competencia de gobiernos regionales, por ejemplo de provincias o de estados. El reparto de poderes está garantizado generalmente por una constitución.

fetua
En el *islam*, pronunciamiento, en especial de un clérigo, para emitir una opinión y/o dar instrucciones para una acción.

feudalismo
Sistema social de la Europa medieval, en que el *estado* se concebía como una pirámide jerárquica con el rey en la cima. Cada nivel o estamento de la sociedad podía reclamar derechos de la inferior y, a su vez, tenía la obligación de prestar distintos servicios al estamento superior en la jerarquía.

feudo
Tierra concedida por un soberano o un gran *señor* a un *vasallo* (o feudatario) a cambio de fidelidad y prestaciones de servicios en el sistema feudal (véase *feudalismo*).

fideicomiso
Situación de un territorio que es administrado por otro país en nombre de las Naciones Unidas, en beneficio de sus habitantes.

fundamentalismo
Creencia estricta en todas las enseñanzas tradicionales de una religión.

genocidio
Exterminio sistemático de un grupo racial o étnico (véase *etnicidad*).

globalización
Proceso impulsado por la mejora de las comunicaciones y de los vínculos internacionales que ha conducido a la creciente difusión e interconexión de ideas, culturas, mercados de trabajo y estilos de vida en todo el mundo.

gnosticismo o nosticismo
Ideología religiosa o movimiento que enfatiza la adquisición de conocimientos de carácter secreto o místico como vía de salvación. Tuvo una importante difusión en los inicios del cristianismo, pero acabó siendo considerado herético (véase *herejía*) por la Iglesia.

golpe (de estado)
Toma ilegal y rápida del poder por un grupo reducido de personas.

gótico, ca
(1) Relativo a los godos, miembros de una tribu germánica que invadió el Imperio romano en los siglos III y IV d. C. (2) Se dice del estilo arquitectónico que floreció en la Europa cristiana del siglo XIII al siglo XVI, y que se caracteriza por el arco apuntado (ojival), la bóveda de crucería y otros elementos que hicieron posible levantar edificios más altos, ligeros y estilizados. La mayoría de las grandes catedrales medievales se construyeron en este estilo.

gremio
Corporación medieval de artesanos y mercaderes de las ciudades. A menudo, los individuos solo estaban autorizados a practicar su oficio si pertenecían al gremio correspondiente.

guerra de guerrillas
Guerra en la que los contendientes combaten en pequeñas unidades, con frecuencia sin uniformes ni estructura militar oficiales.

Guerra Fría
Periodo de hostilidad entre los países occidentales y los comunistas dominados por la extinta Unión Soviética (URSS), que se prolongó desde poco después del fin de la Segunda Guerra Mundial hasta la caída del *comunismo* en Europa oriental en el año 1989.

hegemonía
Situación en la que un país poderoso ejerce una influencia significativa sobre sus vecinos más débiles.

herejía
Creencia o tendencia, por lo general minoritaria, dentro de una religión, considerada heterodoxa (no conforme al dogma) e inaceptable por otros miembros de dicha religión.

homininos
Miembros del grupo biológico que comprende a todos los humanos y sus antepasados extintos y parientes hasta el punto en que se separan de la línea que conduce a los chimpancés.

hugonotes
Nombre que recibían los protestantes franceses (véase *protestantismo*).

humanista
(1) Estudioso de latín y griego, sobre todo durante la época del *Renacimiento*. La obra de los humanistas renacentistas contribuyó al redescubrimiento de los textos clásicos, así como de sus valores, centrados en el ser humano frente a la importancia concedida a la teología y a Dios durante la *Edad Media*. (2) Persona que propugna un enfoque ético de la vida humana que no implica la creencia en ningún dios.

Iglesia griega
Rama de la Iglesia cristiana asociada al Imperio bizantino (de lengua griega), donde el griego era la lengua de la liturgia. Véase también *Iglesia ortodoxa*.

Iglesia ortodoxa
Grupo de iglesias cristianas que se separaron de la Iglesia occidental *(católica)* en el año 1054. Importante en Europa oriental y suroriental, comprende diferentes tradiciones e iglesias nacionales. Véase también *cisma*.

Iglesia romana
Rama occidental de la Iglesia cristiana que permaneció fiel a la autoridad del papa de Roma a raíz del *cisma de Oriente* y cuya lengua litúrgica fue el latín. Véase también *católico, ca*.

imperialismo
Sistema de gobierno de un imperio. En la actualidad se da este nombre a la política de adquisición de territorios lejanos por las potencias occidentales a lo largo del siglo XIX y a la ideología que la sustentaba.

islam
Religión monoteísta (que reconoce a un único dios) fundada en el siglo VII d. C. en Arabia por el profeta Mahoma y el conjunto de los creyentes que la profesan **(musulmanes)**. La palabra islam significa sumisión (a Dios). Se divide en dos ramas principales: **suní** y **chií**, que difieren en la autoridad y legitimidad que otorgan a distintos miembros de la familia del Profeta tras la muerte de este.

islamismo
Tendencia del *islam* que propugna el establecimiento tanto de la ley como de los valores islámicos en las sociedades de todo el mundo.

jacobino, na
Miembro de un grupo revolucionario extremista durante la Revolución Francesa. Su nombre procede del convento de frailes dominicos, llamados jacobinos en la época, donde se reunían en París.

jacobita
Partidario de la *restauración* de los monarcas de la casa Estuardo en Gran Bretaña después de que Jacobo II se viera obligado a huir y a abdicar en 1689.

jedive
Título que llevaron desde 1867 hasta 1914 los gobernadores de Egipto, nominalmente sujetos a la autoridad del Imperio otomano (turco), aunque en la práctica gozaban de una amplia independencia.

judicatura
(1) Conjunto de los jueces en activo de un país. (2) Empleo de juez y tiempo durante el cual se ejerce.

legión
Unidad del ejército romano compuesta por tres mil a seis mil hombres.

legislatura
(1) Institución o conjunto de instituciones de gobierno encargadas de aprobar leyes. (2) Tiempo durante el cual funcionan los cuerpos legislativos.

Levante
Nombre con que se conocía sobre todo en la *Edad Media* al Mediterráneo oriental y territorios ribereños.

liberalismo
Tendencia *política* o ideología que defiende la libertad individual, así como aquellas formas de gobierno que se proponen limitar los poderes del *estado* frente a los individuos (en contraste con el *absolutismo*). El **liberalismo económico** propugna el *capitalismo* de libre mercado. En EE. UU., el término liberal en ocasiones también implica una postura izquierdista favorable al aumento de la intervención del gobierno y del gasto en el *estado* del bienestar.

libre comercio
Intercambio de bienes y servicios entre países sin que exista ningún tipo de limitación o restricción, como cuotas de importación o impuestos sobre las mercancías importadas. Véase también *proteccionismo*.

liga
Asociación de individuos o estados con el fin de prestarse ayuda mutua o perseguir intereses comunes.

mandato
Orden o encargo legal, en especial el conferido por la antigua Sociedad de Naciones a un país para gobernar un territorio determinado por el interés de sus habitantes. Véase también *fideicomiso*.

manifiesto
Declaración escrita de un plan o de principios e intenciones, especialmente por un partido político o un movimiento de otro tipo.

marxista
Se dice de las distintas doctrinas derivadas de las ideas del filósofo y teórico del *socialismo* de origen alemán Karl Marx. Marx estaba convencido de haber descubierto las leyes históricas que demostraban que el *capitalismo* finalmente caería y sería sustituido por el *comunismo*.

mercenario
Soldado a sueldo que combate a favor de un país que no es el suyo.

minoría o minoridad real
Años de la vida de un monarca durante los cuales se considera menor de edad para reinar.

monofisismo
Doctrina que afirma que Jesucristo solo tenía una naturaleza (la divina habría absorbido la humana). Fue minoritaria en la Iglesia cristiana primitiva y hoy es sostenida principalmente por la Iglesia copta y otras iglesias cuyo origen se sitúa en Oriente Próximo.

nación
(1) País independiente. (2) Pueblo definido por sus vínculos históricos, culturales y lingüísticos, tanto si constituye un *estado* independiente como si no.

nacionalismo
Ideología y movimiento político que apoyan los intereses y la personalidad de una *nación*.

nacionalización
Conversión de una propiedad privada en pública por el *estado*, especialmente a gran escala, como una empresa o incluso un sector industrial.

nazismo
Doctrina del Partido Nacionalsocialista (Nazi) alemán, en el poder bajo Adolf Hitler de 1933 a 1945. Similar al *fascismo*, era además racista, basándose en la supremacía de una supuesta raza «aria», de la cual el pueblo alemán se consideraba el más puro representante. Véase también *totalitarismo*.

neoclasicismo
Tendencia de las artes y la literatura europeas del siglo XVIII inspirada por un renovado interés en los valores de las antiguas Grecia y Roma; también hace referencia a cualquier movimiento cultural que recupera estilos y puntos de vista de un periodo *clásico*.

neocolonialismo
Situación en que un país desarrollado y poderoso ejerce su influencia sobre un país menos desarrollado (en especial una antigua colonia) de manera similar al antiguo *colonialismo*.

oligarquía
Sistema político en que unos pocos individuos poderosos, con frecuencia adinerados, se unen para gobernar un país. La antigua *República* de Venecia es un ejemplo histórico. Muchos de los antiguos países comunistas (véase *comunismo*) eran de hecho oligarquías en las que los dirigentes del partido comunista monopolizaban el poder.

OTAN
Siglas de Organización del Tratado del Atlántico Norte, alianza militar internacional establecida en 1949 por las potencias occidentales.

pacifismo
Oposición a la guerra en general.

peregrinación
Viaje por motivos religiosos a un santuario u otro lugar sagrado.

plebiscito
Referéndum, especialmente sobre una cuestión constitucional importante.

pirata
Persona que asalta, generalmente con violencia, un barco en el mar para obtener un botín o para hacer prisioneros. Los **berberiscos** eran piratas procedentes de Berbería (norte de África) que actuaban principalmente en el área mediterránea. Los **corsarios** actuaban con autorización (patente de corso) para interceptar naves y quedarse con parte de sus bienes, según reglas previstas en la legislación; así las campañas de sir Francis Drake estaban financidas por Isabel I de Inglaterra. Se denominaron **filibusteros** o **bucaneros** los piratas franceses, ingleses y holandeses que asaltaban barcos españoles en el área de las Antillas.

pogromo
Matanza organizada, en particular la de judíos en Europa oriental a finales del siglo XIX y principios del siglo XX.

política
Actividad relacionada con el gobierno; forma de gobierno, orientación o medidas adoptadas por un gobierno o un soberano.

populista
Se dice, generalmente con intención crítica, del político que basa su poder en la aceptación de la población general mediante medidas destinadas a ganarse su simpatía. Con frecuencia un populista simplemente dice a la gente aquello que desea oír.

precolombino, na
Relativo a las culturas americanas antes de que entrasen en contacto con los exploradores y conquistadores europeos.

prefecto del pretorio
Alto funcionario de la administración romana durante la *República* y el Imperio, originalmente jefe de los guardias de la máxima autoridad (el pretor, y luego el emperador), o guardia pretoriana.

presbiterianos
Miembros de las Iglesias *protestantes* que no tienen una jerarquía episcopal, sino que están regidas por **presbíteros** (ancianos) elegidos por congregaciones.

proletariado
Conjunto de las personas asalariadas de la clase obrera que no poseen el capital (véase *capitalismo*), a menudo contrapuesto a la *burguesía* (véase *burgués*) dentro de la teoría *marxista*.

proteccionismo
Política cuyo objetivo es la defensa de las industrias de un país mediante barreras a la competencia exterior, por ejemplo, limitando las importaciones.

protectorado
Colonia en la que tanto la defensa como los asuntos exteriores son responsabilidad de la potencia colonial, en beneficio de la población del territorio.

protestantismo
Conjunto de las doctrinas y las formas de cristianismo surgidas a raíz de la *Reforma* del siglo XVI y posteriores, que no reconocen la autoridad del papa de Roma.

purga
Expulsión de una organización de las personas consideradas indeseables por los líderes, generalmente en los regímenes totalitarios (véase *totalitarismo*).

puritanismo
En origen fue un movimiento de la Iglesia de Inglaterra (o anglicana) durante los siglos XVI y XVII que propugnaba cambios a nivel organizativo y doctrinal, más allá de la simple ruptura con la Iglesia *católica* que se produjo bajo Enrique VIII. Más tarde, se dio el nombre de **puritanos** a grupos religiosos no anglicanos que defendían puntos de vista similares y, finalmente, a cualquier persona o ideología que desaprueba el placer y la indulgencia.

Putsch
Intento de derrocar a un gobierno por medios violentos.

recesión
Reducción de la actividad económica de un país, menos grave que una depresión. Se suele considerar que una economía ha entrado en recesión cuando el PIB (producto interior bruto) desciende en dos trimestres sucesivos.

Reforma
Movimiento a favor de la renovación cristiana del siglo XVI cuya consecuencia fue la ruptura de muchos individuos e iglesias con la Iglesia occidental *(católica)* liderada por el papa de Roma.

Renacimiento
Etapa cultural de la historia europea iniciada en Italia y centrada en Roma durante el siglo XV y principios del siglo XVI, que supuso el paso de la *Edad Media* a la Edad Moderna gracias al redescubrimiento de los logros culturales de la Antigüedad grecorromana.

reparaciones de guerra
Término acuñado tras la Primera Guerra Mundial para referirse a los pagos exigidos a los países vencidos por los vencedores como compensación **(indemnización)** de los daños causados por su agresión.

república / República
Sistema de gobierno y país no encabezado por un rey, un príncipe o un emperador hereditario. Actualmente, las repúblicas están gobernadas por presidentes y pueden comprender desde regímenes democráticos hasta dictaduras.

republicanismo
(1) Apoyo de la *república* como sistema de gobierno. (2) Conjunto de ideas y valores asociados a los partidos republicanos. (3) Dentro del contexto irlandés, corriente favorable a la independencia total respecto al Reino Unido.

restauración
Reanudación o restablecimiento de una situación anterior. En España, la **Restauración borbónica** fue la reposición en el trono de la casa de Borbón en 1875, con Alfonso XII como rey. En Inglaterra, la Restauración supuso el regreso a la monarquía en 1660, tras las guerras civiles y la *Commonwealth*.

romanticismo
Movimiento cultural y artístico europeo con múltiples matices nacionales que alcanzó su punto culminante a principios del siglo XIX, caracterizado por el interés por la naturaleza y por la prevalencia de los sentimientos y de las emociones sobre la razón.

Sacro Imperio Romano Germánico
Imperio establecido en Europa durante la *Edad Media* y cuyo territorio estaba centrado en la actual Alemania. Vinculado al papado y también su rival, poco a poco fue adquiriendo la estructura de una serie de estados inconexos. Cuando Napoleón Bonaparte abolió el Sacro Imperio, en 1806, el poder del emperador era ya meramente nominal.

sátrapa
(1) Gobernador de una provincia del antiguo Imperio persa. (2) Referente a un gobernante sagaz y despótico.

secta
Grupo u organización religiosa que sostiene creencias o ideas distintas o no estándares, sobre todo si estas se consideran dudosas, no aceptables e incluso heréticas.

sectario, ria
Se dice de la persona que muestra actitudes hostiles hacia otras ideas o grupos sociales, en especial de una *confesión* distinta de la misma religión.

secular
(1) Que dura un siglo o más, o que ocurre cada siglo. (2) Seglar, no religioso.

segregación
Separación, en especial de una raza de otra en una sociedad racista y en un sistema de *apartheid*.

senado / Senado
(1) Asamblea que actuaba como principal órgano de gobierno en la antigua Roma (aunque finalmente perdió la mayor parte de sus poderes en favor del emperador). (2) Una de las asambleas parlamentarias. En España, el Senado es una cámara de representación territorial que forma parte de las Cortes Generales junto con el **Congreso de los Diputados**. En Estados Unidos recibe este nombre la cámara alta legislativa del *Congreso*.

señor
En el sistema feudal (véase *feudalismo*), poseedor de tierras y lugares con *dominio* y autoridad sobre ellos o solo con derecho a percibir rentas y otras prestaciones territoriales.

señorío
Dignidad y territorio de un *señor* feudal.

siervo de la gleba
Campesino que vivía en condiciones de semiesclavitud, sin derecho a dejar la tierra o al *señor* para el cual trabajaba.

sindicato
Asociación de trabajadores con el objetivo de defender sus intereses económicos y prestarse apoyo mutuo.

sínodo
Asamblea o junta de *eclesiásticos*, principalmente constituida por obispos o por ministros protestantes.

sionista
Partidario de la creación de un *estado* independiente para los judíos. Después de la fundación de Israel en 1948, firme partidario de la continuidad de Israel como *estado* judío.

soberanía
(1) Autoridad legítima plena sobre un territorio. (2) Supremacía de un *estado* sobre otro menos poderoso.

socialdemocracia
Antiguamente era sinónimo de *socialismo* o de *comunismo*. En la actualidad se da este nombre a una forma moderada de socialismo compatible con la *democracia* y el *liberalismo*.

socialismo
Denominación de diversas ideologías y movimientos que suponen en mayor o menor grado la intervención del gobierno en la sociedad y en la economía con el fin de redistribuir la riqueza para el bien común. Los movimientos socialistas van desde los moderados y democráticos hasta los comunistas revolucionarios (véase *democracia* y *comunismo*).

sogún
Jefe militar japonés. En varios periodos de la historia de Japón fueron los sogunes hereditarios, y no los emperadores, quienes gobernaron.

sóviet
Cada uno de los numerosos consejos electos que actuaban en todos los niveles sociales en la antigua URSS **(Unión Soviética)**. El **Sóviet Supremo** era el órgano superior del gobierno *federal*, y cada *república* tenía el suyo propio.

sufragio
Derecho de voto, especialmente en las elecciones públicas. Se denomina **sufragista** a aquella persona que lucha por conseguir el derecho a votar, en particular de las mujeres.

sultán
Título equivalente al de rey o emperador en algunos contextos y culturas islámicos. (véase *islam*).

tecnócrata
(1) Miembro perteneciente a una élite técnica. (2) Persona que enfoca los problemas políticos buscando soluciones técnicas en lugar de mediante ideologías o juicios de valor.

Telón de Acero
Barrera imaginaria entre los países comunistas dominados por la URSS (véase *comunismo*) de Europa oriental y los no comunistas occidentales durante la *Guerra Fría*.

teocracia
Gobierno encabezado por un sacerdote o una autoridad religiosa cuyo poder se considera procedente de Dios.

tetrarquía
Sistema de gobierno de un territorio dividido en cuatro sectores, cada uno con su propio gobernante **(tetrarca)**; también, jurisdicción o territorio gobernado por un tetrarca. En el Imperio romano fue instaurado por Diocleciano.

totalitarismo
Forma de gobierno *autoritario* que trata de controlar los detalles de la vida privada y del pensamiento de la gente, restando importancia a la libertad individual frente al *estado*.

tribuno
Título de distintos funcionarios de la antigua Roma: el **tribuno de la plebe** era uno de los dos magistrados (después más) cuya misión era defender los derechos de las personas corrientes (plebeyos) frente a los nobles (patricios). El **tribuno militar** era un oficial adscrito a una *legión*.

triunfo
En la antigua Roma, desfile solemne de un general vencedor.

Ultramar
Conjunto de los estados medievales establecidos por los *caballeros* cruzados en Oriente Próximo.

usurpar
Arrebatar el poder a un gobernante legítimo, a veces de manera violenta.

utopía
Plan de gobierno o sistema ideal pero irrealizable. El término, que significa literalmente «no lugar», o lugar que no existe, procede del título de una obra de Tomás Moro publicada en 1516.

valido
Persona de confianza de un monarca en la que este delega el ejercicio del poder.

vasallo
En el sistema feudal (véase *feudalismo*), persona que recibía tierras de un superior a cambio de fidelidad y diversos servicios; por extensión, sirviente o subordinado.

Vietcong
Organización *política* y militar que llevó a cabo una *guerra de guerrillas* y otras actividades durante la guerra del Vietnam. Pese a proclamarse como un movimiento rebelde independiente en el seno del Vietnam del Sur no comunista, de hecho estaba controlado por el Vietnam del Norte comunista (véase *comunismo*).

virrey
Persona que gobierna en representación o en nombre del rey en una colonia, región o provincia.

yihad
Lucha o guerra emprendida en defensa de la fe islámica (véase *islam*).

zar
Título de los emperadores de Rusia y de los soberanos de Bulgaria. En Rusia, tanto las emperatrices por propio derecho como la esposa del zar ostentaban el título de **zarina**.

ÍNDICE

Las páginas donde se trata el tema con detalle figuran en **negrita**; aquellas en que está ilustrado se indican en *cursiva*.

A

N

O

R

S

U

V

W

Z

AGRADECIMIENTOS

Dorling Kindersley desea expresar su agradecimiento a las siguientes personas: Irene Lyford por la revisión; Jonny Burrows, Philip Fitzgerald, Spencer Holbrook, Clare Joyce, Maxine Pedliham, Hugh Schermuly y Jackie Swan por su ayuda en el diseño; Steve Crozier por el tratamiento del color; Amy Smith y Jen Allison del Ure Museum of Classical Archaeology, Universidad de Reading; Rachel Grocke y Helen Armstrong del Oriental Museum, Universidad de Durham; Catherine Harvey del Hastings Museum, y Gary Ombler por la fotografía.

New Photography: Durham University Oriental Museum
El Oriental Museum es el único museo del norte de Inglaterra dedicado íntegramente al arte y la arqueología de Oriente. Sus colecciones incluyen más de 23 000 objetos relacionados con Egipto, China, Japón, India y otras grandes culturas de Asia y Oriente Próximo y Medio. Fundado en 1960 para promover la educación y la investigación en la Universidad de Durham, el museo está ahora abierto a todo el mundo.

DK India agradece a Dharini, Sreshtha Bhattacharya, Archana Ramachandran, Anita Kakad, Aisvarya Misra y Vineetha Mokkil su asistencia editorial; Ira Sharma, Priyabrata Roy Chowdhury y Niyati Gosain su ayuda con el diseño; Neeraj Bhatia, Nityanand Kumad y Mohd Rizwan por el retoque de imágenes; y Aditya Katyal por la búsqueda de imágenes.

Los editores agradecen a las siguientes personas e instituciones el permiso para reproducir sus imágenes:

(Clave de las abreviaturas: a-arriba; b-abajo; c-centro; d-derecha; e-extremo; i-izquierda; s-superior.)

© 1982 MJJ Productions, Inc.: Reproducido con autorización. Fotógrafo: Dick Zimmerman 439ca.
Cortesía de 3M: 282cd.
akg-images: British Library, London 222bi, 232sd; CDA / Guillemot 188-189s, 192ci, 206sc, 218cd; DEA Picture Library 188ci; François Guénet 77s; Joseph Martin 200si; Nimatallah 208-209b, 223b; North Wind Picture Archives 292sc; Russian Picture Service 319si, 351si; Sotheby's 233sd; Yvan Travert 137sd; Tretjakov Gallery 235d, 309sd, 318s; Ullstein Bild 334bd; World History Archive / IAM 28cd, 154cb, 186bi; Erich Lessing 40ci, 108sc, 182ebd, 183s.
Alamy Stock Photo: AAA Photostock 193ci; Akademie 135sd; Nir Alon 301cd; Ayhan Altun 94-95s, Ancient Art & Architecture Collection Ltd 41s, 70c, 146c; Antiques & Collectables 240bd, 244bc; Arco Images GmbH 25s; Art Directors & TRIP 36-37s, 78i, 213sd; The Art Archive 30bi, 34si, 35bd, 36c, 41cd, 48si, 64bc, 65c, 92s, 112c, 114sc, 116sc, 138ci, 142sc, 143ci, 156ci, 160ci, 170bi, 171b, 192b, 193c, 194-195s, 195sd, 195ci, 196si, 201sd, 201c, 206-207s, 211ci, 216cdb, 218si, 220sc, 226cd, 234sd, 242sd, 259si, 272ci, 273sd, 284sc, 288si, 292sd, 294ca, 296si, 302-303sc, 304sd, 313sc, 332cib, 335si, 358bi, 402esd, 410cdb, 411cda; The Art Gallery Collection 7si, 18cda, 50si, 68sd, 80ci, 102ci, 114ci, 114c, 129cd, 143c, 159c, 179sd, 181sc, 196ca, 201si, 202sc, 212si, 238ci, 265sc, 285c; ASP Religion 131si; Authors Image 142bi; Greg Balfour Evans 114si; Peter Barritt 137si; Paul Bevitt 282cib; Anders Blomqvist 35sd; BrazilPhotos.com 224-225s; Vlad Breazu 80b; CBW 65bi; Charistoone-Images 149sd; B. Christopher 41ci; Cinematic 374ca; Classic Image 329sd; Dennis Cox 153sd; Stephen Coyne 116ci; Craig Joiner Photography 26-27s; CuboImages srl 76b; Gianni Dagli Orti / The Art Archive 312bd, 318cda; DBI Studio 326cda; Dinodia Photos 225b; Michael Doolittle 333bd; EmmePi Travel 177sd; Eye Ubiquitous 19cda; Stuart Forster 149b; Robert Fried 169cd; GL Archive 334si; Globuss Images 26si; Tim Graham 153sc; The Granger Collection 238bd; Spencer Grant 332cda; Mike Greenslade 284-285s; Handout 464cb; Sonia Halliday Photographs 116-117s; Mark Harmel FAP 283cdb; Hemis 279sd; Peter Horree 34ca, 52c; Imagebroker 132si; ImageClick, Inc. 127sd; Images and Stories 195c; Interfoto 27bi, 55bi, 94cd, 99s, 147b, 153b, 159sd, 167ca, 170-171s, 211b, 212sd, 220si, 229bi, 267sd, 323si; Hanan Isachar 139si; F. Jack Jackson 248si; Martin Jenkinson 70-71s; Jon Arnold Images / Demetrio Carrasco 7esd; Wolfgang Kaehler 34-35s; LatitudeStock 151bd; Lebrecht Music and Arts Photo Library 185c, 207sd, 225sd, 234bd, 289ca, 364cb; David Lyons 88ci; Celia Mannings 288sc; Mary Evans Picture Library 51b, 98c, 99cd, 157si, 163cd, 181sd, 232si, 240bi, 259sc, 261sc, 306s, 318bd, 323cd, 330sc, 364cib; Steven May 330bd; John Mitchell 305sd; Carver Mostardi 136si; Niday Picture Library 222sc, 303sd; North Wind Picture Archives 126sc, 150c, 211sd, 224bd, 244cd, 270sd, 277si, 285sc, 301sc, 321sd, 322si, 329ca; B O'Kane 147si; Oasis / Photos 12 336bd; Olivier Parent 73cd; David Paterson 245s; PhotoEdit 454cib; Photos-12 150sd, 329si; Pictorial Press Ltd. 197si, 220-221s, 295cda, 296sc, 414cib; Pictures Colour Library 118c; Paris Pierce 320sd; Mark Pink 140-141s; Pink Sun Media 215sd; PjrStudio 88sc; Niels Poulsen DK 239bd; The Print Collector 31bd, 112sd, 151sd, 162si, 166c, 175ca, 194bi, 251bc, 289cdb, 305b, 313cda; Prisma Archivo 319bd; Prisma Bildagentur AG 249sd; Ria Novosti 143si, 207bi; Rolf Richardson 163sc; Robert Estall Photo Agency 109sc; Robert Harding World Imagery 108-109s; Robert Preston Photography 92bi; Russ Images 146b; Kumar Sriskandan 365bi; Stock Montage, Inc. 206c; Homer Sykes Archive 434-435s; Vintage Power and Transport / Mark Sykes 332cdb; Giovanni Tagini 194sc; TAO Images Limited 120s; The Natural History Museum 216fcib; TTL Images 152c; V&A Images 136cd, 280sc; Ivan Vdovin 323bi; Visions of America, LLC 220bi; Janine Wiedel Photolibrary 425si; Pete M. Wilson 296sd; World History 4-5, 65sd, 113si, 176si, 252s, 278si, 309sc, 320si, 326sd, 327bi, 415cda.
www.BibleLandPictures.com 21sd, 40si, 64c.
Ancient Art & Architecture Collection: 148b; Prisma 100si.
The Art Archive: Bibliothèque Nationale Paris 62ci, British Library 196b; catedral de Santiago de Compostela / Gianni Dagli Orti 127c; Edinburgh University Library 146sd, Galleria d'Arte Moderna Rome / Alfredo Dagli Orti 71bd; Genius of China Exhibition 27cd; Musée du Louvre (París) / Gianni Dagli Orti 94ci; Musée Guimet Paris / Gianni Dagli Orti 99b; Museum of the City of New York, donación de Murray Hartstein (inv 96.13.1) 210sd; Naval Museum Genoa / Alfredo Dagli Orti 205sd; Royal Horticultural Society / Eileen Tweedy 257si; V&A Images 259cdb.
Bibliothèque Nationale de France (París): 154cdb;
The Bridgeman Art Library: 103d, 143sd, 184sd, 253sd, 264cda, 269cd, 271sd, 374bc; Archives Charmet 157sd, 167sd, 208bi, 236cd, 253ci, 277sd, 288sd, 328sd; Art Gallery of New South Wales (Sídney) 319sd; Ashmolean Museum, University of Oxford (RU) 40cd, 243s; Bibliothèque de l'Institut de France 205bc; Bibliothèque Nationale (París) 6esd, 129si, 130ci, 140si, 152sc, 156sd; Bildarchiv Steffens Henri Stierlin 40sd; Bonhams (Londres) 314si; William Bradley 273cd; Bristol City Museum and Art Gallery (RU) 297ca; © British Library Board. All Rights Reserved 118sc, 132sc, 141cia, 200sd, 272sd, 301si; Brooklyn Museum of Ars (Nueva York) 169cb; Brooklyn Museum of Ars (Nueva York)/donación de K. Thomas y Sharon Elghanayan 110-111s; catedral de Burgos (España) 175sd; Museo del Prado (Madrid) 112sc; Chester Beatty Library, Dublin 220bd; Chicago History Museum 312bi; Chiostro dei Morti, Santissima Annunziata (Florencia) 149si; Christie's Images 243si; City of Edinburgh Museums and Art Galleries (Escocia) 264sd; English Heritage Photo Library 72si; G. Dagli Orti / © NPL - DeA Picture Library 72b; Giraudon 50-51s, 102si, 102-103s, 115ci, 187d; Harappan 26bi; Index 88sd; Indian School 68ci; Patrick Lorette Giraudon 295si; Louvre (París) 189b; Massachusetts Historical Society (Boston) 236c; Ministere des Affaires Etrangeres (París) / Flammarion Giraudon 218bi; Mucha Trust 119sd; Musée de la Presse (París) / Giraudon 337si; Museo Histórico Nacional (Buenos Aires) / Index 312si; National Gallery (Londres) 205bd; National Museums of Scotland 316sd; Palacio del Senado (Madrid) 141sc; Palazzo Ducale (Venecia) Cameraphoto Arte Venezia 156si; Peabody Essex Museum (Salem, Massachusetts) 300sc; Peter Newark Historical Pictures 151si; Peter Newark Military Pictures 196sd; Colección privada 257cdb; Colección privada / Heini Schneebeli 203bd; Colección privada / The Stapleton Collection 204bi; RIA Novosti 224c; The Royal Collection © 2011 Her Majesty Queen Elizabeth II 229s; Science Museum (Londres) 154bd; Sumy Art Museum (Sumy, Ucrania) 168si; The Board of Trinity College (Dublín) 29bi; Ernest Tristram 67si; Universitetskaya Naberezhnaya (San Petersburgo) / Bernard Cox 244si; Victoria & Albert Museum (Londres) 198bi; Wallace Collection (Londres) 214bi; cortesía del New College (Oxford) 131b; © Albaceas de la Watts Gallery (Compton, Surrey) 301sd.
The Trustees of the British Museum: 2, 6sc, 8b, 25c, 27sd, 54bi, 64s, 67c, 84-85 sc, 87bi, 93c, 108si, 149cd, 176-177b, 257cib.
ChinaFotoPress: 30cd.
Corbis: 7sc, 7d, 89ci, 186bd, 205bi, 222si, 238bi, 252bd, 256sc, 278cib, 282bi, 284ca, 330si, 348cia, 350sd, 373cia, 393cda, 404c, 414ca, 426s, 439cda, 441sd, 444-445, 450s, 456cia, 457c, 459si, 459cia, 460cib; Mike Agliolo 238cdb, Albright-Knox Art Gallery / © Succession Miro/ADAGP, Paris and DACS, London 2023 366bi; Alinari Archives 357cia; Paul Almasy 88bc, 128bi, 213c; Amanaimages 192si; Mladen Antonov, 455cda; H. Armstrong Roberts / ClassicStock 433cdb; Tony Arruza 161cd; Arte & Immagini 205sc; 237ci; Asian Art & Archaeology, Inc. 105bd, 138si; Atlantide Phototravel 87cd; Maher Attar / Sygma 444cib; Nathan Benn 21cb, 21bc; Bettmann 29bc, 47c, 65bd, 68c, 87s, 139sd, 175cd, 176ci, 201cd, 208sc, 210cd, 225si, 229bd, 264si, 266sd, 267cib, 278sd, 278cdb, 289si, 289sd, 300si, 306cda, 308b, 309bc, 315si, 328bi, 329sc, 329cia, 334sc, 340cib, 342si, 343bd, 350bc, 358sd, 360si, 362bi, 363si, 365cib, 366sd, 369si, 370-371s, 371cdb, 375bd, 377sd, 378bi, 381sd, 391cda, 393si, 397i, 399s, 400si, 404bi, 407s, 412sd, 419s, 421cdb, 428cb, 430, 433ci, 446ca; Stefano Bianchetti 228sd, 374cd; Bernard Bisson / Sygma 447sd; Brooklyn Museum 30-31s, 126cd, 241bi; Henri Bureau, 437cb; Alexander Burkatovski 41bi; Burstein Collection 66s, 127ci, 180c, 191c, 227cd; Car Culture 333bi; Charles Caratini 450-451s, Jacques M. Chenes, 440-441s; Christie's Images 163sd, 240si; Elio Ciol 95ca, 105bi; Pierre Colombel 46-47s, 105s; Christopher Cormack 266sc; Marco Cristofori 152si; Gianni Dagli Orti 28bi, 45b, 46cd, 49sc, 50c, 53cd, 57cd, 61si, 62-63s, 259sd, 314b; Keith Dannemiller 158si; David J. & Janice L. Frent Collection 337cib; Araldo de Luca 73bi, 77b, 81bi, 86cd, 89cd, 91cd, 374bi; Leonard de Selva 374bd; Destinations 207sc; Dennis di Cicco 183bi; DPA / Agentur Voller Ernst / Yevgeny Khaldei 404-405; Richard Dudman / Sygma 435d; EFE 386s, 406s, 427cb; Anatoly Maltsev / EPA 118bi, EPA 226b, 462cia; Waltraud Grubitzsch / EPA 29ci; Patrick Escudero / Hemis 67sd; Dominique Fages, 438-439cb; Najlah Feanny-Hicks, 454si; Fine Art Photographic Library 180b; Werner Forman 69b, 83b, 156b, 238cib; Michael Freeman 129ci, 236bi; The Gallery Collection 6si, 17cdb, 17bd, 47bd, 54bc, 61cda, 124sc, 128sd, 142si, 158-159b, 184c, 197cd, 204sc, 204bc, 205ci, 210bi, 218sd, 261sd, 287sd, 295cb, 303bd, 312-313sc; Christel Gerstenberg 362cib; Karie Hamilton, 455sd; Blaine Harrington III 287si; Ron Haviv / VII, 449sd; Gavin Hellier / JAI 215c, Hemis / Tuul 142sd; Heritage Images 117bc, 132-133s, 185bi; Jon Hicks 73sc; Historical Picture Archive 46si, 60si, 108sd, 304si, 304sc, 323sc; Hoberman Collection 204sd; Angelo Hornak 101cd, 199ca, 199bc, 199bd; Hulton-Deutsch Collection 260si, 335bd, 341si, 342bc, 343bd, 364bd, 406cdb; iStock 456bd; Mimmo Jodice 64bd; Dewitt Jones 126si; Mark Karrass 63sd; Karen Kasmauski 405bc; Alain Keler / Sygma 436sd; Keystone 340s;

Lebrecht Authors / Lebrecht Music & Arts 130si; Lebrecht Music & Arts 202-203s, 246s; Danny Lehman 52-53s; Charles & Josette Lenars 93s; Diego Lezama Orezzoli 269si; Philippe Lissac / GODONG 150b; Yi Lu 174-175si; Frank Lukasseck 115sd; Macduff Everton / Science Faction 144bi; Rick Maiman, 456si; Luis Marden / National Geographic Society 287cb; John Marian / Transtock 333bc; Francis G. Mayer 52cd, 63ci, 211si; Ulli Michel / Reuters 448sc; Momatiuk - Eastcott 28ci; David Muench 70si, 206bi; NASA 458bi; NASA / Science Faction 55cdb; National Gallery (Londres) 280si, 280sd, 281si, 281cib, 283bd, 284si, 284sd, 284cdb, 285sd, 292si, 293sd, 296-297s, 297sd, 297cb; Michael Nicholson 57cb, 350si, 350bi, 351bi, 351bd, 380ci; Richard S. Nowitz 203sd; Christine Osborne 130sc; Nigel Pavitt / JAI 8–9; Jacques Pavlovsky / Sygma 434ca; Philadelphia Museum of Art 327bd; PictureNet 265sd; Matthew Polak, 451cia; Radius Images 174c; Enzo & Paolo Ragazzini 182cdb; Vittoriano Rastelli 80sd; Carmen Redondo 72-73sc, 200bi; Reuters 108b, 171sd, 183bd; Bertrand Rieger / Hemis 126-127s; Robert Harding World Imagery 224si; Royal Ontario Museum 90bi, 236-237s; David Rubinger 408cdb; Michael Runkel / Robert Harding World Imagery 182bd; Brendan Ryan / Gallo Images 12-13s; Rykoff Collection 416sd; Sakamoto Photo Research Laboratory 37bd, 66b; Michael S. Sedam 82sc; Paul Seheult / Eye Ubiquitous 83ci; Smithsonian Institution 116bc, 259cda; Hubert Stadler 124si; Stapleton Collection 86si, 159sc, 160-161s, 214si, 260sd, 288cb; museo del Hermitage (San Petersburgo) 238bi, 327sd; George Steinmetz 147sc; Keren Su 117sd, 136sd, 461cib; Summerfield Press 153si, 161sd; Swim Ink 2, LLC 301cia, 328cda, 343cia, 351cd, 390cia, 399i; Frédéric Soltan / Sygma 147sd, 160sc, 270si, Sygma 2-3, 351sd; Homer Sykes 115sc; Luca Tettoni 104b, 137ci; The Art Archive 63bd, 95sc, 120ci, 131sd, 150cd, 160si, 162-163s, 166sd, 173cdb, 189sd, 193si, 200c, 211cd, 214sd, 228si, 246cd; The Print Collector 112si; Arthur Thévenart 166cib; Travelasia / Asia Images 157bd; Peter Turnley 438si, 446s, 448ca; Underwood & Underwood 352cda, 356bd, 361si; US Air Force 460-461s; Ruggero Vanni 45s, 77cd, 117sc; Sandro Vannini 24bc, 40bi, 56ca, 75bd; Brian A. Vikander 58cia; Nik Wheeler 83si, 126cb; Roger Wood 84bi; Adam Woolfitt 77ci, 132bc, 157c.

Christie's Images Ltd: © Estate of Cassandre. All Rights Reserved, DACS, London 2023 379bd.

Depositphotos Inc: 360ber 465cib.

Dorling Kindersley: 412si; The American Museum of Natural History 291cdb; The Board of Trustees of the Armouries 48ca, 139c, 168-169b, 217bi, 242bd, 306b, 306cb, 402cb, 436cda, 438cd, 440cda; Ashmolean Museum (Oxford) 135cd; Sarah Ashun 425ca; Bayerische Verwaltung der staatlichen Schlössed, Gärten und Seen 256cdb; BFI Stills, Posters and Designs 334bi; Birmingham Museum and Art Galleries 144sd; British Airways 365cdb; con permiso de la British Library 28bc, 173cib; The Trustees of the British Museum 20sc, 25b, 28s, 29cib, 48sd, 48cb, 48cdb, 48bi, 48bd, 49sd, 49bi, 54si, 54ca, 54cb, 54bd, 59ci, 65cd, 84si, 84sc, 84cda, 84bc, 84bd, 84esd, 85sc, 85sd, 85bd, 92bd, 108ca, 109cd, 122d, 123ci, 134d, 140-141b, 145sc, 162b, 198bc, 204si, 216ci, 216cib, 216cb, 279cda, 290sd, 317cdb, 374cb, 406cda; © CONACULTA-INAH-MEX. Reproducción autorizada por el Instituto Nacional de Antropología e Historia 111d, 113c, 119sc, 119bd, 144sc, 144cda, 144c, 144cd, 144bd, 145c, 145ci, 145cd, 145b, 170s; Captain Cook Birthplace Museum, Middlesbrough Council 269cda; Andrew L Chernack 434cb; City Palace Museum (Jaipur) 198bd; Joe Cornish 286cdb; cortesía del Charlestown Shipwreck and Heritage Centre (Cornwall) 251bi; cortesía del RAF Museum (Hendon) 355cd, 355cdb; Andy Crawford 383c, 413sd, 413cb, 447cda; Danish National Museum 115cd, 119ca, 122si, 122sd, 122cd, 123sd, 123sc, 123c, 123cda, 123cd; The Eden Camp Museum (Yorkshire) 374cdb, 375cdb, 375bc, 386cdb; English Civil War Society 198c; English Heritage 112bi; Ermine Street Guard 85ca, 85cd, 216bd; Bob Gathany 412bi, 416ca; Steve Gorton 413bi, 413bc, 413bd; Ellen Howdon 291cda; Wilberforce House, Hull City Museums 208bc; Imperial War Museum (Duxford) 459b; Imperial War Museum (Londres) 217bd, 349cda, 356bi, 354sd, 354cia, 355si, 355sc, 355sd, 355bi, 355bc, 355bd, 397cd, 402si, 402cd, 402bi, 402bd, 402esi, 403si, 403i, 403sd, 403cda, 403c, 403cdb, 403bd, 403ecdb; Prem Kapoor 411cia; Colin Keates 298cib; James Mann 418cib; Jamie Marshall 82ci, 98si, 219b, 299cdb; Mary Rose Truss, Portsmouth 55cb, 55cib; Andrew McRobb 250bc; Judith Miller 190bd, Judith Miller / Bath Antiquities Centre 124ci, Judith Miller / Kevin Conru 148c, Judith Miller / Lyon and Turnbull Ltd. 313b, Judith Miller / Sloan's 29c, 190sd, 316si, 316sc, Judith Miller / VinMagCo 412bd, Judith Miller / Wallis and Wallis 134cib; The Ministry of Defence Pattern Room (Nottingham) 387ca; Museo Archeologico Nazionale di Napoli 79c; Museu da Cidade (Lisboa) 256ci, 257sd; cortesía del Museum of English Rural Life, The University of Reading 250cb, 251cib; Museum of London 20bi, 20bd, 21bi, 21bd, 21ebd, 28cd; Museum of Mankind Museum of Mankind / The Trustees of the British Museum 21cd; Museo de la Revolución (Moscú) 370cib; Royal Museum of Scotland 144-145s; NASA 412ci, 440i, 275bc; 125b, 135sd, 182ca, 198si, 198tc 275bc; Museo Nacional del Motor (Beaulieu) 332bi, 354bi, 354bc; National Museum (Nueva Delhi) 199sd, 199sc, 199ci, 199cd, 247bi; Trustees of the National Museums of Scotland 215bd, 252ca; National Railway Museum (York) 384-385b; Natural History Museum 12cd, 13cd, 54cib; New York City Police Museum 368cda; Gary Ombler 268cda, 290si, 290sc, 290c, 290cd, 290bi, 290ca, 290cda, 290bc, 290ebi, 291si, 291sc, 291sd, 291ca, 291ca/2, 291cd, 291bi, 291esi, 291esd, 375bi, 391cb, 392c, 398cdb, 402cia, 402bc, 403cb, 449c; Gary Ombler / Collection of Jean-Pierre Verney 354si, 354sc, 355ca, 355ci; Opera di S. Maria del Fiore di Firenze 150si; Pitt Rivers Museum (Oxford) 20ca, 326c, 145cda; Pitt Rivers Museum, University of Oxford / David King 20cb, 20bc, 64ci; Martin Plomer 401cb; Rob Reichenfeld 256si; Alex Robinson 271si; Rough Guides 133sd, 141sd, 433sc; Royal Green Jackets Museum (Winchester) 329cdb; cortesía del Science Museum (Londres) 123bd, 134c, 182sd, 207bd, 250-251, 268ci, 274s, 274bi, 296cd, 298cb, 298cdb, 298bi, 298-299c, 299cb, 299bi, 299bc, 318bi, 328cia, 332cb, 361cda, 428bi, 413si; Dave Shayler / Astro Info Service Ltd 413c; Shuttleworth Collection, Bedfordshire 364sd, 364-365c; Spink and Son Lsd (Londres) 358cda; James Stevenson 412-413, 413ci, 413cd; Jane Stockman 283bc; Harry Taylor 253cda; Universitets Oldsaksamling 123bi, 123bc; University Museum of Archaeology and Anthropology (Cambridge) 20sd, 20-21ca, 21si, 21cda, 145sd; Lorenzo Vecchia 250bi; Jean-Pierre Verney 342cda, 346ca; Vietnam Rolling Thunder 426cia, 426ca, 428cib, 428bc; Vikings of Middle England 122bc, 122bd; Wallace Collection (Londres) 160cd, 198sd, 198cia, 216-217, 217cdb, 233b, 266cia; Matthew Ward 400ca, 401cda; Warwick Castle (Warwick), 17bc, 132ci, 132cd, 303cda; York Archaeological Trust for Excvation and Research Ltd 28bd; Michel Zabe 144si.

Dreamstime.com: Gianni Pasquini 464si; Seregal 130sd.

Éditions Gallimard: Simone de Beauvoid, Le Deuxième Sexe I Les Faits et Les Mythes, 1949 421ci.

ESO: EHT Collaboration 463cda.

John Frost Historical Newspapers: 426cdb.

Getty Images: 336 si; Sylvester Adams 78-79s; AFP 86sd, 284cib, 347sd, 370cda, 420-421s, 424si, 444si, 451c, 458s, 463cia; AFP / Marty Melville 463bc; AFP / Claudio Santana 19sd; AFP / Saul Loeb 464-465sc; AFP / STR 464si; Alterndo Images 243b; Altrendo Travel 91s; Anadolu Agency / Emin Sansar 465si; Marilyn Angel Wynn / Nativestock.com 70bi; Apic / Hulton Archive 331sd, 335cda, 337cda, 347cda, Edward A. Armitage 94si; Arthur Barrett / Hulton Archive 337sd; Allan Baxter 454-455cb; Pietro Benvenuti 286si; Stefano Bianchetti 363b; Bloomberg 396ci, 398si, 398sd, 398cib, 399cda, 400-401b, 401si, 456-457s, 459cda, 460si, 460cdb, 461sd, 462cdb; Bridgeman Art Library 101c, 180-181s, 184si; Sisse Brimberg 16-17s; Bronze Age 19cdb; Father Browne / Universal Images Group / Hulton Archive 186-187s, 189ci, 209sd, 300sd, 315sd; Michelangelo Buonarroti 178; Buyenlarge 331cia; Central Press / Hulton Archive 302si, 321b, 359cda, 362si, 363sd, 380sd, 381ci; Philippe Chery 60cb; Manuel Cohen 51cd, 336bi; Cosmo Condina 111sd; Cover 373s, 373cd, 376sd, 379si, © Succession Picasso/DACS London 2023 382b; 382b; De Agostini Picture Library 34ci, 34-35c, 37bi, 56s, 100ca, 110bi, 175cib, 232ci, 294cib, 385sd; DEA / W.Buss 168-169s; DEA / A. Jemolo 44bi; DEA / G. Dagli Orti 26cd, 44bc, 56-57s, 76ca, 120c, 250bd; DEA / L. Pedicini 250ebd, 258s, 258ci, 259cib; Danita Delimont 83sd, 223si; Patrick Dieudonne 18-19s; Dinodia Photos / Brand X Pictures 307ci; Macduff Everton 81s, 104s; Gallo Images / Orbital Horizon / NASA Landsat data / USGS 457si; Gamma-Keystone 286sd, 293si, 293ca, 293cib, 296cib, 299cib, 353bd, 371ca, 372-373s, 392cib, 397s, 405s, 410sd, 431cia; Gamma-Rapho 407cda, 408s, 408cib, 409cd, 417s, 417cda, 418ca, 425sd, 432sd, 437si, 438-439s, 441ci, 462si, 462-463s, Kenneth Garrett 44-45s; Giraudon 102cd; Deborah Lynn Guber 67b; Henry Guttmann / Hulton Archive 349sd; Hulton Archive 58bi, 118cd, 136sc, 179cd, 188b, 193sd, 202si, 222sd, 223sd, 228b, 229c, 237s, 244ci, 248sd, 280bd, 301bi, 305sc, 314sd, 320cia, 326sc, 330sd, 334sd, 336sd, 342sd, 342cia, 404si; Iberfoto / BeBa 182cb; Imagno 261cia, 267cda, 269cb, 372i; Islamic School 46b; Jean I. Juste 179si; Keystone-France / Gamma-Keystone 332ci, 341cda, 346cd, 366sc; Michael Langford 270cib; Gottfried Lindauer / The Bridgeman Art Library 300cia; London Stereoscopic Company / Hulton Archive 315bd; Michael Melford 81cd, 120-121s, 138cd, 142c, 148si; Nakshi 209bd; National Archive / Newsmakers 331si; New York Daily News 353sd, 356s; National Geographic 69s, 315ca; Nativestock / Marilyn Angel Wynn 227bi, 376ci; New York Daily News Archive 367sd; Richard S. Nowitz 89sd; NurPhoto / Debajyoti Chakraborty 464c; NurPhoto / STR 463si; Panoramic Images 90sd; Paris Match / Philippe Petit 463sc; Per-Anders Pettersson 376cda; 377cda, 377cib, 432cd, 433sd, 448-449s, David Poole 128si, 435sc, 435cia; Popperfoto 269esi, 309ci, 341bi, 347bi, 348s, 348bi, 371sd, 383sd, 390cib, 393cib, 396s, 398ca, 411si, 414-415s, 419c, 431sd; Emile Prisse d'Avennes 286cb; Rischgitz / Hulton Archive 322sd; Roger Viollet 405cd; Science Photo Library 275bd; Science & Society Picture Library / NMeM / Kodak Collection 319cia; DEA / M. Seemuller 54cdb, Frank Siteman 24s; Sports Illustrated 451cda, 451cib; SSPL 180-181b, 225ci, 238bc, 261cdb, 265ca, 268si, 268cd, 270cda, 271sc, 272sc, 274bc, 275ci, 275cd, 275cb, 275bi, 276si, 276ci, 276cd, 282c, 282bd, 283s, 283cb, 293cdb, 366cda, 378si, 412sc, 440si, 428sd; STR / AFP 465cda; Keren Su 36si; SuperStock 188sd, 267si, 368si, 368cd; David Sutherland 79sd; Jane Sweeney 113sd, 256sd; The Bridgeman Art Library 39bi, 59bd, 114-115s, 130cd, 131c, 132sd, 140c, 158sd, 161sc, 168ci, 176-177s, 184bi, 185s, 186s, 192sd, 193bd, 197bd, 219s, 221c, 226-227s, 232bd, 233cd, 247s, 248b, 249cd, 274cib, 304esd; Time & Life Pictures 58-59s, 120-121b, 218bd, 235si, 257sc, 265si, 277cia, 280cib, 346bi, 382s, 384s, 385cda, 386cda, 387s, 387cdb, 390si, 391si, 407bd, 409sd, 415sd, 418sd, 424cda, 424cib, 432cia, 445cdb; Time & Life Pictures / Mansell 236si, 241si, 313cia, 321si, 348bd; Topical Press Agency / Hulton Archive 357sd, 359sd, 361bi, 368bi; Travel Ink 69ci; Universal History Archive 225sc; Roger Viollet 101s, 272cdb, 352s, 352bi, 357cd, 362cda, 379cia, 392si, 425cda; Art Wolfe 233si; WPA Pool / Frank Augstein 465bc.

Robert Hooke, Micrographia, London 1665: Ant from Scbem. XXXII and p203 222cda.

International Instituut voor Sociale Geschiedenis (http://www.iisg.nl/): Take steel as the key link for a leap forward in all fields, Tianjin People's Fine Arts Publishing House, 1958; offses, 53 x 77 cms, inv. nr. BG E12 / 530 417bi.

Riccie Janus: 461cd.

David King Collection: 350bd, 351bc.

The Kobal Collection: Paramount 369bi; Warner Bros 367bd.

Library Of Congress, Washington, D.C.: 266si, Battelle Memorial Institute / 126770pu, 155bd.

Magnum Photos: Rene Burri 420s; Steve McCurry 447i.

Mary Evans Picture Library: 287sc; AISA Media 234c; Alinari Archives, Florence 160-161b; IBL Collections 247cd; Suddeutsche Zeitung 170bd, 203bi.

Moviestore Collection: 420b.

NASA: 365bd, 441cb; GSFC / JPI, MISR Team 245ci.

National Maritime Museum, Greenwich, London: 238bc, 379cd; 238sd, 239c, 239s.

NRAO / AUI / NSF: 183bc.

David Parfitt: 251cdb.

Photolibrary: Wayne Fogden 125sd; Erwin Bud Nielsen 155cdb; Sites & Photos 56-57b.

Press Association Images: 416sc; AP / Zoran Bozicevic 438cib, 450cib.
Rex Shutterstock: 455si; P.G.P.
Royal Geographical Society: Alfred Gregory, 414cdb.
The Royal Bank of Scotland Group: © 2011 65bc.
Giovanni Sarbia: 90c.
Photo Scala (Florencia): 269sc; BPK, Bildagentur fuer Kunss, Kultur und Geschichte (Berlín) 212b; Heritage Images 110cd; The Metropolitan Museum of Art / Art Resource 182ebi, 195bd; Vorderasiatisches Museum, Staatliche Museen zu Berlin 31ci; White Images 154bc, 155si.
Science Museum / Science & Society Picture Library: 55bd, 155bi, 183ci, 214bd, 222bd, 239bi, 239bc, 251cd, 253bi, 269esd, 299cd, 332bd, 365cb, 381cdb, 429s.
Science Photo Library: Martin Bond 275cdb; Jean-Loup Charmet 282bc; Eye of Science 429bc; John Greim 283bi; NASA 436cib; National Institutes Of Health 464sc; Science Source 208sd.
Cortesía de la Schøyen Collection (Oslo y Londres): 154cib, 154bi.
Socialdemokraterna (www. socialdemokraterna.se): 441cda.
SuperStock: De Agostini 55cd; Science and Society 233ci, 332bc, 375ci.
TopFoto.co.uk: The Granger Collection 125cia, 182bi, 264cib, 272si, 272ca, 307si, 307sc, 308s, 326si; Public Record Office / HIP 300bc; RIA Novosti 294si; World History Archive 271cb.
US Naval History & Heritage Command: almirante Isoroku Yamamoto, Armada Imperial Japonesa (1884-1943) retrato oficial de Shugaku Homma, 1943 (inv NH 79462-KN) 393cb.
Werner Forman Archive: Biblioteca Nacional (Madrid) 127sc.
Wikipedia: 65ci; Apple Inc. (http://en.wikipedia.org/wiki/File:Apple_Computer_Logo_rainbow.svg) 434cdb; cortesía de Rare Book Room/Andreas Vesalii, De Humani corporis fabrica pp. 184-185, impreso por Johannes Oporinus c1543 282cdb.
Yale University Art Gallery: Préstamo del Yale Peabody Museum of Natural History 279bi.
Agradecimientos a **Sumedha Chopra** por su ayuda en la búsqueda de imágenes y la documentación con DACS para esta ecición.

Para más información www.dkimages.com